Sports Illustrated 2005 Almanac

By the Editors of Sports Illustrated

Sports Illustrated

2005 Almanac

SPORTS ILLUSTRATED is a registered trademark of Time Inc.

First Edition
ISBN 1-932273-34-4

SPORTS ILLUSTRATED Executive Editor: Rob Fleder
SPORTS ILLUSTRATED Director, New Product Development: Bruce Kaufman

Sports Illustrated 2005 Almanac was prepared by
TPG Sports, Bishop Publishing, of White Plains, N.Y.

Cover photography credits :
Tom Brady: John Biever
Phil Mickelson: Elise Amendola/AP
Ben Wallace: David E. Klutho
Lance Armstrong: Peter Dejong/AP

Back cover photography credits (left to right):
Michael Phelps: Simon Bruty
Johnny Damon: Doug Pensinger/Getty Images
Dale Earnhardt Jr.: Rusty Jarrett/Getty Images

Spine photography credit: Simon Bruty

Title page photography credit: John Biever

TIME INC. HOME ENTERTAINMENT

President . . . . Rob Gursha
Vice President, New Product Development . . . . Richard Fraiman
Executive Director, Marketing Services . . . . Carol Pittard
Director, Retail & Special Sales . . . . : . Tom Mifsud
Director of Finance . . . . Tricia Griffin
Marketing Director . . . . Ann Marie Doherty
Prepress Manager . . . . Emily Rabin
Marketing Manager . . . . Kristin Rivela
Associate Book Production Manager . . . . Suzanne Janso

Special thanks: Bozena Bannett, Alexandra Bliss, Bernadette Corbie, Robert Dente, Anne-Michelle Gallero, Peter Harper, Robert Marasco, Natalie McCrea, Brooke McGuire Jonathan Polsky, Margarita Quiogue, Mary Jane Rigoroso, Steven Sandonato

We welcome your comments and suggestions about Sports Illustrated Books. Please write to us at: Sports Illustrated Books, Attention: Book Editors, PO Box 11016, Des Moines, IA 50336-1016

If you would like to order any of our hardcover Collector's Edition books, please call us at 1-800-327-6388. (Monday through Friday, 7:00 a.m.–8:00 p.m. or Saturday, 7:00 a.m.–6:00 p.m. Central Time).

CONTENTS

SOURCES

In compiling the *Sports Illustrated 2005 Almanac*, the editors would like to extend their gratitude to the media relations offices of the following organizations for their help in providing information and materials relating to their sports: Major League Baseball; the Canadian Football League; the National Football League; the National Collegiate Athletic Association; the National Basketball Association; the National Hockey League; the Association of Tennis Professionals; the Women's Tennis Association; the U.S. Tennis Association; the U.S. Golf Association; the Ladies Professional Golf Association; the Professional Golfers Association; National Thoroughbred Racing Association; the U.S. Trotting Association; the Breeders' Cup; Churchill Downs; the New York Racing Association, Inc.; the Jockey's Guild, Inc.; Championship Auto Racing Teams; the National Hot Rod Association; the International Motor Sports Association; the National Association for Stock Car Auto Racing; the Professional Bowlers Association; the Ladies Professional Bowlers Tour; the United Soccer Leagues; Major League Soccer; the Women's United Soccer Association; the *Fédération Internationale de Football Association*; the U.S. Soccer Federation; the U.S. Olympic Committee; USA Track & Field; U.S. Swimming; U.S. Diving; U.S. Skiing; U.S. Figure Skating Association; the U.S. Chess Federation; U.S. Curling; the Iditarod Trail Committee; the International Game Fish Association; the USA Gymnastics; U.S. Handball Association; the Lacrosse Foundation; the American Power Boat Association; the Unlimited Hydroplane Racing Association; the Professional Rodeo Cowboys Association; U.S. Rowing; the American Amateur Softball Association; the U.S. Speed Skating ; U.S. Rugby Football Union; USA Triathlon; the National Archery Association; USA Wrestling; the U.S. Squash Racquets Association; the U.S. Polo Association; ABC Sports; and the U.S. Volleyball Association.

The following sources were consulted in gathering information:

Baseball *The Baseball Encyclopedia*, Macmillan Publishing Co., 1990; *Total Baseball*, Viking Penguin, 1995; *Baseballistics*, St. Martin's Press, 1990; *The Book of Baseball Records*, Seymour Siwoff, publisher, 1991; *The Complete Baseball Record Book*, The Sporting News Publishing Co., 1992; *The Sporting News Baseball Guide*, The Sporting News Publishing Co., 1996; *The Sporting News Official Baseball Register*, The Sporting News Publishing Co., 1996; *National League Green Book—1994*, The Sporting News Publishing Co., 1993; *American League Red Book—1994*, The Sporting News Publishing Co., 1993; *The Scouting Report: 1996*, Harper Perennial, 1996.

Pro Football *The Official 1997 National Football League Record & Fact Book*, The National Football League, 1997; *The Official National Football League Encyclopedia*, New American Library, 1990; *The Sporting News Football Guide*, The Sporting News Publishing Co., 1996; *The Sporting News Football Register*, The Sporting News Publishing Co., 1996; *The 1993 National Football League Record & Fact Book*, Workman Publishing, 1993; *The Football Encyclopedia*, David Neft and Richard Cohen, St. Martin's Press, 1991.

Pro Football Venues *Ticketmaster*

College Football *1997 NCAA Football*, The National Collegiate Athletic Association, 1997.

Pro Basketball *The Official NBA Basketball Encyclopedia*, Villard Books, 1994; *The Sporting News Official NBA Guide*, The Sporting News Publishing Co., 1996; *The Sporting News Official NBA Register*, The Sporting News Publishing Co., 1996.

College Basketball *1997 NCAA Basketball*, The National Collegiate Athletic Association, 1996.

Hockey   *The National Hockey League Official Guide & Record Book 1997–98*, The National Hockey League, 1997; *The Sporting News Complete Hockey Book,* The Sporting News Publishing Co., 1993; *The Complete Encyclopedia of Hockey,* Visible Ink Press, 1993.

Tennis   *1997 Official USTA Tennis Yearbook,* H.O. Zimman, Inc., 1997; *IBM/ATP Tour 1997 Player Guide,* Association of Tennis Professionals, 1997; *1997 Corel WTA Tour Media Guide,* Corel WTA Tour, 1997.

Golf   *PGA Tour Book 1997,* PGA Tour Creative Services, 1997; *LPGA 1997 Player Guide,* LPGA Communications Department, 1997; *Senior PGA Tour Book 1997,* PGA Tour Creative Services, 1997; *USGA Yearbook 1997,* U.S. Golf Association, 1997.

Boxing   *The Ring 1986–87 Record Book and Boxing Encyclopedia,* The Ring Publishing Corp., 1987. *Computer Boxing Update,* Ralph Citro, Inc., 1992; Bob Yalen, boxing statistician.

Horse Racing   *The American Racing Manual 1994,* Daily Racing Form, Inc., 1994; *1994 Directory and Record Book,* The Thoroughbred Racing Association, 1994; *The Trotting and Pacing Guide 1994,* United States Trotting Association, 1994; *Breeders' Cup 1993 Statistics,* Breeders' Cup Limited, 1993; *NYRA Media Guide 1993,* The New York Racing Association, 1994; *The 120th Kentucky Derby Media Guide, 1994,* Churchill Downs Public Relations Dept., 1994; *The 120th Preakness Press Guide, 1994,* Maryland Jockey Club, 1994; *Harness Racing News,* Harness Racing Communications.

Motor Sports   *The Official NASCAR Yearbook and Press Guide 1997,* UMI Publications, Inc., 1997; *1994 Indianapolis 500 Media Fact Book,* Indy 500 Publications, 1994; *IMSA Yearbook 1995 Season Review,* International Motor Sports Association, 1995; *1994 Winston Drag Racing Series Media Guide,* Sports Marketing Enterprises, 1994.

Bowling   *1994 Professional Bowlers Association Press, Radio and Television Guide,* Professional Bowlers Association, Inc., 1994; *The Professional Women's Bowling Association Tour Guide 1997.*

Soccer   *Rothmans Football Yearbook 1993–94,* Headline Book Publishing, 1993; *American Professional Soccer League 1992 Media Guide,* APSL Media Relations Department, 1992; *The European Football Yearbook,* Facer Publications Limited, 1988; *Soccer America,* Burling Communications; Dan Goldstein, editor of *Football Europe.*

NCAA Sports   *1997–98 National Collegiate Championships,* The National Collegiate Athletic Association, 1998; *1993–94 National Directory of College Athletics,* Collegiate Directories Inc., 1993.

Olympics   *The Complete Book of the Olympics,* Little, Brown and Co., 1991; *The Complete Book of the Summer Olympics,* Little, Brown and Co., 1996.

Track and Field   *American Athletics Annual 1996,* The Athletics Congress/USA, 1996.

Swimming   *6th World Swimming Championships Media Guide,* The World Swimming Championships Organizing Committee, 1991.

Skiing   *U.S. Ski Team 1994 Media Guide / USSA Directory,* U.S. Ski Association, 1993; *Ski Racing Annual Competition Guide 1993–94,* Ski Racing International, 1993; *Ski Magazine's Encyclopedia of Skiing,* Harper & Row, 1974; *Caffe Lavazza Ski World Cup Press Kit,* Biorama, 1991.

PHELPS

U.S. swimmer Michael
Phelps makes history at
the 2004 Olympics

The Year
In Sports

Something for Everyone

A smorgasbord of success stories, 2004 provided inspiration for even the most finicky of sports fans

BY HANK HERSCH

HOW DO YOU like your success stories? Because 2004 had them in just about every variety you can imagine. Call it the Baskin-Robbins of sporting seasons. There were historic deeds delivered in the face of daunting expectations (U.S. swimmer Michael Phelps). There was a remarkable feat that became tarnished after the fact (U.S. gymnast Paul Hamm). There were encouraging tales about rising stars grasping the benefits of teamwork (Chauncey Billups and the Detroit Pistons), and about legendary veterans demonstrating it one last time, before gracefully exiting the world stage (Mia Hamm and her four longstanding teammates from the U.S. women's soccer team). There were the epic achievements of a humble, soon-to-be-well-known artist (tennis ace

Roger Federer) and those of a not-so-humble, very well known one (baseball slugger Barry Bonds).

Those were only a few of the variations in 2004's smorgasbord of success stories. The year began with an up-and-coming quarterback (Tom Brady) winning his second Super Bowl championship—as well as his second Super Bowl MVP award—and ended with that same QB leading his team to an NFL-record unbeaten streak. A late-charging veteran (golfer Vijay Singh) took the PGA by storm in 2004, winning eight titles and supplanting Tiger Woods as the world No. 1. That set up the tasty prospect of the once unchallenged Woods embroiled in a genuine rivalry in 2005.

Had enough? Well save room for the main course: This was the year the Olympics

The workmanlike Wallace typified the Pistons' team-first approach as they stunned the Lakers for the NBA title.

returned to their ancestral home of Athens and, after a shaky run-up, delivered a competition that ranked with the best Games in Olympic history. Providing an hors d'oeuvre of sorts to the Games was the Tour de France in July, when an American cyclist with an appetite for climbing, not to mention unsurpassed greatness, took home a record sixth title in a row.

While Armstrong was tasting glory in France, the Greek national soccer team, which had never won a single game in a major international competition, seized one of the sport's biggest plums, the European Championship, in Portugal. A few months before that, hungry college basketball fans in Storrs, Conn.—and there are many— savored a rare treat: both the UConn men's team and women's team brought home national championships, a first in NCAA history.

So whatever your preference, if you were

FRANCOIS GUILLOT/AFP/GETTY IMAGES

Euro 2004 champs, and gracious Olympic hosts: It was a banner year for Greece.

a sports fan, 2004 had something to satisfy you. But it wasn't all sweet, to be sure. There were some bitter tastes—most notably the possible end of the 2004–05 NHL season before it could get started. After the upstart Tampa Bay Lightning defeated the Calgary Flames 2–1 in Game 7 of the finals—allowing left wing Dave Andreychuk to hoist the Stanley Cup for the first time in his 22-year career—the league's owners and players reached an impasse in negotiations on a new collective bargaining agreement. The crux of their disagreement: the dreaded salary cap. Claiming 20 of its 30 teams were losing money, management demanded economic reform, starting with a cap. By October, players had begun to scramble for jobs in leagues across the globe, an ominous diaspora at a time when the NHL's attendance and TV ratings were in decline.

Athens wasn't all sweetness and light, either. Two old reliables took it on the chin at the Summer Games: the U.S. men's basketball team and track star Marion Jones. Bereft of three-point shooters and befuddled by the international rules and officiating, the U.S. team, led by NBA All-Stars Tim Duncan and Allen Iverson, lost to Puerto Rico—Puerto Rico!—by 19 points in its opening game. The Yanks lost to Lithuania a few nights later, thereby equaling the U.S. loss total in all of the previous Games (the United States was 109–2 in Olympic

competition before Athens 2004). A semifinal loss to Argentina put the U.S. in the third-place game, where it bounced back to beat Lithuania and salvage the bronze medal.

The 28-year-old Jones, who won three gold medals and two bronzes at the 2000 Games, entered the 2004 Olympic trials under suspicion of using performance-enhancing drugs. (No charges were filed.) She had a poor trials, only qualifying for the long jump (in which she finished fifth at Athens) and, after being named to the 4 x 100 relay team at the Games, she and Lauryn Williams flubbed the baton exchange, causing the U.S. to be disqualified in an event they are long accustomed to winning. "When I woke up this morning, this is not the way that I figured the day to end," Jones said. "It exceeded my wildest dreams, in a negative sense."

There were other sour notes at the Olympics—including the withdrawal, under suspicious, drug-related circumstances, of the host nation's two top sprinters—but for the most part, the Athens Games were a glorious affair. And earning the most glory, by far, was Phelps, a jug-eared 19-year-old swimmer from Towson, Md. Before Athens he'd been positioned as a new *and improved* version of Mark Spitz, the legendary swimmer who won a record seven gold medals in 1972. After winning the 400-meter individual medley, Phelps quickly lost his chance of overhauling Spitz's pot of gold, with third-place finishes in the 400-meter freestyle relay and the 200-meter free. But he happily plowed on, despite having to race 17 times in seven days. One night he stood on the medal stand after winning the 200 IM, the strains of *The Star-Spangled Banner* sounding in the arena—and his first 100-butterfly heat was nine minutes away. "The whole time on the podium," said Phelps, "I'm thinking, How fast can I go in the fly?"

Entering the 400-meter medley relay Phelps had racked up five golds and two

El Guerrouj earned sweet redemption in Athens, taking the 1,500 and the 5,000.

bronzes and needed one more piece of hardware to set a record for medals in a single, nonboycotted Games. That's when he ceded his butterfly leg in the final to Ian Crocker, who had swum poorly in the 400-meter free relay (and whom Phelps had beaten in the 100-meter fly) earlier in the Games. Since he swam in one of the preliminary heats, Phelps would receive whatever the U.S. earned in the race. Duly inspired by Phelps's generosity, Crocker swam a tremendous butterfly leg, and the U.S. won gold, giving Phelps his record eighth medal of the Olympics. The gesture allowed Crocker to appear on the victory stand, and provided a sweet grace note to these Games. "Ian's one of the greatest relay swimmers in history," said Phelps. "I was willing to give him another chance."

Another chance. That was certainly a fitting theme for many of the best Olympic success stories. There was 29-year-old Hicham El Guerrouj of Morocco, the world record holder in the 1,500 meters, who, after bitter Olympic disappointments in 1996 and 2000, outkicked Kenya's Bernard Lagat to finally claim gold. In the 5,000 four days later, he calmly tailed 10,000-meter winner Ken Bekele of Ethiopia. "I said to myself, 'Hicham, for the people to look at you as a legend, you have to win this race'" El Guerrouj recalled. He breezed by Bekele and became the first 1,500–5,000 double gold medalist since Paavo Nurmi in 1924.

U.S. gymnast Hamm achieved redemption, too, but he didn't have to wait quite as long. The reigning world champ, Hamm was weak-legged after helping the U.S. team win the silver medal (by competing in 11 of 12 events), and he tumbled into the judges' table on his vault landing in the overall competition. His score of 9.137 was 22nd out of 24 vaulters and dropped him to 12th overall with just two rotations left. "I thought, That's it. I'm done," said Hamm. "Maybe I had a small chance of winning a bronze." But he earned a 9.837 on the parallel bars—the highest score of the week on that apparatus—then matched that mark with a near-flawless performance on the high bar. Though a scoring error lowered the start value of South Korean bronze medalist Tae Young Yang's parallel bars routine, prompting a controversy that lingered long after the Games had ended, Hamm had soared all the way to gold. As Peter Vidmar, the only other American male to have earned an

Olympic all-around medal (a silver in 1984), put it, "This is the greatest comeback in the history of gymnastics."

Joining Hamm on the comeback trail in Athens was the core group of the U.S. women's soccer team, five 17-year veterans known as the '91ers who, for the first time since 1996, failed to hold the title of either Women's World Cup or Olympic champion. Many doubted that the Yanks' fab five—forward Mia Hamm, 32; midfielder Julie Foudy, 33; midfielder Kristine Lilly, 33; and 36-year-old defenders Brandi Chastain and Joy Fawcett—could, in their final major international competition together, reassert a dominance that lasted for a decade, beginning in 1991 with their victory at the inaugural Women's Cup. But in a thrilling display of grit and guile, the U.S. outlasted a younger, better-rested Brazil team, winning the final 2–1 in overtime on a header by Abby Wambach. "No other outcome was possible tonight," the 24-year-old Wambach said. "This is the way these girls needed to go out."

That sort of team spirit was the overriding characteristic of two domestic champions, the Pistons and the Patriots. Heeding the mantra of new coach Larry Brown to "play the right way," Detroit's selfless roster constituted a sum greater than its parts: a shooting guard wearing a face mask to protect his surgically repaired nose (Richard Hamilton), an intimidating 6'9" center (Ben Wallace), a breadstick-thin small forward (Tayshaun Prince), a volatile and hobbled power forward (Rasheed Wallace) and a closet gunner at the point (Billups, the Finals MVP). Detroit combined the Wallaces' shot-blocking and rebounding, the backcourt's productivity and good old-fashioned teamwork—a quaint notion in today's NBA—to dispatch the Lakers in five games, a thoroughly unexpected wipeout yet one so persuasive that it prompted the trade of Shaquille O'Neal to the Miami Heat and the departure of coach Phil Jackson. Several weeks after the Finals, the L.A. franchise could claim a victory of sorts, but it had to be cold comfort indeed: a Colorado judge dismissed sexual assault charges against superstar Kobe Bryant,

leaving him facing a civil suit in the matter.

Having lost its starters to injuries for a league-high 87 games—including marquee free agent signing Rosevelt Colvin, who lined up at linebacker just twice—New England seemed an unhealthy candidate to win its second title in three years. But with the help of underrated veterans, such as linebackers Mike Vrabel and Willie McGinest and safety Rodney Harrison, the Patriots improved all season long and not only defeated Carolina 32–29 in Super Bowl XXXVIII in Houston, but also ended the season on a 15-game winning streak. (A run they extended to a record 19 in October.) Displaying the poise of his idol, Joe Montana, Brady dissected the Panthers for 354 yards and three touchdowns to win his second Super Bowl MVP trophy at the tender age of 26; only Montana, with three, has more. Said Patriots linebacker Ted Johnson, "I told Tommy after the game, 'Your coattails are getting heavy, and I apologize. Right now I'm hanging on for dear life.' "

Coattails were on prominent display at UConn, where a pair of Players of the Year led their teams to an unprecedented double: the men's and women's basketball championships. When chiseled 6'10" junior Emeka Okafor had to write a term paper for his favorite college course, an honors class called Roman Civilization, he chose as his topic the life and culture of gladiators. "Combat, man, combat," he said, explaining his interest in those ancient warriors. "No guts, no glory." Okafor used ample amounts of the former to seize the latter. Despite spasms in his lower back, he scored 18 points—all in the second half—to rally the Huskies past Duke 79–78 in the NCAA semifinals, then racked up 24 points, 15 rebounds, and two blocked shots in a 82–73 defeat of Georgia Tech in the final.

In the midst of his brutish run through the Final Four in San Antonio, Okafor placed a call to his distaff counterpart, do-it-all senior Diana Taurasi, in New Orleans. "You guys better hold up your side," he said. To win their third straight title the Huskies women's team would have to knock off the only other school to have achieved a threepeat: archri-

Brady and the Patriots won in February and were still winning in October.

val Tennessee (1996–98). While Taurasi scored a team-high 17 points, she ceded some of the heavy lifting to Jessica Moore, Barbara Turner and Ann Strother, each of whom scored in double figures for a relatively ho-hum 70–61 victory. When he wasn't teasing her for a couple of missed free throws, UConn coach Geno Auriemma could only marvel at Taurasi, who was named the finals' most outstanding player for the second consecutive year. "If it wasn't

for the way Diana plays the game and the way she comes to practice and the kind of teammate she is," he said, "there is no way her teammates would have been able to do what they did tonight."

Yet there is a limit to one player's influence on a team's fortunes, as a 40-year-old leftfielder in San Francisco would attest. Though he began the season embroiled in the BALCO scandal, which led to four indictments for the distribution of performance-enhancing drugs, Bonds produced numbers both ridiculous and sublime during the 2004 baseball season. He almost singlehandedly kept the Giants in the playoff chase until the season's final day. He led the National League in hitting (.362) and the majors in slugging (.812) and on-base (.609) percentage, and despite receiving 232 walks—a whopping 34 more than the record he'd set in 2002—he still hit the 45-homer mark for the fifth consecutive year and finished the season with a career total of 703 dingers. This, of course, put him in one of baseball's most exclusive clubs—he is now third alltime behind Babe Ruth (714) and Henry Aaron (755).

Bonds hit 45 home runs and joined Ruth and Aaron in the career 700-homer club.

Seattle rightfielder Ichiro Suzuki also made baseball history, and he did it with a more dismal team. The Mariners finished 29 games off the pace in the American League West, but Ichiro smacked 262 hits, five more than the single-season record that had belonged to George Sisler of the St. Louis Browns for 84 years.

Supporting casts were not a problem for Federer and Singh. A 23-year-old from Switzerland, Federer parlayed artistry and style into the most complete tennis game on the planet—and one of the most dominating seasons in the sport's history. He won all 10

ROBERT BECK

tember, birdieing three of the last four holes to edge Woods and defending champ Adam Scott by three strokes. It was Singh's sixth win of the season and gave him the top spot in the world rankings. "I've played pretty good for the last two years," said the understated Singh. "I'm just trying to win tournaments, plodding along, and here I am." By October, the 41-year-old Fijian had plodded to a record in earnings and eight Tour victories, including the PGA championship at Whistling Straits in Kohler, Wisc. And for the first time in his career, Woods had gone two years without winning a major title.

At the start of the 2004 Tour de France, the 32-year-old Armstrong seemed vulnerable as well. True, he had won the event

finals in which he appeared, took more than one title on every major surface and, most importantly, took three of the four Grand Slam titles. Were it not for a loss to Brazil's Gustavo Kuerten in the third round of the French Open, the unassuming Federer might have been the first man to win the Grand Slam since 1969. The last man to accomplish that feat believes Federer could one day pull it off. "He has all the ingredients," Rod Laver said. "With the way he plays under pressure, he has every chance of real greatness."

That's a quality that can be as hard to maintain as it is to achieve in the first place. Just ask Tiger Woods: For 264 consecutive weeks he held golf's No. 1 ranking; at 28, he seemed unlikely to relinquish it for another 264. But like a dogged detective in a British mystery novel, Singh zeroed, in ever so patiently, on his quarry. After failing twice to overtake Tiger, he pounced at the Deutsche Bank Championship in Sep-

for the fifth straight time the year before, but by a scant 61 seconds. "It was a very serious wake-up call," said U.S. Postal Service team director Johan Bruyneel. "I think Lance took a few things for granted." To win a record-setting sixth yellow jersey he put in grueling seven- and eight-hour training sessions in the Pyrenees before the race, working himself into peak condition. Then he produced perhaps his most dominating Tour performance: He won the prologue along with five of the 20 stages—while conceding a seventh to a friend—and defeated runner-up Andreas Klöden of Germany by 6:19.

Though he had hinted at retirement before the Tour, Armstrong made it clear afterward that he would try to burnish his legend. "I'm more excited to race than I've ever been," he said.

Despite what he's already accomplished, Armstrong sounded hungry for more. Could be the the the start of a success story for 2005.

Late October- November 2003

PHIL COALE

OCT 25 Bobby Bowden (above) gets doused by his Florida State players late in the fourth quarter of the Seminoles' 48–24 win over Wake Forest. The victory was Bowden's 339th and moved him to the top of the Division I-A list for career coaching victories.

THIS MONTH'S SIGN OF THE
APOCALYPSE

A Florida Rabbi is delivering a public lecture, titled
The Curses of the Billygoat and the Bambino:
Exploring the Talmudic View on Curses.

GO FIGURE

$1 million Bonus promised to swimmer Michael Phelps, who set seven world records in the summer of 2003, by a swimsuit manufacturer if he wins seven golds at either the 2004 or the 2008 Olympics.

20 Age of Brian Vickers, who won the 2003 Busch series to become the youngest driver to win a NASCAR title.

159 Pitches clocked at 100 mph or faster thrown by Astros closer Billy Wagner during the 2003 season.

BILL FRAKES

JOHN BIEVER

NOV 18 Fourteen-year-old U.S. soccer prodigy Freddy Adu (above) spurns lucrative offers from the likes of Chelsea and Manchester United to sign a four-year deal with Major League Soccer.

NOV 22 In front of 112,118 fans in Ann Arbor, Michigan and running back Chris Perry (23) down Ohio State 35–21 to eliminate the Buckeyes from the national title race and claim a Rose Bowl berth.

THEY SAID IT

Yao Ming, Rockets sophomore center, talking to reporters in late November 2003:

"Thanksgiving just passed, so you should probably know what I'm thankful for: LeBron James."

DAMIAN STROHMEYER

DEC 13 One year after a knee injury almost ended his career, Oklahoma quarterback Jason White (18) wins the Heisman Trophy as the nation's top college football player. White, who finishes the regular season with 40 touchdown passes, outpoints Pittsburgh receiver Larry Fitzgerald 1,481–1,353 to win the award.

THEY SAID IT

Jeff Bzdelik, Nuggets coach, on how the sudden improvement of his team has affected him: "When I crossed the street last year, people would accelerate. Some brake now."

GO FIGURE

3 Times since 1999 that both Super Bowl teams missed the next year's playoffs, including the Bucs and the Raiders in 2003–04.

1 Time before '99 that both Super Bowl teams missed the next year's playoffs.

$106,600 Price Chicago restaurateur Grant DePorter paid at auction for the baseball that Cubs fan Steve Bartman knocked away from Moises Alou in the 2003 NLCS; DePorter planned to publicly destroy the ball to "create some closure to the way the season ended."

DEC 15 Seeking the right mix of players to complement its superstar rookie, LeBron James (23), Cleveland trades Ricky Davis and two players to Boston for Eric Williams, Tony Battie and Kedrick Brown.

DEC 20 Wide receiver Blake Elliott (2) leads St. John's, of Collegeville, Minn., to a 24–6 upset of Alliance, Ohio's Mount Union in the Amos Alonzo Stagg Bowl. The win gives St. John's the Division III national title and breaks Mount Union's NCAA-record 55-game winning streak.

THIS MONTH'S SIGN OF THE APOCALYPSE

More than 100 runners wearing headlamps ran in an underground marathon in the caves of Valkenburg in the Netherlands.

January 2004

GO FIGURE

4 Overtime goals scored in 44 games by New Jersey's Patrik Elias, who tied the NHL single-season record with the mark.

1,000 Astros season tickets sold within a day of the team's signing Roger Clemens to a one-year deal.

6.5 million Video copies of *Seabiscuit* sold in its first four weeks in release.

THEY SAID IT

Marquise Hill, LSU defensive end, after the Tigers won the Sugar Bowl: "People are going to start respecting LSU—if you don't, we're going to hit you in your mouth."

JAN I Matt Leinart (11) and Southern Cal defeat Michigan 28–14 in the Rose Bowl to finish the season at 12–1 and secure a share of the national title. With 327 yards passing, Leinart is the game's MVP.

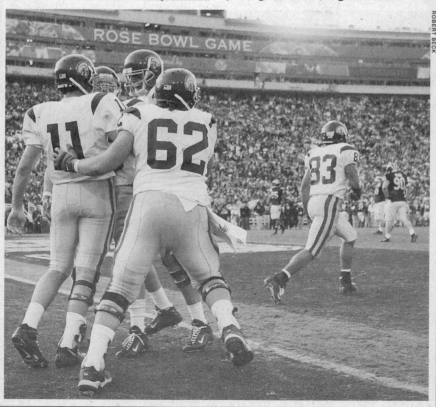

ROBERT BECK

AL TIELEMANS

JAN 4 Skyler Green (5) and Louisiana State defeat Oklahoma 21–14 in the Sugar Bowl to win the BCS championship. The Tigers finish the season ranked No. I in the *USA Today*/ESPN poll and No. 2 in the AP poll, behind USC.

BOB MARTIN

JAN 3I Justine Henin-Hardenne wins the Australian Open, giving her three of the previous four Grand Slam titles. She won the 2003 French and U.S. Opens.

February 2004

THEY SAID IT

Del Harris, Mavericks assistant, after being hired to coach the Chinese Olympic basketball team: "Pick-and-roll is really pick-and-roll in any language."

FEB 1 With wide receiver Deion Branch (83) leading the way, New England edges Carolina 32–29 to win Super Bowl XXXVIII in Houston. Carolina makes the Super Bowl only two years after going 1–15.

$2.4 million
Amount by which the Yankees' payroll increased after they shed the salaries of third basemen Drew Henson and Aaron Boone and traded Alfonso Soriano for Alex Rodriguez.

$4.4 million
Value of tickets sold by the Yankees in the four days after they traded for Rodriguez.

9 Straight 30-win seasons for Devils goalie Martin Brodeur, an NHL record.

FEB 15 The Yankees conclude a whirlwind 72-hour negotiating process to sign All-Star infielder Alex Rodriguez (above). The deal comes less than two months after the Yankees' archrival, Boston, had failed—after five weeks of talks—to sign the slugger.

FEB 15 Dale Earnhardt Jr. (right) wins the Daytona 500, the premier NASCAR event that was the scene of his father's death in 2001.

THIS MONTH'S SIGN OF THE
APOCALYPSE

The father of a basketball player at Colorado Springs' St. Mary's High was cited for misdemeanor assault after allegedly biting two referees in a postgame fracas.

TODD WARSHAW

March 2004

JED JACOBSOHN/ GETTY IMAGES

MARCH 13 With a unanimous decision over Shane Mosley in Las Vegas, Winky Wright (above right) wins the junior middleweight title, unifying the division and spoiling Mosley's prospective $10 million matchup with Felix Trinidad.

ROBERT BECK

THEY SAID IT

Chi Chi Rodriguez, golfer, on what it is like to play with a U.S. president:

"They yell fore, shoot 6 and write down 5."

MARCH 21 The second round of the NCAA tournament features three shockers as Stanford, Kentucky and Gonzaga, the top three teams in the latest AP poll, fall to Alabama (a No. 8 seed, right), UAB (9) and Nevada (10), respectively.

GO FIGURE

66 Years Harvard went without having an NCAA wrestling champ before Jesse Jantzen won the 149-pound title on March 20, 2004.

303 Percentage increase in the Cleveland Cavaliers' local and national television ratings from the 2002–03 season to 2003–04.

6 Coaches in NBA history who have won at least 50 games in each of their first three seasons, after the Indiana Pacers' Rick Carlisle won his 50th on March 17, 2004, to join Rick Adelman, Phil Jackson, Gregg Popovich, Pat Riley and Paul Westphal.

MARCH 30 The 2004 Major League Baseball season gets under way as the Yankees and Tampa Bay square off at the Tokyo Dome (above) in Japan. The Devil Rays upend the defending American League champs 8–3 as former Yankee Tino Martinez belts a two-run homer in the seventh inning.

THIS MONTH'S SIGN OF THE APOCALYPSE

The Braves will have a Lexus-only parking lot at Turner Field during the 2004 season.

KENT SMITH/NBAE VIA GETTY IMAGES

APRIL 5 Two months before he goes to Charlotte as the No. 2 pick in the NBA draft, Emeka Okafor (above) leads Connecticut to an 82–73 win over Georgia Tech for the NCAA title. The UConn women beat Tennessee to make it a double for the Huskies.

ROBERT BECK

GO FIGURE

0 Coaching changes made by Nashville's two major league franchises, the Tennessee Titans of the NFL and the NHL's Nashville Predators, in their six seasons of play in the city.

$40,000 One time fee the University of Tennessee will charge for the right to purchase a pair of courtside women's basketball season tickets.

2.5 Seconds it took Marc Burrows to score for British amateur side Cowes Sports in a game in March 2004. The feat was certified in late April by England's Football Association as the world's fastest goal.

4 Intentional walks—one short of Andre Dawson's major league record—received by San Francisco's Barry Bonds during the Giants' 5–4 loss to the Dodgers on April 23, 2004.

APRIL 11 Draining an 18-foot birdie putt on the final hole of the tournament, Phil Mickelson (left) wins the Masters, edging Ernie Els by a stroke and ending his quest for a major, which had involved countless near-misses and lasted more than a decade.

THIS MONTH'S SIGN OF THE APOCALYPSE

Studios in New York, Miami and Hollywood have begun offering yoga classes for dogs.

APRIL 13 In the seventh inning of San Francisco's eventual 4–2 win over Milwaukee, Giants slugger Barry Bonds (above) belts a 1-2 pitch over the rightfield fence for the 661st home run of his career, surpassing his godfather, Willie Mays, on the alltime list and moving into third place, behind Babe Ruth and Hank Aaron.

THEY SAID IT

Pat Quinn, Maple Leafs coach, on the possibility of top teams losing early in the 2004 NHL playoffs: "Good teams will be dropped out in that first round, and whether it is an upset or not, it will be upsetting to somebody."

ADAM COGLIANESE/AP PHOTO/ NEW YORK RACING ASSOCIATION

THEY SAID IT

Aree Song, 18-year-old golfer, on why she turned pro so early: "So I could retire early."

MAY 1 A 4–1 favorite despite his humble pedigree, the chestnut colt Smarty Jones (above), ridden by Kentucky Derby rookie Stewart Elliott, wins the 130th Run for the Roses, pulling away from runner-up Lion Heart to win by 2¾ lengths.

MAY 18 Arizona lefthander Randy Johnson (left), 40, becomes the oldest pitcher in baseball history to throw a perfect game when he retires 27 consecutive Braves in the Diamondbacks' 2–0 road win over Atlanta.

MAY 30 Buddy Rice (above) becomes the first U.S.-born driver since Eddie Cheever in 1998 to win the Indy 500, taking the checkered flag in a Honda co-owned by talk-show host David Letterman.

GO FIGURE

28-0-2 The Tampa Bay Lightning's NHL record in the 2003–04 season—including 6-0 in the playoffs—when center Brad Richards scores a goal.

2 Perfect games that have been broadcast on national television: Don Larsen's in the 1956 World Series and Randy Johnson's, which aired on May 18, 2004, on TBS.

1–11 The Colorado Rockies' record in 2004 when Todd Greene starts at catcher.

15–10 The Rockies' record in 2004 when Todd Greene does not start at catcher.

June 2004

BILL FRAKES

JEFF GROSS/GETTY IMAGES

JUNE 7 Tampa Bay completes a rally from a three-games-to-two deficit with a 2–1 victory over the Calgary Flames in Game 7 to clinch the Stanley Cup. Lightning center Brad Richards (above) wins the Conn Smythe Trophy as MVP of the playoffs.

GO FIGURE

26 Strikeouts by Brewers hitters in a 17-inning 1–0 win against Anaheim on June 8, 2004, tying the major league record.

20,000 Fans who paid tribute to the 2004 Stanley Cup champion Lightning by attending a June 8 parade in Tampa.

30,000 Fans who paid tribute to the 2004 Stanley Cup runner-up Flames by attending a June 8 parade in Calgary.

66.1 Percentage of 2004 Olympics tickets that remained unsold in early June.

BOB ROSATO

JUNE 15 Chauncey Billups (above left) and the Detroit Pistons dispatch Kobe Bryant and the heavily favored Lakers 100–87 in Game 5 to win the NBA championship.

July 2004

PHIL COLE/GETTY IMAGES

JULY 4 Switzerland's Roger Federer (left) defeats Andy Roddick of the U.S. 4–6, 7–5, 7–6, 6–4 to win a stirring Wimbledon final and claim his second Grand Slam of 2004, after the Australian Open, which he won in January. Seventeen-year-old Maria Sharapova of Russia is the women's champ at Wimbledon.

JULY 4 Angelos Charisteas (right, scoring against France) and Greece, which previously had never won a game in a major tournament, win the 2004 European Championship, stunning hosts Portugal 1–0 in the final in Lisbon.

BEN RADFORD/GETTY IMAGES

GO FIGURE

43 Babies born in Britain in 2003 who were named Wayne.

500 Expected percentage increase in British babies named Wayne this year after England's Wayne Rooney, 17, scored four goals in the Euro 2004 soccer championship.

18 Homers allowed by Kansas City's Darrell May, the third most in the AL as of late June.

0 Homers May has allowed to cleanup hitters.

JULY 25 Cancer survivor Lance Armstrong (above) wins the Tour de France for the sixth straight year, setting a new record for both consecutive Tour triumphs and total Tour victories, surpassing the legendary likes of Belgian Eddy Merckx, Spaniard Miguel Indurain and Frenchmen Jacques Anquetil and Bernard Hinault.

AUG 7 Chicago righthander Greg Maddux (above) secures the 300th win of his career, allowing four runs in five-plus innings during the Cubs' 8–4 win over San Francisco. Maddux is the 22nd—and some predict last—member of baseball's 300-win club.

THEY SAID IT

Terry Francona, Red Sox manager, on rotund infielder Kevin Youkilis, called the "Greek God of Walks" in the book Moneyball: "I've seen him in the shower, and I wouldn't call him the Greek god of anything."

DAVID BERGMAN

0.14 Decrease in Red Sox righthander Derek Lowe's ERA, from 5.47 to 5.33, when centerfielder Johnny Damon asked to be charged with an error on a play that had been ruled a hit in a 14–4 win over the Devil Rays on Aug. 11.

$60 Cost of the Stanley Cup tattoo Lightning coach John Tortorella had inked onto his left ankle.

16 Olympic swimsuits—the team's entire supply—that the British women's triathlon squad sent for emergency alterations because the white garments became translucent when wet.

AUG 15 Vijay Singh (above) defeats Justin Leonard and Chris DiMarco in a playoff to win the PGA Championship in Kohler, Wisc. The victory is part of a remarkable streak in which Singh wins five times in 10 events and unseats Tiger Woods as the world No. 1.

AUG 16 Pieter Van den Hoogenband of the Netherlands, Michael Phelps of the U.S. and Ian Thorpe of Australia (right, l to r) square off in an epic 200-meter freestyle final at the Olympics in Athens. Thorpe, the world record holder, finishes first while Van den Hoogenband, the defending Olympic champ, holds off Phelps at the wall for the silver medal.

HEINZ KLUETMEIER

August 2004

BILL FRAKES

GO FIGURE

44 Consecutive games without a loss by Arsenal, a record for English soccer's top flight.

0 Number of men's basketball teams at the 2004 Games that shot at least 75% from the free throw line.

4 Two-hundred-hit seasons for Mariners rightfielder Ichiro Suzuki, the first player ever to reach that plateau in the first four years of his career.

AUG 19 With an athletic, mistake-free floor exercise, 16-year-old Carly Patterson of the U.S. (above) wins the gold medal in the all-around gymnastics competition at Athens. She is the first American woman to do so since Mary Lou Retton in 1984.

AUG 22 Justin Gatlin of the U.S. (above right) wins the gold medal in the men's 100-meter dash at the Athens Games, clocking 9.85 to edge three other sprinters who also break 9.9 in the race. It is the fastest 100-meter final in Olympic history.

THIS MONTH'S SIGN OF THE
APOCALYPSE

A South African soccer referee shot and killed a coach during an argument over a call.

AUG 29 The Olympics come to a close in Athens, and while swimmer Michael Phelps is the story for the U.S., winning an Olympic-record eight medals, U.S. women also dominate, taking gold medals in soccer, basketball and softball (right).

SEPT 7 Roger Federer (above) beats Lleyton Hewitt 6–0, 7–6, 6–0 to win the U.S. Open and become the first man since Mats Wilander in 1988 to win three Grand Slam titles in one season.

EZRA SHAW/GETTY IMAGES

SCOTT CUNNINGHAM/GETTY IMAGES

GO FIGURE

291 Increase in the number of high schools that offered bowling as a varsity sport from 2003 to '04, making it the country's fastest-growing high school sport.

4.9% Increase in the NFL's average ticket price since last season, from $52.19 to $54.74, according to a Team Marketing Report survey.

$75.33 Average ticket price for the New England Patriots, the NFL's most expensive team to watch.

SEPT 24 The Braves (above) clinch the NL East title with an 8–7 win over Florida. It is a record 13th consecutive division title for Atlanta, which many preseason prognosticators had picked to finish third.

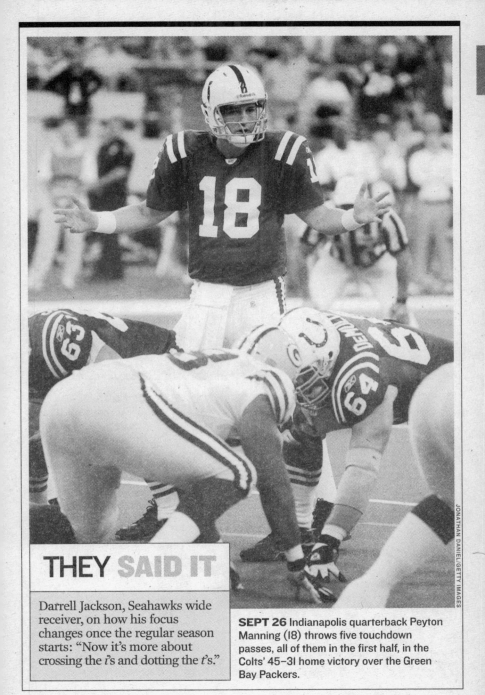

JONATHAN DANIEL/GETTY IMAGES

THEY SAID IT

Darrell Jackson, Seahawks wide receiver, on how his focus changes once the regular season starts: "Now it's more about crossing the *t*'s and dotting the *t*'s."

SEPT 26 Indianapolis quarterback Peyton Manning (18) throws five touchdown passes, all of them in the first half, in the Colts' 45–31 home victory over the Green Bay Packers.

October 2004

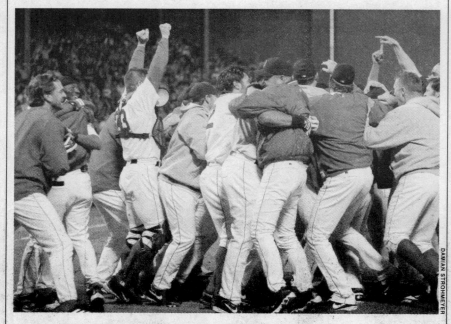

DAMIAN STROHMEYER

AL TIELEMANS

OCT 8 The Red Sox (above) celebrate David Ortiz's two-run walkoff homer in the bottom of the 10th inning of Game 3 of the American League Division Series against Anaheim. The win seals a series sweep for Boston and sends them to a rematch with the Yankees in the ALCS.

OCT 10 Quarterback Tom Brady (12) leads the Patriots to an NFL-record 19th consecutive win, a 24–10 home triumph over the Miami Dolphins.

JOHN MCDONOUGH

OCT 13 Led by freshman running back Adrian Peterson (above), who rushes for 225 yards in the game, second-ranked Oklahoma blanks its fierce rival, fifth-ranked Texas, 12–0 at the Cotton Bowl to improve its record to 5–0.

GO FIGURE

10 Minutes per day, on average, that fantasy football players spend tracking their teams at work, according to the consulting firm Challenger Gray & Christmas.

$2.7 billion Annual cost in lost productivity to employers of fantasy football players.

119 RBIs in the 2004 season by well-traveled Yankees outfielder Gary Sheffield, the first player to drive in 100 runs for five different teams.

12–1 Patriots quarterback Tom Brady's career record in games decided by a field goal or less.

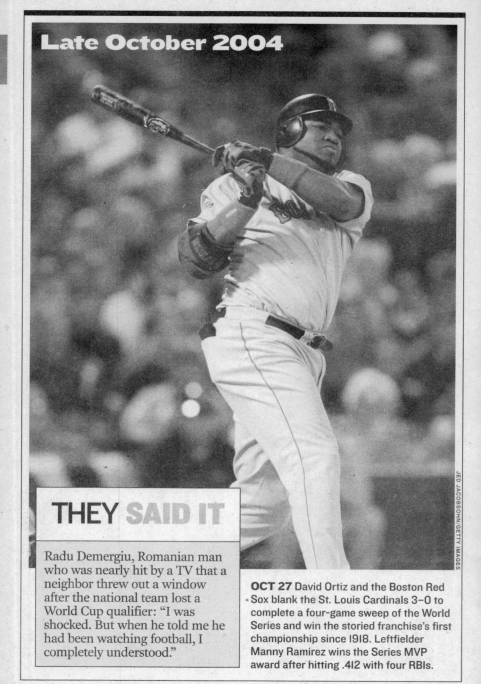

JED JACOBSOHN/GETTY IMAGES

THEY SAID IT

Radu Demergiu, Romanian man who was nearly hit by a TV that a neighbor threw out a window after the national team lost a World Cup qualifier: "I was shocked. But when he told me he had been watching football, I completely understood."

OCT 27 David Ortiz and the Boston Red Sox blank the St. Louis Cardinals 3–0 to complete a four-game sweep of the World Series and win the storied franchise's first championship since 1918. Leftfielder Manny Ramirez wins the Series MVP award after hitting .412 with four RBIs.

Baseball

STEPHEN DUNN/GETTY IMAGES

The World Series champion Boston Red Sox

Boston Glee Party

All of New England celebrated the beloved Red Sox, who won their first championship in 86 years

BY MARK BECHTEL

LET THE RECORD show that on the morning of October 28, 2004, the sun, as scheduled, rose in Boston at 7:13. The were no plagues of locusts and the Charles River did not flow backward. No acts of God that indicated the end might be nigh, just raucous displays from fans celebrating the first World Series championship by the Red Sox since 1918 and the demise of the much ballyhooed Curse of the Bambino.

But except for a strikingly anticlimactic World Series sweep of St. Louis, it didn't come easy for the Sox. Given their history, this was to be expected. In Game 4 of the American League Championship Series they were three outs away from being swept to yet another defeat by—who else?—the New York Yankees. Mariano Rivera, who had blown only three saves in 35 postseason chances, was on the hill, and Boston teetered on the brink of an ingnominious sweep at the hands of their hated rivals. But Red Sox first baseman Kevin Millar drew a walk from Rivera to lead off the inning, then pinch runner Dave Roberts stole second. Third base-

man Bill Mueller, the 2003 AL batting champ whose average had dipped to .283 in '04, came to bat next and singled up the middle, scoring Roberts and tying the game. The Red Sox went on to win when David Ortiz hit a two-run homer into the Boston bullpen in the 12th inning, and they would look back on Millar's walk as a key thread in their postseason lifeline.

For that Game 4 comeback went a long way toward convincing the Sox and their fans that Ruth's ghost might be ready to release its grip on the franchise. And Ruth wasn't the only contributor from beyond the grave in this remarkable journey. After Boston won Game 5 to send the series back to Yankee Stadium, Red Sox righthander Curt Schilling, who was suffering from a displaced tendon in his right ankle, underwent a stopgap operation to try to salvage his postseason. Schilling had the tendon secured with sutures by Sox physician Dr. Bill Morgan, who first tested the procedure on a cadaver at a local hospital. The pitcher responded with one of the great postseason pitching performances in baseball history,

Ramirez hit safely in each of Boston's 14 playoff games and won the World Series MVP award.

allowing just four base runners in seven innings in front of a hostile crowd, evening the series and putting the Yankees on their heels for Game 7.

The victory was a landmark one, since no team in major league history had ever forced a Game 7 after falling behind three games to none—to say nothing of overcoming that deficit and *winning* the seven-game series. (Such a comeback had never happened in the NBA either, and only twice in the history of the NHL.) With Schilling spent and Pedro Martinez on short rest (he pitched Game 5), Boston manager Terry Francona turned to Derek Lowe, who had fallen out of favor during the season, getting relegated to the bullpen after a series of poor performances. For their part, the Yankees sent out one of their blockbuster offseason free-agent signings, Kevin Brown, who had been shelled in Game 3. Brown struggled from the start, and got into real trouble in the second inning, walking Orlando Cabrera to load the bases with one out and the Sox leading 2–0. Johnny Damon was due up next, and New York manager Joe Torre pulled Brown in favor of Javier Vazquez, who had surrendered two homers to Damon in Yankee Stadium earlier in the year. Damon sent Vazquez's first pitch into the right field seats for a grand slam that made it 6–0 (he added a solo shot two innings later for good measure). Boston switched on the cruise control and, after surviving a bumpy relief spell from Martinez (who had declared following a September loss to New York that the Yankees were his "daddy") went on to win 10–3. It was arguably the greatest comeback in sports history. "Not many people get the opportunity to shock the world," said Millar, making a point but perhaps exaggerating the audience

commanded by the ALCS. "We came out and did it. We beat the Yankees. Now they get to watch us on the tube."

The drama between the Red Sox and Yankees is of course an age-old one, whose previous installment came in their memorable 2003 ALCS showdown. Aaron Boone won that series for New York with a homer in the bottom of the 11th inning, making it seem unfathomable that he could become more unpopular in New England.

But on Jan. 16 of the following year, Boone blew out his left knee in a pickup basketball game, setting off a chain of events that would enhance the animosity in baseball's fiercest rivalry, and yes, increase the venom with which Aaron F------ Boone's name was uttered in New England.

Red Sox GM Theo Epstein had spent a good part of the offseason trying to pry Alex Rodriguez away from the Rangers. Texas was floundering—the Rangers finished last in each of A-Rod's first three seasons with the club—and the idea of rebuilding around a high-priced shortstop looked less and less viable with each passing year. Epstein's only problem was that he already had a shortstop: five-time All-Star Nomar Garciaparra. Rodriguez insisted that he didn't want to switch to third base, which meant that Epstein had to pull off two trades to acquire the best player in baseball—one with Texas for the $252 million shortstop and an another to offload Garciaparra. Epstein came close to brokering a deal for Rodriguez, but the players union refused to rubber stamp the restructuring of Rodriguez's mammoth contract. The trade was pronounced dead, leaving Rodriguez in Texas, where he was made captain, and Garciaparra in Boston, where he felt slighted by the attempts to move him. (After sulking for much of the season, Garciaparra was eventually shipped to the Cubs at the trading deadline.)

Then Boone decided to hoop it up. Suddenly, the Yankees needed a third baseman. New York GM Brian Cashman was on the phone with Rodriguez's agent about another client when A-Rod's name came up. About 72 hours later, Rodriguez was a Yankee, and Boone was more hated in the Hub than Bucky F------ Dent. "I only wish to God," one Red Sox official said after the trade, "that Aaron Boone never picked up a basketball."

In baseball's most heated—and one-sided—rivalry, this off-the-field result went true to form: The Sox came out on the losing end, and embarrassingly so. It amounted to yet more bad blood between the two franchises, and the simmering enmity boiled over again in July, when Boston righthander Bronson Arroyo plunked Rodriguez during a game at Fenway. A-Rod began jawing at Arroyo, and Red Sox catcher Jason Varitek interjected. "I told him, in choice words, to get to first base," Varitek said. That triggered a shoving match between Rodriguez and Varitek, and then the benches and bullpens emptied and several skirmishes broke out. "There's no question it wasn't just a generic fight," said Rodriguez, who was ejected along with Varitek. "You could tell there was some residual passion from the past. . . . I think it escalated the rivalry, if

that's possible." Boston won the game on Bill Mueller's ninth-inning homer off Mariano Rivera, but the Sox were losing the war—they would fall 10 games behind New York during the summer.

By September, though, Boston had crept back to within two games of the first-place Yankees, thereby reviving the seemingly annual ritual of raising their fans' hopes only to dash them at the end. This would be the year they finally fulfilled those hopes, and in glorious fashion, but Boston played New York six times in September with a shot at overtaking them for the division title and failed to get the job done. Though fortune would smile on them one month later, Boston fans must have had a here-we-go-again feeling as New York clinched the AL East for the seventh straight year.

The star of the Yankees' run was another high-priced preseason acquisition, rightfielder Gary Sheffield. New York owner George Steinbrenner had personally decided that the team would pursue Sheffield, a 35-year-old with a reputation for surliness, instead of Vladimir Guerrero, a 28-year-old superstar who'd hit .330 with Montreal in 2003. (Guerrero signed with the Angels and went on to lead them to a thrilling, down-to-the-wire win over Oakland for the AL West crown.) The move put a fair amount of pressure on Sheffield, and he didn't handle it well at first. After 44 games he had just three home runs, 18 RBIs and a .265 average. But then the struggling Sheffield decided to confront manager Joe Torre, who had wanted the team to pursue Guerrero instead. The two talked, and Torre convinced Sheffield that he was wanted in the Bronx. "I was a new man," Sheffield said, and set about proving it immediately: That night he drove in six runs, and he would finish the season with 36 homers and 121 RBIs, many of them of the clutch variety.

Sheffield and Rodriguez weren't the only new faces on major league clubs this year. After the 2003 season, New York pitcher Roger Clemens retired and his teammate Andy Pettitte filed for free agency. When Pettitte signed with the Astros—in Clemens's hometown of Houston—the

Ichiro smacked 262 hits to break Sisler's 84-year-old record.

which already featured NL home run champ Adrian Beltre—some added pop, but the team's strength was its pitching. Eric Gagne was his usual dominant self out of the bullpen, but he did see his record streak of saves end after 84 straight chances, giving up two runs to Arizona in the top of the ninth inning on July 5. "Everybody says you have to be real lucky," said Gagne. "I was real lucky for a long time. It just came to an end. I made some great pitches. They beat me."

Said teammate Shawn Green, "It's unbelievable. It's one of those records that will be with all the other huge records of baseball." One such record that fell during the 2004 season was George Sisler's 84-year-old mark of 257 hits in a season. Seattle's Ichiro Suzuki toppled it, smacking 262 hits. "It was a big relief, felt like something I got off my shoulders," Ichiro said through an interpreter. "It is a very exciting time for me. Definitely the highlight of my career." Ichiro's accomplishment was even more impressive considering he was hitting .255 at the end of April. He hit .429 after the All-Star break en route to the record and the AL batting crown.

Ichiro, who slapped 225 singles during his quest, stood in stark contrast to the NL batting champ, Barry Bonds, a power hitter extraordinaire, who, at age 40, still strikes fear in the heart of opposing pitchers. To put it mildly: Bonds received 120 intentional walks and 112 unintentional passes, giving him an on-base percentage of .609, which shattered his major league record of .582, set in 2002. Despite hardly ever being pitched to, Bonds batted .362 and belted 45 homers, including number 661, which moved him past Willie Mays on the all-time list. Bonds also hit career home run No. 700, which put him in the exclusive company of Babe Ruth and Hank Aaron as the only men to have reached that milestone.

Reds outfielder Adam Dunn broke an old

Rocket decided to come out of retirement and join him. To fill their spots, the Yankees dealt for righthanders Vazquez and Brown, from Montreal and Los Angeles, respectively. While Vazquez, Brown and Pettitte all struggled at times, Clemens seemed thoroughly inspired by his new setting, going 18–4 with a 2.98 ERA.

But for the better part of the season, Clemens was the lone bright spot on the Astros, who had spent a lot of money in the offseason trying to transform themselves into a contender. Unhappy with the results, the team's management fired manager Jimy Williams at the All-Star break and replaced him with Phil Garner. As late as the last week of July, the Astros remained in fifth place in the NL Central. But Garner righted the ship: Houston won 36 of its last 46 games to edge the Giants and Cubs for the NL wild card.

The Giants controlled their postseason destiny, arriving in L.A. three games behind the Dodgers with three to play. San Francisco won the first game and led the second one 3–0 in the bottom of the ninth, only to allow Los Angeles to rally and win the game—and the division—on a walk-off grand slam from Steve Finley. Finley had been acquired at the trading deadline in a flurry of deals that were initially unpopular in L.A.

Finley's bat gave the Dodgers lineup—

JONATHAN DANIEL/GETTY IMAGES

a slow start to win their record 13th consecutive division title.

In the AL Central, unsung Minnesota defended its division title behind 25-year-old lefty Johan Santana, who went 20–6 with a 2.61 ERA. He led the Twinkies into their division series against New York on Oct. 5. In a familiar pattern, New York lost the opener of that series then won three straight to elminate the Twins and advance to its ALCS meeting with Boston. That one, of course, did not conform to the timeworn script, and Boston's victory sent the Sox to the World Series, where they faced St Louis.

The Cardinals had vanquished Houston in an exciting seven-game NLCS in which Pujols and Astros centerfielder Carlos Beltran had played a spectacular game of Can-you-top-this? St. Louis was the last one standing when the slugfest was over, and most observers figured the World Series would feature plenty of offensive fireworks. But After his teammates banged out an 11–9 win in Game 1, Schilling took the mound in Game 2 and neutralized the potent Cardinals bats en route to a 6–2 win. Martinez did the same in Game 3, and Lowe wrapped things up the following night, pitching in his third series-clinching game of the playoffs. The Cardinals would go with a whimper instead of a bang. Damon opened the game with a home run and Lowe threw seven innings of three-hit ball in a 3–0 win as Boston sealed a dominating sweep.

"Any time you don a Red Sox uniform, you have to talk about the history of this team and not having a World Series championship since 1918," said rightfielder Trot Nixon. "Sooner or later, that hex had to stop. Everybody thought it was a curse, but to us it was just a five-letter word."

record, but might have wished he didn't: he struck out 195 times in 2004, eclipsing the mark set by Bonds's father, Bobby. "At least I beat a Bonds at something," said Dunn.

Reds fans may have looked at Dunn's dubious distinction as emblematic of their season: they finished 29 games behind St. Louis in the NL Central. They certainly were not alone in eating St. Louis's dust, though, as the Cardinals, with Albert Pujols (.331, 46 HRs, 123 RBIs), Scott Rolen (.314, 34, 124) and Jim Edmonds (.301, 42, 111) leading the way, took the NL Central lead in June and never looked back. They added Larry Walker to their lineup late in the season, and won 105 games, finishing 13 ahead of wild-card winner Houston. The Cardinals' double-digit margin in the Central paralleled Atlanta's 10-game lead in the NL East. Picked by many observers to finish third in the division, the Braves rallied from

Final Standings

National League

EASTERN DIVISION

Team	Won	Lost	Pct	GB	Home	Away
Atlanta	96	66	.593	--	49-32	47-34
Philadelphia	86	76	.531	10.0	42-39	44-37
Florida	83	79	.512	13.0	42-38	41-41
New York	71	91	.438	25.0	38-43	33-48
Montreal	67	95	.414	29.0	35-45	32-50

CENTRAL DIVISION

Team	Won	Lost	Pct	GB	Home	Away
St. Louis	105	57	.648	--	53-28	52-29
†Houston	92	70	.568	13.0	48-33	44-37
Chi Cubs	89	73	.549	16.0	45-37	44-36
Cincinnati	76	86	.469	29.0	40-41	36-45
Pittsburgh	72	89	.447	32.5	39-41	33-48
Milwaukee	67	94	.416	37.5	36-45	31-49

WESTERN DIVISION

Team	Won	Lost	Pct	GB	Home	Away
Los Angeles	93	69	.574	--	49-32	44-37
San Francisco	91	71	.562	2.0	47-35	44-36
San Diego	87	75	.537	6.0	42-39	45-36
Colorado	68	94	.420	25.0	38-43	30-51
Arizona	51	111	.315	42.0	29-52	22-59

†Wild-card team.

American League

EASTERN DIVISION

Team	Won	Lost	Pct	GB	Home	Away
New York	101	61	.623	--	57-24	44-37
†Boston	98	64	.605	3.0	55-26	43-38
Baltimore	78	84	.481	23.0	38-43	40-41
Tampa Bay	70	91	.435	30.5	41-39	29-52
Toronto	67	94	.416	33.5	40-41	27-53

CENTRAL DIVISION

Team	Won	Lost	Pct	GB	Home	Away
Minnesota	92	70	.568	--	49-32	43-38
Chicago	83	79	.512	9.0	46-35	37-44
Cleveland	80	82	.494	12.0	44-37	36-45
Detroit	72	90	.444	20.0	38-43	34-47
Kansas City	58	104	.358	34.0	33-47	25-57

WESTERN DIVISION

Team	Won	Lost	Pct	GB	Home	Away
Anaheim	92	70	.568	--	45-36	47-34
Oakland	91	71	.562	1.0	52-29	39-42
Texas	89	73	.549	3.0	51-30	38-43
Seattle	63	99	.389	29.0	38-44	25-55

2004 Playoffs

National League Division Playoffs

Oct 5 ....Los Angeles 3 at St. Louis 8
Oct 7 ....Los Angeles 3 at St. Louis 8
Oct 9 ....St. Louis 0 at Los Angeles 4
Oct 10 ....St. Louis 6 at Los Angeles 2

(St. Louis won series 3–1)

Oct 6 ....Houston 9 at Atlanta 3
Oct 7 ....Houston 2 at Atlanta 4 (11 innings)
Oct 9 ....Atlanta 5 at Houston 8
Oct 10 ....Atlanta 6 at Houston 5
Oct 11 ....Houston 12 at Atlanta 3

(Houston won series 3–2)

National League Championship Series

Oct 13 ....Houston 7 at St. Louis 10
Oct 14 ....Houston 4 at St. Louis 6
Oct 16 ....St. Louis 2 at Houston 5
Oct 17 ....St. Louis 5 at Houston 6
Oct 18 ....St. Louis 0 at Houston 3
Oct 20 ....Houston 4 at St. Louis 6
Oct 21 ....Houston 2 at St. Louis 5

(St. Louis won series 4–3)

GAME 1

													R	H	E
Houston	2	0	0	2	0	0	0	2	1				**7**	**10**	**1**
St. Louis	2	0	0	0	2	6	0	0	x				**10**	**12**	**0**

W—Williams. **L**—Qualls. **SV**—Isringhausen.
E—Hou: Vizcaino. **LOB**—Hou: 4; StL: 6. **2B**—Hou: Palmeiro, Biggio; StL: Williams, Walker, Edmonds. **3B**—StL: Walker. **HR**—Hou: Beltran, Kent, Berkman, Lamb; StL: Pujols. **S**—StL: Matheny. **SB**—StL: Womack. **GIDP**—StL: Sanders. **T**—3:15. **A**—52,323.

Recap: After Houston centerfielder Carlos Beltran hit a two-run homer to deep right in the visiting half of the first, St. Louis's Albert Pujols answered right back with a two-run shot of his own, serving notice that St. Louis's lineup could stand toe-to-toe, and then some, with Houston's sluggers. The teams traded blows until the sixth, when St. Louis broke the game open with six runs, three of them on a double by Jim Edmonds. Woody Williams went six innings for the win, giving up four runs on four hits, and striking out five.

GAME 2

													R	H	E
Houston	1	0	0	1	1	0	1	0	0				**4**	**10**	**1**
St. Louis	0	0	0	0	4	0	0	2	x				**6**	**9**	**0**

W—Tavarez. **L**—Miceli. **SV**—Isringhausen.
E—Hou: Munro. **LOB**—Hou: 11; StL: 4. **2B**—Hou: Kent, Berkman; StL: Edmonds. **HR**—Hou: Beltran, Ensberg; StL: Walker, Pujols, Rolen 2. **S**—StL: Morris. **SB**—Hou: Berkman StL: Womack. **WP**—StL: Morris. **Balk**—StL: Morris. **CS**—Hou: Bagwell, Ensberg. **T**—3:02. **A**—52,347.

Recap: The Astros' prize late-season pickup, Carlos Beltran, reprised his Game 1 performance, blasting a home run in the first inning, and Houston took a 3–0 lead into the fifth. But St. Louis again countered with firepower of its own, getting homers from Larry Walker and Scott Rolen to take a 4–3 lead in the home half. And after Morgan Ensberg tied it for Houston with an RBI single in the seventh, Albert Pujols and Scott Rolen went deep in the eighth to seal it for the Cardinals.

National League Championship Series (Cont.)

GAME 3

St. Louis	1	1	0	0	0	0	0	0	0	**2**	**5**	**0**
Houston	3	0	0	0	0	0	0	2	x	**5**	**8**	**0**

W—Clemens. **L**—Suppan. **SV**—Lidge.
LOB—StL: 7; Hou: 5. **2B**—Hou: Beltran. **HR**—StL: Walker, Edmonds; Hou: Kent, Beltran, Berkman. **GIDP**—Hou: Bagwell. **T**—2:57. **A**—42,896.

Recap: Needing a win to avoid falling into an 0–3 series hole, the Astros turned to six-time Cy Young Award winner Roger Clemens. The 42-year-old righthander delivered, pitching seven innings and allowing only four hits and two runs while striking out seven. Carlos Beltran, Jeff Kent and Lance Berkman provided the offense for Houston, as each man homered in the 5–2 win.

GAME 4

St. Louis	3	0	1	1	0	0	0	0	0	**5**	**9**	**0**
Houston	1	0	2	0	0	2	0	1	0	x	**6**	**9**	**0**

W—Wheeler. **L**—Tavarez. **SV**—Lidge.
LOB—StL: 8; Hou: 6. **2B**—StL: Rolen; Hou: Bagwell, Berkman, Vizcaino. **HR**—StL: Pujols; Hou: Berkman, Beltran. **S**—StL: Taguchi. **SF**—StL: Edmonds. **GIDP**—Hou: Ensberg. **CS**—Hou: Biggio. **PB**—Hou: Chavez. **T**—3:01. **A**—42,760.

Recap: St. Louis first baseman Albert Pujols blasted his third home run of the series and John Mabry hit a run-scoring single to give the Cardinals a 3–0 lead in the first. They took a 5–3 lead to the bottom of the sixth, when Houston rightfielder Lance Berkman smashed a home run (*his* third of the series) and Raul Chavez singled in Jose Vizcaino to tie it. That set the stage for Astros centerfielder Carlos Beltran to go deep yet again—marking a record fifth straight playoff game in which he has homered—as he golfed Julian Tavarez's low 2–2 slider over the wall in rightfield. Said Tavarez: "Barry Bonds is the best hitter in baseball. I don't think he could have hit that pitch. I can't believe he hit it." Brad Lidge pitched two hitless innings to save it for Houston and tie the series.

GAME 5

St. Louis	0	0	0	0	0	0	0	0	0	**0**	**1**	**0**
Houston	0	0	0	0	0	0	0	0	3	**3**	**3**	**0**

W—Lidge. **L**—Isringhausen. **LOB**—StL: 3; Hou: 4.
HR—Hou: Kent. **HBP**—Hou: Ensberg. **SB**—Hou: Beltran. **T**—2:33. **A**—43,045.

Recap: The bats suddenly went quiet in a series that had been marked by the long ball, and lots of it (19 home runs through four games). Houston starter

GAME 5 *(CONT.)*

Recap (Cont.): Brandon Backe took a no-hitter into the sixth inning, and his counterpart, Woody Williams, nearly kept pace, allowing just one hit through eight innings of work. When Houston came to bat in the bottom of the ninth, the teams had mustered only one single each. That changed when Astros second baseman Jeff Kent belted a three-run walkoff homer against Jason Isringhausen to win the game in dramatic fashion for Houston.

GAME 6

Houston	1	0	1	1	0	0	0	0	1	0	0	0	**4**	**10**	**0**
St. Louis	2	0	2	0	0	0	0	0	0	0	0	2	**6**	**15**	**0**

W—Tavarez. **L**—Miceli. **LOB**—Hou: 9; StL: 10. **2B**—Hou: Bagwell, Kent; StL: Pujols, Sanders, Rolen. **HR**—Hou: Lamb; StL: Pujols, Edmonds. **S**—Hou: Bruntlett. **SF**—Hou: Berkman. **GIDP**—Hou: Lamb. **HBP**—Hou: Ensberg. **SB**—Hou: Beltran, Bagwell. **CS**—Hou: Vizcaino. **T**—3:54. **A**—52,144.

Recap: After Houston first baseman Jeff Bagwell tied the game with an RBI single in the top of the ninth, St. Louis centerfielder Jim Edmonds answered with a two-run walkoff homer in the bottom of the 12th inning to win it and force a Game 7. St. Louis first baseman Albert Pujols continued his torrid run through the NLCS, belting a two-run homer (his sixth of the playoffs), a double and a single. Cardinals reliever Julian Tavarez, who broke his nonpitching hand in a dugout tantrum in Houston during Game 4, pitched two scoreless innings to get the win.

GAME 7

Houston	1	0	1	0	0	0	0	0	0	**2**	**3**	**0**
St. Louis	0	0	1	0	0	3	0	1	x	**5**	**9**	**1**

W—Suppan. **L**—Clemens. **SV**—Isringhausen.
LOB—Hou: 5; StL: 2. **2B**—StL: Womack, Pujols, Anderson. **HR**—Hou: Biggio; StL: Rolen. **S**—StL: Renteria 2, Suppan. **GIDP**—StL: Rolen. **E**—StL: Edmonds. **SB**—Hou: Beltran. **PO**—StL: Womack. **T**—2:51. **A**—52,140.

Recap: With a trip to the World Series on the line, Houston again turned to 42-year-old Roger Clemens, but this time the future Hall of Famer could not get the job done. A run-scoring double by NLCS MVP Albert Pujols and a two-run homer by third baseman Scott Rolen, both in the sixth, did the damage as St. Louis rallied from 2–1 down to go ahead 4–2. Cardinals rightfielder Larry Walker singled home another run in the eighth, and the St. Louis bullpen held the lead, sending the Cards to their first World Series since 1987.

American League Division Playoffs

Oct 5 ....Boston 9 at Anaheim 3
Oct 6 ....Boston 8 at Anaheim 3
Oct 8 ....Boston 8 at Anaheim 6 (10 innings)

(Boston won series 3–0)

Oct 5 ....Minnesota 2 at New York 0
Oct 6 ....Minnesota 6 at New York 7 (12 innings)
Oct 8 ....New York 8 at Minnesota 4
Oct 9 ....New York 6 at Minnesota 5 (11 innings)

(New York won series 3–1)

American League Championship Series

Oct 12 ....Boston 7 at New York 10
Oct 13 ....Boston 1 at New York 3
Oct 16 ....New York 19 at Boston 8
Oct 17 ....New York 4 at Boston 6 (12 innings)
Oct 18 ....New York 4 at Boston 5 (14 innings)
Oct 19 ....Boston 4 at New York 2
Oct 20 ....Boston 10 at New York 3

(Boston won series 4–3)

American League Championship Series (Cont.)

GAME 1

Boston	0	0	0	0	0	0	5	2	0	**7**	**10**	**0**
New York	2	0	4	0	0	2	2	2	0	**10**	**14**	**0**

W—Mussina. **L**—Schilling. **SV**—Rivera.
LOB—Bos 2, NY 8. **2B**—Bos: Bellhorn, Millar; NY: Sheffield 2, Matsui 2, Williams. **HR**—NY: Lofton. **S**—NY: Posada. **HBP**—NY: Posada. **GIDP**—Bos: Mueller; NY: Rodriguez. **T**—3:20. **A**—56,135.

Recap: Boston's effort to reverse the tides of baseball history—if not an outright curse against the franchise—got off to a poor start as the Yankees touched Red Sox ace Curt Schilling for two runs in the first inning and, on Hideki Matsui's second double of the game, three more in the third. While Schilling struggled, New York's Mike Mussina had his very best stuff, pitching a perfect game through six innings as the Yankees built an 8–0 lead. In the seventh, however, the game took a remarkable turn, as games in this rivalry often do: Boston broke up Mussina's perfect game, then broke open the floodgates, scoring five runs in the inning to get back in the game. The Sox added two more in the eighth, nearly tying the score as David Ortiz missed a homer by inches, settling for the triple that made it 8–7. Bernie Williams provided the Yanks with two insurance runs in the bottom of the eighth, doubling over Manny Ramirez's outstretched glove in left, then Mariano Rivera, who arrived in the Yankee bullpen in the fifth inning from Panama, where he'd attended the funeral of two relatives, closed it out in the ninth.

GAME 2

Boston	0	0	0	0	0	0	0	1	0	**1**	**5**	**0**
New York	1	0	0	0	2	0	0	x		**3**	**7**	**0**

W—Lieber. **L**—Martinez. **SV**—Rivera. **LOB**—Bos: 4; NY: 11. **2B**—Bos: Varitek, Ramirez. **HR**—NY: Olerud. **GIDP**—Bos: Millar. **HBP**—NY: Rodriguez, Cairo. **SB**—NY: Jeter. **T**—3:15. **A**—56,136.

Recap: New York starter Jon Lieber was just a shade better than Boston's Pedro Martinez, pitching a three-hitter and allowing only one run in seven innings of work. Martinez gave up only four hits through six innings, but one of them was a two-run homer to first baseman John Olerud, and that provided the difference for New York. The decision also produced a noteworthy stat: In his last 12 starts against the Yankees, Martinez had just two wins.

GAME 3

New York	3	0	3	5	2	0	4	0	2	**19**	**22**	**1**
Boston	0	4	2	0	0	0	2	0	0	**8**	**15**	**0**

W—Vazquez. **L**—Mendoza.
LOB—NY: 7; Bos: 9. **2B**—NY: Rodriguez, Sierra, Matsui, Sheffield, Williams, Posada; Bos: Mueller, Millar, Cabrera, Nixon. **3B**—NY: Sierra. **HR**—NY: Matsui, Rodriguez, Sheffield; Bos: Nixon, Varitek. **HBP**—NY: Cairo. **GIDP**—NY: Posada. **Balk**—Bos: Mendoza. **E**—NY: Jeter. **T**—4:20. **A**—35,126.

Recap: The Yankees jumped on Boston starter Bronson Arroyo in the first inning as third baseman Alex Rodriguez doubled and leftfielder Hideki Matsui homered to stake the Bombers to a 3–0 lead and set the tone for a record night of offense (37 hits between the two sides). The teams traded heavy blows until the sixth, when New York broke it open on a three-run homer by Gary Sheffield and a two-run triple from Ruben Sierra. Up 11–6, the

GAME 3 (CONT.)

Recap (Cont.): Yankees never looked back. Matsui finished with five hits, five RBIs and five runs scored in the rout, which gave New York a 3–0 series edge. No major league baseball team has ever overcome a 3–0 deficit in a best-of-seven series.

GAME 4

New York	0	0	2	0	0	2	0	0	0	0	0	0	**4**	**12**	**1**
Boston	0	0	0	3	0	0	1	0	0	2			**6**	**8**	**0**

W—Leskanic. **L**—Quantrill.
LOB—NY: 14; Bos: 10 **2B**—NY: Matsui. **3B**—NY: Matsui. **HR**—NY: Rodriguguez; Bos: Ortiz. **S**—NY: Jeter, Cairo; Bos: Mintkiewicz. **GIDP**—Bos: Mueller. **SB**—Bos: Roberts, Damon. **E**—NY: Clark. **T**—5:02. **A**—34,826.

Recap: With his team down to the last three outs of their season, Boston's Bill Mueller lined a pitch from Mariano Rivera up the middle, scoring Dave Roberts in the bottom of the ninth and tying the game at 4–4. Rivera held it there, and the old rivals went to extra innings, where Red Sox DH David Ortiz won it with a two-run shot into the right field bullpen, sending the Fenway faithful into a frenzy and ensuring that Boston would play another day.

GAME 5

New York	0	1	0	0	0	3	0	0	0	0	0	0	0	0	**4**	**12**	**1**
Boston	2	0	0	0	0	2	0	0	0	0	0	0	0	1	**5**	**13**	**1**

W—Wakefield. **L**—Loaiza.
LOB—NY: 18; Bos:12. **2B**—NY: Jeter, Cairo, Clark; Bos: Bellhorn, Mientkiewicz. **HR**—NY: Williams; Bos: Ortiz. **S**—NY: Jeter. **SF**—Bos: Varitek. **GIDP**—NY: Sheffield; Bos: Ramirez, Cabrera. **CS**—Bos: Damon, Ortiz. **E**—NY: Jeter; Bos: Ramirez. **PB**—Bos: Varitek 3. **T**—5:49. **A**—35,120.

Recap: A stirring 14-inning endurance test that set a record for the longest game, by time (5:49), in playoff history, Game 5 featured Boston DH David Ortiz in the hero's role again as he blooped a pitch from Esteban Loaiza into centerfield with two out in the bottom of the 14th, sending Johnny Damon home from second with the winning run and giving Boston its second straight come-from-behind, extra-inning victory. Despite giving his catcher, Jason Varitek, fits, causing three passed balls in one inning, Boston knuckleballer Tim Wakefield pitched three scoreless innings to get the win.

GAME 6

Boston	0	0	0	4	0	0	0	0	0	**4**	**11**	**0**
New York	0	0	0	0	0	0	1	1	0	**2**	**6**	**0**

W—Schilling. **L**—Lieber. **SV**—Foulke. **LOB**—Bos: 7; NY: 6. **2B**—Bos: Millar; NY: Cairo 2. **HR**—Bos: Bellhorn; NY: Williams. **GIDP**—Bos: Bellhorn, Mueller. **HBP**—Bos: Mueller. **SB**—Bos: Cabrera. **T**—3:50. **A**—56,128.

Recap: Boston ace Curt Schilling produced a performance that may live forever in New England, pitching on the injured right ankle that had contributed to his poor outing in Game 1 and going seven superb innings, striking out four while allowing only one run. Television viewers could see blood staining Schilling's sock near his right ankle, the result of seepage through three sutures that had been sewn into the joint to stabilize its injured tendons. Schilling's counterpart, Jon Lieber, had one rocky inning, the fourth, when he gave up a three-run

American League Championship Series (Cont.)

GAME 6 (CONT.)

Recap (Cont.): homer to Mark Bellhorn and Boston took a 4–0 lead. Lieber and the New York bullpen held the Red Sox scoreless the rest of the way, but the Yankees were unable to rally, despite a seventh-inning homer by Bernie Williams and a couple of hits and one run off reliever Bronson Arroyo in the eighth. Boston closer Keith Foulke, taking the mound for the third consecutive night, sent a few waves of anxiety through the Boston faithful by giving up two walks in the ninth, but he eventually settled down and subdued the Yankees, striking out Tony Clark on a 3-2 pitch to end the game. The victory made the Red Sox the first team in major league history to rally from an 0–3 deficit to tie a seven-game series at 3–3, and added yet another intriguing chapter to baseball's most storied rivalry as the teams prepared for the climactic tilt at Yankee Stadium the following night.

GAME 7

Boston	2	4	0	2	0	0	0	1	1	**10**	**13**	**0**
New York	0	0	1	0	0	0	2	0	0	**3**	**5**	**1**

W—Lowe. **L**—Brown. **E**—NY: Loaiza. **LOB**—Bos: 9; NY: 5. **2B**—NY: Matsui, Williams. **HR**—Bos: Ortiz, Damon 2, Bellhorn. **SF**—Bos: Cabrera. **HBP**—NY: Cairo. **GIDP**—Bos: Damon. **SB**—Bos: Damon; NY: Cairo, Lofton. **T**—3:31. **A**—56,129.

Recap: Boston set the tone by jumping on New York starter Kevin Brown immediately, getting a two-run homer from David Ortiz in the first inning. While Brown

GAME 7 (CONT.)

Recap (Cont.): struggled, Red Sox righthander Derek Lowe, who'd been an inconsistent performer in 2004, sparkled despite pitching on two days' rest. Lowe thoroughly redeemed himself for any failings during the regular season, twirling a one-hitter over six innings and holding the mighty New York offense to one run. Another Boston player who seized redemption was leadoff man Johnny Damon, whose ALCS average stood at .106 at the start of the game. He exploded out of that slump by sending the first pitch from reliever Javier Vazquez—who had replaced Brown with the bases loaded and one out in the second inning—into the seats in rightfield for a grand slam that made it 6–0 Boston. The Sox never looked back: Damon added another first-pitch blast off Vazquez, a two-run shot in the third, and second baseman Mark Bellhorn went deep in the eighth. Bernie Williams and Kenny Lofton drove in runs for New York in the seventh, but there would be no Yankee miracle this time: The Red Sox slammed the door on years of bad memories in grand style, not only routing their archnemesis to advance to the World Series, but also becoming the first team in baseball history to win a seven-game series after falling behind three games to none. Ortiz was named MVP of the series, in which he smacked two game-winning hits and batted .387 with three home runs and 11 RBIs. Boston advanced to the Fall Classic for the first time since 1986.

2004 World Series

(Boston won series 4–0)

GAME 1

St. Louis	0	1	1	3	0	2	0	2	0	**9**	**11**	**1**
Boston	4	0	3	0	0	0	2	2	x	**11**	**13**	**4**

W—Foulke. **L**—Tavarez. **LOB**—Stl: 9, Bos: 12. **2B**—StL: Walker 2, Renteria, Anderson; Bos: Damon, Millar. **HR**—StL: Walker; Bos: Ortiz, Bellhorn. **S**—Stl: Womack. **SF**—Stl: Matheny 2. **GIDP**—Stl: Rolen. **HBP**—Stl: Pujols; Bos: Cabrera. **E**—StL: Renteria; Bos: Millar, Arroyo, Ramirez 2. **PB**—Bos: Mirabelli. **T**—4:00. **A**—35,035.

Recap: Boston second baseman Mark Bellhorn launched a two-run shot off the foul pole in right field in the bottom of the eighth to provide the difference in this one, the highest scoring opener in the history of the Fall Classic. The Red Sox jumped out to a 4–0 lead in the first, powered by David Ortiz's three-run homer. They added three more in the third to take a 7–2 lead, but the Cardinals answered in the fourth with three of their own, aided by Boston third baseman Kevin Millar's throwing error. Two errors in the top of the eighth by Red Sox leftfielder Manny Ramirez allowed St. Louis to tie the score at 9, setting the stage for Bellhorn's heroics. Keith Foulke pitched an inning and two-thirds of scoreless relief for the win.

GAME 2

St. Louis	0	0	0	1	0	0	0	1	0	**2**	**5**	**0**
Boston	2	0	0	2	0	2	0	0	x	**6**	**8**	**4**

W—Schilling. **L**—Morris. **LOB**—Stl: 6; Bos: 9. **2B**—StL: Pujols 2; Bos: Mueller, Bellhorn. **3B**—StL: Varitek. **SF**—StL: Rolen. **GIDP**—Stl: Renteria; Bos: Bellhorn. **HBP**—Bos: Millar, Varitek. **E**—Bos: Mueller 3, Bellhorn. **T**—3:20. **A**—35,001.

Recap: As he did in Game 6 of the ALCS against New York, Boston stopper Curt Schilling underwent a pregame procedure on his right ankle to secure its damaged tendons with sutures. With blood once again seeping through his sock, the righthander pitched six solid innings, giving up four hits and one unearned run while striking out four. His teammates scored two runs in the first and took a 6–1 lead into the eighth before turning to relievers Mike Timlin and Keith Foulke.

GAME 3

Boston	1 0 0	1 2 0	0 0 0	**4 9 0**
St. Louis	0 0 0	0 0 0	0 0 1	**1 4 0**

W—Martinez. **L**—Suppan.
LOB—Bos: 8; Stl: 3. **2B**—Bos: Mueller, Damon, Cabrera; Stl: Renteria. **HR**—Bos: Ramirez; StL: Walker. **GIDP**—Bos: Damon, Mueller. **HBP**—Bos: Bellhorn. **T**—2:58. **A**—52,015.

Recap: Boston leftfielder Manny Ramirez crushed a solo home run in the top of the first, then threw out Larry Walker at home plate in the bottom of the inning as the St. Louis rightfielder tried to score from third on a fly ball with the bases loaded and one out. Making his first World Series appearance, Red Sox righthander Pedro Martinez produced an excellent performance, holding the Cardinals scoreless through seven innings and giving up only three hits. Ramirez drove in another run in the fifth, and Boston took a 4–0 lead into the bottom of the ninth, when closer Keith Foulke surrendered his first run of the postseason, a home run to Walker, before recovering to strike out St. Louis third baseman Scott Rolen to end the game and put the Red Sox one win away from their first title in 86 years.

GAME 4

Boston	1 0 2	0 0 0	0 0 0	**3 9 0**
St. Louis	0 0 0	0 0 0	0 0 0	**0 4 0**

W—Lowe. **L**—Marquis. **SV**—Foulke.
LOB—Bos: 12; Stl: 6. **2B**—Bos: Nixon 2, Ortiz; Stl: Renteria. **3B**—Bos: Damon. **HR**—Bos: Damon. **S**—Bos: Lowe; StL: Walker. **SB**—StL: Sanders. **WP**—Bos: Lowe. **T**—3:14. **A**—52,037.

Recap: Taking the mound with a chance to clinch a series for the third time in the 2004 playoffs, Boston righthander Derek Lowe delivered, pitching seven shutout innings and giving up only three hits while striking out four. Boston leadoff man Johnny Damon ensured that the Red Sox got off on the right foot in the last stage of their quest to win their first title in 86 years, blasting a home run on the fourth pitch of the game. Trot Nixon belted a two-run double in the third and that was all the offense Boston needed as Lowe and the bullpen shut down the Cardinals. Red Sox closer Keith Foulke got the save and finished the postseason with only one run allowed in 14 innings. Said Game 2 winner Curt Schilling, "I'm happy for the fans in Boston, I'm happy for Johnny Pesky, for Bill Buckner, for [Bob] Stanley and [Calvin] Schiraldi and all the great Red Sox players who can now be remembered for the great players that they were." Lowe, who redeemed a rocky regular season with his postseason heroics, said, "Unbelievable—no more going to Yankee Stadium and having to listen to '1918.'"

2004 World Series Composite Box Score

ST. LOUIS

BATTING	AB	R	H	HR	RBI	Avg
Walker	14	2	5	2	3	.357
Pujols	15	1	5	0	0	.333
Renteria	15	2	5	0	1	.333
Matheny	8	0	2	0	2	.250
Cedeno	4	1	1	0	0	.250
Taguchi	4	1	1	0	1	.250
Womack	11	1	2	0	0	.182
Anderson	6	0	1	0	0	.167
Edmonds	15	2	1	0	0	.067
Rolen	15	0	0	0	1	.000
Molina	3	0	0	0	0	.000
Mabry	4	0	0	0	0	.000
Sanders	9	1	0	0	0	.000
Luna	1	0	0	0	0	.000
Pitchers	3	0	1	0	0	.333
Totals	**126**	**12**	**24**	**2**	**8**	**.190**

PITCHING	G	IP	H	BB	SO	ERA
Haren	2	4⅔	4	3	2	0.00
King	3	2⅔	1	1	1	0.00
Isringhausen	1	2	1	1	2	0.00
Reyes	2	1⅓	0	0	0	0.00
Marquis (0–1)	2	7	6	7	4	3.86
Tavarez (0–1)	2	2	1	0	1	4.50
Suppan (0–1)	1	4⅔	8	1	4	7.71
Morris (0–1)	1	4⅓	4	4	3	8.31
Eldred	2	1⅔	4	0	2	10.80
Calero	2	1⅓	2	4	0	13.50
Williams	1	2⅓	8	3	1	27.00
Totals	**4**	**34**	**39**	**24**	**20**	**6.09**

BOSTON

BATTING	AB	R	H	HR	RBI	Avg
Mueller	14	3	6	0	2	.429
Ramirez	17	2	7	1	4	.412
Nixon	14	1	5	0	3	.357
Mirabelli	3	1	1	0	0	.333
Ortiz	13	3	4	1	4	.308
Bellhorn	10	3	3	1	4	.300
Damon	21	4	6	1	2	.286
Cabrera	17	3	4	0	3	.235
Varitek	13	2	2	0	2	.154
Millar	8	2	1	0	0	.125
Kapler	2	0	0	0	0	.000
Mientkiewicz	1	0	0	0	0	.000
Reese	1	0	0	0	0	.000
Pitchers	4	0	0	0	0	.000
Totals	**138**	**24**	**39**	**4**	**24**	**.283**

PITCHING	G	IP	H	BB	SO	ERA
Martinez (1–0)	1	7	3	2	6	0.00
Lowe (1–0)	1	7	3	1	4	0.00
Schilling (1–0)	1	6	4	1	4	0.00
Embree	3	1⅔	1	0	4	0.00
Foulke (1-0, 1 sv)	4	5	4	1	8	1.80
Timlin	3	3	2	1	0	6.00
Arroyo	2	2⅔	4	1	4	6.75
Wakefield	1	3⅔	3	5	2	12.27
Totals	**4**	**36**	**24**	**12**	**32**	**2.50**

National League Batting

BATTING AVERAGE

Barry Bonds, SF .... .362
Todd Helton, Col .... .347
Mark Loretta, SD .... .335
Adrian Beltre, LA .... .334
Albert Pujols, StL .... .331
Juan Pierre, Fla .... .326
Sean Casey, Cin .... .324
Jason Kendall, Pitt .... .319
Aramis Ramirez, Chi .... .318
Lance Berkman, Hou .... .316

HITS

Juan Pierre, Fla 221
Mark Loretta, SD 208
Jack Wilson, Pitt 201
Adrian Beltre, LA 200
Albert Pujols, StL 196
Cesar Izturis, LA 193
Jimmy Rollins, Phil 190
Todd Helton, Col 190
Sean Casey, Cin 185
Jason Kendall, Pitt 183

DOUBLES

Lyle Overbay, Mil 53
Albert Pujols, StL 51
Todd Helton, Col 49
Mark Loretta, SD 47
Bobby Abreu, Phil 47
Craig Biggio, Hou 47

TRIPLES

Jimmy Rollins, Phil 12
Jack Wilson, Pitt 12
Juan Pierre, Fla 12
Cesar Izturis, LA 9
Carlos Beltran, Hou 9

HOME RUNS

Adrian Beltre, LA 48
Adam Dunn, Cin 46
Albert Pujols, StL 46
Barry Bonds, SF 45
Jim Edmonds, StL 42
Jim Thome, Phil 42
Moises Alou, Chi 39
Carlos Beltran, Hou 38
Jeromy Burnitz, Col 37
Steve Finley, LA 36
Aramis Ramirez, Chi 36

RUNS SCORED

Albert Pujols, StL 133
Barry Bonds, SF 129
Carlos Beltran, Hou 121
Jimmy Rollins, Phil 119
J.D. Drew, Atl 118
Bobby Abreu, Phil 118
Todd Helton, Col 115
Brad Wilkerson, Mtl 112
Scott Rolen, StL 109
Mark Loretta, SD 108

STOLEN BASES

Scott Podsednik, Mil 70
Juan Pierre, Fla 45
Carlos Beltran, Hou 42
Bobby Abreu, Phil 40
Ryan Freel, Cin 37

RUNS BATTED IN

Vinny Castilla, Col 131
Scott Rolen, StL 124
Albert Pujols, StL 123
Adrian Beltre, LA 121
Miguel Cabrera, Fla 112
Jim Edmonds, StL 111
Tony Batista, Mtl 110

RUNS BATTED IN (CONT.)

Jeromy Burnitz, Col 110
Jeff Kent, Hou 107
Lance Berkman, Hou 106
Moises Alou, Chi 106

SLUGGING PERCENTAGE

Barry Bonds, SF .... .812
Albert Pujols, StL .... .657
Jim Edmonds, StL .... .643
Adrian Beltre, LA .... .629
Todd Helton, Col .... .620

ON-BASE PERCENTAGE

Barry Bonds, SF .... .609
Todd Helton, Col .... .469
Lance Berkman, Hou .... .450
J.D. Drew, Atl .... .436
Bobby Abreu, Phil .... .428

BASES ON BALLS

Barry Bonds, SF 232
Todd Helton, Col 127
Lance Berkman, Hou 127
Bobby Abreu, Phil 127
J.D. Drew, Atl 118

National League Pitching

EARNED RUN AVERAGE

Jake Peavy, SD 2.27
Randy Johnson, Ariz 2.60
Ben Sheets, Mil 2.70
Carlos Zambrano, Chi 2.75
Roger Clemens, Hou 2.98
Oliver Perez, Pitt 2.98
Carl Pavano, Fla 3.00
Jason Schmidt, SF 3.20
Al Leiter, NY 3.21
Odalis Perez, LA 3.25

SAVES

Armando Benitez, Fla 47
Jason Isringhausen, StL 47
Eric Gagne, LA 45
John Smoltz, Atl 44
Jose Mesa, Pitt 43
Trevor Hoffman, SD 41
Danny Graves, Cin 41
Dan Kolb, Mil 39
Shawn Chacon, Col 35
Brad Lidge, Hou 29

WINS

Roy Oswalt, Hou 20
Carl Pavano, Fla 18
Jason Schmidt, SF 18
Roger Clemens, Hou 18
Jeff Suppan, StL 16
Randy Johnson, Ariz 16
Carlos Zambrano, Chi 16
Greg Maddux, Chi 16

Eight tied with 15.

GAMES PITCHED

Jim Brower, SF 89
Ray King, StL 86
Salomon Torres, Pitt 84
Rheal Cormier, Phil 84
Chris Reitsma, Atl 84

INNINGS PITCHED

Livan Hernandez, Mtl 255
Randy Johnson, Ariz 245⅔
Ben Sheets, Mil 237
Roy Oswalt, Hou 237
Jason Schmidt, SF 225

STRIKEOUTS

Randy Johnson, Ariz 290
Ben Sheets, Mil 264
Jason Schmidt, SF 251
Oliver Perez, Pitt 239
Roger Clemens, Hou 218
Roy Oswalt, Hou 206
Matt Clement, Chi 190
Carlos Zambrano, Chi 188
Livan Hernandez, Mtl 186
Jake Peavy, SD 173

COMPLETE GAMES

Livan Hernandez, Mtl 9
Cory Lidle, Phil 5
Ben Sheets, Mil 5
Jason Schmidt, SF 4
Randy Johnson, Ariz 4

SHUTOUTS

Jason Schmidt, SF 3
Cory Lidle, Phil 3

Six tied with 2.

American League Batting

BATTING AVERAGE

Ichiro Suzuki, Sea	.372
Melvin Mora, Balt	.340
Vladimir Guerrero, Ana	.337
Ivan Rodriguez, Det	.334
Erubiel Durazo, Oak	.321
Carlos Guillen, Det	.318
Javy Lopez, Balt	.316
Mark Kotsay, Oak	.314
Michael Young, Tex	.313
Travis Hafner, Clev	.311
Miguel Tejada, Balt	.311

HITS

Ichiro Suzuki, Sea	262
Michael Young, Tex	216
Vladimir Guerrero, Ana	206
Miguel Tejada, Balt	203
Mark Kotsay, Oak	190
Johnny Damon, Bos	189
Derek Jeter, NY	188
Melvin Mora, Balt	187
Carl Crawford, TB	185
Javy Lopez, Balt	183

DOUBLES

Brian Roberts, Balt	50
Ronnie Belliard, Clev	48
David Ortiz, Bos	47
Manny Ramirez, Bos	44
Derek Jeter, NY	44

TRIPLES

Carl Crawford, TB	19
Chone Figgins, Ana	17
Carlos Guillen, Det	10
Michael Young, Tex	9
Omar Infante, Det	9

HOME RUNS

Manny Ramirez, Bos	43
David Ortiz, Bos	41
Paul Konerko, Chi	41
Vladimir Guerrero, Ana	39
Mark Teixeira, Tex	38
Alex Rodriguez, NY	36
Gary Sheffield, NY	36
Miguel Tejada, Balt	34
Hank Blalock, Tex	32
Carlos Delgado, Tor	32

RUNS SCORED

Vladimir Guerrero, Ana	124
Johnny Damon, Bos	123
Gary Sheffield, NY	117
Michael Young, Tex	114
Alex Rodriguez, NY	112
Melvin Mora, Balt	111
Derek Jeter, NY	111
Hideki Matsui, NY	109
Matt Lawton, Clev	109
Manny Ramirez, Bos	108

STOLEN BASES

Carl Crawford, TB	59
Dave Roberts, Bos	38
Ichiro Suzuki, Sea	36
Chone Figgins, Ana	34
Brian Roberts, Balt	29

RUNS BATTED IN

Miguel Tejada, Balt	150
David Ortiz, Bos	139
Manny Ramirez, Bos	130
Vladimir Guerrero, Ana	126
Gary Sheffield, NY	121

RUNS BATTED IN *(CONT.)*

Paul Konerko, Chi	117
Mark Teixeira, Tex	112
Hank Blalock, Tex	110
Travis Hafner, Clev	109
Hideki Matsui, NY	108
Victor Martinez, Clev	108

SLUGGING PERCENTAGE

Manny Ramirez, Bos	.613
David Ortiz, Bos	.603
Vladimir Guerrero, Ana	.598
Travis Hafner, Clev	.583
Melvin Mora, Balt	.562

ON-BASE PERCENTAGE

Melvin Mora, Balt	.419
Ichiro Suzuki, Sea	.414
Travis Hafner, Clev	.410
Jorge Posada, NY	.400
Manny Ramirez, Bos	.397
Eric Chavez, Oak	.397

BASES ON BALLS

Eric Chavez, Oak	95
Gary Sheffield, NY	92
Jorge Posada, NY	88
Mark Bellhorn, Bos	88
Hideki Matsui, NY	88

American League Pitching

EARNED RUN AVERAGE

Johan Santana, Minn	2.61
Curt Schilling, Bos	3.26
Jake Westbrook, Clev	3.38
Brad Radke, Minn	3.48
Tim Hudson, Oak	3.53
Rodrigo Lopez, Balt	3.59
Mark Buehrle, Chi	3.89
Pedro Martinez, Bos	3.90
Kelvim Escobar, Ana	3.93
Rich Harden, Oak	3.99

SAVES

Mariano Rivera, NY	53
Francisco Cordero, Tex	49
Joe Nathan, Minn	44
Octavio Dotel, Oak	36
Troy Percival, Ana	33
Keith Foulke, Bos	32
Danys Baez, TB	30
Jorge Julio, Balt	22
Ugueth Urbina, Det	21
Shingo Takatsu, Chi	19

WINS

Curt Schilling, Bos	21
Johan Santana, Minn	20
Kenny Rogers, Tex	18
Bartolo Colon, Ana	18
Mark Mulder, Oak	17
Pedro Martinez, Bos	16
Mark Buehrle, Chi	16

Nine tied with 14.

GAMES PITCHED

Paul Quantrill, NY	86
Tom Gordon, NY	80
Octavio Dotel, Oak	77
Juan Rincon, Minn	77
B.J. Ryan, Balt	76
Mike Timlin, Bos	76

SHUTOUTS

Jeremy Bonderman, Det	2
Sidney Ponson, Balt	2
Tim Hudson, Oak	2

STRIKEOUTS

Johan Santana, Minn	265
Pedro Martinez, Bos	227
Curt Schilling, Bos	203
Kelvim Escobar, Ana	191
Freddy Garcia, Chi	184
Ted Lilly, Tor	168
Jeremy Bonderman, Det	168
Rich Harden, Oak	167
Mark Buehrle, Chi	165
Barry Zito, Oak	163

INNINGS PITCHED

Mark Buehrle, Chi	245⅓
Johan Santana, Minn	228
Curt Schilling, Bos	226⅔
Mark Mulder, Oak	225⅔
Brad Radke, Minn	219⅔

COMPLETE GAMES

Sidney Ponson, Balt	5
Mark Mulder, Oak	5
Jake Westbrook, Clev	5
Mark Buehrle, Chi	4

Three tied with 3.

National League

TEAM BATTING

TEAM BATTING	G	AB	R	H	2B	3B	HR	TB	RBI	BA	OBP	SLG	OPS
St. Louis	162	5555	855	1544	319	24	214	2553	817	.278	.344	.460	.804
Colorado	162	5577	833	1531	331	34	202	2536	795	.275	.345	.455	.800
San Diego	162	5573	768	1521	304	32	139	2306	722	.273	.342	.414	.756
San Francisco	162	5546	850	1500	314	33	183	2429	805	.270	.357	.438	.795
Atlanta	162	5570	803	1503	304	37	178	2415	767	.270	.343	.434	.777
Chicago	162	5628	789	1508	308	29	235	2579	755	.268	.328	.458	.786
Philadelphia	162	5643	840	1505	303	23	215	2499	802	.267	.345	.443	.788
Houston	162	5468	803	1458	294	36	187	2385	756	.267	.342	.436	.778
Florida	162	5486	718	1447	275	32	148	2230	677	.264	.329	.406	.736
Los Angeles	162	5542	761	1450	226	30	203	2345	731	.262	.332	.423	.755
Pittsburgh	161	5483	680	1428	267	39	142	2199	648	.260	.321	.401	.722
Arizona	162	5544	615	1401	295	38	135	2177	582	.253	.310	.393	.703
Cincinnati	162	5518	750	1380	287	28	194	2305	713	.250	.331	.418	.749
NY Mets	162	5532	684	1376	289	20	185	2260	658	.249	.317	.409	.726
Montreal	162	5474	635	1361	276	27	151	2144	605	.249	.313	.392	.705
Milwaukee	161	5483	634	1358	295	32	135	2122	601	.248	.321	.387	.708

TEAM PITCHING

TEAM PITCHING	GP	W	L	SV	SVO	CG	SO	R	ERA	IP	Ks	BB
Atlanta	162	96	66	48	68	4	13	668	3.74	1450.0	1025	523
St. Louis	162	105	57	57	73	4	12	659	3.75	1453.2	1041	440
Chicago	162	89	73	42	66	3	6	665	3.81	1465.1	1346	545
Los Angeles	162	93	69	51	60	2	6	684	4.01	1453.1	1066	521
San Diego	162	87	75	44	64	3	8	705	4.03	1441.0	1079	422
Houston	162	92	70	47	70	2	13	698	4.05	1443.0	1282	525
New York	162	71	91	31	53	2	6	731	4.09	1449.0	977	592
Florida	162	83	79	53	75	6	14	700	4.10	1439.0	1116	513
Milwaukee	161	67	94	42	64	6	10	757	4.24	1442.0	1098	476
Pittsburgh	161	72	89	46	69	3	8	744	4.29	1428.0	1079	576
San Francisco	162	91	71	46	74	8	8	770	4.29	1457.0	1020	548
Montreal	162	67	95	31	49	11	11	769	4.33	1447.0	1032	582
Philadelphia	162	86	76	43	68	4	5	781	4.45	1462.2	1070	502
Arizona	162	51	111	33	55	5	6	899	4.98	1436.0	1153	668
Cincinnati	162	76	86	47	78	5	8	907	5.19	1443.2	992	572
Colorado	162	68	94	36	70	3	2	923	5.54	1435.1	947	697

Note: OPS is on-base percentage plus slugging percentage.

American League

TEAM BATTING

TEAM BATTING	G	AB	R	H	2B	3B	HR	TB	RBI	BA	OBP	SLG	OPS
Boston	162	5720	949	1613	373	25	222	2702	912	.282	.360	.472	.832
Anaheim	162	5675	836	1603	272	37	162	2435	783	.282	.341	.429	.770
Baltimore	162	5736	842	1614	319	18	169	2476	803	.281	.345	.432	.776
Cleveland	162	5676	858	1565	345	29	184	2520	820	.276	.351	.444	.795
Detroit	162	5623	827	1531	284	54	201	2526	800	.272	.337	.449	.786
Seattle	162	5722	698	1544	276	20	136	2268	658	.270	.331	.396	.727
Oakland	162	5728	793	1545	336	15	189	2478	752	.270	.343	.433	.776
New York	162	5527	897	1483	281	20	242	2530	863	.268	.353	.458	.811
Chicago	162	5534	865	1481	284	19	242	2529	823	.268	.333	.457	.790
Texas	162	5615	860	1492	323	34	227	2564	825	.266	.329	.457	.786
Minnesota	162	5623	780	1494	310	24	191	2425	735	.266	.332	.431	.763
Toronto	161	5531	719	1438	290	34	145	2231	680	.260	.328	.403	.732
Kansas City	162	5538	720	1432	261	29	150	2201	675	.259	.322	.397	.720
Tampa Bay	162	5483	714	1416	278	46	145	2221	685	.258	.320	.405	.725

TEAM PITCHING

TEAM PITCHING	GP	W	L	SV	SVO	CG	SO	R	ERA	IP	Ks	BB
Minnesota	162	92	70	48	68	4	9	715	4.03	1476.0	1123	431
Oakland	162	91	71	35	63	10	8	742	4.17	1471.1	1034	544
Boston	162	98	64	36	49	4	12	768	4.18	1451.1	1132	447
Anaheim	162	92	70	50	67	2	11	734	4.28	1454.1	1164	502
Texas	162	89	73	52	66	5	9	794	4.53	1439.2	979	547
New York	162	101	61	59	76	1	5	808	4.69	1443.2	1058	445
Baltimore	162	78	84	27	47	8	10	830	4.70	1455.1	1090	687
Seattle	162	63	99	28	49	7	7	823	4.76	1459.1	1036	575
Cleveland	162	80	82	32	60	8	8	857	4.81	1466.2	1115	579
Tampa Bay	161	70	91	35	45	3	5	842	4.81	1417.0	923	580
Chicago	162	83	79	34	46	8	8	831	4.91	1432.1	1013	527
Toronto	161	67	94	37	53	6	11	823	4.91	1421.0	956	608
Detroit	162	72	90	35	64	7	9	844	4.93	1439.2	995	530
Kansas City	162	58	104	25	47	6	3	905	5.15	1420.1	887	518

Note: OPS is on-base percentage plus slugging percentage.

National League Team-by-Team Statistical Leaders

Arizona Diamondbacks

BATTING	G	AB	R	H	2B	3B	HR	RBI	TB	BB	SO	SB	OBP	SLG	BA
Alex Cintron	154	564	56	148	31	7	4	49	205	31	59	3	.301	.363	.262
Shea Hillenbrand	148	562	68	174	36	3	15	80	261	24	49	2	.348	.464	.310
Danny Bautista	141	539	64	154	27	1	11	65	216	35	66	6	.332	.401	.286
Chad Tracy	143	481	45	137	29	3	8	53	196	45	60	2	.343	.407	.285
Luis Gonzalez	105	379	69	98	28	5	17	48	187	68	58	2	.373	.493	.259
Scott Hairston	101	339	39	84	15	6	13	29	150	21	88	3	.293	.442	.248
Luis Terrero	62	229	21	56	14	0	4	14	82	20	78	10	.319	.358	.245
Robby Hammock	62	195	22	47	16	2	4	18	79	13	39	3	.287	.405	.241
Juan Brito	54	171	17	35	7	0	3	12	51	9	41	1	.246	.298	.205
Matt Kata	42	162	17	40	9	2	2	13	59	13	29	4	.301	.364	.247
Quinton McCracken	55	156	20	45	11	1	2	13	64	13	23	2	.341	.410	.288
Roberto Alomar	38	110	14	34	5	2	3	16	52	12	18	0	.382	.473	.309

PITCHING	GP	GS	W–L	SV	SHO	R	ERA	IP	Ks	BB
Randy Johnson	35	35	16–14	0	2	88	2.60	245.2	290	44
Brandon Webb	35	35	7–16	0	0	111	3.59	208.0	164	119
Casey Fossum	27	27	4–15	0	0	111	6.65	142.0	117	63
Steve W. Sparks	29	18	3–7	0	0	89	6.04	120.2	57	45
Jeff Fassero	41	12	3–8	0	0	73	5.46	112.0	60	44
Mike Koplove	76	0	4–4	2	0	42	4.05	86.2	55	37
Stephen Randolph	45	6	2–5	0	0	56	5.51	81.2	62	76
Chad Durbin	24	8	6–7	0	0	50	6.97	60.2	48	35
Randy Choate	74	0	2–4	0	0	26	4.62	50.2	49	28

Atlanta Braves

BATTING	G	AB	R	H	2B	3B	HR	RBI	TB	BB	SO	SB	OBP	SLG	BA
Andruw Jones	154	570	85	149	34	4	29	91	278	71	147	6	.345	.488	.261
Rafael Furcal	143	563	103	157	24	5	14	59	233	58	71	29	.344	.414	.279
J.D. Drew	145	518	118	158	28	8	31	93	295	118	116	12	.436	.569	.305
Chipper Jones	137	472	69	117	20	1	30	96	229	84	96	2	.362	.485	.248
Johnny Estrada	134	462	56	145	36	0	9	76	208	39	66	0	.378	.450	.314
Marcus Giles	102	379	61	118	22	2	8	48	168	36	70	17	.378	.444	.311
Adam LaRoche	110	324	45	90	27	1	13	45	158	27	78	0	.333	.488	.278
Julio Franco	125	320	37	99	18	3	6	57	141	36	68	4	.378	.441	.309
Mark DeRosa	118	309	33	74	16	0	3	31	99	23	53	1	.293	.320	.239
Nick Green	95	264	40	72	15	3	3	26	102	12	63	1	.312	.386	.273
Eli Marrero	90	250	37	80	18	1	10	40	130	23	50	4	.374	.520	.320
Charles Thomas	83	236	35	68	8	4	7	31	105	21	45	3	.368	.445	.288
Eddie Perez	74	170	14	39	12	0	3	13	60	11	29	0	.286	.353	.229

PITCHING	GP	GS	W–L	SV	SHO	R	ERA	IP	Ks	BB
Russ Ortiz	34	34	15–9	0	1	98	4.13	204.2	143	112
John Thomson	33	33	14–8	0	0	93	3.72	198.1	133	52
Jaret Wright	32	32	15–8	0	0	79	3.28	186.1	159	70
Mike Hampton	29	29	13–9	0	0	86	4.28	172.1	87	65
Paul Byrd	19	19	8–7	0	0	57	3.94	114.1	79	19
John Smoltz	73	0	0–1	44	0	25	2.76	81.2	85	13
Chris Reitsma	84	0	6–4	2	0	38	4.07	79.2	60	20
Antonio Alfonseca	79	0	6–4	0	0	24	2.57	73.2	45	28
Juan Cruz	50	0	6–0	0	0	24	2.75	72.0	70	30
Horacio Ramirez	10	9	2–4	0	0	24	2.39	60.1	31	30
Kevin Gryboski	69	0	3–2	2	0	22	2.84	50.2	24	23
Tom Martin	76	0	0–2	1	0	20	3.97	45.1	30	19

Chicago Cubs

BATTING	G	AB	R	H	2B	3B	HR	RBI	TB	BB	SO	SB	OBP	SLG	BA
Corey Patterson	157	631	91	168	33	6	24	72	285	45	168	32	.320	.452	.266
Derrek Lee	161	605	90	168	39	1	32	98	305	68	128	12	.356	.504	.278
Moises Alou	155	601	106	176	36	3	39	106	335	68	80	3	.361	.557	.293
Aramis Ramirez	145	547	99	174	32	1	36	103	316	49	62	0	.373	.578	.318
Sammy Sosa	126	478	69	121	21	0	35	80	247	56	133	0	.332	.517	.253
Michael Barrett	134	456	55	131	32	6	16	65	223	33	64	1	.337	.489	.287
Neifi Perez	126	381	40	97	17	1	4	39	128	24	41	1	.296	.336	.255
Todd Walker	129	372	60	102	19	4	15	50	174	43	52	0	.352	.468	.274
Ramon Martinez	102	260	22	64	15	1	3	30	90	26	40	1	.313	.346	.246
Mark Grudzielanek	81	257	32	79	12	1	6	23	111	15	32	1	.347	.432	.307
Ben Grieve	123	250	30	65	17	0	8	35	106	39	70	0	.361	.424	.260
Jose Macias	98	194	23	52	6	3	3	22	73	5	38	4	.292	.376	.268
Nomar Garciaparra	43	165	28	49	14	0	4	20	75	16	14	2	.364	.455	.297
Todd Hollandsworth	57	148	28	47	6	2	8	22	81	17	26	1	.392	.547	.318

Chicago Cubs *(Cont.)*

PITCHING	GP	GS	W–L	SV	SHO	R	ERA	IP	Ks	BB
Greg Maddux	33	33	16–11	0	1	103	4.02	212.2	151	33
Carlos Zambrano	31	31	16–8	0	1	73	2.75	209.2	188	81
Matt Clement	30	30	9–13	0	0	79	3.68	181.0	190	77
Kerry Wood	22	22	8–9	0	0	62	3.72	140.1	144	51
Glendon Rusch	32	16	6–2	2	0	54	3.47	129.2	90	33
Mark Prior	21	21	6–4	0	0	53	4.02	118.2	139	48
LaTroy Hawkins	77	0	5–4	25	0	27	2.63	82.0	69	14
Kyle Farnsworth	72	0	4–5	0	0	39	4.73	66.2	78	33
Kent Mercker	71	0	3–1	0	0	15	2.55	53.0	51	27

Cincinnati Reds

BATTING	G	AB	R	H	2B	3B	HR	RBI	TB	BB	SO	SB	OBP	SLG	BA
Sean Casey	146	571	101	185	44	2	24	99	305	46	36	2	.381	.534	.324
Adam Dunn	161	568	105	151	34	0	46	102	323	108	195	6	.388	.569	.266
D'Angelo Jimenez	152	563	76	152	28	3	12	67	222	82	99	13	.364	.394	.270
Ryan Freel	143	505	74	140	21	8	3	28	186	67	88	37	.375	.368	.277
Jason LaRue	114	390	46	98	24	2	14	55	168	26	108	0	.334	.431	.251
Barry Larkin	111	346	55	100	15	3	8	44	145	34	39	2	.352	.419	.289
Wily Mo Pena	110	336	45	87	10	1	26	66	177	22	108	5	.316	.527	.259
Ken Griffey Jr.	83	300	49	76	18	0	20	60	154	44	67	1	.351	.513	.253
Juan Castro	111	299	36	73	21	2	5	26	113	14	51	1	.277	.378	.244
Felipe Lopez	79	264	35	64	18	2	7	31	107	25	81	1	.314	.405	.242
Austin Kearns	64	217	28	50	10	2	9	32	91	28	71	2	.321	.419	.230
Javier Valentin	82	202	18	47	10	1	6	20	77	17	36	0	.293	.381	.233
Jacob Cruz	96	147	22	33	8	0	3	28	50	16	43	0	.317	.340	.224

PITCHING	GP	GS	W–L	SV	SHO	R	ERA	IP	Ks	BB
Paul Wilson	29	29	11–6	0	0	93	4.36	183.2	117	63
Aaron Harang	28	28	10–9	0	1	90	4.86	161.0	125	53
Jose Acevedo	39	27	5–12	0	0	108	5.94	157.2	117	45
Todd Van Poppel	48	11	4–6	0	0	80	6.09	115.1	72	32
John Riedling	70	0	5–3	0	0	54	5.10	77.2	46	40
Danny Graves	68	0	1–6	41	0	39	3.95	68.1	40	13
Brandon Claussen	14	14	2–8	0	0	50	6.14	66.0	45	35
Phil Norton	69	0	2–5	0	0	41	5.07	65.2	48	38
Josh Hancock	16	11	5–2	0	0	43	5.09	63.2	36	28
Gabe White	64	0	1–3	1	0	46	6.94	59.2	41	12
Ryan Wagner	49	0	3–2	0	0	31	4.70	51.2	37	27

Colorado Rockies

BATTING	G	AB	R	H	2B	3B	HR	RBI	TB	BB	SO	SB	OBP	SLG	BA
Vinny Castilla	148	583	93	158	43	3	35	131	312	51	113	0	.332	.535	.271
Royce Clayton	146	574	95	160	36	4	8	54	228	48	125	10	.338	.397	.279
Todd Helton	154	547	115	190	49	2	32	96	339	127	72	3	.469	.620	.347
Jeromy Burnitz	150	540	94	153	30	4	37	110	302	58	124	5	.356	.559	.283
Aaron Miles	134	522	75	153	15	3	6	47	192	29	53	12	.329	.368	.293
Matt Holliday	121	400	53	116	31	3	14	57	195	31	86	3	.349	.488	.290
Luis Gonzalez	102	322	42	94	17	2	12	40	151	15	67	1	.330	.469	.292
Charles Johnson	109	305	42	72	20	0	13	47	131	49	91	2	.350	.430	.236
Preston Wilson	58	202	24	50	11	0	6	29	79	17	49	2	.315	.391	.248
Todd Greene	75	195	23	55	14	0	10	35	99	13	38	0	.325	.508	.282
Mark Sweeney	122	177	25	47	12	2	9	40	90	32	51	1	.377	.508	.266

PITCHING	GP	GS	W–L	SV	SHO	R	ERA	IP	Ks	BB
Shawn Estes	34	34	15–8	0	0	133	5.84	202.0	117	105
Jason Jennings	33	33	11–12	0	0	125	5.51	201.0	133	101
Joe Kennedy	27	27	9–7	0	0	68	3.66	162.1	117	67
Aaron Cook	16	16	6–4	0	0	47	4.28	96.2	40	39
Jamey Wright	14	14	2–3	0	0	39	4.12	78.2	41	45
Steve Reed	65	0	3–8	0	0	29	3.68	66.0	38	17
Shawn Chacon	66	0	1–9	35	0	52	7.11	63.1	52	52
Tim Harikkala	55	0	6–6	0	0	34	4.74	62.2	30	23

Florida Marlins

BATTING	G	AB	R	H	2B	3B	HR	RBI	TB	BB	SO	SB	OBP	SLG	BA
Juan Pierre	162	678	100	221	22	12	3	49	276	45	35	45	.374	.407	.326
Miguel Cabrera	160	603	101	177	31	1	33	.112	309	68	148	5	.366	.512	.294
Mike Lowell	158	598	87	175	44	1	27	85	302	64	77	5	.365	.505	.293
Luis Castillo	150	564	91	164	12	7	2	47	196	75	68	21	.373	.348	.291
Alex Gonzalez	159	561	67	130	30	3	23	79	235	27	126	3	.270	.419	.232
Paul Lo Duca	143	535	68	153	29	2	13	80	225	36	49	4	.338	.421	.286
Jeff Conine	140	521	55	146	35	1	14	83	225	48	78	5	.340	.432	.280
Juan Encarnacion	135	484	63	114	30	2	16	62	196	38	86	5	.299	.405	.236
Mike Redmond	81	246	19	63	15	0	2	25	84	14	28	1	.315	.341	.256
Damion Easley	98	223	26	53	20	1	9	43	102	24	36	4	.331	.457	.238

PITCHING	GP	GS	W–L	SV	SHO	R	ERA	IP	Ks	BB
Carl Pavano	31	31	18–8	0	2	80	3.00	222.1	139	49
Dontrelle Willis	32	32	10–11	0	0	99	4.02	197.0	139	61
Ismael Valdez	34	31	14–9	0	1	105	5.19	170.0	67	49
Josh Beckett	26	26	9–9	0	1	72	3.79	156.2	152	54
A.J. Burnett	20	19	7–6	0	0	50	3.68	120.0	113	38
Guillermo Mota	78	0	9–8	4	0	33	3.07	96.2	85	37
David Weathers	66	2	7–7	0	0	44	4.15	82.1	61	35
Nate Bump	50	2	2–4	1	0	46	5.01	73.2	44	32
Armando Benitez	64	0	2–2	47	0	11	1.29	69.2	62	21
Billy Koch	47	0	2–3	8	0	25	4.41	49.0	50	36
Matt Perisho	66	0	5–3	0	0	23	4.40	47.0	42	26

Houston Astros

BATTING	G	AB	R	H	2B	3B	HR	RBI	TB	BB	SO	SB	OBP	SLG	BA
Craig Biggio	156	633	100	178	47	0	24	63	297	40	94	7	.331	.469	.281
Jeff Bagwell	156	572	104	152	29	2	27	89	266	96	131	6	.377	.465	.266
Lance Berkman	160	544	104	172	40	3	30	106	308	127	101	9	.450	.566	.316
Jeff Kent	145	540	96	156	34	8	27	107	287	49	96	7	.348	.531	.289
Morgan Ensberg	131	411	51	113	20	3	10	66	169	36	46	6	.330	.411	.275
Brad Ausmus	129	403	38	100	14	1	5	31	131	33	56	2	.306	.325	.248
Adam Everett	104	384	66	105	15	2	8	31	148	17	56	13	.317	.385	.273
Jose Vizcaino	138	356	34	98	21	3	3	33	134	20	39	1	.311	.374	.274
Carlos Beltran	90	333	70	86	17	7	23	53	186	55	57	28	.368	.559	.258
Mike Lamb	112	278	38	80	14	3	14	58	142	31	63	1	.356	.511	.288
Raul Chavez	64	162	9	34	8	0	0	23	42	10	38	0	.256	.259	.210
Jason Lane	107	136	21	37	10	2	4	19	63	16	33	1	.348	.463	.272

PITCHING	GP	GS	W–L	SV	SHO	R	ERA	IP	Ks	BB
Roy Oswalt	36	35	20–10	0	2	100	3.49	237.0	206	62
Roger Clemens	33	33	18–4	0	0	76	2.98	214.1	218	79
Tim Redding	27	17	5–7	0	0	73	5.72	100.2	56	43
Pete Munro	21	19	4–7	0	0	59	5.15	99.2	63	26
Brad Lidge	80	0	6–5	29	0	21	1.90	94.2	157	30
Wade Miller	15	15	7–7	0	0	35	3.35	88.2	74	44
Andy Pettitte	15	15	6–4	0	0	37	3.90	83.0	79	31
Danny Miceli	74	0	6–6	2	0	34	3.59	77.2	83	27
Darren Oliver	27	10	3–3	0	0	50	5.94	72.2	46	21
Brandon Backe	33	9	5–3	0	0	33	4.30	67.0	54	27
Dan Wheeler	46	1	3–1	0	0	33	4.29	65.0	55	30
Chad Harville	59	0	3–2	0	0	36	4.69	55.2	46	27
Mike D. Gallo	69	0	2–0	0	0	27	4.74	49.1	34	20

Los Angeles Dodgers

BATTING	G	AB	R	H	2B	3B	HR	RBI	TB	BB	SO	SB	OBP	SLG	BA
Cesar Izturis	159	670	90	193	32	9	4	62	255	43	70	25	.330	.381	.288
Steve Finley	162	628	92	170	28	1	36	94	308	61	82	9	.333	.490	.271
Adrian Beltre	156	598	104	200	32	0	48	121	376	53	87	7	.388	.629	.334
Shawn Green	157	590	92	157	28	1	28	86	271	71	114	5	.352	.459	.266
Milton Bradley	141	516	72	138	24	6	19	67	219	71	123	15	.362	.424	.267
Alex Cora	138	405	47	107	9	4	10	47	154	47	41	3	.364	.380	.264
Hee Seop Choi	126	343	53	86	21	1	15	46	154	63	96	1	.370	.449	.251
Jayson Werth	89	290	56	76	11	3	16	47	141	30	85	4	.338	.486	.262
D Roberts	68	233	45	59	4	7	2	21	83	28	31	33	.340	.356	.253
Jose Hernandez	95	211	32	61	12	1	13	29	114	26	61	3	.370	.540	.289
Brent Mayne	83	190	14	42	6	1	0	15	50	27	41	1	.314	.263	.221
Jason Grabowski	113	173	18	38	7	0	7	20	66	19	50	0	.297	.382	.220
David Ross	70	165	13	28	3	1	5	15	48	15	62	0	.253	.291	.170
Robin Ventura	102	152	19	37	3	0	5	28	55	22	31	0	.337	.362	.243

Los Angeles Dodgers *(Cont.)*

PITCHING	GP	GS	W–L	SV	SHO	R	ERA	IP	Ks	BB
Jeff Weaver	34	34	13–13	0	0	103	4.01	220.0	153	67
Odalis Perez	31	31	7–6	0	0	76	3.25	196.1	128	44
Kazuhisa Ishii	31	31	13–8	0	2	97	4.71	172.0	99	98
Jose Lima	36	24	13–5	0	0	81	4.07	170.1	93	34
Brad Penny	24	24	9–10	0	0	55	3.15	143.0	111	45
Wilson Alvarez	40	15	7–6	1	0	56	4.03	120.2	102	31
Elmer Dessens	50	10	2–6	2	0	61	4.46	105.0	73	31
Hideo Nomo	18	18	4–11	0	0	77	8.25	84.0	54	42
Eric Gagne	70	0	7–3	45	0	24	2.19	82.1	114	22
Duaner Sanchez	67	0	3–1	0	0	34	3.38	80.0	44	27
Giovanni Carrara	42	0	5–2	2	0	15	2.18	53.2	48	20
Darren Dreifort	60	0	1–4	1	0	25	4.44	50.2	63	362

Milwaukee Brewers

BATTING	G	AB	R	H	2B	3B	HR	RBI	TB	BB	SO	SB	OBP	SLG	BA
Scott Podsednik	154	640	85	156	27	7	12	39	233	58	105	70	.313	.364	.244
Geoff Jenkins	157	617	88	163	36	6	27	93	292	46	152	3	.325	.473	.264
Lyle Overbay	159	579	83	174	53	1	16	87	277	81	128	2	.385	.478	.301
Craig Counsell	140	473	59	114	19	5	2	23	149	59	88	17	.330	.315	.241
Bill Hall	126	390	43	93	20	3	9	53	146	20	119	12	.276	.374	.238
Keith Ginter	113	386	47	101	23	2	19	60	185	37	100	8	.333	.479	.262
Brady Clark	138	353	41	99	18	1	7	46	140	53	48	15	.385	.397	.280
Chad Moeller	101	317	25	66	13	1	5	27	96	21	74	0	.265	.303	.208
Wes Helms	92	274	24	72	13	1	4	28	99	24	60	0	.331	.361	.263
Junior Spivey	59	228	33	62	13	0	7	28	96	25	48	5	.359	.421	.272
Gary Bennett	75	219	18	49	14	0	3	20	72	22	32	1	.297	.329	.224
Russell Branyan	51	158	21	37	11	1	11	27	83	20	68	1	.324	.525	.234

PITCHING	GP	GS	W–L	SV	SHO	R	ERA	IP	Ks	BB
Ben Sheets	34	34	12–14	0	0	85	2.70	237.0	264	32
Doug Davis	34	34	12–12	0	0	84	3.39	207.1	166	79
Victor Santos	31	28	11–12	0	0	95	4.97	154.0	115	57
Wes Obermueller	25	20	6–8	0	1	80	5.80	118.0	59	42
Chris Capuano	17	17	6–8	0	0	55	4.99	88.1	80	37
Luis Vizcaino	73	0	4–4	1	0	35	3.75	72.0	63	24
Jeff Bennett	60	0	1–5	0	0	43	4.79	71.1	45	26
Danny Kolb	64	0	0–4	39	0	22	2.98	57.1	21	15
Mike Adams	46	0	2–3	0	0	21	3.40	53.0	39	14

Montreal Expos

BATTING	G	AB	R	H	2B	3B	HR	RBI	TB	BB	SO	SB	OBP	SLG	BA
Tony Batista	157	606	76	146	30	2	32	110	276	26	78	14	.272	.455	.241
Brad Wilkerson	160	572	112	146	39	2	32	67	285	106	152	13	.374	.498	.255
Endy Chavez	132	502	65	139	20	6	5	34	186	30	40	32	.318	.371	.277
Brian Schneider	135	436	40	112	20	3	12	49	174	42	63	0	.325	.399	.257
Jose Vidro	110	412	51	121	24	0	14	60	187	49	43	3	.367	.454	.294
Terrmel Sledge	133	398	45	107	20	6	15	62	184	40	66	3	.336	.462	.269
Juan Rivera	134	391	48	120	24	1	12	49	182	34	45	6	.364	.465	.307
Orlando Cabrera	103	390	41	96	19	2	4	31	131	28	31	12	.298	.336	.246
Nick Johnson	73	251	35	63	16	0	7	33	100	40	58	6	.359	.398	.251
Jamey Carroll	102	218	36	63	14	2	0	16	81	32	21	5	.378	.372	.289
E Diaz	55	139	9	31	6	1	1	11	42	11	10	2	.293	.302	.223
C Everett	39	127	8	32	10	0	2	14	48	8	19	0	.319	.378	.252
Maicer Izturis	32	107	10	22	5	2	1	4	34	10	20	4	.286	.318	.206

PITCHING	GP	GS	W–L	SV	SHO	R	ERA	IP	Ks	BB
Livan Hernandez	35	35	11–15	0	2	105	3.60	255.0	186	83
Sun-Woo Kim	43	17	4–6	0	0	80	4.58	135.2	87	55
Claudio Vargas	45	14	5–5	0	0	75	5.25	118.1	89	64
Zach Day	19	19	5–10	0	1	53	3.93	116.2	61	45
John Patterson	19	19	4–7	0	0	58	5.03	98.1	99	46
Luis Ayala	81	0	6–12	2	0	30	2.69	90.1	63	15
Tomo Ohka	15	15	3–7	0	0	40	3.40	84.2	38	20
Chad Cordero	69	0	7–3	14	0	28	2.94	82.2	83	43
Rocky Biddle	47	9	4–8	0	0	69	6.92	78.0	51	31
Tony Armas	16	16	2–4	0	0	41	4.88	72.0	56	45
T.J. Tucker	54	1	4–2	0	0	28	3.72	67.2	44	17
Scott Downs	12	12	3–6	0	1	47	5.14	63.0	38	23
Francis Beltran	45	0	2–2	1	0	31	5.47	49.1	48	27
Joe Horgan	47	0	4–1	0	0	18	3.15	40.0	30	22

New York Mets

BATTING	G	AB	R	H	2B	3B	HR	RBI	TB	BB	SO	SB	OBP	SLG	BA
Richard Hidalgo	144	523	67	125	26	3	25	82	232	44	129	4	.301	.444	.239
Mike Cameron	140	493	76	114	30	1	30	76	236	57	143	22	.319	.479	.231
Kazuo Matsui	114	460	65	125	32	2	7	44	182	40	97	14	.331	.396	.272
Mike Piazza	129	455	47	121	21	0	20	54	202	68	78	0	.362	.444	.266
Cliff Floyd	113	396	55	103	26	4	18	63	183	47	103	11	.352	.462	.260
Jason Phillips	128	362	34	79	18	0	7	34	118	35	42	0	.298	.326	.218
Todd Zeile	137	348	30	81	16	0	9	35	124	44	83	0	.319	.356	.233
Eric Valent	130	270	39	72	15	2	13	34	130	28	61	0	.337	.481	.267
David Wright	69	263	41	77	17	1	14	40	138	14	40	6	.332	.525	.293
Jose Reyes	53	220	33	56	16	2	2	14	82	5	31	19	.271	.373	.255
Karim Garcia	62	192	24	45	7	2	7	22	77	10	35	3	.272	.401	.234
Shane Spencer	74	185	21	52	10	1	4	26	76	13	37	6	.332	.411	.281
Vance Wilson	79	157	18	43	10	1	4	21	67	11	24	1	.335	.427	.274
Danny Garcia	58	138	23	32	7	1	3	17	50	22	34	3	.371	.362	.232
Joe McEwing	75	138	17	35	3	1	1	16	43	9	32	4	.297	.312	.254
Wilson Delgado	42	130	11	38	4	1	2	13	50	15	29	1	.366	.385	.292

PITCHING	GP	GS	W–L	SV	SHO	R	ERA	IP	Ks	BB
Tom Glavine	33	33	11–14	0	1	94	3.60	212.1	109	70
Steve Trachsel	33	33	12–13	0	0	104	4.00	202.2	117	83
Kris Benson	31	31	12–12	0	1	106	4.31	200.1	134	61
Al Leiter	30	30	10–8	0	0	65	3.21	173.2	117	97
Victor Zambrano	26	25	11–7	0	0	77	4.37	142.0	123	102
Jae Seo	24	21	5–10	0	0	67	4.90	117.2	54	50
Braden Looper	71	0	2–5	29	0	28	2.70	83.1	60	16
Mike Stanton	83	0	2–6	0	0	32	3.16	77.0	58	33
Matt Ginter	15	14	1–3	0	0	41	4.54	69.1	38	20
Ricky Bottalico	60	0	3–2	0	0	30	3.38	69.1	61	34
Mike DeJean	54	0	0–5	0	0	34	4.57	61.0	60	33
Tyler Yates	21	7	2–4	0	0	36	6.36	46.2	35	25
John Franco	52	0	2–7	0	0	28	5.28	46.0	36	24

Philadelphia Phillies

BATTING	G	AB	R	H	2B	3B	HR	RBI	TB	BB	SO	SB	OBP	SLG	BA
Jimmy Rollins	154	657	119	190	43	12	14	73	299	57	73	30	.348	.455	.289
Bobby Abreu	159	574	118	173	47	1	30	105	312	127	116	40	.428	.544	.301
David Bell	143	533	67	155	33	1	18	77	244	57	75	1	.363	.458	.291
Jim Thome	143	508	97	139	28	1	42	105	295	104	144	0	.396	.581	.274
Placido Polanco	126	503	74	150	21	0	17	55	222	27	39	7	.345	.441	.298
Mike Lieberthal	131	476	58	129	31	1	17	61	213	37	69	1	.335	.447	.271
Pat Burrell	127	448	66	115	17	0	24	84	204	78	130	2	.365	.455	.257
Marlon Byrd	106	346	48	79	13	2	5	33	111	22	68	2	.287	.321	.228
Jason Michaels	115	299	44	82	12	0	10	40	124	42	80	2	.364	.415	.274
Chase Utley	94	267	36	71	11	2	13	57	125	15	40	4	.308	.468	.266
Tomas Perez	86	176	22	38	13	2	6	21	73	9	44	0	.257	.415	.216
Doug Glanville	87	162	21	34	1	1	2	14	43	8	21	8	.244	.265	.210
Todd Pratt	45	128	16	33	5	0	3	16	47	18	38	0	.351	.367	.258

PITCHING	GP	GS	W–L	SV	SHO	R	ERA	IP	Ks	BB
Cory Lidle	34	34	12–12	0	3	123	4.90	211.1	126	61
Eric Milton	34	34	14–6	0	0	110	4.75	201.0	161	75
Brett Myers	32	31	11–11	0	1	113	5.52	176.0	116	62
Kevin Millwood	25	25	9–6	0	0	81	4.85	141.0	125	51
Randy Wolf	23	23	5–8	0	1	73	4.28	136.2	89	36
Vicente Padilla	20	20	7–7	0	0	63	4.53	115.1	82	36
Paul Abbott	20	19	3–11	0	0	76	6.47	96.0	46	58
Todd Jones	78	0	11–5	2	0	39	4.15	82.1	59	33
Rheal Cormier	84	0	4–5	0	0	32	3.56	81.0	46	26
Tim Worrell	77	0	5–6	19	0	36	3.68	78.1	64	21
Ryan Madson	52	1	9–3	1	0	23	2.34	77.0	55	19
Felix Rodriguez	76	0	5–8	1	0	25	3.29	65.2	59	29
Roberto Hernandez	63	0	3–5	0	0	39	4.76	56.2	44	29
Amaury Telemaco	42	0	0–2	0	0	27	4.31	54.1	32	19
Billy Wagner	45	0	4–0	21	0	16	2.42	48.1	59	6

Pittsburgh Pirates

BATTING	G	AB	R	H	2B	3B	HR	RBI	TB	BB	SO	SB	OBP	SLG	BA
Jack Wilson	157	652	82	201	41	12	11	59	299	26	71	8	.335	.459	.308
Jason Kendall	147	574	86	183	32	0	3	51	224	60	41	11	.399	.390	.319
Craig Wilson	155	561	97	148	35	5	29	82	280	50	169	2	.354	.499	.264
Tike Redman	155	546	65	153	19	4	8	51	204	23	52	18	.310	.374	.280
Ty Wigginton	144	494	63	129	30	2	17	66	214	45	82	7	.324	.433	.261
Rob Mackowiak	155	491	65	121	22	6	.17	75	206	50	114	13	.319	.420	.246
Jason Bay	120	411	61	116	24	4	26	82	226	41	129	4	.358	.550	.282
Jose Castillo	129	383	44	98	15	2	8	39	141	23	92	3	.298	.368	.256
Daryle Ward	79	293	39	73	17	2	15	57	139	22	45	0	.305	.474	.249
Bobby Hill	126	233	28	62	7	2	2	27	79	20	39	0	.353	.339	.266
Abraham Nunez	112	182	17	43	9	0	2	13	58	10	36	1	.275	.319	.236
Randall Simon	61	175	14	34	6	0	3	14	49	15	17	0	.264	.280	.194
C Stynes	74	162	16	35	10	0	1	16	48	9	23	0	.266	.296	.216
Raul Mondesi	26	99	8	28	8	0	2	14	42	11	27	0	.355	.424	.283

PITCHING	GP	GS	W–L	SV	SHO	R	ERA	IP	Ks	BB
Oliver Perez	30	30	12–10	0	1	71	2.98	196.0	239	81
Josh Fogg	32	32	11–10	0	0	98	4.64	178.1	82	66
Kip Wells	24	24	5–7	0	0	71	4.55	138.1	116	66
Ryan Vogelsong	31	26	6–13	0	0	97	6.50	133.0	92	67
Salomon Torres	84	0	7–7	0	0	33	2.64	92.0	62	22
Brian Meadows	68	0	2–4	1	0	40	3.58	78.0	46	19
Sean Burnett	13	13	5–5	0	1	41	5.02	71.2	30	28
Jose Mesa	70	0	5–2	43	0	26	3.25	69.1	37	20
John Grabow	68	0	2–5	1	0	39	5.11	61.2	64	28
Mike Gonzalez	47	0	3–1	1	0	7	1.25	43.1	55	6

St. Louis Cardinals

BATTING	G	AB	R	H	2B	3B	HR	RBI	TB	BB	SO	SB	OBP	SLG	BA
Albert Pujols	154	592	133	196	51	2	46	123	389	84	52	5	.415	.657	.331
Edgar Renteria	149	586	84	168	37	0	10	72	235	39	78	17	.327	.401	.287
Tony Womack	145	553	91	170	22	3	5	38	213	36	60	26	.349	.385	.307
Scott Rolen	142	500	109	157	32	4	34	124	299	72	92	4	.409	.598	.314
Jim Edmonds	153	498	102	150	38	3	42	111	320	101	150	8	.418	.643	.301
Reggie Sanders	135	446	64	116	27	3	22	67	215	33	118	21	.315	.482	.260
Mike Matheny	122	385	28	95	22	1	5	50	134	23	83	0	.292	.348	.247
Larry Walker	82	258	51	77	16	4	17	47	152	49	57	6	.424	.589	.298
Marlon Anderson	113	253	31	60	12	0	8	28	96	12	38	6	.269	.379	.237
John Mabry	87	240	32	71	11	0	13	40	121	26	63	0	.363	.504	.296
Roger Cedeno	95	200	22	53	9	2	3	23	75	19	41	5	.327	.375	.265
Ray Lankford	92	200	36	51	14	1	6	22	85	29	55	2	.349	.425	.255
So Taguchi	109	179	26	52	10	2	3	25	75	12	23	6	.337	.419	.291
Hector Luna	83	173	25	43	7	2	3	22	63	13	37	6	.304	.364	.249
Yadier Molina	51	135	12	36	6	0	2	15	48	13	20	0	.329	.356	.267

PITCHING	GP	GS	W–L	SV	SHO	R	ERA	IP	Ks	BB
Matt Morris	32	32	15–10	0	2	116	4.72	202.0	131	56
Jason Marquis	32	32	15–7	0	0	90	3.71	201.1	138	70
Woody Williams	31	31	11–8	0	0	93	4.18	189.2	131	58
Jeff Suppan	31	31	16–9	0	0	98	4.16	188.0	110	65
Chris Carpenter	28	28	15–5	0	0	75	3.46	182.0	152	38
Jason Isringhausen	74	0	4–2	47	0	27	2.87	75.1	71	23
Cal Eldred	52	0	4–2	1	0	31	3.76	67.0	54	17
Julian Tavarez	77	0	7–4	4	0	21	2.38	64.1	48	19
Ray King	86	0	5–2	0	0	19	2.61	62.0	40	24
Steve Kline	67	0	2–2	3	0	12	1.79	50.1	35	17
Dan Haren	14	5	3–3	0	0	23	4.50	46.0	32	17
Kiko Calero	41	0	3–1	2	0	14	2.78	45.1	47	10

San Diego Padres

BATTING	G	AB	R	H	2B	3B	HR	RBI	TB	BB	SO	SB	OBP	SLG	BA
Mark Loretta	154	620	108	208	47	2	16	76	307	58	45	5	.391	.495	.335
Brian Giles	159	609	97	173	33	7	23	94	289	89	80	10	.374	.475	.284
Phil Nevin	147	547	78	158	31	1	26	105	269	66	121	0	.368	.492	.289
Sean Burroughs	130	523	76	156	23	3	2	47	191	31	52	5	.348	.365	.298
Khalil Greene	139	484	67	132	31	4	15	65	216	53	94	4	.349	.446	.273
Jay Payton	143	458	57	119	17	4	8	55	168	43	56	2	.326	.367	.260
Ryan Klesko	127	402	58	117	32	2	9	66	180	73	67	3	.399	.448	.291
Ramon Hernandez	111	384	45	106	23	0	18	63	183	35	45	1	.341	.477	.276
Terrence Long	136	288	31	85	19	4	3	28	121	19	51	3	.335	.420	.295
Alex Gonzalez	83	285	36	64	18	1	7	27	105	14	64	2	.263	.368	.225
Miguel Ojeda	62	156	23	40	3	0	8	26	67	15	34	0	.322	.429	.256
Rich Aurilia	51	138	22	35	8	2	2	16	53	15	28	0	.331	.384	.254
Ramon Vazquez	52	115	12	27	3	2	1	13	37	11	24	1	.297	.322	.235

PITCHING	GP	GS	W–L	SV	SHO	R	ERA	IP	Ks	BB
Brian Lawrence	34	34	15–14	0	1	101	4.12	203.0	121	55
Adam Eaton	33	33	11–14	0	0	113	4.61	199.1	153	52
David Wells	31	31	12–8	0	0	85	3.73	195.2	101	20
Jake Peavy	27	27	15–6	0	0	49	2.27	166.1	173	53
Scott Linebrink	73	0	7–3	0	0	22	2.14	84.0	83	26
Akinori Otsuka	73	0	7–2	2	0	16	1.75	77.1	87	26
Jay Witasick	44	0	0–1	1	0	28	3.21	61.2	57	26
Trevor Hoffman	55	0	3–3	41	0	14	2.30	54.2	53	8
Ricky Stone	43	0	2–2	0	0	39	6.45	51.2	38	16

San Francisco Giants

BATTING	G	AB	R	H	2B	3B	HR	RBI	TB	BB	SO	SB	OBP	SLG	BA
Marquis Grissom	145	562	78	157	26	2	22	90	253	37	83	3	.323	.450	.279
Edgardo Alfonzo	139	519	66	150	26	1	11	77	211	46	40	1	.350	.407	.289
Pedro Feliz	144	503	72	139	33	3	22	84	244	23	85	5	.305	.485	.276
Ray Durham	120	471	95	133	28	8	17	65	228	57	60	10	.364	.484	.282
A.J. Pierzynski	131	471	45	128	28	2	11	77	193	19	27	0	.319	.410	.272
Michael Tucker	140	464	77	119	21	6	13	62	191	70	106	5	.353	.412	.256
Deivi Cruz	127	397	46	116	30	2	7	55	171	17	32	1	.322	.431	.292
Barry Bonds	147	373	129	135	27	3	45	101	303	232	41	6	.609	.812	.362
J.T. Snow	107	346	62	113	32	1	12	60	183	58	61	4	.429	.529	.327
Dustan Mohr	117	263	52	72	20	1	7	28	115	46	64	0	.394	.437	.274
Ricky Ledee	104	176	25	41	9	0	7	30	71	27	47	3	.337	.403	.233
Yorvit Torrealba	64	172	19	39	7	3	6	23	70	17	31	2	.302	.407	.227

PITCHING	GP	GS	W–L	SV	SHO	R	ERA	IP	Ks	BB
Jason Schmidt	32	32	18–7	0	3	84	3.20	225.0	251	77
Brett Tomko	32	31	11–7	0	1	98	4.04	194.0	108	64
Kirk Rueter	33	33	9–12	0	0	108	4.73	190.1	56	66
Dustin Hermanson	47	18	6–9	17	0	71	4.53	131.0	102	46
Jerome Williams	22	22	10–7	0	0	69	4.24	129.1	80	44
Jim Brower	89	0	7–7	1	0	42	3.29	93.0	83	36
Noah Lowry	16	14	6–0	0	1	41	3.82	92.0	72	28
Dave Burba	51	0	4–1	2	0	40	4.21	77.0	50	26
Matt Herges	70	0	4–5	23	0	44	5.23	65.1	39	21
Tyler Walker	52	0	5–1	1	0	31	4.24	63.2	48	24
Scott Eyre	83	0	2–2	1	0	26	4.10	52.2	49	27
Wayne Franklin	43	2	2–1	0	0	37	6.39	50.2	40	22
Jason Christiansen	60	0	4–3	3	0	20	4.50	36.0	22	26

American League Team-by-Team Statistical Leaders

Anaheim Angels

BATTING	G	AB	R	H	2B	3B	HR	RBI	TB	BB	SO	SB	OBP	SLG	BA
Vladimir Guerrero	156	612	124	206	39	2	39	126	366	52	74	15	.391	.598	.337
Chone Figgins	148	577	83	171	22	17	5	60	242	49	94	34	.350	.419	.296
David Eckstein	142	566	92	156	24	1	2	35	188	42	49	16	.339	.332	.276
Jose Guillen	148	565	88	166	28	3	27	104	281	37	92	5	.352	.497	.294
Darin Erstad	125	495	79	146	29	1	7	69	198	37	74	16	.346	.400	.295
Adam Kennedy	144	468	70	130	20	5	10	48	190	41	92	15	.351	.406	.278
Garret Anderson	112	442	57	133	20	1	14	75	197	29	75	2	.343	.446	.301
Bengie Molina	97	337	36	93	13	0	10	54	136	18	35	0	.313	.404	.276
Jeff DaVanon	108	285	41	79	11	4	7	34	119	46	54	18	.372	.418	.277
Troy Glaus	58	207	47	52	11	1	18	42	119	31	52	2	.355	.575	.251
Jose Molina	73	203	26	53	10	2	3	25	76	10	52	4	.296	.374	.261
Tim Salmon	60	186	15	47	7	0	2	23	60	14	41	1	.306	.323	.253
R Quinlan	56	160	23	55	14	0	5	23	84	14	26	3	.401	.525	.344

PITCHING	GP	GS	W–L	SV	SHO	R	ERA	IP	Ks	BB
Kelvim Escobar	33	33	11–12	0	0	91	3.93	208.1	191	76
Bartolo Colon	34	34	18–12	0	0	122	5.01	208.1	158	71
John Lackey	33	32	14–13	0	1	108	4.67	198.1	144	60
Jarrod Washburn	25	25	11–8	0	1	81	4.64	149.1	86	40
Aaron Sele	28	24	9–4	0	0	84	5.05	132.0	51	51
Ramon Ortiz	34	14	5–7	0	0	64	4.43	128.0	82	38
Scot Shields	60	0	8–2	4	0	42	3.33	105.1	109	40
Kevin Gregg	55	0	5–2	1	0	43	4.21	87.2	84	28
Francisco Rodriguez	69	0	4–1	12	0	21	1.82	84.0	123	33
Troy Percival	52	0	2–3	33	0	19	2.90	49.2	33	19

Baltimore Orioles

BATTING	G	AB	R	H	2B	3B	HR	RBI	TB	BB	SO	SB	OBP	SLG	BA
Miguel Tejada	162	653	107	203	40	2	34	150	349	48	73	4	.360	.534	.311
Brian Roberts	159	641	107	175	50	2	4	53	241	71	95	29	.344	.376	.273
Javy Lopez	150	579	83	183	33	3	23	86	291	47	97	0	.370	.503	.316
Melvin Mora	140	550	111	187	41	0	27	104	309	66	95	11	.419	.562	.340
Rafael Palmeiro	154	550	68	142	29	0	23	88	240	86	61	2	.359	.436	.258
Larry Bigbie	139	478	76	134	23	1	15	68	204	45	113	8	.341	.427	.280
David Newhan	95	373	66	116	15	7	8	54	169	27	72	11	.361	.453	.311
Jay Gibbons	97	346	36	85	14	1	10	47	131	29	64	1	.303	.379	.246
B.J. Surhoff	100	343	49	106	12	1	8	50	144	30	46	2	.365	.420	.309
Luis Matos	89	330	36	74	18	0	6	28	110	19	60	12	.275	.333	.224
J Hairston	86	287	43	87	19	1	2	24	114	29	29	13	.378	.397	.303
Tim Raines Jr.	48	94	14	24	6	0	0	5	30	4	16	7	.293	.319	.255

PITCHING	GP	GS	W–L	SV	SHO	R	ERA	IP	Ks	BB
Sidney Ponson	33	33	11–15	0	2	136	5.30	215.2	115	69
Rodrigo Lopez	37	23	14–9	0	1	71	3.59	170.2	121	54
Daniel Cabrera	28	27	12–8	1	1	85	5.00	147.2	76	89
Erik Bedard	27	26	6–10	0	0	83	4.59	137.1	121	71
B.J. Ryan	76	0	4–6	3	0	24	2.28	87.0	122	35
John Parrish	56	1	6–3	1	0	39	3.46	78.0	71	55
Eric DuBose	14	14	4–6	0	0	55	6.39	74.2	48	44
Jorge Julio	65	0	2–5	22	0	35	4.57	69.0	70	39
Matt Riley	14	13	3–4	0	0	43	5.63	64.0	60	44
Jason Grimsley	73	0	5–7	0	0	36	3.86	63.0	39	35
Dave Borkowski	17	8	3–4	0	0	37	5.14	56.0	45	15
Rick Bauer	23	2	2–1	0	0	31	4.70	53.2	37	20
Buddy Groom	60	0	4–1	0	0	30	4.78	52.2	32	16

Boston Red Sox

BATTING	G	AB	R	H	2B	3B	HR	RBI	TB	BB	SO	SB	OBP	SLG	BA
Johnny Damon	150	621	123	189	35	6	20	94	296	76	71	19	.380	.477	.304
David Ortiz	150	582	94	175	47	3	41	139	351	75	133	0	.380	.603	.301
Manny Ramirez	152	568	108	175	44	0	43	130	348	82	124	2	.397	.613	.308
Mark Bellhorn	138	523	93	138	37	3	17	82	232	88	177	6	.373	.444	.264
Kevin Millar	150	508	74	151	36	0	18	74	241	57	91	1	.383	.474	.297
Jason Varitek	137	463	67	137	30	1	18	73	223	62	126	10	.390	.482	.296
Bill Mueller	110	399	75	113	27	1	12	57	178	51	56	2	.365	.446	.283
Doug Mientkiewicz	127	391	47	93	24	1	6	35	137	48	56	2	.326	.350	.238
Gabe Kapler	136	290	51	79	14	1	6	33	113	15	49	5	.311	.390	.272
Pokey Reese	96	244	32	54	7	2	3	29	74	17	60	6	.271	.303	.221
Orlando Cabrera	58	228	33	67	19	1	6	31	106	11	23	4	.320	.465	.294
Kevin Youkilis	72	208	38	54	11	0	7	35	86	33	45	0	.367	.413	.260
Doug Mirabelli	59	160	27	45	12	0	9	32	84	19	46	0	.368	.525	.281
Nomar Garciaparra	38	156	24	50	7	3	5	21	78	8	16	2	.367	.500	.321
D McCarty	91	151	24	39	8	1	4	17	61	14	40	1	.327	.404	.258
Trot Nixon	48	149	24	47	9	1	6	23	76	15	24	0	.377	.510	.315

PITCHING	GP	GS	W–L	SV	SHO	R	ERA	IP	Ks	BB
Curt Schilling	32	32	21–6	0	0	84	3.26	226.2	203	35
Pedro Martinez	33	33	16–9	0	1	99	3.90	217.0	227	61
Tim Wakefield	32	30	12–10	0	0	121	4.87	188.1	116	63
Derek Lowe	33	33	14–12	0	0	138	5.42	182.2	105	71
Bronson Arroyo	32	29	10–9	0	0	99	4.03	178.2	142	47
Keith Foulke	72	0	5–3	32	0	22	2.17	83.0	79	15
Mike Timlin	76	0	5–4	1	0	35	4.13	76.1	56	19
Terry Adams	61	0	6–4	3	0	39	4.76	70.0	56	28
Alan Embree	71	0	2–2	0	0	28	4.13	52.1	37	11
Curtis Leskanic	51	0	3–5	4	0	27	5.19	43.1	37	30
Mike Myers	75	0	5–1	0	0	22	4.64	42.2	32	23

Chicago White Sox

BATTING	G	AB	R	H	2B	3B	HR	RBI	TB	BB	SO	SB	OBP	SLG	BA
Carlos Lee	153	591	103	180	37	0	31	99	310	54	86	11	.366	.525	.305
Paul Konerko	155	563	84	156	22	0	41	117	301	69	107	1	.359	.535	.277
Juan Uribe	134	502	82	142	31	6	23	74	254	32	96	9	.327	.506	.283
Joe Crede	144	490	67	117	25	0	21	69	205	34	81	1	.299	.418	.239
Aaron Rowand	140	487	94	151	38	2	24	69	265	30	91	17	.361	.544	.310
Jose Valentin	125	450	73	97	20	3	30	70	213	43	139	8	.287	.473	.216
Willie Harris	129	409	68	107	15	2	2	27	132	51	79	19	.343	.323	.262
Timo Perez	103	293	38	72	12	0	5	40	99	15	29	3	.285	.338	.246
Frank Thomas	74	240	53	65	16	0	18	49	135	64	57	0	.434	.563	.271
Ross Gload	110	234	28	75	16	0	7	44	112	20	37	0	.375	.479	.321
Magglio Ordonez	52	202	32	59	8	2	9	37	98	16	22	0	.351	.485	.292
Joe Borchard	63	201	26	35	4	1	9	20	68	19	57	1	.249	.338	.174
Ben Davis	68	193	22	40	9	0	6	18	67	12	49	1	.256	.347	.207
Carl Everett	43	154	21	41	7	1	5	21	65	8	26	1	.320	.422	.266
Sandy Alomar	50	146	15	35	4	0	2	14	45	11	13	0	.298	.308	.240
Jamie Burke	57	120	22	40	9	0	0	15	49	10	13	0	.386	.408	.333

PITCHING	GP	GS	W–L	SV	SHO	R	ERA	IP	Ks	BB
Mark Buehrle	35	35	16–10	0	1	119	3.89	245.1	165	51
Jon Garland	34	33	12–11	0	0	125	4.89	217.0	113	76
Freddy Garcia	31	31	13–11	0	0	92	3.81	210.0	184	64
Jose Contreras	31	31	13–9	0	0	114	5.50	170.1	150	84
Scott Schoeneweis	20	19	6–9	0	0	74	5.59	112.2	69	49
Damaso Marte	74	0	6–5	6	0	28	3.42	73.2	68	34
Neal Cotts	56	1	4–4	0	0	45	5.65	65.1	58	30
Shingo Takatsu	59	0	6–4	19	0	17	2.31	62.1	50	21
Jon Adkins	50	0	2–3	0	0	35	4.65	62.0	44	20
Cliff Politte	54	0	0–3	1	0	26	4.38	51.1	48	22

Cleveland Indians

BATTING	G	AB	R	H	2B	3B	HR	RBI	TB	BB	SO	SB	OBP	SLG	BA
Ronnie Belliard	152	599	78	169	48	1	12	70	255	60	98	3	.348	.426	.282
Matt Lawton	150	591	109	164	25	0	20	70	249	74	84	23	.366	.421	.277
Casey Blake	152	587	93	159	36	3	28	88	285	68	139	5	.354	.486	.271
Omar Vizquel	148	567	82	165	28	3	7	59	220	57	62	19	.353	.388	.291
Victor Martinez	141	520	77	147	38	1	23	108	256	60	69	0	.359	.492	.283
Coco Crisp	139	491	78	146	24	2	15	71	219	36	69	20	.344	.446	.297
Travis Hafner	140	482	96	150	41	3	28	109	281	68	111	3	.410	.583	.311
J Gerut	134	481	72	121	31	5	11	51	195	54	59	13	.334	.405	.252
Ben Broussard	139	418	57	115	28	5	17	82	204	52	95	4	.370	.488	.275
Josh Phelps	103	371	51	93	19	2	17	61	167	22	93	0	.304	.450	.251
Lou Merloni	71	190	25	55	12	1	4	28	81	14	41	1	.343	.426	.289
A Escobar	46	152	20	32	8	2	1	12	47	23	42	1	.318	.309	.211
Grady Sizemore	43	138	15	34	6	2	4	24	56	14	34	2	.333	.406	.246

PITCHING	GP	GS	W–L	SV	SHO	R	ERA	IP	Ks	BB
Jake Westbrook	33	30	14–9	0	1	95	3.38	215.2	116	61
C.C. Sabathia	30	30	11–10	0	0	90	4.12	188.0	139	72
Cliff Lee	33	33	14–8	0	0	113	5.43	179.0	161	81
Scott Elarton	29	29	3–11	0	1	107	5.90	158.2	103	62
Jason T. Davis	26	19	2–7	0	0	81	5.51	114.1	72	51
Rick White	59	0	5–5	1	0	52	5.29	78.1	44	29
David Riske	72	0	7–3	5	0	32	3.72	77.1	78	41
Rafael Betancourt	68	0	5–6	4	0	32	3.92	66.2	76	18
Matt J. Miller	57	0	4–1	1	0	22	3.09	55.1	55	23
Kazuhito Tadano	14	4	1–1	0	0	30	4.65	50.1	39	18

Detroit Tigers

BATTING	G	AB	R	H	2B	3B	HR	RBI	TB	BB	SO	SB	OBP	SLG	BA
Ivan Rodriguez	135	527	72	176	32	2	19	86	269	41	91	7	.383	.510	.334
Carlos Guillen	136	522	97	166	37	10	20	97	283	52	87	12	.379	.542	.318
Omar Infante	142	503	69	133	27	9	16	55	226	40	112	13	.317	.449	.264
Carlos Pena	142	481	89	116	22	4	27	82	227	70	146	7	.338	.472	.241
Bobby Higginson	131	448	63	110	24	2	12	64	174	70	84	5	.353	.388	.246
Rondell White	121	448	76	121	21	2	19	67	203	39	77	1	.337	.453	.270
Craig Monroe	128	447	65	131	27	3	18	72	218	29	79	3	.337	.488	.293
Brandon Inge	131	408	43	117	15	7	13	64	185	32	72	5	.340	.453	.287
Dimitri Young	104	389	72	106	23	2	18	60	187	33	71	0	.336	.481	.272
A Sanchez	79	332	41	107	9	3	2	26	128	7	50	19	.335	.386	.322
Eric Munson	109	321	36	68	14	2	19	49	143	29	90	1	.289	.445	.212
Marcus Thames	61	165	24	42	12	0	10	33	84	16	42	0	.326	.509	.255
Jason Smith	61	155	20	37	7	4	5	19	67	8	37	1	.280	.432	.239
Nook Logan	47	133	12	37	5	2	0	10	46	13	24	8	.340	.346	.278

PITCHING	GP	GS	W–L	SV	SHO	R	ERA	IP	Ks	BB
Mike Maroth	33	33	11–13	0	1	112	4.31	217.0	108	59
Nate Robertson	34	32	12–10	1	0	116	4.90	196.2	155	66
Jason M. Johnson	33	33	8–15	0	1	121	5.13	196.2	125	60
Jeremy Bonderman	33	32	11–13	0	2	101	4.89	184.0	168	73
Gary Knotts	36	19	7–6	2	0	83	5.25	135.1	81	58
Esteban Yan	69	0	3–6	7	0	43	3.83	87.0	69	32
Al Levine	65	0	3–4	0	0	37	4.58	70.2	32	24
Jamie Walker	70	0	3–4	1	0	28	3.20	64.2	53	12
Ugueth Urbina	54	0	4–6	21	0	28	4.50	54.0	56	32
Wil Ledezma	15	8	4–3	0	0	28	4.39	53.1	29	18

Kansas City Royals

BATTING	G	AB	R	H	2B	3B	HR	RBI	TB	BB	SO	SB	OBP	SLG	BA
Angel Berroa	134	512	72	134	27	6	8	43	197	23	87	14	.308	.385	.262
Joe Randa	128	485	65	139	31	2	8	56	198	40	77	0	.343	.408	.287
Ken Harvey	120	456	47	131	20	1	13	55	192	28	89	1	.338	.421	.287
Matt Stairs	126	439	48	117	21	3	18	66	198	49	92	1	.345	.451	.267
Mike Sweeney	106	411	56	118	23	0	22	79	207	33	44	3	.347	.504	.287
Desi Relaford	114	380	45	84	14	0	6	34	116	34	56	5	.296	.305	.221
David DeJesus	96	363	58	104	15	3	7	39	146	33	53	8	.360	.402	.287
Tony Graffanino	75	278	37	73	11	0	3	26	93	27	38	10	.332	.335	.263
Carlos Beltran	69	266	51	74	19	2	15	51	142	37	44	14	.367	.534	.278
John Buck	71	238	36	56	9	0	12	30	101	15	79	1	.280	.424	.235
Abraham Nunez	59	221	31	50	9	0	5	29	74	25	48	0	.304	.335	.226
Dee Brown	59	195	19	49	7	0	4	24	68	11	50	2	.293	.349	.251
B Santiago	49	175	15	48	10	0	6	23	76	8	32	1	.312	.434	.274
Ruben Gotay	44	152	17	41	7	3	1	16	57	9	36	0	.315	.375	.270

PITCHING	GP	GS	W–L	SV	SHO	R	ERA	IP	Ks	BB
Darrell May	31	31	9–19	0	1	130	5.61	186.0	120	55
Brian J. Anderson	35	26	6–12	0	1	123	5.64	166.0	70	53
Jimmy Gobble	25	24	9–8	0	0	94	5.35	148.0	49	43
Zack Greinke	24	24	8–11	0	0	64	3.97	145.0	100	26
Dennys Reyes	40	12	4–8	0	0	64	4.75	108.0	91	50
Mike Wood	17	17	3–8	0	0	67	5.94	100.0	54	28
Matt Kinney	43	6	3–5	0	0	55	6.06	78.2	73	30
Jeremy Affeldt	38	8	3–4	13	0	49	4.95	76.1	49	32
Shawn Camp	42	0	2–2	2	0	37	3.92	66.2	51	16
Scott Sullivan	49	0	3–4	0	0	34	4.77	60.1	45	24
Jaime Cerda	53	0	1–4	2	0	21	3.15	45.2	33	30

Minnesota Twins

BATTING	G	AB	R	H	2B	3B	HR	RBI	TB	BB	SO	SB	OBP	SLG	BA
Cristian Guzman	145	576	84	158	31	4	8	46	221	30	64	10	.309	.384	.274
Lew Ford	154	569	89	170	31	4	15	72	254	67	75	20	.381	.446	.299
Jacque Jones	151	555	69	141	22	1	24	80	237	40	117	13	.315	.427	.254
Torii Hunter	138	520	79	141	37	0	23	81	247	40	101	21	.330	.475	.271
Corey Koskie	118	422	68	106	24	2	25	71	209	49	103	9	.342	.495	.251
Shannon Stewart	92	378	46	115	17	2	11	47	169	47	44	6	.380	.447	.304
Michael Cuddyer	115	339	49	89	22	1	12	45	149	37	74	5	.339	.440	.263
Luis Rivas	109	336	44	86	19	5	10	34	145	13	53	15	.283	.432	.256
Henry Blanco	114	315	36	65	19	1	10	37	116	21	56	0	.260	.368	.206
Justin Morneau	74	280	39	76	17	0	19	58	150	28	54	0	.340	.536	.271
Matt LeCroy	88	264	25	71	14	0	9	39	112	16	60	0	.321	.424	.269
Jose Offerman	77	172	22	44	14	2	2	22	68	29	31	1	.363	.395	.256
Joe Mauer	35	107	18	33	8	1	6	17	61	11	14	1	.369	.570	.308

PITCHING	GP	GS	W–L	SV	SHO	R	ERA	IP	Ks	BB
Johan Santana	34	34	20–6	0	1	70	2.61	228.0	265	54
Brad Radke	34	34	11–8	0	1	92	3.48	219.2	143	26
Carlos Silva	33	33	14–8	0	1	100	4.21	203.0	76	35
Kyle Lohse	35	34	9–13	0	1	128	5.34	194.0	111	76
Terry Mulholland	39	15	5–9	0	0	76	5.18	123.1	60	33
Juan Rincon	77	0	11–6	2	0	27	2.63	82.0	106	32
J.C. Romero	74	0	7–4	1	0	32	3.51	74.1	69	38
Joe Nathan	73	0	1–2	44	0	14	1.62	72.1	89	23
Joe Roa	48	0	2–3	0	0	38	4.50	70.0	47	24
Seth Greisinger	12	9	2–5	0	0	40	6.18	51.0	36	15
Aaron Fultz	55	0	3–3	1	0	28	5.04	50.0	37	23

New York Yankees

BATTING	G	AB	R	H	2B	3B	HR	RBI	TB	BB	SO	SB	OBP	SLG	BA
Derek Jeter	154	643	111	188	44	1	23	78	303	46	99	23	.352	.471	.292
Alex Rodriguez	155	601	112	172	24	2	36	106	308	80	131	28	.375	.512	.286
Hideki Matsui	162	584	109	174	34	2	31	108	305	88	103	3	.390	.522	.298
Gary Sheffield	154	573	117	166	30	1	36	121	306	92	83	5	.393	.534	.290
Bernie Williams	148	561	105	147	29	1	22	70	244	85	96	1	.360	.435	.262
Jorge Posada	137	449	72	122	31	0	21	81	216	88	92	1	.400	.481	.272
John Olerud	127	425	45	110	20	1	9	48	159	61	61	0	.359	.374	.259
Miguel Cairo	122	360	48	105	17	5	6	42	150	18	49	11	.346	.417	.292
Ruben Sierra	107	307	40	75	12	1	17	65	140	25	55	1	.296	.456	.244
Kenny Lofton	83	276	51	76	10	.7	3	18	109	31	27	7	.346	.395	.275
Jason Giambi	80	264	33	55	9	0	12	40	100	47	62	0	.342	.379	.208
Tony Clark	106	253	37	56	12	0	16	49	116	26	92	0	.297	.458	.221
Enrique Wilson	93	240	19	51	9	0	6	31	78	15	20	1	.254	.325	.213
John Flaherty	47	127	11	32	9	0	6	16	59	5	25	0	.286	.465	.252

PITCHING	GP	GS	W–L	SV	SHO	R	ERA	IP	Ks	BB
Javier Vazquez	32	32	14–10	0	0	114	4.91	198.0	150	60
Esteban Loaiza	31	27	10–7	0	1	124	5.70	183.0	117	71
Jon Lieber	27	27	14–8	0	0	95	4.33	176.2	102	18
Mike Mussina	27	27	12–9	0	0	91	4.59	164.2	132	40
Kevin Brown	22	22	10–6	0	0	65	4.09	132.0	83	35
Paul Quantrill	86	0	7–3	1	0	54	4.72	95.1	37	20
Tom Gordon	80	0	9–4	4	0	23	2.21	89.2	96	23
Orlando Hernandez	15	15	8–2	0	0	31	3.30	84.2	84	36
Mariano Rivera	74	0	4–2	53	0	17	1.94	78.2	66	20
Tanyon Sturtze	28	3	6–2	1	0	49	5.47	77.1	56	33
Felix Heredia	47	0	1–1	0	0	28	6.28	38.2	25	20

Oakland Athletics

BATTING	G	AB	R	H	2B	3B	HR	RBI	TB	BB	SO	SB	OBP	SLG	BA
Mark Kotsay	148	606	78	190	37	3	15	63	278	55	70	8	.370	.459	.314
Eric Byrnes	143	569	91	161	39	3	20	73	266	46	111	17	.347	.467	.283
Scott Hatteberg	152	550	87	156	30	0	15	82	231	72	48	0	.367	.420	.284
Bobby Crosby	151	545	70	130	34	1	22	64	232	58	141	7	.319	.426	.239
Jermaine Dye	137	532	87	141	29	4	23	80	247	49	128	4	.329	.464	.265
Erubiel Durazo	142	511	80	164	35	1	22	88	267	56	104	3	.396	.523	.321
Eric Chavez	125	475	87	131	20	0	29	77	238	95	99	6	.397	.501	.276
Marco Scutaro	137	455	50	124	32	1	7	43	179	16	58	0	.297	.393	.273
Damian Miller	110	397	39	108	25	0	9	58	160	39	87	0	.339	.403	.272
Mark McLemore	77	250	29	62	14	0	2	21	82	41	33	0	.355	.328	.248
Bobby Kielty	83	238	29	51	14	1	7	31	88	35	47	1	.321	.370	.214
Adam Melhuse	69	214	23	55	11	0	11	31	99	16	47	0	.309	.463	.257

PITCHING	GP	GS	W–L	SV	SHO	R	ERA	IP	Ks	BB
Mark Mulder	33	33	17–8	0	1	119	4.43	225.2	140	83
Barry Zito	34	34	11–11	0	0	116	4.48	213.0	163	81
Mark Redman	32	32	11–12	0	0	110	4.71	191.0	102	68
Rich Harden	31	31	11–7	0	0	90	3.99	189.2	167	81
Tim Hudson	27	27	12–6	0	2	82	3.53	188.2	103	44
Justin Duchscherer	53	0	7–6	0	0	37	3.27	96.1	59	32
Octavio Dotel	77	0	6–6	36	0	38	3.69	85.1	122	33
Chad Bradford	68	0	5–7	1	0	32	4.42	59.0	34	24
Chris Hammond	41	0	4–1	1	0	21	2.68	53.2	34	13
Jim Mecir	65	0	0–5	2	0	21	3.59	47.2	49	19
Ricardo Rincon	67	0	1–1	0	0	22	3.68	44.0	40	22
Arthur Rhodes	37	0	3–3	9	0	23	5.12	38.2	34	21

Seattle Mariners

BATTING

	G	AB	R	H	2B	3B	HR	RBI	TB	BB	SO	SB	OBP	SLG	BA
Ichiro Suzuki	161	704	101	262	24	5	8	60	320	49	63	36	.414	.455	.372
Randy Winn	157	626	84	179	34	6	14	81	267	53	98	21	.346	.427	.286
Bret Boone	148	593	74	149	30	0	24	83	251	56	135	10	.317	.423	.251
Edgar Martinez	141	486	45	128	23	0	12	63	187	58	107	1	.342	.385	.263
Raul Ibanez	123	481	67	146	31	1	16	62	227	36	72	1	.353	.472	.304
Scott Spiezio	112	367	38	79	12	3	10	41	127	36	60	4	.288	.346	.215
Jolbert Cabrera	113	359	38	97	19	2	6	47	138	16	70	10	.312	.384	.270
Dan Wilson	103	319	23	80	13	0	2	33	99	26	57	0	.305	.310	.251
Miguel Olivo	96	301	46	70	15	4	13	40	132	20	84	7	.286	.439	.233
Rich Aurilia	73	261	27	63	13	0	4	28	88	22	43	1	.304	.337	.241
J Lopez	57	207	28	48	13	0	5	22	76	8	31	0	.263	.367	.232
Willie Bloomquist	93	188	27	46	10	0	2	18	62	10	48	13	.283	.330	.245
Buddy Jacobsen	42	160	17	44	9	0	9	28	80	14	47	0	.335	.500	.275

PITCHING

	GP	GS	W–L	SV	SHO	R	ERA	IP	Ks	BB
Jamie Moyer	34	33	7–13	0	0	127	5.21	202.0	125	63
Ryan Franklin	32	32	4–16	0	1	116	4.90	200.1	104	61
Joel Pineiro	21	21	6–11	0	0	77	4.67	140.2	111	43
Gil Meche	23	23	7–7	0	1	73	5.01	127.2	99	47
Ron Villone	56	10	8–6	0	0	64	4.08	117.0	86	64
Bobby Madritsch	15	11	6–3	0	0	33	3.27	88.0	60	33
Shigetoshi Hasegawa	68	0	4–6	0	0	42	5.16	68.0	46	31
J.J. Putz	54	0	0–3	9	0	35	4.71	63.0	47	24
Julio Mateo	45	0	1–2	1	0	30	4.68	57.2	43	16
Eddie Guardado	41	0	2–2	18	0	14	2.78	45.1	45	14

Tampa Bay Devil Rays

BATTING

	G	AB	R	H	2B	3B	HR	RBI	TB	BB	SO	SB	OBP	SLG	BA
Carl Crawford	152	626	104	185	26	19	11	55	282	35	81	59	.331	.450	.296
Aubrey Huff	157	600	92	178	27	2	29	104	296	56	74	5	.360	.493	.297
Julio Lugo	157	581	83	160	41	4	7	75	230	54	106	21	.338	.396	.275
Jose Cruz	153	545	76	132	25	8	21	78	236	76	117	11	.333	.433	.242
Rocco Baldelli	136	518	79	145	27	3	16	74	226	30	88	17	.326	.436	.280
Tino Martinez	138	458	63	120	20	1	23	76	211	66	72	3	.362	.461	.262
Toby Hall	119	404	35	103	21	0	8	60	148	24	41	0	.300	.366	.255
Geoff Blum	112	339	38	73	21	0	8	35	118	24	58	2	.266	.348	.215
Rey Sanchez	91	285	23	70	14	3	2	26	96	12	28	0	.281	.337	.246
Robert Fick	76	214	12	43	5	2	6	26	70	20	32	0	.273	.327	.201
Jorge Cantu	50	173	25	52	20	1	2	17	80	9	44	0	.341	.462	.301
B.J. Upton	45	159	19	41	8	2	4	12	65	15	46	4	.324	.409	.258
Brook Fordyce	54	151	14	31	6	0	2	9	43	9	34	0	.259	.285	.205

PITCHING

	GP	GS	W–L	SV	SHO	R	ERA	IP	Ks	BB
Mark Hendrickson	32	30	10–15	0	0	113	4.81	183.1	87	46
Rob Bell	24	19	8–8	0	0	71	4.46	123.0	57	41
Dewon Brazelton	22	21	6–8	0	0	71	4.77	120.2	64	53
John Halama	34	14	7–6	0	0	68	4.70	118.2	59	27
Jorge Sosa	43	8	4–7	1	0	67	5.53	99.1	94	54
Lance Carter	56	0	3–3	0	0	32	3.47	80.1	36	23
Travis Harper	52	0	6–2	0	0	37	3.89	78.2	59	23
Doug Waechter	14	14	5–7	0	0	54	6.01	70.1	36	33
Danys Baez	62	0	4–4	30	0	31	3.57	68.0	52	29
Jeremi Gonzalez	11	8	0–5	0	0	42	6.97	50.1	22	20
Trever Miller	60	0	1–1	1	0	21	3.12	49.0	43	15

Texas Rangers

BATTING

	G	AB	R	H	2B	3B	HR	RBI	TB	BB	SO	SB	OBP	SLG	BA
Michael Young	160	690	114	216	33	9	22	99	333	44	89	12	.353	.483	.313
Hank Blalock	159	624	107	172	38	3	32	110	312	75	149	2	.355	.500	.276
Alfonso Soriano	145	608	77	170	32	4	28	91	294	33	121	18	.324	.484	.280
Mark Teixeira	145	545	101	153	34	2	38	112	305	68	117	4	.370	.560	.281
Kevin Mench	125	438	69	122	30	3	26	71	236	33	63	0	.335	.539	.279
Laynce Nix	115	371	58	92	20	4	14	46	162	23	113	1	.293	.437	.248
Rod Barajas	108	358	50	89	26	1	15	58	162	13	63	0	.276	.453	.249
Eric Young	104	344	55	99	25	2	1	27	131	43	28	14	.377	.381	.288
David Dellucci	107	331	59	80	13	1	17	61	146	47	88	9	.342	.441	.242
Gary Matthews Jr.	87	280	37	77	17	1	11	36	129	33	64	5	.350	.461	.275
Brad Fullmer	76	258	41	60	19	1	11	33	114	27	30	1	.310	.442	.233
Brian Jordan	61	212	27	47	13	1	5	23	77	16	35	2	.275	.363	.222

PITCHING

	GP	GS	W–L	SV	SHO	R	ERA	IP	Ks	BB
Kenny Rogers	35	35	18–9	0	1	117	4.76	211.2	126	66
Ryan Drese	34	33	14–10	0	0	104	4.20	207.2	98	58
R.A. Dickey	25	15	6–7	1	0	77	5.61	104.1	57	33
Joaquin Benoit	28	15	3–5	0	0	67	5.68	103.0	95	31
Chan Ho Park	16	16	4–7	0	0	63	5.46	95.2	63	33
Carlos Almanzar	67	0	7–3	0	0	32	3.72	72.2	44	19
Francisco Cordero	67	0	3–4	49	0	19	2.13	71.2	79	32
Ron Mahay	60	0	3–0	0	0	23	2.55	67.0	54	29
John Wasdin	15	10	2–4	0	0	52	6.78	65.0	36	23
Doug Brocail	43	0	4–1	1	0	29	4.13	52.1	43	20
Frank Francisco	45	0	5–1	0	0	19	3.33	51.1	60	28
Brian Shouse	53	0	2–0	0	0	12	2.23	44.1	34	18
Chris Young	7	7	3–2	0	0	21	4.71	36.1	27	10

Toronto Blue Jays

BATTING

	G	AB	R	H	2B	3B	HR	RBI	TB	BB	SO	SB	OBP	SLG	BA
Eric Hinske	155	570	66	140	23	3	15	69	214	54	109	12	.312	.375	.246
Reed Johnson	141	537	68	145	25	2	10	61	204	28	98	6	.320	.380	.270
Vernon Wells	134	536	82	146	34	2	23	67	253	51	83	9	.337	.472	.272
Orlando Hudson	135	489	73	132	32	7	12	58	214	51	98	7	.341	.438	.270
Carlos Delgado	128	458	74	123	26	0	32	99	245	69	115	0	.372	.535	.269
Alexis Rios	111	426	55	122	24	7	1	28	163	31	84	15	.338	.383	.286
Chris Gomez	109	341	41	96	11	1	3	37	118	28	41	3	.337	.346	.282
Gregg Zaun	107	338	46	91	24	0	6	36	133	47	61	0	.367	.393	.269
Frank Menechino	84	269	40	74	13	4	9	26	122	37	52	0	.371	.454	.275
Frank Catalanotto	75	249	27	73	19	1	1	26	97	17	33	1	.344	.390	.293
Chris Woodward	69	213	21	50	13	4	1	24	74	14	46	1	.283	.347	.235
Kevin Cash	60	181	18	35	9	0	4	21	56	10	59	0	.249	.309	.193

PITCHING

	GP	GS	W–L	SV	SHO	R	ERA	IP	Ks	BB
Miguel Batista	38	31	10–13	5	1	115	4.80	198.2	104	96
Ted Lilly	32	32	12–10	0	1	92	4.06	197.1	168	89
Roy Halladay	21	21	8–8	0	1	66	4.20	133.0	95	39
Josh Towers	21	21	9–9	0	0	70	5.11	116.1	51	26
David Bush	16	16	5–4	0	1	47	3.69	97.2	64	25
Justin Miller	19	15	3–4	0	0	58	6.06	81.2	47	42
Pat Hentgen	18	16	2–9	0	0	67	6.95	80.1	33	42
Justin Speier	62	0	3–8	7	0	32	3.91	69.0	52	25
Jason Frasor	63	0	4–6	17	0	31	4.08	68.1	54	36
Vinny Chulk	47	0	1–3	2	0	30	4.66	56.0	44	27
Kerry Ligtenberg	57	0	1–6	3	0	40	6.38	55.0	49	25

The World Series

Results

1903 ....Boston (A) 5, Pittsburgh (N) 3	1954 ....New York (N) 4, Cleveland (A) 0
1904 ....No series	1955 ....Brooklyn (N) 4, New York (A) 3
1905 ....New York (N) 4, Philadelphia (A) 1	1956 ....New York (A) 4, Brooklyn (N) 3
1906 ....Chicago (A) 4, Chicago (N) 2	1957 ....Milwaukee (N) 4, New York (A) 3
1907 ....Chicago (N) 4, Detroit (A) 0; 1 tie	1958 ....New York (A) 4, Milwaukee (N) 3
1908 ....Chicago (N) 4, Detroit (A) 1	1959 ....Los Angeles (N) 4, Chicago (A) 2
1909 ....Pittsburgh (N) 4, Detroit (A) 3	1960 ....Pittsburgh (N) 4, New York (A) 3
1910 ....Philadelphia (A) 4, Chicago (N) 1	1961 ....New York (A) 4, Cincinnati (N) 1
1911 ....Philadelphia (A) 4, New York (N) 2	1962 ....New York (A) 4, San Francisco (N) 3
1912 ....Boston (A) 4, New York (N) 3; 1 tie	1963 ....Los Angeles (N) 4, New York (A) 0
1913 ....Philadelphia (A) 4, New York (N) 1	1964 ....St. Louis (N) 4, New York (A) 3
1914 ....Boston (N) 4, Philadelphia (A) 0	1965 ....Los Angeles (N) 4, Minnesota (A) 3
1915 ....Boston (A) 4, Philadelphia (N) 1	1966 ....Baltimore (A) 4, Los Angeles (N) 0
1916 ....Boston (A) 4, Brooklyn (N) 1	1967 ....St. Louis (N) 4, Boston (A) 3
1917 ....Chicago (A) 4, New York (N) 2	1968 ....Detroit (A) 4, St. Louis (N) 3
1918 ....Boston (A) 4, Chicago (N) 2	1969 ....New York (N) 4, Baltimore (A) 1
1919 ....Cincinnati (N) 5, Chicago (A) 3	1970 ....Baltimore (A) 4, Cincinnati (N) 1
1920 ....Cleveland (A) 5, Brooklyn (N) 2	1971 ....Pittsburgh (N) 4, Baltimore (A) 3
1921 ....New York (N) 5, New York (A) 3	1972 ....Oakland (A) 4, Cincinnati (N) 3
1922 ....New York (N) 4, New York (A) 0; 1 tie	1973 ....Oakland (A) 4, New York (N) 3
1923 ....New York (A) 4, New York (N) 2	1974 ....Oakland (A) 4, Los Angeles (N) 1
1924 ....Washington (A) 4, New York (N) 3	1975 ....Cincinnati (N) 4, Boston (A) 3
1925 ....Pittsburgh (N) 4, Washington (A) 3	1976 ....Cincinnati (N) 4, New York (A) 0
1926 ....St. Louis (N) 4, New York (A) 3	1977 ....New York (A) 4, Los Angeles (N) 2
1927 ....New York (A) 4, Pittsburgh (N) 0	1978 ....New York (A) 4, Los Angeles (N) 2
1928 ....New York (A) 4, St. Louis (N) 0	1979 ....Pittsburgh (N) 4, Baltimore (A) 3
1929 ....Philadelphia (A) 4, Chicago (N) 1	1980 ....Philadelphia (N) 4, Kansas City (A) 2
1930 ....Philadelphia (A) 4, St. Louis (N) 2	1981 ....Los Angeles (N) 4, New York (A) 2
1931 ....St. Louis (N) 4, Philadelphia (A) 3	1982 ....St. Louis (N) 4, Milwaukee (A) 3
1932 ....New York (A) 4, Chicago (N) 0	1983 ....Baltimore (A) 4, Philadelphia (N) 1
1933 ....New York (N) 4, Washington (A) 1	1984 ....Detroit (A) 4, San Diego (N) 1
1934 ....St. Louis (N) 4, Detroit (A) 3	1985 ....Kansas City (A) 4, St. Louis (N) 3
1935 ....Detroit (A) 4, Chicago (N) 2	1986 ....New York (N) 4, Boston (A) 3
1936 ....New York (A) 4, New York (N) 2	1987 ....Minnesota (A) 4, St. Louis (N) 3
1937 ....New York (A) 4, New York (N) 1	1988 ....Los Angeles (N) 4, Oakland (A) 1
1938 ....New York (A) 4, Chicago (N) 0	1989 ....Oakland (A) 4, San Francisco (N) 0
1939 ....New York (A) 4, Cincinnati (N) 0	1990 ....Cincinnati (N) 4, Oakland (A) 0
1940 ....Cincinnati (N) 4, Detroit (A) 3	1991 ....Minnesota (A) 4, Atlanta (N) 3
1941 ....New York (A) 4, Brooklyn (N) 1	1992 ....Toronto (A) 4, Atlanta (N) 2
1942 ....St. Louis (N) 4, New York (A) 1	1993 ....Toronto (A) 4, Philadelphia (N) 2
1943 ....New York (A) 4, St. Louis (N) 1	1994 ....Series canceled due to players' strike.
1944 ....St. Louis (N) 4, St. Louis (A) 2	1995 ....Atlanta (N) 4, Cleveland (A) 2
1945 ....Detroit (A) 4, Chicago (N) 3	1996 ....New York (A) 4, Atlanta (N) 2
1946 ....St. Louis (N) 4, Boston (A) 3	1997 ....Florida (N) 4, Cleveland (A) 3
1947 ....New York (A) 4, Brooklyn (N) 3	1998 ....New York (A) 4, San Diego (N) 0
1948 ....Cleveland (A) 4, Boston (N) 2	1999 ....New York (A) 4, Atlanta (N) 0
1949 ....New York (A) 4, Brooklyn (N) 1	2000 ....New York (A) 4 , New York (N) 1
1950 ....New York (A) 4, Philadelphia (N) 0	2001 ....Arizona (N) 4, New York (A) 3
1951 ....New York (A) 4, New York (N) 2	2002 ....Anaheim (A) 4, San Francisco (N) 3
1952 ....New York (A) 4, Brooklyn (N) 3	2003 ....Florida (N) 4, New York (A) 2
1953 ....New York (A) 4, Brooklyn (N) 2	2004 ....Boston (A) 4, St. Louis (N) 0

Most Valuable Players

1955	Johnny Podres, Bklyn	1981	Ron Cey, LA; Steve Yeager, LA; Pedro Guerrero, LA
1956	Don Larsen, NY (A)	1982	Darrell Porter, StL
1957	Lew Burdette, Mil	1983	Rick Dempsey, Balt
1958	Bob Turley, NY (A)	1984	Alan Trammell, Det
1959	Larry Sherry, LA	1985	Bret Saberhagen, KC
1960	Bobby Richardson, NY (A)	1986	Ray Knight, NY (N)
1961	Whitey Ford, NY (A)	1987	Frank Viola, Minn
1962	Ralph Terry, NY (A)	1988	Orel Hershiser, LA
1963	Sandy Koufax, LA	1989	Dave Stewart, Oak
1964	Bob Gibson, StL	1990	Jose Rijo, Cin
1965	Sandy Koufax, LA	1991	Jack Morris, Minn
1966	Frank Robinson, Balt	1992	Pat Borders, Tor
1967	Bob Gibson, StL	1993	Paul Molitor, Tor
1968	Mickey Lolich, Det	1994	Series canceled due to strike.
1969	Donn Clendenon, NY (N)	1995	Tom Glavine, Atl
1970	Brooks Robinson, Balt	1996	John Wetteland, NY (A)
1971	Roberto Clemente, Pitt	1997	Livan Hernandez, Fla
1972	Gene Tenace, Oak	1998	Scott Brosius, NY (A)
1973	Reggie Jackson, Oak	1999	Mariano Rivera, NY (A)
1974	Rollie Fingers, Oak	2000	Derek Jeter, NY (A)
1975	Pete Rose, Cin	2001	Randy Johnson, Ariz; Curt Schilling, Ariz
1976	Johnny Bench, Cin	2002	Troy Glaus, Ana
1977	Reggie Jackson, NY (A)	2003	Josh Beckett, Fla
1978	Bucky Dent, NY (A)	2004	Manny Ramirez, Bos
1979	Willie Stargell, Pitt		
1980	Mike Schmidt, Phil		

Career Batting Leaders (Minimum 40 at bats)

GAMES

Yogi Berra	75
Mickey Mantle	65
Elston Howard	54
Hank Bauer	53
Gil McDougald	53
Phil Rizzuto	52
Joe DiMaggio	51
Frankie Frisch	50
Pee Wee Reese	44
Roger Maris	41
Babe Ruth	41

AT BATS

Yogi Berra	259
Mickey Mantle	230
Joe DiMaggio	199
Frankie Frisch	197
Gil McDougald	190
Hank Bauer	188
Phil Rizzuto	183
Elston Howard	171
Pee Wee Reese	169
Roger Maris	152

HITS

Yogi Berra	71
Mickey Mantle	59
Frankie Frisch	58
Joe DiMaggio	54
Pee Wee Reese	46
Hank Bauer	46
Phil Rizzuto	45
Gil McDougald	45
Lou Gehrig	43
Eddie Collins	42
Babe Ruth	42
Elston Howard	42

BATTING AVERAGE

Bobby Brown	.439
Paul Molitor	.418
Pepper Martin	.418
Hal McRae	.400
Lou Brock	.391
Marquis Grissom	.390
Thurman Munson	.373
George Brett	.373
Pat Borders	.372
Hank Aaron	.364

HOME RUNS

Mickey Mantle	18
Babe Ruth	15
Yogi Berra	12
Duke Snider	11
Reggie Jackson	10
Lou Gehrig	10
Frank Robinson	8
Bill Skowron	8
Joe DiMaggio	8
Goose Goslin	7
Hank Bauer	7
Gil McDougald	7

RUNS BATTED IN

Mickey Mantle	40
Yogi Berra	39
Lou Gehrig	35
Babe Ruth	33
Joe DiMaggio	30
Bill Skowron	29
Duke Snider	26
Reggie Jackson	24
Bill Dickey	24
Hank Bauer	24
Gil McDougald	24

RUNS

Mickey Mantle	42
Yogi Berra	41
Babe Ruth	37
Lou Gehrig	30
Joe DiMaggio	27
Derek Jeter	27
Roger Maris	26
Elston Howard	25
Gil McDougald	23
Jackie Robinson	22

STOLEN BASES

Lou Brock	14
Eddie Collins	14
Frank Chance	10
Davey Lopes	10
Phil Rizzuto	10
Honus Wagner	9
Frankie Frisch	9
Johnny Evers	8
Kenny Lofton	8
Roberto Alomar	7
Joe Tinker	7
Pepper Martin	7
Joe Morgan	7
Rickey Henderson	7

Career Batting Leaders (Cont.)

TOTAL BASES

Mickey Mantle	123
Yogi Berra	117
Babe Ruth	96
Lou Gehrig	87
Joe DiMaggio	84
Duke Snider	79
Hank Bauer	75
Reggie Jackson	74
Frankie Frisch	74
Gil McDougald	72

SLUGGING AVERAGE

Reggie Jackson	.755
Babe Ruth	.744
Lou Gehrig	.731
Bobby Brown	.707
Lenny Dykstra	.700
Al Simmons	.658
Lou Brock	.655
Pepper Martin	.636
Paul Molitor	.636
Joe Harris	.625

STRIKEOUTS

Mickey Mantle	54
Elston Howard	37
Duke Snider	33
Derek Jeter	33
Babe Ruth	30
David Justice	30
Gil McDougald	29
Bill Skowron	26
Bernie Williams	26
Hank Bauer	25
Reggie Jackson	24
Bob Meusel	24
Jorge Posada	24

Career Pitching Leaders

GAMES

Whitey Ford	22
Mariano Rivera	20
Mike Stanton	19
Jeff Nelson	16
Rollie Fingers	16
Allie Reynolds	15
Bob Turley	15
Clay Carroll	14
Clem Labine	13
Mark Wohlers	13

LOSSES

Whitey Ford	8
Eddie Plank	5
Schoolboy Rowe	5
Joe Bush	5
Rube Marquard	5
Christy Mathewson	5

COMPLETE GAMES

Christy Mathewson	10
Chief Bender	9
Bob Gibson	8
Red Ruffing	7
Whitey Ford	7
George Mullin	6
Eddie Plank	6
Art Nehf	6
Waite Hoyt	6

INNINGS PITCHED

Whitey Ford	146
Christy Mathewson	101⅔
Red Ruffing	85⅔
Chief Bender	85
Waite Hoyt	83⅔
Bob Gibson	81
Art Nehf	79
Allie Reynolds	77
Jim Palmer	65
Catfish Hunter	63

SAVES

Mariano Rivera	9
Rollie Fingers	6
Allie Reynolds	4
Johnny Murphy	4
John Wetteland	4
Robb Nen	4

STRIKEOUTS

Whitey Ford	94
Bob Gibson	92
Allie Reynolds	62
Sandy Koufax	61
Red Ruffing	61
Chief Bender	59
George Earnshaw	56
John Smoltz	52
Waite Hoyt	49
Christy Mathewson	48
Roger Clemens	48

*EARNED RUN AVERAGE

Jack Billingham	0.35
Harry Brecheen	0.83
Babe Ruth	0.87
Sherry Smith	0.89
Sandy Koufax	0.95
Hippo Vaughn	1.00
Monte Pearson	1.01
Christy Mathewson	1.06
Mariano Rivera	1.16
Babe Adams	1.29

BASES ON BALLS

Whitey Ford	34
Allie Reynolds	32
Art Nehf	32
Jim Palmer	31
Bob Turley	29
Paul Derringer	27
Red Ruffing	27
Don Gullett	26
Burleigh Grimes	26
Vic Raschi	25

WINS

Whitey Ford	10
Bob Gibson	7
Red Ruffing	7
Allie Reynolds	7
Lefty Gomez	6
Chief Bender	6
Waite Hoyt	6
Jack Coombs	5
Three Finger Brown	5
Herb Pennock	5
Christy Mathewson	5
Vic Raschi	5
Catfish Hunter	5

SHUTOUTS

Christy Mathewson	4
Three Finger Brown	3
Whitey Ford	3
Bill Hallahan	2
Lew Burdette	2
Bill Dinneen	2
Sandy Koufax	2
Allie Reynolds	2
Art Nehf	2
Bob Gibson	2

*Minimum 25 innings pitched.

Alltime Team Rankings (by championships)

Team	W	L	Appearances	Pct.	Most Recent	Last Championship
New York Yankees	26	13	39	.666	2003	2000
Phil/KC/Oakland Athletics	9	5	14	.643	1990	1989
St. Louis Cardinals	9	7	16	.563	2004	1982
Brooklyn/LA Dodgers	6	12	18	.333	1988	1988
Boston Red Sox	6	4	10	.600	2004	2004
Pittsburgh Pirates	5	2	7	.714	1979	1979
Cincinnati Reds	5	4	9	.556	1990	1990
New York/San Francisco Giants	5	12	17	.294	2002	1954
Detroit Tigers	4	5	9	.444	1984	1984
Washington/Minnesota Twins	3	3	6	.500	1991	1991
St. Louis/Baltimore Orioles	3	4	7	.429	1983	1983
Boston/Milwaukee/Atlanta Braves	3	6	9	.333	1999	1995
Florida Marlins	2	0	2	1.000	2003	2003
Toronto Blue Jays	2	0	2	1.000	1993	1993
New York Mets	2	2	4	.500	2000	1986
Chicago White Sox	2	2	4	.500	1959	1917
Cleveland Indians	2	3	5	.400	1997	1948
Chicago Cubs	2	8	10	.200	1945	1908
Anaheim Angels	1	0	1	1.000	2002	2002
Arizona Diamondbacks	1	0	1	1.000	2001	2001
Kansas City Royals	1	1	2	.500	1985	1985
Philadelphia Phillies	1	4	5	.200	1993	1980
Seattle/Milwaukee Brewers	0	1	1	.000	1982	—
San Diego Padres	0	2	2	.000	1998	—

League Championship Series

National League

1969	New York (E) 3, Atlanta (W) 0
1970	Cincinnati (W) 3, Pittsburgh (E) 0
1971	Pittsburgh (E) 3, San Francisco (W) 1
1972	Cincinnati (W) 3, Pittsburgh (E) 2
1973	New York (E) 3, Cincinnati (W) 2
1974	Los Angeles (W) 3, Pittsburgh (E) 1
1975	Cincinnati (W) 3, Pittsburgh (E) 0
1976	Cincinnati (W) 3, Philadelphia (E) 0
1977	Los Angeles (W) 3, Philadelphia (E) 1
1978	Los Angeles (W) 3, Philadelphia (E) 1
1979	Pittsburgh (E) 3, Cincinnati (W) 0
1980	Philadelphia (E) 3, Houston (W) 2
1981	Los Angeles (W) 3, Montreal (E) 2
1982	St. Louis (E) 3, Atlanta (W) 0
1983	Philadelphia (E) 3, Los Angeles (W) 1
1984	San Diego (W) 3, Chicago (E) 2
1985	St. Louis (E) 4, Los Angeles (W) 2
1986	New York (E) 4, Houston (W) 2
1987	St. Louis (E) 4, San Francisco (W) 3
1988	Los Angeles (W) 4, New York (E) 3
1989	San Francisco (W) 4, Chicago (E) 1
1990	Cincinnati (W) 4, Pittsburgh (E) 2
1991	Atlanta (W) 4, Pittsburgh (E) 3
1992	Atlanta (W) 4, Pitsburgh (E) 3
1993	Philadelphia (E) 4, Atlanta (W) 2
1994	Playoffs canceled due to players' strike.
1995	Atlanta (E) 4, Cincinnati (C) 0
1996	Atlanta (E) 4, St. Louis (C) 3
1997	Florida (E) 4, Atlanta (E) 2
1998	San Diego (W) 4, Atlanta (E) 2
1999	Atlanta (E) 4, New York (wc) 2
2000	New York (wc) 4, St. Louis (C) 1
2001	Arizona (W) 4, Atlanta (E) 1
2002	San Francisco (wc) 4, St. Louis (C) 1
2003	Florida (wc) 4, Chicago (C) 3
2004	St. Louis (C) 4, Houston (wc) 3

American League

1969	Baltimore (E) 3, Minnesota (W) 0
1970	Baltimore (E) 3, Minnesota (W) 0
1971	Baltimore (E) 3, Oakland (W) 0
1972	Oakland (W) 3, Detroit (E) 2
1973	Oakland (W) 3, Baltimore (E) 2
1974	Oakland (W) 3, Baltimore (E) 1
1975	Boston (E) 3, Oakland (W) 0
1976	New York (E) 3, Kansas City (W) 2
1977	New York (E) 3, Kansas City (W) 2
1978	New York (E) 3, Kansas City (W) 1
1979	Baltimore (E) 3, California (W) 1
1980	Kansas City (W) 3, New York (E) 0
1981	New York (E) 3, Oakland (W) 0
1982	Milwaukee (E) 3, California (W) 2
1983	Baltimore (E) 3, Chicago (W) 1
1984	Detroit (E) 3, Kansas City (W) 0
1985	Kansas City (W) 4, Toronto (E) 3
1986	Boston (E) 4, California (W) 3
1987	Minnesota (W) 4, Detroit (E) 1
1988	Oakland (W) 4, Boston (E) 0
1989	Oakland (W) 4, Toronto (E) 1
1990	Oakland (W) 4, Boston (E) 0
1991	Minnesota (W) 4, Toronto (E) 1
1992	Toronto (E) 4, Oakland (W) 2
1993	Toronto (E) 4, Chicago (W) 2
1994	Playoffs canceled due to players' strike.
1995	Cleveland (C) 4, Seattle (W) 2
1996	New York (E) 4, Baltimore (wc) 1
1997	Cleveland (C) 4, Baltimore (E) 2
1998	New York (E) 4, Cleveland (C) 2
1999	New York (E) 4, Boston (wc) 1
2000	New York (E) 4, Seattle (wc) 2
2001	New York (E) 4, Seattle (W) 1
2002	Anaheim (wc) 4, Minnesota (C) 1
2003	New York (E) 4, Boston (wc) 3
2004	Boston (wc) 4, New York (E) 3

NLCS Most Valuable Player

1977........Dusty Baker, LA	1987........Jeffrey Leonard, SF	1996........Javier Lopez, Atl
1978........Steve Garvey, LA	1988........Orel Hershiser, LA	1997........Livan Hernandez, Fla
1979........Willie Stargell, Pitt	1989........Will Clark, SF	1998........Sterling Hitchcock, SD
1980........Manny Trillo, Phil	1990........R. Myers/R. Dibble, Cin	1999........Eddie Perez, Atl
1981........Burt Hooton, LA	1991........Steve Avery, Atl	2000........Mike Hampton, NY
1982........Darrell Porter, StL	1992........John Smoltz, Atl	2001........Craig Counsell, Ariz
1983........Gary Matthews, Phil	1993........Curt Schilling, Phil	2002........Benito Santiago, SF
1984........Steve Garvey, SD	1994........Playoffs canceled	2003........Ivan Rodriguez, Fla
1985........Ozzie Smith, StL	1995........Mike Devereaux, Atl	2004........Albert Pujols, StL
1986........Mike Scott, Hou		

ALCS Most Valuable Player

1980........Frank White, KC	1988........Dennis Eckersley, Oak	1997........Marquis Grissom, Clev
1981........Graig Nettles, NY	1989........Rickey Henderson, Oak	1998........David Wells, NY
1982........Fred Lynn, Calif	1990........Dave Stewart, Oak	1999........Orlando Hernandez, NY
1983........Mike Boddicker, Balt	1991........Kirby Puckett, Minn	2000........David Justice, NY
1984........Kirk Gibson, Det	1992........Roberto Alomar, Tor	2001........Andy Pettitte, NY
1985........George Brett, KC	1993........Dave Stewart, Tor	2002........Adam Kennedy, Ana
1986........Marty Barrett, Bos	1994........Playoffs canceled	2003........Mariano Rivera, NY
1987........Gary Gaetti, Minn	1995........Orel Hershiser, Clev	2004........David Ortiz, Bos
	1996........Bernie Williams, NY	

Divisional Playoffs

National League

1995	Atlanta (E) 3, Colorado (wc) 1
	Cincinnati (C) 3, Los Angeles (W) 0
1996	St. Louis (C) 3, San Diego (W) 0
	Atlanta (E) 3, Los Angeles (wc) 0
1997	Atlanta (E) 3, Houston (C) 0
	Florida (wc) 3, San Francisco (W) 0
1998	San Diego (W) 3, Houston (C) 1
	Atlanta (E) 3, Chicago (wc) 0
1999	Atlanta (E) 3, Houston (C) 1
	New York (wc) 3, Arizona (W) 1
2000	St. Louis (C) 3, Atlanta (E) 0
	New York (wc) 3, San Francisco (W) 1
2001	Atlanta (E) 3, Houston (C) 0
	Arizona (W) 3, St. Louis (wc) 2
2002	St. Louis (C) 3, Arizona (W) 0
	San Francisco (wc) 3, Atlanta (E) 2
2003	Chicago (C) 3, Atlanta (E) 2
	Florida (wc) 3, San Francisco (W) 1
2004	St. Louis (C) 3, Los Angeles (W) 1
	Houston (wc) 3, Atlanta (E) 2

American League

1995	Cleveland (C) 3, Boston (E) 0
	Seattle (W) 3, New York (wc) 2
1996	Baltimore (wc) 3, Cleveland (C) 1
	New York (E) 3, Texas (W) 1
1997	Baltimore (E) 3, Seattle (W) 1
	Cleveland (C) 3, New York (wc) 2
1998	New York (E) 3, Texas (W) 0
	Cleveland (C) 3, Boston (wc) 1
1999	New York (E) 3, Texas (W) 1
	Boston (wc) 3, Cleveland (C) 2
2000	New York (E) 3, Oakland (W) 2
	Seattle (wc) 3, Chicago (C) 0
2001	Seattle (W) 3, Cleveland (wc) 2
	New York (E) 3, Oakland (wc) 2
2002	Minnesota (C) 3, Oakland (W) 2
	Anaheim (wc) 3, New York (E) 1
2003	New York (E) 3, Minnesota (C) 1
	Boston (wc) 3, Oakland (W) 2
2004	New York (E) 3, Minnesota (C) 1
	Boston (wc) 3 Anaheim (W) 0

The All-Star Game

Results

Date	Winner	Score	Site	Date	Winner	Score	Site
7-6-33	American	4–2	Comiskey Park, Chi	7-14-53	National	5–1	Crosley Field, Cin
7-10-34	American	9–7	Polo Grounds, NY	7-13-54	American	11–9	Municipal Stadium, Clev
7-8-35	American	4–1	Municipal Stadium, Clev	7-12-55	National	6–5	County Stadium, Mil
7-7-36	National	4–3	Braves Field, Bos	7-10-56	National	7–3	Griffith Stadium, Wash
7-7-37	American	8–3	Griffith Stadium, Wash	7-9-57	American	6–5	Busch Stadium, StL
7-6-38	National	4–1	Crosley Field, Cin	7-8-58	American	4–3	Memorial Stadium, Balt
7-11-39	American	3–1	Yankee Stadium, NY	7-7-59	National	5–4	Forbes Field, Pitt
7-10-40	National	4–0	Sportsman's Park, StL	8-3-59	American	5–3	Memorial Coliseum, LA
7-8-41	American	7–5	Briggs Stadium, Det	7-11-60	National	5–3	Municipal Stadium, KC
7-6-42	American	3–1	Polo Grounds, NY	7-13-60	National	6–0	Yankee Stadium, NY
7-13-43	American	5–3	Shibe Park, Phil	7-11-61	National	5–4	Candlestick Park, SF
7-11-44	National	7–1	Forbes Field, Pitt	7-31-61	Tie*	1–1	Fenway Park, Bos
1945	No game due to wartime travel restrictions.			7-10-62	National	3–1	D.C. Stadium, Wash
7-9-46	American	12–0	Fenway Park, Bos	7-30-62	American	9–4	Wrigley Field, Chi
7-8-47	American	2–1	Wrigley Field, Chi	7-9-63	National	5–3	Municipal Stadium, Clev
7-13-48	American	5–2	Sportsman's Park, StL	7-7-64	National	7–4	Shea Stadium, NY
7-12-49	American	11–7	Ebbets Field, Bklyn	7-13-65	National	6–5	Metro. Stadium, Minn
7-11-50	National	4–3	Comiskey Park, Chi	7-12-66	National	2–1	Busch Stadium, StL
7-10-51	National	8–3	Briggs Stadium, Det	7-11-67	National	2–1	Anaheim Stadium, Cal
7-8-52	National	3–2	Shibe Park, Phil	7-9-68	National	1–0	Astrodome, Hou

*Game called because of rain after nine innings.

Results *(Cont.)*

Date	Winner	Score	Site	Date	Winner	Score	Site
7-23-69	National	9–3	R.F.K. Stadium, Wash.	7-12-88	American	2–1	Riverfront Stadium, Cin
7-14-70	National	5–4	Riverfront Stadium, Cin	7-11-89	American	5–3	Anaheim Stadium, Cal
7-13-71	American	6–4	Tiger Stadium, Det	7-10-90	American	2–0	Wrigley Field, Chi
7-25-72	National	4–3	Atlanta Stadium, Atl	7-9-91	American	4–2	SkyDome, Tor
7-24-73	National	7–1	Royals Stadium, KC	7-14-92	American	13–6	Jack Murphy Stadium, SD
7-23-74	National	7–2	Three Rivers Stadium, Pitt	7-13-93	American	9–3	Camden Yards, Balt
7-15-75	National	6–3	County Stadium, Mil	7-12-94	National	8–7	Three Rivers Stadium, Pitt
7-13-76	National	7–1	Veterans Stadium, Phil	7-11-95	National	3–2	The Ballpark in
7-19-77	National	7–5	Yankee Stadium, NY				Arlington, Tex
7-11-78	National	7–3	Jack Murphy Stadium, SD	7-9-96	National	6–0	Veterans Stadium, Phil
7-17-79	National	7–6	Kingdome, Sea	7-8-97	American	3–1	Jacobs Field, Clev
7-8-80	National	4–2	Dodger Stadium, LA	7-7-98	American	13–8	Coors Field, Col
8-9-81	National	5–4	Municipal Stadium, Clev	7-13-99	American	4–1	Fenway Park, Bos
7-13-82	National	4–1	Olympic Stadium, Mtl	7-11-00	American	6–3	Turner Field, Atl
7-6-83	American	13–3	Comiskey Park, Chi	7-10-01	American	4–1	Safeco Field, Sea
7-10-84	National	3–1	Candlestick Park, SF	7-9-02	Tie (11 inn)	7–7	Miller Park, Milwaukee
7-16-85	National	6–1	Metrodome, Minn	7-15-03	American	7–6	Comiskey Park, Chicago
7-15-86	American	3–2	Astrodome, Hou	7-13-04	American	9–4	Minute Maid Park, Hou
7-14-87	National	2–0	Oakland Coliseum, Oak				

Most Valuable Players

1962	Maury Wills, LA	NL	1976	George Foster, Cin	NL	1992	Ken Griffey Jr., Sea	AL
	Leon Wagner, LA	AL	1977	Don Sutton, LA	NL	1993	Kirby Puckett, Minn	AL
1963	Willie Mays, SF	NL	1978	Steve Garvey, LA	NL	1994	Fred McGriff, Atl	NL
1964	Johnny Callison, Phil	NL	1979	Dave Parker, Pitt	NL	1995	Jeff Conine, Fla	NL
1965	Juan Marichal, SF	NL	1980	Ken Griffey, Cin	NL	1996	Mike Piazza, LA	NL
1966	Brooks Robinson, Balt	AL	1981	Gary Carter, Mtl	NL	1997	Sandy Alomar, Clev	AL
1967	Tony Perez, Cin	NL	1982	Dave Concepcion, Cin	NL	1998	Roberto Alomar, Balt	AL
1968	Willie Mays, SF	NL	1983	Fred Lynn, Calif	AL	1999	Pedro Martinez, Bos	AL
1969	Willie McCovey, SF	NL	1984	Gary Carter, Mtl	NL	2000	Derek Jeter, NY	AL
1970	Carl Yastrzemski, Bos	AL	1985	LaMarr Hoyt, SD	NL	2001	Cal Ripken Jr., Balt	AL
1971	Frank Robinson, Balt	AL	1986	Roger Clemens, Bos	AL	2002	None selected	
1972	Joe Morgan, Cin	NL	1987	Tim Raines, Mtl	NL	2003	Garret Anderson, Ana	AL
1973	Bobby Bonds, SF	NL	1988	Terry Steinbach, Oak	AL	2004	Alfonso Soriano, Tex	AL
1974	Steve Garvey, LA	NL	1989	Bo Jackson, KC	AL			
1975	Bill Madlock, Chi	NL	1990	Julio Franco, Tex	AL			
	Jon Matlack, NY	NL	1991	Cal Ripken Jr., Balt	AL			

The Regular Season

Most Valuable Players

NATIONAL LEAGUE

Year	Name and Team	Position	Noteworthy
1911	*Wildfire Schulte, Chi	Outfield	21 HR†, 121 RBI†, .300
1912	*Larry Doyle, NY	Second base	10 HR, 90 RBI, .330
1913	Jake Daubert, Bklyn	First base	52 RBI, .350†
1914	*Johnny Evers, Bos	Second base	FA .976†, .279
1915–23	No selection		
1924	Dazzy Vance, Bklyn	Pitcher	28†–6, 2.16 ERA†, 262 K†
1925	Rogers Hornsby, StL	Second base, Manager	39 HR†, 143 RBI†, .403†
1926	*Bob O'Farrell, StL	Catcher	7 HR, 68 RBI, .293
1927	*Paul Waner, Pitt	Outfield	237 hits†, 131 RBI†, .380†
1928	*Jim Bottomley, StL	First base	31 HR†, 136 RBI†, .325
1929	*Rogers Hornsby, Chi	Second base	39 HR, 149 RBI, 156 runs†, .380
1930	No selection		
1931	*Frankie Frisch, StL	Second base	4 HR, 82 RBI, 28 SB†, .311
1932	Chuck Klein, Phil	Outfield	38 HR†, 137 RBI, 226 hits†, .348
1933	*Carl Hubbell, NY	Pitcher	23†–12, 1.66 ERA†, 10 SO†
1934	*Dizzy Dean, StL	Pitcher	30†–7, 2.66 ERA, 195 K†
1935	*Gabby Hartnett, Chi	Catcher	13 HR, 91 RBI, .344
1936	*Carl Hubbell, NY	Pitcher	26†–6, 2.31 ERA†
1937	Joe Medwick, StL	Outfield	31 HR‡, 154 RBI†, 111 runs†, .374†
1938	Ernie Lombardi, Cin	Catcher	19 HR, 95 RBI, .342†
1939	*Bucky Walters, Cin	Pitcher	27†–11, 2.29 ERA†, 137 K‡
1940	*Frank McCormick, Cin	First base	19 HR, 127 RBI, 191 hits†, .309
1941	*Dolph Camilli, Bklyn	First base	34 HR†, 120 RBI†, .285

*Played for pennant or, after 1968, division winner. †Led league. ‡Tied for league lead.

Most Valuable Players *(Cont.)*
NATIONAL LEAGUE *(Cont.)*

Year	Name and Team	Position	Noteworthy
1942	*Mort Cooper, StL	Pitcher	22†–7, 1.78 ERA†, 10 SO†
1943	*Stan Musial, StL	Outfield	13 HR, 81 RBI, 220 hits†, .357†
1944	*Marty Marion, StL	Shortstop	FA .972†, 63 RBI
1945	*Phil Cavarretta, Chi	First base	6 HR, 97 RBI, .355†
1946	*Stan Musial, StL	First base, Outfield	103 RBI, 124 runs†, 228 hits†, .365†
1947	Bob Elliott, Bos	Third base	22 HR, 113 RBI, .317
1948	Stan Musial, StL	Outfield	39 HR, 131 RBI†, .376†
1949	*Jackie Robinson, Bklyn	Second base	16 HR, 124 RBI, 37 SB†, .342†
1950	*Jim Konstanty, Phil	Pitcher	16–7, 22 saves†, 2.66 ERA
1951	Roy Campanella, Bklyn	Catcher	33 HR, 108 RBI, .325
1952	Hank Sauer, Chi	Outfield	37 HR‡, 121 RBI†, .270
1953	*Roy Campanella, Bklyn	Catcher	41 HR, 142 RBI†, .312
1954	*Willie Mays, NY	Outfield	41 HR, 110 RBI, 13 3B†, .345†
1955	*Roy Campanella, Bklyn	Catcher	32 HR, 107 RBI, .318
1956	*Don Newcombe, Bklyn	Pitcher	27†–7, 3.06 ERA
1957	*Hank Aaron, Mil	Outfield	44 HR†, 132 RBI†, .322
1958	Ernie Banks, Chi	Shortstop	47 HR†, 129 RBI†, .313
1959	Ernie Banks, Chi	Shortstop	45 HR, 143 RBI†, .304
1960	*Dick Groat, Pitt	Shortstop	2 HR, 50 RBI, .325†
1961	*Frank Robinson, Cin	Outfield	37 HR, 124 RBI, .323
1962	Maury Wills, LA	Shortstop	104 SB†, 208 hits, .299, GG
1963	*Sandy Koufax, LA	Pitcher	25‡–5, 1.88 ERA†, 306 K†
1964	*Ken Boyer, StL	Third Base	24 HR, 119 RBI†, .295
1965	Willie Mays, SF	Outfield	52 HR†, 112 RBI, .317, GG
1966	Roberto Clemente, Pitt	Outfield	29 HR, 119 RBI, 202 hits, .317, GG
1967	*Orlando Cepeda, StL	First base	25 HR, 111 RBI†, .325
1968	*Bob Gibson, StL	Pitcher	22–9, 1.12 ERA†, 268 K†, 13 SO†, GG
1969	Willie McCovey, SF	First base	45 HR†, 126 RBI†, .320
1970	*Johnny Bench, Cin	Catcher	45 HR†, 148 RBI†, .293, GG
1971	Joe Torre, StL	Third base	24 HR, 137 RBI†, .363†
1972	*Johnny Bench, Cin	Catcher	40 HR†, 125 RBI†, .270, GG
1973	*Pete Rose, Cin	Outfield	5 HR, 64 RBI, .338†, 230 hits†
1974	*Steve Garvey, LA	First base	21 HR, 111 RBI, 200 hits, .312, GG
1975	*Joe Morgan, Cin	Second base	17 HR, 94 RBI, 67 SB, .327, GG
1976	*Joe Morgan, Cin	Second base	27 HR, 111 RBI, 60 SB, .320, GG
1977	George Foster, Cin	Outfield	52 HR†, 149 RBI†, .320
1978	Dave Parker, Pitt	Outfield	30 HR, 117 RBI, .334†, GG
1979	Keith Hernandez, StL	First base	11 HR, 105 RBI, 210 hits, .344†, GG
	*Willie Stargell, Pitt	First base	32 HR, 82 RBI, .281
1980	*Mike Schmidt, Phil	Third base	48 HR†, 121 RBI†, .286, GG
1981	Mike Schmidt, Phil	Third base	31 HR†, 91 RBI†, 78 runs†, .316, GG
1982	*Dale Murphy, Atl	Outfield	36 HR, 109 RBI†, .281, GG
1983	Dale Murphy, Atl	Outfield	36 HR, 121 RBI†, .302, GG
1984	*Ryne Sandberg, Chi	Second base	19 HR, 84 RBI, 114 runs†, .314, GG
1985	*Willie McGee, StL	Outfield	10 HR, 82 RBI, 18 3B†, .353†, GG
1986	Mike Schmidt, Phil	Third base	37 HR†, 119 RBI†, .290, GG
1987	Andre Dawson, Chi	Outfield	49 HR†, 137 RBI†, .287, GG
1988	*Kirk Gibson, LA	Outfield	25 HR, 76 RBI, 106 runs, .290
1989	*Kevin Mitchell, SF	Outfield	47 HR†, 125 RBI†, .291
1990	*Barry Bonds, Pitt	Outfield	33 HR, 114 RBI, .301
1991	*Terry Pendleton, Atl	Third base	23 HR, 86 RBI, .319†
1992	Barry Bonds, Pitt	Outfield	34 HR, 103 RBI, .311
1993	Barry Bonds, SF	Outfield	46 HR†, 123 RBI†, .336
1994	Jeff Bagwell, Hou	First base	39 HR, 116 RBI†, .368
1995	*Barry Larkin, Cin	Shortstop	15 HR, 66 RBI, 51 SB, .319
1996	*Ken Caminiti, SD	Third base	40 HR, 130 RBI, .326
1997	Larry Walker, Col	Outfield	49 HR†, 130 RBI, .452 OBA†, .366, GG
1998	Sammy Sosa, Chi	Outfield	66 HR, 158 RBI†, 134 runs†, 416 TB†, .308
1999	*Chipper Jones, Atl	Third Base	45 HR, 110 RBI, 116 runs, .319
2000	*Jeff Kent, SF	Second Base	33 HR, 125 RBI, 114 runs, .334
2001	Barry Bonds, SF	Outfield	73 HR†, 137 RBI. 177 BB†, .328, .863 SLG†
2002	Barry Bonds, SF	Outfield	46 HR, 110 RBI, .582 OBP, .370
2003	*Barry Bonds, SF	Outfield	45 HR, .341 avg, .529 OBP†, .749 SLG†

*Played for pennant or, after 1968, division winner. †Led league. ‡Tied for league lead.

Most Valuable Players (Cont.)

AMERICAN LEAGUE

Year	Name and Team	Position	Noteworthy
1911	Ty Cobb, Det	Outfield	8 HR, 144 RBI†, 24 3B†, .420†
1912	*Tris Speaker, Bos	Outfield	10 HR‡, 98 RBI, 53 2B†, .383
1913	Walter Johnson, Wash	Pitcher	36†–7, 1.09 ERA†, 11 SO†, 243 K†
1914	*Eddie Collins, Phil	Second base	2 HR, 85 RBI, 122 runs†, .344
1915–21	No selection		
1922	George Sisler, StL	First base	8 HR, 105 RBI, 246 hits†, .420†
1923	*Babe Ruth, NY	Outfield	41 HR†, 131 RBI†, .393
1924	*Walter Johnson, Wash	Pitcher	23†–7, 2.72 ERA†, 158 K†
1925	*Roger Peckinpaugh, Wash	Shortstop	4 HR, 64 RBI, .294
1926	George Burns, Clev	First base	114 RBI, 216 hits‡, 64 2B†, .358
1927	*Lou Gehrig, NY	First base	47 HR, 175 RBI†, 52 2B†, .373
1928	Mickey Cochrane, Phil	Catcher	10 HR, 57 RBI, .293
1929	No selection		
1930	No selection		
1931	*Lefty Grove, Phil	Pitcher	31†–4, 2.06 ERA†, 175 K†
1932	Jimmie Foxx, Phil	First base	58 HR†, 169 RBI†, 151 runs†, .364
1933	Jimmie Foxx, Phil	First base	48 HR†, 163 RBI†, .356†
1934	*Mickey Cochrane, Det	Catcher	2 HR, 76 RBI, .320
1935	*Hank Greenberg, Det	First base	36 HR†, 170 RBI†, 203 hits, .328
1936	*Lou Gehrig, NY	First base	49 HR†, 152 RBI, 167 runs†, .354
1937	Charlie Gehringer, Det	Second base	14 HR, 96 RBI, 133 runs, .371†
1938	Jimmie Foxx, Phil	First base	50 HR, 175 RBI†, .349†
1939	*Joe DiMaggio, NY	Outfield	30 HR, 126 RBI, .381†
1940	*Hank Greenberg, Det	Outfield	41 HR†, 150 RBI†, 50 2B†, .340
1941	*Joe DiMaggio, NY	Outfield	30 HR, 125 RBI†, .357
1942	*Joe Gordon, NY	Second base	18 HR, 103 RBI, .322
1943	*Spud Chandler, NY	Pitcher	20†–4, 1.64 ERA†, 5 SO‡
1944	Hal Newhouser, Det	Pitcher	29†–9, 2.22 ERA†, 187 K†
1945	*Hal Newhouser, Det	Pitcher	25†–9, 1.81 ERA†, 8 SO†, 212 K†
1946	*Ted Williams, Bos	Outfield	38 HR, 123 RBI, 142 runs†, .342
1947	*Joe DiMaggio, NY	Outfield	20 HR, 97 RBI, .315
1948	*Lou Boudreau, Clev	Shortstop	18 HR, 106 RBI, .355
1949	Ted Williams, Bos	Outfield	43 HR†, 159 RBI†, 150 runs†, .343
1950	*Phil Rizzuto, NY	Shortstop	125 runs, 200 hits, .324
1951	*Yogi Berra, NY	Catcher	27 HR, 88 RBI, .294
1952	Bobby Shantz, Phil	Pitcher	24†–7, 2.48 ERA
1953	Al Rosen, Clev	Third base	43 HR†, 145 RBI†, 115 runs†, .336
1954	Yogi Berra, NY	Catcher	22 HR, 125 RBI, .307
1955	*Yogi Berra, NY	Catcher	27 HR, 108 RBI, .272
1956	*Mickey Mantle, NY	Outfield	52 HR†, 130 RBI†, 132 runs†, .353†
1957	*Mickey Mantle, NY	Outfield	34 HR, 94 RBI, 121 runs†, .365
1958	Jackie Jensen, Bos	Outfield	35 HR, 122 RBI†, .286
1959	*Nellie Fox, Chi	Second base	2 HR, 70 RBI, .306, GG
1960	*Roger Maris, NY	Outfield	39 HR, 112 RBI†, .283, GG
1961	*Roger Maris, NY	Outfield	61 HR†, 142 RBI†, .269
1962	*Mickey Mantle, NY	Outfield	30 HR, 89 RBI, .321, GG
1963	*Elston Howard, NY	Catcher	28 HR, 85 RBI, .287, GG
1964	Brooks Robinson, Balt	Third base	28 HR, 118 RBI†, .317, GG
1965	*Zoilo Versalles, Minn	Shortstop	126 runs†, 45 2B‡, 12 3B‡, GG
1966	*Frank Robinson, Balt	Outfield	49 HR†, 122 RBI†, 122 runs†, .316†
1967	*Carl Yastrzemski, Bos	Outfield	44 HR‡, 121 RBI†, 112 runs†, .326†, GG
1968	*Denny McLain, Det	Pitcher	31†–6, 1.96 ERA, 280 K
1969	*Harmon Killebrew, Minn	Third base, First base	49 HR†, 140 RBI†, .276
1970	*Boog Powell, Balt	First base	35 HR, 114 RBI, .297
1971	*Vida Blue, Oak	Pitcher	24–8, 1.82 ERA†, 8 SO†, 301 K
1972	Dick Allen, Chi	First base	37 HR†, 113 RBI†, .308
1973	*Reggie Jackson, Oak	Outfield	32 HR†, 117 RBI†, 99 runs†, .293
1974	Jeff Burroughs, Tex	Outfield	25 HR, 118 RBI†, .301
1975	Fred Lynn, Bos	Outfield	21 HR, 105 RBI, 103 runs†, .331, GG
1976	*Thurman Munson, NY	Catcher	17 HR, 105 RBI, .302
1977	Rod Carew, Minn	First base	100 RBI, 128 runs†, 239 hits†, .388†
1978	Jim Rice, Bos	Outfield, DH	46 HR†, 139 RBI†, 213 hits†, .315
1979	*Don Baylor, Calif	Outfield, DH	36 HR, 139 RBI†, 120 runs†, .296
1980	*George Brett, KC	Third base	24 HR, 118 RBI, .390†
1981	*Rollie Fingers, Mil	Pitcher	6–3, 28 saves†, 1.04 ERA
1982	*Robin Yount, Mil	Shortstop	29 HR, 114 RBI, 210 hits†, .331, GG

Most Valuable Players (Cont.)
AMERICAN LEAGUE (Cont.)

Year	Name and Team	Position	Noteworthy
1983	*Cal Ripken Jr., Balt	Shortstop	27 HR, 102 RBI, 121 runs†, 211 hits†, .318
1984	*Willie Hernandez, Det	Pitcher	9–3, 32 saves, 1.92 ERA
1985	Don Mattingly, NY	First base	35 HR, 145 RBI†, 48 2B†, .324, GG
1986	*Roger Clemens, Bos	Pitcher	24†–4, 2.48 ERA†, 238 K
1987	George Bell, Tor	Outfield	47 HR, 134 RBI†, .308
1988	*Jose Canseco, Oak	Outfield	42 HR†, 124 RBI†, 40 SB, .307
1989	Robin Yount, Mil	Outfield	21 HR, 103 RBI, 101 runs, .318
1990	*Rickey Henderson, Oak	Outfield	28 HR, 119 runs†, 65 SB†, .325
1991	Cal Ripken Jr., Balt	Shortstop	34 HR, 114 RBI, .323
1992	Dennis Eckersley, Oak	Pitcher	7–1, 1.91 ERA, 51 saves
1993	Frank Thomas, Chi	First base	41 HR, 128 RBI, .317
1994	Frank Thomas, Chi	First base	38 HR, 101 RBI, .353
1995	*Mo Vaughn, Bos	First base	39 HR, 126 RBI, .300
1996	*Juan Gonzalez, Tex	Outfield	47 HR, 144 RBI, .314
1997	*Ken Griffey Jr., Sea	Outfield	56 HR†, 125 runs†, 393 TB†, 147 RBI†, .304
1998	*Juan Gonzalez, Tex	Outfield	45 HR, 157 RBI†, 50 2B†, .318
1999	*Ivan Rodriguez, Tex	Catcher	35 HR, 113 RBI, 116 runs, .332, GG
2000	*Jason Giambi, Oak	First Base	43 HR, 137 RBI, .333
2001	*Ichiro Suzuki, Sea	Outfield	.350†, 242 H†, 127 R, 56 SB†
2002	*Miguel Tejada, Oak	Shortstop	34 HR, 131 RBI, .308
2003	Alex Rodriguez, Tex	Shortstop	47 HR†, 118 RBI, .600 SLG†

*Played for pennant or, after 1968, division winner. †Led league. ‡Tied for league lead.

Notes: 2B=doubles; 3B=triples; FA=fielding average; GG=won Gold Glove, award begun in 1957; K=strikeouts; SO=shutouts; SB=stolen bases; TB=total bases.

Rookies of the Year

NATIONAL LEAGUE

1947*	Jackie Robinson, Bklyn (1B)
1948*	Alvin Dark, Bos (SS)
1949	Don Newcombe, Bklyn (P)
1950	Sam Jethroe, Bos (OF)
1951	Willie Mays, NY (OF)
1952	Joe Black, Bklyn (P)
1953	Junior Gilliam, Bklyn (2B)
1954	Wally Moon, StL (OF)
1955	Bill Virdon, StL (OF)
1956	Frank Robinson, Cin (OF)
1957	Jack Sanford, Phil (P)
1958	Orlando Cepeda, SF (1B)
1959	Willie McCovey, SF (1B)
1960	Frank Howard, LA (OF)
1961	Billy Williams, Chi (OF)
1962	Ken Hubbs, Chi (2B)
1963	Pete Rose, Cin (2B)
1964	Dick Allen, Phil (3B)
1965	Jim Lefebvre, LA (2B)
1966	Tommy Helms, Cin (2B)
1967	Tom Seaver, NY (P)
1968	Johnny Bench, Cin (C)
1969	Ted Sizemore, LA (2B)
1970	Carl Morton, Mtl(P)
1971	Earl Williams, Atl (C)
1972	Jon Matlack, NY (P)
1973	Gary Matthews, SF (OF)
1974	Bake McBride, StL (OF)
1975	John Montefusco, SF (P)
1976	Pat Zachry, Cin (P)
	Butch Metzger, SD (P)
1977	Andre Dawson, Mtl (OF)
1978	Bob Horner, Atl (3B)
1979	Rick Sutcliffe, LA (P)
1980	Steve Howe, LA (P)
1981	Fernando Valenzuela, LA (P)
1982	Steve Sax, LA (2B)
1983	Darryl Strawberry, NY (OF)
1984	Dwight Gooden, NY (P)

AMERICAN LEAGUE

1949	Roy Sievers, StL (OF)
1950	Walt Dropo, Bos (1B)
1951	Gil McDougald, NY (3B)
1952	Harry Byrd, Phil (P)
1953	Harvey Kuenn, Det (SS)
1954	Bob Grim, NY (P)
1955	Herb Score, Clev (P)
1956	Luis Aparicio, Chi (SS)
1957	Tony Kubek, NY (OF, SS)
1958	Albie Pearson, Wash (OF)
1959	Bob Allison, Wash (OF)
1960	Ron Hansen, Balt (SS)
1961	Don Schwall, Bos (P)
1962	Tom Tresh, NY (SS)
1963	Gary Peters, Chi (P)
1964	Tony Oliva, Minn (OF)
1965	Curt Blefary, Balt (OF)
1966	Tommie Agee, Chi (OF)
1967	Rod Carew, Minn (2B)
1968	Stan Bahnsen, NY (P)
1969	Lou Piniella, KC (OF)
1970	Thurman Munson, NY (C)
1971	Chris Chambliss, Clev (1B)
1972	Carlton Fisk, Bos (C)
1973	Al Bumbry, Balt (OF)
1974	Mike Hargrove, Tex (1B)
1975	Fred Lynn, Bos (OF)
1976	Mark Fidrych, Det (P)
1977	Eddie Murray, Balt (DH)
1978	Lou Whitaker, Det (2B)
1979	Alfredo Griffin, Tor (SS)
	John Castino, Minn (3B)
1980	Joe Charboneau, Clev (OF)
1981	Dave Righetti, NY (P)
1982	Cal Ripken Jr., Balt (SS)
1983	Ron Kittle, Chi (OF)
1984	Alvin Davis, Sea (1B)

*Just one selection for both leagues.

Rookies of the Year (Cont.)

NATIONAL LEAGUE (Cont.)

1985	Vince Coleman, StL (OF)
1986	Todd Worrell, StL (P)
1987	Benito Santiago, SD (C)
1988	Chris Sabo, Cin (3B)
1989	Jerome Walton, Chi (OF)
1990	Dave Justice, Atl (OF)
1991	Jeff Bagwell, Hou (3B)
1992	Eric Karros, LA (1B)
1993	Mike Piazza, LA (C)
1994	Raul Mondesi, LA (OF)
1995	Hideo Nomo, LA (P)
1996	Todd Hollandsworth, LA (OF)
1997	Scott Rolen, Phil (3B)
1998	Kerry Wood, Chi (P)
1999	Scott Williamson, Cin-(P)
2000	Rafael Furcal, Atl (SS)
2001	Albert Pujols, StL (OF)
2002	Jason Jennings, Col (P)
2003	Dontrelle Willis, Fla (P)

AMERICAN LEAGUE (Cont.)

1985	Ozzie Guillen, Chi (SS)
1986	Jose Canseco, Oak (OF)
1987	Mark McGwire, Oak (1B)
1988	Walt Weiss, Oak (SS)
1989	Gregg Olson, Balt (P)
1990	Sandy Alomar Jr, Clev (C)
1991	Chuck Knoblauch, Minn (2B)
1992	Pat Listach, Mil (SS)
1993	Tim Salmon, Calif (OF)
1994	Bob Hamelin, KC (DH)
1995	Marty Cordova, Minn (OF)
1996	Derek Jeter, NY (SS)
1997	Nomar Garciaparra, Bos (SS)
1998	Ben Grieve, Oak (OF)
1999	Carlos Beltran, KC (OF)
2000	Kazuhiro Sasaki, Sea (P)
2001	Ichiro Suzuki, Sea (OF)
2002	Eric Hinske, Tor (3B)
2003	Angel Berroa, KC (SS)

Cy Young Award

Year		W–L	Sv	ERA	Year		W–L	Sv	ERA
1956	*Don Newcombe, Bklyn (NL)	27–7	0	3.06	1962	Don Drysdale, LA (NL)	25–9	1	2.83
1957	Warren Spahn, Mil (NL)	21–11	3	2.69	1963	*Sandy Koufax, LA (NL)	25–5	0	1.88
1958	Bob Turley, NY (AL)	21–7	1	2.97	1964	Dean Chance, LA (AL)	20–9	4	1.65
1959	Early Wynn, Chi (AL)	22–10	0	3.17	1965	Sandy Koufax, LA (NL)	26–8	2	2.04
1960	Vernon Law, Pitt (NL)	20–9	0	3.08	1966	Sandy Koufax, LA (NL)	27–9	0	1.73
1961	Whitey Ford, NY (AL)	25–4	0	3.21					

NATIONAL LEAGUE

Year		W–L	Sv	ERA
1967	Mike McCormick, SF	22–10	0	2.85
1968	*Bob Gibson, StL	22–9	0	1.12
1969	Tom Seaver, NY	25–7	0	2.21
1970	Bob Gibson, StL	23–7	0	3.12
1971	Ferguson Jenkins, Chi	24–13	0	2.77
1972	Steve Carlton, Phil	27–10	0	1.97
1973	Tom Seaver, NY	19–10	0	2.08
1974	Mike Marshall, LA	15–12	21	2.42
1975	Tom Seaver, NY	22–9	0	2.38
1976	Randy Jones, SD	22–14	0	2.74
1977	Steve Carlton, Phil	23–10	0	2.64
1978	Gaylord Perry, SD	21–6	0	2.72
1979	Bruce Sutter, Chi	6–6	37	2.23
1980	Steve Carlton, Phil	24–9	0	2.34
1981	Fernando Valenzuela, LA	13–7	0	2.48
1982	Steve Carlton, Phil	23–11	0	3.10
1983	John Denny, Phil	19–6	0	2.37
1984	†Rick Sutcliffe, Chi	16–1	0	2.69
1985	Dwight Gooden, NY	24–4	0	1.53
1986	Mike Scott, Hou	18–10	0	2.22
1987	Steve Bedrosian, Phil	5–3	40	2.83
1988	Orel Hershiser, LA	23–8	1	2.26
1989	Mark Davis, SD	4–3	44	1.85
1990	Doug Drabek, Pitt	22–6	0	2.76
1991	Tom Glavine, Atl	20–11	0	2.55
1992	Greg Maddux, Chi	20–11	0	2.18
1993	Greg Maddux, Atl	20–10	0	2.36
1994	Greg Maddux, Atl	16–6	0	1.56
1995	Greg Maddux, Atl	19–2	0	1.63
1996	John Smoltz, Atl	24–8	0	2.94
1997	Pedro Martinez, Mtl	17–8	0	1.90
1998	Tom Glavine, Atl	20–6	0	2.47
1999	Randy Johnson, Ariz	17–9	0	2.48
2000	Randy Johnson, Ariz	19–7	0	2.64
2001	Randy Johnson, Ariz	21–6	0	2.49
2002	Randy Johnson, Ariz	24–5	0	2.32
2003	Eric Gagne, LA	2–3	55	1.20

AMERICAN LEAGUE

Year		W–L	Sv	ERA
1967	Jim Lonborg, Bos	22–9	0	3.16
1968	*Denny McLain, Det	31–6	0	1.96
1969	Denny McLain, Det	24–9	0	2.80
	Mike Cuellar, Balt	23–11	0	2.38
1970	Jim Perry, Minn	24–12	0	3.03
1971	*Vida Blue, Oak	24–8	0	1.82
1972	Gaylord Perry, Clev	24–16	1	1.92
1973	Jim Palmer, Balt	22–9	1	2.40
1974	Catfish Hunter, Oak	25–12	0	2.49
1975	Jim Palmer, Balt	23–11	1	2.09
1976	Jim Palmer, Balt	22–13	0	2.51
1977	Sparky Lyle, NY	13–5	26	2.17
1978	Ron Guidry, NY	25–3	0	1.74
1979	Mike Flanagan, Balt	23–9	0	3.08
1980	Steve Stone, Balt	25–7	0	3.23
1981	*Rollie Fingers, Mil	6–3	28	1.04
1982	Pete Vuckovich, Mil	18–6	0	3.34
1983	LaMarr Hoyt, Chi	24–10	0	3.66
1984	*Willie Hernandez, Det	9–3	32	1.92
1985	Bret Saberhagen, KC	20–6	0	2.87
1986	*Roger Clemens, Bos	24–4	0	2.48
1987	Roger Clemens, Bos	20–9	0	2.97
1988	Frank Viola, Minn	24–7	0	2.64
1989	Bret Saberhagen, KC	23–6	0	2.16
1990	Bob Welch, Oak	27–6	0	2.95
1991	Roger Clemens, Bos	18–10	0	2.62
1992	*Dennis Eckersley, Oak	7–1	51	1.91
1993	Jack McDowell, Chi	22–10	0	3.37
1994	David Cone, KC	16–4	0	2.94
1995	Randy Johnson, Sea	18–2	0	2.48
1996	Pat Hentgen, Tor	20–10	0	3.22
1997	Roger Clemens, Tor	21–7	0	2.05
1998	Roger Clemens, Tor	20–6	0	2.65
1999	Pedro Martinez, Bos	23–4	0	1.55
2000	Pedro Martinez, Bos	18–6	0	1.74
2001	Roger Clemens, NY	20–3	0	3.51
2002	Barry Zito, Oak	23–5	0	2.75
2003	Roy Halladay, Tor	22–7	0	3.25

*Won the MVP and Cy Young awards in the same season.

†NL games only. Sutcliffe pitched 15 games with Cleveland before being traded to the Cubs.

Career Individual Batting

GAMES

Pete Rose	3562
Carl Yastrzemski	3308
Hank Aaron	3298
Rickey Henderson	3081
Ty Cobb	3034
Stan Musial	3026
Eddie Murray	3026
Cal Ripken Jr.	3001
Willie Mays	2992
Dave Winfield	2973
Rusty Staub	2951
Brooks Robinson	2896
Robin Yount	2856
Al Kaline	2834
Harold Baines	2830
Eddie Collins	2826
Reggie Jackson	2820
Frank Robinson	2808
Honus Wagner	2792
Tris Speaker	2789

AT BATS

Pete Rose	14053
Hank Aaron	12364
Carl Yastrzemski	11988
Cal Ripken Jr.	11551
Ty Cobb	11429
Eddie Murray	11336
Robin Yount	11008
Dave Winfield	11003
Stan Musial	10972
Rickey Henderson	10961
Willie Mays	10881
Paul Molitor	10835
Brooks Robinson	10654
Honus Wagner	10427
George Brett	10349
Lou Brock	10332
Cap Anson	10278
Luis Aparicio	10230
Tris Speaker	10208
Al Kaline	10116

HOME RUNS

Hank Aaron	755
Babe Ruth	714
*Barry Bonds	703
Willie Mays	660
Frank Robinson	586
Mark McGwire	583
*Sammy Sosa	574
Harmon Killebrew	573
Reggie Jackson	563
*Rafael Palmeiro	551
Mike Schmidt	548
Mickey Mantle	536
Jimmie Foxx	534
Ted Williams	521
Willie McCovey	521
Eddie Mathews	512
Ernie Banks	512
Mel Ott	511
Eddie Murray	504
*Ken Griffey Jr.	501

* Active in 2004.

HITS

Pete Rose	4256
Ty Cobb	4189
Hank Aaron	3771
Stan Musial	3630
Tris Speaker	3515
Carl Yastrzemski	3419
Cap Anson	3418
Honus Wagner	3415
Paul Molitor	3319
Eddie Collins	3313
Willie Mays	3283
Eddie Murray	3255
Nap Lajoie	3251
Cal Ripken Jr.	3184
George Brett	3154
Paul Waner	3152
Robin Yount	3142
Tony Gwynn	3141
Dave Winfield	3110
Rickey Henderson	3055

BATTING AVERAGE (5,000 AB)

Ty Cobb	.367
Rogers Hornsby	.358
Ed Delahanty	.346
Tris Speaker	.345
Ted Williams	.344
Billy Hamilton	.344
Dan Brouthers	.342
Jesse Burkett	.342
Babe Ruth	.342
Harry Heilmann	.342
Willie Keeler	.341
Bill Terry	.341
George Sisler	.340
Lou Gehrig	.340
Jesse Burkett	.338
Tony Gwynn	.338
Nap Lajoie	.338
Al Simmons	.334
Paul Waner	.333
Eddie Collins	.333

RUNS

Rickey Henderson	2295
Ty Cobb	2246
Babe Ruth	2174
Hank Aaron	2174
Pete Rose	2165
*Barry Bonds	2070
Willie Mays	2062
Cap Anson	1996
Stan Musial	1949
Lou Gehrig	1888
Tris Speaker	1882
Mel Ott	1859
Frank Robinson	1829
Eddie Collins	1821
Carl Yastrzemski	1816
Ted Williams	1798
Paul Molitor	1782
Charlie Gehringer	1774
Jimmie Foxx	1751
Honus Wagner	1736

DOUBLES

Tris Speaker	793
Pete Rose	746
Stan Musial	725
Ty Cobb	724
George Brett	665
Nap Lajoie	657
Carl Yastrzemski	646
Honus Wagner	640
Hank Aaron	624
Paul Molitor	605
Paul Waner	604
Cal Ripken Jr.	603
Robin Yount	583
Cap Anson	581
Wade Boggs	578
Charlie Gehringer	574
*Rafael Palmeiro	572
*Craig Biggio	564
*Barry Bonds	563
Eddie Murray	560

TRIPLES

Sam Crawford	309
Ty Cobb	295
Honus Wagner	252
Jake Beckley	243
Roger Connor	233
Tris Speaker	222
Fred Clarke	220
Dan Brouthers	205
Joe Kelley	194
Paul Waner	191
Bid McPhee	188
Eddie Collins	187
Ed Delahanty	185
Sam Rice	184
Jesse Burkett	182
Edd Roush	182
Ed Konetchy	182
Buck Ewing	178
Rabbit Maranville	177
Stan Musial	177

BASES ON BALLS

*Barry Bonds	2302
Rickey Henderson	2190
Babe Ruth	2062
Ted Williams	2021
Joe Morgan	1865
Carl Yastrzemski	1845
Mickey Mantle	1733
Mel Ott	1708
Eddie Yost	1614
Darrell Evans	1605
Stan Musial	1599
Pete Rose	1566
Harmon Killebrew	1559
Lou Gehrig	1508
Mike Schmidt	1507
Eddie Collins	1499
Willie Mays	1464
Jimmie Foxx	1452
*Frank Thomas	1450
Eddie Mathews	1444

Career Individual Batting (Cont.)

RUNS BATTED IN

Hank Aaron	2297
•Babe Ruth	2213
Cap Anson	2076
Lou Gehrig	1995
Stan Musial	1951
Ty Cobb	1937
Jimmie Foxx	1922
Eddie Murray	1917
Willie Mays	1903
Mel Ott	1860
Carl Yastrzemski	1844
*Barry Bonds	1843
Ted Williams	1839
Dave Winfield	1833
Al Simmons	1827
Frank Robinson	1812
*Rafael Palmeiro	1775
Honus Wagner	1732
Reggie Jackson	1702
Cal Ripken Jr.	1695

SLUGGING AVERAGE (5,000 AB)

Babe Ruth	.690
Ted Williams	.634
Lou Gehrig	.632
*Barry Bonds	.611
Jimmie Foxx	.609
Hank Greenberg	.605
*Manny Ramirez	.599
Mark McGwire	.588
Joe DiMaggio	.579
Rogers Hornsby	.577
*Alex Rodriguez	.574
*Jim Thome	.569
*Larry Walker	.568
*Frank Thomas	.567
Albert Belle	.564
Johnny Mize	.562
*Mike Piazza	.562
*Juan Gonzalez	.561
*Ken Griffey Jr.	.560
Stan Musial	.559

*Active in 2004.

STOLEN BASES

Rickey Henderson	1406
Lou Brock	938
Billy Hamilton	912
Ty Cobb	892
Tim Raines	808
Vince Coleman	752
Eddie Collins	744
Arlie Latham	739
Max Carey	738
Honus Wagner	722
Joe Morgan	689
Willie Wilson	668
Tom Brown	657
Bert Campaneris	649
Otis Nixon	620
George Davis	616
Dummy Hoy	594
Maury Wills	586
George Van Haltren	583
Ozzie Smith	580

ON-BASE PERCENTAGE (5,000 AB)

Ted Williams	.483
Babe Ruth	.474
Billy Hamilton	.455
Lou Gehrig	.447
*Barry Bonds	.443
Rogers Hornsby	.434
Ty Cobb	.433
*Frank Thomas	.429
Tris Speaker	.428
Jimmie Foxx	.428
Eddie Collins	.424
Dan Brouthers	.423
Mickey Mantle	.420
Mickey Cochrane	.419
*Edgar Martinez	.418
Stan Musial	.418
Cupid Childs	.416
Jesse Burkett	.415
Wade Boggs	.415
Mel Ott	.414

TOTAL BASES

Hank Aaron	6856
Stan Musial	6134
Willie Mays	6066
Ty Cobb	5854
Babe Ruth	5793
Pete Rose	5752
*Barry Bonds	5556
Carl Yastrzemski	5539
Eddie Murray	5397
Frank Robinson	5373
*Rafael Palmeiro	5223
Dave Winfield	5221
Cal Ripken Jr.	5168
Tris Speaker	5101
Lou Gehrig	5060
George Brett	5044
Mel Ott	5041
Jimmie Foxx	4956
Ted Williams	4884
Honus Wagner	4862

STRIKEOUTS

Reggie Jackson	2597
*Sammy Sosa	2110
*Andres Galarraga	2003
Jose Canseco	1942
Willie Stargell	1936
Mike Schmidt	1883
*Fred McGriff	1882
Tony Perez	1867
Dave Kingman	1816
Bobby Bonds	1757
Dale Murphy	1748
Lou Brock	1730
Mickey Mantle	1710
*Jim Thome	1703
Harmon Killebrew	1699
Chili Davis	1698
Dwight Evans	1697
Rickey Henderson	1694
Dave Winfield	1686
Gary Gaetti	1602

The 30–30 Club (30 HR, 30 SB in single season)

Year	Player	HR	SB	Year	Player	HR	SB
1922	Kenny Williams, StL	39	37	1995	Sammy Sosa, ChiC	36	34
1956	Willie Mays, NYG	36	40	1996	Barry Bonds, SF	42	40
1957	Willie Mays, NYG	35	38	1996	Ellis Burks, Col	40	32
1963	Hank Aaron, Mil	44	31	1996	Barry Larkin, Cin	33	36
1969	Bobby Bonds, SF	32	45	1996	Dante Bichette, Col	31	31
1970	Tommy Harper, Mil	31	38	1997	Larry Walker, Col	49	33
1973	Bobby Bonds, SF	39	43	1997	Jeff Bagwell, Hou	43	31
1975	Bobby Bonds, NYY	32	30	1997	Raul Mondesi, LA	30	32
1977	Bobby Bonds, Cal	37	41	1997	Barry Bonds, SF	40	37
1978	Bobby Bonds, Chi/Tex	31	43	1998	Alex Rodriguez, Sea	42	46
1983	Dale Murphy, Atl	36	30	1998	Shawn Green, Tor	35	35
1987	Joe Carter, Clev	32	31	1999	Jeff Bagwell, Hou	42	30
1987	Eric Davis, Cin	37	50	1999	Raul Mondesi, LA	33	36
1987	Darryl Strawberry, NYM	39	36	2000	Preston Wilson, Fla	31	36
1987	Howard Johnson, NYM	36	32	2001	Vladimir Guerrero, Mtl	34	37
1988	Jose Canseco, Oak	42	40	2001	Jose Cruz Jr., Tor	34	32
1989	Howard Johnson, NYM	36	41	2001	Bobby Abreu, Phil	31	36
1990	Ron Gant, Atl	32	33	2002	Alfonso Soriano, NYY	39	41
1990	Barry Bonds, Pitt	33	52	2002	Vladimir Guerrero, Mtl	39	40
1991	Ron Gant, Atl	32	34	2003	Alfonso Soriano, NYY	38	35
1991	Howard Johnson, NYM	38	30	2004	Carlos Beltran, KC/Hou	38	42
1992	Barry Bonds, Pitt	34	39	2004	Bobby Abreu, Phil	30	40
1993	Sammy Sosa, ChiC	33	36				
1995	Barry Bonds, SF	33	31				

Career Individual Pitching

GAMES

Jesse Orosco	1252
*John Franco	1088
Dennis Eckersley	1071
Hoyt Wilhelm	1070
Dan Plesac	1064
Kent Tekulve	1050
Lee Smith	1022
*Mike Jackson	1005
Goose Gossage	1002
Lindy McDaniel	987
*Mike Stanton	968
Rollie Fingers	944
Gene Garber	931
Cy Young	906
Sparky Lyle	899
Jim Kaat	898
Paul Assenmacher	884
Jeff Reardon	880
Don McMahon	874
Phil Niekro	864

LOSSES

Cy Young	316
Pud Galvin	308
Nolan Ryan	292
Walter Johnson	279
Phil Niekro	274
Gaylord Perry	265
Don Sutton	256
Jack Powell	254
Eppa Rixey	251
Bert Blyleven	250
Bobby Mathews	248
Robin Roberts	245
Warren Spahn	245
Steve Carlton	244
Early Wynn	244
Jim Kaat	237
Frank Tanana	236
Gus Weyhing	232
Tommy John	231
Bob Friend	230
Ted Lyons	230

EARNED RUN AVERAGE (2,000 IP)

Ed Walsh	1.82
Addie Joss	1.89
Al Spalding	2.04
Three Finger Brown	2.06
John Ward	2.10
Christy Mathewson	2.13
Tommy Bond	2.14
Rube Waddell	2.16
Walter Johnson	2.17
Ed Reulbach	2.28
Will White	2.28
Eddie Plank	2.35
Larry Corcoran	2.36
Eddie Cicotte	2.38
Candy Cummings	2.39
Doc White	2.39
Nap Rucker	2.42
George Bradley	2.43
Jim McCormick	2.43
Chief Bender	2.46

INNINGS PITCHED

Cy Young	7356⅔
Pud Galvin	5941⅓
Walter Johnson	5914⅓
Phil Niekro	5404⅓
Nolan Ryan	5386
Gaylord Perry	5350⅓
Don Sutton	5282⅓
Warren Spahn	5243⅔
Steve Carlton	5217⅓
Grover Alexander	5190
Kid Nichols	5056½
Tim Keefe	5047⅓
Bert Blyleven	4970
Bobby Mathews	4956
Mickey Welch	4802
Tom Seaver	4782⅔
Christy Mathewson	4780⅔
Tommy John	4710⅓
Robin Roberts	4688⅔
Early Wynn	4564

WINNING PERCENTAGE**

Al Spalding	.796
Spud Chandler	.717
*Pedro Martinez	.705
Whitey Ford	.690
Dave Foutz	.690
Bob Caruthers	.688
Don Gullett	.686
Lefty Grove	.680
Joe Wood	.671
Vic Raschi	.667
*Roger Clemens	.667
Larry Corcoran	.665
Christy Mathewson	.665
Sam Leever	.660
*Randy Johnson	.658
Sal Maglie	.658
Dick McBride	.656
Sandy Koufax	.655
*Andy Pettitte	.654
Johnny Allen	.654

SHUTOUTS

Walter Johnson	110
Grover Alexander	90
Christy Mathewson	79
Cy Young	76
Eddie Plank	69
Warren Spahn	63
Nolan Ryan	61
Tom Seaver	61
Bert Blyleven	60
Don Sutton	58
Pud Galvin	57
Ed Walsh	57
Bob Gibson	56
Three Finger Brown	55
Steve Carlton	55
Jim Palmer	53
Gaylord Perry	53
Juan Marichal	52
Rube Waddell	50
Vic Willis	50

WINS

Cy Young	511
Walter Johnson	417
Grover Alexander	373
Christy Mathewson	373
Pud Galvin	365
Warren Spahn	363
Kid Nichols	361
Tim Keefe	342
Steve Carlton	329
John Clarkson	328
*Roger Clemens	328
Eddie Plank	326
Nolan Ryan	324
Don Sutton	324
Phil Niekro	318
Gaylord Perry	314
Tom Seaver	311
Charley Radbourn	309
Mickey Welch	307
*Greg Maddux	305

SAVES

Lee Smith	478
*John Franco	424
*Trevor Hoffman	393
Dennis Eckersley	390
Jeff Reardon	367
Randy Myers	347
Rollie Fingers	341
*Mariano Rivera	336
John Wetteland	330
*Roberto Hernandez	320
Rick Aguilera	318
*Troy Percival	316
*Robb Nen	314
Tom Henke	311
Goose Gossage	310
Jeff Montgomery	304
Doug Jones	303
Bruce Sutter	300
*Rod Beck	286
Todd Worrell	256

COMPLETE GAMES

Cy Young	749
Pud Galvin	639
Tim Keefe	554
Walter Johnson	531
Kid Nichols	531
Mickey Welch	525
Bobby Mathews	525
Charley Radbourn	489
John Clarkson	485
Tony Mullane	468
Jim McCormick	466
Gus Weyhing	448
Grover Alexander	437
Christy Mathewson	434
Jack Powell	422
Eddie Plank	410
Will White	394
Amos Rusie	392
Vic Willis	388
Tommy Bond	386

* Active in 2004.   ** Minimum 100 victories.

Career Individual Pitching (Cont.)

STRIKEOUTS		BASES ON BALLS	
Nolan Ryan	5714	Nolan Ryan	2795
*Roger Clemens	4317	Steve Carlton	1833
*Randy Johnson	4161	Phil Niekro	1809
Steve Carlton	4136	Early Wynn	1775
Bert Blyleven	3701	Bob Feller	1764
Tom Seaver	3640	Bobo Newsom	1732
Don Sutton	3574	Amos Rusie	1704
Gaylord Perry	3534	Charlie Hough	1665
Walter Johnson	3509	Gus Weyhing	1566
Phil Niekro	3342	Red Ruffing	1541
Ferguson Jenkins	3192	*Roger Clemens	1458
Bob Gibson	3117	Bump Hadley	1442
*Greg Maddux	2916	Warren Spahn	1434
Jim Bunning	2855	Earl Whitehill	1431
Mickey Lolich	2832	Tony Mullane	1408
Cy Young	2803	Sad Sam Jones	1396
Frank Tanana	2773	Jack Morris	1390
David Cone	2668	Tom Seaver	1390
Chuck Finley	2610	Gaylord Perry	1379
Warren Spahn	2583	Bobby Witt	1375

Alltime Winningest Managers

CAREER

	W	L	Pct	Yrs		W	L	Pct	Yrs
Connie Mack	3755	3967	.486	53	Gene Mauch	1907	2044	.483	26
John McGraw	2810	1987	.586	33	Bill McKechnie	1904	1737	.523	25
Sparky Anderson	2238	1855	.547	26	*Joe Torre	1787	1575	.532	23
Bucky Harris	2168	2228	.493	29	Ralph Houk	1627	1539	.514	20
Joe McCarthy	2155	1346	.616	24	Fred Clarke	1609	1189	.575	19
*Tony LaRussa	2121	1854	.536	26	Dick Williams	1592	1474	.519	21
Walter Alston	2063	1634	.558	23	Tommy Lasorda	1589	1434	.526	20
Leo Durocher	2015	1717	.540	24	Earl Weaver	1506	1080	.582	17
*Bobby Cox	2004	1534	.566	23	Clark Griffith	1491	1367	.522	20
Casey Stengel	1942	1868	.510	25	*Lou Piniella	1475	1346	.523	18

REGULAR SEASON

	W	L	Pct	Yrs		W	L	Pct	Yrs
Connie Mack	3731	3948	.486	53	Gene Mauch	1902	2037	.483	26
John McGraw	2784	1959	.587	33	Bill McKechnie	1896	1723	.524	25
Sparky Anderson	2194	1834	.545	26	*Joe Torre	1781	1570	.532	23
Bucky Harris	2157	2218	.493	29	Ralph Houk	1619	1531	.514	20
Joe McCarthy	2125	1333	.615	24	Fred Clarke	1602	1181	.576	19
*Tony La Russa	2114	1846	.534	26	Dick Williams	1571	1451	.520	21
Walter Alston	2040	1613	.558	23	Tommy Lasorda	1558	1404	.526	20
Leo Durocher	2008	1709	.540	24	Clark Griffith	1491	1367	.522	20
*Bobby Cox	2002	1531	.567	23	Earl Weaver	1480	1060	.583	17
Casey Stengel	1905	1842	.508	25	*Lou Piniella	1452	1325	.523	18

WORLD SERIES

	W	L	T	Pct	App	WS		W	L	T	Pct	App	WS
Casey Stengel	37	26	0	.587	10	7	Bucky Harris	11	10	0	.524	3	2
Joe McCarthy	30	13	0	.698	9	7	Billy Southworth	11	11	0	.500	4	2
John McGraw	26	28	2	.482	9	2	Earl Weaver	11	13	0	.458	4	1
Connie Mack	24	19	0	.558	8	5	*Bobby Cox	11	18	0	.379	5	1
*Joe Torre	21	11	0	.657	6	4	Whitey Herzog	10	11	0	.476	3	1
Walter Alston	20	20	0	.500	7	4	Bill Carrigan	8	2	0	.800	2	2
Miller Huggins	18	15	1	.544	6	3	Cito Gaston	8	4	0	.667	2	2
Sparky Anderson	16	12	0	.571	5	3	Danny Murtaugh	8	6	0	.571	2	2
Tommy Lasorda	12	11	0	.522	4	2	Tom Kelly	8	6	0	.571	2	2
Dick Williams	12	14	0	.462	4	2	Ralph Houk	8	8	0	.500	3	2
Frank Chance	11	9	1	.548	4	2	Bill McKechnie	8	14	0	.364	4	2

*Active in 2004.

Individual Batting (Single Season)

HITS

Ichiro Suzuki, 2004 262
George Sisler, 1920.............257
Lefty O'Doul, 1929 254
Bill Terry, 1930....................254
Al Simmons, 1925................253
Rogers Hornsby, 1922.........250
Chuck Klein, 1930 250
Ty Cobb, 1911 248
George Sisler, 1922.............246
Ichiro Suzuki, 2001 242

BATTING AVERAGE

Hugh Duffy, 1894............... .440
Tip O'Neill, 1887 .... .435
Ross Barnes, 1876 .... .429
Nap Lajoie, 1901 .... .426
Willie Keeler, 1897............. .424
Rogers Hornsby, 1924....... .424
George Sisler, 1922............ .420
Ty Cobb, 1911 .... .420
Fred Dunlap, 1884............. .412
Ed Delahanty, 1899 .... .410

DOUBLES

Earl Webb, 1931 67
George Burns, 1926 64
Joe Medwick, 1936...............64
Hank Greenberg, 1934.........63
Paul Waner, 1932 62
Charlie Gehringer, 1936 60
Tris Speaker, 1923...............59
Chuck Klein, 1930 59
Todd Helton, 2000................59
Billy Herman, 1936 57
Billy Herman, 1935 57
Carlos Delgado, 2000...........57

TOTAL BASES

Babe Ruth, 1921..................457
Rogers Hornsby, 1922.........450
Lou Gehrig, 1927 447
Chuck Klein, 1930 445
Jimmie Foxx, 1932...............438
Stan Musial, 1948 429
Sammy Sosa, 2001..............425
Hack Wilson, 1930...............423
Chuck Klein, 1930 420
Luis Gonzalez, 2001............419
Lou Gehrig, 1930.................419

TRIPLES

Chief Wilson, 1912................36
Dave Orr, 1886.....................31
Heinie Reitz, 1894.................31
Perry Werden, 1893...............29
Harry Davis, 1897.................28
George Davis, 1893...............27
Sam Thompson, 1894............27
Jimmy Williams, 1899 27
John Reilly, 1890 26
George Treadway, 1894........26
Joe Jackson, 1912.................26
Sam Crawford, 1914..............26
Kiki Cuyler, 1925...................26

HOME RUNS

Barry Bonds, 2001................73
Mark McGwire, 1998..............70
Sammy Sosa, 1998................66
Mark McGwire, 1999 65
Sammy Sosa, 2001................64
Sammy Sosa, 1999................63
Roger Maris, 1961.................61
Babe Ruth, 1927...................60
Babe Ruth, 1921...................59
Jimmie Foxx, 1932................58
Hank Greenberg, 1938..........58
Mark McGwire, 1997..............58

RUNS BATTED IN

Hack Wilson, 1930................190
Lou Gehrig, 1931..................184
Hank Greenberg, 1937..........183
Lou Gehrig, 1927..................175
Jimmie Foxx, 1938................175
Lou Gehrig, 1930..................174
Babe Ruth, 1921...................171
Chuck Klein, 1930 170
Hank Greenberg, 1935..........170
Jimmie Foxx, 1932................169

STRIKEOUTS

Adam Dunn, 2004..................195
Bobby Bonds, 1970..............189
Jose Hernandez, 2002 188
Bobby Bonds, 1969...............187
Preston Wilson, 2000............187
Rob Deer, 1987 186
Jose Hernandez, 2001 185
Jim Thome, 2001 185
Pete Incaviglia, 1986 185
Cecil Fielder, 1990................182
Jim Thome, 2003 182

RUNS

Billy Hamilton, 1894 192
Tom Brown, 1891..................177
Babe Ruth, 1921...................177
Tip O'Neill, 1887 167
Lou Gehrig, 1936..................167
Billy Hamilton, 1895..............166
Willie Keeler, 1894 165
Joe Kelley, 1894 165
Arlie Latham, 1887...............163
Babe Ruth, 1928...................163
Lou Gehrig, 1931..................163

STOLEN BASES

Hugh Nicol, 1887.................138
Rickey Henderson, 1982 130
Arlie Latham, 1887...............129
Lou Brock, 1974 118
Charlie Comiskey, 1887........117
John Ward, 1887 111
Billy Hamilton, 1889.............111
Billy Hamilton, 1891.............111
Vince Coleman, 1985 110
Arlie Latham, 1888...............109
Vince Coleman, 1987 109

BASES ON BALLS

Barry Bonds, 2004...............232
Barry Bonds, 2002...............198
Barry Bonds, 2001...............177
Babe Ruth, 1923...................170
Ted Williams, 1947 162
Ted Williams, 1949 162
Mark McGwire, 1998.............162
Ted Williams, 1946 156
Eddie Yost, 1956 ....:151
Jeff Bagwell, 1999................149
Eddie Joost, 1949:................149

SLUGGING AVERAGE

Barry Bonds, 2001............ .863
Babe Ruth, 1920................ .847
Babe Ruth, 1921................ .846
Barry Bonds, 2004............. .812
Barry Bonds, 2002............. .799
Babe Ruth, 1927................ .772
Lou Gehrig, 1927................ .765
Babe Ruth, 1923................ .764
Rogers Hornsby, 1925....... .756
Mark McGwire, 1998 .... .752

Individual Pitching (Single Season)

GAMES

Mike Marshall, 1974	106
Kent Tekulve, 1979	94
Mike Marshall, 1973	92
Kent Tekulve, 1978	91
Wayne Granger, 1969	90
Mike Marshall, 1979	90
Kent Tekulve, 1987	90
Steve Kline, 2001	89
Mark Eichhorn, 1987	89
Paul Quantrill, 2003	89
Jim Brower, 2004	89

GAMES STARTED

Will White, 1879	75
Jim Galvin, 1883	75
Jim McCormick, 1880	74
Charley Radbourn, 1884	73
Guy Hecker, 1884	73
Jim Galvin, 1884	72
John Clarkson, 1889	72
Bill Hutchison, 1892	71
John Clarkson, 1885	70
Matt Kilroy, 1887	69

INNINGS PITCHED

Will White, 1878	680.0
Charley Radbourn, 1884	678.2
Guy Hecker, 1884	670.2
Jim McCormick, 1880	657.2
Jim Galvin, 1883	656.1
Jim Galvin, 1884	636.1
Charley Radbourn, 1883	632.1
Bill Hutchison, 1892	627.0
John Clarkson, 1885	623.0
Jim Devlin, 1876	622.0

WINS

Charley Radbourn, 1884	59
John Clarkson, 1885	53
Guy Hecker, 1884	52
John Clarkson, 1889	49
Charley Radbourn, 1883	48
Charlie Buffinton, 1884	48
Al Spalding, 1876	47
John Ward, 1879	47
Jim Galvin, 1883	46
Jim Galvin, 1884	46
Matt Kilroy, 1887	46

LOSSES

John Coleman, 1883	48
Will White, 1880	42
Larry McKeon, 1884	41
George Bradley, 1879	40
Jim McCormick, 1879	40
Henry Porter, 1888	37
Kid Carsey, 1891	37
George Cobb, 1892	37
Stump Weidman, 1886	36
Bill Hutchison, 1892	36

WINNING PERCENTAGE

Roy Face, 1959	.947
Johnny Allen, 1937	.938
Greg Maddux, 1995	.905
Randy Johnson, 1995	.900
Ron Guidry, 1978	.893
Freddie Fitzsimmons, 1940	.889
Lefty Grove, 1931	.886
Bob Stanley, 1978	.882
Preacher Roe, 1951	.880
Fred Goldsmith, 1880	.875
Tom Seaver, 1981	.875

SAVES

Bobby Thigpen, 1990	57
John Smoltz, 2002	55
Eric Gagne, 2003	55
Mariano Rivera, 2004	53
Randy Myers, 1993	53
Trevor Hoffman, 1998	53
Eric Gagne, 2002	52
Dennis Eckersley, 1992	51
Rod Beck, 1998	51
Mariano Rivera, 2001	50
Francisco Cordero, 2004	49

EARNED RUN AVERAGE

Tim Keefe, 1880	0.86
Dutch Leonard, 1914	0.96
Three Finger Brown, 1906	1.04
Bob Gibson, 1968	1.12
Christy Mathewson, 1909	1.14
Walter Johnson, 1913	1.14
Jack Pfiester, 1907	1.15
Addie Joss, 1908	1.16
Carl Lundgren, 1907	1.17
Denny Driscoll, 1882	1.21

SHUTOUTS

George Bradley, 1876	16
Grover Alexander, 1916	16
Jack Coombs, 1910	13
Bob Gibson, 1968	13
Jim Galvin, 1884	12
Ed Morris, 1886	12
Grover Alexander, 1915	12
Tommy Bond, 1879	11
Charley Radbourn, 1884	11
Dave Foutz, 1886	11
Christy Mathewson, 1908	11
Ed Walsh, 1908	11
Walter Johnson, 1913	11
Sandy Koufax, 1963	11
Dean Chance, 1964	11

COMPLETE GAMES

Will White, 1879	75
Charley Radbourn, 1884	73
Jim McCormick, 1880	72
Jim Galvin, 1883	72
Guy Hecker, 1884	72
Jim Galvin, 1884	71
Tim Keefe, 1883	68
John Clarkson, 1885	68
John Clarkson, 1889	68
Bill Hutchison, 1892	67

STRIKEOUTS

Matt Kilroy, 1886	513
Toad Ramsey, 1886	499
Hugh Daily, 1884	483
Dupee Shaw, 1884	451
Charley Radbourn, 1884	441
Charlie Buffinton, 1884	417
Guy Hecker, 1884	385
Nolan Ryan, 1973	383
Sandy Koufax, 1965	382
Bill Sweeney, 1884	374

BASES ON BALLS

Amos Rusie, 1890	289
Mark Baldwin, 1889	274
Amos Rusie, 1892	267
Amos Rusie, 1891	262
Mark Baldwin, 1890	249
Jack Stivetts, 1891	232
Mark Baldwin, 1891	227
Phil Knell, 1891	226
Bob Barr, 1890	219
Amos Rusie 1893	218

Manager of the Year

NATIONAL LEAGUE	AMERICAN LEAGUE
1983 ....Tommy Lasorda, LA	1983 ....Tony La Russa, Chi
1984 ....Jim Frey, Chi	1984 ....Sparky Anderson, Det
1985 ....Whitey Herzog, StL	1985 ....Bobby Cox, Tor
1986 ....Hal Lanier, Hou	1986 ....John McNamara, Bos
1987 ....Buck Rodgers, Mtl	1987 ....Sparky Anderson, Det
1988 ....Tommy Lasorda, LA	1988 ....Tony La Russa, Oak
1989 ....Don Zimmer, Chi	1989 ....Frank Robinson, Balt
1990 ....Jim Leyland, Pitt	1990 ....Jeff Torborg, Chi
1991 ....Bobby Cox, Atl	1991 ....Tom Kelly, Minn
1992 ....Jim Leyland, Pitt	1992 ....Tony La Russa, Oak
1993 ....Dusty Baker, SF	1993 ....Gene Lamont, Chi
1994 ....Felipe Alou, Mtl	1994 ....Buck Showalter, NY
1995 ....Don Baylor, Col	1995 ....Lou Piniella, Sea
1996 ....Bruce Bochy, SD	1996 ....Joe Torre, NY/Johnny Oates, Tex
1997 ....Dusty Baker, SF	1997 ....Davey Johnson, Balt
1998 ....Larry Dierker, Hou	1998 ....Joe Torre, NY
1999 ....Jack McKeon, Cin	1999 ....Jimy Williams, Bos
2000 ....Dusty Baker, SF	2000 ....Jerry Manuel, Chi
2001 ....Larry Bowa, Phil	2001 ....Lou Piniella, Sea
2002 ....Tony La Russa, StL	2002 ....Mike Scioscia, Ana
2003 ....Jack McKeon, Fla	2003 ....Tony Pena, KC

Individual Batting (Single Game)

MOST RUNS

7 ....Guy Hecker, Lou   Aug 15, 1886

MOST HITS

7 ....Wilbert Robinson, Balt   June 10, 1892
         Rennie Stennett, Pitt   Sept 16, 1975

MOST HOME RUNS

4 ......Bobby Lowe, Bos (N)	May 30, 1894
Ed Delahanty, Phil	July 13, 1896
Lou Gehrig, NY (A)	June 3, 1932
Gil Hodges, Bklyn	Aug 31, 1950
Joe Adcock, Mil (N)	July 31, 1954
Rocky Colavito, Clev	June 10, 1959
Willie Mays, SF	April 30, 1961
Mike Schmidt, Phil	April 17, 1976
Bob Horner, Atl	July 6, 1986
Mark Whiten, StL	Sept 7, 1993
Mike Cameron, Sea	May 2, 2002
Shawn Green, LA	May 23, 2002
Carlos Delgado, Tor	Sept 25, 2003

MOST GRAND SLAMS

2 ......Tony Lazzeri, NY (A)	May 24, 1936
Jim Tabor, Bos (A)	July 4, 1939
Rudy York, Bos (A)	July 27, 1946
Jim Gentile, Balt	May 9, 1961
Tony Cloninger, Atl	July 3, 1966
Jim Northrup, Det	June 24, 1968
Frank Robinson, Balt	June 26, 1970
Robin Ventura, Chi (A)	Sept 4, 1995
Chris Hoiles, Balt	Aug 14, 1998
Fernando Tatis, StL	Apr 23, 1999
N. Garciaparra, Bos	May 10, 1999
Bill Mueller, Bos	July 29, 2003

MOST RBIs

12 .....Jim Bottomley, StL	Sept 16, 1924
Mark Whiten, StL	Sept 7, 1993

Individual Batting (Single Inning)

MOST RUNS

3 ....Tommy Burns, Chi (N)	Sept 6, 1883, 7th inning
Ned Williamson, Chi (N)	Sept 6, 1883, 7th inning
Sammy White, Bos (A)	June 18, 1953, 7th inning

MOST RBIs

8.......Fernando Tatis, StL   Apr 23, 1999, 3rd inning

MOST HITS

3 ....Tommy Burns, Chi (N)	Sept 6, 1883, 7th inning
Fred Pfeiffer, Chi (N)	Sept 6, 1883, 7th inning
Ned Williamson, Chi (N)	Sept 6, 1883, 7th inning
Gene Stephens, Bos (A)	June 18, 1953, 7th inning

Note: All single-game hitting records for a nine-inning game.

Individual Pitching (Single Game)

MOST INNINGS PITCHED		
26	Leon Cadore, Bklyn	May 1, 1920, tie 1–1
	Joe Oeschger, Bos (N)	May 1, 1920, tie 1–1

MOST RUNS ALLOWED		
24	Al Travers, Det	May 18, 1912

MOST HITS ALLOWED		
36	Jack Wadsworth, Lou	Aug 17, 1894

MOST STRIKEOUTS		
20	Roger Clemens, Bos	April 29, 1986
20	Roger Clemens, Bos	Sept 18, 1996
20	Kerry Wood, Chi (N)	May 6, 1998
20	Randy Johnson, Ariz	May 8, 2001

MOST WALKS ALLOWED		
16	Bill George, NY (N)	May 30, 1887
	George Van Haltren, Chi (N)	June 27, 1887
	Henry Gruber, Clev	Apr 19, 1890
	Bruno Haas, Phil (A)	June 2, 1915

MOST WILD PITCHES		
6	J.R. Richard, Hou	April 10, 1979
	Phil Niekro, Atl	Aug 14, 1979
	Bill Gullickson, Mtl	April 10, 1982

Individual Pitching (Single Inning)

MOST RUNS ALLOWED		
13	Lefty O'Doul, Bos (A)	July 7, 1923

MOST WALKS ALLOWED		
8	Dolly Gray, Wash	Aug 28, 1909

MOST WILD PITCHES		
4	Walter Johnson, Wash	Sept 21, 1914
	Phil Niekro, Atl	Aug 14, 1979
	Kevin Gregg, Ana	July 25, 2004

Miscellaneous

LONGEST GAME, BY INNINGS		
26	Brooklyn 1, Boston 1	May 1, 1920

LONGEST NINE-INNING GAME, BY TIME	
4:27	Los Angeles 11, San Francisco 10 Oct 5, 2001

Baseball Hall of Fame

Players

	Position	Career	Selected		Position	Career	Selected
Hank Aaron	OF	1954–76	1982	Orlando Cepeda	1B	1958–74	1999
Grover Alexander	P	1911–30	1938	Frank Chance	1B	1898–1914	1946
Cap Anson	1B	1876–97	1939	Oscar Charleston*	OF		1976
Luis Aparicio	SS	1956–73	1984	Jack Chesbro	P	1899–1909	1946
Luke Appling	SS	1930–50	1964	Fred Clarke	OF	1894–1915	1945
Richie Ashburn	OF	1948–62	1995	John Clarkson	P	1882–94	1963
Earl Averill	OF	1929–41	1975	Roberto Clemente	OF	1955–72	1973
Frank Baker	3B	1908–22	1955	Ty Cobb	OF	1905–28	1936
Dave Bancroft	SS	1915–30	1971	Mickey Cochrane	C	1925–37	1947
Ernie Banks	SS-1B	1953–71	1977	Eddie Collins	2B	1906–30	1939
Jake Beckley	1B	1888–1907	1971	Jimmy Collins	3B	1895–1908	1945
Cool Papa Bell*	OF		1974	Earle Combs	OF	1924–35	1970
Johnny Bench	C	1967–83	1989	Roger Connor	1B	1880–97	1976
Chief Bender	P	1903–25	1953	Stan Coveleski	P	1912–28	1969
Yogi Berra	C	1946–65	1972	Sam Crawford	OF	1899–1917	1957
Jim Bottomley	1B	1922–37	1974	Joe Cronin	SS	1926–45	1956
Lou Boudreau	SS	1938–52	1970	Candy Cummings	P	1872–77	1939
Roger Bresnahan	C	1897–1915	1945	Kiki Cuyler	OF	1921–38	1968
George Brett	3B	1973–93	1999	Ray Dandridge*	3B		1987
Lou Brock	OF	1961–79	1985	George Davis	SS	1890–1909	1998
Dan Brouthers	1B	1879–1904	1945	Leon Day*	P		1995
Three Finger Brown	P	1903–16	1949	Dizzy Dean	P	1930–47	1953
Jim Bunning	P	1955–71	1996	Ed Delahanty	OF	1888–1903	1945
Jesse Burkett	OF	1890–1905	1946	Bill Dickey	C	1928–46	1954
Roy Campanella	C	1948–57	1969	Martin Dihigo*	P-OF		1977
Rod Carew	1B-2B	1967–85	1991	Joe DiMaggio	OF	1936–51	1955
Max Carey	OF	1910–29	1961	Larry Doby	OF	1947–59	1998
Steve Carlton	P	1965–88	1994	Bobby Doerr	2B	1937–51	1986
Gary Carter	C	1974–92	2003	Don Drysdale	P	1956–69	1984

Note: Career dates indicate first and last appearances in the majors.
*Elected on the basis of his career in the Negro leagues.

Players (Cont.)

	Position	Career	Selected
Hugh Duffy	OF	1888–1906	1945
Dennis Eckersley	P	1975–98	2004
Johnny Evers	2B	1902–29	1939
Buck Ewing	C	1880–97	1946
Red Faber	P	1914–33	1964
Bob Feller	P	1936–56	1962
Rick Ferrell	C	1929–47	1984
Rollie Fingers	P	1968–85	1992
Carlton Fisk	C	1969–93	2000
Elmer Flick	OF	1898–1910	1963
Whitey Ford	P	1950–67	1974
Bill Foster*	P		1996
Nellie Fox	2B	1947–65	1997
Jimmie Foxx	1B	1925–45	1951
Frankie Frisch	2B	1919–37	1947
Pud Galvin	P	1879–92	1965
Lou Gehrig	1B	1923–39	1939
Charlie Gehringer	2B	1924–42	1949
Bob Gibson	P	1959–75	1981
Josh Gibson*	C		1972
Lefty Gomez	P	1930–43	1972
Goose Goslin	OF	1921–38	1968
Hank Greenberg	1B	1930–47	1956
Burleigh Grimes	P	1916–34	1964
Lefty Grove	P	1925–41	1947
Chick Hafey	OF	1924–37	1971
Jesse Haines	P	1918–37	1970
Billy Hamilton	OF	1888–1901	1961
Gabby Hartnett	C	1922–41	1955
Harry Heilmann	OF	1914–32	1952
Billy Herman	2B	1931–47	1975
Harry Hooper	OF	1909–25	1971
Rogers Hornsby	2B	1915–37	1942
Waite Hoyt	P	1918–38	1969
Carl Hubbell	P	1928–43	1947
Catfish Hunter	P	1965–79	1987
Monte Irvin*	OF	1949–56	1973
Reggie Jackson	OF	1967–87	1993
Travis Jackson	SS	1922–36	1982
Ferguson Jenkins	P	1965–83	1991
Hugh Jennings	SS	1891–1918	1945
Judy Johnson*	3B		1975
Walter Johnson	P	1907–27	1936
Addie Joss	P	1902–10	1978
Al Kaline	OF	1953–74	1980
Tim Keefe	P	1880–93	1964
Willie Keeler	OF	1892–1910	1939
George Kell	3B	1943–57	1983
Joe Kelley	OF	1891–1908	1971
George Kelly	1B	1915–32	1973
King Kelly	C	1878–93	1945
Harmon Killebrew	1B-3B	1954–75	1984
Ralph Kiner	OF	1946–55	1975
Chuck Klein	OF	1928–44	1980
Sandy Koufax	P	1955–66	1972
Nap Lajoie	2B	1896–1916	1937
Tony Lazzeri	2B	1926–39	1991
Bob Lemon	P	1941–58	1976
Buck Leonard*	1B		1977
Fred Lindstrom	3B	1924–36	1976
Pop Lloyd*	SS-1B		1977
Ernie Lombardi	C	1931–47	1986
Ted Lyons	P	1923–46	1955
Mickey Mantle	OF	1951–68	1974
Heinie Manush	OF	1923–39	1964
Rabbit Maranville	SS-2B	1912–35	1954
Juan Marichal	P	1960–75	1983
Rube Marquard	P	1908–25	1971
Eddie Mathews	3B	1952–68	1978
Christy Mathewson	P	1900–16	1936
Willie Mays	OF	1951–73	1979
Bill Mazeroski	2B	1956–72	2001
Tommy McCarthy	OF	1884–96	1946
Willie McCovey	1B	1959–80	1986
Joe McGinnity	P	1899–1908	1946
Bid McPhee	2B	1882–99	2000
Joe Medwick	OF	1932–48	1968
Johnny Mize	1B	1936–53	1981
Paul Molitor	3B	1978–98	2004
Joe Morgan	2B	1963–84	1990
Eddie Murray	1B	1977–97	2003
Stan Musial	OF-1B	1941–63	1969
Hal Newhouser	P	1939–55	1992
Kid Nichols	P	1890–1906	1949
Phil Niekro	P	1964–87	1997
Jim O'Rourke	OF	1876–1904	1945
Mel Ott	OF	1926–47	1951
Satchel Paige*	P	1948–65	1971
Jim Palmer	P	1965–84	1990
Herb Pennock	P	1912–34	1948
Tony Perez	1B	1964–86	2000
Gaylord Perry	P	1962–83	1991
Eddie Plank	P	1901–17	1946
Kirby Puckett	OF	1984–95	2001
Charley Radbourn	P	1880–91	1939
Pee Wee Reese	SS	1940–58	1984
Sam Rice	OF	1915–35	1963
Eppa Rixey	P	1912–33	1963
Phil Rizzuto	SS	1941–56	1994
Robin Roberts	P	1948–66	1976
Brooks Robinson	3B	1955–77	1983
Frank Robinson	OF	1956–76	1982
Jackie Robinson	2B	1947–56	1962
Joe (Bullet) Rogan*	P		1998
Edd Roush	OF	1913–31	1962
Red Ruffing	P	1924–47	1967
Amos Rusie	P	1889–1901	1977
Babe Ruth	OF	1914–35	1936
Nolan Ryan	P	1966–93	1999
Ray Schalk	C	1912–29	1955
Mike Schmidt	3B	1972–89	1995
Red Schoendienst	2B	1945–63	1989
Tom Seaver	P	1967–86	1992
Joe Sewell	SS	1920–33	1977
Al Simmons	OF	1924–44	1953
George Sisler	1B	1915–30	1939
Enos Slaughter	OF	1938–59	1985
Hilton Smith*	P		2001
Ozzie Smith	SS	1978–96	2002
Duke Snider	OF	1947–64	1980
Warren Spahn	P	1942–65	1973
Al Spalding	P	1871–78	1939
Tris Speaker	OF	1907–28	1937
Willie Stargell	OF-1B	1962–82	1988
Turkey Stearns*	CF		2000
Don Sutton	P	1966–88	1998
Bill Terry	1B	1923–36	1954
Sam Thompson	OF	1885–1906	1974
Joe Tinker	SS	1902–16	1946
Pie Traynor	3B	1920–37	1948
Dazzy Vance	P	1915–35	1955
Arky Vaughan	SS	1932–48	1985
Rube Waddell	P	1897–1910	1946
Honus Wagner	SS	1897–1917	1936
Bobby Wallace	SS	1894–1918	1953
Ed Walsh	P	1904–17	1946

*Elected on the basis of his career in the Negro leagues.

Players (Cont.)

	Position	Career	Selected
Lloyd Waner	OF	1927–45	1967
Paul Waner*	OF	1926–45	1952
John Ward	2B-P	1878–94	1964
Mickey Welch	P	1880–92	1973
Willie Wells*	SS	1924–49	1997
Zach Wheat	OF	1909–27	1959
Hoyt Wilhelm	P	1952–72	1985
Billy Williams	OF	1959–76	1987
Ted Williams	OF	1939–60	1966
Vic Willis	P	1898–1910	1995
Hack Wilson	OF	1923–34	1979
Dave Winfield	OF	1973–95	2001
Early Wynn	P	1939–63	1972
Carl Yastrzemski	OF	1961–83	1989
Cy Young	P	1890–1911	1937
Ross Youngs	OF	1917–26	1972
Robin Yount	SS	1974–93	1999

Umpires

	Selected
Al Barlick	1989
Nestor Chylak	1999
Jocko Conlan	1974
Tom Connolly	1953
Billy Evans	1973
Cal Hubbard	1976
Bill Klem	1953
Bill McGowan	1992

Pioneers/Executives

	Selected
Ed Barrow (manager-executive)	1953
Morgan Bulkeley (executive)	1937
Alexander Cartwright (executive)	1938
Henry Chadwick (writer-executive)	1938

*Elected on the basis of his career in the Negro leagues.

Pioneers/Executives (Cont.)

	Selected
Happy Chandler (commissioner)	1982
Charles Comiskey (manager-executive)	1939
Rube Foster (player-manager-executive)	1981
Ford Frick (commissioner-executive)	1970
Warren Giles (executive)	1979
Will Harridge (executive)	1972
William Hulbert (executive)	1995
Ban Johnson (executive)	1937
Kenesaw M. Landis (commissioner)	1944
Larry MacPhail (executive)	1978
Lee MacPhail Jr. (executive)	1998
Branch Rickey (manager-executive)	1967
Al Spalding (player-executive)	1939
Bill Veeck (owner)	1991
George Weiss (executive)	1971
George Wright (player-manager)	1937
Harry Wright (player-manager-executive)	1953
Tom Yawkey (executive)	1980

Managers

	Managed	Selected
Walt Alston	1954–76	1983
Sparky Anderson	1970–94	2000
Leo Durocher	1939–73	1994
Clark Griffith	1901–20	1946
Bucky Harris	1924–56	1975
Ned Hanlon	1899–1907	1996
Miller Huggins	1913–29	1964
Tommy Lasorda	1977–96	1997
Al Lopez	1951–69	1977
Connie Mack	1894–1950	1937
Joe McCarthy	1926–50	1957
John McGraw	1899–1932	1937
Bill McKechnie	1915–46	1962
Wilbert Robinson	1902–31	1945
Frank Selee	1890–1905	1999
Casey Stengel	1934–65	1966
Earl Weaver	1968–82, 85–86	1996

Notable Achievements

No-Hit Games, Nine Innings or More

NATIONAL LEAGUE

Pitcher and Game	
1876......July 15	George Bradley, StL vs Hart 2–0
1880......June 12	John Richmond, Wor vs Clev 1–0 (perfect game)
June 17	Monte Ward, Prov vs Buff 5–0 (perfect game)
Aug 19	Larry Corcoran, Chi vs Bos 6–0
Aug 20	Pud Galvin, Buff vs Wor 1–0
1882......Sept 20	Larry Corcoran, Chi vs Wor 5–0
Sept 22	Tim Lovett, Bklyn vs NY 4–0
1883......July 25	Hoss Radbourn, Prov vs Clev 8–0
Sept 13	Hugh Daily, Clev vs Phil 1–0
1884......June 27	Larry Corcoran, Chi vs Prov 6–0
Aug 4	Pud Galvin, Buff vs Det 18–0
1885......July 27	John Clarkson, Chi vs Prov 4–0
Aug 29	Charles Ferguson, Phil vs Prov 1–0
1891......July 31	Amos Rusie, NY vs Bklyn 6–0
June 22	Tom Lovett, Bklyn vs NY 4–0
1892......Aug 6	Jack Stivetts, Bos vs Bklyn 11–0
Aug 22	Alex Sanders, Lou vs Balt 6–2

Date	Pitcher and Game
1892......Oct 15	Bumpus Jones, Cin vs Pitt 7–1 (first major league game)
1893......Aug 16	Bill Hawke, Balt vs Wash 5–0
1897......Sept 18	Cy Young, Clev vs Cin 6–0
1898......Apr 22	Ted Breitenstein, Cin vs Pitt 11–0
Apr 22	Jim Hughes, Balt vs Bos 8–0
July 8	Frank Donahue, Phil vs Bos 5–0
Aug 21	Walter Thornton, Chi vs Bklyn 2–0
1899......May 25	Deacon Phillippe, Lou vs NY 7–0
Aug 7	Vic Willis, Bos vs Wash 7–1
1900......July 12	Noodles Hahn, Cin vs Phil 4–0
1901......July 15	Christy Mathewson, NY vs StL 5–0
1903......Sept 18	Chick Fraser, Phil vs Chi 10–0
1904......June 11	Bob Wicker, Chi at NY 1–0 (hit in 10th; won in 12th)
1905......June 13	Christy Mathewson, NY vs Chi 1–0
1906......May 1	John Lush, Phil vs Bklyn 6–0
July 20	Mal Eason, Bklyn vs StL 2–0

No-Hit Games, Nine Innings or More (Cont.)

NATIONAL LEAGUE (Cont.)

Date	Pitcher and Game	Date	Pitcher and Game
1906......Aug 1	Harry McIntire, Bklyn vs Pitt 0–1 (hit in 11th; lost in 13th)	1968......July 29	George Culver, Cin vs Phil 6–1
1907......May 8	Frank Pfeffer, Bos vs Cin 6–0	Sept 17	Gaylord Perry, SF vs StL 1–0
Sept 20	Nick Maddox, Pitt vs Bklyn 2–1	Sept 18	Ray Washburn, StL vs SF 2–0
1908......July 4	George Wiltse, NY vs Phil 1–0 (10 innings)	1969......Apr 17	Bill Stoneman, Mtl vs Phil 7–0
		Apr 30	Jim Maloney, Cin vs Hou 10–0
Sept 5	Nap Rucker, Bklyn vs Bos 6–0	May 1	Don Wilson, Hou vs Cin 4–0
1909......Apr 15	Leon Ames, NY vs Bklyn 0–3 (hit in 10th; lost in 13th)	Aug 19	Ken Holtzman, Chi vs Atl 3–0
		Sept 20	Bob Moose, Pitt vs NY 4–0
1912......Sept 6	Jeff Tesreau, NY vs Phil 3–0	1970......June 12	Dock Ellis, Pitt vs SD 2–0
1914......Sept 9	George Davis, Bos vs Phil 7–0	July 20	Bill Singer, LA vs Phil 5–0
1915......Apr 15	Rube Marquard, NY vs Bklyn 2–0	1971......June 3	Ken Holtzman, Chi vs Cin 1–0
Aug 31	Jimmy Lavender, Chi vs NY 2–0	June 23	Rick Wise, Phil vs Cin 4–0
1916......June 16	Tom Hughes, Bos vs Pitt 2–0	Aug 14	Bob Gibson, StL vs Pitt 11–0
1917......May 2	Jim Vaughn, Chi vs Cin 0–1 (hit in 10th; lost in 10th)	1972......Apr 16	Burt Hooton, Chi vs Phil 4–0
		Sept 2	Milt Pappas, Chi vs SD 8–0
May 2	Fred Toney, Cin vs Chi 1–0 (10 innings)	Oct 2	Bill Stoneman, Mtl vs NY 7–0
1919......May 11	Hod Eller, Cin vs StL 6–0	1973......Aug 5	Phil Niekro, Atl vs SD 9–0
1922......May 7	Jesse Barnes, NY vs Phil 6–0	1975......Aug 24	Ed Halicki, SF vs NY 6–0
1924......July 17	Jesse Haines, StL vs Bos 5–0	1976......July 9	Larry Dierker, Hou vs Mtl 6–0
1925......Sept 13	Dazzy Vance, Bklyn vs Phil 10–1	Aug 9	John Candelaria, Pitt vs LA 2–0
1929......May 8	Carl Hubbell, NY vs Pitt 11–0	Sept 29	John Montefusco, SF vs Atl 9–0
1934......Sept 21	Paul Dean, StL vs Bklyn 3–0	1978......Apr 16	Bob Forsch, StL vs Phil 5–0
1938......June 11	Johnny Vander Meer, Cin vs Bos 3–0	June 16	Tom Seaver, Cin vs StL 4–0
June 15	Johnny Vander Meer, Cin vs Bklyn 6–0	1979......Apr 7	Ken Forsch, Hou vs Atl 6–0
1940......Apr 30	Tex Carleton, Bklyn vs Cin, 3–0	1980......June 27	Jerry Reuss, LA vs SF 8–0
1941......Aug 30	Lon Warneke, StL vs Cin 2–0	1981......May 10	Charlie Lea, Mtl vs SF 4–0
1944......Apr 27	Jim Tobin, Bos vs Bklyn 2–0	Sept 26	Nolan Ryan, Hou vs LA 5–0
May 15	Clyde Shoun, Cin vs Bos 1–0	1983......Sept 26	Bob Forsch, StL vs Mtl 3–0
1946......Apr 23	Ed Head, Bklyn vs Bos 5–0	1986......Sept 25	Mike Scott, Hou vs SF 2–0
1947......June 18	Ewell Blackwell, Cin vs Bos 6–0	1988......Sept 16	Tom Browning, Cin vs LA 1–0 (perfect game)
1948......Sept 9	Rex Barney, Bklyn vs NY 2–0		
1950......Aug 11	Vern Bickford, Bos vs Bklyn 7–0	1990......June 29	Fernando Valenzuela, LA vs StL 6–0
1951......May 6	Cliff Chambers, Pitt vs Bos 3–0	1990......Aug 15	Terry Mulholland, Phil vs SF 6–0
1952......June 19	Carl Erskine, Bklyn vs Chi 5–0	1991......May 23	Tommy Greene, Phil vs Mtl 2–0
1954......June 12	Jim Wilson, Mil vs Phil 2–0	July 26	Mark Gardner, LA vs Mtl 0–1 (hit in 10th, lost in 10th)
1955......May 12	Sam Jones, Chi vs Pitt 4–0		
1956......May 12	Carl Erskine, Bklyn vs NY 3–0	July 28	Dennis Martinez, Mtl vs LA 2–0 (perfect game)
Sept 25	Sal Maglie, Bklyn vs Phil 5–0		
1959......May 26	Harvey Haddix, Pitt vs Mil 0–1 (hit in 13th; lost in 13th)	Sept 11	Kent Mercker (6), Mark Wohlers (2), and Alejandro Pena (1), Atl vs SD 1–0
		1992......Aug 17	Kevin Gross, LA vs SF 2–0
1960......May 15	Don Cardwell, Chi vs StL 4–0	1993......Sept 8	Darryl Kile, Hou vs NY 7–1
Aug 18	Lew Burdette, Mil vs Phil 1–0	1994......Apr 8	Kent Mercker, Atl vs LA 6–0
Sept 16	Warren Spahn, Mil vs Phil 4–0	1995......June 3	Pedro Martinez, Mtl vs SD 1–0 (perfect through nine, hit in 10th)
1961......Apr 28	Warren Spahn, Mil vs SF 1–0		
1962......June 30	Sandy Koufax, LA vs NY 5–0	July 14	Ramon Martinez, LA vs Fla 7–0
1963......May 11	Sandy Koufax, LA vs SF 8–0	1996......May 11	Al Leiter, Fla vs Col 11–0
May 17	Don Nottebart, Hou vs Phil 4–1	Sept 17	Hideo Nomo, LA vs Col 9–0
June 15	Juan Marichal, SF vs Hou 1–0	1997......June 10	Kevin Brown, Fla vs SF 9–0
1964......Apr 23	Ken Johnson, Hou vs Cin 0–1	July 12	Francisco Cordova (9) and Ricardo Rincon (1), Pitt vs Col 3–0
June 4	Sandy Koufax, LA vs Phil 3–0		
June 21	Jim Bunning, Phil vs NY 6–0 (perfect game)	1999......June 25	Jose Jimenez, StL vs Ariz 1–0
		2001......May 12	A.J. Burnett, Fla vs SD 3–0
1965......June 14	Jim Maloney, Cin vs NY 0–1 (hit in 10th; lost in 11th)	Sept 3	Bud Smith, StL vs SD 4–0
		2003......June 11	R. Oswalt (1), P. Munro (2.2), K. Saarloos (1.1), B. Lidge (2), O. Dotel (1), B. Wagner (1), Hou vs NYY 8–0
Aug 19	Jim Maloney, Cin vs Chi 1–0 (10 innings)		
Sept 9	Sandy Koufax, LA vs Chi 1–0 (perfect game)	April 27	Kevin Millwood, Phil vs SF 1–0
		2004......May 18	Randy Johnson, Ariz vs Atl 2–0 (perfect game)
1967......June 18	Don Wilson, Hou vs Atl 2–0		

Note: Includes the games struck from the official record book on Sept. 4, 1991, when baseball's committee on statistical accuracy voted to define no-hitters as games of nine innings or more that end with a team getting no hits.

No-Hit Games, Nine Innings or More *(Cont.)*

AMERICAN LEAGUE

Date	Pitcher and Game	Date	Pitcher and Game
1901......May 9	Earl Moore, Clev vs Chi 2–4 (hit in 10th; lost in 10th)	1966......Oct 8	Don Larsen, NY (A) vs Bklyn (N) 2–0 (World Series) (perfect game)
1902......Sept 20	Jimmy Callahan, Chi vs Det 3–0	1957......Aug 20	Bob Keegan, Chi vs Wash 6–0
1904......May 5	Cy Young, Bos vs Phil 3–0 (perfect game)	1958......July 20	Jim Bunning, Det vs Bos 3–0
		Sept 20	Hoyt Wilhelm, Balt vs NY 1–0
Aug 17	Jesse Tannehill, Bos vs Chi 6–0	1962......May 5	Bo Belinsky, LA vs Balt 2–0
1905......July 22	Weldon Henley, Phil vs StL 6–0	June 26	Earl Wilson, Bos vs LA 2–0
Sept 6	Frank Smith, Chi vs Det 15–0	Aug 1	Bill Monbouquette, Bos vs Chi 1–0
Sept 27	Bill Dinneen, Bos vs Chi 2–0	Aug 26	Jack Kralick, Minn vs KC 1–0
1908......June 30	Cy Young, Bos vs NY 8–0	1965......Sept 16	Dave Morehead, Bos vs Clev 2–0
Sept 18	Bob Rhoades, Clev vs Bos 2–1	1966......June 10	Sonny Siebert, Clev vs Wash 2–0
Sept 20	Frank Smith, Chi vs Phil 1–0	1967......Apr 30	Steve Barber (8⅔) and Stu Miller (⅓), Balt vs Det 1–2
1908......Oct 2	Addie Joss, Clev vs Chi 1–0 (perfect game)	Aug 25	Dean Chance, Minn vs Clev 2–1
1910......Apr 20	Addie Joss, Clev vs Chi 1–0	Sept 10	Joel Horlen, Chi vs Det 6–0
May 12	Chief Bender, Phil vs Clev 4–0	1968......Apr 27	Tom Phoebus, Balt vs Bos 6–0
Aug 30	Tom Hughes, NY vs Clev 0–5 (hit in 10th; lost in 11th)	May 8	Catfish Hunter, Oak vs Minn 4–0 (perfect game)
1911......July 29	Joe Wood, Bos vs StL 5–0	1969......Aug 13	Jim Palmer, Balt vs Oak 8–0
Aug 27	Ed Walsh, Chi vs Bos 5–0	1970......July 3	Clyde Wright, Cal vs Oak 4–0
1912......July 4	George Mullin, Det vs StL 7–0	Sept 21	Vida Blue, Oak vs Minn 6–0
Aug 30	Earl Hamilton, StL vs Det 5–1	1973......Apr 27	Steve Busby, KC vs Det 3–0
1914......May 14	Jim Scott, Chi vs Wash 0–1 (hit in 10th; lost in 10th)	May 15	Nolan Ryan, Cal vs KC 3–0
		July 15	Nolan Ryan, Cal vs Det 6–0
May 31	Joe Benz, Chi vs Clev 6–1	July 30	Jim Bibby, Tex vs Oak 6–0
1916......June 21	George Foster, Bos vs NY 2–0	1974......June 19	Steve Busby, KC vs Mil 2–0
Aug 26	Joe Bush, Phil vs Clev 5–0	July 19	Dick Bosman, Clev vs Oak 4–0
Aug 30	Dutch Leonard, Bos vs StL 4–0	Sept 28	Nolan Ryan, Cal vs Minn 4–0
1917......Apr 14	Ed Cicotte, Chi vs StL 11–0	1975......June 1	Nolan Ryan, Cal vs Balt 1–0
Apr 24	George Mogridge, NY vs Bos 2–1	Sept 28	Vida Blue (5), Glenn Abbott and Paul Lindblad (1), Rollie Fingers (2), Oak vs Cal 5–0
May 5	Ernie Koob, StL vs Chi 1–0		
May 6	Bob Groom, StL vs Chi 3–0		
June 23	Ernie Shore, Bos vs Wash 4–0 (perfect game)	1976......July 28	John Odom (5) and Francisco Barrios (4), Chi vs Oak 2–1
1918......June 3	Dutch Leonard, Bos vs Det 5–0	1977......May 14	Jim Colborn, KC vs Tex 6–0
1919......Sept 10	Ray Caldwell, Clev vs NY 3–0	May 30	Dennis Eckersley, Clev vs Cal 1–0
1920......July 1	Walter Johnson, Wash vs Bos 1–0		
1922......Apr 30	Charlie Robertson, Chi vs Det 2–0 (perfect game)	Sept 22	Bert Blyleven, Tex vs Cal 6–0
		1981......May 15	Len Barker, Clev vs Tor 3–0 (perfect game)
1923......Sept 4	Sam Jones, NY vs Phil 2–0	1983......July 4	Dave Righetti, NY vs Bos 4–0
Sept 7	Howard Ehmke, Bos vs Phil 4–0	Sept 29	Mike Warren, Oak vs Chi 3–0
1926......Aug 21	Ted Lyons, Chi vs Bos 6–0	1984......Apr 7	Jack Morris, Det vs Chi 4–0
1931......Apr 29	Wes Ferrell, Clev vs StL 9–0	Sept 30	Mike Witt, Cal vs Tex 1–0 (perfect game)
Aug 8	Bob Burke, Wash vs Bos 5–0		
1934......Sept 18	Bobo Newsom, StL vs Bos 1–2 (hit in 10th; lost in 10th)	1986......Sept 19	Joe Cowley, Chi vs Cal 7–1
		1987......Apr 15	Juan Nieves, Mil vs Balt 7–0
1935......Aug 31	Vern Kennedy, Chi vs Clev 5–0	1990......Apr 11	Mark Langston (7), Mike Witt (2), Cal vs Sea 1–0
1937......June 1	Bill Dietrich, Chi vs StL 8–0		
1938......Aug 27	Mtle Pearson, NY vs Clev 13–0	June 2	Randy Johnson, Sea vs Det 2–0
1940......Apr 16	Bob Feller, Clev vs Chi 1–0 (opening day)	June 11	Nolan Ryan, Tex vs Oak 5–0
		June 29	Dave Stewart, Oak vs Tor 5–0
1945......Sept 9	Dick Fowler, Phil vs StL 1–0	1990......July 1	Andy Hawkins, NY vs Chi 0–4 (pitched eight of nine–innning game)
1946......Apr 30	Bob Feller, Clev vs NY 1–0		
1947......July 10	Don Black, Clev vs Phil 3–0	Sept 2	Dave Stieb, Tor vs Clev 3–0
Sep 3	Bill McCahan, Phil vs Wash 3–0	1991......May 1	Nolan Ryan, Tex vs Tor 3–0
1948......June 30	Bob Lemon, Clev vs Det 2–0	July 13	Bob Milacki (6), Mike Flanagan (1), Mark Williamson (1), and Gregg Olson (1), Balt vs Oak 2–0
1951......July 1	Bob Feller, Clev vs Det 2–1		
July 12	Allie Reynolds, NY vs Clev 1–0		
Sept 28	Allie Reynolds, NY vs Bos 8–0	Aug 11	Wilson Alvarez, Chi vs Balt 7–0
1952......May 15	Virgil Trucks, Det vs Wash 1–0	Aug 26	Bret Saberhagen, KC vs Chi 7–0
Aug 25	Virgil Trucks, Det vs NY 1–0	1993......Apr 22	Chris Bosio, Sea vs Bos 7–0
1953......May 6	Bobo Holloman, StL vs Phil 6–0 (first major league start)	Sept 4	Jim Abbott, NY vs Clev 4–0
1956......July 14	Mel Parnell, Bos vs Chi 4–0		

No-Hit Games, Nine Innings or More (Cont.)

AMERICAN LEAGUE (Cont.)

Date	Pitcher and Game	Date	Pitcher and Game
1994......Apr 27	Scott Erickson, Minn vs Mil 6–0	1999......July 18	David Cone, NY vs Mtl 6–0 (perfect game)
July 28	Kenny Rogers, Texas vs Cal 4–0 (perfect game)	Sept 11	Eric Milton, Minn vs Ana 7–0
1996......May 14	Dwight Gooden, NY vs Sea 2–0	2001......Apr 4	Hideo Nomo, Bos vs Balt 3–0
1998......May 17	David Wells, NY vs Minn 4–0 (perfect game)	2002......Apr 27	Derek Lowe, Bos vs TB 10–0

Longest Hitting Streaks

NATIONAL LEAGUE

Player and Team	Year	G
Willie Keeler, Balt	1897	44
Pete Rose, Cin	1978	44
Bill Dahlen, Chi	1894	42
Tommy Holmes, Bos	1945	37
Billy Hamilton, Phil	1894	36
Luis Castillo, Fla	2002	35
Fred Clarke, Lou	1895	35
Benito Santiago, SD	1987	34
George Davis, NY	1893	33
Rogers Hornsby, StL	1922	32

AMERICAN LEAGUE

Player and Team	Year	G
Joe DiMaggio, NY	1941	56
George Sisler, StL	1922	41
Ty Cobb, Det	1911	40
Paul Molitor, Mil	1987	39
Ty Cobb, Det	1917	35
Ty Cobb, Det	1912	34
George Sisler, StL	1925	34
John Stone, Det	1930	34
George McQuinn, StL	1938	34
Dom DiMaggio, Bos	1949	34

Triple Crown Hitters

NATIONAL LEAGUE

Player and Team	Year	HR	RBI	BA
Paul Hines, Prov	1878	4	50	.358
Hugh Duffy, Bos	1894	18	145	.438
Heinie Zimmerman*, Chi	1912	14	103	.372
Rogers Hornsby, StL	1922	42	152	.401
	1925	39	143	.403
Chuck Klein, Phil	1933	28	120	.368
Joe Medwick, StL	1937	31	154	.374

AMERICAN LEAGUE

Player and Team	Year	HR	RBI	BA
Nap Lajoie, Phil	1901	14	125	.422
Ty Cobb, Det	1909	9	115	.377
Jimmie Foxx, Phil	1933	48	163	.356
Lou Gehrig, NY	1934	49	165	.363
Ted Williams, Bos	1942	36	137	.356
	1947	32	114	.343
Mickey Mantle, NY	1956	52	130	.353
Frank Robinson, Balt	1966	49	122	.316
Carl Yastrzemski, Bos	1967	44	121	.326

*Zimmerman ranked first in RBIs as calculated by Ernie Lanigan, but only third as calculated by Information Concepts Inc.

THEY SAID IT

Kevin Towers, Padres general manager, after Matt Bush was arrested for allegedly biting a bouncer 13 days after San Diego made him the top pick overall in the amateur draft: "This is not a very good early indicator."

Triple Crown Pitchers

NATIONAL LEAGUE						AMERICAN LEAGUE					
Player and Team	Year	W	L	SO	ERA	Player and Team	Year	W	L	SO	ERA
Tommy Bond, Bos	1877	40	17	170	2.11	Cy Young, Bos	1901	33	10	158	1.62
Hoss Radbourn, Prov	1884	60	12	441	1.38	Rube Waddell, Phil	1905	26	11	287	1.48
Tim Keefe, NY	1888	35	12	333	1.74	Walter Johnson, Wash	1913	36	7	303	1.09
John Clarkson, Bos	1889	49	19	284	2.73		1918	23	13	162	1.27
Amos Rusie, NY	1894	36	13	195	2.78		1924	23	7	158	2.72
Christy Mathewson, NY	1905	31	8	206	1.27	Lefty Grove, Phil	1930	28	5	209	2.54
	1908	37	11	259	1.43		1931	31	4	175	2.06
Grover Alexander, Phil	1915	31	10	241	1.22	Lefty Gomez, NY	1934	26	5	158	2.33
	1916	33	12	167	1.55		1937	21	11	194	2.33
	1917	30	13	201	1.86	Hal Newhouser, Det	1945	25	9	212	1.81
Hippo Vaughn, Chi	1918	22	10	148	1.74	Roger Clemens, Tor	1997	21	7	292	2.05
Grover Alexander, Chi	1920	27	14	173	1.91		1998	20	6	271	2.64
Dazzy Vance, Bklyn	1924	28	6	262	2.16	Pedro Martinez, Bos	1999	23	4	313	2.07
Bucky Walters, Cin	1939	27	11	137	2.29						
Sandy Koufax, LA	1963	25	5	306	1.88						
	1965	26	8	382	2.04						
	1966	27	9	317	1.73						
Steve Carlton, Phil	1972	27	10	310	1.97						
Dwight Gooden, NY	1985	24	4	268	1.53						
Randy Johnson, Ariz	2002	24	5	334	2.32						

Consecutive Games Played, 500 or More Games

Cal Ripken Jr.	2,632	Sandy Alomar Sr.	648
Lou Gehrig	2,130	Eddie Brown	618
Everett Scott	1,307	Miguel Tejada	599
Steve Garvey	1,207	Roy McMillan	585
Billy Williams	1,117	George Pinckney	577
Joe Sewell	1,103	Steve Brodie	574
Stan Musial	895	Aaron Ward	565
Eddie Yost	829	Alex Rodriguez	546
Gus Suhr	822	Candy LaChance	540
Nellie Fox	798	Buck Freeman	535
Pete Rose	745	Fred Luderus	533
Dale Murphy	740	Clyde Milan	511
Richie Ashburn	730	Charlie Gehringer	511
Ernie Banks	717	Vada Pinson	508
Pete Rose	678	Tony Cuccinello	504
Earl Averill	673	Charlie Gehringer	504
Frank McCormick	652	Omar Moreno	503

Unassisted Triple Plays

Player and Team	Date	Pos	Opp	Opp Batter
Neal Ball, Clev	7-19-09	SS	Bos	Amby McConnell
Bill Wambsganss, Clev	10-10-20	2B	Bklyn	Clarence Mitchell
George Burns, Bos	9-14-23	1B	Clev	Frank Brower
Ernie Padgett, Bos	10-6-23	SS	Phil	Walter Holke
Glenn Wright, Pitt	5-7-25	SS	StL	Jim Bottomley
Jimmy Cooney, Chi	5-30-27	SS	Pitt	Paul Waner
Johnny Neun, Det	5-31-27	1B	Clev	Homer Summa
Ron Hansen, Wash	7-30-68	SS	Clev	Joe Azcue
Mickey Morandini, Phil	9-20-92	2B	Pitt	Jeff King
John Valentin, Bos	7-15-94	SS	Minn	Marc Newfield
Randy Velarde, Oak	5-29-00	2B	NYY	Shane Spencer
Rafael Furcal, Atl	8-10-03	SS	StL	Woody Williams

Pennant Winners

Year	Team	Manager	W	L	Pct	GA
1900	Brooklyn	Ned Hanlon	82	54	.603	4½
1901	Pittsburgh	Fred Clarke	90	49	.647	7½
1902	Pittsburgh	Fred Clarke	103	36	.741	27½
1903	Pittsburgh	Fred Clarke	91	49	.650	6½
1904	New York	John McGraw	106	47	.693	13
1905	New York	John McGraw	105	48	.686	9
1906	Chicago	Frank Chance	116	36	.763	20
1907	Chicago	Frank Chance	107	45	.704	17
1908	Chicago	Frank Chance	99	55	.643	1
1909	Pittsburgh	Fred Clarke	110	42	.724	6½
1910	Chicago	Frank Chance	104	50	.675	13
1911	New York	John McGraw	99	54	.647	7½
1912	New York	John McGraw	103	48	.682	10
1913	New York	John McGraw	101	51	.664	12½
1914	Boston	George Stallings	94	59	.614	10½
1915	Philadelphia	Pat Moran	90	62	.592	7
1916	Brooklyn	Wilbert Robinson	94	60	.610	2½
1917	New York	John McGraw	98	56	.636	10
1918	Chicago	Fred Mitchell	84	45	.651	10½
1919	Cincinnati	Pat Moran	96	44	.686	9
1920	Brooklyn	Wilbert Robinson	93	61	.604	7
1921	New York	John McGraw	94	59	.614	4
1922	New York	John McGraw	93	61	.604	7
1923	New York	John McGraw	95	58	.621	4½
1924	New York	John McGraw	93	60	.608	1½
1925	Pittsburgh	Bill McKechnie	95	58	.621	8½
1926	St. Louis	Rogers Hornsby	89	65	.578	2
1927	Pittsburgh	Donie Bush	94	60	.610	1½
1928	St. Louis	Bill McKechnie	95	59	.617	2
1929	Chicago	Joe McCarthy	98	54	.645	10½
1930	St. Louis	Gabby Street	92	62	.597	2
1931	St. Louis	Gabby Street	101	53	.656	13
1932	Chicago	Charlie Grimm	90	64	.584	4
1933	New York	Bill Terry	91	61	.599	5
1934	St. Louis	Frankie Frisch	95	58	.621	2
1935	Chicago	Charlie Grimm	100	54	.649	4
1936	New York	Bill Terry	92	62	.597	5
1937	New York	Bill Terry	95	57	.625	3
1938	Chicago	Gabby Hartnett	89	63	.586	2
1939	Cincinnati	Bill McKechnie	97	57	.630	4½
1940	Cincinnati	Bill McKechnie	100	53	.654	12
1941	Brooklyn	Leo Durocher	100	54	.649	2½
1942	St. Louis	Billy Southworth	106	48	.688	2
1943	St. Louis	Billy Southworth	105	49	.682	18
1944	St. Louis	Billy Southworth	105	49	.682	14½
1945	Chicago	Charlie Grimm	98	56	.636	3
1946	St. Louis*	Eddie Dyer	98	58	.628	2
1947	Brooklyn	Burt Shotton	94	60	.610	5
1948	Boston	Billy Southworth	91	62	.595	6½
1949	Brooklyn	Burt Shotton	97	57	.630	1
1950	Philadelphia	Eddie Sawyer	91	63	.591	2
1951	New York†	Leo Durocher	98	59	.624	1
1952	Brooklyn	Chuck Dressen	96	57	.627	4½
1953	Brooklyn	Chuck Dressen	105	49	.682	13
1954	New York	Leo Durocher	97	57	.630	5
1955	Brooklyn	Walt Alston	98	55	.641	13½
1956	Brooklyn	Walt Alston	93	61	.604	1
1957	Milwaukee	Fred Haney	95	59	.617	8
1958	Milwaukee	Fred Haney	92	62	.597	8
1959	Los Angeles‡	Walt Alston	88	68	.564	2
1960	Pittsburgh	Danny Murtaugh	95	59	.617	7
1961	Cincinnati	Fred Hutchinson	93	61	.604	4
1962	San Francisco#	Al Dark	103	62	.624	1
1963	Los Angeles	Walt Alston	99	63	.611	6
1964	St. Louis	Johnny Keane	93	69	.574	1
1965	Los Angeles	Walt Alston	97	65	.599	2

Pennant Winners (Cont.)

Year	Team	Manager	W	L	Pct	GA
1966	Los Angeles	Walt Alston	95	67	.586	1½
1967	St. Louis	Red Schoendienst	101	60	.627	10½
1968	St. Louis	Red Schoendienst	97	65	.599	9
1969	New York (E)††	Gil Hodges	100	62	.617	8
1970	Cincinnati (W)††	Sparky Anderson	102	60	.630	14½
1971	Pittsburgh (E)††	Danny Murtaugh	97	65	.599	7
1972	Cincinnati (W)††	Sparky Anderson	95	59	.617	10½
1973	New York (E)††	Yogi Berra	82	79	.509	1½
1974	Los Angeles (W)††	Walt Alston	102	60	.630	4
1975	Cincinnati (W)††	Sparky Anderson	108	54	.667	20
1976	Cincinnati (W)††	Sparky Anderson	102	60	.630	10
1977	Los Angeles (W)††	Tommy Lasorda	98	64	.605	10
1978	Los Angeles (W)††	Tommy Lasorda	95	67	.586	2½
1979	Pittsburgh (E)††	Chuck Tanner	98	64	.605	2
1980	Philadelphia (E)††	Dallas Green	91	71	.562	1
1981	Los Angeles (W)††	Tommy Lasorda	63	47	.573	**
1982	St. Louis (E)††	Whitey Herzog	92	70	.568	3
1983	Philadelphia (E)††	Pat Corrales/ Paul Owens	90	72	.556	6
1984	San Diego (W)††	Dick Williams	92	70	.568	12
1985	St. Louis (E)††	Whitey Herzog	101	61	.623	3
1986	New York (E)††	Dave Johnson	108	54	.667	21½
1987	St. Louis (E)††	Whitey Herzog	95	67	.586	3
1988	Los Angeles (W)††	Tommy Lasorda	94	67	.584	7
1989	San Francisco (W)††	Roger Craig	92	70	.568	3
1990	Cincinnati (W)††	Lou Piniella	91	71	.562	5
1991	Atlanta (W)††	Bobby Cox	94	68	.580	1
1992	Atlanta (W)††	Bobby Cox	98	64	.605	8
1993	Philadelphia (E)††	Jim Fregosi	97	65	.599	3
1994	Season ended Aug. 11 due to players' strike.					
1995	Atlanta (E)††	Bobby Cox	90	54	.625	21
1996	Atlanta (E)††	Bobby Cox	96	66	.593	8
1997	Florida (wc)††	Jim Leyland	92	70	.568	-9
1998	San Diego (W)††	Bruce Bochy	98	64	.605	9½
1999	Atlanta Braves (E)††	Bobby Cox	103	59	.636	6½
2000	New York Mets (wc)††	Bobby Valentine	94	68	.580	-6½
2001	Arizona (W)††	Bob Brenly	92	70	.568	2
2002	San Francisco (wc)††	Dusty Baker	95	66	.590	-2½
2003	Florida (wc)††	Jack McKeon	91	71	.562	-10
2004	St. Louis (C)††	Tony La Russa	105	57	.648	13

*Defeated Brooklyn, two games to none, in playoff for pennant. †Defeated Brooklyn, two games to one, in playoff for pennant. ‡Defeated Milwaukee, two games to none, in playoff for pennant. #Defeated Los Angeles, two games to one, in playoff for pennant. ††Won Championship Series. **First half 36–21; second half 27–26, in season split by strike; defeated Houston in playoff for Western Division title.

THEY SAID IT

Ron Gardenhire, Twins manager, after learning that Atlanta's Chipper Jones named his son Shea because he hits so well in New York: "I should have named my kid Tidewater."

Leading Batsmen

Year	Player and Team	BA	Year	Player and Team	BA
1900	Honus Wagner, Pitt	.381	1953	Carl Furillo, Bklyn	.344
1901	Jesse Burkett, StL	.382	1954	Willie Mays, NY	.345
1902	Ginger Beaumtl, Pitt	.357	1955	Richie Ashburn, Phil	.338
1903	Honus Wagner, Pitt	.355	1956	Hank Aaron, Mil	.328
1904	Honus Wagner, Pitt	.349	1957	Stan Musial, StL	.351
1905	Cy Seymour, Cin	.377	1958	Richie Ashburn, Phil	.350
1906	Honus Wagner, Pitt	.339	1959	Hank Aaron, Mil	.355
1907	Honus Wagner, Pitt	.350	1960	Dick Groat, Pitt	.325
1908	Honus Wagner, Pitt	.354	1961	Roberto Clemente, Pitt	.351
1909	Honus Wagner, Pitt	.339	1962	Tommy Davis, LA	.346
1910	Sherry Magee, Phil	.331	1963	Tommy Davis, LA	.326
1911	Honus Wagner, Pitt	.334	1964	Roberto Clemente, Pitt	.339
1912	Heinie Zimmerman, Chi	.372	1965	Roberto Clemente, Pitt	.329
1913	Jake Daubert, Bklyn	.350	1966	Matty Alou, Pitt	.342
1914	Jake Daubert, Bklyn	.329	1967	Roberto Clemente, Pitt	.357
1915	Larry Doyle, NY	.320	1968	Pete Rose, Cin	.335
1916	Hal Chase, Cin	.339	1969	Pete Rose, Cin	.348
1917	Edd Roush, Cin	.341	1970	Rico Carty, Atl	.366
1918	Zach Wheat, Bklyn	.335	1971	Joe Torre, StL	.363
1919	Edd Roush, Cin	.321	1972	Billy Williams, Chi	.333
1920	Rogers Hornsby, StL	.370	1973	Pete Rose, Cin	.338
1921	Rogers Hornsby, StL	.397	1974	Ralph Garr, Atl	.353
1922	Rogers Hornsby, StL	.401	1975	Bill Madlock, Chi	.354
1923	Rogers Hornsby, StL	.384	1976	Bill Madlock, Chi	.339
1924	Rogers Hornsby, StL	.424	1977	Dave Parker, Pitt	.338
1925	Rogers Hornsby, StL	.403	1978	Dave Parker, Pitt	.334
1926	Bubbles Hargrave, Cin	.353	1979	Keith Hernandez, StL	.344
1927	Paul Waner, Pitt	.380	1980	Bill Buckner, Chi	.324
1928	Rogers Hornsby, Bos	.387	1981	Bill Madlock, Pitt	.341
1929	Lefty O'Doul, Phil	.398	1982	Al Oliver, Mtl	.331
1930	Bill Terry, NY	.401	1983	Bill Madlock, Pitt	.323
1931	Chick Hafey, StL	.349	1984	Tony Gwynn, SD	.351
1932	Lefty O'Doul, Bklyn	.368	1985	Willie McGee, StL	.353
1933	Chuck Klein, Phil	.368	1986	Tim Raines, Mtl	.334
1934	Paul Waner, Pitt	.362	1987	Tony Gwynn, SD	.370
1935	Arky Vaughan, Pitt	.385	1988	Tony Gwynn, SD	.313
1936	Paul Waner, Pitt	.373	1989	Tony Gwynn, SD	.336
1937	Joe Medwick, StL	.374	1990	Willie McGee, StL	.335
1938	Ernie Lombardi, Cin	.342	1991	Terry Pendleton, Atl	.319
1939	Johnny Mize, StL	.349	1992	Gary Sheffield, SD	.330
1940	Debs Garms, Pitt	.355	1993	Andres Galarraga, Col	.370
1941	Pete Reiser, Bklyn	.343	1994	Tony Gwynn, SD	.394
1942	Ernie Lombardi, Bos	.330	1995	Tony Gwynn, SD	.368
1943	Stan Musial, StL	.357	1996	Tony Gwynn, SD	.353
1944	Dixie Walker, Bklyn	.357	1997	Tony Gwynn, SD	.372
1945	Phil Cavarretta, Chi	.355	1998	Larry Walker, Col	.363
1946	Stan Musial, StL	.365	1999	Larry Walker, Col	.379
1947	Harry Walker, StL-Phil	.363	2000	Todd Helton, Col	.372
1948	Stan Musial, StL	.376	2001	Larry Walker, Col	.350
1949	Jackie Robinson, Bklyn	.342	2002	Barry Bonds, SF	.370
1950	Stan Musial, StL	.346	2003	Albert Pujols, StL	.359
1951	Stan Musial, StL	.355	2004	Barry Bonds, SF	.362
1952	Stan Musial, StL	.336			

Leaders in Runs Scored

Year	Player and Team	Runs	Year	Player and Team	Runs
1900	Roy Thomas, Phil	131	1953	Duke Snider, Bklyn	132
1901	Jesse Burkett, StL	139	1954	Stan Musial, StL	120
1902	Honus Wagner, Pitt	105		Duke Snider, Bklyn	120
1903	Ginger Beaumont, Pitt	137	1955	Duke Snider, Bklyn	126
1904	George Browne, NY	99	1956	Frank Robinson, Cin	122
1905	Mike Donlin, NY	124	1957	Hank Aaron, Mil	118
1906	Honus Wagner, Pitt	103	1958	Willie Mays, SF	121
	Frank Chance, Chi	103	1959	Vada Pinson, Cin	131
1907	Spike Shannon, NY	104	1960	Bill Bruton, Mil	112
1908	Fred Tenney, NY	101	1961	Willie Mays, SF	129
1909	Tommy Leach, Pitt	126	1962	Frank Robinson, Cin	134
1910	Sherry Magee, Phil	110	1963	Hank Aaron, Mil	121
1911	Jimmy Sheckard, Chi	121	1964	Dick Allen, Phil	125
1912	Bob Bescher, Cin	120	1965	Tommy Harper, Cin	126
1913	Tommy Leach, Chi	99	1966	Felipe Alou, Atl	122
	Max Carey, Pitt	99	1967	Hank Aaron, Atl	113
1914	George Burns, NY	100		Lou Brock, StL	113
1915	Gavvy Cravath, Phil	89	1968	Glenn Beckert, Chi	98
1916	George Burns, NY	105	1969	Bobby Bonds, SF	120
1917	George Burns, NY	103		Pete Rose, Cin	120
1918	Heinie Groh, Cin	88	1970	Billy Williams, Chi	137
1919	George Burns, NY	86	1971	Lou Brock, StL	126
1920	George Burns, NY	115	1972	Joe Morgan, Cin	122
1921	Rogers Hornsby, StL	131	1973	Bobby Bonds, SF	131
1922	Rogers Hornsby, StL	141	1974	Pete Rose, Cin	110
1923	Ross Youngs, NY	121	1975	Pete Rose, Cin	112
1924	Frankie Frisch, NY	121	1976	Pete Rose, Cin	130
	Rogers Hornsby, StL	121	1977	George Foster, Cin	124
1925	Kiki Cuyler, Pitt	144	1978	Ivan DeJesus, Chi	104
1926	Kiki Cuyler, Pitt	113	1979	Keith Hernandez, StL	116
1927	Lloyd Waner, Pitt	133	1980	Keith Hernandez, StL	111
	Rogers Hornsby, NY	133	1981	Mike Schmidt, Phil	78
1928	Paul Waner, Pitt	142	1982	Lonnie Smith, StL	120
1929	Rogers Hornsby, Chi	156	1983	Tim Raines, Mtl	133
1930	Chuck Klein, Phil	158	1984	Ryne Sandberg, Chi	114
1931	Bill Terry, NY	121	1985	Dale Murphy, Atl	118
	Chuck Klein, Phil	121	1986	Von Hayes, Phil	107
1932	Chuck Klein, Phil	152		Tony Gwynn, SD	107
1933	Pepper Martin, StL	122	1987	Tim Raines, Mtl	123
1934	Paul Waner, Pitt	122	1988	Brett Butler, SF	109
1935	Augie Galan, Chi	133	1989	Howard Johnson, NY	104
1936	Arky Vaughan, Pitt	122		Will Clark, SF	104
1937	Joe Medwick, StL	111		Ryne Sandberg, Chi	104
1938	Mel Ott, NY	116	1990	Ryne Sandberg, Chi	116
1939	Billy Werber, Cin	115	1991	Brett Butler, LA	112
1940	Arky Vaughan, Pitt	113	1992	Barry Bonds, Pitt	109
1941	Pete Reiser, Bklyn	117	1993	Lenny Dykstra, Phil	143
1942	Mel Ott, NY	118	1994	Jeff Bagwell, Hou	104
1943	Arky Vaughan, Bklyn	112	1995	Craig Biggio, Hou	123
1944	Bill Nicholson, Chi	116	1996	Ellis Burks, Col	142
1945	Eddie Stanky, Bklyn	128	1997	Craig Biggio, Hou	146
1946	Stan Musial, StL	124	1998	Sammy Sosa, Chi	134
1947	Johnny Mize, NY	137	1999	Jeff Bagwell, Hou	143
1948	Stan Musial, StL	135	2000	Jeff Bagwell, Hou	152
1949	Pee Wee Reese, Bklyn	132	2001	Sammy Sosa, Chi	146
1950	Earl Torgeson, Bos	120	2002	Sammy Sosa, Chi	122
1951	Stan Musial, StL	124	2003	Albert Pujols, StL	137
	Ralph Kiner, Pitt	124	2004	Albert Pujols, StL	133
1952	Stan Musial, StL	105			
	Solly Hemus, StL	105			

Leaders in Hits

Year	Player and Team	Hits	Year	Player and Team	Hits
1900	Willie Keeler, Bklyn	208	1955	Ted Kluszewski, Cin	192
1901	Jesse Burkett, StL	228	1956	Hank Aaron, Mil	200
1902	Ginger Beaumont, Pitt	194	1957	Red Schoendienst, NY-Mil	200
1903	Ginger Beaumont, Pitt	209	1958	Richie Ashburn, Phil	215
1904	Ginger Beaumont, Pitt	185	1959	Hank Aaron, Mil	223
1905	Cy Seymour, Cin	219	1960	Willie Mays, SF	190
1906	Harry Steinfeldt, Chi	176	1961	Vada Pinson, Cin	208
1907	Ginger Beaumont, Bos	187	1962	Tommy Davis, LA	230
1908	Honus Wagner, Pitt	201	1963	Vada Pinson, Cin	204
1909	Larry Doyle, NY	172	1964	Roberto Clemente, Pitt	211
1910	Honus Wagner, Pitt	178		Curt Flood, StL	211
	Bobby Byrne, Pitt	178	1965	Pete Rose, Cin	209
1911	Doc Miller, Bos	192	1966	Felipe Alou, Atl	218
1912	Heinie Zimmerman, Chi	207	1967	Roberto Clemente, Pitt	209
1913	Gavvy Cravath, Phil	179	1968	Felipe Alou, Atl	210
1914	Sherry Magee, Phil	171		Pete Rose, Cin	210
1915	Larry Doyle, NY	189	1969	Matty Alou, Pitt	231
1916	Hal Chase, Cin	184	1970	Pete Rose, Cin	205
1917	Heinie Groh, Cin	182		Billy Williams, Chi	205
1918	Charlie Hollocher, Chi	161	1971	Joe Torre, StL	230
1919	Ivy Olson, Bklyn	164	1972	Pete Rose, Cin	198
1920	Rogers Hornsby, StL	218	1973	Pete Rose, Cin	230
1921	Rogers Hornsby, StL	235	1974	Ralph Garr, Atl	214
1922	Rogers Hornsby, StL	250	1975	Dave Cash, Phil	213
1923	Frankie Frisch, NY	223	1976	Pete Rose, Cin	215
1924	Rogers Hornsby, StL	227	1977	Dave Parker, Pitt	215
1925	Jim Bottomley, StL	227	1978	Steve Garvey, LA	202
1926	Eddie Brown, Bos	201	1979	Garry Templeton, StL	211
1927	Paul Waner, Pitt	237	1980	Steve Garvey, LA	200
1928	Freddy Lindstrom, NY	231	1981	Pete Rose, Phil	140
1929	Lefty O'Doul, Phil	254	1982	Al Oliver, Mtl	204
1930	Bill Terry, NY	254	1983	Jose Cruz, Hou	189
1931	Lloyd Waner, Pitt	214		Andre Dawson, Mtl	189
1932	Chuck Klein, Phil	226	1984	Tony Gwynn, SD	213
1933	Chuck Klein, Phil	223	1985	Willie McGee, StL	216
1934	Paul Waner, Pitt	217	1986	Tony Gwynn, SD	211
1935	Billy Herman, Chi	227	1987	Tony Gwynn, SD	218
1936	Joe Medwick, StL	223	1988	Andres Galarraga, Mtl	184
1937	Joe Medwick, StL	237	1989	Tony Gwynn, SD	203
1938	Frank McCormick, Cin	209	1990	Brett Butler, SF	192
1939	Frank McCormick, Cin	209		Lenny Dykstra, Phil	192
1940	Stan Hack, Chi	191	1991	Terry Pendleton, Atl	187
	Frank McCormick, Cin	191	1992	Terry Pendleton, Atl	199
1941	Stan Hack, Chi	186		Andy Van Slyke, Pitt	199
1942	Enos Slaughter, StL	188	1993	Lenny Dykstra, Phil	194
1943	Stan Musial, StL	220	1994	Tony Gwynn, SD	165
1944	Stan Musial, StL	197	1995	Dante Bichette, Col	197
	Phil Cavarretta, Chi	197		Tony Gwynn, SD	197
1945	Tommy Holmes, Bos	224	1996	Lance Johnson, NY	227
1946	Stan Musial, StL	228	1997	Tony Gwynn, SD	220
1947	Tommy Holmes, Bos	191	1998	Dante Bichette, Col	219
1948	Stan Musial, StL	230	1999	Luis Gonzalez, Ariz	206
1949	Stan Musial, StL	207	2000	Todd Helton, Col	216
1950	Duke Snider, Bklyn	199	2001	Rich Aurilia, SF	206
1951	Richie Ashburn, Phil	221	2002	Vladimir Guerrero	206
1952	Stan Musial, StL	194	2003	Albert Pujols, StL	212
1953	Richie Ashburn, Phil	205	2004	Juan Pierre, Fla	221
1954	Don Mueller, NY	212			

Home Run Leaders

Year	Player and Team	HR	Year	Player and Team	HR
1900	Herman Long, Bos	12	1949	Ralph Kiner, Pitt	54
1901	Sam Crawford, Cin	16	1950	Ralph Kiner, Pitt	47
1902	Tommy Leach, Pitt	6	1951	Ralph Kiner, Pitt	42
1903	Jimmy Sheckard, Bklyn	9	1952	Ralph Kiner, Pitt	37
1904	Harry Lumley, Bklyn	9		Hank Sauer, Chi	37
1905	Fred Odwell, Cin	9	1953	Eddie Mathews, Mil	47
1906	Tim Jordan, Bklyn	12	1954	Ted Kluszewski, Cin	49
1907	Dave Brain, Bos	10	1955	Willie Mays, NY	51
1908	Tim Jordan, Bklyn	12	1956	Duke Snider, Bklyn	43
1909	Red Murray, NY	7	1957	Hank Aaron, Mil	44
1910	Fred Beck, Bos	10	1958	Ernie Banks, Chi	47
	Wildfire Schulte, Chi	10	1959	Eddie Mathews, Mil	46
1911	Wildfire Schulte, Chi	21	1960	Ernie Banks, Chi	41
1912	Heinie Zimmerman, Chi	14	1961	Orlando Cepeda, SF	46
1913	Gavvy Cravath, Phil	19	1962	Willie Mays, SF	49
1914	Gavvy Cravath, Phil	19	1963	Hank Aaron, Mil	44
1915	Gavvy Cravath, Phil	24		Willie McCovey, SF	44
1916	Dave Robertson, NY	12	1964	Willie Mays, SF	47
	Cy Williams, Chi	12	1965	Willie Mays, SF	52
1917	Dave Robertson, NY	12	1966	Hank Aaron, Atl	44
	Gavvy Cravath, Phil	12	1967	Hank Aaron, Atl	39
1918	Gavvy Cravath, Phil	8	1968	Willie McCovey, SF	36
1919	Gavvy Cravath, Phil	12	1969	Willie McCovey, SF	45
1920	Cy Williams, Phil	15	1970	Johnny Bench, Cin	45
1921	George Kelly, NY	23	1971	Willie Stargell, Pitt	48
1922	Rogers Hornsby, StL	42	1972	Johnny Bench, Cin	40
1923	Cy Williams, Phil	41	1973	Willie Stargell, Pitt	44
1924	Jack Fournier, Bklyn	27	1974	Mike Schmidt, Phil	36
1925	Rogers Hornsby, StL	39	1975	Mike Schmidt, Phil	38
1926	Hack Wilson, Chi	21	1976	Mike Schmidt, Phil	38
1927	Hack Wilson, Chi	30	1977	George Foster, Cin	52
	Cy Williams, Phil	30	1978	George Foster, Cin	40
1928	Hack Wilson, Chi	31	1979	Dave Kingman, Chi	48
	Jim Bottomley, StL	31	1980	Mike Schmidt, Phil	48
1929	Chuck Klein, Phil	43	1981	Mike Schmidt, Phil	31
1930	Hack Wilson, Chi	56	1982	Dave Kingman, NY	37
1931	Chuck Klein, Phil	31	1983	Mike Schmidt, Phil	40
1932	Chuck Klein, Phil	38	1984	Dale Murphy, Atl	36
	Mel Ott, NY	38		Mike Schmidt, Phil	36
1933	Chuck Klein, Phil	28	1985	Dale Murphy, Atl	37
1934	Ripper Collins, StL	35	1986	Mike Schmidt, Phil	37
	Mel Ott, NY	35	1987	Andre Dawson, Chi	49
1935	Wally Berger, Bos	34	1988	Darryl Strawberry, NY	39
1936	Mel Ott, NY	33	1989	Kevin Mitchell, SF	47
1937	Mel Ott, NY	31	1990	Ryne Sandberg, Chi	40
	Joe Medwick, StL	31	1991	Howard Johnson, NY	38
1938	Mel Ott, NY	36	1992	Fred McGriff, SD	35
1939	Johnny Mize, StL	28	1993	Barry Bonds, SF	46
1940	Johnny Mize, StL	43	1994	Matt Williams, SF	43
1941	Dolph Camilli, Bklyn	34	1995	Dante Bichette, Col	40
1942	Mel Ott, NY	30	1996	Andres Galarraga, Col	47
1943	Bill Nicholson, Chi	29	1997	Larry Walker, Col	49
1944	Bill Nicholson, Chi	33	1998	Mark McGwire, StL	70
1945	Tommy Holmes, Bos	28	1999	Mark McGwire, StL	65
1946	Ralph Kiner, Pitt	23	2000	Sammy Sosa, Chi	50
1947	Ralph Kiner, Pitt	51	2001	Barry Bonds, SF	73
	Johnny Mize, NY	51	2002	Sammy Sosa, Chi	49
1948	Ralph Kiner, Pitt	40	2003	Jim Thome, Phil	47
	Johnny Mize, NY	40	2004	Adrian Beltre, LA	48

Runs Batted In Leaders

Year	Player and Team	RBI	Year	Player and Team	RBI
1900	Elmer Flick, Phil	110	1953	Roy Campanella, Bklyn	142
1901	Honus Wagner, Pitt	126	1954	Ted Kluszewski, Cin	141
1902	Honus Wagner, Pitt	91	1955	Duke Snider, Bklyn	136
1903	Sam Mertes, NY	104	1956	Stan Musial, StL	109
1904	Bill Dahlen, NY	80	1957	Hank Aaron, Mil	132
1905	Cy Seymour, Cin	121	1958	Ernie Banks, Chi	129
1906	Jim Nealon, Pitt	83	1959	Ernie Banks, Chi	143
	Harry Steinfeldt, Chi	83	1960	Hank Aaron, Mil	126
1907	Sherry Magee, Phil	85	1961	Orlando Cepeda, SF	142
1908	Honus Wagner, Pitt	109	1962	Tommy Davis, LA	153
1909	Honus Wagner, Pitt	100	1963	Hank Aaron, Mil	130
1910	Sherry Magee, Phil	123	1964	Ken Boyer, StL	119
1911	Wildfire Schulte, Chi	121	1965	Deron Johnson, Cin	130
1912	Heinie Zimmerman, Chi	103	1966	Hank Aaron, Atl	127
1913	Gavvy Cravath, Phil	128	1967	Orlando Cepeda, StL	111
1914	Sherry Magee, Phil	103	1968	Willie McCovey, SF	105
1915	Gavvy Cravath, Phil	115	1969	Willie McCovey, SF	126
1916	Heinie Zimmerman, Chi-NY	83	1970	Johnny Bench, Cin	148
1917	Heinie Zimmerman, NY	102	1971	Joe Torre, StL	137
1918	Sherry Magee, Phil	76	1972	Johnny Bench, Cin	125
1919	Hi Myers, Bklyn	73	1973	Willie Stargell, Pitt	119
1920	George Kelly, NY	94	1974	Johnny Bench, Cin	129
	Rogers Hornsby, StL	94	1975	Greg Luzinski, Phil	120
1921	Rogers Hornsby, StL	126	1976	George Foster, Cin	121
1922	Rogers Hornsby, StL	152	1977	George Foster, Cin	149
1923	Irish Meusel, NY	125	1978	George Foster, Cin	120
1924	George Kelly, NY	136	1979	Dave Winfield, SD	118
1925	Rogers Hornsby, StL	143	1980	Mike Schmidt, Phil	121
1926	Jim Bottomley, StL	120	1981	Mike Schmidt, Phil	91
1927	Paul Waner, Pitt	131	1982	Dale Murphy, Atl	109
1928	Jim Bottomley, StL	136		Al Oliver, Mtl	109
1929	Hack Wilson, Chi	159	1983	Dale Murphy, Atl	121
1930	Hack Wilson, Chi	190	1984	Gary Carter, Mtl	106
1931	Chuck Klein, Phil	121		Mike Schmidt, Phil	106
1932	Don Hurst, Phil	143	1985	Dave Parker, Cin	125
1933	Chuck Klein, Phil	120	1986	Mike Schmidt, Phil	119
1934	Mel Ott, NY	135	1987	Andre Dawson, Chi	137
1935	Wally Berger, Bos	130	1988	Will Clark, SF	109
1936	Joe Medwick, StL	138	1989	Kevin Mitchell, SF	125
1937	Joe Medwick, StL	154	1990	Matt Williams, SF	122
1938	Joe Medwick, StL	122	1991	Howard Johnson, NY	117
1939	Frank McCormick, Cin	128	1992	Darren Daulton, Phil	109
1940	Johnny Mize, StL	137	1993	Barry Bonds, SF	123
1941	Dolph Camilli, Bklyn	120	1994	Jeff Bagwell, Hou	116
1942	Johnny Mize, NY	110	1995	Dante Bichette, Col	128
1943	Bill Nicholson, Chi	128	1996	Andres Galarraga, Col	150
1944	Bill Nicholson, Chi	122	1997	Andres Galarraga, Col	140
1945	Dixie Walker, Bklyn	124	1998	Sammy Sosa, Chi	158
1946	Enos Slaughter, StL	130	1999	Mark McGwire, StL	147
1947	Johnny Mize, NY	138	2000	Todd Helton, Col	147
1948	Stan Musial, StL	131	2001	Sammy Sosa, Chi	160
1949	Ralph Kiner, Pitt	127	2002	Lance Berkman, Hou	128
1950	Del Ennis, Phil	126	2003	Preston Wilson, Col	141
1951	Monte Irvin, NY	121	2004	Vinny Castilla, Col	131
1952	Hank Sauer, Chi	121			

Leading Base Stealers

Year	Player and Team	SB	Year	Player and Team	SB
1900	George Van Haltren, NY	45	1951	Sam Jethroe, Bos	35
	Patsy Donovan, StL	45	1952	Pee Wee Reese, Bklyn	30
1901	Honus Wagner, Pitt	48	1953	Bill Bruton, Mil	26
1902	Honus Wagner, Pitt	43	1954	Bill Bruton, Mil	34
1903	Jimmy Sheckard, Bklyn	67	1955	Bill Bruton, Mil	35
	Frank Chance, Chi	67	1956	Willie Mays, NY	40
1904	Honus Wagner, Pitt	53	1957	Willie Mays, NY	38
1905	Billy Maloney, Chi	59	1958	Willie Mays, SF	31
	Art Devlin, NY	59	1959	Willie Mays, SF	27
1906	Frank Chance, Chi	57	1960	Maury Wills, LA	50
1907	Honus Wagner, Pitt	61	1961	Maury Wills, LA	35
1908	Honus Wagner, Pitt	53	1962	Maury Wills, LA	104
1909	Bob Bescher, Cin	54	1963	Maury Wills, LA	40
1910	Bob Bescher, Cin	70	1964	Maury Wills, LA	53
1911	Bob Bescher, Cin	80	1965	Maury Wills, LA	94
1912	Bob Bescher, Cin	67	1966	Lou Brock, StL	74
1913	Max Carey, Pitt	61	1967	Lou Brock, StL	52
1914	George Burns, NY	62	1968	Lou Brock, StL	62
1915	Max Carey, Pitt	36	1969	Lou Brock, StL	53
1916	Max Carey, Pitt	63	1970	Bobby Tolan, Cin	57
1917	Max Carey, Pitt	46	1971	Lou Brock, StL	64
1918	Max Carey, Pitt	58	1972	Lou Brock, StL	63
1919	George Burns, NY	40	1973	Lou Brock, StL	70
1920	Max Carey, Pitt	52	1974	Lou Brock, StL	118
1921	Frankie Frisch, NY	49	1975	Davey Lopes, LA	77
1922	Max Carey, Pitt	51	1976	Davey Lopes, LA	63
1923	Max Carey, Pitt	51	1977	Frank Taveras, Pitt	70
1924	Max Carey, Pitt	49	1978	Omar Moreno, Pitt	71
1925	Max Carey, Pitt	46	1979	Omar Moreno, Pitt	77
1926	Kiki Cuyler, Pitt	35	1980	Ron LeFlore, Mtl	97
1927	Frankie Frisch, StL	48	1981	Tim Raines, Mtl	71
1928	Kiki Cuyler, Chi	37	1982	Tim Raines, Mtl	78
1929	Kiki Cuyler, Chi	43	1983	Tim Raines, Mtl	90
1930	Kiki Cuyler, Chi	37	1984	Tim Raines, Mtl	75
1931	Frankie Frisch, StL	28	1985	Vince Coleman, StL	110
1932	Chuck Klein, Phil	20	1986	Vince Coleman, StL	107
1933	Pepper Martin, StL	26	1987	Vince Coleman, StL	109
1934	Pepper Martin, StL	23	1988	Vince Coleman, StL	81
1935	Augie Galan, Chi	22	1989	Vince Coleman, StL	65
1936	Pepper Martin, StL	23	1990	Vince Coleman, StL	77
1937	Augie Galan, Chi	23	1991	Marquis Grissom, Mtl	76
1938	Stan Hack, Chi	16	1992	Marquis Grissom, Mtl	78
1939	Stan Hack, Chi	17	1993	Chuck Carr, Fla	58
	Lee Handley, Pitt	17	1994	Craig Biggio, Hou	39
1940	Lonny Frey, Cin	22	1995	Quilvio Veras, Fla	56
1941	Danny Murtaugh, Phil	18	1996	Eric Young, Col	53
1942	Pete Reiser, Bklyn	20	1997	Tony Womack, Pitt	60
1943	Arky Vaughan, Bklyn	20	1998	Tony Womack, Pitt	58
1944	Johnny Barrett, Pitt	28	1999	Tony Womack, Ariz	72
1945	Red Schoendienst, StL	26	2000	Luis Castillo, Fla	62
1946	Pete Reiser, Bklyn	34	2001	Juan Pierre, Col	46
1947	Jackie Robinson, Bklyn	29	2002	Luis Castillo, Fla	48
1948	Richie Ashburn, Phil	32	2003	Juan Pierre, Fla	65
1949	Jackie Robinson, Bklyn	37	2004	Scott Podsednik, Mil	70
1950	Sam Jethroe, Bos	35			

Leading Pitchers—Winning Percentage

Year	Pitcher and Team	W	L	Pct	Year	Pitcher and Team	W	L	Pct
1900	Jesse Tannehill, Pitt	20	6	.769	1954	Johnny Antonelli, NY	21	7	.750
1901	Jack Chesbro, Pitt	21	10	.677	1955	Don Newcombe, Bklyn	20	5	.800
1902	Jack Chesbro, Pitt	28	6	.824	1956	Don Newcombe, Bklyn	27	7	.794
1903	Sam Leever, Pitt	25	7	.781	1957	Bob Buhl, Mil	18	7	.720
1904	Joe McGinnity, NY	35	8	.814	1958	Warren Spahn, Mil	22	11	.667
1905	Sam Leever, Pitt	20	5	.800		Lew Burdette, Mil	20	10	.667
1906	Ed Reulbach, Chi	19	4	.826	1959	Roy Face, Pitt	18	1	.947
1907	Ed Reulbach, Chi	17	4	.810	1960	Ernie Broglio, StL	21	9	.700
1908	Ed Reulbach, Chi	24	7	.774	1961	Johnny Podres, LA	18	5	.783
1909	Christy Mathewson, NY	25	6	.806	1962	Bob Purkey, Cin	23	5	.821
	Howie Camnitz, Pitt	25	6	.806	1963	Ron Perranoski, LA	16	3	.842
1910	King Cole, Chi	20	4	.833	1964	Sandy Koufax, LA	19	5	.792
1911	Rube Marquard, NY	24	7	.774	1965	Sandy Koufax, LA	26	8	.765
1912	Claude Hendrix, Pitt	24	9	.727	1966	Juan Marichal, SF	25	6	.806
1913	Bert Humphries, Chi	16	4	.800	1967	Dick Hughes, StL	16	6	.727
1914	Bill James, Bos	26	7	.788	1968	Steve Blass, Pitt	18	6	.750
1915	Grover Alexander, Phil	31	10	.756	1969	Tom Seaver, NY	25	7	.781
1916	Tom Hughes, Bos	16	3	.842	1970	Bob Gibson, StL	23	7	.767
1917	Ferdie Schupp, NY	21	7	.750	1971	Don Gullett, Cin	16	6	.727
1918	Claude Hendrix, Chi	19	7	.731	1972	Gary Nolan, Cin	15	5	.750
1919	Dutch Ruether, Cin	19	6	.760	1973	Tommy John, LA	16	7	.696
1920	Burleigh Grimes, Bklyn	23	11	.676	1974	Andy Messersmith, LA	20	6	.769
1921	Bill Doak, StL	15	6	.714	1975	Don Gullett, Cin	15	4	.789
1922	Pete Donohue, Cin	18	9	.667	1976	Steve Carlton, Phil	20	7	.741
1923	Dolf Luque, Cin	27	8	.771	1977	John Candelaria, Pitt	20	5	.800
1924	Emil Yde, Pitt	16	3	.842	1978	Gaylord Perry, SD	21	6	.778
1925	Bill Sherdel, StL	15	6	.714	1979	Tom Seaver, Cin	16	6	.727
1926	Ray Kremer, Pitt	20	6	.769	1980	Jim Bibby, Pitt	19	6	.760
1927	Larry Benton, Bos-NY	17	7	.708	1981*	Tom Seaver, Cin	14	2	.875
1928	Larry Benton, NY	25	9	.735	1982	Phil Niekro, Atl	17	4	.810
1929	Charlie Root, Chi	19	6	.760	1983	John Denny, Phil	19	6	.760
1930	Freddie Fitzsimmons, NY	19	7	.731	1984	Rick Sutcliffe, Chi	16	1	.941
1931	Paul Derringer, StL	18	8	.692	1985	Orel Hershiser, LA	19	3	.864
1932	Lon Warneke, Chi	22	6	.786	1986	Bob Ojeda, NY	18	5	.783
1933	Ben Cantwell, Bos	20	10	.667	1987	Dwight Gooden, NY	15	7	.682
1934	Dizzy Dean, StL	30	7	.811	1988	David Cone, NY	20	3	.870
1935	Bill Lee, Chi	20	6	.769	1989	Mike Bielecki, Chi	18	7	.720
1936	Carl Hubbell, NY	26	6	.813	1990	Doug Drabeck, Pitt	22	6	.786
1937	Carl Hubbell, NY	22	8	.733	1991	John Smiley, Pitt	20	8	.714
1938	Bill Lee, Chi	22	9	.710		Jose Rijo, Cin	15	6	.714
1939	Paul Derringer, Cin	25	7	.781	1992	Bob Tewksbury, StL	16	5	.762
1940	Freddie Fitzsimmons, Bklyn	16	2	.889	1993	Tom Glavine, Atl	22	6	.786
1941	Elmer Riddle, Cin	19	4	.826	1994	Ken Hill, Mtl	16	5	.762
1942	Larry French, Bklyn	15	4	.789	1995	Greg Maddux, Atl	19	2	.905
1943	Mort Cooper, StL	21	8	.724	1996	John Smoltz, Atl	24	8	.750
1944	Ted Wilks, StL	17	4	.810	1997	Denny Neagle, Atl	20	5	.800
1945	Harry Brecheen, StL	15	4	.789	1998	John Smoltz, Atl	17	3	.850
1946	Murray Dickson, StL	15	6	.714	1999	Mike Hampton, Hou	22	4	.846
1947	Larry Jansen, NY	21	5	.808	2000	Randy Johnson, Ariz	19	7	.730
1948	Harry Brecheen, StL	20	7	.741	2001	Curt Schilling, Ariz	22	6	.786
1949	Preacher Roe, Bklyn	15	6	.714	2002	Randy Johnson, Ariz	24	5	.828
1950	Sal Maglie, NY	18	4	.818	2003	Jason Schmidt, SF	17	5	.773
1951	Preacher Roe, Bklyn	22	3	.880	2004	Roger Clemens, Hou	18	4	.818
1952	Hoyt Wilhelm, NY	15	3	.833					
1953	Carl Erskine, Bklyn	20	6	.769					

*1981 percentages based on 10 or more victories. Note: Percentages based on 15 or more victories in all other years.

Leading Pitchers—Earned Run Average

Year	Player and Team	ERA	Year	Player and Team	ERA
1900	Rube Waddell, Pitt	2.37	1953	Warren Spahn, Mil	2.10
1901	Jesse Tannehill, Pitt	2.18	1954	Johnny Antonelli, NY	2.29
1902	Jack Taylor, Chi	1.33	1955	Bob Friend, Pitt	2.84
1903	Sam Leever, Pitt	2.06	1956	Lew Burdette, Mil	2.71
1904	Joe McGinnity, NY	1.61	1957	Johnny Podres, Bklyn	2.66
1905	Christy Mathewson, NY	1.27	1958	Stu Miller, SF	2.47
1906	Three Finger Brown, Chi	1.04	1959	Sam Jones, SF	2.82
1907	Jack Pfiester, Chi	1.15	1960	Mike McCormick, SF	2.70
1908	Christy Mathewson, NY	1.43	1961	Warren Spahn, Mil	3.01
1909	Christy Mathewson, NY	1.14	1962	Sandy Koufax, LA	2.54
1910	George McQuillan, Phil	1.60	1963	Sandy Koufax, LA	1.88
1911	Christy Mathewson, NY	1.99	1964	Sandy Koufax, LA	1.74
1912	Jeff Tesreau, NY	1.96	1965	Sandy Koufax, LA	2.04
1913	Christy Mathewson, NY	2.06	1966	Sandy Koufax, LA	1.73
1914	Bill Doak, StL	1.72	1967	Phil Niekro, Atl	1.87
1915	Grover Alexander, Phil	1.22	1968	Bob Gibson, StL	1.12
1916	Grover Alexander, Phil	1.55	1969	Juan Marichal, SF	2.10
1917	Grover Alexander, Phil	1.83	1970	Tom Seaver, NY	2.81
1918	Hippo Vaughn, Chi	1.74	1971	Tom Seaver, NY	1.76
1919	Grover Alexander, Chi	1.72	1972	Steve Carlton, Phil	1.98
1920	Grover Alexander, Chi	1.91	1973	Tom Seaver, NY	2.08
1921	Bill Doak, StL	2.58	1974	Buzz Capra, Atl	2.28
1922	Rosy Ryan, NY	3.00	1975	Randy Jones, SD	2.24
1923	Dolf Luque, Cin	1.93	1976	John Denny, StL	2.52
1924	Dazzy Vance, Bklyn	2.16	1977	John Candelaria, Pitt	2.34
1925	Dolf Luque, Cin	2.63	1978	Craig Swan, NY	2.43
1926	Ray Kremer, Pitt	2.61	1979	J.R. Richard, Hou	2.71
1927	Ray Kremer, Pitt	2.47	1980	Don Sutton, LA	2.21
1928	Dazzy Vance, Bklyn	2.09	1981	Nolan Ryan, Hou	1.69
1929	Bill Walker, NY	3.08	1982	Steve Rogers, Mtl	2.40
1930	Dazzy Vance, Bklyn	2.61	1983	Atlee Hammaker, SF	2.25
1931	Bill Walker, NY	2.26	1984	Alejandro Pena, LA	2.48
1932	Lon Warneke, Chi	2.37	1985	Dwight Gooden, NY	1.53
1933	Carl Hubbell, NY	1.66	1986	Mike Scott, Hou	2.22
1934	Carl Hubbell, NY	2.30	1987	Nolan Ryan, Hou	2.76
1935	Cy Blanton, Pitt	2.59	1988	Joe Magrane, StL	2.18
1936	Carl Hubbell, NY	2.31	1989	Scott Garrelts, SF	2.28
1937	Jim Turner, Bos	2.38	1990	Danny Darwin, Hou	2.21
1938	Bill Lee, Chi	2.66	1991	Dennis Martinez, Mtl	2.39
1939	Bucky Walters, Cin	2.29	1992	Bill Swift, SF	2.08
1940	Bucky Walters, Cin	2.48	1993	Greg Maddux, Atl	2.36
1941	Elmer Riddle, Cin	2.24	1994	Greg Maddux, Atl	1.56
1942	Mort Cooper, StL	1.77	1995	Greg Maddux, Atl	1.63
1943	Howie Pollet, StL	1.75	1996	Kevin Brown, Fla	1.89
1944	Ed Heusser, Cin	2.38	1997	Pedro Martinez, Mtl	1.90
1945	Hank Borowy, Chi	2.14	1998	Greg Maddux, Atl	1.98
1946	Howie Pollet, StL	2.10	1999	Randy Johnson, Ariz	2.48
1947	Warren Spahn, Bos	2.33	2000	Kevin Brown, LA	2.58
1948	Harry Brecheen, StL	2.24	2001	Randy Johnson, Ariz	2.49
1949	Dave Koslo, NY	2.50	2002	Randy Johnson, Ariz	2.32
1950	Jim Hearn, StL-NY	2.49	2003	Jason Schmidt, SF	2.34
1951	Chet Nichols, Bos	2.88	2004	Jake Peavy, SD	2.27
1952	Hoyt Wilhelm, NY	2.43			

Note: Based on 10 complete games through 1950, then 154 innings until National League expanded in 1962, when it became 162 innings. In strike-shortened 1981, one inning per game required.

Leading Pitchers—Strikeouts

Year	Player and Team	SO	Year	Player and Team	SO
1900	Rube Waddell, Pitt	133	1952	Warren Spahn, Bos	183
1901	Noodles Hahn, Cin	233	1953	Robin Roberts, Phil	198
1902	Vic Willis, Bos	226	1954	Robin Roberts, Phil	185
1903	Christy Mathewson, NY	267	1955	Sam Jones, Chi	198
1904	Christy Mathewson, NY	212	1956	Sam Jones, Chi	176
1905	Christy Mathewson, NY	206	1957	Jack Sanford, Phil	188
1906	Fred Beebe, Chi-StL	171	1958	Sam Jones, StL	225
1907	Christy Mathewson, NY	178	1959	Don Drysdale, LA	242
1908	Christy Mathewson, NY	259	1960	Don Drysdale, LA	246
1909	Orval Overall, Chi	205	1961	Sandy Koufax, LA	269
1910	Christy Mathewson, NY	190	1962	Don Drysdale, LA	232
1911	Rube Marquard, NY	237	1963	Sandy Koufax, LA	306
1912	Grover Alexander, Phil	195	1964	Bob Veale, Pitt	250
1913	Tom Seaton, Phil	168	1965	Sandy Koufax, LA	382
1914	Grover Alexander, Phil	214	1966	Sandy Koufax, LA	317
1915	Grover Alexander, Phil	241	1967	Jim Bunning, Phil	253
1916	Grover Alexander, Phil	167	1968	Bob Gibson, StL	268
1917	Grover Alexander, Phil	200	1969	Ferguson Jenkins, Chi	273
1918	Hippo Vaughn, Chi	148	1970	Tom Seaver, NY	283
1919	Hippo Vaughn, Chi	141	1971	Tom Seaver, NY	289
1920	Grover Alexander, Chi	173	1972	Steve Carlton, Phil	310
1921	Burleigh Grimes, Bklyn	136	1973	Tom Seaver, NY	251
1922	Dazzy Vance, Bklyn	134	1974	Steve Carlton, Phil	240
1923	Dazzy Vance, Bklyn	197	1975	Tom Seaver, NY	243
1924	Dazzy Vance, Bklyn	262	1976	Tom Seaver, NY	235
1925	Dazzy Vance, Bklyn	221	1977	Phil Niekro, Atl	262
1926	Dazzy Vance, Bklyn	140	1978	J.R. Richard, Hou	303
1927	Dazzy Vance, Bklyn	184	1979	J.R. Richard, Hou	313
1928	Dazzy Vance, Bklyn	200	1980	Steve Carlton, Phil	286
1929	Pat Malone, Chi	166	1981	Fernando Valenzuela, LA	180
1930	Bill Hallahan, StL	177	1982	Steve Carlton, Phil	286
1931	Bill Hallahan, StL	159	1983	Steve Carlton, Phil	275
1932	Dizzy Dean, StL	191	1984	Dwight Gooden, NY	276
1933	Dizzy Dean, StL	199	1985	Dwight Gooden, NY	268
1934	Dizzy Dean, StL	195	1986	Mike Scott, Hou	306
1935	Dizzy Dean, StL	182	1987	Nolan Ryan, Hou	270
1936	Van Lingle Mungo, Bklyn	238	1988	Nolan Ryan, Hou	228
1937	Carl Hubbell, NY	159	1989	Jose DeLeon, StL	201
1938	Clay Bryant, Chi	135	1990	David Cone, NY	233
1939	Claude Passeau, Phil-Chi	137	1991	David Cone, NY	241
	Bucky Walters, Cin	137	1992	John Smoltz, Atl	215
1940	Kirby Higbe, Phil	137	1993	Jose Rijo, Cin	227
1941	Johnny Vander Meer, Cin	202	1994	Andy Benes, SD	189
1942	Johnny Vander Meer, Cin	186	1995	Hideo Nomo, LA	236
1943	Johnny Vander Meer, Cin	174	1996	John Smoltz, Atl	276
1944	Bill Voiselle, NY	161	1997	Curt Schilling, Phil	319
1945	Preacher Roe, Pitt	148	1998	Curt Schilling, Phil	300
1946	Johnny Schmitz, Chi	135	1999	Randy Johnson, Ariz	364
1947	Ewell Blackwell, Cin	193	2000	Randy Johnson, Ariz	347
1948	Harry Brecheen, StL	149	2001	Randy Johnson, Ariz	372
1949	Warren Spahn, Bos	151	2002	Randy Johnson, Ariz	334
1950	Warren Spahn, Bos	191	2003	Kerry Wood, Chi	266
1951	Warren Spahn, Bos	164	2004	Randy Johnson, Ariz	290
	Don Newcombe, Bklyn	164			

Leading Pitchers—Saves

Year	Player and Team	SV	Year	Player and Team	SV
1947	Hugh Casey, Bklyn	18	1976	Rawly Eastwick, Cin	26
1948	Harry Gumpert, Cin	17	1977	Rollie Fingers, SD	35
1949	Ted Wilks, StL	9	1978	Rollie Fingers, SD	37
1950	Jim Konstanty, Phil	22	1979	Bruce Sutter, Chi	37
1951	Ted Wilks, StL, Pitt	13	1980	Bruce Sutter, Chi	28
1952	Al Brazle, StL	16	1981	Bruce Sutter, StL	25
1953	Al Brazle, StL	18	1982	Bruce Sutter, StL	36
1954	Jim Hughes, Bklyn	24	1983	Lee Smith, Chi	29
1955	Jack Meyer, Phil	16	1984	Bruce Sutter, StL	45
1956	Clem Labine, Bklyn	19	1985	Jeff Reardon, Mtl	41
1957	Clem Labine, Bklyn	17	1986	Todd Worrell, StL	36
1958	Roy Face, Pitt	20	1987	Steve Bedrosian, Phil	40
1959	Lindy McDaniel, StL	15	1988	John Franco, Cin	39
	Don McMahon, Mil	15	1989	Mark Davis, SD	44
1960	Lindy McDaniel, StL	26	1990	John Franco, NY	33
1961	Stu Miller, SF	17	1991	Lee Smith, StL	47
	Roy Face, Pitt	17	1992	Lee Smith, StL	42
1962	Roy Face, Pitt	28	1993	Randy Myers, Chi	53
1963	Lindy McDaniel, Chi	22	1994	John Franco, NY	30
1964	Hal Woodeshick, Hou	23	1995	Randy Myers, Chi	38
1965	Ted Abernathy, Chi	31	1996	Jeff Brantley, Cin	44
1966	Phil Regan, LA	21		Todd Worrell, LA	44
1967	Ted Abernathy, Cin	28	1997	Jeff Shaw, Cin	42
1968	Phil Regan, Chi, LA	25	1998	Trevor Hoffman, SD	53
1969	Fred Gladding, Hou	29	1999	Ugueth Urbina, Mtl	41
1970	Wayne Granger, Cin	35	2000	Antonio Alfonseca, Fla	45
1971	Dave Giusti, Pitt	30	2001	Robb Nen, SF	45
1972	Clay Carroll, Cin	37	2002	John Smoltz, Atl	55
1973	Mike Marshall, Mtl	13	2003	Eric Gagne, LA	55
1974	Mike Marshall, LA	21	2004	Armando Benitez, Fla	47
1975	Al Hrabosky, StL	22		Jason Isringhausen, StL	47
	Rawly Eastwick, Cin	22			

YET ANOTHER SIGN OF THE APOCALYPSE

Photos of Juan Marichal purposely hitting Johnny Roseboro on the head with a bat in 1965, autographed by both men, are selling on the Internet for $449.

Pennant Winners

Year	Team	Manager	W	L	Pct	GA
1901	Chicago	Clark Griffith	83	53	.610	4
1902	Philadelphia	Connie Mack	83	53	.610	5
1903	Boston	Jimmy Collins	91	47	.659	14½
1904	Boston	Jimmy Collins	95	59	.617	1½
1905	Philadelphia	Connie Mack	92	56	.622	2
1906	Chicago	Fielder Jones	93	58	.616	3
1907	Detroit	Hughie Jennings	92	58	.613	1½
1908	Detroit	Hughie Jennings	90	63	.588	½
1909	Detroit	Hughie Jennings	98	54	.645	3½
1910	Philadelphia	Connie Mack	102	48	.680	14½
1911	Philadelphia	Connie Mack	101	50	.669	13½
1912	Boston	Jake Stahl	105	47	.691	14
1913	Philadelphia	Connie Mack	96	57	.627	6½
1914	Philadelphia	Connie Mack	99	53	.651	8½
1915	Boston	Bill Carrigan	101	50	.669	2½
1916	Boston	Bill Carrigan	91	63	.591	2
1917	Chicago	Pants Rowland	100	54	.649	9
1918	Boston	Ed Barrow	75	51	.595	2½
1919	Chicago	Kid Gleason	88	52	.629	3½
1920	Cleveland	Tris Speaker	98	56	.636	2
1921	New York	Miller Huggins	98	55	.641	4½
1922	New York	Miller Huggins	94	60	.610	1
1923	New York	Miller Huggins	98	54	.645	16
1924	Washington	Bucky Harris	92	62	.597	2
1925	Washington	Bucky Harris	96	55	.636	8½
1926	New York	Miller Huggins	91	63	.591	3
1927	New York	Miller Huggins	110	44	.714	19
1928	New York	Miller Huggins	101	53	.656	2½
1929	Philadelphia	Connie Mack	104	46	.693	18
1930	Philadelphia	Connie Mack	102	52	.662	8
1931	Philadelphia	Connie Mack	107	45	.704	13½
1932	New York	Joe McCarthy	107	47	.695	13
1933	Washington	Joe Cronin	99	53	.651	7
1934	Detroit	Mickey Cochrane	101	53	.656	7
1935	Detroit	Mickey Cochrane	93	58	.616	3
1936	New York	Joe McCarthy	102	51	.667	19½
1937	New York	Joe McCarthy	102	52	.662	13
1938	New York	Joe McCarthy	99	53	.651	9½
1939	New York	Joe McCarthy	106	45	.702	17
1940	Detroit	Del Baker	90	64	.584	1
1941	New York	Joe McCarthy	101	53	.656	17
1942	New York	Joe McCarthy	103	51	.669	9
1943	New York	Joe McCarthy	98	56	.636	13½
1944	St. Louis	Luke Sewell	89	65	.578	1
1945	Detroit	Steve O'Neill	88	65	.575	1½
1946	Boston	Joe Cronin	104	50	.675	12
1947	New York	Bucky Harris	97	57	.630	12
1948	Cleveland†	Lou Boudreau	97	58	.626	1
1949	New York	Casey Stengel	97	57	.630	1
1950	New York	Casey Stengel	98	56	.636	3
1951	New York	Casey Stengel	98	56	.636	5
1952	New York	Casey Stengel	95	59	.617	2
1953	New York	Casey Stengel	99	52	.656	8½
1954	Cleveland	Al Lopez	111	43	.721	8
1955	New York	Casey Stengel	96	58	.623	3
1956	New York	Casey Stengel	97	57	.630	9
1957	New York	Casey Stengel	98	56	.636	8
1958	New York	Casey Stengel	92	62	.597	10
1959	Chicago	Al Lopez	94	60	.610	5
1960	New York	Casey Stengel	97	57	.630	8
1961	New York	Ralph Houk	109	53	.673	8
1962	New York	Ralph Houk	96	66	.593	5
1963	New York	Ralph Houk	104	57	.646	10½
1964	New York	Yogi Berra	99	63	.611	1
1965	Minnesota	Sam Mele	102	60	.630	7
1966	Baltimore	Hank Bauer	97	63	.606	9

Pennant Winners (Cont.)

Year	Team	Manager	W	L	Pct	GA
1967	Boston	Dick Williams	92	70	.568	1
1968	Detroit	Mayo Smith	103	59	.636	12
1969	Baltimore (E)‡	Earl Weaver	109	53	.673	19
1970	Baltimore (E)‡	Earl Weaver	108	54	.667	15
1971	Baltimore (E)‡	Earl Weaver	101	57	.639	12
1972	Oakland (W)‡	Dick Williams	93	62	.600	5½
1973	Oakland (W)‡	Dick Williams	94	68	.580	6
1974	Oakland (W)‡	Al Dark	90	72	.556	5
1975	Boston (E)‡	Darrell Johnson	95	65	.594	4½
1976	New York (E)‡	Billy Martin	97	62	.610	10½
1977	New York (E)‡	Billy Martin	100	62	.617	2½
1978	New York (E)†‡	Billy Martin, Bob Lemon	100	63	.613	1
1979	Baltimore (E)‡	Earl Weaver	102	57	.642	8
1980	Kansas City (W)‡	Jim Frey	97	65	.599	14
1981	New York (E)‡	Gene Michael/Bob Lemon	59	48	.551	#
1982	Milwaukee (E)‡	Buck Rodgers, Harvey Kuenn	95	67	.586	1
1983	Baltimore (E)‡	Joe Altobelli	98	64	.605	6
1984	Detroit (E)‡	Sparky Anderson	104	58	.642	15
1985	Kansas City (W)‡	Dick Howser	91	71	.562	1
1986	Boston (E)‡	John McNamara	95	66	.590	5½
1987	Minnesota (W)‡	Tom Kelly	85	77	.525	2
1988	Oakland (W)‡	Tony La Russa	104	58	.642	13
1989	Oakland (W)‡	Tony La Russa	99	63	.611	7
1990	Oakland (W)‡	Tony La Russa	103	59	.636	9
1991	Minnesota (W)‡	Tom Kelly	95	67	.586	8
1992	Toronto‡	Cito Gaston	96	66	.593	4
1993	Toronto‡	Cito Gaston	95	67	.586	7
1994	Season ended Aug. 11 due to players' strike.					
1995	Cleveland (C)‡	Mike Hargrove	100	44	.694	30
1996	New York (E)‡	Joe Torre	92	70	.568	4
1997	Cleveland (C)‡	Mike Hargrove	86	75	.534	6
1998	New York (E)‡	Joe Torre	114	48	.704	22
1999	New York (E)‡	Joe Torre	98	64	.605	4
2000	New York (E)‡	Joe Torre	87	74	.540	2½
2001	New York (E)‡	Joe Torre	95	65	.594	13½
2002	Anaheim (wc)‡	Mike Scioscia	99	63	.611	-4
2003	New York (E)‡	Joe Torre	101	61	.623	6
2004	Boston (wc)‡	Terry Francona	98	64	.605	-3

†Defeated Boston in one-game playoff. ‡Won championship series.
#First half 34–22; second half 25–26, in season split by strike; defeated Milwaukee in playoff for Eastern Division title.

Leading Batsmen

Year	Player and Team	BA	Year	Player and Team	BA
1901	Nap Lajoie, Phil	.422	1923	Harry Heilmann, Det	.403
1902	Ed Delahanty, Wash	.376	1924	Babe Ruth, NY	.378
1903	Nap Lajoie, Clev	.355	1925	Harry Heilmann, Det	.393
1904	Nap Lajoie, Clev	.381	1926	Heinie Manush, Det	.378
1905	Elmer Flick, Clev	.306	1927	Harry Heilmann, Det	.398
1906	George Stone, StL	.358	1928	Goose Goslin, Wash	.379
1907	Ty Cobb, Det	.350	1929	Lew Fonseca, Clev	.369
1908	Ty Cobb, Det	.324	1930	Al Simmons, Phil	.381
1909	Ty Cobb, Det	.377	1931	Al Simmons, Phil	.390
1910	Nap Lajoie, Clev*	.383	1932	Dale Alexander, Det-Bos	.367
1911	Ty Cobb, Det	.420	1933	Jimmie Foxx, Phil	.356
1912	Ty Cobb, Det	.410	1934	Lou Gehrig, NY	.363
1913	Ty Cobb, Det	.390	1935	Buddy Myer, Wash	.349
1914	Ty Cobb, Det	.368	1936	Luke Appling, Chi	.388
1915	Ty Cobb, Det	.369	1937	Charlie Gehringer, Det	.371
1916	Tris Speaker, Clev	.386	1938	Jimmie Foxx, Bos	.349
1917	Ty Cobb, Det	.383	1939	Joe DiMaggio, NY	.381
1918	Ty Cobb, Det	.382	1940	Joe DiMaggio, NY	.352
1919	Ty Cobb, Det	.384	1941	Ted Williams, Bos	.406
1920	George Sisler, StL	.407	1942	Ted Williams, Bos	.356
1921	Harry Heilmann, Det	.394	1943	Luke Appling, Chi	.328
1922	George Sisler, StL	.420	1944	Lou Boudreau, Clev	.327

*League president Ban Johnson declared Ty Cobb batting champion with a .385 average, beating Lajoie's .384. However, subsequent research has led to the revision of Lajoie's average to .383 and Cobb's to .382.

Leading Batsmen (Cont.)

Year	Player and Team	BA	Year	Player and Team	BA
1945	Snuffy Stirnweiss, NY	.309	1975	Rod Carew, Minn	.359
1946	Mickey Vernon, Wash	.353	1976	George Brett, KC	.333
1947	Ted Williams, Bos	.343	1977	Rod Carew, Minn	.388
1948	Ted Williams, Bos	.369	1978	Rod Carew, Minn	.333
1949	George Kell, Det	.343	1979	Fred Lynn, Bos	.333
1950	Billy Goodman, Bos	.354	1980	George Brett, KC	.390
1951	Ferris Fain, Phil	.344	1981	Carney Lansford, Bos	.336
1952	Ferris Fain, Phil	.327	1982	Willie Wilson, KC	.332
1953	Mickey Vernon, Wash	.337	1983	Wade Boggs, Bos	.361
1954	Bobby Avila, Clev	.341	1984	Don Mattingly, NY	.343
1955	Al Kaline, Det	.340	1985	Wade Boggs, Bos	.368
1956	Mickey Mantle, NY	.353	1986	Wade Boggs, Bos	.357
1957	Ted Williams, Bos	.388	1987	Wade Boggs, Bos	.363
1958	Ted Williams, Bos	.328	1988	Wade Boggs, Bos	.366
1959	Harvey Kuenn, Det	.353	1989	Kirby Puckett, Minn	.339
1960	Pete Runnels, Bos	.320	1990	George Brett, KC	.329
1961	Norm Cash, Det	.361	1991	Julio Franco, Tex	.341
1962	Pete Runnels, Bos	.326	1992	Edgar Martinez, Sea	.343
1963	Carl Yastrzemski, Bos	.321	1993	John Olerud, Tor	.363
1964	Tony Oliva, Minn	.323	1994	Paul O'Neill, NY	.359
1965	Tony Oliva, Minn	.321	1995	Edgar Martinez, Sea	.356
1966	Frank Robinson, Balt	.316	1996	Alex Rodriguez, Sea	.358
1967	Carl Yastrzemski, Bos	.326	1997	Frank Thomas, Chi	.347
1968	Carl Yastrzemski, Bos	.301	1998	Bernie Williams, NY	.339
1969	Rod Carew, Minn	.332	1999	Nomar Garciaparra, Bos	.357
1970	Alex Johnson, Cal	.329	2000	Nomar Garciaparra, Bos	.372
1971	Tony Oliva, Minn	.337	2001	Ichiro Suzuki, Sea	.350
1972	Rod Carew, Minn	.318	2002	Manny Ramirez, Bos	.349
1973	Rod Carew, Minn	.350	2003	Bill Mueller, Bos	.326
1974	Rod Carew, Minn	.364	2004	Ichiro Suzuki, Sea	.372

Leaders in Runs Scored

Year	Player and Team	Runs	Year	Player and Team	Runs
1901	Nap Lajoie, Phil	145	1936	Lou Gehrig, NY	167
1902	Dave Fultz, Phil	110	1937	Joe DiMaggio, NY	151
1903	Patsy Dougherty, Bos	108	1938	Hank Greenberg, Det	144
1904	Patsy Dougherty, Bos-NY	113	1939	Red Rolfe, NY	139
1905	Harry Davis, Phil	92	1940	Ted Williams, Bos	134
1906	Elmer Flick, Clev	98	1941	Ted Williams, Bos	135
1907	Sam Crawford, Det	102	1942	Ted Williams, Bos	141
1908	Matty McIntyre, Det	105	1943	George Case, Wash	102
1909	Ty Cobb, Det	116	1944	Snuffy Stirnweiss, NY	125
1910	Ty Cobb, Det	106	1945	Snuffy Stirnweiss, NY	107
1911	Ty Cobb, Det	147	1946	Ted Williams, Bos	142
1912	Eddie Collins, Phil	137	1947	Ted Williams, Bos	125
1913	Eddie Collins, Phil	125	1948	Tommy Henrich, NY	138
1914	Eddie Collins, Phil	122	1949	Ted Williams, Bos	150
1915	Ty Cobb, Det	144	1950	Dom DiMaggio, Bos	131
1916	Ty Cobb, Det	113	1951	Dom DiMaggio, Bos	113
1917	Donie Bush, Det	112	1952	Larry Doby, Clev	104
1918	Ray Chapman, Clev	84	1953	Al Rosen, Clev	115
1919	Babe Ruth, Bos	103	1954	Mickey Mantle, NY	129
1920	Babe Ruth, NY	158	1955	Al Smith, Clev	123
1921	Babe Ruth, NY	177	1956	Mickey Mantle, NY	132
1922	George Sisler, StL	134	1957	Mickey Mantle, NY	121
1923	Babe Ruth, NY	151	1958	Mickey Mantle, NY	127
1924	Babe Ruth, NY	143	1959	Eddie Yost, Det	115
1925	Johnny Mostil, Chi	135	1960	Mickey Mantle, NY	119
1926	Babe Ruth, NY	139	1961	Mickey Mantle, NY	132
1927	Babe Ruth, NY	158		Roger Maris, NY	132
1928	Babe Ruth, NY	163	1962	Albie Pearson, LA	115
1929	Charlie Gehringer, Det	131	1963	Bob Allison, Minn	99
1930	Al Simmons, Phil	152	1964	Tony Oliva, Minn	109
1931	Lou Gehrig, NY	163	1965	Zoilo Versalles, Minn	126
1932	Jimmie Foxx, Phil	151	1966	Frank Robinson, Balt	122
1933	Lou Gehrig, NY	138	1967	Carl Yastrzemski, Bos	112
1934	Charlie Gehringer, Det	134	1968	Dick McAuliffe, Det	95
1935	Lou Gehrig, NY	125			

Leaders in Runs Scored (Cont.)

Year	Player and Team	Runs	Year	Player and Team	Runs
1969	Reggie Jackson, Oak	123	1988	Wade Boggs, Bos	128
1970	Carl Yastrzemski, Bos	125	1989	Rickey Henderson, NY-Oak	113
1971	Don Buford, Balt	99		Wade Boggs, Bos	113
1972	Bobby Murcer, NY	102	1990	Rickey Henderson, Oak	119
1973	Reggie Jackson, Oak	99	1991	Paul Molitor, Mil	133
1974	Carl Yastrzemski, Bos	93	1992	Tony Phillips, Det	114
1975	Fred Lynn, Bos	103	1993	Rafael Palmeiro, Tex	124
1976	Roy White, NY	104	1994	Frank Thomas, Chi	106
1977	Rod Carew, Minn	128	1995	Albert Belle, Clev	121
1978	Ron LeFlore, Det	126		Edgar Martinez, Sea	121
1979	Don Baylor, Cal	120	1996	Alex Rodriguez, Sea	141
1980	Willie Wilson, KC	133	1997	Ken Griffey Jr., Sea	125
1981	Rickey Henderson, Oak	89	1998	Derek Jeter, NY	127
1982	Paul Molitor, Mil	136	1999	Roberto Alomar, Clev	138
1983	Cal Ripken, Balt	121	2000	Johnny Damon, KC	136
1984	Dwight Evans, Bos	121	2001	Alex Rodriguez, Tex	133
1985	Rickey Henderson, NY	146	2002	Alfonso Soriano, NY	128
1986	Rickey Henderson, NY	130	2003	Alex Rodriguez, Tex	124
1987	Paul Molitor, Mil	114	2004	Vladimir Guerrero, Ana	124

Leaders in Hits

Year	Player and Team	Hits	Year	Player and Team	Hits
1901	Nap Lajoie, Phil	229	1944	Snuffy Stirnweiss, NY	205
1902	Piano Legs Hickman, Bos-Clev	194	1945	Snuffy Stirnweiss, NY	195
1903	Patsy Dougherty, Bos	195	1946	Johnny Pesky, Bos	208
1904	Nap Lajoie, Clev	211	1947	Johnny Pesky, Bos	207
1905	George Stone, StL	187	1948	Bob Dillinger, StL	207
1906	Nap Lajoie, Clev	214	1949	Dale Mitchell, Clev	203
1907	Ty Cobb, Det	212	1950	George Kell, Det	218
1908	Ty Cobb, Det	188	1951	George Kell, Det	191
1909	Ty Cobb, Det	216	1952	Nellie Fox, Chi	192
1910	Nap Lajoie, Clev	227	1953	Harvey Kuenn, Det	209
1911	Ty Cobb, Det	248	1954	Nellie Fox, Chi	201
1912	Ty Cobb, Det	227		Harvey Kuenn, Det	201
1913	Joe Jackson, Clev	197	1955	Al Kaline, Det	200
1914	Tris Speaker, Bos	193	1956	Harvey Kuenn, Det	196
1915	Ty Cobb, Det	208	1957	Nellie Fox, Chi	196
1916	Tris Speaker, Clev	211	1958	Nellie Fox, Chi	187
1917	Ty Cobb, Det	225	1959	Harvey Kuenn, Det	198
1918	George Burns, Phil	178	1960	Minnie Minoso, Chi	184
1919	Ty Cobb, Det	191	1961	Norm Cash, Det	193
	Bobby Veach, Det	191	1962	Bobby Richardson, NY	209
1920	George Sisler, StL	257	1963	Carl Yastrzemski, Bos	183
1921	Harry Heilmann, Det	237	1964	Tony Oliva, Minn	217
1922	George Sisler, StL	246	1965	Tony Oliva, Minn	185
1923	Charlie Jamieson, Clev	222	1966	Tony Oliva, Minn	191
1924	Sam Rice, Wash	216	1967	Carl Yastrzemski, Bos	189
1925	Al Simmons, Phil	253	1968	Bert Campaneris, Oak	177
1926	George Burns, Clev	216	1969	Tony Oliva, Minn	197
	Sam Rice, Wash	216	1970	Tony Oliva, Minn	204
1927	Earle Combs, NY	231	1971	Cesar Tovar, Minn	204
1928	Heinie Manush, StL	241	1972	Joe Rudi, Oak	181
1929	Dale Alexander, Det	215	1973	Rod Carew, Minn	203
	Charlie Gehringer, Det	215	1974	Rod Carew, Minn	218
1930	Johnny Hodapp, Clev	225	1975	George Brett, KC	195
1931	Lou Gehrig, NY	211	1976	George Brett, KC	215
1932	Al Simmons, Phil	216	1977	Rod Carew, Minn	239
1933	Heinie Manush, Wash	221	1978	Jim Rice, Bos	213
1934	Charlie Gehringer, Det	214	1979	George Brett, KC	212
1935	Joe Vosmik, Clev	216	1980	Willie Wilson, KC	230
1936	Earl Averill, Clev	232	1981	Rickey Henderson, Oak	135
1937	Beau Bell, StL	218	1982	Robin Yount, Mil	210
1938	Joe Vosmik, Bos	201	1983	Cal Ripken Jr., Balt	211
1939	Red Rolfe, NY	213	1984	Don Mattingly, NY	207
1940	Rip Radcliff, StL	200	1985	Wade Boggs, Bos	240
	Barney McCosky, Det	200	1986	Don Mattingly, NY	238
	Doc Cramer, Bos	200	1987	Kirby Puckett, Minn	207
1941	Cecil Travis, Wash	218		Kevin Seitzer, KC	207
1942	Johnny Pesky, Bos	205	1988	Kirby Puckett, Minn	234
1943	Dick Wakefield, Det	200			

Leaders in Hits *(Cont.)*

Year	Player and Team	Hits	Year	Player and Team	Hits
1989	Kirby Puckett, Minn	215	1997	Nomar Garciaparra, Bos	209
1990	Rafael Palmeiro, Tex	191	1998	Alex Rodriguez, Sea	213
1991	Paul Molitor, Mil	216	1999	Derek Jeter, NY	219
1992	Kirby Puckett, Minn	210	2000	Darin Erstad, Ana	240
1993	Paul Molitor, Tor	211	2001	Ichiro Suzuki, Sea	242
1994	Kenny Lofton, Clev	160	2002	Alfonso Soriano, NY	209
1995	Lance Johnson, Chi	186	2003	Vernon Wells, Tor	215
1996	Paul Molitor, Minn	225	2004	Ichiro Suzuki, Sea	262

Home Run Leaders

Year	Player and Team	HR	Year	Player and Team	HR
1901	Nap Lajoie, Phil	13	1956	Mickey Mantle, NY	52
1902	Socks Seybold, Phil	16	1957	Roy Sievers, Wash	42
1903	Buck Freeman, Bos	13	1958	Mickey Mantle, NY	42
1904	Harry Davis, Phil	10	1959	Rocky Colavito, Clev	42
1905	Harry Davis, Phil	8		Harmon Killebrew, Wash	42
1906	Harry Davis, Phil	12	1960	Mickey Mantle, NY	40
1907	Harry Davis, Phil	8	1961	Roger Maris, NY	61
1908	Sam Crawford, Det	7	1962	Harmon Killebrew, Minn	48
1909	Ty Cobb, Det	9	1963	Harmon Killebrew, Minn	45
1910	Jake Stahl, Bos	10	1964	Harmon Killebrew, Minn	49
1911	Frank Baker, Phil	9	1965	Tony Conigliaro, Bos	32
1912	Frank Baker, Phil	10	1966	Frank Robinson, Balt	49
	Tris Speaker, Bos	10	1967	Harmon Killebrew, Minn	44
1913	Frank Baker, Phil	13		Carl Yastrzemski, Bos	44
1914	Frank Baker, Phil	9	1968	Frank Howard, Wash	44
1915	Braggo Roth, Chi-Clev	7	1969	Harmon Killebrew, Minn	49
1916	Wally Pipp, NY	12	1970	Frank Howard, Wash	44
1917	Wally Pipp, NY	9	1971	Bill Melton, Chi	33
1918	Babe Ruth, Bos	11	1972	Dick Allen, Chi	37
	Tilly Walker, Phil	11	1973	Reggie Jackson, Oak	32
1919	Babe Ruth, Bos	29	1974	Dick Allen, Chi	32
1920	Babe Ruth, NY	54	1975	Reggie Jackson, Oak	36
1921	Babe Ruth, NY	59		George Scott, Mil	36
1922	Ken Williams, StL	39	1976	Graig Nettles, NY	32
1923	Babe Ruth, NY	41	1977	Jim Rice, Bos	39
1924	Babe Ruth, NY	46	1978	Jim Rice, Bos	46
1925	Bob Meusel, NY	33	1979	Gorman Thomas, Mil	45
1926	Babe Ruth, NY	47	1980	Reggie Jackson, NY	41
1927	Babe Ruth, NY	60		Ben Oglivie, Mil	41
1928	Babe Ruth, NY	54	1981	Tony Armas, Oak	22
1929	Babe Ruth, NY	46	1981	Dwight Evans, Bos	22
1930	Babe Ruth, NY	49		Bobby Grich, Cal	22
1931	Babe Ruth/ Lou Gehrig NY	46		Eddie Murray, Balt	22
1932	Jimmie Foxx, Phil	58	1982	Reggie Jackson, Cal	39
1933	Jimmie Foxx, Phil	48		Gorman Thomas, Mil	39
1934	Lou Gehrig, NY	49	1983	Jim Rice, Bos	39
1935	Jimmie Foxx, Phil	36	1984	Tony Armas, Bos	43
	Hank Greenberg, Det	36	1985	Darrell Evans, Det	40
1936	Lou Gehrig, NY	49	1986	Jesse Barfield, Tor	40
1937	Joe DiMaggio, NY	46	1987	Mark McGwire, Oak	49
1938	Hank Greenberg, Det	58	1988	Jose Canseco, Oak	42
1939	Jimmie Foxx, Bos	35	1989	Fred McGriff, Tor	36
1940	Hank Greenberg, Det	41	1990	Cecil Fielder, Det	51
1941	Ted Williams, Bos	37	1991	Jose Canseco, Oak	44
1942	Ted Williams, Bos	36		Cecil Fielder, Det	44
1943	Rudy York, Det	34	1992	Juan Gonzalez, Tex	43
1944	Nick Etten, NY	22	1993	Juan Gonzalez, Tex	46
1945	Vern Stephens, StL	24	1994	Ken Griffey Jr., Sea	40
1946	Hank Greenberg, Det	44	1995	Albert Belle, Clev	50
1947	Ted Williams, Bos	32	1996	Mark McGwire, Oak	52
1948	Joe DiMaggio, NY	39	1997	Ken Griffey Jr., Sea	56
1949	Ted Williams, Bos	43	1998	Ken Griffey Jr., Sea	56
1950	Al Rosen, Clev	37	1999	Ken Griffey Jr., Sea	48
1951	Gus Zernial, Chi-Phil	33	2000	Troy Glaus, Ana	47
1952	Larry Doby, Clev	32	2001	Alex Rodriguez, Tex	52
1953	Al Rosen, Clev	43	2002	Alex Rodriguez, Tex	57
1954	Larry Doby, Clev	32	2003	Alex Rodriguez, Tex	47
1955	Mickey Mantle, NY	37	2004	Manny Ramirez, Bos	43

Runs Batted In Leaders

Year	Player and Team	RBI	Year	Player and Team	RBI
1907	Ty Cobb, Det	116	1956	Mickey Mantle, NY	130
1908	Ty Cobb, Det	108	1957	Roy Sievers, Wash	114
1909	Ty Cobb, Det	107	1958	Jackie Jensen, Bos	122
1910	Sam Crawford, Det	120	1959	Jackie Jensen, Bos	112
1911	Ty Cobb, Det	144	1960	Roger Maris, NY	112
1912	Frank Baker, Phil	133	1961	Roger Maris, NY	142
1913	Frank Baker, Phil	126	1962	Harmon Killebrew, Minn	126
1914	Sam Crawford, Det	104	1963	Dick Stuart, Bos	118
1915	Sam Crawford, Det	112	1964	Brooks Robinson, Balt	118
	Bobby Veach, Det	112	1965	Rocky Colavito, Clev	108
1916	Del Pratt, StL	103	1966	Frank Robinson, Balt	122
1917	Bobby Veach, Det	103	1967	Carl Yastrzemski, Bos	121
1918	Bobby Veach, Det	78	1968	Ken Harrelson, Bos	109
1919	Babe Ruth, Bos	114	1969	Harmon Killebrew, Minn	140
1920	Babe Ruth, NY	137	1970	Frank Howard, Wash	126
1921	Babe Ruth, NY	171	1971	Harmon Killebrew, Minn	119
1922	Ken Williams, StL	155	1972	Dick Allen, Chi	113
1923	Babe Ruth, NY	131	1973	Reggie Jackson, Oak	117
1924	Goose Goslin, Wash	129	1974	Jeff Burroughs, Tex	118
1925	Bob Meusel, NY	138	1975	George Scott, Mil	109
1926	Babe Ruth, NY	145	1976	Lee May, Balt	109
1927	Lou Gehrig, NY	175	1977	Larry Hisle, Minn	119
1928	Babe Ruth/ Lou Gehrig, NY	142	1978	Jim Rice, Bos	139
1929	Al Simmons, Phil	157	1979	Don Baylor, Cal	139
1930	Lou Gehrig, NY	174	1980	Cecil Cooper, Mil	122
1931	Lou Gehrig, NY	184	1981	Eddie Murray, Balt	78
1932	Jimmie Foxx, Phil	169	1982	Hal McRae, KC	133
1933	Jimmie Foxx, Phil	163	1983	Cecil Cooper, Mil	126
1934	Lou Gehrig, NY	165		Jim Rice, Bos	126
1935	Hank Greenberg, Det	170	1984	Tony Armas, Bos	123
1936	Hal Trosky, Clev	162	1985	Don Mattingly, NY	145
1937	Hank Greenberg, Det	183	1986	Joe Carter, Clev	121
1938	Jimmie Foxx, Bos	175	1987	George Bell, Tor	134
1939	Ted Williams, Bos	145	1988	Jose Canseco, Oak	124
1940	Hank Greenberg, Det	150	1989	Ruben Sierra, Tex	119
1941	Joe DiMaggio, NY	125	1990	Cecil Fielder, Det	132
1942	Ted Williams, Bos	137	1991	Cecil Fielder, Det	133
1943	Rudy York, Det	118	1992	Cecil Fielder, Det	124
1944	Vern Stephens, StL	109	1993	Albert Belle, Clev	129
1945	Nick Etten, NY	111	1994	Kirby Puckett, Minn	112
1946	Hank Greenberg, Det	127	1995	Albert Belle, Clev	126
1947	Ted Williams, Bos	114		Mo Vaughn, Bos	126
1948	Joe DiMaggio, NY	155	1996	Albert Belle, Clev	148
1949	Ted Williams, Bos	159	1997	Ken Griffey Jr., Sea	147
	Vern Stephens, Bos	159	1998	Juan Gonzales, Tex	157
1950	Walt Dropo, Bos	144	1999	Manny Ramirez, Clev	165
	Vern Stephens, Bos	144	2000	Edgar Martinez, Sea	145
1951	Gus Zernial, Chi-Phil	129	2001	Bret Boone, Sea	141
1952	Al Rosen, Clev	105	2002	Alex Rodriguez, Tex	142
1953	Al Rosen, Clev	145	2003	Carlos Delgado, Tor	145
1954	Larry Doby, Clev	126	2004	Miguel Tejada, Balt	150
1955	Ray Boone, Det	116			
	Jackie Jensen, Bos	116			

Note: Runs Batted In not compiled before 1907; officially adopted in 1920.

Leading Base Stealers

Year	Player and Team	SB	Year	Player and Team	SB
1901	Frank Isbell, Chi	48	1912	Clyde Milan, Wash	88
1902	Topsy Hartsel, Phil	54	1913	Clyde Milan, Wash	75
1903	Harry Bay, Clev	46	1914	Fritz Maisel, NY	74
1904	Elmer Flick, Clev	42	1915	Ty Cobb, Det	96
	Harry Bay, Clev	42	1916	Ty Cobb, Det	68
1905	Danny Hoffman, Phil	46	1917	Ty Cobb, Det	55
1906	Elmer Flick, Clev	39	1918	George Sisler, StL	45
	John Anderson, Wash	39	1919	Eddie Collins, Chi	33
1907	Ty Cobb, Det	49	1920	Sam Rice, Wash	63
1908	Patsy Dougherty, Chi	47	1921	George Sisler, StL	35
1909	Ty Cobb, Det	76	1922	George Sisler, StL	51
1910	Eddie Collins, Phil	81	1923	Eddie Collins, Chi	49
1911	Ty Cobb, Det	83	1924	Eddie Collins, Chi	42

Leading Base Stealers (Cont.)

Year	Player and Team	SB	Year	Player and Team	SB
1925	John Mostil, Chi	43	1965	Bert Campaneris, KC	51
1926	John Mostil, Chi	35	1966	Bert Campaneris, KC	52
1927	George Sisler, StL	27	1967	Bert Campaneris, KC	55
1928	Buddy Myer, Bos	30	1968	Bert Campaneris, Oak	62
1929	Charlie Gehringer, Det	27	1969	Tommy Harper, Sea	73
1930	Marty McManus, Det	23	1970	Bert Campaneris, Oak	42
1931	Ben Chapman, NY	61	1971	Amos Otis, KC	52
1932	Ben Chapman, NY	38	1972	Bert Campaneris, Oak	52
1933	Ben Chapman, NY	27	1973	Tommy Harper, Bos	54
1934	Bill Werber, Bos	40	1974	Bill North, Oak	54
1935	Bill Werber, Bos	29	1975	Mickey Rivers, Cal	70
1936	Lyn Lary, StL	37	1976	Bill North, Oak	75
1937	Bill Werber, Phil	35	1977	Freddie Patek, KC	53
	Ben Chapman, Wash-Bos	35	1978	Ron LeFlore, Det	68
1938	Frank Crosetti, NY	27	1979	Willie Wilson, KC	83
1939	George Case, Wash	51	1980	Rickey Henderson, Oak	100
1940	George Case, Wash	35	1981	Rickey Henderson, Oak	56
1941	George Case, Wash	33	1982	Rickey Henderson, Oak	130
1942	George Case, Wash	44	1983	Rickey Henderson, Oak	108
1943	George Case, Wash	61	1984	Rickey Henderson, Oak	66
1944	Snuffy Stirnweiss, NY	55	1985	Rickey Henderson, NY	80
1945	Snuffy Stirnweiss, NY	33	1986	Rickey Henderson, NY	87
1946	George Case, Clev	28	1987	Harold Reynolds, Sea	60
1947	Bob Dillinger, StL	34	1988	Rickey Henderson, NY	93
1948	Bob Dillinger, StL	28	1989	Rickey Henderson, NY-Oak	77
1949	Bob Dillinger, StL	20	1990	Rickey Henderson, Oak	65
1950	Dom DiMaggio, Bos	15	1991	Rickey Henderson, Oak	58
1951	Minnie Minoso, Clev-Chi	31	1992	Kenny Lofton, Clev	66
1952	Minnie Minoso, Chi	22	1993	Kenny Lofton, Clev	70
1953	Minnie Minoso, Chi	25	1994	Kenny Lofton, Clev	60
1954	Jackie Jensen, Bos	22	1995	Kenny Lofton, Clev	54
1955	Jim Rivera, Chi	25	1996	Kenny Lofton, Clev	75
1956	Luis Aparicio, Chi	21	1997	Brian Hunter, Det	74
1957	Luis Aparicio, Chi	28	1998	Rickey Henderson, Oak	66
1958	Luis Aparicio, Chi	29	1999	Brian Hunter, Sea	44
1959	Luis Aparicio, Chi	56	2000	Johnny Damon, KC	46
1960	Luis Aparicio, Chi	51	2001	Ichiro Suzuki, Sea	56
1961	Luis Aparicio, Chi	53	2002	Alfonso Soriano, NY	41
1962	Luis Aparicio, Chi	31	2003	Carl Crawford, TB	55
1963	Luis Aparicio, Balt	40	2004	Carl Crawford, TB	59
1964	Luis Aparicio, Balt	57			

Leading Pitchers—Winning Percentage

Year	Pitcher and Team	W	L	Pct	Year	Pitcher and Team	W	L	Pct
1901	Clark Griffith, Chi	24	7	.774	1925	Stan Coveleski, Wash	20	5	.800
1902	Bill Bernhard, Phil-Clev	18	5	.783	1926	George Uhle, Clev	27	11	.711
1903	Earl Moore, Clev	22	7	.759	1927	Waite Hoyt, NY	22	7	.759
1904	Jack Chesbro, NY	41	12	.774	1928	General Crowder, StL	21	5	.808
1905	Jess Tannehill, Bos	22	9	.710	1929	Lefty Grove, Phil	20	6	.769
1906	Eddie Plank, Phil	19	6	.760	1930	Lefty Grove, Phil	28	5	.848
1907	Wild Bill Donovan, Det	25	4	.862	1931	Lefty Grove, Phil	31	4	.886
1908	Ed Walsh, Chi	40	15	.727	1932	Johnny Allen, NY	17	4	.810
1909	George Mullin, Det	29	8	.784	1933	Lefty Grove, Phil	24	8	.750
1910	Chief Bender, Phil	23	5	.821	1934	Lefty Gomez, NY	26	5	.839
1911	Chief Bender, Phil	17	5	.773	1935	Eldon Auker, Det	18	7	.720
1912	Smoky Joe Wood, Bos	34	5	.872	1936	Monte Pearson, NY	19	7	.731
1913	Walter Johnson, Wash	36	7	.837	1937	Johnny Allen, Clev	15	1	.938
1914	Chief Bender, Phil	17	3	.850	1938	Red Ruffing, NY	21	7	.750
1915	Smoky Joe Wood, Bos	15	5	.750	1939	Lefty Grove, Bos	15	4	.789
1916	Eddie Cicotte, Chi	15	7	.682	1940	Schoolboy Rowe, Det	16	3	.842
1917	Reb Russell, Chi	15	5	.750	1941	Lefty Gomez, NY	15	5	.750
1918	Sad Sam Jones, Bos	16	5	.762	1942	Ernie Bonham, NY	21	5	.808
1919	Eddie Cicotte, Chi	29	7	.806	1943	Spud Chandler, NY	20	4	.833
1920	Jim Bagby, Clev	31	12	.721	1944	Tex Hughson, Bos	18	5	.783
1921	Carl Mays, NY	27	9	.750	1945	Hal Newhouser, Det	25	9	.735
1922	Joe Bush, NY	26	7	.788	1946	Boo Ferriss, Bos	25	6	.806
1923	Herb Pennock, NY	19	6	.760	1947	Allie Reynolds, NY	19	8	.704
1924	Walter Johnson, Wash	23	7	.767	1948	Jack Kramer, Bos	18	5	.783

Leading Pitchers—Winning Percentage (Cont.)

Year	Pitcher and Team	W	L	Pct	Year	Pitcher and Team	W	L	Pct
1949	Ellis Kinder, Bos	23	6	.793	1977	Paul Splittorff, KC	16	6	.727
1950	Vic Raschi, NY	21	8	.724	1978	Ron Guidry, NY	25	3	.893
1951	Bob Feller, Clev	22	8	.733	1979	Mike Caldwell, Mil	16	6	.727
1952	Bobby Shantz, Phil	24	7	.774	1980	Steve Stone, Balt	25	7	.781
1953	Ed Lopat, NY	16	4	.800	1981*	Pete Vuckovich, Mil	14	4	.778
1954	Sandy Consuegra, Chi	16	3	.842	1982	Pete Vuckovich, Mil	18	6	.750
1955	Tommy Byrne, NY	16	5	.762		Jim Palmer, Balt	15	5	.750
1956	Whitey Ford, NY	19	6	.760	1983	Richard Dotson, Chi	22	7	.759
1957	Dick Donovan, Chi	16	6	.727	1984	Doyle Alexander, Tor	17	6	.739
	Tom Sturdivant, NY	16	6	.727	1985	Ron Guidry, NY	22	6	.786
1958	Bob Turley, NY	21	7	.750	1986	Roger Clemens, Bos	24	4	.857
1959	Bob Shaw, Chi	18	6	.750	1987	Roger Clemens, Bos	20	9	.690
1960	Jim Perry, Clev	18	10	.643	1988	Frank Viola, Minn	24	7	.774
1961	Whitey Ford, NY	25	4	.862	1989	Bret Saberhagen, KC	23	6	.793
1962	Ray Herbert, Chi	20	9	.690	1990	Bob Welch, Oak	27	6	.818
1963	Whitey Ford, NY	24	7	.774	1991	Scott Erickson, Minn	20	8	.714
1964	Wally Bunker, Balt	19	5	.792	1992	Mike Mussina, Balt	18	5	.783
1965	Mudcat Grant, Minn	21	7	.750	1993	Jimmy Key, NY	18	6	.750
1966	Sonny Siebert, Clev	16	8	.667	1994	Jimmy Key, NY	17	4	.810
1967	Joel Horlen, Chi	19	7	.731	1995	Randy Johnson, Sea	18	2	.900
1968	Denny McLain, Det	31	6	.838	1996	Charles Nagy, Clev	17	5	.773
1969	Jim Palmer, Balt	16	4	.800	1997	Randy Johnson, Sea	20	4	.833
1970	Mike Cuellar, Balt	24	8	.750	1998	David Wells, NY	18	4	.818
1971	Dave McNally, Balt	21	5	.808	1999	Pedro Martinez, Bos	23	4	.852
1972	Catfish Hunter, Oak	21	7	.750	2000	Tim Hudson, Oak	20	6	.769
1973	Catfish Hunter, Oak	21	5	.808	2001	Roger Clemens, NY	20	3	.870
1974	Mike Cuellar, Balt	22	10	.688	2002	Pedro Martinez, Bos	20	4	.833
1975	Mike Torrez, Balt	20	9	.690	2003	Roy Halladay, Tor	22	7	.759
1976	Bill Campbell, Minn	17	5	.773	2004	Curt Schilling, Bos	21	6	.778

*1981 percentages based on 10 or more victories. Note: Percentages based on 15 or more victories in all other years.

Leading Pitchers—Earned Run Average

Year	Player and Team	ERA	Year	Player and Team	ERA
1913	Walter Johnson, Wash	1.14	1946	Hal Newhouser, Det	1.94
1914	Dutch Leonard, Bos	1.01	1947	Spud Chandler, NY	2.46
1915	Smoky Joe Wood, Bos	1.49	1948	Gene Bearden, Clev	2.43
1916	Babe Ruth, Bos	1.75	1949	Mel Parnell, Bos	2.78
1917	Eddie Cicotte, Chi	1.53	1950	Early Wynn, Clev	3.20
1918	Walter Johnson, Wash	1.27	1951	Saul Rogovin, Det-Chi	2.78
1919	Walter Johnson, Wash	1.49	1952	Allie Reynolds, NY	2.07
1920	Bob Shawkey, NY	2.46	1953	Ed Lopat, NY	2.43
1921	Red Faber, Chi	2.47	1954	Mike Garcia, Clev	2.64
1922	Red Faber, Chi	2.80	1955	Billy Pierce, Chi	1.97
1923	Stan Coveleski, Clev	2.76	1956	Whitey Ford, NY	2.47
1924	Walter Johnson, Wash	2.72	1957	Bobby Shantz, NY	2.45
1925	Stan Coveleski, Wash	2.84	1958	Whitey Ford, NY	2.01
1926	Lefty Grove, Phil	2.51	1959	Hoyt Wilhelm, Balt	2.19
1927	Wilcy Moore, NY#	2.28	1960	Frank Baumann, Chi	2.68
1928	Garland Braxton, Wash	2.52	1961	Dick Donovan, Wash	2.40
1929	Lefty Grove, Phil	2.81	1962	Hank Aguirre, Det	2.21
1930	Lefty Grove, Phil	2.54	1963	Gary Peters, Chi	2.33
1931	Lefty Grove, Phil	2.06	1964	Dean Chance, LA	1.65
1932	Lefty Grove, Phil	2.84	1965	Sam McDowell, Clev	2.18
1933	Monte Pearson, Clev	2.33	1966	Gary Peters, Chi	1.98
1934	Lefty Gomez, NY	2.33	1967	Joe Horlen, Chi	2.06
1935	Lefty Grove, Bos	2.70	1968	Luis Tiant, Clev	1.60
1936	Lefty Grove, Bos	2.81	1969	Dick Bosman, Wash	2.19
1937	Lefty Gomez, NY	2.33	1970	Diego Segui, Oak	2.56
1938	Lefty Grove, Bos	3.07	1971	Vida Blue, Oak	1.82
1939	Lefty Grove, Bos	2.54	1972	Luis Tiant, Bos	1.91
1940	Bob Feller, Clev†	2.62	1973	Jim Palmer, Balt	2.40
1941	Thornton Lee, Chi	2.37	1974	Catfish Hunter, Oak	2.49
1942	Ted Lyons, Chi	2.10	1975	Jim Palmer, Balt	2.09
1943	Spud Chandler, NY	1.64	1976	Mark Fidrych, Det	2.34
1944	Dizzy Trout, Det	2.12	1977	Frank Tanana, Cal	2.54
1945	Hal Newhouser, Det	1.81	1978	Ron Guidry, NY	1.74

Leading Pitchers—Earned Run Average *(Cont.)*

Year	Player and Team	ERA	Year	Player and Team	ERA
1979	Ron Guidry, NY	2.78	1992	Roger Clemens, Bos	2.41
1980	Rudy May, NY	2.47	1993	Kevin Appier, KC	2.56
1981	Steve McCatty, Oak	2.32	1994	Steve Ontiveros, Oak	2.65
1982	Rick Sutcliffe, Clev	2.96	1995	Randy Johnson, Sea	2.48
1983	Rick Honeycutt, Tex	2.42	1996	Juan Guzman, Tor	2.93
1984	Mike Boddicker, Balt	2.79	1997	Roger Clemens, Tor	2.05
1985	Dave Stieb, Tor	2.48	1998	Roger Clemens, Tor	2.64
1986	Roger Clemens, Bos	2.48	1999	Pedro Martinez, Bos	2.07
1987	Jimmy Key, Tor	2.76	2000	Pedro Martinez, Bos	1.74
1988	Allan Anderson, Minn	2.45	2001	Freddy Garcia, Sea	3.05
1989	Bret Saberhagen, KC	2.16	2002	Pedro Martinez, Bos	2.26
1990	Roger Clemens, Bos	1.93	2003	Pedro Martinez, Bos	2.22
1991	Roger Clemens, Bos	2.62	2004	Johan Santana, Minn	2.61

Note: Based on 10 complete games through 1950, then 154 innings until the American League expanded in 1961, when it became 162 innings. In strike-shortened 1981, one inning per game required. Earned runs not tabulated in American League prior to 1913.

#Wilcy Moore pitched only six complete games—he started 12—in 1927 but was recognized as leader because of 213 innings pitched. †Ernie Bonham, New York, had 1.91 ERA and 10 complete games in 1940 but appeared in only 12 games and 99 innings, and Bob Feller was recognized as leader.

Leading Pitchers—Strikeouts

Year	Player and Team	SO	Year	Player and Team	SO
1901	Cy Young, Bos	159	1946	Bob Feller, Clev	348
1902	Rube Waddell, Phil	210	1947	Bob Feller, Clev	196
1903	Rube Waddell, Phil	301	1948	Bob Feller, Clev	164
1904	Rube Waddell, Phil	349	1949	Virgil Trucks, Det	153
1905	Rube Waddell, Phil	286	1950	Bob Lemon, Clev	170
1906	Rube Waddell, Phil	203	1951	Vic Raschi, NY	164
1907	Rube Waddell, Phil	226	1952	Allie Reynolds, NY	160
1908	Ed Walsh, Chi	269	1953	Billy Pierce, Chi	186
1909	Frank Smith, Chi	177	1954	Bob Turley, Balt	185
1910	Walter Johnson, Wash	313	1955	Herb Score, Clev	245
1911	Ed Walsh, Chi	255	1956	Herb Score, Clev	263
1912	Walter Johnson, Wash	303	1957	Early Wynn, Clev	184
1913	Walter Johnson, Wash	243	1958	Early Wynn, Chi	179
1914	Walter Johnson, Wash	225	1959	Jim Bunning, Det	201
1915	Walter Johnson, Wash	203	1960	Jim Bunning, Det	201
1916	Walter Johnson, Wash	228	1961	Camilo Pascual, Minn	221
1917	Walter Johnson, Wash	188	1962	Camilo Pascual, Minn	206
1918	Walter Johnson, Wash	162	1963	Camilo Pascual, Minn	202
1919	Walter Johnson, Wash	147	1964	Al Downing, NY	217
1920	Stan Coveleski, Clev	133	1965	Sam McDowell, Clev	325
1921	Walter Johnson, Wash	143	1966	Sam McDowell, Clev	225
1922	Urban Shocker, StL	149	1967	Jim Lonborg, Bos	246
1923	Walter Johnson, Wash	130	1968	Sam McDowell, Clev	283
1924	Walter Johnson, Wash	158	1969	Sam McDowell, Clev	279
1925	Lefty Grove, Phil	116	1970	Sam McDowell, Clev	304
1926	Lefty Grove, Phil	194	1971	Mickey Lolich, Det	308
1927	Lefty Grove, Phil	174	1972	Nolan Ryan, Cal	329
1928	Lefty Grove, Phil	183	1973	Nolan Ryan, Cal	383
1929	Lefty Grove, Phil	170	1974	Nolan Ryan, Cal	367
1930	Lefty Grove, Phil	209	1975	Frank Tanana, Cal	269
1931	Lefty Grove, Phil	175	1976	Nolan Ryan, Cal	327
1932	Red Ruffing, NY	190	1977	Nolan Ryan, Cal	341
1933	Lefty Gomez, NY	163	1978	Nolan Ryan, Cal	260
1934	Lefty Gomez, NY	158	1979	Nolan Ryan, Cal	223
1935	Tommy Bridges, Det	163	1980	Len Barker, Clev	187
1936	Tommy Bridges, Det	175	1981	Len Barker, Clev	127
1937	Lefty Gomez, NY	194	1982	Floyd Bannister, Sea	209
1938	Bob Feller, Clev	240	1983	Jack Morris, Det	232
1939	Bob Feller, Clev	246	1984	Mark Langston, Sea	204
1940	Bob Feller, Clev	261	1985	Bert Blyleven, Clev-Minn	206
1941	Bob Feller, Clev	260	1986	Mark Langston, Sea	245
1942	Bobo Newsom, Wash Tex Hughson, Bos	113	1987	Mark Langston, Sea	262
			1988	Roger Clemens, Bos	291
1943	Allie Reynolds, Clev	151	1989	Nolan Ryan, Tex	301
1944	Hal Newhouser, Det	187	1990	Nolan Ryan, Tex	232
1945	Hal Newhouser, Det	212	1991	Roger Clemens, Bos	241

Leading Pitchers—Strikeouts (Cont.)

Year	Player and Team	SO	Year	Player and Team	SO
1992	Randy Johnson, Sea	241	1999	Pedro Martinez, Bos	313
1993	Randy Johnson, Sea	308	2000	Pedro Martinez, Bos	284
1994	Randy Johnson, Sea	204	2001	Hideo Nomo, Bos	220
1995	Randy Johnson, Sea	294	2002	Pedro Martinez, Bos	239
1996	Roger Clemens, Bos	257	2003	Esteban Loaiza, Chi	207
1997	Roger Clemens, Tor	292	2004	Johan Santana, Minn	265
1998	Roger Clemens, Tor	271			

Leading Pitchers—Saves

Year	Player and Team	SV	Year	Player and Team	SV
1947	Joe Page, NY	17	1977	Bill Campbell, Bos	31
1948	Russ Christopher, Clev	17	1978	Goose Gossage, NY	27
1949	Joe Page, NY	29	1979	Mike Marshall, Minn	32
1950	Mickey Harris, Wash	15	1980	Dan Quisenberry, KC	33
1951	Ellis Kinder, Bos	14	1981	Rollie Fingers, Mil	28
1952	Harry Dorish, Chi	11	1982	Dan Quisenberry, KC	35
1953	Ellis Kinder, Bos	27	1983	Dan Quisenberry, KC	35
1954	Johnny Sain, NY	22	1984	Dan Quisenberry, KC	44
1955	Ray Narleski, Clev	19	1985	Dan Quisenberry, KC	37
1956	George Zuverink, Bal	16	1986	Dave Righetti, NY	46
1957	Bob Grim, NY	19	1987	Tom Henke, Tor	34
1958	Ryne Duren, NY	20	1988	Dennis Eckersley, Oak	45
1959	Turk Lown, Chi	15	1989	Jeff Russell, Tex	38
1960	Mike Fornieles, Bos	14	1990	Bobby Thigpen, Chi	57
	Johnny Klippstein, Clev	14	1991	Bryan Harvey, Cal	46
1961	Luis Arroyo, NY	29	1992	Dennis Eckersley, Oak	51
1962	Dick Radatz, Bos	24	1993	Jeff Montgomery, KC	45
1963	Stu Miller, Bal	27		Duane Ward, Tor	45
1964	Dick Radatz, Bos	29	1994	Lee Smith, Bal	33
1965	Ron Kline, Wash	29	1995	Jose Mesa, Clev	46
1966	Jack Aker, KC	32	1996	John Wetteland, NY	43
1967	Minnie Rojas, Cal	27	1997	Randy Myers, Balt	45
1968	Al Worthington, Minn	18	1998	Tom Gordon, Bos	46
1969	Ron Perranoski, Minn	31	1999	Mariano Rivera, NY	45
1970	Ron Perranoski, Minn	34	2000	Todd Jones, Det	42
1971	Ken Sanders, Mil	31	2001	Mariano Rivera, NY	50
1972	Sparky Lyle, NY	35	2002	Eddie Guardado, Minn	45
1973	John Hiller, Det	38	2003	Keith Foulke, Oak	43
1974	Terry Forster, Chi	24	2004	Mariano Rivera, NY	53
1975	Goose Gossage, Chi	26			
1976	Sparky Lyle, NY	23			

The Commissioners of Baseball

Kenesaw Mountain Landis .... Elected Nov. 12, 1920. Served until his death on Nov. 25, 1944.

Happy Chandler .... Elected April 24, 1945. Served until July 15, 1951.

Ford Frick .... Elected Sept. 20, 1951. Served until Nov. 16, 1965.

William Eckert .... Elected Nov. 17, 1965. Served until Dec. 20, 1968.

Bowie Kuhn .... Elected Feb. 8, 1969. Served until Sept. 30, 1984.

Peter Ueberroth .... Elected March 3, 1984. Took office Oct. 1, 1984. Served through March 31, 1989.

A. Bartlett Giamatti .... Elected Sept. 8, 1988. Took office April 1, 1989. Served until his death on Sept. 1, 1989.

Francis Vincent Jr. .... Appointed Acting Commissioner Sept. 2, 1989. Elected Commissioner Sept. 13, 1989. Served through Sept. 7, 1992.

Allan H. (Bud) Selig .... Elected chairman of the executive council and given the powers of interim commissioner on Sept. 9, 1992. Unanimously elected Commissioner July 9, 1998.

Pro Football

Tom Brady of the
Super Bowl champion
New England Patriots

Quarterback Draw

With Peyton Manning, Steve McNair and Tom Brady leading the way, 2003 was the year of the quarterback

BY HANK HERSCH

D URING THE MARCH of Sundays, it seemed that every NFL quarterback took a turn in the spotlight, whether because of injury or controversy, rapid ascent or decline, displays of brawn or brain. As they so often do, the quarterbacks dictated the terms of the 2003 season, even obscuring epic rushing achievements, an axe-impaled punter and, yes, an exposed breast. As the schedule plunged into winter, one passer separated himself from the elite pack, not with gaudy statistics or flashy play, but with his remarkable knack for stringing together win after win after win. And so, for the second time in three seasons, the NFL season and the most important hardware that goes with it belonged to Tom Brady and the New England Patriots.

The saga of the quarterbacks began before the first official snap of the year. By the end of the 2002 season, when he engineered the first playoff victory by a visiting team at Green Bay's Lambeau Field, Michael Vick had established himself as the sport's most electrifying player, a dazzling open-field runner with a nuclear left arm. "You're the future of this league," his opposite number with the Packers, Brett Favre, told Vick after the upset. But in an August 2003 exhibition game, Vick broke his right leg, dooming the Atlanta Falcons to a 2–9 start. Even his return on Nov. 30 couldn't lift his team—or save the job of 59-year-old Dan Reeves, who became one of seven coaches to get the axe or resign during or after the 2003 season.

A week after Vick went down, the other quarterbacking revelation of 2002, the New York Jets' Chad Pennington, broke his left wrist in an exhibition game, causing him to miss his team's first six games. (But Jets coach Herman Edwards didn't suffer Reeves's fate, despite a 6–10 finish.) While the quarterbacks were dropping, and just before the season kicked off, Pittsburgh's All-Pro linebacker Joey Porter went down as well—from a 9-mm bullet that entered his left buttock and lodged in his right thigh. Porter had been hanging out in the

The injury to Vick deprived the league of its biggest star, and doomed Atlanta's season.

GARY BOGDON

parking lot of a Denver sports bar when the shots rang out. Doctors removed the bullet the following day, and three weeks later Porter returned to the field and made a sack in the Steelers' 17–10 victory over the Cincinnati Bengals. "For him to come out and play like he played today, it's unbelievable," said Pittsburgh defensive end Kimo von Oelhoffen. "I mean, who does that?"

The same question could have been posed to Jacksonville coach Jack Del Rio, who, to help right the Jaguars after an 0–3 start, put a massive tree stump in the locker room and encouraged the players to "keep chopping wood." Taking him at his word, punter Chris Hanson took a whack with the axe and sliced his right (non-kicking) leg. He needed surgery to repair the damage to his shin, and he missed the rest of the season. "Specialists," Del Rio said, "have more time on their hands."

Another specialist had a happier fate: 5'8" Chiefs return man Dante Hall, who returned a punt or kickoff for a touchdown in an NFL-record three straight games. None of his runs was shorter than 73 yards and two of them were game-winners, including a 93-yard scamper—during which Hall gave ground to his own goal line— that beat the Broncos. "I don't know if I've ever faced an athlete that dominant in Lit-

tle League, college or the pros," said Denver linebacker Ian Gold.

Aided by the maturation of quarterback Trent Green (who would rack up 4,039 yards passing, second in the NFL) and the brilliant running of Priest Holmes (1,420 yards and a league-record 27 touchdowns), the Chiefs stayed unbeaten until Week 11, when they lost 24–19 in a surprising location: Cincinnati. The Bengals would finish 8–8 for their first non-losing season in eight years, thanks in part to Jon Kitna, who was the only quarterback in the league to take every snap for his team. The 31-year-old passer provided poise and leadership for the Bengals while the No. 1 pick of the 2003 draft, Heisman Trophy winner Carson

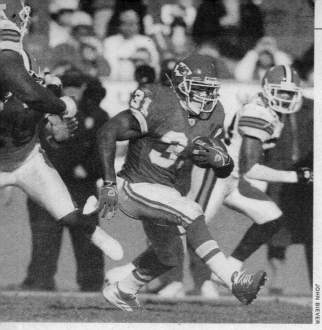

JOHN BIEVER

Carter stepped forward as the Cowboys' quarterback and ignited a passing attack that had ranked 31st in the league the previous year. But then, that was before owner Jerry Jones hired a new coach: the ornery and extraordinary Bill Parcells. "I knew it would be great to play for a coach who will make you better even when you're having success," said Carter. "Plus, he's going to be harder on your mistakes. I have a mother who doesn't take any mess, so I was ready for him. He knows how to push the right buttons." A team that had only five wins in each of the three previous seasons, Dallas reached that total in the first six games en route to a 10–6 record and the franchise's first playoff berth since 1999.

With quarterback Rich Gannon sidelined for more than half the season by a shoulder injury, Oakland's offense struggled, and the Raiders, who came within one win of the championship after the 2002 season, mustered only four wins. The team that beat Oakland in Super Bowl XXXVII in San Diego, the Tampa Bay Buccaneers, also failed to make the playoffs following a rash of late-game collapses. In Week 2, Bucs kicker Martin Gramatica had an extra point blocked on the final play of regulation, clearing the way for the Carolina Panthers to win 12–9 in overtime. Three weeks later, in a home game on *Monday Night Football*, the Bucs held a 35–14 lead over the Indianapolis Colts with 5:09 to play—and *lost the game* 38–35 in overtime. Before facing the Packers in Week 11, Tampa Bay coach Jon Gruden brought in fiery Devil Rays manager Lou Piniella to rally the troops. They were insufficiently rallied: Green Bay marched 98 yards against

Palmer, waited in the wings. In December, Kitna made another, different kind of stand, sporting a cap emblazoned with a Christian cross to a press conference. The NFL levied a $5,000 fine (which it later rescinded) because Kitna wasn't wearing official league apparel, sparking some fans to show their support by buying similar caps or sending fine-defraying checks—not that a multimillionaire professional athlete would need help paying what amounts to a drop in the bucket for him.

Rams quarterback Kurt Warner also felt singled out for his religious convictions: Late in the season he claimed the St. Louis coaches criticized him for reading the Bible too much. Once the embodiment of a rags-to-riches fable—he rose from supermarket stock boy to MVP and Super Bowl champ—Warner saw his honeymon with the Rams end in 2003, when injuries and the ascendancy of a 2001 waiver-wire pick-up Marc Bulger relegated him to the sidelines. After winning the battle of the Horatio Alger QB's, the 26-year-old Bulger kept the Rams' Greatest Show on Turf offense running until the NFC divisional playoffs.

Out of a crowded field in Dallas, Quincy

them in the fourth quarter to win 20–13.

As the season wound down, three obvious MVP candidates surfaced. On Sept. 14, Baltimore Ravens running back Jamal Lewis rambled for a single-game record 295 yards against the Cleveland Browns; by the schedule's midpoint, Lewis had rushed for 1,045 yards, putting him on pace to break Eric Dickerson's 19-year-old single-season mark of 2,105. "He doesn't use a lot of moves, and he's not a nifty cut-back type, but he doesn't have to be," said Tennessee Titans executive vice president Floyd Reese. "Just look at his yards after initial contact. I imagine he's broken more tackles than any back." Despite facing eight- and nine-man fronts, Lewis, 24, took advantage of the league's largest offensive line (average weight: 329.5 pounds) and finished just 39 yards shy of Dickerson's record.

Nipping at Brady's heels in the race to rule the league from the quarterback position were Steve McNair of the Titans and Peyton Manning of the Colts, who offered contrasting styles but equally compelling cases for MVP. Battling through a variety of injuries (ankle, calf and knee), the 6'2", 235-pound McNair produced an NFL-best passer rating of 100.4 and willed a team with no rushing attack to speak of (3.3 yards per carry, tied for worst in the league) to a 12–4 record. "To me, he's almost a mirror image of Brett Favre," said Philadelphia Eagles cornerback Troy Vincent. "They approach the game the same way, they're extremely difficult to bring down, and man, they are tough." Manning announced his MVP candidacy in Week 4 at New Orleans, throwing six touchdown passes in three quarters of a 55–21 rout. A preparation fanatic, Manning passed for a league-high 4,267 yards while steering Indy to a 12–4 record as well. "I've never left the field saying, 'I could've done more to get ready,'" he said, "and that gives me peace of mind."

Manning and McNair would end up as the award's co-winners; Brady came from

off the pace to finish third. The Patriots had entered the season on a controversial note: the release of strong safety Lawyer Milloy. A stalwart on the 2001 championship team, Milloy signed with the Buffalo Bills after being released by New England. In his first game for Buffalo, the Bills waxed none other than New England, 31–0. When the Pats bowed 20–17 in Washington three weeks later, New England fans grumbled loudly. But they would not lose again: With an opportunistic defense, Adam Vinatieri's clutch kicking, the tactical wizardry of coach Bill Belichick and the 26-year-old Brady's

NICK WASS

Lewis rambled for 295 yards against Cleveland on Sept. 14, breaking Corey Dillon's single-game record.

flair for the dramatic, New England roared into the playoffs with 12 straight victories, the most stirring a 38–34 triumph after a goal-line stand at Indianapolis.

After edging McNair and Tennessee 17–14 in the divisional playoffs, New England defeated the Colts again, in the AFC title game, picking off Manning four times. In the NFC, the Eagles reached their third straight conference title game after quarterback Donovan McNabb found wideout Freddie Mitchell for a 28-yard gain on a fourth-and-26 during a last-gasp drive against the Packers. That set up a game-tying 37-yard field goal, and Philadelphia won it in overtime on a 31-yarder after Brian Dawkins picked off a wobbly Favre pass. McNabb ran for 107 yards in the game, a playoff record for a quarterback, but much of that was for his life—he was sacked eight times. Said Philadelphia fullback Jon Ritchie, "Our success remains a mystery."

The intrigue ended one week later. The unsung Panthers entered Philly fresh from a 29–23 double-overtime defeat of the Rams. Quarterback Jake Delhomme found streaking wide receiver Steve Smith for a 69-yard pass to win that game. Though he'd thrown only 86 passes as a backup in New Orleans before signing with the Panthers as a free agent, Delhomme proved every bit the discovery that Brady had been two years before. But the Panthers' bruising running game and smashmouth D (five sacks, four picks) did most of the damage in the 14–3 defeat of the Eagles for the NFC title.

The resourcefulness of the two quarterbacks was on full display at Houston's Reliant

With 10 catches for 143 yards and a TD, Branch led all receivers in Supe XXXVIII.

Stadium during the Super Bowl. (So, too, was the right breast of singer Janet Jackson, which became exposed during the halftime extravaganza, sending shockwaves through the entire culture, it seemed.) During the first 26:55 of Supe XXXVIII neither team scored, and Delhomme completed only 1 of 9 passes for a single yard while Vinatieri uncharacteristically missed a field goal from 31 yards and had a 36-yarder blocked. But after Brady hit wideout Deion Branch for a five-yard TD, the floodgates opened. The teams would combine for 61 points during the next 33:05. Trailing 21–10 in the fourth quarter, Delhomme marched Carolina 81 yards to paydirt, then took advantage of a Brady interception with a Super Bowl–record 85-yard scoring pass to Muhsin Muhammad. After a failed two-point attempt (their second), the Pats trailed 22–21 with 6:53 left. Safety Rodney Harrison told cornerback Ty Law, "Hey, man, there's no reason for us to worry. We've got Tom Brady."

Four minutes later, Brady put the Pats in the end zone with a one-yard pass to linebacker Mike Vrabel, who was moonlighting as a tight end. The Patriots went for two and made it, to take a seven-point lead. But Delhomme responded, taking Carolina 80 yards for a touchdown on seven plays, the last a 12-yard bullet to Ricky Proehl. John Kasay shanked the subsequent kickoff out of bounds, allowing the Pats to start at their own 40 with 1:08 remaining. That turned out to be too little distance and more than enough time for Brady. On third-and-three from the Panthers' 40 he connected with Branch for 17 yards, setting up Vinatieri's game-winning 41-yarder with four seconds on the clock.

Delhomme had been brilliant, finishing 16 of 33 for 323 yards and three touchdowns. But Brady, the Super Bowl MVP for the second time, was slightly better: 32 of 48 for 354 yards and three TDs. "You don't ever dream about this," Brady said. "I mean, you dream about playing football, and you have your fantasies, but you don't dream about winning Super Bowls like this." With 15 straight wins and counting, Brady's fantasy world may only get bigger.

FOR THE RECORD · 2003 – 2004

2003 NFL Final Standings

American Football Conference

EAST DIVISION

	W	L	T	Pct	Pts	OP
New England	14	2	0	.875	348	238
Miami	10	6	0	.625	311	261
Buffalo	6	10	0	.375	243	279
NY Jets	6	10	0	.375	283	299

NORTH DIVISION

	W	L	T	Pct	Pts	OP
Baltimore	10	6	0	.625	391	281
Cincinnati	8	8	0	.500	346	384
Pittsburgh	6	10	0	.375	300	327
Cleveland	5	11	0	.313	254	322

SOUTH DIVISION

	W	L	T	Pct	Pts	OP
Indianapolis	12	4	0	.750	447	336
†Tennessee	12	4	0	.750	435	324
Jacksonville	5	11	0	.313	276	331
Houston	5	11	0	.313	255	380

WEST DIVISION

	W	L	T	Pct	Pts	OP
Kansas City	13	3	0	.813	484	332
†Denver	10	6	0	.625	381	301
Oakland	4	12	0	.250	270	379
San Diego	4	12	0	.250	313	441

† Wild-card team.

National Football Conference

EAST DIVISION

	W	L	T	Pct	Pts	OP
Philadelphia	12	4	0	.750	374	287
†Dallas	10	6	0	.625	289	260
Washington	5	11	0	.313	287	372
NY Giants	4	12	0	.250	243	387

NORTH DIVISION

	W	L	T	Pct	Pts	OP
Green Bay	10	6	0	.625	442	307
Minnesota	9	7	0	.563	416	353
Chicago	7	9	0	.438	283	346
Detroit	5	11	0	.313	270	379

SOUTH DIVISION

	W	L	T	Pct	Pts	OP
Carolina	11	5	0	.688	325	304
New Orleans	8	8	0	.500	340	326
Tampa Bay	7	9	0	.438	301	264
Atlanta	5	11	0	.313	299	422

WEST DIVISION

	W	L	T	Pct	Pts	OP
St. Louis	12	4	0	.750	447	328
†Seattle	10	6	0	.625	404	327
San Francisco	7	9	0	.438	384	337
Arizona	4	12	0	.250	225	452

† Wild-card team.

2003–04 NFL Playoffs

| AFC FIRST ROUND | AFC DIVISIONAL PLAYOFF | AFC CHAMPIONSHIP | NFC CHAMPIONSHIP | NFC DIVISIONAL PLAYOFF | NFC FIRST ROUND |

SUPER BOWL XXXVIII
February 1, 2004

Tennessee 20
Baltimore 17
Tennessee 14
New England 24
New England 17

Denver 10
Indianapolis 41
Indianapolis 38
Indianapolis 14
Kansas City 31

Carolina 29
NEW ENGLAND 32

Carolina 29 (2ot)
Carolina 14
Carolina 29

St. Louis 23
Green Bay 17
Philadelphia 3
Philadelphia 20 (ot)

Dallas 10
Carolina 29
Seattle 27
Green Bay 33 (ot)

NFL Playoff Box Scores

AFC Wild-card Games

Tennessee	7	0	7	6—20
Baltimore	7	3	0	7—17

FIRST QUARTER

Tennessee: Brown 6 run (Anderson kick), 8:58.
Baltimore: Demps 56 int. return (Stover kick), 6:50.

SECOND QUARTER

Baltimore: FG Stover 43, 2:00.

THIRD QUARTER

Tennessee: McCareins 49 pass from McNair (Anderson kick), 8:16.

FOURTH QUARTER

Tennessee: FG Anderson 45, 9:27.
Baltimore: Heap 35 pass from Wright (Stover kick), 4:37.
Tennessee: FG Anderson 46, 0:33.

A: 69,084; T: 3:11.

Denver	3	0	0	7—10
Indianapolis	14	17	10	0—41

FIRST QUARTER

Indianapolis: Stokley 31 pass from Manning (Vanderjagt kick), 12:15.
Denver: FG Elam 49, 4:30.
Indianapolis: Harrison 46 pass from Manning (Vanderjagt kick), 0:35.

SECOND QUARTER

Indianapolis: Harrison 23 pass from Manning (Vanderjagt kick), 7:40.
Indianapolis: Stokley 87 pass from Manning (Vanderjagt kick), 2:01.
Indianapolis: FG Vanderjagt 27, 0:10.

THIRD QUARTER

Indianapolis: Wayne 7 pass from Manning (Vanderjagt kick), 5:24.
Indianapolis: FG Vanderjagt 20, 1:47.

FOURTH QUARTER

Denver: Smith 7 pass from Plummer (Elam kick), 7:24.

A: 56,127; T: 3:19.

NFC Wild-card Games

Dallas	0	3	0	7—10
Carolina	6	10	7	6—29

FIRST QUARTER

Carolina: FG Kasay 18, 8:52.
Carolina: FG Kasay 38, 1:07.

SECOND QUARTER

Carolina: Davis 23 run (Kasay kick), 6:17.
Dallas: FG Cundiff 37, 1:25.
Carolina: FG Kasay 19, 0:04.

THIRD QUARTER

Carolina: Smith 32 pass from Delhomme (Kasay kick), 9:52.

FOURTH QUARTER

Carolina: FG Kasay 32, 12:50.
Dallas: Carter 9 run (Cundiff kick), 7:42.
Carolina: FG Kasay 34, 3:17.

A: 73,258; T: 3:07.

Seattle	3	3	14	7	0—27
Green Bay	0	13	0	14	6—33

FIRST QUARTER

Seattle: FG Brown 30, 7:05

SECOND QUARTER

Green Bay: FG Longwell 31, 9:17.
Seattle: FG Brown 35, 6:55.
Green Bay: Franks 23 pass from Favre (Longwell kick), 4:45.
Green Bay: FG Longwell 27, 0:50.

THIRD QUARTER

Seattle: Alexander 1 run (Brown kick), 9:35.
Seattle: Alexander 1 run (Brown kick), 2:03.

FOURTH QUARTER

Green Bay: Green 1 run (Longwell kick), 10:15.
Green Bay: Green 1 run (Longwell kick), 2:48.
Seattle: Alexander 1 run (Brown kick), 0:55.

OVERTIME

Green Bay: Harris 52 int. return, 10:44.

A: 72,515; T: 3:41.

AFC Divisional Games

Tenessee 7	0	7	0—14
New England..........7	7	0	3—17

FIRST QUARTER

New England: Johnson 41 pass from Brady (Vinatieri kick), 11:10.
Tennessee: Brown 5 run (Anderson kick), 8:13.

SECOND QUARTER

New England: Smith 1 run (Vinatieri kick), 14:44.

THIRD QUARTER

Tennessee: Mason 11 pass from McNair (Anderson kick), 4:27.

FOURTH QUARTER

New England: FG Vinatieri 46, 4:17.

A: 68,436; T: 3:16.

Indianapolis.........14	7	10	7—38
Kansas City............3	7	14	7—31

FIRST QUARTER

Indianapolis: Stokley 29 pass from Manning (Vanderjagt kick), 9:35.
Kansas City: FG Andersen 22, 4:19.
Indianapolis: James 11 run (Vanderjagt kick), 0:51.

SECOND QUARTER

Kansas City: Hall 9 pass from Green (Andersen kick), 8:57.
Indianapolis: Lopienski 2 pass from Manning (Vanderjagt kick), 4:41.

THIRD QUARTER

Indianapolis: FG Vanderjagt 45, 10:08.
Kansas City: Holmes 1 run (Andersen kick), 5:30.
Indianapolis: Wayne 19 pass from Manning (Vanderjagt kick), 2:33.
Kansas City: Hall 92 kickoff return (Andersen kick), 1:48.

FOURTH QUARTER

Indianapolis: James 1 run (Vanderjagt kick), 12:10.
Kansas City: Holmes 1 run (Andersen kick), 4:30.

A: 79,451; T: 3:32.

NFC Divisional Games

Carolina............0	10	6	7	0	6—29
St. Louis 3	6	3	11	0	0—23

FIRST QUARTER

St. Louis: FG Wilkins 20, 5:50.

SECOND QUARTER

St. Louis: FG Wilkins 26, 13:30.
Carolina: Muhammad fum. recovery in end zone (Kasay kick), 12:13.
St. Louis: FG Wilkins 24, 7:00.
Carolina: FG Kasay 45, 1:12.

THIRD QUARTER

St. Louis: FG Wilkins 51, 11:30.
Carolina: FG Kasay 52, 7:55.
Carolina: FG Kasay 34, 1:00.

FOURTH QUARTER

Carolina: Hoover 7 run (Kasay kick), 9:20.
St. Louis: Faulk 1 run (Looker pass from Bulger for 2), 2:44.
St. Louis: FG Wilkins 33, 0:03.

SECOND OVERTIME

Carolina: Smith 69 pass from Delhomme, 14:30.

A: 66,163; T: 4:06.

Green Bay............14	0	0	3	0—17
Philadelphia 0	7	0	10	3—20

FIRST QUARTER

Green Bay: Ferguson 40 pass from Favre (Longwell kick), 7:54.
Green Bay: Ferguson 17 pass from Favre (Longwell kick), 1:31.

SECOND QUARTER

Philadelphia: Staley 7 pass from McNabb (Akers kick), 6:32.

FOURTH QUARTER

Philadelphia: Pinkston 12 pass from McNabb (Akers kick), 15:00.
Green Bay: FG Longwell 21, 10:45.
Philadelphia: FG Akers 37, 0:10.

OVERTIME

Philadelphia: FG Akers 31, 10:18.

A: 68,532; T: 3:39.

NFL Playoff Box Scores *(Cont.)*

AFC Championship

Indianapolis............0	0	7	7—14
New England..........7	8	6	3—24

FIRST QUARTER
New England: Givens 7 pass from Brady (Vinatieri kick), 8:22.

SECOND QUARTER
New England: FG Vinatieri 31, 12:54.
New England: FG Vinatieri 25, 8:36.
New England: Safety,Smith tackled in end zone.

THIRD QUARTER
Indianapolis: James 2 run (Vanderjagt kick), 9:49.
New England: FG Vinatieri 27, 7:50.
New England: FG Vinatieri 21, 1:47.

FOURTH QUARTER
Indianapolis: Pollard 7 pass from Manning (Vanderjagt kick), 2:57.
New England: FG Vinatieri 34, 0:55.

A: 68,522; T: 3:21.

NFC Championship

Carolina 0	7	7	0—14
Philadelphia............0	3	0	0— 3

SECOND QUARTER
Carolina: Muhammad 24 pass from Delhomme (Kasay kick), 10:20.
Philadelphia: FG Akers 41, 3:12.

THIRD QUARTER
Carolina: Foster 1 run (Kasay kick), 4:18.

A: 68,603; T: 3:16.

Super Bowl Box Score

Carolina 0	10	0	19—29
New England..........0	14	0	18—32

SECOND QUARTER
New England: Branch 5 pass from Brady (Vinatieri kick), 3:11. **New England 7–0**.

Carolina: Smith 39 pass from Delhomme (Kasay kick), 1:14. **7–7**

New England: Givens 5 pass from Brady (Vinatieri kick), 0:23. **New England 14–7**

Carolina: FG Kasay 50, 0:05.
New England 14–10.

FOURTH QUARTER
New England: Smith 2 run (Vinatieri kick), 14:55. **New England 21–10**.

Carolina: Foster 33 run (2-pt. conversion failed), 12:48. **New England 21–16**.

Carolina: Muhammad 85 pass from Delhomme (2-pt. conversion failed), 7:12. **Carolina 22–21**.

New England: Vrabel 1 pass from Brady (Faulk ran for 2), 2:58. **New England 29–22**.

Carolina: Proehl 12 pass from Delhomme (Kasay kick), 1:16. **29–29**.

New England: FG Vinatieri 41, 0:09. **New England 32–29**.

Att: 71,323; T: 4:00.

Team Statistics

	Carolina	New England
FIRST DOWNS	17	29
Rushing	3	7
Passing	12	19
Penalty	2	3
THIRD DOWN EFF	4–12	8–17
FOURTH DOWN EFF	0–0	1–1
TOTAL NET YARDS	387	481
Total plays	53	83
Avg gain	7.3	5.8
NET YARDS RUSHING	92	127
Rushes	16	35
Avg per rush	5.8	3.6
NET YARDS PASSING	295	354
Completed–Att	16–33	32–48
Yards per pass	8.0	7.4
Sacked–yards lost	4–28	0–0
Had intercepted	0	1
PUNTS–Avg	7–44.3	5–34.6
PENALTIES–Yds	12–73	8–60
FUMBLES–Lost	1–1	1–0

Passing

CAROLINA

	Comp	Att	Yds	Int	TD
Delhomme	16	33	323	0	3

NEW ENGLAND

	Comp	Att	Yds	Int	TD
Brady	32	48	354	1	3

Rushing

CAROLINA

	No.	Yds	Lg	TD
Davis	13	49	21	0
Foster	3	43	33t	1

NEW ENGLAND

	No.	Yds	Lg	TD
Smith	26	83	9	1
Faulk	6	42	23	0
Brady	2	12	12	0
Brown	1	-10	-10	0

Receiving

CAROLINA

	No.	Yds	Lg	TD
Muhammad	4	140	85	1
Smith	4	80	39	1
Proehl	4	71	31	1
Wiggins	2	21	15	0
Foster	1	9	9	0
Mangum	1	2	2	0

NEW ENGLAND

	No.	Yds	Lg	TD
Branch	10	143	52	1
Brown	8	76	13	0
Givens	5	69	25	1
Graham	4	46	33	0
Faulk	4	19	7	0
Vrabel	1	1	1	1

Defense

CAROLINA

	Tck	Ast	Int	Sack
Morgan	11	7	0	0
Minter	9	5	0	0
Witherspoon	7	6	0	0
Howard	6	0	1	0
Manning	4	2	0	0
Wallace	3	3	0	0
Burton	3	2	0	0
Grant	3	2	0	0
Jenkins	3	0	0	0
Favors	3	0	0	0
Cousin	2	4	0	0
Peppers	2	0	0	0
Buckner	1	2	0	0
Rucker	1	1	0	0
Ciurciu	0	1	0	0
Wesley	0	1	0	0
Willig	0	1	0	0

NEW ENGLAND

	Tck	Ast	Int	Sack
Harrison	8	1	0	1
Law	5	0	0	0
Vrabel	4	2	0	2
Phifer	4	1	0	0
Hamilton	3	1	0	0
Bruschi	2	2	0	0
Seymour	2	0	0	0
McGinest	1	3	0	1
Poole	1	2	0	0
Mayer	1	0	0	0

2003 Associated Press All-Pro Team

OFFENSE

Peyton Manning, Indianapolis	Quarterback
Jamal Lewis, Baltimore	Running Back
Priest Holmes, Kansas City	Running Back
Tony Gonzalez, Kansas City	Tight End
Torry Holt, St. Louis	Wide Receiver
Randy Moss, Minnesota	Wide Receiver
Jonathan Ogden, Baltimore	Tackle
Willie Roaf, Kansas City	Tackle
Orlando Pace, St. Louis	Tackle
Steve Hutchinson, Seattle	Guard
Will Shields, Kansas City	Guard
Tom Nalen, Denver	Center

DEFENSE

Michael Strahan, NY Giants	Defensive End
Leonard Little, St. Louis	Defensive End
Kris Jenkins, Carolina	Defensive Tackle
Richard Seymour, New England	Defensive Tackle
Keith Bulluck, Tennessee	Linebacker
Julian Peterson, San Francisco	Linebacker
Zach Thomas, Miami	Linebacker
Ray Lewis, Baltimore	Linebacker
Ty Law, New England	Cornerback
Chris McAlister, Baltimore	Cornerback
Roy Williams, Dallas	Safety
Rodney Harrison, New England	Safety

SPECIALISTS

Mike Vanderjagt, Indianapolis	Kicker
Shane Lechler, Oakland	Punter
Dante Hall, Kansas City	Kick Returner

2003 AFC Team-by-Team Results

BALTIMORE RAVENS (10–6)

15	at Pittsburgh	34
33	CLEVELAND	13
24	at San Diego	10
10	KANSAS CITY	17
26	at Arizona	18
26	at Cincinnati	34
26	DENVER	6
24	JACKSONVILLE	17
22	at St. Louis	33
6	at Miami	9
44	SEATTLE	41
44	SAN FRANCISCO	6
31	CINCINNATI	13
12	at Oakland	20
35	at Cleveland	0
13	PITTSBURGH	10
391		281

BUFFALO BILLS (6–10)

31	NEW ENGLAND	0
38	at Jacksonville	17
7	at Miami	17
13	PHILADELPHIA	23
22	CINCINNATI	16
3	at NY Jets	30
24	WASHINGTON	7
5	at Kansas City	38
6	at Dallas	10
10	HOUSTON	12
14	INDIANAPOLIS	17
24	at NY Giants	7
17	NY JETS	6
26	at Tennessee	28
3	MIAMI	20
0	at NEW ENGLAND	31
243		279

CINCINNATI BENGALS (8–8)

10	DENVER	30
20	at Oakland	23
10	PITTSBURGH	17
21	at Cleveland	14
16	at Buffalo	22
34	BALTIMORE	26
27	SEATTLE	24
14	at Arizona	17
34	HOUSTON	27
24	KANSAS CITY	19
34	at San Diego	27
24	at Pittsburgh	20
13	at Baltimore	31
41	SAN FRANCISCO	38
10	at St. Louis	27
14	CLEVELAND	22
346		384

CLEVELAND BROWNS (5–11)

6	INDIANAPOLIS	9
13	at Baltimore	33
13	at San Francisco	12
14	CINCINNATI	21
33	at Pittsburgh	13
13	OAKLAND	7
20	SAN DIEGO	26
3	at New England	9
20	at Kansas City	41
44	ARIZONA	6
6	PITTSBURGH	13
7	at Seattle	34
20	ST. LOUIS	26
20	at Denver	23
0	BALTIMORE	35
22	at Cincinnati	14
254		322

DENVER BRONCOS (10-6)

30	at Cincinnati	10
37	at San Diego	13
31	OAKLAND	10
20	DETROIT	16
23	at Kansas City	24
17	PITTSBURGH	14
20	at Minnesota	28
6	at Baltimore	26
26	NEW ENGLAND	30
37	SAN DIEGO	8
10	CHICAGO	19
22	at Oakland	8
45	KANSAS CITY	27
23	CLEVELAND	20
31	at Indianapolis	17
3	at Green Bay	31
381		**301**

HOUSTON TEXANS (5-11)

21	at Miami	20
10	at New Orleans	31
14	KANSAS CITY	42
24	JACKSONVILLE	20
17	at Tennessee	38
14	NY JETS	19
21	at Indianapolis	30
14	CAROLINA	10
27	at Cincinnati	34
12	at Buffalo	10
20	NEW ENGLAND	23
17	ATLANTA	13
0	at Jacksonville	27
3	at Tampa Bay	16
24	TENNESSEE	27
17	INDIANAPOLIS	20
255		**380**

INDIANAPOLIS COLTS (12-4)

9	at Cleveland	6
33	TENNESSEE	7
23	JACKSONVILLE	13
55	at New Orleans	21
38	at Tampa Bay	35
20	CAROLINA	23
30	HOUSTON	21
23	at Miami	17
23	at Jacksonville	28
38	NY Jets	31
17	at Buffalo	14
34	NEW ENGLAND	38
29	at Tennessee	27
38	ATLANTA	7
17	DENVER	31
20	at Houston	17
447		**336**

JACKSONVILLE JAGUARS (5-11)

23	at Carolina	24
17	BUFFALO	38
13	at Indianapolis	23
20	at Houston	24
27	SAN DIEGO	21
10	MIAMI	24
17	TENNESSEE	30
17	at Baltimore	24
28	INDIANAPOLIS	23
3	at Tennessee	10
10	at NY Jets	13
17	TAMPA BAY	10
27	HOUSTON	0
13	at New England	27
20	NEW ORLEANS	19
14	at Atlanta	21
276		**331**

KANSAS CITY CHIEFS (13-3)

27	SAN DIEGO	14
41	PITTSBURGH	20
42	at Houston	14
17	at Baltimore	10
24	DENVER	23
40	at Green Bay	34
17	at Oakland	10
38	BUFFALO	5
41	CLEVELAND	20
19	at Cincinnati	24
27	OAKLAND	24
28	at San Diego	24
27	at Denver	45
45	DETROIT	17
20	at Minnesota	45
31	CHICAGO	3
484		**332**

MIAMI DOLPHINS (10-6)

20	HOUSTON	21
21	at NY JETS	10
17	BUFFALO	7
23	at NY Giants	10
24	at Jacksonville	10
13	NEW ENGLAND	19
26	at San Diego	10
17	INDIANAPOLIS	23
7	at Tennessee	31
9	BALTIMORE	6
24	WASHINGTON	23
40	at Dallas	21
0	at New England	12
27	PHILADELPHIA	34
20	at Buffalo	3
23	NY JETS	21
311		**261**

NEW ENGLAND PATRIOTS (14-2)

0	at Buffalo	31
31	at Philadelphia	10
23	NY JETS	16
17	at Washington	20
38	TENNESSEE	30
17	NY GIANTS	6
19	at Miami	13
9	CLEVELAND	3
30	at Denver	26
12	DALLAS	0
23	at Houston	20
38	at Indianapolis	34
12	MIAMI	0
27	JACKSONVILLE	13
21	at NY Jets	16
31	BUFFALO	0
348		**238**

NEW YORK JETS (6-10)

13	at Washington	16
10	MIAMI	21
16	at New England	23
6	DALLAS	17
30	BUFFALO	3
19	at Houston	14
17	at Philadelphia	24
28	NY GIANTS	31
27	at Oakland	24
31	at Indianapolis	38
13	JACKSONVILLE	10
24	TENNESSEE	17
6	at Buffalo	17
6	PITTSBURGH	0
16	NEW ENGLAND	21
21	at Miami	23
283		**299**

OAKLAND RAIDERS (4-12)

20	at Tennessee	25
23	CINCINNATI	20
10	at Denver	31
34	SAN DIEGO	31
21	at Chicago	24
7	at Cleveland	13
10	KANSAS CITY	17
13	at Detroit	23
24	NY JETS	27
28	MINNESOTA	18
24	at Kansas City	27
8	DENVER	22
7	at Pittsburgh	27
20	BALTIMORE	12
7	GREEN BAY	41
14	at San Diego	21
270		**379**

PITTSBURGH STEELERS (6–10)

34	BALTIMORE	15
20	at Kansas City	41
17	at Cincinnati	10
13	TENNESSEE	30
13	CLEVELAND	33
14	at Denver	17
21	ST. LOUIS	33
16	at Seattle	23
28	ARIZONA	15
14	at San Francisco	30
13	at Cleveland	6
20	CINCINNATI	24
27	OAKLAND	7
0	at NY Jets	6
40	San Diego	24
10	at Baltimore	13
300		327

SAN DIEGO CHARGERS (4–12)

14	at Kansas City	27
13	DENVER	37
10	BALTIMORE	24
31	at Oakland	34
21	at Jacksonville	27
26	at Cleveland	20
10	MIAMI	26
7	at Chicago	20
42	MINNESOTA	28
8	at Denver	37
27	CINCINNATI	34
24	KANSAS CITY	28
14	at Detroit	7
21	GREEN BAY	38
24	at Pittsburgh	40
21	OAKLAND	14
313		441

TENNESSEE TITANS (12–4)

25	OAKLAND	20
7	at Indianapolis	33
27	NEW ORLEANS	12
30	at Pittsburgh	13
30	at New England	38
38	HOUSTON	17
37	at Carolina	17
30	at Jacksonville	17
31	MIAMI	7
10	JACKSONVILLE	3
38	at Atlanta	31
17	at NY Jets	24
27	INDIANAPOLIS	29
28	BUFFALO	26
27	at Houston	24
33	TAMPA BAY	13
435		324

2003 NFC Team-by-Team Results

ARIZONA CARDINALS (4–12)

24	at Detroit	42
0	SEATTLE	38
20	GREEN BAY	13
13	at St. Louis	37
7	at Dallas	24
18	BALTIMORE	26
16	SAN FRANCISCO	13
17	CINCINNATI	14
15	at Pittsburgh	28
6	at Cleveland	44
27	ST. LOUIS	30
3	at Chicago	28
14	at San Francisco	50
17	CAROLINA	20
10	at Seattle	28
18	MINNESOTA	17
225		452

ATLANTA FALCONS (5–11)

27	at Dallas	13
31	WASHINGTON	33
10	TAMPA BAY	31
3	at Carolina	23
26	MINNESOTA	39
0	at St. Louis	36
17	NEW ORLEANS	45
16	PHILADELPHIA	23
27	at NY Giants	7
20	at New Orleans	23
31	TENNESSEE	38
13	at Houston	17
20	CAROLINA	14
7	at Indianapolis	38
30	at Tampa Bay	28
21	JACKSONVILLE	14
299		422

CAROLINA PANTHERS (11–5)

24	JACKSONVILLE	23
12	at Tampa Bay	9
23	ATLANTA	3
19	NEW ORLEANS	13
23	at Indianapolis	20
17	TENNESSEE	37
23	at New Orleans	20
10	at Houston	14
27	TAMPA BAY	24
20	WASHINGTON	17
20	at Dallas	24
16	PHILADELPHIA	25
14	at ATLANTA	20
20	at Arizona	17
20	DETROIT	14
37	at NY Giants	24
325		304

CHICAGO BEARS (7–9)

7	at San Francisco	49
13	at Minnesota	24
23	GREEN BAY	38
24	OAKLAND	21
13	at New Orleans	20
17	at Seattle	24
24	DETROIT	16
20	SAN DIEGO	7
10	at Detroit	12
21	ST. LOUIS	23
19	at Denver	10
28	ARIZONA	3
21	at Green Bay	34
13	MINNESOTA	10
27	WASHINGTON	24
3	at Kansas City	31
283		346

DALLAS COWBOYS (10–6)

13	ATLANTA	27
35	at NY Giants	32
17	at NY Jets	6
24	ARIZONA	7
23	PHILADELPHIA	21
38	at Detroit	7
0	at Tampa Bay	16
21	WASHINGTON	14
10	BUFFALO	6
0	at New England	12
24	CAROLINA	20
21	MIAMI	40
10	at Philadelphia	36
27	at Washington	0
19	NY GIANTS	3
7	at New Orleans	13
289		260

DETROIT LIONS (5–11)

42	ARIZONA	24
6	at Green Bay	31
13	MINNESOTA	23
16	at Denver	20
17	at San Francisco	24
7	DALLAS	38
16	at Chicago	24
23	OAKLAND	13
12	CHICAGO	10
14	at Seattle	35
14	at Minnesota	24
22	GREEN BAY	14
7	SAN DIEGO	14
17	at Kansas City	45
14	at Carolina	20
30	ST. LOUIS	20
270		379

GREEN BAY PACKERS (10–6)

25	MINNESOTA	30
31	DETROIT	6
13	at Arizona	20
38	at Chicago	23
35	SEATTLE	13
34	KANSAS CITY	40
24	at St. Louis	34
30	at Minnesota	27
14	PHILADELPHIA	17
20	at Tampa Bay	13
20	SAN FRANCISCO	10
14	at Detroit	22
34	CHICAGO	21
38	at San Diego	21
41	at Oakland	7
31	DENVER	3
442		**307**

MINNESOTA VIKINGS (9–7)

30	at Green Bay	25
24	CHICAGO	13
23	at Detroit	13
35	SAN FRANCISCO	7
39	at Atlanta	26
28	DENVER	20
17	NY GIANTS	29
27	GREEN BAY	30
28	at San Diego	42
18	at Oakland	28
24	DETROIT	14
17	at St. Louis	48
34	SEATTLE	7
10	at Chicago	13
45	KANSAS CITY	20
17	at Arizona	18
416		**353**

NEW ORLEANS SAINTS (8–8)

10	at Seattle	27
31	HOUSTON	10
12	at Tennessee	27
21	Indianapolis	55
13	at Carolina	19
20	CHICAGO	13
45	at Atlanta	17
20	CAROLINA	23
17	at Tampa Bay	14
23	ATLANTA	20
20	at Philadelphia	33
24	at Washington	20
7	TAMPA BAY	14
45	NY Giants	7
19	at Jacksonville	20
13	DALLAS	7
340		**326**

NEW YORK GIANTS (4–12)

23	ST. LOUIS	13
32	DALLAS	35
24	at Washington	21
10	MIAMI	23
6	at New England	17
10	PHILADELPHIA	14
29	at Minnesota	17
31	at NY Jets	28
7	ATLANTA	27
10	at Philadelphia	28
13	at Tampa Bay	19
7	BUFFALO	24
7	WASHINGTON	20
7	at New Orleans	45
3	at Dallas	19
24	CAROLINA	37
243		**387**

PHILADELPHIA EAGLES (12–4)

0	TAMPA BAY	17
10	NEW ENGLAND	31
23	at Buffalo	13
27	WASHINGTON	25
21	at Dallas	23
14	at NY Giants	10
24	NY JETS	17
23	at Atlanta	16
17	at Green Bay	14
28	NY GIANTS	10
33	NEW ORLEANS	20
25	at Carolina	16
36	DALLAS	10
34	at Miami	27
28	SAN FRANCISCO	31
31	at Washington	7
374		**287**

ST. LOUIS RAMS (12–4)

13	at NY Giants	23
27	SAN FRANCISCO	24
23	at Seattle	24
37	ARIZONA	13
36	ATLANTA	0
34	GREEN BAY	24
33	at Pittsburgh	21
10	at San Francisco	30
33	BALTIMORE	22
23	at Chicago	21
30	at Arizona	27
48	MINNESOTA	17
26	at Cleveland	20
27	SEATTLE	22
27	CINCINNATI	10
20	at Detroit	30
447		**328**

SAN FRANCISCO 49ERS (7–9)

49	CHICAGO	7
24	at St. Louis	27
12	CLEVELAND	13
7	at Minnesota	35
24	DETROIT	17
19	at Seattle	20
24	TAMPA BAY	7
13	at Arizona	16
30	ST. LOUIS	10
30	PITTSBURGH	14
10	at Green Bay	20
6	at Baltimore	44
50	ARIZONA	14
38	at Cincinnati	41
31	at Philadelphia	28
17	SEATTLE	24
384		**337**

SEATTLE SEAHAWKS (10–6)

27	NEW ORLEANS	10
38	at Arizona	0
24	ST. LOUIS	23
13	at Green Bay	35
20	SAN FRANCISCO	19
24	CHICAGO	17
24	at Cincinnati	27
23	PITTSBURGH	16
20	at Washington	27
35	DETROIT	14
41	at Baltimore	44
34	CLEVELAND	7
7	at Minnesota	34
22	at St. Louis	27
28	ARIZONA	10
24	at San Francisco	17
404		**327**

TAMPA BAY BUCCANEERS (7–9)

17	at Philadelphia	0
9	CAROLINA	12
31	at Atlanta	10
35	INDIANAPOLIS	38
35	at Washington	13
7	at San Francisco	24
16	DALLAS	0
14	NEW ORLEANS	17
24	at Carolina	27
13	GREEN BAY	20
19	NY GIANTS	13
10	at Jacksonville	17
14	at New Orleans	7
16	HOUSTON	3
28	ATLANTA	30
13	at Tennessee	33
301		**264**

WASHINGTON REDSKINS (5–11)

16	NY JETS	13	17	at Carolina	20
33	at Atlanta	31	23	at Miami	24
21	NY GIANTS	24	20	NEW ORLEANS	24
20	NEW ENGLAND	17	20	at NY Giants	7
25	at Philadelphia	27	0	DALLAS	27
13	TAMPA BAY	35	24	at Chicago	27
7	at Buffalo	24	7	PHILADELPHIA	31
14	at Dallas	21	**287**		**372**
27	SEATTLE	20			

American Football Conference

Scoring

TOUCHDOWNS	TD	Rush	Rec	Ret	2PT	Pts	KICKING	PAT	FG	Pts
Holmes, KC	27	27	0	0	0	162	Vanderjagt, Ind	46	37	157
Tomlinson, SD	17	13	4	0	0	102	Stover, Balt	35	33	134
Portis, Den	14	14	0	0	1	86	Anderson, Tenn	42	27	123
Lewis, Balt	14	14	0	0	0	84	Elam, Den	39	27	120
Henry, Buff	11	10	1	0	0	66	Vinatieri, NE	27	25	112
James, Ind	11	11	0	0	0	66	Graham, Cin	40	22	106
Chambers, Mia	11	0	11	0	0	66	Andersen, KC	58	16	106
Six tied with 60.							Brien, NYJ	24	27	105
							Reed, Pitt	31	23	100
							Mare, Mia	33	22	99

Passing

	Att	Comp	Yds	TD	Int	Lg	Rating Pts
McNair, Tenn	400	250	3215	24	7	73	100.4
Manning, Ind	566	379	4267	29	10	79	99.0
Green, KC	523	330	4039	24	12	67	92.6
Plummer, Den	302	189	2182	15	7	60	91.2
Kitna, Cin	520	324	3591	26	15	82	87.4
Brady, NE	527	317	3620	23	12	82	85.9
Pennington, NYJ	297	189	2139	13	12	65	82.9
Maddux, Pitt	519	298	3414	18	17	53	75.3
Holcomb, Clev	302	193	1797	10	12	68	74.6
Gannon, Oak	225	125	1274	6	4	46	73.5

Pass Receiving

RECEPTIONS	No.	Yds	Avg	Lg	TD	YARDS	No.	Yds	Avg	Lg	TD
Tomlinson, SD	100	725	7.3	73	4	Johnson, Cin	90	1355	15.1	82	10
Ward, Pitt	95	1163	12.2	50	10	Mason, Tenn	95	1303	13.7	50	8
Mason, Tenn	95	1303	13.7	50	8	Harrison, Ind	94	1272	13.5	79	10
Harrison, Ind	94	1272	13.5	79	10	Ward, Pitt	95	1163	12.2	50	10
Johnson, Cin	90	1355	15.1	82	10	Moss, NYJ	74	1105	14.9	65	10
Warrick, Cin	79	819	10.4	77	7	Johnson, Hou	66	976	14.8	46	4
Moss, NYJ	74	1105	14.9	65	10	Chambers, Mia	64	963	15.0	57	11
Smith, Den	74	845	11.4	38	3	Gonzalez, KC	71	916	12.9	67	10
Holmes, KC	74	690	9.3	36	0	Boston, SD	70	880	12.6	46	7
Gonzalez, KC	71	916	12.9	67	10	Rice, Oak	63	869	13.8	47	2

Rushing

	Att	Yds	Avg	Lg	TD
Lewis, Balt	387	2066	5.3	82	14
Tomlinson, SD	313	1645	5.3	73	13
Portis, Den	290	1591	5.5	65	14
Taylor, Jax	345	1572	4.6	62	6
Holmes, KC	320	1420	4.4	31	27
Williams, Mia	392	1372	3.5	45	9
Henry, Buff	331	1356	4.1	64	10
Martin, NYJ	323	1308	4.0	56	2
James, Ind	310	1259	4.1	43	11
George, Tenn	312	1031	3.3	27	5

Interceptions

	No.	Yds	Lg	TD
Surtain, Mia	7	59	32	0
Reed, Balt	7	132	54	1
Coleman, Hou	7	95	41	0

Eight tied with six.

Sacks

Ogunleye, Mia	15
Taylor, Mia	13
Ellis, NYJ	12.5
Suggs, Balt	12
Schobel, Buff	11.5
Berry, Den	11.5

American Football Conference (Cont.)
Punting

	No.	Yds	Avg	Net Avg	TB	In 20	Lg	Blk	Ret	Ret Avg
Lechler, Oak	96	4503	46.9	37.2	13	27	73	0	52	12.9
Moorman, Buff	85	3788	44.6	37.1	3	20	71	0	52	11.1
Hentrich, Tenn	71	3117	43.9	37.8	8	26	58	0	30	9.2
Knorr, Den	68	2937	43.2	32.2	6	14	62	0	46	12.2
Smith, Ind	62	2617	42.2	35.5	3	20	55	0	32	10.0

Punt Returns

	No.	Yds	Avg	Lg	TD
Hall, KC	29	472	16.3	93	2
Buchanon, Oak	36	491	13.6	80	2
Allen, Jax	27	324	12.0	52	0
Randle El, Pitt	45	542	12.0	84	2
McCareins, Tenn	29	330	11.4	58	1

Kickoff Returns

	No.	Yds	Avg	Lg	TD
Johnson, NE	30	847	28.2	92	1
Bates, NYJ	22	596	27.1	48	0
Hall, KC	57	1478	25.9	100	2
Brightful, Balt	29	716	24.7	75	0
Cole, Den	30	714	23.8	34	0

National Football Conference
Scoring

TOUCHDOWNS	TD	Rush	Rec	Ret	2PT	Pts	KICKING	PAT	FG	Pts
Green, GB	20	15	5	0	0	120	Wilkins, StL	46	39	163
Moss, Minn	17	0	17	0	0	102	Kasay, Car	29	32	125
Alexander, Sea	16	14	2	0	0	96	Longwell, GB	51	23	120
Westbrook, Phil	13	7	4	2	0	78	Brown, Sea	48	22	114
Holt, StL	12	0	12	0	0	72	Akers, Phil	42	24	114
Duckett, Atl	11	11	0	0	0	66	Edinger, Chi	27	26	105
Faulk, StL	11	10	1	0	0	66	Elling, Minn	48	18	102
Horn, NO	10	0	10	0	0	60	Carney, NO	36	22	102
							Hall, Wash	26	25	101
Five tied with 54.							Cundiff, Dall	30	23	99

Passing

	Att	Comp	Yds	TD	Int	Lg	Rating Pts
Culpepper, Minn	454	295	3479	25	11	59	96.4
Favre, GB	471	308	3361	32	21	66	90.4
Hasselbeck, Sea	513	313	3841	26	15	80	88.8
Brooks, NO	518	306	2546	24	8	76	88.8
Johnson, TB	570	354	3811	26	21	76	81.5
Bulger, StL	532	336	3845	22	22	48	81.4
Delhomme, Car	449	266	3219	19	16	67	80.6
Garcia, SF	392	225	2705	18	13	75	80.1
McNabb, Phil	478	275	3216	16	11	59	79.6
Ramsey, Wash	337	179	2166	14	9	64	75.8

Pass Receiving

RECEPTIONS	No.	Yds	Avg	Lg	TD	YARDS	Yds	No.	Avg	Lg	TD
Holt, StL	117	1696	14.5	48	12	Holt, StL	1696	117	14.5	48	12
Moss, Minn	111	1632	14.7	72	17	Moss, Minn	1632	111	14.7	72	17
Boldin, Ariz	101	1377	13.6	71	8	Boldin, Ariz	1377	101	13.6	71	8
Smith, Car	88	1110	12.6	67	7	Coles, Wash	1204	82	14.7	64	6
McCardell, TB	84	1174	14.0	76	8	McCardell, TB	1174	84	14.0	76	8
Coles, Wash	82	1204	14.7	64	6	Jackson, Sea	1137	68	16.7	80	9
Owens, SF	80	1102	13.8	75	9	Smith, Car	1110	88	12.6	67	7
Horn, NO	78	973	12.5	50	10	Owens, SF	1102	80	13.8	75	9
Pittman, TB	75	597	8.0	68	2	Toomer, NYG	1057	63	16.8	77	5
Barber, NYG	69	461	6.7	36	1	Bruce, StL	981	69	14.2	41	5

National Football Conference (Cont.)

Rushing

	Att	Yds	Avg	Lg	TD
Green, GB	355	1883	5.3	98	15
McAllister, NO	351	1641	4.7	76	8
Davis, Car	318	1444	4.5	40	8
Alexander, Sea	326	1435	4.4	55	14
Barber, NYG	278	1216	4.4	27	2
Thomas, Chi	244	1024	4.2	67	6
Barlow, SF	201	1024	5.1	78	6
Hambrick, Dall	275	972	3.5	42	5
Shipp, Ariz	228	830	3.6	36	0
Faulk, StL	209	818	3.9	52	10

Interceptions

	No.	Yds	Lg	TD
Russell, Minn	9	185	50	0
Parrish, SF	9	202	49	0
Chavous, Minn	8	143	39	1
Jackson, Ariz	6	122	30	0
Bly, Det	6	89	48	1

Sacks

Strahan, NYG	18.5
Rice, TB	15
Little, StL	12.5
Rucker, Car	12
Williams, Minn	10.5

Punting

	No.	Yds	Avg	Net Avg	TB	In 20	Lg	Blk	Ret	Ret Avg
Sauerbrun, Car	77	3433	44.6	35.6	9	22	64	0	35	11.5
Berger, NO	71	3144	44.3	38.2	5	28	59	0	36	8.2
Tupa, TB	83	3590	43.3	35.9	6	26	60	0	39	12.5
Player, Ariz	82	3511	42.8	34.4	9	19	64	0	41	11.5
Landeta, StL	59	2525	42.8	32.9	5	14	57	0	32	15.1

Punt Returns

	No.	Yds	Avg	Lg	TD
Westbrook, Phil	20	306	15.3	84	2
Rossum, Atl	39	545	14.0	72	1
Swinton, Det	23	318	13.8	89	1
McQuarters, Chi	37	452	12.2	60	1
Engram, Sea	31	320	10.3	83	1

Kickoff Returns

	No.	Yds	Avg	Lg	TD
Azumah, Chi	41	1191	29.0	89	2
Swinton, Det	40	964	24.1	96	1
Thrash, Phil	34	815	24.0	54	0
Lewis, NO	45	1068	23.7	53	0
Morton, Wash	44	1029	23.4	94	1

2003 NFL Team Leaders

AFC Total Offense

	Total Plays	Yds/ Game	Yds/ Play	F Dwns/ Game	Time of Poss
Kansas City	1003	369.4	5.9	21.8	29:23
Indianapolis	1041	367.1	5.6	21.8	30:54
Denver	1047	349.9	5.3	20.9	33:53
Tennessee	1013	343.8	5.4	19.4	32:52
Jacksonville	1024	334.9	5.2	19.1	30:09
Cincinnati	1038	333.1	5.1	19.6	30:52
San Diego	971	322.9	5.3	18.1	27:52
New England	1042	314.9	4.8	18.4	30:50
NY Jets	936	309.4	5.3	17.1	27:50
Baltimore	1009	308.1	4.9	16.2	30:14
Pittsburgh	1020	299.5	4.7	17.2	30:42
Miami	968	288.1	4.8	16.6	29:49
Oakland	987	285.8	4.6	16.1	27:41
Cleveland	961	281.5	4.7	17.2	29:21
Buffalo	980	271.8	4.4	16.8	29:40
Houston	896	269.1	4.8	14.8	27:39

AFC Total Defense

	Opp Total Plays	Opp Yds/ Game	Opp Yds/ Play	Opp T of Poss
Buffalo	1010	269.6	4.3	30:20
Baltimore	1026	271.3	4.2	29:46
Denver	910	277.1	4.9	26:07
Jacksonville	976	291.1	4.8	29:51
New England	1060	291.6	4.4	29:10
Pittsburgh	968	298.9	4.9	29:18
Miami	1014	299.3	4.7	30:11
Indianapolis	913	299.3	5.2	29:06
Tennessee	926	306.3	5.3	27:08
Cleveland	994	309.9	5.0	30:39
NY Jets	1032	332.4	5.2	32:10
San Diego	1072	349.6	5.2	32:08
Cincinnati	999	351.2	5.6	29:08
Kansas City	1054	356.7	5.4	30:37
Oakland	1036	369.0	5.7	32:19
Houston	1054	380.1	5.8	32:21

NFC Total Offense

	Total Plays	Yds/ Game	Yds/ Play	F Dwns/ Game	Time of Poss
Minnesota	1055	393.4	6.0	21.0	32:52
Green Bay	999	362.4	5.8	19.7	30:52
San Francisco	1038	355.4	5.5	19.6	30:54
Seattle	1017	351.7	5.5	21.1	28:33
St. Louis	1054	341.1	5.2	20.9	31:53
Tampa Bay	1036	340.8	5.3	19.2	31:36
New Orleans	1019	339.9	5.3	18.9	30:18
Dallas	1062	322.6	4.9	17.9	32:34
Carolina	1008	321.3	5.1	17.8	30:27
Philadelphia	944	314.7	5.3	18.9	28:17
NY Giants	1047	308.9	4.7	18.8	28:04
Washington	991	291.2	4.7	17.0	28:45
Arizona	981	280.6	4.6	16.0	29:41
Chicago	1001	273.8	4.4	16.5	29:39
Atlanta	930	272.3	4.7	15.8	27:38
Detroit	975	266.4	4.4	15.6	28:21

NFC Total Defense

	Opp Total Plays	Opp Yds/ Game	Opp Yds/ Play	Opp T of Poss
Dallas	937	253.5	4.3	27:26
Tampa Bay	962	279.1	4.6	28:24
Carolina	996	295.3	4.7	29:33
San Francisco	976	308.0	5.0	29:06
Chicago	992	309.2	5.0	30:21
St. Louis	964	315.8	5.2	28:07
Green Bay	1036	318.8	4.9	29:08
New Orleans	997	327.1	5.2	29:42
Seattle	1069	327.4	4.9	31:27
Philadelphia	1058	331.7	5.0	31:43
NY Giants	1060	332.5	5.0	31:56
Minnesota	955	334.8	5.6	27:08
Detroit	997	335.0	5.4	31:39
Washington	1014	338.2	5.3	31:15
Arizona	993	344.0	5.5	30:19
Atlanta	1043	381.8	5.9	32:22

Takeaways/Giveaways

American Football Conference

	Takeaways			Giveaways			Net Diff
	Int	Fum	Total	Int	Fum	Total	
Kansas City	25	12	37	12	6	18	19
New England	29	12	41	13	11	24	17
Tennessee	21	13	34	9	12	21	13
Indianapolis	15	15	30	10	10	20	10
Baltimore	24	17	41	19	19	38	3
Miami	22	14	36	19	15	34	2
Cincinnati	14	10	24	15	7	22	2
NY Jets	11	9	20	14	6	20	0
Oakland	14	11	25	14	12	26	-1
Pittsburgh	14	11	25	17	11	28	-3
Jacksonville	15	12	27	17	14	31	-4
Denver	9	11	20	18	6	24	-4
Houston	14	8	22	18	9	27	-5
Cleveland	15	7	22	18	15	33	-11
San Diego	13	7	20	19	12	31	-11
Buffalo	10	8	18	17	17	34	-16

National Football Conference

	Takeaways			Giveaways			Net Diff
	Int	Fum	Total	Int	Fum	Total	
Minnesota	28	7	35	13	11	24	11
San Francisco	23	13	36	15	10	25	11
St. Louis	24	22	46	23	16	39	7
Philadelphia	13	13	26	11	11	22	4
Washington	17	13	30	16	12	28	2
Tampa Bay	20	13	33	22	9	31	2
Green Bay	21	11	32	21	11	32	0
Detroit	15	13	28	24	4	28	0
Atlanta	15	16	31	21	10	31	0
Seattle	16	12	28	16	13	29	-1
New Orleans	14	13	27	8	20	28	-1
Dallas	13	12	25	21	8	29	-4
Carolina	16	10	26	16	15	31	-5
Chicago	15	5	20	20	9	29	-9
Arizona	13	10	23	22	14	36	-13
NY Giants	10	12	22	20	18	38	-16

THEY SAID IT

Mike Heimerdinger, Titans offensive coordinator, on why he hasn't been a candidate for an NFL head coaching job: "They're looking for big names, not long names."

Baltimore Ravens

SCORING

	TD Rush	Rec	Ret	PAT	FG	S	Pts
Stover	0	0	0	35/35	33/38	0	134
J. Lewis	14	0	0	0	0	0	84
Robinson	0	6	0	0	0	0	36
Heap	0	3	0	4	0	0	26

RUSHING

	No.	Yds	Avg	Lg	TD
J. Lewis	387	2066	5.3	82	14
C. Taylor	63	276	4.4	32	2

PASSING

	Att	Comp	Pct Comp	Yds	Avg Gain	TD	Int	Rating Pts
Boller	224	116	51.8	1260	5.63	7	9	62.4
Wright	178	94	52.8	1199	6.74	9	8	72.3

RECEIVING

	No.	Yds	Avg	Lg	TD
Heap	57	693	12.2	33	3
T. Taylor	39	632	16.2	73	3
Robinson	31	451	14.5	50	6
J. Lewis	26	205	7.9	26	0
C. Taylor	20	132	6.6	23	0

INTERCEPTIONS: Reed, 7

PUNTING

	No.	Yds	Avg	Net Avg	TB	In 20	Lg	Blk
Zastudil	89	3649	41.0	35.2	8	21	67	0

SACKS: Suggs, 12

Buffalo Bills

SCORING

	TD Rush	Rec	Ret	PAT	FG	S	Pts
Lindell	0	0	0	24/24	17/24	0	75
Henry	10	1	0	0	0	0	66
Shaw	0	4	0	0	0	0	24

RUSHING

	No.	Yds	Avg	Lg	TD
Henry	331	1356	4.1	64	10
Burns	39	113	2.9	12	0

PASSING

	Att	Comp	Pct Comp	Yds	Avg Gain	TD	Int	Rating Pts
Bledsoe	471	274	58.2	2860	6.07	11	12	73.0

RECEIVING

	No.	Yds	Avg	Lg	TD
Moulds	64	780	12.2	49	1
Reed	58	588	10.1	26	2
Shaw	56	732	13.1	54	4
Campbell	34	339	10.0	31	1
Henry	28	158	5.6	18	1

INTERCEPTIONS: Clements, 3

PUNTING

	No.	Yds	Avg	Net Avg	TB	In 20	Lg	Blk
Moorman	85	3788	44.6	37.1	3	20	71	0

SACKS: Schobel, 11.5

Cincinnati Bengals

SCORING

	TD Rush	Rec	Ret	PAT	FG	S	Pts
Graham	0	0	0	40/40	22/25	0	106
C. Johnson	0	10	0	0	0	0	60
R. Johnson	9	0	0	0	0	0	54
Warrick	0	7	1	0	0	0	48
Washington	0	4	0	0	0	0	24

RUSHING

	No.	Yds	Avg	Lg	TD
R. Johnson	215	957	4.5	54	9
Dillon	138	541	3.9	39	2
Bennett	56	173	3.1	19	0
Warrick	18	157	8.7	50	0

PASSING

	Att	Comp	Pct Comp	Yds	Avg Gain	TD	Int	Rating Pts
Kitna	520	324	62.3	3591	6.91	26	15	87.4

RECEIVING

	No.	Yds	Avg	Lg	TD
C. Johnson	90	1355	15.1	82	10
Warrick	79	819	10.4	77	7
Bennett	25	176	7.0	16	1
Schobel	24	332	13.8	45	2
Washington	22	299	13.6	51	4

INTERCEPTIONS: James, 4

PUNTING

	No.	Yds	Avg	Net Avg	TB	In 20	Lg	Blk
Rich'dson	49	1961	40.0	33.5	5	9	58	0
Harris	28	1084	38.7	30.0	3	5	53	0

SACKS: Clemons and Thornton, 6

Cleveland Browns

SCORING

	TD Rush	Rec	Ret	PAT	FG	S	Pts
Dawson	0	0	0	20/21	18/21	0	74
Davis	0	5	0	0	0	0	30
Conway	0	0	0	3/3	5/7	0	18
J. Jackson	3	0	0	0	0	0	18
Morgan	0	3	0	0	0	0	18

RUSHING

	No.	Yds	Avg	Lg	TD
Green	142	559	3.9	26	1
J. Jackson	102	382	3.7	18	3
Suggs	56	289	5.2	78	2
White	70	266	3.8	23	1

PASSING

	Att	Comp	Pct Comp	Yds	Avg Gain	TD	Int	Rating Pts
Holcomb	302	193	63.9	1797	5.95	10	12	74.6
Couch	203	120	59.1	1319	6.50	7	6	77.6

RECEIVING

	No.	Yds	Avg	Lg	TD
Northcutt	62	729	11.8	44	2
White	46	303	6.6	22	1
Johnson	41	381	9.3	41	2
Davis	40	576	14.4	49	5
Morgan	38	516	13.6	71	3

INTERCEPTIONS: Little, 6

PUNTING

	No.	Yds	Avg	Net Avg	TB	In 20	Lg	Blk
Gardocki	72	3019	41.9	34.8	10	18	60	0

SACKS: Lang, 8

Denver Broncos

SCORING	Rush	Rec	Ret	PAT	FG	S	Pts
Elam	0	0	0	39/39	27/31	0	120
Portis	14	0	0	1	0	0	86
Sharpe	0	8	0	0	0	0	48
Anderson	3	2	0	0	0	0	30
Smith	0	3	1	0	0	0	24

RUSHING	No.	Yds	Avg	Lg	TD
Portis	290	1591	5.5	65	14
Griffin	94	345	3.7	23	0
Anderson	70	257	3.7	44	3
Plummer	37	205	5.5	40	3

PASSING	Att	Comp	Pct Comp	Yds	Avg Gain	TD	Int	Rating Pts
Plummer	302	189	62.6	2182	7.23	15	7	91.2
Kanell	103	53	51.5	442	4.29	2	5	49.1
Beuerlein	63	33	52.4	389	6.17	2	5	49.0

RECEIVING	No.	Yds	Avg	Lg	TD
Smith	74	845	11.4	38	3
Sharpe	62	770	12.4	28	8
Portis	38	314	8.3	72	0
Lelie	37	628	17.0	60	2

INTERCEPTIONS: Herndon, 3

PUNTING	No.	Yds	Avg	Net Avg	TB	In 20	Lg	Blk
Knorr	68	2937	43.2	32.2	6	14	62	2

SACKS: Berry, 11.5

Houston Texans

SCORING	Rush	Rec	Ret	PAT	FG	S	Pts
K. Brown	0	0	0	27/27	18/22	0	81
D. Davis	8	0	0	0	0	0	48
Bradford	0	4	0	0	0	0	24
Johnson	0	4	0	0	0	0	24
Mack	4	0	0	0	0	0	24

RUSHING	No.	Yds	Avg	Lg	TD
D. Davis	238	1031	4.3	51	8
Mack	93	253	2.7	13	4

PASSING	Att	Comp	Pct Comp	Yds	Avg Gain	TD	Int	Rating Pts
Carr	295	167	56.6	2013	6.82	9	13	69.5
Banks	102	61	59.8	693	6.79	5	3	84.3

RECEIVING	No.	Yds	Avg	Lg	TD
Johnson	66	976	14.8	46	4
D. Davis	47	351	7.5	17	0
Miller	40	355	8.9	25	3
Gaffney	34	402	11.8	33	2
Bradford	24	460	19.2	78	4

INTERCEPTIONS: Coleman, 7

PUNTING	No.	Yds	Avg	Net Avg	TB	In 20	Lg	Blk
Stanley	97	4028	41.5	36.7	3	36	58	0

SACKS: Sharper, 4

Indianapolis Colts

SCORING	Rush	Rec	Ret	PAT	FG	S	Pts
Vanderjagt	0	0	0	46/46	37/37	0	157
James	11	0	0	0	0	0	66
Harrison	0	10	0	0	0	0	60
Wayne	0	7	0	0	0	0	42

Four tied with 18.

RUSHING	No.	Yds	Avg	Lg	TD
James	310	1259	4.1	43	11
Rhodes	37	157	4.2	25	0
R. Williams	48	155	3.2	19	2

PASSING	Att	Comp	Pct Comp	Yds	Avg Gain	TD	Int	Rating Pts
Manning	566	379	67.0	4267	7.54	29	10	99.0

RECEIVING	No.	Yds	Avg	Lg	TD
Harrison	94	1272	13.5	79	10
Wayne	68	838	12.3	57	7
James	51	292	5.7	17	0
Pollard	40	541	13.5	70	3
Walters	36	456	12.7	46	3
Clark	29	340	11.7	42	1
Stokley	22	211	9.6	37	3

INTERCEPTIONS: Harper, 4

PUNTING	No.	Yds	Avg	Net Avg	TB	In 20	Lg	Blk
H. Smith	62	2617	42.2	35.5	3	20	55	1

SACKS: Freeney, 11

Jacksonville Jaguars

SCORING	Rush	Rec	Ret	PAT	FG	S	Pts
Marler	0	0	0	30/30	20/33	0	90
F. Taylor	6	1	0	0	0	0	42
J. Smith	0	4	0	0	0	0	24
T. Edwards	0	3	0	0	0	0	18
Toefield	2	1	0	0	0	0	18

RUSHING	No.	Yds	Avg	Lg	TD
F. Taylor	345	1572	4.6	62	6
Toefield	53	212	4.0	30	2

PASSING	Att	Comp	Pct Comp	Yds	Avg Gain	TD	Int	Rating Pts
Leftwich	418	239	57.2	2819	6.74	14	16	73.0
Brunell	82	54	65.9	484	5.90	2	0	89.7

RECEIVING	No.	Yds	Avg	Lg	TD
J. Smith	54	805	14.9	67	4
F. Taylor	48	370	7.7	60	1
T. Edwards	35	487	13.9	84	3
M. Edwards	31	226	7.3	32	0
Brady	29	281	9.7	26	1

INTERCEPTIONS: Peterson, 3

PUNTING	No.	Yds	Avg	Net Avg	TB	In 20	Lg	Blk
Royals	45	1852	41.2	34.8	5	9	51	0
Hanson	23	1001	43.5	31.1	1	4	58	1

SACKS: Brackens, 6

Kansas City Chiefs

SCORING

		TD					
SCORING	Rush	Rec	Ret	PAT	FG	S	Pts
Holmes	27	0	0	0	0	0	162
Andersen	0	0	0	58/59	16/20	0	106
Gonzalez	0	10	0	0	0	0	60
Hall	0	1	4	0	0	0	30
Kennison	0	5	0	0	0	0	30
Morton	0	4	0	0	0	0	24

RUSHING	No.	Yds	Avg	Lg	TD
Holmes	320	1420	4.4	31	27
Blaylock	22	112	5.1	25	2

PASSING	Att	Comp	Pct Comp	Yds	Avg Gain	TD	Int	Rating Pts
Green	523	330	63.1	4039	7.72	24	12	92.6

RECEIVING	No.	Yds	Avg	Lg	TD
Holmes	74	690	9.3	36	0
Gonzalez	71	916	12.9	67	10
Kennison	56	853	15.2	51	5
Morton	50	740	14.8	50	4
Hall	40	423	10.6	67	1

INTERCEPTIONS: Wesley and McCleon, 6

PUNTING	No.	Yds	Avg	Net Avg	TB	In 20	Lg	Blk
Baker	80	3156	39.5	33.2	7	21	68	1

SACKS: Holliday, 5.5

Miami Dolphins

		TD					
SCORING	Rush	Rec	Ret	PAT	FG	S	Pts
Mare	0	0	0	33/34	22/29	0	99
Chambers	0	11	0	0	0	0	66
R. Williams	9	1	0	0	0	0	60
Fiedler	3	0	0	0	0	0	18
McKnight	1	2	0	0	0	0	18
McMichael	0	2	1	0	0	0	18

RUSHING	No.	Yds	Avg	Lg	TD
R. Williams	392	1372	3.5	45	9
Minor	41	193	4.7	26	1

PASSING	Att	Comp	Pct Comp	Yds	Avg Gain	TD	Int	Rating Pts
Fiedler	314	179	57.0	2138	6.81	11	13	72.4
Griese	130	74	56.9	813	6.25	5	6	69.2

RECEIVING	No.	Yds	Avg	Lg	TD
Chambers	64	963	15.0	57	11
R. Williams	50	351	7.0	59	1
McMichael	49	598	12.2	46	2
Thompson	26	359	13.8	31	0
McKnight	23	285	12.4	80	2

INTERCEPTIONS: Surtain, 7

PUNTING	No.	Yds	Avg	Net Avg	TB	In 20	Lg	Blk
Turk	68	2631	38.7	34.5	7	23	57	0
Royals	16	643	40.2	36.3	1	5	50	0

SACKS: Ogunleye, 15

New England Patriots

		TD					
SCORING	Rush	Rec	Ret	PAT	FG	S	Pts
Vinatieri	0	0	0	37/38	25/34	0	112
Givens	0	6	0	0	0	0	36
Cloud	5	0	0	0	0	0	30
T. Brown	0	4	0	0	0	0	24
Graham	0	4	0	0	0	0	24

Three tied with 18.

RUSHING	No.	Yds	Avg	Lg	TD
Smith	182	642	3.5	30	3
Faulk	178	638	3.6	23	0
Cloud	27	118	4.4	42	5

PASSING	Att	Comp	Pct Comp	Yds	Avg Gain	TD	Int	Rating Pts
Brady	527	317	60.2	3620	6.87	23	12	85.9

RECEIVING	No.	Yds	Avg	Lg	TD
Branch	57	803	14.1	66	3
Faulk	48	440	9.2	27	0
T. Brown	40	472	11.8	82	4
Graham	28	409	10.8	38	4
Givens	34	510	15.0	57	6
Fauria	28	285	10.2	28	2

INTERCEPTIONS: Law and Poole, 6

PUNTING	No.	Yds	Avg	Net Avg	TB	In 20	Lg	Blk
Walter	76	2865	37.7	33.6	3	25	52	1

SACKS: Vrabel, 9.5

New York Jets

		TD					
SCORING	Rush	Rec	Ret	PAT	FG	S	Pts
Brien	0	0	0	24/24	27/32	0	105
Moss	0	10	0	0	0	0	60
Becht	0	4	1	0	0	0	26
Jordan	4	0	0	0	0	0	24

Four tied with 12.

RUSHING	No.	Yds	Avg	Lg	TD
Martin	323	1308	4.0	56	2
Jordan	46	190	4.1	39	4

PASSING	Att	Comp	Pct Comp	Yds	Avg Gain	TD	Int	Rating Pts
Pennington	297	189	63.6	2139	7.20	13	12	82.9
Testaverde	198	123	62.1	1385	6.99	7	2	90.6

RECEIVING	No.	Yds	Avg	Lg	TD
Moss	74	1105	14.9	65	10
Sowell	47	436	9.3	44	1
Conway	46	640	13.9	45	2
Martin	42	262	6.2	29	0
Becht	40	356	8.9	29	4
Chrebet	27	289	10.7	29	1

INTERCEPTIONS: Beasley, 3

PUNTING	No.	Yds	Avg	Net Avg	TB	In 20	Lg	Blk
Stryzinski	71	2655	37.4	31.3	4	22	55	1

SACKS: Ellis, 12.5

Oakland Raiders

SCORING

		TD					
SCORING	Rush	Rec	Ret	PAT	FG	S	Pts
Janikowski	0	0	0	28/29	22/25	0	94
Crockett	7	0	0	0	0	0	42
Buchanon	0	0	4	0	0	0	24
Garner	3	1	0	0	0	0	24
Wheatley	4	0	0	0	0	0	24
Brown	0	2	0	0	0	0	12
Rice	0	2	0	0	0	0	12

RUSHING

RUSHING	No.	Yds	Avg	Lg	TD
Wheatley	159	678	4.3	41	4
Garner	120	553	4.6	33	3
Fargas	40	203	5.1	53	0
Crockett	48	145	3.0	44	7

PASSING

PASSING	Att	Comp	Pct Comp	Yds	Avg Gain	TD	Int	Rating Pts
Gannon	225	125	55.6	1274	5.66	6	4	73.5
Mirer	221	116	52.5	1267	5.73	3	5	64.8

RECEIVING

RECEIVING	No.	Yds	Avg	Lg	TD
Rice	63	869	13.8	47	2
Brown	52	567	10.9	36	2
Garner	48	386	8.0	46	1
Jolley	31	250	8.1	26	1
Porter	28	361	12.9	35	1

INTERCEPTIONS: Buchanon, 6

PUNTING

PUNTING	No.	Yds	Avg	Net Avg	TB	In 20	Lg	Blk
Lechler	96	4503	46.9	37.2	13	27	73	0

SACKS: Coleman, 5.5

San Diego Chargers

SCORING

		TD					
SCORING	Rush	Rec	Ret	PAT	FG	S	Pts
Tomlinson	13	4	0	0	0	0	102
Christie	0	0	0	36/36	15/20	0	81
Boston	0	7	0	1	0	0	44
Parker	0	3	0	0	0	0	18

RUSHING

RUSHING	No.	Yds	Avg	Lg	TD
Tomlinson	313	1645	5.3	73	13
Flutie	33	168	5.1	17	2

PASSING

PASSING	Att	Comp	Pct Comp	Yds	Avg Gain	TD	Int	Rating Pts
Brees	357	205	57.6	2108	5.92	11	15	67.5
Flutie	167	91	54.5	1097	6.57	9	4	82.8

RECEIVING

RECEIVING	No.	Yds	Avg	Lg	TD
Tomlinson	100	725	7.3	73	4
Boston	70	880	12.6	46	7
Gates	24	389	16.2	48	2
E. Parker	18	244	13.6	33	3

INTERCEPTIONS: Jammer, 4

PUNTING

PUNTING	No.	Yds	Avg	Net Avg	TB	In 20	Lg	Blk
Bennett	82	3436	41.9	36.2	3	28	56	0

SACKS: Scott, 6.5

Pittsburgh Steelers

SCORING

		TD					
SCORING	Rush	Rec	Ret	PAT	FG	S	Pts
Reed	0	0	0	31/32	23/32	0	100
Ward	0	10	0	0	0	0	60
Bettis	7	0	0	1	0	0	44
Burress	0	4	0	0	0	0	24
Randle El	0	1	2	0	0	0	18

RUSHING

RUSHING	No.	Yds	Avg	Lg	TD
Bettis	246	811	3.3	21	7
Zereoue	132	433	3.3	22	2

PASSING

PASSING	Att	Comp	Pct Comp	Yds	Avg Gain	TD	Int	Rating Pts
Maddox	519	298	57.4	3414	6.58	18	17	75.3

RECEIVING

RECEIVING	No.	Yds	Avg	Lg	TD
Ward	95	1163	12.2	50	10
Burress	60	860	14.3	47	4
Zereoue	40	310	7.8	29	0
Randle El	37	364	9.8	32	1
Doering	18	240	13.3	53	1

INTERCEPTIONS: Alexander, 4

PUNTING

PUNTING	No.	Yds	Avg	Net Avg	TB	In 20	Lg	Blk
Miller	84	3521	41.9	36.0	8	27	72	1

SACKS: von Oelhoffen, 8.0

Tennessee Titans

SCORING

		TD					
SCORING	Rush	Rec	Ret	PAT	FG	S	Pts
Anderson	0	0	0	42/42	27/31	0	123
Mason	0	8	0	0	0	0	48
McCareins	0	7	1	0	0	0	48
George	5	0	0	0	0	0	30
Calico	0	4	0	1	0	0	26
McNair	4	0	0	1	0	0	26

RUSHING

RUSHING	No.	Yds	Avg	Lg	TD
George	312	1031	3.3	27	5
Brown	56	221	3.9	28	0
Holcombe	63	201	3.2	21	1
McNair	38	138	3.6	23	4

PASSING

PASSING	Att	Comp	Pct Comp	Yds	Avg Gain	TD	Int	Rating Pts
McNair	400	250	62.5	3215	8.04	24	7	100.4
Volek	69	44	63.8	545	7.90	4	1	101.4

RECEIVING

RECEIVING	No.	Yds	Avg	Lg	TD
Mason	95	1303	13.7	50	8
McCareins	47	813	17.3	73	7
Kinney	41	381	9.3	28	3
Bennett	32	504	15.8	48	4
George	22	163	7.4	22	0
Holcombe	19	121	6.4	11	1
Calico	18	297	16.5	45	4

INTERCEPTIONS: Rolle, 6

PUNTING

PUNTING	No.	Yds	Avg	Net Avg	TB	In 20	Lg	Blk
Hentrich	71	3117	43.9	37.8	8	26	58	0

SACKS: Kearse, 9.5

Arizona Cardinals

SCORING

	TD						
SCORING	Rush	Rec	Ret	PAT	FG	S	Pts
Boldin	0	8	0	0	0	0	48
Rackers	0	0	0	8/8	9/12	0	35
Duncan	0	0	0	5/6	6/10	0	23
Jones	0	3	0	0	0	0	18
Gramatica	0	0	0	6/6	3/4	0	15

RUSHING

RUSHING	No.	Yds	Avg	Lg	TD
Shipp	228	830	3.6	36	0
Smith	90	256	2.8	22	2
Blake	30	177	5.9	19	2
McCown	28	158	5.6	16	1

PASSING

PASSING	Att	Comp	Pct Comp	Yds	Avg Gain	TD	Int	Rating Pts
Blake	367	208	56.7	2247	6.12	13	15	69.6
McCown	166	95	57.2	1018	6.13	5	6	70.3

RECEIVING

RECEIVING	No.	Yds	Avg	Lg	TD
Boldin	101	1377	13.6	71	8
Jones	55	517	9.4	34	3
B. Johnson	35	438	12.5	54	1
Shipp	30	184	6.1	34	0

INTERCEPTIONS: Jackson, 6

PUNTING	No.	Yds	Avg	Net Avg	TB	In 20	Lg	Blk
Player	82	3511	42.8	34.4	9	19	64	1

SACKS: D. Johnson and Thompson, 3

Carolina Panthers

SCORING

	TD						
SCORING	Rush	Rec	Ret	PAT	FG	S	Pts
Kasay	0	0	0	29/30	32/38	0	125
Davis	8	0	0	0	0	0	48
Smith	0	7	1	0	0	0	48
Proehl	0	4	0	0	0	0	24
Muhammad	0	3	0	0	0	0	18

RUSHING

RUSHING	No.	Yds	Avg	Lg	TD
Davis	318	1444	4.5	40	8
Foster	113	429	3.8	21	0

PASSING

PASSING	Att	Comp	Pct Comp	Yds	Avg Gain	TD	Int	Rating Pts
Delhomme	449	266	59.2	3219	7.17	19	16	80.6

RECEIVING

RECEIVING	No.	Yds	Avg	Lg	TD
S. Smith	88	1110	12.6	67	7
Muhammad	54	837	15.5	60	3
Proehl	27	389	14.4	66	4
Foster	26	207	8.0	47	2

INTERCEPTIONS: Minter, Manning, and Grant, 3

PUNTING	No.	Yds	Avg	Net Avg	TB	In 20	Lg	Blk
S'rbrun	77	3433	44.6	35.6	9	22	64	3

SACKS: Rucker, 12

Atlanta Falcons

SCORING

	TD						
SCORING	Rush	Rec	Ret	PAT	FG	S	Pts
Feely	0	0	0	32/33	19/27	0	89
Duckett	11	0	0	0	0	0	66
Dunn	3	2	0	0	0	0	30
Crumpler	0	3	0	0	0	0	18
Price	0	3	0	0	0	0	18

RUSHING

RUSHING	No.	Yds	Avg	Lg	TD
Duckett	197	779	4.0	55	11
Dunn	125	672	5.4	69	3
Vick	50	255	6.4	43	1

PASSING

PASSING	Att	Comp	Pct Comp	Yds	Avg Gain	TD	Int	Rating Pts
D. Johnson	243	136	56.0	1655	6.81	8	12	67.5
Kittner	114	44	38.6	391	3.43	2	6	32.5
Vick	100	50	50.0	585	5.85	4	3	69.0

RECEIVING

RECEIVING	No.	Yds	Avg	Lg	TD
Price	64	838	13.1	49	3
Crumpler	44	552	12.5	63	3
Dunn	37	336	9.1	86	2
Finnetan	26	368	14.2	38	2
Griffith	21	122	5.8	24	2

INTERCEPTIONS: Bolden, McBride, and Carpenter, 3

PUNTING	No.	Yds	Avg	Net Avg	TB	In 20	Lg	Blk
Mohr	87	3473	39.9	36.0	2	19	54	0

SACKS: E. Johnson, 8

Chicago Bears

SCORING

	TD						
SCORING	Rush	Rec	Ret	PAT	FG	S	Pts
Edinger	0	0	0	27/27	26/36	0	105
Thomas	6	0	0	0	0	0	36
Booker	0	4	0	0	0	0	24
Stewart	3	0	0	1	0	0	20
White	0	3	0	0	0	0	18

RUSHING

RUSHING	No.	Yds	Avg	Lg	TD
Thomas	244	1024	4.2	67	6
Stewart	59	290	4.9	25	3
Forsey	50	191	3.8	17	2

PASSING

PASSING	Att	Comp	Pct Comp	Yds	Avg Gain	TD	Int	Rating Pts
Stewart	251	126	50.2	1418	5.65	7	12	56.8
Chandler	192	107	55.7	1050	5.47	3	7	61.3

RECEIVING

RECEIVING	No.	Yds	Avg	Lg	TD
Booker	52	715	13.8	61	4
White	49	583	11.9	49	3
Clark	44	433	9.8	31	2
Terrell	43	361	8.4	35	1

INTERCEPTIONS: Azumah and Tillman, 4

PUNTING	No.	Yds	Avg	Net Avg	TB	In 20	Lg	Blk
Maynard	79	3258	41.2	34.6	9	23	53	2

SACKS: A. Brown, 5

Dallas Cowboys

SCORING

SCORING	Rush	Rec	TD Ret	PAT	FG	S	Pts
Cundiff	0	0	0	30/31	23/29	0	99
Anderson	1	4	0	0	0	0	30
Glenn	0	5	0	0	0	0	30
Hambrick	5	0	0	0	0	0	30

RUSHING

RUSHING	No.	Yds	Avg	Lg	TD
Hambrick	275	972	3.5	42	5
Anderson	70	306	4.4	19	1
Carter	68	257	3.8	19	2
Cason	40	220	5.5	63	2

PASSING

PASSING	Att	Comp	Pct Comp	Yds	Avg Gain	TD	Int	Rating Pts
Carter	505	292	57.8	3302	6.54	17	21	71.4

RECEIVING

RECEIVING	No.	Yds	Avg	Lg	TD
Anderson	69	493	7.1	37	4
Glenn	52	754	14.5	51	5
Bryant	39	550	14.1	55	2
Witten	35	347	9.9	36	1
Galloway	34	672	19.8	64	2

INTERCEPTIONS: Newman, 4

PUNTING	No.	Yds	Avg	Net Avg	TB	In 20	Lg	Blk
Gowin	94	3665	39.0	34.9	8	25	59	0

SACKS: Ellis, 8

Green Bay Packers

SCORING

SCORING	Rush	Rec	TD Ret	PAT	FG	S	Pts
Green	15	5	0	0	0	0	120
Longwell	0	0	0	51/51	23/26	0	120
J. Walker	0	9	0	0	0	0	54
Franks	0	4	0	2	0	0	28
Ferguson	0	4	0	0	0	0	24

RUSHING

RUSHING	No.	Yds	Avg	Lg	TD
Green	355	1883	5.3	98	15
Davenport	77	420	5.5	76	2
Fisher	40	200	5.0	19	1

PASSING

PASSING	Att	Comp	Pct Comp	Yds	Avg Gain	TD	Int	Rating Pts
Favre	471	308	65.4	3361	7.14	32	21	90.4

RECEIVING

RECEIVING	No.	Yds	Avg	Lg	TD
Driver	52	621	11.9	41	2
Green	50	367	7.3	27	5
J. Walker	41	716	17.5	66	9
Ferguson	38	520	13.7	47	4
Franks	30	241	8.0	24	4
Henderson	24	214	8.9	22	3

INTERCEPTIONS: Sharper, 5

PUNTING	No.	Yds	Avg	Net Avg	TB	In 20	Lg	Blk
Bidwell	69	2875	41.7	35.1	7	16	60	0

SACKS: Gbaja-Biamila, 10

Detroit Lions

SCORING

SCORING	Rush	Rec	TD Ret	PAT	FG	S	Pts
Hanson	0	0	0	26/27	22/23	0	92
Hakim	0	4	0	1	0	0	26
Bryson	3	0	0	0	0	0	18
C. Rogers	0	3	0	0	0	0	18

RUSHING

RUSHING	No.	Yds	Avg	Lg	TD
Bryson	158	606	3.8	39	3
Gary	113	384	3.4	27	2

PASSING

PASSING	Att	Comp	Pct Comp	Yds	Avg Gain	TD	Int	Rating Pts
Harrington	554	309	55.8	2880	5.20	17	22	63.9

RECEIVING

RECEIVING	No.	Yds	Avg	Lg	TD
Bryson	54	340	6.3	26	0
Hakim	49	449	9.2	28	4
Ricks	37	434	11.7	38	2
Schroeder	36	397	11.0	26	2
Schlesinger	34	247	7.3	33	2
Fitzsimmons	23	160	7.0	22	2
C. Rogers	22	243	11.0	33	3

INTERCEPTIONS: Bly, 6

PUNTING	No.	Yds	Avg	Net Avg	TB	In 20	Lg	Blk
N. Harris	63	2531	40.2	33.1	5	11	51	1
Jett	25	995	39.8	35.6	3	8	58	0
Hanson	7	264	37.7	33.4	0	1	50	0

SACKS: Hall and Porcher, 4.5

Minnesota Vikings

SCORING

SCORING	Rush	Rec	TD Ret	PAT	FG	S	Pts
Elling	0	0	0	48/48	18/25	0	102
Moss	0	17	0	0	0	0	102
M. Williams	5	3	0	0	0	0	48
O. Smith	5	0	0	1	0	0	32
Campbell	0	4	0	0	0	0	24
Culpepper	4	0	0	0	0	0	24
Kleinsasser	0	4	0	0	0	0	24

RUSHING

RUSHING	No.	Yds	Avg	Lg	TD
M. Williams	174	745	4.3	61	5
O. Smith	107	579	5.4	47	5
Bennett	90	447	5.0	28	1
Culpepper	73	422	5.8	42	4

PASSING

PASSING	Att	Comp	Pct Comp	Yds	Avg Gain	TD	Int	Rating Pts
Culpepper	454	295	65.0	3479	7.66	25	11	96.4
Frerotte	65	38	58.5	690	10.62	7	2	118.1

RECEIVING

RECEIVING	No.	Yds	Avg	Lg	TD
Moss	111	1632	14.7	72	17
M. Williams	65	644	9.9	42	3
Kleinsasser	46	401	8.7	19	4
Burleson	29	455	15.7	52	2
Campbell	25	522	20.9	72	4

INTERCEPTIONS: Russell, 9

PUNTING	No.	Yds	Avg	Net Avg	TB	In 20	Lg	Blk
Johnson	56	2191	39.1	32.6	5	12	55	1
Araguz	7	271	38.7	27.7	0	1	44	0

SACKS: K. Williams, 10.5

New Orleans Saints

SCORING	Rush	Rec	Ret	PAT	FG	S	Pts
			TD				
Carney	0	0	0	36/37	22/30	0	102
Horn	0	10	0	0	0	0	60
McAllister	8	0	0	0	0	0	48
B. Williams	0	5	0	0	0	0	30
Pathon	0	4	0	0	0	0	24
Stallworth	0	3	0	0	0	0	18

RUSHING	No.	Yds	Avg	Lg	TD
McAllister	351	1641	4.7	76	8
Brooks	54	175	3.2	15	2

PASSING	Att	Comp	Pct Comp	Yds	Avg Gain	TD	Int	Rating Pts
Brooks........	518	306	59.1	3546	6.85	24	8	88.8

RECEIVING	No.	Yds	Avg	Lg	TD
Horn	78	973	12.5	50	10
McAllister	69	516	7.5	39	0
Pathon	44	578	13.1	40	4
B. Williams................	41	436	10.6	31	5
Conwell	26	290	11.2	32	2
Stallworth	25	485	19.5	76	3

INTERCEPTIONS: Thomas, 4

PUNTING	No.	Yds	Avg	Net Avg	TB	In 20	Lg	Blk
Berger	71	3144	44.3	38.2	5	28	59	1

SACKS: Grant, 10

Philadelphia Eagles

SCORING	Rush	Rec	Ret	PAT	FG	S	Pts
			TD				
Akers	0	0	0	42/42	24/29	0	114
Westbrook............	7	4	2	0	0	0	78
Buckhalter	8	1	0	0	0	0	54
Staley..................	5	2	0	0	0	0	42
McNabb	3	0	0	0	0	0	18
Ritchie	0	3	0	0	0	0	18

RUSHING	No.	Yds	Avg	Lg	TD
Westbrook	117	613	5.2	62	7
Buckhalter	126	542	4.3	64	8
Staley........................	96	463	4.8	22	5
McNabb	71	355	5.0	34	3

PASSING	Att	Comp	Pct Comp	Yds	Avg Gain	TD	Int	Rating Pts
McNabb......	478	275	57.5	3216	6.73	16	11	79.6

RECEIVING	No.	Yds	Avg	Lg	TD
Thrash	49	558	11.4	51	1
Westbrook	37	332	9.0	38	4
Pinkston...................	36	575	16.0	59	2
Staley	36	382	10.6	52	2
Mitchell....................	35	498	14.2	39	2
Smith	27	321	11.9	36	1
C. Lewis	23	293	12.7	29	1

INTERCEPTIONS: M. Lewis and Vincent, 3

PUNTING	No.	Yds	Avg	Net Avg	TB	In 20	Lg	Blk
D. Johnson..	79	3207	40.6	34.6	10	27	60	0

SACKS: Simon, 7.5

New York Giants

SCORING	Rush	Rec	Ret	PAT	FG	S	Pts
			TD				
Bryant..................	0	0	0	17/17	11/14	0	50
Hilliard	0	6	0	0	0	0	36
Conway	0	0	0	6/6	9/12	0	33
Toomer	0	5	0	0	0	0	30
Barber	2	1	0	1	0	0	20
Levens	3	0	0	0	0	0	18

RUSHING	No.	Yds	Avg	Lg	TD
Barber	278	1216	4.4	27	2
Levens......................	68	197	2.9	17	3

PASSING	Att	Comp	Pct Comp	Yds	Avg Gain	TD	Int	Rating Pts
Collins.........	500	284	56.8	3110	6.22	13	16	70.7
Palmer.........	116	60	51.7	532	4.59	3	4	58.5

RECEIVING	No.	Yds	Avg	Lg	TD
Barber	69	461	6.7	36	1
Toomer	63	1057	16.8	77	5
Hilliard	60	608	10.1	38	6
Shockey	48	535	11.1	46	2
Carter	26	309	11.9	30	0

INTERCEPTIONS: Four tied with 2.

PUNTING	No.	Yds	Avg	Net Avg	TB	In 20	Lg	Blk
Feagles	90	3641	40.5	33.9	6	31	59	1

SACKS: Strahan, 18.5

St. Louis Rams

SCORING	Rush	Rec	Ret	PAT	FG	S	Pts
			TD				
Wilkins..................	0	0	0	46/46	39/42	0	163
Holt.....................	0	12	0	0	0	0	72
Faulk	10	1	0	0	0	0	66
Bruce	0	5	0	0	0	0	30
Bulger	4	0	0	0	0	0	24
Harris	4	0	0	0	0	0	24
Looker	0	3	0	0	0	0	18

RUSHING	No.	Yds	Avg	Lg	TD
Faulk.........................	209	818	3.9	52	10
Gordon	71	298	4.2	20	1
Harris........................	85	255	3.0	18	4

PASSING	Att	Comp	Pct Comp	Yds	Avg Gain	TD	Int	Rating Pts
Bulger	532	336	63.2	3845	7.23	22	22	81.4
Warner.........	65	38	58.5	365	5.62	1	1	72.9

RECEIVING	No.	Yds	Avg	Lg	TD
Holt..........................	117	1696	14.5	48	12
Bruce.:......................	69	981	14.2	41	5
Looker	47	495	10.5	41	3
Faulk.........................	45	290	6.4	30	1
Manumaleuna	29	238	8.2	39	2

INTERCEPTIONS: Four tied with 4.

PUNTING	No.	Yds	Avg	Net Avg	TB	In 20	Lg	Blk
Landeta....	59	2525	42.8	32.9	5	14	57	0

SACKS: Little, 12.5

San Francisco 49ers

SCORING	TD Rush	Rec	Ret	PAT	FG	S	Pts
Peterson	0	0	0	22/23	12/15	0	58
Owens	0	9	0	0	0	0	54
Barlow	6	1	0	0	0	0	42
Garcia	7	0	0	0	0	0	42
Streets	0	7	0	0	0	0	42
Pochman	0	0	0	9/10	8/15	0	33
Chandler	0	0	0	7/8	6/7	0	25
Hearst	3	1	0	0	0	0	24

RUSHING	No.	Yds	Avg	Lg	TD
Barlow	201	1024	5.1	78	6
Hearst	178	768	4.3	36	3
Garcia	56	319	5.7	21	7

PASSING	Att	Comp	Pct Comp	Yds	Avg Gain	TD	Int	Rating Pts
Garcia	392	225	57.4	2704	6.90	18	13	80.1
Rattay	118	73	61.9	856	7.25	7	2	96.6

RECEIVING	No.	Yds	Avg	Lg	TD
Owens	80	1102	13.8	75	9
Streets	47	595	12.7	41	7
Weaver	35	437	12.5	30	1
Wilson	35	396	11.3	29	2
Barlow	35	307	8.8	48	1
Hearst	25	211	8.4	26	1

INTERCEPTIONS: Parrish, 9

PUNTING	No.	Yds	Avg	Net Avg	TB	In 20	Lg	Blk
Lafleur	68	2629	38.7	33.5	3	17	56	1

SACKS: Peterson, 7

Tampa Bay Buccaneers

SCORING	TD Rush	Rec	Ret	PAT	FG	S	Pts
Gramatica	0	0	0	33/34	16/26	0	81
McCardell	0	8	1	0	0	0	54
K. Johnson	0	3	0	0	0	0	18
Jones	3	0	0	0	0	0	18

RUSHING	No.	Yds	Avg	Lg	TD
Pittman	187	751	4.0	17	0
Jones	137	627	4.6	61	3
Stecker	37	125	3.4	15	0

PASSING	Att	Comp	Pct Comp	Yds	Avg Gain	TD	Int	Rating Pts
B. Johnson	570	354	62.1	3811	6.69	26	21	81.5

RECEIVING	No.	Yds	Avg	Lg	TD
McCardell	84	1174	14.0	76	8
Pittman	75	597	8.0	68	2
K. Johnson	45	600	13.3	39	3
Lee	33	432	13.1	72	2
Jones	24	180	7.5	29	0
Dilger	22	244	11.1	48	1

INTERCEPTIONS: D. Smith, 5

PUNTING	No.	Yds	Avg	Net Avg	TB	In 20	Lg	Blk
Tupa	83	3590	43.3	35.9	6	26	60	0

SACKS: Rice, 15

Seattle Seahawks

SCORING	TD Rush	Rec	Ret	PAT	FG	S	Pts
J. Brown	0	0	0	48/48	22/30	0	114
Alexander	14	2	0	0	0	0	96
Jackson	0	9	0	0	0	0	54
Engram	0	6	1	0	0	0	42
K. Robinson	0	4	1	0	0	0	30
Mili	0	4	0	0	0	0	24

RUSHING	No.	Yds	Avg	Lg	TD
Alexander	326	1435	4.4	55	14
Morris	38	239	6.3	43	0
Strong	37	174	4.7	21	1

PASSING	Att	Comp	Pct Comp	Yds	Avg Gain	TD	Int	Rating Pts
Hasselbeck	513	313	61.0	3841	7.49	26	15	88.8

RECEIVING	No.	Yds	Avg	Lg	TD
Jackson	68	1137	16.7	80	9
K. Robinson	65	896	13.8	38	4
Engram	52	637	12.3	34	6
Mili	46	492	10.7	46	4
Alexander	42	295	7.0	22	2
Strong	29	216	7.4	32	0

INTERCEPTIONS: Tongue, 4

PUNTING	No.	Yds	Avg	Net Avg	TB	In 20	Lg	Blk
Rouen	67	2762	41.2	37.1	3	29	61	2

SACKS: Okeafor, 8

Washington Redskins

SCORING	TD Rush	Rec	Ret	PAT	FG	S	Pts
Hall	0	0	0	26/27	25/33	0	101
McCants	0	6	0	2	0	0	40
Coles	0	6	0	0	0	0	36
Gardner	0	5	0	0	0	0	30
Cartwright	4	0	0	0	0	0	24

RUSHING	No.	Yds	Avg	Lg	TD
Canidate	142	600	4.2	38	1
Cartwright	107	411	3.8	22	4
Betts	77	255	3.3	13	2
Morton	48	216	4.5	27	0

PASSING	Att	Comp	Pct Comp	Yds	Avg Gain	TD	Int	Rating Pts
Ramsey	337	179	53.1	2166	6.43	14	9	75.8
Hasselbeck	177	95	53.7	1012	5.72	5	7	63.6

RECEIVING	No.	Yds	Avg	Lg	TD
Coles	82	1204	14.7	64	6
Gardner	59	600	10.2	35	5
McCants	27	360	13.3	32	6
Cartwright	18	176	9.8	40	0

INTERCEPTIONS: Smoot, 4

PUNTING	No.	Yds	Avg	Net Avg	TB	In 20	Lg	Blk
Barker	84	3377	40.2	34.3	5	24	69	0

SACKS: Armstead, 6.5

First two rounds of the 69th annual NFL Draft, held April 25–26 in New York City.

First Round

Team	Selection	Position
1. ....San Diego (to NYG)	Eli Manning, Mississippi	QB
2. ....Oakland	Robert Gallery, Iowa	OT
3. ....Arizona	Larry Fitzgerald, Pittsburgh	WR
4. ....NY Giants (to San Diego)	Philip Rivers, N Carolina St	QB
5. ....Washington	Sean Taylor, Miami (FL)	FS
6. .,......Cleveland, (from Detroit)	Kellen Winslow Jr., Miami (FL)	TE
7. ....Detroit (from Clev)	Roy Williams, Texas	WR
8. ....Atlanta	DeAngelo Hall, Va. Tech	CB
9. ....:Jacksonville	Reggie Williams, Washington	WR
10. ......Houston	Dunta Robinson, S Carolina	CB
11. ......Pittsburgh	Ben Roethlisberger Miami (OH)	QB
12. ......NY Jets	Jonathan Vilma, Miami (FL)	LB
13. ......Buffalo	Lee Evans, Wisconsin	WR
14. ......Chicago	Tommie Harris, Oklahoma	DT
15. ......Tampa Bay	Michael Clayton, Louisiana St	WR
16. ......Philadelphia (from SF)	Shawn Andrews, Arkansas	OT
17. ......Denver (from Cin)	D.J. Williams, Miami (FL)	LB
18. ......New Orleans	Will Smith, Ohio St	DE
19. ......Miami (from Minn)	Vernon Carey, Miami (FL)	G
20. ......Minnesota (from Mia)	Kenechi Udeze, Southern Cal	DE
21. ......New England (from Balt)	Vince Wilfork, Miami (FL)	DT
22. ......Buffalo (from Dallas)	J.P. Losman, Tulane	QB
23. ......Seattle	Marcus Tubbs, Texas,	DT
24. ......St. Louis (from Den via Cin)	Steven Jackson, Ore. St	RB
25. ......Green Bay	Ahmad Carroll, Arkansas	CB
26. ......Cincinnati (from StL)	Chris Perry, Michigan	RB
27. ......Houston (from Tenn)	Jason Babin, Western Michigan	DE
28. ......Carolina (from Phil via SF)	Chris Gamble, Ohio St	CB
29. ......Atlanta (from Ind)	Michael Jenkins, Ohio St	WR
30. ......Detroit (from KC)	Kevin Jones, Virginia Tech	RB
31. ......San Francisco (from Car)	Rashaun Woods, Oklahoma St	WR
32. ......New England	Ben Watson, Georgia	TE

Second Round

Team	Selection	Position
33. ......Arizona	Karlos Dansby, Auburn	LB
34. ......NY Giants	Chris Snee, Boston Coll ·	G
35. ......San Diego	Igor Olshansky, Oregon	DT
36. ......Kansas City (from Detroit)	Junior Siavii, Oregon	DT
37. ......Detroit (from Clev)	Teddy Lehman, Oklahoma	LB
38. ......Pittsburgh (from Atl via Ind)	Ricardo Colclough, Tusculum	CB
39. ......Jacksonville	Daryl Smith, Georgia Tech	LB
40. ......Tennessee (from Hou)	Ben Troupe, Florida	TE
41. ......Denver (from Wash)	Tatum Bell, Oklahoma St	RB
42. ......Tennessee (from NYJ)	Travis LaBoy, Hawaii	DE
43. ......Dallas (from Buff)	Julius Jones, Notre Dame	RB
44. ......Indianapolis (from Pitt)	Bob Sanders, Iowa	SS
45. ......Oakland (from TB)	Jake Grove, Virginia Tech	C
46. ......San Francisco	Justin Smiley, Alabama	G
47. ......Chicago	Terry Johnson, Washington	DT
48. ......Minnesota (from NO)	Dontarrious Thomas, Auburn	LB
49. ......Cincinnati	Keiwan Ratliff, Florida	CB
50. ......New Orleans (from Minn)	Devery Henderson, Louisiana St	WR
51. ......Baltimore (reacq. from SF)	Dwan Edwards, Ore. St	DT
52. ......Dallas	Jacob Rogers, Southern Cal	OT
53. ......Seattle	Michael Boulware, Florida St	LB
54. ......Denver	Darius Watts, Marshall	WR
55. ......Jacksonville (from GB)	Greg Jones, Florida St	RB
56. ......Cincinnati (from Mia via NE)	Madieu Williams, Maryland	FS
57. ......Tennessee	Antwan Odom, Alabama	DE
58. ......San Francisco (from Phil)	Shawntae Spencer, Pittsburgh	CB
59. ......Cleveland (from Ind)	Sean Jones, Georgia	FS
60. ......New Orleans (from StL)	Courtney Watson, Notre Dame	LB
61. ......Kansas City	Kris Wilson, Pittsburgh	TE
62. ......Carolina	Keary Colbert, Southern Cal	WR
63. ......New England	Marquise Hill, Louisiana St	DE

Final Standings

	W	L	T	Pct	Pts	OP
Berlin*	9	1	0	.900	289	195
Frankfurt*	7	3	0	.700	212	192
Amsterdam	5	5	0	.500	173	191
Cologne	4	6	0	.400	191	201
Rhein	3	7	0	.300	161	178
Scotland	2	8	0	.200	128	197

*Clinched World Bowl 2004 berth.

2004 World Bowl

June 12, 2004, in Gelsenkirchen, Germany

Berlin Thunder	7	3	13	7—30
Frankfurt Galaxy	3	7	0	14—24

FIRST QUARTER
Berlin: Sharpe 28 int return (Quast kick), 12:35.
Frankfurt: FG Kleinmann 28, 7:18

SECOND QUARTER
Frankfurt: Lewis 8 pass from O'Sullivan (Kleinmann kick), 0:59.
Berlin: FG Ruffin 38, 0:00.

THIRD QUARTER
Berlin: Gessner 60 pass from Alston (Quast kick), 11:25.
Berlin: FG Ruffin 42, 2:37.
Berlin: FG Ruffin 40, 0:53.

FOURTH QUARTER
Berlin: McCoo 69 run (Quast kick), 6:26.
Frankfurt: Haddad 17 pass from O'Sullivan (Kleinmann kick), 4:05.
Frankfurt: Lewis 19 pass from O'Sullivan (Kleinmann kick), 2:31.

A: 35,413. T: 3:04.

NFL Europe Individual Leaders

PASSING

	Att	Comp	Pct Comp	Yds	Avg Gain	TD	Pct TD	Int	Pct Int	Lg	Rating Pts
Davey, Berlin	206	126	61.2	1,676	8.14	19	9.2	6	2.9	52	105.6
O'Sullivan, Frankfurt	196	120	61.2	1,527	7.79	10	5.1	5	2.6	72	91.9
Van Dyke, Cologne	280	174	62.1	2,003	7.15	16	5.7	14	5.0	81	81.9
Hutchinson, Rhein	207	126	60.9	1,356	6.55	5	2.4	4	1.9	54	80.1
Stoerner, Amsterdam	259	147	56.8	1,788	6.90	11	4.2	10	3.9	57	76.2

RECEIVING

RECEPTIONS	No.	Yds	Avg	Lg	TD	YARDS	Yds	No.	Avg	Lg	TD
McCready, Scotland	59	472	8.0	32	1	Herzing, Rhein	656	49	13.4	54	1
Herzing, Rhein	49	656	13.4	54	1	Horn, Amsterdam	593	34	17.4	54	1
Quinnie, Rhein	46	408	8.9	22	3	Taylor, Amsterdam	573	42	13.6	39	5
Taylor, Amsterdam	42	573	13.6	39	5	Gessner, Berlin	566	38	14.9	47	6
Gessner, Berlin	38	566	14.9	47	6	Morris, Cologne	530	35	15.1	49	4

RUSHING

	Att	Yds	Avg	Lg	TD
McCoo, Berlin	148	669	4.5	46	4
Hicks, Frankfurt	183	661	3.6	59	10
Cobourne, Cologne	134	570	4.3	33	0
Downs, Amsterdam	118	511	4.3	34	3
Reynolds, Rhein	120	405	3.4	21	4

Other Statistical Leaders

Points (TDs)	Hicks, Frankfurt	72
Points (Kicking)	Quast, Berlin	55
Yards from Scrimmage	McCoo, Berlin	1,037
Interceptions	Howard, Rhein	5
Sacks	Claybrooks, Cologne	10.0
Punting Avg	Murphy, Scotland	41.0
Punt Return Avg	Johnson, Cologne	12.4
Kickoff Return Avg	Davis, Rhein	30.1

THEY SAID IT

Dwight Smith, Buccaneers safety, speaking to The Tampa Tribune *about whether his teammates could make Mr. Blackwell's best-dressed list: "A lot of us aren't going to make anybody's anything, besides who can eat the most or who can smell the worst."*

EASTERN DIVISION

	W	L	T	Pts	PF	PA
†Montreal	13	5	0	26	562	409
*Toronto	9	9	0	18	473	433
Ottawa	7	11	0	14	467	581
Hamilton	1	17	0	2	293	583

WESTERN DIVISION

	W	L	T	Pts	PF	PA
†Edmonton	13	5	0	26	569	414
*Winnipeg	11	7	0	22	514	487
*Saskatchewan	11	7	0	22	535	430
*British Columbia	11	7	0	22	531	430
Calgary	5	13	0	10	323	502

†Clinched division title.

*Clinched playoff berth.

2003 Playoff Results

FIRST ROUND

TORONTO 28, British Columbia 7
Saskatchewan 37, WINNIPEG 21

SEMI-FINALS

MONTREAL 30, Toronto 26
EDMONTON 30, Saskatchewan 23

Home team in caps.

2003 Grey Cup Championship

Nov. 16, 2003, at Regina, Saskatchewan

Montreal Alouettes	0	21	1	0—22
Edmonton Eskimos	7	17	0	10—34

A: 50,909.

THEY SAID IT

Jim Haslett, Saints coach, on receiver Joe Horn, who was penalized during the 2003 season for behavior such as an incident in which he called his mother from the end zone on his cellphone. "He'll learn. He's only 32."

The Super Bowl

Results

	Date	Winner (Share)	Loser (Share)	Score	Site (Attendance)
I	1-15-67	Green Bay ($15,000)	Kansas City ($7,500)	35–10	Los Angeles (61,946)
II	1-14-68	Green Bay ($15,000)	Oakland ($7,500)	33–14	Miami (75,546)
III	1-12-69	NY Jets ($15,000)	Baltimore ($7,500)	16–7	Miami (75,389)
IV	1-11-70	Kansas City ($15,000)	Minnesota ($7,500)	23–7	New Orleans (80,562)
V	1-17-71	Baltimore ($15,000)	Dallas ($7,500)	16–13	Miami (79,204)
VI	1-16-72	Dallas ($15,000)	Miami ($7,500)	24–3	New Orleans (81,023)
VII	1-14-73	Miami ($15,000)	Washington ($7,500)	14–7	Los Angeles (90,182)
VIII	1-13-74	Miami ($15,000)	Minnesota ($7,500)	24–7	Houston (71,882)
IX	1-12-75	Pittsburgh ($15,000)	Minnesota ($7,500)	16–6	New Orleans (80,997)
X	1-18-76	Pittsburgh ($15,000)	Dallas ($7,500)	21–17	Miami (80,187)
XI	1-9-77	Oakland ($15,000)	Minnesota ($7,500)	32–14	Pasadena (103,438)
XII	1-15-78	Dallas ($18,000)	Denver ($9,000)	27–10	New Orleans (75,583)
XIII	1-21-79	Pittsburgh ($18,000)	Dallas ($9,000)	35–31	Miami (79,484)
XIV	1-20-80	Pittsburgh ($18,000)	Los Angeles ($9,000)	31–19	Pasadena (103,985)
XV	1-25-81	Oakland ($18,000)	Philadelphia ($9,000)	27–10	New Orleans (76,135)
XVI	1-24-82	San Francisco ($18,000)	Cincinnati ($9,000)	26–21	Pontiac, MI (81,270)
XVII	1-30-83	Washington ($36,000)	Miami ($18,000)	27–17	Pasadena (103,667)
XVIII	1-22-84	LA Raiders ($36,000)	Washington ($18,000)	38–9	Tampa (72,920)
XIX	1-20-85	San Francisco ($36,000)	Miami ($18,000)	38–16	Stanford (84,059)
XX	1-26-86	Chicago ($36,000)	New England ($18,000)	46–10	New Orleans (73,818)
XXI	1-25-87	NY Giants ($36,000)	Denver ($18,000)	39–20	Pasadena (101,063)
XXII	1-31-88	Washington ($36,000)	Denver ($18,000)	42–10	San Diego (73,302)
XXIII	1-22-89	San Francisco ($36,000)	Cincinnati ($18,000)	20–16	Miami (75,129)
XXIV	1-28-90	San Francisco ($36,000)	Denver ($18,000)	55–10	New Orleans (72,919)
XXV	1-27-91	NY Giants ($36,000)	Buffalo ($18,000)	20–19	Tampa (73,813)
XXVI	1-26-92	Washington ($36,000)	Buffalo ($18,000)	37–24	Minneapolis (63,130)
XXVII	1-31-93	Dallas ($36,000)	Buffalo ($18,000)	52–17	Pasadena (98,374)
XXVIII	1-30-94	Dallas ($38,000)	Buffalo ($23,500)	30–13	Atlanta (72,817)
XXIX	1-29-95	San Francisco ($42,000)	San Diego ($26,000)	49–26	Miami (74,107)
XXX	1-28-96	Dallas ($42,000)	Pittsburgh ($27,000)	27–17	Tempe, AZ (76,347)
XXXI	1-26-97	Green Bay ($48,000)	New England ($29,000)	35–21	New Orleans (72,301)
XXXII	1-25-98	Denver ($48,000)	Green Bay ($27,500)	31–24	San Diego (68,912)
XXXIII	1-31-99	Denver ($53,000)	Atlanta ($32,500)	34–19	Miami (74,803)
XXXIV	1-30-00	St. Louis ($58,000)	Tennessee ($33,000)	23–16	Atlanta (72,625)
XXXV	1-28-01	Baltimore ($58,000)	NY Giants ($34,500)	34–7	Tampa (71,921)
XXXVI	2-3-02	New England ($63,000)	St. Louis ($34,500)	20–17	New Orleans (72,922)
XXXVII	1-26-03	Tampa Bay ($64,000)	Oakland ($35,000)	48–21	San Diego (67,603)
XXXVIII	2-1-04	New England ($64,000)	Carolina ($35,000)	32–29	Houston (71,525)

Most Valuable Players

Super Bowl	Player/ Team	Position	Super Bowl	Player/ Team	Position
I	Bart Starr, GB	QB	XX	Richard Dent, Chi	DE
II	Bart Starr, GB	QB	XXI	Phil Simms, NYG	QB
III	Joe Namath, NYJ	QB	XXII	Doug Williams, Wash	QB
IV	Len Dawson, KC	QB	XXIII	Jerry Rice, SF	WR
V	Chuck Howley, Dall	LB	XXIV	Joe Montana, SF	QB
VI	Roger Staubach, Dall	QB	XXV	Ottis Anderson, NYG	RB
VII	Jake Scott, Mia	S	XXVI	Mark Rypien, Wash	QB
VIII	Larry Csonka, Mia	RB	XXVII	Troy Aikman, Dall	QB
IX	Franco Harris, Pitt	RB	XXVIII	Emmitt Smith, Dall	RB
X	Lynn Swann, Pitt	WR	XXIX	Steve Young, SF	QB
XI	Fred Biletnikoff, Oak	WR	XXX	Larry Brown, Dall	DB
XII	Randy White, Dall	DT	XXXI	Desmond Howard, GB	KR
	Harvey Martin, Dall	DE	XXXII	Terrell Davis, Den	RB
XIII	Terry Bradshaw, Pitt	QB	XXXIII	John Elway, Den	QB
XIV	Terry Bradshaw, Pitt	QB	XXXIV	Kurt Warner, StL	QB
XV	Jim Plunkett, Oak	QB	XXXV	Ray Lewis, Balt	LB
XVI	Joe Montana, SF	QB	XXXVI	Tom Brady, NE	QB
XVII	John Riggins, Wash	RB	XXXVII	Dexter Jackson, TB	S
XVIII	Marcus Allen, Rai	RB	XXXVIII	Tom Brady, NE	QB
XIX	Joe Montana, SF	QB			

Composite Standings

	W	L	Pct	Pts	Opp Pts
San Francisco 49ers	5	0	1.000	188	89
Baltimore Ravens	1	0	1.000	34	7
Chicago Bears	1	0	1.000	46	10
New York Jets	1	0	1.000	16	7
Tampa Bay Buccaneers	1	0	1.000	48	21
Pittsburgh Steelers	4	1	.800	120	100
Green Bay Packers	3	1	.750	127	76
Oakland/LA Raiders	3	2	.600	132	114
New York Giants	2	1	.667	66	73
Dallas Cowboys	5	3	.625	221	132
Washington Redskins	3	2	.600	122	103
New England Patriots	2	2	.500	83	127
Baltimore Colts	1	1	.500	23	29
Kansas City Chiefs	1	1	.500	33	42
Miami Dolphins	2	3	.400	74	103
Denver Broncos	2	4	.333	115	206
Los Angeles/St. Louis Rams	1	2	.333	59	67
Carolina Panthers	0	1	.000	29	32
San Diego Chargers	0	1	.000	26	49
Atlanta Falcons	0	1	.000	19	34
Tennesse Titans	0	1	.000	16	23
Philadelphia Eagles	0	1	.000	10	27
Cincinnati Bengals	0	2	.000	37	46
Buffalo Bills	0	4	.000	73	139
Minnesota Vikings	0	4	.000	34	95

Career Leaders

Passing

	GP	Att	Comp	Pct Comp	Yds	Avg Gain	TD	Pct TD	Int	Pct Int	Lg	Rating Pts
Joe Montana, SF	4	122	83	68.0	1142	9.36	11	9.0	0	0.0	44	127.8
Jim Plunkett, Rai	2	46	29	63.0	433	9.41	4	8.7	0	0.0	t80	122.8
Terry Bradshaw, Pitt	4	84	49	58.3	932	11.10	9	10.7	4	4.8	t75	112.8
Troy Aikman, Dall	3	80	56	70.0	689	8.61	5	6.3	1	1.3	t56	111.9
Bart Starr, GB	2	47	29	61.7	452	9.62	3	6.4	1	2.1	t62	106.0
Brett Favre, GB	2	69	39	56.5	502	7.28	5	7.2	1	1.4	t81	97.7
Roger Staubach, Dall	4	98	61	62.2	734	7.49	8	8.2	4	4.1	t45	95.4
Tom Brady, NE	2	75	48	64.0	499	6.65	4	5.3	1	1.3	52	95.4
Kurt Warner, StL	2	89	52	58.4	779	8.75	3	3.4	1	1.1	t73	93.8
Len Dawson, KC	2	44	28	63.6	353	8.02	2	4.5	2	4.5	t46	84.8

Note: Minimum 40 attempts.

Rushing

	GP	Yds	Att	Avg	Lg	TD
Franco Harris, Pitt	4	354	101	3.5	25	4
Larry Csonka, Mia	3	297	57	5.2	9	2
Emmitt Smith, Dall	3	289	70	4.1	38	5
Terrell Davis, Den	2	259	75	4.1	15	3
John Riggins, Wash	2	230	64	3.6	43	2
Timmy Smith, Wash	1	204	22	9.3	58	2
Thurman Thomas, Buff	4	204	52	3.9	31	4
Roger Craig, SF	3	198	52	3.8	18	2
Marcus Allen, Rai	1	191	20	9.6	t74	2
Antowain Smith, NE	2	175	44	4.0	17	2

Receiving

	GP	No.	Yds	Avg	Lg	TD
Jerry Rice, SF	4	33	589	17.9	t48	8
Andre Reed, Buff	4	27	323	11.9	40	0
Roger Craig, SF	3	20	212	10.6	40	2
Thurman Thomas, Buff	4	20	144	7.2	24	0
Jay Novacek, Dall	3	17	178	10.5	23	2
Lynn Swann, Pitt	4	16	364	22.8	t64	3
Michael Irvin, Dall	3	16	256	16.0	25	2
Chuck Foreman, Minn	3	15	139	9.3	26	0
Cliff Branch, Rai	3	14	181	12.9	50	3
Troy Brown, NE	2	14	165	11.8	23	0
Preston Pearson, Balt-Pitt-Dall	5	12	105	8.8	14	0
Don Beebe, Buff-GB	5	12	171	14.3	43	2
Kenneth Davis, Buff	4	12	72	6.0	19	0
Antonio Freeman, GB	2	12	231	19.3	t81	3
Torry Holt, StL	2	12	158	13.2	32	1

Single-Game Leaders

Scoring

	Pts
Roger Craig: XIX, San Francisco vs Miami (1 R, 2 P)	18
Jerry Rice: XXIV, San Francisco vs Denver (3 P); XXIX, SF vs San Diego (3 P)	18
Ricky Watters: XXIX, San Francisco vs San Diego (1 R, 2 P)	18
Terrell Davis: XXXII, Denver vs Green Bay (3 R)	18

Rushing Yards

	Yds
Timmy Smith: XXII, Washington vs Denver	204
Marcus Allen: XVIII, LA Raiders vs Washington	191
John Riggins: XVII, Washington vs Miami	166
Franco Harris: IX, Pittsburgh vs Minnesota	158
Terrell Davis: XXXII, Denver vs Green Bay	157
Larry Csonka: VIII, Miami vs Minnesota	145
Clarence Davis: XI, Oakland vs Minnesota	137
Thurman Thomas: XXV, Buffalo vs NY Giants	135
Emmitt Smith: XXVIII, Dallas vs Buffalo	132
Michael Pittman: XXXVII, Tampa Bay vs Oakland	124

Receptions

	No.
Dan Ross: XVI, Cincinnati vs San Francisco	11
Jerry Rice: XXIII, San Francisco vs Cincinnati	11
Tony Nathan: XIX, Miami vs San Francisco	10
Jerry Rice: XXIX, San Francisco vs San Diego	10
Andre Hastings: XXX, Pittsburgh vs Dallas	10
Deion Branch: XXXVIII, New England vs Carolina	10
Ricky Sanders: XXII, Washington vs Denver	9
Antonio Freeman: XXXII, Green Bay vs Denver	9
Seven tied with eight.	

Touchdown Passes

	No.
Steve Young: XXIX, San Francisco vs San Diego	6
Joe Montana: XXIV, San Francisco vs Denver	5
Terry Bradshaw: XIII, Pittsburgh vs Dallas	4
Doug Williams: XXII, Washington vs Denver	4
Troy Aikman: XXVII, Dallas vs Buffalo	4
Seven tied with three.	

Passing Yards

	Yds
Kurt Warner: XXXIV, St. Louis vs Tennessee	414
Kurt Warner: XXXVI, St. Louis vs New England	365
Joe Montana: XXIII, San Francisco vs Cincinnati	357
Tom Brady: XXXVIII, New England vs. Carolina	354
Doug Williams: XXII, Washington vs Denver	340
John Elway: XXXIII, Denver vs Atlanta	336
Joe Montana: XIX, San Francisco vs Miami	331
Steve Young: XXIX, San Francisco vs San Diego	325
Jake Delhomme: XXXVIII Carolina vs New England	323
Terry Bradshaw: XIII, Pittsburgh vs Dallas	318
Dan Marino: XIX, Miami vs San Francisco	318

Receiving Yards

	Yds
Jerry Rice: XXIII, San Francisco vs Cincinnati	215
Ricky Sanders: XXII, Washington vs Denver	193
Isaac Bruce: XXXIV, St. Louis vs Tennessee	162
Lynn Swann: X, Pittsburgh vs Dallas	161
Andre Reed: XXVII, Buffalo vs Dallas	152
Rod Smith: XXXIII, Denver vs Atlanta	152
Jerry Rice: XXIX, San Francisco vs San Diego	149
Jerry Rice: XXIV, San Francisco vs Denver	148
Deion Branch: XXXVIII, New England vs Carolina	143
Max McGee: I, Green Bay vs Kansas City	138

NFL Playoff History

1933
NFL championship	Chicago Bears 23, NY Giants 21

1934
NFL championship	NY Giants 30, Chicago Bears 13

1935
NFL championship	Detroit 26, NY Giants 7

1936
NFL championship	Green Bay 21, Boston 6

1937
NFL championship	Washington 28, Chicago Bears 21

1938
NFL championship	NY Giants 23, Green Bay 17

1939
NFL championship	Green Bay 27, NY Giants 0

1940
NFL championship	Chicago Bears 73, Washington 0

1941
W. div. playoff	Chicago Bears 33, Green Bay 14
NFL championship	Chicago Bears 37, NY Giants 9

1942
NFL championship	Washington 14, Chicago Bears 6

1943
E. div. playoff	Washington 28, NY Giants 0
NFL championship	Chicago Bears 41, Washington 21

1944
NFL championship	Green Bay 14, NY Giants 7

1945
NFL championship	Cleveland 15, Washington 14

1946
NFL championship	Chicago Bears 24, NY Giants 14

1947
E. div. playoff	Philadelphia 21, Pittsburgh 0
NFL championship	Chi Cardinals 28, Philadelphia 21

1948
NFL championship	Philadelphia 7, Chi Cardinals 0

1949
NFL championship	Philadelphia 14, Los Angeles 0

1950
Am. Conf. playoff	Cleveland 8, NY Giants 3
Nat. Conf. playoff	Los Angeles 24, Chicago Bears 14
NFL championship	Cleveland 30, Los Angeles 28

1951
NFL championship	Los Angeles 24, Cleveland 17

NFL Playoff History (Cont.)

1952
Nat. Conf. playoff	Detroit 31, Los Angeles 21
NFL championship	Detroit 17, Cleveland 7

1953
NFL championship	Detroit 17, Cleveland 16

1954
NFL championship	Cleveland 56, Detroit 10

1955
NFL championship	Cleveland 38, Los Angeles 14

1956
NFL championship	NY Giants 47, Chicago Bears 7

1957
W. Conf. playoff	Detroit 31, San Francisco 27
NFL championship	Detroit 59, Cleveland 14

1958
E. Conf. playoff	NY Giants 10, Cleveland 0
NFL championship	Baltimore 23, NY Giants 17

1959
NFL championship	Baltimore 31, NY Giants 16

1960
NFL championship	Philadelphia 17, Green Bay 13
AFL championship	Houston 24, LA Chargers 16

1961
NFL championship	Green Bay 37, NY Giants 0
AFL championship	Houston 10, San Diego 3

1962
NFL championship	Green Bay 16, NY Giants 7
AFL championship	Dallas Texans 20, Houston 17

1963
NFL championship	Chicago 14, NY Giants 10
AFL E. div. playoff	Boston 26, Buffalo 8
AFL championship	San Diego 51, Boston 10

1964
NFL championship	Cleveland 27, Baltimore 0
AFL championship	Buffalo 20, San Diego 7

1965
NFL W. Conf. playoff	Green Bay 13, Baltimore 10
NFL championship	Green Bay 23, Cleveland 12
AFL championship	Buffalo 23, San Diego 0

1966
NFL championship	Green Bay 34, Dallas 27
AFL championship	Kansas City 31, Buffalo 7

1967
NFL E. Conf. championship	Dallas 52, Cleveland 14
NFL W. Conf. championship	Green Bay 28, Los Angeles 7
NFL championship	Green Bay 21, Dallas 17
AFL championship	Oakland 40, Houston 7

1968
NFL E. Conf. championship	Cleveland 31, Dallas 20
NFL W. Conf. championship	Baltimore 24, Minnesota 14
NFL championship	Baltimore 34, Cleveland 0

1968 *(Cont.)*
AFL W. div. playoff	Oakland 41, Kansas City 6
AFL championship	NY Jets 27, Oakland 23

1969
NFL E. Conf. championship	Cleveland 38, Dallas 14
NFL W. Conf. championship	Minnesota 23, Los Angeles 20
NFL championship	Minnesota 27, Cleveland 7
AFL div. playoffs	Kansas City 13, NY Jets 6
	Oakland 56, Houston 7
AFL championship	Kansas City 17, Oakland 7

1970
AFC div. playoffs	Baltimore 17, Cincinnati 0
	Oakland 21, Miami 14
AFC championship	Baltimore 27, Oakland 17
NFC div. playoffs	Dallas 5, Detroit 0
	San Francisco 17, Minnesota 14
NFC championship	Dallas 17, San Francisco 10

1971
AFC div. playoffs	Miami 27, Kansas City 24
	Baltimore 20, Cleveland 3
AFC championship	Miami 21, Baltimore 0
NFC div. playoffs	Dallas 20, Minnesota 12
	San Francisco 24, Washington 20
NFC championship	Dallas 14, San Francisco 3

1972
AFC div. playoffs	Pittsburgh 13, Oakland 7
	Miami 20, Cleveland 14
AFC championship	Miami 21, Pittsburgh 17
NFC div. playoffs	Dallas 30, San Francisco 28
	Washington 16, Green Bay 3
NFC championship	Washington 26, Dallas 3

1973
AFC div. playoffs	Oakland 33, Pittsburgh 14
	Miami 34, Cincinnati 16
AFC championship	Miami 27, Oakland 10
NFC div. playoffs	Minnesota 27, Washington 20
	Dallas 27, Los Angeles 16
NFC championship	Minnesota 27, Dallas 10

1974
AFC div. playoffs	Oakland 28, Miami 26
	Pittsburgh 32, Buffalo 14
AFC championship	Pittsburgh 24, Oakland 13
NFC div. playoffs	Minnesota 30, St Louis 14
	Los Angeles 19, Washington 10
NFC championship	Minnesota 14, Los Angeles 10

1975
AFC div. playoffs	Pittsburgh 28, Baltimore 10
	Oakland 31, Cincinnati 28
AFC championship	Pittsburgh 16, Oakland 10
NFC div. playoffs	Los Angeles 35, St Louis 23
	Dallas 17, Minnesota 14
NFC championship	Dallas 37, Los Angeles 7

1976
AFC div. playoffs	Oakland 24, New England 21
	Pittsburgh 40, Baltimore 14
AFC championship	Oakland 24, Pittsburgh 7
NFC div. playoffs	Minnesota 35, Washington 20
	Los Angeles 14, Dallas 12
NFC championship	Minnesota 24, Los Angeles 13

1977

AFC div. playoffs	Denver 34, Pittsburgh 21
	Oakland 37, Baltimore 31
AFC championship	Denver 20, Oakland 17
NFC div. playoffs	Dallas 37, Chicago 7
	Minnesota 14, Los Angeles 7
NFC championship	Dallas 23, Minnesota 6

1978

AFC 1st-rd. playoff	Houston 17, Miami 9
AFC div. playoffs	Houston 31, New England 14
	Pittsburgh 33, Denver 10
AFC championship	Pittsburgh 34, Houston 5
NFC 1st-rd. playoff	Atlanta 14, Philadelphia 13
NFC div. playoffs	Dallas 27, Atlanta 20
	Los Angeles 34, Minnesota 10
NFC championship	Dallas 28, Los Angeles 0

1979

AFC 1st-rd. playoff	Houston 13, Denver 7
AFC div. playoffs	Houston 17, San Diego 14
	Pittsburgh 34, Miami 14
AFC championship	Pittsburgh 27, Houston 13
NFC 1st-rd. playoff	Philadelphia 27, Chicago 17
NFC div. playoffs	Tampa Bay 24, Philadelphia 17
	Los Angeles 21, Dallas 19
NFC championship	Los Angeles 9, Tampa Bay 0

1980

AFC 1st-rd. playoff	Oakland 27, Houston 7
AFC div. playoffs	San Diego 20, Buffalo 14
	Oakland 14, Cleveland 12
AFC championship	Oakland 34, San Diego 27
NFC 1st-rd. playoff	Dallas 34, Los Angeles 13
NFC div. playoffs	Philadelphia 31, Minnesota 16
	Dallas 30, Atlanta 27
NFC championship	Philadelphia 20, Dallas 7

1981

AFC 1st-rd. playoff	Buffalo 31, NY Jets 27
AFC div. playoffs	San Diego 41, Miami 38
	Cincinnati 28, Buffalo 21
AFC championship	Cincinnati 27, San Diego 7
NFC 1st-rd. playoff	NY Giants 27, Philadelphia 21
NFC div. playoffs	Dallas 38, Tampa Bay 0
	San Francisco 38, NY Giants 24
NFC championship	San Francisco 28, Dallas 27

1982

AFC 1st-rd. playoffs	Miami 28, New England 13
	LA Raiders 27, Cleveland 10
	NY Jets 44, Cincinnati 17
	San Diego 31, Pittsburgh 28
AFC div. playoffs	NY Jets 17, LA Raiders 14
	Miami 34, San Diego 13
AFC championship	Miami 14, NY Jets 0
NFC 1st-rd. playoffs	Washington 31, Detroit 7
	Green Bay 41, St Louis 16
	Minnesota 30, Atlanta 24
	Dallas 30, Tampa Bay 17
NFC div. playoffs	Washington 21, Minnesota 7
	Dallas 37, Green Bay 26
NFC championship	Washington 31, Dallas 17

1983

AFC 1st-rd. playoff	Seattle 31, Denver 7
AFC div. playoffs	Seattle 27, Miami 20
	LA Raiders 38, Pittsburgh 10
AFC championship	LA Raiders 30, Seattle 14
NFC 1st-rd. playoff	LA Rams 24, Dallas 17
NFC div. playoffs	San Francisco 24, Detroit 23
	Washington 51, LA Rams 7
NFC championship	Washington 24, San Francisco 21

1984

AFC 1st-rd. playoff	Seattle 13, LA Raiders 7
AFC div. playoffs	Miami 31, Seattle 10
	Pittsburgh 24, Denver 17
AFC championship	Miami 45, Pittsburgh 28
NFC 1st-rd. playoff	NY Giants 16, LA Rams 13
NFC div. playoffs	San Francisco 21, NY Giants 10
	Chicago 23, Washington 19
NFC championship	San Francisco 23, Chicago 0

1985

AFC 1st-rd. playoff	New England 26, NY Jets 14
AFC div. playoffs	Miami 24, Cleveland 21
	New England 27, LA Raiders 20
AFC championship	New England 31, Miami 14
NFC 1st-rd. playoff	NY Giants 17, San Francisco 3
NFC div. playoffs	LA Rams 20, Dallas 0
	Chicago 21, NY Giants 0
NFC championship	Chicago 24, LA Rams 0

1986

AFC 1st-rd. playoff	NY Jets 35, Kansas City 15
AFC div. playoffs	Cleveland 23, NY Jets 20
	Denver 22, New England 17
AFC championship	Denver 23, Cleveland 20
NFC 1st-rd. playoff	Washington 19, LA Rams 7
NFC div playoffs	Washington 27, Chicago 13
	NY Giants 49, San Francisco 3
NFC championship	NY Giants 17, Washington 0

1987

AFC 1st-rd. playoff	Houston 23, Seattle 20
AFC div. playoffs	Cleveland 38, Indianapolis 21
	Denver 34, Houston 10
AFC championship	Denver 38, Cleveland 33
NFC 1st-rd. playoff	Minnesota 44, New Orleans 10
NFC div playoffs	Minnesota 36, San Francisco 24
	Washington 21, Chicago 17
NFC championship	Washington 17, Minnesota 10

1988

AFC 1st-rd. playoff	Houston 24, Cleveland 23
AFC div. playoffs	Cincinnati 21, Seattle 13
	Buffalo 17, Houston 10
AFC championship	Cincinnati 21, Buffalo 10
NFC 1st-rd. playoff	Minnesota 28, LA Rams 17
NFC div. playoffs	Chicago 20, Philadelphia 12
	San Francisco 34, Minnesota 9
NFC championship	San Francisco 28, Chicago 3

1989

AFC 1st-rd. playoff	Pittsburgh 26, Houston 23
AFC div. playoffs	Cleveland 34, Buffalo 30
	Denver 24, Pittsburgh 23
AFC championship	Denver 37, Cleveland 21
NFC 1st-rd. playoff	LA Rams 21, Philadelphia 7
NFC div. playoffs	LA Rams 19, NY Giants 13
	San Francisco 41, Minnesota 13
NFC championship	San Francisco 30, LA Rams 3

1990

AFC 1st-rd. playoffs	Miami 17, Kansas City 16
	Cincinnati 41, Houston 14
AFC div. playoffs	Buffalo 44, Miami 34
	LA Raiders 20, Cincinnati 10
AFC championship	Buffalo 51, LA Raiders 3
NFC 1st-rd. playoffs	Chicago 16, New Orleans 6
NFC 1st-rd playoffs	Washington 20, Philadelphia 6
NFC div. playoffs	NY Giants 31, Chicago 3
	San Francisco 28, Washington 10
NFC championship	NY Giants 15, San Francisco 13

1991

AFC 1st-rd. playoffs	Houston 17, NY Jets 10
	Kansas City 10, LA Raiders 6
AFC div. playoffs	Denver 26, Houston 24
	Buffalo 37, Kansas City 14
AFC championship	Buffalo 10, Denver 7
NFC 1st-rd. playoffs	Atlanta 27, New Orleans 20
	Dallas 17, Chicago 13
NFC div. playoffs	Washington 24, Atlanta 7
	Detroit 38, Dallas 6
NFC championship	Washington 41, Detroit 10

1992

AFC 1st-rd. playoffs	San Diego 17, Kansas City 0
	Buffalo 41, Houston 38 (OT)
AFC div. playoffs	Buffalo 24, Pittsburgh 3
	Miami 31, San Diego 0
AFC championship	Buffalo 29, Miami 10
NFC 1st-rd. playoffs	Washington 24, Minnesota 7
	Philadelphia 36, New Orleans 20
NFC div. playoffs	San Francisco 20, Washington 13
	Dallas 34, Philadelphia 10
NFC championship	Dallas 30, San Francisco 20

1993

AFC 1st-rd. playoffs	LA Raiders 42, Denver 24
	Kansas City 27, Pittsburgh 24 (OT)
AFC div. playoffs	Buffalo 29, LA Raiders 23
	Kansas City 28, Houston 20
AFC championship	Buffalo 30, Kansas City 13
NFC 1st-rd. playoffs	NY Giants 17, Minnesota 10
	Green Bay 28, Detroit 24
NFC div. playoffs	San Francisco 44, NY Giants 3
	Dallas 27, Green Bay 17
NFC championship	Dallas 38, San Francisco 21

1994

AFC 1st-rd. playoffs	Miami 27, Kansas City 17
	Cleveland 20, New England 13
AFC div. playoffs	San Diego 22, Miami 21
	Pittsburgh 29, Cleveland 9
AFC championship	San Diego 17, Pittsburgh 13
NFC 1st-rd. playoffs	Green Bay 16, Detroit 12
	Chicago 35, Minnesota 18
NFC div. playoffs	Dallas 35, Green Bay 9
	San Francisco 44, Chicago 15
NFC championship	San Francisco 38, Dallas 28

1995

AFC 1st-rd. playoffs	Buffalo 37, Miami 22
	Indianapolis 35, San Diego 20
AFC div. playoffs	Pittsburgh 40, Buffalo 21
	Indianapolis 10, Kansas City 7
AFC championship	Pittsburgh 20, Indianapolis 16
NFC 1st-rd. playoffs	Philadelphia 58, Detroit 37
	Green Bay 37, Atlanta 20
NFC div. playoffs	Dallas 30, Philadelphia 11
	Green Bay 27, San Francisco 17
NFC championship	Dallas 38, Green Bay 27

1996

AFC 1st-rd. playoffs	Jacksonville 30, Buffalo 27
	Pittsburgh 42, Indianapolis 14
AFC div. playoffs	Jacksonville 30, Denver 27
	New England 28, Pittsburgh 3
AFC championship	New England 20, Jacksonville 6
NFC 1st-rd. playoffs	Dallas 40, Minnesota 15
	San Francisco 14, Philadelphia 0
NFC div. playoffs	Green Bay 35, San Francisco 14
	Carolina 26, Dallas 17
NFC championship	Green Bay 30, Carolina 13

1997

AFC 1st-rd. playoffs	Denver 42, Jacksonville 17
	New England 17, Miami 3
AFC div. playoffs	Denver 14, Kansas City 0
	Pittsburgh 7, New England 6
AFC championship	Denver 24, Pittsburgh 21

1997 (Cont.)

NFC 1st-rd. playoffs	Minnesota 23, NY Giants 22
	Tampa Bay 20, Detroit 10
NFC div. playoffs	Green Bay 21, Tampa Bay 7
	San Francisco 38, Minnesota 22
NFC championship	Green Bay 23, San Francisco 10

1998

AFC 1st-rd. playoffs	Miami 24, Buffalo 17
	Jacksonville 25, New England 10
AFC div. playoffs	Denver 38, Miami 3
	NY Jets 34, Jacksonville 24
AFC championship	Denver 23, NY Jets 10
NFC 1st-rd. playoffs	Arizona 20, Dallas 7
	San Francisco 30, Green Bay 27
NFC div. playoffs	Atlanta 20, San Francisco 18
	Minnesota 41, Arizona 21
NFC championship	Atlanta 30, Minnesota 27 (ot)

1999

AFC 1st-rd. playoffs	Tennessee 22, Buffalo 16
	Miami 20, Seattle 17
AFC div. playoffs	Jacksonville 62, Miami 7
	Tennessee 19, Indianapolis 16
AFC championship	Tennessee 33, Jacksonville 14
NFC 1st-rd. playoffs	Washington 27, Detroit 13
	Minnesota 27, Dallas 10
NFC div. playoffs	Tampa Bay 14, Washington 13
	St Louis 49, Minnesota 37
NFC championship	St Louis 11, Tampa Bay 6

2000

AFC 1st-rd. playoffs	Baltimore 21, Denver 3
	Miami 23, Indianapolis 17 (ot)
AFC div. playoffs	Baltimore 24, Tennessee 10
	Oakland 27, Miami 0
AFC championship	Baltimore 16, Oakland 3
NFC 1st-rd. playoffs	New Orleans 31, St. Louis 28
	Philadelphia 21, Tampa Bay 3
NFC div. playoffs	NY Giants 20, Philadelphia 10
	Minnesota 34, New Orleans 16
NFC championship	NY Giants 41, Minnesota 0

2001

AFC 1st-rd. playoffs	Oakland 38, NY Jets 24
	Baltimore 20, Miami 3
AFC div. playoffs	New England 16, Oakland 13(ot)
	Pittsburgh 27, Baltimore 10
AFC championship	New England 24, Pittsburgh 17
NFC 1st-rd. playoffs	Philadelphia 31, Tampa Bay 9
	Green Bay 25, San Francisco 15
NFC div. playoffs	Philadelphia 33, Chicago 19
	St. Louis 45, Green Bay 17
NFC championship	St. Louis 29, Philadelphia 24

2002

AFC 1st-rd. playoffs	NY Jets 41, Indianapolis 0
	Pittsburgh 36, Cleveland 33
AFC div. playoffs	Tennessee 34, Pittsburgh 31 (ot)
	Oakland 30, NY Jets 10
AFC championship	Oakland 41, Tennessee 24
NFC 1st-rd. playoffs	Atlanta 27, Green Bay 7
	San Francisco 39, NY Giants 38
NFC div. playoffs	Philadelphia 20, Atlanta 6
	Tampa Bay 31, San Francisco 6
NFC championship	Tampa Bay 27, Philadelphia 10

2003

AFC 1st-rd. playoffs	Tennessee 20, Baltimore 17
	Indianapolis 41, Denver 10
AFC div. playoffs	New England 17, Tennessee 14
	Indianapolis 38, Kansas City 31
AFC championship	New England 24, Indianapolis 14
NFC 1st-rd. playoffs	Carolina 29, Dallas 10
	Green Bay 33, Seattle 27 (ot)
NFC div. playoffs	Carolina 29, St. Louis 23
	Philadelphia 20, Green Bay 17 (ot)
NFC championship	Carolina 14, Philadelphia 3

Career Leaders

Scoring

	Yrs	TD	FG	PAT	Pts
†Gary Anderson	22	0	521	783	2,346
†Morten Andersen	22	0	502	753	2,259
George Blanda	26	9	335	943	2,002
Norm Johnson	18	0	366	638	1,736
Nick Lowery	18	0	383	562	1,711
Jan Stenerud	19	0	373	580	1,699
Eddie Murray	19	0	352	539	1,595
Al Del Greco	17	0	347	543	1,584
Pat Leahy	18	0	304	558	1,470
Jim Turner	16	1	304	521	1,439
†John Carney	16	0	343	404	1,433
Matt Bahr	17	0	300	522	1,422
Mark Moseley	16	0	300	482	1,382
Jim Bakken	17	0	282	534	1,380
†Steve Christie	14	0	314	435	1,377
Fred Cox	15	0	282	519	1,365
†Matt Stover	13	0	321	401	1,364
Lou Groza	17	1	234	641	1,349
†Jason Elam	11	0	288	449	1,313
Jim Breech	14	0	243	517	1,246

Rushing

	Yrs	Att	Yds	Avg	Lg	TD
†Emmitt Smith	14	4,142	17,418	4.2	75	152
Walter Payton	13	3,838	16,726	4.4	76	110
Barry Sanders	10	3,062	15,269	5.0	85	99
Eric Dickerson	11	2,996	13,259	4.4	85	90
Tony Dorsett	12	2,936	12,739	4.3	99	77
†Jerome Bettis	11	3,119	12,353	4.0	71	69
Jim Brown	9	2,359	12,312	5.2	80	106
Marcus Allen	16	3,022	12,243	4.1	61	123
Franco Harris	13	2,949	12,120	4.1	75	91
Thurman Thomas	13	2,877	12,074	4.2	80	66
†Curtis Martin	9	2,927	11,669	4.0	70	73
John Riggins	14	2,916	11,352	3.9	66	104
O.J. Simpson	11	2,404	11,236	4.7	94	61
†Marshall Faulk	10	2,576	11,213	4.4	71	97
Ricky Watters	9	2,550	10,325	4.1	57	77
Ottis Anderson	14	2,562	10,273	4.0	76	81
†Eddie George	8	2,733	10,009	3.7	76	64
Earl Campbell	8	2,187	9,407	4.3	81	74
Terry Allen	12	2,152	8,614	4.0	55	73
Jim Taylor	10	1,941	8,597	4.4	84	83

Touchdowns

	Yrs	Rush	Rec	Ret	Total TD
†Jerry Rice	19	10	194	1	205
†Emmitt Smith	14	155	11	0	166
Marcus Allen	16	123	21	1	145
Cris Carter	15	0	130	1	131
†Marshall Faulk	10	97	34	0	131
Jim Brown	9	106	20	0	126
Walter Payton	13	110	15	0	125
John Riggins	14	104	12	0	116
Lenny Moore	12	63	48	2	113
Barry Sanders	10	99	10	0	109

	Yrs	Rush	Rec	Ret	Total TD
Don Hutson	11	3	99	3	105
†Tim Brown	16	1	99	3	103
Steve Largent	14	1	100	0	101
Franco Harris	13	91	9	0	100
Eric Dickerson	11	90	6	0	96
Jim Taylor	10	83	10	0	93
Tony Dorsett	12	77	13	1	91
Bobby Mitchell	11	18	65	8	91
Ricky Watters	10	78	13	0	91

Two tied with 90.

Combined Yards Gained

	Yrs	Total	Rush	Rec	Int Ret	Punt Ret	Kickoff Ret	Fum Ret
†Brian Mitchell	14	23,330	1,967	2,336	0	4,999	14,014	14
†Jerry Rice	19	23,117	645	22,466	0	0	6	0
Walter Payton	13	21,803	16,726	4,538	0	0	539	0
†Emmitt Smith	14	20,537	17,418	3,119	0	0	0	0
†Tim Brown	16	19,434	190	14,734	0	3,272	1,235	3
Barry Sanders	10	18,308	15,269	2,921	0	0	118	0
Herschel Walker	12	18,168	8,225	4,859	0	0	5,084	0
Marcus Allen	16	17,648	12,243	5,411	0	0	0	-6
†Marshall Faulk	10	17,523	11,213	6,274	0	0	18	18
Eric Metcalf	13	17,230	2,392	5,572	0	3,453	5,813	0
Thurman Thomas	13	16,532	12,074	4,458	0	0	0	0
Tony Dorsett	12	16,326	12,739	3,554	0	0	0	33
Henry Ellard	16	15,718	50	13,777	0	1,527	364	0
Irving Fryar	17	15,594	242	12,785	0	2055	505	7
Jim Brown	9	15,459	12,312	2,499	0	0	648	0
Eric Dickerson	11	15,411	13,259	2,137	0	0	0	15
Glyn Milburn	9	14,911	817	1,322	0	2,984	9,788	0
James Brooks	12	14,910	7,962	3,621	0	565	2,762	0
Ricky Watters	10	14,891	10,643	4,248	0	0	0	0
†Curtis Martin	9	14,635	11,669	2,966	0	0	0	0

† Active in 2003.

Career Leaders *(Cont.)*

Passing

PASSING EFFICIENCY*

	Yrs	Att	Comp	Pct Comp	Yds	Avg Gain	TD	Pct TD	Int	Pct Int	Rating Pts
†Kurt Warner	6	1,688	1,121	66.4	14,447	8.56	102	6.0	65	3.9	97.2
Steve Young	15	4,149	2,667	64.3	33,124	7.98	232	5.6	107	2.6	96.8
Joe Montana	15	5,391	3,409	63.2	40,551	7.52	273	5.1	139	2.6	92.3
†Jeff Garcia	5	2,360	1,449	61.4	16,408	6.95	113	4.8	56	2.4	88.3
†Peyton Manning	6	3,383	2,128	62.9	24,885	7.36	167	4.9	110	3.3	88.1
†Daunte Culpepper	5	1,843	1,160	62.9	13,881	7.53	90	4.9	63	3.4	88.0
†Brett Favre	13	6,464	3,960	61.3	45,646	7.06	346	5.4	209	3.2	86.9
Dan Marino	17	8,358	4,967	59.4	61,361	7.34	420	5.0	252	3.0	86.4
†Trent Green	11	2,266	1,336	59.0	17,016	7.51	106	4.7	65	2.9	86.1
†Tom Brady	4	1,544	955	61.9	10,233	6.63	69	4.5	38	2.5	85.9
†Mark Brunell	11	3,643	2,196	60.3	25,793	7.08	144	4.0	86	2.4	85.2
†Rich Gannon	17	4,138	2,492	60.2	28,219	6.82	177	4.3	102	2.5	84.7
Jim Kelly	11	4,779	2,874	60.1	35,467	7.42	237	5.0	175	3.7	84.4
†Steve McNair	9	3,180	1,884	59.2	22,637	7.12	132	4.2	83	2.6	84.1
†Brad Johnson	12	3,401	2,101	61.8	23,239	6.83	140	4.1	95	2.8	84.1
Roger Staubach	11	2,958	1,685	57.0	22,700	7.67	153	5.2	109	3.7	83.4
†Brian Griese	6	1,808	1,118	61.8	12,576	6.96	76	4.2	59	3.3	83.0
Neil Lomax	8	3,153	1,817	57.6	22,771	7.22	136	4.3	90	2.9	82.7
Sonny Jurgensen	18	4,262	2,433	57.1	32,224	7.56	255	6.0	189	4.4	82.6
Len Dawson	19	3,741	2,136	57.1	28,711	7.67	239	6.4	183	4.9	82.6

*1,500 or more attempts. The passer ratings are based on performance standards established for completion percentage, interception percentage, touchdown percentage and average gain. Passers are allocated points according to how their marks compare with those standards.

YARDS

	Yrs	Att	Comp	Pct Comp	Yds		Yrs	Att	Comp	Pct Comp	Yds
Dan Marino	17	8,358	4,967	59.4	61,361	Boomer Esiason	14	5,205	2,969	57.0	37,920
John Elway	16	7,250	4,123	56.9	51,475	†Drew Bledsoe	11	5,599	3,193	57.0	36,876
Warren Moon	17	6,823	3,988	58.5	49,325	Jim Kelly	11	4,779	2,874	60.1	35,467
Fran Tarkenton	18	6,467	3,686	57.0	47,003	Jim Everett	12	4,923	2,841	57.7	34,837
†Brett Favre	13	6,464	3,960	61.3	45,646	Jim Hart	19	5,076	2,593	51.1	34,665
Dan Fouts	15	5,604	3,297	58.8	43,040	Steve DeBerg	17	4,746	2,924	61.6	34,241
†Vinny Testaverde	17	5,925	3,334	56.3	40,943	John Hadl	16	4,687	2,363	50.4	33,503
Joe Montana	15	5,391	3,409	63.2	40,551	Phil Simms	14	4,647	2,576	55.4	33,462
Johnny Unitas	18	5,186	2,830	54.6	40,239	Steve Young	15	4,149	2,667	64.3	33,124
Dave Krieg	19	5,311	3,105	58.5	38,147	Troy Aikman	12	4,715	2,898	61.5	32,942

TOUCHDOWNS

	No.		No.		No.
Dan Marino	420	†Vinny Testaverde	251	Jim Hart	209
†Brett Favre	346	Boomer Esiason	247	Randall Cunningham	207
Fran Tarkenton	342	John Hadl	244	Jim Everett	203
John Elway	300	Len Dawson	239	Phil Simms	199
Warren Moon	291	Jim Kelly	237	Ken Anderson	197
Johnny Unitas	290	George Blanda	236	Joe Ferguson	196
Joe Montana	273	Steve Young	232	Bobby Layne	196
Dave Krieg	261	John Brodie	214	Norm Snead	196
Sonny Jurgensen	255	Terry Bradshaw	212	Steve DeBerg	196
Dan Fouts	254	Y.A. Tittle	212	Ken Stabler	194

† Active in 2003.

Career Leaders (Cont.)

Receiving

RECEPTIONS

	Yrs	No.	Yds	Avg	Lg	TD		Yrs	No.	Yds	Avg	Lg	TD
†Jerry Rice	19	1,519	22,466	14.8	96	194	James Lofton	16	764	14,004	18.3	80	75
Cris Carter	16	1,101	13,899	12.6	80	130	†Marvin Harrison	8	759	10,072	13.8	79	83
†Tim Brown	16	1,070	14,734	13.8	80	99	Michael Irvin	12	750	11,904	15.9	87	65
Andre Reed	16	951	13,198	13.9	83	87	Charlie Joiner	18	750	12,146	16.2	87	65
Art Monk	16	940	12,721	13.5	79	68	Andre Rison	12	743	10,205	13.7	80	84
Irving Fryar	17	851	12,785	15.0	80	84	†Keenan McCardell	13	724	9,370	12.9	76	52
†Larry Centers	14	827	6,797	8.2	54	28	†Jimmy Smith	11	718	10,092	14.1	75	55
Steve Largent	14	819	13,089	16.0	74	100	Gary Clark	11	699	10,856	15.5	84	65
†Shannon Sharpe	15	815	10,060	12.3	82	62	Terance Mathis	13	689	8,809	12.8	81	63
Henry Ellard	16	814	13,777	16.9	81	65	Herman Moore	12	670	9,174	13.7	93	62

YARDS

†Jerry Rice	22,466	Irving Fryar	12,785	†Isaac Bruce	10,461
†Tim Brown	14,734	Art Monk	12,721	Harold Jackson	10,372
James Lofton	14,004	Charlie Joiner	12,146	Lance Alworth	10,266
Cris Carter	13,899	Michael Irvin	11,904	Andre Rison	10,205
Henry Ellard	13,777	Don Maynard	11,834	†Jimmy Smith	10,092
Andre Reed	13,198	Gary Clark	10,856	†Marvin Harrison	10,072
Steve Largent	13,089	Stanley Morgan	10,716		

Sacks

†Bruce Smith	200.0	Chris Doleman	150.5
Reggie White	198.0	†John Randle	137.5
Kevin Greene	160.0	Richard Dent	137.5

Note: Officially compiled since 1982.

Interceptions

	Yrs	No.	Yds	Avg	Lg	TD
Paul Krause	16	81	1185	14.6	81	3
Emlen Tunnell	14	79	1282	16.2	55	4
†Rod Woodson	17	71	1483	20.9	98	17
Dick (Night Train) Lane	14	68	1207	17.8	80	5
Ken Riley	15	65	596	9.2	66	5

Punt Returns

	Yrs	No.	Yds	Avg	Lg	TD
George McAfee	8	112	1431	12.8	74	2
Jack Christiansen	8	85	1084	12.8	89	8
Claude Gibson	5	110	1381	12.6	85	3
Bill Dudley	9	124	1515	12.2	96	3
Rick Upchurch	9	248	3008	12.1	92	8
Desmond Howard	11	244	2895	11.9	95	8

Note: 75 or more returns.

Punting

	Yrs	No.	Yds	Avg	Lg	Blk
†Shane Lechler	4	287	13,113	45.7	73	2
Sammy Baugh	16	338	15,245	45.1	85	9
Tommy Davis	11	511	22,833	44.7	82	2
Yale Lary	11	503	22,279	44.3	74	4
†Todd Sauerbrun	9	684	30,092	44.0	73	5

Note: 250 or more punts.

Kickoff Returns

	Yrs	No.	Yds	Avg	Lg	TD
Gale Sayers	7	91	2781	30.6	103	6
Lynn Chandnois	7	92	2720	29.6	93	3
Abe Woodson	9	193	5538	28.7	105	5
Claude (Buddy) Young	6	90	2514	27.9	104	2
Travis Williams	5	102	2801	27.5	105	6

Note: 75 or more returns.

† Active in 2003.

Single-Season Leaders
Scoring

POINTS

	Year	TD	PAT	FG	Pts
Paul Hornung, GB	1960	15	41	15	176
Gary Anderson, Minn	1998	0	59	35	164
Jeff Wilkins, StL	2003	0	46	39	163
Priest Holmes, KC	2003	27	0	0	162
Mark Moseley, Wash	1983	0	62	33	161
Mike Vanderjagt, Ind	2003	0	46	37	157
Marshall Faulk, StL	2000	26	0	0	156
Gino Cappelletti, Bos	1964	7	38	25	155
Emmitt Smith, Dall	1995	25	0	0	150
Chip Lohmiller, Wash	1991	0	56	31	149

Note: Cappelletti's total includes a two-point conversion.

TOUCHDOWNS

	Year	Rush	Rec	Ret	Total
Priest Holmes, KC	2003	27	0	0	27
Marshall Faulk, StL	2000	18	8	0	26
Emmitt Smith, Dall	1995	25	0	0	25
John Riggins, Wash	1983	24	0	0	24
Priest Holmes, KC	2002	21	3	0	24
O.J. Simpson, Buff	1975	16	7	0	23
Jerry Rice, SF	1987	1	22	0	23
Terrell Davis, Den	1998	21	2	0	23

FIELD GOALS

	Year	Att	No.
Olindo Mare, Mia	1999	46	39
Jeff Wilkins, StL	2003	42	39
John Kasay, Car	1996	45	37
Mike Vanderjagt, Ind	2003	37	37
Cary Blanchard, Ind	1996	40	36
Al Del Greco, Tenn	1998	39	36

Rushing

YARDS GAINED

	Year	Att	Yds	Avg
Eric Dickerson, LA Rams	1984	379	2105	5.6
Jamal Lewis, Balt	2003	387	2066	5.3
Barry Sanders, Det	1997	335	2053	6.1
Terrell Davis, Den	1998	392	2008	5.1
O.J. Simpson, Buff	1973	332	2003	6.0
Earl Campbell, Hou	1980	373	1934	5.2
Jim Brown, Clev	1963	291	1883	6.4
Ahman Green, GB	2003	355	1883	5.3
Barry Sanders, Det	1994	331	1883	5.7
Ricky Williams, Mia	2002	383	1853	4.8

AVERAGE GAIN

	Year	Avg
Beattie Feathers, Chi	1934	8.44
Randall Cunningham, Phil	1990	7.98
Michael Vick, Atl	2002	6.88
Bobby Douglass, Chi	1972	6.87

Minimum 100 attempts.

TOUCHDOWNS

	Year	No.
Priest Holmes, KC	2003	27
Emmitt Smith, Dall	1995	25
John Riggins, Wash	1983	24
Priest Holmes, KC	2002	24
Emmitt Smith, Dall	1994	21
Joe Morris, NYG	1985	21
Terry Allen, Wash	1996	21
Terrell Davis, Den	1998	21

Passing

YARDS GAINED

	Year	Att	Comp	Pct	Yds
Dan Marino, Mia	1984	564	362	64.2	5084
Kurt Warner, StL	2001	546	375	68.7	4830
Dan Fouts, SD	1981	609	360	59.1	4802
Dan Marino, Mia	1986	623	378	60.7	4746
Dan Fouts, SD	1980	589	348	59.1	4715
Warren Moon, Hou	1991	655	404	61.7	4690
Warren Moon, Hou	1990	584	362	62.0	4689
Rich Gannon, Oak	2002	618	418	67.6	4689
Neil Lomax, StL Cards	1984	560	345	61.6	4614
Drew Bledsoe, NE	1994	691	400	57.9	4555

PASSER RATING

	Year	Rat.
Steve Young, SF	1994	112.8
Joe Montana, SF	1989	112.4
Milt Plum, Clev	1960	110.4
Sammy Baugh, Wash	1945	109.9
Kurt Warner, Rams	1999	109.2

TOUCHDOWNS

	Year	No.
Dan Marino, Mia	1984	48
Dan Marino, Mia	1986	44
Kurt Warner, StL	1999	41
Brett Favre, GB	1995	38

Four tied with 36.

Single-Season Leaders (Cont.)
Receiving

RECEPTIONS

	Year	No.	Yds
Marvin Harrison, Ind	2002	143	1722
Herman Moore, Det	1995	123	1686
Cris Carter, Minn	1994	122	1256
Jerry Rice, SF	1995	122	1848
Cris Carter, Minn	1995	122	1371
Isaac Bruce, Rams	1995	119	1781
Torry Holt, StL	2003	117	1696
Jimmy Smith, Jax	1999	116	1636
Marvin Harrison, Ind	1999	115	1663
Rod Smith, Den	2001	113	1343

YARDS GAINED

	Year	Yds
Jerry Rice, SF	1995	1848
Isaac Bruce, Rams	1995	1781
Charley Hennigan, Hou	1961	1746
Marvin Harrison, Ind	2002	1722
Torry Holt, StL	2003	1696

TOUCHDOWNS

	Year	No.
Jerry Rice, SF	1987	22
Mark Clayton, Mia	1984	18
Sterling Sharpe, GB	1994	18
Seven tied with 17.		

All-Purpose Yards

	Year	Run	Rec	Ret	Total
Michael Lewis, NO	2002	15	200	2432	2647
Lionel James, SD	1985	516	1027	992	2535
Terry Metcalf, StL Cards	1975	816	378	1268	2462
Mack Herron, NE	1974	824	474	1146	2444
Gale Sayers, Chi	1966	1231	447	762	2440
Marshall Faulk, Rams	1999	1381	1048	0	2429
Timmy Brown, Phil	1963	841	487	1100	2428
Barry Sanders, Det	1997	2053	305	0	2358
Tim Brown, Rai	1988	50	725	1542	2317
Marcus Allen, Rai	1985	1759	555	-6	2308
Timmy Brown, Phil	1962	545	849	912	2306
Edgerrin James, Ind	2000	1709	594	0	2303

Punting

	Year	No.	Yds	Avg
Sammy Baugh, Wash	1940	35	1799	51.4
Yale Lary, Det	1963	35	1713	48.9
Sammy Baugh, Wash	1941	30	1462	48.7
Yale Lary, Det	1961	52	2516	48.4
Sammy Baugh, Wash	1942	37	1783	48.2

Sacks

	Year	No.
Michael Strahan, NYG	2001	22.5
Mark Gastineau, NYJ	1984	22
Reggie White, Phil	1987	21
Chris Doleman, Minn	1989	21
Lawrence Taylor, NYG	1986	20.5

Interceptions

	Year	No.
Dick (Night Train) Lane, Rams	1952	14
Dan Sandifer, Wash	1948	13
Spec Sanders, NY Yanks	1950	13
Lester Hayes, Oak	1980	13
Nine tied with 12.		

Kickoff Returns

	Year	Avg
Travis Williams, GB	1967	41.1
Gale Sayers, Chi	1967	37.7
Ollie Matson, Chi Cards	1958	35.5
Jim Duncan, Balt Colts	1970	35.4
Lynn Chandnois, Pitt	1952	35.2

Punt Returns

	Year	Avg
Herb Rich, Balt Colts	1950	23.0
Jack Christiansen, Det	1952	21.5
Dick Christy, NY Titans	1961	21.3
Bob Hayes, Dall	1968	20.8

Single-Game Leaders
Scoring

POINTS

	Date	Pts
Ernie Nevers, Chi Cards vs Chi	11-28-29	40
Dub Jones, Clev vs Chi	11-25-51	36
Gale Sayers, Chi vs SF	12-12-65	36
Paul Hornung, GB vs Balt Colts	10-8-61	33

On Thanksgiving Day, 1929, Nevers scored all the Cardinals' points on six rushing TDs and four PATs. The Cards defeated Red Grange and the Bears, 40–6. Jones and Sayers each rushed for four touchdowns and scored two more on returns in their teams' victories. Hornung scored four touchdowns and kicked 6 PATs and a field goal in a 45-7 win over the Colts.

FIELD GOALS

	Date	No.
Jim Bakken, StL Cards vs Pitt	9-24-67	7
Rich Karlis, Minn vs Rams	11-5-89	7
Chris Boniol, Dall vs GB	11-18-96	7
Billy Cundiff, Dall vs NYG	9-15-03	7

Bakken was 7 for 9; Cundiff was 7 for 8; and Karlis and Boniol 7 for 7.

Single-Game Leaders (Cont.)

Scoring (Cont.)

TOUCHDOWNS

	Date	No.
Ernie Nevers, Chi Cards vs Chi	11-28-29	6
Dub Jones, Clev vs Chi	11-25-51	6
Gale Sayers, Chi vs SF	12-12-65	6
Bob Shaw, Chi Cards vs Balt Colts	10-2-50	5
Jim Brown, Clev vs Balt Colts	11-1-59	5
Abner Haynes, Dall Texans vs Oak	11-26-61	5
Billy Cannon, Hou vs NY Titans	12-10-61	5
Cookie Gilchrist, Buff vs NYJ	12-8-63	5
Paul Hornung, GB vs Balt Colts	12-12-65	5
Kellen Winslow, SD vs Oak	11-22-81	5
Jerry Rice, SF vs Atl	10-14-90	5
James Stewart, Jax vs Phil	10-12-97	5
Shaun Alexander, Sea vs Minn	9-29-02	5

Rushing

YARDS GAINED

	Date	Yds
Jamal Lewis, Balt vs Clev	9-14-03	295
Corey Dillon, Cin vs Den	10-22-00	278
Walter Payton, Chi vs Minn	11-20-77	275
O.J. Simpson, Buff vs Det	11-25-76	273
Shaun Alexander, Sea vs Oak	11-11-01	266

CARRIES

	Date	No.
Jamie Morris, Wash vs Cin	12-17-88	45
Butch Woolfolk, NYG vs Phil	11-20-83	43
James Wilder, TB vs GB	9-30-84	43
Rudi Johnson, Cin vs Hou	11-9-03	43
James Wilder, TB vs Pitt	10-30-83	42
Terrell Davis, Den vs Buff	10-26-97	42
Ricky Williams, Mia vs Buff	9-21-03	42

TOUCHDOWNS

	Date	No.
Ernie Nevers, Chi Cards vs Chi	11-28-29	6
Jim Brown, Clev vs Balt Colts	11-1-59	5
Cookie Gilchrist, Buff vs NYJ	12-8-63	5
James Stewart, Jax vs Phil	10-12-97	5

Passing

YARDS GAINED

	Date	Yds
N. Van Brocklin, Rams vs NY Yanks	9-28-51	554
Warren Moon, Hou vs KC	12-16-90	527
Boomer Esiason, Ariz vs Wash	11-10-96	522
Dan Marino, Mia vs NYJ	10-23-88	521
Phil Simms, NYG vs Cin	10-13-85	513

COMPLETIONS

	Date	No.
Drew Bledsoe, NE vs Minn	11-13-94	45
Rich Gannon, Oak vs Pitt	9-15-02	43
Richard Todd, NYJ vs SF	9-21-80	42
Vinny Testaverde, NYJ vs Sea	12-6-98	42
Warren Moon, Hou vs Dall	11-10-91	41
Ken Anderson, Cin vs SD	12-20-82	40
Phil Simms, NYG vs Cin	10-13-85	40
Brad Johnson, TB vs Chi	11-18-01	40

TOUCHDOWNS

	Date	No.
Sid Luckman, Chi vs NYG	11-14-43	7
Adrian Burk, Phil vs Wash	10-17-54	7
George Blanda, Hou vs NY Titans	11-19-61	7
Y. A. Tittle, NYG vs Wash	10-28-62	7
Joe Kapp, Minn vs Balt Colts	9-28-69	7

Receiving

YARDS GAINED

	Date	Yds
Flipper Anderson, Rams vs NO	11-26-89	336
Stephone Paige, KC vs SD	12-22-85	309
Jim Benton, Clev vs Det	11-22-45	303
Cloyce Box, Det vs Balt Colts	12-3-50	302
Jimmy Smith, Jax vs Balt Ravens	9-10-00	291

RECEPTIONS

	Date	No.
Terrell Owens, SF vs Chi	12-17-00	20
Tom Fears, Rams vs GB	12-3-50	18
Clark Gaines, NYJ vs SF	9-21-80	17
Sonny Randle, StL Cards vs NYG	11-4-62	16
Jerry Rice, SF vs Rams	11-20-94	16
Keenan McCardell, Jax vs Rams	10-20-96	16
Troy Brown, NE vs KC	9-22-02	16

Five tied with 15.

Single-Game Leaders (Cont.)

Receiving (Cont.)

TOUCHDOWNS

	Date	No.
Bob Shaw, Chi Cards vs Balt Colts	10-2-50	5
Kellen Winslow, SD vs Oak	11-22-81	5
Jerry Rice, SF vs Atl	10-14-90	5

All-Purpose Yards

	Date	Yds
Glyn Milburn, Den vs Sea	12-10-95	404
Billy Cannon, Hou vs NY Titans	12-10-61	373
Tyrone Hughes, NO vs LA Rams	10-23-94	347
Lionel James, SD vs LA Rai	11-10-85	345
Timmy Brown, Phil vs StL Cards	12-16-62	341

Longest Plays

RUSHING	Opponent	Year	Yds
Tony Dorsett, Dall	Minn	1983	99
Ahman Green, GB	Den	2003	98
Andy Uram, GB	Chi Cards	1939	97
Bob Gage, Pitt	Chi	1949	97
Jim Spavital, Balt Colts	GB	1950	96
Bob Hoernschemeyer, Det	NY Yanks	1950	96
Garrison Hearst, SF	NYJ	1998	96
Corey Dillon, Cin	Det	2001	96

PASSING	Opponent	Year	Yds
Frank Filchock to Andy Farkas, Wash	Pitt	1939	99
George Izo to Bobby Mitchell, Wash	Clev	1963	99
Karl Sweetan to Pat Studstill, Det	Balt Colts	1966	99
Sonny Jurgensen to Gerry Allen, Wash	Chi	1968	99
Jim Plunkett to Cliff Branch, LA Rai	Wash	1983	99
Ron Jaworski to Mike Quick, Phil	Atl	1985	99
Stan Humphries to Tony Martin, SD	Sea	1994	99
Brett Favre to Robert Brooks, GB	Chi	1995	99
Trent Green to Marc Boerigter, KC	SD	2002	99

FIELD GOALS	Opponent	Year	Yds
Tom Dempsey, NO	Det	1970	63
Jason Elam, Den	Jax	1998	63
Steve Cox, Clev	Cin	1984	60
Morten Andersen, NO	Chi	1991	60

PUNTS	Opponent	Year	Yds
Steve O'Neal, NYJ	Den	1969	98
Joe Lintzenich, Chi	NYG	1931	94
Shawn McCarthy, NE	Buff	1991	93
Randall Cunningham, Phil	NYG	1989	91

INTERCEPTION RETURNS	Opponent	Year	Yds
Vencie Glenn, SD	Den	1987	103
Louis Oliver, Mia	Buff	1992	103
Seven players tied at 102.			

KICKOFF RETURNS	Opponent	Year	Yds
Al Carmichael, GB	Chi	1956	106
Noland Smith, KC	Den	1967	106
Roy Green, StL Cards	Dall	1979	106

PUNT RETURNS	Opponent	Year	Yds
Robert Bailey, LA Rams	NO	1994	103
Gil LeFebvre, Cin	Brooklyn	1933	98
Charlie West, Minn	Wash	1968	98
Dennis Morgan, Dall	StL Cards	1974	98
Terance Mathis, NYJ	Dall	1990	98

YET ANOTHER SIGN OF THE APOCALYPSE

Ravens receiver Travis Taylor and his wife, Rashidah, attended the team's 2003 Halloween party dressed as Kobe Bryant and the woman who accused him of sexual assault.

Rushing

Year	Player, Team	Att	Yards	Avg	TD
1932	Cliff Battles, Bos	148	576	3.9	3
1933	Jim Musick, Bos	173	809	4.7	5
1934	Beattie Feathers, Chi	101	1004	9.9	8
1935	Doug Russell, Chi Cards	140	499	3.6	0
1936	Alphonse Leemans, NY	206	830	4.0	2
1937	Cliff Battles, Wash	216	874	4.0	5
1938	Byron White, Pitt	152	567	3.7	4
1939	Bill Osmanski, Chi	121	699	5.8	7
1940	Byron White, Det	146	514	3.5	5
1941	Clarence Manders, Bklyn	111	486	4.4	5
1942	Bill Dudley, Pitt	162	696	4.3	5
1943	Bill Paschal, NY	147	572	3.9	10
1944	Bill Paschal, NY	196	737	3.8	9
1945	Steve Van Buren, Phil	143	832	5.8	15
1946	Bill Dudley, Pitt	146	604	4.1	3
1947	Steve Van Buren, Phil	217	1008	4.6	13
1948	Steve Van Buren, Phil	201	945	4.7	10
1949	Steve Van Buren, Phil	263	1146	4.4	11
1950	Marion Motley, Clev	140	810	5.8	3
1951	Eddie Price, NY	271	971	3.6	7
1952	Dan Towler, LA	156	894	5.7	10
1953	Joe Perry, SF	192	1018	5.3	10
1954	Joe Perry, SF	173	1049	6.1	8
1955	Alan Ameche, Balt	213	961	4.5	9
1956	Rick Casares, Chi	234	1126	4.8	12
1957	Jim Brown, Clev	202	942	4.7	9
1958	Jim Brown, Clev	257	1527	5.9	17
1959	Jim Brown, Clev	290	1329	4.6	14
1960	Jim Brown, Clev, NFL	215	1257	5.8	9
	Abner Haynes, Dall Texans, AFL	156	875	5.6	9
1961	Jim Brown, Clev, NFL	305	1408	4.6	8
	Billy Cannon, Hou, AFL	200	948	4.7	6
1962	Jim Taylor, GB, NFL	272	1474	5.4	19
	Cookie Gilchrist, Buff, AFL	214	1096	5.1	13
1963	Jim Brown, Clev, NFL	291	1863	6.4	12
	Clem Daniels, Oak, AFL	215	1099	5.1	3
1964	Jim Brown, Clev, NFL	280	1446	5.2	7
	Cookie Gilchrist, Buff, AFL	230	981	4.3	6
1965	Jim Brown, Clev, NFL	289	1544	5.3	17
	Paul Lowe, SD, AFL	222	1121	5.0	7
1966	Jim Nance, Bos, AFL	299	1458	4.9	11
	Gale Sayers, Chi, NFL	229	1231	5.4	8
1967	Jim Nance, Bos, AFL	269	1216	4.5	7
	Leroy Kelly, Clev, NFL	235	1205	5.1	11
1968	Leroy Kelly, Clev, NFL	248	1239	5.0	16
	Paul Robinson, Cin, AFL	238	1023	4.3	8
1969	Gale Sayers, Chi, NFL	236	1032	4.4	8
	Dickie Post, SD, AFL	182	873	4.8	6
1970	Larry Brown, Wash, NFC	237	1125	4.7	5
	Floyd Little, Den, AFC	209	901	4.3	3
1971	Floyd Little, Den, AFC	284	1133	4.0	6
	John Brockington, GB, NFC	216	1105	5.1	4
1972	O.J. Simpson, Buff, AFC	292	1251	4.3	6
	Larry Brown, Wash, NFC	285	1216	4.3	8
1973	O.J. Simpson, Buff, AFC	332	2003	6.0	12
	John Brockington, GB, NFC	265	1144	4.3	3
1974	Otis Armstrong, Den, AFC	263	1407	5.3	9
	Lawrence McCutcheon, LA, NFC	236	1109	4.7	3
1975	O.J. Simpson, Buff, AFC	329	1817	5.5	16
	Jim Otis, StL, NFC	269	1076	4.0	5
1976	O.J. Simpson, Buff, AFC	290	1503	5.2	8
	Walter Payton, Chi, NFC	311	1390	4.5	13
1977	Walter Payton, Chi, NFC	339	1852	5.5	14
	Mark van Eeghen, Oak, AFC	324	1273	3.9	7
1978	Earl Campbell, Hou, AFC	302	1450	4.8	13
	Walter Payton, Chi, NFC	333	1395	4.2	11
1979	Earl Campbell, Hou, AFC	368	1697	4.6	19
	Walter Payton, Chi, NFC	369	1610	4.4	14
1980	Earl Campbell, Hou, AFC	373	1934	5.2	13
	Walter Payton, Chi, NFC	317	1460	4.6	6
1981	George Rogers, NO, NFC	378	1674	4.4	13
	Earl Campbell, Hou, AFC	361	1376	3.8	10
1982	Freeman McNeil, NY Jets, AFC	151	786	5.2	6
	Tony Dorsett, Dall, NFC	177	745	4.2	5
1983	Eric Dickerson, LA Rams, NFC	390	1808	4.6	18
	Curt Warner, Sea, AFC	335	1449	4.3	13
1984	Eric Dickerson, LA Rams, NFC	379	2105	5.6	14
	Earnest Jackson, SD, AFC	296	1179	4.0	8
1985	Marcus Allen, LA Raiders, AFC	380	1759	4.6	11
	Gerald Riggs, Atl, NFC	397	1719	4.3	10
1986	Eric Dickerson, LA Rams, NFC	404	1821	4.5	11
	Curt Warner, Sea, AFC	319	1481	4.6	13
1987	Charles White, LA Rams, NFC	324	1374	4.2	11
	Eric Dickerson, Ind, AFC	223	1011	4.5	5
1988	Eric Dickerson, Ind, AFC	388	1659	4.3	14
	Herschel Walker, Dall, NFC	361	1514	4.2	5
1989	Christian Okoye, KC, AFC	370	1480	4.0	12
	Barry Sanders, Det, NFC	280	1470	5.3	14
1990	Barry Sanders, Det, NFC	255	1304	5.1	13
	Thurman Thomas, Buff, AFC	271	1297	4.8	11
1991	Emmitt Smith, Dall, NFC	365	1563	4.3	12
	Thurman Thomas, Buff, AFC	288	1407	4.9	7
1992	Emmitt Smith, Dall, NFC	373	1713	4.6	18
	Barry Foster, Pitt, AFC	390	1690	4.3	11
1993	Emmitt Smith, Dall, NFC	283	1486	5.3	9
	T. Thomas, Buff, AFC	355	1315	3.7	6
1994	Barry Sanders, Det, NFC	331	1883	5.7	7
	Chris Warren, Sea, AFC	333	1545	4.6	9

Rushing *(Cont.)*

Year	Player, Team	Att	Yards	Avg	TD
1995	Emmitt Smith, Dall, NFC	377	1773	4.7	25
	Curtis Martin, NE, AFC	368	1487	4.0	14
1996	Barry Sanders, Det, NFC	307	1553	5.1	11
	Terrell Davis, Den, AFC	345	1538	4.5	13
1997	Barry Sanders, Det, NFC	335	2053	6.1	11
	Terrell Davis, Den, AFC	369	1730	4.7	15
1998	Terrell Davis, Den, AFC	392	2008	5.1	21
	Jamal Anderson, Atl, NFC	410	1846	4.5	14
1999	Edgerrin James, Ind, AFC	369	1553	4.2	13
	Stephen Davis, Wash, NFC	290	1405	4.8	17
2000	Edgerrin James, Ind, AFC	387	1709	4.4	13
	Robert Smith, Minn, NFC	295	1521	5.2	7
2001	Priest Holmes, Kan, AFC	327	1555	4.8	8
	Stephen Davis, Wash, NFC	356	1432	4.0	5
2002	Ricky Williams, Mia, AFC	383	1853	4.8	16
	Deuce McAllister, NO, NFC	325	1388	4.3	13
2003	Jamal Lewis, Balt, AFC	387	2066	5.3	14
	Ahman Green, GB, NFC	355	1883	5.3	15

Passing*

Year	Player, Team	Att	Comp	Yards	TD	Int
1932	Arnie Herber, GB	101	37	639	9	9
1933	Harry Newman, NY	136	53	973	11	17
1934	Arnie Herber, GB	115	42	799	8	12
1935	Ed Danowski, NY	113	57	794	10	9
1936	Arnie Herber, GB	173	77	1239	11	13
1937	Sammy Baugh, Wash	171	81	1127	8	14
1938	Ed Danowski, NY	129	70	848	7	8
1939	Parker Hall, Clev	208	106	1227	9	13
1940	Sammy Baugh, Wash	177	111	1367	12	10
1941	Cecil Isbell, GB	206	117	1479	15	11
1942	Cecil Isbell, GB	268	146	2021	24	14
1943	Sammy Baugh, Wash	239	133	1754	23	19
1944	Frank Filchock, Wash	147	84	1139	13	9
1945	Sammy Baugh, Wash	182	128	1669	11	4
	Sid Luckman, Chi	217	117	1725	14	10
1946	Bob Waterfield, LA	251	127	1747	18	17
1947	Sammy Baugh, Wash	354	210	2938	25	15
1948	Tommy Thompson, Phil	246	141	1965	25	11
1949	Sammy Baugh, Wash	255	145	1903	18	14
1950	Norm Van Brocklin, LA	233	127	2061	18	14
1951	Bob Waterfield, LA	176	88	1566	13	10
1952	Norm Van Brocklin, LA	205	113	1736	14	17
1953	Otto Graham, Clev	258	167	2722	11	9
1954	Norm Van Brocklin, LA	260	139	2637	13	21
1955	Otto Graham, Clev	185	98	1721	15	8
1956	Ed Brown, Chi	168	96	1667	11	12
1957	Tommy O'Connell, Clev	110	63	1229	9	8
1958	Eddie LeBaron, Wash	145	79	1365	11	10
1959	Charlie Conerly, NY	194	113	1706	14	4
1960	Milt Plum, Clev, NFL	250	151	2297	21	5
	Jack Kemp, LA, AFL	406	211	3018	20	25
1961	George Blanda, Hou, AFL	362	187	3330	36	22
	Milt Plum, Clev, NFL	302	177	2416	18	10
1962	Len Dawson, Dall, AFL	310	189	2759	29	17
	Bart Starr, GB, NFL	285	178	2438	12	9
1963	Y.A. Tittle, NY, NFL	367	221	3145	36	14
	Tobin Rote, SD, AFL	286	170	2510	20	17
1964	Len Dawson, KC, AFL	354	199	2879	30	18
	Bart Starr, GB, NFL	272	163	2144	15	4
1965	Rudy Bukich, Chi, NFL	312	176	2641	20	9
	John Hadl, SD, AFL	348	174	2798	20	21
1966	Bart Starr, GB, NFL	251	156	2257	14	3
	Len Dawson, KC, AFL	284	159	2527	26	10
1967	Sonny Jurgensen, Wash, NFL	508	288	3747	31	16
	Daryle Lamonica, Oakland, AFL	425	220	3228	30	20
1968	Len Dawson, KC, AFL	224	131	2109	17	9
	Earl Morrall, Balt, NFL	317	182	2909	26	17
1969	S. Jurgensen, Wash, NFL	442	274	3102	22	15
	Greg Cook, Cin, AFL	197	106	1854	15	11
1970	John Brodie, SF, NFC	378	223	2941	24	10
	Daryle Lamonica, Oak, AFC	356	179	2516	22	15
1971	Roger Staubach, Dall, NFC	211	126	1882	15	4
	Bob Griese, Mia, AFC	263	145	2089	19	9
1972	Norm Snead, NY, NFC	325	196	2307	17	12
	Earl Morrall, Mia, AFC	150	83	1360	11	7
1973	Roger Staubach, Dall, NFC	286	179	2428	23	15
	Ken Stabler, Oak, AFC	260	163	1997	14	10
1974	Ken Anderson, Cin, AFC	328	213	2667	18	10
	Sonny Jurgensen, Wash, NFC	167	107	1185	11	5
1975	Ken Anderson, Cin, AFC	377	228	3169	21	11
	Fran Tarkenton, Minn, NFC	425	273	2994	25	13
1976	Ken Stabler, Oak, AFC	291	194	2737	27	17
	James Harris, LA, AFC	158	91	1460	8	6
1977	Bob Griese, Mia, AFC	307	180	2252	22	13
	Roger Staubach, Dall, NFC	361	210	2620	18	9
1978	Roger Staubach, Dall, NFC	413	231	3190	25	16
	Terry Bradshaw, Pitt, AFC	368	207	2915	28	20
1979	Roger Staubach, Dall, NFC	461	267	3586	27	11
	Dan Fouts, SD, AFC	530	332	4082	24	24
1980	Brian Sipe, Clev, AFC	554	337	4132	30	14
	Ron Jaworski, Phi, NFC	451	257	3529	27	12
1981	Ken Anderson, Cin, AFC	479	300	3754	29	10
	Joe Montana, SF, NFC	488	311	3565	19	12
1982	Ken Anderson, Cin, AFC	309	218	2495	12	9
	Joe Theismann, Wash, NFC	252	161	2033	13	9
1983	Steve Bartkowski, Atl, NFC	432	274	3167	22	5
	Dan Marino, Mia, AFC	296	173	2210	20	6
1984	Dan Marino, Mia, AFC	564	362	5084	48	17
	Joe Montana, SF, NFC	432	279	3630	28	10
1985	Ken O'Brien, NY, AFC	488	297	3888	25	8
	Joe Montana, SF, NFC	494	303	3653	27	13
1986	Tommy Kramer, Minn, NFC	372	208	3000	24	10
	Dan Marino, Mia, AFC	623	378	4746	44	23
1987	Joe Montana, SF, NFC	398	266	3054	31	13
	Bernie Kosar, Clev, AFC	389	241	3033	22	9

Passing *(Cont.)*

Year	Player, Team	Att	Comp	Yards	TD	Int
1988	Boomer Esiason, Cin, AFC	388	223	3572	28	14
	Wade Wilson, Minn, NFC	332	204	2746	15	9
1989	Joe Montana, SF, NFC	386	271	3521	26	8
	Boomer Esiason, Cin, AFC	455	258	3525	28	11
1990	Jim Kelly, Buffalo, AFC	346	219	2829	24	9
	Phil Simms, NY, NFC	311	184	2284	15	4
1991	Steve Young, SF, NFC	279	180	2517	17	8
	Jim Kelly, Buff, AFC	474	304	3844	33	17
1992	Steve Young, SF, NFC	402	268	3465	25	7
	Warren Moon, Hou, AFC	346	224	2521	18	12
1993	Steve Young, SF, NFC	462	314	4023	29	16
	John Elway, Den, AFC	551	348	4030	25	10
1994	Steve Young, SF, NFC	461	324	3969	35	10
	Dan Marino, Mia, AFC	615	385	4453	30	17
1995	Brett Favre, GB, NFC	570	359	4413	38	13
	Jeff Blake, Cin, AFC	567	326	3822	28	17
1996	Vinny Testaverde, Balt, AFC	549	325	4177	33	19
	Brett Favre, GB, NFC	543	325	3899	39	13
1997	Steve Young, SF, NFC	356	241	3029	19	6
	Mark Brunell, Jax, AFC	435	264	3281	18	7
1998	Randall Cunningham, Minn, NFC	425	259	3704	34	10
	Vinny Testaverde, NYJ, AFC	421	259	3256	29	7
1999	Kurt Warner, StL, NFC	499	325	4353	41	13
	Peyton Manning, Ind, AFC	533	331	4135	26	15
2000	Trent Green, StL, NFC	240	145	2063	16	5
	Brian Griese, Den, AFC	336	216	2688	19	4
2001	Kurt Warner, StL, NFC	546	375	4830	36	22
	Rich Gannon, Oak, AFC	549	361	3828	27	9
2002	Brad Johnson, TB, NFC	451	281	3049	22	6
	Chad Pennington, NYJ, AFC	399	275	3120	22	6
2003	Steve McNair, Tenn, AFC	400	250	3215	24	7
	Daunte Culpepper, Minn, NFC	454	295	3479	25	11

*Since 1973, the annual passing leaders have been determined by a passer rating system that compares individual performances to a fixed performance standard.

Pass Receiving*

Year	Player, Team	No.	Yds	Avg	TD
1932	Ray Flaherty, NY	21	350	16.7	3
1933	John Kelly, Brooklyn	22	246	11.2	3
1934	Joe Carter, Phil	16	238	14.9	4
	Morris Badgro, NY	16	206	12.9	1
1935	Tod Goodwin, NY	26	432	16.6	4
1936	Don Hutson, GB	34	536	15.8	8
1937	Don Hutson, GB	41	552	13.5	7
1938	Gaynell Tinsley, Chi Cards	41	516	12.6	1
1939	Don Hutson, GB	34	846	24.9	6
1940	Don Looney, Phil	58	707	12.2	4
1941	Don Hutson, GB	58	738	12.7	10
1942	Don Hutson, GB	74	1211	16.4	17
1943	Don Hutson, GB	47	776	16.5	11
1944	Don Hutson, GB	58	866	14.9	9
1945	Don Hutson, GB	47	834	17.7	9
1946	Jim Benton, LA	63	981	15.6	6
1947	Jim Keane, Chi	64	910	14.2	10
1948	Tom Fears, LA	51	698	13.7	4
1949	Tom Fears, LA	77	1013	13.2	9
1950	Tom Fears, LA	84	1116	13.3	7
1951	Elroy Hirsch, LA	66	1495	22.7	17
1952	Mac Speedie, Clev	62	911	14.7	5
1953	Pete Pihos, Phil	63	1049	16.7	10
1954	Pete Pihos, Phil	60	872	14.5	10
	Billy Wilson, SF	60	830	13.8	5
1955	Pete Pihos, Phil	62	864	13.9	7
1956	Billy Wilson, SF	60	889	14.8	5
1957	Billy Wilson, SF	52	757	14.6	6
1958	Raymond Berry, Balt	56	794	14.2	9
	Pete Retzlaff, Phil	56	766	13.7	2
1959	Raymond Berry, Balt	66	959	14.5	14
1960	Lionel Taylor, Den, AFL	92	1235	13.4	12
	Raymond Berry, Balt, NFL	74	1298	17.5	10
1961	Lionel Taylor, Den, AFL	100	1176	11.8	4
	Jim Phillips, LA, NFL	78	1092	14.0	5
1962	Lionel Taylor, Den, AFL	77	908	11.8	4
	Bobby Mitchell, Wash, NFL	72	1384	19.2	11
1963	Lionel Taylor, Den, AFL	78	1101	14.1	10
	Bobby Joe Conrad, St. Louis, NFL	73	967	13.2	10
1964	Charley Hennigan, Houston, AFL	101	1546	15.3	8
	Johnny Morris, Chi, NFL	93	1200	12.9	10
1965	Lionel Taylor, Den, AFL	85	1131	13.3	6
	Dave Parks, SF, NFL	80	1344	16.8	12
1966	Lance Alworth, SD, AFL	73	1383	18.9	13
	Charley Taylor, Wash, NFL	72	1119	15.5	12
1967	George Sauer, NY, AFL	75	1189	15.9	6
	Charley Taylor, Wash, NFL	70	990	14.1	9
1968	Clifton McNeil, SF, NFL	71	994	14.0	7
	Lance Alworth, SD, AFL	68	1312	19.3	10
1969	Dan Abramowicz, NO, NFL	73	1015	13.9	7
	Lance Alworth, SD, AFL	64	1003	15.7	4
1970	Dick Gordon, Chi, NFC	71	1026	14.5	13
	Marlin Briscoe, Buff, AFC	57	1036	18.2	8
1971	Fred Biletnikoff, Oak, AFC	61	929	15.2	9
	Bob Tucker, NY, NFC	59	791	13.4	4
1972	Harold Jackson, Phil, NFC	62	1048	16.9	4
	Fred Biletnikoff, Oak, AFC	58	802	13.8	7
1973	Harold Carmichael, Phil, NFC	67	1116	16.7	9
	Fred Willis, Hou, AFC	57	371	6.5	1
1974	Lydell Mitchell, Balt, AFC	72	544	7.6	2
	Charles Young, Phil, NFC	63	696	11.0	3

*Most catches.

Pass Receiving *(Cont.)*

Year	Player, Team	No.	Yds	Avg	TD
1975	Chuck Foreman, Minn, NFC	73	691	9.5	9
	Reggie Rucker, Clev, AFC	60	770	12.8	3
	Lydell Mitchell, Balt, AFC	60	544	9.1	4
1976	MacArthur Lane, KC, AFC	66	686	10.4	1
	Drew Pearson, Dall, NFC	58	806	13.9	6
1977	Lydell Mitchell, Balt, AFC	71	620	8.7	4
	Ahmad Rashad, Minn, NFC	51	681	13.4	2
1978	Rickey Young, Minn, NFC	88	704	8.0	5
	Steve Largent, Sea, AFC	71	1168	16.5	8
1979	Joe Washington, Balt, AFC	82	750	9.1	3
	Ahmad Rashad, Minn, NFC	80	1156	14.5	9
1980	Kellen Winslow, SD, AFC	89	1290	14.5	9
	Earl Cooper, SF, NFC	83	567	6.8	4
1981	Kellen Winslow, SD, AFC	88	1075	12.2	10
	Dwight Clark, SF, NFC	85	1105	13.0	4
1982	Dwight Clark, SF, NFC	60	913	15.2	5
	Kellen Winslow, SD, AFC	54	721	13.4	6
1983	Todd Christensen, LA, AFC	92	1247	13.6	12
	Roy Green, StL, NFC	78	1227	15.7	14
	Charlie Brown, Wash, NFC	78	1225	15.7	8
	Earnest Gray, NY, NFC	78	1139	14.6	5
1984	Art Monk, Wash, NFC	106	1372	12.9	7
	Ozzie Newsome, Clev, AFC	89	1001	11.2	5
1985	Roger Craig, SF, NFC	92	1016	11.0	6
	Lionel James, SD, AFC	86	1027	11.9	6
1986	Todd Christensen, LA Rai, AFC	95	1153	12.1	8
	Jerry Rice, SF, NFC	86	1570	18.3	15
1987	J.T. Smith, StL Card, NFC	91	1117	12.3	8
	Al Toon, NY, AFC	68	976	14.4	5
1988	Al Toon, NY, AFC	93	1067	11.5	5
	Henry Ellard, LA Rams, NFC	86	1414	16.4	10
1989	Sterling Sharpe, GB, NFC	90	1423	15.8	12
	Andre Reed, Buff, AFC	88	1312	14.9	9
1990	Jerry Rice, SF, NFC	100	1502	15.0	13
	Haywood Jeffires, Hou, AFC	74	1048	14.2	8
	Drew Hill, Hou, AFC	74	1019	13.8	5
1991	Haywood Jeffires, Hou, AFC	100	1181	11.8	7
	Michael Irvin, Dall, NFC	93	1523	16.4	8
1992	Sterling Sharpe, GB, NFC	108	1461	13.5	13
	Haywood Jeffires, Hou, AFC	90	913	10.1	9
1993	Sterling Sharpe, GB, NFC	112	1274	11.4	11
	Reggie Langhorne, Ind, AFC	85	1038	12.2	3
1994	Cris Carter, Minn, NFC	122	1256	10.3	7
	Ben Coates, NE, AFC	96	1174	12.2	7
1995	Herman Moore, Det, NFC	123	1686	13.7	14
	Carl Pickens, Cin, AFC	99	1234	12.5	17
1996	Jerry Rice, SF, NFC	108	1254	11.6	8
	Carl Pickens, Cin, AFC	100	1180	11.8	12
1997	Herman Moore, Det, NFC	104	1293	12.4	8
	Tim Brown, Oak, AFC	104	1408	13.5	5
1998	Frank Sanders, Ariz, NFC	89	1145	12.9	3
	O.J. McDuffie, Mia, AFC	90	1050	11.7	7
1999	Mushin Muhammad, Car, NFC	96	1253	13.1	8
	Jimmy Smith, Jax, AFC	116	1636	14.1	6
2000	Mushin Muhammad, Car, NFC	102	1183	11.6	6
	Marvin Harrison, Ind, AFC	102	1413	13.9	14
2001	Rod Smith, Den, AFC	113	1343	11.9	11
	Keyshawn Johnson, TB, NFC	106	1266	11.9	1
2002	Marvin Harrison, Ind, AFC	143	1722	12.0	11
	Randy Moss, Minn, NFC	106	1347	12.7	7
2003	LaDainian Tomlinson, SD, AFC	100	725	7.3	4
	Torry Holt, StL, NFC	117	1696	14.5	12

YET ANOTHER SIGN OF THE APOCALYPSE

Democratic presidential candidate Joe Lieberman announced that he received the endorsement of ESPN sportscaster Chris Berman.

Scoring

Year	Player, Team	TD	FG	PAT	TP
1932	Earl Clark, Portsmouth	6	3	10	55
1933	Ken Strong, NY	6	5	13	64
	Glenn Presnell, Ports	6	6	10	64
1934	Jack Manders, Chi	3	10	31	79
1935	Earl Clark, Det	6	1	16	55
1936	Earl Clark, Det	7	4	19	73
1937	Jack Manders, Chi	5	18	15	69
1938	Clarke Hinkle, GB	7	3	7	58
1939	Andy Farkas, Wash	11	0	2	68
1940	Don Hutson, GB	7	0	15	57
1941	Don Hutson, GB	12	1	20	95
1942	Don Hutson, GB	17	1	33	138
1943	Don Hutson, GB	12	3	36	117
1944	Don Hutson, GB	9	0	31	85
1945	Steve Van Buren, Phil	18	0	2	110
1946	Ted Fritsch, GB	10	9	13	100
1947	Pat Harder, Chicago Cards	7	7	39	102
1948	Pat Harder, Chicago Cards	6	7	53	110
1949	Pat Harder, Chicago Cards	8	3	45	102
	Gene Roberts, NY	17	0	0	102
1950	Doak Walker, Det	11	8	38	128
1951	Elroy Hirsch, LA	17	0	0	102
1952	Gordy Soltau, SF	7	6	34	94
1953	Gordy Soltau, SF	6	10	48	114
1954	Bobby Walston, Phil	11	4	36	114
1955	Doak Walker, Det	7	9	27	96
1956	Bobby Layne, Det	5	12	33	99
1957	Sam Baker, Wash	1	14	29	77
	Lou Groza, Clev	0	15	32	77
1958	Jim Brown, Clev	18	0	0	108
1959	Paul Hornung, GB	7	7	31	94
1960	Paul Hornung, GB, NFL	15	15	41	176
	Gene Mingo, Den, AFL	6	18	33	123
1961	Gino Cappelletti, Bos, AFL	8	17	48	147
	Paul Hornung, GB, NFL	10	15	41	146
1962	Gene Mingo, Den, AFL	4	27	32	137
	Jim Taylor, GB, NFL	19	0	0	114
1963	Gino Cappelletti, Bos, AFL	2	22	35	113
	Don Chandler, NY, NFL	0	18	52	106
1964	Gino Cappelletti, Bos, AFL	7	25	36	155
	Lenny Moore, Balt, NFL	20	0	0	120
1965	Gale Sayers, Chi, NFL	22	0	0	132
	Gino Cappelletti, Bos, AFL	9	17	27	132
1966	Gino Cappelletti, Bos, AFL	6	16	35	119
	Bruce Gossett, LA, NFL	0	28	29	113
1967	Jim Bakken, StL, NFL	0	27	36	117
	George Blanda, Oak, AFL	0	20	56	116
1968	Jim Turner, NY, AFL	0	34	43	145
	Leroy Kelly, Clev, NFL	20	0	0	120
1969	Jim Turner, NY, AFL	0	32	33	129
	Fred Cox, Minn, NFL	0	26	43	121
1970	Fred Cox, Minn, NFC	0	30	35	125
	Jan Stenerud, KC, AFC	0	30	26	116
1971	Garo Yepremian, Mia, AFC	0	28	33	117
	Curt Knight, Wash, NFC	0	29	27	114
1972	Chester Marcol, GB, NFC	0	33	29	128
	Bobby Howfield, NY AFC	0	27	40	121
1973	David Ray, LA, NFC	0	30	40	130
	Roy Gerela, Pitt, AFC	0	29	36	123
1974	Chester Marcol, GB, NFC	0	25	19	94
	Roy Gerela, Pitt, AFC	0	20	33	93
1975	O.J. Simpson, Buff, AFC	23	0	0	138
	Chuck Foreman, Minn, NFC	22	0	0	132
1976	Toni Linhart, Balt, AFC	0	20	49	109
	Mark Moseley, Wash, NFC	0	22	31	97

Year	Player, Team	TD	FG	PAT	TP
1977	Errol Mann, Oak, AFC	0	20	39	99
	Walter Payton, Chi, NFC	16	0	0	96
1978	Frank Corral, LA, NFC	0	29	31	118
	Pat Leahy, NY, AFC	0	22	41	107
1979	John Smith, NE, AFC	0	23	46	115
	Mark Moseley, Wash, NFC	0	25	39	114
1980	John Smith, NE, AFC	0	26	51	129
	Ed Murray, Det, NFC	0	27	35	116
1981	Ed Murray, Det, NFC	0	25	46	121
	Rafael Septien, Dall, NFC	0	27	40	121
	Jim Breech, Cin, AFC	0	22	49	115
	Nick Lowery, KC, AFC	0	26	37	115
1982	Marcus Allen, LA, AFC	14	0	0	84
	Wendell Tyler, LA, NFC	13	0	0	78
1983	Mark Moseley, Wash, NFC	0	33	62	161
	Gary Anderson, Pitt, AFC	0	27	38	119
1984	Ray Wersching, SF, NFC	0	25	56	131
	Gary Anderson, Pitt, AFC	0	24	45	117
1985	Kevin Butler, Chi, NFC	0	31	51	144
	Gary Anderson, Pitt, AFC	0	33	40	139
1986	Tony Franklin, NE, AFC	0	32	44	140
	Kevin Butler, Chi, NFC	0	28	36	120
1987	Jerry Rice, SF, NFC	23	0	0	138
	Jim Breech, Cin, AFC	0	24	25	97
1988	Scott Norwood, Buff, AFC	0	32	33	129
	Mike Cofer, SF, NFC	0	27	40	121
1989	Mike Cofer, SF, NFC	0	29	49	136
	David Treadwell, Den, AFC	0	27	39	120
1990	Nick Lowery, KC, AFC	0	34	37	139
	Chip Lohmiller, Wash, NFC	0	30	41	131
1991	Chip Lohmiller, Wash, NFC	0	31	56	149
	Pete Stoyanovich, Mia, AFC	0	31	28	121
1992	Pete Stoyanovich, Mia, AFC	0	30	34	124
	Morten Anderson, NO, NFC	0	29	33	120
	Chip Lohmiller, Wash, NFC	0	30	30	120
1993	Jeff Jaeger, Rai, AFC	0	35	27	132
	Jason Hanson, Det, NFC	0	34	28	130
1994	John Carney, SD, AFC	0	34	33	135
	Fuad Reveiz, Minn, NFC	0	34	30	132
	Emmitt Smith, Dall, NFC	22	0	0	132
1995	Emmitt Smith, Dall, NFC	25	0	0	150
	Norm Johnson, Pitt, AFC	0	34	39	141
1996	John Kasay, Car, NFC	0	37	34	145
	Cary Blanchard, Ind, AFC	0	36	27	135
1997	Richie Cunningham, Dall, NFC	0	34	24	126
	Mike Hollis, Jax, AFC	0	41	31	134
1998	Gary Anderson, Minn, NFC	0	35	59	164
	Steve Christie, Buff, AFC	0	33	41	140
1999	Jeff Wilkins, StL, NFC	0	20	28	124
	Mike Vanderjagt, Ind, AFC	0	34	38	145
2000	Marshall Faulk, StL, NFC	26	0	0	156
	Matt Stover, Balt, AFC	0	35	30	135
2001	Marshall Faulk, StL, NFC	21	0	2	128
	Mike Vanderjagt, Ind, AFC	0	28	41	125
2002	Jay Feely, Atl, NFC	0	32	43	138
	Priest Holmes, KC, AFC	24	0	0	144
2003	Jeff Wilkins StL, NFC	0	39	46	163
	Priest Holmes, KC, AFC	27	0	0	162

Pro Bowl Alltime Results

Date	Result
1-15-39	NY Giants 13, Pro All-Stars 10
1-14-40	Green Bay 16, NFL All-Stars 7
12-29-40	Chi Bears 28, NFL All-Stars 14
1-4-42	Chi Bears 35, NFL All-Stars 24
12-27-42	NFL All-Stars 17, Washington 14
1-14-51	A. Conf. 28, N. Conf. 27
1-12-52	N. Conf. 30, A. Conf. 13
1-10-53	N. Conf. 27, A. Conf. 7
1-17-54	East 20, West 9
1-16-55	West 26, East 19
1-15-56	East 31, West 30
1-13-57	West 19, East 10
1-12-58	West 26, East 7
1-11-59	East 28, West 21
1-17-60	West 38, East 21
1-15-61	West 35, East 31
1-7-62	AFL West 47, East 27
1-14-62	NFL West 31, East 30
1-13-63	AFL West 21, East 14
1-13-63	NFL East 30, West 20

Date	Result
1-12-64	NFL West 31, East 17
1-19-64	AFL West 27, East 24
1-10-65	AFL West 34, East 14
1-16-65	AFL West 38, East 14
1-15-66	AFL All-Stars 30, Buffalo 19
1-15-66	NFL East 36, West 7
1-21-67	AFL East 30, West 23
1-22-67	NFL East 20, West 10
1-21-68	AFL East 25, West 24
1-21-68	NFL West 38, East 20
1-19-69	AFL West 38, East 25
1-19-69	NFL West 10, East 7
1-17-70	AFL West 26, East 3
1-18-70	NFL West 16, East 13
1-24-71	NFC 27, AFC 6
1-23-72	AFC 26, NFC 13
1-21-73	AFC 33, NFC 28
1-20-74	AFC 15, NFC 13
1-20-75	NFC 17, AFC 10
1-26-76	NFC 23, AFC 20
1-17-77	AFC 24, NFC 14
1-23-78	NFC 14, AFC 13
1-29-79	NFC 13, AFC 7
1-27-80	NFC 37, AFC 27

Date	Result
2-1-81	NFC 21, AFC 7
1-31-82	AFC 16, NFC 13
2-6-83	NFC 20, AFC 19
1-29-84	NFC 45, AFC 3
1-27-85	AFC 22, NFC 14
2-2-86	NFC 28, AFC 24
2-1-87	AFC 10, NFC 6
2-7-88	AFC 15, NFC 6
1-29-89	NFC 34, AFC 3
2-4-90	NFC 27, AFC 21
2-3-91	AFC 23, NFC 21
2-2-92	NFC 21, AFC 15
2-7-93	AFC 23, NFC 20
2-6-94	NFC 17, AFC 3
2-5-95	AFC 41, NFC 13
2-4-96	NFC 20, AFC 13
2-2-97	AFC 26, NFC 23
2-1-98	AFC 29, NFC 24
2-7-99	AFC 23, NFC 10
2-6-00	NFC 51, AFC 31
2-4-01	AFC 38, NFC 17
2-9-02	AFC 38, NFC 30
2-2-03	AFC 45, NFC 20
2-8-04	NFC 55, AFC 52

Chicago All-Star Game* Results

Date	Result (Attendance)
8-31-34	Chi Bears 0, All-Stars 0 (79,432)
8-29-35	Chi Bears 5, All-Stars 0 (77,450)
9-3-36	All-Stars 7, Detroit 7 (76,000)
9-1-37	All-Stars 6, Green Bay 0 (84,560)
8-31-38	All-Stars 28, Washington 16 (74,250)
8-30-39	NY Giants 9, All-Stars 0 (81,456)
8-29-40	Green Bay 45, All-Stars 28 (84,567)
8-28-41	Chi Bears 37, All-Stars 13 (98,203)
8-28-42	Chi Bears 21, All-Stars 0 (101,100)
8-25-43	All-Stars 27, Washington 7 (48,471)
8-30-44	Chi Bears 24, All-Stars 21 (48,769)
8-30-45	Green Bay 19, All-Stars 7 (92,753)
8-23-46	All-Stars 16, Los Angeles 0 (97,380)
8-22-47	All-Stars 16, Chi Bears 0 (105,840)
8-20-48	Chi Cardinals 28, All-Stars 0 (101,220)
8-12-49	Philadelphia 38, All-Stars 0 (93,780)
8-11-50	All-Stars 17, Philadelphia 7 (88,885)
8-17-51	Cleveland 33, All-Stars 0 (92,180)
8-15-52	Los Angeles 10, All-Stars 7 (88,316)
8-14-53	Detroit 24, All-Stars 10 (93,818)
8-13-54	Detroit 31, All-Stars 6 (93,470)
8-12-55	All-Stars 30, Cleveland 27 (75,000)

Date	Result (Attendance)
8-10-56	Cleveland 26, All-Stars 0 (75,000)
8-9-57	NY Giants 22, All-Stars 12 (75,000)
8-15-58	All-Stars 35, Detroit 19 (70,000)
8-14-59	Baltimore 29, All-Stars 0 (70,000)
8-12-60	Baltimore 32, All-Stars 7 (70,000)
8-4-61	Philadelphia 28, All-Stars 14 (66,000)
8-3-62	Green Bay 42, All-Stars 20 (65,000)
8-2-63	All-Stars 20, Green Bay 17 (65,000)
8-7-64	Chicago 28, All-Stars 17 (65,000)
8-6-65	Cleveland 24, All-Stars 16 (68,000)
8-5-66	Green Bay 38, All-Stars 0 (72,000)
8-4-67	Green Bay 27, All-Stars 0 (70,934)
8-2-68	Green Bay 34, All-Stars 17 (69,917)
8-1-69	NY Jets 26, All-Stars 24 (74,208)
7-31-70	Kansas City 24, All-Stars 3 (69,940)
7-30-71	Baltimore 24, All-Stars 17 (52,289)
7-28-72	Dallas 20, All-Stars 7 (54,162)
7-27-73	Miami 14, All-Stars 3 (54,103)
1974	No game
8-1-75	Pittsburgh 21, All-Stars 14 (54,103)
7-23-76	Pittsburgh 24, All-Stars 0 (52,895)

*Discontinued.

YET ANOTHER SIGN OF THE APOCALYPSE

Joe Theismann and Lawrence Taylor are selling autographed photos of Taylor snapping Theismann's shinbone in a 1985 game.

Alltime Winningest NFL Coaches

Most Career Wins

Coach	Yrs	Teams	Regular Season W	L	T	Pct	Career W	L	T	Pct
Don Shula	33	Colts, Dolphins	328	156	6	.676	347	173	6	.665
George Halas	40	Bears	318	148	31	.671	324	151	31	.671
Tom Landry	29	Cowboys	250	162	6	.605	270	178	6	.601
Curly Lambeau	33	Packers, Cardinals, Redskins	226	132	22	.624	229	134	22	.623
Chuck Noll	23	Steelers	193	148	1	.566	209	156	1	.572
†Dan Reeves	21	Broncos, Giants, Falcons	190	165	2	.535	201	174	2	.536
Chuck Knox	22	Rams, Bills, Seahawks	186	147	1	.558	193	158	1	.550
Paul Brown	21	Browns, Bengals	166	100	6	.621	170	108	6	.609
†M. Schottenheimer	17	Browns, Chiefs, Redskins, Chargers	165	113	1	.593	170	124	1	.578
Bud Grant	18	Vikings	158	96	5	.620	168	108	5	.607
†Bill Parcells	16	Giants, Patriots, Jets, Cowboys	148	106	1	.582	159	113	1	.584
Marv Levy	17	Chiefs, Bills	143	112	0	.561	154	120	0	.562
Steve Owen	23	Giants	151	100	17	.595	153	108	17	.581
Joe Gibbs	12	Redskins	124	60	0	.674	140	65	0	.683
Hank Stram	17	Chiefs, Saints	131	97	10	.571	136	100	10	.573
Weeb Ewbank	20	Colts, Jets	130	129	7	.502	134	130	7	.507
Mike Ditka	14	Bears, Saints	121	95	0	.560	127	101	0	.557
Jim Mora	15	Saints, Colts	125	106	0	.541	125	112	0	.527
Mike Holmgren	12	Green Bay, Seattle	116	76	0	.604	125	83	0	.601
George Seifert	10	49ers, Panthers	114	62	0	.648	124	67	0	.649

†Active in 2003.

Top Winning Percentages

	W	L	T	Pct		W	L	T	Pct
Vince Lombardi	105	35	6	.740	Don Shula	347	173	6	.665
John Madden	112	39	7	.731	George Seifert	124	67	0	.649
Joe Gibbs	140	65	0	.683	Curly Lambeau	229	134	22	.623
George Allen	118	54	5	.681	Bill Walsh	102	63	1	.617
George Halas	324	151	31	.671	†Mike Shanahan	106	68	0	.609

Note: Minimum 100 victories.

†Active in 2003.

Alltime Number-One Draft Choices

Year	Team	Selection	Position
1936	Philadelphia	Jay Berwanger, Chicago	HB
1937	Philadelphia	Sam Francis, Nebraska	FB
1938	Cleveland	Corbett Davis, Indiana	FB
1939	Chicago Cardinals	Ki Aldrich, Texas Christian	C
1940	Chicago Cardinals	George Cafego, Tennessee	HB
1941	Chicago Bears	Tom Harmon, Michigan	HB
1942	Pittsburgh	Bill Dudley, Virginia	HB
1943	Detroit	Frank Sinkwich, Georgia	HB
1944	Boston	Angelo Bertelli, Notre Dame	QB
1945	Chicago Cardinals	Charley Trippi, Georgia	HB
1946	Boston	Frank Dancewicz, Notre Dame	QB
1947	Chicago Bears	Bob Fenimore, Oklahoma A&M	HB
1948	Washington	Harry Gilmer, Alabama	QB
1949	Philadelphia	Chuck Bednarik, Pennsylvania	C
1950	Detroit	Leon Hart, Notre Dame	E
1951	New York Giants	Kyle Rote, Southern Methodist	HB
1952	Los Angeles	Bill Wade, Vanderbilt	QB
1953	San Francisco	Harry Babcock, Georgia	E
1954	Cleveland	Bobby Garrett, Stanford	QB
1955	Baltimore	George Shaw, Oregon	QB
1956	Pittsburgh	Gary Glick, Colorado A&M	DB
1957	Green Bay	Paul Hornung, Notre Dame	HB
1958	Chicago Cardinals	King Hill, Rice	QB
1959	Green Bay	Randy Duncan, Iowa	QB
1960	Los Angeles	Billy Cannon, Louisiana St	RB
1961	Minnesota	Tommy Mason, Tulane	RB
	Buffalo (AFL)	Ken Rice, Auburn	G

Year	Team	Player	Pos
1962	Washington	Ernie Davis, Syracuse	RB
	Oakland (AFL)	Roman Gabriel, N Carolina St	QB
1963	LA Rams	Terry Baker, Oregon St	QB
	Kansas City (AFL)	Buck Buchanan, Grambling	DT
1964	San Francisco	Dave Parks, Texas Tech	E
	Boston (AFL)	Jack Concannon, Boston College	QB
1965	NY Giants	Tucker Frederickson, Auburn	RB
	Houston (AFL)	Lawrence Elkins, Baylor	E
1966	Atlanta	Tommy Nobis, Texas	LB
	Miami (AFL)	Jim Grabowski, Illinois	RB
1967	Baltimore	Bubba Smith, Michigan St	DT
1968	Minnesota	Ron Yary, Southern California	T
1969	Buffalo (AFL)	O.J. Simpson, Southern California	RB
1970	Pittsburgh	Terry Bradshaw, Louisiana Tech	QB
1971	New England	Jim Plunkett, Stanford	QB
1972	Buffalo	Walt Patulski, Notre Dame	DE
1973	Houston	John Matuszak, Tampa	DE
1974	Dallas	Ed Jones, Tennessee St	DE
1975	Atlanta	Steve Bartkowski, California	QB
1976	Tampa Bay	Lee Roy Selmon, Oklahoma	DE
1977	Tampa Bay	Ricky Bell, Southern California	RB
1978	Houston	Earl Campbell, Texas	RB
1979	Buffalo	Tom Cousineau, Ohio St	LB
1980	Detroit	Billy Sims, Oklahoma	RB
1981	New Orleans	George Rogers, South Carolina	RB
1982	New England	Kenneth Sims, Texas	DT
1983	Baltimore	John Elway, Stanford	QB
1984	New England	Irving Fryar, Nebraska	WR
1985	Buffalo	Bruce Smith, Virginia Tech	DE
1986	Tampa Bay	Bo Jackson, Auburn	RB
1987	Tampa Bay	Vinny Testaverde, Miami (FL)	QB
1988	Atlanta	Aundray Bruce, Auburn	LB
1989	Dallas	Troy Aikman, UCLA	QB
1990	Indianapolis	Jeff George, Illinois	QB
1991	Dallas	Russell Maryland, Miami (FL)	DT
1992	Indianapolis	Steve Emtman, Washington	DT
1993	New England	Drew Bledsoe, Washington St	QB
1994	Cincinnati	Dan Wilkinson, Ohio St	DT
1995	Cincinnati	Ki-Jana Carter, Penn St	RB
1996	New York Jets	Keyshawn Johnson, Southern California	WR
1997	St Louis	Orlando Pace, Ohio St	OT
1998	Indianapolis	Peyton Manning, Tennessee	QB
1999	Cleveland	Tim Couch, Kentucky	QB
2000	Cleveland	Courtney Brown, Penn St	DE
2001	Atlanta	Michael Vick, Virginia Tech	QB
2002	Houston	David Carr, Fresno St	QB
2003	Cincinnati	Carson Palmer, Southern California	QB
2004	San Diego	Eli Manning, Mississippi	QB

From 1947 through 1958, the first selection in the draft was a bonus pick, awarded to the winner of a random draw. That club, in turn, forfeited its last-round draft choice. The winner of the bonus choice was eliminated from future draws. The system was abolished after 1958, by which time all clubs had received a bonus choice.

Members of the Pro Football Hall of Fame

Herb Adderley
George Allen
Marcus Allen
Lance Alworth
Doug Atkins
Morris (Red) Badgro
Lem Barney
Cliff Battles
Sammy Baugh
Chuck Bednarik
Bert Bell
Bobby Bell
Raymond Berry

Elvin Bethea
Charles W. Bidwill Sr.
Fred Biletnikoff
George Blanda
Mel Blount
Terry Bradshaw
Bob (the Boomer) Brown
Jim Brown
Paul Brown
Roosevelt Brown
Willie Brown
Buck Buchanan
Nick Buoniconti

Dick Butkus
Earl Campbell
Tony Canadeo
Joe Carr
Dave Casper
Guy Chamberlin
Jack Christiansen
Earl (Dutch) Clark
George Connor
Jimmy Conzelman
Lou Creekmur
Larry Csonka
Al Davis

Willie Davis
Len Dawson
Joe DeLamielleure
Eric Dickerson
Dan Dierdorf
Mike Ditka
Art Donovan
Tony Dorsett
John (Paddy) Driscoll
Bill Dudley
Albert Glen (Turk) Edwards
Carl Eller
John Elway
Weeb Ewbank
Tom Fears
Jim Finks
Ray Flaherty
Len Ford
Dan Fortmann
Dan Fouts
Frank Gatski
Bill George
Joe Gibbs
Frank Gifford
Sid Gillman
Otto Graham
Harold (Red) Grange
Bud Grant
Joe Greene
Forrest Gregg
Bob Griese
Lou Groza
Joe Guyon
George Halas
Jack Ham
Dan Hampton
John Hannah
Franco Harris
Mike Haynes
Ed Healey
Mel Hein
Ted Hendricks
Wilbur (Pete) Henry
Arnie Herber
Bill Hewitt
Clarke Hinkle
Elroy (Crazylegs) Hirsch
Paul Hornung
Ken Houston
Cal Hubbard
Sam Huff
Lamar Hunt
Don Hutson
Jimmy Johnson
John Henry Johnson
Charlie Joiner
David (Deacon) Jones
Stan Jones
Henry Jordan
Sonny Jurgensen
Jim Kelly
Leroy Kelly

Walt Kiesling
Frank (Bruiser) Kinard
Paul Krause
Earl (Curly) Lambeau
Jack Lambert
Tom Landry
Dick (Night Train) Lane
Jim Langer
Willie Lanier
Steve Largent
Yale Lary
Dante Lavelli
Bobby Layne
Alphonse (Tuffy) Leemans
Marv Levy
Bob Lilly
Larry Little
James Lofton
Vince Lombardi
Howie Long
Ronnie Lott
Sid Luckman
William Roy (Link) Lyman
Tom Mack
John Mackey
Tim Mara
Wellington Mara
Gino Marchetti
George Preston Marshall
Ollie Matson
Don Maynard
George McAfee
Mike McCormack
Tommy McDonald
Hugh McElhenny
Johnny (Blood) McNally
Mike Michalske
Wayne Millner
Bobby Mitchell
Ron Mix
Joe Montana
Lenny Moore
Marion Motley
Mike Munchak
Anthony Munoz
George Musso
Bronko Nagurski
Joe Namath
Earle (Greasy) Neale
Ernie Nevers
Ozzie Newsome
Ray Nitschke
Chuck Noll
Leo Nomellini
Merlin Olsen
Jim Otto
Steve Owen
Alan Page
Clarence (Ace) Parker
Jim Parker
Walter Payton
Joe Perry

Pete Pihos
Hugh (Shorty) Ray
Dan Reeves
Mel Renfro
John Riggins
Jim Ringo
Andy Robustelli
Art Rooney
Dan Rooney
Pete Rozelle
Bob St. Clair
Barry Sanders
Gale Sayers
Joe Schmidt
Tex Schramm
Lee Roy Selmon
Billy Shaw
Art Shell
Don Shula
O.J. Simpson
Mike Singletary
Jackie Slater
Jackie Smith
John Stallworth
Bart Starr
Roger Staubach
Ernie Stautner
Jan Stenerud
Dwight Stephenson
Hank Stram
Ken Strong
Joe Stydahar
Lynn Swann
Fran Tarkenton
Charley Taylor
Jim Taylor
Lawrence Taylor
Jim Thorpe
Y.A. Tittle
George Trafton
Charley Trippi
Emlen Tunnell
Clyde (Bulldog) Turner
Johnny Unitas
Gene Upshaw
Norm Van Brocklin
Steve Van Buren
Doak Walker
Bill Walsh
Paul Warfield
Bob Waterfield
Mike Webster
Arnie Weinmeister
Randy White
Dave Wilcox
Bill Willis
Larry Wilson
Kellen Winslow
Alex Wojciechowicz
Willie Wood
Ron Yary
Jack Youngblood

Canadian Football League Grey Cup

Year	Results	Site	Attendance
1909	U of Toronto 26, Parkdale 6	Toronto	3,807
1910	U of Toronto 16, Hamilton Tigers 7	Hamilton	12,000
1911	U of Toronto 14, Toronto 7	Toronto	13,687
1912	Hamilton Alerts 11, Toronto 4	Hamilton	5,337
1913	Hamilton Tigers 44, Parkdale 2	Hamilton	2,100
1914	Toronto 14, U of Toronto 2	Toronto	10,500
1915	Hamilton Tigers 13, Toronto RAA 7	Toronto	2,808
1916–19	No game	—	—
1920	U of Toronto 16, Toronto 3	Toronto	10,088
1921	Toronto 23, Edmonton 0	Toronto	9,558
1922	Queen's U 13, Edmonton 1	Kingston	4,700
1923	Queen's U 54, Regina 0	Toronto	8,629
1924	Queen's U 11, Balmy Beach 3	Toronto	5,978
1925	Ottawa Senators 24, Winnipeg 1	Ottawa	6,900
1926	Ottawa Senators 10, Toronto U 7	Toronto	8,276
1927	Balmy Beach 9, Hamilton Tigers 6	Toronto	13,676
1928	Hamilton Tigers 30, Regina 0	Hamilton	4,767
1929	Hamilton Tigers 14, Regina 3	Hamilton	1,906
1930	Balmy Beach 11, Regina 6	Toronto	3,914
1931	Montreal AAA 22, Regina 0	Montreal	5,112
1932	Hamilton Tigers 25, Regina 6	Hamilton	4,806
1933	Toronto 4, Sarnia 3	Sarnia	2,751
1934	Sarnia 20, Regina 12	Toronto	8,900
1935	Winnipeg 18, Hamilton Tigers 12	Hamilton	6,405
1936	Sarnia 26, Ottawa RR 20	Toronto	5,883
1937	Toronto 4, Winnipeg 3	Toronto	11,522
1938	Toronto 30, Winnipeg 7	Toronto	18,778
1939	Winnipeg 8, Ottawa 7	Ottawa	11,738
1940	Ottawa 12, Balmy Beach 5	Ottawa	1,700
1940	Ottawa 8, Balmy Beach 2	Toronto	4,998
1941	Winnipeg 18, Ottawa 16	Toronto	19,065
1942	Toronto RCAF 8, Winnipeg RCAF 5	Toronto	12,455
1943	Hamilton F Wild 23, Winnipeg RCAF 14	Toronto	16,423
1944	Montreal St H-D Navy 7, Hamilton F Wild 6	Hamilton	3,871
1945	Toronto 35, Winnipeg 0	Toronto	18,660
1946	Toronto 28, Winnipeg 6	Toronto	18,960
1947	Toronto 10, Winnipeg 9	Toronto	18,885
1948	Calgary 12, Ottawa 7	Toronto	20,013
1949	Montreal Als 28, Calgary 15	Toronto	20,087
1950	Toronto 13, Winnipeg 0	Toronto	27,101
1951	Ottawa 21, Saskatchewan 14	Toronto	27,341
1952	Toronto 21, Edmonton 11	Toronto	27,391
1953	Hamilton Ticats 12, Winnipeg 6	Toronto	27,313
1954	Edmonton 26, Montreal 25	Toronto	27,321
1955	Edmonton 34, Montreal 19	Vancouver	39,417
1956	Edmonton 50, Montreal 27	Toronto	27,425
1957	Hamilton 32, Winnipeg 7	Toronto	27,051
1958	Winnipeg 35, Hamilton 28	Vancouver	36,567
1959	Winnipeg 21, Hamilton 7	Toronto	33,133
1960	Ottawa 16, Edmonton 6	Vancouver	38,102
1961	Winnipeg 21, Hamilton 14	Toronto	32,651
1962	Winnipeg 28, Hamilton 27	Toronto	32,655
1963	Hamilton 21, British Columbia 10	Vancouver	36,545
1964	British Columbia 34, Hamilton 24	Toronto	32,655
1965	Hamilton 22, Winnipeg 16	Toronto	32,655
1966	Saskatchewan 29, Ottawa 14	Vancouver	36,553
1967	Hamilton 24, Saskatchewan 1	Ottawa	31,358
1968	Ottawa 24, Calgary 21	Toronto	32,655
1969	Ottawa 29, Saskatchewan 11	Montreal	33,172
1970	Montreal 23, Calgary 10	Toronto	32,669
1971	Calgary 14, Toronto 11	Vancouver	34,484
1972	Hamilton 13, Saskatchewan 10	Hamilton	33,993
1973	Ottawa 22, Edmonton 18	Toronto	36,653
1974	Montreal 20, Edmonton 7	Vancouver	34,450
1975	Edmonton 9, Montreal 8	Calgary	32,454

Canadian Football League Grey Cup (Cont.)

Year	Results	Site	Attendance
1976	Ottawa 23, Saskatchewan 20	Toronto	53,467
1977	Montreal 41, Edmonton 6	Montreal	68,318
1978	Edmonton 20, Montreal 13	Toronto	54,695
1979	Edmonton 17, Montreal 9	Montreal	65,113
1980	Edmonton 48, Hamilton 10	Toronto	54,661
1981	Edmonton 26, Ottawa 23	Montreal	52,478
1982	Edmonton 32, Toronto 16	Toronto	54,741
1983	Toronto 18, British Columbia 17	Vancouver	59,345
1984	Winnipeg 47, Hamilton 17	Edmonton	60,081
1985	British Columbia 37, Hamilton 24	Montreal	56,723
1986	Hamilton 39, Edmonton 15	Vancouver	59,621
1987	Edmonton 38, Toronto 36	Vancouver	59,478
1988	Winnipeg 22, British Columbia 21	Ottawa	50,604
1989	Saskatchewan 43, Hamilton 40	Toronto	54,088
1990	Winnipeg 50, Edmonton 11	Vancouver	46,968
1991	Toronto 36, Calgary 21	Winnipeg	51,985
1992	Calgary 24, Winnipeg 10	Toronto	45,863
1993	Edmonton 33, Winnipeg 23	Calgary	50,035
1994	British Columbia 26, Baltimore 23	Vancouver	55,097
1995	Baltimore 37, Calgary 20	Regina, Saskatchewan	52,564
1996	Toronto 43, Edmonton 37	Hamilton, Ontario	38,595
1997	Toronto 47, Saskatchewan 23	Edmonton	60,431
1998	Calgary 26, Hamilton 24	Winnipeg	34,157
1999	Hamilton 32, Calgary 21	Vancouver	45,118
2000	British Columbia 28, Montreal 26	Calgary	43,822
2001	Calgary 27, Winnipeg 19	Montreal	65,255
2002	Montreal 25, Edmonton 16	Edmonton	62,531
2003	Edmonton 34, Montreal 22	Regina, Saskatchewan	50,909

In 1909, Earl Grey, the Governor-General of Canada, donated a trophy for the Rugby Football Championship of Canada. The trophy, which subsequently became known as the Grey Cup, was originally open only to teams registered with the Canada Rugby Union. Since 1954, it has been awarded to the winner of the Canadian Football League's championship game.

AMERICAN FOOTBALL LEAGUE I

Year	Champion	Record
1926	Philadelphia Quakers	7-2

AMERICAN FOOTBALL LEAGUE II

Year	Champion	Record
1936	Boston Shamrocks	8-3
1937	LA Bulldogs	8-0

AMERICAN FOOTBALL LEAGUE III

Year	Champion	Record
1940	Columbus Bullies	8-1-1
1941	Columbus Bullies	5-1-2

ALL-AMERICAN FOOTBALL CONFERENCE

Year	Championship Game
1946	Cleveland 14, NY Yankees 9
1947	Cleveland 14, NY Yankees 3
1948	Cleveland 49, Buffalo 7
1949	Cleveland 21, San Francisco 7

WORLD FOOTBALL LEAGUE

Year	World Bowl Championship
1974	Birmingham 22, Florida 21
1975	Disbanded midseason

UNITED STATES FOOTBALL LEAGUE

Year	Championship Game
1983	Michigan 24, Philadelphia 22
1984	Philadelphia 23, Arizona 3
1985	Baltimore 28, Oakland 24

NFL EUROPE

Year	Champion	Record
1991	London	9-1-0
1992	Sacramento	8-2-0
1995	Frankfurt	6-4-0
1996	Scotland	7-3-0
1997	Barcelona	5-5-0
1998	Rhein	7-3-0
1999	Frankfurt	6-4-0
2000	Rhein	7-3-0
2001	Berlin	6-4-0
2002	Berlin	6-4-0
2003	Frankfurt	6-4-0
2004	Berlin	9-1-0

Known as World League of American Football until 1998.

College Football

Matt Mauck of
co-national champion
Louisiana State

BOB ROSATO

Unhappy Returns

Faced with three contenders at the end of the regular season, the BCS produced a championship matchup that satisfied no one

BY B.J. SCHECTER

SINCE ITS INCEPTION in 1998, the Bowl Championship Series (BCS) system has been embroiled in controversy. The idea seemed good enough—to pair the nation's top two teams in a national championship game—but the execution has lacked common sense. Instead of implementing a playoff, or some sort of "selection committee" to determine the top two teams, the conference commissioners decided to leave it to an arcane formula, which they poured into a a set of computers, which in turn spat out a national-championship pairing. Against all odds, the system actually worked for the first five years of its existence—or at least it avoided catastrophic controversy, an outcome that seemed inevitable under its strait-jacketed criteria.

Yes, the BCS produced an undisputed (or not *seriously* disputed) national champion from 1998 to 2002, but it did so almost in spite of itself. A late-season upset or two and a major team with an unblemished record were always required to avert total disaster—and every year they arrived, providing an unassailable BCS matchup for the national title. But it was like an old car that is fixed a little bit every year—and indeed the BCS formula *was* tweaked several times—so it continues to run, delaying the inevitable: a breakdown.

In 2003 the BCS broke down. At end of the season, there were three teams with one loss each—Oklahoma, which had just been whipped 35–7 by Kansas State in the Big 12 championship game, SEC champion Louisiana State and Pac-10 champion Southern Cal, which had just taken over the No. 1 ranking in both polls. When the BCS computers stopped whirring, the matchup they produced was Oklahoma–Louisiana State.

That meant the No. 1 team in the nation would not be playing in the national championship game. Under the BCS formula—which considers poll average, computer average (from seven computer rankings), strength of schedule, number of losses, and "quality wins"—the Trojans

ROBERT BECK

Carroll kept his team focused despite the distractions of the BCS controversy.

finished third, behind BCS No. 1 Oklahoma and No. 2 LSU.

Many fans—particularly those in Southern California—were up in arms over the Trojans' exclusion. USC recovered so impressively after losing to Cal on Sept. 27 that many observers seemed to dismiss the loss altogether, even though it came against a team that finished the regular season at 7–6 and was 2–3 going into the game. Oklahoma's loss in the Big 12 championship, though, that was fresh in everyone's mind, despite the Sooners' utter dominance up to that point. Louisiana State, meanwhile, battled back from an Oct. 11 loss to Florida to finish 12–1.

But when it comes to rankings, it seems the college football nation has a *What have you done for me lately?* mentality. See, the problem was not so much that USC got robbed as that all three teams had a legitimate claim to be in the national title game. They all had one loss, regardless of when it came. There was not enough juice in the BCS formula to solve this problem. For all we know, the computers may have come grinding to a halt, smoke funneling out of the monitors. But the human guardians of those computers assured us that Oklahoma

White, the Heisman Trophy winner, completed 64.0% of his passes and threw for 40 touchdowns.

should play LSU in the Sugar Bowl for the national title. They placed the Trojans in the Rose Bowl against No. 4 Michigan. It amounted to a throwback to the pre-1998 days of the imperfect poll system. If USC won, they certainly would hold on to the top spot in the Associated Press poll, and could legitimately call themselves champions (voters in the Coaches' Poll were obligated to declare the winner of the BCS title game their champion). A split vote—exactly what the BCS was created to prevent—loomed as a dark cloud over bowl season.

USC coach Pete Carroll did not rant or rave. Nor did he liken the BCS to a cancer, as Oregon coach Mike Bellotti did—with much less cause—when the Ducks missed out after the 2001 season. Carroll took the high road, shrugged his shoulders and said that his team would be happy to play in whichever bowl game they were sent to. "We're real proud of where we are, excited as we can be to be playing in the Rose Bowl, and to be the No. 1 team in America," he said. "This is a national-championship game for us."

It was a perfectly sensible response, on several levels. If he'd gotten all excited and emotional, the Trojans may been distracted by the controversy. His let's-take-care-of-business attitude suited the occasion, because, regardless of what happened in the Sugar Bowl, regardless of the BCS jumble, if his team produced a solid victory in the Rose Bowl, they'd be recognized as co-champs, at least. "Our kids have mostly grown up in the BCS generation," Carroll said. "But look down the halls here. It's Rose Bowl, Rose Bowl, Rose Bowl. USC

has won eight national championships. [Seven] of them [have] come after winning the Rose Bowl. When we play Michigan in the Rose Bowl, we'll be playing for a championship. If you look at the top of both polls, USC is the name you'll see."

With the entire college football nation watching, USC wasted little time in demonstrating its worthiness. The Trojans scored 37 seconds into the game, and thoroughly dominated Michigan en rotue to a 28–14 win. USC showed a little of everything—a prolific offense, an air-tight defense and a little razzle-dazzle. Late in the third quarter, Trojans offensive coordinator Norm Chow noticed that Michigan was stacking the box. He called a reverse pass. Even though the play hadn't worked in practice all week, Carroll was more than willing to give it a try. "That's an awesome call," he said. "Let's go for it."

The play worked perfectly. Quarterback Matt Leinart pitched to tailback Hershel Dennis, who ran right before giving the ball to star wideout Mike Williams, who ran left in an apparent reverse. But then Williams stopped and threw a perfect pass to Leinart, who was alone on the left side and ran untouched for a 15-yard touchdown. The score all but assured victory for the Trojans and at least a share of their first national championship since 1978.

"They can have their trophy," USC defensive end Omar Nazel said after the game, referring to the crystal ball that would be awarded to the winner of the Sugar Bowl. "Everybody knows who the people's champion is."

Down in New Orleans, LSU and Oklahoma were trying to stay out of the fray, and, like USC, focus on a big game. Playing in its home state, LSU relished the opportunity to win its first national championship since 1958. Oklahoma, which had been ranked No. 1 for most of the season, was trying to recover from the Kansas State debacle. The Sooners had so thoroughly dominated their opponents during the regular season that many fans claimed they should be mentioned with the greatest teams of all time. Following routs of Texas (65–13) and Oklahoma State (52–9), among others, that talk didn't seem so farfetched, but it died down after the Big 12 championship game. The Sugar Bowl, then, became the perfect opportunity for Oklahoma to prove that the Kansas State game had been an aberration.

Publicly, LSU coach Nick Saban likened the Sooners' complex schemes to those of the NFL's Green Bay Packers, but privately he devised a game plan to win the Sugar Bowl. It would accentuate the strengths of his defense, which had allowed just 10.8 points per game during the regular season, fewest in the nation. Saban figured that if his team could get pressure on Oklahoma's quarterback, Jason White, and make the game a defensive battle, then LSU would have a shot. And that's exactly what the Tigers did. LSU held Oklahoma to 154 yards of offense and pressured White into his worst game of the season (13 for 37, 102 yards, two interceptions). LSU's freshman tailback Justin Vincent (16 carries, 117 yards, 1 TD) and 24-year-old junior quarterback Matt Mauck (13 of 22 passes completed) provided the offense. It wasn't pretty, but LSU won, earning as much right as USC to call itself national champion. The polls reflected the dual claims, as the AP named USC No. 1 and the coaches poll picked LSU.

Of course, the fourth split title since 1990 spelled failure for the BCS, so it went back to the drawing board again, vowing to improve the system. (The BCS runs through the 2005 season; perhaps in the intervening two years a playoff system can be devised, but college football fans probably shouldn't hold their breath.)

The Heisman Trophy race didn't have as much controversy as the BCS, but there was some lively debate. Would the voters select Pittsburgh's sensational sophomore receiver Larry Fitzgerald, who was the nation's best individual player (87 catches for 1,595 yards and 22 touchdowns)? Or would they pick Oklahoma's White, who completed 64.0% of his passes for 3,744 yards and 40 TDs and was the MVP of the regular-season's juggernaut? Fitzgerald had two things going against him: He was a sophomore, and a sophomore had never won the award; and his team finished the regular season at 8–4. In the end, the award went to White, who then carried on a long-standing Heisman tradition of flaming out in his bowl game.

Still, White's rise from relative unknown to star was one of the best stories of the season. After blowing out his left knee in 2001, and his right in 2002, White faced an uphill climb, to say the least. But after deciding to commit himself to a vigorous rehabilitation program he came back better than ever. He gained confidence with each game in 2003, and by the end of the year he was the most prolific single-season passer in Sooner history. "There are so many guys who would have given up and decided that their career just wasn't meant to be," said Oklahoma offensive coordinator Chuck Long, a Heisman runner-up at Iowa in 1985. "But Jason is a very tough-minded young man. His attitude is, I don't care how hard the job is, just tell me what has to be done, and I'll do it."

That same workmanlike attitude was evident at several non-BCS schools who threatened to crash the party in '03. While mid-majors have often been sacrificial lambs for schools from power conferences, who entice the smaller schools to travel to

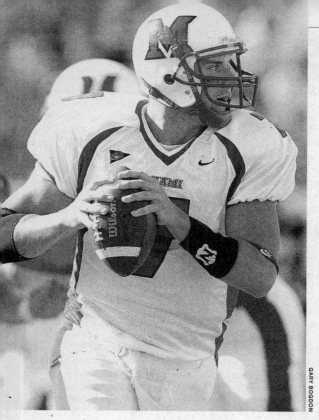

GARY BOGDON

had stayed in the top six then not even the high-powered BCS schools could have kept them out of a big bowl game. But like so many teams before them, the Horned Frogs fell short, losing to Southern Mississippi and then losing 34–31 to Boise State in the Fort Worth Bowl, leading many doubters to say that they never belonged in the first place.

That, of course, couldn't be further from the truth. The mid-majors showed that the gap was shrinking and that there was some pretty darn good football being played at the "lower" levels. Mid-major Miami (Ohio) finished 10th in the AP poll (Bowling Green was 23rd, TCU 25th), and its quarterback, Ben Roethlisberger, was the third passer taken in the NFL draft in April, going 11th to the Pittsburgh Steelers. He threw for 4,486 yards and 37 touchdowns during the season, and led the Redhawks to a 13–1 record, including a 49–28 victory over Louisville in the GMAC Bowl.

Roethlisberger and Miami offered further proof that the gap between majors and mid-majors is closing, and lent credence to the idea that a playoff with champions from all the conferences would attract intense national interest—and might even produce a few of the stunning upsets that make the the NCAA men's basketball tournament so compelling. But that won't happen until 2006 at the earliest, if it ever does. Until a playoff arrives to crown a genuine champion, college football will limp along with the unsatisfying BCS, which, six years in, hardly seems an improvement over the poll system. No, the BCS doesn't work—and you don't need a computer to tell you so.

their cavernous stadiums for huge paydays, this was the season the little guys fought back. Northern Illinois led the way, beating three teams from BCS conferences.

Loaded with players who had been told that they weren't good enough to play at bigger schools, Northern Illinois opened the season in style with wins over Maryland, Iowa State and Alabama (in Tusculoosa). Coach Joe Novak's crew climbed to No. 12 in the nation before falling to Bowling Green, another mid-major that made some noise, putting a scare into Ohio State earlier in the season. But one loss is all it takes to end the title chances of a mid-major (if not of a major), and the Bowling Green defeat banished the Huskies from the national spotlight.

Texas Christian made an even stronger run, going 10–0, rising to No. 10 in the polls and actually climbing into the top six in the BCS rankings. If the Horned Frogs

Final Polls

Associated Press

		Record	Pts	Head Coach	SI Preseason Rank
1.	Southern Cal (48)	12–1	1608	Pete Carroll	10
2.	Louisiana St (17)	13–1	1576	Nick Saban	20
3.	Oklahoma	12–2	1476	Bob Stoops	2
4.	Ohio St	11–2	1411	Jim Tressel	1
5.	Miami [FL]	11–2	1329	Larry Coker	3
6.	Michigan	10–3	1281	Lloyd Carr	13
7.	Georgia	11–3	1255	Mark Richt	5
8.	Iowa	10–3	1107	Kirk Ferentz	39
9.	Washington St	10–3	1060	Bill Doba	43
10.	Miami [OH]	13–1	932	Terry Hoeppner	42
11.	Florida St	10–3	905	Bobby Bowden	11
12.	Texas	10–3	887	Mack Brown	4
13.	Kansas St	11–4	833	Bill Snyder	7
13.	Mississippi	10–3	845	David Cutcliffe	36
15.	Tennessee	10–3	695	Phillip Fulmer	16
16.	Boise St	13–1	645	Dan Hawkins	61
17.	Maryland	10–3	564	Ralph Friedgen	18
18.	Nebraska	10–3	520	Frank Solich/Bo Pelini	32
18.	Purdue	9–4	526	Joe Tiller	26
20.	Minnesota	10–3	368	Glen Mason	31
21.	Utah	10–2	308	Urban Meyer	76
22.	Clemson	9–4	230	Tommy Bowden	48
23.	Bowling Green	11–3	189	Gregg Brandon	66
24.	Florida	8–5	165	Ron Zook	34
25.	Texas Christian	11–2	126	Gary Patterson	28

Note: As voted by a panel of 72 sportswriters and broadcasters following bowl games (1st-place votes in parentheses).

USA Today/ESPN

		Pts	SI Preseason Rank			Pts	SI Preseason Rank
1.	Louisiana St	1572	20	14.	Mississippi	730	36
2.	Southern Cal	1514	10	15.	Boise St	704	61
3.	Oklahoma	1429	2	16.	Tennessee	684	16
4.	Ohio St	1370	1	17.	Minnesota	553	31
5.	Miami (FL)	1306	3	18.	Nebraska	532	32
6.	Georgia	1183	5	19.	Purdue	510	26
7.	Michigan	1140	13	20.	Maryland	462	18
8.	Iowa	1119	39	21.	Utah	327	76
9.	Washington St	983	43	22.	Clemson	219	48
10.	Florida St	929	11	23.	Bowling Green	170	66
11.	Texas	894	4	24.	Texas Christian	145	28
12.	Miami (OH)	800	42	25.	Florida	124	34
13.	Kansas St	746	7				

Note: As voted by a panel of 60 Division I-A head coaches; 25 points for 1st, 24 for 2nd, etc. (1st-place votes in parentheses).

Bowls and Playoffs

NCAA Division I-A Bowl Results

Date	Bowl	Result	Payout/Team ($)	Attendance
12-16-03	New Orleans	Memphis 27, N Texas 17	750,000	25,184
12-18-03	GMAC	Miami (OH) 49, Louisville 28	750,000	40,620
12-22-03	Tangerine	N Carolina St 56, Kansas 26	750,000	26,482
12-23-03	Fort Worth	Boise St 34, Texas Christian 31	800,000	38,028
12-24-03	Las Vegas	Oregon St 55, New Mexico 14	800,000	25,437
12-25-03	Hawaii	Hawaii 54, Houston 48 [3 OT]	750,000	29,005
12-26-03	Motor City	Bowling Green 28, Northwestern 24	780,000	51,286
12-26-03	Insight.com	California 52, Virginia Tech 49	750,000	42,364
12-27-03	Continental Tire	Virginia 23, Pittsburgh 16	750,000	51,236
12-29-03	Alamo	Nebraska 17, Michigan St 3	1.35 million	56,226

NCAA Division I-A Bowl Results (Cont.)

Date	Bowl	Result	Payout/Team ($)	Attendance
12-30-03	Houston	Texas Tech 38, Navy 14	750,000	51,068
12-30-03	Holiday	Washington St 28, Texas 20	2 million	61,102
12-30-03	Silicon Valley	Fresno St 17, UCLA 9	750,000	20,126
12-31-03	Music City	Auburn 28, Wisconsin 14	750,000	55,219
12-31-03	Sun	Minnesota 31, Oregon 30	1.35 million	49,894
12-31-03	Liberty	Utah 17, Southern Miss 0	1.3 million	55,989
12-31-03	Independence	Arkansas 27, Missouri 14	1.2 million	49,625
12-31-03	San Francisco	Boston College 35, Colorado St 21	800,000	25,621
1-1-04	Outback	Iowa 37, Florida 17	2 million	65,372
1-1-04	Gator	Maryland 41, W Virginia 7	1.6 million	78,892
1-1-04	Capital One	Georgia 34, Purdue 27 [OT]	5.125 million	64,565
1-1-04	Rose	Southern Cal 28, Michigan 14	13.5 million	93,849
1-1-04	Orange	Miami (FL) 16, Florida St 14	13.5 million	76,739
1-2-04	Cotton	Mississippi 31, Oklahoma St 28	3 million	73,928
1-2-04	Peach	Clemson 27, Tennessee 14	1.6 million	75,125
1-2-04	Fiesta	Ohio St 35, Kansas St 28	13.5 million	73,425
1-3-04	Humanitarian	Georgia Tech 52, Tulsa 10	750,000	23,118
1-4-04	Sugar	Louisiana St 21, Oklahoma 14	13.5 million	79,342

NCAA Division I-AA Championship Box Score

Colgate	0	0	0	0	—0
Delaware	13	7	14	6	—40

FIRST QUARTER
Del: Jenkins 3 run (Shushman kick), 7:29.
Del: Bennett 1 run (kick failed), 2:35.

SECOND QUARTER
Del: Boler 5 pass from Hall (Shushman kick), 14:55.

THIRD QUARTER
Del: Boler 9 pass from Hall (Shushman kick), 7:30.
Del: Bennett 1 run (Shushman kick), 2:52.

FOURTH QUARTER
Del: Jenkins 2 run (kick failed), 12:22.

	COLGATE	DELAWARE
First downs	10	20
Rushes-yards	32–36	55–165
Passing yards	111	183
Comp/Att/Int	10-22-0	12-20-0
Punts	8–29.0	4–38.0
Fumbles-lost	2–1	0–0
Penalties-yards	3–35	5–45
Time of possession	25:08	34:40

Att: 14,281.

Small College Championship Summaries

NCAA DIVISION II

First round: N Dakota 24, Pittsburg St 14; Winona St 10, Emporia St 3; N Alabama 48, Southern Ark 24; Carson-Newman 35, Valdosta St 29; Saginaw Valley 33, Edinboro 9; Grand Valley St 65, Bentley 36; Central Oklahoma 20, Mesa St 15; Texas A&M–Kingsville 34, Tarleton St 10.
Quarterfinals: N Dakota 36, Winona St 29; N Alabama 41, Carson-Newman 9; Grand Valley St 10, Saginaw Valley 3; Texas A&M–Kingsville 49, Central Oklahoma 6.
Semifinals: N Dakota 29, N Alabama 22; Grand Valley St 31, Texas A&M–Kingsville 3.
Championship: 12-13-03 Florence, AL

N Dakota	0	0	0	3–3
Grand Valley St	3	0	7	0—10

NCAA DIVISION III

First round: WI-La Crosse 52, Concordia (WI) 13; Baldwin-Wallace 54, Hanover 32; Wheaton (IL) 55, Hope 45; E Texas Baptist 42, Trinity (TX) 41 [OT]; Bridgewater (VA) 28, Waynesburg 24; Christopher Newport 24, Muhlenberg 20; Rensselaer 34, Curry 20; Ithaca 14, Brockport St 9; Montclair St 20, Allegheny 19; St. Norbert 26, Simpson 20 [2OT]; Wartburg 21, Bethel (MN) 7; Linfield 31, Redlands 23.

NCAA DIVISION III (CONT.)

Second round: Mount Union 39, WI-La Crosse 14; Wheaton 16, Baldwin-Wallace 12; Lycoming 13, E Texas Baptist 7 [OT]; Bridgewater 26, Christopher Newport 3; Rensselaer 40, Springfield 34; Ithaca 33, Montclair St 13; St. John's (MN) 38, St. Norbert 13; Linfield 23, Wartburg 20.
Quarterfinals: Mount Union 56, Wheaton 10; Bridgewater 13, Lycoming 9; Rensselaer 21, Ithaca 16; St. John's 31, Linfield 25..
Semifinals: Mount Union 66, Bridgewater 0; St. John's 38, Rensselaer 10.
Championship: 12-20-03 Salem, VA

St. John's	0	7	3	14—24
Mount Union	0	6	0	0—6

NAIA CHAMPIONSHIP

12-20-03 Hardin County, TN

NW Oklahoma St	7	0	7	14—28
Carroll	3	14	24	0—41

Awards

Heisman Memorial Trophy

Player, School	Class	Pos	1st	2nd	3rd	Total
Jason White, Oklahoma	Sr	QB	319	204	116	1481
Larry Fitzgerald, Pittsburgh	So	WR	253	233	128	1353
Eli Manning, Mississippi	Sr	QB	95	132	161	710
Chris Perry, Michigan	Sr	RB	27	66	128	341
Darren Sproles, Kansas St	Jr	RB	15	30	29	134

Note: Former Heisman winners and the media vote, with ballots allowing for three names (3 points for 1st, 2 for 2nd, 1 for 3rd).

Other Awards

Maxwell Award (Player)..Eli Manning, Mississippi, QB
Sporting News Player of the Year.............................Jason White, Oklahoma, QB
Walter Camp Player of the Year..........................Larry Fitzgerald, Pittsburgh, WR
Chuck Bednarik Award (Defense).......................Teddy Lehman, Oklahoma, LB
Vince Lombardi/Rotary Award (Lineman/LB)........Tommie Harris, Oklahoma, DL
Outland Trophy (Interior Lineman) ....Robert Gallery, Iowa, OL
Davey O'Brien Award (QB)......................................Jason White, Oklahoma, QB
Unitas Golden Arm Award (Senior QB)..................Eli Manning, Mississippi, QB
Doak Walker Award (RB)...Chris Perry, Michigan, RB
Biletnikoff Award (WR)..Larry Fitzgerald, Pittsburgh, WR
Butkus Award (Linebacker)..................................Teddy Lehman, Oklahoma, LB
Jim Thorpe Award (Defensive Back) ....Derrick Strait, Oklahoma, DB
Associated Press Player of the Year........................Jason White, Oklahoma, QB
Walter Payton Award (Div I-AA Player)....................Jamaal Branch, Colgate, RB
Harlon Hill Trophy (Div II Player) ....Will Hall, N Alabama, QB
Gagliardi Trophy (Div III Player) ....Blake Elliot, St. John's (MN), WR

Coaches' Awards

Walter Camp Award.....................................Bob Stoops, Oklahoma
Eddie Robinson Award (Div I-AA) ....Mike Ayers, Wofford
Bobby Dodd Award ....Bob Stoops, Oklahoma
Bear Bryant Award.....................................Nick Saban, Louisiana St

AFCA COACHES OF THE YEAR

Division I-A ....Pete Carroll, Southern California
Division I-AA..Dick Biddle, Colgate
Division II..Brian Kelly, Grand Valley St
Division III...John Gagliardi, St. John's (MN)

Football Writers Association of America All-America Team

OFFENSE

QB.......Jason White, Oklahoma, Sr
RB........Kevin Jones, Virginia Tech, Jr
WR ......Mark Clayton, Oklahoma, Jr
WR .....Larry Fitzgerald, Pittsburgh, So
WR ......Mike Williams, Southern Cal, So
TE ....Kellen Winslow Jr, Miami, Jr
OL ....Shawn Andrews, Arkansas, Jr
OL ....Alex Barron, Florida St, Jr
OL ....Robert Gallery, Iowa, Sr
OL ....Jacob Rogers, Southern Cal, Sr
OL ....Jake Grove, Virginia Tech, Sr
K ....Nick Browne, Texas Christian, Sr
KR ....Antonio Perkins, Oklahoma, Jr

DEFENSE

DL ....Dave Ball, UCLA, Sr
DL ....Kenechi Udeze, Southern Cal, Jr
DL ....Tommie Harris, Oklahoma, Jr
DL ....Chad Lavalais, Louisiana St, Sr
LB ....Derrick Johnson, Texas, Jr
LB ....Teddy Lehman, Oklahoma, Sr
LB ....Grant Wiley, W Virginia, Sr
DB........Will Allen, Ohio St, Sr
DB........Keiwan Ratliff, Florida, Sr
DB........Derrick Strait, Oklahoma, Sr
DB........Sean Taylor, Miami (FL), Jr
P ....Dustin Colquitt, Tennessee, Jr

Division I-A

ATLANTIC COAST CONFERENCE

	Conference		Full Season		
	W	L	W	L	Pct
Florida St	7	1	10	3	.769
Maryland	6	2	10	3	.769
Clemson	5	3	9	4	.692
N Carolina St	4	4	8	5	.615
Virginia	4	4	8	5	.615
Georgia Tech	4	4	7	6	.538
Wake Forest	3	5	5	7	.417
Duke	2	6	4	8	.333
N Carolina	1	7	2	10	.167

BIG EAST CONFERENCE

	Conference		Full Season		
	W	L	W	L	Pct
Miami (FL)	6	1	11	2	.846
W Virginia	6	1	8	5	.615
Pittsburgh	5	2	8	5	.615
Virginia Tech	4	3	8	5	.615
Boston College	3	4	8	5	.615
Syracuse	2	5	6	6	.500
Rutgers	2	5	5	7	.417
Temple	0	7	1	11	.083

BIG TEN CONFERENCE

	Conference		Full Season		
	W	L	W	L	Pct
Michigan	7	1	10	3	.769
Ohio St	6	2	11	2	.846
Purdue	6	2	9	4	.692
Iowa	5	3	10	3	.769
Minnesota	5	3	10	3	.769
Michigan St	5	3	8	5	.615
Wisconsin	4	4	7	6	.539
Northwestern	4	4	6	7	.462
Penn St	1	7	3	9	.250
Indiana	1	7	2	10	.167
Illinois	0	8	1	11	.083

BIG 12 CONFERENCE

	Conference		Full Season		
NORTH	W	L	W	L	Pct
*Kansas St	6	2	11	4	.733
Nebraska	5	3	10	3	.769
Missouri	4	4	8	5	.615
Kansas	3	5	6	7	.462
Colorado	3	5	5	7	.417
Iowa St	0	8	2	10	.167
SOUTH					
*Oklahoma	8	0	12	2	.857
Texas	7	1	10	3	.769
Oklahoma St	5	3	9	4	.692
Texas Tech	4	4	8	5	.615
Texas A&M	2	6	4	8	.333
Baylor	1	7	3	9	.250

*Full season record includes Big 12 Championship Game in which Kansas St defeated Oklahoma 35–7 on Dec. 6.

Division I-A *(Cont.)*

CONFERENCE USA

| | Conference | | Full Season | | |
	W	L	W	L	Pct
Southern Mississippi	8	0	9	4	.692
Texas Christian	7	1	11	2	.846
Louisville	5	3	9	4	.692
Memphis	5	3	9	4	.692
South Florida	5	3	7	4	.636
Houston	4	4	7	6	.539
Alabama-Birmingham	4	4	5	7	.417
Tulane	3	5	5	7	.417
Cincinnati	2	6	5	7	.417
E Carolina	1	7	1	11	.083
Army	0	8	0	13	.000

MID-AMERICAN ATHLETIC CONFERENCE

| | Conference | | Full Season | | |
EAST	W	L	W	L	Pct
*Miami (OH)	8	0	13	1	.929
Marshall	6	2	8	4	.667
Akron	5	3	7	5	.583
Kent St	4	4	5	7	.417
Central Florida	2	6	3	9	.250
Ohio	1	7	2	10	.167
Buffalo	1	7	1	11	.083
WEST					
*Bowling Green	7	1	11	3	.786
Northern Illinois	6	2	10	2	.833
Toledo	6	2	8	4	.667
Western Michigan	4	4	5	7	.417
Ball St	3	5	4	8	.333
Eastern Michigan	2	6	3	9	.250
Central Michigan	1	7	3	9	.250

*Full season record includes MAC Championship Game in which Miami (OH) defeated Bowling Green 49–27 on Dec 6.

MOUNTAIN WEST CONFERENCE

| | Conference | | Full Season | | |
	W	L	W	L	Pct
Utah	6	1	10	2	.833
New Mexico	5	2	8	5	.615
Colorado St	4	3	7	6	.539
Air Force	3	4	7	5	.583
San Diego St	3	4	6	6	.500
Brigham Young	3	4	4	8	.333
Nevada–Las Vegas	2	5	6	6	.500
Wyoming	2	5	4	8	.333

PACIFIC 10 CONFERENCE

| | Conference | | Full Season | | |
	W	L	W	L	Pct
Southern California	7	1	12	1	.923
Washington St	6	2	10	3	.769
Oregon	5	3	8	5	.615
California	5	3	8	6	.571
Oregon St	4	4	8	5	.615
UCLA	4	4	6	7	.462
Washington	4	4	6	6	.500
Arizona St	2	6	5	7	.417
Stanford	2	6	4	7	.364
Arizona	1	7	2	10	.167

Division I-A (Cont.)

SOUTHEASTERN CONFERENCE

EAST	Conference		Full Season		
	W	L	W	L	Pct
*Georgia	6	2	11	3	.786
Tennessee	6	2	10	3	.769
Florida	6	2	8	5	.615
S Carolina	2	6	5	7	.417
Kentucky	1	7	4	8	.333
Vanderbilt	1	7	2	10	.167
WEST					
*Louisiana St	7	1	13	1	.929
Mississippi	7	1	10	3	.769
Auburn	5	3	8	5	.615
Arkansas	4	4	9	4	.692
Mississippi St	1	7	2	10	.167
Alabama†	2	6	4	9	.308

*Full season record includes SEC Championship Game in which Louisiana St defeated Georgia 34–13, on Dec. 6.
† Ineligible for SEC championship due to probation.

SUN BELT CONFERENCE

	Conference		Full Season		
	W	L	W	L	Pct
N Texas	7	0	9	4	.692
Louisiana-Lafayette	4	3	4	8	.333
Middle Tennessee St	4	3	4	8	.333
Arkansas St	3	4	5	7	.417
Idaho	3	4	3	9	.250
Utah St	3	4	3	9	.250
New Mexico St	2	5	3	9	.250
Louisiana-Monroe	1	6	1	11	.083

WESTERN ATHLETIC CONFERENCE

	Conference		Full Season		
	W	L	W	L	Pct
Boise St	8	0	13	1	.929
Fresno St	6	2	9	5	.643
Tulsa	6	2	8	5	.615
Hawaii	5	3	9	5	.643
Rice	5	3	5	7	.417
Nevada	4	4	6	6	.500
Louisiana Tech	3	5	5	7	.417
San Jose St	2	6	3	8	.273
Texas–El Paso	1	7	2	11	.154
Southern Methodist	0	8	0	12	.000

INDEPENDENTS

	Full Season		
	W	L	Pct
Connecticut	9	3	.750
Navy	8	5	.615
Troy St	6	6	.500
Notre Dame	5	7	.417

Division I-AA

ATLANTIC 10 CONFERENCE

	Conference		Full Season		
	W	L	W	L	Pct
Massachusetts	9	1	10	3	.769
Delaware	8	1	15	1	.938
Northeastern	6	3	8	4	.667
Villanova	5	4	7	4	.636
Maine	4	4	6	5	.546
William & Mary	4	4	5	5	.500
James Madison	4	5	6	6	.500
New Hampshire	3	6	5	7	.417
Rhode Island	3	6	4	8	.333
Hofstra	2	7	2	10	.167
Richmond	1	8	2	9	.182

BIG SKY CONFERENCE

	Conference		Full Season		
	W	L	W	L	Pct
Montana	5	2	9	4	.692
Northern Arizona	5	2	9	4	.692
Montana St	5	2	7	6	.538
Idaho St	4	3	9	4	.692
Weber St	4	3	8	4	.667
Eastern Washington	3	4	6	5	.546
Portland St	1	6	4	7	.364
Sacramento St	1	6	2	9	.182

BIG SOUTH CONFERENCE

	Conference		Full Season		
	W	L	W	L	Pct
Gardner-Webb	4	0	8	4	.667
Liberty	3	1	6	6	.500
Virginia Military	2	2	6	6	.500
Coastal Carolina	1	3	6	5	.546
Charleston Southern	0	4	1	11	.083

GATEWAY COLLEGIATE ATHLETIC CONFERENCE

	Conference		Full Season		
	W	L	W	L	Pct
Southern Illinois	6	1	10	2	.833
Northern Iowa	6	1	10	3	.769
Western Kentucky	5	2	9	4	.692
Illinois St	3	4	6	6	.500
Youngstown St	2	5	5	7	.417
SW Missouri St	1	6	4	7	.364
Indiana St	0	7	3	10	.231

IVY LEAGUE

	Conference		Full Season		
	W	L	W	L	Pct
Pennsylvania	7	0	10	0	1.000
Harvard	4	3	7	3	.700
Yale	4	3	6	4	.600
Brown	4	3	5	5	.500
Dartmouth	4	3	5	5	.500
Columbia	3	4	4	6	.400
Princeton	2	5	2	8	.200
Cornell	0	7	1	9	.100

METRO ATLANTIC ATHLETIC CONFERENCE

	Conference		Full Season		
	W	L	W	L	Pct
Duquesne	5	0	8	3	.727
Iona	4	1	6	5	.546
Marist	2	3	4	6	.400
La Salle	2	3	3	8	.273
St. Peter's	2	3	2	8	.200
Siena	0	5	0	11	.000

Division I-AA (Cont.)

MID-EASTERN ATHLETIC CONFERENCE

	Conference		Full Season		
	W	L	W	L	Pct
N Carolina A&T	7	1	10	3	.769
Bethune Cookman	6	2	9	3	.750
S Carolina St	6	2	8	4	.667
Hampton	5	3	7	4	.636
Morgan St	4	4	6	5	.546
Florida A&M	4	4	6	6	.500
Howard	3	5	4	7	.364
Delaware St	1	7	1	10	.091
Norfolk St	0	8	1	11	.083

NORTHEAST CONFERENCE

	Conference		Full Season		
	W	L	W	L	Pct
Monmouth (NJ)	6	1	10	2	.833
Albany	6	1	7	4	.636
Stony Brook	4	3	6	4	.600
Robert Morris	4	3	6	4	.600
Sacred Heart	3	4	6	5	.546
Wagner	3	4	6	5	.546
Central Conn	2	5	3	8	.273
St. Francis (PA)	0	7	1	9	.100

OHIO VALLEY CONFERENCE

	Conference		Full Season		
	W	L	W	L	Pct
Jacksonville St	7	1	8	4	.667
Eastern Kentucky	6	2	7	5	.583
Samford	5	3	7	4	.636
Tennessee St	5	3	7	5	.583
SE Missouri St	5	3	5	7	.417
Murray St	3	5	4	8	.333
Eastern Illinois	3	5	4	8	.333
Tennessee Tech	1	7	2	9	.182
Tennessee Martin	1	7	2	10	.167

PATRIOT LEAGUE

	Conference		Full Season		
	W	L	W	L	Pct
Colgate	7	0	15	1	.938
Lehigh	6	1	8	3	.727
Fordham	4	3	9	3	.750
Bucknell	4	3	6	6	.500
Towson	3	4	6	6	.500
Lafayette	2	5	5	6	.455
Georgetown	1	6	4	8	.333
Holy Cross	1	6	1	11	.083

PIONEER LEAGUE

	Conference		Full Season		
NORTH	W	L	W	L	Pct
San Diego	4	1	8	2	.800
Dayton	5	2	9	2	.818
Valparaiso	5	3	8	4	.667
Drake	2	4	6	6	.500
Butler	1	5	2	9	.182
SOUTH					
Morehead St	5	2	8	3	.727
Jacksonville	2	3	5	6	.455
Austin Peay	2	4	4	7	.364
Davidson	2	4	3	8	.273

*Full season record includes Pioneer League Championship in which Valparaiso def. Morehead St 54–42 on Nov. 22.

Division I-AA (Cont.)

SOUTHERN CONFERENCE

	Conference		Full Season		
	W	L	W	L	Pct
Wofford	8	0	12	2	.857
Appalachian St	6	2	7	4	.636
Georgia Southern	5	3	7	4	.636
Furman	4	4	6	5	.546
The Citadel	4	4	6	6	.500
Western Carolina	3	5	5	7	.417
Chattanooga	3	5	3	9	.250
E Tenn St	2	6	5	7	.417
Elon	1	7	2	10	.167

SOUTHLAND CONFERENCE

	Conference		Full Season		
	W	L	W	L	Pct
McNeese St	5	0	10	2	.833
Stephen F. Austin	4	1	7	4	.636
Nicholls St	3	2	5	6	.455
Northwestern St	1	4	6	6	.500
Texas St	1	4	4	8	.333
Sam Houston St	1	4	2	9	.182

SOUTHWESTERN ATHLETIC CONFERENCE

	Conference		Full Season		
EASTERN	W	L	W	L	Pct
Alabama A&M	6	3	8	4	.667
Alcorn St	6	3	7	5	.583
Alabama St	6	4	8	5	.615
Jackson St	2	6	2	10	.167
Mississippi Valley St	1	8	2	9	.182
WESTERN					
Southern	9	1	12	1	.923
Grambling	8	1	9	3	.750
Texas Southern	4	5	5	6	.455
Arkansas–Pine Bluff	3	6	5	6	.455
Prairie View A&M	0	8	1	10	.091

*Full season record includes SWAC Championship Game in which Southern defeated Alabama St. 20–9 on Dec. 13.

INDEPENDENTS

	Full Season		
	W	L	Pct
Northern Colorado	9	2	.818
Florida Atlantic	11	3	.786
Cal Poly	7	4	.636
SE Louisiana	5	7	.417
Southern Utah	4	7	.364
Florida International	2	10	.167
St. Mary's (CA)	1	11	.083
Savannah St	0	12	.000

Division I-A

SCORING

	Class	GP	TD	XP	FG	Pts	Pts/Game
Patrick Cobbs, N Texas	Jr	11	21	0	0	126	11.45
Cedric Benson, Texas	Jr	12	22	1	0	134	11.17
Walter Reyes, Syracuse	Jr	12	21	1	0	128	10.67
Larry Fitzgerald, Pittsburgh	So	13	22	0	0	132	10.15
Steven Jackson, Oregon St	Jr	13	22	0	0	132	10.15
Jason Wright, Northwestern	Sr	13	21	0	0	126	9.69
Kevin Jones, Virginia Tech	Jr	13	21	0	0	126	9.69
DonTrell Moore, New Mexico	So	13	21	0	0	126	9.69
Nick Browne, Texas Christian	Sr	13	0	38	28	124	9.54
Jonathan Nichols, Mississippi	Jr	13	0	49	25	124	9.54

FIELD GOALS

	Class	GP	FGA	FG	Pct	FG/Game
Billy Bennett, Georgia	Sr	14	38	31	.816	2.21
Nick Browne, Texas Christian	Sr	13	33	28	.848	2.15
Drew Dunning, Washington St	Sr	13	31	27	.871	2.08
Ben Jones, Purdue	So	13	30	25	.833	1.92
Jonathan Nichols, Mississippi	Jr	13	29	25	.862	1.92

TOTAL OFFENSE

			Rushing		Passing		Total Offense		
	Class	GP	Car	Net	Att	Yds	Yds	Yds/Play	Yds/Game
B.J. Symons, Texas Tech	Sr	13	79	143	719	5833	5976	7.49	459.7
Philip Rivers, N Carolina St	Sr	13	78	109	483	4491	4600	8.20	353.8
Josh Harris, Bowling Green	Sr	14	215	830	494	3813	4643	6.55	331.6
Ben Roethlisberger, Miami (OH)	Jr	14	67	111	495	4486	4597	8.18	328.4
Charlie Frye, Akron	Jr	12	111	228	421	3549	3837	7.21	319.8
Timmy Chang, Hawaii	Jr	13	43	-60	601	4199	4139	6.43	218.4
Ryan Dinwiddie, Boise St	Sr	14	81	43	446	4356	4399	8.35	314.2
Bruce Gradkowski, Toledo	So	12	91	504	389	3210	3714	7.74	309.5
Derek Anderson, Oregon St	Jr	13	57	-125	510	4058	3933	6.94	302.5
Rod Rutherford, Pittsburgh	Sr	13	136	150	413	3679	3829	6.97	294.5

RUSHING

	Class	GP	Car	Yds	TD	Avg	Yds/Game
Patrick Cobbs, N Texas	Jr	11	307	1680	19	5.47	152.73
Michael Turner, Northern Illinois	Sr	12	310	1648	14	5.32	137.33
Darren Sproles, Kansas St	Jr	15	306	1986	16	6.49	132.40
Derrick Knight, Boston College	Sr	13	321	1721	11	5.36	132.38
DeAngelo Williams, Memphis	So	11	243	1430	10	5.88	130.00
Chris Perry, Michigan	Sr	13	338	1674	18	4.95	128.77
Anthony Sherrell, Eastern Michigan	Jr	12	338	1531	12	4.53	127.58
Kevin Jones, Virginia Tech	Jr	13	281	1647	21	5.86	126.69
Jerry Seymour, Central Michigan	Fr	9	205	1117	8	5.45	124.11
Steven Jackson, Oregon St	Jr	13	350	1545	19	4.41	118.85

PASSING EFFICIENCY

	Class	GP	Att	Comp	Pct Comp	Yds	Yds/Att	TD	Int	Rating Pts
Philip Rivers, N Carolina St	Sr	13	483	348	72.05	4491	9.30	34	7	170.5
Ben Roethlisberger, Miami (OH)	Jr	14	495	342	69.09	4486	9.06	37	10	165.8
Matt Leinart, Southern California	So	13	402	255	63.43	3556	8.85	38	9	164.5
Ryan Dinwiddie, Boise St	Sr	14	446	276	61.88	4356	9.77	31	7	163.7
Asad Abdul-Khaliq, Minnesota	Sr	13	250	158	63.20	2401	9.60	17	5	162.3
Bruce Gradkowski, Toledo	So	12	389	277	71.21	3210	8.25	29	7	161.5
Jason White, Oklahoma	Sr	14	451	278	61.64	3846	8.53	40	10	158.1
Rod Rutherford, Pittsburgh	Sr	13	413	247	59.81	3679	8.91	37	14	157.4
Bill Whittemore, Kansas	Sr	10	263	159	60.46	2385	9.07	18	6	154.7
Kevin Kolb, Houston	Fr	13	360	220	61.11	3131	8.70	25	6	153.8

Note: Minimum 15 attempts per game.

Division I-A (Cont.)

RECEPTIONS PER GAME

	Class	GP	No.	Yds	TD	R/Game
Lance Moore, Toledo	Jr	12	103	1194	9	8.58
Chad Owens, Hawaii	Jr	11	85	1134	9	7.73
Wes Welker, Texas Tech	Sr	13	97	1099	9	7.46
Dante Ridgeway, Ball St	So	12	89	1075	10	7.42
Reggie Williams, Washington	Jr	12	89	1109	8	7.42

RECEIVING YARDS PER GAME

	Class	GP	No.	Yds	TD	Yds/Game
Larry Fitzgerald, Pittsburgh	So	13	92	1672	22	128.63
Geoff McArthur, California	Jr	13	85	1504	10	115.69
James Newson, Oregon St	Sr	12	81	1306	3	108.83
Martin Nance, Miami (OH)	Jr	14	90	1498	11	107.00
Kerry Wright, Middle Tennessee St	Jr	12	73	1280	9	106.67

ALL-PURPOSE RUNNERS

	Class	GP	Rush	Rec	PR	KOR	Yds	Yds/Game
DeAngelo Williams, Memphis	So	11	1430	384	0	299	2113	192.09
Darren Sproles, Kansas St	Jr	15	1986	287	190	272	2735	182.33
Jerry Seymour, Central Michigan	Fr	9	1117	103	0	330	1550	172.22
Howard Jackson, Texas–El Paso	Jr	13	1146	391	0	609	2146	165.08
Michael Turner, Northern Illinois	Sr	12	1648	230	0	58	1936	161.33

INTERCEPTIONS

	Class	GP	No.	Int/Game
Sean Taylor, Miami (FL)	Jr	12	10	.83
Josh Bullocks, Nebraska	So	13	10	.77
Derrick Ansley, Troy St	Jr	12	9	.75
Jonathan Burke, Arkansas St	Sr	12	9	.75
Keiwan Ratliff, Florida	Sr	13	9	.69

PUNTING

	Class	No.	Avg
Matt Prater, Central Florida	So	58	47.95
Brandon Fields, Michigan St	So	62	46.42
Joel Stelly, Louisiana-Monroe	So	67	46.25
Jared Scruggs, Rice	Fr	51	45.90
R. Plackemeier, Wake Forest	So	57	45.61

Note: Minimum of 3.6 per game.

PUNT RETURNS

	Class	No.	Yds	TD	Avg
Skyler Green, Louisiana St	So	25	462	2	18.48
Ryne Robinson, Miami (OH)	Fr	38	654	3	17.21
Mark Jones, Tennessee	Sr	20	303	1	15.15
Gabe Lindsay, Oklahoma St	Sr	26	393	1	15.12
DeAngelo Hall, Virginia Tech	Jr	33	487	3	14.76

Note: Minimum 1.2 per game.

KICKOFF RETURNS

	Class	No.	Yds	TD	Avg
Michael Waddell, N Carolina	Sr	15	475	1	31.67
J.R. Reed, S Florida	Sr	18	570	1	31.67
Mike Imoh, Virginia Tech	So	18	549	1	30.50
John Eubanks, Southern Miss	So	17	499	1	29.35
Dexter Wynn, Colorado St	Sr	27	782	0	28.96

Note: Minimum of 1.2 per game.

Division I-A Team Single-Game Highs

RUSHING AND PASSING

Rushing and passing yards: 681—B.J. Symons, Texas Tech, QB, Sept 27, 2003 (vs. Mississippi)
Rushing and passing plays: 77—Timmy Chang, Hawaii, QB, Sept 27, 2003 (vs. Rice)
Rushing plays: 51—Chris Perry, Michigan, RB, Nov 1, 2003 (vs Michigan St)
Net rushing yards: 307—P.J. Daniels, Georgia Tech, RB, Jan 3, 2004 (vs Tulsa)
Passes attempted: 70—Timmy Chang, Hawaii, QB, Sept 27, 2003 (vs Rice)
Passes completed: 49—Bruce Gradkowski, Toledo, QB, Sept 20, 2003 (vs Pittsburgh)
Passing yards: 661—B.J. Symons, Texas Tech, QB, Sept 27, 2003 (vs Mississippi)

RECEIVING AND RETURNS

Passes caught: Six tied with 16.
Receiving yards: 258—Lee Evans, Wisconsin, WR, Nov 15, 2003 (vs Michigan St)
Punt return yards: 277—Antonio Perkins, Oklahoma, Sept 20, 2003 (vs UCLA)
Kickoff return yards: 206—Eric Newman, Louisiana Tech, Nov 15, 2003 (vs Tulsa)

Division I-AA

SCORING

	Class	GP	TD	XP	FG	Pts	Pts/Game
Evan Harney, San Diego	Fr	10	20	1	0	122	12.20
Rob Giancola, Valparaiso	Jr	12	23	1	0	140	11.67
Jamaal Branch, Colgate	Jr	16	29	0	0	174	10.88
Kirwin Watson, Fordham	Sr	12	21	0	0	126	10.50
Gary Jones, Albany	Sr	11	19	0	0	114	10.36

FIELD GOALS

	Class	GP	FGA	FG	Pct	FG/Game
Chris Snyder, Montana	Sr	13	30	25	.833	1.92
Matt Lange, Western Kentucky	Sr	13	28	23	.821	1.77
Jeremy Hershey, Idaho St.	Sr	12	26	18	.692	1.50
John Troost, Yale	Jr	10	19	15	.789	1.50
Danny Marshall, Furman	Sr	11	20	16	.800	1.45

TOTAL OFFENSE

			Rushing		Passing		Total Offense		
	Class	GP	Car	Net	Att	Yds	Yds	Yds/Play	Yds/Game
Bruce Eugene, Grambling	Jr	12	94	412	528	3808	4220	6.78	351.7
Alvin Cowan, Yale	Sr	10	136	451	381	2994	3445	6.66	344.5
David Macchi, Valparaiso	Sr	12	113	316	412	3763	4079	7.77	339.9
Eric Rasmussen, San Diego	Sr	10	38	29	318	2982	3011	8.46	301.1
Ben Dougherty, Florida A&M	Jr	11	155	674	368	2502	3176	6.07	288.7

RUSHING

	Class	GP	Car	Yds	Avg	TD	Yds/Game
Nick Hartigan, Brown	So	10	275	1498	5.45	15	149.80
Evan Harney, San Diego	Fr	10	285	1475	5.18	17	147.50
Jamaal Branch, Colgate	Jr	16	450	2326	5.17	29	145.38
Charles Anthony, Tennessee St	Jr	12	322	1708	5.30	13	142.33
Mike Hilliard, Duquesne	Sr	11	306	1544	5.05	15	140.36

PASSING EFFICIENCY

					Pct					Rating
	Class	GP	Att	Comp	Comp	Yds	Yds/Att	TD	Int	Pts
Eric Rasmussen, San Diego	Sr	10	318	195	61.32	2982	9.38	35	3	174.5
Quincy Richard, Southern	Sr	13	389	256	65.81	3427	8.81	33	15	160.1
David Macchi, Valparaiso	Sr	12	412	238	57.77	3763	9.13	38	10	160.1
Jared Allen, Florida Atlantic	Jr	14	346	218	63.01	3003	8.68	24	9	153.6
Scott Pendarvis, McNeese St.	Jr	12	244	142	58.20	2186	8.96	18	6	152.9

Note: Minimum 15 attempts per game.

RECEPTIONS PER GAME

	Class	GP	No.	Yds	TD	R/G
Javarus Dudley, Fordham	Sr	12	101	1439	14	8.42
Efren Hill, Samford	Jr	11	92	1387	15	8.36
Lorenza Hill, Brown	So	10	76	869	5	7.60
Alonzo Nix, Chattanooga	Jr	12	90	1060	7	7.50
Ari Confesor, Holy Cross	Sr	12	90	1213	9	7.50

INTERCEPTIONS

	Class	GP	No.	Yds	TD	Int/G
Brandon Martin, Butler	Sr	11	8	76	0	.73
James Niklos, R. Morris	Fr	9	6	53	2	.67
Levy Brown, Florida A&M	Sr	11	7	90	0	.64
Corey Lynch, App. St	Fr	10	6	61	0	.60
Steve Costello, UMass	Jr	10	6	24	0	.60

RECEIVING YARDS PER GAME

	Class	GP	No.	Yds	TD	Yds/G
Efrem Hill, Samford	Jr	11	92	1387	15	126.1
Rob Giancola, Valparaiso	Jr	12	57	1496	23	124.7
Javarus Dudley, Fordham	Sr	12	101	1439	14	119.9
Adam Hannula, San Diego	So	10	72	1161	13	116.1
Dan Castles, Penn	Jr	10	71	1067	13	106.7

PUNTING

	Class	No.	Avg
Graham Whitlock, Gardner-Webb	Jr	57	45.49
Mark Gould, Northern Arizona	Sr	58	45.00
Nate McKinney, Appalachian St.	Sr	74	44.51
Jesse Nicassio, Eastern Wash.	Sr	53	44.42
Kyle McQuown, Idaho St	Fr	71	43.92

Division I-AA (Cont)

ALL-PURPOSE RUNNERS

	Class	GP	Rush	Rec	PR	KOR	Yds	Yds/Game
Luke McArdle, Georgetown	Sr	11	0	1118	506	407	2031	184.64
Nick Hartigan, Brown	So	10	1498	308	0	0	1806	180.60
Javarus Dudley, Fordham	Sr	12	34	1439	169	496	2138	178.17
Evan Harney, San Diego	Fr	10	1475	259	0	0	1734	173.40
Ari Confesor, Holy Cross	Sr	12	7	1213	152	700	2072	172.67

Division II

SCORING

	Class	GP	TD	XP	FG	Pts	Pts/Game
D. Green, Minnesota-Morris	Jr	10	20	1	0	122	12.20
John Kuhn, Shippensburg	Jr	11	22	0	0	132	12.00
Dave Rufledt, Minnesota-Duluth	Jr	11	22	0	0	132	12.00
Luke Struble, W Virginia Wesleyan	Sr	10	20	0	0	120	12.00
Vincent Jackson, Northern Colorado	Jr	11	21	0	0	126	11.50
Adam Matthews, Northern Colorado	Sr	11	21	0	0	126	11.50

FIELD GOALS

	Class	GP	FGA	FG	Pct	FG/Game
Travis Snyder, Western St	Jr	11	26	21	.808	1.90
Jessup Pfeifer, Nebraska-Kearney	Fr	10	23	18	.783	1.80
Trey Crum, Delta St	Jr	11	26	19	.731	1.70
David Hendrix, Grand Valley St	Sr	15	32	25	.781	1.70
Eric Houle, Saginaw Valley	Sr	13	32	21	.656	1.60

TOTAL OFFENSE

	Class	GP	Yds	Yds/Game
Cory Allred, Arkansas-Monticello	Sr	11	4267	387.9
Matt Kohn, Indianapolis	Jr	10	3380	338.0
Pat Korth, Nebraska-Kearney	Sr	10	3274	327.4
Scott Eyster, Delta St	Fr	11	3548	322.5
Joey Conrad, Glenville St	So	11	3458	316.8

RUSHING

	Class	GP	Car	Yds	TD	Yds/Game
Justin Kammrad, Nebraska-Omaha	Sr	11	293	1866	14	169.6
D. Green, Minnesota-Morris	Jr	10	286	1669	20	166.9
Chaumont Bouknight, Western St	Jr	10	305	1543	9	154.3
Earnest McNeal, Mansfield	Fr	11	279	1684	17	153.1
Adam Matthews, Northern Colorado	Sr	11	263	1653	18	150.3

PASSING EFFICIENCY

	Class	GP	Att	Comp	Yds	TD	Int	Rating Pts
Will Hall, North Alabama	Sr	14	372	267	3531	30	9	173.3
Brad Nelson, S Dakota St	Jr	11	341	221	3141	27	5	165.4
Drew Beard, SE Oklahoma	Jr	10	228	118	2279	23	8	162.0
Darmel Whitfield, Gannon	Jr	10	248	160	2255	20	8	161.1
Brian Masek, Nebraska-Omaha	So	11	268	160	2336	24	8	156.5

Note: Minimum 15 attempts per game.

RECEPTIONS PER GAME

	Class	GP	No.	Yds	TD	Rec/G
Kevin Wolcott, Tusculum	Sr	11	92	1159	6	8.4
Antonio Carter, Glenville St	Jr	10	81	1168	13	8.1
V. Mayfield, Northern Mich	So	11	85	1019	7	7.7
Chris White, Humboldt St	Sr	10	77	916	4	7.7
Cesare Manning, Ind.	Sr	11	84	1220	9	7.6

RECEIVING YARDS PER GAME

	Class	GP	No.	Yds	TD	Yds/G
Ellis Debrow, Delta St	So	11	77	1637	18	148.8
Richie Ross, NE-Kearney	So	10	75	1482	11	148.2
V. Jackson N. Colorado	Jr	11	66	1462	21	132.9
Nate Washington, Tiffin	Jr	11	70	1286	15	116.9
Antonio Carter, Glenville St	Jr	10	81	1168	13	116.8

Division II (Cont.)

INTERCEPTIONS

	Class	GP	No.	Yds	Int/Game
Shawn Woodward, Shaw	So	9	13	184	1.4
Pierre Thomas, MO Western St.	Sr	12	14	362	1.2
Ricardo Colclough, Tusculum	Sr	11	11	111	1.0
Walt William, Fayetteville St	Fr	9	9	158	1.0

Four tied at 0.8.

PUNTING

	Class	No.	Avg
Joe Smith, Central Washington	Sr	36	44.2
Chris Miller, TX-A&M-Commerce	Jr	54	44.1
Lucas Taroli, Western Oregon	Sr	76	43.7
Michael Koenen, Western Wash.	Jr	52	43.4
Jeff Williams, Adams St	So	55	43.3

Note: Minimum 3.6 per game.

Division III

SCORING

	Class	GP	TD	XP	FG	Pts	Pts/Game
Tony Sutton, Wooster	Jr	9	31	0	0	186	20.7
Brett Trichilo, Wilkes	Jr	11	27	0	0	162	14.7
C.W. Clemmons, Hampden-Sydney	Jr	10	24	1	0	146	14.6
Aaron Binger, Pacific Lutheran	Sr	7	15	0	0	90	12.9
Brad Stanley, Carnegie Mellon	Sr	10	21	0	0	126	12.6

FIELD GOALS

	Class	GP	FGA	FG	Pct	FG/Game
Rhett Soltas, Norwich	Jr	11	22	18	.818	1.6
Cliff Eisenhut, Union (NY)	Sr	10	21	16	.762	1.6
Garrett Wales, Linfield	So	12	22	18	.818	1.5
Matt Verenini, Rensselaer	Sr	13	23	18	.783	1.4

Two tied with 1.3.

TOTAL OFFENSE

	Class	GP	Yds	Yds/Game
Brett Dietz, Hanover	Sr	11	4186	380.5
Jay Macias, Colorado College	Sr	8	2951	368.9
Joel Steele, Anderson (IN)	Sr	10	3664	366.4
John Port, Albright	Jr	10	3358	335.8
Phil Butler, Hope	Sr	11	3628	329.8

RUSHING

	Class	GP	Car	Yds	TD	Yds/Game
Tony Sutton, Wooster	Jr	9	271	1955	30	217.2
Brett Trichilo, Wilkes	Jr	11	332	2175	27	197.7
Dante Washington, Carthage	Jr	10	308	1838	12	183.8
Andrew Mocadlo, WI-La Crosse	Sr	12	327	1942	14	161.8
Jason Meyers, St. John Fisher	Sr	10	308	1585	12	158.5

PASSING EFFICIENCY

	Class	GP	Att	Comp	Pct Comp	Yds	TD	Int	Rating Pts
Zac Bruney, Mount Union	Jr	14	234	148		2439	28	8	182.2
Scott Krause, WI-Stevens Point	Sr	10	310	205		2963	37	9	180.0
Rob Purlee, Monmouth (IL)	Sr	10	264	160		2561	25	10	165.8
Frank Borba, Menlo	Jr	10	316	201		2748	28	9	160.2
Cody Fredenburg, Mary Hardin-Baylor	Sr	10	152	82		1535	14	7	160.0
Ryan Holmes, Wittenberg	Jr	10	202	118		1775	20	5	160.0

Note: Minimum 15 attempts per game.

Division III *(Cont.)*

RECEPTIONS PER GAME

	Class	GP	No.	Yds	TD	Rec/Game
Conrad Singh, Hampden-Sydney	Sr	10	98	1419	11	9.80
Flynn Cochran, Rensselaer	Sr	12	109	1274	15	9.10
Denny Kimmel, Anderson (IN)	Fr	10	88	735	3	8.80
Dusty Kain, Simpson	So	11	93	1466	14	8.50

Two tied with 8.40.

RECEIVING YARDS PER GAME

	Class	GP	No.	Yds	TD	Yds/Game
Conrad Singh, Hampden-Sydney	Sr	10	98	1419	11	141.9
Dusty Kain, Simpson	So	11	93	1466	14	133.3
Mark Bartosic, Susquehanna	Sr	10	78	1313	13	131.3
Eric White, IL-Wesleyan	Jr	10	74	1215	14	121.5
Erik Ferguson, WI-Eau Claire	Sr	10	60	1157	6	115.7

INTERCEPTIONS

	Class	GP	No.	Yds	Int/G
Seth Kopf, Knox	Sr	10	11	58	1.1
Quammi Semper, Oberlin	Sr	10	10	168	1.0
Kyle Westphal, Simpson	Jr	11	10	93	0.9
Tim Mullaney, Trinity (CT)	Sr	8	7	51	0.9

Six tied with 0.8.

PUNTING

	Class	No.	Avg
Cory Ohnesorge, Occidental	So	34	44.4
James Wilson, Linfield	Sr	51	43.8
Nick Schlieman, Augsburg	So	57	42.0
Christian Adams, Guilford	Jr	66	41.6
Erik Naglee, Greensboro	Sr	68	41.4

Note: Minimum 3.6 per game.

2003 NCAA Division I-A Team Leaders

Offense

SCORING

	GP	Pts	Avg
Boise St	14	602	43.00
Miami (OH)	14	602	43.00
Oklahoma	14	601	42.93
Texas Tech	13	552	42.46
Southern California	13	534	41.08
Texas	13	533	41.00
Minnesota	13	503	38.69
N Carolina St	13	489	37.62
Kansas St	15	549	36.60
Akron	12	435	36.25

RUSHING

	GP	Car	Yds	Avg	TD	Yds/Game
Navy	13	760	4202	5.53	44	323.23
Rice	12	687	3800	5.53	35	316.67
Minnesota	13	683	3759	5.50	46	289.15
Air Force	12	716	3367	4.70	31	280.58
Arkansas	13	626	3145	5.02	34	241.92
Missouri	13	551	3087	5.60	38	237.46
Nebraska	13	716	3063	4.28	28	235.62
Texas	13	587	3023	5.15	41	232.54
Kansas St	15	688	3429	4.98	42	228.60
Louisville	14	518	2966	5.73	35	228.15

TOTAL OFFENSE

	GP	Plays	Yds	Avg	TD*	Yds/Game
Texas Tech	13	1088	7576	6.96	76	582.77
Miami (OH)	14	1053	7016	6.66	82	501.14
Bowling Green	14	1111	6954	6.26	61	496.71
Minnesota	13	970	6430	6.63	66	494.62
Louisville	13	913	6355	6.96	58	488.85
Hawaii	14	1072	6834	6.38	63	488.14
Boise St	14	1061	6809	6.42	77	486.36
Connecticut	12	946	5730	6.06	54	477.50
Akron	12	923	5643	6.11	55	470.25
Oregon St	13	1060	6019	5.68	53	463.00

*Defensive and special teams TDs not included.

Offense (Cont.)

PASSING

	GP	Att	Comp	Int	Pct Comp	Yds	Yds/att	TD
Texas Tech	13	780	506	23	64.87	6179	7.92	53
Hawaii	14	754	444	27	58.89	5382	7.14	42
N Carolina St	13	496	357	7	71.98	4580	9.23	35
Miami (OH)	14	535	363	11	67.85	4772	8.92	38
Boise St.	14	489	295	9	60.33	4708	9.63	33
Oregon St.	13	534	274	25	51.31	4265	7.99	25
Akron	12	449	287	10	63.92	3736	8.32	22
Western Michigan	12	450	272	20	60.44	3701	8.22	31
Bowling Green	14	528	345	13	65.34	4206	7.97	32
Connecticut	12	483	283	14	58.59	3575	7.40	33

Single-Game Highs

Points Scored: 77—Boise St, Oct 25, 2003 (vs San Jose St).
77—Oklahoma, Nov 8, 2003 (vs Texas A&M).
Net Rushing Yards: 672—Rice, Nov 29, 2003 (vs Louisiana Tech)
Passing Yards: 661—Texas Tech, Sept 27, 2003 (vs Mississippi)
Rushing and Passing Yards: 782—Texas Christian, Oct 25, 2003 (vs Houston)
Fewest Rushing and Passing Yards Allowed: 54—Oklahoma, Nov 8, 2003 (vs Texas A&M)

Defense

SCORING

	GP	Pts	Avg
Louisiana St	14	154	11.0
Nebraska	13	188	14.5
Georgia	14	203	14.5
Miami (FL)	13	196	15.1
Oklahoma	14	214	15.3
Maryland	13	206	15.8
Iowa	13	210	16.2
Kansas St	15	244	16.3
Auburn	13	212	16.3
Florida St	13	217	16.7

TOTAL DEFENSE

	GP	Plays	Yds	Avg	Yds/Game
Louisiana St	14	877	3528	4.02	252.00
Miami (FL)	13	786	3348	4.26	257.54
Oklahoma	14	881	3635	4.13	259.64
Georgia	14	880	3876	4.40	276.86
Auburn	13	802	3661	4.56	281.62
Kansas St	15	996	4246	4.26	283.07
Oregon St	13	914	3753	4.11	288.69
San Diego St	12	813	3477	4.28	289.75
Memphis	13	879	3845	4.37	295.77
Ohio St	13	930	3859	4.15	296.85

RUSHING

	GP	Car	Yds	Avg	TD	Yds/Game
Southern Cal	13	425	782	1.84	9	60.2
Ohio St	13	415	810	1.95	12	62.3
Louisiana St	14	400	938	2.35	5	67.0
Oregon St	13	447	1097	2.45	11	84.4
New Mexico	13	428	1119	2.61	11	86.1
Washington St	13	441	1181	2.68	8	90.8
Auburn	13	440	1204	2.74	8	92.6
Iowa	13	480	1205	2.51	10	92.7
Texas Christian	13	443	1218	2.75	13	93.7
Purdue	13	467	1260	2.70	9	96.9

TURNOVER MARGIN

		Turnovers Gained			Turnovers Lost			Margin/
	GP	Fum	Int	Total	Fum	Int	Total	Game
Nebraska	13	15	32	47	14	10	24	1.77
Southern Cal	13	20	22	42	13	9	22	1.54
Miami (OH)	14	18	21	39	8	11	19	1.43
W Virginia	13	15	21	36	12	8	20	1.23
Oklahoma	14	12	22	34	6	11	17	1.21
Northern IL	12	8	23	31	7	10	17	1.17
UNLV	12	19	16	35	12	11	23	1.00
Purdue	13	14	14	28	9	7	16	0.92
Toledo	12	10	15	25	6	8	14	0.92

Four tied with 0.85.

PASSING EFFICIENCY

	GP	Att	Comp	Yds	Pct Comp	Yds/Att	TD	Pct TD	Int	Pct Int	Rating Pts
Nebraska	13	430	218	2312	50.70	5.38	10	2.33	32	7.44	88.66
Louisiana St	14	477	213	2590	44.65	5.43	12	2.52	21	4.40	89.81
Oklahoma	14	419	218	2050	52.03	4.89	11	2.63	22	5.25	91.26
Miami (FL)	13	328	167	1866	50.91	5.69	9	2.74	19	5.79	96.16
Washington St	13	547	263	2960	48.08	5.41	19	3.47	24	4.39	96.24
Oregon St	13	467	206	2656	44.11	5.69	22	4.71	20	4.28	98.85
Boise St	14	614	302	3470	49.19	5.65	17	2.77	21	3.42	98.97
S Florida	11	352	173	1979	49.15	5.62	14	3.98	13	3.69	102.06
Michigan	13	411	221	2347	53.77	5.71	9	2.19	14	3.41	102.18
San Diego St	12	345	176	1923	51.01	5.57	12	3.48	12	3.48	102.34

National Champions

Year	Champion	Record	Bowl Game	Head Coach
1883	Yale	8-0-0	No bowl	Ray Tompkins (Captain)
1884	Yale	9-0-0	No bowl	Eugene L. Richards (Captain)
1885	Princeton	9-0-0	No bowl	Charles DeCamp (Captain)
1886	Yale	9-0-1	No bowl	Robert N. Corwin (Captain)
1887	Yale	9-0-0	No bowl	Harry W. Beecher (Captain)
1888	Yale	13-0-0	No bowl	Walter Camp
1889	Princeton	10-0-0	No bowl	Edgar Poe (Captain)
1890	Harvard	11-0-0	No bowl	George A. Stewart/George C. Adams
1891	Yale	13-0-0	No bowl	Walter Camp
1892	Yale	13-0-0	No bowl	Walter Camp
1893	Princeton	11-0-0	No bowl	Tom Trenchard (Captain)
1894	Yale	16-0-0	No bowl	William C. Rhodes
1895	Pennsylvania	14-0-0	No bowl	George Woodruff
1896	Princeton	10-0-1	No bowl	Garrett Cochran
1897	Pennsylvania	15-0-0	No bowl	George Woodruff
1898	Harvard	11-0-0	No bowl	W. Cameron Forbes
1899	Harvard	10-0-1	No bowl	Benjamin H. Dibblee
1900	Yale	12-0-0	No bowl	Malcolm McBride
1901	Michigan	11-0-0	Won Rose	Fielding Yost
1902	Michigan	11-0-0	No bowl	Fielding Yost
1903	Princeton	11-0-0	No bowl	Art Hillebrand
1904	Pennsylvania	12-0-0	No bowl	Carl Williams
1905	Chicago	11-0-0	No bowl	Amos Alonzo Stagg
1906	Princeton	9-0-1	No bowl	Bill Roper
1907	Yale	9-0-1	No bowl	Bill Knox
1908	Pennsylvania	11-0-1	No bowl	Sol Metzger
1909	Yale	10-0-0	No bowl	Howard Jones
1910	Harvard	8-0-1	No bowl	Percy Houghton
1911	Princeton	8-0-2	No bowl	Bill Roper
1912	Harvard	9-0-0	No bowl	Percy Houghton
1913	Harvard	9-0-0	No bowl	Percy Houghton
1914	Army	9-0-0	No bowl	Charley Daly
1915	Cornell	9-0-0	No bowl	Al Sharpe
1916	Pittsburgh	8-0-0	No bowl	Pop Warner
1917	Georgia Tech	9-0-0	No bowl	John Heisman
1918	Pittsburgh	4-1-0	No bowl	Pop Warner
1919	Harvard	9-0-1	Won Rose	Bob Fisher
1920	California	9-0-0	Won Rose	Andy Smith
1921	Cornell	8-0-0	No bowl	Gil Dobie
1922	Cornell	8-0-0	No bowl	Gil Dobie
1923	Illinois	8-0-0	No bowl	Bob Zuppke
1924	Notre Dame	10-0-0	Won Rose	Knute Rockne
1925	Alabama (H)	10-0-0	Won Rose	Wallace Wade
	Dartmouth (D)	8-0-0	No bowl	Jesse Hawley
1926	Alabama (H)	9-0-1	Tied Rose	Wallace Wade
	Stanford (D)(H)	10-0-1	Tied Rose	Pop Warner
1927	Illinois	7-0-1	No bowl	Bob Zuppke
1928	Georgia Tech (H)	10-0-0	Won Rose	Bill Alexander
	Southern Cal (D)	9-0-1	No bowl	Howard Jones
1929	Notre Dame	9-0-0	No bowl	Knute Rockne
1930	Notre Dame	10-0-0	No bowl	Knute Rockne
1931	Southern Cal	10-1-0	Won Rose	Howard Jones
1932	Southern Cal (H)	10-0-0	Won Rose	Howard Jones
	Michigan (D)	8-0-0	No bowl	Harry Kipke
1933	Michigan	7-0-1	No bowl	Harry Kipke
1934	Minnesota	8-0-0	No bowl	Bernie Bierman
1935	Minnesota (H)	8-0-0	No bowl	Bernie Bierman
	Southern Methodist (D)	12-1-0	Lost Rose	Matty Bell
1936	Minnesota	7-1-0	No bowl	Bernie Bierman
1937	Pittsburgh	9-0-1	No bowl	Jock Sutherland
1938	Texas Christian (AP)	11-0-0	Won Sugar	Dutch Meyer
	Notre Dame (D)	8-1-0	No bowl	Elmer Layden
1939	Southern Cal (D)	8-0-2	Won Rose	Howard Jones
	Texas A&M (AP)	11-0-0	Won Sugar	Homer Norton
1940	Minnesota	8-0-0	No bowl	Bernie Bierman
1941	Minnesota	8-0-0	No bowl	Bernie Bierman
1942	Ohio St	9-1-0	No bowl	Paul Brown

Year	Champion	Record	Bowl Game	Head Coach
1943	Notre Dame	9-1-0	No bowl	Frank Leahy
1944	Army	9-0-0	No bowl	Red Blaik
1945	Army	9-0-0	No bowl	Red Blaik
1946	Notre Dame	8-0-1	No bowl	Frank Leahy
1947	Notre Dame	9-0-0	No bowl	Frank Leahy
	Michigan*	10-0-0	Won Rose	Fritz Crisler
1948	Michigan	9-0-0	No bowl	Bennie Oosterbaan
1949	Notre Dame	10-0-0	No bowl	Frank Leahy
1950	Oklahoma	10-1-0	Lost Sugar	Bud Wilkinson
1951	Tennessee	10-1-0	Lost Sugar	Bob Neyland
1952	Michigan St	9-0-0	No bowl	Biggie Munn
1953	Maryland	10-1-0	Lost Orange	Jim Tatum
1954	Ohio St	10-0-0	Won Rose	Woody Hayes
	UCLA (UPI)	9-0-0	No bowl	Red Sanders
1955	Oklahoma	11-0-0	Won Orange	Bud Wilkinson
1956	Oklahoma	10-0-0	No bowl	Bud Wilkinson
1957	Auburn	10-0-0	No bowl	Shug Jordan
	Ohio St (UPI)	9-1-0	Won Rose	Woody Hayes
1958	Louisiana St	11-0-0	Won Sugar	Paul Dietzel
1959	Syracuse	11-0-0	Won Cotton	Ben Schwartzwalder
1960	Minnesota	8-2-0	Lost Rose	Murray Warmath
1961	Alabama	11-0-0	Won Sugar	Bear Bryant
1962	Southern Cal	11-0-0	Won Rose	John McKay
1963	Texas	11-0-0	Won Cotton	Darrell Royal
1964	Alabama	10-1-0	Lost Orange	Bear Bryant
1965	Alabama	9-1-1	Won Orange	Bear Bryant
	Michigan St (UPI)	10-1-0	Lost Rose	Duffy Daugherty
1966	Notre Dame	9-0-1	No bowl	Ara Parseghian
1967	Southern Cal	10-1-0	Won Rose	John McKay
1968	Ohio St	10-0-0	Won Rose	Woody Hayes
1969	Texas	11-0-0	Won Cotton	Darrell Royal
1970	Nebraska	11-0-1	Won Orange	Bob Devaney
	Texas (UPI)	10-1-0	Lost Cotton	Darrell Royal
1971	Nebraska	13-0-0	Won Orange	Bob Devaney
1972	Southern Cal	12-0-0	Won Rose	John McKay
1973	Notre Dame	11-0-0	Won Sugar	Ara Parseghian
	Alabama (UPI)	11-1-0	Lost Sugar	Bear Bryant
1974	Oklahoma	11-0-0	No bowl	Barry Switzer
	Southern Cal (UPI)	10-1-1	Won Rose	John McKay
1975	Oklahoma	11-1-0	Won Orange	Barry Switzer
1976	Pittsburgh	12-0-0	Won Sugar	Johnny Majors
1977	Notre Dame	11-1-0	Won Cotton	Dan Devine
1978	Alabama	11-1-0	Won Sugar	Bear Bryant
	Southern Cal (UPI)	12-1-0	Won Rose	John Robinson
1979	Alabama	12-0-0	Won Sugar	Bear Bryant
1980	Georgia	12-0-0	Won Sugar	Vince Dooley
1981	Clemson	12-0-0	Won Orange	Danny Ford
1982	Penn St	11-1-0	Won Sugar	Joe Paterno
1983	Miami (FL)	11-1-0	Won Orange	Howard Schnellenberger
1984	Brigham Young	13-0-0	Won Holiday	LaVell Edwards
1985	Oklahoma	11-1-0	Won Orange	Barry Switzer
1986	Penn St	12-0-0	Won Fiesta	Joe Paterno
1987	Miami (FL)	12-0-0	Won Orange	Jimmy Johnson
1988	Notre Dame	12-0-0	Won Fiesta	Lou Holtz
1989	Miami (FL)	11-1-0	Won Sugar	Dennis Erickson
1990	Colorado	11-1-1	Won Orange	Bill McCartney
	Georgia Tech (UPI)	11-0-1	Won Citrus	Bobby Ross
1991	Miami (FL)	12-0-0	Won Orange	Dennis Erickson
	Washington (CNN)	12-0-0	Won Rose	Don James
1992	Alabama	13-0-0	Won Sugar	Gene Stallings
1993	Florida St	12-1-0	Won Orange	Bobby Bowden
1994	Nebraska	13-0-0	Won Orange	Tom Osborne
1995	Nebraska	12-0-0	Won Fiesta	Tom Osborne
†1996	Florida	12–1	Won Sugar	Steve Spurrier
1997	Michigan	12–0	Won Rose	Lloyd Carr
	Nebraska (ESPN)	13–0	Won Orange	Tom Osborne
1998	Tennessee	13–0	Won Fiesta	Phillip Fulmer
1999	Florida St	12–0	Won Sugar	Bobby Bowden
2000	Oklahoma	13–0	Won Orange	Bob Stoops
2001	Miami (FL)	12–0	Won Rose	Larry Coker

Year	Champion	Record	Bowl Game	Head Coach
2002	Ohio St	14–0	Won Fiesta	Jim Tressel
2003	Louisiana St	13–1	Won Sugar	Nick Saban
	Southern California	12–1	Won Rose	Pete Carroll

*The AP, which had voted Notre Dame No. 1, took a second vote, giving the national title to Michigan after its 49–0 win over Southern Cal in the Rose Bowl. Note: Selectors: Helms Athletic Foundation (H) 1883–1935, The Dickinson System (D) 1924–40, The Associated Press (AP) 1936–present, United Press International (UPI) 1958–90, *USA Today*/CNN (CNN) 1991–96, and *USA Today*/ESPN (ESPN) 1997–present. †In 1996 the NCAA introduced overtime to break ties.

Results of Major Bowl Games

Rose Bowl

1-1-02	Michigan 49, Stanford 0	1-1-66	UCLA 14, Michigan St 12
1-1-16	Washington St 14, Brown 0	1-2-67	Purdue 14, Southern Cal 13
1-1-17	Oregon 14, Pennsylvania 0	1-1-68	Southern Cal 14, Indiana 3
1-1-18	Mare Island 19, Camp Lewis 7	1-1-69	Ohio St 27, Southern Cal 16
1-1-19	Great Lakes 17, Mare Island 0	1-1-70	Southern Cal 10, Michigan 3
1-1-20	Harvard 7, Oregon 6	1-1-71	Stanford 27, Ohio St 17
1-1-21	California 28, Ohio St 0	1-1-72	Stanford 13, Michigan 12
1-2-22	Washington & Jefferson 0, California 0	1-1-73	Southern Cal 42, Ohio St 17
1-1-23	Southern Cal 14, Penn St 3	1-1-74	Ohio St 42, Southern Cal 21
1-1-24	Navy 14, Washington 14	1-1-75	Southern Cal 18, Ohio St 17
1-1-25	Notre Dame 27, Stanford 10	1-1-76	UCLA 23, Ohio St 10
1-1-26	Alabama 20, Washington 19	1-1-77	Southern Cal 14, Michigan 6
1-1-27	Alabama 7, Stanford 7	1-2-78	Washington 27, Michigan 20
1-2-28	Stanford 7, Pittsburgh 6	1-1-79	Southern Cal 17, Michigan 10
1-1-29	Georgia Tech 8, California 7	1-1-80	Southern Cal 17, Ohio St 16
1-1-30	Southern Cal 47, Pittsburgh 14	1-1-81	Michigan 23, Washington 6
1-1-31	Alabama 24, Washington St 0	1-1-82	Washington 28, Iowa 0
1-1-32	Southern Cal 21, Tulane 12	1-1-83	UCLA 24, Michigan 14
1-2-33	Southern Cal 35, Pittsburgh 0	1-2-84	UCLA 45, Illinois 9
1-1-34	Columbia 7, Stanford 0	1-1-85	Southern Cal 20, Ohio St 17
1-1-35	Alabama 29, Stanford 13	1-1-86	UCLA 45, Iowa 28
1-1-36	Stanford 7, Southern Methodist 0	1-1-87	Arizona St 22, Michigan 15
1-1-37	Pittsburgh 21, Washington 0	1-1-88	Michigan St 20, Southern Cal 17
1-1-38	California 13, Alabama 0	1-2-89	Michigan 22, Southern Cal 14
1-2-39	Southern Cal 7, Duke 3	1-1-90	Southern Cal 17, Michigan 10
1-1-40	Southern Cal 14, Tennessee 0	1-1-91	Washington 46, Iowa 34
1-1-41	Stanford 21, Nebraska 13	1-1-92	Washington 34, Michigan 14
1-1-42	Oregon St 20, Duke 16	1-1-93	Michigan 38, Washington 31
1-1-43	Georgia 9, UCLA 0	1-1-94	Wisconsin 21, UCLA 16
1-1-44	Southern Cal 29, Washington 0	1-2-95	Penn St 38, Oregon 20
1-1-45	Southern Cal 25, Tennessee 0	1-1-96	Southern Cal 41, Northwestern 32
1-1-46	Alabama 34, Southern Cal 14	1-1-97	Ohio St 20, Arizona St 17
1-1-47	Illinois 45, UCLA 14	1-1-98	Michigan 21, Washington St 16
1-1-48	Michigan 49, Southern Cal 0	1-1-99	Wisconsin 38, UCLA 31
1-1-49	Northwestern 20, California 14	1-1-2000	Wisconsin 17, Stanford 9
1-2-50	Ohio St 17, California 14	1-1-2001	Washington 34, Purdue 24
1-1-51	Michigan 14, California 6	1-3-2002	Miami 37, Nebraska 14
1-1-52	Illinois 40, Stanford 7	1-1-2003	Oklahoma 34, Washington St 14
1-1-53	Southern Cal 7, Wisconsin 0	1-1-2004	Southern Cal 28, Michigan 14
1-1-54	Michigan St 28, UCLA 20		
1-1-55	Ohio St 20, Southern Cal 7		
1-2-56	Michigan St 17, UCLA 14		
1-1-57	Iowa 35, Oregon St 19		
1-1-58	Ohio St 10, Oregon 7		
1-1-59	Iowa 38, California 12		
1-1-60	Washington 44, Wisconsin 8		
1-2-61	Washington 17, Minnesota 7		
1-1-62	Minnesota 21, UCLA 3		
1-1-63	Southern Cal 42, Wisconsin 37		
1-1-64	Illinois 17, Washington 7		
1-1-65	Michigan 34, Oregon St 7		

City: Pasadena. Stadium: Rose Bowl, capacity 96,576.
Playing Sites: Tournament Park (1902, 1916–22), Rose Bowl (1923–41, since 1943), Duke Stadium, Durham, NC (1942).

Orange Bowl

1-1-35	Bucknell 26, Miami (FL) 0
1-1-36	Catholic 20, Mississippi 19
1-1-37	Duquesne 13, Mississippi St 12
1-1-38	Auburn 6, Michigan St 0
1-2-39	Tennessee 17, Oklahoma 0
1-1-40	Georgia Tech 21, Missouri 7

Note: The Fiesta, Orange, Rose and Sugar Bowls constitute the Bowl Alliance, formed in 1995. The Alliance holds eight berths: one each for the champions of the ACC, Big 10, Big 12, Big East, Pac 10 and SEC, and two at-large, reserved for any Division I-A team with at least nine wins and ranked in the top 12 of the BCS rankings. Of the eight teams, the two highest-ranked go to the Fiesta Bowl in 2003, and the Sugar Bowl in 2004. Once these four BCS matches have been set conferences may place the remaining qualified teams in the other bowls. Teams that have won at least six games against Division I-A teams qualify.

Orange Bowl (Cont.)

1-1-41	Mississippi St 14, Georgetown 7
1-1-42	Georgia 40, Texas Christian 26
1-1-43	Alabama 37, Boston College 21
1-1-44	Louisiana St 19, Texas A&M 14
1-1-45	Tulsa 26, Georgia Tech 12
1-1-46	Miami (FL) 13, Holy Cross 6
1-1-47	Rice 8, Tennessee 0
1-1-48	Georgia Tech 20, Kansas 14
1-1-49	Texas 41, Georgia 28
1-2-50	Santa Clara 21, Kentucky 13
1-1-51	Clemson 15, Miami (FL) 14
1-1-52	Georgia Tech 17, Baylor 14
1-1-53	Alabama 61, Syracuse 6
1-1-54	Oklahoma 7, Maryland 0
1-1-55	Duke 34, Nebraska 7
1-2-56	Oklahoma 20, Maryland 6
1-1-57	Colorado 27, Clemson 21
1-1-58	Oklahoma 48, Duke 21
1-1-59	Oklahoma 21, Syracuse 6
1-1-60	Georgia 14, Missouri 0
1-2-61	Missouri 21, Navy 14
1-1-62	Louisiana St 25, Colorado 7
1-1-63	Alabama 17, Oklahoma 0
1-1-64	Nebraska 13, Auburn 7
1-1-65	Texas 21, Alabama 17
1-1-66	Alabama 39, Nebraska 28
1-2-67	Florida 27, Georgia Tech 12
1-1-68	Oklahoma 26, Tennessee 24
1-1-69	Penn St 15, Kansas 14
1-1-70	Penn St 10, Missouri 3
1-1-71	Nebraska 17, Louisiana St 12
1-1-72	Nebraska 38, Alabama 6
1-1-73	Nebraska 40, Notre Dame 6
1-1-74	Penn St 16, Louisiana St 9
1-1-75	Notre Dame 13, Alabama 11
1-1-76	Oklahoma 14, Michigan 6
1-1-77	Ohio St 27, Colorado 10
1-2-78	Arkansas 31, Oklahoma 6
1-1-79	Oklahoma 31, Nebraska 24
1-1-80	Oklahoma 24, Florida St·7
1-1-81	Oklahoma 18, Florida St 17
1-1-82	Clemson 22, Nebraska 15
1-1-83	Nebraska 21, Louisiana St 20
1-2-84	Miami (FL) 31, Nebraska 30
1-1-85	Washington 28, Oklahoma 17
1-1-86	Oklahoma 25, Penn St 10
1-1-87	Oklahoma 42, Arkansas 8
1-1-88	Miami (FL) 20, Oklahoma 14
1-2-89	Miami (FL) 23, Nebraska 3
1-1-90	Notre Dame 21, Colorado 6
1-1-91	Colorado 10, Notre Dame 9
1-1-92	Miami (FL) 22, Nebraska 0
1-1-93	Florida St 27, Nebraska 14
1-1-94	Florida St 18, Nebraska 16
1-1-95	Nebraska 24, Miami (FL) 17
1-1-96	Florida St 31, Notre Dame 26
12-31-96	Nebraska 41, Virginia Tech 21
1-2-98	Nebraska 42, Tennessee 17
1-2-99	Florida 31, Syracuse 10
1-1-00	Michigan 35, Alabama 34 (ot)
1-3-01	Oklahoma 13, Florida St 2
1-2-02	Florida 56, Maryland 23
1-2-03	Southern Cal 38, Iowa 17
1-1-04	Miami (FL) 16, Florida St 15

City: Miami. Stadium: Pro Player Stadium, capacity 75,192.
Playing Sites: Orange Bowl (1935–96), Pro Player Stadium
(since 1996).

Sugar Bowl

1-1-35	Tulane 20, Temple 14
1-1-36	Texas Christian 3, Louisiana St 2
1-1-37	Santa Clara 21, Louisiana St 14
1-1-38	Santa Clara 6, Louisiana St 0
1-2-39	Texas Christian 15, Carnegie Tech 7
1-1-40	Texas A&M 14, Tulane 13
1-1-41	Boston Col 19, Tennessee 13
1-1-42	Fordham 2, Missouri 0
1-1-43	Tennessee 14, Tulsa 7
1-1-44	Georgia Tech 20, Tulsa 18
1-1-45	Duke 29, Alabama 26
1-1-46	Oklahoma St 33, St. Mary's (CA) 13
1-1-47	Georgia 20, N Carolina 10
1-1-48	Texas 27, Alabama 7
1-1-49	Oklahoma 14, N Carolina 6
1-2-50	Oklahoma 35, Louisiana St 0
1-1-51	Kentucky 13, Oklahoma 7
1-1-52	Maryland 28, Tennessee 13
1-1-53	Georgia Tech 24, Mississippi 7
1-1-54	Georgia Tech 42, W Virginia 19
1-1-55	Navy 21, Mississippi 0
1-2-56	Georgia Tech 7, Pittsburgh 0
1-1-57	Baylor 13, Tennessee 7
1-1-58	Mississippi 39, Texas 7
1-1-59	Louisiana St 7, Clemson 0
1-1-60	Mississippi 21, Louisiana St 0
1-2-61	Mississippi 14, Rice 6
1-1-62	Alabama 10, Arkansas 3
1-1-63	Mississippi 17, Arkansas 13
1-1-64	Alabama 12, Mississippi 7
1-1-65	Louisiana St 13, Syracuse 10
1-1-66	Missouri 20, Florida 18
1-2-67	Alabama 34, Nebraska 7
1-1-68	Louisiana St 20, Wyoming 13
1-1-69	Arkansas 16, Georgia 2
1-1-70	Mississippi 27, Arkansas 22
1-1-71	Tennessee 34, Air Force 13
1-1-72	Oklahoma 40, Auburn 22
12-31-72	Oklahoma 14, Penn St 0
12-31-73	Notre Dame 24, Alabama 23
12-31-74	Nebraska 13, Florida 10
12-31-75	Alabama 13, Penn St 6
1-1-77	Pittsburgh 27, Georgia 3
1-2-78	Alabama 35, Ohio St 6
1-1-79	Alabama 14, Penn St 7
1-1-80	Alabama 24, Arkansas 9
1-1-81	Georgia 17, Notre Dame 10
1-1-82	Pittsburgh 24, Georgia 20
1-1-83	Penn St 27, Georgia 23
1-2-84	Auburn 9, Michigan 7
1-1-85	Nebraska 28, Louisiana St 10
1-1-86	Tennessee 35, Miami (FL) 7
1-1-87	Nebraska 30, Louisiana St 15
1-1-88	Syracuse 16, Auburn 16
1-2-89	Florida St 13, Auburn 7
1-1-90	Miami (FL) 33, Alabama 25
1-1-91	Tennessee 23, Virginia 22
1-1-92	Notre Dame 39, Florida 28
1-1-93	Alabama 34, Miami (FL) 13
1-1-94	Florida 41, West Virginia 7
1-2-95	Florida St 23, Florida 17
12-31-95	Virginia Tech 28, Texas 10
1-2-97	Florida 52, Florida St 20
1-1-98	Florida St 31, Ohio St 14
1-1-99	Ohio St 24, Texas A&M 14
1-4-00	Florida St 46, Virginia Tech 29
1-2-01	Miami (FL) 37, Florida 20
1-1-02	Louisiana St 47, Illinois 34
1-1-03	Georgia 26, Florida St 13

Sugar Bowl (Cont.)

1-4-04 ....Louisiana St 21, Oklahoma 14

City: New Orleans. Stadium: Louisiana Superdome, capacity 76,791.

Playing Sites: Tulane Stadium (1935–74), Louisiana Superdome (since 1975).

Cotton Bowl

1-1-37 ....Texas Christian 16, Marquette 6
1-1-38 ....Rice 28, Colorado 14
1-2-39 ....St. Mary's (CA) 20, Texas Tech 13
1-1-40 ....Clemson 6, Boston Col 3
1-1-41 ....Texas A&M 13, Fordham 12
1-1-42 ....Alabama 29, Texas A&M 21
1-1-43 ....Texas 14, Georgia Tech 7
1-1-44 ....Texas 7, Randolph Field 7
1-1-45 ....Oklahoma St 34, Texas Christian 0
1-1-46 ....Texas 40, Missouri 27
1-1-47 ....Arkansas 0, Louisiana St 0
1-1-48 ....Southern Methodist 13, Penn St 13
1-1-49 ....Southern Methodist 21, Oregon 13
1-2-50 ....Rice 27, N Carolina 13
1-1-51 ....Tennessee 20, Texas 14
1-1-52 ....Kentucky 20, Texas Christian 7
1-1-53 ....Texas 16, Tennessee 0
1-1-54 ....Rice 28, Alabama 6
1-1-55 ....Georgia Tech 14, Arkansas 6
1-2-56 ....Mississippi 14, Texas Christian 13
1-1-57 ....Texas Christian 28, Syracuse 27
1-1-58 ....Navy 20, Rice 7
1-1-59 ....Texas Christian 0, Air Force 0
1-1-60 ....Syracuse 23, Texas 14
1-2-61 ....Duke 7, Arkansas 6
1-1-62 ....Texas 12, Mississippi 7
1-1-63 ....Louisiana St 13, Texas 0
1-1-64 ....Texas 28, Navy 6
1-1-65 ....Arkansas 10, Nebraska 7
1-1-66 ....Louisiana St 14, Arkansas 7
12-31-66 ....Georgia 24, Southern Methodist 9
1-1-68 ....Texas A&M 20, Alabama 16
1-1-69 ....Texas 36, Tennessee 13
1-1-70 ....Texas 21, Notre Dame 17
1-1-71 ....Notre Dame 24, Texas 11
1-1-72 ....Penn St 30, Texas 6
1-1-73 ....Texas 17, Alabama 13
1-1-74 ....Nebraska 19, Texas 3
1-1-75 ....Penn St 41, Baylor 20
1-1-76 ....Arkansas 31, Georgia 10
1-1-77 ....Houston 30, Maryland 21
1-2-78 ....Notre Dame 38, Texas 10
1-1-79 ....Notre Dame 35, Houston 34
1-1-80 ....Houston 17, Nebraska 14
1-1-81 ....Alabama 30, Baylor 2
1-1-82 ....Texas 14, Alabama 12
1-1-83 ....SMU 7, Pittsburgh 3
1-2-84 ....Georgia 10, Texas 9
1-1-85 ....Boston Col 45, Houston 28
1-1-86 ....Texas A&M 36, Auburn 16
1-1-87 ....Ohio St 28, Texas A&M 12
1-1-88 ....Texas A&M 35, Notre Dame 10
1-2-89 ....UCLA 17, Arkansas 3
1-1-90 ....Tennessee 31, Arkansas 27
1-1-91 ....Miami (FL) 46, Texas 3
1-1-92 ....Florida St 10, Texas A&M 2
1-1-93 ....Notre Dame 28, Texas A&M 3
1-1-94 ....Notre Dame 24, Texas A&M 21
1-2-95 ....Southern Cal 55, Texas Tech 14
1-1-96 ....Colorado 38, Oregon 6
1-1-97 ....Brigham Young 19, Kansas St 15

Cotton Bowl (Cont.)

1-1-98 ....UCLA 29, Texas A&M 23
1-1-99 ....Texas 38, Mississippi St 11
1-1-00 ....Arkansas 27, Texas 6
1-1-01 ....Kansas St 35, Tennessee 21
1-1-02 ....Oklahoma 10, Arkansas 3
1-1-03 ....Texas 35, Louisiana St 20
1-2-04 ....Mississippi 31, Oklahoma St 28

City: Dallas. Stadium: Cotton Bowl, capacity 68,252.

Sun Bowl

1-1-36 ....Hardin-Simmons 14, New Mexico St 14
1-1-37 ....Hardin-Simmons 34, UTEP 6
1-1-38 ....W Virginia 7, Texas Tech 6
1-2-39 ....Utah 26, New Mexico 0
1-1-40 ....Catholic 0, Arizona St 0
1-1-41 ....Case Reserve 26, Arizona St 13
1-1-42 ....Tulsa 6, Texas Tech 0
1-1-43 ....2nd Air Force 13, Hardin-Simmons 7
1-1-44 ....Southwestern (TX) 7, New Mexico 0
1-1-45 ....Southwestern (TX) 35, New Mexico 0
1-1-46 ....New Mexico 34, Denver 24
1-1-47 ....Cincinnati 18, Virginia Tech 6
1-1-48 ....Miami (OH) 13, Texas Tech 12
1-1-49 ....W Virginia 21, UTEP 12
1-2-50 ....UTEP 33, Georgetown 20
1-1-51 ....W Texas St 14, Cincinnati 13
1-1-52 ....Texas Tech 25, Pacific 14
1-1-53 ....Pacific 26, Southern Miss 7
1-1-54 ....UTEP 37, Southern Miss 14
1-1-55 ....UTEP 47, Florida St 20
1-2-56 ....Wyoming 21, Texas Tech 14
1-1-57 ....George Washington 13, UTEP 0
1-1-58 ....Louisville 34, Drake 20
12-31-58 ....Wyoming 14, Hardin-Simmons 6
12-31-59 ....New Mexico St 28, N Texas 8
12-31-60 ....New Mexico St 20, Utah St 13
12-30-61 ....Villanova 17, Wichita St 9
12-31-62 ....W Texas St 15, Ohio 14
12-31-63 ....Oregon 21, Southern Methodist 14
12-26-64 ....Georgia 7, Texas Tech 0
12-31-65 ....UTEP 13, Texas Christian 12
12-24-66 ....Wyoming 28, Florida St 20
12-30-67 ....UTEP 14, Mississippi 7
12-28-68 ....Auburn 34, Arizona 10
12-20-69 ....Nebraska 45, Georgia 6
12-19-70 ....Georgia Tech 17, Texas Tech 9
12-18-71 ....Louisiana St 33, Iowa St 15
12-30-72 ....N Carolina 32, Texas Tech 28
12-29-73 ....Missouri 34, Auburn 17
12-28-74 ....Mississippi St 26, N Carolina 24
12-26-75 ....Pittsburgh 33, Kansas 19
1-2-77 ....Texas A&M 37, Florida 14
12-31-77 ....Stanford 24, Louisiana St 14
12-23-78 ....Texas 42, Maryland 0
12-22-79 ....Washington 14, Texas 7
12-27-80 ....Nebraska 31, Mississippi St 17
12-26-81 ....Oklahoma 40, Houston 14
12-25-82 ....N Carolina 26, Texas 10
12-24-83 ....Alabama 28, Southern Methodist 7
12-22-84 ....Maryland 28, Tennessee 27
12-28-85 ....Georgia 13, Arizona 13
12-25-86 ....Alabama 28, Washington 6
12-25-87 ....Oklahoma St 35, W Virginia 33
12-24-88 ....Alabama 29, Army 28
12-30-89 ....Pittsburgh 31, Texas A&M 28
12-31-90 ....Michigan St 17, Southern Cal 16
12-31-91 ....UCLA 6, Illinois 3
12-31-92 ....Baylor 20, Arizona 15
12-24-93 ....Oklahoma 41, Texas Tech 10

Sun Bowl (Cont.)

12-30-94.........Texas 35, N Carolina 31
12-29-95.........Iowa 38, Washington 18
12-31-96.........Stanford 38, Michigan St 0
12-31-97.........Arizona St 17, Iowa 7
12-31-98.........Texas Christian 28, Southern Cal 19
12-31-99.........Oregon 24, Minnesota 20
12-29-00.........Wisconsin 21, UCLA 20
12-31-01.........Washington St 33, Purdue 27
12-31-02.........Purdue 34, Washington 24
12-31-03.........Minnesota 31, Oregon 30

City: El Paso. Stadium: Sun Bowl, capacity 51,270.

Name Changes: Sun Bowl (1936–86; 94–), John Hancock Sun Bowl (1987–88), John Hancock Bowl (1989–93).

Playing Sites: Kidd Field (1936–62), Sun Bowl (since 1963).

Gator Bowl

1-1-46.............Wake Forest 26, S Carolina 14
1-1-47.............Oklahoma 34, N Carolina St 13
1-1-48.............Maryland 20, Georgia 20
1-1-49.............Clemson 24, Missouri 23
1-2-50.............Maryland 20, Missouri 7
1-1-51.............Wyoming 20, Washington & Lee 7
1-1-52.............Miami (FL) 14, Clemson 0
1-1-53.............Florida 14, Tulsa 13
1-1-54.............Texas Tech 35, Auburn 13
12-31-54.........Auburn 33, Baylor 13
12-31-55.........Vanderbilt 25, Auburn 13
12-29-56.........Georgia Tech 21, Pittsburgh 14
12-28-57.........Tennessee 3, Texas A&M 0
12-27-58.........Mississippi 7, Florida 3
1-2-60.............Arkansas 14, Georgia Tech 7
12-31-60.........Florida 13, Baylor 12
12-30-61.........Penn St 30, Georgia Tech 15
12-29-62.........Florida 17, Penn St 7
12-28-63.........N Carolina 35, Air Force 0
1-2-65.............Florida St 36, Oklahoma 19
12-31-65.........Georgia Tech 31, Texas Tech 21
12-31-66.........Tennessee 18, Syracuse 12
12-30-67.........Penn St 17, Florida St 17
12-28-68.........Missouri 35, Alabama 10
12-27-69.........Florida 14, Tennessee 13
1-2-71.............Auburn 35, Mississippi 28
12-31-71.........Georgia 7, N Carolina 3
12-30-72.........Auburn 24, Colorado 3
12-29-73.........Texas Tech 28, Tennessee 19
12-30-74.........Auburn 27, Texas 3
12-29-75.........Maryland 13, Florida 0
12-27-76.........Notre Dame 20, Penn St 9
12-30-77.........Pittsburgh 34, Clemson 3
12-29-78.........Clemson 17, Ohio St 15
12-28-79.........N Carolina 17, Michigan 15
12-29-80.........Pittsburgh 37, S Carolina 9
12-28-81.........N Carolina 31, Arkansas 27
12-30-82.........Florida St 31, W Virginia 12
12-30-83.........Florida 14, Iowa 6
12-28-84.........Oklahoma St 21, S Carolina 14
12-30-85.........Florida St 34, Oklahoma St 23
12-27-86.........Clemson 27, Stanford 21
12-31-87.........Louisiana St 30, S Carolina 13
1-1-89.............Georgia 34, Michigan St 27
12-30-89.........Clemson 27, W Virginia 7
1-1-91.............Michigan 35, Mississippi 3
12-29-91.........Oklahoma 48, Virginia 14
12-31-92.........Florida 27, N Carolina St 10
12-31-93.........Alabama 24, North Carolina 10
12-30-94.........Tennessee 45, Virginia Tech 23
1-1-96.............Syracuse 41, Clemson 0
1-1-97.............N Carolina 20, W Virginia 13
1-1-98.............N Carolina 42, Viginia Tech 13
1-1-99.............Georgia Tech 35, Notre Dame 28
1-1-00.............Miami 27, Georgia Tech 13

Gator Bowl (Cont.)

1-1-01.............Virginia Tech 41, Clemson 20
1-1-02.............Florida St 30, Virginia Tech 17
1-1-03.............N Carolina St 28, Notre Dame 6
1-1-04.............Maryland 41, W Virginia 7

City: Jacksonville, FL. Stadium: Alltel Stadium, capacity 76,976.

Florida Citrus Bowl

1-1-47.............Catawba 31, Maryville (TN) 6
1-1-48.............Catawba 7, Marshall 0
1-1-49.............Murray St 21, Sul Ross St 21
1-2-50.............St. Vincent 7, Emory & Henry 6
1-1-51.............Morris Harvey 35, Emory & Henry 14
1-1-52.............Stetson 35, Arkansas St 20
1-1-53.............E Texas St 33, Tennessee Tech 0
1-1-54.............E Texas St 7, Arkansas St 7
1-1-55.............NE-Omaha 7, Eastern Kentucky 6
1-2-56.............Juniata 6, Missouri Valley 6
1-1-57.............W Texas St 20, Southern Miss 13
1-1-58.............E Texas St 10, Southern Miss 9
12-27-58.........E Texas St 26, Missouri Valley 7
1-1-60.............Middle Tennessee St 21, Presbyterian 12
12-30-60.........Citadel 27, Tennessee Tech 0
12-29-61.........Lamar 21, Middle Tennessee St 14
12-22-62.........Houston 49, Miami (OH) 21
12-28-63.........Western Kentucky 27, Coast Guard 0
12-12-64.........E Carolina 14, Massachusetts 13
12-11-65.........E Carolina 31, Maine 0
12-10-66.........Morgan St 14, W Chester 6
12-16-67.........TN-Martin 25, W Chester 8
12-27-68.........Richmond 49, Ohio 42
12-26-69.........Toledo 56, Davidson 33
12-28-70.........Toledo 40, William & Mary 12
12-28-71.........Toledo 28, Richmond 3
12-29-72.........Tampa 21, Kent St 18
12-22-73.........Miami (OH) 16, Florida 7
12-21-74.........Miami (OH) 21, Georgia 10
12-20-75.........Miami (OH) 20, S Carolina 7
12-18-76.........Oklahoma St 49, Brigham Young 21
12-23-77.........Florida St 40, Texas Tech 17
12-23-78.........N Carolina St 30, Pittsburgh 17
12-22-79.........Louisiana St 34, Wake Forest 10
12-20-80.........Florida 35, Maryland 20
12-19-81.........Missouri 19, Southern Miss 17
12-18-82.........Auburn 33, Boston Col 26
12-17-83.........Tennessee 30, Maryland 23
12-22-84.........Georgia 17, Florida St 17
12-28-85.........Ohio St 10, Brigham Young 7
1-1-87.............Auburn 16, Southern Cal 7
1-1-88.............Clemson 35, Penn St 10
1-2-89.............Clemson 13, Oklahoma 6
1-1-90.............Illinois 31, Virginia 21
1-1-91.............Georgia Tech 45, Nebraska 21
1-1-92.............California 37, Clemson 13
1-1-93.............Georgia 21, Ohio State 14
1-1-94.............Penn State 31, Tennessee 13
1-2-95.............Alabama 24, Ohio St 17
1-1-96.............Tennessee 20, Ohio St 14
1-1-97.............Tennessee 48, Northwestern 28
1-1-98.............Florida 21, Penn St 6
1-1-99.............Michigan 45, Arkansas 31
1-1-00.............Michigan 37, Florida 34
1-1-01.............Michigan 31, Auburn 28
1-1-02.............Tennessee 45, Michigan 17
1-1-03.............Auburn 13, Penn St 9
1-1-04.............Georgia 34, Purdue 27 (OT)

City: Orlando, FL. Stadium: Florida Citrus Bowl, capacity 70,000.

Name Change: Tangerine Bowl (1947–82).

Playing Sites: Tangerine Bowl (1947–72, 1974–82); Florida Field, Gainesville (1973); Orlando Stadium/Florida Citrus Bowl-Orlando (since 1983).

Liberty Bowl

12-19-59.........Penn St 7, Alabama 0
12-17-60.........Penn St 41, Oregon 12
12-16-61.........Syracuse 15, Miami (FL) 14
12-15-62.........Oregon St 6, Villanova 0
12-21-63.........Mississippi St 16, N Carolina St 12
12-19-64.........Utah 32, W Virginia 6
12-18-65.........Mississippi 13, Auburn 7
12-10-66.........Miami (FL) 14, Virginia Tech 7
12-16-67.........N Carolina St 14, Georgia 7
12-14-68.........Mississippi 34, Virginia Tech 17
12-13-69.........Colorado 47, Alabama 33
12-12-70.........Tulane 17, Colorado 3
12-20-71.........Tennessee 14, Arkansas 13
12-18-72.........Georgia Tech 31, Iowa St 30
12-17-73.........N Carolina 31, Kansas 18
12-16-74.........Tennessee 7, Maryland 3
12-22-75.........Southern Cal 20, Texas A&M 0
12-20-76.........Alabama 36, UCLA 6
12-19-77.........Nebraska 21, N Carolina 17
12-23-78.........Missouri 20, Louisiana St 15
12-22-79.........Penn St 9, Tulane 6
12-27-80.........Purdue 28, Missouri 25
12-30-81.........Ohio St 31, Navy 28
12-29-82.........Alabama 21, Illinois 15
12-29-83.........Notre Dame 19, Boston Col 18
12-27-84.........Auburn 21, Arkansas 15
12-27-85.........Baylor 21, Louisiana St 7
12-29-86.........Tennessee 21, Minnesota 14
12-29-87.........Georgia 20, Arkansas 17
12-28-88.........Indiana 34, S Carolina 10
12-28-89.........Mississippi 42, Air Force 29
12-27-90.........Air Force 23, Ohio St 11
12-29-91.........Air Force 38, Mississippi St 15
12-31-92.........Mississippi 13, Air Force 0
12-28-93.........Louisville 18, Michigan St 7
12-31-94.........Illinois 30, E Carolina 0
12-30-95.........East Carolina 19, Stanford 13
12-27-96.........Syracuse 30, Houston 17
12-31-97.........Southern Miss 41, Pittsburgh 7
12-31-98.........Tulane 41, Brigham Young 27
12-31-99.........Southern Miss 23, Colorado St 17
12-29-01.........Colorado St 22, Louisville 17
12-31-01.........Louisville 28, Brigham Young 10
12-31-02.........Texas Christian 17, Colorado St 3
12-31-03.........Utah 17, Southern Mississippi 0

City: Memphis (since 1965). Stadium: Liberty Bowl Memorial Stadium, capacity 62,921.

Playing Sites: Philadelphia (Municipal Stadium, 1959–63), Atlantic City (Convention Center, 1964).

Bluebonnet Bowl

12-19-59.........Clemson 23, Texas Christian 7
12-17-60.........Texas 3, Alabama 3
12-16-61.........Kansas 33, Rice 7
12-22-62.........Missouri 14, Georgia Tech 10
12-21-63.........Baylor 14, LSU 7
12-19-64.........Tulsa 14, Mississippi 7
12-18-65.........Tennessee 27, Tulsa 6
12-17-66.........Texas 19, Mississippi 0
12-23-67.........Colorado 31, Miami (FL) 21
12-31-68.........Southern Methodist 28, Oklahoma 27
12-31-69.........Houston 36, Auburn 7
12-31-70.........Alabama 24, Oklahoma 24
12-31-71.........Colorado 29, Houston 17
12-30-72.........Tennessee 24, Louisiana St 17
12-29-73.........Houston 47, Tulane 7
12-23-74.........N Carolina St 31, Houston 31
12-27-75.........Texas 38, Colorado 21
12-31-76.........Nebraska 27, Texas Tech 24
12-31-77.........Southern Cal 47, Texas A&M 28
12-31-78.........Stanford 25, Georgia 22
12-31-79.........Purdue 27, Tennessee 22

Bluebonnet Bowl *(Cont.)*

12-31-80.........N Carolina 16, Texas 7
12-31-81.........Michigan 33, UCLA 14
12-31-82.........Arkansas 28, Florida 24
12-31-83.........Oklahoma St 24, Baylor 14
12-31-84.........W Virginia 31, Texas Christian 14
12-31-85.........Air Force 24, Texas 16
12-31-86.........Baylor 21, Colorado 9
12-31-87.........Texas 32, Pittsburgh 27

City: Houston. Playing sites: Rice Stadium (1959–67; 1985–86), Astrodome (1968–84, 1987).

Name change: Astro-Bluebonnet Bowl (1968–76). Bowl was discontinued after 1987.

Peach Bowl

12-30-68.........Louisiana St 31, Florida St 27
12-30-69.........W Virginia 14, S Carolina 3
12-30-70.........Arizona St 48, N Carolina 26
12-30-71.........Mississippi 41, Georgia Tech 18
12-29-72.........N Carolina St 49, W Virginia 13
12-28-73.........Georgia 17, Maryland 16
12-28-74.........Vanderbilt 6, Texas Tech 6
12-31-75.........W Virginia 13, N Carolina St 10
12-31-76.........Kentucky 21, N Carolina 0
12-31-77.........N Carolina St 24, Iowa St 14
12-25-78.........Purdue 41, Georgia Tech 21
12-31-79.........Baylor 24, Clemson 18
1-2-81.............Miami (FL) 20, Virginia Tech 10
12-31-81.........W Virginia 26, Florida 6
12-31-82.........Iowa 28, Tennessee 22
12-30-83.........Florida St 28, N Carolina 3
12-31-84.........Virginia 27, Purdue 24
12-31-85.........Army 31, Illinois 29
12-31-86.........Virginia Tech 25, N Carolina St 24
1-2-88.............Tennessee 27, Indiana 22
12-31-88.........N Carolina St 28, Iowa 23
12-30-89.........Syracuse 19, Georgia 18
12-29-90.........Auburn 27, Indiana 23
1-1-92.............E Carolina 37, N Carolina St 34
1-2-93.............N Carolina 21, Mississippi St 17
12-31-93.........Clemson 14, Kentucky 13
1-1-95.............N Carolina St 28, Mississippi St 24
12-30-95.........Virginia 34, Georgia 27
12-28-96.........Louisiana St 10, Clemson 7
1-2-98.............Auburn 21, Clemson 17
12-31-98.........Georgia 35, Virginia 33
12-30-99.........Mississippi St 17, Clemson 7
12-29-00.........Louisiana St 28, Georgia Tech 14
12-31-01.........N Carolina 16, Auburn 10
12-31-02.........Maryland 30, Tennessee 3
1-2-04.............Clemson 27, Tennessee 14

City: Atlanta. Stadium: Georgia Dome, capacity 71,500. Playing Sites: Grant Field (1968–70), Atlanta–Fulton County Stadium (1971–92), Georgia Dome (since 1993).

Fiesta Bowl

12-27-71.........Arizona St 45, Florida St 38
12-23-72.........Arizona St 49, Missouri 35
12-21-73.........Arizona St 28, Pittsburgh 7
12-28-74.........Oklahoma St 16, Brigham Young 6
12-26-75.........Arizona St 17, Nebraska 14
12-25-76.........Oklahoma 41, Wyoming 7
12-25-77.........Penn St 42, Arizona St 30
12-25-78.........Arkansas 10, UCLA 10
12-25-79.........Pittsburgh 16, Arizona 10
12-26-80.........Penn St 31, Ohio St 19
1-1-82.............Penn St 26, Southern Cal 10
1-1-83.............Arizona St 32, Oklahoma 21
1-2-84.............Ohio St 28, Pittsburgh 23
1-1-85.............UCLA 39, Miami (FL) 37
1-1-86.............Michigan 27, Nebraska 23
1-2-87.............Penn St 14, Miami (FL) 10
1-1-88.............Florida St 31, Nebraska 28

Fiesta Bowl *(Cont.)*

1-2-89 ....Notre Dame 34, W Virginia 21
1-1-90 ....Florida St 41, Nebraska 17
1-1-91 ....Louisville 34, Alabama 7
1-1-92 ....Penn St 42, Tennessee 17
1-1-93 ....Syracuse 26, Colorado 22
1-1-94 ....Arizona 29, Miami (FL) 0
1-2-95 ....Colorado 41, Notre Dame 24
1-2-96 ....Nebraska 62, Florida 24
1-1-97 ....Penn St 38, Texas 15
12-31-97 ....Kansas St 35, Syracuse 18
1-4-99 ....Tennessee 23, Florida St 16
1-2-00 ....Nebraska 31, Tennessee 21
1-1-01 ....Oregon St 41, Notre Dame 9
1-1-02 ....Oregon 38, Colorado 16
1-3-03 ....Ohio St 31, Miami (FL) 24 [2 OT]
1-2-04 ....Ohio St 35, Kansas St 28

City: Tempe, AZ. Stadium: Sun Devil Stadium, capacity 73,471.

Independence Bowl

12-13-76 ....McNeese St 20, Tulsa 16
12-17-77 ....Louisiana Tech 24, Louisville 14
12-16-78 ....E Carolina 35, Louisiana Tech 13
12-15-79 ....Syracuse 31, McNeese St 7
12-13-80 ....Southern Miss 16, McNeese St 14
12-12-81 ....Texas A&M 33, Oklahoma St 16
12-11-82 ....Wisconsin 14, Kansas St 3
12-10-83 ....Air Force 9, Mississippi 3
12-15-84 ....Air Force 23, Virginia Tech 7
12-21-85 ....Minnesota 20, Clemson 13
12-20-86 ....Mississippi 20, Texas Tech 17
12-19-87 ....Washington 24, Tulane 12
12-23-88 ....Southern Miss 38, UTEP 18
12-16-89 ....Oregon 27, Tulsa 24
12-15-90 ....Louisiana Tech 34, Maryland 34
12-29-91 ....Georgia 24, Arkansas 15
12-31-92 ....Wake Forest 39, Oregon 35
12-31-93 ....Virginia Tech 45, Indiana 20
12-28-94 ....Virginia 20, Texas Christian 10
12-29-95 ....Louisiana St 45, Michigan St 26
12-31-96 ....Auburn 32, Army 29
12-28-97 ....Louisiana St 27, Notre Dame 9
12-31-98 ....Mississippi 35, Texas Tech 18
12-31-99 ....Mississippi 27, Oklahoma 25
12-31-00 ....Mississippi St 43, Texas A&M 41
12-27-01 ....Alabama 14, Iowa St 13
12-27-02 ....Mississippi 27, Nebraska 23
12-31-03 ....Arkansas 27, Missouri 14

City: Shreveport, LA. Stadium: Independence Stadium, capacity 50,459.

All-American Bowl

12-22-77 ....Maryland 17, Minnesota 7
12-20-78 ....Texas A&M 28, Iowa St 12
12-29-79 ....Missouri 24, S Carolina 14
12-27-80 ....Arkansas 34, Tulane 15
12-31-81 ....Mississippi St 10, Kansas 0
12-31-82 ....Air Force 36, Vanderbilt 28
12-22-83 ....W Virginia 20, Kentucky 16
12-29-84 ....Kentucky 20, Wisconsin 19
12-31-85 ....Georgia Tech 17, Michigan St 14
12-31-86 ....Florida St 27, Indiana 13
12-22-87 ....Virginia 22, Brigham Young 16
12-29-88 ....Florida 14, Illinois 10
12-28-89 ....Texas Tech 49, Duke 21
12-28-90 ....N Carolina St 31, Southern Miss. 27

City: Birmingham, AL. Stadium: Legion Field.
Name Change: Hall of Fame Classic (1977–84). Bowl was discontinued after 1990.

Holiday Bowl

12-22-78 ....Navy 23, Brigham Young 16
12-21-79 ....Indiana 38, Brigham Young 37
12-19-80 ....Brigham Young 46, SMU45
12-18-81 ....Brigham Young 38, Washington St 36
12-17-82 ....Ohio St 47, Brigham Young 17
12-23-83 ....Brigham Young 21, Missouri 17
12-21-84 ....Brigham Young 24, Michigan 17
12-22-85 ....Arkansas 18, Arizona St 17
12-30-86 ....Iowa 39, San Diego St 38
12-30-87 ....Iowa 20, Wyoming 19
12-30-88 ....Oklahoma St 62, Wyoming 14
12-29-89 ....Penn St 50, Brigham Young 39
12-29-90 ....Texas A&M 65, Brigham Young 14
12-30-91 ....Iowa 13, Brigham Young 13
12-30-92 ....Hawaii 27, Illinois 17
12-30-93 ....Ohio St 28, Brigham Young 21
12-30-94 ....Michigan 24, Colorado St 14
12-29-95 ....Kansas St 54, Colorado St 21
12-30-96 ....Colorado 33, Washington 21
12-29-97 ....Colorado St 35, Missouri 24
12-30-98 ....Arizona 23, Nebraska 20
12-29-99 ....Kansas St 24, Washington 20
12-29-00 ....Oregon 35, Texas 30
12-28-01 ....Texas 47, Washington 43
12-27-02 ....Kansas St 34, Arizona St 27
12-30-03 ....Washington St 28, Texas 20

City: San Diego. Stadium: Qualcomm Stadium, capacity 70,000.

Las Vegas Bowl

12-19-81 ....Toledo 27, San Jose St 25
12-18-82 ....Fresno St 29, Bowling Green 28
12-17-83 ....Northern Illinois 20, Cal St–Fullerton 13
12-15-84 ....UNLV 30, Toledo 13*
12-14-85 ....Fresno St 51, Bowling Green 7
12-13-86 ....San Jose St 37, Miami (OH) 7
12-12-87 ....Eastern Michigan 30, San Jose St 27
12-10-88 ....Fresno St 35, Western Michigan 30
12-9-89 ....Fresno St 27, Ball St 6
12-8-90 ....San Jose St 48, Central Michigan 24
12-14-91 ....Bowling Green 28, Fresno St 21
12-18-92 ....Bowling Green 35, Nevada 34
12-17-93 ....Utah St 42, Ball St 33
12-15-94 ....UNLV 52, Central Michigan 24
12-14-95 ....Toledo 40, Nevada 37
12-19-96 ....Nevada 18, Ball St 15
12-19-97 ....Oregon 41, Air Force 13
12-19-98 ....N Carolina 20, San Diego St 13
12-18-99 ....Utah 17, Fresno St 16
12-21-00 ....UNLV 31, Arkansas 14
12-25-01 ....Utah 10, Southern Cal 6
12-25-02 ....UCLA 27, New Mexico 13
12-24-03 ....Oregon St 55, New Mexico 14

* Toledo won later by forfeit. City: Las Vegas (since 1992).
Stadium: Sam Boyd Silver Bowl Stadium, capacity 40,000.
Name change: California Bowl (1981–91).
Playing sites: Fresno, CA (Bulldog Stadium, 1981–91), Las Vegas.

Aloha Bowl

12-25-82 ....Washington 21, Maryland 20
12-26-83 ....Penn St 13, Washington 10
12-29-84 ....Southern Methodist 27, Notre Dame 20
12-28-85 ....Alabama 24, Southern Cal 3
12-27-86 ....Arizona 30, N Carolina 21
12-25-87 ....UCLA 20, Florida 16
12-25-88 ....Washington St 24, Houston 22
12-25-89 ....Michigan St 33, Hawaii 13
12-25-90 ....Syracuse 28, Arizona 0
12-25-91 ....Georgia Tech 18, Stanford 17
12-25-92 ....Kansas 23, Brigham Young 20

Aloha Bowl *(Cont.)*

12-25-93 ....Colorado 41, Fresno St 30
12-25-94 ....Boston College 12, Kansas St 7
12-25-95 ....Kansas 51, UCLA 30
12-25-96 ....Navy 42, California 38
12-25-97 ....Washington 51, Michigan St 23
12-25-98 ....Colorado 51, Oregon 43
12-25-99 ....Wake Forest 23, Arizona St 3
12-25-00 ....Boston College 31, Arizona St 17

City: Honolulu. Stadium: Aloha Stadium. Bowl was discontinued after 2000.

Freedom Bowl

12-16-84 ....Iowa 55, Texas 17
12-30-85 ....Washington 20, Colorado 17
12-30-86 ....UCLA 31, Brigham Young 10
12-30-87 ....Arizona St 33, Air Force 28
12-29-88 ....Brigham Young 20, Colorado 17
12-30-89 ....Washington 34, Florida 7
12-29-90 ....Colorado St 32, Oregon 31
12-30-91 ....Tulsa 28, San Diego St 17
12-29-92 ....Fresno St 24, Southern Cal 7
12-30-93 ....Southern Cal 28, Utah 21
12-29-94 ....Utah 16, Arizona 13

City: Anaheim. Stadium: Anaheim Stadium. Bowl was discontinued after 1994.

Outback Bowl

12-23-86 ....Boston College 27, Georgia 24
1-2-88 ....Michigan 28, Alabama 24
1-2-89 ....Syracuse 23, Louisiana St 10
1-1-90 ....Auburn 31, Ohio St 14
1-1-91 ....Clemson 30, Illinois 0
1-1-92 ....Syracuse 24, Ohio St 17
1-1-93 ....Tennessee 38, Boston College 23
1-1-94 ....Michigan 42, N Carolina St 7
1-2-95 ....Wisconsin 34, Duke 20
1-1-96 ....Penn St 43, Auburn 14
1-1-97 ....Alabama 17, Michigan 14
1-1-98 ....Georgia 33, Wisconsin 6
1-1-99 ....Penn St 26, Kentucky 14
1-1-00 ....Georgia 28, Purdue 25
1-1-01 ....S Carolina 24, Ohio St 7
1-1-02 ....S Carolina 31, Ohio St 28
1-1-03 ....Michigan 38, Florida 30
1-1-04 ....Iowa 37, Florida 17

City: Tampa. Stadium: Raymond James Stadium, capacity 75,000. Name change: Hall of Fame Bowl (1986–95).

Insight.com Bowl

12-31-89 ....Arizona 17, N Carolina St 10
12-31-90 ....California 17, Wyoming 15
12-31-91 ....Indiana 24, Baylor 0
12-29-92 ....Washington St 31, Utah 28
12-29-93 ....Kansas St 52, Wyoming 17
12-29-94 ....Brigham Young 31, Oklahoma 6
12-27-95 ....Texas Tech 55, Air Force 41
12-27-96 ....Wisconsin 38, Utah 10
12-27-97 ....Arizona 20, New Mexico 14
12-26-98 ....Missouri 34, W Virginia 31
12-31-99 ....Colorado 62, Boston College 28
12-28-00 ....Iowa St 37, Pittsburgh 29
12-29-01 ....Syracuse 26, Kansas St 3
12-26-02 ....Pittsburgh 38, Oregon St 13
12-26-03 ....California 52, Virginia Tech 49

City: Tucson. Stadium: Arizona Stadium, capacity 55,883.
Name change: Copper Bowl 1989–97.

Tangerine Bowl

12-28-90 ....Florida St 24, Penn St 17
12-28-91 ....Alabama 30, Colorado 25
1-1-93 ....Stanford 24, Penn St 3
1-1-94 ....Boston College 31, Virginia 13
1-2-95 ....S Carolina 24, W Virginia 21
12-30-95 ....N Carolina 20, Arkansas 10
12-27-96 ....Miami (FL) 31, Virginia 21
12-29-97 ....Georgia Tech 35, W Virginia 30
12-29-98 ....Miami (FL) 46, N Carolina St 23
12-30-99 ....Illinois 62, Virginia 21
12-28-00 ....N Carolina St 38, Minnesota 30
12-20-01 ....Pittsburgh 34, N Carolina St 19
12-23-02 ....Texas Tech 55, Clemson 15
12-22-03 ....N Carolina 56, Kansas 26

City: Miami. Stadium: Pro Player Stadium, capacity 75,192. Name change: Blockbuster Bowl (1990–93), Carquest Bowl (1994–97), Micron PC Bowl (1998–00).

Alamo Bowl

12-31-93 ....California 37, Iowa 3
12-31-94 ....Washington St 10, Baylor 3
12-28-95 ....Texas A&M 22, Michigan 20
12-29-96 ....Iowa 27, Texas Tech 0
12-30-97 ....Purdue 33, Oklahoma St 20
12-29-98 ....Purdue 37, Kansas St 34
12-28-99 ....Penn St 24, Texas A&M 0
12-30-00 ....Nebraska 66, Northwestern 17
12-29-01 ....Iowa 16, Texas Tech 13
12-28-02 ....Wisconsin 31, Colorado 28 (OT)
12-29-03 ....Nebraska 17, Michigan St 3

City: San Antonio, TX. Stadium: Alamodome, capacity 67,000.

THEY SAID IT

Bobby Johnson, Vanderbilt coach, after students spent five minutes tearing down one goalpost, then 30 seconds tearing down the other, following a 28–17 win over Kentucky: "We're fast learners at Vanderbilt."

1936

		Record	Coach
1.	Minnesota	7-1-0	Bernie Bierman
2.	Louisiana St	9-0-1	Bernie Moore
3.	Pittsburgh	7-1-1	Jack Sutherland
4.	Alabama	8-0-1	Frank Thomas
5.	Washington	7-1-1	Jimmy Phelan
6.	Santa Clara	7-1-0	Buck Shaw
7.	Northwestern	7-1-0	Pappy Waldorf
8.	Notre Dame	6-2-1	Elmer Layden
9.	Nebraska	7-2-0	Dana X. Bible
10.	Pennsylvania	7-1-0	Harvey Harman
11.	Duke	9-1-0	Wallace Wade
12.	Yale	7-1-0	Ducky Pond
13.	Dartmouth	7-1-1	Red Blaik
14.	Duquesne	7-2-0	John Smith
15.	Fordham	5-1-2	Jim Crowley
16.	Texas Christian	8-2-2	Dutch Meyer
17.	Tennessee	6-2-2	Bob Neyland
18.	Arkansas	7-3-0	Fred Thomsen
19.	Navy	6-3-0	Tom Hamilton
20.	Marquette	7-1-0	Frank Murray

1937

		Record	Coach
1.	Pittsburgh	9-0-1	Jack Sutherland
2.	California	9-0-1	Stub Allison
3.	Fordham	7-0-1	Jim Crowley
4.	Alabama	9-0-0	Frank Thomas
5.	Minnesota	6-2-0	Bernie Bierman
6.	Villanova	8-0-1	Clipper Smith
7.	Dartmouth	7-0-2	Red Blaik
8.	Louisiana St	9-1-0	Bernie Moore
9.	Notre Dame	6-2-1	Elmer Layden
	Santa Clara	8-0-0	Buck Shaw
11.	Nebraska	6-1-2	Biff Jones
12.	Yale	6-1-1	Ducky Pond
13.	Ohio St	6-2-0	Francis Schmidt
14.	Holy Cross	8-0-2	Eddie Anderson
	Arkansas	6-2-2	Fred Thomsen
16.	Texas Christian	4-2-2	Dutch Meyer
17.	Colorado	8-1-0	Bunnie Oakes
18.	Rice	5-3-2	Jimmy Kitts
19.	N Carolina	7-1-1	Ray Wolf
20.	Duke	7-2-1	Wallace Wade

1938

		Record	Coach
1.	Texas Christian	10-0-0	Dutch Meyer
2.	Tennessee	10-0-0	Bob Neyland
3.	Duke	9-0-0	Wallace Wade
4.	Oklahoma	10-0-0	Tom Stidham
5.	#Notre Dame	8-1-0	Elmer Layden
6.	Carnegie Tech	7-1-0	Bill Kern
7.	Southern Cal	8-2-0	Howard Jones
8.	Pittsburgh	8-2-0	Jack Sutherland
9.	Holy Cross	8-1-0	Eddie Anderson
10.	Minnesota	6-2-0	Bernie Bierman
11.	Texas Tech	10-0-0	Pete Cawthon
12.	Cornell	5-1-1	Carl Snavely
13.	Alabama	7-1-1	Frank Thomas
14.	California	10-1-0	Stub Allison
15.	Fordham	6-1-2	Jim Crowley
16.	Michigan	6-1-1	Fritz Crisler
17.	Northwestern	4-2-2	Pappy Waldorf

1938 (Cont.)

		Record	Coach
18.	Villanova	8-0-1	Clipper Smith
19.	Tulane	7-2-1	Red Dawson
20.	Dartmouth	7-2-0	Red Blaik

#Selected No. 1 by the Dickinson System.

1939

		Record	Coach
1.	Texas A&M	10-0-0	Homer Norton
2.	Tennessee	10-0-0	Bob Neyland
3.	#Southern Cal	7-0-2	Howard Jones
4.	Cornell	8-0-0	Carl Snavely
5.	Tulane	8-0-1	Red Dawson
6.	Missouri	8-1-0	Don Faurot
7.	UCLA	6-0-4	Babe Horrell
8.	Duke	8-1-0	Wallace Wade
9.	Iowa	6-1-1	Eddie Anderson
10.	Duquesne	8-0-1	Buff Donelli
11.	Boston College	9-1-0	Frank Leahy
12.	Clemson	8-1-0	Jess Neely
13.	Notre Dame	7-2-0	Elmer Layden
14.	Santa Clara	5-1-3	Buck Shaw
15.	Ohio St	6-2-0	Francis Schmidt
16.	Georgia Tech	7-2-0	Bill Alexander
17.	Fordham	6-2-0	Jim Crowley
18.	Nebraska	7-1-1	Biff Jones
19.	Oklahoma	6-2-1	Tom Stidham
20.	Michigan	6-2-0	Fritz Crisler

#Selected No. 1 by the Dickinson System.

1940

		Record	Coach
1.	Minnesota	8-0-0	Bernie Bierman
2.	Stanford	9-0-0	C. Shaughnessy
3.	Michigan	7-1-0	Fritz Crisler
4.	Tennessee	10-0-0	Bob Neyland
5.	Boston College	10-0-0	Frank Leahy
6.	Texas A&M	8-1-0	Homer Norton
7.	Nebraska	8-1-0	Biff Jones
8.	Northwestern	6-2-0	Pappy Waldorf
9.	Mississippi St	9-0-1	Allyn McKeen
10.	Washington	7-2-0	Jimmy Phelan
11.	Santa Clara	6-1-1	Buck Shaw
12.	Fordham	7-1-0	Jim Crowley
13.	Georgetown	8-1-0	Jack Hagerty
14.	Pennsylvania	6-1-1	George Munger
15.	Cornell	6-2-0	Carl Snavely
16.	SMU	8-1-1	Matty Bell
17.	Hard.-Simmons	9-0-0	Abe Woodson
18.	Duke	7-2-0	Wallace Wade
19.	Lafayette	9-0-0	Hooks Mylin
20.			

Only 19 teams selected.

1941

		Record	Coach
1.	Minnesota	8-0-0	Bernie Bierman
2.	Duke	9-0-0	Wallace Wade
3.	Notre Dame	8-0-1	Frank Leahy
4.	Texas	8-1-1	Dana X. Bible
5.	Michigan	6-1-1	Fritz Crisler
6.	Fordham	7-1-0	Jim Crowley
7.	Missouri	8-1-0	Don Faurot
8.	Duquesne	8-0-0	Buff Donelli
9.	Texas A&M	9-1-0	Homer Norton
10.	Navy	7-1-1	Swede Larson
11.	Northwestern	5-3-0	Pappy Waldorf
12.	Oregon St	7-2-0	Lon Stiner
13.	Ohio St	6-1-1	Paul Brown
14.	Georgia	8-1-1	Wally Butts
15.	Pennsylvania	7-1-1	George Munger
16.	Mississippi St	8-1-1	Allyn McKeen
17.	Mississippi	6-2-1	Harry Mehre
18.	Tennessee	8-2-0	John Barnhill
19.	Washington St	6-4-0	Babe Hollingbery
20.	Alabama	8-2-0	Frank Thomas

1942

		Record	Coach
1.	Ohio St	9-1-0	Paul Brown
2.	Georgia	10-1-0	Wally Butts
3.	Wisconsin	8-1-1	H. Stuhldreher
4.	Tulsa	10-0-0	Henry Frnka
5.	Georgia Tech	9-1-0	Bill Alexander
6.	Notre Dame	7-2-2	Frank Leahy
7.	Tennessee	8-1-1	John Barnhill
8.	Boston College	8-1-0	Denny Myers
9.	Michigan	7-3-0	Fritz Crisler
10.	Alabama	7-3-0	Frank Thomas
11.	Texas	8-2-0	Dana X. Bible
12.	Stanford	6-4-0	Marchie Schwartz
13.	UCLA	7-3-0	Babe Horrell
14.	William & Mary	9-1-1	Carl Voyles
15.	Santa Clara	7-2-0	Buck Shaw
16.	Auburn	6-4-1	Jack Meagher
17.	Washington St	6-2-2	Babe Hollingbery
18.	Mississippi St	8-2-0	Allyn McKeen
19.	Minnesota	5-4-0	George Hauser
	Holy Cross	5-4-1	Ank Scanlon
	Penn St	6-1-1	Bob Higgins

1943

		Record	Coach
1.	Notre Dame	9-1-0	Frank Leahy
2.	Iowa Pre-Flight	9-1-0	Don Faurot
3.	Michigan	8-1-0	Fritz Crisler
4.	Navy	8-1-0	Billick Whelchel
5.	Purdue	9-0-0	Elmer Burnham
6.	Great Lakes	10-2-0	Tony Hinkle
7.	Duke	8-1-0	Eddie Cameron
8.	Del Monte P-F	7-1-0	Bill Kern
9.	Northwestern	6-2-0	Pappy Waldorf
10.	March Field	9-1-0	Paul Schissler
11.	Army	7-2-1	Red Blaik
12.	Washington	4-0-0	Ralph Welch
13.	Georgia Tech	7-3-0	Bill Alexander

1943 (Cont.)

		Record	Coach
14.	Texas	7-1-0	Dana X. Bible
15.	Tulsa	6-0-1	Henry Frnka
16.	Dartmouth	6-1-0	Earl Brown
17.	Bainbridge NTS	7-0-0	Joe Maniaci
18.	Colorado College	7-0-0	Hal White
19.	Pacific	7-2-0	Amos A. Stagg
20.	Pennsylvania	6-2-1	George Munger

1944

		Record	Coach
1.	Army	9-0-0	Red Blaik
2.	Ohio St	9-0-0	Carroll Widdoes
3.	Randolph Field	11-0-0	Frank Tritico
4.	Navy	6-3-0	Oscar Hagberg
5.	Bainbridge NTS	9-0-0	Joe Maniaci
6.	Iowa Pre-Flight	10-1-0	Jack Meagher
7.	Southern Cal	7-0-2	Jeff Cravath
8.	Michigan	8-2-0	Fritz Crisler
9.	Notre Dame	8-2-0	Ed McKeever
10.	March Field	7-1-2	Paul Schissler
11.	Duke	5-4-0	Eddie Cameron
12.	Tennessee	8-0-1	John Barnhill
13.	Georgia Tech	8-2-0	Bill Alexander
	Norman P-F	6-0-0	John Gregg
15.	Illinois	5-4-1	Ray Eliot
16.	El Toro Marines	8-1-0	Dick Hanley
17.	Great Lakes	9-2-1	Paul Brown
18.	Fort Pierce	9-0-0	Hamp Pool
19.	St. Mary's P-F	4-4-0	Jules Sikes
20.	2nd Air Force	7-2-1	Bill Reese

1945

		Record	Coach
1.	Army	9-0-0	Red Blaik
2.	Alabama	9-0-0	Frank Thomas
3.	Navy	7-1-1	Oscar Hagberg
4.	Indiana	9-0-1	Bo McMillan
5.	Oklahoma A&M	8-0-0	Jim Lookabaugh
6.	Michigan	7-3-0	Fritz Crisler
7.	St. Mary's (CA)	7-1-0	Jimmy Phelan
8.	Pennsylvania	6-2-0	George Munger
9.	Notre Dame	7-2-1	Hugh Devore
10.	Texas	9-1-0	Dana X. Bible
11.	Southern Cal	7-3-0	Jeff Cravath
12.	Ohio St	7-2-0	Carroll Widdoes
13.	Duke	6-2-0	Eddie Cameron
14.	Tennessee	8-1-0	John Barnhill
15.	Louisiana St	7-2-0	Bernie Moore
16.	Holy Cross	8-1-0	John DeGrosa
17.	Tulsa	8-2-0	Henry Frnka
18.	Georgia	8-2-0	Wally Butts
19.	Wake Forest	4-3-1	Peahead Walker
20.	Columbia	8-1-0	Lou Little

1946

		Record	Coach
1.	Notre Dame	8-0-1	Frank Leahy
2.	Army	9-0-1	Red Blaik
3.	Georgia	10-0-0	Wally Butts
4.	UCLA	10-0-0	B. LaBrucherie

Note: Except where indicated with an asterisk, the polls from 1936 through 1964 were taken before the bowl games and those from 1965 through the present were taken after the bowl games.

1946 (Cont.)

		Record	Coach
5.	Illinois	7-2-0	Ray Eliot
6.	Michigan	6-2-1	Fritz Crisler
7.	Tennessee	9-1-0	Bob Neyland
8.	Louisiana St	9-1-0	Bernie Moore
9.	N Carolina	8-1-1	Carl Snavely
10.	Rice	8-2-0	Jess Neely
11.	Georgia Tech	8-2-0	Bobby Dodd
12.	Yale	7-1-1	Howard Odell
13.	Pennsylvania	6-2-0	George Munger
14.	Oklahoma	7-3-0	Jim Tatum
15.	Texas	8-2-0	Dana X. Bible
16.	Arkansas	6-3-1	John Barnhill
17.	Tulsa	9-1-0	J.O. Brothers
18.	N Carolina St	8-2-0	Beattie Feathers
19.	Delaware	9-0-0	Bill Murray
20.	Indiana	6-3-0	Bo McMillan

1947

		Record	Coach
1.	Notre Dame	9-0-0	Frank Leahy
2.	#Michigan	9-0-0	Fritz Crisler
3.	SMU	9-0-1	Matty Bell
4.	Penn St	9-0-0	Bob Higgins
5.	Texas	9-1-0	Blair Cherry
6.	Alabama	8-2-0	Red Drew
7.	Pennsylvania	7-0-1	George Munger
8.	Southern Cal	7-1-1	Jeff Cravath
9.	N Carolina	8-2-0	Carl Snavely
10.	Georgia Tech	9-1-0	Bobby Dodd
11.	Army	5-2-2	Red Blaik
12.	Kansas	8-0-2	George Sauer
13.	Mississippi	8-2-0	Johnny Vaught
14.	William & Mary	9-1-0	Rube McCray
15.	California	9-1-0	Pappy Waldorf
16.	Oklahoma	7-2-1	Bud Wilkinson
17.	N Carolina St	5-3-1	Beattie Feathers
18.	Rice	6-3-1	Jess Neely
19.	Duke	4-3-2	Wallace Wade
20.	Columbia	7-2-0	Lou Little

#The AP, which had voted Notre Dame No. 1 before the bowl games, took a second vote, giving the title to Michigan after its 49–0 win over Southern Cal in the Rose Bowl.

1948

		Record	Coach
1.	Michigan	9-0-0	Bennie Oosterbaan
2.	Notre Dame	9-0-1	Frank Leahy
3.	N Carolina	9-0-1	Carl Snavely
4.	California	10-0-0	Pappy Waldorf
5.	Oklahoma	9-1-0	Bud Wilkinson
6.	Army	8-0-1	Red Blaik
7.	Northwestern	7-2-0	Bob Voigts
8.	Georgia	9-1-0	Wally Butts
9.	Oregon	9-1-0	Jim Aiken
10.	SMU	8-1-1	Matty Bell
11.	Clemson	10-0-0	Frank Howard
12.	Vanderbilt	8-2-1	Red Sanders
13.	Tulane	9-1-0	Henry Frnka
14.	Michigan St	6-2-2	Biggie Munn
15.	Mississippi	8-1-0	Johnny Vaught
16.	Minnesota	7-2-0	Bernie Bierman
17.	William & Mary	6-2-2	Rube McCray
18.	Penn St	7-1-1	Bob Higgins
19.	Cornell	8-1-0	Lefty James
20.	Wake Forest	6-3-0	Peahead Walker

1949

		Record	Coach
1.	Notre Dame	10-0-0	Frank Leahy
2.	Oklahoma	10-0-0	Bud Wilkinson
3.	California	10-0-0	Pappy Waldorf
4.	Army	9-0-0	Red Blaik
5.	Rice	9-1-0	Jess Neely
6.	Ohio St	6-1-2	Wes Fesler
7.	Michigan	6-2-1	Bennie Oosterbaan
8.	Minnesota	7-2-0	Bernie Bierman
9.	Louisiana St	8-2-0	Gaynell Tinsley
10.	Pacific	11-0-0	Larry Siemering
11.	Kentucky	9-2-0	Bear Bryant
12.	Cornell	8-1-0	Lefty James
13.	Villanova	8-1-0	Jim Leonard
14.	Maryland	8-1-0	Jim Tatum
15.	Santa Clara	7-2-1	Len Casanova
16.	N Carolina	7-3-0	Carl Snavely
17.	Tennessee	7-2-1	Bob Neyland
18.	Princeton	6-3-0	Charlie Caldwell
19.	Michigan St	6-3-0	Biggie Munn
20.	Missouri	7-3-0	Don Faurot
	Baylor	8-2-0	Bob Woodruff

1950

		Record	Coach
1.	Oklahoma	10-0-0	Bud Wilkinson
2.	Army	8-1-0	Red Blaik
3.	Texas	9-1-0	Blair Cherry
4.	Tennessee	10-1-0	Bob Neyland
5.	California	9-0-1	Pappy Waldorf
6.	Princeton	9-0-0	Charlie Caldwell
7.	Kentucky	10-1-0	Bear Bryant
8.	Michigan St	8-1-0	Biggie Munn
9.	Michigan	5-3-1	Bennie Oosterhaan
10.	Clemson	8-0-1	Frank Howard
11.	Washington	8-2-0	Howard Odell
12.	Wyoming	9-0-0	Bowden Wyatt
13.	Illinois	7-2-0	Ray Eliot
14.	Ohio St	6-3-0	Wes Fesler
15.	Miami (FL)	9-0-1	Andy Gustafson
16.	Alabama	9-2-0	Red Drew
17.	Nebraska	6-2-1	Bill Glassford
18.	Washington & Lee	8-2-0	George Barclay
19.	Tulsa	9-1-1	J.O. Brothers
20.	Tulane	6-2-1	Henry Frnka

1951

		Record	Coach
1.	Tennessee	10-1-0	Bob Neyland
2.	Michigan St	9-0-0	Biggie Munn
3.	Maryland	9-0-0	Jim Tatum
4.	Illinois	8-0-1	Ray Eliot
5.	Georgia Tech	10-0-1	Bobby Dodd
6.	Princeton	9-0-0	Charlie Caldwell
7.	Stanford	9-1-0	Chuck Taylor
8.	Wisconsin	7-1-1	Ivy Williamson
9.	Baylor	8-1-1	George Sauer
10.	Oklahoma	8-2-0	Bud Wilkinson
11.	Texas Christian	6-4-0	Dutch Meyer
12.	California	8-2-0	Pappy Waldorf
13.	Virginia	8-1-0	Art Guepe
14.	San Francisco	9-0-0	Joe Kuharich
15.	Kentucky	7-4-0	Bear Bryant
16.	Boston University	6-4-0	Buff Donelli
17.	UCLA	5-3-1	Red Sanders
18.	Washington St	7-3-0	Forest Evashevski

1951 (Cont.)

		Record	Coach
19.	Holy Cross	8-2-0	Eddie Anderson
20.	Clemson	7-2-0	Frank Howard

1952

		Record	Coach
1.	Michigan St	9-0-0	Biggie Munn
2.	Georgia Tech	11-0-0	Bobby Dodd
3.	Notre Dame	7-2-1	Frank Leahy
4.	Oklahoma	8-1-1	Bud Wilkinson
5.	Southern Cal	9-1-0	Jess Hill
6.	UCLA	8-1-0	Red Sanders
7.	Mississippi	8-0-2	Johnny Vaught
8.	Tennessee	8-1-1	Bob Neyland
9.	Alabama	9-2-0	Red Drew
10.	Texas	8-2-0	Ed Price
11.	Wisconsin	6-2-1	Ivy Williamson
12.	Tulsa	8-1-1	J.O. Brothers
13.	Maryland	7-2-0	Jim Tatum
14.	Syracuse	7-2-0	Ben Schwartzwalder
15.	Florida	7-3-0	Bob Woodruff
16.	Duke	8-2-0	Bill Murray
17.	Ohio St	6-3-0	Woody Hayes
18.	Purdue	4-3-2	Stu Holcomb
19.	Princeton	8-1-0	Charlie Caldwell
20.	Kentucky	5-4-2	Bear Bryant

1953

		Record	Coach
1.	Maryland	10-0-0	Jim Tatum
2.	Notre Dame	9-0-1	Frank Leahy
3.	Michigan St	8-1-0	Biggie Munn
4.	Oklahoma	8-1-1	Bud Wilkinson
5.	UCLA	8-1-0	Red Sanders
6.	Rice	8-2-0	Jess Neely
7.	Illinois	7-1-1	Ray Eliot
8.	Georgia Tech	8-2-1	Bobby Dodd
9.	Iowa	5-3-1	Forest Evashevski
10.	W Virginia	8-1-0	Art Lewis
11.	Texas	7-3-0	Ed Price
12.	Texas Tech	10-1-0	DeWitt Weaver
13.	Alabama	6-2-3	Red Drew
14.	Army	7-1-1	Red Blaik
15.	Wisconsin	6-2-1	Ivy Williamson
16.	Kentucky	7-2-1	Bear Bryant
17.	Auburn	7-2-1	Shug Jordan
18.	Duke	7-2-1	Bill Murray
19.	Stanford	6-3-1	Chuck Taylor
20.	Michigan	6-3-0	Bennie Oosterbaan

1954

		Record	Coach
1.	Ohio St	9-0-0	Woody Hayes
2.	#UCLA	9-0-0	Red Sanders
3.	Oklahoma	10-0-0	Bud Wilkinson
4.	Notre Dame	9-1-0	Terry Brennan
5.	Navy	7-2-0	Eddie Erdelatz
6.	Mississippi	9-1-0	Johnny Vaught
7.	Army	7-2-0	Red Blaik
8.	Maryland	7-2-1	Jim Tatum
9.	Wisconsin	7-2-0	Ivy Williamson
10.	Arkansas	8-2-0	Bowden Wyatt

1954 (Cont.)

		Record	Coach
11.	Miami (FL)	8-1-0	Andy Gustafson
12.	W Virginia	8-1-0	Art Lewis
13.	Auburn	7-3-0	Shug Jordan
14.	Duke	7-2-1	Bill Murray
15.	Michigan	6-3-0	Bennie Oosterbaan
16.	Virginia Tech	8-0-1	Frank Moseley
17.	Southern Cal	8-3-0	Jess Hill
18.	Baylor	7-3-0	George Sauer
19.	Rice	7-3-0	Jess Neely
20.	Penn St	7-2-0	Rip Engle

#Selected No. 1 by UP.

1955

		Record	Coach
1.	Oklahoma	10-0-0	Bud Wilkinson
2.	Michigan St	8-1-0	Duffy Daugherty
3.	Maryland	10-0-0	Jim Tatum
4.	UCLA	9-1-0	Red Sanders
5.	Ohio St	7-2-0	Woody Hayes
6.	Texas Christian	9-1-0	Abe Martin
7.	Georgia Tech	8-1-1	Bobby Dodd
8.	Auburn	8-1-1	Shug Jordan
9.	Notre Dame	8-2-0	Terry Brennan
10.	Mississippi	9-1-0	Johnny Vaught
11.	Pittsburgh	7-3-0	John Michelosen
12.	Michigan	7-2-0	Bennie Oosterbaan
13.	Southern Cal	6-4-0	Jess Hill
14.	Miami (FL)	6-3-0	Andy Gustafson
15.	Miami (OH)	9-0-0	Ara Parseghian
16.	Stanford	6-3-1	Chuck Taylor
17.	Texas A&M	7-2-1	Bear Bryant
18.	Navy	6-2-1	Eddie Erdelatz
19.	W Virginia	8-2-0	Art Lewis
20.	Army	6-3-0	Red Blaik

1956

		Record	Coach
1.	Oklahoma	10-0-0	Bud Wilkinson
2.	Tennessee	10-0-0	Bowden Wyatt
3.	Iowa	8-1-0	Forest Evashevski
4.	Georgia Tech	9-1-0	Bobby Dodd
5.	Texas A&M	9-0-1	Bear Bryant
6.	Miami (FL)	8-1-1	Andy Gustafson
7.	Michigan	7-2-0	Bennie Oosterbaan
8.	Syracuse	7-1-0	Ben Schwartzwalder
9.	Michigan St	7-2-0	Duffy Daugherty
10.	Oregon St	7-2-1	Tommy Prothro
11.	Baylor	8-2-0	Sam Boyd
12.	Minnesota	6-1-2	Murray Warmath
13.	Pittsburgh	7-2-1	John Michelosen
14.	Texas Christian	7-3-0	Abe Martin
15.	Ohio St	6-3-0	Woody Hayes
16.	Navy	6-1-2	Eddie Erdelatz
17.	Geo Washington	7-1-1	Gene Sherman
18.	Southern Cal	8-2-0	Jess Hill
19.	Clemson	7-1-2	Frank Howard
20.	Colorado	7-2-1	Dallas Ward
	Penn St	6-2-1	Rip Engle

1957

		Record	Coach
1.	Auburn	10-0-0	Shug Jordan
2.	#Ohio St	8-1-0	Woody Hayes
3.	Michigan St	8-1-0	Duffy Daugherty
4.	Oklahoma	9-1-0	Bud Wilkinson
5.	Navy	8-1-1	Eddie Erdelatz
6.	Iowa	7-1-1	Forest Evashevski
7.	Mississippi	8-1-1	Johnny Vaught
8.	Rice	7-3-0	Jess Neely
9.	Texas A&M	8-2-0	Bear Bryant
10.	Notre Dame	7-3-0	Terry Brennan
11.	Texas	6-3-1	Darrell Royal
12.	Arizona St	10-0-0	Dan Devine
13.	Tennessee	7-3-0	Bowden Wyatt
14.	Mississippi St	6-2-1	Wade Walker
15.	N Carolina St	7-1-2	Earle Edwards
16.	Duke	6-2-2	Bill Murray
17.	Florida	6-2-1	Bob Woodruff
18.	Army	7-2-0	Red Blaik
19.	Wisconsin	6-3-0	Milt Brunt
20.	VMI	9-0-1	John McKenna

#Selected No. 1 by UP.

1958

		Record	Coach
1.	Louisiana St	10-0-0	Paul Dietzel
2.	Iowa	7-1-1	Forest Evashevski
3.	Army	8-0-1	Red Blaik
4.	Auburn	9-0-1	Shug Jordan
5.	Oklahoma	9-1-0	Bud Wilkinson
6.	Air Force	9-0-1	Ben Martin
7.	Wisconsin	7-1-1	Milt Bruhn
8.	Ohio St	6-1-2	Woody Hayes
9.	Syracuse	8-1-0	Ben Schwartzwalder
10.	Texas Christian	8-2-0	Abe Martin
11.	Mississippi	8-2-0	Johnny Vaught
12.	Clemson	8-2-0	Frank Howard
13.	Purdue	6-1-2	Jack Mollenkopf
14.	Florida	6-3-1	Bob Woodruff
15.	S Carolina	7-3-0	Warren Giese
16.	California	7-3-0	Pete Elliott
17.	Notre Dame	6-4-0	Terry Brennan
18.	SMU	6-4-0	Bill Meek
19.	Oklahoma St	7-3-0	Cliff Speegle
20.	Rutgers	8-1-0	John Stiegman

1959

		Record	Coach
1.	Syracuse	10-0-0	Ben Schwartzwalder
2.	Mississippi	9-1-0	Johnny Vaught
3.	Louisiana St	9-1-0	Paul Dietzel
4.	Texas	9-1-0	Darrell Royal
5.	Georgia	9-1-0	Wally Butts
6.	Wisconsin	7-2-0	Milt Bruhn
7.	Texas Christian	8-2-0	Abe Martin
8.	Washington	9-1-0	Jim Owens
9.	Arkansas	8-2-0	Frank Broyles
10.	Alabama	7-1-2	Bear Bryant
11.	Clemson	8-2-0	Frank Howard

1959 (Cont.)

		Record	Coach
12.	Penn St	8-2-0	Rip Engle
13.	Illinois	5-3-1	Ray Eliot
14.	Southern Cal	8-2-0	Don Clark
15.	Oklahoma	7-3-0	Bud Wilkinson
16.	Wyoming	9-1-0	Bob Devaney
17.	Notre Dame	5-5-0	Joe Kuharich
18.	Missouri	6-4-0	Dan Devine
19.	Florida	5-4-1	Bob Woodruff
20.	Pittsburgh	6-4-0	John Michelosen

1960

		Record	Coach
1.	Minnesota	8-1-0	Murray Warmath
2.	Mississippi	9-0-1	Johnny Vaught
3.	Iowa	8-1-0	Forest Evashevski
4.	Navy	9-1-0	Wayne Hardin
5.	Missouri	9-1-0	Dan Devine
6.	Washington	9-1-0	Jim Owens
7.	Arkansas	8-2-0	Frank Broyles
8.	Ohio St	7-2-0	Woody Hayes
9.	Alabama	8-1-1	Bear Bryant
10.	Duke	7-3-0	Bill Murray
11.	Kansas	7-2-1	Jack Mitchell
12.	Baylor	8-2-0	John Bridgers
13.	Auburn	8-2-0	Shug Jordan
14.	Yale	9-0-0	Jordan Oliver
15.	Michigan St	6-2-1	Duffy Daugherty
16.	Penn St	6-3-0	Rip Engle
17.	New Mexico St	10-0-0	Warren Woodson
18.	Florida	8-2-0	Ray Graves
19.	Syracuse	7-2-0	Ben Schwartzwalder
	Purdue	4-4-1	Jack Mollenkopf

1961

		Record	Coach
1.	Alabama	10-0-0	Bear Bryant
2.	Ohio St	8-0-1	Woody Hayes
3.	Texas	9-1-0	Darrell Royal
4.	Louisiana St	9-1-0	Paul Dietzel
5.	Mississippi	9-1-0	Johnny Vaught
6.	Minnesota	7-2-0	Murray Warmath
7.	Colorado	9-1-0	Sonny Grandelius
8.	Michigan St	7-2-0	Duffy Daugherty
9.	Arkansas	8-2-0	Frank Broyles
10.	Utah St	9-0-1	John Ralston
11.	Missouri	7-2-1	Dan Devine
12.	Purdue	6-3-0	Jack Mollenkopf
13.	Georgia Tech	7-3-0	Bobby Dodd
14.	Syracuse	7-3-0	Ben Schwartzwalder
15.	Rutgers	9-0-0	John Bateman
16.	UCLA	7-3-0	Bill Barnes
17.	Rice	7-3-0	Jess Neely
	Penn St	7-3-0	Rip Engle
	Arizona	8-1-1	Jim LaRue
20.	Duke	7-3-0	Bill Murray

1962

		Record	Coach
1.	Southern Cal	10-0-0	John McKay
2.	Wisconsin	8-1-0	Milt Bruhn
3.	Mississippi	9-0-0	Johnny Vaught
4.	Texas	9-0-1	Darrell Royal
5.	Alabama	9-1-0	Bear Bryant
6.	Arkansas	9-1-0	Frank Broyles
7.	Louisiana St	8-1-1	Charlie McClendon
8.	Oklahoma	8-2-0	Bud Wilkinson
9.	Penn St	9-1-0	Rip Engle
10.	Minnesota	6-2-1	Murray Warmath
11–20: UPI			
11.	Georgia Tech	7-2-1	Bobby Dodd
12.	Missouri	7-1-2	Dan Devine
13.	Ohio St	6-3-0	Woody Hayes
14.	Duke	8-2-0	Bill Murray
	Washington	7-1-2	Jim Owens
16.	Northwestern	7-2-0	Ara Parseghian
	Oregon St	8-2-0	Tommy Prothro
18.	Arizona St	7-2-1	Frank Kush
	Miami (FL)	7-3-0	Andy Gustafson
	Illinois	2-7-0	Pete Elliott

1963

		Record	Coach
1.	Texas	10-0-0	Darrell Royal
2.	Navy	9-1-0	Wayne Hardin
3.	Illinois	7-1-1	Pete Elliott
4.	Pittsburgh	9-1-0	John Michelosen
5.	Auburn	9-1-0	Shug Jordan
6.	Nebraska	9-1-0	Bob Devaney
7.	Mississippi	7-0-2	Johnny Vaught
8.	Alabama	8-2-0	Bear Bryant
9.	Oklahoma	8-2-0	Bud Wilkinson
10.	Michigan St	6-2-1	Duffy Daugherty
11–20: UPI			
11.	Mississippi St	6-2-2	Paul Davis
12.	Syracuse	8-2-0	Ben Schwartzwalder
13.	Arizona St	8-1-0	Frank Kush
14.	Memphis St	9-0-1	Billy J. Murphy
15.	Washington	6-4-0	Jim Owens
16.	Penn St	7-3-0	Rip Engle
	Southern Cal	7-3-0	John McKay
	Missouri	7-3-0	Dan Devine
19.	N Carolina	8-2-0	Jim Hickey
20.	Baylor	7-3-0	John Bridgers

1964

		Record	Coach
1.	Alabama	10-0-0	Bear Bryant
2.	Arkansas	10-0-0	Frank Broyles
3.	Notre Dame	9-1-0	Ara Parseghian
4.	Michigan	8-1-0	Bump Elliott
5.	Texas	9-1-0	Darrell Royal
6.	Nebraska	9-1-0	Bob Devaney
7.	Louisiana St	7-2-1	Charlie McClendon
8.	Oregon St	8-2-0	Tommy Prothro
9.	Ohio St	7-2-0	Woody Hayes
10.	Southern Cal	7-3-0	John McKay

1964 *(Cont.)*

		Record	Coach
11–20: UPI			
11.	Florida St	8-1-1	Bill Peterson
12.	Syracuse	7-3-0	Ben Schwartzwalder
13.	Princeton	9-0-0	Dick Colman
14.	Penn St	6-4-0	Rip Engle
	Utah	8-2-0	Ray Nagel
16.	Illinois	6-3-0	Pete Elliott
	New Mexico	9-2-0	Bill.Weeks
18.	Tulsa	8-2-0	Glenn Dobbs
19.	Missouri	6-3-1	Dan Devine
20.	Mississippi	5-4-1	Johnny Vaught
	Michigan St	4-5-1	Duffy Daugherty

1965

		Record	Coach
1.	Alabama	9-1-1	Bear Bryant
2.	#Michigan St	10-1-0	Duffy Daugherty
3.	Arkansas	10-1-0	Frank Broyles
4.	UCLA	8-2-1	Tommy Prothro
5.	Nebraska	10-1-0	Bob Devaney
6.	Missouri	8-2-1	Dan Devine
7.	Tennessee	8-1-2	Doug Dickey
8.	Louisiana St	8-3-0	Charlie McClendon
9.	Notre Dame	7-2-1	Ara Parseghian
10.	Southern Cal	7-2-1	John McKay
11–20: UPI			
11.	Texas Tech	8-2-0	J.T. King
12.	Ohio St	7-2-0	Woody Hayes
13.	Florida	7-3-0	Ray Graves
14.	Purdue	7-2-1	Jack Mollenkopf
15.	Georgia	6-4-0	Vince Dooley
16.	Tulsa	8-2-0	Glenn Dobbs
17.	Mississippi	6-4-0	Johnny Vaught
18.	Kentucky	6-4-0	Charlie Bradshaw
19	Syracuse	7-3-0	Ben Schwartzwalder
20.	Colorado	6-2-2	Eddie Crowder

#Selected No. 1 by UPI.

1966*

		Record	Coach
1.	Notre Dame	9-0-1	Ara Parseghian
2.	Michigan St	9-0-1	Duffy Daugherty
3.	Alabama	10-0-0	Bear Bryant
4.	Georgia	9-1-0	Vince Dooley
5.	UCLA	9-1-0	Tommy Prothro
6.	Nebraska	9-1-0	Bob Devaney
7.	Purdue	8-2-0	Jack Mollenkopf
8.	Georgia Tech	9-1-0	Bobby Dodd
9.	Miami (FL)	7-2-1	Charlie Tate
10.	SMU	8-2-0	Hayden Fry
11–20: UPI			
11.	Florida	8-2-0	Ray Graves
12.	Mississippi	8-2-0	Johnny Vaught
13.	Arkansas	8-2-0	Frank Broyles
14.	Tennessee	7-3-0	Doug Dickey
15.	Wyoming	9-1-0	Lloyd Eaton
16.	Syracuse	8-2-0	Ben Schwartzwalder
17.	Houston	8-2-0	Bill Yeoman
18.	Southern Cal	7-3-0	John McKay
19.	Oregon St	7-3-0	Dee Andros
20.	Virginia Tech	8-1-1	Jerry Claiborne

Note: Except where indicated with an asterisk, the polls from 1936 through 1964 were taken before the bowl games and those from 1965 through the present were taken after the bowl games. Additionally, the AP ranked only ten teams in its polls from 1962–67; positions 11–20 from those years are from the UPI poll.

1967*

		Record	Coach
1.	Southern Cal	9-1-0	John McKay
2.	Tennessee	9-1-0	Doug Dickey
3.	Oklahoma	9-1-0	Chuck Fairbanks
4.	Indiana	9-1-0	John Pont
5.	Notre Dame	8-2-0	Ara Parseghian
6.	Wyoming	10-0-0	Lloyd Eaton
7.	Oregon St	7-2-1	Dee Andros
8.	Alabama	8-1-1	Bear Bryant
9.	Purdue	8-2-0	Jack Mollenkopf
10.	Penn St	8-2-0	Joe Paterno

11–20: UPI†

		Record	Coach
11.	UCLA	7-2-1	Tommy Prothro
12.	Syracuse	8-2-0	Ben Schwartzwalder
13.	Colorado	8-2-0	Eddie Crowder
14.	Minnesota	8-2-0	Murray Warmath
15.	Florida St	7-2-1	Bill Peterson
16.	Miami (FL)	7-3-0	Charlie Tate
17.	N Carolina St	8-2-0	Earle Edwards
18.	Georgia	7-3-0	Vince Dooley
19.	Houston	9-2-0	Bill Yeoman
20.	Arizona St	8-2-0	Frank Kush

†UPI ranked Penn St 11th and did not rank Alabama, which was on probation.

1968

		Record	Coach
1.	Ohio St	10-0-0	Woody Hayes
2.	Penn St	11-0-0	Joe Paterno
3.	Texas	9-1-1	Darrell Royal
4.	Southern Cal	9-1-1	John McKay
5.	Notre Dame	7-2-1	Ara Parseghian
6.	Arkansas	10-1-0	Frank Broyles
7.	Kansas	9-2-0	Pepper Rodgers
8.	Georgia	8-1-2	Vince Dooley
9.	Missouri	8-3-0	Dan Devine
10.	Purdue	8-2-0	Jack Mollenkopf
11.	Oklahoma	7-4-0	Chuck Fairbanks
12.	Michigan	8-2-0	Bump Elliott
13.	Tennessee	8-2-1	Doug Dickey
14.	SMU	8-3-0	Hayden Fry
15.	Oregon St	7-3-0	Dee Andros
16.	Auburn	7-4-0	Shug Jordan
17.	Alabama	8-3-0	Bear Bryant
18.	Houston	6-2-2	Bill Yeoman
19.	Louisiana St	8-3-0	Charlie McClendon
20.	Ohio	10-1-0	Bill Hess

1969

		Record	Coach
1.	Texas	11-0-0	Darrell Royal
2.	Penn St	11-0-0	Joe Paterno
3.	Southern Cal	10-0-1	John McKay
4.	Ohio St	8-1-0	Woody Hayes
5.	Notre Dame	8-2-1	Ara Parseghian
6.	Missouri	9-2-0	Dan Devine
7.	Arkansas	9-2-0	Frank Broyles
8.	Mississippi	8-3-0	Johnny Vaught
9.	Michigan	8-3-0	Bo Schembechler
10.	Louisiana St	9-1-0	Charlie McClendon
11.	Nebraska	9-2-0	Bob Devaney
12.	Houston	9-2-0	Bill Yeoman
13.	UCLA	8-1-1	Tommy Prothro
14.	Florida	9-1-1	Ray Graves
15.	Tennessee	9-2-0	Doug Dickey
16.	Colorado	8-3-0	Eddie Crowder
17.	W Virginia	10-0-1	Jim Carlen
18.	Purdue	8-2-0	Jack Mollenkopf
19.	Stanford	7-2-1	John Ralston
20.	Auburn	8-3-0	Shug Jordan

1970

		Record	Coach
1.	Nebraska	11-0-1	Bob Devaney
2.	Notre Dame	10-1-0	Ara Parseghian
3.	#Texas	10-1-0	Darrell Royal
4.	Tennessee	11-1-0	Bill Battle
5.	Ohio St	9-1-0	Woody Hayes
6.	Arizona St	11-0-0	Frank Kush
7.	Louisiana St	9-3-0	Charlie McClendon
8.	Stanford	9-3-0	John Ralston
9.	Michigan	9-1-0	Bo Schembechler
10.	Auburn	9-2-0	Shug Jordan
11.	Arkansas	9-2-0	Frank Broyles
12.	Toledo	12-0-0	Frank Lauterbur
13.	Georgia Tech	9-3-0	Bud Carson
14.	Dartmouth	9-0-0	Bob Blackman
15.	Southern Cal	6-4-1	John McKay
16.	Air Force	9-3-0	Ben Martin
17.	Tulane	8-4-0	Jim Pittman
18.	Penn St	7-3-0	Joe Paterno
19.	Houston	8-3-0	Bill Yeoman
20.	Oklahoma	7-4-1	Chuck Fairbanks
	Mississippi	7-4-0	Johnny Vaught

#Selected No. 1 by UPI.

1971

		Record	Coach
1.	Nebraska	13-0-0	Bob Devaney
2.	Oklahoma	11-1-0	Chuck Fairbanks
3.	Colorado	10-2-0	Eddie Crowder
4.	Alabama	11-1-0	Bear Bryant
5.	Penn St	11-1-0	Joe Paterno
6.	Michigan	11-1-0	Bo Schembechler
7.	Georgia	11-1-0	Vince Dooley
8.	Arizona St	11-1-0	Frank Kush
9.	Tennessee	10-2-0	Bill Battle
10.	Stanford	9-3-0	John Ralston
11.	Louisiana St	9-3-0	Charlie McClendon
12.	Auburn	9-2-0	Shug Jordan
13.	Notre Dame	8-2-0	Ara Parseghian
14.	Toledo	12-0-0	John Murphy
15.	Mississippi	10-2-0	Billy Kinard
16.	Arkansas	8-3-1	Frank Broyles
17.	Houston	9-3-0	Bill Yeoman
18.	Texas	8-3-0	Darrell Royal
19.	Washington	8-3-0	Jim Owens
20.	Southern Cal	6-4-1	John McKay

1972

		Record	Coach
1.	Southern Cal	12-0-0	John McKay
2.	Oklahoma	11-1-0	Chuck Fairbanks
3.	Texas	10-1-0	Darrell Royal
4.	Nebraska	9-2-1	Bob Devaney
5.	Auburn	10-1-0	Shug Jordan
6.	Michigan	10-1-0	Bo Schembechler
7.	Alabama	10-2-0	Bear Bryant
8.	Tennessee	10-2-0	Bill Battle
9.	Ohio St	9-2-0	Woody Hayes
10.	Penn St	10-2-0	Joe Paterno
11.	Louisiana St	9-2-1	Charlie McClendon
12.	N Carolina	11-1-0	Bill Dooley
13.	Arizona St	10-2-0	Frank Kush
14.	Notre Dame	8-3-0	Ara Parseghian
15.	UCLA	8-3-0	Pepper Rodgers
16.	Colorado	8-4-0	Eddie Crowder
17.	N Carolina St	8-3-1	Lou Holtz
18.	Louisville	9-1-0	Lee Corso
19.	Washington St	7-4-0	Jim Sweeney
20.	Georgia Tech	7-4-1	Bill Fulcher

1973

		Record	Coach
1.	Notre Dame	11-0-0	Ara Parseghian
2.	Ohio St	10-0-1	Woody Hayes
3.	Oklahoma	10-0-1	Barry Switzer
4.	#Alabama	11-1-0	Bear Bryant
5.	Penn St	12-0-0	Joe Paterno
6.	Michigan	10-0-1	Bo Schembechler
7.	Nebraska	9-2-1	Tom Osborne
8.	Southern Cal	9-2-1	John McKay
9.	Arizona St	11-1-0	Frank Kush
	Houston	11-1-0	Bill Yeoman
11.	Texas Tech	11-1-0	Jim Carlen
12.	UCLA	9-2-0	Pepper Rodgers
13.	Louisiana St	9-3-0	Charlie McClendon
14.	Texas	8-3-0	Darrell Royal
15.	Miami (OH)	11-0-0	Bill Mallory
16.	N Carolina St	9-3-0	Lou Holtz
17.	Missouri	8-4-0	Al Onofrio
18.	Kansas	7-4-1	Don Fambrough
19.	Tennessee	8-4-0	Bill Battle
20.	Maryland	8-4-0	Jerry Claiborne
	Tulane	9-3-0	Bennie Ellender

#Selected No. 1 by UPI.

1974

		Record	Coach
1.	Oklahoma	11-0-0	Barry Switzer
2.	#Southern Cal	10-1-1	John McKay
3.	Michigan	10-1-0	Bo Schembechler
4.	Ohio St	10-2-0	Woody Hayes
5.	Alabama	11-1-0	Bear Bryant
6.	Notre Dame	10-2-0	Ara Parseghian
7.	Penn St	10-2-0	Joe Paterno
8.	Auburn	10-2-0	Shug Jordan
9.	Nebraska	9-3-0	Tom Osborne
10.	Miami (OH)	10-0-1	Dick Crum
11.	N Carolina St	9-2-1	Lou Holtz
12.	Michigan St	7-3-1	Denny Stolz
13.	Maryland	8-4-0	Jerry Claiborne
14.	Baylor	8-4-0	Grant Teaff
15.	Florida	8-4-0	Doug Dickey
16.	Texas A&M	8-3-0	Emory Ballard
17.	Mississippi St	9-3-0	Bob Tyler
	Texas	8-4-0	Darrell Royal
19.	Houston	8-3-1	Bill Yeoman
20.	Tennessee	7-3-2	Bill Battle

#Selected No. 1 by UPI.

1975

		Record	Coach
1.	Oklahoma	11-1-0	Barry Switzer
2.	Arizona St	12-0-0	Frank Kush
3.	Alabama	11-1-0	Bear Bryant
4.	Ohio St	11-1-0	Woody Hayes
5.	UCLA	9-2-1	Dick Vermeil
6.	Texas	10-2-0	Darrell Royal
7.	Arkansas	10-2-0	Frank Broyles
8.	Michigan	8-2-2	Bo Schembechler
9.	Nebraska	10-2-0	Tom Osborne
10.	Penn St	9-3-0	Joe Paterno
11.	Texas A&M	10-2-0	Emory Bellard

1975(Cont.)

		Record	Coach
12.	Miami (OH)	11-1-0	Dick Crum
13.	Maryland	9-2-1	Jerry Claiborne
14.	California	8-3-0	Mike White
15.	Pittsburgh	8-4-0	Johnny Majors
16.	Colorado	9-3-0	Bill Mallory
17.	Southern Cal	8-4-0	John McKay
18.	Arizona	9-2-0	Jim Young
19.	Georgia	9-3-0	Vince Dooley
20.	W Virginia	9-3-0	Bobby Bowden

1976

		Record	Coach
1.	Pittsburgh	12-0-0	Johnny Majors
2.	Southern Cal	11-1-0	John Robinson
3.	Michigan	10-2-0	Bo Schembechler
4.	Houston	10-2-0	Bill Yeoman
5.	Oklahoma	9-2-1	Barry Switzer
6.	Ohio St	9-2-1	Woody Hayes
7.	Texas A&M	10-2-0	Emory Bellard
8.	Maryland	11-1-0	Jerry Claiborne
9.	Nebraska	9-3-1	Tom Osborne
10.	Georgia	10-2-0	Vince Dooley
11.	Alabama	9-3-0	Bear Bryant
12.	Notre Dame	9-3-0	Dan Devine
13.	Texas Tech	10-2-0	Steve Sloan
14.	Oklahoma St	9-3-0	Jim Stanley
15.	UCLA	9-2-1	Terry Donahue
16.	Colorado	8-4-0	Bill Mallory
17.	Rutgers	11-0-0	Frank Burns
18.	Kentucky	9-3-0	Fran Curci
19.	Iowa St	8-3-0	Earle Bruce
20.	Mississippi St	9-2-0	Bob Tyler

1977

		Record	Coach
1.	Notre Dame	11-1-0	Dan Devine
2.	Alabama	11-1-0	Bear Bryant
3.	Arkansas	11-1-0	Lou Holtz
4.	Texas	11-1-0	Fred Akers
5.	Penn St	11-1-0	Joe Paterno
6.	Kentucky	10-1-0	Fran Curci
7.	Oklahoma	10-2-0	Barry Switzer
8.	Pittsburgh	9-2-1	Jackie Sherrill
9.	Michigan	10-2-0	Bo Schembechler
10.	Washington	10-2-0	Don James
11.	Ohio St	9-3-0	Woody Hayes
12.	Nebraska	9-3-0	Tom Osborne
13.	Southern Cal	8-4-0	John Robinson
14.	Florida St	10-2-0	Bobby Bowden
15.	Stanford	9-3-0	Bill Walsh
16.	San Diego St	10-1-0	Claude Gilbert
17.	N Carolina	8-3-1	Bill Dooley
18.	Arizona St	9-3-0	Frank Kush
19.	Clemson	8-3-1	Charley Pell
20.	Brigham Young	9-2-0	LaVell Edwards

1978

		Record	Coach
1.	Alabama	11-1-0	Bear-Bryant
2.	#Southern Cal	12-1-0	John Robinson
3.	Oklahoma	11-1-0	Barry Switzer
4.	Penn St	11-1-0	Joe Paterno
5.	Michigan	10-2-0	Bo Schembechler
6.	Clemson	11-1-0	Charley Pell
7.	Notre Dame	9-3-0	Dan Devine
8.	Nebraska	9-3-0	Tom Osborne
9.	Texas	9-3-0	Fred Akers
10.	Houston	9-3-0	Bill Yeoman
11.	Arkansas	9-2-1	Lou Holtz
12.	Michigan St	8-3-0	Darryl Rogers
13.	Purdue	9-2-1	Jim Young
14.	UCLA	8-3-1	Terry Donahue
15.	Missouri	8-4-0	Warren Powers
16.	Georgia	9-2-1	Vince Dooley
17.	Stanford	8-4-0	Bill Walsh
18.	N Carolina St	9-3-0	Bo Rein
19.	Texas A&M	8-4-0	Emory Bellard (4–2)
			Tom Wilson (4–2)
20.	Maryland	9-3-0	Jerry Claiborne

#Selected No. 1 by UPI.

1979

		Record	Coach
1.	Alabama	12-0-0	Bear Bryant
2.	Southern Cal	11-0-1	John Robinson
3.	Oklahoma	11-1-0	Barry Switzer
4.	Ohio St	11-1-0	Earle Bruce
5.	Houston	11-1-0	Bill Yeoman
6.	Florida St	11-1-0	Bobby Bowden
7.	Pittsburgh	11-1-0	Jackie Sherrill
8.	Arkansas	10-2-0	Lou Holtz
9.	Nebraska	10-2-0	Tom Osborne
10.	Purdue	10-2-0	Jim Young
11.	Washington	10-1-0	Don James
12.	Texas	9-3-0	Fred Akers
13.	Brigham Young	11-1-0	LaVell Edwards
14.	Baylor	8-4-0	Grant Teaff
15.	N Carolina	8-3-1	Dick Crum
16.	Auburn	8-3-0	Doug Barfield
17.	Temple	10-2-0	Wayne Hardin
18.	Michigan	8-4-0	Bo Schembechler
19.	Indiana	8-4-0	Lee Corso
20.	Penn St	8-4-0	Joe Paterno

1980

		Record	Coach
1.	Georgia	12-0-0	Vince Dooley
2.	Pittsburgh	11-1-0	Jackie Sherrill
3.	Oklahoma	10-2-0	Barry Switzer
4.	Michigan	10-2-0	Bo Schembechler
5.	Florida St	10-2-0	Bobby Bowden
6.	Alabama	10-2-0	Bear Bryant
7.	Nebraska	10-2-0	Tom Osborne
8.	Penn St	10-2-0	Joe Paterno
9.	Notre Dame	9-2-1	Dan Devine
10.	N Carolina	11-1-0	Dick Crum
11.	Southern Cal	8-2-1	John Robinson
12.	Brigham Young	12-1-0	LaVell Edwards
13.	UCLA	9-2-0	Terry Donahue
14.	Baylor	10-2-0	Grant Teaff
15.	Ohio St	9-3-0	Earle Bruce
16.	Washington	9-3-0	Don James
17.	Purdue	9-3-0	Jim Young

1980 *(Cont.)*

		Record	Coach
18.	Miami (FL)	9-3-0	H. Schnellenberger
19.	Mississippi St	9-3-0	Emory Bellard
20.	SMU	8-4-0	Ron Meyer

1981

		Record	Coach
1.	Clemson	12-0-0	Danny Ford
2.	Texas	10-1-1	Fred Akers
3.	Penn St	10-2-0	Joe Paterno
4.	Pittsburgh	11-1-0	Jackie Sherrill
5.	SMU	10-1-0	Ron Meyer
6.	Georgia	10-2-0	Vince Dooley
7.	Alabama	9-2-1	Bear Bryant
8.	Miami (FL)	9-2-0	H. Schnellenberger
9.	N Carolina	10-2-0	Dick Crum
10.	Washington	10-2-0	Don James
11.	Nebraska	9-3-0	Tom Osborne
12.	Michigan	9-3-0	Bo Schembechler
13.	Brigham Young	11-2-0	LaVell Edwards
14.	Southern Cal	9-3-0	John Robinson
15.	Ohio St	9-3-0	Earle Bruce
16.	Arizona St	9-2-0	Darryl Rogers
17.	W Virginia	9-3-0	Don Nehlen
18.	Iowa	8-4-0	Hayden Fry
19.	Missouri	8-4-0	Warren Powers
20.	Oklahoma	7-4-1	Barry Switzer

1982

		Record	Coach
1.	Penn St	11-1-0	Joe Paterno
2.	SMU	11-0-1	Bobby Collins
3.	Nebraska	12-1-0	Tom Osborne
4.	Georgia	11-1-0	Vince Dooley
5.	UCLA	10-1-1	Terry Donahue
6.	Arizona St	10-2-0	Darryl Rogers
7.	Washington	10-2-0	Don James
8.	Clemson	9-1-1	Danny Ford
9.	Arkansas	9-2-1	Lou Holtz
10.	Pittsburgh	9-3-0	Foge Fazio
11.	Louisiana St	8-3-1	Jerry Stovall
12.	Ohio St	9-3-0	Earle Bruce
13.	Florida St	9-3-0	Bobby Bowden
14.	Auburn	9-3-0	Pat Dye
15.	Southern Cal	8-3-0	John Robinson
16.	Oklahoma	8-4-0	Barry Switzer
17.	Texas	9-3-0	Fred Akers
18.	N Carolina	8-4-0	Dick Crum
19.	W Virginia	9-3-0	Don Nehlen
20.	Maryland	8-4-0	Bobby Ross

1983

		Record	Coach
1.	Miami (FL)	11-1-0	H. Schnellenberger
2.	Nebraska	12-1-0	Tom Osborne
3.	Auburn	11-1-0	Pat Dye
4.	Georgia	10-1-1	Vince Dooley
5.	Texas	11-1-0	Fred Akers
6.	Florida	9-2-1	Charlie Pell
7.	Brigham Young	11-1-0	LaVell Edwards
8.	Michigan	9-3-0	Bo Schembechler
9.	Ohio St	9-3-0	Earle Bruce
10.	Illinois	10-2-0	Mike White
11.	Clemson	9-1-1	Danny Ford
12.	SMU	10-2-0	Bobby Collins

1983 *(Cont.)*

		Record	Coach
13.	Air Force	10-2-0	Ken Hatfield
14.	Iowa	9-3-0	Hayden Fry
15.	Alabama	8-4-0	Ray Perkins
16.	W Virginia	9-3-0	Don Nehlen
17.	UCLA	7-4-1	Terry Donahue
18.	Pittsburgh	8-3-1	Foge Fazio
19.	Boston College	9-3-0	Jack Bicknell
20.	E Carolina	8-3-0	Ed Emory

1984

		Record	Coach
1.	Brigham Young	13-0-0	LaVell Edwards
2.	Washington	11-1-0	Don James
3.	Florida	9-1-1	Chas Pell (0-1-1) Galen Hall (9-0)
4.	Nebraska	10-2-0	Tom Osborne
5.	Boston College	10-2-0	Jack Bicknell
6.	Oklahoma	9-2-1	Barry Switzer
7.	Oklahoma St	10-2-0	Pat Jones
8.	SMU	10-2-0	Bobby Collins
9.	UCLA	9-3-0	Terry Donahue
10.	Southern Cal	10-3-0	Ted Tollner
11.	S Carolina	10-2-0	Joe Morrison
12.	Maryland	9-3-0	Bobby Ross
13.	Ohio St	9-3-0	Earle Bruce
14.	Auburn	9-4-0	Pat Dye
15.	Louisiana St	8-3-1	Bill Arnsparger
16.	Iowa	8-4-1	Hayden Fry
17.	Florida St	7-3-2	Bobby Bowden
18.	Miami (FL)	8-5-0	Jimmy Johnson
19.	Kentucky	9-3-0	Jerry Claiborne
20.	Virginia	8-2-2	George Welsh

1985

		Record	Coach
1.	Oklahoma	11-1-0	Barry Switzer
2.	Michigan	10-1-1	Bo Schembechler
3.	Penn St	11-1-0	Joe Paterno
4.	Tennessee	9-1-2	Johnny Majors
5.	Florida	9-1-1	Galen Hall
6.	Texas A&M	10-2-0	Jackie Sherrill
7.	UCLA	9-2-1	Terry Donahue
8.	Air Force	12-1-0	Fisher DeBerry
9.	Miami (FL)	10-2-0	Jimmy Johnson
10.	Iowa	10-2-0	Hayden Fry
11.	Nebraska	9-3-0	Tom Osborne
12.	Arkansas	10-2-0	Ken Hatfield
13.	Alabama	9-2-1	Ray Perkins
14.	Ohio St	9-3-0	Earle Bruce
15.	Florida St	9-3-0	Bobby Bowden
16.	Brigham Young	11-3-0	LaVell Edwards
17.	Baylor	9-3-0	Grant Teaff
18.	Maryland	9-3-0	Bobby Ross
19.	Georgia Tech	9-2-1	Bill Curry
20.	Louisiana St	9-2-1	Bill Arnsparger

1986

		Record	Coach
1.	Penn St	12-0-0	Joe Paterno
2.	Miami (FL)	11-1-0	Jimmy Johnson
3.	Oklahoma	11-1-0	Barry Switzer
4.	Arizona St	10-1-1	John Cooper
5.	Nebraska	10-2-0	Tom Osborne
6.	Auburn	10-2-0	Pat Dye
7.	Ohio St	10-3-0	Earle Bruce

1986 *(Cont.)*

		Record	Coach
8.	Michigan	11-2-0	Bo Schembechler
9.	Alabama	10-3-0	Ray Perkins
10.	Louisiana St	9-3-0	Bill Arnsparger
11.	Arizona	9-3-0	Larry Smith
12.	Baylor	9-3-0	Grant Teaff
13.	Texas A&M	9-3-0	Jackie Sherrill
14.	UCLA	8-3-1	Terry Donahue
15.	Arkansas	9-3-0	Ken Hatfield
16.	Iowa	9-3-0	Hayden Fry
17.	Clemson	8-2-2	Danny Ford
18.	Washington	8-3-1	Don James
19.	Boston College	9-3-0	Jack Bicknell
20.	Virginia Tech	9-2-1	Bill Dooley

1987

		Record	Coach
1.	Miami (FL)	12-0-0	Jimmy Johnson
2.	Florida St	11-1-0	Bobby Bowden
3.	Oklahoma	11-1-0	Barry Switzer
4.	Syracuse	11-0-1	Dick MacPherson
5.	Louisiana St	10-1-1	Mike Archer
6.	Nebraska	10-2-0	Tom Osborne
7.	Auburn	9-1-2	Pat Dye
8.	Michigan St	9-2-1	George Perles
9.	UCLA	10-2-0	Terry Donahue
10.	Texas A&M	10-2-0	Jackie Sherrill
11.	Oklahoma St	10-2-0	Pat Jones
12.	Clemson	10-2-0	Danny Ford
13.	Georgia	9-3-0	Vince Dooley
14.	Tennessee	10-2-1	Johnny Majors
15.	S Carolina	8-4-0	Joe Morrison
16.	Iowa	10-3-0	Hayden Fry
17.	Notre Dame	8-4-0	Lou Holtz
18.	Southern Cal	8-4-0	Larry Smith
19.	Michigan	8-4-0	Bo Schembechler
20.	Arizona St	7-4-1	John Cooper

1988

		Record	Coach
1.	Notre Dame	12-0-0	Lou Holtz
2.	Miami (FL)	11-1-0	Jimmy Johnson
3.	Florida St	11-1-0	Bobby Bowden
4.	Michigan	9-2-1	Bo Schembechler
5.	W Virginia	11-1-0	Don Nehlen
6.	UCLA	10-2-0	Terry Donahue
7.	Southern Cal	10-2-0	Larry Smith
8.	Auburn	10-2-0	Pat Dye
9.	Clemson	10-2-0	Danny Ford
10.	Nebraska	11-2-0	Tom Osborne
11.	Oklahoma St	10-2-0	Pat Jones
12.	Arkansas	10-2-0	Ken Hatfield
13.	Syracuse	10-2-0	Dick MacPherson
14.	Oklahoma	9-3-0	Barry Switzer
15.	Georgia	9-3-0	Vince Dooley
16.	Washington St	9-3-0	Dennis Erickson
17.	Alabama	9-3-0	Bill Curry
18.	Houston	9-3-0	Jack Pardee
19.	Louisiana St	8-4-0	Mike Archer
20.	Indiana	8-3-1	Bill Mallory

†1989

		Record	Coach
1.	Miami (FL)	11-1-0	Dennis Erickson
2.	Notre Dame	12-1-0	Lou Holtz
3.	Florida St	10-2-0	Bobby Bowden
4.	Colorado	11-1-0	Bill McCartney
5.	Tennessee	11-1-0	Johnny Majors
6.	Auburn	10-2-0	Pat Dye
7.	Michigan	10-2-0	Bo Schembechler
8.	Southern Cal	9-2-1	Larry Smith
9.	Alabama	10-2-0	Bill Curry
10.	Illinois	10-2-0	John Mackovic
11.	Nebraska	10-2-0	Tom Osborne
12.	Clemson	10-2-0	Danny Ford
13.	Arkansas	10-2-0	Ken Hatfield
14.	Houston	9-2-0	Jack Pardee
15.	Penn St	8-3-1	Joe Paterno
16.	Michigan St	8-4-0	George Perles
17.	Pittsburgh	8-3-1	Mike Gottfried
18.	Virginia	10-3-0	George Welsh
19.	Texas Tech	9-3-0	Spike Dykes
20.	Texas A&M	8-4-0	R.C. Slocum
21.	W Virginia	8-3-1	Don Nehlen
22.	Brigham Young	10-3-0	LaVell Edwards
23.	Washington	8-4-0	Don James
24.	Ohio St	8-4-0	John Cooper
25.	Arizona	8-4-0	Dick Tomey

1990

		Record	Coach
1.	Colorado	11-1-1	Bill McCartney
2.	#Georgia Tech	11-0-1	Bobby Ross
3.	Miami (FL)	10-2-0	Dennis Erickson
4.	Florida St	10-2-0	Bobby Bowden
5.	Washington	10-2-0	Don James
6.	Notre Dame	9-3-0	Lou Holtz
7.	Michigan	9-3-0	Gary Moeller
8.	Tennessee	9-2-2	Johnny Majors
9.	Clemson	10-2-0	Ken Hatfield
10.	Houston	10-1-0	John Jenkins
11.	Penn St	9-3-0	Joe Paterno
12.	Texas	10-2-0	David McWilliams
13.	Florida	9-2-0	Steve Spurrier
14.	Louisville	10-1-1	H. Schnellenberger
15.	Texas A&M	9-3-1	R.C. Slocum
16.	Michigan St	8-3-1	George Perles
17.	Oklahoma	8-3-0	Gary Gibbs
18.	Iowa	8-4-0	Hayden Fry
19.	Auburn	8-3-1	Pat Dye
20.	Southern Cal	8-4-1	Larry Smith
21.	Mississippi	9-3-0	Billy Brewer
22.	Brigham Young	10-3-0	LaVell Edwards
23.	Virginia	8-4-0	George Wells
24.	Nebraska	9-3-0	Tom Osborne
25.	Illinois	8-4-0	John Mackovic

#Selected No. 1 by UPI.

1991

		Record	Coach
1.	Miami (FL)	12-0-0	Dennis Erickson
2.	#Washington	12-0-0	Don James
3.	Penn St	11-2-0	Joe Paterno
4.	Florida St	11-2-0	Bobby Bowden
5.	Alabama	11-1-0	Gene Stallings
6.	Michigan	10-2-0	Gary Moeller
7.	Florida	10-2-0	Steve Spurrier
8.	California	10-2-0	Bruce Snyder
9.	E Carolina	11-1-0	Bill Lewis
10.	Iowa	10-1-1	Hayden Fry

1991 (Cont.)

		Record	Coach
11.	Syracuse	10-2-0	Paul Pasqualoni
12.	Texas A&M	10-2-0	R.C. Slocum
13.	Notre Dame	10-3-0	Lou Holtz
14.	Tennessee	9-3-0	Johnny Majors
15.	Nebraska	9-2-1	Tom Osborne
16.	Oklahoma	9-3-0	Gary Gibbs
17.	Georgia	9-3-0	Ray Goff
18.	Clemson	9-2-1	Ken Hatfield
19.	UCLA	9-3-0	Terry Donahue
20.	Colorado	8-3-1	Bill McCartney
21.	Tulsa	10-2-0	David Rader
22.	Stanford	8-4-0	Dennis Green
23.	Brigham Young	8-3-2	LaVell Edwards
24.	N Carolina St	9-3-0	Dick Sheridan
25.	Air Force	10-3-0	Fisher DeBerry

#Selected No. 1 by *USA Today*/ CNN.

1992

		Record	Coach
1.	Alabama	13-0-0	Gene Stallings
2.	Florida St	11-1-0	Bobby Bowden
3.	Miami	11-1-0	Dennis Erickson
4.	Notre Dame	10-1-1	Lou Holtz
5.	Michigan	9-0-3	Gary Moeller
6.	Syracuse	10-2-0	Paul Pasqualoni
7.	Texas A&M	12-1-0	R.C. Slocum
8.	Georgia	10-2-0	Ray Goff
9.	Stanford	10-3-0	Bill Walsh
10.	Florida	9-4-0	Steve Spurrier
11.	Washington	9-3-0	Don James
12.	Tennessee	9-3-0	Johnny Majors
13.	Colorado	9-2-1	Bill McCartney
14.	Nebraska	9-3-0	Tom Osborne
15.	Washington St	9-3-0	Mike Price
16.	Mississippi	9-3-0	Billy Brewer
17.	N Carolina St	9-3-1	Dick Sheridan
18.	Ohio St	8-3-1	John Cooper
19.	N Carolina	9-3-0	Mack Brown
20.	Hawaii	11-2-0	Bob Wagner
21.	Boston College	8-3-1	Tom Coughlin
22.	Kansas	8-4-0	Glen Mason
23.	Mississippi St	7-5-0	Jackie Sherrill
24.	Fresno St	9-4-0	Jim Sweeney
25.	Wake Forest	8-4-0	Bill Dooley

1993

		Record	Coach
1.	Florida St	12-1-0	Bobby Bowden
2.	Notre Dame	11-1-0	Lou Holtz
3.	Nebraska	11-1-0	Tom Osborne
4.	Auburn	11-0-0	Terry Bowden
5.	Florida	11-2-0	Steve Spurrier
6.	Wisconsin	10-1-1	Barry Alvarez
7.	W Virginia	11-1-0	Don Nehlen
8.	Penn St	10-2-0	Joe Paterno
9.	Texas A&M	10-2-0	R.C. Slocum
10.	Arizona	10-2-0	Dick Tomey
11.	Ohio St	10-1-1	John Cooper
12.	Tennessee	9-2-1	Phil Fulmer
13.	Boston College	9-3-0	Tom Coughlin
14.	Alabama	9-3-1	Gene Stallings
15.	Miami	9-3-0	Dennis Erickson
16.	Colorado	8-3-1	Bill McCartney
17.	Oklahoma	9-3-0	Gary Gibbs
18.	UCLA	8-4-0	Terry Donahue
19.	N Carolina	10-3-0	Mack Brown
20.	Kansas St	9-2-1	Bill Snyder
21.	Michigan	8-4-0	Gary Moeller
22.	Virginia Tech	9-3-0	Frank Beamer
23.	Clemson	9-3-0	Ken Hatfield
24.	Louisville	9-3-0	H. Schnellenberger
25.	California	9-4-0	Keith Gilbertson

1994

		Record	Coach
1.	Nebraska	13-0-0	Tom Osborne
2.	Penn St	12-0-0	Joe Paterno
3.	Colorado	11-1-0	Bill McCartney
4.	Florida St	10-1-1	Bobby Bowden
5.	Alabama	12-1-0	Gene Stallings
6.	Miami (FL)	10-2-0	Dennis Erickson
7.	Florida	10-2-1	Steve Spurrier
8.	Texas A&M	10-0-1	R.C. Slocum
9.	Auburn	9-1-1	Terry Bowden
10.	Utah	10-2-0	Ron McBride
11.	Oregon	9-4-0	Rich Brooks
12.	Michigan	8-4-0	Gary Moeller
13.	Southern Cal	8-3-1	John Robinson
14.	Ohio St	9-4-0	John Cooper
15.	Virginia	9-3-0	George Welsh
16.	Colorado St	10-2-0	Sonny Lubick
17.	N Carolina St	9-3-0	Mike O'Cain
18.	Brigham Young	10-3-0	LaVell Edwards
19.	Kansas St	9-3-0	Bill Snyder
20.	Arizona	8-4-0	Dick Tomey
21.	Washington St	8-4-0	Mike Price
22.	Tennessee	8-4-0	Phillip Fulmer
23.	Boston College	7-4-1	Dan Henning
24.	Mississippi St	8-4-0	Jackie Sherrill
25.	Texas	8-4-0	John Mackovic

1995

		Record	Coach
1.	Nebraska	12-0-0	Tom Osborne
2.	Florida	12-1-0	Steve Spurrier
3.	Tennessee	11-1-0	Phillip Fulmer
4.	Florida St	10-2-0	Bobby Bowden
5.	Colorado	10-2-0	Rick Neuheisel
6.	Ohio St	11-2-0	John Cooper
7.	Kansas St	10-2-0	Bill Snyder
8.	Northwestern	10-2-0	Gary Barnett
9.	Kansas	10-2-0	Glen Mason
10.	Virginia Tech	10-2-0	Frank Beamer
11.	Notre Dame	9-3-0	Lou Holtz
12.	Southern Cal	9-2-1	John Robinson
13.	Penn St	9-3-0	Joe Paterno
14.	Texas	10-2-1	John Mackovic
15.	Texas A&M	9-3-0	S.C. Slocum
16.	Virginia	9-4-0	George Welsh
17.	Michigan	9-4-0	Lloyd Carr
18.	Oregon	9-3-0	Mike Bellotti
19.	Syracuse	9-3-0	Paul Pasqualoni
20.	Miami (FL)	8-3-0	Butch Davis
21.	Alabama	8-3-0	Gene Stallings
22.	Auburn	8-4-0	Terry Bowden
23.	Texas Tech	9-3-0	Spike Dykes
24.	Toledo	11-0-1	Gary Pinkel
25.	Iowa	8-4-0	Hayden Fry

1996

		Record*	Coach
1.	Florida	12-1	Steve Spurrier
2.	Ohio St	11-1	John Cooper
3.	Florida St	11-1	Bobby Bowden
4.	Arizona St	11-1	Bruce Snyder
5.	Brigham Young	14-1	LaVell Edwards
6.	Nebraska	11-2	Tom Osborne
7.	Penn St	11-2	Joe Paterno
8.	Colorado	10-2	Rick Neuheisel
9.	Tennessee	10-2	Phillip Fulmer
10.	N Carolina	10-2	Mack Brown
11.	Alabama	10-3	Gene Stallings

†In 1989 the AP expanded its final poll to 25 teams.
*In 1996 the NCAA introduced overtime to break ties.

1996 (Cont.)

		Record	Coach
12.	Louisiana St	10-2	Gerry DiNardo
13.	Virginia Tech	10-2	Frank Beamer
14.	Miami (FL)	9-3	Butch Davis
15.	Northwestern	9-3	Gary Barnett
16.	Washington	9-3	Jim Lambright
17.	Kansas St	9-3	Bill Snyder
18.	Iowa	9-3	Hayden Fry
19.	Notre Dame	8-3	Lou Holtz
20.	Michigan	8-4	Lloyd Carr
21.	Syracuse	9-3	Paul Pasqualoni
22.	Wyoming	10-2	Joe Tiller
23.	Texas	8-5	John Mackovic
24.	Auburn	8-4	Terry Bowden
25.	Army	10-2	Bob Sutton

1997

		Record	Coach
1.	Michigan	12-0	Lloyd Carr
2.	Nebraska	13-0	Tom Osborne
3.	Florida St	11-1	Bobby Bowden
4.	Florida	10-2	Steve Spurrier
5.	UCLA	10-2	Bob Toledo
6.	N Carolina	11-1	Mack Brown
7.	Tennessee	11-2	Phillip Fulmer
8.	Kansas St	11-1	Bill Snyder
9.	Washington St	10-2	Mike Price
10.	Georgia	10-2	Jim Donnan
11.	Auburn	10-3	Terry Bowden
12.	Ohio St	10-3	John Cooper
13.	Louisiana St	9-3	Gerry DiNardo
14.	Arizona St	8-3	Bruce Snyder
15.	Purdue	9-3	Joe Tiller
16.	Penn St	9-3	Joe Paterno
17.	Colorado St	11-2	Sonny Lubick
18.	Washington	8-4	Jim Lambright
19.	Southern Mississippi	9-3	Jeff Bower
20.	Texas A&M	9-4	R. C. Slocum
21.	Syracuse	9-4	Paul Pasqualoni
22.	Mississippi	8-4	Tommy Tuberville
23.	Missouri	7-5	Larry Smith
24.	Oklahoma St	8-4	Bob Simmons
25.	Georgia Tech	7-5	George O'Leary

1998

		Record	Coach
1.	Tennessee	13-0	Phillip Fulmer
2.	Ohio St	11-1	John Cooper
3.	Florida St	11-2	Bobby Bowden
4.	Arizona	12-1	Dick Tomey
5.	Florida	10-2	Steve Spurrier
6.	Wisconsin	11-1	Barry Alvarez
7.	Tulane	12-0	Tommy Bowden
8.	UCLA	10-2	Bob Toledo
9.	Georgia Tech	10-2	George O'Leary
10.	Kansas St	11-2	Bill Snyder
11.	Texas A&M	11-3	R.C. Slocum
12.	Michigan	10-3	Lloyd Carr
13.	Air Force	12-1	Fisher DeBerry
14.	Georgia	9-3	Jim Donnan
15.	Texas	9-3	Mack Brown
16.	Arkansas	9-3	Houston Nutt
17.	Penn St	9-3	Joe Paterno
18.	Virginia	9-3	George Welsh
19.	Nebraska	9-4	Frank Solich
20.	Miami (FL)	9-3	Butch Davis
21.	Missouri	8-4	Larry Smith
22.	Notre Dame	9-3	Bob Davie
23.	Virginia Tech	9-3	Frank Beamer
24.	Purdue	9-4	Joe Tiller
25.	Syracuse	8-4	Paul Pasqualoni

1999

		Record	Coach
1.	Florida St	12–0	Bobby Bowden
2.	Virginia Tech	11–1	Frank Beamer
3.	Nebraska	12–1	Frank Solich
4.	Wisconsin	10–2	Barry Alvarez
5.	Michigan	10–2	Lloyd Carr
6.	Kansas St	11–1	Bill Snyder
7.	Michigan St	10–2	Nick Saban
8.	Alabama	10–3	Mike DuBose
9.	Tennessee	9–3	Phillip Fulmer
10.	Marshall	13–0	Bob Pruett
11.	Penn St	10–3	Joe Paterno
12.	Florida	9–4	Steve Spurrier
13.	Mississippi St	10–2	Jackie Sherrill
14.	Southern Miss	9–3	Jeff Bower
15.	Miami (FL)	9–4	Butch Davis
16.	Georgia	8–4	Jim Donnan
17.	Arkansas	8–4	Houston Nutt
18.	Minnesota	8–4	Glen Mason
19.	Oregon	9–3	Mike Bellotti
20.	Georgia Tech	8–4	Goerge O'Leary
21.	Texas	9–5	Mack Brown
22.	Mississippi	8–4	David Cutcliffe
23.	Texas A&M	8–4	R.C. Slocum
24.	Illinois	8–4	Ron Turner
25.	Purdue	7–5	Joe Tiller

2000

		Record	Coach
1.	Oklahoma	13–0	Bob Stoops
2.	Miami (FL)	11–1	Butch Davis
3.	Washington	11–1	Rick Neuheisel
4.	Oregon St	11–1	Dennis Erickson
5.	Florida St	11–2	Bobby Bowden
6.	Virginia Tech	11–1	Frank Beamer
7.	Oregon	10–2	Mike Belotti
8.	Nebraska	10–2	Frank Solich
9.	Kansas St	11–3	Bill Snyder
10.	Florida	10–3	Steve Spurrier
11.	Michigan	9–3	Lloyd Carr
12.	Texas	9–3	Mack Brown
13.	Purdue	8–4	Joe Tiller
14.	Colorado St	10–2	Sonny Lubeck
15.	Notre Dame	9–3	Bob Davie
16.	Clemson	9–3	Tommy Bowden
17.	Georgia Tech	9–3	George O'Leary
18.	Auburn	9–4	Tommy Tuberville
19.	S Carolina	8–4	Lou Holtz
20.	Georgia	8–4	Jim Donnan
21.	Texas Christian	10–2	Dennis Franchione
22.	Louisiana State	8–4	Nick Saban
23.	Wisconsin	9–4	Barry Alvarez
24.	Mississippi St	8–4	Jackie Sherrill
25.	Iowa St	9–3	Dan McCarney

2001

		Record	Coach
1.	Miami (FL)	12–0	Larry Coker
2.	Oregon	11–1	Mike Belotti
3.	Florida	10–2	Steve Spurrier
4.	Tennessee	11–2	Phillip Fulmer
5.	Texas	11–2	Mack Brown
6.	Oklahoma	11–2	Bob Stoops
7.	Louisiana St	10–3	Nick Saban
8.	Nebraska	11–2	Frank Solich
9.	Colorado	10–3	Gary Barnett
10.	Washington St	10–2	Mike Price
11.	Maryland	10–2	Ralph Friedgen
12.	Illinois	10–2	Ron Turner
13.	S Carolina	9–3	Lou Holtz

2001 (Cont.)

		Record	Coach
14.	Syracuse	10–3	Paul Pasqualoni
15.	Florida St	8–4	Bobby Bowden
16.	Stanford	9–3	Tyrone Willingham
17.	Louisville	11–2	John Smith
18.	Virginia Tech	8–4	Frank Beamer
19.	Washington	8–4	Rick Neuheisel
20.	Michigan	8–4	Lloyd Carr
21.	Boston College	8–4	Tom O'Brien
22.	Georgia	8–4	Mark Richt
23.	Toledo	10–2	Tom Amstutz
24.	Georgia Tech	8–5	George O'Leary
25.	Brigham Young	12–2	Gary Crowton

2002

		Record	Coach
1.	Ohio St	14–0	Jim Tressel
2.	Miami (FL)	12–1	Larry Coker
3.	Georgia	13–1	Mark Richt
4.	Southern Cal	11–2	Pete Carroll
5.	Oklahoma	12–2	Bob Stoops
6.	Texas	11–2	Mack Brown
7.	Kansas St	11–2	Bill Snyder
8.	Iowa	11–2	Kirk Ferentz
9.	Michigan	10–3	Lloyd Carr
10.	Washington St	10–3	Mike Price
11.	Alabama	10–3	Dennis Franchione
12.	N Carolina St	11–3	Chuck Amato
13.	Maryland	11–3	Ralph Friedgen
14.	Auburn	9–4	Tommy Tuberville
15.	Boise St	12–1	Dan Hawkins
16.	Penn St	9–4	Joe Paterno
17.	Notre Dame	10–3	Tyrone Willingham
18.	Virginia Tech	10–4	Frank Beamer
19.	Pittsburgh	9–4	Walt Harris
20.	Colorado	9–5	Gary Barnett
21.	Florida St	9–5	Bobby Bowden
22.	Viriginia	9–5	Al Groh
23.	Texas Christian	10–2	Gary Patterson
24.	Marshall	11–2	Bob Pruett
25.	W Virginia	9–4	Rich Rodriguez

2003

		Record	Coach
1.	Southern Cal	12–1	Pete Carroll
2.	Louisiana St*	13–1	Nick Saban
3.	Oklahoma	12–2	Bob Stoops
4.	Ohio St	11–2	Jim Tressel
5.	Miami (FL)	11–2	Larry Coker
6.	Michigan	10–3	Lloyd Carr
7.	Georgia	11–3	Mark Richt
8.	Iowa	10–3	Kirk Ferentz
9.	Washington St	10–3	Bill Doba
10.	Miami (OH)	13–1	Terry Hoeppner
11.	Florida St	10–3	Bobby Bowden
12.	Texas	10–3	Mack Brown
13.	Kansas St	11–4	Bill Snyder
	Mississippi	10–3	David Cutcliffe
15.	Tennessee	10–3	Phillip Fulmer
16.	Boise St	13–1	Dan Hawkins
17.	Maryland	10–3	Ralph Friedgen
18.	Nebraska	10–3	Frank Solich/Bo Pelini
	Purdue	9–4	Joe Tiller
20.	Minnesota	10–3	Glen Mason
21.	Utah	10–2	Urban Meyer
22.	Clemson	9–4	Tommy Bowden
23.	Bowling Green	11–3	Gregg Brandon
24.	Florida	8–5	Ron Zook
25.	Texas Christian	11–2	Gary Patterson

*Ranked No. 1 in *USAToday*/ESPN Poll.

NCAA Divisional Championships

Division I-AA

Year	Winner	Runner-Up	Score
1978	Florida A&M	Massachusetts	35–28
1979	Eastern Kentucky	Lehigh	30–7
1980	Boise St	Eastern Kentucky	31–29
1981	Idaho St	Eastern Kentucky	34–23
1982	Eastern Kentucky	Delaware	17–14
1983	Southern Illinois	Western Carolina	43–7
1984	Montana St	Louisiana Tech	19–6
1985	Georgia Southern	Furman	44–42
1986	Georgia Southern	Arkansas St	48–21
1987	NE Louisiana	Marshall	43–42
1988	Furman	Georgia Southern	17–12
1989	Georgia Southern	Stephen F. Austin St	37–34
1990	Georgia Southern	NV-Reno	36–13
1991	Youngstown St	Marshall	25–17
1992	Marshall	Youngstown St	31–28
1993	Youngstown St	Marshall	17–5
1994	Youngstown St	Boise St	28–14
1995	Montana	Marshall	22–20
1996	Marshall	Montana	49–29
1997	Youngstown St	McNesse St	10–9
1998	Massachusetts	Georgia Southern	55–43
1999	Georgia Southern	Youngstown St	59–24
2000	Georgia Southern	Montana	27–25
2001	Montana	Furman	13–6
2002	Western Kentucky	McNeese St	34–14
2003	Delaware	Colgate	40–0

Division II

Year	Winner	Runner-Up	Score
1973	Louisiana Tech	Western Kentucky	34–0
1974	Central Michigan	Delaware	54–14
1975	Northern Michigan	Western Kentucky	16–14
1976	Montana St	Akron	24–13
1977	Lehigh	Jacksonville St	33–0
1978	Eastern Illinois	Delaware	10–9
1979	Delaware	Youngstown St	38–21
1980	Cal Poly SLO	Eastern Illinois	21–13
1981	SW Texas St	N Dakota St	42–13
1982	SW Texas St	UC–Davis	34–9
1983	N Dakota St	Central St (OH)	41–21
1984	Troy St	N Dakota St	18–17
1985	N Dakota St	N Alabama	35–7
1986	N Dakota St	S Dakota	27–7
1987	Troy St	Portland St	31–17
1988	N Dakota St	Portland St	35–21
1989	Mississippi College	Jacksonville St	3–0
1990	N Dakota St	Indiana (PA)	51–11
1991	Pittsburg St	Jacksonville St	23–6
1992	Jacksonville St	Pittsburg St	17–13
1993	N Alabama	Indiana (PA)	41–34
1994	N Alabama	Texas A&M–Kingsville	16–10
1995	N Alabama	Pittsburg St	27–7
1996	Northern Colorado	Carson-Newman	23–14
1997	Northern Colorado	New Haven	51–0
1998	NW Missouri St	Carson-Newman	24–6
1999	NW Missouri St	Carson-Newman	58–52 (OT)
2000	Delta St	Bloomsburg	63–34
2001	Grand Valley St	N Dakota	17–14
2002	Grand Valley St	Valdosta St	31–24
2003	Grand Valley St	N Dakota	10–3

Division III

Year	Winner	Runner-Up	Score
1973	Wittenberg	Juniata	41–0
1974	Central (IA)	Ithaca	10–8
1975	Wittenberg	Ithaca	28–0
1976	St. John's (MN)	Towson St	31–28
1977	Widener	Wabash	39–36
1978	Baldwin-Wallace	Wittenberg	24–10
1979	Ithaca	Wittenberg	14–10
1980	Dayton	Ithaca	63–0
1981	Widener	Dayton	17–10
1982	W Georgia	Augustana (IL)	14–0
1983	Augustana (IL)	Union (NY)	21–17
1984	Augustana (IL)	Central (IA)	21–12
1985	Augustana (IL)	Ithaca	20–7

Division III *(Cont.)*

Year	Winner	Runner-Up	Score
1986	Augustana (IL)	Salisbury St	31–3
1987	Wagner	Dayton	19–3
1988	Ithaca	Central (IA)	39–24
1989	Dayton	Union (NY)	17–7
1990	Allegheny	Lycoming	21–14 (OT)
1991	Ithaca	Dayton	34–20
1992	WI-LaCrosse	Washington & Jefferson	16–12
1993	Mount Union	Rowan	34–24
1994	Albion	Washington & Jefferson	38–15
1995	WI-LaCrosse	Rowan	36–7
1996	Mount Union	Rowan	56–24
1997	Mount Union	Lycoming	61–12
1998	Mount Union	Rowan	44–24
1999	Pacific Lutheran	Rowan	42–13
2000	Mount Union	St. John's	10–7
2001	Mount Union	Bridgewater	30–27
2002	Mount Union	Trinity (TX)	48–7
2003	St. John's (MN)	Mount Union	24–6

NAIA Divisional Championships

Division I

Year	Winner	Runner-Up	Score
1956	St. Joseph's (IN)/ Montana St		0–0
1957	Pittsburg St (KS)	Hillsdale (MI)	27–26
1958	NE Oklahoma	Northern Arizona	19–13
1959	Texas A&I	Lenoir-Rhyne (NC)	20–7
1960	Lenoir-Rhyne (NC)	Humboldt St (CA)	15–14
1961	Pittsburg St (KS)	Linfield (OR)	12–7
1962	Central St (OK)	Lenoir-Rhyne (NC)	28–13
1963	St. John's (MN)	Prairie View (TX)	33–27
1964	Concordia-Moorhead/ Sam Houston		7–7
1965	St. John's (MN)	Linfield (OR)	33–0
1966	Waynesburg (PA)	WI-Whitewater	42–21
1967	Fairmont St (WV)	Eastern Washington	28–21
1968	Troy St (MI)	Texas A&I	43–35
1969	Texas A&I	Concordia-Moorhead (MN)	32–7
1970	Texas A&I	Wofford (SC)	48–7
1971	Livingston (AL)	Arkansas Tech	14–12
1972	E Texas St	Carson-Newman (TN)	21–18
1973	Abilene Christian	Elon (NC)	42–14
1974	Texas A&I	Henderson St (AR)	34–23
1975	Texas A&I	Salem (WV)	37–0
1976	Texas A&I	Central Arkansas	26–0
1977	Abilene Christian	SW Oklahoma	24–7
1978	Angelo St (TX)	Elon (NC)	34–14
1979	Texas A&I	Central St (OK)	20–14
1980	Elon (NC)	NE Oklahoma	17–10
1981	Elon (NC)	Pittsburg St	3–0
1982	Central St (OK)	Mesa (CO)	14–11
1983	Carson-Newman (TN)	Mesa (CO)	36–28
1984	Carson-Newman (TN)/Central Arkansas		19–19
1985	Central Arkansas/ Hillsdale (MI)		10–10
1986	Carson-Newman (TN)	Cameron (OK)	17–0
1987	Cameron (OK)	Carson-Newman (TN)	30–2
1988	Carson-Newman (TN)	Adams St (CO)	56–21
1989	Carson-Newman (TN)	Emporia St (KS)	34–20
1990	Central St (OH)	Mesa St (CO)	38–16
1991	Central Arkansas	Central St (OH)	19–16
1992	Central St (OH)	Gardner-Webb (NC)	19–16
1993	E Central (OK)	Glenville St (WV)	49–35
1994	Northeastern St (OK)	Arkansas–Pine Bluff	13–12
1995	Central St (OH)	Northeastern St (OK)	37–7
1996	SW Oklahoma St	Montana Tech	33–31
1997	Findlay (OH)	Willamette (OR)	14–7
1998	Azusa Pacific	Olivet Nazarene	17–14
1999	Northwestern Oklahoma St	Georgetown (KY)	34–26
2000	Georgetown (KY)	Northwestern Oklahoma St	20–0
2001	Georgetown (KY)	Sioux Falls	49–27
2002	Carroll (MN)	Georgetown (KY)	28–7
2003	Carroll (MN)	Northwestern Oklahoma St	41–28

Division II†

Year	Winner	Runner-Up	Score
1970	Westminster (PA)	Anderson (IN)	21–16
1971	California Lutheran	Westminster (PA)	30–14
1972	Missouri Southern	Northwestern (IA)	21–14
1973	Northwestern (IA)	Glenville St (WV)	10–3
1974	Texas Lutheran	Missouri Valley	42–0
1975	Texas Lutheran	California Lutheran	34–8
1976	Westminster (PA)	Redlands (CA)	20–13
1977	Westminster (PA)	California Lutheran	17–9
1978	Concordia-Moorhead (MN)	Findlay (OH)	7–0
1979	Findlay (OH)	Northwestern (IA)	51–6
1980	Pacific Lutheran	Wilmington (OH)	38–10
1981	Austin Coll./ Conc.-Moorhead (MN)		24–24
1982	Linfield (OR)	William Jewell (MO)	33–15
1983	Northwestern (IA)	Pacific Lutheran	25–21
1984	Linfield (OR)	Northwestern (IA)	33–22
1985	WI-La Crosse	Pacific Lutheran	24–7
1986	Linfield (OR)	Baker (KS)	17–0
1987	Pacific Lutheran	WI-Stevens Point*	16–16
1988	Westminster (PA)	WI-La Crosse	21–14
1989	Westminster (PA)	WI-La Crosse	51–30
1990	Peru St (NE)	Westminster (PA)	17–7
1991	Georgetown (KY)	Pacific Lutheran	28–20
1992	Findlay (OH)	Linfield (OR)	26–13
1993	Pacific Lutheran (WA)	Westminster (PA)	50–20
1994	Westminster (PA)	Pacific Lutheran	27–7
1995	Findlay (OH)/ Central Washington		21–21
1996	Sioux Falls (SD)	Western Washington	47–25

*Forfeited 1987 season due to use of an ineligible player.   †In 1997 the NAIA consolidated its two divisions into one.

Awards

Heisman Memorial Trophy

Awarded to the best college player by the Downtown Athletic Club of New York City. The trophy is named after John W. Heisman, who coached Georgia Tech to the national championship in 1917 and later served as DAC athletic director.

Year	Winner, College, Position	Winner's Season Statistics	Runner-Up, College
1935	Jay Berwanger, Chicago, HB	Rush: 119 Yds: 577 TD: 6	Monk Meyer, Army
1936	Larry Kelley, Yale, E	Rec: 17 Yds: 372 TD: 6	Sam Francis, Nebraska
1937	Clint Frank, Yale, HB	Rush: 157 Yds: 667 TD: 11	Byron White, Colorado*
1938	†Davey O'Brien, Texas Christian, QB	Att/Comp: 194/110 Yds: 1733 TD: 19	Marshall Goldberg, Pittsburgh
1939	Nile Kinnick, Iowa, HB	Rush: 106 Yds: 374 TD: 5	Tom Harmon, Michigan
1940	Tom Harmon, Michigan, HB	Rush: 191 Yds: 852 TD: 16	John Kimbrough, Texas A&M
1941	†Bruce Smith, Minnesota, HB	Rush: 98 Yds: 480 TD: 6	Angelo Bertelli, Notre Dame
1942	Frank Sinkwich, Georgia, HB	Att/Comp: 166/84 Yds: 1392 TD: 10	Paul Governali, Columbia
1943	Angelo Bertelli, Notre Dame, QB	Att/Comp: 36/25 Yds: 511 TD: 10	Bob Odell, Pennsylvania
1944	Les Horvath, Ohio State, QB	Rush: 163 Yds: 924 TD: 12	Glenn Davis, Army
1945	*†Doc Blanchard, Army, FB	Rush: 101 Yds: 718 TD: 13	Glenn Davis, Army
1946	Glenn Davis, Army, HB	Rush: 123 Yds: 712 TD: 7	Charley Trippi, Georgia
1947	†John Lujack, Notre Dame, QB	Att/Comp: 109/61 Yds: 777 TD: 9	Bob Chappius, Michigan
1948	*Doak Walker, Southern Methodist, HB	Rush: 108 Yds: 532 TD: 8	Charlie Justice, N Carolina
1949	†Leon Hart, Notre Dame, E	Rec: 19 Yds: 257 TD: 5	Charlie Justice, N Carolina
1950	*Vic Janowicz, Ohio St, HB	Att/Comp: 77/32 Yds: 561 TD: 12	Kyle Rote, Southern Methodist
1951	Dick Kazmaier, Princeton, HB	Rush: 149 Yds: 861 TD: 9	Hank Lauricella, Tennessee
1952	Billy Vessels, Oklahoma, HB	Rush: 167 Yds: 1072 TD: 17	Jack Scarbath, Maryland
1953	John Lattner, Notre Dame, HB	Rush: 134 Yds: 651 TD: 6	Paul Giel, Minnesota
1954	Alan Ameche, Wisconsin, FB	Rush: 146 Yds: 641 TD: 9	Kurt Burris, Oklahoma
1955	Howard Cassady, Ohio St, HB	Rush: 161 Yds: 958 TD: 15	Jim Swink, Texas Christian
1956	Paul Hornung, Notre Dame, QB	Att/Comp: 111/59 Yds: 917 TD: 3	Johnny Majors, Tennessee
1957	John David Crow, Texas A&M, HB	Rush: 129 Yds: 562 TD: 10	Alex Karras, Iowa
1958	Pete Dawkins, Army, HB	Rush: 78 Yds: 428 TD: 6	Randy Duncan, Iowa

Heisman Memorial Trophy (Cont.)

Year	Winner, College, Position	Winner's Season Statistics	Runner-Up, College
1959	Billy Cannon, Louisiana St, HB	Rush: 139 Yds: 598 TD: 6	Rich Lucas, Penn St
1960	Joe Bellino, Navy, HB	Rush: 168 Yds: 834 TD: 18	Tom Brown, Minnesota
1961	Ernie Davis, Syracuse, HB	Rush: 150 Yds: 823 TD: 15	Bob Ferguson, Ohio St
1962	Terry Baker, Oregon St, QB	Att/Comp: 203/112 Yds: 1738 TD: 15	Jerry Stovall, Louisiana St
1963	*Roger Staubach, Navy, QB	Att/Comp: 161/107 Yds: 1474 TD: 7	Billy Lothridge, Georgia Tech
1964	John Huarte, Notre Dame, QB	Att/Comp: 205/114 Yds: 2062 TD: 16	Jerry Rhome, Tulsa
1965	Mike Garrett, Southern Cal, HB	Rush: 267 Yds: 1440 TD: 16	Howard Twilley, Tulsa
1966	Steve Spurrier, Florida, QB	Att/Comp: 291/179 Yds: 2012 TD: 16	Bob Griese, Purdue
1967	Gary Beban, UCLA, QB	Att/Comp: 156/87 Yds: 1359 TD: 8	O.J. Simpson, Southern Cal
1968	O.J. Simpson, Southern Cal, HB	Rush: 383 Yds: 1880 TD: 23	Leroy Keyes, Purdue
1969	Steve Owens, Oklahoma, FB	Rush: 358 Yds: 1523 TD: 23	Mike Phipps, Purdue
1970	Jim Plunkett, Stanford, QB	Att/Comp: 358/191 Yds: 2715 TD: 18	Joe Theismann, Notre Dame
1971	Pat Sullivan, Auburn, QB	Att/Comp: 281/162 Yds: 2012; 20 TD	Ed Marinaro, Cornell
1972	Johnny Rodgers, Nebraska, FL	Rec: 55 Yds: 942 TD: 17	Greg Pruitt, Oklahoma
1973	John Cappelletti, Penn St, HB	Rush: 286 Yds: 1522 TD: 17	John Hicks, Ohio St
1974	*Archie Griffin, Ohio St, HB	Rush: 256 Yds: 1695 TD: 12	Anthony Davis, Southern Cal
1975	Archie Griffin, Ohio St, HB	Rush: 262 Yds: 1450 TD: 4	Chuck Muncie, California
1976	†Tony Dorsett, Pittsburgh, HB	Rush: 370 Yds: 2150 TD: 23	Ricky Bell, Southern Cal
1977	Earl Campbell, Texas, FB	Rush: 267 Yds: 1744 TD: 19	Terry Miller, Oklahoma St
1978	*Billy Sims, Oklahoma, HB	Rush: 231 Yds: 1762 TD: 20	Chuck Fusina, Penn St
1979	Charles White, Southern Cal, HB	Rush: 332 Yds: 1803 TD: 19	Billy Sims, Oklahoma
1980	George Rogers, S Carolina, HB	Rush: 324 Yds: 1894 TD: 14	Hugh Green, Pittsburgh
1981	Marcus Allen, Southern Cal, HB	Rush: 433 Yds: 2427 TD: 23	Herschel Walker, Georgia
1982	*Herschel Walker, Georgia, HB	Rush: 335 Yds: 1752 TD: 17	John Elway, Stanford
1983	Mike Rozier, Nebraska, HB	Rush: 275 Yds: 2148 TD: 29	Steve Young, Brigham Young
1984	Doug Flutie, Boston College, QB	Att/Comp: 396/233 Yds: 3454 TD: 27	Keith Byars, Ohio St
1985	Bo Jackson, Auburn, HB	Rush: 278 Yds: 1786 TD: 17	Chuck Long, Iowa
1986	Vinny Testaverde, Miami (FL), QB	Att/Comp: 276/175 Yds: 2557 TD: 26	Paul Palmer, Temple
1987	Tim Brown, Notre Dame, WR	Rec: 39 Yds: 846 TD: 7	Don McPherson, Syracuse
1988	*Barry Sanders, Oklahoma St, RB	Rush: 344 Yds: 2628 TD: 39	Rodney Peete, Southern Cal
1989	*Andre Ware, Houston, QB	Att/Comp: 578/365 Yds: 4699 TD: 46	Anthony Thompson, Indiana
1990	*Ty Detmer, Brigham Young, QB	Att/Comp: 562/361 Yds: 5188 TD: 41	Raghib Ismail, Notre Dame
1991	*Desmond Howard, Michigan, WR	Rec: 61 Yds: 950 TD: 23	Casey Weldon, Florida St
1992	Gino Torretta, Miami (FL), QB	Att/Comp: 402/228 Yds: 3060 TD: 19	Marshall Faulk, San Diego St
1993	†Charlie Ward, Florida St, QB	Att/Comp: 380/264 Yds: 3032 TD: 27	Heath Shuler, Tennessee
1994	Rashaan Salaam, Colorado, RB	Rush: 298 Yds: 2055 TD: 24	Ki-Jana Carter, Penn St
1995	Eddie George, Ohio State, RB	Rush: 303 Yds: 1826 TD: 23	Tommie Frazier, Nebraska
1996	†Danny Wuerffel, Florida, QB	Att/Comp: 360/207 Yds: 3625 TD: 39	Troy Davis, Iowa St
1997	†Charles Woodson, Michigan, CB/ WR	7 interceptions; Rec: 11 Yds: 231 TD: 4	Peyton Manning, Tennessee
1998	Ricky Williams, Texas, RB	Rush: 361 Yds: 2124 TD: 28	Michael Bishop, Kansas St
1999	Ron Dayne, Wisconsin, RB	Rush: 303 Yds: 1834 TD: 19	Joe Hamilton, Georgia Tech
2000	Chris Weinke, Florida St, QB	Att/Comp: 431/266 Yds: 4167 TD: 33	Josh Heupel, Oklahoma
2001	Eric Crouch, Nebraska, QB	Att/Comp: 189/105 Yds: 1510 TD: 7; Rush: 1115 Yds: 18 TD	Rex Grossman, Florida
2002	Carson Palmer, Southern Cal, QB	Att/Comp: 450/228 Yds: 3639 TD: 32	Brad Banks, Iowa
2003	Jason White, Oklahoma, QB	Pct. Comp: 64; 3744 Yds; TD: 40	Larry Fitzgerald, Pittsburgh

*Juniors (all others seniors).   †Winners who played for national championship teams the same year.

Note: Former Heisman winners and national media cast votes, with ballots allowing for three names (3 points for first, 2 for second and 1 for third).

Maxwell Award

Given to the nation's outstanding college football player by the Maxwell Football Club of Philadelphia.

Year	Player, College, Position	Year	Player, College, Position
1937	Clint Frank, Yale, HB	1971	Ed Marinaro, Cornell, RB
1938	Davey O'Brien, Texas Christian, QB	1972	Brad Van Pelt, Michigan St, DB
1939	Nile Kinnick, Iowa, HB	1973	John Cappelletti, Penn St, RB
1940	Tom Harmon, Michigan, HB	1974	Steve Joachim, Temple, QB
1941	Bill Dudley, Virginia, HB	1975	Archie Griffin, Ohio St, RB
1942	Paul Governali, Columbia, QB	1976	Tony Dorsett, Pittsburgh, RB
1943	Bob Odell, Pennsylvania, HB	1977	Ross Browner, Notre Dame, DE
1944	Glenn Davis, Army, HB	1978	Chuck Fusina, Penn St, QB
1945	Doc Blanchard, Army, FB	1979	Charles White, Southern Cal, RB
1946	Charley Trippi, Georgia, HB	1980	Hugh Green, Pittsburgh, DE
1947	Doak Walker, Southern Meth, HB	1981	Marcus Allen, Southern Cal, RB
1948	Chuck Bednarik, Pennsylvania, C	1982	Herschel Walker, Georgia, RB
1949	Leon Hart, Notre Dame, E	1983	Mike Rozier, Nebraska, RB
1950	Reds Bagnell, Pennsylvania, HB	1984	Doug Flutie, Boston College, QB
1951	Dick Kazmaier, Princeton, HB	1985	Chuck Long, Iowa, QB
1952	John Lattner, Notre Dame, HB	1986	Vinny Testaverde, Miami (FL), QB
1953	John Lattner, Notre Dame, HB	1987	Don McPherson, Syracuse, QB
1954	Ron Beagle, Navy, E	1988	Barry Sanders, Oklahoma St, RB
1955	Howard Cassady, Ohio St, HB	1989	Anthony Thompson, Indiana, RB
1956	Tommy McDonald, Oklahoma, HB	1990	Ty Detmer, Brigham Young, QB
1957	Bob Reifsnyder, Navy, T	1991	Desmond Howard, Michigan, WR
1958	Pete Dawkins, Army, HB	1992	Gino Torretta, Miami (FL), QB
1959	Rich Lucas, Penn St, QB	1993	Charlie Ward, Florida St, QB
1960	Joe Bellino, Navy, HB	1994	Kerry Collins, Penn St, QB
1961	Bob Ferguson, Ohio St, FB	1995	Eddie George, Ohio St, RB
1962	Terry Baker, Oregon St, QB	1996	Danny Wuerffel, Florida, QB
1963	Roger Staubach, Navy, QB	1997	Peyton Manning, Tennessee, QB
1964	Glenn Ressler, Penn St, C	1998	Ricky Williams, Texas, RB
1965	Tommy Nobis, Texas, LB	1999	Ron Dayne, Wisconsin, RB
1966	Jim Lynch, Notre Dame, LB	2000	Drew Brees, Purdue, QB
1967	Gary Beban, UCLA, QB	2001	Ken Dorsey, Miami (FL), QB
1968	O.J. Simpson, Southern Cal, RB	2002	Larry Johnson, Penn St, RB
1969	Mike Reid, Penn St, DT	2003	Eli Manning, Mississippi, QB
1970	Jim Plunkett, Stanford, QB		

Davey O'Brien National Quarterback Award

Given to the top quarterback in the nation by the Davey O'Brien Educational and Charitable Trust of Fort Worth. Named for Texas Christian Hall of Fame quarterback Davey O'Brien (1936–38).

Year	Player, College	Year	Player, College
1981	Jim McMahon, Brigham Young	1993	Charlie Ward, Florida St
1982	Todd Blackledge, Penn St	1994	Kerry Collins, Penn St
1983	Steve Young, Brigham Young	1995	Danny Wuerffel, Florida
1984	Doug Flutie, Boston College	1996	Danny Wuerffel, Florida
1985	Chuck Long, Iowa	1997	Peyton Manning, Tennessee
1986	Vinny Testaverde, Miami (FL)	1998	Michael Bishop, Kansas St
1987	Don McPherson, Syracuse	1999	Joe Hamilton, Georgia Tech
1988	Troy Aikman, UCLA	2000	Chris Weinke, Florida St
1989	Andre Ware, Houston	2001	Eric Crouch, Nebraska
1990	Ty Detmer, Brigham Young	2002	Brad Banks, Iowa
1991	Ty Detmer, Brigham Young	2003	Jason White, Oklahoma
1992	Gino Torretta, Miami (FL)		

Note: Originally honored the outstanding football player in the Southwest as follows: 1977—Earl Campbell, Texas, RB; 1978—Billy Sims, Oklahoma, RB; 1979—Mike Singletary, Baylor, LB; 1980—Mike Singletary, Baylor, LB.

Vince Lombardi/Rotary Award

Given to the outstanding college lineman of the year, the award is sponsored by the Rotary Club of Houston.

Year	Player, College, Position	Year	Player, College, Position
1970	Jim Stillwagon, Ohio St, MG	1985	Tony Casillas, Oklahoma, NG
1971	Walt Patulski, Notre Dame, DE	1986	Cornelius Bennett, Alabama, LB
1972	Rich Glover, Nebraska, MG	1987	Chris Spielman, Ohio St, LB
1973	John Hicks, Ohio St, OT	1988	Tracy Rocker, Auburn, DT
1974	Randy White, Maryland, DT	1989	Percy Snow, Michigan St, LB
1975	Lee Roy Selmon, Oklahoma, DT	1990	Chris Zorich, Notre Dame, NG
1976	Wilson Whitley, Houston, DT	1991	Steve Emtman, Washington, DT
1977	Ross Browner, Notre Dame, DE	1992	Marvin Jones, Florida St, LB
1978	Bruce Clark, Penn St, DT	1993	Aaron Taylor, Notre Dame, OT
1979	Brad Budde, Southern Cal, G	1994	Warren Sapp, Miami (FL), DT
1980	Hugh Green, Pittsburgh, DE	1995	Orlando Pace, Ohio St, OT
1981	Kenneth Sims, Texas, DT	1996	Orlando Pace, Ohio St, OT
1982	Dave Rimington, Nebraska, C	1997	Grant Wistrom, Nebraska, DE
1983	Dean Steinkuhler, Nebraska, G	1998	Dat Nguyen, Texas A&M, LB
1984	Tony Degrate, Texas, DT	1999	Corey Moore, Virginia Tech, DE

Lombardi Award (Cont.)

Year	Player, College, Position	Year	Player, College, Position
2000	Jamal Reynolds, Florida St, DE	2002	Terrell Suggs, Arizona St, DL
2001	Julius Peppers, N Carolina, DE	2003	Tommie Harris, Oklahoma, DT

Outland Trophy

Given to the outstanding interior lineman, selected by the Football Writers Association of America.

Year	Player, College, Position	Year	Player, College, Position
1946	George Connor, Notre Dame, T	1976	Ross Browner, Notre Dame, DE
1947	Joe Steffy, Army, G	1977	Brad Shearer, Texas, DT
1948	Bill Fischer, Notre Dame, G	1978	Greg Roberts, Oklahoma, G
1949	Ed Bagdon, Michigan St, G	1979	Jim Ritcher, N Carolina St, C
1950	Bob Gain, Kentucky, T	1980	Mark May, Pittsburgh, OT
1951	Jim Weatherall, Oklahoma, T	1981	Dave Rimington, Nebraska, C
1952	Dick Modzelewski, Maryland, T	1982	Dave Rimington, Nebraska, C
1953	J.D. Roberts, Oklahoma, G	1983	Dean Steinkuhler, Nebraska, G
1954	Bill Brooks, Arkansas, G	1984	Bruce Smith, Virginia Tech, DT
1955	Calvin Jones, Iowa, G	1985	Mike Ruth, Boston College, NG
1956	Jim Parker, Ohio St, G	1986	Jason Buck, Brigham Young, DT
1957	Alex Karras, Iowa, T	1987	Chad Hennings, Air Force, DT
1958	Zeke Smith, Auburn, G	1988	Tracy Rocker, Auburn, DT
1959	Mike McGee, Duke, T	1989	Mohammed Elewonibi, Brigham Young, G
1960	Tom Brown, Minnesota, G	1990	Russell Maryland, Miami (FL), DT
1961	Merlin Olsen, Utah St, T	1991	Steve Emtman, Washington, DT
1962	Bobby Bell, Minnesota, T	1992	Will Shields, Nebraska, G
1963	Scott Appleton, Texas, T	1993	Rob Waldrop, Arizona, NG
1964	Steve DeLong, Tennessee, T	1994	Zach Wiegert, Nebraska, G
1965	Tommy Nobis, Texas, G	1995	Jonathan Ogden, UCLA, OT
1966	Loyd Phillips, Arkansas, T	1996	Orlando Pace, Ohio St, OT
1967	Ron Yary, Southern Cal, T	1997	Aaron Taylor, Nebraska, G
1968	Bill Stanfill, Georgia, T	1998	Kris Farris, UCLA, OL
1969	Mike Reid, Penn St, DT	1999	Chris Samuels, Alabama, OL
1970	Jim Stillwagon, Ohio St, MG	2000	John Henderson, Tennessee, DT
1971	Larry Jacobson, Nebraska, DT	2001	Bryant McKinnie, Miami (FL), OT
1972	Rich Glover, Nebraska, MG	2002	Rien Long, Washington St, DL
1973	John Hicks, Ohio St, OT	2003	Robert Gallery, Iowa, OT
1974	Randy White, Maryland, DE		
1975	Lee Roy Selmon, Oklahoma, DT		

Butkus Award

Given to the top collegiate linebacker, the award was established by the Downtown Athletic Club of Orlando and named for college Hall of Famer Dick Butkus of Illinois.

Year	Player, College	Year	Player, College
1985	Brian Bosworth, Oklahoma	1995	Kevin Hardy, Illinois
1986	Brian Bosworth, Oklahoma	1996	Matt Russell, Colorado
1987	Paul McGowan, Florida St	1997	Andy Katzenmoyer, Ohio St
1988	Derrick Thomas, Alabama	1998	Chris Claiborne, Southern Cal
1989	Percy Snow, Michigan St	1999	LaVar Arrington, Penn St
1990	Alfred Williams, Colorado	2000	Dan Morgan, Miami (FL)
1991	Erick Anderson, Michigan	2001	Rocky Calmus, Oklahoma
1992	Marvin Jones, Florida St	2002	E.J. Henderson, Maryland
1993	Trev Alberts, Nebraska	2003	Teddy Lehman, Oklahoma
1994	Dana Howard, Illinois		

Jim Thorpe Award

Given to the best defensive back of the year, the award is presented by the Jim Thorpe Athletic Club of Oklahoma City.

Year	Player, College	Year	Player, College
1986	Thomas Everett, Baylor	1995	Greg Myers, Colorado St
1987	Bennie Blades, Miami (FL)	1996	Lawrence Wright, Florida
	Rickey Dixon, Oklahoma	1997	Charles Woodson, Michigan
1988	Deion Sanders, Florida St	1998	Antoine Winfield, Ohio St
1989	Mark Carrier, Southern Cal	1999	Tyrone Carter, Minnesota
1990	Darryl Lewis, Arizona	2000	Jamar Fletcher, Wisconsin
1991	Terrell Buckley, Florida St	2001	Roy Williams, Oklahoma
1992	Deon Figures, Colorado	2002	Terence Newman, Kansas St
1993	Antonio Langham, Alabama	2003	Derrick Strait, Oklahoma
1994	Chris Hudson, Colorado		

Walter Payton Player of the Year Award

Given to the top Division I-AA player as voted by Division I-AA sports information directors. Sponsored by Sports Network.

Year	Player, College, Position	Year	Player, College, Position
1987	Kenny Gamble, Colgate, RB	1996	Archie Amerson, Northern Arizona, RB
1988	Dave Meggett, Towson St, RB	1997	Brian Finneran, Villanova, WR
1989	John Friesz, Idaho, QB	1998	Jerry Azumah, New Hampshire, RB
1990	Walter Dean, Grambling, RB	1999	Adrian Peterson, Georgia Southern, RB
1991	Jamie Martin, Weber St, QB	2000	Louis Ivory, Furman, RB
1992	Michael Payton, Marshall, QB	2001	Brian Westbrook, Villanova, RB
1993	Doug Nussmeier, Idaho, QB	2002	Tony Romo, Eastern Ilinois, QB
1994	Steve McNair, Alcorn St, QB	2003	Jamaal Branch, Colgate, RB
1995	Dave Dickenson, Montana, QB		

NCAA Division I-A Individual Records

Career

SCORING

Most Points Scored: 468—Travis Prentice, Miami (OH), 1996–99
Most Points Scored per Game: 12.1—Marshall Faulk, San Diego St, 1991–93
Most Touchdowns Scored: 73—Travis Prentice, Miami (OH), 1996–99
Most Touchdowns Scored per Game: 2.0—Marshall Faulk, San Diego St, 1991–93
Most Touchdowns Scored, Rushing: 73—Travis Prentice, Miami (OH), 1996–99
Most Touchdowns Scored, Passing: 121—Ty Detmer, Brigham Young, 1988–91
Most Touchdowns Scored, Receiving: 50—Troy Edwards, Louisiana Tech, 1996–98
Most Touchdowns Scored, Interception Returns: 5—Ken Thomas, San Jose St, 1979–82; Jackie Walker, Tennessee, 1969–71; Deltha O'Neal, California, 1996–99
Most Touchdowns Scored, Punt Returns: 7—Johnny Rodgers, Nebraska, 1970–72; Jack Mitchell, Oklahoma, 1946–48; David Allen, Kansas St, 1997–99
Most Touchdowns Scored, Kickoff Returns: 6—Anthony Davis, Southern Cal, 1972–74

TOTAL OFFENSE

Most Plays: 2,156—Kliff Kingsbury, Texas Tech, 1999–2002
Most Plays per Game: 48.5—Doug Gaynor, Long Beach St, 1984–85
Most Yards Gained: 14,665—Ty Detmer, Brigham Young, 1988–91 (15,031 passing, -366 rushing)
Most Yards Gained per Game: 382.4—Tim Rattay, Louisiana Tech, 1997–99
Most 300+ Yard Games: 33 —Ty Detmer, Brigham Young, 1988–91

RUSHING

Most Rushes: 1,215—Steve Bartalo, Colorado St, 1983–86 (4813 yds)
Most Rushes per Game: 34.0—Ed Marinaro, Cornell, 1969–71
Most Yards Gained: 6,397—Ron Dayne, Wisconsin, 1996–99
Most Yards Gained per Game: 174.6—Ed Marinaro, Cornell, 1969–71

RUSHING *(CONT.)*

Most 100+ Yard Games: 33—Tony Dorsett, Pittsburgh, 1973–76; Archie Griffin, Ohio St, 1972–75
Most 200+ Yard Games: 11—Marcus Allen, Southern Cal, 1978–81; Ricky Williams, Texas, 1995–98; Ron Dayne, Wisconsin, 1996–99

PASSING

Highest Passing Efficiency Rating: 168.4—Ryan Dinwiddie, Boise St, 2000–03 (992 attempts, 622 completions, 82 touchdown passes, 21 interceptions, 9,819 yards)
Most Passes Attempted: 1,679—Chris Redman, Louisville, 1996–99
Most Passes Attempted per Game: 47.0—Tim Rattay, Louisiana Tech, 1997–99
Most Passes Completed: 1,031—Chris Redman, Louisville, 1996–99
Most Passes Completed per Game: 30.8—Tim Rattay, Louisiana Tech, 1997–99
*Highest Completion Percentage: 67.1—Tim Couch, Kentucky, 1996-98
Most Yards Gained: 15,031—Ty Detmer, Brigham Young, 1988–91
Most Yards Gained per Game: 386.2—Tim Rattay, Louisiana Tech, 1997–99

*Minimum 1,000 attempts.

RECEIVING

Most Passes Caught: 300—Arnold Jackson, Louisville, 1997–00
Most Passes Caught per Game: 10.5—Emmanuel Hazard, Houston, 1989–90
Most Yards Gained: 5,005—Trevor Insley, Nevada, 1996–99
Most Yards Gained per Game: 140.9—Alex Van Dyke, Nevada, 1994–95
Highest Average Gain per Reception: 25.7—Wesley Walker, California, 1973–75

Career *(Cont.)*

ALL-PURPOSE RUNNING

Most Plays: 1,347—Steve Bartalo, Colorado St, 1983-86 (1,215 rushes, 132 receptions)
Most Yards Gained: 7,206—Ricky Williams, Texas, 1995–98 (6,279 rushing, 927 receiving)
Most Yards Gained per Game: 237.8—Ryan Benjamin, Pacific, 1990–92
Highest Average Gain per Play: 17.4—Anthony Carter, Michigan, 1979–82

INTERCEPTIONS

Most Passes Intercepted: 29—Al Brosky, Illinois, 1950–52
Most Passes Intercepted per Game: 1.1—Al Brosky, Illinois, 1950–52
Most Yards on Interception Returns: 501—Terrell Buckley, Florida St, 1989–91
Highest Average Gain per Interception: 26.5—Tom Pridemore, W Virginia, 1975–77

SPECIAL TEAMS

Highest Punt Return Average: 23.6—Jack Mitchell, Oklahoma, 1946–48
Highest Kickoff Return Average: 35.1—Anthony Davis, Southern Cal, 1972–74
Highest Average Yards per Punt: 46.3—Todd Sauerbrun, W Virginia, 1991–94
Note: 150–249 punts.

Single Season

SCORING

Most Points Scored: 234—Barry Sanders, Oklahoma St, 1988
Most Points Scored per Game: 21.3—Barry Sanders, Oklahoma St, 1988
Most Touchdowns Scored: 39—Barry Sanders, Oklahoma St, 1988
Most Touchdowns Scored, Rushing: 37—Barry Sanders, Oklahoma St, 1988
Most Touchdowns Scored, Passing: 54—David Klingler, Houston, 1990
Most Touchdowns Scored, Receiving: 27—Troy Edwards, Louisiana Tech, 1998
Most Touchdowns Scored, Interception Returns: 4—Deltha O'Neal, California, 1999
Most Touchdowns Scored, Punt Returns: 4—Santana Moss, Miami (FL), 2000; David Allen, Kansas St, 1998; Quinton Spotwood, Syracuse, 1997; Tinker Keck, Cincinnati, 1997; James Henry, Southern Miss, 1987; Golden Richards, Brigham Young, 1971; Cliff Branch, Colorado, 1971
Most Touchdowns Scored, Kickoff Returns: 3—Leland McElroy, Texas A&M, 1993; Terance Mathis, New Mexico, 1989; Willie Gault, Tennessee, 1980; Anthony Davis, Southern Cal, 1974; Stan Brown, Purdue, 1970; Forrest Hall, San Francisco, 1946

TOTAL OFFENSE

Most Plays: 814—Kliff Kingsbury, Texas Tech, 2002
Most Yards Gained: 5,976—B.J. Symons, Texas Tech, 2003
Most Yards Gained per Game: 474.6—David Klingler, Houston, 1990
Most 300+ Yard Games: 12—Ty Detmer, Brigham Young, 1990

RUSHING

Most Rushes: 403—Marcus Allen, Southern Cal, 1981
Most Rushes per Game: 39.6—Ed Marinaro, Cornell, 1971
Most Yards Gained: 2,628—Barry Sanders, Oklahoma St, 1988
Most Yards Gained per Game: 238.9—Barry Sanders, Oklahoma St, 1988
Most 100+ Yard Games: 11—By 14 players, most recently Ahman Green, Nebraska, 1997

PASSING

Highest Passing Efficiency Rating: 183.3—Shaun King, Tulane, 1998 (328 attempts, 223 completions, 6 interceptions, 3,232 yards, 36 TD passes)
Most Passes Attempted: 719—B.J. Symons, Texas Tech, 2003
Most Passes Attempted per Game: 58.5—David Klingler, Houston, 1990
Most Passes Completed: 479—Kliff Kingsbury, Texas Tech, 2002
Most Passes Completed per Game: 36.4—Tim Couch, Kentucky, 1998
Highest Completion Percentage: 73.6—Daunte Culpepper, Central Florida, 1998
Most Yards Gained: 5,833—B.J. Symons, Texas Tech, 2003
Most Yards Gained per Game: 467.3—David Klingler, Houston, 1990

RECEIVING

Most Passes Caught: 142—Emmanuel Hazard, Houston, 1989
Most Passes Caught per Game: 13.4—Howard Twilley, Tulsa, 1965
Most Yards Gained: 2,060—Trevor Insley, Nevada, 1999
Most Yards Gained per Game: 187.3—Trevor Insley, Nevada, 1999
Highest Average Gain per Reception: 27.9—Elmo Wright, Houston, 1968 (min. 30 receptions)

ALL-PURPOSE RUNNING

Most Plays: 432—Marcus Allen, Southern Cal, 1981
Most Yards Gained: 3,250—Barry Sanders, Oklahoma St, 1988
Most Yards Gained per Game: 295.5—Barry Sanders, Oklahoma St, 1988
Highest Average Gain per Play: 18.5—Henry Bailey, UNLV, 1992

Single Season (Cont.)

INTERCEPTIONS

Most Passes Intercepted: 14 — Al Worley, Washington, 1968
Most Yards on Interception Returns: 302 — Charles Phillips, Southern Cal, 1974
Highest Average Gain per Interception: 50.6 — Norm Thompson, Utah, 1969

SPECIAL TEAMS

Highest Punt Return Average: 25.9 — Bill Blackstock, Tennessee, 1951
Highest Kickoff Return Average: 40.1 — Paul Allen, Brigham Young, 1961
Highest Average Yards per Punt: 50.3 — Chad Kessler, Louisiana St, 1997

Single Game

SCORING

Most Points Scored: 48—Howard Griffith, Illinois, 1990 (vs Southern Illinois)
Most Field Goals: 7—Dale Klein, Nebraska, 1985 (vs Missouri); Mike Prindle, Western Michigan, 1984 (vs Marshall)
Most Extra Points (Kick): 13—Derek Mahoney, Fresno St, 1991 (vs New Mexico); Terry Leiweke, Houston, 1968 (vs Tulsa)
Most Extra Points (2-Pts): 6—Jim Pilot, New Mexico St, 1961 (vs Hardin-Simmons)

TOTAL OFFENSE

Most Yards Gained: 732—David Klingler, Houston, 1990 (vs Arizona St)

RUSHING

Most Yards Gained: 406—LaDainian Tomlinson, Texas Christian, 1999 (vs UTEP)
Most Touchdowns Rushed: 8—Howard Griffith, Illinois, 1990 (vs Southern Illinois)

PASSING

Most Passes Completed: 55—Rusty LaRue, Wake Forest, 1995 (vs Duke); Drew Brees, Purdue, 1998 (vs Wisconsin)
Most Yards Gained: 716—David Klingler, Houston, 1990 (vs Arizona St)
Most Touchdown Passes: 11—David Klingler, Houston, 1990 [vs Eastern Washington (I-AA)]

RECEIVING

Most Passes Caught: 23—Randy Gatewood, UNLV, 1994 (vs Idaho)
Most Yards Gained: 405—Troy Edwards, Louisiana Tech, 1998 (vs Nebraska)
Most Touchdown Catches: 7—Rashaun Woods, Oklahoma St, 2003 (vs Southern Methodist)

NCAA Division I-AA Individual Records

Career

SCORING

Most Points Scored: 544—Brian Westbrook, Villanova, 1998-01
Most Touchdowns Scored: 89—Brian Westbrook, Villanova, 1998-01
Most Touchdowns Scored, Rushing: 84—Adrian Peterson, Georgia Southern, 1998–01
Most Touchdowns Scored, Passing: 139—Willie Totten, Mississippi Valley, 1982–85
Most Touchdowns Scored, Receiving: 50—Jerry Rice, Mississippi Valley, 1981–84

RUSHING

Most Rushes: 1,124—Charles Roberts, Cal St–Sacramento, 1997–00
Most Rushes per Game: 38.2—Arnold Mickens, Butler, 1994–95
Most Yards Gained: 6,559—Adrian Peterson, Georgia Southern, 1998–01
Most Yards Gained per Game: 190.7—Arnold Mickens, Butler, 1994–95

PASSING

Highest Passing Efficiency Rating: 170.8—Shawn Knight, William & Mary, 1991–94
Most Passes Attempted: 1,680—Marcus Brady, Cal St—Northridge, 1998-01; Steve McNair, Alcorn St, 1991–94
Most Passes Completed: 1,039—Marcus Brady, Cal St—Northridge, 1998-01
Most Passes Completed per Game: 26.5—Chris Sanders, Chattanooga, 1999–00
Highest Completion Percentage: 67.3—Dave Dickenson, Montana, 1992–95
Most Yards Gained: 14,496—Steve McNair, Alcorn St, 1991–94
Most Yards Gained per Game: 350.0—Neil Lomax, Portland St, 1978–80

RECEIVING

Most Passes Caught: 317—Jacquay Nunnally, Florida A&M, 1997–00
Most Yards Gained: 4,693—Jerry Rice, Mississippi Valley, 1981–84
Most Yards Gained per Game: 119.1—Tramon Douglas, Grambling, 2002–03
Highest Average Gain per Reception: 24.3—John Taylor, Delaware St, 1982–85

Single Season

SCORING

Most Points Scored: 176—Brian Westbrook, Villanova, 2001
Most Touchdowns Scored: 29—Adrian Peterson, Georgia Southern, 1999; Brian Westbrook, Villanova, 2001
Most Touchdowns Scored, Rushing: 28—Adrian Peterson, Georgia Southern, 1999
Most Touchdowns Scored, Passing: 56—Willie Totten, Mississippi Valley, 1984
Most Touchdowns Scored, Receiving: 27—Jerry Rice, Mississippi Valley, 1984

RUSHING

Most Rushes: 409—Arnold Mickens, Butler, 1994
Most Rushes per Game: 40.9—Arnold Mickens, Butler, 1994
Most Yards Gained: 2,326—Jamaal Branch, Colgate, 2003
Most Yards Gained per Game: 225.5—Arnold Mickens, Butler, 1994

PASSING

Highest Passing Efficiency Rating: 204.6—Shawn Knight, William & Mary, 1993
Most Passes Attempted: 577—Joe Lee, Towson, 1999
Most Passes Completed: 324—Willie Totten, Mississippi Valley, 1984
Most Passes Completed per Game: 32.4—Willie Totten, Mississippi Valley, 1984
Highest Completion Percentage: 70.6—Giovanni Carmazzi, Hofstra, 1997
Most Yards Gained: 4,863—Steve McNair, Alcorn St, 1994
Most Yards Gained per Game: 455.7—Willie Totten, Mississippi Valley, 1984

RECEIVING

Most Passes Caught: 120—Stephen Campbell, Brown, 2000
Most Yards Gained: 1,712—Eddie Conti, Delaware, 1998
Most Yards Gained per Game: 168.2—Jerry Rice, Mississippi Valley, 1984
Highest Average Gain per Reception: 28.9—Mikhael Ricks, Stephen F. Austin, 1997; (min. 35 receptions)

Single Game

SCORING

Most Points Scored: 42—Jesse Burton, McNeese St, 1998 (vs Southern Utah); Archie Amerson, Northern Arizona, 1996 (vs Weber St)
Most Field Goals: 8—Goran Lingmerth, Northern Arizona, 1986 (vs Idaho)

RUSHING

Most Yards Gained: 437—Maurice Hicks, N Carolina A&T, 2001 (vs Morgan St)
Most Touchdowns Rushed: 7—Archie Amerson, Northern Arizona, 1996 (vs Weber St)

PASSING

Most Passes Completed: 48—Clayton Millis, Cal St–Northridge, 1995 (vs St. Mary's [CA])
Most Yards Gained: 624—Jamie Martin, Weber St, 1991 (vs Idaho St)
Most Touchdown Passes: 9—Willie Totten, Mississippi Valley, 1984 (vs Kentucky St)

RECEIVING

Most Passes Caught: 24—Chas Gessner, Brown, 2002, (vs Rhode Island); Jerry Rice, Mississippi Valley, 1983 (vs Southern–BR)
Most Yards Gained: 376—Kassim Osgood, Cal Poly, 2000 (vs Northern Iowa)
Most Touchdown Catches: 6—Cos DeMatteo, Chattanooga, 2000 (vs Mississippi Valley)

NCAA Division II Individual Records

Career

SCORING

Most Points Scored: 570—Ian Smart, C.W. Post, 1999–2002
Most Touchdowns Scored: 95—Ian Smart, C.W. Post, 1999–2002
Most Touchdowns Scored, Rushing: 94—Ian Smart, C.W. Post, 1999–2002
Most Touchdowns Scored, Passing: 116—Chris Hatcher, Valdosta St, 1991–94
Most Touchdowns Scored, Receiving: 76—David Kircus, Grand Valley St, 1999–2002

RUSHING

Most Rushes: 1,131—Josh Ranek, S Dakota St, 1997–01
Most Rushes per Game: 29.8—Bernie Peeters, Luther, 1968–71
Most Yards Gained: 6,958—Brian Shay, Emporia St, 1995–98
Most Yards Gained per Game: 183.4—Anthony Gray, Western NM, 1997–98

Career *(Cont.)*

PASSING

Highest Passing Efficiency Rating: 190.8—Dusty Bonner, Valdosta St, 2000–01
Most Passes Attempted: 1,898—Andrew Webb, Fort Lewis, 2000–03
Most Passes Completed: 1,007—Andrew Webb, Fort Lewis, 2000–03
Most Passes Completed per Game: 25.7—Chris Hatcher, Valdosta St, 1991–94
Highest Completion Percentage: 72.7—Dusty Bonner, Valdosta St, 2000–01
Most Yards Gained: 11,742—Andrew Webb, Fort Lewis, 2000–03
Most Yards Gained per Game: 323.7—Dusty Bonner, Valdosta St, 2000–01

RECEIVING

Most Passes Caught: 323—Clarence Coleman, Ferris St, 1998–01
Most Yards Gained: 4,983—Clarence Coleman, Ferris St, 1998–01
Most Yards Gained per Game: 160.8—Chris George, Glenville St, 1993–94
Highest Average Gain per Reception: 22.8—Tyrone Johnson, Western St (CO), 1990–93

Single Season

SCORING

Most Points Scored: 212—David Kircus, Grand Valley St, 2002
Most Touchdowns Scored: 35—David Kircus, Grand Valley St, 2002
Most Touchdowns Scored, Rushing: 33—Ian Smart, C.W. Post, 2001
Most Touchdowns Scored, Passing: 54—Dusty Bonner, Valdosta St, 2000
Most Touchdowns Scored, Receiving: 35—David Kircus, Grand Valley St, 2002

RUSHING

Most Rushes: 385—Joe Gough, Wayne St (MI), 1994
Most Rushes per Game: 38.6—Mark Perkins, Hobart, 1968
Most Yards Gained: 2,653—Kavin Gailliard, American International, 1999
Most Yards Gained per Game: 222.0—Anthony Gray, Western New Mexico, 1997

PASSING

Highest Passing Efficiency Rating: 221.63—Curt Anes, Grand Valley St, 2001
Most Passes Attempted: 544—Lance Funderburk, Valdosta St, 1995
Most Passes Completed: 356—Lance Funderburk, Valdosta St, 1995
Most Passes Completed per Game: 32.4—Lance Funderburk, Valdosta St, 1995
Highest Completion Percentage: 74.7—Chris Hatcher, Valdosta St, 1994
Most Yards Gained: 4,189—Wilkie Perez, Glenville St, 1997
Most Yards Gained per Game: 393.4—Grady Benton, W Texas A&M, 1994

RECEIVING

Most Passes Caught: 119—Brad Bailey, W Texas A&M, 1994
Most Yards Gained: 1,876—Chris George, Glenville St, 1993
Most Yards Gained per Game: 187.6—Chris George, Glenville St, 1993
Highest Average Gain per Reception: 32.5—Tyrone Johnson, Western St, 1991 (min. 30 receptions)

Single Game

SCORING

Most Points Scored: 48—Paul Zaeske, N Park, 1968 (vs N Central); Junior Wolf, Panhandle St, 1958 (vs St. Mary [KS])
Most Field Goals: 6—Steve Huff, Central Missouri St, 1985 (vs SE Missouri St)

RUSHING

Most Yards Gained: 405—Alvon Brown, Kentucky St, 2000 (vs Kentucky Wesleyan)
Most Touchdowns Rushed: 8—Junior Wolf, Panhandle St, 1958 (vs St. Mary [KS])

PASSING

Most Passes Completed: 56—Jarrod DeGeorgia, Wayne St (NE),1996 (vs Drake)
Most Yards Gained: 645—Matt Kohn, Indianapolis, 2003 (vs Michigan Tech)
Most Touchdowns Passed: 10—Bruce Swanson, N Park, 1968 (vs N Central)

RECEIVING

Most Passes Caught: 23—Chris George, Glenville St, 1994 (vs WV Wesleyan); Barry Wagner, Alabama A&M, 1989 (vs Clark Atlanta)
Most Yards Gained: 401—Kevin Ingram, W Chester, 1998 (vs Clarion)
Most Touchdown Catches: 8—Paul Zaeske, N Park, 1968 (vs N Central)

NCAA Division III Individual Records

Career

SCORING

Most Points Scored: 562—R.J. Bowers, Grove City, 1997–00
Most Touchdowns Scored: 92—R.J. Bowers, Grove City, 1997–00
Most Touchdowns Scored, Rushing: 91—R.J. Bowers, Grove City, 1997–00
Most Touchdowns Scored, Passing: 148—Justin Peery, Westminster (MO), 1996–99
Most Touchdowns Scored, Receiving: 75—Scott Pingel, Westminster (MO), 1996–99

RUSHING

Most Rushes: 1,190—Steve Tardif, Maine Maritime, 1996–99
Most Rushes per Game: 32.7—Chris Sizemore, Bridgewater (VA), 1972–74
Most Yards Gained: 7,353—R.J. Bowers, Grove City, 1997–00
Most Yards Gained per Game: 183.8—R.J. Bowers, Grove City, 1997–00

PASSING

Highest Passing Efficiency Rating: 194.2—Bill Borchert, Mount Union, 1994–97
Most Passes Attempted: 1,696—Kirk Baumgartner, WI–Stevens Point, 1986–89
Most Passes Completed: 1,012—Justin Peery, Westminster (MO), 1996–99
Most Passes Completed per Game: 25.9—Justin Peery, Westminster (MO), 1996–99
Highest Completion Percentage: 67.0—Gary Smeck, Mount Union, 1997–00
Most Yards Gained: 13,262—Justin Peery, Westminster (MO), 1996–99
Most Yards Gained per Game: 340.1—Justin Peery, Westminster (MO), 1996–99

RECEIVING

Most Passes Caught: 436—Scott Pingel, Westminster (MO), 1996–99
Most Yards Gained: 6,108—Scott Pingel, Westminster (MO), 1996–99
Most Yards Gained per Game: 156.6—Scott Pingel, Westminster (MO), 1996–99
Highest Average Gain per Reception: 22.9—Kirk Aikens, Hartwick, 1995–98

Single Season

SCORING

Most Points Scored: 250—Dan Pugh, Mount Union, 2002
Most Points Scored per Game: 20.8—James Regan, Pomona-Pitzer, 1997
Most Touchdowns Scored: 41—Dan Pugh Mount Union, 2002
Most Touchdowns Scored, Rushing: 35—Dan Pugh, Mount Union, 2002
Most Touchdowns Scored, Passing: 54—Justin Peery, Westminster (MO), 1999
Most Touchdowns Scored, Receiving: 26—Scott Pingel, Westminster (MO), 1998

RUSHING

Most Rushes: 380—Mike Birosak, Dickinson, 1989
Most Rushes per Game: 38.0—Mike Birosak, Dickinson, 1989
Most Yards Gained: 2,385—Dante Brown, Marietta, 1996

PASSING

Highest Passing Efficiency Rating: 225.0—Mike Simpson, Eureka, 1994
Most Passes Attempted: 527—Kirk Baumgartner, WI–Stevens Point, 1988
Most Passes Completed: 329—Justin Peery, Westminster (MO), 1999
Most Passes Completed per Game: 32.9—Justin Peery, Westminster (MO), 1999
Highest Completion Percentage: 72.9—Jim Ballard, Mount Union, 1993
Most Yards Gained: 4,501—Justin Peery, Westminster (MO), 1998
Most Yards Gained per Game: 450.1—Justin Peery, Westminster (MO), 1998

RECEIVING

Most Passes Caught: 136—Scott Pingel, Westminster (MO), 1999
Most Yards Gained: 2,157—Scott Pingel, Westminster, (MO), 1998
Most Yards Gained per Game: 215.7—Scott Pingel, Westminster, (MO), 1998
Highest Average Gain per Reception: 26.9—Marty Redlawsk, Concordia (IL), 1985

Single Game

SCORING

Most Field Goals: 6—Jim Hever, Rhodes, 1984 (vs Millsaps)

PASSING

Most Passes Completed: 51—Scott Kello, Sul Ross St, 2002 (vs Howard Payne)
Most Yards Gained: 731—Zamir Amin, Menlo, 2000 (vs California Lutheran)
Most Touchdown Passes: 9—Joe Zarlinga, Ohio Northern, 1998 (vs Capital)

RUSHING

Most Yards Gained: 441—Dante Brown, Marietta, 1996 (vs Baldwin-Wallace)
Most Touchdowns Rushed: 8—Carey Bender, Coe, 1994 (vs Beloit)

RECEIVING

Most Passes Caught: 23—Sean Munroe, Mass-Boston, 1992 (vs Mass-Maritime)
Most Yards Gained: 418—Lewis Howes, Principia, 2002 (vs Martin Luther)
Most Touchdown Catches: 7—Matt Perceval, Wesleyan (CT), 1998 (vs Middlebury)

Career

Scoring

POINTS (KICKERS)

	Years	Pts
Roman Anderson, Houston	1988–91	423
Billy Bennett, Georgia	2000–03	409
Carlos Huerta, Miami (FL)	1988–91	397
Jason Elam, Hawaii	1988–92	395
Derek Schmidt, Florida St	1984–87	393

POINTS (NON-KICKERS)

	Years	Pts
Travis Prentice, Miami (OH)	1996–99	468
Ricky Williams, Texas	1995–98	452
Brock Forsey, Boise St	1999–02	408
Anthony Thompson, Indiana	1986–89	394
Ron Dayne, Wisconsin	1996–99	378

POINTS PER GAME (NON-KICKERS)

	Years	Pts/Game
Marshall Faulk, San Diego St	1991–93	12.1
Ed Marinaro, Cornell	1969–71	11.8
Bill Burnett, Arkansas	1968–70	11.3
Steve Owens, Oklahoma	1967–69	11.2
Eddie Talboom, Wyoming	1948–50	10.8

Total Offense

YARDS GAINED

	Years	Yds
Ty Detmer, Brigham Young	1988–91	14,665
Philip Rivers, N Carolina St	2000–03	13,582
Luke McCown, Louisiana Tech	2000–03	12,731
Timmy Chang, Hawaii	2000–03	12,637
Tim Rattay, Louisiana Tech	1997–99	12,618

YARDS PER GAME

	Years	Yds/Game
Tim Rattay, Louisiana Tech	1997–99	382.4
Chris Vargas, Nevada	1992–93	320.9
Ty Detmer, Brigham Young	1988–91	318.8
Daunte Culpepper, Central Florida	1996–98	313.5
Mike Perez, San Jose St	1986–87	309.1

Rushing

YARDS GAINED

	Years	Yds
Ron Dayne, Wisconsin	1996–99	6,397
Ricky Williams, Texas	1995–98	6,279
Tony Dorsett, Pittsburgh	1973–76	6,082
Charles White, Southern Cal	1976–79	5,598
Travis Prentice, Miami (OH)	1996–99	5,596

YARDS PER GAME

	Years	Yds/Game
Ed Marinaro, Cornell	1969–71	174.6
O.J. Simpson, Southern Cal	1967–68	164.4
Herschel Walker, Georgia	1980–82	159.4
LeShon Johnson, Northern Illinois	1992–93	150.6
Ron Dayne, Wisconsin	1996–99	148.8

TOUCHDOWNS RUSHING

	Years	TD
Travis Prentice, Miami (OH)	1996–99	73
Ricky Williams, Texas	1995–98	72
Anthony Thompson, Indiana	1986–89	64
Ron Dayne, Wisconsin	1996–99	63
Eric Crouch, Nebraska	1998–01	59

Passing

PASSING EFFICIENCY

	Years	Rating
Ryan Dinwiddie, Boise St	2000–03	168.4
Danny Wuerffel, Florida	1993–96	163.6
Ty Detmer, Brigham Young	1988–91	162.7
Steve Sarkisian, Brigham Young	1995–96	162.0
Billy Blanton, San Diego St	1993–96	157.1

Note: Minimum 500 completions.

YARDS GAINED

	Years	Yds
Ty Detmer, Brigham Young	1988–91	15,031
Philip Rivers, N Carolina St	2000–03	13,484
Timmy Chang, Hawaii	2000–03	12,814
Tim Rattay, Louisiana Tech	1997–99	12,746
Luke McCown, Louisiana Tech	2000–03	12,666

COMPLETIONS

	Years	Comp
Kliff Kingsbury, Texas Tech	1999–02	1,231
Chris Redman, Louisville	1996–99	1,031
Tim Rattay, Louisiana Tech	1997–99	1,015
Ty Detmer, Brigham Young	1988–91	958
Drew Brees, Purdue	1997–00	942

TOUCHDOWNS PASSING

	Years	TD
Ty Detmer, Brigham Young	1988–91	121
Tim Rattay, Louisiana Tech	1997–99	115
Danny Wuerffel, Florida	1993–96	114
Chad Pennington, Marshall	1997–99	100
Kliff Kingsbury, Texas Tech	1999–02	95
Philip Rivers, N Carolina St	2000–03	95

Receiving

CATCHES

	Years	No.
Arnold Jackson, Louisville	1997–00	300
Trevor Insley, Nevada	1996–99	298
Geoff Noisy, Nevada	1995–98	295
Rashaun Woods, Oklahoma St	2000–03	293
Troy Edwards, Louisiana Tech	1996–98	280

CATCHES PER GAME

	Years	No./Game
Emmanuel Hazard, Houston	1989–90	10.5
Alex Van Dyke, Nevada	1994–95	10.3
Howard Twilley, Tulsa	1963–65	10.0
Jason Phillips, Houston	1987–88	9.4
Troy Edwards, Louisiana Tech	1996–98	8.2
Bryan Reeves, Nevada	1992–93	8.2

YARDS GAINED

	Years	Yds
Trevor Insley, Nevada	1996–99	5,005
Marcus Harris, Wyoming	1993–96	4,518
Rashaun Woods, Oklahoma St	2000–03	4,412
Ryan Yarborough, Wyoming	1990–93	4,357
Troy Edwards, Louisiana Tech	1996–98	4,352

TOUCHDOWN CATCHES

	Years	TD
Troy Edwards, Louisiana Tech	1996–98	50
Darius Watts, Marshall	2000–03	47
Aaron Turner, Pacific	1989–92	43
Ryan Yarborough, Wyoming	1990–93	42
Rashaun Woods, Oklahoma St	2000–03	42
Marcus Harris, Wyoming	1993–96	38
Clarkston Hines, Duke	1986–89	38

Career (Cont.)

All-Purpose Running

YARDS GAINED	Years	Yds
Ricky Williams, Texas	1996–98	7,206
Napoleon McCallum, Navy	1981–85	7,172
Darrin Nelson, Stanford	1977–78, 80–81	6,885
Kevin Faulk, Louisiana St	1995–98	6,833
Ron Dayne, Wisconsin	1996–99	6,701

YARDS PER GAME	Years	Yds/Game
Ryan Benjamin, Pacific	1990–92	237.8
Sheldon Canley, San Jose St	1988–90	205.8
Howard Stevens, Louisville	1971–72	193.7
O.J. Simpson, Southern Cal	1967–68	192.9
Alex Van Dyke, Nevada	1994–95	188.5

Interceptions

PLAYER/SCHOOL	Years	Int
Al Brosky, Illinois	1950–52	29
John Provost, Holy Cross	1972–74	27
Martin Bayless, Bowling Green	1980–83	27
Tom Curtis, Michigan	1967–69	25
Tony Thurman, Boston Col	1981–84	25
Tracy Saul, Texas Tech	1989–92	25

Punting Average

PLAYER/SCHOOL	Years	Avg
Todd Sauerbrun, W Virginia	1991–94	46.3
Reggie Roby, Iowa	1979–82	45.6
Greg Montgomery, Michigan St	1985–87	45.4
Tom Tupa, Ohio St	1984–87	45.2
Barry Helton, Colorado	1984–87	44.9

Note: 150–249 punts.

Punt Return Average

PLAYER/SCHOOL	Years	Avg
Jack Mitchell, Oklahoma	1946–48	23.6
Gene Gibson, Cincinnati	1949–50	20.5
Eddie Macon, Pacific	1949–51	18.9
Jackie Robinson, UCLA	1939–40	18.8
Bobby Dillon, Texas	1949–51	17.7
Mike Fuller, Auburn	1972–74	17.7

Note: At least 30 returns.

Kickoff Return Average

PLAYER/SCHOOL	Years	Avg
Anthony Davis, Southern Cal	1972–74	35.1
Eric Booth, Southern Miss	1994–97	32.4
Overton Curtis, Utah St	1957–58	31.0
Fred Montgomery, New Mexico St	1991–92	30.5
Altie Taylor, Utah St	1966–68	29.3

Note: At least 30 returns.

Single Season

Scoring

POINTS	Year	Pts
Barry Sanders, Oklahoma St	1988	234
Brock Forsey, Boise St	2002	192
Troy Edwards, Louisiana Tech	1998	188
Mike Rozier, Nebraska	1983	174
Lydell Mitchell, Penn St	1971	174

FIELD GOALS	Year	FG
Billy Bennett, Georgia	2003	31
John Lee, UCLA	1984	29
Paul Woodside, W Virginia	1982	28
Luis Zendejas, Arizona St	1983	28
Nick Browne, Texas Christian	2003	28

Three tied with 27.

All-Purpose Running

YARDS GAINED	Year	Yds
Barry Sanders, Oklahoma St	1988	3,250
Ryan Benjamin, Pacific	1991	2,995
Troy Edwards, Louisiana Tech	1998	2,794
Darren Sproles, Kansas St	2003	2,735
Mike Pringle, Fullerton St	1989	2,690

All-Purpose Running (Cont.)

YARDS PER GAME	Year	Yds/Game
Barry Sanders, Oklahoma St	1988	295.5
Ryan Benjamin, Pacific	1991	249.6
Byron (Whizzer) White, Colorado	1937	246.3
Mike Pringle, Fullerton St	1989	244.6
Paul Palmer, Temple	1986	239.4

Total Offense

YARDS GAINED	Year	Yds
B.J. Symons, Texas Tech	2003	5,976
David Klingler, Houston	1990	5,221
Ty Detmer, Brigham Young	1990	5,022
Kliff Kingsbury, Texas Tech	2002	4,903
Tim Rattay, Louisiana Tech	1998	4,840

YARDS PER GAME	Year	Yds/Game
David Klingler, Houston	1990	474.6
B.J. Symons, Texas Tech	2003	459.7
Andre Ware, Houston	1989	423.7
Ty Detmer, Brigham Young	1990	418.5
Tim Rattay, Louisiana Tech	1998	403.3

Single Season *(Cont.)*

Rushing

YARDS GAINED

	Year	Yds
Barry Sanders, Oklahoma St	1988	2,628
Marcus Allen, Southern Cal	1981	2,342
Troy Davis, Iowa St	1996	2,185
LaDainian Tomlinson, Texas Christian	2000	2,158
Mike Rozier, Nebraska	1983	2,148

YARDS PER GAME

	Year	Yds/Game
Barry Sanders, Oklahoma St	1988	238.9
Marcus Allen, Southern Cal	1981	212.9
Ed Marinaro, Cornell	1971	209.0
Troy Davis, Iowa St	1996	198.6
LaDainian Tomlinson, Texas Christian	2000	196.2

TOUCHDOWNS RUSHING

	Year	TD
Barry Sanders, Oklahoma St	1988	37
Mike Rozier, Nebraska	1983	29
Willis McGahee, Miami (FL)	2002	28
Ricky Williams, Texas	1998	27
Lee Suggs, Virginia Tech	2000	27
Brock Forsey, Boise St	2002	26

Passing

PASSING EFFICIENCY

	Year	Rating
Shaun King, Tulane	1998	183.3
Michael Vick, Virginia Tech	1999	180.4
Danny Wuerffel, Florida	1995	178.4
Jim McMahon, Brigham Young	1980	176.9
Ty Detmer, Brigham Young	1989	175.6

YARDS GAINED

	Year	Yds
B.J. Symons, Texas Tech	2003	5,833
Ty Detmer, Brigham Young	1990	5,188
David Klingler, Houston	1990	5,140
Kliff Kingsbury, Texas Tech	2002	5,017
Tim Rattay, Louisiana Tech	1998	4,943

COMPLETIONS

	Year	Att	Comp
Kliff Kingsbury, Texas Tech	2002	712	479
B.J. Symons, Texas Tech	2003	719	470
Tim Couch, Kentucky	1998	553	400
Tim Rattay, Louisiana Tech	1998	559	380
David Klingler, Houston	1990	643	374

Passing *(Cont.)*

TOUCHDOWNS PASSING

	Year	TD
David Klingler, Houston	1990	54
B.J. Symons, Texas Tech	2003	52
Jim McMahon, Brigham Young	1980	47
Andre Ware, Houston	1989	46
Tim Rattay, Louisiana Tech	1998	46

Receiving

CATCHES

	Year	GP	No.
Emmanuel Hazard, Houston	1989	11	142
Troy Edwards, Louisiana Tech	1998	12	140
Nate Burleson, Nevada	2002	12	138
Howard Twilley, Tulsa	1965	10	134
Trevor Insley, Nevada	1999	11	134

CATCHES PER GAME

	Year	No.	No./Game
Howard Twilley, Tulsa	1965	134	13.4
Emmanuel Hazard, Houston	1989	142	12.9
Trevor Insley, Nevada	1999	134	12.2
Troy Edwards, Louisiana Tech	1998	140	11.7
Alex Van Dyke, Nevada	1995	129	11.7

YARDS GAINED

	Year	Yds
Trevor Insley, Nevada	1999	2,060
Troy Edwards, Louisiana Tech	1998	1,996
Alex Van Dyke, Nevada	1995	1,854
J.R. Tolver, San Diego St	2002	1,785
Howard Twilley, Tulsa	1965	1,779

TOUCHDOWN CATCHES

	Year	TD
Troy Edwards, Louisiana Tech	1998	27
Randy Moss, Marshall	1997	25
Emmanuel Hazard, Houston	1989	22
Larry Fitzgerald, Pittsburgh	2003	22
Desmond Howard, Michigan	1991	19
Ashley Lelie, Hawaii	2001	19

Single Game

Scoring

POINTS

	Opponent	Year	Pts
Howard Griffith, Illinois	Southern Illinois	1990	48
Marshall Faulk, San Diego St	Pacific	1991	44
Jim Brown, Syracuse	Colgate	1956	43
Showboat Boykin, Mississippi	Mississippi St	1951	42
Fred Wendt, UTEP*	New Mexico St	1948	42
Rashaun Woods, Oklahoma St	SMU	2003	42

*UTEP was Texas Mines in 1948.

FIELD GOALS

	Opponent	Year	FG
Dale Klein, Nebraska	Missouri	1985	7
Mike Prindle, Western Michigan	Marshall	1984	7

Note: 14 tied with 6.

Klein's distances were 32-22-43-44-29-43-43. Prindle's distances were 32-44-42-23-48-41-27.

Single Game (Cont.)

Total Offense

YARDS GAINED	Opponent	Year	Yds
David Klingler, Houston	Arizona St	1990	732
Matt Vogler, TCU	Houston	1990	696
B.J. Symons, Texas Tech	Mississippi	2003	681
Brian Lindgren, Idaho	Middle Tenn St	2001	657
David Klingler, Houston	Texas Christian	1990	625
Scott Mitchell, Utah	Air Force	1988	625

Passing

YARDS GAINED	Opponent	Year	Yds
David Klingler, Houston	Arizona St	1990	716
Matt Vogler, TCU	Houston	1990	690
B.J. Symons, Texas Tech	Mississippi	2003	661
Brian Lindgren, Idaho	Middle Tenn St	2001	637
Scott Mitchell, Utah	Air Force	1988	631

COMPLETIONS	Opponent	Year	Comp
Drew Brees, Purdue	Wisconsin	1998	55
Rusty LaRue, Wake Forest	Duke	1995	55
Rusty LaRue, Wake Forest	NC St	1995	50
Brian Lindgren, Idaho	Middle Tenn St	2001	49
Kliff Kingsbury, Texas Tech	Missouri	2002	49
Kliff Kingsbury, Texas Tech	Texas A&M	2002	49
Bruce Gradkowski, Toledo	Pittsburgh	2003	49

TOUCHDOWNS PASSING	Opponent	Year	TD
David Klingler, Houston	E Wash	1990	11

Note: Klingler's TD passes were 5-48-29-7-3-7-40-10-7-8-51.

Rushing

YARDS GAINED	Opponent	Year	Yds
LaDainian Tomlinson	UTEP	1999	406
Texas Christian			
Tony Sands, Kansas	Missouri	1991	396
Marshall Faulk,			
San Diego St	Pacific	1991	386
Troy Davis, Iowa St	Missouri	1996	378
Anthony Thompson,			
Indiana	Wisconsin	1989	377
Robbie Mixon,			
Central Michigan	Eastern Mich	2002	377

TOUCHDOWNS RUSHING	Opponent	Year	TD
Howard Griffith, Illinois	Southern Illinois	1990	8

Note: Griffith's TD runs were 5-51-7-41-5-18-5-3.

Receiving

CATCHES	Opponent	Year	No.
Randy Gatewood, UNLV	Idaho	1994	23
Jay Miller, Brigham Young	New Mexico	1973	22
Troy Edwards, La. Tech	Nebraska	1998	21
Chris Daniels, Purdue	Michigan St	1999	21
Rick Eber, Tulsa	Idaho St	1967	20
Kenny Christian,			
Eastern Michigan	Temple	2000	20

YARDS GAINED	Opponent	Year	Yds
Troy Edwards, Louisiana Tech	Nebraska	1998	405
Randy Gatewood, UNLV	Idaho	1994	363
Chuck Hughes, UTEP*	N Texas St	1965	349
Nate Burleson, Nevada	San Jose St	2001	326
Rick Eber, Tulsa	Idaho St	1967	322

*UTEP was Texas Western in 1965.

TOUCHDOWN CATCHES	Opponent	Year	TD
Rashaun Woods, Okla. St	SMU	2003	7
Tim Delaney, San Diego St	New Mex. St	1969	6

Longest Plays (since 1941)

PASSING	Opponent	Year	Yds
Fred Owens to Jack Ford, Portland	St. Mary's (CA)	1947	99
Bo Burris to Warren McVea, Houston	Washington St	1966	99
Colin Clapton to Eddie Jenkins, Holy Cross	Boston U	1970	99
Terry Peel to Robert Ford, Houston	Syracuse	1970	99
Terry Peel to Robert Ford, Houston	San Diego St	1972	99
Cris Collinsworth to Derrick Gaffney, Florida	Rice	1977	99
Scott Ankrom to James Maness, Texas Christian	Rice	1984	99
Gino Toretta to Horace Copeland, Miami (FL)	Arkansas	1991	99
John Paci to Thomas Lewis, Indiana	Penn St	1993	99
Troy DeGar to Wes Caswell, Tulsa	Oklahoma	1996	99
Drew Brees to Vinny Sutherland, Purdue	Northwestern	1999	99
Dan Urban to Justin McCariens, Northern Illinois	Ball St	2000	99
Jason Johnson to Brandon Marshall, Arizona	Idaho	2001	99
Dondrial Pinkins to Troy Williamson, S Carolina	Virginia	2003	99

RUSHING	Opponent	Year	Yd
Gale Sayers, Kansas	Nebraska	1963	99
Max Anderson, Arizona St	Wyoming	1967	99
Ralph Thompson, W Texas St	Wichita St	1970	99
Kelsey Finch, Tennessee	Florida	1977	99
Eric Vann, Kansas	Oklahoma	1997	99

FIELD GOALS	Opponent	Year	Yds
Steve Little, Arkansas	Texas	1977	67
Russell Erxleben, Texas	Rice	1977	67
Joe Williams, Wichita St	Southern IL	1978	67
Martin Gramatica, Kansas St	Northern IL	1998	65
Tony Franklin, Texas A&M	Baylor	1976	65

PUNTS	Opponent	Year	Yds
Pat Brady, Nevada*	Loyola (CA)	1950	99
George O'Brien, Wisconsin	Iowa	1952	96
John Hadl, Kansas	Oklahoma	1959	94
Carl Knox, Texas Christian	Oklahoma St	1947	94
Preston Johnson, SMU	Pittsburgh	1940	94

*Nevada was Nevada-Reno in 1950.

DIVISION I-A WINNINGEST TEAMS

Alltime Winning Percentage

	Yrs	W	L	T	Pct	GP	Bowl Record
Notre Dame	115	796	257	42	.746	1,095	13-12-0
Michigan	125	833	272	36	.746	1,141	17-17-0
Alabama	109	758	293	43	.713	1,094	29-19-3
Oklahoma	109	737	284	53	.711	1,074	22-13-1
Texas	111	776	309	33	.709	1,118	20-21-2
Ohio St	114	756	294	53	.709	1,103	16-19-0
Nebraska	114	781	311	40	.708	1,132	21-21-0
Tennessee	107	736	302	52	.699	1,090	23-21-0
Southern Cal	111	707	297	54	.694	1,058	27-15-0
Penn St	117	756	331	41	.688	1,128	23-12-2
Boise St	36	284	135	2	.677	421	4-0-0
Florida St	57	419	197	17	.675	633	18-12-2
Miami (OH)	115	624	343	44	.639	1,011	6-2-0
Georgia	110	673	370	54	.638	1,097	21-15-3
Washington	114	638	353	50	.637	1,041	14-14-1
Miami (FL)	77	507	285	19	.637	811	16-12-0
Louisiana St	110	649	369	47	.632	1,065	17-17-1
Auburn	111	634	379	47	.620	1,060	16-12-2
Arizona St	91	507	310	24	.617	841	10-8-1
Florida	97	590	359	40	.617	989	13-17-0
Colorado	114	635	391	36	.615	1,062	11-14-0
Central Michigan	103	522	326	36	.611	884	0-2-0
Texas A&M	109	627	404	48	.603	1,079	13-14-0
Army	114	622	406	51	.600	1,079	2-2-0
UCLA	85	505	330	37	.600	872	12-10-1

Note: Includes bowl games.

Alltime Victories

Michigan	833	Georgia	673	Army	622
Notre Dame	796	Syracuse	658	N Carolina	621
Nebraska	781	Louisiana St	649	Pittsburgh	620
Texas	776	Washington	638	Arkansas	619
Alabama	758	Colorado	635	Minnesota	609
Penn St	756	Auburn	634	Virginia Tech	605
Ohio St	756	Texas A&M	627	Clemson	594
Oklahoma	737	Miami (OH)	624	Florida	590
Tennessee	736	Georgia Tech	623	Navy	589
Southern Cal	707	W Virginia	623	Mississippi	583

NUMBER ONE VS NUMBER TWO

The No. 1 and No. 2 teams, according to the Associated Press Poll, have met 33 times, including 13 bowl games, since the poll's inception in 1936. The No. 1 teams have a 20-11-2 record in these matchups. Notre Dame (4-3-2) has played in nine of the games.

Date	Results	Stadium
10-9-43	No. 1 Notre Dame 35, No. 2 Michigan 12	Michigan (Ann Arbor)
11-20-43	No. 1 Notre Dame 14, No. 2 Iowa Pre-Flight 13	Notre Dame (South Bend)
12-2-44	No. 1 Army 23, No. 2 Navy 7	Municipal (Baltimore)
11-10-45	No. 1 Army 48, No. 2 Notre Dame 0	Yankee (New York)
12-1-45	No. 1 Army 32, No. 2 Navy 13	Municipal (Philadelphia)
11-9-46	No. 1 Army 0, No. 2 Notre Dame 0	Yankee (New York)
1-1-63	No. 1 Southern Cal 42, No. 2 Wisconsin 37 (Rose Bowl)	Rose Bowl (Pasadena)
10-12-63	No. 2 Texas 28, No. 1 Oklahoma 7	Cotton Bowl (Dallas)
1-1-64	No. 1 Texas 28, No. 2 Navy 6 (Cotton Bowl)	Cotton Bowl (Dallas)
11-19-66	No. 1 Notre Dame 10, No. 2 Michigan St 10	Spartan (E Lansing)
9-28-68	No. 1 Purdue 37, No. 2 Notre Dame 22	Notre Dame (South Bend)
1-1-69	No. 1 Ohio St 27, No. 2 Southern Cal 16 (Rose Bowl)	Rose Bowl (Pasadena)
12-6-69	No. 1 Texas 15, No. 2 Arkansas 14	Razorback (Fayetteville)
11-25-71	No. 1 Nebraska 35, No. 2 Oklahoma 31	Owen Field (Norman)
1-1-72	No. 1 Nebraska 38, No. 2 Alabama 6 (Orange Bowl)	Orange Bowl (Miami)
1-1-79	No. 2 Alabama 14, No. 1 Penn St 7 (Sugar Bowl)	Sugar Bowl (New Orleans)
9-26-81	No. 1 Southern Cal 28, No. 2 Oklahoma 24	Coliseum (Los Angeles)
1-1-83	No. 2 Penn St 27, No. 1 Georgia 23 (Sugar Bowl)	Sugar Bowl (New Orleans)

NUMBER ONE VS NUMBER TWO *(Cont.)*

Date	Results	Stadium
10-19-85	No. 1 Iowa 12, No. 2 Michigan 10	Kinnick (Iowa City)
9-27-86	No. 2 Miami (FL) 28, No. 1 Oklahoma 16	Orange Bowl (Miami)
1-2-87	No. 2 Penn St 14, No. 1 Miami (FL) 10 (Fiesta Bowl)	Sun Devil (Tempe)
11-21-87	No. 2 Oklahoma 17, No. 1 Nebraska 7	Memorial (Lincoln)
1-1-88	No. 2 Miami (FL) 20, No. 1 Oklahoma 14 (Orange Bowl)	Orange Bowl (Miami)
11-26-88	No. 1 Notre Dame 27, No. 2 Southern Cal 10	Coliseum (Los Angeles)
9-16-89	No. 1 Notre Dame 24, No. 2 Michigan 19	Michigan (Ann Arbor)
11-16-91	No. 2 Miami (FL) 17, No. 1 Florida St 16	Campbell (Tallahassee)
1-1-93	No. 2 Alabama 34, No. 1 Miami (FL) 13 (Sugar Bowl)	Superdome (New Orleans)
11-13-93	No. 2 Notre Dame 31, No. 1 Florida St 24	Notre Dame (South Bend)
1-1-94	No. 1 Florida St 18, No. 2 Nebraska 16 (Orange Bowl)	Orange Bowl (Miami)
1-2-96	No. 1 Nebraska 62, No. 2 Florida 24 (Fiesta Bowl)	Sun Devil (Tempe)
11-30-96	No. 2 Florida St 24, No. 1 Florida 21	Campbell (Tallahassee)
1-4-99	No. 1 Tennessee 23, No. 2 Florida St 16 (Fiesta Bowl)	Sun Devil (Tempe)
1-4-00	No. 1 Florida St 46, No. 2 Virginia Tech 29 (Sugar Bowl)	Superdome (New Orleans)
1-3-03	No. 2 Ohio St 31, Miami (FL) 24 [2OT] (Fiesta Bowl)	Sun Devil (Tempe)

LONGEST DIVISION I-A WINNING STREAKS

Wins	Team	Yrs	Ended by	Score
47	Oklahoma	1953–57	Notre Dame	7–0
39	Washington	1908–14	Oregon St	0–0
37	Yale	1890–93	Princeton	6–0
37	Yale	1887–89	Princeton	10–0
35	Toledo	1969–71	Tampa	21–0
34	Miami	2000–03	Ohio St	31–24 (2ot)
34	Pennsylvania	1894–96	Lafayette	6–4
31	Oklahoma	1948–50	Kentucky	13–7
31	Pittsburgh	1914–18	Cleveland Naval Reserve	10–9
31	Pennsylvania	1896–98	Harvard	10–0
30	Texas	1968–70	Notre Dame	24–11

LONGEST DIVISION I-A UNBEATEN STREAKS

No.	W	T	Team	Yrs	Ended by	Score
63	59	4	Washington	1907–17	California	27–0
56	55	1	Michigan	1901–05	Chicago	2–0
50	46	4	California	1920–25	Olympic Club	15–0
48	47	1	Oklahoma	1953–57	Notre Dame	7–0
48	47	1	Yale	1885–89	Princeton	10–0
47	42	5	Yale	1879–85	Princeton	6–5
44	42	2	Yale	1894–96	Princeton	24–6
42	39	3	Yale	1904–08	Harvard	4–0
39	37	2	Notre Dame	1946–50	Purdue	28–14
37	36	1	Oklahoma	1972–75	Kansas	23–3
37	37	0	Yale	1890–93	Princeton	6–0
35	35	0	Toledo	1969–71	Tampa	21–0
35	34	1	Minnesota	1903–05	Wisconsin	16–12
34	34	0	Miami	2000–03	Ohio St	31–24 (2ot)
34	33	1	Nebraska	1912–16	Kansas	7–3
34	34	0	Pennsylvania	1894–96	Lafayette	6–4
34	32	2	Princeton	1884–87	Harvard	12–0
34	29	5	Princeton	1877–82	Harvard	1–0
33	30	3	Tennessee	1926–30	Alabama	18–6
33	31	2	Georgia Tech	1914–18	Pittsburgh	32–0
33	30	3	Harvard	1911–15	Cornell	10–0
32	31	1	Nebraska	1969–71	UCLA	20–17
32	30	2	Army	1944–47	Columbia	21–20
32	31	1	Harvard	1898–1900	Yale	28–0
31	30	1	Penn St	1967–70	Colorado	41–13
31	30	1	San Diego St	1967–70	Long Beach St	27–11
31	29	2	Georgia Tech	1950–53	Notre Dame	27–14
31	31	0	Oklahoma	1948–50	Kentucky	13–7
31	31	0	Pittsburgh	1914–18	Cleveland Naval	10–9
31	31	0	Pennsylvania	1896–98	Harvard	10–0

Note: Includes bowl games.

LONGEST DIVISION I-A LOSING STREAKS

Losses		Seasons	Ended Against	Score
34	Northwestern	1979–82	Northern Illinois	31–6
28	Virginia	1958–61	William & Mary	21–6
28	Kansas St	1945–48	Arkansas St	37–6
27	New Mexico St	1988–90	Cal St–Fullerton	43–9
27	Eastern Michigan	1980–82	Kent St	9–7

MOST-PLAYED DIVISION I-A RIVALRIES

GP	Opponents (Series Leader Listed First)	Record	First Game	GP	Opponents (Series Leader Listed First)	Record	First Game
113	Minnesota–Wisconsin	59-46-8	1890	101	Clemson–S Carolina	61-36-4	1896
112	Missouri–Kansas	52-51-9	1891	101	Kansas–Kansas St	61-35-5	1902
110	Nebraska-Kansas	86-21-3	1892	100	Mississippi–Miss St	57-37-6	1901
110	Texas–Texas A&M	71-34-5	1894	100	N Carolina–Wake Forest	66-31-2	1888
108	Miami (OH)–Cincinnati	58-43-7	1888	99	Michigan–Ohio St	57-37-6	1897
108	N Carolina–Virginia	†56-48-4	1892	99	Tennessee–Kentucky	67-23-9	1893
107	Auburn–Georgia	51-48-8	1892	98	Georgia–Georgia Tech	55-38-5	1893
107	Oregon–Oregon St	54-43-10	1894	98	Nebraska–Iowa St	81-15-2	1896
106	Purdue–Indiana	65-35-6	1891	98	Texas–Oklahoma	55-38-5	1900
106	Stanford–California	54-41-11	1892	98	Oklahoma–Oklahoma St	75-16-7	1904
104	Army–Navy	49-48-7	1890	97	Oklahoma–Kansas	63-28-6	1903
103	Baylor–Texas Christian*	49-47-7	1899				
103	Utah–Utah St	71-28-4	1892				

*Have not met since 1995.
†Disputed series record: Virginia claims N Carolina leads series 54-49-4 based on a forfeited game in 1956.

NCAA Coaches' Records

ALLTIME WINNINGEST DIVISION I-A COACHES

Coach (Alma Mater)	Colleges Coached	Yrs	W	L	T	Pct
Knute Rockne (Notre Dame '14)†	Notre Dame 1918–30	13	105	12	5	.881
Frank W. Leahy (Notre Dame '31)†	Boston Col 1939–40; Notre Dame 1941–43, 1946–53	13	107	13	9	.864
George W. Woodruff (Yale 1889)†	Pennsylvania 1892–01; Illinois 1903; Carlisle 1905	12	142	25	2	.846
Barry Switzer (Arkansas '60)	Oklahoma 1973–88	16	157	29	4	.837
Tom Osborne (Hastings '59)†	Nebraska 1973–98	25	255	49	3	.836
Percy D. Haughton (Harvard 1899)†	Cornell 1899–1900; Harvard 1908–16; Columbia 1923–24	13	96	17	6	.832
Bob Neyland (Army '16)†	Tennessee 1926–34, 1936–40, 1946–52	21	173	31	12	.829
Fielding Yost (W Virginia 1895)†	Ohio Wesleyan 1897; Nebraska 1898; Kansas 1899; Stanford 1900; Michigan 1901–23, 1925–26	29	196	36	12	.828
Bud Wilkinson (Minnesota '37)†	Oklahoma 1947–63	17	145	29	4	.826
Jock Sutherland (Pittsburgh '18)†	Lafayette 1919–23; Pittsburgh 1924–38	20	144	28	14	.812
Bob Devaney (Alma, MI '39)†	Wyoming 1957–61; Nebraska 1962–72	16	136	30	7	.806
*Phillip Fulmer (Tennessee '71)	Tennessee 1992–	12	113	28	0	.801
Frank W. Thomas (Notre Dame '23)†	Tenn.-Chattanooga 1925–28; Alabama 1931–42, 1944–46	19	141	33	9	.795
Henry L. Williams (Yale 1891)†	Army 1891; Minnesota 1900–21	23	141	34	12	.786
Gil Dobie (Minnesota '02)†	N Dakota St 1906–07; Washington 1908-16; Navy 1917–19; Cornell 1920–35; Boston College 1936–38	33	180	45	15	.781
Bear Bryant (Alabama '36)†	Maryland 1945, Kentucky 1946–53, Texas A&M 1954–57, Alabama 1958–82	38	323	85	17	.780

*Active in 2003. †Hall of Fame member.
Note: Minimum 10 years as head coach at Division I institutions; record at four-year colleges only; bowl games included; ranked by percentage, ties computed as half won, half lost.

ALLTIME WINNINGEST DIVISION I-A COACHES (Cont.)

By Victories

	Yrs	W	L	T	Pct		Yrs	W	L	T	Pct
*Bobby Bowden	38	342	99	4	.773	Bo Schembechler	27	234	65	8	.775
*Joe Paterno	38	339	109	3	.755	Hayden Fry	37	232	178	10	.564
Paul (Bear) Bryant	38	323	85	17	.780	Jess Neely	40	207	176	19	.539
Glenn (Pop) Warner	44	319	106	32	.733	Warren Woodson	31	203	95	14	.673
Amos Alonzo Stagg	57	314	199	35	.605	Don Nehlen	30	202	128	8	.609
LaVell Edwards	29	257	100	3	.718	Vince Dooley	25	201	77	10	.715
Tom Osborne	25	255	49	3	.836	Eddie Anderson	39	201	128	15	.606
*Lou Holtz	32	243	127	7	.654	*Active in 2003.					
Woody Hayes	33	238	72	10	.759						

Most Bowl Victories

	W	L	T		W	L	T
*Joe Paterno	20	10	1	Barry Switzer	8	5	0
*Bobby Bowden	18	8	1	*Jackie Sherrill	8	6	0
Paul (Bear) Bryant	15	12	2	Darrell Royal	8	7	1
Jim Wacker	13	2	0	Vince Dooley	8	10	2
*Lou Holtz	12	8	2	Pat Dye	7	2	1
Tom Osborne	12	13	0	Bob Devaney	7	3	0
Don James	10	5	0	Dan Devine	7	3	0
John Vaught	10	8	0	Earle Bruce	7	5	0
Bobby Dodd	9	4	0	Charlie McClendon	7	6	0
Johnny Majors	9	7	0	Hayden Fry	7	9	1
*John Robinson	8	1	0	LaVell Edwards	7	14	1
Terry Donahue	8	4	1	*Active in 2003.			

WINNINGEST ACTIVE DIVISION I-A COACHES
By Percentage

						Bowls		
Coach, College	Yrs	W	L	T	Pct#	W	L	T
Bob Pruett, Marshall	8	88	17	0	.838	5	1	0
Phillip Fulmer, Tennessee	12	113	28	0	.801	6	6	0
Bobby Bowden, Florida St	38	342	99	4	.773	18	8	1
Lloyd Carr, Michigan	9	86	26	0	.768	5	4	0
Joe Paterno, Penn St	38	339	109	3	.755	20	10	1
Bill Snyder, Kansas St	15	127	55	1	.697	6	5	0
Nick Saban, Louisiana St	10	82	39	1	.676	3	4	0
Tommy Bowden, Clemson	7	56	28	0	.667	2	3	0
Dennis Franchione, Texas A&M	21	159	81	2	.661	5	2	0
Paul Pasqualoni, Syracuse	18	135	70	1	.658	6	2	0

#Bowl games included in overall record. Ties computed as half win, half loss.

Note: Minimum five years as Division I-A head coach; record at four-year colleges only.

YET ANOTHER SIGN OF THE APOCALYPSE

A 46-year-old Alabama man was charged with attempted murder after he allegedly fired a gun at his son while stewing over the Tide's 2003 loss to Arkansas.

WINNINGEST ACTIVE DIVISION I-A COACHES *(Cont.)*

By Victories

Bobby Bowden, Florida St	342	Ken Hatfield, Rice	164
Joe Paterno, Penn St	339	Dennis Franchione, Texas A&M	159
Lou Holtz, S Carolina	243	Fisher DeBerry, Air Force	156
Jackie Sherrill, Mississippi St	180	Mack Brown, Texas	145
Frank Beamer, Virginia Tech	167	Paul Pasqualoni, Syracuse	135

WINNINGEST ACTIVE DIVISION I-AA COACHES
By Percentage

Coach, College	Yrs	W	L	T	Pct*
Mike Kelly, Dayton	23	215	43	1	.832
Al Bagnoli, Pennsylvania	22	173	51	0	.772
Greg Gattuso, Duquesne	11	90	28	0	.763
Pete Richardson, Southern	16	138	48	1	.741
Dick Biddle, Colgate	8	69	27	0	.719
Roy Kidd, Eastern Kentucky	40	322	128	8	.712
Billy Joe, Florida A&M	30	234	100	4	.698
Joe Taylor, Hampton	21	160	68	4	.698
Alvin Wyatt, Bethune-Cookman	7	54	25	0	.684
Walt Hameline, Wagner	23	163	76	2	.681

*Playoff games included.

Note: Minimum five years as a Division I-A and/or Division I-AA head coach; record at four-year colleges only.

By Victories

Roy Kidd, Eastern Kentucky	322	Al Bagnoli, Pennsylvania	173
Billy Joe, Florida A&M	234	Walt Hameline, Wagner	163
Mike Kelly, Dayton	215	Joe Taylor, Hampton	160
Ron Randleman, Sam Houston St	207	Jimmye Laycock, William & Mary	159
Bill Hayes, N Carolina A&T	205	Andy Talley, Villanova	159

WINNINGEST ACTIVE DIVISION II COACHES
By Percentage

Coach, College	Yrs	W	L	T	Pct*
Bryan Collins, C.W. Post	6	55	11	0	.833
Chuck Broyles, Pittsburg St (KS)	14	140	29	2	.825
Ken Sparks, Carson-Newman	24	234	54	2	.810
Bill Zwaan, West Chester	7	62	17	0	.785
Brian Kelly, Grand Valley St	13	118	35	2	.768
John Luckhardt, California (PA)	19	147	49	2	.748
Peter Yetten, Bentley	16	118	41	1	.741
Danny Hale, Bloomsburg	16	128	48	1	.726
Frank Cignetti, Indiana (PA)	22	186	70	1	.726
Dale Lennon, N Dakota	7	60	23	0	.723

*Ties computed as half win, half loss. Playoff games included.

Note: Minimum five years as a college head coach; record at four-year colleges only.

By Victories

Ken Sparks, Carson-Newman	234	Gary Howard, Central Oklahoma	170
Willard Bailey, Virginia Union	211	Mel Tjeerdsma, NW Missouri St	155
Bud Elliott, Eastern New Mexico	199	John Luckhardt, California (PA)	147
Frank Cignetti, Indiana (PA)	186	Jerry Vandergriff, Angelo St	141
Dennis Douds, E Stroudsburg	178	Monte Cater, Shepherd	141

WINNINGEST ACTIVE DIVISION III
By Percentage

Coach, College	Yrs	W	L	T	Pct*
Larry Kehres, Mount Union	18	205	18	3	.914
Joe Fincham, Wittenberg	8	81	11	0	.880
Rick Willis, Wartburg	7	64	11	0	.853
Dick Farley, Williams	17	114	19	3	.849
Chris Creighton, Wabash	7	59	13	0	.819
Rich Kacmarynski, Central (IA)	7	62	15	0	.805
Jay Locey, Linfield	8	61	17	0	.782
John Gagliardi, St. John's (MN)	55	414	114	11	.778
Jimmie Keeling, Hardin-Simmons	14	117	36	0	.765
Frank Girardi, Lycoming	32	241	74	5	.761

*Ties computed as half won, half lost. Playoff games included.

Note: Minimum five years as a college head coach; record at four-year colleges only.

By Victories

John Gagliardi, St John's (MN)	414	Eric Hamilton, College of New Jersey	172
Frosty Westering, Pacific Lutheran	305	Lou Wacker, Emory & Henry	160
Frank Girardi, Lycoming	241	Wayne Perry, Hanover	158
Larry Kehres, Mount Union	205	Rick Giancola, Montclair St	148
Peter Mazzaferro, Bridgewater (MA)	204	Bob Bierie, Loras	140

NAIA Coaches' Records

WINNINGEST ACTIVE NAIA COACHES
By Percentage

Coach, College	Yrs	W	L	T	Pct*
Bill Cronin, Georgetown (KY)	7	73	13	0	.849
Myron Schulz, Mary (ND)	5	46	10	0	.821
Mike Van Diest, Carroll (MT)	5	52	14	0	.788
Hank Biesiot, Dickinson St (ND)	28	202	69	1	.744
Peter Shinnick, Azusa Pacific (CA)	5	36	15	0	.706
Carl Poelker, McKendree (IL)	22	148	63	1	.700
Bob Young, Sioux Falls (SD)	22	161	68	3	.700
Paul Troth, Missouri Valley	7	51	25	0	.671
Larry Wilcox, Benedictine (KS)	25	177	88	0	.668
Orv Otten, Northwestern (IA)	9	64	32	0	.667
Geno DeMarco, Geneva (PA)	11	78	39	0	.667

*Playoff games included.

Note: Minimum five years as a collegiate head coach and includes record against four-year institutions only.

By Victories

Hank Biesiot, Dickinson St (ND)	202	Carl Poelker, McKendree (IL)	148
Larry Wilcox, Benedictine (KS)	177	Jim Dennison, Walsh (OH)	143
Kevin Donley, St. Francis (IN)	167	Fran Schwenk, Doane (NE)	114
Bob Young, Sioux Falls (SD)	161	Bob Green, Montana Tech	98
Vic Wallace, Lambuth (TN)	154		

Rasheed Wallace
of the NBA champion
Detroit Pistons

Pro Basketball

Under The Radar

While their opponents in the NBA Finals grabbed all the headlines, the Detroit Pistons took home the championship trophy

BY STEPHEN CANNELLA

IN THE END, THE 2003–04 NBA season was about the Detroit Pistons and their surprising run to the NBA championship. Detroit's five-game pasting of the Los Angeles Lakers for the title was one of the biggest upsets in Finals history, and it returned the championship to the blue-collar Eastern Conference for the first-time since 1998, when Michael Jordan dropped the curtain on an era in Chicago.

Yet, as is proven time and time again in Hollywood, the best performances aren't always the ones that draw the most attention. So, for the second year in a row, the carnival caravan that was the Los Angeles Laker basketball team dominated the year's hoop headlines. Never mind that the Lakers failed to win the NBA championship (also for the second year in a row). Forget that they did not finish with the best regular-season record, or suit up the league's leading scorer, rebounder or assist man. And set aside the fact that on many nights, the Lakers' play was maddeningly uninspired, more befitting of an over-40 rec league than a team with four future Hall of Famers in the lineup (Shaquille O'Neal, Gary Payton, Karl Malone and Kobe Bryant) and another (coach Phil Jackson) pulling strings on the bench.

In spite (or because?) of these factors, the Lakers owned the spotlight for most of the season, overshadowing less dysfunctional stories like the unexpected success of Chauncey Billups, Tayshaun Prince, Rasheed Wallace and the rest of the Pistons; the dominating performance of league MVP Kevin Garnett of the Minnesota Timberwolves; and the emergence of two of the most scintillating rookies to come along in years, LeBron James and Carmelo Anthony, who rekindled memories of the league-saving rivalry that blossomed when Larry Bird and Magic Johnson arrived in 1979.

If the NBA were the network schedule, those stories would be the equivalent of *Masterpiece Theater* and *Meet the Press*— quality programs that have trouble drawing an audience. The Lakers, undoubtedly, would be a ratings-devouring reality series. But which one? *The Real World*, perhaps,

Finals MVP Billups soared for 21 points a game against L.A.

with its multiple internecine feuds (see Shaq vs. Kobe), and potentially-awkward romantic plotline (Jackson was dating owner Jerry Buss's daughter, Jeanie). Or maybe a real-life edition of *Law & Order*, considering the year-long legal circus that enveloped Bryant, who spent the season with one foot in the L.A. backcourt and the other in an Eagle, Col., courtroom. He was scheduled to stand trial in August 2004 on charges that he sexually assaulted a woman in June of the previous year, and faced four years to life in prison if convicted.

In the end, though, *Survivor* may have matched most closely the fate of our favorite characters in Purple and Gold, whose dynasty quickly unraveled after the season. Three days after his team was dispatched 100–87 by the Pistons in Game 5, Jackson walked away from his coaching duties. O'Neal was voted off the the island, traded to the Miami Heat in a multi-player deal, a few weeks later. Bryant, who opted out of the final year of his contract and became a free agent, toyed with the idea of signing elsewhere, but ultimately agreed to a seven-year, $136.4 million contract. That made him the last man standing on the Lakers' island of dysfunction. And with his criminal trial pending, Bryant was hardly a rock upon which to build a new dynasty. Ratings could be down next season for the NBA's premier reality show.

The erosion of the Lakers was a season-long process—several seasons, actually—but things truly uraveled in the Finals against Detroit. The matchup was a culture clash. The low-profile Pistons, who finished second in the Central Division in their first season under coach Larry Brown, were the league's stingiest defensive team during the regular season, holding opponents to 84.3 points per game. They were a gritty team of castoffs and nomads, including Brown and point guard Billups, who had made six and five other stops, respectively, in the NBA during their peripatetic careers. Forward Rasheed Wallace, Detroit's most talented player, joined the team in February in a trade with the Atlanta Hawks, bringing with him a reputation for moodiness and inconsistency.

ANDREW D. BERNSTEIN/NBAE VIA GETTY IMAGES

made Payton look old and slow by comparison. Said Brown after Game 1, "I'm not sure we can play any better."

It turned out they could. The Lakers tied the series with a 99–91 overtime win in Game 2, thanks to a game-tying, buzzer-beating three-pointer by Bryant at the end of regulation. But the Pistons re-took control of the series with a lopsided 88–68 win in Game 3 at the Palace at Auburn Hills, then sat back and watched the Lakers—at their schismatic worst—implode in Game 4.

On the one hand there was O'Neal, rumbling around the court from the opening tip, imposing his will and his 345-pound body on any Piston defender who considered getting in his way. He finished with 20 rebounds and a game-high 36 points. He should have had more, but the other half of the Lakers' self-defeating equation, Bryant, came to the fore in the second half. To the Big Diesel's visible dismay, Bryant denied the hothanded O'Neal the ball, and hoisted shot after misguided shot himself. It was a desperate and selfish performance, the self-immolation of a star unwilling to sublimate his offensive urges to the confines of the game plan. Bryant, who finished with 20 points, ended up missing 17 of the 25 shots he took, which was four more than O'Neal (16 of 21) attempted. The Lakers lost 88–80 (Rasheed Wallace led Detroit with 26 points) and tumbled into a 3–1 hole. After the game, Shaq was asked why the bricklaying Bryant got more looks than he did. "You tell me," he replied testily.

After that debacle, Game 5 was a formality. The Pistons rolled to a series-clinching 13-point victory. It was a textbook performance by a team that prided itself on its democratic style. All five starters scored in double figures, led by Hamilton's 21. Center and rebounder extraordinaire Ben Wallace grabbed 22 boards and chipped in a surprising 18 points. The series MVP award, though, went to Billups, who averaged 21.0 points a

The Pistons entered the Finals as heavy underdogs to the star-studded Lakers, having struggled and scraped past Indiana in a decidedly unglamorous, defense-heavy rust-belt of an Eastern Conference final. Most observers believed that Detroit would be no match for the high-fliers from Tinseltown, would have no answer for Kobe and Shaq. Even if they could bottle up L.A.'s two stars, the consensus was, how would the offensively-challenged Pistons cobble together enough points to win? The answer came in Game 1, a stunning 87–75 Pistons victory at the Staples Center. Other than O'Neal, who had 11 points in the first quarter, the Lakers came out flat, while Detroit defended well and ran its screen-heavy offense with precision. Playing with a plastic facemask to protect his broken nose, the Pistons leading scorer, Richard Hamilton, had an off night, but his teammates compensated with a balanced attack. Four of them scored in double figures, led by Billups's 22.

Los Angeles, meanwhile, got meaningful contributions from Shaq (34 points), Kobe (25)—and no one else. It was becoming clear that the Lakers aging supporting cast (Malone was 40, Payton 35) was out of gas. Jackson had to be particularly troubled by the advantage the Pistons seemed to have at point guard, where the energetic Billups

game and directed Detroit's balanced attack with aplomb.

General manager Joe Dumars called the Detroit locker room "the most functional in the NBA," and the Pistons were indeed a harmonious bunch. They enjoyed hanging together on the road—bowling was a favorite diversion, and the entire team spent one night during the Easern Conference finals cavorting at an Indianapolis pool hall—and they reveled in their underdog status. "They may have had better individual players," Billups said through a champagne-spray haze in the home locker room at the Palace of Auburn Hills, "but we always felt we were the better team."

The Pistons may have been unlikely champions, but their rugged style and defense-first philosophy were emblematic of the 21st-century NBA. A sport once known for creativity and showmanship seemed bogged down by complex defensive schemes and micromanaging coaches. Only two teams—the Dallas Mavericks (105.2) and the Sacramento Kings (102.8)—averaged more than 100 points per game; five franchises checked in with scoring averages below 90. (During the 1973–74 season, all 17 NBA teams averaged more than 100.) A handful of teams, notably the New Jersey Nets and the Denver Nuggets, played with the pedal to the metal, but for the most part, fast-break, firewagon basketball was a rarity in 2003–04.

There was the excitement of the dawning of the LeBron James era, however. Following a year of hype, including millions in endorsement dollars before he played an NBA minute, the top pick in the 2003 draft debuted with the Cleveland Cavaliers. The 19-year-old proved to be worth the hype—and more. He joined Oscar Robertson and Michael Jordan as the only players to average 20 points, five rebounds and five assists in their first year in the league. In perhaps the best measure of his impact, the 6'8" swingman helped the Cavs improve from a record of 17–65 in 2002–03 to 35–47 this season.

The Cavs narrowly missed the playoffs, but the league's other marquee rookie, Anthony, led his team, the Nuggets, to a first-round series with Minnesota. After guiding Syracuse to the NCAA championship as a college freshman in 2003, the 19-year-old jumped to the NBA and electrifed the league, injecting drama into the Rookie of the Year chase, which most observers had assumed would go to James in a walk. In traning camp, Anthony announced that the perenially hapless Nuggets would double their win total (they had 17 in 2002–03) and be a playoff contender. They did better than that, going 43-39 and edging the Utah Jazz by one game for the final Western Conference playoff spot.

The 6'8" Anthony was every bit as sensational as James. He scored more points per game (21.0 to 20.9) than James, and became the first rookie to lead a playoff team in scoring since David Robinson in 1989–90. He also easily scaled the proverbial rookie wall, seeming to get stronger, not weaker, as the season wore on. His shooting percentage in his final 33 games (44.4%) was better than it was in the previous 49 (41.1%). Ditto for his scoring average (24.7 ppg vs 18.6).

Anthony also took his sudden celebrity—his jersey was the league's second-best seller, behind James's—in stride. By the end of the season there was widespread sentiment that he, not James, was the league's best rookie. Nuggets guard Jon Barry called it "a complete sham" when the hardware went to LeBron. Anthony graciously said all the right things to reporters, but he also lobbed a subtle jibe at James and those who voted for him. "I'm really happy for LeBron," Anthony said in a statement after the balloting was announced on the eve of the playoffs. "But I'm not real worried about the Rookie of the Year Award right now. My focus is on Minnesota."

He didn't have to keep his focus for very long. The young Nuggets were crushed in five games by the Timberwolves, who finished the regular season with the league's second-best record (58–24) and advanced past the first round for the first time in franchise history. The T-wolves were led, predictably, by Garnett, who joined the NBA's elite echelon in 2003–04. Da Kid led the league in rebounding (13.9 per game) and trailed only Tracy McGrady of the Orlando

NATHANIEL BUTLER/NBAE/GETTY IMAGES

After helping Cleveland double its 2002–03 win total, James edged Anthony for the rookie of the year award.

seven-game, second round series against the Sacramento Kings: In Game 7 he scored 14 of his 32 points in the fourth quarter to seal an 83–80 win and give the T-wolves their first trip to the conference finals.

Garnett wasn't enough to derail the Lakers, however; Los Angeles dispatched Minnesota in six games to advance to the Finals for the fourth time in five years. It was the last moment of glory for what, on paper, looked to be one of the most talented teams ever assembled. When it was announced that Jackson, owner of nine championship rings, would not return, O'Neal decried the decision while Bryant met it with a telling silence. Kobe had begun to chafe under the constraints of Jackson's triangle offense, and the minimal effort the LA front office made to keep Jackson was seen as a bow to Bryant. Shaq, resentful of the sway Bryant held in the organization, immediately demanded a trade. Meanwhile, in a move approved by Bryant, the Lakers tried to lure Duke coach Mike Krzyzewski to replace Jackson.

After a very public dalliance, Krzyzewski decided to stay in the college ranks, and former Houston Rockets coach Rudy Tomjanovich was hired to preside over the gutted Los Angeles roster (Malone had not re-signed by early August, and Payton was dealt to Boston along with Rick Fox). The Lakers' offseason radically shifted the league's balance of power, suddenly making the West a wide-open conference. In the East, Shaq made the Heat instant contenders, but the defending champion Pistons, who were set to return virtually intact, entered the 2004–05 season as the favorites.

The league also braced for another influx of young, straight-from-high-school talent. A record eight prep players were chosen in the first round of the draft in June, led by No. 1 pick Dwight Howard, who went to the Orlando Magic. The Lakers' run as the league's top dog had ended. A new generation, led by Garnett, James and Anthony, was poised to assume their place in the spotlight.

Magic in scoring average (24.2 ppg).

Minnesota received a huge boost from the inspired play of two newcomers, small forward Latrell Sprewell (16.8 ppg) and point guard Sam Cassell (7.3 assists per game), but there was no question whose team the Timberwolves were. In 2003, Garnett was the MVP runner-up to San Antonio's Tim Duncan. In '04, in the first year of a five-year, $100-million contract extension, he grabbed the award with both of his famously powdered hands.

Garnett continued his dominance when the playoffs began, leading the team in scoring, rebounding and assists against the Nuggets. He was immense in a thrilling

FOR THE RECORD • 2003 – 2004

NBA Final Standings

Eastern Conference

ATLANTIC DIVISION

Team	W	L	Pct	GB
New Jersey	47	35	.573	—
Miami	42	40	.512	5
New York	39	43	.476	8
Boston	36	46	.439	11
Philadelphia	33	49	.402	14
Washington	25	57	.305	22
Orlando	21	61	.256	26

CENTRAL DIVISION

Team	W	L	Pct	GB
Indiana	61	21	.744	—
Detroit	54	28	.659	7
New Orleans	41	41	.500	20
Milwaukee	41	41	.500	20
Cleveland	35	47	.427	26
Toronto	33	49	.402	28
Atlanta	28	54	.341	33
Chicago	23	59	.280	38

Western Conference

MIDWEST DIVISION

Team	W	L	Pct	GB
Minnesota	58	24	.707	—
San Antonio	57	25	.695	1
Dallas	52	30	.634	6
Memphis	50	32	.610	8
Houston	45	37	.549	13
Denver	43	39	.524	15
Utah	42	40	.512	16

PACIFIC DIVISION

Team	W	L	Pct	GB
LA Lakers	56	26	.683	—
Sacramento	55	27	.671	1
Portland	41	41	.500	15
Golden State	37	45	.451	19
Seattle	37	45	.451	19
Phoenix	29	53	.354	27
LA Clippers	28	54	.341	28

2004 NBA Playoffs

EASTERN CONFERENCE — WESTERN CONFERENCE

1st ROUND — SEMIFINALS — FINALS — FINALS — SEMIFINALS — 1st ROUND

NBA FINALS

Indiana — Boston — Miami — New Orleans — Detroit — Milwaukee — New Jersey — New York

Indiana (4–0) — Miami (4–3) — Detroit (4–1) — New Jersey (4–0)

Indiana (4–2) — Detroit (4–2) — Detroit (4–3)

DETROIT (4–1)

Minnesota (4–1) — Sacramento (4–1) — San Antonio (4–0) — LA Lakers (4–1)

Minnesota (4–3) — LA Lakers (4–2)

Minnesota — Denver — Dallas — Sacramento — San Antonio — Memphis — Houston — LA Lakers

Eastern Conference First Round

Game 1......Boston	88	at Indiana	104
Game 2......Boston	90	at Indiana	103
Game 3......Indiana	108	at Boston	85
Game 4......Indiana	90	at Boston	75

Indiana won series 4–0.

Game 1......New York	83	at New Jersey	107
Game 2......New York	81	at New Jersey	99
Game 3......New Jersey	81	at New York	78
Game 4......New Jersey	100	at New York	94

New Jersey won series 4–0.

Game 1......Milwaukee	82	at Detroit	108
Game 2......Milwaukee	92	at Detroit	88
Game 3......Detroit	95	at Milwaukee	85
Game 4......Detroit	109	at Milwaukee	92
Game 5......Milwaukee	77	at Detroit	91

Detroit won series 4–1.

Game 1......New Orleans	79	at Miami	81
Game 2......New Orleans	63	at Miami	93
Game 3......Miami	71	at New Orleans	77
Game 4......Miami	85	at New Orleans	96
Game 5......New Orleans	83	at Miami	87
Game 6......Miami	83	at New Orleans	89
Game 7......New Orleans	77	at Miami	85

Miami won series 4–3.

Western Conference First Round

Game 1......Denver	92	at Minnesota	106
Game 2......Denver	81	at Minnesota	95
Game 3......Minnesota	86	at Denver	107
Game 4......Minnesota	84	at Denver	82
Game 5......Denver	91	at Minnesota	102

Minnesota won series 4–1.

Game 1......Houston	71	at LA Lakers	72
Game 2......Houston	84	at LA Lakers	98
Game 3......LA Lakers	91	at Houston	102
Game 4......LA Lakers	92	at Houston	88*
Game 5......Houston	78	at LA Lakers	97

LA Lakers won series 4–1.

Game 1......Memphis	74	at San Antonio	98
Game 2......Memphis	70	at San Antonio	87
Game 3......San Antonio	95	at Memphis	93
Game 4......San Antonio	110	at Memphis	97

San Antonio won series 4–0.

Game 1......Dallas	105	at Sacramento	116
Game 2......Dallas	79	at Sacramento	83
Game 3......Sacramento	79	at Dallas	104
Game 4......Sacramento	94	at Dallas	92
Game 5......Dallas	118	at Sacramento	119

Sacramento won series 4–1.

Eastern Conference Semifinals

Game 1......Miami	81	at Indiana	94
Game 2......Miami	80	at Indiana	91
Game 3......Indiana	87	at Miami	94
Game 4......Indiana	88	at Miami	100
Game 5......Miami	83	at Indiana	94
Game 6......Indiana	73	at Miami	70

Indiana won series 4–2.

Game 1......New Jersey	56	at Detroit	78
Game 2......New Jersey	80	at Detroit	95
Game 3......Detroit	64	at New Jersey	82
Game 4......Detroit	79	at New Jersey	94
Game 5......New Jersey	127	at Detroit	120†
Game 6......Detroit	81	at New Jersey	75
Game 7......New Jersey	69	at Detroit	90

Detroit won series 4–3.

Western Conference Semifinals

Game 1......Sacramento	104	at Minnesota	98
Game 2......Sacramento	89	at Minnesota	94
Game 3......Minnesota	114	at Sacramento	113*
Game 4......Minnesota	81	at Sacramento	87
Game 5......Sacramento	74	at Minnesota	86
Game 6......Minnesota	87	at Sacramento	104
Game 7......Sacramento	80	at Minnesota	83

Minnesota won series 4–3.

Game 1......LA Lakers	78	at San Antonio	88
Game 2......LA Lakers	85	at San Antonio	95
Game 3......San Antonio	81	at LA Lakers	105
Game 4......San Antonio	90	at LA Lakers	98
Game 5......LA Lakers	74	at San Antonio	73
Game 6......San Antonio	76	at LA Lakers	88

LA Lakers won series 4–2.

Eastern Conference Finals

Game 1......Detroit	74	at Indiana	78
Game 2......Detroit	72	at Indiana	67
Game 3......Indiana	78	at Detroit	85
Game 4......Indiana	83	at Detroit	68
Game 5......Detroit	83	at Indiana	65
Game 6......Indiana	65	at Detroit	69

Detroit won series 4–2.

Western Conference Finals

Game 1......LA Lakers	97	at Minnesota	88
Game 2......LA Lakers	71	at Minnesota	89
Game 3......Minnesota	89	at LA Lakers	100
Game 4......Minnesota	85	at LA Lakers	92
Game 5......LA Lakers	96	at Minnesota	98
Game 6......Minnesota	90	at LA Lakers	96

LA Lakers won series 4–2.

Finals

Game 1......Detroit	87	at LA Lakers	75
Game 2......Detroit	91	at LA Lakers	99*
Game 3......LA Lakers	68	at Detroit	88
Game 4......LA Lakers	80	at Detroit	88
Game 5......LA Lakers	87	at Detroit	100

Detroit won series 4–1.

*Overtime. †Triple overtime.

NBA Finals Composite Box Score

DETROIT PISTONS

Player	GP	FG%	3FG%	FT%	Rebounds Off	Total	A	Stl	TO	BS	Ppg	Hi
Hamilton	5	40.2	40.0	85.3	12	26	20	4	23	0	21.4	31
Billups	5	50.9	47.1	92.9	3	16	26	6	13	0	21.0	27
R. Wallace	5	45.3	25.0	77.8	7	39	7	2	4	8	13.0	26
B. Wallace	5	47.8	0.0	29.4	19	68	7	9	6	5	10.8	18
Prince	5	38.9	18.8	45.5	15	34	10	9	2	2	10.0	17
Williamson	5	40.0	—	90.0	4	12	1	0	4	0	4.2	7
Hunter	5	29.4	25.0	100.0	1	7	4	3	1	2	3.6	5
Campbell	5	37.5	—	50.0	6	13	8	5	3	3	3.4	6
Okur	4	44.4	100.0	50.0	1	6	2	0	4	0	2.8	7
James	5	50.0	—	—	2	4	4	0	1	0	1.2	4
Ham	4	100.0	—	—	1	1	0	0	1	0	0.5	2
Milicic	3	0.0	—	—	1	2	0	1	1	0	0.0	0
Totals	5	42.9	31.8	69.6	72	228	89	39	69	20	90.8	100

LOS ANGELES LAKERS

Player	GP	FG%	3FG%	FT%	Rebounds Off	Total	A	Stl	TO	BS	Ppg	Hi
O'Neal	5	63.1	—	49.1	15	54	8	2	14	3	26.6	36
Bryant	5	38.1	17.4	92.0	2	14	22	9	18	3	22.6	33
Fisher	5	30.6	37.5	57.1	5	15	9	5	4	0	6.4	10
George	5	39.3	33.3	50.0	3	14	3	5	2	2	5.8	8
Malone	4	33.3	0.0	66.7	8	29	9	1	4	1	5.0	9
Payton	5	32.1	20.0	50.0	6	15	22	6	7	2	4.2	8
Medvedenko	5	35.3	—	75.0	6	18	3	0	2	1	3.6	10
Rush	5	31.8	25.0	—	0	5	2	1	5	0	3.6	8
Walton	4	38.5	16.7	100.0	3	12	18	6	7	2	3.3	7
Rick Fox	3	57.1	0.0	—	0	3	7	0	1	0	2.7	6
Cook	3	16.7	—	100.0	3	8	0	1	2	0	1.3	4
Russell	3	0.0	0.0	—	1	1	0	0	0	0	0.0	0
Totals	5	41.6	24.7	64.0	52	188	103	36	68	14	81.8	99

NBA Finals Box Scores

Game 1

DETROIT 87

Player	Min	FG M-A	FT M-A	Reb O-T	A	PF	S	TO	TP
Hamilton	43	5-16	2-4	3-7	6	0	1	6	12
Billups	39	8-14	4-4	1-3	4	1	3	2	22
Prince	35	5-10	0-0	1-6	4	3	2	0	11
R. Wallace	29	3-4	6-6	1-8	1	3	0	1	14
B. Wallace	41	4-8	1-2	1-8	0	1	1	2	9
Campbell	18	2-5	2-6	1-1	4	1	2	1	6
Hunter	13	1-5	2-2	0-1	0	2	0	1	5
Williamson	11	2-3	3-4	1-2	1	3	0	0	7
Okur	6	0-0	1-2	0-0	0	1	0	1	1
Ham	4	0-0	0-0	0-0	0	2	0	0	0
James	1	0-0	0-0	0-0	0	0	0	0	0
Totals	240	33-89	19-25	13-45	19	26	5	8	89

Percentages: FG—.462, FT—.700. 3-pt goals: 6–12, .500 (Billups 2–4, R. Wallace 2–2, Prince 1–4, Hunter 1–2). Team rebounds: 11. Blocked shots: 4 (Campbell 2, R. Wallace, B. Wallace).

LOS ANGELES 75

Player	Min	FG M-A	FT M-A	Reb O-T	A	PF	S	TO	TP
Bryant	47	10-27	4-4	1-4	4	2	4	3	25
Payton	31	1-4	0-0	1-2	3	5	2	2	3
Malone	44	2-9	0-0	3-11	3	1	0	0	4
George	27	2-5	0-0	0-3	0	2	1	1	5
O'Neal	45	13-16	8-12	5-11	1	4	0	6	34
Fisher	20	1-9	0-0	3-3	3	2	1	1	2
M'denko	6	0-0	2-2	0-1	0	3	0	0	2
Fox	4	0-0	0-0	0-0	1	2	0	0	0
Totals	240	29-73	14-18	13-37	15	25	8	15	75

Percentages: FG—.397, FT—.778. 3-pt goals: 3–13, .231 (Bryant 1–6, Payton 1–1, George 1–2, Fisher 0–2, Rush 0–2). Team rebounds: 8. Blocked shots: 4 (Bryant 2, Malone 1, O'Neal).

A: 18,997. Officials: Crawford, Delaney, Fryer.

Game 2

DETROIT 91

Player	Min	FG M-A	FT M-A	Reb O-T	A	PF	S	TO	TP
Hamilton	47	10-25	4-5	5-8	2	2	0	5	26
Billups	47	6-15	13-14	2-4	9	1	0	3	27
Prince	47	2-6	0-0	4-5	0	2	3	0	5
R. Wallace	34	5-14	1-2	1-7	3	4	0	0	11
B. Wallace	43	5-11	2-8	4-14	1	5	2	0	12
Okur	18	0-2	1-2	0-2	1	2	0	3	1
Hunter	12	2-4	0-0	0-0	2	1	1	0	5
Campbell	9	1-2	0-0	2-4	1	4	0	1	2
Williamson	7	1-2	0-0	1-2	0	2	0	2	2
James	1	0-0	0-0	0-0	0	0	0	0	0
Totals	265	32-81	21-31	19-46	19	23	6	14	91

Percentages: FG—.395, FT—.677. 3-pt goals: 6-12, .500 (Hamilton 2-2, Billups 2-2, Prince 1-2, Hunter 1-3, R. Wallace 0-3). Team rebounds:12. Blocked shots: 6 (Prince 2, R. Wallace 2, B. Wallace 2).

LOS ANGELES 99

Player	Min	FG M-A	FT M-A	Reb O-T	A	PF	S	TO	TP
Bryant	49	14-27	4-5	0-4	7	5	2	5	33
Payton	28	1-3	0-0	1-3	3	4	1	3	2
Malone	39	3-9	3-4	3-9	2	3	1	1	9
George	21	3-7	0-0	0-2	1	2	1	0	7
O'Neal	48	10-20	9-14	3-7	3	5	0	3	29
Walton	27	3-3	0-0	1-5	8	3	0	0	7
Fisher	25	2-6	1-2	0-3	2	4	2	0	7
Rush	18	2-4	0-0	0-2	2	0	0	1	5
M'enko	9	0-1	0-0	1-3	0	1	0	0	0
Cook	1	0-0	0-0	0-0	0	0	0	1	0
Totals	265	38-80	17-25	9-38	28	27	7	14	99

Percentages: FG—.475, FT—.680. 3-pt goals: 6-17, .353 (Fisher 2-4, Bryant 1-5, George 1-3, Walton 1-1, Rush 1-2, Payton 0-1, Malone 0-1). Team rebounds: 13. Blocked shots: 3 (O'Neal, Walton 2).

A: 18,997. Officials: DeRosa, Javie, Salvatore.

Game 3

LOS ANGELES 68

Player	Min	FG M-A	FT M-A	Reb O-T	A	PF	S	TO	TP
Bryant	45	4-13	3-3	0-3	5	3	1	4	11
Payton	35	2-7	1-2	1-4	7	2	1	0	6
George	21	3-8	0-0	0-3	0	3	2	1	8
Malone	18	2-4	1-2	0-4	2	2	0	1	5
O'Neal	38	7-14	0-2	2-8	1	5	1	2	14
M'enko	21	1-3	1-2	2-8	1	4	0	1	3
Walton	19	1-5	2-2	1-3	2	4	1	2	4
Rush	18	3-8	0-0	0-1	0	2	1	2	8
Fisher	16	4-9	0-0	1-2	1	1	0	3	9
Cook	8	0-3	0-0	0-3	0	2	0	0	0
Russell	1	0-0	0-0	0-0	0	0	0	0	0
Totals	240	27-74	8-13	7-39	19	28	7	16	68

Percentages: FG—.365, FT—.615. 3-pt goals: 6-27, .222 (George 2-6, Rush 2-7, Payton 1-5, Fisher 1-3, Walton 0-2, Bryant 0-4). Team rebounds:8. Blocked shots: 4 (Bryant, Payton, George, Medvedenko).

DETROIT 88

Player	Min	FG M-A	FT M-A	Reb O-T	A	PF	S	TO	TP
Hamilton	43	11-22	7-7	3-6	3	1	2	3	31
Billups	36	5-17	7-7	0-2	3	1	1	2	19
Prince	36	5-13	0-2	3-6	2	1	3	1	11
R. Wallace	26	1-4	1-4	2-10	1	3	0	1	3
B. Wallace	38	3-9	1-4	2-11	3	2	3	3	7
Hunter	16	1-3	0-0	1-5	2	4	0	0	2
Williamson	15	2-4	2-2	0-3	0	0	0	1	6
Campbell	13	1-4	3-4	2-2	1	3	3	0	5
Okur	8	1-4	0-0	1-4	1	0	0	0	2
James	4	0-0	0-0	1-1	1	0	0	0	0
Ham	3	1-1	0-0	0-0	0	0	0	0	2
Milicic	2	0-1	0-0	0-0	0	0	0	0	0
Totals	240	31-76	21-30	15-51	17	16	11	11	88

Percentages: FG—.408, FT—.700. 3-pt goals: 5-15, .333 (Hamilton 2-4, Billups 2-5, Prince 1-5, B. Wallace 0-1). Team rebounds: 8. Blocked shots: 4 (R. Wallace 2, Hunter 2).

A: 22,076. Officials: Callahan, Crawford, Garretson.

Game 4

LOS ANGELES 80

Player	Min	FG M-A	FT M-A	Reb O-T	A	PF	S	TO	TP
Bryant	45	8-25	2-2	0-0	2	3	1	3	20
Payton	43	4-11	0-0	1-2	5	4	0	1	8
Malone	21	1-2	0-0	2-5	2	2	0	2	2
George	15	1-2	2-4	1-3	0	5	1	0	5
O'Neal	47	16-21	4-11	3-20	2	4	0	2	36
Fisher	21	1-6	0-3	1-5	2	4	0	0	4
Fox	16	1-4	0-0	0-1	6	3	0	0	2
M'enko	13	1-5	1-2	1-1	1	3	0	0	3
Walton	12	0-1	0-0	3-6	3	6	2	2	0
Rush	6	0-1	0-0	0-0	0	1	0	0	0
Russell	1	0-0	0-0	0-0	0	0	0	0	0
Totals	240	33-78	11-22	9-38	23	35	4	10	80

Percentages: FG—.423, FT—.500. 3-pt goals: 3-16, .188 (Bryant 2-6, George 1-2, Payton 0-2, Fisher 0-3, Fox 0-1, Walton 0-1, Rush 0-1). Team rebounds: 10. Blocked shots: 1 (O'Neal).

DETROIT 88

Player	Min	FG M-A	FT M-A	Reb O-T	A	PF	S	TO	TP
Hamilton	44	5-11	7-7	1-2	6	5	0	5	17
Billups	37	7-12	7-9	0-4	4	3	2	3	23
R. Wallace	41	10-23	6-6	2-13	2	4	2	2	26
Prince	40	3-10	0-1	4-7	2	1	0	0	6
B. Wallace	39	2-5	4-14	2-13	2	3	1	1	8
Campbell	14	0-3	0-0	0-2	0	2	0	0	0
Hunter	11	0-1	4-4	0-0	0	1	0	0	4
James	6	2-2	0-0	0-2	0	0	0	1	4
Williamson	5	0-1	0-0	0-0	0	1	0	0	0
Ham	2	0-0	0-0	0-0	0	1	0	0	0
Milicic	1	0-0	0-0	0-0	0	0	0	0	0
Totals	240	29-68	28-41	9-45	16	20	5	12	88

Percentages: FG—.426, FT—.683. 3-pt goals: 2-13, .154 (Billups 2-5, R. Wallace 0-5, Prince 0-3). Team rebounds: 15. Blocked shots: 4 (R. Wallace 2, B. Wallace, Campbell).

A: 22,076. Officials: Bavetta, Nies, Rush.

Game 5

LOS ANGELES 87

Player	Min	FG M–A	FT M–A	Reb O–T	A	PF	S	TO	TP
Bryant	45	7–21	10–11	1–3	4	2	1	3	24
Payton	31	1–3	0–0	2–4	4	2	2	1	2
M'enko	23	4–8	2–2	2–5	1	1	0	1	10
George	20	2–6	0–0	2–3	2	4	0	0	4
O'Neal	35	7–13	6–16	2–8	1	4	1	1	20
Rush	20	2–6	0–0	0–0	0	3	0	0	5
Walton	19	1–4	0–0	1–3	5	2	3	3	2
Fisher	19	3–6	1–2	0–2	1	5	2	0	10
Cook	12	1–3	2–2	3–5	0	2	1	1	4
Fox	10	3–3	0–0	0–2	0	1	0	1	6
Russell	6	0–2	0–0	1–1	0	1	0	0	0
Totals	240	31–75	21–33	14–36	18	27	10	11	87

Percentages: FG—.413, FT—.636. 3-pt goals: 4–16, .250 (Fisher 3–4, Rush 1–4, Bryant 0–2, Payton 0–1, George 0–2, Walton 0–2, Russell 0–1). Team rebounds: 12. Blocked shots: 2 (Payton, George).

DETROIT 100

Player	Min	FG M–A	FT M–A	Reb O–T	A	PF	S	TO	TP
Hamilton	45	6–18	9–11	0–3	4	1	1	4	21
Billups	33	3–5	8–8	0–3	6	2	0	3	14
Prince	38	6–15	5–8	3–10	2	2	1	1	17
R. Wallace	21	5–8	0–0	1–1	0	5	0	0	11
B. Wallace	42	8–13	2–6	10–22	1	3	3	0	18
Campbell	14	2–2	0–0	1–4	2	3	0	1	4
Williamson	14	1–5	4–4	2–3	0	2	0	1	6
Hunter	13	1–4	0–0	0–1	0	3	2	0	2
James	10	0–2	0–0	1–1	3	2	0	0	0
Okur	7	3–3	0–0	0–0	0	4	0	0	7
Milicic	2	0–1	0–2	1–1	0	0	1	1	0
Ham	1	0–0	0–0	1–1	0	0	0	1	0
Totals	240	35–76	28–39	20–50	18	27	8	12	100

Percentages: FG—.461, FT—.718. 3-pt goals: 2–14, .143 (R. Wallace 1–2, Okur 1–1, Hamilton 0–4, Billups 0–1, Prince 0–2, B. Wallace 0–1, Hunter 0–3). Team rebounds: 10. Blocked shots: 2 (R. Wallace, B. Wallace).

A: 22,076. Officials: Crawford, Fryer, Salvatore.

All-NBA Teams

FIRST TEAM	SECOND TEAM	THIRD TEAM
G Kobe Bryant, LA Lakers	Tracy McGrady, Orlando	Michael Redd, Milwaukee
G Jason Kidd, New Jersey	Sam Cassell, Minnesota	Baron Davis, New Orleans
C Shaquille O'Neal, LA Lakers	Ben Wallace, Detroit	Yao Ming, Houston
F Kevin Garnett, Minnesota	Jermaine O'Neal, Indiana	Dirk Nowitzki, Dallas
F Tim Duncan, San Antonio	Peja Stojakovic, Sacramento	Ron Artest, Indiana

All-Defensive Team

FIRST TEAM	SECOND TEAM
G Bruce Bowen, San Antonio	Doug Christie, Sacramento
G Kobe Bryant, LA Lakers	Jason Kidd, New Jersey
C Ben Wallace, Detroit	Theo Ratliff, Portland
F Ron Artest, Indiana	Andrei Kirilenko, Utah
F Kevin Garnett, Minnesota	Tim Duncan, San Antonio

All-Rookie Teams

FIRST TEAM	SECOND TEAM
Carmelo Anthony, Denver	Josh Howard, Dallas
LeBron James, Cleveland	T.J. Ford, Milwaukee
Dwyane Wade, Miami	Udonis Haslem, Miami
Chris Bosh, Toronto	Jarvis Hayes, Washington
Kirk Hinrich, Chicago	Marquis Daniels, Dallas

NBA Individual Leaders

Scoring

	GP	Pts	Avg
Tracy McGrady, Orl	67	1,878	28.0
Peja Stojakovic, Sac	81	1,964	24.2
Kevin Garnett, Minn	82	1,987	24.2
Kobe Bryant, LAL	65	1,557	24.0
Paul Pierce, Bos	80	1,836	23.0
Baron Davis, NO	67	1,532	22.9
Vince Carter, Tor	73	1,645	22.5
Tim Duncan, SA	69	1,538	22.3
Dirk Nowitzki, Dall	77	1,680	21.8
Michael Redd, Mil	82	1,776	21.7

Rebounds

	GP	Reb	Avg
Kevin Garnett, Minn	82	1,139	13.9
Tim Duncan, SA	69	859	12.4
Ben Wallace, Det	81	1,006	12.4
Erick Dampier, GS	74	887	12.0
Carlos Boozer, Clev	75	857	11.4
Zach Randolph, Port	81	851	10.5
Jamaal Magloire, NO	82	847	10.3
Brad Miller, Sac	72	743	10.3
Kenny Thomas, Phil	74	750	10.1
Marcus Camby, Den	72	727	10.1

Assists

	GP	Assists	Avg
Jason Kidd, NJ	67	618	9.2
Stephon Marbury, NY	81	719	8.9
Steve Nash, Dall	78	687	8.8
Baron Davis, NO	67	501	7.5
Sam Cassell, Minn	81	592	7.3
Eric Snow, Phil	82	563	6.9
Jason Williams, Mem	72	492	6.8
Kirk Hinrich, Chi	76	517	6.8
Steve Francis, Hou	79	493	6.2

Three tied with 6.1.

Field-Goal Percentage

	FGA	FGM	Pct
Shaquille O'Neal, LAL	948	554	.584
Mark Blount, Bos	604	342	.566
Erick Dampier, GS	650	348	.535
Antawn Jamison, Dall	913	488	.535
Nenê, Den	630	334	.530
Carlos Boozer, Clev	900	471	.523
Yao Ming, Hou	1025	535	.522
Brad Miller, Sac	731	373	.510
Corliss Williamson, Det	602	304	.505
Tim Duncan, SA	1181	592	.501

Free-Throw Percentage

	FTA	FTM	Pct
Peja Stojakovic, Sac	425	394	.927
Steve Nash, Dall	251	230	.916
Allan Houston, NY	172	157	.913
Ray Allen, Sea	271	245	.904
Reggie Miller, Ind	165	146	.885
Chauncey Billups, Det	460	404	.878
Brian Cardinal, GS	271	238	.878
Dirk Nowitzki, Dall	423	371	.877
Earl Boykins, Den	162	142	.877
Damon Stoudamire, Port	145	127	.876

Three-Point Field-Goal Percentage

	3FGM	3FGA	Pct
Anthony Peeler, Sac	68	141	.482
Brent Barry, Sea	114	252	.452
Brian Cardinal, GS	55	124	.444
Fred Hoiberg, Minn	76	172	.442
Aaron McKie, Phil	75	172	.436
Peja Stojakovic, Sac	240	554	.433
Allan Houston, NY	87	202	.431
Hidayet Turkoglu, SA	101	241	.419
Casey Jacobsen, Phoe	75	180	.417
Charlie Ward, SA	84	206	.408

Steals

	GP	Steals	Avg
Baron Davis, NO	67	158	2.36
Shawn Marion, Phoe	79	167	2.11
Ron Artest, Ind	73	152	2.08
Andrei Kirilenko, Utah	78	150	1.92
Doug Christie, Sac	82	151	1.84
Stephen Jackson, Atl	80	142	1.78
Emanuel Ginobili, SA	77	136	1.77
Ben Wallace, Det	81	143	1.77
Steve Francis, Hou	79	139	1.76
Andre Miller, Den	82	142	1.73

Blocked Shots

	GP	BS	Avg
Theo Ratliff, Port	85	307	3.61
Ben Wallace, Det	81	246	3.04
Andrei Kirilenko, Utah	78	215	2.76
Tim Duncan, SA	69	185	2.68
Marcus Camby, Den	72	187	2.60
Jermaine O'Neal, Ind	78	199	2.55
Zadrunas Ilgauskas, Clev	81	201	2.48
Shaquille O'Neal, LAL	67	166	2.48
Samuel Dalembert, Phil	82	189	2.30
Elton Brand, LAC	69	154	2.23

NBA Team Statistics

Offense

Team	FG Pct	3FG Pct	FT Pct	Rebound Avg Off	Rebound Avg Total	A	TO	Stl	Scoring Avg
Dallas	46.0	34.8	79.6	14.3	45.3	23.9	11.8	8.0	105.2
Sacramento	46.2	40.1	79.6	10.8	41.2	26.2	13.5	8.7	102.8
LA Lakers	45.4	32.7	69.4	12.2	43.1	23.8	13.4	8.3	98.2
Milwaukee	44.7	35.0	77.5	11.7	42.2	22.8	13.0	6.8	98.0
Denver	44.3	33.6	76.5	13.2	42.3	21.9	14.7	9.1	97.2
Seattle	44.6	37.4	76.5	11.1	39.3	21.7	13.8	8.1	97.1
Memphis	44.5	34.0	72.7	12.8	41.8	23.4	14.4	9.7	96.7
Boston	44.3	34.6	75.0	10.4	40.1	20.5	15.7	9.4	95.3
LA Clippers	42.8	32.1	78.5	14.0	43.5	20.2	15.6	7.2	94.8
Minnesota	46.2	36.3	78.1	10.7	42.9	23.1	12.2	6.8	94.6
Phoenix	44.3	34.5	74.6	11.3	40.6	19.3	14.7	9.0	94.2
Orlando	42.9	34.4	73.7	12.2	40.9	19.3	13.0	6.7	94.0
Golden St	44.2	33.4	72.5	12.2	43.1	20.5	14.1	7.0	93.3
Cleveland	43.3	31.4	75.3	13.6	45.6	22.1	14.2	7.1	92.9
Atlanta	43.3	33.6	77.6	12.2	42.7	20.1	15.6	7.7	92.8
New York	44.2	36.4	79.3	11.6	42.6	20.7	15.3	7.4	92.0
Washington	42.1	34.1	71.4	13.6	42.8	18.7	16.7	8.9	91.8
New Orleans	42.0	31.9	75.1	13.3	42.8	20.9	14.1	8.6	91.8
San Antonio	44.2	35.8	68.1	12.6	45.1	20.4	14.1	8.1	91.5
Indiana	43.6	35.1	76.4	11.8	41.7	21.6	13.5	8.9	91.4
Portland	44.8	34.6	73.1	12.7	41.7	21.6	13.8	7.5	90.7
New Jersey	44.2	33.6	75.3	10.5	40.7	24.5	14.1	8.7	90.3
Miami	42.5	35.7	76.2	11.5	41.5	19.1	13.1	7.2	90.3
Detroit	43.5	34.4	75.3	12.4	42.8	20.8	14.4	8.0	90.1
Houston	44.2	36.6	77.3	10.3	42.6	19.3	15.8	6.8	89.8
Chicago	41.4	34.2	72.5	12.8	43.5	21.9	15.2	8.0	89.7
Utah	43.6	32.1	74.6	13.5	41.2	20.4	15.3	7.1	88.7
Philadelphia	42.8	34.2	75.3	11.5	40.8	20.0	14.7	8.0	88.0
Toronto	41.8	35.6	75.0	10.1	39.6	19.2	13.3	7.4	85.4

Defense (Opponent's Statistics)

Team	FG Pct	3FG Pct	FT Pct	Rebound Avg. Off	Rebound Avg. Total	A	TO	Stl	Scoring Avg
Detroit	41.3	30.2	74.4	12.0	40.7	19.0	14.7	7.9	84.3
San Antonio	40.9	32.7	74.4	11.1	41.1	17.3	14.6	7.7	84.3
Indiana	43.2	32.5	75.0	10.6	40.1	20.1	15.2	7.1	85.6
New Jersey	42.7	35.0	76.1	10.7	40.8	19.8	15.2	8.0	87.8
Houston	41.2	37.3	73.7	11.1	39.7	20.6	12.8	8.7	88.1
Toronto	42.8	30.7	74.7	12.6	45.1	18.5	13.9	7.2	88.5
Minnesota	41.4	33.5	75.3	12.2	41.5	20.7	12.8	6.7	89.1
Miami	42.8	34.3	76.8	10.9	41.2	18.6	14.2	7.1	89.7
Utah	43.2	34.3	77.1	10.6	36.6	18.6	14.8	8.1	89.9
Philadelphia	43.2	33.3	74.4	12.2	41.4	21.3	14.5	8.3	90.5
New Orleans	44.1	34.1	75.0	11.9	42.1	21.8	14.7	7.5	91.9
Portland	45.0	34.1	75.3	12.4	40.3	23.3	13.0	8.0	92.0
New York	42.9	33.8	76.3	11.6	41.4	20.4	13.2	8.2	93.5
Golden St	44.5	37.4	74.6	12.0	42.8	21.5	13.4	8.1	94.0
LA Lakers	44.0	33.7	75.0	11.2	42.4	20.8	14.5	7.5	94.3
Memphis	43.7	33.8	76.4	13.4	44.0	20.4	16.1	8.2	94.3
Cleveland	43.7	37.1	74.9	11.8	42.0	21.7	12.4	7.7	95.5
Chicago	43.6	35.6	74.8	12.3	45.0	23.1	14.5	8.5	96.1
Denver	45.3	35.6	72.8	12.9	42.9	23.6	16.4	8.1	96.2
Boston	43.7	36.2	73.6	13.0	43.8	23.0	16.3	8.8	96.7
Milwaukee	45.2	35.2	73.9	12.0	42.7	22.8	13.6	7.5	97.0
Washington	45.4	34.3	77.1	12.8	43.5	24.0	15.5	9.6	97.4
Atlanta	44.0	35.8	76.0	12.8	43.1	22.0	13.2	8.9	97.5
Seattle	45.0	34.9	77.4	13.0	42.7	21.1	14.1	7.7	97.8
Sacramento	45.4	33.9	74.9	13.2	43.9	21.3	14.3	7.9	97.8
Phoenix	44.6	34.9	76.5	12.7	43.8	21.5	15.0	7.9	97.9
LA Clippers	46.0	36.0	74.1	12.6	41.4	22.9	13.1	8.5	99.4
Dallas	45.9	36.3	74.6	12.3	43.6	23.6	14.4	7.1	100.8
Orlando	46.6	37.7	74.2	13.1	44.4	24.4	12.9	7.6	101.1

Atlanta Hawks

Player	GP	MPG	FG%	3Pt%	FT%	OFF	DEF	Total	APG	SPG	BPG	TO	PF	PPG
			Field Goals			Rebounds								
Stephen Jackson...80		36.8	.425	.340	.785	1.20	3.40	4.60	3.1	1.78	.25	2.79	2.70	18.1
Jason Terry..........81		37.3	.417	.347	.827	.60	3.50	4.10	5.4	1.53	.20	2.83	2.40	16.8
Bob Sura 80		20.8	.416	.266	.757	1.30	2.80	4.10	2.9	.78	.18	1.31	2.00	7.5
Jason Collier 20		27.3	.479	.250	.788	1.80	3.80	5.60	.9	.55	.55	1.55	3.60	11.3
Chris Crawford 56		21.6	.448	.389	.866	1.00	2.10	3.10	.8	.66	.36	.98	2.30	10.2
Zeljko Rebraca.....24		11.4	.442	.000	.767	1.00	1.50	2.40	.3	.21	.46	.71	2.20	3.8
Bob Sura 80		20.8	.416	.266	.757	1.30	2.80	4.10	2.9	.78	.18	1.31	2.00	7.5
Wesley Person 58		17.9	.401	.399	.795	.30	1.70	2.00	1.1	.33	.16	.66	.70	5.8
Boris Diaw 76		25.3	.447	.231	.602	1.50	3.00	4.50	2.4	.78	.49	1.66	2.50	4.5
Alan Henderson 6		11.3	.476	.000	.667	1.80	1.70	3.50	.3	.17	.33	.50	.20	4.0
Joel Przybilla......17		20.4	.360	.000	.419	1.90	4.60	6.50	.4	.29	1.00	1.06	3.10	2.9
Jacque Vaughn 71		17.9	.386	.150	.779	.20	1.50	1.60	2.7	.62	.03	1.18	1.80	3.8
M. N'diaye 28		13.1	.391	.000	.746	1.50	2.50	4.00	.0	.29	.89	.64	2.10	3.5
Travis Hansen......41		12.4	.354	.300	.815	.70	1.00	1.70	.5	.24	.22	.37	1.60	3.0
Hawks...............82		**242.7**	**.433**	**.335**	**.776**	**12.1**	**30.6**	**42.7**	**20.1**	**7.7**	**5.0**	**16.5**	**22.3**	**92.8**
Opponents 82		**242.7**	**.440**	**.358**	**.760**	**12.8**	**30.3**	**43.1**	**22.0**	**8.9**	**5.1**	**14.0**	**20.7**	**97.5**

Boston Celtics

Player	GP	MPG	FG%	3Pt%	FT%	OFF	DEF	Total	APG	SPG	BPG	TO	PF	PPG
			Field Goals			Rebounds								
Paul Pierce..........80		38.7	.402	.299	.819	.90	5.70	6.50	5.1	1.64	.65	3.79	2.90	23.0
Ricky Davis 79		31.3	.469	.371	.718	1.00	3.60	4.50	3.3	1.22	.28	2.39	2.20	14.4
Chucky Atkins 24		24.1	.397	.336	.753	.10	1.30	1.50	3.5	.70	.03	1.44	1.60	8.4
Mark Blount 82		29.3	.566	.000	.719	2.50	4.70	7.20	.9	.98	1.29	1.83	3.10	10.3
Jiri Welsch..........81		26.9	.428	.381	.743	.70	2.90	3.70	2.3	1.25	.09	1.59	2.20	9.2
Walter McCarty 77		24.7	.388	.374	.756	.40	2.70	3.10	1.6	.94	.29	1.18	2.30	7.9
Raef LaFrentz.......17		19.3	.460	.200	.769	1.80	2.90	4.60	1.4	.47	.76	.65	2.80	7.8
Chris Mihm..........76		17.5	.488	.000	.663	2.10	3.40	5.40	.3	.49	.83	1.18	2.70	6.3
Dana Barros 1		11.0	.667	.000	1.000	.00	.00	.00	.0	.00	.00	.00	2.00	6.0
Marcus Banks 81		17.1	.400	.314	.756	.40	1.30	1.60	2.2	1.09	.16	1.54	2.10	5.9
Brandon Hunter 36		11.3	.457	.000	.442	1.40	1.90	3.30	.5	.36	.03	.61	1.10	3.5
Jumaine Jones 42		8.9	.344	.295	.609	.60	1.00	1.60	.3	.29	.21	.45	1.10	2.2
Kendrick Perkins ..10		3.5	.533	.000	.667	.50	.90	1.40	.3	.00	.20	.50	.60	2.2
Michael Stewart 2		5.9	.417	.000	.750	.30	.90	1.20	.0	.00	.40	.12	1.40	.5
Celtics 82		**240.3**	**.443**	**.346**	**.750**	**10.4**	**29.8**	**40.1**	**20.5**	**9.4**	**4.0**	**16.2**	**22.4**	**95.3**
Opponents 82		**240.3**	**.437**	**.362**	**.736**	**13.0**	**30.8**	**43.8**	**23.0**	**8.8**	**5.0**	**17.2**	**22.2**	**96.7**

Chicago Bulls

Player	GP	MPG	FG%	3Pt%	FT%	OFF	DEF	Total	APG	SPG	BPG	TO	PF	PPG
			Field Goals			Rebounds								
Jalen Rose...........82		40.9	.406	.370	.854	.80	3.50	4.30	4.8	.88	.28	3.48	3.30	22.1
Donyell Marshall ...78		30.5	.459	.379	.756	3.00	6.00	9.00	1.8	1.22	1.09	1.73	3.00	13.4
Marcus Fizer 38		21.3	.465	.167	.657	2.10	3.60	5.70	1.3	.37	.45	1.50	2.30	11.7
Jamal Crawford ...80		24.9	.413	.355	.806	.30	2.10	2.30	4.2	.96	.31	1.68	1.60	10.7
Eddy Curry 81		19.4	.585	.000	.624	1.40	2.90	4.40	.5	.22	.77	1.69	2.80	10.5
Jay Williams..........75		26.1	.399	.322	.640	.40	2.20	2.60	4.7	1.15	.23	2.28	2.40	9.5
Tyson Chandler 75		24.4	.531	.000	.608	2.30	4.60	6.90	1.0	.49	1.41	1.80	2.90	9.2
Eddie Robinson 64		21.2	.492	.214	.810	1.20	1.90	3.10	1.0	.97	.20	.81	1.90	5.7
Lonny Baxter 55		12.4	.466	.000	.680	1.20	1.80	3.00	.3	.16	.40	.84	2.50	4.8
Trenton Hassell 82		24.4	.367	.325	.745	.50	2.70	3.10	1.8	.55	.74	1.01	2.40	4.2
Rick Brunson 17		11.5	.460	.667	.833	.20	.90	1.10	2.1	.59	.18	1.00	1.20	3.5
Corie Blount..........50		16.7	.485	.000	.571	1.40	2.70	4.10	1.0	.66	.38	.86	2.40	3.0
Fred Hoiberg 63		12.4	.389	.238	.820	.20	2.00	2.20	1.1	.63	.08	.40	.90	2.3
Dalibor Bagaric 10		7.6	.308	.000	.750	.70	1.30	2.00	.4	.30	.30	.50	1.10	1.9
Roger Mason Jr. ...17		6.6	.355	.333	1.000	.10	.60	.70	.7	.24	.00	.29	1.20	1.8
Bulls................82		**241.8**	**.414**	**.342**	**.725**	**12.8**	**30.7**	**43.5**	**21.9**	**8.0**	**4.8**	**16.1**	**23.3**	**89.7**
Opponents 82		**241.8**	**.436**	**.355**	**.748**	**12.3**	**32.7**	**45.0**	**23.0**	**8.5**	**5.4**	**15.2**	**20.5**	**96.0**

Cleveland Cavaliers

Player	GP	MPG	FG%	3Pt%	FT%	OFF	DEF	Total	APG	SPG	BPG	TO	PF	PPG
LeBron James	79	39.5	.417	.290	.754	1.30	4.20	5.50	5.9	1.65	.73	3.46	1.90	20.9
Carlos Boozer	75	34.6	.523	.167	.768	3.10	8.40	11.40	2.0	.99	.73	1.79	2.70	15.5
Z. Ilgauskas	81	31.3	.483	.286	.746	3.40	4.60	8.10	1.3	.48	2.48	2.01	3.40	15.3
Jeff McInnis	70	33.8	.447	.362	.797	.50	2.00	2.50	6.1	1.03	.09	1.71	2.30	11.8
Eric Williams	71	26.6	.386	.276	.760	.90	3.10	4.00	1.7	.99	.13	1.24	2.50	10.0
Lee Nailon	57	13.7	.450	.000	.810	1.10	1.40	2.50	.7	.26	.14	.79	1.60	6.0
Dajuan Wagner	44	16.1	.366	.360	.681	.20	1.10	1.30	1.2	.59	.16	.93	2.00	6.5
Tony Battie	73	20.2	.443	.222	.742	1.60	3.30	4.90	.8	.36	.92	.86	2.20	5.6
Kedrick Brown	55	17.6	.461	.384	.630	.70	1.90	2.70	1.2	.55	.13	.53	1.50	5.3
Kevin Ollie	82	17.1	.370	.444	.835	.30	1.80	2.10	2.9	.62	.10	.99	1.50	4.2
Ira Newble	64	19.5	.391	.105	.783	1.00	1.40	2.40	1.1	.39	.30	.84	1.70	4.0
Jason Kapono	41	10.4	.403	.477	.833	.50	.90	1.30	.3	.32	.05	.51	1.00	3.5
DeSagana Diop	55	13.0	.388	.000	.600	1.30	2.30	3.60	.6	.46	.91	.52	2.10	2.3
Cavaliers	82	242.1	.433	.314	.753	13.6	31.9	45.6	22.0	7.1	6.6	14.8	21.3	92.9
Opponents	82	242.1	.437	.371	.749	11.8	30.2	42.0	21.7	7.7	5.3	13.1	20.2	95.5

Dallas Mavericks

Player	GP	MPG	FG%	3Pt%	FT%	OFF	DEF	Total	APG	SPG	BPG	TO	PF	PPG
Dirk Nowitzki	77	37.9	.462	.341	.877	1.20	7.50	8.70	2.7	1.19	1.35	1.75	2.80	21.8
Michael Finley	72	38.6	.443	.405	.850	1.10	3.40	4.50	2.9	1.17	.54	1.15	1.60	18.6
Antawn Jamison	82	29.0	.535	.400	.748	2.80	3.50	6.30	.9	1.01	.37	.99	2.10	14.8
Steve Nash	78	33.5	.470	.405	.916	.80	2.20	3.00	8.8	.86	.10	2.68	1.80	14.5
Antoine Walker	82	34.6	.428	.269	.554	2.40	5.90	8.30	4.5	.79	.79	2.46	2.60	14.0
Josh Howard	67	23.7	.430	.303	.703	2.20	3.30	5.50	1.4	1.03	.81	1.00	2.50	8.6
Marquis Daniels	56	18.6	.494	.306	.769	1.20	1.40	2.60	2.1	.95	.21	.79	.90	8.5
Tony Delk	33	15.4	.380	.303	.841	.50	1.30	1.80	.8	.82	.21	.52	1.40	6.0
Danny Fortson	56	11.2	.511	.000	.815	2.00	2.40	4.50	.2	.21	.20	.66	2.60	3.9
Shawn Bradley	66	11.7	.473	.000	.837	1.10	1.50	2.60	.3	.50	1.12	.26	2.00	3.3
Eduardo Najera	58	12.4	.444	.500	.652	1.20	1.50	2.70	.4	.60	.33	.50	1.60	3.0
Scott Williams	43	12.3	.484	.667	.593	.90	2.20	3.10	.4	.47	.37	.37	2.20	4.6
Travis Best	61	12.5	.372	.150	.870	.30	.80	1.10	1.8	.51	.07	.54	1.10	2.8
Mavericks	82	241.5	.459	.348	.796	14.3	31.0	45.3	23.9	8.0	5.3	12.2	19.6	105.2
Opponents	82	241.5	.459	.363	.746	12.3	31.2	43.5	23.6	7.1	4.7	15.2	20.6	100.8

Denver Nuggets

Player	GP	MPG	FG%	3Pt%	FT%	OFF	DEF	Total	APG	SPG	BPG	TO	PF	PPG
Carmelo Anthony	82	36.5	.426	.322	.777	2.20	3.80	6.10	2.8	1.18	.50	3.01	2.70	21.0
Andre Miller	82	34.6	.457	.185	.832	1.50	2.90	4.50	6.1	1.73	.30	2.62	2.40	14.8
Voshon Lenard	73	30.6	.422	.367	.791	.60	2.10	2.70	2.1	.84	.16	1.38	2.40	14.2
Nenê	77	32.5	.530	.000	.682	2.00	4.50	6.50	2.2	1.51	.53	2.38	3.60	11.8
Earl Boykins	82	22.5	.419	.322	.877	.50	1.20	1.70	3.6	.62	.04	1.22	1.00	10.2
Marcus Camby	72	30.0	.477	.000	.721	2.90	7.20	10.10	1.8	1.19	2.60	1.36	3.30	8.6
Rodney White	72	13.7	.459	.379	.750	.60	1.70	2.30	.8	.44	.28	1.08	1.50	7.5
Jon Barry	57	19.3	.404	.370	.845	.40	1.70	2.20	2.6	1.00	.14	.93	1.20	6.2
Michael Doleac	26	13.2	.412	.000	.875	1.10	1.80	2.90	.5	.23	.23	.42	2.20	3.6
Michael Doleac	72	14.3	.435	.000	.865	1.20	2.50	3.70	.6	.32	.50	.67	2.00	4.5
Francisco Elson	62	14.1	.472	.000	.667	1.00	2.20	3.30	.5	.56	.63	.56	2.30	3.5
Chris Andersen	71	14.5	.443	.000	.589	1.30	2.90	4.20	.5	.48	1.61	.68	1.70	3.4
N. Tskitishvili	39	7.9	.328	.273	.793	.60	1.00	1.60	.3	.15	.21	.44	1.30	2.7
Jeff Trepagnier	11	8.7	.263	.500	.500	.50	.80	1.40	.4	.27	.00	.55	.60	2.3
Ryan Bowen	52	7.5	.340	.000	.833	.80	.90	1.70	.3	.35	.31	.12	.90	.9
Mark Pope	4	5.0	.500	.000	.000	.00	.80	.80	.0	.25	.00	.75	2.00	.5
Nuggets	82	240.6	.443	.336	.767	13.2	29.1	42.3	21.9	9.1	6.3	15.6	22.0	97.2
Opponents	82	240.6	.453	.356	.728	12.9	30.1	42.9	23.5	8.1	5.8	17.1	23.1	96.1

Detroit Pistons

Player	GP	MPG	FG%	3Pt%	FT%	OFF	DEF	Total	APG	SPG	BPG	TO	PF	PPG
			Field Goals			Rebounds								
Richard Hamilton...78		35.5	.455	.265	.868	1.00	2.60	3.60	4.0	1.32	.22	2.69	2.80	17.6
C. Billups..............78		35.4	.394	.388	.878	.40	3.10	3.50	5.7	1.08	.10	2.42	2.30	16.9
R. Wallace............68		35.1	.436	.331	.736	1.50	5.30	6.80	2.3	.90	1.79	1.75	2.80	16.0
Tayshaun Prince....82		32.9	.467	.363	.766	1.10	3.60	4.80	2.3	.77	.84	1.45	1.80	10.3
Mehmet Okur 71		22.3	.463	.375	.775	2.30	3.70	5.90	1.0	.51	.89	1.42	1.90	9.6
Ben Wallace 81		37.7	.421	.125	.490	4.00	8.40	12.40	1.7	1.77	3.04	1.52	2.00	9.5
C. Williamson 79		19.9	.505	.000	.731	1.10	2.10	3.20	.7	.38	.25	1.43	2.60	9.5
Mike James..........26		19.7	.401	.364	.844	.30	1.90	2.20	3.7	1.00	.04	1.58	1.70	6.3
Mike James..........81		27.1	.414	.377	.811	.30	2.50	2.90	4.2	1.19	.04	1.53	1.90	9.3
Elden Campbell...65		13.7	.439	.000	.685	.80	2.40	3.20	.7	.32	.77	.97	2.10	5.6
Lindsey Hunter.....33		20.0	.343	.280	.625	.40	1.60	2.00	2.6	1.18	.18	1.03	1.40	3.5
Darvin Ham..........54		9.0	.493	.500	.600	.90	.90	1.70	.3	.24	.15	.57	1.20	1.8
Darko Milicic 34		4.7	.262	.000	.583	.30	.90	1.30	.2	.21	.44	.38	1.00	1.4
T. Fowlkes............36		7.3	.313	.125	.722	.50	1.00	1.50	.4	.25	.08	.33	1.00	1.2
Pistons..............82		**241.2**	**.435**	**.344**	**.753**	**12.4**	**30.4**	**42.8**	**20.8**	**8.0**	**7.0**	**15.1**	**20.3**	**90.1**
Opponents 82		**241.2**	**.413**	**.302**	**.744**	**12.0**	**28.7**	**40.6**	**19.0**	**7.9**	**5.0**	**16.0**	**22.9**	**84.3**

Golden State Warriors

Player	GP	MPG	FG%	3Pt%	FT%	OFF	DEF	Total	APG	SPG	BPG	TO	PF	PPG
			Field Goals			Rebounds								
J. Richardson.......78		37.6	.438	.282	.684	1.60	5.10	6.70	2.9	1.10	.53	2.51	2.30	18.7
Nick Van Exel 39		32.2	.390	.307	.707	.40	2.30	2.70	5.3	.51	.05	2.00	1.50	12.6
Erick Dampier 74		32.5	.535	.000	.654	4.60	7.30	12.00	.8	.45	1.85	1.77	3.10	12.3
Clifford Robinson ..82		34.7	.387	.357	.711	.70	3.30	3.90	3.3	.83	.89	2.11	2.90	11.8
Mike Dunleavy ...75		31.1	.449	.370	.741	1.20	4.70	5.90	2.9	.91	.17	1.91	2.30	11.7
Speedy Claxton ...60		26.6	.427	.182	.813	.60	2.00	2.60	4.5	1.62	.15	1.70	2.40	10.6
Troy Murphy 28		21.8	.440	.294	.750	1.70	4.50	6.20	.7	.43	.61	1.21	2.10	10.0
Brian Cardinal 76		21.5	.472	.444	.878	1.30	2.90	4.20	1.4	.87	.26	1.11	2.70	9.6
Calbert Cheaney.79		26.2	.481	.000	.610	1.00	2.30	3.30	1.7	.76	.15	1.08	2.30	7.6
Mickael Pietrus.....53		14.1	.416	.333	.693	.90	1.30	2.20	.5	.60	.23	.75	1.90	5.3
Avery Johnson ...46		13.8	.402	.000	.667	.10	.70	.70	2.4	.57	.07	1.11	.70	4.6
Sean Lampley 10		6.3	.650	.000	.667	.20	.90	1.10	.2	.00	.10	.30	.20	3.4
Adonal Foyle 44		13.0	.454	.000	.543	1.20	2.60	3.80	.4	.14	1.05	.48	1.50	3.1
J.R. Bremer 36		12.3	.272	.257	.650	.30	.80	1.00	1.4	.50	.11	.67	.90	3.3
Cherokee Parks...12		5.3	.400	.000	.667	.30	.50	.80	.1	.00	.25	.17	.60	1.0
Rusty LaRue .....:..4		5.5	.333	1.000	.500	.00	.80	.80	.5	.50	.00	1.00	.50	1.0
Popeye Jones 5		2.0	.000	.000	.000	.20	.00	.20	.0	.00	.00	.00	.40	.0
Warriors 82		**242.1**	**.442**	**.334**	**.725**	**12.2**	**30.9**	**43.1**	**20.5**	**7.0**	**4.7**	**14.8**	**20.6**	**93.3**
Opponents 82		**242.1**	**.445**	**.374**	**.746**	**12.0**	**30.9**	**42.8**	**21.5**	**8.1**	**5.1**	**14.0**	**22.0**	**94.0**

Houston Rockets

Player	GP	MPG	FG%	3Pt%	FT%	OFF	DEF	Total	APG	SPG	BPG	TO	PF	PPG
			Field Goals			Rebounds								
Yao Ming 82		32.8	.522	.000	.809	2.40	6.60	9.00	1.5	.27	1.90	2.49	3.30	17.5
Steve Francis 79		40.4	.403	.292	.775	1.50	4.00	5.50	6.2	1.76	.44	3.72	3.30	16.6
Cuttino Mobley......80		40.4	.426	.390	.811	.50	4.00	4.50	3.2	1.34	.41	2.25	2.20	15.8
Jim Jackson 80		39.0	.424	.400	.843	.70	5.40	6.10	2.8	1.08	.29	2.19	2.80	12.9
Maurice Taylor......75		27.7	.480	.000	.736	1.70	3.40	5.10	1.4	.57	.63	1.99	3.40	11.5
Kelvin Cato...........69		25.3	.447	.000	.676	2.20	4.60	6.80	1.0	.75	1.39	1.22	2.90	6.1
C. Weatherspoon .52		16.7	.493	.000	.736	1.40	2.50	3.90	.6	.58	.29	.67	1.40	5.0
Eric Piatkowski.....49		14.3	.377	.352	.855	.20	1.30	1.50	.5	.33	.10	.59	.90	4.1
Scott Padgett........58		9.4	.443	.431	.750	.80	1.60	2.40	.4	.21	.22	.38	1.30	3.4
Bostjan Nachbar ..45		11.5	.356	.365	.724	.20	1.40	1.60	.7	.31	.31	.51	1.60	3.1
Mark Jackson.......42		13.7	.340	.171	.718	.20	1.40	1.70	2.8	.40	.02	1.26	1.00	2.5
Mike Wilks 26		5.6	.472	.600	.833	.10	.50	.60	.7	.12	.00	.27	.60	1.9
Alton Ford.............9		4.6	.545	.000	.500	.30	.90	1.20	.3	.00	.11	.33	1.00	1.7
Charles Oakley 7		3.6	.333	.000	.833	.00	.70	.70	.3	.00	.00	.14	1.10	1.3
Adrian Griffin 19		7.0	.278	.500	.000	.10	.90	1.00	.5	.37	.11	.16	.90	.6
Rockets 82		**243.0**	**.442**	**.366**	**.773**	**10.3**	**32.3**	**42.6**	**19.3**	**6.8**	**5.4**	**16.7**	**21.5**	**89.8**
Opponents 82		**243.0**	**.412**	**.372**	**.737**	**11.1**	**28.7**	**39.7**	**20.6**	**8.7**	**4.4**	**13.5**	**20.7**	**88.0**

Indiana Pacers

Player	GP	MPG	Field Goals FG%	Field Goals 3Pt%	FT%	Rebounds OFF	Rebounds DEF	Total	APG	SPG	BPG	TO	PF	PPG
Jermaine O'Neal ...78		35.7	.434	.111	.757	2.50	7.50	10.00	2.1	.76	2.55	2.32	3.20	20.1
Ron Artest 73		37.2	.421	.310	.733	1.40	3.90	5.30	3.7	2.08	.68	2.77	2.70	18.3
Al Harrington 79		30.9	.463	.273	.734	2.10	4.40	6.40	1.7	1.01	.28	2.06	3.20	13.3
Reggie Miller 80		28.2	.438	.401	.885	.20	2.10	2.40	3.1	.81	.14	.85	1.20	10.0
Jamaal Tinsley 52		26.5	.414	.372	.731	.50	2.10	2.60	5.8	1.62	.33	2.12	2.50	8.3
J. Bender 21		12.9	.472	.409	.830	.40	1.50	1.90	.4	.24	.52	1.57	1.10	7.0
Anthony Johnson ...73		21.9	.406	.336	.798	.40	1.40	1.80	2.8	.88	.11	1.03	1.90	6.2
Jeff Foster 82		23.9	.544	.000	.669	3.00	4.40	7.40	.8	.87	.33	.73	2.30	6.1
Kenny Anderson ...44		20.6	.441	.250	.729	.40	1.40	1.80	2.8	.59	.11	1.14	1.70	6.0
Austin Croshere ...77		13.6	.388	.389	.894	.80	2.40	3.20	.7	.31	.18	.71	1.30	5.0
Fred Jones 81		18.6	.395	.303	.832	.30	1.20	1.60	2.1	.80	.22	.90	1.60	4.9
Jamison Brewer ...13		12.3	.371	.357	.167	.20	.70	.80	1.3	.54	.00	.77	.70	2.5
Scot Pollard.........61		11.1	.412	.000	.571	1.10	1.60	2.70	.2	.38	.43	.36	1.80	1.7
Primoz Brezec......18		4.0	.462	.000	.667	.30	.60	.80	.2	.00	.17	.33	.70	1.6
James Jones 6		4.3	.222	.250	1.000	.00	.30	.30	.0	.17	.00	.00	.20	1.2
Pacers................82		**241.5**	**.435**	**.351**	**.764**	**11.8**	**29.9**	**41.7**	**21.6**	**8.9**	**5.0**	**14.4**	**20.8**	**91.4**
Opponents 82		**241.5**	**.432**	**.324**	**.750**	**10.6**	**29.5**	**40.1**	**20.1**	**7.1**	**6.2**	**15.9**	**21.9**	**85.6**

Los Angeles Clippers

Player	GP	MPG	Field Goals FG%	Field Goals 3Pt%	FT%	Rebounds OFF	Rebounds DEF	Total	APG	SPG	BPG	TO	PF	PPG
Corey Maggette ...73		36.0	.447	.329	.848	1.30	4.60	5.90	3.1	.89	.22	2.84	3.00	20.7
Elton Brand 69		38.7	.493	.000	.773	3.90	6.40	10.30	3.3	.93	2.23	2.80	3.30	20.0
Q. Richardson......65		36.0	.398	.352	.740	2.20	4.10	6.40	2.1	1.03	.29	2.17	2.00	17.2
Chris Wilcox 65		20.6	.521	.000	.700	1.90	2.80	4.70	.8	.45	.31	1.23	2.80	8.6
Marko Jaric 58		30.3	.388	.340	.733	.80	2.30	3.00	4.8	1.60	.34	1.98	2.30	8.5
Bobby Simmons...56		24.6	.394	.167	.834	2.10	2.60	4.70	1.7	.91	.30	1.30	3.00	7.8
Eddie House 60		19.8	.359	.375	.800	.50	1.80	2.30	2.5	1.08	.07	1.05	1.50	6.8
P. Drobnjak..........61		15.6	.393	.306	.849	.90	2.30	3.20	.6	.36	.39	.79	1.40	6.3
Keyon Dooling 58		19.6	.389	.174	.830	.30	1.10	1.40	2.2	.78	.10	1.12	1.90	6.2
Chris Kaman 82		22.5	.460	.000	.697	1.50	4.10	5.60	1.0	.28	.89	1.89	2.60	6.1
Matt Barnes.........38		18.9	.457	.154	.705	1.40	2.60	4.00	1.3	.71	.08	1.16	2.00	4.5
Melvin Ely 42		12.1	.431	.000	.595	1.10	1.30	2.40	.5	.21	.40	.48	1.60	3.7
Glen Rice 18		14.6	.289	.179	1.000	.50	1.80	2.30	1.3	.33	.00	.72	1.20	3.7
Doug Overton 61		16.9	.404	.130	.742	.30	1.10	1.40	2.3	.43	.03	.95	1.50	3.7
Randy Livingston ...4		12.0	.200	.000	.667	.50	1.30	1.80	1.0	.50	.00	1.00	1.80	2.0
Olden Polynice....2		6.0	.000	.000	.000	.50	.50	1.00	.5	.50	.00	2.00	1.00	.0
Clippers 82		**241.5**	**.428**	**.321**	**.785**	**14.0**	**29.5**	**43.5**	**20.2**	**7.2**	**4.6**	**16.4**	**22.1**	**94.8**
Opponents 82		**241.5**	**.460**	**.360**	**.741**	**12.6**	**28.8**	**41.4**	**22.9**	**8.5**	**5.3**	**13.7**	**22.7**	**99.4**

Los Angeles Lakers

Player	GP	MPG	Field Goals FG%	Field Goals 3Pt%	FT%	Rebounds OFF	Rebounds DEF	Total	APG	SPG	BPG	TO	PF	PPG
Kobe Bryant.........65		37.6	.438	.327	.852	1.60	3.90	5.50	5.1	1.72	.43	2.63	2.70	24.0
Shaquille O'Neal ...67		36.8	.584	.000	.490	3.70	7.80	11.50	2.9	.51	2.48	2.91	3.40	21.5
Gary Payton 82		34.5	.471	.333	.714	.90	3.30	4.20	5.5	1.17	.23	1.84	2.10	14.6
Karl Malone 42		32.7	.483	.000	.747	1.50	7.30	8.70	3.9	1.19	.48	2.45	2.80	13.2
S. Medvedenko ...68		21.2	.441	.000	.767	2.20	2.90	5.00	.8	.56	.26	.87	2.80	8.3
Devean George ...82		23.8	.408	.349	.760	1.10	3.00	4.00	1.4	.99	.46	1.07	2.30	7.4
Derek Fisher 82		21.6	.352	.291	.797	.40	1.50	1.90	2.3	1.26	.05	.96	1.40	7.1
Kareem Rush 72		17.3	.440	.348	.596	.30	1.10	1.30	.8	.46	.28	.67	1.50	6.4
Rick Fox 38		22.3	.392	.246	.733	.80	1.90	2.70	2.6	.76	.11	1.26	2.60	4.8
Brian Cook 35		12.6	.475	.000	.750	.90	2.00	2.90	.6	.46	.46	.49	1.80	4.4
Horace Grant 55		20.1	.411	.000	.722	1.40	2.80	4.20	1.3	.44	.38	.53	1.30	4.1
Bryon Russell 72		13.1	.402	.384	.769	.40	1.40	1.80	1.0	.44	.17	.51	1.50	4.0
Jamal Sampson ...10		13.0	.478	.000	.583	2.30	2.90	5.20	.7	.20	.40	.60	1.60	2.9
Luke Walton 72		10.1	.425	.333	.705	.50	1.20	1.80	1.6	.39	.11	.61	1.00	2.4
Ime Udoka 4		7.0	.333	.000	.500	.30	1.00	1.30	.5	.50	.25	.75	.80	2.0
Lakers................82		**242.1**	**.454**	**.327**	**.693**	**12.2**	**30.9**	**43.1**	**23.8**	**8.3**	**4.6**	**13.8**	**21.1**	**98.2**
Opponents 82		**242.1**	**.440**	**.337**	**.749**	**11.2**	**31.2**	**42.4**	**20.8**	**7.5**	**3.8**	**15.3**	**24.7**	**94.3**

Memphis Grizzlies

Player	GP	MPG	FG%	3Pt%	FT%	OFF	DEF	Total	APG	SPG	BPG	TO	PF	PPG
Pau Gasol	78	31.5	.482	.267	.714	2.60	5.10	7.70	2.5	.56	1.69	2.40	2.40	17.7
James Posey	82	29.9	.478	.386	.830	1.10	3.80	4.90	1.5	1.67	.49	1.37	3.00	13.7
Bonzi Wells	59	24.9	.437	.344	.750	1.00	2.40	3.40	1.8	1.20	.27	2.19	2.70	12.3
Bonzi Wells	72	26.0	.427	.319	.754	1.10	2.50	3.60	1.9	1.26	.26	2.24	2.70	12.3
Mike Miller	65	27.2	.438	.372	.723	.60	2.70	3.30	3.6	.91	.22	1.65	2.50	11.1
Jason Williams	72	29.4	.407	.330	.837	.30	1.70	2.00	6.8	1.28	.07	1.89	1.30	10.9
Stromile Swift	77	19.8	.469	.250	.725	1.80	3.10	4.90	.5	.73	1.53	1.14	2.40	9.4
Lorenzen Wright	65	25.8	.439	.000	.733	2.20	4.60	6.80	1.1	.69	.89	1.18	3.00	9.4
Shane Battier	79	24.6	.446	.349	.732	1.30	2.50	3.80	1.3	1.28	.73	.71	2.40	8.5
Earl Watson	81	20.6	.371	.245	.652	.60	1.60	2.20	5.0	1.12	.23	1.80	2.20	5.7
Bo Outlaw	82	19.6	.510	.000	.526	1.50	2.60	4.20	1.1	.89	.85	.84	2.10	4.6
Jake Tsakalidis	40	13.3	.504	.000	.590	.90	2.30	3.20	.5	.23	.55	.58	2.00	4.3
Theron Smith	20	8.9	.372	.500	.750	.70	1.40	2.10	.4	.25	.25	.70	.90	2.2
Dahntay Jones	20	7.7	.283	.250	.455	.40	.80	1.20	.6	.25	.30	.60	1.20	1.8
Troy Bell	6	5.7	.222	.000	1.000	.50	.20	.70	.7	.17	.00	1.00	1.00	1.8
Ryan Humphrey	2	5.5	.250	.000	.000	1.00	.50	1.50	.5	.50	.00	1.00	1.50	1.0
Grizzlies	82	242.4	.445	.340	.727	12.8	29.0	41.8	23.4	9.7	6.9	15.0	23.2	96.7
Opponents	82	242.4	.436	.338	.764	13.4	30.6	44.0	20.4	8.2	5.6	17.0	23.1	94.3

Miami Heat

Player	GP	MPG	FG%	3Pt%	FT%	OFF	DEF	Total	APG	SPG	BPG	TO	PF	PPG
Eddie Jones	81	37.0	.409	.370	.835	.50	3.30	3.80	3.2	1.14	.42	1.59	2.80	17.3
Lamar Odom	80	37.5	.430	.298	.742	2.00	7.70	9.70	4.1	1.06	.89	2.95	3.40	17.1
Dwyane Wade	61	34.9	.465	.302	.747	1.40	2.70	4.00	4.5	1.41	.56	3.21	2.30	16.2
Rafer Alston	82	31.5	.376	.371	.769	.30	2.40	2.80	4.5	1.39	.22	1.56	2.60	10.2
Caron Butler	68	29.9	.380	.238	.756	1.40	3.40	4.80	1.9	1.10	.19	1.34	2.40	9.2
Brian Grant	76	30.3	.471	.000	.782	2.30	4.60	6.90	.9	.67	.46	1.08	3.30	8.7
Udonis Haslem	75	23.9	.459	.000	.765	2.50	3.80	6.30	.7	.44	.32	.99	2.60	7.3
Rasual Butler	45	15.0	.474	.463	.762	.10	1.30	1.40	.5	.22	.29	.62	1.60	6.8
John Wallace	37	9.9	.421	.385	.775	.30	1.30	1.60	.4	.14	.22	.65	1.00	4.3
Malik Allen	45	13.7	.419	.000	.758	.90	1.70	2.60	.4	.27	.62	.60	1.80	4.2
Samaki Walker	33	12.7	.384	.000	.659	1.30	2.10	3.40	.2	.27	.33	.45	1.60	3.2
Loren Woods	38	13.3	.458	.000	.600	1.70	1.80	3.50	.3	.29	.50	.68	1.40	3.2
Wang Zhizhi	16	7.1	.370	.286	.900	.30	.90	1.10	.1	.19	.31	.38	.80	2.9
Tyrone Hill	5	7.6	.600	.000	.750	1.00	.60	1.60	.0	.00	.20	.40	2.00	1.8
Kirk Penney	2	9.0	.167	.333	.000	.00	.50	.50	.5	.50	.00	1.50	.50	1.5
Bimbo Coles	22	7.7	.353	.000	.667	.10	.40	.50	.7	.14	.00	.41	1.20	1.3
Jerome Beasley	2	2.5	.333	.000	.000	.00	.50	.50	.0	.00	.00	.00	.00	1.0
Heat	82	240.9	.425	.357	.762	11.5	30.0	41.5	19.1	7.2	3.8	13.9	22.1	90.3
Opponents	82	240.9	.428	.343	.768	10.9	30.3	41.2	18.6	7.1	5.4	14.7	21.1	89.7

Milwaukee Bucks

Player	GP	MPG	FG%	3Pt%	FT%	OFF	DEF	Total	APG	SPG	BPG	TO	PF	PPG
Michael Redd	82	36.8	.440	.350	.868	1.40	3.50	5.00	2.3	.99	.07	1.41	1.90	21.7
Keith Van Horn	62	32.5	.454	.399	.859	2.10	4.90	7.00	1.7	.94	.46	2.35	3.00	16.1
Desmond Mason	82	30.9	.472	.231	.769	1.10	3.20	4.40	1.9	.73	.29	1.80	2.30	14.4
Joe Smith	76	29.7	.439	.200	.859	3.00	5.40	8.50	1.0	.62	1.24	1.08	2.80	10.9
Brian Skinner	56	28.2	.497	.000	.572	2.10	5.20	7.30	.9	.54	1.09	1.39	2.90	10.5
Toni Kukoc	73	20.8	.417	.292	.729	.80	2.90	3.70	2.7	.81	.29	1.51	1.50	8.4
T.J. Ford	55	26.8	.384	.238	.816	.70	2.50	3.20	6.5	1.09	.05	2.53	2.20	7.1
Damon Jones	82	24.6	.401	.359	.764	.20	1.90	2.10	5.8	.37	.05	1.26	1.10	7.0
Brevin Knight	56	18.5	.427	.250	.754	.30	1.80	2.00	3.6	1.50	.02	1.29	1.90	4.7
Dan Gadzuric	75	16.8	.524	.000	.492	1.70	2.90	4.60	.4	.68	1.40	.60	2.50	5.7
Erick Strickland	43	13.3	.403	.439	.863	.90	1.30	1.70	2.1	.60	.05	1.26	1.50	5.4
Daniel Santiago	54	13.1	.479	.000	.678	.60	1.80	2.40	.4	.35	.39	.59	1.80	4.0
Dan Langhi	6	6.2	.357	.500	1.000	.00	.70	.70	.0	.00	.00	.33	1.20	2.2
Marcus Haislip	31	8.5	.486	.500	.714	.70	1.00	1.70	.1	.19	.39	.29	.80	3.0
Bucks	82	241.2	.447	.350	.775	11.7	30.5	42.2	22.8	6.8	4.7	13.5	20.3	98.0
Opponents	82	241.2	.452	.352	.739	12.0	30.7	42.7	22.8	7.5	5.0	14.2	22.9	97.0

Minnesota Timberwolves

Player	GP	MPG	FG%	3Pt%	FT%	OFF	DEF	Total	APG	SPG	BPG	TO	PF	PPG
			Field Goals			Rebounds								
Kevin Garnett	82	40.5	.502	.282	.751	3.00	10.50	13.40	6.0	1.38	1.57	2.79	2.40	23.0
Wally Szczerbiak	52	35.3	.481	.421	.867	1.00	3.60	4.60	2.6	.85	.42	1.67	2.40	17.6
Troy Hudson	79	32.9	.428	.365	.900	.50	1.80	2.30	5.7	.76	.09	2.30	2.00	14.2
R. Nesterovic	77	30.4	.525	.000	.642	1.90	4.60	6.50	1.5	.51	1.51	1.29	3.30	11.2
Kendall Gill	82	25.2	.422	.322	.764	.60	2.40	3.00	1.9	.95	.18	1.32	2.10	8.7
Anthony Peeler	82	27.4	.414	.410	.780	.50	2.50	2.90	3.0	.88	.16	1.00	2.00	7.7
Joe Smith	54	20.7	.460	.000	.779	2.10	2.90	5.00	.7	.26	1.02	.80	3.20	7.5
Rod Strickland	47	20.3	.432	.091	.738	.40	1.60	2.00	4.6	.98	.13	1.62	1.20	6.8
Gary Trent	80	15.3	.535	.000	.594	1.30	2.30	3.60	1.0	.40	.29	.74	1.80	6.0
Marc Jackson	77	13.5	.438	1.000	.765	1.10	1.80	2.90	.5	.31	.39	.77	1.80	5.5
Reggie Slater	26	5.4	.540	.000	.600	.70	.50	1.20	.2	.23	.04	.35	1.20	3.1
Loren Woods	38	9.3	.382	.333	.778	.70	1.80	2.50	.5	.26	.34	.61	1.00	2.1
Mike Wilks	46	15.0	.338	.286	.787	.40	1.10	1.50	2.0	.59	.09	.61	1.50	3.2
Igor Rakocevic	42	5.8	.379	.417	.806	.10	.30	.40	.8	.10	.00	.55	.60	1.9
Timberwolves	**82**	**241.5**	**.466**	**.368**	**.770**	**11.7**	**31.9**	**43.6**	**25.2**	**6.7**	**5.3**	**13.7**	**20.8**	**98.1**
Opponents	**82**	**241.5**	**.437**	**.347**	**.752**	**11.9**	**29.8**	**41.7**	**22.8**	**7.0**	**4.9**	**13.6**	**20.6**	**96.0**

New Jersey Nets

Player	GP	MPG	FG%	3Pt%	FT%	OFF	DEF	Total	APG	SPG	BPG	TO	PF	PPG
			Field Goals			Rebounds								
Richard Jefferson	82	38.2	.498	.364	.763	1.30	4.30	5.70	3.8	1.12	.34	2.41	2.70	18.5
Kenyon Martin	65	34.6	.488	.280	.684	2.00	7.40	9.50	2.5	1.46	1.26	2.58	3.50	16.7
Jason Kidd	67	36.6	.384	.321	.827	1.30	5.10	6.40	9.2	1.82	.21	3.19	1.60	15.5
Kerry Kittles	82	34.7	.453	.351	.787	.70	3.30	4.00	2.5	1.52	.49	1.16	1.80	13.1
Alonzo Mourning	12	17.9	.465	.000	.882	.70	1.60	2.30	.7	.17	.50	.83	2.70	8.0
Rodney Rogers	69	20.4	.410	.329	.765	1.40	3.00	4.40	2.0	.86	.39	1.42	2.70	7.8
Lucious Harris	69	21.8	.404	.376	.846	.60	1.50	2.00	2.0	.59	.03	.77	1.10	6.9
Aaron Williams	72	18.6	.503	.333	.677	1.40	2.70	4.10	1.1	.47	.64	1.24	2.60	6.3
Jason Collins	78	28.5	.424	.000	.739	1.80	3.30	5.10	2.0	.86	.72	1.24	3.20	5.9
Brian Scalabrine	69	13.4	.394	.244	.829	.60	1.90	2.50	.9	.30	.20	.61	1.60	3.5
Zoran Planinic	49	9.7	.411	.281	.633	.30	.80	1.10	1.4	.27	.06	.73	1.40	3.1
B. Armstrong	56	7.8	.371	.365	.500	.20	.60	.80	.3	.21	.04	.43	.90	2.7
Tamar Slay	22	7.5	.350	.333	.500	.50	.70	1.10	.6	.32	.05	.50	.90	2.4
Robert Pack	26	8.5	.423	.000	.833	.20	.50	.70	1.0	.46	.04	.62	.80	1.9
Damone Brown	3	5.7	.100	.000	.500	1.00	.70	1.70	.0	.67	.00	.33	.70	1.0
A. Goldwire	11	7.7	.318	.250	1.000	.10	.50	.60	1.0	.45	.00	.27	.50	1.5
Hubert Davis	17	4.6	.091	.000	1.000	.10	.40	.50	.2	.12	.00	.18	.70	.2
Nets	**82**	**240.3**	**.441**	**.336**	**.753**	**10.5**	**30.2**	**40.7**	**24.5**	**8.7**	**3.9**	**14.7**	**21.0**	**90.3**
Opponents	**82**	**240.3**	**.427**	**.350**	**.761**	**10.6**	**30.1**	**40.8**	**19.8**	**8.0**	**4.6**	**16.1**	**21.2**	**87.8**

New Orleans Hornets

Player	GP	MPG	FG%	3Pt%	FT%	OFF	DEF	Total	APG	SPG	BPG	TO	PF	PPG
			Field Goals			Rebounds								
Baron Davis	67	40.1	.395	.321	.673	1.00	3.30	4.30	7.5	2.36	.40	3.21	2.70	22.9
Jamal Mashburn	19	38.4	.392	.284	.813	1.00	5.20	6.20	2.5	.74	.26	1.95	2.20	20.8
David Wesley	61	32.8	.389	.323	.753	.50	1.70	2.20	2.9	1.16	.23	1.64	2.40	14.0
Jamaal Magloire	82	33.9	.473	.000	.751	3.30	7.10	10.30	1.0	.52	1.23	2.45	3.40	13.6
Darrell Armstrong	79	28.4	.395	.315	.854	.80	2.10	2.90	3.9	1.68	.20	1.96	1.90	10.6
P.J. Brown	80	34.4	.476	.000	.854	3.00	5.70	8.60	1.9	.98	.91	1.26	2.50	10.5
Stacey Augmon	69	20.5	.412	.143	.791	.80	1.80	2.50	1.2	.80	.22	1.10	1.70	5.8
Robert Traylor	71	13.3	.505	.400	.547	1.50	2.20	3.70	.6	.55	.52	.87	2.30	5.1
Steve Smith	71	13.1	.406	.402	.928	.40	.80	1.10	.8	.21	.08	.59	1.30	5.0
George Lynch	78	21.8	.397	.309	.667	1.20	2.80	4.00	1.5	.62	.23	.82	2.00	4.8
S. Williams	53	14.4	.375	.300	.879	.20	1.00	1.10	2.2	.70	.04	.89	1.20	4.8
David West	71	13.1	.474	.000	.713	1.60	2.50	4.20	.8	.38	.39	.68	1.60	3.8
Maurice Carter	10	11.0	.314	.364	.800	.20	.90	1.10	.4	.00	.00	.90	1.00	4.2
Tierre Brown	3	5.7	.500	.000	.500	.00	.30	.30	.7	.00	.00	2.33	.30	2.0
Bryce Drew	15	5.2	.222	.143	1.000	.00	.40	.40	.9	.27	.00	.53	.10	.8
Hornets	**82**	**241.8**	**.420**	**.319**	**.751**	**13.3**	**29.5**	**42.8**	**20.9**	**8.6**	**4.2**	**15.0**	**20.9**	**91.8**
Opponents	**82**	**241.8**	**.441**	**.341**	**.750**	**11.9**	**30.2**	**42.1**	**21.8**	**7.5**	**5.2**	**15.6**	**21.1**	**91.9**

New York Knicks

Player	GP	MPG	Field Goals		FT%	Rebounds			APG	SPG	BPG	TO	PF	PPG
			FG%	3Pt%		OFF	DEF	Total						
Stephon Marbury...81		40.2	.431	.318	.817	.70	2.50	3.20	8.9	1.59	.11	3.07	2.10	20.2
Allan Houston.......50		36.0	.435	.431	.913	.40	2.00	2.40	2.0	.76	.04	2.04	2.10	18.5
Tim Thomas 66		31.7	.446	.376	.784	1.00	3.90	4.80	1.9	.97	.30	1.76	3.00	14.7
Kurt Thomas......80		31.9	.473	.000	.835	1.80	6.50	8.30	1.9	.70	1.00	1.65	3.70	11.1
A. Hardaway 76		27.6	.411	.380	.804	.90	2.90	3.80	2.3	.92	.26	1.41	1.90	9.2
Nazr Mohammed...80		20.1	.521	.000	.592	2.20	3.70	5.90	.5	.69	.65	1.20	2.40	7.4
S. Anderson 80		24.7	.422	.281	.764	.70	2.10	2.80	1.5	.85	.21	1.48	2.30	7.9
Vin Baker..............54		24.3	.481	.333	.726	2.10	3.10	5.20	1.2	.54	.59	1.43	3.00	9.8
D. Mutombo 65		23.0	.478	.000	.681	2.20	4.50	6.70	.4	.26	1.89	.83	2.20	5.6
DerMarr Johnson...21		13.7	.371	.361	.903	.20	1.60	1.90	.5	.38	.33	.76	1.50	5.4
O. Harrington 56		15.6	.495	.000	.744	1.00	2.10	3.20	.5	.21	.25	1.16	2.40	4.6
Mike Sweetney....42		11.8	.493	.000	.724	1.60	2.10	3.70	.3	.43	.29	.76	1.40	4.3
Moochie Norris.....66		12.8	.369	.345	.761	.20	.80	1.00	1.8	.67	.08	.97	.80	3.5
Frank-Williams....56		12.8	.385	.300	.854	.10	.80	.90	2.2	.45	.11	1.13	1.00	3.9
Bruno Sundov........5		6.6	.400	.000	.500	.40	1.60	2.00	.2	.00	.00	.60	1.80	2.2
Cezary Trybanski ...7		2.1	.000	.000	.500	.00	.10	.10	.0	.14	.14	.29	.40	.1
Knicks...............82		**242.4**	**.442**	**.364**	**.793**	**11.6**	**31.0**	**42.6**	**20.7**	**7.4**	**4.8**	**15.7**	**23.1**	**92.0**
Opponents 82		**242.4**	**.429**	**.338**	**.763**	**11.6**	**29.8**	**41.4**	**20.4**	**8.2**	**4.7**	**13.8**	**19.5**	**93.5**

Orlando Magic

Player	GP	MPG	Field Goals		FT%	Rebounds			APG	SPG	BPG	TO	PF	PPG
			FG%	3Pt%		OFF	DEF	Total						
Tracy McGrady 67		39.9	.417	.339	.796	1.40	4.60	6.00	5.5	1.39	.63	2.67	1.90	28.0
Juwan Howard 81		35.5	.453	.000	.809	2.10	4.90	7.00	2.0	.67	.27	2.20	3.50	17.0
Drew Gooden 79		27.0	.445	.214	.637	2.00	4.50	6.50	1.1	.78	.91	1.59	2.50	11.6
D. Stevenson.......80		30.6	.432	.268	.676	1.00	2.70	3.70	2.0	.65	.21	1.50	1.80	11.4
Tyronn Lue 76		30.7	.433	.383	.771	.30	2.10	2.50	4.2	.80	.07	1.63	2.40	10.5
Keith Bogans 73		24.5	.403	.358	.631	1.50	2.90	4.30	1.3	.63	.14	1.03	1.80	6.8
Zaza Pachulia 59		11.3	.389	.000	.644	1.20	1.80	2.90	.2	.36	.20	.58	1.50	3.3
A. DeClercq 71		17.1	.477	.000	.815	1.80	2.60	4.50	.6	.66	.45	.76	3.10	3.2
D. Penigar............10		8.9	.500	.000	1.000	.60	1.80	2.40	.3	.20	.20	.60	1.40	3.2
Steven Hunter.....59		13.4	.529	.000	.333	.90	2.00	2.90	.2	.08	1.24	.49	1.70	3.2
Derrick Dial 9		9.6	.321	.222	.750	.60	.90	1.40	.2	.67	.00	.11	.70	2.9
Sean Rooks..........55		10.8	.358	.000	.892	.40	1.30	1.80	.5	.25	.18	.40	1.60	2.6
Britton Johnsen....20		14.5	.288	.083	.438	.80	1.50	2.30	.6	.35	.05	.70	1.40	2.1
Reece Gaines.......38		9.6	.291	.300	.640	.20	.80	1.00	1.1	.29	.05	.47	.60	1.8
Mengke Bateer 7		5.7	.571	.000	.000	.70	.40	1.10	.1	.14	.00	.29	1.40	1.1
Pat Garrity.............2		11.0	.333	.000	.000	.00	.00	.00	.5	.00	.00	.00	1.00	1.0
Magic 82		**241.8**	**.429**	**.344**	**.737**	**12.2**	**28.7**	**40.9**	**19.3**	**6.7**	**3.8**	**13.7**	**21.3**	**94.0**
Opponents 82		**241.8**	**.466**	**.377**	**.742**	**13.1**	**31.3**	**44.4**	**24.4**	**7.6**	**5.5**	**13.6**	**20.6**	**101.1**

Philadelphia 76ers

Player	GP	MPG	Field Goals		FT%	Rebounds			APG	SPG	BPG	TO	PF	PPG
			FG%	3Pt%		OFF	DEF	Total						
Allen Iverson 48		42.5	.387	.286	.745	.70	3.00	3.70	6.8	2.40	.10	4.35	1.80	26.4
Glenn Robinson....42		31.8	.448	.340	.832	1.10	3.40	4.50	1.4	1.00	.21	2.52	2.30	16.6
Kenny Thomas 74		36.5	.469	.200	.752	3.50	6.60	10.10	1.5	1.11	.45	2.32	3.00	13.6
Eric Snow 82		36.2	.413	.111	.797	.80	2.70	3.40	6.9	1.18	.07	2.28	2.60	10.3
Marc Jackson........22		27.2	.415	.000	.790	2.00	3.70	5.70	.8	.55	.27	1.09	2.00	9.4
Aaron McKie 75		28.2	.459	.436	.757	.60	2.80	3.40	2.6	1.13	.31	1.37	1.90	9.2
Derrick Coleman...34		24.8	.413	.222	.754	1.30	4.30	5.60	1.4	.68	.76	1.68	2.30	8.0
S. Dalembert 82		26.8	.541	.000	.644	2.40	5.30	7.60	.3	.54	2.30	1.05	3.30	8.0
Willie Green..........53		14.5	.401	.311	.728	.30	.90	1.20	1.0	.49	.09	1.11	1.60	6.9
John Salmons 77		20.8	.387	.340	.772	.50	2.10	2.50	1.7	.81	.21	1.00	1.60	5.8
Kyle Korver 74		11.9	.352	.391	.792	.40	1.10	1.50	.5	.34	.11	.55	1.40	4.5
Zendon Hamilton...45		10.5	.537	.000	.698	1.10	2.20	3.20	.3	.18	.18	.60	1.60	3.8
Greg Buckner........53		13.3	.377	.273	.741	.50	1.40	1.90	.8	.40	.08	.64	1.50	3.1
Amal McCaskill 59		10.8	.402	.000	.704	.80	1.40	2.30	.3	.20	.34	.42	1.50	1.9
76ers.................82		**242.1**	**.428**	**.342**	**.753**	**11.5**	**29.4**	**40.8**	**20.0**	**8.0**	**4.4**	**15.9**	**20.7**	**88.0**
Opponents 82		**242.1**	**.432**	**.333**	**.744**	**12.1**	**29.2**	**41.4**	**21.3**	**8.3**	**5.7**	**15.2**	**21.4**	**90.5**

Phoenix Suns

Player	GP	MPG	FG%	3Pt%	FT%	OFF	DEF	Total	APG	SPG	BPG	TO	PF	PPG
A. Stoudemire	55	36.8	.475	.200	.713	2.90	6.20	9.00	1.4	1.16	1.62	3.22	3.40	20.6
Shawn Marion	79	40.7	.440	.340	.851	2.70	6.60	9.30	2.7	2.11	1.32	1.97	2.60	19.0
Joe Johnson	82	40.6	.430	.305	.750	1.00	3.70	4.70	4.4	1.13	.32	2.43	2.20	16.7
L. Barbosa	70	21.4	.447	.395	.770	.30	1.40	1.80	2.4	1.33	.10	1.71	2.60	7.9
Howard Eisley	67	21.7	.368	.319	.854	.30	1.60	1.90	4.1	.84	.07	1.46	2.00	6.9
Jake Voskuhl	66	24.3	.507	.000	.740	1.90	3.30	5.20	.9	.64	.38	1.17	3.90	6.6
Casey Jacobsen	78	23.4	.417	.417	.820	.50	2.00	2.60	1.3	.62	.12	.87	1.80	6.0
A. McDyess	42	22.1	.470	.000	.551	1.70	4.50	6.10	.9	.88	.57	1.36	2.80	6.9
Maciej Lampe	21	10.7	.489	.000	.769	.40	1.70	2.10	.4	.14	.14	.71	1.30	4.6
Jahidi White	62	14.0	.521	.000	.500	1.60	2.60	4.20	.1	.40	.82	1.06	2.80	4.2
Z. Cabarkapa	49	11.6	.411	.188	.660	.50	1.50	2.00	.8	.20	.27	1.10	1.50	4.1
Donnell Harvey	60	13.1	.443	.000	.735	.80	1.90	2.70	.4	.40	.45	.75	2.20	4.0
Suns	**82**	**240.6**	**.443**	**.345**	**.746**	**11.3**	**29.3**	**40.6**	**19.3**	**9.0**	**4.7**	**15.2**	**22.7**	**94.2**
Opponents	**82**	**240.6**	**.446**	**.349**	**.765**	**12.7**	**31.1**	**43.8**	**21.5**	**7.9**	**5.3**	**15.9**	**19.4**	**97.9**

Portland Trail Blazers

Player	GP	MPG	FG%	3Pt%	FT%	OFF	DEF	Total	APG	SPG	BPG	TO	PF	PPG
Zach Randolph	81	37.9	.485	.200	.761	3.00	7.50	10.50	2.0	.84	.51	3.05	2.80	20.1
Derek Anderson	51	35.5	.376	.305	.824	.50	3.10	3.60	4.5	1.29	.06	1.76	1.50	13.6
D. Stoudamire	82	38.0	.401	.365	.876	.60	3.10	3.80	6.1	1.21	.11	2.20	2.10	13.4
Darius Miles	79	26.3	.485	.175	.642	1.40	3.10	4.50	2.1	.85	.77	1.65	2.10	10.9
S. Abdur-Rahim	56	31.6	.475	.265	.869	2.20	5.30	7.50	2.0	.80	.44	2.16	2.60	16.3
Theo Ratliff	85	31.3	.485	.000	.645	2.30	4.90	7.20	.8	.64	3.61	1.41	3.50	7.9
R. Patterson	73	22.6	.506	.167	.553	1.80	1.90	3.70	1.9	1.15	.29	1.44	2.10	6.9
Dale Davis	76	22.1	.473	.000	.613	2.10	3.20	5.20	.9	.57	.82	.53	2.00	4.4
Qyntel Woods	62	10.9	.371	.345	.633	.70	1.50	2.20	.7	.32	.23	.84	1.40	3.6
Vladimir Stepania	42	11.8	.417	.000	.611	1.20	1.80	3.00	.5	.26	.36	.45	1.50	2.6
Kaniel Dickens	3	4.0	1.000	.000	.500	.70	.00	.70	.0	.00	.00	.33	1.00	2.3
Dan Dickau	43	6.8	.378	.333	.786	.20	.40	.60	.9	.40	.00	.60	1.00	2.2
Eddie Gill	22	7.1	.417	.375	.850	.20	.60	.80	.7	.41	.05	.55	.70	2.3
D. Ferguson	7	4.6	.417	.375	.000	.00	.60	.60	.1	.00	.00	.14	.00	1.9
Tracy Murray	7	5.0	.250	.400	.000	.40	.30	.70	.1	.14	.00	.29	.40	1.1
Travis Outlaw	8	2.4	.429	.000	.500	.30	.30	.50	.1	.13	.00	.13	.10	1.0
Omar Cook	17	8.2	.259	.000	.000	.20	.20	.40	1.4	.59	.00	.59	.80	.8
Slavko Vranes	1	3.0	.000	.000	.000	.00	.00	.00	.0	.00	.00	.00	1.00	.0
Trail Blazers	**82**	**243.7**	**.448**	**.346**	**.731**	**12.7**	**29.0**	**41.7**	**21.6**	**7.5**	**5.4**	**14.8**	**19.0**	**90.7**
Opponents	**82**	**243.7**	**.450**	**.341**	**.753**	**12.4**	**28.0**	**40.3**	**23.3**	**8.0**	**4.8**	**13.7**	**18.7**	**92.0**

Sacramento Kings

Player	GP	MPG	FG%	3Pt%	FT%	OFF	DEF	Total	APG	SPG	BPG	TO	PF	PPG
P. Stojakovic	81	40.3	.480	.433	.927	1.10	5.10	6.30	2.1	1.33	.17	1.89	2.00	24.2
Chris Webber	23	36.1	.413	.200	.711	2.10	6.60	8.70	4.6	1.35	.87	2.61	3.30	18.7
Mike Bibby	82	36.3	.450	.392	.815	.80	2.60	3.40	5.4	1.37	.22	2.13	1.80	18.4
Brad Miller	72	36.4	.510	.316	.778	2.70	7.70	10.30	4.3	.94	1.19	2.00	3.40	14.1
Bobby Jackson	50	23.7	.444	.370	.752	1.10	2.40	3.50	2.1	.98	.16	1.26	2.10	13.8
Doug Christie	82	33.9	.461	.345	.860	.80	3.20	4.00	4.2	1.84	.50	1.89	2.30	10.1
Vlade Divac	81	28.6	.470	.154	.654	1.70	4.00	5.70	5.3	.70	.95	2.14	2.70	9.9
Anthony Peeler	75	18.5	.448	.482	.836	.40	1.60	2.00	1.6	.75	.13	1.03	1.40	5.7
Darius Songaila	73	13.4	.487	.000	.807	1.20	1.80	3.10	.7	.58	.16	.59	1.70	4.6
T. Massenburg	59	13.4	.475	.000	.683	1.00	2.20	3.20	.5	.24	.31	.76	2.40	4.3
Jabari Smith	31	5.4	.371	.000	.600	.40	.60	1.00	.4	.06	.19	.23	.80	2.1
Gerald Wallace	37	9.1	.360	.000	.458	.90	1.10	2.00	.5	.38	.38	.22	1.00	2.0
Rodney Buford	22	6.4	.339	.000	.500	.30	.40	.70	.3	.27	.05	.18	.40	1.9
Kings	**82**	**241.2**	**.462**	**.401**	**.796**	**10.8**	**30.4**	**41.2**	**26.2**	**8.7**	**4.0**	**13.9**	**19.3**	**102.8**
Opponents	**82**	**241.2**	**.454**	**.339**	**.749**	**13.2**	**30.7**	**43.9**	**21.3**	**7.9**	**5.0**	**14.9**	**22.2**	**97.8**

San Antonio Spurs

Player	GP	MPG	FG%	3Pt%	FT%	OFF	DEF	Total	APG	SPG	BPG	TO	PF	PPG
Tim Duncan	69	36.6	.501	.167	.599	3.30	9.20	12.40	3.1	.90	2.68	2.65	2.40	22.3
Tony Parker	75	34.4	.447	.312	.702	.60	2.60	3.20	5.5	.81	.09	2.39	2.00	14.7
Emanuel Ginobili	77	29.4	.418	.359	.802	1.10	3.40	4.50	3.8	1.77	.21	2.09	2.40	12.8
Hidayet Turkoglu	80	25.9	.406	.419	.708	.70	3.80	4.50	1.9	1.00	.40	1.18	2.10	9.2
R. Nesterovic	82	28.7	.469	.000	.474	3.10	4.60	7.70	1.4	.62	2.01	1.30	3.00	8.7
Malik Rose	67	18.7	.428	.000	.813	1.60	3.10	4.80	1.0	.54	.36	1.67	2.40	7.9
Bruce Bowen	82	32.0	.420	.363	.579	.50	2.50	3.10	1.4	1.02	.40	1.10	2.00	6.9
Charlie Ward	71	17.6	.410	.408	.741	.20	1.90	2.00	3.0	.90	.15	1.35	1.50	6.0
Ron Mercer	39	13.2	.427	.286	.765	.30	1.00	1.30	.6	.36	.13	.67	.90	5.0
Robert Horry	81	15.9	.405	.380	.645	1.30	2.00	3.40	1.2	.59	.60	.68	2.00	4.8
Anthony Carter	5	17.4	.297	.000	.000	.40	1.80	2.20	2.4	.80	.00	2.40	1.80	4.4
Devin Brown	58	10.8	.434	.286	.811	.70	1.60	2.20	.6	.26	.07	.66	1.10	4.0
Shane Heal	6	12.0	.292	.222	.800	.20	.50	.70	.8	.17	.00	.83	.30	3.7
Kevin Willis	48	7.8	.467	.000	.615	.80	1.30	2.00	.2	.44	.19	.67	1.30	3.4
Jason Hart	53	12.5	.447	.222	.767	.20	1.30	1.50	1.5	.53	.09	.55	1.10	3.3
Alex Garcia	2	6.5	.143	.000	.500	.00	.00	.00	.0	1.00	.00	.50	.00	1.5
Matt Carroll	16	4.4	.438	.333	.667	.10	.30	.40	.1	.06	.00	.38	.50	1.2
Spurs	82	240.9	.442	.358	.681	12.5	32.5	45.1	20.4	8.1	6.6	14.7	20.3	91.5
Opponents	82	240.9	.409	.327	.744	11.1	30.0	41.1	17.3	7.7	4.6	15.3	22.4	84.3

Seattle SuperSonics

Player	GP	MPG	FG%	3Pt%	FT%	OFF	DEF	Total	APG	SPG	BPG	TO	PF	PPG
Ray Allen	56	38.4	.440	.392	.904	1.20	3.90	5.10	4.8	1.27	.20	2.79	2.40	23.0
Rashard Lewis	80	36.6	.435	.376	.763	1.70	4.80	6.50	2.2	1.24	.68	1.69	2.90	17.8
Ronald Murray	82	24.6	.425	.293	.715	.50	1.90	2.50	2.5	.99	.34	1.82	1.90	12.4
V. Radmanovic	77	30.1	.425	.371	.748	1.40	3.90	5.30	1.8	1.04	.55	1.42	2.40	12.0
Brent Barry	59	30.6	.504	.452	.827	.40	3.10	3.50	5.8	1.44	.27	2.36	2.10	10.8
Antonio Daniels	71	21.3	.470	.362	.842	.30	1.70	2.00	4.2	.63	.08	.86	.90	8.0
Vitaly Potapenko	65	21.8	.489	.000	.641	1.60	2.90	4.40	.8	.34	.43	1.18	2.50	7.1
Luke Ridnour	82	16.1	.414	.338	.823	.50	1.10	1.60	2.4	.75	.10	1.16	1.50	5.5
Jerome James	65	15.2	.498	.000	.660	1.20	2.30	3.50	.5	.31	.92	1.26	2.80	5.0
Calvin Booth	71	17.0	.466	.000	.798	1.20	2.70	3.90	.4	.24	1.42	.63	2.10	4.9
Ansu Sesay	57	10.2	.455	.286	.696	.80	.90	1.60	.3	.33	.35	.40	1.20	3.5
Richie Frahm	54	8.7	.453	.370	.885	.20	.80	1.00	.4	.30	.07	.13	.90	3.4
Reggie Evans	75	17.1	.406	.000	.561	2.10	3.40	5.40	.4	.72	.13	.87	2.30	2.9
Leon Smith	1	4.0	.500	.000	.000	1.00	1.00	2.00	.0	.00	.00	.00	1.00	2.0
Sonics	82	241.5	.446	.373	.765	11.1	28.3	39.3	21.7	8.1	4.7	14.5	21.8	97.1
Opponents	82	241.5	.450	.349	.774	13.0	29.6	42.7	21.1	7.7	4.7	14.8	20.2	97.8

Toronto Raptors

Player	GP	MPG	FG%	3Pt%	FT%	OFF	DEF	Total	APG	SPG	BPG	TO	PF	PPG
Vince Carter	73	38.2	.417	.383	.806	1.30	3.50	4.80	4.8	1.21	.89	3.05	2.90	22.5
Donyell Marshall	82	36.4	.461	.403	.736	2.60	7.30	9.90	1.5	1.13	1.51	1.43	3.00	14.7
Jalen Rose	66	37.8	.402	.342	.810	.50	3.50	4.00	5.0	.77	.33	3.15	2.80	15.5
Chris Bosh	75	33.5	.459	.357	.701	2.50	4.90	7.40	1.0	.79	1.41	1.43	2.90	11.5
Alvin Williams	56	30.9	.405	.292	.776	.30	2.40	2.70	4.0	.98	.18	1.39	2.00	8.8
Morris Peterson	82	26.2	.405	.371	.809	.40	2.80	3.20	1.4	1.07	.17	.84	2.50	8.3
Lamond Murray	33	15.7	.353	.350	.686	.40	2.30	2.70	.8	.45	.21	1.15	1.40	6.0
Rod Strickland	61	19.6	.425	.278	.735	.60	2.00	2.50	4.0	.57	.18	1.39	1.20	6.3
Dion Glover	69	23.8	.390	.336	.769	.80	3.00	3.90	1.9	.72	.28	1.48	1.80	9.0
Milt Palacio	59	20.5	.349	.154	.662	.30	1.50	1.70	3.1	.69	.19	1.47	1.50	4.4
Roger Mason Jr.	26	12.6	.327	.333	.864	.00	1.20	1.20	1.0	.42	.23	.77	1.40	3.7
Michael Curry	70	17.6	.388	.200	.845	.30	.90	1.20	.8	.33	.07	.69	2.20	2.9
Jerome Moiso	35	11.9	.476	.000	.579	1.20	2.10	3.20	.2	.49	.34	.71	1.20	2.9
Corie Blount	62	16.9	.455	.000	.556	1.60	2.90	4.40	.9	.79	.39	.69	2.20	4.0
Robert Archibald	32	8.0	.273	.000	.452	.70	1.00	1.60	.4	.44	.09	.31	1.60	1.0
Raptors	82	243.7	.418	.356	.750	10.1	29.5	39.6	19.2	7.4	4.9	14.2	21.3	85.4
Opponents	82	243.7	.428	.307	.747	12.6	32.5	45.1	18.5	7.2	4.1	14.6	19.7	88.5

Utah Jazz

Player	GP	MPG	FG%	3Pt%	FT%	OFF	DEF	Total	APG	SPG	BPG	TO	PF	PPG
				Field Goals			**Rebounds**							
Andrei Kirilenko	78	37.1	.443	.338	.790	2.90	5.20	8.10	3.1	1.92	2.76	2.76	2.20	16.5
Matt Harpring	31	36.6	.471	.242	.688	2.90	5.00	8.00	2.0	.71	.06	2.10	3.30	16.2
Gordan Giricek	73	28.0	.436	.395	.854	.70	2.40	3.10	1.7	.77	.21	1.41	2.00	11.3
Carlos Arroyo	71	28.3	.441	.325	.804	.60	2.00	2.60	5.0	.89	.07	2.20	2.30	12.6
Raja Bell	82	24.6	.409	.373	.786	.70	2.20	2.90	1.3	.77	.16	1.35	3.20	11.2
Raul Lopez	82	19.7	.431	.294	.863	.30	1.60	1.90	3.7	.76	.02	2.12	2.40	7.0
Greg Ostertag	78	27.6	.476	.000	.579	2.80	4.60	7.40	1.6	.38	1.78	1.27	2.90	6.8
Jarron Collins	81	21.4	.498	.000	.718	1.40	2.50	3.90	1.0	.32	.22	.98	3.10	6.0
Maurice Williams	57	13.5	.380	.256	.786	.40	.90	1.30	1.3	.49	.04	.89	1.50	5.0
A. Pavlovic	79	14.5	.396	.271	.774	.60	1.50	2.00	.8	.52	.20	.85	2.40	4.8
Mikki Moore	32	12.3	.505	.000	.857	.90	1.70	2.60	.6	.22	.41	.69	2.00	4.1
Ben Handlogten	17	10.1	.532	.000	.667	1.30	1.90	3.20	.4	.18	.24	.59	1.90	4.0
Tom Gugliotta	55	14.9	.345	.250	.714	1.20	2.20	3.40	1.1	.56	.22	.71	1.50	2.9
Curtis Borchardt	16	16.1	.393	.000	.778	.80	2.60	3.40	.9	.25	.88	1.13	2.50	3.6
Michael Ruffin	41	17.9	.325	.000	.421	1.90	3.10	5.00	1.0	.54	.51	1.02	2.50	2.2
Jazz	**82**	**241.2**	**.436**	**.321**	**.746**	**13.5**	**27.7**	**41.2**	**20.4**	**7.1**	**6.0**	**16.7**	**25.6**	**88.7**
Opponents	**82**	**241.2**	**.432**	**.343**	**.771**	**10.6**	**26.0**	**36.6**	**18.6**	**8.1**	**6.5**	**15.4**	**24.4**	**89.9**

Washington Wizards

Player	GP	MPG	FG%	3Pt%	FT%	OFF	DEF	Total	APG	SPG	BPG	TO	PF	PPG
				Field Goals			**Rebounds**							
Gilbert Arenas	55	37.6	.392	.375	.748	1.00	3.60	4.60	5.0	1.87	.22	4.11	3.20	19.6
Larry Hughes	61	33.8	.397	.341	.797	1.60	3.80	5.30	2.4	1.56	.43	2.49	2.40	18.8
Jerry Stackhouse	26	29.8	.399	.354	.806	.60	3.00	3.60	4.0	.92	.12	3.38	1.90	13.9
Kwame Brown	74	30.3	.489	.500	.683	2.40	5.00	7.40	1.5	.89	.70	1.89	1.90	10.9
Jarvis Hayes	70	29.2	.400	.305	.786	1.00	2.80	3.80	1.5	1.01	.16	1.57	2.20	9.6
Juan Dixon	71	20.8	.388	.298	.799	.40	1.70	2.10	1.9	1.15	.06	1.46	1.60	9.4
Etan Thomas	79	24.1	.489	.000	.647	2.30	4.40	6.70	.9	.46	1.56	1.43	2.80	8.9
B. Haywood	77	19.3	.515	.000	.585	2.40	2.60	5.00	.6	.42	1.30	1.04	2.00	7.0
Steve Blake	75	18.6	.386	.371	.821	.20	1.30	1.60	2.8	.76	.09	1.71	1.30	5.9
Christian Laettner	48	20.5	.465	.286	.800	1.00	3.80	4.80	1.9	.77	.58	.88	2.10	5.9
Jared Jeffries	82	23.3	.377	.167	.614	2.20	3.00	5.20	1.1	.59	.34	1.30	2.60	5.7
Lonny Baxter	62	12.4	.493	.333	.579	1.00	2.00	3.00	.3	.27	.47	.61	2.00	4.0
Mitchell Butle	41	13.5	.435	.367	.625	.60	1.10	1.70	.8	.54	.10	.59	1.30	3.3
Chris Whitney	16	11.6	.378	.444	1.000	.20	.80	.90	1.9	.38	.13	.38	.40	2.9
Torraye Braggs	15	10.3	.485	.000	.667	1.20	1.40	2.60	.5	.27	.13	.87	1.90	2.7
Wizards	**82**	**241.8**	**.421**	**.341**	**.714**	**13.6**	**29.2**	**42.8**	**18.7**	**8.9**	**5.0**	**17.6**	**20.9**	**91.8**
Opponents	**82**	**241.8**	**.454**	**.342**	**.771**	**12.8**	**30.7**	**43.5**	**24.0**	**9.6**	**5.5**	**16.1**	**21.7**	**97.4**

2004 NBA Draft

The 2004 NBA Draft was held on June 24 in New York City.

First Round

1. Dwight Howard, Orlando
2. Emeka Okafor, Charlotte (from LAC)
3. Ben Gordon, Chicago
4. Shaun Livingston, LA Clippers
5. Devin Harris, Washington
6. Josh Childress, Atlanta
7. Luol Deng, Phoenix
8. Rafael Araujo, Toronto
9. Andre Iguodala, Philadelphia
10. Luke Jackson, Cleveland
11. Andris Biedrins, Golden State
12. Robert Swift, Seattle
13. Sebastian Telfair, Portland
14. Kris Humphries, Utah
15. Al Jefferson, Boston
16. Kirk Snyder, Utah (from New York/Phoenix)
17. Josh Smith, Atlanta
18. J.R. Smith, New Orleans
19. Dorell Wright, Miami
20. Jameer Nelson, Denver
21. P. Podkolzine, Utah (from Hou)
22. Viktor Khryapa, New Jersey

23. Sergie Monia, Port (from Mem)
24. Delonte West, Boston (from Dall)
25. Tony Allen, Boston (from Det)
26. Kevin Martin, Sacramento
27. Sasha Vujacic, LA Lakers
28. Beno Udrih, San Antonio
29. David Harrison, Indiana

Second Round

30. Anderson Varejao, Orlando
31. Jackson Vroman, Chicago
32. Peter John Ramos, Wash
33. Lionel Chalmers, LA Clippers (from Charlotte)
34. Donta Smith, Atlanta
35. Andre Emmett, Seattle (from LA Clippers)
36. Antonio Burks, Orlando (from Phoenix)
37. Royal Ivey, Atlanta (from Phil)
38. Chris Duhon, Chicago (from Tor)
39. Albert Miralles, Toronto (from Cleveland)
40. Justin Reed, Boston
41. David Young, Seattle

42. Viktor Sanikidze, Atlanta (from Orl/Phil/GS)
43. Trevor Ariza, New York
44. Tim Pickett, New Orleans
45. Bernard Robinson, Charlotte (from Milwaukee)
46. Ha Seung-Jin, Portland
47. Pape Sow, Miami
48. Ricky Minard, Sacramento (from Utah)
49. Sergei Lishouk, Memphis (from Denver/Orlando)
50. Vassillis Spanoulis, Dallas (from Houston/Denver)
51. Christian Drejer, New Jersey
52. Romain Sato, San Antonio (from Memphis)
53. Matt Freije, Miami (from Dall)
54. Rickey Paulding, Detroit
55. Luis Flores, Houston (from Sacramento/Utah)
56. Marcus Douthit, LA Lakers
57. Sergei Karaulov, SA
58. Blake Stepp, Minnesota
59. Rashad Wright, Indiana

Women's National Basketball Association

2003 Final Standings

EASTERN CONFERENCE

Team	W	L	Pct	GB
†Detroit	25	9	.735	—
*Charlotte	18	16	.529	7
*Connecticut	18	16	.529	7
*Cleveland	17	17	.500	8
Indiana	16	18	.471	9
New York	16	18	.471	9
Washington	9	25	.265	16

WESTERN CONFERENCE

Team	W	L	Pct	GB
†Los Angeles	24	10	.706	—
*Houston	20	14	.588	4
*Sacramento	19	15	.559	5
*Minnesota	18	16	.529	6
Seattle	18	16	.529	6
San Antonio	12	22	.353	12
Phoenix	8	26	.235	16

†Clinched conference title.   *Clinched playoff berth.

2003 Playoffs

FIRST ROUND

EASTERN CONFERENCE

Game 1	Cleveland	74	at Detroit	76
Game 2	Detroit	59	at Cleveland	66
Game 3	Cleveland	63	at Detroit	77

Detroit won series 2–1.

| Game 1 | Connecticut | 68 | at Charlotte | 66 |
| Game 2 | Charlotte | 62 | at Connecticut | 68 |

Connecticut won series 2–0.

WESTERN CONFERENCE

Game 1	Minnesota	74	at Los Angeles	72
Game 2	Los Angeles	80	at Minnesota	69
Game 3	Minnesota	64	at Los Angeles	74

Los Angeles won series 2–1.

Game 1	Sacramento	65	at Houston	59
Game 2	Houston	69	at Sacramento	48
Game 3	Sacramento	70	at Houston	68

Sacramento won series 2–1.

EASTERN CONFERENCE FINALS

| Game 1 | Connecticut | 63 | at Detroit | 73 |
| Game 2 | Detroit | 79 | at Connecticut | 73 |

Detroit won series 2–0.

WESTERN CONFERENCE FINALS

Game 1	Sacramento	77	at Los Angeles	69
Game 2	Los Angeles	79	at Sacramento	54
Game 3	Sacramento	63	at Los Angeles	66

Los Angeles won series 2–1.

WNBA FINALS

Game 1	Los Angeles	75	at Detroit	63
Game 2	Detroit	62	at Los Angeles	61
Game 3	Los Angeles	78	at Detroit	83

Detroit won series 2–1.

THEY SAID IT

Dion Glover, Raptors guard, after being surrounded by 10 reporters covering his first practice with the team after he was waived by the Hawks: "This is like our crowds in Atlanta."

FOR THE RECORD · Year by Year

NBA Champions

Season	Winner	Series	Runner-Up	Winning Coach	Finals MVP
1946–47	Philadelphia	4–1	Chicago	Eddie Gottlieb	—
1947–48	Baltimore	4–2	Philadelphia	Buddy Jeannette	—
1948–49	Minneapolis	4–2	Washington	John Kundla	—
1949–50	Minneapolis	4–2	Syracuse	John Kundla	—
1950–51	Rochester	4–3	New York	Les Harrison	—
1951–52	Minneapolis	4–3	New York	John Kundla	—
1952–53	Minneapolis	4–1	New York	John Kundla	—
1953–54	Minneapolis	4–3	Syracuse	John Kundla	—
1954–55	Syracuse	4–3	Ft Wayne	Al Cervi	—
1955–56	Philadelphia	4–1	Ft Wayne	George Senesky	—
1956–57	Boston	4–3	St Louis	Red Auerbach	—
1957–58	St Louis	4–2	Boston	Alex Hannum	—
1958–59	Boston	4–0	Minneapolis	Red Auerbach	—
1959–60	Boston	4–3	St Louis	Red Auerbach	—
1960–61	Boston	4–1	St Louis	Red Auerbach	—
1961–62	Boston	4–3	LA Lakers	Red Auerbach	—
1962–63	Boston	4–2	LA Lakers	Red Auerbach	—
1963–64	Boston	4–1	San Francisco	Red Auerbach	—
1964–65	Boston	4–1	LA Lakers	Red Auerbach	—
1965–66	Boston	4–3	LA Lakers	Red Auerbach	—
1966–67	Philadelphia	4–2	San Francisco	Alex Hannum	—
1967–68	Boston	4–2	LA Lakers	Bill Russell	—
1968–69	Boston	4–3	LA Lakers	Bill Russell	Jerry West, LA
1969–70	New York	4–3	LA Lakers	Red Holzman	Willis Reed, NY
1970–71	Milwaukee	4–0	Baltimore	Larry Costello	Kareem Abdul-Jabbar, Mil
1971–72	LA Lakers	4–1	New York	Bill Sharman	Wilt Chamberlain, LA
1972–73	New York	4–1	LA Lakers	Red Holzman	Willis Reed, NY
1973–74	Boston	4–3	Milwaukee	Tommy Heinsohn	John Havlicek, Bos
1974–75	Golden State	4–0	Washington	Al Attles	Rick Barry, GS
1975–76	Boston	4–2	Phoenix	Tommy Heinsohn	JoJo White, Bos
1976–77	Portland	4–2	Philadelphia	Jack Ramsay	Bill Walton, Port
1977–78	Washington	4–3	Seattle	Dick Motta	Wes Unseld, Wash
1978–79	Seattle	4–1	Washington	Lenny Wilkens	Dennis Johnson, Sea
1979–80	LA Lakers	4–2	Philadelphia	Paul Westhead	Magic Johnson, LA
1980–81	Boston	4–2	Houston	Bill Fitch	Cedric Maxwell, Bos
1981–82	LA Lakers	4–2	Philadelphia	Pat Riley	Magic Johnson, LA
1982–83	Philadelphia	4–0	LA Lakers	Billy Cunningham	Moses Malone, Phil
1983–84	Boston	4–3	LA Lakers	K.C. Jones	Larry Bird, Bos
1984–85	LA Lakers	4–2	Boston	Pat Riley	Kareem Abdul-Jabbar, LA
1985–86	Boston	4–2	Houston	K.C. Jones	Larry Bird, Bos
1986–87	LA Lakers	4–2	Boston	Pat Riley	Magic Johnson, LA
1987–88	LA Lakers	4–3	Detroit	Pat Riley	James Worthy, LA
1988–89	Detroit	4–0	LA Lakers	Chuck Daly	Joe Dumars, Det
1989–90	Detroit	4–1	Portland	Chuck Daly	Isiah Thomas, Det
1990–91	Chicago	4–1	LA Lakers	Phil Jackson	Michael Jordan, Chi
1991–92	Chicago	4–2	Portland	Phil Jackson	Michael Jordan, Chi
1992–93	Chicago	4–2	Phoenix	Phil Jackson	Michael Jordan, Chi
1993–94	Houston	4–3	New York	Rudy Tomjanovich	Hakeem Olajuwon, Hou
1994–95	Houston	4–0	Orlando	Rudy Tomjanovich	Hakeem Olajuwon, Hou
1995–96	Chicago	4–2	Seattle	Phil Jackson	Michael Jordan, Chi
1996–97	Chicago	4–2	Utah	Phil Jackson	Michael Jordan, Chi
1997–98	Chicago	4–2	Utah	Phil Jackson	Michael Jordan, Chi
1998–99	San Antonio	4–1	New York	Gregg Popovich	Tim Duncan, SA
1999–00	LA Lakers	4–2	Indiana	Phil Jackson	Shaquille O'Neal, LA
2000–01	LA Lakers	4–1	Philadelphia	Phil Jackson	Shaquille O'Neal, LA
2001–02	LA Lakers	4–0	New Jersey	Phil Jackson	Shaquille O'Neal, LA
2002–03	San Antonio	4–2	New Jersey	Gregg Popovich	Tim Duncan, SA
2003–04	Detroit	4–1	LA Lakers	Larry Brown	Chauncey Billups, Det

Most Valuable Player: Maurice Podoloff Trophy

Season	Player, Team	GP	Field Goals		3-Pt FG		Free Throws		Rebounds		A	Stl	BS	Avg
			FGM	Pct	FGM	Pct	FTM	Pct	Off	Total				
1955–56	Bob Pettit, StL	72	646	42.9	–	–	557	73.6	–	1,164	189	–	–	25.7
1956–57	Bob Cousy, Bos	64	478	37.8	–	–	363	82.1	–	309	478	–	–	20.6
1957–58	Bill Russell, Bos	69	456	44.2	–	–	230	51.9	–	1,564	202	–	–	16.6
1958–59	Bob Pettit, StL	72	719	43.8	–	–	667	75.9	–	1,182	221	–	–	29.2
1959–60	Wilt Chamberlain, Phil	72	1,065	46.1	–	–	577	58.2	–	1,941	168	–	–	37.6
1960–61	Bill Russell, Bos	78	532	42.6	–	–	258	55.0	–	1,868	264	–	–	16.9
1961–62	Bill Russell, Bos	76	575	45.7	–	–	286	59.5	–	1,891	341	–	–	18.9
1962–63	Bill Russell, Bos	78	511	43.2	–	–	287	55.5	–	1,843	348	–	–	16.8
1963–64	Oscar Robertson, Cin	79	840	48.3	–	–	800	85.3	–	783	868	–	–	31.4
1964–65	Bill Russell, Bos	78	429	43.8	–	–	244	57.3	–	1,878	410	–	–	14.1
1965–66	Wilt Chamberlain, Phil	79	1,074	54.0	–	–	501	51.3	–	1,943	414	–	–	33.5
1966–67	Wilt Chamberlain, Phil	81	785	68.3	–	–	386	44.1	–	1,957	630	–	–	24.1
1967–68	Wilt Chamberlain, Phil	82	819	59.5	–	–	354	38.0	–	1,952	702	–	–	24.3
1968–69	Wes Unseld, Balt	82	427	47.6	–	–	277	60.5	–	1,491	213	–	–	13.8
1969–70	Willis Reed, NY	81	702	50.7	–	–	351	75.6	–	1,126	161	–	–	21.7
1970–71	Kareem Abdul-Jabbar, Mil	82	1,063	57.7	–	–	470	69.0	–	1,311	272	–	–	31.7
1971–72	Kareem Abdul-Jabbar, Mil	81	1,159	57.4	–	–	504	68.9	–	1,346	370	–	–	34.8
1972–73	Dave Cowens, Bos	82	740	45.2	–	–	204	77.9	–	1,329	333	–	–	20.5
1973–74	Kareem Abdul-Jabbar, Mil	81	948	53.9	–	–	295	70.2	287	1,178	386	112	283	27.0
1974–75	Bob McAdoo, Buff	82	1,095	51.2	–	–	641	80.5	307	1,155	179	92	174	34.5
1975–76	Kareem Abdul-Jabbar, LA	82	914	52.9	–	–	447	70.3	272	1,383	413	119	338	27.7
1976–77	Kareem Abdul-Jabbar, LA	82	888	57.9	–	–	376	70.1	266	1,090	319	101	261	26.2
1977–78	Bill Walton, Port	58	460	52.2	–	–	177	72.0	118	766	291	60	146	18.9
1978–79	Moses Malone, Hou	82	716	54.0	–	–	599	73.9	587	1,444	147	79	119	24.8
1979–80	Kareem Abdul-Jabbar, LA	82	835	60.4	0	00.0	364	76.5	190	886	371	81	280	24.8
1980–81	Julius Erving, Phil	82	794	52.1	4	22.2	422	78.7	244	657	364	173	147	24.6
1981–82	Moses Malone, Hou	81	945	51.9	0	00.0	630	76.2	558	1,188	142	76	125	31.1
1982–83	Moses Malone, Phil	78	654	50.1	0	00.0	600	76.1	445	1,194	101	89	157	24.5
1983–84	Larry Bird, Bos	79	758	49.2	18	24.7	374	88.8	181	796	520	144	69	24.2
1984–85	Larry Bird, Bos	80	918	52.2	56	42.7	403	88.2	164	842	531	129	98	28.7
1985–86	Larry Bird, Bos	82	796	49.6	82	42.3	441	89.6	190	805	557	166	51	25.8
1986–87	Magic Johnson, LA Lakers	80	683	52.2	8	20.5	535	84.8	122	504	977	138	36	23.9
1987–88	Michael Jordan, Chi	82	1,069	53.5	7	13.2	723	84.1	139	449	485	259	131	35.0
1988–89	Magic Johnson, LA Lakers	77	579	50.9	59	31.4	513	91.1	111	607	988	138	22	22.5
1989–90	Magic Johnson, LA Lakers	79	546	48.0	106	38.4	567	89.0	128	522	907	132	34	22.3
1990–91	Michael Jordan, Chi	82	990	53.9	29	31.2	571	85.1	118	492	453	223	83	31.5
1991–92	Michael Jordan, Chi	80	943	51.9	27	27.0	491	83.2	91	511	489	182	75	30.1
1992–93	Charles Barkley, Phoe	76	716	52.0	67	30.5	445	76.5	237	928	385	119	74	25.6
1993–94	Hakeem Olajuwon, Hou	80	894	52.8	8	42.1	388	71.6	229	955	287	128	297	27.3
1994–95	David Robinson, SA	81	788	53.0	6	30.0	656	77.4	234	877	236	134	262	27.6
1995–96	Michael Jordan, Chi	82	916	49.5	111	42.7	548	83.4	148	543	352	180	42	30.4
1996–97	Karl Malone, Utah	82	864	55.0	0	00.0	521	75.5	193	809	368	113	48	27.4
1997–98	Michael Jordan, Chi	82	881	46.5	30	23.8	565	78.4	130	475	283	141	45	28.7
1998–99	Karl Malone, Utah	49	393	49.3	0	00.0	378	78.8	107	463	201	62	28	23.8
1999–00	Shaquille O'Neal, LA Lakers	79	956	57.4	0	00.0	432	52.4	336	1078	299	36	239	29.7
2000–01	Allen Iverson, Phil	71	762	42.0	98	32.0	585	81.4	50	273	325	78	20	31.1
2001–02	Tim Duncan, SA	82	764	50.8	1	10.0	560	79.9	268	1042	307	61	203	25.5
2002–03	Tim Duncan, SA	81	714	51.3	6	27.3	450	71.0	260	1045	316	55	237	23.3
2003–04	Kevin Garnett, Minn	82	804	49.9	11	25.6	368	79.1	245	1139	409	120	178	24.2

Coach of the Year: Arnold (Red) Auerbach Trophy

1962–63...Harry Gallatin, StL
1963–64...Alex Hannum, SF
1964–65...Red Auerbach, Bos
1965–66...Dolph Schayes, Chi
1966–67...Johnny Kerr, Chi
1967–68...Richie Guerin, StL
1968–69...Gene Shue, Balt
1969–70...Red Holzman, NY
1970–71...Dick Motta, Chi
1971–72...Bill Sharman, LA
1972–73...Tom Heinsohn, Bos
1973–74...Ray Scott, Det
1974–75...Phil Johnson, KC-Oma
1975–76...Bill Fitch, Clev

1976–77...Tom Nissalke, Hou
1977–78...Hubie Brown, Atl
1978–79...Cotton Fitzsimmons, KC
1979–80...Bill Fitch, Bos
1980–81...Jack McKinney, Ind
1981–82...Gene Shue, Wash
1982–83...Don Nelson, Mil
1983–84...Frank Layden, Utah
1984–85...Don Nelson, Mil
1985–86...Mike Fratello, Atl
1986–87...Mike Schuler, Port
1987–88...Doug Moe, Den
1988–89...Cotton Fitzsimmons, Phoe
1989–90...Pat Riley, LA Lakers

1990–91...Don Chaney, Hou
1991–92...Don Nelson, GS
1992–93...Pat Riley, NY
1993–94...Lenny Wilkens, Atl
1994–95...Del Harris, LA Lakers
1995–96...Phil Jackson, Chi
1996–97...Pat Riley, Mia
1997–98...Larry Bird, Ind
1998–99...Mike Dunleavy, Port
1999–00...Glenn (Doc) Rivers, Orl
2000–01...Larry Brown, Phil
2001–02...Rick Carlisle, Det
2002–03...Gregg Popovich, SA
2003–04...Hubie Brown, Mem

Note: Award named after Auerbach in 1986.

Rookie of the Year: Eddie Gottlieb Trophy

1952–53...Don Meineke, FW
1953–54...Ray Felix, Balt
1954–55...Bob Pettit, Mil
1955–56...Maurice Stokes, Roch
1956–57...Tom Heinsohn, Bos
1957–58...Woody Sauldsberry, Phil
1958–59...Elgin Baylor, Minn
1959–60...Wilt Chamberlain, Phil
1960–61...Oscar Robertson, Cin
1961–62...Walt Bellamy, Chi
1962–63...Terry Dischinger, Chi
1963–64...Jerry Lucas, Cin
1964–65...Willis Reed, NY
1965–66...Rick Barry, SF
1966–67...Dave Bing, Det
1967–68...Earl Monroe, Balt
1968–69...Wes Unseld, Balt
1969–70...K. Abdul-Jabbar, Mil

1970–71...Dave Cowens, Bos
　　　　　Geoff Petrie, Port
1971–72...Sidney Wicks, Port
1972–73...Bob McAdoo, Buff
1973–74...Ernie DiGregorio, Buff
1974–75...Keith Wilkes, GS
1975–76...Alvan Adams, Phoe
1976–77...Adrian Dantley, Buff
1977–78...Walter Davis, Phoe
1978–79...Phil Ford, KC
1979–80...Larry Bird, Bos
1980–81...Darrell Griffith, Utah
1981–82...Buck Williams, NJ
1982–83...Terry Cummings, SD
1983–84...Ralph Sampson, Hou
1984–85...Michael Jordan, Chi
1985–86...Patrick Ewing, NY
1986–87...Chuck Person, Ind

1987–88...Mark Jackson, NY
1988–89...Mitch Richmond, GS
1989–90...David Robinson, SA
1990–91...Derrick Coleman, NJ
1991–92...Larry Johnson, Char
1992–93...Shaquille O'Neal, Orl
1993–94...Chris Webber, GS
1994–95...J. Kidd, Dall/G. Hill, Det
1995–96...Damon Stoudamire, Tor
1996–97...Allen Iverson, Phil
1997–98...Tim Duncan, SA
1998–99...Vince Carter, Tor
1999–00..Steve Francis, Hou
　　　　　Elton Brand, Chi
2000–01 ..Mike Miller, Orl
2001–02..Pau Gasol, Mem
2002–03 ..Amare Stoudemire, Phoe
2003–04 ..LeBron James, Clev

Defensive Player of the Year

1982–83...Sidney Moncrief, Mil
1983–84...Sidney Moncrief, Mil
1984–85...Mark Eaton, Utah
1985–86...Alvin Robertson, SA
1986–87...Michael Cooper, Lakers
1987–88...Michael Jordan, Chi
1988–89...Mark Eaton, Utah
1989–90...Dennis Rodman, Det

1990–91...Dennis Rodman, Det
1991–92...David Robinson, SA
1992–93...Hakeem Olajuwon, Hou
1993–94...Hakeem Olajuwon, Hou
1994–95...Dikembe Mutombo, Den
1995–96...Gary Payton, Sea
1996–97...Dikembe Mutombo, Den

1997–98...Dikembe Mutombo, Atl
1998–99...Alonzo Mourning, Mia
1999–00...Alonzo Mourning, Mia
2000–01...Dikembe Mutombo, Phil
2001–02...Ben Wallace, Det
2002–03...Ben Wallace, Det
2003–04...Ron Artest, Ind

Sixth Man Award

1982–83...Bobby Jones, Phil
1983–84...Kevin McHale, Bos
1984–85...Kevin McHale, Bos
1985–86...Bill Walton, Bos
1986–87...Ricky Pierce, Mil
1987–88...Roy Tarpley, Dall
1988–89...Eddie Johnson, Phoe
1989–90...Ricky Pierce, Mil

1990–91...Detlef Schrempf, Ind
1991–92...Detlef Schrempf, Ind
1992–93...Cliff Robinson, Port
1993–94...Dell Curry, Char
1994–95...Anthony Mason, NY
1995–96...Tony Kukoc, Chi
1996–97...John Starks, NY

1997–98...Danny Manning, Phoe
1998–99...Darrell Armstrong, Orl
1999–00...Rodney Rogers, Phoe
2000–01...Aaron McKie, Phil
2001–02...Corliss Williamson, Det
2002–03...Bobby Jackson, Sac
2003–04...Antawn Jamison, Dall

J. Walter Kennedy Citizenship Award

1974–75...Wes Unseld, Wash
1975–76...Slick Watts, Sea
1976–77...Dave Bing, Wash
1977–78...Bob Lanier, Det
1978–79...Calvin Murphy, Hou
1979–80...Austin Carr, Clev
1980–81...Mike Glenn, NY
1981–82...Kent Benson, Det
1982–83...Julius Erving, Phil
1983–84...Frank Layden, Utah
1984–85...Dan Issel, Den

1985–86...Michael Cooper, Lakers
　　　　　Rory Sparrow, NY
1986–87...Isiah Thomas, Det
1987–88...Alex English, Den
1988–89...Thurl Bailey, Utah
1989–90...Glenn Rivers, Atl
1990–91...Kevin Johnson, Phoe
1991–92...Magic Johnson, Lakers
1992–93...Terry Porter, Port
1993–94...Joe Dumars, Det

1994–95...Joe O'Toole, Atl
1995–96...Chris Dudley, Port
1996–97...P.J. Brown, Mia
1997–98...Steve Smith, Atl
1998–99...Brian Grant, Port
1999–00...Vlade Divac, Sac
2000–01...Dikembe Mutombo, Phil
2001–02...Alonzo Mourning, Mia
2002–03...David Robinson, SA
2003–04...Reggie Miller, Ind

Most Improved Player

1985–86...Alvin Robertson, SA
1986–87...Dale Ellis, Sea
1987–88...Kevin Duckworth, Port
1988–89...Kevin Johnson, Phoe
1989–90...Rony Seikaly, Mia
1990–91...Scott Skiles, Orl
1991–92...Pervis Ellison, Wash

1992–93...Chris Jackson, Den
1993–94...Don MacLean, Wash
1994–95...Dana Barros, Phil
1995–96...Gheorghe Muresan, Wash
1996–97...Isaac Austin, Mia
1997–98...Alan Henderson, Atl

1998–99...Darrell Armstrong, Orl
1999–00...Jalen Rose, Ind
2000–01...Tracy McGrady, Orl
2001–02...Jermaine O'Neal, Ind
2002–03...Gilbert Arenas, GS
2003–04...Zach Randolph, Port

Executive of the Year

1972–73...Joe Axelson, KC-Oma
1973–74...Eddie Donovan, Buff
1974–75...Dick Vertlieb, GS
1975–76...Jerry Colangelo, Phoe
1976–77...Ray Patterson, Hou
1977–78...Angelo Drossos, SA
1978–79...Bob Ferry, Wash
1979–80...Red Auerbach, Bos
1980–81...Jerry Colangelo, Phoe
1981–82...Bob Ferry, Wash
1982–83...Zollie Volchok, Sea

1983–84...Frank Layden, Utah
1984–85...Vince Boryla, Den
1985–86...Stan Kasten, Atl
1986–87...Stan Kasten, Atl
1987–88...Jerry Krause, Chi
1988–89...Jerry Colangelo, Phoe
1989–90...Bob Bass, SA
1990–91...Bucky Buckwalter, Port
1991–92...Wayne Embry, Clev
1992–93...Jerry Colangelo, Phoe
1993–94...Bob Whitsitt, Sea

1994–95...Jerry West, LA Lakers
1995–96...Jerry Krause, Chi
1996–97...Bob Bass, Char
1997–98...Wayne Embry, Clev
1998–99...Geoff Petrie, Sac
1999–00...John Gabriel, Orl
2000–01...Geoff Petrie, Sac
2001–02...Rod Thorn, NJ
2002–03...Joe Dumars, Det
2003–04...Jerry West, Mem

Sponsored by *The Sporting News.*

NBA Alltime Individual Leaders

Scoring

MOST POINTS, CAREER

	Pts	Avg
Kareem Abdul-Jabbar	38,387	24.6
Karl Malone	36,928	25.0
Michael Jordan	32,292	30.1
Wilt Chamberlain	31,419	30.1
Moses Malone	27,409	20.6
Elvin Hayes	27,313	21.0
Hakeem Olajuwon	26,946	21.8
Oscar Robertson	26,710	25.7
Dominique Wilkins	26,669	24.8
John Havlicek	26,395	20.8

MOST POINTS, SEASON

Wilt Chamberlain, Phil	4,029	1961–62
Wilt Chamberlain, SF	3,586	1962–63
Michael Jordan, Chi	3,041	1986–87
Wilt Chamberlain, Phil	3,033	1960–61
Wilt Chamberlain, SF	2,948	1963–64
Michael Jordan, Chi	2,868	1987–88
Bob McAdoo, Buff	2,831	1974–75
Rick Barry, SF	2,775	1966–67
Michael Jordan, Chi	2,753	1989–90
Elgin Baylor, LA	2,719	1962–63

HIGHEST SCORING AVERAGE, CAREER

Michael Jordan	30.1	1,072 games
Wilt Chamberlain	30.1	1,045 games
Elgin Baylor	27.4	846 games
Shaquille O'Neal	27.1	809 games
Jerry West	27.0	932 games
Allen Iverson	27.0	535 games
Bob Pettit	26.4	792 games
George Gervin	26.2	791 games
Oscar Robertson	25.7	1,040 games
Karl Malone	25.0	1,476 games

Note: Minimum 400 games.

HIGHEST SCORING AVERAGE, SEASON

Wilt Chamberlain, Phil	50.4	1961–62
Wilt Chamberlain, SF	44.8	1962–63
Wilt Chamberlain, Phil	38.4	1960–61
Wilt Chamberlain, Phil	37.6	1959–60
Michael Jordan, Chi	37.1	1986–87
Wilt Chamberlain, SF	36.9	1963–64
Rick Barry, SF	35.6	1966–67
Michael Jordan, Chi	35.0	1987–88
Elgin Baylor, LA	34.8	1960–61

Note: Minimum 70 games.

MOST POINTS, GAME

	Player, Team	Opp	Date
100	Wilt Chamberlain, Phil	NY	3/2/62
78	Wilt Chamberlain, Phil	LA	12/8/61
73	Wilt Chamberlain, Phil	Chi	1/13/62
73	Wilt Chamberlain, SF	NY	11/16/62
73	David Thompson, Den	Det	4/9/78
72	Wilt Chamberlain, SF	LA	11/3/62
71	David Robinson, SA	LAC	4/24/94
71	Elgin Baylor, LA	NY	11/15/60
70	Wilt Chamberlain, SF	Syr	3/10/63
69	Michael Jordan, Chi	Clev	3/28/90

Field-Goal Percentage

Highest FG Percentage, Career: .599—Artis Gilmore
Highest FG Percentage, Season: .727—Wilt
  Chamberlain, LA Lakers, 1972–73 (426/586)

Free Throws

HIGHEST FREE-THROW PERCENTAGE, CAREER

Mark Price	.904
Rick Barry	.900
Steve Nash	.893
Calvin Murphy	.892
Scott Skiles	.889

Note: Minimum 1200 free throws made.

HIGHEST FREE-THROW PERCENTAGE, SEASON

Calvin Murphy, Hou	.958	1980–81
Mahmoud Abdul-Rauf, Den	.956	1993–94
Jeff Hornacek, Utah	.950	1999–00
Mark Price, Clev	.948	1992–93
Mark Price, Clev	.947	1991–92

MOST FREE THROWS MADE, CAREER

	No.	Yrs	Pct
Karl Malone	9,787	19	.742
Moses Malone	8,531	19	.769
Oscar Robertson	7,694	14	.838
Michael Jordan	7,327	15	.835
Jerry West	7,160	14	.814

Three-Point Field Goals

Most Three-Point Field-Goals, Career: 2,464—Reggie
  Miller
Highest Three-Point Field-Goal Percentage, Career:
  .454—Steve Kerr
Most Three-Point Field Goals, Season: 267—Dennis
  Scott, Orl, 1995–96
Highest Three-Point Field-Goal Percentage, Season:
  .524—Steve Kerr, Chi, 1994–95
Most Three-Point Field Goals, Game: 12—Kobe
  Bryant, LA Lakers vs Seattle, 1/7/03

Note: First year of shot: 1979–80.

Steals

Most Steals, Career: 3,265—John Stockton
Most Steals, Season: 301—Alvin Robertson, San
  Antonio, 1985–86
Most Steals, Game: 11—Kendall Gill, New Jersey vs
  Miami, 4/3/99; Larry Kenon, San Antonio
  vs Kansas City, 12/26/76

Rebounds

MOST REBOUNDS, CAREER

	No.	Yrs	Avg
Wilt Chamberlain	23,924	14	22.9
Bill Russell	21,620	13	22.5
Kareem Abdul-Jabbar	17,440	20	11.4
Elvin Hayes	16,279	16	12.5
Moses Malone	16,212	19	12.2
Karl Malone	14,968	19	10.1
Robert Parish	14,715	21	9.1
Nate Thurmond	14,464	14	15.0
Walt Bellamy	14,241	14	13.7
Wes Unseld	13,769	13	14.0

Rebounds (Cont.)
MOST REBOUNDS, SEASON

Wilt Chamberlain, Phil	2,149	1960–61
Wilt Chamberlain, Phil	2,052	1961–62
Wilt Chamberlain, Phil	1,957	1966–67
Wilt Chamberlain, Phil	1,952	1967–68
Wilt Chamberlain, SF	1,946	1962–63
Wilt Chamberlain, Phil	1,943	1965–66
Wilt Chamberlain, Phil	1,941	1959–60
Bill Russell, Bos	1,930	1963–64
Bill Russell, Bos	1,878	1964–65
Bill Russell, Bos	1,868	1960–61

MOST REBOUNDS, GAME

	Player, Team	Opp	Date
55	Wilt Chamberlain, Phil	Bos	11/24/60
51	Bill Russell, Bos	Syr	2/5/60
49	Bill Russell, Bos	Phil	11/16/57
49	Bill Russell, Bos	Det	3/11/65
45	Wilt Chamberlain, Phil	Syr	2/6/60
45	Wilt Chamberlain, Phil	LA	1/21/61

Assists
MOST ASSISTS, CAREER

John Stockton	15,806
Mark Jackson	10,334
Magic Johnson	10,141
Oscar Robertson	9,887
Isiah Thomas	9,061

Assists (Cont.)
MOST ASSISTS, SEASON

John Stockton, Utah	1,164	1990–91
John Stockton, Utah	1,134	1989–90
John Stockton, Utah	1,128	1987–88
John Stockton, Utah	1,126	1991–92
Isiah Thomas, Det	1,123	1984–85

MOST ASSISTS, GAME: 30—Scott Skiles, Orlando vs Denver, 12/30/90

Blocked Shots
MOST BLOCKED SHOTS, CAREER

Hakeem Olajuwon	3,830
Kareem Abdul-Jabbar	3,189
Mark Eaton	3,064
Dikembe Mutombo	2,996
David Robinson	2,954

MOST BLOCKED SHOTS, SEASON

Mark Eaton, Utah	456	1984–85
Manute Bol, Wash	397	1985–86
Elmore Smith, LA	393	1973–74

MOST BLOCKED SHOTS, GAME: 17—Elmore Smith, LA Lakers vs Portland, 10/28/73

Scoring
MOST POINTS, CAREER

	Pts	Yrs	Avg
Michael Jordan	5,987	13	33.4
Kareem Abdul-Jabbar	5,762	18	24.3
Karl Malone	4,761	19	24.7
Jerry West	4,457	13	29.1
Shaquille O'Neal	4,294	11	27.2
Larry Bird	3,897	12	23.8
John Havlicek	3,776	13	22.0
Hakeem Olajuwon	3,755	15	25.9
Magic Johnson	3,701	13	19.5
Scottie Pippen	3,642	15	17.7

*HIGHEST SCORING AVERAGE, CAREER

	Avg	Games
Michael Jordan	33.4	179
Allen Iverson	30.6	57
Jerry West	29.1	153
Shaquille O'Neal	27.2	158
Elgin Baylor	27.0	134
George Gervin	27.0	59
Hakeem Olajuwon	25.9	145
Dirk Nowitzki	25.6	40
Bob Pettit	25.5	88
Dominique Wilkins	25.4	55

*Minimum of 25 games.

Scoring (Cont.)
MOST POINTS, GAME

	Player, Team	Opp	Date
†63	Michael Jordan, Chi	Bos	4/20/86
61	Elgin Baylor, LA	Bos	4/14/62
56	Wilt Chamberlain, Phil	Syr	3/22/62
56	Michael Jordan, Chi	Mia	4/29/92
56	Charles Barkley, Phoe	GS	5/4/94
55	Rick Barry, SF	Phil	4/18/67
55	Michael Jordan, Chi	Clev	5/1/88
55	Michael Jordan, Chi	Phoe	4/16/95
55	Michael Jordan, Chi	Wash	4/27/97

†Double overtime game.

Rebounds
MOST REBOUNDS, CAREER

	No.	Yrs	Avg
Bill Russell	4,104	13	24.9
Wilt Chamberlain	3,913	13	24.5
Kareem Abdul-Jabbar	2,481	18	10.5
Karl Malone	2,062	19	10.7
Shaquille O'Neal	2,040	11	12.9

MOST REBOUNDS, GAME

	Player, Team	Opp	Date
41	Wilt Chamberlain, Phil	Bos	4/5/67
40	Bill Russell, Bos	Phil	3/23/58
40	Bill Russell, Bos	StL	3/29/60
*40	Bill Russell, Bos	LA	4/18/62

Three tied at 39.
*Overtime game.

Assists

MOST ASSISTS, CAREER

	No.	Games
Magic Johnson	2,346	190
John Stockton	1,839	182
Larry Bird	1,062	164
Scottie Pippen	1,035	204
Michael Jordan	1,022	179

MOST ASSISTS, GAME

Player, Team	Opp	Date
24 ....Magic Johnson, LAL	Pho	5/15/84
24 ....John Stockton, Utah	LAL	5/17/88
23 ....Magic Johnson, LAL	Port	5/3/85
22 ....Doc Rivers, Atl	Bos	5/16/88
Four tied at 21.		

Games played

Kareem Abdul-Jabbar	237
Scottie Pippen	204
Danny Ainge	193
Karl Malone	193
Magic Johnson	190

Appearances

John Stockton	19
Karl Malone	19
Kareem Abdul-Jabbar	18
Robert Parish	16
Dolph Schayes	15
Clyde Drexler	15
Tree Rollins	15
Jerome Kersey	15
Hakeem Olajuwon	15

NBA Season Leaders

Scoring

1946–47	Joe Fulks, Phil	1389	1975–76	Bob McAdoo, Buff	31.1
1947–48	Max Zaslofsky, Chi	1007	1976–77	Pete Maravich, NO	31.1
1948–49	George Mikan, Minn	1698	1977–78	George Gervin, SA	27.2
1949–50	George Mikan, Minn	1865	1978–79	George Gervin, SA	29.6
1950–51	George Mikan, Minn	1932	1979–80	George Gervin, SA	33.1
1951–52	Paul Arizin, Phil	1674	1980–81	Adrian Dantley, Utah	30.7
1952–53	Neil Johnston, Phil	1564	1981–82	George Gervin, SA	32.3
1953–54	Neil Johnston, Phil	1759	1982–83	Alex English, Den	28.4
1954–55	Neil Johnston, Phil	1631	1983–84	Adrian Dantley, Utah	30.6
1955–56	Bob Pettit, StL	1849	1984–85	Bernard King, NY	32.9
1956–57	Paul Arizin, Phil	1817	1985–86	Dominique Wilkins, Atl	30.3
1957–58	George Yardley, Det	2001	1986–87	Michael Jordan, Chi	37.1
1958–59	Bob Pettit, StL	2105	1987–88	Michael Jordan, Chi	35.0
1959–60	Wilt Chamberlain, Phil	2707	1988–89	Michael Jordan, Chi	32.5
1960–61	Wilt Chamberlain, Phil	3033	1989–90	Michael Jordan, Chi	33.6
1961–62	Wilt Chamberlain, Phil	4029	1990–91	Michael Jordan, Chi	31.5
1962–63	Wilt Chamberlain, SF	3586	1991–92	Michael Jordan, Chi	30.1
1963–64	Wilt Chamberlain, SF	2948	1992–93	Michael Jordan, Chi	32.6
1964–65	Wilt Chamberlain, SF-Phil	2534	1993–94	David Robinson, SA	29.8
1965–66	Wilt Chamberlain, Phil	2649	1994–95	Shaquille O'Neal, Orl	29.3
1966–67	Rick Barry, SF	2775	1995–96	Michael Jordan, Chi	30.4
1967–68	Dave Bing, Det	2142	1996–97	Michael Jordan, Chi	29.6
1968–69	Elvin Hayes, SD	2327	1997–98	Michael Jordan, Chi	28.7
1969–70	Jerry West, LA	*31.2	1998–99	Allen Iverson, Phil	26.8
1970–71	Kareem Abdul-Jabbar, Mil	31.7	1999–00	Shaquille O'Neal, LA Lakers	29.7
1971–72	Kareem Abdul-Jabbar, Mil	34.8	2000–01	Allen Iverson, Phil	31.1
1972–73	Nate Archibald, KC-Oma	34.0	2001–02	Allen Iverson, Phil	31.4
1973–74	Bob McAdoo, Buff	30.6	2002–03	Tracy McGrady, Orl	32.1
1974–75	Bob McAdoo, Buff	34.5	2003–04	Tracy McGrady, Orl	28.0

*Based on per game average since 1969–70.

Rebounding

1950–51	Dolph Schayes, Syr	1080	1963–64	Bill Russell, Bos	1930
1951–52	Larry Foust, FW	880	1964–65	Bill Russell, Bos	1878
	Mel Hutchins, Mil	880	1965–66	Wilt Chamberlain, Phil	1943
1952–53	George Mikan, Minn	1007	1966–67	Wilt Chamberlain, Phil	1957
1953–54	Harry Gallatin, NY	1098	1967–68	Wilt Chamberlain, Phil	1952
1954–55	Neil Johnston, Phil	1085	1968–69	Wilt Chamberlain, LA	1712
1955–56	Bob Pettit, StL	1164	1969–70	Elvin Hayes, SD	*16.9
1956–57	Maurice Stokes, Roch	1256	1970–71	Wilt Chamberlain, LA	18.2
1957–58	Bill Russell, Bos	1564	1971–72	Wilt Chamberlain, LA	19.2
1958–59	Bill Russell, Bos	1612	1972–73	Wilt Chamberlain, LA	18.6
1959–60	Wilt Chamberlain, Phil	1941	1973–74	Elvin Hayes, Capital	18.1
1960–61	Wilt Chamberlain, Phil	2149	1974–75	Wes Unseld, Wash	14.8
1961–62	Wilt Chamberlain, Phil	2052	1975–76	Kareem Abdul-Jabbar, LA	16.9
1962–63	Wilt Chamberlain, SF	1946	1976–77	Bill Walton, Port	14.4

Rebounding (Cont.)

1977–78	Len Robinson, NO	15.7	1991–92	Dennis Rodman, Det	18.7
1978–79	Moses Malone, Hou	17.6	1992–93	Dennis Rodman, Det	18.3
1979–80	Swen Nater, SD	15.0	1993–94	Dennis Rodman, SA	17.3
1980–81	Moses Malone, Hou	14.8	1994–95	Dennis Rodman, SA	16.8
1981–82	Moses Malone, Hou	14.7	1995–96	Dennis Rodman, Chi	14.9
1982–83	Moses Malone, Phil	15.3	1996–97	Dennis Rodman, Chi	16.1
1983–84	Moses Malone, Phil	13.4	1997–98	Dennis Rodman, Chi	15.0
1984–85	Moses Malone, Phil	13.1	1998–99	Chris Webber, Sac	13.0
1985–86	Bill Laimbeer, Det	13.1	1999–00	Dikembe Mutombo, Atl	14.1
1986–87	Charles Barkley, Phil	14.6	2000–01	Dikembe Mutombo, Atl	13.5
1987–88	Michael Cage, LA Clippers	13.0	2001–02	Ben Wallace, Det	13.0
1988–89	Hakeem Olajuwon, Hou	13.5	2002–03	Ben Wallace, Det	15.4
1989–90	Hakeem Olajuwon, Hou	14.0	2003–04	Kevin Garnett, Minn	13.9
1990–91	David Robinson, SA	13.0			

*Based on per game average since 1969–70.

Assists

1946–47	Ernie Calverly, Prov	202	1975–76	Don Watts, Sea	8.1
1947–48	Howie Dallmar, Phil	120	1976–77	Don Buse, Ind	8.5
1948–49	Bob Davies, Roch	321	1977–78	Kevin Porter, NJ-Det	10.2
1949–50	Dick McGuire, NY	386	1978–79	Kevin Porter, Det	13.4
1950–51	Andy Phillip, Phil	414	1979–80	Micheal Richardson, NY	10.1
1951–52	Andy Phillip, Phil	539	1980–81	Kevin Porter, Wash	9.1
1952–53	Bob Cousy, Bos	547	1981–82	Johnny Moore, SA	9.6
1953–54	Bob Cousy, Bos	578	1982–83	Magic Johnson, LA	10.5
1954–55	Bob Cousy, Bos	557	1983–84	Magic Johnson, LA	13.1
1955–56	Bob Cousy, Bos	642	1984–85	Isiah Thomas, Det	13.9
1956–57	Bob Cousy, Bos	478	1985–86	Magic Johnson, LA Lakers	12.6
1957–58	Bob Cousy, Bos	463	1986–87	Magic Johnson, LA Lakers	12.2
1958–59	Bob Cousy, Bos	557	1987–88	John Stockton, Utah	13.8
1959–60	Bob Cousy, Bos	715	1988–89	John Stockton, Utah	13.6
1960–61	Oscar Robertson, Cin	690	1989–90	John Stockton, Utah	14.5
1961–62	Oscar Robertson, Cin	899	1990–91	John Stockton, Utah	14.2
1962–63	Guy Rodgers, SF	825	1991–92	John Stockton, Utah	13.7
1963–64	Oscar Robertson, Cin	868	1992–93	John Stockton, Utah	12.0
1964–65	Oscar Robertson, Cin	861	1993–94	John Stockton, Utah	12.6
1965–66	Oscar Robertson, Cin	847	1994–95	John Stockton, Utah	12.3
1966–67	Guy Rodgers, Chi	908	1995–96	John Stockton, Utah	11.2
1967–68	Wilt Chamberlain, Phil	702	1996–97	Mark Jackson, Ind	11.4
1968–69	Oscar Robertson, Cin	772	1997–98	Rod Strickland, Wash	10.1
1969–70	Len Wilkens, Sea	*9.1	1998–99	Jason Kidd, Phoe	10.8
1970–71	Norm Van Lier, Cin	10.1	1999–00	Jason Kidd, Phoe	10.1
1971–72	Jerry West, LA	9.7	2000–01	Jason Kidd, Phoe	9.8
1972–73	Nate Archibald, KC-Oma	11.4	2001–02	Andre Miller, Clev	10.9
1973–74	Ernie DiGregorio, Buff	8.2	2002–03	Jason Kidd, NJ	8.9
1974–75	Kevin Porter, Wash	8.0	2003–04	Jason Kidd, NJ	9.2

*Based on per game average since 1969–70.

Field-Goal Percentage

1946–47	Bob Feerick, Wash	40.1	1967–68	Wilt Chamberlain, Phil	59.5
1947–48	Bob Feerick, Wash	34.0	1968–69	Wilt Chamberlain, LA	58.3
1948–49	Arnie Risen, Roch	42.3	1969–70	Johnny Green, Cin	55.9
1949–50	Alex Groza, Ind	47.8	1970–71	Johnny Green, Cin	58.7
1950–51	Alex Groza, Ind	47.0	1971–72	Wilt Chamberlain, LA	64.9
1951–52	Paul Arizin, Phil	44.8	1972–73	Wilt Chamberlain, LA	72.7
1952–53	Neil Johnston, Phil	45.2	1973–74	Bob McAdoo, Buff	54.7
1953–54	Ed Macauley, Bos	48.6	1974–75	Don Nelson, Bos	53.9
1954–55	Larry Foust, FW	48.7	1975–76	Wes Unseld, Wash	56.1
1955–56	Neil Johnston, Phil	45.7	1976–77	Kareem Abdul-Jabbar, LA	57.9
1956–57	Neil Johnston, Phil	44.7	1977–78	Bobby Jones, Den	57.8
1957–58	Jack Twyman, Cin	45.2	1978–79	Cedric Maxwell, Bos	58.4
1958–59	Ken Sears, NY	49.0	1979–80	Cedric Maxwell, Bos	60.9
1959–60	Ken Sears, NY	47.7	1980–81	Artis Gilmore, Chi	67.0
1960–61	Wilt Chamberlain, Phil	50.9	1981–82	Artis Gilmore, Chi	65.2
1961–62	Walt Bellamy, Chi	51.9	1982–83	Artis Gilmore, SA	62.6
1962–63	Wilt Chamberlain, SF	52.8	1983–84	Artis Gilmore, SA	63.1
1963–64	Jerry Lucas, Cin	52.7	1984–85	James Donaldson, LA Clippers	63.7
1964–65	Wilt Chamberlain, SF-Phil	51.0	1985–86	Steve Johnson, SA	63.2
1965–66	Wilt Chamberlain, Phil	54.0	1986–87	Kevin McHale, Bos	60.4
1966–67	Wilt Chamberlain, Phil	68.3	1987–88	Kevin McHale, Bos	60.4

Field-Goal Percentage (Cont.)

1988–89	Dennis Rodman, Det	59.5	1996–97	Gheorghe Muresan, Wash	60.4
1989–90	Mark West, Phoe	62.5	1997–98	Shaquille O'Neal, LA Lakers	58.4
1990–91	Buck Williams, Port	60.2	1998–99	Shaquille O'Neal, LA Lakers	57.6
1991–92	Buck Williams, Port	60.4	1999–00	Shaquille O'Neal, LA Lakers	57.4
1992–93	Cedric Ceballos, Phoe	57.6	2000–01	Shaquille O'Neal, LA Lakers	57.2
1993–94	Shaquille O'Neal, Orl	59.9	2001–02	Shaquille O'Neal, LA Lakers	57.9
1994–95	Chris Gatling, GS	63.3	2002–03	Eddy Curry, Chi	58.5
1995–96	Gheorghe Muresan, Wash	58.4	2003–04	Shaquille O'Neal, LA Lakers	58.4

Free-Throw Percentage

1946–47	Fred Scolari, Wash	81.1	1975–76	Rick Barry, GS	92.3
1947–48	Bob Feerick, Wash	78.8	1976–77	Ernie DiGregorio, Buff	94.5
1948–49	Bob Feerick, Wash	85.9	1977–78	Rick Barry, GS	92.4
1949–50	Max Zaslofsky, Chi	84.3	1978–79	Rick Barry, Hou	94.7
1950–51	Joe Fulks, Phil	85.5	1979–80	Rick Barry, Hou	93.5
1951–52	Bob Wanzer, Roch	90.4	1980–81	Calvin Murphy, Hou	95.8
1952–53	Bill Sharman, Bos	85.0	1981–82	Kyle Macy, Phoe	89.9
1953–54	Bill Sharman, Bos	84.4	1982–83	Calvin Murphy, Hou	92.0
1954–55	Bill Sharman, Bos	89.7	1983–84	Larry Bird, Bos	88.8
1955–56	Bill Sharman, Bos	86.7	1984–85	Kyle Macy, Phoe	90.7
1956–57	Bill Sharman, Bos	90.5	1985–86	Larry Bird, Bos	89.6
1957–58	Dolph Schayes, Syr	90.4	1986–87	Larry Bird, Bos	91.0
1958–59	Bill Sharman, Bos	93.2	1987–88	Jack Sikma, Mil	92.2
1959–60	Dolph Schayes, Syr	89.2	1988–89	Magic Johnson, LA Lakers	91.1
1960–61	Bill Sharman, Bos	92.1	1989–90	Larry Bird, Bos	93.0
1961–62	Dolph Schayes, Syr	89.6	1990–91	Reggie Miller, Ind	91.8
1962–63	Larry Costello, Syr	88.1	1991–92	Mark Price, Clev	94.7
1963–64	Oscar Robertson, Cin	85.3	1992–93	Mark Price, Clev	94.8
1964–65	Larry Costello, Phil	87.7	1993–94	Mahmoud Abdul-Rauf, Den	95.6
1965–66	Larry Siegfried, Bos	88.1	1994–95	Spud Webb, Sac	93.4
1966–67	Adrian Smith, Cin	90.3	1995–96	Mahmoud Abdul-Rauf, Den	93.0
1967–68	Oscar Robertson, Cin	87.3	1996–97	Mark Price, Clev	90.6
1968–69	Larry Siegfried, Bos	86.4	1997–98	Chris Mullin, Ind	93.9
1969–70	Flynn Robinson, Mil	89.8	1998–99	Reggie Miller, Ind	91.5
1970–71	Chet Walker, Chi	85.9	1999–00	Jeff Hornacek, Utah	95.0
1971–72	Jack Marin, Balt	89.4	2000–01	Reggie Miller, Ind	92.8
1972–73	Rick Barry, GS	90.2	2001–02	Reggie Miller, Ind	91.1
1973–74	Ernie DiGregorio, Buff	90.2	2002–03	Allan Houston, NY	91.9
1974–75	Rick Barry, GS	90.4	2003–04	Peja Stojakovic, Sac	92.7

Three-Point Field-Goal Percentage

1979–80	Fred Brown, Sea	44.3	1992–93	B.J. Armstrong, Chi	45.3
1980–81	Brian Taylor, SD	38.3	1993–94	Tracy Murray, Por	45.9
1981–82	Campy Russell, NY	43.9	1994–95	Steve Kerr, Chi	52.4
1982–83	Mike Dunleavy, SA	34.5	1995–96	Tim Legler, Wash	52.2
1983–84	Darrell Griffith, Utah	36.1	1996–97	Kevin Gamble, Sac	48.2
1984–85	Byron Scott, LA Lakers	43.3	1997–98	Dale Ellis, Sea	46.0
1985–86	Craig Hodges, Mil	45.1	1998–99	Dell Curry, Char	47.6
1986–87	Kiki Vandeweghe, Por	48.1	1999–00	Hubert Davis, Dall	49.1
1987–88	Craig Hodges, Mil-Phoe	49.1	2000–01	Brent Barry, Sea	47.6
1988–89	Jon Sundvold, Mia	52.2	2001–02	Steve Smith, SA	47.2
1989–90	Steve Kerr, Clev	50.7	2002–03	Bruce Bowen, SA	44.1
1990–91	Jim Les, Sac	46.1	2003–04	Anthony Peeler, Sac	48.2
1991–92	Dana Barros, Sea	44.6			

Steals

1973–74	Larry Steele, Por	2.68	1989–90	Michael Jordan, Chi	2.77
1974–75	Rick Barry, GS	2.85	1990–91	Alvin Robertson, Mil	3.04
1975–76	Don Watts, Sea	3.18	1991–92	John Stockton, Utah	2.98
1976–77	Don Buse, Ind	3.47	1992–93	Michael Jordan, Chi	2.83
1977–78	Ron Lee, Phoe	2.74	1993–94	Nate McMillan, Sea	2.96
1978–79	M.L. Carr, Det	2.46	1994–95	Scottie Pippen, Chi	2.94
1979–80	Micheal Richardson, NY	3.23	1995–96	Gary Payton, Sea	2.85
1980–81	Magic Johnson, LA	3.43	1996–97	Mookie Blaylock, Atl	2.72
1981–82	Magic Johnson, LA	2.67	1997–98	Mookie Blaylock, Atl	2.61
1982–83	Micheal Richardson, GS-NJ	2.84	1998–99	Kendall Gill, NJ	2.68
1983–84	Rickey Green, Utah	2.65	1999–00	Eddie Jones, Char	2.67
1984–85	Micheal Richardson, NJ	2.96	2000–01	Allen Iverson, Phil	2.51
1985–86	Alvin Robertson, SA	3.67	2001–02	Allen Iverson, Phil	2.80
1986–87	Alvin Robertson, SA	3.21	2002–03	Allen Iverson, Phil	2.74
1987–88	Michael Jordan, Chi	3.16	2003–04	Baron Davis, NO	2.36
1988–89	John Stockton, Utah	3.21			

Blocked Shots

1973–74	Elmore Smith, LA	4.85	1989–90	Hakeem Olajuwon, Hou	4.59
1974–75	Kareem Abdul-Jabbar, Mil	3.26	1990–91	Hakeem Olajuwon, Hou	3.95
1975–76	Kareem Abdul-Jabbar, LA	4.12	1991–92	David Robinson, SA	4.49
1976–77	Bill Walton, Port	3.25	1992–93	Hakeem Olajuwon, Hou	4.17
1977–78	George Johnson, NJ	3.38	1993–94	Dikembe Mutombo, Den	4.10
1978–79	Kareem Abdul-Jabbar, LA	3.95	1994–95	Dikembe Mutombo, Den	3.91
1979–80	Kareem Abdul-Jabbar, LA	3.41	1995–96	Dikembe Mutombo, Den	4.49
1980–81	George Johnson, SA	3.39	1996–97	Shawn Bradley, NJ	3.40
1981–82	George Johnson, SA	3.12	1997–98	Marcus Camby, Tor	3.65
1982–83	Wayne Rollins, Atl	4.29	1998–99	Alonzo Mourning, Mia	3.91
1983–84	Mark Eaton, Utah	4.28	1999–00	Alonzo Mourning, Mia	3.72
1984–85	Mark Eaton, Utah	5.56	2000–01	Theo Ratliff, Phil/Atl	3.74
1985–86	Manute Bol, Wash	4.96	2001–02	Ben Wallace, Det	3.48
1986–87	Mark Eaton, Utah	4.06	2002–03	Theo Ratliff, Atl	3.23
1987–88	Mark Eaton, Utah	3.71	2003–04	Theo Ratliff, Port	3.61
1988–89	Manute Bol, GS	4.31			

NBA All-Star Game Results

Year	Result	Site	Winning Coach	Most Valuable Player
1951	East 111, West 94	Boston	Joe Lapchick	Ed Macauley, Bos
1952	East 108, West 91	Boston	Al Cervi	Paul Arizin, Phil
1953	West 79, East 75	Ft Wayne	John Kundla	George Mikan, Minn
1954	East 98, West 93 (OT)	New York	Joe Lapchick	Bob Cousy, Bos
1955	East 100, West 91	New York	Al Cervi	Bill Sharman, Bos
1956	West 108, East 94	Rochester	Charley Eckman	Bob Pettit, StL
1957	East 109, West 97	Boston	Red Auerbach	Bob Cousy, Bos
1958	East 130, West 118	St Louis	Red Auerbach	Bob Pettit, StL
1959	West 124, East 108	Detroit	Ed Macauley	B. Pettit, StL/ E. Baylor, Minn
1960	East 125, West 115	Philadelphia	Red Auerbach	Wilt Chamberlain, Phil
1961	West 153, East 131	Syracuse	Paul Seymour	Oscar Robertson, Cin
1962	West 150, East 130	St Louis	Fred Schaus	Bob Pettit, StL
1963	East 115, West 108	Los Angeles	Red Auerbach	Bill Russell, Bos
1964	East 111, West 107	Boston	Red Auerbach	Oscar Robertson, Cin
1965	East 124, West 123	St Louis	Red Auerbach	Jerry Lucas, Cin
1966	East 137, West 94	Cincinnati	Red Auerbach	Adrian Smith, Cin
1967	West 135, East 120	San Francisco	Fred Schaus	Rick Barry, SF
1968	East 144, West 124	New York	Alex Hannum	Hal Greer, Phil
1969	East 123, West 112	Baltimore	Gene Shue	Oscar Robertson, Cin
1970	East 142, West 135	Philadelphia	Red Holzman	Willis Reed, NY
1971	West 108, East 107	San Diego	Larry Costello	Lenny Wilkens, Sea
1972	West 112, East 110	Los Angeles	Bill Sharman	Jerry West, LA
1973	East 104, West 84	Chicago	Tom Heinsohn	Dave Cowens, Bos
1974	West 134, East 123	Seattle	Larry Costello	Bob Lanier, Det
1975	East 108, West 102	Phoenix	K.C. Jones	Walt Frazier, NY
1976	East 123, West 109	Philadelphia	Tom Heinsohn	Dave Bing, Wash
1977	West 125, East 124	Milwaukee	Larry Brown	Julius Erving, Phil
1978	East 133, West 125	Atlanta	Billy Cunningham	Randy Smith, Buff
1979	West 134, East 129	Detroit	Lenny Wilkens	David Thompson, Den
1980	East 144, West 135 (OT)	Washington	Billy Cunningham	George Gervin, SA
1981	East 123, West 120	Cleveland	Billy Cunningham	Nate Archibald, Bos
1982	East 120, West 118	New Jersey	Bill Fitch	Larry Bird, Bos
1983	East 132, West 123	Los Angeles	Billy Cunningham	Julius Erving, Phil
1984	East 154, West 145 (OT)	Denver	K.C. Jones	Isiah Thomas, Det
1985	West 140, East 129	Indiana	Pat Riley	Ralph Sampson, Hou
1986	East 139, West 132	Dallas	K.C. Jones	Isiah Thomas, Det
1987	West 154, East 149 (OT)	Seattle	Pat Riley	Tom Chambers, Sea
1988	East 138, West 133	Chicago	Mike Fratello	Michael Jordan, Chi
1989	West 143, East 134	Houston	Pat Riley	Karl Malone, Utah
1990	East 130, West 113	Miami	Chuck Daly	Magic Johnson, LA Lakers
1991	East 116, West 114	Charlotte	Chris Ford	Charles Barkley, Phil
1992	West 153, East 113	Orlando	Don Nelson	Magic Johnson, LA Lakers
1993	West 135, East 132	Salt Lake City	Paul Westphal	K. Malone/ J. Stockton ,Utah
1994	East 127, West 118	Minneapolis	Lenny Wilkens	Scottie Pippen, Chi
1995	West 139, East 112	Phoenix	Paul Westphal	Mitch Richmond, Sac
1996	East 129, West 118	San Antonio	Phil Jackson	Michael Jordan, Chi
1997	East 132, West 120	Cleveland	Doug Collins	Glen Rice, Char
1998	East 135, West 114	New York	Larry Bird	Michael Jordan, Chi
1999	Cancelled due to lockout.			
2000	West 137, East 126	Oakland	Phil Jackson	O'Neal, Lakers/T. Duncan, SA
2001	East 111, West 110	Washington	Larry Brown	Allen Iverson, Phil
2002	West 135, East 120	Philadelphia	Don Nelson	Kobe Bryant, LA Lakers
2003	West 155, East 145 (2OT)	Atlanta	Rick Adelman	Kevin Garnett, Minn
2004	West 136, East 132	Los Angeles	Flip Saunders	Shaquille O'Neal, LA Lakers

Contributors

Senda Abbott (1984)
Forest C. (Phog) Allen (1959)
Clair F. Bee (1967)
Danny Biasone (2000)
Walter A. Brown (1965)
John W. Bunn (1964)
Jerry Colangelo (2004)
Bob Douglas (1971)
Al Duer (1981)
Wayne Embry (1999)
Clifford Fagan (1983)
Harry A. Fisher (1973)
Larry Fleisher (1991)
Edward Gottlieb (1971)
Luther H. Gulick (1959)
Lester Harrison (1979)
Chick Hearn (2003)
Ferenc Hepp (1980)

Edward J. Hickox (1959)
Paul D. (Tony) Hinkle (1965)
Ned Irish (1964)
R. William Jones (1964)
J. Walter Kennedy (1980)
Meadowlark Lemon (2003)
Emil S. Liston (1974)
Earl Lloyd (2003)
John B. McLendon (1978)
Bill Mokray (1965)
Ralph Morgan (1959)
Frank Morgenweck (1962)
James Naismith (1959)
Peter F. Newell (1978)
C.M. Newton (2000)
John J. O'Brien (1961)
Larry O'Brien (1991)

Harold G. Olsen (1959)
Maurice Podoloff (1973)
H. V. Porter (1960)
William A. Reid (1963)
Elmer Ripley (1972)
Lynn W. St. John (1962)
Abe Saperstein (1970)
Arthur A. Schabinger (1961)
Amos Alonzo Stagg (1959)
Boris Stankovic (1991)
Edward Steitz (1983)
Chuck Taylor (1968)
Oswald Tower (1959)
Arthur L. Trester (1961)
Clifford Wells (1971)
Lou Wilke (1982)
Fred Zollner (1999)

Players

Kareem Abdul-Jabbar (1995)
Nate (Tiny) Archibald (1991)
Paul J. Arizin (1977)
Thomas B. Barlow (1980)
Rick Barry (1987)
Elgin Baylor (1976)
John Beckman (1972)
Walt Bellamy (1993)
Sergei Belov (1992)
Dave Bing (1990)
Larry Bird (1998)
Carol Blazejowski (1994)
Bennie Borgmann (1961)
Bill Bradley (1982)
Joseph Brennan (1974)
Al Cervi (1984)
Wilt Chamberlain (1978)
Charles (Tarzan) Cooper (1976)
Kresimir Cosic (1996)
Bob Cousy (1970)
Dave Cowens (1991)
Joan Crawford (1997)
Billy Cunningham (1986)
Denise Curry (1997)
Drazen Dalipagic (2004)
Bob Davies (1969)
Forrest S. DeBernardi (1961)
Dave DeBusschere (1982)
Anne Donovan (1995)
Clyde Drexler (2004)
Paul Endacott (1971)
Alex English (1997)
Julius Erving (1993)
Harold (Bud) Foster (1964)
Walter (Clyde) Frazier (1987)
Max (Marty) Friedman (1971)
Joe Fulks (1977)
Lauren (Laddie) Gale (1976)
Harry (the Horse) Gallatin (1991)
William Gates (1989)
George Gervin (1996)
Tom Gola (1975)

Gail Goodrich (1996)
Hal Greer (1981)
Robert (Ace) Gruenig (1963)
Clifford O. Hagan (1977)
Victor Hanson (1960)
John Havlicek (1983)
Connie Hawkins (1992)
Elvin Hayes (1990)
Marques Haynes (1998)
Tom Heinsohn (1986)
Nat Holman (1964)
Robert J. Houbregs (1987)
Bailey Howell (1997)
Chuck Hyatt (1959)
Dan Issel (1993)
Harry (Buddy) Jeannette (1994)
Earvin (Magic) Johnson (2002)
William C. Johnson (1976)
D. Neil Johnston (1990)
K.C. Jones (1989)
Sam Jones (1983)
Edward (Moose) Krause (1975)
Bob Kurland (1961)
Bob Lanier (1992)
Joe Lapchick (1966)
Nancy Lieberman-Cline (1996)
Clyde Lovellette (1988)
Jerry Lucas (1979)
Angelo (Hank) Luisetti (1959)
C. Edward Macauley (1960)
Moses Malone (2001)
Peter P. Maravich (1987)
Slater Martin (1981)
Bob McAdoo (2000)
Branch McCracken (1960)
Jack McCracken (1962)
Bobby McDermott (1988)
Dick McGuire (1993)
Kevin McHale (1999)
Dino Meneghin (2003)
Ann Meyers (1993)
George L. Mikan (1959)
Vern Mikkelsen (1995)

Cheryl Miller (1995)
Earl Monroe (1990)
Calvin Murphy (1993)
Charles (Stretch) Murphy (1960)
H. O. (Pat) Page (1962)
Robert Parish (2003)
Drazen Petrovic (2002)
Bob Pettit (1970)
Andy Phillip (1961)
Jim Pollard (1977)
Frank Ramsey (1981)
Willis Reed (1981)
Arnie Risen (1998)
Oscar Robertson (1979)
John S. Roosma (1961)
Bill Russell (1974)
John (Honey) Russell (1964)
Adolph Schayes (1972)
Ernest J. Schmidt (1973)
John J. Schommer (1959)
Barney Sedran (1962)
Uljana Semjonova (1993)
Bill Sharman (1975)
Christian Steinmetz (1961)
Lusia Harris Stewart (1992)
Maurice Stokes (2004)
Isiah Thomas (2000)
David Thompson (1996)
John A. (Cat) Thompson (1962)
Nate Thurmond (1984)
Jack Twyman (1982)
Wes Unseld (1988)
Robert (Fuzzy) Vandivier (1974)
Edward A. Wachter (1961)
Bill Walton (1993)
Robert F. Wanzer (1987)
Jerry West (1979)
Nera White (1992)
Lenny Wilkens (1989)
Lynette Woodard (2004)
John R. Wooden (1960)
James Worthy (2003)
George (Bird) Yardley (1996)

Coaches

Harold Anderson (1984)
Red Auerbach (1968)
Leon Barmore (2003)
Sam Barry (1978)
Ernest A. Blood (1960)
Larry Brown (2002)
Howard G. Cann (1967)

H. Clifford Carlson (1959)
Lou Carnesecca (1992)
Ben Carnevale (1969)
Pete Carril (1997)
Everett Case (1981)
John Chaney (2001)
Jody Conradt (1998)

Denny Crum (1994)
Chuck Daly (1994)
Everett S. Dean (1966)
Antonio Diaz-Miguel (1997)
Edgar A. Diddle (1971)
Bruce Drake (1972)
Clarence Gaines (1981)

Note: Year of election in parentheses.

Coaches *(Cont.)*

Jack Gardner (1983)
Amory T. (Slats) Gill (1967)
Aleksandr Gomelsky (1995)
Alex Hannum (1998)
Marv Harshman (1984)
Don Haskins (1997)
Edgar S. Hickey (1978)
Howard A. Hobson (1965)
Red Holzman (1986)
Hank Iba (1968)
Alvin F. (Doggie) Julian (1967)
Frank W. Keaney (1960)
George E. Keogan (1961)
Bob Knight (1991)
Mike Krzyzewski (2001)
John Kundla (1995)

Ward L. Lambert (1960)
Harry Litwack (1975)
Kenneth D. Loeffler (1964)
A.C. (Dutch) Lonborg (1972)
Arad A. McCutchan (1980)
Al McGuire (1992)
Frank McGuire (1976)
Walter E. Meanwell (1959)
Raymond J. Meyer (1978)
Ralph Miller (1988)
Billie Moore (1999)
Aleksandar Nikolic (1998)
Lute Olson (2002)
Jack Ramsay (1992)
Cesare Rubini (1994)
Adolph F. Rupp (1968)

Leonard D. Sachs (1961)
Bill Sharman (2004)
Everett F. Shelton (1979)
Dean Smith (1982)
Pat Summitt (2000)
Fred R. Taylor (1985)
Bertha Teague (1984)
John Thompson (1999)
Margaret Wade (1984)
Stanley H. Watts (1985)
Lenny Wilkens (1998)
John R. Wooden (1972)
Morgan Wooten (2000)
Phil Woolpert (1992)
Kay Yow (2002)

Referees

James E. Enright (1978)
George T. Hepbron (1960)
George Hoyt (1961)
Matthew P. Kennedy (1959)
Lloyd Leith (1982)
Zigmund J. Mihalik (1985)

John P. Nucatola (1977)
Ernest C. Quigley (1961)
J. Dallas Shirley (1979)
Earl Strom (1995)
David Tobey (1961)
David H. Walsh (1961)

Teams

Buffalo Germans (1961)
First Team (1959)
Harlem Globetrotters (2002)
Original Celtics (1959)
Renaissance (1963)

ABA Champions

Year	Champion	Series	Runner-up	Winning Coach
1968	Pittsburgh Pipers	4–3	New Orleans Bucs	Vince Cazetta
1969	Oakland Oaks	4–1	Indiana Pacers	Alex Hannum
1970	Indiana Pacers	4–2	Los Angeles Stars	Bob Leonard
1971	Utah Stars	4–3	Kentucky Colonels	Bill Sharman
1972	Indiana Pacers	4–2	New York Nets	Bob Leonard
1973	Indiana Pacers	4–3	Kentucky Colonels	Bob Leonard
1974	New York Nets	4–1	Utah Stars	Kevin Loughery
1975	Kentucky Colonels	4–1	Indiana Pacers	Hubie Brown
1976	New York Nets	4–2	Denver Nuggets	Kevin Loughery

ABA Postseason Awards

Most Valuable Player

1967–68 ....Connie Hawkins, Pitt
1968–69 ....Mel Daniels, Ind
1969–70 ....Spencer Haywood, Den
1970–71 ....Mel Daniels, Ind
1971–72 ....Artis Gilmore, Ken
1972–73 ....Billy Cunningham, Car
1973–74 ....Julius Erving, NY
1974–75 ....Julius Erving, NY
               George McGinnis, Ind
1975–76 ....Julius Erving, NY

Rookie of the Year

1967–68 ....Mel Daniels, Minn
1968–69 ....Warren Armstrong, Oak
1969–70 ....Spencer Haywood, Den
1970–71 ....Charlie Scott, Vir
               Dan Issel, Ken
1971–72 ....Artis Gilmore, Ken
1972–73 ....Brian Taylor, NY
1973–74 ....Swen Nater, SA
1974–75 ....Marvin Barnes, StL
1975–76 ....David Thompson, Den

Coach of the Year

1967–68 ....Vince Cazetta, Pitt
1968–69 ....Alex Hannum, Oak
1969–70 ....Bill Sharman, LA
               Joe Belmont, Den
1970–71 ....Al Bianchi, Vir
1971–72 ....Tom Nissalke, Dall
1972–73 ....Larry Brown, Car
1973–74 ....Babe McCarthy, Ken
               Joe Mullaney, Utah
1974–75 ....Larry Brown, Den
1975–76 ....Larry Brown, Den

ABA Season Leaders

Scoring

		GP	Pts	Avg
1967–68	Connie Hawkins, Pitt	70	1875	26.8
1968–69	Rick Barry, Oak	35	1190	34.0
1969–70	Spencer Haywood, Den	84	2519	30.0
1970–71	Dan Issel, Ken	83	2480	29.4
1971–72	Charlie Scott, Vir	73	2524	34.6
1972–73	Julius Erving, Vir	71	2268	31.9
1973–74	Julius Erving, NY	84	2299	27.4
1974–75	George McGinnis, Ind	79	2353	29.8
1975–76	Julius Erving, NY	84	2462	29.3

Rebounds

1967–68	Mel Daniels, Minn	15.6
1968–69	Mel Daniels, Ind	16.5
1969–70	Spencer Haywood, Den	19.5
1970–71	Mel Daniels, Ind	18.0
1971–72	Artis Gilmore, Ken	17.8
1972–73	Artis Gilmore, Ken	17.5
1973–74	Artis Gilmore, Ken	18.3
1974–75	Swen Nater, SA	16.4
1975–76	Artis Gilmore, Ken	15.5

Assists

1967–68	Larry Brown, NO	6.5
1968–69	Larry Brown, Oak	7.1
1969–70	Larry Brown, Wash	7.1
1970–71	Bill Melchionni, NY	8.3
1971–72	Bill Melchionni, NY	8.4
1972–73	Bill Melchionni, NY	7.5
1973–74	Al Smith, Den	8.2
1974–75	Mack Calvin, Den	7.7
1975–76	Don Buse, Ind	8.2

Steals

1973–74	Ted McClain, Car	2.98
1974–75	Brian Taylor, NY	2.80
1975–76	Don Buse, Ind	4.12

Blocked Shots

1973–74	Caldwell Jones, SD	4.00
1974–75	Caldwell Jones, SD	3.24
1975–76	Billy Paultz, SA	3.05

World Championship of Basketball

Year	Winner	Runner-Up	Score	Site
1950	Argentina	United States	†	Rio de Janeiro
1954	United States	Brazil	†	Rio de Janeiro
1959	Brazil	United States	†	Santiago, Chile
1963	Brazil	Yugoslavia	†	Rio de Janeiro
1967	Soviet Union	Yugoslavia	†	Montevideo, Uruguay
1970	Yugoslavia	Brazil	†	Ljubljana, Yugoslavia
1974	Soviet Union	Yugoslavia	†	San Juan
1978	Yugoslavia	Soviet Union	82–81 (OT)	Manila
1982	Soviet Union	United States	95–94	Cali, Colombia
1986	United States	Soviet Union	87–85	Madrid
1990	Yugoslavia	Soviet Union	92–75	Buenos Aires
1994*	United States	Russia	137–91	Toronto
1998	Yugoslavia	Russia	64–62	Athens
2002	Yugoslavia	Argentina	84–77 (OT)	Indianapolis

*U.S. professionals began competing in 1994. In 1998, a labor dispute resulted in a boycott of the World Championship by NBA stars; the U.S. roster was filled by members of the CBA and European professional leagues and college players.

†Result determined by overall record in final round of competition.

THEY SAID IT

Bonzi Wells, Trail Blazers guard, on flipping off a fan during a game despite a pledge to behave more maturely: "I was probably wrong. But I don't remember doing nothing like that. I black out sometimes."

College Basketball

Emeka Okafor
of national champion
Connecticut

Husky Double

Connecticut made college basketball history as both its men's and women's programs won national championships

BY B.J. SCHECTER

HIS MISSION WAS accomplished, but a fire still burned inside Emeka Okafor. He had just reached his ultimate goal, winning the national championship with his Connecticut teammates, but as those teammates whooped it up on the Alamodome floor, confetti raining down from the rafters, following their 82–73 win over Georgia Tech in the NCAA final, Okafor had one more thing to take care of: He wanted the game ball.

Across the court, UConn swingman Rashad Anderson was holding that very prize. Okafor went after it like it was the most important rebound of his career. Only problem was, Anderson didn't want to give up the rock. Okafor first pleaded, then threatened ("I'm 6'9", 250-pounds," he said later. "I was either going to come away with it peacefully or I was going to get it with force.") before finally brokering a trade: his shoes for the game ball. Okafor cradled it all night, and in the wee hours of the morning, as the Huskies were celebrating on the balcony of their San Antonio hotel, Okafor was still holding the ball tightly, like a young child clinging to a teddy bear.

"I wanted something to remember this by," he said. "I've been plotting this for a long time. Ben [Gordon] got the ball after we won the Big East tournament. I was going to get the championship ball."

After putting an exclamation point on UConn's roller coaster season by dominating the Yellow Jackets with 24 points and 15 rebounds, Okafor deserved the game ball. But it was fitting that he had to struggle for it because he and the Huskies had to fight all season to stay on top. They started off well enough, as the unanimous preseason No. 1, but the Huskies had trouble dealing with the pressure and expectations from the start. When they played well and used all of their weapons, there was no better team. But too often the Huskies coasted, and coach Jim Calhoun was left shaking his head. There were other obstacles as well. In the preseason NIT, Okafor injured his back, limiting him to just nine points in a 77–61 loss to Georgia Tech at Madison Square Garden. He returned for the next game but the injury caused problems for him all season long.

BOB ROSATO

Gordon (4) played Mr. Outside to Okafor's Mr. Inside, then followed his teammate in the NBA draft, going third to Chicago.

And the Huskies were dogged by inconsistency. One game they would look like national champions and a few nights later they'd play like a middle-of-the-pack Big East team. "Expectations were so high at the beginning of the year that we were made almost godlike," said Calhoun. "People wrote that we were not going to lose a game in the Big East. We had the returning national champs [Syracuse] in our league. We had Pittsburgh who many people thought were stronger and more physical than we were. [But] at some point during the season we started to forget about the expectations."

Still, Calhoun struggled to push the right buttons, and the Huskies' inconsistent play was causing his blood to boil. After back-to-back losses at Notre Dame and Pittsburgh in February, Calhoun lost it. During UConn's next home game, against Miami,

Calhoun decided that his team was going to understand what he expected of them, whether they liked it or not. Even though the Huskies won easily, 76–63, Calhoun rode them harder than he had all season.

"We won by 13, but we really didn't play well at all," said Calhoun. "I went bonkers on the sideline. No matter what we did, it wasn't right. The team walked into the locker room afterward looking like they'd lost by 40. Everyone was expecting Attila the Hun."

However, when Calhoun entered the locker room he dropped the madman act, and started cracking jokes. He apologized to his players for over criticizing them, then pleaded with them to play with emotion and passion. He would try to control his temper, he said, if they could meet him half-way. "It was corny and funny," said Calhoun, "and they just started laughing at me and enjoying themselves. They do have emotion and passion. I just had to back off and let it come out. I showed up at practice the next day and we had a lot of fun. From that point on we were a really fun, relaxed basketball team."

But were they a championship team? Calhoun really didn't know as the Huskies rolled into New York City for the Big East tournament after an ugly loss at Syracuse. Okafor was sidelined by his cranky back, so it was up to Gordon to provide the Huskies' starpower. Calhoun had long believed that Gordon could be a dominant player, and he often rode Gordon hard in practice, labelling him "Gentle Ben." Calhoun wanted to fire up his top guard, to instill a take-charge mentality in him.

In New York, the message finally got through. Gordon came in with an aggressive, you-can't-stop-me attitude and set a Big East tournament record with 81 points in three games. In the Big East final, UConn trailed Pittsburgh 51–40 with 8:23 remaining, and Gordon sparked a 21–7 run with 11 points, helping the Huskies scrape and claw to a 61–58 victory.

"I mean, I had no choice [but to take over]," said Gordon, who was named the tournament's MVP. "I knew that was the only way that we would get to where we wanted to go. I've kind of been playing up and down this year, and I knew this was the best time of the year to have one of my best performances."

Seeded No. 2 in the West out of the Phoenix region—the same one UConn came out of in 1999 to win the national championship—the Huskies rolled through the early rounds of the NCAA tournament. And when top seeded Stanford was upset by Alabama in the second round, UConn's path was clear. The Huskies rolled over the Crimson Tide 87–71 behind Gordon's 36 points, and advanced to the Final Four. UConn had won its first four tournament games by an

average of 17.5 points, but waiting for the Huskies in San Antonio was Duke, which finished the regular season at 27–5, ranked sixth in the national polls.

From the opening tip, this game had all the makings of a classic heavyweight fight. Duke landed the first blow, getting Okafor into early foul trouble: the big man went to the bench after only four minutes with his second personal. Duke immediately took advantage, embarking on a 15–1 run. Calhoun went over to Okafor while Duke was running wild and told him to be ready, he might be going back in. Later, Calhoun conceded that statement had been a "blatant lie."

Calhoun knew that if the Huskies could keep the game close, they could make their run in the second half. With Duke's lead at seven points heading into the break, Calhoun couldn't help but grin as he left the court. In the second half, Calhoun moved Okafor off of Duke center Shelden Williams and put him on forward Luol Deng, who was less inclined to post up Okafor and possibly entice him to foul out of the game. Sure enough, Okafor stepped up and single-handedly took over the game. He scored all 18 of his points in the second half, and helped UConn overcome an eight-point deficit with 3:28 remaining. The Huskies won, 79–78.

"It wasn't who we beat," said Okafor. "It was how we beat them. Down eight points, not many minutes left, the whole country probably thought we were out of it except us. I don't remember the comeback, to tell you the truth. I just know we all believed, and the next thing you know we're up, game over, we're all hopping around."

As the UConn bus arrived at their hotel after the game, Calhoun got up and addressed the team. "Words cannot express how I feel about you guys right now and the effort that we made tonight," he said. "I just have two numbers for you guys: 4, 0. Those are the minutes that we have left to play our very best basketball." Less than 48 hours later, the Huskies would take care of business, knocking off Georgia Tech—which beat Oklahoma

State on a last-second shot in the other semifinal—with that nine-point victory that was not as close as its score suggested.

The following night in New Orleans, the UConn women made it a Huskies sweep, winning their third consecutive national title and making Connecticut the first program in the history of college basketball to win both the men's and women's championships in the same season. It was a fitting end for UConn star Diana Taurasi, arguably the best player ever in the women's game. "Coming in as a freshman, I never expected this," said Taurasi. "Three in a row? You just don't do that!"

And she almost didn't: Taurasi's third and final championship season was certainly her toughest. UConn was more vulnerable than ever, and after it lost to Boston College in the Big East tournament semifinal at the Hartford Civic Center, opponents could smell blood. For the first time in six years, UConn didn't receive a No. 1 seed, but the Huskies used the snub as motivation and easily advanced to the Final Four. There, UConn earned a spot in the final with archrival Tennessee—which the Huskies had beaten to win three of their four titles—after a hard-fought 67–58 win over scrappy Minnesota.

Taurasi (3) and the Huskies blew past all comers to win their third consecutive title.

Before the championship game, UConn guard Ashley Valley received an e-mail from Gordon that was equal parts prophesy and encouragement: "We're making history," Gordon wrote. "It's the year of the 2-seeds." It seemed to be, indeed, as the UConn women started to run away with the game in the first half, opening up a 17-point lead. But Tennessee clawed back and cut the deficit to two points with just under 10 minutes remaining. In the end, Taurasi & Co. wouldn't be denied. UConn pulled away again and held on for an 70–61 victory. After the final buzzer sounded, a joyous Taurasi punted the ball into the stands.

While Taurasi celebrated with her teammates, many Huskies supporters, including coach Geno Auriemma's teenage son, Michael, were crying. "Not because we won but because D's leaving," said the younger Auriemma. "She just has a connection with a lot of people."

The men's team at tiny Saint Joseph's developed a connection with a lot of people, too, captivating the nation with a season-long, Cinderella-like run. The

DAMIAN STROHMEYER

The king of the St. Joe's bashers was CBS analyst Billy Packer, who argued that there were many other teams who were more deserving of a No. 1 seed than the Hawks. And when St. Joe's was given a No. 1, Packer and Hawks coach Phil Martelli engaged in a spirited debate on the Selection Show after which Martelli called Packer "a jackass."

Once the tournament began, St. Joe's proved it was indeed deserving of a top seed. With Nelson showing why he was the best guard in the country, his backcourt partner Delonte West and swingman Pat Carroll showing deadly form from the outside, and Tyrone Barley locking up opposing scorers on defense, the Hawks rolled into the Sweet 16.

In a touch of irony, St. Joe's faced Wake Forest (Packer's alma mater) in the East Rutherford regional semifinal, and Packer was on hand to call the game. The Hawks won in impressive fashion, 84–80, winning over an egg-faced Packer and proving beyond any doubt that they were a worthy No. 1 seed. They were only one win away from the Final Four. Oklahoma State stood in the way, and in one of the best games of the tournament, the Cowboys knocked the Hawks off their perch. This one came down to the wire, and after Carroll hit a three pointer to give St. Joe's a one-point lead, Oklahoma State guard John Lucas Jr. hit a three with 6.9 seconds remaining. When Nelson's last-second shot attempt fell short, the Hawks were grounded.

"Just leaving these guys hurts me more than the loss," said Nelson. "It hasn't just been a magical season. It's been a magical team."

In the end, little St. Joe's proved that it could play with the big boys and the Hawks left the court with their heads help high. But the year belonged to UConn. On the game's biggest stage, Okafor and Taurasi helped the Huskies hit an unprecedented double.

Philadelphia school with only 3,800 students knocked off bigger schools, and doubters, all season. Led by 5'11" senior point guard Jameer Nelson, the Hawks kept on winning, but the skeptics kept on doubting. As the regular season entered the home stretch, St. Joe's and Stanford were the only two undefeated teams in the country, but many observers questioned Saint Joseph's schedule, and the strength of their conference, the Atlantic 10.

St. Joe's beat St. Bonaventure and Stanford lost its final game of the regular season to Washington, leaving St. Joe's as the only undefeated team in the nation heading into the conference tournaments, which the NCAA considers part of the regular season. (The last team to finish the regular season undefeated was UNLV in 1990–91.) But the Hawks had nearly been upset by Rhode Island before the St. Bonaventure victory, and after they were blown out by Xavier in the first round of the Atlantic-10 tournament, the debate rekindled anew: Some wags claimed that St. Joe's, despite its 27–1 record, did not deserve a No. 1 seed.

NCAA Championship Game Box Score

Connecticut 82

CONNECTICUT	Min	FG M–A	FT M–A	Reb O–T	A	PF	TP
Boone	29	4-6	1-4	5-6	1	2	9
Anderson	31	5-10	6-8	2-6	1	1	18
Okafor	38	10-17	4-8	7-15	1	3	24
Gordon	30	5-17	8-9	0-2	2	4	21
Brown	37	2-6	5-8	0-6	4	3	9
Villanueva	7	0-0	0-0	0-1	1	1	0
Armstrong	7	0-1	1-2	0-6	0	1	1
Tooles	2	0-0	0-0	0-0	0	0	0
Brown	19	0-4	0-0	3-6	0	3	0
Totals	200	26-61	25-39	17-48	10	18	82

Percentages: FG-.426, FT-.641. 3-Point Goals: 5-17, .294 (Anderson 2-7, Gordon 3-8, Brown 0-2). Team Rebounds: 2. Blocked Shots: 2 (Okafor 2). Turnovers: 16 (Okafor 6, Gordon 4, Brown 2, Brown 2, Anderson, Armstrong). Steals: 5 (Gordon, Anderson 2, Okafor).

Halftime: Connecticut 41, Gergia Tech 26.
A: 44,468.

Georgia Tech 73

GEORGIA TECH	Min	FG M–A	FT M–A	Reb O–T	A	PF	TP
Lewis	23	3-9	0-0	0-1	1	3	6
Mchenry	20	1-3	0-0	2-4	0	4	3
Schenscher	28	4-7	1-2	7-11	0	2	9
Elder	28	4-15	3-4	2-4	0	4	14
Jack	26	1-8	5-6	0-4	3	3	7
Muhammad	16	5-12	0-0	4-5	0	3	10
Bynum	23	6-11	2-6	0-2	5	4	17
Brooks	1	0-0	0-0	0-0	0	0	0
Moore	24	3-5	1-3	2-10	0	2	7
Tarver	11	0-1	0-0	1-2	0	1	0
Totals	200	27-71	12-21	18-43	9	26	73

Percentages: FG-.380, FT-.571. 3-Point Goals:7-22, .318 (Lewis 0-5, Mchenry 1-1, Elder 3-8, Jack 0-1, Bynum 3-6, Moore 0-1). Team Rebounds: 0. Blocked Shots: 1 (Mchenry). Turnovers: 14 (Jack 5, Lewis 2, Schenscher 2, Mchenry 2, Elder, Muhammad, Bynum). Steals: 10 (Jack 4, Muhammad 2, Tarver 2, Lewis, Bynum).

Officials: Dick Cartmell, Randy McCall, Verne Harris.

Final AP Top 25

Poll taken before NCAA Tournament.

1. Stanford (55)	29–1		14. Georgia Tech	23–9
2. Kentucky (9)	26–4		15. N Carolina St	20–9
3. Gonzaga (2)	27–2		16. Kansas	21–8
4. Oklahoma St (4)	27–3		17. Wake Forest	19–9
5. Saint Joseph's (1)	27–1		18. N Carolina	18–10
6. Duke	27–5		19. Maryland	19–11
7. Connecticut (1)	27–6		20. Syracuse	21–7
8. Mississippi St	25–3		21. Providence	20–8
9. Pittsburgh	29–4		22. Arizona	20–9
10. Wisconsin	24–6		23. Southern Illinois	25–4
11. Cincinnati	24–6		24. Memphis	21–7
12. Texas	23–7		25. (tie) Boston College	23–9
13. Illinois	24–6		25. (tie) Utah St	25–3

National Invitation Tournament Scores

Opening round: Nebraska 71, Creighton 70; Niagara 87, Troy St 83; George Mason 58, Tennessee 55; West Virginia 65, Kent St 54; Rhode Island 80, Boston University 52; Austin Peay 65, Belmont 59;WI-Milwaukee 91, Rice 53; Boise St 84, Nevada–Las Vegas 69.
First round: Marquette 87, Toledo 72; Saint Louis 70, Iowa 69; Michigan 65, Missouri 64; Notre Dame 71, Purdue 59; Virginia 79, George Washington 66; Rutgers 76, Temple 71; Villanova 85, Drexel 60; Florida St 91, Wichita St 84 (2OT); Hawaii 85, Utah St 74; Iowa St 82, Georgia 74; Oklahoma 70, LSU 61;Oregon 77, Colorado 72 (OT); West Virginia 79, Rhode Island 72; George Mason 66, Austin Peay 60; Nebraska 78, Niagara 70; Boise St 73, WI-Milwaukee 70.
Second round: Villanova 73, Virginia 63; Notre Dame 77, Saint Louis 66; Rutgers 67, West Virginia 64; Michigan 63, Oklahoma 52; Hawaii 84, Nebraska 83; Iowa St 62, Florida St 59; Marquette 66, Boise St 53; Oregon 68, George Mason 54.
Quarterfinals: Rutgers 72, Villanova 60; Michigan 88, Hawaii 73; Iowa St 77, Marquette 69; Oregon 65, Notre Dame 61.
Semifinals: Rutgers 84, Iowa St 81(OT); Michigan 78, Oregon 53.
Championship Game: Michigan 62, Rutgers 55.

2004 NCAA Basketball Men's Division I Tournament

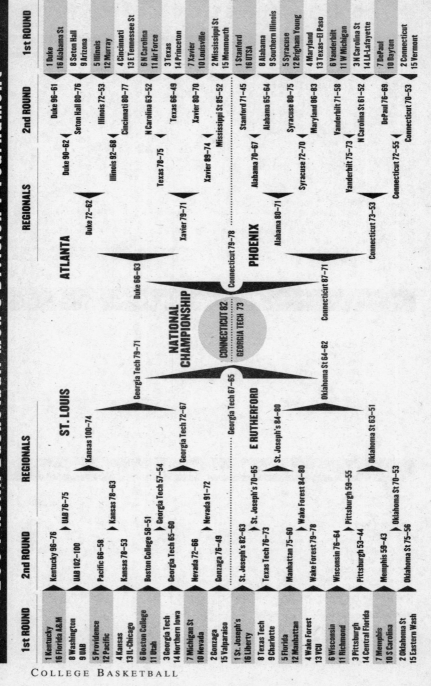

NCAA Men's Division I Conference Standings

America East

	Conference			All Games		
	W	L	Pct	W	L	Pct
Boston U	17	1	.944	23	6	.793
Vermont	15	3	.833	22	9	.710
Northeastern	13	5	.722	19	11	.633
Maine	12	6	.667	20	10	.667
Binghamton	10	8	.556	14	16	.467
Hartford	6	12	.333	12	17	.414
New Hampshire	5	13	.278	10	20	.333
Stony Brook	5	13	.278	10	20	.333
UMBC	4	14	.222	7	21	.250
Albany (NY)	3	15	.167	5	23	.179

Atlantic Coast

	Conference			All Games		
	W	L	Pct	W	L	Pct
Duke	13	3	.812	31	6	.838
N Carolina St	11	5	.688	21	10	.677
Georgia Tech	9	7	.562	28	10	.737
Wake Forest	9	7	.562	21	10	.677
N Carolina	8	8	.500	19	11	.633
Maryland	7	9	.438	20	12	.625
Virginia	6	10	.375	18	13	.581
Florida St	6	10	.375	19	14	.576
Clemson	3	13	.188	10	18	.357
Florida St	4	12	.250	14	15	.483

Atlantic Sun

	Conference			All Games		
	W	L	Pct	W	L	Pct
Troy St	18	2	.900	24	7	.774
Central Florida	17	3	.850	25	6	.806
Belmont	15	5	.750	21	9	.700
Georgia St	14	6	.700	20	9	.690
Stetson	10	10	.500	12	15	.444
Mercer	9	11	.450	12	18	.400
Jacksonville	8	12	.400	13	15	.464
Florida Atlantic	6	14	.300	9	19	.321
Gardner Webb	6	14	.300	9	20	.310
Lipscomb	4	16	.200	7	21	.250
Campbell	3	17	.150	3	24	.111

Atlantic 10

	Conference			All Games		
	W	L	Pct	W	L	Pct
EAST						
St Joseph's	16	0	1.000	30	2	.938
Temple	9	7	.562	15	14	.517
Rhode Island	7	9	.438	20	14	.588
Massachusetts	4	12	.250	10	19	.345
St Bonaventure	3	13	.188	7	21	.250
Fordham	3	13	.188	6	22	.214
WEST						
Dayton	12	4	.750	24	9	.727
George Washington	11	5	.688	18	12	.600
Xavier	10	6	.625	26	11	.703
Richmond	10	6	.625	20	13	.606
Duquesne	6	10	.375	12	17	.414
La Salle	5	11	.312	10	20	.333

Big East

	Conference			All Games		
	W	L	Pct	W	L	Pct
EAST						
Pittsburgh	13	3	.812	31	5	.861
Connecticut	12	4	.750	33	6	.846
Syracuse	11	5	.688	23	8	.742
Providence	11	5	.688	20	9	.690
Boston College	10	6	.625	24	10	.706
Seton Hall	10	6	.625	21	10	.677
Notre Dame	9	7	.562	19	13	.594
Rutgers	8	9	.471	20	13	.606
West Virginia	7	9	.438	17	14	.548
Virginia Tech	7	9	.438	15	14	.517
Villanova	6	11	.353	18	17	.514
Miami (FL)	4	12	.250	14	16	.467
Georgetown	4	12	.250	13	15	.464
St John's	1	15	.062	6	21	.222

Big Sky

	Conference			All Games		
	W	L	Pct	W	L	Pct
Eastern Wash	11	3	.786	17	13	.567
Northern Arizona	7	7	.500	15	14	.517
Weber St	7	7	.500	15	14	.517
Sacramento St	7	7	.500	13	15	.464
Idaho St	7	7	.500	13	18	.419
Montana St	6	8	.429	14	13	.519
Montana	6	8	.429	10	18	.357
Portland St	5	9	.357	11	16	.407

Big South

	Conference			All Games		
	W	L	Pct	W	L	Pct
Birm'ham Southern	12	4	.750	20	7	.741
Liberty	12	4	.750	18	15	.545
High Point	10	6	.625	19	11	.633
Winthrop	10	6	.625	16	12	.571
Coastal Carolina	8	8	.500	14	15	.483
Radford	7	9	.438	12	16	.429
UNC-Asheville	6	10	.375	9	20	.310
VMI	4	12	.250	6	22	.214
Charleston Southern	3	13	.188	6	22	.214

Big 10

	Conference			All Games		
	W	L	Pct	W	L	Pct
Illinois	13	3	.812	26	7	.788
Wisconsin	12	4	.750	25	7	.781
Michigan St	12	4	.750	18	12	.600
Iowa	9	7	.562	16	13	.552
Michigan	8	8	.500	23	11	.676
Northwestern	8	8	.500	14	15	.483
Purdue	7	9	.438	17	14	.548
Indiana	7	9	.438	14	15	.483
Ohio State	6	10	.375	14	16	.467
Minnesota	3	13	.188	12	18	.400
Penn St	3	13	.188	9	19	.321

Note: Standings based on regular-season conference play only; overall records include all tournament play.

Big 12

	Conference			All Games		
	W	L	Pct	W	L	Pct
Oklahoma St	14	2	.875	31	4	.886
Texas	12	4	.750	25	8	.758
Kansas	12	4	.750	24	9	.727
Colorado	10	6	.625	18	11	.621
Texas Tech	9	7	.562	23	11	.676
Missouri	9	7	.562	16	14	.533
Oklahoma	8	8	.500	20	11	.645
Iowa St	7	9	.438	20	13	.606
Nebraska	6	10	.375	18	13	.581
Kansas St	6	10	.375	14	14	.500
Baylor	3	13	.188	8	21	.276
Texas A&M	0	16	.000	7	21	.250

Big West

	Conference			All Games		
	W	L	Pct	W	L	Pct
Utah St	17	1	.944	25	4	.862
Pacific	17	1	.944	25	8	.758
Santa Barbara	10	8	.556	16	12	.571
Idaho	9	9	.500	14	16	.467
Cal St Northridge	7	11	.389	14	16	.467
Cal St Fullerton	7	11	.389	11	17	.393
UC Riverside	7	11	.389	11	17	.393
Cal Poly	6	12	.333	11	16	.407
UC Irvine	6	12	.333	11	17	.393
Long Beach St	4	14	.222	6	21	.222

Colonial

	Conference			All Games		
	W	L	Pct	W	L	Pct
Va. Commonwealth	14	4	.778	23	8	.742
Drexel	13	5	.722	18	11	.621
George Mason	12	6	.667	23	10	.697
Old Dominion	11	7	.611	17	12	.586
Delaware	10	8	.556	16	12	.571
Hofstra	10	8	.556	14	15	.483
UNC-Wilmington	9	9	.500	15	15	.500
Towson	4	14	.222	8	21	.276
William & Mary	4	14	.222	7	21	.250
James Madison	3	15	.167	7	21	.250

Conference USA

	Conference			All Games		
AMERICAN	W	L	Pct	W	L	Pct
Cincinnati	12	4	.750	25	7	.781
Charlotte	12	4	.750	21	9	.700
Depaul	12	4	.750	22	10	.688
Louisville	9	7	.562	20	10	.667
Saint Louis	9	7	.562	19	13	.594
Marquette	8	8	.500	19	12	.613
E Carolina	5	11	.312	13	14	.481
NATIONAL						
Memphis	12	4	.750	22	8	.733
UAB	12	4	.750	22	10	.688
Texas Christian	7	9	.438	12	17	.414
Southern Miss	6	10	.375	13	15	.464
Tulane	4	12	.250	11	17	.393
Houston	3	13	.188	9	18	.333
S Florida	1	15	.062	7	20	.259

Horizon League

	Conference			All Games		
	W	L	Pct	W	L	Pct
WI-Milwaukee	13	3	.812	20	11	.645
IL-Chicago	12	4	.750	24	8	.750
WI-Green Bay	11	5	.688	17	11	.607
Detroit	10	6	.625	19	11	.633
Wright St	10	6	.625	14	14	.500
Butler	8	8	.500	16	14	.533
Loyola Chicago	4	12	.250	9	20	.310
Youngstown St	4	12	.250	8	20	.286
Cleveland St	0	16	.000	4	25	.138

Ivy League

	Conference			All Games		
	W	L	Pct	W	L	Pct
Princeton	13	1	.929	20	8	.714
Pennsylvania	10	4	.714	17	10	.630
Brown	10	4	.714	14	13	.519
Yale	7	7	.500	12	15	.444
Cornell	6	8	.429	11	16	.407
Columbia	6	8	.429	10	17	.370
Harvard	3	11	.214	4	23	.148
Dartmouth	1	13	.071	3	25	.107

Metro Atlantic

	Conference			All Games		
	W	L	Pct	W	L	Pct
Manhattan	16	2	.889	25	6	.806
Niagara	13	5	.722	22	10	.688
St Peter's	12	6	.667	17	12	.586
Fairfield	12	7	.632	19	11	.633
Rider	10	8	.556	17	14	.548
Siena	10	9	.526	14	16	.467
Iona	8	10	.444	11	18	.379
Canisius	5	13	.278	10	20	.333
Marist	4	14	.222	6	22	.214
Loyola (MD)	1	17	.056	1	27	.036

Mid-American

	Conference			All Games		
EAST	W	L	Pct	W	L	Pct
Kent State	13	5	.722	22	9	.710
Miami Ohio	12	6	.667	18	11	.621
Buffalo	11	7	.611	17	12	.586
Marshall	8	10	.444	12	17	.414
Akron	7	11	.389	13	15	.464
Ohio	7	11	.389	10	20	.333
WEST						
Western Michigan	15	3	.833	26	5	.839
Toledo	12	6	.667	20	11	.645
Ball St	10	8	.556	14	15	.483
Bowling Green	8	10	.444	14	17	.452
Eastern Mich	7	11	.389	13	15	.464
Northern Illinois	5	13	.278	10	20	.333
Central Michigan	2	16	.111	6	24	.200

Mid-Continent

	Conference			All Games		
	W	L	Pct	W	L	Pct
Valparaiso	11	5	.688	18	13	.581
Indiana-Purdue	10	6	.625	21	11	.656
Oral Roberts	10	6	.625	17	11	.607
Centenary	10	6	.625	16	12	.571
MO-Kansas City	9	7	.562	15	14	.517
Chicago St	9	7	.562	12	20	.375
Oakland	6	10	.375	13	17	.433
Southern Utah	6	10	.375	10	18	.357
Western Illinois	1	15	.062	3	25	.107

Mid-Eastern Athletic

	Conference			All Games		
	W	L	Pct	W	L	Pct
S Carolina St	14	4	.778	18	11	.621
Coppin St	14	4	.778	18	14	.562
Delaware St	11	7	.611	13	15	.464
Hampton	11	7	.611	13	17	.433
Florida A&M	10	8	.556	15	17	.469
Norfolk St	10	8	.556	12	17	.414
Morgan St	9	9	.500	11	16	.407
Bethune Cookman	7	11	.389	8	21	.276
MD-Eastern Shore	6	12	.333	8	21	.276
Howard	4	14	.222	6	22	.214
N Carolina A&T	3	15	.167	3	25	.107

Missouri Valley

	Conference			All Games		
	W	L	Pct	W	L	Pct
Southern Illinois	17	1	.944	25	5	.833
Creighton	12	6	.667	20	9	.690
Northern Iowa	12	6	.667	21	10	.677
Wichita St	12	6	.667	21	11	.656
SW Missouri St	9	9	.500	19	14	.576
Bradley	7	11	.389	15	16	.484
Drake	7	11	.389	12	16	.429
Indiana St	5	13	.278	9	19	.321
Evansville	5	13	.278	7	22	.241
Illinois St	4	14	.222	10	19	.345

Mountain West

	Conference			All Games		
	W	L	Pct	W	L	Pct
Air Force	12	2	.857	22	7	.759
Brigham Young	10	4	.714	21	9	.700
Utah	9	5	.643	24	9	.727
Nevada–Las Vegas	7	7	.500	18	13	.581
New Mexico	5	9	.357	14	14	.500
San Diego St	5	9	.357	14	16	.467
Colorado St	4	10	.286	13	16	.448
Wyoming	4	10	.286	11	17	.393

Northeast

	Conference			All Games		
	W	L	Pct	W	L	Pct
Monmouth (NJ)	12	6	.667	21	12	.636
St Francis (NY)	12	6	.667	15	13	.536
Fairleigh Dickinson	11	7	.611	17	12	.586
Robert Morris	10	8	.556	14	15	.483
St Francis (PA)	10	8	.556	13	15	.464
Wagner	10	8	.556	13	16	.448
Central Conn	9	9	.500	14	14	.500
Sacred Heart	8	10	.444	12	15	.444
Mt St Mary's	8	10	.444	10	19	.345
Quinnipiac	5	13	.278	9	20	.310
LIU-Brooklyn	4	14	.222	8	19	.296

Ohio Valley

	Conference			All Games		
	W	L	Pct	W	L	Pct
Austin Peay	16	0	1.000	22	10	.688
Murray St	14	2	.875	28	6	.824
Morehead St	10	6	.625	16	13	.552
Eastern Ky	8	8	.500	14	15	.483
Jacksonville St	7	9	.438	14	14	.500
Tennessee Tech	7	9	.438	13	15	.464
Samford	7	9	.438	12	16	.429
Tennessee St	6	10	.375	7	21	.250
Tennessee-Martin	5	11	.312	10	18	.357
SE Missouri St	4	12	.250	11	16	.407
Eastern Illinois	4	12	.250	6	21	.222

Pac 10

	Conference			All Games		
	W	L	Pct	W	L	Pct
Stanford	17	1	.944	30	2	.938
Washington	12	6	.667	19	12	.613
Arizona	11	7	.611	20	10	.667
Oregon	9	9	.500	18	13	.581
California	9	9	.500	13	15	.464
Southern Cal	8	10	.444	13	15	.464
Washington St	7	11	.389	13	16	.448
UCLA	7	11	.389	11	17	.393
Oregon St	6	12	.333	12	16	.429
Arizona St	4	14	.222	10	17	.370

Patriot League

	Conference			All Games		
EAST	W	L	Pct	W	L	Pct
Lehigh	10	4	.714	20	11	.645
American	10	4	.714	18	13	.581
Lafayette	9	5	.643	18	10	.643
Bucknell	9	5	.643	14	15	.483
Holy Cross	7	7	.500	13	15	.464
Colgate	6	8	.429	15	14	.517
Army	3	11	.214	6	21	.222
Navy	2	12	.143	5	23	.179

Southeastern

EAST	Conference			All Games		
	W	L	Pct	W	L	Pct
Kentucky	13	3	.812	27	5	.844
Florida	9	7	.562	20	11	.645
Vanderbilt	8	8	.500	23	10	.697
S Carolina	8	8	.500	23	11	.676
Georgia	7	9	.438	16	14	.533
Tennessee	7	9	.438	15	14	.517
WEST						
Mississippi St	14	2	.875	26	4	.867
Louisiana St	8	8	.500	18	11	.621
Alabama	8	8	.500	20	13	.606
Auburn	5	11	.312	14	14	.500
Mississippi	5	11	.312	13	15	.464
Arkansas	4	12	.250	12	16	.429

Southern

NORTH	Conference			All Games		
	W	L	Pct	W	L	Pct
E Tennessee St	15	1	.938	27	6	.818
Chattanooga	10	6	.625	19	11	.633
Elon	7	9	.438	12	18	.400
UNC-Greensboro	7	9	.438	11	17	.393
Western Carolina	6	10	.375	13	15	.464
Appalachian St	4	12	.250	9	21	.300
WEST						
Georgia Southern	11	5	.688	21	8	.724
Charleston	11	5	.688	20	9	.690
Davidson	11	5	.688	17	12	.586
Furman	8	8	.500	17	12	.586
Wofford	4	12	.250	9	20	.310
The Citadel	2	14	.125	6	22	.214

Southland

	Conference			All Games		
	W	L	Pct	W	L	Pct
SE Louisiana	11	5	.688	20	9	.690
Texas Arlington	11	5	.688	17	12	.586
Texas–San Antonio	11	5	.688	19	14	.576
S.F. Austin	10	6	.625	21	9	.700
Sam Houston	8	8	.500	13	15	.464
Texas St	8	8	.500	13	15	.464
Northwestern St	8	8	.500	11	17	.393
Louisiana-Monroe	8	8	.500	12	19	.387
McNeese St	7	9	.438	11	16	.407
Lamar	5	11	.312	11	18	.379
Nicholls St	1	15	.062	6	21	.222

Southwestern Athletic

	Conference			All Games		
	W	L	Pct	W	L	Pct
Miss. Valley St	16	2	.889	22	7	.759
Texas Southern	11	7	.611	15	14	.517
Alabama St	11	7	.611	16	15	.516
Alabama A&M	9	9	.500	13	17	.433
Jackson St	9	9	.500	12	17	.414
Alcorn St	9	9	.500	11	18	.379
Grambling	9	9	.500	11	18	.379
Southern	8	10	.444	11	17	.393
Prairie View	7	11	.389	7	20	.259
AR–Pine Bluff	1	17	.056	1	26	.037

Sun Belt

EAST	Conference			All Games		
	W	L	Pct	W	L	Pct
AR–Little Rock	9	5	.643	17	12	.586
Middle Tennessee St	8	6	.571	17	12	.586
Western Kentucky	8	6	.571	15	13	.536
Arkansas St	7	7	.500	17	11	.607
Florida Int'l	1	13	.071	5	22	.185
WEST						
Louisiana-Lafayette	12	3	.800	20	9	.690
New Orleans	9	6	.600	17	14	.548
N Texas	8	7	.533	13	15	.464
Denver	6	9	.400	14	13	.519
New Mexico St	6	9	.400	13	14	.481
S Alabama	6	9	.400	12	16	.429

West Coast

	Conference			All Games		
	W	L	Pct	W	L	Pct
Gonzaga	14	0	1.000	28	3	.903
St Mary's (CA)	9	5	.643	19	12	.613
Pepperdine	9	5	.643	15	16	.484
San Francisco	7	7	.500	17	14	.548
Santa Clara	6	8	.429	16	16	.500
Loyola-Marymount	5	9	.357	15	14	.517
Portland	5	9	.357	11	17	.393
San Diego	1	13	.071	4	26	.133

Western Athletic

	Conference			All Games		
	W	L	Pct	W	L	Pct
Texas–El Paso	13	5	.722	24	8	.750
Nevada	13	5	.722	25	9	.735
Boise St	12	6	.667	23	10	.697
Rice	12	6	.667	22	11	.667
Hawaii	11	7	.611	21	12	.636
Fresno St	10	8	.556	14	15	.483
Louisiana Tech	8	10	.444	15	15	.500
Southern Methodist	5	13	.278	12	18	.400
Tulsa	5	13	.278	9	20	.310
San Jose St	1	17	.056	6	23	.207

Independents

	All Games		
	W	L	Pct
TX A&M–Corpus Christi	15	11	.577
TX–Pan America	14	14	.500
Savannah St	4	24	.143
IU–PU Fort Wayne	3	25	.107

Scoring

	Class	GP	FG	3FG	FT	Pts	Avg
Keydren Clark, St. Peter's	So.	29	233	112	197	775	26.7
Kevin Martin, Western Caro.	Jr.	27	208	51	206	673	24.9
David Hawkins, Temple	Sr.	29	224	84	177	709	24.4
Taylor Coppenrath, Vermont	Jr.	24	203	14	159	579	24.1
Luis Flores, Manhattan	Sr.	31	234	68	208	744	24.0
Michael Watson, UMKC	Sr.	29	225	96	134	680	23.4
Mike Helms, Oakland	Sr.	30	224	79	168	695	23.2
Odell Bradley, IUPUI	Sr.	29	235	31	170	671	23.1
Ike Diogu, Arizona St.	So.	27	179	14	243	615	22.8
Derrick Tarver, Akron	Sr.	27	196	47	173	612	22.7
Bryant Matthews, Va. Tech	Sr.	29	219	31	172	641	22.1
Andrew Wisniewski, Centenary	Sr.	28	196	66	154	612	21.9
Ricky Minard, Morehead St.	Sr.	29	210	45	166	631	21.8
Kris Humphries, Minn.	Fr.	29	221	17	170	629	21.7
Luke Jackson, Oregon	Sr.	31	210	73	163	656	21.2
Dylan Page, WI-Mil	Sr.	31	227	59	134	647	20.9
Jose Juan Barea, Northeastern	So.	26	180	73	105	538	20.7
Ken Tutt, Oral Roberts	Fr.	28	193	101	92	579	20.7
Andre Emmett, Texas Tech	Sr.	34	260	16	165	701	20.6
Jameer Nelson, St. Joseph's	Sr.	32	234	73	118	659	20.6
Juan Mendez, Niagara	Jr.	32	208	17	223	656	20.5
Adam Hess, William & Mary	Sr.	28	194	57	123	568	20.3
Terrence Woods, Florida A&M	Sr.	31	192	140	104	628	20.3
Ka'Ron Barnes, Cornell	Sr.	27	184	56	120	544	20.1
Maurice Bailey, Sacred Heart	Sr.	27	174	40	154	542	20.1

FIELD-GOAL PERCENTAGE

	Class	GP	FG	FGA	Pct
Nigel Dixon, Western Ky.	Sr	28	179	264	67.8
Sean Finn, Dayton	Sr	33	175	264	66.3
Adam Mark, Belmont	Sr	30	233	352	66.2
David Harrison, Colorado	Jr	29	186	295	63.1
Cuthbert Victor, Murray St.	Sr	34	190	302	62.9
Jon Bentley, Eastern Ky.	Sr	29	154	245	62.9
Michael Harris, Rice	Jr	33	217	360	60.3
Dominick Martin, Yale	Jr	27	138	229	60.3
Emeka Okafor, Connecticut	Jr	36	261	436	59.9
Jai Lewis, George Mason	So	33	187	313	59.7

Note: Minimum 5 made per game.

FREE-THROW PERCENTAGE

	Class	GP	FT	FTA	Pct
Blake Ahearn, SW Mo. St	Fr	33	117	120	97.5
J.J. Redick, Duke	So	37	143	150	95.3
Jake Sullivan, Iowa St.	Sr	33	83	89	93.3
Steve Drabyn, Belmont	Sr	30	96	105	91.4
Chris Hernandez, Stanford	So	30	96	105	91.4
Scooter McFadgon, Tenn	Jr	28	134	147	91.2
Terry Williams, Ga. Southern	Jr	29	81	90	90.0
Delonte West, St. Joseph's	Jr	32	124	139	88.7
Antoine Jordan, Siena	So	25	63	71	88.7
Leon Pattman, Dartmouth	Fr	26	70	79	88.6

Note: Minimum 2.5 made per game.

REBOUNDS

	Class	GP	Reb	Avg
Paul Millsap, Louisiana Tech	Fr	30	374	12.5
Jaime Lloreda, Louisiana St	Sr	22	256	11.6
Emeka Okafor, Connecticut	Jr	36	415	11.5
Nate Lofton, SE Louisiana.	Jr	29	315	10.9
Nigel Wyatte, Wagner	Sr	28	292	10.4
Charles Gaines, Southern Miss.	Sr	28	290	10.4
Nigel Dixon, Western Kentucky	Sr	28	287	10.3
Cuthbert Victor, Murray St.	Sr	34	347	10.2
Odartey Blankson, UNLV	Jr	31	315	10.2
Kris Humphries, Minnesota	Fr	29	293	10.1

ASSISTS

	Class	GP	A	Avg
Greg Davis, Troy St.	Sr	31	256	8.3
Martell Bailey, IL-Chicago	Sr	32	250	7.8
Aaron Miles, Kansas	Jr	33	242	7.3
Andres Rodriguez, American	Sr	31	225	7.3
Raymond Felton, N Carolina	So	30	212	7.1
Maurice Searight, Grambling	So	28	195	7.0
Blake Stepp, Gonzaga	Sr	31	207	6.7
Jerel Blassingame, UNLV	Jr	31	205	6.6
Walker Russell, Jacksonville St.	So	28	182	6.5
Mike McGrain, San Diego	Jr	26	169	6.5

*Includes games played in tournaments.

THREE-POINT FIELD-GOAL PERCENTAGE

	Class	GP	FG	FGA	Pct
Brad Lechtenberg, San Diego	Sr	23	71	139	51.1
James Odoms, Mercer	Jr	23	59	121	48.8
Tyson Dorsey, Samford	Sr	28	74	152	48.7
Antonio Burks, S.F. Austin	Sr	30	78	164	47.6
Trey Guidry, Illinois St.	Jr	29	86	187	46.0
Pat Carroll, St. Joseph's	Jr	32	81	177	45.8
Dewarick Spencer, Arkansas St.	Jr	28	86	188	45.7
Aaron Thomas, Robert Morris	Sr	29	78	171	45.6
Tim Begley, Pennsylvania	Jr	27	83	182	45.6
Chris Hill, Michigan St.	Jr	30	84	185	45.4

Note: Minimum 1.5 made per game.

BLOCKED SHOTS

	Class	GP	BS	Avg
Anwar Ferguson, Houston	Sr	27	111	4.1
Emeka Okafor, Connecticut	Jr	36	147	4.1
D'or Fischer, West Virginia	Jr	31	124	4.0
Gerrick Morris, S Florida	Sr	27	108	4.0
Nick Billings, Binghamton	Jr	30	105	3.5
Moussa Badiane, E Carolina	Jr	27	90	3.3
Marcus Douthit, Providence	Sr	29	92	3.2
Herve Lamizana, Rutgers	Sr	33	102	3.1
Shelden Williams, Duke	So	37	111	3.0
Haminn Quaintance, Jacksonville	Fr	28	84	3.0
Shawnson Johnson, N Texas	Sr	23	69	3.0

THREE-POINT FIELD GOALS MADE PER GAME

	Class	GP	FG	Avg
Terrence Woods, Florida A&M	Sr	31	140	4.5
Keydren Clark, St. Peter's	So	29	112	3.9
Marques Green, St. Bonaventure	Sr	27	98	3.6
Ken Tutt, Oral Roberts	Fr	28	101	3.6
Erik Benzel, Denver	Jr	27	97	3.6
Akeem Clark, IUPUI	Jr	32	109	3.4
Gerry McNamara, Syracuse	So	31	105	3.4
Ed McCants, WI-Milwaukee	Jr	31	104	3.4
Brendan Plavich, Charlotte	Jr	29	97	3.3
Tim Pickett, Florida St.	Sr	33	110	3.3

STEALS

	Class	GP	S	Avg
Marques Green, St. Bonaventure	Sr	27	107	4.0
Obie Trotter, Alabama A&M	So	29	88	3.0
Chakowby Hicks, Norfolk St.	Jr	29	86	3.0
Zakee Wadood, E Tennessee St.	Sr	33	92	2.8
Jameer Nelson, St. Joseph's	Sr	32	89	2.8
Louis Ford, Howard	So	28	77	2.8
Jamon Gordon, Virginia Tech	Fr	24	66	2.8
Chris Paul, Wake Forest	Fr	31	84	2.7
David Hawkins, Temple	Sr	29	78	2.7
Tory Cavalieri, St. Francis (N.Y.)	Jr	28	75	2.7

Single-Game Highs

POINTS

45 .....Alex Loughton, Old Dominion, Dec 6, 2003 (vs Charlotte)
44 .....Derrick Tarver, Akron, Dec 30, 2003 (vs Wright St)
44 .....Derrick Tarver, Akron, Dec 1, 2003 (vs Hampton)
44 .....Kevin Martin, Western Carolina, Nov 21, 2003 (vs Georgia)

REBOUNDS

22 .....Nate Lofton, SE Louisiana, March 10, 2004 (vs Texas–San Antonio
22 .....Caleb Green, Oral Roberts, Feb 28, 2004 (vs Southern Utah)
22 .....Emeka Okafor, Connecticut, Feb 21, 2004 (vs Notre Dame)

Nine tied with 21.

ASSISTS

19 .....Andres Rodriguez, American, Jan 14, 2004 (vs Navy)
18.....Raymond Felton, N Carolina, Dec 7, 2003 (vs George Mason)
15 .....Francisco Garcia, Louisville, Jan 3, 2004 (vs Murray St)
15 .....Jay Straight, Wyoming, Dec 20, 2003 (vs Winthrop)
15 .....Maurice Searight, Grambling, Dec 11, 2003 (vs Texas College)
15 .....Marfell Bailey, IL-Chicago, Nov 25, 2003 (vs Evansville)

THREE-POINT FIELD GOALS

11 .....Earnest Crumbley, Florida Atlantic, Feb 26, 2004 (vs Campbell)
11 .....Kevin Bettencourt, Bucknell, Dec 6, 2003 (vs St. Francis)

STEALS

9 ....Linas Lekavicius, American, Feb 7, 2004 (vs Bucknell)
9 ....James Denson, Jacksonville St, Jan 24, 2004 (vs Morehead St)
9 ....Edward O'Neil, Charleston Southern, Jan 13, 2004 (vs Coastal Carol
9 ....Derrick Obasohan, Texas-Arlington, Dec 22, 2003 (vs Wichita St)
9 ....Ryan Price, McNeese St, Dec 18, 2003 (vs George Mason)
9 ....Michael Ross, Eastern Michigan, Nov 25, 2003 (vs Concordia [MI])

BLOCKED SHOTS

10.....Gerrick Morris, S Florida, Feb 21, 2004 (vs Houston)
10 .....Nick Billings, Binghamton, Jan 31, 2004 (vs Hartford)
10.....Emeka Okafor, Connecticut, Dec 6, 2003 (vs Army)
10.....Gerrick Morris, S Florida, Nov 29, 2003 (vs Wright St)

SCORING OFFENSE

	GP	W	L	Pts	Avg
Arizona	30	20	10	2614	87.1
Troy St.	31	24	7	2624	84.6
Wake Forest	31	21	10	2590	83.5
North Carolina	30	19	11	2464	82.1
Chattanooga	30	19	11	2463	82.1
Washington	31	19	12	2543	82.0
Gonzaga	31	28	3	2536	81.8
Niagara	32	22	10	2611	81.6
Oral Roberts	28	17	11	2265	80.9
Georgia Southern	29	21	8	2337	80.6

SCORING DEFENSE

	GP	W	L	Pts	Avg
Air Force	29	22	7	1475	50.9
Pittsburgh	36	31	5	2031	56.4
Princeton	28	20	8	1591	56.8
Wisconsin	32	25	7	1823	57.0
Utah	33	24	9	1893	57.4
Utah St.	29	25	4	1684	58.1
Holy Cross	28	13	15	1641	58.6
Richmond	33	20	13	1964	59.5
Boston U.	29	23	6	1726	59.5
Detroit	30	19	11	1787	59.6
UNC Wilmington	30	15	15	1787	59.6

SCORING MARGIN

	Off	Def	Mar
Gonzaga	81.8	66.2	15.6
St. Joseph's	77.4	62.3	15.1
Connecticut	78.8	63.9	14.9
Duke	79.8	65.0	14.8
Oklahoma St.	77.1	62.5	14.6
Stanford	73.6	60.5	13.1
Cincinnati	76.7	64.3	12.5
Western Mich.	78.5	66.1	12.4
Troy St.	84.6	72.7	12.0
Louisville	73.2	61.5	11.6

FIELD-GOAL PERCENTAGE

	FG	FGA	Pct
Oklahoma St.	1002	1953	51.3
Gonzaga	899	1765	50.9
Utah St.	711	1397	50.9
Murray St.	994	2009	49.5
Michigan St.	748	1519	9.2
Chattanooga	861	1751	49.2
Samford	644	1318	48.9
Brigham Young	764	1571	48.6
Arizona	942	1938	48.6
Lafayette	731	1513	48.3

FIELD-GOAL PERCENTAGE DEFENSE

	FG	FGA	Pct
Connecticut	924	2502	36.9
Louisville	638	1672	38.2
Gonzaga	725	1890	38.4
Stanford	671	1745	38.5
Pittsburgh	765	1984	38.6
Georgia Tech	865	2228	38.8
Mississippi Valley	588	1509	39.0
Kansas	766	1959	39.1
Maine	680	1730	39.3
E Carolina	601	1526	39.4

FREE-THROW PERCENTAGE

	FT	FTA	Pct
North Carolina St.	481	602	79.9
Arizona	511	650	78.6
Bowling Green	551	711	77.5
Michigan St.	452	586	77.1
Butler	335	439	76.3
Manhattan	607	798	76.1
Oral Roberts	492	647	76.0
Robert Morris	384	509	75.4
UTEP	614	817	75.2
Stanford	489	651	75.1

THREE-POINT FIELD GOALS MADE PER GAME

	GP	FG	Avg
Troy St.	31	364	11.7
St. Joseph's	32	313	9.8
Belmont	30	293	9.8
Samford	28	264	9.4
St. Francis (N.Y.)	28	258	9.2
Oregon	31	280	9.0
Birmingham-So.	27	243	9.0
Florida St.	33	296	9.0
St. Peter's	29	259	8.9
Pennsylvania	27	236	8.7

REBOUNDING MARGIN

	GP	REB	Opp REB	Margin /G
Connecticut	39	1742	1363	9.7
Gonzaga	31	1230	975	8.2
Mississippi St.	30	1231	992	8.0
Rhode Island	34	1381	1127	7.5
Utah	33	1140	896	7.4
Western Ky.	28	1085	884	7.2
Louisiana Tech	30	1180	969	7.0
Dayton	33	1266	1037	6.9
TX. A&M-Corp. Chris	26	969	790	6.9
Stanford	32	1178	962	6.8

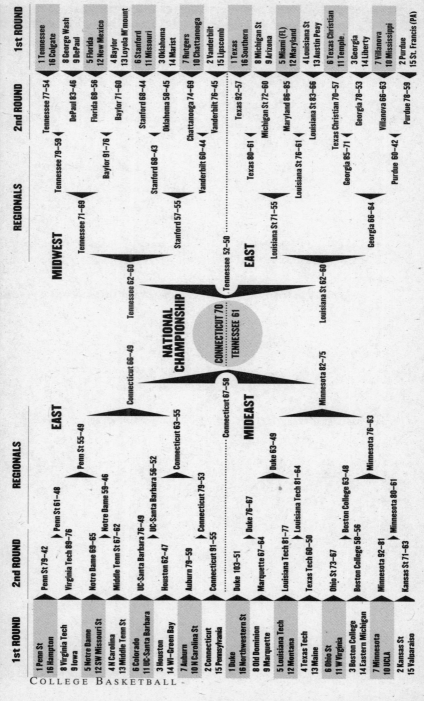

2004 NCAA Basketball Women's Division I Tournament

EAST

1st ROUND

1 Penn St
16 Hampton
8 Virginia Tech
9 Iowa
5 Notre Dame
12 SW Missouri St
4 N Carolina
13 Middle Tenn St
6 Colorado
11 UC-Santa Barbara
3 Houston
14 WI-Green Bay
7 Auburn
10 N Carolina St
2 Connecticut
15 Pennsylvania

2nd ROUND

Penn St 79–42
Virginia Tech 89–76
Notre Dame 69–65
Middle Tenn St 67–62
UC-Santa Barbara 76–49
Houston 62–47
Auburn 79–59
Connecticut 91–55

REGIONALS

Penn St 61–48
Notre Dame 59–46
UC-Santa Barbara 56–52
Connecticut 79–53

Penn St 55–49
Connecticut 63–55

Connecticut 67–58

MIDEAST

1st ROUND

1 Duke
16 Northwestern St
8 Old Dominion
9 Marquette
5 Louisiana Tech
12 Montana
4 Texas Tech
13 Maine
6 Ohio St
11 W Virginia
3 Boston College
14 Eastern Michigan
7 Minnesota
10 UCLA
2 Kansas St
15 Valparaiso

2nd ROUND

Duke 103–51
Marquette 67–64
Louisiana Tech 81–77
Texas Tech 60–50
Ohio St 73–67
Boston College 58–56
Minnesota 92–81
Kansas St 71–63

REGIONALS

Duke 76–67
Louisiana Tech 81–64
Boston College 63–48
Minnesota 80–61

Duke 63–49
Minnesota 76–63

Minnesota 82–75

NATIONAL CHAMPIONSHIP

Connecticut 66–49

Minnesota 82–75

CONNECTICUT 70
TENNESSEE 61

Tennessee 62–60

Louisiana St 62–60

MIDWEST

REGIONALS

Tennessee 71–69
Stanford 57–55

Vanderbilt 60–44

Tennessee 79–59
Baylor 91–76

Stanford 68–43
Chattanooga 74–69

2nd ROUND

Tennessee 77–54
DePaul 83–46
Florida 68–56
Baylor 71–60
Stanford 68–44
Oklahoma 58–45
Chattanooga 74–69
Vanderbilt 76–45

1st ROUND

1 Tennessee
16 Colgate
8 George Wash
9 DePaul
5 Florida
12 New Mexico
4 Baylor
13 Loyola M'mount
6 Stanford
11 Missouri
3 Oklahoma
14 Marist
7 Rutgers
10 Chattanooga
2 Vanderbilt
15 Lipscomb

EAST

Tennessee 52–50

REGIONALS

Texas 80–61
Louisiana St 71–55

Georgia 66–64

Texas 92–57
Maryland 86–85

Louisiana St 83–66
Georgia 78–53

2nd ROUND

Texas 92–57
Michigan St 72–60
Maryland 86–85
Louisiana St 83–66
Texas Christian 70–57
Georgia 78–53
Villanova 66–63
Purdue 78–59

1st ROUND

1 Texas
16 Southern
8 Michigan St
9 Arizona
5 Miami (FL)
12 Maryland
4 Louisiana St
13 Austin Peay
6 Texas Christian
11 Temple
3 Georgia
14 Liberty
7 Villanova
10 Mississippi
2 Purdue
15 St. Francis (PA)

Georgia 85–71
Purdue 60–42

NCAA Women's Championship Game Box Score

Connecticut 70

Connecticut	Min	FG M-A	FT M-A	Reb O-T	A	PF	TP
Turner	33	4-12	3-6	1-9	4	2	12
Moore	30	6-9	2-2	6-9	1	3	14
Taurasi	37	6-11	2-4	0-3	2	1	17
Conlon	33	1-4	4-4	0-2	5	0	7
Strother	37	5-8	3-3	0-2	2	1	14
Battle	15	1-4	0-0	0-1	0	1	3
Crockett	15	1-3	1-1	0-2	1	2	3
Totals	200	24-51	15-20	7-28	15	10	70

Percentages: FG—.471, FT—750. 3-pt goals: 7–14, .500 (Turner 1–2, Taurasi 3–7, Conlon 1–2, Strother 1–2, Battle 1–1). Team rebounds: 3. Blocked shots: 2 (Turner 2). Turnovers: 10 (Taurasi 3, Moore 2, Crockett 2, Battle, Conlon, Strother). Steals: 7 (Conlon 2, Moore 2, Turner 2, Battle).

Halftime: Connecticut 30, Tennessee 24.
A: 18,211. Officials: Mattingly, Kantner, Enterline.

Tennessee 61

Tennessee	Min	FG M-A	FT M-A	Reb O-T	A	PF	TP
Davis	30	3-8	0-0	1-1	7	5	6
Ely	26	4-10	2-4	2-7	0	2	10
Robinson	39	6-10	1-4	4-7	1	1	13
Butts	32	1-10	6-6	3-6	2	2	8
Zolman	37	6-11	4-4	2-9	1	2	19
Spencer	14	0-1	0-0	0-1	0	4	0
Redding	3	0-1	0-0	0-0	1	0	0
Jackson	11	1-7	0-0	0-1	1	2	3
Fluker	8	1-3	0-0	1-1	0	0	2
Totals	200	22-61	13-18	13-33	13	18	61

Percentages: FG—.361, FT—.722. 3-pt goals: 4–16, .250 (Butts 0–6, Zolman 3–6, Jackson 1–4). Team rebounds: 6. Blocked shots: 2 (Robinson 2). Turnovers: 11 (Davis 3, Ely 3, Jackson 2, Butts, Robinson, Zolman). Steals: 8 (Davis 4, Butts 3, Zolman).

NCAA Women's Division I Individual Leaders

SCORING

Player and Team	Class	GP	TFG	3FG	FT	Pts	Avg
Emily Faurholt, Idaho	So	29	261	43	172	737	25.4
Hana Peljito, Harvard	Sr	27	246	37	112	641	23.7
Chandi Jones, Houston	Sr	32	255	71	146	727	22.7
Cyndy Wilks, Virginia Commonwealth	Sr	28	215	58	130	618	22.1
Shameka Christon, Arkansas	Sr	28	219	47	126	611	21.8
Candace Futrell, Duquesne	Sr	29	214	74	119	621	21.4
Giuliana Mendiola, Washington	Sr	31	244	48	125	661	21.3
Jennifer Smith, Michigan	Sr	31	218	13	210	659	21.3
Beth Swink, St. Francis	Jr	31	260	0	139	659	21.3
Katie Feenstra, Liberty	Jr	32	291	0	92	674	21.1
Lindsay Whalen, Minnesota	Sr	27	185	40	144	554	20.5
Crystal Kitt, Alabama St.	Jr	28	209	0	155	573	20.5
Emily Christian, Tennessee Tech	So	27	202	14	134	552	20.4
Khara Smith, DePaul	So	30	261	6	83	611	20.4
Nicole Powell, Stanford	Sr	31	204	58	161	627	20.2

Miracle Worker

Facing the prospect of losing his 15th straight Big Ten game, Minnesota basketball coach Dan Monson turned to Hollywood. After practice on Feb. 10, 2004, Monson took the Gophers to a matinee of *Miracle*, the film based on the 1980 U.S. men's Olympic hockey team. "I was a senior in high school when that Lake Placid event happened," said Monson. "If anything ever epitomized a team, it was them, and I wanted our guys to see that." The next night Minnesota rallied from a nine-point halftime deficit to beat Michigan 81–78.

NCAA Women's Division I Individual Leaders (Cont.)

FIELD-GOAL PERCENTAGE

Player and Team	Class	GP	FG	FGA	Pct
Katie Feenstra, Liberty	Jr	32	291	443	65.7
Janel McCarville, Minnesota	Jr	34	212	344	61.6
Gerlonda Hardin, Austin Peay	Sr	31	223	367	60.8
Le'Coe Willingham, Auburn	Sr	31	192	316	60.8
Khara Smith, DePaul	So	30	261	430	60.7
Pam O'Connor, Eastern Ill.	Jr	27	166	276	60.1
Colleen Fitzpatrick, Lafayette	Jr	25	125	208	60.1
Beth Swink, St. Francis (PA)	Jr	31	260	433	60.0
Kate Flavin, Richmond	Jr	33	251	424	59.2
Tera Bjorklund, Colorado	Sr	30	211	359	58.8

Note: Minimum 5 made per game.

REBOUNDS

Player and Team	Class	GP	Reb	Avg
Ashlee Kelly, Quinnipiac	Sr	29	392	13.5
Desire Almind, Bucknell	Sr	29	390	13.4
Sandora Irvin, TCU	Jr	30	366	12.2
Rebekkah Brunson, Georgetown	Sr	28	336	12.0
Khara Smith, DePaul	So	30	351	11.7
Rosalee Mason, Manhattan	Jr	28	325	11.6
Crystal Kitt, Alabama St.	Jr	28	323	11.5
Angela Buckner, Wichita St.	Sr	28	318	11.4
Nicole Powell, Stanford	Sr	31	346	11.2
Katie Feenstra, Liberty	Jr	32	353	11.0

FREE-THROW PERCENTAGE

Player and Team	Class	GP	FT	FTA	Pct
Shanna Zolman, Tennessee	So	35	88	92	95.7
Cyndi Valentin, Indiana	So	29	99	107	92.5
Seimone Augustus, LSU	So	35	100	111	90.1
Jill Marano, La Salle	Jr	28	95	106	89.6
Kari Koch, SW Mo. St.	So	32	107	120	89.2
Kandi Brown, Morehead St.	Sr	28	104	117	88.9
Kate Murray, Loyola Marym't	Sr	30	106	120	88.3
Lindsay Boyett, Birm'ham-So.	Sr	30	81	92	88.0
Anne O'Neil, Iowa St.	Jr	33	127	145	87.6
Michelle Fahy, Iona	Sr	28	147	168	87.5
Jessalyn Deveny, Boston Coll.	Jr	34	119	136	87.5

Note: Minimum 2.5 made per game.

ASSISTS

Player and Team	Class	GP	A	Avg
La'Terrica Dobin, Northwestern St.	Sr	26	249	9.6
Temeka Johnson, LSU	Sr	35	289	8.3
Leah Cannon, Oral Roberts	So	28	231	8.3
Yolanda Paige, West Virginia	Jr	32	253	7.9
Brooklynn Lorenzen, Montana	Jr	32	251	7.8
Toccara Williams, Texas A&M	Sr	27	192	7.1
Tanara Golston, Brown	Sr	27	188	7.0
Latesha Lee, Jackson St.	Sr	30	202	6.7
Malika Willoughby, Kent St.	So	29	194	6.7
Nancy Bowden, Butler	Sr	29	193	6.7

THREE-POINT FIELD-GOAL PERCENTAGE

Player and Team	Class	GP	FG	FGA	Pct
Marion Crandall, Eastern Mich.	Sr	30	77	152	50.7
K.C. Cowgill, SW Mo. St.	Jr	32	65	138	47.1
S. Collins, St. Bonaventure	Jr	26	75	161	46.6
Tory Mauseth, Yale	Jr	27	55	120	45.8
Cathy Joens, George Wash.	Sr	30	96	218	44.0
Chelsee Insell, Samford	So	27	62	141	44.0
Emily Niemann, Baylor	Fr	35	75	171	43.9
Laurie Koehn, Kansas St.	Jr	31	100	230	43.5
Kate Fagan, Colorado	Sr	30	79	184	42.9
Jeannie Cullen, Dartmouth	So	27	82	191	42.9

Note: Minimum 1.5 made per game.

BLOCKED SHOTS

Player and Team	Class	GP	BS	Avg
Brooke McAfee, IUPUI	So	27	130	4.8
Amie Williams, Jackson St.	Sr	30	127	4.2
Sandora Irvin, TCU	Jr	30	117	3.9
Zane Teilane, Western Ill.	So	29	112	3.9
Katie Beth Pate, Lipscomb	So	31	113	3.6
Ashley Sparkman, Northw'rn St.	Jr	31	110	3.5
Vanessa Hayden, Florida	Sr	30	106	3.5
Ugo Oha, George Wash.	Sr	30	100	3.3
Jennyffer Vargas, Morgan St.	So	22	69	3.1
Andrea Csaszar, Kent St.	Jr	29	82	2.8

NCAA Men's Division II Individual Leaders

SCORING

Player and Team	Class	GP	TFG	3FG	FT	Pts	Avg
Lewis Muse, Concord	Jr.	26	308	0	125	741	28.5
Rasheim Wright, Dist. Columbia	Jr.	27	263	45	155	726	26.9
Ron Christy, Teikyo Post	Sr.	31	293	69	172	827	26.7
Kenneth Barrett, Okla. Panhandle	Sr.	24	195	80	132	602	25.1
Darnell Hinson, Northeastern St.	Sr.	26	209	79	138	635	24.4
Mike Taylor, West Virginia St.	Sr.	32	250	140	141	781	24.4
Flem Tucker, Albany St. (GA)	Sr.	28	205	54	197	661	23.6
Jake Chrisman, BYU-Hawaii	Jr.	29	270	23	112	675	23.3
Yandel Brown, Columbus St.	Jr.	31	254	116	88	712	23.0
Carl Edwards, Charleston (WV)	Sr.	25	215	24	118	572	22.9

REBOUNDS

Player and Team	Class	GP	Reb	Avg
Jack Bain, UC-Colorado Springs.	...Sr	27	336	12.4
Jakim Donaldson, Edinboro	...........Jr	28	322	11.5
Nick Wallery, Albany St. (GA)	.........Jr	28	319	11.4
Omari Pearson, Mansfield	...............Sr	26	295	11.3
Jason.Chivers, Seattle Pacific	.........Jr	26	293	11.3
D. Peoples, St. Augustine's	............Sr	28	308	11.0
Demond Cowins, N.J.I.T.	................Sr	28	306	10.9
Gordon James, Bridgeport	............Sr	28	305	10.9
Billy McDaniel, AR-Monticello	.......So	27	294	10.9
Allen Early, Fort Valley St.	...............Sr	29	301	10.4

ASSISTS

Player and Team	Class	GP	A	Avg
Deshawn Bowman, Columbus St.	..Sr	27	220	8.1
Jamie Holden, St. Joseph's (IN)	.....Sr	27	208	7.7
Josh Mueller, S Dakota	...................Jr	32	246	7.7
Te'Ron Reed, Cal St. San B'dino	...Sr	29	212	7.3
Darnell Miller, W Georgia.	...............Jr	30	208	6.9
Mark White, Humboldt St.	................Sr	34	235	6.9
Ben Fordham, Charleston (WV)	....Sr	30	202	6.7
Eric Faber, Rollins	...........................Jr	33	215	6.5
Leon Pursoo, Southampton	.............Jr	24	156	6.5
Alex Carlson, St. Cloud St.	...............Sr	28	180	6.4

FIELD-GOAL PERCENTAGE

Player and Team	Class	GP	FG	FGA	Pct
Anthony Greenup, Shaw	..........Sr.	24	210	296	70.9
Ralph Brown, Virginia Union	.....Jr.	30	175	252	69.4
Brian Robinson, Assumption	....Jr.	28	188	273	68.9
Turner Trofholz, S Dakota	........So.	32	165	241	68.5
Damien Argrett, Pfeiffer	............Jr.	34	190	299	63.5
Brad Hawks, Tusculum	..............Jr.	27	173	276	62.7
Nick Brooks, Fort Lewis	............Jr.	28	141	225	62.7
Lester Strong, Metro St.	.............Sr.	35	189	303	62.4
Kofi Danquah, West Chester	...Sr.	28	155	249	62.2
Pat Schumacher, Cent Mo. St.	..Jr.	23	117	188	62.2

Note: Minimum 5 made per game.

FREE-THROW PERCENTAGE

Player and Team	Class	GP	FT	FTA	Pct
Ralph Steele, Seattle Pacific	...Jr	27	82	90	91.1
T. Mirabal, NM Highlands	........So	21	56	62	90.3
Dusty Smith, Wayne St. (NE)	...So	28	72	80	90.0
Victor Pierson, Bellarmine	........Sr	27	69	77	89.6
Luqman Jaaber, Va. Union	.......Jr	30	91	102	89.2
Rico Grier, Pfeiffer	......................Jr	34	157	176	89.2
Jajuan Davis, Slippery Rock	....Jr	23	66	74	89.2
John Green, Barton	..................Sr	27	98	110	89.1
Brett Longpre', Mansfield	........Sr	28	98	110	89.1
Cory Coe, Hillsdale	..................So	26	86	97	88.7

Note: Minimum 2.5 made per game.

SCORING

Player and Team	Class	GP	TFG	3FG	FT	Pts	Avg
Candice Allen, Cal Poly Pomona	............................Sr	30	254	29	197	734	24.5
Mandy Koupal, S Dakota	....Sr	33	282	33	209	806	24.4
Allyson Hardy, Bowie St.	....Jr	29	231	35	156	653	22.5
September Harrison, St. Leo	...................................Sr	28	215	8	172	610	21.8
Crystal Clary, Lenoir-Rhyne	.....................................Fr	28	256	0	88	600	21.4
Tasha Washington, Armstrong Atlantic	....................Sr	30	205	41	190	641	21.4
Marisa Leighton, N Dakota	....Sr	32	265	11	141	682	21.3
Jodi Young, Wayne St. (MI)	....Sr	27	196	74	109	575	21.3
Lucresia West, Fla. Southern	...................................Jr	26	229	0	89	547	21.0
Sherika Tarpkins, Fort Valley St.	..............................Jr	31	189	63	205	646	20.8

REBOUNDS

Player and Team	Class	GP	Reb	Avg
Crystal Clary, Lenoir-Rhyne	...........Fr	28	357	12.8
Marita Meldere, Longwood	.............Jr	26	320	12.3
Keauna Vinson, Barton	..................So	30	367	12.2
Heather Cigich, Clarion	...................Jr	27	328	12.1
Jel-ani Armstrong, Midwestern St.	...Sr	27	317	11.7
Rosa Masler, Mesa St	....................Sr	28	327	11.7
Robyn Milne, Montana St–Billings	...Jr	27	313	11.6
Ivana Stojkovic, Western NM	.........Jr	22	255	11.6
Mandy Koupal, S Dakota	...............Sr	33	381	11.5
Genai Walker, Central Arkansas	...Sr	32	358	11.2

ASSISTS

Player and Team	Class	GP	A	Avg
Princess Wimsatt, Bellarmine	.........Jr	30	253	8.4
Kelly West, W Liberty St.	.................Sr	31	255	8.2
Megan Storck, California (PA)	.......So	36	285	7.9
Heidi Buehler, NW Nazarene	........So	27	194	7.2
Jen Gwin, Gannon	.........................Jr	29	203	7.0
Zulmary Andino, Dowling	...............Sr	29	202	7.0
Ebony Vincent, Wayne St. (MI)	......Sr	27	188	7.0
Laura Hensley, Augustana (SD)	....Jr	27	186	6.9
Kim Abts, Cal St. Chico	..................Jr	28	191	6.8
Amber McFeely, Slippery Rock	.....So	27	180	6.7

FIELD-GOAL PERCENTAGE

Player and Team	Class	GP	FGA	FG	Pct
Nina Smith, Holy Family	Sr	26	191	279	68.5
Crystal Clary, Lenoir-Rhyne	Fr	28	256	390	65.6
Sameera Philyaw, Calif. (PA)	Sr	36	245	377	65.0
Lucresia West, FL Southern	Jr	26	229	362	63.3
Ashlea Bland, W Liberty St	Sr	31	258	409	63.1
Kim Davis, Southern Ark.	Fr	27	190	303	62.7
Katelyn Dwyer, Assumption	Sr	30	228	364	62.6
Marisa Leighton, N Dakota	Sr	32	265	437	60.6
Shevon Gibbons, Bentley	Jr	31	160	264	60.6
Candice Ferrell, Valdosta St	So	25	154	257	59.9

Note: Minimum 5 made per game.

FREE-THROW PERCENTAGE

Player and Team	Class	GP	FTA	FT	Pct
Kiesha Mack, West Chester	So	29	73	80	91.3
Kim Omer, UC Davis	Sr	28	78	88	88.6
S Conner, Pitt.-Johnstown	So	28	89	101	88.1
Katie Spieker, Pittsburg St.	Sr	27	95	108	88.0
Bethanie Bentz, SW Okla.	Jr	24	102	116	87.9
L. Chiles, Anderson (SC)	Jr	31	84	96	87.5
S Rance, Phila. Sciences	Fr	30	83	95	87.4
Heidi Buehler, NW Nazarene	So	27	151	173	87.3
Apryl Brown, Clayton St.	Jr	24	67	77	87.0
Maggie Gernbacher, Bemidji St	Fr	29	109	126	86.5
Lesli Shores, East Central	Sr	26	109	126	86.5

Note: Minimum 2.5 made per game.

SCORING

Player and Team	Class	GP	TFG	3FG	FT	Pts	Avg
Dennis Stanton, Ursinus	Sr	27	261	140	217	879	32.6
Steve Wood, Grinnell	Sr	24	235	61	188	719	30.0
Rohan Russell, Johnson & Wales	Sr	29	266	110	141	783	27.0
Rich Melzer, WI-River Falls	Sr	27	280	5	162	727	26.9
Josh Hinz, Beloit	So	23	227	10	114	578	25.1
Justin Call, Emory & Henry	Sr	27	249	76	95	669	24.8
Derek Suttles, MacMurray	Sr	25	234	30	115	613	24.5
Jeremy Coleman, Philadelphia Bible	Jr	25	236	2	138	612	24.5
Bryan Depew, Whitworth	Sr	25	198	33	162	591	23.6
Benny West, Howard Payne	Sr	25	205	20	154	584	23.4

REBOUNDS

Player and Team	Class	GP	Reb	Avg
Matt Clement, Maine Maritime	Sr	19	303	15.9
Anthony Fitzgerald, Villa Julie	So	25	374	15.0
T. Stolhandske, Texas Lutheran	Jr	21	293	14.0
Chris Braier, Lawrence	So	29	388	13.4
J. Coleman, Philadelphia Bible	Jr	25	324	13.0
Badou Gaye, Gwynedd-Mercy	Jr	29	352	12.1
Dan Sheppard, Coast Guard	So	23	273	11.9
John Danielski, Manhattanville	Sr	28	329	11.8
John Mietus, Lewis & Clark	Sr	23	264	11.5
Josef Woldense, Bard	So	24	274	11.4

FIELD-GOAL PERCENTAGE

Player and Team	Class	GP	FG	FGA	Pct
J. Konzelman, Bapt. Bible (PA)	So	26	144	212	67.9
D. Nawrocki, Johns Hopkins	Fr	25	138	207	66.7
Phil Sander, Susquehanna	So	22	116	174	66.7
Adam Novak, Adrian	Sr	28	142	215	66.0
Ryan Hodges, Cal Lutheran	Sr	22	137	210	65.2
Stephen Bash, Maryville (MO)	Jr	25	131	207	63.3
F. Beckford, Lake Forest	So	24	154	245	62.9
C. Hendershot, FDU-Florham	Jr	25	160	255	62.7
Matt Rowles, Pitt.-Bradford	Sr	25	182	292	62.3
Andreas Pope, Plymouth St.	Fr	27	137	220	62.3

Note: Minimum 5 made per game.

ASSISTS

Player and Team	Class	GP	A	Avg
Michael Crotty, Williams	Sr	32	249	7.8
Andre Bagot, Lehman	Jr	28	205	7.3
Cliff Foster, La Roche	Sr	28	201	7.2
Ryan Anderson, Bridgewater St	Sr	26	184	7.1
Ben Fisher, Emory & Henry	Sr	26	183	7.0
Gabe Perez, Rochester	Jr	26	183	7.0
Mike McGarvey, Ursinus	So	27	186	6.9
J.D. Henderson, Dubuque	Sr	25	165	6.6
Jesse Farrell, Trinity (CT)	Jr	27	175	6.5
Bobby Jenkins, N.C. Wesleyan	Sr	25	159	6.4

FREE-THROW PERCENTAGE

Player and Team	Class	GP	FT	FTA	Pct
Joe Bueckers, Conc.-M'head	Sr	26	71	75	94.7
Aaron Faulkner, St. Norbert	Jr	23	64	68	94.1
C. Taggatz, WI-La Crosse	Sr	25	67	72	93.1
Casey Stitzel, Widener	Jr	25	70	76	92.1
Blair Mills, Catholic	Sr	30	102	112	91.1
Ryan Wietor, Concordia (WI)	Jr	26	150	166	90.4
Ryan Grabill, Frostburg St	Sr	27	84	93	90.3
B. Constantine, W. Paterson	Sr	24	70	78	89.7
Kyle Lefebvre, LaGrange	So	27	70	78	89.7
S. Tamargo, Johnson & Wales	Jr	29	86	96	89.6

Note: Minimum 2.5 made per game.

SCORING

Player and Team	Class	GP	TFG	3FG	FT	Pts	Avg
Camille Manning, NYCCT	Jr	23	173	70	139	555	24.1
Karen Hall, Alma	Sr	25	199	2	161	561	22.4
Angel Hall, Anderson (IN)	Sr	27	205	95	97	602	22.3
Patrece Carter, Louisiana College	Sr	25	201	9	138	549	22.0
Hayley Smith, Maryville (TN)	Sr	29	237	70	83	627	21.6
Melody Bongiorno, Chapman	Sr	26	215	10	120	560	21.5
Tiffany Speer, Whitworth	Jr	25	179	24	145	527	21.1
DeeDee Arnall, Pacific (OR)	So	23	186	0	112	484	21.0
Kelly Heil, Ohio Wesleyan	Jr	27	191	44	128	554	20.5
Chasity Vaughan, Chowan	Sr	26	180	28	143	531	20.4

REBOUNDS

Player and Team	Class	GP	Reb	Avg
Jacclyn Rock, Staten Island	Jr	30	452	15.1
Amy Abernathy, Frank. & Marsh.	Sr	24	330	13.8
Shervon James, Kean	Sr	27	333	12.3
Cheyenne Noble, Wentworth Inst.	Fr	24	296	12.3
Brooke Schmidt, WI-Eau Claire	Fr	27	332	12.3
Melissa Escalara, Lehman	So	25	305	12.2
Nichola Hall, NYCCT	Jr	23	271	11.8
Kate Puschak, Marywood	Sr	21	245	11.7
Kendra Ryl, Augustana (IL)	Sr	24	276	11.5
Shermika Harris, Ferrum	Sr	26	298	11.5

ASSISTS

Player and Team	Class	GP	A	Avg
Brooke Johnson, Peace	Sr	26	253	9.7
Diana Esterkamp, Otterbein	Sr	28	224	8.0
Lisa Belmonte, Norwich	Sr	30	210	7.0
Kira Peterson, Coast Guard	Jr	23	158	6.9
Casey Ridge, Mass.-Dartmouth	Jr	27	179	6.6
Tara Toland, Ferrum	Jr	26	167	6.4
C. Argentina, St. Joseph's (L.I.)	So	26	164	6.3
Allison Coleman, Eastern Conn St	Sr	31	195	6.3
Mandy Pearson, Conc.-M'head	Jr	28	176	6.3
Sheemea Carr, Rowan	So	26	162	6.2

Four tied with 5.8.

FIELD-GOAL PERCENTAGE

Player and Team	Class	GP	FG	FGA	Pct
Alicia Davis, Loras	Sr	27	219	322	68.0
Kayla Smiley, Austin	Jr	23	135	215	62.8
Selina Theisen, Augsburg	Fr	24	159	259	61.4
Karen Hall, Alma	Sr	25	199	327	60.9
Tara Rohde, Trinity (TX)	Jr	27	142	236	60.2
Lindsey Chappell, Earlham	Sr	25	132	220	60.0
Heather Gepper, Otterbein	Sr	28	165	277	59.6
Elizabeth Klotz, Fontbonne	Sr	24	183	308	59.4
Lisa Winkle, Calvin	Fr	27	143	241	59.3
DeeDee Arnall, Pacific (OR)	So	23	186	315	59.0

Note: Minimum 5 made per game.

FREE-THROW PERCENTAGE

Player and Team	Class	GP	FT	FTA	Pct
Sarah Kuhn, Defiance	Sr	27	74	80	92.5
Angel Hall, Anderson (IN)	Sr	27	97	105	92.4
Ashley Edwards, Conc.-Austin	Jr	25	120	130	92.3
Joanie Hammer, Ripon	Sr	27	77	86	89.5
Beth Bergmann, Emory	Fr	25	63	71	88.7
Lish Yoder, Marietta	Sr	26	73	83	88.0
D. Chewning, Emory & Henry	Sr	26	65	74	87.8
E. Greeno, Westminster (MO)	So	22	64	73	87.7
Jess Unick, Messiah	Sr	27	83	95	87.4
Jessica Reardon, Eureka	Jr	26	160	184	87.0

Note: Minimum 2.5 made per game.

YET ANOTHER SIGN OF THE APOCALYPSE

At its men's basketball game against Seton Hall on Valentine's Day 2004, Notre Dame planned to give away oven mitts to the first 1,000 female fans.

NCAA Men's Division I Championship Results

NCAA Final Four Results

Year	Winner	Score	Runner-up	Third Place	Fourth Place	Winning Coach
1939	Oregon	46–33	Ohio St	*Oklahoma	*Villanova	Howard Hobson
1940	Indiana	60–42	Kansas	*Duquesne	*Southern Cal	Branch McCracken
1941	Wisconsin	39–34	Washington St	*Pittsburgh	*Arkansas	Harold Foster
1942	Stanford	53–38	Dartmouth	*Colorado	*Kentucky	Everett Dean
1943	Wyoming	46–34	Georgetown	*Texas	*DePaul	Everett Shelton
1944	Utah	42–40 (OT)	Dartmouth	*Iowa St	*Ohio St	Vadal Peterson
1945	Oklahoma St	49–45	NYU	*Arkansas	*Ohio St	Hank Iba
1946	Oklahoma St	43–40	N Carolina	Ohio St	California	Hank Iba
1947	Holy Cross	58–47	Oklahoma	Texas	CCNY	Alvin Julian
1948	Kentucky	58–42	Baylor	Holy Cross	Kansas St	Adolph Rupp
1949	Kentucky	46–36	Oklahoma St	Illinois	Oregon St	Adolph Rupp
1950	CCNY	71–68	Bradley	N Carolina St	Baylor	Nat Holman
1951	Kentucky	68–58	Kansas St	Illinois	Oklahoma St	Adolph Rupp
1952	Kansas	80–63	St. John's (NY)	Illinois	Santa Clara	Forrest Allen
1953	Indiana	69–68	Kansas	Washington	Louisiana St	Branch McCracken
1954	La Salle	92–76	Bradley	Penn St	Southern Cal	Kenneth Loeffler
1955	San Francisco	77–63	La Salle	Colorado	Iowa	Phil Woolpert
1956	San Francisco	83–71	Iowa	Temple	Southern Meth	Phil Woolpert
1957	N Carolina	54–53 (3OT)	Kansas	San Francisco	Michigan St	Frank McGuire
1958	Kentucky	84–72	Seattle	Temple	Kansas St	Adolph Rupp
1959	California	71–70	W Virginia	Cincinnati	Louisville	Pete Newell
1960	Ohio St	75–55	California	Cincinnati	NYU	Fred Taylor
1961	Cincinnati	70–65 (OT)	Ohio St	Vacated‡	Utah	Edwin Jucker
1962	Cincinnati	71–59	Ohio St	Wake Forest	UCLA	Edwin Jucker
1963	Loyola (IL)	60–58 (OT)	Cincinnati	Duke	Oregon St	George Ireland
1964	UCLA	98–83	Duke	Michigan	Kansas St	John Wooden
1965	UCLA	91–80	Michigan	Princeton	Wichita St	John Wooden
1966	UTEP	72–65	Kentucky	Duke	Utah	Don Haskins
1967	UCLA	79–64	Dayton	Houston	N Carolina	John Wooden
1968	UCLA	78–55	N Carolina	Ohio St	Houston	John Wooden
1969	UCLA	92–72	Purdue	Drake	N Carolina	John Wooden
1970	UCLA	80–69	Jacksonville	New Mexico St	St. Bonaventure	John Wooden
1971	UCLA	68–62	Vacated‡	Vacated‡	Kansas	John Wooden
1972	UCLA	81–76	Florida St	N Carolina	Louisville	John Wooden
1973	UCLA	87–66	Memphis St	Indiana	Providence	John Wooden
1974	N Carolina St	76–64	Marquette	UCLA	Kansas	Norm Sloan
1975	UCLA	92–85	Kentucky	Louisville	Syracuse	John Wooden
1976	Indiana	86–68	Michigan	UCLA	Rutgers	Bob Knight
1977	Marquette	67–59	N Carolina	UNLV	NC-Charlotte	Al McGuire
1978	Kentucky	94–88	Duke	Arkansas	Notre Dame	Joe Hall
1979	Michigan St	75–64	Indiana St	DePaul	Penn	Jud Heathcote
1980	Louisville	59–54	Vacated‡	Purdue	Iowa	Denny Crum
1981	Indiana	63–50	N Carolina	Virginia	Louisiana St	Bob Knight
1982	N Carolina	63–62	Georgetown	*Houston	*Louisville	Dean Smith
1983	N Carolina St	54–52	Houston	*Georgia	*Louisville	Jim Valvano
1984	Georgetown	84–75	Houston	*Kentucky	*Virginia	John Thompson
1985	Villanova	66–64	Georgetown	St. John's (NY)	Vacated‡	Rollie Massimino
1986	Louisville	72–69	Duke	*Kansas	*Louisiana St	Denny Crum
1987	Indiana	74–73	Syracuse	*UNLV	*Providence	Bob Knight
1988	Kansas	83–79	Oklahoma	*Arizona	*Duke	Larry Brown
1989	Michigan	80–79 (OT)	Seton Hall	*Duke	*Illinois	Steve Fisher
1990	UNLV	103–73	Duke	*Arkansas	*Georgia Tech	Jerry Tarkanian
1991	Duke	72–65	Kansas	*UNLV	*N Carolina	Mike Krzyzewski
1992	Duke	71–51	Michigan	*Cincinnati	*Indiana	Mike Krzyzewski
1993	N Carolina	77–71	Michigan	*Kansas	*Kentucky	Dean Smith
1994	Arkansas	76–72	Duke	*Arizona	*Florida	Nolan Richardson
1995	UCLA	89–78	Arkansas	*N Carolina	*Oklahoma St	Jim Harrick
1996	Kentucky	76–67	Syracuse	Vacated‡	Mississippi St	Rick Pitino
1997	Arizona	84–79 (OT)	Kentucky	*Minnesota	*N Carolina	Lute Olson
1998	Kentucky	78–69	Utah	*Stanford	*N Carolina	Tubby Smith
1999	Connecticut	77–74	Duke	*Michigan St	*Ohio St	Jim Calhoun
2000	Michigan St	89–76	Florida	*Wisconsin	*N Carolina	Tom Izzo
2001	Duke	82–72	Arizona	*Maryland	*Michigan St	Mike Krzyzewski
2002	Maryland	64–52	Indiana	*Kansas	*Oklahoma	Gary Williams
2003	Syracuse	81–78	Kansas	*Marquette	*Texas	Jim Boeheim
2004	Connecticut	82–73	Georgia Tech	*Oklahoma St	*Duke	Jim Calhoun

*Tied for third place. ‡Student-athletes representing St. Joseph's (PA) in 1961, Villanova in 1971, Western Kentucky in 1971, UCLA in 1980, Memphis State in 1985 and Massachusetts in 1996 were declared ineligible subsequent to the tournament. Under NCAA rules, the teams' and ineligible student-athletes' records were deleted, and the teams' places in the standings were vacated.

NCAA Final Four MVPs

Year	Winner, School	GP	Field Goals		3-Pt FG		Free Throws		Reb	A	Stl	BS	Avg
			FGM	Pct	FGA	FGM	FTM	Pct					
1939	....None selected												
1940	....Marv Huffman, Indiana	2	7	—	—	—	4	—	—	—	—	—	9.0
1941	....John Kotz, Wisconsin	2	8	—	—	—	6	—	—	—	—	—	11.0
1942	....Howard Dallmar, Stanford	2	8	—	—	—	4	66.7	—	—	—	—	10.0
1943	....Ken Sailors, Wyoming	2	10	—	—	—	8	72.7	—	—	—	—	14.0
1944	....Arnie Ferrin, Utah	2	11	—	—	—	6	—	—	—	—	—	14.0
1945	....Bob Kurland, Oklahoma St	2	16	—	—	—	5	—	—	—	—	—	18.5
1946	....Bob Kurland, Oklahoma St	2	21	—	—	—	10	66.7	—	—	—	—	26.0
1947	....George Kaftan, Holy Cross	2	18	—	—	—	12	70.6	—	—	—	—	24.0
1948	....Alex Groza, Kentucky	2	16	—	—	—	5	—	—	—	—	—	18.5
1949	....Alex Groza, Kentucky	2	19	—	—	—	14	—	—	—	—	—	26.0
1950	....Irwin Dambrot, CCNY	2	12	42.9	—	—	4	50.0	—	—	—	—	14.0
1951	....None selected												
1952	....Clyde Lovellette, Kansas	2	24	—	—	—	18	—	—	—	—	—	33.0
1953	....*B.H. Horn, Kansas	2	17	—	—	—	17	—	—	—	—	—	25.5
1954	....Tom Gola, La Salle	2	12	—	—	—	14	—	—	—	—	—	19.0
1955	....Bill Russell, San Francisco	2	19	—	—	—	9	—	—	—	—	—	23.5
1956	....*Hal Lear, Temple	2	32	—	—	—	16	—	—	—	—	—	40.0
1957	....*Wilt Chamberlain, Kansas	2	18	51.4	—	—	19	70.4	25	—	—	—	32.5
1958	....*Elgin Baylor, Seattle	2	18	34.0	—	—	12	75.0	41	—	—	—	24.0
1959	....*Jerry West, West Virginia	2	22	66.7	—	—	22	68.8	25	—	—	—	33.0
1960	....Jerry Lucas, Ohio State	2	16	66.7	—	—	3	100.0	23	—	—	—	17.5
1961	....*Jerry Lucas, Ohio State	2	20	71.4	—	—	16	94.1	25	—	—	—	28.0
1962	....Paul Hogue, Cincinnati	2	23	63.9	—	—	12	63.2	38	—	—	—	29.0
1963	....Art Heyman, Duke	2	18	41.0	—	—	15	68.2	19	—	—	—	25.5
1964	....Walt Hazzard, UCLA	2	11	55.0	—	—	8	66.7	10	—	—	—	15.0
1965	....*Bill Bradley, Princeton	2	34	63.0	—	—	19	95.0	24	—	—	—	43.5
1966	....*Jerry Chambers, Utah	2	25	53.2	—	—	20	83.3	35	—	—	—	35.0
1967	....Lew Alcindor, UCLA	2	14	60.9	—	—	11	45.8	38	—	—	—	19.5
1968	....Lew Alcindor, UCLA	2	22	62.9	—	—	9	90.0	34	—	—	—	26.5
1969	....Lew Alcindor, UCLA	2	23	67.7	—	—	16	64.0	41	—	—	—	31.0
1970	....Sidney Wicks, UCLA	2	15	71.4	—	—	9	60.0	34	—	—	—	19.5
1971	....*†Howard Porter, Villanova	2	20	48.8	—	—	7	77.8	24	—	—	—	23.5
1972	....Bill Walton, UCLA	2	20	69.0	—	—	17	73.9	41	—	—	—	28.5
1973	....Bill Walton, UCLA	2	28	82.4	—	—	2	40.0	30	—	—	—	29.0
1974	....David Thompson, NC State	2	19	51.4	—	—	11	78.6	17	—	—	—	24.5
1975	....Richard Washington, UCLA	2	23	54.8	—	—	8	72.7	20	—	—	—	27.0
1976	....Kent Benson, Indiana	2	17	50.0	—	—	7	63.6	18	—	—	—	20.5
1977	....Butch Lee, Marquette	2	11	34.4	—	—	8	100.0	6	2	1	1	15.0
1978	....Jack Givens, Kentucky	2	28	65.1	—	—	8	66.7	17	4	1	3	32.0
1979	....Earvin Johnson, Michigan St	2	17	68.0	—	—	19	86.4	17	3	0	2	26.5
1980	....Darrell Griffith, Louisville	2	23	62.2	—	—	11	68.8	7	15	0	2	28.5
1981	....Isiah Thomas, Indiana	2	14	56.0	—	—	9	81.8	4	9	3	4	18.5
1982	....James Worthy, N Carolina	2	20	74.1	—	—	2	28.6	8	9	0	4	21.0
1983	....*Akeem Olajuwon, Houston	2	16	55.2	—	—	9	64.3	40	3	2	5	20.5
1984	....Patrick Ewing, Georgetown	2	8	57.1	—	—	2	100.0	18	1	1	15	9.0
1985	....Ed Pinckney, Villanova	2	8	57.1	—	—	12	75.0	15	6	3	0	14.0
1986	....Pervis Ellison, Louisville	2	15	60.0	—	—	6	75.0	24	2	3	1	18.0
1987	....Keith Smart, Indiana	2	14	63.6	1	0	7	77.8	7	7	0	2	17.5
1988	....Danny Manning, Kansas	2	25	55.6	1	0	6	66.7	17	4	8	9	28.0
1989	....Glen Rice, Michigan	2	24	49.0	16	7	4	100.0	16	1	0	3	29.5
1990	....Anderson Hunt, UNLV	2	19	61.3	16	9	2	50.0	4	9	1	1	24.5
1991	....Christian Laettner, Duke	2	12	54.5	1	1	21	91.3	17	2	1	2	23.0
1992	....Bobby Hurley, Duke	2	10	41.7	12	7	8	80.0	3	11	0	3	17.5
1993	....Donald Williams, N Carolina	2	15	65.2	14	10	10	100.0	4	2	2	0	25.0
1994	....Corliss Williamson, Arkansas	2	21	50.0	0	0	10	71.4	21	8	4	3	26.0
1995	....Ed O'Bannon, UCLA	2	16	45.7	8	3	10	76.9	25	3	7	1	22.5
1996	....Tony Delk, Kentucky	2	15	41.7	16	8	6	54.6	9	2	3	2	22.0
1997	....Miles Simon, Arizona	2	17	45.9	10	3	17	77.3	8	6	0	1	27.0
1998	....Jeff Sheppard, Kentucky	2	16	55.2	10	4	7	77.8	10	7	4	0	21.5
1999	....Richard Hamilton, Connecticut	2	20	51.3	7	3	8	72.7	12	4	2	1	25.5
2000	....Mateen Cleaves, Michigan St	2	8	44.4	4	3	10	83.3	6	5	2	0	14.5
2001	....Shane Battier, Duke	2	13	50.0	12	5	12	70.6	19	8	2	6	21.5
2002	....Juan Dixon, Maryland	2	16	59.3	15	7	12	80.0	8	5	7	0	25.5
2003	....Carmelo Anthony, Syracuse	2	19	54.3	6	9	9	81.1	24	8	4	0	26.5
2004	....Emeka Okafor, Connecticut	2	17	65.4	0	0	8	53.3	22	2	1	4	21.0

*Not a member of the championship-winning team.   †Record later vacated.

Best NCAA Tournament Single-Game Scoring Performances

Player and Team	Year	Round	FG	3FG	FT	TP
Austin Carr, Notre Dame vs Ohio	1970	1st	25	—	11	61
Bill Bradley, Princeton vs Wichita St	1965	C*	22	—	14	58
Oscar Robertson, Cincinnati vs Arkansas	1958	C	21	—	14	56
Austin Carr, Notre Dame vs Kentucky	1970	2nd	22	—	8	52
Austin Carr, Notre Dame vs Texas Christian	1971	1st	20	—	12	52
David Robinson, Navy vs Michigan	1987	1st	22	0	6	50
Elvin Hayes, Houston vs Loyola (IL)	1968	1st	20	—	9	49
Hal Lear, Temple vs SMU	1956	C*	17	—	14	48
Austin Carr, Notre Dame vs Houston	1971	C	17	—	13	47
Dave Corzine, DePaul vs Louisville	1978	2nd	18	—	10	46

C=regional third place; C*=third-place game.

NIT Championship Results

Year	Winner	Score	Runner-up	Year	Winner	Score	Runner-up
1938	Temple	60–36	Colorado	1972	Maryland	100–69	Niagara
1939	Long Island U	44–32	Loyola (IL)	1973	Virginia Tech	92–91 (OT)	Notre Dame
1940	Colorado	51–40	Duquesne	1974	Purdue	97–81	Utah
1941	Long Island U	56–42	Ohio U	1975	Princeton	80–69	Providence
1942	W Virginia	47–45	W Kentucky	1976	Kentucky	71–67	NC-Charlotte
1943	St. John's (NY)	48–27	Toledo	1977	St. Bonaventure	94–91	Houston
1944	St. John's (NY)	47–39	DePaul	1978	Texas	101–93	N Carolina St
1945	DePaul	71–54	Bowling Green	1979	Indiana	53–52	Purdue
1946	Kentucky	46–45	Rhode Island	1980	Virginia	58–55	Minnesota
1947	Utah	49–45	Kentucky	1981	Tulsa	86–84 (OT)	Syracuse
1948	St. Louis	65–52	NYU	1982	Bradley	67–58	Purdue
1949	San Francisco	48–47	Loyola (IL)	1983	Fresno St	69–60	DePaul
1950	CCNY	69–61	Bradley	1984	Michigan	83–63	Notre Dame
1951	BYU	62–43	Dayton	1985	UCLA	65–62	Indiana
1952	La Salle	75–64	Dayton	1986	Ohio St	73–63	Wyoming
1953	Seton Hall	58–46	St. John's (NY)	1987	Southern Miss	84–80	La Salle
1954	Holy Cross	71–62	Duquesne	1988	Connecticut	72–67	Ohio St
1955	Duquesne	70–58	Dayton	1989	St. John's (NY)	73–65	St. Louis
1956	Louisville	93–80	Dayton	1990	Vanderbilt	74–72	St. Louis
1957	Bradley	84–83	Memphis St	1991	Stanford	78–72	Oklahoma
1958	Xavier (OH)	78–74 (OT)	Dayton	1992	Virginia	81–76	Notre Dame
1959	St. John's (NY)	76–71 (OT)	Bradley	1993	Minnesota	62–61	Georgetown
1960	Bradley	88–72	Providence	1994	Villanova	80–73	Vanderbilt
1961	Providence	62–59	St. Louis	1995	Virginia Tech	65–64 (OT)	Marquette
1962	Dayton	73–67	St. John's (NY)	1996	Nebraska	60–56	St. Joseph's
1963	Providence	81–66	Canisius	1997	Michigan	82–73	Florida St
1964	Bradley	86–54	New Mexico	1998	Minnesota	79–72	Penn St
1965	St. John's (NY)	55–51	Villanova	1999	California	61–60	Clemson
1966	BYU	97–84	NYU	2000	Wake Forest	71–61	Notre Dame
1967	Southern Illinois	71–56	Marquette	2001	Tulsa	79–60	Alabama
1968	Dayton	61–48	Kansas	2002	Memphis	72–62	S Carolina
1969	Temple	89–76	Boston College	2003	St. John's	70–67	Georgetown
1970	Marquette	65–53	St. John's (NY)	2004	Michigan	62–55	Rutgers
1971	N Carolina	84–66	Georgia Tech				

NCAA Men's Division I Season Leaders

Scoring Average

Year	Player and Team	Ht	Class	GP	FG	3FG	FT	Pts	Avg
1948	Murray Wier, Iowa	5-9	Sr	19	152	—	95	399	21.0
1949	Tony Lavelli, Yale	6-3	Sr	30	228	—	215	671	22.4
1950	Paul Arizin, Villanova	6-3	Sr	29	260	—	215	735	25.3
1951	Bill Mlkvy, Temple	6-4	Sr	25	303	—	125	731	29.2
1952	Clyde Lovellette, Kansas	6-9	Sr	28	315	—	165	795	28.4
1953	Frank Selvy, Furman	6-3	Jr	25	272	—	194	738	29.5
1954	Frank Selvy, Furman	6-3	Sr	29	427	—	355	1209	41.7
1955	Darrell Floyd, Furman	6-1	Jr	25	344	—	209	897	35.9
1956	Darrell Floyd, Furman	6-1	Sr	28	339	—	268	946	33.8
1957	Grady Wallace, S Carolina	6-4	Sr	29	336	—	234	906	31.2
1958	Oscar Robertson, Cincinnati	6-5	So	28	352	—	280	984	35.1
1959	Oscar Robertson, Cincinnati	6-5	Jr	30	331	—	316	978	32.6
1960	Oscar Robertson, Cincinnati	6-5	Sr	30	369	—	273	1011	33.7
1961	Frank Burgess, Gonzaga	6-1	Sr	26	304	—	234	842	32.4
1962	Billy McGill, Utah	6-9	Sr	26	394	—	221	1009	38.8
1963	Nick Werkman, Seton Hall	6-3	Jr	22	221	—	208	650	29.5
1964	Howard Komives, Bowling Green	6-1	Sr	23	292	—	260	844	36.7

Scoring Average (Cont.)

Year	Player and Team	Ht	Class	GP	FG	3FG	FT	Pts	Avg
1965	Rick Barry, Miami (FL)	6-7	Sr	26	340	—	293	973	37.4
1966	Dave Schellhase, Purdue	6-4	Sr	24	284	—	213	781	32.5
1967	Jim Walker, Providence	6-3	Sr	28	323	—	205	851	30.4
1968	Pete Maravich, Louisiana St	6-5	So	26	432	—	274	1138	43.8
1969	Pete Maravich, Louisiana St	6-5	Jr	26	433	—	282	1148	44.2
1970	Pete Maravich, Louisiana St	6-5	Sr	31	522	—	337	1381	44.5
1971	Johnny Neumann, Mississippi	6-6	So	23	366	—	191	923	40.1
1972	Dwight Lamar, Southwestern Louisiana	6-1	Jr	29	429	—	196	1054	36.3
1973	William Averitt, Pepperdine	6-1	Sr	25	352	—	144	848	33.9
1974	Larry Fogle, Canisius	6-5	So	25	326	—	183	835	33.4
1975	Bob McCurdy, Richmond	6-7	Sr	26	321	—	213	855	32.9
1976	Marshall Rodgers, TX-Pan American	6-2	Sr	25	361	—	197	919	36.8
1977	Freeman Williams, Portland St	6-4	Jr	26	417	—	176	1010	38.8
1978	Freeman Williams, Portland St	6-4	Sr	27	410	—	149	969	35.9
1979	Lawrence Butler, Idaho St	6-3	Sr	27	310	—	192	812	30.1
1980	Tony Murphy, Southern-BR	6-3	Sr	29	377	—	178	932	32.1
1981	Zam Fredrick, S Carolina	6-2	Sr	27	300	—	181	781	28.9
1982	Harry Kelly, Texas Southern	6-7	Jr	29	336	—	190	862	29.7
1983	Harry Kelly, Texas Southern	6-7	Sr	29	333	—	169	835	28.8
1984	Joe Jakubick, Akron	6-5	Sr	27	304	—	206	814	30.1
1985	Xavier McDaniel, Wichita St	6-8	Sr	31	351	—	142	844	27.2
1986	Terrance Bailey, Wagner	6-2	Jr	29	321	—	212	854	29.4
1987	Kevin Houston, Army	5-11	Sr	29	311	63	268	953	32.9
1988	Hersey Hawkins, Bradley	6-3	Sr	31	377	87	284	1125	36.3
1989	Hank Gathers, Loyola Marymount	6-7	Jr	31	419	0	177	1015	32.7
1990	Bo Kimble, Loyola Marymount	6-5	Sr	32	404	92	231	1131	35.3
1991	Kevin Bradshaw, U.S. Int'l	6-6	Sr	28	358	60	278	1054	37.6
1992	Brett Roberts, Morehead St	6-8	Sr	29	278	66	193	815	28.1
1993	Greg Guy, TX-Pan American	6-1	Jr	19	189	67	111	556	29.3
1994	Glenn Robinson, Purdue	6-8	Jr	34	368	79	215	1030	30.3
1995	Kurt Thomas, Texas Christian	6-9	Sr	27	288	3	202	781	28.9
1996	Kevin Granger, Texas Southern	6-3	Sr	24	194	30	230	648	27.0
1997	Charles Jones, LIU-Brooklyn	6-3	Jr	30	338	109	118	903	30.1
1998	Charles Jones, LIU-Brooklyn	6-3	Sr	30	326	116	101	869	29.0
1999	Alvin Young, Niagara	6-3	Sr	29	253	65	157	728	25.1
2000	Courtney Alexander, Fresno St	6-6	Sr	27	252	58	107	669	24.8
2001	Ronnie McCollum, Centenary	6-4	Sr	27	244	85	214	787	29.1
2002	Jason Conley, Virginia Military	6-5	Fr	28	285	79	171	820	29.3
2003	Ruben Douglas, New Mexico	6-5	Sr	28	218	94	253	783	28.0
2004	Keydren Clark, St. Peter's	5-8	So	29	233	112	197	775	26.7

Rebounds

Year	Player and Team	Ht	Class	GP	Reb	Avg
1951	Ernie Beck, Pennsylvania	6-4	So	27	556	20.6
1952	Bill Hannon, Army	6-3	So	17	355	20.9
1953	Ed Conlin, Fordham	6-5	So	26	612	23.5
1954	Art Quimby, Connecticut	6-5	Jr	26	588	22.6
1955	Charlie Slack, Marshall	6-5	Jr	21	538	25.6
1956	Joe Holup, George Washington	6-6	Sr	26	604	†.256
1957	Elgin Baylor, Seattle	6-6	Jr	25	508	†.235
1958	Alex Ellis, Niagara	6-5	Sr	25	536	†.262
1959	Leroy Wright, Pacific	6-8	Jr	26	652	†.238
1960	Leroy Wright, Pacific	6-8	Sr	17	380	†.234
1961	Jerry Lucas, Ohio St	6-8	Jr	27	470	†.198
1962	Jerry Lucas, Ohio St	6-8	Sr	28	499	†.211
1963	Paul Silas, Creighton	6-7	Sr	27	557	20.6
1964	Bob Pelkington, Xavier (OH)	6-7	Sr	26	567	21.8
1965	Toby Kimball, Connecticut	6-8	Sr	23	483	21.0
1966	Jim Ware, Oklahoma City	6-8	Sr	29	607	20.9
1967	Dick Cunningham, Murray St	6-10	Jr	22	479	21.8
1968	Neal Walk, Florida	6-10	Jr	25	494	19.8
1969	Spencer Haywood, Detroit	6-8	So	22	472	21.5
1970	Artis Gilmore, Jacksonville	7-2	Jr	28	621	22.2
1971	Artis Gilmore, Jacksonville	7-2	Sr	26	603	23.2
1972	Kermit Washington, American	6-8	Jr	23	455	19.8
1973	Kermit Washington, American	6-8	Sr	22	439	20.0
1974	Marvin Barnes, Providence	6-9	Sr	32	597	18.7
1975	John Irving, Hofstra	6-9	So	21	323	15.4
1976	Sam Pellom, Buffalo	6-8	So	26	420	16.2
1977	Glenn Mosley, Seton Hall	6-8	Sr	29	473	16.3
1978	Ken Williams, N Texas St	6-7	Sr	28	411	14.7
1979	Monti Davis, Tennessee St	6-7	Jr	26	421	16.2
1980	Larry Smith, Alcorn St	6-8	Sr	26	392	15.1
1981	Darryl Watson, Miss Valley	6-7	Sr	27	379	14.0

Rebounds (Cont.)

Year	Player and Team	Ht	Class	GP	Reb	Avg
1982	LaSalle Thompson, Texas	6-10	Jr	27	365	13.5
1983	Xavier McDaniel, Wichita St	6-7	So	28	403	14.4
1984	Akeem Olajuwon, Houston	7-0	Jr	37	500	13.5
1985	Xavier McDaniel, Wichita St	6-8	Sr	31	460	14.8
1986	David Robinson, Navy	6-11	Jr	35	455	13.0
1987	Jerome Lane, Pittsburgh	6-6	So	33	444	13.5
1988	Kenny Miller, Loyola (IL)	6-9	Fr	29	395	13.6
1989	Hank Gathers, Loyola (CA)	6-7	Jr	31	426	13.7
1990	Anthony Bonner, St. Louis	6-8	Sr	33	456	13.8
1991	Shaquille O'Neal, Louisiana St	7-1	So	28	411	14.7
1992	Popeye Jones, Murray St	6-8	Sr	30	431	14.4
1993	Warren Kidd, Middle Tenn St	6-9	Sr	26	386	14.8
1994	Jerome Lambert, Baylor	6-8	Jr	24	355	14.8
1995	Kurt Thomas, Texas Christian	6-9	Sr	27	393	14.6
1996	Marcus Mann, Mississippi Valley	6-8	Sr	29	394	13.6
1997	Tim Duncan, Wake Forest	6-11	Sr	31	457	14.7
1998	Ryan Perryman, Dayton	6-7	Sr	33	412	12.5
1999	Ian McGinnis, Dartmouth	6-8	So	26	317	12.2
2000	Darren Phillips, Fairfield	6-7	Sr	29	405	14.0
2001	Chris Marcus, Western Kentucky	7-1	Jr	31	374	12.1
2002	Jeremy Bishop, Quinnipiac	6-6	Jr	29	347	12.0
2003	Brandon Hunter, Ohio	6-7	Sr	30	378	12.6
2004	Paul Millsap, Louisiana Tech	6-7	Fr	30	374	12.5

†From 1956–1962, title was based on highest individual recoveries out of total by both teams in all games.

Assists

Year	Player and Team	Class	GP	A	Avg
1984	Craig Lathen, IL-Chicago	Jr	29	274	9.45
1985	Rob Weingard, Hofstra	Sr	24	228	9.50
1986	Mark Jackson, St. John's (NY)	Jr	36	328	9.11
1987	Avery Johnson, Southern-BR	Jr	31	333	10.74
1988	Avery Johnson, Southern-BR	Sr	30	399	13.30
1989	Glenn Williams, Holy Cross	Sr	28	278	9.93
1990	Todd Lehmann, Drexel	Sr	28	260	9.29
1991	Chris Corchiani, N Carolina St	Sr	31	299	9.65
1992	Van Usher, Tennessee Tech	Sr	29	254	8.76
1993	Sam Crawford, New Mex St	Sr	34	310	9.12
1994	Jason Kidd, California	So	30	272	9.06
1995	Nelson Haggerty, Baylor	Sr	28	284	10.10
1996	Raimonds Miglinieks, UC-Irvine	Sr	27	230	8.52
1997	Kenny Mitchell, Dartmouth	Sr	26	203	7.81
1998	Ahlon Lewis, Arizona St	Sr	32	294	9.19
1999	Doug Gottlieb, Oklahoma St	Jr	34	299	8.79
2000	Mark Dickel, UNLV	Sr	31	280	9.03
2001	Markus Carr, Cal St–Northridge	Jr	32	286	8.94
2002	T.J. Ford, Texas	Fr	33	273	8.27
2003	Martell Bailey, IL-Chicago	Jr	30	244	8.13
2004	Greg Davis, Troy St	Sr	31	256	8.26

Blocked Shots

Year	Player and Team	Class	GP	BS	Avg
1986	David Robinson, Navy	Jr	35	207	5.91
1987	David Robinson, Navy	Sr	32	144	4.50
1988	Rodney Blake, St. Joseph's (PA)	Sr	29	116	4.00
1989	Alonzo Mourning, Georgetown	Fr	34	169	4.97
1990	Kenny Green, Rhode Island	Sr	26	124	4.77
1991	Shawn Bradley, Brigham Young	Fr	34	177	5.21
1992	Shaquille O'Neal, Louisiana St	Jr	30	157	5.23
1993	Theo Ratliff, Wyoming	Jr	28	124	4.43
1994	Grady Livingston, Howard	Jr	26	115	4.42
1995	Keith Closs, Central Conn St	Fr	26	139	5.35
1996	Keith Closs, Central Conn St	So	28	178	6.36
1997	Adonal Foyle, Colgate	Jr	28	180	6.43
1998	Jerome James, Florida A&M	Sr	27	125	4.63
1999	Tarvis Williams, Hampton	Jr	27	135	5.00
2000	Ken Johnson, Ohio St	Sr	30	161	5.37
2001	Tarvis Williams, Hampton	Sr	32	147	4.59
2002	Wojciech Myrda, LA-Monroe	Sr	32	172	5.38
2003	Emeka Okafor, Connecticut	So	33	156	4.73
2004	Anwar Ferguson, Houston	Sr	27	111	4.11

Steals

Year	Player and Team	Class	GP	S	Avg
1986	Darron Brittman, Chicago St	Sr	28	139	4.96
1987	Tony Fairley, Charleston Sou	Sr	28	114	4.07
1988	Aldwin Ware, Florida A&M	Sr	29	142	4.90

Steals (Cont.)

Year	Player and Team	Class	GP	S	Avg
1989	Kenny Robertson, Cleveland St	Jr	28	111	3.96
1990	Ronn McMahon, E Washington	Sr	29	130	4.48
1991	Van Usher, Tennessee Tech	Jr	28	104	3.71
1992	Victor Snipes, NE Illinois	So	25	86	3.44
1993	Jason Kidd, California	Fr	29	110	3.80
1994	Shawn Griggs, SW Louisiana	Sr	30	120	4.00
1995	Roderick Anderson, Texas	Sr	30	101	3.37
1996	Pointer Williams, McNeese St	Sr	27	118	4.37
1997	Joel Hoover, MD-Eastern Shore	Fr	28	90	3.21
1998	Bonzi Wells, Ball St	Sr	29	103	3.55
1999	Shawnta Rogers, George Wash	Sr	29	103	3.55
2000	Carl Williams, Liberty	Sr	28	107	3.82
2001	Greedy Daniels, Texas Christian	Jr	25	108	4.32
2002	Desmond Cambridge, AL A&M	Sr	29	160	5.52
2003	Alexis McMillan, Stetson	Sr	22	87	3.95
2004	Marques Green, St. Bonaventure	Sr	27	107	3.96

Single Game Records

SCORING HIGHS VS DIVISION I OPPONENT

Pts	Player and Team vs Opponent	Date
72	Kevin Bradshaw, U.S. Int'l vs Loyola Marymount	1-5-91
69	Pete Maravich, Louisiana St vs Alabama	2-7-70
68	Calvin Murphy, Niagara vs Syracuse	12-7-68
66	Jay Handlan, Washington & Lee vs Furman	2-17-51
66	Pete Maravich, Louisiana St vs Tulane	2-10-69
66	Anthony Roberts, Oral Roberts vs N Carolina A&T	2-19-77
65	Anthony Roberts, Oral Roberts vs Oregon	3-9-77
65	Scott Haffner, Evansville vs Dayton	2-18-89
64	Pete Maravich, Louisiana St vs Kentucky	2-21-70
63	Johnny Neumann, Mississippi vs Louisiana St	1-30-71
63	Hersey Hawkins, Bradley vs Detroit	2-22-88

SCORING HIGHS VS NON-DIVISION I OPPONENT

Pts	Player and Team vs Opponent	Date
100	Frank Selvy, Furman vs Newberry	2-13-54
85	Paul Arizin, Villanova vs Philadelphia NAMC	2-12-49
81	Freeman Williams, Portland St vs Rocky Mountain	2-3-78
73	Bill Mlkvy, Temple vs Wilkes	3-3-51
71	Freeman Williams, Portland St vs Southern Oregon	2-9-77

REBOUNDING HIGHS BEFORE 1973

Reb	Player and Team vs Opponent	Date
51	Bill Chambers, William & Mary vs Virginia	2-14-53
43	Charlie Slack, Marshall vs Morris Harvey	1-12-54
42	Tom Heinsohn, Holy Cross vs Boston College	3-1-55
40	Art Quimby, Connecticut vs Boston U	1-11-55
39	Maurice Stokes, St. Francis (PA) vs John Carroll	1-28-55
39	Dave DeBusschere, Detroit vs Central Michigan	1-30-60
39	Keith Swagerty, Pacific vs UC-Santa Barbara	3-5-65

REBOUNDING HIGHS SINCE 1973*

Reb	Player and Team vs Opponent	Date
35	Larry Abney, Fresno St vs Southern Methodist	2-17-00
34	David Vaughn, Oral Roberts vs Brandeis	1-8-73
32	Jervaughn Scales, Southern-BR vs Grambling	2-7-94
32	Durand Macklin, Louisiana St vs Tulane	11-26-76
31	Jim Bradley, Northern Illinois vs WI-Milwaukee	2-19-73
31	Calvin Natt, NE Louisiana vs Georgia Southern	12-29-76

ASSISTS

A	Player and Team vs Opponent	Date
22	Tony Fairley, Baptist vs Armstrong St	2-9-87
22	Avery Johnson, Southern-BR vs Texas Southern	1-25-88
22	Sherman Douglas, Syracuse vs Providence	1-28-89
21	Mark Wade, UNLV vs Navy	12-29-86
21	Kelvin Scarborough, New Mexico vs Hawaii	2-13-87
21	Anthony Manuel, Bradley vs UC-Irvine	12-19-87
21	Avery Johnson, Southern-BR vs Alabama St	1-16-88

Single Game Records *(Cont.)*

STEALS

S	Player and Team vs Opponent	Date
13	Mookie Blaylock, Oklahoma vs Centenary	12-12-87
13	Mookie Blaylock, Oklahoma vs Loyola Marymount	12-17-88
12	Kenny Robertson, Cleveland St vs Wagner	12-3-88
12	Terry Evans, Oklahoma vs Florida A&M	1-27-93
12	Richard Duncan, Middle Tenn St vs Eastern Kentucky	2-20-99
12	Greedy Daniels, Texas Christian vs AR–Pine Bluff	12-30-00
12	Jehiel Lewis, Navy vs Bucknell	1-12-02

BLOCKED SHOTS

BS	Player and Team vs Opponent	Date
14	David Robinson, Navy vs NC–Wilmington	1-4-86
14	Shawn Bradley, Brigham Young vs Eastern Kentucky	12-7-90
14	Roy Rogers, Alabama vs Georgia	2-10-96
14	Loren Woods, Arizona vs Oregon	2-3-00
13	Kevin Roberson, Vermont vs New Hampshire	1-9-92
13	Jim McIlvaine, Marquette vs Northeastern (IL)	12-9-92
13	Keith Closs, Central Conn. St vs St. Francis (PA)	12-21-94
13	D'or Fischer, Northwestern St vs SW Texas St	1-22-01
13	Wojciech Myrda, LA–Monroe vs Texas–San Antonio	1-17-02

Single Season Records

POINTS

Player and Team	Year	GP	FG	3FG	FT	Pts
Pete Maravich, Louisiana St	1970	31	522	—	337	1381
Elvin Hayes, Houston	1968	33	519	—	176	1214
Frank Selvy, Furman	1954	29	427	—	355	1209
Pete Maravich, Louisiana St	1969	26	433	—	282	1148
Pete Maravich, Louisiana St	1968	26	432	—	274	1138
Bo Kimble, Loyola Marymount	1990	32	404	92	231	1131
Hersey Hawkins, Bradley	1988	31	377	87	284	1125
Austin Carr, Notre Dame	1970	29	444	—	218	1106
Austin Carr, Notre Dame	1971	29	430	—	241	1101
Otis Birdsong, Houston	1977	36	452	—	186	1090

SCORING AVERAGE

Player and Team	Year	GP	FG	3FG	FT	Pts	Avg
Pete Maravich, Louisiana St	1970	31	522		337	1381	44.5
Pete Maravich, Louisiana St	1969	26	433		282	1148	44.2
Pete Maravich, Louisiana St	1968	26	432		274	1138	43.8
Frank Selvy, Furman	1954	29	427		355	1209	41.7
Johnny Neumann, Mississippi	1971	23	366	191	923		40.1
Freeman Williams, Portland St	1977	26	417	176	1010		38.8
Billy McGill, Utah	1962	26	394	221	1009		38.8
Calvin Murphy, Niagara	1968	24	337	242	916		38.2
Austin Carr, Notre Dame	1970	29	444	218	1106		38.1
Austin Carr, Notre Dame	1971	29	430	241	1101		38.0

REBOUNDS

Player and Team	Year	GP	Reb	Player and Team	Year	GP	Reb
Walt Dukes, Seton Hall	1953	33	734	Artis Gilmore, Jacksonville	1970	28	621
Leroy Wright, Pacific	1959	26	652	Tom Gola, La Salle	1955	31	618
Tom Gola, La Salle	1954	30	652	Ed Conlin, Fordham	1953	26	612
Charlie Tyra, Louisville	1956	29	645	Art Quimby, Connecticut	1955	25	611
Paul Silas, Creighton	1964	29	631	Bill Russell, San Francisco	1956	29	609
Elvin Hayes, Houston	1968	33	624	Jim Ware, Oklahoma City	1966	29	607

REBOUND AVERAGE BEFORE 1973 / REBOUND AVERAGE SINCE 1973*

Player and Team	Year	GP	Reb	Avg	Player and Team	Year	GP	Reb	Avg
Charlie Slack, Marshall	1955	21	538	25.6	Kermit Washington, American	1973	22	439	20.0
Leroy Wright, Pacific	1959	26	652	25.1	Marvin Barnes, Providence	1973	30	571	19.0
Art Quimby, Connecticut	1955	25	611	24.4	Marvin Barnes, Providence	1974	32	597	18.7
Charlie Slack, Marshall	1956	22	520	23.6	Pete Padgett, NV-Reno	1973	26	462	17.8
Ed Conlin, Fordham	1953	26	612	23.5	Jim Bradley, Northern Illinois	1973	24	426	17.8

*Freshmen became eligible for varsity play in 1973.

Single Season Records (Cont.)

ASSISTS

Player and Team	Year	GP	A	Player and Team	Year	GP	A
Mark Wade, UNLV	1987	38	406	Sherman Douglas, Syracuse	1989	38	326
Avery Johnson, Southern-BR	1988	30	399	Sam Crawford, New Mex. St	1993	34	310
Anthony Manuel, Bradley	1988	31	373	Greg Anthony, UNLV	1991	35	310
Avery Johnson, Southern-BR	1987	31	333	Reid Gettys, Houston	1984	37	309
Mark Jackson, St. John's (NY)	1986	32	328	Carl Golston, Loyola (IL)	1985	33	305

ASSIST AVERAGE

Player and Team	Year	GP	A	Avg	Player and Team	Year	GP	A	Avg
Avery Johnson, Southern-BR	1988	30	399	13.3	Chris Corchiani, N Carolina St	1991	31	299	9.6
Anthony Manuel, Bradley	1988	31	373	12.0	Tony Fairley, Charleston So.*	1987	28	270	9.6
Avery Johnson, Southern-BR	1987	31	333	10.7	Tyrone Bogues, Wake Forest	1987	29	276	9.5
Mark Wade, UNLV	1987	38	406	10.7	Ron Weingard, Hofstra	1985	24	228	9.5
Nelson Haggerty, Baylor	1995	28	284	10.1	Craig Neal, Georgia Tech	1988	32	303	9.5
Glenn Williams, Holy Cross	1989	28	278	9.9	*Formerly Baptist.				

FIELD-GOAL PERCENTAGE

Player and Team	Year	GP	FG	FGA	Pct
Steve Johnson, Oregon St	1981	28	235	315	74.6
Dwayne Davis, Florida	1989	33	179	248	72.2
Keith Walker, Utica	1985	27	154	216	71.3
Steve Johnson, Oregon St	1980	30	211	297	71.0
Adam Mark, Belmont	2002	26	150	212	70.8
Oliver Miller, Arkansas	1991	38	254	361	70.4
Alan Williams, Princeton	1987	25	163	232	70.3
Mark McNamara, California	1982	27	231	329	70.2
Warren Kidd, Middle Tennessee St	1991	30	173	247	70.0
Pete Freeman, Akron	1991	28	175	250	70.0

Based on qualifiers for annual championship.

FREE-THROW PERCENTAGE

Player and Team	Year	GP	FT	FTA	Pct
Blake Ahearn SW Mo. St	2004	33	117	120	97.5
Craig Collins, Penn St	1985	27	94	98	95.9
J.J. Redick, Duke	2004	37	143	150	95.3
Steve Drabyn, Belmont	2003	29	78	82	95.1
Rod Foster, UCLA	1982	27	95	100	95.0
Clay McKnight, Pacific	2000	24	74	78	94.9
Matt Logie, Lehigh	2003	28	91	96	94.8
Danny Basile, Marist	1994	27	84	89	94.4
Carlos Gibson, Marshall	1978	28	84	89	94.4
Jim Barton, Dartmouth	1986	26	65	69	94.2

Based on qualifiers for annual championship.

THREE-POINT FIELD-GOAL PERCENTAGE

Player and Team	Year	GP	3FG	3FGA	Pct
Glenn Tropf, Holy Cross	1988	29	52	82	63.4
Sean Wightman, Western Michigan	1992	30	48	76	63.2
Keith Jennings, E Tennessee St	1991	33	84	142	59.2
Dave Calloway, Monmouth (NJ)	1989	28	48	82	58.5
Steve Kerr, Arizona	1988	38	114	199	57.3
Reginald Jones, Prairie View	1987	28	64	112	57.1
Jim Cantamessa, Siena	1998	29	66	117	56.4
Joel Tribelhorn, Colorado St	1989	33	76	135	56.3
Mike Joseph, Bucknell	1988	28	65	116	56.0
Brian Jackson, Evansville	1995	27	53	95	55.8
Amory Sanders, SE Missouri St	2001	24	53	95	55.8

Based on qualifiers for annual championship.

Single Season Records (Cont.)

STEALS

Player and Team	Year	GP	S
Desmond Cambridge, Alabama A&M	2002	29	160
Mookie Blaylock, Oklahoma	1988	39	150
Aldwin Ware, Florida A&M	1988	29	142
Darron Brittman, Chicago St	1986	28	139
John Linehan, Providence	2002	31	139

BLOCKED SHOTS

Player and Team	Year	GP	BS
David Robinson, Navy	1986	35	207
Adonal Foyle, Colgate	1997	28	180
Keith Closs, Central Conn St	1996	28	178
Shawn Bradley, BYU	1991	34	177
Wojiech Myrda, LA–Monroe	2002	32	172

STEAL AVERAGE

Player and Team	Year	GP	S	Avg
D. Cambridge, Alabama A&M	2002	29	160	5.52
Darron Brittman, Chicago St	1986	28	139	4.96
Aldwin Ware, Florida A&M	1988	29	142	4.90
John Linehan, Providence	2002	31	139	4.48
Ronn McMahon, E Washington	1990	29	130	4.48

BLOCKED-SHOT AVERAGE

Player and Team	Year	GP	BS	Avg
Adonal Foyle, Colgate	1997	28	180	6.43
Keith Closs, Central Conn St	1996	28	178	6.36
David Robinson, Navy	1986	35	207	5.91
Adonal Foyle, Colgate	1996	29	165	5.69
Wojiech Myrda, LA–Monroe	2002	32	172	5.37

Career Records

POINTS

Player and Team	Ht	Final Year	GP	FG	3FG*	FT	Pts
Pete Maravich, Louisiana St	6-5	1970	83	1387	—	893	3667
Freeman Williams, Portland St	6-4	1978	106	1369	—	511	3249
Lionel Simmons, La Salle	6-7	1990	131	1244	56	673	3217
Alphonso Ford, Mississippi Valley	6-2	1993	109	1121	333	590	3165
Harry Kelly, Texas Southern	6-7	1983	110	1234	—	598	3066
Hersey Hawkins, Bradley	6-3	1988	125	1100	118	690	3008
Oscar Robertson, Cincinnati	6-5	1960	88	1052	—	869	2973
Danny Manning, Kansas	6-10	1988	147	1216	10	509	2951
Alfredrick Hughes, Loyola (IL)	6-5	1985	120	1226	—	462	2914
Elvin Hayes, Houston	6-8	1968	93	1215	—	454	2884
Larry Bird, Indiana St	6-9	1979	94	1154	—	542	2850
Otis Birdsong, Houston	6-4	1977	116	1176	—	480	2832
Kevin Bradshaw, Bethune-Cookman, U.S. Int'l	6-6	1991	111	1027	132	618	2804
Allan Houston, Tennessee	6-6	1993	128	902	346	651	2801
Hank Gathers, Southern Cal, Loyola Marymount	6-7	1990	117	1127	0	469	2723
Reggie Lewis, Northeastern	6-7	1987	122	1043	30 (1)	592	2708
Daren Queenan, Lehigh	6-5	1988	118	1024	29	626	2703
Byron Larkin, Xavier (OH)	6-3	1988	121	1022	51	601	2696
David Robinson, Navy	7-1	1987	127	1032	1	604	2669
Wayman Tisdale, Oklahoma	6-9	1985	104	1077	—	507	2661

*Listed is the number of three-pointers scored since it became the national rule in 1987; the number in the parentheses is number scored prior to 1987—these counted as three points in the game but counted as two-pointers in the national rankings. The three-pointers in the parentheses are not included in total points.

SCORING AVERAGE

Player and Team	Final Year	GP	FG	FT	Pts	Avg
Pete Maravich, Louisiana St	1968	83	1387	893	3667	44.2
Austin Carr, Notre Dame	1971	74	1017	526	2560	34.6
Oscar Robertson, Cincinnati	1960	88	1052	869	2973	33.8
Calvin Murphy, Niagara	1970	77	947	654	2548	33.1
Dwight Lamar, Southwestern Louisiana	1973	57	768	326	1862	32.7
Frank Selvy, Furman	1954	78	922	694	2538	32.5
Rick Mount, Purdue	1970	72	910	503	2323	32.3
Darrell Floyd, Furman	1956	71	868	545	2281	32.1
Nick Werkman, Seton Hall	1964	71	812	649	2273	32.0
Willie Humes, Idaho St	1971	48	565	380	1510	31.5
William Averitt, Pepperdine	1973	49	615	311	1541	31.4
Elgin Baylor, Coll. of Idaho, Seattle	1958	80	956	588	2500	31.3
Elvin Hayes, Houston	1968	93	1215	454	2884	31.0
Freeman Williams, Portland St	1978	106	1369	511	3249	30.7
Larry Bird, Indiana St	1979	94	1154	542	2850	30.3

Career Records (Cont.)

REBOUNDS BEFORE 1973

Player and Team	Final Year	GP	Reb
Tom Gola, La Salle	1955	118	2201
Joe Holup, George Washington	1956	104	2030
Charlie Slack, Marshall	1956	88	1916
Ed Conlin, Fordham	1955	102	1884
Dickie Hemric, Wake Forest	1955	104	1802

REBOUNDS SINCE 1973*

Player and Team	Final Year	GP	Reb
Tim Duncan, Wake Forest	1997	128	1570
Derrick Coleman, Syracuse	1990	143	1537
Malik Rose, Drexel	1996	120	1514
Ralph Sampson, Virginia	1983	132	1511
Pete Padgett, NV-Reno	1976	104	1464

ASSISTS

Player and Team	Final Year	GP	A
Bobby Hurley, Duke	1993	140	1076
Chris Corchiani, N Carolina St	1991	124	1038
Ed Cota, N Carolina	2000	138	1030
Keith Jennings, E Tennessee St	1991	127	983
Steve Blake, Maryland	2003	138	972

FIELD-GOAL PERCENTAGE

Player and Team	Final Year	FG	FGA	Pct
Steve Johnson, Oregon St	1981	828	1222	67.8
Michael Bradley, Kentucky/Villanova	2001	441	651	67.7
Murray Brown, Florida St	1980	566	847	66.8
Lee Campbell, SW Missouri St	1990	411	618	66.5
Warren Kidd, Middle Tennessee St	1993	496	747	66.4

Note: Minimum 400 field goals and 4 FG made per game.

FREE-THROW PERCENTAGE

Player and Team	Final Year	FT	FTA	Pct
Gary Buchanan, Villanova	2003	324	355	91.3
Greg Starrick, Kentucky; Southern Illinois	1972	341	375	90.9
Jack Moore, Nebraska	1982	446	495	90.1
Steve Henson, Kansas St	1990	361	401	90.0
Steve Alford, Indiana	1987	535	596	89.8

Note: Minimum 300 free throws made.

*Freshmen became eligible for varsity play in 1973.

THEY SAID IT

Former Louisiana State basketball coach Dale Brown, on his home state of North Dakota: "I once asked my father-in-law, who worked on the railroad outdoors on the border of North Dakota and Canada, how he could stand the cold. He told me, 'It surely keeps the riffraff out.'"

Career Records (Cont.)

THREE-POINT FIELD GOALS MADE

Player and Team	Final Year	GP	3FG
Curtis Staples, Virginia	1998	122	413
Keith Veney, Lamar; Marshall	1997	111	409
Doug Day, Radford	1993	117	401
Michael Watson, MO–Kansas City	2004	117	391
Ronnie Schmitz, MO–Kansas City	1993	112	378

THREE-POINT FIELD-GOAL PERCENTAGE

Player and Team	Final Year	3FG	3FGA	Pct
Tony Bennett, WI–Green Bay	1992	290	584	49.7
David Olson, Eastern Illinois	1992	262	562	46.6
Ross Land, Northern Arizona	2000	308	664	46.4
Dan Dickau, Washington/Gonzaga	2002	215	465	46.2
Sean Jackson, Ohio/Princeton	1992	243	528	46.0

Note: Minimum 200 3-point field goals and 2.0 3FG/G.

STEALS

Player and Team	Final Year	GP	S
John Linehan, Providence	2002	122	385
Eric Murdock, Providence	1991	117	376
Pepe Sanchez, Temple	2000	116	365
Cookie Belcher, Nebraska	2001	131	353
Kevin Braswell, Georgetown	2002	128	349

BLOCKED SHOTS

Player and Team	Final Year	GP	BS
Wojciech Myrda, Louisiana-Monroe	2002	115	535
Adonal Foyle, Colgate	1997	87	492
Tim Duncan, Wake Forest	1997	128	481
Alonzo Mourning, Georgetown	1992	120	453
Tarvis Williams, Hampton	2001	114	452

NCAA Men's Division I Team Leaders

Division I Team Alltime Wins

Team	First Year	Yrs	W	L	T
Kentucky	1903	101	1876	577	1
N Carolina	1911	94	1827	677	0
Kansas	1899	106	1825	762	0
Duke	1906	99	1737	781	0
St. John's (NY)	1908	97	1667	784	0
Syracuse	1901	103	1625	745	0
Temple	1895	108	1622	888	0
Pennsylvania	1897	104	1572	886	2
Indiana	1901	104	1554	840	0
Notre Dame	1898	99	1548	851	1
UCLA	1920	85	1531	689	0
Oregon St	1902	103	1529	1083	0
Utah	1909	96	1516	784	0
Princeton	1901	104	1495	904	0
Purdue	1897	106	1470	863	0
Washington	1896	102	1463	992	0

Note: Minimum of 25 years in Division I.

Division I Alltime Winning Percentage

Team	First Year	Yrs	W	L	T	Pct
Kentucky	1903	101	1876	577	1	.765
N Carolina	1911	94	1827	677	0	.730
UNLV	1959	46	943	376	0	.715
Kansas	1899	106	1825	762	0	.706
Duke	1906	99	1737	781	0	.690
UCLA	1920	85	1531	689	0	.690
Syracuse	1901	103	1625	745	0	.686
St. John's (NY)	1908	97	1667	784	0	.680
Western Kentucky	1915	85	1481	736	0	.668
Utah	1909	97	1516	784	0	.659
Indiana	1901	104	1554	840	0	.649
Arkansas	1924	81	1389	758	0	.647
Temple	1895	108	1622	888	0	.646
Louisville	1912	90	1451	788	0	.648
Notre Dame	1898	99	1548	851	1	.645

NCAA Men's Division I Winning Streaks

Longest—Full Season

Team	Games	Years	Ended by
UCLA	88	1971–74	Notre Dame (71–70)
San Francisco	60	1955–57	Illinois (62–33)
UCLA	47	1966–68	Houston (71–69)
UNLV	45	1990–91	Duke (79–77)
Texas	44	1913–17	Rice (24–18)
Seton Hall	43	1939–41	LIU-Brooklyn (49–26)
LIU-Brooklyn	43	1935–37	Stanford (45–31)
UCLA	41	1968–69	Southern Cal (46–44)
Marquette	39	1970–71	Ohio St (60–59)
Cincinnati	37	1962–63	Wichita St (65–64)
N Carolina	37	1957–58	W Virginia (75–64)

Longest—Regular Season

Team	Games	Years	Ended by
UCLA	76	1971–74	Notre Dame (71–70)
Indiana	57	1975–77	Toledo (59–57)
Marquette	56	1970–72	Detroit (70–49)
Kentucky	54	1952–55	Georgia Tech (59–58)
San Francisco	51	1955–57	Illinois (62–33)
Pennsylvania	48	1970–72	Temple (57–52)
Ohio State	47	1960–62	Wisconsin (86–67)
Texas	44	1913–17	Rice (24–18)
UCLA	43	1966–68	Houston (71–69)
LIU-Brooklyn	43	1935–37	Stanford (45–31)
Seton Hall	42	1939–41	LIU-Brooklyn (49–26)

Longest—Home Court

Team	Games	Years	Team	Games	Years
Kentucky	129	1943–55	Lamar	80	1978–84
St. Bonaventure	99	1948–61	Long Beach St	75	1968–74
UCLA	98	1970–76	UNLV	72	1974–78
Cincinnati	86	1957–64	Arizona	71	1987–92
Marquette	81	1967–73	Cincinnati	68	1972–78
Arizona	81	1945–51	Western Kentucky	67	1949–55

NCAA Men's Division I Winningest Coaches

Active Coaches*

WINS

Coach and Team	W
Bob Knight, Texas Tech	832
Lou Henson, New Mexico St	775
Eddie Sutton, Oklahoma St	755
Lute Olson, Arizona	710
John Chaney, Temple	707
Mike Krzyzewski, Duke	694
Jim Calhoun, Connecticut	680
Jim Boeheim, Syracuse	676
Hugh Durham, Jacksonville	617
Billy Tubbs, Lamar	606

Note: Minimum 5 years as a Division I head coach; includes record at 4-year colleges only.
*Active in 2003–04.

WINNING PERCENTAGE

Coach and Team	Yrs	W	L	Pct
Roy Williams, N Carolina	16	437	112	.796
Mike Krzyzewski, Duke	29	694	240	.743
Jim Boeheim, Syracuse	28	676	234	.743
Rick Majerus, Utah	20	422	147	.742
Lute Olson, Arizona	31	710	250	.740
Bob Huggins, Cincinnati	23	542	191	.739
Rick Pitino, Louisville	18	415	154	.729
Bob Knight, Texas Tech	38	832	322	.721
John Chaney, Temple	32	707	283	.714
Tom Izzo, Michigan St	8	207	90	.697

Note: Minimum 5 years as a Division I head coach; includes record at 4-year colleges only.
*Active in 2003–04.

Alltime Winningest Men's Division I Coaches

	W
Dean Smith (N Carolina)	879
Adolph Rupp (Kentucky)	876
Bob Knight (Army, Indiana, Texas Tech)	832
Jim Phelan (Mt. St. Mary's)	830
Lefty Driesell (Davidson, Maryland, James Madison, Georgia St)	786
Jerry Tarkanian (Long Beach St, UNLV, Fresno St)	778
Lou Henson (Hardin-Simmons, New Mexico St, Illinois)	775
Hank Iba (NW Missouri St, Colorado, Oklahoma St)	767
Ed Diddle (Western Kentucky)	759
Eddie Sutton (Creighton, Arkansas, Kentucky, Oklahoma St)	755
Phog Allen (Baker, Kansas, Haskell, Central Missouri St, Kansas)	746
Norm Stewart (Northern Iowa, Missouri)	731
Ray Meyer (DePaul)	724
Don Haskins (UTEP)	719
John Chaney (Cheyney St, Temple)	707
Denny Crum (Louisville)	675

Note: Minimum 10 head coaching seasons in Division I.

Alltime Winningest Men's Division I Coaches *(Cont.)*
WINNING PERCENTAGE

Coach (Team, Years)	Yrs	W	L	Pct
Clair Bee (Rider 29–31, LIU-Brooklyn 32–45, 46–51)	.21	412	87	.826
Adolph Rupp (Kentucky 31–72)	.41	876	190	.822
John Wooden (Indiana St 47–48, UCLA 49–75)	.29	664	162	.804
John Kresse (Charleston 80–02)	.23	560	143	.797
Roy Williams (Kansas 89–2003, N Carolina 2003–)	.16	437	112	.796
Jerry Tarkanian (Long Beach St 69–73, UNLV 74–92, Fresno St 95–02)	.31	778	202	.794
Dean Smith (N Carolina 62–97)	.36	879	254	.776
Harry Fisher (Columbia 07–16, Army 22–23, 25)	.13	147	44	.770
Frank Keaney (Rhode Island 21–48)	.27	387	117	.768
George Keogan (St. Louis 16, Allegheny 19, Valparaiso 20–21, Notre Dame 24–43)	.24	385	117	.767
Jack Ramsay (St. Joseph's [PA] 56–66)	.11	231	71	.765
Vic Bubas (Duke 60–69)	.10	213	67	.761
Charles (Chick) Davies (Duquesne 25–43, 47–48)	.21	314	106	.748
Ray Mears (Wittenberg 57–62, Tennessee 63–77)	.21	399	135	.747
Mike Krzyzewski (Army 76–80, Duke 81–)	.29	694	240	.743
Jim Boeheim (Syracuse 77–)	.28	676	234	.743
Rick Majerus (Marquette 84–86, Ball St 88–89, Utah 90–)	.20	422	147	.742
Lute Olson (Long Beach St 73–74, Iowa 74–83, Arizona 83–)	.31	710	250	.740
Al McGuire (Belmont Abbey 58–64, Marquette 65–77)	.20	405	143	.739
Everett Case (N Carolina St 47–64)	.18	376	133	.739
Phog Allen (Baker 06–08, Kansas 08–09, Haskell 09, Cent MO St 13–19, Kansas 20–56)	.48	746	264	.739

Note: Minimum 10 head coaching seasons in Division I.

NCAA Women's Division I Championship Results

Year	Winner	Score	Runner-up	Winning Coach
1982	Louisiana Tech	76–62	Cheyney	Sonja Hogg
1983	Southern Cal	69–67	Louisiana Tech	Linda Sharp
1984	Southern Cal	72–61	Tennessee	Linda Sharp
1985	Old Dominion	70–65	Georgia	Marianne Stanley
1986	Texas	97–81	Southern Cal	Jody Conradt
1987	Tennessee	67–44	Louisiana Tech	Pat Summitt
1988	Louisiana Tech	56–54	Auburn	Leon Barmore
1989	Tennessee	76–60	Auburn	Pat Summitt
1990	Stanford	88–81	Auburn	Tara VanDerveer
1991	Tennessee	70–67 (OT)	Virginia	Pat Summitt
1992	Stanford	78–62	Western Kentucky	Tara VanDerveer
1993	Texas Tech	84–82	Ohio State	Marsha Sharp
1994	N Carolina	60–59	Louisiana Tech	Sylvia Hatchell
1995	Connecticut	70–64	Tennessee	Geno Auriemma
1996	Tennessee	83–65	Georgia	Pat Summitt
1997	Tennessee	68–59	Old Dominion	Pat Summitt
1998	Tennessee	93–75	Louisiana Tech	Pat Summitt
1999	Purdue	62–45	Duke	Carolyn Peck
2000	Connecticut	71–52	Tennessee	Geno Auriemma
2001	Notre Dame	68–66	Purdue	Muffet McGraw
2002	Connecticut	82–70	Oklahoma	Geno Auriemma
2003	Connecticut	73–68	Tennessee	Geno Auriemma
2004	Connecticut	70–61	Tennessee	Geno Auriemma

NCAA Women's Division I Alltime Individual Leaders

Single-Game Records
SCORING HIGHS

Pts	Player and Team vs Opponent	Year
60	Cindy Brown, Long Beach St vs San Jose St	1987
58	Kim Perrot, SW Louisiana vs SE Louisiana	1990
58	Lorri Bauman, Drake vs SW Missouri St	1984
56	Jackie Stiles, SW Missouri St vs Evansville	2000
55	Patricia Hoskins, Mississippi Valley vs Southern-BR	1989
55	Patricia Hoskins, Mississippi Valley vs Alabama St	1989
54	Anjinea Hopson, Grambling vs Jackson St	1994
54	Mary Lowry, Baylor vs Texas	1994
54	Wanda Ford, Drake vs SW Missouri St	1986

Three tied with 53.

Single-Game Records *(Cont.)*
REBOUNDS

Reb	Player and Team vs Opponent	Year
40	Deborah Temple, Delta St vs AL-Birmingham	1983
37	Rosina Pearson, Bethune-Cookman vs Florida Memorial	1985
33	Maureen Formico, Pepperdine vs Loyola (CA)	1985
31	Darlene Beale, Howard vs S Carolina St	1987
30	Cindy Bonforte, Wagner vs Queens (NY)	1983
30	Kayone Hankins, New Orleans vs. Nicholls St	1994
30	Wanda Ford, Drake vs Eastern Illinois	1985
30	Jennifer Butler, Massachusetts vs Florida	2003

Three tied with 29.

ASSISTS

A	Player and Team vs Opponent	Year
23	Michelle Burden, Kent St vs Ball St	1991
22	Shawn Monday, Tennessee Tech vs Morehead St	1988
22	Veronica Pettry, Loyola (IL) vs Detroit	1989
22	Tine Freil, Pacific vs Wichita St	1991
21	Tine Freil, Pacific vs Fresno St	1992
21	Amy Bauer, Wisconsin vs Detroit	1989
21	Neacole Hall, Alabama St vs Southern-BR	1989

Six tied with 20.

Single Season Records
POINTS

Player and Team	Year	GP	FG	3FG	FT	Pts
Jackie Stiles, SW Missouri St	2001	35	365	65	267	1062
Cindy Brown, Long Beach St	1987	35	362	—	250	974
Genia Miller, Cal St-Fullerton	1991	33	376	0	217	969
Sheryl Swoopes, Texas Tech	1993	34	356	32	211	955
Andrea Congreaves, Mercer	1992	28	353	77	142	925
Wanda Ford, Drake	1986	30	390	—	139	919
Chamique Holdsclaw, Tennessee	1998	39	370	9	166	915
Barbara Kennedy, Clemson	1982	31	392	—	124	908
Patricia Hoskins, Mississippi Valley	1989	27	345	13	205	908
LaTaunya Pollard, Long Beach St	1983	31	376	—	155	907

SEASON SCORING AVERAGE

Player and Team	Year	GP	FG	3FG	FT	Pts	Avg
Patricia Hoskins, Mississippi Valley	1989	27	345	13	205	908	33.6
Andrea Congreaves, Mercer	1992	28	353	77	142	925	33.0
Deborah Temple, Delta St	1984	28	373	—	127	873	31.2
Andrea Congreaves, Mercer	1993	26	302	51	150	805	31.0
Wanda Ford, Drake	1986	30	390	—	139	919	30.6
Anucha Browne, Northwestern	1985	28	341	—	173	855	30.5
LeChandra LeDay, Grambling	1988	28	334	36	146	850	30.4
Jackie Stiles, SW MIssouri St	2001	35	365	65	267	1062	30.3
Kim Perrot, Southwestern Louisiana	1990	28	308	95	128	839	30.0
Tina Hutchinson, San Diego St	1984	30	383	—	132	898	29.9
Jan Jensen, Drake	1991	30	358	6	166	888	29.6
Genia Miller, Cal St-Fullerton	1991	33	376	0	217	969	29.4
Barbara Kennedy, Clemson	1982	31	392	—	124	908	29.3
LaTaunya Pollard, Long Beach St	1983	31	376	—	155	907	29.3
Lisa McMullen, Alabama St	1991	28	285	126	119	815	29.1

Single Season Records *(Cont.)*

REBOUNDS

Player and Team	Year	GP	Reb	Player and Team	Year	GP	Reb
Wanda Ford, Drake	1985	30	534	R. Pearson, Beth.-Cookman	1985	26	480
Wanda Ford, Drake	1986	30	506	Patricia Hoskins, Miss Valley	1987	28	476
Anne Donovan, Old Dominion	1983	35	504	Cheryl Miller, Southern Cal	1985	30	474
Darlene Jones, Miss Valley	1983	31	487	Darlene Beale, Howard	1987	29	459
Melanie Simpson, Okla. City	1982	37	481	Olivia Bradley, W Virginia	1985	30	458

REBOUND AVERAGE

Player and Team	Year	GP	Reb	Avg
Rosina Pearson, Bethune-Cookman	1985	26	480	18.5
Wanda Ford, Drake	1985	30	534	17.8
Katie Beck, E Tennessee St	1988	25	441	17.6
DeShawne Blocker, E Tennessee St	1994	26	450	17.3
Patricia Hoskins, Mississippi Valley	1987	28	476	17.0
Wanda Ford, Drake	1986	30	506	16.9
Patricia Hoskins, Mississippi Valley	1989	27	440	16.3
Joy Kellogg, Oklahoma City	1984	23	373	16.2
Deborah Mitchell, Mississippi Coll.	1983	28	447	16.0
Cheryl Miller, Southern California	1985	30	474	15.8

FIELD-GOAL PERCENTAGE

Player and Team	Year	GP	FG	FGA	Pct
Myndee Larsen, Southern Utah	1998	28	249	344	72.4
Chantelle Anderson, Vanderbilt	2001	34	292	404	72.3
Deneka Knowles, Southeastern La.	1996	26	199	276	72.1
Barbara Farris, Tulane	1998	27	151	210	71.9
Renay Adams, Tennessee Tech	1991	30	185	258	71.7
Regina Days, Georgia Southern	1986	27	234	332	70.5
Kim Wood, WI-Green Bay	1994	27	188	271	69.4
Kelly Lyons, Old Dominion	1990	31	308	444	69.4
Alisha Hill, Howard	1995	28	194	281	69.0
Ruth Riley, Notre Dame	1999	31	198	290	68.3

Based on qualifiers for annual championship.

FREE-THROW PERCENTAGE

Player and Team	Year	GP	FT	FTA	Pct
Shanna Zolman, Tennessee	2004	35	88	92	95.7
Ginny Doyle, Richmond	1992	29	96	101	95.0
Jill Marano, La Salle	2003	29	88	93	94.6
Sue Bird, Connecticut	2002	39	98	104	94.2
Paula Corder-King, SE Missouri St	1999	28	111	118	94.1
Kandi Brown, Morehead St	2003	28	104	111	93.7
Linda Cyborski, Delaware	1991	29	74	79	93.7
Kandi Brown, Morehead St	2002	29	74	79	93.7
Paula Corder-King, SE Missouri St	2000	27	69	74	93.2
Jennifer Howard, N Carolina St	1994	27	118	127	92.9

Based on qualifiers for annual championship.

Career Records
POINTS

Player and Team	Yrs	GP	Pts
Jackie Stiles, SW Missouri St	1997–01	129	3393
Patricia Hoskins, Mississippi Valley	1985–89	110	3122
Lorri Bauman, Drake	1981–84	120	3115
Chamique Holdsclaw, Tennessee	1995–99	148	3025
Cheryl Miller, Southern Cal	1983–86	128	3018
Cindy Blodgett, Maine	1994–98	118	3005
Valorie Whiteside, Appalachian St	1984–88	116	2944
Joyce Walker, Louisiana St	1981–84	117	2906
Sandra Hodge, New Orleans	1981–84	107	2860
Andrea Congreaves, Mercer	1989–93	108	2796

SCORING AVERAGE

Player and Team	Yrs	GP	FG	3FG	FT	Pts	Avg
Patricia Hoskins, Mississippi Valley	1985–89	110	1196	24	706	3122	28.4
Sandra Hodge, New Orleans	1981–84	107	1194	—	472	2860	26.7
Jackie Stiles, SW Missouri St	1997–01	129	1160	221	852	3393	26.3
Lorri Bauman, Drake	1981–84	120	1104	—	907	3115	26.0
Andrea Congreaves, Mercer	1989–93	108	1107	153	429	2796	25.9
Cindy Blodgett, Maine	1994–98	118	1055	219	676	3005	25.5
Valorie Whiteside, Appalachian St	1984–88	116	1153	0	638	2944	25.4
Joyce Walker, Louisiana St	1981–84	117	1259	—	388	2906	24.8
Tarcha Hollis, Grambling	1988–91	85	904	3	247	2058	24.2
Korie Hlede, Duquesne	1994–98	109	1045	162	379	2631	24.1

NCAA Men's Division II Championship Results

Year	Winner	Score	Runner-up	Third Place	Fourth Place
1957	Wheaton (IL)	89–65	Kentucky Wesleyan	Mount St Mary's (MD)	Cal St-Los Angeles
1958	S Dakota	75–53	St. Michael's	Evansville	Wheaton (IL)
1959	Evansville	83–67	SW Missouri St	N Carolina A&T	Cal St-Los Angeles
1960	Evansville	90–69	Chapman	Kentucky Wesleyan	Cornell College
1961	Wittenberg	42–38	SE Missouri St	S Dakota St	Mount St Mary's (MD)
1962	Mount St Mary's (MD)	58–57 (OT)	Cal St-Sacramento	Southern Illinois	Nebraska Wesleyan
1963	S Dakota St	44–42	Wittenberg	Oglethorpe	Southern Illinois
1964	Evansville	72–59	Akron	N Carolina A&T	Northern Iowa
1965	Evansville	85–82 (OT)	Southern Illinois	N Dakota	St Michael's
1966	Kentucky Wesleyan	54–51	Southern Illinois	Akron	N Dakota
1967	Winston-Salem	77–74	SW Missouri St	Kentucky Wesleyan	Illinois St
1968	Kentucky Wesleyan	63–52	Indiana St	Trinity (TX)	Ashland
1969	Kentucky Wesleyan	75–71	SW Missouri St	†Vacated	Ashland
1970	Philadelphia Textile	76–65	Tennessee St	UC-Riverside	Buffalo St
1971	Evansville	97–82	Old Dominion	†Vacated	Kentucky Wesleyan
1972	Roanoke	84–72	Akron	Tennessee St	Eastern Mich
1973	Kentucky Wesleyan	78–76 (OT)	Tennessee St	Assumption	Brockport St
1974	Morgan St	67–52	SW Missouri St	Assumption	New Orleans
1975	Old Dominion	76–74	New Orleans	Assumption	TN-Chattanooga
1976	Puget Sound	83–74	TN-Chattanooga	Eastern Illinois	Old Dominion
1977	TN-Chattanooga	71–62	Randolph-Macon	N Alabama	Sacred Heart
1978	Cheyney	47–40	WI-Green Bay	Eastern Illinois	Central Florida
1979	N Alabama	64–50	WI-Green Bay	Cheyney	Bridgeport
1980	Virginia Union	80–74	New York Tech	Florida Southern	N Alabama
1981	Florida Southern	73–68	Mount St Mary's (MD)	Cal Poly-SLO	WI-Green Bay
1982	District of Columbia	73–63	Florida Southern	Kentucky Wesleyan	Cal St-Bakersfield
1983	Wright St	92–73	District of Columbia	*Cal St-Bakersfield	*Morningside
1984	Central Missouri St	81–77	St. Augustine's	*Kentucky Wesleyan	*N Alabama
1985	Jacksonville St	74–73	S Dakota St	*Kentucky Wesleyan	*Mount St. Mary's (MD)
1986	Sacred Heart	93–87	SE Missouri St	*Cheyney	*Florida Southern
1987	Kentucky Wesleyan	92–74	Gannon	*Delta St	*Eastern Montana
1988	Lowell	75–72	AK-Anchorage	Florida Southern	Troy St
1989	N Carolina Central	73–46	SE Missouri St	UC-Riverside	Jacksonville St
1990	Kentucky Wesleyan	93–79	Cal St-Bakersfield	N Dakota	Morehouse
1991	N Alabama	79–72	Bridgeport (CT)	*Cal St-Bakersfield	*Virginia Union
1992	Virginia Union	100–75	Bridgeport (CT)	*Cal St-Bakersfield	*California (PA)
1993	Cal St-Bakersfield	85–72	Troy St (AL)	*New Hampshire Coll	*Wayne St (MI)

*Indicates tied for third. †Student-athletes representing American International in 1969 and Southwestern Louisiana in 1971 were declared ineligible subsequent to the tournament. Under NCAA rules, the teams' and ineligible student-athletes' records were deleted, and the teams' places in the final standings were vacated.

Year	Winner	Score	Runner-up	Third Place	Fourth Place
1994	Cal St-Bakersfield	92–86	Southern Indiana	*New Hampshire Coll	*Washburn
1995	Southern Indiana	71–63	UC–Riverside	*Norfolk St	*Indiana (PA)
1996	Fort Hays St	70–63	Northern Kentucky	*California (PA)	*Virginia Union
1997	Cal St-Bakersfield	57–56	Northern Kentucky	*Lynn	*Salem-Teikyo
1998	UC-Davis	83–77	Kentucky Wesleyan	*St. Rose	*Virginia Union
1999	Kentucky Wesleyan	75–60	Metropolitan St	*Truman St	*Florida Southern
2000	Metropolitan St	97–79	Kentucky Wesleyan	*Missouri Southern	*Seattle Pacific
2001	Kentucky Wesleyan	72–63	Washburn	*Western Washington	*Tampa
2002	Metropolitan St	80–72	Kentucky Wesleyan	*Shaw	*Indiana (PA)
2003	Northeastern St (OK)	75–64	vacated	*Bowie St	*Queens (NC)
2004	Kennesaw St	84–59	Southern Indiana	*Humboldt St	*Metropolitan St

NCAA Men's Division II Alltime Individual Leaders

SINGLE-GAME SCORING HIGHS

Pts	Player and Team vs Opponent	Date
113	Bevo Francis, Rio Grande vs Hillsdale	1954
84	Bevo Francis, Rio Grande vs Alliance	1954
82	Bevo Francis, Rio Grande vs Bluffton	1954
80	Paul Crissman, Southern Cal Col vs Pacific Christian	1966
77	William English, Winston-Salem vs Fayetteville St	1968

Single Season Records

SCORING AVERAGE

Player and Team	Year	GP	FG	FT	Pts	Avg
Bevo Francis, Rio Grande	1954	27	444	367	1255	46.5
Earl Glass, Mississippi Industrial	1963	19	322	171	815	42.9
Earl Monroe, Winston-Salem	1967	32	509	311	1329	41.5
John Rinka, Kenyon	1970	23	354	234	942	41.0
Willie Shaw, Lane	1964	18	303	121	727	40.4

REBOUND AVERAGE

Player and Team	Year	GP	Reb	Avg
Tom Hart, Middlebury	1956	21	620	29.5
Tom Hart, Middlebury	1955	22	649	29.5
Frank Stronczek, American Int'l	1966	26	717	27.6
R.C. Owens, College of Idaho	1954	25	677	27.1
Maurice Stokes, St Francis (PA)	1954	26	689	26.5

ASSISTS

Player and Team	Year	GP	A
Steve Ray, Bridgeport	1989	32	400
Steve Ray, Bridgeport	1990	33	385
Tony Smith, Pfeiffer	1992	35	349
Jim Ferrer, Bentley	1989	31	309
Rob Paternostro, New Hamp. Coll.	1995	33	309

ASSIST AVERAGE

Player and Team	Year	GP	A	Avg
Steve Ray, Bridgeport	1989	32	400	12.5
Steve Ray, Bridgeport	1990	33	385	11.7
Demetri Beekman, Assumption	1993	23	264	11.5
Ernest Jenkins, NM Highlands	1995	27	291	10.8
Brian Gregory, Oakland	1989	28	300	10.7

FIELD-GOAL PERCENTAGE

Player and Team	Year	Pct
Todd Linder, Tampa	1987	75.2
Maurice Stafford, N Alabama	1984	75.0
Matthew Cornegay, Tuskegee	1982	74.8
Brian Moten, W Georgia	1992	73.4
Ed Phillips, Alabama A&M	1968	73.3

FREE-THROW PERCENTAGE

Player and Team	Year	Pct
Paul Cluxton, Northern Kentucky	1997	100.0
Tomas Rimkus, Pace	1997	95.6
C.J. Cowgill, Chaminade	2001	95.0
Billy Newton, Morgan St	1976	94.4
Kent Andrews, McNeese St	1968	94.4

Career Records

POINTS

Player and Team	Yrs	Pts
Travis Grant, Kentucky St	1969–72	4045
Bob Hopkins, Grambling	1953–56	3759
Tony Smith, Pfeiffer	1989–92	3350
Earnest Lee, Clark Atlanta	1984–87	3298
Joe Miller, Alderson-Broaddus	1954–57	3294

Career Records *(Cont.)*

CAREER SCORING AVERAGE

Player and Team	Yrs	GP	Pts	Avg
Travis Grant, Kentucky St	1969–72	121	4045	33.4
John Rinka, Kenyon	1967–70	99	3251	32.8
Florindo Vieira, Quinnipiac	1954–57	69	2263	32.8
Willie Shaw, Lane	1961–64	76	2379	31.3
Mike Davis, Virginia Union	1966–69	89	2758	31.0

REBOUND AVERAGE

Player and Team	Yrs	GP	Reb	Avg
Tom Hart, Middlebury	1953, 55–56	63	1738	27.6
Maurice Stokes, St. Francis (PA)	1953–55	72	1812	25.2
Frank Stronczek, American Int'l	1965–67	62	1549	25.0
Bill Thieben, Hofstra	1954–56	76	1837	24.2
Hank Brown, Lowell Tech	1965–67	49	1129	23.0

ASSISTS

Player and Team	Yrs	A
Demetri Beekman, Assumption	1990–93	1044
Adam Kaufman, Edinboro	1998–01	936
Rob Paternostro, New Hamp. Coll.	1992–95	919
Tony Smith, Pfeiffer	1989–92	828
Jamie Stevens, Montana St-Billings	1996–99	805

ASSIST AVERAGE

Player and Team	Yrs	GP	A	Avg
Steve Ray, Bridgeport	1989–90	65	785	12.1
Demetri Beekman, Assumption	1990–93	119	1044	8.8
Ernest Jenkins, NM Highlands	1992–95	84	699	8.3
Adam Kaufman, Edinboro	1998–01	116	936	8.1
Mark Benson, Texas A&I	1989–91	86	674	7.8

Note: Minimum 550 Assists.

FIELD-GOAL PERCENTAGE

Player and Team	Yrs	Pct
Todd Linder, Tampa	1984–87	70.8
Tom Schurfranz, Bellarmine	1989–92	70.2
Chad Scott, California (PA)	1991–94	70.0
Ed Phillips, Alabama, A&M	1968–71	68.9
Ulysses Hackett, SC-Spartanburg	1990–92	67.9

Note: Minimum 400 FGM.

FREE-THROW PERCENTAGE

Player and Team	Yrs	Pct
Paul Cluxton, Northern Kentucky	1994–97	93.5
Kent Andrews, McNeese St	1967–69	91.6
Jon Hagen, Minn St–Mankato	1963–65	90.0
Dave Reynolds, Davis & Elkins	1986–89	89.3
Michael Shue, Lock Haven	1994–97	88.5

Note: Minimum 250 FTM.

NCAA Men's Division III Championship Results

Year	Winner	Score	Runner-up	Third Place	Fourth Place
1975	LeMoyne-Owen	57–54	Glassboro St	Augustana (IL)	Brockport St
1976	Scranton	60–57	Wittenberg	Augustana (IL)	Plattsburgh St
1977	Wittenberg	79–66	Oneonta St	Scranton	Hamline
1978	North Park	69–57	Widener	Albion	Stony Brook
1979	North Park	66–62	Potsdam St	Franklin & Marshall	Centre
1980	North Park	83–76	Upsala	Wittenberg	Longwood
1981	Potsdam St	67–65 (OT)	Augustana (IL)	Ursinus	Otterbein
1982	Wabash	83–62	Potsdam St	Brooklyn	Cal St-Stanislaus
1983	Scranton	64–63	Wittenberg	Roanoke	WI–Whitewater
1984	WI–Whitewater	103–86	Clark (MA)	DePauw	Upsala
1985	North Park	72–71	Potsdam St	Nebraska Wesleyan	Widener
1986	Potsdam St	76–73	LeMoyne-Owen	Nebraska Wesleyan	Jersey City St
1987	North Park	106–100	Clark (MA)	Wittenberg	Stockton St
1988	Ohio Wesleyan	92–70	Scranton	Nebraska Wesleyan	Hartwick
1989	WI–Whitewater	94–86	Trenton St	Southern Maine	Centre
1990	Rochester	43–42	DePauw	Washington (MD)	Calvin
1991	WI–Platteville	81–74	Franklin & Marshall	Otterbein	Ramapo (NJ)
1992	Calvin	62–49	Rochester	WI–Platteville	Jersey City St
1993	Ohio Northern	71–68	Augustana	Mass–Dartmouth	Rowan
1994	Lebanon Valley Coll	66–59 (OT)	New York University	Wittenberg	St Thomas (MN)
1995	WI–Platteville	69–55	Manchester	Rowan	Trinity (CT)
1996	Rowan	100–93	Hope (MI)	Illinois Wesleyan	Franklin & Marshall
1997	Illinois Wesleyan	89–86	Nebraska Wesleyan	Williams	Alvernia
1998	WI–Platteville	69–56	Hope (MI)	Williams	Wilkes
1999	WI–Platteville	76–75 (2 OT)	Hampden-Sydney	William Paterson	Connecticut Coll.
2000	Calvin	79–74	WI-Eau Claire	Salem St	Franklin & Marshall
2001	Catholic	76–62	William Paterson	*Illinois Wesleyan	*Ohio Northern
2002	Otterbein	102–83	Elizabethtown	Carthage	Rochester
2003	Williams	67–65	Gustavus Adolphus	Wooster	Hampden Sydney
2004	WI–Stevens Point	84–82	Williams	John Carroll	Amherst

SINGLE-GAME SCORING HIGHS

Pts	Player and Team vs Opponent	Year
77	Jeff Clement, Grinnell vs Illinois College	1998
69	Steve Diekmann, Grinnell vs Simpson	1995
63	Joe DeRoche, Thomas vs St. Joseph's (ME)	1988
62	Shannon Lilly, Bishop vs Southwest Assembly of God	1983
61	Steve Honderd, Calvin vs Kalamazoo	1993
61	Dana Wilson, Husson vs Ricker	1974
61	Joshua Metzger, Wisconsin Lutheran vs Grinnell	2000

Single Season Records

SCORING AVERAGE

Player and Team	Year	GP	FG	FT	Pts	Avg
Steve Diekmann, Grinnell	1995	20	223	162	745	37.3
Rickey Sutton, Lyndon St	1976	14	207	93	507	36.2
Shannon Lilly, Bishop	1983	26	345	218	908	34.9
Dana Wilson, Husson	1974	20	288	122	698	34.9
Rickey Sutton, Lyndon St	1977	16	223	112	558	34.9

REBOUND AVERAGE

Player and Team	Year	GP	Reb	Avg
Joe Manley, Bowie St	1976	29	579	20.0
Fred Petty, New Hampshire College	1974	22	436	19.8
Larry Williams, Pratt	1977	24	457	19.0
Charles Greer, Thomas	1977	17	318	18.7
Larry Parker, Plattsburgh St	1975	23	430	18.7

ASSISTS

Player and Team	Year	GP	A
Robert James, Kean	1989	29	391
Tennyson Whitted, Ramapo	2002	29	319
Ricky Spicer, WI-Whitewater	1989	31	295
Joe Marcotte, New Jersey Tech	1995	30	292
Andre Bolton, Chris. Newport	1996	30	289

ASSIST AVERAGE

Player and Team	Year	GP	A	Avg
Robert James, Kean	1989	29	391	13.5
Albert Kirchner, Mt. St. Vincent	1990	24	267	11.1
Tennyson Whitted, Ramapo	2002	29	319	11.0
Ron Torgalski, Hamilton	1989	26	275	10.6
Louis Adams, Rust	1989	22	227	10.3

FIELD-GOAL PERCENTAGE

Player and Team	Year	Pct
Travis Weiss, St. John's (MN)	1994	76.6
Pete Metzelaars, Wabash	1982	75.3
Tony Rychlec, Mass. Maritime	1981	74.9
Tony Rychlec, Mass. Maritime	1982	73.1
Russ Newnan, Menlo	1991	73.0

FREE-THROW PERCENTAGE

Player and Team	Year	Pct
Korey Coon, IL Wesleyan	2000	96.3
Chanse Young, Manchester	1998	95.6
Andy Enfield, Johns Hopkins	1991	95.3
Nick Wilkins, Coe	2003	95.7
Chris Carideo, Widener	1992	95.2
Yudi Teichman, Yeshiva	1989	95.2

Career Records

POINTS

Player and Team	Yrs	Pts
Andre Foreman, Salisbury St	1989–92	2940
Willie Chandler, Misericordia	2000–03	2898
Lamont Strothers, Chris. Newport	1988–91	2709
Matt Hancock, Colby	1987–90	2678
Scott Fitch, Geneseo St	1990–94	2634

CAREER SCORING AVERAGE

Player and Team	Yrs	GP	Avg
Dwain Govan, Bishop	1974–75	55	32.8
Dave Russell, Shepherd	1974–75	60	30.6
Rickey Sutton, Lyndon St	1976–79	80	29.7
John Atkins, Knoxville	1976–78	70	28.7
Steve Petnik, Windham	1974–77	76	27.6

REBOUND AVERAGE

Player and Team	Yrs	GP	Reb	Avg
Larry Parker, Plattsburgh St	1975–78	85	1482	17.4
Charles Greer, Thomas	1975–77	58	926	16.0
Willie Parr, LeMoyne-Owen	1974–76	76	1182	15.6
Michael Smith, Hamilton	1989–92	107	1632	15.2
Dave Kufeld, Yeshiva	1977–80	81	1222	15.1

ASSIST AVERAGE

Player and Team	Yrs	Avg
Phil Dixon, Shenandoah	1993–96	8.6
Tennyson Whitted, Ramapo	2000–03	8.5
Steve Artis, Chris. Newport	1990–93	8.1
David Genovese, Mt. St. Vincent	1992–95	7.5
Kevin Root, Eureka	1989–91	7.1

Vincent Lecavalier of the Stanley Cup champion Tampa Bay Lightning

Hockey

Lightning Strike

After Tampa Bay defeated Calgary in an exciting (but low-profile) Stanley Cup, the league faced an imminent work stoppage

BY B.J. SCHECTER

THE NATIONAL HOCKEY LEAGUE certainly has its share of problems—dreadful television ratings in the U.S., an impending lockout and an on-ice ethos that promotes violent retribution are chief among them—but when its players get down to the business of deciding a championship, the league shines as bright as any of its more glamorous counterparts in major sports. Every year, without fail, the NHL playoffs produce a series of taut showdowns, during which premeditated violence is rare and the action is quick, skillful and downright exciting. Further, the league has just the right amount of parity: The teams with the lowest payrolls often challenge, and occasionally beat, big-market teams, and expansion teams, if they are run wisely, can become powerhouses.

Witness the 2003–04 Tampa Bay Lightning. Though the team's original owners nearly ran it into the ground, the Lightning has since become a model franchise. Tampa entered the league in 1992 and quickly became recognized as one of the worst-run franchises in all of sports. By 1998, the Lightning had a lifetime record of nearly 100 games below .500, and the team was sold for a loss in June of the following year. Its new owner, William Davidson, who also owns the 2003–04 NBA champion Detroit Pistons, quickly began to turn things around. (Davidson also owns the 2003 WNBA champion Detroit Shock, giving him a trio of reigning titlists.)

In 2003, Tampa Bay won its first playoff series; this season the Lightning topped the Eastern Conference with 106 points. They entered the 2004 playoffs as the No. 1 seed, and with a group of budding stars leading the way, they dispatched the Islanders, Montreal and Philadelphia en route to the finals. Martin St. Louis—who won the Hart Trophy as the regular-season MVP—Vincent Lecavalier and Brad Richards spearheaded Tampa's run along with steady goaltender Nikolai Khabibulin and fiery coach John Tortorella. The Lightning stood poised to become the first expansion franchise since 1991 to win North America's oldest professional trophy.

Standing in their way were the Calgary Flames, an underdog story in their own right. The Flames won the Stanley Cup in 1989 and had been a contender for much of the 1980s, but had missed the playoffs for seven consecutive seasons before this one. They had the 12th-best record of all of the playoff contenders, yet fought their way to the last round, becoming the first team to beat three division winners to reach the Stanley Cup finals.

Canada quickly rallied around Calgary, not only because the Flames were trying to become the first Canadian team since Montreal in 1993 to win the Cup, but also because they played an exciting, up-and-down style of hockey that was fun to watch (Tampa Bay employed a similar style, making the Finals a wide-open affair). With hot goaltender Miikka Kiprusoff and high-scoring right winger Jarome Iginla, who established himself as one of the game's biggest stars in the playoffs, Calgary had all the ingredients of a championship team.

DAVID E. KLUTHO

With 41 goals during the regular season, and a superb playoff performance, Iginla established himself as an NHL superstar.

Though the Flames outplayed the Lightning in the early part of the series, Tampa Bay managed to stay in it with its quick-strike ability. The series was dead-locked at two games apiece when Calgary came into the St. Pete Times Forum for a critical Game 5. In one of the best games of the series, Calgary fought and clawed and created scoring chances, but Tampa refused to buckle. Finally, Iginla corralled the puck in the Flames' zone and raced up ice, blasting a shot whose rebound Oleg Saprykin tucked away for the game-winner at 14:40 of overtime. Iginla had played an astounding 31 minutes in the game, including seven in overtime, and brought his team to within one win of the Cup.

On the brink of defeat, the Lightning

DAVID E. KLUTHO

At 40, Andreychuk got a sweet taste of Cup glory.

staff and later played the message for his teammates.

"He said not to give up, and he told us what to do and what not to do in the next game," said Taylor. "It was almost like he was coaching us." Taylor's teammates, many of whom grew up idolizing Bourque, were stunned when they heard Bourque's voice. It immediately fired them up. Said Tampa Bay forward Brad Richards, "Hearing that message sent chills down my body."

History wasn't on Tampa Bay's side—only four of the 18 teams that had lost the fifth game in a finals series that was tied had come back to win—but the Lightning were undaunted by the rabid Calgary fans and matched the Flames' every move. In an exciting and hard-fought game, Tampa Bay staved off elimination with a 3–2 victory in double overtime, thanks to Richards, who scored two

traveled in silence to Calgary, where red-clad fans in the Saddledome were ready to cheer their team to its first Stanley Cup in 15 years. But Tampa Bay was hardly ready to concede, and received an unexpected piece of encouragement upon arriving in Calgary. When he got off the plane, Lightning veteran center Tim Taylor turned on his cell phone and retrieved a message from former teammate Ray Bourque. Bourque, a future hall of famer, played 21 years in the NHL before finally winning a title, in 2001 with the Colorado Avalanche. His team had trailed three games to two. He called to encourage Taylor and the rest of the Lightning. Taylor borrowed a tape recorder from Tampa Bay's public relations'

power-play goals in the second period, and St. Louis, who assisted on Richard's first goal and scored the game-winner 33 seconds into the second overtime.

It was a sweet moment for Richards, who failed to score in 11 postseason games in 2003 and took his share of the blame for the Lightning's second-round loss to the Devils that season. In 2003–04, Tampa Bay was undefeated (31-0-2) in games in which Richards scored, and he finished as the leading scorer in the playoffs with 26 points. "When I didn't play well in [last year's] playoffs it was because I didn't want the puck," said Richards, who would go on to win the Conn Smythe Trophy as the playoff MVP. "I want the puck more now and want to get

318   H O C K E Y

through some of the things that are tougher than in the regular season."

Tampa Bay was tough went it counted in Game 7, keeping Iginla in check and feeding off its own excitable South Florida fans, many of whom didn't know the difference between the blue line and a tanline. Lightning right wing Ruslan Fedotenko, who had missed Game 4 after getting driven into the boards in Game 3, was the hero, scoring both Lightning goals in a 2–1 victory that delivered the Stanley Cup to sunny Tampa Bay.

It was a shining moment for the Lightning's 40-year-old captain Dave Andreychuk, who had been the NHL's current leader in games played without a title. To delirious cheers from the Tampa Bay crowd, Andreychuk took the famous trophy from commissioner Gary Bettman and skated around the ice, tears welling in his eyes. "I can't put it into words the way I feel," said Andreychuk, who took 1,759 games to win his first NHL championship (compared with Bourque's 1,826 games). "This is the pinnacle. This is what we play for and it's taken me a while to get here. It was a moment that's gone through my head lots of times and it finally happened."

Though his team fell short, Iginla cemented his status as a bona fide superstar. During the past three seasons nobody has scored more goals. Iginla tied for the league lead in 2003–04 with 41, then Iginla added 13 more (and nine assists) in the playoffs.

"You can argue who is the best player," said Calgary defenseman Andrew Ference. "but there's no doubt Jarome's the best role model. He's a superstar because of his talent, but beyond that his greatest asset is his work ethic. I played with Mario [Lemieux] and Jaromir [Jagr], and they had the talent the rest of us could only dream of. But the way Jarome has made himself great, by his willingness to fight through the challenges, he makes it seem that greatness isn't beyond our reach."

As impressive as Iginla was, the Stanley Cup finals flew well below the radar of the average U.S. sports fan. In Canada, Game 6 was the most watched hockey broadcast on CBC in the last 10 years, with 4.7 million viewers. But with two small-market teams squaring off, television ratings hit an alltime low in the U.S., on ABC. And during the regular season, U.S. ratings for the NHL were often lower than those of the Arena Football League. As a result, the NHL was forced to sign a television deal with NBC with no guaranteed money (its previous contract had been with ABC and ESPN for five years and $600 million).

When people did tune in it usually wasn't because of good news. On March 8, Canucks forward Todd Bertuzzi brutally assaulted Colorado rookie Steve Moore during a game in Vancouver. The video clip of the ugly incident was played over and over at the top of newscasts, no doubt deepening some viewers' impression of the league as a WWF on skates. But the incident had a context: Earlier in the season, Moore had knocked the Canucks' best player and captain, Markus Naslund, out of a game. While Moore did not draw a penalty on the play, many observers questioned the hit, and Bertuzzi was determined to get revenge. He approached Moore from behind, sucker-punched him with a haymaker, and then drove his head into the ice, leaving Moore with a broken neck.

Bertuzzi's overreaction (he later tearfully apologized, saying he never meant to hurt Moore) sparked anew the age-old debate over fighting in the NHL, the only league in the world that doesn't punish fisticuffs with an automatic ejection. The purists argued that fighting was crucial to the self-policing of the game by players, saying that the league's instigator rule actually creates incidents like the Bertuzzi hit on Moore, because it prevents players from settling disputes as they happen, for fear of drawing an extra two-minute minor penalty and an additional 10-minute misconduct as the instigator of a fight. Others contended that a sport which promotes—or at least tacitly approves—violence is asking for trouble. Canadian Prime Minister Paul Martin said the NHL "must clean up [its] act," and the president-elect of the American College of Sports Medicine issued a statement saying, "It's time to stop these muggings mas-

Bertuzzi's assault on Moore left an ugly mark on an otherwise entertaining season.

querading as sport." The NHL came down appropriately hard on Bertuzzi, suspending him for the final 13 games of the regular season and the playoffs. The punishment cost him more than $500,000 in lost wages, and he had to apply for reinstatement before being allowed back into the league.

But Bertuzzi may not have a league to reenter in the fall as the NHL's Collective Bargaining Agreement was set to expire on Sept. 15 with the league and the players' union worlds apart in terms of agreeing on a new one. A lockout seemed inevitable. The major sticking point was a salary cap, which the league said was necessary given that losses were approaching $273 million annually, according to an independent audit paid for by the league. The union said that they wouldn't accept a cap under any conditions, and both sides seemed ready to dig their heels in for a long work stoppage.

This of course is not good news for the NHL, which receives roughly 60% of its $2 billion in revenue from the gate, and already has an image problem. Hockey is a national obsession in Canada, but with 24 of the 30 franchises located in the U.S., the league needs to have a strong image in the States to survive. Will the majority of American sports fans care if there is no hockey for a year? A prolonged work stoppage will undoubtedly alienate the precious few fans the NHL has in the United States.

So remember the sparkling Iginla and the rousing Stanley Cup staged by Calgary and the Tampa Bay Lightning. It may be a while before there's another one.

NHL Final Standings

Eastern Conference

NORTHEAST DIVISION

	GP	W	L	T	OTL	Pts	GF	GA
Boston	82	41	19	15	7	104	209	188
Toronto	82	45	24	10	3	103	242	204
Ottawa	82	43	23	10	6	102	262	189
Montreal	82	41	30	7	4	93	208	192
Buffalo	82	37	34	7	4	85	220	221

ATLANTIC DIVISION

	GP	W	L	T	OTL	Pts	GF	GA
Philadelphia	82	40	21	15	6	101	229	186
New Jersey	82	43	25	12	2	100	213	164
NY Islanders	82	38	29	11	4	91	237	210
NY Rangers	82	27	40	7	8	69	206	250
Pittsburgh	82	23	47	8	4	58	190	303

SOUTHEAST DIVISION

	GP	W	L	T	OTL	Pts	GF	GA
Tampa Bay	82	48	21	11	6	106	245	192
Atlanta	82	33	37	8	4	78	214	243
Carolina	82	28	34	14	6	76	172	209
Florida	82	28	35	15	4	75	188	221
Washington	82	23	46	10	3	59	186	253

Western Conference

CENTRAL DIVISION

	GP	W	L	T	OTL	Pts	GF	GA
Detroit	82	48	21	11	2	109	255	189
St. Louis	82	39	30	11	2	91	191	198
Nashville	82	38	29	11	4	91	216	217
Columbus	82	25	45	8	4	62	177	238
Chicago	82	20	43	11	8	59	188	259

NORTHWEST DIVISION

	GP	W	L	T	OTL	Pts	GF	GA
Vancouver	82	43	24	10	5	101	235	194
Colorado	82	40	22	13	7	100	236	198
Calgary	82	42	30	7	3	94	200	176
Edmonton	82	36	29	12	5	89	221	208
Minnesota	82	30	29	20	3	83	188	183

PACIFIC DIVISION

	GP	W	L	T	OTL	Pts	GF	GA
San Jose	82	43	21	12	6	104	219	183
Dallas	82	41	26	13	2	97	194	175
Los Angeles	82	28	29	16	9	81	205	217
Anaheim	82	29	35	10	8	76	184	213
Phoenix	82	22	36	18	6	68	188	245

OTL=overtime loss; worth 1 pt.

2004 Stanley Cup Playoffs

EASTERN CONFERENCE

QUARTERFINALS SEMIFINALS CONFERENCE FINAL

WESTERN CONFERENCE

CONFERENCE FINAL SEMIFINALS QUARTERFINALS

STANLEY CUP

Tampa Bay (4-3)

Eastern			Western		
NY Islanders	Tampa Bay (4-1)		Detroit (4-2)		Nashville
Tampa Bay		Tampa Bay (4-0)		Calgary (4-2)	Detroit
Montreal	Montreal (4-3)			Calgary (4-3)	Calgary
Boston		Tampa Bay (4-3)			Vancouver
New Jersey	Philadelphia (4-1)		Calgary (4-2)		St. Louis
Philadelphia		Philadelphia (4-2)		San Jose (4-1)	San Jose
Ottawa	Toronto (4-3)		San Jose (4-2)		Dallas
Toronto				Colorado (4-1)	Colorado

Stanley Cup Playoff Results

Conference Quarterfinals

EASTERN CONFERENCE

April 8	NY Islanders	0	at Tampa Bay	3	April 14	Tampa Bay	3	at NY Islanders	0
April 10	NY Islanders	3	at Tampa Bay	0	April 16	NY Islanders	2	at Tampa Bay	3*
April 12	Tampa Bay	3	at NY Islanders	0		Tampa Bay won series 4-1.		

Conference Quarterfinals *(Cont.)*

EASTERN CONFERENCE *(Cont.)*

April 7	Montreal	0	at Boston	3
April 9	Montreal	1	at Boston	2*
April 11	Boston	2	at Montreal	3
Aoril 13	Boston	4	at Montreal	3†

April 8	New Jersey	2	at Philadelphia	3
April 10	New Jersey	2	at Philadelphia	3
April 12	Philadelphia	2	at New Jersey	4
April 14	Philadelphia	3	at New Jersey	0
April 17	New Jersey	1	at Philadelphia	3

Philadelphia won series 4–1.

April 15	Montreal	5	at Boston	1
April 17	Boston	2	at Montreal	5
April 19	Montreal	2	at Boston	0

Montreal won series 4–3.

April 8	Ottawa	4	at Toronto	2
April 10	Ottawa	0	at Toronto	2
April 12	Toronto	2	at Ottawa	0
April 14	Toronto	1	at Ottawa	4
April 16	Ottawa	0	at Toronto	2
April 18	Toronto	1	at Ottawa	2†
April 20	Ottawa	1	at Toronto	4

Toronto won series 4–3.

WESTERN CONFERENCE

April 7	Nashville	1	at Detroit	3
April 10	Nashville	1	at Detroit	2
April 11	Detroit	1	at Nashville	3
April 13	Detroit	0	at Nashville	3
April 15	Nashville	1	at Detroit	4
April 17	Detroit	2	at Nashville	0

Detroit won series 4–2.

April 8	St. Louis	0	at San Jose	1*
April 10	St. Louis	1	at San Jose	3
April 12	San Jose	1	at St. Louis	4
April 13	San Jose	4	at St. Louis	3
April 15	St. Louis	1	at San Jose	3

San Jose won series 4–1.

April 7	Calgary	3	at Vancouver	5
April 9	Calgary	2	at Vancouver	1
April 11	Vancouver	2	at Calgary	1
April 13	Vancouver	0	at Calgary	4
April 15	Calgary	2	at Vancouver	1
April 17	Vancouver	5	at Calgary	4*
April 19	Calgary	3	at Vancouver	2*

Calgary won series 4–3.

April 7	Dallas	1	at Colorado	3
April 9	Dallas	2	at Colorado	5
April 12	Colorado	3	at Dallas	4*
April 14	Colorado	3	at Dallas	2†
April 17	Dallas	1	at Colorado	5

Colorado won series 4–1.

Conference Semifinals

EASTERN CONFERENCE

April 23	Montreal	0	at Tampa Bay	4
April 25	Montreal	1	at Tampa Bay	3
April 27	Tampa Bay	4	at Montreal	3*
April 29	Tampa Bay	3	at Montreal	1

Tampa Bay won series 4–0.

April 22	Toronto	1	at Philadelphia	3
April 25	Toronto	1	at Philadelphia	2
April 28	Philadelphia	1	at Toronto	4
April 30	Philadelphia	1	at Toronto	3
May 2	Toronto	2	at Philadelphia	7
May 4	Philadelphia	3	at Toronto	2*

Philadelphia won series 4–2.

WESTERN CONFERENCE

April 22	Calgary	2	at Detroit	1*
April 24	Calgary	2	at Detroit	5
April 27	Detroit	2	at Calgary	3
April 29	Detroit	4	at Calgary	2
May 1	Calgary	1	at Detroit	0
May 3	Detroit	0	at Calgary	1

Calgary won series 4–2.

April 22	Colorado	2	at San Jose	5
April 24	Colorado	1	at San Jose	4
April 26	San Jose	1	at Colorado	0
April 28	San Jose	0	at Colorado	1*
May 1	Colorado	2	at San Jose	1*
May 4	San Jose	3	at Colorado	1

San Jose won series 4–2.

Eastern Finals

May 8	Philadelphia	1	at Tampa Bay	3
May 10	Philadelphia	6	at Tampa Bay	2
May 13	Tampa Bay	4	at Philadelphia	1
May 15	Tampa Bay	2	at Philadelphia	3
May 18	Philadelphia	2	at Tampa Bay	4
May 20	Tampa Bay	4	at Philadelphia	5*
May 22	Philadelphia	1	at Tampa Bay	2

Tampa Bay won series 4–3.

Western Finals

May 9	Calgary	4	at San Jose	3*
May 11	Calgary	4	at San Jose	1
May 13	San Jose	3	at Calgary	0
May 16	San Jose	4	at Calgary	2
May 17	Calgary	3	at San Jose	0
May 19	San Jose	1	at Calgary	3

Calgary won series 4–2.

Stanley Cup Finals

May 25	Calgary	4	at Tampa Bay	1
May 27	Calgary	1	at Tampa Bay	4
May 29	Tampa Bay	0	at Calgary	3
May 31	Tampa Bay	1	at Calgary	0
June 3	Calgary	3	at Tampa Bay	2*
June 5	Tampa Bay	3	at Calgary	2†
June 7	Calgary	1	at Tampa Bay	2

Tampa Bay won series 4–3.

*Overtime game. †Double overtime game.

Game 1

Calgary	1	2	1—4
Tampa Bay	0	0	1—1

FIRST PERIOD

Scoring: 1, Calgary, Martin Gelinas 7 (Craig Conroy, Andrew Ference), 3:02. Penalties: S Yelle, Cgy (int), 11:32; P Kubina, TB (holding), 18:52.

SECOND PERIOD

Scoring: 2, Calgary, Jarome Iginla 11 (shorthanded) (Unassisted), 15:21. 3, Calgary, Stephane Yelle 3 (Unassisted), 18:08. Penalties: R Regehr, Cgy (holding), 9:22; A Ference, Cgy (hooking), 14:48.

THIRD PERIOD

Scoring: 4, Tampa Bay, Martin St. Louis 6 (power play) (Brad Richards, Dan Boyle), 4:13. 5, Calgary, Chris Simon 4 (power play) (Oleg Saprykin, Robyn

THIRD PERIOD (CONT.)

Regehr), 19:40. Penalties: V Nieminen, Cgy (roughing), 3:05; S Donovan, Cgy (roughing), 4:30; C Stillman, TB (roughing), 4:30; A Roy, TB (roughing), 4:30; O Saprykin, Cgy (unsportsmanlike cond), 7:55; R Fedotenko, TB (roughing), 17:50; M St. Louis, TB (high sticking), 19:06.

Shots on goal: CGY 5-10-4—19; TB 10-8-6—24

Power-play opportunities: CGY:1 of 4, TB 1 of 5.

Goalies: Cgy, Miikka Kiprusoff (24 shots, 23 saves). TB, Nikolai Khabibulin (19 shots, 15 saves).

Referees: McCreary, Walkom. Linesmen: Murphy, Driscoll. A: 21,674.

Game 2

Calgary	0	0	1—1
Tampa Bay	1	0	3—4

FIRST PERIOD

Scoring: 1, Tampa Bay, Ruslan Fedotenko 10 (Jassen Cullimore, Vincent Lecavalier), 7:10. Penalties: A Roy, TB (interference), 2:00; D Afanasenkov, TB (boarding), 7:58; D Lowry, Cgy (obstruction hooking), 10:21; V Lecavalier, Tam (high sticking), 13:33; S Donovan, Cgy (holding), 15:04; Bench, Tam (too many men; served by D Afanasenkov), 16:59.

SECOND PERIOD

Scoring: None. Penalties: F Modin, Tam (obstr hooking), 0:53; O Saprykin, Cgy (goalie interference), 19:22.

THIRD PERIOD

Scoring: 2, Tampa Bay, Brad Richards 9 (Dave Andreychuk, Martin St. Louis), 2:51. 3, Tampa Bay, Dan Boyle 2 (Brad Richards, Fredrik Modin), 4:00. 4, Tampa Bay, Martin St. Louis 7 (power play) (Vincent Lecavalier, Dave Andreychuk), 5:58. 5, Calgary, Ville Nieminen 4 (power play) (Shean Donovan, Robyn Regehr), 12:21. Penalties: S Yelle, Cgy (cross

THIRD PERIOD (CONT.)

checking), 0:37; C Kobasew, Cgy (roughing), 5:50; C Clark, Cgy (roughing), 5:50; B Richards, TB (roughing), 5:50; C Stillman, Tam (major fighting), 5:50; D Boyle, TB (roughing), 5:50; C Simon, Cgy (cross checking), 5:50; A Ference, Cgy (unsportsmanlike cond, fighting major), 5:50; A Roy, TB (major fighting), 8:31; C Dingman, Tam (double minor roughing, misconduct, game misconduct), 8:31; C Simon, Cgy (instigator, fighting major, misconduct), 8:31; T Taylor, Tam (holding), 10:35; C Kobasew, Cgy (interference), 14:27; R Regehr, Cgy (holding), 15:13; M Gelinas, Cgy (cross checking, game misconduct), 19:48; C Kobasew, Cgy (misconduct), 20:00; P Kubina, Tam (misconduct), 20:00.

Shots on goal: Cgy 6-9-4—19; TB 8-10-13—31

Power-play opportunities: CGY 1 of 7, TB 1 of 9.

Goalies: Cgy, Miikka Kiprusoff (31 shots, 27 saves). TB, Nikolai Khabibulin (19 shots, 18 saves).

Referees: Watson, Walkom. Linesmen: Murphy, Scapinello. A: 22,222.

Game 3

Tampa Bay	0	0	0—0
Calgary	0	2	1—3

FIRST PERIOD

Scoring: None. Penalties: M Gelinas, Cgy (elbowing), 0:21; B Lukowich, Tam (cross checking), 3:50; V Lecavalier, Tam (major fighting), 6:17; J Iginla, Cgy (major fighting), 6:17; C Clark, Cgy (tripping), 7:10; D Boyle, Tam (hooking), 9:36; M Gelinas, Cgy (holding stick), 17:03.

SECOND PERIOD

Scoring: 1, Calgary, Chris Simon 5 (power play) (Jarome Iginla, Jordan Leopold), 13:53. 2, Calgary, Shean Donovan 5 (Unassisted), 17:09. Penalties: B Lukowich, Tam (slashing), 13:03.

THIRD PERIOD

Scoring: 3, Calgary, Jarome Iginla 12 (power play) (Robyn Regehr, Chris Simon), 18:28. Penalties: S Donovan, Cgy (holding), 4:05; C Sarich, Tam (slashing), 17:23; C Sarich, TB (misconduct), 19:16.

Shots on goal: TB 5-6-10—21; Cgy 2-12-4—18

Power-play opportunities: TB 0 of 4, Cgy 2 of 4.

Goalies: Tampa Bay, Nikolai Khabibulin (18 shots, 15 saves). Cgy Miikka Kiprusoff (21 shots, 21 saves).

Referees: McCreary, Fraser. Linesmen: Wheler, Driscoll. A: 19,221.

Game 4

Tampa Bay	1	0	0—1
Calgary	0	0	0—0

FIRST PERIOD

Scoring: 1, Tampa Bay, Brad Richards 10 (power play) (Dave Andreychuk, Dan Boyle), 2:48. Penalties: C Clark, Cgy (cross checking), 1:52; M Commodore, Cgy (holding), 1:52; V Lecavalier, TB (tripping), 7:50; D Afanasenkov, Tam (elbowing), 12:52; C Kobasew, Cgy (holding), 16:40.

SECOND PERIOD

Scoring: None. Penalties: K Oliwa, Cgy (holding), 5:07.

THIRD PERIOD

Scoring: None. Penalties: V Nieminen, Cgy (major boarding, game misconduct), 15:47.

Shots on goal: TB 12-7-5—24; Cgy 12-5-12—29.

Power-play opportunities: TB 1 of 5, Cgy 0 of 2.

Goalies: TB, N. Khabibulin (29 shots, 29 saves). Cgy, M. Kiprusoff (24 shots, 23 saves). Referees: Watson, Fraser. Linesmen: Murphy, Wheler. A: 19,221.

Game 5

```
Calgary ..............1    1    0    1 —3
Tampa Bay .........1    0    1    0 —2
```

FIRST PERIOD

Scoring: 1, Calgary, Martin Gelinas 8 (power play) (Toni Lydman, Steve Montador) 2:13. 2, Tampa Bay, Martin St. Louis 8 (Martin Cibak, Chris Dingman),19:26. Penalties: F Modin, TB (high sticking), 1:43; D Lowry, Cgy (interference), 8:41; A Roy, TB (roughing), 13:18.

SECOND PERIOD

Scoring: 3, Calgary, Jarome Iginla 13 (Unassisted), 5:10.

THIRD PERIOD

Scoring: 4, Tampa Bay, Fredrik Modin 8 (power play) (Brad Richards, Dave Andreychuk)0:37. Penalties: R Warrener, Cgy (holding stick), 0:31.

OVERTIME

Scoring: 5, Calgary, Oleg Saprykin 3 (Jarome Iginla, Marcus Nilson),14:40.

Shots on goal: Cgy 11-14-4-7—36; TB 9-3-8-8—28

Power-play Opportunities: Cgy 1 of 2, TB 1 of 2.

Goalies : Cgy, Miikka Kiprusoff (28 shots, 26 saves).

Tampa Bay, Nikolai Khabibulin (36 shots, 33 saves).

Referees: Bill McCreary, Stephen Walkom. Linesmen: Ray Scapinello, Scott Driscoll. A: 22,426.

Game 6

```
Tampa Bay .........0    2    0    0    1 —3
Calgary ...............0    2    0    0    0 —2
```

FIRST PERIOD

Scoring: None. Penalties: D Andreychuk, Tam (elbowing), 11:59; A Ference, Cgy (hooking), 11:59; C Sarich, Tam (interference), 16:34; R Fedotenko, Tam (interference), 19:01.

SECOND PERIOD

Scoring: 1, Tampa Bay, Brad Richards 11 (power play) (Martin St. Louis, Ruslan Fedotenko) 4:17. 2, Calgary, Chris Clark 3 (Stephane Yelle, Ville Nieminen), 9:05. 3, Tampa Bay, Brad Richards 12 (power play) (Unassisted)10:52. 4, Calgary, Marcus Nilson 4 (Oleg Saprykin, Andrew Ference),17:49. Penalties: J Leopold, Cgy (interference), 2:34; C Conroy, Cgy (obstruction hooking), 9:25.

THIRD PERIOD

Scoring: None. Penalties: C Conroy, Cgy (hooking), 0:45; C Simon, Cgy (cross checking), 8:38; J Cullimore, Tam (interference), 11:18.

OVERTIME

Scoring: None. Penalties: None.

SECOND OVERTIME

Scoring: 5, Tampa Bay, Martin St. Louis 9 (Tim Taylor, Jassen Cullimore),0:33.

Shots on goal: TB 6-5-7-7-2—27; Cgy 6-13-7-7-0—33

Power-play opportunities: TB 2 of 4, Cgy 0 of 3.

Goalies : TB, Nikolai Khabibulin (33 shots, 31 saves). Cgy, Miikka Kiprusoff (27 shots, 24 saves).

Referees: McCreary, Walkom. Linesmen: Wheler, Scapinello. A: 19,221.

Game 7

```
Calgary .............0    0    1 —1
Tampa Bay .......1    1    0 —2
```

FIRST PERIOD

Scoring: 1, Tampa Bay, Ruslan Fedotenko 11 (power play) (Brad Richards, Fredrik Modin), 13:31. Penalties: M Nilson, Cgy (slashing), 1:10; O Saprykin, Cgy (tripping), 11:59; J Cullimore, TB (int.), 19:42.

SECOND PERIOD

Scoring: 2, Tampa Bay, Ruslan Fedotenko 12 (Vincent Lecavalier, Cory Stillman), 14:38. Penalties: M Gelinas, Cgy (boarding), 4:16; C Clark, Cgy (tripping), 18:46.

THIRD PERIOD

Scoring: 3, Calgary, Craig Conroy 6 (power play) (Jordan Leopold), 9:21. Penalties: N Pratt, Tam (interference), 8:50; A Ference, Cgy (charging), 18:59; D Andreychuk, Tam (tripping), 19:37.

Shots on goal: Cgy 3-4 -10—17; TB 6-4-5—15

Power-play opportunities: Cgy 1 of 2; TB 1 of 5.

Goalies : Calgary, Miikka Kiprusoff (15 shots, 13 saves). Tampa Bay, Nikolai Khabibulin (17 shots, 16 saves).

Referees: McCreary, Fraser. Linesmen: Murphy, Wheler. A: 22,717.

Individual Playoff Leaders

Scoring

POINTS

Player and Team	GP	G	A	Pts	+/–	PM	Player and Team	GP	G	A	Pts	+/–	PM
Brad Richards, TB	23	12	14	26	5	4	V. Damphousse, SJ	17	7	7	14	0	20
Martin St. Louis, TB	23	9	15	24	6	14	Dave Andreychuk, TB	23	1	13	14	-2	14
Jarome Iginla, Cgy	26	13	9	22	13	45	Jeremy Roenick, Phil	18	4	9	13	4	8
Fredrik Modin, TB	23	8	11	19	7	10	Patrick Marleau, SJ	17	8	4	12	0	6
Craig Conroy, Cgy	26	6	11	17	12	12	Joe Sakic, Col	11	7	5	12	0	8
Vincent Lecavalier, TB	23	9	7	16	-2	25	Marcus Nilson, Cgy	26	4	7	11	0	12
Keith Primeau, Phil	18	9	7	16	11	22	Peter Forsberg, Col	11	4	7	11	6	12
Martin Gelinas, Cgy	26	8	7	15	10	35	Saku Koivu, Mtl	11	3	8	11	1	10
Alexei Zhamnov, Phil	18	4	10	14	-1	8							
Ruslan Fedotenko, TB	22	12	2	14	0	14							

GOALS

Player and Team	GP	G
Jarome Iginla, Cgy	26	13
Brad Richards, TB	23	12
Ruslan Fedotenko, TB	22	12
Martin St. Louis, TB	23	9
Vincent Lacavalier, TB	23	9
Keith Primeau, Phil	18	9

GAME-WINNING GOALS

Player and Team	GP	GW
Brad Richards, TB	23	7

Six tied with 3.

POWER PLAY GOALS

Player and Team	GP	PP
Brad Richards, TB	23	7
Ruslan Fedotenko, TB	22	5
Jarome Iginla, Cgy	26	4
Patrick Marleau, SJ	17	4
Chris Simon, Cgy	16	4

SHORT-HANDED GOALS

Player and Team	GP	SH
Jarome Iginla, Cgy	26	2
Keith Primeau, Phil	18	2

ASSISTS

Player and Team	GP	A
Martin St. Louis, TB	23	15
Brad Richards, TB	23	14
Dave Andreychuk, TB	23	13
Fredrik Modin, TB	23	11
Craig Conroy, Cgy	26	11

PLUS/MINUS

Player and Team	GP	+/−
Jarome Iginla, Cgy	26	13
Craig Conroy, Cgy	26	12
Keith Primeau, Phil	18	11
Martin Gelinas, Cgy	26	10
Simon Gagne, Phil	18	10

Goaltending (Minimum 420 minutes)

GOALS AGAINST AVERAGE

Player and Team	GP	W - L -T	Avg
Curtis Joseph, Det	9	4- 4- 0	1.39
N. Khabibulin, TB	23	16- 7- 0	1.71
Evgeni Nabokov, SJ	17	10- 7- 0	1.71
Miikka Kiprusoff, Cgy	26	15-11- 0	1.85
David Aebischer, Col	11	6- 5- 0	2.08

SAVE PERCENTAGE

Player and Team	GP	W-L-T	GAA	GA	SV	SV%	SA
Curtis Joseph, Det	9	4-4-0	1.39	12	185	.939	197
E. Nabokov, SJ	17	10-7-0	1.71	30	431	.935	461
N. Khabibulin, TB	23	16-7-0	1.71	40	558	.933	598
Ed Belfour, Tor	13	6-7-0	2.09	27	352	.929	379
M. Kiprusoff, Cgy	26	15-11-0	1.85	51	659	.928	710

NHL Awards

Award	Player and Team	Award	Player and Team
Hart Trophy (MVP)	Martin St. Louis, TB	Selke Trophy (top defensive forward)	Kris Draper, Det
Calder Trophy (top rookie)	Andrew Raycroft, Bos	Jennings Trophy (goaltender on club allowing fewest goals)	Martin Brodeur, NJ
Vezina Trophy (top goaltender)	Martin Brodeur, NJ	Conn Smythe Trophy (playoff MVP)	Brad Richards, TB
Norris Trophy (top defenseman)	Scott Niedermayer, NJ		
Lady Byng Trophy (for gentlemanly play)	Brad Richards, TB		
Adams Award (top coach)	John Tortorella, TB		

Individual Regular Season Leaders

Scoring
POINTS

Player and Team	GP	G	A	Pts	+/−	PM
Martin St. Louis, TB	82	38	56	94	35	24
Ilya Kovalchuk, Atl	81	41	46	87	-10	63
Joe Sakic, Col	81	33	54	87	11	42
Markus Naslund, Van	78	35	49	84	24	58
Marian Hossa, Ott	81	36	46	82	4	46
Patrik Elias, NJ	82	38	43	81	26	44
Daniel Alfredsson, Ott	77	32	48	80	12	24
Cory Stillman, TB	81	25	55	80	18	36
Robert Lang, Det	69	30	49	79	4	24
Alex Tanguay, Col	69	25	54	79	30	42
Brad Richards, TB	82	26	53	79	14	12
Mats Sundin, Tor	81	31	44	75	11	52
Mark Recchi, Phil	82	26	49	75	18	47
Milan Hejduk, Col	82	35	40	75	19	20
Jaromir Jagr, NYR	77	31	43	74	-5	38
Jarome Iginla, Cgy	81	41	32	73	21	84
Joe Thornton, Bos	77	23	50	73	18	98
Steve Sullivan, Nash	80	24	49	73	1	48
Keith Tkachuk, StL	75	33	38	71	8	83
Scott Gomez, NJ	80	14	56	70	18	70

GOALS

Player and Team	GP	G
Jarome Iginla, Cgy	81	41
Rick Nash, Clb	80	41
Ilya Kovalchuk, Atl	81	41
Martin St. Louis, TB	82	38
Patrik Elias, NJ	82	38

POWER PLAY GOALS

Player and Team	GP	PP
Rick Nash, Clb	80	19
Keith Tkachuk, StL	75	18
Milan Hejduk, Col	82	16
Ilya Kovalchuk, Atl	81	16

GAME-WINNING GOALS

Player and Team	GP	GW
Mats Sundin, Tor	81	10
Bill Guerin, Dal	82	10
Jarome Iginla, Cgy	81	10
Richard Zednik, Mon	81	9
Glen Murray, Bos	81	9
Patrik Elias, NJ	82	9
J. Cheechoo, SJ	81	9

SHORT-HANDED GOALS

Player and Team	GP	SHG
Martin St. Louis, TB	82	8
Kris Draper, Det	67	5
Kevyn Adams, Car	73	5

ASSISTS

Player and Team	GP	A
Scott Gomez, NJ	80	56
Martin St. Louis, TB	82	56
Cory Stillman, TB	81	55
Alex Tanguay, Col	69	54
Joe Sakic, Col	81	54
Brad Richards, TB	82	53

PLUS/MINUS

Player and Team	GP	+/−
Martin St. Louis, TB	82	35
Marek Malik, Van	78	35
Zdeno Chara, Ott	79	33
Fredrik Modin, TB	82	31
Nils Ekman, SJ	82	30
Alex Tanguay, Col	69	30

Goaltending
(Minimum 25 games)

GOALS AGAINST AVERAGE

Player and Team	GP	W-L-T	GAA	TGA
Miikka Kiprusoff, Cgy	...38	24-10-4	1.70	65
Dwayne Roloson, Minn.	.48	19-18-11	1.88	89
Marty Turco, Dall	...73	37-21-13	1.98	144
Martin Brodeur, NJ	...75	38-26-11	2.03	154
Robert Esche, Phil	40	21-11-7	2.04	79

SAVE PERCENTAGE

Player and Team	GP	W-L-T	GA	SA	Pct
Miikka Kiprusoff, Cgy	...38	24-10-4	65	966	.933
D. Roloson, Minn	48	19-18-11	89	1323	.933
Roberto Luongo, Fla	..72	25-33-14	172	2475	.931
Vesa Toskala, SJ	28	12-8-4	53	760	.930
A. Raycroft, Bos	57	29-18-9	117	1586	.926

WINS

Player and Team	GP	GAA	W	L	T
Martin Brodeur, NJ	75	2.03	38	26	11
Marty Turco, Dall	73	1.98	37	21	13
Tomas Vokoun, Nash	73	2.53	34	29	10
Ed Belfouor, Tor	59	2.13	34	19	6
Jose Theodore, Mtl	67	2.27	33	28	5
Dan Cloutier, Van	60	2.27	33	21	6

SHUTOUTS

Player and Team	GP	W	L	T	SO
Martin Brodeur, NJ	75	38	26	11	11
Ed Belfour, Tor	59	34	19	6	10
Evgeni Nabokov, SJ	59	31	19	8	9
Marty Turco, Dall	73	37	21	13	9
Roberto Luongo, Fla	72	25	33	14	7

NHL Team-by-Team Statistical Leaders

Anaheim Mighty Ducks
SCORING

Player	GP	G	A	Pts	+/-	PM
Sergei Fedorov, C	80	31	34	65	-5	2
Vaclav Prospal, LW	82	19	35	54	-9	54
Petr Sykora, RW	81	23	29	52	-9	34
Steve Rucchin, C	82	20	23	43	-14	12
Joffrey Lupul, C	75	13	21	34	-6	28
Andy McDonald, LW	79	9	21	30	-13	24
Rob Niedermayer, C	55	12	16	28	-6	34
Niclas Havelid, D	79	6	20	26	-28	28
Samuel Pahlsson, C	82	8	14	22	-2	52
Stanislav Chistov, LW	56	2	16	18	-16	26
Jason Krog, LW	80	6	12	18	-4	16
Vitaly Vishnevski, D	...73	6	10	16	0	51
Sandis Ozolinsh, D	36	5	11	16	-7	24
Ruslan Salei, D	82	4	11	15	-1	110
Martin Skoula, D	21	2	7	9	3	2
Todd Simpson, D	46	4	3	7	-6	105
Keith Carney, D	69	2	5	7	-5	42
Chris Kunitz, LW	21	0	6	6	1	12
Kurt Sauer, D	55	1	4	5	-8	32
Lance Ward, D	46	0	4	4	-1	94
Mike Leclerc, LW	10	1	3	4	-1	4
Cam Severson, LW	31	3	0	3	-3	50
Garrett Burnett, LW	39	1	2	3	0	184
Craig Johnson, LW	39	1	2	3	-4	14
Tony Martensson, C	6	1	1	2	-2	0
Mikael Holmqvist, C	21	2	0	2	-6	25
Petr Schastlivy, LW	22	2	0	2	-3	4
JS Giguere, G	55	0	2	2	0	4

GOALTENDING

Player	GP	Mins	W	L	T	Avg	SO
J.S. Giguere	55	3210	17	31	6	2.62	3
Martin Gerber	32	1698	11	12	4	2.26	2
Ilya Bryzgalov	1	60	1	0	0	1.98	0

Atlanta Thrashers
SCORING

Player	GP	G	A	Pts	+/-	PM
Ilya Kovalchuk, LW	81	41	46	87	-10	63
S. McEachern, RW	82	17	38	55	5	76
Marc Savard, C	45	19	33	52	-8	85
Slava Kozlov, LW	76	20	32	52	-12	74
Patrik Stefan, C	82	14	26	40	-7	26
Randy Robitaille, C	69	11	26	37	-12	20
R. Petrovicky, RW	78	16	15	31	-9	123
Frantisek Kaberle, D	...67	3	26	29	2	30
Dany Heatley, RW	31	13	12	25	-8	18
Serge Aubin, LW	66	10	15	25	0	73
Jeff Cowan, LW	58	9	15	24	2	68
Andy Sutton, D	65	8	13	21	0	94
Daniel Tjarnqvist, D	68	5	15	20	-4	20
J.P. Vigier, RW	70	10	8	18	-18	22
Garnet Exelby, D	71	1	9	10	-10	134
Ivan Majesky, D	63	3	7	10	-7	76
Yannick Tremblay, D	38	2	8	10	-13	13
Chris Tamer, D	38	2	5	7	-9	55
J.L. Grand-Pierre, RW	...27	2	2	4	-7	26
Shawn Heins, D	17	0	4	4	-1	16
Ben Simon, C	52	3	0	3	-10	2
Tommi Santala, C	33	1	2	3	-7	22
Zdenek Blatny, LW	16	3	0	3	0	6
Francis Lessard, RW	62	1	1	2	-5	181
Pasi Nurminen, G	64	0	2	2	0	35
Kyle Rossiter, D	2	0	1	1	1	0
Derek MacKenzie, C	...12	0	1	1	0	10
Kamil Piros, RW	14	0	1	1	-3	4

GOALTENDING

Player	GP	Mins	W	L	T	Avg	SO
Pasi Nurminen	64	3738	25	30	7	2.78	3
Kari Lehtonen	4	240	4	0	0	1.25	1
Byron Dafoe	16	973	4	11	1	3.15	0

Boston Bruins
SCORING

Player	GP	G	A	Pts	+/-	PM
Joe Thornton, C	77	23	50	73	18	98
Glen Murray, RW	81	32	28	60	17	56
Brian Rolston, C	82	19	29	48	9	40
Mike Knuble, RW	82	21	25	46	19	32
S. Samsonov, LW	58	17	23	40	12	4
Patrice Bergeron, C	71	16	23	39	5	22
Nick Boynton, D	81	6	24	30	17	98
Dan McGillis, D	80	5	23	28	-1	65
Martin Lapointe, RW	78	15	10	25	-5	67
P.J. Axelsson, LW	68	6	14	20	2	42
Jiri Slegr, D	36	4	15	19	5	27
Travis Green, C	64	11	5	16	-6	67
Jeff Jillson, D	50	4	10	14	-1	35
Michael Nylander, C	15	1	11	12	3	14
Sean O'Donnell, D	82	1	10	11	10	110
Ted Donato, LW	63	6	5	11	2	18
Hal Gill, D	82	2	7	9	16	99
Sergei Gonchar, D	15	4	5	9	6	12
Rob Zamuner, LW	57	4	5	9	3	16
Shaone Morrisonn, D	30	1	7	8	10	10
Ian Moran, D	35	1	4	5	3	28
Michal Grosek, LW	33	3	2	5	1	33
Sandy McCarthy, RW	37	3	1	4	0	28
Craig MacDonald, C	18	0	3	3	0	8
Andy Hilbert, C	18	2	0	2	1	9
Carl Corazzini, C	12	2	0	2	2	0
Andrew Raycroft, G	57	0	2	2	0	0
Sergei Zinovjev, C	10	0	1	1	1	2
Doug Doull, LW	35	0	1	1	2	132

GOALTENDING

Player	GP	Mins	W	L	T	Avg	SO
Andrew Raycroft	57	3420	29	18	9	2.05	3
Felix Potvin	28	1605	12	8	6	2.50	4

Buffalo Sabres
SCORING

Player	GP	G	A	Pts	+/-	PM
Daniel Briere, C	82	28	37	65	-7	70
Miroslav Satan, RW	82	29	28	57	-15	30
Chris Drury, C	76	18	35	53	8	68
J.P. Dumont, RW	77	22	31	53	-9	40
Jochen Hecht, LW	64	15	37	52	17	49
Dmitri Kalinin, D	77	10	24	34	0	42
M. Afinogenov, RW	73	17	14	31	-4	57
Alexei Zhitnik, D	68	4	24	28	-13	102
Ales Kotalik, RW	62	15	11	26	-1	41
Curtis Brown, C	68	9	12	21	2	30
Taylor Pyatt, LW	63	8	12	20	-7	25
Adam Mair, C	81	6	14	20	-3	146
Derek Roy, C	49	9	10	19	-8	12
Chris Taylor, C	54	6	6	12	-2	22
Rory Fitzpatrick, D	60	4	7	11	-5	44
James Patrick, D	55	4	7	11	11	12
Brian Campbell, D	53	3	8	11	-8	12
Henrik Tallinder, D	72	1	9	10	5	26
Milan Bartovic, RW	23	1	8	9	1	18
Mike Grier, RW	14	1	8	9	10	4
Andy Delmore, D	37	2	5	7	-5	29
Jay McKee, D	43	2	3	5	6	41
Jeff Jillson, D	14	0	3	3	-3	19
Eric Boulton, LW	44	1	2	3	-2	110
Jason Botterill, LW	19	2	1	3	0	14
Andrew Peters, LW	42	2	0	2	-3	151
Brad Brown, D	13	0	2	2	3	12
Martin Biron, G	52	0	2	2	0	10
Mika Noronen, G	35	1	0	1	0	0

GOALTENDING

Player	GP	Mins	W	L	T	Avg	SO
Martin Biron	52	2972	26	18	5	2.52	2
Mika Noronen	35	1796	11	17	2	2.57	2
Ryan Miller	3	178	0	3	0	5.06	0

Calgary Flames
SCORING

Player	GP	G	A	Pts	+/-	PM
Jarome Iginla, RW	81	41	32	73	21	84
Craig Conroy, C	63	8	39	47	13	44
Shean Donovan, RW	82	18	24	42	14	72
Martin Gelinas, LW	76	17	18	35	10	70
Jordan Leopold, D	82	9	24	33	8	24
D. McAmmond, C	64	17	13	30	9	18
Steve Reinprecht, C	44	7	22	29	1	4
M. Lombardi, C	79	16	13	29	4	32
Oleg Saprykin, LW	69	12	17	29	1	41
Chris Clark, RW	82	10	15	25	-3	106
Toni Lydman, D	67	4	16	20	6	30
Robyn Regehr, D	82	4	14	18	14	74
Stephane Yelle, C	53	4	13	17	1	24
Chuck Kobasew, RW	70	6	11	17	-12	51
Rhett Warrener, D	77	3	14	17	8	97
Andrew Ference, D	72	4	12	16	5	53

SCORING *(CONT.)*

Player	GP	G	A	Pts	+/-	PM
Denis Gauthier, D	80	1	15	16	4	113
Ville Nieminen, LW	19	3	5	8	6	18
Josh Green, LW	36	2	4	6	-3	24
Marcus Nilson, LW	14	5	0	5	3	14
Chris Simon, LW	13	3	2	5	1	25
Krzysztof Oliwa, LW	65	3	2	5	-8	247

GOALTENDING

Player	GP	Mins	W	L	T	Avg	SO
Miikka Kiprusoff	38	2301	24	10	4	1.70	4
J. McLennan	26	1446	12	9	3	2.20	4
Roman Turek	18	1031	6	11	0	2.33	3
Dany Sabourin	4	169	0	3	0	3.56	0

Carolina Hurricanes
SCORING

Player	GP	G	A	Pts	+/-	PM
Josef Vasicek, C	82	19	26	45	-3	60
Erik Cole, LW	80	18	24	42	-4	93
Sean Hill, D	80	13	26	39	-2	84
Rod Brind'Amour, C	78	12	26	38	0	28
Jeff O'Neill, RW	67	14	20	34	-12	607
Eric Staal, C	81	11	20	31	-6	40
Ron Francis, C	68	10	20	30	-12	14
Radim Vrbata, RW	80	12	13	25	-10	24
Bret Hedican, D	81	7	17	24	-10	64
Kevyn Adams, C	73	10	12	22	6	43
Justin Williams, RW	32	5	13	18	2	32
Craig Adams, RW	80	7	10	17	-5	69
Danny Markov, D	44	4	10	14	-6	37
Marty Murray, C	66	5	7	12	6	8
Niclas Wallin, D	57	3	7	10	-8	51
Aaron Ward, D	49	3	5	8	1	37
Pavel Brendl, RW	18	5	3	8	0	8
Jesse Boulerice, RW	76	6	1	7	-5	127
Glen Wesley, D	74	0	6	6	18	32
Ryan Bayda, LW	44	3	3	6	-14	22
Bob Boughner, D	43	0	5	5	-9	80
J. Svoboda, RW	33	3	1	4	3	6

GOALTENDING

Player	GP	Mins	W	L	T	Avg	SO
Kevin Weekes	66	3765	23	30	11	2.33	6
Arturs Irbe	10	564	5	2	1	2.45	0
Jamie Storr	14	660	0	8	2	2.91	0

Colorado Avalanche
SCORING

Player	GP	G	A	Pts	+/-	PM
Joe Sakic, C	81	33	54	87	11	2
Alex Tanguay, LW	69	25	54	79	30	42
Milan Hejduk, RW	82	35	40	75	19	20
Peter Forsberg, C	39	18	37	55	16	30
Rob Blake, D	74	13	33	46	6	61
S. Konowalchuk, LW	76	19	20	39	2	70
Paul Kariya, LW	51	11	25	36	-5	22
John-Michael Liles, D	79	10	24	34	7	28
Teemu Selanne, RW	78	16	16	32	2	32
Adam Foote, D	73	8	22	30	13	87
Derek Morris, D	69	6	22	28	4	47
Martin Skoula, D	58	2	14	16	2	30
Karlis Skrastins, D	82	5	8	13	18	26
Steve Moore, C	57	5	7	12	-5	37
Andrei Nikolishin, C	49	5	7	12	3	24
Dan Hinote, RW	59	4	7	11	-6	57
Matthew Barnaby, RW	13	4	5	9	3	37
Travis Brigley, LW	36	3	4	7	0	10
Cody McCormick, C	44	2	3	5	-4	73
Brad Larsen, LW	26	2	2	4	2	11
Peter Worrell, LW	49	3	1	4	2	179
D. Hendrickson, C	20	1	3	4	-8	6
Jim Cummins, RW	55	1	2	3	-5	147

GOALTENDING

Player	GP	Mins	W	L	T	Avg	SO
David Aebischer	62	3703	32	19	9	2.09	4
Philippe Sauve	17	986	7	7	3	3.04	0
Tommy Salo	5	304	1	3	1	2.37	0

Chicago Blackhawks
SCORING

Player	GP	G	A	Pts	+/-	PM
Tyler Arnason, C	82	22	33	55	-13	16
Bryan Berard, D	58	13	34	47	-24	53
Mark Bell, LW	82	21	24	45	-14	106
Tuomo Ruutu, C	82	23	21	44	-31	58
Steve Sullivan, RW	56	15	28	43	-7	36
Kyle Calder, LW	66	21	18	39	-18	29
Brett McLean, C	76	11	20	31	-11	54
Nathan Dempsey, D	58	8	17	25	-5	30
Alexei Zhamnov, C	23	6	12	18	-8	14
Scott Nichol, C	75	7	11	18	-16	145
Igor Korolev, C	62	3	10	13	-15	22
Ville Nieminen, LW	60	2	11	13	-15	40
S. Robidas, D	45	2	10	12	6	33
Jim Vandermeer, D	23	2	10	12	-6	58
Eric Daze, LW	19	4	7	11	-7	0
Deron Quint, D	51	4	7	11	-26	18
Igor Radulov, LW	36	4	7	11	-2	18
Mikhail Yakubov, C	30	1	7	8	-12	8
A. Karpovtsev, D	24	0	7	7	-17	14
Travis Moen, LW	82	4	2	6	-17	142
Burke Henry, D	23	2	4	6	0	24
VandenBussche, RW	65	4	1	5	-10	120

GOALTENDING

Player	GP	Mins	W	L	T	Avg	SO
Craig Anderson	21	1205	6	14	0	2.84	1
Michael Leighton	34	1988	6	18	8	2.99	2
Jocelyn Thibault	14	821	5	7	2	2.85	1
Steve Passmore	9	478	2	6	0	2.89	0
Adam Munro	7	426	1	5	1	3.66	0

Columbus Blue Jackets
SCORING

Player	GP	G	A	Pts	+/-	PM
Rick Nash, LW	80	41	16	57	-35	87
David Vyborny, RW	82	22	31	53	-26	40
Todd Marchant, C	77	9	25	34	-17	34
Nikolai Zherdev, RW	57	13	21	34	-11	54
Trevor Letowski, RW	73	15	17	32	-12	16
Geoff Sanderson, LW	67	13	16	29	-9	34
Anders Eriksson, D	66	7	20	27	-6	18
Andrew Cassels, C	58	6	20	26	-24	26
Manny Malhotra, C	56	12	13	25	-5	24
Jaroslav Spacek, D	58	5	17	22	-13	45
Tyler Wright, RW	68	9	9	18	-19	63
Darryl Sydor, D	49	2	13	15	-19	26
Rostislav Klesla, D	47	2	11	13	-16	27
Lasse Pirjeta, C	57	2	8	10	-6	20
Derrick Walser, D	27	1	8	9	-6	22
Aaron Johnson, D	29	2	6	8	-2	32
Alexander Svitov, C	29	2	6	8	-8	16
Duvie Westcott, D	34	0	7	7	-15	39
Luke Richardson, D	64	1	5	6	-11	48
Jody Shelley, LW	76	3	3	6	-10	228
Scott Lachance, D	77	0	4	4	-23	44
Mark Hartigan, C	9	1	3	4	-2	6
Espen Knutsen, C	14	0	4	4	-5	2
Kent McDonell, RW	29	1	2	3	-7	36
Tim Jackman, RW	19	1	2	3	-7	16
David Ling, RW	50	1	2	3	-3	98

GOALTENDING

Player	GP	Mins	W	L	T	Avg	SO
Marc Denis	66	3796	21	36	7	2.56	5
Fred Brathwaite	21	1050	4	11	1	3.37	0
Pascal Leclaire	2	119	0	2	0	3.52	0

Dallas Stars

SCORING

Player	GP	G	A	Pts	+/-	PM
Bill Guerin, RW	82	34	35	69	14	109
Jason Arnott, C	73	21	36	57	23	66
Brenden Morrow, LW	81	25	24	49	10	121
Mike Modano, C	76	14	30	44	-21	46
Sergei Zubov, D	77	7	35	42	0	20
Pierre Turgeon, C	76	15	25	40	17	20
Stu Barnes, C	77	11	18	29	7	18
Jere Lehtinen, RW	58	13	13	26	0	20
Philippe Boucher, D	70	8	16	24	15	64
Rob DiMaio, RW	69	9	15	24	2	52
R. Matvichuk, D	75	1	20	21	0	36
Teppo Numminen, D	62	3	14	17	-5	18
Scott Young, RW	53	8	8	16	-15	14
Steve Ott, C	73	2	10	12	-2	152
David Oliver, RW	36	7	5	12	6	12
Don Sweeney, D	63	0	11	11	22	18
Shayne Corson, LW	17	5	5	10	12	29
Valeri Bure, RW	13	2	5	7	3	6
Trevor Daley, D	27	1	5	6	-6	14
Jon Klemm, D	58	2	4	6	10	24
Niko Kapanen, C	67	1	5	6	-15	16
Aaron Downey, RW	37	1	1	2	2	77

GOALTENDING

Player	GP	Mins	W	L	T	Avg	SO
Marty Turco	73	4359	37	21	13	1.98	9
Ron Tugnutt	11	548	3	7	0	2.41	1
Dan Ellis	1	60	1	0	0	3.00	0

Detroit Red Wings

SCORING

Player	GP	G	A	Pts	+/-	PM
Brett Hull, RW	81	25	43	68	-4	2
Pavel Datsyuk, C	75	30	38	68	-2	35
B Shanahan, LW	82	25	28	53	15	117
Steve Yzerman, C	75	18	33	51	10	46
Mathieu Schneider, D	78	14	32	46	22	56
Ray Whitney, LW	67	14	29	43	7	22
Henrik Zetterberg, LW	61	15	28	43	15	14
Kris Draper, C	67	24	16	40	22	31
Nicklas Lidstrom, D	81	10	28	38	19	18
Kirk Maltby, LW	79	14	19	33	24	80
Tomas Holmstrom, LW	67	15	15	30	8	38
Steve Thomas, RW	44	10	12	22	8	25
Chris Chelios, D	69	2	19	21	12	61
Jiri Fischer, D	81	4	15	19	0	75
Jason Woolley, D	55	4	15	19	19	28
Boyd Devereaux, C	61	6	9	15	-1	20
Jason Williams, C	49	6	7	13	1	15
Mathieu Dandenault, D	65	3	9	12	9	40
Mark Mowers, RW	52	3	8	11	3	4
Darren McCarty, RW	43	6	5	11	2	50
Jamie Rivers, D	50	3	4	7	9	41
Niklas Kronwall, D	20	1	4	5	5	16
Robert Lang, C	6	1	4	5	2	0
Derian Hatcher, D	15	0	4	4	4	8
Jiri Hudler, C	12	1	2	3	-1	10
Dominik Hasek, G	14	0	2	2	0	2

GOALTENDING

Player	GP	Mins	W	L	T	Avg	SO
Manny Legace	41	2325	23	10	5	2.12	3
Curtis Joseph	31	1708	16	10	3	2.39	2
Dominik Hasek	14	817	8	3	2	2.20	2
Marc Lamothe	2	125	1	0	1	1.45	0

Edmonton Oilers

SCORING

Player	GP	G	A	Pts	+/-	PM
Ryan Smyth, LW	82	23	36	59	11	70
Radek Dvorak, RW	78	15	35	50	18	26
Mike York, C	61	16	26	42	18	15
Shawn Horcoff, C	80	15	25	40	0	73
Ales Hemsky, RW	71	12	22	34	-7	14
Raffi Torres, LW	80	20	14	34	12	65
Ethan Moreau, LW	81	20	12	32	7	96
F. Pisani, RW	76	16	14	30	14	46
Steve Staios, D	82	6	22	28	17	8
M.A. Bergeron, D	54	9	17	26	13	26
Eric Brewer, D	77	7	18	25	-6	67
Cory Cross, D	68	7	14	21	9	56
Jarret Stoll, C	68	10	11	21	8	42
Jason Smith, D	68	7	12	19	13	98
Igor Ulanov, D	42	5	13	18	19	28

Player	GP	G	A	Pts	+/-	PM
Adam Oates, C	60	2	16	18	0	8
Brad Isbister, LW	51	10	8	18	-2	54
G. Laraque, RW	66	6	11	17	7	99
Petr Nedved, C	16	5	10	15	1	4
Jason Chimera, LW	60	4	8	12	-1	57
Marty Reasoner, C	17	2	6	8	5	10
Scott Ferguson, D	52	1	5	6	-5	80
Alexei Semenov, D	46	2	3	5	8	32

GOALTENDING

Player	GP	Mins	W	L	T	Avg	SO
Ty Conklin	38	2086	17	14	4	2.42	1
Tommy Salo	44	2487	17	18	6	2.58	3
Jussi Markkanen	7	394	2	2	2	1.83	0
S. Valiquette	1	14	0	0	0	8.65	0

Florida Panthers

SCORING

Player	GP	G	A	Pts	+/–	PM
Olli Jokinen, C	82	26	32	58	-16	81
Valeri Bure, RW	55	20	25	45	0	20
Mike Van Ryn, D	79	13	24	37	-16	52
Kristian Huselius, LW	76	10	21	31	-6	24
Stephen Weiss, C	50	12	17	29	-10	10
Viktor Kozlov, RW	48	11	16	27	-4	16
Juraj Kolnik, RW	53	14	11	25	-7	14
Niklas Hagman, LW	75	10	13	23	-5	22
Nathan Horton, C	55	14	8	22	-5	57
Jay Bouwmeester, D	61	2	18	20	-15	30
Matt Cullen, C	56	6	13	19	-2	24
Marcus Nilson, LW	69	6	13	19	-9	26
Lyle Odelein, D	82	4	12	16	-7	88
Pavel Trnka, D	67	3	13	16	2	51
Donald Audette, RW	28	6	7	13	-9	22
Mathieu Biron, D	57	3	10	13	-13	51
Byron Ritchie, C	50	5	6	11	-10	84
M. Samuelsson, RW	37	3	6	9	0	35
Vaclav Nedorost, C	32	4	3	7	-6	12
Lukas Krajicek, D	18	1	6	7	-2	12
Andreas Lilja, D	79	3	4	7	-8	90
Branislav Mezei, D	45	0	7	7	-4	80
Eric Beaudoin, LW	30	2	4	6	-6	12
I. Novoseltsev, RW	17	1	4	5	-6	8

GOALTENDING

Player	GP	Mins	W	L	T	Avg	SO
Roberto Luongo	72	4252	25	33	14	2.43	7
Steve Shields	16	732	3	6	1	3.44	0

Los Angeles Kings

SCORING

Player	GP	G	A	Pts	+/–	PM
Luc Robitaille, LW	80	22	29	51	4	56
A. Frolov, LW	77	24	24	48	8	24
Trent Klatt, RW	82	17	26	43	2	46
Zigmund Palffy, RW	35	16	25	41	18	12
Jozef Stumpel, C	64	8	29	37	5	16
Derek Armstrong, C	57	14	21	35	4	33
Eric Belanger, C	81	13	20	33	-16	44
Jaroslav Modry, D	79	5	27	32	11	44
L. Visnovsky, D	58	8	21	29	8	26
Sean Avery, C	76	9	19	28	2	261
Joe Corvo, D	72	8	17	25	7	36
Ian Laperriere, RW	62	10	12	22	-4	58
M. Cammalleri, C	31	9	6	15	1	20
Martin Straka, C	32	6	8	14	-9	4
Mattias Norstrom, D	74	1	13	14	-3	44
Jon Sim, LW	48	6	7	13	0	27
Scott Barney, RW	19	5	6	11	3	4
Esa Pirnes, C	57	3	8	11	-9	12
Brad Chartrand, LW	53	3	4	7	-3	30
Nathan Dempsey, D	17	4	3	7	-7	2
Tim Gleason, D	47	0	7	7	1	21
Jason Holland, D	52	3	3	6	5	24
John Tripp, RW	34	1	5	6	-4	33
Tomas Zizka, D	15	2	3	5	-4	12

GOALTENDING

Player	GP	Mins	W	L	T	Avg	SO
R. Cechmanek	49	2701	18	21	6	2.51	5
Cristobal Huet	41	2199	10	16	10	2.43	3
Milan Hnilicka	2	80	0	1	0	3.76	0

Minnesota Wild

SCORING

Player	GP	G	A	Pts	+/–	PM
A. Daigle, RW	78	20	31	51	4	14
A. Brunette, LW	82	15	34	49	3	12
M. Gaborik, RW	65	18	22	40	10	20
Sergei Zholtok, C	59	13	16	29	4	19
Pascal Dupuis, LW	59	11	15	26	5	20
Antti Laaksonen, LW	77	12	14	26	0	20
Richard Park, RW	73	13	12	25	0	28
Wes Walz, C	57	12	13	25	5	32
Jim Dowd, C	55	4	20	24	6	38
Filip Kuba, D	77	5	19	24	-7	28
P.M. Bouchard, LW	61	4	18	22	-7	22
Marc Chouinard, C	45	11	10	21	4	17
Andrei Zyuzin, D	65	8	13	21	4	48
Jason Wiemer, C	62	7	11	18	-6	106
Nick Schultz, D	79	6	10	16	12	16
Willie Mitchell, D	70	1	13	14	12	83
S. Veilleux, LW	19	2	8	10	0	20
Rickard Wallin, C	15	5	4	9	1	14
C. Brandner, LW	35	4	5	9	-2	8
Matt Johnson, LW	57	7	1	8	4	177
Eric Chouinard, RW	31	3	4	7	-7	6
Brent Burns, RW	36	1	5	6	-10	12
Alex Henry, D	71	2	4	6	4	106
Jason Marshall, D	12	1	4	5	-1	18

GOALTENDING

Player	GP	Mins	W	L	T	Avg	SO
D. Roloson	48	2847	19	18	11	1.88	5
M. Fernandez	37	2166	11	14	9	2.49	2

Montreal Canadiens

SCORING

Player	GP	G	A	Pts	+/–	PM
Mike Ribeiro, LW	81	20	45	65	15	34
Michael Ryder, RW	81	25	38	63	10	26
Saku Koivu, C	68	14	41	55	-5	52
Richard Zednik, RW	81	26	24	50	5	63
Sheldon Souray, D	63	15	20	35	4	104
Yanic Perreault, C	69	16	15	31	-10	40
Patrice Brisebois, D	71	4	27	31	17	22
Jan Bulis, C	72	13	17	30	-8	30
Andrei Markov, D	69	6	22	28	-2	20
Pierre Dagenais, LW	50	17	10	27	15	24
Niklas Sundstrom, RW	66	8	12	20	3	18
Francis Bouillon, D	73	2	16	18	1	70
Joe Juneau, C	70	5	10	15	-4	20
Steve Begin, C	52	10	5	15	6	41
Craig Rivet, D	80	4	8	12	-1	98
Jason Ward, RW	53	5	7	12	3	21
Andreas Dackell, RW	60	4	8	12	8	10
Stephane Quintal, D	73	3	5	8	10	82
Donald Audette, RW	23	3	5	8	-4	16
Jim Dowd, C	14	3	2	5	6	6
Chad Kilger, LW	36	2	2	4	2	14
Mike Komisarek, D	46	0	4	4	4	34
Jose Theodore, G	67	0	3	3	0	4
Alexei Kovalev, RW	12	1	2	3	-4	12
Darren Langdon, LW	64	0	3	3	-2	135

GOALTENDING

Player	GP	Mins	W	L	T	Avg	SO
Jose Theodore	67	3961	33	28	5	2.27	6
Mathieu Garon	19	1003	8	6	2	2.27	0

Nashville Predators

SCORING

Player	GP	G	A	Pts	+/–	PM
Scott Walker, RW	75	25	42	67	4	94
Marek Zidlicky, D	82	14	39	53	-16	82
Martin Erat, LW	76	16	33	49	10	38
David Legwand, C	82	18	29	47	9	46
Kimmo Timonen, D	77	12	32	44	-7	52
Vladimir Orszagh, RW	82	16	21	37	-4	74
Scott Hartnell, LW	59	18	15	33	-5	87
Greg Johnson, C	82	14	18	32	-21	33
Steve Sullivan, RW	24	9	21	30	8	12
A. Johansson, LW	47	12	15	27	-2	26
Adam Hall, RW	79	13	14	27	-8	37
Dan Hamhuis, D	80	7	19	26	-12	57
Denis Arkhipov, C	72	9	12	21	-2	22
Rem Murray, C	39	8	9	17	-1	12
Jason York, D	67	2	13	15	-4	64
Mark Eaton, D	75	4	9	13	16	26
J. Stevenson, LW	53	5	4	9	-2	103
A.Hutchinson, D	18	4	4	8	1	4
Jordin Tootoo, RW	70	4	4	8	-6	137
Jim McKenzie, LW	61	1	3	4	-13	88
Wyatt Smith, C	18	3	1	4	2	2
Jamie Allison, D	47	0	3	3	-7	76
Robert Schnabel, D	20	0	3	3	6	34

GOALTENDING

Player	GP	Mins	W	L	T	Avg	SO
Tomas Vokoun	73	4221	34	29	10	2.53	3
Chris Mason	17	744	4	4	1	2.18	1

New Jersey Devils

SCORING

Player	GP	G	A	Pts	+/–	PM
Patrik Elias, LW	82	38	43	81	26	44
Scott Gomez, C	80	14	56	70	18	70
Scott Niedermayer, D	81	14	40	54	20	44
Jeff Friesen, LW	81	17	20	37	8	26
Brian Rafalski, D	69	6	30	36	6	24
John Madden, C	80	12	23	35	7	22
Sergei Brylin, C	82	14	19	33	10	20
Brian Gionta, RW	75	21	8	29	19	36
T. Stevenson, RW	61	14	13	27	0	76
Jay Pandolfo, LW	82	13	13	26	5	14
J.Langenbrunner, RW	53	10	16	26	-9	43
Paul Martin, D	70	6	18	24	12	4
Grant Marshall, RW	65	8	7	15	-9	67
Colin White, D	75	2	11	13	10	96
Erik Rasmussen, C	69	7	6	13	5	41
Scott Stevens, D	38	3	9	12	3	22
Igor Larionov, C	49	1	10	11	3	20
Michael Rupp, RW	51	6	5	11	-1	41
Jan Hrdina, C	13	1	6	7	4	10
Viktor Kozlov, RW	11	2	4	6	0	2
C. Berglund, LW	23	2	3	5	-4	4
David Hale, D	65	0	4	4	12	72
Tommy Albelin, D	45	1	3	4	7	4

GOALTENDING

Player	GP	Mins	W	L	T	Avg	SO
Martin Brodeur	75	4555	38	26	11	2.03	11
S. Clemmensen	4	238	3	1	0	1.01	2
Corey Schwab	3	187	2	0	1	0.64	1

New York Islanders

SCORING

Player	GP	G	A	Pts	+/–	PM
Trent Hunter, RW	77	25	26	51	23	16
Oleg Kvasha, LW	81	15	36	51	4	48
M. Czerkawski, RW	81	25	24	49	8	16
Jason Blake, LW	75	22	25	47	11	56
Adrian Aucoin, D	81	13	31	44	29	54
Michael Peca, C	76	11	29	40	17	71
Mark Parrish, RW	59	24	11	35	8	18
Alexei Yashin, C	47	15	19	34	-1	10
Shawn Bates, LW	69	9	23	32	-8	46
Kenny Jonsson, D	79	5	24	29	25	22
Roman Hamrlik, D	81	7	22	29	2	68
Janne Niinimaa, D	82	9	19	28	12	64
Dave Scatchard, C	61	9	16	25	12	78
Arron Asham, RW	79	12	12	24	-12	92
Cliff Ronning, C	40	9	15	24	3	2
M. Weinhandl, RW	55	8	12	20	9	26
Justin Papineau, C	64	8	5	13	4	8
Eric Cairns, D	72	2	6	8	-5	189
Radek Martinek, D	47	4	3	7	-9	43
Sven Butenschon, D	41	1	6	7	-3	30
Justin Mapletoft, C	27	1	4	5	-1	6

GOALTENDING

Player	GP	Mins	W	L	T	Avg	SO
Rick DiPietro	50	2844	23	18	5	2.36	5
Garth Snow	39	2015	14	15	5	2.80	1
W. Dubielewicz	2	105	1	0	1	1.72	0

New York Rangers

SCORING

Player	GP	G	A	Pts	+/–	PM
Bobby Holik, C	82	25	31	56	4	96
Mark Messier, C	76	18	25	43	3	42
Alexei Kovalev, RW	66	13	29	42	-5	54
Martin Rucinsky, LW	69	13	29	42	13	62
Brian Leetch, D	57	13	23	36	-5	24
Matthew Barnaby, RW	69	12	20	32	15	120
Eric Lindros, C	39	10	22	32	7	60
Petr Nedved, C	65	14	17	31	-9	42
Jaromir Jagr, RW	31	15	14	29	-1	12
Jan Hlavac, LW	72	5	21	26	-8	16
Tom Poti, D	67	10	14	24	-1	47
Chris Simon, LW	65	14	9	23	14	225
Vladimir Malakhov, D	56	3	15	18	-5	53
Anson Carter, RW	43	10	7	17	-12	14
Boris Mironov, D	75	3	13	16	1	86\
Greg de Vries, D	53	3	12	15	12	37
Darius Kasparaitis, D	44	1	9	10	11	48
Jamie Lundmark, C	56	2	8	10	-8	33
Joel Bouchard, D	28	1	7	8	2	10
Dan LaCouture, LW	59	5	2	7	-13	82
Fedor Tyutin, D	25	2	5	7	-4	14
Jed Ortmeyer, RW	58	2	4	6	-10	16
Jozef Balej, RW	13	1	4	5	0	4
Josh Green, LW	14	3	2	5	0	8

GOALTENDING

Player	GP	Mins	W	L	T	Avg	SO
Mike Dunham	57	3148	16	30	6	3.03	2
Jussi Markkanen	26	1244	8	12	1	2.56	2
Jason Labarbera	4	198	1	2	0	4.84	0
S. Valiquette	2	120	1	1	0	3.00	0
Jamie McLennan	4	244	1	3	0	2.96	0

Ottawa Senators

SCORING

Player	GP	G	A	Pts	+/-	PM
Marian Hossa, RW	81	36	46	82	4	46
Daniel Alfredsson, RW	77	32	48	80	12	24
Martin Havlat, RW	68	31	37	68	12	46
Jason Spezza, C	78	22	33	55	22	71
Bryan Smolinski, C	80	19	27	46	22	49
Radek Bonk, C	66	12	32	44	2	66
Wade Redden, D	81	17	26	43	21	65
Zdeno Chara, D	79	16	25	41	33	147
Peter Schaefer, LW	81	15	24	39	22	26
Todd White, C	53	9	20	29	12	22
Chris Phillips, D	82	7	16	23	15	46
Josh Langfeld, RW	38	7	10	17	6	16
Karel Rachunek, D	60	1	16	17	17	29
Chris Neil, RW	82	8	8	16	13	194
Antoine Vermette, LW	57	7	7	14	5	16
Peter Bondra, RW	23	5	9	14	1	16
Shaun Van Allen, C	73	2	10	12	6	80
Vaclav Varada, LW	30	5	5	10	2	26
Mike Fisher, C	24	4	6	10	-3	39
Brian Pothier, D	55	2	6	8	6	24
Petr Schastlivy, LW	43	2	4	6	-1	14
Curtis Leschyshyn, D	56	1	4	5	13	16
Shane Hnidy, D	37	0	5	5	2	72

GOALTENDING

Player	GP	Mins	W	L	T	Avg	SO
Patrick Lalime	57	3324	25	23	7	2.29	5
Martin Prusek	29	1528	16	6	3	2.12	3
Ray Emery	3	126	2	0	0	2.38	0

Philadelphia Flyers

SCORING

Player	GP	G	A	Pts	+/-	PM
Mark Recchi, LW	82	26	49	75	18	47
Michal Handzus, C	82	20	38	58	18	82
John LeClair, LW	75	23	32	55	20	51
Tony Amonte, RW	80	20	33	53	13	38
Jeremy Roenick, C	62	19	28	47	1	62
Simon Gagne, LW	80	24	21	45	12	29
Kim Johnsson, D	80	13	29	42	16	26
Sami Kapanen, RW	74	12	18	30	9	14
Joni Pitkanen, D	71	8	19	27	15	44
Justin Williams, RW	47	6	20	26	10	32
Keith Primeau, C	54	7	15	22	11	80
Alexei Zhamnov, C	20	5	13	18	7	14
M. Ragnarsson, D	70	7	9	16	12	58
Radovan Somik, LW	53	4	10	14	-2	17
Donald Brashear, LW	64	6	7	13	-1	212
Eric Desjardins, D	48	1	11	12	11	28
Chris Therien, D	56	1	9	10	2	50
Mike Comrie, C	21	4	5	9	2	12
Eric Weinrich, D	54	2	7	9	11	32
B. Radivojevic, RW	24	1	8	9	0	36
Claude Lapointe, C	42	5	3	8	2	32
Patrick Sharp, C	41	5	2	7	-3	55

GOALTENDING

Player	GP	Mins	W	L	T	Avg	SO
Robert Esche	40	2322	21	11	7	2.04	3
Jeff Hackett	27	1630	10	10	6	2.39	3
Sean Burke	15	825	6	5	2	2.55	1
Antero Niittymaki	3	180	3	0	0	1.00	0

Phoenix Coyotes

SCORING

Player	GP	G	A	Pts	+/-	PM
Shane Doan, LW	79	27	41	68	-11	47
Ladislav Nagy, LW	55	24	28	52	11	46
Daymond Langkow, C	81	21	31	52	4	40
Paul Mara, D	81	6	36	42	-11	48
Chris Gratton, C	68	11	18	29	-19	93
Jan Hrdina, C	55	11	15	26	-10	30
Brian Savage, LW	61	12	13	25	-5	36
B. Radivojevic, RW	53	9	14	23	-5	36
Radoslav Suchy, D	82	7	14	21	1	8
Cale Hulse, D	82	3	17	20	-4	123
Jeff Taffe, C	59	8	10	18	-8	20
Daniel Cleary, RW	68	6	11	17	-8	42
Mike Comrie, C	28	8	7	15	-8	16
Mike Sillinger, C	60	8	6	14	-14	54
Fredrik Sjostrom, RW	57	7	6	13	-7	22
David Tanabe, D	45	5	7	12	4	22
Krystofer Kolanos, C	41	4	6	10	-9	24
Mike Johnson, RW	11	1	9	10	-1	10
Tyson Nash, LW	69	3	5	8	-6	110
Ossi Vaananen, D	67	2	4	6	-10	87
Brad Ference, D	63	0	5	5	-19	103
Landon Wilson, RW	35	1	3	4	-3	16
Derek Morris, D	14	0	4	4	-5	2

GOALTENDING

Player	GP	Mins	W	L	T	Avg	SO
Sean Burke	32	1795	10	15	5	2.81	1
Brian Boucher	40	2364	10	19	10	2.74	5
J.M. Pelletier	4	175	1	1	0	4.12	0
Brent Johnson	8	486	1	6	1	2.59	0
Zac Bierk	4	190	0	1	2	3.79	0

Pittsburgh Penguins
SCORING

Player	GP	G	A	Pts	+/–	PM
Dick Tarnstrom, D	80	16	36	52	-37	38
Aleksey Morozov, RW	75	16	34	50	-24	24
Ryan Malone, LW	81	22	21	43	-23	64
Milan Kraft, C	66	19	21	40	-22	18
Rico Fata, RW	73	16	18	34	-46	54
Konstantin Koltsov, LW	82	9	20	29	-30	30
Ric Jackman, D	25	7	17	24	-5	14
Tomas Surovy, LW	47	11	12	23	-8	16
Tom Kostopoulos, RW	60	9	13	22	-14	67
Drake Berehowsky,D	47	5	16	21	-16	50
Brian Holzinger, C	61	6	15	21	-27	38
Mike Eastwood, C	82	4	15	19	-18	40
Matt Bradley, RW	82	7	9	16	-27	65
Martin Strbak, D	44	3	11	14	-11	38
Lasse Pirjeta, C	13	6	6	12	3	0
Martin Straka, C	22	4	8	12	-16	16
Eric Meloche, RW	25	3	7	10	-6	20
Brooks Orpik, D	79	1	9	10	-36	127
Marc Bergevin, D	52	1	8	9	-8	27
Mario Lemieux, C	10	1	8	9	-2	6
Josef Melichar, D	82	3	5	8	-17	62
Patrick Boileau, D	16	3	4	7	-16	8
Landon Wilson, RW	19	5	1	6	0	31
Jon Sim, LW	16	2	3	5	-4	6
Ramzi Abid, LW	16	3	2	5	-5	27
Dan Focht, D	52	2	3	5	-23	105
Kelly Buchberger, C	71	1	3	4	-19	109

Player	GP	Mins	W	L	T	Avg	SO
Sebastien Caron	40	2213	9	24	5	3.74	1
J.S. Aubin	22	1067	7	9	0	2.98	1
M.A. Fleury	21	1154	4	14	2	3.64	1
Andy Chiodo	8	486	3	4	1	3.46	0
Martin Brochu	1	33	0	0	0	1.84	0

St. Louis Blues
SCORING

Player	GP	G	A	Pts	+/–	PM
Keith Tkachuk, LW	75	33	38	71	8	83
Doug Weight, C	75	14	51	65	-3	37
Pavol Demitra, C	68	23	35	58	1	18
Chris Pronger, D	80	14	40	54	-1	88
Dallas Drake, RW	79	13	22	35	10	65
Scott Mellanby, RW	68	14	17	31	-7	76
Petr Cajanek, C	70	12	14	26	12	16
Mark Rycroft, RW	71	9	12	21	2	32
Christian Backman, D	66	5	13	18	3	16
Eric Nickulas, RW	44	7	11	18	-2	44
Mike Danton, C	68	7	5	12	-8	141
Ryan Johnson, C	69	4	7	11	-2	8
Jamal Mayers, RW	80	6	5	11	-19	91
Eric Boguniecki, RW	27	6	4	10	-1	20
Mike Sillinger, C	16	5	5	10	4	14
A. Khavanov, D	48	3	7	10	2	18
Eric Weinrich, D	26	2	8	10	1	14
Bryce Salvador, D	69	3	5	8	-4	47
Brian Savage, LW	13	4	3	7	-3	2
Murray Baron, D	80	1	5	6	-6	61
Pascal Rheaume, C	25	1	3	4	-3	4
Peter Sejna, LW	20	2	2	4	-9	4
Jeff Heerema, RW	22	1	2	3	-5	4
Barret Jackman, D	15	1	2	3	-1	41

GOALTENDING

Player	GP	Mins	W	L	T	Avg	SO
Chris Osgood	67	3861	31	25	8	2.24	3
Reinhard Divis	13	629	4	4	2	2.76	0
Brent Johnson	10	493	4	3	1	2.43	1

San Jose Sharks
SCORING

Player	GP	G	A	Pts	+/–	PM
Patrick Marleau, C	80	28	29	57	-5	24
Nils Ekman, LW	82	22	33	55	30	34
Alyn McCauley, C	82	20	27	47	23	28
J. Cheechoo, RW	81	28	19	47	5	33
Marco Sturm, LW	64	21	20	41	0	36
V. Damphousse, C	82	12	29	41	-5	66
Brad Stuart, D	77	9	30	39	9	34
Alex Korolyuk, LW	63	19	18	37	20	18
Wayne Primeau, C	72	9	20	29	4	90
Scott Thornton, LW	80	13	14	27	-6	84
Mike Ricci, C	71	7	19	26	8	40
Niko Dimitrakos, RW	68	9	15	24	6	49
Kyle McLaren, D	64	2	22	24	10	60
Scott Hannan, D	82	6	15	21	10	48
Mike Rathje, D	80	2	17	19	18	46
Tom Preissing, D	69	2	17	19	8	12
Christian Ehrhoff, D	41	1	11	12	4	14
Todd Harvey, RW	47	4	5	9	3	38
Scott Parker, RW	50	1	3	4	0	101
Mark Smith, C	36	1	3	4	-5	72
Curtis Brown, C	12	2	2	4	1	6
Rob Davison, D	55	0	3	3	-3	92

GOALTENDING

Player	GP	Mins	W	L	T	Avg	SO
Evgeni Nabokov	59	3456	31	19	8	2.21	9
Vesa Toskala	28	1541	12	8	4	2.06	1

Tampa Bay Lightning
SCORING

Player	GP	G	A	Pts	+/-	PM
Martin St. Louis, RW	82	38	56	94	35	24
Cory Stillman, LW	81	25	55	80	18	36
Brad Richards, C	82	26	53	79	14	12
Vincent Lecavalier, C	...81	32	34	66	23	52
Fredrik Modin, LW	82	29	28	57	31	32
Dan Boyle, D,	78	9	30	39	23	60
Ruslan Fedotenko, RW...	77	17	22	39	14	30
Dave Andreychuk, LW...82		21	18	39	-9	42
Pavel Kubina, D	81	17	18	35	9	85
Tim Taylor, C	82	7	15	22	-5	25
Cory Sarich, D	82	3	16	19	5	89
Brad Lukowich, D	79	5	14	19	29	24
D. Afanasenkov, LW.....71		6	10	16	-4	12
Ben Clymer, RW	66	2	8	10	5	50
Martin Cibak, C	63	2	7	9	-1	30
Darryl Sydor, D	31	1	6	7	3	6
Jassen Cullimore, D.....79		2	5	7	8	58
Shane Willis, RW	12	0	6	6	1	2
Chris Dingman, LW.....74		1	5	6	-9	140
Nolan Pratt, D	58	1	3	4	11	42

GOALTENDING

Player	GP	Mins	W	L	T	Avg	SO
N. Khabibulin	55	3274	28	19	7	2.33	3
John Grahame	29	1688	18	9	1	2.06	1

Toronto Maple Leafs
SCORING

Player	GP	G	A	Pts	+/-	PM
Mats Sundin, C	81	31	44	75	.11	52
Bryan McCabe, D	75	16	37	53	22	86
Joe Nieuwendyk, C.....64		22	28	50	7	26
Gary Roberts, LW	72	28	20	48	9	84
Owen Nolan, RW	65	19	29	48	4	110
Darcy Tucker, RW	64	21	11	32	4	68
Nik Antropov, C	62	13	18	31	7	62
Tomas Kaberle, D	71	3	28	31	16	18
Robert Reichel, C	69	11	19	30	2	30
A. Mogilny, RW	37	8	22	30	9	12
Ken Klee, D	66	4	25	29	-1	36
A Ponikarovsky, LW....73		9	19	28	14	44
Matthew Stajan, C.....69		14	13	27	7	22
Mikael Renberg,RW....59		12	13	25	-1	50
Tie Domi, RW	80	7	13	20	-2	208
Karel Pilar, D	50	2	17	19	2	22
Tom Fitzgerald, RW......69		7	10	17	-2	52
Brian Leetch, D	15	2	13	15	11	10
Ron Francis, C	12	3	7	10	3	0
Aki Berg, D	79	2	7	9	-1	40
Ric Jackman, D	29	2	4	6	-11	13
Calle Johansson, D.......8		0	6	6	5	0
Bryan Marchment, D...75		1	3	4	4	106
Harold Druken, C	9	0	4	4	4	2

GOALTENDING

Player	GP	Mins	W	L	T	Avg	SO
Ed Belfour	59	3444	34	19	6	2.13	10
Trevor Kidd	15	883	6	5	2	3.26	1
Mikael Tellqvist	11	647	5	3	2	2.87	0

Vancouver Canucks
SCORING

Player	GP	G	A	Pts	+/-	PM
Markus Naslund, LW....78		35	49	84	24	58
Todd Bertuzzi, RW	69	17	43	60	21	122
Brendan Morrison, C ...82		22	38	60	16	50
Daniel Sedin, LW	82	18	36	54	18	18
Brent Sopel, D	80	10	32	42	11	36
Henrik Sedin, LW	76	11	31	42	23	32
Trevor Linden, C	82	14	22	36	-6	26
Mattias Ohlund, D.........82		14	20	34	14	73
Sami Salo, D	74	7	19	26	8	22
Ed Jovanovski, D	56	7	16	23	2	64
Matt Cooke, C	53	11	12	23	5	73
Jason King, RW	47	12	9	21	0	8
Marek Malik, D	78	3	16	19	35	45
Artem Chubarov, C 65		12	7	19	1	14
Mike Keane, LW	64	9	9	17	7	20
Magnus Arvedson, LW...41		8	7	15	7	12
Jarkko Ruutu, LW	71	6	8	14	-13	133
Brad May, LW	70	5	6	11	-2	137
Geoff Sanderson, LW...13		3	4	7	-1	4
Bryan Allen, D	74	2	5	7	-10	94
Jiri Slegr, D	16	2	5	7	6	8
Ryan Kesler, C	28	2	3	5	-2	16
Nolan Baumgartner, D ...9		0	3	3	3	2
Tyler Bouck, RW	18	1	2	3	-4	23
Martin Rucinsky, LW ...13		1	2	3	2	10

GOALTENDING

layer	GP	Mins	W	L	T	Avg	SO
Dan Cloutier	60	3539	33	21	6	2.27	5
Johan Hedberg	21	1098	8	6	2	2.51	3
Alexander Auld	6	349	2	2	2	2.06	0

Washington Capitals
SCORING

Player	GP	G	A	Pts	+/-	PM
Robert Lang, C	63	29	45	74	2	24
Sergei Gonchar, D	56	7	42	49	-20	44
Jeff Halpern, C	79	19	27	46	-21	56
Jaromir Jagr, RW	46	16	29	45	-4	26
Peter Bondra, RW	54	21	14	35	-17	22
Kip Miller, LW	66	9	22	31	-10	8
Dainius Zubrus, RW.....54		12	15	27	-16	38
Alexander Semin, LW...52		10	12	22	-2	36
Mike Grier, RW	68	8	12	20	-19	32
Brian Willsie, RW	49	10	5	15	-7	18
Josef Boumedienne, D...37		2	12	14	-10	30
Brendan Witt, D	72	2	10	12	-22	123
Matt Pettinger, LW	71	7	5	12	-9	37
Joel Kwiatkowski, D 80		6	6	12	-28	89
Jason Doig, D	65	2	9	11	-12	105
Trent Whitfield, C	44	6	5	11	-2	14
Anson Carter, RW	19	5	5	10	2	6
Bates Battaglia, LW	66	4	6	10	-23	38
Boyd Gordon, RW	41	1	5	6	-9	8
Craig Johnson, LW	15	0	6	6	-6	8
Rick Berry, D	65	0	6	6	-5	108
Stephen Peat, RW	64	5	0	5	-10	90

GOALTENDING

Player	GP	Mins	W	L	T	Avg	SO
Olaf Kolzig	63	3738	19	35	9	2.89	2
Maxime Ouellet	6	365	2	3	1	3.12	1
Rastislav Stana	6	211	1	2	0	3.12	0
Matt Yeats	5	258	1	3	0	3.03	0
S. Charpentier	7	369	0	6	0	3.41	0

First Round

The opening round of the 2004 NHL draft was held on June 26 in Raleigh, NC.

Team	Selection	Position	Team	Selection	Position
1.....Washington	Alexander Ovechkin	F	16...NY Islanders	Petteri Nokelainen	F
2.....Pittsburgh	Evgeni Malkin	F	17...St. Louis	Marek Schwarz	G
3.....Chicago	Cam Barker	D	18...Montreal	Kyle Chipchura	F
4.....Carolina	Andrew Ladd	F	19...NY Rangers	Lauri Korpikoski	F
5.....Phoenix	Blake Wheeler	F	20...New Jersey	Travis Zajac	F
6.....NY Rangers	Al Montoya	G	21...Colorado	Wojtek Wolski	F
7.....Florida	Rostislav Olesz	F	22...San Jose	Lukas Kaspar	F
8.....Columbus	Alexandre Picard	F	23...Ottawa	Andrej Meszaros	D
9.....Anaheim	Ladislav Smid	D	24...Calgary	Kris Chucko	F
10...Atlanta	Boris Valabik	D	25...Edmonton	Robbie Schremp	F
11...Los Angeles	Lauri Tukonen	F	26...Vancouver	Cory Schneider	G
12...Minnesota	A.J. Thelen	D	27...Washington	Jeff Schultz	D
13...Buffalo	Drew Stafford	F	28...Dallas	Mark Fistric	D
14...Edmonton	Devan Dubnyk	G	29...Washington	Mike Green	D
15...Nashville	Alexander Radulov	F	30...Tampa Bay	Andy Rogers	D

FOR THE RECORD · Year by Year

The Stanley Cup

Awarded annually to the team that wins the NHL's best-of-seven final-round playoffs. The Stanley Cup is the oldest trophy competed for by professional athletes in North America. It was donated in 1893 by Frederick Arthur, Lord Stanley of Preston.

Results

1892–93.....Montreal A.A.A.	1900–01.....Winnipeg Victorias	1907–08.....Montreal Wanderers
1893–94.....Montreal A.A.A.	1901–02.....Winnipeg Victorias (Jan)	1908–09.....Ottawa Senators
1894–95.....Montreal Victorias	1901–02.....Montreal A.A.A. (Mar)	1909–10.....Montreal Wanderers
1895–96.....Winnipeg Victorias (Feb)	1902–03.....Montreal A.A.A. (Feb)	1910–11.....Ottawa Senators
1895–96.....Montreal Victorias (Dec)	1902–03.....Ottawa Silver Seven (Mar)	1911–12.....Quebec Bulldogs
1896–97.....Montreal Victorias	1903–04.....Ottawa Silver Seven	1912–13.....Quebec Bulldogs
1897–98.....Montreal Victorias	1904–05.....Ottawa Silver Seven	1913–14.....Toronto Blueshirts
1898–99.....Montreal Victorias (Feb)	1905–06.....Ottawa Silver Seven (Feb)	1914–15.....Vancouver Millionaires
1898–99.....Montreal Shamrocks (Mar)	1905–06.....Montreal Wanderers (Mar)	1915–16.....Montreal Canadiens
1899–1900...Montreal Shamrocks	1906–07.....Kenora Thistles (Jan)	1916–17.....Seattle Metropolitans
	1906–07.....Montreal Wanderers (Mar)	

NHL WINNERS AND FINALISTS

Season	Champion	Finalist	GP in Final
1917–18.....................Toronto Arenas		Vancouver Millionaires	5
1918–19.....................No decision*		No decision*	5
1919–20.....................Ottawa Senators		Seattle Metropolitans	5
1920–21.....................Ottawa Senators		Vancouver Millionaires	5
1921–22.....................Toronto St. Pats		Vancouver Millionaires	5
1922–23.....................Ottawa Senators		Vancouver Maroons, Edmonton Eskimos	2, 4
1923–24.....................Montreal Canadiens		Vancouver Maroons, Calgary Tigers	2, 2
1924–25.....................Victoria Cougars		Montreal Canadiens	4
1925–26.....................Montreal Maroons		Victoria Cougars	4
1926–27.....................Ottawa Senators		Boston Bruins	4
1927–28.....................New York Rangers		Montreal Maroons	5
1928–29.....................Boston Bruins		New York Rangers	2
1929–30.....................Montreal Canadiens		Boston Bruins	2
1930–31.....................Montreal Canadiens		Chicago Blackhawks	5
1931–32.....................Toronto Maple Leafs		New York Rangers	3
1932–33.....................New York Rangers		Toronto Maple Leafs	4
1933–34.....................Chicago Blackhawks		Detroit Red Wings	4
1934–35.....................Montreal Maroons		Toronto Maple Leafs	3

NHL WINNERS AND FINALISTS *(CONT.)*

Season	Champion	Finalist	GP in Final
1935–36	Detroit Red Wings	Toronto Maple Leafs	4
1936–37	Detroit Red Wings	New York Rangers	5
1937–38	Chicago Blackhawks	Toronto Maple Leafs	4
1938–39	Boston Bruins	Toronto Maple Leafs	5
1939–40	New York Rangers	Toronto Maple Leafs	6
1940–41	Boston Bruins	Detroit Red Wings	4
1941–42	Toronto Maple Leafs	Detroit Red Wings	7
1942–43	Detroit Red Wings	Boston Bruins	4
1943–44	Montreal Canadiens	Chicago Blackhawks	4
1944–45	Toronto Maple Leafs	Detroit Red Wings	7
1945–46	Montreal Canadiens	Boston Bruins	5
1946–47	Toronto Maple Leafs	Montreal Canadiens	6
1947–48	Toronto Maple Leafs	Detroit Red Wings	4
1948–49	Toronto Maple Leafs	Detroit Red Wings	4
1949–50	Detroit Red Wings	New York Rangers	7
1950–51	Toronto Maple Leafs	Montreal Canadiens	5
1951–52	Detroit Red Wings	Montreal Canadiens	4
1952–53	Montreal Canadiens	Boston Bruins	5
1953–54	Detroit Red Wings	Montreal Canadiens	7
1954–55	Detroit Red Wings	Montreal Canadiens	7
1955–56	Montreal Canadiens	Detroit Red Wings	5
1956–57	Montreal Canadiens	Boston Bruins	5
1957–58	Montreal Canadiens	Boston Bruins	6
1958–59	Montreal Canadiens	Toronto Maple Leafs	5
1959–60	Montreal Canadiens	Toronto Maple Leafs	4
1960–61	Chicago Blackhawks	Detroit Red Wings	6
1961–62	Toronto Maple Leafs	Chicago Blackhawks	6
1962–63	Toronto Maple Leafs	Detroit Red Wings	5
1963–64	Toronto Maple Leafs	Detroit Red Wings	7
1964–65	Montreal Canadiens	Chicago Blackhawks	7
1965–66	Montreal Canadiens	Detroit Red Wings	6
1966–67	Toronto Maple Leafs	Montreal Canadiens	6
1967–68	Montreal Canadiens	St. Louis Blues	4
1968–69	Montreal Canadiens	St. Louis Blues	4
1969–70	Boston Bruins	St. Louis Blues	4
1970–71	Montreal Canadiens	Chicago Blackhawks	7
1971–72	Boston Bruins	New York Rangers	6
1972–73	Montreal Canadiens	Chicago Blackhawks	6
1973–74	Philadelphia Flyers	Boston Bruins	6
1974–75	Philadelphia Flyers	Buffalo Sabres	6
1975–76	Montreal Canadiens	Philadelphia Flyers	4
1976–77	Montreal Canadiens	Boston Bruins	4
1977–78	Montreal Canadiens	Boston Bruins	6
1978–79	Montreal Canadiens	New York Rangers	5
1979–80	New York Islanders	Philadelphia Flyers	6
1980–81	New York Islanders	Minnesota North Stars	5
1981–82	New York Islanders	Vancouver Canucks	4
1982–83	New York Islanders	Edmonton Oilers	4
1983–84	Edmonton Oilers	New York Islanders	5
1984–85	Edmonton Oilers	Philadelphia Flyers	5
1985–86	Montreal Canadiens	Calgary Flames	6
1986–87	Edmonton Oilers	Philadelphia Flyers	7
1987–88	Edmonton Oilers	Boston Bruins	4
1988–89	Calgary Flames	Montreal Canadiens	6
1989–90	Edmonton Oilers	Boston Bruins	5
1990–91	Pittsburgh Penguins	Minnesota North Stars	6
1991–92	Pittsburgh Penguins	Chicago Blackhawks	4
1992–93	Montreal Canadiens	Los Angeles Kings	5
1993–94	New York Rangers	Vancouver Canucks	7
1994–95	New Jersey Devils	Detroit Red Wings	4
1995–96	Colorado Avalanche	Florida Panthers	4
1996–97	Detroit Red Wings	Philadelphia Flyers	4
1997–98	Detroit Red Wings	Washington Capitals	4
1998–99	Dallas Stars	Buffalo Sabres	6
1999–2000	New Jersey Devils	Dallas Stars	6

NHL WINNERS AND FINALISTS *(CONT.)*

Season	Champion	Finalist	GP in Final
2000–01	Colorado Avalanche	New Jersey Devils	7
2001–02	Detroit Red Wings	Carolina Hurricanes	5
2002–03	New Jersey Devils	Anaheim Mighty Ducks	7
2003–04	Tampa Bay	Calgary	7

*In 1919 the Montreal Canadiens traveled to meet Seattle, the PCHL champions. After 5 games had been played—the teams were tied at 2 wins and 1 tie—the series was called off by the local Department of Health because of the influenza epidemic and the death of Canadiens defenseman Joe Hall from influenza.

Conn Smythe Trophy

Awarded to the Most Valuable Player of the Stanley Cup playoffs, as selected by the Professional Hockey Writers Association. The trophy is named after the former coach, general manager, president and owner of the Toronto Maple Leafs.

1965	Jean Beliveau, Mtl	1985	Wayne Gretzky, Edm
1966	Roger Crozier, Det	1986	Patrick Roy, Mtl
1967	Dave Keon, Tor	1987	Ron Hextall, Phil
1968	Glenn Hall, StL	1988	Wayne Gretzky, Edm
1969	Serge Savard, Mtl	1989	Al MacInnis, Cgy
1970	Bobby Orr, Bos	1990	Bill Ranford, Edm
1971	Ken Dryden, Mtl	1991	Mario Lemieux, Pitt
1972	Bobby Orr, Bos	1992	Mario Lemieux, Pitt
1973	Yvan Cournoyer, Mtl	1993	Patrick Roy, Mtl
1974	Bernie Parent, Phil	1994	Brian Leetch, NYR
1975	Bernie Parent, Phil	1995	Claude Lemieux, NJ
1976	Reggie Leach, Phil	1996	Joe Sakic, Col
1977	Guy Lafleur, Mtl	1997	Mike Vernon, Det
1978	Larry Robinson, Mtl	1998	Steve Yzerman, Det
1979	Bob Gainey, Mtl	1999	Joe Nieuwendyk, Dall
1980	Bryan Trottier, NYI	2000	Scott Stevens, NJ
1981	Butch Goring, NYI	2001	Patrick Roy, Col
1982	Mike Bossy, NYI	2002	Nicklas Lidstrom, Det
1983	Bill Smith, NYI	2003	J.-S. Giguere, Ana
1984	Mark Messier, Edm	2004	Brad Richards, TB

Alltime Stanley Cup Playoff Leaders
Points

	Yrs	GP	G	A	Pts		Yrs	GP	G	A	Pts
Wayne Gretzky, four teams	16	208	122	260	382	Denis Savard, Chi, Mtl	16	169	66	109	175
*Mark Messier, Edm, Van, NYR	18	236	109	186	295	*Mario Lemieux, Pitt	8	107	76	96	172
Jari Kurri, four teams	15	200	106	127	233	Denis Potvin, NYI	14	185	56	108	164
Glenn Anderson, four teams	15	225	93	121	214	*Sergei Fedorov, Det, Ana	13	162	50	113	163
Paul Coffey, six teams	16	198	59	137	196	Mike Bossy, NYI	10	129	85	75	160
*Brett Hull, four teams	19	202	103	87	190	Gordie Howe, Det, Hart	20	157	68	92	160
Doug Gilmour, seven teams	18	182	60	128	188	Bobby Smith, Minn, Mtl	13	184	64	96	160
Bryan Trottier, NYI, Pitt	17	221	71	113	184	*Al MacInnis, Cgy, StL	19	177	39	121	160
*Steve Yzerman, Det	19	192	70	111	181	*Claude Lemieux, six teams	17	233	80	77	157
Ray Bourque, Bos, Col	21	214	41	139	180	*Active in 2003–04 season.					
Jean Beliveau, Mtl	17	162	79	97	176						

Goals

	Yrs	GP	G
Wayne Gretzky, four teams	17	208	122
*Mark Messier, Edm, NYR	18	236	109
Jari Kurri, five teams	15	200	106
*Brett Hull, Cgy, StL, Dall, Det	19	202	103
Glenn Anderson, four teams	15	225	93
Mike Bossy, NYI	10	129	85
Maurice Richard, Mtl	15	133	82
*Claude Lemieux, six teams	17	233	80
Jean Beliveau, Mtl	17	162	79
*Joe Sakic, Col	11	153	78

*Active in 2003–04.

Assists

	Yrs	GP	A
Wayne Gretzky, four teams	17	208	260
*Mark Messier, Edm, NYR	18	236	186
Ray Bourque, Bos, Col	21	214	139
Paul Coffey, six teams	16	198	137
Doug Gilmour, seven teams	18	182	128
Jari Kurri, five teams	15	196	127
Glenn Anderson, four teams	15	225	121
*Al MacInnis, Cgy, StL	19	177	121
Larry Robinson, Mtl, LA	20	227	116
Larry Murphy, six teams	15	215	115

*Active in 2003–04.

Alltime Stanley Cup Playoff Goaltending Leaders

WINS	W	L	Pct
Patrick Roy, Mtl, Col	151	94	.616
Grant Fuhr, five teams	92	50	.648
Billy Smith, LA, NYI	88	36	.710
*Martin Brodeur, NJ	84	60	.583
*Ed Belfour, four teams	88	68	.564
Ken Dryden, Mtl	80	32	.714
Mike Vernon, four teams	77	56	.579
Jacques Plante, five teams	71	37	.657
Andy Moog, four teams	68	57	.544
*Curtis Joseph, four teams	62	66	.484

*Active in 2003–04.

SHUTOUTS	GP	W	SO
Patrick Roy, Mtl, Col	247	151	23
*Martin Brodeur, NJ	144	84	20
*Curtis Joseph, four teams	133	62	16
Clint Benedict, Ott, Mtl M	48	25	15
*Ed Belfour, four teams	161	88	14
Jacques Plante, five teams	112	71	14

GOALS AGAINST AVG			Avg
*Martin Brodeur, NJ			1.87
George Hainsworth, Mtl, Tor			1.93
Turk Broda, Tor			1.98
*Dominik Hasek, Chi, Buff, Det			2.03
*Ed Belfour, four teams			2.17

Note: At least 50 games played.
*Active in 2003–04.

Alltime Stanley Cup Playoff Wins

TEAM	W	L	Pct	TEAM	W	L	Pct
Montreal	391	262	.599	Buffalo	99	110	.474
Detroit	257	236	.521	Calgary*	84	98	.462
Toronto	251	269	.483	Washington	69	85	.448
Boston	242	264	.478	Vancouver	66	89	.426
Chicago	188	218	.463	Los Angeles	65	101	.392
NY Rangers	183	195	.484	San Jose	39	45	.464
Philadelphia	178	161	.525	Carolina§	35	49	.417
St. Louis	138	165	.455	Ottawa	31	38	.449
Dallas#	137	137	.500	Phoenix††	28	63	.308
Edmonton	135	90	.600	Tampa Bay	23	17	.575
NY Islanders	131	102	.562	Anaheim	19	17	.528
Colorado**	122	102	.545	Florida	13	18	.419
Pittsburgh	109	99	.524	Minnesota	8	10	.444
New Jersey†	107	86	.549	Nashville	2	4	.333

*Atlanta Flames 1972–80. †Colorado Rockies 1976–82. #Minnesota North Stars 1967–93. **Quebec Nordiques 1979–95. ††Winnipeg Jets 1979–96. §Hartford Whalers 1979–97. Note: Teams ranked by playoff victories.

Stanley Cup Playoff Coaching Records

Coach	Team	Yrs	Series			Games				Cups	Pct
			Series	W	L	Games	W	L	T		
†Glen Sather	Edm	10	27	21	6	*126	89	37	0	4	.706
Toe Blake	Mtl	13	23	18	5	119	82	37	0	8	.689
Scott Bowman	Five teams	28	68	49	19	353	223	130	0	9	.632
Bob Hartley	Col	4	13	10	3	80	49	31	0	1	.613
Hap Day	Tor	9	14	10	4	80	49	31	0	5	.613
Al Arbour	StL, NYI	16	42	30	12	209	123	86	0	4	.589
†Ken Hitchcock	Dall, Phil	7	19	13	6	111	64	47	0	1	.577
Mike Keenan	five teams	11	28	18	10	160	91	69	0	1	.569
Fred Shero	Phil, NYR	8	21	15	6	108	61	47	0	2	.565
†Jacques Lemaire	Mtl, NJ, Minn	7	18	12	6	101	57	44	0	1	.564

*Does not include suspended game, May 24, 1988. †Active in 2003–04.
Note: Coaches ranked by winning percentage. Minimum: 65 games.

The 10 Longest Overtime Games

Date	Result	OT	Scorer	Series	Series Winner
3-24-36	Det 1 vs Mtl M 0	116:30	Mud Bruneteau	SF	Det
4-3-33	Tor 1 vs Bos 0	104:46	Ken Doraty	SF	Tor
5-4-00	Phil 2 vs Pitt 1	92:01	Keith Primeau	CSF	Phil
4-24-03	Ana 4 vs Dall 3	80:48	Petr Sykora	CSF	Ana
4-24-96	Pitt 3 vs Wash 2	79:15	Petr Nedved	CQF	Pitt
3-23-43	Tor 3 vs Det 2	70:18	Jack McLean	SF	Det
3-28-30	Mtl 2 vs NYR 1	68:52	Gus Rivers	SF	Mtl
4-18-87	NYI 3 vs Wash 2	68:47	Pat LaFontaine	DSF	NYI
4-27-94	Buff 1 vs NJ 0	65:43	Dave Hannan	CQF	NJ
3-27-51	Mtl 3 vs Det 2	61:09	Maurice Richard	SF	Mtl

Hart Memorial Trophy

Awarded annually "to the player adjudged to be the most valuable to his team." The original trophy was donated by Dr. David A. Hart, father of Cecil Hart, former manager-coach of the Montreal Canadiens. In the 1980s Wayne Gretzky won the award nine times.

Year	Winner	Key Statistics	Runner-Up
1924	Frank Nighbor, Ott	10 goals, 3 assists in 20 games	Sprague Cleghorn, Mtl
1925	Billy Burch, Ham	20 goals, 4 assists in 27 games	Howie Morenz, Mtl
1926	Nels Stewart, Mtl M	42 points in 36 games	Sprague Cleghorn, Mtl
1927	Herb Gardiner, Mtl	12 points in 44 games as defenseman	Bill Cook, NYR
1928	Howie Morenz, Mtl	33 goals, 18 assists	Roy Worters, Pitt
1929	Roy Worters, NYA	1.21 goals against, 13 shutouts	Ace Bailey, Tor
1930	Nels Stewart, Mtl M	39 goals, 16 assists	Lionel Hitchman, Bos
1931	Howie Morenz, Mtl	28 goals, 23 assists	Eddie Shore, Bos
1932	Howie Morenz, Mtl	24 goals, 25 assists	Ching Johnson, NYR
1933	Eddie Shore, Bos	27 assists in 48 games as defenseman	Bill Cook, NYR
1934	Aurel Joliat, Mtl	27 points	Lionel Conacher, Chi
1935	Eddie Shore, Bos	26 assists in 48 games as defenseman	Charlie Conacher, Tor
1936	Eddie Shore, Bos	16 assists in 46 games as defenseman	Hooley Smith, Mtl M
1937	Babe Siebert, Mtl	28 points	Lionel Conacher, Mtl M
1938	Eddie Shore, Bos	17 points in 47 games as defenseman	Paul Thompson, Chi
1939	Toe Blake, Mtl	led NHL in points (47)	Syl Apps, Tor
1940	Ebbie Goodfellow, Det	28 points	Syl Apps, Tor
1941	Bill Cowley, Bos	led NHL in assists (45) and points (62)	Dit Clapper, Bos
1942	Tom Anderson, Bos	41 points	Syl Apps, Tor
1943	Bill Cowley, Bos	led NHL in assists (45)	Doug Bentley, Chi
1944	Babe Pratt, Tor	57 points in 50 games	Bill Cowley, Bos
1945	Elmer Lach, Mtl	led NHL in assists (54) and points (80)	Maurice Richard, Mtl
1946	Max Bentley, Chi	61 points in 47 games	Gaye Stewart, Tor
1947	Maurice Richard, Mtl	led NHL in goals (45); 26 assists	Milt Schmidt, Bos
1948	Buddy O'Connor, NYR	60 points in 60 games	Frank Brimsek, Bos
1949	Sid Abel, Det	28 goals, 26 assists	Bill Durnan, Mtl
1950	Charlie Rayner, NYR	6 shutouts	Ted Kennedy, Tor
1951	Milt Schmidt, Bos	61 points in 62 games	Maurice Richard, Mtl
1952	Gordie Howe, Det	led NHL in goals (47) and points (86)	Elmer Lach, Mtl
1953	Gordie Howe, Det	led NHL in goals (49) and points (95)	Al Rollins, Chi
1954	Al Rollins, Chi	5 shutouts	Red Kelly, Det
1955	Ted Kennedy, Tor	52 points	Harry Lumley, Tor
1956	Jean Beliveau, Mtl	led NHL in goals (47) and points (88)	Tod Sloan, Tor
1957	Gordie Howe, Det	led NHL in goals (44) and points (89)	Jean Beliveau, Mtl
1959	Andy Bathgate, NYR	74 points in 70 games	Gordie Howe, Det
1960	Gordie Howe, Det	45 assists, 73 points	Bobby Hull, Chi
1961	Bernie Geoffrion, Mtl	50 goals, 95 points	Johnny Bower, Tor
1962	Jacques Plante, Mtl	42 wins, 2.37 goals against avg.	Doug Harvey, NYR
1963	Gordie Howe, Det	47 assists, 73 points	Stan Mikita, Chi
1964	Jean Beliveau, Mtl	50 assists, 78 points	Bobby Hull, Chi
1965	Bobby Hull, Chi	39 goals, 32 assists	Norm Ullman, Det
1966	Bobby Hull, Chi	led NHL in goals (54) and points (97)	Jean Beliveau, Mtl
1967	Stan Mikita, Chi	led NHL in assists (62) and points (97)	Ed Giacomin, NYR
1968	Stan Mikita, Chi	40 goals, 47 assists	Jean Beliveau, Mtl
1969	Phil Esposito, Bos	led NHL in assists (77) and points (126)	Jean Beliveau, Mtl
1970	Bobby Orr, Bos	led NHL in assists (87) and points (120)	Tony Esposito, Chi
1971	Bobby Orr, Bos	102 assists, 139 points	Tony Esposito, Chi
1972	Bobby Orr, Bos	80 assists, 117 points	Ken Dryden, Mtl
1973	Bobby Clarke, Phil	67 assists, 104 points	Phil Esposito, Bos
1974	Phil Esposito, Bos	led NHL in goals (68) and points (145)	Bernie Parent, Phil
1975	Bobby Clarke, Phil	89 assists, 116 points	Rogatien Vachon, LA
1976	Bobby Clarke, Phil	89 assists, 119 points	Denis Potvin, NYI
1977	Guy Lafleur, Mtl	led NHL in assists (80) and points (136)	Bobby Clarke, Phil
1978	Guy Lafleur, Mtl	led NHL in goals (60) and points (132)	Bryan Trottier, NYI
1979	Bryan Trottier, NYI	led NHL in assists (87) and points (134)	Guy Lafleur, Mtl
1980	Wayne Gretzky, Edm	51 goals, 86 assists	Marcel Dionne, LA
1981	Wayne Gretzky, Edm	led NHL in assists (109) and points (164)	Mike Liut, StL
1982	Wayne Gretzky, Edm	NHL-record 92 goals and 212 points	Bryan Trottier, NYI
1983	Wayne Gretzky, Edm	led NHL in goals (71) and points (196)	Pete Peeters, Bos
1984	Wayne Gretzky, Edm	led NHL in goals (87) and points (205)	Rod Langway, Wash
1985	Wayne Gretzky, Edm	led NHL in goals (73) and points (208)	Dale Hawerchuk, Winn
1986	Wayne Gretzky, Edm	NHL-record 163 assists and 215 points	Mario Lemieux, Pitt

Hart Memorial Trophy (Cont.)

Year	Winner	Key Statistics	Runner-Up
1987	Wayne Gretzky, Edm	led NHL in assists (121) and points (183)	Ray Bourque, Bos
1988	Mario Lemieux, Pitt	led NHL in goals (70) and points (168)	Grant Fuhr, Edm
1989	Wayne Gretzky, LA	114 assists, 168 points	Mario Lemieux, Pitt
1990	Mark Messier, Edm	84 assists, 129 points	Ray Bourque, Bos
1991	Brett Hull, StL	led NHL in goals (86); 131 points	Wayne Gretzky, LA
1992	Mark Messier, NYR	72 assists, 107 points	Patrick Roy, Mtl
1993	Mario Lemieux, Pitt	69 goals, 91 assists in 60 games	Doug Gilmour, Tor
1994	Sergei Fedorov, Det	56 goals, 64 assists	Dominik Hasek, Buff
1995	Eric Lindros, Phil	29 goals, 41 assists in 46 games	Jaromir Jagr, Pitt
1996	Mario Lemieux, Pitt	led NHL in goals (69) and points (161)	Mark Messier, NYR
1997	Dominik Hasek, Buff	5 shutouts, 2.27 goals against avg.	Paul Kariya, Ana
1998	Dominik Hasek, Buff	13 shutouts, 2.09 goals against avg.	Jaromir Jagr, Pitt
1999	Jaromir Jagr, Pitt	44 goals, 127 points	Alexei Yashin, Ott
2000	Chris Pronger, StL	62 points, +52 plus/minus rating	Jaromir Jagr, Pitt
2001	Joe Sakic, Col	118 points, +45 plus/minus rating	Mario Lemieux, Pitt
2002	Jose Theodore, Mtl	2.11 goals against avg./7 shutouts	Jarome Iginla, Cal
2003	Peter Forsberg, Col	77 assists, +52 plus/minus rating	Markus Naslund, Van
2004	Martin St. Louis, TB	94 points, +35 plus/minus rating	Jarome Iginla, Cal

Art Ross Trophy

Awarded annually "to the player who leads the league in scoring points at the end of the regular season." The trophy was presented to the NHL in 1947 by Arthur Howie Ross, former manager-coach of the Boston Bruins. The tie-breakers, in order, are as follows: (1) player with most goals, (2) player with fewer games played, (3) player scoring first goal of the season. Bobby Orr is the only defenseman in NHL history to win this trophy, and he won it twice (1970 and 1975).

Year	Winner	Pts	Year	Winner	Pts
1919	Newsy Lalonde, Mtl	44	1957	Gordie Howe, Det	89
1920	Joe Malone, Que	30	1958	Dickie Moore, Mtl	84
1921	Newsy Lalonde, Mtl	48	1959	Dickie Moore, Mtl	96
1922	Punch Broadbent, Ott	41	1960	Bobby Hull, Chi	81
1923	Babe Dye, Tor	46	1961	Bernie Geoffrion, Mtl	95
1924	Cy Denneny, Ott	37	1962	Bobby Hull, Chi	84
1925	Babe Dye, Tor	23	1963	Gordie Howe, Det	86
1926	Nels Stewart, Mtl M	44	1964	Stan Mikita, Chi	89
1927	Bill Cook, NYR	42	1965	Stan Mikita, Chi	87
1928	Howie Morenz, Mtl	37	1966	Bobby Hull, Chi	97
1929	Ace Bailey, Tor	51	1967	Stan Mikita, Chi	97
1930	Cooney Weiland, Bos	32	1968	Stan Mikita, Chi	87
1931	Howie Morenz, Mtl	73	1969	Phil Esposito, Bos	126
1932	Harvey Jackson, Tor	51	1970	Bobby Orr, Bos	120
1933	Bill Cook, NYR	53	1971	Phil Esposito, Bos	152
1934	Charlie Conacher, Tor	50	1972	Phil Esposito, Bos	133
1935	Charlie Conacher, Tor	57	1973	Phil Esposito, Bos	130
1936	Sweeney Schriner, NYA	45	1974	Phil Esposito, Bos	145
1937	Sweeney Schriner, NYA	46	1975	Bobby Orr, Bos	135
1938	Gordie Drillon, Tor	52	1976	Guy Lafleur, Mtl	125
1939	Toe Blake, Mtl	47	1977	Guy Lafleur, Mtl	136
1940	Milt Schmidt, Bos	52	1978	Guy Lafleur, Mtl	132
1941	Bill Cowley, Bos	62	1979	Bryan Trottier, NYI	134
1942	Bryan Hextall, NYR	56	1980	Marcel Dionne, LA	137
1943	Doug Bentley, Chi	73	1981	Wayne Gretzky, Edm	164
1944	Herb Cain, Bos	82	1982	Wayne Gretzky, Edm	212
1945	Elmer Lach, Mtl	80	1983	Wayne Gretzky, Edm	196
1946	Max Bentley, Chi	61	1984	Wayne Gretzky, Edm	205
1947	*Max Bentley, Chi	72	1985	Wayne Gretzky, Edm	208
1948	Elmer Lach, Mtl	61	1986	Wayne Gretzky, Edm	215
1949	Roy Conacher, Chi	68	1987	Wayne Gretzky, Edm	183
1950	Ted Lindsay, Det	78	1988	Mario Lemieux, Pitt	168
1951	Gordie Howe, Det	86	1989	Mario Lemieux, Pitt	199
1952	Gordie Howe, Det	86	1990	Wayne Gretzky, LA	142
1953	Gordie Howe, Det	95	1991	Wayne Gretzky, LA	163
1954	Gordie Howe, Det	81	1992	Mario Lemieux, Pitt	131
1955	Bernie Geoffrion, Mtl	75	1993	Mario Lemieux, Pitt	160
1956	Jean Beliveau, Mtl	88	1994	Wayne Gretzky, LA	130
			1995	Jaromir Jagr, Pitt	70

Art Ross Trophy (Cont.)

Year	Winner	Pts	Year	Winner	Pts
1996	Mario Lemieux, Pitt	161	2001	Jaromir Jagr, Pitt	121
1997	Mario Lemieux, Pitt	122	2002	Jarome Iginla, Cgy	96
1998	Jaromir Jagr, Pitt	102	2003	Peter Forsberg, Col	106
1999	Jaromir Jagr, Pitt	127	2004	Martin St. Louis, TB	94
2000	Jaromir Jagr, Pitt	96			

Note: Listing includes scoring leaders prior to inception of Art Ross Trophy in 1947–48.

Lady Byng Memorial Trophy

Awarded annually "to the player adjudged to have exhibited the best type of sportsmanship and gentlemanly conduct combined with a high standard of playing ability." Lady Byng, who first presented the trophy in 1925, was the wife of Canada's Governor-General. She donated a second trophy in 1936 after the first was given permanently to Frank Boucher of the New York Rangers, who won it seven times in eight seasons. Stan Mikita, one of the league's most penalized players during his early years in the NHL, won the trophy twice late in his career (1967 and 1968).

Year	Winner	Year	Winner	Year	Winner
1925	Frank Nighbor, Ott	1952	Sid Smith, Tor	1979	Bob MacMillan, Atl
1926	Frank Nighbor, Ott	1953	Red Kelly, Det	1980	Wayne Gretzky, Edm
1927	Billy Burch, NYA	1954	Red Kelly, Det	1981	Rick Kehoe, Pitt
1928	Frank Boucher, NYR	1955	Sid Smith, Tor	1982	Rick Middleton, Bos
1929	Frank Boucher, NYR	1956	Earl Reibel, Det	1983	Mike Bossy, NYI
1930	Frank Boucher, NYR	1957	Andy Hebenton, NYR	1984	Mike Bossy, NYI
1931	Frank Boucher, NYR	1958	Camille Henry, NYR	1985	Jari Kurri, Edm
1932	Joe Primeau, Tor	1959	Alex Delvecchio, Det	1986	Mike Bossy, NYI
1933	Frank Boucher, NYR	1960	Don McKenney, Bos	1987	Joe Mullen, Cgy
1934	Frank Boucher, NYR	1961	Red Kelly, Tor	1988	Mats Naslund, Mtl
1935	Frank Boucher, NYR	1962	Dave Keon, Tor	1989	Joe Mullen, Cgy
1936	Doc Romnes, Chi	1963	Dave Keon, Tor	1990	Brett Hull, StL
1937	Marty Barry, Det	1964	Ken Wharram, Chi	1991	Wayne Gretzky, LA
1938	Gordie Drillon, Tor	1965	Bobby Hull, Chi	1992	Wayne Gretzky, LA
1939	Clint Smith, NYR	1966	Alex Delvecchio, Det	1993	Pierre Turgeon, NYI
1940	Bobby Bauer, Bos	1967	Stan Mikita, Chi	1994	Wayne Gretzky, LA
1941	Bobby Bauer, Bos	1968	Stan Mikita, Chi	1995	Ron Francis, Pitt
1942	Syl Apps, Tor	1969	Alex Delvecchio, Det	1996	Paul Kariya, Ana
1943	Max Bentley, Chi	1970	Phil Goyette, StL	1997	Paul Kariya, Ana
1944	Clint Smith, Chi	1971	John Bucyk, Bos	1998	Ron Francis, Pitt
1945	Billy Mosienko, Chi	1972	Jean Ratelle, NYR	1999	Wayne Gretzky, NYR
1946	Toe Blake, Mtl	1973	Gilbert Perreault, Buff	2000	Pavol Demitra, StL
1947	Bobby Bauer, Bos	1974	John Bucyk, Bos	2001	Joe Sakic, Col
1948	Buddy O'Connor, NYR	1975	Marcel Dionne, Det	2002	Ron Francis, Car
1949	Bill Quackenbush, Det	1976	Jean Ratelle, NYR-Bos	2003	Alexander Mogilny, Det
1950	Edgar Laprade, NYR	1977	Marcel Dionne, LA	2004	Brad Richards, TB
1951	Red Kelly, Det	1978	Butch Goring, LA		

James Norris Memorial Trophy

Awarded annually "to the defense player who demonstrates throughout the season the greatest all-around ability in the position." James Norris was the former owner-president of the Detroit Red Wings. Bobby Orr holds the record for most consecutive times winning the award (eight, 1968–1975).

Year	Winner	Year	Winner	Year	Winner
1954	Red Kelly, Det	1971	Bobby Orr, Bos	1988	Ray Bourque, Bos
1955	Doug Harvey, Mtl	1972	Bobby Orr, Bos	1989	Chris Chelios, Mtl
1956	Doug Harvey, Mtl	1973	Bobby Orr, Bos	1990	Ray Bourque, Bos
1957	Doug Harvey, Mtl	1974	Bobby Orr, Bos	1991	Ray Bourque, Bos
1958	Doug Harvey, Mtl	1975	Bobby Orr, Bos	1992	Brian Leetch, NYR
1959	Tom Johnson, Mtl	1976	Denis Potvin, NYI	1993	Chris Chelios, Chi
1960	Doug Harvey, Mtl	1977	Larry Robinson, Mtl	1994	Ray Bourque, Bos
1961	Doug Harvey, Mtl	1978	Denis Potvin, NYI	1995	Paul Coffey, Det
1962	Doug Harvey, NYR	1979	Denis Potvin, NYI	1996	Chris Chelios, Chi
1963	Pierre Pilote, Chi	1980	Larry Robinson, Mtl	1997	Brian Leetch, NYR
1964	Pierre Pilote, Chi	1981	Randy Carlyle, Pitt	1998	Rob Blake, LA
1965	Pierre Pilote, Chi	1982	Doug Wilson, Chi	1999	Al MacInnis, StL
1966	Jacques Laperriere, Mtl	1983	Rod Langway, Wash	2000	Chris Pronger, StL
1967	Harry Howell, NYR	1984	Rod Langway, Wash	2001	Nicklas Lidstrom, Det
1968	Bobby Orr, Bos	1985	Paul Coffey, Edm	2002	Nicklas Lidstrom, Det
1969	Bobby Orr, Bos	1986	Paul Coffey, Edm	2003	Nicklas Lidstrom, Det
1970	Bobby Orr, Bos	1987	Ray Bourque, Bos	2004	Scott Niedermayer, NJ

Calder Memorial Trophy

Awarded annually "to the player selected as the most proficient in his first year of competition in the National Hockey League." Frank Calder was a former NHL president. Sergei Makarov, who won the award in 1989–90, was the oldest recipient of the trophy, at 31. Players are no longer eligible for the award if they are 26 or older as of September 15th of the season in question.

1933 ....Carl Voss, Det	1957 ....Larry Regan, Bos	1981 ....Peter Stastny, Que
1934 ....Russ Blinko, Mtl M	1958 ....Frank Mahovlich, Tor	1982 ....Dale Hawerchuk, Winn
1935 ....Dave Schriner, NYA	1959 ....Ralph Backstrom, Mtl	1983 ....Steve Larmer, Chi
1936 ....Mike Karakas, Chi	1960 ....Bill Hay, Chi	1984 ....Tom Barrasso, Buff
1937 ....Syl Apps, Tor	1961 ....Dave Keon, Tor	1985 ....Mario Lemieux, Pitt
1938 ....Cully Dahlstrom, Chi	1962 ....Bobby Rousseau, Mtl	1986 ....Gary Suter, Cgy
1939 ....Frank Brimsek, Bos	1963 ....Kent Douglas, Tor	1987 ....Luc Robitaille, LA
1940 ....Kilby MacDonald, NYR	1964 ....Jacques Laperriere, Mtl	1988 ....Joe Nieuwendyk, Cgy
1941 ....Johnny Quilty, Mtl	1965 ....Roger Crozier, Det	1989 ....Brian Leetch, NYR
1942 ....Grant Warwick, NYR	1966 ....Brit Selby, Tor	1990 ....Sergei Makarov, Cgy
1943 ....Gaye Stewart, Tor	1967 ....Bobby Orr, Bos	1991 ....Ed Belfour, Chi
1944 ....Gus Bodnar, Tor	1968 ....Derek Sanderson, Bos	1992 ....Pavel Bure, Van
1945 ....Frank McCool, Tor	1969 ....Danny Grant, Minn	1993 ....Teemu Selanne, Winn
1946 ....Edgar Laprade, NYR	1970 ....Tony Esposito, Chi	1994 ....Martin Brodeur, NJ
1947 ....Howie Meeker, Tor	1971 ....Gilbert Perreault, Buff	1995 ....Peter Forsberg, Que
1948 ....Jim McFadden, Det	1972 ....Ken Dryden, Mtl	1996 ....Daniel Alfredsson, Ott
1949 ....Pentti Lund, NYR	1973 ....Steve Vickers, NYR	1997 ....Bryan Berard, NYI
1950 ....Jack Gelineau, Bos	1974 ....Denis Potvin, NYI	1998 ....Sergei Samsonov, Bos
1951 ....Terry Sawchuk, Det	1975 ....Eric Vail, Atl	1999 ....Chris Drury, Col
1952 ....Bernie Geoffrion, Mtl	1976 ....Bryan Trottier, NYI	2000 ....Scott Gomez, NJ
1953 ....Gump Worsley, NYR	1977 ....Willi Plett, Atl	2001 ....Evgeni Nabakov, SJ
1954 ....Camille Henry, NYR	1978 ....Mike Bossy, NYI	2002 ....Dany Heatley, Atl
1955 ....Ed Litzenberger, Chi	1979 ....Bobby Smith, Minn	2003 ....Barret Jackman, StL
1956 ....Glenn Hall, Det	1980 ....Ray Bourque, Bos	2004 ....Andrew Raycroft, Bos

Vezina Trophy

Awarded annually "to the goalkeeper adjudged to be the best at his position." The trophy is named after Georges Vezina, an outstanding goalie for the Montreal Canadiens who collapsed during a game on November 28, 1925, and died four months later of tuberculosis. The general managers of the NHL teams vote on the award.

1927 ....George Hainsworth, Mtl	1958 ....Jacques Plante, Mtl	1980 ....Bob Sauve, Buff
1928 ....George Hainsworth, Mtl	1959 ....Jacques Plante, Mtl	Don Edwards, Buff
1929 ....George Hainsworth, Mtl	1960 ....Jacques Plante, Mtl	1981 ....Richard Sevigny, Mtl
1930 ....Tiny Thompson, Bos	1961 ....Johnny Bower, Tor	Denis Herron, Mtl
1931 ....Roy Worters, NYA	1962 ....Jacques Plante, Mtl	Michel Larocque, Mtl
1932 ....Charlie Gardiner, Chi	1963 ....Glenn Hall, Chi	1982 ....Billy Smith, NYI
1933 ....Tiny Thompson, Bos	1964 ....Charlie Hodge, Mtl	1983 ....Pete Peeters, Bos
1934 ....Charlie Gardiner, Chi	1965 ....Terry Sawchuk, Tor	1984 ....Tom Barrasso, Buff
1935 ....Lorne Chabot, Chi	Johnny Bower, Tor	1985 ....Pelle Lindbergh, Phil
1936 ....Tiny Thompson, Bos	1966 ....Gump Worsley, Mtl	1986 ....John Vanbiesbrouck,
1937 ....Normie Smith, Det	Charlie Hodge, Mtl	NYR
1938 ....Tiny Thompson, Bos	1967 ....Glenn Hall, Chi	1987 ....Ron Hextall, Phil
1939 ....Frank Brimsek, Bos	Rogie Vachon, Mtl	1988 ....Grant Fuhr, Edm
1940 ....Dave Kerr, NYR	1969 ....Jacques Plante, StL	1989 ....Patrick Roy, Mtl
1941 ....Turk Broda, Tor	Glenn Hall, StL	1990 ....Patrick Roy, Mtl
1942 ....Frank Brimsek, Bos	1970 ....Tony Esposito, Chi	1991 ....Ed Belfour, Chi
1943 ....Johnny Mowers, Det	1971 ....Ed Giacomin, NYR	1992 ....Patrick Roy, Mtl
1944 ....Bill Durnan, Mtl	Gilles Villemure, NYR	1993 ....Ed Belfour, Chi
1945 ....Bill Durnan, Mtl	1972 ....Tony Esposito, Chi	1994 ....Dominik Hasek, Buff
1946 ....Bill Durnan, Mtl	Gary Smith, Chi	1995 ....Dominik Hasek, Buff
1947 ....Bill Durnan, Mtl	1973 ....Ken Dryden, Mtl	1996 ....Jim Carey, Wash
1948 ....Turk Broda, Tor	1974 ....Bernie Parent, Phil	1997 ....Dominik Hasek, Buff
1949 ....Bill Durnan, Mtl	Tony Esposito, Chi	1998 ....Dominik Hasek, Buff
1950 ....Bill Durnan, Mtl	1975 ....Bernie Parent, Phil	1999 ....Dominik Hasek, Buff
1951 ....Al Rollins, Tor	1976 ....Ken Dryden, Mtl	2000 ....Olaf Kolzig, Wash
1952 ....Terry Sawchuk, Det	1977 ....Ken Dryden, Mtl	2001 ....Dominik Hasek, Buff
1953 ....Terry Sawchuk, Det	Michel Larocque, Mtl	2002 ....Jose Theodore, Mtl
1954 ....Harry Lumley, Tor	1978 ....Ken Dryden, Mtl	2003 ....Martin Brodeur, NJ
1955 ....Terry Sawchuk, Det	Michel Larocque, Mtl	2004 ....Martin Brodeur, NJ
1956 ....Jacques Plante, Mtl	1979 ....Ken Dryden, Mtl	
1957 ....Jacques Plante, Mtl	Michel Larocque, Mtl	

Selke Trophy

Awarded annually "to the forward who best excels in the defensive aspects of the game." The trophy is named after Frank J. Selke, the architect of the Montreal Canadians dynasty that won five consecutive Stanley Cups in the late '50s. The winner is selected by a vote of the Professional Hockey Writers Association.

1978........Bob Gainey, Mtl	1987........Dave Poulin, Phil	1996........Sergei Fedorov, Det
1979........Bob Gainey, Mtl	1988........Guy Carbonneau, Mtl	1997........Michael Peca, Buff
1980........Bob Gainey, Mtl	1989........Guy Carbonneau, Mtl	1998........Jere Lehtinen, Dall
1981........Bob Gainey, Mtl	1990........Rick Meagher, StL	1999........Jere Lehtinen, Dall
1982........Steve Kasper, Bos	1991........Dirk Graham, Chi	2000........Steve Yzerman, Det
1983........Bobby Clarke, Phil	1992........Guy Carbonneau, Mtl	2001........John Madden, NJ
1984........Doug Jarvis, Wash	1993........Doug Gilmour, Tor	2002........Michael Peca, NYI
1985........Craig Ramsay, Buff	1994........Sergei Fedorov, Det	2003........Jere Lehtinen, Dall
1986........Troy Murray, Chi	1995........Ron Francis, Pitt	2004........Kris Draper, Det

Adams Award

Awarded annually "to the NHL coach adjudged to have contributed the most to his team's success." The trophy is named in honor of Jack Adams, longtime coach and general manager of the Detroit Red Wings. The winner is selected by a vote of the National Hockey League Broadcasters' Association.

1974.....Fred Shero, Phil	1985.....Mike Keenan, Phil	1996.....Scotty Bowman, Det
1975.....Bob Pulford, LA	1986.....Glen Sather, Edm	1997.....Ted Nolan, Buff
1976.....Don Cherry, Bos	1987.....Jacques Demers, Det	1998.....Pat Burns, Bos
1977.....Scott Bowman, Mtl	1988.....Jacques Demers, Det	1999.....Jacques Martin, Ott
1978.....Bobby Kromm, Det	1989.....Pat Burns, Mtl	2000.....Joel Quenneville, StL
1979.....Al Arbour, NYI	1990.....Bob Murdoch, Winn	2001.....Bill Barber, Phil
1980.....Pat Quinn, Phil	1991.....Brian Sutter, StL	2002.....Bob Francis, Phoe
1981.....Red Berenson, StL	1992.....Pat Quinn, Van	2003.....Jacques Lemaire, Minn
1982.....Tom Watt, Winn	1993.....Pat Burns, Tor	2004.....John Tortorella, TB
1983.....Orval Tessier, Chi	1994.....Jacques Lemaire, NJ	
1984.....Bryan Murray, Wash	1995.....Marc Crawford, Que	

THEY SAID IT

Sheldon Souray, Canadiens defenseman, on his candidacy for the Norris Trophy as the NHL's best blueliner: "The only Norris I know is Chuck."

Alltime Point Leaders

	Player	Yrs	GP	G	A	Pts	Pts/game
1.	Wayne Gretzky, Edm, LA, StL, NYR	20	1487	894	1963	2857	1.921
2.	*Mark Messier, Edm, NYR, Van	25	1756	694	1193	1887	1.074
3.	Gordie Howe, Det, Hart	26	1767	801	1049	1850	1.047
4.	*Ron Francis, four teams	23	1731	549	1249	1798	1.038
5.	Marcel Dionne, Det, LA, NYR	18	1348	731	1040	1771	1.314
6.	*Steve Yzerman, Det	21	1453	678	1043	1721	1.184
7.	*Mario Lemieux, Pitt	16	889	683	1018	1701	1.913
8.	Phil Esposito, Chi, Bos, NYR	18	1282	717	873	1590	1.240
9.	Ray Bourque, Bos, Col	22	1612	410	1169	1579	.980
10.	Paul Coffey, eight teams	21	1409	396	1135	1531	1.087
11.	Stan Mikita, Chi	22	1394	541	926	1467	1.052
12.	Bryan Trottier, NYI, Pitt	18	1279	524	901	1425	1.114
13.	*Adam Oates, seven teams	19	1337	341	1079	1420	1.062
14.	Doug Gilmour, seven teams	20	1474	450	964	1414	.959
15.	Dale Hawerchuk, Winn, Buff, StL, Phil	16	1188	518	891	1409	1.186

*Active in 2003–04.

Alltime Goal-Scoring Leaders

	Player	Yrs	GP	G	G/game
1.	Wayne Gretzky, Edm, LA, StL, NYR	20	1487	894	.601
2.	Gordie Howe, Det, Hart	26	1767	801	.453
3.	*Brett Hull, Cal, StL, Dall, Det	19	1264	741	.586
4.	Marcel Dionne, Det, LA, NYR	18	1348	731	.542
5.	Phil Esposito, Chi, Bos, NYR	18	1282	717	.559
6.	Mike Gartner, Wash, Minn, NYR, Tor, Phoe	19	1432	708	.494
7.	*Mark Messier, Edm, NYR, Van	25	1756	694	.395
8.	*Mario Lemieux, Pitt	16	889	683	.768
9.	*Steve Yzerman, Det	21	1453	678	.467
10.	*Luc Robitaille, LA, Pitt, NYR, Det	18	1366	653	.478

*Active in 2003–04.

Alltime Assist Leaders

	Player	Yrs	GP	A	A/game
1.	Wayne Gretzky, Edm, LA, StL, NYR	20	1487	1963	1.320
2.	*Ron Francis, Hart, Pitt, Car	23	1731	1249	.721
3.	*Mark Messier, Edm, NYR, Van	25	1756	1193	.679
4.	Ray Bourque, Bos, Col	22	1612	1169	.725
5.	Paul Coffey, eight teams	21	1409	1135	.806
6.	*Adam Oates, seven teams	19	1337	1079	.807
7.	Gordie Howe, Det, Hart	26	1767	1049	.594
8.	*Steve Yzerman, Det	21	1453	1043	.718
9.	Marcel Dionne, Det, LA, NYR	18	1348	1040	.771
10.	*Mario Lemieux, Pitt	16	889	1018	1.145

*Active player in 2003–04.

Alltime Penalty Minutes Leaders

Player		Yrs	GP	PIM	Min/game
1.	Dave Williams, Tor, Van, Det, LA, Hart	14	962	3966	4.12
2.	Dale Hunter, Que, Wash, Col	19	1407	3565	2.53
3.	*Tie Domi, Tor, NYR, Winn	15	943	3406	3.61
4.	Marty McSorley, Pitt, Edm, LA, NYR, SJ, Bos	17	961	3381	3.52
5.	Bob Probert, Det, Chi	16	935	3300	3.53
6.	*Rob Ray, Buff, Ott	15	900	3207	3.56
7.	Craig Berube, Phil, Tor, Cgy, Wash, NYI	17	1054	3149	2.99
8.	Tim Hunter, Cgy, Que, Van, SJ	16	815	3146	3.86
9.	Chris Nilan, Mtl, NYR, Bos	13	688	3043	4.42
10.	Rick Tocchet, Phil, Pitt, LA, Bos, Wash, Phoe	18	1144	2974	2.60

*Active in 2003–04.

Goaltending Records

ALLTIME WIN LEADERS

Goaltender	W	L	T	Pct
Patrick Roy, Mtl, Col	551	315	131	.618
Terry Sawchuk, five teams	447	330	173	.562
*Ed Belfour, Chi, SJ, Dall, Tor	435	281	111	.593
Jacques Plante, five teams	434	246	147	.614
Tony Esposito, Mtl, Chi	423	306	152	.566
Glenn Hall, Det, Chi, StL	407	327	163	.545
*Martin Brodeur, NJ	403	217	105	.628
Grant Fuhr, six teams	403	295	114	.567
*Curtis Joseph, StL, Edm, Tor, Det	396	289	90	.569
Mike Vernon, Cgy, Det, SJ, Fla	385	273	92	.575

*Active in 2003–04.

ACTIVE GOALTENDING LEADERS

Goaltender	W	L	T	Pct
Martin Brodeur, NJ	403	217	105	.628
Chris Osgood, Det, NYI, StL	305	177	66	.617
Ed Belfour, Chi, SJ, Dall, Tor	435	281	111	.593
Dominik Hasek, Chi, Buff, Det	296	192	82	.591
Patrick Lalime, Pitt, Ott	167	112	32	.588
Roman Turek, Dall, StL, Cgy	159	115	43	.569
Curtis Joseph, StL, Edm, Tor, Det	396	289	90	.569
Nikolai Khabibulin, Phoe, TB	209	187	58	.524
Olaf Kolzig, Wash	234	220	63	.514
Felix Potvin, five teams	266	260	85	.505

Note: Ranked by winning percentage; minimum 250 games played. All players active in 2003–04.

ALLTIME SHUTOUT LEADERS

Goaltender	Team	Yrs	GP	SO
Terry Sawchuk	Det, Bos, Tor, LA, NYR	21	971	103
George Hainsworth	Mtl, Tor	11	465	94
Glenn Hall	Det, Chi, StL	18	906	84
Jacques Plante	Mtl, NYR, StL, Tor, Bos	18	837	82
Tiny Thompson	Bos, Det	12	553	81
Alex Connell	Ott, Det, NYA, Mtl M	12	417	81
Tony Esposito	Mtl, Chi	16	886	76
*Martin Brodeur	NJ	12	740	75
*Ed Belfour	Chi, SJ, Dall, Tor	15	856	75
Lorne Chabot	NYR, Tor, Mtl, Chi, Mtl M, NYA	11	411	73

*Active in 2003–04.

ALLTIME GOALS AGAINST AVERAGE LEADERS (PRE-1950)

Goaltender	Team	Yrs	GP	GA	GAA
George Hainsworth	Mtl, Tor	11	465	937	1.91
Alex Connell	Ott, Det, NYA, Mtl M	12	417	830	1.91
Chuck Gardiner	Chi	7	316	664	2.02
Lorne Chabot	NYR, Tor, Mtl, Chi, Mtl M, NYA	11	411	861	2.04
Tiny Thompson	Bos, Det	12	553	1183	2.08

ALLTIME GOALS AGAINST AVERAGE LEADERS (POST-1950)

Goaltender	Team	Yrs	GP	GA	GAA
*Martin Brodeur	NJ	12	740	1573	2.17
*Dominik Hasek	Chi, Buff, Det	13	595	1284	2.23
Ken Dryden	Mtl	8	397	870	2.24
*Roman Turek	Dall, StL, Cgy	8	328	734	2.31
Jacques Plante	Mtl, NYR, StL, Tor, Bos	18	837	1965	2.38

*Active in 2003–04.

Note: Minimum 250 games played. Goals against average equals goals against per 60 minutes played.

Coaching Records

Coach	Team	Seasons	W	L	T	Pct
Scott Bowman.............five teams		1967–87, 91–2002	1244	583	314	.654
Toe Blake ....Mtl		1955–68	500	255	159	.634
*Ken Hitchcock...........Dall, Phil		1995–	362	211	94	.613
Fred Shero ....Phil, NYR		1971–81	390	225	119	.612
*Glen Sather................Edm, NYR		1979-89, 93-94, 2003-04	497	310	125	.600
Emile Francis ....NYR, StL		1965–77, 81–83	388	273	117	.574
Billy Reay ....Tor, Chi		1957–59, 63–77	542	385	175	.571
*Marc Crawford..........Que, Col, Van		1994–	369	264	108	.571
*Pat Burns..................Mtl, Tor, Bos, NJ		1988–2001, 2002–	501	359	153	.570
Al Arbour....................StL, NYI		1970–94	781	577	248	.564
*Pat Quinn..................Phil, LA, Van, Tor		1978–	616	460	157	.563

Note: Minimum 600 regular-season games. Ranked by percentage. *Active in 2003–04.

Adam at Ease

After a 19-year NHL career in which he had 1,079 assists and 1,420 points, center Adam Oates retired. Mike Adessa, who coached Oates at RPI, once affectionately called him a "stumpy, heavy-footed, poor-skating, no-shooting kid." But Oates was one of the smartest players and greatest passers the game has ever known. Playing for the Bruins in the 1992–93 season, Oates had 97 assists, a total only Wayne Gretzky, Mario Lemieux and Bobby Orr have surpassed. He played with several top teams—he broke in with the Red Wings and also played for Washington, Philadelphia and St.Louis—but Oates didn't reach the Stanley Cup finals until last year, with the Mighty Ducks. In his final game, for Edmonton in April 2004, Oates set up Igor Ulanov for a goal.

Single-Season Records

Goals

Player	Season	GP	G	Player	Season	GP	G
Wayne Gretzky, Edm	1981–82	80	92	Wayne Gretzky, Edm	1982–83	80	71
Wayne Gretzky, Edm	1983–84	74	87	Brett Hull, StL	1991–92	73	70
Brett Hull, StL	1990–91	78	86	Mario Lemieux, Pitt	1987–88	77	70
Mario Lemieux, Pitt	1988–89	76	85	Bernie Nicholls, LA	1988–89	79	70
Alexander Mogilny, Buff	1992–93	77	76	Mario Lemieux, Pitt	1992–93	60	69
Phil Esposito, Bos	1970–71	78	76	Mario Lemieux, Pitt	1995–96	70	69
Teemu Selanne, Winn	1992–93	84	76	Mike Bossy, NYI	1978–79	80	69
Wayne Gretzky, Edm	1984–85	80	73	Phil Esposito, Bos	1973–74	78	68
Brett Hull, StL	1989–90	80	72	Jari Kurri, Edm	1985–86	78	68
Jari Kurri, Edm	1984–85	73	71	Mike Bossy, NYI	1980–81	79	68

Assists

Player	Season	GP	A	Player	Season	GP	A
Wayne Gretzky, Edm	1985–86	80	163	Wayne Gretzky, LA	1989–90	73	102
Wayne Gretzky, Edm	1984–85	80	135	Bobby Orr, Bos	1970–71	78	102
Wayne Gretzky, Edm	1982–83	80	125	Mario Lemieux, Pitt	1987–88	77	98
Wayne Gretzky, LA	1990–91	78	122	Adam Oates, Bos	1992–93	84	97
Wayne Gretzky, Edm	1986–87	79	121	Doug Gilmour, Tor	1992–93	83	95
Wayne Gretzky, Edm	1981–82	80	120	Pat LaFontaine, Buff	1992–93	84	95
Wayne Gretzky, Edm	1983–84	74	118	Mario Lemieux, Pitt	1985–86	79	93
Mario Lemieux, Pitt	1988–89	76	114	Peter Stastny, Que	1981–82	80	93
Wayne Gretzky, LA	1988–89	78	114	Wayne Gretzky, LA	1993–94	81	92
Wayne Gretzky, Edm	1987–88	64	109	Mario Lemieux, Pitt	1995–96	70	92
Wayne Gretzky, Edm	1980–81	80	109	Ron Francis, Pitt	1995–96	77	92

Points

Player	Season	G	A	Pts	Player	Season	G	A	Pts
Wayne Gretzky, Edm	1985–86	52	163	215	Wayne Gretzky, LA	1990–91	41	122	163
Wayne Gretzky, Edm	1981–82	92	120	212	Mario Lemieux, Pitt	1995–96	69	92	161
Wayne Gretzky, Edm	1984–85	73	135	208	Mario Lemieux, Pitt	1992–93	69	91	160
Wayne Gretzky, Edm	1983–84	87	118	205	Steve Yzerman, Det	1988–89	65	90	155
Mario Lemieux, Pitt	1988–89	85	114	199	Phil Esposito, Bos	1970–71	76	76	152
Wayne Gretzky, Edm	1982–83	71	125	196	Bernie Nicholls, LA	1988–89	70	80	150
Wayne Gretzky, Edm	1986–87	62	121	183	Wayne Gretzky, Edm	1987–88	40	109	149
Mario Lemieux, Pitt	1987–88	70	98	168	Pat LaFontaine, Buff	1992–93	53	95	148
Wayne Gretzky, LA	1988–89	54	114	168	Mike Bossy, NYI	1981–82	64	83	147
Wayne Gretzky, Edm	1980–81	55	109	164	Phil Esposito, Bos	1973–74	68	77	145

Points per Game

Player	Season	GP	Pts	Avg	Player	Season	GP	Pts	Avg
Wayne Gretzky, Edm	1983–84	74	205	2.77	Mario Lemieux, Pitt	1987–88	77	168	2.18
Wayne Gretzky, Edm	1985–86	80	215	2.69	Wayne Gretzky, LA	1988–89	78	168	2.15
Mario Lemieux, Pitt	1992–93	60	160	2.67	Wayne Gretzky, LA	1990–91	78	163	2.09
Wayne Gretzky, Edm	1981–82	80	212	2.65	Mario Lemieux, Pitt	1989–90	59	123	2.08
Mario Lemieux, Pitt	1988–89	76	199	2.62	Wayne Gretzky, Edm	1980–81	80	164	2.05
Wayne Gretzky, Edm	1984–85	80	208	2.60	Mario Lemieux, Pitt	1991–92	64	131	2.05
Wayne Gretzky, Edm	1982–83	80	196	2.45	Bill Cowley, Bos	1943–44	36	71	1.97
Wayne Gretzky, Edm	1987–88	64	149	2.33	Phil Esposito, Bos	1970–71	78	152	1.95
Wayne Gretzky, Edm	1986–87	79	183	2.32	Wayne Gretzky, LA	1989–90	73	142	1.95
Mario Lemieux, Pitt	1995–96	70	161	2.30	Steve Yzerman, Det	1988–89	80	155	1.94

Note: Minimum 50 points in one season.

Goals per Game

Player	Season	GP	G	Avg
Joe Malone, Mtl	1917–18	20	44	2.20
Cy Denneny, Ott	1917–18	22	36	1.64
Newsy Lalonde, Mtl	1917–18	14	23	1.64
Joe Malone, Que	1919–20	24	39	1.63
Newsy Lalonde, Mtl	1919–20	23	36	1.57
Joe Malone, Ham	1920–21	20	30	1.50
Babe Dye, Ham-Tor	1920–21	24	35	1.46
Cy Denneny, Ott	1920–21	24	34	1.42
Reg Noble, Tor	1917–18	20	28	1.40
Newsy Lalonde, Mtl	1920–21	24	33	1.38

Note: Minimum 20 goals in one season.

Assists per Game

Player	Season	GP	A	Avg
Wayne Gretzky, Edm	1985–86	80	163	2.04
Wayne Gretzky, Edm	1987–88	64	109	1.70
Wayne Gretzky, Edm	1984–85	80	135	1.69
Wayne Gretzky, Edm	1983–84	74	118	1.59
Wayne Gretzky, Edm	1982–83	80	125	1.56
Wayne Gretzky, LA	1990–91	78	122	1.56
Wayne Gretzky, Edm	1986–87	79	121	1.53
Mario Lemieux, Pitt	1992–93	60	91	1.52
Wayne Gretzky, Edm	1981–82	80	120	1.50
Mario Lemieux, Pitt	1988–89	76	114	1.50

Note: Minimum 35 assists in one season.

Shutout Leaders

	Season	SO	Length of Schedule
George Hainsworth, Mtl	1928–29	22	44
Alex Connell, Ott	1925–26	15	36
Alex Connell, Ott	1927–28	15	44
Hal Winkler, Bos	1927–28	15	44
Tony Esposito, Chi	1969–70	15	76
George Hainsworth, Mtl	1926–27	14	44
Clint Benedict, Mtl M	1926–27	13	44
Alex Connell, Ott	1926–27	13	44
George Hainsworth, Mtl	1927–28	13	44
John Roach, NYR	1928–29	13	44
Roy Worters, NYA	1928–29	13	44
Harry Lumley, Tor	1953–54	13	70
Dominik Hasek, Buff	1997–98	13	82
Tiny Thompson, Bos	1928–29	12	44
Lorne Chabot, Tor	1928–29	12	44
Chuck Gardiner, Chi	1930–31	12	44
Terry Sawchuk, Det	1951–52	12	70
Terry Sawchuk, Det	1953–54	12	70
Terry Sawchuk, Det	1954–55	12	70
Glenn Hall, Det	1955–56	12	70
Bernie Parent, Phil	1973–74	12	78
Bernie Parent, Phil	1974–75	12	80
Lorne Chabot, NYR	1927–28	11	44
Harry Holmes, Det	1927–28	11	44

	Season	SO	Length of Schedule
Clint Benedict, Mtl M	1928–29	11	44
Joe Miller, Pitt Pirates	1928–29	11	44
Tiny Thompson, Bos	1932–33	11	48
Terry Sawchuck, Det	1950–51	11	70
Dominik Hasek, Buff	2000–01	11	82
Martin Brodeur, NJ	2003–04	11	82
Lorne Chabot, NYR	1926–27	10	44
Roy Worters, Pitt Pirates	1927–28	10	44
Clarence Dolson, Det	1928–29	10	44
John Roach, Det	1932–33	10	48
Chuck Gardiner, Chi	1933–34	10	48
Tiny Thompson, Bos	1935–36	10	48
Frank Brimsek, Bos	1938–39	10	48
Bill Durnan, Mtl	1948–49	10	60
Gerry McNeil, Mtl	1952–53	10	70
Harry Lumley, Tor	1952–53	10	70
Tony Esposito, Chi	1973–74	10	78
Ken Dryden, Mtl	1976–77	10	80
Martin Brodeur, NJ	1996–97	10	82
Martin Brodeur, NJ	1997–98	10	82
Roman Cechmanek, Phil	2000–01	10	82
Byron Dafoe, Bos	1998–99	10	82
Ed Belfour, Tor	2003–04	10	82

Wins

	Season	Record
Bernie Parent, Phil	1973–74	47-13-12
Bernie Parent, Phil	1974–75	44-14-9
Terry Sawchuk, Det	1950–51	44-13-13
Terry Sawchuk, Det	1951–52	44-14-12
Tom Barasso, Pitt	1992–93	43-14-5
Ed Belfour, Chi	1990–91	43-19-7
Martin Brodeur, NJ	1997–98	43-17-8
Martin Brodeur, NJ	1999–00	43-20-8
Jacques Plante, Mtl	1955–56	42-12-10
Jacques Plante, Mtl	1961–62	42-14-14
Ken Dryden, Mtl	1975–76	42-10-8
Mike Richter, NYR	1993–94	42-12-6
Roman Turek, StL	1999–00	42-15-9
Martin Brodeur, NJ	2000–01	42-17-11

Goals Against Average

(PRE-1950)

	Season	GP	GAA
George Hainsworth, Mtl	1928–29	44	0.92
George Hainsworth, Mtl	1927–28	44	1.05
Alex Connell, Ott	1925–26	36	1.12
Tiny Thompson, Bos	1928–29	44	1.18
Roy Worters, NYA	1928–29	38	1.21

(POST-1950)

	Season	GP	GAA
Miika Kiprusoff, Cal	2003–04	38	1.6949
Marty Turco, Dall	2002–03	55	1.7287
Tony Esposito, Chi	1971–72	48	1.7698
Al Rollins, Tor	1950–51	40	1.7744
Ron Tugnutt, Ott	1998–99	43	1.7943

Single-Game Records

Goals

	Date	G
Joe Malone, Que vs Tor	1-31-20	7
Newsy Lalonde, Mtl vs Tor	1-10-20	6
Joe Malone, Que vs Ott	3-10-20	6
Corb Denneny, Tor vs Ham	1-26-21	6
Cy Denneny, Ott vs Ham	3-7-21	6
Syd Howe, Det vs NYR	2-3-44	6
Red Berenson, StL vs Phil	11-7-68	6
Darryl Sittler, Tor vs Bos	2-7-76	6

Assists

	Date	A
Billy Taylor, Det vs Chi	3-16-47	7
Wayne Gretzky, Edm vs Wash	2-15-80	7
Wayne Gretzky, Edm vs Chi	12-11-85	7
Wayne Gretzky, Edm vs Que	2-14-86	7

Note: 24 tied with 6.

Points

	Date	G	A	Pts
Darryl Sittler, Tor vs Bos	2-7-76	6	4	10
Maurice Richard, Mtl vs Det	12-28-44	5	3	8
Bert Olmstead, Mtl vs Chi	1-9-54	4	4	8
Tom Bladon, Phil vs Clev	12-11-77	4	4	8
Bryan Trottier, NYI vs NYR	12-23-78	5	3	8
Peter Stastny, Que vs Wash	2-22-81	4	4	8
Anton Stastny, Que vs Wash	2-22-81	3	5	8
Wayne Gretzky, Edm vs NJ	11-19-83	3	5	8
Wayne Gretzky, Edm vs Minn	1-4-84	4	4	8
Paul Coffey, Edm vs Det	3-14-86	2	6	8
Mario Lemieux, Pitt vs StL	10-15-88	2	6	8
Bernie Nicholls, LA vs Tor	12-1-88	2	6	8
Mario Lemieux, Pitt vs NJ	12-31-88	5	3	8

NHL Season Leaders

Points

Season	Player and Club	Pts	Season	Player and Club	Pts
1917–18	Joe Malone, Mtl	44	1956–57	Gordie Howe, Det	89
1918–19	Newsy Lalonde, Mtl	30	1957–58	Dickie Moore, Mtl	84
1919–20	Joe Malone, Que	48	1958–59	Dickie Moore, Mtl	96
1920–21	Newsy Lalonde, Mtl	41	1959–60	Bobby Hull, Chi	81
1921–22	Punch Broadbent, Ott	46	1960–61	Bernie Geoffrion, Mtl	95
1922–23	Babe Dye, Tor	37	1961–62	Andy Bathgate, NY	84
1923–24	Cy Denneny, Ott	23		Bobby Hull, Chi	84
1924–25	Babe Dye, Tor	44	1962–63	Gordie Howe, Det	86
1925–26	Nels Stewart, Mtl M	42	1963–64	Stan Mikita, Chi	89
1926–27	Bill Cook, NY	37	1964–65	Stan Mikita, Chi	87
1927–28	Howie Morenz, Mtl	51	1965–66	Bobby Hull, Chi	97
1928–29	Ace Bailey, Tor	32	1966–67	Stan Mikita, Chi	97
1929–30	Cooney Weiland, Bos	73	1967–68	Stan Mikita, Chi	87
1930–31	Howie Morenz, Mtl	51	1968–69	Phil Esposito, Bos	126
1931–32	Harvey Jackson, Tor	53	1969–70	Bobby Orr, Bos	120
1932–33	Bill Cook, NY	50	1970–71	Phil Esposito, Bos	152
1933–34	Charlie Conacher, Tor	52	1971–72	Phil Esposito, Bos	133
1934–35	Charlie Conacher, Tor	57	1972–73	Phil Esposito, Bos	130
1935–36	Sweeney Schriner, NYA	45	1973–74	Phil Esposito, Bos	145
1936–37	Sweeney Schriner, NYA	46	1974–75	Bobby Orr, Bos	135
1937–38	Gord Drillon, Tor	52	1975–76	Guy Lafleur, Mtl	125
1938–39	Hector Blake, Mtl	47	1976–77	Guy Lafleur, Mtl	136
1939–40	Milt Schmidt, Bos	52	1977–78	Guy Lafleur, Mtl	132
1940–41	Bill Cowley, Bos	62	1978–79	Bryan Trottier, NYI	134
1941–42	Bryan Hextall, NY	54	1979–80	Marcel Dionne, LA	137
1942–43	Doug Bentley, Chi	73		Wayne Gretzky, Edm	137
1943–44	Herb Cain, Bos	82	1980–81	Wayne Gretzky, Edm	164
1944–45	Elmer Lach, Mtl	80	1981–82	Wayne Gretzky, Edm	212
1945–46	Max Bentley, Chi	61	1982–83	Wayne Gretzky, Edm	196
1946–47	Max Bentley, Chi	72	1983–84	Wayne Gretzky, Edm	205
1947–48	Elmer Lach, Mtl	61	1984–85	Wayne Gretzky, Edm	208
1948–49	Roy Conacher, Chi	68	1985–86	Wayne Gretzky, Edm	215
1949–50	Ted Lindsay, Det	78	1986–87	Wayne Gretzky, Edm	183
1950–51	Gordie Howe, Det	86	1987–88	Mario Lemieux, Pitt	168
1951–52	Gordie Howe, Det	86	1988–89	Mario Lemieux, Pitt	199
1952–53	Gordie Howe, Det	95	1989–90	Wayne Gretzky, LA	142
1953–54	Gordie Howe, Det	81	1990–91	Wayne Gretzky, LA	163
1954–55	Bernie Geoffrion, Mtl	75	1991–92	Mario Lemieux, Pitt	131
1955–56	Jean Beliveau, Mtl	88	1992–93	Mario Lemieux, Pitt	160

Points (Cont.)

Season	Player and Club	Pts	Season	Player and Club	Pts
1993–94	Wayne Gretzky, LA	130	1999–00	Jaromir Jagr, Pitt	96
1994–95	Jaromir Jagr, Pitt	70	2000–01	Jaromir Jagr, Pitt	121
1995–96	Mario Lemieux, Pitt	161	2001–02	Jarome Iginla, Cgy	96
1996–97	Mario Lemieux, Pitt	122	2002–03	Peter Forsberg, Col	106
1997–98	Jaromir Jagr, Pitt	102	2003–04	Martin St. Louis, TB	94
1998–99	Jaromir Jagr, Pitt	127			

Goals

Season	Player and Club	G	Season	Player and Club	G
1917–18	Joe Malone, Mtl	44	1961–62	Bobby Hull, Chi	50
1918–19	Odie Cleghorn, Mtl	23	1962–63	Gordie Howe, Det	38
1919–20	Joe Malone, Que	39	1963–64	Bobby Hull, Chi	43
1920–21	Babe Dye, Ham-Tor	35	1964–65	Norm Ullman, Det	42
1921–22	Punch Broadbent, Ott	32	1965–66	Bobby Hull, Chi	54
1922–23	Babe Dye, Tor	26	1966–67	Bobby Hull, Chi	52
1923–24	Cy Denneny, Ott	22	1967–68	Bobby Hull, Chi	44
1924–25	Babe Dye, Tor	38	1968–69	Bobby Hull, Chi	58
1925–26	Nels Stewart, Mtl	34	1969–70	Phil Esposito, Bos	43
1926–27	Bill Cook, NY	33	1970–71	Phil Esposito, Bos	76
1927–28	Howie Morenz, Mtl	33	1971–72	Phil Esposito, Bos	66
1928–29	Ace Bailey, Tor	22	1972–73	Phil Esposito, Bos	55
1929–30	Cooney Weiland, Bos	43	1973–74	Phil Esposito, Bos	68
1930–31	Bill Cook, NY	30	1974–75	Phil Esposito, Bos	61
1931–32	Charlie Conacher, Tor	34	1975–76	Guy Lafleur, Mtl	56
	Bill Cook, NY	34	1976–77	Steve Shutt, Mtl	60
1932–33	Bill Cook, NY	28	1977–78	Guy Lafleur, Mtl	60
1933–34	Charlie Conacher, Tor	32	1978–79	Mike Bossy, NYI	69
1934–35	Charlie Conacher, Tor	36	1979–80	Charlie Simmer, LA	56
1935–36	Charlie Conacher, Tor	23		Blaine Stoughton, Hart	56
	Bill Thoms, Tor	23	1980–81	Mike Bossy, NYI	68
1936–37	Larry Aurie, Det	23	1981–82	Wayne Gretzky, Edm	92
	Nels Stewart, Bos-NYA	23	1982–83	Wayne Gretzky, Edm	71
1937–38	Gord Drill, Tor	26	1983–84	Wayne Gretzky, Edm	87
1938–39	Roy Conacher, Bos	26	1984–85	Wayne Gretzky, Edm	73
1939–40	Bryan Hextall, NY	24	1985–86	Jari Kurri, Edm	68
1940–41	Bryan Hextall, NY	26	1986–87	Wayne Gretzky, Edm	62
1941–42	Lynn Patrick, NY	32	1987–88	Mario Lemieux, Pitt	70
1942–43	Doug Bentley, Chi	43	1988–89	Mario Lemieux, Pitt	85
1943–44	Doug Bentley, Chi	38	1989–90	Brett Hull, StL	72
1944–45	Maurice Richard, Mtl	50	1990–91	Brett Hull, StL	78
1945–46	Gaye Stewart, Tor	37	1991–92	Brett Hull, StL	70
1946–47	Maurice Richard, Mtl	50	1992–93	Alexander Mogilny, Buff	76
1947–48	Ted Lindsay, Det	33		Teemu Selanne, Winn	76
1948–49	Sid Abel, Det	28	1993–94	Pavel Bure, Van	60
1949–50	Maurice Richard, Mtl	43	1994–95	Peter Bondra, Wash	34
1950–51	Gordie Howe, Det	43	1995–96	Mario Lemieux, Pitt	69
1951–52	Gordie Howe, Det	47	1996–97	Keith Tkachuk, Phoe	52
1952–53	Gordie Howe, Det	49	1997–98	Teemu Selanne, Ana	52
1953–54	Maurice Richard, Mtl	37		Peter Bondra, Wash	52
1954–55	Bernie Geoffrion, Mtl	38	1998–99	Teemu Selanne, Ana	47
	Maurice Richard, Mtl	38	1999–00	Pavel Bure, Fla	58
1955–56	Jean Beliveau, Mtl	47	2000–01	Pavel Bure, Fla	59
1957–58	Dickie Moore, Mtl	36	2001–02	Jarome Iginla, Cgy	52
1956–57	Gordie Howe, Det	44	2002–03	Milan Hejduk, Col	50
1958–59	Jean Beliveau, Mtl	45	2003–04	Jarome Iginla, Cgy	41
1959–60	Bobby Hull, Chi	39		Rick Nash, Clb	41
	Bronco Horvath, Bos	39		Ilya Kovalchuk, Atl	41
1960–61	Bernie Geoffrion, Mtl	50			

Assists

Season	Player and Club	A	Season	Player and Club	A
1917–18	statistic not kept		1964–65	Stan Mikita, Chi	59
1918–19	Newsy Lalonde, Mtl	9	1965–66	Stan Mikita, Chi	48
1919–20	Corbett Denneny, Tor	12		Bobby Rousseau, Mtl	48
1920–21	Louis Berlinquette, Mtl	9		Jean Beliveau, Mtl	48
1921–22	Punch Broadbench, Ott	14	1966–67	Stan Mikita, Chi	62
1922–23	Babe Dye, Tor	11	1967–68	Phil Esposito, Bos	49
1923–24	Billy Boucher, Mtl	6	1968–69	Phil Esposito, Bos	77
1924–25	Cy Denneny, Ott	15	1969–70	Bobby Orr, Bos	87
1925–26	Cy Denneny, Ott	12	1970–71	Bobby Orr, Bos	102
1926–27	Dick Irvin, Chi	18	1971–72	Bobby Orr, Bos	80
1927–28	Howie Morenz, Mtl	18	1972–73	Phil Esposito, Bos	75
1928–29	Frank Boucher, NY	16	1973–74	Bobby Orr, Bos	89
1929–30	Frank Boucher, NY	36	1974–75	Bobby Clarke, Phil	89
1930–31	Joe Primeau, Tor	36		Bobby Orr, Bos	89
1931–32	Joe Primeau, Tor	37	1975–76	Bobby Clarke, Phil	89
1932–33	Frank Boucher, NY	28	1976–77	Guy Lafleur, Mtl	80
1933–34	Joe Primeau, Tor	32	1977–78	Bryan Trottier, NYI	77
1934–35	Art Chapman, NYA	28	1978–79	Bryan Trottier, NYI	87
1935–36	Art Chapman, NYA	28	1979–80	Wayne Gretzky, Edm	86
1936–37	Syl Apps, Tor	29	1980–81	Wayne Gretzky, Edm	109
1937–38	Syl Apps, Tor	29	1981–82	Wayne Gretzky, Edm	120
1938–39	Bill Cowley, Bos	34	1982–83	Wayne Gretzky, Edm	125
1939–40	Milt Schmidt, Bos	30	1983–84	Wayne Gretzky, Edm	118
1940–41	Bill Cowley, Bos	45	1984–85	Wayne Gretzky, Edm	135
1941–42	Phil Watson, NY	37	1985–86	Wayne Gretzky, Edm	163
1942–43	Bill Cowley, Bos	45	1986–87	Wayne Gretzky, Edm	121
1943–44	Clint Smith, Chi	49	1987–88	Wayne Gretzky, Edm	109
1944–45	Elmer Lach, Mtl	54	1988–89	Wayne Gretzky, LA	114
1945–46	Elmer Lach, Mtl	34		Mario Lemieux, Pitt	114
1946–47	Billy Taylor, Det	46	1989–90	Wayne Gretzky, LA	102
1947–48	Doug Bentley, Chi	37	1990–91	Wayne Gretzky, LA	122
1948–49	Doug Bentley, Chi	43	1991–92	Wayne Gretzky, LA	90
1949–50	Ted Lindsay, Det	55	1992–93	Adam Oates, Bos	97
1950–51	Gordie Howe, Det	43	1993–94	Wayne Gretzky, LA	92
	Ted Kennedy, Tor	43	1994–95	Ron Francis, Pitt	48
1951–52	Elmer Lach, Mtl	50	1995–96	Mario Lemieux, Pitt	92
1952–53	Gordie Howe, Det	46		Ron Francis, Pitt	92
1953–54	Gordie Howe, Det	48	1996–97	Mario Lemieux, Pitt	72
1954–55	Bert Olmstead, Mtl	48	1997–98	Jaromir Jagr, Pitt	67
1955–56	Bert Olmstead, Mtl	56		Wayne Gretzky, NYR	67
1956–57	Ted Lindsay, Det	55	1998–99	Jaromir Jagr, Pitt	83
1957–58	Henri Richard, Mtl	52	1999–00	Mark Recchi, Phil	63
1958–59	Dickie Moore, Mtl	55	2000–01	Jaromir Jagr, Pitt	69
1959–60	Bobby Hull, Chi	42		Adam Oates, Wash	69
1960–61	Jean Beliveau, Mtl	58	2001–02	Adam Oates, Wash	57
1961–62	Andy Bathgate, NY	56	2002–03	Peter Forsberg, Col	77
1962–63	Henri Richard, Mtl	50	2003–04	Scott Gomez, NJ	56
1963–64	Andy Bathgate, NY-Tor	58		Martin St. Louis, TB	56

THEY SAID IT

David Letterman, CBS talk show host, on being a new father: "I can hardly wait until I beat up on my first hockey coach."

Goals Against Average

Season	Goaltender and Club	GP	Min	GA	SO	Avg
1917–18	Georges Vezina, Mtl	21	1282	84	1	3.93
1918–19	Clint Benedict, Ott	18	1113	53	2	2.86
1919–20	Clint Benedict, Ott	24	1444	64	5	2.66
1920–21	Clint Benedict, Ott	24	1457	75	2	3.09
1921–22	Clint Benedict, Ott	24	1508	84	2	3.34
1922–23	Clint Benedict, Ott	24	1478	54	4	2.19
1923–24	Georges Vezina, Mtl	24	1459	48	3	1.97
1924–25	Georges Vezina, Mtl	30	1860	56	5	1.81
1925–26	Alex Connell, Ott	36	2251	42	15	1.12
1926–27	Clint Benedict, Mtl M	43	2748	65	13	1.42
1927–28	George Hainsworth, Mtl	44	2730	48	13	1.05
1928–29	George Hainsworth, Mtl	44	2800	43	22	0.92
1929–30	Tiny Thompson, Bos	44	2680	98	3	2.19
1930–31	Roy Worters, NYA	44	2760	74	8	1.61
1931–32	Chuck Gardiner, Chi	48	2989	92	4	1.85
1932–33	Tiny Thompson, Bos	48	3000	88	11	1.76
1933–34	Wilf Cude, Det-Mtl	30	1920	47	5	1.47
1934–35	Lorne Chabot, Chi	48	2940	88	8	1.80
1935–36	Tiny Thompson, Bos	48	2930	82	10	1.68
1936–37	Normie Smith, Det	48	2980	102	6	2.05
1937–38	Tiny Thompson, Bos	48	2970	89	7	1.80
1938–39	Frank Brimsek, Bos	43	2610	68	10	1.56
1939–40	Dave Kerr, NYR	48	3000	77	8	1.54
1940–41	Turk Broda, Tor	48	2970	99	5	2.00
1941–42	Frank Brimsek, Bos	47	2930	115	3	2.35
1942–43	Johnny Mowers, Det	50	3010	124	6	2.47
1943–44	Bill Durnan, Mtl	50	3000	109	2	2.18
1944–45	Bill Durnan, Mtl	50	3000	121	1	2.42
1945–46	Bill Durnan, Mtl	40	2400	104	4	2.60
1946–47	Bill Durnan, Mtl	60	3600	138	4	2.30
1947–48	Turk Broda, Tor	60	3600	143	5	2.38
1948–49	Bill Durnan, Mtl	60	3600	126	10	2.10
1949–50	Bill Durnan, Mtl	64	3840	141	8	2.20
1950–51	Al Rollins, Tor	40	2367	70	5	1.77
1951–52	Terry Sawchuk, Det	70	4200	133	12	1.90
1952–53	Terry Sawchuk, Det	63	3780	120	9	1.90
1953–54	Harry Lumley, Tor	69	4140	128	13	1.86
1954–55	Harry Lumley, Tor	69	4140	134	8	1.94
	Terry Sawchuk, Det	68	4060	132	12	1.94
1955–56	Jacques Plante, Mtl	64	3840	119	7	1.86
1956–57	Jacques Plante, Mtl	61	3660	123	9	2.02
1957–58	Jacques Plante, Mtl	57	3386	119	9	2.11
1958–59	Jacques Plante, Mtl	67	4000	144	9	2.16
1959–60	Jacques Plante, Mtl	69	4140	175	3	2.54
1960–61	Johnny Bower, Tor	58	3480	145	2	2.50
1961–62	Jacques Plante, Mtl	70	4200	166	4	2.37
1962–63	Jacques Plante, Mtl	56	3320	138	5	2.49
1963–64	Johnny Bower, Tor	51	3009	106	5	2.11
1964–65	Johnny Bower, Tor	34	2040	81	3	2.38
1965–66	Johnny Bower, Tor	35	1998	75	3	2.25
1966–67	Glenn Hall, Chi	32	1664	66	2	2.38
1967–68	Gump Worsley, Mtl	40	2213	73	6	1.98
1968–69	Jacques Plante, StL	37	2139	70	5	1.96
1969–70	Ernie Wakely, StL	30	1651	58	4	2.11
1970–71	Jacques Plante, Tor	40	2329	73	4	1.88
1971–72	Tony Esposito, Chi	48	2780	82	9	1.77
1972–73	Ken Dryden, Mtl	54	3165	119	6	2.26
1973–74	Bernie Parent, Phil	73	4314	136	12	1.89
1974–75	Bernie Parent, Phil	68	4041	137	12	2.03
1975–76	Ken Dryden, Mtl	62	3580	121	8	2.03
1976–77	Michael Larocque, Mtl	26	1525	53	4	2.09
1977–78	Ken Dryden, Mtl	52	3071	105	5	2.05
1978–79	Ken Dryden, Mtl	47	2814	108	5	2.30
1979–80	Bob Sauve, Buff	32	1880	74	4	2.36
1980–81	Richard Sevigny, Mtl	33	1777	71	2	2.40
1981–82	Denis Herron, Mtl	27	1547	68	3	2.64
1982–83	Pete Peeters, Bos	62	3611	142	8	2.36
1983–84	Pat Riggin, Wash	41	2299	102	4	2.66

Goals Against Average (Cont.)

Season	Goaltender and Club	GP	Min	GA	SO	Avg
1984–85	Tom Barrasso, Buff	54	3248	144	5	2.66
1985–86	Bob Froese, Phil	51	2728	116	5	2.55
1986–87	Brian Hayward, Mtl	37	2178	102	1	2.81
1987–88	Pete Peeters, Wash	35	1896	88	2	2.78
1988–89	Patrick Roy, Mtl	48	2744	113	4	2.47
1989–90	Patrick Roy, Mtl	54	3173	134	3	2.53
	Mike Liut, Hart-Wash	37	2161	91	4	2.53
1990–91	Ed Belfour, Chi	74	4127	170	4	2.47
1991–92	Patrick Roy, Mtl	67	3935	155	5	2.36
1992–93	Felix Potvin, Tor	48	2781	116	2	2.50
1993–94	Dominik Hasek, Buff	58	3358	109	7	1.95
1994–95	Dominik Hasek, Buff	41	2416	85	5	2.11
1995–96	Ron Hextall, Phil	53	3102	112	4	2.17
	Chris Osgood, Det	50	2933	106	5	2.17
1996–97	Martin Brodeur, NJ	67	3838	120	10	1.88
1997–98	Ed Belfour, Dall	61	3581	112	9	1.88
1998–99	Ron Tugnutt, Ott	43	2508	75	3	1.79
1999–00	Brian Boucher, Phil	35	2038	65	4	1.91
2000–01	Marty Turco, Dall	26	1266	40	3	1.90
2001–02	Patrick Roy, Col	63	3774	122	9	1.94
2002–03	Marty Turco, Dall	55	3193	92	7	1.72
2003–04	Miikka Kiprusoff, Cgy	38	2301	65	4	1.70

Penalty Minutes

Season	Player and Club	GP	PIM	Season	Player and Club	GP	PIM
1918–19	Joe Hall, Mtl	17	85	1961–62	Lou Fontinato, Mtl	54	167
1919–20	Cully Wilson, Tor	23	79	1962–63	Howie Young, Det	64	273
1920–21	Bert Corbeau, Mtl	24	86	1963–64	Vic Hadfield, NYR	69	151
1921–22	Sprague Cleghorn, Mtl	24	63	1964–65	Carl Brewer, Tor	70	177
1922–23	Billy Boucher, Mtl	24	52	1965–66	Reggie Fleming, Bos-NYR	69	166
1923–24	Bert Corbeau, Tor	24	55	1966–67	John Ferguson, Mtl	67	177
1924–25	Billy Boucher, Mtl	30	92	1967–68	Barclay Plager, StL	49	153
1925–26	Bert Corbeau, Tor	36	121	1968–69	Forbes Kennedy, Phil-Tor	77	219
1926–27	Nels Stewart, Mtl M	44	133	1969–70	Keith Magnuson, Chi	76	213
1927–28	Eddie Shore, Bos	44	165	1970–71	Keith Magnuson, Chi	76	291
1928–29	Red Dutton, Mtl M	44	139	1971–72	Brian Watson, Pitt	75	212
1929–30	Joe Lamb, Ott	44	119	1972–73	Dave Schultz, Phil	76	259
1930–31	Harvey Rockburn, Det	42	118	1973–74	Dave Schultz, Phil	73	348
1931–32	Red Dutton, NYA	47	107	1974–75	Dave Schultz, Phil	76	472
1932–33	Red Horner, Tor	48	144	1975–76	Steve Durbano, Pitt-KC	69	370
1933–34	Red Horner, Tor	42	126	1976–77	Dave Williams, Tor	77	338
1934–35	Red Horner, Tor	46	125	1977–78	Dave Schultz, LA-Pitt	74	405
1935–36	Red Horner, Tor	43	167	1978–79	Dave Williams, Tor	77	298
1936–37	Red Horner, Tor	48	124	1979–80	Jimmy Mann, Winn	72	287
1937–38	Red Horner, Tor	47	82	1980–81	Dave Williams, Van	77	343
1938–39	Red Horner, Tor	48	85	1981–82	Paul Baxter, Pitt	76	409
1939–40	Red Horner, Tor	30	87	1982–83	Randy Holt, Wash	70	275
1940–41	Jimmy Orlando, Det	48	99	1983–84	Chris Nilan, Mtl	76	338
1941–42	Jimmy Orlando, Det	48	81	1984–85	Chris Nilan, Mtl	77	358
1942–43	Jimmy Orlando, Det	40	89	1985–86	Joey Kocur, Det	59	377
1943–44	Mike McMahon, Mtl	42	98	1986–87	Tim Hunter, Cgy	73	361
1944–45	Pat Egan, Bos	48	86	1987–88	Bob Probert, Det	74	398
1945–46	Jack Stewart, Det	47	73	1988–89	Tim Hunter, Cgy	75	375
1946–47	Gus Mortson, Tor	60	133	1989–90	Basil McRae, Minn	66	351
1947–48	Bill Barilko, Tor	57	147	1990–91	Bob Ray, Buff	66	350
1948–49	Bill Ezinicki, Tor	52	145	1991–92	Mike Peluso, Chi	63	408
1949–50	Bill Ezinicki, Tor	67	144	1992–93	Marty McSorley, LA	81	399
1950–51	Gus Mortson, Tor	60	142	1993–94	Tie Domi, Winn	81	347
1951–52	Gus Kyle, Bos	69	127	1994–95	Enrico Ciccone, TB	41	225
1952–53	Maurice Richard, Mtl	70	112	1995–96	Matthew Barnaby, Buff	73	335
1953–54	Gus Mortson, Chi	68	132	1996–97	Gino Odjick, Van	70	371
1954–55	Fern Flaman, Bos	70	150	1997–98	Donald Brashear, Van	77	372
1955–56	Lou Fontinato, NYR	70	202	1998–99	Rob Ray, Buff	76	261
1956–57	Gus Mortson, Chi	70	147	1999–00	Denny Lambert, Atl	73	219
1957–58	Lou Fontinato, NYR	70	152	2000–01	Matthew Barnaby, TB	76	265
1958–59	Ted Lindsay, Chi	70	184	2001–02	Peter Worrell, Fla	79	354
1959–60	Carl Brewer, Tor	67	150	2002–03	Jody Shelley, Clb	68	249
1960–61	Pierre Pilote, Chi	70	165	2003–04	Sean Avery, LA	76	261

NHL All-Star Game

First played in 1947, this game was scheduled before the start of the regular season and used to match the defending Stanley Cup Champions against a squad made up of the league All-stars from other teams. In 1966 the games were moved to mid-season, although there was no game that year. The format changed to a conference versus conference showdown in 1969.

Results

Year	Site	Score	MVP	Attendance
1947	Toronto	All-Stars 4, Toronto 3	None named	14,169
1948	Chicago	All-Stars 3, Toronto 1	None named	12,794
1949	Toronto	All-Stars 3, Toronto 1	None named	13,541
1950	Detroit	Detroit 7, All-Stars 1	None named	9,166
1951	Toronto	1st team 2, 2nd team 2	None named	11,469
1952	Detroit	1st team 1, 2nd team 1	None named	10,680
1953	Montreal	All-Stars 3, Montreal 1	None named	14,153
1954	Detroit	All-Stars 2, Detroit 2	None named	10,689
1955	Detroit	Detroit 3, All-Stars 1	None named	10,111
1956	Montreal	All-Stars 1, Montreal 1	None named	13,095
1957	Montreal	All-Stars 5, Montreal 3	None named	13,003
1958	Montreal	Montreal 6, All-Stars 3	None named	13,989
1959	Montreal	Montreal 6, All-Stars 1	None named	13,818
1960	Montreal	All-Stars 2, Montreal 1	None named	13,949
1961	Chicago	All-Stars 3, Chicago 1	None named	14,534
1962	Toronto	Toronto 4, All-Stars 1	Eddie Shack, Tor	14,236
1963	Toronto	All-Stars 3, Toronto 3	Frank Mahovlich, Tor	14,034
1964	Toronto	All-Stars 3, Toronto 2	Jean Beliveau, Mtl	14,232
1965	Montreal	All-Stars 5, Montreal 2	Gordie Howe, Det	13,529
1967	Montreal	Montreal 3, All-Stars 0	Henri Richard, Mtl	14,284
1968	Toronto	Toronto 4, All-Stars 3	Bruce Gamble, Tor	15,753
1969	Montreal	East 3, West 3	Frank Mahovlich, Det	16,260
1970	St Louis	East 4, West 1	Bobby Hull, Chi	16,587
1971	Boston	West 2, East 1	Bobby Hull, Chi	14,790
1972	Minnesota	East 3, West 2	Bobby Orr, Bos	15,423
1973	NY Rangers	East 5, West 4	Greg Polis, Pitt	16,986
1974	Chicago	West 6, East 4	Garry Unger, StL	16,426
1975	Montreal	Wales 7, Campbell 1	Syl Apps Jr, Pitt	16,080
1976	Philadelphia	Wales 7, Campbell 5	Pete Mahovlich, Mtl	16,436
1977	Vancouver	Wales 4, Campbell 3	Rick Martin, Buff	15,607
1978	Buffalo	Wales 3, Campbell 2 (OT)	Billy Smith, NYI	16,433
1980	Detroit	Wales 6, Campbell 3	Reg Leach, Phil	21,002
1981	Los Angeles	Campbell 4, Wales 1	Mike Liut, StL	15,761
1982	Washington	Wales 4, Campbell 2	Mike Bossy, NYI	18,130
1983	NY Islanders	Campbell 9, Wales 3	Wayne Gretzky, Edm	15,230
1984	New Jersey	Wales 7, Campbell 6	Don Maloney, NYR	18,939
1985	Calgary	Wales 6, Campbell 4	Mario Lemieux, Pitt	16,825
1986	Hartford	Wales 4, Campbell 3 (OT)	Grant Fuhr, Edm	15,100
1988	St Louis	Wales 6, Campbell 5 (OT)	Mario Lemieux, Pitt	17,878
1989	Edmonton	Campbell 9, Wales 5	Wayne Gretzky, LA	17,503
1990	Pittsburgh	Wales 12, Campbell 7	Mario Lemieux, Pitt	16,236
1991	Chicago	Campbell 11, Wales 5	Vince Damphousse, Tor	18,472
1992	Philadelphia	Campbell 10, Wales 6	Brett Hull, StL	17,380
1993	Montreal	Wales 16, Campbell 6	Mike Gartner, NYR	17,137
1994	NY Rangers	East 9, West 8	Mike Richter, NYR	18,200
1996	Boston	East 5, West 4	Ray Bourque, Bos	17,565
1997	San Jose	East 11, West 7	Mark Recchi, Mtl	17,565
1998	Vancouver	N America 8, World 7	Teemu Selanne, Ana (World)	18,422
1999	Tampa Bay	N America 8, World 6	Wayne Gretzky, NYR (N America)	19,758
2000	Toronto	World 9, N America 4	Pavel Bure, Fla (World)	19,300
2001	Denver	N America 14, World 12	Bill Guerin, Bos (N America)	18,646
2002	Los Angeles	World 8, N America 5	Eric Daze, Chi (N America)	18,118
2003	Sunrise, Fla.	West 6, East 5 (shootout)	Dany Heatley, Atl (East)	19,250
2004	St. Paul, Minn.	East 6, West 4	Joe Sakic, Col (West)	19,434

Note: The Challenge Cup, a series between the NHL All-Stars and the Soviet Union, was played instead of the All-Star Game in 1979. Eight years later, Rendez-Vous '87, a two-game series matching the Soviet Union and the NHL All-Stars, replaced the All-Star Game. The 1995 NHL All-Star game was cancelled due to a labor dispute. The 1998 NHL All-Star game, billed as a preview to the 1998 Winter Olympics in Nagano, Japan, matched North Amercian–born All-Stars and All-Stars born elsewhere.

Hockey Hall of Fame

Located in Toronto, the Hockey Hall of Fame was officially opened on August 26, 1961. The current chairman is William C. Hay. There are, at present, 306 members of the Hockey Hall of Fame—209 players, 84 "builders," and 14 on-ice officials. (One member, Alan Eagleson, resigned from the Hall 3-25-98.) To be eligible, player and referee/linesman candidates should have been out of the game for three years, but the Hall's Board of Directors can make exceptions.

Players

Sid Abel (1969)
Jack Adams (1959)
Charles (Syl) Apps (1961)
George Armstrong (1975)
Irvine (Ace) Bailey (1975)
Donald H. (Dan) Bain (1945)
Hobey Baker (1945)
Bill Barber (1990)
Marty Barry (1965)
Andy Bathgate (1978)
Bobby Bauer (1996)
Jean Beliveau (1972)
Clint Benedict (1965)
Douglas Bentley (1964)
Max Bentley (1966)
Hector (Toe) Blake (1966)
Leo Boivin (1986)
Dickie Boon (1952)
Mike Bossy (1991)
Emile (Butch) Bouchard (1966)
Frank Boucher (1958)
George (Buck) Boucher (1960)
Ray Bourque (2004)
Johnny Bower (1976)
Russell Bowie (1945)
Frank Brimsek (1966)
Harry L. (Punch) Broadbent (1962)
Walter (Turk) Broda (1967)
John Bucyk (1981)
Billy Burch (1974)
Harry Cameron (1962)
Gerry Cheevers (1985)
Francis (King) Clancy (1958)
Aubrey (Dit) Clapper (1947)
Bobby Clarke (1987)
Sprague Cleghorn (1958)
Paul Coffey (2004)
Neil Colville (1967)
Charlie Conacher (1961)
Lionel Conacher (1994)
Roy Conacher (1998)
Alex Connell (1958)
Bill Cook (1952)
Fred (Bun) Cook (1995)
Arthur Coulter (1974)
Yvan Cournoyer (1982)
Bill Cowley (1968)
Samuel (Rusty) Crawford (1962)
Jack Darragh (1962)
Allan M. (Scotty) Davidson (1950)
Clarence (Hap) Day (1961)
Alex Delvecchio (1977)
Cy Denneny (1959)
Marcel Dionne (1992)
Gordie Drillon (1975)
Charles Drinkwater (1950)

Ken Dryden (1983)
Woody Dumart (1992)
Thomas Dunderdale (1974)
Bill Durnan (1964)
Mervyn A. (Red) Dutton (1958)
Cecil (Babe) Dye (1970)
Phil Esposito (1984)
Tony Esposito (1988)
Arthur F. Farrell (1965)
Bernie Federko (2002)
Viacheslav Fetisov (2001)
Ferdinand (Fern) Flaman (1990)
Frank Foyston (1958)
Frank Frederickson (1958)
Grant Fuhr (2003)
Bill Gadsby (1970)
Bob Gainey (1992)
Chuck Gardiner (1945)
Herb Gardiner (1958)
Jimmy Gardner (1962)
Mike Gartner (2001)
Bernie (Boom Boom) Geoffrion (1972)
Eddie Gerard (1945)
Ed Giacomin (1987)
Rod Gilbert (1982)
Clark Gilles (2002)
Hamilton (Billy) Gilmour (1962)
Frank (Moose) Goheen (1952)
Ebenezer R. (Ebbie) Goodfellow (1963)
Michel Goulet (1998)
Mike Grant (1950)
Wilfred (Shorty) Green (1962)
Wayne Gretzky (1999)
Si Griffis (1950)
George Hainsworth (1961)
Glenn Hall (1975)
Joe Hall (1961)
Doug Harvey (1973)
Dale Hawerchuk (2001)
George Hay (1958)
William (Riley) Hern (1962)
Bryan Hextall (1969)
Harry (Hap) Holmes (1972)
Tom Hooper (1962)
George (Red) Horner (1965)
Miles (Tim) Horton (1977)
Gordie Howe (1972)
Syd Howe (1965)
Harry Howell (1979)
Bobby Hull (1983)
John (Bouse) Hutton (1962)
Harry M. Hyland (1962)
James (Dick) Irvin (1958)
Harvey (Busher) Jackson (1971)

Ernest (Moose) Johnson (1952)
Ivan (Ching) Johnson (1958)
Tom Johnson (1970)
Aurel Joliat (1947)
Gordon (Duke) Keats (1958)
Leonard (Red) Kelly (1969)
Ted (Teeder) Kennedy (1966)
Dave Keon (1986)
Jari Kurri (2001)
Elmer Lach (1966)
Guy Lafleur (1988)
Pat LaFonaine (2003)
Edouard (Newsy) Lalonde (1950)
Rod Langway (2002)
Jacques Laperriere (1987)
Guy LaPointe (1993)
Edgar Laprade (1993)
Reed Larson (1996)
Jean (Jack) Laviolette (1962)
Hugh Lehman (1958)
Jacques Lemaire (1984)
Mario Lemieux (1997)
Percy LeSueur (1961)
Herbert A. Lewis (1989)
Ted Lindsay (1966)
Harry Lumley (1980)
Lanny McDonald (1992)
Frank McGee (1945)
Billy McGimsie (1962)
George McNamara (1958)
Duncan (Mickey) MacKay (1952)
Frank Mahovlich (1981)
Joe Malone (1950)
Sylvio Mantha (1960)
Jack Marshall (1965)
Fred G. (Steamer) Maxwell (1962)
Stan Mikita (1983)
Dicky Moore (1974)
Patrick (Paddy) Moran (1958)
Howie Morenz (1945)
Billy Mosienko (1965)
Joe Mullen (2000)
Larry Murphy (2004)
Frank Nighbor (1947)
Reg Noble (1962)
Herbert (Buddy) O'Connor (1988)
Harry Oliver (1967)
Bert Olmstead (1985)
Bobby Orr (1979)
Bernie Parent (1984)
Brad Park (1988)
Lester Patrick (1947)
Lynn Patrick (1980)
Gilbert Perreault (1990)
Tommy Phillips (1945)
Pierre Pilote (1975)

Players *(Cont.)*

Didier (Pit) Pitre (1962)
Jacques Plante (1978)
Denis Potvin (1991)
Walter (Babe) Pratt (1966)
Joe Primeau (1963)
Marcel Pronovost (1978)
Bob Pulford (1991)
Harvey Pulford (1945)
Hubert (Bill) Quackenbush (1976)
Frank Rankin (1961)
Jean Ratelle (1985)
Claude (Chuck) Rayner (1973)
Kenneth Reardon (1966)
Henri Richard (1979)
Maurice (Rocket) Richard (1961)
George Richardson (1950)
Gordon Roberts (1971)
Larry Robinson (1995)
Art Ross (1945)
Blair Russel (1965)
Ernest Russell (1965)
Jack Ruttan (1962)
Borje Salming (1996)
Denis Savard (2000)
Serge Savard (1986)
Terry Sawchuk (1971)
Fred Scanlan (1965)
Milt Schmidt (1961)
Dave (Sweeney) Schriner (1962)
Earl Seibert (1963)
Oliver Seibert (1961)
Eddie Shore (1947)
Steve Shutt (1993)
Albert C. (Babe) Siebert (1964)
Harold (Bullet Joe) Simpson (1962)
Daryl Sittler (1989)
Alfred E. Smith (1962)
Billy Smith (1993)
Clint Smith (1991)
Reginald (Hooley) Smith (1972)
Thomas Smith (1973)
Allan Stanley (1981)
Russell (Barney) Stanley (1962)
Peter Stastny (1998)
John (Black Jack) Stewart (1964)
Nels Stewart (1962)
Bruce Stuart (1961)
Hod Stuart (1945)
Frederic (Cyclone) (O.B.E.)
   Taylor (1947)
Cecil R. (Tiny) Thompson (1959)
Vladislav Tretiak (1989)
Harry J. Trihey (1950)
Bryan Trottier (1997)
Norm Ullman (1982)
Georges Vezina (1945)
Jack Walker (1960)
Marty Walsh (1962)
Harry Watson (1994)
Harry E. Watson (1962)

Players *(Cont.)*

Ralph (Cooney) Weiland (1971)
Harry Westwick (1962)
Fred Whitcroft (1962)
Gordon (Phat) Wilson (1962)
Lorne (Gump) Worsley (1980)
Roy Worters (1969)

Builders

Charles Adams (1960)
Weston W. Adams (1972)
Thomas (Frank) Ahearn (1962)
John (Bunny) Ahearne (1977)
Montagu Allan (C.V.O.) (1945)
Keith Allen (1992)
Al Arbour (1996)
Harold Ballard (1977)
David Bauer (1989)
John Bickell (1978)
Scott Bowman (1991)
George V. Brown (1961)
Walter A. Brown (1962)
Frank Buckland (1975)
Walter L. Bush (2000)
Jack Butterfield (1980)
Frank Calder (1947)
Angus D. Campbell (1964)
Clarence Campbell (1966)
Joe Cattarinich (1977)
Bob Cole (1996)
Joseph (Leo) Dandurand (1963)
Francis Dilio (1964)
George S. Dudley (1958)
James A. Dunn (1968)
Robert Alan Eagleson (1989–98*)
Cliff Fletcher (2004)
Sergio Gambucci (1996)
Emile Francis (1982)
Jack Gibson (1976)
Tommy Gorman (1963)
Frank Griffiths (1993)
William Hanley (1986)
Charles Hay (1974)
James C. Hendy (1968)
Foster Hewitt (1965)
William Hewitt (1947)
Fred J. Hume (1962)
Mike Ilitch (2003)
George (Punch) Imlach (1984)
Tommy Ivan (1974)
William M. Jennings (1975)
Bob Johnson (1992)
Gordon W. Juckes (1979)
John Kilpatrick (1960)
Brian Kilrea (2003)
Seymour Knox III (1993)
George Leader (1969)
Robert LeBel (1970)
Thomas F. Lockhart (1965)
Paul Loicq (1961)
Frederic McLaughlin (1963)

Builders *(Cont.)*

John Mariucci (1985)
Frank Mathers (1992)
John (Jake) Milford (1984)
Hartland Molson (1973)
Scotty Morrison (1999)
Mngr. Athol (Pere) Murray (1998)
Roger Neilson (2002)
Francis Nelson (1947)
Bruce A. Norris (1969)
James Norris, Sr. (1958)
James D. Norris (1962)
William M. Northey (1947)
John O'Brien (1962)
Brian O'Neill (1994)
Fred Page (1993)
Craig Patrick (1996)
Frank Patrick (1958)
Allan W. Pickard (1958)
Rudy Pilous (1985)
Norman (Bud) Poile (1990)
Samuel Pollock (1978)
Donat Raymond (1958)
John Robertson (1947)
Claude C. Robinson (1947)
Philip D. Ross (1976)
Gunther Sabetzki (1995)
Glen Sather (1997)
Frank J. Selke (1960)
Harry Sinden (1983)
Frank D. Smith (1962)
Conn Smythe (1958)
Edward M. Snider (1988)
Lord Stanley of Preston (1945)
James T. Sutherland (1947)
Anatoli V. Tarasov (1974)
Bill Torrey (1995)
Lloyd Turner (1958)
William Tutt (1978)
Carl Potter Voss (1974)
Fred C. Waghorn (1961)
Arthur Wirtz (1971)
Bill Wirtz (1976)
John A. Ziegler, Jr. (1987)

Referees/Linesmen

Neil Armstrong (1991)
John Ashley (1981)
William L. Chadwick (1964)
John D'Amico (1993)
Chaucer Elliott (1961)
George Hayes (1988)
Robert W. Hewitson (1963)
Fred J. (Mickey) Ion (1961)
Matt Pavelich (1987)
Mike Rodden (1962)
J. Cooper Smeaton (1961)
Roy (Red) Storey (1967)
Frank Udvari (1973)
Andy van Hellemond (1999)

Note: Year of election to the Hall of Fame is in parentheses after the member's name.
*Eagleson resigned from Hall March 25, 1998.

Tennis

**Triple major winner
Roger Federer**

Russian Revolution

While Roger Federer held court in the men's game, a talented crop of young Russians overthrew women's tennis

BY B.J. SCHECTER

THERE'S A NEW king in men's tennis, one who operates and strikes with the precision of an assassin. Roger Federer may not have the flair or the movie star looks of American Andy Roddick, and his stoic on-court demeanor exceeds even that of Pete Sampras, but his game provokes excitement in all who see it. Four-time U.S. Open champ John McEnroe has been moved on more than one occasion to say that Federer is "the most talented player I've ever laid eyes on." With efficient ground strokes, skill at the net and a solid serve, Federer has no flaws as a player.

And lest anyone think McEnroe's assessment a bit hyperbolic, Federer won three of the four majors in 2004. He positively rolled through the U.S. Open in September, dropping only three sets and rarely getting challenged. In his 6–0, 7–6, 6–0 victory over former world No. 1 Lleyton Hewitt in the final, Federer lost just five points in the first set.

"He's setting the new standard for every-

one right now," said Tim Henman, who lost to Federer 6–3, 6–4, 6–4 in the Open semifinal. "He's so difficult [to beat] because he's so complete in every area." After Marat Safin lost to Federer in the final of the Australian Open he said, "I just lost to a magician."

Once regarded as an underachiever for bowing out in the early rounds of big tournaments, Federer was at his best in 2004 when the stakes were highest. His U.S. Open victory was the 11th consecutive time he made a final and won, and his defeat of Hewitt was Federer's 17th straight win over a Top 10 player. What's more, Federer had ascended to the top without the benefit of a coach or a full-time agent. Federer's girlfriend handles his schedule and travel arrangements and one of his childhood friends serves as his hitting partner. "I guess I've discovered that I like being my own boss."

On the court, Federer showed opponents who was boss. He faced Roddick in a classic Wimbledon final, one that marked the

The 17-year-old Sharapova dispatched Serena Williams 6–1, 6–4 to win Wimbledon.

BOB MARTIN

first time in 22 years that the top two seeds had met for the championship at the All-England Club. Roddick came out determined, unleashing 145-mph serves and taking the first set. Federer fought back and went up two breaks in the second set, but Roddick wouldn't relent and gained them back. Federer dug in and broke Roddick to win the second set with a beautiful forehand down the line, and in a rare display of emotion screamed, "Yesss!" After Roddick stormed out to a 4–2 lead in the third set, Federer composed himself during a rain delay—remember he has no coach—and decided to switch to more of a serve-and-volley game. The strategy worked and helped him force a tiebreaker, which he won 7–3 to take the third set. Momentum his, he won the fourth set 6–4 to close out the match and defend his Wimbledon title.

It was the best match of the year, and went a way toward establishing Federer-Roddick as the best rivalry in men's tennis since Sampras-Andre Agassi. "He pushed me to the limit," said Federer of Roddick. "I really had to give everything I had because it looked like he was going to crush me. Luckily I could fight hard and stay in contention. This is the only way I could [win] and I'm very proud of it."

When Federer served up an ace to seal the match, he fell to his knees and began to cry. Physically exhausted and emotionally drained, Roddick walked around the net, embraced his opponent and said, "Hopefully we'll get to do this again sometime."

Members of the Russian Tennis Federation must have had similar thoughts after Anastasia Myskina beat Elena Dementieva in an all-Russian French Open final. With stars Venus and Serena Williams dogged by injuries or disinterest, the door has been open to other contenders since mid-2003. Justine Henin-Hardenne of Belgium started through it, winning the 2003 French and U.S. Opens, and kicking off 2004 by winning the Australian Open. But that's when the talented and telegenic young Russian women burst past her. After Myskina's triumph over Dementieva at Roland Garros, their countrywoman Maria Sharapova won Wimbledon, defeating Serena Williams, and Svetlana Kuznetsova downed Dementieva in the U.S. Open final—the second all-Russian Grand Slam final of the season. It was truly a Russian revolution in women's tennis.

The biggest hit was the 17-year-old

Sharapova. Six-feet tall, gorgeous and graceful on and off the court, Sharapova looked more like a fashion model than an athlete. But at Wimbledon she showed that she could be tennis's next big thing. With remarkable grace and poise, Sharapova came back from a set down to beat Ai Sugiyama in the quarterfinals and Lindsay Davenport in the semifinals. "I had control of the match," said Davenport, "and she took it from me."

In the final against two-time defending champion Serena Williams, Sharapova cruised to a 6–1, 6–4 victory, even making Serena look silly at times. At the end of one key rally Serena slipped and fell on her rear end while trying to chase down a blistering Sharapova return. In her postmatch press conference, the normally talkative Serena was at a loss for words. "I just didn't . . . I don't know what happened," she said.

What happened was that Sharapova played a near perfect match. She showed both power and touch and constantly kept Williams on her heels with a deadly serve-and-volley game. And like Federer she won admirers among former and current players. "She reminds me a bit of myself," said five-time Grand Slam champion Martina Hingis. Even Williams was impressed. "She's kind of like me: she doesn't back off," Serena said.

For Sharapova, Wimbledon was a spectacular coming-out party. She prepared for the tournament like she knew she could win, and appeared undaunted as she marched through the draw. In the final, she looked as comfortable as she would on a Sunday at a country club. "I wasn't nervous at all," she said. "I knew I had the power within me. Whatever I wanted to achieve I could do it—and I did."

The combination of her looks, talent and a stirring rags-to-riches life story made Sharapova a media darling. When she was two years old, her father, Yuri, moved the family from Siberia to the resort city of Sochi to escape the fallout of the Chernobyl nuclear disaster. Five years later, he moved with Maria to Florida with $700 in his pocket, and enrolled her in the Bollettieri Tennis Academy in Bradenton, where she began to impress some of the world's top coaches. She lost to veteran Mary Pierce in the third round of the U.S. Open but Sharapova, like her promising compatriots, figures to be around for some time to come.

While Sharapova's Wimbledon triumph was a surprise, 19-year-old Kuznetsova's U.S. Open victory was practically a bolt from the blue. Sharapova had at least attracted the buzz of a promising prospect; Kuznetsova was best known for being Martina Navratilova's doubles partner. She does come from an athletic family—her brother Nikolai won a silver medal in cylcing at the 1996 Olympics—and possesses a tremendous work ethic, often practicing after matches. But she wasn't exactly an odds-on favorite in New York. She quietly worked her way to the semifinals, dismissing Pierce and Nadia Petrova, yet another Russian, in straight sets along the way. When 2002 champion Serena Williams bowed out in the quarterfinals to Jennifer Capriati, at least partly due to some horrible line calls, the title seemed up for grabs. Kuznetsova lost 6–1 in the first set of her semifinal against Lindsay Davenport but after Davenport strained a hip flexor, the young Russian rallied to win the next two, 6–2 and 6–4. In the final she dismantled Dementieva 6–3, 7–5, and served notice that she would be a force on the tour for years to come.

"She hits harder than Venus or Serena," said Navratilova of Kuznetsova. "[Her title] won't seem strange in a few years. She's the real deal."

So is Federer, who will be the No. 1 player in the world for as long as he maintains his current form, and could challenge for a place among the greats when the curtain falls on his career. "People underestimate the role of confidence and self-belief in tennis," said Federer. "When you feel like you can trust your game, it makes all the difference in the world. I'm proud of myself for really reaching that point."

Roger that.

FOR THE RECORD · 2003–2004

2004 Grand Slam Champions

Australian Open

Men's Singles

	Winner	Runner-up	Score
Quarterfinals	Marat Safin	Andy Roddick	2–6, 6–3, 7–5, 6–7 (0-7), 6–4
	Andre Agassi	Sebastien Grosjean	6–2, 2–0, ret.
	Juan Carlos Ferrero	Hicham Arazi	6–1, 7–6 (8-6), 7–6 (7-5)
	Roger Federer	David Nalbandian	7–5, 6–4, 5–7, 6–3
Semifinals	Marat Safin	Andre Agassi	7–6 (8-6), 7–6 (8-6) 5–7, 1–6, 6–3
	Roger Federer	Juan Carlos Ferrero	6–4, 6–1, 6–4
Final	Roger Federer	Marat Safin	7–6 (7-3), 6–4, 6–2

Women's Singles

	Winner	Runner-up	Score
Quarterfinals	Justine Henin-Hardenne	Lindsay Davenport	7–5, 6–3
	Fabiola Zuluaga	Amelie Mauresmo	walkover
	Patty Schnyder	Lisa Raymond	7–6 (7-2), 6–3
	Kim Clijsters	Anastasia Myskina	6–2, 7–6 (11-9)
Semifinals	Justine Henin-Hardenne	Fabiola Zuluaga	6–2, 6–2
	Kim Clijsters	Patty Schnyder	6–2, 7–6 (7-2)
Final	Justine Henin-Hardenne	Kim Clijsters	6–3, 4–6, 6–3

Doubles

	Winner	Runner-up	Score
Men's Final	Michael Llodra/ Fabrice Santoro	Bob Bryan/ Mike Bryan	7–6 (7-4), 6–3
Women's Final	Virginia Ruano Pasqual/ Paola Suarez	Svetlana Kuznetsova/ Elena Likhovtseva	6–4, 6–3
Mixed Final	Nenad Zimonjic/ Elena Bovina	Leander Paes/ Martina Navratilova	6–1, 7–6 (7-3)

French Open

Men's Singles

	Winner	Runner-up	Score
Quarterfinals	David Nalbandian	Gustavo Kuerten	6–2, 3–6, 6–4, 7–6 (8-6)
	Gaston Gaudio	Lleyton Hewitt	6–3, 6–2, 6–2
	Guillermo Coria	Carlos Moya	7–5, 7–6 (7-3), 6–3
	Tim Henman	Juan Ignacio Chela	6–2, 6–4, 6–4
Semifinals	Gaston Gaudio	David Nalbandian	6–3, 7–6 (7-5), 6–0
	Guillermo Coria	Tim Henman	3–6, 6–4, 6–0, 7–5
Final	Gaston Gaudio	Guillermo Coria	8–6, 0–6, 3–6, 6–4, 6–1

Women's Singles

	Winner	Runner-up	Score
Quarterfinals	Paola Suarez	Maria Sharapova	6–1, 6–3
	Elena Dementieva	Amelie Mauresmo	6–4, 6–3
	Anastasia Myskina	Venus Williams	6–3, 6–4
	Jennifer Capriati	Serena Williams	6–3, 2–6, 6–3
Semifinals	Elena Dementieva	Paola Suarez	6–0, 7–5
	Anastasia Myskina	Jennifer Capriati	6–2, 6–2
Final	Anastasia Myskina	Elena Dementieva	6–1, 6–2

French Open (Cont.)
Doubles

	Winner	Runner-Up	Score
Men's Final	Xavier Malisse/ Olivier Rochus	Michael Llodra/ Fabrice Santoro	7–5, 7–5
Women's Final	Virginia Ruano Pasqual/ Paola Suarez	Svetlana Kuznetsova Elena Likhovtseva	6–0, 6–3
Mixed Final	Tatiana Golovin/ Richard Gasquet	Cara Black/ Wayne Black	6–3, 6–4

Wimbledon
Men's Singles

	Winner	Runner-Up	Score
Quarterfinals	Roger Federer	Lleyton Hewitt	6–1, 6–7 (1-7), 6–0, 6–4
	Sebastien Grosjean	Florian Mayer	7–5, 6–4, 6–2
	Mario Ancic	Tim Henman	7–6 (7-5), 6–4, 6–2
	Andy Roddick	Sjeng Schalken	7–6 (7-4), 7–6 (11-9), 6–3
Semifinals	Roger Federer	Sebastien Grosjean	6–2, 6–3, 7–6 (8-6)
	Andy Roddick	Mario Ancic	6–4, 4–6, 7–5, 7–5
Final	Roger Federer	Andy Roddick	4–6, 7–5, 7–6 (7-3), 6–4

Women's Singles

	Winner	Runner-Up	Score
Quarterfinals	Serena Williams	Jennifer Capriati	6–1, 6–1
	Amelie Mauresmo	Paola Suarez	6–0, 5–7, 6–1
	Lindsay Davenport	Karolina Sprem	6–2, 6–2
	Maria Sharapova	Ai Sugiyama	5–7, 7–5, 6–1
Semifinals	Serena Williams	Amelie Mauresmo	6–7 (4-7), 7–5, 6–4
	Maria Sharapova	Lindsay Davenport	2–6, 7–6 (7-5), 6–1
Final	Maria Sharapova	Serena Williams	6–1, 6–4

Doubles

	Winner	Runner-Up	Score
Men's Final	Jonas Bjorkman/ Todd Woodbridge	Julian Knowle/ Nenad Zimonjic	6–1, 6–4, 4–6, 6–4
Women's Final	Cara Black/ Rennae Stubbs	Liezel Huber/ Ai Sugiyama	6–3, 7–6 (7-5)
Mixed Final	Wayne Black/ Cara Black	Todd Woodbridge/ Alicia Molik	3–6, 7–6 (10-8), 6–4

U.S. Open
Men's Singles

	Winner	Runner-Up	Score
Quarterfinals	Roger Federer	Andre Agassi	6–3, 2–6, 7–5, 3–6, 6–3
	Tim Henman	Dominik Hrbaty	6–1, 7–5, 5–7, 6–2
	Lleyton Hewitt	Tommy Haas	6–2, 6–2, 6–2
	Joachim Johansson	Andy Roddick	6–4, 6–4, 3–6, 2–6, 6–4
Semifinals	Roger Federer	Tim Henman	6–3, 6–4, 6–4
	Lleyton Hewitt	Joachim Johansson	6–4, 7–5, 6–3
Final	Roger Federer	Lleyton Hewitt	6–0, 7–6 (7-3), 6–0

U.S. Open *(Cont.)*

Women's Singles

	Winner	Runner-Up	Score
Quarterfinals	Svetlana Kuznetsova	Nadia Petrova	7–6 (7-4), 6–3
	Lindsay Davenport	Shinobu Asagoe	6–1, 6–1
	Jennifer Capriati	Serena Williams	2–6, 6–4, 6–4
	Elena Dementieva	Amelie Mauresmo	4–6, 6–4, 7–6 (7-1)
Semifinals	Svetlana Kuznetsova	Lindsay Davenport	1–6, 6–2, 6–4
	Elena Dementieva	Jennifer Capriati	6–0, 2–6, 7–6 (7-5)
Final	Svetlana Kuznetsova	Elena Dementieva	6–3, 7–5

Doubles

	Winner	Runner-Up	Score
Men's Final	Mark Knowles/ Daniel Nestor	Leander Paes/ David Rikl	6–3, 6–3
Women's Final	Virginia Ruano Pascual/ Paola Suarez	Svetlana Kuznetsova/ Elena Likhovtseva	6–4, 7–5
Mixed Final	Vera Zvonareva/ Bob Bryan	Alicia Molik/ Todd Woodbridge	6–3, 6–4

Major Tournament Results

Men's Tour (late 2003)

Date	Tournament	Site	Singles Winner	Surface	Prize Money ($)
Oct 6	CA Trophy	Vienna	Roger Federer	Indoor Hard	765,000
Oct 6	Lyon Grand Prix	Lyon, France	Rainer Schuettler	Indoor Carpet	800,000
Oct 20	Swiss Indoors	Basel, Switzerland	Guillermo Coria	Indoor Carpet	1,000,000
Oct 20	St. Petersburg Open	St. Petersburg, Russia	Gustavo Kuerten	Indoor Hard	1,000,000
Oct 20	Stockholm Open	Stockholm	Mardy Fish	Indoor Hard	650,000
Oct 27	Paris Masters	Paris	Tim Henman	Indoor Carpet	2,240,000
Nov 10	Tennis Masters Cup	Houston	Roger Federer	Outdoor	3,700,000

Men's Tour (through September 19, 2004)

Date	Tournament	Site	Winner	Surface	Prize Money ($)
Jan 5	Qatar Open	Doha, Qatar	Nicolas Escude	Outdoor Hard	1,000,000
Jan 19	Australian Open	Melbourne	Roger Federer	Outdoor Hard	6,737,000
Feb 16	ABN/Amro	Rotterdam	Lleyton Hewitt	Indoor Hard	875,505
Feb 16	Kroger St. Jude	Memphis	Joachim Johansson	Indoor Hard	690,000
Feb 23	Marseille Open	Marseille, France	Dominik Hrbaty	Indoor Hard	600,000
Mar 1	Dubai Open	Dubai, UAE	Roger Federer	Outdoor Hard	1,000,000
Mar 8	Pacific Life Open	Indian Wells, California	Roger Federer	Outdoor Hard	2,779,000
Mar 22	NASDAQ 100 Open	Miami	Andy Roddick	Outdoor Hard	3,450,000
Apr 12	Estoril Open	Estoril, Portugal	Juan Ignacio Chela	Outdoor Clay	525,000
Apr 19	Monte Carlo Masters	Monte Carlo	Guillermo Coria	Outdoor Clay	2,450,000
Apr 26	BMW Open	Munich	Nikolay Davydenko	Outdoor Clay	380,000
Apr 26	Open SEAT Godó	Barcelona	Tommy Robredo	Outdoor Clay	1,000,000
May 3	Italian Masters	Rome	Carlos Moya	Outdoor Clay	2,450,000
May 10	Hamburg Masters	Hamburg	Roger Federer	Outdoor Clay	2,450,000

Men's Tour (through September 19, 2004) (Cont.)

Start Date	Tournament	Site	Winner	Surface	Prize Money
May 24	French Open	Paris	Gaston Gaudio	Outdoor Clay	7,462,318
June 7	Gerry Weber Open	Halle, Germany	Roger Federer	Outdoor Grass	791,750
June 14	Ordina Open	'S-Hertog'bosch Netherlands	Michael Llodra	Outdoor Grass	380,000
June 21	Wimbledon	Wimbledon	Roger Federer	Outdoor Grass	8,328,704
July 5	Swiss Open	Gstaad, Switzerland	Roger Federer	Outdoor Clay	544,750
July 12	Mercedes Cup	Stuttgart, Germany	Guillermo Canas	Outdoor Clay	614,750
July 19	Generali Open	Kitzbuhel, Austria	Nicolas Massu	Outdoor Clay	800,000
July 19	RCA Championships	Indianapolis	Andy Roddick	Outdoor Hard	600,000
Aug 2	Tennis Masters Series	Cincinnati	Andre Agassi	Outdoor Hard	2,450,000
Aug 16	Legg Mason Classic	Wash., D.C.	Lleyton Hewitt	Outdoor Hard	500,000
Aug 30	U.S. Open	New York City	Roger Federer	Outdoor Hard	7,946,000
Sept 13	China Open	Beijing	Marat Safin	Outdoor Hard	500,000

Women's Tour (Late 2003)

Date	Tournament	Site	Winner	Runner-Up	Score
Sept 22	Sparkassen Cup	Leipzig, Germany	Anastasia Myskina	Justine Henin-Hardenne	3–6, 6–3, 6–3
Sept 29	Ladies Kremlin Cup	Moscow	Anastasia Myskina	Amelie Mauresmo	6–2, 6–4
Sept 29	Japan Open	Tokyo	Maria Sharapova	Anikò Kapros	2–6, 6–2, 7–6 (7-5)
Oct 13	Swisscom Challenge	Zurich	Justine Henin-Hardenne	Jelena Dokic	6–0, 6–4
Oct 20	Generali Ladies Open	Linz, Aust.	Ai Sugiyama	Nadia Petrova	7–5, 6–4
Nov 3	Sanex Championships	Los Angeles	Kim Clijsters	Amelie Mauresmo	6–2, 6–0

Women's Tour (through September 11, 2004)

Start Date	Tournament	Site	Winner	Runner-Up	Score
Jan 12	Adidas International	Sydney	Justine Henin-Hardenne	Amelie Mauresmo	6–4, 6–4
Jan 19	Australian Open	Melbourne	Justine Henin-Hardenne	Kim Clijsters	6–3, 4–6, 6–3
Feb 2	Pan Pacific Open	Tokyo	L. Davenport	M. Maleeva	6–4, 6–1
Feb 9	Open Gaz de France	Paris	Kim Clijsters	Mary Pierce	6–2, 6–1
Mar 1	Qatar Open	Doha, Qatar	Anastasia Myskina	Svetlana Kuznetsova	4–6,6–4, 6–4
Mar 8	Pacific Life Open	Indian Wells, California	Justine Henin-Hardenne	Lindsay Davenport	6–1, 6–4
Mar 22	NASDAQ-100 Open	Miami	Serena Williams	Elena Dementieva	6–1, 6–1
Apr 5	Bausch & Lomb Championships	Amelia Island, Florida	Lindsay Davenport	Amelie Mauresmo	6–4, 6–4
Apr 12	Family Circle Cup	Charleston, S Carolina	Venus Williams	Conchita Martinez	2–6, 6–2, 6–1
Apr 26	J&S Cup	Warsaw	Venus Williams	S. Kuznetsova	6–1, 6–4
May 3	German Open	Berlin	Amelie Mauresmo	Venus Williams	walkover
May 10	Italia Masters	Rome	Amelie Mauresmo	Jennifer Capriati	3–6, 6–3, 7–6 (7-6)
May 17	Int'l de Strasbourg	Strasbourg,Fra	Claudine Schaul	L. Davenport	2–6, 6–0, 6–3
May 24	French Open	Paris	Anastasia Myskina	Elena Dementieva	6–1, 6–2
June 14	Hastings Direct Int'l Championships	Eastbourne, England	Svetlana Kuznetsova	Daniela Hantuchova	2–6, 7–6 (7-2), 6–4
June 21	Wimbledon	Wimbledon	Maria Sharapova	Serena Williams	6–1, 6–4
July 12	Bank of the West	Stanford	L. Davenport	Venus Williams	7-6 (7-4), 5-7, 7-6 (7-4)
July 19	JP Morgan Chase Open	Los Angeles	L. Davenport	Serena Williams	6–1, 6–3
July 26	Acura Classic	San Diego	L. Davenport	A. Myskina	6–1, 6–4
Aug 2	Rogers AT&T Cup	Montreal	Amelie Mauresmo	Elena Likhovtseva	6–1, 6–0
Aug 23	Pilot Pen Int'l	New Haven,CT	Elena Bovina	Nathalie Dechy	6–2, 2–6, 7–5
Aug 30	U.S. Open	New York City	Svetlana Kuznetsova	Elena Dementieva	6–3, 7–5

Men

Rank	Player	Country	Points	Events
1. ......Andy Roddick	USA	4535	23
2. ......Roger Federer	SUI	4375	24
3. ......Juan Carlos Ferrero	ESP	4205	20
4. ......Andre Agassi	USA	3425	19
5. ......Guillermo Coria	ARG	3330	22
6. ......Rainer Schuettler	GER	3205	29
7. ......Carlos Moya	ESP	2280	24
8. ......David Nalbandian	ARG	2060	21
9. ......Mark Philippoussis	AUS	1615	20
10. ....Sebastien Grosjean	FRA	1610	22

Note: Compiled by the ATP Tour, through 2003 season.

Women

Rank	Player	Country	Points
1. ......Justine Henin-Hardenne	BGM	6628
2. ......Kim Clijsters	BGM	6553
3. ......Serena Williams	USA	3916
4. ......Amelie Mauresmo	FRA	3194
5. ......Lindsay Davenport	USA	2990
6. ......Jennifer Capriati	USA	2766
7. ......Anastasia Myskina	RUS	2581
8. ......Elena Dementieva	RUS	2383
9. ......Chanda Rubin	USA	2328
10. ....Ai Sugiyama	JAP	2235

Note: Compiled by the WTA, as of Nov 10, 2003.

Helping Hand

Andy Roddick woke up to the smell of acrid smoke at 5:15 on Sunday, May 2, 2004, in Rome's Grand Hotel Parco dei Principi. When the 2003 U.S. Open champ, in town for the Italian Open, went into the hall, he saw about a dozen guests amid thick black smoke. He ushered them into his room, took them onto his balcony, then did what any 21-year-old in a tight spot would do: He called Mom. From Boca Raton, Fla., Blanche Roddick told her son to wet towels and put them under the door, but Andy said, "It's way beyond that." When Roddick realized that fire truck ladders could not reach the balcony above him, he helped seven people from that floor down to his balcony, including Sjeng Schalken, whom Roddick caught when the Dutch player jumped 10 feet. The blaze killed three guests, but everyone on Roddick's balcony made it to safety. "I think it was instinctive, and there was a lot of adrenaline going," he said.

National Team Competition

2003 Davis Cup World Group Final

Australia def. Spain 3–1, Nov. 28–30, 2003 in Melbourne
  Hewitt (Aus) def. Ferrero (Esp) 3–6, 6–3, 3–6, 7–6, 6–2
  Moya (Esp) def. Philippoussis (Aus) 6–4, 6–4, 4–6, 7–6
  Arthurs and Woodbridge (Aus) def. Corretja and Lopez (Esp) 6–3, 6–1, 6–3
  Philippoussis (Aus) def Ferrerro (Esp) 7–5, 6–3, 1–6, 2–6, 6–0

2004 Davis Cup World Group Tournament

FIRST ROUND

United States def. Austria 5–0
Sweden def. Australia 4–1
Belarus def. Russia 3–2
Argentina def. Morocco 5–0
Switzerland def. Romania 3–2
France def. Croatia 4–1
Netherlands def. Canada 4–1
Spain def. Czech Republic 3–2

QUARTERFINAL ROUND

United States def. Sweden 4–1
Belarus def. Argentina 5–0
France def. Switzerland 3–2
Spain def. Netherlands 4–1

SEMIFINALS

United States def. Belarus 4–0
  Andy Roddick (U.S.) def. Vladimir Voltchkov (Bel)
  6–1, 6–4, 6–4
  Mardy Fish (U.S.) def. Max Mirnyi (Bel)
  7–5, 6–2, 3–6, 6–3
  Bob Bryan and Mike Bryan (U.S.) def Max Mirnyi
  and Vladimir Voltchkov (Bel) 6–1, 6–3, 7–5
  Andy Roddick (U.S.) def. Alexander Skrypko (Bel)
  6–4, 6–2.

Spain def. France, 4–1
  Paul-Henri Mathieu (Fra) def. Carlos Moya (Esp),
  6–3, 3–6, 2–6, 6–3, 6–3
  Juan Carlos Ferrero (Esp) def. Fabrice Santoro (Fra)
  6–3, 6–1, 1–6, 6–3
  Tommy Robredo and Rafael Nadal (Esp) def. Michael
  Llodra and Arnaud Clement (Fra) 7–6 (7-4), 4–6,
  6–2, 2–6, 6–3
  Rafael Nadal (Esp) def. Arnaud Clement (Fra) 6–4,
  6–1, 6–2
  Tommy Robredo (Esp) def. Paul-Henri Mathieu (Fra)
  6–4, 6–4

FINAL: United States versus Spain to be held Dec. 3–5, 2004.

2004 Federation Cup World Group Tournament

FIRST ROUND

United States def. Slovenia 4–1
Austria def. Slovakia 3–2
Russia def. Australia 4–1
Argentina def. Japan 4–1
Italy def. Czech Republic 3–1
France def. Germany 5–0
Spain def. Switzerland 3–2
Belgium def. Croatia 3–2

QUARTERFINALS

Austria def. United States 4–1
Russia def. Argentina 4–1
France def. Italy 3–2
Spain def. Belgium 3–2

Note: Semifinals to be held Nov 22–23, 2004, in Moscow.

Grand Slam Tournaments

MEN
Australian Championships

Year	Winner	Finalist	Score
1905	Rodney Heath	A. H. Curtis	4–6, 6–3, 6–4, 6–4
1906	Tony Wilding	H. A. Parker	6–0, 6–4, 6–4
1907	Horace M. Rice	H. A. Parker	6–3, 6–4, 6–4
1908	Fred Alexander	A. W. Dunlop	3–6, 3–6, 6–0, 6–2, 6–3
1909	Tony Wilding	E. F. Parker	6–1, 7–5, 6–2
1910	Rodney Heath	Horace M. Rice	6–4, 6–3, 6–2
1911	Norman Brookes	Horace M. Rice	6–1, 6–2, 6–3
1912	J. Cecil Parke	A. E. Beamish	3–6, 6–3, 1–6, 6–1, 7–5
1913	E. F. Parker	H. A. Parker	2–6, 6–1, 6–2, 6–3
1914	Pat O'Hara Wood	G. L. Patterson	6–4, 6–3, 5–7, 6–1
1915	Francis G. Lowe	Horace M. Rice	4–6, 6–1, 6–1, 6–4
1916–18	No tournament		
1919	A. R. F. Kingscote	E. O. Pockley	6–4, 6–0, 6–3
1920	Pat O'Hara Wood	Ron Thomas	6–3, 4–6, 6–8, 6–1, 6–3
1921	Rhys H. Gemmell	A. Hedeman	7–5, 6–1, 6–4
1922	Pat O'Hara Wood	Gerald Patterson	6–0, 3–6, 3–6, 6–3, 6–2
1923	Pat O'Hara Wood	C. B. St John	6–1, 6–1, 6–3
1924	James Anderson	R. E. Schlesinger	6–3, 6–4, 3–6, 5–7, 6–3
1925	James Anderson	Gerald Patterson	11–9, 2–6, 6–2, 6–3
1926	John Hawkes	J. Willard	6–1, 6–3, 6–1
1927	Gerald Patterson	John Hawkes	3–6, 6–4, 3–6, 18–16, 6–3
1928	Jean Borotra	R. O. Cummings	6–4, 6–1, 4–6, 5–7, 6–3
1929	John C. Gregory	R. E. Schlesinger	6–2, 6–2, 5–7, 7–5
1930	Gar Moon	Harry C. Hopman	6–3, 6–1, 6–3
1931	Jack Crawford	Harry C. Hopman	6–4, 6–2, 2–6, 6–1
1932	Jack Crawford	Harry C. Hopman	4–6, 6–3, 3–6, 6–3, 6–1
1933	Jack Crawford	Keith Gledhill	2–6, 7–5, 6–3, 6–2
1934	Fred Perry	Jack Crawford	6–3, 7–5, 6–1
1935	Jack Crawford	Fred Perry	2–6, 6–4, 6–4, 6–4
1936	Adrian Quist	Jack Crawford	6–2, 6–3, 4–6, 3–6, 9–7
1937	Vivian B. McGrath	John Bromwich	6–3, 1–6, 6–0, 2–6, 6–1
1938	Don Budge	John Bromwich	6–4, 6–2, 6–1
1939	John Bromwich	Adrian Quist	6–4, 6–1, 6–3
1940	Adrian Quist	Jack Crawford	6–3, 6–1, 6–2
1941–45	No tournament		
1946	John Bromwich	Dinny Pails	5–7, 6–3, 7–5, 3–6, 6–2
1947	Dinny Pails	John Bromwich	4–6, 6–4, 3–6, 7–5, 8–6
1948	Adrian Quist	John Bromwich	6–4, 3–6, 6–3, 2–6, 6–3
1949	Frank Sedgman	Ken McGregor	6–3, 6–3, 6–2
1950	Frank Sedgman	Ken McGregor	6–3, 6–4, 4–6, 6–1
1951	Richard Savitt	Ken McGregor	6–3, 2–6, 6–3, 6–1
1952	Ken McGregor	Frank Sedgman	7–5, 12–10, 2–6, 6–2
1953	Ken Rosewall	Mervyn Rose	6–0, 6–3, 6–4
1954	Mervyn Rose	Rex Hartwig	6–2, 0–6, 6–4, 6–2
1955	Ken Rosewall	Lew Hoad	9–7, 6–4, 6–4
1956	Lew Hoad	Ken Rosewall	6–4, 3–6, 6–4, 7–5
1957	Ashley Cooper	Neale Fraser	6–3, 9–11, 6–4, 6–2
1958	Ashley Cooper	Mal Anderson	7–5, 6–3, 6–4
1959	Alex Olmedo	Neale Fraser	6–1, 6–2, 3–6, 6–3
1960	Rod Laver	Neale Fraser	5–7, 3–6, 6–3, 8–6, 8–6
1961	Roy Emerson	Rod Laver	1–6, 6–3, 7–5, 6–4
1962	Rod Laver	Roy Emerson	8–6, 0–6, 6–4, 6–4
1963	Roy Emerson	Ken Fletcher	6–3, 6–3, 6–1
1964	Roy Emerson	Fred Stolle	6–3, 6–4, 6–2
1965	Roy Emerson	Fred Stolle	7–9, 2–6, 6–4, 7–5, 6–1
1966	Roy Emerson	Arthur Ashe	6–4, 6–8, 6–2, 6–3
1967	Roy Emerson	Arthur Ashe	6–4, 6–1, 6–1
1968	Bill Bowrey	Juan Gisbert	7–5, 2–6, 9–7, 6–4
1969*	Rod Laver	Andres Gimeno	6–3, 6–4, 7–5
1970	Arthur Ashe	Dick Crealy	6–4, 9–7, 6–2

*Became Open (amateur and professional) in 1969.

MEN *(Cont.)*

Australian Championships *(Cont.)*

Year	Winner	Finalist	Score
1971	Ken Rosewall	Arthur Ashe	6–1, 7–5, 6–3
1972	Ken Rosewall	Mal Anderson	7–6, 6–3, 7–5
1973	John Newcombe	Onny Parun	6–3, 6–7, 7–5, 6–1
1974	Jimmy Connors	Phil Dent	7–6, 6–4, 4–6, 6–3
1975	John Newcombe	Jimmy Connors	7–5, 3–6, 6–4, 7–5
1976	Mark Edmondson	John Newcombe	6–7, 6–3, 7–6, 6–1
1977 (Jan)	Roscoe Tanner	Guillermo Vilas	6–3, 6–3, 6–3
1977 (Dec)	Vitas Gerulaitis	John Lloyd	6–3, 7–6, 5–7, 3–6, 6–2
1978	Guillermo Vilas	John Marks	6–4, 6–4, 3–6, 6–3
1979	Guillermo Vilas	John Sadri	7–6, 6–3, 6–2
1980	Brian Teacher	Kim Warwick	7–5, 7–6, 6–3
1981	Johan Kriek	Steve Denton	6–2, 7–6, 6–7, 6–4
1982	Johan Kriek	Steve Denton	6–3, 6–3, 6–2
1983	Mats Wilander	Ivan Lendl	6–1, 6–4, 6–4
1984	Mats Wilander	Kevin Curren	6–7, 6–4, 7–6, 6–2
1985 (Dec)	Stefan Edberg	Mats Wilander	6–4, 6–3, 6–3
1987 (Jan)	Stefan Edberg	Pat Cash	6–3, 6–4, 3–6, 5–7, 6–3
1988	Mats Wilander	Pat Cash	6–3, 6–7, 3–6, 6–1, 8–6
1989	Ivan Lendl	Miloslav Mecir	6–2, 6–2, 6–2
1990	Ivan Lendl	Stefan Edberg	4–6, 7–6, 5–2, ret.
1991	Boris Becker	Ivan Lendl	1–6, 6–4, 6–4, 6–4
1992	Jim Courier	Stefan Edberg	6–3, 3–6, 6–4, 6–2
1993	Jim Courier	Stefan Edberg	6–2, 6–1, 2–6, 7–5
1994	Pete Sampras	Todd Martin	7–6, 6–4, 6–4
1995	Andre Agassi	Pete Sampras	4–6, 6–1, 7–6, 6–4
1996	Boris Becker	Michael Chang	6–2, 6–4, 2–6, 6–2
1997	Pete Sampras	Carlos Moya	6–2, 6–3, 6–3
1998	Petr Korda	Marcelo Rios	6–2, 6–2, 6–2
1999	Yevgeny Kafelnikov	Thomas Enqvist	4–6, 6–0, 6–3, 7–6
2000	Andre Agassi	Yevgeny Kafelnikov	3–6, 6–3, 6–2, 6–4
2001	Andre Agassi	Arnaud Clement	6–4, 6–2, 6–2
2002	Thomas Johansson	Marat Safin	3–6, 6–4, 6–4, 7–6 (7-4)
2003	Andre Agassi	Rainer Schuettler	6–2, 6–2, 6–1
2004	Roger Federer	Marat Safin	7–6 (7-3), 6–4, 6–2

French Championships

Year	Winner	Finalist	Score
1925†	Rene Lacoste	Jean Borotra	7–5, 6–1, 6–4
1926	Henri Cochet	Rene Lacoste	6–2, 6–4, 6–3
1927	Rene Lacoste	Bill Tilden	6–4, 4–6, 5–7, 6–3, 11–9
1928	Henri Cochet	Rene Lacoste	5–7, 6–3, 6–1, 6–3
1929	Rene Lacoste	Jean Borotra	6–3, 2–6, 6–0, 2–6, 8–6
1930	Henri Cochet	Bill Tilden	3–6, 8–6, 6–3, 6–1
1931	Jean Borotra	Claude Boussus	2–6, 6–4, 7–5, 6–4
1932	Henri Cochet	Giorgio de Stefani	6–0, 6–4, 4–6, 6–3
1933	Jack Crawford	Henri Cochet	8–6, 6–1, 6–3
1934	Gottfried von Cramm	Jack Crawford	6–4, 7–9, 3–6, 7–5, 6–3
1935	Fred Perry	Gottfried von Cramm	6–3, 3–6, 6–1, 6–3
1936	Gottfried von Cramm	Fred Perry	6–0, 2–6, 6–2, 2–6, 6–0
1937	Henner Henkel	Henry Austin	6–1, 6–4, 6–3
1938	Don Budge	Roderick Menzel	6–3, 6–2, 6–4
1939	Don McNeill	Bobby Riggs	7–5, 6–0, 6–3
1940	No tournament		
1941‡	Bernard Destremau	n/a	n/a
1942‡	Bernard Destremau	n/a	n/a
1943‡	Yvon Petra	n/a	n/a
1944‡	Yvon Petra	n/a	n/a
1945‡	Yvon Petra	Bernard Destremau	7–5, 6–4, 6–2
1946	Marcel Bernard	Jaroslav Drobny	3–6, 2–6, 6–1, 6–4, 6–3
1947	Joseph Asboth	Eric Sturgess	8–6, 7–5, 6–4
1948	Frank Parker	Jaroslav Drobny	6–4, 7–5, 5–7, 8–6
1949	Frank Parker	Budge Patty	6–3, 1–6, 6–1, 6–4
1950	Budge Patty	Jaroslav Drobny	6–1, 6–2, 3–6, 5–7, 7–5
1951	Jaroslav Drobny	Eric Sturgess	6–3, 6–3, 6–3
1952	Jaroslav Drobny	Frank Sedgman	6–2, 6–0, 3–6, 6–4
1953	Ken Rosewall	Vic Seixas	6–3, 6–4, 1–6, 6–2

MEN *(Cont.)*

French Championships *(Cont.)*

Year	Winner	Finalist	Score
1954	Tony Trabert	Arthur Larsen	6–4, 7–5, 6–1
1955	Tony Trabert	Sven Davidson	2–6, 6–1, 6–4, 6–2
1956	Lew Hoad	Sven Davidson	6–4, 8–6, 6–3
1957	Sven Davidson	Herbie Flam	6–3, 6–4, 6–4
1958	Mervyn Rose	Luis Ayala	6–3, 6–4, 6–4
1959	Nicola Pietrangeli	Ian Vermaak	3–6, 6–3, 6–4, 6–1
1960	Nicola Pietrangeli	Luis Ayala	3–6, 6–3, 6–4, 4–6, 6–3
1961	Manuel Santana	Nicola Pietrangeli	4–6, 6–1, 3–6, 6–0, 6–2
1962	Rod Laver	Roy Emerson	3–6, 2–6, 6–3, 9–7, 6–2
1963	Roy Emerson	Pierre Darmon	3–6, 6–1, 6–4, 6–4
1964	Manuel Santana	Nicola Pietrangeli	6–3, 6–1, 4–6, 7–5
1965	Fred Stolle	Tony Roche	3–6, 6–0, 6–2, 6–3
1966	Tony Roche	Istvan Gulyas	6–1, 6–4, 7–5
1967	Roy Emerson	Tony Roche	6–1, 6–4, 2–6, 6–2
1968*	Ken Rosewall	Rod Laver	6–3, 6–1, 2–6, 6–2
1969	Rod Laver	Ken Rosewall	6–4, 6–3, 6–4
1970	Jan Kodes	Zeljko Franulovic	6–2, 6–4, 6–0
1971	Jan Kodes	Ilie Nastase	8–6, 6–2, 2–6, 7–5
1972	Andres Gimeno	Patrick Proisy	4–6, 6–3, 6–1, 6–1
1973	Ilie Nastase	Nikki Pilic	6–3, 6–3, 6–0
1974	Bjorn Borg	Manuel Orantes	6–7, 6–0, 6–1, 6–1
1975	Bjorn Borg	Guillermo Vilas	6–2, 6–3, 6–4
1976	Adriano Panatta	Harold Solomon	6–1, 6–4, 4–6, 7–6
1977	Guillermo Vilas	Brian Gottfried	6–0, 6–3, 6–0
1978	Bjorn Borg	Guillermo Vilas	6–1, 6–1, 6–3
1979	Bjorn Borg	Victor Pecci	6–3, 6–1, 6–7, 6–4
1980	Bjorn Borg	Vitas Gerulaitis	6–4, 6–1, 6–2
1981	Bjorn Borg	Ivan Lendl	6–1, 4–6, 6–2, 3–6, 6–1
1982	Mats Wilander	Guillermo Vilas	1–6, 7–6, 6–0, 6–4
1983	Yannick Noah	Mats Wilander	6–2, 7–5, 7–6
1984	Ivan Lendl	John McEnroe	3–6, 2–6, 6–4, 7–5, 7–5
1985	Mats Wilander	Ivan Lendl	3–6, 6–4, 6–2, 6–2
1986	Ivan Lendl	Mikael Pernfors	6–3, 6–2, 6–4
1987	Ivan Lendl	Mats Wilander	7–5, 6–2, 3–6, 7–6
1988	Mats Wilander	Henri Leconte	7–5, 6–2, 6–1
1989	Michael Chang	Stefan Edberg	6–1, 3–6, 4–6, 6–4, 6–2
1990	Andres Gomez	Andre Agassi	6–3, 2–6, 6–4, 6–4
1991	Jim Courier	Andre Agassi	3–6, 6–4, 2–6, 6–1, 6–4
1992	Jim Courier	Petr Korda	7–5, 6–2, 6–1
1993	Sergi Bruguera	Jim Courier	6–4, 2–6, 6–2, 3–6, 6–3
1994	Sergi Bruguera	Alberto Berasategui	6–3, 7–5, 2–6, 6–1
1995	Thomas Muster	Michael Chang	7–5, 6–2, 6–4
1996	Yevgeny Kafelnikov	Michael Stich	7–6, 7–5, 7–6
1997	Gustavo Kuerten	Sergi Bruguera	6–3, 6–4, 6–2
1998	Carlos Moya	Alex Corretja	6–3, 7–5, 6–3
1999	Andre Agassi	Andrei Medvedev	1–6, 2–6, 6–4, 6–3, 6–4
2000	Gustavo Kuerten	Magnus Norman	6–2, 6–3, 2–6, 7–6
2001	Gustavo Kuerten	Alex Corretja	6–7, 7–5, 6–2, 6–0
2002	Albert Costa	Juan Carlos Ferrero	6–1, 6–0, 4–6, 6–3
2003	Juan Carlos Ferrero	Martin Verkerk	6–1, 6–3, 6–2
2004	Gaston Gaudio	Guillermo Coria	8–6, 0–6, 3–6, 6–4, 6–1

*Became Open (amateur and professional) in 1968 but closed to contract professionals in 1972.

†1925 was the first year that entries were accepted from all countries.‡From 1941 to 1945 the event was called Tournoi de France and was closed to all foreigners.

Wimbledon Championships

Year	Winner	Finalist	Score
1877	Spencer W. Gore	William C. Marshall	6–1, 6–2, 6–4
1878	P. Frank Hadow	Spencer W. Gore	7–5, 6–1, 9–7
1879	John T. Hartley	V. St Leger Gould	6–2, 6–4, 6–2
1880	John T. Hartley	Herbert F. Lawford	6–0, 6–2, 2–6, 6–3
1881	William Renshaw	John T. Hartley	6–0, 6–2, 6–1
1882	William Renshaw	Ernest Renshaw	6–1, 2–6, 4–6, 6–2, 6–2
1883	William Renshaw	Ernest Renshaw	2–6, 6–3, 6–3, 4–6, 6–3
1884	William Renshaw	Herbert F. Lawford	6–0, 6–4, 9–7

MEN (Cont.)

Wimbledon Championship (Cont.)

Year	Winner	Finalist	Score
1885	William Renshaw	Herbert F. Lawford	7–5, 6–2, 4–6, 7–5
1886	William Renshaw	Herbert F. Lawford	6–0, 5–7, 6–3, 6–4
1887	Herbert F. Lawford	Ernest Renshaw	1–6, 6–3, 3–6, 6–4, 6–4
1888	Ernest Renshaw	Herbert F. Lawford	6–3, 7–5, 6–0
1889	William Renshaw	Ernest Renshaw	6–4, 6–1, 3–6, 6–0
1890	William J. Hamilton	William Renshaw	6–8, 6–2, 3–6, 6–1, 6–1
1891	Wilfred Baddeley	Joshua Pim	6–4, 1–6, 7–5, 6–0
1892	Wilfred Baddeley	Joshua Pim	4–6, 6–3, 6–3, 6–2
1893	Joshua Pim	Wilfred Baddeley	3–6, 6–1, 6–3, 6–2
1894	Joshua Pim	Wilfred Baddeley	10–8, 6–2, 8–6
1895	Wilfred Baddeley	Wilberforce V. Eaves	4–6, 2–6, 8–6, 6–2, 6–3
1896	Harold S. Mahoney	Wilfred Baddeley	6–2, 6–8, 5–7, 8–6, 6–3
1897	Reggie F. Doherty	Harold S. Mahoney	6–4, 6–4, 6–3
1898	Reggie F. Doherty	H. Laurie Doherty	6–3, 6–3, 2–6, 5–7, 6–1
1899	Reggie F. Doherty	Arthur W. Gore	1–6, 4–6, 6–2, 6–3, 6–3
1900	Reggie F. Doherty	Sidney H. Smith	6–8, 6–3, 6–1, 6–2
1901	Arthur W. Gore	Reggie F. Doherty	4–6, 7–5, 6–4, 6–4
1902	H. Laurie Doherty	Arthur W. Gore	6–4, 6–3, 3–6, 6–0
1903	H. Laurie Doherty	Frank L. Riseley	7–5, 6–3, 6–0
1904	H. Laurie Doherty	Frank L. Riseley	6–1, 7–5, 8–6
1905	H. Laurie Doherty	Norman E. Brookes	8–6, 6–2, 6–4
1906	H. Laurie Doherty	Frank L. Riseley	6–4, 4–6, 6–2, 6–3
1907	Norman E. Brookes	Arthur W. Gore	6–4, 6–2, 6–2
1908	Arthur W. Gore	H. Roper Barrett	6–3, 6–2, 4–6, 3–6, 6–4
1909	Arthur W. Gore	M. J. G. Ritchie	6–8, 1–6, 6–2, 6–2, 6–2
1910	Anthony F. Wilding	Arthur W. Gore	6–4, 7–5, 4–6, 6–2
1911	Anthony F. Wilding	H. Roper Barrett	6–4, 4–6, 2–6, 6–2 ret
1912	Anthony F. Wilding	Arthur W. Gore	6–4, 6–4, 4–6, 6–4
1913	Anthony F. Wilding	Maurice E. McLoughlin	8–6, 6–3, 10–8
1914	Norman E. Brookes	Anthony F. Wilding	6–4, 6–4, 7–5
1915–18	No tournament		
1919	Gerald L. Patterson	Norman E. Brookes	6–3, 7–5, 6–2
1920	Bill Tilden	Gerald L. Patterson	2–6, 6–3, 6–2, 6–4
1921	Bill Tilden	Brian I. C. Norton	4–6, 2–6, 6–1, 6–0, 7–5
1922	Gerald L. Patterson	Randolph Lycett	6–3, 6–4, 6–2
1923	Bill Johnston	Francis T. Hunter	6–0, 6–3, 6–1
1924	Jean Borotra	Rene Lacoste	6–1, 3–6, 6–1, 3–6, 6–4
1925	Rene Lacoste	Jean Borotra	6–3, 6–3, 4–6, 8–6
1926	Jean Borotra	Howard Kinsey	8–6, 6–1, 6–3
1927	Henri Cochet	Jean Borotra	4–6, 4–6, 6–3, 6–4, 7–5
1928	Rene Lacoste	Henri Cochet	6–1, 4–6, 6–4, 6–2
1929	Henri Cochet	Jean Borotra	6–4, 6–3, 6–4
1930	Bill Tilden	Wilmer Allison	6–3, 9–7, 6–4
1931	Sidney B. Wood Jr	Francis X. Shields	walkover
1932	Ellsworth Vines	Henry Austin	6–4, 6–2, 6–0
1933	Jack Crawford	Ellsworth Vines	4–6, 11–9, 6–2, 2–6, 6–4
1934	Fred Perry	Jack Crawford	6–3, 6–0, 7–5
1935	Fred Perry	Gottfried von Cramm	6–2, 6–4, 6–4
1936	Fred Perry	Gottfried von Cramm	6–1, 6–1, 6–0
1937	Don Budge	Gottfried von Cramm	6–3, 6–4, 6–2
1938	Don Budge	Henry Austin	6–1, 6–0, 6–3
1939	Bobby Riggs	Elwood Cooke	2–6, 8–6, 3–6, 6–3, 6–2
1940–45	No tournament		
1946	Yvon Petra	Geoff E. Brown	6–2, 6–4, 7–9, 5–7, 6–4
1947	Jack Kramer	Tom P. Brown	6–1, 6–3, 6–2
1948	Bob Falkenburg	John Bromwich	7–5, 0–6, 6–2, 3–6, 7–5
1949	Ted Schroeder	Jaroslav Drobny	3–6, 6–0, 6–3, 4–6, 6–4
1950	Budge Patty	Frank Sedgman	6–1, 8–10, 6–2, 6–3
1951	Dick Savitt	Ken McGregor	6–4, 6–4, 6–4
1952	Frank Sedgman	Jaroslav Drobny	4–6, 6–3, 6–2, 6–3
1953	Vic Seixas	Kurt Nielsen	9–7, 6–3, 6–4
1954	Jaroslav Drobny	Ken Rosewall	13–11, 4–6, 6–2, 9–7
1955	Tony Trabert	Kurt Nielsen	6–3, 7–5, 6–1
1956	Lew Hoad	Ken Rosewall	6–2, 4–6, 7–5, 6–4
1957	Lew Hoad	Ashley Cooper	6–2, 6–1, 6–2
1958	Ashley Cooper	Neale Fraser	3–6, 6–3, 6–4, 13–11
1959	Alex Olmedo	Rod Laver	6–4, 6–3, 6–4

MEN (Cont.)

Wimbledon Championships (Cont.)

Year	Winner	Finalist	Score
1960	Neale Fraser	Rod Laver	6–4, 3–6, 9–7, 7–5
1961	Rod Laver	Chuck McKinley	6–3, 6–1, 6–4
1962	Rod Laver	Martin Mulligan	6–2, 6–2, 6–1
1963	Chuck McKinley	Fred Stolle	9–7, 6–1, 6–4
1964	Roy Emerson	Fred Stolle	6–4, 12–10, 4–6, 6–3
1965	Roy Emerson	Fred Stolle	6–2, 6–4, 6–4
1966	Manuel Santana	Dennis Ralston	6–4, 11–9, 6–4
1967	John Newcombe	Wilhelm Bungert	6–3, 6–1, 6–1
1968*	Rod Laver	Tony Roche	6–3, 6–4, 6–2
1969	Rod Laver	John Newcombe	6–4, 5–7, 6–4, 6–4
1970	John Newcombe	Ken Rosewall	5–7, 6–3, 6–2, 3–6, 6–1
1971	John Newcombe	Stan Smith	6–3, 5–7, 2–6, 6–4, 6–4
1972	Stan Smith	Ilie Nastase	4–6, 6–3, 6–3, 4–6, 7–5
1973	Jan Kodes	Alex Metreveli	6–1, 9–8, 6–3
1974	Jimmy Connors	Ken Rosewall	6–1, 6–1, 6–4
1975	Arthur Ashe	Jimmy Connors	6–1, 6–1, 5–7, 6–4
1976	Bjorn Borg	Ilie Nastase	6–4, 6–2, 9–7
1977	Bjorn Borg	Jimmy Connors	3–6, 6–2, 6–1, 5–7, 6–4
1978	Bjorn Borg	Jimmy Connors	6–2, 6–2, 6–3
1979	Bjorn Borg	Roscoe Tanner	6–7, 6–1, 3–6, 6–3, 6–4
1980	Bjorn Borg	John McEnroe	1–6, 7–5, 6–3, 6–7, 8–6
1981	John McEnroe	Bjorn Borg	4–6, 7–6, 7–6, 6–4
1982	Jimmy Connors	John McEnroe	3–6, 6–3, 6–7, 7–6, 6–4
1983	John McEnroe	Chris Lewis	6–2, 6–2, 6–2
1984	John McEnroe	Jimmy Connors	6–1, 6–1, 6–2
1985	Boris Becker	Kevin Curren	6–3, 6–7, 7–6, 6–4
1986	Boris Becker	Ivan Lendl	6–4, 6–3, 7–5
1987	Pat Cash	Ivan Lendl	7–6, 6–2, 7–5
1988	Stefan Edberg	Boris Becker	4–6, 7–6, 6–4, 6–2
1989	Boris Becker	Stefan Edberg	6–0, 7–6, 6–4
1990	Stefan Edberg	Boris Becker	6–2, 6–2, 3–6, 3–6, 6–4
1991	Michael Stich	Boris Becker	6–4, 7–6, 6–4
1992	Andre Agassi	Goran Ivanisevic	6–7, 6–4, 6–4, 1–6, 6–4
1993	Pete Sampras	Jim Courier	7–6, 7–6, 3–6, 6–3
1994	Pete Sampras	Goran Ivanisevic	7–6, 7–6, 6–0
1995	Pete Sampras	Boris Becker	6–7, 6–2, 6–4, 6–2
1996	Richard Krajicek	MaliVai Washington	6–3, 6–4, 6–3
1997	Pete Sampras	Cedric Pioline	6–4, 6–2, 6–4
1998	Pete Sampras	Goran Ivanisevic	6–7, 7–6, 6–4, 3–6, 6–2
1999	Pete Sampras	Andre Agassi	6–3, 6–4, 7–5
2000	Pete Sampras	Patrick Rafter	6–7, 7–6, 6–4, 6–2
2001	Goran Ivanisevic	Patrick Rafter	6–3, 3–6, 6–3, 2–6, 9–7
2002	Lleyton Hewitt	David Nalbandian	6–1, 6–3, 6–2
2003	Roger Federer	Mark Philippoussis	7–6 (7–5), 6–2, 7–6 (7–3)
2004	Roger Federer	Andy Roddick	4–6, 7–5, 7–6 (7–3), 6–4

*Became Open (amateur and professional) in 1968 but closed to contract professionals in 1972

Note: Prior to 1922 the tournament was run on a challenge-round system. The previous year's winner "stood out" of an All Comers event, which produced a challenger to play him for the title.

United States Championships

Year	Winner	Finalist	Score
1881	Richard D. Sears	W.E. Glyn	6–0, 6–3, 6–2
1882	Richard D. Sears	C.M. Clark	6–1, 6–4, 6–0
1883	Richard D. Sears	James Dwight	6–2, 6–0, 9–7
1884	Richard D. Sears	H.A. Taylor	6–0, 1–6, 6–0, 6–2
1885	Richard D. Sears	G.M. Brinley	6–3, 4–6, 6–0, 6–3
1886	Richard D. Sears	R.L. Beeckman	4–6, 6–1, 6–3, 6–4
1887	Richard D. Sears	H.W. Slocum Jr	6–1, 6–3, 6–2
1888‡	H. W. Slocum Jr	H.A. Taylor	6–4, 6–1, 6–0
1889	H. W. Slocum Jr	Q.A. Shaw	6–3, 6–1, 4–6, 6–2
1890	Oliver S. Campbell	H.W. Slocum Jr	6–2, 4–6, 6–3, 6–1
1891	Oliver S. Campbell	Clarence Hobart	2–6, 7–5, 7–9, 6–1, 6–2
1892	Oliver S. Campbell	Frederick H. Hovey	7–5, 3–6, 6–3, 7–5
1893‡	Robert D. Wrenn	Frederick H. Hovey	6–4, 3–6, 6–4, 6–4
1894	Robert D. Wrenn	M.F. Goodbody	6–8, 6–1, 6–4, 6–4

MEN *(Cont.)*

United States Championships *(Cont.)*

Year	Winner	Finalist	Score
1895	Frederick H. Hovey	Robert D. Wrenn	6–3, 6–2, 6–4
1896	Robert D. Wrenn	Frederick H. Hovey	7–5, 3–6, 6–0, 1–6, 6–1
1897	Robert D. Wrenn	Wilberforce V. Eaves	4–6, 8–6, 6–3, 2–6, 6–2
1898‡	Malcolm D. Whitman	Dwight F. Davis	3–6, 6–2, 6–2, 6–1
1899	Malcolm D. Whitman	J. Parmly Paret	6–1, 6–2, 3–6, 7–5
1900	Malcolm D. Whitman	William A. Larned	6–4, 1–6, 6–2, 6–2
1901‡	William A. Larned	Beals C. Wright	6–2, 6–8, 6–4, 6–4
1902	William A. Larned	Reggie F. Doherty	4–6, 6–2, 6–4, 8–6
1903	H. Laurie Doherty	William A. Larned	6–0, 6–3, 10–8
1904‡	Holcombe Ward	William J. Clothier	10–8, 6–4, 9–7
1905	Beals C. Wright	Holcombe Ward	6–2, 6–1, 11–9
1906	William J. Clothier	Beals C. Wright	6–3, 6–0, 6–4
1907‡	William A. Larned	Robert LeRoy	6–2, 6–2, 6–4
1908	William A. Larned	Beals C. Wright	6–1, 6–2, 8–6
1909	William A. Larned	William J. Clothier	6–1, 6–2, 5–7, 1–6, 6–1
1910	William A. Larned	Thomas C. Bundy	6–1, 5–7, 6–0, 6–8, 6–1
1911	William A. Larned	Maurice E. McLoughlin	6–4, 6–4, 6–2
1912†	Maurice E. McLoughlin	Bill Johnson	3–6, 2–6, 6–2, 6–4, 6–2
1913	Maurice E. McLoughlin	Richard N. Williams	6–4, 5–7, 6–3, 6–1
1914	Richard N. Williams	Maurice E. McLoughlin	6–3, 8–6, 10–8
1915	Bill Johnston	Maurice E. McLoughlin	1–6, 6–0, 7–5, 10–8
1916	Richard N. Williams	Bill Johnston	4–6, 6–4, 0–6, 6–2, 6–4
1917#	R.L. Murray	N. W. Niles	5–7, 8–6, 6–3, 6–3
1918	R.L. Murray	Bill Tilden	6–3, 6–1, 7–5
1919	Bill Johnston	Bill Tilden	6–4, 6–4, 6–3
1920	Bill Tilden	Bill Johnston	6–1, 1–6, 7–5, 5–7, 6–3
1921	Bill Tilden	Wallace F. Johnson	6–1, 6–3, 6–1
1922	Bill Tilden	Bill Johnston	4–6, 3–6, 6–2, 6–3, 6–4
1923	Bill Tilden	Bill Johnston	6–4, 6–1, 6–4
1924	Bill Tilden	Bill Johnston	6–1, 9–7, 6–2
1925	Bill Tilden	Bill Johnston	4–6, 11–9, 6–3, 4–6, 6–3
1926	Rene Lacoste	Jean Borotra	6–4, 6–0, 6–4
1927	Rene Lacoste	Bill Tilden	11–9, 6–3, 11–9
1928	Henri Cochet	Francis T. Hunter	4–6, 6–4, 3–6, 7–5, 6–3
1929	Bill Tilden	Francis T. Hunter	3–6, 6–3, 4–6, 6–2, 6–4
1930	John H. Doeg	Francis X. Shields	10–8, 1–6, 6–4, 16–14
1931	Ellsworth Vines	George M. Lott Jr	7–9, 6–3, 9–7, 7–5
1932	Ellsworth Vines	Henri Cochet	6–4, 6–4, 6–4
1933	Fred Perry	Jack Crawford	6–3, 11–13, 4–6, 6–0, 6–1
1934	Fred Perry	Wilmer L. Allison	6–4, 6–3, 1–6, 8–6
1935	Wilmer L. Allison	Sidney B. Wood Jr	6–2, 6–2, 6–3
1936	Fred Perry	Don Budge	2–6, 6–2, 8–6, 1–6, 10–8
1937‡	Don Budge	Gottfried von Cramm	6–1, 7–9, 6–1, 3–6, 6–1
1938	Don Budge	Gene Mako	6–3, 6–8, 6–2, 6–1
1939	Bobby Riggs	Welby Van Horn	6–4, 6–2, 6–4
1940	Don McNeill	Bobby Riggs	4–6, 6–8, 6–3, 6–3, 7–5
1941	Bobby Riggs	Francis Kovacs II	5–7, 6–1, 6–3, 6–3
1942	Ted Schroeder	Frank Parker	8–6, 7–5, 3–6, 4–6, 6–2
1943	Joseph R. Hunt	Jack Kramer	6–3, 6–8, 10–8, 6–0
1944	Frank Parker	William F. Talbert	6–4, 3–6, 6–3, 6–3
1945	Frank Parker	William F. Talbert	14–12, 6–1, 6–2
1946	Jack Kramer	Tom P. Brown	9–7, 6–3, 6–0
1947	Jack Kramer	Frank Parker	4–6, 2–6, 6–1, 6–0, 6–3
1948	Pancho Gonzales	Eric W. Sturgess	6–2, 6–3, 14–12
1949	Pancho Gonzales	Ted Schroeder	16–18, 2–6, 6–1, 6–2, 6–4
1950	Arthur Larsen	Herbie Flam	6–3, 4–6, 5–7, 6–4, 6–3
1951	Frank Sedgman	Vic Seixas	6–4, 6–1, 6–1
1952	Frank Sedgman	Gardnar Mulloy	6–1, 6–2, 6–3
1953	Tony Trabert	Vic Seixas	6–3, 6–2, 6–3
1954	Vic Seixas	Rex Hartwig	3–6, 6–2, 6–4, 6–4
1955	Tony Trabert	Ken Rosewall	9–7, 6–3, 6–3
1956	Ken Rosewall	Lew Hoad	4–6, 6–2, 6–3, 6–3
1957	Mal Anderson	Ashley J. Cooper	10–8, 7–5, 6–4

MEN (Cont.)
United States Championships (Cont.)

Year	Winner	Finalist	Score
1958	Ashley J. Cooper	Mal Anderson	6–2, 3–6, 4–6, 10–8, 8–6
1959	Neale Fraser	Alex Olmedo	6–3, 5–7, 6–2, 6–4
1960	Neale Fraser	Rod Laver	6–4, 6–4, 9–7
1961	Roy Emerson	Rod Laver	7–5, 6–3, 6–2
1962	Rod Laver	Roy Emerson	6–2, 6–4, 5–7, 6–4
1963	Rafael Osuna	Frank Froehling III	7–5, 6–4, 6–2
1964	Roy Emerson	Fred Stolle	6–4, 6–2, 6–4
1965	Manuel Santana	Cliff Drysdale	6–2, 7–9, 7–5, 6–1
1966	Fred Stolle	John Newcombe	4–6, 12–10, 6–3, 6–4
1967	John Newcombe	Clark Graebner	6–4, 6–4, 8–6
1968*	Arthur Ashe	Tom Okker	14–12, 5–7, 6–3, 3–6, 6–3
1968**	Arthur Ashe	Bob Lutz	4–6, 6–3, 8–10, 6–0, 6–4
1969	Rod Laver	Tony Roche	7–9, 6–1, 6–3, 6–2
1969**	Stan Smith	Bob Lutz	9–7, 6–3, 6–1
1970	Ken Rosewall	Tony Roche	2–6, 6–4, 7–6, 6–3
1971	Stan Smith	Jan Kodes	3–6, 6–3, 6–2, 7–6
1972	Ilie Nastase	Arthur Ashe	3–6, 6–3, 6–7, 6–4, 6–3
1973	John Newcombe	Jan Kodes	6–4, 1–6, 4–6, 6–2, 6–3
1974	Jimmy Connors	Ken Rosewall	6–1, 6–0, 6–1
1975	Manuel Orantes	Jimmy Connors	6–4, 6–3, 6–3
1976	Jimmy Connors	Bjorn Borg	6–4, 3–6, 7–6, 6–4
1977	Guillermo Vilas	Jimmy Connors	2–6, 6–3, 7–6, 6–0
1978	Jimmy Connors	Bjorn Borg	6–4, 6–2, 6–2
1979	John McEnroe	Vitas Gerulaitis	7–5, 6–3, 6–3
1980	John McEnroe	Bjorn Borg	7–6, 6–1, 6–7, 5–7, 6–4
1981	John McEnroe	Bjorn Borg	4–6, 6–2, 6–4, 6–3
1982	Jimmy Connors	Ivan Lendl	6–3, 6–2, 4–6, 6–4
1983	Jimmy Connors	Ivan Lendl	6–3, 6–7, 7–5, 6–0
1984	John McEnroe	Ivan Lendl	6–3, 6–4, 6–1
1985	Ivan Lendl	John McEnroe	7–6, 6–3, 6–4
1986	Ivan Lendl	Miloslav Mecir	6–4, 6–2, 6–0
1987	Ivan Lendl	Mats Wilander	6–7, 6–0, 7–6, 6–4
1988	Mats Wilander	Ivan Lendl	6–4, 4–6, 6–3, 5–7, 6–4
1989	Boris Becker	Ivan Lendl	7–6, 1–6, 6–3, 7–6
1990	Pete Sampras	Andre Agassi	6–4, 6–3, 6–2
1991	Stefan Edberg	Jim Courier	6–2, 6–4, 6–0
1992	Stefan Edberg	Pete Sampras	3–6, 6–4, 7–6, 6–2
1993	Pete Sampras	Cedric Pioline	6–4, 6–4, 6–3
1994	Andre Agassi	Michael Stich	6–1, 7–6, 7–5
1995	Pete Sampras	Andre Agassi	6–4, 6–3, 4–6, 7–5
1996	Pete Sampras	Michael Chang	6–1, 6–4, 7–6
1997	Patrick Rafter	Greg Rusedski	6–3, 6–2, 4–6, 7–5
1998	Patrick Rafter	Mark Philippoussis	6–3, 3–6, 6–2, 6–0
1999	Andre Agassi	Todd Martin	6–4, 6–7, 6–7, 6–3, 6–2
2000	Marat Safin	Pete Sampras	6–4, 6–3, 6–3
2001	Lleyton Hewitt	Pete Sampras	7–6, 6–1, 6–1
2002	Pete Sampras	Andre Agassi	6–3, 6–4, 5–7, 6–4
2003	Andy Roddick	Juan Carlos Ferrero	6–3, 7–6 (7-2), 6–3
2004	Roger Federer	Lleyton Hewitt	6–0, 7–6 (7-3), 6–0

‡No challenge round played.*Became Open (amateur and professional) in 1968.†Challenge round abolished; #National Patriotic Tournament.**Amateur event held.

WOMEN
Australian Championships

Year	Winner	Finalist	Score
1922	Margaret Molesworth	Esna Boyd	6–3, 10–8
1923	Margaret Molesworth	Esna Boyd	6–1, 7–5
1924	Sylvia Lance	Esna Boyd	6–3, 3–6, 6–4
1925	Daphne Akhurst	Esna Boyd	1–6, 8–6, 6–4
1926	Daphne Akhurst	Esna Boyd	6–1, 6–3
1927	Esna Boyd	Sylvia Harper	5–7, 6–1, 6–2
1928	Daphne Akhurst	Esna Boyd	7–5, 6–2
1929	Daphne Akhurst	Louise Bickerton	6–1, 5–7, 6–2
1930	Daphne Akhurst	Sylvia Harper	10–8, 2–6, 7–5
1931	Coral Buttsworth	Margorie Crawford	1–6, 6–3, 6–4

WOMEN (Cont.)

Australian Championships (Cont.)

Year	Winner	Finalist	Score
1932	Coral Buttsworth	Kathrine Le Messurier	9–7, 6–4
1933	Joan Hartigan	Coral Buttsworth	6–4, 6–3
1934	Joan Hartigan	Margaret Molesworth	6–1, 6–4
1935	Dorothy Round	Nancye Wynne Bolton	1–6, 6–1, 6–3
1936	Joan Hartigan	Nancye Wynne Bolton	6–4, 6–4
1937	Nancye Wynne Bolton	Emily Westacott	6–3, 5–7, 6–4
1938	Dorothy Bundy	D. Stevenson	6–3, 6–2
1939	Emily Westacott	Nell Hopman	6–1, 6–2
1940	Nancye Wynne Bolton	Thelma Coyne	5–7, 6–4, 6–0
1941–45	No tournament		
1946	Nancye Wynne Bolton	Joyce Fitch	6–4, 6–4
1947	Nancye Wynne Bolton	Nell Hopman	6–3, 6–2
1948	Nancye Wynne Bolton	Marie Toomey	6–3, 6–1
1949	Doris Hart	Nancye Wynne Bolton	6–3, 6–4
1950	Louise Brough	Doris Hart	6–4, 3–6, 6–4
1951	Nancye Wynne Bolton	Thelma Long	6–1, 7–5
1952	Thelma Long	H. Angwin	6–2, 6–3
1953	Maureen Connolly	Julia Sampson	6–3, 6–2
1954	Thelma Long	J. Staley	6–3, 6–4
1955	Beryl Penrose	Thelma Long	6–4, 6–3
1956	Mary Carter	Thelma Long	3–6, 6–2, 9–7
1957	Shirley Fry	Althea Gibson	6–3, 6–4
1958	Angela Mortimer	Lorraine Coghlan	6–3, 6–4
1959	Mary Carter-Reitano	Renee Schuurman	6–2, 6–3
1960	Margaret Smith	Jan Lehane	7–5, 6–2
1961	Margaret Smith	Jan Lehane	6–1, 6–4
1962	Margaret Smith	Jan Lehane	6–0, 6–2
1963	Margaret Smith	Jan Lehane	6–2, 6–2
1964	Margaret Smith	Lesley Turner	6–3, 6–2
1965	Margaret Smith	Maria Bueno	5–7, 6–4, 5–2 ret.
1966	Margaret Smith	Nancy Richey	Default
1967	Nancy Richey	Lesley Turner	6–1, 6–4
1968	Billie Jean King	Margaret Smith	6–1, 6–2
1969*	Margaret Smith Court	Billie Jean King	6–4, 6–1
1970	Margaret Smith Court	Kerry Melville Reid	6–3, 6–1
1971	Margaret Smith Court	Evonne Goolagong	2–6, 7–6, 7–5
1972	Virginia Wade	Evonne Goolagong	6–4, 6–4
1973	Margaret Smith Court	Evonne Goolagong	6–4, 7–5
1974	Evonne Goolagong	Chris Evert	7–6, 4–6, 6–0
1975	Evonne Goolagong	Martina Navratilova	6–3, 6–2
1976	Evonne Goolagong Cawley	Renata Tomanova	6–2, 6–2
1977 (Jan)	Kerry Melville Reid	Dianne Balestrat	7–5, 6–2
1977 (Dec)	Evonne Goolagong Cawley	Helen Gourlay	6–3, 6–0
1978	Chris O'Neil	Betsy Nagelsen	6–3, 7–6
1979	Barbara Jordan	Sharon Walsh	6–3, 6–3
1980	Hana Mandlikova	Wendy Turnbull	6–0, 7–5
1981	Martina Navratilova	Chris Evert Lloyd	6–7, 6–4, 7–5
1982	Chris Evert Lloyd	Martina Navratilova	6–3, 2–6, 6–3
1983	Martina Navratilova	Kathy Jordan	6–2, 7–6
1984	Chris Evert Lloyd	Helena Sukova	6–7, 6–1, 6–3
1985 (Dec)	Martina Navratilova	Chris Evert Lloyd	6–2, 4–6, 6–2
1987 (Jan)	Hana Mandlikova	Martina Navratilova	7–5, 7–6
1988	Steffi Graf	Chris Evert	6–1, 7–6
1989	Steffi Graf	Helena Sukova	6–4, 6–4
1990	Steffi Graf	Mary Joe Fernandez	6–3, 6–4
1991	Monica Seles	Jana Novotna	5–7, 6–3, 6–1
1992	Monica Seles	Mary Joe Fernandez	6–2, 6–3
1993	Monica Seles	Steffi Graf	4–6, 6–3, 6–2
1994	Steffi Graf	Arantxa Sánchez Vicario	6–0, 6–2
1995	Mary Pierce	Arantxa Sánchez Vicario	6–3, 6–2
1996	Monica Seles	Anke Huber	6–4, 6–1
1997	Martina Hingis	Mary Pierce	6–2, 6–2
1998	Martina Hingis	Conchita Martinez	6–3, 6–3
1999	Martina Hingis	Amelie Mauresmo	6–2, 6–3
2000	Lindsay Davenport	Martina Hingis	6–1, 7–5
2001	Jennifer Capriati	Martina Hingis	6–4, 6–3

WOMEN *(Cont.)*

Australian Championships *(Cont.)*

Year	Winner	Finalist	Score
2002	Jennifer Capriati	Martina Hingis	4–6, 7–6 (9–7), 6–2
2003	Serena Williams	Venus Williams	7–6 (7-4), 3–6, 6–4
2004	Justine Henin-Hardenne	Kim Clijsters	6–3, 4–6, 6–3

*Became Open (amateur and professional) in 1969.

French Championships

Year	Winner	Finalist	Score
1925†	Suzanne Lenglen	Kathleen McKane	6–1, 6–2
1926	Suzanne Lenglen	Mary K. Browne	6–1, 6–0
1927	Kea Bouman	Irene Peacock	6–2, 6–4
1928	Helen Wills	Eileen Bennett	6–1, 6–2
1929	Helen Wills	Simone Mathieu	6–3, 6–4
1930	Helen Wills Moody	Helen Jacobs	6–2, 6–1
1931	Cilly Aussem	Betty Nuthall	8–6, 6–1
1932	Helen Wills Moody	Simone Mathieu	7–5, 6–1
1933	Margaret Scriven	Simone Mathieu	6–2, 4–6, 6–4
1934	Margaret Scriven	Helen Jacobs	7–5, 4–6, 6–1
1935	Hilde Sperling	Simone Mathieu	6–2, 6–1
1936	Hilde Sperling	Simone Mathieu	6–3, 6–4
1937	Hilde Sperling	Simone Mathieu	6–2, 6–4
1938	Simone Mathieu	Nelly Landry	6–0, 6–3
1939	Simone Mathieu	Jadwiga Jedrzejowska	6–3, 8–6
1940–45	No tournament		
1946	Margaret Osborne	Pauline Betz	1–6, 8–6, 7–5
1947	Patricia Todd	Doris Hart	6–3, 3–6, 6–4
1948	Nelly Landry	Shirley Fry	6–2, 0–6, 6–0
1949	Margaret Osborne duPont	Nelly Adamson	7–5, 6–2
1950	Doris Hart	Patricia Todd	6–4, 4–6, 6–2
1951	Shirley Fry	Doris Hart	6–3, 3–6, 6–3
1952	Doris Hart	Shirley Fry	6–4, 6–4
1953	Maureen Connolly	Doris Hart	6–2, 6–4
1954	Maureen Connolly	Ginette Bucaille	6–4, 6–1
1955	Angela Mortimer	Dorothy Knode	2–6, 7–5, 10–8
1956	Althea Gibson	Angela Mortimer	6–0, 12–10
1957	Shirley Bloomer	Dorothy Knode	6–1, 6–3
1958	Zsuzsi Kormoczi	Shirley Bloomer	6–4, 1–6, 6–2
1959	Christine Truman	Zsuzsi Kormoczi	6–4, 7–5
1960	Darlene Hard	Yola Ramirez	6–3, 6–4
1961	Ann Haydon	Yola Ramirez	6–2, 6–1
1962	Margaret Smith	Lesley Turner	6–3, 3–6, 7–5
1963	Lesley Turner	Ann Haydon Jones	2–6, 6–3, 7–5
1964	Margaret Smith	Maria Bueno	5–7, 6–1, 6–2
1965	Lesley Turner	Margaret Smith	6–3, 6–4
1966	Ann Jones	Nancy Richey	6–3, 6–1
1967	Francoise Durr	Lesley Turner	4–6, 6–3, 6–4
1968*	Nancy Richey	Ann Jones	5–7, 6–4, 6–1
1969	Margaret Smith Court	Ann Jones	6–1, 4–6, 6–3
1970	Margaret Smith Court	Helga Niessen	6–2, 6–4
1971	Evonne Goolagong	Helen Gourlay	6–3, 7–5
1972	Billie Jean King	Evonne Goolagong	6–3, 6–3
1973	Margaret Smith Court	Chris Evert	6–7, 7–6, 6–4
1974	Chris Evert	Olga Morozova	6–1, 6–2
1975	Chris Evert	Martina Navratilova	2–6, 6–2, 6–1
1976	Sue Barker	Renata Tomanova	6–2, 0–6, 6–2
1977	Mima Jausovec	Florenza Mihai	6–2, 6–7, 6–1
1978	Virginia Ruzici	Mima Jausovec	6–2, 6–2
1979	Chris Evert Lloyd	Wendy Turnbull	6–2, 6–0
1980	Chris Evert Lloyd	Virginia Ruzici	6–0, 6–3
1981	Hana Mandlikova	Sylvia Hanika	6–2, 6–4
1982	Martina Navratilova	Andrea Jaeger	7–6, 6–1
1983	Chris Evert Lloyd	Mima Jausovec	6–1, 6–2
1984	Martina Navratilova	Chris Evert Lloyd	6–3, 6–1
1985	Chris Evert Lloyd	Martina Navratilova	6–3, 6–7, 7–5
1986	Chris Evert Lloyd	Martina Navratilova	2–6, 6–3, 6–3

WOMEN (Cont.)

French Championships (Cont.)

Year	Winner	Finalist	Score
1987	Steffi Graf	Martina Navratilova	6–4, 4–6, 8–6
1988	Steffi Graf	Natalia Zvereva	6–0, 6–0
1989	Arantxa Sánchez Vicario	Steffi Graf	7–6, 3–6, 7–5
1990	Monica Seles	Steffi Graf	7–6, 6–4
1991	Monica Seles	Arantxa Sánchez Vicario	6–3, 6–4
1992	Monica Seles	Steffi Graf	6–2, 3–6, 10–8
1993	Steffi Graf	Mary Joe Fernandez	4–6, 6–2, 6–4
1994	Arantxa Sánchez Vicario	Mary Pierce	6–4, 6–4
1995	Steffi Graf	Arantxa Sánchez Vicario	7–5, 4–6, 6–0
1996	Steffi Graf	Arantxa Sánchez Vicario	6–3, 6–7 (4–7), 10–8
1997	Iva Majoli	Martina Hingis	6–4, 6–2
1998	Arantxa Sánchez Vicario	Monica Seles	7–6 (7–5), 0–6, 6–2
1999	Steffi Graf	Martina Hingis	4–6, 7–5, 6–2
2000	Mary Pierce	Conchita Martinez	6–2, 7–5
2001	Jennifer Capriati	Kim Clijsters	1–6, 6–4, 12–10
2002	Serena Williams	Venus Williams	7–5, 6–3
2003	Justine Henin-Hardenne	Kim Clijsters	6–0, 6–4
2004	Anastasia Myskina	Elena Dementieva	6–1, 6–2

†1925 was the first year that entries were accepted from all countries. *Became Open (amateur and professional) in 1968 but closed to contract professionals in 1972.

Wimbledon Championships

Year	Winner	Finalist	Score
1884	Maud Watson	Lilian Watson	6–8, 6–3, 6–3
1885	Maud Watson	Blanche Bingley	6–1, 7–5
1886	Blanche Bingley	Maud Watson	6–3, 6–3
1887	Charlotte Dod	Blanche Bingley	6–2, 6–0
1888	Charlotte Dod	Blanche Bingley Hillyard	6–3, 6–3
1889	Blanche Bingley Hillyard	n/a	n/a
1890	Lena Rice	n/a	n/a
1891	Charlotte Dod	n/a	n/a
1892	Charlotte Dod	Blanche Bingley Hillyard	6–1, 6–1
1893	Charlotte Dod	Blanche Bingley Hillyard	6–8, 6–1, 6–4
1894	Blanche Bingley Hillyard	n/a	n/a
1895	Charlotte Cooper	n/a	
1896	Charlotte Cooper	Mrs. W. H. Pickering	6–2, 6–3
1897	Blanche Bingley Hillyard	Charlotte Cooper	5–7, 7–5, 6–2
1898	Charlotte Cooper	n/a	n/a
1899	Blanche Bingley Hillyard	Charlotte Cooper	6–2, 6–3
1900	Blanche Bingley Hillyard	Charlotte Cooper	4–6, 6–4, 6–4
1901	Charlotte Cooper Sterry	Blanche Bingley Hillyard	6–2, 6–2
1902	Muriel Robb	Charlotte Cooper Sterry	7–5, 6–1
1903	Dorothea Douglass	n/a	n/a
1904	Dorothea Douglass	Charlotte Cooper Sterry	6–0, 6–3
1905	May Sutton	Dorothea Douglass	6–3, 6–4
1906	Dorothea Douglass	May Sutton	6–3, 9–7
1907	May Sutton	Dorothea Douglass Lambert Chambers	6–1, 6–4
1908	Charlotte Cooper Sterry	n/a	n/a
1909	Dora Boothby	n/a	n/a
1910	Dorothea Douglass Lambert Chambers	Dora Boothby	6–2, 6–2
1911	Dorothea Douglass Lambert Chambers	Dora Boothby	6–0, 6–0
1912	Ethel Larcombe	n/a	n/a
1913	Dorothea Douglass Lambert Chambers		
1914	Dorothea Douglass Lambert Chambers	Ethel Larcombe	7–5, 6–4
1915–18	No tournament		
1919	Suzanne Lenglen	Dorothea Douglass Lambert Chambers	10–8, 4–6, 9–7
1920	Suzanne Lenglen	Dorothea Douglass Lambert Chambers	6–3, 6–0
1921	Suzanne Lenglen	Elizabeth Ryan	6–2, 6–0
1922	Suzanne Lenglen	Molla Mallory	6–2, 6–0

WOMEN *(Cont.)*

Wimbledon Championships *(Cont.)*

Year	Winner	Finalist	Score
1923	Suzanne Lenglen	Kathleen McKane	6–2, 6–2
1924	Kathleen McKane	Helen Wills	4–6, 6–4, 6–2
1925	Suzanne Lenglen	Joan Fry	6–2, 6–0
1926	Kathleen McKane Godfree	Lili de Alvarez	6–2, 4–6, 6–3
1927	Helen Wills	Lili de Alvarez	6–2, 6–4
1928	Helen Wills	Lili de Alvarez	6–2, 6–3
1929	Helen Wills	Helen Jacobs	6–1, 6–2
1930	Helen Wills Moody	Elizabeth Ryan	6–2, 6–2
1931	Cilly Aussem	Hilde Kranwinkel	7–5, 7–5
1932	Helen Wills Moody	Helen Jacobs	6–3, 6–1
1933	Helen Wills Moody	Dorothy Round	6–4, 6–8, 6–3
1934	Dorothy Round	Helen Jacobs	6–2, 5–7, 6–3
1935	Helen Wills Moody	Helen Jacobs	6–3, 3–6, 7–5
1936	Helen Jacobs	Hilde Kranwinkel Sperling	6–2, 4–6, 7–5
1937	Dorothy Round	Jadwiga Jedrzejowska	6–2, 2–6, 7–5
1938	Helen Wills Moody	Helen Jacobs	6–4, 6–0
1939	Alice Marble	Kay Stammers	6–2, 6–0
1940–45	No tournament		
1946	Pauline Betz	Louise Brough	6–2, 6–4
1947	Margaret Osborne	Doris Hart	6–2, 6–4
1948	Louise Brough	Doris Hart	6–3, 8–6
1949	Louise Brough	Margaret Osborne duPont	10–8, 1–6, 10–8
1950	Louise Brough	Margaret Osborne duPont	6–1, 3–6, 6–1
1951	Doris Hart	Shirley Fry	6–1, 6–0
1952	Maureen Connolly	Louise Brough	6–4, 6–3
1953	Maureen Connolly	Doris Hart	8–6, 7–5
1954	Maureen Connolly	Louise Brough	6–2, 7–5
1955	Louise Brough	Beverly Fleitz	7–5, 8–6
1956	Shirley Fry	Angela Buxton	6–3, 6–1
1957	Althea Gibson	Darlene Hard	6–3, 6–2
1958	Althea Gibson	Angela Mortimer	8–6, 6–2
1959	Maria Bueno	Darlene Hard	6–4, 6–3
1960	Maria Bueno	Sandra Reynolds	8–6, 6–0
1961	Angela Mortimer	Christine Truman	4–6, 6–4, 7–5
1962	Karen Hantze Susman	Vera Sukova	6–4, 6–4
1963	Margaret Smith	Billie Jean Moffitt	6–3, 6–4
1964	Maria Bueno	Margaret Smith	6–4, 7–9, 6–3
1965	Margaret Smith	Maria Bueno	6–4, 7–5
1966	Billie Jean King	Maria Bueno	6–3, 3–6, 6–1
1967	Billie Jean King	Ann Haydon Jones	6–3, 6–4
1968*	Billie Jean King	Judy Tegart	9–7, 7–5
1969	Ann Haydon Jones	Billie Jean King	3–6, 6–3, 6–2
1970	Margaret Smith Court	Billie Jean King	14–12, 11–9
1971	Evonne Goolagong	Margaret Smith Court	6–4, 6–1
1972	Billie Jean King	Evonne Goolagong	6–3, 6–3
1973	Billie Jean King	Chris Evert	6–0, 7–5
1974	Chris Evert	Olga Morozova	6–0, 6–4
1975	Billie Jean King	Evonne Goolagong Cawley	6–0, 6–1
1976	Chris Evert	Evonne Goolagong Cawley	6–3, 4–6, 8–6
1977	Virginia Wade	Betty Stove	4–6, 6–3, 6–1
1978	Martina Navratilova	Chris Evert	2–6, 6–4, 7–5
1979	Martina Navratilova	Chris Evert Lloyd	6–4, 6–4
1980	Evonne Goolagong Cawley	Chris Evert Lloyd	6–1, 7–6
1981	Chris Evert Lloyd	Hana Mandlikova	6–2, 6–2
1982	Martina Navratilova	Chris Evert Lloyd	6–1, 3–6, 6–2
1983	Martina Navratilova	Andrea Jaeger	6–0, 6–3
1984	Martina Navratilova	Chris Evert Lloyd	7–6, 6–2
1985	Martina Navratilova	Chris Evert Lloyd	4–6, 6–3, 6–2
1986	Martina Navratilova	Hana Mandlikova	7–6, 6–3
1987	Martina Navratilova	Steffi Graf	7–5, 6–3
1988	Steffi Graf	Martina Navratilova	5–7, 6–2, 6–1
1989	Steffi Graf	Martina Navratilova	6–2, 6–7, 6–1
1990	Martina Navratilova	Zina Garrison	6–4, 6–1
1991	Steffi Graf	Gabriela Sabatini	6–4, 3–6, 8–6

WOMEN *(Cont.)*

Wimbledon Championships *(Cont.)*

Year	Winner	Finalist	Score
1992	Steffi Graf	Monica Seles	6–2, 6–1
1993	Steffi Graf	Jana Novotna	7–6, 1–6, 6–4
1994	Conchita Martinez	Martina Navratilova	6–4, 3–6, 6–3
1995	Steffi Graf	Arantxa Sánchez Vicario	4–6, 6–1, 7–5
1996	Steffi Graf	Arantxa Sánchez Vicario	6–3, 7–5
1997	Martina Hingis	Jana Novotna	2–6, 6–3, 6–3
1998	Jana Novotna	Nathalie Tauziat	6–4, 7–6
1999	Lindsay Davenport	Steffi Graf	6–4, 7–5
2000	Venus Williams	Lindsay Davenport	6–3, 7–6
2001	Venus Williams	Justine Henin	6–1, 3–6, 6–0
2002	Serena Williams	Venus Williams	7–6 (7–4), 6–3
2003	Serena Williams	Venus Williams	4–6, 6–4, 6–2
2004	Maria Sharapova	Serena Williams	6–1, 6–4

*Became Open (amateur and professional) in 1968 but closed to contract professionals in 1972.

Note: Prior to 1922 the tournament was run on a challenge-round system. The previous year's winner "stood out" of an All-Comers event, which produced a challenger to play her for the title.

United States Championships

Year	Winner	Finalist	Score
1887	Ellen Hansell	Laura Knight	6–1, 6–0
1888	Bertha L. Townsend	Ellen Hansell	6–3, 6–5
1889	Bertha L. Townsend	Louise Voorhes	7–5, 6–2
1890	Ellen C. Roosevelt	Bertha L. Townsend	6–2, 6–2
1891	Mabel Cahill	Ellen C. Roosevelt	6–4, 6–1, 4–6, 6–3
1892	Mabel Cahill	Elisabeth Moore	5–7, 6–3, 6–4, 4–6, 6–2
1893	Aline Terry	Alice Schultze	6–1, 6–3
1894	Helen Hellwig	Aline Terry	7–5, 3–6, 6–0, 3–6, 6–3
1895	Juliette Atkinson	Helen Hellwig	6–4, 6–2, 6–1
1896	Elisabeth Moore	Juliette Atkinson	6–4, 4–6, 6–2, 6–2
1897	Juliette Atkinson	Elisabeth Moore	6–3, 6–3, 4–6, 3–6, 6–3
1898	Juliette Atkinson	Marion Jones	6–3, 5–7, 6–4, 2–6, 7–5
1899	Marion Jones	Maud Banks	6–1, 6–1, 7–5
1900	Myrtle McAteer	Edith Parker	6–2, 6–2, 6–0
1901	Elisabeth Moore	Myrtle McAteer	6–4, 3–6, 7–5, 2–6, 6–2
1902**	Marion Jones	Elisabeth Moore	6–1, 1–0, ret.
1903	Elisabeth Moore	Marion Jones	7–5, 8–6
1904	May Sutton	Elisabeth Moore	6–1, 6–2
1905	Elisabeth Moore	Helen Homans	6–4, 5–7, 6–1
1906	Helen Homans	Maud Barger-Wallach	6–4, 6–3
1907	Evelyn Sears	Carrie Neely	6–3, 6–2
1908	Maud Barger–Wallach	Evelyn Sears	6–3, 1–6, 6–3
1909	Hazel Hotchkiss	Maud Barger–Wallach	6–0, 6–1
1910	Hazel Hotchkiss	Louise Hammond	6–4, 6–2
1911	Hazel Hotchkiss	Florence Sutton	8–10, 6–1, 9–7
1912†	Mary K. Browne	Eleanora Sears	6–4, 6–2
1913	Mary K. Browne	Dorothy Green	6–2, 7–5
1914	Mary K. Browne	Marie Wagner	6–2, 1–6, 6–1
1915	Molla Bjurstedt	Hazel Hotchkiss Wightman	4–6, 6–2, 6–0
1916	Molla Bjurstedt	Louise Hammond Raymond	6–0, 6–1
1917‡	Molla Bjurstedt	Marion Vanderhoef	4–6, 6–0, 6–2
1918	Molla Bjurstedt	Eleanor Goss	6–4, 6–3
1919	Hazel Hotchkiss Wightman	Marion Zinderstein	6–1, 6–2
1920	Molla Bjurstedt Mallory	Marion Zinderstein	6–3, 6–1
1921	Molla Bjurstedt Mallory	Mary K. Browne	4–6, 6–4, 6–2
1922	Molla Bjurstedt Mallory	Helen Wills	6–3, 6–1
1923	Helen Wills	Molla Bjurstedt Mallory	6–2, 6–1
1924	Helen Wills	Molla Bjurstedt Mallory	6–1, 6–3
1925	Helen Wills	Kathleen McKane	3–6, 6–0, 6–2
1926	Molla Bjurstedt Mallory	Elizabeth Ryan	4–6, 6–4, 9–7
1927	Helen Wills	Betty Nuthall	6–1, 6–4
1928	Helen Wills	Helen Jacobs	6–2, 6–1
1929	Helen Wills	Phoebe Holcroft Watson	6–4, 6–2
1930	Betty Nuthall	Anna McCune Harper	6–1, 6–4
1931	Helen Wills Moody	Eileen Whitingstall	6–4, 6–1
1932	Helen Jacobs	Carolin Babcock	6–2, 6–2
1933	Helen Jacobs	Helen Wills Moody	8–6, 3–6, 3–0, ret.
1934	Helen Jacobs	Sarah Palfrey	6–1, 6–4
1935	Helen Jacobs	Sarah Palfrey Fabyan	6–2, 6–4

WOMEN (Cont.)

United States Championships (Cont.)

Year	Winner	Finalist	Score
1936	Alice Marble	Helen Jacobs	4–6, 6–3, 6–2
1937	Anita Lizane	Jadwiga Jedrzejowska	6–4, 6–2
1938	Alice Marble	Nancye Wynne	6–0, 6–3
1939	Alice Marble	Helen Jacobs	6–0, 8–10, 6–4
1940	Alice Marble	Helen Jacobs	6–2, 6–3
1941	Sarah Palfrey Cooke	Pauline Betz	7–5, 6–2
1942	Pauline Betz	Louise Brough	4–6, 6–1, 6–4
1943	Pauline Betz	Louise Brough	6–3, 5–7, 6–3
1944	Pauline Betz	Margaret Osborne	6–3, 8–6
1945	Sarah Palfrey Cooke	Pauline Betz	3–6, 8–6, 6–4
1946	Pauline Betz	Patricia Canning	11–9, 6–3
1947	Louise Brough	Margaret Osborne	8–6, 4–6, 6–1
1948	Margaret Osborne duPont	Louise Brough	4–6, 6–4, 15–13
1949	Margaret Osborne duPont	Doris Hart	6–4, 6–1
1950	Margaret Osborne duPont	Doris Hart	6–4, 6–3
1951	Maureen Connolly	Shirley Fry	6–3, 1–6, 6–4
1952	Maureen Connolly	Doris Hart	6–3, 7–5
1953	Maureen Connolly	Doris Hart	6–2, 6–4
1954	Doris Hart	Louise Brough	6–8, 6–1, 8–6
1955	Doris Hart	Patricia Ward	6–4, 6–2
1956	Shirley Fry	Althea Gibson	6–3, 6–4
1957	Althea Gibson	Louise Brough	6–3, 6–2
1958	Althea Gibson	Darlene Hard	3–6, 6–1, 6–2
1959	Maria Bueno	Christine Truman	6–1, 6–4
1960	Darlene Hard	Maria Bueno	6–4, 10–12, 6–4
1961	Darlene Hard	Ann Haydon	6–3, 6–4
1962	Margaret Smith	Darlene Hard	9–7, 6–4
1963	Maria Bueno	Margaret Smith	7–5, 6–4
1964	Maria Bueno	Carole Graebner	6–1, 6–0
1965	Margaret Smith	Billie Jean Moffitt	8–6, 7–5
1966	Maria Bueno	Nancy Richey	6–3, 6–1
1967*	Billie Jean King	Ann Haydon Jones	11–9, 6–4
1968*	Virginia Wade	Billie Jean King	6–4, 6–4
1968#	Margaret Smith Court	Maria Bueno	6–2, 6–2
1969	Margaret Smith Court	Nancy Richey	6–2, 6–2
1969#	Margaret Smith Court	Virginia Wade	4–6, 6–3, 6–0
1970	Margaret Smith Court	Rosie Casals	6–2, 2–6, 6–1
1971	Billie Jean King	Rosie Casals	6–4, 7–6
1972	Billie Jean King	Kerry Melville	6–3, 7–5
1973	Margaret Smith Court	Evonne Goolagong	7–6, 5–7, 6–2
1974	Billie Jean King	Evonne Goolagong	3–6, 6–3, 7–5
1975	Chris Evert	Evonne Goolagong Cawley	5–7, 6–4, 6–2
1976	Chris Evert	Evonne Goolagong Cawley	6–3, 6–0
1977	Chris Evert	Wendy Turnbull	7–6, 6–2
1978	Chris Evert	Pam Shriver	7–6, 6–4
1979	Tracy Austin	Chris Evert Lloyd	6–4, 6–3
1980	Chris Evert Lloyd	Hana Mandlikova	5–7, 6–1, 6–1
1981	Tracy Austin	Martina Navratilova	1–6, 7–6, 7–6
1982	Chris Evert Lloyd	Hana Mandlikova	6–3, 6–1
1983	Martina Navratilova	Chris Evert Lloyd	6–1, 6–3
1984	Martina Navratilova	Chris Evert Lloyd	4–6, 6–4, 6–4
1985	Hana Mandlikova	Martina Navratilova	7–6, 1–6, 7–6
1986	Martina Navratilova	Helena Sukova	6–3, 6–2
1987	Martina Navratilova	Steffi Graf	7–6, 6–1
1988	Steffi Graf	Gabriela Sabatini	6–3, 3–6, 6–1
1989	Steffi Graf	Martina Navratilova	3–6, 6–4, 6–2
1990	Gabriela Sabatini	Steffi Graf	6–2, 7–6
1991	Monica Seles	Martina Navratilova	7–6, 6–1
1992	Monica Seles	Arantxa Sánchez Vicario	6–3, 6–2
1993	Steffi Graf	Helena Sukova	6–3, 6–3
1994	Arantxa Sánchez Vicario	Steffi Graf	1–6, 7–6, 6–4
1995	Steffi Graf	Monica Seles	7–6, 0–6, 6–3
1996	Steffi Graf	Monica Seles	7–5, 7–4
1997	Martina Hingis	Venus Williams	6–0, 6–4
1998	Lindsay Davenport	Martina Hingis	6–3, 7–5
1999	Serena Williams	Martina Hingis	6–3, 7–6
2000	Venus Williams	Lindsay Davenport	6–4, 7–5
2001	Venus Williams	Serena Williams	6–2, 6–4
2002	Serena Williams	Venus Williams	6–4, 6–3

WOMEN (Cont.)
United States Championships (Cont.)

Year	Winner	Finalist	Score
2003	Justine Henin-Hardenne	Kim Clijsters	7–5, 6–1
2004	Svetlana Kuznetsova	Elena Dementieva	6–3, 7–5

**Five-set final abolished; †Challenge round abolished. *Became Open (amateur and professional) in 1968. ‡National Patriotic Tournament; #Amateur event held.

Grand Slams

Singles

Don Budge, 1938
Maureen Connolly, 1953
Rod Laver, 1962, 1969
Margaret Smith Court, 1970
Steffi Graf, 1988

Doubles

Frank Sedgman and Ken McGregor, 1951
Martina Navratilova and Pam Shriver, 1984
Maria Bueno and two partners: Christine Truman
(Australian), Darlene Hard (French, Wimbledon
and U.S. Championships), 1960
Martina Hingis and two partners: Mirjana Lucic
(Australian), Jana Novotna (French, Wimbledon
and U.S. Championships), 1998

Mixed Doubles

Margaret Smith and Ken Fletcher, 1963
Owen Davidson and two partners: Lesley Turner
(Australian), Billie Jean King (French, Wimbledon
and U.S. Championships), 1967

Alltime Grand Slam Champions

MEN

Player	Aus. S-D-M	French S-D-M	Wim. S-D-M	U.S. S-D-M	Total
Roy Emerson	6-3-0	2-6-0	2-3-0	2-4-0	28
John Newcombe	2-5-0	0-3-0	3-6-0	2-3-1	25
Frank Sedgman	2-2-2	0-2-2	1-3-2	2-2-2	22
Bill Tilden	†	0-0-1	3-1-0	7-5-4	21
Rod Laver	3-4-0	2-1-1	4-1-2	2-0-0	20
John Bromwich	2-8-1	0-0-0	0-2-2	0-3-1	19
Jean Borotra	1-1-1	1-5-2	2-3-1	0-0-1	18
Fred Stolle	0-3-1	1-2-0	0-2-3	1-3-2	18
Ken Rosewall	4-3-0	2-2-0	0-2-0	2-2-1	18
Neale Fraser	0-3-1	0-3-0	1-2-0	2-3-3	18
Adrian Quist	3-10-0	0-1-0	0-2-0	0-1-0	17
John McEnroe	0-0-0	0-0-1	3-4-0	4-5-0	17
Jack Crawford	4-4-3	1-1-1	1-1-1	0-0-0	17
Mark Woodforde	0-2-2	0-1-1	0-6-1	0-3-1	17

†Did not compete.

WOMEN

Player	Aus. S-D-M	French S-D-M	Wim. S-D-M	U.S. S-D-M	Total
Margaret Smith Court	11-8-2	5-4-4	3-2-5	5-5-8	62
*Martina Navratilova	3-8-1	2-7-2	9-7-4	4-9-2	58
Billie Jean King	1-0-1	1-1-2	6-10-4	4-5-4	39
Doris Hart	1-1-2	2-5-3	1-4-5	2-4-5	35
Helen Wills Moody	†	4-2-0	8-3-1	7-4-2	31
Louise Brough	1-1-0	0-3-0	4-5-4	1-8-3	30**
Margaret Osborne duPont	†	2-3-0	1-5-1	3-8-6	29**
Elizabeth Ryan	†	0-4-0	0-12-7	0-1-2	26
Steffi Graf	4-0-0	6-0-0	7-1-0	5-0-0	23
Pam Shriver	0-7-0	0-4-1	0-5-0	0-5-0	22
Chris Evert	2-0-0	7-2-0	3-1-0	6-0-0	21
Darlene Hard	†	1-3-2	0-4-3	2-6-0	21
Suzanne Lenglen	†	2-2-2#	6-6-3	0-0-0	21
Nancye Wynne Bolton	6-10-4	0-0-0	0-0-0	0-0-0	20
Maria Bueno	0-1-0	0-1-1	3-5-0	4-4-0	19
Thelma Coyne Long	2-12-4	0-0-1	0-0-0	0-0-0	19

*Active player. †Did not compete. #Suzanne Lenglen also won four singles titles at the French Championships before 1925, when competition was first opened to entries from all nations.**From 1940–45, with competition in the U.S. Championships thinned due to wartime constraints, Louise Brough Clapp also won four doubles titles (1942–45) and one mixed doubles title (1942); and Margaret Osborne duPont won five doubles titles (1941–45) and three mixed doubles titles (1943–45).

Alltime Grand Slam Singles Champions

MEN

Player	Aus.	French	Wim.	U.S.	Total
Pete Sampras	2	0	7	5	14
Roy Emerson	6	2	2	2	12
Bjorn Borg	0	6	5	0	11
Rod Laver	3	2	4	2	11
Bill Tilden	†	0	3	7	10
Jimmy Connors	1	0	2	5	8
Ivan Lendl	2	3	0	3	8
Fred Perry	1	1	3	3	8
Ken Rosewall	4	2	0	2	8
*Andre Agassi	4	1	1	2	8
Henri Cochet	†	4	2	1	7
Rene Lacoste	†	3	2	2	7
Bill Larned	†	†	0	7	7
John McEnroe	0	0	3	4	7
John Newcombe	2	0	3	2	7
Willie Renshaw	†	†	7	†	7
Dick Sears	†	†	0	7	7

*Active player. †Did not compete.

WOMEN

Player	Aus.	French	Wim.	U.S.	Total
Margaret Smith Court	11	5	3	5	24
Steffi Graf	4	6	7	5	22
Helen Wills Moody	†	4	8	7	19
Chris Evert	2	7	3	6	18
Martina Navratilova	3	2	9	4	18
Billie Jean King	1	1	6	4	12
Maureen Connolly	1	2	3	3	9
*Monica Seles	4	3	0	2	9
Suzanne Lenglen	†	2#	6	0	8
Molla Bjurstedt Mallory	†	†	0	8	8
Maria Bueno	0	0	3	4	7
Evonne Goolagong	4	1	2	0	7
Dorothea D.L. Chambers	†	†	7	0	7
Nancye Wynne Bolton	6	0	0	0	6
Louise Brough	1	0	4	1	6
Margaret Osborne duPont	†	2	1	3	6
Doris Hart	1	2	1	2	6
Blanche Bingley Hillyard	†	†	6	†	6
*Serena Williams	1	1	2	2	6

*Active player. †Did not compete.

#Suzanne Lenglen also won four singles titles at the French Championships before 1925, when competition was first opened to entries from all nations.

Davis Cup

the 1898 U.S. Championships. A Davis Cup meeting between two countries is known as a tie and is a three-day event consisting of two singles matches, followed by one doubles match and then two more singles matches. The United States boasts the greatest number of wins (31), followed by Australia (20).

Year	Winner	Finalist	Site	Score
1900	United States	Great Britain	Boston	3–0
1901	No tournament			
1902	United States	Great Britain	New York	3–2
1903	Great Britain	United States	Boston	4–1
1904	Great Britain	Belgium	Wimbledon	5–0
1905	Great Britain	United States	Wimbledon	5–0
1906	Great Britain	United States	Wimbledon	5–0
1907	Australasia	Great Britain	Wimbledon	3–2
1908	Australasia	United States	Melbourne	3–2
1909	Australasia	United States	Sydney	5–0
1910	No tournament			
1911	Australasia	United States	Christchurch, NZ	5–0
1912	Great Britain	Australasia	Melbourne	3–2
1913	United States	Great Britain	Wimbledon	3–2
1914	Australasia	United States	New York	3–2
1915–18	No tournament			
1919	Australasia	Great Britain	Sydney	4–1
1920	United States	Australasia	Auckland, NZ	5–0
1921	United States	Japan	New York	5–0
1922	United States	Australasia	New York	4–1
1923	United States	Australasia	New York	4–1
1924	United States	Australia	Philadelphia	5–0
1925	United States	France	Philadelphia	5–0
1926	United States	France	Philadelphia	4–1
1927	France	United States	Philadelphia	3–2
1928	France	United States	Paris	4–1
1929	France	United States	Paris	3–2
1930	France	United States	Paris	4–1
1931	France	Great Britain	Paris	3–2
1932	France	United States	Paris	3–2
1933	Great Britain	France	Paris	3–2
1934	Great Britain	United States	Wimbledon	4–1
1935	Great Britain	United States	Wimbledon	5–0
1936	Great Britain	Australia	Wimbledon	3–2
1937	United States	Great Britain	Wimbledon	4–1
1938	United States	Australia	Philadelphia	3–2
1939	Australia	United States	Philadelphia	3–2
1940–45	No tournament			
1946	United States	Australia	Melbourne	5–0
1947	United States	Australia	New York	4–1
1948	United States	Australia	New York	5–0
1949	United States	Australia	New York	4–1
1950	Australia	United States	New York	4–1
1951	Australia	United States	Sydney	3–2
1952	Australia	United States	Adelaide	4–1
1953	Australia	United States	Melbourne	3–2
1954	United States	Australia	Sydney	3–2
1955	Australia	United States	New York	5–0
1956	Australia	United States	Adelaide	5–0
1957	Australia	United States	Melbourne	3–2
1958	United States	Australia	Brisbane	3–2
1959	Australia	United States	New York	3–2
1960	Australia	Italy	Sydney	4–1
1961	Australia	Italy	Melbourne	5–0
1962	Australia	Mexico	Brisbane	5–0
1963	United States	Australia	Adelaide	3–2
1964	Australia	United States	Cleveland	3–2
1965	Australia	Spain	Sydney	4–1
1966	Australia	India	Melbourne	4–1
1967	Australia	Spain	Brisbane	4–1
1968	United States	Australia	Adelaide	4–1
1969	United States	Romania	Cleveland	5–0
1970	United States	W Germany	Cleveland	5–0
1971	United States	Romania	Charlotte, NC	3–2
1972	United States	Romania	Bucharest	3–2

Davis Cup *(Cont.)*

Year	Winner	Finalist	Site	Score
1973	Australia	United States	Cleveland	5–0
1974	South Africa	India	*	walkover
1975	Sweden	Czechoslovakia	Stockholm	3–2
1976	Italy	Chile	Santiago	4–1
1977	Australia	Italy	Sydney	3–1
1978	United States	Great Britain	Palm Springs	4–1
1979	United States	Italy	San Francisco	5–0
1980	Czechoslovakia	Italy	Prague	4–1
1981	United States	Argentina	Cincinnati	3–1
1982	United States	France	Grenoble, France	4–1
1983	Australia	Sweden	Melbourne	3–2
1984	Sweden	United States	Göteborg, Sweden	4–1
1985	Sweden	W Germany	Munich	3–2
1986	Australia	Sweden	Melbourne	3–2
1987	Sweden	India	Göteborg, Sweden	5–0
1988	West Germany	Sweden	Göteborg, Sweden	4–1
1989	West Germany	Sweden	Stuttgart	3–2
1990	United States	Australia	St. Petersburg	3–2
1991	France	United States	Lyon	3–1
1992	United States	Switzerland	Fort Worth, TX	3–1
1993	Germany	Australia	Dusseldorf	4–1
1994	Sweden	Russia	Moscow	4–1
1995	United States	Russia	Moscow	3–2
1996	France	Sweden	Malmö, Sweden	3–2
1997	Sweden	United States	Göteborg, Sweden	5–0
1998	Sweden	Italy	Milan	4–1
1999	Australia	France	Nice, France	3–2
2000	Spain	Australia	Barcelona	3–1
2001	France	Australia	Melbourne	3–2
2002	Russia	France	Paris	3–2
2003	Australia	Spain	Melbourne	3–1

*India refused to play the final in protest over South Africa's governmental policy of apartheid.
Note: Prior to 1972 the challenge-round system was in effect, with the previous year's winner "standing out" of the competition until the finals. A straight 16-nation tournament has been held since 1981.

Federation Cup

The Federation Cup was started in 1963 by the International Lawn Tennis Federation (now the ITF). Until 1991 all entrants gathered at one site at one time for a tournament that was concluded within one week. Since 1995 the Fed Cup, as it is now called, has been contested in three rounds by a World Group of eight nations. A meeting between two countries now consists of five matches: four singles and one doubles. The United States has the most wins (15), followed by Australia (7).

Year	Winner	Finalist	Site	Score
1963	United States	Australia	London	2–1
1964	Australia	United States	Philadelphia	2–1
1965	Australia	United States	Melbourne	2–1
1966	United States	W Germany	Turin	3–0
1967	United States	Great Britain	W Berlin	2–0
1968	Australia	Netherlands	Paris	3–0
1969	United States	Australia	Athens	2–1
1970	Australia	Great Britain	Freiburg	3–0
1971	Australia	Great Britain	Perth	3–0
1972	South Africa	Great Britain	Johannesburg	2–1
1973	Australia	South Africa	Bad Homburg	3–0
1974	Australia	United States	Naples	2–1
1975	Czechoslovakia	Australia	Aix-en-Provence	3–0
1976	United States	Australia	Philadelphia	2–1
1977	United States	Australia	Eastbourne, G.B.	2–1
1978	United States	Australia	Melbourne	2–1
1979	United States	Australia	Madrid	3–0
1980	United States	Australia	W Berlin	3–0
1981	United States	Great Britain	Nagoya	3–0
1982	United States	W Germany	Santa Clara, CA	3–0
1983	Czechoslovakia	W Germany	Zurich	2–1
1984	Czechoslovakia	Australia	Sao Paulo	2–1
1985	Czechoslovakia	United States	Tokyo	2–1
1986	United States	Czechoslovakia	Prague	3–0
1987	W Germany	United States	Vancouver	2–1
1988	Czechoslovakia	USSR	Melbourne	2–1

Federation Cup (Cont.)

Year	Winner	Finalist	Site	Score
1989	United States	Spain	Tokyo	3–0
1990	United States	USSR	Atlanta	2–1
1991	Spain	United States	Nottingham	2–1
1992	Germany	Spain	Frankfurt	2–1
1993	Spain	Australia	Frankfurt	3–0
1994	Spain	United States	Frankfurt	3–0
1995	Spain	United States	Valencia, Spain	3–2
1996	United States	Spain	Atlantic City	5–0
1997	France	Netherlands	Hertogenbosch, Neth.	4–1
1998	Spain	Switzerland	Geneva	3–2
1999	United States	Russia	Palo Alto, California	4–1
2000	United States	Spain	Las Vegas, Nevada	5–0
2001	Belgium	Russia	Barcelona	2–1
2002	Slovak Republic	Spain	Maspalomas, C. Isles	3–1
2003	France	United States	Moscow	4–1

Rankings

ATP Computer Year-End Top 10
MEN

1973
1 ....Ilie Nastase
2 ...John Newcombe
3 ...Jimmy Connors
4 ...Tom Okker
5 ...Stan Smith
6 ...Ken Rosewall
7 ...Manuel Orantes
8 ...Rod Laver
9 ...Jan Kodes
10 ..Arthur Ashe

1974
1 ....Jimmy Connors
2 ...John Newcombe
3 ...Bjorn Borg
4 ...Rod Laver
5 ...Guillermo Vilas
6 ...Tom Okker
7 ...Arthur Ashe
8 ...Ken Rosewall
9 ...Stan Smith
10 ..Ilie Nastase

1975
1 ....Jimmy Connors
2 ...Guillermo Vilas
3 ...Bjorn Borg
4 ...Arthur Ashe
5 ...Manuel Orantes
6 ...Ken Rosewall
7 ...Ilie Nastase
8 ...John Alexander
9 ...Roscoe Tanner
10 ..Rod Laver

1976
1 ....Jimmy Connors
2 ....Bjorn Borg
3 ...Ilie Nastase
4 ...Manuel Orantes
5 ...Raul Ramirez
6 ...Guillermo Vilas
7 ....Adriano Panatta
8 ...Harold Solomon
9 ...Eddie Dibbs
10 ..Brian Gottfried

1977
1 ....Jimmy Connors
2 ....Guillermo Vilas
3 ....Bjorn Borg
4 ....Vitas Gerulaitis
5 ....Brian Gottfried
6 ....Eddie Dibbs
7 ....Manuel Orantes
8 ....Raul Ramirez
9 ....Ilie Nastase
10 ..Dick Stockton

1978
1 ....Jimmy Connors
2 ....Bjorn Borg
3 ....Guillermo Vilas
4 ....John McEnroe
5 ....Vitas Gerulaitis
6 ....Eddie Dibbs
7 ....Brian Gottfried
8 ....Raul Ramirez
9 ....Harold Solomon
10 ..Corrado Barazzutti

1979
1 ....Bjorn Borg
2 ....Jimmy Connors
3 ....John McEnroe
4 ....Vitas Gerulaitis
5 ....Roscoe Tanner
6 ....Guillermo Vilas
7 ....Arthur Ashe
8 ....Harold Solomon
9 ....Jose Higueras
10 ..Eddie Dibbs

1980
1 ....Bjorn Borg
2 ....John McEnroe
3 ....Jimmy Connors
4 ....Gene Mayer
5 ....Guillermo Vilas
6 ....Ivan Lendl
7 ....Harold Solomon
8 ....Jose–Luis Clerc
9 ....Vitas Gerulaitis
10 ..Eliot Teltscher

1981
1 ....John McEnroe
2 ....Ivan Lendl
3 ....Jimmy Connors
4 ....Bjorn Borg
5 ....Jose–Luis Clerc
6 ....Guillermo Vilas
7 ....Gene Mayer
8 ....Eliot Teltscher
9 ....Vitas Gerulaitis
10 ..Peter McNamara

1982
1 ....John McEnroe
2 ....Jimmy Connors
3 ....Ivan Lendl
4 ....Guillermo Vilas
5 ....Vitas Gerulaitis
6 ....Jose–Luis Clerc
7 ....Mats Wilander
8 ....Gene Mayer
9 ....Yannick Noah
10 ..Peter McNamara

1983
1 ....John McEnroe
2 ....Ivan Lendl
3 ....Jimmy Connors
4 ....Mats Wilander
5 ....Yannick Noah
6 ....Jimmy Arias
7 ....Jose Higueras
8 ....Jose–Luis Clerc
9 ....Kevin Curren
10 ..Gene Mayer

ATP Computer Year-End Top 10 *(Cont.)*
MEN *(CONT.)*

1984
1 ....John McEnroe
2 ....Jimmy Connors
3 ....Ivan Lendl
4 ....Mats Wilander
5 ....Andres Gomez
6 ....Anders Jarryd
7 ....Henrik Sundstrom
8 ....Pat Cash
9 ....Eliot Teltscher
10 ..Yannick Noah

1985
1 ....Ivan Lendl
2 ....John McEnroe
3 ....Mats Wilander
4 ....Jimmy Connors
5 ....Stefan Edberg
6 ....Boris Becker
7 ....Yannick Noah
8 ....Anders Jarryd
9 ....Miloslav Mecir
10 ..Kevin Curren

1986
1 ....Ivan Lendl
2 ....Boris Becker
3 ....Mats Wilander
4 ....Yannick Noah
5 ....Stefan Edberg
6 ....Henri Leconte
7 ....Joakim Nystrom
8 ....Jimmy Connors
9 ....Miloslav Mecir
10 ..Andres Gomez

1987
1 ....Ivan Lendl
2 ....Stefan Edberg
3 ....Mats Wilander
4 ....Jimmy Connors
5 ....Boris Becker
6 ....Miloslav Mecir
7 ....Pat Cash
8 ....Yannick Noah
9 ....Tim Mayotte
10 ..John McEnroe

1988
1 ....Mats Wilander
2 ....Ivan Lendl
3 ....Andre Agassi
4 ....Boris Becker
5 ....Stefan Edberg
6 ....Kent Carlsson
7 ....Jimmy Connors
8 ....Jakob Hlasek
9 ....Henri Leconte
10 ..Tim Mayotte

1989
1 ....Ivan Lendl
2 ....Boris Becker
3 ....Stefan Edberg
4 ....John McEnroe
5 ....Michael Chang
6 ....Brad Gilbert
7 ....Andre Agassi
8 ....Aaron Krickstein
9 ....Alberto Mancini
10 ..Jay Berger

1990
1 ....Stefan Edberg
2 ....Boris Becker
3 ....Ivan Lendl
4 ....Andre Agassi
5 ....Pete Sampras
6 ....Andres Gomez
7 ....Thomas Muster
8 ....Emilio Sanchez
9 ....Goran Ivanisevic
10 ..Brad Gilbert

1991
1 ....Stefan Edberg
2 ....Jim Courier
3 ....Boris Becker
4 ....Michael Stich
5 ....Ivan Lendl
6 ....Pete Sampras
7 ....Guy Forget
8 ....Karel Novacek
9 ....Petr Korda
10 ...Andre Agassi

1992
1 ....Jim Courier
2 ....Stefan Edberg
3 ....Pete Sampras
4 ....Goran Ivanisevic
5 ....Boris Becker
6 ...Michael Chang
7 ....Petr Korda
8 ....Ivan Lendl
9 ....Andre Agassi
10 ...Richard Krajicek

1993
1 ....Pete Sampras
2 ....Michael Stich
3 ....Jim Courier
4 ....Sergi Bruguera
5 ....Stefan Edberg
6 ....Andrei Medvedev
7 ....Goran Ivanisevic
8 ....Michael Chang
9 ....Thomas Muster
10 ...Cedric Pioline

1994
1 ....Pete Sampras
2 ....Andre Agassi
3 ....Boris Becker
4 ....Sergi Bruguera
5 ....Goran Ivanisevic
6 ....Michael Chang
7 ....Stefan Edberg
8 ....Alberto Berasategui
9 ....Michael Stich
10 ...Todd Martin

1995
1 ....Pete Sampras
2 ....Andre Agassi
3 ....Thomas Muster
4 ....Boris Becker
5 ....Michael Chang
6 ....Yevgeny Kafelnikov
7 ....Thomas Enqvist
8 ....Jim Courier
9 ....Wayne Ferreira
10 ...Goran Ivanisevic

1996
1 ....Pete Sampras
2 ....Michael Chang
3 ....Yevgeny Kafelnikov
4 ....Goran Ivanisevic
5 ....Thomas Muster
6 ....Boris Becker
7 ....Richard Krajicek
8 ....Andre Agassi
9 ....Thomas Enqvist
10 ...Wayne Ferreira

1997
1 ....Pete Sampras
2 ....Patrick Rafter
3 ....Michael Chang
4 ....Jonas Bjorkman
5 ....Yevgeny Kafelnikov
6 ....Greg Rusedski
7 ....Carlos Moya
8 ....Sergei Bruguera
9 ....Thomas Muster
10 ...Marcelo Ríos

ATP Computer Year-End Top 10 (Cont.)
MEN (CONT.)

1998
1 ....Pete Sampras
2 ....Marcelo Rios
3 ....Alex Corretja
4 ....Patrick Rafter
5 ....Carlos Moya
6 ....Andre Agassi
7 ....Tim Henman
8 ....Karol Kucera
9 ....Greg Rusedski
10..Richard Krajicek

1999
1 ....Andre Agassi
2 ....Yevgeny Kafelnikov
3 ....Pete Sampras
4 ....Thomas Enqvist
5 ....Gustavo Kuerten
6 ....Nicolas Kiefer
7 ....Todd Martin
8 ....Nicolas Lapentti
9 ....Marcelo Rios
10..Richard Krajicek

2000
1 ....Gustavo Kuerten
2 ....Marat Safin
3 ....Pete Sampras
4 ....Magnus Norman
5 ....Yevgeny Kafelnikov
6 ....Andre Agassi
7 ....Lleyton Hewitt
8 ....Alex Corretja
9 ....Thomas Enqvist
10 ..Tim Henman

2001
1 ....Lleyton Hewitt
2 ....Gustavo Kuerten
3 ....Andre Agassi
4 ....Yevgeny Kafelnikov
5 ....Juan Carlos Ferrero
6 ....Sebastien Grosjean
7 ....Patrick Rafter
8 ....Tommy Haas
9 ....Tim Henman
10 ..Pete Sampras

2002
1 ....Lleyton Hewitt
2 ....Andre Agassi
3 ....Marat Safin
4 ....Juan Carlos Ferrero
5 ....Carlos Moya
6 ....Roger Federer
7 ....Jiri Novak
8 ....Tim Henman
9 ....Albert Costa
10 ..Andy Roddick

2003
1 ....Andy Roddick
2 ....Roger Federer
3 ....Juan Carlos Ferrero
4 ....Andre Agassi
5 ....Guillermo Coria
6 ....Rainer Schuettler
7 ....Carlos Moya
8 ....David Nalbandian
9 ....Mark Philippoussis
10 ..Sebastien Grosjean

WTA Computer Year-End Top 10
WOMEN

1973
1 ....Margaret Smith
       Court
2 ....Billie Jean King
3 ....Evonne Goolagong
4 ....Chris Evert
5 ....Rosie Casals
6 ....Virginia Wade
7 ....Kerry Reid
8 ....Nancy Gunter
9 ....Julie Heldman
10..Helga Masthoff

1974
1 ....Billie Jean King
2 ....Evonne Goolagong
3 ....Chris Evert
4 ....Virginia Wade
5 ....Julie Heldman
6 ....Rosie Casals
7 ....Kerry Reid
8 ....Olga Morozova
9 ....Lesley Hunt
10..Francoise Durr

1975
1 ....Chris Evert
2 ....Billie Jean King
3 ....Evonne Goolagong
       Cawley
4 ....Martina Navratilova
5 ....Virginia Wade
6 ....Margaret Smith
       Court
7 ....Olga Morozova
8 ....Nancy Gunter
9 ....Francoise Durr
10..Rosie Casals

1976
1 ....Chris Evert
2 ....Evonne Goolagong
       Cawley
3 ....Virginia Wade
4 ....Martina Navratilova
5 ....Sue Barker
6 ....Betty Stove
7 ....Dianne Balestrat
8 ....Mima Jausovec
9 ....Rosie Casals
10...Francoise Durr

1977
1 ....Chris Evert
2 ....Billie Jean King
3 ....Martina Navratilova
4 ....Virginia Wade
5 ....Sue Barker
6 ....Rosie Casals
7 ....Betty Stove
8 ....Dianne Balestrat
9 ....Wendy Turnbull
10...Kerry Reid

1978
1 ....Martina Navratilova
2 ....Chris Evert
3 ....Evonne Goolagong
       Cawley
4 ....Virginia Wade
5 ....Billie Jean King
6 ....Tracy Austin
7 ....Wendy Turnbull
8 ....Kerry Reid
9 ....Betty Stove
10...Dianne Balestrat

1979
1 ....Martina Navratilova
2 ....Chris Evert Lloyd
3 ....Tracy Austin
4 ....Evonne Goolagong
       Cawley
5 ....Billie Jean King
6 ....Dianne Balestrat
7 ....Wendy Turnbull
8 ....Virginia Wade
9 ....Kerry Reid
10...Sue Barker

1980
1 ....Chris Evert Lloyd
2 ....Tracy Austin
3 ....Martina Navratilova
4 ....Hana Mandlikova
5 ....Evonne Goolagong
       Cawley
6 ....Billie Jean King
7 ....Andrea Jaeger
8 ....Wendy Turnbull
9 ....Pam Shriver
10...Greer Stevens

1981
1 ....Chris Evert Lloyd
2 ....Tracy Austin
3 ....Martina Navratilova
4 ....Andrea Jaeger
5 ....Hana Mandlikova
6 ....Sylvia Hanika
7 ....Pam Shriver
8 ....Wendy Turnbull
9 ....Bettina Bunge
10...Barbara Potter

1982
1 ....Martina Navratilova
2 ....Chris Evert Lloyd
3 ....Andrea Jaeger
4 ....Tracy Austin
5 ....Wendy Turnbull
6 ....Pam Shriver
7 ....Hana Mandlikova
8 ....Barbara Potter
9 ....Bettina Bunge
10...Sylvia Hanika

1983
1 ....Martina Navratilova
2 ....Chris Evert Lloyd
3 ....Andrea Jaeger
4 ....Pam Shriver
5 ....Sylvia Hanika
6 ....Jo Durie
7 ....Bettina Bunge
8 ....Wendy Turnbull
9 ....Tracy Austin
10...Zina Garrison

1984
1 ....Martina Navratilova
2 ....Chris Evert Lloyd
3 ....Hana Mandlikova
4 ....Pam Shriver
5 ....Wendy Turnbull
6 ....Manuela Maleeva
7 ....Helena Sukova
8 ....Claudia Kohde-
       Kilsch
9 ....Zina Garrison
10...Kathy Jordan

WTA Computer Year-End Top 10 (Cont.)
WOMEN (CONT.)

1985
1 ....Martina Navratilova
2 ....Chris Evert Lloyd
3 ....Hana Mandlikova
4 ....Pam Shriver
5 ....Claudia Kohde-
 Kilsch
6 ....Steffi Graf
7 ....Manuela Maleeva
8 ....Zina Garrison
9 ....Helena Sukova
10...Bonnie Gadusek

1986
1 ....Martina Navratilova
2 ....Chris Evert Lloyd
3 ....Pam Shriver
4 ....Hana Mandlikova
5 ....Helena Sukova
6 ....Pam Shriver
7 ....Claudia Kohde-
 Kilsch
8 ....Manuela Maleeva
9 ....Kathy Rinaldi
10...Gabriela Sabatini

1987
1 ....Steffi Graf
2 ....Martina Navratilova
3 ....Chris Evert
4 ....Pam Shriver
5 ....Hana Mandlikova
6 ....Gabriela Sabatini
7 ....Helena Sukova
8 ....Manuela Maleeva
9 ....Zina Garrison
10...Claudia Kohde-
 Kilsch

1988
1 ....Steffi Graf
2 ....Martina Navratilova
3 ....Chris Evert
4 ....Gabriela Sabatini
5 ....Pam Shriver
6 ....Manuela Maleeva-
 Fragniere
7 ....Natalia Zvereva
8 ....Helena Sukova
9 ....Zina Garrison
10...Barbara Potter

1989
1 ....Steffi Graf
2 ....Martina Navratilova
3 ....Gabriela Sabatini
4 ....Zina Garrison
5 ....A.S. Vicario
6 ....Monica Seles
7 ....Conchita Martinez
8 ....Helena Sukova
9 ....Manuela Maleeva-
 Fragniere
10...Chris Evert*

1990
1 ....Steffi Graf
2 ....Monica Seles
3 ....Martina Navratilova
4 ....Mary Joe Fernandez
5 ....Gabriela Sabatini
6 ....Katerina Maleeva
7 ....A.S. Vicario
8 ....Jennifer Capriati
9 ....M. Maleeva-Fragniere
10...Zina Garrison

1991
1 ....Monica Seles
2 ....Steffi Graf
3 ....Gabriela Sabatini
4 ....Martina Navratilova
5 ....Arantxa Sánchez
 Vicario
6 ....Jennifer Capriati
7 ....Jana Novotna
8 ....Mary Joe Fernandez
9 ....Conchita Martinez
10...M. Maleeva-Fragniere

1992
1 ....Monica Seles
2 ....Steffi Graf
3 ....Gabriela Sabatini
4 ....Arantxa Sánchez
 Vicario
5 ....Martina Navratilova
6 ....Mary Joe Fernandez
7 ....Jennifer Capriati
8 ....Conchita Martinez
9 ....M. Maleeva-Fragniere
10...Jana Novotna

1993
1 ....Steffi Graf
2 ....Arantxa Sánchez
 Vicario
3 ....Martina Navratilova
4 ....Conchita Martinez
5 ....Gabriela Sabatini
6 ....Jana Novotna
7 ....Mary Joe Fernandez
8 ....Monica Seles
9 ....Jennifer Capriati
10 ..Anke Huber

1994
1 ....Steffi Graf
2 ....Arantxa Sánchez
 Vicario
3 ....Conchita Martinez
4 ....Jana Novotna
5 ....Mary Pierce
6 ....Lindsay Davenport
7 ....Gabriela Sabatini
8 ....Martina Navratilova
9 ....Kimiko Date
10 ..Natasha Zvereva

1995
1 ....Steffi Graf (co-No. 1)
1 ....Monica Seles
 (co-No. 1)
2 ....Conchita Martinez
3 ....A. S.Vicario
4 ....Kimiko Date
5 ....Mary Pierce
6 ....Magdalena Maleeva
7 ....Gabriela Sabatini
8 ....Mary Joe Fernandez
9 ....Iva Majoli
10 ..Anke Huber

1996
1 ....Steffi Graf
2 ....Monica Seles
3 ....Jana Novotna
4 ....Lindsay Davenport
5 ....Martina Hingis
6 ....Stephanie de Ville
7 ....Tamarine
 Tanasugarn
8 ....Anke Huber
9 ....Conchita Martinez
10 ..Julie Halard-
 Decugis

1997
1 ....Martina Hingis
2 ....Jana Novotna
3 ....Lindsay Davenport
4 ....Amanda Coetzer
5 ....Monica Seles
6 ....Iva Majoli
7 ....Mary Pierce
8 ....Irina Spirlea
9 ....Arantxa Sánchez
 Vicario
10...Mary Joe Fernandez

1998
1 ....Lindsay Davenport
2 ....Martina Hingis
2 ....Jana Novotna
4 ....A.S. Vicario
5 ....Venus Williams
6 ....Monica Seles
7 ....Mary Pierce
8 ....Conchita Martinez
9 ....Steffi Graf
10...Nathalie Tauziat

1999
1 ....Martina Hingis
2 ....Lindsay Davenport
3 ....Venus Williams
4 ....Serena Williams
5 ....Mary Pierce
6 ....Monica Seles
7 ....Nathalie Tauziat
8 ....Barbara Schett
9 ....J. Halard-Decugis
10 ..Amelie Mauresmo

2000
1-...Martina Hingis
2 ....Lindsay Davenport
3 ....Venus Williams
4 ....Monica Seles
5 ....Conchita Martinez
6 ....Serena Williams
7 ....Mary Pierce
8 ....Anna Kournikova
9 ....Arantxa
 Sánchez Vicario
10 ..Nathalie Tauziat

2001
1 ....Lindsay Davenport
2 ....Jennifer Capriati
3 ....Venus Williams
4 ....Martina Hingis
5 ....Kim Clijsters
6 ....Serena Williams
7 ....Justine Henin
8 ....Jelena Dokic
9 ....Amelie Mauresmo
10 ..Monica Seles

2002
1 ....Serena Williams
2 ....Venus Williams
3 ....Jennifer Capriati
4 ....Kim Clijsters
5 ....Justine Henin
6 ....Amelie Mauresmo
7 ....Monica Seles
8 ....Daniela Hantuchova
9 ....Jelena Dokic
10 ..Martina Hingis

2003
1 ....Justine Henin-
 Hardenne
2 ....Kim Clijsters
3 ....Serena Williams
4 ....Amelie Mauresmo
5 ....Lindsay Davenport
6 ....Jennifer Capriati
7 ....Anastasia Myskina
8 ....Elena Dementieva
9 ....Chandra Rubin
10 ..Ai Sugiyama

*When Chris Evert announced her retirement at the 1989 United States Open, she was ranked fourth in the world. That was her last official series tournament.

Prize Money

Top 25 Men's Career Prize Money Leaders

Note: From arrival of Open tennis in 1968 through September 20, 2004.

	Earnings ($)
Pete Sampras	43,280,489
Andre Agassi	29,200,579
Boris Becker	25,080,956
Yevgeny Kafelnikov	23,883,797
Ivan Lendl	21,262,417
Stefan Edberg	20,630,941
Goran Ivanisevic	19,876,579
Michael Chang	19,145,632
Gustavo Kuerten	14,609,954
Jim Courier	14,033,132
Lleyton Hewitt	13,713,820
Michael Stich	12,592,483
John McEnroe	12,539,622
Roger Federer	12,491,230
Thomas Muster	12,224,410
Sergi Bruguera	11,632,199
Patrick Rafter	11,127,058
Carlos Moya	10,937,296
Jonas Bjorkman	10,915,233
Petr Korda	10,448,450
Alex Corretja	10,338,209
Tim Henman	10,321,240
Thomas Enqvist	10,290,743
Richard Krajicek	10,077,425
Wayne Ferreira	9,969,617

Top 25 Women's Career Prize Money Leaders

Note: From arrival of Open tennis in 1968 through September 19, 2004.

	Earnings ($)
Steffi Graf	21,895,277
Martina Navratilova	21,194,804
Martina Hingis	18,344,660
Lindsay Davenport	18,171,981
Arantxa Sánchez Vicario	16,938,363
Monica Seles	14,891,762
Venus Williams	13,784,491
Serena Williams	13,771,061
Jana Novotna	11,249,284
Conchita Martinez	11,005,339
Jennifer Capriati	9,726,539
Chris Evert	8,896,195
Gabriela Sabatini	8,785,850
Kim Clijsters	8,711,741
Natasha Zvereva	7,792,503
Justine Henin-Hardenne	7,518,086
Mary Pierce	7,009,293
Nathalie Tauziat	6,649,907
Helena Sukova	6,391,245
Amelie Mauresmo	6,024,213
Amanda Coetzer	5,582,821
Lisa Raymond	5,501,821
Pam Shriver	5,460,566
Mary Joe Fernandez	5,258,471
Ai Sugiyama	5,020,457

Ungentlemanly Quarterly?

For those who like to keep abreast of the tennis news: French Open winner Anastasia Myskina filed an $8 million suit against *GQ* claiming the magazine did not prevent topless shots taken of her during a photo session two years ago from being sold to the Russian glossy *Medved*, which featured them in its August 2004 issue. According to the lawsuit, Myskina, 23, never intended for the pictures to be published and that they "are highly embarrassing and have caused Ms. Myskina great emotional distress and economic harm."

Open Era Overall Wins

Men's Career Leaders—Singles Titles Won

The top tournament-winning men from the institution of Open tennis in 1968 through Sept 26, 2004.

	W		W
Jimmy Connors	109	Thomas Muster	44
Ivan Lendl	94	Stefan Edberg	41
John McEnroe	77	Stan Smith	39
Pete Sampras	64	Michael Chang	34
Bjorn Borg	62	Arthur Ashe	33
Guillermo Vilas	62	Mats Wilander	33
Andre Agassi	59	John Newcombe	32
Ilie Nastase	57	Manuel Orantes	32
Boris Becker	49	Ken Rosewall	32
Rod Laver	47	Tom Okker	31

Women's Career Leaders—Singles Titles Won

The top tournament-winning women from the institution of Open tennis in 1968 through Sept. 26, 2004.

	W		W
Martina Navratilova	167	Martina Hingis	40
Chris Evert	157	Helga Masthoff	37
Steffi Graf	107	Conchita Martinez	32
Evonne Goolagong Cawley	88	Olga Morozova	31
Margaret Smith Court	79	Venus Williams	31
Billie Jean King	67	Tracy Austin	29
Maria Bueno	63	Arantxa Sánchez Vicario	29
Virginia Wade	55	Hana Mandlikova	27
Monica Seles	53	Gabriela Sabatini	27
Lindsay Davenport	44	Francoise Durr-Browning	26

Annual ATP/WTA Champions

Men—ATP Tour World Championship

Year	Player	Year	Player
1970	Stan Smith	1987	Ivan Lendl
1971	Ilie Nastase	1988	Boris Becker
1972	Ilie Nastase	1989	Stefan Edberg
1973	Ilie Nastase	1990	Andre Agassi
1974	Guillermo Vilas	1991	Pete Sampras
1975	Ilie Nastase	1992	Boris Becker
1976	Manuel Orantes	1993	Michael Stich
1977	Not held	1994	Pete Sampras
1978	Jimmy Connors	1995	Boris Becker
1979	John McEnroe	1996	Pete Sampras
1980	Bjorn Borg	1997	Pete Sampras
1981	Bjorn Borg	1998	Alex Corretja
1982	Ivan Lendl	1999	Pete Sampras
1983	Ivan Lendl	2000	Gustavo Kuerten
1984	John McEnroe	2001	Lleyton Hewitt
1985	John McEnroe	2002	Lleyton Hewitt
1986 (Jan)	Ivan Lendl	2003	Roger Federer
1986 (Dec)	Ivan Lendl		

Note: Event held twice in 1986. *Since 1984 the final has been best-of-five sets.

Women—WTA Tour Championship

Year	Player	Year	Player
1972	Chris Evert	1988	Gabriela Sabatini
1973	Chris Evert	1989	Steffi Graf
1974	Evonne Goolagong	1990	Monica Seles
1975	Chris Evert	1991	Monica Seles
1976	Evonne Goolagong Cawley	1992	Monica Seles
1977	Chris Evert	1993	Steffi Graf
1978	Martina Navratilova	1994	Gabriela Sabatini
1979	Martina Navratilova	1995	Steffi Graf
1980	Tracy Austin	1996	Steffi Graf
1981	Martina Navratilova	1997	Jana Novotna
1982	Sylvia Hanika	1998	Martina Hingis
1983	Martina Navratilova	1999	Lindsay Davenport
1984*	Martina Navratilova	2000	Martina Hingis
1985	Martina Navratilova	2001	Serena Williams
1986 (Mar)	Martina Navratilova	2002	Kim Clijsters
1986 (Nov)	Martina Navratilova	2003	Kim Clijsters
1987	Steffi Graf		

YET ANOTHER SIGN OF THE APOCALYPSE

Former tennis star Pat Cash said he was "50 percent sure" he had an affair with a woman who claims to have slept with David Beckham.

Pauline Betz Addie (1965)
George T. Adee (1964)
Fred B. Alexander (1961)
Wilmer L. Allison (1963)
Manuel Alonso (1977)
Malcolm Anderson (2000)
Arthur Ashe (1985)
Juliette Atkinson (1974)
H.W. Bunny Austin (1997)
Tracy Austin (1992)
Lawrence A. Baker Sr. (1975)
Maud Barger-Wallach (1958)
Angela Mortimer Barrett (1993)
Boris Becker (2003)
Karl Behr (1969)
Bjorn Borg (1987)
Jean Borotra (1976)
Lesley Turner Bowrey (1997)
Maureen Connolly Brinker (1968)
John Bromwich (1984)
Norman Everard Brookes (1977)
Mary K. Browne (1957)
Jacques Brugnon (1976)
J. Donald Budge (1964)
Maria E. Bueno (1978)
May Sutton Bundy (1956)
Mabel E. Cahill (1976)
Rosie Casals (1996)
Oliver S. Campbell (1955)
Malcolm Chace (1961)
Dorothy (Dodo) Cheney (2004)
Dorothea Douglass
   Chambers (1981)
Philippe Chatrier (1992)
Louise Brough Clapp (1967)
Clarence Clark (1983)
Joseph S. Clark (1955)
William J. Clothier (1956)
Henri Cochet (1976)
Arthur W. (Bud) Collins Jr. (1994)
Jimmy Connors (1998)
Ashley Cooper (1991)
Margaret Smith Court (1979)
Gottfried von Cramm (1977)
Jack Crawford (1979)
Joseph F. Cullman III (1990)
Allison Danzig (1968)
Sarah Palfrey Danzig (1963)
Herman David (1998)
Dwight F. Davis (1956)
Charlotte Dod (1983)
John H. Doeg (1962)

Lawrence Doherty (1980)
Reginald Doherty (1980)
Jaroslav Drobny (1983)
Margaret Osborne duPont
   (1967)
Francoise Durr (2003)
James Dwight (1955)
Stefan Edberg (2004)
Roy Emerson (1982)
Pierre Etchebaster (1978)
Chris Evert (1995)
Robert Falkenburg (1974)
Neale Fraser (1984)
Shirley Fry-Irvin (1970)
Charles S. Garland (1969)
Althea Gibson (1971)
Kathleen McKane Godfree
   (1978)
Richard A. Gonzales (1968)
Evonne Goolagong Cawley
   (1988)
Steffi Graf (2004)
Bryan M. Grant Jr. (1972)
David Gray (1985)
Clarence Griffin (1970)
King Gustaf V of Sweden
   (1980)
Harold H. Hackett (1961)
Ellen Forde Hansell (1965)
Darlene R. Hard (1973)
Doris J. Hart (1969)
Gladys M. Heldman (1979)
W.E. (Slew) Hester Jr. (1981)
Bob Hewitt (1992)
Lew Hoad (1980)
Harry Hopman (1978)
Fred Hovey (1974)
Joseph R. Hunt (1966)
Lamar Hunt (1993)
Francis T. Hunter (1961)
Helen Hull Jacobs (1962)
William Johnston (1958)
Ann Haydon Jones (1985)
Perry Jones (1970)
Robert Kelleher (2000)
Billie Jean King (1987)
Jan Kodes (1990)
John A. Kramer (1968)
Rene Lacoste (1976)
Al Laney (1979)
William A. Larned (1956)
Arthur D. Larsen (1969)

Rod G. Laver (1981)
Ivan Lendl (2001)
Suzanne Lenglen (1978)
Dorothy Round Little (1986)
George M. Lott Jr. (1964)
Gene Mako (1973)
Molla Bjurstedt Mallory (1958)
Hana Mandlikova (1994)
Alice Marble (1964)
Alastair B. Martin (1973)
Dan Maskell (1996)
William McChesney Martin (1982)
John McEnroe (1999)
Ken McGregor (1999)
Chuck McKinley (1986)
Maurice McLoughlin (1957)
Frew McMillan (1992)
W. Donald McNeill (1965)
Elisabeth H. Moore (1971)
Gardnar Mulloy (1972)
R. Lindley Murray (1958)
Julian S. Myrick (1963)
Ilie Nastase (1991)
Martina Navratilova (2000)
John D. Newcombe (1986)
Arthur C. Nielsen Sr (1971)
Alex Olmedo (1987)
Rafael Osuna (1979)
Mary Ewing Outerbridge (1981)
Frank A. Parker (1966)
Gerald Patterson (1989)
Budge Patty (1977)
Theodore R. Pell (1966)
Fred Perry (1975)
Tom Pettitt (1982)
Nicola Pietrangeli (1986)
Adrian Quist (1984)
Dennis Ralston (1987)
Ernest Renshaw (1983)
William Renshaw (1983)
Vincent Richards (1961)
Nancy Richey (2003)
Bobby Riggs (1967)
Helen Wills Moody Roark
   (1959)
Anthony D. Roche (1986)
Ellen C. Roosevelt (1975)
Mervyn Rose (2001)
Ken Rosewall (1980)
Elizabeth Ryan (1972)
Manuel Santana (1984)
Richard Savitt (1976)

Frederick R. Schroeder (1966)
Eleonora Sears (1968)
Richard D. Sears (1955)
Frank Sedgman (1979)
Pancho Segura (1984)
Vic Seixas Jr. (1971)
Francis X. Shields (1964)
Betty Nuthall Shoemaker (1977)
Pam Shriver (2002)
Henry W. Slocum Jr. (1955)
Stan Smith (1987)
Fred Stolle (1985)
William F. Talbert (1967)
Bill Tilden (1959)

Lance Tingay (1982)
Ted Tinling (1986)
Brian Tobin (2003)
Bertha Townsend Toulmin
  (1974)
Tony Trabert (1970)
James H. Van Alen (1965)
John Van Ryn (1963)
Guillermo Vilas (1991)
Ellsworth Vines (1962)
Virginia Wade (1989)
Marie Wagner (1969)
Holcombe Ward (1956)
Watson Washburn (1965)

Malcolm D. Whitman (1955)
Hazel Hotchkiss Wightman
  (1957)
Mats Wilander (2002)
Anthony Wilding (1978)
Richard Norris Williams II
  (1957)
Major Walter Clopton Wingfield
  (1997)
Sidney B. Wood (1964)
Robert D. Wrenn (1955)
Beals C. Wright (1956)

Note: Years in parentheses are dates of induction.

| Super Soph | Liza Wischer, a sophomore at Red River High in Grand Forks, N. Dak., didn't lose a set in the individual tournament as she won the singles title at the North Dakota State Girls Tennis Tournament for the third straight year. She was 26–0 for the season and led the Roughriders to a 14–0 record. |

Golf

PGA Championship
winner Vijay Singh

The King Is Dead

For now at least, as the game's courtiers, led by Vijay Singh, unseated Tiger Woods from golf's throne

BY STEPHEN CANNELLA

THE FRENCH HAVE 1789. Eastern Europe has 1989. And now the PGA has 2004, the year an autocrat was taken down and democracy bloomed in the world of golf. Well, sort of. After five years Tiger Woods's reign as lord of the links came to an end, and while power didn't exactly go to the people, it was disbursed among a handful of talented noblemen who had spent years trying to dethrone Woods. The emperor still had his swoosh-covered clothes, but by the end of 2004 Tiger had lost his top spot in the world rankings—and, more tellingly, his aura of invincibility. When you go more than a year without winning a stroke-play tournament, opponents tend not to quake at the sight of you striding to the tee box.

It was a year that saw Phil Mickelson win his long-awaited first major (the Masters) and Ernie Els strengthen his credentials as one of the game's five best players. But the title of World's Best was snatched away from Woods by one of his most prickly rivals, Vijay Singh. In his 11th year on the Tour the 41-year-old Fijian put together a season for the ages. With eight tournament wins, including a thrilling playoff triumph at the PGA Championship, Singh had earned $9,455,566 by the end of September, a record. After Singh's win at the Deutsche Bank Championship in Boston on Labor Day weekend, the official rankings finally confirmed what Tour observers had known for months. After 264 consecutive weeks at the top, Woods ceded the No. 1 ranking to Singh.

If Woods, who wouldn't celebrate his 29th birthday until December, was once golf's boy king, Singh was the commoner who infiltrated the royal court and somehow clambered up the social ladder. After a hardscrabble childhood in Fiji, Singh followed his golfing dreams around the globe, spending his 20s giving lessons and hustling oil executives at clubs in Borneo, all the while working odd jobs ranging from carpenter to nightclub bouncer. He tried and failed to qualify for the British Open in 1987, then spent years toiling on the African and European tours. Finally in 1993, at age

Mickelson finally broke through in a major, taking the Masters in style.

30, he qualified for the PGA Tour.

Once there, he impressed his fellow players with a Puritan's work ethic, developing a reputation as a pro's pro who always had a swing tip or practice advice for others on Tour. But even after victories at the 1998 PGA Championship and 2000 Masters, the respect Singh received in the clubhouse didn't translate into love from the public. His aloof manner still left fans cold. It didn't help that he was one of the few Tour members who refused to kowtow to Woods while the younger player was reinventing the game. At the 2000 Presidents Cup, Singh's caddie wore a cap stitched with the words "Tiger Who?" When the rivals were paired together at the 2003 American Express Championship, the following frosty exchange was the extent of their conversation:

Tiger: "Good luck."

Vijay: "Titleist 2."

By then the cracks in Woods's empire had already begun to spread. He finished 2004 winless in his previous 10 major tournaments, his last victory coming at the '02 U.S. Open. He showed once-unthinkable vulnerability even when playing well; after winning 18 straight tournaments when he led after two rounds, Woods coughed up two consecutive post-cut leads early in 2004. Since his bitter parting of the ways with swing coach Butch Harmon in '02, Woods's game had grown increasingly erratic, particularly off the tee. (By the end of September he sank to 173rd on the Tour in driving accuracy.) Only a spectacular short game kept Woods among the PGA elite.

Woods was clearly off his game in April when the Tour pulled into Augusta National, a course that once seemed tailor-made for him. He finished the Masters two over par, tied for 22nd place. Singh finished sixth, but

JOHN BIEVER

the tournament belonged to Mickelson, who at last closed the deal in a major, having been tantalizingly close to a major title more times than he cared to count. But this one, though it turned out differently, was not without its tense moments. Indeed, as the final rounds drew to a close, the gallery cringed at the thought of yet another heartbreaking loss for the talented lefthander.

He began Sunday with his first three-round lead in a major, but after nervous bogeys on the third and fifth holes he found himself down three shots to the charging Els. In years past, Mickelson might have folded under Els's assault. This time he played aggressively—attacking the flag on the devious par-3 12th and scoring a birdie; setting up another birdie on 13 with a magical seven-iron approach—and clawed his way back into the hunt.

Els finished the final round with a blistering 67, but Mickelson was only one shot behind when he arrived at the par-3 16th. He coolly birdied to draw even, and there he stood when he strode onto the 18th green facing an 18-foot putt for birdie—and the Masters championship. Mickelson drained the putt, becoming only the sixth player to win the Masters with a final-hole birdie—and triggering a wild celebration with his family. "It was an amazing, amazing day," he said, wearing his new green jacket, "the fulfillment of all my dreams."

With the ice broken, many golf fans believed that the 33-year-old was primed for a slew of major victories. But they didn't come in 2004. On the contrary, Mickelson reverted to his old ways at the U.S. Open at Shinnecock Hills Golf Club in Southampton, N.Y., three-putting on the 71st hole of the tournament to knock himself out of contention. That opened the door for South Africa's Retief Goosen, who held off Mickelson to win his second U.S. Open. Aside from Goosen's victory, the talk of the tournament was the condition of Shinnecock's rock-hard greens, which drew the ire of several players. Said Els, "This isn't golf. It's crazy."

Crazy was an apt description for what happened a month later at Scotland's Royal Troon, where Todd Hamilton became one of the unlikeliest champions in the British Open's 145-year history. Like Singh, Hamilton, 38, was a latecomer to the PGA Tour, having eked out a modest living playing in India, Pakistan, Thailand and Japan over the last decade. The Oquawka, Ill., native was an anonymous PGA rookie in 2004, despite a win at the Honda Classic in March.

He may have been unknown on Thursday at Royal Troon, but everyone knew who Hamilton was by Sunday. Hamilton's game is ill-suited to most PGA courses, but it fit Royal Troon perfectly: He keeps his irons and chips low—the fierce Scottish winds couldn't wreak havoc with them there—and is a splendid putter, particulary when the greens are slow, as Troon's were. He began the final round with a one-shot lead over Els and a two-shot advantage over Mickelson, Goosen and France's Thomas Levet. Hamilton bogeyed the 18th hole, opening the door for Els to win if he could sink a 10-foot birdie putt. He couldn't, and his bogey on the third

hole of a four-hole playoff gave Hamilton the tournament.

Singh finished 20th at Troon but soon caught fire. After forsaking his trademark belly putter for a conventional model, he won the Buick Open on Aug. 1, beginning a stretch in which he won five times in 10 events. Included in that run was an unlikely victory at the PGA at stunningly beautiful Whistling Straits in Kohler, Wisc. Singh started Sunday with a one-stroke lead over Justin Leonard, only to shoot an ugly 76. Leonard wasn't much better, missing several key putts on the back nine, none bigger than a 10-footer for par on the 72nd hole that would have given him the championship. "He should have put my man away when he had the chance," Singh's caddie, Dave Renwick, would say later.

Leonard missed, setting up a three-way playoff with Singh and Chris DiMarco. Singh fired his only birdie of the day on the first hole and held on to win. Afterward, he was asked if it was the ugliest victory of his career. "It's the prettiest one, I think," Singh said. "I think this is the biggest accomplishment I've had in my career."

Singh added the PGA Player of the Year Award to his 2004 résumé, cementing golf's new world order. The Ryder Cup, on the other hand, took on a decidedly Old World tone. The Europeans dominated the event, held at Oakland Hills Country Club in Bloomfield Township, Mich., despite fielding a lineup entirely bereft of major titleholders. The U.S., by contrast, had five major winners and five of the world's top 11 players. Yet Europe romped, 18½–9½, the worst defeat ever suffered by a U.S. Ryder team. U.S. captain Hal Sutton's decision to create a Dream Team pairing of Mickelson and Woods proved disastrous; they were tight and uninspired in a 2-and-1 loss to Colin Montgomerie and Padraig Harrington in the opening match, setting the tone for America's lost weekend.

Can Woods recover from his lost year, and regain form in 2005? That remains to be seen. For now, golf's social order can be summed up thusly: The King is dead. Long live the Singh.

Men's Majors

The Masters
**Augusta National GC (par 72; 7,290 yds);
Augusta, GA, April 8–11**

Player	Score	Earnings ($)
Phil Mickelson	72-69-69-69—279	1,170,000
Ernie Els	70-72-71-67—280	702,000
K.J. Choi	71-70-72-69—282	442,000
Bernhard Langer	71-73-69-72—285	286,000
Sergio Garcia	72-72-75-66—285	286,000
Fred Couples	73-69-74-70—286	189,893
Davis Love III	75-67-74-70—286	189,893
Nick Price	72-73-71-70—286	189,893
Kirk Triplett	71-74-69-72—286	189,893
Chris DiMarco	69-73-68-76—286	189,893
Vijay Singh	75-73-69-69—286	189,893
Paul Casey	75-69-68-74—286	189,893
Retief Goosen	75-73-70-70—288	125,667
Padraig Harrington	74-74-68-72—288	125,667
Charles Howell III	71-71-76-70—288	125,667
Casey Wittenberg*	76-72-71-69—288	
Jay Haas	69-75-72-73—289	97,500
Steve Flesch	76-67-77-69—289	97,500
Stewart Cink	74-73-69-73—289	97,500
Stephen Leaney	76-71-73-69—289	97,500
Fredrik Jacobson	74-74-67-74—289	97,500

*Amateur.

U.S. Open
**Shinnecock Hills GC, (par 70; 6,996 yds);
Southampton, NY, June 17–20**

Player	Score	Earnings ($)
Retief Goosen	70-66-69-71—276	1,125,000
Phil Mickelson	68-66-73-71—278	675,000
Jeff Maggert	68-67-74-72—281	424,604
Mike Weir	69-70-71-74—284	267,756
Shigeki Maruyama	66-68-74-76—284	267,756
Fred Funk	70-66-72-77—285	212,444
Steve Flesch	68-74-70-74—286	183,828
Robert Allenby	70-72-74-70—286	183,828
Jay Haas	66-74-76-71—287	145,282
Stephen Ames	74-66-73-74—287	145,282
Chris DiMarco	71-71-70-75—287	145,282
Ernie Els	70-67-70-80—287	145,282
Tim Herron	75-66-73-74—288	119,770
Tim Clark	73-70-66-79—288	119,770
Spencer Levin*	69-73-71-75—288	
Angel Cabrera	66-71-77-75—289	109,410
Skip Kendall	68-75-74-73—290	98,477
Corey Pavin	67-71-73-79—290	98,477
Tiger Woods	72-69-73-76—290	98,477

Four tied at 291.

*Amateur.

British Open
**Royal Troon GC (par 71; 7,175 yds);
Troon, Scotland, July 15–18**

Player	Score	Earnings ($)
Todd Hamilton#	71-67-67-69—274	1,348,272
Ernie Els	69-69-68-68—274	805,218
Phil Mickelson	73-66-68-68—275	514,965
Lee Westwood	72-71-68-67—278	393,246
Davis Love III	72-69-71-67—279	298,679
Thomas Levet	66-70-71-72—279	298,679
Scott Verplank	69-70-70-71—280	220,030
Retief Goosen	69-70-68-73—280	220,030
Tiger Woods	70-71-68-72—281	167,597
Mike Weir	71-68-71-71—281	167,597
Mark Calcavecchia	72-73-69-68—282	129,833
Skip Kendall	69-66-75-72—282	129,833
Darren Clarke	69-72-73-68—282	129,833
Barry Lane	69-68-71-75—283	105,801
Stewart Cink	72-71-71-69—283	105,801
Kenny Perry	69-70-72-74—284	88,012
Justin Leonard	70-72-71-71—284	88,012
Joakim Haeggman	69-73-72-70—284	88,012
K.J. Choi	68-69-74-73—284	88,012

Five tied at 285.

Won playoff.

PGA Championship
**Whistling Straits GC (par 72; 7,514 yds),
Kohler, WI, August 12–15**

Player	Score	Earnings ($)
Vijay Singh#	67-68-69-76—280	1,125,000
Chris DiMarco	68-70-71-71—280	550,000
Justin Leonard	66-69-70-75—280	550,000
Ernie Els	66-70-72-73—281	267,500
Chris Riley	69-70-69-73—281	267,500
Paul McGinley	69-74-70-69—282	196,000
K.J. Choi	68-71-73-70—282	196,000
Phil Mickelson	72-67-74-74—282	196,000
Robert Allenby	71-70-72-70—283	152,000
Ben Crane	70-74-69-70—283	152,000
Adam Scott	71-71-69-72—283	152,000
Stephen Ames	68-71-69-75—283	152,000
Arron Oberholser	73-71-70-70—284	110,250
Brad Faxon	71-71-70-72—284	110,250
Brian Davis	70-71-69-74—284	110,250
Darren Clarke	65-71-72-76—284	110,250
Stuart Appleby	68-75-72-70—285	76,857
J.F. Remesy	72-71-70-72—285	76,857
Stewart Cink	73-70-70-72—285	76,857
David Toms	72-72-69-72—285	76,857
Fredrik Jacobson	72-70-70-73—285	76,857
Matt Gogel	71-71-69-74—285	76,857
Loren Roberts	6872-70-75—285	76,857

Won playoff.

Men's Tour Results

Late 2003 PGA Tour Events

Tournament	Final Round	Winner	Score/ Under Par	Earnings ($)
Las Vegas Invitational	Oct 12	Stuart Appleby	328/–31	720,000
Chrysler Classic of Greensboro	Oct 19	Shigeki Maruyama	266/–22	810,000
Funai Classic at Walt Disney World	Oct 26	Vijay Singh	265/–23	720,000
Chrysler Championship	Nov 2	Retief Goosen	272/–12	864,000
The Tour Championship	Nov 9	Chad Campbell	268/–16	1,080,000
Southern Farm Bureau Classic	Nov 3	Luke Donald	201/–15	468,000
WGC World Cup	Nov 16	Trevor Immelman/Rory Sabatini	275/–13	350,000 each
Franklin Templeton Shootout	Nov 16	Jeff Sluman/Hank Kuehne*	193/–23	275,000 each
The Skins Game	Nov 30	Fred Couples	8 skins	605,000
Nedbank Golf Challenge	Nov 30	Sergio Garcia*	274/–14	1,250,050
PGA Grand Slam of Golf	Dec 6	Jim Furyk	135/–9	400,000
Target World Challenge	Dec 14	Davis Love III	277/–11	1,200,000

2004 PGA Tour Events

Tournament	Final Round	Winner	Score/ Under Par	Earnings ($)
Mercedes Championships	Jan 11	Stuart Appleby	270/–22	1,060,000
Sony Open in Hawaii	Jan 18	Ernie Els*	262/–18	864,000
Bob Hope Chrysler Classic	Jan 25	Phil Mickelson*	330/–30	810,000
FBR Open	Feb 1	Jonathan Kaye	266/–18	936,000
AT&T Pebble Beach National Pro-Am	Feb 8	Vijay Singh	272/–16	954,000
Buick Invitational	Feb 15	John Daly*	268/–10	864,000
Nissan Open	Feb 22	Mike Weir	267/–17	864,000
WGC Match Play Championship	Feb 29	Tiger Woods	3 & 2	1,200,000
Chrysler Classic of Tucson	Feb 29	Heath Slocum	266/–22	540,000
Ford Championship	Mar 7	Craig Parry*	271/–17	900,000
Honda Classic	Mar 14	Todd Hamilton	276/–12	900,000
Bay Hill Invitational	Mar 21	Chad Campbell	270/–18	900,000
The Players Championship	Mar 28	Adam Scott	276/–12	1,440,000
BellSouth Classic	Apr 4	Zach Johnson	275/–13	810,000
The Masters	Apr 11	Phil Mickelson	279/–9	1,170,000
MCI Heritage	Apr 18	Stewart Cink*	274/–10	864,000
Shell Houston Open	Apr 25	Vijay Singh	277/–11	900,000
HP Classic of New Orleans	May 2	Vijay Singh	266/–22	918,000
Wachovia Championship	May 9	Joey Sindelar*	277/–11	1,080,000
EDS Byron Nelson Classic	May 16	Sergio Garcia*	270/–10	1,044,000
Bank of America Colonial	May 23	Steve Flesch	269/–11	954,000
FedEx St. Jude Classic	May 30	David Toms	268/–16	846,000
Memorial Tournament	June 6	Ernie Els	270/–18	945,000
Buick Classic	June 13	Sergio Garcia*	272/–12	945,000
U.S. Open	June 20	Retief Goosen	276/–4	1,125,000
Booz Allen Classic	June 27	Adam Scott	263/–21	864,000
Western Open	July 4	Stephen Ames	274/–10	864,000
John Deere Classic	July 11	Mark Hensby	268/–16	684,000
British Open	July 18	Todd Hamilton*	274/–10	1,300,000
B.C. Open	July 18	Jonathan Byrd	268/–20	540,000
U.S. Bank Championship	July 25	Carlos Franco	267/–13	630,000
Buick Open	Aug 1	Vijay Singh	265/–23	810,000
The International	Aug 8	Rod Pampling	+31‡	900,000
PGA Championship	Aug 15	Vijay Singh*	280/–8	1,125,000
WGC-NEC Invitational	Aug 22	Stewart Cink	269/–11	1,200,000
Reno-Tahoe Open	Aug 22	Vaughn Taylor	278/–10	540,000
Buick Championship	Aug 29	Woody Austin*	270/–10	756,000
Deutsche Bank Championship	Sep 6	Vijay Singh	268/–16	900,000
Bell Canadian Open	Sep 13	Vijay Singh*	275/–9	810,000
Valero Texas Open	Sep 19	Bart Bryant	261/–19	630,000
84 Lumber Classic of Pennsylvania	Sep 26	Vijay Singh	273/–15	756,000
WGC-American Express Champ.	Oct 3	Ernie Els	270/–18	1,200,000

* Won playoff. ‡ Revised Stableford scoring.

Kraft Nabisco Championship

Mission Hills CC; Rancho Mirage, CA
(par 72; 6,460 yds) March 25–28

Player	Score	Earnings ($)
Grace Park	72-69-67-69—277	240,000
Aree Song	66-73-69-70—278	146,826
Karrie Webb	68-71-71-69—279	106,512
Michelle Wie*	69-72-69-71—281	
Cristie Kerr	71-71-71-69—282	74,358
Catriona Matthew	67-75-70-70—282	74,359
Mi-Hyun Kim	71-70-71-71—283	54,261
Lorena Ochoa	67-76-74-66—284	36,737
Candie Kung	69-75-71-69—284	36,737
Christina Kim	72-72-70-70—284	36,737
Rosie Jones	67-73-71-73—284	36,737
Jung Yeon Lee	69-69-71-75—284	36,737
Annika Sorenstam	71-76-69-69—285	26,420
Hee-Won Han	72-71-71-71—285	26,420
Stacy Prammanasudh	71-71-69-74—285	26,420
Laura Davies	71-77-70-68—286	20,633
Se Ri Pak	72-73-72-69—286	20,633
Karen Stupples	70-76-68-72—286	20,633
Young Kim	74-72-67-73—286	20,633
Carin Koch	70-72-71-73—286	20,633
Wendy Doolan	70-69-72-75—286	20,633

*Amateur.

McDonald's LPGA Championship

DuPont CC; Wilmington, DE
(par 71; 6,408 yds) June 10–13

Player	Score	Earnings ($)
Annika Sorenstam	68-71-64-72—275	240,000
Shi Hyun Ahn	69-70-69-66—274	144,780
Grace Park	68-70-70-68—276	105,028
Angela Stanford	69-71-67-71—278	73,322
Gloria Park	67-72-68-71—278	73,322
Christina Kim	74-69-64-72—279	49,145
Juli Inkster	70-66-70-73—279	49,145
Wendy Doolan	73-70-65-72—280	35,538
Soo-Yun Kang	69-68-71-72—280	35,538
Lorena Ochoa	71-67-67-75—280	35,538
Carin Koch	69-71-68-73—281	28,734
Reilley Rankin	70-67-71-73—281	28,734
Pat Hurst	69-69-75-69—282	24,466
Mhairi McKay	72-69-69-72—282	24,466
Jennfer Rosales	66-70-74-72—282	24,466
Meg Mallon	69-73-70-71—283	21,718
Betsy King	76-70-70-68—284	18,654
Dawn Coe-Jones	72-72-70-70—284	18,654
Cristi Albers	70-74-69-71—284	18,654
Cristie Kerr	69-73-71-71—284	18,654
Se Ri Pak	69-73-70-72—284	18,654
Michelle Ellis	72-70-69-73—284	18,654

U.S. Women's Open

The Orchards GC; South Hadley, MA
(par 71; 6,473 yds) July 1–4

Player	Score	Earnings ($)
Meg Mallon	73-69-67-65—274	560,000
Annika Sorenstam	71-68-70-67—276	335,000
Kelly Robbins	74-67-68-69—278	208,863
Jennifer Rosales	70-67-69-75—281	145,547
Michele Redman	70-72-73-67—282	111,173
Candie Kung	70-68-74-70—282	111,173
Jeong Jang	72-74-71-66—283	86,744
Moira Dunn	73-67-72-71—283	86,744
Pat Hurst	70-71-71-71—283	86,744
Carin Koch	72-67-75-70—284	68,813
Michelle Ellis	70-69-72-73—284	68,813
Rachel Teske	71-69-70-74—284	68,813
P. Meunier-Lebouc	67-75-74-69—285	60,602
Paula Creamer*	72-69-72-72—285	
Michelle Wie*	71-70-71-73—285	
Suzann Pettersen	74-72-71-69—286	54,052
Mi Hyun Kim	76-68-71-71—286	54,052
Karrie Webb	72-71-71-72—286	54,052
Catriona Matthew	73-71-72-71—287	48,432

Seven players tied at 288.

*Amateur.

Weetabix Women's British Open

The Old Course at Sunningdale; Berjshire,
England, (par 72; 6,392 yds) July 29–Aug. 1

Player	Score	Earnings ($)
Karen Stupples	65-70-70-64—269	290,880
Rachel Teske	70-69-65-70—274	181,800
Heather Bowie	70-69-65-71—275	127,260
Lorena Ochoa	69-71-66-70—276	99,990
Michele Redman	70-71-70-66—277	72,114
Giulia Sergas	72-71-67-67—277	72,114
Beth Daniel	69-69-71-68—277	72,114
Jung Yeon Lee	67-72-70-69—278	52,722
Minea Blomqvist	68-78-62-70—278	52,722
Laura Davies	70-69-69-70—278	52,722
Pat Hurst	72-72-66-69—279	41,814
Cristie Kerr	69-73-63-74—279	41,814
Grace Park	71-70-69-70—280	28,918
Hee-Won Han	72-68-70-70—280	28,918
Carin Koch	70-70-70-70—280	28,918
Christina Kim	73-68-68-71—280	28,918
Laura Diaz	70-69-70-71—280	28,918
Annika Sorenstam	68-71-70-71—280	28,918
Natalie Gulbis	68-71-70-71—280	28,918
Paula Marti	73-66-68-73—280	28,918

Women's Tour Results

Late 2003 LPGA Tour Events

Tournament	Final Round	Winner	Score/ Under Par	Earnings ($)
Samsung World Championship	Oct 12	Sophie Gustafson	274/–14	200,000
Sports Today CJ Nine Bridges Classic	Nov 2	Shi Hyun Ahn	204/–12	187,500
Mizuno Classic	Nov 9	Annika Sorenstam	192/–24	169,500
Mobil LPGA Tournament of Champions	Nov 16	Dorothy Delasin	280/–8	122,000
ADT Championship	Nov 23	Meg Mallon	281/–7	215,000

2004 LPGA Tour Events

Tournament	Final Round	Winner	Score/ Under Par	Earnings ($)
Welch's/Fry's Championship	Mar 14	Karen Stupples	258/–22	120,000
Safeway International	Mar 21	Annika Sorenstam	270/–18	180,000
Kraft Nabisco Championship	Mar 28	Grace Park	277/–11	240,000
Office Depot Championship	Apr 4	Annika Sorenstam	207/–9	262,500
Takefuji Classic	Apr 17	Cristie Kerr	209/–7	165,000
Chick-fil-A Charity Championship	May 2	Jennifer Rosales	274/–14	240,000
Michelob Ultra Open at Kingsmill	May 9	Se Ri Pak	275/–9	330,000
Franklin American Mortgage Champ.	May 16	Lorena Ochoa	272/–16	135,000
Sybase Classic	May 23	Sherri Steinhauer	272/–12	187,500
LPGA Corning Classic	May 30	Annika Sorenstam	270/–18	150,000
Kellogg-Keebler Classic	June 6	Karrie Webb	200/–16	180,000
McDonald's LPGA Championship	June 13	Annika Sorenstam	271/–13	240,000
ShopRite LPGA Classic	June 20	Cristie Kerr	202/–11	195,000
Wegman's Rochester LPGA	June 27	Kim Saiki	274/–14	225,000
U.S. Women's Open	July 4	Meg Mallon	274/–10	560,000
Canadian Women's Open	July 11	Meg Mallon	270/–18	195,000
Giant Eagle LPGA Classic	July 18	Moira Dunn	204/–12	150,000
Evian Masters	July 24	Wendy Doolan	270/–18	375,000
Women's British Open	Aug 1	Karen Stupples	269/–19	290,880
Jamie Farr Owens Corning Classic	Aug 8	Meg Mallon	277/–7	165,000
Wendy's Championship for Children	Aug 22	Catriona Matthew*	278/–10	165,000
Wachovia Classic	Aug 29	Lorena Ochoa	269/–19	150,000
State Farm Classic	Sep 5	Cristie Kerr	264/–24	180,000
John Q. Hammons Hotel Classic	Sep 12	Annika Sorenstam	204/–9	150,000
Safeway Classic	Sep 19	Hee-Won Han*	207/–9	180,000
Longs Drugs Challenge	Sep 26	Christina Kim	266/–18	150,000

* Won playoff.

Late 2003 Senior Tour Events

Tournament	Final Round	Winner	Score/ Under Par	Earnings ($)
Turtle Bay Championship	Oct 12	Hale Irwin	208/–8	225,000
SBC Championship	Oct 19	Craig Stadler	198/–15	225,000
Charles Schwab Cup Championship	Oct 26	Jim Thorpe	268/–20	440,000
Father-Son Challenge	Dec 7	Hale/Steve Irwin	123/–21	100,000 each

2004 Senior Tour Events

Tournament	Final Round	Winner	Score/ Under Par	Earnings ($)
MasterCard Championship	Jan 25	Fuzzy Zoeller	196/–20	268,000
Wendy's Champions Skins Game	Feb 1	Tom Watson	10 skins	400,000
Royal Caribbean Classic	Feb 8	Bruce Fleisher	210/–6	217,500
ACE Group Classic	Feb 15	Craig Stadler*	206/–10	240,000
Outback Steakhouse Pro-Am	Feb 22	Mark McNulty	200/–13	241,000
MasterCard Classic	Mar 7	Ed Fiori	210/–6	300,000
SBC Classic	Mar 14	Gil Morgan	202/–14	225,000
Toshiba Senior Classic	Mar 21	Tom Purtzer	198/–15	240,000
Blue Angels Classic	Apr 18	Tom Jenkins	196/–14	225,000
Liberty Mutual Legends of Golf	April 25	Hale Irwin	205/–11	350,000
Bruno's Memorial Classic	May 2	Bruce Fleisher	200/–16	225,000
FedEx Kinko's Classic	May 9	Larry Nelson	209/–7	240,000
Allianz Championship	May 23	D.A. Weibring	204/–9	225,000
Senior PGA Championship	May 30	Hale Irwin	276/–8	360,000
Farmers Charity Classic	June 6	Jim Thorpe	203/–13	240,000
Bayer Advantage Celebrity Pro-Am	June 13	Allen Doyle	131/–13	247,500
Bank of America Championship	June 27	Craig Stadler	201/–15	232,500
Commerce Bank Long Island Classic	July 4	Jim Thorpe	201/–9	225,000
Ford Senior Players Championship	July 11	Mark James	275/–13	375,000
Senior British Open	July 25	Pete Oakley	284/–4	295,000
U.S. Senior Open	Aug 1	Peter Jacobsen	272/–12	470,000
3M Championship	Aug 8	Tom Kite	203/–13	262,500
Greater Hickory Classic at Rock Barn	Aug 22	Doug Tewell	202/–14	240,000
Jeld-Wen Tradition	Aug 29	Craig Stadler	275/–13	345,000
First Tee Open at Pebble Beach	Sep 5	Craig Stadler	201/–15	300,000
Kroger Classic	Sep 12	Bruce Summerhays	201/–15	225,000
SAS Championship	Sep 26	Craig Stadler	199/–17	270,000
Constellation Energy Classic	Oct 3	Wayne Levi	200/–16	240,000

*Won playoff.

Leonard of the Links

Leonard Cruess, 100, of Goleta, Calif., a retired meat cutter, made a hole in one on the 57-yard par-3 4th hole at the Encina Royale Golf Course and retirement community, where he lives. He has been golfing regularly since the 1920s.

U.S. Amateur Results*

Tournament	Final Round	Winner	Score	Runner-Up
Women's Amateur Public Links	June 27	Ya-Ni Tseng	1 up	Michelle Wie
Men's Amateur Public Links	July 17	Ryan Moore	6 & 5	Dayton Rose
Girls' Junior Amateur	July 24	J. Granada	1 up, 20 holes	Jane Park
Boys' Junior Amateur	July 24	Sihwan Kim	1 up	David Chung
Women's Amateur	Aug 15	Jane Park	1 up	Amanda McCurdy
Men's Amateur	Aug 22	Ryan Moore	2 up	Luke List
Women's Mid-Amateur	Sep 15	Corey Weworski	5 & 4	Virginia Grimes

*Results through 10/3/04.

International Results*

Tournament	Final Round	Winner	Score	Runner-Up
Curtis Cup	June 13	United States	10–8	Great Britain/Ireland
Ryder Cup	Sep 19	Europe	18½–9½	United States

*Results through 10/3/04.

PGA Tour Final 2003 Money Leaders

Name	Events	Best Finish	Scoring Average*	Money ($)
Vijay Singh	27	1 (4)	69.11	7,573,907
Tiger Woods	18	1 (5)	69.38	6,673,413
Davis Love III	23	1 (5)	69.78	6,081,896
Jim Furyk	27	1 (3)	69.28	5,182,863
Mike Weir	21	1 (4)	69.89	4,918,910
Kenny Perry	26	1 (4)	70.02	4,400,121
Chad Campbell	27	1 (1)	69.91	3,912,063
David Toms	25	1 (3)	70.22	3,710,904
Ernie Els	17	1 (3)	69.90	3,371,237
Retief Goosen	19	1 (2)	69.73	3,166,374

*Adjusted for average score of field in each tournament entered.

LPGA Tour Final 2003 Money Leaders

Name	Events	Best Finish	Scoring Average	Money ($)
Annika Sorenstam	17	1 (6)	69.02	2,029,506
Se Ri Pak	26	1 (3)	70.03	1,611,928
Grace Park	26	1 (1)	70.11	1,417,702
Hee-Won Han	27	1 (2)	70.88	1,111,860
Juli Inkster	21	1 (2)	70.55	1,028,205
Candie Kung	30	1 (3)	71.27	938,079
Rachel Teske	27	1 (2)	70.90	924,667
Beth Daniel	22	1 (1)	70.81	917,654
Lorena Ochoa	24	2 (2)	70.97	823,740
Rosie Jones	19	1 (1)	70.29	808,785

Senior Tour Final 2003 Money Leaders

Name	Events	Best Finish	Scoring Average	Money ($)
Tom Watson	14	1 (2)	68.81	1,853,109
Jim Thorpe	30	1 (2)	70.20	1,830,306
Gil Morgan	25	1 (1)	69.71	1,620,206
Bruce Lietzke	22	1 (2)	70.04	1,610,826
Hale Irwin	22	1 (2)	69.59	1,607,390
Tom Kite	27	2 (4)	69.79	1,549,819
Tom Jenkins	30	1 (1)	69.99	1,415,503
Larry Nelson	24	1 (1)	69.82	1,365,973
Allen Doyle	30	1 (1)	70.07	1,349,272
Bruce Fleisher	29	1 (1)	70.02	1,306,012

Tired Tiger?

After more than 80,000 tickets had been sold and full-page ads in local newspapers promoting a showdown between the top two golfers in the world were placed, Tiger Woods pulled of the 84 Lumber Classic in Farmington, Pa., on Sept. 21, 2004, citing post–Ryder Cup fatigue and exhaustion. Still, the day he withdrew, the supposedly drained Woods summoned the energy to chat it up on *The Early Show*, *Live with Regis and Kelly*, *SportsCenter* and *Late Night with Conan O'Brien* to promote his new video game, *Tiger Woods PGA Tour 2005*. The game features several pro golfers, plus Justin Timberlake, who golfs a black 8 ball and breaks out into celebratory dance moves on the greens.

Men's Golf

THE MAJOR TOURNAMENTS

The Masters

Year	Winner	Score	Runner-Up
1934	Horton Smith	284	Craig Wood
1935	Gene Sarazen* (144) (only 36-hole playoff)	282	Craig Wood (149)
1936	Horton Smith	285	Harry Cooper
1937	Byron Nelson	283	Ralph Guldahl
1938	Henry Picard	285	Ralph Guldahl / Harry Cooper
1939	Ralph Guldahl	279	Sam Snead
1940	Jimmy Demaret	280	Lloyd Mangrum
1941	Craig Wood	280	Byron Nelson
1942	Byron Nelson* (69)	280	Ben Hogan (70)
1943–45	No tournament		
1946	Herman Keiser	282	Ben Hogan
1947	Jimmy Demaret	281	Byron Nelson / Frank Stranahan
1948	Claude Harmon	279	Cary Middlecoff
1949	Sam Snead	282	Johnny Bulla / Lloyd Mangrum / Jim Ferrier
1950	Jimmy Demaret	283	
1951	Ben Hogan	280	Skee Riegel
1952	Sam Snead	286	Jack Burke Jr..
1953	Ben Hogan	274	Ed Oliver Jr.
1954	Sam Snead* (70)	289	Ben Hogan (71)
1955	Cary Middlecoff	279	Ben Hogan
1956	Jack Burke Jr.	289	Ken Venturi
1957	Doug Ford	282	Sam Snead
1958	Arnold Palmer	284	Doug Ford / Fred Hawkins
1959	Art Wall Jr.	284	Cary Middlecoff
1960	Arnold Palmer	282	Ken Venturi
1961	Gary Player	280	Charles R. Coe / Arnold Palmer
1962	Arnold Palmer* (68)	280	Gary Player (71) / D. Finsterwald (77)
1963	Jack Nicklaus	286	Tony Lema
1964	Arnold Palmer	276	Dave Marr / Jack Nicklaus
1965	Jack Nicklaus	271	Arnold Palmer / Gary Player
1966	Jack Nicklaus* (70)	288	Tommy Jacobs (72) / Gay Brewer Jr. (78)
1967	Gay Brewer Jr.	280	Bobby Nichols
1968	Bob Goalby	277	Roberto DeVicenzo
1969	George Archer	281	Billy Casper / George Knudson / Tom Weiskopf
1970	Billy Casper* (69)	279	Gene Littler (74)
1971	Charles Coody	279	Johnny Miller / Jack Nicklaus
1972	Jack Nicklaus	286	Bruce Crampton / Bobby Mitchell / Tom Weiskopf
1973	Tommy Aaron	283	J.C. Snead
1974	Gary Player	278	Tom Weiskopf / Dave Stockton
1975	Jack Nicklaus	276	Johnny Miller / Tom Weiskopf
1976	Ray Floyd	271	Ben Crenshaw
1977	Tom Watson	276	Jack Nicklaus
1978	Gary Player	277	Hubert Green / Rod Funseth / Tom Watson
1979	Fuzzy Zoeller* (4–3)†	280	Ed Sneed (4–4) / Tom Watson (4–4)
1980	Seve Ballesteros	275	Gibby Gilbert / Jack Newton
1981	Tom Watson	280	Johnny Miller / Jack Nicklaus
1982	Craig Stadler* (4)	284	Dan Pohl (5)
1983	Seve Ballesteros	280	Ben Crenshaw / Tom Kite
1984	Ben Crenshaw	277	Tom Watson
1985	Bernhard Langer	282	Curtis Strange / Seve Ballesteros / Ray Floyd
1986	Jack Nicklaus	279	Greg Norman / Tom Kite
1987	Larry Mize* (4–3)	285	Seve Ballesteros (5) / Greg Norman (4–4)
1988	Sandy Lyle	281	Mark Calcavecchia
1989	Nick Faldo* (5–3)	283	Scott Hoch (5–4)
1990	Nick Faldo* (4–4)	278	Ray Floyd (4–x)
1991	Ian Woosnam	277	José María Olazábal
1992	Fred Couples	275	Ray Floyd
1993	Bernhard Langer	277	Chip Beck
1994	José María Olazábal	279	Tom Lehman
1995	Ben Crenshaw	274	Davis Love III
1996	Nick Faldo	276	Greg Norman
1997	Tiger Woods	270	Tom Kite
1998	Mark O'Meara	279	David Duval / Fred Couples
1999	José María Olazábal	280	Davis Love III
2000	Vijay Singh	278	Ernie Els
2001	Tiger Woods	272	David Duval
2002	Tiger Woods	276	Retief Goosen
2003	Mike Weir	281	Len Mattiace
2004	Phil Mickelson	279	Ernie Els

*Winner in playoff. Playoff scores are in parentheses. †Playoff cut from 18 holes to sudden death.
Note: Played at Augusta National Golf Club, Augusta, GA.

United States Open Championship

Year	Winner	Score	Runner-Up	Site
1895	Horace Rawlins	†173	Willie Dunn	Newport GC, Newport, RI
1896	James Foulis	†152	Horace Rawlins	Shinnecock Hills GC, Southampton, NY
1897	Joe Lloyd	†162	Willie Anderson	Chicago GC, Wheaton, IL
1898	Fred Herd	328	Alex Smith	Myopia Hunt Club, Hamilton, MA
1899	Willie Smith	315	George Low / Val Fitzjohn / W.H. Way	Baltimore CC, Baltimore
1900	Harry Vardon	313	John H. Taylor	Chicago GC, Wheaton, IL
1901	Willie Anderson* (85)	331	Alex Smith (86)	Myopia Hunt Club, Hamilton, MA
1902	Laurie Auchterlonie	307	Stewart Gardner	Garden City GC, Garden City, NY
1903	Willie Anderson* (82)	307	David Brown (84)	Baltusrol GC, Springfield, NJ
1904	Willie Anderson	303	Gil Nicholls	Glen View Club, Golf, IL
1905	Willie Anderson	314	Alex Smith	Myopia Hunt Club, Hamilton, MA
1906	Alex Smith	295	Willie Smith	Onwentsia Club, Lake Forest, IL
1907	Alex Ross	302	Gil Nicholls	Philadelphia Cricket Club, Chestnut Hill, PA
1908	Fred McLeod* (77)	322	Willie Smith (83)	Myopia Hunt Club, Hamilton, MA
1909	George Sargent	290	Tom McNamara	Englewood GC, Englewood, NJ
1910	Alex Smith* (71)	298	John McDermott (75) / Macdonald Smith (77)	Philadelphia Cricket Club, Chestnut Hill, PA
1911	John McDermott* (80)	307	Mike Brady (82) / George Simpson (85)	Chicago GC, Wheaton, IL
1912	John McDermott	294	Tom McNamara	CC of Buffalo, Buffalo
1913	Francis Ouimet* (72)	304	Harry Vardon (77) / Edward Ray (78)	The Country Club, Brookline, MA
1914	Walter Hagen	290	Chick Evans	Midlothian CC, Blue Island, IL
1915	Jerry Travers	297	Tom McNamara	Baltusrol GC, Springfield, NJ
1916	Chick Evans	286	Jock Hutchison	Minikahda Club, Minneapolis
1917–18	No tournament			
1919	Walter Hagen* (77)	301	Mike Brady (78)	Brae Burn CC, West Newton, MA
1920	Edward Ray	295	Harry Vardon / Jack Burke / Leo Diegel / Jock Hutchison	Inverness CC, Toledo
1921	Jim Barnes	289	Walter Hagen / Fred McLeod	Columbia CC, Chevy Chase, MD
1922	Gene Sarazen	288	John L. Black / Bobby Jones	Skokie CC, Glencoe, IL
1923	Bobby Jones* (76)	296	Bobby Cruickshank (78)	Inwood CC, Inwood, NY
1924	Cyril Walker	297	Bobby Jones	Oakland Hills CC, Birmingham, MI
1925	W. MacFarlane* (75–72)	291	Bobby Jones (75–73)	Worcester CC, Worcester, MA
1926	Bobby Jones	293	Joe Turnesa	Scioto CC, Columbus, OH
1927	Tommy Armour* (76)	301	Harry Cooper (79)	Oakmont CC, Oakmont, PA
1928	Johnny Farrell* (143)	294	Bobby Jones (144)	Olympia Fields CC, Matteson, IL
1929	Bobby Jones* (141)	294	Al Espinosa (164)	Winged Foot GC, Mamaroneck, NY
1930	Bobby Jones	287	Macdonald Smith	Interlachen CC, Hopkins, MN
1931	Billy Burke* (149–148)	292	George Von Elm (149–149)	Inverness Club, Toledo
1932	Gene Sarazen	286	Phil Perkins / Bobby Cruickshank	Fresh Meadows CC, Flushing, NY
1933	Johnny Goodman	287	Ralph Guldahl	North Shore CC, Glenview, IL
1934	Olin Dutra	293	Gene Sarazen	Merion Cricket Club, Ardmore, PA
1935	Sam Parks Jr.	299	Jimmy Thompson	Oakmont CC, Oakmont, PA
1936	Tony Manero	282	Harry Cooper	Baltusrol GC (Upper Course), Springfield, NJ
1937	Ralph Guldahl	281	Sam Snead	Oakland Hills CC, Birmingham, MI
1938	Ralph Guldahl	284	Dick Metz	Cherry Hills CC, Denver
1939	Byron Nelson* (68–70)	284	Craig Wood (68–73) / Denny Shute (76)	Philadelphia CC, Philadelphia
1940	Lawson Little* (70)	287	Gene Sarazen (73)	Canterbury GC, Cleveland
1941	Craig Wood	284	Denny Shute	Colonial Club, Fort Worth
1942–45	No tournament			
1946	Lloyd Mangrum* (72–72)	284	Vic Ghezzi (72–73) / Byron Nelson (72–73)	Canterbury GC, Cleveland

United States Open Championship (Cont.)

Year	Winner	Score	Runner-Up	Site
1947	Lew Worsham* (69)	282	Sam Snead (70)	St. Louis CC, Clayton, MO
1948	Ben Hogan	276	Jimmy Demaret	Riviera CC, Los Angeles
1949	Cary Middlecoff	286	Sam Snead	Medinah CC, Medinah, IL
			Clayton Heafner	
1950	Ben Hogan* (69)	287	Lloyd Mangrum (73)	Merion GC, Ardmore, PA
			George Fazio (75)	
1951	Ben Hogan	287	Clayton Heafner	Oakland Hills CC, Birmingham, MI
1952	Julius Boros	281	Ed Oliver	Northwood CC, Dallas
1953	Ben Hogan	283	Sam Snead	Oakmont CC, Oakmont, PA
1954	Ed Furgol	284	Gene Littler	Baltusrol GC (Lower Course), Springfield, NJ
1955	Jack Fleck* (69)	287	Ben Hogan (72)	Olympic Club (Lake Course), San Francisco
1956	Cary Middlecoff	281	Ben Hogan	Oak Hill CC, Rochester, NY
			Julius Boros	
1957	Dick Mayer* (72)	282	Cary Middlecoff (79)	Inverness Club, Toledo
1958	Tommy Bolt	283	Gary Player	Southern Hills CC, Tulsa
1959	Billy Casper	282	Bob Rosburg	Winged Foot GC, Mamaroneck, NY
1960	Arnold Palmer	280	Jack Nicklaus	Cherry Hills CC, Denver
1961	Gene Littler	281	Bob Goalby	Oakland Hills CC, Birmingham, MI
			Doug Sanders	
1962	Jack Nicklaus* (71)	283	Arnold Palmer (74)	Oakmont CC, Oakmont, PA
1963	Julius Boros* (70)	293	Jacky Cupit (73)	The Country Club, Brookline, MA
			Arnold Palmer (76)	
1964	Ken Venturi	278	Tommy Jacobs	Congressional CC, Bethesda, MD
1965	Gary Player* (71)	282	Kel Nagle (74)	Bellerive CC, St. Louis
1966	Billy Casper* (69)	278	Arnold Palmer (73)	Olympic Club (Lake Course), San Francisco
1967	Jack Nicklaus	275	Arnold Palmer	Baltusrol GC (Lower Course), Springfield, NJ
1968	Lee Trevino	275	Jack Nicklaus	Oak Hill CC, Rochester, NY
1969	Orville Moody	281	Deane Beman	Champions GC (Cypress Creek Course),
			Al Geiberger	Houston
			Bob Rosburg	
1970	Tony Jacklin	281	Dave Hill	Hazeltine GC, Chaska, MN
1971	Lee Trevino* (68)	280	Jack Nicklaus (71)	Merion GC (East Course), Ardmore, PA
1972	Jack Nicklaus	290	Bruce Crampton	Pebble Beach GL, Pebble Beach, CA
1973	Johnny Miller	279	John Schlee	Oakmont CC, Oakmont, PA
1974	Hale Irwin	287	Forrest Fezler	Winged Foot GC, Mamaroneck, NY
1975	Lou Graham* (71)	287	John Mahaffey (73)	Medinah CC, Medinah, IL
1976	Jerry Pate	277	Tom Weiskopf	Atlanta Athletic Club, Duluth, GA
			Al Geiberger	
1977	Hubert Green	278	Lou Graham	Southern Hills CC, Tulsa
1978	Andy North	285	Dave Stockton	Cherry Hills CC, Denver
			J.C. Snead	
1979	Hale Irwin	284	Gary Player	Inverness Club, Toledo
			Jerry Pate	
1980	Jack Nicklaus	272	Isao Aoki	Baltusrol GC (Lower Course), Springfield, NJ
1981	David Graham	273	George Burns	Merion GC, Ardmore, PA
			Bill Rogers	
1982	Tom Watson	282	Jack Nicklaus	Pebble Beach GL, Pebble Beach, CA
1983	Larry Nelson	280	Tom Watson	Oakmont CC, Oakmont, PA
1984	Fuzzy Zoeller* (67)	276	Greg Norman (75)	Winged Foot GC, Mamaroneck, NY
1985	Andy North	279	Dave Barr	Oakland Hills CC, Birmingham, MI
			T.C. Chen	
			Denis Watson	
1986	Ray Floyd	279	Lanny Wadkins	Shinnecock Hills GC, Southampton, NY
			Chip Beck	
1987	Scott Simpson	277	Tom Watson	Olympic Club (Lake Course), San Francisco
1988	Curtis Strange* (71)	278	Nick Faldo (75)	The Country Club, Brookline, MA
1989	Curtis Strange	278	Chip Beck	Oak Hill CC, Rochester, NY
			Mark McCumber	
			Ian Woosnam	
1990	Hale Irwin* (74) (3)	280	Mike Donald (74) (4)	Medinah CC, Medinah, IL
1991	Payne Stewart* (75)	282	Scott Simpson (77)	Hazeltine GC, Chaska, MN
1992	Tom Kite	285	Jeff Sluman	Pebble Beach GL, Pebble Beach, CA
1993	Lee Janzen	272	Payne Stewart	Baltusrol GC, Springfield, NJ
1994	Ernie Els*	279	Loren Roberts	Oakmont CC, Oakmont, PA
			Colin Montgomerie	

United States Open Championship *(Cont.)*

Year	Winner	Score	Runner-Up	Site
1995	Corey Pavin	280	Greg Norman	Shinnecock Hills GC, Southampton, NY
1996	Steve Jones	278	Davis Love III	Oakland Hills CC, Birmingham, MI
			Tom Lehman	
1997	Ernie Els	276	Colin Montgomerie	Congressional CC, Bethesda, MD
1998	Lee Janzen	280	Payne Stewart	The Olympic Club, San Francisco
1999	Payne Stewart	279	Phil Mickelson	Pinehurst Resort and CC, Pinehurst, NC
2000	Tiger Woods	272	Miguel Angel Jiménez	Pebble Beach GL, Pebble Beach, CA
			Ernie Els	
2001	Retief Goosen* (70)	276	Mark Brooks (72)	Southern Hills CC, Tulsa
2002	Tiger Woods	277	Phil Mickelson	Bethpage Black Course, Bethpage, NY
2003	Jim Furyk	272	Stephen Leaney	Olympia Fields CC, Olympia Fields, IL
2004	Retief Goosen	276	Phil Mickelson	Shinnecock Hills GC, Southampton, NY

*Winner in playoff. Playoff scores are in parentheses. The 1990 playoff went to one hole of sudden death after an 18-hole playoff. In the 1994 playoff, Montgomerie was eliminated after 18 playoff holes, and Els beat Roberts on the 20th.
†Before 1898, 36 holes. From 1898 on, 72 holes.

British Open

Year	Winner	Score	Runner-Up	Site
1860†	Willie Park	174	Tom Morris Sr.	Prestwick, Scotland
1861‡	Tom Morris Sr.	163	Willie Park	Prestwick, Scotland
1862	Tom Morris Sr.	163	Willie Park	Prestwick, Scotland
1863	Willie Park	168	Tom Morris Sr.	Prestwick, Scotland
1864	Tom Morris, Sr.	160	Andrew Strath	Prestwick, Scotland
1865	Andrew Strath	162	Willie Park	Prestwick, Scotland
1866	Willie Park	169	David Park	Prestwick, Scotland
1867	Tom Morris Sr.	170	Willie Park	Prestwick, Scotland
1868	Tom Morris Jr.	154	Tom Morris Sr.	Prestwick, Scotland
1869	Tom Morris Jr.	157	Tom Morris Sr.	Prestwick, Scotland
1870	Tom Morris Jr.	149	David Strath	Prestwick, Scotland
			Bob Kirk	
1871	No tournament			
1872	Tom Morris Jr.	166	David Strath	Prestwick, Scotland
1873	Tom Kidd	179	Jamie Anderson	St. Andrews, Scotland
1874	Mungo Park	159	No record	Musselburgh, Scotland
1875	Willie Park	166	Bob Martin	Prestwick, Scotland
1876	Bob Martin#	176	David Strath	St. Andrews, Scotland
1877	Jamie Anderson	160	Bob Pringle	Musselburgh, Scotland
1878	Jamie Anderson	157	Robert Kirk	Prestwick, Scotland
1879	Jamie Anderson	169	Andrew Kirkaldy	St. Andrews, Scotland
			James Allan	
1880	Robert Ferguson	162	No record	Musselburgh, Scotland
1881	Robert Ferguson	170	Jamie Anderson	Prestwick, Scotland
1882	Robert Ferguson	171	Willie Fernie	St. Andrews, Scotland
1883	Willie Fernie*	159	Robert Ferguson	Musselburgh, Scotland
1884	Jack Simpson	160	Douglas Rolland	Prestwick, Scotland
			Willie Fernie	
1885	Bob Martin	171	Archie Simpson	St. Andrews, Scotland
1886	David Brown	157	Willie Campbell	Musselburgh, Scotland
1887	Willie Park Jr.	161	Bob Martin	Prestwick, Scotland
1888	Jack Burns	171	Bernard Sayers	St. Andrews, Scotland
			David Anderson	
1889	Willie Park Jr.* (158)	155	Andrew Kirkaldy (163)	Musselburgh, Scotland
1890	John Ball	164	Willie Fernie	Prestwick, Scotland
1891	Hugh Kirkaldy	166	Andrew Kirkaldy	St. Andrews, Scotland
			Willie Fernie	
1892	Harold Hilton	**305	John Ball	Muirfield, Scotland
			Hugh Kirkaldy	
1893	William Auchterlonie	322	John E. Laidlay	Prestwick, Scotland
1894	John H. Taylor	326	Douglas Rolland	Royal St. George's, England
1895	John H. Taylor	322	Alexander Herd	St. Andrews, Scotland
1896	Harry Vardon* (157)	316	John H. Taylor (161)	Muirfield, Scotland
1897	Harold Hilton	314	James Braid	Hoylake, England
1898	Harry Vardon	307	Willie Park Jr.	Prestwick, Scotland
1899	Harry Vardon	310	Jack White	Royal St. George's, England
1900	John H. Taylor	309	Harry Vardon	St. Andrews, Scotland

British Open (Cont.)

Year	Winner	Score	Runner-Up	Site
1901	James Braid	309	Harry Vardon	Muirfield, Scotland
1902	Alexander Herd	307	Harry Vardon	Hoylake, England
1903	Harry Vardon	300	Tom Vardon	Prestwick, Scotland
1904	Jack White	296	John H. Taylor	Royal St. George's, England
1905	James Braid	318	John H. Taylor	St. Andrews, Scotland
			Rolland Jones	
1906	James Braid	300	John H. Taylor	Muirfield, Scotland
1907	Arnaud Massy	312	John H. Taylor	Hoylake, England
1908	James Braid	291	Tom Ball	Prestwick, Scotland
1909	John H. Taylor	295	James Braid	Deal, England
			Tom Ball	
1910	James Braid	299	Alexander Herd	St. Andrews, Scotland
1911	Harry Vardon	303	Arnaud Massy	Royal St. George's, England
1912	Ted Ray	295	Harry Vardon	Muirfield, Scotland
1913	John H. Taylor	304	Ted Ray	Hoylake, England
1914	Harry Vardon	306	John H. Taylor	Prestwick, Scotland
1915–19	No tournament			
1920	George Duncan	303	Alexander Herd	Deal, England
1921	Jock Hutchison* (150)	296	Roger Wethered (159)	St. Andrews, Scotland
1922	Walter Hagen	300	George Duncan	Royal St. George's, England
			Jim Barnes	
1923	Arthur G. Havers	295	Walter Hagen	Troon, Scotland
1924	Walter Hagen	301	Ernest Whitcombe	Hoylake, England
1925	Jim Barnes	300	Archie Compston	Prestwick, Scotland
			Ted Ray	
1926	Bobby Jones	291	Al Watrous	Royal Lytham & St. Annes, England
1927	Bobby Jones	285	Aubrey Boomer	St. Andrews, Scotland
1928	Walter Hagen	292	Gene Sarazen	Royal St. George's, England
1929	Walter Hagen	292	Johnny Farrell	Muirfield, Scotland
1930	Bobby Jones	291	Macdonald Smith	Hoylake, England
			Leo Diegel	
1931	Tommy Armour	296	Jose Jurado	Carnoustie, Scotland
1932	Gene Sarazen	283	Macdonald Smith	Prince's, England
1933	Denny Shute* (149)	292	Craig Wood (154)	St. Andrews, Scotland
1934	Henry Cotton	283	Sidney F. Brews	Royal St. George's, England
1935	Alfred Perry	283	Alfred Padgham	Muirfield, Scotland
1936	Alfred Padgham	287	James Adams	Hoylake, England
1937	Henry Cotton	290	Reginald A. Whitcombe	Carnoustie, Scotland
1938	Reginald A. Whitcombe	295	James Adams	Royal St. George's, England
1939	Richard Burton	290	Johnny Bulla	St. Andrews, Scotland
1940–45	No tournament			
1946	Sam Snead	290	Bobby Locke	St. Andrews, Scotland
			Johnny Bulla	
1947	Fred Daly	293	Reginald W. Horne	Hoylake, England
			Frank Stranahan	
1948	Henry Cotton	294	Fred Daly	Muirfield, Scotland
1949	Bobby Locke* (135)	283	Harry Bradshaw (147)	Royal St. George's, England
1950	Bobby Locke	279	Roberto DeVicenzo	Troon, Scotland
1951	Max Faulkner	285	Tony Cerda	Portrush, Ireland
1952	Bobby Locke	287	Peter Thomson	Royal Lytham & St. Annes, England
1953	Ben Hogan	282	Frank Stranahan	Carnoustie, Scotland
			Dai Rees	
			Peter Thomson	
			Tony Cerda	
1954	Peter Thomson	283	Sidney S. Scott	Royal Birkdale, England
			Dai Rees	
			Bobby Locke	
1955	Peter Thomson	281	John Fallon	St. Andrews, Scotland
1956	Peter Thomson	286	Flory Van Donck	Hoylake, England
1957	Bobby Locke	279	Peter Thomson	St. Andrews, Scotland
1958	Peter Thomson* (139)	278	Dave Thomas (143)	Royal Lytham & St. Annes, England
1959	Gary Player	284	Fred Bullock	Muirfield, Scotland
			Flory Van Donck	
1960	Kel Nagle	278	Arnold Palmer	St. Andrews, Scotland
1961	Arnold Palmer	284	Dai Rees	Royal Birkdale, England
1962	Arnold Palmer	276	Kel Nagle	Troon, Scotland

British Open (Cont.)

Year	Winner	Score	Runner-Up	Site
1963	Bob Charles* (140)	277	Phil Rodgers (148)	Royal Lytham & St. Annes, England
1964	Tony Lema	279	Jack Nicklaus	St. Andrews, Scotland
1965	Peter Thomson	285	Brian Huggett	Southport, England
			Christy O'Connor	
1966	Jack Nicklaus	282	Doug Sanders	Muirfield, Scotland
			Dave Thomas	
1967	Robert DeVicenzo	278	Jack Nicklaus	Hoylake, England
1968	Gary Player	289	Jack Nicklaus	Carnoustie, Scotland
			Bob Charles	
1969	Tony Jacklin	280	Bob Charles	Royal Lytham & St. Annes, England
1970	Jack Nicklaus* (72)	283	Doug Sanders (73)	St. Andrews, Scotland
1971	Lee Trevino	278	Lu Liang Huan	Royal Birkdale, England
1972	Lee Trevino	278	Jack Nicklaus	Muirfield, Scotland
1973	Tom Weiskopf	276	Johnny Miller	Troon, Scotland
1974	Gary Player	282	Peter Oosterhuis	Royal Lytham & St. Annes, England
1975	Tom Watson* (71)	279	Jack Newton (72)	Carnoustie, Scotland
1976	Johnny Miller	279	Jack Nicklaus	Royal Birkdale, England
			Seve Ballesteros	
1977	Tom Watson	268	Jack Nicklaus	Turnberry, Scotland
1978	Jack Nicklaus	281	Ben Crenshaw	St. Andrews, Scotland
			Tom Kite	
			Ray Floyd	
			Simon Owen	
1979	Seve Ballesteros	283	Ben Crenshaw	Royal Lytham & St. Annes, England
			Jack Nicklaus	
1980	Tom Watson	271	Lee Trevino	Muirfield, Scotland
1981	Bill Rogers	276	Bernhard Langer	Royal St. George's, England
1982	Tom Watson	284	Nick Price	Troon, Scotland
			Peter Oosterhuis	
1983	Tom Watson	275	Andy Bean	Royal Birkdale, England
1984	Seve Ballesteros	276	Tom Watson	St. Andrews, Scotland
			Bernhard Langer	
1985	Sandy Lyle	282	Payne Stewart	Royal St. George's, England
1986	Greg Norman	280	Gordon Brand	Turnberry, Scotland
1987	Nick Faldo	279	Paul Azinger	Muirfield, Scotland
			Rodger Davis	
1988	Seve Ballesteros	273	Nick Price	Royal Lytham & St. Annes, England
1989††	Mark Calcavecchia* (4-3-3-3)	275	Wayne Grady (4-4-4-4)	Troon, Scotland
			Greg Norman (3-3-4-x)	
1990	Nick Faldo	270	Payne Stewart	St. Andrews, Scotland
			Mark McNulty	
1991	Ian Baker-Finch	272	Mike Harwood	Royal Birkdale, England
1992	Nick Faldo	272	John Cook	Muirfield, Scotland
1993	Greg Norman	267	Nick Faldo	Royal St. George's, England
1994	Nick Price	268	Jesper Parnevik	Turnberry, Scotland
1995	John Daly* (4-3-4-4)	282	C. Rocca (5-4-7-3)	St. Andrews, Scotland
1996	Tom Lehman	271	Mark McCumber	Royal Lytham & St. Annes, England
			Ernie Els	
1997	Justin Leonard	272	Jesper Parnevik	Troon, Scotland
			Darren Clarke	
1998	Mark O'Meara* (4-4-5-4)	280	Brian Watts (5-4-5-5)	Southport, England
1999	Paul Lawrie* (5-4-3-3)	290	Jean Van de Velde (6-4-3-5)	Carnoustie GC, Carnoustie,
			Justin Leonard (5-4-4-5)	Scotland
2000	Tiger Woods	269	Thomas Bjorn	St. Andrews, Scotland
			Ernie Els	
2001	David Duval	274	Niclas Fasth	Royal Lytham & St. Annes, England
2002	Ernie Els*	278	Stuart Appleby	Muirfield, Scotland
2003	Ben Curtis	283	Vijay Singh	Royal St. George's, England
2004	Todd Hamilton*	274	Ernie Els	Troon, Scotland

*Winner in playoff. †The first event was open only to professional golfers.
‡The second annual open was open to amateurs and pros. #Tied, but refused playoff.
**Championship extended from 36 to 72 holes. ††Playoff cut from 18 holes to 4 holes.

PGA Championship

Year	Winner	Score	Runner-Up	Site
1916	Jim Barnes	1 up	Jock Hutchison	Siwanoy CC, Bronxville, NY
1917–18	No tournament			
1919	Jim Barnes	6 & 5	Fred McLeod	Engineers CC, Roslyn, NY
1920	Jock Hutchison	1 up	J. Douglas Edgar	Flossmoor CC, Flossmoor, IL
1921	Walter Hagen	3 & 2	Jim Barnes	Inwood CC, Far Rockaway, NY
1922	Gene Sarazen	4 & 3	Emmet French	Oakmont CC, Oakmont, PA
1923	Gene Sarazen	1 up 38 holes	Walter Hagen	Pelham CC, Pelham, NY
1924	Walter Hagen	2 up	Jim Barnes	French Lick CC, French Lick, IN
1925	Walter Hagen	6 & 5	William Mehlhorn	Olympia Fields CC, Olympia Fields, IL
1926	Walter Hagen	5 & 3	Leo Diegel	Salisbury GC, Westbury, NY
1927	Walter Hagen	1 up	Joe Turnesa	Cedar Crest CC, Dallas
1928	Leo Diegel	6 & 5	Al Espinosa	Five Farms CC, Baltimore
1929	Leo Diegel	6 & 4	Johnny Farrell	Hillcrest CC, Los Angeles
1930	Tommy Armour	1 up	Gene Sarazen	Fresh Meadow CC, Flushing, NY
1931	Tom Creavy	2 & 1	Denny Shute	Wannamoisett CC, Rumford, RI
1932	Olin Dutra	4 & 3	Frank Walsh	Keller GC, St. Paul
1933	Gene Sarazen	5 & 4	Willie Goggin	Blue Mound CC, Milwaukee
1934	Paul Runyan	1 up	Craig Wood	Park CC, Williamsville, NY
1935	Johnny Revolta	5 & 4 38 holes	Tommy Armour	Twin Hills CC, Oklahoma City
1936	Denny Shute	3 & 2	Jimmy Thomson	Pinehurst CC, Pinehurst, NC
1937	Denny Shute	1 up 37 holes	Harold McSpaden	Pittsburgh FC, Aspinwall, PA
1938	Paul Runyan	8 & 7	Sam Snead	Shawnee CC, Shawnee-on-Delaware, PA
1939	Henry Picard	1 up 37 holes	Byron Nelson	Pomonok CC, Flushing, NY
1940	Byron Nelson	1 up	Sam Snead	Hershey CC, Hershey, PA
1941	Vic Ghezzi	1 up 38 holes	Byron Nelson	Cherry Hills CC, Denver
1942	Sam Snead	2 & 1	Jim Turnesa	Seaview CC, Atlantic City
1943	No tournament			
1944	Bob Hamilton	1 up	Byron Nelson	Manito G & CC, Spokane, WA
1945	Byron Nelson	4 & 3	Sam Byrd	Morraine CC, Dayton
1946	Ben Hogan	6 & 4	Ed Oliver	Portland GC, Portland, OR
1947	Jim Ferrier	2 & 1	Chick Harbert	Plum Hollow CC, Detroit
1948	Ben Hogan	7 & 6	Mike Turnesa	Norwood Hills CC, St. Louis
1949	Sam Snead	3 & 2	Johnny Palmer	Hermitage CC, Richmond
1950	Chandler Harper	4 & 3	Henry Williams Jr.	Scioto CC, Columbus, OH
1951	Sam Snead	7 & 6	Walter Burkemo	Oakmont CC, Oakmont, PA
1952	Jim Turnesa	1 up	Chick Harbert	Big Spring CC, Louisville
1953	Walter Burkemo	2 & 1	Felice Torza	Birmingham CC, Birmingham, MI
1954	Chick Harbert	4 & 3	Walter Burkemo	Keller GC, St. Paul
1955	Doug Ford	4 & 3	Cary Middlecoff	Meadowbrook CC, Detroit
1956	Jack Burke	3 & 2	Ted Kroll	Blue Hill CC, Boston
1957	Lionel Hebert	2 & 1	Dow Finsterwald	Miami Valley CC, Dayton
1958	Dow Finsterwald	276	Billy Casper	Llanerch CC, Havertown, PA
1959	Bob Rosburg	277	Jerry Barber Doug Sanders	Minneapolis GC, St. Louis Park, MN
1960	Jay Hebert	281	Jim Ferrier	Firestone CC, Akron
1961	Jerry Barber* (67)	277	Don January (68)	Olympia Fields CC, Olympia Fields, IL
1962	Gary Player	278	Bob Goalby	Aronimink GC, Newton Square, PA
1963	Jack Nicklaus	279	Dave Ragan Jr.	Dallas Athletic Club, Dallas
1964	Bobby Nichols	271	Jack Nicklaus Arnold Palmer	Columbus CC, Columbus, OH
1965	Dave Marr	280	Billy Casper Jack Nicklaus	Laurel Valley CC, Ligonier, PA
1966	Al Geiberger	280	Dudley Wysong	Firestone CC, Akron
1967	Don January* (69)	281	Don Massengale (71)	Columbine CC, Littleton, CO
1968	Julius Boros	281	Bob Charles Arnold Palmer	Pecan Valley CC, San Antonio
1969	Ray Floyd	276	Gary Player	NCR CC, Dayton
1970	Dave Stockton	279	Arnold Palmer Bob Murphy	Southern Hills CC, Tulsa

PGA Championship (Cont.)

Year	Winner	Score	Runner-Up	Site
1971	Jack Nicklaus	281	Billy Casper	PGA Nat'l GC, Palm Beach Gardens, FL
1972	Gary Player	281	Tommy Aaron	Oakland Hills CC, Birmingham, MI
			Jim Jamieson	
1973	Jack Nicklaus	277	Bruce Crampton	Canterbury GC, Cleveland
1974	Lee Trevino	276	Jack Nicklaus	Tanglewood GC, Winston-Salem, NC
1975	Jack Nicklaus	276	Bruce Crampton	Firestone CC, Akron
1976	Dave Stockton	281	Ray Floyd	Congressional CC, Bethesda, MD
			Don January	
1977†	Lanny Wadkins* (4-4-4)	282	Gene Littler (4-4-5)	Pebble Beach GL, Pebble Beach, CA
1978	John Mahaffey* (4–3)	276	Jerry Pate (4–4)	Oakmont CC, Oakmont, PA
			Tom Watson (4–5)	
1979	David Graham* (4-4-2)	272	Ben Crenshaw (4-4-4)	Oakland Hills CC, Birmingham, MI
1980	Jack Nicklaus	274	Andy Bean	Oak Hill CC, Rochester, NY
1981	Larry Nelson	273	Fuzzy Zoeller	Atlanta Athletic Club, Duluth, GA
1982	Raymond Floyd	272	Lanny Wadkins	Southern Hills CC, Tulsa
1983	Hal Sutton	274	Jack Nicklaus	Riviera CC, Pacific Palisades, CA
1984	Lee Trevino	273	Gary Player	Shoal Creek, Birmingham, AL
			Lanny Wadkins	
1985	Hubert Green	278	Lee Trevino	Cherry Hills CC, Denver
1986	Bob Tway	276	Greg Norman	Inverness CC, Toledo
1987	Larry Nelson* (4)	287	Lanny Wadkins (5)	PGA Natl GC, Palm Beach Gardens, FL
1988	Jeff Sluman	272	Paul Azinger	Oak Tree GC, Edmond, OK
1989	Payne Stewart	276	Mike Reid	Kemper Lakes GC, Hawthorn Woods, IL
1990	Wayne Grady	282	Fred Couples	Shoal Creek, Birmingham, AL
1991	John Daly	276	Bruce Lietzke	Crooked Stick GC, Carmel, IN
1992	Nick Price	278	Jim Gallagher Jr.	Bellerive CC, St. Louis
1993	Paul Azinger* (4–4)	272	Greg Norman (4–5)	Inverness CC, Toledo
1994	Nick Price	269	Corey Pavin	Southern Hills CC, Tulsa
1995	Steve Elkington* (3)	267	Colin Montgomerie (4)	Riviera CC, Pacific Palisades, CA
1996	Mark Brooks* (3)	277	Kenny Perry (x)	Valhalla GC, Louisville
1997	Davis Love III	269	Justin Leonard	Winged Foot GC, Mamaroneck, NY
1998	Vijay Singh	271	Steve Stricker	Sahalee CC, Redmond, WA
1999	Tiger Woods	277	Sergio Garcia	Medinah CC, Medinah, IL
2000	Tiger Woods* (3-4-5)	270	Bob May (4-4-x)	Valhalla GC, Louisville
2001	David Toms	265	Phil Mickelson	Atlanta AC, Duluth, GA
2002	Rich Beem	278	Tiger Woods	Hazeltine National GC, Shaska, MN
2003	Shaun Micheel	276	Chad Campbell	Oak Hill CC, Rochester, NY
2004	Vijay Singh*	280	Chris DiMarco	Whistling Straits GC, Kohler, WI
			Justin Leonard	

*Winner in playoff. †Playoff changed from 18 holes to sudden death.

Alltime Major Championship Winners

	Masters	U.S. Open	British Open	PGA Champ.	U.S. Amateur	British Amateur	Total
†Jack Nicklaus	6	4	3	5	2	0	20
Bobby Jones	0	4	3	0	5	1	13
Walter Hagen	0	2	4	5	0	0	11
*Tiger Woods	3	2	1	2	3	0	11
Ben Hogan	2	4	1	2	0	0	9
†Gary Player	3	1	3	2	0	0	9
John Ball	0	0	1	0	0	8	9
†Arnold Palmer	4	1	2	0	1	0	8
†Tom Watson	2	1	5	0	0	0	8
Harold Hilton	0	0	2	0	1	4	7
Gene Sarazen	1	2	1	3	0	0	7
Sam Snead	3	0	1	3	0	0	7
Harry Vardon	0	1	6	0	0	0	7

*Active PGA player. †Active Senior PGA player.

Alltime Multiple Professional Major Winners

MASTERS		U.S. OPEN (Cont.)		BRITISH OPEN (Cont.)		PGA CHAMPIONSHIP	
Jack Nicklaus	6	Hale Irwin	3	J.H. Taylor	5	Walter Hagen	5
Arnold Palmer	4	Julius Boros	2	Peter Thomson	5	Jack Nicklaus	5
Jimmy Demaret	3	Billy Casper	2	Tom Watson	5	Gene Sarazen	3
Nick Faldo	3	Ernie Els	2	Walter Hagen	4	Sam Snead	3
Gary Player	3	Retief Goosen	2	Bobby Locke	4	Jim Barnes	2
Sam Snead	3	Ralph Guldahl	2	Tom Morris Sr.	4	Leo Diegel	2
Tiger Woods	3	Walter Hagen	2	Tom Morris Jr.	4	Raymond Floyd	2
Seve Ballesteros	2	Lee Janzen	2	Willie Park	4	Ben Hogan	2
Ben Crenshaw	2	John McDermott	2	Jamie Anderson	3	Byron Nelson	2
Ben Hogan	2	Cary Middlecoff	2	Seve Ballesteros	3	Larry Nelson	2
Bernhard Langer	2	Andy North	2	Henry Cotton	3	Gary Player	2
Byron Nelson	2	Gene Sarazen	2	Nick Faldo	3	Paul Runyan	2
José María Olazábal	2	Alex Smith	2	Robert Ferguson	3	Denny Shute	2
Horton Smith	2	Payne Stewart	2	Bobby Jones	3	Dave Stockton	2
Tom Watson	2	Curtis Strange	2	Jack Nicklaus	3	Lee Trevino	2
		Lee Trevino	2	Gary Player	3	Tiger Woods	2
U.S. OPEN		Tiger Woods	2	Harold Hilton	2	Vijay Singh	2
				Bob Martin	2		
Willie Anderson	4			Greg Norman	2		
Ben Hogan	4	**BRITISH OPEN**		Arnold Palmer	2		
Bobby Jones	4			Willie Park Jr.	2		
Jack Nicklaus	4	Harry Vardon	6	Lee Trevino	2		
		James Braid	5				

THE PGA TOUR

Most Career Wins*

	Wins		Wins		Wins
Sam Snead	82	Billy Casper	51	Tom Watson	39
Jack Nicklaus	73	Walter Hagen	44	Lloyd Mangrum	36
Ben Hogan	64	Cary Middlecoff	40	Horton Smith	32
Arnold Palmer	62	Tiger Woods	40	Harry Cooper	31
Byron Nelson	52	Gene Sarazen	39	Jimmy Demaret	31

* Through 10/3/04

Season Money Leaders

	Earnings ($)		Earnings ($)		Earnings ($)
1934 ...Paul Runyan	6,767.00	1958 ...Arnold Palmer	42,607.50	1982 ...Craig Stadler	446,462.00
1935 ...Johnny Revolta	9,543.00	1959 ...Art Wall	53,167.60	1983 ...Hal Sutton	426,668.00
1936 ...Horton Smith	7,682.00	1960 ...Arnold Palmer	75,262.85	1984 ...Tom Watson	476,260.00
1937 ...Harry Cooper	14,138.69	1961 ...Gary Player	64,540.45	1985 ...Curtis Strange	542,321.00
1938 ...Sam Snead	19,534.49	1962 ...Arnold Palmer	81,448.33	1986 ...Greg Norman	653,296.00
1939 ...Henry Picard	10,303.00	1963 ...Arnold Palmer	128,230.00	1987 ...Curtis Strange	925,941.00
1940 ...Ben Hogan	10,655.00	1964 ...Jack Nicklaus	113,284.50	1988 ...Curtis Strange	1,147,644.00
1941 ...Ben Hogan	18,358.00	1965 ...Jack Nicklaus	140,752.14	1989 ...Tom Kite	1,395,278.00
1942 ...Ben Hogan	13,143.00	1966 ...Billy Casper	121,944.92	1990 ...Greg Norman	1,165,477.00
1943 ...No statistics compiled		1967 ...Jack Nicklaus	188,998.08	1991 ...Corey Pavin	979,430.00
1944 ...Byron Nelson*	37,967.69	1968 ...Billy Casper	205,168.67	1992 ...Fred Couples	1,344,188.00
1945 ...Byron Nelson*	63,335.66	1969 ...Frank Beard	164,707.11	1993 ...Nick Price	1,478,557.00
1946 ...Ben Hogan	42,556.16	1970 ...Lee Trevino	157,037.63	1994 ...Nick Price	1,499,927.00
1947 ...Jimmy Demaret	27,936.83	1971 ...Jack Nicklaus	244,490.50	1995 ...Greg Norman	1,654,959.00
1948 ...Ben Hogan	32,112.00	1972 ...Jack Nicklaus	320,542.26	1996 ...Tom Lehman	1,780,159.00
1949 ...Sam Snead	31,593.83	1973 ...Jack Nicklaus	308,362.10	1997 ...Tiger Woods	2,066,833.00
1950 ...Sam Snead	35,758.83	1974 ...Johnny Miller	353,021.59	1998 ...David Duval	2,591,031.00
1951 ...Lloyd Mangrum	26,088.83	1975 ...Jack Nicklaus	298,149.17	1999 ...Tiger Woods	6,616,585.00
1952 ...Julius Boros	37,032.97	1976 ...Jack Nicklaus	266,438.57	2000 ...Tiger Woods	9,188,321.00
1953 ...Lew Worsham	34,002.00	1977 ...Tom Watson	310,653.16	2001 ...Tiger Woods	5,687,777.00
1954 ...Bob Toski	65,819.81	1978 ...Tom Watson	362,428.93	2002 ...Tiger Woods	6,912,625.00
1955 ...Julius Boros	63,121.55	1979 ...Tom Watson	462,636.00	2003 ...Vijay Singh	7,573,907.00
1956 ...Ted Kroll	72,835.83	1980 ...Tom Watson	530,808.33		
1957 ...Dick Mayer	65,835.00	1981 ...Tom Kite	375,698.84		

* War bonds. Note: Total money listed from 1968 through 1974. Official money listed from 1975 on.

Career Money Leaders*

		Earnings ($)
1.	Tiger Woods	$44,494,737
2.	Vijay Singh	$35,310,489
3.	Phil Mickelson	$29,445,428
4.	Davis Love III	$29,207,838
5.	Ernie Els	$24,308,792
6.	Nick Price	$19,715,533
7.	Jim Furyk	$19,643,382
8.	Scott Hoch	$18,455,984
9.	David Toms	$18,408,565
10.	Justin Leonard	$17,586,648
11.	Fred Couples	$16,544,574
12.	David Duval	$16,339,549
13.	M. Calcavecchia	$16,240,545
14.	Kenny Perry	$15,671,778
15.	Jeff Sluman	$15,403,402
16.	Mike Weir	$15,358,744
17.	Brad Faxon	$15,295,723
18.	Hal Sutton	$15,249,365
19.	Fred Funk	$14,859,518
20.	Tom Lehman	$14,836,499
21.	Loren Roberts	$14,035,943
22.	Stewart Cink	$13,998,988
23.	Greg Norman	$13,946,089
24.	Mark O'Meara	$13,687,545
25.	Jay Haas	$13,500,059
26.	Chris DiMarco	$13,453,962
27.	Scott Verplank	$13,333,736
28.	Paul Azinger	$13,265,171
29.	Bob Tway	$13,109,040
30.	Bob Estes	$13,109,032
31.	Stuart Appleby	$13,069,215
32.	John Huston	$12,897,764
33.	Jeff Maggert	$12,272,206
34.	Lee Janzen	$11,878,849
35.	Payne Stewart	$11,737,008
36.	Kirk Triplett	$11,614,711
37.	Rocco Mediate	$11,330,978
38.	John Cook	$11,286,291
39.	Corey Pavin	$11,106,994
40.	Tom Kite	$10,937,613
41.	Jesper Parnevik	$10,925,025
42.	Sergio Garcia	$10,921,684
43.	Jerry Kelly	$10,745,408
44.	Robert Allenby	$10,568,677
45.	Steve Lowery	$10,520,120
46.	Billy Mayfair	$10,440,462
47.	Steve Flesch	$10,366,721
48.	Steve Elkington	$10,262,170
49.	Duffy Waldorf	$10,083,701
50.	Retief Goosen	$9,981,209

*Through 10/3/04.

Year by Year Statistical Leaders

SCORING AVERAGE

1980	Lee Trevino	69.73
1981	Tom Kite	69.80
1982	Tom Kite	70.21
1983	Raymond Floyd	70.61
1984	Calvin Peete	70.56
1985	Don Pooley	70.36
1986	Scott Hoch	70.08
1987	David Frost	70.09
1988	Greg Norman	69.38
1989	Payne Stewart	69.485†
1990	Greg Norman	69.10
1991	Fred Couples	69.59
1992	Fred Couples	69.38
1993	Greg Norman	68.90
1994	Greg Norman	68.81
1995	Greg Norman	69.06
1996	Tom Lehman	69.32
1997	Nick Price	68.98
1998	David Duval	69.13
1999	Tiger Woods	68.43
2000	Tiger Woods	67.79
2001	Tiger Woods	68.81
2002	Tiger Woods	68.13
2003	Tiger Woods	68.41

Note: Scoring average per round, with adjustments made at each round for the field's course scoring average.

DRIVING DISTANCE

		Yds
1980	Dan Pohl	274.3
1981	Dan Pohl	280.1
1982	Bill Calfee	275.3
1983	John McComish	277.4
1984	Bill Glasson	276.5
1985	Andy Bean	278.2
1986	Davis Love III	285.7
1987	John McComish	283.9
1988	Steve Thomas	284.6
1989	Ed Humenik	280.9
1990	Tom Purtzer	279.6
1991	John Daly	288.9
1992	John Daly	283.4

DRIVING DISTANCE (Cont.)

1993	John Daly	288.9
1994	Davis Love III	283.8
1995	John Daly	289.0
1996	John Daly	288.8
1997	John Daly	302.0
1998	John Daly	299.4
1999	John Daly	305.6
2000	John Daly	301.4
2001	John Daly	306.7
2002	John Daly	306.8
2003	Hank Kuehne	321.4

Note: Average computed by charting distance of two tee shots on a predetermined par-four or par-five hole (one on front nine, one on back nine).

DRIVING ACCURACY

1980	Mike Reid	79.5
1981	Calvin Peete	81.9
1982	Calvin Peete	84.6
1983	Calvin Peete	81.3
1984	Calvin Peete	77.5
1985	Calvin Peete	80.6
1986	Calvin Peete	81.7
1987	Calvin Peete	83.0
1988	Calvin Peete	82.5
1989	Calvin Peete	82.6
1990	Calvin Peete	83.7
1991	Hale Irwin	78.3
1992	Doug Tewell	82.3
1993	Doug Tewell	82.5
1994	David Edwards	81.6
1995	Fred Funk	81.3
1996	Fred Funk	78.7
1997	Allen Doyle	80.8
1998	Bruce Fleisher	81.4
1999	Fred Funk	80.2
2000	Fred Funk	79.7
2001	Joe Durant	81.1
2002	Fred Funk	81.2
2003	Fred Funk	77.9

Note: Percentage of fairways hit on number of par-four and par-five holes played; par-three holes excluded.

GREENS IN REGULATION

1980	Jack Nicklaus	72.1
1981	Calvin Peete	73.1
1982	Calvin Peete	72.4
1983	Calvin Peete	71.4
1984	Andy Bean	72.1
1985	John Mahaffey	71.9
1986	John Mahaffey	72.0
1987	Gil Morgan	73.3
1988	John Adams	73.9
1989	Bruce Lietzke	72.6
1990	Doug Tewell	70.9
1991	Bruce Lietzke	73.3
1992	Tim Simpson	74.0
1993	Fuzzy Zoeller	73.6
1994	Bill Glasson	73.0
1995	Lenny Clements	72.3
1996	Fred Couples	71.8
	Mark O'Meara	71.8
1997	Tom Lehman	72.7
1998	Hal Sutton	71.3
1999	Tiger Woods	71.4
2000	Tiger Woods	75.2
2001	Tom Lehman	74.5
2002	Tiger Woods	74.0
2003	Joe Durant	72.9

Note: Average of greens reached in regulation out of total holes played; hole is considered hit in regulation if any part of the ball rests on the putting surface in two shots less than the hole's par—a par-5 hit in two shots is one green in regulation.

PUTTING

1980	Jerry Pate	28.81
1981	Alan Tapie	28.70
1982	Ben Crenshaw	28.65
1983	Morris Hatalsky	27.96
1984	Gary McCord	28.57
1985	Craig Stadler	28.627†
1986	Greg Norman	1.736
1987	Ben Crenshaw	1.743
1988	Don Pooley	1.729
1989	Steve Jones	1.734

† Number had to be carried to extra decimal place to determine winner.

Year by Year Statistical Leaders (Cont.)

PUTTING (Cont.)

1990	Larry Rinker	1.7467†	1995	Jim Furyk	1.708	2000	Brad Faxon	1.704
1991	Jay Don Blake	1.7326†	1996	Brad Faxon	1.709	2001	David Frost	1:708
1992	Mark O'Meara	1.731	1997	Don Pooley	1.718	2002	Bob Heintz	1.682
1993	David Frost	1.739	1998	Rick Fehr	1.722	2003	John Huston	1.713
1994	Loren Roberts	1.737	1999	Brad Faxon	1.723			

Note: Average number of putts taken on greens reached in regulation; prior to 1986, based on average number of putts per 18 holes.

SAND SAVES

1980	Bob Eastwood	65.4	1988	Greg Powers	63.5	1996	Gary Rusnak	64.0
1981	Tom Watson	60.1	1989	Mike Sullivan	66.0	1997	Bob Estes	70.3
1982	Isao Aoki	60.2	1990	Paul Azinger	67.2	1998	Keith Fergus	71.0
1983	Isao Aoki	62.3	1991	Ben Crenshaw	64.9	1999	Jeff Sluman	67.3
1984	Peter Oosterhuis	64.7	1992	Mitch Adcock	66.9	2000	Fred Couples	67.0
1985	Tom Purtzer	60.8	1993	Ken Green	64.4	2001	Franklin Langham	68.9
1986	Paul Azinger	63.8	1994	Corey Pavin	65.4	2002	J. Olazabal	64.9
1987	Paul Azinger	63.2	1995	Billy Mayfair	68.6	2003	Stuart Appleby	62.1

Note: Percentage of up-and-down efforts from greenside sand traps only—fairway bunkers excluded.

PAR BREAKERS

1980	Tom Watson	.213	1984	Craig Stadler	.220	1988	Ken Green	.236
1981	Bruce Lietzke	.225	1985	Craig Stadler	.218	1989	Greg Norman	.224
1982	Tom Kite	.2154†	1986	Greg Norman	.248	1990	Greg Norman	.219
1983	Tom Watson	.211	1987	Mark Calcavecchia	.221			

Note: Average based on total birdies and eagles scored out of total holes played. Discontinued as an official category after 1990.

EAGLES

1980	Dave Eichelberger	16	1987	Phil Blackmar	20	1995	Kelly Gibson	16
1981	Bruce Lietzke	12	1988	Ken Green	21	1996	Tom Watson	97.2
1982	Tom Weiskopf	10	1989	Lon Hinkle	14	1997	Tiger Woods	104.1
	J.C. Snead	10		Duffy Waldorf	14	1998	Davis Love III	83.3
	Andy Bean	10	1990	Paul Azinger	14	1999	Vijay Singh	104.8
1983	Chip Beck	15	1991	Andy Bean	15	2000	Tiger Woods	72.0
1984	Gary Hallberg	15	1992	Dan Forsman	18	2001	Phil Mickelson	73.8
1985	Larry Rinker	14	1993	Davis Love III	15	2002	John Daly	78.4
1986	Joey Sindelar	16	1994	Davis Love III	18	2003	Tiger Woods	76.5

Note: Total of eagles scored 1980–1995. Since 1996 winner determined by number of holes played per eagle.

BIRDIES

1980	Andy Bean	388	1988	Dan Forsman	465	1996	Fred Couples	4.20
1981	Vance Heafner	388	1989	Ted Schulz	415	1997	Tiger Woods	4.25
1982	Andy Bean	392	1990	Mike Donald	401	1998	David Duval	4.29
1983	Hal Sutton	399	1991	Scott Hoch	446	1999	Tiger Woods	4.46
1984	Mark O'Meara	419	1992	Jeff Sluman	417	2000	Tiger Woods	4.92
1985	Joey Sindelar	411	1993	John Huston	426	2001	Phil Mickelson	4.49
1986	Joey Sindelar	415	1994	Brad Bryant	397	2002	Tiger Woods	4.47
1987	Dan Forsman	409	1995	Steve Lowery	410	2003	Vijay Singh	4.41

Note: Total of birdies scored 1980–95. Since 1996, winner determined by average number of birdies per round.

ALL-AROUND

1987	Dan Pohl	170	1993	Gil Morgan	252	1999	Tiger Woods	120
1988	Payne Stewart	170	1994	Bob Estes	227	2000	Tiger Woods	113
1989	Paul Azinger	250	1995	Justin Leonard	323	2001	Phil Mickelson	174
1990	Paul Azinger	162	1996	Fred Couples	214	2002	Phil Mickelson	259
1991	Scott Hoch	283	1997	Bill Glasson	282	2003	Tiger Woods	206
1992	Fred Couples	256	1998	John Huston	151			

Note: Sum of the places of standing from the other statistical categories; the player with the number closest to zero leads.

† Number had to be carried to extra decimal place to determine winner.

PGA Player of the Year Award

1948 ....Ben Hogan	1967 ....Jack Nicklaus	1986 ....Bob Tway
1949 ....Sam Snead	1968 ....Not awarded	1987 ....Paul Azinger
1950 ....Ben Hogan	1969 ....Orville Moody	1988 ....Curtis Strange
1951 ....Ben Hogan	1970 ....Billy Casper	1989 ....Tom Kite
1952 ....Julius Boros	1971 ....Lee Trevino	1990 ....Wayne Levi
1953 ....Ben Hogan	1972 ....Jack Nicklaus	1991 ....Fred Couples
1954 ....Ed Furgol	1973 ....Jack Nicklaus	1992 ....Fred Couples
1955 ....Doug Ford	1974 ....Johnny Miller	1993 ....Nick Price
1956 ....Jack Burke	1975 ....Jack Nicklaus	1994 ....Nick Price
1957 ....Dick Mayer	1976 ....Jack Nicklaus	1995 ....Greg Norman
1958 ....Dow Finsterwald	1977 ....Tom Watson	1996 ....Tom Lehman
1959 ....Art Wall	1978 ....Tom Watson	1997 ....Tiger Woods
1960 ....Arnold Palmer	1979 ....Tom Watson	1998 ....David Duval
1961 ....Jerry Barber	1980 ....Tom Watson	1999 ....Tiger Woods
1962 ....Arnold Palmer	1981 ....Bill Rogers	2000 ....Tiger Woods
1963 ....Julius Boros	1982 ....Tom Watson	2001 ....Tiger Woods
1964 ....Ken Venturi	1983 ....Hal Sutton	2002 ....Tiger Woods
1965 ....Dave Marr	1984 ....Tom Watson	2003 ....Tiger Woods
1966 ....Billy Casper	1985 ....Lanny Wadkins	2004 ....Vijay Singh

Vardon Trophy: Scoring Average

Year	Winner	Avg	Year	Winner	Avg	Year	Winner	Avg
1937	Harry Cooper	*500	1962	Arnold Palmer	70.27	1983	Raymond Floyd	70.61
1938	Sam Snead	520	1963	Billy Casper	70.58	1984	Calvin Peete	70.56
1939	Byron Nelson	473	1964	Arnold Palmer	70.01	1985	Don Pooley	70.36
1940	Ben Hogan	423	1965	Billy Casper	70.85	1986	Scott Hoch	70.08
1941	Ben Hogan	494	1966	Billy Casper	70.27	1987	Don Pohl	70.25
1942-46	No award		1967	Arnold Palmer	70.18	1988	Chip Beck	69.46
1947	Jimmy Demaret	69.90	1968	Billy Casper	69.82	1989	Greg Norman	69.49
1948	Ben Hogan	69.30	1969	Dave Hill	70.34	1990	Greg Norman	69.10
1949	Sam Snead	69.37	1970	Lee Trevino	70.64	1991	Fred Couples	69.59
1950	Sam Snead	69.23	1971	Lee Trevino	70.27	1992	Fred Couples	69.38
1951	Lloyd Mangrum	70.05	1972	Lee Trevino	70.89	1993	Nick Price	69.11
1952	Jack Burke	70.54	1973	Bruce Crampton	70.57	1994	Greg Norman	68.81
1953	Lloyd Mangrum	70.22	1974	Lee Trevino	70.53	1995	Steve Elkington	69.62
1954	E.J. Harrison	70.41	1975	Bruce Crampton	70.51	1996	Tom Lehman	69.32
1955	Sam Snead	69.86	1976	Don January	70.56	1997	Nick Price	68.98
1956	Cary Middlecoff	70.35	1977	Tom Watson	70.32	1998	David Duval	69.13
1957	Dow Finsterwald	70.30	1978	Tom Watson	70.16	1999	Tiger Woods	68.43
1958	Bob Rosburg	70.11	1979	Tom Watson	70.27	2000	Tiger Woods	67.79
1959	Art Wall	70.35	1980	Lee Trevino	69.73	2001	Tiger Woods	68.81
1960	Billy Casper	69.95	1981	Tom Kite	69.80	2002	Tiger Woods	68.13
1961	Arnold Palmer	69.85	1982	Tom Kite	70.21	2003	Tiger Woods	68.41

*Point system used, 1937–41.
Note: As of 1988, based on minimum of 60 rounds per year. Adjusted for average score of field in tournaments entered.

Alltime PGA Tour Records*

Scoring

90 HOLES

324—(65-61-67-66-65) by Joe Durant, at four courses, La Quinta, CA, to win the 2001 Bob Hope Classic (36 under par).

72 HOLES

254—(64-62-63-65) by Tommy Armour III, at LaCantera GC, San Antonio, TX, to win the 2003 Valero Texas Open (26 under par).

54 HOLES, OPENING ROUNDS

189—(64-62-63) by John Cook, at the TPC at Southwind, Memphis, en route to winning the 1996 St. Jude Classic.

189—(65-60-64) Mark Calcavecchia, at the TPC at Scottsdale, Scottsdale, AZ, en route to winning the 2001 Phoenix Open.

54 HOLES, OPENING ROUNDS (Cont.)

189—(64-62-63) by Tommy Armour III, at LaCantera GC, San Antonio, TX, en route to winning the 2003 Valero Texas Open.

54 HOLES, CONSECUTIVE ROUNDS

189—(63-63-63) by Chandler Harper in the last three rounds to win the 1954 Texas Open at Brackenridge Park GC, San Antonio.

189—(64-62-63) by John Cook, at the TPC at Southwind, Memphis, in the first three rounds en route to winning the 1996 St. Jude Classic.

189—(65-60-64) Mark Calcavecchia, at the TPC at Scottsdale, Scottsdale, AZ, in the first three rounds en route to winning the 2001 Phoenix Open.

Alltime PGA Tour Records *(Cont.)**

Scoring *(Cont.)*

54 HOLES, CONSECUTIVE ROUNDS *(Cont.)*

189—(64-62-63) by Tommy Armour III, at LaCantera GC, San Antonio, TX, in the first three rounds en route to winning the 2003 Valero Texas Open.

36 HOLES, OPENING ROUNDS

125—(64–61) by Tiger Woods, in the 2000 World Golf Championships/ NEC Invitational, which he won, at Firestone CC, Akron.

125—(65–60) by Mark Calcavecchia, in the 2001 Phoenix Open, which he won, at TPC at Scottsdale, Scottsdale, AZ.

36 HOLES, CONSECUTIVE ROUNDS

125—(64–61) by Gay Brewer, in the middle rounds of the 1967 Pensacola Open, which he won, at Pensacola CC, Pensacola, FL.

125—(63–62) by Ron Streck, in the last two rounds to win the 1978 Texas Open at Oak Hills CC, San Antonio.

125—(62–63) by Blaine McCallister, in the middle two rounds of the 1988 Hardee's Golf Classic, which he won at Oakwood CC, Coal Valley, IL.

125—(62–63) by John Cook, in the middle two rounds of the 1996 St. Jude Classic, which he won at the TPC at Southwind, Memphis.

125—(62–63) by John Cook, in the fourth and fifth rounds in winning the 1997 Bob Hope Chrysler Classic at Indian Wells CC, Indian Hills, CA.

125—(64–61) by Tiger Woods, in the first two rounds of the 2000 World Golf Championship/ NEC Invitational, which he won, at Firestone CC, Akron.

125—(65–60) by Mark Calcavecchia, in the first two rounds of the 2001 Phoenix Open, which he won, at TPC at Scottsdale, Scottsdale, AZ.

125—(62-63) by Tommy Armour III, in the middle two rounds of the 2003 Valero Texas Open, which he won at LaCantera GC, San Antonio, TX.

18 HOLES

59—by Al Geiberger, at Colonial Country Club, Memphis, in second round in winning the 1977 Memphis Classic.

59—by Chip Beck, at Sunrise Golf Club, Las Vegas, in third round of the 1991 Las Vegas Invitational.

59—by David Duval, on the Palmer Course at PGA West, La Quinta, CA, in the fifth round of the 1999 Bob Hope Chrysler Classic.

9 HOLES

27—by Mike Souchak, at Brackenridge Park GC, San Antonio, on par-35 second nine of first round in the 1955 Texas Open.

27—by Andy North, at En-Joie GC, Endicott, NY, on par-34 second nine of first round in the 1975 BC Open.

27—by Billy Mayfair, at Warwick Hills, Grand Blanc, MI, on par-36 back nine of fourth round, 2001 Buick Open.

MOST CONSECUTIVE ROUNDS UNDER 70

19—Byron Nelson in 1945.

Scoring *(Cont.)*

MOST BIRDIES IN A ROW

8—Bob Goalby, at Pasadena GC, St. Petersburg, FL, during fourth round in winning the 1961 St Petersburg Open.

8—Fuzzy Zoeller, at Oakwood CC, Coal Valley, IL, during first round of 1976 Quad Cities Open.

8—Dewey Arnette, at Warwick Hills GC, Grand Blanc, MI, during first round of the 1987 Buick Open.

8—Edward Fryatt, at the Blue Course of the Doral Resort and Spa, Miami, during second round of the 2000 Doral-Ryder Open.

MOST BIRDIES IN A ROW TO WIN

5—Jack Nicklaus, to win 1978 Jackie Gleason Inverrary Classic (last 5 holes).

Wins

MOST CONSECUTIVE YEARS WINNING AT LEAST ONE TOURNAMENT

17—Jack Nicklaus, 1962–78.
17—Arnold Palmer, 1955–71.
16—Billy Casper, 1956–71.

MOST CONSECUTIVE WINS

11—Byron Nelson, from Miami Four Ball, March 8–11, 1945, through Canadian Open, August 2–4, 1945.

MOST WINS IN A SINGLE EVENT

8—Sam Snead, Greater Greensboro Open, 1938, 1946, 1949, 1950, 1955, 1956, 1960, and 1965.

MOST CONSECUTIVE WINS IN A SINGLE EVENT

4—Walter Hagen, PGA Championships, 1924–27.
4—Gene Sarazen, Miami Open, 1926, (schedule change) 1928–30.
4—Tiger Woods, Bay Hill Invitational, 2000–03.

MOST WINS IN A CALENDAR YEAR

18—Byron Nelson, 1945

MOST YEARS BETWEEN WINS

15 yrs, 5 mos—Butch Baird, 1961–76.

MOST YEARS FROM FIRST WIN TO LAST

28 yrs, 11 mos, 20 days—Raymond Floyd, 1963–92.

YOUNGEST WINNERS

19 yrs, 10 mos—John McDermott, 1911 U.S. Open.

OLDEST WINNER

52 yrs, 10 mos—Sam Snead, 1965 Greater Greensboro Open.

WIDEST WINNING MARGIN: STROKES

16—Bobby Locke, 1948 Chicago Victory National Championship.

*Through 12/31/03.

THE MAJOR TOURNAMENTS

LPGA Championship

Year	Winner	Score	Runner-Up	Site
1955	Beverly Hanson† (4 & 3)	220	Louise Suggs	Orchard Ridge CC, Ft Wayne, IN
1956	Marlene Hagge*	291	Patty Berg	Forest Lake CC, Detroit
1957	Louise Suggs	285	Wiffi Smith	Churchill Valley CC, Pittsburgh
1958	Mickey Wright	288	Fay Crocker	Churchill Valley CC, Pittsburgh
1959	Betsy Rawls	288	Patty Berg	Sheraton Hotel CC, French Lick, IN
1960	Mickey Wright	292	Louise Suggs	Sheraton Hotel CC, French Lick, IN
1961	Mickey Wright	287	Louise Suggs	Stardust CC, Las Vegas
1962	Judy Kimball	282	Shirley Spork	Stardust CC, Las Vegas
1963	Mickey Wright	294	Mary Lena Faulk Mary Mills Louise Suggs	Stardust CC, Las Vegas
1964	Mary Mills	278	Mickey Wright	Stardust CC, Las Vegas
1965	Sandra Haynie	279	Clifford A. Creed	Stardust CC, Las Vegas
1966	Gloria Ehret	282	Mickey Wright	Stardust CC, Las Vegas
1967	Kathy Whitworth	284	Shirley Englehorn	Pleasant Valley CC, Sutton, MA
1968	Sandra Post*	294	Kathy Whitworth (75)	Pleasant Valley CC, Sutton, MA
1969	Betsy Rawls	293	Susie Berning Carol Mann	Concord GC, Kiameshia Lake, NY
1970	Shirley Englehorn*	285	Kathy Whitworth (78)	Pleasant Valley CC, Sutton, MA
1971	Kathy Whitworth	288	Kathy Ahern	Pleasant Valley CC, Sutton, MA
1972	Kathy Ahern	293	Jane Blalock	Pleasant Valley CC, Sutton, MA
1973	Mary Mills	288	Betty Burfeindt	Pleasant Valley CC, Sutton, MA
1974	Sandra Haynie	288	JoAnne Carner	Pleasant Valley CC, Sutton, MA
1975	Kathy Whitworth	288	Sandra Haynie	Pine Ridge GC, Baltimore
1976	Betty Burfeindt	287	Judy Rankin	Pine Ridge GC, Baltimore
1977	Chako Higuchi	279	Pat Bradley Sandra Post Judy Rankin	Bay Tree Golf Plantation, N Myrtle Beach, SC
1978	Nancy Lopez	275	Amy Alcott	Jack Nicklaus GC, Kings Island, OH
1979	Donna Caponi	279	Jerilyn Britz	Jack Nicklaus GC, Kings Island, OH
1980	Sally Little	285	Jane Blalock	Jack Nicklaus GC, Kings Island, OH
1981	Donna Caponi	280	Jerilyn Britz Pat Meyers	Jack Nicklaus GC, Kings Island, OH
1982	Jan Stephenson	279	JoAnne Carner	Jack Nicklaus GC, Kings Island, OH
1983	Patty Sheehan	279	Sandra Haynie	Jack Nicklaus GC, Kings Island, OH
1984	Patty Sheehan	272	Beth Daniel Pat Bradley	Jack Nicklaus GC, Kings Island, OH
1985	Nancy Lopez	273	Alice Miller	Jack Nicklaus GC, Kings Island, OH
1986	Pat Bradley	277	Patty Sheehan	Jack Nicklaus GC, Kings Island, OH
1987	Jane Geddes	275	Betsy King	Jack Nicklaus GC, Kings Island, OH
1988	Sherri Turner	281	Amy Alcott	Jack Nicklaus GC, Kings Island, OH
1989	Nancy Lopez	274	Ayako Okamoto	Jack Nicklaus GC, Kings Island, OH
1990	Beth Daniel	280	Rosie Jones	Bethesda CC, Bethesda, MD
1991	Meg Mallon	274	Pat Bradley Ayako Okamoto	Bethesda CC, Bethesda, MD
1992	Betsy King	267	Karen Noble	Bethesda CC, Bethesda, MD
1993	Patty Sheehan	275	Lauri Merten	Bethesda CC, Bethesda, MD
1994	Laura Davies	279	Alice Ritzman	DuPont CC, Wilmington, DE
1995	Kelly Robbins	274	Laura Davies	DuPont CC, Wilmington, DE
1996	Laura Davies	213†	Julie Piers	DuPont CC, Wilmington, DE
1997	Chris Johnson*	281	Leta Lindley	DuPont CC, Wilmington, DE
1998	Se Ri Pak	273	Donna Andrews	DuPont CC, Wilmington, DE
1999	Juli Inkster	268	Liselotte Neumann	DuPont CC, Wilmington, DE
2000	Juli Inkster*	281	Stefania Croce	DuPont CC, Wilmington, DE
2001	Karrie Webb	270	Laura Diaz	DuPont CC, Wilmington, DE
2002	Se Ri Pak	279	Beth Daniel	DuPont CC, Wilmington, DE
2003	Annika Sorenstam*	278	Grace Park	DuPont CC, Wilmington, DE
2004	Annika Sorenstam	271	Shi Hyun Ahn	DuPont CC, Wilmington, DE

*Won playoff. †Won match-play final. #Shortened due to rain.

U.S. Women's Open

Year	Winner	Score	Runner-Up	Site
1946	Patty Berg	5 & 4	Betty Jameson	Spokane CC, Spokane, WA
1947	Betty Jameson	295	Sally Sessions	Starmount Forest CC, Greensboro, NC
			Polly Riley	
1948	Babe Zaharias	300	Betty Hicks	Atlantic City CC, Northfield, NJ
1949	Louise Suggs	291	Babe Zaharias	Prince George's G & CC, Landover, MD
1950	Babe Zaharias	291	Betsy Rawls	Rolling Hills CC, Wichita, KS
1951	Betsy Rawls	293	Louise Suggs	Druid Hills GC, Atlanta
1952	Louise Suggs	284	Marlene Bauer	Bala GC, Philadelphia
			Betty Jameson	
1953	Betsy Rawls* (71)	302	Jackie Pung (77)	CC of Rochester, Rochester, NY
1954	Babe Zaharias	291	Betty Hicks	Salem CC, Peabody, MA
1955	Fay Crocker	299	Mary Lena Faulk	Wichita CC, Wichita, KS
			Louise Suggs	
1956	Kathy Cornelius* (75)	302	Barbara McIntire (82)	Northland CC, Duluth, MN
1957	Betsy Rawls	299	Patty Berg	Winged Foot GC, Mamaroneck, NY
1958	Mickey Wright	290	Louise Suggs	Forest Lake CC, Detroit
1959	Mickey Wright	287	Louise Suggs	Churchill Valley CC, Pittsburgh
1960	Betsy Rawls	292	Joyce Ziske	Worcester CC, Worcester, MA
1961	Mickey Wright	293	Betsy Rawls	Baltusrol GC (Lower Course), Springfield, NJ
1962	Murle Breer	301	Jo Ann Prentice	Dunes GC, Myrtle Beach, SC
			Ruth Jessen	
1963	Mary Mills	289	Sandra Haynie	Kenwood CC, Cincinnati
			Louise Suggs	
1964	Mickey Wright* (70)	290	Ruth Jessen (72)	San Diego CC, Chula Vista, CA
1965	Carol Mann	290	Kathy Cornelius	Atlantic City CC, Northfield, NJ
1966	Sandra Spuzich	297	Carol Mann	Hazeltine Natl GC, Chaska, MN
1967	Catherine LaCoste	294	Susie Berning	Hot Springs GC (Cascades Course),
			Beth Stone	Hot Springs, VA
1968	Susie Berning	289	Mickey Wright	Moslem Springs GC, Fleetwood, PA
1969	Donna Caponi	294	Peggy Wilson	Scenic Hills CC, Pensacola, FL
1970	Donna Caponi	287	Sandra Haynie	Muskogee CC, Muskogee, OK
			Sandra Spuzich	
1971	JoAnne Carner	288	Kathy Whitworth	Kahkwa CC, Erie, PA
1972	Susie Berning	299	Kathy Ahern	Winged Foot GC, Mamaroneck, NY
			Pam Barnett	
			Judy Rankin	
1973	Susie Berning	290	Gloria Ehret	CC of Rochester, Rochester, NY
			Shelley Hamlin	
1974	Sandra Haynie	295	Carol Mann	La Grange CC, La Grange, IL
			Beth Stone	
1975	Sandra Palmer	295	JoAnne Carner	Atlantic City CC, Northfield, NJ
			Sandra Post	
			Nancy Lopez	
1976	JoAnne Carner* (76)	292	Sandra Palmer (78)	Rolling Green CC, Springfield, PA
1977	Hollis Stacy	292	Nancy Lopez	Hazeltine Natl GC, Chaska, MN
1978	Hollis Stacy	289	JoAnne Carner	CC of Indianapolis, Indianapolis
			Sally Little	
1979	Jerilyn Britz	284	Debbie Massey	Brooklawn CC, Fairfield, CT
			Sandra Palmer	
1980	Amy Alcott	280	Hollis Stacy	Richland CC, Nashville
1981	Pat Bradley	279	Beth Daniel	La Grange CC, La Grange, IL
1982	Janet Anderson	283	Beth Daniel	Del Paso CC, Sacramento
			Sandra Haynie	
			Donna White	
			JoAnne Carner	
1983	Jan Stephenson	290	JoAnne Carner	Cedar Ridge CC, Tulsa
			Patty Sheehan	
1984	Hollis Stacy	290	Rosie Jones	Salem CC, Peabody, MA
1985	Kathy Baker	280	Judy Dickinson	Baltusrol GC (Upper Course), Springfield, NJ
1986	Jane Geddes* (71)	287	Sally Little (73)	NCR GC, Dayton
1987	Laura Davies* (71)	285	Ayako Okamoto (73)	Plainfield CC, Plainfield, NJ
			JoAnne Carner (74)	
1988	Liselotte Neumann	277	Patty Sheehan	Baltimore CC, Baltimore
1989	Betsy King	278	Nancy Lopez	Indianwood G & CC, Lake Orion, MI
1990	Betsy King	284	Patty Sheehan	Atlanta Athletic Club, Duluth, GA
1991	Meg Mallon	283	Pat Bradley	Colonial Club, Fort Worth

U.S. Women's Open (Cont.)

Year	Winner	Score	Runner-Up	Site
1992	Patty Sheehan* (72)	280	Juli Inkster	Oakmont CC, Oakmont, PA
1993	Lauri Merten	280	Donna Andrew Helen Alfredsson	Crooked Stick, Carmel, IN
1994	Patty Sheehan	277	Tammie Green	Indianwood G & CC, Lake Orion, MI
1995	Annika Sorenstam	278	Meg Mallon	The Broadmoor GC, Colorado Springs, CO
1996	Annika Sorenstam	272	Kris Tschetter	Pine Needles GC, Southern Pines, NC
1997	Alison Nicholas	274	Nancy Lopez	Pumpkin Ridge CC, North Plains, OR
1998	Se Ri Pak†	290	Jenny Chuasiriporn	Blackwolf Run Golf Resort, Kohler, WI
1999	Juli Inkster	272	Sherri Turner	Old Waverly GC, West Point, MS
2000	Karrie Webb	282	Cristie Kerr/ Meg Mallon	Merit GC, Libertyville, IL
2001	Karrie Webb	273	Se Ri Pak	Pine Needles GC, Southern Pines, NC
2002	Juli Inkster	276	Annika Sorenstam	Prairie Dunes CC, Hutchinson, KS
2003	Hilary Lunke*	283	Kelly Robbins	Pumpkin Ridge GC, North Plains, OR
2004	Meg Mallon	274	Annika Sorenstam	The Orchards GC, South Hadley, MA

* Winner in playoff. † Winner on second hole of sudden death after 18-hole playoff ended in a tie.

Nabisco Championship

Year	Winner	Score	Runner-Up	Year	Winner	Score	Runner-Up
1972	Jane Blalock	213	Carol Mann Judy Rankin	1989	Juli Inkster	279	Tammie Green JoAnne Carner
1973	Mickey Wright	284	Joyce Kazmierski	1990	Betsy King	283	Kathy Postlewait Shirley Furlong
1974	Jo Ann Prentice*	289	Jane Blalock Sandra Haynie	1991	Amy Alcott	273	Dottie Mochrie
1975	Sandra Palmer	283	Kathy McMullen	1992	Dottie Mochrie*	279	Juli Inkster
1976	Judy Rankin	285	Betty Burfeindt	1993	Helen Alfredsson	284	Amy Benz Tina Barrett
1977	Kathy Whitworth	289	JoAnne Carner Sally Little				Betsy King
1978	Sandra Post*	283	Penny Pulz	1994	Donna Andrews	276	Laura Davies
1979	Sandra Post	276	Nancy Lopez	1995	Nanci Bowen	285	Susie Redman
1980	Donna Caponi	275	Amy Alcott	1996	Patti Sheehan	281	Kelly Robbins Meg Mallon
1981	Nancy Lopez	277	Carolyn Hill				Annika Sörenstam
1982	Sally Little	278	Hollis Stacy Sandra Haynie	1997	Betsy King	276	Kris Tschetter
1983	Amy Alcott	282	Beth Daniel Kathy Whitworth	1998	Pat Hurst	281	Helen Dobson
				1999	Dottie Pepper	269	Meg Mallon
1984	Juli Inkster*	280	Pat Bradley	2000	Karrie Webb	274	Dottie Pepper
1985	Alice Miller	275	Jan Stephenson	2001	Annika Sorenstam	281	five players
1986	Pat Bradley	280	Val Skinner	2002	Annika Sorenstam	280	Liselotte Neumann
1987	Betsy King*	283	Patty Sheehan	2003	P. Meunier-Lebouc	281	Annika Sorenstam
1988	Amy Alcott	274	Colleen Walker	2004	Grace Park	277	Aree Song

*Winner in sudden-death playoff. Note: Designated fourth major in 1983; played at Mission Hills CC, Rancho Mirage, CA.

du Maurier Classic

Year	Winner	Score	Runner-Up	Site
1973	Jocelyne Bourassa*	214	Sandra Haynie Judy Rankin	Montreal GC, Montreal
1974	Carole Jo Callison	208	JoAnne Carner	Candiac GC, Montreal
1975	JoAnne Carner*	214	Carol Mann	St. George's GC, Toronto
1976	Donna Caponi*	212	Judy Rankin	Cedar Brae G & CC, Toronto
1977	Judy Rankin	214	Pat Meyers Sandra Palmer	Lachute G & CC, Montreal
1978	JoAnne Carner	278	Hollis Stacy	St. George's CC, Toronto
1979	Amy Alcott	285	Nancy Lopez	Richelieu Valley CC, Montreal
1980	Pat Bradley	277	JoAnne Carner	St. George's GC, Toronto
1981	Jan Stephenson	278	Nancy Lopez Pat Bradley	Summerlea CC, Dorion, Quebec
1982	Sandra Haynie	280	Beth Daniel	St. George's GC, Toronto
1983	Hollis Stacy	277	JoAnne Carner Alice Miller	Beaconsfield GC, Montreal
1984	Juli Inkster	279	Ayako Okamoto	St. George's G & CC, Toronto
1985	Pat Bradley	278	Jane Geddes	Beaconsfield CC, Montreal
1986	Pat Bradley*	276	Ayako Okamoto	Board of Trade CC, Toronto
1987	Jody Rosenthal	272	Ayako Okamoto	Islesmere GC, Laval, Quebec
1988	Sally Little	279	Laura Davies	Vancouver GC, Coquitlam, British Columbia
1989	Tammie Green	279	Pat Bradley Betsy King	Beaconsfield GC, Montreal

du Maurier Classic (Cont.)

Year	Winner	Score	Runner-Up	Site
1990	Cathy Johnston	276	Patty Sheehan	Westmount G & CC, Kitchener, Ontario
1991	Nancy Scranton	279	Debbie Massey	Vancouver GC, Coquitlam, British Columbia
1992	Sherri Steinhauer	277	Judy Dickinson	St. Charles CC, Winnipeg, Manitoba
1993	Brandie Burton	277	Betsy King	London Hunt and CC, London, Ontario
1994	Martha Nause	279	Michelle McGann	Ottawa Hunt and GC, Ottawa, Ont.
1995	Jenny Lidback	280	Liselotte Neumann	Beaconsfield GC, Pointe-Claire, Quebec
1996	Laura Davies	277	Nancy Lopez	Edmonton CC, Edmonton, Alberta
			Karrie Webb	
1997	Colleen Walker	278	Liselotte Neumann	Glen Abbey GC, Oakville, Ontario
1998	Brandie Burton	270	Annika Sorenstam	Essex G & CC, Windsor, Ontario
1999	Karrie Webb	277	Laura Davies	Priddis Greens G & CC, Calgary, Alberta
2000	Meg Mallon	282	Rosie Jones	Royal Ottawa GC, Aylmer, Quebec

*Winner in sudden-death playoff. Note: Designated third major in 1979; discontinued in 2001.

Women's British Open

Year	Winner	Score	Runner-Up	Site
2001	Se Ri Pak	277	Mi Hyun Kim	Sunningdale GC, Berkshire, England
2002	Karrie Webb	273	Michelle Ellis	Turnberry GC, Ailsa, Scotland
			Paula Marti	
2003	Annika Sorenstam	278	Se Ri Pak	Royal Lytham & St. Annes, England
2004	Karen Stupples	269	Rachel Teske	Sunningdale GC, Berkshire, England

Note: Designated fourth major in 2001.

Alltime Major Championship Winners

	LPGA	U.S. Open	Nabisco	Brit. Open	‡du Maurier	#Titleholders	†Western	U.S. Am	Brit. Am	Total
Patty Berg	0	1	0	0	0	7	7	1	0	16
Mickey Wright	4	4	0	0	0	2	3	0	0	13
Louise Suggs	1	2	0	0	0	4	4	1	1	13
Babe Zaharias	0	3	0	0	0	3	4	1	1	12
*Juli Inkster	2	2	2	0	1	0	0	3	0	10
Betsy Rawls	2	4	0	0	0	0	2	0	0	8
*JoAnne Carner	0	2	0	0	0	0	0	5	0	7
*Annika Sorenstam	2	2	2	1	0	0	0	0	0	7
Kathy Whitworth	3	0	0	0	0	2	1	0	0	6
Pat Bradley	1	1	1	0	3	0	0	0	0	6
*Patty Sheehan	3	2	1	0	0	0	0	0	0	6
Glenna Vare	0	0	0	0	0	0	0	6	0	6
*Betsy King	1	2	3	0	0	0	0	0	0	6

*Active LPGA player.
#Major from 1937–1972. †Major from 1937–1967. ‡Major from 1979–2000.

Alltime Multiple Professional Major Winners

LPGA
Mickey Wright	4
Nancy Lopez	3
Patty Sheehan	3
Kathy Whitworth	3
Donna Caponi	2
Sandra Haynie	2
Mary Mills	2
Betsy Rawls	2
Laura Davies	2
Juli Inkster	2
Se Ri Pak	2
Annika Sorenstam	2

U.S. OPEN
Betsy Rawls	4
Mickey Wright	4
Susie Maxwell Berning	3

U.S. OPEN (Cont.)
Hollis Stacy	3
Babe Zaharias	3
JoAnne Carner	2
Donna Caponi	2
Betsy King	2
Meg Mallon	2
Patty Sheehan	2
Louise Suggs	2
Annika Sorenstam	2
Karrie Webb	2
Juli Inkster	2

NABISCO/DINAH SHORE
Amy Alcott	3
Betsy King	3
Juli Inkster	2
Annika Sorenstam	2

DU MAURIER
Pat Bradley	3
Brandie Burton	2
JoAnne Carner	2

TITLEHOLDERS
Patty Berg	7
Louise Suggs	4
Babe Zaharias	3
Dorothy Kirby	2
Marilynn Smith	2
Kathy Whitworth	2
Mickey Wright	2

WESTERN OPEN
Patty Berg	7
Louise Suggs	4
Babe Zaharias	4
Mickey Wright	3
June Beebe	2
Opal Hill	2
Betty Jameson	2
Betsy Rawls	2

THE LPGA TOUR

Most Career Wins†

	Wins		Wins		Wins
Kathy Whitworth	88	JoAnne Carner*	42	Pat Bradley	31
Mickey Wright	82	Sandra Haynie	42	Juli Inkster*	30
Patty Berg	57	Babe Zaharias	41	Karrie Webb*	30
Betsy Rawls	55	Carol Mann	40	Amy Alcott*	29
Annika Sorenstam*	53	Patty Sheehan*	35	Jane Blalock	29
Louise Suggs	50	Betsy King*	34	Judy Rankin	26
Nancy Lopez	48	Beth Daniel*	33		

*Active player.

Season Money Leaders

	Earnings ($)		Earnings ($)		Earnings ($)
1950...Babe Zaharias	14,800	1968...Kathy Whitworth	48,379	1986...Pat Bradley	492,021
1951...Babe Zaharias	15,087	1969...Carol Mann	49,152	1987...Ayako Okamoto	466,034
1952...Betsy Rawls	14,505	1970...Kathy Whitworth	30,235	1988...Sherri Turner	350,851
1953...Louise Suggs	19,816	1971...Kathy Whitworth	41,181	1989...Betsy King	654,132
1954...Patty Berg	16,011	1972...Kathy Whitworth	65,063	1990...Beth Daniel	863,578
1955...Patty Berg	16,492	1973...Kathy Whitworth	82,864	1991...Pat Bradley	763,118
1956...Marlene Hagge	20,235	1974...JoAnne Carner	87,094	1992...Dottie Mochrie	693,335
1957...Patty Berg	16,272	1975...Sandra Palmer	76,374	1993...Betsy King	595,992
1958...Beverly Hanson	12,639	1976...Judy Rankin	150,734	1994...Laura Davies	687,201
1959...Betsy Rawls	26,774	1977...Judy Rankin	122,890	1995...Annika Sorenstam	666,533
1960...Louise Suggs	16,892	1978...Nancy Lopez	189,814	1996...Karrie Webb	1,002,000
1961...Mickey Wright	22,236	1979...Nancy Lopez	197,489	1997...Annika Sorenstam	1,236,789
1962...Mickey Wright	21,641	1980...Beth Daniel	231,000	1998...Annika Sorenstam	1,092,748
1963...Mickey Wright	31,269	1981...Beth Daniel	206,998	1999...Karrie Webb	1,591,959
1964...Mickey Wright	29,800	1982...JoAnne Carner	310,400	2000...Karrie Webb	1,876,853
1965...Kathy Whitworth	28,658	1983...JoAnne Carner	291,404	2001...Annika Sorenstam	2,105,868
1966...Kathy Whitworth	33,517	1984...Betsy King	266,771	2002...Annika Sorenstam	2,863.904
1967...Kathy Whitworth	32,937	1985...Nancy Lopez	416,472	2003...Annika Sorenstam	2,029,506

Career Money Leaders†

	Earnings ($)		Earnings ($)		Earnings ($)
1. Annika Sorenstam	15,064,482	11. Pat Bradley	5,750,965	21. Tammie Green	4,097,260
2. Karrie Webb	10,096,940	12. Kelly Robbins	5,709,625	22. Brandie Burton	4,021,171
3. Juli Inkster	9,283,419	13. Patty Sheehan	5,513,409	23. Michele Redman	3,970,115
4. Meg Mallon	8,507,707	14. Lorie Kane	5,433,284	24. Jane Geddes	3,805,553
5. Beth Daniel	8,213,870	15. Nancy Lopez	5,320,877	25. Pat Hurst	3,744,958
6. Se Ri Pak	7,985,550	16. Liselotte Neumann	4,720,207	26. Cristie Kerr	3,588,773
7. Rosie Jones	7,654,780	17. Mi-Hyun Kim	4,620,118	27. Donna Andrews	3,583,648
8. Betsy King	7,622,549	18. Sherri Steinhauer	4,305,838	28. Chris Johnson	3,581,345
9. Dottie Pepper	6,827,284	19. Rachel Teske	4,255,660	29. D. Ammaccapane	3,548,167
10. Laura Davies	6,816,525	20. Grace Park	4,157,215	30. Catriona Matthew	3,489,868

LPGA Player of the Year

1966	Kathy Whitworth	1979	Nancy Lopez	1992	Dottie Mochrie
1967	Kathy Whitworth	1980	Beth Daniel	1993	Betsy King
1968	Kathy Whitworth	1981	JoAnne Carner	1994	Beth Daniel
1969	Kathy Whitworth	1982	JoAnne Carner	1995	Annika Sörenstam
1970	Sandra Haynie	1983	Patty Sheehan	1996	Laura Davies
1971	Kathy Whitworth	1984	Betsy King	1997	Annika Sorenstam
1972	Kathy Whitworth	1985	Nancy Lopez	1998	Annika Sorenstam
1973	Kathy Whitworth	1986	Pat Bradley	1999	Karrie Webb
1974	JoAnne Carner	1987	Ayako Okamoto	2000	Karrie Webb
1975	Sandra Palmer	1988	Nancy Lopez	2001	Annika Sorenstam
1976	Judy Rankin	1989	Betsy King	2002	Annika Sorenstam
1977	Judy Rankin	1990	Beth Daniel	2003	Annika Sorenstam
1978	Nancy Lopez	1991	Pat Bradley		

†Through 10/3/04.

Vare Trophy: Best Scoring Average*

Year	Player	Avg	Year	Player	Avg	Year	Player	Avg
1953	Patty Berg	75.00	1970	Kathy Whitworth	72.26	1987	Betsy King	71.14
1954	Babe Zaharias	75.48	1971	Kathy Whitworth	72.88	1988	Colleen Walker	71.26
1955	Patty Berg	74.47	1972	Kathy Whitworth	72.38	1989	Beth Daniel	70.38
1956	Patty Berg	74.57	1973	Judy Rankin	73.08	1990	Beth Daniel	70.54
1957	Louise Suggs	74.64	1974	JoAnne Carner	72.87	1991	Pat Bradley	70.76
1958	Beverly Hanson	74.92	1975	JoAnne Carner	72.40	1992	Dottie Mochrie	70.80
1959	Betsy Rawls	74.03	1976	Judy Rankin	72.25	1993	Nancy Lopez	70.83
1960	Mickey Wright	73.25	1977	Judy Rankin	72.16	1994	Beth Daniel	70.90
1961	Mickey Wright	73.55	1978	Nancy Lopez	71.76	1995	Annika Sorenstam	71.00
1962	Mickey Wright	73.67	1979	Nancy Lopez	71.20	1996	Annika Sorenstam	70.47
1963	Mickey Wright	72.81	1980	Amy Alcott	71.51	1997	Karrie Webb	70.00
1964	Mickey Wright	72.46	1981	JoAnne Carner	71.75	1998	Annika Sorenstam	69.99
1965	Kathy Whitworth	72.61	1982	JoAnne Carner	71.49	1999	Karrie Webb	69.43
1966	Kathy Whitworth	72.60	1983	JoAnne Carner	71.41	2000	Karrie Webb	70.05
1967	Kathy Whitworth	72.74	1984	Patty Sheehan	71.40	2001	Annika Sorenstam	69.42
1968	Carol Mann	72.04	1985	Nancy Lopez	70.73	2002	Annika Sorenstam	68.70
1969	Kathy Whitworth	72.38	1986	Pat Bradley	71.10	2003	Se Ri Pak	70.03

Alltime LPGA Tour Records†

Scoring

72 HOLES

259—(65-62-67-65) by Wendy Doolan to win at the Dell Urich GC, Tucson, AZ, in the 2003 Welch's/Fry's Champ. (21 under par).

261—(71-61-63-66) by Se Ri Pak to win at the Highland Meadows CC, Sylvania, OH, in the 1998 Jamie Farr Kroger Classic (23 under par).

261—(65-59-69-68) by Annika Sorenstam to win at the Moon Valley CC, Phoenix, in the 2001 Standard Register PING (27 under par).

54 HOLES

192—(63-63-66) by Annika Sorenstam to win at the Seta GC, Otsu-shi, Shiga, Japan in the 2003 Mizuno Classic (24 under par).

193—(66-61-66) by Karrie Webb to lead at the Walnut Hills CC, East Lansing, MI, in the 2000 Oldsmobile Classic (23 under par).

193—(65-59-69) by Annika Sorenstam to lead at the Moon Valley CC, Phoenix, in the 2001 Standard Register PING (23 under par)

36 HOLES

124—(65-59) by Annika Sorenstam to lead at the Moon Valley CC, Phoenix, in the 2001 Standard Register PING (20 under par).

18 HOLES

59—by Annika Sorenstam at the Moon Valley CC, Phoenix, in the second round in winning the 2001 Standard Register PING (13 under par).

9 HOLES

28—by Mary Beth Zimmerman at Rail GC, 1984 Rail Charity Golf Classic, Springfield, IL (par 36). Zimmerman shot 64.

28—by Pat Bradley at Green Gables CC, Denver, 1984 Columbia Savings Classic (par 35). Bradley shot 65.

28—by Muffin Spencer-Devlin at Knollwood CC, Elmsford, NY, in winning the 1985 MasterCard International Pro-Am (par 35). Spencer-Devlin shot 64.

Scoring (Cont.)

9 HOLES (Cont.)

28—by Peggy Kirsch at Squaw Creek CC, Vienna, OH, in the 1991 Phar-Mor (par 35).

28—by Renee Heiken at Highland Meadows CC, Sylvania, OH, in the 1996 Jamie Farr Kroger Classic (par 34).

28—by Annika Sorenstam at the Moon Valley CC, Phoenix, in the 2001 Standard Register PING (par 36).

28—by Danielle Ammaccapane at Highland Meadows GC, Sylvania, OH, in the 2002 Jamie Farr Kroger Classic (par 34)

28—by Young Kim at Dell Urich GC, Tucson, AZ, in the 2003 Welch's/Fry's Championship (par 35)

28—by Chris Johnson at Highland Meadows GC, Sylvania, OH, in the 2003 Jamie Farr Kroger Classic (par 34)

MOST CONSECUTIVE ROUNDS UNDER 70

11—Annika Sorenstam, in 2002.

MOST BIRDIES IN A ROW

9—Beth Daniel at Onion Creek Club in Austin, in the second round of the 1999 Philips Invitational. Daniel shot 62 (8 under par).

Wins

MOST CONSECUTIVE WINS IN SCHEDULED EVENTS

4—Mickey Wright, in 1962.

4—Mickey Wright, in 1963.

4—Kathy Whitworth, in 1969.

4—Annika Sorenstam in 2001.

MOST CONSECUTIVE WINS IN ENTERED TOURNAMENTS

5—Nancy Lopez, in 1978.

MOST WINS IN A CALENDAR YEAR

13—Mickey Wright, in 1963.

WIDEST WINNING MARGIN, STROKES

14—Louise Suggs, 1949 U.S. Women's Open.

14—Cindy Mackey, 1986 MasterCard Int'l Pro-Am.

†Through 10/3/04. *Must play 70 rounds in order to qualify; Annika Sorenstam compiled an average of 69.02 in 60 rounds in 2003.

U.S. Senior Open

Year	Winner	Score	Runner-Up	Site
1980	Roberto DeVicenzo	285	William C. Campbell	Winged Foot GC, Mamaroneck, NY
1981	Arnold Palmer* (70)	289	Bob Stone (74)	Oakland Hills CC, Birmingham, MI
			Billy Casper (77)	
1982	Miller Barber	282	Gene Littler	Portland GC, Portland, OR
			Dan Sikes, Jr.	
1983	Billy Casper* (75) (3)	288	Rod Funseth (75) (4)	Hazeltine GC, Chaska, MN
1984	Miller Barber	286	Arnold Palmer	Oak Hill CC, Rochester, NY
1985	Miller Barber	285	Roberto DeVicenzo	Edgewood Tahoe GC, Stateline, NV
1986	Dale Douglass	279	Gary Player	Scioto CC, Columbus, OH
1987	Gary Player	270	Doug Sanders	Brooklawn CC, Fairfield, CT
1988	Gary Player* (68)	288	Bob Charles (70)	Medinah CC, Medinah, IL
1989	Orville Moody	279	Frank Beard	Laurel Valley GC, Ligonier, PA
1990	Lee Trevino	275	Jack Nicklaus	Ridgewood CC, Paramus, NJ
1991	Jack Nicklaus (65)	282	Chi Chi Rodriguez (69)	Oakland Hills CC, Birmingham, MI
1992	Larry Laoretti	275	Jim Colbert	Saucon Valley CC, Bethlehem, PA
1993	Jack Nicklaus	278	Tom Weiskopf	Cherry Hills CC, Englewood, CO
1994	Simon Hobday	274	Jim Albus	Pinehurst Resort & CC, Pinehurst, NC
1995	Tom Weiskopf	275	Jack Nicklaus	Congressional CC, Bethesda, MD
1996	Dave Stockton	277	Hale Irwin	Canterbury GC, Beachwood, OH
1997	Graham Marsh	280	Hale Irwin	Olympia Fields CC, Olympia Fields, IL
1998	Hale Irwin	285	Vicente Fernandez	Riviera CC, Pacific Palisades, CA
1999	Dave Eichelberger	281	Ed Dougherty	Des Moines G & CC, Des Moines, IA
2000	Hale Irwin	267	Bruce Fleisher	Saucon Valley CC, Bethlehem, PA
2001	Bruce Fleisher	280	Isao Aoki	Salem CC, Peabody, MA
			Gil Morgan	
2002	Don Pooley*	274	Tom Watson	Caves Valley GC, Owings Mill, MD
2003	Bruce Lietzke	277	Tom Watson	Inverness GC, Toledo, OH
2004	Peter Jacobsen	272	Hale Irwin	Bellerive CC, St. Louis, MO

*Winner in playoff. Playoff scores are in parentheses. The 1983 playoff went to one hole of sudden death after an 18-hole playoff.

SENIOR TOUR
Season Money Leaders

Year	Winner	Earnings ($)	Year	Winner	Earnings ($)	Year	Winner	Earnings ($)
1980	Don January	44,100	1988	Bob Charles	533,929	1996	Jim Colbert	1,627,890
1981	Miller Barber	83,136	1989	Bob Charles	725,887	1997	Hale Irwin	2,449,420
1982	Miller Barber	106,890	1990	Lee Trevino	1,190,518	1998	Hale Irwin	2,861,945
1983	Don January	237,571	1991	Mike Hill	1,065,657	1999	Bruce Fleisher	2,515,705
1984	Don January	328,597	1992	Lee Trevino	1,027,002	2000	Larry Nelson	2,708,005
1985	Peter Thomson	386,724	1993	Dave Stockton	1,175,944	2001	Allen Doyle	2,553,582
1986	Bruce Crampton	454,299	1994	Dave Stockton	1,402,519	2002	Hale Irwin	3,028,304
1987	Chi Chi Rodriguez	509,145	1995	Jim Colbert	1,444,386	2003	Tom Watson	1,853,108

Career Money Leaders†

#	Player	Earnings ($)	#	Player	Earnings ($)	#	Player	Earnings ($)
1.	Hale Irwin	20,329,465	11.	Isao Aoki	8,917,390	21.	John Jacobs	7,501,819
2.	Gil Morgan	14,249,619	12.	Jim Thorpe	8,891,160	22.	Tom Kite	7,239,419
3.	Bruce Fleisher	11,873,051	13.	Raymond Floyd	8,797,506	23.	Vicente Fernandez	7,197,427
4.	Larry Nelson	11,708,819	14.	Jim Dent	8,641,889	24.	J.C. Snead	7,145,996
5.	Jim Colbert	11,302,900	15.	Jay Sigel	8,554,889	25.	Doug Tewell	7,145,822
6.	Dave Stockton	10,433,865	16.	George Archer	8,329,648	26.	Bob Murphy	6,997,579
7.	Dana Quigley	10,044,993	17.	Mike Hill	8,257,545	27.	Dale Douglass	6,915,081
8.	Allen Doyle	9,838,091	18.	Graham Marsh	8,236,554	28.	Tom Wargo	6,883,834
9.	Lee Trevino	9,758,773	19.	Tom Jenkins	7,778,606	29.	Jose Maria Canizares	6,745,179
10.	Bob Charles	8,951,920	20.	Bruce Summerhays	7,681,091	30.	John Bland	6,692,468

Most Career Wins†

Player	Wins	Player	Wins
Hale Irwin	40	Jim Colbert	20
Lee Trevino	29	Bruce Crampton	20
Miller Barber	24	George Archer	19
Bob Charles	23	Gary Player	19
Gil Morgan	23	Bruce Fleisher	18
Don January	22	Mike Hill	18
Chi Chi Rodriguez	22	Larry Nelson	18

†Through 10/3/04.

MAJOR MEN'S AMATEUR CHAMPIONSHIPS

U.S. Amateur

Year	Winner	Score	Runner-Up	Site
1895	Charles B. Macdonald	12 & 11	Charles E. Sands	Newport GC, Newport, RI
1896	H.J. Whigham	8 & 7	J.G Thorp	Shinnecock Hills GC, Southampton, NY
1897	H.J. Whigham	8 & 6	W. Rossiter Betts	Chicago GC, Wheaton, IL
1898	Findlay S. Douglas	5 & 3	Walter B. Smith	Morris County GC, Morristown, NJ
1899	H.M. Harriman	3 & 2	Findlay S. Douglas	Onwentsia Club, Lake Forest, IL
1900	Walter Travis	2 up	Findlay S. Douglas	Garden City GC, Garden City, NY
1901	Walter Travis	5 & 4	Walter E. Egan	CC of Atlantic City, NJ
1902	Louis N. James	4 & 2	Eben M. Byers	Glen View Club, Golf, IL
1903	Walter Travis	5 & 4	Eben M. Byers	Nassau CC, Glen Cove, NY
1904	H. Chandler Egan	8 & 6	Fred Herreshoff	Baltusrol GC, Springfield, NJ
1905	H. Chandler Egan	6 & 5	D.E. Sawyer	Chicago GC, Wheaton, IL
1906	Eben M. Byers	2 up	George S. Lyon	Englewood GC, Englewood, NJ
1907	Jerry Travers	6 & 5	Archibald Graham	Euclid Club, Cleveland, OH
1908	Jerry Travers	8 & 7	Max H. Behr	Garden City GC, Garden City, NY
1909	Robert A. Gardner	4 & 3	H. Chandler Egan	Chicago GC, Wheaton, IL
1910	William C. Fownes Jr.	4 & 3	Warren K. Wood	The Country Club, Brookline, MA
1911	Harold Hilton	1 up	Fred Herreshoff	The Apawamis Club, Rye, NY
1912	Jerry Travers	7 & 6	Charles Evans Jr.	Chicago GC, Wheaton, IL
1913	Jerry Travers	5 & 4	John G. Anderson	Garden City GC, Garden City, NY
1914	Francis Ouimet	6 & 5	Jerry Travers	Ekwanok CC, Manchester, VT
1915	Robert A. Gardner	5 & 4	John G. Anderson	CC of Detroit, Grosse Pt. Farms, MI
1916	Chick Evans	4 & 3	Robert A. Gardner	Merion Cricket Club, Haverford, PA
1917–18	No tournament			
1919	S. Davidson Herron	5 & 4	Bobby Jones	Oakmont CC, Oakmont, PA
1920	Chick Evans	7 & 6	Francis Ouimet	Engineers' Club, Roslyn, NY
1921	Jesse P. Guilford	7 & 6	Robert A. Gardner	St. Louis CC, Clayton, MO
1922	Jess W. Sweetser	3 & 2	Chick Evans	The Country Club, Brookline, MA
1923	Max R. Marston	1 up	Jess W. Sweetser	Flossmoor CC, Flossmoor, IL
1924	Bobby Jones	9 & 8	George Von Elm	Merion Cricket Club, Ardmore, PA
1925	Bobby Jones	8 & 7	Watts Gunn	Oakmont CC, Oakmont, PA
1926	George Von Elm	2 & 1	Bobby Jones	Baltusrol GC, Springfield, NJ
1927	Bobby Jones	8 & 7	Chick Evans	Minikahda Club, Minneapolis
1928	Bobby Jones	10 & 9	T. Phillip Perkins	Brae Burn CC, West Newton, MA
1929	Harrison R. Johnston	4 & 3	Dr. O.F. Willing	Del Monte G & CC, Pebble Beach, CA
1930	Bobby Jones	8 & 7	Eugene V. Homans	Merion Cricket Club, Ardmore, PA
1931	Francis Ouimet	6 & 5	Jack Westland	Beverly CC, Chicago, IL
1932	C. Ross Somerville	2 & 1	John Goodman	Baltimore CC, Timonium, MD
1933	George T. Dunlap Jr.	6 & 5	Max R. Marston	Kenwood CC, Cincinnati, OH
1934	Lawson Little	8 & 7	David Goldman	The Country Club, Brookline, MA
1935	Lawson Little	4 & 2	Walter Emery	The Country Club, Cleveland, OH
1936	John W. Fischer	1 up	Jack McLean	Garden City GC, Garden City, NY
1937	John Goodman	2 up	Raymond E. Billows	Alderwood CC, Portland, OR
1938	William P. Turnesa	8 & 7	B. Patrick Abbott	Oakmont CC, Oakmont, PA
1939	Marvin H. Ward	7 & 5	Raymond E. Billows	North Shore CC, Glenview, IL
1940	Richard D. Chapman	11 & 9	W. McCullough Jr.	Winged Foot GC, Mamaroneck, NY
1941	Marvin H. Ward	4 & 3	B. Patrick Abbott	Omaha Field Club, Omaha, NE
1942–45	No tournament			
1946	Ted Bishop	1 up	Smiley L. Quick	Baltusrol GC, Springfield, NJ
1947	Skee Riegel	2 & 1	John W. Dawson	Del Monte G & CC, Pebble Beach, CA
1948	William P. Turnesa	2 & 1	Raymond E. Billows	Memphis CC, Memphis, TN
1949	Charles R. Coe	11 & 10	Rufus King	Oak Hill CC, Rochester, NY
1950	Sam Urzetta	1 up	Frank Stranahan	Minneapolis GC, Minneapolis, MN
1951	Billy Maxwell	4 & 3	Joseph F. Gagliardi	Saucon Valley CC, Bethlehem, PA
1952	Jack Westland	3 & 2	Al Mengert	Seattle GC, Seattle, WA
1953	Gene Littler	1 up	Dale Morey	Oklahoma City G & CC, Oklahoma City
1954	Arnold Palmer	1 up	Robert Sweeny	CC of Detroit, Grosse Pt. Farms, MI
1955	E. Harvie Ward Jr.	9 & 8	William Hyndman III	CC of Virginia, Richmond, VA
1956	E. Harvie Ward Jr.	5 & 4	Charles Kocsis	Knollwood Club, Lake Forest, IL
1957	Hillman Robbins Jr.	5 & 4	Dr. Frank M. Taylor	The Country Club, Brookline, MA
1958	Charles R. Coe	5 & 4	Tommy Aaron	Olympic Club, San Francisco, CA
1959	Jack Nicklaus	1 up	Charles R. Coe	Broadmoor GC, Colorado Springs, CO
1960	Deane Beman	6 & 4	Robert W. Gardner	St. Louis CC, Clayton, MO
1961	Jack Nicklaus	8 & 6	H. Dudley Wysong	Pebble Beach GL, Pebble Beach, CA

U.S. Amateur (Cont.)

Year	Winner	Score	Runner-Up	Site
1962	Labron E. Harris Jr.	1 up	Downing Gray	Pinehurst CC, Pinehurst, NC
1963	Deane Beman	2 & 1	Richard H. Sikes	Wakonda Club, Des Moines, IA
1964	William C. Campbell	1 up	Edgar M. Tutwiler	Canterbury GC, Cleveland, OH
1965	Robert J. Murphy Jr.	291	Robert B. Dickson	Southern Hills, CC, Tulsa
1966	Gary Cowan	285–75	Deane Beman	Merion GC, Ardmore, PA
1967	Robert B. Dickson	285	Marvin Giles III	Broadmoor GC, Colorado Springs
1968	Bruce Fleisher	284	Marvin Giles III	Scioto CC, Columbus, OH
1969	Steven N. Melnyk	286	Marvin Giles III	Oakmont CC, Oakmont, PA
1970	Lanny Wadkins	279	Tom Kite	Waverley CC, Portland, OR
1971	Gary Cowan	280	Eddie Pearce	Wilmington CC, Wilmington DE
1972	Marvin Giles III	285	two tied	Charlotte CC, Charlotte, NC
1973	Craig Stadler	6 & 5	David Strawn	Inverness Club, Toledo
1974	Jerry Pate	2 & 1	John P. Grace	Ridgewood CC, Ridgewood, NJ
1975	Fred Ridley	2 up	Keith Fergus	CC of Virginia, Richmond
1976	Bill Sander	8 & 6	C. Parker Moore Jr.	Bel Air CC, Los Angeles
1977	John Fought	9 & 8	Doug Fischesser	Aronimink GC, Newton Square, PA
1978	John Cook	5 & 4	Scott Hoch	Plainfield CC, Plainfield, NJ
1979	Mark O'Meara	8 & 7	John Cook	Canterbury GC, Cleveland
1980	Hal Sutton	9 & 8	Bob Lewis	CC of North Carolina, Pinehurst, NC
1981	Nathaniel Crosby	1 up	Brian Lindley	Olympic Club, San Francisco
1982	Jay Sigel	8 & 7	David Tolley	The Country Club, Brookline, MA
1983	Jay Sigel	8 & 7	Chris Perry	North Shore CC, Glenview, IL
1984	Scott Verplank	4 & 3	Sam Randolph	Oak Tree GC, Edmond, OK
1985	Sam Randolph	1 up	Peter Persons	Montclair GC, West Orange, NJ
1986	Buddy Alexander	5 & 3	Chris Kite	Shoal Creek, Shoal Creek, AL
1987	Bill Mayfair	4 & 3	Eric Rebmann	Jupiter Hills Club, Jupiter, FL
1988	Eric Meeks	7 & 6	Danny Yates	Va. Hot Springs G & CC, VA
1989	Chris Patton	3 & 1	Danny Green	Merion GC, Ardmore, PA
1990	Phil Mickelson	5 & 4	Manny Zerman	Cherry Hills CC, Englewood, CO
1991	Mitch Voges	7 & 6	Manny Zerman	The Honors Course, Ooltewah, TN
1992	Justin Leonard	8 & 7	Tom Scherrer	Muirfield Village GC, Dublin, OH
1993	John Harris	5 & 3	Danny Ellis	Champions GC, Houston
1994	Tiger Woods	2 up	Trip Kuehne	TPC-Sawgrass, Ponte Vedre, FL
1995	Tiger Woods	2 up	Buddy Marucci	Newport Country Club, Newport, RI
1996	Tiger Woods	38 holes	Steve Scott	Pumpkin Ridge GC, Cornelius, OR
1997	Matthew Kuchar	2 & 1	Joel Kribel	Cog Hill G & CC, Lemont, IL
1998	Hank Kuehne	2 & 1	Tom McKnight	Oak Hill CC, Rochester, NY
1999	David Gossett	9 & 8	Sung Yoon Kim	Pebble Beach GL, Pebble Beach, CA
2000	Jeff Quinney	39 holes	James Driscoll	Baltusrol GC, Upper Springfield, NJ
2001	Bubba Dickerson	1 up	Robert Hamilton	East Lake CC, Atlanta
2002	Ricky Barnes	2 & 1	Hunter Mahan	Oakland Hills CC, Bloomfield Hills, MI
2003	Nick Flanagan	37 holes	Frank Abbott	East Lake CC, Atlanta
2004	Ryan Moore	2 up	Luke List	Winged Foot GC, Mamaroneck, NY

Note: All stroke play from 1965 to 1972.

U.S. Junior Amateur

1948...Dean Lind	1963...Gregg McHatton	1978...Don Hurter	1993...Tiger Woods
1949...Gay Brewer	1964...Johnny Miller	1979...Jack Larkin	1994...Terry Noe
1950...Mason Rudolph	1965...James Masserio	1980...Eric Johnson	1995...D. Scott Hailes
1951...Tommy Jacobs	1966...Gary Sanders	1981...Scott Erickson	1996...Shane McMenamy
1952...Don Bisplinghoff	1967...John Crooks	1982...Rich Marik	1997...Jason Allred
1953...Rex Baxter	1968...Eddie Pearce	1983...Tim Straub	1998...James Oh
1954...Foster Bradley	1969...Aly Trompas	1984...Doug Martin	1999...Hunter Mahan
1955...William Dunn	1970...Gary Koch	1985...Charles Rymer	2000...Matthew Rosenfeld
1956...Harlan Stevenson	1971...Mike Brannan	1986...Brian Montgomery	2001...Henry Liaw
1957...Larry Beck	1972...Bob Byman	1987...Brett Quigley	2002...Charlie Beljan
1958...Buddy Baker	1973...Jack Renner	1988...Jason Widener	2003...Brian Harman
1959...Larry Lee	1974...David Nevatt	1989...David Duval	2004...Sihwan Kim
1960...Bill Tindall	1975...Brett Mullin	1990...Mathew Todd	
1961...Charles McDowell	1976...Madden Hatcher III	1991...Tiger Woods	
1962...Jim Wiechers	1977...Willie Wood Jr.	1992...Tiger Woods	

Mid-Amateur Championship

1981...Jim Holtgrieve	1987...Jay Sigel	1993...Jeff Thomas	1999...Danny Green
1982...William Hoffer	1988...David Eger	1994...Tim Jackson	2000...Greg Puga
1983...Jay Sigel	1989...James Taylor	1995...Jerry Courville Jr.	2001...Tim Jackson
1984...Mike Podolak	1990...Jim Stuart	1996...John Miller	2002...George Zahringer
1985...Jay Sigel	1991...Jim Stuart	1997...Ken Bakst	2003...Nathan Smith
1986...Bill Loeffler	1992...Danny Yates	1998...John Miller	

British Amateur

1887	H. G. Hutchinson	1928	T.P. Perkins
1888	John Ball	1929	C.J.H. Tolley,
1889	J.E. Laidlay	1930	Robert T. Jones Jr
1890	John Ball	1931	E. Martin Smith
1891	J.E. Laidlay	1932	J. DeForest
1892	John Ball	1933	M. Scott
1893	Peter Anderson	1934	W. Lawson Little
1894	John Ball	1935	W. Lawson Little
1895	L.M.B. Melville	1936	H. Thomson
1896	F.G. Tait	1937	R. Sweeney Jr
1897	A.J.T. Allan	1938	C.R. Yates
1898	F.G. Tait	1939	A.T. Kyle
1899	John Ball	1940–45	not held
1900	H.H. Hilton	1946	J. Bruen
1901	H.H. Hilton	1947	Willie D. Turnesa
1902	C. Hutchings	1948	Frank R. Stranahan
1903	R. Maxwell	1949	S.M. McReady
1904	W.J. Travis	1950	Frank R. Stranahan
1905	A.G. Barry	1951	Richard D. Chapman
1906	James Robb	1952	E.H. Ward
1907	John Ball	1953	J.B. Carr
1908	E.A. Lassen	1954	D.W. Bachli
1909	R. Maxwell	1955	J.W. Conrad
1910	John Ball	1956	J.C. Beharrel
1911	H.H. Hilton	1957	R. Reid Jack
1912	John Ball	1958	J.B. Carr
1913	H.H. Hilton	1959	Deane Beman
1914	J.L.C. Jenkins	1960	J.B. Carr
1915–19	not held	1961	M. Bonallack
1920	C.J.H. Tolley	1962	R. Davies
1921	W.I. Hunter	1963	M. Lunt
1922	E.W.E. Holderness	1964	C. Clark
1923	R.H. Wethered	1965	M. Bonallack
1924	E.W.E. Holderness	1966	C.R. Cole
1925	R. Harris	1967	R. Dickson
1926	Jess Sweetser	1968	M. Bonallack
1927	Dr. W. Tweddell	1969	M. Bonallack

1970	M. Bonallack
1971	Steve Melnyk
1972	Trevor Homer
1973	R. Siderowf
1974	Trevor Homer
1975	M. Giles
1976	R. Siderowf
1977	P. McEvoy
1978	P. McEvoy
1979	J. Sigel
1980	D. Evans
1981	P. Ploujoux
1982	M. Thompson
1983	A. Parkin
1984	J.M. Olazabal
1985	G. McGimpsey
1986	D. Curry
1987	P. Mayo
1988	C. Hardin
1989	S. Dodd
1990	R. Muntz
1991	G. Wolstenholme
1992	S. Dundas
1993	I. Pyman
1994	L. James
1995	G. Sherry
1996	W. Bladon
1997	C. Watson
1998	Sergio Garcia
1999	Graeme Storm
2000	Mikko Ilonen
2001	Michael Hoey
2002	Alejandro Larrazabal
2003	Gary Wolstenholme
2004	Stuart Wilson

Amateur Public Links

1922	Edmund R. Held	1951	Dave Stanley
1923	Richard J. Walsh	1952	Omer L. Bogan
1924	Joseph Coble	1953	Ted Richards Jr
1925	Raymond J. McAuliffe	1954	Gene Andrews
		1955	Sam D. Kocsis
1926	Lester Bolstad	1956	James H. Buxbaum
1927	Carl F. Kauffmann	1957	Don Essig III
1928	Carl F. Kauffmann	1958	Daniel D. Sikes Jr
1929	Carl F. Kauffmann	1959	William A. Wright
1930	Robert E. Wingate	1960	Verne Callison
1931	Charles Ferrera	1961	Richard H. Sikes
1932	R.L. Miller	1962	Richard H. Sikes
1933	Charles Ferrera	1963	Robert Lunn
1934	David A. Mitchell	1964	William McDonald
1935	Frank Strafaci	1965	Arne Dokka
1936	B. Patrick Abbott	1966	Lamont Kaser
1937	Bruce N. McCormick	1967	Verne Callison
1938	Al Leach	1968	Gene Towry
1939	Andrew Szwedko	1969	John M. Jackson Jr
1940	Robert C. Clark	1970	Robert Risch
1941	William M. Welch Jr	1971	Fred Haney
1942–45	not held	1972	Bob Allard
1946	Smiley L. Quick	1973	Stan Stopa
1947	Wilfred Crossley	1974	Charles Barenaba
1948	Michael A. Ferentz	1975	Randy Barenaba
1949	Kenneth J. Towns	1976	Eddie Mudd
1950	Stanley Bielat	1977	Jerry Vidovic

1978	Dean Prince
1979	Dennis Walsh
1980	Jodie Mudd
1981	Jodie Mudd
1982	Billy Tuten
1983	Billy Tuten
1984	Bill Malley
1985	Jim Sorenson
1986	Bill Mayfair
1987	Kevin Johnson
1988	Ralph Howe III
1989	Tim Hobby
1990	Michael Combs
1991	David Berganio Jr
1992	Warren Schulte
1993	David Berganio Jr
1994	Guy Yamamoto
1995	Chris Wollmann
1996	Tim Hogarth
1997	Tim Clark
1998	Trevor Immelman
1999	Hunter Haas
2000	D.J. Trahan
2001	Chez Reavie
2002	Ryan Moore
2003	Brandt Snedeker
2004	Ryan Moore

U.S. Senior Golf

1955 ....J. Wood Platt	1971 ....Tom Draper	1987 ....John Richardson
1956 ....Frederick J. Wright	1972 ....Lewis W. Oehmig	1988 ....Clarence Moore
1957 ....J. Clark Espie	1973 ....William Hyndman III	1989 ....Bo Williams
1958 ....Thomas C. Robbins	1974 ....Dale Morey	1990 ....Jackie Cummings
1959 ....J. Clark Espie	1975 ....William F. Colm	1991 ....Bill Bosshard
1960 ....Michael Cestone	1976 ....Lewis W. Oehmig	1992 ....Clarence Moore
1961 ....Dexter H. Daniels	1977 ....Dale Morey	1993 ....Joe Ungvary
1962 ....Merrill L. Carlsmith	1978 ..........K.K. Compton	1994 ....O. Gordon Brewer
1963 ....Merrill L. Carlsmith	1979 ....William C. Campbell	1995 ....James Stahl Jr.
1964 ....William D. Higgins	1980 ....William C. Campbell	1996 ....O. Gordon Brewer
1965 ....Robert B. Kiersky	1981 ....Ed Updegraff	1997 ....Cliff Cunningham
1966 ....Dexter H. Daniels	1982 ....Alton Duhon	1998 ....Bill Shean Jr.
1967 ....Ray Palmer	1983 ....William Hyndman III	1999 ....Bill Ploeger
1968 ....Curtis Person Sr.	1984 ....Bob Rawlins	2000 ....Bill Shean Jr.
1969 ....Curtis Person Sr.	1985 ....Lewis W. Oehmig	2001 ....Kemp Richardson
1970 ....Gene Andrews	1986 ....Bo Williams	2002 ....Greg Reynolds
		2003 ....Kemp Richardson

Note: Event is for amateur golfers at least 55 years of age.

MAJOR WOMEN'S AMATEUR CHAMPIONSHIPS

U.S. Women's Amateur

Year	Winner	Score	Runner-Up	Site
1895 ....Mrs. Charles S. Brown		132	Nellie Sargent	Meadow Brook Club, Hempstead, NY
1896 ....Beatrix Hoyt		2 & 1	Mrs. Arthur Turnure	Morris Couty GC, Morristown, NJ
1897 ....Beatrix Hoyt		5 & 4	Nellie Sargent	Essex County Club, Manchester, MA
1898 ....Beatrix Hoyt		5 &3	Maude Wetmore	Ardsley Club, Ardsley-on-Hudson, NY
1899 ....Ruth Underhill		2 & 1	Margaret Fox	Philadelphia CC, Philadelphia, PA
1900 ....Frances C. Griscom		6 & 5	Margaret Curtis	Shinnecock Hills GC, Shinnecock Hills, NY
1901 ....Genevieve Hecker		5 & 3	Lucy Herron	Baltusrol GC, Springfield, NJ
1902 ....Genevieve Hecker		4 & 3	Louisa A. Wells	The Country Club, Brookline, MA
1903 ....Bessie Anthony		7 & 6	J. Anna Carpenter	Chicago GC, Wheaton, IL
1904 ....Georgianna M. Bishop		5 & 3	Mrs. E.F. Sanford	Merion Cricket Club, Haverford, PA
1905 ....Pauline Mackay		1 up	Margaret Curtis	Morris County GC, Convent, NJ
1906 ....Harriot S. Curtis		2 & 1	Mary B. Adams	Brae Burn CC, West Newton, MA
1907 ....Margaret Curtis		7 & 6	Harriot S. Curtis	Midlothian CC, Blue Island, IL
1908 ....Katherine C. Harley		6 & 5	Mrs. T.H. Polhemus	Chevy Chase Club, Chevy Chase, MD
1909 ....Dorothy I. Campbell		3 & 2	Nonna Barlow	Merion Cricket Club, Haverford, PA
1910 ....Dorothy I. Campbell		2 & 1	Mrs. G.M. Martin	Homewood CC, Flossmoor, IL
1911 ....Margaret Curtis		5 & 3	Lillian B. Hyde	Baltusrol GC, Springfield, NJ
1912 ....Margaret Curtis		3 & 2	Nonna Barlow	Essex County Club, Manchester, MA
1913 ....Gladys Ravenscroft		2 up	Marion Hollins	Wilmington CC, Wilmington, DE
1914 ....Katherine Harley		1 up	Elaine V. Rosenthal	Nassau CC, Glen Cove, NY
1915 ....Florence Vanderbeck		3 & 2	Margaret Gavin	Onwentsia Club, Lake Forest, IL
1916 ....Alexa Stirling		2 & 1	Mildred Caverly	Belmont Springs CC, Waverley, MA
1917–18 .....No tournament				
1919..........Alexa Stirling		6 & 5	Margaret Gavin	Shawnee CC, Shawnee-on-Delaware, PA
1920 ....Alexa Stirling		5 & 4	Dorothy Campbell	Mayfield CC, Cleveland
1921 ....Marion Hollins		5 & 4	Alexa Stirling	Hollywood GC, Deal, NJ
1922..........Glenna Collett		5 & 4	Margaret Gavin	Greenbriar GC, White Sulphur Springs, WV
1923 ....Edith Cummings		3 & 2	Alexa Stirling	Westchester-Biltmore CC, Rye, NY
1924 ....Dorothy Campbell		7 & 6	Mary K. Browne	Rhode Island CC, Nyatt, RI
1925 ....Glenna Collett		9 & 8	Alexa Stirling	St. Louis CC, Clayton, MO
1926 ....Helen Stetson		3 & 1	Elizabeth Goss	Merion Cricket Club, Ardmore, PA
1927 ....Miiriam Burns Horn		5 & 4	Maureen Orcutt	Cherry Valley Club, Garden City, NY
1928 ....Glenna Collett		13 & 12	Virginia Van Wie	Va. Hot Springs G & TC, Hot Springs, VA
1929 ....Glenna Collett		4 & 3	Leona Pressler	Oakland Hills CC, Birmingham, MI
1930 ....Glenna Collett		6 & 5	Virginia Van Wie	Los Angeles CC, Beverly Hills, CA
1931 ....Helen Hicks		2 & 1	Glenna Collet Vare	CC of Buffalo, Williamsville, NY
1932 ....Virginia Van Wie		10 & 8	Glenna Collet Vare	Salem CC, Peabody, MA
1933 ....Virginia Van Wie		4 & 3	Helen Hicks	Exmoor CC, Highland Park, IL
1934 ....Virginia Van Wie		2 & 1	Dorothy Traung	Whitemarsh Valley CC, Chestnut Hill, PA
1935 ....Glenna Collett Vare		3 & 2	Patty Berg	Interlachen CC, Hopkins, MN
1936 ....Pamela Barton		4 & 3	Maureen Orcutt	Canoe Brook CC, Summit, NJ
1937 ....Estelle Lawson		7 & 6	Patty Berg	Memphis CC, Memphis, TN
1938 ....Patty Berg		6 & 5	Estelle Lawson	Westmoreland CC, Wilmette, IL

U.S. Women's Amateur (Cont.)

Year	Winner	Score	Runner-Up	Site
1939	Betty Jameson	3 & 2	Dorothy Kirby	Wee Burn Club, Darien, CT
1940	Betty Jameson	6 & 5	Jane S. Cothran	Del Monte G & CC, Pebble Beach, CA
1941	Elizabeth Hicks	5 & 3	Helen Sigel	The Country Club, Brookline, MA
1942–45	No tournament			
1946	Babe Zaharias	11 & 9	Clara Sherman	Southern Hills CC, Tulsa
1947	Louise Suggs	2 up	Dorothy Kirby	Franklin Hills CC, Franklin, MI
1948	Grace S. Lenczyk	4 & 3	Helen Sigel	Del Monte G & CC, Pebble Beach, CA
1949	Dorothy Porter	3 & 2	Dorothy Kielty	Merion GC, Ardmore, PA
1950	Beverly Hanson	6 & 4	Mae Murray	Atlanta AC, Atlanta
1951	Dorothy Kirby	2 & 1	Claire Doran	Town & CC, St. Paul
1952	Jacqueline Pung	2 & 1	Shirley McFedters	Waverley CC, Portland, OR
1953	Mary Lena Faulk	3 & 2	Polly Riley	Rhode Island CC, West Barrington, RI
1954	Barbara Romack	4 & 2	Mickey Wright	Allegheny CC, Sewickley, PA
1955	Patricia A. Lesser	7 & 6	Jane Nelson	Myers Park CC, Charlotte
1956	Marlene Stewart	2 & 1	JoAnne Gunderson	Meridian Hills CC, Indianapolis
1957	JoAnne Gunderson	8 & 6	Ann Casey Johnstone	Del Paso CC, SacramentoA
1958	Anne Quast	3 & 2	Barbara Romack	Wee Burn CC, Darien, CT
1959	Barbara McIntire	4 & 3	Joanne Goodwin	Congressional CC, Washington, D.C.
1960	JoAnne Gunderson	6 & 5	Jean Ashley	Tulsa CC, Tulsa
1961	Anne Quast Decker	14 & 13	Phyllis Preuss	Tacoma G & CC, Tacoma, WA
1962	JoAnne Gunderson	9 & 8	Anne Baker	CC of Rochester, Rochester, NY
1963	Anne Quast Decker	2 & 1	Peggy Conley	Taconic GC, Williamstown, MA
1964	Barbara McIntire	3 & 2	JoAnne Gunderson	Prairie Dunes CC, Hutchinson, KS
1965	Jean Ashley	5 & 4	Anne Quast Decker	Lakewood CC, Denver
1966	JoAnne Gunderson	1 up	Marlene Stewart Streit	Sewickley Heights GC, Sewickley, PA
1967	Mary Lou Dill	5 & 4	Jean Ashley	Annandale GC, Pasadena
1968	JoAnne Gunderson Carner	5 & 4	Anne Quast Decker	Birmingham CC, Birmingham, MI
1969	Catherine Lacoste	3 & 2	Shelley Hamling	Las Colinas CC, Irving, TX
1970	Martha Wilkinson	3 & 2	Cynthia Hall	Wee Burn CC, Darien, CT
1971	Laura Baugh	1 up	Beth Barry	Atlanta CC, Atlanta
1972	Mary Budke	5 & 4	Cynthia Hill	St. Louis CC, St. Louis
1973	Carol Semple	1 up	Anne Quast Decker	Montclair GC, Montclair, NJ
1974	Cynthia Hill	5 & 4	Carol Semple	Broadmoor GC, Seattle
1975	Beth Daniel	3 & 2	Donna Horton	Brae Burn, West Newton, MA
1976	Donna Horton	2 & 1	Marianne Bretton	Del Paso CC, Sacramento
1977	Beth Daniel	3 & 1	Cathy Sherk	Cincinnati CC, Cincinnati
1978	Cathy Sherk	4 & 3	Judith Oliver	Sunnybrook GC, Plymouth Meeting, PA
1979	Carolyn Hill	7 & 6	Patty Sheehan	Memphis CC, Memphis
1980	Juli Inkster	2 up	Patti Rizzo	Prairie Dunes CC, Hutchinson, KS
1981	Juli Inkster	1 up	Lindy Goggin	Waverley CC, Portland, OR
1982	Juli Inkster	4 & 3	Cathy Hanlon	Broadmoor GC, Colorado Springs, CO
1983	Joanne Pacillo	2 & 1	Sally Quinlan	Canoe Brook CC, Summit, NJ
1984	Deb Richard	1 up	Kimberly Williams	Broadmoor GC, Seattle
1985	Michiko Hattori	5 & 4	Cheryl Stacy	Fox Chapel CC, Pittsburgh
1986	Kay Cockerill	9 & 7	Kathleen McCarthy	Pasatiempo GC, Santa Cruz, CA
1987	Kay Cockerill	3 & 2	Tracy Kerdyk	Rhode Island CC, Barrington, RI
1988	Pearl Sinn	6 & 5	Karen Noble	Minikahda Club, Minneapolis
1989	Vicki Goetze	4 & 3	Brandie Burton	Pinehurst CC (No. 2), Pinehurst, NC
1990	Pat Hurst	37 holes	Stephanie Davis	Canoe Brook CC, Summit, NJ
1991	Amy Fruhwirth	5 & 4	Heidi Voorhees	Prairie Dunes CC, Hutchinson, KN
1992	Vicki Goetz	1 up	Annika Sorensteam	Kemper Lakes GC, Hawthorne Hills, IL
1993	Jill McGill	1 up	Sarah Ingram	San Diego CC, Chula Vista, CA
1994	Wendy Ward	2 & 1	Jill McGill	The Homestead, Hot Springs, WV
1995	Kelli Kuehne	4 & 3	Anne-Marie Knight	The Country Club, Brookline, MA
1996	Kelli Kuehne	2 & 1	Marisa Baena	Firethorn GC, Lincoln, NE
1997	Silvia Cavalleri	5 & 4	Robin Burke	Brae Burn CC, West Newton, MA
1998	Grace Park	7 & 6	Jenny Chuasiriporn	Barton Hills CC, Ann Arbor, MI
1999	Dorothy Delasin	4 & 3	Jimin Kang	Biltmore Forest CC, Asheville, NC
2000	Marcy Newton	8 & 7	Laura Myerscough	Waverley CC, Portland, OR
2001	Meredith Duncan	37 holes	Nicole Perrot	Flint Hills GC, Wichita, KA
2002	Becky Lucidi	3 & 2	Brandi Jackson	Sleepy Hollow CC, Scarborough, NY
2003	Virada Nirapathpongporn	2 & 1	Jane Park	Philadelphia CC, Gladwyne, PA
2004	Jane Park	1 up	Amanda McCurdy	Kahkwa Club, Erie, PA

U.S. Girls' Junior Amateur

1949 ....Marlene Bauer	1969 ....Hollis Stacy	1989 ....Brandie Burton
1950 ....Patricia Lesser	1970 ....Hollis Stacy	1990 ....Sandrine Mendiburu
1951 ....Arlene Brooks	1971 ....Hollis Stacy	1991 ....Emilee Klein
1952 ....Mickey Wright	1972 ....Nancy Lopez	1992 ....Jamie Koizumi
1953 ....Millie Meyerson	1973 ....Amy Alcott	1993 ....Kellee Booth
1954 ....Margaret Smith	1974 ....Nancy Lopez	1962 ....Maureen Orcutt
1955 ....Carole Jo Kabler	1975 ....Dayna Benson	1963 ....Sis Choate
1956 ....JoAnne Gunderson	1976 ....Pilar Dorado	1994 ....Kelli Kuehne
1957 ....Judy Eller	1977 ....Althea Tome	1995 ....Marcy Newton
1958 ....Judy Eller	1978 ....Lori Castillo	1996 ....Dorothy Delasin
1959 ....Judy Rand	1979 ....Penny Hammel	1997 ....Beth Bauer
1960 ....Carol Sorenson	1980 ....Laurie Rinker	1998 ....Leigh Anne Hardin
1961 ....Mary Lowell	1981 ....Kay Cornelius	1999 ....Aree Wongluekiet
1962 ....Mary Lou Daniel	1982 ....Heather Farr	2000 ....Lisa Ferrero
1963 ....Janis Ferraris	1983 ....Kim Saiki	2001 ....Nicole Perrot
1964 ....Peggy Conley	1984 ....Cathy Mockett	2002 ....In-Bee Park
1965 ....Gail Sykes	1985 ....Dana Lofland	2003 ....Sukjin-Lee Wuesthoff
1966 ....Claudia Mayhew	1986 ....Pat Hurst	2004 ....J. Granada
1967 ....Elizabeth Story	1987 ....Michelle McGann	
1968 ....Peggy Harmon	1988 ....Jamille Jose	

Women's British Open Amateur

1893 ....Lady Margaret Scott	1929 ....Miss J. Wethered	1966 ....E. Chadwick
1894 ....Lady Margaret Scott	1930 ....Miss D. Fishwick	1967 ....E. Chadwick
1895 ....Lady Margaret Scott	1931 ....Miss E. Wilson	1968 ....B. Varangot
1896 ....Miss Pascoe	1932 ....Miss E. Wilson	1975 ....C. Lacoste
1897 ....Miss E.C. Orr	1933 ....Miss E. Wilson	1976 ....D. Oxley
1898 ....Miss L. Thomson	1934 ....Mrs. A.M. Holm	1977 ....A. Uzielli
1899 ....Miss M. Hezlet	1935 ....Miss W. Morgan	1978 ....E. Kennedy
1900 ....Miss Adair	1936 ....Miss P. Barton	1979 ....M. Madill
1901 ....Miss Graham	1937 ....Miss J. Anderson	1980 ....A. Quast
1902 ....Miss M. Hezlet	1938 ....Mrs. A.M. Holm	1981 ..........I.C. Robertson
1903 ....Miss Adair	1939 ....Miss P. Barton	1982 ....K. Douglas
1904 ....Miss L. Dod	1940–45 ....not held	1983 ....J. Thornhill
1905 ....Miss B. Thompson	1946 ..........G.W. Hetherington	1984 ....J. Rosenthal
1906 ....Mrs. Kennon	1947 ....B. Zaharias	1985 ....L. Beman
1907 ....Miss M. Hezlet	1948 ....L. Suggs	1986 ....M. McGuire
1908 ....Miss M. Titterton	1949 ....F. Stephens	1987 ....J. Collingham
1909 ....Miss D. Campbell	1950 ....Vicomtesse de Saint	1988 ....J. Furby
1910 ....Miss Grant Suttie	..................Sauveur	1989 ....H. Dobson
1911 ....Miss D. Campbell	1951 ..........P.J. MacCann	1990 ....J. Hall
1912 ....Miss G. Ravenscroft	1952 ....M. Paterson	1991 ....V. Michaud
1913 ....Miss M. Dodd	1953 ....M. Stewart	1992 ....P. Pedersen
1914 ....Miss C. Leitch	1954 ....F. Stephens	1993 ....Catriona Lambert
1915–19 ....not held	1955 ....J. Valentine	1994 ....Emma Duggleby
1920 ....Miss C. Leitch	1956 ....M. Smith	1995 ....Julie Hall
1921 ....Miss C. Leitch	1957 ....P. Garvey	1996 ....Kelli Kuehne
1922 ....Miss J. Wethered	1958 ....J. Valentine	1997 ....Alison Rose
1923 ....Miss D. Chambers	1959 ....E. Price	1998 ....K. Rostron
1924 ....Miss J. Wethered	1960 ....B. McIntyre	1999 ....Marine Monnet
1925 ....Miss J. Wethered	1961 ....M. Spearman	2000 ....Rebecca Hudson
1926 ....Miss C. Leitch	1962 ....M. Spearman	2001 ....Rebecca Hudson
1927 ....Miss Thion de la	1963 ....B. Varangot	2002 ....Rebecca Hudson
..................Chaume	1964 ....C. Sorenson	2003 ....Elisa Serramia
1928 ....Miss N. Le Blan	1965 ....B. Varangot	2004 ....Louise Stahle

Women's Amateur Public Links

1977 ....Kelly Fuiks	1986 ....Cindy Schreyer	1996 ....Heather Graff
1978 ....Kelly Fuiks	1987 ....Tracy Kerdyk	1997 ....Jo Jo Robertson
1979 ....Lori Castillo	1988 ....Pearl Sinn	1998 ....Amy Spooner
1980 ....Lori Castillo	1989 ....Pearl Sinn	1999 ....Jody Niemann
1981 ....Mary Enright	1990 ....Cathy Mockett	2000 ....Catherine Cartwright
1982 ....Nancy Taylor	1991 ....Tracy Hanson	2001 ....Candie Kung
1983 ....Kelli Antolock	1992 ....Amy Fruhwirth	2002 ....Annie Thurman
1984 ....Heather Farr	1993 ....Connie Masterson	2003 ....Michelle Wie
1985 ....Danielle	1994 ....Jill McGill	2004 ....Ya-Ni Tseng
..................Ammaccapane	1995 ....Jo Jo Robertson	

U.S. Senior Women's Amateur

1964 ....Loma Smith	1977 ....Dorothy Porter	1990 ....Anne Sander
1965 ....Loma Smith	1978 ....Alice Dye	1991 ....Phyllis Preuss
1966 ....Maureen Orcutt	1979 ....Alice Dye	1992 ....Rosemary Thompson
1967 ....Marge Mason	1980 ....Dorothy Porter	1993 ....Anne Sander
1968 ....Carolyn Cudone	1981 ....Dorothy Porter	1994 ....Marlene Streit
1969 ....Carolyn Cudone	1982 ....Edean Ihlanfeldt	1995 ....Jean Smith
1970 ....Carolyn Cudone	1983 ....Dorothy Porter	1996 ....Gayle Borthwick
1971 ....Carolyn Cudone	1984 ....Constance Guthrie	1997 ....Nancy Fitzgerald
1972 ....Carolyn Cudone	1985 ....Marlene Streit	1998 ....Gayle Borthwick
1973 ....Gwen Hibbs	1986 ....Connie Guthrie	1999 ....C. Semple Thompson
1974 ....Justine Cushing	1987 ....Anne Sander	2000 ....C. Semple Thompson
1975 ....Alberta Bower	1988 ....Lois Hodge	2001 ....C. Semple Thompson
1976 ....Cecile H. Maclaurin	1989 ....Anne Sander	2002 ....C. Semple Thompson
		2003 ....Marlene Streit

Women's Mid-Amateur Championship

1987 ....Cindy Scholefield	1993 ....Sarah Ingram	1999 ....Alissa Herron
1988 ....Martha Lang	1994 ....Sarah Ingram	2000 ....Ellen Port
1989 ....Robin Weiss	1995 ....Ellen Port	2001 ....Laura Shanahan
1990 ....C. Semple Thompson	1996 ....Ellen Port	2002 ....Kathy Hartwiger
1991 ....Sarah LeBrun Ingram	1997 ....C. Semple Thompson	2003 ....Amber Marsh
1992 ....M. Mamey-McInerney	1998 ....Virginia Derby Grimes	2004 ....Corey Weworski

International Golf

Ryder Cup Matches

Year	Results	Site
1927 ....United States 9½, Great Britain 2½		Worcester CC, Worcester, MA
1929 ....Great Britain 7, United States 5		Moortown GC, Leeds, England
1931 ....United States 9, Great Britain 3		Scioto CC, Columbus, OH
1933 ....Great Britain 6½, United States 5½		Southport and Ainsdale Courses, Southport, England
1935 ....United States 9, Great Britain 3		Ridgewood CC, Ridgewood, NJ
1937 ....United States 8, Great Britain 4		Southport and Ainsdale Courses, Southport, England
1939–1945.....No tournament		
1947 ....United States 11, Great Britain 1		Portland GC, Portland, OR
1949 ....United States 7, Great Britain 5		Ganton GC, Scarborough, England
1951 ....United States 9½, Great Britain 2½		Pinehurst CC, Pinehurst, NC
1953 ....United States 6½, Great Britain 5½		Wentworth Club, Surrey, England
1955 ....United States 8, Great Britain 4		Thunderbird Ranch & CC, Palm Springs, CA
1957 ....Great Britain 7½, United States 4½		Lindrick GC, Yorkshire, England
1959 ....United States 8½, Great Britain 3½		Eldorado CC, Palm Desert, CA
1961 ....United States 14½, Great Britain 9½		Royal Lytham & St. Annes GC, St Anne's-on-the-Sea, England
1963 ....United States 23, Great Britain 9		East Lake CC, Atlanta
1965 ....United States 19½, Great Britain 12½		Royal Birkdale GC, Southport, England
1967 ....United States 23½, Great Britain 8½		Champions GC, Houston
1969 ....United States 16, Great Britain 16		Royal Birkdale GC, Southport, England
1971 ....United States 18½, Great Britain 13½		Old Warson CC, St. Louis
1973 ....United States 19, Great Britain 13		Hon Co of Edinburgh Golfers, Muirfield, Scotland
1975 ....United States 21, Great Britain 11		Laurel Valley GC, Ligonier, PA
1977 ....United States 12½, Great Britain 7½		Royal Lytham & St. Annes GC, St. Annes-on-the-Sea, Eng.
1979 ....United States 17, Europe 11		Greenbrier, White Sulphur Springs, WV
1981 ....United States 18½, Europe 9½		Walton Heath GC, Surrey, England
1983 ....United States 14½, Europe 13½		PGA National GC, Palm Beach Gardens, FL
1985 ....Europe 16½, United States 11½		Belfry GC, Sutton Coldfield, England
1987 ....Europe 15, United States 13		Muirfield GC, Dublin, OH
1989 ....Europe 14, United States 14		Belfry GC, Sutton Coldfield, England
1991 ....United States 14½, Europe 13½		Ocean Course, Kiawah Island, SC
1993 ....United States 15, Europe 13		Belfry GC, Sutton Coldfield, England
1995 ....Europe 14½, United States 13½		Oak Hill CC, Rochester, NY
1997 ....Europe 14½, United States 13½		Valderrama GC, Sotogrande, Spain
1999 ....United States 14½, Europe 13½		The Country Club, Brookline, MA
2002 ....Europe 15½, Unites States 12½		Belfry GC, Sutton Coldfield, England
2004 ....Europe 18½, United States 9½		Oakland Hills CC, Bloomfield Hills, MI

Team matches held every odd year between U.S. professionals and those of Great Britain/Europe. Team members selected on basis of finishes in PGA and European tour events. Match in 2001 canceled due to 9/11 terrorist attacks.

Walker Cup Matches

Year	Results	Site
1922	United States 8, Great Britain 4	Nat'l Golf Links of America, Southampton, NY
1923	United States 6, Great Britain 5	St. Andrews, Scotland
1924	United States 9, Great Britain 3	Garden City GC, Garden City, NY
1926	United States 6, Great Britain 5	St. Andrews, Scotland
1928	United States 11, Great Britain 1	Chicago GC, Wheaton, IL
1930	United States 10, Great Britain 2	Royal St. George GC, Sandwich, England
1932	United States 8, Great Britain 1	The Country Club, Brookline, MA
1934	United States 9, Great Britain 2	St. Andrews, Scotland
1936	United States 9, Great Britain 0	Pine Valley GC, Clementon, NJ
1938	Great Britain 7, United States 4	St. Andrews, Scotland
1940–46	No tournament	
1947	United States 8, Great Britain 4	St. Andrews, Scotland
1949	United States 10, Great Britain 2	Winged Foot GC, Mamaroneck, NY
1951	United States 6, Great Britain 3	Birkdale GC, Southport, England
1953	United States 9, Great Britain 3	The Kittansett Club, Marion, MA
1955	United States 10, Great Britain 2	St. Andrews, Scotland
1957	United States 8, Great Britain 3	Minikahda Club, Minneapolis
1959	United States 9, Great Britain 3	Muirfield, Scotland
1961	United States 11, Great Britain 1	Seattle GC, Seattle
1963	United States 12, Great Britain 8	Ailsa Course, Turnberry, Scotland
1965	Great Britain 11, United States 11	Baltimore CC, Five Farms, Baltimore, MD
1967	United States 13, Great Britain 7	Royal St. George's GC, Sandwich, England
1969	United States 10, Great Britain 8	Milwaukee CC, Milwaukee, WI
1971	Great Britain 13, United States 11	St. Andrews, Scotland
1973	United States 14, Great Britain 10	The Country Club, Brookline, MA
1975	United States 15½, Great Britain 8½	St. Andrews, Scotland
1977	United States 16, Great Britain 8	Shinnecock Hills GC, Southampton, NY
1979	United States 15½, Great Britain 8½	Muirfield, Scotland
1981	United States 15, Great Britain 9	Cypress Point Club, Pebble Beach, CA
1983	United States 13½, Great Britain 10½	Royal Liverpool GC, Hoylake, England
1985	United States 13, Great Britain 11	Pine Valley GC, Pine Valley, NJ
1987	United States 16½, Great Britain 7½	Sunningdale GC, Berkshire, England
1989	Great Britain 12½, United States 11½	Peachtree Golf Club, Atlanta
1991	United States 14, Great Britain 10	Portmarnock GC, Dublin, Ireland
1993	United States 19, Great Britain 5	Interlachen CC, Edina, MN
1995	Great Britain/Ireland 14, United States 10	Royal Porthcawl, Porthcawl, Wales
1997	United States 18, Great Britain/Ireland 6	Quaker Ridge GC, Scarsdale, NY
1999	Great Britain/Ireland 15, United States 9	Nairn GC, Nairn, Scotland
2001	Great Britain/Ireland 15, United States 9	Ocean Forest GC, Sea Island, GA
2003	Great Britain/Ireland 12½, United States 11½	Ganton GC, Ganton, England

Men's amateur team competition every other year between United States and Great Britain/Ireland. U.S. team members selected by USGA.

Solheim Cup Matches

Year	Results	Site
1990	United States 11½, Europe 4½	Lake Nona GC, Orlando, FL
1992	Europe 11½, United States 6½	Dalmahoy Hotel GC, Edinburgh
1994	United States 13, Europe 7	The Greenbriar, White Sulpher Springs, WV
1996	United States 17, Europe 11	Marriot St Pierre Hotel & CC, Chepstow, Wales
1998	United States 16, Europe 12	Muirfield Village GC, Dublin, OH
2000	Europe 14½, United States 11½	Loch Lomond GC, Luss, Scotand
2002	United States 15½, Europe 12½	Interlachen CC, Minneapolis, MN
2003	Europe 17½, United States 10½	Barseback G&CC, Malmo, Sweden

Women's team matches held every other year between U.S. professionals and those of Europe. Team members selected on the basis of finishes in LPGA and European tour events.

Curtis Cup Matches

Year	Results	Site
1932	United States 5½, British Isles 3½	Wentworth GC, Wentworth, England
1934	United States 6½, British Isles 2½	Chevy Chase Club, Chevy Chase, MD
1936	United States 4½, British Isles 4½	King's Course, Gleneagles, Scotland
1938	United States 5½, British Isles 3½	Essex CC, Manchester, MA
1940–46	No tournament	
1948	United States 6½, British Isles 2½	Birkdale GC, Southport, England
1950	United States 7½, British Isles 1½	CC of Buffalo, Williamsville, NY

Curtis Cup Matches *(Cont.)*

Year	Results	Site
1952	British Isles 5, United States 4	Muirfield, Scotland
1954	United States 6, British Isles 3	Merion GC, Ardmore, PA
1956	British Isles 5, United States 4	Prince's GC, Sandwich Bay, England
1958	British Isles 4½, United States 4½	Brae Burn CC, West Newton, Mass.
1960	United States 6½, British Isles 2½	Lindrick GC, Worksop, England
1962	United States 8, British Isles 1	Broadmoor CG, Colorado Springs,CO
1964	United States 10½, British Isles 7½	Royal Porthcawl GC, Porthcawl, South Wales
1966	United States 13, British Isles 5	Va. Hot Springs G & TC, Hot Springs, VA
1968	United States 10½, British Isles 7½	Royal County Down GC, Newcastle, N. Ire.
1970	United States 11½, British Isles 6½	Brae Burn CC, West Newton, MA
1972	United States 10, British Isles 8	Western Gailes, Ayrshire, Scotland
1974	United States 13, British Isles 5	San Francisco GC, San Francisco
1976	United States 11½, British Isles 6½	Royal Lytham & St. Annes GC, England
1978	United States 12, British Isles 6	Apawamis Club, Rye, NY
1980	United States 13, British Isles 5	St. Pierre G & CC, Chepstow, Wales
1982	United States 14½, British Isles 3½	Denver CC, Denver
1984	United States 9½, British Isles 8½	Muirfield, Scotland
1986	British Isles 13, United States 5	Prairie Dunes CC, Hutchinson, KS
1988	British Isles 11, United States 7	Royal St. George's GC, Sandwich, England
1990	United States 14, British Isles 4	Somerset Hills CC, Bernardsville, NJ
1992	Great Britain/Ireland 10, United States 8	Royal Liverpool GC, Hoylake, England
1994	Great Britain/Ireland 9, United States 9	The Honors Course, Ooltewah, TN
1996	Great Britain/Ireland 11½, United States 6½	Killarney Golf & Fishing Club, Killarney, Ireland
1998	United States 10, Great Britain/Ireland 8	The Minikahda Club, Minneapolis
2000	United States 10, Great Britain/Ireland 8	Ganton GC, North Yorkshire, England
2002	United States 11, Great Britain/Ireland 7	Fox Chapel GC, Pittsburgh, PA
2004	United States 10, Great Britain/Ireland 8	Formby GC, Merseyside, England

Women's amateur team competition every other year between the United States and Great Britain/Ireland. U.S. team members selected by USGA.

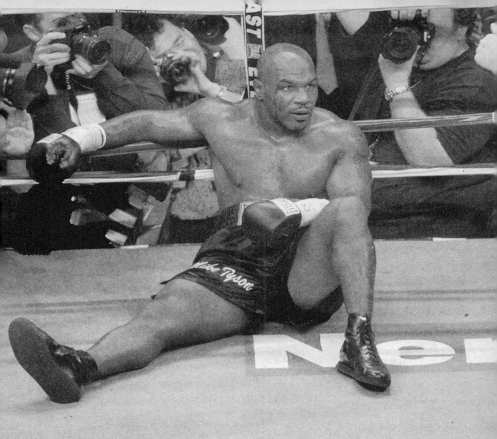

Former
heavyweight champion
Mike Tyson

NEAL PRESTON

Boxing

Alphabet Soup

With too many sanctioning bodies and too few undisputed champions, the sport was a confusing muddle to most fans

BY STEPHEN CANNELLA

STOP US IF YOU'VE heard this one before, but on a steamy July night in Louisville, the spectacular career of Mike Tyson came to a crashing end. Yes, boxing fans had assumed that to be the case several times before, only to be burned when Tyson, like an unkillable sidewalk weed, popped back into the ring. But what other conclusion could be drawn upon seeing the once-fearsome fighter, now 38 years old and deeply in debt, seated on the canvas with left leg bent, right arm hanging over a rope and the hint of a woozy smile tugging at his lips?

That Iron Mike had been flattened in the fourth round by an unknown Brit named Danny Williams only underscored the notion that it was time for the nearly destitute Tyson to begin looking for a day job. The fact that the former champ could be envisioned as a title contender if things had gone as planned against Williams spoke volumes about the state of the heavyweights in 2004. The division has devolved into a motley collection of no-names and lesser-talents lacking in ring panache and box office punch. By the end of

the summer four fighters could lay claim to the title of best heavyweight, with Vitali Klitschko holding the WBC belt, Chris Byrd the IBF's, John Ruiz the WBA's and Lamon Brewster the dubious WBO's.

In a division drowning in alphabet soup and lacking in marquee personalities after Lennox Lewis retired in February, Tyson's was a familiar name for fans to cling to as they searched for order in the sport. He hadn't fought since February of 2003, when he needed just 49 seconds to level Clifford Etienne, and since then his outlaw image had softened a bit. In the weeks leading up to the Williams bout Tyson's tone with reporters bordered on gracious. He seemed to have quelled the inner rage that had always been his calling card, and he sounded like a man intent on polishing his tarnished boxing legacy. He even joked about his concerted effort to stay on his best behavior. "My kids are on the Internet now," he said. "I don't want them reading anything bad about me."

If the Tyson tykes wandered onto the financial pages, they might read some per-

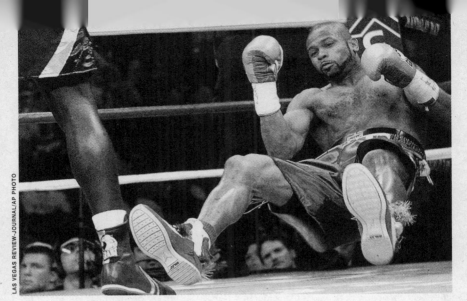

Jones Jr.'s unofficial reign as the pound-for-pound world champion may be over.

ilous news indeed about papa: The news that he had squandered several lifetimes' worth of riches and, spending freely on cars, houses, and exotic animals, had run up a debt of $38 million. In bankruptcy court his lawyers unveiled a plan in which Tyson would fight seven times, keeping the pauper's sum of $2 million per fight for himself and funneling the rest to his many creditors. Promoter Bob Arum helped the cause by signing Tyson to a $100 million contract.

In a division thin on talent, surely the twin engines of financial need and an apparent rededication to his craft could propel Tyson back into title contention. Early in the bout against Williams, whose previous claim to fame was his habit of crying before fights, the idea seemed to have merit. Tyson battered his larger opponent—who, at 265 pounds, outweighed Tyson by 32—in the first round, briefly staggering Williams with a vicious uppercut and then bludgeoning him with a series of body-blow left hooks.

But Williams withstood these opening sallies, and soon began to make his size advantage work for him. He leaned in close to Tyson, tying him up, pushing him around and

sapping his energy. In the third round Williams opened a cut above Tyson's right eye. In the fourth he moved in for the kill, at one point peppering the former champ with at least 25 unanswered blows. The final punch was barely knockout grade. It glanced off Tyson's glove, yet sank him onto the ropes and into an uncertain future, both in and out of the ring.

In Tyson's defense, he was hobbled by a torn knee ligament he suffered in the first round, and, to his credit, he refused to use the injury as an excuse for his poor showing. But in the end, Williams's postfight comments succinctly summed up why this had to be the end for Iron Mike (knowing boxing though, whether it *will* be the end is another question). "People forget this isn't a peak Mike Tyson," he said after the bout. "This was a Mike Tyson who was 38 years old."

And whatever luster Tyson had provided the division was dimmed even further, if not smudged out entirely, with the defeat. Upon securing the WBC title with a knockout of Corrie Sanders in Los Angeles in April, Klitschko proclaimed, "Since I was 15 years old, I've had a dream to fight Iron Mike. And I always try to make my dreams come true." That dream, like Tyson, is not what it once was, but the 6'8" Klitschko, from Ukraine, remains the best hope for a dominant heavyweight. (Even if the sanctioning body whose belt he held spent 2004 teetering on the financial brink.) He's big and, though stiff, packs a wallop. As the holder of a Ph.D., the speaker of four languages and the older brother of another contender, Wladimir, Klitschko also has the potential to develop into a seat-filling personality. By decking Sanders, who had knocked out Wladmir in 2003, Vitali gained a measure of familial revenge—and, he hoped, recognition. "I feel a huge weight off of my shoulders," he said. "Now I am out of the shadows."

Lack of publicity has never been a problem for Oscar De La Hoya but, as his June match with the lightly regarded Felix Sturm suggested, his conditioning and diminishing skill may be concerns. In preparation for their September bout, De La Hoya and undisputed middleweight champion Bernard Hopkins fought a dual card in Las Vegas. The 39-year-old Hopkins successfully defended his title for the 18th time, taking out Robert Allen in the first fight, a rugged if lackluster affair. In the main event, De La Hoya, fighting at 160 pounds for the first time in his storied career, needed a furious final-round rally to pull out a slim victory on points.

One of the reasons for the exhibition was to prove that De La Hoya was up to the task of taking on middleweights. He won, but his performance only created more questions before his showdown with Hopkins. De La Hoya looked a bit soft and was slow to defend himself against Sturm's punches. His ring strategy—he tried to wear down Sturm with a barrage of body blows—was questionable. He took more of a beating than a man warming up for a $40 million bout—a record for a non-heavyweight fight—should be expected to take. Afterward his handlers dropped hints that he was suffering from a back injury. "Everything went wrong tonight," he said. Things failed to improve when De La Hoya met Hopkins in mid-September: He was KO'd by a body punch in Round 9.

Another one of boxing's biggest names faded considerably in 2004. In May, Roy Jones Jr.—long considered the best fighter, pound-for-pound, in any ring—was the victim of a stunning knockout by light heavyweight Antonio Tarver. A year earlier Jones, looking for a challenge after years of dominating the middle divisions, bulked up and swiped the WBA heavyweight crown from John Ruiz. (Ruiz later regained the title.) In November 2003, Jones barely won a decision against Tarver. He blamed his uninspired performance on the fact that he had to quickly shed 25 pounds to meet Tarver as a light heavyweight.

During introductions before their rematch at the Mandalay Bay Events Center in Las Vegas, Tarver growled at Jones, "Got any excuses tonight, Roy?" It's unclear what Jones said to that, but he had no response for the sudden left hand that Tarver delivered in the second round. The blow flattened Jones and won the light heavyweight belt for Tarver, who said before the fight that Jones's legacy would be on the line. He may have been right: At age 35, after a decade of dominance, was Jones losing his touch?

Jones took on IBF light heavyweight champ Glen Johnson in September and was knocked out in the ninth, all but eliminating the possibility of another showdown with Tarver. Fight fans jonesing for a juicy rematch turned their eyes to the November junior middleweight showdown between Winky Wright and Shane Mosley. In March Wright, 32, unified the 154-pound crown with a surprising decision over Mosley. The bout was supposed to be a cakewalk for Sugar Shane, nothing more than a bone thrown to the under-the-radar Wright to help him gain some recognition. Against all expectations, Wright thoroughly outboxed Mosley, ruining his plans for a fight against Felix Trinidad, who had pledged to come out of retirement to face Mosley.

Speaking of truncated retirements, former heavyweight champ Riddick Bowe announced in August that he was ready to re-enter the ring after an almost eight-year absence. Bowe had looked old and overmatched when he lost to Andrew Golota in 1996, and may have ring-related neurological problems to boot, but given the current heavyweight scene, who could blame him for a little misguided optimism?

FOR THE RECORD · 2003 – 2004

Current Champions

Division	Weight Limit	WBA Champion	WBC Champion	IBF Champion
Heavyweight	None	John Ruiz	Vitali Klitschko	Chris Byrd
Cruiserweight	190	Jean-Marc Mormeck	Wayne Braithwaite	Kelvin Davis
Light Heavyweight	175	Fabrice Tiozzo	Antonio Tarver	Glencoffe Johnson
Super Middleweight	168	Manny Siaca	Cristian Sanavia	Sven Ottke
Middleweight	160	Bernard Hopkins	Bernard Hopkins	Bernard Hopkins
Junior Middleweight	154	Winky Wright	Winky Wright	Verno Phillips
Welterweight	147	Cory Spinks	Cory Spinks	Cory Spinks
Junior Welterweight	140	Vivian Harris	Arturo Gatti	Kostya Tszyu
Lightweight	135	Juan Diaz	Jose Luis Castillo	Julio Diaz
Junior Lightweight	130	Yodsanan Nanthachai	Erik Morales	Erik Morales
Featherweight	126	Juan Manuel Marquez	In Jin Chi	Juan Manuel Marquez
Junior Featherweight	122	Mahyar Monshipour	Oscar Larios	Israel Vazquez
Bantamweight	118	Johnny Bredahl	Veerapol Sahaprom	Rafael Marquez
Junior Bantamweight	115	Alexander Munoz	Katsushige Kawashima	Luis Perez
Flyweight	112	Lorenzo Parra	Pongsaklek Wonjongkam	Irene Pacheco
Junior Flyweight	108	Rosendo Alvarez	Jorge Arce	Jose Victor Burgos
Strawweight	105	Yukata Niida	Eagle Akakura	Daniel Reyes

Note: WBC=World Boxing Council; WBA=World Boxing Association; IBF=International Boxing Federation. Champions as of August 24, 2004.

Championship and Major Fights of 2003 and 2004

Abbreviations: WBC=World Boxing Council; WBA= World Boxing Association; IBF=International Boxing Federation; KO=knockout; TKO=technical knockout; UD=unanimous decision; SD=split decision; DQ=disqualification; MD=majority decision; TD=technical decision. Bouts from Oct 1, 2003 to Sept 1, 2004.

Heavyweight

Date	Winner	Loser	Result	Title	Site
Oct 4	James Toney	Evander Holyfield	TKO 9	—	Las Vegas
Dec 6	Vitali Klitschko	Kirk Johnson	KO 2	—	New York City
April 17	Chris Byrd	Andrew Golota	DRAW	IBF	New York City
April 17	John Ruiz	Fres Oquendo	TKO 11	WBA	New York City
April 24	Vitali Klitschko	Corrie Sanders	TKO 8	WBC	Los Angeles
July 30	Danny Williams	Mike Tyson	KO 4	—	Louisville

Cruiserweight

Date	Winner	Loser	Result	Title	Site
April 17	Wayne Braithwaite	Louis Azille	UD	WBC	New York City
May 1	Kelvin Davis	Ezra Sellers	TKO 8	IBF	Miami
May 22	Jean-Marc Mormeck	Virgil Hill	UD	WBA	Carnival City, S Africa

Light Heavyweight

Date	Winner	Loser	Result	Title	Site
Nov 7	Glencoffe Johnson/Clinton Woods	Draw	vacant IBF	Sheffield, England	
Nov 8	Roy Jones Jr.	Antonio Tarver	MD	WBC	Las Vegas
Feb 6	Glencoffe Johnson	Clinton Woods	UD	IBF	Sheffield, England
Mar 20	Fabrice Tiozzo	Silvio Branco	MD	WBA	Lyon
May 15	Antonio Tarver	Roy Jones Jr.	TKO 2	WBC	Las Vegas

Super Middleweight

Date	Winner	Loser	Result	Title	Site
Dec 13	Sven Ottke	Robin Reid	UD	IBF	Nuremberg
Feb 28	Markus Beyer	Andre Thysse	UD	WBC	Dresden
Mar 27	Sven Ottke	Armand Krajnc	UD	IBF	Magdeburg, Germany
May 5	Manny Siaca	Anthony Mundine	Split	WBA	Sydney
June 5	Cristian Sanavia	Markus Beyer	MD	WBC	Chemnitz, Germany

Middleweight

Date	Winner	Loser	Result	Title	Site
Dec 13	Bernard Hopkins	William Joppy	UD	WBC/WBA/IBF	Atlantic City
May 1	Maselino Masoe	Evans Ashira	TKO 2	Interim WBA	Miami
June 5	Bernard Hopkins	Robert Allen	UD	WBC/WBA/IBF	Las Vegas

Junior Middleweight (Super Welterweight)

Date	Winner	Loser	Result	Title	Site
Nov 8	Winky Wright	Angel Hernandez	UD	IBF	Las Vegas
Mar 13	Winky Wright	Shane Mosley	UD	WBC/WBA/IBF	Las Vegas
June 5	Verno Phillips	Carlos Bojorquez	TKO 6	IBF	Joplin, Missouri

Welterweight

Date	Winner	Loser	Result	Title	Site
Dec 13	Cory Spinks	Ricardo Mayorga	MD	WBC/WBA/IBF	Atlantic City
April 10	Cory Spinks	Zab Judah	UD	WBC/WBA/IBF	Las Vegas

Junior Welterweight (Super Lightweight)

Date	Winner	Loser	Result	Title	Site
Jan 24	Arturo Gatti	Gianluca Branco	UD	WBC	Atlantic City
Feb 7	Sharmba Mitchell	Lovemore Ndou	UD	Interim IBF	Las Vegas
April 3	Sharmba Mitchell	Michael Stewart	UD	Interim IBF	Manchester, England
April 17	Vivian Harris	Oktay Urkal	Split	Interim WBA	Berlin
May 22	Floyd Mayweather	DeMarcus Corley	UD	WBC	Atlantic City
July 24	Arturo Gatti	Leonard Dorin	KO 2	WBC	Atlantic City
Aug 7	Sharmba Mitchell	Moises Pedroza	KO 2	Interim IBF	Mashantucket, Conn.

Lightweight

Date	Winner	Loser	Result	Title	Site
Nov 1	Floyd Mayweather	Phillip N'Dou	TKO 7	WBC	Grand Rapids, Mich.
Nov 22	Javier Jauregui	Levander Johnson	TKO 11	IBF	Los Angeles
April 10	Lakva Sim	Miguel Callist	TKO 5	WBA	Las Vegas
May 13	Julio Diaz	Javier Jauregui	MD	IBF	San Diego, Calif.
June 5	Jose Luis Castillo	Juan Lazcano	UD	WBC	Las Vegas
July 17	Juan Diaz	Lakva Sim	UD	WBA	Houston

Junior Lightweight (Super Featherweight)

Date	Winner	Loser	Result	Title	Site
Feb 28	Erik Morales	Jesus Chavez	UD	WBC	Las Vegas
July 31	Erik Morales	Carlos Hernandez	UD	WBC/IBF	Las Vegas
Aug 7	Yodsanan Nanthachai	Steve Forbes	UD	WBA	Mashantucket, Conn.

Featherweight

Date	Winner	Loser	Result	Title	Site
Oct 18	In Jin Chi/Michael Brodie		DRAW	vacant WBC	Manchester, England
Nov 1	Juan Manuel Marquez	Derrick Gainer	TKO 7	WBA/IBF	Grand Rapids, Mich.
April 10	In Jin Chi	Michael Brodie	KO 7	WBC	Manchester, England
May 8	Juan Manuel Marquez	Manny Pacquiao	DRAW	WBA/IBF	Las Vegas
June 4	Chris John	Osamu Sato	UD	Interim WBA	Tokyo
June 19	Marco Antonio Barrera	Paulie Ayala	TKO 10	—	Los Angeles
July 24	In Jin Chi	Eiichi Sugama	TKO 10	WBC	Seoul

Junior Featherweight (Super Bantamweight)

Date	Winner	Loser	Result	Title	Site
Nov 22	Oscar Larios	N. Kiattisakchocchoi	TKO 10	WBC	Los Angeles
Dec 19	Mayhar Monshipour	Jairo Tagliafero	TKO 8	WBA	Levallaois, France
Mar 6	Oscar Larios	Shigeru Nakazato	UD	WBC	Saitama, Japan
Mar 25	Israel Vazquez	Jose Luis Valbuena	TKO 12	vacant IBF	Los Angeles
May 28	Mahyar Monshipour	Salim Medjkoune	TKO 8	WBA	Claremon-Ferrrand, Fr

Bantamweight

Date	Winner	Loser	Result	Title	Site
Oct 24	Johnny Bredahl	David Guerault	UD	WBA	Copenhagen, Denmark
Jan 31	Rafael Marquez	Pete Frissina	TKO 2	IBF	Phoenix
Mar 6	Veeraphol Sahaprom	Toshiaki Nishioaka	UD	WBC	Saitama, Japan
Mar 6	Julio Zarate	Hideki Todaka	Split	Interim WBA	Saitama, Japan
Mar 13	Johnny Bredahl	Nobuaki Naka	UD	WBA	Copenhagen, Denmark
May 1	Veeraphol Sahaprom	Julio Cesar Avila	KO 12	WBC	Nongkhai, Thailand
July 31	Rafael Marquez	Heriberto Ruiz	KO 3	IBF	Las Vegas

Junior Bantamweight (Super Flyweight)

Date	Winner	Loser	Result	Title	Site
Dec 13	Luis Perez	Felix Machado	UD	IBF	Atlantic City
Jan 3	Masamori Tokuyama	Dimitri Kirilov	UD	WBC	Yokohama
Jan 3	Alexander Munoz	Eiji Kojima	KO 10	WBA	Yokohama
May 16	Martin Castillo	Hideyasu Ishihara	TKO 11	Interim WBA	Gifu, Japan
June 28	Katsushige Kawashima	Masamori Tokuyama	KO 1	WBC	Yokohama

Flyweight

Date	Winner	Loser	Result	Title	Site
Nov 14	Pongsaklek Wonjongkam	Hussein Hussein	UD	WBC	Bangkok
Dec 6	Lorenzo Parra	Eric Morel	UD	WBA	Bayamon, Puerto Rico
Jan 3	Pongsaklek Wonjongkam	Masaki Nakanuma	UD	WBC	Yokohama
June 4	Lorenzo Parra	Takefumi Sakata	MD	WBA	Tokyo
July 15	Pongsaklek Wonjongkam	Luis Angel Martinez	TKO 5	WBC	Khonkaen, Thailand

Junior Flyweight

Date	Winner	Loser	Result	Title	Site
Nov 15	Beibis Mendoza	Choi Yosam	UD	WBA	Seoul
Dec 13	Rosendo Alvarez/ Victor Burgos		DRAW	WBA/IBF	Atlantic City
Jan 10	Jorge Arce	Jamo Gamboa	KO 2	WBC	Mexico City
April 24	Jorge Arce	Melchor Cob Castro	KO 5	WBC	Chiapas, Mexico
May 15	Victor Burgos	Fahlan Sakkreerin	TKO 6	IBF	Las Vegas

Strawweight (Mini Flyweight)

Date	Winner	Loser	Result	Title	Site
Jan 10	Eagle Akakura	Jose Antonio Aguirre	MD	WBC	Tokyo
May 5	Juan Landaeta/ Chana Porpaoin		DRAW	WBA	Bangkok
June 28	Eagle Akakura	Satoshi Kogumazaka	Tech D 8	WBC	Yokohama
July 3	Yukata Niida	Noel Arambulet	UD	WBA	Tokyo

World Champions

Sanctioning bodies: the National Boxing Association (NBA), the New York State Athletic Commission (NY), the World Boxing Association (WBA), the World Boxing Council (WBC), and the International Boxing Federation (IBF).

Heavyweights
(Weight: Unlimited)

Champion	Reign	Champion	Reign	Champion	Reign
John L. Sullivan*	1885–92	Joe Frazier* NY	1968–70	Evander Holyfield*	1990–92
James J. Corbett*	1892–97	Jimmy Ellis WBA	1968–70	Lennox Lewis WBC	1993–95
Bob Fitzsimmons*	1897–99	Joe Frazier*	1970–73	Riddick Bowe*	1992–93
James J. Jeffries*	1899–05†	George Foreman*	1973–74	Evander Holyfield*	1993–94
Marvin Hart*	1905–06	Muhammad Ali*	1974–78	Michael Moorer*	1994
Tommy Burns*	1906–08	Leon Spinks*	1978	George Foreman*	1994–95
Jack Johnson*	1908–15	Ken Norton WBC	1978	Oliver McCall WBC	1995
Jess Willard*	1915–19	Larry Holmes WBC	1978–80	Frank Bruno WBC	1995–96
Jack Dempsey*	1919–26	Muhammad Ali*	1978–79†	Bruce Seldon WBA	1995–96
Gene Tunney*	1926–28†	John Tate WBA	1979–80	Mike Tyson WBA	1996
Max Schmeling*	1930–32	Mike Weaver WBA	1980–82	Michael Moorer IBF	1996–97
Jack Sharkey*	1932–33	Larry Holmes*	1980–85	Shannon Briggs*	1997–98
Primo Carnera*	1933–34	Michael Dokes WBA	1982–83	Lennox Lewis* WBC	1997–01
Max Baer*	1934–35	Gerrie Coetzee WBA	1983–84	E. Holyfield WBA, IBF	1996–99
James J. Braddock*	1935–37	Tim Witherspoon WBC	1984	Lennox Lewis	1999–01
Joe Louis*	1937–49†	Pinklon Thomas WBC	1984–86	E. Holyfield WBA	2000–01
Ezzard Charles*	1949–51	Greg Page WBA	1984–85	John Ruiz WBA	2001–03
Jersey Joe Walcott*	1951–52	Michael Spinks*	1985–87	Hasim Rahman*	
Rocky Marciano*	1952–56†	Tim Witherspoon WBA	1986	WBC, IBF	2001
Floyd Patterson*	1956–59	Trevor Berbick WBC	1986	Chris Byrd IBF	2002–
Ingemar Johansson*	1959–60	Mike Tyson WBC	1986–87	Roy Jones Jr.. WBA	2003–04
Floyd Patterson*	1960–62	James Smith WBA	1986–87	Lennox Lewis*	
Sonny Liston*	1962–64	Tony Tucker IBF	1987	WBC	2001–04
Muhammad Ali*	1964–70†	Mike Tyson*	1987–90	John Ruiz, WBA	2004–
Ernie Terrell WBA	1965–67	Buster Douglas*	1990	Vitali Klitschko, WBC	2004–

Cruiserweights
(Weight Limit: 190 pounds)

Champion	Reign	Champion	Reign	Champion	Reign
Marvin Camel* WBC	1980	E. Holyfield* WBA, IBF	1987–88	Nate Miller WBA	1995–97
Carlos De Leon* WBC	1980–82	Evander Holyfield*	1988†	M. Dominguez* WBC	1996–98
Ossie Ocasio WBA	1982–84	Toufik Belbouli WBA	1989	A. Washington IBF	1996–97
S.T. Gordon* WBC	1982–83	Robert Daniels WBA	1989–91	Uriah Grant IBF	1997
Carlos De Leon* WBC	1983–85	Carlos De Leon* WBC	1989–90	Imamu Mayfield IBF	1997–98
Marvin Camel IBF	1983–84	Glenn McCrory IBF	1989–90	Fabrice Tiozzo WBA	1997–00
Lee Roy Murphy IBF	1984–86	Jeff Lampkin IBF	1990	J.C. Gomez* WBC	1998–02†
Piet Crous WBA	1984–85	M. Duran* WBC	1990–91	Arthur Williams IBF	1998–99
Alfonso Ratliff* WBC	1985	Bobby Czyz WBA	1991–92†	Vassiliy Girov* IBF	1999–03
Dwight Braxton WBA	1985–86	Anaclet Wamba* WBC	1991–95†	James Toney* IBF	2003
Bernard Benton* WBC	1985–86	James Pritchard IBF	1991	Virgil Hill WBA	2000–02
Carlos De Leon* WBC	1986–88	James Warring IBF	1991–92	Wayne Braithwaite WBC	2002–
Evander Holyfield* WBA	1986–88	Alfred Cole IBF	1992–96	J.M. Mormeck WBA	2002–
Ricky Parkey IBF	1986–87	Orlin Norris WBA	1993–95	Kelvin Davis IBF	2004–

*Lineal champion.
†Champion relinquished title to retire or switch weight classes, or had title stripped by boxing organization.

Light Heavyweights
(Weight Limit: 175 pounds)

Champion	Reign
Jack Root*	1903
George Gardner*	1903
Bob Fitzsimmons*	1903–05
Jack O'Brien*	1905–12†
Jack Dillon*	1914–16
Battling Levinsky*	1916–20
Georges Carpentier*	1920–22
Battling Siki*	1922–23
Mike McTigue*	1923–25
Paul Berlenbach*	1925–26
Jack Delaney*	1926–27†
Jimmy Slattery NBA	1927
Tommy Loughran*	1927–29†
Maxie Rosenbloom*	1930–34
George Nichols NBA	1932
Bob Godwin NBA	1933
Bob Olin*	1934–35
John Henry Lewis*	1935–38†
Melio Bettina	1939
Billy Conn*	1939–40†
Anton Christoforidis	1941
Gus Lesnevich*	1941–48
Freddie Mills*	1948–50
Joey Maxim*	1950–52
Archie Moore*	1952–62†
Harold Johnson NBA	1961
Harold Johnson*	1962–63

Champion	Reign
Willie Pastrano*	1963–65
Jose Torres*	1965–66
Dick Tiger*	1966–68
Bob Foster*	1968–74†
Vicente Rondon WBA	1971–72
John Conteh WBC	1974–77
Victor Galindez* WBA	1974–78
Miguel A. Cuello WBC	1977–78
Mate Parlov WBC	1978
Mike Rossman* WBA	1978–79
Victor Galindez* WBA	1979
Marvin Johnson* WBC	1978–79
M.S. Muhammad* WBC	1979–81
Marvin Johnson WBA	1979–80
E.M. Muhammad* WBA	1980–81
Michael Spinks* WBA	1981–83
Dwight Qawi WBC	1981–83
Michael Spinks*	1983–85†
J. B. Williamson WBC	1985–86
Slobodan Kacar IBF	1985–86
Marvin Johnson* WBA	1986–87
Dennis Andries WBC	1986–87
Bobby Czyz IBF	1986–87
Leslie Stewart WBA	1987
Virgil Hill* WBA	1987–91
Pr Charles Williams IBF	1987–93
Thomas Hearns WBC	1987†

Champion	Reign
Donny Lalonde WBC	1987–88
Sugar Ray Leonard WBC	1988
Dennis Andries WBC	1989
Jeff Harding WBC	1989–90
Dennis Andries WBC	1990–91
Thomas Hearns* WBA	1991–92
Jeff Harding WBC	1991–94
Iran Barkley* WBA	1992
Virgil Hill* WBA	1992–97
Henry Maske IBF	1993–96
Mike McCallum WBC	1994–95
Fabrice Tiozzo WBC	1995–96
D. Michalczewski* IBF	1997†
Roy Jones Jr. WBC, WBA	1997–03
William Guthrie IBF	1997–98
Reggie Johnson IBF	1998–99
Roy Jones Jr.*	1999–03
Bruno Girard WBA	2001–03
Mehdi Sahnoune WBA	2003
Silvio Branco WBA	2003–
Antonio Tarver WBC, IBF	2003
Roy Jones Jr. WBC	...,..2003
Glencoffe Johnson IBF	2004–
Fabrice Tiozzo WBA	2004–
Antonio Tarver* WBC	2004–

Super Middleweights
(Weight Limit: 168 pounds)

Champion	Reign
Murray Sutherland* IBF	1984
Chong-Pal Park* IBF	1984–87
Chong-Pal Park* WBA	1987–88
G. Rocchigiani IBF	1988–89
F. Obelmejias* WBA	1988–89
Sugar Ray Leonard WBC	1988–90†
In-Chul Baek* WBA	1989–90
Lindell Holmes IBF	1990–91
Chris Tiozzo* WBA	1990–91
Mauro Galvano WBC	1990–92
Victor Cordova* WBA	1991
Darrin Van Horn IBF	1991–92
Iran Barkley IBF	1992

Champion	Reign
Nigel Benn WBC	1992–96
James Toney IBF	1992–94
Michael Nunn* WBA	1992–94
Steve Little* WBA	1994
Frank Liles* WBA	1994–99
Roy Jones Jr. IBF	1994–96
Thulane Malinga WBC	1996
V. Nardiello WBC	1996
Robin Reid WBC	1996–97
Charles Brewer IBF	1997–98
Thulane Malinga WBC	1997–98
Richie Woodhall WBC	1998–99
Sven Ottke IBF	1998–03

Champion	Reign
Byron Mitchell* WBA	1999–00
Markus Beyer WBC	1999–00
Bruno Girard* WBA	2000–01†
Glenn Catley WBC	2000–01
Eric Lucas WBC	2000–03
Byron Mitchell WBA	2000–03
Sven Ottke WBA	2003†
Anthony Mundine WBA	2003
Markus Beyer WBC	2003
Sven Ottke, IBF	2003–
Cristian Sanavia WBC	2004–
Manny Siaca, WBA	2004–

*Lineal champion. †Champion retired or relinquished title.

Middleweights
(Weight Limit: 160 pounds)

Champion	Reign	Champion	Reign	Champion	Reign
Jack Dempsey*	1884–91	Jake La Motta*	1949–51	Sugar Ray Leonard*	1987†
Bob Fitzsimmons*	1891–97†	Sugar Ray Robinson*	1951	Frank Tate IBF	1987–88
Kid McCoy	1897–98	Randy Turpin*	1951	Sumbu Kalambay WBA	1987–89
Tommy Ryan*	1898–07†	Sugar Ray Robinson*	1951–52†	Thomas Hearns* WBC	1987–88
Stanley Ketchel*	1908	Bobo Olson*	1953–55	Iran Barkley* WBC	1988–89
Billy Papke*	1908	Sugar Ray Robinson*	1955–57	Michael Nunn IBF	1988–91
Stanley Ketchel*	1908–10†	Gene Fullmer*	1957	Roberto Duran* WBC	1989–90†
Frank Klaus*	1913	Sugar Ray Robinson*	1957	Michael Nunn* IBF	1991
George Chip*	1913–14	Carmen Basilio*	1957–58	Mike McCallum WBA	1989–91
Al McCoy*	1914–17	Sugar Ray Robinson*	1958–60	Julian Jackson WBC	1990–93
Mike O'Dowd*	1917–20	Gene Fullmer NBA	1959–62	James Toney* IBF	1991–93†
Johnny Wilson*	1920–23	Paul Pender*	1960–61	Reggie Johnson WBA	1992–94
Harry Greb*	1923–26	Terry Downes*	1961–62	Roy Jones Jr.* IBF	1993–95†
Tiger Flowers*	1926	Paul Pender*	1962–63†	G. McClellan WBC	1993–95†
Mickey Walker*	1926–31†	Dick Tiger WBA	1962–63	Jorge Castro WBA	1994–95
Gorilla Jones*	1931–32	Dick Tiger*	1963	Shinji Takehara WBA	1995–96
Marcel Thil*	1932–37	Joey Giardello*	1963–65	Jullian Jackson WBC	1995
Fred Apostoli*	1937–39	Dick Tiger*	1965–66	Quincy Taylor WBC	1995–96
Al Hostak NBA	1938	Emile Griffith*	1966–67	Bernard Hopkins* IBF	1994–
Solly Krieger NBA	1938–39	Nino Benvenuti*	1967	Keith Holmes WBC	1996–98
Al Hostak NBA	1939–40	Emile Griffith*	1967–68	William Joppy WBA	1996–97
Ceferino Garcia*	1939–40	Nino Benvenuti*	1968–70	J.C. Green WBA	1997
Ken Overlin*	1940–41	Carlos Monzon*	1970–77†	William Joppy WBA	1998–01
Tony Zale NBA	1940–41	Rodrigo Valdez WBC	1974–76	Hassine Cherifi WBC	1998–99
Billy Soose*	1941	Rodrigo Valdez*	1977–78	Keith Holmes WBC	1999–00
Tony Zale*	1941–47	Hugo Corro*	1978–79	Felix Trinidad WBA	2001
Rocky Graziano*	1947–48	Vito Antuofermo*	1979–80	Bernard Hopkins*	2001–
Tony Zale*	1948	Alan Minter*	1980	William Joppy WBA	2001–03
Marcel Cerdan*	1948–49	Marvin Hagler*	1980–87		

Junior Middleweights
(Weight Limit: 154 pounds)

Champion	Reign	Champion	Reign	Champion	Reign
Emile Griffith (EBU)	1962–63	Tadashi Mihara WBA	1981–82	Luis Santana* WBC	1995–95
Dennis Moyer*	1962–63	Davey Moore WBA	1982–83	Vincent Pettway IBF	1994–95
Ralph Dupas*	1963	Thomas Hearns* WBC	1982–84	Paul Vaden IBF	1995
Sandro Mazzinghi*	1963–65	Roberto Duran WBA	1983–84	Carl Daniels WBA	1995
Nino Benvenuti*	1965–66	Mark Medal IBF	1984	Terry Norris* WBC	1995–97
Ki-Soo Kim*	1966–68	Thomas Hearns*	1984–86†	Terry Norris* IBF	1995–96†
Sandro Mazzinghi*	1968	Mike McCallum* WBA	1984–87†	L. Boudouani WBA	1996–99
Freddie Little*	1969–70	Carlos Santos IBF	1984–86	Raul Marquez IBF	1997
Carmelo Bossi*	1970–71	Buster Drayton IBF	1986–87	Keith Mullings* WBC	1997–99
Koichi Wajima*	1971–74	Duane Thomas WBC	1986–87	Yori Boy Campas IBF	1997–98
Oscar Albarado*	1974–75	Matthew Hilton IBF	1987–88	Fernando Vargas IBF	1998–00
Koichi Wajima*	1975	Lupe Aquino WBC	1987	F. Javier Castillejo* WBC	1999–01
Miguel de Oliveira WBC	1975–76	Gianfranco Rosi WBC	1987–88	David Reid WBA	1999–00
Jae-Do Yuh*	1975–76	Julian Jackson WBA	1987–90	Felix Trinidad WBA	2000–01
Elisha Obed WBC	1975–76	Donald Curry WBC	1988–89	Felix Trinidad WBA	2001†
Koichi Wajima*	1976	Robert Hines IBF	1988–89	Oscar De La Hoya*	
Jose Duran*	1976	Darrin Van Horn IBF	1989	WBC	2001–03
Eckhard Dagge WBC	1976–77	Rene Jacquot WBC	1989	Fernando Vargas WBA	2001–02
Miguel Angel Castellini*	1976–77	John Mugabi* WBC	1989–90	Ronald Wright IBF†	2001–04
Eddie Gazo*	1977–78	Gianfranco Rosi IBF	1989–94	Oscar De La Hoya*	
Rocky Mattioli WBC	1977–79	Terry Norris* WBC	1990–93	WBC/WBA	2002–03
Masashi Kudo*	1978–79	Gilbert Dele WBA	1991	Shane Mosley* WBC	2003–04
Maurice Hope WBC	1979–81	Vinny Pazienza WBA	1991–92	Alejandro Garcia WBA	2003–
Ayub Kalule*	1979–81	Julio C. Vasquez WBA	1992–95	Ronald Wright WBA,	
Wilfred Benitez WBC	1981–82	Simon Brown* WBC	1993–94	WBC	2004–
Sugar Ray Leonard*	1981–82†	Terry Norris* WBC	1994	Verno Phillips IBF	2004–

*Lineal champion.
†Champion relinquished title to retire or switch weight classes, or had title stripped by boxing organization.

Welterweights
(Weight Limit: 147 pounds)

Champion	Reign
Paddy Duffy*	1888–90†
Mysterious Billy Smith*	1892–94
Tommy Ryan*	1894–98†
Mysterious Billy Smith*	1898–1900
Rube Ferns*	1900
Matty Matthews*	1900–01
Rube Ferns*	1901
Joe Walcott*	1901–04
The Dixie Kid*	1904–05†
Honey Mellody*	1906–07
Mike Sullivan*	1907–08†
Jimmy Gardner*	1908†
Jimmy Clabby*	1910–1†
Waldemar Holberg*	1914
Tom McCormick*	1914
Matt Wells*	1914–15
Mike Glover*	1915
Jack Britton*	1915
Ted "Kid" Lewis*	1915–16
Jack Britton*	1916–17
Ted "Kid" Lewis*	1917–19
Jack Britton*	1919–22
Mickey Walker*	1922–26
Pete Latzo*	1926–27
Joe Dundee*	1927–29
Jackie Fields*	1929–30
Young Jack Thompson*	1930
Tommy Freeman*	1930–31
Young Jack Thompson*	1931
Lou Brouillard*	1931–32
Jackie Fields*	1932–33
Young Corbett III*	1933
Jimmy McLarnin*	1933–34
Barney Ross*	1934
Jimmy McLarnin*	1934–35

Champion	Reign
Barney Ross*	1935–38
Henry Armstrong*	1938–40
Fritzie Zivic*	1940–41
Red Cochrane*	1941–46
Marty Servo*	1946
Sugar Ray Robinson*	1946–51†
Johnny Bratton	1951
Kid Gavilan*	1951–54
Johnny Saxton*	1954–55
Tony DeMarco*	1955
Carmen Basilio*	1955–56
Johnny Saxton*	1956
Carmen Basilio*	1956–57†
Virgil Akins*	1958
Don Jordan*	1958–60
Kid Paret*	1960–61
Emile Griffith*	1961
Kid Paret*	1961–62
Emile Griffith*	1962–63
Luis Rodriguez*	1963
Emile Griffith*	1963–66†
Curtis Cokes*	1966–69
Jose Napoles*	1969–70
Billy Backus*	1970–71
Jose Napoles*	1971–75
Hedgemon Lewis NY	1972–73
Angel Espada WBA	1975–76
John H. Stracey*	1975–76
Carlos Palomino*	1976–79
Pipino Cuevas WBA	1976–80
Wilfredo Benitez*	1979
Sugar Ray Leonard*	1979–80
Roberto Duran*	1980
Thomas Hearns WBA	1980–81
Sugar Ray Leonard*	1980–82†

Champion	Reign
Donald Curry* WBA	1983–85
Milton McCrory WBC	1983–85
Donald Curry*	1985–86
Lloyd Honeyghan*	1986–87
Jorge Vaca* WBC	1987–88
Lloyd Honeyghan* WBC	1988–89
Mark Breland WBA	1987
Marlon Starling WBA	1987–88
Tomas Molinares WBA	1988–89
Simon Brown IBF	1988–91
Mark Breland WBA	1989–90
Marlon Starling* WBC	1989–90
Aaron Davis WBA	1990–91
Maurice Blocker* WBC	1990–91
Meldrick Taylor WBA	1991–92
Simon Brown* WBC	1991
Buddy McGirt* WBC	1991–93
Felix Trinidad IBF	1993–00
Pernell Whitaker* WBC	1993–97
Crisanto Espana WBA	1992–94
Ike Quartey WBA	1994–97†
Oscar De La Hoya* WBC	1997–99
James Page WBA	1998–01
Felix Trinidad* IBF, WBC	1999–00†
Shane Mosley* WBC	2000–02
Andrew Lewis WBA	2001–02
Vernon Forrest IBF	2001
Vernon Forrest* WBC	2001–03
Ricardo Mayorga WBA	2002
Ricardo Mayroga* WBC	2003–
Michele Piccirillo IBF	2002–03
Jose Rivera WBA	2003
Cory Spinks IBF, WBC, WBA	2003–

Junior Welterweights
(Weight Limit: 140 pounds)

Champion	Reign
Pinkey Mitchell*	1922–25
Red Herring	1925
Mushy Callahan*	1926–30
Jack (Kid) Berg*	1930–31
Tony Canzoneri*	1931–32
Johnny Jadick*	1932–33
Sammy Fuller	1932–33
Battling Shaw*	1933
Tony Canzoneri*	1933
Barney Ross*	1933–35†
Tippy Larkin*	1946
Carlos Ortiz*	1959–60
Duilio Loi*	1960–62
Eddie Perkins*	1962
Duilio Loi*	1962–63†
Roberto Cruz WBA	1963
Eddie Perkins*	1963–65
Carlos Hernandez*	1965–66
Sandro Lopopolo*	1966–67
Paul Fujii*	1967–68
Nicolino Loche*	1968–72
Pedro Adigue WBC	1968–70
Bruno Arcari WBC	1970–74
Alfonso Frazer*	1972
Antonio Cervantes*	1972–76
Perico Fernandez WBC	1974–75
S. Muangsurin WBC	1975–76
Wilfred Benitez*	1976–79†

Champion	Reign
M. Velasquez WBC	1976
S. Muangsurin WBC	1976–78
A. Cervantes WBA	1977–80
Sang-Hyun Kim WBC	1978–80
Saoul Mamby WBC	1980–82
Aaron Pryor* WBA	1980–83
Leroy Haley WBC	1982–83
Aaron Pryor* IBF	1983–85†
Bruce Curry WBC	1983–84
Johnny Bumphus WBA	1984
Bill Costello WBC	1984–85
Gene Hatcher WBA	1984–85
Ubaldo Sacco WBA	1985–86
Lonnie Smith* WBC	1985–86
Patrizio Oliva WBA	1986–87
Gary Hinton IBF	1986
Rene Arredondo* WBC	1986
Tsuyoshi Hamada WBC	1986–87
Joe Louis Manley IBF	1986–87
Terry Marsh IBF	1987
Juan Coggi WBA	1987–90
Rene Arredondo WBC	1987
R. Mayweather* WBC	1987–89
James McGirt IBF	1988
Meldrick Taylor IBF	1988–90
Julio César Chávez* WBC	1989–94
Julio César Chávez* IBF	1990–91
Loreto Garza WBA	1990–91

Champion	Reign
Juan Coggi WBA	1991
Edwin Rosario WBA	1991–92
Rafael Pineda IBF	1991–92
Akinobu Hiranaka WBA	1992
Pernell Whitaker IBF	1992–93†
Charles Murray IBF	1993–94
Jake Rodriguez IBF	1994–95
Juan Coggi WBA	1993–94
Frankie Randall* WBC	1994
Frankie Randall WBA	1994–96
Juan Coggi WBA	1996
Julio César Chávez* WBC	1994–96
Kostya Tszyu IBF	1995–97
Frankie Randall WBA	1996–97
Oscar De La Hoya* WBC	1996–97†
Khalid Rahilou WBA	1997–98
Vincent Phillips* IBF	1997–99
Sharmba Mitchell WBA	1998–01
Kostya Tszyu WBC	1998–
Terronn Millett* IBF	1999–00
Zab Judah* IBF	2000–01
Kostya Tszyu*† WBA/WBC	2001–03
Kostya Tszyu*	2001–
Kostya Tszyu* IBF	2003–
Vivian Harris WBA	2003–
Arturo Gatti WBC	2004–

Lightweights
(Weight Limit: 135 pounds)

Champion	Reign
Jack McAuliffe*	1886–94†
Kid Lavigne*	1896–99
Frank Erne*	1899–1902
Joe Gans*	1902–04
Jimmy Britt*	1904–05
Battling Nelson*	1905–06
Joe Gans*	1906–08
Battling Nelson*	1908–10
Ad Wolgast*	1910–12
Willie Ritchie*	1912–14
Freddie Welsh*	1915–17
Benny Leonard*	1917–25†
Jimmy Goodrich*	1925
Rocky Kansas*	1925–26
Sammy Mandell*	1926–30
Al Singer*	1930
Tony Canzoneri*	1930–33
Barney Ross*	1933–35†
Tony Canzoneri*	1935–36
Lou Ambers*	1936–38
Henry Armstrong*	1938–39
Lou Ambers*	1939–40
Sammy Angott* NBA	1940–41
Lew Jenkins*	1940–41
Sammy Angott*	1941–42†
Beau Jack* NY	1942–43
Bob Montgomery* NY	1943
Sammy Angott NBA	1943–44
Beau Jack* NY	1943–44
Bob Montgomery* NY	1944–47
Juan Zurita NBA	1944–45
Ike Williams*	1947–51
James Carter*	1951–52
Lauro Salas*	1952
James Carter*	1952–54
Paddy DeMarco*	1954
James Carter*	1954–55
Wallace Smith*	1955–56

Champion	Reign
Joe Brown*	1956–62
Carlos Ortiz*	1962–65
Ismael Laguna*	1965
Carlos Ortiz*	1965–68
Carlos Teo Cruz*	1968–69
Mando Ramos*	1969–70
Ismael Laguna*	1970
Ken Buchanan*	1970–72
Roberto Duran*	1972–79†
Chango Carmona WBC	1972
Rodolfo Gonzalez WBC	1972–74
Ishimatsu Suzuki WBC	1974–76
Estaban DeJesus WBC	1976–78
Jim Watt WBC*	1979–81
Ernesto Espana WBA	1979–80
Hilmer Kenty WBA	1980–81
Sean O'Grady WBA	1981
Claude Noel WBA	1981
Alexis Arguello* WBC	1981–82†
Arturo Frias WBA	1981–82
Ray Mancini* WBA	1982–84
Alexis Arguello	1982–83
Edwin Rosario WBC	1983–84
Choo Choo Brown IBF	1984
L. Bramble* WBA	1984–86
Jose Luis Ramirez WBC	1984–85
Harry Arroyo IBF	1984–85
Jimmy Paul IBF	1985–86
Hector Camacho WBC	1985–86
Greg Haugen IBF	1986–87
Edwin Rosario* WBA	1986–87
Julio César Chávez* WBA	1987–88
Jose Luis Ramirez WBC	1987–88
Julio César Chávez*	1988–89†
Vinny Pazienza IBF	1987–88
Greg Haugen IBF	1988–89
P. Whitaker* WBC, IBF	1989–90

Champion	Reign
Edwin Rosario WBA	1989–90
Juan Nazario WBA	1990
P. Whitaker* WBA, WBC	1990–92†
Pernell Whitaker* IBF	1991–92†
Julio César Chávez IBF	1990–91
Edwin Rosario WBA	1991–92
Julio César Chávez WBC	1990–92
Miguel Gonzalez WBC	1992–95
Joey Gamache WBA	1992–93
Dingaan Thobela WBA	1993
Fred Pendleton* IBF	1993–94
Orzubek Nazarov WBA	1993–98
Rafael Ruelas* IBF	1994–95
Oscar De La Hoya* IBF	1995†
Phillip Holiday IBF	1995–97
Jean B. Mendy* WBC	1996–97
Steve Johnston* WBC	1997–98
Shane Mosley IBF	1997–99†
Jean B. Mendy WBA	1998–99
Cesar Bazan* WBC	1998–99
Steve Johnston* WBC	1999–00
Julien Lorcy WBA	1999
Stefano Zoff WBA	1999
Paul Spadafora IBF	1999–03
Gilbert Serrano WBA	1999–00
T. Hatakeyama WBA	2000–01
Jose Luis Castillo* WBC	2000–02
Julien Lorcy WBA	2001
Raul Balbi WBA	2001
F. Mayweather* WBC	2002–03
Leonard Dorin WBA	2002–03
Javier Jauregui IBF	2003–04
Julio Diaz IBF	2004–
Lakva Sim WBA	2004
Juan Diaz WBA	2004–
Jose Luis Castillo WBC	2004–

Junior Lightweights
(Weight Limit: 130 pounds)

Champion	Reign
Johnny Dundee*	1921–23
Jack Bernstein*	1923
Johnny Dundee*	1923–24
Steve (Kid) Sullivan*	1924–25
Mike Ballerino*	1925
Tod Morgan*	1925–29
Benny Bass*	1929–31
Kid Chocolate*	1931–33
Frankie Klick*	1933–34†
Sandy Saddler*	1949–50†
Harold Gomes*	1959–60
Gabriel (Flash) Elorde*	1960–67
Yoshiaki Numata*	1967
Hiroshi Kobayashi*	1967–71
Rene Barrientos WBC	1969–70
Yoshiaki Numata WBC	1970–71
Alfredo Marcano*	1971–72
R. Arredondo WBC	1971–74
Ben Villaflor*	1972–73
Kuniaki Shibata*	1973
Ben Villaflor*	1973–76
Kuniaki Shibata WBC	1974–75
Alfredo Escalera WBC	1975–78
Samuel Serrano*	1976–80
Alexis Arguello WBC	1978–80

Champion	Reign
Yasutsune Uehara*	1980–81
Rafael Limon WBC	1980–81
C. Boza-Edwards WBC	1981
Samuel Serrano*	1981–83
R. Navarrete WBC	1981–82
Rafael Limon WBC	1982
Bobby Chacon WBC	1982–83
Roger Mayweather*	1983–84
Hector Camacho WBC	1983–84
Rocky Lockridge*	1984–85
Hwan-Kil Yuh IBF	1984–85
Julio César Chávez WBC	1984–87
Lester Ellis IBF	1985
Wilfredo Gomez*	1985–86
Barry Michael IBF	1985–87
Alfredo Layne* WBA	1986
Brian Mitchell* WBA	1986–91†
Rocky Lockridge IBF	1987–88
Azumah Nelson* WBC	1988–94
Tony Lopez IBF	1988–89
Juan Molina IBF	1989–90
Tony Lopez IBF	1990–91
Joey Gamache WBA	1991
Brian Mitchell IBF	1991

Champion	Reign
Genaro Hernandez WBA	1991–95
James Leija* WBC	1994
Juan Molina IBF	1991–95
Gabriel Ruelas* WBC	1994–95
Eddie Hopson IBF	1995
Tracy Patterson IBF	1995
Azumah Nelson* WBC	1995–97
Choi Yong-Soo WBA	1995–98
Arturo Gatti IBF	1995–98†
Genaro Hernandez* WBC	1997–98
Roberto Garcia IBF	1998–99
Floyd Mayweather* WBC	1998–01†
T. Hatakeyama WBA	1998–99
Lakva Sim WBA	1999
Diego Corrales IBF	1999–01
Jong Kwon Baek WBA	1999–00
Joel Casamayor WBA	2000–02
Steve Forbes IBF	2000–02†
Acelino Freitas* WBA	2002–04
Y. Nantchachai WBA	2002–
S. Singmanassak WBA	2002–03
Jesus Chavez WBC	2003–04
Carlos Hernandez IBF	2003–04
Erik Morales WBC/IBF	2004–

Featherweights
(Weight Limit: 126 pounds)

Champion	Reign
Torpedo Billy Murphy*	1890
Young Griffo*	1890–92†
George Dixon*	1892–97
Solly Smith*	1897–98
Dave Sullivan*	1898
George Dixon*	1898–1900
Terry McGovern*	1900–01
Young Corbett II*	1901–03†
Abe Attell*	1903–04
Tommy Sullivan*	1904–05†
Abe Attell*	1906–12
Johnny Kilbane*	1912–23
Eugene Criqui*	1923
Johnny Dundee*	1923–24†
"Kid" Kaplan*	1925–26†
Tony Canzoneri*	1927–28
Andre Routis*	1928–29
Battling Battalino*	1929–32†
Tommy Paul NBA	1932–33
Kid Chocolate NY	1932–33†
Freddie Miller NBA	1933–36
Mike Beloise NY	1936–37
Petey Sarron NBA	1936–37
Maurice Holtzer	1937–38
Henry Armstrong*	1937–38†
Joey Archibald* NY	1938–39
Leo Rodak NBA	1938–39
Joey Archibald	1939–40
Petey Scalzo NBA	1940–41
Harry Jeffra*	1940–41
Joey Archibald*	1941
Richie Lamos NBA	1941
Chalky Wright*	1941–42
Jackie Wilson NBA	1941–43
Willie Pep*	1942–48
Jackie Callura NBA	1943
Phil Terranova NBA	1943–44
Sal Bartolo NBA	1944–46

Champion	Reign
Sandy Saddler*	1948–49
Willie Pep*	1949–50
Sandy Saddler*	1950–57†
Kid Bassey*	1957–59
Davey Moore*	1959–63
Sugar Ramos*	1963–64
Vicente Saldivar*	1964–67†
Paul Rojas WBA	1968
Jose Legra WBC	1968–69
Shozo Saijyo WBA	1968–71
J. Famechon* WBC	1969–70
Vicente Saldivar* WBC	1970
Kuniaki Shibata* WBC	1970–72
Antonio Gomez WBA	1971–72
C. Sanchez* WBC	1972
Ernesto Marcel WBA	1972–74
Jose Legra* WBC	1972–73
Eder Jofre* WBC	1973–74†
Ruben Olivares WBA	1974
Bobby Chacon WBC	1974–75
Alexis Arguello* WBA	1974–76†
Ruben Olivares WBA	1975
Poison Kotey WBC	1975–76
Danny Lopez* WBC	1976–80
Rafael Ortega WBA	1977
Cecilio Lastra WBA	1977–78
Eusebio Pedroza* WBA	1978–85
S. Sanchez* WBC	1980–82†
Juan LaPorte WBC	1982–84
Wilfredo Gomez WBC	1984
Min-Keun Oh IBF	1984–85
Azumah Nelson WBC	1984–88
Barry McGuigan* WBA	1985–86
Ki Young Chung IBF	1985–86
Steve Cruz* WBA	1986–87
Antonio Rivera IBF	1986–88
A. Esparragoza* WBA	1987–91
Calvin Grove IBF	1988

Champion	Reign
Jorge Paez IBF	1988–91
Jeff Fenech WBC	1988–90†
Marcos Villasana WBC	1990–91
Paul Hodkinson WBC	1991–93
Troy Dorsey IBF	1991
Manuel Medina IBF	1991–93
Yung Kyun Park* WBA	1991–93
Gregorio Vargas WBC	1993
Tom Johnson IBF	1993–97†
Eloy Rojas* WBA	1993–96
Kevin Kelley WBC	1993–95
A. Gonzalez WBC	1995
Manuel Medina WBC	1995–95
Luisito Espinosa WBC	1995–99
Wilfredo Vazquez* WBA	1996–98
Hector Lizarraga IBF	1997–98
Naseem Hamed* WBA	1998†
Naseem Hamed*	1998–01
Freddy Norwood WBA	1998
Manuel Medina IBF	1998–99
Antonio Cermeno WBA	1998–99
Cesar Soto WBC	1999
Freddy Norwood WBA	1999–00
Naseem Hamed* WBC	1999†
Paul Ingle IBF	1999–00
Guty Espadas WBC	2000–01
Erik Morales WBC	2000–02
Derrick Gainer WBA	2000–03
Mbulelo Botile IBF	2001
Frankie Toledo IBF	2001
Manuel Medina IBF	2001–02
Marco A. Barrera*	2001–
Johnny Tapia IBF	2002
Marco A. Barrera* WBC	2002†
Erik Morales WBC	2002–03
Juan Marquez IBF, WBA	2003–
In Jin Chi WBC	2004–

Junior Featherweights
(Weight Limit: 122 pounds)

Champion	Reign
Jack (Kid) Wolfe*	1922–23
Carl Duane*	1923–24
Rigoberto Riasco* WBC	1976
R. Kobayashi* WBC	1976
Dong-Kyun Yum* WBC	1976–77
Wilfredo Gomez* WBC	1977–83†
Soo-Hwan Hong WBA	1977–78
Ricardo Cardona WBA	1978–80
Leo Randolph WBA	1980
Sergio Palma WBA	1980–82
Leonardo Cruz WBA	1982–84
Jaime Garza* WBC	1983
Bobby Berna IBF	1983–84
Loris Stecca WBA	1984
Seung-Il Suh IBF	1984–85
Victor Callejas WBA	1984–86
Juan Meza* WBC	1984–85
Ji-Won Kim IBF	1985–86
Lupe Pintor* WBC	1985–86
S. Payakaroon* WBC	1986–87

Champion	Reign
Seung-Hoon Lee IBF	1987–88
Louie Espinoza WBA	1987
Jeff Fenech* WBC	1987†
Julio Gervacio WBA	1987–88
Daniel Zaragoza* WBC	1988–90
Jose Sanabria IBF	1988–89
B. Pinango WBA	1988
J.J. Estrada WBA	1988–89
Fabrice Benichou IBF	1989–90
Jesus Salud WBA	1989–90
Welcome Ncita IBF	1990–92
Paul Banke* WBC	1990
Luis Mendoza WBA	1990–91
Raul Perez WBA	1992
Pedro Decima* WBC	1990–91
K. Hatanaka* WBC	1991
Daniel Zaragoza* WBC	1991–92
Thiery Jacob* WBC	1992
Tracy Patterson* WBC	1992–94
Kennedy McKinney IBF	1993–94

Champion	Reign
Wilfredo Vasquez WBA	1992–95
Vuyani Bungu IBF	1994–99†
H. Acero* Sanchez WBC	1994–95
Antonio Cermeno WBA	1995–98†
Daniel Zaragoza* WBC	1995–97
Erik Morales* WBC	1997–00†
Enrique Sanchez WBA	1998
Nestor Garza WBA	1998–00
Benedict Ledwaba IBF	1999–01
Clarence Adams WBA	2000–01†
Willie Jorrin WBC	2000–02
Manny Pacquiao IBF	2001–04
Yober Ortega WBA	2001–02
Y. Sithyodthong WBC	2002
Osamu Sato WBA	2002
Salim Medjkoune WBA	2002–03
Mahyar Monshipour WBA	2003–
Oscar Larios WBC	2002–
Israel Vazquez IBF	2004–

*Lineal champion.
†Champion relinquished title to retire or switch weight classes, or had title stripped by boxing organization.

Bantamweights
(Weight Limit: 118 pounds)

Champion	Reign	Champion	Reign	Champion	Reign
Spider Kelly	1887	Sixto Escobar*	1938–39†	Daniel Zaragoza WBC	1985
Hughey Boyle	1887–88	Georgie Pace NBA	1939–40	Miguel Lora WBC	1985–88
Spider Kelly	1889	Lou Salica*	1940–42	Gaby Canizales*	1986
Chappie Moran	1889–90	Manuel Ortiz*	1942–47	Bernardo Pinango*	1986–87†
George Dixon	1890–91	Harold Dade*	1947	W. Vasquez WBA	1987–88
Pedlar Palmer	1895–99	Manuel Ortiz*	1947–50	Kevin Seabrooks* IBF	1987–88
Terry McGovern*	1899–00†	Vic Toweel*	1950–52	Kaokor Galaxy WBA	1988
Harry Harris	1901	Jimmy Carruthers*	1952–54†	Moon Sung-Kil WBA	1988–89
Harry Forbes*	1901–03	Robert Cohen*	1954–56	Kaokor Galaxy WBA	1989
Frankie Neil*	1903–04	Paul Macias NBA	1955–57	Raul Perez WBC	1988–91
Joe Bowker*	1904–05†	Mario D'Agata*	1956–57	O. Canizales* IBF	1988–95†
Jimmy Walsh*	1905–06†	Alphonse Halimi*	1957–59	Luisito Espinosa WBA	1989–91
Owen Moran	1907–08	Joe Becerra*	1959–60†	Israel Contreras WBA	1991–92
Monte Attell	1909–10	Eder Jofre*	1961–65	Eddie Cook WBA	1992–93
Frankie Conley	1910–11	Fighting Harada*	1965–68	Greg Richardson WBC	1991
Johnny Coulon*	1910–14	Lionel Rose*	1968–69	J. Tatsuyoshi, WBC	1991–92
Kid Williams*	1914–17	Ruben Olivares*	1969–70	Victor Rabanales WBC	1992–93
Kewpie Ertle	1915	Chucho Castillo*	1970–71	Jung-Il Byun WBC	1993
Pete Herman*	1917–20	Ruben Olivares*	1971–72	Jorge Julio WBA	1993
Joe Lynch*	1920–21	Rafael Herrera*	1972	Yasuei Yakushiji WBC	1993–95
Pete Herman*	1921	Enrique Pinder*	1972–73	Junior Jones WBA	1994
Johnny Buff*	1921–22	Romeo Anaya*	1973	John M. Johnson WBA	1994
Joe Lynch*	1922–24	Arnold Taylor*	1973–74	D. Chuvatana WBA	1994–95
Abe Goldstein*	1924	Rafael Herrera WBC	1973–74	V. Sahaprom* WBA	1995–96
Cannonball Martin*	1924–25	Soo-Hwan Hong*	1974–75	W. McCullough WBC	1995–96
Phil Rosenberg*	1925–27†	Rodolfo Martinez WBC	1974–76	Harold Mestre IBF	1995
Bud Taylor NBA	1927–28	Alfonso Zamora*	1975–77	Mbulelo Botile IBF	1995–97
Bushy Graham NY	1928–29	Carlos Zarate* WBC	1976–79	Nana Konadu* WBA	1996–98
Panama Al Brown*	1929–35	Jorge Lujan	1977–80	S. Singmanassak WBC	1996–97
Sixto Escobar NBA	1934–35	Lupe Pintor* WBC	1979–83†	Tim Austin IBF	1997–03
Baltazar Sangchilli*	1935–36	Julian Solis	1980	J.Tatsuyoshi WBC	1997–98
Lou Salica NBA	1935	Jeff Chandler*	1980–84	Johnny Tapia* WBA	1998–99
Sixto Escobar NBA	1935–36	Albert Davila WBC	1983–85	V. Sahaprom* WBC	1998–
Tony Marino*	1936	Richard Sandoval*	1984–86	Paulie Ayala* WBA	1999–01†
Sixto Escobar*	1936–37	Satoshi Shingaki IBF	1984–85	Eidy Moya WBA	2001–02
Harry Jeffra*	1937–38	Jeff Fenech IBF	1985	Johnny Bredahl WBA	2002–
				Rafael Marquez IBF	2003–

Junior Bantamweights
(Weight Limit: 115 pounds)

Champion	Reign	Champion	Reign	Champion	Reign
Rafael Orono* WBC	1980–81	Ellyas Pical IBF	1987–89	Gerry Penalosa* WBC	1997–98
Chul-Ho Kim* WBC	1981–82	Giberto Roman* WBC	1988–89	Johnny Tapia IBF	1997–99†
Gustavo Ballas WBA	1981	Juan Polo Perez IBF	1989–90	Satoshi Iida WBA	1997–98
Rafael Pedroza WBA	1981–82	Nana Konadu* WBC	1989–90	In-Joo Cho* WBC	1998–00
Jiro Watanabe WBA	1982–84	Sung-Kil Moon* WBC	1990–93	Jesus Rojas WBA	1998–99
Rafael Orono* WBC	1982–83	Robert Quiroga IBF	1990–93	Mark Johnson IBF	1999–00
Payao Poontarat* WBC	1983–84	Julio Borboa IBF	1993–94	Hideki Todaka WBA	1999–00
Joo-Do Chun IBF	1983–85	Katsuya Onizuka WBA	1993–94	Felix Machado IBF	2000–03
Jiro Watanabe*	1984–86	Lee Hyung-Chul WBA	1994–95	M. Tokuyama* WBC	2000–04
Kaosai Galaxy WBA	1984	Jose Luis Bueno* WBC	1993–94	Leo Gamez WBA	2000–01
Ellyas Pica IBF	1985–86	H. Kawashima* WBC	1994–97	Celes Kobayashi WBA	2001–02
Cesar Polanco IBF	1986	Harold Grey IBF	1994–95	Alexander Munoz WBA	2002–
Gilberto Roman* WBC	1986–87	Alimi Goitia WBA	1995–96	Luis Perez IBF	2003–
Ellyas Pical IBF	1986	Yokthai Sith-Oar WBA	1996–97	Katsushige	
Santos Laciar* WBC	1987	Carlos Salazar IBF	1995–96	Kawashima WBC	2004–
Tae-Il Chang IBF	1987	Harold Grey IBF	1996		
Sugar Rojas* WBC	1987–88	Danny Romero IBF	1996–97		

*Lineal champion.
†Champion relinquished title to retire or switch weight classes, or had title stripped by boxing organization.

Flyweights
(Weight Limit: 112 pounds)

Champion	Reign	Champion	Reign	Champion	Reign
Sid Smith*	1913	Chartchai Chionoi*	1970	Chong-Kwan Chung IBF	1985–86
Bill Ladbury*	1913–14	B. Chartvanchai WBA	1970	Bi-Won Chung IBF	1986
Percy Jones*	1914†	Masao Ohba WBA	1970–73	Hi-Sup Shin IBF	1986–87
Joe Symonds*	1914–16	Erbito Salavarria*	1970–73†	Dodie Penalosa IBF	1987
Jimmy Wilde*	1916–23	B. Gonzalez WBA	1972	Fidel Bassa WBA	1987–89
Pancho Villa*	1923–25†	V. Borkorsor WBC	1972–73†	Choi-Chang Ho IBF	1987–88
Fidel La Barba*	1925–27†	Venice Borkorsor*	1973†	Rolando Bohol IBF	1988
Frenchy Belanger* NBA	1927–28	Chartchai Chionoi WBA	1973–74	Yong-Kang Kim* WBC	1988–89
Izzy Schwartz NY	1927–29	B. Gonzalez* WBA	1973–74	Duke McKenzie IBF	1988–89
Frankie Genaro* NBA	1928–29	Shoji Oguma* WBC	1974–75	Sot Chitalada* WBC	1989–91
Spider Pladner* NBA	1929	S. Hanagata WBA	1974–75	Dave McAuley IBF	1989–92
Frankie Genaro* NBA	1929–31	Miguel Canto* WBC	1975–79	Jesus Rojas WBA	1989–90
Midget Wolgast NY	1930–35	Erbito Salavarria WBA	1975–76	Yul-Woo Lee WBA	1990
Young Perez* NBA	1931–32	Alfonso Lopez WBA	1976	L. Tamakuma WBA	1990–91
Jackie Brown* NBA	1932–35	G. Espadas WBA	1976–78	M. Kittikasem* WBC	1991–92
Benny Lynch*	1935–38†	B. Gonzalez WBA	1978–79	Yuri Arbachakov* WBC	1992–97
Small Montana NY	1935–37	Chan-Hee Park* WBC	1979–80	Yong Kang Kim WBA	1991–92
Peter Kane*	1938–43	Luis Ibarra WBA	1979–80	Rodolfo Blanco IBF	1992–93
Little Dado NY	1938–40	Tae-Shik Kim WBA	1980	P. Sithbangprachan IBF	1993–95
Jackie Paterson*	1943–48	Shoji Oguma* WBC	1980–81	David Griman WBA	1992–94
Rinty Monaghan*	1948–50†	Peter Mathebula WBA	1980–81	S.S. Ploenchit WBA	1994–96
Terry Allen*	1950	Santos Laciar WBA	1981	Francisco Tejedor IBF	1995
Dado Marino*	1950–52	Antonio Avelar* WBC	1981–82	Danny Romero IBF	1995–96
Yoshio Shirai*	1952–54	Luis Ibarra WBA	1981	Mark Johnson IBF	1996–99†
Pascual Perez*	1954–60	Juan Herrera WBA	1981–82	Jose Bonilla WBA	1996–98
Pone Kingpetch*	1960–62	P. Cardona* WBC	1982	Chatchai Sasakul* WBC	1997–98
Masahiko Harada*	1962–63	Santos Laciar WBA	1982–85	Hugo Soto WBA	1998–99
Pone Kingpetch*	1963	Freddie Castillo* WBC	1982	Manny Pacquiao* WBC	1998–99
Hiroyuki Ebihara*	1963–64	E. Mercedes* WBC	1982–83	Leo Gamez WBA	1999
Pone Kingpetch*	1964–65	Charlie Magri* WBC	1983	Irene Pacheco IBF	1999–
Salvatore Burrini*	1965–66	Frank Cedeno* WBC	1983–84	S. Pisnurachan WBA	1999–00
H. Accavallo WBA	1966–68	Soon-Chun Kwon IBF	1983–85	M. Sinsurat* WBC	1999–00
Walter McGowan*	1966	Koji Kobayashi* WBC	1984	Malcolm Tunacao* WBC	2000–01
Chartchai Chionoi*	1966–69	Gabriel Bernal* WBC	1984	Eric Morel WBA	2000–03
Efren Torres*	1969–70	Sot Chitalada* WBC	1984–88	P. Wonjongkam* WBC	2001–
Hiroyuki Ebihara WBA	1969	Hilario Zapate WBA	1985–87	Lorenzo Parra WBA	2003–
B. Villacampo WBA	1969–70				

Junior Flyweights
(Weight Limit: 108 pounds)

Champion	Reign	Champion	Reign	Champion	Reign
Franco Udella WBC	1975	Dodie Penalosa IBF	1983–86	H. Gonzalez* WBC, IBF	1994–95
Jaime Rios WBA	1975–76	Francisco Quiroz WBA	1984–85	Choi Hi-Yong WBA	1995–96
Luis Estaba* WBC	1975–78	Joey Olivo WBA	1985	S. Sor Jaturong WBC, IBF	1995–96
Juan Guzman WBA	1976	Myung-Woo Yuh* WBA	1985–91	Carlos Murillo WBA	1996
Yoko Gushiken WBA	1976–81	Jum-Hwan Choi IBF	1986–88	Keiji Yamaguchi WBA	1996
Freddy Castillo* WBC	1978	Tacy Macalos IBF	1988–89	Michael Carbajal IBF	1996–97
Sor Vorasingh* WBC	1978	German Torres WBC	1988–89	Saman Jaturong* WBC	1995–99
Sung-Jun Kim* WBC	1978–80	Yul-Woo Lee WBC	1989	Phichitchor Siriwat WBA	1996–00
Shigeo Nakajima* WBC	1980	M. Kittikasem IBF	1989–90	Mauricio Pastrana IBF	1997–98†
Hilario Zapata* WBC	1980–82	H. Gonzalez WBC	1989–90	Will Grigsby IBF	1998–99
Pedro Flores WBA	1981	Michael Carbajal IBF	1990–94	Ricardo Lopez IBF	1999–02
Hwan-Jin Kim WBA	1981	R. Pascua WBC	1990	Yo-Sam Choi* WBC	1999–02
Katsuo Tokashiki WBA	1981–83	M. C. Castro WBC	1991	Beibis Mendoza WBA	2000–01
Amado Urzua* WBC	1982	H. Gonzalez WBC	1991–93	Rosendo Alvarez WBA	2001–
Tadashi Tomori* WBC	1982	Hirokia Ioka* WBA	1991–92	Jorge Arce* WBC	2002–
Hilario Zapata* WBC	1982–83	Myung-Woo Yuh* WBA	1993†	Jose Burgos IBF	2003–
Jung-Koo Chang* WBC	1983–88†	Michael Carbajal* WBC	1993–94		
Lupe Madera WBA	1983–84	Leo Gamez WBA	1993–95		

Strawweights
(Weight Limit: 105 pounds)

Champion	Reign	Champion	Reign	Champion	Reign
Kyung-Yun Lee* IBF	1987	Manny Melchor IBF	1992	Keitaro Hoshino WBA	2000–01
Hiroki Ioka* WBC	1987–88	Hideyuki Ohashi WBA	1992–93	Chana Porpaoin WBA	2001
Leo Gamez WBA	1988–89	R.S. Voraphin IBF	1992–96	Roberto Leyva IBF	2001–02
S. Sithnaruepol IBF	1988–89	Chana Porpaoin WBA	1993–95	Yutaka Niida WBA	2001†
N. Kiatwanchai* WBC	1988–89	Rosendo Alvarez WBA	1995–98	Miguel Barrera IBF	2002–03
Bong-Jun Kim WBA	1989–91	R. Sor Vorapin IBF	1996–97	Edgar Cardenas IBF	2003
Nico Thomas IBF	1989	Zolani Petelo* IBF	1997–00†	Noel Arambulet WBA	2002–04
Eric Chavez IBF	1989–90	W. Chor Charoen WBC	1998–00	Daniel Reyes IBF	2003–
Jum-Hwan Choi* WBC	1989–90	R. Lopez* WBA, WBC	1998–99†	Eagle Akakura WBC	2004–
Hideyuki Ohashi* WBC	1990	Songkram Popaoin WBA	1999	Yukata Niida WBA	2004–
F. Lookmingwan IBF	1990–92	Noel Arambulet WBA	1999–00		
Ricardo Lopez* WBC	1990–98†	Jose Aguirre* WBC	2000–04		
Hi-Yong Choi WBA	1991–92	Joma Gamboa WBA	2000		

*Lineal champion.
†Champion relinquished title to retire or switch weight classes, or had title stripped by boxing organization.

Reality Rocky	Sylvester Stallone is hoping Americans still have a soft spot for unknown fighters who come out of nowhere for their one big shot. He's producing *The Contender*, a TV show that will search for a real-life Rocky Balboa and which NBC has bought for a staggering $2 million per episode. In addition to a nationwide search for a sweet scientist, the producers will manage the fighter and are planning to form a boxing federation to rival the WBO, the WBC and the IBF. "Sly will be the heart and soul of the show," said producer Mark Burnett, the mastermind behind *Survivor*.

Alltime Career Leaders

Total Bouts

ame	Years Active	Bouts	Name	Years Active	Bouts
Len Wickwar	1928–47	463	Maxie Rosenbloom	1923–39	299
Jack Britton	1905–30	350	Harry Greb	1913–26	298
Johnny Dundee	1910–32	333	Young Stribling	1921–33	286
Billy Bird	1920–48	318	Battling Levinsky	1910–29	282
George Marsden	1928–46	311	Ted (Kid) Lewis	1909–29	279

Note: Based on records in *The Ring Record Book* and *Boxing Encyclopedia*.

Most Knockouts

Name	Years Active	KOs	Name	Years Active	KOs
Archie Moore	1936–63	130	Sandy Saddler	1944–56	103
Young Stribling	1921–33	126	Sam Langford	1902–26	102
Billy Bird	1920–48	125	Henry Armstrong	1931–45	100
George Odwell	1930–45	114	Jimmy Wilde	1911–23	98
Sugar Ray Robinson	1940–65	110	Len Wickwar	1928–47	93

Note: Based on records in *The Ring Record Book* and *Boxing Encyclopedia*.

Riddick's Return

In August 2004, former heavyweight champ Riddick Bowe, 37, announced his intention to return to the ring, where he hadn't appeared competitively in nearly eight years. Bowe was released from prison in May 2004 after serving a 17-month sentence for abducting his first wife and their five children. In announcing his bout against 38-year-old journeyman Jeff Lally (23-23-1) at an Indian casino in Oklahoma, Bowe said, "I truly believe I'm the best fighter out there, especially when I get in good shape. The division is wide open, so why not?"

There's a host of reasons to be skeptical of a Bowe comeback, not the least of which is that he appeared neurologically shaky when he hung up his gloves in 1997. In his last two fights Bowe (40–1; his only loss was to Evander Holyfield) absorbed savage beatings from Andrew Golota, who lost both bouts because he was DQ'd for low blows. Bowe's speech was slurred in interviews afterward, and he was essentially browbeaten into retirement by his handlers. "His strength was diminished, his reflexes were diminished, and he was starting to get hit and dropped in training," said former manager Rock Newman. "I told him he had too much wealth to jeopardize his health."

Bowe made a reported $20 million in the ring and is financially sound. But in 1999, after his abduction conviction, his lawyers said his judgment was impaired by trauma sustained in the ring. Bowe now calls the brain-damage defense a ruse, a claim Newman disputed: "He was told he was impaired, but if he led a normal life it would repair itself." In late August, Bowe got a clean bill of health from neurologists hired by the Citizens Potawatomi Nation boxing commission, which is set to oversee his bout with Lally. The ex-champ—who lost 70 pounds in prison, bringing him to 255—said he wants to fight 15 times and contend for the title in 18 months. "If he got in the ring I'd root for him," said Newman. "But I'd be scared while I was cheering."

World Heavyweight Championship Fights

Date	Winner	Wgt	Loser	Wgt	Result	Site
Sept 7, 1892	James J. Corbett*	178	John L. Sullivan	212	KO 21	New Orleans
Jan 25, 1894	James J. Corbett*	184	Charley Mitchell	158	KO 3	Jacksonville
Mar 17, 1897	Bob Fitzsimmons*	167	James J. Corbett	183	KO 14	Carson City, NV
June 9, 1899	James J. Jeffries*	206	Bob Fitzsimmons	167	KO 11	Coney Island, NY
Nov 3, 1899	James J. Jeffries*	215	Tom Sharkey	183	Ref 25	Coney Island, NY
Apr 6, 1900	James J. Jeffries*	n/a	Jack Finnegan	n/a	KO 1	Detroit
May 11, 1900	James J. Jeffries*	218	James J. Corbett	188	KO 23	Coney Island, NY
Nov 15, 1901	James J. Jeffries*	211	Gus Ruhlin	194	TKO 6	San Francisco
July 25, 1902	James J. Jeffries*	219	Bob Fitzsimmons	172	KO 8	San Francisco
Aug 14, 1903	James J. Jeffries*	220	James J. Corbett	190	KO 10	San Francisco
Aug 25, 1904	James J. Jeffries*	219	Jack Munroe	186	TKO 2	San Francisco
July 3, 1905	Marvin Hart*	190	Jack Root	171	KO 12	Reno
Feb 23, 1906	Tommy Burns*	180	Marvin Hart	188	Ref 20	Los Angeles
Oct 2, 1906	Tommy Burns*	n/a	Jim Flynn	n/a	KO 15	Los Angeles
Nov 28, 1906	Tommy Burns*	172	Jack O'Brien	163½	Draw 20	Los Angeles
May 8, 1907	Tommy Burns*	180	Jack O'Brien	167	Ref 20	Los Angeles
Jul 4, 1907	Tommy Burns*	181	Bill Squires	180	KO 1	Colma, CA
Dec 2, 1907	Tommy Burns*	177	Gunner Moir	204	KO 10	London
Feb 10, 1908	Tommy Burns*	n/a	Jack Palmer	n/a	KO 4	London
Mar 17, 1908	Tommy Burns*	n/a	Jem Roche	n/a	KO 1	Dublin
Apr 18, 1908	Tommy Burns*	n/a	Jewey Smith	n/a	KO 5	Paris
June 13, 1908	Tommy Burns*	184	Bill Squires	183	KO 8	Paris
Aug 24, 1908	Tommy Burns*	181	Bill Squires	184	KO 13	Sydney
Sept 2, 1908	Tommy Burns*	183	Bill Lang	187	KO 6	Melbourne
Dec 26, 1908	Jack Johnson*	192	Tommy Burns	168	TKO 14	Sydney
Mar 10, 1909	Jack Johnson*	n/a	Victor McLaglen	n/a	ND 6	Vancouver
May 19, 1909	Jack Johnson*	205	Jack O'Brien	161	ND 6	Philadelphia
June 30, 1909	Jack Johnson*	207	Tony Ross	214	ND 6	Pittsburgh
Sept 9, 1909	Jack Johnson*	209	Al Kaufman	191	ND 10	San Francisco
Oct 16, 1909	Jack Johnson*	205½	Stanley Ketchel	170¼	KO 12	Colma, CA
July 4, 1910	Jack Johnson*	208	James J. Jeffries	227	KO 15	Reno
July 4, 1912	Jack Johnson*	195½	Jim Flynn	175	TKO 9	Las Vegas
Dec 19, 1913	Jack Johnson*	n/a	Jim Johnson	n/a	Draw 10	Paris
June 27, 1914	Jack Johnson*	221	Frank Moran	203	Ref 20	Paris
Apr 5, 1915	Jess Willard*	230	Jack Johnson	205½	KO 26	Havana
Mar 25, 1916	Jess Willard*	225	Frank Moran	203	ND 10	New York City
July 4, 1919	Jack Dempsey*	187	Jess Willard	245	TKO 4	Toledo, OH
Sept 6, 1920	Jack Dempsey*	185	Billy Miske	187	KO 3	Benton Harbor, MI
Dec 14, 1920	Jack Dempsey*	188¼	Bill Brennan	197	KO 12	New York City
July 2, 1921	Jack Dempsey*	188	Georges Carpentier	172	KO 4	Jersey City
July 4, 1923	Jack Dempsey*	188	Tommy Givvons	175½	Ref 15	Shelby, MT
Sept 14, 1923	Jack Dempsey*	192½	Luis Firpo	216½	KO 2	New York City
Sept 23, 1926	Gene Tunney*	189½	Jack Dempsey	190	UD 10	Philadelphia
Sept 22, 1927	Gene Tunney*	189½	Jack Dempsey	192½	UD 10	Chicago
July 26, 1928	Gene Tunney*	192	Tom Heeney	203½	TKO 11	New York City
June 12, 1930	Max Schmeling*	188	Jack Sharkey	197	DQ 4	New York City
July 3, 1931	Max Schmeling*	189	Young Stribling	186½	TKO 15	Cleveland
June 21, 1932	Jack Sharkey*	205	Max Schmeling	188	Split 15	Long Island City
June 29, 1933	Primo Carnera*	260½	Jack Sharkey	201	KO 6	Long Island City
Oct 22, 1933	Primo Carnera*	259½	Paulino Uzcudun	229¼	UD 15	Rome
Mar 1, 1934	Primo Carnera*	270	Tommy Loughran	184	UD 15	Miami
June 14, 1934	Max Baer*	209½	Primo Carnera	263¼	TKO 11	Long Island City
June 13, 1935	James J. Braddock*	193¾	Max Baer	209½	UD 15	Long Island City
June 22, 1937	Joe Louis*	197¼	James J. Braddock	197	KO 8	Chicago
Aug 30, 1937	Joe Louis*	197	Tommy Farr	204¼	UD 15	New York City
Feb 23, 1938	Joe Louis*	200	Nathan Mann	193½	KO 3	New York City
Apr 1, 1938	Joe Louis*	202½	Harry Thomas	196	KO 5	Chicago
June 22, 1938	Joe Louis*	198¾	Max Schmeling	193	KO 1	New York City
Jan 25, 1939	Joe Louis*	200¼	John Henry Lewis	180¾	KO 1	New York City
Apr 17, 1939	Joe Louis*	201¼	Jack Roper	204¾	KO 1	Los Angeles
June 28, 1939	Joe Louis*	200¾	Tony Galento	233¾	TKO 4	New York City
Sept 20, 1939	Joe Louis*	200	Bob Pastor	183	KO 11	Detroit
Feb 9, 1940	Joe Louis*	203	Arturo Godoy	202	Split 15	New York City
Mar 29, 1940	Joe Louis*	201½	Johnny Paychek	187½	KO 2	New York City
June 20, 1940	Joe Louis*	199	Arturo Godoy	201¼	TKO 8	New York City
Dec 16, 1940	Joe Louis*	202¼	Al McCoy	180¾	TKO 6	Boston
Jan 31, 1941	Joe Louis*	202½	Red Burman	188	KO 5	New York City

Date	Winner	Wgt	Loser	Wgt	Result	Site
Feb 17, 1941	Joe Louis*	203½	Gus Dorazio	193½	KO 2	Philadelphia
Mar 21, 1941	Joe Louis*	202	Abe Simon	254½	TKO 13	Detroit
Apr 8, 1941	Joe Louis*	203½	Tony Musto	199½	TKO 9	St Louis
May 23, 1941	Joe Louis*	201½	Buddy Baer	237½	DQ 7	Washington, D.C.
June 18, 1941	Joe Louis*	199½	Billy Conn	174	KO 13	New York City
Sept 29, 1941	Joe Louis*	202¼	Lou Nova	202½	TKO 6	New York City
Jan 9, 1942	Joe Louis*	206¾	Buddy Baer	250	KO 1	New York City
Mar 27, 1942	Joe Louis*	207½	Abe Simon	255½	KO 6	New York City
June 9, 1946	Joe Louis*	207	Billy Conn	187	KO 8	New York City
Sept 18, 1946	Joe Louis*	211	Tami Mauriello	198½	KO 1	New York City
Dec 5, 1947	Joe Louis*	211½	Jersey Joe Walcott	194½	Split 15	New York City
June 25, 1948	Joe Louis*	213½	Jersey Joe Walcott	194¾	KO 11	New York City
June 22, 1949	Ezzard Charles*	181¾	Jersey Joe Walcott	195½	UD 15	Chicago
Aug 10, 1949	Ezzard Charles*	180	Gus Lesnevich	182	TKO 8	New York City
Oct 14, 1949	Ezzard Charles*	182	Pat Valentino	188½	KO 8	San Francisco
Aug 15, 1950	Ezzard Charles*	183¼	Freddie Beshore	184½	TKO 14	Buffalo
Sept 27, 1950	Ezzard Charles*	184½	Joe Louis	218	UD 15	New York City
Dec 5, 1950	Ezzard Charles*	185	Nick Barone	178½	KO 11	Cincinnati
Jan 12, 1951	Ezzard Charles*	185	Lee Oma	193	TKO 10	New York City
Mar 7, 1951	Ezzard Charles*	186	Jersey Joe Walcott	193	UD 15	Detroit
May 30, 1951	Ezzard Charles*	182	Joey Maxim	181½	UD 15	Chicago
July 18, 1951	Jersey Joe Walcott*	194	Ezzard Charles	182	KO 7	Pittsburgh
June 5, 1952	Jersey Joe Walcott*	196	Ezzard Charles	191½	UD 15	Philadelphia
Sept 23, 1952	Rocky Marciano*	184	Jersey Joe Walcott	196	KO 13	Philadelphia
May 15, 1953	Rocky Marciano*	184½	Jersey Joe Walcott	197¾	KO 1	Chicago
Sept 24, 1953	Rocky Marciano*	185	Roland LaStarza	184¾	TKO 11	New York City
June 17, 1954	Rocky Marciano*	187½	Ezzard Charles	185½	UD 15	New York City
Sept 17, 1954	Rocky Marciano*	187	Ezzard Charles	192½	KO 8	New York City
May 16, 1955	Rocky Marciano*	189	Don Cockell	205	TKO 9	San Francisco
Sept 21, 1955	Rocky Marciano*	188¼	Archie Moore	188	KO 9	New York City
Nov 30, 1956	Floyd Patterson*	182¼	Archie Moore	187¾	KO 5	Chicago
July 29, 1957	Floyd Patterson*	184	Tommy Jackson	192½	TKO 10	New York City
Aug 22, 1957	Floyd Patterson*	187¼	Pete Rademacher	202	KO 6	Seattle
Aug 18, 1958	Floyd Patterson*	184½	Roy Harris	194	TKO 13	Los Angeles
May 1, 1959	Floyd Patterson*	182½	Brian London	206	KO 11	Indianapolis
June 26, 1959	Ingemar Johansson*	196	Floyd Patterson	182	TKO 3	New York City
June 20, 1960	Floyd Patterson*	190	Ingemar Johansson	194¾	KO 5	New York City
Mar 13, 1961	Floyd Patterson*	194¾	Ingemar Johansson	206½	KO 6	Miami Beach
Dec 4, 1961	Floyd Patterson*	188½	Tom McNeeley	197	KO 4	Toronto
Sept 25, 1962	Sonny Liston*	214	Floyd Patterson	189	KO 1	Chicago
July 22, 1963	Sonny Liston*	215	Floyd Patterson	194½	KO 1	Las Vegas
Feb 25, 1964	Cassius Clay*	210½	Sonny Liston	218	TKO 7	Miami Beach
Mar 5, 1965	Ernie Terrell	199	Eddie Machen	192	UD 15	Chicago
May 25, 1965	Muhammad Ali*	206	Sonny Liston	215¼	KO 1	Lewiston, ME
Nov 1, 1965	Ernie Terrell	206	George Chuvalo	209	UD 15	Toronto
Nov 22, 1965	Muhammad Ali*	210	Floyd Patterson	196¾	TKO 12	Las Vegas
Mar 29, 1966	Muhammad Ali*	214½	George Chuvalo	216	UD 15	Toronto
May 21, 1966	Muhammad Ali*	201½	Henry Cooper	188	TKO 6	London
June 28, 1966	Ernie Terrell	209½	Doug Jones	187½	UD 15	Houston
Aug 6, 1966	Muhammad Ali*	209½	Brian London	201½	KO 3	London
Sept 10, 1966	Muhammad Ali*	203½	Karl Mildenberger	194¼	TKO 12	Frankfurt
Nov 14, 1966	Muhammad Ali*	212¾	Cleveland Williams	210½	TKO 3	Houston
Feb 6, 1967	Muhammad Ali*	212¼	Ernie Terrell	212½	UD 15	Houston
Mar 22, 1967	Muhammad Ali*	211½	Zora Folley	202½	KO 7	New York City
Mar 4, 1968	Joe Frazier	204½	Buster Mathis	243½	TKO 11	New York City
Apr 27, 1968	Jimmy Ellis	197	Jerry Quarry	195	Maj 15	Oakland
June 24, 1968	Joe Frazier NY	203½	Manuel Ramos	208	TKO 2	New York City
Aug 14, 1968	Jimmy Ellis	198	Floyd Patterson	188	Ref 15	Stockholm
Dec 10, 1968	Joe Frazier NY	203	Oscar Bonavena	207	UD 15	Philadelphia
Apr 22, 1969	Joe Frazier NY	204½	Dave Zyglewicz	190½	KO 1	Houston
June 23, 1969	Joe Frazier NY	203½	Jerry Quarry	198½	TKO 8	New York City
Feb 16, 1970	Joe Frazier NY	205	Jimmy Ellis	201	TKO 5	New York City
Nov 18, 1970	Joe Frazier	209	Bob Foster	188	KO 2	Detroit
Mar 8, 1971	Joe Frazier*	205½	Muhammad Ali	215	UD 15	New York City
Jan 15, 1972	Joe Frazier*	215½	Terry Daniels	195	TKO 4	New Orleans
May 26, 1972	Joe Frazier*	217½	Ron Stander	218	TKO 5	Omaha
Jan 22, 1973	George Foreman*	217½	Joe Frazier	214	TKO 2	Kingston, Jam.

Date	Winner	Wgt	Loser	Wgt	Result	Site
Sept 1, 1973	George Foreman*	219½	Jose Roman	196½	KO 1	Tokyo
Mar 26, 1974	George Foreman*	224¼	Ken Norton	212¼	TKO 2	Caracas
Oct 30, 1974	Muhammad Ali*	216½	George Foreman	220	KO 8	Kinshasa, Zaire
Mar 24, 1975	Muhammad Ali*	223½	Chuck Wepner	225	TKO 15	Cleveland
May 16, 1975	Muhammad Ali*	224½	Ron Lyle	219	TKO 11	Las Vegas
July 1, 1975	Muhammad Ali*	224½	Joe Bugner	230	UD 15	Kuala Lumpur, Malay.
Oct 1, 1975	Muhammad Ali*	224½	Joe Frazier	215	TKO 15	Manila
Feb 20, 1976	Muhammad Ali*	226	Jean Pierre Coopman	206	KO 5	San Juan
Apr 30, 1976	Muhammad Ali*	230	Jimmy Young	209	UD 15	Landover, MD
May 24, 1976	Muhammad Ali*	230	Richard Dunn	206½	TKO 5	Munich
Sept 28, 1976	Muhammad Ali*	221	Ken Norton	217½	UD 15	New York City
May 16, 1977	Muhammad Ali*	221¼	Alfredo Evangelista	209¼	UD 15	Landover, MD
Sept 29, 1977	Muhammad Ali*	225	Earnie Shavers	211¼	UD 15	New York City
Feb 15, 1978	Leon Spinks*	197¼	Muhammad Ali	224¼	Split 15	Las Vegas
June 9, 1978	Larry Holmes	209	Ken Norton	220	Split 15	Las Vegas
Sept 15, 1978	Muhammad Ali*	221	Leon Spinks	201	UD 15	New Orleans
Nov 10, 1978	Larry Holmes*	214	Alfredo Evangelista	208¼	KO 7	Las Vegas
Mar 23, 1979	Larry Holmes*	214	Osvaldo Ocasio	207	TKO 7	Las Vegas
June 22, 1979	Larry Holmes*	215	Mike Weaver	202	TKO 12	New York City
Sept 28, 1979	Larry Holmes*	210	Earnie Shavers	211	TKO 11	Las Vegas
Oct 20, 1979	John Tate	240	Gerrie Coetzee	222	UD 15	Pretoria
Feb 3, 1980	Larry Holmes *	213½	Lorenzo Zanon	215	TKO 6	Las Vegas
Mar 31, 1980	Mike Weaver	232	John Tate	232	KO 15	Knoxville
Mar 31, 1980	Larry Holmes*	211	Leroy Jones	254½	TKO 8	Las Vegas
July 7, 1980	Larry Holmes*	214¼	Scott LeDoux	226	TKO 7	Minneapolis
Oct 2, 1980	Larry Holmes*	211¼	Muhammad Ali	217½	TKO 11	Las Vegas
Oct 25, 1980	Mike Weaver	210	Gerrie Coetzee	226½	KO 13	Sun City, S.A.
Apr 11, 1981	Larry Holmes*	215	Trevor Berbick	215½	UD 15	Las Vegas
June 12, 1981	Larry Holmes*	212¼	Leon Spinks	200¼	TKO 3	Detroit
Oct 3, 1981	Mike Weaver	215	James Quick Tillis	209	UD 15	Rosemont, IL
Nov 6, 1981	Larry Holmes*	213¼	Renaldo Snipes	215¾	TKO 11	Pittsburgh
June 11, 1982	Larry Holmes*	212½	Gerry Cooney	225½	TKO 13	Las Vegas
Nov 26, 1982	Larry Holmes*	217½	Tex Cobb	234¼	UD 15	Houston
Dec 10, 1982	Michael Dokes	216	Mike Weaver	209¾	TKO 1	Las Vegas
Mar 27, 1983	Larry Holmes*	221	Lucien Rodriguez	209	UD 12	Scranton, PA
May 20, 1983	Michael Dokes	223	Mike Weaver	218½	Draw 15	Las Vegas
May 20, 1983	Larry Holmes*	213	Tim Witherspoon	219½	Split 12	Las Vegas
Sept 10, 1983	Larry Holmes*	223	Scott Frank	211¼	TKO 5	Atlantic City
Sept 23, 1983	Gerrie Coetzee	215	Michael Dokes	217	KO 10	Richfield, OH
Nov 25, 1983	Larry Holmes*	219	Marvis Frazier	200	TKO 1	Las Vegas
Mar 9, 1984	Tim Witherspoon	220¼	Greg Page	239½	Maj 12	Las Vegas
Aug 31, 1984	Pinklon Thomas	216	Tim Witherspoon	217	Maj 12	Las Vegas
Nov 9, 1984	Larry Holmes* IBF	221½	James Smith	227	TKO 12	Las Vegas
Dec 1, 1984	Greg Page	236½	Gerrie Coetzee	218	KO 8	Sun City, S.A.
Mar 15, 1985	Larry Holmes*	223½	David Bey	233¼	TKO 10	Las Vegas
Apr 29, 1985	Tony Tubbs	229	Greg Page	239½	UD 15	Buffalo
May 20, 1985	Larry Holmes*	224¼	Carl Williams	215	UD 15	Las Vegas
June 15, 1985	Pinklon Thomas	220¼	Mike Weaver	221¼	KO 8	Las Vegas
Sept 21, 1985	Michael Spinks*	200	Larry Holmes	221½	UD 15	Las Vegas
Jan 17, 1986	Tim Witherspoon	227	Tony Tubbs	229	Maj 15	Atlanta
Mar 22, 1986	Trevor Berbick	218½	Pinklon Thomas	222¾	UD 15	Las Vegas
Apr 19, 1986	Michael Spinks*	205	Larry Holmes	223	Split 15	Las Vegas
July 19, 1986	Tim Witherspoon	234¾	Frank Bruno	228	TKO 11	Wembley, Eng.
Sept 6, 1986	Michael Spinks*	201	Steffen Tangstad	214¾	TKO 4	Las Vegas
Nov 22, 1986	Mike Tyson	221¼	Trevor Berbick	218½	TKO 2	Las Vegas
Dec 12, 1986	James Smith	228½	Tim Witherspoon	233½	TKO 1	New York City
Mar 7, 1987	Mike Tyson	219	James Smith	233	UD 12	Las Vegas
May 30, 1987	Mike Tyson	218¾	Pinklon Thomas	217¾	TKO 6	Las Vegas
May 30, 1987	Tony Tucker	222¼	Buster Douglas	227¼	TKO 10	Las Vegas
June 15, 1987	Michael Spinks*	208¾	Gerry Cooney	238	TKO 5	Atlantic City
Aug 1, 1987	Mike Tyson	221	Tony Tucker	221	UD 12	Las Vegas
Oct 16, 1987	Mike Tyson	216	Tyrell Biggs	228¾	TKO 7	Atlantic City
Jan 22, 1988	Mike Tyson	215¾	Larry Holmes	225¾	TKO 4	Atlantic City
Mar 20, 1988	Mike Tyson	216¼	Tony Tubbs	238¼	KO 2	Tokyo
June 27, 1988	Mike Tyson*	218¼	Michael Spinks	212¼	KO 1	Atlantic City
Feb 25, 1989	Mike Tyson*	218	Frank Bruno	228	TKO 5	Las Vegas
July 21, 1989	Mike Tyson*	219¼	Carl Williams	218	TKO 1	Atlantic City

Date	Winner	Wgt	Loser	Wgt	Result	Site
Feb 10, 1990	Buster Douglas*	231½	Mike Tyson	220½	KO 10	Tokyo
Oct 25, 1990	Evander Holyfield*	208	Buster Douglas	246	KO 3	Las Vegas
Apr 19, 1991	Evander Holyfield*	212	George Foreman	257	UD 12	Atlantic City
Nov 23, 1991	Evander Holyfield*	210	Bert Cooper	215	TKO 7	Atlanta
June 19, 1992	Evander Holyfield*	210	Larry Holmes	233	UD 12	Las Vegas
Nov 13, 1992	Riddick Bowe*	235	Evander Holyfield	205	UD 12	Las Vegas
Feb 6, 1993	Riddick Bowe*	243	Michael Dokes	244	KO 1	New York City
May 8, 1993	Lennox Lewis	235	Tony Tucker	235	UD 12	Las Vegas
May 22, 1993	Riddick Bowe*	244	Jesse Ferguson	224	KO 2	Washington, D.C.
Oct 2, 1993	Lennox Lewis	229	Frank Bruno	233	KO 7	London
Nov 6, 1993	Evander Holyfield*	217	Riddick Bowe	246	Split 12	Las Vegas
Apr 22, 1994	Michael Moorer*	214	Evander Holyfield	214	Split 12	Las Vegas
May 6, 1994	Lennox Lewis	235	Phil Jackson	218	TKO 8	Atlantic City
Nov 6, 1994	George Foreman*	250	Michael Moorer	222	KO 10	Las Vegas
Mar 11, 1995	Riddick Bowe	241	Herbie Hide	214	KO 6	Las Vegas
Apr 8, 1995	Oliver McCall	231	Larry Holmes	236	UD 12	Las Vegas
Apr 8, 1995	Bruce Seldon	236	Tony Tucker	243	TKO 7	Las Vegas
Apr 22, 1995	George Foreman*	256	Axel Schulz	221	Split 12	Las Vegas
Jun 17, 1995	Riddick Bowe	243	Jorge Luis Gonzalez	237	KO 6	Las Vegas
Aug 19, 1995	Bruce Seldon	234	Joe Hipp	233	TKO 10	Las Vegas
Sept 2, 1995	Frank Bruno	247¾	Oliver McCall	234¾	UD 12	London
Dec 9, 1995	Frans Botha	237	Axel Shulz	223	Split 12	Stuttgart
Mar 16, 1996	Mike Tyson	220	Frank Bruno	247	TKO 3	Las Vegas
June 22, 1996	Michael Moorer	222¼	Axel Shulz	222¾	Split 12	Dortmund, Ger.
Sept 7, 1996	Mike Tyson	219	Bruce Seldon	229	TKO 1	Las Vegas
Nov 3, 1996	George Foreman*	253	Crawford Grimsley		UD 12	Tokyo
Nov 9, 1996	Evander Holyfied	215	Mike Tyson	222	TKO 11	Las Vegas
Feb 7, 1997	Lennox Lewis	251	Oliver McCall	237	TKO 5	Las Vegas
Apr 26, 1997	George Foreman*	253	Lou Savarese		Split 12	Atlantic City
June 28, 1997	Evander Holyfied	218	Mike Tyson	218	DQ 4	Las Vegas
Oct 4, 1997	Lennox Lewis	244	Andrew Golota	244	TKO 1	Atlantic City
Nov 8, 1997	Evander Holyfied	214	Michael Moorer	223	TKO 8	Las Vegas
Nov 22, 1997	Shannon Briggs*		George Foreman		MD 12	Atlantic City
Mar 28, 1998	Lennox Lewis*	243	Shannon Briggs	228	TKO 5	Atlantic City
Mar 13, 1999	Evander Holyfield	215	Lennox Lewis*	246	Draw 12	New York City
Nov 13, 1999	Lennox Lewis*	242	Evander Holyfield	217	UD 12	Las Vegas
Apr 29, 2000	Lennox Lewis*	247	Michael Grant	250	KO 2	New York
July 15, 2000	Lennox Lewis*	250	Frans Botha	236	TKO 2	London
Aug 12, 2000	Evander Holyfield	221	John Ruiz	224	UD 12	Las Vegas
Nov 11, 2000	Lennox Lewis*	249	David Tua	245	UD 12	Las Vegas
Mar 3, 2001	John Ruiz	227	Evander Holyfield	217	UD 12	Las Vegas
Apr 22, 2001	Hasim Rahman*	238	Lennox Lewis	253½	KO 5	Brakpan, S Africa
Nov 17, 2001	Lennox Lewis*	246½	Hasim Rahman	236	KO 4	Las Vegas
Dec 15, 2001	John Ruiz	232	Evander Holyfield	219	Draw 12	Mashantucket, CT
June 8, 2002	Lennox Lewis*	249¼	Mike Tyson	234½	KO 8	Memphis, TN
July 27, 2002	John Ruiz	233	Kirk Johnson	238	DQ 10	Las Vegas
Dec 14, 2002	Chris Byrd	214	Evander Holyfield	220	UD 12	Atlantic City
Mar 1, 2003	Roy Jones Jr.	193	John Ruiz	226	UD 12	Las Vegas
June 21, 2003	Lennox Lewis*	256½	Vitali Klitschko	248	TKO 6	Los Angeles
Sept 20, 2003	Chris Byrd	211½	Fres Oquendo	224	UD 12	Uncasville, CT
April 17, 2004	Chris Byrd	210½	Andrew Golota	237½	Draw 12	New York City
April 17, 2004	John Ruiz	240	Fres Oquendo	225	TKO 11	New York City
April 24, 2004	Vitali Klitschko	245	Corrie Sanders	235	TKO 8	Los Angeles

*Lineal champion. KO=knockout; TKO=technical knockout; UD=unanimous decision; Split=split decision; Ref=referee's decision; MD=majority decision; DQ=disqualification; ND=no decision.

Year	Fighter	Year	Fighter	Year	Fighter
1928	Gene Tunney	1935	Barney Ross	1940	Billy Conn
1929	Tommy Loughran	1936	Joe Louis	1941	Joe Louis
1930	Max Schmeling	1937	Henry Armstrong	1942	Ray Robinson
1932	Jack Sharkey	1938	Joe Louis	1943	Fred Apostoli
1934	T. Canzoneri/B. Ross	1939	Joe Louis	1944	Beau Jack

Note: No award in 1933; no fight of the year named until 1945

Year	Fighter	Fight	Winner	Site
1945	Willie Pep	Rocky Graziano–Freddie Cochrane	Rocky Graziano	New York City
1946	Tony Zale	Tony Zale–Rocky Graziano	Tony Zale	New York City
1947	Gus Lesnevich	Rocky Graziano–Tony Zale	Rocky Graziano	Chicago
1948	Ike Williams	Marcel Cerdan–Tony Zale	Marcel Cerdan	Jersey City
1949	Ezzard Charles	Willie Pep–Sandy Saddler	Willie Pep	New York City
1950	Ezzard Charles	Jake LaMotta–Laurent Dauthuille	Jake LaMotta	Detroit
1951	Ray Robinson	Jersey Joe Walcott–Ezzard Charles	Jersey Joe Walcott	Pittsburgh
1952	Rocky Marciano	Rocky Marciano–Jersey Joe Walcott	Rocky Marciano	Philadelphia
1953	Carl Olson	Rocky Marciano–Roland LaStarza	Rocky Marciano	New York City
1954	Rocky Marciano	Rocky Marciano–Ezzard Charles	Rocky Marciano	New York City
1955	Rocky Marciano	Carmen Basilio–Tony DeMarco	Carmen Basilio	Boston
1956	Floyd Patterson	Carmen Basilio–Johnny Saxton	Carmen Basilio	Syracuse
1957	Carmen Basilio	Carmen Basilio–Ray Robinson	Carmen Basilio	New York City
1958	Ingemar Johansson	Ray Robinson–Carmen Basilio	Ray Robinson	Chicago
1959	Ingemar Johansson	Gene Fullmer–Carmen Basilio	Gene Fullmer	San Francisco
1960	Floyd Patterson	Floyd Patterson–Ingemar Johansson	Floyd Patterson	New York City
1961	Joe Brown	Joe Brown–Dave Charnley	Joe Brown	London
1962	Dick Tiger	Joey Giardello–Henry Hank	Joey Giardello	Philadelphia
1963	Cassius Clay	Cassius Clay–Doug Jones	Cassius Clay	New York City
1964	Emile Griffith	Cassius Clay–Sonny Liston	Cassius Clay	Miami Beach
1965	Dick Tiger	Floyd Patterson–George Chuvalo	Floyd Patterson	New York City
1966	No award	Jose Torres–Eddie Cotton	Jose Torres	Las Vegas
1967	Joe Frazier	Nino Benvenuti–Emile Griffith	Nino Benvenuti	New York City
1968	Nino Benvenuti	Dick Tiger–Frank DePaula	Dick Tiger	New York City
1969	Jose Napoles	Joe Frazier–Jerry Quarry	Joe Frazier	New York City
1970	Joe Frazier	Carlos Monzon–Nino Benvenuti	Carlos Monzon	Rome
1971	Joe Frazier	Joe Frazier–Muhammad Ali	Joe Frazier	New York City
1972	Muhammad Ali Carlos Monzon	Bob Foster–Chris Finnegan	Bob Foster	London
1973	George Foreman	George Foreman–Joe Frazier	George Foreman	Kingston, Jam.
1974	Muhammad Ali	Muhammad Ali–George Foreman	Muhammad Ali	Kinshasa, Zaire
1975	Muhammad Ali	Muhammad Ali–Joe Frazier	Muhammad Ali	Manila
1976	George Foreman	George Foreman–Ron Lyle	George Foreman	Las Vegas
1977	Carlos Zarate	Joe Young–George Foreman	Joe Young	San Juan
1978	Muhammad Ali	Leon Spinks–Muhammad Ali	Leon Spinks	Las Vegas
1979	Ray Leonard	Danny Lopez–Mike Ayala	Danny Lopez	San Antonio
1980	Thomas Hearns	Saad Muhammad–Yaqui Lopez	Saad Muhammad	McAfee, NJ
1981	Ray Leonard Salvador Sanchez	Ray Leonard–Tommy Hearns	Ray Leonard	Las Vegas
1982	Larry Holmes	Bobby Chacon–Rafael Limon	Bobby Chacon	Sacramento
1983	Marvin Hagler	Bobby Chacon–Cornelius Boza-Edwards	Bobby Chacon	Las Vegas
1984	Thomas Hearns	Jose Luis Ramirez–Edwin Rosario	Jose Luis Ramirez	San Juan
1985	Donald Curry Marvin Hagler	Marvin Hagler–Tommy Hearns	Marvin Hagler	Las Vegas
1986	Mike Tyson	Stevie Cruz–Barry McGuigan	Stevie Cruz	Las Vegas
1987	Evander Holyfield	Ray Leonard–Marvin Hagler	Ray Leonard	Las Vegas
1988	Mike Tyson	Tony Lopez–Rocky Lockridge	Tony Lopez	Inglewood, CA
1989	Pernell Whitaker	Roberto Duran–Iran Barkley	Roberto Duran	Atlantic City
1990	Julio César Chávez	Julio César Chávez–Meldrick Taylor	Julio César Chávez	Las Vegas
1991	James Toney	Robert Quiroga–Kid Akeem Anifowoshe	Robert Quiroga	San Antonio
1992	Riddick Bowe	Riddick Bowe–Evander Holyfield	Riddick Bowe	Las Vegas
1993	Michael Carbajal	Michael Carbajal–Humberto Gonzalez	Michael Carbajal	Las Vegas
1994	Roy Jones	Jorge Castro–John David Jackson	Jorge Castro	Monterrey, Mex.
1995	Oscar De La Hoya	Saman Sor Jaturong–Chiquita Gonzalez	Saman Sor Jaturong	Inglewood, CA
1996	Evander Holyfield	Evander Holyfield–Mike Tyson	Evander Holyfield	Las Vegas
1997	Evander Holyfield	Arturo Gatti–Gabriel Ruelas	Arturo Gatti	Atlantic City
1998	Floyd Mayweather	Ivan Robinson–Arturo Gatti	Ivan Robinson	Atlantic City
1999	Paulie Ayala	Paulie Ayala–Johnny Tapia	Paulie Ayala	Las Vegas
2000	Felix Trinidad	Erik Morales–Marco Antonio Barrera	Erik Morales	Las Vegas
2001	Bernard Hopkins	Micky Ward–Emanuel Burton	Micky Ward	Las Vegas
2002	Vernon Forrest	Micky Ward–Arturo Gatti	Micky Ward	Uncasville, CT
2003	James Toney	Micky Ward–Arturo Gatti	Arturo Gatti	Atlantic City

U.S. Olympic Gold Medalists

LIGHT FLYWEIGHT
1984 ....Paul Gonzales

FLYWEIGHT
1904 ....George Finnegan
1920 ....Frank Di Gennara
1024 ....Fidel LaBarba
1952 ....Nathan Brooks
1976 ....Leo Randolph
1984 ....Steve McCrory

BANTAMWEIGHT
1904 ....Oliver Kirk
1988 ....Kennedy McKinney

FEATHERWEIGHT
1904 ....Oliver Kirk
1924 ....John Fields
1984 ....Meldrick Taylor

LIGHTWEIGHT
1904 ....Harry Spanger
1920 ....Samuel Mosberg
1968 ....Ronald W. Harris
1976 ....Howard Davis
1984 ....Pernell Whitaker
1992 ....Oscar De La Hoya

LIGHT WELTERWEIGHT
1952 ....Charles Adkins
1972 ....Ray Seales
1976 ....Ray Leonard
1984 ....Jerry Page

WELTERWEIGHT
1904 ....Albert Young
1932 ....Edward Flynn
1984 ....Mark Breland

LIGHT MIDDLEWEIGHT
1960 ....Wilbert McClure
1984 ....Frank Tate
1996 ....David Reid

MIDDLEWEIGHT
1904 ....Charles Mayer
1932 ....Carmen Bath
1952 ....Floyd Patterson
1960 ....Edward Crook
1976 ....Michael Spinks

LIGHT HEAVYWEIGHT
1920 ....Eddie Eagan
1952 ....Norvel Lee
1956 ....James Boyd
1960 ....Cassius Clay
1976 ....Leon Spinks
1988 ....Andrew Maynard
2004 ....Andre Ward

HEAVYWEIGHT
1984 ....Henry Tillman
1988 ....Ray Mercer

SUPER HEAVYWEIGHT
1904 ....Samuel Berger
1952 ....H. Edward Sanders
1956 ....T. Peter
          Rademacher
1964 ....Joe Frazier
1968 ....George Foreman
1984 ....Tyrell Biggs

THEY SAID IT

*Don King, boxing promoter, on
learning that Top Rank, the
organization run by rival
Bob Arum, has been the subject
of a federal investigation:
"I always feel sorry for people who
are raided by the FBI."*

Lineal Heavyweight Champions

Champion	Reign	Age*	Career	W-L-D (KO)	Successful Defenses
John L. Sullivan	1885–92	26	1878–92	38-1-3 (33)	0
James J. Corbett	1892–97	26	1884–03	11-4-2 (7)	1
Bob Fitzsimmons	1897–99	33	1880–16	74-8-3 (67)	0
James J. Jeffries†	1899–05	24	1896–10	18-1-2 (15)	7
Marvin Hart	1905–06	28	1899–10	28-7-4 (19)	0
Tommy Burns	1906–08	24	1900–20	46-5-8 (37)	11
Jack Johnson	1908–15	30	1894–28	77-13-14 (48)	9
Jess Willard	1915–19	33	1911–23	23-6-1 (20)	1
Jack Dempsey	1919–26	24	1914–27	60-6-8 (50)	5
Gene Tunney†	1926–28	29	1915–28	61-1-1 (45)	2
Max Schmeling	1930–32	24	1924–48	56-10-4 (39)	1
Jack Sharkey	1932–33	29	1924–36	38-13-3 (14)	0
Primo Carnera	1933–34	26	1928–37	88-14-0 (69)	2
Max Baer	1934–35	25	1929–41	72-12-0 (53)	0
James J. Braddock	1935–37	29	1926–38	51-26-7 (26)	0
Joe Louis†	1937–49	23	1934–51	68-3-0 (54)	25
Ezzard Charles	1949–51	27	1940–59	96-25-1 (59)	8
Jersey Joe Walcott	1951–52	37	1930–53	53-18-1 (33)	1
Rocky Marciano†	1952–56	29	1947–56	49-0-0 (43)	6
Floyd Patterson	1956–59	21	1952–72	55-8-1 (40)	4
Ingemar Johansson	1959–60	26	1952–63	26-2-0 (17)	0
Floyd Patterson	1960–62	25	1952–72	55-8-1 (40)	2
Sonny Liston	1962–64	30	1953–70	50-4-0 (39)	1
Muhammad Ali	1964–71	22	1960–81	56-5-0 (37)	9
Joe Frazier	1971–73	27	1965–81	32-4-1 (27)	2
George Foreman	1973–74	24	1969–97	76-5-0 (68)	2
Muhammad Ali	1974–78	32	1960–81	56-5-0 (37)	10
Leon Spinks	1978	24	1977–95	26-17-3 (14)	0
Muhammad Ali†	1978–79	36	1960–81	56-5-0 (37)	0
Larry Holmes	1980–85	29	1973–	69-6-0 (44)	20
Michael Spinks	1985–88	29	1977–88	32-1-0 (21)	3
Mike Tyson	1988–90	21	1985–	49-4-0 (43)	2
Buster Douglas	1990	29	1981–99	38-6-1 (25)	0
Evander Holyfield	1990–92	28	1984–	38-5-2 (26)	3
Riddick Bowe	1992–93	25	1989–96	40-1-0 (32)	2
Evander Holyfield	1993–94	31	1984–	38-5-2 (26)	0
Michael Moorer	1994	26	1988–97	39-2-0 (31)	0
George Foreman	1994–97	45	1969–97	76-5-0 (68)	3
Shannon Briggs	1997–98	25	1992–00	32-3-1 (25)	0
Lennox Lewis	1998–01	32	1989–	40-2-1 (31)	5
Hasim Rahman	2001	28	1994–	35-4-0 (29)	0
Lennox Lewis†	2001–04	36	1989–	41-2-1 (32)	2
Vitali Klitschko	2004	32	1996–	34-2-0 (32)	

*Age when boxer won world championship.
† Boxer retired or relinquished world title.

Horse Racing

BILL FRAKES

Kentucky Derby and
Preakness winner
Smarty Jones

So Close, Yet...

For the second year in a row, and sixth in the last eight, there was a Triple Crown teaser

BY STEPHEN CANNELLA

IT'S COME TO THIS: The sport of kings yearns so deeply for a horse to wear its crown that upset winners of the Belmont Stakes apologize for denying a favorite his chance at history. The wait for another Triple Crown champion—Affirmed was the last, in 1978—is, at 26 years and counting, the longest drought since Sir Barton became the first thoroughbred to sweep the Kentucky Derby, the Preakness and the Belmont in 1919. In six of the last eight years, and each of the last two, a horse has entered the Belmont with a shot at glory, only to fall short. As the list of near-misses lengthens, the Crown takes on the aura of the supermodel who lives next door: It's tantalizingly close yet impossibly out of reach.

Little wonder, then, that veteran trainer Nick Zito sounded sheepish after Birdstone, his 36-1 longshot, outran Smarty Jones, the latest Triple Crown contender and a beloved fan favorite, and the rest of the field at the 2004 Belmont. "I'm sorry, man," Zito said to John Servis, his counterpart in the Smarty Jones camp. But his words might have been directed to the record 120,139 railbirds in the grandstand and the millions more watching on television, most of whom hoped if not expected to witness a coronation on the first Saturday in June.

In 2003, Funny Cide energized a downtrodden sport with a Triple Crown bid of his own and a rags-to-riches biography seemingly concocted in a Hollywood pitch meeting. In 2004, Smarty Jones went a step further, luring casual fans back to racing and grabbing the nation's imagination like no other horse in recent memory. Television ratings for the Belmont were the event's highest since Seattle Slew won the Triple Crown in 1977. Licensed Smarty merchandise flew off the shelves in the weeks leading up to the race. In the days before the race, negotiations to syndicate Smarty Jones's breeding rights began with a number of blueblood Kentucky farms, with the price expected to approach $40 million. Despite the Belmont loss, they eventually sold for $48 million.

Smarty's allure was rooted in his supreme talent, which was on full display in his sweeping victories in the first two Triple Crown legs. The three-year-old chestnut colt possessed brilliant speed, a pilot's knack for controlling it and a steam engine's stamina. To track veterans he was a nearly perfect racehorse. "He's a gift from God," enthused rival trainer Bob Baffert. "He's a freak of nature."

By the sport's standards he was an accident of breeding as well. A small-time outsider in the insular world of elite racing, Smarty Jones was born at little-known Someday Farm in Chester County, Pa., and made his home at past-its-prime Philadelphia Park. The middle-class colt carried more than the weight of

history into the Belmont: He also bore a seemingly endless cache of gripping and feel-good backstories. His septuagenarian owner, Roy (Chappie) Chapman, a car salesman who opened Someday Farm in 1988, was a Triple Crown rookie who spent two decades as a self-described "ham-and-egger" in racing's minor leagues. Chapman and his wife, Pat, met in 1976 and lived a storybook sportsman's life full of deep-sea fishing trips and fox hunts in the Pennsylvania countryside. But during the last decade Chapman developed emphysema, a disease that left the kindly owner confined to a wheelchair and lashed to a portable oxygen tank. "It's a bitch when you've been as active as I was," he said, "but I can't complain. I've had a hell of a good life."

An emotionally devastated Chapman nearly left the racing game in 2001 when Bob Camac, the longtime trainer at Someday Farm, was murdered by Camac's stepson. After selling most of his breeding stock, Chapman hired Servis, a regular at Philadelphia Park. Servis had been a respected but small-time trainer in the Northeast for 20 years, barely a blip on the big-time racing radar screen. Ditto for Smarty's jockey, Stewart Elliott, 39, a previously anonymous

Elliott won the Derby in his first attempt, the first jockey to do so since 1979.

lifer who quit school at 16 to ride in Canada and spent two decades piecing together a living in front of sparse crowds at midlevel tracks. When he was 19, Elliott suffered a career-threatening back injury when a horse flipped him onto the inner rail. He was unable to ride for 18 months; when he recovered he bounced around minor-league tracks and eventually became an alcoholic and a petty criminal. Elliott sobered up in 2000, and late in 2003 Servis asked him to ride a promising two-year-old named Smarty Jones. "I knew what Stew was going through," said Servis, who, like the rest of the Smarty Jones principals, made his Triple Crown debut at the Derby. "He opened his eyes, got dedicated and decided that he wanted to be a top rider."

The horse, too, overcame significant obstacles. Smarty's career nearly ended before it began: In 2003, less than a month after Servis began training him, Smarty banged his head on a starting gate. He spent nearly a month in the hospital and didn't enter his first 2-year-old race until Novem-

BILL FRAKES

Birdstone (4) overtook Smarty Jones in the stretch and ran away with the Belmont.

ber. He won that, as well as his next five outings, and went off as a 4–1 favorite at the Kentucky Derby. But because Servis had run him against lesser competition in Arkansas and not the top-tier races in Florida and California, many skeptics weren't sold on his chances.

On the stormy first Saturday in May, the Churchill Downs track a quagmire, the doubters were silenced. Elliott prodded his mount to close Lion Heart's four-length lead as they approached the final turn. Smarty took control of the race just inside the quarter pole, winning in 2:04.06, a moderate pace but an impresssive one for such a muddy track. Elliott became the first jockey to win the Derby in his first try since 1979. Smarty, the first unbeaten Derby winner since Seattle Slew in 1977, was just the second favorite to win the Run for the Roses since '79.

The Smarty party turned its focus to Pimlico Race Course in Baltimore two weeks later. Before a record crowd of 112,668, Smarty Jones and Elliott thoroughly demolished the Preakness field with an 11½-length win, the largest margin of victory in the 129 runnings of the race. Once again he trailed Lion Heart in the early stages, but Elliott calmly guided the colt wide around the first turn and, at the ⅜ pole, coaxed a burst of

speed from Smarty. He ducked to the rail, eased past Lion Heart and set a clear course for history. Said Patrick Biancone, Lion Heart's trainer, "Smarty Jones swallowed him in two jumps."

Having won his eight career races by a total of 47½ lengths, Smarty Jones seemed unbeatable heading into the Belmont. He had barely broken a sweat in the Derby and Preakness wins, and thanks to his relatively soft pre-Triple Crown schedule he was fit and running on a full tank. Elliott had proven to be a steady pilot with a steadfast heart, someone who could handle the pressure of history bearing down upon the Smarty camp.

Yet like so many before him, Smarty saw his bid for immortality die on the eternal homestretch of the Belmont's 1½-mile track. The 1–5 favorite blazed to an early lead, briefly fell behind Purge, then went back ahead as the field approached the backstretch, where he was pressed by Eddington and Preakness runner-up Rock Hard Ten. The Belmont is not kind to horses drunk on early speed, and holding off the challengers took its toll on Smarty. After running the opening half mile in 48.65 seconds and the second third in a blistering 46.79, he weakened down the stretch and was easily overtaken by Birdstone, who ran to victory over the final 100 yards.

The one-length loss was a gallant effort, less a refelction of Smarty's shortcomings than a stark reminder of how difficult it is to grasp the final jewel in the Triple Crown. "Smarty Jones ran a huge race," said Rock Hard Ten trainer Jason Orman. "He had to fight off those horses early and then just barely got beat at the finish."

It would be Smarty Jones's last race, the final lap in a thrilling eight-month joyride. In August he was retired after Servis discovered bruising on his hooves. It was a relatively minor injury, one that Smarty could have recovered from, but there are no risks to be taken with a horse with such lucrative breeding rights. One of history's most beloved horses would never race again. And fans were left to wonder if the sport would ever see another Triple Crown winner as well.

THOROUGHBRED RACING

The Triple Crown

130th Kentucky Derby

May 1, 2004. Grade I, 3-year-olds; 10th race, Churchill Downs, Louisville. All 126 lbs. Distance: 1¼ miles. Purse: $1,000,000 guaranteed. Track: Sloppy. Off: 6:12 p.m. Winner: Smarty Jones (By Elusive Quality out of I'll Get Along by Smile); Times: 0:22.99, 0:46.73, 1:11.80, 1:37.35, 2:04.06. Won: Driving. Breeder: Someday Farm.

Horse	Finish-PP	Margin	Jockey/Trainer
Smarty Jones	1–13	2¾	Stewart Elliott/John Servis
Lion Heart	2–3	3¼	Mike Smith/Patrick Biancone
Imperialism	3–8	2	Kent Desormeaux/Kristin Mulhall
Limehouse	4–1	4½	Jose Santos/Todd Pletcher
The Cliff's Edge	5–9	1¼	Shane Sellers/Nick Zito
Action This Day	6–4	1	David Flores/Richard Mandella
Read the Footnotes	7–12	½	Robbie Albarado/Richard Violette Jr
Birdstone	8–11	½	Edgar Prado/Nick Zito
Tapit	9–16	½	Ramon Dominguez/Michael Dickinson
Borrego	10–10	1¼	Victor Espinoza/C. Greely
Song of the Sword	11–2	1	Norberto Arroyo Jr/Jennifer Pedersen
Master David	12–7	1½	Alex Solis/Robert Frankel
Pro Prado	13–17	5¼	John McKee/Robert Holthus
Castledale	14–14	11½	Jose Valdivia Jr/Jeff Mullins
Friends Lake	15–5	½	Richard Migliore/John Kimmel
Minister Eric	16–6	3½	Pat Day/Richard Mandella
Pollard's Vision	17–15	—	John Velazquez/Todd Pletcher
Quintons Gold Rush	18–18	—	Corey Nakatani/Steven Asmussen

129th Preakness Stakes

May 15, 2004. Grade I, 3-year-olds; 12th race, Pimlico Race Course, Baltimore. All 126 lbs. Distance: 1³⁄₁₆ miles; Stakes value: $1,000,000. Track: Fast. Off: 6:25 p.m. Winner: Smarty Jones (By Elusive Quality out of I'll Get Along by Smile); Times: 0:23.65, 0:47.32, 1:11.53, 1:36.44, 1:55.59. Won: Driving. Breeder: Someday Farm.

Horse	Finish-PP	Margin	Jockey/Trainer
Smarty Jones	1–6	11½	Stewart Elliott/John Servis
Rock Hard Ten	2–9	2	Gary Stevens/J. Orman
Eddington	3–8	head	Jerry Bailey/M. Hennig
Lion Heart	4–1	head	Mike Smith/Patrick Biancone
Imperialism	5–7	1	Kent Desormeaux/Kristin Mulhall
Sir Shackleton	6–5	¾	R. Bejarano/Nick Zito
Borrego	7–2	5½	Victor Espinoza/C. Greely
Little Matth Man	8–3	2	Richard Migliore/M. Ciresa
Song of the Sword	9–4	3½	Jorge Chavez/Jennifer Pedersen
Water Cannon	10–10	—	R. Fogelsonger/L. Albert

136th Belmont Stakes

June 5, 2004. Grade I, 3-year-olds; 11th race, Belmont Park, Elmont, NY. All 126 lbs. Distance: 1½ miles. Stakes value: $1,000,000. Track: Fast. Off: 6:48 p.m. Winner: Birdstone (By Grindstone out of Dear Birdie by Storm Bird); Times: 0:24.33, 48.65, 1:11.76, 1:35.44, 2:00.52, 2:27.50. Won: Driving. Breeder: Marylou Whitney Stables.

Horse	Finish-PP	Margin	Jockey/Trainer
Birdstone	1–4	1	Edgar Prado/Nick Zito
Smarty Jones	2–9	8	Stewart Elliott/John Servis
Royal Assault	3–6	3	Pat Day/Nick Zito
Eddington	4–8	nose	Jerry Bailey/Mark Hennig
Rock Hard Ten	5–5	14	Alex Solis/Jason Orman
Tap Dancer	6–7	4¼	Javier Castellano/Edward Allard
Master David	7–1	1	Jose Santos/Robert Frankel
Caiman	8–3	6¼	Ramon Dominguez/Angel Medina
Purge	9–9	—	John Velazquez/Todd Pletcher

Major Stakes Races

Late 2003

Date	Race	Track	Distance	Winner	Jockey/Trainer	Purse ($)
Sept 20	Super Derby	Louisiana Downs	1⅛ miles	Ten Most Wanted	Pat Day/ W. Dollase	500,000
Sept 27	Vosburgh Stakes	Belmont Park	6½ furlongs	Ghostzapper	J. Castellano/ Robert Frankel	500,000
Sept 27	Jockey Club Gold Cup	Belmont Park	1¼ miles	Mineshaft	Robbie Albarado/ N. Howard	1,000,000
Sept 27	Tuf Classic Invitational	Belmont Park	1½ miles	Sulamani	Jerry Bailey/ S. bin Suroor	750,000
Sept 27	Flower Bowl Invitational	Belmont Park	1¼ miles	Dimitrova	Jerry Bailey/ D. Weld	750,000
Sept 28	Yellow Ribbon Stakes	Santa Anita	1¼ miles	Tates Creek	Pat Valenzuela/ Robert Frankel	500,000
Sept 28	Hawthorne Gold Cup Handicap	Hawthorne	1¼ miles	Perfect Drift	Pat Day/ M. Johnson	750,000
Oct 3	Meadowlands BC Stakes	Meadowlands	1⅛ miles	Bowman's Band	R. Dominguez/ H. Jerkens	400,000
Oct 4	Indiana Derby	Hoosier Park	1¹⁄₁₆ miles	Excessive-pleasure	K. Court/ D. O'Neill	411,800
Oct 4	Beldame Stakes	Belmont Park	1⅛ miles	Sightseek	Jerry Bailey/ Robert Frankel	750,000
Oct 4	Shadwell Turf Mile Stakes	Keeneland	1 mile	Perfect Soul	Edgar Prado/ R. Attfield	600,000
Oct 4	Frizette Stakes	Belmont Park	1¹⁄₁₆ miles	Society Selection	R. Ganpath/ H. Jerkens	500,000
Oct 4	Champagne Stakes	Belmont Park	1¹⁄₁₆ miles	Birdstone	Jerry Bailey/ Nick Zito	500,000
Oct 5	Overbrook Spinster Stakes	Keeneland	1⅛ miles	Take Charge Lady	Edgar Prado/ K. McPeek	500,000
Oct 5	Winstar Galaxy Stakes	Keeneland	1³⁄₁₆ miles	Bien Nicole	D. Pettinger/ D. Von Hemel	500,000
Oct 19	Pattison Canadian International	Woodbine	1½ miles	Phoenix Reach	M. Dwyer/ A. Balding	1,500,000
Oct 19	Taylor Stakes	Woodbine	1¼ miles	Volga	Richard Migliore/ K. McLaughlin	750,000
Oct 25	Breeders' Cup Classic	Santa Anita	1¼ miles	Pleasantly Perfect	Alex Solis/ Richard Mandella	4,000,000
Oct 25	Breeders' Cup Turf	Santa Anita	1½ miles	High Chaparral	M. Kinane/ A. O'Brien	2,110,100
Oct 25	Breeders' Cup Turf	Santa Anita	1½ miles	Johar	Alex Solis/ Richard Mandella	2,110,100
Oct 25	Breeders' Cup Juvenile	Santa Anita	1¹⁄₁₆ miles	Action This Day	David Flores/ Richard Mandella	1,500,000
Oct 25	Breeders' Cup Sprint	Santa Anita	6 furlongs	Cajun Beat	C. Velasqeuz/ S. Margoli	1,180,000
Oct 25	Breeders' Cup Filly and Mare Turf	Santa Anita	1¼ miles	Islington	K. Fallon/ M. Stoute	1,060,000
Oct 25	Breeders' Cup Mile	Santa Anita	1 mile	Six Perfections	Jerry Bailey/ E. Bary	1,500,000
Oct 25	Breeders' Cup Juvenile Fillies	Santa Anita	1¹⁄₁₆ miles	Halfbridled	Julie Krone/ Richard Mandella	1,000,000
Oct 25	Breeders' Cup Distaff	Santa Anita	1⅛ miles	Adoration	Pat Valenzuela/ D. Hoffmans	1,834,000
Nov 28	Clark Handicap	Churchill Downs	1⅛ miles	Quest	J. Castellano/ Nick Zito	582,000
Nov 29	Cigar Mile	Aqueduct	1 mile	Congaree	Jerry Bailey/ Bob Baffert	350,000
Nov 29	Citation Handicap	Hollywood Park	1¹⁄₁₆ miles	Redattore	Julie Krone/ Richard Mandella	400,000
Nov 30	Matriarch Stakes	Hollywood Park	1 mile	Heat Haze	John Velazquez/ Robert Frankel	500,000
Nov 30	Hollywood Derby	Hollywood Park	1¼ miles	Sweet Return	Julie Krone/ R. McAnally	600,000
Dec 5	Delta Jackpot	Delta Downs	1¹⁄₁₆ miles	Mr. Jester	R. Chapa/ S. Wren	1,000,000

2004 (through August 22)

Date	Race	Track	Distance	Winner	Jockey/Trainer	Purse ($)
Jan 24	Franks Farm Turf	Gulfstream	1⅛ miles	Proud Man	Rene Douglas/ C. Clement	400,000
Jan 24	John Deere Filly and Mare Turf	Santa Anita	1⅛ miles	Valentine Dancer	Jon Court/ C. Lewis	500,000
Jan 24	Distaff Stakes	Gulfstream	1¹⁄₁₆ miles	Secret Request	E. Coa/ D. Brownlee	500,000
Feb 7	Donn Handicap	Gulfstream	1⅛ miles	Medaglia d'Oro	Jerry Bailey/ Robert Frankel	500,000
Feb 29	New Orleans Handicap	Fair Grounds	1⅛ miles	Peace Rules	Jerry Bailey/ Robert Frankel	500,000
Mar 6	Santa Anita Handicap	Santa Anita	1¼ miles	Southern Image	Victor Espinoza/ M. Machowsky	1,000,000
Mar 7	Louisiana Derby	Fair Grounds	1¹⁄₁₆ miles	Wimbledon	J. Santiago/ Bob Baffert	600,000
Mar 13	Florida Derby Handicap	Gulfstream	1⅛ miles	Friends Lake	Richard Migliore/ J. Kimmel	1,000,000
Mar 20	Lane's End Stakes	Turfway Park	1⅛ miles	Sinister G	Paul Toscano/ J. Toscano Jr.	500,000
Mar 21	Mervin Muniz Handicap	Fair Grounds Park	1⅛ miles	Mystery Giver	Robbie Albarado/ R. Scherer	500,000
Mar 27	Dubai World Cup	Nad al Sheba	1¼ miles	Pleasantly Perfect	Alex Solis/ Richard Mandella	6,000,000
Apr 3	Santa Anita Derby	Santa Anita	1⅛ miles	Castledale	J. Valdivia/ J. Mullins	750,000
Apr 3	Ashland Stakes	Keeneland	1¹⁄₁₆ miles	Madcap Escapade	Rene Douglas/ F. Brothers	485,000
Apr 3	Apple Blossom Handicap	Oaklawn	1¹⁄₁₆ miles	Azeri	Mike Smith/ D. Wayne Lukas	500,000
Apr 3	Illinois Derby	Hawthorne	1⅛ miles	Pollard's Vision	E. Coa/ Todd Pletcher	500,000
Apr 3	Oaklawn Handicap	Oaklawn	1⅛ miles	Peace Rules	Jerry Bailey/ Robert Frankel	500,000
Apr 10	Keeneland Bluegrass	Keeneland	1⅛ miles	The Cliff's Edge	Shane Sellers/ Nick Zito	750,000
Apr 10	Wood Memorial	Aqueduct	1⅛ miles	Tapit	R. Dominguez/ M. Dickinson	750,000
Apr 10	Arkansas Derby	Oaklawn	1⅛ miles	Smarty Jones	Stewart Elliott/ John Servis	1,000,000
Apr 30	Kentucky Oaks	Churchill Downs	1⅛ miles	Ashado	John Velazquez/ Todd Pletcher	572,000
May 1	Kentucky Derby	Churchill Downs	1¼ miles	Smarty Jones	Stewart Elliott/ John Servis	1,154,800
May 1	Woodford Reserve Classic	Churchill Downs	1⅛ miles	Stroll	Jerry Bailey/ William Mott	453,900
May 14	Pimlico Special	Pimlico	1³⁄₁₆ miles	Southern Image	Victor Espinoza/ M. Machowsky	500,000
May 15	Preakness Stakes	Pimlico	1³⁄₁₆ miles	Smarty Jones	Stewart Elliott/ John Servis	1,000,000
May 31	Metropolitan Handicap	Belmont Park	1 mile	Pico Central	Alex Solis/ P. Lobo	750,000
May 31	Shoemaker B.C. Mile	Hollywood Park	1 mile	Designed For Luck	Pat Valenzuela/ V. Cerin	456,000
June 5	Belmont Stakes	Belmont Park	1½ miles	Birdstone	Edgar Prado/ Nick Zito	1,000,000
June 19	Massachusetts Handicap	Suffolk Downs	1⅛ miles	Offlee Wild	Edgar Prado/ R. Dutrow Jr.	500,000
June 27	Queen's Plate	Woodbine	1¼ miles	Niigon	Robert Landry/ E. Coatrieux	1,000,000
July 3	American Oaks	Hollywood Park	1¼ miles	Ticker Tape	Kent Desormeaux/ J. Cassidy	750,000
July 3	United Nations Stakes	Monmouth Park	1⅜ miles	Request For Parole	Edgar Prado/ S. Hough	750,000
July 3	Suburban Handicap	Belmont Park	1¼ miles	Peace Rules	Jerry Bailey/ Robert Frankel	500,000
July 10	Princess Rooney Handicap	Calder	6 furlongs	Ema Bovary	R. Gonzalez/ L. Ross	500,000

2004 (through August 22) (Cont.)

Date	Race	Track	Distance	Winner	Jockey/Trainer	Purse ($)
July 10	Hollywood Gold Cup	Hollywood Park	1¼ miles	Total Impact	Mike Smith/ L. de Seroux	750,000
July 10	Smile Sprint	Calder	6 furlongs	Champali	Jerry Bailey/ G. Foley	500,000
July 10	Swaps B.C. Stakes	Hollywood Park	1⅛ miles	Rock Hard Ten	Corey Nakatani/ J. Orman	409,300
July 10	Virginia Derby	Colonial Downs	1¼ miles	Kitten's Joy	Edgar Prado/ D. Romans	500,000
July 17	Delaware Oaks	Delaware Park	1¹⁄₁₆ miles	Yearly Report	Jerry Bailey/ Bob Baffert	500,000
July 18	Delaware Handicap	Delaware Park	1¼ miles	Summer Wind Dancer	Victor Espinoza/ J. Mullins	750,900
July 24	Coaching Club American Oaks	Belmont Park	1¼ miles	Ashado	J. Velazquez/ Todd Pletcher	500,000
July 31	Diana Handicap	Saratoga	1⅛ miles	Wonder Again	Edgar Prado/ J.J. Toner	500,000
Aug 7	Whitney Handicap	Saratoga	1⅛ miles	Roses in May	Edgar Prado/ D. Romans	750,000
Aug 14	Arlington Million	Arlington	1¼ miles	Kicken Kris	Kent Desormeaux/ M. Matz	1,000,000
Aug 14	Beverly D. Stakes	Arlington	1³⁄₁₆ miles	Crimson Palace	Frankie Dettori/ S. bin Suroor	750,000
Aug 14	Secretariat Stakes	Arlington	1¼ miles	Kitten's Joy	Jerry Bailey/ D. Romans	400,000
Aug 14	Sword Dancer Invitational	Saratoga	1½ miles	Better Talk Now	R. Dominguez/ G. Motion	500,000
Aug 21	Alabama Stakes	Saratoga	1¼ miles	Society Selection	C. Velasquez/ H. Jerkens	750,000
Aug 22	Pacific Classic	Del Mar	1¼ miles	Pleasantly Perfect	Jerry Bailey/ Richard Mandella	1,000,000

2003 Statistical Leaders

Horses

Horse	Starts	1st	2nd	3rd	Purses ($)	Horse	Starts	1st	2nd	3rd	Purses ($)
Pleasantly Perfect	4	2	0	1	2,470,000	Empire Maker	6	3	3	0	1,936,200
Mineshaft	9	7	2	0	2,209,686	Peace Rules	7	3	1	1	1,850,000
Wando	8	5	1	1	2,017,323	Congaree	9	5	2	0	1,608,000
Medaglia d'Oro	5	3	2	0	1,990,000	Ten Most Wanted	10	4	2	1	1,544,860
Funny Cide	8	2	2	2	1,963,200	Perfect Drift	8	5	0	0	1,505,388

Jockeys

Jockey	Mounts	1st	2nd	3rd	Purses ($)	Win Pct	$ Pct*
Jerry Bailey	726	206	149	97	23,354,960	.27	.58
Edgar Prado	1478	259	235	207	18,475,582	.18	.47
Alex Solis	1115	203	170	175	16,304,252	.18	.49
Pat Valenzuela	1447	287	266	237	15,697,352	.20	.55
John Velazquez	1308	306	193	175	15,425,501	.23	.52
Pat Day	985	215	175	110	13,378,292	.22	.51
Jose Santos	1157	176	183	162	11,472,287	.15	.45
Ramon Dominguez	1627	453	316	252	11,359,767	.28	.63
Todd Kabel	836	160	163	110	11,323,313	.19	.52
Patrick Husbands	882	168	144	117	11,168,817	.19	.49

*Percentage in the Money (1st, 2nd, and 3rd).

Trainers

Trainer	Starts	1st	2nd	3rd	Purses ($)	Win Pct	$ Pct*
Robert Frankel...........411		114	79	57	19,143,289	.28	.61
Todd Pletcher............826		199	132	105	12,356,924	.24	.53
Steven Asmussen ...1949		452	352	301	11,725,782	.23	.57
Richard Mandella......253		51	40	38	9,869,548	.20	.51
Bob Baffert...............674		127	119	80	9,442,281	.19	.48
Scott Lake 2009		455	344	280	9,163,599	.23	.54
William Mott...............718		138	101	85	6,866,920	.19	.45
Doug O'Neill..............760		133	119	109	6,438,799	.18	.48
Jerry Hollendorfer ...1216		282	211	193	6,260,305	.23	.56
Mark Shuman 1105		225	177	128	5,633,150	.20	.48

*Percentage in the Money (1st, 2nd, and 3rd).

Owners

Owner	Starts	1st	2nd	3rd	Purses ($)
Michael Gill 2235		425	339	267	9,236,530
Stronach Stables...........................622		126	112	63	7,289,114
Juddmonte Farms, Inc..................122		33	21	12	6,265,030
Edmund Gann................................83		25	19	8	5,848,681
Richard Englander......................1182		226	190	163	5,347,231
Eugene & Laura McInyk 455		92	65	60	4,123,765
John Franks 988		143	134	120	4,083,255
Sam-Son Farms 201		44	31	31	3,864,116
The Thoroughbred Corporation.....227		44	41	26	3,486,782
Gustav Schickedanz.....................106		29	9	8	3,361,790

HARNESS RACING

Major Stakes Races

Late 2003

Date	Race	Location	Winner	Driver/Trainer	Purse ($)
Oct 18	Goldsmith Maid	Mohawk	Peaceful Way	Chris Christoforou/ David Tingley	622,610
Oct 18	Governor's Cup	Mohawk	I Am A Fool	Ron Pierce/ Brett Pelling	652,898
Oct 18	Three Diamonds	Mohawk	Glowing Report	George Brennan/ Jerry Silverman	588,363
Oct 18	Valley Victory	Mohawk	Beardmore	John Campbell/ Lyle Anderson	557.668
Nov 29	BC Two-year-old Filly Trot	Meadowlands	Forever Starlet	David Miller/ Brett Pelling	480,000
Nov 29	BC Two-year-old Filly Pace	Meadowlands	Pans Culottes	Daniel Dube/. Ben Wallace	470,000
Nov 29	BC Two-year-old Colt Trot	Meadowlands	Cantab Hall	Michel Lachance/ Ron Gurfein	420,000
Nov 29	BC Two-year-old Colt Pace	Meadowlands	I Am A Fool	Ron Pierce/ Brett Pelling	540,000
Nov 29	BC Three-year-old Filly Trot	Meadowlands	Stroke Play	Brian Sears/ Trond Smedshammer	500,000
Nov 29	BC Three-year-old Filly Pace	Meadowlands	Burning Point	Kevin Wallis/ Linda Wallis	670,000
Nov 29	BC Three-year-old Colt Trot	Meadowlands	Mr. Muscleman	Ron Pierce/ Noel Daley	585,000
Nov 29	BC Three-year-old Colt Pace	Meadowlands	No Pan Intended	David Miller/ Ivan Sugg	542,000

2004 (through September 23)

Date	Race	Location	Winner	Driver/Trainer	Purse ($)
May 29	New Jersey Classic	Meadowlands	Modern Art	David Miller/ Joe Holloway	500,000
June 19	North America Cup	Woodbine	Mantacular	Cat Manzi/ Larry Rathbone	1,189,535

2004 (through September 23) (Cont.)

Date	Race	Location	Winner	Driver/Trainer	Purse ($)
July 16	Stanley Dancer	Meadowlands	Windsong's Legacy	Trond Smedshammer	382,000
July 17	Meadowlands Pace	Meadowlands	Holborn Hanover	Jim Morrill Jr/ Mark Harder	1,000,000
July 31	BC Open Pace	Meadowlands	Boulder Creek	Ron Pierce/ Mark Silva	552,500
July 31	BC Mare Trot	Meadowlands	Armbro Affair	Ron Pierce/ Bob McIntosh	250,000
July 31	BC Mare Pace	Meadowlands	Always Cam	David Miller/ Bill Zendt	300,000
July 31	BC Open Trot	Meadowlands	H P Paque	Brian Sears/ Trond Smedshammer	800,000
Aug 5	Peter Haughton	Meadowlands	New York Yank	Ron Pierce/ Noel Daley	420,000
Aug 5	Merrie Annabelle	Meadowlands	Reinvent	Ron Pierce/ Brett Pelling	450,620
Aug 6	Woodrow Wilson	Meadowlands	Village Jolt	Ron Pierce/ Ed Hart	432,000
Aug 6	Sweetheart	Meadowlands	Fox Valley Shaker	George Brennan/ Ervin Miller	443,200
Aug 7	Hambletonian Oaks	Meadowlands	Silver Springs	George Brennan/ Jan Johnson	500,000
Aug 7	Hambletonian	Meadowlands	Windsong's Legacy	Trond Smedshammer	1,000,000
Sept 23	Little Brown Jug	Delaware, OH	Timesarea- changing	Ron Pierce/ Brett Pelling	308,617

Major Races

The Hambletonian
Raced at The Meadowlands, East Rutherford, NJ, on August 7, 2004

Horse	Driver	PP	¼	½	¾	Stretch	Finish
Windsong's Legacy	Trond Smedshammer	7	7°/5Q	4°/1T	4°/2	1/NS	1/1
Cantab Hall	Michel Lachance	1	2/1T	3/1H	3/1H	3/1H	2/1
Cash Hall	John Campbell	5	5°/3T	2°/H	2°/H	2/NS	3/3T
Coventry	R. Douglas Ackerman	10	9°/7Q	6°/2T	6°/3T	5/4	4/6H
Justice Hall	James Morrill Jr.	4	6/4Q	8/4H	8/5Q	7/5	5/8Q
American Mike	Brian Sears	8	8/6	7°/4H	7°/5	8/5Q	6/8T
Castle of Fortune	Luc Ouellette	2	4/3	5/2T	5/3T	6/5	7/13T
Tom Ridge	Ronald Pierce	6	1/1T	1/H	1/H	4/1T	8/18Q
Lantern's Law	Trevor Ritchie	9	3°X/2Q	X9/14	9/11	9/12T	9/23
Eilean Donon	David Miller	X3	10/dis	10/dis	10/dis	10/dis	10/32Q

Times: 0:28.2, 0:57.2, 1:26.3, 1:54.1

The Little Brown Jug
Raced at the Delaware County Fairgrounds, in Delaware, OH, on September 23, 2004

Horse	Driver	PP	¼	½	¾	Stretch	Finish
Timesareachanging	Ron Pierce	2	5/7	4°/2H	2°/T	2/H	1/H
Western Terror	Brian Sears	1	2/1H	2/1Q	3/1Q	3/1.	2/H
Metropolitan	John Campbell	5	8/12H	7°/4H	6°/3H	6/2T	3/1Q
Blissed Out	Luc Ouellette	3	1/1H	1/1Q	1/T	1/H	4/1Q
Driven To Win	David Miller	9	3/3H	3/2Q	5/2H	5/2Q	5/2
Maltese Artist	David Palone	4	6/8H	5°/3H	4°/2	4/2	6/3Q
Four Starzzz King	Michel Lachance	8	4/5H	6/4	8/5H	7/3T	7/4T
Town Champion	Richard Silverman	6	7/10H	8/6H	7°/5H	8/5T	8/6
The Preacher Pan	Daniel Dube	7	9/15H	9/8H	9/7H	9/6T	9/7Q

Times: 0:27.1, 0:55.1, 1:23.2, 1:51.3.

2003 Leading Moneywinners by Age, Sex and Gait

Division	Horse	Starts	1st	2nd	3rd	Earnings ($)
2-Year-Old Pacing Colts	I Am A Fool	15	9	2	2	1,159,062
2-Year-Old Pacing Fillies	Kikikatie	15	14	1	0	788,044
3-Year-Old Pacing Colts	No Pan Intended	21	17	3	0	1,465,852
3-Year-Old Pacing Fillies	Burning Point	29	22	4	1	861,252
Older Pacing Horses	Art Major	11	8	3	0	1,082,930
Older Pacing Mares	Eternal Camnation	20	11	4	0	908,346
2-Year-Old Trotting Colts	Cantab Hall	10	10	0	0	461,337
2-Year-Old Trotting Fillies	Peaceful Way	10	8	0	1	733,726
3-Year-Old Trotting Colts	Mr. Muscleman	17	8	4	2	1,178,115
3-Year-Old Trotting Fillies	Southwind Allaire	16	6	3	4	596,153
Older Trotting Horses	Rotation	10	4	3	0	760,590
Older Trotting Mares	Scully FBI	35	5	7	7	221,052

Drivers

Driver	Earnings ($)	Driver	Earnings ($)
David Miller	11,490,590	John Campbell	6,035,930
Ron Pierce	9,361,745	Randy Waples	6,011,275
Chris Christoforou	8,492,464	George Brennan	5,578,214
Luc Ouellette	8,120,602	Cat Manzi	5,509,422
Michel Lachance	7,876,334	Jim Morrill Jr.	5,233,189

Who's Her Daddy?

Horse owners Bill and Lynda Gallagher will never know how they were blessed with Amazing Philly, a 4-year-old fatherless filly who finished third in her debut at Philadelphia Park in February 2004. Amazing's mom, Speak Compelling, was once a fast 3-year-old—maybe a little too fast. Though she'd been kept away from the males stabled near her, she ended up pregnant, a condition no one knew about until she gave birth, on Jan. 30, 2000, 11 days after finishing 38 lengths back in a race. Blood tests on all 52 horses with access to her have failed to turn up Amazing's dad. Maybe when she wins a big purse, he'll come forward.

FOR THE RECORD · Year by Year

THOROUGHBRED RACING

Kentucky Derby

Run at Churchill Downs, Louisville, KY, on the first Saturday in May.

Year	Winner (Margin)	Jockey	Second	Third	Time
1875	Aristides (1)	Oliver Lewis	Volcano	Verdigris	2:37¾
1876	Vagrant (2)	Bobby Swim	Creedmoor	Harry Hill	2:38¼
1877	Baden-Baden (2)	William Walker	Leonard	King William	2:38
1878	Day Star (2)	Jimmie Carter	Himyar	Leveler	2:37¼
1879	Lord Murphy (1)	Charlie Shauer	Falsetto	Strathmore	2:37
1880	Fonso (1)	George Lewis	Kimball	Bancroft	2:37½
1881	Hindoo (4)	Jimmy McLaughin	Lelex	Alfambra	2:40
1882	Apollo (½)	Babe Hurd	Runnymede	Bengal	2:40¼
1883	Leonatus (3)	Billy Donohue	Drake Carter	Lord Raglan	2:43
1884	Buchanan (2)	Isaac Murphy	Loftin	Audrain	2:40¼
1885	Joe Cotton (Neck)	Erskine Henderson	Bersan	Ten Booker	2:37¼
1886	Ben Ali (½)	Paul Duffy	Blue Wing	Free Knight	2:36½
1887	Montrose (2)	Isaac Lewis	Jim Gore	Jacobin	2:39¼
1888	MacBeth II (1)	George Covington	Gallifet	White	2:38¼
1889	Spokane (Nose)	Thomas Kiley	Proctor Knott	Once Again	2:34½
1890	Riley (2)	Isaac Murphy	Bill Letcher	Robespierre	2:45
1891	Kingman (1)	Isaac Murphy	Balgowan	High Tariff	2:52¼
1892	Azra (Nose)	Alonzo Clayton	Huron	Phil Dwyer	2:41½
1893	Lookout (5)	Eddie Kunze	Plutus	Boundless	2:39¼
1894	Chant (2)	Frank Goodale	Pearl Song	Sigurd	2:41
1895	Halma (3)	Soup Perkins	Basso	Laureate	2:37½
1896	Ben Brush (Nose)	Willie Simms	Ben Eder	Semper Ego	2:07¾
1897	Typhoon II (Head)	Buttons Garner	Ornament	Dr. Catlett	2:12½
1898	Plaudit (Neck)	Willie Simms	Lieber Karl	Isabey	2:09
1899	Manuel (2)	Fred Taral	Corsini	Mazo	2:12
1900	Lieut. Gibson (4)	Jimmy Boland	Florizar	Thrive	2:06¼
1901	His Eminence (2)	Jimmy Winkfield	Sannazarro	Driscoll	2:07¾
1902	Alan-a-Dale (Nose)	Jimmy Winkfield	Inventor	The Rival	2:08¾
1903	Judge Himes (¾)	Hal Booker	Early	Bourbon	2:09
1904	Elwood (½)	Frankie Prior	Ed Tierney	Brancas	2:08½
1905	Agile (3)	Jack Martin	Ram's Horn	Layson	2:10¾
1906	Sir Huon (2)	Roscoe Troxler	Lady Navarre	James Reddick	2:08⅕
1907	Pink Star (2)	Andy Minder	Zal	Ovelando	2:12⅗
1908	Stone Street (1)	Arthur Pickens	Sir Cleges	Dunvegan	2:15⅕
1909	Wintergreen (4)	Vincent Powers	Miami	Dr. Barkley	2:08⅕
1910	Donau (½)	Fred Herbert	Joe Morris	Fighting Bob	2:06⅖
1911	Meridian (¾)	George Archibald	Governor Gray	Colston	2:05
1912	Worth (Neck)	Carroll H. Schilling	Duval	Flamma	2:09⅖
1913	Donerail (½)	Roscoe Goose	Ten Point	Gowell	2:04⅘
1914	Old Rosebud (8)	John McCabe	Hodge	Bronzewing	2:03⅖
1915	Regret (2)	Joe Notter	Pebbles	Sharpshooter	2:05⅖
1916	George Smith (Neck)	Johnny Loftus	Star Hawk	Franklin	2:04
1917	Omar Khayyam (2)	Charles Borel	Ticket	Midway	2:04⅗
1918	Exterminator (1)	William Knapp	Escoba	Viva America	2:10⅘
1919	Sir Barton (5)	Johnny Loftus	Billy Kelly	Under Fire	2:09⅘
1920	Paul Jones (Head)	Ted Rice	Upset	On Watch	2:09
1921	Behave Yourself (Head)	Charles Thompson	Black Servant	Prudery	2:04⅕
1922	Morvich (½)	Albert Johnson	Bet Mosie	John Finn	2:04⅗
1923	Zev (1½)	Earl Sande	Martingale	Vigil	2:05⅖
1924	Black Gold (½)	John Mooney	Chilhowee	Beau Butler	2:05⅕
1925	Flying Ebony (1½)	Earl Sande	Captain Hal	Son of John	2:07⅗
1926	Bubbling Over (5)	Albert Johnson	Bagenbaggage	Rock Man	2:03⅗
1927	Whiskery (Head)	Linus McAtee	Osmond	Jock	2:06
1928	Reigh Count (3)	Chick Lang	Misstep	Toro	2:10⅖
1929	Clyde Van Dusen (2)	Linus McAtee	Naishapur	Panchio	2:10⅘
1930	Gallant Fox (2)	Earl Sande	Gallant Knight	Ned O.	2:07⅗
1931	Twenty Grand (4)	Charles Kurtsinger	Sweep All	Mate	2:01⅘
1932	Burgoo King (5)	Eugene James	Economic	Stepenfetchit	2:05⅕
1933	Brokers Tip (Nose)	Don Meade	Head Play	Charley O.	2:06⅘
1934	Cavalcade (2½)	Mack Garner	Discovery	Agrarian	2:04
1935	Omaha (1½)	Willie Saunders	Roman Soldier	Whiskolo	2:05
1936	Bold Venture (Head)	Ira Hanford	Brevity	Indian Broom	2:03⅗

Kentucky Derby *(Cont.)*

Year	Winner (Margin)	Jockey	Second	Third	Time
1937	War Admiral (1¾)	Charles Kurtsinger	Pompoon	Reaping Reward	2:03⅕
1938	Lawrin (1)	Eddie Arcaro	Dauber	Can't Wait	2:04⅘
1939	Johnstown (8)	James Stout	Challedon	Heather Broom	2:03⅗
1940	Gallahadion (1½)	Carroll Bierman	Bimelech	Dit	2:05
1941	Whirlaway (8)	Eddie Arcaro	Staretor	Market Wise	2:01⅖
1942	Shut Out (2½)	Wayne Wright	Alsab	Valdina Orphan	2:04⅖
1943	Count Fleet (3)	John Longden	Blue Swords	Slide Rule	2:04
1944	Pensive (4½)	Conn McCreary	Broadcloth	Stir Up	2:04⅕
1945	Hoop Jr. (6)	Eddie Arcaro	Pot o' Luck	Darby Dieppe	2:07
1946	Assault (8)	Warren Mehrtens	Spy Song	Hampden	2:06⅗
1947	Jet Pilot (Head)	Eric Guerin	Phalanx	Faultless	2:06⅘
1948	Citation (3½)	Eddie Arcaro	Coaltown	My Request	2:05⅖
1949	Ponder (3)	Steve Brooks	Capot	Palestinian	2:04⅕
1950	Middleground (1¼)	William Boland	Hill Prince	Mr. Trouble	2:01⅗
1951	Count Turf (4)	Conn McCreary	Royal Mustang	Ruhe	2:02⅗
1952	Hill Gail (2)	Eddie Arcaro	Sub Fleet	Blue Man	2:01⅗
1953	Dark Star (Head)	Hank Moreno	Native Dancer	Invigorator	2:02
1954	Determine (1½)	Ray York	Hasty Road	Hasseyampa	2:03
1955	Swaps (1½)	Bill Shoemaker	Nashua	Summer Tan	2:01⅘
1956	Needles (¾)	Dave Erb	Fabius	Come On Red	2:03⅖
1957	Iron Liege (Nose)	Bill Hartack	Gallant Man	Round Table	2:02⅕
1958	Tim Tam (½)	Ismael Valenzuela	Lincoln Road	Noureddin	2:05
1959	Tomy Lee (Nose)	Bill Shoemaker	Sword Dancer	First Landing	2:02⅕
1960	Venetian Way (3½)	Bill Hartack	Bally Ache	Victoria Park	2:02⅖
1961	Carry Back (¾)	John Sellers	Crozier	Bass Clef	2:04
1962	Decidedly (2¼)	Bill Hartack	Roman Line	Ridan	2:00⅖
1963	Chateaugay (1¼)	Braulio Baeza	Never Bend	Candy Spots	2:01⅘
1964	Northern Dancer (Neck)	Bill Hartack	Hill Rise	The Scoundrel	2:00
1965	Lucky Debonair (Neck)	Bill Shoemaker	Dapper Dan	Tom Rolfe	2:01⅕
1966	Kauai King (½)	Don Brumfield	Advocator	Blue Skyer	2:02
1967	Proud Clarion (1)	Bobby Ussery	Barbs Delight	Damascus	2:00⅗
1968	Forward Pass (Disq.)	Ismael Valenzuela	Francie's Hat	T.V. Commercial	2:02⅕
1969	Majestic Prince (Neck)	Bill Hartack	Arts and Letters	Dike	2:01⅘
1970	Dust Commander (5)	Mike Manganello	My Dad George	High Echelon	2:03⅖
1971	Canonero II (3¾)	Gustavo Avila	Jim French	Bold Reason	2:03⅕
1972	Riva Ridge (3¼)	Ron Turcotte	No Le Hace	Hold Your Peace	2:01⅘
1973	Secretariat (2½)	Ron Turcotte	Sham	Our Native	1:59⅖
1974	Cannonade (2¼)	Angel Cordero Jr.	Hudson County	Agitate	2:04
1975	Foolish Pleasure (1¾)	Jacinto Vasquez	Avatar	Diabolo	2:02
1976	Bold Forbes (1)	Angel Cordero Jr.	Honest Pleasure	Elocutionist	2:01⅗
1977	Seattle Slew (1¾)	Jean Cruguet	Run Dusty Run	Sanhedrin	2:02⅕
1978	Affirmed (1¼)	Steve Cauthen	Alydar	Believe It	2:01⅕
1979	Spectacular Bid (2¾)	Ronald J. Franklin	General Assembly	Golden Act	2:02⅖
1980	Genuine Risk (1)	Jacinto Vasquez	Rumbo	Jaklin Klugman	2:02
1981	Pleasant Colony (¾)	Jorge Velasquez	Woodchopper	Partez	2:02
1982	Gato Del Sol (2½)	Eddie Delahoussaye	Laser Light	Reinvested	2:02⅕
1983	Sunny's Halo (2)	Eddie Delahoussaye	Desert Wine	Caveat	2:02⅕
1984	Swale (3¼)	Laffit Pincay Jr.	Coax Me Chad	At the Threshold	2:02⅖
1985	Spend A Buck (5)	Angel Cordero Jr.	Stephan's Odyssey	Chief's Crown	2:00⅕
1986	Ferdinand (2¼)	Bill Shoemaker	Bold Arrangement	Broad Brush	2:02⅘
1987	Alysheba (¾)	Chris McCarron	Bet Twice	Avies Copy	2:03⅖
1988	Winning Colors (Neck)	Gary Stevens	Forty Niner	Risen Star	2:02⅕
1989	Sunday Silence (2½)	Pat Valenzuela	Easy Goer	Awe Inspiring	2:05
1990	Unbridled (3½)	Craig Perret	Summer Squall	Pleasant Tap	2:02
1991	Strike the Gold (1¾)	Chris Antley	Best Pal	Mane Minister	2:03
1992	Lil E. Tee (1)	Pat Day	Casual Lies	Dance Floor	2:03
1993	Sea Hero (2½)	Jerry Bailey	Prairie Bayou	Wild Gale	2:02⅖
1994	Go for Gin (2½)	Chris McCarron	Strodes Creek	Blumin Affair	2:03⅗
1995	Thunder Gulch (2¼)	Gary Stevens	Tejano Run	Timber Country	2:01⅕
1996	Grindstone (Nose)	Jerry Bailey	Cavonnier	Prince of Thieves	2:01
1997	Silver Charm (Head)	Gary Stevens	Captain Bodgit	Free House	2:02⅖
1998	Real Quiet (½)	Kent Desormeaux	Victory Gallop	Indian Charlie	2:02⅒
1999	Charismatic (Neck)	Chris Antley	Menifee	Cat Thief	2:03⅕
2000	Fusaichi Pegasus (1½)	Kent Desormeaux	Aptitude	Impeachment	2:01.12
2001	Monarchos (4 ¾)	Jorge Chavez	Invisible Ink	Congaree	1:59.97
2002	War Emblem (4)	Victor Espinoza	Proud Citizen	Perfect Drift	2:01.13
2003	Funny Cide (1¾)	Jose Santos	Empire Maker	Peace Rules	2:01.19
2004	Smarty Jones (2¾)	Stewart Elliott	Lion Heart	Imperialism	2:04.06

Note: Distance: 1½ miles (1875–95), 1¼ miles (1896–present).

Preakness

Run at Pimlico Race Course, Baltimore, Md., two weeks after the Kentucky Derby.

Year	Winner (Margin)	Jockey	Second	Third	Time
1873	Survivor (10)	G. Barbee	John Boulger	Artist	2:43
1874	Culpepper (¾)	W. Donohue	King Amadeus	Scratch	2:56½
1875	Tom Ochiltree (2)	L. Hughes	Viator	Bay Final	2:43½
1876	Shirley (4)	G. Barbee	Rappahannock	Algerine	2:44¾
1877	Cloverbrook (4)	C. Holloway	Bombast	Lucifer	2:45½
1878	Duke of Magenta (6)	C. Holloway	Bayard	Albert	2:41¾
1879	Harold (3)	L. Hughes	Jericho	Rochester	2:40½
1880	Grenada (¾)	L. Hughes	Oden	Emily F.	2:40½
1881	Saunterer (½)	T. Costello	Compensation	Baltic	2:40½
1882	Vanguard (Neck)	T. Costello	Heck	Col Watson	2:44½
1883*	Jacobus (4)	G. Barbee	Parnell		2:42½
1884*	Knight of Ellerslie (2)	S. Fisher	Welcher		2:39½
1885	Tecumseh (2)	Jim McLaughlin	Wickham	John C.	2:49
1886	The Bard (3)	S. Fisher	Eurus	Elkwood	2:45
1887	Dunboyne (1)	W. Donohue	Mahoney	Raymond	2:39½
1888	Refund (3)	F. Littlefield	Judge Murray	Glendale	2:49
1889*	Buddhist (8)	W. Anderson	Japhet	*	2:17½
1890*	Montague (3)	W. Martin	Philosophy	Barrister	2:36¾
1894	Assignee (3)	Fred Taral	Potentate	Ed Kearney	1:49¼
1895	Belmar (1)	Fred Taral	April Fool	Sue Kittie	1:50½
1896	Margrave (1)	H. Griffin	Hamilton II	Intermission	1:51
1897	Paul Kauvar (1½)	C. Thorpe	Elkins	On Deck	1:51¼
1898	Sly Fox (2)	C. W. Simms	The Huguenot	Nuto	1:49⅗
1899	Half Time (1)	R. Clawson	Filigrane	Lackland	1:47
1900	Hindus (Head)	H. Spencer	Sarmation	Ten Candles	1:48⅖
1901	The Parader (2)	F. Landry	Sadie S.	Dr. Barlow	1:47⅕
1902	Old England (Nose)	L. Jackson	Major Daingerfield	Namtor	1:45⅘
1903	Flocarline (½)	W. Gannon	Mackey Dwyer	Rightful	1:44⅘
1904	Bryn Mawr (1)	E. Hildebrand	Wotan	Dolly Spanker	1:44⅕
1905	Cairngorm (Head)	W. Davis	Kiamesha	Coy Maid	1:45⅘
1906	Whimsical (4)	Walter Miller	Content	Larabie	1:45
1907	Don Enrique (1)	G. Mountain	Ethon	Zambesi	1:45⅖
1908	Royal Tourist (4)	E. Dugan	Live Wire	Robert Cooper	1:46⅖
1909	Effendi (1)	Willie Doyle	Fashion Plate	Hilltop	1:39⅘
1910	Layminster (½)	R. Estep	Dalhousie	Sager	1:40⅗
1911	Watervale (1)	E. Dugan	Zeus	The Nigger	1:51
1912	Colonel Holloway (5)	C. Turner	Bwana Tumbo	Tipsand	1:56⅗
1913	Buskin (Neck)	J. Butwell	Kleburne	Barnegat	1:53⅖
1914	Holiday (¾)	A. Schuttinger	Brave Cunarder	Defendum	1:53⅘
1915	Rhine Maiden (1½)	Douglas Hoffman	Half Rock	Runes	1:58
1916	Damrosch (1½)	Linus McAtee	Greenwood	Achievement	1:54⅘
1917	Kalitan (2)	E. Haynes	Al M. Dick	Kentucky Boy	1:54⅖
1918*	War Cloud (¾)	Johnny Loftus	Sunny Slope	Lanius	1:53⅗
1918*	Jack Hare, Jr (2)	C. Peak	The Porter	Kate Bright	1:53⅖
1919	Sir Barton (4)	Johnny Loftus	Eternal	Sweep On	1:53
1920	Man o' War (1½)	Clarence Kummer	Upset	Wildair	1:51⅗
1921	Broomspun (¾)	F. Coltiletti	Polly Ann	Jeg	1:54⅕
1922	Pillory (Head)	L. Morris	Hea	June Grass	1:51⅗
1923	Vigil (1¼)	B. Marinelli	General Thatcher	Rialto	1:53⅗
1924	Nellie Morse (1½)	J. Merimee	Transmute	Mad Play	1:57⅕
1925	Coventry (4)	Clarence Kummer	Backbone	Almadel	1:59
1926	Display (Head)	J. Maiben	Blondin	Mars	1:59⅘
1927	Bostonian (½)	A. Abel	Sir Harry	Whiskery	2:01⅗
1928	Victorian (Nose)	Sonny Workman	Toro	Solace	2:00⅕
1929	Dr. Freeland (1)	Louis Schaefer	Minotaur	African	2:01⅗
1930	Gallant Fox (¾)	Earl Sande	Crack Brigade	Snowflake	2:00⅗
1931	Mate (1½)	G. Ellis	Twenty Grand	Ladder	1:59
1932	Burgoo King (Head)	E. James	Tick On	Boatswain	1:59⅘
1933	Head Play (4)	Charles Kurtsinger	Ladysman	Utopian	2:02
1934	High Quest (Nose)	R. Jones	Cavalcade	Discovery	1:58⅕
1935	Omaha (6)	Willie Saunders	Firethorn	Psychic Bid	1:58⅖
1936	Bold Venture (Nose)	George Woolf	Granville	Jean Bart	1:59
1937	War Admiral (Head)	Charles Kurtsinger	Pompoon	Flying Scot	1:58⅖
1938	Dauber (7)	M. Peters	Cravat	Menow	1:59⅘
1939	Challedon (1¼)	George Seabo	Gilded Knight	Volitant	1:59⅘
1940	Bimelech (3)	F. A. Smith	Mioland	Gallahadion	1:58⅗
1941	Whirlaway (5½)	Eddie Arcaro	King Cole	Our Boots	1:58⅘

Preakness (Cont.)

Year	Winner (Margin)	Jockey	Second	Third	Time
1942	Alsab (1)	B. James	Requested Sun Again	(dead heat for second)	1:57
1943	Count Fleet (8)	Johnny Longden	Blue Swords	Vincentive	1:57⅖
1944	Pensive (¾)	Conn McCreary	Platter	Stir Up	1:59⅕
1945	Polynesian (2½)	W. D. Wright	Hoop Jr.	Darby Dieppe	1:58⅘
1946	Assault (Neck)	Warren Mehrtens	Lord Boswell	Hampden	2:01⅖
1947	Faultless (1¼)	Doug Dodson	On Trust	Phalanx	1:59
1948	Citation (5½)	Eddie Arcaro	Vulcan's Forge	Boyard	2:02⅖
1949	Capot (Head)	Ted Atkinson	Palestinian	Noble Impulse	1:56
1950	Hill Prince (5)	Eddie Arcaro	Middleground	Dooley	1:59⅕
1951	Bold (7)	Eddie Arcaro	Counterpoint	Alerted	1:56⅖
1952	Blue Man (3½)	Conn McCreary	Jampol	One Count	1:57⅖
1953	Native Dancer (Neck)	Eric Guerin	Jamie K.	Royal Bay Gem	1:57⅘
1954	Hasty Road (Neck)	Johnny Adams	Correlation	Hasseyampa	1:57⅖
1955	Nashua (1)	Eddie Arcaro	Saratoga	Traffic Judge	1:54⅗
1956	Fabius (¾)	Bill Hartack	Needles	No Regrets	1:58⅖
1957	Bold Ruler (2)	Eddie Arcaro	Iron Liege	Inside Tract	1:56⅕
1958	Tim Tam (1½)	I. Valenzuela	Lincoln Road	Gone Fishin'	1:57⅕
1959	Royal Orbit (4)	William Harmatz	Sword Dancer	Dunce	1:57
1960	Bally Ache (4)	Bobby Ussery	Victoria Park	Celtic Ash	1:57⅗
1961	Carry Back (¾)	Johnny Sellers	Globemaster	Crozier	1:57⅗
1962	Greek Money (Nose)	John Rotz	Ridan	Roman Line	1:56⅕
1963	Candy Spots (3½)	Bill Shoemaker	Chateaugay	Never Bend	1:56⅕
1964	Northern Dancer (2¼)	Bill Hartack	The Scoundrel	Hill Rise	1:56⅘
1965	Tom Rolfe (Neck)	Ron Turcotte	Dapper Dan	Hail to All	1:56⅕
1966	Kauai King (1¾)	Don Brumfield	Stupendous	Amberoid	1:55⅖
1967	Damascus (2¼)	Bill Shoemaker	In Reality	Proud Clarion	1:55⅕
1968	Forward Pass (6)	I. Valenzuela	Out of the Way	Nodouble	1:56⅘
1969	Majestic Prince (Head)	Bill Hartack	Arts and Letters	Jay Ray	1:55⅗
1970	Personality (Neck)	Eddie Belmonte	My Dad George	Silent Screen	1:56⅕
1971	Canonero II (1½)	Gustavo Avila	Eastern Fleet	Jim French	1:54
1972	Bee Bee Bee (1¼)	Eldon Nelson	No Le Hace	Key to the Mint	1:55⅗
1973	Secretariat (2½)	Ron Turcotte	Sham	Our Native	1:54⅖
1974	Little Current (7)	Miguel Rivera	Neapolitan Way	Cannonade	1:54⅗
1975	Master Derby (1)	Darrel McHargue	Foolish Pleasure	Diabolo	1:56⅖
1976	Elocutionist (3)	John Lively	Play the Red	Bold Forbes	1:55
1977	Seattle Slew (1½)	Jean Cruguet	Iron Constitution	Run Dusty Run	1:54⅖
1978	Affirmed (Neck)	Steve Cauthen	Alydar	Believe It	1:54⅖
1979	Spectacular Bid (5½)	Ron Franklin	Golden Act	Screen King	1:54⅕
1980	Codex (4¾)	Angel Cordero Jr.	Genuine Risk	Colonel Moran	1:54⅕
1981	Pleasant Colony (1)	Jorge Velasquez	Bold Ego	Paristo	1:54⅗
1982	Aloma's Ruler (½)	Jack Kaenel	Linkage	Cut Away	1:55⅖
1983	Deputed Testamony (2¾)	Donald Miller Jr.	Desert Wine	High Honors	1:55⅖
1984	Gate Dancer (1½)	Angel Cordero Jr.	Play On	Fight Over	1:53⅗
1985	Tank's Prospect (Head)	Pat Day	Chief's Crown	Eternal Prince	1:53⅖
1986	Snow Chief (4)	Alex Solis	Ferdinand	Broad Brush	1:54⅘
1987	Alysheba (½)	Chris McCarron	Bet Twice	Cryptoclearance	1:55⅘
1988	Risen Star (1¼)	E. Delahoussaye	Brian's Time	Winning Colors	1:56⅕
1989	Sunday Silence (Nose)	Pat Valenzuela	Easy Goer	Rock Point	1:53⅘
1990	Summer Squall (2¼)	Pat Day	Unbridled	Mister Frisky	1:53⅗
1991	Hansel (Head)	Jerry Bailey	Corporate Report	Mane Minister	1:54
1992	Pine Bluff (¾)	Chris McCarron	Alydeed	Casual Lies	1:55⅗
1993	Prairie Bayou (½)	Mike Smith	Cherokee Run	El Bakan	1:56⅗
1994	Tabasco Cat (¾)	Pat Day	Go For Gin	Concern	1:56⅖
1995	Timber Country (½)	Pat Day	Oliver's Twist	Thunder Gulch	1:54⅖
1996	Louis Quatorze (3¼)	Pat Day	Skip Away	Editor's Note	1:53⅖
1997	Silver Charm (Head)	Gary Stevens	Free House	Captain Bodgit	1:54⅖
1998	Real Quiet (2¼)	Kent Desormeaux	Victory Gallop	Classic Cat	1:54⅗
1999	Charismatic (1½)	Chris Antley	Menifee	Badge	1:55⅕
2000	Red Bullet (3¾)	Jerry Bailey	Fusaichi Pegasus	Impeachment	1:56.04
2001	Point Given (2¼)	Gary Stevens	A P Valentine	Congaree	1:55.51
2002	War Emblem (¾)	Victor Espinoza	Magic Weisner	Proud Citizen	1:56.36
2003	Funny Cide (9¾)	Jose Santos	Midway Road	Scrimshaw	1:55.61
2004	Smarty Jones (11½)	Stewart Elliott	Rock Hard Ten	Eddington	1:55.59

*Preakness was a two-horse race in 1883, '84 and '89. It was not run 1891–1893; and in 1918, it was run in two divisions.

Note: Distance: 1½ miles (1873–88), 1¼ miles (1889), 1½ miles (1890), 1 1/16 miles (1894–1900), 1 mile and 70 yards (1901–1907), 1 1/16 miles (1908), 1 mile (1909–10), 1⅛ miles (1911–24), 1 3/16 miles (1925–present).

Belmont

Run at Belmont Park, Elmont, NY, three weeks after the Preakness Stakes. Held previously at two locations in the Bronx (NY): Jerome Park (1867–1889) and Morris Park (1890–1904).

Year	Winner (Margin)	Jockey	Second	Third	Time
1867	Ruthless (Head)	J. Gilpatrick	De Courcy	Rivoli	3:05
1868	General Duke (2)	R. Swim	Northumberland	Fannie Ludlow	3:02
1869	Fenian (Unknown)	C. Miller	Glenelg	Invercauld	3:04¼
1870	Kingfisher (½)	E. Brown	Foster	Midday	2:59½
1871	Harry Bassett (3)	W. Miller	Stockwood	By-the-Sea	2:56
1872	Joe Daniels (¾)	James Rowe	Meteor	Shylock	2:58¼
1873	Springbok (4)	James Rowe	Count d'Orsay	Strachino	3:01¾
1874	Saxon (Neck)	G. Barbee	Grinstead	Aaron Pennington	2:39½
1875	Calvin (2)	R. Swim	Aristides	Milner	2:40¼
1876	Algerine (Head)	W. Donahue	Fiddlestick	Barricade	2:40½
1877	Cloverbrook (1)	C. Holloway	Loiterer	Baden-Baden	2:46
1878	Duke of Magenta (2)	L. Hughes	Bramble	Sparta	2:43½
1879	Spendthrift (5)	S. Evans	Monitor	Jericho	2:42¾
1880	Grenada (½)	L. Hughes	Ferncliffe	Turenne	2:47
1881	Saunterer (Neck)	T. Costello	Eole	Baltic	2:47
1882	Forester (5)	James McLaughlin	Babcock	Wyoming	2:43
1883	George Kinney (2)	James McLaughlin	Trombone	Renegade	2:42½
1884	Panique (½)	James McLaughlin	Knight of Ellerslie	Himalaya	2:42
1885	Tyrant (3½)	Paul Duffy	St. Augustine	Tecumseh	2:43
1886	Inspector B (1)	James McLaughlin	The Bard	Linden	2:41
1887*	Hanover (28-32)	James McLaughlin	Oneko		2:43½
1888*	Sir Dixon (12)	James McLaughlin	Prince Royal		2:40¼
1889	Eric (Head)	W. Hayward	Diable	Zephyrus	2:47
1890	Burlington (1)	S. Barnes	Devotee	Padishah	2:07¾
1891	Foxford (Neck)	E. Garrison	Montana	Laurestan	2:08¾
1892*	Patron (Unknown)	W. Hayward	Shellbark		2:17
1893	Comanche (Head)	Willie Simms	Dr. Rice	Rainbow	1:53¼
1894	Henry of Navarre (2-4)	Willie Simms	Prig	Assignee	1:56½
1895	Belmar (Head)	Fred Taral	Counter Tenor	Nanki Pooh	2:11½
1896	Hastings (Neck)	H. Griffin	Handspring	Hamilton II	2:24½
1897	Scottish Chieftain (1)	J. Scherrer	On Deck	Octagon	2:23¼
1898	Bowling Brook (8)	P. Littlefield	Previous	Hamburg	2:32
1899	Jean Bereaud (Head)	R. R. Clawson	Half Time	Glengar	2:23
1900	Ildrim (Head)	N. Turner	Petrucio	Missionary	2:21½
1901	Commando (½)	H. Spencer	The Parader	All Green	2:21
1902	Masterman (2)	John Bullmann	Ranald	King Hanover	2:22½
1903	Africander (2)	John Bullmann	Whorler	Red Knight	2:23⅕
1904	Delhi (3½)	George Odom	Graziallo	Rapid Water	2:06⅗
1905	Tanya (1/2)	E. Hildebrand	Blandy	Hot Shot	2:08
1906	Burgomaster (4)	L. Lyne	The Quail	Accountant	2:20
1907	Peter Pan (1)	G. Mountain	Superman	Frank Gill	Unknown
1908	Colin (Head)	Joe Notter	Fair Play	King James	Unknown
1909	Joe Madden (8)	E. Dugan	Wise Mason	Donald MacDonald	2:21⅗
1910*	Sweep (6)	J. Butwell	Duke of Ormonde		2:22
1913	Prince Eugene (½)	Roscoe Troxler	Rock View	Flying Fairy	2:18
1914	Luke McLuke (8)	M. Buxton	Gainer	Charlestonian	2:20
1915	The Finn (4)	G. Byrne	Half Rock	Pebbles	2:18⅖
1916	Friar Rock (3)	E. Haynes	Spur	Churchill	2:22
1917	Hourless (10)	J. Butwell	Skeptic	Wonderful	2:17⅘
1918	Johren (2)	Frank Robinson	War Cloud	Cum Sah	2:20⅖
1919	Sir Barton (5)	Johnny Loftus	Sweep On	Natural Bridge	2:17⅖
1920*	Man o' War (20)	Clarence Kummer	Donnacona		2:14⅕
1921	Grey Lag (3)	Earl Sande	Sporting Blood	Leonardo II	2:16⅘
1922	Pillory (2)	C. H. Miller	Snob II	Hea	2:18⅘
1923	Zev (1½)	Earl Sande	Chickvale	Rialto	2:19
1924	Mad Play (2)	Earl Sande	Mr. Mutt	Modest	2:18⅘
1925	American Flag (8)	Albert Johnson	Dangerous	Swope	2:16⅘
1926	Crusader (1)	Albert Johnson	Espino	Haste	2:32⅕
1927	Chance Shot (1½)	Earl Sande	Bois de Rose	Flambino	2:32⅖
1928	Vito (3)	Clarence Kummer	Genie	Diavolo	2:33⅕
1929	Blue Larkspur (¾)	Mack Garner	African	Jack High	2:32⅘
1930	Gallant Fox (3)	Earl Sande	Whichone	Questionnaire	2:31⅗

Belmont (Cont.)

Year	Winner (Margin)	Jockey	Second	Third	Time
1931	Twenty Grand (10)	Charles Kurtsinger	Sun Meadow	Jamestown	2:29⅗
1932	Faireno (1½)	T. Malley	Osculator	Flag Pole	2:32⅘
1933	Hurryoff (1½)	Mack Garner	Nimbus	Union	2:32⅗
1934	Peace Chance (6)	W. D. Wright	High Quest	Good Goods	2:29⅕
1935	Omaha (1½)	Willie Saunders	Firethorn	Rosemont	2:30⅗
1936	Granville (Nose)	James Stout	Mr. Bones	Hollyrood	2:30
1937	War Admiral (3)	Charles Kurtsinger	Sceneshifter	Vamoose	2:28⅗
1938	Pasteurized (Neck)	James Stout	Dauber	Cravat	2:29⅖
1939	Johnstown (5)	James Stout	Belay	Gilded Knight	2:29⅗
1940	Bimelech (¾)	F. A. Smith	Your Chance	Andy K	2:29⅗
1941	Whirlaway (2½)	Eddie Arcaro	Robert Morris	Yankee Chance	2:31
1942	Shut Out (2)	Eddie Arcaro	Alsab	Lochinvar	2:29⅕
1943	Count Fleet (25)	Johnny Longden	Fairy Manhurst	Deseronto	2:28⅕
1944	Bounding Home (½)	G. L. Smith	Pensive	Bull Dandy	2:32⅕
1945	Pavot (5)	Eddie Arcaro	Wildlife	Jeep	2:30⅕
1946	Assault (3)	Warren Mehrtens	Natchez	Cable	2:30⅘
1947	Phalanx (5)	R. Donoso	Tide Rips	Tailspin	2:29⅖
1948	Citation (8)	Eddie Arcaro	Better Self	Escadru	2:28⅕
1949	Capot (½)	Ted Atkinson	Ponder	Palestinian	2:30⅕
1950	Middleground (1)	William Boland	Lights Up	Mr. Trouble	2:28⅗
1951	Counterpoint (4)	D. Gorman	Battlefield	Battle Morn	2:29
1952	One Count (2½)	Eddie Arcaro	Blue Man	Armageddon	2:30⅕
1953	Native Dancer (Neck)	Eric Guerin	Jamie K.	Royal Bay Gem	2:38⅗
1954	High Gun (Neck)	Eric Guerin	Fisherman	Limelight	2:30⅘
1955	Nashua (9)	Eddie Arcaro	Blazing Count	Portersville	2:29
1956	Needles (Neck)	David Erb	Career Boy	Fabius	2:29⅘
1957	Gallant Man (8)	Bill Shoemaker	Inside Tract	Bold Ruler	2:26⅗
1958	Cavan (6)	Pete Anderson	Tim Tam	Flamingo	2:30⅕
1959	Sword Dancer (¾)	Bill Shoemaker	Bagdad	Royal Orbit	2:28⅖
1960	Celtic Ash (5½)	Bill Hartack	Venetian Way	Disperse	2:29⅗
1961	Sherluck (2¼)	Braulio Baeza	Globemaster	Guadalcanal	2:29⅕
1962	Jaipur (Nose)	Bill Shoemaker	Admiral's Voyage	Crimson Satan	2:28⅘
1963	Chateaugay (2½)	Braulio Baeza	Candy Spots	Choker	2:30⅕
1964	Quadrangle (2)	Manuel Ycaza	Roman Brother	Northern Dancer	2:28⅖
1965	Hail to All (Neck)	John Sellers	Tom Rolfe	First Family	2:28⅖
1966	Amberold (2½)	William Boland	Buffle	Advocator	2:29⅗
1967	Damascus (2½)	Bill Shoemaker	Cool Reception	Gentleman James	2:28⅘
1968	Stage Door Johnny (1¼)	Hellodoro Gustines	Forward Pass	Call Me Prince	2:27⅕
1969	Arts and Letters (5½)	Braulio Baeza	Majestic Prince	Dike	2:28⅘
1970	High Echelon (¾)	John L. Rotz	Needles N Pins	Naskra	2:34
1971	Pass Catcher (¾)	Walter Blum	Jim French	Bold Reason	2:30⅖
1972	Riva Ridge (7)	Ron Turcotte	Ruritania	Cloudy Dawn	2:28
1973	Secretariat (31)	Ron Turcotte	Twice a Prince	My Gallant	2:24
1974	Little Current (7)	Miguel A. Rivera	Jolly Johu	Cannonade	2:29⅕
1975	Avatar (Neck)	Bill Shoemaker	Foolish Pleasure	Master Derby	2:28⅕
1976	Bold Forbes (Neck)	Angel Cordero Jr.	McKenzie Bridge	Great Contractor	2:29
1977	Seattle Slew (4)	Jean Cruguet	Run Dusty Run	Sanhedrin	2:29⅗
1978	Affirmed (Head)	Steve Cauthen	Alydar	Darby Creek Road	2:26⅘
1979	Coastal (3¼)	Ruben Hernandez	Golden Act	Spectacular Bid	2:28⅗
1980	Temperence Hill (2)	Eddie Maple	Genuine Risk	Rockhill Native	2:29⅘
1981	Summing (Neck)	George Martens	Highland Blade	Pleasant Colony	2:29
1982	Conquistador Cielo (14½)	Laffit Pincay, Jr.	Gato Del Sol	Illuminate	2:28⅕
1983	Caveat (3½)	Laffit Pincay Jr.	Slew o'Gold	Barberstown	2:27⅘
1984	Swale (4)	Laffit Pincay Jr.	Pine Circle	Morning Bob	2:27⅕
1985	Creme Fraiche (½)	Eddie Maple	Stephan's Odyssey	Chief's Crown	2:27
1986	Danzig Connection (1¼)	Chris McCarron	Johns Treasure	Ferdinand	2:29⅘
1987	Bet Twice (14)	Craig Perret	Cryptoclearance	Gulch	2:28⅕
1988	Risen Star (14¾)	Eddie Delahoussaye	Kingpost	Brian's Time	2:26⅖
1989	Easy Goer (8)	Pat Day	Sunday Silence	Le Voyageur	2:26
1990	Go and Go (8¼)	Michael Kinane	Thirty Six Red	Baron de Vaux	2:27⅕
1991	Hansel (Head)	Jerry Bailey	Strike the Gold	Mane Minister	2:28
1992	A.P. Indy (¾)	Eddie Delahoussaye	My Memoirs	Pine Bluff	2:26
1993	Colonial Affair (2¼)	Julie Krone	Kissin Kris	Wild Gale	2:29⅘
1994	Tabasco Cat (2)	Pat Day	Go For Gin	Strodes Creek	2:26⅘

Belmont (Cont.)

Year	Winner (Margin)	Jockey	Second	Third	Time
1995..........	Thunder Gulch (2)	Gary Stevens	Star Standard	Citadeed	2:32
1996..........	Editor's Note (1)	Rene Douglas	Skip Away	My Flag	2:28⅘
1997..........	Touch Gold (¾)	Chris McCarron	Silver Charm	Free House	2:28⅘
1998..........	Victory Gallop (Nose)	Gary Stevens	Real Quiet	Thomas Jo	2:28⅘
1999..........	Lemon Drop Kid (Head)	Jose Santos	Vision and Verse	Charismatic	2:27⅘
2000..........	Commendable (1½)	Pat Day	Aptitude	Unshaded	2:31.19
2001..........	Point Given (12¼)	Gary Stevens	A P Valentine	Monarchos	2:26.56
2002..........	Sarava (½)	Edgar Prado	Medaglia d'Oro	Sunday Break	2:29.71
2003..........	Empire Maker (¾)	Jerry Bailey	Ten Most Wanted	Funny Cide	2:28.26
2004..........	Birdstone (1)	Edgar Prado	Smarty Jones	Royal Assault	2:27.59

*Belmont was a two-horse race in 1887, '88, '92, 1910 and '20; and was not held in 1911–1912.
Note: Distance: 1 mile 5 furlongs (1867–89), 1¼ miles (1890–1905), 1⅜ miles (1906–25), 1½ miles (1926–present).

Triple Crown Winners

Year	Horse	Jockey	Owner	Trainer
1919..........	Sir Barton	John Loftus	J. K. L. Ross	H. G. Bedwell
1930..........	Gallant Fox	Earle Sande	Belair Stud	James Fitzsimmons
1935..........	Omaha	William Saunders	Belair Stud	James Fitzsimmons
1937..........	War Admiral	Charles Kurtsinger	Samuel D. Riddle	George Conway
1941..........	Whirlaway	Eddie Arcaro	Calumet Farm	Ben Jones
1943..........	Count Fleet	John Longden	Mrs J. D. Hertz	Don Cameron
1946..........	Assault	Warren Mehrtens	King Ranch	Max Hirsch
1948..........	Citation	Eddie Arcaro	Calumet Farm	Jimmy Jones
1973..........	Secretariat	Ron Turcotte	Meadow Stable	Lucien Laurin
1977..........	Seattle Slew	Jean Cruguet	Karen L. Taylor	William H. Turner Jr.
1978..........	Affirmed	Steve Cauthen	Harbor View Farm	Laz Barrera

Belmont Bill

The last time a horse won the Triple Crown, Bill Murray was a long way from New York's Belmont Park—way up in the woods of Ontario, in fact, filming the summer-camp comedy *Meatballs*. On June 5, 2004, he was among the record crowd of 120,139 who crammed the track to cheer on Smarty Jones in the Belmont Stakes. Shortly before the big race, Murray mingled in the paddock with the family and friends of Smarty's sizable entourage, posing for pictures with everyone who asked. When asked whom he was rooting for, Murray declared, "Oh, I'm for Smarty Jones. Aren't you? You wanna fight?" Murray—who watched the race in a box with Penny Chenery, who owned Secretariat—took Smarty's loss hard, staring in stunned silence across the track after the race.

Horse of the Year

Year	Horse	Owner	Trainer	Breeder
1936	Granville	Belair Stud	James Fitzsimmons	Belair Stud
1937	War Admiral	Samuel D. Riddle	George Conway	Mrs. Samuel D. Riddle
1938	Seabiscuit	Charles S. Howard	Tom Smith	Wheatley Stable
1939	Challedon	William L. Brann	Louis J. Schaefer	Branncastle Farm
1940	Challedon	William L. Brann	Louis J. Schaefer	Branncastle Farm
1941	Whirlaway	Calumet Farm	Ben Jones	Calumet Farm
1942	Whirlaway	Calumet Farm	Ben Jones	Calumet Farm
1943	Count Fleet	Mrs. John D. Hertz	Don Cameron	Mrs. John D. Hertz
1944	Twilight Tear	Calumet Farm	Ben Jones	Calumet Farm
1945	Busher	Louis B. Mayer	George Odom	Idle Hour Stock Farm
1946	Assault	King Ranch	Max Hirsch	King Ranch
1947	Armed	Calumet Farm	Jimmy Jones	Calumet Farm
1948	Citation	Calumet Farm	Jimmy Jones	Calumet Farm
1949	Capot	Greentree Stable	John M. Gaver Sr.	Greentree Stable
1950	Hill Prince	C.T. Chenery	Casey Hayes	C.T. Chenery
1951	Counterpoint	C.V. Whitney	Syl Veitch	C.V. Whitney
1952	One Count	Mrs. W. M. Jeffords	O. White	W M. Jeffords
1953	Tom Fool	Greentree Stable	John M. Gaver Sr.	D.A. Headley
1954	Native Dancer	A.G. Vanderbilt	Bill Winfrey	A.G. Vanderbilt
1955	Nashua	Belair Stud	James Fitzsimmons	Belair Stud
1956	Swaps	Ellsworth-Galbreath	Mesh Tenney	R. Ellsworth
1957	Bold Ruler	Wheatley Stable	James Fitzsimmons	Wheatley Stable
1958	Round Table	Kerr Stables	Willy Molter	Claiborne Farm
1959	Sword Dancer	Brookmeade Stable	Elliott Burch	Brookmeade Stable
1960	Kelso	Bohemia Stable	C. Hanford	Mrs. R.C. duPont
1961	Kelso	Bohemia Stable	C. Hanford	Mrs. R.C. duPont
1962	Kelso	Bohemia Stable	C. Hanford	Mrs. R.C. duPont
1963	Kelso	Bohemia Stable	C. Hanford	Mrs. R.C. duPont
1964	Kelso	Bohemia Stable	C. Hanford	Mrs. R.C. duPont
1965	Roman Brother	Harbor View Stable	Burley Parke	Ocala Stud
1966	Buckpasser	Ogden Phipps	Eddie Neloy	Ogden Phipps
1967	Damascus	Mrs. E. W. Bancroft	Frank Y. Whiteley Jr.	Mrs. E. W. Bancroft
1968	Dr. Fager	Tartan Stable	John A. Nerud	Tartan Farms
1969	Arts and Letters	Rokeby Stable	Elliott Burch	Paul Mellon
1970	Fort Marcy	Rokeby Stable	Elliott Burch	Paul Mellon
1971	Ack Ack	E.E. Fogelson	Charlie Whittingham	H.F. Guggenheim
1972	Secretariat	Meadow Stable	Lucien Laurin	Meadow Stud
1973	Secretariat	Meadow Stable	Lucien Laurin	Meadow Stud
1974	Forego	Lazy F Ranch	Sherrill W. Ward	Lazy F Ranch
1975	Forego	Lazy F Ranch	Sherrill W. Ward	Lazy F Ranch
1976	Forego	Lazy F Ranch	Frank Y. Whiteley Jr.	Lazy F Ranch
1977	Seattle Slew	Karen L. Taylor	Billy Turner Jr.	B.S. Castleman
1978	Affirmed	Harbor View Farm	Laz Barrera	Harbor View Farm
1979	Affirmed	Harbor View Farm	Laz Barrera	Harbor View Farm
1980	Spectacular Bid	Hawksworth Farm	Bud Delp	Mmes. Gilmore and Jason
1981	John Henry	Dotsam Stable	Ron McAnally and Lefty Nickerson	Golden Chance Farm
1982	Conquistador Cielo	H. de Kwiatkowski	Woody Stephens	L.E. Landoli
1983	All Along	Daniel Wildenstein	P.L. Biancone	Dayton
1984	John Henry	Dotsam Stable	Ron McAnally	Golden Chance Farm
1985	Spend a Buck	Hunter Farm	Cam Gambolati	Irish Hill & R.W. Harper
1986	Lady's Secret	Mr. & Mrs. Eugene Klein	D. Wayne Lukas	R.H. Spreen
1987	Ferdinand	Mrs. H.B. Keck	Charlie Whittingham	H.B. Keck
1988	Alysheba	D. & P. Scharbauer	Jack Van Berg	Preston Madden
1989	Sunday Silence	Gaillard, Hancock, & Whittingham	Charlie Whittingham	Oak Cliff Thoroughbreds
1990	Criminal Type	Calumet Farm	D. Wayne Lukas	Calumet Farm
1991	Black Tie Affair	Jeffrey Sullivan	Ernie Poulos	Stephen D. Peskoff
1992	A.P. Indy	Tomonori Tsurumaki	Neil Drysdale	W.S. Farish & W.S. Kilroy
1993	Kotashaan	La Presle Farm	Richard Mandella	La Presle Farm
1994	Holy Bull	Jimmy Croll	Jimmy Croll	Pelican Stable
1995	Cigar	Allen E. Paulson	William Mott	Allen E. Paulson
1996	Cigar	Allen E. Paulson	William Mott	Allen E. Paulson
1997	Favorite Trick	Joseph LaCombe	William Mott	Mr. & Mrs. M.L. Wood
1998	Skip Away	Carolyn Hine	Hubert Hine	Anna Marie Barnhart

Horse of the Year (Cont.)

Year	Horse	Owner	Trainer	Breeder
1999	Charismatic	Robert & Beverly Lewis	D. Wayne Lukas	William Farish/Partners
2000	Tiznow	Michael Cooper and Cecilia Straub-Rubens	Jay M. Robbins	Cecilia Straub-Rubens
2001	Point Given	The Thoroughbred Corp.	Bob Baffert	The Thoroughbred Corp.
2002	Azeri	Allen Paulson Living Trust	Laura de Seroux	Allen Paulson
2003	Mineshaft	William Farish	Neil Howard	William Farish

Note: From 1936 to 1970, the *Daily Racing Form* annually selected a "Horse of the Year." In 1971 the *Daily Racing Form*, with the Thoroughbred Racing Association and the National Turf Writers Association, jointly created the Eclipse Awards.

Eclipse Award Winners

2-YEAR-OLD COLT

1971	Riva Ridge
1972	Secretariat
1973	Protagonist
1974	Foolish Pleasure
1975	Honest Pleasure
1976	Seattle Slew
1977	Affirmed
1978	Spectacular Bid
1979	Rockhill Native
1980	Lord Avie
1981	Deputy Minister
1982	Roving Boy
1983	Devil's Bag
1984	Chief's Crown
1985	Tasso
1986	Capote
1987	Forty Niner
1988	Easy Goer
1989	Rhythm
1990	Fly So Free
1991	Arazi
1992	Gilded Time
1993	Dehere
1994	Timber Country
1995	Maria's Mon
1996	Boston Harbor
1997	Favorite Trick
1998	Answer Lively
1999	Anees
2000	Macho Uno
2001	Johannesburg
2002	Vindication
2003	Action This Day

2-YEAR-OLD FILLY

1971	Numbered Account
1972	La Prevoyante
1973	Talking Picture
1974	Ruffian
1975	Dearly Precious
1976	Sensational
1977	Lakeville Miss
1978	Candy Eclair, It's in the Air
1979	Smart Angle
1980	Heavenly Cause
1981	Before Dawn
1982	Landaluce
1983	Althea
1984	Outstandingly
1985	Family Style
1986	Brave Raj
1987	Epitome
1988	Open Mind
1989	Go for Wand
1990	Meadow Star
1991	Pleasant Stage
1992	Eliza
1993	Phone Chatter
1994	Flanders
1995	Golden Attraction
1996	Storm Song
1997	Countess Diana
1998	Silverbulletday
1999	Chilukki
2000	Caressing
2001	Tempera
2002	Storm Flag Flying
2003	Halfbridled

3-YEAR-OLD COLT

1971	Canonero II
1972	Key to the Mint
1973	Secretariat
1974	Little Current
1975	Wajima
1976	Bold Forbes
1977	Seattle Slew
1978	Affirmed
1979	Spectacular Bid
1980	Temperence Hill
1981	Pleasant Colony
1982	Conquistador Cielo
1983	Slew o' Gold
1984	Swale
1985	Spend A Buck
1986	Snow Chief
1987	Alysheba
1988	Risen Star
1989	Sunday Silence
1990	Unbridled
1991	Hansel
1992	A.P. Indy
1993	Prairie Bayou
1994	Holy Bull
1995	Thunder Gulch
1996	Skip Away
1997	Silver Charm
1998	Real Quiet
1999	Charismatic
2000	Tiznow
2001	Point Given
2002	War Emblem
2003	Funny Cide

CHAMPION TURF HORSE

1971	Run the Gantlet (3)
1972	Cougar II (6)
1973	Secretariat (3)
1974	Dahlia (4)
1975	Snow Knight (4)
1976	Youth (3)
1977	Johnny D (3)
1978	Mac Diarmida (3)

CHAMPION MALE TURF HORSE

1979	Bowl Game (5)
1980	John Henry (5)
1981	John Henry (6)
1982	Perrault (5)
1983	John Henry (8)
1984	John Henry (9)
1985	Cozzene (4)
1986	Manila (3)
1987	Theatrical (5)
1988	Sunshine Forever (3)
1989	Steinlen (6)
1990	Itsallgreektome (3)

CHAMPION MALE TURF HORSE (Cont.)

1991	Tight Spot (4)
1992	Sky Classic (5)
1993	Kotashaan (5)
1994	Paradise Creek (5)
1995	Northern Spur (4)
1996	Singspiel (4)
1997	Chief Bearhart (4)
1998	Buck's Boy (5)
1999	Daylami (5)
2000	Kalanisi (4)
2001	Fantastic Light (5)
2002	High Chaparral (3)
2003	High Chaparral (4)

CHAMPION FEMALE TURF HORSE

1979	Trillion (5)
1980	Just a Game II (4)
1981	De La Rose (3)
1982	April Run (4)
1983	All Along (4)
1984	Royal Heroine (4)
1985	Pebbles (4)

CHAMPION FEMALE TURF HORSE (Cont.)

1986	Estrapade (6)
1987	Miesque (3)
1988	Miesque (4)
1989	Brown Bess (7)
1990	Laugh and Be Merry (5)
1991	Miss Alleged (4)
1992	Flawlessly (4)
1993	Flawlessly (5)
1994	Hatoof (5)
1995	Possibly Perfect (5)
1996	Wandesta (5)
1997	Ryafan (3)
1998	Fiji (4)
1999	Soaring Softly (4)
2000	Perfect Sting (4)
2001	Banks Hill (3)
2002	Golden Apples (4)
2003	Islington (4)

Eclipse Award Winners (Cont.)

3-YEAR-OLD FILLY

1971 ....Turkish Trousers
1972 ....Susan's Girl
1973 ....Desert Vixen
1974 ....Chris Evert
1975 ....Ruffian
1976 ....Revidere
1977 ....Our Mims
1978 ....Tempest Queen
1979 ....Davona Dale
1980 ....Genuine Risk
1981 ....Wayward Lass
1982 ....Christmas Past
1983 ....Heartlight No. One
1984 ....Life's Magic
1985 ....Mom's Command
1986 ....Tiffany Lass
1987 ....Sacahuista
1988 ....Winning Colors
1989 ....Open Mind
1990 ....Go for Wand
1991 ....Dance Smartly
1992 ....Saratoga Dew
1993 ....Hollywood Wildcat
1994 ....Heavenly Prize
1995 ....Serena's Song
1996 ....Yank's Music
1997 ....Ajina
1998 ....Banshee Breeze
1999 ....Silverbulletday
2000 ....Surfside
2001 ....Xtra Heat
2002 ....Farda Amiga
2003 ....Bird Town

OLDER COLT, HORSE OR GELDING

1971 ....Ack Ack (5)
1972 ....Autobiography (4)
1973 ....Riva Ridge (4)
1974 ....Forego (4)
1975 ....Forego (5)
1976 ....Forego (6)
1977 ....Forego (7)
1978 ....Seattle Slew (4)
1979 ....Affirmed (4)
1980 ....Spectacular Bid (4)
1981 ....John Henry (6)
1982 ....Lemhi Gold (4)
1983 ....Bates Motel (4)
1984 ....Slew o'Gold (4)
1985 ....Vanlandingham (4)
1986 ....Turkoman (4)
1987 ....Ferdinand (4)
1988 ....Alysheba (4)
1989 ....Blushing John (4)
1990 ....Criminal Type (5)
1991 ....Black Tie Affair (5)
1992 ....Pleasant Tap (5)
1993 ....Bertrando (4)
1994 ....The Wicked North (5)
1995 ....Cigar (5)
1996 ....Cigar (6)
1997 ....Skip Away (4)
1998 ....Skip Away (5)
1999 ....Victory Gallop (4)
2000 ....Lemon Drop Kid (4)
2001 ....Tiznow (4)
2002 ....Left Bank (5)
2003 ....Mineshaft (4)

Note: Number in parentheses is horse's age.

OLDER FILLY OR MARE

1971 ....Shuvee (5)
1972 ....Typecast (6)
1973 ....Susan's Girl (4)
1974 ....Desert Vixen (4)
1975 ....Susan's Girl (6)
1976 ....Proud Delta (4)
1977 ....Cascapedia (4)
1978 ....Late Bloomer (4)
1979 ....Waya (5)
1980 ....Glorious Song (4)
1981 ....Relaxing (5)
1982 ....Track Robbery (6)
1983 ....Ambassador of Luck (4)
1984 ....Princess Rooney (4)
1985 ....Life's Magic (4)
1986 ....Lady's Secret (4)
1987 ....North Sider (5)
1988 ....Personal Ensign (4)
1989 ....Bayakoa (5)
1990 ....Bayakoa (6)
1991 ....Queena (5)
1992 ....Paseana (5)
1993 ....Paseana (6)
1994 ....Sky Beauty (4)
1995 ....Inside Information (4)
1996 ....Jewel Princess (4)
1997 ....Hidden Lake (4)
1998 ....Escena (5)
1999 ....Beautiful Pleasure (4)
2000 ....Riboletta (6)
2001 ....Gourmet Girl (6)
2002 ....Azeri (4)
2003 ....Azeri (4)

STEEPLECHASE OR HURDLE HORSE

1971 .....Shadow Brook (7)
1972 .....Soothsayer (5)
1973 .....Athenian Idol (7)
1974 .....Gran Kan (8)
1975 .....Life's Illusion (4)
1976 .....Straight & True (6)
1977 .....Cafe Prince (7)
1978 .....Cafe Prince (8)
1979 .....Martie's Anger (4)
1980 .....Zaccio (4)
1981 .....Zaccio (5)
1982 .....Zaccio (6)
1983 .....Flatterer (4)
1984 .....Flatterer (5)
1985 .....Flatterer (6)
1986 .....Flatterer (7)
1987 .....Inlander (6)
1988 .....Jimmy Lorenzo (6)
1989 .....Highland Bud (4)
1990 .....Morley Street (7)
1991 .....Morley Street (8)
1992 .....Lonesome Glory (4)
1993 .....Lonesome Glory (5)
1994 .....Warm Spell (6)
1995 .....Lonesome Glory (7)
1996 .....Correggio (5)
1997 .....Lonesome Glory (9)
1998 .....Flat Top (5)
1999 .....Lonesome Glory (11)
2000 .....All Gong (6)
2001 .....Pompeyo (7)
2002 .....Flat Top (9)
2003 .....McDynamo (6)

SPRINTER

1971 .....Ack Ack (5)
1972 .....Chou Croute (4)
1973 .....Shecky Greene (3)
1974 .....Forego (4)
1975 .....Gallant Bob (3)
1976 .....My Juliet (4)
1977 .....What a Summer (4)
1978 .....Dr. Patches (4)
         J.O. Tobin (4)
1979 .....Star de Naskra (4)
1980 .....Plugged Nickel (3)
1981 .....Guilty Conscience (5)
1982 .....Gold Beauty (3)
1983 .....Chinook Pass (4)
1984 .....Eillo (4)
1985 .....Precisionist (4)
1986 .....Smile (4)
1987 .....Groovy (4)
1988 .....Gulch (4)
1989 .....Safely Kept (3)
1990 .....Housebuster (3)
1991 .....Housebuster (4)
1992 .....Rubiano (5)
1993 .....Cardmania (7)
1994 .....Cherokee Run (4)
1995 .....Not Surprising (5)
1996 .....Lit de Justice (6)
1997 .....Smoke Glacken (3)
1998 .....Reraise (3)
1999 .....Artax (4)
2000 .....Kona Gold (6)
2001 .....Squirtle Squirt (3)
2002 .....Orientate (4)
2003 .....Aldebaran (5)

OUTSTANDING OWNER

1971 .....Mr. & Mrs. E. E. Fogleson
1974 .....Dan Lasater
1975 .....Dan Lasater
1976 .....Dan Lasater
1977 .....Maxwell Gluck
1978 .....Harbor View Farm
1979 .....Harbor View Farm
1980 .....Mr. & Mrs. Bertram
1981 .....Dotsam Stable
1982 .....Viola Sommer
1983 .....John Franks
1984 .....John Franks
1985 .....Mr. & Mrs. Eugene Klein
1986 .....Mr. & Mrs. Eugene Klein
1987 .....Mr. & Mrs. Eugene Klein
1988 .....Ogden Phipps
1989 .....Ogden Phipps
1990 .....Frances Genter
1991 .....Sam-Son Farm
1992 .....Juddmonte Farms
1993 .....John Franks
1994 .....John Franks
1995 .....Allen E. Paulson
1996 .....Allen E. Paulson
1997 .....Carolyn Hine
1998 .....Frank Stronach
1999 .....Frank Stronach
2000 .....Frank Stronach
2001 .....Richard Englander
2002 .....Richard Englander
2003 .....Juddmonte Farms

Eclipse Award Winners (Cont.)

OUTSTANDING TRAINER	OUTSTANDING JOCKEY	OUTSTANDING APPRENTICE JOCKEY
1971.....Charlie Whittingham	1971.....Laffit Pincay Jr.	1971.....Gene St. Leon
1972.....Lucien Laurin	1972.....Braulio Baeza	1972.....Thomas Wallis
1973.....H. Allen Jerkens	1973.....Laffit Pincay Jr	1973.....Steve Valdez
1974.....Sherrill Ward	1974.....Laffit Pincay Jr	1974.....Chris McCarron
1975.....Steve DiMauro	1975.....Braulio Baeza	1975.....Jimmy Edwards
1976.....Lazaro Barrera	1976.....Sandy Hawley	1976.....George Martens
1977.....Lazaro Barrera	1977.....Steve Cauthen	1977.....Steve Cauthen
1978.....Lazaro Barrera	1978.....Darrel McHargue	1978.....Ron Franklin
1979.....Lazaro Barrera	1979.....Laffit Pincay Jr.	1979.....Cash Asmussen
1980.....Bud Delp	1980.....Chris McCarron	1980.....Frank Lovato Jr.
1981.....Ron McAnally	1981.....Bill Shoemaker	1981.....Richard Migliore
1982.....Charlie Whittingham	1982.....Angel Cordero Jr	1982.....Alberto Delgado
1983.....Woody Stephens	1983.....Angel Cordero Jr	1983.....Declan Murphy
1984.....Jack Van Berg	1984.....Pat Day	1984.....Wesley Ward
1985.....D. Wayne Lukas	1985.....Laffit Pincay Jr	1985.....Art Madrid Jr.
1986.....D. Wayne Lukas	1986.....Pat Day	1986.....Allen Stacy
1987.....D. Wayne Lukas	1987.....Pat Day	1987.....Kent Desormeaux
1988.....Claude R. McGaughey III	1988.....Jose Santos	1988.....Steve Capanas
1989.....Charlie Whittingham	1989.....Kent Desormeaux	1989.....Michael Luzzi
1990.....Carl Nafzger	1990.....Craig Perret	1990.....Mark Johnston
1991.....Ron McAnally	1991.....Pat Day	1991.....Mickey Walls
1992.....Ron McAnally	1992.....Kent Desormeaux	1992.....Jesus A. Bracho
1993.....Bobby Frankel	1993.....Mike Smith	1993.....Juan Umana
1994.....D. Wayne Lukas	1994.....Mike Smith	1994.....Dale Beckner
1995.....William Mott	1995.....Jerry Bailey	1995.....Ramon Perez
1996.....William Mott	1996.....Jerry Bailey	1996.....Neil Pozansky
1997.....Bob Baffert	1997.....Jerry Bailey	1997.....Phil Teator
1998.....Bob Baffert	1998.....Gary Stevens	Roberto Rosado
1999.....Bob Baffert	1999.....Jorge Chavez	1998.....Shaun Bridgmohan
2000.....Robert Frankel	2000.....Jerry Bailey	1999.....Ariel Smith
2001.....Robert Frankel	2001.....Jerry Bailey	2000.....Tyler Baze
2002.....Robert Frankel	2002.....Jerry Bailey	2001.....Jeremy Rose
2003.....Robert Frankel	2003.....Jerry Bailey	2002.....Ryan Fogelsonger
		2003.....Eddie Castro

Eclipse Award Winners (Cont.)

OUTSTANDING BREEDER

1974.....John W. Galbreath
1975.....Fred W. Hooper
1976.....Nelson Bunker Hunt
1977.....Edward Plunket Taylor
1978.....Harbor View Farm
1979.....Claiborne Farm
1980.....Mrs. Henry D. Paxson
1981.....Golden Chance Farm
1982.....Fred W. Hooper
1983.....Edward Plunket Taylor
1984.....Claiborne Farm
1985.....Nelson Bunker Hunt
1986.....Paul Mellon
1987.....Nelson Bunker Hunt
1988.....Ogden Phipps
1989.....North Ridge Farm
1990.....Calumet Farm
1991.....John and Betty Mabee
1992.....William S. Farish III
1993.....Allen Paulson
1994.....William T. Young
1995.....Juddmonte Farms
1996.....Fansworth Farms

OUTSTANDING BREEDER (Cont.)

1997.....Golden Eagle Farm
1998.....John and Betty Mabee
1999.....William Farish/Partners
2000.....Frank Stronach/Adena
         Springs
2001.....Juddmonte Farms
2002.....Juddmonte Farms
2003.....Juddmonte Farms

AWARD OF MERIT

1976.....Jack J. Dreyfus
1977.....Steve Cauthen
1978.....Ogden Phipps
1979.....Frank E. Kilroe
1980.....John D. Schapiro
1981.....Bill Shoemaker
1984.....John Gaines
1985.....Keene Daingerfield
1986.....Herman Cohen
1987.....J. B. Faulconer
1988.....John Forsythe
1989.....Michael P. Sandler
1991.....Fred W. Hooper
1994.....Alfred G. Vanderbilt
1996.....Allen E. Paulson
2002.....Howard Battle
         Ogden Phipps

SPECIAL AWARD

1971.....Robert J. Kleberg
1974.....Charles Hatton
1976.....Bill Shoemaker
1980.....John T. Landry
         Pierre E. Bellocq (Peb)
1984.....C. V. Whitney
1985.....Arlington Park
1987.....Anheuser-Busch
1988.....Edward J. DeBartolo Sr.
1989.....Richard Duchossois
1994.....John Longden
         Edward Arcaro
1998.....Oak Tree Racing
         Association
2002.....Keeneland Library

Note: Special Award and Award of Merit, for long-term and/or outstanding service to the industry, not presented annually.

Reporting for Duty

Sgt. York, a 13-year-old standardbred, was selected to serve as the riderless horse escorting the body of President Ronald Reagan to the Capitol in June 2004. The black gelding had a modest career as a harness racehorse named Allaboard Jules, winning five of 23 races and $14,881 at New York and New Jersey tracks in the 1990s. When his career ended, an employee of the New Jersey Racing Commission who had a son in the Army got him a job at Fort Myer, an Army base near Arlington National Cemetery. He was rechristened Sgt. York and made a caparisoned horse, which trails the caisson without a rider as a tribute to a fallen hero.

Breeders' Cup

Location: Hollywood 1984, '87, '97; Aqueduct 1985; Santa Anita 1986, '93, '03; Churchill Downs 1988, '91, '98,'00; Gulfstream (FL) 1989, '92, '99; Belmont 1990, '95, '01; Woodbine (Toronto) 1996; Arlington 2002.

Juveniles

Year	Winner (Margin)	Jockey	Second	Third	Time
1984	Chief's Crown (¾)	Don MacBeth	Tank's Prospect	Spend a Buck	1:36⅕
1985	Tasso (Nose)	Laffit Pincay Jr.	Storm Cat	Scat Dancer	1:36⅕
1986	Capote (1¼)	Laffit Pincay Jr.	Qualify	Alysheba	1:43⅘
1987	Success Express (1¾)	Jose Santos	Regal Classic	Tejano	1:35⅕
1988	Is It True (1¼)	Laffit Pincay Jr.	Easy Goer	Tagel	1:46⅗
1989	Rhythm (2)	Craig Perret	Grand Canyon	Slavic	1:43⅗
1990	Fly So Free (3)	Jose Santos	Take Me Out	Lost Mountain	1:43⅖
1991	Arazi (4¾)	Pat Valenzuela	Bertrando	Snappy Landing	1:44⅗
1992	Gilded Time (¾)	Chris McCarron	It'sali'lknownfact	River Special	1:43⅖
1993	Brocco (5)	Gary Stevens	Blumin Affair	Tabasco Cat	1:42⅘
1994	Timber Country (½)	Pat Day	Eltish	Tejano Run	1:44⅖
1995	Unbridled's Song (Neck)	Mike Smith	Hennessy	Editor's Note	1:41⅗
1996	Boston Harbor (Neck)	Jerry Bailey	Acceptable	Ordway	1:43⅖
1997	Favorite Trick (5½)	Pat Day	Dawson's Legacy	Nationalore	1:41⅗
1998	Answer Lively (Head)	Jerry Bailey	Aly's Alley	Cat Thief	1:44
1999	Anees (2½)	Gary Stevens	Chief Seattle	High Yield	1:42.29
2000	Macho Uno (Nose)	Jerry Bailey	Point Given	Street Cry	1:42.05
2001	Johannesburg (1¼)	Michael Kinane	Repent	Siphonic	1:42.27
2002	Vindication (2¾)	Mike Smith	Kafwain	Hold That Tiger	1:49.61
2003	Action This Day (2¼)	David Flores	Minister Eric	Chapel Royal	1:43.62

Note: One mile (1984–85, '87), 1 1/16 miles (1986 and 1988–2001, '03), 1⅛ miles (2002).

Juvenile Fillies

Year	Winner (Margin)	Jockey	Second	Third	Time
1984	Outstandingly*	Walter Guerra	Dusty Heart	Fine Spirit	1:37⅘
1985	Twilight Ridge (1)	Jorge Velasquez	Family Style	Steal a Kiss	1:35⅘
1986	Brave Raj (5½)	Pat Valenzuela	Tappiano	Saros Brig	1:43⅕
1987	Epitome (Nose)	Pat Day	Jeanne Jones	Dream Team	1:36⅖
1988	Open Mind (1¾)	Angel Cordero Jr.	Darby Shuffle	Lea Lucinda	1:46⅗
1989	Go for Wand (2¾)	Randy Romero	Sweet Roberta	Stella Madrid	1:44⅕
1990	Meadow Star (5)	Jose Santos	Private Treasure	Dance Smartly	1:44
1991	Pleasant Stage (Neck)	Eddie Delahoussaye	La Spia	Cadillac Women	1:46⅖
1992	Eliza (1½)	Pat Valenzuela	Educated Risk	Boots 'n Jackie	1:42⅘
1993	Phone Chatter (Head)	Laffit Pincay	Sardula	Heavenly Prize	1:43
1994	Flanders (Head)	Pat Day	Serena's Song	Stormy Blues	1:45⅕
1995	My Flag (½)	Jerry Bailey	Cara Rafaela	Golden Attraction	1:42⅖
1996	Storm Song (4½)	Craig Perret	Love That Jazz	Critical Factor	1:43⅗
1997	Countess Diana (8½)	Shane Sellers	Career Collection	Primaly	1:42⅕
1998	Silverbulletday (½)	Gary Stevens	Excellent Meeting	Three Ring	1:43⅗
1999	Cash Run (1¼)	Jerry Bailey	Chilukki	Surfside	1:43.31
2000	Caressing (½)	John Velazquez	Platinum Tiara	Shes a Devil Due	1:42.72
2001	Tempera (1½)	David Flores	Imperial Gesture	Bella Bellucci	1:41.49
2002	Storm Flag Flying (½)	John Velazquez	Composure	Santa Catarina	1:49.60
2003	Halfbridled (2½)	Julie Krone	Ashado	Victory U.S.A.	1:42.75

*In 1984, winner Fran's Valentine dq'd. Note: One mile (1984-85, '87), 1 1/16 miles (1986 and 1988-01, '03), 1⅛ miles (02).

Sprint

Year	Winner (Margin)	Jockey	Second	Third	Time
1984	Eillo (Nose)	Craig Perret	Commemorate	Fighting Fit	1:10⅕
1985	Precisionist (¾)	Chris McCarron	Smile	Mt. Livermore	1:08⅖
1986	Smile (1¼)	Jacinto Vasquez	Pine Tree Lane	Bedside Promise	1:08⅖
1987	Very Subtle (4)	Pat Valenzuela	Groovy	Exclusive Enough	1:08⅘
1988	Gulch (¾)	Angel Cordero Jr	Play the King	Afleet	1:10⅖
1989	Dancing Spree (Neck)	Angel Cordero Jr	Safely Kept	Dispersal	1:09
1990	Safely Kept (Neck)	Craig Perret	Dayjur	Black Tie Affair	1:09⅗
1991	Sheikh Albadou (Neck)	Pat Eddery	Pleasant Tap	Robyn Dancer	1:09⅕
1992	Thirty Slews (Neck)	Eddie Delahoussaye	Meafara	Rubiano	1:08⅕
1993	Cardmania (Neck)	Eddie Delahoussaye	Meafara	Gilded Time	1:08⅗
1994	Cherokee Run (Head)	Mike Smith	Soviet Problem	Cardmania	1:09⅖
1995	Desert Stormer (Neck)	Kent Desormeaux	Mr. Greeley	Lit de Justice	1:09
1996	Lit de Justice (1¼)	Corey Nakatani	Paying Dues	Honour and Glory	1:08⅗
1997	Elmhurst (½)	Corey Nakatani	Hesabull	Bet on Sunshine	1:08
1998	Reraise (2)	Corey Nakatani	Grand Slam	Kona Gold	1:09
1999	Artax (½)	Jorge Chavez	Kona Gold	Big Jag	1:07.89
2000	Kona Gold (½)	Alex Solis	Honest Lady	Bet on Sunshine	1:07.77
2001	Squirtle Squirt (½)	Jerry Bailey	Xtra Heat	Caller One	1:08.41
2002	Orientate (½)	Jerry Bailey	Thunderello	Crafty C.T.	1:08.89
2003	Cajun Beat (2¼)	Cornelio Velasquez	Bluesthestandard	Shake You Down	1:07.95

Note: Six furlongs (since 1984).

Breeders' Cup *(Cont.)*

Mile

Year	Winner (Margin)	Jockey	Second	Third	Time
1984	Royal Heroine (1½)	Fernando Toro	Star Choice	Cozzene	1:32⅗
1985	Cozzene (2¼)	Walter Guerra	Al Mamoon*	Shadeed	1:35
1986	Last Tycoon (Head)	Yves St-Martin	Palace Music	Fred Astaire	1:35⅕
1987	Miesque (3½)	Freddie Head	Show Dancer	Sonic Lady	1:32⅘
1988	Miesque (4)	Freddie Head	Steinlen	Simply Majestic	1:38⅗
1989	Steinlen (¾)	Jose Santos	Sabona	Most Welcome	1:37⅕
1990	Royal Academy (Neck)	Lester Piggott	Itsallgreektome	Priolo	1:35⅕
1991	Opening Verse (2¼)	Pat Valenzuela	Val de Bois	Star of Cozzene	1:37⅖
1992	Lure (3)	Mike Smith	Paradise Creek	Brief Truce	1:32⅘
1993	Lure (2¼)	Mike Smith	Ski Paradise	Fourstars Allstar	1:33⅖
1994	Barathea (Head)	Frankie Dettori	Johann Quatz	Unfinished Symph	1:34⅖
1995	Ridgewood Pearl (2)	John Murtagh	Fastness	Sayyedati	1:43⅗
1996	Da Hoss (1½)	Gary Stevens	Spinning World	Same Old Wish	1:35⅘
1997	Spinning World (2)	Cash Asmussen	Geri	Decorated Hero	1:32⅘
1998	Da Hoss (Head)	John Velazquez	Hawksley Hill	Labeeb	1:35⅕
1999	Silic (Neck)	Corey Nakatani	Tuzla	Docksider	1:34.26
2000	War Chant (Neck)	Gary Stevens	North East Bound	Dansili	1:34.67
2001	Val Royal (1¾)	Jose Valdivia	Forbidden Apple	Bach	1:32.05
2002	Domedriver (¾)	Thierry Thulliez	Rock of Gibraltar	Good Journey	1:36.92
2003	Six Perfections (¾)	Jerry Bailey	Touch of the Blues	Century City	1:33.86

*2nd place finisher Palace Music was disqualified for interference and placed 9th.

Distaff

Year	Winner (Margin)	Jockey	Second	Third	Time
1984	Princess Rooney (7)	Eddie Delahoussaye	Life's Magic	Adored	2:02⅖
1985	Life's Magic (6¼)	Angel Cordero Jr.	Lady's Secret	Dontstop Themusic	2:02
1986	Lady's Secret (2½)	Pat Day	Fran's Valentine	Outstandingly	2:01⅕
1987	Sacahuista (2¼)	Randy Romero	Clabber Girl	Oueee Bebe	2:02⅘
1988	Personal Ensign (Nose)	Randy Romero	Winning Colors	Goodbye Halo	1:52
1989	Bayakoa (1½)	Laffit Pincay Jr.	Gorgeous	Open Mind	1:47⅖
1990	Bayakoa (6¾)	Laffit Pincay Jr.	Colonial Waters	Valay Maid	1:49⅕
1991	Dance Smarty (½)	Pat Day	Versailles Treaty	Brought to Mind	1:50⅘
1992	Paseana (4)	Chris McCarron	Versailles Treaty	Magical Maiden	1:48
1993	Hollywood Wildcat (Nose)	Eddie Delahoussaye	Paseana	Re Toss	1:48⅕
1994	One Dreamer (Neck)	Gary Stevens	Heavenly Prize	Miss Dominique	1:50⅗
1995	Inside Information (13½)	Mike Smith	Heavenly Prize	Lakeway	1:46
1996	Jewel Princess (1½)	Corey Nakatani	Serena's Song	Different	1:48⅖
1997	Ajina (2)	Mike Smith	Sharp Cat	Escena	1:47⅕
1998	Escena (Nose)	Gary Stevens	Banshee Breeze	Keeper Hill	1:49⅘
1999	Beautiful Pleasure (¾)	Jorge Chavez	Banshee Breeze	Heritage of Gold	1:47.56
2000	Spain (1½)	Victor Espinoza	Surfside	Heritage of Gold	1:47.66
2001	Unbridled Elaine (head)	Pat Day	Spain	Too Item Limit	1:49.21
2002	Azeri (5)	Mike Smith	Farda Amiga	Imperial Gesture	1:48.64
2003	Adoration (4½)	Pat Valenzuela	Elloluv	Got Koko	1:49.17

Note: 1¼ miles (1984–87), 1⅛ miles (since 1988).

Turf

Year	Winner (Margin)	Jockey	Second	Third	Time
1984	Lashkari (Neck)	Yves St. Martin	All Along	Raami	2:25⅕
1985	Pebbles (Neck)	Pat Eddery	Strawberry Rd II	Mourjane	2:27
1986	Manila (Neck)	Jose Santos	Theatrical	Estrapade	2:25⅖
1987	Theatrical (½)	Pat Day	Trempolino	Village Star II	2:24⅖
1988	Great Communicator (½)	Ray Sibille	Sunshine Forever	Indian Skimmer	2:35⅕
1989	Prized (Head)	Eddie Delahoussaye	Sierra Roberta	Star Lift	2:28
1990	In the Wings (½)	Gary Stevens	With Approval	El Senor	2:29⅗
1991	Miss Alleged (2)	Eric Legrix	Itsallgreektome	Quest for Fame	2:30⅘
1992	Fraise (Nose)	Pat Valenzuela	Sky Classic	Quest For Fame	2:24
1993	Kotashaan (½)	Kent Desormeaux	Bien Bien	Luazar	2:25
1994	Tikkanen (1 ½)	Mike Smith	Hatoof	Paradise Creek	2:26⅖
1995	Northern Spur (Neck)	Chris McCarron	Freedom Cry	Carnegie	2:42
1996	Pilsudski (1 ¼)	Walter Swinburn	Singspiel	Swain	2:30⅕
1997	Chief Bearhart (¾)	Jose Santos	Borgia	Flag Down	2:23⅘
1998	Buck's Boy (1 ¼)	Shane Sellers	Yagli	Dushyantor	2:28⅗
1999	Daylami (2½)	Frankie Dettori	Royal Anthem	Buck's Boy	2:24.73
2000	Kalanisi (½)	John Murtagh	Quiet Resolve	John's Call	2:26.96
2001	Fantastic Light (¾)	Frankie Dettori	Milan	Timboroa	2:24.36
2002	High Chaparral (1¾)	Michael Kinane	With Anticipation	Falcon Flight	2:30.14
2003	High Chaparral/Johar	Michael Kinane/Alex Solis		Falbrav	2:24.24

Note: 1½ miles.

Breeders' Cup (Cont.)

Classic

Year	Winner (Margin)	Jockey	Second	Third	Time
1984	Wild Again (Head)	Pat Day	Slew o' Gold*	Gate Dancer	2:03⅖
1985	Proud Truth (Head)	Jorge Velasquez	Gate Dancer	Turkoman	2:00⅘
1986	Skywalker (1¼)	Laffit Pincay Jr.	Turkoman	Precisionist	2:00⅖
1987	Ferdinand (Nose)	Bill Shoemaker	Alysheba	Judge Angelucci	2:01⅖
1988	Alysheba (Nose)	Chris McCarron	Seeking the Gold	Waquoit	2:04⅘
1989	Sunday Silence (½)	Chris McCarron	Easy Goer	Blushing John	2:00⅕
1990	Unbridled (1)	Pat Day	Ibn Bey	Thirty Six Red	2:02⅕
1991	Black Tie Affair (1¼)	Jerry Bailey	Twilight Agenda	Unbridled	2:02⅘
1992	A.P. Indy (2)	Eddie Delahoussaye	Pleasant Tap	Jolypha	2:00⅕
1993	Arcangues (2)	Jerry Bailey	Bertrando	Kissin Kris	2:00⅘
1994	Concern (Neck)	Jerry Bailey	Tabasco Cat	Dramatic Gold	2:02⅖
1995	Cigar (2½)	Jerry Bailey	L'Carriere	Unaccounted For	1:59⅖
1996	Alphabet Soup (Nose)	Chris McCarron	Louis Quatorze	Cigar	2:01
1997	Skip Away (6)	Mike Smith	Deputy Commander	Dowty	1:59⅕
1998	Awesome Again (¾)	Pat Day	Silver Charm	Swain	2:02
1999	Cat Thief (1¼)	Pat Day	Budroyale	Golden Missile	1:59.52
2000	Tiznow (Neck)	Chris McCarron	Giant's Causeway	Captain Steve	2:00.75
2001	Tiznow (Nose)	Chris McCarron	Sakhee	Albert the Great	2:00.62
2002	Volponi (6½)	Jose Santos	Medaglia d'Oro	Milwaukee Brew	2:01.39
2003	Pleasantly Perfect (1½)	Alex Solis	Medaglia d'Oro	Dynever	1:59.88

*2nd place finisher Gate Dancer was disqualified for interference and placed 3rd.

Note: 1¼ miles.

England's Triple Crown Winners

England's Triple Crown consists of the Two Thousand Guineas, held at Newmarket; the Epsom Derby, held at Epsom Downs; and the St. Leger Stakes, held at Doncaster.

Year	Horse	Owner
1853	West Australian	Mr. Bowes
1865	Gladiateur	F. DeLagrange
1866	Lord Lyon	R. Sutton
1886	*Ormonde	Duke of Westminster
1891	Common	†F. Johnstone
1893	Isinglass	H. McCalmont
1897	Galtee More	J. Gubbins
1899	Flying Fox	Duke of Westminster
1900	Diamond Jubilee	Prince of Wales
1903	*Rock Sand	J. Miller
1915	Pommern	S. Joel
1917	Gay Crusader	Mr. Fairie
1918	Gainsborough	Lady James Douglas
1935	*Bahram	Aga Khan
1970	‡Nijinsky II	C. W. Engelhard

*Imported into United States. †Raced in name of Lord Alington in Two Thousand Guineas. ‡Canadian-bred.

Horse—Money Won

Year	Horse	Age	Starts	1st	2nd	3rd	Winnings ($)
1919	Sir Barton	3	13	8	3	2	88,250
1920	Man o' War	3	11	11	0	0	166,140
1921	Morvich	2	11	11	0	0	115,234
1922	Pillory	3	7	4	1	1	95,654
1923	Zev	3	14	12	1	0	272,008
1924	Sarzen	3	12	8	1	1	95,640
1925	Pompey	2	10	7	2	0	121,630
1926	Crusader	3	15	9	4	0	166,033
1927	Anita Peabody	2	7	6	0	1	111,905
1928	High Strung	2	6	5	0	0	153,590
1929	Blue Larkspur	3	6	4	1	0	153,450
1930	Gallant Fox	3	10	9	1	0	308,275
1931	Gallant Flight	2	7	7	0	0	219,000
1932	Gusto	3	16	4	3	2	145,940
1933	Singing Wood	2	9	3	2	2	88,050
1934	Cavalcade	3	7	6	1	0	111,235
1935	Omaha	3	9	6	1	2	142,255
1936	Granville	3	11	7	3	0	110,295
1937	Seabiscuit	4	15	11	2	2	168,580
1938	Stagehand	3	15	8	2	3	189,710
1939	Challedon	3	15	9	2	3	184,535
1940	Bimelech	3	7	4	2	1	110,005
1941	Whirlaway	3	20	13	5	2	272,386
1942	Shut Out	3	12	8	2	0	238,872
1943	Count Fleet	3	6	6	0	0	174,055
1944	Pavot	2	8	8	0	0	179,040
1945	Busher	3	13	10	2	1	273,735
1946	Assault	3	15	8	2	3	424,195
1947	Armed	6	17	11	4	1	376,325
1948	Citation	3	20	19	1	0	709,470
1949	Ponder	3	21	9	5	2	321,825
1950	Noor	5	12	7	4	1	346,940
1951	Counterpoint	3	15	7	2	1	250,525
1952	Crafty Admiral	4	16	9	4	1	277,225
1953	Native Dancer	3	10	9	1	0	513,425
1954	Determine	3	15	10	3	2	328,700
1955	Nashua	3	12	10	1	1	752,550
1956	Needles	3	8	4	2	0	440,850
1957	Round Table	3	22	15	1	3	600,383
1958	Round Table	4	20	14	4	0	662,780
1959	Sword Dancer	3	13	8	4	0	537,004
1960	Bally Ache	3	15	10	3	1	445,045
1961	Carry Back	3	16	9	1	3	565,349
1962	Never Bend	2	10	7	1	2	402,969
1963	Candy Spots	3	12	7	2	1	604,481
1964	Gun Bow	4	16	8	4	2	580,100
1965	Buckpasser	2	11	9	1	0	568,096
1966	Buckpasser	3	14	13	1	0	669,078
1967	Damascus	3	16	12	3	1	817,941
1968	Forward Pass	3	13	7	2	0	546,674
1969	Arts and Letters	3	14	8	5	1	555,604
1970	Personality	3	18	8	2	1	444,049
1971	Riva Ridge	2	9	7	0	0	503,263
1972	Droll Role	4	19	7	3	4	471,633
1973	Secretariat	3	12	9	2	1	860,404
1974	Chris Evert	3	8	5	1	2	551,063
1975	Foolish Pleasure	3	11	5	4	1	716,278
1976	Forego	6	8	6	1	1	401,701
1977	Seattle Slew	3	7	6	0	1	641,370
1978	Affirmed	3	11	8	2	0	901,541
1979	Spectacular Bid	3	12	10	1	1	1,279,334
1980	Temperence Hill	3	17	8	3	1	1,130,452
1981	John Henry	6	10	8	0	0	1,798,030
1982	Perrault	5	8	4	1	2	1,197,400
1983	All Along	4	7	4	1	1	2,138,963
1984	Slew o'Gold	4	6	5	1	0	2,627,944
1985	Spend A Buck	3	7	5	1	1	3,552,704

Horse—Money Won (Cont.)

Year	Horse	Age	Starts	1st	2nd	3rd	Winnings ($)
1986	Snow Chief	3	9	6	1	1	1,875,200
1987	Alysheba	3	10	3	3	1	2,511,156
1988	Alysheba	4	9	7	1	0	3,808,600
1989	Sunday Silence	3	9	7	2	0	4,578,454
1990	Unbridled	3	11	4	3	2	3,718,149
1991	Dance Smartly	3	8	8	0	0	2,876,821
1992	A.P. Indy	3	7	5	0	1	2,622,560
1993	Kotashaan	3	10	6	3	0	2,619,014
1994	Paradise Creek	5	11	8	2	1	2,610,187
1995	Cigar	5	10	10	0	0	4,819,800
1996	Cigar	6	8	5	2	1	4,910,000
1997	Skip Away	4	11	4	5	2	4,089,000
1998	Silver Charm	4	9	6	2	0	4,696,506
1999	Almutawakel	4	4	1	1	1	3,290,000
2000	Dubai Millennium	4	1	1	0	0	3,600,000
2001	Captain Steve	4	6	2	1	1	4,201,200
2002	War Emblem	4	10	5	0	0	3,455,000
2003	Pleasantly Perfect	5	4	2	0	1	2,470,000

Trainer—Money Won

Year	Trainer	Wins	Winnings ($)	Year	Trainer	Wins	Winnings ($)
1908	James Rowe, Sr.	50	284,335	1956	Willie Molter	142	1,227,402
1909	Sam Hildreth	73	123,942	1957	Jimmy Jones	70	1,150,910
1910	Sam Hildreth	84	148,010	1958	Willie Molter	69	1,116,544
1911	Sam Hildreth	67	49,418	1959	Willie Molter	71	847,290
1912	John F. Schorr	63	58,110	1960	Hirsch Jacobs	97	748,349
1913	James Rowe, Sr.	18	45,936	1961	Jimmy Jones	62	759,856
1914	R. C. Benson	45	59,315	1962	Mesh Tenney	58	1,099,474
1915	James Rowe, Sr.	19	75,596	1963	Mesh Tenney	40	860,703
1916	Sam Hildreth	39	70,950	1964	Bill Winfrey	61	1,350,534
1917	Sam Hildreth	23	61,698	1965	Hirsch Jacobs	91	1,331,628
1918	H. Guy Bedwell	53	80,296	1966	Eddie Neloy	93	2,456,250
1919	H. Guy Bedwell	63	208,728	1967	Eddie Neloy	72	1,776,089
1920	L. Feustal	22	186,087	1968	Eddie Neloy	52	1,233,101
1921	Sam Hildreth	85	262,768	1969	Elliott Burch	26	1,067,936
1922	Sam Hildreth	74	247,014	1970	Charlie Whittingham	82	1,302,354
1923	Sam Hildreth	75	392,124	1971	Charlie Whittingham	77	1,737,115
1924	Sam Hildreth	77	255,608	1972	Charlie Whittingham	79	1,734,020
1925	G. R. Tompkins	30	199,245	1973	Charlie Whittingham	85	1,865,385
1926	Scott P. Harlan	21	205,681	1974	Pancho Martin	166	2,408,419
1927	W. H. Bringloe	63	216,563	1975	Charlie Whittingham	93	2,437,244
1928	John F. Schorr	65	258,425	1976	Jack Van Berg	496	2,976,196
1929	James Rowe, Jr.	25	314,881	1977	Laz Barrera	127	2,715,848
1930	Sunny Jim Fitzsimmons	47	397,355	1978	Laz Barrera	100	3,307,164
1931	Big Jim Healey	33	297,300	1979	Laz Barrera	98	3,608,517
1932	Sunny Jim Fitzsimmons	68	266,650	1980	Laz Barrera	99	2,969,151
1933	Humming Bob Smith	53	135,720	1981	Charlie Whittingham	74	3,993,300
1934	Humming Bob Smith	43	249,938	1982	Charlie Whittingham	63	4,587,457
1935	Bud Stotler	87	303,005	1983	D. Wayne Lukas	78	4,267,261
1936	Sunny Jim Fitzsimmons	42	193,415	1984	D. Wayne Lukas	131	5,835,921
1937	Robert McGarvey	46	209,925	1985	D. Wayne Lukas	218	11,155,188
1938	Earl Sande	15	226,495	1986	D. Wayne Lukas	259	12,345,180
1939	Sunny Jim Fitzsimmons	45	266,205	1987	D. Wayne Lukas	343	17,502,110
1940	Silent Tom Smith	14	269,200	1988	D. Wayne Lukas	318	17,842,358
1941	Plain Ben Jones	70	475,318	1989	D. Wayne Lukas	305	16,103,998
1942	John M. Gaver Sr.	48	406,547	1990	D. Wayne Lukas	267	14,508,871
1943	Plain Ben Jones	73	267,915	1991	D. Wayne Lukas	289	15,942,223
1944	Plain Ben Jones	60	601,660	1992	D. Wayne Lukas	230	9,806,436
1945	Silent Tom Smith	52	510,655	1993	Robert Frankel	79	8,883,252
1946	Hirsch Jacobs	99	560,077	1994	D. Wayne Lukas	147	9,247,457
1947	Jimmy Jones	85	1,334,805	1995	D. Wayne Lukas	194	12,842,866
1948	Jimmy Jones	81	1,118,670	1996	D. Wayne Lukas	192	15,966,344
1949	Jimmy Jones	76	978,587	1997	D. Wayne Lukas	175	10,338,957
1950	Preston Burch	96	637,754	1998	Bob Baffert	139	15,000,870
1951	John M. Gaver Sr.	42	616,392	1999	Bob Baffert	169	16,934,607
1952	Plain Ben Jones	29	662,137	2000	Bob Baffert	146	11,831,605
1953	Harry Trotsek	54	1,028,873	2001	Bob Baffert	138	16,354,996
1954	Willie Molter	136	1,107,860	2002	Robert Frankel	117	17,748,340
1955	Sunny Jim Fitzsimmons	66	1,270,055	2003	Robert Frankel	114	19,143,289

Jockey—Money Won

Year	Jockey	Mts	1st	2nd	3rd	Pct	Winnings ($)
1919	John Loftus	177	65	36	24	.37	252,707
1920	Clarence Kummer	353	87	79	48	.25	292,376
1921	Earl Sande	340	112	69	59	.33	263,043
1922	Albert Johnson	297	43	57	40	.14	345,054
1923	Earl Sande	430	122	89	79	.28	569,394
1924	Ivan Parke	844	205	175	121	.24	290,395
1925	Laverne Fator	315	81	54	44	.26	305,775
1926	Laverne Fator	511	143	90	86	.28	361,435
1927	Earl Sande	179	49	33	19	.27	277,877
1928	Pony McAtee	235	55	43	25	.23	301,295
1929	Mack Garner	274	57	39	33	.21	314,975
1930	Sonny Workman	571	152	88	79	.27	420,438
1931	Charles Kurtsinger	519	93	82	79	.18	392,095
1932	Sonny Workman	378	87	48	55	.23	385,070
1933	Robert Jones	471	63	57	70	.13	226,285
1934	Wayne D. Wright	919	174	154	114	.19	287,185
1935	Silvio Coucci	749	141	125	103	.19	319,760
1936	Wayne D. Wright	670	100	102	73	.15	264,000
1937	Charles Kurtsinger	765	120	94	106	.16	384,202
1938	Nick Wall	658	97	94	82	.15	385,161
1939	Basil James	904	191	165	105	.21	353,333
1940	Eddie Arcaro	783	132	143	112	.17	343,661
1941	Don Meade	1,164	210	185	158	.18	398,627
1942	Eddie Arcaro	687	123	97	89	.18	481,949
1943	John Longden	871	173	140	121	.20	573,276
1944	Ted Atkinson	1,539	287	231	213	.19	899,101
1945	John Longden	778	180	112	100	.23	981,977
1946	Ted Atkinson	1,377	233	213	173	.17	1,036,825
1947	Douglas Dodson	646	141	100	75	.22	1,429,949
1948	Eddie Arcaro	726	188	108	98	.26	1,686,230
1949	Steve Brooks	906	209	172	110	.23	1,316,817
1950	Eddie Arcaro	888	195	153	144	.22	1,410,160
1951	Bill Shoemaker	1,161	257	197	161	.22	1,329,890
1952	Eddie Arcaro	807	188	122	109	.23	1,859,591
1953	Bill Shoemaker	1,683	485	302	210	.29	1,784,187
1954	Bill Shoemaker	1,251	380	221	142	.30	1,876,760
1955	Eddie Arcaro	820	158	126	108	.19	1,864,796
1956	Bill Hartack	1,387	347	252	184	.25	2,343,955
1957	Bill Hartack	1,238	341	208	178	.28	3,060,501
1958	Bill Shoemaker	1,133	300	185	137	.26	2,961,693
1959	Bill Shoemaker	1,285	347	230	159	.27	2,843,133
1960	Bill Shoemaker	1,227	274	196	158	.22	2,123,961
1961	Bill Shoemaker	1,256	304	186	175	.24	2,690,819
1962	Bill Shoemaker	1,126	311	156	128	.28	2,916,844
1963	Bill Shoemaker	1,203	271	193	137	.22	2,526,925
1964	Bill Shoemaker	1,056	246	147	133	.23	2,649,553
1965	Braulio Baeza	1,245	270	200	201	.22	2,582,702
1966	Braulio Baeza	1,341	298	222	190	.22	2,951,022
1967	Braulio Baeza	1,064	256	184	127	.24	3,088,888
1968	Braulio Baeza	1,089	201	184	145	.18	2,835,108
1969	Jorge Velasquez	1,442	258	230	204	.18	2,542,315
1970	Laffit Pincay Jr.	1,328	269	208	187	.20	2,626,526
1971	Laffit Pincay Jr.	1,627	380	288	214	.23	3,784,377
1972	Laffit Pincay Jr.	1,388	289	215	205	.21	3,225,827
1973	Laffit Pincay Jr.	1,444	350	254	209	.24	4,093,492
1974	Laffit Pincay Jr.	1,278	341	227	180	.27	4,251,060
1975	Braulio Baeza	1,190	196	208	180	.16	3,674,398
1976	Angel Cordero Jr.	1,534	274	273	235	.18	4,709,500
1977	Steve Cauthen	2,075	487	345	304	.23	6,151,750
1978	Darrel McHargue	1,762	375	294	263	.21	6,188,353
1979	Laffit Pincay Jr.	1,708	420	302	261	.25	8,183,535
1980	Chris McCarron	1,964	405	318	282	.20	7,666,100
1981	Chris McCarron	1,494	326	251	207	.22	8,397,604
1982	Angel Cordero Jr.	1,838	397	338	227	.22	9,702,520
1983	Angel Cordero Jr.	1,792	362	296	237	.20	10,116,807
1984	Chris McCarron	1,565	356	276	218	.23	12,038,213
1985	Laffit Pincay Jr.	1,409	289	246	183	.21	13,415,049
1986	Jose Santos	1,636	329	237	222	.20	11,329,297
1987	Jose Santos	1,639	305	268	208	.19	12,407,355
1988	Jose Santos	1,867	370	287	265	.20	14,877,298

Jockey—Money Won (Cont.)

Year	Jockey	Mts	1st	2nd	3rd	Pct	Winnings ($)
1989	Jose Santos	1,459	285	238	220	.20	13,847,003
1990	Gary Stevens	1,504	283	245	202	.19	13,881,198
1991	Chris McCarron	1,440	265	228	206	.18	14,441,083
1992	Kent Desormeaux	1,568	361	260	208	.23	14,193,006
1993	Mike Smith	1,510	343	235	214	.23	14,008,148
1994	Mike Smith	1,484	317	250	196	.21	15,979,820
1995	Jerry Bailey	1,265	287	193	144	.23	16,308,230
1996	Jerry Bailey	1,187	298	189	165	.25	19,465,376
1997	Jerry Bailey	1,143	272	186	178	.26	18,260,553
1998	Gary Stevens	869	178	145	122	.20	19,358,840
1999	Pat Day	1,265	254	209	209	.20	18,092,845
2000	Pat Day	1,219	267	206	186	.22	17,479,838
2001	Jerry Bailey	912	227	194	137	.25	22,597,720
2002	Jerry Bailey	832	213	139	118	.26	19,271,814
2003	Jerry Bailey	776	206	149	97	.27	23,354,960

Jockey—Races Won

Year	Jockey	Mts	1st	2nd	3rd	Pct
1895	J. Perkins	762	192	177	129	.25
1896	J. Scherrer	1,093	271	227	172	.24
1897	H. Martin	803	173	152	116	.21
1898	T. Burns	973	277	213	149	.28
1899	T. Burns	1,064	273	173	266	.26
1900	C. Mitchell	874	195	140	139	.23
1901	W. O'Connor	1,047	253	221	192	.24
1902	J. Ranch	1,069	276	205	181	.26
1903	G.C. Fuller	918	229	152	122	.25
1904	E. Hildebrand	1,169	297	230	171	.25
1905	D. Nicol	861	221	143	136	.26
1906	W. Miller	1,384	388	300	199	.28
1907	W. Miller	1,194	334	226	170	.28
1908	V. Powers	1,260	324	204	185	.26
1909	V. Powers	704	173	121	114	.25
1910	G. Garner	947	200	188	153	.20
1911	T. Koerner	813	162	133	112	.20
1912	P. Hill	967	168	141	129	.17
1913	M. Buxton	887	146	131	136	.16
1914	J. McTaggart	787	157	132	106	.20
1915	M. Garner	775	151	118	90	.19
1916	F. Robinson	791	178	131	124	.23
1917	W. Crump	803	151	140	101	.19
1918	F. Robinson	864	185	140	108	.21
1919	C. Robinson	896	190	140	126	.21
1920	J. Butwell	721	152	129	139	.21
1921	C. Lang	696	135	110	105	.19
1922	M. Fator	859	188	153	116	.22
1923	I. Parke	718	173	105	95	.24
1924	I. Parke	844	205	175	121	.24
1925	A. Mortensen	987	187	145	138	.19
1926	R. Jones	1,172	190	163	152	.16
1927	L. Hardy	1,130	207	192	151	.18
1928	J. Inzelone	1,052	155	152	135	.15
1929	M. Knight	871	149	132	133	.17
1930	H.R. Riley	861	177	145	123	.21
1931	H. Roble	1,174	173	173	155	.15
1932	J. Gilbert	1,050	212	144	160	.20
1933	J. Westrope	1,224	301	235	166	.25
1934	M. Peters	1,045	221	179	147	.21
1935	C. Stevenson	1,099	206	169	146	.19
1936	B. James	1,106	245	195	161	.22
1937	J. Adams	1,265	260	186	177	.21
1938	J. Longden	1,150	236	168	171	.21
1939	D. Meade	1,284	255	221	180	.20
1940	E. Dew	1,377	287	201	180	.21
1941	D. Meade	1,164	210	185	158	.18
1942	J. Adams	1,120	245	185	150	.22
1943	J. Adams	1,069	228	159	171	.21

Jockey—Races Won *(Cont.)*

Year	Jockey	Mts	1st	2nd	3rd	Pct
1944	T. Atkinson	1,539	287	231	213	.19
1945	J.D. Jessop	1,085	290	182	168	.27
1946	T. Atkinson	1,377	233	213	173	.17
1947	J. Longden	1,327	316	250	195	.24
1948	J. Longden	1,197	319	233	161	.27
1949	G. Glisson	1,347	270	217	181	.20
1950	W. Shoemaker	1,640	388	266	230	.24
1951	C. Burr	1,319	310	232	192	.24
1952	A. DeSpirito	1,482	390	247	212	.26
1953	W. Shoemaker	1,683	485	302	210	.29
1954	W. Shoemaker	1,251	380	221	142	.30
1955	W. Hartack	1,702	417	298	215	.25
1956	W. Hartack	1,387	347	252	184	.25
1957	W. Hartack	1,238	341	208	178	.28
1958	W. Shoemaker	1,133	300	185	137	.26
1959	W. Shoemaker	1,285	347	230	159	.27
1960	W. Hartack	1,402	307	247	190	.22
1961	J. Sellers	1,394	328	212	227	.24
1962	R. Ferraro	1,755	352	252	226	.20
1963	W. Blum	1,704	360	286	215	.21
1964	W. Blum	1,577	324	274	170	.21
1965	J. Davidson	1,582	319	228	190	.20
1966	A. Gomez	996	318	173	142	.32
1967	J. Velasquez	1,939	438	315	270	.23
1968	A. Cordero Jr.	1,662	345	278	219	.21
1969	L. Snyder	1,645	352	290	243	.21
1970	S. Hawley	1,908	452	313	265	.24
1971	L Pincay Jr.	1,627	380	288	214	.23
1972	S. Hawley	1,381	367	269	200	.27
1973	S. Hawley	1,925	515	336	292	.27
1974	C.J. McCarron	2,199	546	392	297	.25
1975	C.J. McCarron	2,194	458	389	305	.21
1976	S. Hawley	1,637	413	245	201	.25
1977	S. Cauthen	2,075	487	345	304	.23
1978	E. Delahoussaye	1,666	384	285	238	.23
1979	D. Gall	2,146	479	396	326	.22
1980	C.J. McCarron	1,964	405	318	282	.20
1981	D. Gall	1,917	376	305	297	.20
1982	Pat Day	1,870	399	326	255	.21
1983	Pat Day	1,725	454	321	251	.26
1984	Pat Day	1,694	399	296	259	.24
1985	C.W. Antley	2,335	469	371	288	.20
1986	Pat Day	1,417	429	246	202	.30
1987	Kent Desormeaux	2,207	450	370	294	.28
1988	Kent Desormeaux	1,897	474	295	276	.25
1989	Kent Desormeaux	2,312	598	385	309	.25
1990	Pat Day	1,421	364	265	222	.26
1991	Pat Day	1,405	430	256	213	.31
1992	Russell Baze	1,691	433	296	237	.25
1993	Russell Baze	1,579	410	297	225	.26
1994	Russell Baze	1,588	415	301	266	.26
1995	Russell Baze	1,531	445	310	232	.29
1996	Russell Baze	1,482	415	297	200	.28
1997	Edgar S. Prado	2,037	533	384	308	.26
1998	Edgar S. Prado	1,969	470	377	285	.23
1999	Edgar S. Prado	1,902	402	307	276	.21
2000	Ramon Dominguez	1,586	361	293	238	.23
2001	Ramon Dominguez	1,864	431	368	278	.23
2002	Russell Baze	1,508	431	302	219	.29
2003	Ramon Dominguez	1,627	453	316	252	.28

Leading Jockeys—Career Records

Jockey	Years Riding	Mts	1st	2nd	3rd	Win Pct	Winnings ($)
Laffit Pincay Jr. (2003)	39	48,485	9,531	7,784	6,650	.197	236,851,825
Bill Shoemaker (1990)	42	40,350	8,833	6,136	4,987	.219	123,375,524
Pat Day	32	39,442	8,615	6,708	5,573	.218	285,701,004
Russell Baze	31	39,070	8,504	6,600	5,566	.218	125,611,779
Dave Gall (1999)	41	41,775	7,396	6,525	6,131	.177	24,547,584
Chris McCarron (2002)	28	34,244	7,141	5,670	4,673	.209	264,351,679
Angel Cordero (1992)	31	38,656	7,057	6,136	5,359	.183	164,561,227
Jorge Velasquez (1998)	35	40,852	6,795	6,178	5,755	.166	125,544,379
Sandy Hawley (1998)	31	31,455	6,449	4,825	4,159	.205	88,681,292
Larry Snyder (1994)	35	35,681	6,388	5,030	3,440	.179	47,207,289
Eddie Delahoussaye (2002)	32	39,213	6,384	5,676	5,585	.163	195,881,170
Carl Gambardella (1994)	39	39,018	6,349	5,953	5,353	.163	29,389,041
Earlie Fires	40	43,643	6,296	5,381	5,200	.144	81,486,627
John Longden (1966)	40	32,413	6,032	4,914	4,273	.186	24,665,800
Jerry Bailey	31	29,672	5,600	4,358	3,754	.189	265,110,451
Mario Pino	25	33,083	5,329	4,859	4,529	.161	83,473,139
Jacinto Vasquez (1998)	38	37,337	5,228	4,714	4,510	.140	82,754,115
Ron Ardoin (2003)	31	32,335	5,226	4,298	3,793	.162	58,908,059
Edgar Prado	21	26,180	4,994	4,251	3,720	.190	132,239,542
Rick Wilson	33	24,637	4,928	4,243	3,458	.200	77,040,815
Rodolfo Baez (1999)	26	28,609	4,875	4,291	4,103	.170	30,474,225
Eddie Arcaro (1961)	31	24,092	4,779	3,807	3,302	.198	30,039,543
Gary Stevens	30	26,942	4,767	4,278	3,863	.177	209,889,473
Anthony Black	28	31,156	4,715	4,095	3,994	.151	52,793,398
Don Brumfield (1989)	37	33,223	4,573	4,076	3,758	.138	43,567,861

Note: Jockeys ranked by wins. Records go through March 11, 2004, and include available statistics for races ridden in foreign countries. Figures in parentheses after jockey's name indicate last year in which he rode.

Leading jockeys courtesy of *National Thoroughbred Racing Association*.

Two Legs Better than Four?	Finishing in a time of 2:05:19, Englishman Huw Lobb, 27, became the first human to win the annual 22-mile Man versus Horse marathon in Wales. Lobb, from South London, bested 499 of his fellow men and 40 horses to claim the £25,000 first prize.

HORSES

Ack Ack (1986, 1966)
Affectionately (1989, 1960)
Affirmed (1980, 1975)
All Along (1990, 1979)
Alsab (1976, 1939)
Alydar (1989, 1975)
Alysheba (1993, 1984)
American Eclipse (1970, 1814)
A.P. Indy (2000, 1989)
Armed (1963, 1941)
Artful (1956, 1902)
Arts and Letters (1994, 1966)
Assault (1964, 1943)
Battleship (1969, 1927)
Bayakoa (1998, 1984)
Bed o' Roses (1976, 1947)
Beldame (1956, 1901)
Ben Brush (1955, 1893)
Bewitch (1977, 1945)
Bimelech (1990, 1937)
Black Gold (1989, 1921)
Black Helen (1991, 1932)
Blue Larkspur (1957, 1926)
Bold 'n Determined (1997, 1977)
Bold Ruler (1973, 1954)
Bon Nouvel (1976, 1960)
Boston (1955, 1833)
Broomstick (1956, 1901)
Buckpasser (1970, 1963)
Busher (1964, 1942)
Bushranger (1967, 1930)
Cafe Prince (1985, 1970)
Carry Back (1975, 1958)
Cavalcade (1993, 1931)
Challedon (1977, 1936)
Chris Evert (1988, 1971)
Cicada (1967, 1959)
Cigar (2002, 1990)
Citation (1959, 1945)
Coaltown (1983, 1945)
Colin (1956, 1905)
Commando (1956, 1898)
Count Fleet (1961, 1940)
Crusader (1995, 1923)
Dahlia (1981, 1970)
Damascus (1974, 1964)
Dance Smartly (2003, 1988)
Dark Mirage (1974, 1965)
Davona Dale (1985, 1976)
Desert Vixen (1979, 1970)
Devil Diver (1980, 1939)
Discovery (1969, 1931)
Domino (1955, 1891)
Dr. Fager (1971, 1964)
Easy Goer (1997, 1986)
Eight Thirty (1994, 1936)
Elkridge (1966, 1938)

Emperor of Norfolk (1988, 1885)
Equipoise (1957, 1928)
Exceller (1999, 1973)
Exterminator (1957, 1915)
Fairmount (1985, 1921)
Fair Play (1956, 1905)
Fashion (1980, 1837)
Firenze (1981, 1884)
Flatterer (1994, 1979)
Flawlessly (2004, 1988)
Foolish Pleasure (1995, 1972)
Forego (1979, 1970)
Fort Marcy (1998, 1964)
Gallant Bloom (1977, 1966)
Gallant Fox (1957, 1927)
Gallant Man (1987, 1954)
Gallorette (1962, 1942)
Gamely (1980, 1964)
Genuine Risk (1986, 1977)
Go For Wand (1996, 1987)
Good and Plenty (1956, 1900)
Grandville (1997, 1933)
Grey Lag (1957, 1918)
Gun Bow (1999, 1960)
Hamburg (1986, 1895)
Hanover (1955, 1884)
Henry of Navarre (1985, 1891)
Hill Prince (1991, 1947)
Hindoo (1955, 1878)
Holy Bull (2001, 1991)
Imp (1965, 1894)
Jay Trump (1971, 1957)
John Henry (1990, 1975)
Johnstown (1992, 1936)
Jolly Roger (1965, 1922)
Kelso (1967, 1957)
Kentucky (1983, 1861)
Kingston (1955, 1884)
Lady's Secret (1992, 1982)
La Prevoyante (1995, 1970)
L'Escargot (1977, 1963)
Lexington (1955, 1850)
Longfellow (1971, 1867)
Luke Blackburn (1956, 1877)
Majestic Prince (1988, 1966)
Man o' War (1957, 1917)
Maskette (2001, 1908)
Miesque (1999, 1984)
Miss Woodford (1967, 1880)
Myrtlewood (1979, 1932)
Nashua (1965, 1952)
Native Dancer (1963, 1950)
Native Diver (1978, 1959)
Needles (2000, 1953)
Neji (1966, 1950)
Noor (2002, 1945)
Northern Dancer (1976, 1961)

Oedipus (1978, 1946)
Old Rosebud (1968, 1911)
Omaha (1965, 1932)
Pan Zareta (1972, 1910)
Parole (1984, 1873)
Paseana (2001, 1987)
Personal Ensign (1993, 1984)
Peter Pan (1956, 1904)
Precisionist (2003, 1981)
Princess Doreen (1982, 1921)
Princess Rooney (1991, 1980)
Real Delight (1987, 1949)
Regret (1957, 1912)
Reigh Count (1978, 1923)
Riva Ridge (1998, 1969)
Roamer (1981, 1911)
Roseben (1956, 1901)
Round Table (1972, 1954)
Ruffian (1976, 1972)
Ruthless (1975, 1864)
Salvator (1955, 1886)
Sarazen (1957, 1921)
Seabiscuit (1958, 1933)
Searching (1978, 1952)
Seattle Slew (1981, 1974)
Secretariat (1974, 1970)
Serena's Song (2002, 1992)
Shuvee (1975, 1966)
Silver Spoon (1978, 1956)
Sir Archy (1955, 1805)
Sir Barton (1957, 1916)
Skip Away (2004, 1993)
Slew o' Gold (1992, 1980)
Spectacular Bid (1982, 1976)
Stymie (1975, 1941)
Sun Beau (1996, 1925)
Sunday Silence (1996, 1986)
Susan's Girl (1976, 1969)
Swaps (1966, 1952)
Sword Dancer (1977, 1956)
Sysonby (1956, 1902)
Ta Wee (1994, 1967)
Ten Broeck (1982, 1872)
Tim Tam (1985, 1955)
Tom Fool (1960, 1949)
Top Flight (1966, 1929)
Tosmah (1984, 1961)
Twenty Grand (1957, 1928)
Twilight Tear (1963, 1941)
Two Lea (1982, 1946)
War Admiral (1958, 1934)
Whirlaway (1959, 1938)
Whisk Broom II (1979, 1907)
Winning Colors (2000, 1985)
Zaccio (1990, 1976)
Zev (1983, 1920)

Note: Years of election and foaling in parentheses.

HARNESS RACING

Major Races

Hambletonian

Year	Winner	Driver	Year	Winner	Driver
1926	Guy McKinney	Nat Ray	1967	Speedy Streak	Del Cameron
1927	Iosola's Worthy	Marvin Childs	1968	Nevele Pride	Stanley Dancer
1928	Spenser	W. H. Leese	1969	Lindy's Pride	H. Beissinger
1929	Walter Dear	Walter Cox	1970	Timothy T.	J. Simpson Jr.
1930	Hanover's Bertha	Tom Berry	1971	Speedy Crown	H. Beissinger
1931	Calumet Butler	R. D. McMahon	1972	Super Bowl	Stanley Dancer
1932	The Marchioness	William Caton	1973	Flirth	Ralph Baldwin
1933	Mary Reynolds	Ben White	1974	Christopher T.	Bill Haughton
1934	Lord Jim	Doc Parshall	1975	Bonefish	Stanley Dancer
1935	Greyhound	Sep Palin	1976	Steve Lobell	Bill Haughton
1936	Rosalind	Ben White	1977	Green Speed	Bill Haughton
1937	Shirley Hanover	Henry Thomas	1978	Speedy Somolli	H. Beissinger
1938	McLin Hanover	Henry Thomas	1979	Legend Hanover	George Sholty
1939	Peter Astra	Doc Parshall	1980	Burgomeister	Bill Haughton
1940	Spencer Scott	Fred Egan	1981	Shiaway St. Pat	Ray Remmen
1941	Bill Gallon	Lee Smith	1982	Speed Bowl	Tom Haughton
1942	The Ambassador	Ben White	1983	Duenna	Stanley Dancer
1943	Volo Song	Ben White	1984	Historic Freight	Ben Webster
1944	Yankee Maid	Henry Thomas	1985	Prakas	Bill O'Donnell
1945	Titan Hanover	H. Pownall Sr.	1986	Nuclear Kosmos	Ulf Thoresen
1946	Chestertown	Thomas Berry	1987	Mack Lobell	John Campbell
1947	Hoot Mon	Sep Palin	1988	Armbro Goal	John Campbell
1948	Demon Hanover	Harrison Hoyt	1989	Park Ave. Joe/Probe*	R. Waples/B. Fahy
1949	Miss Tilly	Fred Egan	1990	Harmonious	John Campbell
1950	Lusty Song	Del Miller	1991	Giant Victory	Jack Moiseyev
1951	Mainliner	Guy Crippen	1992	Alf Palema	Mickey McNichol
1952	Sharp Note	Bion Shively	1993	American Winner	Ron Pierce
1953	Helicopter	Harry Harvey	1994	Victory Dream	Michel Lachance
1954	Newport Dream	Del Cameron	1995	Tagliabue	John Campbell
1955	Scott Frost	Joe O'Brien	1996	Continentalvictory	Michel Lachance
1956	The Intruder	Ned Bower	1997	Malabar Man	Mal Burroughs
1957	Hickory Smoke	J. Simpson Sr.	1998	Muscles Yankee	John Campbell
1958	Emily's Pride	Flave Nipe	1999	Self Possessed	Michel Lachance
1959	Diller Hanover	Frank Ervin	2000	Yankee Paco	T.J. Ritchie
1960	Blaze Hanover	Joe O'Brien	2001	Scarlet Knight	Stefan Melander
1961	Harlan Dean	James Arthur	2002	Chip Chip Hooray	Eric Ledford
1962	A. C.'s Viking	Sanders Russell	2003	Amigo Hall	Mike Lachance
1963	Speedy Scot	Ralph Baldwin	2004	Windsong's Legacy	Trond Smedshammer
1964	Ayres	J. Simpson Sr.			
1965	Egyptian Candor	Del Cameron			
1966	Kerry Way	Frank Ervin			

*Park Avenue Joe and Probe dead-heated for win. Park Avenue finished first in the summary 2-1-1 to Probe's 1-9-1 finish.
Note: Run at 1 mile since 1947.

Little Brown Jug

Year	Winner	Driver	Year	Winner	Driver
1946	Ensign Hanover	Wayne Smart	1976	Keystone Ore	Stanley Dancer
1947	Forbes Chief	Del Cameron	1977	Governor Skipper	John Chapman
1948	Knight Dream	Frank Safford	1978	Happy Escort	William Popfinger
1949	Good Time	Frank Ervin	1979	Hot Hitter	Herve Filion
1950	Dudley Hanover	Del Miller	1980	Niatross	Clint Galbraith
1951	Tar Heel	Del Cameron	1981	Fan Hanover	Glen Garnsey
1952	Meadow Rice	Wayne Smart	1982	Merger	John Campbell
1953	Keystoner	Frank Ervin	1983	Ralph Hanover	Ron Waples
1954	Adios Harry	Morris MacDonald	1984	Colt Fortysix	Chris Boring
1955	Quick Chief	Bill Haughton	1985	Nihilator	Bill O'Donnell
1956	Noble Adios	John Simpson Sr.	1986	Barberry Spur	Bill O'Donnell
1957	Torpid	John Simpso Sr.	1987	Jaguar Spur	Dick Stillings
1958	Shadow Wave	Joe O'Brien	1988	B. J. Scoot	Michel Lachance
1959	Adios Butler	Clint Hodgins	1989	Goalie Jeff	Michel Lachance
1960	Bullet Hanover	John Simpson Sr.	1990	Beach Towel	Ray Remmen
1961	Henry T. Adios	Stanley Dancer	1991	Precious Bunny	Jack Moiseye
1962	Lehigh Hanover	Stanley Dancer	1992	Fake Left	Ron Waples
1963	Overtrick	John Patterson	1993	Life Sign	John Campbell
1964	Vicar Hanover	Bill Haughton	1994	Magical Mike	Michel Lachance
1965	Bret Hanover	Frank Ervin	1995	Nick's Fantasy	John Campbell
1966	Romeo Hanover	George Sholty	1996	Armbro Operative	Jack Moiseyev
1967	Best of All	James Hackett	1997	Western Dreamer	Michel Lachance
1968	Rum Customer	Bill Haughton	1998	Shady Character	Ron Pierce
1969	Laverne Hanover	Bill Haughton	1999	Blissful Hall	Ron Pierce
1970	Most Happy Fella	Stanley Dancer	2000	Astreos	Chris Christoforou
1971	Nansemond	Herve Filion	2001	Bettor's Delight	Michel Lachance
1972	Strike Out	Keith Waples	2002	Million Dollar Cam	Luc Ouellette
1973	Melvin's Woe	Joe O'Brien	2003	No Pan Intended	David S. Miller
1974	Armbro Omaha	Bill Haughton	2004	Timesareachanging	Ron Pierce
1975	Seatrain	Ben Webster			

Smart Investment

Three Chimneys Farm of Midway, Ky., paid $24 million to be the retirement home of 2004 Kentucky Derby and Preakness champ Smarty Jones. Owners Pat and Roy Chapman will decide when the horse retires, and when he does, they will retain half ownership.[Smarty retired in August 2004—*Ed.*] The stud farm, which is located on 1,500 acres, will syndicate the other half, bringing Smarty's overall value to $48 million—second only to the reported $60 million Fusaichi Pegasus was syndicated for in 2000.

Breeders' Crown

1984

Div	Winner	Driver
2PC	Dragon's Lair	Jeff Mallet
2PF	Amneris	John Campbell
3PC	Troublemaker	Bill O'Donnell
3PF	Naughty But Nice	Tommy Haughton
2TC	Workaholic	Berndt Lindstedt
2TF	Conifer	George Sholty
3TC	Baltic Speed	Jan Nordin
3TF	Fancy Crown	Bill O'Donnell

1985

Div	Winner	Driver
2PC	Robust Hanover	John Campbell
2PF	Caressable	Hervé Filion
3PC	Nihilator	Bill O'Donnell
3PF	Stienam	Buddy Gilmour
2TC	Express Ride	John Campbell
2TF	JEF's Spice	Mickey McNichol
3TC	Prakas	John Campbell
3TF	Armbro Devona	Bill O'Donnell
AP	Division Street	Michel Lachance
AT	Sandy Bowl	John Campbell

1986

Div	Winner	Driver
2PC	Sunset Warrior	Bill Gale
2PF	Halcyon	Ray Remmen
3PC	Masquerade	Richard Silverman
3PF	Glow Softly	Ron Waples
2TC	Mack Lobell	John Campbell
2TF	Super Flora	Ron Waples
3TC	Sugarcane Hanover	Ron Waples
3TF	JEF's Spice	Bill O'Donnell
APM	Samshu Bluegrass	Michel Lachance
ATM	Grades Singing	Herve Filion
APH	Forrest Skipper	Lucien Fontaine
ATH	Nearly Perfect	Mickey McNichol

1987

Div	Winner	Driver
2PC	Camtastic	Bill O'Donnell
2PF	Leah Almahurst	Bill Fahy
3PC	Call For Rain	Clint Galbraith
3PF	Pacific	Tom Harmer
2TC	Defiant One	Howard Beissinger
2TF	Nan's Catch	Berndt Lindstedt
3TC	Mack Lobell	John Campbell
3TF	Armbro Fling	George Sholty
APM	Follow My Star	John Campbell
ATM	Grades Singing	Olle Goop
APH	Armbro Emerson	Walter Whelan
ATH	Sugarcane Hanover	Ron Waples

1988

Div	Winner	Driver
2PC	Kentucky Spur	Dick Stillings
2PF	Central Park West	John Campbell
3PC	Camtastic	Bill O'Donnell
3PF	Sweet Reflection	Bill O'Donnell
2TC	Valley Victory	Bill O'Donnell
2TF	Peace Corps	John Campbell
3TC	Firm Tribute	Mark O'Mara
3TF	Nalda Hanover	Mickey McNichol
APM	Anniecrombie	Dave Magee
ATM	Armbro Flori	Larry Walker
APH	Call For Rain	Clint Galbraith
ATH	Mack Lobell	John Campbell

1989

Div	Winner	Driver
2PC	Till We Meet Again	Mickey McNichol
2PF	Town Pro	Doug Brown
3PC	Goalie Jeff	Michel Lachance
3PF	Cheery Hello	John Campbell
2TC	Royal Troubador	Carl Allen
2TF	Delphi's Lobell	Ron Waples
3TC	Esquire Spur	Dick Stillings
3TF	Pace Corps	John Campbell
APM	Armbro Feather	John Kopas
ATM	Grades Singing	Olle Goop
APH	Matt's Scooter	Michel Lachance
ATH	Delray Lobell	John Campbell

1990

Div	Winner	Driver
2PC	Artsplace	John Campbell
2PF	Miss Easy	John Campbell
3PC	Beach Towel	Ray Remmen
3PF	Town Pro	Doug Brown
2TC	Crysta's Best	Dick Richardson Jr.
2TF	Jean Bi	Jan Nordin
3TC	Embassy Lobell	Michel Lachance
3TF	Me Maggie	Berndt Lindstedt
APM	Caesar's Jackpot	Bill Fahy
ATM	Peace Corps	Stig Johansson
APH	Bay's Fella	Paul MacDonell
ATH	No Sex Please	Ron Waples

1991

Div	Winner	Driver
2PC	Digger Almahurst	Doug Brown
2PF	Hazleton Kay	John Campbell
3PC	Three Wizzards	Bill Gale
3PF	Miss Easy	John Campbell
2TC	King Conch	Bill Gale
2TF	Armbro Keepsake	John Campbell
3TC	Giant Victory	Ron Pierce
3TF	Twelve Speed	Ron Waples
APM	Delinquent Account	Bill O'Donnell
ATM	Me Maggie	Berndt Lindstedt
APH	Camluck	Michel Lachance
ATH	Billyjojimbob	Paul MacDonell

1992

Div	Winner	Driver
2PC	Village Jiffy	Ron Waples
2PF	Immortality	John Campbell
3PC	Kingsbridge	Roger Mayotte
3PF	So Fresh	John Campbell
2TC	Giant Chill	John Patterson Jr.
2TF	Winky's Goal	Cat Manzi
3TC	Baltic Striker	Michel Lachance
3TF	Imperfection	Michel Lachance
APM	Shady Daisy	Ron Pierce
ATM	Peace Corps	Torbjorn Jansson
APH	Artsplace	John Campbell
ATH	No Sex Please	Ron Waples

Note: 2=Two-year-old; T=Trotter; C=Colt; 3=Three-year-old; P=Pacer; F=Filly; A=Aged; H=Horse; M=Mare.

Breeders' Crown *(Cont.)*

1993

Div	Winner	Driver
2PC	Expensive Scooter	Jack Moiseyev
2PF	Electric Scooter	Mike Lachance
3PC	Life Sign	John Campbell
3PF	Immortality	John Campbell
2TC	Westgate Crown	John Campbell
2TF	Gleam	Jimmy Takter
3TC	Pine Chip	John Campbell
3TF	Expressway Hanover	Per Henriksen
APM	Swing Back	Kelly Sheppard
ATM	Lifetime Dream	Paul MacDonnell
APH	Staying Together	Bill O'Donnell
ATH	Earl	Chris Christoforou Jr.

1994

Div	Winner	Driver
2PC	Jenna's Beach Boy	Bill Fahy
2PF	Yankee Cashmere	Peter Wrenn
3PC	Magical Mike	Michel Lachance
3PF	Hardie Hanover	Tim Twaddle
2TC	Eager Seelster	Teddy Jacobs
2TF	Lookout Victory	John Patterson
3TC	Incredible Abe	Italo Tamborrino
3TF	Imageofa Clear Day	Bill O'Donnell
APM	Shady Daisy	Michel Lachance
ATM	Armbro Keepsake	Stig Johansson
APH	Village Jiffy	Paul MacDonell
ATH	Pine Chip	John Campbell

1995

Div	Winner	Driver
2PC	John Street North	Jack Moiseyev
2PF	Paige Nicole Q	John Campbell
3PC	Jenna's Beach Boy	Bill Fahy
3PF	Headline Hanover	Doug Brown
2TC	Armbro Officer	Steve Condren
2TF	Continentalvictory	Michel Lachance
3TC	Abundance	Bill O'Donnell
3TF	Lookout Victory	Sonny Patterson
APM	Ellamony	Mike Saftic
ATM	CR Kay Suzie	Rod Allen
APH	That'll Be Me	Roger Mayotte
ATH	Panifesto	Luc Ouellette

1996

Div	Winner	Driver
2PC	His Mattjesty	Doug Brown
2PF	Before Sunrise	Steve Condren
3PC	Armbro Operative	Michel Lachance
3PF	Mystical Maddy	Michel Lachance
2TC	Malabar Man	Mal Burroughs
2TF	Armbro Prowess	Jimmy Takter
3TC	Running Sea	Wally Hennessey
3TF	Personal Banner	Peter Wrenn
APM	She's A Great Lady	John Campbell
APH	Jenna's Beach Boy	Bill Fahy
AT	CR Kay Suzie	Rod Allen

1997

Div	Winner	Driver
2PC	Artiscape	Michel Lachance
2PF	Take Flight	Luc Ouellette
3PC	Village Jasper	Paul McDonnell
3PF	Stienam's Place	Jack Moiseyev
2TC	Catch As Catch Can	Wally Hennessey
2TF	My Dolly	Wally Hennessey
3TC	Malabar Man	Malvern Burroughs
3TF	No Nonsense Woman	Jim Doherty
APM	Jay's Table	John Campbell
APH	Red Bow Tie	Luc Ouellette
AT	Moni Maker	Wally Hennessey

1998

Div	Winner	Driver
2PC	Badlands Hanover	Ron Pierce
2PF	Juliet's Fate	George Brennan
3PC	Artiscape	Michel Lachance
3PF	Galleria	George Brennan
2TC	CR Commando	Carl Allen
2TF	Musical Victory	Luc Ouellette
3TC	Muscles Yankee	John Campbell
3TF	Lassie's Goal	Mark O'Mara
APM	Shore By Five	Daniel Dube
APH	Red Bow Tie	Luc Ouellette
AT	Supergrit	Ron Pierce

1999

Div	Winner	Driver
2PC	Tyberwood	Richard Silverman
2PF	Eternal Camnation	Eric Ledford
3PC	Grinfromeartoear	Chris Christoforou
3PF	Odies Fame	David Wall
2TC	Master Lavec	Daniel Daley
2TF	Dream of Joy	James Meittinis
3TC	CR Renegade	Rodney Allen
3TF	Oolong	Ronald Pierce
APM	Shore By Five	Daniel Dube
APH	Red Bow Tie	Luc Ouellette
AT	Supergrit	Ronald Pierce

2000

Div	Winner	Driver
2PC	Bettor's Delight	Michel Lachance
2PF	Lady MacBeach	Luc Ouellette
3PC	Gallo Blue Chip	Daniel Dube
3PF	Popcorn Penny	Ryan Anderson
2TC	Banker Hall	Trevor Ritchie
2TF	Syrinx Hanover	Trevor Ritchie
3TC	Fast Photo	Michel Lachance
3TF	Aviano	Trevor Ritchie
APM	Ron's Girl	Michel Lachance
APH	Western Ideal	Michel Lachance
AT	Magician	David Miller

2001

Div	Winner	Driver
2PC	Western Shooter	John Campbell
2PF	Cam Swifty	Jim Meittinis
3PC	Real Desire	John Campbell
3PF	Bunny Lake	John Stark Jr.
2TC	Duke Of York	Paul MacDonnell
2TF	Cameron Hall	Michel Lachance
3TC	Liberty Balance	Randall Waples
3TF	Syrinx Hanover	John Campbell
APM	Eternal Camnation	Eric Ledford
APH	Goliath Bayama	Sylvain Filion
AT	Varenne	G. Minnucci

Breeders' Crown (Cont.)

	2002			2003	
Div	Winner	Driver	Div	Winner	Driver
2PC	Totally Western	Mario Baillargeon	2PC	I Am A Fool	Ron Pierce
2PF	Armbro Amoretto	Luc Ouellette	2PF	Pans Culottes	Daniel Dube
3PC	Art Major	John Campbell	3PC	No Pan Intended	David Miller
3PF	Allamerican Nadia	Chris Christoforou	3PF	Burning Point	Kevin Wallis
2TC	Broadway Hall	John Campbell	2TC	Cantab Hall	Michel Lachance
2TF	Pick Me Up	Luc Ouellette	2TF	Forever Starlet	David Miller
3TC	Kadabra	David S. Miller	3TC	Mr. Muscleman	Ron Pierce
3TF	Cameron Hall	Trevor Ritchie	3TF	Stroke Play	Brian Sears
APM	Molly Can Do It	Jack Moiseyev	APM	Eternal Camnation	Eric Ledford
APH	Real Desire	John Campbell	APH	Art Major	John Campbell
AT	Fool's Goal	Jack Moiseyev	AT	Fool's Goal	Jack Moiseyev

Note: 2=Two-year-old; T=Trotter; C=Colt; 3=Three-year-old; P=Pacer; F=Filly; A=Aged; H=Horse; M=Mare.

Triple Crown Winners

Trotting

Trotting's Triple Crown consists of the Hambletonian (first run in 1926), the Kentucky Futurity (first run in 1893) and the Yonkers Trot (known as the Yonkers Futurity when it began in 1955).

Year	Horse	Owner	Breeder	Trainer & Driver
1955	Scott Frost	S.A. Camp Farms	Est of W.N. Reynolds	Joe O'Brien
1963	Speedy Scot	Castleton Farms	Castleton Farms	Ralph Baldwin
1964	Ayres	Charlotte Sheppard	Charlotte Sheppard	John Simpson Sr
1968	Nevele Pride	Nevele Acres & Lou Resnick	Mr & Mrs E.C. Quin	Stanley Dancer
1969	Lindy's Pride	Lindy Farm	Hanover Shoe Farms	Howard Beissinger
1972	Super Bowl	Rachel Dancer & Rose Hild Breeding Farm	Stoner Creek Stud	Stanley Dancer

Pacing

Pacing's Triple Crown consists of the Cane Pace (called the Cane Futurity when it began in 1955), the Little Brown Jug (first run in 1946) and the Messenger Stakes (first run in 1956).

Year	Horse	Owner	Breeder	Trainer/Driver
1959	Adios Butler	Paige West & Angelo Pellillo	R.C. Carpenter	Paige West/Clint Hodgins
1965	Bret Hanover	Richard Downing	Hanover Shoe Farms	Frank Ervin
1966	Romeo Hanover	Lucky Star Stables & Morton Finder	Hanover Shoe Farms	Jerry Silverman/ William Meyer (Cane) & George Sholty (Jug & Messenger)
1968	Rum Customer	Kennilworth Farms & L. C. Mancuso	Mr. & Mrs. R.C. Larkin	Bill Haughton
1970	Most Happy Fella	Egyptian Acres Stable	Stoner Creek Stud	Stanley Dancer
1980	Niatross	Niagara Acres, C. Galbraith & Niatross Stables	Niagara Acres	Clint Galbraith
1983	Ralph Hanover	Waples Stable, Pointsetta Stable, Grant's Direct Stable & P. J. Baugh	Hanover Shoe Farms	Stew Firlotte/Ron Waples
1997	Western Dreamer	Daniel and Matthew Daly and Patrick Daly Jr.	Kentuckiana Farms	Bill Robinson/Michel Lachance
1999	Blissful Hall	Daniel Plouffe	Walnut Hall Limited	Ben Wallace/Ron Pierce
2003	No Pan Intended	Peter Pan Stables, Inc.	Winbak Farm	Ivan Sugg/David Miller

Horse of the Year

Year	Horse	Gait	Owner
1947	Victory Song	T	Castleton Farm
1948	Rodney	T	R.H. Johnston
1949	Good Time	P	William Cane
1950	Proximity	T	Ralph and Gordon Verhurst
1951	Pronto Don	T	Hayes Fair Acres Stable
1952	Good Time	P	William Cane
1953	Hi Lo's Forbes	P	Mr. and Mrs. Earl Wagner
1954	Stenographer	T	Max Hempt
1955	Scott Frost	T	S.A. Camp Farms
1956	Scott Frost	P	S.A. Camp Farms
1957	Torpid	P	Sherwood Farm
1958	Emily's Pride	T	Walnut Hall and Castleton Farms
1959	Bye Bye Byrd	P	Mr. and Mrs. Rex Larkin
1960	Adios Butler	P	Adios Butler Syndicate
1961	Adios Butler	P	Adios Butler Syndicate
1962	Su Mac Lad	T	I.W. Berkemeyer
1963	Speedy Scot	T	Castleton Farm
1964	Bret Hanover	P	Richard Downing
1965	Bret Hanover	P	Richard Downing
1966	Bret Hanover	P	Richard Downing
1967	Nevele Pride	T	Nevele Acres
1968	Nevele Pride	T	Nevele Acres, Louis Resnick
1969	Nevele Pride	T	Nevele Acres, Louis Resnick
1970	Fresh Yankee	T	Duncan MacDonald
1971	Albatross	P	Albatross Stable
1972	Albatross	P	Amicable Stable
1973	Sir Dalrae	P	A La Carte Racing Stable
1974	Delmonica Hanover	T	Delvin Miller, W. Arnold Hanger
1975	Savoir	T	Allwood Stable
1976	Keystone Ore	P	Mr. and Mrs. Stanley Dancer, Rose Hild Farms, Robert Jones
1977	Green Speed	T	Beverly Lloyds
1978	Abercrombie	P	Shirley Mitchell, L. Keith Bulen
1979	Niatross	P	Niagara Acres, Clint Galbraith

Year	Horse	Gait	Owner
1980	Niatross	P	Niatross Syndicate, Niagara Acres, Clint Galbraith
1981	Fan Hanover	P	Dr. J. Glen Brown
1982	Cam Fella	P	Norm Clements, Norm Faulkner
1983	Cam Fella	P	JEF's Standardbred, Norm Clements, Norm Faulkner
1984	Fancy Crown	T	Fancy Crown Stable
1985	Nihilator	P	Wall Street-Nihilator Syndicate
1986	Forrest Skipper	P	Forrest L. Bartlett
1987	Mack Lobell	T	One More Time Stable and Fair Wind Farm
1988	Mack Lobell	T	John Erik Magnusson
1989	Matt's Scooter	P	Gordon and Illa Rumpel, Charles Jurasvinski
1990	Beach Towel	P	Uptown Stables
1991	Precious Bunny	P	R. Peter Heffering
1992	Artsplace	P	George Segal
1993	Staying Together	P	Robert Hamather
1994	Cam's Card Shark	P	Jeffrey S. Snyder
1995	CR Kay Suzie	T	Carl & Rod Allen Stable, Inc.
1996	Continental-victory	T	Continentalvictory Stables
1997	Malabar Man	T	Malvern Burroughs
1998	Moni Maker	T	Moni Maker Stable
1999	Moni Maker	T	Moni Maker Stable
2000	Gallo Blue Chip	P	Dan Gernatt Farms
2001	Bunny Lake	P	W. Springtime Racing Stable
2002	Real Desire	P	Brittany Farms
2003	No Pan Intended	P	Peter Pan Stables, Inc.

Driver of the Year

Year	Driver
1968	Stanley Dancer
1969	Herve Filion
1970	Herve Filion
1971	Herve Filion
1972	Herve Filion
1973	Herve Filion
1974	Herve Filion
1975	Joe O'Brien
1976	Herve Filion
1977	Donald Dancer
1978	Carmine Abbatiello Herve Filion
1979	Ron Waples

Year	Driver
1980	Ron Waples
1981	Herve Filion
1982	Bill O'Donnell
1983	John Campbell
1984	Bill O'Donnell
1985	Michel Lachance
1986	Michel Lachance
1987	Michel Lachance
1988	John Campbell
1989	Herve Filion
1990	John Campbell
1991	Walter Case Jr.
1992	Walter Case Jr.

Year	Driver
1993	Jack Moiseyev
1994	Dave Magee
1995	Luc Ouellette
1996	Tony Morgan Luc Ouellette
1997	Tony Morgan
1998	Walter Case Jr.
1999	Dave Palone
2000	Dave Palone
2001	Stephane Bouchard
2002	Tony Morgan
2003	Dave Palone

Note: Balloting is conducted by the U.S Trotting Association for the U.S. Harness Writers Association.

Leading Drivers—Money Won

Year	Driver	Winnings ($)	Year	Driver	Winnings ($)
1946	Thomas Berry	121,933	1975	Carmine Abbatiello	2,275,093
1947	H.C. Fitzpatrick	133,675	1976	Herve Filion	2,278,634
1948	Ralph Baldwin	153,222	1977	Herve Filion	2,551,058
1949	Clint Hodgins	184,108	1978	Carmine Abbatiello	3,344,457
1950	Del Miller	306,813	1979	John Campbell	3,308,984
1951	John Simpson Sr.	333,316	1980	John Campbell	3,732,306
1952	Bill Haughton	311,728	1981	Bill O'Donnell	4,065,608
1953	Bill Haughton	374,527	1982	Bill O'Donnell	5,755,067
1954	Bill Haughton	415,577	1983	John Campbell	6,104,082
1955	Bill Haughton	599,455	1984	Bill O'Donnell	9,059,184
1956	Bill Haughton	572,945	1985	Bill O'Donnell	10,207,372
1957	Bill Haughton	586,950	1986	John Campbell	9,515,055
1958	Bill Haughton	816,659	1987	John Campbell	10,186,495
1959	Bill Haughton	771,435	1988	John Campbell	11,148,565
1960	Del Miller	567,282	1989	John Campbell	9,738,450
1961	Stanley Dancer	674,723	1990	John Campbell	11,620,878
1962	Stanley Dancer	760,343	1991	Jack Moiseyev	9,568,468
1963	Bill Haughton	790,086	1992	John Campbell	8,202,108
1964	Stanley Dancer	1,051,538	1993	John Campbell	9,926,482
1965	Bill Haughton	889,943	1994	John Campbell	9,834,139
1966	Stanley Dancer	1,218,403	1995	John Campbell	9,469,797
1967	Bill Haughton	1,305,773	1996	Michel Lachance	8,408,231
1968	Bill Haughton	1,654,463	1997	Michel Lachance	9,215,388
1969	Del Insko	1,635,463	1998	John Campbell	10,768,771
1970	Herve Filion	1,647,837	1999	Luc Ouellette	10,841,495
1971	Herve Filion	1,915,945	2000	John Campbell	11,160,462
1972	Herve Filion	2,473,265	2001	John Campbell	14,184,863
1973	Herve Filion	2,233,303	2002	John Campbell	11,967,597
1974	Herve Filion	3,474,315	2003	David Miller	11,490,590

Motor Sports

RABIH MOGHRABI/AFP/GETTY IMAGES

Formula One champ
Michael Schumach

Engine Overhaul

While NASCAR revamped its system to create drama, F/I made changes to counter the dominance of Michael Schumacher

BY MARK BECHTEL

NASCAR'S POPULARITY has grown by leaps and bounds during the past several years, thanks to the circuit's marketing savvy, its personable drivers and its on-track action. What it hasn't offered its fans—surprisingly enough—is much down-to-the-wire drama in its season points races. Matt Kenseth waltzed to the 2003 Winston Cup Championship, building a lead so impressive that, if he felt like it, he could have run the season's last two races in a beat-up Pinto and still won the title. And Kenseth's runaway victory was no aberration: Four of the last five NASCAR points races failed to come down to the wire.

Yet NASCAR resisted calls to revamp its championship points system, which rewarded consistency over the long haul more than wins. In 2003, though, the winds of change upgraded to near Hurricane levels. Winston, which had sponsored NASCAR's top series since 1971—a symbiotic relationship that allowed stock car racing to grow from a fringe sport to a major

player with a television contract worth $2.4 billion—announced it was pulling out because federal regulation of tobacco advertising hamstrung its ability to take full advantage of its sponsorship. (The new sponsor, Nextel, wasted little time rolling out products and services with NASCAR tie-ins.) Then Bill France, whose father founded NASCAR in 1947, announced he was stepping down as CEO and chairman of the board. France's son, Brian, would take over. Next NASCAR announced that it was moving its traditional Labor Day race from Darlington Raceway, in South Carolina, the heart of stock-car country, to California Speedway, a cookie-cutter track located an hour east of Los Angeles.

Against that backdrop of change, NASCAR announced in January that it was going to completely overhaul its points system. Under the new scheme, after 26 of the season's 36 races, the top 10 drivers (along with any other driver within 400 points of the leader) advance to a 10-race playoff called the Chase for the Championship. In

FRED VUICH

Under NASCAR's new system, Gordon saw his points lead trimmed come playoff time.

this phase, their point totals would be reset, with each driver staggered five points behind the driver in front of him in the standings.

The announcement provoked mixed reactions. "Having 10 guys with a shot at the championship with 10 races to go is a story," said driver Michael Waltrip. "If I'm the networks, I love it. If I'm a race fan, I love it." While it guaranteed a tight finish, it failed to address the biggest flaw in the previous system: its arbitrariness. (In 2003, Kenseth won one race and made 11 top-five finishes; Ryan Newman, by contrast, had eight wins and 17 top fives, but finished in sixth place over all. If anything, the change made things more arbitrary for the drivers, and placed even less of an emphasis on going all out for the win. "If you think you're solidly within the points window they're gonna use for the playoffs, you do a Dean Smith and go into a four-corners," driver Elliott Sadler said.

Yet, as Waltrip predicted, the new system did give the fans and networks the injection of drama they craved: By the time the 26th race, in Richmond, rolled around, 15 drivers had a shot at qualifying for the playoffs. During the race, crew chiefs, drivers and fans kept a constant eye on the up-to-the-minute standings. Jeremy Mayfield, who started the race in 14th place in the standings, took the checkered flag to vault to ninth place, knocking rookie Kasey Kahne, who spun out early and finished 24th in Richmond, out of the top ten. Kahne wasn't the only driver feeling a little glum after the race. Thanks to the new system, points leader Jeff Gordon saw a handful of drivers suddenly pop up on his tail. (Mayfield came to Richmond 479 points behind Gordon; he left just 40 back.) "I could go from leading the points right now to finishing 10th, and I don't know that anybody would say that's really fair," Gordon said.

Fair or not, the new system also proved beneficial for Dale Earnhardt Jr. At the season-opening event, the Daytona 500, Junior won the race that was the scene of his father's death in 2001. "The things that have happened here [at Daytona] affected so many people who are close to me," said

Junior. "Every time we come to Daytona it feels like I'm closer to Dad. But at the same time, it's a reminder of losing him. So I wanted to come down here and win."

Earnhardt Jr.'s dramatic victory was the most universally popular triumph in NASCAR since his father finally won at Daytona in 1998, on his 20th attempt to win the famous race. "Considering what this kid has gone through, losing his father here at the Daytona 500, it's nice to see him get this victory," said Tony Stewart, who finished second. "I think his father's really proud today." The win turned out to be a springboard to the most consistent stretch of the younger Earnhardt's career. His season was sailing along until he decided to take part in a sports car race at Sonoma on a rare Nextel Cup off-weekend. Earnhardt crashed during practice, and his car caught fire, burning his face and legs. Two weeks later he still couldn't bend his left leg, and he had to spend 45 minutes a day soaking in a bath. He didn't miss a race, but he did cede to a relief driver in two events—getting pulled from his car during pit stops like a rag doll by his gasman, Jeff Clark. By the time the playoff rolled around, though, Earnhardt, who had fallen 267 points off the lead at one point, was healed and—thanks to the new scoring system—only 10 points out of the lead.

While NASCAR was charging toward its most wide-open finish ever, Formula One saw—depending on your point of view— either the most dominating performance in its history or the most boring one. Michael Schumacher won the season's first five races, sending early notice that he didn't plan on easing up after the 2003 season, when he surpassed Juan-Manuel Fangio's record of five career world championships. Schumacher was so clearly the class of the field that after the fifth race, one Irish bookmaker, Paddy Power, paid out to anyone who had bet on the German to win the season title—even though there were 13 races left on the schedule. Schumacher finally failed to win a race, at Monaco, when he was taken out in a wreck with Juan Pablo Montoya. But Schumacher's loss wasn't the biggest of the weekend. As part of a promotion for the forthcoming heist film *Ocean's 12*, a luxury car company placed $350,000-diamonds in the noses of two of its cars. With the film's stars George Clooney, Matt Damon and Brad Pitt looking on, driver Christian Klein crashed on the first lap, sending debris—including one of the uninsured 108-carat rocks—onto the street in front of the Hotel Mirabeau. Workers couldn't begin looking for the jewel until the race was over, and despite the car company's offer of one of its $45,000-models as a reward, the diamond never turned up.

Formula One events returned to normal the following week as there were no incidents and Schumacher won in a runaway on the Nurbirgring in his home country of Germany. He went on to win the next six races, wrapping up the driving title with four events left. Concerned that such hegemony was turning the sport into a snooze, the International Automobile Federation announced several rules changes in May, to take effect in 2006. Engines will be simpler and, therefore cheaper. Expensive tire testing will be curtailed with the move to a single tire supplier. And electronic driver aids will eliminated. The moves were made to give the circuit's smaller teams, like Minardi, which operates on an annual budget of $35 million, a chance to compete with Schumacher's Ferrari team, which spends nearly half a billion dollars a year.

Until the changes are enacted, though, nothing short of an overhaul of the points system, a lá NASCAR, is going to bring F/1 a wide-open points race. And even though NASCAR's new scheme has its detractors, that might not be a bad idea. For the first time in NASCAR history, more than 10 drivers left the Labor Day weekend race with a legitimate chance to win the title, much to the delight of fans and, naturally, the drivers who qualified for the Chase for the Championship. "Man, I love your new points system," Mayfield gushed to Brian France after his win in Richmond. "You couldn't have come up with anything better than this."

Then again, he may have to.

FOR THE RECORD · 2003 – 2004

Indy Racing League

Indianapolis 500

Results of the 88th running of the Indianapolis 500 and fourth race of the 2004 Indy Racing League season. Held Sunday, May 30, 2004, at the 2.5-mile Indianapolis Motor Speedway in Indianapolis.

Distance, 500 miles; starters, 33; time of race, 3 hours, 14 mins., 55.2395 seconds; average speed, 138.518 mph; margin of victory, 0.1559 seconds; caution flags, 8 for 56 laps; lead changes, 17 among nine drivers.

TOP 10 FINISHERS

Pos.	Driver (start pos.)	C/E/T	Qual. Speed	Laps	Status
1	Buddy Rice (1)	G/H/F	222.024	180	running
2	Tony Kanaan (5)	D/H/F	221.200	180	running
3	Dan Wheldon (2)	D/H/F	221.524	180	running
4	Bryan Herta (23)	D/H/F	219.871	180	running
5	Bruno Junqueira (4)	G/H/F	221.379	180	running
6	Vitor Meira (7)	G/H/F	220.958	180	running
7	Adrian Fernandez (6)	G/H/F	220.999	180	running
8	Scott Dixon (13)	G/T/F	219.319	180	running
9	Helio Castroneves (8)	D/T/F	220.882	180	running
10	Roger Yasukawa (12)	G/H/F	220.030	180	running

2004 Indy Racing League Results (through September 12)

Date	Race	Winner (start pos.)	C/E/T	Qual. Speed
Feb 29	Miami 300	Sam Hornish Jr. (7)	D/T/F	216.322
Mar 21	Phoenix 200	Tony Kanaan (2)	D/H/F	174.291
Apr 17	Japan 300	Dan Wheldon (1)	D/H/F	205.762
May 30	Indianapolis 500	Buddy Rice (1)	G/H/F	222.024
June 12	Texas 500	Tony Kanaan (3)	D/H/F	208.511
June 26	Richmond 250*	Dan Wheldon (20)	D/H/F	164.935
July 4	Kansas 300	Buddy Rice (1)	G/H/F	210.141
July 17	Nashville 200	Tony Kanaan (5)	D/H/F	199.804
July 25	Milwaukee 225	Dario Franchitti (7)	D/T/F	167.312
Aug 1	Michigan 400	Buddy Rice (6)	G/H/F	214.018
Aug 15	Kentucky 300	Adrian Fernandez (4)	G/H/F	215.326
Aug 22	Pikes Peak 225*	Dario Franchitti (4)	D/H/F	172.916
Aug 29	Nazareth 225*	Dan Wheldon (8)	D/H/F	165.093
Sept 12	Chicago 300	Adrian Fernandez (10)	G/H/F	212.871

Note: Distances are in miles unless followed by K (kilometers) or * (laps).

2003 Final Championship Standings

Driver	Pts
Scott Dixon	507
Gil de Ferran	489
Helio Castroneves	484
Tony Kanaan	476
Sam Hornish Jr.	461
Al Unser Jr.	374
Tomas Scheckter	356
Scott Sharp	351
Kenny Brack	342
Tora Takagi	317

2004 CART Championship Series Results (through September 26)

Date	Event	Winner (start pos.)	Car	Avg Speed
April 18	Grand Prix of Long Beach	Paul Tracy (3)	Lola-Ford	91.785
May 23	Grand Prix of Monterrey	Sebastien Bourdais (1)	Lola-Ford	86.544
June 5	Milwaukee 250	Ryan Hunter-Reay (1)	Lola-Ford	129.85
June 20	Grand Prix of Portland	Sebastien Bourdais (1)	Lola-Ford	104.923
July 3	Grand Prix of Cleveland	Sebastien Bourdais (3)	Lola-Ford	113.209
July 11	Molson Indy Toronto	Sebastien Bourdais (1)	Lola-Ford	83.749
July 25	Molson Indy Vancouver	Paul Tracy (1)	Lola-Ford	95.900
Aug 8	Elkhart Lake Road America	Alex Tagliani (13)	Lola-Ford	110.903
Aug 15	Grand Prix of Denver	Sebastien Bourdais (1)	Lola-Ford	88.566
Aug 29	Molson Indy Montreal	Bruno Junqueira (4)	Lola-Ford	113.049
Sept 12	Grand Prix of Monterey	Patrick Carpentier (2)	Lola-Ford	100.217
Sept 26	Las Vegas 400	Sebastien Bourdais (3)	Lola-Ford	167.832

2003 Championship Standings

Driver	Overall	Road	Oval
Paul Tracy	226	224	2
Bruno Junqueira	199	187	12
Michel Jourdain Jr.	195	160	35
Sebastien Bourdais	159	133	26
Patrick Carpentier	146	126	20
Mario Dominguez	118	97	21
Oriol Servia	108	82	26
Adrian Fernandez	105	97	8
Darren Manning	103	83	20
Alex Tagliani	97	87	10

National Association for Stock Car Auto Racing

Daytona 500

Results of the 46th Daytona 500, the opening round of the 2004 Nextel Cup series. Held Sunday, February 15, 2004, at the 2.5-mile high-banked Daytona International Speedway.

Distance, 500 miles; starters, 43; time of race, 3:11:53; average speed, 156.345 mph; margin of victory, .273 seconds; caution flags, four for 23 laps; lead changes, 28.

TOP 10 FINISHERS

Pos.	Driver (start pos.)	Car	Laps	Winnings ($)
1	Dale Earnhardt Jr. (3)	Chevrolet	200	1,495,070
2	Tony Stewart (5)	Chevrolet	200	1,096,160
3	Scott Wimmer (26)	Dodge	200	758,839
4	Kevin Harvick (10)	Chevrolet	200	610,792
5	Jimmie Johnson (6)	Chevrolet	200	472,189
6	Joe Nemechek (14)	Chevrolet	200	358,839
7	Elliott Sadler (2)	Ford	200	358,772
8	Jeff Gordon (39)	Chevrolet	200	318,490
9	Matt Kenseth (12)	Ford	200	307,917
10	Dale Jarrett (31)	Ford	200	279,529

Late 2003 Winston Cup* Series Results

Date	Track/Distance	Winner (start pos.)	Car	Laps	Winnings ($)
Oct 5	Kansas 400	Ryan Newman (11)	Dodge	267	191,000
Oct 11	Lowe's 500	Tony Stewart (6)	Chevrolet	334	312,478
Oct 19	Martinsville 500	Jeff Gordon (1)	Chevrolet	500	183,018
Oct 27	Atlanta 500	Jeff Gordon (19)	Chevrolet	325	249,978
Nov 2	Phoenix 500	Dale Earnhardt Jr. (11)	Chevrolet	312	203,017
Nov 9	N Carolina 400	Bill Elliott (5)	Dodge	393	207,648
Nov 16	Miami 400	Bobby Labonte (2)	Chevrolet	267	331,058

*Series name changed to Nextel Cup after 2003 season.

2004 Nextel Cup Series Results (through September 26)

Date	Track/Distance	Winner (start pos.)	Car	Laps	Winnings ($)
Feb 15	Daytona 500	Dale Earnhardt Jr. (3)	Chevrolet	200	1,495,070
Feb 22	N Carolina 400	Matt Kenseth (23)	Ford	393	222,303
Mar 7	Las Vegas 400	Matt Kenseth (25)	Ford	267	260,775
Mar 14	Atlanta 500	Dale Earnhardt Jr. (7)	Chevrolet	325	180,078
Mar 21	Darlington 400	Jimmie Johnson (11)	Chevrolet	293	151,150
Mar 28	Bristol 500	Kurt Busch (13)	Ford	500	173,465
Apr 4	Texas 500	Elliott Sadler (19)	Ford	334	507,733
Apr 18	Martinsville 500	Rusty Wallace (17)	Dodge	500	170,998
Apr 25	Talladega 499	Jeff Gordon (11)	Chevrolet	188	320,258
May 2	California 500	Jeff Gordon (16)	Chevrolet	250	318,628
May 15	Richmond 400	Dale Earnhardt Jr. (4)	Chevrolet	400	285,053
May 30	Lowe's 600	Jimmie Johnson (1)	Chevrolet	400	426,350
June 6	Dover 400	Mark Martin (7)	Ford	400	271,900
June 13	Pocono 500	Jimmie Johnson (5)	Chevrolet	200	186,950
June 20	Michigan 400	Ryan Newman (4)	Dodge	200	176,367
June 27	Infineon 350	Jeff Gordon (1)	Chevrolet	110	388,103
July 3	Daytona 400	Jeff Gordon (1)	Chevrolet	160	346,703
July 11	Chicagoland 400	Tony Stewart (10)	Chevrolet	267	336,803
July 25	New Hampshire 300	Kurt Busch (32)	Ford	300	222,225
Aug 1	Pennsylvania 500	Jimmie Johnson (14)	Chevrolet	200	276,950
Aug 8	Brickyard 400	Jeff Gordon (11)	Chevrolet	161	518,053
Aug 15	Watkins Glen	Tony Stewart (4)	Chevrolet	90	195,288
Aug 22	Michigan 400	Greg Biffle (24)	Ford	200	190,180
Aug 28	Bristol 500	Dale Earnhardt Jr. (30)	Chevrolet	500	322,443
Sept 5	California 500	Elliott Sadler (17)	Ford	250	279,398
Sept 11	Richmond 400	Jeremy Mayfield (7)	Dodge	400	211,120
Sept 19	New Hampshire 300	Kurt Busch (7)	Ford	300	237,225
Sept 26	Dover 400	Ryan Newman (2)	Dodge	400	195,477

2003 Winston Cup* Final Standings

Driver	Pts	Starts	Wins	Top 5	Top 10
Matt Kenseth	5022	36	1	11	25
Jimmie Johnson	4932	36	3	14	20
Dale Earnhardt Jr.	4815	36	2	13	21
Jeff Gordon	4785	36	3	15	20
Kevin Harvick	4770	36	1	11	18
Ryan Newman	4711	36	8	17	22
Tony Stewart	4549	36	2	12	18
Bobby Labonte	4377	36	2	12	17
Bill Elliott	4303	36	1	9	12
Terry Labonte	4162	36	1	4	9

2003 Winston Cup* Driver Winnings

Driver	Winnings ($)
Jimmie Johnson	5,517,850
Tony Stewart	5,227,500
Jeff Gordon	5,107,760
Kurt Busch	5,020,480
Kevin Harvick	4,994,250
Dale Earnhardt Jr.	4,923,500
Ryan Newman	4,827,380
Bobby Labonte	4,745,260
Michael Waltrip	4,463,840
Bill Elliott	4,321,190

*Series name changed to Nextel Cup after 2003 season.

Formula One Grand Prix Racing

2004 Formula One Results (through September 26)

Grand Prix	Date	Winner	Car	Laps	Time
Australian	Mar 7	Michael Schumacher	Ferrari	58	1:24:15.757
Malaysian	Mar 21	Michael Schumacher	Ferrari	56	1:31:07.490
Bahrain	Apr 4	Michael Schumacher	Ferrari	57	1:28:34.875
San Marino	Apr 25	Michael Schumacher	Ferrari	62	1:26:19.670
Spain	May 9	Michael Schumacher	Ferrari	66	1:27:32.841
Monaco	May 23	Jarno Trulli	Renault	77	1:45:46.601
European	May 30	Michael Schumacher	Ferrari	60	1:32:35.101
Canadian	June 13	Michael Schumacher	Ferrari	70	1:28:24.803
United States	June 20	Michael Schumacher	Ferrari	73	1:40:29.914
French	July 4	Michael Schumacher	Ferrari	70	1:30:18.133
British	July 11	Michael Schumacher	Ferrari	60	1:24:42.700
German	July 25	Michael Schumacher	Ferrari	66	1:23:54.848
Hungarian	Aug 15	Michael Schumacher	Ferrari	70	1:35:26.131
Belgian	Aug 29	Kimi Räikkönen	McLaren-Mercedes	44	1:32:35.274
Italian	Sept 12	Rubens Barrichello	Ferrari	53	1:15:18.448
Chinese	Sept 26	Rubens Barrichello	Ferrari	56	1:29:12.420

2003 World Championship Final Standings

Drivers compete in Grand Prix races for the title of World Driving Champion. Below are the top 10 drivers from the 2003 season. Points are awarded for places 1–6 as follows: 10-6-4-3-2-1.

Driver	Country	Team	Pts
Michael Schumacher	Germany	Ferrari	93
Kimi Räikkönen	Finland	McLaren-Mercedes	91
Juan Pablo Montoya	Colombia	Williams-BMW	82
Rubens Barrichello	Brazil	Ferrari	65
Ralf Schumacher	Germany	Williams-BMW	58
Fernando Alonso	Spain	Renault	55
David Coulthard	Scotland	McLaren-Mercedes	51
Jarno Trulli	Italy	Renault	33
Jenson Button	England	Honda	17
Mark Webber	Australia	Jaguar	17

Professional Sports Car Racing

The 24 Hours of Daytona

Held at the Daytona International Speedway on Jan. 31–Feb. 1, 2004, the 24 Hours of Daytona serves as the opening round of Grand American Road Racing Association's season.

Place	Drivers	Car (Class)	Distance
1	Forest Barber, Terry Borcheller, Andy Pilgrim, Christian Fittipaldi	Pontiac Doran	526 laps (117.651, top mph)
2	Mike Fitzgerald, Joe Policastro, Robin Liddell, Johnny Mowlem	Porsche GT3 RS	523
3	Seth Neiman, Lonnie Pechnik, Johannes van Overbeek, Peter Cunningham, Mike Rockenfeller	Porsche GT3 RS	523
4	Didier Theys, Fredy Lienhard, Jan Lammers, Marc Goossens	Lexus Doran	521
5	Andy Wallace, Tony Stewart, Dale Earnhardt Jr.	Chevrolet Crawford	519

2004 American Le Mans Series—Prototype Class (through September 25)

Date	Race	Winners	Car
Mar 20	12 Hours of Sebring	F. Biela, P. Kaffer, A. McNish	Audi R8
June 27	Mid-Ohio	J.J. Lehto, Marco Werner	Audi R8
July 5	Grand Prix of New England	J.J. Lehto, Marco Werner	Audi R8
July 18	Grand Prix of Sonoma	J.J. Lehto, Marco Werner	Audi R8
July 25	Grand Prix of Portland	J.J. Lehto, Marco Werner	Audi R8
Aug 8	Grand Prix of Toronto	James Weaver, Butch Leitzinger	Lola EX257
Aug 22	Road America 500	J.J. Lehto, Marco Werner	Audi R8
Sept 25	Petit Le Mans	J.J. Lehto, Marco Werner	Audi R8

2004 American Le Mans Series—GTS Class (through September 25)

Date	Race	Winners	Car
Mar 20	12 Hours at Sebring	Ron Fellows, Johnny O'Connell, M. Papis	Corvette C5-R
June 27	Mid-Ohio	Ron Fellows, Johnny O'Connell	Corvette C5-R
July 5	Grand Prix of New England	Oliver Gavin, Olivier Beretta	Corvette C5-R
July 18	Grand Prix of Sonoma	Ron Fellows, Johnny O'Connell	Corvette C5-R
July 25	Grand Prix of Portland	Ron Fellows, Johnny O'Connell	Corvette C5-R
Aug 8	Grand Prix of Toronto	Oliver Gavin, Olivier Beretta	Corvette C5-R
Aug 22	Road America 500	Oliver Gavin, Olivier Beretta	Corvette C5-R
Sept 25	Petit Le Mans	Oliver Gavin, Olivier Beretta, Jan Magnussen	Corvette C5-R

2004 American Le Mans Series—GT Class (through September 25)

Date	Race	Winners	Car
Mar 20	12 Hours at Sebring	Timo Bernhard, Jorg Bergmeister, S. Maassen	Porsche 911 GT3Rs
June 27	Mid-Ohio	Johannes van Overbeek, D. Law	Porsche 911 GT3Rs
July 5	Grand Prix of New England	Ralf Kelleners, Anthony Lazzaro	Ferrari 360 Modena
July 18	Grand Prix of Sonoma	Timo Bernhard, Jorg Bergmeister	Porsche 911 GT3Rs
July 25	Grand Prix of Portland	Romain Dumas, Marc Lieb	Porsche 911 GT3Rs
Aug 8	Grand Prix of Toronto	Jorg Bergmeister, Timo Bernhard	Porsche 911 GT3Rs
Aug 22	Road America 500	Timo Bernhard, Jorg Bergmeister	Porsche 911 GT3Rs
Sept 25	Petit Le Mans	Timo Bernhard, Jorg Bergmeister	Porsche 911 GT3Rs

2003 American Le Mans Series Championship Final Standings

PROTOTYPE CLASS	Pts	GTS CLASS	Pts	GT CLASS	Pts
Frank Biela	170	Ron Fellows	151	Sascha Maassen	164
Marco Werner	170	Johnny O'Connell	151	Lucas Luhr	164
J.J. Lehto	163	David Brabham	118	Timo Bernhard	104
Johnny Herbert	160	Oliver Gavin	115	Jorg Bergmeister	104
Olivier Beretta	160	Kelly Collins	115	Ralf Kelleners	96
David Saelens	101			Anthony Lazzaro	96

24 Hours of Le Mans

Held at Le Mans, France, on June 12–13, 2004, the 24 Hours of Le Mans is the most prestigious international event in endurance racing.

Place	Drivers	Car	Laps
1	Seiji Ara, Rinaldo Capello, Tom Kristensen	Audi R8	379 (133.855 mph)
2	J. Davies, Johnny Herbert, G. Smith	Audi R8	379
3	J.J. Lehto, Marco Werner, E. Pirro	Audi R8	368
4	S. Ayari, E. Comas, B. Treluyer	Pescarolo Judd	361
5	Frank Biela, P. Kaffer, A. McNish	Audi R8	350

National Hot Rod Association

2004 Results (through September 26)

TOP FUEL

Date	Race, Site	Winner
Feb 19–22	Winternationals, Pomona, CA	Tony Schumacher
Mar 5–7	Kragen Nationals, Phoenix	Brandon Bernstein
Mar 18–21	Gatornationals, Gainesville, FL	Tony Schumacher
Apr 1–4	Las Vegas Nationals, Las Vegas	Tony Schumacher
Apr 15–18	Spring Nationals, Houston	Brandon Bernstein
Apr 30–May 2	Thunder Valley Nationals, Bristol, TN	Tony Schumacher
May 13–16	Southern Nationals, Atlanta	Cory McClenathan
May 20–23	Route 66 Nationals, Chicago	Doug Kalitta
May 27–30	Summer Nationals, Topeka, KS	Brandon Bernstein
June 10–13	Pontiac Nationals, Columbus, OH	Darrell Russell
June 17–20	Super Nationals, Englishtown, NJ	Larry Dixon
June 25–27	Sears Nationals, St. Louis	Doug Kalitta
July 16–18	Mile High Nationals, Denver	Scott Kalitta
July 23–25	Carquest Nationals, Seattle	Tony Schumacher
July 30–Aug 1	Autolite Nationals, Sonoma, CA	Doug Kalitta
Aug 12–15	Lucas Oil Nationals, Brainerd, MN	Tony Schumacher
Aug 20–22	Mid-South Nationals, Memphis	Larry Dixon
Sept 1–6	U.S. Nationals, Indianapolis	Tony Schumacher
Sept 23–26	Fall Nationals, Dallas	Tony Schumacher

FUNNY CAR

Date	Race, Site	Winner
Feb 19–22	Winternationals, Pomona, CA	Jerry Toliver
Mar 5–7	Kragen Nationals, Phoenix	Del Worsham
Mar 18–21	Gatornationals, Gainesville, FL	Del Worsham
Apr 1–4	Las Vegas Nationals, Las Vegas	Phil Burkart Jr.
Apr 15–18	Spring Nationals, Houston	Tim Wilkerson
Apr 30–May 2	Thunder Valley Nationals, Bristol, TN	John Force
May 13–16	Southern Nationals, Atlanta	Whit Bazemore

2004 Results (through September 26) *(Cont.)*

FUNNY CAR *(CONT.)*

Date	Race, Site	Winner
May 20–23	Route 66 Nationals, Chicago	John Force
May 27–30	Summer Nationals, Topeka, KS	Whit Bazemore
June 10–13	Pontiac Nationals, Columbus, OH	Del Worsham
June 17–20	Super Nationals, Englishtown, NJ	Gary Densham
June 25–27	Sears Nationals, St. Louis	Gary Scelzi
July 16–18	Mile High Nationals, Denver	Phil Burkart Jr.
July 23–25	Carquest Nationals, Seattle	John Force
July 30–Aug 1	Autolite Nationals, Sonoma, CA	Tim Wilkerson
Aug 12–15	Lucas Oil Nationals, Brainerd, MN	Eric Medlen
Aug 20–22	Mid-South Nationals, Memphis	John Force
Sept 1–6	U.S. Nationals, Indianapolis	Gary Densham
Sept 23–26	Fall Nationals, Dallas	Del Worsham

PRO STOCK

Date	Race, Site	Winner
Feb 19–22	Winternationals, Pomona, CA	Greg Anderson
Mar 5–7	Kragen Nationals, Phoenix	Kurt Johnson
Mar 18–21	Gatornationals, Gainesville, FL	Greg Anderson
Apr 1–4	Las Vegas Nationals, Las Vegas	Greg Anderson
Apr 15–18	Spring Nationals, Houston	Greg Anderson
Apr 30–May 2	Thunder Valley Nationals, Bristol, TN	Greg Anderson
May 13–16	Southern Nationals, Atlanta	Greg Anderson
May 20–23	Route 66 Nationals, Chicago	Jason Line
May 27–30	Summer Nationals, Topeka, KS	Greg Anderson
June 10–13	Pontiac Nationals, Columbus, OH	Greg Anderson
June 17–20	Super Nationals, Englishtown, NJ	Jason Line
June 25–27	Sears Nationals, St. Louis	Greg Anderson
July 16–18	Mile High Nationals, Denver	Greg Anderson
July 23–25	Carquest Nationals, Seattle	Greg Anderson
July 30–Aug 1	Autolite Nationals, Sonoma, CA	Greg Anderson
Aug 12–15	Lucas Oil Nationals, Brainerd, MN	Dave Connolly
Aug 20–22	Mid-South Nationals, Memphis	Jason Line
Sept 1–6	U.S. Nationals, Indianapolis	Greg Anderson
Sept 23–26	Fall Nationals, Dallas	Dave Connolly

2003 Final Standings

TOP FUEL

Driver	Pts
Larry Dixon	1994
Doug Kalitta	1664
Tony Schumacher	1523
Darrell Russell	1301
Cory McClenathan	1150

FUNNY CAR

Driver	Pts
Tony Pedregon	1768
Whit Bazemore	1628
John Force	1504
Del Worsham	1387
Gary Densham	1343

PRO STOCK

Driver	Pts
Greg Anderson	2217
Kurt Johnson	1754
Jeg Coughlin	1611
Warren Johnson	1363
Mike Edwards	985

FOR THE RECORD·Year by Year

Indianapolis 500

First held in 1911, the Indianapolis 500—200 laps of the 2.5-mile Indianapolis Motor Speedway Track (called the Brickyard in honor of its original pavement)—grew to become the most famous auto race in the world. Though the Memorial Day weekend event lost participants and prestige in the mid-1990s due to feuding in the world of U.S. open-wheel racing, it annually attracts crowds of over 100,000.

Year	Winner (start pos.)	Chassis-Engine	Avg Speed	Pole Winner	Speed
1911	Ray Harroun (28)	Marmon-Marmon	74.590	Lewis Strang	First entered
1912	Joe Dawson (7)	National-National	78.720	Gil Anderson	First entered
1913	Jules Goux (7)	Peugeot-Peugeot	75.930	Caleb Bragg	Drew pole
1914	Rene Thomas (15)	Delage-Delage	82.470	Jean Chassagne	Drew pole
1915	Ralph DePalma (2)	Mercedes-Mercedes	89.840	Howard Wilcox	98.90
1916	Dario Resta (4)	Peugeot-Peugeot	84.000	John Aitken	96.69
1917–18	No race				
1919	Howard Wilcox (2)	Peugeot-Peugeot	88.050	Rene Thomas	104.78
1920	Gaston Chevrolet (6)	Frontenac-Frontenac	88.620	Ralph DePalma	99.15
1921	Tommy Milton (20)	Frontenac-Frontenac	89.620	Ralph DePalma	100.75
1922	Jimmy Murphy (1)	Duesenberg-Miller	94.480	Jimmy Murphy	100.50
1923	Tommy Milton (1)	Miller-Miller	90.950	Tommy Milton	108.17
1924	L.L. Corum	Duesenberg-Duesenberg	98.230	Jimmy Murphy	108.037
	Joe Boyer (21)				
1925	Peter DePaolo (2)	Duesenberg-Duesenberg	101.130	Leon Duray	113.196
1926	Frank Lockhart (20)	Miller-Miller	95.904	Earl Cooper	111.735
1927	George Souders (22)	Duesenberg-Duesenberg	97.545	Frank Lockhart	120.100
1928	Louis Meyer (13)	Miller-Miller	99.482	Leon Duray	122.391
1929	Ray Keech (6)	Miller-Miller	97.585	Cliff Woodbury	120.599
1930	Billy Arnold (1)	Summers-Miller	100.448	Billy Arnold	113.268
1931	Louis Schneider (13)	Stevens-Miller	96.629	Russ Snowberger	112.796
1932	Fred Frame (27)	Wetteroth-Miller	104.144	Lou Moore	117.363
1933	Louis Meyer (6)	Miller-Miller	104.162	Bill Cummings	118.524
1934	Bill Cummings (10)	Miller-Miller	104.863	Kelly Petillo	119.329
1935	Kelly Petillo (22)	Wetteroth-Offy	106.240	Rex Mays	120.736
1936	Louis Meyer (28)	Stevens-Miller	109.069	Rex Mays	119.664
1937	Wilbur Shaw (2)	Shaw-Offy	113.580	Bill Cummings	123.343
1938	Floyd Roberts (1)	Wetteroth-Miller	117.200	Floyd Roberts	125.681
1939	Wilbur Shaw (3)	Maserati-Maserati	115.035	Jimmy Snyder	130.138
1940	Wilbur Shaw (2)	Maserati-Maserati	114.277	Rex Mays	127.850
1941	Floyd Davis	Wetteroth-Offy	115.117	Mauri Rose	128.691
	Mauri Rose (17)				
1942–45	No race				
1946	George Robson (15)	Adams-Sparks	114.820	Cliff Bergere	126.471
1947	Mauri Rose (3)	Deidt-Offy	116.338	Ted Horn	126.564
1948	Mauri Rose (3)	Deidt-Offy	119.814	Rex Mays	130.577
1949	Bill Holland (4)	Deidt-Offy	121.327	Duke Nalon	132.939
1950	Johnnie Parsons (5)	Kurtis-Offy	124.002	Walt Faulkner	134.343
1951	Lee Wallard (2)	Kurtis-Offy	126.244	Duke Nalon	136.498
1952	Troy Ruttman (7)	Kuzma-Offy	128.922	Fred Agabashian	138.010
1953	Bill Vukovich (1)	KK500A-Offy	128.740	Bill Vukovich	138.392
1954	Bill Vukovich (19)	KK500A-Offy	130.840	Jack McGrath	141.033
1955	Bob Sweikert (14)	KK500C-Offy	128.209	Jerry Hoyt	140.045
1956	Pat Flaherty (1)	Watson-Offy	128.490	Pat Flaherty	145.596
1957	Sam Hanks (13)	Salih-Offy	135.601	Pat O'Connor	143.948
1958	Jim Bryan (7)	Salih-Offy	133.791	Dick Rathmann	145.974
1959	Rodger Ward (6)	Watson-Offy	135.857	Johnny Thomson	145.908
1960	Jim Rathmann (2)	Watson-Offy	138.767	Eddie Sachs	146.592
1961	A.J. Foyt (7)	Trevis-Offy	139.130	Eddie Sachs	147.481
1962	Rodger Ward (2)	Watson-Offy	140.293	Parnelli Jones	150.370
1963	Parnelli Jones (1)	Watson-Offy	143.137	Parnelli Jones	151.153
1964	A.J. Foyt (5)	Watson-Offy	147.350	Jim Clark	158.828
1965	Jim Clark (2)	Lotus-Ford	150.686	A.J. Foyt	161.233
1966	Graham Hill (15)	Lola-Ford	144.317	Mario Andretti	165.899
1967	A.J. Foyt (4)	Coyote-Ford	151.207	Mario Andretti	168.982
1968	Bobby Unser (3)	Eagle-Offy	152.882	Joe Leonard	171.559
1969	Mario Andretti (2)	Hawk-Ford	156.867	A.J. Foyt	170.568
1970	Al Unser (1)	PJ Colt-Ford	155.749	Al Unser	170.221
1971	Al Unser (5)	PJ Colt-Ford	157.735	Peter Revson	178.696
1972	Mark Donohue (3)	McLaren-Offy	162.962	Bobby Unser	195.940
1973	Gordon Johncock (11)	Eagle-Offy	159.036	Johnny Rutherford	198.413
1974	Johnny Rutherford (25)	McLaren-Offy	158.589	A.J. Foyt	191.632

Year	Winner (start pos.)	Chassis-Engine	Avg speed	Pole Winner	Speed
1975	Bobby Unser (3)	Racers Eagle-Offy	149.213	A.J. Foyt	193.976
1976	Johnny Rutherford (1)	McLaren-Offy	148.725	Johnny Rutherford	188.957
1977	A.J. Foyt (4)	Coyote-Ford	161.331	Tom Sneva	198.884
1978	Al Unser (5)	Lola-Cosworth	161.361	Tom Sneva	202.156
1979	Rick Mears (1)	Penske-Cosworth	158.899	Rick Mears	193.736
1980	Johnny Rutherford (1)	Chaparral-Coswoth	142.862	Johnny Rutherford	192.256
1981	Bobby Unser (1)	Penske-Cosworth	139.084	Bobby Unser	200.546
1982	Gordon Johncock (5)	Wildcat-Cosworth	162.026	Rick Mears	207.004
1983	Tom Sneva (4)	March-Cosworth	162.117	Teo Fabi	207.395
1984	Rick Mears (3)	March-Cosworth	163.612	Tom Sneva	210.029
1985	Danny Sullivan (8)	March-Cosworth	152.982	Pancho Carter	212.583
1986	Bobby Rahal (4)	March-Cosworth	170.722	Rick Mears	216.828
1987	Al Unser (20)	March-Cosworth	162.175	Mario Andretti	215.390
1988	Rick Mears (1)	Penske-Chevrolet	144.809	Rick Mears	219.198
1989	Emerson Fittipaldi (3)	Penske-Chevrolet	167.581	Rick Mears	223.885
1990	Arie Luyendyk (3)	Lola-Chevrolet	185.981*	Emerson Fittipaldi	225.301
1991	Rick Mears (1)	Penske-Chevrolet	176.457	Rick Mears	224.113
1992	Al Unser Jr (12)	Galmer-Chevrolet	134.477	Roberto Guerrero	232.482
1993	Emerson Fittipaldi (9)	Penske-Chevrolet	157.207	Arie Luyendyk	223.967
1994	Al Unser Jr (1)	Penske-Mercedes	160.872	Al Unser Jr	228.011
1995	Jacques Villeneuve (5)	Reynard-Ford	153.616	Scott Brayton	231.616
1996	Buddy Lazier (5)	Reynard-Ford	147.956	Tony Stewart	233.100†
1997	Arie Luyendyk (1)	G Force-Oldsmobile	145.827	Arie Luyendyk	231.468
1998	Eddie Cheever (17)	Dallara-Oldsmobile	145.155	Billy Boat	223.503
1999	Kenny Brack (8)	Dallara-Oldsmobile	153.176	Arie Luyendyk	225.179
2000	Juan Montoya (2)	G Force-Oldsmobile	167.607	Greg Ray	223.471
2001	Helio Castroneves (11)	Dallara-Oldsmobile	153.601	Scott Sharp	226.037
2002	Helio Castroneves (13)	Dallara-Chevrolet	166.499	Bruno Junqueira	231.342
2003	Gil de Ferran	Panoz-Toyota	156.291	Helio Castroneves	231.725
2004	Buddy Rice (1)	G Force-Honda	138.518	Buddy Rice	222.024

*Track record, winning speed. †Track record, qualifying speed.

Indianapolis 500 Rookie of the Year Award

1952	Art Cross	1971	Denny Zimmerman	1989	Bernard Jourdain
1953	Jimmy Daywalt	1972	Mike Hiss		Scott Pruett
1954	Larry Crockett	1973	Graham McRae	1990	Eddie Cheever*
1955	Al Herman	1974	Pancho Carter	1991	Jeff Andretti
1956	Bob Veith	1975	Bill Puterbaugh	1992	Lyn St. James
1957	Don Edmunds	1976	Vern Schuppan	1993	Nigel Mansell
1958	George Amick	1977	Jerry Sneva	1994	Jacques Villeneuve*
1959	Bobby Grim	1978	Rick Mears*	1995	Gil de Ferran
1960	Jim Hurtubise		Larry Rice	1996	Tony Stewart
1961	Parnelli Jones*	1979	Howdy Holmes	1997	Jeff Ward
	Bobby Marshman	1980	Tim Richmond	1998	Steve Knapp
1962	Jimmy McElreath	1981	Josele Garza	1999	Robby McGehee
1963	Jim Clark*	1982	Jim Hickman	2000	Juan Montoya*
1964	Johnny White	1983	Teo Fabi	2001	Helio Castroneves*
1965	Mario Andretti*	1984	Michael Andretti	2002	Alex Barron
1966	Jackie Stewart		Roberto Guerrero		Tomas Scheckter
1967	Denis Hulme	1985	Arie Luyendyk*	2003	Tora Tagaki
1968	Billy Vukovich	1986	Randy Lanier	2004	Kosuke Matsuura
1969	Mark Donohue*	1987	Fabrizio Barbazza		
1970	Donnie Allison	1988	Billy Vukovich III		

*Future winner of Indy 500.

CART Championship Series Champions

From 1909 to 1955, this championship was awarded by the American Automobile Association (AAA), and from 1956 to 1979 by the United States Auto Club (USAC). Since 1979, Championship Auto Racing Teams (CART) has conducted the championship. Known as PPG CART World Series until 1998.

1909 ....George Robertson	1940 ....Rex Mays	1974 ....Bobby Unser
1910 ....Ray Harroun	1941 ....,.....Rex Mays	1975 .............A.J. Foyt
1911 ....Ralph Mulford	1942–45 ....No racing	1976 ....Gordon Johncock
1912 ....Ralph DePalma	1946 ....Ted Horn	1977 ....Tom Sneva
1913 ....Earl Cooper	1947 ....Ted Horn	1978 ....Tom Sneva
1914 ....Ralph DePalma	1948 ....Ted Horn	1979 .............A.J. Foyt
1915 ....Earl Cooper	1949 ....Johnnie Parsons	1979 ....Rick Mears
1916 ....Dario Resta	1950 ....Henry Banks	1980 ....Johnny Rutherford
1917 ....Earl Cooper	1951 ....Tony Bettenhausen	1981 ....Rick Mears
1918 .....,.......Ralph Mulford	1952 ....Chuck Stevenson	1982 ....Rick Mears
1919 ....Howard Wilcox	1953 ....Sam Hanks	1983 ....Al Unser
1920 ....Tommy Milton	1954 ....Jimmy Bryan	1984 ....Mario Andretti
1921 ....Tommy Milton	1955 ....Bob Sweikert	1985 ....Al Unser
1922 ....Jimmy Murphy	1956 ....Jimmy Bryan	1986 ....Bobby Rahal
1923 ....Eddie Hearne	1957 ....Jimmy Bryan	1987 ....Bobby Rahal
1924 ....Jimmy Murphy	1958 ....Tony Bettenhausen	1988 ....Danny Sullivan
1925 ....Peter DePaolo	1959 ....Rodger Ward	1989 ....Emerson Fittipaldi
1926 ....Harry Hartz	1960 .............A.J. Foyt	1990 ....Al Unser Jr.
1927 ....Peter DePaolo	1961 .............A.J. Foyt	1991 ....Michael Andretti
1928 ....Louis Meyer	1962 ....Rodger Ward	1992 ....Bobby Rahal
1929 ....Louis Meyer	1963 .............A.J. Foyt	1993 ....Nigel Mansell
1930 ....Billy Arnold	1964 .............A.J. Foyt	1994 ....Al Unser Jr.
1931 ....Louis Schneider	1965 ....Mario Andretti	1995 ....Jacques Villeneuve
1932 ....Bob Carey	1966 ....Mario Andretti	1996 ....Jimmy Vasser
1933 ....Louis Meyer	1967 .............A.J. Foyt	1997 ....Alex Zanardi
1934 ....Bill Cummings	1968 ....Bobby Unser	1998 ....Alex Zanardi
1935 ....Kelly Petillo	1969 ....Mario Andretti	1999 ....Juan Montoya
1936 ....Mauri Rose	1970 ....Al Unser	2000 ....Gil de Ferran
1937 ....Wilbur Shaw	1971 ....Joe Leonard	2001 ....Gil de Ferran
1938 ....Floyd Roberts	1972 ....Joe Leonard	2002 ....Cristiano da Matta
1939 ....Wilbur Shaw	1973 ....Roger McCluskey	2003 ....Paul Tracy

Alltime CART Leaders

WINS		POLE POSITIONS	
A.J. Foyt	67	Mario Andretti	67
Mario Andretti	52	A.J. Foyt	53
Michael Andretti	42	Bobby Unser	49
Al Unser	39	Rick Mears	40
Bobby Unser	35	Michael Andretti	32
Al Unser Jr	31	Al Unser	27
Rick Mears	29	Johnny Rutherford	23
*Paul Tracy	28	*Paul Tracy	21
Johnny Rutherford	27	Gordon Johncock	20
Rodger Ward	26	Rex Mays	19
Gordon Johncock	25	Danny Sullivan	19
Bobby Rahal	24	Bobby Rahal	18
Ralph DePalma	24	Emerson Fittipaldi	17
Tommy Milton	23	Gil de Ferran	16
Tony Bettenhausen	22	Tony Bettenhausen	14
Emerson Fittipaldi	22	Juan Montoya	14
Earl Cooper	20	Don Branson	14
Jimmy Bryan	19	Tom Sneva	14
Jimmy Murphy	19	Parnelli Jones	12
Danny Sullivan	17	*Sebastien Bourdais	12
Ralph Mulford	17		

*Active driver. Note: Leaders through September 2004.

Stock Car Racing's Major Events

In 1985, Winston began offering a $1 million bonus to any driver to win three of the top four NASCAR events in the same season. A fifth event, the Brickyard 400 (in Indianapolis) was added in 1994. As of 1998 the Winston million was awarded to any driver who won three of the five events. The other four races are the richest (Daytona 500), the fastest (Talladega 500), the longest (Charlotte 600) and the oldest (Southern 500 at Darlington). Only five drivers, Lee Roy Yarbrough (1969), David Pearson (1976), Bill Elliott (1985), Dale Jarrett (1996) and Jeff Gordon (1997, '98) have scored the three-track hat trick.

Daytona 500

Year	Winner	Car	Avg Speed	Pole Winner	Speed
1959	Lee Petty	Oldsmobile	135.520	Cotton Owens	143.198
1960	Junior Johnson	Chevrolet	124.740	Fireball Roberts	151.556
1961	Marvin Panch	Pontiac	149.601	Fireball Roberts	155.709
1962	Fireball Roberts	Pontiac	152.529	Fireball Roberts	156.995
1963	Tiny Lund	Ford	151.566	Johnny Rutherford	165.183
1964	Richard Petty	Plymouth	154.345	Paul Goldsmith	174.910
1965	Fred Lorenzen	Ford	141.539	Darel Dieringer	171.151
1966	Richard Petty	Plymouth	160.627	Richard Petty	175.165
1967	Mario Andretti	Ford	149.926	Curtis Turner	180.831
1968	Cale Yarborough	Mercury	143.251	Cale Yarborough	189.222
1969	Lee Roy Yarbrough	Ford	157.950	David Pearson	190.029
1970	Pete Hamilton	Plymouth	149.601	Cale Yarborough	194.015
1971	Richard Petty	Plymouth	144.462	A.J. Foyt	182.744
1972	A.J. Foyt	Mercury	161.550	Bobby Isaac	186.632
1973	Richard Petty	Dodge	157.205	Buddy Baker	185.662
1974	Richard Petty	Dodge	140.894	David Pearson	185.017
1975	Benny Parsons	Chevrolet	153.649	Donnie Allison	185.827
1976	David Pearson	Mercury	152.181	A.J. Foyt	185.943
1977	Cale Yarborough	Chevrolet	153.218	Donnie Allison	188.048
1978	Bobby Allison	Ford	159.730	Cale Yarborough	187.536
1979	Richard Petty	Oldsmobile	143.977	Buddy Baker	196.049
1980	Buddy Baker	Oldsmobile	177.602*	A.J. Foyt	195.020
1981	Richard Petty	Buick	169.651	Bobby Allison	194.624
1982	Bobby Allison	Buick	153.991	Benny Parsons	196.317
1983	Cale Yarborough	Pontiac	155.979	Ricky Rudd	198.864
1984	Cale Yarborough	Chevrolet	150.994	Cale Yarborough	201.848
1985	Bill Elliott	Ford	172.265	Bill Elliott	205.114
1986	Geoff Bodine	Chevrolet	148.124	Bill Elliott	205.039
1987	Bill Elliott	Ford	176.263	Bill Elliott	210.364†
1988	Bobby Allison	Buick	137.531	Ken Schrader	193.823
1989	Darrell Waltrip	Chevrolet	148.466	Ken Schrader	196.996
1990	Derrike Cope	Chevrolet	165.761	Ken Schrader	196.515
1991	Ernie Irvan	Chevrolet	148.148	Davey Allison	195.955
1992	Davey Allison	Ford	160.256	Sterling Marlin	192.213
1993	Dale Jarrett	Chevrolet	154.972	Kyle Petty	189.426
1994	Sterling Marlin	Chevrolet	156.931	Loy Allen Jr	190.158
1995	Sterling Marlin	Chevrolet	141.710	Dale Jarrett	193.498
1996	Dale Jarrett	Ford	154.308	Dale Earnhardt	189.510
1997	Jeff Gordon	Chevrolet	148.295	Mike Skinner	189.813
1998	Dale Earnhardt	Chevrolet	172.712	Bobby Labonte	192.415
1999	Jeff Gordon	Chevrolet	161.551	Jeff Gordon	195.067
2000	Dale Jarrett	Ford	155.669	Dale Jarrett	191.091
2001	Michael Waltrip	Chevrolet	161.783	Bill Elliott	183.570
2002	Ward Burton	Dodge	142.971	Jimmie Johnson	185.831
2003	Michael Waltrip	Chevrolet	133.87	Jeff Green	186.606
2004	Dale Earnhardt Jr.	Chevrolet	156.345	Greg Biffle	188.387

*Track record, winning speed. †Track record, qualifying speed. Note: The Daytona 500, held annually in February, now opens the NASCAR season with 200 laps around the high-banked Daytona International Speedway.

Charlotte 600

Year	Winner	Car	Avg Speed	Pole Winner
1960	Joe Lee Johnson	Chevrolet	107.752	Joe Lee Johnson
1961	David Pearson	Pontiac	111.634	Richard Petty
1962	Nelson Stacy	Ford	125.552	Fireball Roberts
1963	Fred Lorenzen	Ford	132.418	Junior Johnson
1964	Jim Paschal	Plymouth	125.772	Junior Johnson
1965	Fred Lorenzen	Ford	121.772	Fred Lorenzon
1966	Marvin Panch	Plymouth	135.042	Paul Goldsmith
1967	Jim Paschal	Plymouth	135.832	Cale Yarborough
1968	Buddy Baker	Dodge	104.207	Donnie Allison
1969	Lee Roy Yarbrough	Mercury	134.631	Donnie Allison
1970	Donnie Allison	Ford	129.680	Bobby Isaac
1971	Bobby Allison	Mercury	140.442	Charlie Glotzbach
1972	Buddy Baker	Dodge	142.255	Bobby Allison
1973	Buddy Baker	Dodge	134.890	Buddy Baker
1974	David Pearson	Mercury	135.720	David Pearson
1975	Richard Petty	Dodge	145.327	David Pearson
1976	David Pearson	Mercury	137.352	David Pearson
1977	Richard Petty	Dodge	137.636	David Pearson
1978	Darrell Waltrip	Chevrolet	138.355	David Pearson
1979	Darrell Waltrip	Chevrolet	136.674	Neil Bonnet
1980	Benny Parsons	Chevrolet	119.265	Cale Yarborough
1981	Bobby Allison	Buick	129.326	Neil Bonnett
1982	Neil Bonnett	Ford	130.508	David Pearson
1983	Neil Bonnett	Chevrolet	140.406	Buddy Baker
1984	Bobby Allison	Buick	129.233	Harry Gant
1985	Darrell Waltrip	Chevrolet	141.807	Bill Elliott
1986	Dale Earnhardt	Chevrolet	140.406	Geoff Bodine
1987	Kyle Petty	Ford	131.483	Bill Elliott
1988	Darrell Waltrip	Chevrolet	124.460	Davey Allison
1989	Darrell Waltrip	Chevrolet	144.077	Alan Kulwicki
1990	Rusty Wallace	Pontiac	137.650	Ken Schrader
1991	Davey Allison	Ford	138.951	Mark Martin
1992	Dale Earnhardt	Chevrolet	132.980	Bill Elliott
1993	Dale Earnhardt	Chevrolet	145.504	Ken Schrader
1994	Jeff Gordon	Chevrolet	139.445	Jeff Gordon
1995	Bobby Labonte	Chevrolet	151.952	Jeff Gordon
1996	Dale Jarrett	Ford	147.581	Jeff Gordon
1997	Jeff Gordon	Chevrolet	136.745	Jeff Gordon
1998	Jeff Gordon	Chevrolet	136.424	Jeff Gordon
1999	Jeff Burton	Ford	151.367	Bobby Labonte
2000	Matt Kenseth	Ford	142.640	Dale Earnhardt Jr
2001	Jeff Burton	Ford	138.107	Ryan Newman
2002	Mark Martin	Ford	137.729	Jimmie Johnson
2003	Jimmie Johnson	Chevrolet	126.198	Ryan Newman
2004	Jimmie Johnson	Chevrolet	142.763	Jimmie Johnson

Note: Held at the 1.5-mile high-banked Lowe's Motor Speedway in Charlotte on Memorial Day weekend.

Brickyard 400

Year	Winner	Car	Avg Speed	Pole Winner	Speed
1994	Jeff Gordon	Chevrolet	131.977	Rick Mast	172.414
1995	Dale Earnhardt	Chevrolet	155.206	Jeff Gordon	172.536
1996	Dale Jarrett	Ford	139.508	Jeff Gordon	176.419
1997	Ricky Rudd	Ford	130.814	Ernie Irvan	177.736
1998	Jeff Gordon	Chevrolet	126.772	Ernie Irvan	179.394
1999	Dale Jarrett	Ford	148.194	Jeff Gordon	179.612
2000	Bobby Labonte	Pontiac	155.912	Ricky Rudd	181.068
2001	Jeff Gordon	Chevrolet	130.790	Jimmy Spencer	179.666
2002	Bill Elliott	Dodge	125.033	Tony Stewart	182.960
2003	Kevin Harvick	Chevrolet	134.554	Kevin Harvick	184.343*
2004	Jeff Gordon	Chevrolet	115.037	Casey Mears	186.293*

*Track record.

Talladega 500

Year	Winner	Car	Avg Speed	Pole Winner	Speed
1970	Pete Hamilton	Plymouth	152.321	Bobby Isaac	199.658
1971	Donnie Allison	Mercury	147.419	Donnie Allison	185.869
1972	David Pearson	Mercury	134.400	Bobby Isaac	192.428
1973	David Pearson	Mercury	131.956	Buddy Baker	193.435
1974	David Pearson	Mercury	130.220	David Pearson	186.086
1975	Buddy Baker	Ford	144.94	Buddy Baker	189.947
1976	Buddy Baker	Ford	169.887	Dave Marcis	189.197
1977	Darrell Waltrip	Chevrolet	164.887	A.J. Foyt	192.424
1978	Cale Yarborough	Oldsmobile	155.699	Cale Yarborough	191.904
1979	Bobby Allison	Ford	154.770	Darrell Waltrip	195.644
1980	Buddy Baker	Oldsmobile	170.481	David Pearson	197.704
1981	Bobby Allison	Buick	149.376	Bobby Allison	195.864
1982	Darrell Waltrip	Buick	156.697	Benny Parsons	200.176
1983	Richard Petty	Pontiac	135.936	Cale Yarborough	202.650
1984	Cale Yarborough	Chevrolet	172.988	Cale Yarborough	202.692
1985	Bill Elliott	Ford	186.288	Bill Elliott	209.398
1986	Bobby Allison	Buick	157.698	Bill Elliott	212.229
1987	Davey Allison	Ford	154.228	Bill Elliott	221.809
1988	Phil Parsons	Oldsmobile	156.547	Davey Allison	198.969
1989	Davey Allison	Ford	155.869	Mark Martin	193.061
1990	Dale Earnhardt	Chevrolet	159.571	Bill Elliott	199.388
1991	Harry Gant	Oldsmobile	165.620	Ernie Irvan	195.186
1992	Davey Allison	Ford	167.609	Ernie Irvan	192.831
1993	Ernie Irvan	Chevrolet	155.412	Dale Earnhardt	192.355
1994	Dale Earnhardt	Chevrolet	157.478	Ernie Irvan	193.298
1995	Mark Martin	Ford	178.902	Terry Labonte	196.532
1996	Sterling Marlin	Chevrolet	149.999	Ernie Irvan	192.855
1997	Mark Martin	Ford	188.354	John Andretti	193.627
1998	Dale Jarrett	Ford	159.318	Ken Schrader	196.153
1999	Dale Earnhardt	Chevrolet	166.632	Joe Nemechek	198.331
2000	Dale Earnhardt	Chevrolet	165.681	Joe Nemechek	190.279
2001	Dale Earnhardt Jr.	Chevrolet	164.185	Stacy Compton	185.240
2002	Dale Earnhardt Jr.	Chevrolet	183.665	qualifying cancelled	—
2003	Michael Waltrip	Chevrolet	156.045	Elliot Sadler	189.943
2004	Jeff Gordon	Chevrolet	129.396	Ricky Rudd	191.180

Note: Formerly the Winston 500, held at the 2.66-mile Talladega Superspeedway.

Southern 500

Year	Winner	Car	Avg Speed	Pole Winner
1950	Johnny Mantz	Plymouth	76.260	Wally Campbell
1951	Herb Thomas	Hudson	76.900	Marshall Teague
1952	Fonty Flock	Oldsmobile	74.510	Dick Rathman
1953	Buck Baker	Oldsmobile	92.780	Fonty Flock
1954	Herb Thomas	Hudson	94.930	Buck Baker
1955	Herb Thomas	Chevrolet	92.281	Tim Flock
1956	Curtis Turner	Ford	95.067	Buck Baker
1957	Speedy Thompson	Chevrolet	100.100	Paul Goldsmith
1958	Fireball Roberts	Chevrolet	102.590	Fireball Roberts
1959	Jim Reed	Chevrolet	111.836	Fireball Roberts
1960	Buck Baker	Pontiac	105.901	Cotton Owens
1961	Nelson Stacy	Ford	117.880	Fireball Roberts
1962	Larry Frank	Ford	117.965	Fireball Roberts
1963	Fireball Roberts	Ford	129.784	Fireball Roberts
1964	Buck Baker	Dodge	117.757	Richard Petty
1965	Ned Jarrett	Ford	115.924	Junior Johnson
1966	Darel Dieringer	Mercury	114.830	Lee Yarborough
1967	Richard Petty	Plymouth	131.933	David Pearson
1968	Cale Yarborough	Mercury	126.132	Charlie Glotzbach
1969	Lee Roy Yarbrough	Ford	105.612	Cale Yarborough
1970	Buddy Baker	Dodge	128.817	David Pearson
1971	Bobby Allison	Mercury	131.398	Bobby Allison
1972	Bobby Allison	Chevrolet	128.124	David Pearson
1973	Cale Yarborough	Chevrolet	134.033	David Pearson
1974	Cale Yarborough	Chevrolet	111.075	Richard Petty
1975	Bobby Allison	Matador	116.825	David Pearson
1976	David Pearson	Mercury	120.534	David Pearson
1977	David Pearson	Mercury	106.797	Darrell Waltrip
1978	Cale Yarborough	Oldsmobile	116.828	David Pearson
1979	David Pearson	Chevrolet	126.259	Bobby Allison
1980	Terry Labonte	Chevrolet	115.210	Darrell Waltrip
1981	Neil Bonnett	Ford	126.410	Harry Gant
1982	Cale Yarborough	Buick	126.703	David Pearson
1983	Bobby Allison	Buick	123.343	Neil Bonnett
1984	Harry Gant	Chevrolet	128.270	Harry Gant
1985	Bill Elliott	Ford	121.254	Bill Elliott
1986	Tim Richmond	Chevrolet	121.068	Tim Richmond
1987	Dale Earnhardt	Chevrolet	115.520	Davey Allison
1988	Bill Elliott	Ford	128.297	Bill Elliott
1989	Dale Earnhardt	Chevrolet	135.462	Alan Kulwicki
1990	Dale Earnhardt	Chevrolet	123.141	Dale Earnhardt
1991	Harry Gant	Oldsmobile	133.508	Davey Allison
1992	Darrell Waltrip	Chevrolet	129.114	Sterling Marlin
1993	Mark Martin	Ford	137.932	Ken Schrader
1994	Bill Elliott	Ford	127.915	Geoff Bodine
1995	Jeff Gordon	Chevrolet	121.231	John Andretti
1996	Jeff Gordon	Chevrolet	135.757	Dale Jarrett
1997	Jeff Gordon	Chevrolet	121.149	Bobby Labonte
1998	Jeff Gordon	Chevrolet	139.031	Dale Jarrett
1999	Jeff Burton	Ford	100.816	Kenny Irwin
2000	Bobby Labonte	Pontiac	108.275	Jeremy Mayfield
2001	Ward Burton	Dodge	122.773	Kurt Busch
2002	Jeff Gordon	Chevrolet	118.617	Sterling Marlin
2003	Terry Labonte	Chevrolet	120.744	Ryan Newman

Note: Held at the 1.366-mile Darlington (S.C.) Raceway on Labor Day weekend. The 2004 edition of the race was scheduled for November 12–15.

Winston Cup* NASCAR Champions

Year	Driver	Car	Wins	Poles	Winnings ($)
1949	Red Byron	Oldsmobile	2	1	5,800
1950	Bill Rexford	Oldsmobile	1	0	6,175
1951	Herb Thomas	Hudson	7	4	18,200
1952	Tim Flock	Hudson	8	4	20,210
1953	Herb Thomas	Hudson	11	10	27,300
1954	Lee Petty	Dodge	7	3	26,706
1955	Tim Flock	Chrysler	18	19	33,750
1956	Buck Baker	Chrysler	14	12	29,790
1957	Buck Baker	Chevrolet	10	5	24,712
1958	Lee Petty	Oldsmobile	7	4	20,600
1959	Lee Petty	Plymouth	10	2	45,570
1960	Rex White	Chevrolet	6	3	45,260
1961	Ned Jarrett	Chevrolet	1	4	27,285
1962	Joe Weatherly	Pontiac	9	6	56,110
1963	Joe Weatherly	Mercury	3	6	58,110
1964	Richard Petty	Plymouth	9	8	98,810
1965	Ned Jarrett	Ford	13	9	77,966
1966	David Pearson	Dodge	14	7	59,205
1967	Richard Petty	Plymouth	27	18	130,275
1968	David Pearson	Ford	16	12	118,824
1969	David Pearson	Ford	11	14	183,700
1970	Bobby Isaac	Dodge	11	13	121,470
1971	Richard Petty	Plymouth	21	9	309,225
1972	Richard Petty	Plymouth	8	3	227,015
1973	Benny Parsons	Chevrolet	1	0	114,345
1974	Richard Petty	Dodge	10	7	299,175
1975	Richard Petty	Dodge	13	3	378,865
1976	Cale Yarborough	Chevrolet	9	2	387,173
1977	Cale Yarborough	Chevrolet	9	3	477,499
1978	Cale Yarborough	Oldsmobile	10	8	530,751
1979	Richard Petty	Chevrolet	5	1	531,292
1980	Dale Earnhardt	Chevrolet	5	0	588,926
1981	Darrell Waltrip	Buick	12	11	693,342
1982	Darrell Waltrip	Buick	12	7	873,118
1983	Bobby Allison	Buick	6	0	828,355
1984	Terry Labonte	Chevrolet	2	2	713,010
1985	Darrell Waltrip	Chevrolet	3	4	1,318,735
1986	Dale Earnhardt	Chevrolet	5	1	1,783,880
1987	Dale Earnhardt	Chevrolet	11	1	2,099,243
1988	Bill Elliott	Ford	6	6	1,574,639
1989	Rusty Wallace	Pontiac	6	4	2,247,950
1990	Dale Earnhardt	Chevrolet	9	4	3,083,056
1991	Dale Earnhardt	Chevrolet	4	0	2,396,685
1992	Alan Kulwicki	Ford	2	6	2,322,561
1993	Dale Earnhardt	Chevrolet	6	2	3,353,789
1994	Dale Earnhardt	Chevrolet	4	2	3,400,733
1995	Jeff Gordon	Chevrolet	7	9	4,347,343
1996	Terry Labonte	Chevrolet	2	4	4,030,648
1997	Jeff Gordon	Chevrolet	10	1	4,201,227
1998	Jeff Gordon	Chevrolet	13	7	6,175,867
1999	Dale Jarrett	Ford	4	0	3,608,829
2000	Bobby Labonte	Pontiac	4	2	4,041,750
2001	Jeff Gordon	Chevrolet	6	8	6,649,076
2002	Tony Stewart	Pontiac	3	4	4,695,150
2003	Matt Kenseth	Ford	1	2	4,038,120

*Series name changed to Nextel Cup after 2003 season.

Alltime NASCAR Leaders

WINS		POLE POSITIONS	
Richard Petty	200	Richard Petty	126
David Pearson	105	David Pearson	113
Bobby Allison	84	Cale Yarborough	70
Darrell Waltrip	84	Darrell Waltrip	59
Cale Yarborough	83	Bobby Allison	57
Dale Earnhardt	76	*Jeff Gordon	56
*Jeff Gordon	65	*Bill Elliott	55
Lee Petty	54	Bobby Isaac	51
*Rusty Wallace	54	Junior Johnson	47
Ned Jarrett	50	Buck Baker	44
Junior Johnson	50	*Mark Martin	42
Herb Thomas	48	Buddy Baker	40
Buck Baker	46	Tim Flock	39
*Bill Elliott	44	Herb Thomas	39
Tim Flock	40	Geoff Bodine	37

*Active drivers. Note: NASCAR wins leaders through 2003 season. Pole positions leaders through Sept. 28, 2004.

Formula One Grand Prix Racing

World Driving Champions

Year	Winner	Car	Year	Winner	Car
1950	Guiseppe Farina, Italy	Alfa Romeo	1974	Emerson Fittipaldi, Brazil	McLaren-Ford
1951	Juan-Manuel Fangio, Argentina	Alfa Romeo	1975	Niki Lauda, Austria	Ferrari
			1976	James Hunt, Grt Britain	McLaren-Ford
1952	Alberto Ascari, Italy	Ferrari	1977	Niki Lauda, Austria	Ferrari
1953	Alberto Ascari, Italy	Ferrari	1978	Mario Andretti, U.S.	Lotus-Ford
1954	Juan-Manuel Fangio, Argentina	Maserati-Mercedes	1979	Jody Scheckter, S Africa	Ferrari
			1980	Alan Jones, Australia	Williams-Ford
1955	Juan-Manuel Fangio, Argentina	Mercedes	1981	Nelson Piquet, Brazil	Brabham-Ford
			1982	Keke Rosberg, Finland	Williams-Ford
1956	Juan-Manuel Fangio, Argentina	Ferrari	1983	Nelson Piquet, Brazil	Brabham-BMW
			1984	Niki Lauda, Austria	McLaren-Porsche
1957	Juan-Manuel Fangio, Argentina	Maserati	1985	Alain Prost, France	McLaren-Porsche
			1986	Alain Prost, France	McLaren-Porsche
1958	Mike Hawthorn, Grt Britain	Ferrari	1987	Nelson Piquet, Brazil	Williams-Honda
1959	Jack Brabham, Australia	Cooper-Climax	1988	Ayrton Senna, Brazil	McLaren-Honda
1960	Jack Brabham, Australia	Cooper-Climax	1989	Alain Prost, France	McLaren-Honda
1961	Phil Hill, U.S.	Ferrari	1990	Ayrton Senna, Brazil	McLaren-Honda
1962	Graham Hill, Grt Britain	BRM	1991	Ayrton Senna, Brazil	McLaren-Honda
1963	Jim Clark, Scotland	Lotus-Climax	1992	Nigel Mansell, Grt Britain	Williams-Renault
1964	John Surtees, Grt Britain	Ferrari	1993	Alain Prost, France	Williams-Renault
1965	Jim Clark, Scotland	Lotus-Climax	1994	Michael Schumacher, Ger	Benetton-Ford
1966	Jack Brabham, Australia	Brabham-Repco	1995	Michael Schumacher, Ger	Benetton-Renault
1967	Denny Hulme, New Zealand	Brabham-Repco	1996	Damon Hill, Grt Britain	Williams-Renault
			1997	Jacques Villeneuve, Can	Williams-Renault
1968	Graham Hill, Grt Britain	Lotus-Ford	1998	Mika Hakkinen, Finland	McLaren-Mercedes
1969	Jackie Stewart, Scotland	Matra-Ford	1999	Mika Hakkinen, Finland	McLaren-Mercedes
1970	Jochen Rindt, Austria*	Lotus-Ford	2000	Michael Schumacher, Ger	Ferrari
1971	Jackie Stewart, Scotland	Tyrell-Ford	2001	Michael Schumacher, Ger	Ferrari
1972	Emerson Fittipaldi, Brazil	Lotus-Ford	2002	Michael Schumacher, Ger	Ferrari
1973	Jackie Stewart, Scotland	Tyrell-Ford	2003	Michael Schumacher, Ger	Ferrari

*The championship was awarded posthumously, after Rindt was killed during practice for the Italian Grand Prix.

Alltime Grand Prix Winners

Driver	Wins	Driver	Wins
*Michael Schumacher, Germany	75	Jim Clark, Great Britain	25
Alain Prost, France	51	Niki Lauda, Austria	25
Ayrton Senna, Brazil	41	Juan Manuel Fangio, Argentina	24
Nigel Mansell, Great Britain	31	Nelson Piquet, Brazil	23
Jackie Stewart, Great Britain	27	Damon Hill, Great Britain	22

*Active driver. Note: Grand Prix winners through Sept. 26, 2004.

Alltime Grand Prix Pole Winners

Driver	Poles	Driver	Poles
Ayrton Senna, Brazil	65	Juan Manuel Fangio, Argentina	29
*Michael Schumacher, Germany	59	Mika Hakkinen, Finland	26
Alain Prost, France	33	Niki Lauda, Austria	24
Jim Clark, Great Britain	33	Nelson Piquet, Brazil	24
Nigel Mansell, Great Britain	32	Damon Hill, Great Britain	20

*Active driver. Note: Pole winners through Sept. 26, 2004.

Professional Sports Car Racing

The 24 Hours of Daytona

Year	Winner	Car	Avg Speed	Distance
1962	Dan Gurney	Lotus 19-Class SP11	104.101 mph	3 hrs (312.42 mi)
1963	Pedro Rodriguez	Ferrari-Class 12	102.074 mph	3 hrs (308.61 mi)
1964	Pedro Rodriguez/Phil Hill	Ferrari 250 LM	98.230 mph	2,000 km
1965	Ken Miles/Lloyd Ruby	Ford	99.944 mph	2,000 km
1966	Ken Miles/Lloyd Ruby	Ford Mark II	108.020 mph	24 hrs (2,570.63 mi)
1967	Lorenzo Bandini/Chris Amon	Ferrari 330 P4	105.688 mph	24 hrs (2,537.46 mi)
1968	Vic Elford/Jochen Neerpasch	Porsche 907	106.697 mph	24 hrs (2,565.69 mi)
1969	Mark Donohue/Chuck Parsons	Chevy Lola	99.268 mph	24 hrs (2,383.75 mi)
1970	Pedro Rodriguez/Leo Kinnunen	Porsche 917	114.866 mph	24 hrs (2,758.44 mi)
1971	Pedro Rodriguez/Jackie Oliver	Porsche 917K	109.203 mph	24 hrs (2,621.28 mi)
1972*	Mario Andretti/Jacky Ickx	Ferrari 312/P	122.573 mph	6 hrs (738.24 mi)
1973	Peter Gregg/Hurley Haywood	Porsche Carrera	106.225 mph	24 hrs (2,552.7 mi)
1974	(No race)			
1975	Peter Gregg/Hurley Haywood	Porsche Carrera	108.531 mph	24 hrs (2,606.04 mi)
1976†	Peter Gregg/Brian Redman/ John Fitzpatrick	BMW CSL	104.040 mph	24 hrs (2,092.8 mi)
1977	John Graves/Hurley Haywood/ Dave Helmick	Porsche Carrera	108.801 mph	24 hrs (2,615 mi)
1978	Rolf Stommelen/ Antoine Hezemans/Peter Gregg	Porsche Turbo	108.743 mph	24 hrs (2,611.2 mi)
1979	Ted Field/Danny Ongais/ Hurley Haywood	Porsche Turbo	109.249 mph	24 hrs (2,626.56 mi)
1980	Volkert Meri/Rolf Stommelen/ Reinhold Joest	Porsche Turbo	114.303 mph	24 hrs
1981	Bob Garretson/Bobby Rahal/ Brian Redman	Porsche Turbo	113.153 mph	24 hrs
1982	John Paul Jr/John Paul Sr/ Rolf Stommelen	Porsche Turbo	114.794 mph	24 hrs
1983	Preston Henn/Bob Wollek/ Claude Ballot-Lena/A.J. Foyt	Porsche Turbo	98.781 mph	24 hrs
1984	Sarel van der Merwe/ Graham Duxbury/Tony Martin	Porsche March	103.119 mph	24 hrs (2,476.8 mi)
1985	A.J. Foyt/Bob Wollek/ Al Unser/Thierry Boutsen	Porsche 962	104.162 mph	24 hrs (2,502.68 mi)
1986	Al Holbert/Derek Bell/Al Unser Jr.	Porsche 962	105.484 mph	24 hrs (2,534.72 mi)
1987	Chip Robinson/Derek Bell/ Al Holbert/Al Unser Jr.	Porsche 962	111.599 mph	24 hrs (2,680.68 mi)
1988	Martin Brundle/John Nielsen/ Raul Boesel	Jaguar XJR-9	107.943 mph	24 hrs (2,591.68 mi)

The 24 Hours of Daytona (Cont.)

Year	Winner	Car	Avg Speed	Distance
1989	John Andretti/Derek Bell/ Bob Wollek	Porsche 962	92.009 mph	24 hrs (2,210.76 mi)
1990	Davy Jones/ Jan Lammers/ Andy Wallace	Jaguar XJR-12	112.857 mph	24 hrs (2,709.16 mi)
1991	Hurley Haywood/ John Winter/ Frank Jelinski/ Henri Pescarolo/ Bob Wollek	Porsche 962C	106.633 mph	24 hrs (2,559.64 mi)
1992	Massahiro Hasemi/ Kazuoyshi Hoshino/ Toshio Suzuki/ Anders Olofsson	Nissan R91CP	112.987 mph	24 hrs (2,712.72 mi)
1993	P.J. Jones/Mark Dismore/ Rocky Moran	Toyota Eagle MK III	103.537 mph	24 hrs (2,484.88 mi)
1994	Paul Gentilozzi/ Scott Pruett/ Butch Leitzinger/ Steve Millen	Nissan 300 ZX	104.80 mph	24 hrs (2,693.67 mi)
1995	Jurgen Lassig/ Christophe Buochut/ Giovanni Lavaggi/ Marco Werner	Porsche Spyder K8	102.28 mph	690 laps (2,456.4 mi)
1996	Wayne Taylor/ Scott Sharp/ Jim Pace	Oldsmobile Mark III	103.32 mph	697 laps (2,481.32 mi)
1997	Elliot Forbes-Robinson/ John Schneider/Rob Dyson/ John Paul Jr/Butch Leitzinger/ James Weaver/Andy Wallace	Ford R & S MK III	102.292 mph	690 laps (2,456.4 mi)
1998	Arie Luyendyk/Didier Theys/ Mauro Baldi	Ferrari 333 SP	105.565 mph	711 laps (2,531.16 mi)
1999	Elliott Forbes-Robinson/ Butch Leitzinger/ Andy Wallace	Ford R & S MK III	104.9 mph	708 laps (2,520.48 mi)
2000	Olivier Beretta/Karl Wendlinger/ Dominique Dupuy	Dodge Viper	107.207 mph	723 laps (2,573.88 m)
2001	Ron Fellows/Chris Kneifel/Franck Freon/Johnny O'Connell	Corvette	97.293 mph	656 laps (2,335.360 mi)
2002	Didier Theys/Fredy Lienhard/ Max Papis/Mauro Baldi	Dallara-Judd (SRP)	106.143 mph	716 laps (2,548.96 mi)
2003	Kevin Buckler/Michael Schrom Timo Bernhard/Jorg Bergmeister	Porsche GT3 RS	114.068† mph	694 laps (2,470.64 mi)
2004	Forest Barber/Terry Borcheller Andy Pilgrim/Christian Fittipaldi	Pontiac Doran	117.651	526 laps (1,872.56 mi)

*Race shortened due to fuel crisis. †Course lengthened from 3.81 miles to 3.84 miles. † Top speed.

World SportsCar Champions*

Year	Winner	Car	Year	Winner	Car
1978	Peter Gregg	Porsche 935	1989	Geoff Brabham	Nissan GTP
1979	Peter Gregg	Porsche 935	1990	Geoff Brabham	Nissan GTP
1980	John Fitzpatrick	Porsche 935	1991	Geoff Brabham	Nissan NPT
1981	Brian Redman	Chevy Lola	1992	Juan Fangio II	Toyota EGL MKIII
1982	John Paul Jr	Chevy Lola	1993	Juan Fangio II	Toyota EGL MKIII
1983	Al Holbert	Chevy March	1994	Wayne Taylor	Mazda Kudzu
1984	Randy Lanier	Chevy March	1995	Fermin Velez	Ferrari 333 SP
1985	Al Holbert	Porsche 962	1996	Wayne Taylor	Mazda Kudzu
1986	Al Holbert	Porsche 962	1997	Butch Leitzinger	Ford R&S MKIII
1987	Chip Robinson	Porsche 962	1998	Butch Leitzinger	Ford R&S MKIII
1988	Geoff Brabham	Nissan GTP			

Year	Prototype	GTS	GT
1999	Elliott Forbes-Robinson	Olivier Beretta	Cort Wagner
2000	Allan McNish	Olivier Beretta	Sascha Maassen
2001	Emanuele Pirro	Terry Borcheller	Jörg Müller
2002	Tom Kristensen	Ron Fellows	Lucas Luhr
2003	Frank Biela/Marco Werner	Ron Fellows/John O'Connell	Sascha Maassen/L. Luhr

1978–93 champions raced in the GT series, which in 1994 was replaced by the World SportsCar series. Beginning in 1999, racing was reclassified according to the American Le Mans Series. The Series is comprised of two different types of race cars divided into two categories and five separate classes. The Prototype category features open-cockpit prototype World Sports Cars (WSC) and Le Mans Prototypes (LMP), as well as Grand Touring Prototype (GTP) class cars. The Grand Touring category features the Grand Touring S (GTS) class cars, formerly known as GT2, and Grand Touring(GT) cars, formerly known as GT3. Both classes feature purpose-built race cars with an emphasis on spectator car identification.

Alltime SportsCar Leaders

PROTOTYPE WINS (WSC/GTP ERA: 1994–2003)

James Weaver 14
Butch Leitzinger 13
Frank Biela 11
Rinaldo Capello 9
J.J. Lehto 9
Wayne Taylor 8
David Brabham 8
Gianpiero Moretti 7
Allan McNish 6
Emanuele Pirro 6

Seven tied with five.

Note: Leaders through September 27, 2003.

GTS AND GT WINS (IMSA GT: 1971–1993)

Al Holbert 49
Peter Gregg 41
Hurley Haywood 31
Geoff Brabham 26
Parker Johnstone 25
Jim Downing 23
Irv Hoerr 23
Jack Baldwin 22
Don Devendorf 22
Bob Earl 22
Tommy Riggins 22

24 Hours of Le Mans

Year	Winning Drivers	Car
1923	André Lagache/René Léonard	Chenard & Walker
1924	John Duff/Francis Clement	Bentley
1925	Gérard de Courcelles/André Rossignol	La Lorraine
1926	Robert Bloch/André Rossignol	La Lorraine
1927	J. Dudley Benjafield/Sammy Davis	Bentley
1928	Woolf Barnato/Bernard Rubin	Bentley
1929	Woolf Barnato/Sir Henry Birkin	Bentley Speed 6
1930	Woolf Barnato/Glen Kidston	Bentley Speed 6
1931	Earl Howe/Sir Henry Birkin	Alfa Romeo 8C-2300 sc
1932	Raymond Sommer/Luigi Chinetti	Alfa Romeo 8C-2300 sc
1933	Raymond Sommer/Tazio Nuvolari	Alfa Romeo 8C-2300 sc
1934	Luigi Chinetti/Philippe Etancelin	Alfa Romeo 8C-2300 sc
1935	John Hindmarsh/Louis Fontés	Lagonda M45R
1936	Race cancelled	
1937	Jean-Pierre Wimille/Robert Benoist	Bugatti 57G sc
1938	Eugene Chaboud/Jean Tremoulet	Delahaye 135M
1939	Jean-Pierre Wimille/Pierre Veyron	Bugatti 57G sc
1940–48	Races cancelled	
1949	Luigi Chinetti/Lord Selsdon	Ferrari 166MM
1950	Louis Rosier/Jean-Louis Rosier	Talbot-Lago
1951	Peter Walker/Peter Whitehead	Jaguar C
1952	Hermann Lang/Fritz Reiss	Mercedes-Benz 300 SL
1953	Tony Rolt/Duncan Hamilton	Jaguar C
1954	Froilan Gonzales/Maurice Trintignant	Ferrari 375
1955	Mike Hawthorn/Ivor Bueb	Jaguar D
1956	Ron Flockhart/Ninian Sanderson	Jaguar D
1957	Ron Flockhart/Ivor Bueb	Jaguar D
1958	Olivier Gendebien/Phil Hill	Ferrari 250 TR58
1959	Carroll Shelby/Roy Salvadori	Aston Martin DBR1
1960	Olivier Gendebien/Paul Frère	Ferrari 250 TR59/60
1961	Olivier Gendebien/Phil Hill	Ferrari 250 TR61
1962	Olivier Gendebien/Phil Hill	Ferrari 250P
1963	Lodovico Scarfiotti/Lorenzo Bandini	Ferrari 250P
1964	Jean Guichel/Nino Vaccarella	Ferrari 275P
1965	Jochen Rindt/Masten Gregory	Ferrari 250LM
1966	Chris Amon/Bruce McLaren	Ford Mk2
1967	Dan Gurney/A.J. Foyt	Ford Mk4
1968	Pedro Rodriguez/Lucien Bianchi	Ford GT40
1969	Jacky Ickx/Jackie Oliver	Ford GT40
1970	Hans Herrmann/Richard Attwood	Porsche 917
1971	Helmut Marko/Gijs van Lennep	Porsche 917
1972	Henri Pescarolo/Graham Hill	Matra-Simca MS670
1973	Henri Pescarolo/Gérard Larrousse	Matra-Simca MS670B

Year	Winning Drivers	Car
1974	Henri Pescarolo/Gérard Larrousse	Matra-Simca MS670B
1975	Jacky Ickx/Derek Bell	Mirage-Ford MB
1976	Jacky Ickx/Gijs van Lennep	Porsche 936
1977	Jacky Ickx/Jurgen Barth/Hurley Haywood	Porsche 936
1978	Jean-Pierre Jaussaud/Didier Pironi	Renault-Alpine A442
1979	Klaus Ludwig/Bill Whittington/Don Whittington	Porsche 935
1980	Jean-Pierre Jaussaud/Jean Rondeau	Rondeau-Ford M379B
1981	Jacky Ickx/Derek Bell	Porsche 936-81
1982	Jacky Ickx/Derek Bell	Porsche 956
1983	Vern Schuppan/Hurley Haywood/Al Holbert	Porsche 956-83
1984	Klaus Ludwig/Henri Pescarolo	Porsche 956B
1985	Klaus Ludwig/Paolo Barilla/John Winter	Porsche 956B
1986	Derek Bell/Hans-Joachim Stuck/Al Holbert	Porsche 962C
1987	Derek Bell/Hans-Joachim Stuck/Al Holbert	Porsche 962C
1988	Jan Lammers/Johnny Dumfries/Andy Wallace	Jaguar XJR9LM
1989	Jochen Mass/Manuel Reuter/Stanley Dickens	Sauber-Mercedes C9-88
1990	John Nielsen/Price Cobb/Martin Brundle	TWR Jaguar XJR-12
1991	Volker Weidler/Johnny Herbert/Bertrand Gachot	Mazda 787B
1992	Derek Warwick/Yannick Dalmas/Mark Blundell	Peugeot 905B
1993	Geoff Brabham/Christophe Bouchut/Eric Helary	Peugeot 905
1994	Yannick Dalmas/Hurley Haywood/Mauro Baldi	Porsche 962
1995	Yannick Dalmas/J.J. Lehto/Masanori Sekiya	McLaren BMW
1996	Manuel Reuter/Davy Jones/Alexander Wurz	TWR Porsche
1997	Michele Alboreto/Stefan Johansson/Tom Kristensen	TWR Porsche
1998	Allan McNish/Laurent Aiello/Stephane Ortelli	Porsche GT One
1999	Yannick Dalmas/Joachim Winkelhock/Pierluigi Martini	BMW V12 LMR
2000	Frank Biela/Tom Kristensen/Emanuele Pirro	Audi R8
2001	Frank Biela/Tom Kristensen/Emanuele Pirro	Audi R8
2002	Frank Biela/Tom Kristensen/Emanuele Pirro	Audi R8
2003	Rinaldo Capello/Tom Kristensen/Guy Smith	Bentley EXP Speed 8
2004	Rinaldo Capello/Seiji Ara/Tom Kristensen	Audi R8

Sir Jackie Rates the Yanks

SI's 1973 Sportsman of the Year, Sir Jackie Stewart of Scotland, won 27 Grand Prix races and three World Championships during his F/1 career, from 1964 through '73. A long-time commentator for ABC Sports, he remains a keen observer of the sport. Here are Sir Jackie's picks for the top five U.S. drivers in F/1 history, with the years in which they competed in Grand Prix racing, their number of GP wins and Stewart's comment for each.

1. Dan Gurney, 1959–69, four wins: "A world-class competitor, Dan is hands down the best American driver ever."

2. Mario Andretti, 1968–82, 12 wins plus the 1978 World Championship: "In the late '70s nobody in the world was better than Mario."

3. Phil Hill, 1958–67, three wins plus the 1961 World Championship: "Phil was a balanced driver and never backed down."

4. Eddie Cheever, 1978–89, no wins: "Eddie never won a Grand Prix, but he probably should have."

5. Danny Sullivan, 1983, no wins: "Danny had more desire than almost anyone I've ever met in the sport. He'd always give you his best."

Top Fuel
ELAPSED TIME

Time (Sec.)	Driver	Date	Site
9.00	Jack Chrisman	Feb 18, 1961	Pomona, CA
8.97	Jack Chrisman	May 20, 1961	Empona, VA
7.96	Bobby Vodnick	May 16, 1964	Bayview, MD
6.97	Don Johnson	May 7, 1967	Carlsbad, CA
5.97	Mike Snively	Nov. 17, 1972	Ontario, CA
5.78	Don Garlits	Nov 18, 1973	Ontario, CA
5.698	Gary Beck	Oct 10, 1975	Ontario, CA
5.573	Gary Beck	Oct 18, 1981	Irvine, CA
5.484	Gary Beck	Sept 6, 1982	Clermont, IN
5.391	Gary Beck	Oct 1, 1983	Fremont, CA
5.280	Darrell Gwynn	Sept 25, 1986	Ennis, TX
5.176	Darrell Gwynn	April 4, 1987	Ennis, TX
5.090	Joe Amato	Oct 1, 1987	Ennis, TX
4.990	Eddie Hill	April 9, 1988	Ennis, TX
4.881	Gary Ormsby	Sept 28, 1990	Topeka, KS
4.799	Cory McClenathan	Sept 19, 1992	Mohnton, PA
4.762	Cory McClenathan	Oct 3, 1993	Topeka, KS
4.690	Michael Brotherton	May 20, 1994	Englishtown, NJ
4.595	Joe Amato	July 5,1996	Topeka, KS
4.539	Joe Amato	Mar 21, 1998	Baytown, TX
4.525	Gary Scelzi	Oct 23, 1998	Ennis, TX
4.503	Mike Dunn	Feb 5, 1999	Pomona, CA
4.486	Larry Dixon	Apr 9, 1999	Houston
4.480	Gary Scelzi	Oct 31, 1999	Houston
4.477	Kenny Bernstein	June 2, 2001	Joliet, IL
4.441	Tony Schumacher	Oct 4, 2003	Reading, PA

SPEED

MPH	Driver	Date	Site
180.36	Connie Kalitta	Sept 3, 1962	Indianapolis
190.26	Don Garlits	Sept 21, 1963	East Haddam, CT
201.34	Don Garlits	Aug 1, 1964	Great Meadows, NJ
211.26	Donny Milani	May 15, 1965	Sacramento, CA
223.32	Don Cook	Apr 24, 1965	Fremont, CA
230.17	James Warren	Apr 10, 1967	Fresno, CA
243.24	Don Garlits	Mar 18, 1973	Gainesville, FL
250.69	Don Garlits	Oct 11, 1975	Ontario, CA
260.11	Joe Amato	Mar 18, 1984	Gainesville, FL
272.56	Don Garlits	Mar 23, 1986	Gainesville, FL
282.13	Joe Amato	Sept 5, 1987	Clermont, IN
291.54	Connie Kalitta	Feb 11, 1989	Pomona, CA
301.70	Kenny Bernstein	Mar 20, 1992	Gainesville, FL
311.86	Kenny Bernstein	Oct 30, 1994	Pomona, CA
319.82	Joe Amato	Mar 21, 1998	Baytown, TX
323.50	Joe Amato	May 17, 1998	Englishtown, NJ
326.44	Gary Scelzi	Nov 2, 1998	Houston
326.91	Tony Schumacher	Oct 22, 1999	Dallas
330.55	Mike Dunn	June 2, 2001	Joliet, IL
332.18	Kenny Bernstein	Oct. 7, 2001	Richardson, TX
332.75	Larry Dixon	Apr 3, 2003	Las Vegas
333.41	Brandon Bernstein	May 22, 2004	Joliet, IL

Funny Car
ELAPSED TIME

Time (sec.)	Driver	Date	Site
6.92	Leroy Goldstein	Sept 3, 1970	Clermont, IN
5.987	Don Prudhomme	Oct 12, 1975	Ontario, CA
5.868	Raymond Beadle	July 16, 1981	Englishtown, NJ
5.799	Tom Anderson	Sept 3, 1982	Clermont, IN
5.637	Don Prudhomme	Sept 4, 1982	Clermont, IN
5.588	Rick Johnson	Feb 3, 1985	Pomona, CA
5.425	Kenny Bernstein	Sept 26, 1986	Ennis, TX
5.397	Kenny Bernstein	April 5, 1987	Ennis, TX
5.255	Ed McCulloch	April 17, 1988	Ennis, TX
5.193	Don Prudhomme	Mar 2, 1989	Baytown, TX
5.077	Cruz Pedregon	Sept 20, 1992	Mohnton, PA
4.987	Chuck Etcholis	Oct 2, 1993	Topeka, KS
4.819	Cruz Pedregon	Mar 21, 1998	Baytown, TX
4.807	Cruz Pedregon	Nov 1, 1998	Houston
4.788	John Force	Apr 11, 1999	Houston
4.763	John Force	June 2, 2001	Joliet, IL
4.750	William Bazemore	Sept 28, 2001	Joliet, IL
4.731	John Force	Oct. 7, 2001	Yorba Linda, CA
4.713	Whit Bazemore	May 22, 2004	Joliet, IL

SPEED

MPH	Driver	Date	Site
200.44	Gene Snow	Aug, 1968	Houston
250.00	Don Prudhomme	May 23, 1982	Baton Rouge
260.11	Kenny Bernstein	Mar 18, 1984	Gainesville, FL
271.41	Kenny Bernstein	Aug 30, 1986	Indianapolis
280.72	Mike Dunn	Oct 2, 1987	Ennis, TX
290.13	Jim White	Oct 11, 1991	Ennis, TX
291.82	Jim White	Oct 25, 1991	Pomona, CA
300.40	Jim Epler	Oct 3, 1993	Topeka, KS
303.64	John Force	Sept 2, 1995	Indianapolis
308.74	John Force	Sept 28, 1997	Topeka, KS
317.46	John Force	Mar 21, 1998	Baytown, TX
323.89	John Force	May 17, 1998	Englishtown, NJ
324.05	John Force	Mar 19, 1999	Gainesville, FL
325.45	William Bazemore	Sept 28, 2001	Joliet, IL
326.87	Gary Densham	Feb. 9, 2002	Bellflower, CA
330.55	Gary Scelzi	May 22, 2004	Joliet, IL

Pro Stock
ELAPSED TIME

Time (sec.)	Driver	Date	Site
7.778	Lee Shepherd	Mar 12, 1982	Gainesville, FL
7.655	Lee Shepherd	Oct 1, 1982	Fremont, CA
7.557	Bob Glidden	Feb 2, 1985	Pomona, CA
7.497	Bob Glidden	Sep 13, 1985	Maple Grove, PA
7.377	Bob Glidden	Aug 28, 1986	Clermont, IN
7.294	Frank Sanchez	Oct 7, 1988	Baytown, TX
7.184	Darrell Alderman	Oct 12, 1990	Ennis, TX
7.099	Scott Geoffrion	Sept 19, 1992	Mohnton, PA
6.988	Kurt Johnson	May 20, 1994	Englishtown, NJ
6.873	Warren Johnson	Mar 14, 1998	Gainesville, FL
6.867	Warren Johnson	Oct 23, 1998	Ennis, TX
6.866	Warren Johnson	Mar 19, 1999	Gainesville, FL
6.843	Warren Johnson	Apr 30, 1999	Dinwiddie, VA
6.840	Kurt Johnson	May 1, 1999	Dinwiddie, VA
6.822	Warren Johnson	Oct 23, 1999	Dallas
6.801	Kurt Johnson	Sept 29, 2001	Joliet, IL
6.750	Jeg Coughlin	Oct. 7, 2001	Delaware, OH
6.670	Greg Anderson	May 18, 2003	Englishtown, NJ

Pro Stock *(Cont.)*

SPEED

MPH	Driver	Date	Site
181.08	Warren Johnson	Oct 1, 1982	Fremont, CA
190.07	Warren Johnson	Aug 29, 1986	Clermont, IN
191.32	Bob Glidden	Sept 4, 1987	Clermont, IN
192.18	Warren Johnson	Oct 13, 1990	Ennis, TX
193.21	Bob Glidden	July 28, 1991	Sonoma, CA
194.51	Warren Johnson	July 31, 1992	Sonoma, CA
195.99	Warren Johnson	May 21, 1993	Englishtown, NJ
196.24	Warren Johnson	Mar 19, 1993	Gainesville, FL
197.15	Warren Johnson	Apr 23, 1994	Commerce, GA
199.15	Warren Johnson	Mar 10, 1995	Baytown, TX
201.20	Warren Johnson	Mar 14, 1998	Gainesville, FL
201.34	Warren Johnson	Oct 23, 1998	Ennis, TX
201.37	Warren Johnson	Mar 19, 1999	Gainesville, FL
202.24	Warren Johnson	Apr 30,1999	Dinwiddie, VA
202.33	Warren Johnson	Oct 23, 1999	Dallas
202.36	Warren Johnson	Oct 31, 1999	Houston
202.70	Kurt Johnson	Sept 29, 2001	Joliet, IL
204.35	Mark Osborne	Oct. 6, 2001	Abdingdon, VA
207.18	Greg Anderson	May 18, 2003	Englishtown, NJ

Alltime Drag Racing Leaders

NHRA CAREER WINS

*John Force	113
*Warren Johnson	92
Bob Glidden	85
*Pat Austin	75
Kenny Bernstein	69
Joe Amato	57
*David Rampy	56
*Frank Manzo	55
Don Prudhomme	49
*Bob Newberry	45

*Active driver. Note: Leaders through September 2004.

YET ANOTHER SIGN OF THE APOCALYPSE

English inventor Giuseppe Cannella has developed a jet-powered wheelchair that travels over 60 mph.

Bowling

Mika Koivuniemi
rocks the PBA Tour

Fantastic Finn

Finland's Mika Koivuniemi bowled a perfect game on ESPN, then topped the year-end lists in earnings and average

BY HANK HERSCH

THERE COULD HARDLY have been a more lopsided title matchup for the PBA World Championship in Ypsilanti, Mich.: a 36-year-old Finn who had emerged as the top bowler in 2003–04 entering the tour's ultimate event, against a 49-year-old from Buffalo, N.Y., who hadn't claimed a title in 123 events, had never won a major and had finished no higher that 13th during the season. But righthander Tom Baker had gained much wisdom in his 28 years on the tour, and after an opening spare in the biggest match of his Hall of Fame career, he racked up six straight strikes.

Then, just as he had in his come-from-behind semifinal victory over Wes Malott, Mika Koivuniemi responded with a string of five strikes into the 10th frame to roll a 239 and seize the lead. With a five-year exemption and a $120,000 first prize on the line, Baker needed to mark in the final frame. His solid first shot struck the pocket and, for an instant, left the seven and 10 pins standing as the crowd of 2,086 held its

collective breath. Finally, the 10-pin tumbled. Baker converted the spare and finished with a 246. "I needed a huge break," Koivuniemi said, "and I almost got it."

It was a rare time the pins didn't go Koivuniemi's way in 2003–04, a breakout season for the former electrician known as the Big Finn. Growing up in Tampere, Finland, he dumped his hockey stick and his putter—he was the 1981 national youth miniature golfing champ—for a bowling ball at age 15, then turned pro eight years later while living in Helsinki. On his largely successful travels (Koivuniemi has won titles in nine countries outside the U.S.), he met Team USA bowler Patrick Healey Jr., who persuaded him to move to the States. After arriving in 1996, Koivuniemi soon moved to Michigan, where he trained and taught at the Institute of Bowling Technologies, in Chesterfield.

He began the 2003–04 season with two victories in his four-year PBA career, both at major tournaments. Hence another nickname: Major Mika. But last season Koivu-

Baker won his first major, taking the PBA World Championship in Ypsilanti.

niemi's earnings dipped from $158,550 to $42,400, prompting him to switch to a 15-pound ball. He quickly became the most dominant foreign-born player on the tour since Amleto Monacelli of Venezuela in 1990. In October, he produced back-to-back runner-up finishes at Kansas City and Vernon Hills, Ill. Then in December, the Big Finn enjoyed one of the finest—and most financially beneficial—days in tour history.

At the PBA Cambridge Credit Classic in Windsor Locks, Conn., Koivuniemi opened ESPN's live telecast by rolling the 16th televised perfect game in tour history, defeating Jason Couch, who tossed a 248. Instead of letting down after earning a $30,000 bonus for throwing a televised 300, Koivuniemi went on to rout Peter Hernandez 277–206 in the semifinals, then beat Patrick Allen 259–237 for the title and a $40,000 paycheck. The righthander's three-game total of 836—which included 32 of 35 possible strikes—fell only 14 pins shy of Bob Learn Jr.'s TV record 850 in 1996.

"I was not that concerned about the 300 game," Koivuniemi said afterward. "I was on a mission. Now that I have won, mission accomplished."

That sort of focus paid off handsomely. Koivuniemi finished the season with a pair of victories, also taking the PBA Reno Open title 258–181 over Brad Angelo, the only bowler who would surpass him in the final rankings. Koivuniemi did, however, set the pace in average (222.73) and earnings ($238,590), edging Walter Ray Williams Jr. ($233,950) after pocketing the second-place prize of $50,000 in Ypsilanti.

The winner of that tournament, Baker, earned the 10th title of his career and upped his career winnings to $1,268,882. He had entered the PBA World Championship hoping to crack the top 50 in points and earn an exemption for 2004–05. "Everything after that would be just icing on the cake," said Baker, who finished No. 29 in the rankings. "Who would have thought that I'd win the cake as well?"

The Majors

MEN

2003 Tournament of Champions

	Games	Total	Earnings ($)
Patrick Healey Jr	2	431	100,000
Randy Pedersen	2	466	30,000
Chris Barnes	1	192	10,000
Brian Himmler	1	227	10,000

Playoff Results: Healey def. Barnes 210–192; Pedersen def. Himmler 278–227; Healey def. Pedersen 222–188.

Held at the Mohegan Sun in Uncasville, CT, Dec 11–14, 2003.

2004 U.S. Open

	Games	Total	Earnings ($)
Pete Weber	1	231	100,000
Brian Voss	3	652	50,000
Chris Barnes	1	193	25,000
Walter Ray Williams Jr	2	442	15,000

Playoff Results: Williams def. Palermaa 228–198; Voss def. Williams 260–214; Voss def. Barnes 214–193; Weber def. Voss 231–178.

Held at the Fountain Bowl in Fountain Valley, CA, Feb 2–Feb 8, 2004

2004 ABC Masters
CHAMPIONSHIP ROUND

Bowler	Games	Total	Earnings ($)
Walter Ray Williams Jr	2	500	100,000
Chris Barnes	1	239	50,000
Mika Koivuniemi	3	651	25,000
D.J. Archer	1	149	15,000

Playoff Results: Koivuniemi def. Allen 214–173; Koivuniemi def. Archer 224–149; Williams def. Koivuniemi 237–213; Williams def. Barnes 268–239.

Held at National Bowling Stadium in Reno, NV, Jan 20–25, 2004.

2004 PBA World Championship
CHAMPIONSHIP ROUND

Bowler	Games	Total	Earnings ($)
Tom Baker	2	523	120,000
Mika Koivuniemi	2	464	50,000
Brad Angelo	1	243	20,000
Wes Malott	1	193	20,000

Playoff Results: Baker def. Angelo 277–243; Koivuniemi def. Malott 225–193; Baker def. Koivuniemi 246–239.

Held at Eastern Michigan Convocation Center in Ypsilanti, MI, Mar 15–21, 2004.

WOMEN

2002 Miller High Life National Players Championship

CHAMPIONSHIP ROUND

Bowler	Games	Total	Earnings ($)
Marianne DiRupo	3	689	13,000
Leanne Barrette	1	158	7,000
Michelle Feldman	1	191	4,600
Kelly Kulick	1	152	4,200
Tammy Turner	1	190	3,700

Playoff Results: DiRupo def. Turner and Kulick, 266–190–152; DiRupo def. Feldman, 243–191; DiRupo def. Barrette 180–158.

Held at Funquest Lanes, Collierville, TN, July 21–25, 2002.

2003 WIBC Queens

CHAMPIONSHIP ROUND

Bowler	Games	Total	Earnings ($)
Wendy Macpherson	1	218	14,000
Kendra Gaines	2	415	11,000
Tish Johnson	2	457	8,500
Robin Romeo	1	218	6,500
Lisa Bishop	1	180	5,500

Playoff Results: Johnson def. Romeo and Bishop 242–218–180; Gaines def. Johnson 222–215; Macpherson def. Gaines 218–193.

Held at the National Bowling Stadium in Reno, NV, April 7–11, 2003.

2003 U.S. Open

CHAMPIONSHIP ROUND

Bowler	Games	Total	Earnings ($)
Kelly Kulick	4	951	30,000
Carolyn Dorin-Ballard	1	195	15,000
Michelle Feldman	1	174	11,000
Wendy Macpherson	1	179	9,000
Leanne Barrette	1	213	7,000

Playoff Results: Kulick def. Barrette 213–213 with rolloff 39–35; Kulick def. Macpherson 221–179; Kulick def. Feldman 256–174; Kulick def. Dorin-Ballard 261–195.

Held in Sterling Heights, MI, May 26–June 1, 2003.

Note: The PWBA suspended operations during the 2003 season.

Men
2003–04 Tour

Date	Event	Winner	Earnings ($)	Runner-Up
Sept 19–21	Japan Cup	Chris Barnes	40,000	Tommy Jones
Oct 8–12	Banquet Open	Robert Smith	40,000	Michael Machuga
Oct 15–19	Greater Kansas City Classic	Norm Duke	40,000	Mika Koivuniemi
Oct 22–26	Miller High Life Open	Brian Himmler	40,000	Mika Koivuniemi
Oct 29–Nov 2	Pepsi Open	Jason Couch	40,000	Steve Wilson
Nov 5–9	Toledo Open	Steve Jaros	40,000	Jeff Labrecque
Nov 12–16	Greater Philadelphia Open	Patrick Allen	40,000	Danny Wiseman
Nov 19–23	Empire State Open	Ryan Shafer	40,000	Chris Barnes
Nov 26–30	Geico Open	Patrick Healey Jr	40,000	Ryan Shafer
Dec 3–7	Cambridge Credit Classic	Mika Koivuniemi	50,300	Patrick Allen
Dec 11–14	Tournament of Champions	Patrick Healey Jr	100,000	Randy Pedersen
Jan 7–11	Earl Anthony Classic	Walter Ray Williams Jr	40,000	Lonnie Waliczek
Jan 14–18	Medford Open	Pete Weber	40,000	Tommy Delutz Jr
Jan 20–25	ABC Masters	Walter Ray Williams Jr	100,000	Chris Barnes
Jan 25–29	Reno Open	Mika Koivuniemi	40,000	Brad Angelo
Feb 2–8	U.S. Open	Pete Weber	100,000	Brian Voss
Feb 11–15	Odor-Eaters Open	Robert Smith	40,000	Walter Ray Williams Jr
Feb 18–22	Days Inn Open	Steve Jaros	40,000	David Traber
Feb 25–29	Baby Ruth Real Deal Classic	Mike Scroggins	40,000	Walter Ray Williams Jr
March 3–7	Uniroyal Tire Classic	Steve Jaros	40,000	Dave D'Entremont
March 15–21	PBA World Championship	Tom Baker	120,000	Mika Koivuniemi

2004 Senior Tour

Date	Event	Winner	Earnings ($)	Runner-Up
March 28–31	Epicenter Classic	Robert Glass	8,000	Don Sylvia
April 4–9	ABC Senior Masters	Gary Dickinson	20,000	Roy Buckley
April 24–27	Clarksville Open	Gary Hiday	8,000	Bob Chamberlain
May 1–4	Chillicothe Open	Robert Glass	8,100	Gary Skidmore
May 8–14	Senior U.S. Openn	David Ozio	20,100	Steve Neff
May 16–19	Manassas Open	George Pappas	8,000	Timothy Kauble
Aug 1–4	Don Carter Classic	Doug Evans	8,000	Tommy Nevitt
Aug 8–11	St. Petersburg/Clearwater Open	Jeff Bellinger	8,000	Gary Hiday
Aug 14–18	Jackson Open	Vince Mazzanti Jr	8,000	Roger Bowker
Aug 23–26	Lake County Open	Roger Kossert	8,000	Pete Couture

2002 Fall Tour

Date	Event	Winner	Earnings ($)	Runner-Up
Sep 15–22	Three Rivers Open	Leanne Barrette	9,000	Marianne DiRupo
Sep 22–26	Burlington Open	Carolyn Dorin-Ballard	9,000	Kendra Gaines
Sep 29–Oct 3	Lady Ebonite Classic	Liz Johnson	12,000	Leanne Barrette
Oct 7–10	Greater Pasadena Open	Tish Johnson	9,000	Liz Johnson
Oct 20–24	Wheelchair Awareness Classic	Tiffany Stanbrough	9,000	Kelly Kulick
Oct 27–Nov 1	Greater San Diego Open	Michelle Feldman	9,000	Wendy Macpherson
Nov 3–8	Storm Las Vegas Challenge	Tiffany Stanbrough	12,000	Kendra Gaines

2003 Tour

Date	Event	Winner	Earnings ($)	Runner-Up
April 7–11	WIBC Queens	Wendy Macpherson	14,000	Kendra Gaines
May 26–Jun 1	U.S. Open	Kelly Kulick	30,000	Carolyn Dorin-Ballard
Jun 5–8	Greater Terre Haute Open	Tiffany Stanbrough	15,000	Lisa Bishop
Jun 11–15	Greater Rockford Classic	Tiffany Stanbrough	15,000	Michelle Feldman
Jun 19–22	Greater Cincinnati Open	Carolyn Dorin-Ballard	15,000	Liz Johnson
Jun 26–29	Greater Harrisburg Open	Dede Davidson	15,000	Cara Honeychurch
July 3–6	Greater Memphis Open	Tennelle Milligan	15,000	Cara Honeychurch
July 9–13	Dallas Open	Michelle Feldman	15,000	Kendra Gaines

Note: Remainder of 2003 tour cancelled.

†Known as LBPT until 1998.

Tour Leaders

PBA: 2003–04

MONEY LEADERS				AVERAGE		
Name (Titles)	Events	Earnings ($)		Name	Events	Average
Mika Koivuniemi	20	238,590		Mika Koivuniemi	20	222.73
Walter Ray Williams Jr	21	233,950		Walter Ray Williams Jr	21	222.69
Pete Weber	21	206,217		Chris Barnes	21	222.37
Chris Barnes	21	191,550		Patrick Allen	20	221.98
Patrick Healey Jr	19	174,600		Brad Angelo	20	221.00

Seniors: 2004

MONEY LEADERS				AVERAGE		
Name	Events	Earnings ($)		Name	Events	Average
Robert Glass	9	28,600		David Ozio	6	226.47
David Ozio	6	27,900		Gary Skidmore	6	217.16
Gary Dickinson	6	26,700		Bob Chamberlain	9	216.65
Gary Hiday	10	25,150		George Pappas	8	216.37
Bob Chamberlain	9	24,050		Roger Bowker	9	216.12

PWBA: 2002

MONEY LEADERS				AVERAGE		
Name (Titles)	Tournaments	Earnings ($)		Name	Games	Average
Michelle Feldman (3)	19	82,405		Leanne Barrette	717	216.45
Leanne Barrette (3)	18	72,960		Carolyn Dorin-Ballard	738	215.46
Kim Terrell (1)	19	69,487		Wendy Macpherson	741	214.39
Kendra Gaines (1)	19	68,800		Michelle Feldman	745	213.93
Carolyn Dorin-Ballard (2)	19	65,672		Kendra Gaines	743	213.93

FOR THE RECORD·Year by Year

BPAA United States Open

Year	Winner	Score	Runner-Up	Site
1942	John Crimmins	265.09–262.33	Joe Norris	Chicago
1943	Connie Schwoegler	not available	Frank Benkovic	Chicago
1944	Ned Day	315.21–298.21	Paul Krumske	Chicago
1945	Buddy Bomar	304.46–296.16	Joe Wilman	Chicago
1946	Joe Wilman	310.27–305.37	Therman Gibson	Chicago
1947	Andy Varipapa	314.16–308.04	Allie Brandt	Chicago
1948	Andy Varipapa	309.23–309.06	Joe Wilman	Chicago
1949	Connie Schwoegler	312.31–307.27	Andy Varipapa	Chicago
1950	Junie McMahon	318.37–307.17	Ralph Smith	Chicago
1951	Dick Hoover	305.29–304.07	Lee Jouglard	Chicago
1952	Junie McMahon	309.29–305.41	Bill Lillard	Chicago
1953	Don Carter	304.17–297.36	Ed Lubanski	Chicago
1954	Don Carter	308.02–307.25	Bill Lillard	Chicago
1955	Steve Nagy	307.17–303.34	Ed Lubanski	Chicago
1956	Bill Lillard	304.30–304.22	Joe Wilman	Chicago
1957	Don Carter	308.49–305.45	Dick Weber	Chicago
1958	Don Carter	311.03–308.09	Buzz Fazio	Minneapolis
1959	Billy Welu	311.48–310.26	Ray Bluth	Buffalo
1960	Harry Smith	312.24–308.12	Bob Chase	Omaha
1961	Bill Tucker	318.49–309.11	Dick Weber	San Bernardino, CA
1962	Dick Weber	299.34–297.38	Roy Lown	Miami Beach
1963	Dick Weber	642–591	Billy Welu	Kansas City, MO
1964	Bob Strampe	714–616	Tommy Tuttle	Dallas
1965	Dick Weber	608–586	Jim St. John	Philadelphia
1966	Dick Weber	684–681	Nelson Burton Jr.	Lansing, MI
1967	Les Schissler	613–610	Pete Tountas	St. Ann, MO
1968	Jim Stefanich	12,401–12,104	Billy Hardwick	Garden City, NY
1969	Billy Hardwick	12,585–11,463	Dick Weber	Miami
1970	Bobby Cooper	12,936–12,307	Billy Hardwick	Northbrook, IL
1971	Mike Limongello	397 (2 games)	Teata Semiz	St. Paul, MN
1972	Don Johnson	233 (1 game)	George Pappas	New York City
1973	Mike McGrath	712 (3 games)	Earl Anthony	New York City
1974	Larry Laub	749 (3 games)	Dave Davis	New York City
1975	Steve Neff	279 (1 game)	Paul Colwell	Grand Prairie, TX
1976	Paul Moser	226 (1 game)	Jim Frazier	Grand Prairie, TX
1977	Johnny Petraglia	279 (1 game)	Bill Spigner	Greensboro, NC
1978	Nelson Burton Jr.	873 (4 games)	Jeff Mattingly	Greensboro, NC
1979	Joe Berardi	445 (2 games)	Earl Anthony	Windsor Locks, CT
1980	Steve Martin	930 (4 games)	Earl Anthony	Windsor Locks, CT
1981	Marshall Holman	684 (3 games)	Mark Roth	Houston
1982	Dave Husted	1011 (4 games)	Gil Sliker	Houston
1983	Gary Dickinson	214 (1 game)	Steve Neff	Oak Lawn, IL
1984	Mark Roth	244 (1 game)	Guppy Troup	Oak Hill, IL
1985	Marshall Holman	233 (1 game)	Wayne Webb	Venice, FL
1986	Steve Cook	467 (2 games)	Frank Ellenburg	Venice, FL
1987	Del Ballard Jr.	525 (2 games)	Pete Weber	Tacoma, WA
1988	Pete Weber	929 (4 games)	Marshall Holman	Atlantic City
1989	Mike Aulby	429 (2 games)	Jim Pencak	Edmond, OK
1990	Ron Palombi Jr.	269 (1 game)	Amleto Monacelli	Indianapolis
1991	Pete Weber	956 (4 games)	Mark Thayer	Indianapolis
1992	Robert Lawrence	667 (3 games)	Scott Devers	Canandaigua, NY
1993	Del Ballard Jr.	505 (2 games)	Walter Ray Williams Jr.	Canandaigua, NY
1994	Justin Hromek	267 (1 game)	Parker Bohn III	Troy, MI
1995	Dave Husted	266 (1 game)	Paul Koehler	Troy, MI
1996	Dave Husted	730 (3 games)	George Brooks	Indianapolis
1998	Walter Ray Williams Jr.	466 (2 games)	Tim Criss	Fairfield, CT
1999	Bob Learn Jr.	231 (1 game)	Jason Couch	Uncasville, CT
2000	Robert Smith	202 (1 game)	Norm Duke	Phoenix
2001	Mika Koivuniemi	247 (1 game)	Patrick Healey Jr	Fountain Valley, CA
2003	Walter Ray Williams Jr.	236 (1 game)	Michael Haugen Jr.	Fountain Valley, CA
2004	Pete Weber	231 (1 game)	Brian Voss	Fountain Valley, CA

Note: From 1942 to 1970, the tournament was called the BPAA All-Star. Peterson scoring was used from 1942 through 1962. Under this system, the winner of an individual match game gets one point, plus one point for each 50 pins knocked down. From 1963 through 1967, a three-game championship was held between the two top qualifiers. From 1968 through 1970 total pinfall determined the winner. From 1971 to the present, five qualifiers compete for the championship.

Touring Players Championship

Year	Winner	Score	Runner-Up	Site
1996	Mike Aulby	268 (1 game)	Parker Bohn III	Harmarville, PA
1997	Steve Hoskins	932 (4 games)	Danny Wiseman	Harmarville, PA
1998	Dennis Horan	481 (2 games)	Parker Bohn III	Akron, OH
1999	Steve Hoskins	503 (2 games)	Parker Bohn III	Akron, OH
2000	Dennis Horan	924 (4 games)	Pete Weber	Akron, OH
2001	Tournament discontinued.			

PBA World Championship

Year	Winner	Score	Runner-Up	Site
1960	Don Carter	6512 (30 games)	Ronnie Gaudern	Memphis
1961	Dave Soutar	5792 (27 games)	Morrie Oppenheim	Cleveland
1962	Carmen Salvino	5369 (25 games)	Don Carter	Philadelphia
1963	Billy Hardwick	13,541 (61 games)	Ray Bluth	Long Island, NY
1964	Bob Strampe	13,979 (61 games)	Ray Bluth	Long Island, NY
1965	Dave Davis	13,895 (61 games)	Jerry McCoy	Detroit
1966	Wayne Zahn	14,006 (61 games)	Nelson Burton Jr.	Long Island, NY
1967	Dave Davis	421 (2 games)	Pete Tountas	New York City
1968	Wayne Zahn	14,182 (60 games)	Nelson Burton Jr.	New York City
1969	Mike McGrath	13,670 (60 games)	Bill Allen	Garden City, NY
1970	Mike McGrath	660 (3 games)	Dave Davis	Garden City, NY
1971	Mike Limongello	911 (4 games)	Dave Davis	Paramus, NJ
1972	Johnny Guenther	12,986 (56 games)	Dick Ritger	Rochester, NY
1973	Earl Anthony	212 (1 game)	Sam Flanagan	Oklahoma City
1974	Earl Anthony	218 (1 game)	Mark Roth	Downey, CA
1975	Earl Anthony	245 (1 game)	Jim Frazier	Downey, CA
1976	Paul Colwell	191 (1 game)	Dave Davis	Seattle
1977	Tommy Hudson	206 (1 game)	Jay Robinson	Seattle
1978	Warren Nelson	453 (2 games)	Joseph Groskind	Reno
1979	Mike Aulby	727 (3 games)	Earl Anthony	Las Vegas
1980	Johnny Petraglia	235 (1 game)	Gary Dickinson	Sterling Heights, MI
1981	Earl Anthony	242 (1 game)	Ernie Schlegel	Toledo, OH
1982	Earl Anthony	233 (1 game)	Charlie Tapp	Toledo, OH
1983	Earl Anthony	210 (1 game)	Mike Durbin	Toledo, OH
1984	Bob Chamberlain	961 (4 games)	Dan Eberl	Toledo, OH
1985	Mike Aulby	476 (2 games)	Steve Cook	Toledo, OH
1986	Tom Crites	190 (1 game)	Mike Aulby	Toledo, OH
1987	Randy Pedersen	759 (3 games)	Amleto Monacelli	Toledo, OH
1988	Brian Voss	246 (1 game)	Todd Thompson	Toledo, OH
1989	Pete Weber	221 (1 game)	Dave Ferraro	Toledo, OH
1990	Jim Pencak	900 (4 games)	Chris Warren	Toledo, OH
1991	Mike Miller	450 (2 games)	Norm Duke	Toledo, OH
1992	Eric Forkel	833 (4 games)	Bob Vespi	Toledo, OH
1993	Ron Palombi Jr.	237 (1 game)	Eugene McCune	Toledo, OH
1994	David Traber	196 (1 game)	Dale Traber	Toledo, OH
1995	Scott Alexander	246 (1 game)	Wayne Webb	Toledo, OH
1996	Butch Soper	442 (2 games)	Walter Ray Williams Jr.	Toledo, OH
1997	Rick Steelsmith	888 (4 games)	Brian Voss	Toledo, OH
1998	Pete Weber	277 (1 game)	David Ozio	Toledo, OH
1999	Tim Criss	238 (1 game)	Dave Arnold	Toledo, OH
2000	Norm Duke	492 (2 games)	Jason Couch	Toledo, OH
2001	Walter Ray Williams Jr.	258 (1 game)	Jeff Lizzi	Toledo, OH
2002	Doug Kent	417 (2 games)	Lonnie Waliczek	Toledo, OH
2003	Walter Ray Williams Jr	443 (2 games)	Brian Kretzer	Taylor, MI
2004	Tom Baker	523 (2 games)	Mika Koivuniemi	Ypsilanti, MI

Note: Totals from 1963–66, 1968–69 and 1972 include bonus pins.

Tournament of Champions

Year	Winner	Score	Runner-Up	Site
1965	Billy Hardwick	484 (2 games)	Dick Weber	Akron, OH
1966	Wayne Zahn	595 (3 games)	Dick Weber	Akron, OH
1967	Jim Stefanich	227 (1 game)	Don Johnson	Akron, OH
1968	Dave Davis	213 (1 game)	Don Johnson	Akron, OH
1969	Jim Godman	266 (1 game)	Jim Stefanich	Akron, OH
1970	Don Johnson	299 (1 game)	Dick Ritger	Akron, OH
1971	Johnny Petraglia	245 (1 game)	Don Johnson	Akron, OH
1972	Mike Durbin	775 (3 games)	Tim Harahan	Akron, OH
1973	Jim Godman	451 (2 games)	Barry Asher	Akron, OH
1974	Earl Anthony	679 (3 games)	Johnny Petraglia	Akron, OH
1975	Dave Davis	448 (2 games)	Barry Asher	Akron, OH
1976	Marshall Holman	441 (2 games)	Billy Hardwick	Akron, OH
1977	Mike Berlin	434 (2 games)	Mike Durbin	Akron, OH
1978	Earl Anthony	237 (1 game)	Teata Semiz	Akron, OH
1979	George Pappas	224 (1 game)	Dick Ritger	Akron, OH
1980	Wayne Webb	750 (3 games)	Gary Dickinson	Akron, OH
1981	Steve Cook	287 (1 game)	Pete Couture	Akron, OH
1982	Mike Durbin	448 (2 games)	Steve Cook	Akron, OH
1983	Joe Berardi	865 (4 games)	Henry Gonzalez	Akron, OH
1984	Mike Durbin	950 (4 games)	Mike Aulby	Akron, OH
1985	Mark Williams	616 (3 games)	Bob Handley	Akron, OH
1986	Marshall Holman	233 (1 game)	Mark Baker	Akron, OH
1986	Marshall Holman	233 (1 game)	Mark Baker	Akron, OH
1987	Pete Weber	928 (4 games)	Jim Murtishaw	Akron, OH
1988	Mark Williams	237 (1 game)	Tony Westlake	Fairlawn, OH
1989	Del Ballard Jr.	490 (2 games)	Walter Ray Williams Jr.	Fairlawn, OH
1990	Dave Ferraro	226 (1 game)	Tony Westlake	Fairlawn, OH
1991	David Ozio	476 (2 games)	Amleto Monacelli	Fairlawn, OH
1992	Marc McDowell	471 (2 games)	Don Genalo	Fairlawn, OH
1993	George Branham III	227 (1 game)	Parker Bohn III	Fairlawn, OH
1994	Norm Duke	422 (2 games)	Eric Forkel	Fairlawn, OH
1995	Mike Aulby	502 (2 games)	Bob Spaulding	Lake Zurich, IL
1996	Dave D'Entremont	971 (4 games)	Dave Arnold	Lake Zurich, IL
1997	John Gant	446 (2 games)	Mike Aulby	Reno
1998	Bryan Goebel	245 (1 game)	Steve Hoskins	Overland Park, KS
1999	Jason Couch	427 (2 games)	Chris Barnes	Overland Park, KS
2000	Jason Couch	198 (1 game)	Ryan Shafer	Lake Zurich, IL
2001	Not held			
2002	Jason Couch	478 (2 games)	Ryan Shafer	Uncasville, CT
2003	Patrick Healey Jr	432 (2 games)	Randy Pedersen	Uncasville, CT

ABC Masters Tournament

Year	Winner	Scoring Avg	Runner-Up	Site
1951	Lee Jouglard	201.8	Joe Wilman	St. Paul, MN
1952	Willard Taylor	200.32	Andy Varipapa	Milwaukee
1953	Rudy Habetler	200.13	Ed Brosius	Chicago
1954	Eugene Elkins	205.19	W. Taylor	Seattle
1955	Buzz Fazio	204.13	Joe Kristof	Ft. Wayne, IN
1956	Dick Hoover	209.9	Ray Bluth	Rochester, NY
1957	Dick Hoover	216.39	Bill Lillard	Ft. Worth, TX
1958	Tom Hennessy	209.15	Lou Frantz	Syracuse, NY
1959	Ray Bluth	214.26	Billy Golembiewski	St. Louis
1960	Billy Golembiewski	206.13	Steve Nagy	Toledo, OH
1961	Don Carter	211.18	Dick Hoover	Detroit
1962	Billy Golembiewski	223.12	Ron Winger	Des Moines, IA
1963	Harry Smith	219.3	Bobby Meadows	Buffalo
1964	Billy Welu	227	Harry Smith	Oakland, CA
1965	Billy Welu	202.12	Don Ellis	St. Paul, MN
1966	Bob Strampe	219.80	Al Thompson	Rochester, NY
1967	Lou Scalia	216.9	Bill Johnson	Miami Beach
1968	Pete Tountas	220.15	Buzz Fazio	Cincinnati
1969	Jim Chestney	223.2	Barry Asher	Madison, WI
1970	Don Glover	215.10	Bob Strampe	Knoxville, TN
1971	Jim Godman	229.8	Don Johnson	Detroit
1972	Bill Beach	220.27	Jim Godman	Long Beach, CA
1973	Dave Soutar	218.61	Dick Ritger	Syracuse, NY
1974	Paul Colwell	234.17	Steve Neff	Indianapolis
1975	Eddie Ressler	213.51	Sam Flanagan	Dayton, OH
1976	Nelson Burton Jr.	220.79	Steve Carson	Oklahoma City
1977	Earl Anthony	218.21	Jim Godman	Reno
1978	Frank Ellenburg	200.61	Earl Anthony	St. Louis
1979	Doug Myers	202.9	Bill Spigner	Tampa
1980	Neil Burton	206.69	Mark Roth	Louisville
1981	Randy Lightfoot	218.3	Skip Tucker	Memphis
1982	Joe Berardi	207.12	Ted Hannahs	Baltimore
1983	Mike Lastowski	212.65	Pete Weber	Niagara Falls
1984	Earl Anthony	212.5	Gil Sliker	Reno
1985	Steve Wunderlich	210.4	Tommy Kress	Tulsa
1986	Mark Fahy	206.5	Del Ballard Jr.	Las Vegas
1987	Rick Steelsmith	210.7	Brad Snell	Niagara Falls
1988	Del Ballard Jr.	219.1	Keith Smith	Jacksonville
1989	Mike Aulby	218.5	Mike Edwards	Wichita
1990	Chris Warren	231.6	David Ozio	Reno
1991	Doug Kent	226.8	George Branham III	Toledo, OH
1992	Ken Johnson	230.0	Dave D'Entremont	Corpus Christi, TX
1993	Norm Duke	245.68	Patrick Allen	Tulsa
1994	Steve Fehr	213.09	Steve Anderson	Greenacres, FL
1995	Mike Aulby	230.7	Mark Williams	Reno
1996	Ernie Schlegel	221.2	Mike Aulby	Salt Lake City
1997	Jason Queen	225.5	Eric Forkel	Huntsville, AL
1998	Mike Aulby	224.0	Parker Bohn III	Reno
1999	Brian Boghosian	246.0	Parker Bohn III	Syracuse, NY
2000	Mika Koivuniemi	241.0	Pete Weber	Albuquerque
2001	Parker Bohn III	224.0	Jason Couch	Reno
2002	Brett Wolfe	222.3	Dennis Horan Jr.	Reno
2003	Bryon Smith	236.0	W. R. Williams Jr.	Reno
2004	Walter Ray Williams Jr	252.5	Chris Barnes	Reno

BPAA United States Open

Year	Winner	Score	Runner-Up	Site
1949	Marion Ladewig	113.26–104.26	Catherine Burling	Chicago
1950	Marion Ladewig	151.46–146.06	Stephanie Balogh	Chicago
1951	Marion Ladewig	159.17–148.03	Sylvia Wene	Chicago
1952	Marion Ladewig	154.39–142.05	Shirley Garms	Chicago
1953	Not held			
1954	Marion Ladewig	148.29–143.01	Sylvia Wene	Chicago
1955	Sylvia Wene	142.30–141.11	Sylvia Fanta	Chicago
1955	Anita Cantaline	144.40–144.13	Doris Porter	Chicago
1956	Marion Ladewig	150.16–145.41	Marge Merrick	Chicago
1957	Not held			
1958	Merle Matthews	145.09–143.14	Marion Ladewig	Minneapolis
1959	Marion Ladewig	149.33–143.00	Donna Zimmerman	Buffalo
1960	Sylvia Wene	144.14–143.26	Marion Ladewig	Omaha
1961	Phyllis Notaro	144.13–143.12	Hope Riccilli	San Bernardino, CA
1962	Shirley Garms	138.44–135.49	Joy Abel	Miami Beach
1963	Marion Ladewig	586–578	Bobbie Shaler	Kansas City, MO
1964	LaVerne Carter	683–609	Evelyn Teal	Dallas
1965	Ann Slattery	597–550	Sandy Hooper	Philadelphia
1966	Joy Abel	593–538	Bette Rockwell	Lansing, MI
1967	Gloria Bouvia	578–516	Shirley Garms	St. Ann, MO
1968	Dotty Fothergill	9,000–8,187	Doris Coburn	Garden City, NY
1969	Dotty Fothergill	8,284–8,258	Kayoka Suda	Miami
1970	Mary Baker	8,730–8,465	Judy Cook	Northbrook, IL
1971	Paula Carter	5,660–5,650	June Llewellyn	Kansas City, MO
1972	Lorrie Nichols	5,272–5,189	Mary Baker	Denver
1973	Millie Martorella	5,553–5,294	Patty Costello	Garden City, NY
1974	Patty Costello	219–216	Betty Morris	Irving, TX
1975	Paula Carter	6,500–6,352	Lorrie Nichols	Toledo, OH
1976	Patty Costello	11,341–11,281	Betty Morris	Tulsa
1977	Betty Morris	10,511–10,358	Virginia Norton	Milwaukee
1978	Donna Adamek	236–202	Vesma Grinfelds	Miami
1979	Diana Silva	11,775–11,718	Bev Ortner	Phoenix
1980	Pat Costello	223–199	Shinobu Saitoh	Rockford, IL
1981	Donna Adamek	201–190	Nikki Gianulias	Rockford, IL
1982	Shinobu Saitoh	12,184–12,028	Robin Romeo	Hendersonville, TN
1983	Dana Miller-Mackie	247–200	Aleta Sill	St. Louis
1984	Karen Ellingsworth	236–217	Lorrie Nichols	St. Louis
1985	Pat Mercatani	214–178	Nikki Gianulias	Topeka, KS
1986	Wendy Macpherson	265–179	Lisa Wagner	Topeka, KS
1987	Carol Norman	206–179	Cindy Coburn	Mentor, OH
1988	Lisa Wagner	226–218	Lorrie Nichols	Winston-Salem, NC
1989	Robin Romeo	187–163	Michelle Mullen	Addison, IL
1990	Dana Miller-Mackie	190–189	Tish Johnson	Dearborn Heights, MI
1991	Anne Marie Duggan	196–185	Leanne Barrette	Fountain Valley, CA
1992	Tish Johnson	216–213	Aleta Sill	Fountain Valley, CA
1993	Dede Davidson	213–194	Dana Miller-Mackie	Garland, TX
1994	Aleta Sill	229–170	Anne Marie Duggan	Wichita
1995	Cheryl Daniels	235–180	Tish Johnson	Blaine, MN
1996	Liz Johnson	265–236	Marianne DiRupo	Indianapolis
1997	No event—tournament rescheduled to April, beginning in 1998.			
1998	Aleta Sill	276–151	Tammy Turner	Milford, CT
1999	Kim Adler	213–195	Lynda Barnes	Uncasville, CT
2000	Tennelle Grijalva	239–155	Kelly Kulick	Phoenix
2001	Kim Terrell	234–220	Wendy Macpherson	Laughlin, NV
2003	Kelly Kulick	261–195	Carolyn Dorin-Ballard	Sterling Heights, MI

Note: From 1942 to 1970, tournament was called the BPAA All-Star. Peterson scoring used from 1949 to '62. Under this system, the winner of an individual match game gets one point, plus one point for each 50 pins. From 1963 to '67, a three-game championship was held between the two top qualifiers. From 1968 to '73, 1975 to '77, 1979 and 1982, total pinfall determined the winner. In the other years, five qualifiers competed in a playoff for the championship, with the final listed above.

AMF Gold Cup *(Discontinued)*

Year	Winner	Score	Runner-Up	Site
1997	Aleta Sill	221–179	C. Gianotti-Block	Richmond, VA
1998	Dana Miller-Mackie	278–170	Dede Davidson	Richmond, VA
1999	Dana Miller-Mackie	236–222	Cara Honeychurch	Richmond, VA

WIBC Queens

ear	Winner	Score	Runner-Up	Site
1961	Janet Harman	794–776	Eula Touchette	Fort Wayne, IN
1962	Dorothy Wilkinson	799–794	Marion Ladewig	Phoenix
1963	Irene Monterosso	852–803	Georgette DeRosa	Memphis
1964	D. D. Jacobson	740–682	Shirley Garms	Minneapolis
1965	Betty Kuczynski	772–739	LaVerne Carter	Portland, OR
1966	Judy Lee	771–742	Nancy Peterson	New Orleans
1967	Millie Ignizio	840–809	Phyllis Massey	Rochester, NY
1968	Phyllis Massey	884–853	Marian Spencer	San Antonio
1969	Ann Feigel	832–765	Millie Ignizio	San Diego
1970	Millie Ignizio	807–797	Joan Holm	Tulsa
1971	Millie Ignizio	809–778	Katherine Brown	Atlanta
1972	Dotty Fothergill	890–841	Maureen Harris	Kansas City, MO
1973	Dotty Fothergill	804–791	Judy Soutar	Las Vegas
1974	Judy Soutar	939–705	Betty Morris	Houston
1975	Cindy Powell	758–674	Patty Costello	Indianapolis
1976	Pam Buckner	214–178	Shirley Sjostrom	Denver
1977	Dana Stewart	175–167	Vesma Grinfelds	Milwaukee
1978	Loa Boxberger	197–176	Cora Fiebig	Miami
1979	Donna Adamek	216–181	Shinobu Saitoh	Tucson
1980	Donna Adamek	213–165	Cheryl Robinson	Seattle
1981	Katsuko Sugimoto	166–158	Virginia Norton	Baltimore
1982	Katsuko Sugimoto	160–137	Nikki Gianulias	St. Louis
1983	Aleta Sill	214–188	Dana Miller-Mackie	Las Vegas
1984	Kazue Inahashi	248–222	Aleta Sill	Niagara Falls
1985	Aleta Sill	279–192	Linda Graham	Toledo, OH
1986	Cora Fiebig	223–177	Barbara Thorberg	Orange County, CA
1987	Cathy Almeida	850–817	Lorrie Nichols	Hartford, CT
1988	Wendy Macpherson	213–199	Leanne Barrette	Reno/Carson City, NV
1989	Carol Gianotti	207–177	Sandra Jo Shiery	Bismarck-Mandan, ND
1990	Patty Ann	207–173	Vesma Grinfelds	Tampa
1991	Dede Davidson	231–159	Jeanne Maiden	Cedar Rapids, IA
1992	Cindy Coburn-Carroll	184–170	Dana Miller-Mackie	Lansing, MI
1993	Jan Schmidt	201–163	Pat Costello	Baton Rouge, LA
1994	Anne Marie Duggan	224–177	Wendy Macpherson-Papanos	Salt Lake City
1995	Sandra Postma	226–187	Carolyn Dorin	Tucson
1996	Lisa Wagner	231–226	Tammy Turner	Buffalo
1997	S.J. Shiery-Odom	209–185	Audry Allen	Reno
1998	Lynda Norry	213–157	Karen Stroud	Davenport, IA
1999	Leanne Barrette	256–174	Dede Davidson	Indianapolis
2000	Wendy Macpherson	227–202	Marianne DiRupo	Reno
2001	Carolyn Dorin-Ballard	213–197	Kelly Kulick	Ft. Lauderdale, FL
2002	Kim Terrell	227–214	Kim Adler	Wauwatosa, WI
2003	Wendy Macpherson	218–193	Kendra Gaines	Reno

Sam's Town Invitational *(Discontinued)*

Year	Winner	Score	Runner-Up	Site
1984	Aleta Sill	238 (1 game)	Cheryl Daniels	Las Vegas
1985	Patty Costello	236 (1 game)	Robin Romeo	Las Vegas
1986	Aleta Sill	238 (1 game)	Dina Wheeler	Las Vegas
1987	Debbie Bennett	880 (4 games)	Lorrie Nichols	Las Vegas
1988	Donna Adamek	634 (3 games)	Robin Romeo	Las Vegas
1989	Tish Johnson	210 (1 game)	Dede Davidson	Las Vegas
1990	Wendy Macpherson	900 (4 games)	Jeanne Maiden	Las Vegas
1991	Lorrie Nichols	469 (2 games)	Dana Miller-Mackie	Las Vegas
1992	Tish Johnson	279 (1 game)	Robin Romeo	Las Vegas
1993	Robin Romeo	194 (1 game)	Tammy Turner	Las Vegas
1994	Tish Johnson	178 (1 game)	Carol Gianotti	Las Vegas
1995	Michelle Mullen	202 (1 game)	Cheryl Daniels	Las Vegas
1996	C. Gianotti-Block	892 (4 games)	Leanne Barrette	Las Vegas
1997	Kim Adler	953 (4 games)	Wendy Macpherson	Las Vegas
1998	Julie Gardner	961 (4 games)	Dede Davidson	Las Vegas
1999	Wendy Macpherson	209 (1 game)	Marianne DiRupo	Las Vegas
2000	Dede Davidson	183 (1 game)	Tiffany Stanbrough	Las Vegas

PWBA Championships *(Discontinued)*

1960...Marion Ladewig	1966...Joy Abel	1972...Patty Costello	1978...Toni Gillard
1961...Shirley Garms	1967...Betty Mivalez	1973...Betty Morris	1979...Cindy Coburn
1962...Stephanie Balogh	1968...Dotty Fothergill	1974...Pat Costello	1980...Donna Adamek
1963...Janet Harman	1969...Dotty Fothergill	1975...Pam Buckner	
1964...Betty Kuczynski	1970...Bobbe North	1976...Patty Costello	
1965...Helen Duval	1971...Patty Costello	1977...Vesma Grinfelds	

YET ANOTHER SIGN OF THE APOCALYPSE

Through May 2004, nine of the previous 20 PBA tour events had been won by bowlers using scented balls.

Men's Awards

BWAA Bowler of the Year

1942	Johnny Crimmins	1972	Don Johnson
1943	Ned Day	1973	Don McCune
1944	Ned Day	1974	Earl Anthony
1945	Buddy Bomar	1975	Earl Anthony
1946	Joe Wilman	1976	Earl Anthony
1947	Buddy Bomar	1977	Mark Roth
1948	Andy Varipapa	1978	Mark Roth
1949	Connie Schwoegler	1979	Mark Roth
1950	Junie McMahon	1980	Wayne Webb
1951	Lee Jouglard	1981	Earl Anthony
1952	Steve Nagy	1982	Earl Anthony
1953	Don Carter	1983	Earl Anthony
1954	Don Carter	1984	Mark Roth
1955	Steve Nagy	1985	Mike Aulby
1956	Bill Lillard	1986	Walter Ray Williams Jr.
1957	Don Carter	1987	Marshall Holman
1958	Don Carter	1988	Brian Voss
1959	Ed Lubanski	1989	Mike Aulby/ Amleto Monacelli*
1960	Don Carter	1990	Amleto Monacelli
1961	Dick Weber	1991	David Ozio
1962	Don Carter	1992	Dave Ferraro
1963	Dick Weber	1993	Walter Ray Williams Jr.
	Billy Hardwick*	1994	Norm Duke
1964	Billy Hardwick	1995	Mike Aulby
	Bob Strampe*	1996	Walter Ray Williams Jr.
1965	Dick Weber	1997	Walter Ray Williams Jr.
1966	Wayne Zahn	1998	Walter Ray Williams Jr.
1967	Dave Davis	1999	Parker Bohn III
1968	Jim Stefanich	2000	Norm Duke
1969	Billy Hardwick	2001	Parker Bohn III
1970	Nelson Burton Jr.	2002	Walter Ray Williams Jr.
1971	Don Johnson	2003	Walter Ray Williams Jr.

PBA Bowler of the Year. The PBA began selecting a player of the year in 1963. Its selection has been the same as the BWAA's in all but three years.

Women's Awards

BWAA Bowler of the Year

1948	Val Mikiel	1976	Patty Costello
1949	Val Mikiel	1977	Betty Morris
1950	Marion Ladewig	1978	Donna Adamek
1951	Marion Ladewig	1979	Donna Adamek
1952	Marion Ladewig	1980	Donna Adamek
1953	Marion Ladewig	1981	Donna Adamek
1954	Marion Ladewig	1982	Nikki Gianulias
1955	Marion Ladewig	1983	Lisa Wagner
1956	Sylvia Martin	1984	Aleta Sill
1957	Anita Cantaline	1985	Aleta Sill/Patty Costello*
1958	Marion Ladewig	1986	Lisa Wagner/Jeanne Madden*
1959	Marion Ladewig	1987	Betty Morris
1960	Sylvia Martin	1988	Lisa Wagner
1961	Shirley Garms	1989	Robin Romeo
1962	Shirley Garms	1990	Tish Johnson/Leanne Barrette*
1963	Marion Ladewig	1991	Leanne Barrette
1964	LaVerne Carter	1992	Tish Johnson
1965	Betty Kuczynski	1993	Lisa Wagner
1966	Joy Abel	1994	Anne Marie Duggan
1967	Millie Martorella	1995	Tish Johnson
1968	Dotty Fothergill	1996	Wendy Macpherson
1969	Dotty Fothergill	1997	Wendy Macpherson
1970	Mary Baker	1998	Carol Gianotti-Block
1971	Paula Sperber Carter	1999	Wendy Macpherson
1972	Patty Costello	2000	Wendy Macpherson
1973	Judy Soutar	2001	Carolyn Dorin-Ballard
1974	Betty Morris	2002	Leanne Barrette
1975	Judy Soutar		

*PWBA Bowler of the Year. The PWBA began selecting a player of the year in 1983. Its selection has been the same as the BWAA's in all but three years.

Career Leaders

Earnings

MEN

Walter Ray Williams Jr.	$3,236,132
Pete Weber	$2,585,168
Parker Bohn III	$2,201,964
Mike Aulby	$2,097,253
Brian Voss	$2,055,077

WOMEN

Wendy Macpherson	$1,194,535
Aleta Sill	$1,071,194
Tish Johnson	$1,063,062
Leanne Barrette	$1,010,343
Anne Marie Duggan	$936,421

Titles

MEN

Earl Anthony	41
Walter Ray Williams Jr.	39
Mark Roth	34
Pete Weber	31
Parker Bohn III	29

WOMEN

Lisa Wagner	32
Aleta Sill	31
Leanne Barrette	26
Patty Costello	25
Tish Johnson	25

Note: Leaders through 2003–04 season.

No Joshing

Josh Garner, a 12-year-old seventh-grader at Sprately Middle School in Hampton, Va., became the third youngest person ever to bowl a perfect game and have an 800 series in the same day. He competes in the BBC League at Century Lanes in Hampton.

Soccer

The U.S. women take gold in Athens

ATHENS 2004

Greece Is the Word

After the Greek men pulled a stunner at Euro 2004, the U.S. women traveled to Athens and made history of their own

BY HANK HERSCH

MY GIFT TO THEM," forward Abby Wambach called it, her goal from 10 yards out in the 22nd minute of overtime of the Olympic gold-medal match, a sizzling header that gave the U.S. women's soccer team a 2–1 victory over Brazil. The gift came unwrapped and without a card, but there was no doubting the sentiment behind it. The objects of Wambach's generosity were five teammates—forward Mia Hamm, 32; midfielder Julie Foudy, 33; midfielder Kristine Lilly, 33; and 36-year-old defenders Brandi Chastain and Joy Fawcett—soccer pioneers known as the '91ers who had desperately wanted to strike gold in their last major international competition together. "No other outcome was possible tonight," Wambach said. "This is the way these girls needed to go out."

"An opera," Chastain called it, her 17 years of scintillating highs and lachrymose lows, infused, always, with unbridled passion. The drama took flight in 1991, when Chastain & Co. seized the inaugural Women's World Cup title in China to so lit-

tle fanfare that they had to fax news of their victory to loved ones back home. There was an inaugural Olympic gold as well, at the Atlanta Games in 1996, and another Women's World Cup championship in '99, which Chastain clinched with a penalty kick before memorably doffing her shirt before 90,185 fans at the Rose Bowl. And before the curtain dropped in Athens, the '91ers did their version of the five sopranos, belting out a buoyant if not pitch-perfect version of *The Star-Spangled Banner* on the victory stand.

"A scrapbook full of wonderful memories," Hamm called her remarkable career, which began when she was 15 and ended with 153 goals—a record for international players—in a whopping 266 matches for the U.S. And though in that time Hamm became a sporting icon, arguably the most recognizable female athlete in the world, she never warmed to her leading role, constantly deflecting attention to her teammates—and sometimes underperforming. At Karaiskaki Stadium in Greece, she basked in the U.S. team's success—a tri-

Adu (9), who turned 15 in June, made D.C. United MLS's biggest draw on the road.

umph so inspiring it led the American delegation to name her the flag bearer at the Games' closing ceremony—yet she'd gone, happily, goal-less against Brazil. "Our lives aren't just a series of successes," Hamm said. "There are a lot more failures than everyone sees. And the fact that these players responded in such a positive way says a lot about them."

The perfect ending to a fairy tale, many called it—and it was. Doubters had figured that the '91ers (and their young compatriots) would be 86'ed in Athens . After all, they they lost the 2000 Olympic gold-medal game to Norway (3–2) and took third place in the '03 Women's World Cup, falling to Germany 3–0 in the semifinals. Those results prompted Chastain to approach U.S. Soccer Federation president Bob Contiguglia in December and ask that coach April Heinrichs be fired after four years on the job. But Contiguglia stood by Heinrichs—who had been a star striker on the '91 championship team—and as the Games began, a sense of urgency superseded any dissent: Hamm, Foudy and Fawcett had

announced that this would be their last major tournament. Drawing Germany in the semis helped steel the Americans' resolve. "It's like you've got another chance," Foudy said, "another life almost."

The U.S. exacted sweet revenge with a 2–1 overtime victory. Hamm didn't score, but she set up the decisive goal with a pass to 19-year-old Heather O'Reilly, who'd grown up in East Brunswick, N.J., with posters of Mia splashed on her bedroom wall. Three days later, a much younger and better-rested team from Brazil seemed poised to prematurely snatch the '91ers' torch. After 20-year-old Lindsay Tarpley put the U.S. up 1–0 with a 24-yard drive inside the left post in the 39th minute, the Samba Queens equalized in the 73rd minute when Pretinha cashed in a rebound. Brazil then rattled a couple of potential game-winners off the post. "We were bending but not breaking," said U.S. goalkeeper Briana Scurry. "They were throwing the kitchen sink at us."

Finally, Wambach delivered her present off a corner kick from Lilly in the 22nd minute of overtime. "Thanks for making sure I'm not miserable for the next four years of my life," Foudy screamed. Afterward Fawcett, who with her fellow '91ers played in 1,230 international matches, took an even longer view. "We wanted to leave on top," she said. "To make people take another look at women's soccer and fall in love with it again."

Love for soccer has long existed in Argentina, but it only intensified during the Athens Games. With a goal in the 18th minute against Paraguay, 20-year-old Boca Juniors striker Carlos Tevez gave the nation a 1–0 victory in the men's soccer final, lifting Argentina to its first gold medal in 52 years at the Summer Games. "Victories in football bring happiness to the people," coach Marcelo Bielsa said. "Especially in Argentina."

And so, too, in Greece, the host of the Olympics, yes, but a nation whose greater glory came earlier in the summer, when its national team won the European Championship, producing the biggest soccer story of the year. "All Greeks should celebrate this victory," striker Angelos Charisteas proclaimed after his team upset host Portugal in the final. And celebrate they did, for *upset* is an understatement where their team's accomplishment is concerned. Hellas—as Greece was known to its fans—was a 100-to-1 shot in the 16-team field, having never won so much as a single game at a major event. That streak ended with a 2–1 shocker over Portugal in Greece's opening game. They would go on to tie Spain in group play and book a spot in the quarterfinals on goal difference over those same Spaniards. But there, surely, their surprising run would end as they faced the defending European champions, France. No, not yet: Greece eliminated Les Bleus 1–0 and followed that with a knockout of the potent Czech Republic by the same score to advance to the final. Coach Otto Rehhagel, a 65-year-old German, had instilled a Teutonic unity in an often fractious squad. His handiwork earned him a nickname from his adopted nation: *Rehhakles*, Greek for Hercules.

The moniker was appropriate for the final, in which Hellas faced a Herculean task, squaring off against a talented Portugal team bent on revenge and playing in front of an impassioned home crowd. Portugal had poured $735 million into preparations for Euro 2004, building or refurbishing 10 stadiums. Thousands of people lined the streets of Lisbon to honor their team as TV helicopters tracked the players' bus *before* the championship match. But with impeccable man-marking spearheaded by rugged defender Giourkas Seitaridis, the Greeks pitched yet another shutout. In the 57th minute, they took their first and last shot on goal of the game—a header by Charisteas, off their first and last corner kick. It went in. "Today we played to our strengths," Rehhagel said. "The Greek team has written football history here." It was a rugged, unpretty history, with three consecutive 1–0 victories, but it was history just the same.

MLS hoped for a similarly seismic jolt when it signed a 14-year-old, Freddy Adu. Born in Ghana, raised in Potomac, Md., and schooled at the U.S. Soccer under-17 residency program in Bradenton, Fla., Adu was heralded as the best player his age on the planet. His prodigious talent earned him a $500,000 salary—the highest in the league—and his charismatic way in front of a camera had helped him land myriad endorsements before he suited up for D.C. United. Nike chairman Phil Knight signed him to a $1 million deal and believed he could accomplish more for the company than Michael Jordan, Tiger Woods and LeBron James. "They have done great things within what you'd call established American sports," Knight said. "Freddy has the potential to bring soccer almost for the first time into the public's consciousness."

But Adu struggled to establish himself as a rookie, at times flashing his brilliance, at times looking like a child among men. "I'm going to prove to everybody that I deserve to be here," he said shortly before the midseason All-Star Game. "I will make a difference in this league, and sooner than anyone thinks." As of early October, Adu had five goals and an assist—not world-shaking totals, but not bad either.

Hey, as the '91ers can attest, great things often do take time.

FOR THE RECORD · 2003 – 2004

2004 European Championship

Group Standings

Country	GP	W	L	T	GF	GA	Pts
GROUP A							
*Portugal	3	2	1	0	4	2	6
*Greece	3	1	1	1	4	4	4
Spain	3	1	1	1	2	2	4
Russia	3	1	2	0	2	4	3
GROUP B							
*France	3	2	0	1	7	4	7
*England	3	2	1	0	8	4	6
Croatia	3	0	1	2	4	6	2
Switzerland	3	0	2	1	1	6	1

Country	GP	W	L	T	GF	GA	Pts
GROUP C							
*Sweden	3	1	0	2	8	3	5
*Denmark	3	1	0	2	4	2	5
Italy	3	1	0	2	3	2	5
Bulgaria	3	0	3	0	1	9	0
GROUP D							
*Czech Rep.	3	3	0	0	7	4	9
*Netherlands	3	1	1	1	6	4	4
Germany	3	0	1	2	2	3	2
Latvia	3	0	2	1	1	5	1

*Advanced to second round.

Note: In group play, teams are awarded three points for a victory, one for a tie. The top two in each group advance to the Round of 16. First tiebreaker is head-to-head competition, second is goal differential, third goals scored.

GROUP A	GROUP B	GROUP C	GROUP D
Greece 2, Portugal 1	Switzerland 0, Croatia 0	Denmark 0, Italy 0	Germany 1, Netherlands 1
Spain 1, Russia 0	France 2, England 1	Sweden 5, Bulgaria 0	Czech Rep. 2, Latvia 1
Greece 1, Spain 1	England 3, Switzerland 0	Denmark 2, Bulgaria 0	Latvia 0, Germany 0
Portugal 2, Russia 0	France 2, Croatia 2	Italy 1, Sweden 1	Czech Rep. 3, Neth. 2
Portugal 1, Spain 0	England 4, Croatia 2	Italy 2, Bulgaria 1	Netherlands 3, Latvia 0
Russia 2, Greece 1	France 3, Switzerland 1	Sweden 2, Denmark 2	Czech Rep. 2, Germany 1

Euro 2004—Quarterfinals

*Portugal and the Netherlands advanced on penalties, 6–5 and 5–4; respectively.

Major League Soccer

2003 Final Standings

EASTERN CONFERENCE

Team	GP	W	L	T	Pts	GF	GA
Chicago	30	15	7	8	53	53	43
New England	30	12	9	9	45	55	47
MetroStars	30	11	10	9	42	40	40
D.C. United	30	10	11	9	39	38	36
Columbus	30	10	12	8	38	44	44

WESTERN CONFERENCE

Team	GP	W	L	T	Pts	GF	GA
San Jose	30	14	7	9	51	45	35
Kansas City	30	11	10	9	42	48	44
Colorado	30	11	12	7	40	40	45
Los Angeles	30	9	12	9	36	35	35
Dallas Burn	30	6	19	5	23	35	64

Note: Three points for a win. One point for a tie. †Conference champion. *Qualified for playoffs

SCORING LEADERS

Player, Team	GP	G	A	Pts
Preki, KC	30	12	17	41
Carlos Ruiz, LA	26	15	5	35
Ante Razov, Chi	26	14	6	34
Taylor Twellman, NE	22	15	4	34
John Spencer, Col	27	14	5	33
Landon Donovan, SJ	22	12	6	30

ASSISTS LEADERS

Player, Team	GP	A
Preki, KC	30	17
Mark Lisi, MetroStars	24	11
Amado Guevara, MetroStars	25	10
Brian Mullan, SJ	30	9
Chris Carrieri, Col	30	8
Cobi Jones, LA	28	8

GOALS LEADERS

Player, Team	GP	G
Carlos Ruiz, LA	26	15
Taylor Twellman, NE	22	15
Ante Razov, Chi	26	14
John Spencer, Col	27	14
Landon Donovan, SJ	22	12
Brian McBride, Clb	24	12
Preki, KC	30	12

GOALS-AGAINST-AVERAGE LEADERS

Player, Team	GAA
Jonny Walker, MetroStars	0.95
Pat Onstad, SJ	1.04
Nick Rimando, D.C.	1.13
Kevin Hartman, LA	1.13
Zach Thornton, Chi	1.22

2003 PLAYOFFS

Note: Scores for conference semifinals are two-game aggregates, all others are single games. *Golden-goal overtime.

MLS Cup 2003

CARSON, CALIF., NOVEMBER 23, 2003

San Jose	2	2	—4
Chicago	0	2	—2

Goals: Ekelund 5, Donovan 38; Beasley 49; Mulrooney 50; Roner (og) 54; Donovan 71.

San Jose—Onstad, Dayak, Robinson, Waibel (Roner 51), Agoos, Mullan, Ekelund, Mulrooney, Lagos (Russell 70), Walker (DeRosario 60), Donovan.

Chicago—Thornton, Perez (Gray 46), Curtin (Jacqua 81), Bocanegra, Whitfield, Beasley, Marsch, Armas, Williams (Mapp 70), Ralph, Razov.

Att: 27,000.

2003–2004 U.S. Men's National Team Results

Date	Opponent	Result	U.S. Goals	Site
Jan. 18	Denmark	1-1 T	Donovan	Carson, Calif
Feb. 18	Holland	0-1 L	-	Amsterdam
March 13	Haiti	1-1 T	Califf	Miami, Fla.
March 31	Poland	1-0 W	Beasley	Plock, Poland
Apr. 28	Mexico	1-0 W	Pope	Dallas, Texas
June 2	Honduras	4-0 W	McBride (2), Lewis, Sanneh	Foxboro, Mass.
June 13	Grenada *	3-0 W	Beasley (2), Vanney	Columbus, Ohio
June 20	Grenada *	3-2 W	Donovan, Wolff, Beasley	St. George's, Grenada
July 11	Poland	1-1 T	Bocanegra	Chicago, Ill.
Aug. 18	Jamaica *	1-1 T	Ching	Kingston, Jamaica
Sept. 4	El Salvador*	2-0 W	Ching, Donovan	Foxboro, Mass
Sept 8	Panama*	1–1 T	Jones	Panama City

*CONCACAF World Cup Qualifying game. Record in 2004, through Oct 9: 6-1-5.

2003–2004 U.S. Women's National Team Results

Date	Opponent	Result	U.S. Goals	Site
Jan. 30	Sweden #	3-0 W	Boxx, Tarpley (2)	Shenzhen, China
Feb. 1	China #	0-0 T	-	Shenzhen, China
Feb. 3	Canada #	2-0 W	Tarpley, Fawcett	Shenzhen, China
Feb. 25	Trin & Tob*	7-0 W	Boxx (3), Lilly, Hamm (2) Wambach, Wagner	San Jose, Costa Rica
Feb. 27	Haiti*	8-0 W	Parlow (3), MacMillan Tarpley, Wambach, og	Heredia, Costa Rica
Feb. 29	Mexico*	2-0 W	og, Wambach	San Jose, Costa Rica
March 3	Costa Rica*	4-0 W	Wagner, Wambach, Lilly, Boxx	San Jose, Costa Rica
March 5	Mexico*	3-2 W	Tarpley, Wambach, Foudy	Heredia, Costa Rica
March 14	France @	5-1 W	Wambach, Hamm, Hucles (2)Tarpley	Ferreiras, Portugal
March 16	Denmark @	1-0 W	Hucles	Quarteira, Portugal
March 18	Sweden @	1-3 L	Reddick	Lagos, Portugal
March 20	Norway @	4-1 W	Wambach (3), Tarpley	Faro, Portugal
April 24	Brazil	5-1 W	Foudy, Wambach (2), Welsh, Hamm	Birmingham, Alabama
May 9	Mexico	3-0 W	Parlow, Hamm, Chalupny	Albuquerque, N.M.
June 6	Japan	1-1 T	Wambach	Lousiville, Ky.
July 3	Canada	1-0 W	Mitts	Nashville, Tenn.
July 21	Australia	3-1 W	Boxx, Hamm, Wambach	Blaine, Minn.
Aug. 1	China	3-1 W	Wagner, Hamm, Wambach	East Hartford, Conn.
Aug. 11	Greece^	3-0 W	Boxx, Wambach, Hamm	Heraklio, Greece
Aug. 14	Brazil^	2-0 W	Hamm, Wambach	Thessaloniki, Greece
Aug. 17	Australia^	1-1 T	Lilly	Thessaloniki, Greece
Aug. 20	Japan^	2-1 W	Lilly, Wambach	Thessaloniki, Greece
Aug. 23	Germany^	2-1 W (OT)	Lilly, O'Reilly	Heraklio, Greece
Aug. 26	Brazil^	2-1 W (OT)	Tarpley, Wambach	Athens, Greece

#Four Nations Tournament. * CONCACAF Olympic Qualifying Tournament. @ Algarve Cup. ^ Olympics.
Record in 2004, through Sept 24: 20-1-3.

International Club Competition

Intercontinental Cup

Competition between winners of European Cup and Libertadores Cup.

YOKOHAMA, JAPAN: DECEMBER 14, 2003

Boca Juniors (Arg)	1	0	0	0—1
AC Milan (Ita)	1	0	0	0—1

Boca Juniors won 3–1 on penalty kicks.

Goals: Tomasson 24; Donnet 29.

Att: 67,000.

Boca Jrs.: Abbondanzieri, Schiavi, Perea, Burdisso, Rodriguez, Cagna, Cascini, Donnet, Battaglia, Schelotto (Tevez 72), Iarley.

AC Milan: Dida, Costacurta, Maldini, Cafu, Pancaro, Seedorf, Gattuso (Ambrosini 102), Pirlo, Kaká (Costa 78), Shevchenko, Tomasson (Inzaghi 59).

UEFA Cup

Competition between teams other than league champions and cup-winners from UEFA.

GÖTEBORG, SWEDEN: MAY 19, 2004

Valencia (Esp)	1	1 —2
Marseille (Fra)	0	0 —0

Goals: Vicente 45+3 (pen), Mista 58.

Cautions: Barthez 45, red card.

Att: 43,200.

Valencia: Canizares, Ayala, Marchena (Pellegrino 86), Albelda, Baraja, Angulo (Sissoko 82), Vicente, Carboni, Rufete (Aimar 64), Mista, Curro Torres.

Marseille: Barthez, Ferriera, Dos Santos, Hemdani, N'Diaye (Celestini 84), Drogba, Méité, Meriem (Gavanon 46), Marlet, Beye, Flamini (Batlles 71).

Champions League

League champions of the countries belonging to UEFA (Union of European Football Associations).

GELSENKIRCHEN, GERMANY: MAY 26, 2004

FC Porto (Port)	1	2 —3
Monaco (Fra)	0	0 —0

Goals: Carlos Albert 39, Deco 71, Alenichev 75.

Att: 61,266.

FC Porto: Victor Baía, Jorge Costa, Carvalho, Costinha, Nuno Valente, Deco, Derlei (McCarthy 78), Maniche, Carlos Alberto (Alenichev 60), Paulo Ferreira, Mendes.

Monaco: Roma, Evra, Ibarra, Bernardi, Giuly (Pirsó 23), Morientes, Cissé (Nonda 64), Zikos, Rothen, Rodriguez, Givet (Squillaci 72).

Libertadores Cup

Competition between champion clubs and runners-up of 10 South American National Associations.

(2ND LEG) MANIZALES, COLOMBIA: JULY 1, 2004

Once Caldas* (Col)	1	0—1
Boca Juniors (Arg)	0	1—1

Goals: Viafara 7, Cangele 51.

* Two-game aggregate: 1–1; Once Caldas won 2–0 on penalty kicks.

Att: 40,000.

Once Caldas: Henao, Rojas, Catano, Vanegas, Garcia, Velasquez, Viafara, Valentierra, Soto, Moreno (Diaz 66), Alcazar (Agudelo 79).

Boca Juniors: Abbondanzieri, Perea, Schiavi, Burdisso, Rodriguez, Villareal, Cascini, Vargas, Cagna (Caneo 86), Cangele, Tevez.

2003-2004 Club Champions—Europe

Country	League Champion	League Scoring Leader, Club	Cup Winner
Albania	SK Tirana	Vioresin Sinani, Vllaznia	Partizani Tirana
Andorra	Santa Coloma	Jorge Carneiro, Sant Julià	Santa Coloma
Armenia	Pyunik Yerevan*	Ara Hakobyan, Banants Yerevan	Mika Ashtarak*
Austria	Austria Vienna	Lawaree, Bregenz	Austria Vienna
Azerbaijan	Neftci Baki	Samir Musayev, Qarabag	Neftci Baki
Belarus	FK Homel	Heanadz Bliznyuk, Homel	Dynama Minsk
		Syarhei Karnilenka, Dynama Minsk	
Belgium	Anderlecht	Luigi Pieroni, Mouscron	Club Brugge
Bosnia & Herz	Siroki Brijeg	Alen Skoro, Sarajevo	Modrica Maksima
Bulgaria	Lokomotiv Plovdiv	Martin Kamburov, Lokomotiv	Litex Lovech
Croatia	Hajduk Split	Robert Spehar, Osijek	Dinamo Zagreb
Cyprus	APOEL Nicosia	Lukasz Sosin, Apollonas	AEK Larnaca
		Jozef Kosleg, Omonia	
Czech Republic	FC Baník Ostrava	Marek Heinz, Banik Ostrava	AC Sparta Prague
Denmark	FC Copenhagen	n/a	FC Copenhagen
England	Arsenal	Thierry Henry, Arsenal	Manchester United
Estonia	FC Flora Tallinn*	Tor Henning Hamre, Flora*	TVMK Tallinn
Faroe Islands	HB Tórshavn*	Hjalgrím Elttør, Kí Klaksvík*	B36 Tórshavn*
Finland	HJK Helsinki*	Saku Puhakainen, MyPa Anjalankoski*	HJK Helsinki*
France	Lyon	Djibril Cissé, Auxerre	Paris Saint-Germain
Georgia	WIT Georgi Tbilisi	Suliko Davitashvili, Torpedo Kutaisi	Dinamo Tbilisi
Germany	Werder Bremen	Ailton, Werder Bremen	Werder Bremen
Greece	Panathinaikos	Oliveira Giovanni, Olympiakos	Panathinaikos
Hungary	Ferencváros	n/a	Ferencváros
Iceland	FH Hafnarfjör	Gretar Hjartarson, Grindavik	ÍA Akranes
		Gunnar Thorvaldsson, IBV	
Ireland	Shelbourne	Alan Murphy, Galway United	Longford Town
Israel	Maccabi Haifa	Ofir Haim, Hapoel Beer-Sheva	Hapoel Bnei Sakhnin
		Shai Holtzman, Ashdod SC	
Italy	AC Milan	n/a	Lazio
Kazakhstan	Irtysh Pavlodar*	Andrey Finonchenko, Shakhter Karagandy*	Kairat Almaty*
Latvia	Skonto Riga*	Viktors Dobrecovs, Metalurgs	FK Ventspils*
Lithuania	FBK Kaunas*	Ricardas Beniusis, FBK Kaunus, Atlantas Klaipeda*	Zalgiris Vilnius*
Luxembourg	Jeunesse d'Esch	José Gomes, Spora Luxembourg	F 91 Dudelange
Macedonia	Pobeda Prilep	n/a	Sloga Jugomagnat
Malta	Sliema Wanderers	Adrian Mifsud, Hibernians	Sliema Wanderers
		Danilo Doncic, Sliema	
		Michael Galea, Birkirkara	
Moldova	Sheriff Tiraspol	Vladimir Shishelov, Zimbru Chisinau	Zimbru Chisinau
Netherlands	Ajax Amsterdam	n/a	FC Utrecht
Northern Ireland	Linfield	Glenn Ferguson, Linfield	Glentoran
Norway	Rosenborg*	n/a	Rosenborg*
Poland	Wisla Kraków	n/a	Lech Poznań
Portugal	FC Porto	Benni McCarthy, FC Porto	Benfica
Romania	Dinamo Bucharest	Ionel Daniel Danciulescu, Dinamo Bucharest	Dinamo Bucharest
Russia	CSKA Moscow*	Dmitriy Loskov, Lokomotiv Moscow*	Terek Groznyi*
San Marino	Pennarossa	Damiano Vannucci, Virtus	Pennarossa
Scotland	Glasgow Celtic	n/a	Glasgow Celtic
Serbia and Montenegro	Crvena zvezda Belgrade	Nicola Zigiae, Cz Belgrade	Cz Belgrade
Slovakia	MSK Zilina	Roland Stevko, Ruzomberok	FC A. Petrzalka
Slovenia	ND Gorica	Drazen Zezelj, Primorje Ajdovscina, Olimpija Ljubljana	Maribor
Spain	Valencia	Ronaldo, Real Madrid	Real Zaragoza
Sweden	Djurgårdens IF*	Niklas Skoog, Malmö	IF Elfsborg
Switzerland	FC Basel	Stéphane Chapuisat, BSC Young Boys Bern	FC Basel
Turkey	Fenerbahçe	Zafer Biryol, Konyaspor	Trabzonspor
Ukraine	Dinamo Kiev	G.Demetradze, Metalurh Donetsk	Shakhtar Donestk
Wales	Rhyl FC	Andy Moran, Rhyl FC	Rhyl FC

Note: Results are from 2004 unless followed by *.

The World Cup

Results

Year	Champion	Score	Runner-Up	Winning Coach
1930	Uruguay	4–2	Argentina	Alberto Supicci
1934	Italy	2–1	Czechoslovakia	Vittorio Pozzo
1938	Italy	4–2	Hungary	Vittorio Pozzo
1950	Uruguay	2–1	Brazil	Juan Lopez
1954	W Germany	3–2	Hungary	Sepp Herberger
1958	Brazil	5–2	Sweden	Vicente Feola
1962	Brazil	3–1	Czechoslovakia	Aymore Moreira
1966	England	4–2	W Germany	Alf Ramsey
1970	Brazil	4–1	Italy	Mario Zagalo
1974	W Germany	2–1	Netherlands	Helmut Schoen
1978	Argentina	3–1	Netherlands	César Menotti
1982	Italy	3–1	W Germany	Enzo Bearzot
1986	Argentina	3–2	W Germany	Carlos Bilardo
1990	W Germany	1–0	Argentina	Franz Beckenbauer
1994	Brazil	0–0 (3–2)	Italy	Carlos Alberto Parreira
1998	France	3–0	Brazil	Aime Jacquet
2002	Brazil	2–0	Germany	Luis Felipe Scolari

Alltime World Cup Participation

Of the 69 nations that have taken part in the World Cup Finals, only Brazil has competed in each of the 17 tournaments held to date. West Germany or an undivided Germany (1934, '38, '94 and '98) has played in 15 World Cups. Ranked by victories.

Nation	Matches	W	T	L	Goals For	Goals Against	Nation	Matches	W	T	L	Goals For	Goals Against
Brazil	87	60	14	13	191	82	Costa Rica	7	3	1	3	9	12
*Germany	85	50	18	17	176	106	Wales	5	2	6	1	10	7
Italy	70	39	17	14	110	67	Morocco	10	2	4	4	10	13
Argentina	60	30	11	19	102	70	Senegal	5	2	2	1	7	6
England	50	22	15	13	68	45	Norway	8	2	3	3	7	8
France	44	21	7	16	86	61	Saudi Arabia	10	2	1	7	7	25
Spain	45	19	12	14	71	53	Algeria	6	2	1	3	6	10
Yugoslavia	37	17	6	14	60	46	Japan	7	2	1	4	6	7
†Russia	37	17	6	14	64	44	E Germany	6	2	2	2	5	5
Uruguay	40	15	10	15	65	57	S Africa	6	1	3	2	8	11
Hungary	32	15	3	14	87	57	N Korea	4	1	1	2	5	9
Netherlands	31	14	9	8	55	34	Tunisia	9	1	3	5	5	11
Poland	28	14	5	9	42	36	Cuba	3	1	1	1	5	12
Sweden	41	14	9	18	67	65	Republic of Ireland	13	1	5	3	4	7
Austria	29	12	4	13	42	48	Iran	6	1	1	4	4	12
Czechoslovakia	30	11	5	14	44	45	Jamaica	3	1	0	2	3	9
Belgium	36	10	9	17	46	63	Ecuador	3	1	0	2	2	4
Mexico	41	10	11	20	43	79	Israel	3	1	0	2	1	3
Romania	21	8	5	8	30	32	Egypt	4	0	2	2	3	6
Chile	25	7	6	12	31	40	Honduras	3	0	2	1	2	3
Portugal	12	7	0	5	25	16	Kuwait	3	0	1	2	2	6
Denmark	13	7	2	4	24	18	Slovenia	3	0	0	3	2	7
Switzerland	22	6	3	13	33	51	United Arab Emirates	3	0	0	3	2	11
United States	22	6	2	14	25	45	New Zealand	3	0	0	3	2	12
Paraguay	19	5	7	7	25	34	Haiti	3	0	0	3	2	14
Turkey	10	5	1	4	20	17	Iraq	3	0	0	3	1	4
Croatia	9	5	0	4	11	7	Bolivia	6	0	1	5	1	20
Scotland	23	4	7	12	25	41	El Salvador	6	0	0	6	1	22
Peru	15	4	3	8	19	31	Australia	3	0	1	2	0	5
Cameroon	17	4	7	6	16	28	Dutch East Indies	1	0	0	1	0	6
Nigeria	11	4	1	6	14	16	Canada	3	0	0	3	0	5
Bulgaria	25	3	8	14	22	49	Zaire	3	0	0	3	0	14
S Korea	21	3	6	12	19	49	Greece	3	0	0	3	0	8
Colombia	13	3	2	8	14	23	China	3	0	0	3	0	9
Northern Ireland	13	3	5	5	13	23							

*Includes West Germany 1950–90. †Includes USSR 1930–1990.
Note: Matches decided by penalty kicks are shown as drawn games.

World Cup Final Box Scores

URUGUAY 1930

| Uruguay ....1 | 3 —4 |
| Argentina.........2 | 0 —2 |

FIRST HALF

Scoring: 1, Uruguay, Dorado (12); 2, Argentina, Peucelle (20); 3, Argentina, Stabile (37).

SECOND HALF

Scoring: 4, Uruguay, Cea (57); 5, Uruguay, Iriarte (68); 6, Uruguay, Castro (89).

Argentina: Botosso, Della Toree, Paternoster, J. Evaristo, Monti, Suarez, Peucelle, Varallo, Stabile, Ferreira, M. Evaristo.

Uruguay: Ballesteros, Nasazzi, Mascheroni, Andrade, Fernandez, Gestido, Dorado, Scarone, Castro, Cea, Iriarte.

Referee: Langenus (Belgium).

ITALY 1934

| Italy...................0 | 1 | 1 —2 |
| Czechoslovakia....0 | 1 | 0 —1 |

SECOND HALF

Scoring: 1, Czech., Puc (70); 2, Italy, Orsi (80).

OVERTIME

Scoring: 3, Italy, Schiavio (95).

Italy: Combi, Monzeglio, Allemandi, Ferraris Monti, Monti, Bertolini, Guaita, Meazza, Schiavio, Ferrari, Orsi.

Czechoslovakia: Planicka, Zenisek, Ctyroky, Kostalek, Cambal, Cambal, Krcil, Junek, Svoboda, Sobotka, Nejedly, Puc.

Referee: Eklind (Sweden).

FRANCE 1938

| Italy...................3 | 1 —4 |
| Hungary ....1 | 1 —2 |

FIRST HALF

Scoring: 1, Italy, Colaussi (5); 2, Hungary, Titkos (7); 3, Italy, Piola (16); 4, Italy, Piola (35).

SECOND HALF

Scoring: 5, Hungary, Sarosi (70); 6, Italy, Colaussi (82).

Italy: Olivieri, Foni, Rava, Serantoni, Andreolo, Locatelli, Biavati, Meazza, Piola, Ferrari, Colaussi.

Hungary: Szabo, Polger, Biro, Szalay, Szucs, Lazar, Sas, Vincze, Sarosi, Zsengeller, Titkos.

Referee: Capdeville (France).

BRAZIL 1950

| Uruguay ....0 | 2 —2 |
| Brazil................0 | 1 —1 |

SECOND HALF

Scoring: 1, Brazil, Friaca (47); 2, Uruguay, Schiaffino (66); 3, Uruguay, Ghiggia (79).

Uruguay: Maspoli, Gonzales, Tejera, Gambretta, Varela, Andrade, Ghiggia, Perez, Miguez, Schiffiano, Moran.

Brazil: Barbosa, Augusto, Juvenal, Bauer, Banilo, Bigode, Friaca, Zizinho, Ademir, Jair, Chico.

Referee: Reader (England).

SWITZERLAND 1954

| W Germany ......2 | 1 —3 |
| Hungary ....2 | 0 —2 |

FIRST HALF

Scoring: 1, Hungary, Puskas (6); 2, Hungary, Czibor (8); 3, W Germ., Morlock (10); 4, W Germ., Rahn (18).

SECOND HALF

Scoring: 5, W Germany, Rahn (84).

W Germany: Turek, Posipal, Kohlmeyer, Eckel, Liebrich, Mai, Rahn, Morlock, O.Walter, F. Walter, Schaefer.

Hungary: Grosics, Buzansky, Lantos, Bozsik, Lorant, Zakarias, Czibor, Kocsis, Hidegkuti, Puskas, Toth.

Referee: Ling (England).

SWEDEN 1958

| Brazil.................2 | 3 —5 |
| Sweden.............1 | 1 —2 |

FIRST HALF

Scoring:1, Sweden, Liedholm (3); 2, Brazil, Vava (9); 3, Brazil, Vava (32).

SECOND HALF

Scoring: 4, Brazil, Pelé (55); 5, Brazil, Zagalo (68); 6, Sweden Simonsson (80); 7, Brazil, Pelé (90).

Brazil: Glymar, D. Santos, N. Santos, Zito, Bellini, Orlando, Garrincha, Didi, Vava, Pelé, Zagalo.

Sweden: Svensson, Bergmark, Axbom, Boerjesson, Gustavsson, Parling, Hamrin, Gren, Simonsson, Liedholm, Skoglund.

Referee: Guigue (France).

CHILE 1962

| Brazil...........................1 | 2 —3 |
| Czechoslovakia ....1 | 0 —1 |

FIRST HALF

Scoring: 1, Czech., Masopust (15); 2, Brazil, Amarildo (17).

SECOND HALF

Scoring: 3, Brazil, Zito (68); 4, Brazil, Vava (77).

Brazil: Glymar, D. Santos, N. Santos, Zito, Mauro, Zozimo, Garrincha, Didi, Vava, Amarildo, Zagalo.

Czechoslovakia: Schroiff, Tichy, Novak, Pluskal, Popluhar, Masopust, Pospichal, Scherer, Kvasnak, Kadraba, Jelinek.

Referee: Latychev (USSR).

World Cup Final Box Scores *(Cont.)*

ENGLAND 1966

England	1	1	2 —4
W Germany	1	1	0 —2

FIRST HALF

Scoring: 1, W Germany, Haller (12); 2, England, Hurst (18).

SECOND HALF

Scoring: 3, England, Peters (78); 4, W. Germany, Weber (90).

OVERTIME

Scoring: 5, England, Hurst (101); 6, England, Hurst (120).

England: Banks, Cohen, Wilson, Stiles, J. Charlton, Moore, Ball, Hurst, Hunt, R. Charlton, Peters.

W Germany: Tilkowski, Hottges, Schmellinger, Beckenbauer, Schulz, Weber, Held, Haller, Seeler, Overath, Emmerich.

Referee: Dienst (Switzerland).

W GERMANY 1974

W Germany	2	0 —2
Netherlands	1	0 —1

FIRST HALF

Scoring: 1, Netherlands, Neeskens, PK (1); 2, W Germany, Breitner, PK (26); 3, W Germany, Müller (44).

W Germany: Maier, Vogts, Beckenbauer, Schwarzenbeck, Breitner, Hoeness, Bonhof, Overath, Grabowski, Müller, Holzenbein.

Netherlands: Jongbloed, Suurbier, Rijsbergen (de Jong), Haan, Krol, Jansen, Neeskens, van Hanagem, Cruyff, Rensenbrink (van der Kerkhof).

Referee: Taylor (England).

ITALY 1982

Italy	0	3 —3
W Germany	0	1 —1

SECOND HALF

Scoring: 1, Italy, Rossi (57); 2, Italy, Tardelli (68); 3, Italy, Altobelli (81); 4, W Germany, Breitner (83).

Italy: Zoff, Bergomi, Scirea, Collovati, Cabrini, Oriali, Gentile, Tardelli, Conti, Rossi, Graziani (Altobelli, Causio).

W Germany: Schumacher, Kaltz, Stielike, K. Foerster, B. Foerster, Dremmler (Hrubesch), Breitner, Briegel, Rummenigge (Müller), Fishcher (Littbarski).

Referee: Coelho (Brazil).

MEXICO 1986 *(Cont.)*

Argentina: Pumpido, Brown, Cuciuffo, Ruggeri, Olarticoecha, Bastista, Giusti, Burruchaga (Trobbiani 90), Enrique, Maradona, Valdona.

W Germany: Schumacher, Jakobs, Forster, Eder, Brehme, Matthaus, Berthold, Magath (Hoeness 62), Briegel, Rummenigge, Allofs (Voller 46).

Referee: Filho (Brazil).

MEXICO 1970

Brazil	1	3 —4
Italy	1	0 —1

FIRST HALF

Scoring: 1, Brazil, Pelé (18); 2, Italy, Boninsegna (32).

SECOND HALF

Scoring: 3, Brazil, Gerson (65); 4, Brazil, Jairzinho (70); 5, Brazil, Alberto (86).

Brazil: Feliz, Alberto, Brito, Wilson, Piazza, Everaldo, Clodoaldo, Gerson, Jairzinho, Tostao, Pelé, Rivelino.

Italy: Albertosi, Burgnich, Cera, Rosato, Facchetti, Bertini (Juliano), Mazzola, De Sisti, Domenghini, Boninsegna (Rivera), Riva.

Referee: Glockner (E Germany).

ARGENTINA 1978

Argentina	1	0	2 —3
Netherlands	0	1	0 —1

FIRST HALF

Scoring: 1, Argentina, Kempes (38).

SECOND HALF

Scoring: 2, Netherlands, Nanninga (81).

OVERTIME

Scoring: 3, Arg., Kempes (104); 4, Arg., Bertoni (114).

Argentina: Fillol, Olguin, Galvan, Passarella, Tarantini, Ardiles (Larrosa), Gallego, Kempes, Bertoni, Luque, Ortiz (Houseman).

Netherlands: Jongbloed, Jansen (Suurbier), Krol, Brandts, Poortvliet, Neeskens, Haan, W. van der Kerkhoff, R. van der Kerkhoff, Rep (Nanninga), Rensenbrink.

Referee: Gonella (Italy).

MEXICO 1986

Argentina	1	2 —3
W Germany	0	2 —2

FIRST HALF

Scoring: 1, Argentina, Brown (22).

SECOND HALF

Scoring: 2, Arg., Valdano (55); 3, W Germ., Rummenigge (73); 4, W Germ., Voller (81); 5, Arg., Burruchaga (83).

ITALY 1990

W Germany	0	1 —1
Argentina	0	0 —0

SECOND HALF

Scoring: 1, W Germany, Brehme, PK (84).

W Germany: Illgner, Brehme, Kohler, Augenthaler, Buchwald, Berthold (Reuter), Littbarski, Haessler, Mattaeus, Voeller, Klinsmann.

Argentina: Goychoechea, Lorenzo, Serrizuela, Sensini, Ruggeri (Monzon), Simon, Basualdo, Burruchag (Calderon), Maradona, Troglio, Dezottir.

Referee: Coelho (Brazil).

World Cup Final Box Scores (Cont.)

UNITED STATES 1994

Italy	0	0	0—0
Brazil	0	0	0—0

Scoring: None. Shootout goals: Italy—2: Albertini, Evani; Brazil—3: Romario, Branco, Dunga.

Italy: Pagliuca, Benarrivo, Maldini, Baresi, Mussi (Apolloni 35), Albertini, D. Baggio (Evani 95), Berti, Donadoni, Baggio, Massaro.

Brazil: Taffarel, Jorginho (Cafu 21), Branco, Aldair, Santos, Silva, Dunga, Zinho (Viola 106), Mazinho, Bebeto, Romario.

Referee: Puhl (Hungary).

FRANCE 1998

Brazil	0	0—0
France	2	1—3

FIRST HALF

Scoring: 1, France, Zidane (27); 2, France, Zidane (45).

SECOND HALF

Scoring: 3, France, Petit (90).

Brazil: Taffarel, Cafu, Aldair, Baiano, Carlos, Sampaio (Edmundo 74), Dunga, Rivaldo, Leonardo, (Denilson 46), Bebeto, Ronaldo.

France: Barthez, Lizarazu, Desailly, Thuram, Leboeuf, Djorkaeff (Vieira 75) Deschamps, Zidane, Petit, Karembeu (Boghossian 57), Guivarc'h (Dugarry 66).

Referee: Belqola (Morocco).

KOREA/JAPAN 2002

Brazil	0	2 —2
Germany	0	0 —0

SECOND HALF

Scoring: 1, Brazil, Ronaldo (67); 2, Brazil, Ronaldo (79).

Brazil: Marcos, Cafu, Lucio, Roque Junior, Edmilson, Carlos, Silva, Ronaldo (Denilson, 90), Rivaldo, Ronaldinho (Juninho, 85), Kleberson.

Germany: Kahn, Linke, Ramelow, Neuville, Hamann, Klose (Bierhoff, 74), Jeremies (Asamoah, 77), Bode (Ziege, 84), Schneider, Metzelder, Frings.

Referee: Collina (Italy).

Alltime Leaders

GOALS

Player, Nation	Tournaments	Goals	Player, Nation	Tournaments	Goals
Gerd Müller, W Germany	1970, '74	14	Gary Lineker, England	1986, '90	10
Just Fontaine, France	1958	13	Ademir, Brazil	1950	9
Pelé, Brazil	1958, '62, '66, '70	12	Eusebio, Portugal	1966	9
Ronaldo, Brazil	1998, 2002	12	Jairzinho, Brazil	1970, '74	9
Sandor Kocsis, Hungary	1954	11	Paolo Rossi, Italy	1982, '86	9
Teofilo Cubillas, Peru	1970, '78	10	K.H. Rummenigge, W Ger	1978, '82, '86	9
Gregorz Lato, Poland	1974, '78, '82	10	Uwe Seeler, W Germany	1958, '62, '66, '70	9
Helmut Rahn, W Germany	1954, '58	10	Vava, Brazil	1958, '62	9

LEADING SCORER, CUP BY CUP

Year	Player, Nation	Goals	Year	Player, Nation	Goals
1930	Guillermo Stabile, Argentina	8	1966	Eusebio Ferreira, Portugal	9
1934	Oldrich Nejedly, Czechoslovakia	5	1970	Gerd Müller, W Germany	10
1938	Leonidas da Silva, Brazil	8	1974	Gregorz Lato, Poland	7
1950	Ademir de Menezes, Brazil	9	1978	Mario Kempes, Argentina	6
1954	Sandor Kocsis, Hungary	11	1982	Paolo Rossi, Italy	6
1958	Just Fontaine, France	13	1986	Gary Lineker, England	6
1962	Florian Albert, Hungary	4	1990	Salvatore Schillaci, Italy	6
	Valentin Ivanov, USSR		1994	Hristo Stoichkov, Bulgaria	6
	Garrincha, Brazil; Vava, Brazil			Oleg Salenko, Russia	
	Drazan Jerkovic, Yugoslavia		1998	Davor Suker, Croatia	6
	Leonel Sanchez, Chile		2002	Ronaldo, Brazil	8

Most Goals, Individual, One Game

Goals	Player, Nation	Score	Date
5	Oleg Salenko, Russia	Russia–Cameroon, 6–1	6-28-94
4	Leonidas, Brazil	Brazil–Poland, 6–5	6-5-38
4	Ernest Willimowski, Poland	Brazil–Poland, 6–5	6-5-38
4	Gustav Wetterstrîm, Sweden	Sweden–Cuba, 8–0	6-12-38
4	Juan Alberto Schiaffino, Uruguay	Uruguay–Bolivia, 8–0	7-2-50
4	Ademir, Brazil	Brazil–Sweden, 7–1	7-9-50
4	Sandor Kocsis, Hungary	Hungary–W Germany, 8–3	6-20-54
4	Just Fontaine, France	France–W Germany, 6–3	6-28-58
4	Eusebio, Portugal	Portugal–N Korea, 5–3	7-23-66
4	Emilio Butragueño, Spain	Spain–Denmark, 5–1	6-18-86

Note: 31 players have scored 32 World Cup hat tricks. Gerd Müller of West Germany is the only man to have two World Cup hat tricks, both in 1970. The last hat tricks were 6-1-02, Miroslav Klose (Ger) vs. Saudi Arabia; 6-21-98, Gabriel Batistuta (Arg) vs. Jamaica; 6-23-90, Tomas Skuhravy (Czech) vs. Costa Rica; and 6-17-90, Michel (Spain) vs. S Korea.

Attendance and Goal Scoring, Year by Year

Year	Site	No. of Games	Goals	Goals/Game	Attendance	Avg Att
1930	Uruguay	18	70	3.89	434,500	24,139
1934	Italy	17	70	4.12	395,000	23,235
1938	France	18	84	4.67	483,000	26,833
1950	Brazil	22	88	4.00	1,337,000	60,773
1954	Switzerland	26	140	5.38	943,000	36,269
1958	Sweden	35	126	3.60	868,000	24,800
1962	Chile	32	89	2.78	776,000	24,250
1966	England	32	89	2.78	1,614,677	50,459
1970	Mexico	32	95	2.97	1,673,975	52,312
1974	W Germany	38	97	2.55	1,774,022	46,685
1978	Argentina	38	102	2.68	1,610,215	42,374
1982	Spain	52	146	2.80	1,856,277	35,698
1986	Mexico	52	132	2.54	2,441,731	46,956
1990	Italy	52	115	2.21	2,514,443	48,354
1994	United States	52	140	2.69	3,567,415	68,604
1998	France	64	171	2.67	2,775,400	43,366
2002	Korea/Japan	64	161	2.52	2,705,216	42,269
Totals		580	1,754	3.02	25,064,655	43,215

The United States in the World Cup

URUGUAY 1930: FINAL COMPETITION

Date	Opponent	Result	Scoring
7-13-30	Belgium	3–0 W	U.S.: McGhee 2, Patenaude
7-17-30	Paraguay	3–0 W	U.S.: Patenaude 2, Florie
7-26-30	Argentina	1–6 L	Arg.: Monti 2, Scopelli 2, Stabile 2 U.S.: Brown.

ITALY 1934: FINAL COMPETITION

Date	Opponent	Result	Scoring
5-27-34	Italy	1–7 L	U.S.: Donelli Italy: Schiavio 3, Orsi 2, Meazza, Ferrari

BRAZIL 1950: FINAL COMPETITION

Date	Opponent	Result	Scoring
6-25-50	Spain	1–3 L	U.S.: Pariani Spain: Igoa, Basora, Zarra
6-29-50	England	1–0 W	U.S.: Gaetjens.
7-2-50	Chile	2–5 L	U.S.: Wallace, Maca Chile: Robledo, Cremaschi 3, Prieto

ITALY 1990: FINAL COMPETITION

Date	Opponent	Result	Scoring
6-10-90	Czechoslovakia	1–5 L	U.S.: Caligiuri Czech.: Skuhravy 2, Hasek, Bilek, Luhovy
6-14-90	Italy	0–1 L	Italy: Giannini
6-19-90	Austria	1–2 L	U.S.: Murray Austria: Rodax, Ogris

UNITED STATES 1994: FINAL COMPETITION

Date	Opponent	Result	Scoring
6-18-94	Switzerland	1–1 T	U.S.: Wynalda Switz.: Bregy
6-22-94	Colombia	2–1 W	U.S.: Escobar (own goal), Stewart Colombia: Valencia
6-26-94	Romania	1–0 L	Romania: Petrescu
7-4-94	Brazil	1–0 L	Brazil: Bebeto

FRANCE 1998: FINAL COMPETITION

Date	Opponent	Result	Scoring
6-15-98	Germany	2–0 L	Germany: Möller, Klinsmann
6-21-98	Iran	2–1 L	U.S.: McBride Iran: Estili, Mahdavikia
6-25-98	Yugoslavia	1–0 L	Yugoslavia: Komljenovic

KOREA/JAPAN 2002: FINAL COMPETITION

Date	Opponent	Result	Scoring
6-5-02	Portugal	3–2 W	U.S.: O'Brien, Costa (own goal), McBride Portugal: Beto, Agoos (own goal)
6-10-02	S Korea	1–1 T	U.S.: Mathis S Korea: Ahn
6-14-02	Poland	3–1 L	Poland: Olisadebe, Kryszalowicz, Zewlakow U.S.: Donovan
6-17-02	Mexico	2–0 W	U.S.: McBride, Donovan
6-21-02	Germany	1–0 L	Germany: Ballack

International Competition

European Championship

Official name: the European Football Championship. Held every four years since 1960.

Year	Champion	Score	Runner-up	Year	Champion	Score	Runner-up
1960	USSR	2–1	Yugoslavia	1984	France	2–0	Spain
1964	Spain	2–1	USSR	1988	Holland	2–0	USSR
1968	Italy	2–0	Yugoslavia	1992	Denmark	2–0	Germany
1972	W Germany	3–0	USSR	1996	Germany†	2–1	Czech Republic
1976	Czechoslovakia*	2–2	W Germany	2000	France†	2–1	Italy
1980	W Germany	2–1	Belgium	2004	Greece	1–0	Portugal

*Won on penalty kicks. †Won in sudden-death overtime.

Under-20 World Championship

Year	Host	Champion	Runner-Up
1977	Tunisia	USSR	Mexico
1979	Japan	Argentina	USSR
1981	Australia	W Germany	Qatar
1983	Mexico	Brazil	Argentina
1985	USSR	Brazil	Spain
1987	Chile	Yugoslavia	W Germany
1989	Saudi Arabia	Portugal	Nigeria
1991	Portugal	Portugal	Brazil
1993	Australia	Brazil	Ghana
1995	Qatar	Argentina	Brazil
1997	Malaysia	Argentina	Uruguay
1999	Nigeria	Spain	Japan
2001	Argentina	Argentina	Ghana
2003	UAE	Brazil	Spain

Under-17 World Championship

Year	Champion
1985	Nigeria
1987	USSR
1989	Saudi Arabia
1991	Ghana
1993	Nigeria

Under-17 *(Cont.)*

Year	Champion
1995	Ghana
1997	Brazil
1999	Brazil
2001	France
2003	Brazil

Pan American Games

Year	Champion
1951	Argentina
1955	Argentina
1959	Argentina
1963	Brazil
1967	Mexico
1971	Argentina
1975	Brazil/Mexico (tie)
1979	Brazil
1983	Uruguay
1987	Brazil
1991	United States
1995	Argentina
1999	Mexico
2003	Argentina

South American Championship (Copa America)

Year	Champion	Host	Year	Champion	Host
1916	Uruguay	Argentina	1953	Paraguay	Peru
1917	Uruguay	Uruguay	1955	Argentina	Chile
1919	Brazil	Brazil	1956	Uruguay	Uruguay
1920	Uruguay	Chile	1957	Argentina	Peru
1921	Argentina	Argentina	1958	Argentina	Argentina
1922	Brazil	Brazil	1959	Uruguay	Ecuador
1923	Uruguay	Uruguay	1963	Bolivia	Bolivia
1924	Uruguay	Uruguay	1967	Uruguay	Uruguay
1925	Argentina	Argentina	1975	Peru	Various sites
1926	Uruguay	Chile	1979	Paraguay	Various sites
1927	Argentina	Peru	1983	Uruguay	Various sites
1929	Argentina	Argentina	1987	Uruguay	Argentina
1935	Uruguay	Peru	1989	Brazil	Brazil
1937	Argentina	Argentina	1990	Brazil	Argentina
1939	Peru	Peru	1991	Argentina	Chile
1941	Argentina	Chile	1993	Argentina	Ecuador
1942	Uruguay	Uruguay	1995	Uruguay	Uruguay
1945	Argentina	Chile	1997	Brazil	Bolivia
1946	Argentina	Argentina	1999	Brazil	Paraguay
1947	Argentina	Ecuador	2001	Colombia	Colombia
1949	Brazil	Brazil	2004	Brazil	Peru

Awards

European Footballer of the Year

Year	Player	Club	Year	Player	Club
1956	Stanley Matthews	Blackpool	1976	Franz Beckenbauer	Bayern Munich
1957	Alfredo Di Stefano	Real Madrid	1977	Allan Simonsen	Borussia M'gladbach
1958	Raymond Kopa	Real Madrid	1978	Kevin Keegan	SV Hamburg
1959	Alfredo Di Stefano	Real Madrid	1979	Kevin Keegan	SV Hamburg
1960	Luis Suarez	Barcelona	1980	Karl-Heinz Rummenigge	Bayern Munich
1961	Omar Sivori	Juventus	1981	Karl-Heinz Rummenigge	Bayern Munich
1962	Josef Masopust	Dukla Prague	1982	Paolo Rossi	Juventus
1963	Lev Yashin	Moscow Dynamo	1983	Michel Platini	Juventus
1964	Denis Law	Manchester United	1984	Michel Platini	Juventus
1965	Eusebio	Benfica	1985	Michel Platini	Juventus
1966	Bobby Charlton	Manchester United	1986	Igor Belanov	Dynamo Kiev
1967	Florian Albert	Ferencvaros	1987	Ruud Gullit	AC Milan
1968	George Best	Manchester United	1988	Marco Van Basten	AC Milan
1969	Gianni Rivera	AC Milan	1989	Marco Van Basten	AC Milan
1970	Gerd Mueller	Bayern Munich	1990	Lothar Matthaeus	Inter Milan
1971	Johan Cruyff	Ajax	1991	Jean-Pierre Papin	Olympique Marseille
1972	Franz Beckenbauer	Bayern Munich	1992	Marco Van Basten	AC Milan
1973	Johan Cruyff	Barcelona	1993	Roberto Baggio	Juventus
1974	Johan Cruyff	Barcelona	1994	Hristo Stoichkov	Barcelona
1975	Oleg Blokhin	Dynamo Kiev			

European Footballer of the Year (Cont.)

Year	Player	Club	Year	Player	Club
1995	George Weah	AC Milan	2000	Luis Figo	Real Madrid
1996	Matthias Sammer	Borussia Dortmund	2001	Michael Owen	Liverpool
1997	Ronaldo	Inter Milan	2002	Ronaldo	Real Madrid
1998	Zinedine Zidane	Juventus	2003	Pavel Nedved	Juventus
1999	Rivaldo	Barcelona			

African Footballer of the Year

Year	Player	Club	Year	Player	Club
1970	Salif Keita	St. Etienne	1988	Kalusha Bwalya	Cercle Bruges
1971	Ibrahim Sunday	Asante Kotoko	1989	George Weah	Monaco
1972	Chérif Soueymane	Hafia	1990	Roger Milla	St. Denis
1973	Tshimen Bwanga	TP Mazembe	1991	Abedi Pele Ayew	Marseille
1974	Paul Moukila	CARA Brazzaville	1992	Abedi Pele Ayew	Marseille
1975	Ahmed Faras	Mohammedia	1993	Rashidi Yekini	FC Zurich
1976	Roger Milla	Canon Yaounde	1994	George Weah	Paris St. Germain
1977	Tarak Dhiab	Esperance	1995	George Weah	AC Milan
1978	Karim Abdul Razak	Asante Kotoko	1996	Nwankwo Kanu	Inter Milan
1979	Thomas Nkono	Canon Yaounde	1997	Victor Ikpeba	Monaco
1980	Jean Manga Onguene	Canon Yaounde	1998	Mustapha Hadji	Deportivo Coruna
1981	Lakhdar Belloumi	GCR Mascara	1999	Nwankwo Kanu	Arsenal
1982	Thomas Nkono	Espanol	2000	Patrick Mboma	Parma
1983	Mahmoud Al-Khatib	Al Ahli	2001	El Hadji Diouf	Lens
1984	Theophile Abega	Toulouse	2002	El Hadji Diouf	Lens
1985	Mohamed Timoumi	Royal Armed Forces	2003	Samuel Eto'o	Real Mallorca
1986	Badou Ezaki	Real Mallorca			
1987	Rabah Madjer	FC Porto			

South American Player of the Year

Year	Player	Club	Year	Player	Club
1971	Tostao	Cruzeiro	1988	Ruben Paz	Racing Buenos Aires
1972	Teofilo Cubillas	Alianza Lima	1989	Bebeto	Vasco da Gama
1973	Pelé	Santos	1990	Raul Amarilla	Olimpia
1974	Elias Figueroa	Internacional	1991	Oscar Ruggeri	Velez Sarsfield
1975	Elias Figueroa	Internacional	1992	Rai	São Paulo
1976	Elias Figueroa	Internacional	1993	Carlos Valderrama	Junior Barranquilla
1977	Zico	Flamengo	1994	Cafu	São Paulo
1978	Mario Kempes	Valencia	1995	Enzo Francescoli	River Plate
1979	Diego Maradona	Argentinos Juniors	1996	Jose-Luis Chilavert	Velez Sarsfield
1980	Diego Maradona	Boca Juniors	1997	Marcelo Salas	River Plate
1981	Zico	Flamengo	1998	Martin Palermo	Boca Juniors
1982	Zico	Flamengo	1999	Javier Saviola	River Plate
1983	Socrates	Corinthians	2000	Romario	Vasco da Gama
1984	Enzo Francescoli	River Plate	2001	Juan Riquelme	Boca Juniors
1985	Julio Cesar Romero	Fluminense	2002	Jose Cardozo	Toluca
1986	Antonio Alzamendi	River Plate	2003	Carlos Tevez	Boca Juniors
1987	Carlos Valderrama	Deportivo Cali			

International Club Competition

Intercontinental Cup

Competition between winners of European Cup and Libertadores Cup.

1960...Real Madrid, Spain	1976...Bayern Munich	1992...São Paulo, Brazil
1961...Penarol, Uruguay	1977...Boca Juniors, Argentina	1993...São Paulo, Brazil
1962...Santos, Brazil	1978...No tournament	1994...Velez Sarsfield, Argentina
1963...Santos, Brazil	1979...Olimpia, Paraguay	1995...Ajax Amsterdam, Netherlands
1964...Inter, Italy	1980...Nacional, Uruguay	1996...Juventus, Italy
1965...Inter, Italy	1981...Flamengo, Brazil	1997...Borussia Dortmund, Ger.
1966...Penarol, Uruguay	1982...Penarol, Uruguay	1998...Real Madrid, Spain
1967...Racing Club, Argentina	1983...Gremio, Brazil	1999...Manchester United, England
1968...Estudiantes, Argentina	1984...Independiente, Argentina	2000...Boca Juniors, Argentina
1969...Milan, Italy	1985...Juventus, Italy	2001...Bayern Munich, Germany
1970...Feyenoord, Netherlands	1986...River Plate, Argentina	2002...Real Madrid, Spain
1971...Nacional, Uruguay	1987...Porto, Portugal	2003...Boca Juniors, Argentina
1972...Ajax Amsterdam, Netherlands	1988...Nacional, Uruguay	
1973...Independiente, Argentina	1989...Milan, Italy	
1974...Atletico de Madrid, Spain	1990...Milan, Italy	
1975...No tournament	1991...Red Star Belgrade, Yugos.	

Note: Until 1968 a best-of-three-games format decided the winner. From 1968 to '79: two-game/total-goal format. One-game championship since 1980. The European Cup runner-up substituted for the winner in 1971, 1973, 1974, and 1979.

European Cup (Champions League)

1956...Real Madrid, Spain	1974...Bayern Munich, W Germany	1988...PSV Eindhoven, Netherlands
1957...Real Madrid, Spain	1975...Bayern Munich, W Germany	1989...AC Milan, Italy
1958...Real Madrid, Spain	1976...Bayern Munich, W Germany	1990...AC Milan, Italy
1959...Real Madrid, Spain		1991....Red Star Belgrade, Yugoslav.
1960...Real Madrid, Spain	1977...Liverpool, England	1992...Barcelona, Spain
1961...Benfica, Portugal	1978...Liverpool, England	1993...Olympique Marseille, France
1962...Benfica, Portugal	1979...Nottingham Forest, England	1994...AC Milan, Italy
1963...AC Milan, Italy	1980...Nottingham Forest, England	1995...Ajax Amsterdam, Netherlands
1964...Inter-Milan, Italy		1996...Juventus, Italy
1965...Inter-Milan, Italy	1981...Liverpool, England	1997...Borussia Dortmund, Ger.
1966...Real Madrid, Spain	1982...Aston Villa, England	1998...Real Madrid, Spain
1967...Celtic, Scotland	1983...SV Hamburg, W Germany	1999...Manchester United, England
1968...Manchester United, England	1984...Liverpool, England	2000...Real Madrid, Spain
1969...AC Milan, Italy	1985...Juventus, Italy	2001...Bayern Munich, Germany
1970...Feyenoord, Netherlands	1986...Steaua Bucharest, Romania	2002...Real Madrid, Spain
1971...Ajax Amsterdam, Netherlands	1987...Porto, Portugal	2003...AC Milan, Italy
1972...Ajax Amsterdam, Netherlands		2004...FC Porto, Portugal
1973...Ajax Amsterdam, Netherlands		

Note: On four occasions the European Cup winner has refused to play in the Intercontinental Cup and has been replaced by the runner-up: Panathinaikos (Greece) in 1971, Juventus (Italy) in 1973, Atletico Madrid (Spain) in 1974, and Malmo (Sweden) in 1979.

Libertadores Cup

Competition between champion clubs and runners-up of 10 South American National Associations.

1960...Penarol, Uruguay	1975...Independiente, Argentina	1990...Olimpia, Paraguay
1961...Penarol, Uruguay	1976...Cruzeiro, Brazil	1991...Colo Colo, Chile
1962...Santos, Brazil	1977...Boca Juniors, Argentina	1992...São Paulo, Brazil
1963...Santos, Brazil	1978...Boca Juniors, Argentina	1993...São Paulo, Brazil
1964...Independiente, Argentina	1979...Olimpia, Paraguay	1994...Velez Sarsfield, Argentina
1965...Independiente, Argentina	1980...Nacional, Uruguay	1995...Gremio, Brazil
1966...Penarol, Uruguay	1981...Flamengo, Brazil	1996...River Plate, Argentina
1967...Racing Club, Argentina	1982...Penarol, Uruguay	1997...Cruzeiro, Brazil
1968...Estudiantes, Argentina	1983...Gremio, Brazil	1998...Vasco da Gama, Brazil
1969...Estudiantes, Argentina	1984...Independiente, Argentina	1999...Palmeiras, Brazil
1970...Estudiantes, Argentina	1985...Argentinos Juniors, Arg	2000...Boca Juniors, Argentina
1971...Nacional, Uruguay	1986...River Plate, Argentina	2001...Boca Juniors, Argentina
1972...Independiente, Argentina	1987...Penarol, Uruguay	2002...Olimpia, Paraguay
1973...Independiente, Argentina	1988...Nacional, Uruguay	2003...Boca Juniors, Argentina
1974...Independiente, Argentina	1989...Atletico Nacional, Colombia	2004...Once Caldas, Colombia

UEFA Cup

1958...Barcelona, Spain	1975...Borussia Monchengladbach, W Germany	1989...Naples, Italy
1959...No tournament		1990...Juventus, Italy
1960...Barcelona, Spain	1976...Liverpool, England	1991...Inter-Milan, Italy
1961...AS Roma, Italy	1977...Juventus, Italy	1992...Torino, Italy
1962...Valencia, Spain	1978...PSV Eindhoven, Netherl.	1993...Juventus, Italy
1963...Valencia, Spain	1979...Borussia Monchengladbach, W Germany	1994...Internazionale, Italy
1964...Real Zaragoza, Spain		1995...Parma, Italy
1965...Ferencvaros, Hungary	1980...Eintracht Frankfurt, W Germany	1996...Bayern Munich, Germany
1966...Barcelona, Spain		1997...Schalke 04, Germany
1967...Dynamo Zagreb, Yugoslav.	1981...Ipswich Town, England	1998...Inter Milan, Italy
1968...Leeds United, England	1982...IFK Gothenburg, Sweden	1999...Parma, Italy
1969...Newcastle United, England	1983...Anderlecht, Belgium	2000...Galatasaray, Turkey
1970...Arsenal, England	1984...Tottenham Hotspur, England	2001...Liverpool, England
1971...Leeds United, England	1985...Real Madrid, Spain	2002...Feyenoord, Netherlands
1972...Tottenham Hotspur, England	1986...Real Madrid, Spain	2003...FC Porto, Portugal
1973...Liverpool, England	1987...IFK Gothenburg, Sweden	2004...Valencia, Spain
1974...Feyenoord, Netherlands	1988...Bayer Leverkusen, W Germany	

European Cup-Winners' Cup

1961...AC Fiorentina, Italy	1974...Magdeburg, E Germany	1987...Ajax Amsterdam, Neth.
1962...Atletico Madrid, Spain	1975...Dynamo Kiev, USSR	1988...Mechelen, Belgium
1963...Tottenham Hotspur, England	1976...Anderlecht, Belgium	1989...Barcelona, Spain
1964...Sporting Lisbon, Portugal	1977...SV Hamburg, W Germ.	1990...Sampdoria, Italy
1965...West Ham United, England	1978...Anderlecht, Belgium	1991...Manchester United, England
1966...Borussia Dortmund, W Ger	1979...Barcelona, Spain	1992...Werder Bremen, Germany
1967...Bayern Munich, W Germ.	1980...Valencia, Spain	1993...Parma, Italy
1968...AC Milan, Italy	1981...Dynamo Tbilisi, USSR	1994...Arsenal, England
1969...Slovan Bratislava, Czech.	1982...Barcelona, Spain	1995...Real Zaragoza, Spain
1970...Manchester City, England	1983...Aberdeen, Scotland	1996...Paris St. Germain, France
1971...Chelsea, England	1984...Juventus, Italy	1997...Barcelona, Spain
1972...Glasgow Rangers, Scotland	1985...Everton, England	1998...Chelsea, England
1973...AC Milan, Italy	1986...Dynamo Kiev, USSR	1999...Lazio, Italy

Note: the Cup-Winners Cup was discontinued after 1999.

Major League Soccer

MLS Cup Results

Year	Champion	Score	Runner-up	Regular Season MVP
1996	D.C. United	3–2 (ot)	Los Angeles	Carlos Valderrama, TB
1997	D.C. United	2–1	Colorado	Preki, Kansas City
1998	Chicago	2–0	D.C. United	Marco Etcheverry, D.C.
1999	D.C. United	2–0	Los Angeles	Jason Kreis, Dallas
2000	Kansas City	1–0	Chicago	Tony Meola, Kansas City
2001	San Jose	2–1 (ot)	Los Angeles	Alex Pineda Chacon, Mia
2002	Los Angeles	1–0 (ot)	New England	Carlos Ruiz, Los Angeles
2003	San Jose	4–2	Chicago	Preki, Kansas City

A-League

Year	Champion	Score	Runner-Up	Regular Season MVP
1991	San Francisco	1–3, 2–0 (1–0 on PKs)	Albany	Jean Harbor, Maryland
1992	Colorado	1–0	Tampa Bay	Taifour Diane, Colorado
1993	Colorado	3–1 (OT)	Los Angeles	Taifour Diane, Colorado
1994	Montreal	1–0	Colorado	Paulinho, Los Angeles
1995	Seattle	1–2 (SO), 3–0, 2–1 (SO)	Atlanta	Peter Hattrup, Seattle
1996	Seattle	2–0	Rochester	Wolde Harris, Colorado
1997	Milwaukee	2–1 (SO)	Carolina	Doug Miller, Rochester
1998	Rochester	3–1	Minnesota	Mark Baena, Seattle
1999	Minnesota	2–1	Rochester	John Swallen, Minnesota
2000	Rochester	3–1	Minnesota	Vitalis Takawira, Mil
2001	Rochester	2–0	Vancouver	Paul Conway, Charleston
2002	Milwaukee	2–1 (2ot)	Richmond	Leighton O'Brien, Seattle
2003	Charleston	3–0	Minnesota	Thiago Martins, Pittsburgh
2004	Montreal	2–0	Seattle	Greg Sutton, Montreal

Woman's United Soccer Association

Founders Cup Results

Year	Champion	Score	Runner-up	Regular Season MVP
2001	Bay Area	3–3 (4–2 PKs)	Atlanta	Tiffeny Milbrett, New York
2002	Carolina	3–2	Washington	Marinette Pichon, Philadelphia
2003	Washington	2–1 (ot)	Atlanta	Maren Meinert, Boston

Note: WUSA suspended operations after the 2003 season.

U.S. Open Cup

Open to all amateur and professional teams in the United States, the annual U.S. Open Cup is the oldest cup competition in the country and among the oldest in the world. The tournament is a single-elimination event running concurrent to the MLS season. The winner advances to the CONCACAF Cup, a tournament of the top club teams from North and Central America and the Caribbean.

Year	Champion	Year	Champion
1914	Brooklyn Field Club (NYC)	1961	Ukrainian Nationals (Philadelphia)
1915	Bethlehem Steel FC (PA)		
1916	Bethlehem Steel FC (PA)	1962	New York Hungaria (NYC)
1917	Fall River Rovers (MA)	1963	Ukrainian Nationals (Philadelphia)
1918	Bethlehem Steel FC (PA)		
1919	Bethlehem Steel FC (PA)	1964	Los Angeles Kickers (CA)
1920	Ben Miller FC (St. Louis)	1965	New York Hungaria (NYC)
1921	Robbins Dry Dock FC (Brooklyn)	1966	Ukrainian Nationals (Philadelphia)
1922	Scullin Steel FC (St. Louis)		
1923	Paterson FC (NJ)	1967	Greek American AA (NYC)
1924	Fall River FC (MA)	1968	Greek American AA (NYC)
1925	Shawsheen FC (Andover, MA)	1969	Greek American AA (NYC)
1926	Bethlehem Steel FC (PA)	1970	Elizabeth SC (Union, NJ)
1927	Fall River FC (MA)	1971	Hota SC (NYC)
1928	New York National FC (NYC)	1972	Elizabeth SC (Union, NJ)
1929	Hakoah All Star SC (NYC)	1973	Maccabee SC (Los Angeles)
1930	Fall River FC (MA)	1974	Greek American AA (NYC)
1931	Fall River FC (MA)	1975	Maccabee SC (Los Angeles)
1932	New Bedford FC (MA)	1976	San Francisco AC (CA)
1933	Stix, Baer and Fuller FC (St. Louis)	1977	Maccabee SC (Los Angeles)
		1978	Maccabee SC (Los Angeles)
1934	Stix, Baer and Fuller FC (St. Louis)	1979	Brooklyn Dodgers SC (NYC)
		1980	NY Pancyprian-Freedoms (NYC)
1935	Central Breweries FC (Chicago)	1981	Maccabee SC (Los Angeles)
1936	German-Americans (Philadelphia)	1982	NY Pancyprian-Freedoms (NYC)
		1983	NY Pancyprian-Freedoms (NYC)
1937	New York American FC (NYC)	1984	AO Krete (NYC)
1938	Sparta A and BA (Chicago)	1985	Greek American AC (San Francisco)
1939	St. Mary's Celtic SC (Brooklyn)		
1940	—	1986	Kutis SC (St. Louis)
1941	Pawtucket FC (RI)	1987	Club Espana (Washington, D.C.)
1942	Gallatin SC (PA)	1988	Busch SC (St. Louis)
1943	Brooklyn Hispano SC (NYC)	1989	HRC Kickers (St. Petersburg, FL)
1944	Brooklyn Hispano SC (NYC)	1990	AAC Eagles (Chicago)
1945	Brookhattan FC (NYC)	1991	Brooklyn Italians (East NY)
1946	Chicago Viking FC (IL)	1992	San Jose Oaks (CA)
1947	Ponta Delgada SC (Fall River, MA)	1993	Club Deportivo Mexico (San Francisco)
1948	Simpkins-Ford SC (St. Louis)	1994	Greek American AC (San Francisco)
1949	Morgan SC (PA)		
1950	Simpkins-Ford SC (St. Louis)	1995	Richmond Kickers (VA)
1951	German Hungarian SC (NYC)	1996	D.C. United (MLS)
1952	Harmarville SC (PA)	1997	Dallas Burn (MLS)
1953	Falcons SC (Chicago)	1998	Chicago Fire (MLS)
1954	New York Americans (NYC)	1999	Rochester Rhinos (A-League)
1955	Eintracht Sport Club (NYC)	2000	Chicago Fire (MLS)
1956	Harmarville SC (PA)	2001	Los Angeles Galaxy (MLS)
1957	Kutis SC (St. Louis)	2002	Columbus Crew (MLS)
1958	Los Angeles Kickers (CA)	2003	Chicago Fire (MLS)
1959	McIlvaine Canvasbacks (Los Angeles)	2004	Kansas City Wizards (MLS)
1960	Ukrainian Nationals (Philadelphia)		

North American Soccer League

Formed in 1968 by the merger of the National Professional Soccer League and the USA League, both of which had begun operations a year earlier. The NPSL's lone champion was the Oakland Clippers. The USA League, which brought entire teams in from Europe, was won in 1967 by the L.A. Wolves, who were the English League's Wolverhampton Wanderers.

Year	Champion	Score	Runner-Up	Regular Season MVP
1968	Atlanta	0–0, 3–0	San Diego	John Kowalik, Chi
1969	Kansas City	No game	Atlanta	Cirilio Fernandez, KC
1970	Rochester	3–0,1–3	Washington	Carlos Metidieri, Roch
1971	Dallas	1–2, 4–1, 2–0	Atlanta	Carlos Metidieri, Roch
1972	New York	2–1	St. Louis	Randy Horton, NY
1973	Philadelphia	2–0	Dallas	Warren Archibald, Mia
1974	Los Angeles	4–3*	Miami	Peter Silvester, Balt
1975	Tampa Bay	2–0	Portland	Steve David, Mia
1976	Toronto	3–0	Minnesota	Pelé, NY
1977	New York	2–1	Seattle	Franz Beckenbauer, NY
1978	New York	3–1	Tampa Bay	Mike Flanagan, NE
1979	Vancouver	2–1	Tampa Bay	Johan Cruyff, LA
1980	New York	3–0	Ft. Lauderdale	Roger Davies, Sea
1981	Chicago	1–0*	New York	Giorgio Chinaglia, NY
1982	New York	1–0	Seattle	Peter Ward, Sea
1983	Tulsa	2–0	Toronto	Roberto Cabanas, NY
1984	Chicago	2–1, 3–2	Toronto	Steve Zungul, SJ

*Shootout.

Championship Format: 1968 and 1970: Two games/total goals. 1971 and 1984: Best-of-three series. 1972–1983: One-game championship. Title in 1969 went to the regular-season champion.

Statistical Leaders

SCORING

Year	Player/Team	Pts	Year	Player/Team	Pts
1968	John Kowalik, Chi	69	1977	Steven David, LA	58
1969	Kaiser Motaung, Atl	36	1978	Giorgio Chinaglia, NY	79
1970	Kirk Apostolidis, Dall	35	1979	Oscar Fabbiani, Tampa Bay	58
1971	Carlos Metidieri, Roch	46	1980	Giorgio Chinaglia, NY	77
1972	Randy Horton, NY	22	1981	Giorgio Chinaglia, NY	74
1973	Kyle Rote, Dall	30	1982	Giorgio Chinaglia, NY	55
1974	Paul Child, San Jose	36	1983	Roberto Cabanas, NY	66
1975	Steven David, Miami	52	1984	Slavisa Zungul, Golden Bay	50
1976	Giorgio Chinaglia, NY	49			

Grassroots Soccer

Survivor Australia winner Tina Wesson bought a Harley with part of her $1 million prize money. *Survivor Africa* winner Ethan Zohn is trying to do a little more with his. The former Vassar soccer star is giving some of his reality riches to Grassroots Soccer, an African AIDS and HIV awareness program driven by soccer players. Zohn, who played in Zimbabwe before landing on *Survivor*, will help train professional players as HIV educators and join them in classrooms throughout the African nation, where the life expectancy is 39 years. Says Zohn, 30, "It's the same concept as Charles Barkley going into the innner city to teach kids about drugs."

NCAA Sports

Mark Carroll of Cal State Fullerton

Holding the Fort

The national champions in soccer, hockey and baseball each defended late leads from determined opponents

BY HANK HERSCH

WHETHER IT'S FOR 75 minutes or 94 seconds or three outs, holding a lead with a national title at stake can be a trying experience. Here's how three of the 2003–2004 NCAA champions took hold of those advantages—and clung to them for dear life.

MEN'S SOCCER
The College Cup in Columbus, Ohio, would be the last match for Indiana coach Jerry Yeagley, who had said he would retire following the season, leaving a program he created 31 years ago. Yeagley didn't have to wait long to get the upper hand on St. John's, the Hoosiers' opponent in the final: In the 16th minute, All-America junior forward Ned Grabavoy curled a 18-yard free kick over the Red Storm wall and into the corner of the net for his 11th goal of the season. To deliver that goal at Yeagley's going-away party, Grabavoy had to come a long way: 7,300 miles, give or take a few, in close to 24 hours.

Only two days before the NCAA final, Grabavoy and Indiana defender Drew Moor had been in the United Arab Emirates, playing for the U.S. under-20 team at the World Youth Championship. After the U.S. lost to Argentina 2–1 in the quarterfinals of that tournament (which had been postponed from March because of the war in Iraq), Grabavoy boarded flights from Dubai to Frankfurt, Germany, to Chicago to Columbus, arriving in central Ohio around midnight; Moor was bumped off the Chicago plane and rerouted through New York. He arrived within two hours of kickoff.

The loss to Argentina had been trying enough for Moor: His foul had led to the decisive penalty kick. Now he had to hold together the Hoosiers' back line to protect the narrow lead against a determined St. John's team—in a steady snowfall, no less. Indiana got a bit more relief in the 20th minute, when freshman Jacob Peterson blasted an 18-yard rocket on a breakaway, bringing a roar from the crowd of 5,330 that had braved the nasty weather.

But IU's 2–0 edge dwindled by half with

Yeagley's Hoosiers rebounded from a slow start to give him the perfect send-off.

AP PHOTO/BLOOMINGTON HERALD-TIMES, CHRIS HOWELL

12 minutes remaining, when St. John's sub Ashley Kozicki slipped a shot past goalkeeper Jay Nolly. "I was getting a little nervous toward the end," said Nolly, who tied his season high with 10 saves, "but we stuck together like we have all year." The Hoosiers had gotten off to a 2-3-4 start, the worst in the program's history, before turning their season around, helping Yeagley pass the career record for coaching victories set by San Francisco's Stephen Negoesco. By standing firm over the final minutes to the Red Storm 2–1, the Hoosiers not only gave their coach win No. 544, but they also rewarded him with the sixth national championship of his legendary career, and his third in the last six years.

"I did have the strangest feeling after the game," the 63-year-old Yeagley said. "I asked the guys in the locker room, 'Is this a dream or is this real?'" It was real, alright, and it was the perfect ending to a great career.

MEN'S HOCKEY

With 94 seconds to play in the NCAA ice hockey title game, Denver held a 1–0 edge on the scoreboard but stared at a gaping deficit on the ice: a five-on-three Maine power play that would swell to six-on-three when the Black Bears removed goaltender Jimmy Howard for yet another extra skater. Before play resumed with a face-off in the Denver end at Boston's FleetCenter, Pioneers coach George Gwozdecky turned to his penalty killers and said, "I'm counting on you, and we're going to get through this."

Senior right wing Greg Keith giggled, perhaps in nervous anticipation of the assault that lay ahead. But he also could have been laughing at Denver's improbable journey to that one-goal advantage. The Pioneers earned their first Frozen Four berth in 18 years with a 1–0 defeat of North Dakota, the tournament's top seed, in the West Regional final. Then in the national semifinals they scored four times in the final period to topple Minnesota-Duluth 5–3. The following day, Gwozdecky suspended senior forward Lukas Dora, who had scored the game-winning goal in the semifinal, for a violation of team rules. "I knew it wouldn't be easy for us," said captain Ryan Caldwell, a senior defenseman.

Seven minutes after Maine had a power play goal disallowed, Denver's sophomore center Gabe Gauthier beat Howard on the power play with a blast from the circle that zipped inside the far post. As Maine went on the offensive, Denver parried every thrust; of the 51 shots the Black Bears would attempt, 27 were blocked by forwards or defensemen, sacrificing their bodies by diving in front of the flying pucks. Senior goalie Adam Berkhoel, the Frozen Four MVP, took care of the rest, making 24 saves.

With 2:09 left in the game, junior defenseman Matt Laatsch was sent off for hooking; 35 seconds later Gauthier joined him in the box with a delay of game penalty after gloving a bouncing puck inside the Denver blue line and throwing it down the ice. Laatsch sat through most of the final 94 seconds with his head in his hands, no doubt aware that of Maine's 33 wins, 15 were by one goal, including eight in a row entering the final. "Gabe had to give me the play-by-play," he said. "I couldn't watch."

Laatsch missed one of the most frantic endings in the tournament's 57-year history. The puck hardly left the Pioneers' end during the frenzy, and Berkhoel turned away three shots while another one clanged off a post. When time finally expired, Denver had claimed its first title since 1969, becoming the first 1–0 winner in a finals and the champion with the fewest wins (27) in 23 years. The frustrated Black Bears, who scored only once in 22 postseason power plays, suffered their second one-goal loss in an NCAA final in three years. "You don't have to be real talented to play defense, but you have to have a lot of character and heart to persevere," Gwozdecky said. "We had to learn that to beat a terrific team like Maine."

BASEBALL

He had no command of his curveball, the one that had helped him win 11 straight games entering the College World Series final. His pitch total over nine days in Omaha had surpassed 300. When behind in the count he had to rely on off-speed pitches to keep the opposing hitters off-balance. But now three outs stood between Cal State-Fullerton senior right-hander Jason Windsor and a title-clinching 3–2 win over Texas.

In the vital art of gaining leads and protecting them, no team had been better than Texas. Ranked No. 1 in the country and seeded first in the national tournament, the Longhorns came to Omaha with one of the country's top bullpens, anchored by J. Brent Cox and Huston Street. The Titans' pedigree, on the other hand, was slightly less impressive. They started the season 15–16. Their slogans of "choke and poke" and "hunt and attack" bespoke their paucity of power hitters. A miniature toilet sat in their dugout, the better to "flush away" an error or bad at bat. Some of the players even had little commodes on their keychains. "They call them mini-me's," sports information director Ryan Ermeling explained.

Its less-than-imposing style aside, in Game 1 of the best-of-three final Fullerton showed why it had won 30 of its 36 games after that horrendous start. Sophomore left-fielder Danny Dorn belted a two-run double off Street in the seventh inning to give Fullerton the lead for good in a 6–4 victory. "We all know who Huston Street is," Titans coach George Horton said. "If he had come in and cut us to shreds, that would have had a hangover affect."

The Longhorns took a 2–0 lead in Game 2 against Windsor, but Texas starter Sam LeClure, nicked on the ankle by a hard comebacker in the fifth inning, was unable to finish. Titans pinch hitter Brett Pill hit a triple to drive in one run off Texas reliever Buck Cody, who then threw a wild pitch to allow the Titans to tie the game. With Ronnie Prettyman on second after a throwing error, Cox came on to face All-America catcher Kurt Suzuki, who had gone 2 for 20 during the CWS. He lined a two-out single to left that nudged Fullerton ahead, 3–2. "I just went up there with good thoughts and said, You know, this is my box. I own it. I'm the man, and I want to be the man in this situation," Suzuki said. "I just made it happen."

It came down to the bottom of the ninth, which Windsor took care of with characteristic cool, his weighty pitch total notwithstanding. He finished with a five-hitter, and was named the tournament's most outstanding player. In 21 innings of work in Omaha, Windsor gave up 11 hits and two runs, while striking out 29.

"I still have chills," Horton said, "and it's not from the cold water that was just dropped on my head."

NCAA Team Champions

Fall 2003
Cross-Country

MEN

	Champion	Runner-Up
Division I:	Stanford	Wisconsin
Division II:	Adams St	Abilene Christian
Division III:	Calvin	WI-Stevens Pt

WOMEN

Division I:	Stanford	Brigham Young
Division II:	Adams St	Western St (CO)
Division III:	Middlebury	Trinity (CT)

Field Hockey

WOMEN

	Champion	Runner-Up
Division I:	Wake Forest	Duke
Division II	Bloomsburg	UMass–Lowell
Division III:	Salisbury	Middlebury

Football

MEN

	Champion	Runner-Up
Division I-AA:	Delaware	Colgate
Division II:	Grand Valley St	N Dakota
Division III:	St. John's (MN)	Mount Union

Soccer

MEN

	Champion	Runner-Up
Division I:	Indiana	St. John's (NY)
Division II:	Lynn	Cal St Chico
Division III:	Trinity (TX)	Drew

WOMEN

Division I:	N Carolina	Connecticut
Division II:	Kennesaw St	Franklin Pierce
Division III:	Oneonta St	Chicago

Volleyball

WOMEN

	Champion	Runner-Up
Division I:	Southern Cal	Florida
Division II:	N Alabama	Concordia–St. Paul
Division III:	Washington (MO)	New York University

Water Polo

MEN

Champion	Runner-Up
Southern Cal	Stanford

Winter 2003–2004
Basketball
MEN

	Champion	Runner-Up
Division I:	Connecticut	Georgia Tech
Division II:	Kennesaw St	Southern Indiana
Division III:	WI–Stevens Pt	Williams

WOMEN

	Champion	Runner-Up
Division I:	Connecticut	Tennessee
Division II:	California (PA)	Drury
Division III:	Wilmington	Bowdoin

Fencing

Champion	Runner-Up
Ohio St	Penn St

Gymnastics
MEN

Champion	Runner-Up
Penn St	Oklahoma

WOMEN

Champion	Runner-Up
UCLA	Georgia

Ice Hockey
MEN

	Champion	Runner-Up
Division I:	Denver	Maine
Division III:	Middlebury	St. Norbert

WOMEN

	Champion	Runner-Up
Division I:	Minnesota	Harvard
Division III:	Middlebury	WI–Stevens Pt.

Rifle

Champion	Runner-Up
AK-Fairbanks	Nevada

Skiing

Champion	Runner-Up
New Mexico	Utah

Swimming and Diving
MEN

	Champion	Runner-Up
Division I:	Auburn	Stanford
Division II:	Cal St–Bakersfield	Drury
Division III:	Kenyon	Emory

WOMEN

	Champion	Runner-Up
Division I:	Auburn	Georgia
Division II:	Truman St	Drury
Division III:	Kenyon	Emory

Wrestling
MEN

	Champion	Runner-Up
Division I:	Oklahoma St	Iowa
Division II:	Nebraska-Omaha	N Dakota St
Division III:	Wartburg	Augsburg

Winter 2003–2004 (Cont.)
Indoor Track and Field
MEN

	Champion	Runner-Up
Division I:	Louisiana St	Florida/ Arkansas (tie)
Division II:	Abilene Christian	St. Augustine's
Division III:	WI–La Crosse	WI-Whitewater/ Lincoln (tie)

WOMEN

	Champion	Runner-Up
Division I:	Louisiana St	Florida
Division II:	Lincoln	Adams St
Division III:	WI-Oshkosh	Wheaton (MA)

Spring 2004
Baseball

	Champion	Runner-Up
Division I:	Cal St Fullerton	Texas
Division II:	Delta St	Grand Valley St
Division III:	George Fox University	Eastern Connecticut St

Golf
MEN

	Champion	Runner-Up
Division I:	California	UCLA
Division II:	S Carolina–Aiken	Chico St
Division III:	Gustavus Adolphus	Redlands

WOMEN

	Champion	Runner-Up
Division I:	UCLA	Oklahoma St
Division II:	Rollins (FL)	Ferris St/ Florida Southern (tie)
Division III	Methodist	Mary-Hardin Baylor

Lacrosse
MEN

	Champion	Runner-Up
Division I:	Syracuse	Navy
Division II:	Le Moyne	Limestone
Division III:	Salisbury	Nazareth

WOMEN

	Champion	Runner-Up
Division I:	Virginia	Princeton
Division II	Adelphi	West Chester
Division III:	Middlebury	College of New Jersey

Rowing
WOMEN

	Champion	Runner-Up
Division I:	Brown	Yale
Division II	Mercyhurst	Humboldt St
Division III:	Ithaca	Smith

Softball

	Champion	Runner-Up
Division I:	UCLA	California
Division II:	Angelo St	Florida Southern
Division III:	St. Thomas	Moravian

Tennis
MEN

	Champion	Runner-Up
Division I:	Baylor	UCLA
Division II:	W Florida	Valdosta St
Division III:	Middlebury	Williams

Spring 2004 (Cont.)
Tennis (Cont.)
WOMEN

	Champion	Runner-Up
Division I:	Stanford	UCLA
Division II:	BYU–Hawaii	Lynn
Division III:	Emory	Amherst

Outdoor Track and Field
MEN

	Champion	Runner-Up
Division I:	Arkansas	Florida
Division II:	Abilene Christian	St. Augustine's
Division III:	WI–La Crosse	Nebraska Wesleyan

WOMEN

	Champion	Runner-Up
Division I:	UCLA	Louisiana St
Division II:	Lincoln	Adams St
Division III:	WI-Oshkosh	Calvin

Volleyball
MEN

Champion	Runner-Up
Brigham Young	Long Beach St

Water Polo
WOMEN

Champion	Runner-Up
Southern Cal	Loyola-Marymount

NCAA Division I Individual Champions

Fall 2003
Cross Country
MEN

Champion	Runner-Up
Dathan Ritzenhein, Colorado	Ryan Hall, Stanford

WOMEN

Champion	Runner-Up
Shalane Flanagan, N Carolina	Kim Smith, Providence

Winter 2003–2004
Fencing
MEN

	Champion	Runner-Up
Sabre	Adam Crompton, Ohio St	Sergey Isayenko, Columbia
Foil	Boaz Ellis, Ohio St	Corey Werk, Yale
Épée	Arpad Horvath, St. John's (NY)	Benjamin Bratton, St. John's (NY)

WOMEN

	Champion	Runner-Up
Sabre	Valerie Providenza, Notre Dame	Sophia Hiss, Penn State
Foil	Alicja Kryczalo, Notre Dame	Andrea Ament, Notre Dame
Épée	Anna Garina, Wayne St	Kerry Walton, Notre Dame

Gymnastics
MEN

	Champion	Runner-Up
All-around	Luis Vargas, Penn St	Dan Gill, Stanford
Vault	Graham Ackerman, California	Adam Pummer, Illinois
Parallel bars	Ramon Jackson, William & Mary	Linas Gaveika, Iowa
Horizontal bar	Justin Spring, Illinois	Dan Gill, Stanford
		Graham Ackerman, California
Floor exercise	Graham Ackerman, California	Randall Heflin, California
Pommel horse	Bob Rogers, Illinois	Dan Gill, Stanford
Rings	Kevin Tan, Penn St	Nyika White, Temple

Winter 2003–2004 (Cont.)

Gymnastics (Cont.)

WOMEN

	Champion	Runner-Up
All-around	Jeana Rice, Alabama	Jeanette Antolin, UCLA
Balance beam	Ashley Kelly, Arizona State	Jeana Rice, Alabama
Uneven bars	Elise Ray, Michigan	Kristen Maloney, UCLA
Floor exercise	Ashley Miles, Alabama	Jeanette Antolin, UCLA
	Courtney Bumpers, N Carolina	
Vault	Ashley Miles, Alabama	Annabeth Eberle, Utah

Skiing

MEN

	Champion	Runner-Up
Slalom	Paul McDonald, Dartmouth	Michal Rajcan, Nevada
Giant slalom	BenThornhill, Utah	Petter Roering, New Mexico
10-kilometer free	Henning Dybendal, Utah	Lowell Bailey, Vermont
20-kilometer classic	Henning Dybendal, Utah	Tor Erik Schjellerud, Colorado

WOMEN

	Champion	Runner-Up
Slalom	Pia Rivelsrud, Denver	Courtney Calise, Dartmouth
Giant slalom	Jennifer Delich, New Mexico	Erika Hogan, Colorado
5-kilometer free	Sigrid Aas, AK-Fairbanks	Mandy Kaempf, AK-Anchorage
15-kilometer classic	Sigrid Aas, AK-Fairbanks	Mandy Kaempf, AK-Anchorage

Wrestling

	Champion	Runner-Up
125 lb	Jason Powell, Nebraska	Kyle Ott, Illinois
133 lb	Zach Roberson, Iowa St	Josh Moore, Penn St
141 lb	Cliff Moore, Iowa	Matt Murray, Nebraska
149 lb	Jesse Jantzen, Harvard	Zack Esposito, Oklahoma St
157 lb	Matt Gentry, Stanford	Jake Percival, Ohio
165 lb	Troy Letters, Lehigh	Tyrone Lewis, Oklahoma St
174 lb	Chris Pendleton, Oklahoma St	Ben Askren, Missouri
184 lb	Greg Jones, W Virginia	Ben Heizer, Northern Illinois
197 lb	Damion Hahn, Minnesota	Ryan Fulsaas, Iowa
HWT	Tommy Rowlands, Ohio St.	Pat Cummins, Penn St

Swimming and Diving

MEN

	Champion	Time	Runner-Up	Time
50-m freestyle	Fred Bousquet, Auburn	21.10†#*	Ian Crocker, Texas	21.53
100-m freestyle	Ian Crocker, Texas	46.25†#*	Duge Draganja, California	46.64
200-m freestyle	Jayme Cramer, Stanford	1:45.04	Dan Ketchum, Michigan	1:45.11
400-m freestyle	Peter Vanderkaay, Michigan	3:40.78	Dan Ketchum, Michigan	3:44.92
1500-m freestyle	Peter Vanderkaay, Michigan	14:44.53	Ousama Mellouli, Southern Cal	14:45.49
100-m backstroke	Peter Marshall, Stanford	50.32†#*	Markus Rogan, Stanford	51.60
200-m backstroke	Aaron Peirsol, Texas	1:50.64†#*	Markus Rogan, Stanford	1:51.37
100-m breaststroke	Brendan Hansen, Texas	58.19	Mark Gangloff, Auburn	58.78
200-m breaststroke	Brendan Hansen, Texas	2:04.73*	Scott Usher, Wyoming	2:07.66
100-m butterfly	Ian Crocker, Texas	49.07†#*	Milorad Cavic, California	50.81
200-m butterfly	Rainer Kendrick, Texas	1:54.97*	Jayme Cramer, Stanford	1:55.0
200-m IM	George Bovell, Auburn	1:53.93†#*	Markus Rogan, Stanford	1:55.51
400-m IM	Ryan Lochte, Florida	4:04.52†#*	Ousama Mellouli, Southern Cal	4:04.90

	Champion	Pts	Runner-Up	Pts
1-meter diving	Jevon Tarantino, Tennessee	388.65	Andy Bradley, S Carolina	384.90
3-meter diving	Joona Puhakka, Arizona St	647.30	Phillip Jones, Tennessee	633.50
Platform	Caesar Garcia, Auburn	635.05	Steven Segerlin, Auburn	574.80

†World record. #American record. *NCAA record.

NCAA Division I Individual Champions (Cont.)

Winter 2003–2004 (Cont.)

Swimming and Diving (Cont.)

WOMEN

	Champion	Time	Runner-Up	Time
50-m freestyle	Kara Lynn Joyce, Georgia	24.24	Eileen Coparropa, Auburn	24.11
100-m freestyle	Kara Lynn Joyce, Georgia	53.15*	Jennifer Vanassan, S Carolina	54.38
200-m freestyle	Margaret Hoelzer, Auburn	1:56.16*	Jennifer Vanassan, S Carolina	1:57.66
400-m freestyle	Emily Mason, Arizona	4:01.58*	Kalyn Keller, Southern Cal	4:02.21
1500-m freestyle	Kalyn Keller, Southern Cal	15:49.14#*	Rachael Burke, Virginia	15:55.27
100-m backstroke	Natalie Coughlin, California	57.51	Margaret Hoelzer, Auburn	58.54
200-m backstroke	Kirsty Coventry, Auburn	2:03.86	Margaret Hoelzer, Auburn	2:05.55
100-m breaststroke	Tara Kirk, Stanford	1:04.79†#*	Sarah Poewe, Georgia	1:06.02
200-m breaststroke	Tara Kirk, Stanford	2:20.70#*	Birte Steven, Oregon St	2:22.14
100-m butterfly	Natalie Coughlin, California	56.88	Dana Kirk, Stanford	57.16
200-m butterfly	Mary Descenza, Georgia	2:06.02*	Kaitlin Sandeno, Southern Cal	2:06.07
200-m IM	Kaitlin Sandeno, Southern Cal	2:08.11*	Kirsty Coventry, Auburn	2:08.88
400-m IM	Kaitlin Sandeno, Southern Cal	4:30.44#*	Kirsty Coventry, Auburn	4:34.20

	Champion	Pts	Runner-Up	Pts
1-meter diving	Allison Brennan, S Carolina	307.20	Lane Bassham, Alabama	305.85
3-meter diving	Lane Bassham, Alabama	557.74	Mandy Moran, Arkansas	541.95
Platform	Nicole, Pohorenec, Texas	482.20	Trisha Tumlinson, Arizona St	454.35

† World record. #American record. *NCAA record.

Indoor Track and Field

MEN

	Champion	Time/Mark	Runner-Up	Time/Mark
60-meter dash	DaBryan Blanton, Oklahoma	6.59	Mardy Scales, Middle Tenn St	6.61
60-meter hurdles	Antwon Hicks, Mississippi	7.61	Jermaine Cooper, Texas	7.67
200-meter dash	Leo Bookman, Kansas	20.42	Kenneth Baxter, Purdue	20.57
400-meter dash	Jeremy Wariner, Baylor	45.39	Jerry Harris, Texas Christian	45.52
800-meter run	Nate Brannen, Michigan	1:47.61	Christian Smith, Kansas St	1:48.18
Mile run	Sean Jefferson, Indiana	4:00.16	Nathan Robison, Brigham Young	4:01.99
3,000-meter run	Alistair Cragg, Arkansas	7:55.29	Nick Willis, Michigan	7:56.44
5,000-meter run	Alistair Cragg, Arkansas	13:39.63	Ian Dobson, Stanford	13:40.91
High jump	Andra Manson, Texas	7 ft 3¾ in	Marcus Harris, Texas Southern	7 ft 3¾ in
Pole vault	Brad Walker, Washington	18 ft 8¼ in	Tommy Skipper, Oregon	18 ft 4½ in
Long jump	John Moffitt, Louisiana St	26 ft 9¾ in	Tony Allmond, S Carolina	26 ft 6¼ in
Triple jump	Lejuan Simon, Louisiana St	55 ft 11¼ in	John Moffitt, Louisiana St	55 ft 1 in
Shot put	Dan Taylor, Ohio St	66 ft 7¼ in	Carl Myerscough, Nebraska	66 ft 3 in
35-pound wt throw	Dan Taylor, Ohio St	77 ft 7½ in	Keith McBride, Purdue	71 ft 2¾ in

WOMEN

	Champion	Time/Mark	Runner-Up	Time/Mark
60-meter dash	Muna Lee, Louisiana St	7.21	Toyin Olupona, Tennessee	7.28
60-meter hurdles	Priscilla Lopes, Nebraska	7.96	Lolo Jones, Louisiana St	8.00
200-meter dash	Veronica Campbell, Arkansas	22.43	Sanya Richards, Texas	22.49
400-meter dash	Sanya Richards, Texas	50.82	Tiandra Ponteen, Florida	51.23
800-meter run	Nicole Cook, Tennessee	2:03.27	Neisha Bernard-Thomas, LSU	2:04.36
Mile run	Tiffany McWilliams, Mississippi St	4:32.24	Johanna Nilsson, Northern Ariz	4:32.72
3,000-meter run	Kim Smith, Providence	8:49.18	Sara Bei, Stanford	9:05.02
5,000-meter run	Kim Smith, Providence	15:14.18	Alicia Craig, Stanford	15:45.08
High jump	Chaunte Howard, Georgia Tech	6 ft 3½ in	Sharon Day, Cal Poly SLO	6 ft 1¼ in
Pole vault	Fanni Juhasz, Georgia	13 ft 11¼ in	Chelsea Johnson, UCLA	13 ft 11¼ in
Long jump	Hyleas Fountain, Georgia	21 ft 7¼ in	S. Sowell, Northwestern St	20 ft 10½ in
Triple jump	Ineta Radevica, Nebraska	44 ft 10¾ in	Chaytan Hill, Kansas St	44 ft 8¼ in
Shot put	Laura Gerraughty, N Carolina	62 ft 10 in	Becky Breisch, Nebraska	56 ft 10¼ in
20-pound wt throw	Candice Scott, Florida	75 ft 7½ in	Kim Barrett, Florida	75 ft 3½ in

*NCAA record.

Rifle

	Champion	Pts	Runner-Up	Pts
Smallbore	Matthew Rawlings, AK-Fairbanks	1179	Joseph Hein, AK-Fairbanks	1178
Air rifle	Morgan Hicks, Murray St	398	Matthew Rawlings, AK-Fairbanks	396

*NCAA record.

Spring 2004
Golf

MEN

Champion	Score	Runner-Up	Score
Ryan Moore, Nevada–Las Vegas	267	Bill Haas, Wake Forest	273

WOMEN

Sarah Huarte, California	278	Karin Sjodin, Oklahoma St	279

Outdoor Track and Field

MEN

	Champion	Mark	Runner-Up	Mark
100-meter dash	Tyson Gay, Arkansas	10.06	Michael Frater, Texas Christian	10.06
200-meter dash	Wallace Spearmon, Arkansas	20.12	Stanford Routt, Houston	20.20
400-meter dash	Jeremy Wariner, Baylor	44.71	Kelly Willie, Louisiana St	44.85
800-meter run	Jonathan Johnson, Texas Tech	1:46.39	Jesse O'Connell, Georgetown	1:46.79
1,500-meter run	Chris Mulvaney, Arkansas	3:44.72	Nathan Robison, Brigham Young	3:44.94
5,000-meter run	Robert Cheseret, Arizona	13:49.85	Dathan Ritzenhein, Colorado	13:52.13
10,000-meter run	Alistair Cragg, Arkansas	29:22.43	Robert Cheseret, Arizona	29:26.51
110-meter hurdles	Josh Walker, Florida	13.32	Eric Mitchum, Oregon	13.38
400-meter hurdles	Kerron Clement, Florida	49.05	Bennie Brazell, Louisiana St	49.34
3,000-m steeple	Jordan Desilets, Eastern Michigan	8:42.64	Andy Smith, N Carolina St	8:45.84
High jump	Andra Manson, Texas	7 ft 7¼ in	Kyle Lancaster, Kansas St	7 ft 6 in
Pole vault	Tommy Skipper, Oregon	18 ft 8¼ in	Uyoo Kim, UCLA	18 ft 4½ in
Long jump	John Moffitt, Louisiana St	27 ft 6¾ in	Tony Allmond, S Carolina	27 ft 4¾ in
Triple jump	Leevan Sands, Auburn	56 ft 2 in	Aarik Wilson, Indiana	55 ft 6½ in
Shot put	Carl Myerscough, Nebraska	67 ft 8¾ in	Dan Taylor, Ohio St	65 ft 11¾ in
Discus throw	Hannes Hopley, SMU	203 ft 5 in	Jason Young, Texas Tech	197 ft 8 in
Hammer throw	Thomas Freeman, Manhattan	232 ft 2 in	Spyridon Jullien, Virginia Tech	231 ft 11 in
Javelin throw	Gabriel Wallin, Boise St	264 ft 9 in	Brian Chaput, Pennsylvania	256 ft 2 in
Decathlon	Ryan Harlan, Rice	8171 pts	Trey Hardee, Mississippi St	8041 pts

WOMEN

100-meter dash	Lauryn Williams, Miami	10.97	Muna Lee, Louisiana St	11.12
200-meter dash	LaShaunte'a Moore, Arkansas	22.37	Muna Lee, Louisiana St	22.55
400-meter dash	Dee Dee Trotter, Tennessee	50.32	Monique Henderson, UCLA	50.62
800-meter run	Neisha Bernard-Thomas, LSU	2:02.86	Kameisha Bennett, Tennessee	2:03.11
1,500-meter run	Tiffany McWilliams, Mississippi St	4:11.59	Treniere Clement, Georgetown	4:12.21
5,000-meter run	Kim Smith, Providence	15:48.86	Sara Bei, Stanford	16:24.90
10,000-meter run	Alicia Craig, Stanford	33:58.27	Vicky Gill, Florida St	34:02.31
100-meter hurdles	Nichole Denby, Texas	12.62	Priscilla Lopes, Nebraska	12.64
400-meter hurdles	Sheena Johnson, UCLA	53.54	Lashinda Demus, S Carolina	54.22
3,000-m steeple	Ida Nilsson, Northern Arizona	9:48.29	Briana Shook, Toledo	9:49.44
High jump	Chaunte Howard, Georgia Tech	6 ft 4 in	Sharon Day, Cal Poly SLO	6 ft 2¾ in
Pole vault	Chelsea Johnson, UCLA	14 ft 1¼ in	Kate Soma, Washington	13 ft 9¼ in
Long jump	Tina Harris, Louisiana St	21 ft 1½ in	Amy Menlove, Brigham Young	20 ft 6½ in
Triple jump	Ineta Radevica, Nebraska	45 ft 6¼ in	Nicole Toney, Louisiana St	45 ft 3½ in
Shot put	Laura Gerraughty, N Carolina	59 ft 11 in	Jillian Camarena, Stanford	59 ft 5 in
Discus throw	Carol Stevenson, Cal St N'ridge	178 ft 11 in	LaQuanda Cotten, Florida	169 ft 3 in
Hammer throw	Candice Scott, Florida	225 ft 10 in	Jessica Cosby, UCLA	219 ft 5 in
Javelin throw	Katy Doyle, Texas A&M	185 ft 7 in	Inga Stasiulionyte, Southern Cal	185 ft 4 in
Heptathlon	Jacquelyn Johnson, Arizona St	5807 pts	Hyleas Fountain, Georgia	5785 pts

Tennis

MEN

	Champion	Score	Runner-Up
Singles	Benjamin Becker, Baylor	6–4, 7–6 (10-8)	Michael Kogan, Tulane
Doubles	KC Corkery & Sam Warburg, Stanford	6–2, 6–7, 6–4	Bo Hodge & John Isner, Georgia

WOMEN

Singles	Amber Liu, Stanford	6–4, 0–6, 6–3	Jelena Pandzic, Fresno St
Doubles	Daniela Bercek & Lauren Fisher, UCLA	6–4, 6–4	Jessica Johnson & Ashley Kroh, Marshall

CHAMPIONSHIP RESULTS

Baseball

DIVISION I

Year	Champion	Coach	Score	Runner-Up	Most Outstanding Player
1947	California*	Clint Evans	8–7	Yale	No award
1948	Southern Cal	Sam Barry	9–2	Yale	No award
1949	Texas*	Bibb Falk	10–3	Wake Forest	Charles Teague, Wake Forest, 2B
1950	Texas	Bibb Falk	3–0	Washington St	Ray VanCleef, Rutgers, CF
1951	Oklahoma*	Jack Baer	3–2	Tennnessee	Sidney Hatfield, Tennessee, P-1B
1952	Holy Cross	Jack Barry	8–4	Missouri	James O'Neill, Holy Cross, P
1953	Michigan	Ray Fisher	7–5	Texas	J.L. Smith, Texas, P
1954	Missouri	John (Hi) Simmons	4–1	Rollins	Tom Yewcic, Michigan St, C
1955	Wake Forest	Taylor Sanford	7–6	Western Michigan	Tom Borland, Oklahoma St, P
1956	Minnesota	Dick Siebert	12–1	Arizona	Jerry Thomas, Minnesota, P
1957	California*	George Wolfman	1–0	Penn St	Cal Emery, Penn St, P-1B
1958	Southern Cal	Rod Dedeaux	8–7†	Missouri	Bill Thom, Southern Cal, P
1959	Oklahoma St	Toby Greene	5–3	Arizona	Jim Dobson, Oklahoma St, 3B
1960	Minnesota	Dick Siebert	2–1‡	Southern Cal	John Erickson, Minnesota, 2B
1961	Southern Cal*	Rod Dedeaux	1–0	Oklahoma St	Littleton Fowler, Oklahoma St, P
1962	Michigan	Don Lund	5–4	Santa Clara	Bob Garibaldi, Santa Clara, P
1963	Southern Cal	Rod Dedeaux	5–2	Arizona	Bud Hollowell, Southern Cal, C
1964	Minnesota	Dick Siebert	5–1	Missouri	Joe Ferris, Maine, P
1965	Arizona St	Bobby Winkles	2–1#	Ohio St	Sal Bando, Arizona St, 3B
1966	Ohio St	Marty Karow	8–2	Oklahoma St	Steve Arlin, Ohio St, P
1967	Arizona St	Bobby Winkles	11–2	Houston	Ron Davini, Arizona St, C
1968	Southern Cal*	Rod Dedeaux	4–3	Southern Illinois	Bill Seinsoth, Southern Cal, 1B
1969	Arizona St	Bobby Winkles	10–1	Tulsa	John Dolinsek, Arizona St, LF
1970	Southern Cal	Rod Dedeaux	2–1	Florida St	Gene Ammann, Florida St, P
1971	Southern Cal	Rod Dedeaux	7–2	Southern Illinois	Jerry Tabb, Tulsa, 1B
1972	Southern Cal	Rod Dedeaux	1–0	Arizona St	Russ McQueen, Southern Cal, P
1973	Southern Cal*	Rod Dedeaux	4–3	Arizona St	Dave Winfield, Minnesota, P-OF
1974	Southern Cal	Rod Dedeaux	7–3	Miami (FL)	George Milke, Southern Cal, P
1975	Texas	Cliff Gustafson	5–1	S Carolina	Mickey Reichenbach, Texas, 1B
1976	Arizona	Jerry Kindall	7–1	Eastern Michigan	Steve Powers, Arizona, P-DH
1977	Arizona St	Jim Brock	2–1	S Carolina	Bob Horner, Arizona St, 3B
1978	Southern Cal*	Rod Dedeaux	10–3	Arizona St	Rod Boxberger, Southern Cal, P
1979	Cal St-Fullerton	Augie Garrido	2–1	Arkansas	Tony Hudson, Cal St-Fullerton, P
1980	Arizona	Jerry Kindall	5–3	Hawaii	Terry Francona, Arizona, LF
1981	Arizona St	Jim Brock	7–4	Oklahoma St	Stan Holmes, Arizona St, LF
1982	Miami (FL)*	Ron Fraser	9–3	Wichita St	Dan Smith, Miami (FL), P
1983	Texas*	Cliff Gustafson	4–3	Alabama	Calvin Schiraldi, Texas, P
1984	Cal St-Fullerton	Augie Garrido	3–1	Texas	John Fishel, Cal St-Fullerton, LF
1985	Miami (FL)	Ron Fraser	10–6	Texas	Greg Ellena, Miami (FL), DH
1986	Arizona	Jerry Kindall	10–2	Florida St	Mike Senne, Arizona, LF
1987	Stanford	Mark Marquess	9–5	Oklahoma St	Paul Carey, Stanford, RF
1988	Stanford	Mark Marquess	9–4	Arizona St	Lee Plemel, Stanford, P
1989	Wichita St	Gene Stephenson	5–3	Texas	Greg Brummett, Wichita St, P
1990	Georgia	Steve Webber	2–1	Oklahoma St	Mike Rebhan, Georgia, P
1991	Louisiana St	Skip Bertman	6–3	Wichita St	Gary Hymel, Louisiana St, C
1992	Pepperdine	Andy Lopez	3–2	Cal St-Fullerton	Phil Nevin, Cal St-Fullerton, 3B
1993	Louisiana St	Skip Bertman	8–0	Wichita St	Todd Walker, Louisiana St, 2B
1994	Oklahoma	Larry Cochell	13–5	Georgia Tech	Chip Glass, Oklahoma, CF
1995	Cal St-Fullerton*	Augie Garrido	11–5	Southern Cal	Mark Kotsay, Cal St-Fullerton, CF-P
1996	Louisiana St	Skip Bertman	9–8	Miami (FL)	Pat Burrell, Miami (FL), 3B
1997	Louisiana St*	Skip Bertman	13–6	Alabama	Brandon Larson, Louisiana St, SS
1998	Southern Cal	Mike Gillespie	21–14	Arizona St	Wes Rachels, Southern Cal, 2B
1999	Miami (FL)	Jim Morris	6–5	Florida St	Marshall McDougall, FSU 3B/2B
2000	Louisiana St*	Skip Bertman	6–5	Stanford	Trey Hodges, Louisiana St, P
2001	Miami (FL)*	Jim Morris	12–1	Stanford	Charlton Jimerson, Miami (FL), OF
2002	Texas	Augie Garrido	12–6	S Carolina	Huston Street, Texas, P
2003	Rice	Wayne Graham	14–2^	Stanford	John Hudgins, Stanford, P
2004	Cal St-Fullerton	George Horton	3–2^	Texas	Jason Windsor, Cal St-Fullerton, P

*Undefeated teams in College World Series play. †12 innings. ‡10 innings. #15 innings. ^Score of decisive game of best-of-three series.

DIVISION II

Year	Champion	Year	Champion	Year	Champion
1968	Chapman*	1972	Florida Southern	1976	Cal Poly–Pomona
1969	Illinois St*	1973	UC–Irvine*	1977	UC–Riverside
1970	Cal St-Northridge	1974	UC–Irvine	1978	Florida Southern
1971	Florida Southern	1975	Florida Southern	1979	Valdosta St

Baseball (Cont.)

DIVISION II (Cont.)

Year	Champion	Year	Champion	Year	Champion
1980	Cal Poly–Pomona*	1990	Jacksonville St	1999	Cal St–Chico
1981	Florida Southern*	1991	Jacksonville St	2000	SE Oklahoma St
1982	UC–Riverside*	1992	Tampa*	2001	St. Mary's (TX)
1983	Cal Poly–Pomona*	1993	Tampa	2002	Columbus St
1984	Cal St–Northridge	1994	Central Missouri St	2003	Central Missouri St
1985	Florida Southern*	1995	Florida Southern*	2004	Kennesaw St
1986	Troy St	1996	Kennesaw St*		
1987	Troy St*	1997	Cal St–Chico*		
1988	Florida Southern*	1998	Tampa*		
1989	Cal Poly–SLO				

DIVISION III

Year	Champion	Year	Champion	Year	Champion
1976	Cal St–Stanislaus	1986	Marietta	1996	William Paterson
1977	Cal St–Stanislaus	1987	Montclair St	1997	Southern Maine
1978	Glassboro St	1988	Ithaca	1998	Eastern Connecticut St
1979	Glassboro St	1989	NC Wesleyan	1999	N Carolina Wesleyan
1980	Ithaca	1990	Eastern Connecticut St	2000	Montclair St
1981	Marietta	1991	Southern Maine	2001	St. Thomas (MN)
1982	Eastern Connecticut St	1992	William Paterson	2002	Eastern Connecticut St
1983	Marietta	1993	Montclair St	2003	Chapman
1984	Ramapo	1994	WI–Oshkosh	2004	WI–Stevens Pt
1985	WI–Oshkosh	1995	La Verne		

*Undefeated teams in final series.

Cross-Country

Men
DIVISION I

Year	Champion	Coach	Pts	Runner-Up	Pts	Individual Champion	Time
1938	Indiana	Earle Hayes	51	Notre Dame	61	Greg Rice, Notre Dame	20:12.9
1939	Michigan St	Lauren Brown	54	Wisconsin	57	Walter Mehl, Wisconsin	20:30.9
1940	Indiana	Earle Hayes	65	Eastern Michigan	68	Gilbert Dodds, Ashland	20:30.2
1941	Rhode Island	Fred Tootell	83	Penn St	110	Fred Wilt, Indiana	20:30.1
1942	Indiana	Earle Hayes	57			Oliver Hunter, Notre Dame	20:18.0
	Penn St	Charles Werner	57				
1943	No meet						
1944	Drake	Bill Easton	25	Notre Dame	64	Fred Feiler, Drake	21:04.2
1945	Drake	Bill Easton	50	Notre Dame	65	Fred Feiler, Drake	21:14.2
1946	Drake	Bill Easton	42	NYU	98	Quentin Brelsford, Ohio Wesleyan	20:22.9
1947	Penn St	Charles Werner	60	Syracuse	72	Jack Milne, N Carolina	20:41.1
1948	Michigan St	Karl Schlademan	41	Wisconsin	69	Robert Black, Rhode Island	19:52.3
1949	Michigan St	Karl Schlademan	59	Syracuse	81	Robert Black, Rhode Island	20:25.7
1950	Penn St	Charles Werner	53	Michigan St	55	Herb Semper Jr, Kansas	20:31.7
1951	Syracuse	Robert Grieve	80	Kansas	118	Herb Semper Jr, Kansas	20:09.5
1952	Michigan St	Karl Schlademan	65	Indiana	68	Charles Capozzoli, Georgetown	19:36.7
1953	Kansas	Bill Easton	70	Indiana	82	Wes Santee, Kansas	19:43.5
1954	Oklahoma St	Ralph Higgins	61	Syracuse	118	Allen Frame, Kansas	19:54.2
1955	Michigan St	Karl Schlademan	46	Kansas	68	Charles Jones, Iowa	19:57.4
1956	Michigan St	Karl Schlademan	28	Kansas	88	Walter McNew, Texas	19:55.7
1957	Notre Dame	Alex Wilson	121	Michigan St	127	Max Truex, Southern Cal	19:12.3
1958	Michigan St	Francis Dittrich	79	Western Michigan	104	Crawford Kennedy, Michigan State	20:07.1
1959	Michigan St	Francis Dittrich	44	Houston	120	Al Lawrence, Houston	20:35.7
1960	Houston	John Morriss	54	Michigan St	80	Al Lawrence, Houston	19:28.2
1961	Oregon St	Sam Bell	68	San Jose St	82	Dale Story, Oregon St	19:46.6
1962	San Jose St	Dean Miller	58	Villanova	69	Tom O'Hara, Loyola (IL)	19:20.3
1963	San Jose St	Dean Miller	53	Oregon	68	Victor Zwolak, Villanova	19:35.0
1964	W Michigan	George Dales	86	Oregon	116	Elmore Banton, Ohio	20:07.5
1965	W Michigan	George Dales	81	Northwestern	114	John Lawson, Kansas	29:24.0
1966	Villanova	James Elliott	79	Kansas St	155	Gerry Lindgren, Washington St	29:01.4
1967	Villanova	James Elliott	91	Air Force	96	Gerry Lindgren, Washington St	30:45.6
1968	Villanova	James Elliott	78	Stanford	100	Michael Ryan, Air Force	29:16.8
1969	UTEP	Wayne Vandenburg	74	Villanova	88	Gerry Lindgren, Wash St	28:59.2
1970	Villanova	James Elliott	85	Oregon	86	Steve Prefontaine, Oregon	28:00.2

Men (Cont.)
DIVISION I (Cont.)

Year	Champion	Coach	Pts	Runner-Up	Pts	Individual Champion	Time
1971	Oregon	Bill Dellinger	83	Washington St	122	Steve Prefontaine, Oregon	29:14.0
1972	Tennessee	Stan Huntsman	134	E Tennessee St	148	Neil Cusack, E Tenn St	28:23.0
1973	Oregon	Bill Dellinger	89	UTEP	157	Steve Prefontaine, Oregon	28:14.0
1974	Oregon	Bill Dellinger	77	Western Kentucky	110	Nick Rose, Western Ky	29:22.0
1975	UTEP	Ted Banks	88	Washington St	92	Craig Virgin, Illinois	28:23.3
1976	UTEP	Ted Banks	62	Oregon	117	Henry Rono, Washington St	28:06.6
1977	Oregon	Bill Dellinger	100	UTEP	105	Henry Rono, Washington St	28:33.5
1978	UTEP	Ted Banks	56	Oregon	72	Alberto Salazar, Oregon	29:29.7
1979	UTEP	Ted Banks	86	Oregon	93	Henry Rono, Washington St	28:19.6
1980	UTEP	Ted Banks	58	Arkansas	152	Suleiman Nyambui, UTEP	29:04.0
1981	UTEP	Ted Banks	17	Providence	109	Mathews Motshwarateu,UTEP	28:45.6
1982	Wisconsin	Dan McClimon	59	Providence	138	Mark Scrutton, Colorado	30:12.6
1983	Vacated			Wisconsin	164	Zakarie Barie, UTEP	29:20.0
1984	Arkansas	John McDonnell	101	Arizona	111	Ed Eyestone, Brigham Young	29:28.8
1985	Wisconsin	Martin Smith	67	Arkansas	104	Timothy Hacker, Wisconsin	29:17.88
1986	Arkansas	John McDonnell	69	Dartmouth	141	Aaron Ramirez, Arizona	30:27.53
1987	Arkansas	John McDonnell	87	Dartmouth	119	Joe Falcon, Arkansas	29:14.97
1988	Wisconsin	Martin Smith	105	Northern Arizona	160	Robert Kennedy, Indiana	29:20.0
1989	Iowa St	Bill Bergan	54	Oregon	72	John Nuttall, Iowa St	29:30.55
1990	Arkansas	John McDonnell	68	Iowa St	96	Jonah Koech, Iowa St	29:05.0
1991	Arkansas	John McDonnell	52	Iowa St	114	Sean Dollman, Western Ky	30:17.1
1992	Arkansas	John McDonnell	46	Wisconsin	87	Bob Kennedy, Indiana	30:15.3
1993	Arkansas	John McDonnell	31	Brigham Young	153	Josephat Kapkory, Wash St	29:32.4
1994	Iowa St	Bill Bergan	65	Colorado	88	Martin Keino, Arizona	30:08.7
1995	Arkansas	John McDonnell	100	Northern Arizona	142	Godfrey Siamusiye, Arkansas	30:09
1996	Stanford	Vin Lananna	46	Arkansas	74	Godfrey Siamusiye, Arkansas	29:49
1997	Stanford	Vin Lananna	53	Arkansas	56	Mebrahtom Keflezighi, UCLA	28:54
1998	Arkansas	John McDonnell	97	Stanford	114	Adam Goucher, Colorado	29:26
1999	Arkansas	John McDonnell	58	Wisconsin	185	David Kimani, S Alabama	30:06.6
2000	Arkansas	John McDonnell	83	Colorado	94	Keith Kelly, Providence	30:14.5
2001	Colorado	Mark Wetmore	90	Stanford	91	Boaz Cheboiywo, E Michigan	28:47
2002	Stanford	Andrew Gerard	47	Wisconsin	107	Jorge Torres, Colorado	29:04.7
2003	Stanford	Andrew Gerard	24	Wisconsin	124	Dathan Ritzenhein, Colorado	29:14.1

DIVISION II

Year	Champion	Year	Champion	Year	Champion
1958	Northern Illinois	1973	S Dakota St	1989	S Dakota St
1959	S Dakota St	1974	SW Missouri St	1990	Edinboro
1960	Central St (OH)	1975	UC–Irvine	1991	MA–Lowell
1961	Southern Illinois	1976	UC–Irvine	1992	Adams St
1962	Central St (OH)	1977	Eastern Illinois	1993	Adams St
1963	Emporia St	1978	Cal Poly–SLO	1994	Adams St
1964	Kentucky St	1979	Cal Poly–SLO	1995	Western St
1965	San Diego St	1980	Humboldt St	1996	S Dakota St
1966	San Diego St	1981	Millersville	1997	S Dakota
1967	San Diego St	1982	Eastern Washington	1998	Adams St
1968	Eastern Illinois	1983	Cal Poly–Pomona	1999	Western St
1969	Eastern Illinois	1984	SE Missouri St	2000	Western St
1970	Eastern Michigan	1985	S Dakota St	2001	Western St
1971	Cal St–Fullerton	1986	Edinboro	2002	Western St
1972	N Dakota St	1987	Edinboro	2003	Adams St
		1988	Edinboro/ Mankato St		

DIVISION III

Year	Champion	Year	Champion	Year	Champion
1973	Ashland	1984	St. Thomas (MN)	1994	Williams
1974	Mount Union	1985	Luther	1995	Williams
1975	North Central	1986	St. Thomas (MN)	1996	WI–La Crosse
1976	North Central	1987	N Central	1997	N Central
1977	Occidental	1988	WI–Oshkosh	1998	N Central
1978	N Central	1989	WI–Oshkosh	1999	N Central
1979	N Central	1990	WI–Oshkosh	2000	Calvin
1980	Carleton	1991	Rochester	2001	WI–La Crosse
1981	N Central	1992	N Central	2002	WI–Oshkosh
1982	N Central	1993	N Central	2003	Calvin
1983	Brandeis				

Women
DIVISION I

Year	Champion	Coach	Pts	Runner-Up	Pts	Individual Champion	Time
1981	Virginia	John Vasvary	36	Oregon	83	Betty Springs, N Carolina St	16:19.0
1982	Virginia	Martin Smith	48	Stanford	91	Lesley Welch, Virginia	16:39.7
1983	Oregon	Tom Heinonen	95	Stanford	98	Betty Springs, N Carolina St	16:30.7
1984	Wisconsin	Peter Tegen	63	Stanford	89	Cathy Branta, Wisconsin	16:15.6
1985	Wisconsin	Peter Tegen	58	Iowa St	98	Suzie Tuffey, N Carolina St	16:22.5
1986	Texas	Terry Crawford	62	Wisconsin	64	Angela Chalmers, N Arizona	16:55.49
1987	Oregon	Tom Heinonen	97	N Carolina St	99	Kimberly Betz, Indiana	16:10.85
1988	Kentucky	Don Weber	75	Oregon	128	Michelle Dekkers, Indiana	16:30.0
1989	Villanova	Marty Stern	99	Kentucky	168	Vicki Huber, Villanova	15:59.86
1990	Villanova	Marty Stern	82	Providence	172	Sonia O'Sullivan, Villanova	16:06.0
1991	Villanova	Marty Stern	85	Arkansas	168	Sonia O'Sullivan, Villanova	16:30.3
1992	Villanova	Marty Stern	123	Arkansas	130	Carole Zajac, Villanova	17:01.9
1993	Villanova	Marty Stern	66	Arkansas	71	Carole Zajac, Villanova	16:40.3
1994	Villanova	John Marshall	75	Michigan	108	Jennifer Rhines, Villanova	16:31.2
1995	Providence	Ray Treacy	88	Colorado	123	Kathy Butler, Wisconsin	16:51
1996	Stanford	Beth Alford-Sullivan	101	Villanova	106	Amy Skieresz, Arizona	17:04
1997	BYU	Patrick Shane	100	Stanford	102	Carrie Tollefson, Villanova	16:58
1998	Villanova	Marcus O'Sullivan	106	BYU	110	Katie McGregor, Michigan	16:47.21
1999	BYU	Patrick Shane	72	Arkansas	125	Erica Palmer, Wisconsin	16:39.50
2000	Colorado	Mark Wetmore	117	Brigham Young	167	Kara Grgas-Wheeler, Colorado	20:30.5
2001	BYU	Patrick Shane	62	N Carolina St	148	Tara Chaplin, Arizona	20:24
2002	BYU	Patrick Shane	85	Stanford	113	Shalane Flanagan	19:36.0
2003	Stanford	Dena Evans	120	Brigham Young	128	Shalane Flanagan	19:30.4

DIVISION II

Year	Champion	Year	Champion	Year	Champion
1981	S Dakota St	1989	Cal Poly–SLO	1997	Adams St
1982	Cal Poly–SLO	1990	Cal Poly–SLO	1998	Adams St
1983	Cal Poly–SLO	1991	Cal Poly–SLO	1999	Adams St
1984	Cal Poly–SLO	1992	Adams St	2000	Western St
1985	Cal Poly–SLO	1993	Adams St	2001	Western St
1986	Cal Poly–SLO	1994	Adams St	2002	Western St
1987	Cal Poly–SLO	1995	Adams St	2003	Adams St
1988	Cal Poly–SLO	1996	Adams St		

DIVISION III

Year	Champion	Year	Champion	Year	Champion
1981	Central (IA)	1988	WI–Oshkosh	1996	WI–Oshkosh
1982	St. Thomas (MN)	1989	Cortland St	1997	Cortland St
1983	WI–La Crosse	1990	Cortland St	1998	Calvin
1984	St. Thomas (MN)	1991	WI–Oshkosh	1999	Calvin
1985	Franklin & Marshall	1992	Cortland St	2000	Middlebury
1986	St. Thomas (MN)	1993	Cortland St	2001	Middlebury
1987	St. Thomas (MN)/	1994	Cortland St	2002	Williams
	WI–Oshkosh	1995	Cortland St	2003	Middlebury

Fencing

Men's and Women's Combined
TEAM CHAMPIONS

Year	Champion	Coach	Pts	Runner-Up	Pts
1990	Penn St	Emmanuil Kaidanov	36	Columbia–Barnard	35
1991	Penn St	Emmanuil Kaidanov	4700	Columbia–Barnard	4200
1992	Columbia–Barnard	G. Kolombatovich/A. Kogler	4150	Penn St	3646
1993	Columbia–Barnard	G. Kolombatovich/A. Kogler	4525	Penn St	4500
1994	Notre Dame	Michael DeCicco	4350	Penn St	4075
1995	Penn St	Emmanuil Kaidanov	440	St. John's (NY)	413
1996	Penn St	Emmanuil Kaidanov	1500	Notre Dame	1190
1997	Penn St	Emmanuil Kaidanov	1530	Notre Dame	1470
1998	Penn St	Emmanuil Kaidanov	149	Notre Dame	147
1999	Penn St	Emmanuil Kaidanov	171	Notre Dame	139
2000	Penn St	Emmanuil Kaidanov	175	Notre Dame	171
2001	St. John's (NY)	Yuri Gelman	180	Penn St	172
2002	Penn St	Emmanuil Kaidanov	195	St. John's (NY)	190
2003	Notre Dame	Janusz Bednarski	182	Penn St	179
2004	Ohio St	Vladimir Nazlymov	194	Penn St	160

Men
TEAM CHAMPIONS

Year	Champion	Coach	Pts	Runner-Up	Pts
1941	Northwestern	Henry Zettleman	28½	Illinois	27
1942	Ohio St	Frank Riebel	34	St. John's (NY)	33½
1943–46	No tournament				

Men (Cont.)
TEAM CHAMPIONS (Cont.)

Year	Champion	Coach	Pts	Runner-Up	Pts
1947	NYU	Martinez Castello	72	Chicago	50½
1948	CCNY	James Montague	30	Navy	28
1949	Army/Rutgers	S. Velarde/D. Cetrulo	63		
1950	Navy	Joseph Fiems	67½	NYU/Rutgers	66½
1951	Columbia	Servando Velarde	69	Pennsylvania	64
1952	Columbia	Servando Velarde	71	NYU	69
1953	Pennsylvania	Lajos Csiszar	94	Navy	86
1954	Columbia	Irving DeKoff	61		
	NYU	Hugo Castello	61		
1955	Columbia	Irving DeKoff	62	Cornell	57
1956	Illinois	Maxwell Garret	90	Columbia	88
1957	NYU	Hugo Castello	65	Columbia	64
1958	Illinois	Maxwell Garret	47	Columbia	43
1959	Navy	Andre Deladrier	72	NYU	65
1960	NYU	Hugo Castello	65	Navy	57
1961	NYU	Hugo Castello	79	Princeton	68
1962	Navy	Andre Deladrier	76	NYU	74
1963	Columbia	Irving DeKoff	55	Navy	50
1964	Princeton	Stan Sieja	81	NYU	79
1965	Columbia	Irving DeKoff	76	NYU	74
1966	NYU	Hugo Castello	5–0	Army	5–2
1967	NYU	Hugo Castello	72	Pennsylvania	64
1968	Columbia	Louis Bankuti	92	NYU	87
1969	Pennsylvania	Lajos Csiszar	54	Harvard	43
1970	NYU	Hugo Castello	71	Columbia	63
1971	NYU/Columbia	Hugo Castello/Louis Bankuti	68		
1972	Detroit	Richard Perry	73	NYU	70
1973	NYU	Hugo Castello	76	Pennsylvania	71
1974	NYU	Hugo Castello	92	Wayne St (MI)	87
1975	Wayne St (MI)	Istvan Danosi	89	Cornell	83
1976	NYU	Herbert Cohen	79	Wayne St (MI)	77
1977	Notre Dame	Michael DeCicco	114*	NYU	114
1978	Notre Dame	Michael DeCicco	121	Pennsylvania	110
1979	Wayne St (MI)	Istvan Danosi	119	Notre Dame	108
1980	Wayne St (MI)	Istvan Danosi	111	Pennsylvania/MIT	106
1981	Pennsylvania	Dave Micahnik	113	Wayne St (MI)	111
1982	Wayne St (MI)	Istvan Danosi	85	Clemson	77
1983	Wayne St (MI)	Aladar Kogler	86	Notre Dame	80
1984	Wayne St (MI)	Gil Pezza	69	Penn St	50
1985	Wayne St (MI)	Gil Pezza	141	Notre Dame	140
1986	Notre Dame	Michael DeCicco	151	Columbia	141
1987	Columbia	George Kolombatovich	86	Pennsylvania	78
1988	Columbia	G. Kolombatovich/A. Kogler	90	Notre Dame	83
1989	Columbia	G. Kolombatovich/A. Kogler	88	Penn St	85

*Tie broken by a fence-off. Note: Beginning in 1990, men's and women's combined teams competed for the national championship. See p. 573.

INDIVIDUAL CHAMPIONS

Foil	Sabre	Épée
1941 Edward McNamara, Northwestern	William Meyer, Dartmouth	G.H. Boland, Illinois
1942 Byron Kreiger, Wayne St (MI)	Andre Deladrier, St. John's (NY)	Ben Burtt, Ohio St
1943–46 No tournament		
1947 Abraham Balk, NYU		Abraham Balk, NYU
1948 Albert Axelrod, CCNY	Oscar Parsons, Temple	William Bryan, Navy
1949 Ralph Tedeschi, Rutgers	James Day, Navy	Richard C. Bowman, Army
1950 Robert Nielsen, Columbia	Alex Treves, Rutgers	Thomas Stuart, Navy
1951 Robert Nielsen, Columbia	Alex Treves, Rutgers	Daniel Chafetz, Columbia
1952 Harold Goldsmith, CCNY	Chamberless Johnston, Princeton	James Wallner, NYU
1953 Ed Nober, Brooklyn	Frank Zimolzak, Navy	Jack Tori, Pennsylvania
1954 Robert Goldman, Pennsylvania	Robert Parmacek, Penn	Henry Kolowrat, Princeton
1955 Herman Velasco, Illinois	Steve Sobel, Columbia	Donald Tadrawski, Notre Dame
1956 Ralph DeMarco, Columbia	Barry Pariser, Columbia	Kinmont Hoitsma, Princeton
1957 Bruce Davis, Wayne St (MI)	Gerald Kaufman, Columbia	James Margolis, Columbia
1958 Bruce Davis, Wayne St (MI)	Bernie Balaban, NYU	Roland Wommack, Navy
1959 Joe Paletta, Navy	Art Schankin, Illinois	Roland Wommack, Navy
1960 Gene Glazer, NYU	Al Morales, Navy	Gil Eisner, NYU
1961 Herbert Cohen, NYU	Mike Desaro, NYU	Jerry Halpern, NYU
1962 Herbert Cohen, NYU	Israel Colon, NYU	Thane Hawkins, Navy
1963 Jay Lustig, Columbia	Barton Nisonson, Columbia	Larry Crum, Navy
	Bela Szentivanyi, Wayne St (MI)	

Men (Cont.)
INDIVIDUAL CHAMPIONS (Cont.)

	Foil	Sabre	Épée
1964	Bill Hicks, Princeton	Craig Bell, Illinois	Paul Pesthy, Rutgers
1965	Joe Nalven, Columbia	Howard Goodman, NYU	Paul Pesthy, Rutgers
1966	Al Davis, NYU	Paul Apostol, NYU	Bernhard Hermann, Iowa
1967	Mike Gaylor, NYU	Todd Makler, Pennsylvania	George Masin, NYU
1968	Gerard Esponda, San Francisco	Todd Makler, Pennsylvania	Don Sieja, Cornell
1969	Anthony Kestler, Columbia	Norman Braslow, Penn	James Wetzler, Pennsylvania
1970	Walter Krause, NYU	Bruce Soriano, Columbia	John Nadas, Case Reserve
1971	Tyrone Simmons, Detroit	Bruce Soriano, Columbia	George Szunyogh, NYU
1972	Tyrone Simmons, Detroit	Bruce Soriano, Columbia	Ernesto Fernandez, Penn
1973	Brooke Makler, Pennsylvania	Peter Westbrock, NYU	Risto Hurme, NYU
1974	Greg Benko, Wayne St (MI)	Steve Danosi, Wayne St (MI)	Risto Hurme, NYU
1975	Greg Benko, Wayne St (MI)	Yuri Rabinovich, Wayne St (MI)	Risto Hurme, NYU
1976	Greg Benko, Wayne St (MI)	Brian Smith, Columbia	Randy Eggleton, Pennsylvania
1977	Pat Gerard, Notre Dame	Mike Sullivan, Notre Dame	Hans Wieselgren, NYU
1978	Ernest Simon, Wayne St (MI)	Mike Sullivan, Notre Dame	Bjorne Vaggo, Notre Dame
1979	Andrew Bonk, Notre Dame	Yuri Rabinovich, Wayne St (MI)	Carlos Songini, Cleveland St
1980	Ernest Simon, Wayne St (MI)	Paul Friedberg, Pennsylvania	Gil Pezza, Wayne St (MI)
1981	Ernest Simon, Wayne St (MI)	Paul Friedberg, Pennsylvania	Gil Pezza, Wayne St (MI)
1982	Alexander Flom, George Mason	Neil Hick, Wayne St (MI)	Peter Schifrin, San Jose St
1983	Demetrios Valsamis, NYU	John Friedberg, N Carolina	Ola Harstrom, Notre Dame
1984	Charles Higgs-Coulthard, Notre Dame	Michael Lofton, NYU	Ettore Bianchi, Wayne St (MI)
1985	Stephan Chauvel, Wayne St (MI)	Michael Lofton, NYU	Ettore Bianchi, Wayne St (MI)
1986	Adam Feldman, Penn St	Michael Lofton, NYU	Chris O'Loughlin, Pennsylvania
1987	William Mindel, Columbia	Michael Lofton, NYU	James O'Neill, Harvard
1988	Marc Kent, Columbia	Robert Cottingham, Columbia	Jon Normile, Columbia
1989	Edward Mufel, Penn St	Peter Cox, Penn St	Jon Normile, Columbia
1990	Nick Bravin, Stanford	David Mandell, Columbia	Jubba Beshin, Notre Dame
1991	Ben Atkins, Columbia	Vitali Nazlimov, Penn St	Marc Oshima, Columbia
1992	Nick Bravin, Stanford	Tom Strzalkowski, Penn St	Harald Bauder, Wayne St
1993	Nick Bravin, Stanford	Tom Strzalkowski, Penn St	Ben Atkins, Columbia
1994	Kwame van Leeuwen, Harvard	Tom Strzalkowski, Penn St	Harald Winkman, Princeton
1995	Sean McClain, Stanford	Paul Palestis, NYU	Mike Gattner, Lawrence
1996	Thorstein Becker, Wayne St (MI)	Maxim Pekarev, Princeton	Jeremy Kahn, Duke
1997	Cliff Bayer, Pennsylvania	Keith Smart, St. John's (NY)	Alden Clarke, Stanford
1998	Ayo Griffin, Yale	Luke LaValle, Penn St	George Hentea, St. John's (NY)
1999	Felix Reichling, Stanford	Keeth Smart, St. John's (NY)	Alex Roytblat St. John's (NY)
2000	Felix Reichling, Stanford	Gabor Szelle, Notre Dame	Daniel Landgren, Penn St
2001	William Jed Dupree, Columbia	Ivan Lee, St. John's (NY)	Soren Thompson, Princeton
2002	Nontapat Panchan, Penn St	Ivan Lee, St. John's (NY)	Arpád Horváth, St. John's (NY)
2003	Nontapat Panchan, Penn St	Adam Crompton, Ohio St	Weston Kelsey, Air Force
2004	Boaz Ellis, Ohio St	Adam Crompton, Ohio St	Arpád Horváth, St. John's (NY)

Women
TEAM CHAMPIONS

Year	Champion	Coach	Rec	Runner-Up	Rec
1982	Wayne St (MI)	Istvan Danosi	7–0	San Jose St	6–1
1983	Penn St	Beth Alphin	5–0	Wayne St (MI)	3–2
1984	Yale	Henry Harutunian	3–0	Penn St	2–1
1985	Yale	Henry Harutunian	3–0	Pennsylvania	2–1
1986	Pennsylvania	David Micahnik	3–0	Notre Dame	2–1
1987	Notre Dame	Yves Auriol	3–0	Temple	2–1
1988	Wayne St (MI)	Gil Pezza	3–0	Notre Dame	2–1
1989	Wayne St (MI)	Gil Pezza	3–0	Columbia-Barnard	2–1

Note: Beginning in 1990, men's and women's combined teams competed for the national championship. See p. 573.

INDIVIDUAL CHAMPIONS

	Foil		Foil (Cont.)		Sabre (Cont.)
1982	Joy Ellingson, San Jose St	1996	Olga Kalinovskaya, Penn St	2004	Valerie Providenza, ND

Foil

	Foil
1982	Joy Ellingson, San Jose St
1983	Jana Angelakis, Penn St
1984	Mary Jane O'Neill, Penn
1985	C. Bilodeaux, Columbia-Barn.
1986	M. Sullivan, Notre Dame
1987	C. Bilodeaux, Columbia-Barn.
1988	M. Sullivan, Notre Dame
1989	Yasemin Topcu, Wayne St (MI)
1990	Tzu Moy, Columbia-Barn.
1991	Heidi Piper, Notre Dame
1992	Olga Cheryak, Penn St
1993	Olga Kalinovskaya, Penn St
1994	Olga Kalinovskaya, Penn St
1995	Olga Kalinovskaya, Penn St

Foil (Cont.)

	Foil (Cont.)
1996	Olga Kalinovskaya, Penn St
1997	Yelena Kalkina, Ohio St
1998	F. Zimmermann, Stanford
1999	Monique DeBruin, Stanford
2000	Eva Petschnigg, Princeton
2001	Iris Zimmerman, Stanford
2002	Alicja Kryczalo, Notre Dame
2003	Alicja Kryczalo, Notre Dame
2004	Alicja Kryczalo, Notre Dame

Sabre

	Sabre
2000	Caroline Purcell, MIT
2001	Sada Jacobson, Yale
2002	Sada Jacobson, Yale
2003	Alexis Jemal, Rutgers

Sabre (Cont.)

	Sabre (Cont.)
2004	Valerie Providenza, ND

Épée

	Épée
1995	Tina Loven, St. John's (NY)
1996	N. Dygert, St. John's (NY)
1997	Magda Krol, Notre Dame
1998	Charlotte Walker, Penn St
1999	F. Zimmermann, Stanford
2000	Jessica Burke, Penn St
2001	E. Takács, St. John's (NY)
2002	Stephanie Eim, Penn St
2003	Katarzyna Trzopek, Penn St
2004	Anna Garina, Wayne St

Field Hockey

DIVISION I

Year	Champion	Coach	Score	Runner-Up
1981	Connecticut	Diane Wright	4–1	Massachusetts
1982	Old Dominion	Beth Anders	3–2	Connecticut
1983	Old Dominion	Beth Anders	3–1 (3 OT)	Connecticut
1984	Old Dominion	Beth Anders	5–1	Iowa
1985	Connecticut	Diane Wright	3–2	Old Dominion
1986	Iowa	Judith Davidson	2–1 (2 OT)	New Hampshire
1987	Maryland	Sue Tyler	2–1 (OT)	N Carolina
1988	Old Dominion	Beth Anders	2–1	Iowa
1989	N Carolina	Karen Shelton	2–1 (3 OT)*	Old Dominion
1990	Old Dominion	Beth Anders	5–0	N Carolina
1991	Old Dominion	Beth Anders	2–0	N Carolina
1992	Old Dominion	Beth Anders	4–0	Iowa
1993	Maryland	Missy Meharg	2–1 (3 OT)*	N Carolina
1994	James Madison	Christy Morgan	2–1 (3 OT)*	N Carolina
1995	N Carolina	Karen Shelton-Scroggs	5–1	Maryland
1996	N Carolina	Karen Shelton-Scroggs	3–0	Princeton
1997	N Carolina	Karen Shelton	3–2	Old Dominion
1998	Old Dominion	Beth Anders	3–2	Princeton
1999	Maryland	Missy Meharg	2–1	Michigan
2000	Old Dominion	Beth Anders	3–1	N Carolina
2001	Michigan	Marcia Pankratz	2–0	Maryland
2002	Wake Forest	Jennifer Averill	2–0	Penn St
2003	Wake Forest	Jennifer Averill	3–1	Duke

*Penalty strokes.

DIVISION II (Discontinued, then renewed)

Year	Champion	Coach	Score	Runner-Up
1981	Pfeiffer	Ellen Briggs	5–3	Bentley
1982	Lock Haven	Sharon E. Taylor	4–1	Bloomsburg
1983	Bloomsburg	Jan Hutchinson	1–0	Lock Haven
1992	Lock Haven	Sharon E. Taylor	3–1	Bloomsburg
1993	Bloomsburg	Jan Hutchinson	2–1 (2 OT)	Lock Haven
1994	Lock Haven	Sharon E. Taylor	2–1	Bloomsburg
1995	Lock Haven	Sharon E. Taylor	1–0	Bloomsburg
1996	Bloomsburg	Jan Hutchinson	1–0	Lock Haven
1997	Bloomsburg	Jan Hutchinson	2–0	Kutztown
1998	Bloomsburg	Jan Hutchinson	4–3 (OT)	Lock Haven
1999	Bloomsburg	Jan Hutchinson	2–0	Bentley
2000	Lock Haven	Pat Rudy	2–0	Bentley
2001	Bentley	Kell McGowan	4–2	E Stroudsburg
2002	Bloomsburg	Jan Hutchinson	5–0	Bentley
2003	Bloomsburg	Jan Hutchinson	4–1	UMass–Lowell

DIVISION III

Year	Champion	Year	Champion	Year	Champion
1981	Trenton St	1989	Lock Haven	1997	William Smith
1982	Ithaca	1990	Trenton St	1998	Middelbury
1983	Trenton St	1991	Trenton St	1999	College of New Jersey*
1984	Bloomsburg	1992	William Smith	2000	William Smith
1985	Trenton St	1993	Cortland St	2001	Cortland St
1986	Salisbury St	1994	Cortland St	2002	Rowan
1987	Bloomsburg	1995	Trenton St	2003	Salisbury
1988	Trenton St	1996	College of New Jersey*		*Formerly Trenton St.

Golf

Men

DIVISION I

Results, 1897–1938

Year	Champion	Site	Individual Champion
1897	Yale	Ardsley Casino	Louis Bayard Jr, Princeton
1898	Harvard (spring)		John Reid Jr, Yale
1898	Yale (fall)		James Curtis, Harvard
1899	Harvard		Percy Pyne, Princeton
1900	No tournament		
1901	Harvard	Atlantic City	H. Lindsley, Harvard
1902	Yale (spring)	Garden City	Charles Hitchcock Jr, Yale
1902	Harvard (fall)	Morris County	Chandler Egan, Harvard
1903	Harvard	Garden City	F.O. Reinhart, Princeton
1904	Harvard	Myopia	A.L. White, Harvard
1905	Yale	Garden City	Robert Abbott, Yale
1906	Yale	Garden City	W.E. Clow Jr, Yale
1907	Yale	Nassau	Ellis Knowles, Yale
1908	Yale	Brae Burn	H.H. Wilder, Harvard
1909	Yale	Apawamis	Albert Seckel, Princeton

Men (Cont.)
DIVISION I (Cont.)
Results, 1897–1938 (Cont.)

Year	Champion	Site	Individual Champion
1910	Yale	Essex County	Robert Hunter, Yale
1911	Yale	Baltusrol	George Stanley, Yale
1912	Yale	Ekwanok	F.C. Davison, Harvard
1913	Yale	Huntingdon Valley	Nathaniel Wheeler, Yale
1914	Princeton	Garden City	Edward Allis, Harvard
1915	Yale	Greenwich	Francis Blossom, Yale
1916	Princeton	Oakmont	J.W. Hubbell, Harvard
1917–18	No tournament		
1919	Princeton	Merion	A.L. Walker Jr, Columbia
1920	Princeton	Nassau	Jess Sweetster, Yale
1921	Dartmouth	Greenwich	Simpson Dean, Princeton
1922	Princeton	Garden City	Pollack Boyd, Dartmouth
1923	Princeton	Siwanoy	Dexter Cummings, Yale
1924	Yale	Greenwich	Dexter Cummings, Yale
1925	Yale	Montclair	Fred Lamprecht, Tulane
1926	Yale	Merion	Fred Lamprecht, Tulane
1927	Princeton	Garden City	Watts Gunn, Georgia Tech
1928	Princeton	Apawamis	Maurice McCarthy, Georgetown
1929	Princeton	Hollywood	Tom Aycock, Yale
1930	Princeton	Oakmont	G.T. Dunlap Jr, Princeton
1931	Yale	Olympia Fields	G.T. Dunlap Jr, Princeton
1932	Yale	Hot Springs	J.W. Fischer, Michigan
1933	Yale	Buffalo	Walter Emery, Oklahoma
1934	Michigan	Cleveland	Charles Yates, Georgia Tech
1935	Michigan	Congressional	Ed White, Texas
1936	Yale	North Shore	Charles Kocsis, Michigan
1937	Princeton	Oakmont	Fred Haas Jr, Louisiana St
1938	Stanford	Louisville	John Burke, Georgetown

Results, 1939–2004

Year	Champion (Score)	Coach	Runner-Up (Score)	Host or Site	Individual Champion
1939	Stanford (612)	Eddie Twiggs	Northwestern (614) Princeton (614)	Wakonda	Vincent D'Antoni, Tulane
1940	Princeton (601) Louisiana St (601)	Walter Bourne Mike Donahue		Ekwanok	Dixon Brooke, Virginia
1941	Stanford (580)	Eddie Twiggs	Louisiana St (599)	Ohio St	Earl Stewart, Louisiana St
1942	Louisiana St (590) Stanford (590)	Mike Donahue Eddie Twiggs		Notre Dame	Frank Tatum Jr, Stanford
1943	Yale (614)	William Neale Jr	Michigan (618)	Olympia Fields	Wallace Ulrich, Carleton
1944	Notre Dame (311)	George Holderith	Minnesota (312)	Inverness	Louis Lick, Minnesota
1945	Ohio St (602)	Robert Kepler	Northwestern (621)	Ohio St	John Lorms, Ohio St
1946	Stanford (619)	Eddie Twiggs	Michigan (624)	Princeton	George Hamer, Georgia
1947	Louisiana St (606)	T.P. Heard	Duke (614)	Michigan	Dave Barclay, Michigan
1948	San Jose St (579)	Wilbur Hubbard	Louisiana St (588)	Stanford	Bob Harris, San Jose St
1949	N Texas (590)	Fred Cobb	Purdue (600) Texas (600)	Iowa St	Harvie Ward, N Carolina.
1950	N Texas (573)	Fred Cobb	Purdue (577)	New Mexico	Fred Wampler, Purdue
1951	N Texas (588)	Fred Cobb	Ohio St (589)	Ohio St	Tom Nieporte, Ohio St
1952	N Texas (587)	Fred Cobb	Michigan (593)	Purdue	Jim Vickers, Oklahoma
1953	Stanford (578)	Charles Finger	N Carolina (580)	Broadmoor	Earl Moeller, Oklahoma St
1954	SMU (572)	Graham Ross	N Texas (573)	Houston Hillman Robbins, Memphis St	
1955	Louisiana St (574)	Mike Barbato	N Texas (583)	Tennessee	Joe Campbell, Purdue
1956	Houston (601)	Dave Williams	N Texas (602) Purdue (602)	Ohio St	Rick Jones, Ohio St
1957	Houston (602)	Dave Williams	Stanford (603)	Broadmoor	Rex Baxter Jr., Houston
1958	Houston (570)	Dave Williams	Oklahoma St (582)	Williams	Phil Rodgers, Houston
1959	Houston (561)	Dave Williams	Purdue (571)	Oregon	Dick Crawford, Houston
1960	Houston (603)	Dave Williams	Purdue (607) Oklahoma St (607)	Broadmoor	Dick Crawford, Houston
1961	Purdue (584)	Sam Voinoff	Arizona St (595)	Lafayette	Jack Nicklaus, Ohio St
1962	Houston (588)	Dave Williams	Oklahoma St (598)	Duke	Kermit Zarley, Houston
1963	Oklahoma St (581)	Labron Harris	Houston (582)	Wichita St	R.H. Sikes, Arkansas
1964	Houston (580)	Dave Williams	Oklahoma St (587)	Broadmoor	Terry Small, San Jose St
1965	Houston (577)	Dave Williams	Cal St–LA (582)	Tennessee	Marty Fleckman, Houston
1966	Houston (582)	Dave Williams	San Jose St (586)	Stanford	Bob Murphy, Florida
1967	Houston (585)	Dave Williams	Florida (588)	Shawnee, PA	Hale Irwin, Colorado

Men (Cont.)
DIVISION I (Cont.)
Results, 1939–2004 (Cont.)

Year	Champion (Score)	Coach	Runner-Up (Score)	Host or Site	Individual Champion
1968	Florida (1154)	Buster Bishop	Houston (1156)	New Mexico St	Grier Jones, Oklahoma St
1969	Houston (1223)	Dave Williams	Wake Forest (1232)	Broadmoor	Bob Clark, Cal St–LA
1970	Houston (1172)	Dave Williams	Wake Forest (1182)	Ohio St	John Mahaffey, Houston
1971	Texas (1144)	George Hannon	Houston (1151)	Arizona	Ben Crenshaw, Texas
1972	Texas (1146)	George Hannon	Houston (1159)	Cape Coral	Ben Crenshaw, Texas
					Tom Kite, Texas
1973	Florida (1149)	Buster Bishop	Oklahoma St (1159)	Oklahoma St	Ben Crenshaw, Texas
1974	Wake Forest (1158)	Jess Haddock	Florida (1160)	San Diego St	Curtis Strange, Wake Forest
1975	Wake Forest (1156)	Jess Haddock	Oklahoma St (1189)	Ohio St	Jay Haas, Wake Forest
1976	Oklahoma St (1166)	Mike Holder	Brigham Young (1173)	New Mexico	Scott Simpson, USC
1977	Houston (1197)	Dave Williams	Oklahoma St (1205)	Colgate	Scott Simpson, USC
1978	Oklahoma St (1140)	Mike Holder	Georgia (1157)	Oregon	David Edwards, Oklahoma St
1979	Ohio St (1189)	James Brown	Oklahoma St (1191)	Wake Forest	Gary Hallberg, Wake Forest
1980	Oklahoma St (1173)	Mike Holder	Brigham Young (1177)	Ohio St	Jay Don Blake, Utah St
1981	BYU (1161)	Karl Tucker	Oral Roberts (1163)	Stanford	Ron Commans, USC
1982	Houston (1141)	Dave Williams	Oklahoma St (1151)	Pinehurst	Billy Ray Brown, Houston
1983	Oklahoma St (1161)	Mike Holder	Texas (1168)	Fresno St	Jim Carter, Arizona St
1984	Houston (1145)	Dave Williams	Oklahoma St (1146)	Houston	John Inman, N Carolina
1985	Houston (1172)	Dave Williams	Oklahoma St (1175)	Florida	Clark Burroughs, Ohio St
1986	Wake Forest (1156)	Jess Haddock	Oklahoma St (1160)	Wake Forest	Scott Verplank, Oklahoma St
1987	Oklahoma St (1160)	Mike Holder	Wake Forest (1176)	Ohio St	Brian Watts, Oklahoma St
1988	UCLA (1176)	Eddie Merrins	UTEP (1179)	Southern Cal	E.J. Pfister, Oklahoma St
			Oklahoma (1179)		
			Oklahoma St (1179)		
1989	Oklahoma (1139)	Gregg Grost	Texas (1158)	Oklahoma	Phil Mickelson, Arizona St
				Oklahoma St	
1990	Arizona St (1155)	Steve Loy	Florida (1157)	Florida	Phil Mickelson, Arizona St
1991	Oklahoma (1161)	Mike Holder	N Carolina (1168)	San Jose St	Warren Schutte, UNLV
1992	Arizona (1129)	Rick LaRose	Arizona St (1136)	New Mexico	Phil Mickelson, Arizona St
1993	Florida (1145)	Buddy Alexander	Georgia Tech (1146)	Kentucky	Todd Demsey, Arizona St
1994	Stanford (1129)	Wally Goodwin	Texas (1133)	McKinney, TX	Justin Leonard, Texas
1995	Oklahoma St* (1156)	Mike Holder	Stanford (1156)	Ohio St	Chip Spratlin, Auburn
1996	Arizona St (1186)	Randy Lein	UNLV (1189)	Chattanooga	Tiger Woods, Stanford
1997	Pepperdine (1148)	John Geiberger	Wake Forest (1151)	Evanston, IL	Charles Warren, Clemson
1998	UNLV (1118)	Dwaine Knight	Clemson (1121)	Albuquerque	James McLean, Minnesota
1999	Georgia (1180)	Chris Haack	Oklahoma St (1183)	Chaska, MN	Donald Luke, Northwestern
2000	Oklahoma St* (1116)	Mike Holder	Georgia Tech (1116)	Opelika, AL	Charles Howell, Oklahoma St
2001	Florida (1126)	Buddy Alexander	Clemson (1144)	Durham, NC	Nick Gilliam, Florida
2002	Minnesota (1134)	Brad James	Georgia Tech	Ohio St	Troy Matteson, Ga. Tech
2003	Clemson (1191)	Larry Penley	Oklahoma St	Oklahoma St	A. Canizares, Arizona St
2004	California (1134)	Steve Desimone	UCLA (1140)	Hot Springs, Va	Ryan Moore, UNLV

*Won sudden death playoff. Notes: Match play, 1897–1964; par-70 tournaments held in 1969, 1973 and 1989; par-71 tournaments held in 1968, 1981 and 1988; all other championships par-72 tournaments. Scores are based on 4 rounds instead of 2 after 1967.

DIVISION II

Year	Champion	Year	Champion	Year	Champion
1963	SW Missouri St	1977	Troy St	1991	Florida Southern
1964	Southern Illinois	1978	Columbus St	1992	Columbus St
1965	Middle Tennessee St	1979	UC–Davis	1993	Abilene Christian
1966	Cal St–Chico	1980	Columbus St	1994	Columbus St
1967	Lamar	1981	Florida Southern	1995	Florida Southern
1968	Lamar	1982	Florida Southern	1996	Florida Southern
1969	Cal St–Northridge	1983	SW Texas St	1997	Columbus St
1970	Rollins	1984	Troy St	1998	Florida Southern
1971	New Orleans	1985	Florida Southern	1999	Florida Southern
1972	New Orleans	1986	Florida Southern	2000	Florida Southern
1973	Cal St–Northridge	1987	Tampa	2001	W Florida
1974	Cal St–Northridge	1988	Tampa	2002	Rollins
1975	UC–Irvine	1989	Columbus St	2003	Francis Marion
1976	Troy St	1990	Florida Southern	2004	S Carolina–Aiken

Note: Par-71 tournaments held in 1967, 1970, 1976–78, 1985, 1988 and 2001; par-70 tournament held in 1996; all other championships par-72 tournaments.

Men (Cont.)

DIVISION III

Year	Champion	Year	Champion	Year	Champion
1975	Wooster	1985	Cal St–Stanislaus	1995	Methodist (NC)
1976	Cal St–Stanislaus	1986	Cal St–Stanislaus	1996	Methodist (NC)
1977	Cal St–Stanislaus	1987	Cal St–Stanislaus	1997	Methodist (NC)
1978	Cal St–Stanislaus	1988	Cal St–Stanislaus	1998	Methodist (NC)
1979	Cal St–Stanislaus	1989	Cal St–Stanislaus	1999	Methodist (NC)
1980	Cal St–Stanislaus	1990	Methodist (NC)	2000	Greensboro
1981	Cal St–Stanislaus	1991	Methodist (NC)	2001	WI–Eau Claire
1982	Ramapo	1992	Methodist (NC)	2002	Guilford
1983	Allegheny	1993	UC–San Diego	2003	Averett
1984	Cal St–Stanislaus	1994	Methodist (NC)	2004	Gustavus Adolphus

Note: All championships par-72 except for 1986, 1988 and 2001, which were par-71; fourth round of 1975 championships canceled as a result of bad weather; first round of 1988 championships canceled as a result of rain.

Women

DIVISION I

Year	Champion	Coach	Score	Runner-Up	Score	Individual Champion
1982	Tulsa	Dale McNamara	1191	Texas Christian	1227	Kathy Baker, Tulsa
1983	Texas Christian	Fred Warren	1193	Tulsa	1196	Penny Hammel, Miami (FL)
1984	Miami (FL)	Lela Cannon	1214	Arizona St	1221	Cindy Schreyer, Georgia
1985	Florida	Mimi Ryan	1218	Tulsa	1233	Danielle Ammaccapane, Arizona St
1986	Florida	Mimi Ryan	1180	Miami (FL)	1188	Page Dunlap, Florida
1987	San Jose St	Mark Gale	1187	Furman	1188	Caroline Keggi, New Mexico
1988	Tulsa	Dale McNamara	1175	Georgia	1182	Melissa McNamara, Tulsa
				Arizona	1182	
1989	San Jose St	Mark Gale	1208	Tulsa	1209	Pat Hurst, San Jose St
1990	Arizona St	Linda Vollstedt	1206	UCLA	1222	Susan Slaughter, Arizona
1991	UCLA*	Jackie Steinmann	1197	San Jose St	1197	Annika Sorenstam, Arizona
1992	San Jose St	Mark Gale	1171	Arizona	1175	Vicki Goetze, Georgia
1993	Arizona St	Linda Vollstedt	1187	Texas	1189	Charlotta Sorenstam, Texas
1994	Arizona St	Linda Vollstedt	1189	Southern Cal	1205	Emilee Klein, Arizona St
1995	Arizona St	Linda Vollstedt	1155	San Jose St	1181	Kristel Mourgue d'Algue, Arizona St
1996	Arizona*	Rick LaRose	1240	San Jose St	1240	Marisa Baena, Arizona
1997	Arizona St	Linda Vollstedt	1178	San Jose St	1180	Heather Bowie, Texas
1998	Arizona St	Linda Vollstedt	1155	Florida	1173	Jennifer Rosales, USC
1999	Duke	Dan Brooks	895	Arizona St/Georgia	903	Grace Park, Arizona St
2000	Arizona	Todd McCorkle	1175	Stanford	1196	Jenna Daniels, Arizona
2001	Georgia	Todd McCorkle	1176	Duke	1179	Candy Hannemann, Duke
2002	Duke	Dan Brooks	1164	Arizona/Auburn/Texas	1160	Virada Nirapathpongporn, Duke
2003	Southern Cal	Andrea Gaston	1197	Pepperdine	1212	Mikaela Parmlid, Southern Cal
2004	UCLA	Carrie Forsyth	1148	Oklahoma St	1151	Sarah Huarte, California

*Won sudden death playoff. Note: Par-74 tournaments held in 1983 and 1988; par-72 tournament held in 1990, 2000 and 2001; all other championships par-73 tournaments.

DIVISIONS II AND III

Year	Champion	Year	Champion
1996	Methodist (NC)	1998	Methodist (NC)
1997	Lynn	1999	Methodist (NC)

DIVISION II		DIVISION III	
Year	Champion	Year	Champion
2000	Florida Southern	2000	Methodist (NC)
2001	Florida Southern	2001	Methodist (NC)
2002	Florida Southern	2002	Methodist (NC)
2003	Rollins (FL)	2003	Methodist (NC)
2004	Rollins (FL)	2004	Methodist (NC)

Men
TEAM CHAMPIONS

Year	Champion	Coach	Pts	Runner-Up	Pts
1938	Chicago	Dan Hoffer	22	Illinois	18
1939	Illinois	Hartley Price	21	Army	17
1940	Illinois	Hartley Price	20	Navy	17
1941	Illinois	Hartley Price	68.5	Minnesota	52.5
1942	Illinois	Hartley Price	39	Penn St	30
1943–47	No tournament				
1948	Penn St	Gene Wettstone	55	Temple	34.5
1949	Temple	Max Younger	28	Minnesota	18
1950	Illinois	Charley Pond	26	Temple	25
1951	Florida St	Hartley Price	26	Illinois/ Southern Cal	23.5
1952	Florida St	Hartley Price	89.5	Southern Cal	75
1953	Penn St	Gene Wettstone	91.5	Illinois	68
1954	Penn St	Gene Wettstone	137	Illinois	68
1955	Illinois	Charley Pond	82	Penn St	69
1956	Illinois	Charley Pond	123.5	Penn St	67.5
1957	Penn St	Gene Wettstone	88.5	Illinois	80
1958	Michigan St	George Szypula	79		
	Illinois	Charley Pond	79		
1959	Penn St	Gene Wettstone	152	Illinois	87.5
1960	Penn St	Gene Wettstone	112.5	Southern Cal	65.5
1961	Penn St	Gene Wettstone	88.5	Southern Illinois	80.5
1962	Southern Cal	Jack Beckner	95.5	Southern Illinois	75
1963	Michigan	Newton Loken	129	Southern Illinois	73
1964	Southern Illinois	Bill Meade	84.5	Southern Cal	69.5
1965	Penn St	Gene Wettstone	68.5	Washington	51.5
1966	Southern Illinois	Bill Meade	187.200	California	185.100
1967	Southern Illinois	Bill Meade	189.550	Michigan	187.400
1968	California	Hal Frey	188.250	Southern Illinois	188.150
1969	Iowa	Mike Jacobson	161.175	Penn St	160.450
	Michigan*	Newton Loken		Colorado St	
1970	Michigan	Newton Loken	164.150	Iowa St	164.050
				New Mexico St	
1971	Iowa St	Ed Gagnier	319.075	Southern Illinois	316.650
1972	Southern Illinois	Bill Meade	315.925	Iowa St	312.325
1973	Iowa St	Ed Gagnier	325.150	Penn St	323.025
1974	Iowa St	Ed Gagnier	326.100	Arizona St	322.050
1975	California	Hal Frey	437.325	Louisiana St	433.700
1976	Penn St	Gene Wettstone	432.075	Louisiana St	425.125
1977	Indiana St	Roger Counsil	434.475		
	Oklahoma	Paul Ziert	434.475		
1978	Oklahoma	Paul Ziert	439.350	Arizona St	437.075
1979	Nebraska	Francis Allen	448.275	Oklahoma	446.625
1980	Nebraska	Francis Allen	563.300	Iowa St	557.650
1981	Nebraska	Francis Allen	284.600	Oklahoma	281.950
1982	Nebraska	Francis Allen	285.500	UCLA	281.050
1983	Nebraska	Francis Allen	287.800	UCLA	283.900
1984	UCLA	Art Shurlock	287.300	Penn St	281.250
1985	Ohio St	Michael Willson	285.350	Nebraska	284.550
1986	Arizona St	Don Robinson	283.900	Nebraska	283.600
1987	UCLA	Art Shurlock	285.300	Nebraska	284.750
1988	Nebraska	Francis Allen	288.150	Illinois	287.150
1989	Illinois	Yoshi Hayasaki	283.400	Nebraska	282.300
1990	Nebraska	Francis Allen	287.400	Minnesota	287.300
1991	Oklahoma	Greg Buwick	288.025	Penn St	285.500
1992	Stanford	Sadao Hamada	289.575	Nebraska	288.950
1993	Stanford	Sadao Hamada	276.500	Nebraska	275.500
1994	Nebraska	Francis Allen	288.250	Stanford	285.925
1995	Stanford	Sadao Hamada	232.400	Nebraska	231.525
1996	Ohio St	Peter Kormann	232.150	California	231.775
1997	California	Barry Weiner	233.825	Oklahoma	232.725
1998	Caliornia	Barry Weiner	231.200	Iowa	229.675
1999	Michigan	Kurt Golder	232.550	Ohio St	230.850
2000	Penn St	Randy Jepson	231.975	Michigan	231.850
2001	Ohio St	Miles Avery	218.125	Oklahoma	217.775
2002	Oklahoma	Mark Williams	219.300	Ohio St	218.650
2003	Oklahoma	Mark Williams	222.600	Ohio St	220.700
2004	Penn St	Randy Jepson	223.350	Oklahoma	222.300

*Trampoline.

Men (Cont.)

INDIVIDUAL CHAMPIONS

ALL-AROUND	HORIZONTAL BAR	PARALLEL BARS
1938.....Joe Giallombardo, Illinois	1938.....Bob Sears, Army	1938.....Erwin Beyer, Chicago
1939.....Joe Giallombardo, Illinois	1939.....Adam Walters, Temple	1939.....Bob Sears, Army
1940.....Joe Giallombardo, Illinois	1940.....Norm Boardman, Temple	1940.....Bob Hanning, Minnesota
Paul Fina, Illinois	1941.....Newt Loken, Minnesota	1941.....Caton Cobb, Illinois
1941.....Courtney Shanken, Chicago	1942.....Norm Boardman, Temple	1942.....Hal Zimmerman, Penn St
1942.....Newt Loken, Minnesota	1948.....Joe Calvetti, Illinois	1948.....Ray Sorenson, Penn St
1948.....Ray Sorenson, Penn St	1949.....Bob Stout, Temple	1949.....Joe Kotys, Kent
1949.....Joe Kotys, Kent	1950.....Joe Kotys, Kent	Mel Stout, Michigan St
1950.....Joe Kotys, Kent	1951.....Bill Roetzheim, Florida St	1950.....Joe Kotys, Kent
1951.....Bill Roetzheim, Florida St	1952.....Charles Simms, USC	1951.....Jack Beckner, USC
1952.....Jack Beckner, Southern Cal	1953.....Hal Lewis, Navy	1952.....Jack Beckner, USC
1953.....Jean Cronstedt, Penn St	1954.....Jean Cronstedt, Penn St	1953.....Jean Cronstedt, Penn St
1954.....Jean Cronstedt, Penn St	1955.....Carlton Rintz, Michigan St	1954.....Jean Cronstedt, Penn St
1955.....Karl Schwenzfeier, Penn St	1956.....Ronnie Amster, Florida St	1955.....Carlton Rintz, Michigan St
1956.....Don Tonry, Illinois	1957.....Abie Grossfeld, Illinois	1956.....Armando Vega, Penn St
1957.....Armando Vega, Penn St	1958.....Abie Grossfeld, Illinois	1957.....Armando Vega, Penn St
1958.....Abie Grossfeld, Illinois	1959.....Stanley Tarshis, Mich St	1958.....Tad Muzyczko, Mich St
1959.....Armando Vega, Penn St	1960.....Stanley Tarshis, Mich St	1959.....Armando Vega, Penn St
1960.....Jay Werner, Penn St	1961.....Bruno Klaus, Southern Ill	1960.....Robert Lynn, Southern Cal
1961.....Gregor Weiss, Penn St	1962.....Robert Lynn, USC	1961.....Fred Tijerina, Southern Ill
1962.....Robert Lynn, Southern Cal	1963.....Gil Larose, Michigan	Jeff Cardinalli, Springfield
1963.....Gil Larose, Michigan	1964.....Ron Barak, USC	1962.....Robert Lynn, Southern Cal
1964.....Ron Barak, Southern Cal	1965.....Jim Curzi, Michigan St	1963.....Arno Lascari, Michigan
1965.....Mike Jacobson, Penn St	Mike Jacobsen, Penn St	1964.....Ron Barak, Southern Cal
1966.....Steve Cohen, Penn St	1966.....Rusty Rock, Cal St–	1965.....Jim Curzi, Michigan St
1967.....Steve Cohen, Penn St	Northridge	1966.....Jim Curzi, Michigan St
1968.....Makoto Sakamoto, USC	1967.....Rich Grigsby, Cal St–	1967.....Makoto Sakamoto, USC
1969.....Mauno Nissinen, Wash	Northridge	1968.....Makoto Sakamoto, USC
1970.....Yoshi Hayasaki, Wash	1968.....Makoto Sakamoto, USC	1969.....Ron Rapper, Michigan
1971.....Yoshi Hayasaki, Wash	1969.....Bob Manna, New Mexico	1970.....Ron Rapper, Michigan
1972.....Steve Hug, Stanford	1970.....Yoshi Hayasaki, Wash	1971.....Brent Simmons, Iowa St
1973.....Steve Hug, Stanford	1971.....Brent Simmons, Iowa St	Tom Dunn, Penn St
Marshall Avener, Penn St	1972.....Tom Lindner, Souhern Ill	1972.....Dennis Mazur, Iowa St
1974.....Steve Hug, Stanford	1973.....Jon Aitken, New Mexico	1973.....Steve Hug, Stanford
1975.....Wayne Young, BYU	1974.....Rick Banley, Indiana St	1974.....Steve Hug, Stanford
1976.....Peter Kormann,	1975.....Rich Larsen, Iowa St	1975.....Yoichi Tomita,
Southern Conn St	1976.....Tom Beach, California	Long Beach St
1977.....Kurt Thomas, Indiana St	1977.....John Hart, UCLA	1976.....Gene Whelan, Penn St
1978.....Bart Conner, Oklahoma	1978.....Mel Cooley, Washington	1977.....Kurt Thomas, Indiana St
1979.....Kurt Thomas, Indiana St	1979.....Kurt Thomas, Indiana St	1978.....John Corritore, Michigan
1980.....Jim Hartung, Nebraska	1980.....Philip Cahoy, Nebraska	1979.....Kurt Thomas, Indiana St
1981.....Jim Hartung, Nebraska	1981.....Philip Cahoy, Nebraska	1980.....Philip Cahoy, Nebraska
1982.....Peter Vidmar, UCLA	1982.....Peter Vidmar, UCLA	1981.....Philip Cahoy, Nebraska
1983.....Peter Vidmar, UCLA	1983.....Scott Johnson, Nebraska	Peter Vidmar, UCLA
1984.....Mitch Gaylord, UCLA	1984.....Charles Lakes, Illinois	Jim Hartung, Nebraska
1985.....Wes Suter, Nebraska	1985.....Dan Hayden, Arizona St	1982.....Jim Hartung, Nebraska
1986.....Jon Louis, Stanford	Wes Suter, Nebraska	1983.....Scott Johnson, Nebraska
1987.....Tom Schlesinger, Nebraska	1986.....Dan Hayden, Arizona St	1984.....Tim Daggett, UCLA
1988.....Vacated†	1987.....David Moriel, UCLA	1985.....Dan Hayden, Arizona St
1989.....Patrick Kirsey, Nebraska	1988.....Vacated†	Noah Riskin, Ohio St
1990.....Mike Racanelli, Ohio St	1989.....Vacated†	Seth Riskin, Ohio St
1991.....John Roethlisberger, Minn	1990.....Chris Waller, UCLA	1986.....Dan Hayden, Arizona St
1992.....John Roethlisberger, Minn	1991.....Luis Lopez, New Mexico	1987.....Kevin Davis, Nebraska
1993.....John Roethlisberger, Minn	1992.....Jair Lynch, Stanford	Tom Schlesinger, Nebraska
1994.....Dennis Harrison, Nebraska	1993.....Steve McCain, UCLA	1988.....Kevin Davis, Nebraska
1995.....Richard Grace, Nebraska	1994.....Jim Foody, UCLA	1989.....Vacated†
1996.....Blaine Wilson, Ohio St	1995.....Rick Kieffer, Nebraska	1990.....Patrick Kirksey, Nebraska
1997.....Blaine Wilson, Ohio St	1996.....Carl Imhauser, Temple	1991.....Scott Keswick, UCLA
1998.....Travis Romagnoli, Illinois	1997.....Marshall Nelson,Nebraska	John Roethlisberger, Minn
1999.....Justin Hardabura, Nebraska	1998.....Todd Bishop, Oklahoma	1992.....Dom Minicucci, Temple
2000.....Jamie Natalie, Ohio St	1999.....Todd Bishop, Oklahoma	1993.....Jair Lynch, Stanford
2001.....Jamie Natalie, Ohio St	2000.....Michael Ashe, California	1994....,.Richard Grace, Nebraska
2002.....Raj Bhavsar, Ohio St	2001.....Michael Ashe, California	1995.....Richard Grace, Nebraska
2003.....Daniel Furney, Oklahoma	2002.....Daniel Diaz-Luong, Mich.	1996.....Jamie Ellis, Stanford
2004.....Luis Vargas, Penn St	2003.....Linas Gaveika, Iowa	Blaine Wilson, Ohio St
	2004.....Justin Spring, Illinois	1997.....Marshall Nelson, Nebraska
		1998.....Marshall Nelson, Nebraska

Men (Cont.)
INDIVIDUAL CHAMPIONS (Cont.)

PARALLEL BARS (CONT.)

1999.....Justin Toman, Michigan
2000.....Kris Zimmerman, Michigan
.............Justin Toman, Michigan
2001 ....Raj Bhavsar, Ohio St
2002 ....Cody Moore, California
2003 ....Daniel Furney, Oklahoma
2004 ....Ramon Jackson, Wm & M

VAULT

1938.....Erwin Beyer, Chicago
1939.....Marv Forman, Illinois
1940.....Earl Shanken, Chicago
1941.....Earl Shanken, Chicago
1942.....Earl Shanken, Chicago
1948.....Jim Peterson, Minnesota
1962.....Bruno Klaus, Southern Ill
1963.....Gil Larose, Michigan
1964.....Sidney Oglesby, Syracuse
1965.....Dan Millman, California
1966.....Frank Schmitz, S Illinois
1967.....Paul Mayer, S Illinois
1968.....Bruce Colter, Cal St–LA
1969.....Dan Bowles, California
.............Jack McCarthy, Illinois
1970.....Doug Boger, Arizona
1971.....Pat Mahoney, Cal St–N'rdge
1972.....Gary Morava, Southern Ill
1973.....John Crosby, S Conn St
1974.....Greg Goodhue, Oklahoma
1975.....Tom Beach, California
1976.....Sam Shaw, Cal St-Fullerton
1977.....Steve Wejmar, Wash
1978.....Ron Galimore, Louisiana St
1979.....Leslie Moore, Oklahoma
1980.....Ron Galimore, Iowa St
1981.....Ron Galimore, Iowa St
1982.....Randall Wickstrom, Cal
.............Steve Elliott, Nebraska
1983.....Chris Riegel, Nebraska
.............Mark Oates, Oklahoma
1984.....Chris Riegel, Nebraska
1985.....Derrick Cornelius, Cort. St
1986.....Chad Fox, New Mexico
1987.....Chad Fox, New Mexico
1988.....Chad Fox, New Mexico
1989.....Chad Fox, New Mexico
1990.....Brad Hayashi, UCLA
1991.....Adam Carton, Penn St
1992.....Jason Hebert, Syracuse
1993.....Steve Wiegel, N Mexico
1994.....Steve McCain, UCLA
1995.....Ian Bachrach, Stanford
1996.....Jay Thornton, Iowa
1997.....Blaine Wilson, Ohio St
1998.....Travis Romagnoli, Illinois
1999.....Guard Young, BYU
2000.....Guard Young, BYU
2001.....Daren Lynch, Ohio St
2002.....Dan Gill, Stanford
2003.....Andrew DiGiore, Michigan
2004.....Graham Ackerman, Cal

POMMEL HORSE

1938.....Erwin Beyer, Chicago
1939.....Erwin Beyer, Chicago
1940.....Harry Koehnemann, Illinois
1941.....Caton Cobb, Illinois
1942.....Caton Cobb, Illinois
1948.....Steve Greene, Penn St
1949.....Joe Berenato, Temple
1950.....Gene Rabbitt, Syracuse

POMMEL HORSE (CONT.)

1951.....Joe Kotys, Kent
1952.....Frank Bare, Illinois
1953.....Carlton Rintz, Michigan St
1954.....Robert Lawrence, Penn St
1955.....Carlton Rintz, Michigan St
1956.....James Brown, Cal St–L.A.
1957.....John Davis, Illinois
1958.....Bill Buck, Iowa
1959.....Art Shurlock, California
1960.....James Fairchild, California
1961.....James Fairchild, California
1962.....Mike Aufrecht, Illinois
1963.....Russ Mills, Yale
1964.....Russ Mills, Yale
1965.....Bob Elsinger, Springfield
1966.....Gary Hoskins, Cal St–L.A.
1967.....Keith McCanless, Iowa
1968.....Jack Ryan, Colorado
1969.....Keith McCanless, Iowa
1970.....Russ Hoffman, Iowa St
.............John Russo, Wisconsin
1971.....Russ Hoffman, Iowa St
1972.....Russ Hoffman, Iowa St
1973.....Ed Slezak, Indiana St
1974.....Ted Marcy, Stanford
1975.....Ted Marcy, Stanford
1976.....Ted Marcy, Stanford
1977.....Chuck Walter, New Mexico
1978.....Mike Burke, Northern Ill
1979.....Mike Burke, Northern Ill
1980.....David Stoldt, Illinois
1981.....Mark Bergman, California
.............Steve Jennings, New Mexico
1982 ....Peter Vidmar, UCLA
.............Steve Jennings, New Mexico
1983.....Doug Kieso, Northern Ill
1984.....Tim Daggett, UCLA
1985.....Tony Pineda, UCLA
1986.....Curtis Holdsworth, UCLA
1987.....Li Xiao Ping, Cal St-Fullerton
1988.....Vacated†
.............Mark Sohn, Penn St
1989.....Mark Sohn, Penn St
.............Chris Waller, UCLA
1990.....Mark Sohn, Penn St
1991.....Mark Sohn, Penn St
1992.....Che Bowers, Nebraska
1993.....John Roethlisberger, Minn
1994.....Jason Bertram, California
1995.....Drew Durbin, Ohio St
1996.....Drew Durbin, Ohio St
1997.....Drew Durbin, Ohio St
1998.....Josh Birckelbaw, California
1999.....Brandon Stefaniak, Penn St
2000.....Brandon Stefaniak, Penn St
.............Don Jackson, Iowa
2001.....Clay Strother, Minnesota
2002.....Clay Strother, Minnesota
2003.....Josh Landis, Oklahoma
2004.....Bob Rogers, Illinois

FLOOR EXERCISE

1941 ....Lou Fina, Illinois
1953 ....Bob Sullivan, Illinois
1954 ....Jean Cronstedt, Penn St
1955 ....Don Faber, UCLA
1956 ....Jamile Ashmore, Florida St
1957 ....Norman Marks, Cal St–LA
1958 ....Abie Grossfeld, Illinois
1959 ....Don Tonry, Illinois
1960 ....Ray Hadley, Illinois

FLOOR EXERCISE (CONT.)

1961 .....Robert Lynn, Southern Cal
1962 .....Robert Lynn, Southern Cal
1963 .....Tom Seward, Penn St
.............Mike Henderson, Michigan
1964 .....Rusty Mitchell, S Illinois
1965 .....Frank Schmitz, S Illinois
1966 .....Frank Schmitz, S Illinois
1967 .....Dave Jacobs, Michigan
1968 .....Toby Towson, Michigan St
1969 .....Toby Towson, Michigan St
1970 .....Tom Proulx, Colorado St
1971 ......Stormy Eaton, New Mexico
1972 .....Odessa Lovin, Oklahoma
1973 .....Odessa Lovin, Oklahoma
1974 .....Doug Fitzjarrell, Iowa St
1975 .....Kent Brown, Arizona St
1976 .....Bob Robbins, Colorado St
1977 .....Ron Galimore, Louisiana St
1978 .....Curt Austin, Iowa St
1979 .....Mike Wilson, Oklahoma
.............Bart Conner, Oklahoma
1980 .....Steve Elliott, Nebraska
1981 .....James Yuhashi, Oregon
1982 .....Steve Elliott, Nebraska
1983 .....Scott Johnson, Nebraska
.............David Branch, Arizona St
.............Donnie Hinton, Arizona St
1984 .....Kevin Ekburg, Northern Ill
1985 .....Wes Suter, Nebraska
1986 .....Jerry Burrell, Arizona St
.............Brian Ginsberg, UCLA
1987 .....Chad Fox, New Mexico
1988 .....Chris Wyatt, Temple
1989 .....Jody Newman, Arizona St
1990 .....Mike Racanelli, Ohio St
1991 .....Brad Hayashi, UCLA
1992 .....Brian Winkler, Michigan
1993 .....Richard Grace, Nebraska
1994 .....Mark Booth, Stanford
1995 .....Jay Thornton, Iowa
1996 .....Ian Bachrach, Stanford
1997 .....Jeremy Killen, Oklahoma
1998 .....Darin Gerlach, Temple
1999 ....Jason Hardabura, Nebraska
2000 ....Jamie Natalie, Ohio St
2001 .....Clay Strother, Minnesota
2002 .....Clay Strother, Minnesota
2003 .....Josh Landis, Oklahoma
2004 .....Graham Ackerman, Cal

RINGS

1959 .....Armando Vega, Penn St
1960 .....Sam Garcia, Southern Cal
1961 .....Fred Orlofsky, Southern Ill
1962 .....Dale Cooper, Michigan St
1963 .....Dale Cooper, Michigan St
1964 .....Chris Evans, Arizona St
1965 .....Glenn Gailis, Iowa
1966 .....Ed Gunny, Michigan St
1967 .....Josh Robison, California
1968 .....Pat Arnold, Arizona
1969 .....Paul Vexler, Penn St
.............Ward Maythaler, Iowa St
1970 .....Dave Seal, Indiana St
1971 .....Charles Ropiequet, S Illinois
1972 .....Dave Seal, Indiana St
1973 .....Bob Mahorney, Indiana St
1974 .....Keith Heaver, Iowa St
1975 .....Keith Heaver, Iowa St

Men (Cont.)
INDIVIDUAL CHAMPIONS (Cont.)

RINGS (CONT.)
1976.....Doug Wood, Iowa St
1977.....Doug Wood, Iowa St
1978.....Scott McEldowney, Oregon
1979.....Kirk Mango, Northern Ill
1980.....Jim Hartung, Nebraska
1981.....Jim Hartung, Nebraska
1982.....Jim Hartung, Nebraska
1983.....Alex Schwartz, UCLA
1984.....Tim Daggett, UCLA
1985.....Mark Diab, Iowa St
1986.....Mark Diab, Iowa St
1987.....Paul O'Neill, Hou. Baptist

RINGS (CONT.)
1988.....Paul O'Neill, New Mexico
1989.....Vacated†
        Paul O'Neill, New Mexico
1990.....Wayne Cowden, Penn St
1991.....Adam Carton, Penn St
1992.....Scott Keswick, UCLA
1993.....Chris LaMorte, N Mexico
1994.....Chris LaMorte, N Mexico
1995.....Dave Frank, Temple
1996.....Scott McCall, Will. & Mary
        Blaine Wilson, Ohio St
1997.....Blaine Wilson, Ohio St

RINGS (CONT.)
1998.....Dan Fink, Oklahoma
1999.....Cortney Bramwell, BYU
2000.....Cortney Bramwell, BYU
2001.....Chris Lakeman, Penn St
2002.....Marshall Erwin, Stanford
2003.....Kevin Tan, Penn St
2004.....Kevin Tan, Penn St

†Championships won by Miguel Rubio (All Around, 1988; Horizontal Bar, 1988–89) and Alfonso Rodriguez (Pommel Horse, 1988; Rings, 1989; Parallel Bars, 1989) were vacated by action of the NCAA Committee on Infractions.

DIVISION II (Discontinued)

Year	Champion	Coach	Pts	Runner-Up	Pts
1968	Cal St–Northridge	Bill Vincent	179.400	Springfield	178.050
1969	Cal St–Northridge	Bill Vincent	151.800	Southern Connecticut St	145.075
1970	Northwestern Louisiana	Armando Vega	160.250	Southern Connecticut St	159.300
1971	Cal St–Fullerton	Dick Wolfe	158.150	Springfield	156.987
1972	Cal St–Fullerton	Dick Wolfe	160.550	Southern Connecticut St	153.050
1973	Southern Connecticut St	Abe Grossfeld	160.750	Cal St–Northridge	158.700
1974	Cal St–Fullerton	Dick Wolfe	309.800	Southern Connecticut St	309.400
1975	Southern Connecticut St	Abe Grossfeld	411.650	IL–Chicago	398.800
1976	Southern Connecticut St	Abe Grossfeld	419.200	IL–Chicago	388.850
1977	Springfield	Frank Wolcott	395.950	Cal St–Northridge	381.250
1978	IL–Chicago	C. Johnson/A. Gentile	406.850	Cal St–Northridge	400.400
1979	IL–Chicago	Clarence Johnson	418.550	WI–Oshkosh	385.650
1980	WI–Oshkosh	Ken Allen	260.550	Cal St–Chico	256.050
1981	WI–Oshkosh	Ken Allen	209.500	Springfield	201.550
1982	WI–Oshkosh	Ken Allen	216.050	E Stroudsburg	211.200
1983	E Stroudsburg	Bruno Klaus	258.650	WI–Oshkosh	257.850
1984	E Stroudsburg	Bruno Klaus	270.800	Cortland St	246.350

Women
TEAM CHAMPIONS

Year	Champion	Coach	Pts	Runner-Up	Pts
1982	Utah	Greg Marsden	148.60	Cal St–Fullerton	144.10
1983	Utah	Greg Marsden	184.65	Arizona St	183.30
1984	Utah	Greg Marsden	186.05	UCLA	185.55
1985	Utah	Greg Marsden	188.35	Arizona St	186.60
1986	Utah	Greg Marsden	186.95	Arizona St	186.70
1987	Georgia	Suzanne Yoculan	187.90	Utah	187.55
1988	Alabama	Sarah Patterson	190.05	Utah	189.50
1989	Georgia	Suzanne Yoculan	192.65	UCLA	192.60
1990	Utah	Greg Marsden	194.900	Alabama	194.575
1991	Alabama	Sarah Patterson	195.125	Utah	194.375
1992	Utah	Greg Marsden	195.650	Georgia	194.600
1993	Georgia	Suzanne Yoculan	198.000	Alabama	196.825
1994	Utah	Greg Marsden	196.400	Alabama	196.350
1995	Utah	Greg Marsden	196.650	Alabama	196.425
				Michigan	196.425
1996	Alabama	Sarah Patterson	198.025	UCLA	197.475
1997	UCLA	Valorie Kondos	197.150	Arizona St	196.850
1998	Georgia	Suzanne Yoculan	197.725	Florida	196.350
1999	Georgia	Suzanne Yoculan	196.850	Michigan	196.55
2000	UCLA	Valorie Kondos	197.300	Utah	196.875
2001	UCLA	Valorie Kondos	197.575	Georgia	197.400
2002	Alabama	Sarah Patterson	197.575	Georgia	197.25
2003	UCLA	Valorie Kondos Field	197.825	Alabama	197.275
2004	UCLA	Valorie Kondos Field	198.125	Georgia	197.200

Women (Cont.)
INDIVIDUAL CHAMPIONS

ALL-AROUND

1982.....Sue Stednitz, Utah
1983.....Megan McCunniff, Utah
1984......Megan McCunniff-Marsden, Utah
1985......Penney Hauschild, Alabama
1986......Penney Hauschild, Alabama
      Jackie Brummer, Arizona St
1987.....Kelly Garrison-Steves, Oklahoma
1988.....Kelly Garrison-Steves, Okla
1989.....Corrinne Wright, Georgia
1990.....Dee Dee Foster, Alabama
1991.....Hope Spivey, Georgia
1992.....Missy Marlowe, Utah
1993.....Jenny Hansen, Kentucky
1994.....Jenny Hansen, Kentucky
1995.....Jenny Hansen, Kentucky
1996.....Meredith Willard, Alabama
1997.....Kim Arnold, Georgia
1998.....Kim Arnold, Georgia
1999.....Theresa Kulikowski, Utah
2000.....Mohini Bhardwaj, UCLA
      Heather Brink, Nebraska
2001 ....Onnis Willis, UCLA
      Elise Ray, Michigan
2002 ....Jamie Dantzscher, UCLA
2003 ....Richelle Simpson, Neb.
2004 ....Jeana Rice, Alabama

VAULT

1982.....Elaine Alfano, Utah
1983.....Elaine Alfano, Utah
1984.....Megan Marsden, Utah
1985.....Elaine Alfano, Utah
1986.....Kim Neal, Arizona St
      Pam Loree, Penn St
1987.....Yumi Mordre, Washington
1988.....Jill Andrews, UCLA
1989.....Kim Hamilton, UCLA
1990.....Michele Bryant, Nebraska
1991.....Anna Basaldva, Arizona
1992.....Tammy Marshall, Mass.
      Heather Stepp, Georgia
      Kristein Kenoyer, Utah
1993.....Heather Stepp, Georgia
1994.....Jenny Hansen, Kentucky
1995.....Jenny Hansen, Kentucky
1996.....Leah Brown, Georgia
1997.....Susan Hines, Florida
1998.....Susan Hines, Florida
1999.....Heidi Moneymaker, UCLA
2000.....Heather Brink, Nebraska
2001 ....Cory Fritzinger, Georgia
2002.....Jamie Dantzscher, UCLA

VAULT (Cont.)

2003.....Ashley Miles, Alabama
2004.....Ashley Miles, Alabama

BALANCE BEAM

1982.....Sue Stednitz, Utah
1983.....Julie Goewey, Cal St–Fullerton
1984.....Heidi Anderson, Oregon St
1985.....Lisa Zeis, Arizona St
1986.....Jackie Brummer, Arizona St
1987.....Yumi Mordre, Washington
1988.....Kelly Garrison-Steves, Oklahoma
1989.....Jill Andrews, UCLA
      Joy Selig, Oregon St
1990.....Joy Selig, Oregon St
1991.....Missy Marlowe, Utah
1992.....Missy Marlowe, Utah
1992   Dana Dobransky, Alabama
1993.....Dana Dobransky, Alabama
1994.....Jenny Hansen, Kentucky
1995.....Jenny Hansen, Kentucky
1996.....Summer Reid, UUtah
1997.....Summer Reid, Utah
      Elizabeth Reid, Arizona St
1998   Larissa Fontaine, Stanford
      Susan Hines, Florida
1999.....Theresa Kulikowski, Utah
2000.....Lena Degteva, UCLA
2001.....Theresa Kulikowski, Utah
2002.....Elise Ray, Michigan
2003.....Kate Richardson, UCLA
2004.....Ashley Kelly, Arizona St

FLOOR EXERCISE

1982.....Mary Ayotte-Law, Oregon St
1983.....Kim Neal, Arizona St
1984.....Maria Anz, Florida
1985.....Lisa Mitzel, Utah
1986.....Lisa Zeis, Arizona St
      P. Hauschild, Alabama
1987.....Kim Hamilton, UCLA
1988.....Kim Hamilton, UCLA
1989.....Corrinne Wright, Georgia
      Kim Hamilton, UCLA
1990.....Joy Selig, Oregon St
1991.....Hope Spivey, Georgia
1992.....Missy Marlowe, Utah

FLOOR EXERCISE (Cont.)

1993.....Heather Stepp, Georgia
      Tammy Marshall, Mass.
      Amy Durham, Oregon St
1994......Hope Spivey-Sheeley, UGA
1995.....Jenny Hansen, Kentucky
      Stella Umeh, UCLA
      Leslie Angeles, Georgia
1996.....Heidi Hornbeek, Arizona
      Kim Kelly, Alabama
1997.....Leah Brown, Georgia
1998.....Kim Arnold, Georgia
      Jenni Beathard, Georgia
      Betsy Hamm, Florida
1999.....Marny Oestreng, BGSU
2000.....Suzanne Sears, Georgia
2001.....Mohini Bhardwaj, UCLA
2002.....Jamie Dantzscher, UCLA
      Nicole Arnstad, LSU
2003.....Richelle Simpson, Neb.
2004.....Ashley Miles, Alabama
      Courtney Bumpers, UNC

UNEVEN BARS

1982.....Lisa Shirk, Pittsburgh
1983.....Jeri Cameron, Arizona St
1984.....Jackie Brummer, Arizona St
1985......Penney Hauschild, Alabama
1986.....Lucy Wener, Georgia
1987.....Lucy Wener, Georgia
1988.....Kelly Garrison-Steves, Oklahoma
1989.....Lucy Wener, Georgia
1990.....Marie Roethlisberger, Minnesota
1991.....Kelly Macy, Georgia
1992.....Missy Marlowe, Utah
1993.....Agina Simpkins, Georgia
      Beth Wymer, Michigan
1994.....Sandy Woolsey, Utah
      Beth Wymer, Michigan
      Lori Strong, Georgia
1995.....Beth Wymer, Michigan
1996.....Stephanie Woods, Alabama
1997.....Jenni Beathard, Georgia
1998.....Karin Lichey, Georgia
      Stella Umeh, UCLA
1999.....Angie Leionard, Utah
2000.....Mohini Bhardwaj, UCLA
2001.....Yvonne Tousek, UCLA
2002.....Andree' Pickens, Alabama
2003 ....Jamie Dantzscher, UCLA
      Kate Richardson, UCLA
2004.....Elise Ray, Michigan

Ice Hockey

Men

DIVISION I

Year	Champion	Coach	Score	Runner-Up	Most Outstanding Player
1948	Michigan	Vic Heyliger	8–4	Dartmouth	Joe Riley, Dartmouth, F
1949	Boston College	John Kelley	4–3	Dartmouth	Dick Desmond, Dartmouth, G
1950	Colorado College	Cheddy Thompson	13–4	Boston University	Ralph Bevins, Boston University, G
1951	Michigan	Vic Heyliger	7–1	Brown	Ed Whiston, Brown, G
1952	Michigan	Vic Heyliger	4–1	Colorado College	Kenneth Kinsley, Colorado Coll, G
1953	Michigan	Vic Heyliger	7–3	Minnesota	John Matchefts, Michigan, F
1954	Rensselaer	Ned Harkness	5–4 (OT)	Minnesota	Abbie Moore, Rensselaer, F
1955	Michigan	Vic Heyliger	5–3	Colorado College	Philip Hilton, Colorado College, D
1956	Michigan	Vic Heyliger	7–5	Michigan Tech	Lorne Howes, Michigan, G
1957	Colorado College	Thomas Bedecki	13–6	Michigan	Bob McCusker, Colorado Coll, F
1958	Denver	Murray Armstrong	6–2	N Dakota	Murray Massier, Denver, F
1959	N Dakota	Bob May	4–3 (OT)	Michigan St	Reg Morelli, N Dakota, F
1960	Denver	Murray Armstrong	5–3	Michigan Tech	Bob Marquis, Boston University, F
1961	Denver	Murray Armstrong	12–2	St. Lawrence	Barry Urbanski, Boston Univ, G
1962	Michigan Tech	John MacInnes	7–1	Clarkson	Louis Angotti, Michigan Tech, F
1963	N Dakota	Barney Thorndycraft	6–5	Denver	Al McLean, N Dakota, F
1964	Michigan	Allen Renfrew	6–3	Denver	Bob Gray, Michigan, G
1965	Michigan Tech	John MacInnes	8–2	Boston College	Gary Milroy, Michigan Tech, F
1966	Michigan St	Amo Bessone	6–1	Clarkson	Gaye Cooley, Michigan St, G
1967	Cornell	Ned Harkness	4–1	Boston University	Walt Stanowski, Cornell, D
1968	Denver	Murray Armstrong	4–0	N Dakota	Gerry Powers, Denver, G
1969	Denver	Murray Armstrong	4–3	Cornell	Keith Magnuson, Denver, D
1970	Cornell	Ned Harkness	6–4	Clarkson	Daniel Lodboa, Cornell, D
1971	Boston University	Jack Kelley	4–2	Minnesota	Dan Brady, Boston University, G
1972	Boston University	Jack Kelley	4–0	Cornell	Tim Regan, Boston University, G
1973	Wisconsin	Bob Johnson	4–2	Vacated	Dean Talafous, Wisconsin, F
1974	Minnesota	Herb Brooks	4–2	Michigan Tech	Brad Shelstad, Minnesota, G
1975	Michigan Tech	John MacInnes	6–1	Minnesota	Jim Warden, Michigan Tech, G
1976	Minnesota	Herb Brooks	6–4	Michigan Tech	Tom Vanelli, Minnesota, F
1977	Wisconsin	Bob Johnson	6–5 (OT)	Michigan	Julian Baretta, Wisconsin, G
1978	Boston University	Jack Parker	5–3	Boston College	Jack O'Callahan, Boston Univ, D
1979	Minnesota	Herb Brooks	4–3	N Dakota	Steve Janaszak, Minnesota, G
1980	N Dakota	John Gasparini	5–2	Northern Michigan	Doug Smail, N Dakota, F
1981	Wisconsin	Bob Johnson	6–3	Minnesota	Marc Behrend, Wisconsin, G
1982	N Dakota	John Gasparini	5–2	Wisconsin	Phil Sykes, N Dakota, F
1983	Wisconsin	Jeff Sauer	6–2	Harvard	Marc Behrend, Wisconsin, G
1984	Bowling Green	Jerry York	5–4 (OT)	MN–Duluth	Gary Kruzich, Bowling Green, G
1985	Rensselaer	Mike Addesa	2–1	Providence	Chris Terreri, Providence, G
1986	Michigan St	Ron Mason	6–5	Harvard	Mike Donnelly, Michigan St, F
1987	N Dakota	John Gasparini	5–3	Michigan St	Tony Hrkac, N Dakota, F
1988	Lake Superior St	Frank Anzalone	4–3 (OT)	St. Lawrence	Bruce Hoffort, Lake Superior St, G
1989	Harvard	Bill Cleary	4–3 (OT)	Minnesota	Ted Donato, Harvard, F
1990	Wisconsin	Jeff Sauer	7–3	Colgate	Chris Tancill, Wisconsin, F
1991	N Michigan	Rick Comley	8–7 (3OT)	Boston University	Scott Beattie, N Michigan, F
1992	Lake Superior St	Jeff Jackson	4–2	Wisconsin	Paul Constantin, Lake Superior St, F
1993	Maine	Shawn Walsh	5–4	Lake Superior St	Jim Montgomery, Maine, F
1994	Lake Superior St	Jeff Jackson	9–1	Boston University	Sean Tallaire, Lake Superior St, F
1995	Boston University	Jack Parker	6–2	Maine	Chris O'Sullivan, Boston Univ, F
1996	Michigan	Red Berenson	3–2 (OT)	Colorado College	Brendan Morrison, Michigan, F
1997	N Dakota	Dean Blais	6–4	Boston University	Matt Henderson, N Dakota, F
1998	Michigan	Red Berenson	3–2 (OT)	Boston Coll	Marty Turco, Michigan, G
1999	Maine	Shawn Walsh	3–2 (OT)	New Hampshire	Alfie Michaud, Maine, G
2000	N Dakota	Dean Blais	4–2	Boston College	Lee Goren, N Dakota, F
2001	Boston College	Jerry York	3–2 (OT)	N Dakota	Chuck Kobasew, Boston Coll, F
2002	Minnesota	Don Lucia	4–3 (OT)	Maine	Grant Potulny, Minnesota, F
2003	Minnesota	Don Lucia	5–1	New Hampshire	Thomas Vanek, Minnesota, F
2004	Denver	George Gwozdecky	1–0	Maine	Adam Berkhoel, Denver, G

DIVISION II (*Discontinued*)

Year	Champion	Coach	Score	Runner-Up
1978	Merrimack	Thom Lawler	12–2	Lake Forest
1979	Lowell	Bill Riley Jr	6–4	Mankato St
1980	Mankato St	Don Brose	5–2	Elmira
1981	Lowell	Bill Riley Jr	5–4	Plattsburgh St
1982	Lowell	Bill Riley Jr	6–1	Plattsburgh St
1983	RIT	Brian Mason	4–2	Bemidji St
1984	Bemidji St	R.H. (Bob) Peters	14–4*	Merrimack
1993	Bemidji St	R.H. (Bob) Peters	15–6*	Mercyhurst
1994	Bemidji St	R.H. (Bob) Peters	7–6*	AL–Huntsville
1995	Bemidji St	R.H. (Bob) Peters	11–6*	Mercyhurst

DIVISION II (Cont.)

Year	Champion	Coach	Score	Runner-Up
1996	AL–Huntsville	Doug Ross	10–1*	Bemidji St
1997	Bemidji St	R.H. (Bob) Peters	7–4*	AL–Huntsville
1998	AL–Huntsville	Doug Ross	11–4*	Bemidji St
1999	St. Michael's (VT)	Lou DiMasi	12–9*	New Hamp. Coll

*Two-game, total-goal series.

DIVISION III

Year	Champion	Coach	Score	Runner-Up
1984	Babson	Bob Riley	8–0	Union (NY)
1985	RIT	Bruce Delventhal	5–1	Bemidji St
1986	Bemidji St	R.H. (Bob) Peters	8–5	Vacated
1987	Vacated			Oswego St
1988	WI–River Falls	Rick Kozuback	7–1, 3–5, 3–0	Elmira
1989	WI–Stevens Point	Mark Mazzoleni	3–3, 3–2	RIT
1990	WI–Stevens Point	Mark Mazzoleni	10–1, 3–6, 1–0	Plattsburgh St
1991	WI–Stevens Point	Mark Mazzoleni	6–2	Mankato St
1992	Plattsburgh St	Bob Emery	7–3	WI–Stevens Point
1993	WI–Stevens Point	Joe Baldarotta	4–3	WI–River Falls
1994	WI–River Falls	Dean Talafous	6–4	WI–Superior
1995	Middlebury	Bill Beaney	1–0	Fredonia St
1996	Middlebury	Bill Beaney	3–2	RIT
1997	Middlebury	Bill Beaney	3–2	WI–Superior
1998	Middlebury	Bill Beaney	2–1	WI–Stevens Point
1999	Middlebury	Bill Beaney	5–0	WI–Superior
2000	Norwich	Michael McShane	2–1	St. Thomas (MN)
2001	Plattsburgh	Bob Emery	6–2	RIT
2002	WI–Superior	Dan Stauber	3–2	Norwich
2003	Norwich	Michael McShane	2–1	Oswego St
2004	Middlebury	Bill Beaney	1–0	St. Norbert

Women
DIVISION I

Year	Champion	Coach	Score	Runner-Up
2001	Minnesota-Duluth	Shannon Miller	4–2	St. Lawrence
2002	Minnesota-Duluth	Shannon Miller	3–2	Brown
2003	Minnesota-Duluth	Shannon Miller	4–3 (2 ot)	Harvard
2004	Minnesota	Laura Holldorson	6–2	Harvard

Lacrosse

Men
DIVISION I

Year	Champion	Coach	Score	Runner-Up
1971	Cornell	Richie Moran	12–6	Maryland
1972	Virginia	Glenn Thiel	13–12	Johns Hopkins
1973	Maryland	Bud Beardmore	10–9 (2 OT)	Johns Hopkins
1974	Johns Hopkins	Bob Scott	17–12	Maryland
1975	Maryland	Bud Beardmore	20–13	Navy
1976	Cornell	Richie Moran	16–13 (OT)	Maryland
1977	Cornell	Richie Moran	16–8	Johns Hopkins
1978	Johns Hopkins	Henry Ciccarone	13–8	Cornell
1979	Johns Hopkins	Henry Ciccarone	15–9	Maryland
1980	Johns Hopkins	Henry Ciccarone	9–8 (2 OT)	Virginia
1981	N Carolina	Willie Scroggs	14–13	Johns Hopkins
1982	N Carolina	Willie Scroggs	7–5	Johns Hopkins
1983	Syracuse	Roy Simmons Jr	17–16	Johns Hopkins
1984	Johns Hopkins	Don Zimmerman	13–10	Syracuse
1985	Johns Hopkins	Don Zimmerman	11–4	Syracuse
1986	N Carolina	Willie Scroggs	10–9 (OT)	Virginia
1987	Johns Hopkins	Don Zimmerman	11–10	Cornell
1988	Syracuse	Roy Simmons Jr	13–8	Cornell
1989	Syracuse	Roy Simmons Jr	13–12	Johns Hopkins
1990	Syracuse	Roy Simmons Jr	21–9	Loyola (MD)
1991	N Carolina	Dave Klarmann	18–13	Towson St
1992	Princeton	Bill Tierney	10–9	Syracuse
1993	Syracuse	Roy Simmons Jr	13–12	N Carolina
1994	Princeton	Bill Tierney	9–8 (OT)	Virginia
1995	Syracuse	Roy Simmons Jr	13–9	Maryland
1996	Princeton	Bill Tierney	13–12 (OT)	Virginia
1997	Princeton	Bill Tierney	19–7	Maryland
1998	Princeton	Bill Tierney	15–5	Maryland
1999	Virginia	Dom Starsia	12–10	Syracuse

Men (Cont.)

DIVISION I (Cont.)

Year	Champion	Coach	Score	Runner-Up
2000	Syracuse	John Desko	13–7	Princeton
2001	Princeton	Bill Tierney	10–9 (OT)	Syracuse
2002	Syracuse	John Desko	13–12	Princeton
2003	Virginia	Dom Starsia	9–7	Johns Hopkins
2004	Syracuse	John Desko	14–13	Navy

DIVISION II (Discontinued, then renewed)

Year	Champion	Coach	Score	Runner-Up
1974	Towson St	Carl Runk	18–17 (OT)	Hobart
1975	Cortland St	Chuck Winters	12–11	Hobart
1976	Hobart	Jerry Schmidt	18–9	Adelphi
1977	Hobart	Jerry Schmidt	23–13	Washington (MD)
1978	Roanoke	Paul Griffin	14–13	Hobart
1979	Adelphi	Paul Doherty	17–12	MD–Baltimore County
1980	MD–Baltimore County	Dick Watts	23–14	Adelphi
1981	Adelphi	Paul Doherty	17–14	Loyola (MD)
1993	Adelphi	Kevin Sheehan	11–7	LIU–C.W. Post
1994	Springfield	Keith Bugbee	15–12	New York Tech
1995	Adelphi	Sandy Kapatos	12–10	Springfield
1996	LIU–C.W. Post	Tom Postel	15–10	Adelphi
1997	New York Tech	Jack Kaley	18–11	Adelphi
1998	Adelphi	Sandy Kapatos	18–6	LIU–C.W. Post
1999	Adelphi	Sandy Kapatos	11–8	LIU–C.W. Post
2000	Limestone	Mike Cerino	10–9	LIU–C.W. Post
2001	Adelphi	Sandy Kapatos	14–10	Limestone
2002	Limestone	T.W. Johnson	11–9	New York Tech
2003	New York Tech	Jack Kaley	9–4	Limestone
2004	Le Moyne	Dan Sheehan	11–10 (2OT)	Limestone

DIVISION III

Year	Champion	Coach	Score	Runner-Up
1980	Hobart	Dave Urick	11–8	Cortland St
1981	Hobart	Dave Urick	10–8	Cortland St
1982	Hobart	Dave Urick	9–8 (OT)	Washington (MD)
1983	Hobart	Dave Urick	13–9	Roanoke
1984	Hobart	Dave Urick	12–5	Washington (MD)
1985	Hobart	Dave Urick	15–8	Washington (MD)
1986	Hobart	Dave Urick	13–10	Washington (MD)
1987	Hobart	Dave Urick	9–5	Ohio Wesleyan
1988	Hobart	Dave Urick	18–9	Ohio Wesleyan
1989	Hobart	Dave Urick	11–8	Ohio Wesleyan
1990	Hobart	B.J. O'Hara	18–6	Washington (MD)
1991	Hobart	B.J. O'Hara	12–11	Salisbury St
1992	Nazareth (NY)	Scott Nelson	13–12	Hobart
1993	Hobart	B.J. O'Hara	16–10	Ohio Wesleyan
1994	Salisbury St	Jim Berkman	15–9	Hobart
1995	Salisbury St	Jim Berkman	22–13	Nazareth
1996	Nazareth	Scott Nelson	11–10 (OT)	Washington (MD)
1997	Nazareth	Scott Nelson	15–14 (OT)	Washington (MD)
1998	Washington (MD)	John Haus	16–10	Nazareth
1999	Salisbury St	Jim Berkman	13–6	Middlebury
2000	Middlebury	Erin Quinn	16–12	Salisbury St
2001	Middlebury	Erin Quinn	15–10	Gettysburg
2002	Middlebury	Erin Quinn	14–9	Gettysburg
2003	Salisbury	Jim Berkman	14–13	Middlebury
2004	Salisbury	Jim Berkman	13–9	Nazareth

Women*

DIVISION I

Year	Champion	Coach	Score	Runner-Up
2001	Maryland	Cindy Timchal	14–13 (OT)	Georgetown
2002	Princeton	Chris Sailer	12–7	Georgetown
2003	Princeton	Chris Sailer	8–7 (OT)	Virginia
2004	Virginia	Julie Myers	10–4	Princeton

DIVISION II

Year	Champion	Coach	Score	Runner-Up
2001	LIU–C.W. Post	Karen MacCrate	13–9	W Chester
2002	Westchester	Ginny Martino	11–6	Stonehill
2003	Stonehill	Michael Daly	9–8	Longwood
2004	Adelphi	Jill Lessne	12–11	West Chester

*Divisions I and II competed for a single championship until 2001.

Women (Cont.)
DIVISIONS I AND II

Year	Champion	Coach	Score	Runner-Up
1982	Massachusetts	Pamela Hixon	9–6	Trenton St
1983	Delaware	Janet Smith	10–7	Temple
1984	Temple	Tina Sloan Green	6–4	Maryland
1985	New Hampshire	Marisa Didio	6–5	Maryland
1986	Maryland	Sue Tyler	11–10	Penn St
1987	Penn St	Susan Scheetz	7–6	Temple
1988	Temple	Tina Sloan Green	15–7	Penn St
1989	Penn St	Susan Scheetz	7–6	Harvard
1990	Harvard	Carole Kleinfelder	8–7	Maryland
1991	Virginia	Jane Miller	8–6	Maryland
1992	Maryland	Cindy Timchal	11–10	Harvard
1993	Virginia	Jane Miller	8–6 (OT)	Princeton
1994	Princeton	Chris Sailer	10–7	Virginia
1995	Maryland	Cindy Timchal	13–5	Princeton
1996	Maryland	Cindy Timchal	10–5	Virginia
1997	Maryland	Cindy Timchal	8–7	Loyola (MD)
1998	Maryland	Cindy Timchal	11–5	Virginia
1999	Maryland	Cindy Timchal	16–6	Virginia
2000	Maryland	Cindy Timchal	16–8	Princeton

DIVISION III

Year	Champion	Score	Runner-Up	Year	Champion	Score	Runner-Up
1985	Trenton St	7–4	Ursinus	1995	Trenton St	14–13	William Smith
1986	Ursinus	12–10	Trenton St	1996	Trenton St	15–8	Middlebury
1987	Trenton St	8–7 (ot)	Ursinus	1997	Middlebury	14–9	College of NJ*
1988	Trenton St	14–11	William Smith	1998	Coll of NJ	14–9	Williams
1989	Ursinus	8–6	Trenton St	1999	Middlebury	10–9	Amherst
1990	Ursinus	7–6	St. Lawrence	2000	Coll of NJ	14–8	Williams
1991	Trenton St	7–6	Ursinus	2001	Middlebury	11–10	Amherst
1992	Trenton St	5–3	William Smith	2002	Middlebury	12–6	College of NJ*
1993	Trenton St	10–9	William Smith	2003	Amherst	11–9	Middlebury
1994	Trenton St	29–11	William Smith	2004	Middlebury	13–11 (ot)	College of NJ

*Formerly Trenton St

Rifle

						Individual Champions	
Year	Champion	Coach	Score	Runner-Up	Score	Air Rifle	Smallbore
1980	Tennessee Tech	James Newkirk	6201	W Virginia	6150	Rod Fitz-Randolph, Tennessee Tech	Rod Fitz-Randolph, Tennessee Tech
1981	Tennessee Tech	James Newkirk	6139	W Virginia	6136	John Rost, W Virginia	Kurt Fitz-Randolph, Tennessee Tech
1982	Tennessee Tech	James Newkirk	6138	W Virginia	6136	John Rost, W Virginia	Kurt Fitz-Randolph, Tennessee Tech
1983	W Virginia	Edward Etzel	6166	Tennessee Tech	6148	Ray Slonena, Tennessee Tech	David Johnson, W Virginia
1984	W Virginia	Edward Etzel	6206	E Tennessee St	6142	Pat Spurgin, Murray St	Bob Broughton, W Virginia
1985	Murray St	Elvis Green	6150	W Virginia	6149	Christian Heller, W Virginia	Pat Spurgin, Murray St
1986	W Virginia	Edward Etzel	6229	Murray St	6163	Marianne Wallace, Murray St	Mike Anti, W Virginia
1987	Murray St	Elvis Green	6205	W Virginia	6203	Rob Harbison, TN–Martin	Web Wright, W Virginia
1988	W Virginia	Greg Perrine	6192	Murray St	6183	Deena Wigger, Murray St	Web Wright, W Virginia
1989	W Virginia	Edward Etzel	6234	S Florida	6180	Michelle Scarborough, S Florida	Deb Sinclair, AK–Fairbanks
1990	W Virginia	Marsha Beasley	6205	Navy	6101	Gary Hardy, W Virginia	M. Scarborough, S Florida
1991	W Virginia	Marsha Beasley	6171	AK–Fairbanks	6110	Ann Pfiffner, W Virginia	Soma Dutta, UTEP
1992	W Virginia	Marsha Beasley	6214	AK–Fairbanks	6166	Ann Pfiffner, W Virginia	Tim Manges, W Virginia
1993	W Virginia	Marsha Beasley	6179	AK–Fairbanks	6169	Trevor Gathman, W Virginia	Eric Uptagrafft, W Virginia
1994	AK–Fairbanks	Randy Pitney	6194	W Virginia	6187	Nancy Napolski, Kentucky	Cory Brunetti, AK–Fairbanks
1995	W Virginia	Marsha Beasley	6241	Air Force	6187	Benji Belden, Murray St	Oleg Selezner, AK–Fairbanks
1996	W Virginia	Marsha Beasley	6179	Air Force	6168	T. Gathman, WVa	Joe Johnson, Navy

						Individual Champions	
Year	Champion	Coach	Score	Runner-Up	Score	Air Rifle	Smallbore
1997	W Virginia	Marsha Beasley	6223	Kentucky	6175	Marra Hastings, Murray St	Marcos Scrivner, W Virginia
1998	W Virginia	Marsha Beasley	6214	AK–Fairbanks	6175	Emily Caruso, Norwich	Karen Juzinuk, Xavier
1999	AK-Fairbanks	Randy Pitney	6276	Navy	6168	Kelly Mansfield, AK-Fairbanks	Kelly Mansfield, AK–Fairbanks
2000	AK-Fairbanks	Randy Pitney	6285	Xavier	6156	Kelly Mansfield, AK-Fairbanks	Nicole Allaire, Nebraska
2001	AK-Fairbanks	David Johnson	6283	Kentucky	6175	Matthew Emmons, AK-Fairbanks	Matthew Emmons, AK–Fairbanks
2002	AK-Fairbanks	Randy Pitney	6241	Kentucky	6209	Ryan Tanoue, Nevada	Matthew Emmons AK–Fairbanks
2003	AK-Fairbanks	Glenn Dubis	6287	Xavier	6187	Jamie Beyerle, AK-Fairbanks	Matthew Emmons AK–Fairbanks
2004	AK-Fairbanks	Glenn Dubis	6273	Nevada	6185	Morgan Hicks, Murray St	Matthew Rawlings AK–Fairbanks

Skiing

Year	Champion	Coach	Pts	Runner-Up	Pts	Host or Site
1954	Denver	Willy Schaeffler	384.0	Seattle	349.6	NV–Reno
1955	Denver	Willy Schaeffler	567.05	Dartmouth	558.935	Norwich
1956	Denver	Willy Schaeffler	582.01	Dartmouth	541.77	Winter Park
1957	Denver	Willy Schaeffler	577.95	Colorado	545.29	Ogden Snow Basin
1958	Dartmouth	Al Merrill	561.2	Denver	550.6	Dartmouth
1959	Colorado	Bob Beattie	549.4	Denver	543.6	Winter Park
1960	Colorado	Bob Beattie	571.4	Denver	568.6	Bridger Bowl
1961	Denver	Willy Schaeffler	376.19	Middlebury	366.94	Middlebury
1962	Denver	Willy Schaeffler	390.08	Colorado	374.30	Squaw Valley
1963	Denver	Willy Schaeffler	384.6	Colorado	381.6	Solitude
1964	Denver	Willy Schaeffler	370.2	Dartmouth	368.8	Franconia Notch
1965	Denver	Willy Schaeffler	380.5	Utah	378.4	Crystal Mountain
1966	Denver	Willy Schaeffler	381.02	Western Colorado	365.92	Crested Butte
1967	Denver	Willy Schaeffler	376.7	Wyoming	375.9	Sugarloaf Mountain
1968	Wyoming	John Cress	383.9	Denver	376.2	Mount Werner
1969	Denver	Willy Schaeffler	388.6	Dartmouth	372.0	Mount Werner
1970	Denver	Willy Schaeffler	386.6	Dartmouth	378.8	Cannon Mountain
1971	Denver	Peder Pytte	394.7	Colorado	373.1	Terry Peak
1972	Colorado	Bill Marolt	385.3	Denver	380.1	Winter Park
1973	Colorado	Bill Marolt	381.89	Wyoming	377.83	Middlebury
1974	Colorado	Bill Marolt	176	Wyoming	162	Jackson Hole
1975	Colorado	Bill Marolt	183	Vermont	115	Fort Lewis
1976	Colo/Dart	Bill Marolt/Jim Page	112			Bates
1977	Colorado	Bill Marolt	179	Wyoming	154.5	Winter Park
1978	Colorado	Bill Marolt	152.5	Wyoming	121.5	Cannon Mountain
1979	Colorado	Tim Hinderman	153	Utah	130	Steamboat Springs
1980	Vermont	Chip LaCasse	171	Utah	151	Lake Placid and Stowe
1981	Utah	Pat Miller	183	Vermont	172	Park City
1982	Colorado	Tim Hinderman	461	Vermont	436.5	Lake Placid
1983	Utah	Pat Miller	696	Vermont	650	Bozeman
1984	Utah	Pat Miller	750.5	Vermont	684	New Hampshire
1985	Wyoming	Tim Ameel	764	Utah	744	Bozeman
1986	Utah	Pat Miller	612	Vermont	602	Vermont
1987	Utah	Pat Miller	710	Vermont	627	Anchorage
1988	Utah	Pat Miller	651	Vermont	614	Middlebury
1989	Vermont	Chip LaCasse	672	Utah	668	Jackson Hole
1990	Vermont	Chip LaCasse	671	Utah	571	Vermont
1991	Colorado	Richard Rokos	713	Vermont	682	Park City, UT
1992	Vermont	Chip LaCasse	693.5	New Mexico	642.5	New Hampshire
1993	Utah	Pat Miller	783	Vermont	700.5	Steamboat Springs
1994	Vermont	Chip LaCasse	688	Utah	667	Sugarloaf, ME
1995	Colorado	Richard Rokos	720.5	Utah	711	New Hampshire
1996	Utah	Pat Miller	719	Denver	635.5	Montana St
1997	Utah	Pat Miller	686	Vermont	646.5	Vermont
1998	Colorado	Richard Rokos	654	Utah	651.5	Montana St
1999	Colorado	Richard Rokos	650	Denver	636	Bates College
2000	Denver	Kurt Smitz	720	Colorado	621	Park City, UT
2001	Denver	Kurt Smitz	649	Vermont	605	Middlebury, VT
2002	Denver	Kurt Smitz	656	Colorado	612	Anchorage
2003	Utah	Kevin Sweeney	682	Vermont	551	Hanover, NH
2004	New Mexico	George Brooks	623	Utah	581	Donner Summit, CA

Men
DIVISION I

Year	Champion	Coach	Score	Runner-Up
1959	St. Louis	Bob Guelker	5–2	Bridgeport
1960	St. Louis	Bob Guelker	3–2	Maryland
1961	West Chester	Mel Lorback	2–0	St. Louis
1962	St. Louis	Bob Guelker	4–3	Maryland
1963	St. Louis	Bob Guelker	3–0	Navy
1964	Navy	F.H. Warner	1–0	Michigan St
1965	St. Louis	Bob Guelker	1–0	Michigan St
1966	San Francisco	Steve Negoesco	5–2	LIU–Brooklyn
1967	Michigan St	Gene Kenney	0–0	Game called due to
	St. Louis	Harry Keough		inclement weather
1968	Maryland	Doyle Royal	2–2 (2 OT)	
	Michigan St	Gene Kenney		
1969	St. Louis	Harry Keough	4–0	San Francisco
1970	St. Louis	Harry Keough	1–0	UCLA
1971	Vacated		3–2	St. Louis
1972	St. Louis	Harry Keough	4–2	UCLA
1973	St. Louis	Harry Keough	2–1 (OT)	UCLA
1974	Howard	Lincoln Phillips	2–1 (4 OT)	St. Louis
1975	San Francisco	Steve Negoesco	4–0	SIU–Edwardsville
1976	San Francisco	Steve Negoesco	1–0	Indiana
1977	Hartwick	Jim Lennox	2–1	San Francisco
1978	Vacated		2–0	Indiana
1979	SIU–Edwardsville	Bob Guelker	3–2	Clemson
1980	San Francisco	Steve Negoesco	4–3 (OT)	Indiana
1981	Connecticut	Joe Morrone	2–1 (OT)	Alabama A&M
1982	Indiana	Jerry Yeagley	2–1 (8 OT)	Duke
1983	Indiana	Jerry Yeagley	1–0 (2 OT)	Columbia
1984	Clemson	I.M. Ibrahim	2–1	Indiana
1985	UCLA	Sigi Schmid	1–0 (8 OT)	American
1986	Duke	John Rennie	1–0	Akron
1987	Clemson	I.M. Ibrahim	2–0	San Diego St
1988	Indiana	Jerry Yeagley	1–0	Howard
1989	Santa Clara	Steve Sampson	1–1 (2 OT)	
	Virginia	Bruce Arena		
1990	UCLA	Sigi Schmid	1–0 (OT)	Rutgers
1991	Virginia	Bruce Arena	0–0*	Santa Clara
1992	Virginia	Bruce Arena	2–0	San Diego
1993	Virginia	Bruce Arena	2–0	S Carolina
1994	Virginia	Bruce Arena	1–0	Indiana
1995	Wisconsin	Jim Launder	2–0	Duke
1996	St. John's (NY)	Dave Masur	4–1	Florida International
1997	UCLA	Sigi Schmid	2–1	Virginia
1998	Indiana	Jerry Yeagley	3–1	Stanford
1999	Indiana	Jerry Yeagley	1–0	Santa Clara
2000	Connecticut	Ray Reid	2–0	Creighton
2001	N Carolina	Elmar Bolowich	2–0	Indiana
2002	UCLA	Tom Fitzgerald	1–0	Stanford
2003	Indiana	Jerry Yeagley	2–1	St. John's (NY)

*Under a rule passed in 1991, the NCAA determined that when a score is tied after regulation and overtime, and the championship is determined by penalty kicks, the official score will be 0–0.

DIVISION II

Year	Champion	Year	Champion	Year	Champion
1972	SIU–Edwardsville	1984	Florida International	1996	Grand Canyon
1973	MO–St. Louis	1985	Seattle Pacific	1997	Cal St-Bakersfield
1974	Adelphi	1986	Seattle Pacific	1998	Southern Connecticut St
1975	Baltimore	1987	Southern Connecticut St	1999	Southern Connecticut St
1976	Loyola (MD)	1988	Florida Tech	2000	Cal St–Dominguez Hills
1977	Alabama A&M	1989	New Hampshire College	2001	Tampa
1978	Seattle Pacific	1990	Southern Connecticut St	2002	Sonoma St
1979	Alabama A&M	1991	Florida Tech	2003	Lynn
1980	Lock Haven	1992	Southern Connecticut St		
1981	Tampa	1993	Seattle Pacific		
1982	Florida International	1994	Tampa		
1983	Seattle Pacific	1995	Southern Connecticut St		

Men (Cont.)

DIVISION III

Year	Champion	Year	Champion	Year	Champion
1974	Brockport St	1984	Wheaton (IL)	1994	Bethany (WV)
1975	Babson	1985	NC–Greensboro	1995	Williams
1976	Brandeis	1986	NC–Greensboro	1996	College of New Jersey
1977	Lock Haven	1987	NC–Greensboro	1997	Wheaton (IL)
1978	Lock Haven	1988	UC–San Diego	1998	Ohio Wesleyan
1979	Babson	1989	Elizabethtown	1999	St. Lawrence
1980	Babson	1990	Glassboro St	2000	Messiah
1981	Glassboro St	1991	UC–San Diego	2001	Richard Stockton
1982	NC–Greensboro	1992	Kean	2002	Messiah
1983	NC–Greensboro	1993	UC–San Diego	2003	Trinity (TX)

Women

DIVISION I

Year	Champion	Coach	Score	Runner-Up
1982	N Carolina	Anson Dorrance	2–0	Central Florida
1983	N Carolina	Anson Dorrance	4–0	George Mason
1984	N Carolina	Anson Dorrance	2–0	Connecticut
1985	George Mason	Hank Leung	2–0	N Carolina
1986	N Carolina	Anson Dorrance	2–0	Colorado College
1987	N Carolina	Anson Dorrance	1–0	Massachusetts
1988	N Carolina	Anson Dorrance	4–1	N Carolina St
1989	N Carolina	Anson Dorrance	2–0	Colorado College
1990	N Carolina	Anson Dorrance	6–0	Connecticut
1991	N Carolina	Anson Dorrance	3–1	Wisconsin
1992	N Carolina	Anson Dorrance	9–1	Duke
1993	N Carolina	Anson Dorrance	6–0	George Mason
1994	N Carolina	Anson Dorrance	5–0	Notre Dame
1995	Notre Dame	Chris Petrucelli	1–0	Portland
1996	N Carolina	Anson Dorrance	1–0	Notre Dame
1997	N Carolina	Anson Dorrance	2–0	Connecticut
1998	Florida	Becky Burleigh	1–0	N Carolina
1999	N Carolina	Anson Dorrance	2–0	Notre Dame
2000	N Carolina	Anson Dorrance	2–1	UCLA
2001	Santa Clara	Jerry Smith	1–0	N Carolina
2002	Portland	Clive Charles	2–1	Santa Clara
2003	N Carolina	Anson Dorrance	6–0	Connecticut

DIVISION II

Year	Champion
1988	Cal St–Hayward
1989	Barry
1990	Sonoma St
1991	Cal St–Dominguez Hills
1992	Barry
1993	Barry
1994	Franklin Pierce
1995	Franklin Pierce
1996	Franklin Pierce
1997	Franklin Pierce
1998	Lynn
1999	Franklin Pierce
2000	UC–San Diego
2001	UC–San Diego
2002	Christian Brothers
2003	Kennesaw St

*Formerly Trenton St

DIVISION III

Year	Champion
1986	Rochester
1987	Rochester
1988	William Smith
1989	UC–San Diego
1990	Ithaca
1991	Ithaca
1992	Cortland St
1993	Trenton St
1994	Trenton St
1995	UC–San Diego
1996	UC–San Diego
1997	UC–San Diego
1998	Macalester
1999	UC–San Diego
2000	College of New Jersey*
2001	Ohio Wesleyan
2002	Ohio Wesleyan
2003	Oneonta St

DIVISION I

Year	Champion	Coach	Score	Runner-Up
1982	UCLA*	Sharron Backus	2-0†	Fresno St
1983	Texas A&M	Bob Brock	2-0‡	Cal St-Fullerton
1984	UCLA	Sharron Backus	1-0#	Texas A&M
1985	UCLA	Sharron Backus	2-1**	Nebraska
1986	Cal St-Fullerton*	Judi Garman	3-0	Texas A&M
1987	Texas A&M	Bob Brock	4-1	UCLA
1988	UCLA	Sharron Backus	3-0	Fresno St
1989	UCLA*	Sharron Backus	1-0	Fresno St
1990	UCLA	Sharron Backus	2-0	Fresno St
1991	Arizona	Mike Candrea	5-1	UCLA
1992	UCLA*	Sharron Backus	2-0	Arizona
1993	Arizona	Mike Candrea	1-0	UCLA
1994	Arizona	Mike Candrea	4-0	Cal St-Northridge
1995	Vacated	—		Arizona
1996	Arizona*	Mike Candrea	6-4	Washington
1997	Arizona	Mike Candrea	10-2***	UCLA
1998	Fresno St	Margie Wright	1-0	Arizona
1999	UCLA	Sue Enquist	3-2	Washington
2000	Oklahoma	Patty Gasso	3-1	UCLA
2001	Arizona*	Mike Candrea	1-0	UCLA
2002	California	Diane Ninemire	6-0	Arizona
2003	UCLA	Sue Enquist	1-0**	California
2004	UCLA	Sue Enquist	3-1	California

*Undefeated teams in final series. †Eight innings. ‡12 innings. #13 innings. **Nine innings. ***Five innings.

DIVISION II

Year	Champion	Year	Champion	Year	Champion
1982	Sam Houston St	1990	Cal St-Bakersfield	1998	California (PA)
1983	Cal St-Northridge	1991	Augustana (SD)	1999	Humboldt St
1984	Cal St-Northridge	1992	Missouri Southern	2000	N Dakota St
1985	Cal St-Northridge	1993	Florida Southern	2001	Nebraska-Omaha
1986	SF Austin St	1994	Merrimack	2002	St. Mary's (IA)
1987	Cal St-Northridge	1995	Kennesaw St	2003	UC Davis
1988	Cal St-Bakersfield	1996	Kennesaw St	2004	Angelo St
1989	Cal St-Bakersfield	1997	California (PA)*		

DIVISION III

Year	Champion	Year	Champion	Year	Champion
1982	Sam Houston St	1989	Trenton St*	1997	Simpson (IA)*
1982	Eastern Connecticut St*	1990	Eastern Connecticut St	1998	WI-Stevens Point
1983	Trenton St	1991	Central (IA)	1999	Simpson (IA)
1984	Buena Vista*	1992	Trenton St	2000	St. Mary's
1985	Eastern Connecticut St	1993	Central (IA)	2001	Muskingum*
1986	Eastern Connecticut St	1994	Trenton St	2002	Williams
1987	Trenton St*	1995	Chapman	2003	Central (IA)
1988	Central (IA)	1996	Trenton St*	2004	St. Thomas

*Undefeated teams in final series.

Swimming and Diving

Men
DIVISION I

Year	Champion	Coach	Pts	Runner-Up	Pts
1937	Michigan	Matt Mann	75	Ohio St	39
1938	Michigan	Matt Mann	46	Ohio St	45
1939	Michigan	Matt Mann	65	Ohio St	58
1940	Michigan	Matt Mann	45	Yale	42
1941	Michigan	Matt Mann	61	Yale	58
1942	Yale	Robert J.H. Kiphuth	71	Michigan	39
1943	Ohio St	Mike Peppe	81	Michigan	47
1944	Yale	Robert J.H. Kiphuth	39	Michigan	38
1945	Ohio St	Mike Peppe	56	Michigan	48
1946	Ohio St	Mike Peppe	61	Michigan	37
1947	Ohio St	Mike Peppe	66	Michigan	39
1948	Michigan	Matt Mann	44	Ohio St	41
1949	Ohio St	Mike Peppe	49	Iowa	35
1950	Ohio St	Mike Peppe	64	Yale	43
1951	Yale	Robert J.H. Kiphuth	81	Michigan St	60
1952	Ohio St	Mike Peppe	94	Yale	81
1953	Yale	Robert J.H. Kiphuth	96½	Ohio St	73½
1954	Ohio St	Mike Peppe	94	Michigan	67

Men (Cont.)
DIVISION I (Cont.)

Year	Champion	Coach	Pts	Runner-Up	Pts
1955	Ohio St	Mike Peppe	90	Yale/ Michigan	51
1956	Ohio St	Mike Peppe	68	Yale	54
1957	Michigan	Gus Stager	69	Yale	61
1958	Michigan	Gus Stager	72	Yale	63
1959	Michigan	Gus Stager	137½	Ohio St	44
1960	Southern Cal	Peter Daland	87	Michigan	73
1961	Michigan	Gus Stager	85	Southern Cal	62
1962	Ohio St	Mike Peppe	92	Southern Cal	46
1963	Southern Cal	Peter Daland	81	Yale	77
1964	Southern Cal	Peter Daland	96	Indiana	91
1965	Southern Cal	Peter Daland	285	Indiana	278½
1966	Southern Cal	Peter Daland	302	Indiana	286
1967	Stanford	Jim Gaughran	275	Southern Cal	260
1968	Indiana	James Counsilman	346	Yale	253
1969	Indiana	James Counsilman	427	Southern Cal	306
1970	Indiana	James Counsilman	332	Southern Cal	235
1971	Indiana	James Counsilman	351	Southern Cal	260
1972	Indiana	James Counsilman	390	Southern Cal	371
1973	Indiana	James Counsilman	358	Tennessee	294
1974	Southern Cal	Peter Daland	339	Indiana	338
1975	Southern Cal	Peter Daland	344	Indiana	274
1976	Southern Cal	Peter Daland	398	Tennessee	237
1977	Southern Cal	Peter Daland	385	Alabama	204
1978	Tennessee	Ray Bussard	307	Auburn	185
1979	California	Nort Thornton	287	Southern Cal	227
1980	California	Nort Thornton	234	Texas	220
1981	Texas	Eddie Reese	259	UCLA	189
1982	UCLA	Ron Ballatore	219	Texas	210
1983	Florida	Randy Reese	238	Southern Meth	227
1984	Florida	Randy Reese	287½	Texas	277
1985	Stanford	Skip Kenney	403½	Florida	302
1986	Stanford	Skip Kenney	404	California	335
1987	Stanford	Skip Kenney	374	Southern Cal	296
1988	Texas	Eddie Reese	424	Southern Cal	369½
1989	Texas	Eddie Reese	475	Stanford	396
1990	Texas	Eddie Reese	506	Southern Cal	423
1991	Texas	Eddie Reese	476	Stanford	420
1992	Stanford	Skip Kenney	632	Texas	356
1993	Stanford	Skip Kenney	520½	Michigan	396
1994	Stanford	Skip Kenney	566½	Texas	445
1995	Michigan	Jon Urbanchek	561	Stanford	475
1996	Texas	Eddie Reese	479	Auburn	443½
1997	Auburn	David Marsh	496½	Stanford	340
1998	Stanford	Skip Kenney	594	Auburn	394½
1999	Auburn	David Marsh	467½	Stanford	414½
2000	Texas	Eddie Reese	538	Auburn	385
2001	Texas	Eddie Reese	597½	Stanford	457½
2002	Texas	Eddie Reese	512	Stanford	5011
2003	Auburn	David Marsh	609½	Texas	413
2004	Auburn	David Marsh	634	Stanford	377.5

DIVISION II

Year	Champion	Year	Champion	Year	Champion
1963	SW Missouri St	1977	Cal St–Northridge	1991	Cal St–Bakersfield
1964	Bucknell	1978	Cal St–Northridge	1992	Cal St–Bakersfield
1965	San Diego St	1979	Cal St–Northridge	1993	Cal St–Bakersfield
1966	San Diego St	1980	Oakland (MI)	1994	Oakland (MI)
1967	UC–Santa Barbara	1981	Cal St–Northridge	1995	Oakland (MI)
1968	Long Beach St	1982	Cal St–Northridge	1996	Oakland (MI)
1969	UC–Irvine	1983	Cal St–Northridge	1997	Oakland (MI)
1970	UC–Irvine	1984	Cal St–Northridge	1998	Cal St–Bakersfield
1971	UC–Irvine	1985	Cal St–Northridge	1999	Drury
1972	Eastern Michigan	1986	Cal St–Bakersfield	2000	Cal St–Bakersfield
1973	Cal St–Chico	1987	Cal St–Bakersfield	2001	Cal St–Bakersfield
1974	Cal St–Chico	1988	Cal St–Bakersfield	2002	Cal St–Bakersfield
1975	Cal St–Northridge	1989	Cal St–Bakersfield	2003	Drury
1976	Cal St–Chico	1990	Cal St–Bakersfield	2004	Cal St–Bakersfield

DIVISION III

Year	Champion	Year	Champion	Year	Champion
1975	Cal St–Chico	1985	Kenyon	1995	Kenyon
1976	St. Lawrence	1986	Kenyon	1996	Kenyon
1977	Johns Hopkins	1987	Kenyon	1997	Kenyon
1978	Johns Hopkins	1988	Kenyon	1998	Kenyon
1979	Johns Hopkins	1989	Kenyon	1999	Kenyon
1980	Kenyon	1990	Kenyon	2000	Kenyon
1981	Kenyon	1991	Kenyon	2001	Kenyon
1982	Kenyon	1992	Kenyon	2002	Kenyon
1983	Kenyon	1993	Kenyon	2003	Kenyon
1984	Kenyon	1994	Kenyon	2004	Kenyon

Women

DIVISION I

Year	Champion	Coach	Pts	Runner-Up	Pts
1982	Florida	Randy Reese	505	Stanford	383
1983	Stanford	George Haines	418½	Florida	389½
1984	Texas	Richard Quick	392	Stanford	324
1985	Texas	Richard Quick	643	Florida	400
1986	Texas	Richard Quick	633	Florida	586
1987	Texas	Richard Quick	648½	Stanford	631½
1988	Texas	Richard Quick	661	Florida	542½
1989	Stanford	Richard Quick	610½	Texas	547
1990	Texas	Mark Schubert	632	Stanford	622½
1991	Texas	Mark Schubert	746	Stanford	653
1992	Stanford	Richard Quick	735½	Texas	651
1993	Stanford	Richard Quick	649½	Florida	421
1994	Stanford	Richard Quick	512	Texas	421
1995	Stanford	Richard Quick	497½	Michigan	478½
1996	Stanford	Richard Quick	478	SMU	397
1997	Southern Cal	Mark Schubert	406	Stanford	395
1998	Stanford	Richard Quick	422	Arizona	378
1999	Georgia	Jack Bauerle	504½	Stanford	441
2000	Georgia	Jack Bauerle	490½	Arizona	472
2001	Georgia	Jack Bauerle	389	Stanford	387½
2002	Auburn	David Marsh	474	Georgia	386
2003	Auburn	David Marsh	536	Georgia	373
2004	Auburn	David Marsh	569	Georgia	431

DIVISION II

Year	Champion	Year	Champion	Year	Champion
1982	Cal St–Northridge	1990	Oakland (MI)	1998	Drury
1983	Clarion	1991	Oakland (MI)	1999	Drury
1984	Clarion	1992	Oakland (MI)	2000	Drury
1985	S Florida	1993	Oakland (MI)	2001	Truman St
1986	Clarion	1994	Oakland (MI)	2002	Truman St
1987	Cal St–Northridge	1995	Air Force	2003	Truman St
1988	Cal St–Northridge	1996	Air Force	2004	Truman St
1989	Cal St–Northridge	1997	Drury		

DIVISION III

Year	Champion	Year	Champion	Year	Champion
1982	Williams	1990	Kenyon	1998	Kenyon
1983	Williams	1991	Kenyon	1999	Kenyon
1984	Kenyon	1992	Kenyon	2000	Kenyon
1985	Kenyon	1993	Kenyon	2001	Denison
1986	Kenyon	1994	Kenyon	2002	Kenyon
1987	Kenyon	1995	Kenyon	2003	Kenyon
1988	Kenyon	1996	Kenyon	2004	Kenyon
1989	Kenyon	1997	Kenyon		

Men

INDIVIDUAL CHAMPIONS 1883–1945

Year	Champion	Year	Champion
1883	Joseph Clark, Harvard (spring)	1914	George Church, Princeton
1883	Howard Taylor, Harvard (fall)	1915	Richard Williams II, Harvard
1884	W.P. Knapp, Yale	1916	G. Colket Caner, Harvard
1885	W.P. Knapp, Yale	1917–18	No tournament
1886	G.M. Brinley, Trinity (CT)	1919	Charles Garland, Yale
1887	P.S. Sears, Harvard	1920	Lascelles Banks, Yale
1888	P.S. Sears, Harvard	1921	Philip Neer, Stanford
1889	R.P. Huntington Jr, Yale	1922	Lucien Williams, Yale
1890	Fred Hovey, Harvard	1923	Carl Fischer, Philadelphia Osteo
1891	Fred Hovey, Harvard	1924	Wallace Scott, Washington
1892	William Larned, Cornell	1925	Edward Chandler, California
1893	Malcolm Chace, Brown	1926	Edward Chandler, California
1894	Malcolm Chace, Yale	1927	Wilmer Allison, Texas
1895	Malcolm Chace, Yale	1928	Julius Seligson, Lehigh
1896	Malcolm Whitman, Harvard	1929	Berkeley Bell, Texas
1897	S.G. Thompson, Princeton	1930	Clifford Sutter, Tulane
1898	Leo Ware, Harvard	1931	Keith Gledhill, Stanford
1899	Dwight Davis, Harvard	1932	Clifford Sutter, Tulane
1900	Raymond Little, Princeton	1933	Jack Tidball, UCLA
1901	Fred Alexander, Princeton	1934	Gene Mako, Southern Cal
1902	William Clothier, Harvard	1935	Wilbur Hess, Rice
1903	E.B. Dewhurst, Pennsylvania	1936	Ernest Sutter, Tulane
1904	Robert LeRoy, Columbia	1937	Ernest Sutter, Tulane
1905	E.B. Dewhurst, Pennsylvania	1938	Frank Guernsey, Rice
1906	Robert LeRoy, Columbia	1939	Frank Guernsey, Rice
1907	G. Peabody Gardner Jr, Harvard	1940	Donald McNeil, Kenyon
1908	Nat Niles, Harvard	1941	Joseph Hunt, Navy
1909	Wallace Johnson, Pennsylvania	1942	Frederick Schroeder Jr, Stanford
1910	R.A. Holden Jr, Yale	1943	Pancho Segura, Miami (FL)
1911	E.H. Whitney, Harvard	1944	Pancho Segura, Miami (FL)
1912	George Church, Princeton	1945	Pancho Segura, Miami (FL)
1913	Richard Williams II, Harvard		

DIVISION I

Year	Champion	Coach	Pts	Runner-Up	Pts	Individual Champion
1946	Southern Cal	William Moyle	9	William & Mary	6	Robert Falkenburg, Southern Cal
1947	William & Mary	Sharvey G. Umbeck	10	Rice	4	Gardner Larned, William & Mary
1948	William & Mary	Sharvey G. Umbeck	6	San Francisco	5	Harry Likas, San Francisco
1949	San Francisco	Norman Brooks	7	Rollins/Tulane/ Washington	4	Jack Tuero, Tulane
1950	UCLA	William Ackerman	11	California/ USC	5	Herbert Flam, UCLA
1951	Southern Cal	Louis Wheeler	9	Cincinnati	7	Tony Trabert, Cincinnati
1952	UCLA	J.D. Morgan	11	California/USC	5	Hugh Stewart, Southern Cal
1953	UCLA	J.D. Morgan	11	California	6	Hamilton Richardson, Tulane
1954	UCLA	J.D. Morgan	15	Southern Cal	10	Hamilton Richardson, Tulane
1955	Southern Cal	George Toley	12	Texas	7	Jose Aguero, Tulane
1956	UCLA	J.D. Morgan	15	Southern Cal	14	Alejandro Olmedo, Southern Cal
1957	Michigan	William Murphy	10	Tulane	9	Barry MacKay, Michigan
1958	Southern Cal	George Toley	13	Stanford	9	Alejandro Olmedo, Southern Cal
1959	Notre Dame	Thomas Fallon	8			Whitney Reed, San Jose St
	Tulane	Emmet Pare	8			
1960	UCLA	J.D. Morgan	18	Southern Cal	8	Larry Nagler, UCLA
1961	UCLA	J.D. Morgan	17	Southern Cal	16	Allen Fox, UCLA
1962	Southern Cal	George Toley	22	UCLA	12	Rafael Osuna, Southern Cal
1963	Southern Cal	George Toley	27	UCLA	19	Dennis Ralston, Southern Cal
1964	Southern Cal	George Toley	26	UCLA	25	Dennis Ralston, Southern Cal
1965	UCLA	J.D. Morgan	31	Miami (FL)	13	Arthur Ashe, UCLA
1966	Southern Cal	George Toley	27	UCLA	23	Charles Pasarell, UCLA
1967	Southern Cal	George Toley	28	UCLA	23	Bob Lutz, Southern Cal
1968	Southern Cal	George Toley	31	Rice	23	Stan Smith, Southern Cal
1969	Southern Cal	George Toley	35	UCLA	23	Joaquin Loyo-Mayo, Southern Cal
1970	UCLA	Glenn Bassett	26	Trinity (TX)	22	Jeff Borowiak, UCLA
				Rice	22	
1971	UCLA	Glenn Bassett	35	Trinity (TX)	27	Jimmy Connors, UCLA
1972	Trinity (TX)	Clarence Mabry	36	Stanford	30	Dick Stockton, Trinity (TX)

Men (Cont.)

DIVISION I (Cont.)

Year	Champion	Coach	Pts	Runner-Up	Pts	Individual Champion
1973	Stanford	Dick Gould	33	Southern Cal	28	Alex Mayer, Stanford
1974	Stanford	Dick Gould	30	Southern Cal	25	John Whitlinger, Stanford
1975	UCLA	Glenn Bassett	27	Miami (FL)	20	Bill Martin, UCLA
1976	Southern Cal	George Toley	21			Bill Scanlon, Trinity (TX)
	UCLA	Glenn Bassett	21			
1977	Stanford	Dick Gould		Trinity (TX)		Matt Mitchell, Stanford
1978	Stanford	Dick Gould		UCLA		John McEnroe, Stanford
1979	UCLA	Glenn Bassett		Trinity (TX)		Kevin Curren, Texas
1980	Stanford	Dick Gould		California		Robert Van't Hof, Southern Cal
1981	Stanford	Dick Gould		UCLA		Tim Mayotte, Stanford
1982	UCLA	Glenn Bassett		Pepperdine		Mike Leach, Michigan
1983	Stanford	Dick Gould		SMU		Greg Holmes, Utah
1984	UCLA	Glenn Bassett		Stanford		Mikael Pernfors, Georgia
1985	Georgia	Dan Magill		UCLA		Mikael Pernfors, Georgia
1986	Stanford	Dick Gould		Pepperdine		Dan Goldie, Stanford
1987	Georgia	Dan Magill		UCLA		Andrew Burrow, Miami (FL)
1988	Stanford	Dick Gould		Louisiana St		Robby Weiss, Pepperdine
1989	Stanford	Dick Gould		Georgia		Donni Leaycraft, Louisiana St
1990	Stanford	Dick Gould		Tennessee		Steve Bryan, Texas
1991	Southern Cal	Dick Leach		Georgia		Jared Palmer, Stanford
1992	Stanford	Dick Gould		Notre Dame		Alex O'Brien, Stanford
1993	Southern Cal	Dick Leach		Georgia		Chris Woodruff, Tennessee
1994	Southern Cal	Dick Leach		Stanford		Mark Merklein, Florida
1995	Stanford	Dick Gould		Mississippi		Sargis Sargsian, Arizona St
1996	Stanford	Dick Gould		UCLA		Cecil Mamiit, Southern Cal
1997	Stanford	Dick Gould		Georgia		Luke Smith, UNLV
1998	Stanford	Dick Gould		Georgia		Bob Bryan, Stanford
1999	Georgia	Manuel Diaz		UCLA		Jeff Morrison, Florida
2000	Stanford	Dick Gould		VA–Commonwealth		Alex Kim, Stanford
2001	Georgia	Manuel Diaz		Tennessee		Matias Boeker, Georgia
2002	Southern Cal	Dick Leach		Georgia		Matias Boeker, Georgia
2003	Illinois	Craig Tiley		Vanderbilt		Amer Delic, Illinois
2004	Baylor	Matt Knoll		UCLA		Benjamin Becker, Baylor

Note: Prior to 1977, individual wins counted in the team's total points. In 1977, a dual-match single-elimination team championship was initiated, eliminating the point system.

DIVISION II

Year	Champion		Year	Champion		Year	Champion
1963	Cal St–LA		1977	UC–Irvine		1991	Rollins
1964	Cal St–LA/S Illinois		1978	SIU–Edwardsville		1992	UC–Davis
1965	Cal St–LA		1979	SIU–Edwardsville		1993	Lander
1966	Rollins		1980	SIU–Edwardsville		1994	Lander
1967	Long Beach St		1981	SIU–Edwardsville		1995	Lander
1968	Fresno St		1982	SIU–Edwardsville		1996	Lander
1969	Cal St–Northridge		1983	SIU–Edwardsville		1997	Lander
1970	UC–Irvine		1984	SIU–Edwardsville		1998	Lander
1971	UC–Irvine		1985	Chapman		1999	Lander
1972	UC–Irvine/ Rollins		1986	Cal Poly–SLO		2000	Lander
1973	UC–Irvine		1987	Chapman		2001	Rollins
1974	San Diego		1988	Chapman		2002	BYU–Hawaii
1975	UC–Irvine/San Diego		1989	Hampton		2003	BYU–Hawaii
1976	Hampton		1990	Cal Poly–SLO		2004	W Florida

DIVISION III

Year	Champion		Year	Champion		Year	Champion
1976	Kalamazoo		1985	Swarthmore		1995	UC–Santa Cruz
1977	Swarthmore		1986	Kalamazoo		1996	UC–Santa Cruz
1978	Kalamazoo		1987	Kalamazoo		1997	Washington (MD)
1979	Redlands		1988	Washington & Lee		1998	UC–Santa Cruz
1980	Gustavus Adolphus		1989	UC–Santa Cruz		1999	Williams
1981	Claremont-M-S/ Swarthmore		1990	Swarthmore		2000	Trinity (TX)
			1991	Kalamazoo		2001	Williams
1982	Gustavus Adolphus		1992	Kalamazoo		2002	Williams
1983	Redlands		1993	Kalamazoo		2003	Emory
1984	Redlands		1994	Washington (MD)		2004	Middlebury

Women
DIVISION I

Year	Champion	Coach	Runner-Up	Individual Champion
1982	Stanford	Frank Brennan	UCLA	Alycia Moulton, Stanford
1983	Southern Cal	Dave Borelli	Trinity (TX)	Beth Herr, Southern Cal
1984	Stanford	Frank Brennan	Southern Cal	Lisa Spain, Georgia
1985	Southern Cal	Dave Borelli	Miami (FL)	Linda Gates, Stanford
1986	Stanford	Frank Brennan	Southern Cal	Patty Fendick, Stanford
1987	Stanford	Frank Brennan	Georgia	Patty Fendick, Stanford
1988	Stanford	Frank Brennan	Florida	Shaun Stafford, Florida
1989	Stanford	Frank Brennan	UCLA	Sandra Birch, Stanford
1990	Stanford	Frank Brennan	Florida	Debbie Graham, Stanford
1991	Stanford	Frank Brennan	UCLA	Sandra Birch, Stanford
1992	Florida	Andy Brandi	Texas	Lisa Raymond, Florida
1993	Texas	Jeff Moore	Stanford	Lisa Raymond, Florida
1994	Georgia	Jeff Wallace	Stanford	Angela Lettiere, Georgia
1995	Texas	Jeff Moore	Florida	Keri Phebus, UCLA
1996	Florida	Andy Brandi	Stanford	Jill Craybas, Florida
1997	Stanford	Frank Brennan	Florida	Lilia Osterloh, Stanford
1998	Florida	Andy Brandi	Duke	Vanessa Webb, Duke
1999	Stanford	Frank Brennan	Florida	Zuzana Lesenarova, UC–SD
2000	Georgia	Jeff Wallace	Stanford	Laura Granville, Stanford
2001	Stanford	Lele Forood	Vanderbilt	Laura Granville, Stanford
2002	Stanford	Lele Forood	Florida	Bea Bielek, Wake Forest
2003	Florida	Roland Thornqvist	Stanford	Amber Liu, Stanford
2004	Stanford	Lele Forood	UCLA	Amber Liu, Stanford

DIVISION II

Year	Champion	Year	Champion	Year	Champion
1982	Cal St–Northridge	1990	UC–Davis	1998	Lynn
1983	TN–Chattanooga	1991	Cal Poly–Pomona	1999	BYU–Hawaii
1984	TN–Chattanooga	1992	Cal Poly–Pomona	2000	BYU–Hawaii
1985	TN–Chattanooga	1993	UC–Davis	2001	Lynn
1986	SIU–Edwardsville	1994	N Florida	2002	BYU–Hawaii
1987	SIU–Edwardsville	1995	Armstrong St	2003	BYU–Hawaii
1988	SIU–Edwardsville	1996	Armstrong St	2004	BYU–Hawaii
1989	SIU–Edwardsville	1997	Lynn		

DIVISION III

Year	Champion	Year	Champion	Year	Champion
1982	Occidental	1990	Gustavus Adolphus	1998	Kenyon
1983	Principia	1991	Mary Washington	1999	Amherst
1984	Davidson	1992	Pomona-Pitzer	2000	Trinity (TX)
1985	UC–San Diego	1993	Kenyon	2001	Williams
1986	Trenton St	1994	UC–San Diego	2002	Williams
1987	UC–San Diego	1995	Kenyon	2003	Emory
1988	Mary Washington	1996	Emory	2004	Emory
1989	UC–San Diego	1997	Kenyon		

Indoor Track and Field

Men
DIVISION I

Year	Champion	Coach	Pts	Runner-Up	Pts
1965	Missouri	Tom Botts	14	Oklahoma St	12
1966	Kansas	Bob Timmons	14	Southern Cal	13
1967	Southern Cal	Vern Wolfe	26	Oklahoma	17
1968	Villanova	Jim Elliott	35	Southern Cal	25
1969	Kansas	Bob Timmons	41½	Villanova	33
1970	Kansas	Bob Timmons	27½	Villanova	26
1971	Villanova	Jim Elliott	22	UTEP	19¼
1972	Southern Cal	Vern Wolfe	19	Bowling Green/ Mich St	18
1973	Manhattan	Fred Dwyer	18	Kansas/Kent St/UTEP	12
1974	UTEP	Ted Banks	19	Colorado	18
1975	UTEP	Ted Banks	36	Kansas	17½
1976	UTEP	Ted Banks	23	Villanova	15
1977	Washington St	John Chaplin	25½	UTEP	25
1978	UTEP	Ted Banks	44	Auburn	38
1979	Villanova	Jim Elliott	52	UTEP	51
1980	UTEP	Ted Banks	76	Villanova	42
1981	UTEP	Ted Banks	76	SMU	51
1982	UTEP	John Wedel	67	Arkansas	30

Men (Cont.)
DIVISION I (Cont.)

Year	Champion	Coach	Pts	Runner-Up	Pts
1983	SMU	Ted McLaughlin	43	Villanova	32
1984	Arkansas	John McDonnell	38	Washington St	28
1985	Arkansas	John McDonnell	70	Tennessee	29
1986	Arkansas	John McDonnell	49	Villanova	22
1987	Arkansas	John McDonnell	39	SMU	31
1988	Arkansas	John McDonnell	34	Illinois	29
1989	Arkansas	John McDonnell	34	Florida	31
1990	Arkansas	John McDonnell	44	Texas A&M	36
1991	Arkansas	John McDonnell	34	Georgetown	27
1992	Arkansas	John McDonnell	53	Clemson	46
1993	Arkansas	John McDonnell	66	Clemson	30
1994	Arkansas	John McDonnell	83	UTEP	45
1995	Arkansas	John McDonnell	59	GMU/Tennessee	26
1996	George Mason	John Cook	39	Nebraska	31½
1997	Arkansas	John McDonnell	59	Auburn	27
1998	Arkansas	John McDonnell	56	Stanford	36½
1999	Arkansas	John McDonnell	65	Stanford	42½
2000	Arkansas	John McDonnell	69½	Stanford	52
2001	Louisiana St	Pat Henry	34	Texas Christian	33
2002	Tennessee	Bill Webb	62½	Louisiana St	44
2003	Arkansas	John McDonnell	52	Auburn	28
2004	Louisiana St	Pat Henry	45½	Florida	38

DIVISION II

Year	Champion	Year	Champion	Year	Champion
1985	SE Missouri St	1992	St. Augustine's	1999	Abilene Christian
1986	Not held	1993	Abilene Christian	2000	Abilene Christian
1987	St. Augustine's	1994	Abilene Christian	2001	St. Augustine's
1988	Abil. Christian/St. August.	1995	St. Augustine's	2002	Abilene Christian
1989	St. Augustine's	1996	Abilene Christian	2003	Abilene Christian
1990	St. Augustine's	1997	Abilene Christian	2004	Abilene Christian
1991	St. Augustine's	1998	Abilene Christian		

DIVISION III

Year	Champion	Year	Champion	Year	Champion
1985	St. Thomas (MN)	1992	WI–La Crosse	1999	Lincoln (PA)
1986	Frostburg St	1993	WI–La Crosse	2000	Lincoln (PA)
1987	WI–La Crosse	1994	WI–La Crosse	2001	WI–La Crosse
1988	WI–La Crosse	1995	Lincoln (PA)	2002	WI–La Crosse
1989	N Central	1996	Lincoln (PA)	2003	WI–La Crosse
1990	Lincoln (PA)	1997	WI–La Crosse	2004	WI–La Crosse
1991	WI–La Crosse	1998	Lincoln (PA)		

Women
DIVISION I

Year	Champion	Coach	Pts	Runner-Up	Pts
1983	Nebraska	Gary Pepin	47	Tennessee	44
1984	Nebraska	Gary Pepin	59	Tennessee	48
1985	Florida St	Gary Winckler	34	Texas	32
1986	Texas	Terry Crawford	31	Southern Cal	26
1987	Louisiana St	Loren Seagrave	49	Tennessee	30
1988	Texas	Terry Crawford	71	Villanova	52
1989	Louisiana St	Pat Henry	61	Villanova	34
1990	Texas	Terry Crawford	50	Wisconsin	26
1991	Louisiana St	Pat Henry	48	Texas	39
1992	Florida	Bev Kearney	50	Stanford	26
1993	Louisiana St	Pat Henry	49	Wisconsin	44
1994	Louisiana St	Pat Henry	48	Alabama	29
1995	Louisiana St	Pat Henry	40	UCLA	37
1996	Louisiana St	Pat Henry	52	Georgia	34
1997	Louisiana St	Pat Henry	49	Texas/Wisconsin	39
1998	Texas	Bev Kearney	60	Louisiana St	30
1999	Texas	Bev Kearney	61	Louisiana St	57
2000	UCLA	Jeanette Bolden	51	S Carolina	41
2001	UCLA	Jeanette Bolden	53½	S Carolina	40
2002	Louisiana St	Pat Henry	57	Florida	35
2003	Louisiana St	Pat Henry	62	S Carolina/Florida	44
2004	Lousiana St	Pat Henry	52	Florida	51

Women (Cont.)

DIVISION II

Year	Champion	Year	Champion	Year	Champion
1985	St. Augustine's	1992	Alabama A&M	1999	Abilene Christian
1986	Not held	1993	Abilene Christian	2000	Abilene Christian
1987	St. Augustine's	1994	Abilene Christian	2001	St. Augustine's
1988	Abilene Christian	1995	Abilene Christian	2002	N Dakota St
1989	Abilene Christian	1996	Abilene Christian	2003	St. Augustine's
1990	Abilene Christian	1997	Abilene Christian	2004	Lincoln
1991	Abilene Christian	1998	Abilene Christian		

DIVISION III

Year	Champion	Year	Champion	Year	Champion
1985	MA–Boston	1992	Christopher Newport	1999	Wheaton (MA)
1986	MA–Boston	1993	Lincoln (PA)	2000	Wheaton (MA)
1987	MA–Boston	1994	WI–Oshkosh	2001	Wheaton (MA)
1988	Christopher Newport	1995	WI–Oshkosh	2002	Wheaton (MA)
1989	Christopher Newport	1996	WI–Oshkosh	2003	Wheaton (MA)
1990	Christopher Newport	1997	Christopher Newport	2004	WI–Oshkosh
1991	Cortland St	1998	Christopher Newport		

Outdoor Track and Field

Men

DIVISION I

Year	Champion	Coach	Pts	Runner-Up	Pts
1921	Illinois	Harry Gill	20†	Notre Dame	16†
1922	California	Walter Christie	28†	Penn St	19†
1923	Michigan	Stephen Farrell	29†	Mississippi St	16
1924	No meet				
1925	Stanford*	R.L. Templeton	31†		
1926	Southern Cal*	Dean Cromwell	27†		
1927	Illinois*	Harry Gill	35†		
1928	Stanford	R.L. Templeton	72	Ohio St	31
1929	Ohio St	Frank Castleman	50	Washington	42
1930	Southern Cal	Dean Cromwell	55†	Washington	40
1931	Southern Cal	Dean Cromwell	77†	Ohio St	31†
1932	Indiana	Billy Hayes	56	Ohio St	49†
1933	Louisiana St	Bernie Moore	58	Southern Cal	54
1934	Stanford	R.L. Templeton	63	Southern Cal	54†
1935	Southern Cal	Dean Cromwell	74†	Ohio St	40†
1936	Southern Cal	Dean Cromwell	103†	Ohio St	73
1937	Southern Cal	Dean Cromwell	62	Stanford	50
1938	Southern Cal	Dean Cromwell	67†	Stanford	38
1939	Southern Cal	Dean Cromwell	86	Stanford	44†
1940	Southern Cal	Dean Cromwell	47	Stanford	28†
1941	Southern Cal	Dean Cromwell	81†	Indiana	50
1942	Southern Cal	Dean Cromwell	85†	Ohio St	44†
1943	Southern Cal	Dean Cromwell	46	California	39
1944	Illinois	Leo Johnson	79	Notre Dame	43
1945	Navy	E.J. Thomson	62	Illinois	48†
1946	Illinois	Leo Johnson	78	Southern Cal	42†
1947	Illinois	Leo Johnson	59†	Southern Cal	34†
1948	Minnesota	James Kelly	46	Southern Cal	41†
1949	Southern Cal	Jess Hill	55†	UCLA	31
1950	Southern Cal	Jess Hill	49†	Stanford	28
1951	Southern Cal	Jess Mortenson	56	Cornell	40
1952	Southern Cal	Jess Mortenson	66†	San Jose St	24†
1953	Southern Cal	Jess Mortenson	80	Illinois	41
1954	Southern Cal	Jess Mortenson	66†	Illinois	31†
1955	Southern Cal	Jess Mortenson	42	UCLA	34
1956	UCLA	Elvin Drake	55†	Kansas	51
1957	Villanova	James Elliott	47	California	32
1958	Southern Cal	Jess Mortenson	48†	Kansas	40†
1959	Kansas	Bill Easton	73	San Jose St	48
1960	Kansas	Bill Easton	50	Southern Cal	37

Men (Cont.)
DIVISION I (Cont.)

Year	Champion	Coach	Pts	Runner-Up	Pts
1961	Southern Cal	Jess Mortenson	65	Oregon	47
1962	Oregon	William Bowerman	85	Villanova	40†
1963	Southern Cal	Vern Wolfe	61	Stanford	42
1964	Oregon	William Bowerman	70	San Jose St	40
1965	Oregon	William Bowerman	32		
	Southern Cal	Vern Wolfe	32		
1966	UCLA	Jim Bush	81	Brigham Young	33
1967	Southern Cal	Vern Wolfe	86	Oregon	40
1968	Southern Cal	Vern Wolfe	58	Washington St	57
1969	San Jose St	Bud Winter	48	Kansas	45
1970	Brigham Young	Clarence Robison	35		
	Kansas	Bob Timmons	35		
	Oregon	William Bowerman	35		
1971	UCLA	Jim Bush	52	Southern Cal	41
1972	UCLA	Jim Bush	82	Southern Cal	49
1973	UCLA	Jim Bush	56	Oregon	31
1974	Tennessee	Stan Huntsman	60	UCLA	56
1975	UTEP	Ted Banks	55	UCLA	42
1976	Southern Cal	Vern Wolfe	64	UTEP	44
1977	Arizona St	Senon Castillo	64	UTEP	50
1978	UCLA/UTEP	Jim Bush/Ted Banks	50		
1979	UTEP	Ted Banks	64	Villanova	48
1980	UTEP	Ted Banks	69	UCLA	46
1981	UTEP	Ted Banks	70	SMU	57
1982	UTEP	John Wedel	105	Tennessee	94
1983	SMU	Ted McLaughlin	104	Tennessee	102
1984	Oregon	Bill Dellinger	113	Washington St	94½
1985	Arkansas	John McDonnell	61	Washington St	46
1986	SMU	Ted McLaughlin	53	Washington St	52
1987	UCLA	Bob Larsen	81	Texas	28
1988	UCLA	Bob Larsen	82	Texas	41
1989	Louisiana St	Pat Henry	53	Texas A&M	51
1990	Louisiana St	Pat Henry	44	Arkansas	36
1991	Tennessee	Doug Brown	51	Washington St	42
1992	Arkansas	John McDonnell	60	Tennessee	46½
1993	Arkansas	John McDonnell	69	LSU/Ohio St	45
1994	Arkansas	John McDonnell	83	UTEP	45
1995	Arkansas	John McDonnell	61½	UCLA	55
1996	Arkansas	John McDonnell	55	George Mason	40
1997	Arkansas	John McDonnell	55	Texas	42½
1998	Arkansas	John McDonnell	58½	Stanford	51
1999	Arkansas	John McDonnell	59	Stanford	52
2000	Stanford	Vin Lananna	72	Arkansas	59
2001	Tennessee	Bill Webb	50	Texas Christian	49
2002	Louisiana St	Pat Henry	64	Tennessee	57
2003	Arkansas	John McDonnell	59	Auburn	50
2004	Arkansas	John McDonnell	65½	Florida	49

*Unofficial championship. †Fraction of a point.

DIVISION II

Year	Champion	Year	Champion	Year	Champion
1963	MD–Eastern Shore	1977	Cal St–Hayward	1992	St. Augustine's
1964	Fresno St	1978	Cal St–LA	1993	St. Augustine's
1965	San Diego St	1979	Cal Poly–SLO	1994	St. Augustine's
1966	San Diego St	1980	Cal Poly–SLO	1995	St. Augustine's
1967	Long Beach St	1981	Cal Poly–SLO	1996	Abilene Christian
1968	Cal Poly–SLO	1982	Abilene Christian	1997	Abilene Christian
1969	Cal Poly–SLO	1983	Abilene Christian	1998	St. Augustine's
1970	Cal Poly–SLO	1984	Abilene Christian	1999	Abilene Christian
1971	Kentucky St	1985	Abilene Christian	2000	Abilene Christian
1972	Eastern Michigan	1986	Abilene Christian	2001	St. Augustine's
1973	Norfolk St	1987	Abilene Christian	2002	Abilene Christian
1974	Eastern Illinois	1988	Abilene Christian	2003	Abilene Christian
	Norfolk St	1989	St. Augustine's	2004	Abilene Christian
1975	Cal St–Northridge	1990	St. Augustine's		
1976	UC–Irvine	1991	St. Augustine's		

Men (Cont.)

DIVISION III

Year	Champion	Year	Champion	Year	Champion
1974	Ashland	1985	Lincoln (PA)	1996	Lincoln (PA)
1975	Southern–N Orleans	1986	Frostburg St	1997	WI–La Crosse
1976	Southern–N Orleans	1987	Frostburg St	1998	N Central
1977	Southern–N Orleans	1988	WI–La Crosse	1999	Lincoln (PA)
1978	Occidental	1989	N Central	2000	Nebraska Wesleyan
1979	Slippery Rock	1990	Lincoln (PA)	2001	WI–La Crosse
1980	Glassboro St	1991	WI–La Crosse	2002	WI–La Crosse
1981	Glassboro St	1992	WI–La Crosse	2003	WI–La Crosse
1982	Glassboro St	1993	WI–La Crosse	2004	WI–La Crosse
1983	Glassboro St	1994	N Central		
1984	Glassboro St	1995	Lincoln (PA)		

Women

DIVISION I

Year	Champion	Coach	Pts	Runner-Up	Pts
1982	UCLA	Scott Chisam	153	Tennessee	126
1983	UCLA	Scott Chisam	116½	Florida St	108
1984	Florida St	Gary Winckler	145	Tennessee	124
1985	Oregon	Tom Heinonen	52	Florida St/LSU	46
1986	Texas	Terry Crawford	65	Alabama	55
1987	Louisiana St	Loren Seagrave	62	Alabama	53
1988	Louisiana St	Loren Seagrave	61	UCLA	58
1989	Louisiana St	Pat Henry	86	UCLA	47
1990	Louisiana St	Pat Henry	53	UCLA	46
1991	Louisiana St	Pat Henry	78	Texas	67
1992	Louisiana St	Pat Henry	87	Florida	81
1993	Louisiana St	Pat Henry	93	Wisconsin	44
1994	Louisiana St	Pat Henry	86	Texas	43
1995	Louisiana St	Pat Henry	69	UCLA	58
1996	Louisiana St	Pat Henry	81	Texas	52
1997	Louisiana St	Pat Henry	63	Texas	62
1998	Texas	Bev Kearney	60	UCLA	55
1999	Texas	Bev Kearney	62	UCLA	60
2000	Louisiana St	Pat Henry	59	Southern Cal	56
2001	Southern Cal	Ron Allice	64	UCLA	55
2002	South Carolina	Curtis Frye	82	UCLA	72
2003	Louisiana St	Pat Henry	64	Texas	50
2004	UCLA	Jeanette Bolden	69	Louisiana St	68

DIVISION II

Year	Champion	Year	Champion	Year	Champion
1982	Cal Poly–SLO	1990	Cal Poly–SLO	1998	Abilene Christian
1983	Cal Poly–SLO	1991	Cal Poly–SLO	1999	Abilene Christian
1984	Cal Poly–SLO	1992	Alabama A&M	2000	St. Augustine's
1985	Abilene Christian	1993	Alabama A&M	2001	St. Augustine's
1986	Abilene Christian	1994	Alabama A&M	2002	St. Augustine's
1987	Abilene Christian	1995	Abilene Christian	2003	Lincoln
1988	Abilene Christian	1996	Abilene Christian	2004	Lincoln
1989	Cal Poly–SLO	1997	St. Augustine's		

DIVISION III

Year	Champion	Year	Champion	Year	Champion
1982	Central (IA)	1990	WI–Oshkosh	1998	Chris. Newport
1983	WI–La Crosse	1991	WI–Oshkosh	1999	Lincoln (PA)
1984	WI–La Crosse	1992	Chris. Newport	2000	Lincoln (PA)
1985	Cortland State	1993	Lincoln (PA)	2001	Wheaton (MA)
1986	MA–Boston	1994	Chris. Newport	2002	Wheaton (MA)
1987	Chris. Newport	1995	WI–Oshkosh	2003	Wheaton (MA)
1988	Chris. Newport	1996	WI–Oshkosh	2004	WI-Oshkosh
1989	Chris. Newport	1997	WI–Oshkosh		

Volleyball

Men

Year	Champion	Coach	Score	Runner-Up	Most Outstanding Player
1970	UCLA	Al Scates	3–0	Long Beach St	Dane Holtzman, UCLA
1971	UCLA	Al Scates	3–0	UC–Santa Barbara	K. Kilgore, UCLA/T. Bonynge, UCSB
1972	UCLA	Al Scates	3–2	San Diego St	Dick Irvin, UCLA
1973	San Diego St	Jack Henn	3–1	Long Beach St	Duncan McFarland, San Diego St
1974	UCLA	Al Scates	3–2	UC–Santa Barbara	Bob Leonard, UCLA

Men (Cont.)

Year	Champion	Coach	Score	Runner-Up	Most Outstanding Player
1975	UCLA	Al Scates	3–1	UC–Santa Barbara	John Bekins, UCLA
1976	UCLA	Al Scates	3–0	Pepperdine	Joe Mika, UCLA
1977	Southern Cal	Ernie Hix	3–1	Ohio St	Celso Kalache, Southern Cal
1978	Pepperdine	Marv Dunphy	3–2	UCLA	Mike Blanchard, Pepperdine
1979	UCLA	Al Scates	3–1	Southern Cal	Sinjin Smith, UCLA
1980	Southern Cal	Ernie Hix	3–1	UCLA	Dusty Dvorak, Southern Cal
1981	UCLA	Al Scates	3–2	Southern Cal	Karch Kiraly, UCLA
1982	UCLA	Al Scates	3–0	Penn St	Karch Kiraly, UCLA
1983	UCLA	Al Scates	3–0	Pepperdine	Ricci Luyties, UCLA
1984	UCLA	Al Scates	3–1	Pepperdine	Ricci Luyties, UCLA
1985	Pepperdine	Marv Dunphy	3–1	Southern Cal	Bob Ctvrtlik, Pepperdine
1986	Pepperdine	Rod Wilde	3–2	Southern Cal	Steve Friedman, Pepperdine
1987	UCLA	Al Scates	3–0	Southern Cal	Ozzie Volstad, UCLA
1988	Southern Cal	Bob Yoder	3–2	UC–Santa Barbara	Jen-Kai Liu, Southern Cal
1989	UCLA	Al Scates	3–1	Stanford	Matt Sonnichsen, UCLA
1990	Southern Cal	Jim McLaughlin	3–1	Long Beach St	Bryan Ivie, Southern Cal
1991	Long Beach St	Ray Ratelle	3–1	Southern Cal	Brent Hilliard, Long Beach St
1992	Pepperdine	Marv Dunphy	3–0	Stanford	Alon Grinberg, Pepperdine
1993	UCLA	Al Scates	3–0	Cal St–Northridge	Mike Sealy/Jeff Nygaard, UCLA
1994	Penn St	Tom Peterson	3–2	UCLA	Ramon Hernandez, Penn St
1995	UCLA	Al Scates	3–0	Penn St	Jeff Nygaard, UCLA
1996	UCLA	Al Scates	3–2	Hawaii	Yuval Katz, Hawaii
1997	Stanford	Ruben Nieves	3–2	UCLA	Mike Lambert, Stanford
1998	UCLA	Al Scates	3–2	Pepperdine	George Roumain, Pepperdine
1999	Brigham Young	Carl McGown	3–0	Long Beach St	Ossie Antonetti, Brigham Young
2000	UCLA	Al Scates	3–0	Ohio St	Brandon Taliaferro, UCLA
2001	Brigham Young	Carl McGown	3–0	UCLA	Mike Wall, Brigham Young
2002	Hawaii	Mike Wilton	3–1	Pepperdine	Costas Theochardis, Hawaii
2003	Lewis	Dave Deuser	3–2	Brigham Young	Gustavo Meyer, Lewis
2004	Brigham Young	Tom Peterson	3–2	Long Beach St	Carlos Moreno, Brigham Young

Women

DIVISION I

Year	Champion	Coach	Score	Runner-Up
1981	Southern Cal	Chuck Erbe	3–2	UCLA
1982	Hawaii	Dave Shoji	3–2	Southern Cal
1983	Hawaii	Dave Shoji	3–0	UCLA
1984	UCLA	Andy Banachowski	3–2	Stanford
1985	Pacific	John Dunning	3–1	Stanford
1986	Pacific	John Dunning	3–0	Nebraska
1987	Hawaii	Dave Shoji	3–1	Stanford
1988	Texas	Mick Haley	3–0	Hawaii
1989	Long Beach St	Brian Gimmillaro	3–0	Nebraska
1990	UCLA	Andy Banachowski	3–0	Pacific
1991	UCLA	Andy Banachowski	3–2	Long Beach St
1992	Stanford	Don Shaw	3–1	UCLA
1993	Long Beach St	Brian Gimmillaro	3–1	Penn St
1994	Stanford	Don Shaw	3–1	UCLA
1995	Nebraska	Terry Pettit	3–1	Texas
1996	Stanford	Don Shaw	3–0	Hawaii
1997	Stanford	Don Shaw	3–2	Penn St
1998	Long Beach St	Brian Gimmillaro	3–2	Penn St
1999	Penn St	Russ Rose	3–0	Stanford
2000	Nebraska	John Cook	3–2	Wisconsin
2001	Stanford	Don Shaw	3–0	Long Beach St
2002	Southern Cal	Mick Haley	3–1	Stanford
2003	Southern Cal	Mick Haley	3–1	Florida

DIVISION II

Year	Champion	Year	Champion	Year	Champion
1981	Cal St–Sacramento	1989	Cal St–Bakersfield	1997	West Texas A&M
1982	UC–Riverside	1990	West Texas A&M	1998	Hawaii Pacific
1983	Cal St–Northridge	1991	West Texas A&M	1999	BYU–Hawaii
1984	Portland St	1992	Portland St	2000	Hawaii Pacific
1985	Portland St	1993	Northern Michigan	2001	Barry
1986	UC–Riverside	1994	Northern Michigan	2002	BYU–Hawaii
1987	Cal St–Northridge	1995	Barry	2003	N Alabama
1988	Portland St	1996	Nebraska–Omaha		

DIVISION III

Year	Champion	Year	Champion	Year	Champion	Year	Champion
1981	UC–San Diego	1987	UC–San Diego	1993	Washington (MO)	1999	Central (IA)
1982	La Verne	1988	UC–San Diego	1994	Washington (MO)	2000	Central (IA)
1983	Elmhurst	1989	Washington (MO)	1995	Washington (MO)	2001	La Verne
1984	UC–San Diego	1990	UC–San Diego	1996	Washington (MO)	2002	WI–Whitewater
1985	Elmhurst	1991	Washington (MO)	1997	UC–San Diego	2003	Washington (MO)
1986	UC–San Diego	1992	Washington (MO)	1998	Central (IA)		

Water Polo

Men

Year	Champion	Coach	Score	Runner-Up
1969	UCLA	Bob Horn	5–2	California
1970	UC–Irvine	Ed Newland	7–6 (3 OT)	UCLA
1971	UCLA	Bob Horn	5–3	San Jose St
1972	UCLA	Bob Horn	10–5	UC–Irvine
1973	California	Pete Cutino	8–4	UC–Irvine
1974	California	Pete Cutino	7–6	UC–Irvine
1975	California	Pete Cutino	9–8	UC–Irvine
1976	Stanford	Art Lambert	13–12	UCLA
1977	California	Pete Cutino	8–6	UC–Irvine
1978	Stanford	Dante Dettamanti	7–6 (3 OT)	California
1979	UC–Santa Barbara	Pete Snyder	11–3	UCLA
1980	Stanford	Dante Dettamanti	8–6	California
1981	Stanford	Dante Dettamanti	17–6	Long Beach St
1982	UC–Irvine	Ed Newland	7–4	Stanford
1983	California	Pete Cutino	10–7	Southern Cal
1984	California	Pete Cutino	9–8	Stanford
1985	Stanford	Dante Dettamanti	12–11 (2 OT)	UC–Irvine
1986	Stanford	Dante Dettamanti	9–6	California
1987	California	Pete Cutino	9–8 (OT)	Southern Cal
1988	California	Pete Cutino	14–11	UCLA
1989	UC–Irvine	Ed Newland	9–8	California
1990	California	Steve Heaston	8–7	Stanford
1991	California	Steve Heaston	7–6	UCLA
1992	California	Steve Heaston	12–11	Stanford
1993	Stanford	Dante Dettamanti	11–9	Southern Cal
1994	Stanford	Dante Dettamanti	14–10	Southern Cal
1995	UCLA	Guy Baker	10–8	California
1996	UCLA	Guy Baker	8–7	Southern Cal
1997	Pepperdine	Terry Schroeder	8–7 (OT)	Southern Cal
1998	Southern Cal	John Williams	9–8 (2 OT)	Stanford
1999	UCLA	Guy Baker	6–5	Stanford
2000	UCLA	Guy Baker/Adam Krikorian	11–2	UC–San Diego
2001	Stanford	Dante Dettamanti	8–5	UCLA
2002	Stanford	John Vargas	7–6	California
2003	Southern Cal	Jovan Vavic	9–7	Stanford

Women

Year	Champion	Coach	Score	Runner-Up
2001	UCLA	Adam Krikorian	5–4	Stanford
2002	Stanford	John Tanner	8–4	UCLA
2003	UCLA	Adam Krikorian	4–3	Stanford
2004	Southern Cal	Jovan Vavic	10–8	Loyola-M'mnt.

Wrestling

DIVISION I

Year	Champion	Coach	Pts	Runner-Up	Pts	Most Outstanding Wrestler
1928	Oklahoma St*	E.C. Gallagher				
1929	Oklahoma St	E.C. Gallagher	26	Michigan	18	
1930	Oklahoma St*	E.C. Gallagher	27	Illinois	14	
1931	Oklahoma St*	E.C. Gallagher		Michigan		
1932	Indiana*	W.H. Thom		Oklahoma St		Edwin Belshaw, Indiana
1933	OK St*/Iowa St*	E. Gallagher/H. Otopalik				A. Kelley, OK St/P. Johnson, Harv
1934	Oklahoma St	E.C. Gallagher	29	Indiana	19	Ben Bishop, Lehigh
1935	Oklahoma St	E.C. Gallagher	36	Oklahoma	18	Ross Flood, Oklahoma St
1936	Oklahoma	Paul Keen	14	Central St/ OK St	10	Wayne Martin, Oklahoma
1937	Oklahoma St	E.C. Gallagher	31	Oklahoma	13	Stanley Henson, Oklahoma St
1938	Oklahoma St	E.C. Gallagher	19	Illinois	15	Joe McDaniels, Oklahoma St
1939	Oklahoma St	E.C. Gallagher	33	Lehigh	12	Dale Hanson, Minnesota
1940	Oklahoma St	E.C. Gallagher	24	Indiana	14	Don Nichols, Michigan
1941	Oklahoma St	Art Griffith	37	Michigan St	26	Al Whitehurst, Oklahoma St
1942	Oklahoma St	Art Griffith	31	Michigan St	26	David Arndt, Oklahoma St
1946	Oklahoma St	Art Griffith	25	Northern Iowa	24	Gerald Leeman, Northern Iowa
1947	Cornell	Paul Scott	32	Northern Iowa	19	William Koll, Northern Iowa
1948	Oklahoma St	Art Griffith	33	Michigan St	28	William Koll, Northern Iowa
1949	Oklahoma St	Art Griffith	32	Northern Iowa	27	Charles Hetrick, Oklahoma St
1950	Northern Iowa	David McCuskey	30	Purdue	16	Anthony Gizoni, Waynesburg
1951	Oklahoma	Port Robertson	24	Oklahoma St	23	Walter Romanowski, Cornell
1952	Oklahoma	Port Robertson	22	Northern Iowa	21	Tommy Evans, Oklahoma
1953	Penn St	Charles Speidel	21	Oklahoma	15	Frank Bettucci, Cornell
1954	Oklahoma St	Art Griffith	32	Pittsburgh	17	Tommy Evans, Oklahoma
1955	Oklahoma St	Art Griffith	40	Penn St	31	Edward Eichelberger, Lehigh
1956	Oklahoma St	Art Griffith	65	Oklahoma	62	Dan Hodge, Oklahoma
1957	Oklahoma	Port Robertson	73	Pittsburgh	66	Dan Hodge, Oklahoma
1958	Oklahoma St	Myron Roderick	77	Iowa St	62	Dick Delgado, Oklahoma
1959	Oklahoma St	Myron Roderick	73	Iowa St	51	Ron Gray, Iowa St
1960	Oklahoma	Thomas Evans	59	Iowa St	40	Dave Auble, Cornell

DIVISION I (Cont.)

Year	Champion	Coach	Pts	Runner-Up	Pts	Most Outstanding Wrestler
1961	Oklahoma St	Myron Roderick	82	Oklahoma	63	E. Gray Simons, Lock Haven
1962	Oklahoma St	Myron Roderick	82	Oklahoma	45	E. Gray Simons, Lock Haven
1963	Oklahoma	Thomas Evans	48	Iowa St	45	Mickey Martin, Oklahoma
1964	Oklahoma St	Myron Roderick	87	Oklahoma	58	Dean Lahr, Colorado
1965	Iowa St	Harold Nichols	87	Oklahoma St	86	Yojiro Uetake, Oklahoma St
1966	Oklahoma St	Myron Roderick	79	Iowa St	70	Yojiro Uetake, Oklahoma St
1967	Michigan St	Grady Peninger	74	Michigan	63	Rich Sanders, Portland St
1968	Oklahoma St	Myron Roderick	81	Iowa St	78	Dwayne Keller, Oklahoma St
1969	Iowa St	Harold Nichols	104	Oklahoma	69	Dan Gable, Iowa St
1970	Iowa St	Harold Nichols	99	Michigan St	84	Larry Owings, Washington
1971	Oklahoma St	Tommy Chesbro	94	Iowa St	66	Darrell Keller, Oklahoma St
1972	Iowa St	Harold Nichols	103	Michigan St	72½	Wade Schalles, Clarion
1973	Iowa St	Harold Nichols	85	Oregon St	72½	Greg Strobel, Oregon St
1974	Oklahoma	Stan Abel	69½	Michigan	67	Floyd Hitchcock, Bloomsburg
1975	Iowa	Gary Kurdelmeier	102	Oklahoma	77	Mike Frick, Lehigh
1976	Iowa	Gary Kurdelmeier	123½	Iowa St	85¾	Chuch Yagla, Iowa
1977	Iowa St	Harold Nichols	95½	Oklahoma St	88¾	Nick Gallo, Hofstra
1978	Iowa	Dan Gable	94½	Iowa St	94	Mark Churella, Michigan
1979	Iowa	Dan Gable	122½	Iowa St	88	Bruce Kinseth, Iowa
1980	Iowa	Dan Gable	110¾	Oklahoma St	87	Howard Harris, Oregon St
1981	Iowa	Dan Gable	129¾	Oklahoma	100¼	Gene Mills, Syracuse
1982	Iowa	Dan Gable	131¾	Iowa St	111	Mark Schultz, Oklahoma
1983	Iowa	Dan Gable	155	Oklahoma St	102	Mike Sheets, Oklahoma St
1984	Iowa	Dan Gable	123¾	Oklahoma St	98	Jim Zalesky, Iowa
1985	Iowa	Dan Gable	145¼	Oklahoma	98½	Barry Davis, Iowa
1986	Iowa	Dan Gable	158	Oklahoma	84¼	Marty Kistler, Iowa
1987	Iowa St	Jim Gibbons	133	Iowa	108	John Smith, Oklahoma St
1988	Arizona St	Bobby Douglas	93	Iowa	85½	Scott Turner, N Carolina St
1989	Oklahoma St	Joe Seay	91¼	Arizona St	70½	Tim Krieger, Iowa St
1990	Oklahoma St	Joe Seay	117¾	Arizona St	104¾	Chris Barnes, Oklahoma St
1991	Iowa	Dan Gable	157	Oklahoma St	108¾	Jeff Prescott, Penn St
1992	Iowa	Dan Gable	149	Oklahoma St	100½	Tom Brands, Iowa
1993	Iowa	Dan Gable	123¾	Penn St	87½	Terry Steiner, Iowa
1994	Oklahoma St	John Smith	94¾	Iowa	76½	Pat Smith, Oklahoma St
1995	Iowa	Dan Gable	134	Oregon St	77½	T.J. Jaworsky, N Carolina
1996	Iowa	Dan Gable	122½	Iowa St	78½	Les Gutches, Oregon St
1997	Iowa	Dan Gable	170	Oklahoma St	113½	Lincoln McIlravy, Iowa
1998	Iowa	Jim Zalesky	115	Minnesota	102	Joe Williams, Iowa
1999	Iowa	Jim Zalesky	100½	Minnesota	98½	Cael Sanderson, Iowa St
2000	Iowa	Jim Zalesky	116	Iowa St	109½	Cael Sanderson, Iowa St
2001	Minnesota	J Robinson	138½	Iowa	125½	Cael Sanderson, Iowa St
2002	Minnesota	J Robinson	126½	Iowa St	104	Cael Sanderson, Iowa St
2003	Oklahoma St	John Smith	143	Minnesota	104½	Eric Larkin, Arizona St
2004	Oklahoma St	John Smith	123½	Iowa	82	Jesse Jantzen, Harvard

*Unofficial champions.

DIVISION II

Year	Champion	Year	Champion	Year	Champion
1963	Western St (CO)	1977	Cal St–Bakersfield	1991	NE–Omaha
1964	Western St (CO)	1978	Northern Iowa	1992	Central Oklahoma
1965	Mankato St	1979	Cal St–Bakersfield	1993	Central Oklahoma
1966	Cal Poly–SLO	1980	Cal St–Bakersfield	1994	Central Oklahoma
1967	Portland St	1981	Cal St–Bakersfield	1995	Central Oklahoma
1968	Cal Poly–SLO	1982	Cal St–Bakersfield	1996	Pittsburgh–Johnstown
1969	Cal Poly–SLO	1983	Cal St–Bakersfield	1997	San Francisco St
1970	Cal Poly–SLO	1984	SIU–Edwardsville	1998	N Dakota St
1971	Cal Poly–SLO	1985	SIU–Edwardsville	1999	Pittsburgh–Johnstown
1972	Cal Poly–SLO	1986	SIU–Edwardsville	2000	N Dakota St
1973	Cal Poly–SLO	1987	Cal St–Bakersfield	2001	N Dakota St
1974	Cal Poly–SLO	1988	N Dakota St	2002	Central Oklahoma
1975	Northern Iowa	1989	Portland St	2003	Central Oklahoma
1976	Cal St–Bakersfield	1990	Portland St	2004	Nebraska-Omaha

DIVISION III

Year	Champion	Year	Champion	Year	Champion
1974	Wilkes	1985	Trenton St	1996	Wartburg
1975	John Carroll	1986	Montclair St	1997	Augsburg
1976	Montclair St	1987	Trenton St	1998	Augsburg
1977	Brockport St	1988	St. Lawrence	1999	Wartburg
1978	Buffalo	1989	Ithaca	2000	Augsburg
1979	Trenton St	1990	Ithaca	2001	Augsburg
1980	Brockport St	1991	Augsburg	2002	Augsburg
1981	Trenton St	1992	Brockport	2003	Wartburg
1982	Brockport St	1993	Augsburg	2004	Wartburg
1983	Brockport St	1994	Ithaca		
1984	Trenton St	1995	Augsburg		

INDIVIDUAL CHAMPIONSHIP RECORDS

Swimming

Men

Event	Time	Record Holder	Date
50-yard freestyle	19.08	Neil Walker, Texas	3-27-97
100-yard freestyle	41.62	Anthony Ervin, California	3-20-02
200-yard freestyle	1:33.03	Matt Biondi, California	4-3-87
500-yard freestyle	4:08.75	Tom Dolan, Michigan	3-23-95
1,650-yard freestyle	14:26.62	Chris Thompson, Michigan	3-24-01
100-yard backstroke	45.25	Neil Walker, Texas	3-28-97
200-yard backstroke	1:39.16	Aaron Peirsol, Texas	3-29-03
100-yard breaststroke	52.32	Jeremy Linn, Tennessee	3-28-97
200-yard breaststroke	1:52.62	Brendan Hansen, Texas	3-29-03
100-yard butterfly	45.44	Ian Crocker, Texas	3-29-02
200-yard butterfly	1:41.78	Melvin Stewart, Tennessee	3-30-91
200-yard individual medley	1:42.66	George Bovell, Auburn	3-27-03
400-yard individual medley	3:38.18	Tom Dolan, Michigan	3-24-95

Women

Event	Time	Record Holder	Date
50-yard freestyle	21.69	Maritza Correia, Georgia	3-21-02
100-yard freestyle	47.29	Maritza Correia, Georgia	3-22-03
200-yard freestyle	1:43.08	Martina Moravcova, Southern Methodist	3-28-97
500-yard freestyle	4:34.39	Janet Evans, Stanford	3-15-90
1,650-yard freestyle	15:39.14	Janet Evans, Stanford	3-17-90
100-yard backstroke	49.97	Natalie Coughlin, California	3-22-02
200-yard backstroke	1:49.52	Natalie Coughlin, California	3-22-02
100-yard breaststroke	59.05	Kristy Kowal, Georgia	3-20-98
200-yard breaststroke	2:07.36	Tara Kirk, Stanford	3-22-02
100-yard butterfly	50.01	Natalie Coughlin, California	3-22-02
200-yard butterfly	1:53.36	Limin Liu, Nevada	3-20-99
200-yard individual medley	1:53.91	Maggie Bowen, Auburn	3-21-02
400-yard individual medley	4:02.28	Summer Sanders, Stanford	3-20-92

INDIVIDUAL COLLEGIATE RECORDS

Indoor Track and Field

Men

Event	Mark	Record Holder	Date
55-meter dash	6.00	Lee McRae, Pittsburgh	3-14-86
60-meter dash	6.45	Leonard Myles-Mills, Brigham Young	2-20-99
55-meter hurdles	7.07	Allen Johnson, N Carolina	3-13-92
60-meter hurdles	7.47	Reggie Torian, Wisconsin	2-7-97
200-meter dash	20.26	Shawn Crawford, Clemson	3-10-00
400-meter dash	45.35	Alleyne Francique, Louisiana St	2-24-02
800-meter run	1:44.84	Paul Ereng, Virginia	3-4-89
Mile run	3:55.00	Tony Waldrop, N Carolina	2-17-74
3,000-meter run	7:46.03	Adam Goucher, Colorado	3-14-98
5,000-meter run	13:20.40	Suleiman Nyambui, Texas–El Paso	2-6-81
High jump	7 ft 9¼ in	Hollis Conway, SW Louisiana	3-11-89
Pole vault	19 ft 2¼ in	Jacob Davis, Texas	3-6-99
Long jump	28 ft 2¼ in	Miguel Pate, Alabama	3-1-02
Triple jump	57 ft 5 in	Charlie Simpkins, Baptist	1-17-86
Shot put	70 ft 6½ in	Terry Albritton, Stanford	2-4-77
35-pound weight throw	78 ft 6½ in	Tore Johnsen, Texas–El Paso	2-25-84

INDIVIDUAL COLLEGIATE RECORDS (CONT.)

Indoor Track and Field (Cont.)

Women

Event	Mark	Record Holder	Date
55-meter dash	6.56	Gwen Torrence, Georgia	3-14-87
60-meter dash	7.09	Angela Williams, Southern Cal	3-11-01
55-meter hurdles	7.39	Tiffany Lott, Brigham Young	3-7-97
60-meter hurdles	7.90	Perdita Felicien, Illinois	3-8-02
200-meter dash	22.49	Muna Lee, Louisiana St	3-14-03
400-meter dash	51.05	Maicel Malone, Arizona St	3-9-91
800-meter run	2:01.65	Amy Wickus, Wisconsin	2-12-94
Mile run	4:28.31	Vicki Huber, Villanova	2-5-88
3,000-meter run	8:53.54	PattiSue Plumer, Stanford	2-27-83
5,000-meter run	15:17.28	Sonia O'Sullivan, Villanova	1-26-91
High jump	6 ft 5½ in	Four recordholders	—
Pole vault	14 ft 10 ¼ in	Amy Linnen, Arizona	3-13-02
Long jump	22 ft 8 in	Elva Goulbourne, Auburn	2-23-02
Triple jump	46 ft 9 in	Suzette Lee, Louisiana St	3-8-97
Shot put	61 ft 9½ in	Teri Tunks, Southern Methodist	2-28-98
35-pound weight throw	71 ft 8¾ in	Dawn Ellerbe, S Carolina	3-7-97

Outdoor Track and Field

Men

Event	Mark	Record Holder	Date
100-meter dash	9.92	Ato Bolden, UCLA	6-1-96
200-meter dash	19.86	Justin Gatlin, Tennessee	5-12-02
400-meter dash	44.00	Quincy Watts, Southern Cal	6-6-92
800-meter run	1:44.55	Julius Achon, George Mason	5-4-96
1,500-meter run	3:35.30	Sydney Maree, Villanova	6-6-81
3,000-meter steeplechase	8:05.40	Henry Rono, Washington St	4-8-78
5,000-meter run	13:08.40	Henry Rono, Washington St	4-8-78
10,000-meter run	27:36.20	Gabriel Kamau, Texas–El Paso	4-24-82
110-meter high hurdles	13.00	Renaldo Nehemiah, Maryland	5-6-79
400-meter intermediate hurdles	47.85	Kevin Young, UCLA	6-3-88
High jump	7 ft 9¾ in	Hollis Conway, SW Louisiana	6-3-89
Pole vault	19 ft 7½ in	Lawrence Johnson, Tennessee	5-25-96
Long jump	28 ft 8¼ ft	Erick Walder, Arkansas	4-2-94
Triple jump	57 ft 7¾ in	Keith Connor, Southern Methodist	6-5-82
Shot put	72 ft 2¼ in	John Godina, UCLA	6-3-95
Discus throw	219 ft 6 in	Gábor Máté, Auburn	3-25-00
Hammer throw	268 ft 10 in	Balazs Kiss, Southern Cal	5-19-95
Javelin throw (new javelin)	268 ft 7 in	Esko Mikkola, Arizona	6-3-98
Decathlon	8463 pts	Tom Pappas, Tennessee	3-17/18-99

Women

Event	Mark	Record Holder	Date
100-meter dash	10.78	Dawn Sowell, Louisiana St	6-3-89
200-meter dash	22.04	Dawn Sowell, Louisiana St	6-2-89
400-meter dash	50.18	Pauline Davis, Alabama	6-3-89
800-meter run	1:59.11	Suzy Favor, Wisconsin	6-1-90
1,500-meter run	4:08.26	Suzy Favor, Wisconsin	6-2-90
3,000-meter run	8:47.35	Vicki Huber, Villanova	6-3-88
5,000-meter run	15:23.03	Kathy Hayes, Oregon	5-4-85
10,000-meter run	32:22.97	Carole Zajac, Villanova	4-23-92
100-meter hurdles	12.61	Gail Devers, UCLA	5-21-88
400-meter hurdles	54.54	Ryan Tolbert, Vanderbilt	6-6-97
High jump	6 ft 6 in	Amy Acuff, UCLA/	5-19-95
		Kajsa Bergqvist, Southern Methodist	5-22-99
Pole vault	14 ft 10¼ in	Amy Linnen, Arizona	3-9-02
Long jump	22 ft 11¼ in	Jackie Joyner-Kersee, UCLA	5-4-85
Triple jump	46 ft 9 in	Suzette Lee, Louisiana St	3-8-97
Shot put	62 ft 3¼ in	Meg Ritchie, Arizona	5-7-83
Discus throw	222 ft 5 in	Meg Ritchie, Arizona	4-26-81
Hammer throw	220 ft 6 in	Jamine Moton, Clemson	5-29-02
Javelin throw (new javelin)	197 ft 8 in	Angeliki Tsiolakoudi, Texas–El Paso	6-3-00
Heptathlon	6527 pts	Diane Guthrie-Gresham, George Mason	6-2/3-95

Olympics

The Olympics return to their ancestral home of Athens

Greek Surprise

With American Michael Phelps leading the way, the Athens Games came off swimmingly, defying the skeptics

BY MERRELL NODEN

FROM THE MOMENT the International Olympic Committee awarded the 2004 Olympic Games to Athens, the prospect of the Games' returning to their ancient birthplace caused more concern than excitement: Would the Olympics be targeted by terrorists? Would all of the much-needed construction—of a new highway linking downtown Athens to the airport, not to mention the venues themselves—be finished in time? What about the smog and heat, the wild dogs in the street? And how would Greece, a small, relatively poor country, pay for it all?

For years, the Greeks did little to allay those fears. They looked less like speedy Hermes than like Sisyphus, trying to roll that big rock uphill. Following a stern warning from the IOC in 2000, the Athens organizing committee and its ever-so-chic leader, Gianna Angelopoulos-Daskalaki, spent the last few years on double, not-so-secret probation. Discussed openly was the possibility of returning the Games to Sydney. That would have been an unbearable humiliation for a

proud people still smarting from the IOC's decision to award the centennial Games of 1996 to Atlanta.

But IOC president Jacques Rogge stuck with Athens and, for 17 days in mid-August, he was proven magnificently right. Yes, workers were still pouring concrete and jamming saplings into the ground around venues just days before the Games, and the Olympic swimming pool never did get the roof designed for it. But mother of Zeus! These were spectacular Games, ones that took the whole glorious span of Greek history and culture for a backdrop.

From the Parthenon, floodlit each night atop the Acropolis, to the crumbling ruins of the original Olympic stadium—where for one day shot putters found themselves in the extraordinary position of being the sole focus of an excited crowd of 15,000—the Greeks made splendid use of the one thing no other host city could ever have: its own Olympic past. How could you not love a marathon course that traced the original route taken by Pheidippides? (Unless you were poor Paula

Phelps, whose endurance matched his extraordinary talent, won six gold medals.

Radcliffe of Great Britain, the world record holder, who wilted in the heat and was left sitting weeping on the curb at 23 miles.) And, in case you were still somehow deaf to all the echoes of antiquity, all medalists were crowned with wreaths of olive, an especially nice touch in these turbulent times.

The greatest asset of all was the fervor of the Greek people, though their faith was tested mightily by two terrible events in the run-up to the Games. In the first, a week before the Opening Ceremonies, Greek judo competitor Eleni Ioannou leaped from the window of an Athens apartment, apparently following a lovers' spat with her kickboxer boyfriend. Two nights later he jumped out the same window. He survived, but she died in the second week of the Games.

The second incident was the mysterious, late-night motorcycle accident involving Greece's top male and female sprinters, Kostas Kenteris and Ekaterini Thanou, just hours after they had missed a drug test. There were no witnesses to the purported accident, and both athletes pulled out of the Games under a dark cloud of suspicion. There could hardly have been a more high-profile embarrassment since Kenteris, the defending Olympic champion at the 200 meters, was his country's choice to light the Olympic flame. On the night of the men's 200 final, the Greek faithful who'd bought tickets expecting to see Kenteris defend his Olympic title, booed mercilessly, delaying the start of the race by four minutes. One could understand their frustration, but an investigation revealed that this was hardly the first time Kenteris had missed a drug test.

For the most part, though, the Greeks were generous, exuberant, exceedingly proud hosts. By the time Greece claimed the first of its six gold medals—in men's synchronized diving—they were ready to sing, cheer and get passionate about their ancestors' incomparable gift to the world. Yes, there were many empty seats at some venues. But in the end 3.6 million tickets had been sold, many to Greeks who at the last minute simply couldn't bear not to be part of this once-in-a-lifetime experience.

Each night thousands of visitors thronged the outdoor cafés and winding streets of Athens' old Plaza district. There was much to toast. Along with the usual spheres of dominance—China cleaned up in diving, Cuba in boxing and the U.S. in swimming, track and field and women's team sports—these Games will be remembered above all for a pair of American gymnasts and for one young man, Michael Phelps, who arrived in Athens aiming to surpass Mark Spitz's Olympic record of seven gold medals in a single Games.

Including qualifying rounds of individual events and relays, Phelps swam 17 races in seven days. By comparison, Spitz swam 13 races in eight days to win his seven gold medals in Munich. Phelps, a likeable 19-year-old from Baltimore, won six golds and a record-tying eight medals in all. But he stamped himself as a true champion as much through the two races he didn't win as in those he did. Despite all that he risked by attempting too much, Phelps was eager to swim the 200-meter freestyle, which was not his specialty, in order to race the great Ian Thorpe of Australia, and Pieter van den Hoogenband of the Netherlands. Thorpe won the gold in the classic showdown (his second of the Games), van den Hoogenband silver, and Phelps bronze—but it was still inspiring to see a great athlete taking a risk in the pursuit of new challenges.

And Phelps's big-heartedness didn't end there. With one event left in his exhausting itinerary (and five gold medals under his belt), he gave his spot in the 400 medley final to Ian Crocker. Phelps would still get a gold medal for swimming the prelims, but his generosity in allowing his U.S. teammate to compete for a gold medal did not go unappreciated by Crocker—who'd missed gold medal chances in the 100 fly (to Phelps) and the 400 free relay (in which he swam poorly)—or the viewing public.

It was one of the Games' most uplifting gesture, a welcome counterweight to the Iranian judo champion who refused to fight his first round opponent, an Israeli; the judging controversy in gymnastics; and the 24 drug positives, twice the previous record.

There were a number of historic firsts. Gal Fridman gave Israel something to celebrate, its first Olympic gold medal, in windsurfing, while New York-born Felix Sanchez attained the same honor for the Dominican Republic, winning the men's 400 hurdles.

But the biggest surprise of these Games may have been the utterly unexpected run of the Iraqi soccer team, which had been left in shambles by the nation's sadistic former Olympic chief, Uday Hussein. Shaking off their troubled past, they stunned everyone in their opening match by upsetting Portugal 4–2. They next beat Costa Rica 2–0. They lost to Paraguay in the semis and then to Italy, 1–0, in the bronze medal game, but their performance rivaled Phelps's as the Games' most inspirational.

Numbing is a good word for the latest Olympic judging controversy, which swirled for days, poisoning the historic achievement of the top U.S. gymnast, Paul Hamm. Hamm won the all around title at the 2003 world championships and was given a good chance of doing so in Athens. But when a botched landing in the vault sent him stumbling into the judges' table, he slipped from first to twelfth place. Even Hamm thought the best he could hope for was a bronze. Blocking that thought from his mind, he set out to do a routine for the ages on the high bar, and nailed it, flying breathtakingly high on three consecutive releases. When his score came up, a 9.837, Hamm was, by the smallest margin in history, the all-around Olympic men's gymnastics champion, a U.S. first.

But was he? It turned out that Yang Tae Young of South Korea, who won the bronze medal, had been given too low a start score in his parallel bars routine. If you added the extra one tenth of a point he should have started with, then Young, not Hamm, was the real Olympic champion. Except . . . the Korean delegation hadn't filed its protest in the time frame specified by the rules. Except . . . as U.S. coaches pointed out after examining a tape of Young's performance, he did four holds in his parallel bars routine, rather than the maximum three, and could have suffered a mandatory deduction of .20. On and on the controversy went, casting a pall over Hamm's astounding comeback.

The International Gymnastics Federation showed its cowardice by asking Hamm to give his gold medal to Young. He refused, and the dispute moved on to a court of arbitration. One has to wonder how much the IOC now rues the Pandora's Box it opened two years ago by awarding a second pair of gold medals in pairs figure skating following the revelations of vote swapping in Salt Lake City. If these Games had one unfortunate legacy, it may be their litigiousness.

The U.S. women gymnasts were favorites but finished second to Romania in the team competition. Redemption came in the form of 16-year-old Carly Patterson, whose missteps in the team final had contributed to the U.S.'s second-place finish. Performing the last floor exercise of the evening, Patterson nailed it for 9.712 points and the gold medal.

The U.S. women's teams in basketball, soccer and softball all won gold medals, going a combined 22-0-1. No one was more dominant than the softball team, which

BILL FRAKES

Hamm's all-around gold medal, a U.S. first, was marred by a judging controversy.

outscored its opponents 51–1. The famous soccer team, anchored, it seems, since Homer's day by Mia Hamm, Julie Foudy, Joy Fawcett, Kristine Lilly and Brandi Chastain, gave those veterans a perfect send-off, defeating Brazil in the final, 2–1.

The U.S. men's basketball team, by contrast, was a colossal disappointment. Despite sending a team of NBA All Stars, including Allen Iverson and Tim Duncan, former league MVPs both, the U.S. lost three games, including its opener, in which Puerto Rico ran circles around the hapless Americans, beating them by 19 points. In the semis the U.S. lost to Argentina, the eventual gold medal winner, but came back to claim the bronze against Lithuania. The U.S. men looked bewildered by the international game, which puts a premium on outside shooting and features a wider lane that limits the effectiveness of big men in the low post. With the seven-foot Duncan as its best player, and an utter dearth of outside shooters, the U.S. team was doomed from the start.

There were other disappointments for the U.S. For the first time since 1912, the U.S. did not win a single diving medal. Andre Ward won the U.S. boxing team's only gold medal, and Cael Sanderson won the U.S.'s

only gold in any style of wrestling, fulfilling the promise of his perfect collegiate record at Iowa State. Greco-Roman heavyweight Rulon Gardner, who in Sydney had slain the closest thing the Olympics have to a giant, Alexander Karelin, settled for bronze here.

The most celebrated U.S. Olympian from the Sydney Games, Marion Jones, capped a terrible, controversial year with a fifth-place finish in the long jump, then botched her handoff in the 400-meter relay. For the first time in Olympic history (excluding the boycotted 1980 Games), the U.S. won neither 400 relay. The U.S. men passed poorly and anchor Maurice Greene fell just short of running down Great Britain for the gold.

Still, a new generation of American track stars shone brightly in Athens. The U.S. men won eight of nine medals in the sprints, with Justin Gatlin winning the 100, Shawn Crawford waiting out the crowd's booing to lead a sweep in the 200 and Jeremy Wariner leading another U.S. sweep in the 400. The women were not quite as strong. Lauryn Williams took silver in the 100 and 18-year-old Allyson Felix came second in the 200.

Perhaps the best track and field story in Athens was that of Morocco's Hicham El Guerrouj. Having stumbled in Atlanta eight years ago, El Guerrouj, the world record holder in both the 1500 and the mile, had been the heavy favorite in Sydney but suc-

ROBERTO SCHMIDT/AFP/GETTY IMAGES

cumbed to a paralyzing case of nerves, finishing second. In Athens, after briefly losing the lead to Bernard Lagat of Kenya in the final homestretch, he surged to the front and won his first gold medal. Four days later he claimed a second, winning the 5,000 over Kenenisa Bekele of Ethiopia.

In the men's marathon, the final event of the Games, confusion and controversy surfaced once again. Roughly three miles from the finish, Cornelius Horan, a disturbed and defrocked Irish priest, rushed onto the course in a kilt and beret and steered the visibly terrified leader, Vanderlei de Lima of Brazil, into the crowd. De Lima lost about 10 seconds and who knows how much composure before resuming the race. He was overtaken by Stefano Baldini of Italy, who won the gold, and Meb Keflezighi of the U.S., who claimed silver. Fortunately, de Lima held on to finish third, running delightedly to the finish line with his arms spread wide. It sure looked like de Lima was delighted to have won the bronze, but the Brazilian Olympic federation followed South Korea's example by asking that de Lima be awarded a second gold medal.

It was a strange ending to a superb Olympics. Indeed, there were calls for desig-

nating Athens the permanent host of the Olympics, a change that would have meant all those brand new facilities actually got used again. But that's almost certainly not going to happen. The Greeks themselves may not want the Games again, after they get the bill. By one estimate, Greece will have spent $9 billion on its Games, with $1.5 billion of that going to security. You can buy a lot of security for that, and with surveillance cameras and dirigibles everywhere, scuba divers circling the port and heavily armed soldiers patrolling, the Games went off without problems of the worst kind. That wind at the end of the Closing Ceremonies? That wasn't Aeolus blowing Odysseus home. That was Dr. Rogge, exhaling in relief that nothing too serious had happened.

Rogge seems to have chucked his predecessor's habit of awarding each host city the perfunctory honorific of "best ever" Olympic host in his closing remarks. Certainly, though, you could make a good case that the Athens Games were exactly that. Asked what advice she had for the five cities still vying to host the 2012 Games, Angelopoulos-Daskalaki summed up perfectly what made these Games special: "I don't know if they have the passion of Greece."

And so it's on to Beijing for the next summer Games. In Athens, the Chinese had their best Games ever, winning 63 medals overall, third best behind the U.S. (103) and somewhat deflated Russia (92). Thirty-two of China's medals were gold, second only to the U.S.'s 35. They dominated diving, table tennis and weightlifting, and claimed surprising medals in sports like tennis and women's wrestling. Most impressive of all was Liu Xiang, a 21-year-old from Shanghai who tied the world record (12.91) while easily winning the men's 110-meter hurdles.

The world can expect the Chinese to be well-prepared both in and out of competition four years from now. Still, they will find Athens a tough act to follow. The Greeks, after all, began preparing for these Games many centuries ago.

2004 Summer Games

TRACK AND FIELD
Men

100 METERS
1. ...Justin Gatlin, United States — 9.85
2. ...Francis Obikwelu, Portugal — 9.86
3. ...Maurice Greene, United States — 9.87

200 METERS
1. ...Shawn Crawford, United States — 19.79
2. ...Bernard Williams, United States — 20.01
3. ...Justin Gatlin, United States — 20.03

400 METERS
1. ...Jeremy Wariner, United States — 44.00
2. ...Otis Harris, United States — 44.16
3. ...Derrick Brew, United States — 44.42

800 METERS
1. ...Yuriy Borzakovskiy, Russia — 1:44.45
2. ...Mbulaeni Mulaudzi, S Africa — 1:44.61
3. ...Wilson Kipketer, Denmark — 1:44.65

1,500 METERS
1. ...Hicham El Guerrouj, Morocco — 3:34.18
2. ...Bernard Lagat, Kenya — 3:34.30
3. ...Rui Silva, Portugal — 3:34.68

5,000 METERS
1. ...Hicham El Guerrouj, Morocco — 13:14.39
2. ...Kenenisa Bekele, Ethiopia — 13:14.59
3. ...Eliud Kipchoge, Kenya — 13:15.10

10,000 METERS
1. ...Kenenisa Bekele, Ethiopia — 27:05.10 OR
2. ...Sileshi Sihine, Ethiopia — 27:09.39
3. ...Zersenay Tadesse, Eritrea — 27:22.57

MARATHON
1. ...Stefano Baldini, Italy — 2:10:55
2. ...Mebrahtom Keflezighi, United States — 2:11:29
3. ...Vanderlei de Lima, Brazil — 2:12:11

110-METER HURDLES
1. ...Xiang Liu, China — 12.91 EWR
2. ...Terrence Trammell, United States — 13.18
3. ...Anier García, Cuba — 13.20

400-METER HURDLES
1. ...Felix Sanchez, Dominican Republic — 47.63
2. ...Danny McFarlane, Jamaica — 48.11
3. ...Naman Keita, France — 48.26

3,000-METER STEEPLECHASE
1. ...Ezekiel Kemboi, Kenya — 8:05.81
2. ...Brimin Kipruto, Kenya — 8:06.11
3. ...Paul Kipsiele Koech, Kenya — 8:06.64

4 X 100-METER RELAY
1. ...Great Britian: (Jason Gardener Darren Campbell, Marlon Devonish, Mark Lewis Francis) — 38.07
2. ...United States — 38.08
3. ...Nigeria — 38.23

4 X 400-METER RELAY
1. ...United States: (Otis Harris, Derrick Brew, Jeremy Wariner, Darold Williamson) — 2:55.91
2. ...Australia — 3:00.60
3. ...Nigeria — 3:00.90

20-KILOMETER WALK
1. ...Ivano Brugnetti, Italy — 1:19:40
2. ...Francisco Javier Fernandez, Spain — 1:19:45
3. ...Nathan Deakes, Australian — 1:20:02

50-KILOMETER WALK
1. ...Robert Korzeniowski, Poland — 3:38:46
2. ...Denis Nizhegorodov, Russia — 3:42:50
3. ...Aleksey Voyevodin, Russia — 3:43:34

HIGH JUMP
1. ...Stefan Holm, Sweden — 7 ft 8¾ in
2. ...Matthew Hemingway, United States — 7 ft 8 in
3. ...Yaroslav Baba, Czech Republic — 7 ft 8 in

POLE VAULT
1. ...Timothy Mack, United States — 19 ft 6¼ in
2. ...Toby Stevenson, United States — 19 ft 4¼ in
3. ...Giuseppe Gibilisco, Italy — 19 ft 2¼ in

LONG JUMP
1. ...Dwight Phillips, United States — 28 ft 2¼ in
2. ...John Moffitt, United States — 27 ft 9½ in
3. ...Joan Lino Martinez, Spain — 27 ft 3¾ in

TRIPLE JUMP
1. ...Christian Olsson, Sweden — 58 ft 4½ in
2. ...Marian Oprea, Romania — 57 ft 7 in
3. ...Danila Burkenya, Russia — 57 ft 4¼ in

SHOT PUT
1. ...Yuriy Bilonog, Ukraine — 69 ft 5¼ in
2. ...Adam Nelson, United States — 69 ft 5¼ in
3. ...Joachim Olsen, Denmark — 69 ft 1½ in

DISCUS THROW
1. ...Virgilijus Alekna, Lithuania — 229 ft 3 in
2. ...Zoltan Kovago, Hungary — 219 ft 11 in
3. ...Aleksander Tammert, Estonia — 218 ft 8 in

HAMMER THROW
1. ...Adrian Zsolt, Hungary — 272 ft 11 in
2. ...Koji Murofushi, Japan — 272 ft
3. ...Ivan Tikhon, Belarus — 261 ft 10 in

JAVELIN
1. ...Andreas Thorkildsen, Norway — 283 ft 9 in
2. ...Vadims Vasilevskis, Latvia — 278 ft 8 in
3. ...Sergey Makarov, Russia — 278 ft 4 in

DECATHLON
Pts
1. ...Roman Seberle, Czech Republic — 8893 OR
2. ...Bryan Clay, United States — 8820
3. ...Dmitriy Karpov, Kazakhstan — 8725

Note: OR=Olympic record. WR=world record. EOR=equals Olympic record. EWR=equals world record.

TRACK AND FIELD (Cont.)
Women

100 METERS
1. ...Yuliya Nesterenko, Belarus — 10.93
2. ...Lauryn Williams, United States — 10.96
3. ...Veronica Campbell, Jamaica — 10.97

200 METERS
1. ...Veronica Campbell, Jamaica — 22.05
2. ...Allyson Felix, United States — 22.18
3. ...Debbie Ferguson, Bahamas — 22.30

400 METERS
1. ...Tonique Williams-Darling, Bahamas — 49.41
2. ...Ana Guevara, Mexico — 49.56
3. ...Natalya Antyukh, Russia — 49.89

800 METERS
1. ...Kelly Holmes, Great Britain — 1:56.38
2. ...Hasna Benhassi, Morocco — 1:56.43
3. ...Jolanda Ceplak, Slovenia — 1:56.43

1,500 METERS
1. ...Kelly Holmes, Great Britain — 3:57.90
2. ...Tatyana Tomashova, Russia — 3:58.12
3. ...Maria Cioncan, Romania — 3:58.39

5,000 METERS
1. ...Meseret Defar, Ethiopia — 14:45.65
2. ...Isabella Ochichi, Kenya — 14:48.19
3. ...Tirunesh Dibaba, Ethiopia — 14:51.83

10,000 METERS
1. ...Huina Xing, China — 30:24.36
2. ...Ejegayehu Dibaba, Ethiopia — 30:24.98
3. ...Derartu Tulu, Ethiopia — 30:26.42

MARATHON
1. ...Noguchi Mizuki, Japan — 2:26:20
2 ....Nyambura Wincatherine, Kenya — 2:26:32
3. ...Deena Kastor, United States — 2:27:20

100-METER HURDLES
1. ...Joanna Hayes, United States — 12.37 OR
2. ...Olena Krasovska, Ukraine — 12.45
3. ...Melissa Morrison, United States — 12.56

400-METER HURDLES
1. ...Faní Halkiá, Greece — 52.82
2. ...Ionela Tirlea-Manolache, Romania — 53.38
3. ...Tetiana Tereshuk-Antipova, Ukraine — 53.44

4 X 100-METER RELAY
1. ...Jamaica (T. Lawrence, S. Simpson, — 41.73
    Aleen Bailey, Veronica Campbell)
2. ...Russia — 42.27
3. ...France — 42.54

4 X 400-METER RELAY
1. ...United States (DeeDee Trotter, — 3:19.01
   Monique Henderson, Sanya Richards,
   Monique Hennagan)
2. ...Russia — 3:20.16
3. ...Jamaica — 3:22.00

20-KILOMETER WALK
1. ...Athanasía Tsoumeléka, Greece — 1:29:12
2. ...Olimpiada Ivanova, Russia — 1:29:16
3. ...Jane Saville, Australia — 1:29:25

HIGH JUMP
1. ...Yelena Slesarenko, Russia — 6 ft 9 in
2. ...Hestrie Cloete, S Africa — 6 ft 7½ in
3. ...Vita Styopina, Ukraine — 6 ft 7½ in

POLE VAULT
1. ...Yelena Isinbayeva, Russia — 16 ft 1¼ in WR
2. ...Svetlana Feofanova, Russia — 15 ft 7 in
3. ...Anna Rogowska, Poland — 15 ft 5 in

LONG JUMP
1. ...Tatyana Lebedeva, Russia — 23 ft 2½ in
2. ...Irina Simajina, Russia — 23 ft 1¾ in
3. ...Tatyana Kotova, Russia — 23 ft 1¾ in

TRIPLE JUMP
1. ...Frangoise Mbango Etone, Cameroon — 50 ft 2½ in
2. ...Chrysopigi Devetzi, Greece — 50 ft ½ in
3. ...Tatyana Lebedeva, Russia — 49 ft 8¼ in

SHOT PUT
1. ...Yumileidi Cumba Jay, Cuba — 64 ft 3¾ in
2. ...Nadine Kleinert, Germany — 64 ft 1¾ in
3. ...Svetlana Krivelyova, Russia — 63 ft 11½ in

DISCUS THROW
1. ...Natalya Sadova, Russia — 219 ft 10 in
2. ...Anastasia Kelesidou, Greece — 218 ft 9 in
3. ...Iryna Yatchenko, Belarus — 217 ft 1 in

JAVELIN
1. ...Osleidys Menendez, Cuba — 234 ft 8 in OR
2. ...Steffi Nerius, Germany — 215 ft 11 in
3. ...Mirela Manjani, Greece — 210 ft 11 in

HEPTATHLON — Pts
1. ...Carolina Kluft, Sweden — 6952
2. ...Austra Skujyte, Lithuania — 6435
3. ...Kelly Sotherton, Great Britain — 6424

HAMMER THROW
1. ...Olga Kuzenkova, Russia — 246 ft 1½ in OR
2. ...Yipsi Moreno, Cuba — 240 ft 8¼ in
3. ...Yunaika Crawford, Cuba — 240 ft ½ in

INDIVIDUAL ARCHERY

Men
1. ....Marco Galiazzo, Italy
2. ....Hiroshi Yamamoto, Japan
3. ....Tim Cuddihy, Australia

Women
1. ....Sung Hyun Park, S Korea
2. ....Sung Jin Lee, S Korea
3. ....Alison Williamson, Great Britain

TEAM ARCHERY

Men
1. ....S Korea
2. ....Taiwan
3. ....Ukraine

Women
1. ....S Korea
2. ....China
3. ....Taiwan

Note: OR=Olympic record. WR=world record. EOR=equals Olympic record. EWR=equals world record.

BADMINTON

Men

SINGLES
1. ...Taufik Hidayat, Indonesia
2. ...Seung Mo Shon, S Korea
3. ...Soni Dwi Kuncoro, Indonesia

DOUBLES
1. ...Ha Tae Kwon/ Dong Moon Kim, S Korea
2. ...Dong Soo Lee/ Yoo Yong Sung, S Korea
3. ...Eng Hian/ Limpele Flandy, Indonesia

Women

SINGLES
1. ...Ning Zhang, China
2. ...Mia Audina, Netherlands
3. ...Mi Zhou, China

DOUBLES
1. .....Yang Wei/ Jiewen Zhang, China
2. ...Gao Ling/ Sui Huang, China
3. ...Kyung Min Ra/ Lee Kyung Won, S Korea

MIXED DOUBLES
1. ....Jun Zhang/ Gao Ling, China
2. ....Nathan Robertson/ Gail Emms, Great Britain
3. ....Jens Eriksen/ Schjoldager Mette, Denmark

BASEBALL

1. ....Cuba
2. ....Australia
3. ....Japan

BASKETBALL

Men

Final: Argentina 84, Italy 69
United States (3rd)
Argentina: Juan Sanchez, Emanuel Ginobili, Alejandro Montecchia, Fabricio Oberto, Walter Herrmann, Gabriel Fernandez, Hugo Sconochini, Luis Scola, Leonardo Gutierrez, Andres Nocioni, Carlos Delfino, Ruben Wolkowyski.

Women

Final: United States 74, Australia 63
Russia (3rd)
United States: Shannon Johnson, Dawn Staley, Suzanne Bird, Sheryl Swoopes, Ruth Riley, Lisa Leslie, Tamika Catchings, Tina Thompson, Diana Taurasi, Yolanda Griffith, Katie Smith, Swintayla Cash.

BOXING

LIGHT FLYWEIGHT (106 LB)
1. ....Yan Bhartelemy Varela, Cuba
2. ....Atagun Yal Cinkaya, Turkey
3. ....Shiming Zou, China
3. ....Sergey Kazakov, Russia

FLYWEIGHT (112 LB)
1. ....Yuriokis Gamboa Toledano, Cuba
2. ....Jerome Thomas, France
3. ....Fuad Aslanov, Azerbaijan
3. ....Rustamhodza Rahimov, Germany

BANTAMWEIGHT (119 LB)
1. ....Guillermo Rigondeaux Ortiz, Cuba
2. ....Worapoj Petchkoom, Thailand
3. ....Aghasi Mammadov, Azerbaijan
3. ....Bahodirion Sooltonov, Uzbekistan

FEATHERWEIGHT (125 LB)
1. ....Alexei Tichtchenko, Russia
2. ....Song Guk Kim, N Korea
3. ....Vitali Tajbert, Germany
3. ....Seok Hwan Jo, S Korea

LIGHTWEIGHT (132 LB)
1. ....Mario Kindelan Mesa, Cuba
2. ....Amir Khan, Great Britain
3. ....Serik Yeleuov, Kazakhstan
3. ....Murat Khrachev, Russia

LIGHT WELTERWEIGHT (139 LB)
1. ....Manus Boonjumnong, Thailand
2. ....Yudel Johnson Cedeno, Cuba
3. ....Boris Georgive, Bulgaria
3. ....Ionut Gheorghe, Romania

WELTERWEIGHT (147 LB)
1. ....Bakhtiyar Artayev, Kazakhstan
2. ....Lorenzo Aragon Armenteros, Cuba
3. ....Oleg Saitov, Russia
3. ....Jung Joo Kim, S Korea

MIDDLEWEIGHT (165 LB)
1. ....Gaydarbek Gaydarbekov, Russia
2. ....Gennadiy Golovkin, Kazakhstan
3. ....Suriya Prasathinphimai, Thailand
3. ....Andre Dirrell, United States

LIGHT HEAVYWEIGHT (178 LB)
1. ....Andre Ward, United States
2. ....Magomed Aripgadjiev, Belarus
3. ....Utkirbek Haydarov, Uzbekistan
3. ....Ahmed Ismail, Egypt

HEAVYWEIGHT (201 LB)
1. ....Odlanier Solis Fonte, Cuba
2. ....Viktar Zuyev, Belarus
3. ....Mohamed Elsayed, Egypt
3. ....Naser Al Shami, Syria

SUPERHEAVYWEIGHT (201+ LB)
1. ....Alexander Povetkin, Russia
2. ....Mohamed Aly, Egypt
3. ....Roberto Cammarelle, Italy
3. ....Michel Lopez Nunez, Cuba

CANOE/KAYAK

Men

C-1 FLATWATER 500 METERS

1.	...Andreas Dittmer, Germany	1:46.383
2.	...David Cal, Spain	1:46.723
3.	...Maxim Opalev, Russia	1:47.767

C-1 FLATWATER 1,000 METERS

1.	...David Cal, Spain	3:46.201
2.	...Andreas Dittmer, Germany	3:46.721
3.	...Attila Vajda, Hungary	3:49.025

C-2 FLATWATER 500 METERS

1.	...G. Meng/ W. Yang, China	1:40.278
2.	...I. Blanco/ L. Pajon, Cuba	1:40.350
3.	...A. Kostoglod/ A. Kovalev, Russia	1:40.442

C-2 FLATWATER 1,000 METERS

1.	...C. Gille/ T. Wylenzek, Germany	3:41.802
2.	...A. Kostoglod/ A. Kovalev, Russia	3:42.990
3.	...G. Kolonics/ G. Kozmann, Hungary	3:43.106

C-1 WHITEWATER SLALOM

		Pts
1.	...Tony Estanguet, France	189.16
2.	...Michal Martikan, Slovakia	189.28
3.	...Stefan Pfannmoeller, Germany	191.56

C-2 WHITEWATER SLALOM

		Pts
1.	...Pavel/ Peter Hochschorner, Slovakia	207.16
2.	...M. Becker/ S. Henze, Germany	210.98
3.	...J. Volf/ O. Stepanek, Czech Republic	212.86

K-1 FLATWATER 500 METERS

1.	...Adam Van Koeverden, Canada	1:37.919
2.	...Nathan Baggaley, Australia	1:38.467
3.	...Ian Wynne, Great Britain	1:38.547

K-1 FLATWATER 1,000 METERS

1.	...Eirik Veraas Larsen, Norway	3:25.897
2.	...Ben Fouhy, New Zealand	3:27.413
3.	...Adam Van Koeverden, Canada	3:28.218

Men (Cont.)

K-2 FLATWATER 500 METERS

1.	...R. Rauhe/ T. Wieskoetter, Germany	1:27.040
2.	...C. Robinson/ N. Baggaley, Australia	1:27.920
3.	...R. Piatrushenka/ V. Makhneu, Belarus	1:27.996

K-2 FLATWATER 1,000 METERS

1.	...M. Oscarsson/ H. Nilsson, Sweden	3:18.420
2.	...B. Bonomi/ A. Rossi, Italy	3:19.484
3.	...E.V. Larsen/ N.O. Fjeldheim, Norway	3:19.528

K-4 FLATWATER 1,000 METERS

1.	...Hungary	2:56.919
2.	...Germany	2:58.659
3.	...Slovakia	2:59.314

K-1 WHITEWATER SLALOM

		Pts
1.	...Benoit Peschier, France	187.96
2.	...Campbell Walsh, Great Britain	190.17
3.	...Fabien Lefevre, France	190.99

Women

K-1 FLATWATER 500 METERS

1.	...Natasa Janics, Hungary	1:47.741
2.	...Josefa Idem Guerrini, Italy	1:49.729
3.	...Caroline Brunet, Canada	1:50.601

K-2 FLATWATER 500 METERS

1.	...K. Kovacs/ N. Janics, Hungary	1:38.101
2.	...B. Fischer/ C. Leonhardt, Germany	1:39.533
3.	...A. Pastuszka/ B. Sokoloska, Poland	1:40.077

K-4 FLATWATER 500 METERS

1.	...Germany	1:34.340
2.	...Hungary	1:34.536
3.	...Ukraine	1:36.192

K-1 WHITEWATER SLALOM

		Pts
1.	...Elena Kaliska, Slovakia	210.03
2.	...Rebecca Giddens, United States	214.62
3.	...Helen Reeves, Great Britain	218.77

CYCLING

Men

ROAD RACE

1.	...Paolo Bettini, Italy	5:41:44
2.	...Sergio Paulinho, Portugal	5:41:45
3.	...Axel Merckx, Belgium	5:41:52

INDIVIDUAL TIME TRIAL

1.	...Tyler Hamilton, United States	57:31.74
2.	...Vyatcheslav Ekimov, Russia	57:50.58
3.	...Robert Julich, United States	57:58.19

1KM TIME TRIAL

1.	...Chris Hoy, Great Britain	1:00.711
2.	...Arnaud Tournant, France	1:00.896
3.	...Stefan Nimke, Germany	1:01.186

4,000-METER INDIVIDUAL PURSUIT

1.	...Bradley Wiggins, Great Britain	4:16.304
2.	...Brad McGee, Australia	4:20.436
3.	...Sergi Escobar, Spain	4:17.947

4,000-METER TEAM PURSUIT

1.	...Australia (Graeme Brown, Brett Lancaster, Brad McGee, Luke Roberts)	3:58.233
2.	...Great Britain	4:01.760
3.	...Spain	4:05.523

Men (Cont.)

SPRINT

1.	...Ryan Bayley, Australia	10.743
2.	...Theo Bos, Netherlands	10.710
3.	...Rene Wolff, German	10.612

POINTS RACE

1.	...Mikhail Ignatyev, Russia	93
2.	...Joan Llaneras, Spain	82
3.	...Guido Fulst, Germany	79

KIERIN

1.	...Ryan Bayley, Australia	10.601
2.	...Jose Escuredo, Spain	
3.	...Shane Kelly, Australia	

MADISON

1.	...G. Brown/ S. O'Grady, Australia	22
2.	...F. Marvulli/ B. Risi, Switzerland	15
3.	...R. Hayles/ B. Wiggins, Great Britain	12

OLYMPIC SPRINT

1.	...Germany	43.980
2.	...Japan	44.246
3.	...France	44.359

CYCLING *(Cont.)*

Women

POINTS RACE

1. ...Olga Slyusareva, Russia — 20
2. ...Belem Guerrero Mendez, Mexico — 14
3. ...Erin Mirabella, United States — 9

INDIVIDUAL TIME TRIAL

1. ...L. Zijlaard-van Moorsel, Netherlands — 31:11.53
2. ...Deirdre Demet-Barry, United States — 31:35.62
3. ...Karin Thuerig, Switzerland — 31:54.89

3,000-METER INDIVIDUAL PURSUIT

1. ...Sarah Ulmer, New Zealand — 3:24.537 WR
2. ...Katie Mactier, Australia — 3:27.650
3. ...L. Zijlaard-van Moorsel, Netherlands — 3:27.037

SPRINT

1. ...Lori-Ann Muenzer, Canada — 12.140
2. ...Tamilla Abassova, Russia — —
3. ...Anna Meares, Australia — 11.822

ROAD RACE

1. ...Sara Carrigan, Australia — 3:24:24
2. ...Judith Arndt, Germany — 3:24:31
3. ...Olga Slyusareva, Russia — 3:25:03

500-M TIME TRIAL

1. ...Anna Meares, Australia — 33.952
2. ...Jiang Yonghua, China — 34.112
3. ...Natallia Tsylinskaya, Belarus — 34.167

DIVING

Men

SPRINGBOARD

	Pts
1. ....Bo Peng, China	787.38
2. ....Alexandre Despatie, Canada	755.97
3. ....Dmitry Sautin, Russia	753.27

PLATFORM

	Pts
1. ....Jia Hu, China	748.08
2. ....Matthew Helm, Australia	730.56
3. ....Liang Tian, China	729.66

Women

SPRINGBOARD

	Pts
1. ....Jingjing Guo, China	633.15
2. ....Minxia Wu, China	612.00
3. ....Yulia Pakhalina, Russia	610.62

PLATFORM

	Pts
1. ....Chantelle Newbery, Australia	590.31
2. ....Lishi Lao, China	576.30
3. ....Loudy Tourky, Australia	561.66

EQUESTRIAN

TEAM EVENTING

1. ......France
2. ......Great Britain
3. ......United States

INDIVIDUAL EVENTING

	Pts
1. ......Leslie Law, Great Britain	44.40
2. ......Kim Severson, United States	45.20
3. ......Philippa Funnell, Great Britain	46.60

TEAM DRESSAGE

1. ......Germany
2. ......Spain
3. ......United States

INDIVIDUAL DRESSAGE

	Pts
1. ......Anky van Grunsven, Netherlands	85.825
2. ......Ulla Salzgeber, Germany	83.450
3. ......Beatriz Ferrer-Salat, Spain	79.575

TEAM JUMPING

1. ......Germany
2. ......United States
3. ......Sweden

INDIVIDUAL JUMPING

	Pts
1. ......Cian O'Connor, Ireland	4.00
2. ......Rodrigo Pessoa, Brazil	8.00
3. ......Chris Kappler, United States	8.00

FENCING

Men

FOIL

1. ....Brice Guyart, France
2. ....Salvatore Sanzo, Italy
3. ....Andrea Cassara, Italy

SABRE

1. ....Aldo Montano, Italy
2. ....Zsolt Nemcsik, Hungary
3. ....Vladislav Tretiak, Ukraine

ÉPÉE

1. ....Marcel Fischer, Switzerland
2. ....Lei Wang, China
3. ....Pavel Kolobkov, Russia

TEAM FOIL

1. ....Italy
2. ....China
3. ....Russia

TEAM SABRE

1. ....France
2. ....Italy
3. ....Russia

TEAM ÉPÉE

1. ....France
2. ....Hungary
3. ....Germany

Women

FOIL

1. ....Valentina Vezzali, Italy
2. ....Giovanna Trillini, Italy
3. ....Sylwia Gruchala, Poland

SABRE

1. ....Mariel Zagunis, United States
2. ....Xue Tan, China
3. ....Sada Jacobson, United States

FENCING *(Cont.)*

Women *(Cont.)*

ÉPÉE
1. ....Timea Nagy, Hungary
2. ....Laura Flessel-Colovic, France
3. ....Maureen Nisima, France

TEAM ÉPÉE
1. ....Russia
2. ....Germany
3. ....France

FIELD HOCKEY

Men
1. ....Australia
2. ....Netherlands
3. .,................Germany

Women
1. ....Germany
2. ....Netherlands
3. ....Argentina

GYMNASTICS

Men

ALL-AROUND
		Pts
1.	Paul Hamm, United States	57.823
2.	Dae Eun Kim, S Korea	57.811
3.	Tae Young Yang, S Korea	57.774

HORIZONTAL BAR
		Pts
1.	Igor Cassina, Italy	9.812
2.	Paul Hamm, United States	9.812
3.	Isao Yoneda, Japan	9.787

PARALLEL BARS
		Pts
1.	Valeri Goncharov, Ukraine	9.787
2.	Hiroyuki Tomita, Japan	9.775
3.	Xiaopeng Li, China	9.762

VAULT
		Pts
1.	Gervasio Deferr, Spain	9.737
2.	Evgeni Sapronenko, Latvia	9.706
3.	Marian Dragulescu, Romania	9.612

POMMEL HORSE
		Pts
1.	Haibin Teng, China	9.837
2.	Marius Urzica, Romania	9.825
3.	Takehiro Kashima, Japan	9.787

RINGS
		Pts
1.	Dimosthenis Tampakos, Greece	9.862
2.	Jordan Jovtchev, Bulgaria	9.850
3.	Yuri Chechi, Italy	9.812

FLOOR EXERCISE
		Pts
1.	Kyle Shewfelt, Canada	9.787
2.	Marian Dragulescu, Romania	9.787
3.	Jordan Jovtchev, Bulgaria	9.775

TEAM COMBINED EXERCISES
1. ....Japan
2. ....United States
3. ....Romania

Women

ALL-AROUND
		Pts
1.	Carly Patterson, United States	38.387
2.	Svetlana Khorkina, Russia	38.211
3.	Nan Zhang, China	38.049

VAULT
		Pts
1.	Monica Rosu, Romania	9.656
2.	Annia Hatch, United States	9.481
3.	Anna Pavlova, Russia	9.475

UNEVEN BARS
		Pts
1.	Emilie Lepennec, France	9.687
2.	Terin Humphrey, United States	9.662
2.	Courtney Kupets, United States	9.637

BALANCE BEAM
		Pts
1.	Catalina Ponor, Romania	9.787
2.	Carly Patterson, United States	9.775
3.	Alexandra Eremia, Romania	9.700

FLOOR EXERCISE
		Pts
1.	Catalina Ponor, Romania	9.750
2.	Nicoleta Sofronie, Romania	9.562
3.	Patricia Moreno, Spain	9.487

TEAM COMBINED EXERCISES
1. ....Romania
2. ....United States
3. ....Russia

JUDO

Men	Women

EXTRA-LIGHTWEIGHT

Men	Women
1. Tadahiro Nomura, Japan	1. Ryoko Tani, Japan
2. Nestor Khergiani, Georgia	2. Frederique Jossinet, France
3. Khashbaatar Tsagaanbaatar, Mongolia	3. Feng Gao, China
3. Choi Min-ho, S Korea	3. Julia Matijass, Germany

HALF-LIGHTWEIGHT

Men	Women
1. Masato Uchishiba, Japan	1. Dongmei Xian, China
2. Jozef Krnac, Slovakia	2. Yuki Yokosawa, Japan
3. Georgi Georgiev, Bulgaria	3. Ilse Heylen, Belgium
3. Yordanis Arencibia, Cuba	3. Amarilis Savon, Cuba

LIGHTWEIGHT

Men	Women
1. Won Hee Lee, S Korea	1. Yvonne Boenisch, Germany
2. Vitaliy Makarov, Russia	2. Sun-Hi Kye, N Korea
3. Leandro Guilheiro, Brazil	3. Deborah Gravenstijn, Netherlands
3. James Pedro, United States	3. Yurisleidy Lupetey, Cuba

HALF-MIDDLEWEIGHT

Men	Women
1. Ilias Iliadas, Greece	1. Ayumi Tanimoto, Japan
2. Roman Gontyuk, Ukraine	2. Claudia Heill, Austria
3. Flavio Canto, Brazil	3. Urska Zolnir, Slovenia
3. Dmitri Nossov, Russia	3. Driulys Gonzalez, Cuba

MIDDLEWEIGHT

Men	Women
1. Zurab Zviadauri, Georgia	1. Masae Ueno, Japan
2. Hiroshi Izumi, Japan	2. Edith Bosch, Netherlands
3. Mark Huizinga, Netherlands	3. Dongya Qin, China
3. Khasanbi Taov, Russia	3. Annett Boehm, Germany

HALF-HEAVYWEIGHT

Men	Women
1. Ihar Makarau, Belarus	1. Noriko Anno, Japan
2. Sung Ho Jang, S Korea	2. Xia Liu, China
3. Michael Jurack, Germany	3. Lucia Morico, Italy
3. Ariel Zeevi, Israel	3. Yurisel Laborde, Cuba

HEAVYWEIGHT

Men	Women
1. Keiji Suzuki, Japan	1. Maki Tsukada, Japan
2. Tamerlan Tmenov, Russia	2. Daima Mayelis Beltran, Cuba
3. Indrek Pertelson, Estonia	3. Fuming Sun, China
3. Dennis Van Der Geest, Netherlands	3. Tea Donguzashvili, Russia

MODERN PENTATHLON

Men	Women
1. Andrey Moiseev, Russia	1. Zsuzsanna Voros, Hungary
2. Andrejus Zadneprovskis, Lithuania	2. Jelena Rublevska, Latvia
3. Libor Capalini, Czech Republic	3. Georgina Harland, Great Britain

MOUNTAIN BIKING

Men		Women	
1. Julien Absalon, France	2:15.02	1. Gunn-Rita Dahle, Norway	1:56.51
2. Jose Antonio Hermida, Spain	2:16.02	2. Marie-Helene Premont, Canada	1:57.50
3. Bart Brentjens, Netherlands	2:17.05	3. Sabine Spitz, Germany	1:59.21

ROWING

Men

SINGLE SCULLS		LIGHTWEIGHT DOUBLE SCULLS	
1. Olaf Tufte, Norway	6:49.30	1. T. Kucharski/R. Sycz, Poland	6:20.93
2. Jueri Jaanson, Estonia	6:51.42	2. F. Dufour/ P. Touron, France	6:21.46
3. Ivo Yanakiev, Bulgaria	6:52.80	3. V. Polymeros/ N. Skiathitis, Greece	6:23.23
DOUBLE SCULLS		QUADRUPLE SCULLS	
1. S. Vieilledent/ A. Hardy, France	6:29.00	1. Russia	5:56.85
2. L. Spik/ I. Cop, Slovenia	6:31.72	2. Czech Republic	5:57.43
3. R. Galtarossa/ A. Sartori, Italy	6:32.93	3. Ukraine	5:58.87

ROWING (Cont.)
Men (Cont.)

COXLESS PAIR		LIGHTWEIGHT COXLESS FOUR	
1. ...D. Jinn/ J. Tomkins, Australia	6:30.76	1. ...Denmark	6:01.39
2. ...S. Skelin/ N. Skelin, Croatia	6:32.64	2. ...Australia	6:02.79
3. ...D. Cech/ R. di Clemente, S Africa	6:33.40	3. ...Italy	6:03.74

COXLESS FOUR		EIGHT-OARS	
1. ...Great Britain	6:06.98	1. ...United States	5:42.48
2. ...Canada	6:07.06	2. ...Netherlands	5:43.75
3. ...Italy	6:10.41	3. ...Australia	5:45.38

Women

SINGLE SCULLS		QUADRUPLE SCULLS	
1. ...Katrin Rutschow-Stomporowski, Germany	7:18.12	1. ...Germany	6:29.29
2. ...Yekaterina Karsten, Belarus	7:22.04	2. ...Great Britain	6:31.26
3. ...Rumyana Neykova, Bulgaria	7:23.10	3. ...Australia	6:34.73

DOUBLE SCULLS		COXLESS PAIR	
1. ...C. Evers-Swindell/ G. Evers-Swindell, NZ	7:01.79	1. ...G. Damian/ V. Susanu, Romania	7:06.55
2. ...B. Oppelt/ P. Waleska, Germany	7:02.78	2. ...K. Grainger/ C. Bishop, Great Britain	7:08.66
3. ...E. Laverick/ S. Winckless, Great Britain	7:07.58	3. ...Y. Bichyk/ N. Helakh, Bulgaria	7:09.86

LIGHTWEIGHT DOUBLE SCULLS		EIGHT-OARS	
1. ...C. Burcica/ A. Alupei, Romania	6:56.05	1. ...Romania	6:17.70
2. ...D. Reimer/ C. Blasberg, Germany	6:57.33	2. ...United States	6:19.56
3. ...K. van Der Kolk/ M. van Eupen, Neth	6:58.54	3. ...Netherlands	6:19.85

SHOOTING
Men

RAPID-FIRE PISTOL	Pts	SMALL-BORE RIFLE, PRONE	Pts
1......Ralf Schumann, Germany	694.9	1......Matt Emmons, United States	703.3
2......Sergei Poliakov, Russia	692.7	2......Christian Lusch, Germany	702.2
3......Serguie Alifirenko, Russia	692.3	3......Serguei Martynov, Belarus	701.6

FREE PISTOL	Pts	AIR RIFLE	Pts
1......Mikhail Nestruev, Russia	663.3	1......Qinan Zhu, China	702.7
2......Jong Oh Jin, S Korea	661.5	2......Jie Ling, China	701.3
3......Jong Su Kim, N Korea	657.7	3......Jozef Gonci, Slovakia	697.4

AIR PISTOL	Pts	TRAP	Pts
1......Yifu Wang, China	690.0	1......Alexei Alipov, Russia	149.0
2......Mikhail Nestruev, Russia	689.8	2......Giovanni Pellielo, Italy	146.0
3......Vladimir Isakov, Russia	684.3	3......Adam Vella, Australia	145.0

RUNNING TARGET	Pts	DOUBLE TRAP	Pts
1......Manfred Kurzer, Germany	682.4	1......Ahmed Al Maktoum, UAE	189.0
2......Alexander Blinov, Russia	678.0	2......Rajyavardhan Rathore, India	179.0
3......Dimitri Lykin, Russia	677.1	3......Zheng Wang, China	178.0

SMALL-BORE RIFLE, THREE-POSITION	Pts	SKEET	Pts
1......Zhanbo Gia, China	1264.5	1......Andrea Benelli, Italy	149.0
2......Michael Anti, United States	1263.1	2......Marko Kemppainen, Finland	149.0
3......Christian Planer, Austria	1262.8	3......Juan Miguel Rodriguez, Cuba	147.0

Women

SPORT PISTOL	Pts	AIR PISTOL	Pts
1......Mariya Grozdeva, Bulgaria	688.2	1.,....Olena Kostevych, Ukraine	483.3
2......Lenka Hykova, Czech Republic	687.8	2......Jasna Sekaric, Serbia & Montenegro	483.3
3......Irada Ashumova, Azerbaijan	687.3	3......Mariya Grozdeva, Bulgaria	482.3

SHOOTING (Cont.)

Women (Cont.)

SMALL-BORE RIFLE, THREE-POSITION

	Pts
1......Lioubov Galkina, Russia	688.4
2......Valentina Turisini, Italy	685.9
3......Chengyi Wang, China	685.4

AIR RIFLE

	Pts
1......Li Du, China	502.0
2......Lioubov Galkina, Russia	501.5
3......Katerina Kurkova, Czech Republic	501.1

DOUBLE TRAP

	Pts
1......Kimberly Rhode, United States	146.0
2......Bo Na Lee, S Korea	145.0
3......E Gao, China	142.0

TRAP

	Pts
1......Suzanne Balogh, Australia	88.0
2......Maria Quintanal, Spain	84.0
3......Bo Na Lee, S Korea	83.0

SKEET

	Pts
1......Diana Igaly, Hungary	97.0
2......Ning Wei, China	93.0
3......Zemfina Meftakhetdinova, Azerbaijan	93.0

SOCCER

Men
1. ....Argentina
2. ....Paraguay
3. ....Italy

Women
1. ....United States
2. ....Brazil
3. ....Germany

SOFTBALL
1. ....United States
2. ....Australia
3. ....Japan

SWIMMING

Men

50-METER FREESTYLE

1. ...Gary Hall Jr., United States	21.93
2. ...Duje Draganja, Croatia	21.94
3. ...Roland Schoeman, S Africa	22.02

100-METER FREESTYLE

1. ...Pieter van den Hoogenband, Netherlands	48.17
2. ...Roland Schoeman, S Africa	48.23
3. ...Ian Thorpe, Australia	48.56

200-METER FREESTYLE

1. ...Ian Thorpe, Australia	1:44.71 OR
2. ...Pieter van den Hoogenband, Netherlands	1:45.23
3. ...Michael Phelps, United States	1:45.32

400-METER FREESTYLE

1. ...Ian Thorpe, Australia	3:43.10
2. ...Grant Hackett, Australia	3:43.36
3. ...Klete Keller, United States	3:44.11

1,500-METER FREESTYLE

1. ...Grant Hackett, Australia	14:43.40 OR
2. ...Larsen Jensen, United States	14:45.29
3. ...David Davies, Great Britain	14:45.95

100-METER BACKSTROKE

1. ...Aaron Peirsol, United States	54.06
2. ...Markus Rogan, Austria	54.35
3. ...Tomomi Morita, Japan	54.36

200-METER BACKSTROKE

1. ...Aaron Peirsol, United States	1:54.95 OR
2. ...Markus Rogan, Austria	1:57.35
3. ...Razvan Florea, Romania	1:57.56

100-METER BREASTSTROKE

1. ...Kosuke Kitajima, Japan	1:00.08
2. ...Brendan Hansen, United States	1:00.25
3. ...Hugues Duboscq, France	1:00.88

200-METER BREASTSTROKE

1. ...Kosuke Kitajima, Japan	2:09.44 OR
2. ...Daniel Gyurta, Hungary	2:10.80
3. ...Brendan Hansen, United States	2:10.87

100-METER BUTTERFLY

1. ...Michael Phelps, United States	51.25 OR
2. ...Ian Crocker, United States	51.29
3. ...Andriy Serdinov, Ukraine	51.36

200-METER BUTTERFLY

1. ...Michael Phelps, United States	1:54.04 OR
2. ...Takashi Yamamoto, Japan	1:54.56
3. ...Stephen Parry, Great Britain	1:55.52

200-METER INDIVIDUAL MEDLEY

1. ...Michael Phelps, United States	1:57.14 OR
2. ...Ryan Lochte, United States	1:58.78
3. ...George Bovell, Trinidad & Tobago	1:58.80

400-METER INDIVIDUAL MEDLEY

1. ...Michael Phelps, United States	4:08.26 WR
2. ...Eric Vendt, United States	4:11.81
3. ...Laszlo Cseh, Hungary	4:12.15

4 X 100-METER MEDLEY RELAY

1. ...United States (Aaron Peirsol, Brendan Hanson, Ian Crocker, Jason Lezak)	3:30.68 WR
2. ...Germany	3:33.62
3. ...Japan	3:35.22

4 X 100-METER FREESTYLE RELAY

1. ...S Africa (Schoeman, Ferns, Townsend, Neethling)	3:13.17 WR
2. ...Netherlands	3:14.36
3. ...United States	3:14.62

4 X 200-METER FREESTYLE RELAY

1. ...United States (Phelps, Lochte, Vanderkaay, Keller)	7:07.33
2. ...Australia	7:07.46
3. ...Italy	7:11.83

Note: OR=Olympic record. WR=world record. EOR=equals Olympic record. EWR=equals world record.

SWIMMING (Cont.)

Women

50-METER FREESTYLE
1. ...Inge de Bruijn, Netherlands   24.58
2. ...Malia Metella, France   24.89
3. ...Lisbeth Lenton, Australia   24.91

100-METER FREESTYLE
1. ...Jodie Henry, Australia   53.84
2. ...Inge de Bruijn, Netherlands   54.16
3. ...Natalie Coughlin, United States   54.40

200-METER FREESTYLE
1. ...Camelia Potec, Romania   1:58.03
2. ...Federica Pellegrini, Italy   1:58.22
3. ...Solenne Figues, France   1:58.45

400-METER FREESTYLE
1. ...Laure Manaudou, France   4:05.34
2. ...Otylia Jedrzejczak, Poland   4:05.84
3. ...Kaitlin Sandeno, United States   4:06.19

800-METER FREESTYLE
1. ...Ai Shibata, Japan   8:24.54
2. ...Laure Manaudou, France   8:24.96
3. ...Diana Munz, United States   8:26.61

100-METER BACKSTROKE
1. ...Natalie Coughlin, United States   1:00.37
2. ...Kirsty Coventry, Zimbabwe   1:00.50
3. ...Laure Manaudou, France   1:00.88

200-METER BACKSTROKE
1. ...Kirsty Coventry, Zimbabwe   2:09.19
2. ...Stanislava Komarova, Russia   2:09.72
3. ...Antie Buschschulte, Germany   2:09.88

100-METER BREASTSTROKE
1. ...Xuejuan Luo, China   1:06.64
2. ...Brooke Hanson, Australia   1:07.15
3. ...Leisel Jones, Australia   1:07.16

200-METER BREASTSTROKE
1. ...Amanda Beard, United States   2:23.37 OR
2. ...Leisel Jones, Australia   2:23.60
3. ...Anne Poleska, Germany   2:25.82

100-METER BUTTERFLY
1. ...Petria Thomas, Australia   57.72
2. ...Otylia Jedrzejczak, Poland   57.84
3. ...Inge de Bruijn, Netherlands   57.99

200-METER BUTTERFLY
1. ...Otylia Jedrzejczak, Poland   2:06.05
2. ...Petria Thomas, Australia   2:06.36
3. ...Yuko Nakanishi, Japan   2:08.04

200-METER INDIVIDUAL MEDLEY
1. ...Yana Klochkova, Ukraine   2:11.14
2. ...Amanda Beard, United States   2:11.70
3. ...Kirsty Coventry, Zimbabwe   2:12.72

400-METER INDIVIDUAL MEDLEY
1. ...Yana Klochkova, Ukraine   4:34.83
2. ...Kaitlin Sandeno, United States   4:34.95
3. ...Georgina Bardach, Argentina   4:37.51

4 X 100-METER MEDLEY RELAY
1. ...Australia (Giaan Rooney,   3:57.32 WR
  Leisel Jones, Petria Thomas,
  Jodie Henry)
2. ...United States   3:59.12
3. ...Germany   4:00.72

4 X 100-METER FREESTYLE RELAY
1. ...Australia (Alice Mills,   3:35.94 WR
  Lisbeth Lenton, Petria Thomas,
  Jodie Henry)
2. ...United States   3:36.39
3. ...Netherlands   3:37.59

4 X 200-METER FREESTYLE RELAY
1. ...United States (Natalie Coughlin,   7:53.42 WR
  Carly Piper, Dana Vollmer,
  Kaitlin Sandeno)
2. ...China   7:55.97
3. ...Germany   7:57.35

Note: OR=Olympic record. WR=world record. EOR=equals Olympic record. EWR=equals world record.

SYNCHRONIZED SWIMMING

DUET
1. ....Russia
2. ....Japan
3. ....United States

TEAM
1. ....Russia
2. ......:...................Japan
3. ....United States

SYNCHRONIZED DIVING

Men

3M SPRINGBOARD
	Pts
1. ....N. Siranidis/ T. Bimis, Greece	353.34
2. ....A. Wels/ T. Schellenberg, Germany	350.01
3. ....R. Newbery/ S. Barnett, Australia	349.59

10M PLATFORM
	Pts
1. ....L. Tian/ J. Yang, China	383.88
2. ....P. Waterfield/ L. Taylor, Great Britain	371.52
3. ....M. Helm/ R. Newbery, Australia	366.84

Women

3M SPRINGBOARD
	Pts
1. ....J. Guo/ M. Wu, China	336.90
2. ....V. Ilyina/ Y. Pakhalina, Russia	330.84
3. ....I. Lashko/ C. Newbery, Australia	309.30

10M PLATFORM
	Pts
1. ....L. Lao/ T. Li, China	352.54
2. ....N. Goncharova/ Y. Koltunova, Russia	340.92
3. ....B. Hartley/ E. Heymans, Canada	327.78

TABLE TENNIS

Men

SINGLES
1. ....,.......Seung Min Ryu, S Korea
2. ....Hao Wang, China
3. ....Ligin Wang, China

DOUBLES
1. ....M. Lin/ Q. Chen, China
2. ....L. Chak Ko/ L. Ching, Hong Kong
3. ....M. Maze/ F. Tugwell, Denmark

Women

SINGLES
1. ....Zhang Yining, China
2. ....Hyang Mi Kim, N Korea
3. ....Kim Kyung Ah, S Korea

DOUBLES
1. ....N. Wang/ Z. Yining, China
2. ....................E.-C. Lee/ E. M. Seok, S Korea
3. ....N. Jianfeng/ Y. Guo, China

TAEKWONDO

Men

FLYWEIGHT
1. ....Mu Yen Chu, Taiwan
2. ....Oscar Blanco, Mexico
3. ....Tamer Bayoumi, Egypt

FEATHERWEIGHT
1. ....Hadi Saeibonehkohal, Iran
2. ....Chih-Hsiung Huang, Taiwan
3. ....Myeong Seob Song, S Korea

WELTERWEIGHT
1. ....Steven Lopez, United States
2. ....Bahri Tanrikulu, Turkey
3. ....Yossef Karami, Iran

HEAVYWEIGHT
1. ....Dae Sung Moon, S Korea
2. ....Alexandros Nikolaidis, Greece
3. ....Pascal Gentil, France

Women

FLYWEIGHT
1. ....Shih Hsin Chen, Taiwan
2. ....Yanelis Diaz, Cuba
3. ....Yaowapa Boorapolchai, Thailand

FEATHERWEIGHT
1. ....Ji Won Jang, S Korea
2. ....Nia Abdallah, United States
3. ....Iridia Blanco, Mexico

WELTERWEIGHT
1. ....Wei Luo, China
2. ....Elisavet Mystakidou, Greece
3. ....Kyung Sun Hwang

HEAVYWEIGHT
1. ....Zhong Chen, China
2. ....Myriam Baverel, France
3. ....Adriana Carmona, Brazil

TEAM HANDBALL

Men

1. ....Croatia
2. ....Germany
3. ....Russia

Women

1. ....Denmark
2. ....S Korea
3. ....Ukraine

TENNIS

Men

SINGLES
1. ....Nicolas Massu, Chile
2. ....Mardy Fish, United States
3. ....Fernando Gonzalez, Chile

DOUBLES
1. ....Fernando Gonzalez/ Nicolas Massu Chile
2. ....Rainer Schuettler/ Nicolas Kiefer, Germany
3. ....Mario Ancic/ Ljubicic Ivan, Croatia

Women

SINGLES
1. ....Justine Henin-Hardenne, Belgium
2. ....Amelie Mauresmo, France
3. ....Alicia Molik, Australia

DOUBLES
1. ....Ting Li/ Tian Tian Sun, China
2. ....Conchita Martinez/ Virginia Ruano, Spain
3. ....Paola Suares/ Patricia Tarbabini, Argentina

TRAMPOLINE

Men

1. ....Yuri Nikitin, Ukraine	41.50
2. ....Alexandre Moskalenko, Russia	41.20
3. ....Henrik Stehlik, Germany	40.80

Women

1. ....Anna Dogonadze, Germany	39.60
2. ....Karen Cockburn, Canada	39.20
3. ....Shaohua Huang, China	39.00

TRIATHLON

Men

1. ....Hamish Carter, New Zealand	1:51:07
2. ....Bevan Docherty, New Zealand	1:51:15
3. ....Sven Riederer, Switzerland	1:51:33

Women

1. ....Kate Allen, Austria	2:04:43
2. ....Loretta Harrop, Australia	2:04:50
3. ....Susan Williams, United States	2:05:08

VOLLEYBALL

Men

1. ....Brazil
2. ....Italy
3. ....Russia

Women

1. ....China
2. ....Russia
3. ....Cuba

BEACH VOLLEYBALL

Men

1. ....Emanuel Rigo/ Ricardo Santos, Brazil
2. ....Pablo Herrera/ Javier Bosma, Spain
3. ....Patrick Heuscher/ Stefan Kobel, Switzerland

Women

1. ....Misty May/ Kerri Walsh, United States
2. ....Shelda Bede/ Adriana Behar, Brazil
3. ....Holly McPeak/ Elaine Youngs, United States

WATER POLO

Men

1. ....Hungary
2. ....Serbia & Montenegro
3. ....Russia

Women

1. ....Italy
2. ....Greece
3. ....United States

WEIGHTLIFTING

Men

123 POUNDS

1. ....Halil Mutlu, Turkey — 649 lb
2. ....Meijin Wu, China — 632.5 lb
3. ....Sedat Artuc, Turkey — 616 lb

137 POUNDS

1. ....Zhiyong Shi, China — 715 lb
2. ....Maosheng Le, China — 687.5 lb
3. ....Jose Israel Rubio, Venezuela — 649 lb

152 POUNDS

1. ....Guozheng Zhang, China — 764.5 lb
2. ....Bae Young Lee, S Korea — 753.5 lb
3. ....Nikolay Pechalov, Croatia — 742.5 lb

170 POUNDS

1. ....Taner Sagir, Turkey — 825 lb OR
2. ....Sergei Filimonov, Kazakhstan — 819.5 lb
3. ....Oleg Perepetchenov, Russia — 803 lb

187 POUNDS

1. ....George Asanidze, Georgia — 841.5 lb
2. ....Andrei Rybakou, Belarus — 836 lb
3. ....Pyrros Dimas, Greece — 830.5 lb

207 POUNDS

1. ....Milen Dobrev, Bulgaria — 896.5 lb
2. ....Khadjimourad Akkaev, Russia — 891 lb
3. ....Eduard Tjukin, Russia — 874.5

231 POUNDS

1. ....Dmitry Berestov, Russia — 935 lb
2. ....Igor Razoronov, Ukraine — 924 lb
3. ....Gleb Pisarevskiy, Russia — 924 lb

231+ POUNDS

1. ....Hossein Reza Zadeh, Iran — 1,039.5 lb
2. ....Viktors Scerbatihs, Latvia — 1001 lb
3. ....Velichko Cholakov, Bulgaria — 984.5 lb

Women

106 POUNDS

1. ....Taylan Nurcan, Turkey — 462 lb
2. ....Zhuo Li, China — 451 lb
3. ....Aree Wiratthaworn, Thailand — 440 lb

117 POUNDS

1. ....Udomporn Polsak, Thailand — 490 lb
2. ....Raema Lisa Rumbewas, Indonesia — 462 lb
3. ....Mabel Mosquera, Colombia — 434.4 lb

128 POUNDS

1. ....Yanging Chen, China — 523 lb
2. ....Song Hui Ri, N Korea — 512 lb
3. ....Wandee Kameajm, Thailand — 506 lb

139 POUNDS

1. ....Natalia Skakun, Ukraine — 535 lb
2. ....Hanna Batsiushka, Belarus — 535 lb
3. ....Tatsiana Stukalava, Belarus — 491 lb

152 POUNDS

1. ....Chunhong Liu, China — 606 lb WR
2. ....Eszter Krutzler, Hungary — 579 lb
3. ....Zarema Kasaeva, Russia — 579 lb

165 POUNDS

1. ....Pawina Thongsuk, Thailand — 601 lb
2. ....Natalia Zabolotnaia, Russia — 601 lb WR
3. ....Valentina Popova, Russia — 583 lb

165+ POUNDS

1. ....Gonghong Tang, China — 671 lb
2. ....Mi Ran Jang, S Korea — 666 lb
3. ....Agata Wrobel, Poland — 638

FREESTYLE WRESTLING

121 POUNDS
1. ....Mavlet Batirov, Russia
2. ....Stephen Abas, United States
3. ....Chikara Tanabe, Japan

132 POUNDS
1. ....Yandro Miguel Quintana, Cuba
2. ....Masuod Jokar, Iran
3. ....Kenji Inoue, Japan

145.5 POUNDS
1. ....Elbrus Tedeyev, Ukraine
2. ....Jamill Kelly, United States
3. ....Makhach Murtazaliev, Russia

163 POUNDS
1. ....Buvaysa Saytive, Russia
2. ....Gennadily Laliyev, Kazakhstan
3. ....Ivan Fundora, Cuba

185 POUNDS
1. ....Cael Sanderson, United States
2. ....Evi Jae Moon, S Korea
3. ....Sazhid Sazhidov, Russia

211.5 POUNDS
1. ....Khadjimourat Gatsalov, Russia
2. ....Magomed Ibragimov, Uzbekistan
3. ....Alireza Heidari, Iran

264.5 POUNDS
1. ....Artur Taymazov, Uzbekistan
2. ....Alireza Rezaei, Iran
3. ....Aydin Polatci, Turkey

GRECO-ROMAN WRESTLING

121 POUNDS
1. ....Istvan Majoros, Hungary
2. ....Gueidar Mamedaliev, Russia
3. ....Artiom Kjourejkian, Greece

132 POUNDS
1. ....Ji Hyun Jung, S Korea
2. ....Roberto Monzon, Cuba
3. ....Armen Nazarian, Bulgaria

145.5 POUNDS
1. ....Farid Monsurov, Azerbaijan
2. ....Seref Eroglu, Turkey
3. ....Mkkhitar Manukyan, Kazakhstan

163 POUNDS
1. ....Alexandr Dokturishivili, Uzbekistan
2. ....Marko Yli-Hannuksela, Finland
3. ....Varteres Samourgachev, Russia

185 POUNDS
1. ....Alexei Michine, Russia
2. ....Ara Abrahamian, Sweden
3. ....Viachaslau Makaranka, Belarus

211.5 POUNDS
1. ....Karam Ibrahim, Egypt
2. ....Ramaz Nozadze, Georgia
3. ....Mehmet Ozal, Turkey

264.5 POUNDS
1. ....Khasan Baroev, Russia
2. ....Georgiy Tsurtsumia, Kazakhstan
3. ....Rulon Gardner, United States

YACHTING

Men

MEN'S 470
1. ....United States
2. ....Great Britain
3. ....Japan

MEN'S FINN
1. ....Great Britain
2. ....Spain
3. ....Poland

MISTRAL
1. ....Israel
2. ....Greece
3. ....Great Britain

STAR
1. ....Brazil
2. ....Canada
3. ....France

TORNADO
1. ....Austria
2. ....United States
3. ....Argentina

LASER
1. ....Brazil
2. ....Austria
3. ....Slovenia

49ER
1. ....Spain
2. ....Ukraine
3. ....Great Britain

Women

MISTRAL
1. ....France
2. ....China
3. ....Italy

470
1. ....Greece
2. ....Spain
3. ....Sweden

EUROPE
1. ....Norway
2. ....Czech Republic
3. ....Denmark

KEEL
1. ....Great Britain
2. ....Ukraine
3. ....Denmark

BIATHLON

Men			Women		
10 KILOMETERS			**7.5 KILOMETERS**		
1. ...Ole Einar Bjoerndalen, Norway		24:51.3	1. ...Kati Wilhelm, Germany		20:41.4
2. ...Sven Fisher, Germany		25:20.2	2. ...Uschi Disl, Germany		20:57.0
3. ...Wolfgang Perner, Austria		25:44.4	3. ...Magdalena Forsberg, Sweden		21:20.4
20 KILOMETERS			**15 KILOMETERS**		
1. ...Ole Einar Bjoerndalen, Norway		51:03.3	1. ...Andrea Henkel, Germany		47:29.1
2. ...Frank Luck, Germany		51:39.4	2. ...Liv Grete Poiree, Norway		47:37.0
3. ...Victor Maigovrov, Russia		51:40.6	3. ...Magdalena Forsberg, Sweden		48:08.3
4 X 7.5-KILOMETER RELAY			**4 X 7.5-KILOMETER RELAY**		
1. ...Norway		1:23:42.3	1. ...Germany		1:27:55.0
2. ...Germany		1:24:27.7	2. ...Norway		1:28:25.6
3. ...France		1:24:36.6	3. ...Russia		1:29:19.7

BOBSLED

Men			Women		
TWO-MAN			**TWO-PERSON**		
1. ...Christoph Langen/ Markus Zimmerman, Germany I		3:10.10	1. ...Jill Bakken/ Vonetta Flowers, USA II		1:37.76
2. ...Christian Reich/ Steve Anderhub, Switz.I		3:10.20	2. ...Sandra Prokoff/ Ulrike Holzner, Ger. I		1:38.06
3. ...Martin Annen/ Beat Hefti, Switz II		3:10.62	3. ...S.L. Erdmann/ N. Herschmann, Ger II		1:38.29
FOUR-MAN					
1. ...Germany II		3:07.51			
2. ...USA I		3:07.81			
3. ...USA II		3:07.86			

CURLING

Men		Women	
1. ...Norway		1. ...Britain	
2. ...Canada		2. ...Switzerland	
3. ...Switzerland		3. ...Canada	

FIGURE SKATING

Men		Women	
1. ...Alexei Yagudin, Russia		1. ...Sarah Hughes, United States	
2. ...Evgeni Plushenko, Russia		2. ...Irina Slutskaya, Russia	
3. ...Timothy Goebel, United States		3. ...Michelle Kwan, United States	

Pairs		Ice Dancing	
1. ...Elena Berezhnaya/ Anton Sikharulidze, Russia		1. ...Marina Anissina/ Gwendal Peizerat, France	
1. ...David Pelletier/ Jamie Sale, Canada		2. ...Irina Lobacheva/ Ilia Averbukh, Russia	
3. ...Hongbo Zhao/ Xue Shen, China		3. ...Barbara Fusar Poli/ Maurizio Margaglio, Italy	

ICE HOCKEY

Men		Women	
1. ...Canada		1. ...Canada	
2. ...USA		2. ...USA	
3. ...Russia		3. ...Sweden	

LUGE

Men			Women		
SINGLES			**SINGLES**		
1. ...Armin Zoeggeler, Italy		2:57.941	1. ...Sylke Otto, Germany		2:52.464
2. ...Georg Hackl, Germany		2:58.270	2. ...Barbara Niedernhuber, Germany		2:52.785
3. ...Markus Prock, Austria		2:58.283	3. ...Silke Kraushaar, Germany		2:52.865
DOUBLES					
1. ...Alexander Resch/ P.F. Leitner, Ger		1:26.082			
2. ...Mark Grimmette/ Brian Martin, U.S.		1:26.216			
3. ...Chris Thorpe/ Clay Ives, U.S.		1:26.220			

SKELETON

Men			Women		
1. ...Jim Shea Jr., United States		1:41.96	1. ...Tristan Gale, United States		1:45.11
2. ...Martin Rettl, Austria		1:42.01	2. ...Lea Ann Parsley, United States		1:45.21
3. ...Gregor Staehli, Switzerland		1:42.15	3. ...Alex Coomber, Great Britain		1:45.37

SPEED SKATING

Men

500 METERS
1. ...Casey FitzRandolph, United States 1:09.23
2. ...Hiroyasu Shimizu, Japan 1:09.26
3. ...Kip Carpenter, United States 1:09.47

1,000 METERS
1. ...Gerard Van Velde, Netherlands 1:07.18
2. ...Jan Bos, Netherlands 1:07.53
3. ...Joey Cheek, United States 1:07.61

1,500 METERS
1. ...Derek Parra, United States 1:43.95
2. ...Jochem Uytdehaage, Netherlands 1:44.57
3. ...Adne Sondral, Norway 1:45.26

5,000 METERS
1. ...Jochem Uytdehaage, Netherlands 6:14.66
2. ...Derek Parra, United States 6:17.98
3. ...Jens Boden, Germany 6:21.73

10,000 METERS
1. ...Jochem Uytdenhaage, Netherlands 12:58.92 WR
2. ...Gianni Romme, Netherlands 13:10.03
3. ...Lasse Saetre, Norway 13:16.92

500 METERS SHORT TRACK
1. ...Marc Gagnon, Canada 41.802 OR
2. ...Jonathan Guilmette, Canada 41.994
3. ...Rusty Smith, United States 42.027

1,000 METERS SHORT TRACK
1. ...Steven Bradbury, Austrialia 1:29.109
2. ...Apolo Anton Ohno, United States 1:30.160
3. ...Mathieu Turcotte, Canada 1:30.563

1,500 METERS SHORT TRACK
1. ...Apolo Anton Ohno, United States 2:18.541
2. ...Jiajun Li, China 2:18.731
3. ...Marc Gagnon, Canada 2:18.806

5,000-METER SHORT TRACK RELAY
1. ...Canada 6:51.579
2. ...Italy 6:56.327
3. ...China 6:59.633

Women

500 METERS
1. ...Catriona LeMay Doan, Canada 1:14.75
2. ...Monique Garbrecht-Enfeld, Ger 1:14.94
3. ...Sabine Voelker, Germany 1:15.19

1,000 METERS
1. ...Chris Witty, United States 1:13.83
2. ...Sabine Voelker, Germany 1:13.96
3. ...Jennifer Rodriguez, United States 1:14.24

1,500 METERS
1. ...Anni Friesinger, Germany 1:54.02
2. ...Sabine Voelker, Germany 1:54.94
3. ...Jennifer Rodriguez, United States 1:55.32

3,000 METERS
1. ...Claudia Pechstein, Germany 3:57.70
2. ...Renate Groenwold, Netherlands 3:58.94
3. ...Cindy Klassen, Canada 3:58.94

5,000 METERS
1. ...Claudia Pechstein, Germany 6:46.91 WR
2. ...Gretha Smit, Germany 6:49.22
3. ...Clara Hughes, Canada 6:53.53

500 METERS SHORT TRACK
1. ...Annie Perreault, Canada 46.568
2. ...Yang Yang, China 46.627
3. ...Chun Lee Kyung, S Korea 46.335

1,000 METERS
1. ...Yang A. Yang, China 1:36.391
2. ...Gi-Hyun Ko, Korea 1:36.427
3. ...Yang S. Yang, China 1:37.008

1,500 METERS
1. ...Gi-Hyan Ko, Korea 2:31.581
2. ...Eun-Kyung Choi, Korea 2:31.610
3. ...Evgenia Radanova, Bulgaria 2:31.723

3,000-METER SHORT TRACK RELAY
1. ...Korea 4:12.793
2. ...China 4:13.236
3. ...Canada 4:15.738

Note: OR=Olympic Record. WR=World Record. EOR=Equals Olympic Record. EWR=Equals World Record. WB=World Best.

ALPINE SKIING

Men

DOWNHILL
1. ...Fritz Strobl, Austria 1:39.13
2. ...Lasse Kjus, Norway 1:39.35
3. ...Stephan Eberharter, Austria 1:39.41

SLALOM
1. ...Jean-Pierre Vidal, France 1:41.06
2. ...Sebastien Amiez, France 1:41.82
3. ...Benjamin Raich, Austria 1:42.41

GIANT SLALOM
1. ...Stephan Eberharter, Austria 2:23.28
2. ...Bode Miller, United States 2:24.16
3. ...Lasse Kjus, Norway 2:24.32

SUPER GIANT SLALOM
1. ...Kjetil André Aamodt, Norway 1:21.58
2. ...Stephan Eberharter, Austria 1:21.68
3. ...Andreas Schifferer, Austria 1:21.83

COMBINED
1. ...Kjetil André Aamodt, Norway 3:17.56
2. ...Bode Miller, United States 3:17.84
3. ...Benjamin Raich, Austria 3:18.26

Women

DOWNHILL
1. ...Carole Montillet, France 1:39.56
2. ...Isolde Kostner, Italy 1:40.01
3. ...Renate Goetschl, Austria 1:40.39

SLALOM
1. ...Janica Kostelic, Croatia 1:46.10
2. ...Laure Pequegnot, France 1:46.17
3. ...Anja Paerson, Sweden 1:47.09

GIANT SLALOM
1. ...Janica Kostelic, Croatia 2:30.01
2. ...Anja Paerson, Sweden 2:31.33
3. ...Sonja Nef, Switzerland 2:31.67

SUPER GIANT SLALOM
1. ...Daniela Ceccarelli, Italy 1:13.59
2. ...Janica Kostelic, Croatia 1:13.64
3. ...Karen Putzer, Italy 1:13.86

COMBINED
1. ...Janica Kostelic, Croatia 2:43.28
2. ...Renate Goetschl, Austria 2:44.77
3. ...Martina Ertl, Germany 2:45.16

FREESTYLE SKIING

Men

MOGULS	Pts
1. ...Janne Lahtela, Finland	27.97
2. ...Travis Mayer, United States	27.59
3. ...Richard Gay, France	26.91

AERIALS	Pts
1. ...Ales Valenta, Czech Republic	257.02
2. ...Joe Pack, United States	251.64
3. ...Alexei Grichin, Belarus	251.19

Women

MOGULS	Pts
1. ...Kari Traa, Norway	25.94
2. ...Shannon Bahrke, United States	25.06
3. ...Tae Satoya, Japan	24.85

AERIALS	Pts
1. ...Alisa Camplin, Australia	193.47
2. ...Veronica Brenner, Canada	190.02
3. ...Deidra Dionne, Canada	189.26

NORDIC SKIING

Men

1.5 KILOMETERS SPRINT	
1. ...Tor Arne Hetland, Norway	2:56.9
2. ...Peter Schlickenrieder, Germany	2:57.0
3. ...Cristian Zorzi, Italy	2:57.2

10 KILOMETERS PURSUIT FREESTYLE	
1. ...Johann Muehlegg, Spain	49:20.4
2. ...Frode Estil, Norway	49:48.9
2. ...Thomas Alsgaard, Norway	49:48.9

15 KILOMETERS CLASSICAL	
1. ...Andrus Veerpalu, Estonia	37:07.4
2. ...Frode Estil, Norway	37:43.4
3. ...Jaak Mae, Estonia	37:50.8

30 KILOMETERS FREESTYLE	
1. ...Johann Muelegg, Spain	1:09:28.9
2. ...Christian Hoffman, Austria	1:11:31.0
3. ...Mikhail Botvinov, Austria	1:11:32.3

50 KILOMETERS CLASSICAL	
1. ...Mikhail Ivanov, Russia	2:06:20.8
2. ...Andrus Veerpalu, Estonia	2:06:44.5
3. ...Odd-Bjoern Hjelmeset, Norway	2:08:41.5

4 X 10-KILOMETER RELAY MIXED STYLE	
1. ....Norway	1:32:45.5
2. ....Italy	1:32:45.8
3. ....Germany	1:33:21.0

90-METER HILL SKI JUMPING	Pts
1. ...Simon Ammann, Switzerland	269.0
2. ...Sven Hannawald, Germany	267.5
3. ...Adam Malysz, Poland	263.0

120-METER HILL SKI JUMPING	Pts
1. ...Simon Ammann, Switzerland	281.4
2. ...Adam Malysz, Germany	269.7
3. ...Matti Hautamacki, Finland	256.0

120-METER HILL TEAM SKI JUMPING	Pts
1. ...Germany	974.1
2. ...Finland	974.0
3. ...Slovenia	946.3

INDIVIDUAL COMBINED	Pts
1. ...Samppa Lajunen, Finland	123.8
2. ...Jaakko Tallus, Finland	119.9
3. ...Felix Gottwald, Austria	110.3

INDIVIDUAL SPRINT COMBINED	Pts
1. ...Samppa Lajunen, Finland	123.8
2. ...Ronny Ackermann, Germany	119.9
3. ...Felix Gottwald, Austria	110.3

TEAM COMBINED	
1. ....Finland	48:42.2
2. ....Germany	48:49.7
3. ....Austria	48:53.2

Women

1.5 KILOMETERS SPRINT	
1. ...Julija Tchepalova, Russia	3:10.6
2. ...Evi Sachenbacher, Germany	3:12.2
3. ...Anita Moen, Norway	3:12.7

5 KILOMETERS PURSUIT	
1. ...Olga Danilova, Russia	24:52.1
2. ...Larissa Lazutina, Russia	24:59.0
3. ...Beckie Scott, Canada	25:09.9

10 KILOMETERS CLASSICAL STYLE	
1. ...Bante Skari, Norway	28:05.6
2. ...Olga Danilova, Russia	28:08.1
3. ...Julija Tchepalova, Russia	28:09.9

15 KILOMETERS FREESTYLE	
1. ...Stefania Belmondo, Italy	39:54.4
2. ...Larissa Lazutina, Russia	39:54.4
3. ...Katerina Neumannova, Czech Rep	39:56.2

30 KILOMETERS CLASSICAL STYLE	
1. ...Gabriella Paruzzi, Italy	1:30:57.1
2. ...Stefania Belmondo, Italy	1:31:01.6
3. ...Bente Skari, Norway	1:31:36.3

4 X 5-KILOMETER RELAY MIXED STYLE	
1. ....Germany	49:30.6
2. ....Norway	49:31.9
3. ....Switzerland	50:03.6

SNOWBOARDING

Men

PARALLEL GIANT SLALOM	
1. ...Philipp Schoch, Switzerland	
2. ...Richard Richardsson, Sweden	
3. ...Chris Klug, United States	

HALF-PIPE	Pts
1. ...Ross Powers, United States	46.1
2. ...Danny Kass, United States	42.5
3. ...Jarret Thomas, United States	42.1

Women

PARALLEL GIANT SLALOM	
1. ...Isabelle Blanc, France	
2. ...Karine Ruby, Germany	
3. ...Lidia Trettel, Italy	

HALF-PIPE	Pts
1. ...Kelly Clark, United States	47.9
2. ...Doriane Vidal, France	43.0
3. ...Fabienne Reuteler, Switzerland	39.7

Olympic Games Locations and Dates

Summer

	Year	Site	Dates	Competitors Men	Women	Nations	Most Medals	US Medals
I	1896	Athens, Greece	Apr 6–15	311	0	13	Greece (10-19-18—47)	11-6-2—19 (2nd)
II	1900	Paris, France	May 20–Oct 28	1319	11	22	France (29-41-32—102)	20-14-19—53 (2nd)
III	1904	St Louis, United States	July 1–Nov 23	681	6	12	United States (80-86-72—238)	
—	1906	Athens, Greece	Apr 22–May 28	77	7	20	France (15-9-16—40)	12-6-5—23 (4th)
IV	1908	London, Great Britain	Apr 27–Oct 31	1999	36	23	Britain (56-50-39—145)	23-12-12—47 (2nd)
V	1912	Stockholm, Sweden	May 5–July 22	2490	57	28	Sweden (24-24-17—65)	23-19-19—61 (2nd)
VI	1916	Berlin, Germany	Canceled because of war					
VII	1920	Antwerp, Belgium	Apr 20–Sep 12	2543	64	29	United States (41-27-28—96)	
VIII	1924	Paris, France	May 4–July 27	2956	136	44	United States (45-27-27—99)	
IX	1928	Amsterdam, Netherlands	May 17–Aug 12	2724	290	46	United States (22-18-16—56)	
X	1932	Los Angeles, United States	July 30–Aug 14	1281	127	37	United States (41-32-31—104)	
XI	1936	Berlin, Germany	Aug 1–16	3738	328	49	Germany (33-26-30—89)	24-20-12—56 (2nd)
XII	1940	Tokyo, Japan	Canceled because of war					
XIII	1944	London, Great Britain	Canceled because of war					
XIV	1948	London, Great Britain	July 29–Aug 14	3714	385	59	United States (38-27-19—84)	
XV	1952	Helsinki, Finland	July 19–Aug 3	4407	518	69	United States (40-19-17—76)	
XVI	1956	Melbourne, Australia*	Nov 22–Dec 8	2958	384	67	USSR (37-29-32—98)	32-25-17—74 (2nd)
XVII	1960	Rome, Italy	Aug 25–Sep 11	4738	610	83	USSR (43-29-31—103)	34-21-16—71 (2nd)
XVIII	1964	Tokyo, Japan	Oct 10–24	4457	683	93	United States (36-26-28—90)	
XIX	1968	Mexico City, Mexico	Oct 12–27	4750	781	112	United States (45-28-34—107)	
XX	1972	Munich, W Germany	Aug 26–Sep 10	5848	1299	122	USSR (50-27-22—99)	33-31-30—94 (2nd)
XXI	1976	Montreal, Canada	July 17–Aug 1	4834	1251	92†	USSR (49-41-35—125)	34-35-25—94 (3rd)
XXII	1980	Moscow, USSR	July 19–Aug 3	4265	1088	81‡	USSR (80-69-46—195)	Did not compete
XXIII	1984	Los Angeles, United States	July 28–Aug 12	5458	1620	141#	United States (83-61-30—174)	
XXIV	1988	Seoul, S Korea	Sep 17–Oct 2	7105	2476	160	USSR (55-31-46—132)	36-31-27—94 (3rd)
XXV	1992	Barcelona, Spain	July 25–Aug. 9	7555	3008	172	Unified Team (45-38-29—112)	37-34-37—108 (2nd)
XXVI	1996	Atlanta, United States	July 19–Aug 4	6984	3766	197	United States (44-32-25—101)	
XXVII	2000	Sydney, Australia	Sept 15–Oct 1	6862	4254	199	United States (39-25-33—97)	
XXVIII	2004	Athens, Greece	Aug 11–Aug 29	11099 total		202	United States (35-39-29—103)	

*The equestrian events were held in Stockholm, Sweden, June 10–17, 1956.

†This figure includes Cameroon, Egypt, Morocco, and Tunisia, countries that boycotted the 1976 Olympics after some of their athletes had already competed.

‡The U.S. was among 65 countries that did not participate in the 1980 Summer Games in Moscow.

#The USSR, East Germany, and 14 other countries did not participate in the 1984 Summer Games in Los Angeles.

Winter

	Year	Site	Dates	Men	Competitors Women	Nations	Most Medals	US Medals
I	1924	Chamonix, France	Jan 25–Feb 4	281	13	16	Norway (4-7-6—17)	1-2-1—4 (3rd)
II	1928	St. Moritz, Switzerland	Feb 11–19	366	27	25	Norway (6-4-5—15)	2-2-2—6 (2nd)
III	1932	Lake Placid, United States	Feb 4–13	277	30	17	United States (6-4-2—12)	
IV	1936	Garmisch-Partenkirchen, Germany	Feb 6–16	680	76	28	Norway (7-5-3—15)	1-0-3—4 (T-5th)
—	1940	Garmisch-Partenkirchen, Germany	Canceled because of war					
—	1944	Cortina d'Ampezzo, Italy	Canceled because of war					
V	1948	St. Moritz, Switzerland	Jan 30–Feb 8	636	77	28	Norway (4-3-3—10) Sweden (4-3-3—10) Switzerland (3-4-3—10)	3-4-2—9 (4th)
VI	1952	Oslo, Norway	Feb 14–25	624	108	30	Norway (7-3-6—16)	4-6-1—11 (2nd)
VII	1956	Cortina d'Ampezzo, Italy	Jan 26–Feb 5	687	132	32	USSR (7-3-6—16)	2-3-2—7 (T-4th)
VIII	1960	Squaw Valley, United States	Feb 18–28	502	146	30	USSR (7-5-9—21)	3-4-3—10 (2nd)
IX	1964	Innsbruck, Austria	Jan 29–Feb 9	758	175	36	USSR (11-8-6—25)	1-2-3—6 (7th)
X	1968	Grenoble, France	Feb 6–18	1063	230	37	Norway (6-6-2—14)	1-5-1—7 (T-7th)
XI	1972	Sapporo, Japan	Feb 3–13	927	218	35	USSR (8-5-3—16)	3-2-3—8 (6th)
XII	1976	Innsbruck, Austria	Feb 4–15	1013	248	37	USSR (13-6-8—27)	3-3-4—10 (T-3rd)
XIII	1980	Lake Placid, United States	Feb 13–24	1012	271	37	East Germany (9-7-7—23)	6-4-2—12 (3rd)
XIV	1984	Sarajevo, Yugoslavia	Feb 8–19	1127	283	49	USSR (6-10-9—25)	4-4-0—8 (T-5th)
XV	1988	Calgary, Canada	Feb 13–28	1270	364	57	USSR (11-9-9—29)	2-1-3—6 (T-8th)
XVI	1992	Albertville, France	Feb 8–23	1313	488	65	Germany (10-10-6—26)	5-4-2—11 (6th)
XVII	1994	Lillehammer, Norway	Feb 12–27	1302	542	67	Norway (10-11-5—26)	6-5-2—13 (T-5th)
XVIII	1998	Nagano, Japan	Feb 7–22	2302 (total)		72	Germany (12-9-8—29)	6-3-4—13 (6th)
XIV	2002	Salt Lake City, United States	Feb 8–24	1513	886	77	Germany (12-16-7—35)	10-13-11—34 (2nd)

Alltime Olympic Medal Winners

Summer

NATIONS

Nation	Gold	Silver	Bronze	Total	Nation	Gold	Silver	Bronze	Total
United States	906	698	615	2219	W Germany (1952–88)	77	104	120	301
Soviet Union (1952–88)	395	319	296	1010	Finland	101	83	114	298
Great Britain	189	242	237	668	China	112	96	78	286
France	199	202	230	631	Romania	82	88	114	284
Italy	189	154	168	511	Poland	59	74	118	251
Germany	152	154	178	484	Russia	86	80	85	251
(1896–1936, 1992–)					Canada	54	87	101	242
Sweden	140	157	179	476	The Netherlands	65	76	94	235
Hungary	158	141	161	460	Bulgaria	50	83	74	207
E Germany (1956–88)	159	150	136	445	Switzerland	48	76	64	188
Australia	119	126	154	399	Denmark	42	63	64	169
Japan	113	106	114	333	Cuba	64	51	49	164

Summary *(Cont.)*

INDIVIDUALS — OVERALL

Men

Athlete, Nation	Sport	G	S	B	Tot
Nikolai Andrianov, USSR	Gym	7	5	3	15
Boris Shakhlin, USSR	Gym	7	4	2	13
Edoardo Mangiarotti, Italy	Fen	6	5	2	13
Takashi Ono, Japan	Gym	5	4	4	13
Paavo Nurmi, Finland	Track	9	3	0	12
Sawao Kato, Japan	Gym	8	3	1	12
Alexei Nemov, Russia	Gym	4	2	6	12
Mark Spitz, United States	Swim	9	1	1	11
Matt Biondi, United States	Swim	8	2	1	11
Viktor Chukarin, USSR	Gym	7	3	1	11
Carl Osburn, United States	Shoot	5	4	2	11
Ray Ewry, United States	Track	10	0	0	10
Carl Lewis, United States	Track	9	1	0	10
Aladár Gerevich, Hungary	Fen	7	1	2	10
Akinori Nakayama, Japan	Gym	6	2	2	10
Vitaly Scherbo, UT/Belarus	Gym	6	0	4	10
Aleksandr Dityatin, USSR	Gym	3	6	1	10

Women

Athlete, Nation	Sport	G	S	B	Tot
Larissa Latynina, USSR	Gym	9	5	4	18
Vera Cáslavská, Czech	Gym	7	4	0	11
Agnes Keleti, Hungary	Gym	5	3	2	10
Polina Astakhova, USSR	Gym	5	2	3	10
Nadia Comaneci, Romania	Gym	5	3	1	9
Jenny Thompson, United States	Swim	7	1	1	9
Lyudmila Touricheva, USSR	Gym	4	3	2	9
Kornelia Ender, E Germany	Swim	4	4	0	8
Dawn Fraser, Australia	Swim	4	4	0	8
Shirley Babashoff, United States	Swim	2	6	0	8
Sofia Muratova, USSR	Gym	2	2	4	8
Dara Torres, United States	Swim	4	0	4	8
Inge de Bruijn, Netherlands	Swim	4	2	2	8

Eight tied with seven.

INDIVIDUALS — GOLD

Men

Ray Ewry, United States	10	
Paavo Nurmi, Finland	9	
Carl Lewis, United States	9	
Mark Spitz, United States	9	
Sawao Kato, Japan	8	
Matt Biondi, United States	8	
Nikolai Andrianov, USSR	7	
Boris Shakhlin, USSR	7	
Viktor Chukarin, USSR	7	
Aladár Gerevich, Hungary	7	

Women

Larissa Latynina, USSR	9	
Jenny Thompson, U.S.	8	
Vera Cáslavská, Czech	7	
Kristin Otto, E Germany	6	
Agnes Keleti, Hungary	5	
Nadia Comaneci, Romania	5	
Polina Astakhova, USSR	5	
Krisztina Egerszegi, Hungary	5	
Kornelia Ender, E Germany	4	
Dawn Fraser, Australia	4	
Lyudmila Tourischeva, USSR	4	
Evelyn Ashford, United States	4	
Janet Evans, United States	4	
Fanny Blankers-Koen, Neth	4	
Betty Cuthbert, Australia	4	
Pat McCormick, United States	4	
Bärbel Eckert Wöckel, E Ger	4	
Amy Van Dyken, United States	4	
Inge de Bruijn, Netherlands	4	
Yana Klochkova, Ukraine	4	

Winter

NATIONS

Nation	Gold	Silver	Bronze	Total	Nation	Gold	Silver	Bronze	Total
Norway	94	93	73	260	Finland	41	51	49	141
Soviet Union (1956–88)	78	56	59	193	E Germany (1956–88)	39	37	35	111
United States	70	70	51	191	Sweden	36	28	38	102
Austria	41	57	65	163	Switzerland	32	33	36	101
Germany	54	51	37	142	Canada	30	28	37	95

INDIVIDUALS — OVERALL

Men

Athlete, Nation	Sport	G	S	B	Tot
Bjørn Dæhlie, Norway	N Ski	8	4	0	12
Sixten Jernberg, Sweden	N Ski	4	3	2	9

Seven tied with 7.

Women

Athlete, Nation	Sport	G	S	B	Tot
Raisa Smetanina, USSR/UT	N Ski	4	5	1	10
Lyubov Egorova, UT/Russia	N Ski	6	3	0	9
Larissa Lazutina, UT/Russia	N Ski	5	3	1	9
Stefania Belmondo, Italy	N Ski	2	3	4	9

Four tied with 8.

INDIVIDUALS — GOLD

Men

Bjørn Dæhlie, Norway	8
A. Clas Thunberg, Finland	5
O. Bjoerndalen, Norway	5
Eric Heiden, United States	5

Nine tied with 4.

Women

Lyubov Egorova, UT/Russia	6
Lydia Skoblikova, USSR	6
Larissa Lazutina, UT/Russia	5
Bonnie Blair, United States	5

Four tied with 4.

TRACK AND FIELD
Men

100 METERS

1896	Thomas Burke, United States	12.0
1900	Frank Jarvis, United States	11.0
1904	Archie Hahn, United States	11.0
1906	Archie Hahn, United States	11.2
1908	Reginald Walker, S Africa	10.8 OR
1912	Ralph Craig, United States	10.8
1920	Charles Paddock, United States	10.8
1924	Harold Abrahams, Great Britain	10.6 OR
1928	Percy Williams, Canada	10.8
1932	Eddie Tolan, United States	10.3 OR
1936	Jesse Owens, United States	10.3
1948	Harrison Dillard, United States	10.3
1952	Lindy Remigino, United States	10.4
1956	Bobby Morrow, United States	10.5
1960	Armin Hary, W Germany	10.2 OR
1964	Bob Hayes, United States	10.0 EWR
1968	Jim Hines, United States	9.95 WR
1972	Valery Borzov, USSR	10.14
1976	Hasely Crawford, Trinidad	10.06
1980	Allan Wells, Great Britain	10.25
1984	Carl Lewis, United States	9.99
1988	Carl Lewis, United States*	9.92 WR
1992	Linford Christie, Great Britain	9.96
1996	Donovan Bailey, Canada	9.84 WR
2000	Maurice Greene, United States	9.87
2004	Justin Gatlin, United States	9.85

*Ben Johnson, Canada, disqualified.

200 METERS

1900	John Walter Tewksbury, United States	22.2
1904	Archie Hahn, United States	21.6 OR
1906	Not held	
1908	Robert Kerr, Canada	22.6
1912	Ralph Craig, United States	21.7
1920	Allen Woodring, United States	22.0
1924	Jackson Scholz, United States	21.6
1928	Percy Williams, Canada	21.8
1932	Eddie Tolan, United States	21.2 OR
1936	Jesse Owens, United States	20.7 OR
1948	Mel Patton, United States	21.1
1952	Andrew Stanfield, United States	20.7
1956	Bobby Morrow, United States	20.6 OR
1960	Livio Berruti, Italy	20.5 EWR
1964	Henry Carr, United States	20.3 OR
1968	Tommie Smith, United States	19.83 WR
1972	Valery Borzov, USSR	20.00
1976	Donald Quarrie, Jamaica	20.23
1980	Pietro Mennea, Italy	20.19
1984	Carl Lewis, United States	19.80 OR
1988	Joe DeLoach, United States	19.75 OR
1992	Mike Marsh, United States	20.01
1996	Michael Johnson, United States	19.32 WR
2000	Konstadinos Kederis, Greece	20.09
2004	Shawn Crawford, United States	19.79

400 METERS

1896	Thomas Burke, United States	54.2
1900	Maxey Long, United States	49.4 OR
1904	Harry Hillman, United States	49.2 OR
1906	Paul Pilgrim, United States	53.2
1908	Wyndham Halswelle, Great Britain	50.0
1912	Charles Reidpath, United States	48.2 OR
1920	Bevil Rudd, South Africa	49.6
1924	Eric Liddell, Great Britain	47.6 OR
1928	Ray Barbuti, United States	47.8
1932	William Carr, United States	46.2 WR
1936	Archie Williams, United States	46.5
1948	Arthur Wint, Jamaica	46.2

400 METERS *(CONT.)*

1952	George Rhoden, Jamaica	45.9
1956	Charles Jenkins, United States	46.7
1960	Otis Davis, United States	44.9 WR
1964	Michael Larrabee, United States	45.1
1968	Lee Evans, United States	43.86 WR
1972	Vincent Matthews, United States	44.66
1976	Alberto Juantorena, Cuba	44.26
1980	Viktor Markin, USSR	44.60
1984	Alonzo Babers, United States	44.27
1988	Steve Lewis, United States	43.87
1992	Quincy Watts, United States	43.50 OR
1996	Michael Johnson, United States	43.49 OR
2000	Michael Johnson, United States	43.84
2004	Jeremy Wariner, United States	44.00

800 METERS

1896	Edwin Flack, Australia	2:11
1900	Alfred Tysoe, Great Britain	2:01.2
1904	James Lightbody, United States	1:56 OR
1906	Paul Pilgrim, United States	2:01.5
1908	Mel Sheppard, United States	1:52.8 WR
1912	James Meredith, United States	1:51.9 WR
1920	Albert Hill, Great Britain	1:53.4
1924	Douglas Lowe, Great Britain	1:52.4
1928	Douglas Lowe, Great Britain	1:51.8 OR
1932	Thomas Hampson, Great Britain	1:49.8 WR
1936	John Woodruff, United States	1:52.9
1948	Mal Whitfield, United States	1:49.2 OR
1952	Mal Whitfield, United States	1:49.2 EOR
1956	Thomas Courtney, United States	1:47.7 OR
1960	Peter Snell, New Zealand	1:46.3 OR
1964	Peter Snell, New Zealand	1:45.1 OR
1968	Ralph Doubell, Australia	1:44.3 EWR
1972	Dave Wottle, United States	1:45.9
1976	Alberto Juantorena, Cuba	1:43.50 WR
1980	Steve Ovett, Great Britain	1:45.40
1984	Joaquim Cruz, Brazil	1:43.00 OR
1988	Paul Ereng, Kenya	1:43.45
1992	William Tanui, Kenya	1:43.66
1996	Vebjoern Rodal, Norway	1:42.58 OR
2000	Nils Schumann, Germany	1:45.08
2004	Yuriy Borzakovskiy, Russia	1:44.45

1,500 METERS

1896	Edwin Flack, Australia	4:33.2
1900	Charles Bennett, Great Britain	4:06.2 WR
1904	James Lightbody, United States	4:05.4 WR
1906	James Lightbody, United States	4:12.0
1908	Mel Sheppard, United States	4:03.4 OR
1912	Arnold Jackson, Great Britain	3:56.8 OR
1920	Albert Hill, Great Britain	4:01.8
1924	Paavo Nurmi, Finland	3:53.6 OR
1928	Harry Larva, Finland	3:53.2 OR
1932	Luigi Beccali, Italy	3:51.2 OR
1936	Jack Lovelock, New Zealand	3:47.8 WR
1948	Henri Eriksson, Sweden	3:49.8
1952	Josef Barthel, Luxemburg	3:45.1 OR
1956	Ron Delany, Ireland	3:41.2 OR
1960	Herb Elliott, Australia	3:35.6 WR
1964	Peter Snell, New Zealand	3:38.1
1968	Kipchoge Keino, Kenya	3:34.9 OR
1972	Pekkha Vasala, Finland	3:36.3
1976	John Walker, New Zealand	3:39.17
1980	Sebastian Coe, Great Britain	3:38.4
1984	Sebastian Coe, Great Britain	3:32.53 OR
1988	Peter Rono, Kenya	3:35.96
1992	Fermin Cacho, Spain	3:40.12
1996	Noureddine Morceli, Algeria	3:35.78
2000	Noah Ngeni, Kenya	3:32.07 OR
2004	Hicham El Guerrouj, Morocco	3:34.18

Note: OR=Olympic Record. WR=World Record. EOR=Equals Olympic Record. EWR=Equals World Record. WB=World Best.

TRACK AND FIELD (Cont.)
Men (Cont.)

5,000 METERS

1912	Hannes Kolehmainen, Finland	14:36.6 WR
1920	Joseph Guillemot, France	14:55.6
1924	Paavo Nurmi, Finland	14:31.2 OR
1928	Villie Ritola, Finland	14:38
1932	Lauri Lehtinen, Finland	14:30 OR
1936	Gunnar Hickert, Finland	14:22.2 OR
1948	Gaston Reiff, Belgium	14:17.6 OR
1952	Emil Zatopek, Czechoslovakia	14:06.6 OR
1956	Vladimir Kuts, USSR	13:39.6 OR
1960	Murray Halberg, New Zealand	13:43.4
1964	Bob Schul, United States	13:48.8
1968	Mohamed Gammoudi, Tunisia	14:05.0
1972	Lasse Viren, Finland	13:26.4 OR
1976	Lasse Viren, Finland	13:24.76
1980	Miruts Yifter, Ethiopia	13:21.0
1984	Said Aouita, Morocco	13:05.59 OR
1988	John Ngugi, Kenya	13:11.70
1992	Dieter Baumann, Germany	13:12.52
1996	Venuste Niyongabo, Burundi	13:07.96
2000	Millon Wolde, Ethiopia	13:35.49
2004	Hicham El Guerrouj, Morocco	13:14.39

10,000 METERS

1912	Hannes Kolehmainen, Finland	31:20.8
1920	Paavo Nurmi, Finland	31:45.8
1924	Vilho (Ville) Ritola, Finland	30:23.2 WR
1928	Paavo Nurmi, Finland	30:18.8 OR
1932	Janusz Kusocinski, Poland	30:11.4 OR
1936	Ilmari Salminen, Finland	30:15.4
1948	Emil Zatopek, Czechoslovakia	29:59.6 OR
1952	Emil Zatopek, Czechoslovakia	29:17.0 OR
1956	Vladimir Kuts, USSR	28:45.6 QR
1960	Pyotr Bolotnikov, USSR	28:32.2 OR
1964	Billy Mills, United States	28:24.4 OR
1968	Naftali Temu, Kenya	29:27.4
1972	Lasse Viren, Finland	27:38.4 WR
1976	Lasse Viren, Finland	27:40.38
1980	Miruts Yifter, Ethiopia	27:42.7
1984	Alberto Cova, Italy	27:47.54
1988	Brahim Boutaib, Morocco	27:21.46 OR
1992	Khalid Skah, Morocco	27:46.70
1996	Haile Gebrselassie, Ethiopia	27:07.34 OR
2000	Haile Gebrselassie, Ethiopia	27:18.20
2004	Kenenisa Bekele, Ethiopia	27:05.10 OR

MARATHON

1896	Spiridon Louis, Greece	2:58:50
1900	Michel Theato, France	2:59:45
1904	Thomas Hicks, United States	3:28:53
1906	William Sherring, Canada	2:51:23.6
1908	John Hayes, United States	2:55:18.4 OR
1912	Kenneth McArthur, S Africa	2:36:54.8
1920	Hannes Kolehmainen, Finland	2:32:35.8 WB
1924	Albin Stenroos, Finland	2:41:22.6
1928	Boughera El Ouafi, France	2:32:57
1932	Juan Zabala, Argentina	2:31:36 OR
1936	Kijung Son, Japan (Korea)	2:29:19.2 OR
1948	Delfo Cabrera, Argentina	2:34:51.6
1952	Emil Zatopek, Czechoslovakia	2:23:03.2 OR
1956	Alain Mimoun O'Kacha, France	2:25:00.0
1960	Abebe Bikila, Ethiopia	2:15:16.2 WB
1964	Abebe Bikila, Ethiopia	2:12:11.2 WB
1968	Mamo Wolde, Ethiopia	2:20:26.4
1972	Frank Shorter, United States	2:12:19.8
1976	Waldemar Cierpinski, E Germ.	2:09:55 OR
1980	Waldemar Cierpinski, E Germ.	2:11:03.0
1984	Carlos Lopes, Portugal	2:09:21.0 OR
1988	Gelindo Bordin, Italy	2:10:32
1992	Hwang Young-Cho, S Korea	2:13:23
1996	Josia Thugwane, S Africa	2:12:36
2000	Gezahgne Abera, Ethiopia	2:10:11
2004	Stefano Baldini, Italy	2:10:55

110-METER HURDLES

1896	Thomas Curtis, United States	17.6
1900	Alvin Kraenzlein, United States	15.4 OR
1904	Frederick Schule, United States	16.0
1906	Robert Leavitt, United States	16.2
1908	Forrest Smithson, United States	15.0 WR
1912	Frederick Kelly, United States	15.1
1920	Earl Thomson, Canada	14.8 WR
1924	Daniel Kinsey, United States	15.0
1928	Sydney Atkinson, S Africa	14.8
1932	George Saling, United States	14.6
1936	Forrest Towns, United States	14.2
1948	William Porter, United States	13.9 OR
1952	Harrison Dillard, United States	13.7 OR
1956	Lee Calhoun, United States	13.5 OR
1960	Lee Calhoun, United States	13.8
1964	Hayes Jones, United States	13.6
1968	Willie Davenport, United States	13.3 OR
1972	Rod Milburn, United States	13.24 EWR
1976	Guy Drut, France	13.30
1980	Thomas Munkelt, E Germany	13.39
1984	Roger Kingdom, United States	13.20 OR
1988	Roger Kingdom, United States	12.98 OR
1992	Mark McKoy, Canada	13.12
1996	Allen Johnson, United States	12.95 OR
2000	Anier Garcia, Cuba	13.00
2004	Xiang Liu, China	12.91 EWR

400-METER HURDLES

1900	John Walter Tewksbury, U.S.	57.6
1904	Harry Hillman, United States	53.0
1906	Not held	
1908	Charles Bacon, United States	55.0 WR
1912	Not held	
1920	Frank Loomis, United States	54.0 WR
1924	F. Morgan Taylor, United States	52.6
1928	David Burghley, Great Britain	53.4 OR
1932	Robert Tisdall, Ireland	51.7
1936	Glenn Hardin, United States	52.4
1948	Roy Cochran, United States	51.1 OR
1952	Charles Moore, United States	50.8 OR
1956	Glenn Davis, United States	50.1 EOR
1960	Glenn Davis, United States	49.3 EOR
1964	Rex Cawley, United States	49.6
1968	Dave Hemery, Great Britain	48.12 WR
1972	John Akii-Bua, Uganda	47.82 WR
1976	Edwin Moses, United States	47.64 WR
1980	Volker Beck, E Germany	48.70
1984	Edwin Moses, United States	47.75
1988	Andre Phillips, United States	47.19 OR
1992	Kevin Young, United States	46.78 WR
1996	Derrick Adkins, United States	47.54
2000	Angelo Taylor, United States	47.50
2004	Felix Sanchez, Dominican Rep	47.63

3,000-METER STEEPLECHASE

1920	Percy Hodge, Great Britain	10:00.4 OR
1924	Vilho (Ville) Ritola, Finland	9:33.6 OR
1928	Toivo Loukola, Finland	9:21.8 WR
1932	Volmari Iso-Hollo, Finland	10:33.4*
1936	Volmari Iso-Hollo, Finland	9:03.8 WR
1948	Thore Sjöstrand, Sweden	9:04.6
1952	Horace Ashenfelter, U.S.	8:45.4 WR
1956	Chris Brasher, Great Britain	8:41.2 OR
1960	Zdzislaw Krzyszkowiak, Poland	8:34.2 OR
1964	Gaston Roelants, Belgium	8:30.8 OR
1968	Amos Biwott, Kenya	8:51
1972	Kipchoge Keino, Kenya	8:23.6 OR
1976	Anders Gärderud, Sweden	8:08.2 WR
1980	Bronislaw Malinowski, Poland	8:09.7
1984	Julius Korir, Kenya	8:11.8
1988	Julius Kariuki, Kenya	8:05.51 OR
1992	Matthew Birir, Kenya	8:08.84
1996	Joseph Keter, Kenya	8:07.12
2000	Reuben Kosgei, Kenya	8:21.43

TRACK AND FIELD (Cont.)

Men (Cont.)

3,000-METER STEEPLECHASE *(CONT.)*

2004	Ezekiel Kemboi, Kenya	8:05.81

*About 3,450 meters; extra lap by error.

4 X 100-METER RELAY

1912	Great Britain	42.4 OR
1920	United States	42.2 WR
1924	United States	41.0 EWR
1928	United States	41.0 EWR
1932	United States	40.0 EWR
1936	United States	39.8 WR
1948	United States	40.6
1952	United States	40.1
1956	United States	39.5 WR
1960	W Germany	39.5 EWR
1964	United States	39.0 WR
1968	United States	38.2 WR
1972	United States	38.19 EWR
1976	United States	38.33
1980	USSR	38.26
1984	United States	37.83 WR
1988	USSR	38.19
1992	United States	37.40 WR
1996	Canada	37.69
2000	United States	37.61
2004	Great Britain	38.07

4 X 400-METER RELAY

1908	United States	3:29.4
1912	United States	3:16.6 WR
1920	Great Britain	3:22.2
1924	United States	3:16.0 WR
1928	United States	3:14.2 WR
1932	United States	3:08.2 WR
1936	Great Britain	3:09.0
1948	United States	3:10.4 WR
1952	Jamaica	3:03.9 WR
1956	United States	3:04.8
1960	United States	3:02.2 WR
1964	United States	3:00.7 WR
1968	United States	2:56.16 WR
1972	Kenya	2:59.8
1976	United States	2:58.65
1980	USSR	3:01.1
1984	United States	2:57.91
1988	United States	2:56.16 EWR
1992	United States	2:55.74 WR
1996	United States	2:55.99
2000	United States	2:56.35
2004	United States	2:55.91

20-KILOMETER WALK

1956	Leonid Spirin, USSR	1:31:27.4
1960	Vladimir Golubnichiy, USSR	1:33:07.2
1964	Kenneth Mathews, Great Britain	1:29:34.0 OR
1968	Vladimir Golubnichiy, USSR	1:33:58.4
1972	Peter Frenkel, E Germany	1:26:42.4 OR
1976	Daniel Bautista, Mexico	1:24:40.6 OR
1980	Maurizio Damilano, Italy	1:23:35.5 OR
1984	Ernesto Canto, Mexico	1:23:13.0 OR
1988	Jozef Pribilinec, Czechoslovakia	1:19:57.0 OR
1992	Daniel Plaza, Spain	1:21:45.0
1996	Jefferson Pérez, Ecuador	1:20:07
2000	Robert Korzeniowski, Poland	1:18:59 OR
2004	Ivano Brugnetti, Italy	1:19:40

50-KILOMETER WALK

1932	Thomas Green, Great Britain	4:50:10
1936	Harold Whitlock, Great Britain	4:30:41.4 OR
1948	John Ljunggren, Sweden	4:41:52
1952	Giuseppe Dordoni, Italy	4:28:07.8 OR
1956	Norman Read, New Zealand	4:30:42.8
1960	Donald Thompson, Great Britain	4:25:30 OR
1964	Abdon Parnich, Italy	4:11:12.4 OR

50-KILOMETER WALK *(CONT.)*

1968	Christoph Höhne, E Germany	4:20:13.6
1972	Bernd Kannenberg, W Germany	3:56:11.6 OR
1980	Hartwig Gauder, E Germany	3:49:24.0 OR
1984	Raul Gonzalez, Mexico	3:47:26.0 OR
1988	Viacheslav Ivanenko, USSR	3:38:29.0 OR
1992	Andrey Perlov, Unified Team	3:50:13
1996	Robert Korzeniowski, Poland	3:43:30
2000	Robert Korzeniowski, Poland	3:42:22 OR
2004	Robert Korzeniowski, Poland	3:38:46

HIGH JUMP

1896	Ellery Clark, United States	5 ft 11¼ in
1900	Irving Baxter, United States	6 ft 2¾ in OR
1904	Samuel Jones, United States	5 ft 11 in
1906	Cornelius Leahy, Great Britain/Ireland	5 ft 10 in
1908	Harry Porter, United States	6 ft 3 in OR
1912	Alma Richards, United States	6 ft 4 in OR
1920	Richmond Landon, United States	6 ft 4 in OR
1924	Harold Osborn, United States	6 ft 6 in OR
1928	Robert W. King, United States	6 ft 4½ in
1932	Duncan McNaughton, Canada	6 ft 5½ in
1936	Cornelius Johnson, United States	6 ft 8 in OR
1948	John L. Winter, Australia	6 ft 6 in
1952	Walter Davis, United States	6 ft 8½ in OR
1956	Charles Dumas, United States	6 ft 11½ in OR
1960	Robert Shavlakadze, USSR	7 ft 1 in OR
1964	Valery Brumel, USSR	7 ft 1¾ in OR
1968	Dick Fosbury, United States	7 ft 4¼ in OR
1972	Yuri Tarmak, USSR	7 ft 3¾ in
1976	Jacek Wszola, Poland	7 ft 4½ in OR
1980	Gerd Wessig, E Germany	7 ft 8¾ in WR
1984	Dietmar Mögenburg, W Ger	7 ft 8½ in
1988	Gennadiy Avdeyenko, USSR	7 ft 9¾ in OR
1992	Javier Sotomayor, Cuba	7 ft 8 in.
1996	Charles Austin, United States	7 ft 10 in OR
2000	Sergey Kliugin, Russia	7 ft 8¼ in
2004	Stefan Holm, Sweden	7 ft 8¾ in

POLE VAULT

1896	William Hoyt, United States	10 ft 10 in
1900	Irving Baxter, United States	10 ft 10 in
1904	Charles Dvorak, United States	11 ft 5¾ in
1906	Fernand Gonder, France	11 ft 5¾ in
1908	Alfred Gilbert, United States Edward Cooke Jr., United States	12 ft 2 in OR
1912	Harry Babcock, United States	12 ft 11½ in OR
1920	Frank Foss, United States	13 ft 5 in WR
1924	Lee Barnes, United States	12 ft 11½ in
1928	Sabin Carr, United States	13 ft 9¼ in OR
1932	William Miller, United States	14 ft 1¾ in OR
1936	Earle Meadows, United States	14 ft 3¼ in OR
1948	Guinn Smith, United States	14 ft 1¼ in
1952	Robert Richards, United States	14 ft 11 in OR
1956	Robert Richards, United States	14 ft 11½ in OR
1960	Don Bragg, United States	15 ft 5 in OR
1964	Fred Hansen, United States	16 ft 8¾ in OR
1968	Bob Seagren, United States	17 ft 8½ in OR
1972	Wolfgang Nordwig, E Germany	18 ft ½ in OR
1976	Tadeusz Slusarski, Poland	18 ft ½ in EOR
1980	Wladyslaw Kozakiewicz, Pol	18 ft 11½ in WR
1984	Pierre Quinon, France	18 ft 10¼ in
1988	Sergei Bubka, USSR	19 ft 4¼ in OR
1992	Maksim Tarasov, Unified Team	19 ft ¼ in
1996	Jean Galfione, France	19 ft 5¼ in OR
2000	Nick Hysong, United States	19 ft 4¼ in
2004	Timothy Mack, United States	19 ft 6¼ in

Note: OR=Olympic Record. WR=World Record. EOR=Equals Olympic Record. EWR=Equals World Record. WB=World Best.

TRACK AND FIELD *(Cont.)*

Men *(Cont.)*

LONG JUMP

1896...Ellery Clark, United States	20 ft 10 in	
1900...Alvin Kraenzlein, United States	23 ft 6¾ in OR	
1904...Meyer Prinstein, United States	24 ft 1 in OR	
1906...Meyer Prinstein, United States	23 ft 7½ in	
1908...Frank Irons, United States	24 ft 6½ in OR	
1912...Albert Gutterson, United States	24 ft 11¼ in OR	
1920...William Petersson, Sweden	23 ft 5½ in	
1924...DeHart Hubbard, United States	24 ft 5 in	
1928...Edward B. Hamm, United States	25 ft 4½ in OR	
1932...Edward Gordon, United States	25 ft ¾ in	
1936...Jesse Owens, United States	26 ft 5½ in OR	
1948...William Steele, United States	25 ft 8 in	
1952...Jerome Biffle, United States	24 ft 10 in	
1956...Gregory Bell, United States	25 ft 8¼ in	
1960...Ralph Boston, United States	26 ft 7¾ in OR	
1964...Lynn Davies, Great Britain	26 ft 5¾ in	
1968...Bob Beamon, United States	29 ft 2½ in WR	
1972...Randy Williams, United States	27 ft ½ in	
1976...Arnie Robinson, United States	27 ft 4¾ in	
1980...Lutz Dombrowski, E Germany	28 ft ¼ in	
1984...Carl Lewis, United States	28 ft ¼ in	
1988...Carl Lewis, United States	28 ft 7½ in	
1992...Carl Lewis, United States	28 ft 5½ in	
1996...Carl Lewis, United States	27 ft 10¾ in	
2000...Ivan Pedrosa, Cuba	28 ft ¾ in	
2004...Dwight Phillips, United States	28 ft 2¼ in	

TRIPLE JUMP

1896...James Connolly, United States	44 ft 11¾ in	
1900...Meyer Prinstein, United States	47 ft 5¾ in OR	
1904...Meyer Prinstein, United States	47 ft 1 in	
1906...Peter O'Connor, GB/ Ire	46 ft 2¼ in	
1908...Timothy Ahearne, GB/ Ire	48 ft 11¼ in OR	
1912...Gustaf Lindblom, Sweden	48 ft 5¼ in	
1920...Vilho Tuulos, Finland	47 ft 7 in	
1924...Anthony Winter, Australia	50 ft 11¼ in WR	
1928...Mikio Oda, Japan	49 ft 11 in	
1932...Chuhei Nambu, Japan	51 ft 7 in WR	
1936...Naoto Tajima, Japan	52 ft 6 in WR	
1948...Arne Ahman, Sweden	50 ft 6¼ in	
1952...Adhemar da Silva, Brazil	53 ft 2¾ in WR	
1956...Adhemar da Silva, Brazil	53 ft 7¾ in OR	
1960...Jozef Schmidt, Poland	55 ft 2 in	
1964...Jozef Schmidt, Poland	55 ft 3½ in OR	
1968...Viktor Saneyev, USSR	57 ft ¾ in WR	
1972...Viktor Saneyev, USSR	56 ft 11¾ in	
1976...Viktor Saneyev, USSR	56 ft 8¾ in	
1980...Jaak Uudmae, USSR	56 ft 11¼ in	
1984...Al Joyner, United States	56 ft 7½ in	
1988...Khristo Markov, Bulgaria	57 ft 9½ in OR	
1992...Mike Conley, United States	59 ft 7½ in (w)	
1996...Kenny Harrison, United States	59 ft 4¼ in OR	
2000...Jonathon Edwards, G. Britain	58 ft 1¼ in	
2004...Christian Olsson, Sweden	58 ft 4½ in	

SHOT PUT

1896...Robert Garrett, United States	36 ft 9¾ in	
1900...Richard Sheldon, United States	46 ft 3¼ in OR	
1904...Ralph Rose, United States	48 ft 7 in WR	
1906...Martin Sheridan, United States	40 ft 5¼ in	
1908...Ralph Rose, United States	46 ft 7½ in	
1912...Pat McDonald, United States	50 ft 4 in OR	
1920...Ville Porhola, Finland	48 ft 7¼ in	
1924...Clarence Houser, United States	49 ft 2¼ in	
1928...John Kuck, United States	52 ft ¾ in WR	
1932...Leo Sexton, United States	52 ft 6 in OR	

SHOT PUT *(CONT.)*

1936...Hans Woellke, Germany	53 ft 1¾ in OR	
1948...Wilbur Thompson, United States	56 ft 2 in OR	
1952...Parry O'Brien, United States	57 ft ½ in OR	
1956...Parry O'Brien, United States	60 ft 11¼ in OR	
1960...William Nieder, United States	64 ft 6¾ in OR	
1964...Dallas Long, United States	66 ft 8½ in OR	
1968...Randy Matson, United States	67 ft 4¾ in	
1972...Wladyslaw Komar, Poland	69 ft 6 in OR	
1976...Udo Beyer, E Germany	69 ft ¾ in	
1980...Vladimir Kiselyov, USSR	70 ft ½ in OR	
1984...Alessandro Andrei, Italy	69 ft 9 in	
1988...Ulf Timmermann, E Germany	73 ft 8¾ in OR	
1992...Mike Stulce, United States	71 ft 2½ in	
1996...Randy Barnes, United States	70 ft 11 in	
2000...Arsi Harju, Finland	69 ft 10¼ in	
2004...Yuriy Bilonog, Ukraine	69 ft 5¼ in	

DISCUS THROW

1896...Robert Garrett, United States	95 ft 7½ in	
1900...Rudolf Bauer, Hungary	118 ft 3 in OR	
1904...Martin Sheridan, United States	128 ft 10½ in OR	
1906...Martin Sheridan, United States	136 ft	
1908...Martin Sheridan, United States	134 ft 2 in OR	
1912...Armas Taipele, Finland	148 ft 3 in OR	
1920...Elmer Niklander, Finland	146 ft 7 in	
1924...Clarence Houser, United States	151 ft 4 in OR	
1928...Clarence Houser, United States	155 ft 3 in OR	
1932...John Anderson, United States	162 ft 4 in OR	
1936...Ken Carpenter, United States	165 ft 7 in OR	
1948...Adolfo Consolini, Italy	173 ft 2 in OR	
1952...Sim Iness, United States	180 ft 6 in OR	
1956...Al Oerter, United States	184 ft 11 in OR	
1960...Al Oerter, United States	194 ft 2 in OR	
1964...Al Oerter, United States	200 ft 1 in OR	
1968...Al Oerter, United States	212 ft 6 in OR	
1972...Ludvik Danek, Czechoslovakia	211 ft 3 in	
1976...Mac Wilkins, United States	221 ft 5 in OR	
1980...Viktor Rashchupkin, USSR	218 ft 8 in	
1984...Rolf Dannenberg, W Ger	218 ft 6 in	
1988...Jürgen Schult, E Germany	225 ft 9 in OR	
1992...Romas Ubartas, Lithuania	213 ft 8 in	
1996...Lars Riedel, Germany	227 ft 8 in OR	
2000...Virgilijus Alekna, Lithuania	227 ft 4 in	
2004...Virgilijus Alekna, Lithuania	229 ft 3 in	

HAMMER THROW

1900...John Flanagan, United States	163 ft 1 in	
1904...John Flanagan, United States	168 ft 1 in OR	
1906...Not held		
1908...John Flanagan, United States	170 ft 4 in OR	
1912...Matt McGrath, United States	179 ft 7 in OR	
1920...Pat Ryan, United States	173 ft 5 in	
1924...Fred Tootell, United States	174 ft 10 in	
1928...Patrick O'Callaghan, Ireland	168 ft 7 in	
1932...Patrick O'Callaghan, Ireland	176 ft 11 in	
1936...Karl Hein, Germany	185 ft 4 in OR	
1948...Imre Nemeth, Hungary	183 ft 11 in	
1952...Jozsef Csermak, Hungary	197 ft 11 in WR	
1956...Harold Connolly, United States	207 ft 3 in OR	
1960...Vasily Rudenkov, USSR	220 ft 2 in OR	
1964...Romuald Klim, USSR	228 ft 10 in OR	
1968...Gyula Zsivotsky, Hungary	240 ft 8 in OR	
1972...Anatoli Bondarchuk, USSR	247 ft 8 in OR	
1976...Yuri Sedykh, USSR	254 ft 4 in OR	
1980...Yuri Sedykh, USSR	268 ft 4 in WR	
1984...Juha Tiainen, Finland	256 ft 2 in	
1988...Sergei Litvinov, USSR	278 ft 2 in OR	
1992...Andrey Abduvaliyev, Unified T	270 ft 9 in	

TRACK AND FIELD (Cont.)
Men (Cont.)

HAMMER THROW (CONT.)

1996	Balazs Kiss, Hungary	266 ft 6 in
2000	Szymon Ziolkowski, Poland	262 ft 6 in
2004	Adrian Zsolt, Hungary	272 fr 11 in

JAVELIN

1908	Erik Lemming, Sweden	179 ft 10 in
1912	Erik Lemming, Sweden	198 ft 11 in WR
1920	Jonni Myyrä, Finland	215 ft 10 in OR
1924	Jonni Myyrä, Finland	206 ft 6 in
1928	Eric Lundkvist, Sweden	218 ft 6 in OR
1932	Matti Jarvinen, Finland	238 ft 6 in OR
1936	Gerhard Stöck, Germany	235 ft 8 in
1948	Kai Rautavaara, Finland	228 ft 10½ in
1952	Cy Young, United States	242 ft 1 in OR
1956	Egil Danielson, Norway	281 ft 2¼ in WR
1960	Viktor Tsibulenko, USSR	277 ft 8 in
1964	Pauli Nevala, Finland	271 ft 2 in
1968	Janis Lusis, USSR	295 ft 7 in OR
1972	Klaus Wolfermann, W Ger	296 ft 10 in OR
1976	Miklos Nemeth, Hungary	310 ft 4 in WR
1980	Dainis Kuta, USSR	299 ft 2⅜ in
1984	Arto Härkönen, Finland	284 ft 8 in
1988	Tapio Korjus, Finland	276 ft 6 in
1992	Jan Zelezny, Czechoslovakia	294 ft 2 in OR
1996	Jan Zelezny, Czech Republic	289 ft 3 in
2000	Jan Zelezny, Czech Republic	295 ft 9½ in OR
2004	Andrea Thorkildsen, Norway	283 ft 9 in

DECATHLON

		Pts
1904	Thomas Kiely, Ireland	6036
1912	Jim Thorpe, United States*	8412 WR
1920	Helge Lövland, Norway	6803
1924	Harold Osborn, United States	7711 WR
1928	Paavo Yrjölä, Finland	8053.29 WR
1932	James Bausch, United States	8462 WR
1936	Glenn Morris, United States	7900 WR
1948	Robert Mathias, United States	7139
1952	Robert Mathias, United States	7887 WR
1956	Milton Campbell, United States	7937 OR
1960	Rafer Johnson, United States	8392 OR
1964	Willi Holdorf, W Germany	7887
1968	Bill Toomey, United States	8193 OR
1972	Nikolai Avilov, USSR	8454 WR
1976	Bruce Jenner, United States	8617 WR
1980	Daley Thompson, Great Britain	8495
1984	Daley Thompson, Great Britain	8798 EWR
1988	Christian Schenk, E Germany	8488
1992	Robert Zmelik, Czechoslovakia	8611
1996	Dan O'Brien, United States	8824 OR
2000	Erki Nool, Estonia	8641
2004	Roman Seberle, Czech Rep	8893 OR

*In 1913, Thorpe was disqualified for having played professional baseball in 1910. His record was restored in 1982.

Women

100 METERS

1928	Elizabeth Robinson, United States	12.2 EWR
1932	Stella Walsh, Poland	11.9 EWR
1936	Helen Stephens, United States	11.5
1948	Francina Blankers-Koen, Neth	11.9
1952	Marjorie Jackson, Australia	11.5 EWR
1956	Betty Cuthbert, Australia	11.5 EWR
1960	Wilma Rudolph, United States	11.0
1964	Wyomia Tyus, United States	11.4
1968	Wyomia Tyus, United States	11.0 WR
1972	Renate Stecher, E Germany	11.07
1976	Annegret Richter, W Germany	11.08
1980	Lyudmila Kondratyeva, USSR	11.06
1984	Evelyn Ashford, United States	10.97 OR
1988	Florence Griffith Joyner, United States	10.54 WR
1992	Gail Devers, United States	10.82
1996	Gail Devers, United States	10.94
2000	Marion Jones, United States	10.75
2004	Yuliya Nesterenko, Belarus	10.93

200 METERS

1948	Francina Blankers-Koen, Neth	24.4
1952	Marjorie Jackson, Australia	23.7
1956	Betty Cuthbert, Australia	23.4 EOR
1960	Wilma Rudolph, United States	24.0
1964	Edith McGuire, United States	23.0 OR
1968	Irena Szewinska, Poland	22.5 WR
1972	Renate Stecher, E Germany	22.40 EWR
1976	Bärbel Eckert, E Germany	22.37 OR
1980	Bärbel Wöckel (Eckert), E Germ.	22.03 OR
1984	Valerie Brisco-Hooks, U.S.	21.81 OR
1988	Florence Griffith Joyner, U.S.	21.34 WR

200 METERS (CONT.)

1992	Gwen Torrence, United States	21.81
1996	Marie-José Pérec, France	22.12
2000	Marion Jones, United States	21.84
2004	Veronica Campbell, Jamaica	22.05

400 METERS

1964	Betty Cuthbert, Australia	52.0 OR
1968	Colette Besson, France	52.0 EOR
1972	Monika Zehrt, E Germany	51.08 OR
1976	Irena Szewinska, Poland	49.29 WR
1980	Marita Koch, E Germany	48.88 OR
1984	Valerie Brisco-Hooks, U.S.	48.83 OR
1988	Olga Bryzgina, USSR	48.65 OR
1992	Marie-José Pérec, France	48.83
1996	Marie-José Pérec, France	48.25 OR
2000	Cathy Freeman, Australia	49.11
2004	T. Williams-Darling, Bahamas	49.41

800 METERS

1928	Lina Radke, Germany	2:16.8 WR
1932	Not held 1932–1956	
1960	Lyudmila Shevtsova, USSR	2:04.3 EWR
1964	Ann Packer, Great Britain	2:01.1 OR
1968	Madeline Manning, United States	2:00.9 OR
1972	Hildegard Falck, W Germany	1:58.55 OR
1976	Tatyana Kazankina, USSR	1:54.94 WR
1980	Nadezhda Olizarenko, USSR	1:53.42 WR
1984	Doina Melinte, Romania	1:57.6
1988	Sigrun Wodars, E Germany	1:56.10
1992	Ellen Van Langen, Netherlands	1:55.54
1996	Svetlana Masterkova, Russia	1:57.73
2000	Maria Mutola, Mozambique	1:56.15
2004	Kelly Holmes, Great Britain	1:56.38

Note: OR=Olympic Record. WR=World Record. EOR=Equals Olympic Record. EWR=Equals World Record. WB=World Best.

TRACK AND FIELD (Cont.)

Women (Cont.)

1,500 METERS

1972	Lyudmila Bragina, USSR	4:01.4 WR
1976	Tatyana Kazankina, USSR	4:05.48
1980	Tatyana Kazankina, USSR	3:56.6 OR
1984	Gabriella Dorio, Italy	4:03.25
1988	Paula Ivan, Romania	3:53.96 OR
1992	Hassiba Boulmerka, Algeria	3:55.30
1996	Svetlana Masterkova, Russia	4:00.83
2000	Nouria Merah-Benida, Algeria	4:05.10
2004	Kelly Holmes, Great Britain	3:57.90

3,000 METERS

1984	Maricica Puica, Romania	8:35.96 OR
1988	Tatyana Samolenko, USSR	8:26.53 OR
1992	Elena Romanova, Unified Team	8:46.04

5,000 METERS

1996	Wang Junxia, China	14:57.88
2000	Gabriela Szabo, Romania	14:40.79 OR
2004	Meseret Defar, Ethiopia	14:45.65

10,000 METERS

1988	Olga Bondarenko, USSR	31:05.21 OR
1992	Derartu Tulu, Ethiopia	31:06.02
1996	Fernanda Ribeiro, Portugal	31:01.63 OR
2000	Derartu Tulu, Ethiopia	30:17.49 OR
2004	Huina Xing, China	30:24.36

MARATHON

1984	Joan Benoit, United States	2:24:52 OR
1988	Rosa Mota, Portugal	2:25:40
1992	Valentin Yegorova, Unified Team	2:32:41
1996	Fatuma Roba, Ethiopia	2:26:05
2000	Naoko Takahashi, Japan	2:23:14 OR
2004	Noguchi Mizuki, Japan	2:26:20

80-METER HURDLES

1932	Babe Didrikson, United States	11.7 WR
1936	Trebisonda Valla, Italy	11.7
1948	Francina Blankers-Koen, Neth	11.2 OR
1952	Shirley Strickland, Australia	10.9 WR
1956	Shirley Strickland, Australia	10.7 OR
1960	Irina Press, USSR	10.8
1964	Karin Balzer, E Germany	10.5
1968	Maureen Caird, Australia	10.3 OR

100-METER HURDLES

1972	Annelie Ehrhardt, E Germany	12.59 WR
1976	Johanna Schaller, E Germany	12.77
1980	Vera Komisova, USSR	12.56 OR
1984	Benita Fitzgerald-Brown, U.S.	12.84
1988	Yordanka Donkova, Bulgaria	12.38 OR
1992	Paraskevi Patoulidou, Greece	12.64
1996	Lyudmila Engqvist, Sweden	12.58
2000	Olga Shishigina, Kazakhstan	12.65
2004	Joanna Hayes, United States	12.37 OR

400-METER HURDLES

1984	Nawal el Moutawakel, Morocco	54.61 OR
1988	Debra Flintoff-King, Australia	53.17 OR
1992	Sally Gunnell, Great Britain	53.23
1996	Deon Hemmings, Jamaica	52.82 OR
2000	Irina Privalova, Russia	53.02
2004	Faní Halkiá, Greece	52.82

4 X 100-METER RELAY

1928	Canada	48.4 WR
1932	United States	46.9 WR
1936	United States	46.9
1948	Netherlands	47.5
1952	United States	45.9 WR
1956	Australia	44.5 WR

4 X 100-METER RELAY (CONT.)

1960	United States	44.5
1964	Poland	43.6
1968	United States	42.8 WR
1972	W Germany	42.81 EWR
1976	E Germany	42.55 OR
1980	E Germany	41.60 WR
1984	United States	41.65
1988	United States	41.98
1992	United States	42.11
1996	United States	41.95
2000	Bahamas	41.95
2004	Jamaica	41.73

4 X 400-METER RELAY

1972	E Germany	3:23 WR
1976	E Germany	3:19.23 WR
1980	USSR	3:20.02
1984	United States	3:18.29 OR
1988	USSR	3:15.18 WR
1992	Unified Team	3:20.20
1996	United States	3:20.91
2000	United States	3:22.62
2004	United States	3:19.01

10-KILOMETER WALK

1992	Chen Yueling, China	44:32
1996	Elena Nikolayeva, Russia	41:49 OR

20-KILOMETER WALK

2000	Liping Wang, China	1:29:05
2004	Athanasía Tsoumeléka, Greece	1:29:12

HIGH JUMP

1928	Ethel Catherwood, Canada	5 ft 2½ in
1932	Jean Shiley, United States	5 ft 5¼ in WR
1936	Ibolya Csak, Hungary	5 ft 3 in
1948	Alice Coachman, United States	5 ft 6 in OR
1952	Esther Brand, South Africa	5 ft 5¾ in
1956	Mildred L. McDaniel, U.S.	5 ft 9¼ in WR
1960	Iolanda Balas, Romania	6 ft ¾ in OR
1964	Iolanda Balas, Romania	6 ft 2¾ in OR
1968	Miloslava Reskova, Czech.	5 ft 11½ in
1972	Ulrike Meyfarth, W. Germany	6 ft 3½ in EWR
1976	Rosemarie Ackermann, E Germ	6 ft 4 in OR
1980	Sara Simeoni, Italy	6 ft 5½ in OR
1984	Ulrike Meyfarth, W Germany	6 ft 7½ in OR
1988	Louise Ritter, United States	6 ft 8 in OR
1992	Heike Henkel, Germany	6 ft 7½ in
1996	Stefka Kostadinova, Bulgaria	6 ft 8¾ in OR
2000	Yelena Yelesina, Russia	6 ft 7 in
2004	Yelena Slesarenko, Russia	6 ft 9 in

POLE VAULT

2000	Stacy Dragila, United States	15 ft 1 in OR
2004	Yelena Isinbayeva, Russia	16 ft 1¼ in WR

LONG JUMP

1948	Olga Gyarmati, Hungary	18 ft 8¼ in
1952	Yvette Williams, New Zealand	20 ft 5¾ in OR
1956	Elzbieta Krzeskinska, Poland	20 ft 10 in EWR
1960	Vyera Krepkina, USSR	20 ft 10¾ in OR
1964	Mary Rand, Great Britain	22 ft 2¼ in WR
1968	Viorica Viscopoleanu, Rom	22 ft 4½ in WR
1972	Heidemarie Rosendahl, W Ger	22 ft 3 in
1976	Angela Voigt, E Germany	22 ft ¾ in
1980	Tatyana Kolpakova, USSR	23 ft 2 in OR
1984	Anisoara Stanciu, Romania	22 ft 10 in
1988	Jackie Joyner-Kersee, U.S.	24 ft 3½ in OR
1992	Heike Drechsler, Germany	23 ft 5¼ in
1996	Chioma Ajunwa, Nigeria	23 ft 4½ in
2000	Heike Drechsler, Germany	22 ft 11¼ in
2004	Tatyana Lebedeva, Russia	23 ft 2½ in

Note: OR=Olympic Record; WR=World Record; EOR=Equals Olympic Record; EWR=Equals World Record; WB=World Best.

TRACK AND FIELD (Cont.)
Women (Cont.)

TRIPLE JUMP

1996...Inessa Kravets, Ukraine	50 ft 3½ in	
2000...Tereza Marinova, Bulgaria	49 ft 10½ in	
2004...Frangoise M. Etone, Cameroon	50 ft 2½ in	

SHOT PUT

1948...Micheline Ostermeyer, France	45 ft 1½ in
1952...Galina Zybina, USSR	50 ft 1¾ in WR
1956...Tamara Tyshkevich, USSR	54 ft 5 in
1960...Tamara Press, USSR	56 ft 10 in OR
1964...Tamara Press, USSR	59 ft 6¼ in OR
1968...Margitta Gummel, E Germany	64 ft 4 in WR
1972...Nadezhda Chizhova, USSR	69 ft WR
1976...Ivanka Hristova, Bulgaria	69 ft 5¼ in OR
1980...Ilona Slupianek, E Germany	73 ft 6¼ in
1984...Claudia Losch, W Germany	67 ft 2¼ in
1988...Natalya Lisovskaya, USSR	72 ft 11¾ in
1992...Svetlana Kriveleva, Unified Team	69 ft 1¼ in
1996...Astrid Kumbernuss, Germany	67 ft 5½ in
2000...Yanina Korolchik, Belarus	67 ft 5½ in
2004...Yumileidi Cumba Jay, Cuba	64 ft 3¼ in

DISCUS THROW

1928...Helena Konopacka, Poland	129 ft 11¾ in WR
1932...Lillian Copeland, United States	133 ft 2 in OR
1936...Gisela Mauermayer, Germany	156 ft 3 in OR
1948...Micheline Ostermeyer, France	137 ft 6 in
1952...Nina Romaschkova, USSR	168 ft 8 in OR
1956...Olga Fikotova, Czechoslovakia	176 ft 1 in OR
1960...Nina Ponomaryeva, USSR	180 ft 9 in OR
1964...Tamara Press, USSR	187 ft 10 in OR
1968...Lia Manoliu, Romania	191 ft 2 in OR
1972...Faina Melnik, USSR	218 ft 7 in OR
1976...Evelin Schlaak, E Germany	226 ft 4 in OR
1980...Evelin Jahl (Schlaak), E Germ.	229 ft 6 in OR
1984...Ria Stalman, Netherlands	214 ft 5 in
1988...Martina Hellmann, E Germany	237 ft 2 in OR
1992...Maritza Martén, Cuba	229 ft 10 in
1996...Ilke Wyludda, Germany	228 ft 6 in
2000...Ellina Zvereva, Belarus	224 ft 5 in
2004...Natalya Sadova, Russia	219 ft 10 in

HAMMER THROW

2000...Kamila Skolimowska, Russia	233 ft 5 in OR
2004...Olga Kuzenkova, Russia	246 ft 1½ in OR

JAVELIN THROW

1932...Babe Didrikson, United States	143 ft 4 in OR
1936...Tilly Fleischer, Germany	148 ft 3 in OR
1948...Herma Bauma, Austria	149 ft 6 in
1952...Dana Zatopkova, Czechoslovakia	165 ft 7 in
1956...Inese Jaunzeme, USSR	176 ft 8 in
1960...Elvira Ozolina, USSR	183 ft 8 in OR
1964...Mihaela Penes, Romania	198 ft 7 in
1968...Angela Nemeth, Hungary	198 ft
1972...Ruth Fuchs, E Germany	209 ft 7 in OR
1976...Ruth Fuchs, E Germany	216 ft 4 in OR
1980...Maria Colon, Cuba	224 ft 5 in OR
1984...Tessa Sanderson, Great Britain	228 ft 2 in OR
1988...Petra Felke, E Germany	245 ft OR
1992...Silke Renk, Germany	224 ft 2 in
1996...Heli Rantanen, Finland	222 ft 11 in
2000...Trine Hattestad, Norway	226 ft ½ in OR
2004...Osleidys Menendez, Cuba	234 ft 8 in OR

PENTATHLON

	Pts
1964...Irina Press, USSR	5246 WR
1968...Ingrid Becker, W Germany	5098
1972...Mary Peters, Great Britain	4801 WR*
1976...Siegrun Siegl, E Germany	4745
1980...Nadezhda Tkachenko, USSR	5083 WR

HEPTATHLON

	Pts
1984...Glynis Nunn, Australia	6390 OR
1988...Jackie Joyner-Kersee, U.S.	7291 WR
1992...Jackie Joyner-Kersee, U.S.	7044
1996...Ghada Shouaa, Syria	6780
2000...Denise Lewis, Great Britain	6584
2004...Carolina Kluft, Sweden	6952

*In 1971, the 100-meter hurdles replaced the 80-meter hurdles, requiring a change in scoring tables.

BASKETBALL
Men

1936
Final: United States 19, Canada 8
United States: Ralph Bishop, Joe Fortenberry, Carl Knowles, Jack Ragland, Carl Shy, William Wheatley, Francis Johnson, Samuel Balter, John Gibbons, Frank Lubin, Arthur Mollner, Donald Piper, Duane Swanson, Willard Schmidt

1948
Final: United States 65, France 21
United States: Cliff Barker, Don Barksdale, Ralph Beard, Lewis Beck, Vince Boryla, Gordon Carpenter, Alex Groza, Wallace Jones, Bob Kurland, Ray Lumpp, Robert Pitts, Jesse Renick, Bob Robinson, Ken Rollins

1952
Final: United States 36, USSR 25
United States: Charles Hoag, Bill Hougland, Melvin Dean Kelley, Bob Kenney, Clyde Lovellette, Marcus Freiberger, Victor Wayne Glasgow, Frank McCabe, Daniel Pippen, Howard Williams, Ronald Bontemps, Bob Kurland, William Lienhard, John Keller

1956
Final: United States 89, USSR 55
United States: Carl Cain, Bill Hougland, K.C. Jones, Bill Russell, James Walsh, William Evans, Burdette Haldorson, Ron Tomsic, Dick Boushka, Gilbert Ford, Bob Jeangerard, Charles Darling

1960
Final: United States 90, Brazil 63
United States: Jay Arnette, Walt Bellamy, Bob Boozer, Terry Dischinger, Jerry Lucas, Oscar Robertson, Adrian Smith, Burdette Haldorson, Darrall Imhoff, Allen Kelley, Lester Lane, Jerry West

1964
Final: United States 73, USSR 59
United States: Jim Barnes, Bill Bradley, Larry Brown, Joe Caldwell, Mel Counts, Richard Davies, Walt Hazzard, Lucius Jackson, John McCaffrey, Jeff Mullins, Jerry Shipp, George Wilson

1968
Final: United States 65, Yugoslavia 50
United States: John Clawson, Ken Spain, Jo-Jo White, Michael Barrett, Spencer Haywood, Charles Scott, William Hosket, Calvin Fowler, Michael Silliman, Glynn Saulters, James King, Donald Dee

1972
Final: USSR 51, United States 50
United States: Kenneth Davis, Doug Collins, Thomas Henderson, Mike Bantom, Bobby Jones, Dwight Jones, James Forbes, James Brewer, Tom Burleson, Tom McMillen, Kevin Joyce, Ed Ratleff

BASKETBALL *(Cont.)*
Men *(Cont.)*

1976
Final: United States 95, Yugoslavia 74
United States: Phil Ford, Steve Sheppard, Adrian Dantley, Walter Davis, Quinn Buckner, Ernie Grunfield, Kenny Carr, Scott May, Michel Armstrong, Tom La Garde, Phil Hubbard, Mitch Kupchak

1980
Final: Yugoslavia 86, Italy 77
U.S. participated in boycott.

1984
Final: United States 96, Spain 65
United States: Steve Alford, Leon Wood, Patrick Ewing, Vern Fleming, Alvin Robertson, Michael Jordan, Joe Kleine, Jon Koncak, Wayman Tisdale, Chris Mullin, Sam Perkins, Jeff Turner

1988
Final: USSR 76, Yugoslavia 63
U.S. (3rd): Mitch Richmond, Charles E. Smith IV, Vernell Coles, Hersey Hawkins, Jeff Grayer, Charles D. Smith, Willie Anderson, Stacey Augmon, Dan Majerle, Danny Manning, J.R. Reid, David Robinson

1992
Final: United States 117, Croatia 85
United States: David Robinson, Christian Laettner, Patrick Ewing, Larry Bird, Scottie Pippen, Michael Jordan, Clyde Drexler, Karl Malone, John Stockton, Chris Mullin, Charles Barkley, Earvin Johnson

1996
Final: United States 95, Yugoslavia 69
United States: Charles Barkley, Anfernee Hardaway, Grant Hill, Karl Malone, Reggie Miller, Hakeem Olajuwon, Shaquille O'Neal, Scottie Pippen, Mitch Richmond, John Stockton, David Robinson, Gary Payton

2000
Final: United States 85, France 75
United States: Shareef Abdur-Rahim, Ray Allen, Vin Baker, Vince Carter, Kevin Garnett, Tim Hardaway, Allan Houston, Jason Kidd, Antonio McDyess, Alonzo Mourning, Gary Payton, Steve Smith

2004
Final: Argentina 84, Italy 69
U.S. (3rd): Allen Iverson, LeBron James, Tim Duncan, Carmelo Anthony, Dwyane Wade, Richard Jefferson, Lamar Odom, Stephon Marbury, Carlos Boozer, Emeka Okafor, Amare Stoudemire, Shawn Marion

Women

1976
Gold, USSR; Silver, United States*
United States: Cindy Brogdon, Susan Rojcewicz, Ann Meyers, Lusia Harris, Nancy Dunkle, Charlotte Lewis, Nancy Lieberman, Gail Marquis, Patricia Roberts, Mary Anne O'Connor, Patricia Head, Julienne Simpson
*In 1976 the women played a round-robin tournament, with the gold medal going to the team with the best record. The USSR won with a 5–0 record, and the USA, with a 3–2 record, was given the silver by virtue of a 95–79 victory over Bulgaria, which was also 3–2.

1980
Final: USSR 104, Bulgaria 73
U.S. participated in boycott.

1984
Final: United States 85, Korea 55
United States: Teresa Edwards, Lea Henry, Lynette Woodard, Anne Donovan, Cathy Boswell, Cheryl Miller, Janice Lawrence, Cindy Noble, Kim Mulkey, Denise Curry, Pamela McGee, Carol Menken-Schaudt

1988
Final: United States 77, Yugoslavia 70
United States: Teresa Edwards, Mary Ethridge, Cynthia Brown, Anne Donovan, Teresa Weatherspoon, Bridgette Gordon, Victoria Bullett, Andrea Lloyd, Katrina McClain, Jennifer Gillom, Cynthia Cooper, Suzanne McConnell

1992
Final: Unified Team 76, China 66
United States (3rd): Teresa Edwards, Teresa Weatherspoon, Victoria Bullett, Katrina McClain, Cynthia Cooper, Suzanne McConnell, Daedra Charles, Clarissa Davis, Tammy Jackson, Vickie Orr, Carolyn Jones, Medina Dixon

1996
Final: United States 111, Brazil 87
United States: Jennifer Azzi, Ruthie Bolton, Teresa Edwards, Lisa Leslie, Rebecca Lobo, Katrina McClain, Nikki McCray, Carla McGhee, Dawn Staley, Katy Steding, Sheryl Swoopes, Venus Lacey

2000
Final: United States 76, Australia 54
United States: Ruthie Bolton-Holifield, Teresa Edwards, Yolanda Griffith, Chamique Holdsclaw, Lisa Leslie, Nikki McCray, Delisha Milton, Katie Smith, Dawn Staley, Sheryl Swoopes, Natalie Williams, Kara Wolters

2004
Final: United States 74, Australia 63
United States: Dawn Staley, Diana Taurasi, Lisa Leslie, Sheryl Swoopes, Tamika Catchings, Sue Bird, Ruth Riley, Shannon Johnson, Katie Smith, Yolanda Griffith, Swintayla Cash, Tina Thompson

BOXING

LIGHT FLYWEIGHT (106 LB)	LIGHT FLYWEIGHT *(CONT.)*
1968 ....Francisco Rodriguez, Venezuela	1988 ....Ivailo Hristov, Bulgaria
1972 ....Gyorgy Gedo, Hungary	1992 ....Rogelio Marcelo, Cuba
1976 ....Jorge Hernandez, Cuba	1996 ....,.....Daniel Petrov, Bulgaria
1980 ....Shamil Sabyrov, USSR	2000 ....Brahim Asloum, France
1984 ....Paul Gonzalez, United States	2004 ....Yan Bhartelemy Varela, Cuba

BOXING (Cont.)

FLYWEIGHT (112 LB)

1904	George Finnegan, United States
1920	Frank Di Gennara, United States
1924	Fidel LaBarba, United States
1928	Antal Kocsis, Hungary
1932	Istvan Enekes, Hungary
1936	Willi Kaiser, Germany
1948	Pascual Perez, Argentina
1952	Nathan Brooks, United States
1956	Terence Spinks, Great Britain
1960	Gyula Torok, Hungary
1964	Fernando Atzori, Italy
1968	Ricardo Delgado, Mexico
1972	Georgi Kostadinov, Bulgaria
1976	Leo Randolph, United States
1980	Peter Lessov, Bulgaria
1984	Steve McCrory, United States
1988	Kim Kwang Sun, S Korea
1992	Su Choi Chol, N Korea
1996	Maikro Romero, Cuba
2000	Wijan Ponlid, Thailand
2004	Yuriokis Toledano, Cuba

BANTAMWEIGHT (119 LB)

1904	Oliver Kirk, United States
1908	A. Henry Thomas, Great Britain
1920	Clarence Walker, S Africa
1924	William Smith, S Africa
1928	Vittorio Tamagnini, Italy
1932	Horace Gwynne, Canada
1936	Ulderico Sergo, Italy
1948	Tibor Csik, Hungary
1952	Pentti Hamalainen, Finland
1956	Wolfgang Behrendt, E Germany
1960	Oleg Grigoryev, USSR
1964	Takao Sakurai, Japan
1968	Valery Sokolov, USSR
1972	Orlando Martinez, Cuba
1976	Yong Jo Gu, N Korea
1980	Juan Hernandez, Cuba
1984	Maurizio Stecca, Italy
1988	Kennedy McKinney, United States
1992	Joel Casamayor, Cuba
1996	István Kovács, Hungary
2000	Guillermo Ortiz, Cuba
2004	Guillermo Ortiz, Cuba

FEATHERWEIGHT (125 LB)

1904	Oliver Kirk, United States
1908	Richard Gunn, Great Britain
1920	Paul Fritsch, France
1924	John Fields, United States
1928	Lambertus van Klaveren, Netherlands
1932	Carmelo Robledo, Argentina
1936	Oscar Casanovas, Argentina
1948	Ernesto Formenti, Italy
1952	Jan Zachara, Czechoslovakia
1956	Vladimir Safronov, USSR
1960	Francesco Musso, Italy
1964	Stanislav Stephashkin, USSR
1968	Antonio Roldan, Mexico
1972	Boris Kousnetsov, USSR
1976	Angel Herrera, Cuba
1980	Rudi Fink, E Germany
1984	Meldrick Taylor, United States
1988	Giovanni Parisi, Italy
1992	Andreas Tews, Germany
1996	Somluck Kamsing, Thailand
2000	Bekzat Sattarkhanox, Kazakhsta
2004	Alexei Tichtchenko, Russia

LIGHTWEIGHT (132 LB)

1904	Harry Spanger, United States
1908	Frederick Grace, Great Britain
1920	Samuel Mosberg, United States
1924	Hans Nielsen, Denmark
1928	Carlo Orlandi, Italy
1932	Lawrence Stevens, S Africa
1936	Imre Harangi, Hungary
1948	Gerald Dreyer, S Africa
1952	Aureliano Bolognesi, Italy
1956	Richard McTaggart, Great Britain
1960	Kazimierz Pazdzior, Poland
1964	Jozef Grudzien, Poland
1968	Ronald Harris, United States
1972	Jan Szczepanski, Poland
1976	Howard Davis, United States
1980	Angel Herrera, Cuba
1984	Pernell Whitaker, United States
1988	Andreas Zuelow, E Germany
1992	Oscar De La Hoya, United States
1996	Hocine Soltani, Algeria
2000	Mario Mesa, Cuba
2004	Mario Mesa, Cuba

LIGHT WELTERWEIGHT (139 LB)

1952	Charles Adkins, United States
1956	Vladimir Yengibaryan, USSR
1960	Bohumil Nemecek, Czechoslovakia
1964	Jerzy Kulej, Poland
1968	Jerzy Kulej, Poland
1972	Ray Seales, United States
1976	Ray Leonard, United States
1980	Patrizio Oliva, Italy
1984	Jerry Page, United States
1988	Viatcheslav Janovski, USSR
1992	Hector Vinent, Cuba
1996	Hector Vinent, Cuba
2000	Mahamadkadyz Abdullaev, Uzbekistan
2004	Manus Boonjumnong, Thailand

WELTERWEIGHT (147 LB)

1904	Albert Young, United States
1920	Albert Schneider, Canada
1924	Jean Delarge, Belgium
1928	Edward Morgan, New Zealand
1932	Edward Flynn, United States
1936	Sten Suvio, Finland
1948	Julius Torma, Czechoslovakia
1952	Zygmunt Chychla, Poland
1956	Nicolae Linca, Romania
1960	Giovanni Benvenuti, Italy
1964	Marian Kasprzyk, Poland
1968	Manfred Wolke, E Germany
1972	Emilio Correa, Cuba
1976	Jochen Bachfeld, E Germany
1980	Andres Aldama, Cuba
1984	Mark Breland, United States
1988	Robert Wangila, Kenya
1992	Michael Carruth, Ireland
1996	Oleg Saitov, Russia
2000	Oleg Saitov, Russia
2004	Bakhtiyar Artayev, Kazakhstan

LIGHT MIDDLEWEIGHT (156 LB)

1952	Laszlo Papp, Hungary
1956	Laszlo Papp, Hungary
1960	Wilbert McClure, United States
1964	Boris Lagutin, USSR
1968	Boris Lagutin, USSR
1972	Dieter Kottysch, W Germany
1976	Jerzy Rybicki, Poland
1980	Armando Martinez, Cuba
1984	Frank Tate, United States

BOXING (Cont.)

LIGHT MIDDLEWEIGHT (CONT.)

1988 ....Park Si-Hun, S Korea
1992 ....Juan Lemus, Cuba
1996 ....David Reid, United States
2000 ....Yermakhan Ibraimov, Kazakhstan

MIDDLEWEIGHT (165 LB)

1904 ....Charles Mayer, United States
1908 ....John Douglas, Great Britain
1920 ....Harry Mallin, Great Britain
1924 ....Harry Mallin, Great Britain
1928 ....Piero Toscani, Italy
1932 ....Carmen Barth, United States
1936 ....Jean Despeaux, France
1948 ....Laszlo Papp, Hungary
1952 ....Floyd Patterson, United States
1956 ....Gennady Schatkov, USSR
1960 ....Edward Crook, United States
1964 ....Valery Popenchenko, USSR
1968 ....Christopher Finnegan, Great Britain
1972 ....Vyacheslav Lemechev, USSR
1976 ....Michael Spinks, United States
1980 ....Jose Gomez, Cuba
1984 ....Shin Joon Sup, S Korea
1988 ....Henry Maske, E Germany
1992 ....Ariel Hernandez, Cuba
1996 ....Ariel Hernandez, Cuba
2000 ....Jorge Gutierrez, Cuba
2004 ....Gaydarbek Gaydarbekov, Russia

LIGHT HEAVYWEIGHT (178 LB)

1920 ....Edward Eagan, United States
1924 ....Harry Mitchell, Great Britain
1928 ....Victor Avendano, Argentina
1932 ....David Carstens, S Africa
1936 ....Roger Michelot, France
1948 ....George Hunter, S Africa
1952 ....Norvel Lee, United States
1956 ....James Boyd, United States
1960 ....Cassius Clay, United States
1964 ....Cosimo Pinto, Italy
1968 ....Dan Poznyak, USSR
1972 ....Mate Parlov, Yugoslavia
1976 ....Leon Spinks, United States

LIGHT HEAVYWEIGHT (CONT.)

1980 ....Slobodan Kacer, Yugoslavia
1984 ....Anton Josipovic, Yugoslavia
1988 ....Andrew Maynard, United States
1992 ....Torsten May, Germany
1996 ....Vassili Jirov, Kazakhstan
2000 ....Alexander Lebziak, Russia
2004 ....Andre Ward, United States

HEAVYWEIGHT (OVER 201 LB)

1904 ....Samuel Berger, United States
1908 ....Albert Oldham, Great Britain
1920 ....Ronald Rawson, Great Britain
1924 ....Otto von Porat, Norway
1928 ....Arturo Rodriguez Jurado, Argentina
1932 ....Santiago Lovell, Argentina
1936 ....Herbert Runge, Germany
1948 ....Rafael Inglesias, Argentina
1952 ....H. Edward Sanders, United States
1956 ....T. Peter Rademacher, United States
1960 ....Franco De Piccoli, Italy
1964 ....Joe Frazier, United States
1968 ....George Foreman, United States
1972 ....Teofilo Stevenson, Cuba
1976 ....Teofilo Stevenson, Cuba
1980 ....Teofilo Stevenson, Cuba

HEAVYWEIGHT (201* LB)

1984 ....Henry Tillman, United States
1988 ....Ray Mercer, United States
1992 ....Félix Sávon, Cuba
1996 ....Félix Sávon, Cuba
2000 ....Félix Sávon, Cuba
2004 ....Odlanier Fonte, Cuba

SUPERHEAVYWEIGHT (UNLIMITED)

1984 ....Tyrell Biggs, United States
1988 ....Lennox Lewis, Canada
1992 ....Roberto Balado, Cuba
1996 ....Vladimir Klitchko, Ukraine
2000 ....Audley Harrison, Great Britain
2004 ....Alexander Povetkin, Russia

*Until 1984 the heavyweight division was unlimited. With the addition of the super heavyweight division, a limit of 201 pounds was imposed.

SWIMMING

Men

50-METER FREESTYLE

1904 ...Zoltan Halmay, Hungary (50 yds)	28.0	
1988 ....Matt Biondi, United States	22.14	WR
1992 ....Aleksandr Popov, Unified Team	22.30	
1996 ....Aleksandr Popov, Russia	22.13	
2000 ....Anthony Ervin, United States	21.98	
Gary Hall Jr, United States	21.98	
2004 ....Gary Hall Jr, United States	21.93	

100-METER FREESTLYE

1896 ....Alfred Hajos, Hungary	1:22.2	OR
1904 .....Zoltan Halmay, Hungary (100 yds)	1:02.8	
1906 ....Charles Daniels, United States	1:13.4	
1908 ....Charles Daniels, United States	1:05.6	WR
1912 .....Duke Kahanamoku, United States	1:03.4	
1920 .....Duke Kahanamoku, United States	1:00.4	WR
1924 ....John Weissmuller, United States	59.0	OR
1928 ....John Weissmuller, United States	58.6	OR
1932 ....Yasuji Miyazaki, Japan	58.2	

100-METER FREESTLYE (CONT.)

1936 ....Ferenc Csik, Hungary	57.6	
1948 ....Wally Ris, United States	57.3	OR
1952 ....Clarke Scholes, United States	57.4	
1956 ....Jon Henricks, Australia	55.4	OR
1960 ....John Devitt, Australia	55.2	OR
1964 ....Don Schollander, United States	53.4	OR
1968 ....Mike Wenden, Australia	52.2	WR
1972 ....Mark Spitz, United States	51:22	WR
1976 ....Jim Montgomery, United States	49.99	WR
1980 ....Jörg Woithe, E Germany	50.40	
1984 ....Rowdy Gaines, United States	49.80	OR
1988 ....Matt Biondi, United States	48.63	OR
1992 ....Aleksandr Popov, Unified Team	49.02	
1996 ....Aleksandr Popov, Russia	48.74	
2000 ....P. van den Hoogenband, Neth	48.30	
2004 ....P. van den Hoogenband, Neth	48.17	

Note: OR=Olympic Record. WR=World Record. EOR=Equals Olympic Record. EWR=Equals World Record. WB=World Best.

SWIMMING *(Cont.)*
Men *(Cont.)*

200-METER FREESTYLE

1900	Frederick Lane, Australia	2:25.2 OR
1904	Charles Daniels, United States	2:44.2
1968	Michael Wenden, Australia	1:55.2 OR
1972	Mark Spitz, United States	1:52.78 WR
1976	Bruce Furniss, United States	1:50.29 WR
1980	Sergei Kopliakov, USSR	1:49.81 OR
1984	Michael Gross, W Germany	1:47.44 WR
1988	Duncan Armstrong, Australia	1:47.25 WR
1992	Evgueni Sadovyi, Unified Team	1:46.70 OR
1996	Danyon Loader, New Zealand	1:47.63
2000	Pieter van den Hoogenband, Neth	1:45.35 EWR
2004	Ian Thorpe, Australia	1:44.71 OR

400-METER FREESTYLE

1896	Paul Neumann, Austria (500 yds)	8:12.6
1904	Charles Daniels, U.S. (440 yds)	6:16.2
1906	Otto Scheff, Austria (440 yds)	6:23.8
1908	Henry Taylor, Great Britain	5:36.8
1912	George Hodgson, Canada	5:24.4
1920	Norman Ross, United States	5:26.8
1924	John Weissmuller, United States	5:04.2 OR
1928	Albert Zorilla, Argentina	5:01.6 OR
1932	Buster Crabbe, United States	4:48.4 OR
1936	Jack Medica, United States	4:44.5 OR
1948	William Smith, United States	4:41.0 OR
1952	Jean Boiteux, France	4:30.7 OR
1956	Murray Rose, Australia	4:27.3 OR
1960	Murray Rose, Australia	4:18.3 OR
1964	Don Schollander, United States	4:12.2 WR
1968	Mike Burton, United States	4:09.0 OR
1972	Brad Cooper, Australia	4:00.27 OR
1976	Brian Goodell, United States	3:51.93 WR
1980	Vladimir Salnikov, USSR	3:51.31 OR
1984	George DiCarlo, United States	3:51.23 OR
1988	Uwe Dassler, E Germany	3:46.95 WR
1992	Evgueni Sadovyi, Unified Team	3:45.00 WR
1996	Danyon Loader, New Zealand	3:47.97
2000	Ian Thorpe, Australia	3:40.59 WR
2004	Ian Thorpe, Australia	3:43.10

1,500-METER FREESTYLE

1908	Henry Taylor, Great Britain	22:48.4 WR
1912	George Hodgson, Canada	22:00.0 WR
1920	Norman Ross, United States	22:23.2
1924	Andrew Charlton, Australia	20:06.6 WR
1928	Arne Borg, Sweden	19:51.8 OR
1932	Kusuo Kitamura, Japan	19:12.4 OR
1936	Noboru Terada, Japan	19:13.7
1948	James McLane, United States	19:18.5
1952	Ford Konno, United States	18:30.3 OR
1956	Murray Rose, Australia	17:58.9
1960	John Konrads, Australia	17:19.6 OR
1964	Robert Windle, Australia	17:01.7 OR
1968	Mike Burton, United States	16:38.9 OR
1972	Mike Burton, United States	15:52.58 OR
1976	Brian Goodell, United States	15:02.40 WR
1980	Vladimir Salnikov, USSR	14:58.27 WR
1984	Michael O'Brien, United States	15:05.20
1988	Vladimir Salnikov, USSR	15:00.40
1992	Kieren Perkins, Australia	14:43.48 WR
1996	Kieren Perkins, Australia	14:56.40
2000	Grant Hackett, Australia	14:48.33
2004	Grant Hackett, Australia	14:43.40 OR

100-METER BACKSTROKE

1904	Walter Brack, Germany (100 yds)	1:16.8
1908	Arno Bieberstein, Germany	1:24.6 WR
1912	Harry Hebner, United States	1:21.2

100-METER BACKSTROKE *(CONT.)*

1920	Warren Kealoha, United States	1:15.2
1924	Warren Kealoha, United States	1:13.2 OR
1928	George Kojac, United States	1:08.2 WR
1932	Masaji Kiyokawa, Japan	1:08.6
1936	Adolph Kiefer, United States	1:05.9 OR
1948	Allen Stack, United States	1:06.4
1952	Yoshi Oyakawa, United States	1:05.4 OR
1956	David Thiele, Australia	1:02.2 OR
1960	David Thiele, Australia	1:01.9 OR
1968	Roland Matthes, E Germany	58.7 OR
1972	Roland Matthes, E Germany	56.58 OR
1976	John Naber, United States	55.49 WR
1980	Bengt Baron, Sweden	56.33
1984	Rick Carey, United States	55.79
1988	Daichi Suzuki, Japan	55.05
1992	Mark Tewksbury, Canada	53.98 WR
1996	Jeff Rouse, United States	54.10
2000	Lenny Krayzelburg, United States	53.72 OR
2004	Aaron Peirsol, United States	54.06

200-METER BACKSTROKE

1900	Ernst Hoppenberg, Germany	2:47.0
1964	Jed Graef, United States	2:10.3 WR
1968	Roland Matthes, E Germany	2:09.6 OR
1972	Roland Matthes, E Germany	2:02.82 EWR
1976	John Naber, United States	1:59.19 WR
1980	Sandor Wladar, Hungary	2:01.93
1984	Rick Carey, United States	2:00.23
1988	Igor Polianski, USSR	1:59.37
1992	Martin Lopez-Zubero, Spain	1:58.47 OR
1996	Brad Bridgewater, United States	1:58.54
2000	Lenny Krayzelburg, United States	1:56.76 OR
2004	Aaron Peirsol, United States	1:54.95 OR

100-METER BREASTSTROKE

1968	Don McKenzie, United States	1:07.7 OR
1972	Nobutaka Taguchi, Japan	1:04.94 WR
1976	John Hencken, United States	1:03.11 WR
1980	Duncan Goodhew, Great Britain	1:03.44
1984	Steve Lundquist, United States	1:01.65 WR
1988	Adrian Moorhouse, Great Britain	1:02.04
1992	Nelson Diebel, United States	1:01.50 OR
1996	Fred DeBurghgraeve, Belgium	1:00.65
2000	Domenico Fioravanti, Italy	1:00.46 OR
2004	Kosuke Kitajima, Japan	1:00.08

200-METER BREASTSTROKE

1908	Frederick Holman, Great Britain	3:09.2 WR
1912	Walter Bathe, Germany	3:01.8 OR
1920	Haken Malmroth, Sweden	3:04.4
1924	Robert Skelton, United States	2:56.6
1928	Yoshiyuki Tsuruta, Japan	2:48.8 OR
1932	Yoshiyuki Tsuruta, Japan	2:45.4
1936	Tetsuo Hamuro, Japan	2:41.5 OR
1948	Joseph Verdeur, United States	2:39.3 OR
1952	John Davies, Australia	2:34.4 OR
1956	Masura Furukawa, Japan	2:34.7 OR
1960	William Mulliken, United States	2:37.4
1964	Ian O'Brien, Australia	2:27.8 WR
1968	Felipe Munoz, Mexico	2:28.7
1972	John Hencken, United States	2:21.55 WR
1976	David Wilkie, Great Britain	2:15.11 WR
1980	Robertas Zhulpa, USSR	2:15.85
1984	Victor Davis, Canada	2:13.34 WR
1988	Jozsef Szabo, Hungary	2:13.52
1992	Mike Barrowman, United States	2:10.16 WR
1996	Norbert Rózsa, Hungary	2:12.57
2000	Domenico Fioravanti, Italy	2:10.87
2004	Kosuke Kitajima, Japan	2:09.44 OR

Note: OR=Olympic Record. WR=World Record. EOR=Equals Olympic Record. EWR=Equals World Record. WB=World Best.

SWIMMING (Cont.)

Men (Cont.)

100-METER BUTTERFLY

1968	Doug Russell, United States	55.9 OR
1972	Mark Spitz, United States	54.27 WR
1976	Matt Vogel, United States	54.35
1980	Pär Arvidsson, Sweden	54.92
1984	Michael Gross, W Germany	53.08 WR
1988	Anthony Nesty, Suriname	53.00 OR
1992	Pablo Morales, United States	53.32
1996	Denis Pankratov, Russia	52.27 WR
2000	Lars Froelander, Sweden	52.00
2004	Michael Phelps, United States	51.25 OR

200-METER BUTTERFLY

1956	William Yorzyk, United States	2:19.3 OR
1960	Michael Troy, United States	2:12.8 WR
1964	Kevin Berry, Australia	2:06.6 WR
1968	Carl Robie, United States	2:08.7
1972	Mark Spitz, United States	2:00.70 WR
1976	Mike Bruner, United States	1:59.23 WR
1980	Sergei Fesenko, USSR	1:59.76
1984	Jon Sieben, Australia	1:57.04 WR
1988	Michael Gross, W Germany	1:56.94 OR
1992	Melvin Stewart, United States	1:56.26 OR
1996	Denis Pankratov, Russia	1:56.51
2000	Tom Malchow, United States	1:55.35 OR
2004	Michael Phelps, United States	1:54.04 OR

200-METER INDIVIDUAL MEDLEY

1968	Charles Hickcox, United States	2:12.0 OR
1972	Gunnar Larsson, Sweden	2:07.17 WR
1984	Alex Baumann, Canada	2:01.42 WR
1988	Tamas Darnyi, Hungary	2:00.17 WR
1992	Tamas Darnyi, Hungary	2:00.76
1996	Attila Czene, Hungary	1:59.91 OR
2000	Massimiliano Rosolino, Italy	1:58.98 OR
2004	Michael Phelps, United States	1:57.14 OR

400-METER INDIVIDUAL MEDLEY

1964	Richard Roth, United States	4:45.4 WR
1968	Charles Hickcox, United States	4:48.4
1972	Gunnar Larsson, Sweden	4:31.98 OR
1976	Rod Strachan, United States	4:23.68 WR
1980	Aleksandr Sidorenko, USSR	4:22.89 OR
1984	Alex Baumann, Canada	4:17.41 WR
1988	Tamas Darnyi, Hungary	4:14.75 WR
1992	Tamas Darnyi, Hungary	4:14.23 OR
1996	Tom Dolan United States	4:14.90
2000	Tom Dolan, United States	4:11.76 WR
2004	Michael Phelps, United States	4:08.26 WR

4 X 100-METER MEDLEY RELAY

1960	United States	4:05.4 WR
1964	United States	3:58.4 WR
1968	United States	3:54.9 WR
1972	United States	3:48.16 WR
1976	United States	3:42.22 WR
1980	Australia	3:45.70
1984	United States	3:39.30 WR
1988	United States	3:36.93 WR
1992	United States	3:36.93 EWR
1996	United States	3:34.84 WR
2000	United States	3:33.73 WR
2004	United States	3:30.68 WR

4 X 100-METER FREESTYLE RELAY

1964	United States	3:32.2 WR
1968	United States	3:31.7 WR
1972	United States	3:26.42 WR
1984	United States	3:19.03 WR
1988	United States	3:16.53 WR
1992	United States	3:16.74
1996	United States	3:15.41 OR
2000	Australia	3:13.67 WR
2004	S Africa	3:13.17 WR

4 X 200-METER FREESTYLE RELAY

1906	Hungary (1,000 m)	16:52.4
1908	Great Britain	10:55.6
1912	Australia/New Zealand	10:11.6 WR
1920	United States	10:04.4 WR
1924	United States	9:53.4 WR
1928	United States	9:36.2 WR
1932	Japan	8:58.4 WR
1936	Japan	8:51.5 WR
1948	United States	8:46.0 WR
1952	United States	8:31.1 OR
1956	Australia	8:23.6 WR
1960	United States	8:10.2 WR
1964	United States	7:52.1 WR
1968	United States	7:52.33
1972	United States	7:35.78 WR
1976	United States	7:23.22 WR
1980	USSR	7:23.50
1984	United States	7:15.69 WR
1988	United States	7:12.51 WR
1992	Unified Team	7:11.95 WR
1996	United States	7:14.84
2000	Australia	7:07.05 WR
2004	United States	7:07.33

Women

50-METER FREESTYLE

1988	Kristin Otto, E Germany	25.49 OR
1992	Yang Wenyi, China	24.79 WR
1996	Amy Van Dyken, United States	24.87
2000	Inge de Bruijn, Netherlands	24.32 OR
2004	Inge de Bruijn, Netherlands	24.58

100-METER FREESTYLE

1912	Fanny Durack, Australia	1:22.2
1920	Ethelda Bleibtrey, United States	1:13.6 WR
1924	Ethel Lackie, United States	1:12.4
1928	Albina Osipowich, United States	1:11.0 OR
1932	Helene Madison, United States	1:06.8 OR
1936	Hendrika Mastenbroek, Neth	1:05.9 OR
1948	Greta Andersen, Denmark	1:06.3
1952	Katalin Szöke, Hungary	1:06.8
1956	Dawn Fraser, Australia	1:02.0 WR
1960	Dawn Fraser, Australia	1:01.2 OR
1964	Dawn Fraser, Australia	59.5 OR
1968	Jan Henne, United States	1:00.0

100-METER FREESTYLE (CONT.)

1972	Sandra Neilson, United States	58.59 OR
1976	Kornelia Ender, E Germany	55.65 WR
1980	Barbara Krause, E Germany	54.79 WR
1984	Carrie Steinseifer, United States	55.92
	Nancy Hogshead, United States	55.92
1988	Kristin Otto, E Germany	54.93
1992	Zhuang Yong, China	54.64 OR
1996	Le Jingyi, China	54.50 OR
2000	Inge de Bruijn, Netherlands	53.83 OR
2004	Jodie Henry, Australia	53.84

200-METER FREESTYLE

1968	Debbie Meyer, United States	2:10.5 OR
1972	Shane Gould, Australia	2:03.56 WR
1976	Kornelia Ender, E Germany	1:59.26 WR
1980	Barbara Krause, E Germany	1:58.33 OR
1984	Mary Wayte, United States	1:59.23
1988	Heike Friedrich, E Germany	1:57.65 OR
1992	Nicole Haislett, United States	1:57.90

Note: OR=Olympic Record. WR=World Record. EOR=Equals Olympic Record. EWR=Equals World Record. WB=World Best.

SWIMMING (Cont.)
Women (Cont.)

200-METER FREESTYLE (CONT.)

1996	Claudia Poll, Costa Rica	1:58.16
2000	Susie O'Neill, Australia	1:58.24
2004	Camelia Potec, Romania	1:58.03

400-METER FREESTYLE

1924	Martha Norelius, United States	6:02.2 OR
1928	Martha Norelius, United States	5:42.8 WR
1932	Helene Madison, United States	5:28.5 WR
1936	Hendrika Mastenbroek, Neth	5:26.4 OR
1948	Ann Curtis, United States	5:17.8 OR
1952	Valeria Gyenge, Hungary	5:12.1 OR
1956	Lorraine Crapp, Australia	4:54.6 OR
1960	Chris von Saltza, United States	4:50.6 OR
1964	Virginia Duenkel, United States	4:43.3 OR
1968	Debbie Meyer, United States	4:31.8 OR
1972	Shane Gould, Australia	4:19.44 WR
1976	Petra Thümer, E Germany	4:09.89 WR
1980	Ines Diers, E Germany	4:08.76 WR
1984	Tiffany Cohen, United States	4:07.10 OR
1988	Janet Evans, United States	4:03.85 WR
1992	Dagmar Hase, Germany	4:07.18
1996	Michelle Smith, Ireland	4:07.25
2000	Brooke Bennett, United States	4:05.80
2004	Laure Manaudou, France	4:05.34

800-METER FREESTYLE

1968	Debbie Meyer, United States	9:24.0 OR
1972	Keena Rothhammer, United States	8:53.68 WR
1976	Petra Thümer, E Germany	8:37.14 WR
1980	Michelle Ford, Australia	8:28.90 OR
1984	Tiffany Cohen, United States	8:24.95 OR
1988	Janet Evans, United States	8:20.20 OR
1992	Janet Evans, United States	8:25.52
1996	Brooke Bennett, United States	8:27.89
2000	Brooke Bennett, United States	8:19.67 OR
2004	Ai Shibata, Japan	8:24.54

100-METER BACKSTROKE

1924	Sybil Bauer, United States	1:23.2 OR
1928	Marie Braun, Netherlands	1:22.0
1932	Eleanor Holm, United States	1:19.4
1936	Dina Senff, Netherlands	1:18.9
1948	Karen Harup, Denmark	1:14.4 OR
1952	Joan Harrison, South Africa	1:14.3
1956	Judy Grinham, Great Britain	1:12.9 OR
1960	Lynn Burke, United States	1:09.3 OR
1964	Cathy Ferguson, United States	1:07.7 WR
1968	Kaye Hall, United States	1:06.2 WR
1972	Melissa Belote, United States	1:05.78 OR
1976	Ulrike Richter, E Germany	1:01.83 OR
1980	Rica Reinisch, E Germany	1:00.86 WR
1984	Theresa Andrews, United States	1:02.55
1988	Kristin Otto, E Germany	1:00.89
1992	Krisztina Egerszegi, Hungary	1:00.68 OR
1996	Beth Botsford, United States	1:01.19
2000	Diana Iuliana Mocanu, Romania	1:00.21 OR
2004	Natalie Coughlin, United States	1:00.37

200-METER BACKSTROKE

1968	Pokey Watson, United States	2:24.8 OR
1972	Melissa Belote, United States	2:19.19 WR
1976	Ulrike Richter, E Germany	2:13.43 OR
1980	Rica Reinisch, E Germany	2:11.77 WR
1984	Jolanda De Rover, Netherlands	2:12.38
1988	Krisztina Egerszegi, Hungary	2:09.29 OR
1992	Krisztina Egerszegi, Hungary	2:07.06 OR
1996	Krisztina Egerszegi, Hungary	2:07.83
2000	Diana Iuliana Mocanu, Romania	2:08.16
2004	Kirsty Coventry, Zimbabwe	2:09.19

100-METER BREASTSTROKE

1968	Djurdjica Bjedov, Yugoslavia	1:15.8 OR
1972	Catherine Carr, United States	1:13.58 WR

100-METER BREASTSTROKE (CONT.)

1976	Hannelore Anke, E Germany	1:11.16
1980	Ute Geweniger, E Germany	1:10.22
1984	Petra Van Staveren, Netherlands	1:09.88 OR
1988	Tania Dangalakova, Bulgaria	1:07.95 OR
1992	Elena Roudkovskaia, Unified Team	1:08.00
1996	Penelope Heyns, S Africa	1:07.73
2000	Megan Quann, United States	1:07.05
2004	Xue Juan Luo, China	1:06.64

200-METER BREASTSTROKE

1924	Lucy Morton, Great Britain	3:33.2 OR
1928	Hilde Schrader, Germany	3:12.6
1932	Clare Dennis, Australia	3:06.3 OR
1936	Hideko Maehata, Japan	3:03.6
1948	Petronella Van Vliet, Netherlands	2:57.2
1952	Eva Szekely, Hungary	2:51.7 OR
1956	Ursula Happe, W Germany	2:53.1 OR
1960	Anita Lonsbrough, Great Britain	2:49.5 WR
1964	Galina Prozumenshikova, USSR	2:46.4 OR
1968	Sharon Wichman, United States	2:44.4 OR
1972	Beverly Whitfield, Australia	2:41.71 OR
1976	Marina Koshevaia, USSR	2:33.35 WR
1980	Lina Kaciusyte, USSR	2:29.54 OR
1984	Anne Ottenbrite, Canada	2:30.38
1988	Silke Hoerner, E Germany	2:26.71 WR
1992	Kyoko Iwasaki, Japan	2:26.65 OR
1996	Penelope Heyns, S Africa	2:25.41 OR
2000	Agnes Kovacs, Hungary	2:24.35 OR
2004	Amanda Beard, United States	2:23.37 OR

100-METER BUTTERFLY

1956	Shelley Mann, United States	1:11.0 OR
1960	Carolyn Schuler, United States	1:09.5 OR
1964	Sharon Stouder, United States	1:04.7 WR
1968	Lynn McClements, Australia	1:05.5
1972	Mayumi Aoki, Japan	1:03.34 WR
1976	Kornelia Ender, E Germany	1:00.13 EWR
1980	Caren Metschuck, E Germany	1:00.42
1984	Mary T. Meagher, United States	59.26
1988	Kristin Otto, E Germany	59.00 OR
1992	Qian Hong, China	58.62 OR
1996	Amy Van Dyken, United States	59.13
2000	Inge de Bruijn, Netherlands	56.61 WR
2004	Petria Thomas, Australia	57.72

200-METER BUTTERFLY

1968	Ada Kok, Netherlands	2:24.7 OR
1972	Karen Moe, United States	2:15.57 WR
1976	Andrea Pollack, E Germany	2:11.41 OR
1980	Ines Geissler, E Germany	2:10.44 OR
1984	Mary T. Meagher, United States	2:06.90 OR
1988	Kathleen Nord, E Germany	2:09.51
1992	Summer Sanders, United States	2:08.67
1996	Susan O'Neill, Australia	2:07.76
2000	Misty Hyman, United States	2:05.88 OR
2004	Otylia Jedrzegczak, Poland	2:06.05

200-METER INDIVIDUAL MEDLEY

1968	Claudia Kolb, United States	2:24.7 OR
1972	Shane Gould, Australia	2:23.07 WR
1984	Tracy Caulkins, United States	2:12.64 OR
1988	Daniela Hunger, E Germany	2:12.59 OR
1992	Lin Li, China	2:11.65 WR
1996	Michelle Smith, Ireland	2:13.93
2000	Yana Klochkova, Ukraine	2:10.68 OR
2004	Yana Klochkova, Ukraine	2:11.14

Note: OR=Olympic Record. WR=World Record. EOR=Equals Olympic Record. EWR=Equals World Record. WB=World Best.

SWIMMING (Cont.)

Women (Cont.)

400-METER INDIVIDUAL MEDLEY

1964	Donna de Varona, United States	5:18.7 OR
1968	Claudia Kolb, United States	5:08.5 OR
1972	Gail Neall, Australia	5:02.97 WR
1976	Ulrike Tauber, E Germany	4:42.77 WR
1980	Petra Schneider, E Germany	4:36.29 WR
1984	Tracy Caulkins, United States	4:39.24
1988	Janet Evans, United States	4:37.76
1992	Krisztina Egerszegi, Hungary	4:36.54
1996	Michelle Smith, Ireland	4:39.18
2000	Yana Klochkova, Ukraine	4:33.59 WR
2004	Yana Klochkova, Ukraine	4:34.83

4 X 100-METER MEDLEY RELAY

1960	United States	4:41.1 WR
1964	United States	4:33.9 WR
1968	United States	4:28.3 OR
1972	United States	4:20.75 WR
1976	E Germany	4:07.95 WR
1980	E Germany	4:06.67 WR
1984	United States	4:08.34
1988	E Germany	4:03.74 OR
1992	United States	4:02.54 WR
1996	United States	4:02.88
2000	United States	3:58.30 WR
2004	Australia	3:57.32 WR

4 X 100-METER FREESTYLE RELAY

1912	Great Britain	5:52.8 WR
1920	United States	5:11.6 WR
1924	United States	4:58.8 WR
1928	United States	4:47.6 WR
1932	United States	4:38.0 WR
1936	Netherlands	4:36.0 OR
1948	United States	4:29.2 OR
1952	Hungary	4:24.4 WR
1956	Australia	4:17.1 WR
1960	United States	4:08.9 WR
1964	United States	4:03.8 WR
1968	United States	4:02.5 OR
1972	United States	3:55.19 WR
1976	United States	3:44.82 WR
1980	E Germany	3:42.71 WR
1984	United States	3:43.43
1988	E Germany	3:40.63 OR
1992	United States	3:39.46 WR
1996	United States	3:39.29 OR
2000	United States	3:36.61 WR
2004	Australia	3:35.94 WR

4 X 200-METER FREESTYLE RELAY

1996	United States	7:59.87
2000	United States	7:57.80 OR
2004	United States	7:53.42 WR

DIVING

Men

SPRINGBOARD

		Pts
1908	Albert Zürner, Germany	85.5
1912	Paul Günther, Germany	79.23
1920	Louis Kuehn, United States	675.40
1924	Albert White, United States	97.46
1928	Pete DesJardins, United States	185.04
1932	Michael Galitzen, United States	161.38
1936	Richard Degener, United States	163.57
1948	Bruce Harlan, United States	163.64
1952	David Browning, United States	205.29
1956	Robert Clotworthy, United States	159.56
1960	Gary Tobian, United States	170.00
1964	Kenneth Sitzberger, United States	159.90
1968	Bernie Wrightson, United States	170.15
1972	Vladimir Vasin, USSR	594.09
1976	Phil Boggs, United States	619.05
1980	Aleksandr Portnov, USSR	905.02
1984	Greg Louganis, United States	754.41
1988	Greg Louganis, United States	730.80
1992	Mark Lenzi, United States	676.53
1996	Xiong Ni, China	701.46
2000	Xiong Ni, China	708.72
2004	Bo Peng, China	787.38

PLATFORM

		Pts
1904	George Sheldon, United States	12.66
1906	Gottlob Walz, Germany	156.0
1908	Hjalmar Johansson, Sweden	83.75
1912	Erik Adlerz, Sweden	73.94
1920	Clarence Pinkston, United States	100.67
1924	Albert White, United States	97.46
1928	Pete DesJardins, United States	98.74
1932	Harold Smith, United States	124.80
1936	Marshall Wayne, United States	113.58
1948	Sammy Lee, United States	130.05
1952	Sammy Lee, United States	156.28
1956	Joaquin Capilla, Mexico	152.44
1960	Robert Webster, United States	165.56
1964	Robert Webster, United States	148.58
1968	Klaus Dibiasi, Italy	164.18
1972	Klaus Dibiasi, Italy	504.12
1976	Klaus Dibiasi, Italy	600.51
1980	Falk Hoffmann, E Germany	835.65
1984	Greg Louganis, United States	710.91
1988	Greg Louganis, United States	638.61
1992	Sun Shuwei, China	677.31
1996	Dmitri Sautin, Russia	692.34
2000	Tian Liang, China	724.53
2004	Jia Hu, China	748.08

Women

SPRINGBOARD

		Pts
1920	Aileen Riggin, United States	539.90
1924	Elizabeth Becker, United States	474.50
1928	Helen Meany, United States	78.62
1932	Georgia Coleman, United States	87.52
1936	Marjorie Gestring, United States	89.27
1948	Victoria Draves, United States	108.74
1952	Patricia McCormick, United States	147.30

SPRINGBOARD (CONT.)

		Pts
1956	Patricia McCormick, United States	142.36
1960	Ingrid Krämer, E Germany	155.81
1964	Ingrid Engel Krämer, E Germany	145.00
1968	Sue Gossick, United States	150.77
1972	Micki King, United States	450.03
1976	Jennifer Chandler, United States	506.19
1980	Irina Kalinina, USSR	725.91

DIVING *(Cont.)*
Women *(Cont.)*

SPRINGBOARD *(CONT.)*

		Pts
1984	Sylvie Bernier, Canada	530.70
1988	Gao Min, China	580.23
1992	Gao Min, China	572.40
1996	Fu Mingxia, China	547.68
2000	Fu Mingxia, China	609.42
2004	Jingjing Guo, China	633.15

PLATFORM

		Pts
1912	Greta Johansson, Sweden	39.90
1920	Stefani Fryland-Clausen, Denmark	34.60
1924	Caroline Smith, United States	33.20
1928	Elizabeth B. Pinkston, United States	31.60
1932	Dorothy Poynton, United States	40.26
1936	Dorothy Poynton Hill, United States	33.93
1948	Victoria Draves, United States	68.87

PLATFORM *(CONT.)*

		Pts
1952	Patricia McCormick, United States	79.37
1956	Patricia McCormick, United States	84.85
1960	Ingrid Krämer, E Germany	91.28
1964	Lesley Bush, United States	99.80
1968	Milena Duchkova, Czechoslovakia	109.59
1972	Ulrika Knape, Sweden	390.00
1976	Elena Vaytsekhovskaya, USSR	406.59
1980	Martina Jäschke, E Germany	596.25
1984	Zhou Jihong, China	435.51
1988	Xu Yanmei, China	445.20
1992	Mingxia Fu, China	461.43
1996	Mingxia Fu, China	521.58
2000	Laura Wilkinson, United States	543.75
2004	Chantelle Newbery, Australia	590.31

GYMNASTICS
Men

ALL-AROUND

		Pts
1900	Gustave Sandras, France	302
1904	Julius Lenhart, Austria	69.80
1906	Pierre Paysse, France	97
1908	Alberto Braglia, Italy	317.0
1912	Alberto Braglia, Italy	135.0
1920	Giorgio Zampori, Italy	88.35
1924	Leon Stukelj, Yugoslavia	110.340
1928	Georges Miez, Switzerland	247.500
1932	Romeo Neri, Italy	140.625
1936	Alfred Schwarzmann, Germany	113.100
1948	Veikko Huhtanen, Finland	229.70
1952	Viktor Chukarin, USSR	115.70
1956	Viktor Chukarin, USSR	114.25
1960	Boris Shakhlin, USSR	115.95
1964	Yukio Endo, Japan	115.95
1968	Sawao Kato, Japan	115.90
1972	Sawao Kato, Japan	114.65
1976	Nikolai Andrianov, USSR	116.65
1980	Aleksandr Dityatin, USSR	118.65
1984	Koji Gushiken, Japan	118.70
1988	Vladimir Artemov, USSR	119.125
1992	Vitaly Scherbo, Unified Team	59.025
1996	Li Xiaoshuang, China	58.423
2000	Alexei Nemov, Russia	58.474
2004	Paul Hamm, United States	57.823

HORIZONTAL BAR

		Pts
1896	Hermann Weingärtner, Germany	—
1904	Anton Heida, United States	40
1924	Leon Stukelj, Yugoslavia	19.73
1928	Georges Miez, Switzerland	19.17
1932	Dallas Bixler, United States	18.33
1936	Aleksanteri Saarvala, Finland	19.367
1948	Josef Stafler, Switzerland	19.85
1952	Jack Günthard, Switzerland	19.55
1956	Takashi Ono, Japan	19.60
1960	Takashi Ono, Japan	19.60
1964	Boris Shakhlin, USSR	19.625
1968	Akinori Nakayama, Japan	19.55
1972	Mitsuo Tsukahara, Japan	19.725
1976	Mitsuo Tsukahara, Japan	19.675
1980	Stoyan Deltchev, Bulgaria	19.825
1984	Shinji Morisue, Japan	20.00
1988	Vladimir Artemov, USSR	19.90
1992	Trent Dimas, United States	9.875
1996	Andreas Wecker, Germany	9.850
2000	Alexei Nemov, Russia	9.787
2004	Igor Cassina, Italy	9.812

PARALLEL BARS

		Pts
1896	Alfred Flatow, Germany	—
1904	George Eyser, United States	44
1924	August Güttinger, Switzerland	21.63
1928	Ladislav Vacha, Czechoslovakia	18.83
1932	Romeo Neri, Italy	18.97
1936	Konrad Frey, Germany	19.067
1948	Michael Reusch, Switzerland	19.75
1952	Hans Eugster, Switzerland	19.65
1956	Viktor Chukarin, USSR	19.20
1960	Boris Shakhlin, USSR	19.40
1964	Yukio Endo, Japan	19.675
1968	Akinori Nakayama, Japan	19.475
1972	Sawao Kato, Japan	19.475
1976	Sawao Kato, Japan	19.675
1980	Aleksandr Tkachyov, USSR	19.775
1984	Bart Conner, United States	19.95
1988	Vladimir Artemov, USSR	19.925
1992	Vitaly Scherbo, Unified Team	9.900
1996	Rustan Sharipov, Ukraine	9.837
2000	Xiaopeng Li, China	9.825
2004	Valeri Goncharov, Ukraine	9.787

VAULT

		Pts
1896	Karl Schumann, Germany	—
1904	George Eyser, United States	36
1924	Frank Kriz, United States	9.98
1928	Eugen Mack, Switzerland	9.58
1932	Savino Guglielmetti, Italy	18.03
1936	Alfred Schwarzmann, Germany	19.20
1948	Paavo Aaltonen, Finland	19.55
1952	Viktor Chukarin, USSR	19.20
1956	Helmut Bantz, Germany	18.85
1960	Takashi Ono, Japan	19.35
1964	Haruhiro Yamashita, Japan	19.60
1968	Mikhail Voronin, USSR	19.00
1972	Klaus Köste, E Germany	18.85
1976	Nikolai Andrianov, USSR	19.45
1980	Nikolai Andrianov, USSR	19.825
1984	Lou Yun, China	19.95
1988	Lou Yun, China	19.875
1992	Vitaly Scherbo, Unified Team	9.856
1996	Alexei Nemov, Russia	9.787
2000	Gervasio Deferr, Spain	9.712
2004	Gervasio Deferr, Spain	9.737

GYMNASTICS *(Cont.)*
Men *(Cont.)*

POMMEL HORSE

		Pts
1896	Louis Zutter, Switzerland	—
1904	Anton Heida, United States	42
1924	Josef Wilhelm, Switzerland	21.23
1928	Hermann Hänggi, Switzerland	19.75
1932	Istvan Pelle, Hungary	19.07
1936	Konrad Frey, Germany	19.333
1948	Paavo Aaltonen, Finland	19.35
1952	Viktor Chukarin, USSR	19.50
1956	Boris Shakhlin, USSR	19.25
1960	Eugen Ekman, Finland	19.375
1964	Miroslav Cerar, Yugoslavia	19.525
1968	Miroslav Cerar, Yugoslavia	19.325
1972	Viktor Klimenko, USSR	19.125
1976	Zoltan Magyar, Hungary	19.70
1980	Zoltan Magyar, Hungary	19.925
1984	Li Ning, China	19.95
1988	Dmitri Bilozerchev, USSR	19.95
1992	Vitaly Scherbo, Unified Team	9.925
1996	Donghua Li, Switzerland	9.875
2000	Marius Urzica, Romania	9.862
2004	Haibin Teng, China	9.837

RINGS

		Pts
1896	Ioannis Mitropoulos, Greece	—
1904	Hermann Glass, United States	45
1924	Francesco Martino, Italy	21.553
1928	Leon Stukelj, Yugoslavia	19.25
1932	George Gulack, United States	18.97
1936	Alois Hudec, Czechoslovakia	19.433
1948	Karl Frei, Switzerland	19.80
1952	Grant Shaginyan, USSR	19.75
1956	Albert Azaryan, USSR	19.35
1960	Albert Azaryan, USSR	19.725
1964	Takuji Haytta, Japan	19.475
1968	Akinori Nakayama, Japan	19.45
1972	Akinori Nakayama, Japan	19.35
1976	Nikolai Andrianov, USSR	19.65
1980	Aleksandr Dityatin, USSR	19.875
1984	Koji Gushiken, Japan	19.85
1988	Holger Behrendt, E Germany	19.925
1992	Vitaly Scherbo, Unified Team	9.937
1996	Yuri Chechi, Italy	9.887
2000	Szilveszter Csollany, Hungary	9.862
2004	Dimosthenis Tampakos, Greece	9.862

FLOOR EXERCISE

		Pts
1932	Istvan Pelle, Hungary	9.60

FLOOR EXERCISE *(CONT.)*

		Pts
1936	Georges Miez, Switzerland	18.666
1948	Ferenc Pataki, Hungary	19.35
1952	K. William Thoresson, Sweden	19.25
1956	Valentin Muratov, USSR	19.20
1960	Nobuyuki Aihara, Japan	19.45
1964	Franco Menichelli, Italy	19.45
1968	Sawao Kato, Japan	19.475
1972	Nikolai Andrianov, USSR	19.175
1976	Nikolai Andrianov, USSR	19.45
1980	Roland Brückner, E Germany	19.75
1984	Li Ning, China	19.925
1988	Sergei Kharkov, USSR	19.925
1992	Li Xiaoshuang, China	9.925
1996	Ioannis Melissanidis, Greece	9.850
2000	Igors Vihrovs, Latvia	9.812
2004	Kyle Shewfelt, Canada	9.787

TEAM COMBINED EXERCISES

		Pts
1904	Turngemeinde Philadelphia	374.43
1906	Norway	19.00
1908	Sweden	438
1912	Italy	265.75
1920	Italy	359.855
1924	Italy	839.058
1928	Switzerland	1718.625
1932	Italy	541.850
1936	Germany	657.430
1948	Finland	1358.30
1952	USSR	574.40
1956	USSR	568.25
1960	Japan	575.20
1964	Japan	577.95
1968	Japan	575.90
1972	Japan	571.25
1976	Japan	576.85
1980	USSR	598.60
1984	United States	591.40
1988	USSR	593.35
1992	Unified Team	585.45
1996	Russia	576.778
2000	China	231.919
2004	Japan	173.821

Women

ALL-AROUND

		Pts
1952	Maria Gorokhovskaya, USSR	76.78
1956	Larissa Latynina, USSR	74.933
1960	Larissa Latynina, USSR	77.031
1964	Vera Caslavska, Czechoslovakia	77.564
1968	Vera Caslavska, Czechoslovakia	78.25
1972	Lyudmila Tousischeva, USSR	77.025
1976	Nadia Comaneci, Romania	79.275
1980	Yelena Davydova, USSR	79.15
1984	Mary Lou Retton, United States	79.175
1988	Yelena Shushunova, USSR	79.662
1992	Tatiana Gutsu, Unified Team	39.737
1996	Lilia Podkopayeva, Ukraine	39.255
2000	Simona Amanar, Romania	38.642
2004	Carly Patterson, United States	38.387

VAULT

		Pts
1952	Yekaterina Kalinchuk, USSR	19.20
1956	Larissa Latynina, USSR	18.833
1960	Margarita Nikolayeva, USSR	19.316
1964	Vera Caslavska, Czechoslovakia	19.483
1968	Vera Caslavska, Czechoslovakia	19.775
1972	Karin Janz, E Germany	19.525
1976	Nelli Kim, USSR	19.80
1980	Natalya Shaposhnikova, USSR	19.725
1984	Ecaterina Szabo, Romania	19.875
1988	Svetlana Boginskaya, USSR	19.905
1992	Henrietta Onodi, Hungary	9.925
	Lavinia Milosovici, Romania	9.925
1996	Simona Amanar, Romania	9.825
2000	Yelena Zamolodtchikova, Russia	9.731
2004	Monica Rosu, Romania	9.656

GYMNASTICS (Cont.)
Women (Cont.)

UNEVEN BARS

	Pts
1952 .....Margit Korondi, Hungary	19.40
1956 .....Agnes Keleti, Hungary	18.966
1960 .....Polina Astakhova, USSR	19.616
1964 .....Polina Astakhova, USSR	19.332
1968 .....Vera Caslavska, Czechoslovakia	19.65
1972 .....Karin Janz, E Germany	19.675
1976 .....Nadia Comaneci, Romania	20.00
1980 .....Maxi Gnauck, E Germany	19.875
1984 .....Ma Yanhong, China	19.95
1988 .....Daniela Silivas, Romania	20.00
1992 .....Lu Li, China	10.00
1996 .....Svetlana Khorkina, Russia	9.850
2000 .....Svetlana Khorkina, Russia	9.862
2004 .....Emilie Lepennec, France	9.687

BALANCE BEAM

	Pts
1952 .....Nina Bocharova, USSR	19.22
1956 .....Agnes Keleti, Hungary	18.80
1960 .....Eva Bosakova, Czechoslovakia	19.283
1964 .....Vera Caslavska, Czechoslovakia	19.449
1968 .....Natalya Kuchinskaya, USSR	19.65
1972 .....Olga Korbut, USSR	19.40
1976 .....Nadia Comaneci, Romania	19.95
1980 .....Nadia Comaneci, Romania	19.80
1984 .....Simona Pauca, Romania	19.80
1988 .....Daniela Silivas, Romania	19.924
1992 .....Tatiana Lisenko, Unified Team	9.975
1996 .....Shannon Miller, United States	9.862
2000 .....Xuan Li, China	9.825
2004 .....Catalina Ponor, Romania	9.787

FLOOR EXERCISE

	Pts
1952 .....Agnes Keleti, Hungary	19.36
1956 .....Agnes Keleti, Hungary	18.733
1960 .....Larissa Latynina, USSR	19.583
1964 .....Larissa Latynina, USSR	19.599
1968 .....Vera Caslavska, Czechoslovakia	19.675
1972 .....Olga Korbut, USSR	19.575
1976 .....Nelli Kim, USSR	19.85

FLOOR EXERCISE (Cont.)

	Pts
1980 .....Nadia Comaneci, Romania	19.875
1984 .....Ecaterina Szabo, Romania	19.975
1988 .....Daniela Silivas, Romania	19.937
1992 .....Lavinia Milosovici, Romania	10.00
1996 .....Lilia Podkopayeva, Ukraine	9.887
2000 .....Yelena Zamolodtchikova, Russia	9.850
2004 .....Catalina Ponor, Romania	9.750

TEAM COMBINED EXERCISES

		Pts
1928	.............The Netherlands	316.75
1932	.............Not held	
1936	.............Germany	506.50
1948	.............Czechoslovakia	445.45
1952	.............USSR	527.03
1956	.............USSR	444.800
1960	.............USSR	382.320
1964	.............USSR	280.890
1968	.............USSR	382.85
1972	.............USSR	380.50
1976	.............USSR	466.00
1980	.............USSR	394.90
1984	.............Romania	392.02
1988	.............USSR	395.475
1992	.............Unified Team	395.666
1996	.............United States	389.225
2000	.............Romania	154.608
2004	.............Romania	114.283

RHYTHMIC ALL-AROUND

	Pts
1984 .....Lori Fung, Canada	57.95
1988 .....Marina Lobach, USSR	60.00
1992 .....A. Timoshenko, Unified Team	59.037
1996 .....E. Serebrianskaya, Ukraine	39.683
2000 .....Yulia Barsukova, Russia	39.632
2004 .....Alina Kabaeva, Russia	108.400

RHYTHMIC TEAM COMBINED EXERCISES

	Pts
1996 .....Spain	38.933
2000 .....Russia	39.500
2004 .....China	249.750

SOCCER

Men

1900 .....Great Britain	1928 .....Uruguay	1964 .....Hungary	1988 .....Soviet Union
1904 .....Canada	1936 .....Italy	1968 .....Hungary	1992 .....Spain
1908 .....Great Britain	1948 .....Sweden	1972 .....Poland	1996 .....Nigeria
1912 .....Great Britain	1952 .....Hungary	1976 .....E Germany	2000 .....Cameroon
1920 .....Belgium	1956 .....Soviet Union	1980 .....Czechoslovakia	2004 .....Argentina
1924 .....Uruguay	1960 .....Yugoslavia	1984 .....France	

Women

1996 ....United States	
2000 ....Norway	
2004 ....United States	

BIATHLON
Men

10 KILOMETERS

1980	Frank Ullrich, E Germany	32:10.69
1984	Eirik Kvalfoss, Norway	30:53.8
1988	Frank-Peter Rötsch, W Germany	25:08.1
1992	Mark Kirchner, Germany	26:02.3
1994	Sergei Tchepikov, Russia	28:07.0
1998	Ole Einar Bjorndalen, Norway	27:16.2
2002	Ole Einar Bjorndalen, Norway	24:51.3

20 KILOMETERS

1960	Klas Lestander, Sweden	1:33:21.6
1964	Vladimir Melyanin, Soviet Union	1:20:26.8
1968	Magnar Solberg, Norway	1:13:45.9
1972	Magnar Solberg, Norway	1:15:55.5
1976	Nikolay Kruglov, Soviet Union	1:14:12.26
1980	Anatoliy Alyabiev, Soviet Union	1:08:16.31
1984	Peter Angerer, W Germany	1:11:52.7
1988	Frank-Peter Rötsch, W Germany	56:33.3

20 KILOMETERS *(Cont.)*

1992	Evgueni Redkine, Unified Team	57:34.4
1994	Sergei Tarasov, Russia	57:25.3
1998	Halvard Hanevold, Norway	56:16.4
2002	Ole Einar Bjordalen, Norway	51:03.3

4 X 7.5-KILOMETER RELAY

1968	Soviet Union	2:13:02.4
1972	Soviet Union	1:51:44.92
1976	Soviet Union	1:57:55.64
1980	Soviet Union	1:34:03.27
1984	Soviet Union	1:38:51.7
1988	Soviet Union	1:22:30.0
1992	Germany	1:24:43.5
1994	Germany	1:30:22.1
1998	Germany	1:19:43.3
2002	Norway	1:23:42.3

12.5 KILOMETERS PURSUIT

2002	Ole Einar Bjorndalen	1:23:42.3

Women

7.5 KILOMETERS

1992	Antissa Restzova, Unified Team	24:29.2
1994	Myriam Bedard, Canada	26:08.8
1998	Galina Koukleva, Russia	23:08.0
2002	Kati Wilhemn, Germany	20:41.4

10 KILOMETERS PURSUIT

2002	Olga Pyleva, Russia	31:07.7

15 KILOMETERS

1992	Antje Misersky, Germany	51:47.2
1994	Myriam Bedard, Canada	52:06.6
1998	Ekaterina Dofovska, Bulgaria	54:52.0
2002	Andrea Henkel, Germany	47:29.1

3 X 7.5-KILOMETER RELAY

1992	France	1:15:55.6
1994	Russia	1:47:19.5
1998	Germany	1:40:13.6
2002	Germany	1:27:55.0

BOBSLED

4-MAN

1924	Switzerland (Eduard Scherrer)	5:45.54
1928	United States	3:20.50
	(William Fiske) (5-man)	
1932	United States (William Fiske)	7:53.68
1936	Switzerland (Pierre Musy)	5:19.85
1948	United States (Francis Tyler)	5:20.10
1952	Germany (Andreas Ostler)	5:07.84
1956	Switzerland (Franz Kapus)	5:10.44
1960	Not held	
1964	Canada (Victor Emery)	4:14.46
1968	Italy (Eugenio Monti) (2 runs)	2:17.39
1972	Switzerland (Jean Wicki)	4:43.07
1976	E Germany (Meinhard Nehmer)	3:40.43
1980	E Germany (Meinhard Nehmer)	3:59.92
1984	E Germany (Wolfgang Hoppe)	3:20.22
1988	Switzerland (Ekkehard Fasser)	3:47.51
1992	Austria (Ingo Appelt)	3:53.90
1994	Germany (Harold Czudaj)	3:27.78
1998	Germany (Christoph Langen)	2:39.41
2002	Germany (Andre Lange)	3:10.11

Note: Driver in parentheses.

2-MAN

1932	United States (Hubert Stevens)	8:14.74
1936	United States (Ivan Brown)	5:29.29
1948	Switzerland (Felix Endrich)	5:29.20
1952	Germany (Andreas Ostler)	5:24.54
1956	Italy (Lamberto Dalla Costa)	5:30.14
1960	Not held	
1964	Great Britain (Anthony Nash)	4:21.90
1968	Italy (Eugenio Monti)	4:41.54
1972	W Germany	4:57.07
	(Wolfgang Zimmerer)	
1976	E Germany (Meinhard Nehmer)	3:44.42
1980	Switzerland (Erich Schärer)	4:09.36
1984	E Germany (Wolfgang Hoppe)	3:25.56
1988	USSR (Janis Kipours)	3:53.48
1992	Switzerland (Gustav Weder)	4:03.26
1994	Switzerland (Gustav Weder)	3:30.81
1998	Canada (Pierre Lueders)	3:37.24
	Italy (Guenther Huber)	3:37.24
2002	Germany (Martin Langen)	3:10:11

WOMEN

2-PERSON

2002	United States (Jill Bakken)	1:37:76

Note: Driver in parentheses.

CURLING

Men	Women
1998 .....Switzerland, Canada, Norway	1998 .....Canada, Denmark, Sweden
2002 .....Norway, Canada, Switzerland	2002 .....Britain, Switzerland, Canada
Note: Gold, silver, and bronze medals.	Note: Gold, silver, and bronze medals.

ICE HOCKEY

Men

1920* ....Canada, United States, Czechoslovakia	1972 .....USSR, United States, Czechoslovakia
1924 .....Canada, United States, Great Britain	1976 .....USSR, Czechoslovakia, W Germany
1928 .....Canada, Sweden, Switzerland	1980 .....United States, USSR, Sweden
1932 .....Canada, United States, Germany	1984 .....USSR, Czechoslovakia, Sweden
1936 .....Great Britain, Canada, United States	1988 .....USSR, Finland, Sweden
1948 .....Canada, Czechoslovakia, Switzerland	1992 .....Unified Team, Canada, Czechoslovakia
1952 .....Canada, United States, Sweden	1994 .....Sweden, Canada, Finland
1956 .....USSR, United States, Canada	1998 .....Czech Republic, Russia, Finland
1960 .....United States, Canada, USSR	2002 .....Canada, United States, Russia
1964 .....USSR, Sweden, Czechoslovakia	*Competition held at Summer Games in Antwerp.
1968 .....USSR, Czechoslovakia, Canada	Note: Gold, silver, and bronze medals.

Women

1998 ...:.United States, Canada, Finland	Note: Gold, silver, and bronze medals.
2002 .....Canada, United States, Sweden	

LUGE

Men

SINGLES		DOUBLES	
1964 .....Thomas Köhler, East Germany	3:26.77	1964 ....Austria	1:41.62
1968 .....Manfred Schmid, Austria	2:52.48	1968 ....E Germany	1:35.85
1972 ....Wolfgang Scheidel, W Germany	3:27.58	1972 ....E Germany	1:28.35
1976 .....Detlef Guenther, W Germany	3:27.688	1976 ....E Germany	1:25.604
1980 .....Bernhard Glass, W Germany	2:54.796	1980 ....E Germany	1:19.331
1984 .....Paul Hildgartner, Italy	3:04.258	1984 ....W Germany	1:23.620
1988 .....Jens Müller, W Germany	3:05.548	1988 ....E Germany	1:31.940
1992 .....Georg Hackl, Germany	3:02.363	1992 ....Germany	1:32.053
1994 .....Georg Hackl, Germany	3:21.571	1994 ....Italy	1:36.720
1998 .....Georg Hackl, Germany	3:18.44	1998 ....Germany	1:41.105
2002 .....Armin Zoeggeler, Italy	2:57.941	2002 ....Germany	1:26.082

Women

SINGLES		SINGLES (Cont.)	
1964 .....Ortrun Enderlein, Germany	3:24.67	1984 .....Steffi Martin, E Germany	2:46.570
1968 .....Erica Lechner, Italy	2:28.66	1988 .....Steffi Walter (Martin) E Germany	3:03.973
1972 .....Anna-Maria Müller, E Germany	2:59.18	1992 .....Doris Neuner, Austria	3:06.696
1976 .....Margit Schumann, E Germany	2:50.621	1994 .....Gerda Weissensteiner, Italy	3:15.517
1980 .....Vera Zozulya, USSR	2:36.537	1998 .....Silke Kraushaar, Germany	3:23.779
		2002 .....Sylke Otto, Germany	2:52.464

YET ANOTHER SIGN OF THE APOCALYPSE

The president of Turkmenistan, a poor desert nation in Central Asia, ordered that a palace made of ice be built so "our children can learn to ski."

FIGURE SKATING

Men

1908* ....Ulrich Salchow, Sweden
1920† ....Gillis Grafström, Sweden
1924 ....Gillis Grafström, Sweden
1928 ....Gillis Grafström, Sweden
1932 ....Karl Schäfer, Austria
1936 ....Karl Schäfer, Austria
1948 ....Dick Button, United States
1952 ....Dick Button, United States
1956 ....Hayes Alan Jenkins, United States
1960 ....David Jenkins, United States
1964 ....Manfred Schnelldorfer, W Germany
1968 ....Wolfgang Schwarz, Austria
1972 ....Ondrej Nepela, Czechoslovakia
1976 ....John Curry, Great Britain
1980 ....Robin Cousins, Great Britain
1984 ....Scott Hamilton, United States
1988 ....Brian Boitano, United States
1992 ....Victor Petrenko, Unified Team
1994 :.............Alexei Urmanov, Russia
1998 ....Ilia Kulik, Russia
2002 ....Alexei Yagudin, Russia

*Competition held at Summer Games in London.
†Competition held at Summer Games in Antwerp.

Women

1908* ....Madge Syers, Great Britain
1920† ....Magda Julin, Sweden
1924 ....Herma Szabo-Planck, Austria
1928 ....Sonja Henie, Norway
1932 ....Sonja Henie, Norway
1936 ....Sonja Henie, Norway
1948 ....Barbara Ann Scott, Canada
1952 ....Jeanette Altwegg, Great Britain
1956 ....Tenley Albright, United States
1960 ....Carol Heiss, United States
1964 ....Sjoukje Dijkstra, Netherlands
1968 ....Peggy Fleming, United States
1972 ....Beatrix Schuba, Austria
1976 ....Dorothy Hamill, United States
1980 ....Anett Pötzsch, E Germany
1984 ....Katarina Witt, E Germany
1988 ....Katarina Witt, E Germany
1992 ....Kristi Yamaguchi, United States
1994 ....Oksana Baiul, Ukraine
1998 ....Tara Lipinski, United States
2002 ....Sarah Hughes, United States

Mixed

PAIRS

1908* ..Anna Hübler & Heinrich Burger, Germany
1920† ..Ludovika & Walter Jakobsson, Finland
1924 ....Helene Engelmann & Alfred Berger, Austria
1928 ....Andree Joly & Pierre Brunet, France
1932 ....Andree Brunet (Joly) & Pierre Brunet, France
1936 ....Maxi Herber & Ernst Baier, Germany
1948 ....Micheline Lannoy & Pierre Baugniet, Belgium
1952 ....Ria Falk and Paul Falk, W Germany
1956 ....Elisabeth Schwartz & Kurt Oppelt, Austria
1960 ....Barbara Wagner & Robert Paul, Canada
1964 ....Lyudmila Beloussova & Oleg Protopopov, USSR
1968 ....Lyudmila Beloussova & Oleg Protopopov, USSR
1972 ....Irina Rodnina & Alexei Ulanov, USSR
1976 ....Irina Rodnina & Aleksandr Zaitzev, USSR
1980 ....Irina Rodnina & Aleksandr Zaitzev, USSR
1984 ....Elena Valova & Oleg Vasiliev, USSR
1988 ....Ekaterina Gordeeva & Sergei Grinkov, USSR
1992 ....Natalia Michkouteniok & Artour Dmitriev, Unified Team
1994 ....Ekaterina Gordeeva & Sergei Grinkov, Russia
1998 ....Oksana Kazakova & Artur Dmitriev, Russia
2002 ....Elena Berezhnaya & Anton Sikharulidze, Russia/ Jamie Sale & David Pelletier, Canada

DANCE

1976 ....Lyudmila Pakhomova & Aleksandr Gorshkov, USSR
1980 ....Natalia Linichuk & Gennadi Karponosov, USSR
1984 ....Jayne Torvill & Christopher Dean, Great Britain
1988 ....Natalia Bestemianova & Andrei Bukin, USSR
1992 ....Marina Klimova & Sergei Ponomarenko, Unified Team
1994 ....Oksana Grishuk & Evgeny Platov, Russia
1998 ....Pasha Grishuk & Evgeny Platov, Russia
2002 ....Marina Anissina & Gwendal Peizeralt, France

*Competition held at Summer Games in London.
†Competition held at Summer Games in Antwerp.

SKELETON

Men

1928 .....Jennison Heaton, United States   3:01.8
1948 .....Nino Bibbia, Italy   5:23.2
2002 .....Jim Shea Jr., United States   1:41.96

Women

2002 .....Tristan Gale, United States   1:45.11

SPEED SKATING

Men

500 METERS

1924	Charles Jewtraw, United States	44.0
1928	Clas Thunberg, Finland	43.4 OR
	Bernt Evensen, Norway	43.4 OR
1932	John Shea, United States	43.4 EOR
1936	Ivar Ballangrud, Norway	43.4 EOR
1948	Finn Helgesen, Norway	43.1 OR
1952	Kenneth Henry, United States	43.2
1956	Yevgeny Grishin, USSR	40.2 EWR
1960	Yevgeny Grishin, USSR	40.2 EWR
1964	Terry McDermott, United States	40.1 OR
1968	Erhard Keller, W Germany	40.3
1972	Erhard Keller, W Germany	39.44 OR
1976	Yevgeny Kulikov, USSR	39.17 OR
1980	Eric Heiden, United States	38.03 OR
1984	Sergei Fokichev, USSR	38.19
1988	Uwe-Jens Mey, E Germany	36.45 WR
1992	Uwe-Jens Mey, E Germany	37.14
1994	Aleksandr Golubev, Russia	36.33
1998	Hiroyasu Shimizu, Japan (second run)	35.59 OR
2002	Casey FitzRandolph, U.S.	1:09.23*

1,000 METERS

1976	Peter Mueller, United States	1:19.32
1980	Eric Heiden, United States	1:15.18 OR
1984	Gaetan Boucher, Canada	1:15.80
1988	Nikolai Gulyaev, USSR	1:13.03 OR
1992	Olaf Zinke, Germany	1:14.85
1994	Dan Jansen, United States	1:12.43 WR
1998	Ids Postma, Netherlands	1:10.64 OR
2002	Gerard van Velde, Netherlands	1:07.18

1,500 METERS

1924	Clas Thunberg, Finland	2:20.8
1928	Clas Thunberg, Finland	2:21.1
1932	John Shea, United States	2:57.5
1936	Charles Mathisen, Norway	2:19.2 OR
1948	Sverre Farstad, Norway	2:17.6 OR
1952	Hjalmar Andersen, Norway	2:20.4
1956	Yevgeny Grishin, USSR	2:08.6 WR
	Yuri Mikhailov, USSR	2:08.6 WR
1960	Roald Aas, Norway	2:10.4
	Yevgeny Grishin, USSR	2:10.4
1964	Ants Anston, USSR	2:10.3
1968	Cornelis Verkerk, Netherlands	2:03.4 OR
1972	Ard Schenk, Netherlands	2:02.96 OR
1976	Jan Egil Storholt, Norway	1:59.38 OR
1980	Eric Heiden, United States	1:55.44 OR

1,500 METERS (Cont.)

1984	Gaetan Boucher, Canada	1:58.36
1988	Andre Hoffmann, E Germany	1:52.06 WR
1992	Johann Olav Koss, Norway	1:54.81
1994	Johann Olav Koss, Norway	1:51.29 WR
1998	Aadne Sondral, Norway	1:47.87 WR
2002	Derek Parra, United States	1:43.95

5,000 METERS

1924	Clas Thunberg, Finland	8:39.0
1928	Ivar Ballangrud, Norway	8:50.5
1932	Irving Jaffee, United States	9:40.8
1936	Ivar Ballangrud, Norway	8:19.6 OR
1948	Reidar Liaklev, Norway	8:29.4
1952	Hjalmar Andersen, Norway	8:10.6 OR
1956	Boris Shilkov, USSR	7:48.7 OR
1960	Viktor Kosichkin, USSR	7:51.3
1964	Knut Johannesen, Norway	7:38.4 OR
1968	Fred Anton Maier, Norway	7:22.4 WR
1972	Ard Schenk, Netherlands	7:23.61
1976	Sten Stensen, Norway	7:24.48
1980	Eric Heiden, United States	7:02.29 OR
1984	Sven Tomas Gustafson, Sweden	7:12.28
1988	Tomas Gustafson, Sweden	6:44.63 WR
1992	Geir Karlstad, Norway	6:59.97
1994	Johann Olav Koss, Norway	6:34.96 WR
1998	Gianni Romme, Netherlands	6:22.20 WR
2002	Jochem Uytdehaage, Net	6:41.66

10,000 METERS

1924	Julius Skutnabb, Finland	18:04.8
1928	Not held, thawing of ice	
1932	Irving Jaffee, United States	19:13.6
1936	Ivar Ballangrud, Norway	17:24.3 OR
1948	Ake Seyffarth, Sweden	17:26.3
1952	Hjalmar Andersen, Norway	16:45.8 OR
1956	Sigvard Ericsson, Sweden	16:35.9 OR
1960	Knut Johannesen, Norway	15:46.6 WR
1964	Jonny Nilsson, Sweden	15:50.1
1968	Johnny Höglin, Sweden	15:23.6 OR
1972	Ard Schenk, Netherlands	15:01.35 OR
1976	Piet Kleine, Netherlands	14:50.59 OR
1980	Eric Heiden, United States	14:28.13 WR
1984	Igor Malkov, USSR	14:39.90
1988	Tomas Gustafson, Sweden	13:48.20 WR
1992	Bart Veldkamp, Netherlands	14:12.12
1994	Johann Olav Koss, Norway	13:30.55 WR
1998	Gianni Romme, Netherlands	13:15.33 WR
2002	Jochem Uytdehaage, Neth	12:58.92 WR

Women

500 METERS

1960	Helga Haase, E Germany	45.9
1964	Lydia Skoblikova, USSR	45.0 OR
1968	Lyudmila Titova, USSR	46.1
1972	Anne Henning, United States	43.33 OR
1976	Sheila Young, United States	42.76 OR
1980	Karin Enke, E Germany	41.78 OR
1984	Christa Rothenburger, E Germany	41.02 OR

500 METERS (Cont.)

1988	Bonnie Blair, United States	39.10 WR
1992	Bonnie Blair, United States	40.33
1994	Bonnie Blair, United States	39.25
1998	Catriona LeMay Doan, Canada (second run)	38.21 OR
2002	Catriona LeMay, Canada	1:14.75*

Note: OR=Olympic Record; WR=World Record; EOR=Equals Olympic Record; EWR=Equals World Record; WB=World Best.

*Combined time.

SPEED SKATING (Cont.)
Women (Cont.)

1,000 METERS		
1960	Klara Guseva, USSR	1:34.1
1964	Lydia Skoblikova, USSR	1:33.2 OR
1968	Carolina Geijssen, Netherlands	1:32.6 OR
1972	Monika Pflug, W Germany	1:31.40 OR
1976	Tatiana Averina, USSR	1:28.43 OR
1980	Natalya Petruseva, USSR	1:24.10 OR
1984	Karin Enke, E Germany	1:21.61 OR
1988	Christa Rothenburger, E Germany	1:17.65 WR
1992	Bonnie Blair, United States	1:21.90
1994	Bonnie Blair, United States	1:18.74
1998	Marianne Timmer, Netherlands	1:16.51 OR
2002	Chris Witty, United States	1:13.83

1,500 METERS		
1960	Lydia Skoblikova, USSR	2:25.2 WR
1964	Lydia Skoblikova, USSR	2:22.6 OR
1968	Kaija Mustonen, Finland	2:22.4 OR
1972	Dianne Holum, United States	2:20.85 OR
1976	Galina Stepanskaya, USSR	2:16.58 OR
1980	Anne Borckink, Netherlands	2:10.95 OR
1984	Karin Enke, E Germany	2:03.42 WR
1988	Yvonne van Gennip, Netherlands	2:00.68 OR
1992	Jacqueline Boerner, Germany	2:05.87
1994	Emese Hunyady, Austria	2:02.19
1998	Marianne Timmer, Netherlands	1:57.58 WR

1,500 METERS (Cont.)		
2002	Anni Friesinger, Germany	1:54.02

3,000 METERS		
1960	Lydia Skoblikova, USSR	5:14.3
1964	Lydia Skoblikova, USSR	5:14.9
1968	Johanna Schut, Netherlands	4:56.2 OR
1972	Christina Baas-Kaiser, Netherlands	4:52.14 OR
1976	Tatiana Averina, USSR	4:45.19 OR
1980	Bjorg Eva Jensen, Norway	4:32.13 OR
1984	Andrea Schöne, E Germany	4:24.79 OR
1988	Yvonne van Gennip, Netherlands	4:11.94 WR
1992	Gunda Niemann, Germany	4:19.90
1994	Svetlana Bazhanova, Russia	4:17.43
1998	Gunda Niemann-Stirnemann, Germany	4:07.29 OR
2002	Claudia Pechstein, Germany	3:57.70

5,000 METERS		
1988	Yvonne van Gennip, Netherlands	7:14.13 WR
1992	Gunda Niemann, Germany	7:31.57
1994	Claudia Pechstein, Germany	7:14.37
1998	Claudia Pechstein, Germany	6:59.61 WR
2002	Claudia Pechstein, Germany	6:46.91 WR

SHORT TRACK SPEED SKATING

Men

500 METERS		
1994	Chae Ji-Hoon, S Korea	43.54
1998	Takafumi Nishitani, Japan	42.862
2002	Marc Gagnon, Canada	41.802 OR

1,000 METERS		
1992	Kim Ki-Hoon, S Korea	1:30.76
1994	Kim Ki-Hoon, S Korea	1:34.57
1998	Kim Dong Sung, S Korea	1:32.375
2002	Steve Bradbury, Austrailia	1:29.109

1,500 METERS		
2002	Apolo Anton Ohno, United States	2:18.541

5,000-METER RELAY		
1992	Korea	7:14.02
1994	Italy	7:11.74
1998	Canada	7:06.075
2002	Canada	6:51.579

Women

500 METERS		
1992	Cathy Turner, United States	47.04
1994	Cathy Turner, United States	45.98
1998	Annie Perreault, Canada	46.568
2002	Yang Yang, China	44.187

1,000 METERS		
1994	Chun Lee Kyung, S Korea	1:36.87
1998	Chun Lee Kyung, S Korea	1:42.776
2002	Yang A. Yang, China	1:36.391

1,500 METERS		
2002	Ko Gi-Hyun, Korea	2:31.581

3,000-METER RELAY		
1992	Canada	4:36.62
1994	S Korea	4:26.64
1998	S Korea	4:16.260
2002	S Korea	4:12.793

ALPINE SKIING
Men

DOWNHILL		
1948	Henri Oreiller, France	2:55.0
1952	Zeno Colo, Italy	2:30.8
1956	Anton Sailer, Austria	2:52.2
1960	Jean Vuarnet, France	2:06.0
1964	Egon Zimmermann, Austria	2:18.16
1968	Jean-Claude Killy, France	1:59.85
1972	Bernhard Russi, Switzerland	1:51.43
1976	Franz Klammer, Austria	1:45.73
1980	Leonhard Stock, Austria	1:45.50
1984	Bill Johnson, United States	1:45.59
1988	Pirmin Zurbriggen, Switzerland	1:59.63
1992	Patrick Ortlieb, Austria	1:50.37
1994	Tommy Moe, United States	1:45.75
1998	Jean-Luc Crétier, France	1:50.11
2002	Fritz Strobl, Austria	1:39.13

SLALOM		
1948	Edi Reinalter, Switzerland	2:10.3
1952	Othmar Schneider, Austria	2:00.0
1956	Anton Sailer, Austria	3:14.7
1960	Ernst Hinterseer, Austria	2:08.9
1964	Josef Stiegler, Austria	2:11.13
1968	Jean-Claude Killy, France	1:39.73
1972	F. Fernandez Ochoa, Spain	1:49.27
1976	Piero Gros, Italy	2:03.29
1980	Ingemar Stenmark, Sweden	1:44.26
1984	Phil Mahre, United States	1:39.41
1988	Alberto Tomba, Italy	1:39.47
1992	Finn Christian Jagge, Norway	1:44.39
1994	Thomas Stangassinger, Austria	2:02.02
1998	Hans-Petter Buraas, Norway	1:49.31
2002	Jean-Pierre Vidal, France	1:41.06

ALPINE SKIING

Men (Cont.)

GIANT SLALOM

1952	Stein Eriksen, Norway	2:25.0
1956	Anton Sailer, Austria	3:00.1
1960	Roger Staub, Switzerland	1:48.3
1964	Francois Bonlieu, France	1:46.71
1968	Jean-Claude Killy, France	3:29.28
1972	Gustav Thöni, Italy	3:09.62
1976	Heini Hemmi, Switzerland	3:26.97
1980	Ingemar Stenmark, Sweden	2:40.74
1984	Max Julen, Switzerland	2:41.18
1988	Alberto Tomba, Italy	2:06.37
1992	Alberto Tomba, Italy	2:06.98
1994	Markus Wasmeier, Germany	2:52.46
1998	Hermann Maier, Austria	2:38.51
2002	Stephan Eberharter, Austria	2:23.28

SUPER GIANT SLALOM

1988	Franck Piccard, France	1:39.66
1992	Kjetil André Aamodt, Norway	1:13.04
1994	Markus Wasmeier, Germany	1:32.53
1998	Hermann Maier, Austria	1:34.82
2002	Kjetil André Aamodt, Norway	1:21.58

COMBINED*

1936	Franz Pfnür, Germany	99.25
1948	Henri Oreiller, France	3.27
1988	Hubert Strolz, Austria	36.55
1992	Josef Polig, Italy	14.58
1994	Lasse Kjus, Norway	3:17.53
1998	Mario Reiter, Austria	3:08.06
2002	Kjetil André Aamodt, Norway	3:17.56

Women

DOWNHILL

1948	Hedy Schlunegger, Switzerland	2:28.3
1952	Trude Jochum-Beiser, Austria	1:47.1
1956	Madeleine Berthod, Switzerland	1:40.7
1960	Heidi Biebl, W Germany	1:37.6
1964	Christl Haas, Austria	1:55.39
1968	Olga Pall, Austria	1:40.87
1972	Marie-Theres Nadig, Switzerland	1:36.68
1976	Rosi Mittermaier, W Germany	1:46.16
1980	Annemarie Moser-Pröll, Austria	1:37.52
1984	Michela Figini, Switzerland	1:13.36
1988	Marina Kiehl, W Germany	1:25.86
1992	Kerrin Lee-Gartner, Canada	1:52.55
1994	Katja Seizinger, Germany	1:35.93
1998	Katja Seizinger, Germany	1:28.89
2002	Carole Montillet, France	1:39.56

SLALOM

1948	Gretchen Fraser, United States	1:57.2
1952	Andrea Mead Lawrence, United States	2:10.6
1956	Renee Colliard, Switzerland	1:52.3
1960	Anne Heggtveigt, Canada	1:49.6
1964	Christine Goitschel, France	1:29.86
1968	Marielle Goitschel, France	1:25.86
1972	Barbara Cochran, United States	1:31.24
1976	Rosi Mittermaier, W Germany	1:30.54
1980	Hanni Wenzel, Liechtenstein	1:25.09
1984	Paoletta Magoni, Italy	1:36.47
1988	Vreni Schneider, Switzerland	1:36.69
1992	Petra Kronberger, Austria	1:32.68
1994	Vreni Schneider, Switzerland	1:56.01
1998	Hilde Gerg, Germany	1:32.40
2002	Janica Kostelic, Croatia	1:46.10

GIANT SLALOM

1952	Andrea Mead Lawrence, U.S.	2:06.8
1956	Ossi Reichert, W Germany	1:56.5
1960	Yvonne Rüegg, Switzerland	1:39.9
1964	Marielle Goitschel, France	1:52.24
1968	Nancy Greene, Canada	1:51.97
1972	Marie-Theres Nadig, Switzerland	1:29.90
1976	Kathy Kreiner, Canada	1:29.13
1980	Hanni Wenzel, Liechtenstein (2 runs)	2:41.66
1984	Debbie Armstrong, United States	2:20.98
1988	Vreni Schneider, Switzerland	2:06.49
1992	Pernilla Wiberg, Sweden	2:12.74
1994	Deborah Compagnoni, Italy	2:30.97
1998	Deborah Compagnoni, Italy	2:50.59
2002	Janica Kostelic, Croatia	2:30.01

SUPER GIANT SLALOM

1988	Sigrid Wolf, Austria	1:19.03
1992	Deborah Compagnoni, Italy	1:21.22
1994	Diann Roffe-Steinrotter, U.S.	1:22.15
1998	Picabo Street, United States	1:18.02
2002	Daniela Ceccarelli, Italy	1:13.59

COMBINED*

1988	Anita Wachter, Austria	29.25
1992	Petra Kronberger, Austria	2.55
1994	Pernilla Wiberg, Sweden	3:05.16
1998	Katja Seizinger, Germany	2:40.74
2002	Janica Kostelic, Croatia	2:43.28

*Beginning in 1994, scoring was based on time.

FREESTYLE SKIING

Men

MOGULS

		Pts
1992	Edgar Grospiron, France	25.81
1994	Jean-Luc Brassard, Canada	27.24
1998	Jonny Moseley, United States	26.93
2002	Janne Lahtela, Finland	27.97

AERIALS

		Pts
1994	Andreas Schoenbaechler, Switz	234.67
1998	Eric Bergoust, United States	255.64
2002	Ales Valenta, Czech Republic	257.02

Women

MOGULS

		Pts
1992	Donna Weinbrecht, United States	23.69
1994	Stine Lise Hattestad, Norway	25.97
1998	Tae Satoya, Japan	25.06
2002	Kari Traa, Norway	25.94

AERIALS

		Pts
1994	Lina Cherjazova, Uzbekistan	166.84
1998	Nikki Stone, United States	193.00
2002	Alisa Camplin, Australia	193.47

NORDIC SKIING

Men

10 KILOMETERS CLASSICAL STYLE

1992	Vegard Ulvang, Norway	27:36.0
1994	Bjørn Dæhlie, Norway	24:20.1
1998	Bjørn Dæhlie, Norway	27:24.5

15 KILOMETERS CLASSICAL STYLE

1924	Thorlief Haug, Norway	1:14:31.0*
1928	Johan Gröttumsbraaten, Norway	1:37:01.0†
1932	Sven Utterström, Sweden	1:23:07.0‡
1936	Erik-August Larsson, Sweden	1:14:38.0*
1948	Martin Lundström, Sweden	1:13:50.0*
1952	Hallgeir Brenden, Norway	1:01:34.0*
1956	Hallgeir Brenden, Norway	49:39.0
1960	Haakon Brusveen, Norway	51:55.5
1964	Eero Mantyränta, Finland	50:54.1
1968	Harald Grönningen, Norway	47:54.2
1972	Sven-Ake Lundback, Sweden	45:28.24
1976	Nikolay Bajukov, Unified Team	43:58.47
1980	Thomas Wassberg, Sweden	41:57.63
1984	Gunde Swan, Sweden	41:25.6
1988	Michael Deviatyarov, USSR	41:18.9
2002	Andrus Veerpalu, Estonia	37:07.4

*Distance was 18 km. †Distance was 19.7 km.

‡Distance was 18.2 km.

15 KILOMETERS PURSUIT FREESTYLE

1992	Bjørn Dæhlie, Norway	1:05:37.9
1994	Bjørn Dæhlie, Norway	1:00:08.8
1998	Thomas Alsgaard, Norway	1:07:01.7

30 KILOMETERS CLASSICAL STYLE

1956	Veikko Hakulinen, Finland	1:44:06.0
1960	Sixten Jernberg, Sweden	1:51:03.9
1964	Eero Mantyränta, Finland	1:30:50.7
1968	Franco Nones, Italy	1:35:39.2
1972	Viaceslav Vedenine, USSR	1:36:31.2
1976	Sergei Savelyev, USSR	1:30:29.38
1980	Nikolai Simyatov, USSR	1:27:02.80
1984	Nikolai Simyatov, USSR	1:28:56.3
1988	Alexey Prokororov, USSR	1:24:26.3
1992	Vegard Ulvang, Norway	1:22:27.8
1994	Thomas Alsgaard, Norway	1:12:26.4
1998	Mika Myllylae, Finland	1:33:55.8

50 KILOMETERS FREESTYLE

1924	Thorleif Haug, Norway	3:44:32.0
1928	Per Erik Hedlund, Sweden	4:52:03.0
1932	Veli Saarinen, Finland	4:28:00.0
1936	Elis Wiklund, Sweden	3:30:11.0
1948	Nils Karlsson, Sweden	3:47:48.0
1952	Veikko Hakulinen, Finland	3:33:33.0
1956	Sixten Jernberg, Sweden	2:50:27.0
1960	Kalevi Hämäläinen, Finland	2:59:06.3
1964	Sixten Jernberg, Sweden	2:43:52.6
1968	Olle Ellefsaeter, Norway	2:28:45.8
1972	Paal Tyldrum, Norway	2:43:14.75
1976	Ivar Formo, Norway	2:37:30.50
1980	Nikolai Simyatov, USSR	2:27:24.60
1984	Thomas Wassberg, Sweden	2:15:55.8
1988	Gunde Svan, Sweden	2:04:30.9
1992	Bjørn Dæhlie, Norway	2:03:41.5
1994	Vladimir Smirnov, Kazakhstan	2:07:20.3
1998	Bjørn Dæhlie, Norway	2:05:08.2

4 X 10-KILOMETER RELAY MIXED STYLE

1936	Finland	2:41:33.0
1948	Sweden	2:32:80.0
1952	Finland	2:20:16.0

4 X 10-KILOMETER RELAY MIXED STYLE *(Cont.)*

1956	USSR	2:15:30.0
1960	Finland	2:18:45.6
1964	Sweden	2:18:34.6
1968	Norway	2:08:33.5
1972	USSR	2:04:47.94
1976	Finland	2:07:59.72
1980	USSR	1:57:03.46
1984	Sweden	1:55:06.3
1988	Sweden	1:43:58.6
1992	Norway	1:39:26.0
1994	Italy	1:41:15.0
1998	Norway	1:40:55.7
2002	Norway	1:32:45.5

SKI JUMPING (NORMAL HILL)

		Pts
1964	Veikko Kankkonen, Finland	229.90
1968	Jiri Raska, Czechoslovakia	216.5
1972	Yukio Kasaya, Japan	244.2
1976	Hans-Georg Aschenbach, E Germany	252.0
1980	Toni Innauer, Austria	266.3
1984	Jens Weissflog, E Germany	215.2
1988	Matti Nykänen, Finland	229.1
1992	Ernst Vettori, Austria	222.8
1994	Espen Bredesen, Norway	282.0
1998	Jani Soininen, Finland	234.5
2002	Simon Ammann, Switzerland	269.0

SKI JUMPING (LARGE HILL)

		Pts
1924	Jacob Tullin Thams, Norway	18.960
1928	Alf Andersen, Norway	19.208
1932	Birger Ruud, Norway	228.1
1936	Birger Ruud, Norway	232.0
1948	Petter Hugsted, Norway	228.1
1952	Arnfinn Bergmann, Norway	226.0
1956	Antti Hyvärinen, Finland	227.0
1960	Helmut Recknagel, E Germany	227.2
1964	Toralf Engan, Norway	230.70
1968	Vladimir Beloussov, USSR	231.3
1972	Wojciech Fortuna, Poland	219.9
1976	Karl Schnabl, Austria	234.8
1980	Jouko Tormanen, Finland	271.0
1984	Matti Nykänen, Finland	231.2
1988	Matti Nykänen, Finland	224.0
1992	Toni Nieminen, Finland	239.5
1994	Jens Weissflog, Germany	274.5
1998	Kazuyoshi Funaki, Japan	272.3
2002	Simon Amman, Switzerland	281.4

TEAM SKI JUMPING

		Pts
1988	Finland	634.4
1992	Finland	644.4
1994	Germany	970.1
1998	Japan	933.0
2002	Germany	974.1

NORDIC SKIING *(Cont.)*
Men *(Cont.)*

NORDIC COMBINED	Pts
1924....Thorleif Haug, Norway	18.906*
1928....Johan Gröttumsbraaten, Norway	17.833*
1932....Johan Gröttumsbraaten, Norway	446.0
1936....Oddbjörn Hagen, Norway	430.30
1948....Heikki Hasu, Finland	448.80
1952....Simon Slattvik, Norway	451.621
1956....Sverre Stenersen, Norway	455.0
1960....Georg Thoma, W Germany	457.952
1964....Tormod Knutsen, Norway	469.28
1968....Frantz Keller, W Germany	449.04
1972....Ulrich Wehling, E Germany	413.34
1976....Ulrich Wehling, E Germany	423.39
1980....Ulrich Wehling, E Germany	432.20
1984....Tom Sandberg, Norway	422.595

NORDIC COMBINED *(Cont.)*	Pts
1988....Hippolyt Kempf, Switzerland	432.230
1992....Fabrice Guy, France	426.47
1994....Fred B. Lundberg, Norway	457.970
1998....Bjarte Engen Vik, Norway	41:21.1†
2002....Samppa Lajunen, Finland	38:18.7

TEAM NORDIC COMBINED
1988....W Germany
1992....Japan
1994....Japan
1998....Norway
2002....Finland

SPRINT NORDIC COMBINED	
2002....Samppa Lajunen, Finland	123.8

* Different scoring system; 1924–1952 distance was 18 km; 1952–present, 15 km.

† Times in the cross-country race were not converted into points. According to the Gundersen Method, used since 1988, starting times in the race are staggered in proportion to points earned in the ski jumping segment of the event.

Women

1.5 KILOMETERS SPRINT	
2002....Julija Tchepalova, Russia	3:10.6

5 KILOMETERS PURSUIT	
2002....Olga Danilova, Russia	24:52.1

5 KILOMETERS CLASSICAL STYLE	
1964....Klaudia Boyarskikh, USSR	17:50.5
1968....Toini Gustafsson, Sweden	16:45.2
1972....Galina Kulakova, USSR	17:00.50
1976....Helena Takalo, Finland	15:48.69
1980....Raisa Smetanina, USSR	15:06.92
1984....Marja-Liisa Hamalainen, Finland	17:04.0
1988....Marjo Matikainen, Finland	15:04.0
1992....Marjut Lukkarinen, Finland	14:13.8
1994....Lyubova Egorova, Russia	14:08.8
1998....Larissa Lazhutina, Russia	17:37.9

10 KILOMETERS CLASSICAL STYLE	
1952....Lydia Widemen, Finland	41:40.0
1956....Lyubov Kosyryeva, USSR	38:11.0
1960....Maria Gusakova, USSR	39:46.6
1964....Klaudia Boyarskikh, USSR	40:24.3
1968....Toini Gustafsson, Sweden	36:46.5
1972....Galina Kulakova, USSR	34:17.8
1976....Raisa Smetanina, USSR	30:13.41
1980....Barbara Petzold, E Germany	30:31.54
1984....Marja-Lissa Hamalainen, Finland	31:44.2
1988....Vida Ventsene, USSR	30:08.3
2002....Bante Skari, Norway	28:05.6

30 KILOMETERS CLASSICAL TYLE	
2002....Gabriela Paruzzi, Italy	1:30:57.1

10 KILOMETERS PURSUIT FREESTYLE	
1992....Lyubov Egorova, Unified Team	40:07.7
1994....Lyubov Egorova, Russia	41:38.1
1998....Larissa Lazhutina, Russia	46:06.9

15 KILOMETERS FREESTYLE	
2002....Stefania Belmondo, Italy	39:54.4

15 KILOMETERS CLASSICAL STYLE	
1992....Lyubov Egorova, Unified Team	42:20.8
1994....Manuela Di Centa, Italy	39:44.5
1998....Olga Danilova, Russia	46:55.04

20 KILOMETERS FREESTYLE	
1984....Marja-Liisa Hamalainen, Finland	1:01:45.0
1988....Tamara Tikhonova, USSR	55:53.6

30 KILOMETERS FREESTYLE	
1992....Stefania Belmondo, Italy	1:22:30.1
1994....Manuela Di Centa, Italy	1:25:41.6
1998....Julija Tchepalova, Russia	1:22:01.5

4 X 5-KILOMETER RELAY MIXED STYLE	
1956....Finland	1:9:01.0
1960....Sweden	1:4:21.4
1964....USSR	59:20.0
1968....Norway	57:30.0
1972....USSR	48:46.15
1976....USSR	1:07:49.75
1980....E Germany	1:02:11.10
1984....Norway	1:06:49.7
1988....USSR	59:51.1
1992....Unified Team	59:34.8
1994....Russia	57:12.5
1998....Russia	55:13.5
2002....Germany	49:30.6

SNOWBOARDING

Men

GIANT SLALOM	
1998....Ross Rebagliati, Canada	2:03.96

PARALLEL GIANT SLALOM
2002....Philipp Schoch, Switzerland

HALF-PIPE	Pts
1998....Gian Simmen, Switzerland	85.2
2002....Ross Powers, United States	46.1

Women

GIANT SLALOM	
1998....Karine Ruby, France	2:17.34

PARALLEL GIANT SLALOM
2002....Isabella Blanc, France

HALF-PIPE	Pts
1998....Nicola Thost, Germany	74.6
2002....Kelly Clark, United States	47.9

Track & Field

Hicham El Guerrouj

Dark Days

The shadow of a drug scandal cloaked the sport, obscuring all, including a stirring Olympics

BY MERRELL NODEN

"VAST CHAOS." that's how Marion Jones, superstar of the Sydney Olympics, described the Olympic year of 2004. Jones was talking about her own painful experience, but it's also an apt description of how what should have been a magical year for track fans was poisoned by a drug scandal that tarnished not only Jones, but also many other top athletes, including her boyfriend, 100-meter world record holder Tim Montgomery. A brief, blessed antidote to the depressing news came in mid-August, when fresh faces shone in the bright spotlight of a magnificent Olympic Games in Athens. But the federal investigation of drug distribution by the Bay Area Laboratory Co-operative (BALCO) pushed track and field into a dark tunnel, from which it has yet to emerge.

The scandal began in June of 2003, when a coach—later revealed to be Trevor Graham, former coach of both Jones and Montgomery—gave the U.S. Anti-Doping Agency a syringe containing tetrahydrogestrinone (THG), a designer steroid undetectable by current tests. In the fall of 2003 more than 30 athletes from track and field, baseball and football were subpoenaed to testify before a grand jury in San Francisco. Jones and Montgomery both gave evidence, as did slugger Barry Bonds and a number of Oakland Raiders. This was huge news, fueling investigations by both the IRS and John McCain's Senate Commerce Committee. President Bush even alluded to it in his State of the Union address.

In February, the grand jury handed down a 42-count indictment against four men, including BALCO CEO Victor Conte; Bonds's trainer, Greg Anderson; and Bay-area track coach Remi Korchemny. Jones was not charged, but several track athletes were, including Montgomery and fellow 2000 Olympics sprinters Chryste Gaines and Alvin Harrison. Kelli White, already stripped of the two gold medals she'd won at the 2003 world championships for using a banned substance, agreed to a two-year ban in exchange for her cooperation.

All of this dragged on through the spring, in a kind of water torture of leaks, innuendo and guesses. At the Olympic Trials in Sacramento, none of the athletes charged by the USADA made the U.S. team, which spared USA Track & Field from having to decide whether to cut them from the team. Jones finished fifth in the 100 and fifth in the quarterfinals of the 200, whereupon she withdrew from the event. She won the long jump with a leap of 23-4, her best since 1998, and thus made the team for Athens.

Not surprisingly, the drug news overshadowed some great stories. One, which for a time did a pretty good job of countering the

Gatlin (right) won the gold medal in a blisteringly fast Olympic 100.

deluge of bad news, was the re-emergence of miler Alan Webb. After breaking Jim Ryun's ancient high school mile record in 2001, Webb spent the last few years struggling to run anywhere near as fast. This year he finally broke through. First, Webb trounced his rivals at the Home Depot Invitational, then traveled to Ostrava, in the Czech Republic, and beat a top international 1500 field in 3:32.73, the fastest time of the year to that date. Finally, he ran a 3:50.85 mile at the Pre Classic in June, the fastest mile by an American on U.S. soil. At the Olympic Trials he showed incredible confidence by simply running away from the field.

But because of either nerves or a rookie's bad judgment, Webb ran poorly in Athens, letting himself get outkicked in a slow race. He wasn't the only medal hopeful to fare poorly on the big stage. World decathlon champ Tom Pappas was unable to finish. In the women's vault, Stacy Dragila didn't reach the final. Allen Johnson and Gail Devers both wiped out in early rounds of the hurdles. Finally, after finishing fifth in the long jump, Marion Jones botched the exchange with Lauryn Williams and the U.S. did not finish in the 400 relay final. The men got the stick around safely but finished second to Great Britain by .01. It was the first time the U.S. had not won at least one of the two short relays at an Olympics.

Despite all that, the U.S. had a superb Olympics. Of the 25 medals the team won, eight came in the men's sprints. Justin Gatlin won a fast, deep 100 (9.85); Shawn Crawford (19.79), led a U.S. sweep of the 200, and Jeremy Wariner led a U.S. sweep in the 400 (44.00). Timothy Mack and Toby Stevenson went 1-2 in the vault, while Dwight Phillips won the long jump.

Among the U.S. women, Joanna Hayes won the 100 hurdles, and youngsters Lauryn Williams and Allyson Felix each claimed silver, in the 100 and 200, respectively. None of those results was particularly surprising, but Deena Kastor's bronze and Meb Keflezighi's silver in the marathon were.

There were only two world records broken or tied at the Olympics—which some took as a sign that drug testing was working—and there were only two double individual winners as well. The double winners were Kelly Holmes of Great Britain (800, 1500) and Hicham El Guerrouj (1500, 5,000), the great Moroccan miler. Despite holding multiple world records and losing only four 1500 or mile races since 1996, El Guerrouj had had terrible luck in past Olympics, stumbling and falling on the final lap in Atlanta and being overwhelmed by nerves in Sydney.

Not this time: He beat Bernard Lagat in a stirring homestretch duel in the 1500, then returned to top Kenenisa Bekele in a slow 5,000. El Guerrouj fell to his knees in prayer after the 1500, delighted to find hope and possibility beyond even the worst disasters. Now if only the beleaguered sport can do the same.

U.S. Olympic Trials

Sacramento, July 9–18, 2004

Men

100 METERS

1.	Maurice Green, adidas	9.91
2.	Justin Gatlin, Nike	9.92
3.	Shawn Crawford, Nike	9.93

200 METERS

1.	Shawn Crawford, Nike	19.99
2.	Justin Gatlin, Nike	20.01
3.	Bernard Williams, Nike	20.30

400 METERS

1.	Jeremy Wariner, Baylor	44.37
2.	Otis Harris, Nike	44.67
3.	Derrick Brew, Nike	44.69

800 METERS

1.	Jonathan Johnson, Texas Tech	1:44.77
2.	Khadevis Robinson, Nike	1:44.91
3.	Derrick Peterson, adidas	1:45.08

1,500 METERS

1.	Alan Webb, Nike	3:36.13
2.	Charlie Gruber, Nike	3:38.45
3.	Rob Myers, unattached	3:38.93

3,000 M STEEPLECHASE

1.	Daniel Lincoln, Nike	8:15.02
2.	Anthoney Famiglietti, adidas	8:17.91
3.	Robert Gary, adidas	8:19.46

5,000 METERS

1.	Tim Broe, adidas	13:27.36
2.	Jonathon Riley, Nike	13:30.85
3.	Bolota Asmerom, Nike	13:32.77

10,000 METERS

1.	Meb Keflezighi, Nike	27:36.49
2.	Abdi Abdirahman, Nike	27:55.00
3.	Daniel Browne, Nike	28:07.47

110-METER HURDLES

1.	Terrence Trammell, Mizuno	13.09
2.	Duane Ross, Nike	13.21
3.	Allen Johnson, Nike	13.25

400-METER HURDLES

1.	James Carter, Nike	47.68
2.	Angelo Taylor, Nike	48.03
3.	Bennie Brazell, Louisiana St	48.05

20-KILOMETER RACE WALK

1.	Tim Seaman, NYAC	1:25:40
2.	John Nunn, U.S. Army	1:26:23
3.	Kevin Eastler, U.S. Air Force	1:28:49

HIGH JUMP

1.	Jamie Nieto, Nike	7 ft 7¾ in
2.	Matt Hemingway, adidas	7 ft 6½ in
3.	Tora Harris, Nike	7 ft 5¼ in

POLE VAULT

1.	Timothy Mack, Nike	19 ft 4¼ in
2.	Toby Stevenson, Nike	19 ft 2¼ in
3.	Derek Miles, Nike	19 ft ¼ in

LONG JUMP

1.	Dwight Phillips, Nike	27 ft 2 in
2.	Tony Allmond, unattached	26 ft 7 in
3.	John Moffitt, Nike	26 ft 5¾ in

TRIPLE JUMP

1.	Melvin Lister, unattached	58 ft 4 in
2.	Walter Davis, Nike	57 ft 10¼ in
3.	Kenta Bell, Nike	57 ft 8¼ in

SHOT PUT

1.	Adam Nelson, Nike	71 ft
2.	Reese Hoffa, NYAC	69 ft 4¼ in
3.	John Godina, adidas	69 ft 2 in

DISCUS THROW

1.	Jarred Rome, unattached	215 ft 9 in
2.	Ian Waltz, unattached	212 ft 3 in
3.	Casey Malone, Nike	211 ft 6 in

HAMMER THROW

1.	James Parker, U.S. Air Force	254 ft 6 in
2.	A.G. Kruger, Ashland Elite	249 ft 5 in
3.	Travis Nutter, Pacific Bay TC	237 ft 9 in

JAVELIN THROW

1.	Breaux Greer, adidas	270 ft 4 in
2.	Brian Chaput, Penn	261 ft 10 in
3.	Leigh Smith, Tennessee	250 ft 7 in

DECATHLON

1.	Bryan Clay, Nike	8660
2.	Tom Pappas, Nike	8517
3.	Paul Terek, World's Greatest Ath.	8312

MARATHON*

1.	Alan Culpepper	2:11:42
2.	Meb Keflezighi	2:11:47
3.	Dan Browne	2:12:02

*Held on Feb. 7 in Birmingham, AL

Women

100 METERS

1.	LaTasha Colander, Nike	10.97
2.	Torri Edwards, adidas	11.02
3.	Lauryn Williams, Miami	11.10

200 METERS

1.	Allyson Felix, adidas	22.28
2.	Muna Lee, Nike	22.36
3.	Torri Edwards, adidas	22.39

400 METERS

1.	Monique Hennagan, unattached	49.56
2.	Sanya Richards, Nike	49.89
3.	DeeDee Trotter, Tennessee	50.28

800 METERS

1.	Jearl Miles-Clark, New Balance	1:59.06
2.	Nicole Teter, Nike	2:00.25
3.	Hazel Clark, Nike	2:00.37

1,500 METERS

1.	Carrie Tollefson, adidas	4:08.32
2.	Jennifer Toomey, Nike	4:08.43
3.	Amy Rudolph, adidas	4:08.57

3,000 M STEEPLECHASE

1.	Ann Gaffigan, Nebraska	9:39.35AR
2.	Kathryn Andersen, BYU	9:45.52
3.	Carrie Messner, Asics	9:50.70

5,000 METERS

1.	Shayne Culpepper, adidas	15:07.41
2.	Marla Runyan, Nike	15:07.48
3.	Shalane Flanagan, Nike	15:10.52

10,000 METERS

1.	Deena Kastor, Asics	31:09.65
2.	Elva Dryer, Nike	31:58.14
3.	Kate O'Neill, Nike	32:07.25

20-KILOMETER RACE WALK

1.	Teresa Vaill, Walk U.S.A.	1:35:57
2.	Joanne Dow, adidas	1:38:42
3.	Bobbi Chapman, unattached	1:39:01

100-METER HURDLES

1.	Gail Devers, Nike	12.55
2.	Joanna Hayes, Nike	12.55
3.	Melissa Morrison, adidas	12.61

400-METER HURDLES

1.	Sheena Johnson, Nike	52.95
2.	Brenda Taylor, Nike	53.36
3.	Lashinda Demus, S Carolina	53.43

HIGH JUMP

1.	Tisha Waller, Nike	6 ft 6 in
2.	Chaunte Howard, Georgia Tech	6 ft 4¾ in
3.	Amy Acuff, Asics	6 ft 4¾ in

POLE VAULT

1.	Stacy Dragila, Nike	15 ft 7 in
2.	Jillian Schwartz, Nike	14 ft 11 in
3.	Kellie Suttle, Nike	14 ft 11 in

LONG JUMP

1.	Marion Jones, Nike	23 ft 4 in
2.	Grace Upshaw, Nike	22 ft 5 in
3.	Akiba McKinney, unattached	21 ft 6¾ in

TRIPLE JUMP

1.	Tiombe Hurd, Nike	47 ft 5 in
2.	Shakeema Walker, unattached	46 ft 1½ in
3.	Vanitta Kinard, Nike	45 ft ½ in

SHOT PUT

1.	Laura Gerraughty, N Carolina	60 ft 8½ in
2.	Kristin Heaston, Nike	59 ft 4¾ in
3.	Jillian Camarena, Stanford	58 ft 2 in

DISCUS THROW

1.	Aretha Hill, Nike	208 ft 6 in
2.	Stephanie Brown, Moreno T.	203 ft 1 in
3.	Seilala Sua, Nike	202 ft 1 in

HAMMER THROW

1.	Erin Gilreath, NYAC	231 ft
2.	Anna Mahon, Nike	227 ft 1 in
3.	Amber Campbell, C Carolina	216 ft 6 in

JAVELIN THROW

1.	Kim Kreiner, Nike	182 ft 7 in
2.	Sarah Malone, Oregon	177 ft 11 in
3.	Denise O'Connell, unattached	177 ft 4 in

HEPTATHLON

1.	Shelia Burrell, Nike	6194
2.	Tiffany Lott-Hogan, unattached	6159
3.	Michelle Perry, Nike	6126

MARATHON*

1.	Colleen De Reuck	2:28:25
2.	Deena Kastor	2:29:38
3.	Jen Rhines	2:29:57

*Held on April 3 in St. Louis.

Boston, Feb 27–29

Men

60 METERS

1. ....Shawn Crawford, Nike — 6.47
2. ....John Capel, adidas — 6.52
3. ....Mickey Grimes, Nike — 6.60

200 METERS

1. ....Jimmie Hackley, unattached — 20.83
2. ....Coby Miller, Nike — 21.01
3. ....Kevin Braunskill, unattached — 21.19

400 METERS

1. ....Milton Campbell, Holyfield Int'l. — 46.43
2. ....James Carter, Nike — 46.80
3. ....Joseph Mendel, unattached — 46.94

800 METERS

1. ....Michael Stember, Nike — 1:48.08
2. ....Derrick Peterson, adidas — 1:48.67
3. ....Jesse O'Connell, unattached — 1:49.19

1,500 METERS

1. ....Rob Myers, unattached — 3:40.80
2. ....Charlie Gruber, Nike — 3:40.83
3. ....Jason Long, unattached — 3:42.26

3,000 METERS

1. ....Jonathon Riley, Nike — 7:57.69
2. ....Luke Watson, adidas — 7:57.92
3. ....Bolota Asmerom, Nike — 7:57.98

5,000-METER RACE WALK

1. ....Tim Seaman, NYAC — 19:30.59
2. ....John Nunn, U.S. Army — 19:35.58
3. ....Kevin Eastler, U.S. Air Force — 19:50.36

60-METER HURDLES

1. ....Allen Johnson, Nike — 7.44
2. ....Duane Ross, Nike — 7.59
3. ....Ron Bramlett, Nike — 7.64

HIGH JUMP

1. ....Jamie Nieto, Nike — 7 ft 6½ in
2. ....Adam Shunk, Indiana Invaders — 7 ft 2½ in
2. ....Tora Harris, Shore Athletic — 7 ft 2½ in
2. ....Ryan Fitzpatric, unattached — 7 ft 2½ in
2. ....Henry Patterson, unattached — 7 ft 2½ in

POLE VAULT

1. ....Toby Stevenson, Nike — 19 ft ¼ in
2. ....Jeff Hartwig, Nike — 18 ft 10¼ in
3. ....Russ Buller, Asics — 18 ft 10¼ in

LONG JUMP

1. ....Savante Stringfellow, Nike — 27 ft 1¼ in
2. ....Marcus Thomas, unattached — 25 ft 8 in
3. ....Joseph Allen, unattached — 25 ft 4¾ in

TRIPLE JUMP

1. ....Allen Simms, unattached — 55 ft 4¾ in
2. ....LaMark Carter, unattached — 54 ft 1 in
3. ....Melvin Lister, unattached — 53 ft 5 in

SHOT PUT

1. ....Christian Cantwell, Nike — 69 ft 9 in
1. ....Reese Hoffa, NYAC — 68 ft 9¾ in
3. ....Jesse Roberge, unattached — 62 ft 11½ in

WEIGHT THROW

1. ....James Parker, U.S. Air Force — 76 ft ¾ in
2. ............A.G. Kruger, Ashland Elite — 74 ft ¼ in
3. ....Thomas Freeman, unattached — 72 ft 7¼ in

HEPTATHLON*

1. ....Paul Terek, World's Greatest — 6040
2. ....Stephen Harris, unattached — 5989
3. ....Phil McMullen, Nike — 5898

* Held on March 6-7 in Chapel Hill, N Carolina.

Women

60 METERS

1.	Gail Devers, Nike	7.12
2.	Torri Edwards, adidas	7.12
3.	Lakeisha Backus, U.S. Army	7.18

200 METERS

1.	Crystal Cox, unattached	23.27
2.	Rachelle Boone, Nike	23.53
3.	Debbie Dunn, unattached	23.59

400 METERS

1.	Julian Clay, unattached	52.85
2.	Gigi Miller, unattached	53.33
3.	Demetria Washington, Nike	53.34

800 METERS

1.	Jen Toomey, Nike	2:00.02
2.	Hazel Clark, Nike	2:01.06
3.	Nicole Teter, Nike	2:03.05

1,500 METERS

1.	Jen Toomey, Nike	4:09.82
2.	Amy Rudolph, adidas	4:11.93
3.	Suzy Favor Hamilton, Nike	4:12.87

3,000 METERS

1.	Shayne Culpepper, adidas	9:00.59
2.	Carrie Tollefson, adidas	9:00.93
3.	Sarah Schwald, Nike	9:03.25

3,000-METER RACE WALK

1.	Joanne Dow, adidas	12:36.76
2.	Michelle Rohl, Moving Comfort	13:10.79
3.	Amber Antonia, NYAC	13:28.38

60-METER HURDLES

1.	Gail Devers, Nike	7.81
2.	Joanna Hayes, Nike	7.91
3.	Anjanette Kirkland, Nike	7.99

HIGH JUMP

1.	Amy Acuff, Asics	6 ft 4 in
2.	Tisha Waller, Nike	6 ft 2¾ in
3.	Ifoma Jones, unattached	6 ft 2¾ in

POLE VAULT

1.	Stacy Dragila, Nike	15 ft 5 in
2.	Jillian Schwartz, Nike	14 ft 5¼ in
3.	Lindsay Taylor, unattached	14 ft 3¼ in

LONG JUMP

1.	Tameisha King, unattached	21 ft 2 in
2.	Grace Upshaw, Nike	21 ft 1¼ in
3.	Antoinette Wilks, unattached	20 ft 10½ in

TRIPLE JUMP

1.	Tiombe Hurd, Nike	45 ft 5 in
2.	Yuliana Perez, unattached	45 ft 2½ in
3.	Teresa Bundy, Nike	45 ft 2¼ in

SHOT PUT

1.	Laura Gerraughty, N Carolina	62 ft 9½ in
2.	Kristin Heaston, Nike	58 ft 5¼ in
3.	Stephanie Brown, unattached	57 ft 9½ in

WEIGHT THROW

1.	Erin Gilreath, NYAC	77 ft ½ in
2.	Anna Mahon, Nike	75 ft 11 in
3.	Amber Campbell, C Carolina	72 ft 11¾ in

PENTATHLON*

1.	Tiffany Lott-Hogan, unattached	4224
2.	Michelle Moran, uattached	4093
3.	Fiona Asigbee, unattached	4041

* Held on March 6-7 in Chapel Hill, N Carolina.

2004 IAAF World Cross-Country Championships

Brussels, March 20–21

MEN (12,000 METERS; 7.5 MILES)

1.	Kenenisa Bekele, Ethiopia	35:52
2.	G. Gebremariam, Ethiopia	36:10
3.	Sileshi Sihine, Ethiopia	36:11

WOMEN (8,000 METERS; 5 MILES)

1.	Benita Johnson, Australia	27:17
2.	Egegayehu Dibaba, Ethiopia	27:29
3.	Werknesh Kidane, Ethiopia	27:34

Major Marathons

Chicago: October 12, 2003

MEN

1.	Evans Rutto, Kenya	2:05:50
2.	Paul Koech, Kenya	2:07:07
3.	Daniel Njenga, Kenya	2:07:41

WOMEN

1.	Svetlana Zakharova, Russia	2:23:07
2.	Constantina Tomescu-Dita, Rom	2:23:35
3.	Jelena Prokopcuka, Latvia	2:24:53

New York City: November 2, 2003

MEN

1.	Martin Lel, Kenya	2:10:30
2.	Rodgers Rop, Kenya	2:11:11
3.	Christopher Cheboiboch, Kenya	2:11:23

WOMEN

1.	Margaret Okayo, Kenya	2:22:31
2.	Catherine Ndereba, Kenya	2:23:03
3.	Lornah Kiplagat, Netherlands	2:11:23

Tokyo: November 16, 2003

WOMEN ONLY

1.	Elfenesh Alemu, Ethiopia	2:24:47
2.	Naoko Takahashi, Japan	2:27:21
3.	Kiyoko Shimahara, Japan	2:31:10

Tokyo: February 8, 2004

MEN ONLY

1.	Daniel Njenga, Kenya	2:08:43
2.	Satoshi Osaki, Japan	2:08:46
3.	Ben Kimondiu, Kenya	2:09:27

Rome: March 28, 2004

MEN

1.	Ruggero Pertile, Italy	2:10:13
2.	Migidio Bourifa, Italy	2:11:13
3.	Samuel Kemboi, Kenya	2:11:45

WOMEN

1.	Ornella Ferrara, Italy	2:27:49
2.	Bruna Genovese, Italy	2:29:04
3.	Rosalba Console, Italy	2:32:15

Paris: April 4, 2004

MEN

1.	Ambesa Tolosa, Ethiopia	2:08:56
2.	Raymond Kipkoech, Kenya	2:10:08
3.	Paul Biwott, Kenya	2:10:30

WOMEN

1.	Salina Kosgei, Kenya	2:24:32
2.	Asha Gigi, Ethiopia	2:26:05
3.	Corinne Raux, France	2:29:19

Boston: April 19, 2004

MEN

1.	Timothy Cherigat, Kenya	2:10:37
2.	Robert Cheboror, Kenya	2:11:49
3.	Martin Lel, Kenya	2:13:38

WOMEN

1.	Catherine Ndereba, Kenya	2:24:27
2.	Elfenesh Alemu, Ethiopia	2:24:43
3.	Olivera Jevtic, Serbia	2:27:34

Rotterdam: April 4, 2004

MEN

1.	Felix Limo, Kenya	2:06:14
2.	Michael Rotich, Kenya	2:09:07
3.	Romulo Wagner da Silva, Brazil	2:11:28

WOMEN

1.	Zhor el Kamch, Morocco	2:26:10
2.	Madai Perez, Mexico	2:27:08
3.	Jelena Burykina, Russia	2:30:53

London: April 18, 2004

MEN

1.	Evans Rutto, Kenya	2:06:18
2.	Sammy Korir, Kenya	2:06:48
3.	Jaouad Gharib, Morocco	2:07:02

WOMEN

1.	Margaret Okayo, Kenya	2:22:35
2.	Ludmila Petrova, Russia	2:26:02
3.	Constantina Tomescu-Dita, Rom	2:26:52

TRACK AND FIELD

World Records

As of September 15, 2004. World outdoor records are recognized by the International Amateur Athletics Federation (IAAF).

Men

Event	Mark	Record Holder	Date	Site
100 meters	9.78	Tim Montgomery, United States	9-14-02	Paris
200 meters	19.32	Michael Johnson, United States	8-1-96	Atlanta
400 meters	43.18	Michael Johnson, United States	8-26-99	Seville
800 meters	1:41.11	Wilson Kipketer, Denmark	8-24-97	Cologne
1,000 meters	2:11.96	Noah Ngeny, Kenya	9-5-99	Rieti, Italy
1,500 meters	3:26.00	Hicham El Guerrouj, Morocco	7-14-98	Rome
Mile	3:43.13	Hicham El Guerrouj, Morocco	7-7-99	Rome
2,000 meters	4:44.79	Hicham El Guerrouj, Morocco	9-7-99	Berlin
3,000 meters	7:20.67	Daniel Komen, Kenya	9-1-96	Rieti, Italy
Steeplechase	7:53.63*	Saif Saaeed Shaheen, Qatar	9-3-04	Brussels
5,000 meters	12:37.35	Kenenisa Bekele, Ethiopia	5-31-04	Hengelo, Netherlands
10,000 meters	26:20.31	Kenenisa Bekele, Ehtiopia	6-8-04	Ostrava, Czech Republic
20,000 meters	56:55.6	Arturo Barrios, Mexico	3-30-91	La Flàche, France
Hour	21,101 meters	Arturo Barrios, Mexico	3-30-91	La Flàche, France
25,000 meters	1:13:55.8	Toshihiko Seko, Japan	3-22-81	Christchurch, New Zealand
30,000 meters	1:29:18.8	Toshihiko Seko, Japan	3-22-81	Christchurch, New Zealand
Marathon	2:04:55	Paul Tergat, Kenya	9-28-03	Berlin
110-meter hurdles	12.91	Colin Jackson, Great Britain	8-20-93	Stuttgart, Germany
	12.91*	Xiang Liu, China	8-27-04	Athens
400-meter hurdles	46.78	Kevin Young, United States	8-6-92	Barcelona
20-kilometer walk	1:17:25	Bernardo Segura, Mexico	5-7-94	Bergen, Norway
30-kilometer walk	2:01:44.1	Maurizio Damilano, Italy	10-3-92	Cuneo, Italy
50-kilometer walk	3:40:57.9	Thierry Toutain, France	9-29-96	Héricourt, France
4 x 100-meter relay	37.40	United States (Mike Marsh, Leroy Burrell, Dennis Mitchell, Carl Lewis)	8-8-92	Barcelona
		United States (Jon Drummond, Andre Cason, Dennis Mitchell, Leroy Burrell)	8-21-93	Stuttgart, Germany
4 x 200-meter relay	1:18.68	Santa Monica TC (Mike Marsh, Leroy Burrell, Floyd Heard, Carl Lewis)	4-17-94	Walnut, CA
4 x 400-meter relay	2:54.20	United States (Jerome Young, Antonio Pettigrew, Tyree Washington, Michael Johnson)	7-22-98	New York City
4 x 800-meter relay	7:03.89	Great Britain (Peter Elliott, Garry Cook, Steve Cram, Sebastian Coe)	8-30-82	London
4 x 1,500-meter relay	14:38.8	W Germany (Thomas Wessinghage, Harald Hudak, Michael Lederer, Karl Fleschen)	8-17-77	Cologne
High jump	8 ft ½ in	Javier Sotomayor, Cuba	7-27-93	Salamanca, Spain
Pole vault	20 ft 1¾ in	Sergei Bubka, Ukraine	7-31-94	Sestriere, Italy
Long jump	29 ft 4½ in	Mike Powell, United States	8-30-91	Tokyo
Triple jump	60 ft ¼ in	Jonathan Edwards, Great Britain	8-7-95	Göteborg, Sweden
Shot put	75 ft 10¼ in	Randy Barnes, United States	5-20-90	Westwood, CA
Discus throw	243 ft 0 in	Jürgen Schult, E Germany	6-6-86	Neubrandenburg, Germany
Hammer throw	284 ft 7 in	Yuri Syedikh, USSR	8-30-86	Stuttgart, Germany
Javelin throw	323 ft 1 in	Jan Zelezny, Czech Republic	5-25-96	Jena, Germany
Decathlon	9026 pts	Roman Sebrle, Czech Republic	5-27-01	Götzis

Note: The decathlon consists of 10 events: the 100 meters, long jump, shot put, high jump and 400 meters on the first day; the 110-meter hurdles, discus, pole vault, javelin and 1,500 meters on the second.

*Pending ratification.

Women

Event	Mark	Record Holder	Date	Site
100 meters	10.49	Florence Griffith Joyner, United States	7-16-88	Indianapolis
200 meters	21.34	Florence Griffith Joyner, United States	9-29-88	Seoul
400 meters	47.60	Marita Koch, E Germany	10-6-85	Canberra, Australia
800 meters	1:53.28	Jarmila Kratochvílová, Czechoslovakia	7-26-83	Munich
1,000 meters	2:28.98	Svetlana Masterkova, Russia	8-23-96	Brussels
1,500 meters	3:50.46	Qu Yunxia, China	9-11-93	Beijing
Mile	4:12.56	Svetlana Masterkova, Russia	8-14-96	Zurich
2,000 meters	5:25.36	Sonia O'Sullivan, Ireland	7-8-94	Edinburgh
3,000 meters	8:06.11	Wang Junxia, China	9-13-93	Beijing
Steeplechase	9:01.59	Gulnara Samitova, Russia	7-4-04	Iraklio, Greece
5,000 meters	14:24.68	Elvan Abeylegesse, Turkey	6-11-04	Bergen, Norway
10,000 meters	29:31.78	Wang Junxia, China	9-8-93	Beijing
Hour	18,340 meters	Tegla Loroupe, Kenya	8-8-98	Borgholzhausen, Germany
20,000 meters	1:05:26.6	Tegla Loroupe, Kenya	9-3-00	Borgholzhausen, Germany
25,000 meters	1:27:05.9	Tegla Loroupe, Kenya	9-21-02	Mengerskirchen
30,000 meters	1:45:50.0	Tegla Loroupe, Kenya	6-6-03	Warstein
Marathon	2:15:25	Paula Radcliffe, Great Britain	4-13-03	London
100-meter hurdles	12.21	Yordanka Donkova, Bulgaria	8-20-88	Stara Zagora, Bulgaria
400-meter hurdles	52.34	Yuliya Pechonkina, Russia	8-8-03	Tula
5-kilometer walk	20:02.60	Gillian O'Sullivan, Ireland	7-13-02	Dublin
10-kilometer walk	41:56.23	Nadezhda Ryashkina, URS	7-24-90	Seattle
4 x 100-meter relay	41.37	East Germany (Silke Gladisch, Sabine Reiger, Ingrid Auerswald, Marlies Göhr)	10-6-85	Canberra, Australia
4 x 200-meter relay	1:27.46	United States (LaTasha Jenkins, LaTasha Colander-Richardson, Nanceen Perry, Marion Jones)	4-29-00	Philadelphia
4 x 400-meter relay	3:15.17	USSR (Tatyana Ledovskaya, Olga Nazarova, Maria Pinigina, Olga Bryzgina)	10-1-88	Seoul
4 x 800-meter relay	7:50.17	USSR (Nadezhda Olizarenko, Lyubov Gurina, Lyudmila Borisova, Irina Podyalovskaya)	8-5-84	Moscow
High jump	6 ft 10¼ in	Stefka Kostadinova, Bulgaria	8-30-87	Rome
Pole vault	16 ft 1¾ in*	Yelena Isinbayeva, Russia	9-3-04	Brussels
Long jump	24 ft 8¼ in	Galina Chistyakova, USSR	6-11-88	Leningrad
Triple jump	50 ft 10¼ in	Inessa Kravets, Ukraine	8-10-95	Göteborg, Sweden
Shot put	74 ft 3 in	Natalya Lisovskaya, USSR	6-7-87	Moscow
Discus throw	252 ft	Gabriele Reinsch, E Germany	7-9-88	Neubrandenburg, Germany
Hammer throw	247 ft 3 in	Mihaela Melinte, Romania	8-29-99	Rüdlingen, Switzerland
Javelin throw	234 ft 8 in	Osleidys Menéndez, Cuba	7-1-01	Réthymno, Greece
Heptathlon	7291 pts	Jackie Joyner-Kersee, United States	9-23/24-88	Seoul

Note: The heptathlon consists of 7 events: the 100-meter hurdles, high jump, shot put and 200 meters on the first day; the long jump, javelin and 800 meters on the second.

*Pending ratification.

As of September 15, 2004. American outdoor records are recognized by USA Track and Field (USATF). WR=world record. EWR=equals world record.

Men

Event	Mark	Record Holder	Date	Site
100 meters	9.78 WR	Tim Montgomery	9-14-02	Paris
200 meters	19.32 WR	Michael Johnson	8-1-96	Atlanta
400 meters	43.18 WR	Michael Johnson	8-26-99	Seville
800 meters	1:42.60	Johnny Gray	8-28-85	Koblenz, Germany
1,000 meters	2:13.9	Rick Wohlhuter	7-30-74	Oslo
1,500 meters	3:29.77	Sydney Maree	8-25-85	Cologne
Mile	3:47.69	Steve Scott	7-7-82	Oslo
2,000 meters	4:52.44	Jim Spivey	9-15-87	Lausanne
3,000 meters	7:30.84	Bob Kennedy	8-8-98	Monte Carlo
Steeplechase	8:09.17	Henry Marsh	8-28-85	Koblenz, Germany
5,000 meters	12:58.21	Bob Kennedy	8-14-96	Zurich
10,000 meters	27:13.98	Mebrahtom Keflezighi	5-4-01	Palo Alto, California
20,000 meters	58:25.0	Bill Rodgers	8-9-77	Boston
Hour	20,547 meters	Bill Rodgers	8-9-77	Boston
25,000 meters	1:14:11.8	Bill Rodgers	2-21-79	Saratoga, CA
30,000 meters	1:31:49	Bill Rodgers	2-21-79	Saratoga, CA
Marathon	2:05:38	Khalid Khannouchi	4-14-02	London
110-meter hurdles	12.92	Roger Kingdom	8-16-89	Zurich
		Allen Johnson	6-23-96	Atlanta
		Allen Johnson	8-23-96	Brussels
400-meter hurdles	46.78 WR	Kevin Young	8-6-92	Barcelona
20-kilometer walk	1:23:40	Tim Seaman	8-14-00	La Jolla, CA
30-kilometer walk	2:14:31	Allen James	10-31-93	Atlanta
50-kilometer walk	3:59:41.1	Herman Nelson	6-9-96	Seattle
4x100-meter relay	37.40 WR	United States (Mike Marsh, Leroy Burrell, Dennis Mitchell, Carl Lewis)	8-8-92	Barcelona
		United States (Jon Drummond, Andre Cason, Dennis Mitchell, Leroy Burrell)	8-21-93	Stuttgart, Germany
4x200-meter relay	1:18.68 WR	Santa Monica Track Club (Mike Marsh, Leroy Burrell, Floyd Heard, Carl Lewis)	4-17-94	Walnut, CA
4x400-meter relay	2:54.20 WR	United States (Jerome Young, Antonio Pettigrew, Tyree Washington, Michael Johnson)	7-22-98	New York City
4x800-meter relay	7:06.5	Santa Monica Track Club (James Robinson, David Mack, Earl Jones, Johnny Gray)	4-26-86	Walnut, CA
4x1,500-meter relay	14:46.3	National Team (Dan Aldredge, Andy Clifford, Todd Harbour, Tom Duits)	6-24-79	Bourges, France
High jump	7 ft 10½ in	Charles Austin	8-17-91	Zurich
Pole vault	19 ft 9¼ in	Jeff Hartwig	6-14-00	Jonesboro, AR
Long jump	29 ft 4½ in WR	Mike Powell	8-30-91	Tokyo
Triple jump	59 ft 4¼ in	Kenny Harrison	7-27-96	Atlanta
Shot put	75 ft 10¼ in WR	Randy Barnes	5-20-90	Westwood, CA
Discus throw	237 ft 4 in	Ben Plucknett	7-7-81	Stockholm
Hammer throw	270 ft 9 in	Lance Deal	9-7-96	Milan
Javelin throw	286 ft 8½ in	Breaux Greer	6-11-04	Bergen, Norway
Decathlon	8891 pts	Dan O'Brien	9-4/5-92	Talence, France

Women

Event	Mark	Record Holder	Date	Site
100 meters	10.49 WR	Florence Griffith Joyner	7-16-88	Indianapolis
200 meters	21.34 WR	Florence Griffith Joyner	9-29-88	Seoul
400 meters	48.83	Valerie Brisco-Hooks	8-6-84	Los Angeles
800 meters	1:56.40	Jearl Miles-Clark	8-11-99	Zurich
1,500 meters	3:57.12	Mary Slaney	7-26-83	Stockholm
Mile	4:16.71	Mary Slaney	8-21-85	Zurich
2,000 meters	5:32.7	Mary Slaney	8-3-84	Eugene, OR
3,000 meters	8:25.83	Mary Slaney	9-7-85	Rome
Steeplechase	9:41.94	Elizabeth Jackson	9-4-01	Brisbane
5,000 meters	14:45.38	Regina Jacobs	7-21-00	Sacramento, CA
10,000 meters	30:50.32	Deena Drossin	5-3-02	Palo Alto, CA
Marathon	2:21:21	Joan Samuelson	10-20-85	Chicago
100-meter hurdles	12.33	Gail Devers	7-23-00	Sacramento, CA
400-meter hurdles	52.61 WR	Kim Batten	8-11-95	Göteborg, Sweden
5,000-meter walk	20:56.88	Michelle Rohl	4-27-96	Philadelphia
10,000-meter walk	44:41.87	Michelle Rohl	7-26-94	St. Petersburg
4 x 100-meter relay	41.47	National Team (Chryste Gaines, Marion Jones, Inger Miller, Gail Devers)	8-9-97	Athens
4 x 200-meter relay	1:27.46 WR	USA Blue (LaTasha Jenkins, LaTasha Colander, Nanceen Perry, Marion Jones)	4-29-00	Philadelphia
4 x 400-meter relay	3:15.51	United States (Denean Howard, Diane Dixon, Valerie Brisco, Florence Griffith Joyner)	10-1-88	Seoul
4 x 800-meter relay	8:17.09	Athletics West (Sue Addison, Lee Arbogast, Mary Decker, Chris Mullen)	4-24-83	Walnut, CA
High jump	6 ft 8 in	Louise Ritter	7-9-88	Austin
		Louise Ritter	9-30-88	Seoul
Pole vault	15 ft 9¼ in WR	Stacy Dragila	6-9-01	Palo Alto, CA
Long jump	24 ft 7 in	Jackie Joyner-Kersee	5-22-94	New York City
			7-31-94	Sestriere, Italy
Triple jump	47 ft 3½ in	Sheila Hudson	7-8-96	Stockholm
Shot put	66 ft 2½ in	Ramona Pagel	6-25-88	San Diego
Discus throw	227 ft 10 in	Suzy Powell	4-27-02	La Jolla, CA
Hammer throw	236 ft 3 in	Anna Norgren-Mahon	7-28-02	Walnut, CA
Javelin throw	199 ft 8 in	Kim Kreiner	8-7-03	Santo Domingo, D.R.
Heptathlon	7291 pts WR	Jackie Joyner-Kersee	9-23/24-88	Seoul

World and American Indoor Records

As of September 15, 2004. American indoor records are recognized by USA Track and Field. World Indoor records are recognized by the International Amateur Athletics Federation (IAAF).

Men

Event	Mark	Record Holder	Date	Site
50 meters	5.56	Donovan Bailey, Canada (W)	2-9-96	Reno
	5.56	Maurice Greene (A)	2-13-99	Los Angeles
55 meters*	5.99	Obadele Thompson, Barbados (W)	2-22-97	Colorado Springs
	6.00	Lee McRae (A)	3-14-86	Oklahoma City
60 meters	6.39	Maurice Greene (W, A)	3-1-98	Madrid
	6.39	Maurice Greene (W, A)	3-3-01	Atlanta
200 meters	19.92	Frankie Fredericks, Namibia (W)	2-18-96	Liévin, France
	20.26	Shawn Crawford (A)	3-11-00	Fayetteville, AR
	20.26	John Capel (A)	3-11-00	Fayetteville, AR
400 meters	44.63	Michael Johnson (W, A)	3-4-95	Atlanta
800 meters	1:42.67	Wilson Kipketer, Denmark (W)	3-9-97	Paris
	1:45.00	Johnny Gray (A)	3-8-92	Sindelfingen, Germany
1,000 meters	2:14.96	Wilson Kipketer, Denmark (W)	2-20-00	Birmingham, England
	2:17.85	David Krummenacker (A)	1-27-02	Boston

Men *(Cont.)*

Event	Mark	Record Holder	Date	Site
1,500 meters	3:31.18	Hicham El Guerrouj, Morocco (W)	2-02-97	Stuttgart, Germany
	3:38.12	Jeff Atkinson (A)	3-5-89	Budapest
Mile	3:48.45	Hicham El Guerrouj, Morocco (W)	2-12-97	Ghent, Belgium
	3:51.8	Steve Scott (A)	2-20-81	San Diego
3,000 meters	7:24.90	Daniel Komen, Kenya (W)	2-6-98	Budapest
	7:39.23	Tim Broe (A)	1-27-02	Boston
5,000 meters	12:49.60	Kenenisa Bekele, Ethiopia (W)	2-20-04	Birmingham, England
	13:20.55	Doug Padilla (A)	2-12-82	New York City
50-meter hurdles	6.25	Mark McKoy, Canada (W)	3-5-86	Kobe, Japan
	6.35	Greg Foster (A)	1-27-85	Rosemont, Illinois
55-meter hurdles*	6.89	Renaldo Nehemiah (A)	1-20-79	New York City
60-meter hurdles	7.30	Colin Jackson, Great Britain (W)	3-6-94	Sindelfingen, Germany
	7.36	Greg Foster (A)	1-16-87	Los Angeles
	7.36	Allen Johnson (A)	3-6-04	Budapest
5,000-meter walk	18:07.08	Mikhail Shchennikov, Russia (W)	2-14-95	Moscow
	19:18.40	Tim Lewis (A)	3-7-87	Indianapolis
4 x 200-meter relay	1:22.11	Great Britain (W) (Linford Christie, Darren Braithwaite, Ade Mafe, John Regis)	3-3-91	Glasgow
	1:22.71	National Team (A) (Thomas Jefferson, Raymond Pierre, Antonio McKay Kevin Little)	3-3-91	Glasgow
4 x 400-meter relay	3:02.83	United States (W, A) (Andre Morris, Dameon Johnson, Deon Minor, Milt Campbell)	3-7-99	Maebashi, Japan
4 x 800-meter relay	7:13.94	Global Athletics & Marketing (W, A) (Rich Kenah, Joel Woody, Karl Paranya, David Krummenacker)	2-6-00	Boston
High jump	7 ft 11½ in	Javier Sotomayor, Cuba (W)	3-4-89	Budapest
	7 ft 10½ in	Hollis Conway (A)	3-10-91	Seville
Pole vault	20 ft 2 in	Sergei Bubka, Ukraine (W)	2-21-93	Donetsk, Ukraine
	19 ft 9½ in	Jeff Hartwig (A)	3-10-02	Sindelfingen, Germany
Long jump	28 ft 10¼ in	Carl Lewis (W, A)	1-27-84	New York City
Triple jump	58 ft 6 in	Alicier Urrutia, Cuba (W)	3-1-97	Sindelfingen, Germany
	58 ft 6 in	Christian Olsson, Sweden (W)	3-7-04	Budapest
	58 ft 3¼ in	Mike Conley (A)	2-27-87	New York City
Shot put	74 ft 4¼ in	Randy Barnes (W, A)	1-20-89	Los Angeles
Weight throw*	84 ft 10¼ in	Lance Deal (W, A)	3-4-95	Atlanta
Pentathlon*	4478 pts	Steve Fritz, (W, A)	1-14-95	Lawrence, KS
Heptathlon	6476 pts	Dan O'Brien (W, A)	3-13/14-93	Toronto

*No recognized world record.

†Pending ratification.

THEY SAID IT

Sir Ranulph Fiennes, 59-year-old cousin of actors Joseph and Ralph Fiennes, whose 2003 New York City Marathon was his seventh marathon in seven days on six continents: "This has been enjoyable throughout except for the bits of running."

Women

Event	Mark	Record Holder	Date	Site
50 meters	5.96	Irina Privolova, Russia (W)	2-9-95	Madrid
	6.02	Gail Devers (A)	2-21-99	Liévin, France
55 meters*	6.54	Evelyn Ashford (A)	2-26-82	New York
		Jeanette Bolden (A)	2-21-86	Inglewood, CA
60 meters	6.92	Irina Privalova, Russia (W)	2-11-93	Madrid
	6.92	Irina Privalova, Russia (W)	2-9-95	Madrid
	6.95	Gail Devers (A)	3-12-93	Toronto
	6.95	Marion Jones (A)	3-7-98	Maebashi, Japan
200 meters	21.87	Merlene Ottey, Jamaica (W)	2-13-93	Liévin, France
	22.18	Michell Collins (A)	3-15-03	Birmingham, England
400 meters	49.59	Jarmila Kratochvilová, Czech. (W)	3-7-82	Milan
	50.64	Diane Dixon (A)	3-10-91	Seville
800 meters	1:55.82	Jolanda Ceplak, Slovenia (W)	3-3-02	Vienna
	1:58.71	Nicole Teter (A)	3-2-02	New York
1,000 meters	2:30.94	Maria Mutola, Mozambique (W)	2-25-99	Stockholm
	2:34.19	Jennifer Toomey (A)	2-20-04	Birmingham, England
1,500 meters	3:59.98	Regina Jacobs, United States (W, A)	2-1-03	Boston
Mile	4:17.14	Doina Melinte, Romania (W)	2-9-90	East Rutherford, NJ
	4:20.5	Mary Slaney (A)	2-19-82	San Diego
3,000 meters	8:29.15	Berhane Adere, Ethiopia	2-3-02	Stuttgart
	8:39.14	Regina Jacobs (A)	3-7-99	Maebashi, Japan
5,000 meters	14:39.29	Berhane Adere, Ethiopia (W)	1-31-04	Stuttgart
	15:07.33	Marla Runyan (A)	2-18-01	New York
50-meter hurdles	6.58	Cornelia Oschkenat, E Germany (W)	2-20-88	Berlin
	6.67	Jackie Joyner-Kersee (A)	2-10-95	Reno
55-meter hurdles*	7.30	Tiffany Lott (A)	2-20-97	Air Force Academy, CO
60-meter hurdles	7.69	Lyudmila Narozhilenko, Russia (W)	2-4-90	Chelyabinsk, Russia
	7.74	Gail Devers (A)	3-1-03	Boston
3,000-meter walk	11:40.33	Claudia Stef, Romania	1-30-99	Bucharest
	12:20.79	Debbi Lawrence (A)	3-12-93	Toronto
4 x 200-meter relay	1:32.55	SC Eintracht Hamm, W Gemany (W)	2-20-88	Dortmund, W Germany
	1:32.55	LG Olympia Dortmund, Germany (W)	2-21-99	Karlsruhe
	1:33.24	National Team (A)	2-12-94	Glasgow
		(Flirtisha Harris, Chryste Gaines, Terri Dendy, Michele Collins)		
4 x 400-meter relay	3:23.88	Russia (W)	3-7-04	Budapest
	3:27.59	National Team (A) (Michelle Collins, Monique Hennagan, Zundra Feagin-Alexander, Shanelle Porter)	3-7-99	Maebashi, Japan
4 x 800-meter relay	8:18.71	Russia (W) (Natalya Zaytseva, Olga Kuvnetsova, Yelena Afanasyeva, Yekaterina Podkopayeva)	2-4-94	Moscow
	8:25.50	Villanova (A) (Gina Procaccio, Debbie Grant, Michelle DiMuro, Celeste Halliday)	2-7-87	Gainesville, FL
High jump	6 ft 9½ in	Heike Henkel, Germany (W)	2-8-92	Karlsruhe, Germany
	6 ft 7 in	Tisha Waller (A)	2-28-98	Atlanta
Pole vault	15 ft 11¼ in	Yelena Isinbayeva, Russia (W)	3-6-04	Budapest
	15 ft 9 ½ in	Stacy Dragila (A)	3-6-04	Budapest
Long jump	24 ft 2¼ in	Heike Drechsler, E Germany (W)	2-13-88	Vienna
	23 ft 4¾ in	Jackie Joyner-Kersee (A)	3-5-94	Atlanta
Triple jump	50 ft 4¾ in	Tatyana Lebedeva, Russia (W)	3-6-04	Budapest
	46 ft 8¼ in	Sheila Hudson-Strudwick (A)	3-4-95	Atlanta
Shot put	73 ft 10 in	Helena Fibingerová, Czech. (W)	2-19-77	Jablonec, Czech.
	65 ft ¾ in	Ramona Pagel (A)	2-20-87	Inglewood, CA
Weight throw*	78 ft 7 in	Erin Gilreath (A)	1-25-04	Gainesville, FL
Pentathlon	4991 pts	Irina Byelova, CIS (W)	2-14/15-92	Berlin
	4753	Le Shundra Nathan (A)	3-4/5-99	Maebashi, Japan

*No recognized world record.
†Pending ratification.

Men

100 METERS

1983	Carl Lewis, United States	10.07
1987*	Carl Lewis, United States	9.93 WR
1991	Carl Lewis, United States	9.86 WR
1993	Linford Christie, Great Britain	9.87
1995	Donovan Bailey, Canada	9.97
1997	Maurice Greene, United States	9.86
1999	Maurice Greene, United States	9.80
2001	Maurice Greene, United States	9.82
2003	Kim Collins, St. Kitts & Nevis	10.07

200 METERS

1983	Calvin Smith, United States	20.14
1987	Calvin Smith, United States	20.16
1991	Michael Johnson, United States	20.01
1993	Frank Fredericks, Namibia	19.85
1995	Michael Johnson, United States	19.79
1997	Ato Boldon, Trinidad and Tobago	20.04
1999	Maurice Greene, United States	19.90
2001	Konstadínos Kedéris, Greece	20.04
2003	John Capel, United States	20.30

400 METERS

1983	Bert Cameron, Jamaica	45.05
1987	Thomas Schoenlebe, E Germany	44.33
1991	Antonio Pettigrew, United States	44.57
1993	Michael Johnson, United States	43.65
1995	Michael Johnson, United States	43.39
1997	Michael Johnson, United States	44.12
1999	Michael Johnson, United States	43.18 WR
2001	Avard Moncur, Bahamas	44.64
2003	Jerome Young, United States	44.50

800 METERS

1983	Willi Wulbeck, W Germany	1:43.65
1987	Billy Konchellah, Kenya	1:43.06
1991	Billy Konchellah, Kenya	1:43.99
1993	Paul Ruto, Kenya	1:44.71
1995	Wilson Kipketer, Denmark	1:45.08
1997	Wilson Kipketer, Denmark	1:43.38
1999	Wilson Kipketer, Denmark	1:43.30
2001	André Bucher, Switzerland	1:43.70
2003	Djabir Saïd-Guerni, Algeria	1:44.81

1,500 METERS

1983	Steve Cram, Great Britain	3:41.59
1987	Abdi Bile, Somalia	3:36.80
1991	Noureddine Morceli, Algeria	3:32.84
1993	Noureddine Morceli, Algeria	3:34.24
1995	Noureddine Morceli, Algeria	3:33.73
1997	Hicham El Guerrouj, Morocco	3:35.83
1999	Hicham El Guerrouj, Morocco	3:27.65
2001	Hicham El Guerrouj, Morocco	3:30.68
2003	Hicham El Guerrouj, Morocco	3:31.77

STEEPLECHASE

1983	Patriz Ilg, W Germany	8:15.06
1987	Francesco Panetta, Italy	8:08.57
1991	Moses Kiptanui, Kenya	8:12.59
1993	Moses Kiptanui, Kenya	8:06.36
1995	Moses Kiptanui, Kenya	8:04.16
1997	Wilson Boit Kipketer, Kenya	8:05.84
1999	Christopher Koskei, Kenya	8:11.76
2001	Reuben Kosgei, Kenya	8:15.16
2003	Saif Saaeed Shaheen, Qatar	8:04.39

5,000 METERS

1983	Eamonn Coghlan, Ireland	13:28.53
1987	Said Aouita, Morocco	13:26.44
1991	Yobes Ondieki, Kenya	13:14.45
1993	Ismael Kirui, Kenya	13:02.75
1995	Ismael Kirui, Kenya	13:16.77

WR=World record. *Ben Johnson, Canada, disqualified.

5,000 METERS *(CONT.)*

1997	Daniel Komen, Kenya	13:07.38
1999	Salah Hissou, Morocco	12:58.13
2001	Richard Limo, Kenya	13:00.77
2003	Eliud Kipchoge, Kenya	12:52.79

10,000 METERS

1983	Alberto Cova, Italy	28:01.04
1987	Paul Kipkoech, Kenya	27:38.63
1991	Moses Tanui, Kenya	27:38.74
1993	Haile Gebrselassie, Ethiopia	27:46.02
1995	Haile Gebrselassie, Ethiopia	27:12.95
1997	Haile Gebrselassie, Ethiopia	27:24.58
1999	Haile Gebrselassie, Ethiopia	27:57.27
2001	Charles Kamathi, Kenya	27:53.25
2003	Kenenisa Bekele, Ethiopia	26:49.57

MARATHON

1983	Rob de Castella, Australia	2:10:03
1987	Douglas Wakiihuri, Kenya	2:11:48
1991	Hiromi Taniguchi, Japan	2:14:57
1993	Mark Plaatjes, United States	2:13:57
1995	Martín Fiz, Spain	2:11:41
1997	Abel Anton, Spain	2:13:16
1999	Abel Anton, Spain	2:13:36
2001	Gezahegne Abera, Ethiopia	2:12:42
2003	Jaouad Gharib, Morocco	2:08:31

110-METER HURDLES

1983	Greg Foster, United States	13.42
1987	Greg Foster, United States	13.21
1991	Greg Foster, United States	13.06
1993	Colin Jackson, Great Britain	12.91 WR
1995	Allen Johnson, United States	13.00
1997	Allen Johnson, United States	12.93
1999	Colin Jackson, Great Britain	13.04
2001	Allen Johnson, United States	13.04
2003	Allen Johnson, United States	13.12

400-METER HURDLES

1983	Edwin Moses, United States	47.50
1987	Edwin Moses, United States	47.46
1991	Samuel Matete, Zambia	47.64
1993	Kevin Young, United States	47.18
1995	Derrick Adkins, United States	47.98
1997	Stéphane Diagana, France	47.70
1999	Fabrizio Mori, Italy	47.72
2001	Felix Sánchez, Dominican Rep.	47.49
2003	Felix Sánchez, Dominican Rep.	47.25

20-KILOMETER WALK

1983	Ernesto Canto, Mexico	1:20:49
1987	Maurizio Damilano, Italy	1:20:45
1991	Maurizio Damilano, Italy	1:19:37
1993	Valentin Massana, Spain	1:22:31
1995	Michele Didoni, Italy	1:19:59
1997	Daniel Garcia, Mexico	1:21:43
1999	Ilya Markov, Russia	1:23:34
2001	Roman Rasskazov, Russia	1:20:31
2003	Jefferson Pérez, Ecuador	1:17.21 WR

50-KILOMETER WALK

1983	Ronald Weigel, E Germany	3:43:08
1987	Hartwig Gauder, E Germany	3:40:53
1991	Aleksandr Potashov, USSR	3:53:09
1993	Jesus Angel Garcia, Spain	3:41:41
1995	Valentin Kononen, Finland	3:43:42
1997	Robert Korzeniowski, Poland	3:44:46
1999	German Skurygin, Russia	3:44:23
2001	Robert Korzeniowski, Poland	3:42:08
2003	R. Korzeniowski, Poland	3:36:03 WR

Men *(Cont.)*

4 X 100-METER RELAY

1983	United States (Emmit King, Willie Gault, Calvin Smith, Carl Lewis)	37.86
1987	United States (Lee McRae, Lee McNeil, Harvey Glance, Carl Lewis)	37.90
1991	United States (A. Cason L. Burrell, D. Mitchell, C. Lewis)	37.50 WR
1993	United States (J. Drummond, A. Cason, D. Mitchell, L. Burrell)	37.48
1995	Canada (Robert Esmie, Glenroy Gilbert, Bruny Surin, Donovan Bailey)	38.31
1997	Canada (Robert Esmie, Glenroy Gilbert, Bruny Surin, Donovan Bailey)	37.86
1999	United States (Jon Drummond, Tim Montgomery, Brian Lewis, Maurice Greene)	37.59
2001	United States (Mickey Grimes, Bernard Williams, Dennis Mitchell, Tim Montgomery)	37.96
2003	United States (J. Capel, B. Williams D. Patton, J. Johnson)	38.06

4 X 400-METER RELAY

1983	USSR (S. Lovachev, A. Troschilo, N. Chernyetski, V. Markin)	3:00.79
1987	United States (Danny Everett Rod Haley, Antonio McKay, Butch Reynolds)	2:57.29
1991	Great Britain (Roger Black Derek Redmond, John Regis, Kriss Akabusi)	2:57.53
1993	United States (Andrew Valmon, Quincy Watts, Butch Reynolds, Michael Johnson)	2:54.29 WR
1995	United States (Marlon Ramsey, Derek Mills, Butch Reynolds, Michael Johnson)	2:57.32
1997	United States (J. Young, A. Pettigrew, C. Jones, T. Washington)	2:56.47
1999	United States (Jerome Davis, Antonio Pettigrew, Angelo Taylor, Michael Johnson)	2:56.45
2001	United States (L. Byrd, A. Pettigrew, D. Brew, A. Taylor)	2:57.54
2003	United States (C. Harrison, T. Washington, D. Brew, J. Young)	2:58.88

HIGH JUMP

1983	Gennadi Avdeyenko, USSR	7 ft 7¼ in
1987	Patrik Sjoberg, Sweden	7 ft 9¾ in
1991	Charles Austin, United States	7 ft 9¾ in
1993	Javier Sotomayor, Cuba	7 ft 10½ in
1995	Troy Kemp, Bahamas	7 ft 9¼ in
1997	Javier Sotomayor, Cuba	7 ft 9¼ in
1999	Vyacheslav Voronin, Russia	7 ft 9¼ in
2001	Martin Buss, Germany	7 ft 8¾ in
2003	Jacques Freitag, S Africa	7 ft 8½ in

POLE VAULT

1983	Sergei Bubka, USSR	18 ft 8¼ in
1987	Sergei Bubka, USSR	19 ft 2¼ in
1991	Sergei Bubka, USSR	19 ft 6¼ in
1993	Sergei Bubka, Ukraine	19 ft 8¼ in
1995	Sergei Bubka, Ukraine	19 ft 5 in
1997	Sergei Bubka, Ukraine	19 ft 8½ in
1999	Maksim Tarasov, Russia	19 ft 9 in
2001	Dmitri Markov, Australia	19 ft 10¼ in
2003	Guiseppe Gibilisco, Italy	19 ft 4¼ in

LONG JUMP

1983	Carl Lewis, United States	28 ft ¾ in
1987	Carl Lewis, United States	28 ft 5¼ in
1991	Mike Powell, U.S.	29 ft 4½ in WR

LONG JUMP *(CONT.)*

1993	Mike Powell, United States	28 ft 2¼ in
1995	Iván Pedroso, Cuba	28 ft 6½ in
1997	Iván Pedroso, Cuba	27 ft 7½ in
1999	Iván Pedroso, Cuba	28 ft 1 in
2001	Iván Pedroso, Cuba	27 ft 6¾ in
2003	Dwight Phillips, United States	27 ft 3½ in

TRIPLE JUMP

1983	Zdzislaw Hoffmann, Poland	57 ft 2 in
1987	Khristo Markov, Bulgaria	58 ft 9½ in
1991	Kenny Harrison, United States	58 ft 4 in
1993	Mike Conley, United States	58 ft 7¼ in
1995	Jonathan Edwards, G.B.	60 ft ¼ in WR
1997	Yoelvis Quesada, Cuba	58 ft 6¾ in
1999	Charle Michael Friedek, Ger.	57 ft 8½ in
2001	Jonathan Edwards, G. Britain	58 ft 9½ in
2003	Christian Olsson, Sweden	58 ft 1¾ in

SHOT PUT

1983	Edward Sarul, Poland	70 ft 2¼ in
1987	Werner Günthör, Switz.	72 ft 11¼ in
1991	Werner Günthör, Switz.	71 ft 1¼ in
1993	Werner Günthör, Switz.	72 ft 1 in
1995	John Godina, United States	70 ft 5¼ in
1997	John Godina, United States	70 ft 4¼ in
1999	C.J. Hunter, United States	71 ft 6 in
2001	John Godina, United States	71 ft 9 in
2003	Andrei Mikahnevic, Bulgaria	71 ft 2 in

DISCUS THROW

1983	Imrich Bugar, Czechoslovakia	222 ft 2 in
1987	Juergen Schult, E Germany	225 ft 6 in
1991	Lars Riedel, Germany	217 ft 2 in
1993	Lars Riedel, Germany	222 ft 2 in
1995	Lars Riedel, Germany	225 ft 7 in
1997	Lars Riedel, Germany	224 ft 10 in
1999	Anthony Washington, U.S.	226 ft 8 in
2001	Lars Riedel, Germany	228 ft 9 in
2003	Virgilijus Alekna, Lithuania	228 ft 7¾ in

HAMMER THROW

1983	Sergei Litvinov, USSR	271 ft 3 in
1987	Sergei Litvinov, USSR	272 ft 6 in
1991	Yuriy Sedykh, USSR	268 ft
1993	Andrey Abduvaliyev, Tajikistan	267 ft 10 in
1995	Andrey Abduvaliyev, Tajikistan	267 ft 7 in
1997	Heinz Weis, Germany	268 ft 4 in
1999	Karsten Kobs, Germany	263 ft 3 in
2001	Szymon Kiólkowski, Poland	273 ft 7 in
2003	Ivan Tikhon, Bulgaria	272 ft 5¾ in

JAVELIN

1983	Detlef Michel, E Germany	293 ft 7 in
1987	Seppo Räty, Finland	274 ft 1 in
1991	Kimmo Kinnunen, Finland	297 ft 11 in
1993	Jan Zelezny, Czech Republic	282 ft 1 in
1995	Jan Zelezny, Czech Republic	293 ft 11 in
1997	Marius Corbett, S Africa	290 ft 0 in
1999	Aki Parviainen, Finland	293 ft 8 in
2001	Jan Zelezny, Czech Republic	304 ft 5 in
2003	Sergey Makarov, Russia	280 ft 3¾ in

DECATHLON

1983	Daley Thompson, G. Britain	8666 pts
1987	Torsten Voss, E Germany	8680 pts
1991	Dan O'Brien, United States	8812 pts
1993	Dan O'Brien, United States	8817 pts
1995	Dan O'Brien, United States	8695 pts
1997	Tomás Dvorák, Czech Rep.	8837 pts
1999	Tomás Dvorák, Czech Rep.	8744 pts
2001	Tomás Dvorák, Czech Rep.	8902 pts
2003	Tom Pappas, United States	8750 pts

WR=World record.

Women

100 METERS

1983	Marlies Gohr, E Germany	10.97
1987	Silke Gladisch, E Germany	10.90
1991	Katrin Krabbe, Germany	10.99
1993	Gail Devers, United States	10.82
1995	Gwen Torrence, United States	10.85
1997	Marion Jones, United States	10.83
1999	Marion Jones, United States	10.70
2001	Zhanna Pintusevich-Block, Ukraine	10.82
2003	Kelli White, United States	10.85

200 METERS

1983	Marita Koch, E Germany	22.13
1987	Silke Gladisch, E Germany	21.74
1991	Katrin Krabbe, Germany	22.09
1993	Merlene Ottey, Jamaica	21.98
1995	Merlene Ottey, Jamaica	22.12
1997	Zhanna Pintusevich, Ukraine	22.32
1999	Inger Miller, United States	21.77
2001	Marion Jones, United States	22.39
2003	Kelli White, United States	22.05

400 METERS

1983	Jarmila Kratochvilova, Czech.	47.99
1987	Olga Bryzgina, USSR	49.38
1991	Marie-José Pérec, France	49.13
1993	Jearl Miles, United States	49.82
1995	Marie-José Pérec, France	49.28
1997	Cathy Freeman, Australia	49.77
1999	Cathy Freeman, Australia	49.67
2001	Amy Mbacke Thiam, Senegal	49.86
2003	Ana Guevara, Mexico	48.89

800 METERS

1983	Jarmila Kratochvilova, Czech.	1:54.68
1987	Sigrun Wodars, E Germany	1:55.26
1991	Lilia Nurutdinova, USSR	1:57.50
1993	Maria Mutola, Mozambique	1:55.43
1995	Ana Quirot, Cuba	1:56.11
1997	Ana Quirot, Cuba	1:57.14
1999	Ludmila Formanová, Czech Rep.	1:56.68
2001	Maria Mutola, Mozambique	1:57.17
2003	Maria Mutola, Mozambique	1:59.89

1,500 METERS

1983	Mary Slaney, United States	4:00.90
1987	Tatyana Samolenko, USSR	3:58.56
1991	Hassiba Boulmerka, Algeria	4:02.21
1993	Dong Liu, China	4:00.50
1995	Hassiba Boulmerka, Algeria	4:02.42
1997	Carla Sacramento, Portugal	4:04.24
1999	Svetlana Masterkova, Russia	3:59.53
2001	Gabriela Szabo, Romania	4:00.57
2003	Tatyana Tomashova, Russia	3:58.52

3,000 METERS

1983	Mary Slaney, United States	8:34.62
1987	Tatyana Samolenko, USSR	8:38.73
1991	Tatyana Dorovskikh, USSR	8:35.82
1993	Qu Yunxia, China	8:28.71

5,000 METERS

1995	Sonia O'Sullivan, Ireland	14:46.47
1997	Gabriela Szabo, Romania	14:57.68
1999	Gabriela Szabo, Romania	14:41.82
2001	Olga Yegorova, Russia	15:03.39
2003	Tirunesh Dibaba, Ethiopia	14:51.72

10,000 METERS

1987	Ingrid Kristiansen, Norway	31:05.85
1991	Liz McColgan, Great Britain	31:14.31
1993	Wang Junxia, China	30:49:30
1995	Fernanda Ribeiro, Portugal	31:04.99
1997	Sally Barsosio, Kenya	31:32.92
1999	Gete Wami, Ethiopia	30:24.56
2001	Derartu Tulu, Ethiopia	31:48.81
2003	Berhane Adere, Ethiopia	30:04.18

*400 meters short.

MARATHON

1983	Grete Waitz, Norway	2:28:09
1987	Rosa Mota, Portugal	2:25:17
1991	Wanda Panfil, Poland	2:29:53
1993	Junko Asari, Japan	2:30:03
1995	Manuela Machado, Portugal	2:25:39*
1997	Hiromi Suzuki, Japan	2:29:48
1999	Jong Song-Ok, N Korea	2:26:59
2001	Lidia Simon, Romania	2:26.01
2003	Catherine Ndereba, Kenya	2:23:55

100-METER HURDLES

1983	Bettine Jahn, E Germany	12.35
1987	Ginka Zagorcheva, Bulgaria	12.34
1991	Lyudmila Narozhilenko, USSR	12.59
1993	Gail Devers, United States	12.46
1995	Gail Devers, United States	12.68
1997	Ludmila Engquist, Sweden	12.50
1999	Gail Devers, United States	12.37
2001	Anjanette Kirkland, United States	12.42
2003	Perdita Felicien, Canada	12.53

400-METER HURDLES

1983	Yekaterina Fesenko, USSR	54.14
1987	Sabine Busch, E Germany	53.62
1991	Tatyana Ledovskaya, USSR	53.11
1993	Sally Gunnell, Great Britain	52.74 WR
1995	Kim Batten, United States	52.61
1997	Nezha Bidouane, Morocco	52.97
1999	Daimi Pernia, Cuba	52.89
2001	Nezha Bidouane, Morocco	53.34
2003	Jana Pittman, Australia	53.22

10-KILOMETER WALK

1987	Irina Strakhova, USSR	44:12
1991	Alina Ivanova, USSR	42:57
1993	Sari Essayah, Finland	42:59
1995	Irina Stankina, Russia	42:13
1997	Annarita Sidoti, Italy	42:56

20-KILOMETER WALK

1999	Hongyu Liu, China	1:30:50
2001	Olimpiada Ivanova, Russia	1:27:48
2003	Yelena Nikolayeva, Russia	1:26:52

4 X 100-METER RELAY

1983	E Germany (S. Gladisch, M. Koch, I. Auerswald, M. Gohr)	41.76
1987	United States (A. Brown, D. Williams, F. Griffith, P. Marshall)	41.58
1991	Jamaica (Dalia Duhaney, Juliet Cuthbert, Beverley McDonald, Merlene Ottey)	41.94
1993	Russia (Olga Bogoslovskaya, Galina Malchugina, Natalya Voronova, Irina Privalova)	41.49
1995	United States (Celena Mondie-Milner, Carlette Guidry, Chryste Gaines, Gwen Torrence)	42.12
1997	United States (C. Gaines, M. Jones, I. Miller, G.Devers)	41.47
1999	Bahamas (S. Fynes, C. Sturrup, P. Davis-Thompson, D. Ferguson)	41.92
2001	United States (Kelli White, Chryste Gaines, Inger Miller, Marion Jones)	41.71
2003	France (P. Girard, M. Hurtis, S. Félix, C. Arron)	41.78

4 X 400-METER RELAY

1983	E Germany (Kerstin Walther, Sabine Busch, Marita Koch, Dagmar Rubsam)	3:19.73

Women *(Cont.)*

4 X 400-METER RELAY *(CONT.)*

1987	E Germany (Dagmar Neubauer, Kirsten Emmelmann, Petra Müller, Sabine Busch)	3:18.63
1991	USSR (Tatyana Ledovskaya, Lyudmila Dzhigalova, Olga Nazarova, Olga Bryzgina)	3:18.43
1993	United States (Gwen Torrence, Maicel Malone, Natasha Kaiser-Brown, Jearl Miles)	3:16.71
1995	United States (Kim Graham, Rochelle Stevens, Camara Jones, Jearl Miles)	3:22.39
1997	Germany (A. Feller, U. Rohlander, A. Rucker, G. Breuer)	3:20.92
1999	Russia (Tatyana Chebykina, Svetlana Goncharenko, Olga Kotylarova, Natalya Nazarova)	3:21.98
2001	Jamaica (Sandie Richards, Catherine Scott, Debbie Ann Parris, Lorraine Fenton)	3:20.65
2003	United States (M. Barber, D. Washington, J. Miles-Clark, S. Richards)	3:22.63

HIGH JUMP

1983	Tamara Bykova, USSR	6 ft 7 in
1987	Stefka Kostadinova, Bulgaria	6 ft 10¼ in
1991	Heike Henkel, Germany	6 ft 8¾ in
1993	Ioamnet Quintero, Cuba	6 ft 6¼ in
1995	Stefka Kostadinova, Bulgaria	6 ft 7 in
1997	Hanne Haugland, Norway	6 ft 6¼ in
1999	Inga Babakova, Ukraine	6 ft 6¼ in
2001	Hestrie Cloete, S Africa	6 ft 6¾ in
2003	Hestrie Cloete, S Africa	6 ft 9 in

POLE VAULT

1999	Stacy Dragila, U.S.	15 ft 1 in EWR
2001	Stacy Dragila, United States	15 ft 7 in
2003	Svetlana Feofanova, Russia	15 ft 7 in

LONG JUMP

1983	Heike Daute, E Germany	23 ft 10¼ in
1987	Jackie Joyner-Kersee, U.S.	24 ft 1¾ in
1991	Jackie Joyner-Kersee, U.S.	24 ft ¼ in
1993	Heike Drechsler, Germany	23 ft 4 in
1995	Fiona May, Italy	22 ft 10¾ in
1997	Lyudmila Galkina, Russia	23 ft 1¾ in
1999	Niurka Montalvo, Spain	23 ft 2 in
2001	Fiona May, Italy	23 ft ½ in
2003	Eunice Barber, France	22 ft 11 in

WR=World record. EWR=equals world record.

TRIPLE JUMP

1993	Ana Biryukova, Russia	49 ft 6 ¼ in WR
1995	Inessa Kravets, Ukraine	50 ft 10¼ in WR

TRIPLE JUMP *(CONT.)*

1997	S. Kasparkova, Czech Rep.	49 ft 10½ in
1999	Paraskevi Tsiamíta, Greece	48 ft 10 in
2001	Tatyana Lebedeva, Russia	50 ft ½ in
2003	Tatyana Lebedeva, Russia	49 ft 9½ in

SHOT PUT

1983	Helena Fibingerova, Czech.	69 ft ¾ in
1987	Natalya Lisovskaya, USSR	69 ft 8¼ in
1991	Zhihong Huang, China	68 ft 4¼ in
1993	Zhihong Huang, China	67 ft 6 in
1995	Astrid Kumbernuss, Germany	69 ft 7½ in
1997	Astrid Kumbernuss, Germany	67 ft 11½ in
1999	Astrid Kumbernuss, Germany	65 ft 1½ in
2001	Yanina Korolchik, Belarus	67 ft 7½ in
2003	Svetlana Krivelyova, Russia	67 ft 8 in

HAMMER THROW

1999	Mihaela Melinte, Romania	246 ft 9 in
2001	Yipsi Moreno, Cuba	231 ft 9 in
2003	Yipsi Moreno, Cuba	240 ft 7 in

DISCUS THROW

1983	Martina Opitz, E Germany	226 ft 2 in
1987	Martina Hellmann, E Germany	235 ft
1991	Tsvetanka Khristova, Bulgaria	233 ft
1993	Olga Burova, Russia	221 ft 1 in
1995	Ellina Zvereva, Belarus	225 ft 2 in
1997	Beatrice Faumuina, New Zeal.	219 ft 3 in
1999	Franka Dietzsch, Germany	223 ft 7 in
2001	Natalya Sadova, Russia	224 ft 11 in
2003	Irina Yatchenko, Bulgaria	220 ft 10½ in

JAVELIN

1983	Tiina Lillak, Finland	232 ft 4 in
1987	Fatima Whitbread, G.B.	251 ft 5 in
1991	Demei Xu, China	225 ft 8 in
1993	Trine Hattestad, Finland	227 ft
1995	Natalya Shikolenko, Belarus	221 ft 8 in
1997	Trine Hattestad, Norway	225 ft 8 in
1999	Miréla Manjani-Tzelili, Greece	220 ft 1 in
2001	Osleidys Menéndez, Cuba	228 ft 1 in
2003	Miréla Manjani, Greece	218 ft 3 in

HEPTATHLON

1983	Ramona Neubert, E Germany	6714 pts
1987	Jackie Joyner-Kersee, U.S.	7128 pts
1991	Sabine Braun, Germany	6672 pts
1993	Jackie Joyner-Kersee, U.S.	6837 pts
1995	Ghada Shouaa, Syria	6651 pts
1997	Sabine Braun, Germany	6739 pts
1999	Eunice Barber, France	6861 pts
2001	Yelena Prokhorova, Russia	6694 pts
2003	Carolina Klüft, Sweden	7001 pts

Track and Field News Athlete of the Year

Each year (since 1959 for men and since 1974 for women) *Track and Field News* has chosen the outstanding athlete in the sport.

Year	Athlete	Event	Year	Athlete	Event
1959	Martin Lauer, W Germany	110H/Decath	1973	Ben Jipcho, Kenya	1,500/5K/ST
1960	Rafer Johnson, United States	Decathlon	1974	Rick Wohlhuter, United States	800/1,500
1961	Ralph Boston, United States	Long jump	1975	John Walker, New Zealand	800/1,500
1962	Peter Snell, New Zealand	800/1,500	1976	Alberto Juantorena, Cuba	400/800
1963	C. K. Yang, Taiwan	Decath/PV	1977	Alberto Juantorena, Cuba	400/800
1964	Peter Snell, New Zealand	800/1,500	1978	Henry Rono, Kenya	5K/10K/ST
1965	Ron Clarke, Australia	5K/10K	1979	Sebastian Coe, Great Britain	800/1,500
1966	Jim Ryun, United States	800/1,500	1980	Edwin Moses, United States	400H
1967	Jim Ryun, United States	1,500	1981	Sebastian Coe, Great Britain	800/1,500
1968	Bob Beamon, United States	Long jump	1982	Carl Lewis, United States	100/200/LJ
1969	Bill Toomey, United States	Decathlon	1983	Carl Lewis, United States	100/200/LJ
1970	Randy Matson, United States	Shot put	1984	Carl Lewis, United States	100/200/LJ
1971	Rod Milburn, United States	110H	1985	Said Aouita, Morocco	1,500/5000
1972	Lasse Viren, Finland	5K/10K	1986	Yuri Syedikh, USSR	Hammer

Track and Field News Athlete of the Year (Cont.)

MEN (CONT.)

Year	Athlete	Event
1987	Ben Johnson, Canada	100
1988	Sergei Bubka, USSR	Pole vault
1989	Roger Kingdom, United States	110H
1990	Michael Johnson, United States	200/400
1991	Sergei Bubka, CIS	Pole vault
1992	Kevin Young, United States	400H
1993	Noureddine Morceli, Algeria	1,500/mile/3K
1994	Noureddine Morceli, Algeria	1,500/mile/3K
1995	Haile Gebrselassie, Ethiopia	5K/10K
1996	Michael Johnson, United States	200/400
1997	Wilson Kipketer, Denmark	800
1998	Haile Gebrselassie, Ethiopia	5K/10K
1999	Hicham El Guerrouj, Morocco	1,500/Mile
2000	Virgilijus Alekna, Lithuania	Discus
2001	Hicham El Guerrouj, Morocco	1,500/Mile
2002	Hicham El Guerrouj, Morocco	1,500/Mile
2003	Felix Sanchez, Dominican Rep.	400H

WOMEN

Year	Athlete	Event
1974	Irena Szewinska, Poland	100/200/400
1975	Faina Melnik, USSR	Shot/Discus
1976	Tatyana Kazankina, USSR	800/1,500
1977	R. Ackermann, E Germany	High jump
1978	Marita Koch, E Germany	100/200/400
1979	Marita Koch, E Germany	100/200/400

WOMEN (CONT.)

Year	Athlete	Event
1980	Ilona Briesenick, E Germany	Shot put
1981	Evelyn Ashford, United States	100/200
1982	Marita Koch, E Germany	100/200/400
1983	J. Kratochvilova, Czechoslovakia	200/400/800
1984	Evelyn Ashford, United States	100
1985	Marita Koch, E Germany	100/200/400
1986	Jackie Joyner-Kersee, U.S.	LJ/Hept
1987	Jackie Joyner-Kersee, U.S	100H/LJ/Hept
1988	Florence Griffith Joyner, U.S.	100/200
1989	Ana Quirot, Cuba	400/800
1990	Merlene Ottey, Jamaica	100/200
1991	Heike Henkel, Germany	High jump
1992	Heike Drechsler, Germany	Long Jump
1993	Wang Junxia, China	1.5K/3K/10K
1994	Jackie Joyner-Kersee, U.S.	100H/LJ/Hept
1995	Sonia O'Sullivan, Ireland	1,500/3K/5K
1996	Svetlana Masterkova, Russia	800/1,500
1997	Marion Jones, United States	100/200/LJ
1998	Marion Jones, United States	100/200/LJ
1999	Gabriela Szabo, Romania	1,500/5,000
2000	Marion Jones, United States	100/200/LJ
2001	Stacy Dragila, United States	Pole vault
2002	Paula Radcliffe, Great Britain	Marathon
2003	Maria Mutola, Mozambique	800

Marathon World Record Progression

Men

Record Holder	Time	Date	Site
John Hayes, United States	2:55:18.4	7-24-08	Shepherd's Bush, London
Robert Fowler, United States	2:52:45.4	1-1-09	Yonkers, NY
James Clark, United States	2:46:52.6	2-12-09	New York City
Albert Raines, United States	2:46:04.6	5-8-09	New York City
Frederick Barrett, Great Britain	2:42:31	5-26-09	Shepherd's Bush, London
Harry Green, Great Britain	2:38:16.2	5-12-13	Shepherd's Bush, London
Alexis Ahlgren, Sweden	2:36:06.6	5-31-13	Shepherd's Bush, London
Johannes Kolehmainen, Finland	2:32:35.8	8-22-20	Antwerp, Belgium
Albert Michelsen, United States	2:29:01.8	10-12-25	Port Chester, NY
Fusashige Suzuki, Japan	2:27:49	3-31-35	Tokyo
Yasuo Ikenaka, Japan	2:26:44	4-3-35	Tokyo
Kitei Son, Japan	2:26:42	11-3-35	Tokyo
Yun Bok Suh, Korea	2:25:39	4-19-47	Boston
James Peters, Great Britain	2:20:42.2	6-14-52	Chiswick, England
James Peters, Great Britain	2:18:40.2	6-13-53	Chiswick, England
James Peters, Great Britain	2:18:34.8	10-4-53	Turku, Finland
James Peters, Great Britain	2:17:39.4	6-26-54	Chiswick, England
Sergei Popov, USSR	2:15:17	8-24-58	Stockholm
Abebe Bikila, Ethiopia	2:15:16.2	9-10-60	Rome
Toru Terasawa, Japan	2:15:15.8	2-17-63	Beppu, Japan
Leonard Edelen, United States	2:14:28	6-15-63	Chiswick, England
Basil Heatley, Great Britain	2:13:55	6-13-64	Chiswick, England
Abebe Bikila, Ethiopia	2:12:11.2	6-21-64	Tokyo
Morio Shigematsu, Japan	2:12:00	6-12-65	Chiswick, England
Derek Clayton, Australia	2:09:36.4	12-3-67	Fukuoka, Japan
Derek Clayton, Australia	2:08:33.6	5-30-69	Antwerp, Belgium
Rob de Castella, Australia	2:08:18	12-6-81	Fukuoka, Japan
Steve Jones, Great Britain	2:08:05	10-21-84	Chicago
Carlos Lopes, Portugal	2:07:12	4-20-85	Rotterdam, Netherlands
Belayneh Dinsamo, Ethiopia	2:06:50	4-17-88	Rotterdam, Netherlands
Ronaldo Da Costa, Brazil	2:06:05	9-20-98	Berlin, Germany
Khalid Khannouchi, Morocco	2:05:42	10-24-99	Chicago
Khalid Khannouchi, United States	2:05:38	4-14-02	London
Paul Tergat, Kenya	2:04:55	9-28-03	Berlin

Women

Record Holder	Time	Date	Site
Dale Greig, Great Britain	3:27:45	5-23-64	Ryde, England
Mildred Simpson, New Zealand	3:19:33	7-21-64	Auckland, New Zealand
Maureen Wilton, Canada	3:15:22	5-6-67	Toronto
Anni Pede-Erdkamp, W Germany	3:07:26	9-16-67	Waldniel, W Germany
Caroline Walker, United States	3:02:53	2-28-70	Seaside, OR

Women (Cont.)

Record Holder	Time	Date	Site
Elizabeth Bonner, United States	3:01:42	5-9-71	Philadelphia
Adrienne Beames, Australia	2:46:30	8-31-71	Werribee, Australia
Chantal Langlace, France	2:46:24	10-27-74	Neuf Brisach, France
Jacqueline Hansen, United States	2:43:54.5	12-1-74	Culver City, CA
Liane Winter, W Germany	2:42:24	4-21-75	Boston
Christa Vahlensieck, W Germany	2:40:15.8	5-3-75	Dülmen, W Germany
Jacqueline Hansen, United States	2:38:19	10-12-75	Eugene, OR
Chantal Langlace, France	2:35:15.4	5-1-77	Oyarzun, France
Christa Vahlensieck, W Germany	2:34:47.5	9-10-77	Berlin, W Germany
Grete Waitz, Norway	2:32:29.9	10-22-78	New York City
Grete Waitz, Norway	2:27:32.6	10-21-79	New York City
Grete Waitz, Norway	2:25:41.3	10-26-80	New York City
Grete Waitz, Norway	2:25:29	4-17-83	London
Joan Benoit Samuelson, United States	2:22:43	4-18-83	Boston
Ingrid Kristiansen, Norway	2:21:06	4-21-85	London
Tegla Loroupe, Kenya	2:20:47	4-19-98	Rotterdam, Netherlands
Tegla Loroupe, Kenya	2:20:43	9-26-99	Berlin
Naoko Takahashi, Japan	2:19:46	9-30-01	Berlin
Catherine Ndereba, Kenya	2:18:47	10-7-01	Chicago
Paula Radcliffe, Great Britain	2:17:18	10-13-02	Chicago
Paula Radcliffe, Great Britain	2:15:25	4-13-03	London

Boston Marathon

The Boston Marathon began in 1897 as a local Patriot's Day event. Run every year but 1918 since then, it has grown into one of the world's premier marathons.

Men

Year	Winner	Time	Year	Winner	Time
1897	John J. McDermott, United States	2:55:10	1941	Leslie Pawson, United States	2:30:38
1898	Ronald J. McDonald, United States	2:42:00	1942	Bernard Joseph Smith, United States	2:26:51
1899	Lawrence J. Brignolia, United States	2:54:38	1943	Gerard Cote, Canada	2:28:25
1900	James J. Caffrey, Canada	2:39:44	1944	Gerard Cote, Canada	2:31:50
1901	James J. Caffrey, Canada	2:29:23	1945	John A. Kelley, United States	2:30:40
1902	Sammy Mellor, United States	2:43:12	1946	Stylianos Kyriakides, Greece	2:29:27
1903	John C. Lorden, United States	2:41:29	1947	Yun Bok Suh, Korea	2:25:39
1904	Michael Spring, United States	2:38:04	1948	Gerard Cote, Canada	2:31:02
1905	Fred Lorz, United States	2:38:25	1949	Karl Gosta Leandersson, Sweden	2:31:50
1906	Timothy Ford, United States	2:45:45	1950	Kee Yong Ham, Korea	2:32:39
1907	Tom Longboat, Canada	2:24:24	1951	Shigeki Tanaka, Japan	2:27:45
1908	Thomas Morrissey, United States	2:25:43	1952	Doroteo Flores, Guatemala	2:31:53
1909	Henri Renaud, United States	2:53:36	1953	Keizo Yamada, Japan	2:18:51
1910	Fred Cameron, Canada	2:28:52	1954	Veikko Karvonen, Finland	2:20:39
1911	Clarence H. DeMar, United States	2:21:39	1955	Hideo Hamamura, Japan	2:18:22
1912	Mike Ryan, United States	2:21:18	1956	Antti Viskari, Finland	2:14:14
1913	Fritz Carlson, United States	2:25:14	1957	John J. Kelley, United States	2:20:05
1914	James Duffy, Canada	2:25:01	1958	Franjo Mihalic, Yugoslavia	2:25:54
1915	Edouard Fabre, Canada	2:31:41	1959	Eino Oksanen, Finland	2:22:42
1916	Arthur Roth, United States	2:27:16	1960	Paavo Kotila, Finland	2:20:54
1917	Bill Kennedy, United States	2:28:37	1961	Eino Oksanen, Finland	2:23:39
1919	Carl Linder, United States	2:29:13	1962	Eino Oksanen, Finland	2:23:48
1920	Peter Trivoulidas, Greece	2:29:31	1963	Aurele Vandendriessche, Belgium	2:18:58
1921	Frank Zuna, United States	2:18:57	1964	Aurele Vandendriessche, Belgium	2:19:59
1922	Clarence H. DeMar, United States	2:18:10	1965	Morio Shigematsu, Japan	2:16:33
1923	Clarence H. DeMar, United States	2:23:37	1966	Kenji Kimihara, Japan	2:17:11
1924	Clarence H. DeMar, United States	2:29:40	1967	David McKenzie, New Zealand	2:15:45
1925	Chuck Mellor, United States	2:33:00	1968	Amby Burfoot, United States	2:22:17
1926	John C. Miles, Canada	2:25:40	1969	Yoshiaki Unetani, Japan	2:13:49
1927	Clarence H. DeMar, United States	2:40:22	1970	Ron Hill, England	2:10:30
1928	Clarence H. DeMar, United States	2:37:07	1971	Alvaro Mejia, Colombia	2:18:45
1929	John C. Miles, Canada	2:33:08	1972	Olavi Suomalainen, Finland	2:15:39
1930	Clarence H. DeMar, United States	2:34:48	1973	Jon Anderson, United States	2:16:03
1931	James (Hinky) Henigan, United States	2:46:45	1974	Neil Cusack, Ireland	2:13:39
1932	Paul de Bruyn, Germany	2:33:36	1975	Bill Rodgers, United States	2:09:55
1933	Leslie Pawson, United States	2:31:01	1976	Jack Fultz, United States	2:20:19
1934	Dave Komonen, Canada	2:32:53	1977	Jerome Drayton, Canada	2:14:46
1935	John A. Kelley, United States	2:32:07	1978	Bill Rodgers, United States	2:10:13
1936	Ellison M. (Tarzan) Brown, United States	2:33:40	1979	Bill Rodgers, United States	2:09:27
1937	Walter Young, Canada	2:33:20	1980	Bill Rodgers, United States	2:12:11
1938	Leslie Pawson, United States	2:35:34	1981	Toshihiko Seko, Japan	2:09:26
1939	Ellison M. (Tarzan) Brown, United States	2:28:51	1982	Alberto Salazar, United States	2:08:52
1940	Gerard Cote, Canada	2:28:28	1983	Gregory A. Meyer, United States	2:09:00

Boston Marathon (Cont.)

Year	Winner	Time	Year	Winner	Time
1984...Geoff Smith, England		2:10:34	1974...Miki Gorman, United States		2:47:11
1985...Geoff Smith, England		2:14:05	1975...Liane Winter, W Germany		2:42:24
1986...Rob de Castella, Australia		2:07:51	1976...Kim Merritt, United States		2:47:10
1987...Toshihiko Seko, Japan		2:11:50	1977...Miki Gorman, United States		2:48:33
1988...Ibrahim Hussein, Kenya		2:08:43	1978...Gayle Barron, United States		2:44:52
1989...Abebe Mekonnen, Ethiopia		2:09:06	1979...Joan Benoit, United States		2:35:15
1990...Gelindo Bordin, Italy		2:08:19	1980...Jacqueline Gareau, Canada		2:34:28
1991...Ibrahim Hussein, Kenya		2:11:06	1981...Allison Roe, New Zealand		2:26:46
1992...Ibrahim Hussein, Kenya		2:08:14	1982...Charlotte Teske, W Germany		2:29:33
1993...Cosmas N'Deti, Kenya		2:09:33	1983...Joan Benoit, United States		2:22:43
1994...Cosmas N'Deti, Kenya		2:07:15	1984...Lorraine Moller, New Zealand		2:29:28
1995...Cosmas N'Deti, Kenya		2:09:22	1985...Lisa Larsen Weidenbach, United States		2:34:06
1996...Moses Tanui, Kenya		2:09:16	1986...Ingrid Kristiansen, Norway		2:24:55
1997...Lameck Aguta, Kenya		2:10:34	1987...Rosa Mota, Portugal		2:25:21
1998...Moses Tanui, Kenya		2:07:34	1988...Rosa Mota, Portugal		2:24:30
1999...Joseph Chebet, Kenya		2:09:52	1989...Ingrid Kristiansen, Norway		2:24:33
2000...Elijah Lagat, Kenya		2:09:47	1990...Rosa Mota, Portugal		2:25:24
2001...Lee Bong-Ju, Korea		2:09:43	1991...Wanda Panfil, Poland		2:24:18
2002...Rodgers Rop, Kenya		2:09:02	1992...Olga Markova, Russia		2:23:43
2003...Robert Cheruiyot, Kenya		2:10:11	1993...Olga Markova, Russia		2:25:27
2004...Timothy Cherigat, Kenya		2:10:37	1994...Uta Pippig, Germany		2:21:45

Women

Year	Winner	Time	Year	Winner	Time
			1995...Uta Pippig, Germany		2:25:11
1966...Roberta Gibb, United States		3:21:40*	1996...Uta Pippig, Germany		2:27:12
1967...Roberta Gibb, United States		3:27:17*	1997...Fatuma Roba, Ethiopia		2:26:23
1968...Roberta Gibb, United States		3:30:00*	1998...Fatuma Roba, Ethiopia		2:23:21
1969...Sara Mae Berman, United States		3:22:46*	1999...Fatuma Roba, Ethiopia		2:23:25
1970...Sara Mae Berman, United States		3:05:07*	2000...Catherine Ndereba, Kenya		2:26:11
1971...Sara Mae Berman, United States		3:08:30*	2001...Catherine Ndereba, Kenya		2:23:53
1972...Nina Kuscsik, United States		3:10:36	2002...Margaret Okayo, Kenya		2:20:43
1973...Jacqueline A. Hansen, United States		3:05:59	2003...Svetlana Zakharova, Russia		2:25:20
			2004...Catherine Ndereba, Kenya		2:24:27

Note: Over the years the Boston course has varied in length. The distances have been 24 miles, 1,232 yards (1897–1923); 26 miles, 209 yards (1924–1926); 26 miles, 385 yards (1927–1952); and 25 miles, 958 yards (1953–1956). Since 1957, the course has been certified to be the standard marathon distance of 26 miles, 385 yards. (*Unofficial.)

New York City Marathon

MEN			WOMEN		
Year	Winner	Time	Year	Winner	Time
1970...Gary Muhrcke, United States		2:31:38	1970...No finisher		
1971...Norman Higgins, United States		2:22:54	1971...Beth Bonner, United States		2:55:22
1972...Sheldon Karlin, United States		2:27:52	1972...Nina Kuscsik, United States		3:08:41
1973...Tom Fleming, United States		2:21:54	1973...Nina Kuscsik, United States		2:57:07
1974...Norbert Sander, United States		2:26:30	1974...Katherine Switzer, United States		3:07:29
1975...Tom Fleming, United States		2:19:27	1975...Kim Merritt, United States		2:46:14
1976...Bill Rodgers, United States		2:10:10	1976...Miki Gorman, United States		2:39:11
1977...Bill Rodgers, United States		2:11:28	1977...Miki Gorman, United States		2:43:10
1978...Bill Rodgers, United States		2:12:12	1978...Grete Waitz, Norway		2:32:30
1979...Bill Rodgers, United States		2:11:42	1979...Grete Waitz, Norway		2:27:33
1980...Alberto Salazar, United States		2:09:41	1980...Grete Waitz, Norway		2:25:41
1981...Alberto Salazar, United States		2:08:13	1981...Allison Roe, New Zealand		2:25:29
1982...Alberto Salazar, United States		2:09:29	1982...Grete Waitz, Norway		2:27:14
1983...Rod Dixon, New Zealand		2:08:59	1983...Grete Waitz, Norway		2:27:00
1984...Orlando Pizzolato, Italy		2:14:53	1984...Grete Waitz, Norway		2:29:30
1985...Orlando Pizzolato, Italy		2:11:34	1985...Grete Waitz, Norway		2:28:34
1986...Gianni Poli, Italy		2:11:06	1986...Grete Waitz, Norway		2:28:06
1987...Ibrahim Hussein, Kenya		2:11:01	1987...Priscilla Welch, Great Britain		2:30:17
1988...Steve Jones, Great Britain		2:08:20	1988...Grete Waitz, Norway		2:28:07
1989...Juma Ikangaa, Tanzania		2:08:01	1989...Ingrid Kristiansen, Norway		2:25:30
1990...Douglas Wakiihuri, Kenya		2:12:39	1990...Wanda Panfil, Poland		2:30:45
1991...Salvador Garcia, Mexico		2:09:28	1991...Liz McColgan, Scotland		2:27:23
1992...Willie Mtolo, S Africa		2:09:29	1992...Lisa Ondieki, Australia		2:24:40
1993...Andres Espinosa, Mexico		2:10:04	1993...Uta Pippig, Germany		2:26:24
1994...German Silva, Mexico		2:11:21	1994...Tegla Loroupe, Kenya		2:27:37
1995...German Silva, Mexico		2:11:00	1995...Tegla Loroupe, Kenya		2:28:06
1996...Giacomo Leone, Italy		2:09:54	1996...Anuta Catuna, Romania		2:28:18
1997...John Kagwe, Kenya		2:08:12	1997...Franziska Rochat-Moser, Switzerland		2:28:43
1998...John Kagwe, Kenya		2:08:45	1998...Franca Fiacconi, Italy		2:25:17
1999...Joseph Chebet, Kenya		2:09:14	1999...Adriana Fernandez, Mexico		2:25:06
2000...Abdelkhader El Mouaziz, Morocco		2:10:09	2000...Ludmila Petrova, Russia		2:25:45
2001...Tesfaye Jifar, Ethiopia		2:07:43	2001...Margaret Okayo, Kenya		2:24:21
2002...Rodgers Rop, Kenya		2:08:07	2002...Joyce Chepchumba, Kenya		2:25:56
2003...Martin Lel, Kenya		2:10:30	2003...Margaret Okayo, Kenya		2:22:31

World Cross-Country Championships

Conducted by the International Amateur Athletic Federation (IAAF), this meet draws the best runners in the world at every distance from the mile to the marathon to compete in the same cross-country race.

Men

Year	Winner	Winning Team	Year	Winner	Winning Team
1973	Pekka Paivarinta, Finland	Belgium	1990	Khalid Skah, Morocco	Kenya
1974	Eric DeBeck, Belgium	Belgium	1991	Khalid Skah, Morocco	Kenya
1975	Ian Stewart, Scotland	New Zealand	1992	John Ngugi, Kenya	Kenya
1976	Carlos Lopes, Portugal	England	1993	William Sigei, Kenya	Kenya
1977	Leon Schots, Belgium	Belgium	1994	William Sigei, Kenya	Kenya
1978	John Treacy, Ireland	France	1995	Paul Tergat, Kenya	Kenya
1979	John Treacy, Ireland	England	1996	Paul Tergat, Kenya	Kenya
1980	Craig Virgin, United States	England	1997	Paul Tergat, Kenya	Kenya
1981	Craig Virgin, United States	Ethiopia	1998	Paul Tergat, Kenya	Kenya
1982	Mohammed Kedir, Ethiopia	Ethiopia	1999	Paul Tergat, Kenya	Kenya
1983	Bekele Debele, Ethiopia	Ethiopia	2000	Mohammed Mourhit, Belgium	Kenya
1984	Carlos Lopes, Portugal	Ethiopia	2001	Mohammed Mourhit, Belgium	Kenya
1985	Carlos Lopes, Portugal	Ethiopia	2002	Kenenisa Bekele , Ethiopia	Kenya
1987	John Ngugi, Kenya	Kenya	2003	Kenenisa Bekele, Ethiopia	Kenya
1988	John Ngugi, Kenya	Kenya	2004	Kenenisa Bekele, Ethiopia	Ethiopia
1989	John Ngugi, Kenya	Kenya			

Women

Year	Winner	Winning Team	Year	Winner	Winning Team
1973	Paola Cacchi, Italy	England	1989	Annette Sergent, France	USSR
1974	Paola Cacchi, Italy	England	1990	Lynn Jennings, United States	USSR
1975	Julie Brown, United States	United States	1991	Lynn Jennings, United States	Kenya
1976	Carmen Valero, Spain	USSR	1992	Lynn Jennings, United States	Kenya
1977	Carmen Valero, Spain	USSR	1993	Albertina Dias, Portugal	Kenya
1978	Grete Waitz, Norway	Romania	1994	Helen Chepngeno, Kenya	Portugal
1979	Grete Waitz, Norway	United States	1995	Derartu Tulu, Ethiopia	Kenya
1980	Grete Waitz, Norway	USSR	1996	Gete Wami, Ethiopia	Kenya
1981	Grete Waitz, Norway	USSR	1997	Derartu Tulu, Ethiopia	Ethiopia
1982	Maricica Puica, Romania	USSR	1998	Sonia O'Sullivan, Ireland	Kenya
1983	Grete Waitz, Norway	United States	1999	Gete Wami, Ethiopia	Ethiopia
1984	Maricica Puica, Romania	United States	2000	Derartu Tulu, Ethiopia	Ethiopia
1985	Zola Budd, England	United States	2001	Paula Radcliffe, Great Britain	Kenya
1986	Zola Budd, England	England	2002	Paula Radcliffe, Great Britain	Ethiopia
1987	Annette Sergent, France	United States	2003	Werknesh Kidane, Ethiopia	Ethiopia
1988	Ingrid Kristiansen, Norway	USSR	2004	Benita Johnson, Australia	Ethiopia

Notable Achievements

Longest Winning Streaks

MEN

Event	Name and Nationality	Streak	Years
100 meters	Bob Hayes, United States	49	1962–64
200 meters	Manfred Gemar, Germany	41	1956–60
400 meters	Michael Johnson, United States	58	1989–97
800 meters	Mal Whitfield, United States	40	1951–54
1,500 meters	Hicham El Guerrouj, Morocco	23	1996–00
1,500 meters/mile	Steve Ovett, Great Britain	45	1977–80
Mile	Herb Elliott, Australia	35	1957–60
Steeplechase	Gaston Roelants, Belgium	45	1961–66
5,000 meters	Emil Zátopek, Czechoslovakia	48	1949–52
10,000 meters	Emil Zátopek, Czechoslovakia	38	1948–54
Marathon	Frank Shorter, United States	6	1971–73
110-meter hurdles	Jack Davis, United States	44	1952–55
400-meter hurdles	Edwin Moses, United States	107	1977–87
High jump	Ernie Shelton, United States	46	1953–55
Pole vault	Bob Richards, United States	50	1950–52
Long jump	Carl Lewis, United States	65	1981–91
Triple jump	Adhemar da Silva, Brazil	60	1950–56
Shot put	Parry O'Brien, United States	116	1952–56
Discus throw	Ricky Bruch, Sweden	54	1972–73
Hammer throw	Imre Nemeth, Hungary	73	1946–50
Javelin throw	Janis Lusis, USSR	41	1967–70
Decathlon	Bob Mathias, United States	11	1948–56

Longest Winning Streaks *(Cont.)*

WOMEN

Event	Name and Nationality	Streak	Years
100 meters	Merlene Ottey, Jamaica	56	1987–91
200 meters	Irena Szewinska, Poland	38	1973–75
400 meters	Irena Szewinska, Poland	36	1973–78
800 meters	Ana Fidelia Quirot, Cuba	36	1987–90
1,500 meters	Paula Ivan, Romania	15	1988–91
1,500 meters/mile	Paula Ivan, Romania	19	1988–90
3,000 meters	Mary Slaney, United States	10	1982–84
10,000 meters	Ingrid Kristiansen, Norway	5	1985–87
Marathon	Katrin Dörre, E Germany	10	1982–86
100-meter hurdles	Annelie Ernhardt, E Germany	44	1972–75
400-meter hurdles	Ann-Louise Skoglund, Sweden	18	1981–83
High jump	Iolanda Balas, Romania	140	1956–67
Long jump	Tatyana Shchelkanova, USSR	19	1964–66
Shot put	Nadezhda Chizhova, USSR	57	1969–73
Discus throw	Gisela Mauermeyer, Germany	65	1935–42
Javelin throw	Ruth Fuchs, E Germany	30	1972–73
Multi	Heide Rosendahl, W Germany	15	1969–72

Most Consecutive Years Ranked No. 1 in the World

MEN

No.	Name and Nationality	Event	Years
11	Sergei Bubka, Ukraine	Pole vault	1984–94
9	Viktor Saneyev, USSR	Triple jump	1968–76
8	Bob Richards, United States	Pole vault	1949–56
8	Ralph Boston, United States	Long jump	1960–67

WOMEN

No.	Name and Nationality	Event	Years
9	Iolanda Balas, Romania	High jump	1958–66
8	Ruth Fuchs, E Germany	Javelin	1972–79
7	Faina Melnick, USSR	Discus throw	1971–77

Major Barrier Breakers

MEN

Event	Mark	Name and Nationality	Date	Site
sub 10-second 100 meters	9.95	Jim Hines, United States	Oct. 14, 1968	Mexico City
sub 20-second 200 meters	19.83	Tommie Smith, United States	Oct. 16, 1968	Mexico City
sub 45-second 400 meters	44.9	Otis Davis, United States	Sept. 6, 1960	Rome
sub 1:45 800 meters	1:44.3	Peter Snell, New Zealand	Feb. 3, 1962	Christchurch, New Zealand
sub four minute mile	3:59.4	Roger Bannister, Great Britain	May 6, 1954	Oxford
sub 3:50 mile	3:49.4	John Walker, New Zealand	Aug. 12, 1975	Göteborg, Sweden
sub 13-minute 5,000 meters	12:58.39	Said Aouita, Morocco	July 22, 1986	Rome
sub 27:00 10,000 meters	26:58.38	Yobes Ondieki, Kenya	July 10, 1993	Oslo
sub 13-second 110-meter hurdles	12.93	Renaldo Nehemiah, United States	Aug. 19, 1981	Zurich
sub 50-second 400-meter hurdles	49.5	Glenn Davis, United States	June 29, 1956	Los Angeles
7 ft high jump	7 ft ⅝ in	Charles Dumas, United States	June 29, 1956	Los Angeles
8 ft high jump	8 ft	Javier Sotomayor, Cuba	July 29, 1989	San Juan
60 ft triple jump	60 ft ¼ in	Jonathan Edwards, Great Britain	Aug. 7, 1995	Göteborg, Sweden
20 ft pole vault	20 ft	Sergei Bubka, USSR	March 15, 1991	San Sebastian, Spain
70 ft shot put	70 ft 7¼ in	Randy Matson, United States	May 5, 1965	College Station, Texas
200 ft discus throw	200 ft 5 in	Al Oerter, United States	May 18, 1962	Los Angeles
300 ft (new) javelin	300 ft 1 in	Steve Backley, Great Britain	Jan. 25, 1992	Auckland, New Zealand
9,000-pt decathlon	9026	Roman Sebrle, Czech Republic	May 27, 2001	Gotzis, Austria

Major Barrier Breakers *(Cont.)*
WOMEN

Event	Mark	Name and Nationality	Date	Site
sub 11-second 100 meters	10.88	Marlies Oelsner, E Germany	July 1, 1977	Dresden
sub 22-second 200 meters	21.71	Marita Koch, E Germany	June 10, 1979	Karl Marxstadt, E Germany
sub 50-second 400 meters	49.9	Irena Szewinska, Poland	June 22, 1974	Warsaw
sub 2:00 800 meters	1:59.1	Shin Geum Dan, N Korea	Nov. 12, 1963	Djakarta
sub 4:00 1,500 meters	3:56.0	Tatyana Kazankina, USSR	June 28, 1976	Podolsk, USSR
sub 4:20 mile	4:17.55	Mary Decker, United States	Feb. 16, 1980	Houston
sub 15:00 5,000 meters	14:58.89	Ingrid Kristiansen, Norway	June 28, 1984	Oslo
sub 30:00 10,000 meters	29:31.78	Wang Junxia, China	Sept. 8, 1993	Beijing
sub 2:30 marathon	2:27:33	Grete Waitz, Norway	Oct. 21, 1979	New York City
sub 2:20 marathon	2:19:46	Naoko Takahashi, Japan	Sept. 30, 2001	Berlin
sub 13-second 100-meter hurdles	12.9	Karin Balzer, E Germany	Sept. 5, 1969	Berlin
6 ft high jump	6 ft	Iolanda Balas, Romania	Oct. 18, 1958	Budapest
15 ft pole vault	15 ft ½ in	Emma George, Australia	March 14, 1998	Melbourne
70 ft shot put	70 ft 4½ in	Nadyezhda Chizhova, USSR	Sept. 29, 1973	Varna, Bulgaria
200 ft discus throw	201 ft	Liesel Westermann, W Germany	Nov. 5, 1967	Sao Paulo
200 ft javelin throw	201 ft 4 in	Elvira Ozolina, USSR	Aug. 27, 1964	Kiev
first 7,000-point heptathlon	7,148	Jackie Joyner-Kersee, U.S.	July 6–7, 1986	Moscow

Olympic Accomplishments

Oldest Olympic gold medalist—Patrick (Babe) McDonald, United States, 42 years, 26 days, 56-pound weight throw, 1920.
Oldest Olympic medalist—Tebbs Lloyd Johnson, Great Britain, 48 years, 115 days, 1948 (bronze), 50K walk.
Youngest Olympic gold medalist—Barbara Jones, United States, 15 years 123 days, 1952, 4 x 100 relay.
Youngest gold medalist in individual event—Ulrike Meyfarth, W Germany, 16 years, 123 days, 1972, high jump.

World Record Accomplishments*

Most world records equaled or set in a day—6, Jesse Owens, United States, 5-25-35, (9.4 100 yards; 26' 8¼" long jump; 20.3 200 meters and 220 yards; and 22.6 220-yard hurdles and 200-meter hurdles.
Most records in a year—10, Gunder Hägg, Sweden, 1941–42, 1,500 to 5,000 meters.
Most records in a career—35, Sergei Bubka, 1983–94, pole vault indoors and out.
Longest span of record setting—11 years, 20 days, Irena Szewinska, Poland, 1965–76, 200 meters.
Youngest person to set a set world record—Carolina Gisolf, Holland, 15 years, 5 days, 1928, high jump, 5 ft 3⅜ in.
Youngest man to set a world record—John Thomas, United States, 17 years, 355 days, 1959, high jump, 7 ft 1¼ in.
Oldest person to set world record—Carlos Lopes, Portugal, 38 years, 59 days, marathon, 2:07:12.
Greatest percentage improvement—6.59, Bob Beamon, United States, 1968, long jump.
Longest lasting record—long jump, 26 ft 8¼ in, Jesse Owens, United States, 25 years, 79 days (1935–60).
Highest clearance over head, men—23¼ in, Franklin Jacobs, United States (5' 8"), 1978.
Highest clearance over head, woman—12¾ in, Yolanda Henry, United States (5' 6"), 1990.

*Marks sanctioned by the IAAF.

**Michael Phelps
of the United States**

Swimming

Be Like Mike

Michael Phelps made history in Athens, winning six gold medals and providing a worthy example of sportsmanship

BY MARK BECHTEL

SITTING IN his hotel room on the night of the opening ceremonies of the Athens Olympics, Michael Phelps was ready to go. He was itching to let the Games begin. For him, these Olympics were a quest to make history (he was attempting to equal or surpass Mark Spitz's 1972 take of seven gold medals) and a not insubstantial chunk of change (a swimsuit company offered him $1 million if he equalled the record). "I wish the meet started six months ago," the rangy 19-year-old said. "I feel awesome in the water in training. I need to get in the pool and swim fast *sooo* bad."

When he finally got into the water the next day, he swam very fast indeed, breaking his own world record in the 400-meter individual medley. Soon after that, however, Phelps found himself embroiled in a slight but distracting controversy. His second race was the 4 x 100-meter freestyle relay, an event the U.S. and Australia have turned into a simmering rivalry. When it came time to pick his team, U.S. coach Eddie Reese bypassed Gary Hall Jr., who had anchored three gold

medal–winning relay teams in the past two Games, opting instead to use Ian Crocker and Phelps. Hall was less than pleased, as Crocker was under the weather and Phelps had 17 races in seven days on his itinerary. Hall questioned Phelps's inclusion in the relay, and Hall's agent, David Arluck, said, "Gary is one of the best Olympians of all time. I can't believe they kept him off the relay for some 19-year-old guy who is going after something that he's not going to accomplish anyway."

The remainder of the Games would expose Arluck's "some 19-year-old guy" reference for the absurdity it was when he uttered it, as Phelps put on a performance for the ages, every bit as impressive as Spitz's '72 feat. But first there was the 400 free relay. Phelps's swam his leg in 48.74 seconds—only .01 of a second slower than Hall swam in the prelims—but it became a moot point after Crocker's abysmal 50.05-second opening leg left the U.S. in eighth place. The best his teammates could do was rally for the bronze medal. That meant that eight gold medals were beyond Phelps's reach, and to

Coughlin won five medals in Athens, including the 100-meter backstroke gold.

match Spitz's medal haul he'd have to be flawless for the rest of the Games—a tall order considering his next event was the 200-meter freestyle, which is not his specialty, and, more importantly, which also featured world record holder Ian Thorpe of Australia, and 2000 Olympic gold medalist Pieter van den Hoogenband from the Netherlands. The wisdom of competing in such a race was widely questioned in the media firestorm comparing Phelps to Spitz, but Phelps said his Olympic effort wasn't about trying to eclipse Spitz. "I wanted to race Thorpe in a freestyle before we were both done," he said. Throw in van den Hoogenband and you had an extraordinary race indeed.

Bob Bowman, Phelps's coach, said before the Games, "If this was just about seven gold medals, he would have dropped this event. But that's not the goal. The goal is to see what he can do." What Phelps did was swim the fastest 200 ever by an American, but it still wasn't enough to beat Thorpe, who overtook van den Hoogenband in the last 50 meters. Phelps nearly nipped the Dutchman at the wall, but settled for his second bronze. "It was fun," Phelps said, unperturbed that his chance to tie Spitz's medal total had evaporated. He swam gloriously for the rest of the meet, winning gold medals and setting

Olympic records in the 100 fly, the 200 fly, and the 200 IM. Add his opening 400 IM world record, and Phelps had four individual gold medals (equaling Spitz's record 1972 take on that count) and four records. His overall medal haul stood at seven, and he seemed certain to win an eighth—and tie Russian gymnast Aleksandr Dityatin's record for medals in one Games—in the medley relay. That's when Phelps added a grace note to his performance: He gave his spot in the medley relay final to Crocker, whom he'd narrowly defeated in the 100 fly, and who'd faltered in the 400 free relay. "Ian's one of the greatest relay swimmers in history," Phelps said. "I was willing to give him another chance." Phelps watched from the stands as Crocker swam the second-fastest butterfly split in history and the U.S. romped to the gold. Since he swam in the preliminaries, Phelps would still receive a gold medal, his record-tying eighth medal overall.

There were other record-setters in Athens. Natalie Coughlin won five medals, tying Shirley Babashoff and Dara Torres for the best showing by a U.S. woman. And Hall defended his 50 free title, bringing his career Olympic medal total to 10. But the Games belonged to Phelps, who said of his decision to allow Crocker a shot at redemption, "I wanted him to show the world what he was really made of." In doing so, he showed the world what he was made of as well.

2003–2004 Major Competitions

Men

U.S. Open
Federal Way, Wash., December 4–6, 2003

50 free	Jason Lezak, Irvine Novaquatics	22.34
100 free	Jason Lezak, Irvine Novaquatics	49.20
200 free	Brent Hayden, Canada	1:48.80
400 free	Klete Keller, Wolverine	3:51.87
1,500 free	Sung Mo Cho, Chivas	15:22.91
100 back	Lenny Krayzelburg, Irvine Nov.	55.35
200 back	Cameron Gibson, New Zealand	2:01.31
100 breast	Thijs van Valkengoed, Neth	1:01.52
200 breast	Thijs van Valkengoed, Neth	2:13.32
100 fly	Mike Mintenko, Canada	52.94
200 fly	Tom Malchow, Wolverine	1:57.61
200 IM	Brian Johns, Canada	2:00.91†
400 IM	Brian Johns, Canada	4:18.91†
400 m relay	Canada A	3:42.16†
400 f relay	Canada A	3:19.69
800 f relay	Canada A	7:20.47†

U.S. NATIONAL CHAMPIONSHIPS (SPRING)
Orlando, Fla., February 10–14, 2004

50 free	Roland Schoeman, U of Arizona	22.12
100 free	Michael Phelps, N Baltimore	49.05
200 free	Michael Phelps, N Baltimore	1:46.47
400 free	Chad Carvin, Mission Viejo	3:48.92
800 free	Larsen Jensen, Mission Viejo	7:53.29
1,500 free	David Davies, Great Britain	15:02.63
100 back	Randall Bal, unattached	54.78
200 back	Michael Phelps, N Baltimore	1:55.30
100 breast	Vladislav Polyakov, Coral Sp'gs	1:01.98
200 breast	Vladislav Polyakov, Coral Sp'gs	2:14.36
100 fly	Michael Phelps, N Baltimore	51.84†
200 fly	Michael Phelps, N Baltimore	1:55.30
200 IM	Michael Phelps, N Baltimore	1:56.80
400 IM	Kevin Clements, N Baltimore	4:18.91
400 m relay	Irvine Novaquatics	3:43.53
400 f relay	Irvine Novaquatics	3:19.74
800 f relay	Denmark	7:26.72

U.S. OLYMPIC TRIALS
Long Beach, Calif., July 7–14, 2004

50 free	Gary Hall Jr	21.91
100 free	Jason Lezak	48.41
200 free	Michael Phelps	1:46.27†
400 free	Klete Keller	3:44.19†
1,500 free	Larsen Jensen	14:56.71*
100 back	Aaron Peirsol	53.64†
200 back	Aaron Peirsol	1:54.74 WR
100 breast	Brendan Hansen	59.30 WR
200 breast	Brendan Hansen	2:09.04 WR
100 fly	Ian Crocker	50.76 WR
200 fly	Michael Phelps	1:54.31†
200 IM	Michael Phelps	1:56.71
400 IM	Michael Phelps	4:08.41WR

U.S. OLYMPIC TRIALS—DIVING
St. Peters, Mo., June 7–13, 2004

3-m spgbd	Troy Dumais	1151.37
Platform	Caesar Garcia	1157.94
3-m sync	Troy Dumais/ Justin Dumais	684.33
Platfm sync	Mark Ruiz/ Kyle Prandi	703.98

U.S. NATIONAL CHAMPIONSHIPS (SUMMER)
Stanford, Calif., August 3–7, 2004

50 free	Randall Bal, Stanford	22.75
100 free	Garrett Weber-Gale, Longhorn	49.91
200 free	Justin Mortimer, Mission Viejo	1:50.18
400 free	Michael Klueh, Longhorn	3:54.75
800 free	Justin Mortimer, Mission Viejo	8:02.90
1,500 free	Justin Mortimer, Mission Viejo	15:23.96
100 back	Randall Bal, Stanford	54.67
200 back	Trent Staley, Trojan SC	2:02.02
100 breast	Kevin Swander, Indiana ST	1:02.81
200 breast	Julien Nicolardot, France	2:14.52
100 fly	Daniel Rohleder, Longhorn	54.17
200 fly	William Stovall, Memphis Tiger	2:00.03
200 IM	Mark Stephens, Dynamo SC	2:04.34
400 IM	Justin Mortimer, Mission Viejo	4:21.15
400 m relay	Longhorn Aquatic	3:46.02
400 f relay	Longhorn Aquatic	3:25.59
800 f relay	Mecklenburg NC	7:35.84

†Meet record. *American record. WR World record.

Women

U.S. Open
Federal Way, Wash., December 4-6, 2003

50 free	Marleen Veldhuis, De Whee	25.24
100 free	Marleen Veldhuis, De Whee	54.88†
200 free	Marleen Veldhuis, De Whee	2:00.78
400 free	Sachiko Yamada, Japan	4:10.04
800 free	Sachiko Yamada, Japan	8:30.31
100 back	Hannah McLean, New Zealand	1:02.26
200 back	Jamie Reid, Highlander	2:14.30
100 breast	Megan Quann, S Sound	1:08.13
200 breast	Birte Steven, Oregon St	2:27.71
100 fly	Jennifer Button, Canada	59.97
200 fly	Kimberly Vandenberg, UCLA	2:11.29
200 IM	Yana Klochkova, Ukraine	2:14.34†
400 IM	Sara McLarty, Florida	4:45.38
400 m relay	Irvine Novaquatics	4:09.54
400 f relay	Canada A	3:48.42
800 f relay	Canada A	8:14.56

U.S. NATIONAL CHAMPIONSHIPS (SPRING)
Orlando, Fla., February 10-14, 2004

50 free	Michelle Engelsman, unattached	25.17
100 free	Lindsay Benko, Trojan SC	55.43
200 free	Lindsay Benko, Trojan SC	1:58.62
400 free	Sachiko Yamada, Japan	4:09.37
800 free	Sachiko Yamada, Japan	8:25.62
1,500 free	Sachiko Yamada, Japan	16:06.13
100 back	Haley Cope, unattached	1:01.92
200 back	Pamela Hanson, Tenn. Aquatic	2:13.56
100 breast	Amanda Beard, Tucson Ford	1:08.28
200 breast	Amanda Beard, Tucson Ford	2:24.97
100 fly	Martina Moravcova, SMU	58.76
200 fly	Noelle Bassi, Berkeley Aquatic	2:10.96
200 IM	Amanda Beard, Tucson Ford	2:13.11
400 IM	Katie Hoff, N Baltimore	4:42.32
400 m relay	Irvine Novaquatics	4:09.25
400 f relay	Canada	3:45.38
800 f relay	Denmark	8:13.56

U.S. OLYMPIC TRIALS
Long Beach, Calif., July 7-14, 2004

50 free	Jenny Thompson	25.02
100 free	Kara Lynn Joyce	54.38
200 free	Dana Vollmer	1:59.20
400 free	Kaitlin Sandeno	4:08.07
800 free	Diana Munz	8:26.06
100 back	Natalie Coughlin	59.85†
200 back	Margaret Hoelzer	2:11.88
100 breast	Amanda Beard	1:07.65
200 breast	Amanda Beard	2:22.44 WR
100 fly	Rachel Komisarz	58.77
200 fly	Dana Kirk	2:08.86
200 IM	Katie Hoff	2:12.06
400 IM	Katie Hoff	4:37.67†

U.S. OLYMPIC TRIALS—DIVING
St. Peters, Mo., June 7-13, 2004

3-m spgbd	Kimiko Soldati	884.70
Platform	Laura Wilkinson	878.85
Platfm. sync	Cassandra Cardinell/ Sara Hildenbrand	634.29

U.S. NATIONAL CHAMPIONSHIPS (SUMMER)
Stanford, Calif., August 3-7, 2004

50 free	Brooke Bishop, Palo Alto Stan	26.10
100 free	Tanica Jamison, Longhorn	55.96
200 free	Lauren Medina, Calif. Aquatic	2:01.89
400 free	Kate Ziegler, The Fish-PV	4:12.06
800 free	Alyssa Kiel, Lake Erie Silver	8:33.08
1,500 free	Kate Ziegler, The Fish-PV	16:22.03
100 back	Hayley McGregory, Longhorn	1:02.55
200 back	Hayley McGregory, Longhorn	2:13.59
100 breast	Jessica Hardy, Irvine Novaquat.	1:08.33
200 breast	Lindsey Ertter, Athens Bulldog	2:30.64
100 fly	Tanica Jamison, Longhorn	59.23
200 fly	Kimberly Vandenberg, UCLA	2:11.08
200 IM	Danielle Townsend, Aggie SC	2:15.75
400 IM	Ariana Kukors, King	4:45.41
400 m relay	Longhorn Aquatic	4:10.34
400 f relay	Longhorn Aquatic	3:48.76
800 f relay	Longhorn Aquatic	8:18.05

†Meet record. *American record. WR World record.

World and American Records Set in 2004

Men

Event	Mark	Record Holder	Date	Site
200 free	1:45.32	Michael Phelps, United States (A)	8-16-04	Athens
400 free	3:44.11	Klete Keller, United States (A)	8-14-04	Athens
1500 free	14:45.29	Larsen Jensen, United States (A)	8-21-04	Athens
100 back	53.45	Aaron Peirsol, United States (W, A)	8-21-04	Athens
200 back	1:54.74	Aaron Peirsol, United States (W, A)	7-12-04	Long Beach, CA
100 breast	59.30	Brendan Hansen, United States (W, A)	7-8-04	Long Beach, CA
200 breast	2:09.04	Brendan Hansen, United States (W,A)	7-11-04	Long Beach, CA
50 fly	23.30	Ian Crocker (W, A)	2-29-04	Austin, TX
100 fly	50.76	Ian Crocker, United States (W, A)	7-13-04	Long Beach, CA
400 IM	4:08.26	Michael Phelps, United States (A)	8-14-04	Athens
400 medley relay	3:30.68	United States (W, A) (Aaron Peirsol Brendan Hansen, Ian Crocker Jason Lezak)	8-21-04	Athens
400 free relay	3:13.17	S Africa (W) (Roland Schoeman, Lyndon Ferns, Darian Townsend Ryk Neethling)	8-15-04	Athens
800 free relay	7:07.33	United States (A) (Phelps, Lochte Vanderkaay, Keller)	8-17-04	Athens

Women

Event	Mark	Record Holder	Date	Site
100 free	53.52	Jodie Henry, Australia (W)	8-18-04	Athens
200 breast	2:22.44	Amanda Beard, United States (W, A)	7-12-04	Long Beach, CA
200 IM	2:11.70	Amanda Beard, United States (A)	8-17-04	Athens
400 IM	4:34.95	Kaitlin Sandeno, United States (A)	8-14-04	Athens
400 free relay	3:35.94	Australia (W) (Alice Mills, Lisbeth Lenton, Petria Thomas, Jodie Henry	8-14-04	Athens
400 medley relay	3:57.32	Australia (W) (Giaan Rooney, Leisel Jones, Petria Thomas, Jodie Henry)	8-21-04	Athens
400 free relay	3:35.94	Australia (W) (Alice Mills, Lisbeth Lenton, Petria Thomas, Jodie Henry)	8-14-04	Athens
	3:36.39	United States (A) (Kara Lynn Joyce Natalie Coughlin, Amanda Weir, Jenny Thompson)	8-14-04	Athens
800 free relay	7:53.42	United States (W, A) (Natalie Coughlin, Carly Piper, Dana Vollmer, Kaitlin Sandeno)	8-18-04	Athens

W= world record. A= American record. EW=Equals world record.

Hawaiian Plunge	Ginny Walsh, a senior at St. Andrew's Episcopal School in Austin, Texas, swam the Pailolo Channel between Maui and Molokai, becoming, at 17, the youngest person to swim across a Hawaiian channel. She covered the 9.1-mile distance in five hours.

World and American Records

MEN

Freestyle

Event	Time	Record Holder	Date	Site
50 meters	21.64	Alexander Popov, Russia (W)	6-16-00	Moscow
	21.76	Gary Hall Jr. (A)	8-15-00	Indianapolis
100 meters	47.84	Pieter van den Hoogenband (W) Netherlands	9-19-00	Sydney
	48.33	Anthony Ervin (A)	7-27-01	Fukuoka, Japan
200 meters	1:44.06	Ian Thorpe, Australia (W)	7-25-01	Fukuoka, Japan
	1:45.32	Michael Phelps (A)	8-16-04	Athens
400 meters	3:40.08	Ian Thorpe, Australia (W)	7-30-02	Manchester
	3:44.11	Klete Keller (A)	8-14-04	Athens
800 meters	7:39.16	Ian Thorpe, Australia (W)	7-24-01	Fukuoka, Japan
	7:48.09	Larsen Jensen (A)	7-25-03	Barcelona
1,500 meters	14:34.56	Grant Hackett, Australia (W)	7-30-01	Fukuoka, Japan
	14:45.29	Larsen Jensen (A)	8-21-04	Athens

Backstroke

Event	Time	Record Holder	Date	Site
50 meters	24.80	Thomas Rupprath, Germany (W)	7-27-03	Barcelona
	24.99	Lenny Krayzelburg (A)	8-28-99	Sydney
100 meters	53.45	Aaron Peirsol (W, A)	8-21-04	Athens
200 meters	1:54.74	Aaron Peirsol (W, A)	7-12-04	Long Beach, CA

Breaststroke

Event	Time	Record Holder	Date	Site
50 meters	27.18	Oleg Lisogor, Ukr (W)	8-1-02	Berlin
	27.39	Ed Moses (A)	3-31-01	Austin, TX
100 meters	59.30	Brendan Hansen (W, A)	7-8-04	Long Beach, CA
200 meters	2:09.04	Brendan Hansen (W, A)	7-11-04	Long Beach, CA

Butterfly

Event	Time	Record Holder	Date	Site
50 meters	23.30	Ian Crocker (W, A)	2-29-04	Austin, TX
100 meters	50.76	Ian Crocker (W, A)	7-13-04	Long Beach, CA
200 meters	1:53.93	Michael Phelps (W, A)	7-22-03	Barcelona

Individual Medley

Event	Time	Record Holder	Date	Site
200 meters	1:55.94	Michael Phelps (W, A)	8-9-03	College Park, MD
400 meters	4:08.26	Michael Phelps (W, A)	8-14-04	Athens

Relays

Event	Time	Record Holder	Date	Site
400-meter medley	3:30.68	United States (W,A) (Aaron Peirsol, Brendan Hansen, Ian Crocker, Jason Lezak)	8-21-04	Athens
400-meter freestyle	3:13.17	S Africa (W) (Roland Schoeman, Lyndon Ferns, Darian Townsend, Ryk Neethling)	8-15-04	Athens
	3:13.86	United States (A) (Anthony Ervin, Neil Walker, Jason Lezak, Gary Hall Jr	9-16-00	Sydney
800-meter freestyle	7:04.66	Australia (W) (Ian Thorpe, Michael Klim, Bill Kirby, Grant Hackett)	7-27-01	Fukuoka, Japan
	7:07.33	United States (A) (Phelps, Lochte, Vanderkaay, Keller)	8-17-04	Athens

Note: Records through Sept. 9, 2004.

WOMEN

Freestyle

Event	Time	Record Holder	Date	Site
50 meters	24.13	Inge de Bruijn, Netherlands (W)	9-22-00	Sydney
	24.63	Dara Torres (A)	9-23-00	Sydney
100 meters	53.52	Jodie Henry, Australia (W)	8-18-04	Athens
	53.99	Natalie Coughlin (A)	8-29-02	Yokohama, Japan
200 meters	1:56.64	Franziska van Almsick, Germany (W)	8-3-02	Berlin
	1:57.41	Lindsay Benko (A)	7-24-03	Barcelona
400 meters	4:03.85	Janet Evans (W, A)	9-22-88	Seoul
800 meters	8:16.22	Janet Evans (W, A)	8-20-89	Tokyo
1,500 meters	15:52.10	Janet Evans (W, A)	3-26-88	Orlando, FL

Backstroke

Event	Time	Record Holder	Date	Site
50 meters	28.25	Sandra Volker, Germany (W)	6-17-00	Berlin
	28.49	Natalie Coughlin (A)	7-23-01	Fukuoka, Japan
100 meters	59.58	Natalie Coughlin (W, A)	8-13-02	Fort Lauderdale, FL
200 meters	2:06.62	Krisztina Egerszegi, Hungary (W)	8-25-91	Athens, Greece
	2:08.53	Natalie Coughlin (A)	8-16-02	Fort Lauderdale, FL

Breaststroke

Event	Time	Record Holder	Date	Site
50 meters	30.57	Zoe Baker, Great Britain (W)	7-30-02	Berlin
	31.34	Megan Quann (A)	8-11-00	Indianapolis
100 meters	1:06.37	Leisel Jones, Australia (W)	7-21-03	Barcelona
	1:07.05	Megan Quann (A)	9-18-00	Sydney
200 meters	2:22.44	Amanda Beard (W, A)	7-12-04	Long Beach, CA

Butterfly

Event	Time	Record Holder	Date	Site
50 meters	25.57	Anna-Karin Kammerling, Sweden (W)	7-30-02	Berlin
	26.50	Dara Torres (A)	8-9-00	Indianapolis
100 meters	56.61	Inge de Bruijn, Netherlands (W)	9-17-00	Sydney
	57.58	Dara Torres (A)	8-9-00	Indianapolis
200 meters	2:05.78	Otylia Jedrejczak, Poland (W)	8-4-02	Berlin
	2:05.88	Misty Hyman (A)	9-20-00	Sydney

Individual Medley

Event	Time	Record Holder	Date	Site
200 meters	2:09.72	Yanyan Wu, China (W)	10-17-97	Shanghai
	2:11.70	Amanda Beard (A)	8-17-04	Athens
400 meters	4:33.59	Yana Klochkova, Ukraine (W)	9-16-00	Sydney
	4:34.95	Kaitlin Sandeno (A)	8-14-04	Athens

Relays

Event	Time	Record Holder	Date	Site
400-meter medley	3:57.32	Australia (W) (Giaan Rooney, Leisel Jones, Petria Thomas, Jodie Henry)	8-21-04	Athens
	3:58.30	United States (A) (BJ Bedford, Megan Quann, Jenny Thompson, Dana Torres)	9-23-00	Sydney
400-meter freestyle	3:35.94	Australia (W) (Alice Mills, Lisbeth Lenton, Petria Thomas, Jodie Henry)	8-14-04	Athens
	3:36.39	United States (A) (Kara Lynn Joyce, Natalie Coughlin, Amanda Weir, Jenny Thompson)	8-14-04	Athens
800-meter freestyle	7:53.42	United States (W, A) (Natalie Coughlin, Carly Piper, Dana Vollmer, Kaitlin Sandeno)	8-18-04	Athens

MEN

50-meter Freestyle

1986	Tom Jager, United States	22.49‡
1991	Tom Jager, United States	22.16‡
1994	Alexander Popov, Russia	22.17
1998	Bill Pilczuk, United States	22.29
2001	Anthony Ervin, United States	22.09
2003	Alexander Popov, Russia	21.92‡

100-meter Freestyle

1973	Jim Montgomery, United States	51.70
1975	Andy Coan, United States	51.25
1978	David McCagg, United States	50.24
1982	Jorg Woithe, E Germany	50.18
1986	Matt Biondi, United States	48.94
1991	Matt Biondi, United States	49.18
1994	Alexander Popov, Russia	49.12
1998	Alexander Popov, Russia	48.93‡
2001	Anthony Ervin, United States	48.33‡
2003	Alexander Popov, Russia	48.42

200-meter Freestyle

1973	Jim Montgomery, United States	1:53.02
1975	Tim Shaw, United States	1:52.04‡
1978	Billy Forrester, United States	1:51.02‡
1982	Michael Gross, W Germany	1:49.84
1986	Michael Gross, W Germany	1:47.92
1991	Giorgio Lamberti, Italy	1:47.27‡
1994	Antti Kasvio, Finland	1:47.32
1998	Michael Klim, Australia	1:47.41
2001	Ian Thorpe, Australia	1:44.06*
2003	Ian Thorpe, Australia	1:45.14

400-meter Freestyle

1973	Rick DeMont, United States	3:58.18‡
1975	Tim Shaw, United States	3:54.88‡
1978	Vladimir Salnikov, USSR	3:51.94‡
1982	Vladimir Salnikov, USSR	3:51.30‡
1986	Rainer Henkel, W Germany	3:50.05
1991	Joerg Hoffman, Germany	3:48.04‡
1994	Kieran Perkins, Australia	3:43.80*
1998	Ian Thorpe, Australia	3:46.29
2001	Ian Thorpe, Australia	3:40.17*
2003	Ian Thorpe, Australia	3:42.58

1,500-meter Freestyle

1973	Stephen Holland, Australia	15:31.85
1975	Tim Shaw, United States	15:28.92‡
1978	Vladimir Salnikov, USSR	15:03.99‡
1982	Vladimir Salnikov, USSR	15:01.77‡
1986	Rainer Henkel, W Germany	15:05.31
1991	Joerg Hoffman, Germany	14:50.36*
1994	Kieran Perkins, Australia	14:50.52
1998	Grant Hackett, Australia	14:51.70
2001	Grant Hackett, Australia	14:34.56*
2003	Grant Hackett, Australia	14:43.14

100-meter Backstroke

1973	Roland Matthes, E Germany	57.47
1975	Roland Matthes, E Germany	58.15
1978	Bob Jackson, United States	56.36‡
1982	Dirk Richter, E Germany	55.95
1986	Igor Polianski, USSR	55.58‡
1991	Jeff Rouse, United States	55.23‡
1994	Martin Lopez Zubero, Spain	55.17‡
1998	Lenny Krayzelburg, United States	55.00‡
2001	Matt Welsh, Australia	54.31‡
2003	Aaron Peirsol, United States	53.61‡

200-meter Backstroke

1973	Roland Matthes, E Germany	2:01.87‡
1975	Zoltan Varraszto, Hungary	2:05.05
1978	Jesse Vassallo, United States	2:02.16
1982	Rick Carey, United States	2:00.82‡
1986	Igor Polianski, USSR	1:58.78‡
1991	Martin Zubero, Spain	1:59.52
1994	Vladimir Selkov, Russia	1:57.42‡
1998	Lenny Krayzelburg, United States	1:58.84

200-meter Backstroke (Cont.)

2001	Aaron Peirsol, United States	1:57.13‡
2003	Aaron Peirsol, United States	1:55.92

100-meter Breaststroke

1973	John Hencken, United States	1:04.02‡
1975	David Wilkie, Great Britain	1:04.26‡
1978	Walter Kusch, W Germany	1:03.56‡
1982	Steve Lundquist, United States	1:02.75‡
1986	Victor Davis, Canada	1:02.71
1991	Norbert Rozsa, Hungary	1:01.45*
1994	Norbert Rozsa, Hungary	1:01.24‡
1998	Frederik Deburghgraeve, Belgium	1:01.34
2001	Roman Sloudnov, Russia	1:00.16
2003	Kosuke Kitajima, Japan	59.78*

200-meter Breaststroke

1973	David Wilkie, Great Britain	2:19.28‡
1975	David Wilkie, Great Britain	2:18.23‡
1978	Nick Nevid, United States	2:18.37
1982	Victor Davis, Canada	2:14.77*
1986	Jozsef Szabo, Hungary	2:14.27‡
1991	Mike Barrowman, United States	2:11.23*
1994	Norbert Rozsa, Hungary	2:12.81
1998	Kurt Grote, United States	2:13.40
2001	Brendan Hansen, United States	2:10.69‡
2003	Kosuke Kitajima, Japan	2:09.42*

100-meter Butterfly

1973	Bruce Robertson, Canada	55.69
1975	Greg Jagenburg, United States	55.63
1978	Joe Bottom, United States	54.30
1982	Matt Gribble, United States	53.88‡
1986	Pablo Morales, United States	53.54‡
1991	Anthony Nesty, Suriname	53.29‡
1994	Rafal Szukala, Poland	53.51
1998	Michael Klim, Australia	52.25‡
2001	Lars Frolander, Sweden	52.10‡
2003	Ian Crocker, United States	50.98*

200-meter Butterfly

1973	Robin Backhaus, United States	2:03.32
1975	Bill Forrester, United States	2:01.95‡
1978	Mike Bruner, United States	1:59.38‡
1982	Michael Gross, E Germany	1:58.85‡
1986	Michael Gross, E Germany	1:56.53‡
1991	Melvin Stewart, United States	1:55.69*
1994	Denis Pankratov, Russia	1:56.54
1998	Denys Sylantyev, Ukraine	1:56.61
2001	Michael Phelps, United States	1:54.58*
2003	Michael Phelps, United States	1:54.35

200-meter Individual Medley

1973	Gunnar Larsson, Sweden	2:08.36
1975	Andras Hargitay, Hungary	2:07.72
1978	Graham Smith, Canada	2:03.65*
1982	Aleksandr Sidorenko, USSR	2:03.30‡
1986	Tamás Darnyi, Hungary	2:01.57‡
1991	Tamás Darnyi, Hungary	1:59.36*
1994	Jani Sievin, Finland	1:58.16*
1998	Marcel Wouda, Netherlands	2:01.18
2001	Massimiliano Rosolino, Italy	1:59.71
2003	Michael Phelps, United States	1:56.04*

400-meter Individual Medley

1975	Andras Hargitay, Hungary	4:32.57
1978	Jesse Vassallo, United States	4:20.05*
1982	Ricardo Prado, Brazil	4:19.78*
1986	Tamás Darnyi, Hungary	4:18.98‡
1991	Tamás Darnyi, Hungary	4:12.36*
1994	Tom Dolan, United States	4:12.30*
1998	Tom Dolan, United States	4:14.95
2001	Alessio Boggiatto, Italy	4:13.15
2003	Michael Phelps, United States	4:09.09*

* World record. ‡Meet record.

MEN (Cont.)

400-meter Medley Relay

1973.....United States (Mike Stamm,   3:49.49
John Hencken, Joe Bottom,
Jim Montgomery)
1975.....United States (John Murphy,   3:49.00
Rick Colella, Greg Jagenburg,
Andy Coan)
1978.....United States (Robert Jackson,   3:44.63
Nick Nevid, Joe Bottom,
David McCagg)
1982.....United States (Rick Carey,   3:40.84*
Steve Lundquist, Matt Gribble,
Rowdy Gaines)
1986.....United States (Dan Veatch,   3:41.25
David Lundberg, Pablo Morales,
Matt Biondi)
1991.....United States (Jeff Rouse,   3:39.66‡
Eric Wunderlich, Mark Henderson
Matt Biondi)
1994.....United States (Jeff Rouse, Eric   3:37.74‡
Wunderlich, Mark Henderson,
Gary Hall)
1998.....Australia (Matt Welsh, Phil Rogers,   3:37.98
Robin Backhaus, Rick Klatt,
Jim Montgomery)
2001.....Australia (Matt Welsh, Ian Thorpe,   3:35.35
Geoff Huegill, Regan Harrison)
2003.....United States (Aaron Peirsol   3:31.54*
Brendan Hansen,Ian Crocker,
Jason Lezak)

400-meter Freestyle Relay

1973.....United States (Mel Nash,   3:27.18
Joe Bottom, Jim Montgomery,
John Murphy)
1975.....United States (Bruce Furniss,   3:24.85
Jim Montgomery, Andy Coan,
John Murphy)
1978.....United States (Jack Babashoff,   3:19.74
Rowdy Gaines, Jim Montgomery,
David McCagg)
1982.....United States (Chris Cavanaugh,   3:19.26*
Robin Leamy, David McCagg,
Rowdy Gaines)
1986.....United States (Tom Jager,   3:19.89
Mike Heath, Paul Wallace,
Matt Biondi)
1991.....United States (Tom Jager,   3:17.15‡
Brent Lang, Doug Gjertsen,
Matt Biondi)
1994.....United States (Jon Olsen,   3:16.90‡
Josh Davis, Ugur Taner, Gary Hall Jr.)
1998.....United States (Bryan Jones,   3:16.69‡
Jon Olsen, Bradley Schumacher,
Gary Hall Jr.)
2001.....Australia (Michael Klim, Ian Thorpe,   3:14.10‡
Todd Pearson, Ashley Callus)
2003.....Russia (Andrei Kapralov, Ivan   3:14.06‡
Usov, Denis Pimankov
Alexander Popov)

800-meter Freestyle Relay

1973.....United States (Kurt Krumpholz,   7:33.22*
Robin Backhaus, Rick Klatt,
Jim Montgomery)
1975.....W Germany (Klaus Steinbach,   7:39.44
Werner Lampe, Hans Joachim
Geisler, Peter Nocke)
1978.....United States (Bruce Furniss,   7:20.82
Billy Forrester, Bobby Hackett,
Rowdy Gaines)
1982.....United States (Rich Saeger,   7:21.09
Jeff Float, Kyle Miller,
Rowdy Gaines)
1986.....E Germany (Lars Hinneburg,   7:15.91‡
Thomas Flemming, Dirk Richter,
Sven Lodziewski)

1991.....Germany (Peter Sitt,   7:13.50‡
Steffan Zesner, Stefan Pfeiffer,
Michael Gross)
1994.....Sweden (Christer Waller,   7:17.34
Tommy Werner, Lars Frolander,
Anders Holmertz)
1998.....Australia (Daniel Kowalski,   7:12.48‡
Grant Hackett, Ian Thorpe,
Anthony Rogis)
2001.....Australia (Michael Klim, Ian Thorpe,   7:04.66*
William Kirby, Grant Hackett)
2003.....Australia (Grant Hackett, Craig,   7:08.58
Stevens, N. Springer, Ian Thorpe)

WOMEN

50-meter Freestyle

1986....Tamara Costache, Romania	25.28*
1991....Zhuang Yong, China	25.47
1994....Le Jingyi, China	24.51*
1998....Amy Van Dyken, United States	25.15
2001....Inge de Bruijn, Netherlands	24.47
2003....Inge de Bruijn, Netherlands	24.47

100-meter Freestyle

1973....Kornelia Ender, E Germany	57.54
1975....Kornelia Ender, E Germany	56.50
1978....Barbara Krause, E Germany	55.68‡
1982....Birgit Meineke, E Germany	55.79
1986....Kristin Otto, E Germany	55.05‡
1991....Nicole Haislett, United States	55.17
1994....Le Jingyi, China	54.01*
1998....Jenny Thompson, United States	54.95
2001....Inge de Bruijn, Netherlands	54.18
2003....Hanna-Maria Seppälä, Finland	54.37

* World record; ‡Meet record.

200-meter Freestyle

1973.....Keena Rothhammer, United States	2:04.99
1975.....Shirley Babashoff, United States	2:02.50
1978.....Cynthia Woodhead, United States	1:58.53*
1982.....Annemarie Verstappen, Netherlands	1:59.53‡
1986....Heike Friedrich, E Germany	1:58.26‡
1991....Hayley Lewis, Australia	2:00.48
1994....Franziska Van Almsick, Germany	1:56.78*
1998....Claudia Poll, Costa Rica	1:58.90
2001....Giaan Rooney, Australia	1:58.57
2003....Alena Popchanka, Bulgaria	1:58.32

400-meter Freestyle

1973.....Heather Greenwood, United States	4:20.28
1975.....Shirley Babashoff, United States	4:22.70
1978.....Tracey Wickham, Australia	4:06.28*
1982.....Carmela Schmidt, E Germany	4:08.98
1986....Heike Friedrich, E Germany	4:07.45
1991....Janet Evans, United States	4:08.63
1994....Yang Aihua, China	4:09.64
1998....Chen Yan, China	4:06.72
2001....Yana Klochkova, Ukraine	4:07.30
2003....Hannah Stockbauer, Germany	4:06.75

WOMEN *(Cont.)*

800-meter Freestyle

1973	Novella Calligaris, Italy	8:52.97
1975	Jenny Turrall, Australia	8:44.75‡
1978	Tracey Wickham, Australia	8:24.94‡
1982	Kim Linehan, United States	8:27.48
1986	Astrid Strauss, E Germany	8:28.24
1991	Janet Evans, United States	8:24.05‡
1994	Janet Evans, United States	8:29.85
1998	Brooke Bennett, United States	8.28.71
2001	Hannah Stockbauer, Germany	8:24.66
2003	Hannah Stockbauer, Germany	8:23.66‡

100-meter Backstroke

1973	Ulrike Richter, E Germany	1:05.42
1975	Ulrike Richter, E Germany	1:03.30‡
1978	Linda Jezek, United States	1:02.55‡
1982	Kristin Otto, E Germany	1:01.30‡
1986	Betsy Mitchell, United States	1:01.74
1991	Krisztina Egerszegi, Hungary	1:01.78
1994	He Cihong, China	1:00.57
1998	Lea Maurer, United States	1:01.16
2001	Natalie Coughlin, United States	1:00.37
2003	Antje Buschschulte, Germany	1:00.50

200-meter Backstroke

1973	Melissa Belote, United States	2:20.52
1975	Birgit Treiber, E Germany	2:15.46*
1978	Linda Jezek, United States	2:11.93*
1982	Cornelia Sirch, E Germany	2:09.91*
1986	Cornelia Sirch, E Germany	2:11.37
1991	Krisztina Egerszegi, Hungary	2:09.15‡
1994	He Cihong, China	2:07.40
1998	Roxanna Maracineanu, France	2:11.26
2001	Diana Mocanu, Romania	2:09.94
2003	Katy Sexton, Great Britain	2:08.74

100-meter Breaststroke

1973	Renate Vogel, E Germany	1:13.74
1975	Hannalore Anke, E Germany	1:12.72
1978	Julia Bogdanova, USSR	1:10.31*
1982	Ute Geweniger, E Germany	1:09.14‡
1986	Sylvia Gerasch, E Germany	1:08.11*
1991	Linley Frame, Australia	1:08.81
1994	Samantha Riley, Australia	1:07.96*
1998	Kristy Kowal, United States	1:08.42
2001	Xuejuan Luo, China	1:07.18‡
2003	Xuejuan Luo, China	1:06.80

200-meter Breaststroke

1973	Renate Vogel, E Germany	2:40.01
1975	Hannalore Anke, E Germany	2:37.25‡
1978	Lina Kachushite, USSR	2:31.42*
1982	Svetlana Varganova, USSR	2:28.82‡
1986	Silke Hoerner, E Germany	2:27.40*
1991	Elena Volkova, USSR	2:29.53
1994	Samantha Riley, Australia	2:26.87‡
1998	Agnes Kovacs, Hungary	2:25.45‡
2001	Agnes Kovacs, Hungary	2:24.90
2003	Amanda Beard, United States	2:22.99*

100-meter Butterfly

1973	Kornelia Ender, E Germany	1:02.53
1975	Kornelia Ender, E Germany	1:01.24*
1978	Joan Pennington, United States	1:00.20‡
1982	Mary T. Meagher, United States	59.41‡
1986	Kornelia Gressler, E Germany	59.51
1991	Qian Hong, China	59.68
1994	Liu Limin, China	58.98‡
1998	Jenny Thompson, United States	58.46‡
2001	Petria Thomas, Australia	58:27
2003	Jenny Thompson, United States	57.96‡

200-meter Butterfly

1973	Rosemarie Kother, E Germany	2:13.76‡
1975	Rosemarie Kother, E Germany	2:15.92
1978	Tracy Caulkins, United States	2:09.87*
1982	Ines Geissler, E Germany	2:08.66‡
1986	Mary T. Meagher, United States	2:08.41‡
1991	Summer Sanders, United States	2:09.24
1994	Liu Limin, China	2:07.25‡
1998	Susie O'Neill, Australia	2:07.93‡
2001	Petria Thomas, Australia	2:06.73‡
2003	Otylia Jedrzejczak, Poland	2:07.56

200-meter Individual Medley

1973	Andrea Huebner, E Germany	2:20.51
1975	Kathy Heddy, United States	2:19.80
1978	Tracy Caulkins, United States	2:14.07*
1982	Petra Schneider, E Germany	2:11.79
1986	Kristin Otto, E Germany	2:15.56
1991	Li Lin, China	2:13.40
1994	Lu Bin, China	2:12.34‡
1998	Wu Yanyan, China	2:10.88
2001	Martha Bowen, United States	2:11.93
2003	Yana Klochkova, Ukraine	2:10.75‡

400-meter Individual Medley

1973	Gudrun Wegner, E Germany	4:57.71
1975	Ulrike Tauber, E Germany	4:52.76‡
1978	Tracy Caulkins, United States	4:40.83*
1982	Petra Schneider, E Germany	4:36.10*
1986	Kathleen Nord, E Germany	4:43.75
1991	Lin Li, China	4:41.45
1994	Dai Guohong, China	4:39.14
1998	Chen Yan, China	4:36.66
2001	Yana Klochkova, Ukraine	4:36.98
2003	Yana Klochkova, Ukraine	4:36.74

400-meter Medley Relay

1973	E Germany (Ulrike Richter, Renate Vogel, Rosemarie Kother, Kornelia Ender)	4:16.84
1975	E Germany (Ulrike Richter, Hannelore Anke, Rosemarie Kother, Kornelia Ender)	4:14.74
1978	United States (Linda Jezek, Tracy Caulkins, Joan Pennington, Cynthia Woodhead)	4:08.21‡
1982	E Germany (Kristin Otto, Ute Gewinger, Ines Geissler, Birgit Meineke)	4:05.8*
1986	E Germany (Kathrin Zimmermann, Sylvia Gerasch, Kornelia Gressler, Kristin Otto)	4:04.82
1991	United States (Janie Wagstaff, Tracey McFarlane, Crissy Ahmann-Leighton, Nicole Haislett)	4:06.51
1994	China (He Cihong, Dai Guohong, Liu Limin, Lu Bin)	4:01.67*
1998	United States (Kristy Kowal, Lea Maurer, Jenny Thompson, Amy Van Dyken)	4:01.93
2001	Australia (Dyana Calub, Sarah Ryan, Petria Thomas, Leisel Jones)	4:07.30
2003	China (Shu Xhan, Xuejuan Luo Yafei Zhou, Yu Yang)	3:59.89‡

400-meter Freestyle Relay

1973	E Germany (Kornelia Ender, Andrea Eife, Andrea Huebner, Sylvia Eichner)	3:52.45
1975	E Germany (Kornelia Ender, Barbara Krause, Claudia Hempel, Ute Bruckner)	3:49.37
1978	United States (Tracy Caulkins, Stephanie Elkins, Joan Pennington, Cynthia Woodhead)	3:43.43*

World Championships (Cont.)

WOMEN (Cont.)

400-meter Freestyle Relay (Cont.)

1982	E Germany (Birgit Meineke, Susanne Link, Kristin Otto, Caren Metschuk)	3:43.97
1986	E Germany (Kristin Otto, Manuela Stellmach, Sabine Schulze, Heike Friedrich)	3:40.57*
1991	United States (Nicole Haislett, Julie Cooper, Whitney Hedgepeth, Jenny Thompson)	3:43.26
1994	China (Le Jingyi, Ying Shan, Le Ying, Lu Bin)	3:37.91*
1998	United States (Catherine Fox, Lindsey Farella, Melanie Valerio, B.J. Bedford)	3:42.11
2001	Germany (Petra Dallman, Antje Buschschulter, Katrin Meissner, Sandra Volkner)	3:39.58
2003	United States (Natalie Coughlin, Lindsay Benko, Rhiannon Jeffrey, Jenny Thompson)	3:38.09

800-meter Freestyle Relay

1986	E Germany (Manuela Stellmach, Astrid Strauss, Nadja Bergknecht, Heike Friedrich)	7:59.33*
1991	Germany (Kerstin Kielgass, Manuela Stellmach, Dagmar Hase, Stephanie Ortwig)	8:02.56
1994	China (Le Ying, Yang Alhua, Zhou Guabin, Lu Bin)	7:57.96
1998	Germany (Silvia Szalai, Antje Buschschulte, Janina Goetz, Franziska Van Almsick)	8:02.56
2001	Great Britain (Nicola Jackson, Janine Belton, Karen Legg, Karen Pickering)	7:58.69
2003	United States (Lindsay Benko, Rachel Komisarz, Rhiannon Jeffrey, Diana Munz)	7:55.70‡

* World record; ‡Meet record.

World Diving Championships

MEN

1-meter Springboard

		Pts
1991	Edwin Jongejans, Netherlands	588.51
1994	Evan Stewart, Zimbabwe	382.14
1998	Yu Zhuocheng, China	417.54
2001	Wang Feng, China	444.03
2003	Xiang Xu, China	431.94

3-meter Springboard

		Pts
1973	Phil Boggs, United States	618.57
1975	Phil Boggs, United States	597.12
1978	Phil Boggs, United States	913.95
1982	Greg Louganis, United States	752.67
1986	Greg Louganis, United States	750.06
1991	Kent Ferguson, United States	650.25
1994	Wu Zhuocheng, China	655.44
1998	Dmitry Sautin, Russia	746.79
2001	Dmitry Sautin, Russia	725.82
2003	Alexander Dobrosok, Russia	788.37

Platform

		Pts
1973	Klaus Dibiasi, Italy	559.53
1975	Klaus Dibiasi, Italy	547.98
1978	Greg Louganis, United States	844.11
1982	Greg Louganis, United States	634.26
1986	Greg Louganis, United States	668.58
1991	Sun Shuwei, China	626.79
1994	Dmitry Sautin, Russia	634.71
1998	Dmitry Sautin, Russia	750.90
2001	Tian Lang, China	688.77
2003	Alexandre Despatie, Canada	716.91

3-meter Synchronized

		Pts
1998	China (Sun Shuwei, Tian Liang)	313.50
2001	China (Bo Peng, Kenan Wang)	342.63
2003	Russia (A. Dobrosok, D. Sautin)	369.18

10-meter Synchronized

1998	China (Xu Hao, Yu Zhuocheng)	326.34
2001	China (Jian Tian, Jia Bu)	361.41
2003	Australia (M. Helm, R. Newbery)	384.6

WOMEN

1-meter Springboard

		Pts
1991	Gao Min, China	478.26
1994	Chen Lixia, China	279.30
1998	Irina Lashko, Russia	296.07
2001	Blythe Hartley, Canada	300.81
2003	Irina Lashko, Australia	299.97

3-meter Springboard

		Pts
1973	Christa Koehler, E Germany	442.17
1975	Irina Kalinina, USSR	489.81
1978	Irina Kalinina, USSR	691.43
1982	Megan Neyer, United States	501.03
1986	Gao Min, China	582.90
1991	Gao Min, China	539.01
1994	Tan Shuping, China	548.49
1998	Yulia Pakhalina, Russia	544.62
2001	Jingjing Guo, China	596.67
2003	Jingjing Guo, China	617.94

Platform

1973	Ulrike Knape, Sweden	406.77
1975	Janet Ely, United States	403.89
1978	Irina Kalinina, USSR	412.71
1982	Wendy Wyland, United States	438.79
1986	Chen Lin, China	449.67
1991	Fu Mingxia, China	426.51
1994	Fu Mingxia, China	434.04
1998	Olena Zhupyna, Ukraine	550.41
2001	Mian Xu, China	532.65
2003	Emilie Heymans, Canada	597.45

3-meter Synchronized

		Pts
1998	Russia (Irina Lashko, Yulia Pakhalina)	282.30
2001	China (Minxia Wu, Jingjing Guo)	347.31
2003	China (Minxia Wu, Jingjing Guo)	357.30

10-meter Synchronized

		Pts
1998	Ukraine (O. Zhupyna, S. Serbina)	278.28
2001	China (Qing Duan, Xue Sang)	329.94
2003	China (Lishi Lao, Ting Li)	344.58

Men

50-METER FREESTYLE

1988 ....Matt Biondi	22.14*
2000 .....Gary Hall Jr. and Anthony Ervin	21.98
2004 ....Gary Hall Jr.	21.93

100-METER FREESTLYE

1906 ....Charles Daniels	1:13.4
1908 ....Charles Daniels	1:05.6*
1912 ....Duke Kahanamoku	1:03.4
1920 ....Duke Kahanamoku	1:00.4
1924 ....John Weissmuller	59.0‡
1928 ....John Weissmuller	58.6‡
1948 ....Wally Ris	57.3‡
1952 ....Clarke Scholes	57.4
1964 ....Don Schollander	53.4‡
1972 ....Mark Spitz	51.22*
1976 ....Jim Montgomery	49.99*
1984 ....Rowdy Gaines	49.80‡
1988 ....Matt Biondi	48.63‡

200-METER FREESTYLE

1904 ....Charles Daniels	2:44.2
1906–1964 Not held	
1972 ....Mark Spitz	1:52.78*
1976 ....Bruce Furniss	1:50.29*

400-METER FREESTYLE

1904 ....Charles Daniels (440 yds)	6:16.2
1920 ....Norman Ross	5:26.8
1924 ....John Weissmuller	5:04.2‡
1932 ....Buster Crabbe	4:48.4‡
1936 ....Jack Medica	4:44.5‡
1948 ....William Smith	4:41.0‡
1964 ....Don Schollander	4:12.2*
1968 ....Mike Burton	4:09.0‡
1976 ....Brian Goodell	3:51.93*
1984 ....George DiCarlo	3:51.23‡

1,500-METER FREESTYLE

1920 ....Norman Ross	22:23.2
1948 ....James McLane	19:18.5
1952 ....Ford Konno	18:30.3‡
1968 ....Mike Burton	16:38.9‡
1972 ....Mike Burton	15:52.58‡
1976 .....Brian Goodell	15:02.40*
1984 ....Michael O'Brien	15:05.20

100-METER BACKSTROKE

1912 ....Harry Hebner	1:21.2
1920 ....Warren Kealoha	1:15.2
1924 ....Warren Kealoha	1:13.2‡
1928 ....George Kojac	1:08.2*
1936 ....Adolph Kiefer	1:05.9‡
1948 ....Allen Stack	1:06.4
1952 ....Yoshi Oyakawa	1:05.4‡
1976 ....John Naber	55.49*
1984 ....Rick Carey	55.79
1996 ....Jeff Rouse	54.10
2000 ....Lenny Krayzelburg	53.60‡
2004 ....Aaron Peirsol	54.06

200-METER BACKSTROKE

1964 ....Jed Graef	2:10.3*
1976 ....John Naber	1:59.19*
1984 ....Rick Carey	2:00.23
1996 .....Brad Bridgewater	1:58.54
2000 .....Lenny Krayzelburg	1:56.76‡
2004 .....Aaron Peirsol	1:54.95‡

* World record. ‡Meet (Olympic) record.

100-METER BREASTSTROKE

1968 ....Donald McKenzie	1:07.7‡
1976 ....John Hencken	1:03.11*
1984 ....Steve Lundquist	1:01.65 *
1992 ....Nelson Diebel	1:01.50‡

200-METER BREASTSTROKE

1924 ....Robert Skelton	2:56.6
1948 ....Joseph Verdeur	2:39.3‡
1960 ....William Mulliken	2:37.4
1972 ....John Hencken	2:21.55
1992 ....Mike Barrowman	2:10.16*

100-METER BUTTERFLY

1968 ....Douglas Russell	55.9‡
1972 ....Mark Spitz	54.27*
1976 ....Matt Vogel	54.35
1992 ....Pablo Morales	53.32
2004 ....Michael Phelps	51.24‡

200-METER BUTTERFLY

1956 ....William Yorzyk	2:19.3‡
1960 ....Michael Troy	2:12.8*
1968 ....Carl Robie	2:08.7
1972 ....Mark Spitz	2:00.70*
1976 ....Mike Bruner	1:59.23*
1992 ....Melvin Stewart	1:56.26
2000 ....Tom Malchow	1:55.35‡
2004 ....Michael Phelps	1:54.04‡

200-METER INDIVIDUAL MEDLEY

1968 ....Charles Hickcox	2:12.0‡
2004 ....Michael Phelps	1:57.14‡

400-METER INDIVIDUAL MEDLEY

1964 ....Richard Roth	4:45.4*
1968 ....Charles Hickcox	4:48.4
1976 ....Rod Strachan	4:23.68*
1996 ....Tom Dolan	4:14.90
2000 ....Tom Dolan	4:11.76‡
2004 ....Michael Phelps	4:08.26*

3-METER SPRINGBOARD DIVING

1920 ....Louis Kuehn	675.4 points
1924 ....Albert White	696.4
1928 ....Pete Desjardins	185.04
1932 ....Michael Galitzen	161.38
1936 ....Richard Degener	163.57
1948 ....Bruce Harlan	163.64
1952 ....David Browning	205.29
1956 ....Robert Clotworthy	159.56
1960 ....Gary Tobian	170.00
1964 ....Kenneth Sitzberger	159.90
1968 ....Bernard Wrightson	170.15
1976 ....Philip Boggs	619.05
1984 ....Greg Louganis	754.41
1988 ....Greg Louganis	730.80

PLATFORM DIVING

1904 ....George Sheldon	12.66 points
1920 ....Clarence Pinkston	100.67
1924 ....Albert White	97.46
1928 ....Pete Desjardins	98.74
1932 ....Harold Smith	124.80
1936 ....Marshall Wayne	113.58
1948 ....Sammy Lee	130.05
1952 ....Sammy Lee	156.28
1960 ....Robert Webster	165.56
1964 ....Robert Webster	148.58
1984 ....Greg Louganis	576.99
1988 ....Greg Louganis	638.61

Women

50-METER FREESTYLE

1996	Amy Van Dyken	24.87

100-METER FREESTLYE

1920	Ethelda Bleibtrey	1:13.6*
1924	Ethel Lackie	1:12.4
1928	Albina Osipowich	1:11.0‡
1932	Helene Madison	1:06.8‡
1968	Jan Henne	1:00.0
1972	Sandra Neilson	58.59‡
1984	Carrie Steinseifer	55.92
	Nancy Hogshead	55.92

200-METER FREESTYLE

1968	Debbie Meyer	2:10.5‡
1984	Mary Wayte	1:59.23
1992	Nicole Haislett	1:57.90

400-METER FREESTYLE

1924	Martha Norelius	6:02.2‡
1928	Martha Norelius	5:42.8*
1932	Helene Madison	5:28.5*
1948	Ann Curtis	5:17.8‡
1960	Chris von Saltza	4:50.6
1964	Virginia Duenkel	4:43.3‡
1968	Debbie Meyer	4:31.8‡
1984	Tiffany Cohen	4:07.10‡
1988	Janet Evans	4:03.85*

800-METER FREESTYLE

1968	Debbie Meyer	9:24.0‡
1972	Keena Rothhammer	8:53.86*
1984	Tiffany Cohen	8:24.95‡
1988	Janet Evans	8:20.20‡
1992	Janet Evans	8:25.52
1996	Brooke Bennett	8:27.89
2000	Brooke Bennett	8:19.67

100-METER BACKSTROKE

1924	Sybil Bauer	1:23.2‡
1932	Eleanor Holm	1:19.4
1960	Lynn Burke	1:09.3‡
1964	Cathy Ferguson	1:07.7*
1968	Kaye Hall	1:06.2*
1972	Melissa Belote	1:05.78‡
1984	Theresa Andrews	1:02.55
1996	Beth Botsford	1:01.19
2004	Natalie Coughlin	1:00.37

200-METER BACKSTROKE

1968	Pokey Watson	2:24.8‡
1972	Melissa Belote	2:19.19*

* World record; ‡Meet (Olympic) record.

100-METER BREASTSTROKE

1972	Catherine Carr	1:13.58*
2000	Megan Quann	1:07.05

200-METER BREASTSTROKE

1968	Sharon Wichman	2:44.4‡
2004	Amanda Beard	2:23.37‡

100-METER BUTTERFLY

1956	Shelley Mann	1:11.0‡
1960	Carolyn Schuler	1:09.5‡
1964	Sharon Stouder	1:04.7*
1984	Mary T. Meagher	59.26
1996	Amy Van Dyken	59.13

200-METER BUTTERFLY

1972	Karen Moe	2:15.57*
1984	Mary T. Meagher	2:06.90‡
1992	Summer Sanders	2:08.67
2000	Misty Hyman	2:05.88‡

200-METER INDIVIDUAL MEDLEY

1968	Sharon Wichman	2:44.4‡
1984	Tracy Caulkins	2:12.64‡

400-METER INDIVIDUAL MEDLEY

1964	Donna De Varona	5:18.7‡
1968	Claudia Kolb	5:08.5‡
1984	Tracy Caulkins	4:39.24
1988	Janet Evans	4:37.76

3-METER SPRINGBOARD DIVING

1920	Aileen Riggin	539.9 points
1924	Elizabeth Becker	474.5
1928	Helen Meany	78.62
1932	Georgia Coleman	87.52
1936	Marjorie Gestring	89.27
1948	Victoria Draves	108.74
1952	Patricia McCormick	147.30
1956	Patricia McCormick	142.36
1968	Sue Gossick	150.77
1972	Micki King	450.03
1976	Jennifer Chandler	506.19

PLATFORM DIVING

1924	Caroline Smith	33.2 points
1928	Elizabeth Becker Pinkston	31.6
1932	Dorothy Poynton	40.26
1936	Dorothy Poynton Hill	33.93
1948	Victoria Draves	68.87
1952	Patricia McCormick	79.37
1956	Patricia McCormick	84.85
1964	Lesley Bush	99.80
2000	Laura Wilkinson	543.75

Notable Achievements

Barrier Breakers

MEN

Event	Barrier	Athlete and Nation	Time	Date
100 Freestyle	1:00	Johnny Weissmuller, United States	58.6	7-9-22
100 Freestyle	:50	James Montgomery, United States	49.99	7-25-76
200 Freestyle	2:00	Don Schollander, United States	1:58.8	7-27-63
200 Freestyle	1:50	Sergei Kopliakov, USSR	1:49.83	4-7-79
200 Freestyle	1:45	Ian Thorpe, Australia	1:44.06	7-25-01
400 Freestyle	4:00	Rick DeMont, United States	3:58.18	9-6-73
400 Freestyle	3:50	Vladimir Salnikov, USSR	3:49.57	3-12-82
800 Freestyle	8:00	Vladimir Salnikov, USSR	7:56.49	3-23-79
800 Freestyle	7:40	Ian Thorpe, Australia	7:39.16	7-24-01
1500 Freestyle	15:00	Vladimir Salnikov, USSR	14:58.27	7-22-80
1500 Freestyle	14:35	Grant Hackett, Australia	14:34.56	7-29-01
100 Backstroke	1:00	Thompson Mann, United States	59.6	10-16-64
200 Backstroke	2:00	John Naber, United States	1:59.19	7-24-76
100 Breaststroke	1:00	Roman Sloudnov, Russia	59.97	6-28-01
200 Breaststroke	2:30	Chester Jastremski, United States	2:29.6	8-19-61
200 Breaststroke	2:10	Kosuke Kitajima, Japan	2:09.42	7-24-03
100 Butterfly	1:00	Lance Larson, United States	59.0	6-29-60
200 Butterfly	2:00	Roger Pyttel, E Germany	1:59.63	6-3-76

WOMEN

Event	Barrier	Athlete and Nation	Time	Date
100 Freestyle	1:00	Dawn Fraser, Australia	59.9	10-27-62
200 Freestyle	2:00	Kornelia Ender, E Germany	1:59.78	6-2-76
400 Freestyle	4:30	Debbie Meyer, United States	4:29.0	8-18-67
800 Freestyle	10:00	Jane Cederqvist, Sweden	9:55.6	8-17-60
800 Freestyle	9:00	Ann Simmons, United States	8:59.4	9-10-71
1500 Freestyle	20:00	Ilsa Konrads, Australia	19:25.7	1-14-60
	16:00	Janet Evans, United States	15:52.10	3-26-88
100 Backstroke	1:00	Natalie Coughlin, United States	59.58	8-16-02
200 Backstroke	2:30	Satoko Tanaka, Japan	2:29.6	2-10-63
100 Butterfly	1:00	Christiane Knacke, E Germany	59.78	8-28-77
400 Individual Medley	5:00	Gudrun Wegner, E Germany	4:57.51	9-6-73

Olympic Achievements

MOST INDIVIDUAL GOLDS IN SINGLE OLYMPICS

MEN

No.	Athlete and Nation	Olympic Year	Events
4	Mark Spitz, United States	1972	100, 200 Free; 100, 200 Fly
4	Michael Phelps, United States	2004	100, 200 fly, 200 IM, 400 IM

WOMEN

No.	Athlete and Nation	Olympic Year	Events
4	Kristin Otto, E Germany	1988	50, 100 Free; 100 Back; 100 Fly
3	Debbie Meyer, United States	1968	200, 400, 800 Free
3	Shane Gould, Australia	1972	200, 400 Free; 200 IM
3	Kornelia Ender, E Germany	1976	100, 200 Free; 100 Fly
3	Janet Evans, United States	1988	400, 800 Free; 400 IM
3	Krisztina Egerszegi, Hungary	1992	100, 200 Back; 400 IM
3	Michelle Smith, Ireland	1996	400 Free; 200, 400 IM
3	Inge de Bruijn, Netherlands	2000	50, 100 Free; 100 Fly

Olympic Achievements *(Cont.)*

MOST INDIVIDUAL OLYMPIC GOLD MEDALS, CAREER
MEN

No.	Athlete and Nation	Olympic Years and Events
4	Charles Meldrum Daniels, United States	1904 (220, 440 Free); 1906 (100 Free) 1908 (100 Free)
4	Roland Matthes, E Germany	1968 (100, 200 Back); 1972 (100, 200 Back)
4	Mark Spitz, United States	1972 (100, 200 Free; 100, 200 Fly)
4	Michael Phelps, United States	2004 (100, 200 fly; 200, 400 IM)

WOMEN

No.	Athlete and Nation	Olympic Years and Events
4	Kristin Otto, E Germany	1988 (50 Free; 100 Free, Back and Fly)
4	Janet Evans, United States	1988 (400, 800 Free; 400 IM); 1992 (800 Free)
4	Krisztina Egerszegi, Hungary	1992 (100, 200 Back; 400 IM); 1996 (200 Back)
4	Inge de Bruijn, Netherlands	2000 (50, 100 free; 100 fly); 2004 (50 free)
4	Yana Klochkova, Ukraine	2000 (200, 400 IM); 2004 (200, 400 IM)

Most Olympic Gold Medals in a Single Olympics, Men—7, Mark Spitz, United States, 1972: 100, 200 Free; 100, 200 Fly; 4 x 100, 4 x 200 Free Relays; 4 x 100 Medley Relay.
Most Olympic Gold Medals in a Single Olympics, Women—6, Kristin Otto, E Germany, 1988: 50, 100 Free; 100 Back; 100 Fly; 4 x 100 Free Relay; 4 x 100 Medley Relay.
Most Olympic Medals in a Single Olympics, Men—8, Michael Phelps, United States, 2004: (six gold, two bronze).
Most Olympic Medals in a Career, Men—11, Matt Biondi, United States: 1984 (one gold), '88 (five gold, one silver, one bronze), '92 (two gold, one silver); 11, Mark Spitz, United States: 1968 (two gold, one silver, one bronze), '72 (seven gold); 10, Gary Hall Jr., United States 1996 (one gold, three silver), 2000 (three gold, one bronze) 2004 (two gold).
Most Olympic Medals in a Career, Women—11, Jenny Thompson, United States: 1992 (two gold, one silver), 1996 (three gold), 2000 (three gold, one bronze); 2004 (one silver); 8, Dawn Fraser, Australia: 1956 (two gold, one silver), '60 (one gold, two silver), '64 (one gold, one silver); 8, Kornelia Ender, E Germany: 1972 (three silver), '76 (four gold, one silver); 8, Shirley Babashoff, United States: 1972 (one gold, two silver); '76 (one gold, four silver); 8, Inge de Bruijn, Netherlands: 2000 (three gold, one silver), 2004 (one gold, one silver, two bronze).
Winner, Same Event, Three Consecutive Olympics—Dawn Fraser, Australia, 100 Freestyle, 1956, '60, '64; Krisztina Egerszegi, Hungary, 200 Back, 1988, '92, '96.
Youngest Person to Win an Olympic Diving Gold—Marjorie Gestring, United States, 1936, 13 years, 9 months, springboard diving.
Youngest Person to Win an Olympic Swimming Gold—Krisztina Egerszegi, Hungary, 1988, 14 years, one month, 200 backstroke.

World Record Achievements

Most World Records, Career, Women—42, Ragnhild Hveger, Denmark, 1936–42.
Most World Records, Career, Men—32, Arne Borg, Sweden, 1921–29.
Most Freestyle Records Held Concurrently—5, Helene Madison, United States, 1931–33; 5, Shane Gould, Australia, 1972.
Most Consecutive Lowerings of a Record—10, Kornelia Ender, E Germany, 100 Freestyle, 7-13-73 to 7-19-76.
Longest Duration of World Record—19 years, 359 days, 1:04.6 in 100 Free, Willy den Ouden, Netherlands.

Skiing

World Cup overall champion Hermann Maier of Austria

"I'll Be Back"

Fulfilling the cinematic vow of his Hollywood namesake, Hermann Maier, aka the Herminator, made a stunning return

BY MARK BECHTEL

WHEN HE BECAME THE 2004 overall World Cup champion, Hermann Maier was napping in his hotel in the Italian Alps. That was fitting, for if anyone deserved a rest it was the 31-year-old Maier, who strung together one solid performance after another in the speed events to win his fourth overall title in his first full season back from a motorcycle crash that nearly killed him.

Maier wrapped up the crown when heavy snow and fog forced the abandonment of the men's giant slalom at Sestriere, Italy—the site of the 2006 Olympic skiing competition. The cancellation gave Maier an insurmountable lead over fellow Austrian Benjamin Raich, whose first run, before the storm swirled in, had put him in position to challenge Maier for the overall championship. "Of course I feel sorry for Benjamin," Maier said. "But there's no need to remind you that in 1999 there was a giant slalom and a super-G late in the season that were can-celed, and I lost the World Cup by only a few points. So I was lucky today, but I was also unlucky in the past."

Maier had been extremely unlucky in the summer of 2001, when a car hit his motorcycle and left him with a crushed right leg and severe internal bleeding. He underwent seven hours of surgery, came dangerously close to kidney failure and almost lost the leg. But after months of gruelling rehabilitation, Maier made an impressive return to the slopes in January 2003. But he was a different skier than the "Herminator," the dominant, powerful skier who bounced back from a horrific crash in the downhill at the Nagano Games of 1998 to win two gold medals. The new Maier could no longer blow away the competition, and had to rely on guts and grit instead. He also wasn't afraid to talk about the doubts he now faced. "All I can tell you is that 100 percent of the Hermann today was used," he said at Sestriere. "The only difference is that I don't have that 1.5-second margin anymore over the others. It doesn't exist anymore."

Pärson won the super G, the slalom and ran away with the women's overall title.

So, deprived of the Herminator of old, the 2003–04 World Cup season was predictably wide open. American Bode Miller, who finished second in both the overall and the giant slalom last season, arrived in Sestriere with the lead in the giant slalom standings and an outside shot at the overall title, which before the season began he had boldly predicted he would win. But Miller crashed on the upper section in his first run, opening the door for Finland's Kalle Palander. Then the snow storm that gave Maier his overall title ensured that Miller would win the giant slalom as well. "I think I deserved the GS title, but I would have been happier to see that race go off and see what Palander would do," said Miller, who became the first American man since Phil Mahre in 1983 to win the giant slalom season title. But after beginning the season with his prediction of overall glory—something many observers thought he could achieve after his showing last season—Miller wound up a disappointing fourth in the standings, with last year's champion, Stephan Eberharter finishing second and Raich third, giving Austria a 1-2-3 sweep.

The women's overall title was won by 22-year-old Swede Anja Pärson. A slalom specialist—she won her first slalom race six years ago—Pärson wrapped up the slalom and super-G titles by the time she arrived in Sestriere. Her domination of those two fields, along with her improvement in the speed events, made for a one-woman race in the overall standings. (Pärson also benefitted from the absence of Janica Kostelic, the Croatian technical specialist who won the overall title in 2003 but sat out last season with a thyroid condition.) "Anja had a super season," said Austrian Renate Götschl, the overall winner in 2000 who finished second to Pärson this year. "She proved that she was super consistent."

Pärson's performance was reminiscent of the way Maier won the overall titles in 1998, 2000 and 2001. Maier's last championship before his injury came by a whopping 743 points over Eberharter. He had grown accustomed to winning, and to *expecting* to win, but the wreck caused Maier to alter his approach, to lower his expectations. So the 2003–04 season came as one long, and very pleasant, surprise for the legendary Austrian. "At the start of the season my goal was to finish the season, to race as many races as possible," he said. "So you can imagine how surprised I am."

Given Maier's starry track record, though, few skiing fans shared that surprise.

FOR THE RECORD·2003–2004

World Cup Alpine Racing Season Results

Men

Date	Event	Site	Winner
10-26-03	Giant Slalom	Sölden, Austria	Bode Miller, United States
11-22-03	Giant Slalom	Park City, Utah	Bode Miller, United States
11-23-03	Slalom	Park City, Utah	Kalle Palander, Finland
11-29-03	Downhill	Lake Louise, Alberta	Michael Walchhofer, Austria
11-30-03	Super G	Lake Louise, Alberta	Hermann Maier, Austria
12-5-03	Downhill	Vail/Beaver Creek, Colorado	Daron Rahlves, United States
12-6-03	Downhill	Vail/Beaver Creek, Colorado	Hermann Maier, Austria
12-7-03	Super G	Vail/Beaver Creek, Colorado	Bjarne Solbakken, Norway
12-14-03	Giant Slalom	Alta Badia, Italy	Kalle Palander, Finland
12-15-03	Slalom	Madonna di Campiglio, Italy	Ivica Kostelic, Croatia
12-19-03	Super G	Val Gardena/Groeden, Italy	Lasse Kjus, Norway
12-20-03	Downhill	Val Gardena/Groeden, Italy	Antoine Deneriaz, France
12-21-03	Giant Slalom	Alta Badia, Italy	Davide Simoncelli, Italy
1-3-04	Giant Slalom	Flachau, Austria	Benjamin Raich, Austria
1-4-04	Slalom	Flachau, Austria	Kalle Palander, Finland
1-10-04	Downhill	Chamonix, France	Stephan Eberharter, Austria
1-11-04	Slalom	Chamonix, France	Giorgio Rocca, Italy
1-11-04	Combined	Chamonix, France	Bode Miller, United States
1-18-04	Slalom	Wengen, Switzerland	Benjamin Raich, Austria
1-22-04	Downhill	Kitzbühel, Austria	Lasse Kjus, Norway
1-23-04	Super G	Kitzbühel, Austria	Daron Rahlves, United States
1-24-04	Downhill	Kitzbühel, Austria	Stephan Eberharter, Austria
1-25-04	Slalom	Kitzbühel, Austria	Kalle Palander, Finland
1-25-04	Combined	Kitzbühel, Austria	Bode Miller, United States
1-27-04	Slalom	Schladming, Austria	Benjamin Raich, Austria
1-30-04	Downhill	Garmisch, Germany	Didier Cuche, Switzerland
1-31-04	Downhill	Garmisch, Germany	Stephan Eberharter, Austria
2-1-04	Super G	Garmisch, Germany	Hermann Maier, Austria
2-7-04	Giant Slalom	Adelboden, Switzerland	Kalle Palander, Finland
2-8-04	Slalom	Adelboden, Switzerland	Rainer Schoenfelder, Austria
2-14-04	Downhill	Sankt Anton, Austria	Hermann Maier, Austria
2-15-04	Slalom	Sankt Anton, Austria	Bode Miller, United States
2-28-04	Giant Slalom	Kranjska Gora, Slovenia	Bode Miller, United States
2-29-04	Slalom	Kranjska Gora, Slovenia	Truls Ove Karlsen, Norway
3-6-04	Downhill	Kvitfjell, Norway	Stephan Eberharter, Norway
3-7-04	Super G	Kvitfjell, Norway	Daron Rahlves, United States
3-10-04	Downhill	Sestriere, Italy	Daron Rahlves, United States
3-11-04	Super G	Sestriere, Italy	Hermann Maier, Austria
3-14-04	Slalom	Sestriere, Italy	Kalle Palander, Finland

Women

Date	Event	Site	Winner
10-25-03	Giant Slalom	Sölden, Austria	Martina Ertl, Germany
11-28-03	Giant Slalom	Park City, Utah	Anja Pärson, Sweden
11-29-03	Slalom	Park City, Utah	Anja Pärson, Sweden
12-5-03	Downhill	Lake Louise, Alberta	Carole Montillet, France
12-6-03	Downhill	Lake Louise, Alberta	Carole Montillet, France
12-7-03	Super G	Lake Louise, Alberta	Renate Götschl, Austria
12-13-03	Giant Slalom	Alta Badia, Italy	Denise Karbon, Italy
12-16-03	Slalom	Madonna di Campiglio, Italy	Anja Pärson, Sweden
12-17-03	Slalom	Madonna di Campiglio, Italy	Nicole Hosp, Austria
12-20-03	Downhill	St. Moritz, Switzerland	Renate Götschl, Austria
12-27-03	Giant Slalom	Lienz, Austria	Nicole Hosp, Austria
12-28-03	Slalom	Lienz, Austria	Anja Pärson, Sweden
1-4-04	Super G	Megeve, France	Alexandra Meissnitzer, Austria
1-5-04	Slalom	Megeve, France	Anja Pärson, Sweden
1-10-04	Downhill	Veysonnaz, Switzerland	Renate Götschl, Austria
1-11-04	Super G	Veysonnaz, Switzerland	Hilde Gerg, Germany
1-14-04	Super G	Cortina d'Ampezzo, Italy	Genevieve Simard, Canada
1-16-04	Super G	Cortina d'Ampezzo, Italy	Renate Götschl, Austria
1-17-04	Downhill	Cortina d'Ampezzo, Italy	Hilde Gerg, Germany
1-18-04	Downhill	Cortina d'Ampezzo, Italy	Carole Montillet, France
1-24-04	Giant Slalom	Maribor, Slovenia	Anja Pärson, Sweden
1-25-04	Slalom	Maribor, Slovenia	Anja Pärson, Sweden
1-30-04	Downhill	Haus/Ennstal, Austria	Maria Riesch, Germany
1-31-04	Downhill	Haus/Ennstal, Austria	Isolde Kostner, Italy
2-1-04	Super G	Haus/Ennstal, Austria	Carole Montillet, France
			Maria Riesch, Germany
2-7-04	Giant Slalom	Region Arber, Germany	Anja Pärson, Sweden

World Cup Alpine Racing Season Results (Cont.)

Women (Cont.)

Date	Event	Site	Winner
2-8-04	Slalom	Region Arber, Germany	Anja Pärson, Sweden
2-21-04	Super G	Are, Sweden	Renate Götschl, Austria
2-22-04	Giant Slalom	Are, Sweden	Anja Pärson, Sweden
2-28-04	Slalom	Levi, Finland	Tanja Poutiainen, Finland
2-29-04	Slalom	Levi, Finland	Maria Fiesch, Germany
3-10-04	Downhill	Sestriere, Italy	Renate Götschl, Austria
3-11-04	Super G	Sestriere, Italy	Nadia Styger, Switzerland
3-13-04	Slalom	Sestriere, Italy	Marlies Schild, Austria
3-14-04	Giant Slalom	Sestriere, Italy	Anja Pärson, Sweden

World Cup Alpine Racing Final Standings

Men

OVERALL

	Pts
Hermann Maier, Austria	1,265
Stephan Eberharter, Austria	1,223
Benjamin Raich, Austria	1,139
Bode Miller, United States	1,134
Daron Rahlves, U.S.	1,004
Kalle Palander, Finland	944
Michael Walchhofer, Austria	828
Lasse Kjus, Norway	824
Hans Knauss, Austria	796
Rainer Schoenfelder, Austria	727

DOWNHILL

	Pts
Stephan Eberharter, Austria	831
Daron Rahlves, United States	627
Hermann Maier, Austria	537
Fritz Strobl, Austria	512
Michael Walchhofer, Austria	503
Hans Knauss, Austria	421
Antoine Deneriaz, France	367
Ambrosi Hoffman, Switzerland	317
Lasse Kjus, Norway	316
Didier Cuche, Switzerland	316

SLALOM

	Pts
Rainer Schoenfelder, Austria	630
Kalle Palander, Finland	595
Benjamin Raich, Austria	468
Giorgio Rocca, Italy	429
Bode Miller, United States	376
Mario Matt, Austria	352
Manfred Pranger, Austria	347
Truls Ove Karlsen, Norway	262
Manfred Mölgg, Italy	236
Thomas Grandi, Canada	221

GIANT SLALOM

	Pts
Bode Miller, United States	410
Kalle Palander, Finland	349
Massimiliano Blardone, Italy	266
Benjamin Raich, Austria	255
Davide Simoncelli, Italy	238
Heinz Schilchegger, Austria	210
Frederic Covili, France	190
Joel Chenal, France	187
Andreas Schifferer, Austria	186
Christoph Gruber, Austria	181

SUPER G

	Pts
Hermann Maier, Austria	580
Daron Rahlves, United States	340
Stephan Eberharter, Austria	312
Bjarne Solbakken, Norway	298
Michael Walchhofer, Austria	243
Hans Knauss, Austria	237
Lasse Kjus, Norway	230
Benjamin Raich, Austria	215
Andreas Schifferer, Austria	212
Didier Cuche, Switzerland	211

Women

OVERALL

	Pts
Anja Pärson, Sweden	1,561
Renate Götschl, Austria	1,344
Maria Riesch, Germany	977
Hilde Gerg, Germany	962
Carole Montillet, France	957
Michaela Dorfmeister, Austria	943
Martina Ertl, Germany	770
Alexandra Meissnitzer, Austria	734
Tanja Poutiainen, Finland	669
Elisabeth Görgl, Austria	654

DOWNHILL

	Pts
Renate Götschl, Austria	680
Hilde Gerg, Germany	546
Carole Montillet, France	492
Isolde Kostner, Italy	348
Michaela Dorfmeister, Austria	334
Sylviane Berthod, Switzerland	300
Maria Riesch, Germany	283
Nadia Styger, Switzerland	252
Kirsten Clark, United States	228
Alexandra Meissnitzer, Austria	225

SLALOM

	Pts
Anja Pärson, Sweden	770
Marlies Schild, Austria	455
M. B.-Schmuderer, Germany	437
Tanja Poutiainen, Finland	390
Elisabeth Görgl, Austria	339
Nicole Hosp, Austria	306
Martina Ertl, Germany	299
Kristina Koznick, United States	297
Maria Riesch, Germany	245
Sarka Zahrobska, Czech Rep.	244

GIANT SLALOM

	Pts
Anja Pärson, Sweden	630
Denise Karbon, Italy	343
M. J. Rienda Contreras, Spain	339
Elisabeth Görgl, Austria	293
Tanja Poutiainen, Finland	279
Nicole Hosp, Austria	260
Alexandra Meissnitzer, Aus	242
Tina Maze, Slovenia	234
Martina Ertl, Germany	230
Michaela Dorfmeister, Austria	218

SUPER G

	Pts
Renate Götschl, Austria	467
Carole Montillet, France	402
Michael Dorfmeister, Austria	391
Hilde Gerg, Germany	390
Maria Riesch, Germany	338
Nadia Styger, Switzerland	292
Alexandra Meissnitzer, Austria	267
Silvia Berger, Austria	219
Melanie Suchet, France	207
Brigitte Obermoser, Austria	195

Event Descriptions

Downhill: A speed event entailing a single run on a course with a minimum vertical drop of 500 meters (800 for men's World Cup) and very few control gates.
Slalom: A technical event in which times for runs on two courses are totaled to determine the winner. Skiers must make many quick, short turns through a combination of gates (55–75 gates for men, 40–60 for women) over a short course (140–220-meter vertical drop for men, 120–180 for women).
Combined: An event in which scores from designated slalom and downhill races are combined to determine finish order.

Giant Slalom: A faster technical event with fewer, more broadly spaced gates than in the slalom. Times for runs on two courses with vertical drops of 250–400 meters for men and 250–300 meters for women are combined to determine the winner.
Super Giant Slalom: A speed event that is a cross between the downhill and the giant slalom.
Parallel Slalom: A technical event that combines slalom and giant slalom turns.

FIS World Championships

Sites

1931	Mürren, Switzerland	1936	Innsbruck, Austria
1932	Cortina d'Ampezzo, Italy	1937	Chamonix, France
1933	Innsbruck, Austria	1938	Engelberg, Switzerland
1934	St. Moritz, Switzerland	1939	Zakopane, Poland
1935	Mürren, Switzerland		

Men

DOWNHILL

1931	Walter Prager, Switzerland
1932	Gustav Lantschner, Austria
1933	Walter Prager, Switzerland
1934	David Zogg, Switzerland
1935	Franz Zingerle, Austria
1936	Rudolf Rominger, Switzerland
1937	Émile Allais, France
1938	James Couttet, France
1939	Hans Lantschner, Germany

SLALOM

1931	David Zogg, Switzerland
1932	Friedrich Dauber, Germany
1933	Anton Seelos, Austria
1934	Franz Pfnür, Germany
1935	Anton Seelos, Austria
1936	Rudi Matt, Austria
1937	Émile Allais, France
1938	Rudolf Rominger, Switzerland
1939	Rudolf Rominger, Switzerland

Women

DOWNHILL

1931	Esme Mackinnon, Great Britain
1932	Paola Wiesinger, Italy
1933	Inge Wersin-Lantschner, Austria
1934	Anni Rüegg, Switzerland
1935	Christel Cranz, Germany
1936	Evie Pinching, Great Britain
1937	Christel Cranz, Germany
1938	Lisa Resch, Germany
1939	Christel Cranz, Germany

SLALOM

1931	Esme Mackinnon, Great Britain
1932	Rösli Streiff, Switzerland
1933	Inge Wersin-Lantschner, Austria
1934	Christel Cranz, Germany
1935	Anni Rüegg, Switzerland
1936	Gerda Paumgarten, Austria
1937	Christel Cranz, Germany
1938	Christel Cranz, Germany
1939	Christel Cranz, Germany

FIS World Alpine Ski Championships

Sites

1950	Aspen, Colorado	1985	Bormio, Italy
1954	Are, Sweden	1987	Crans-Montana, Switzerland
1958	Badgastein, Austria	1989	Vail, Colorado
1962	Chamonix, France	1991	Saalbach-Hinterglemm, Austria
1966	Portillo, Chile	1993	Morioka-Shizukuishi, Japan
1970	Val Gardena, Italy	1996	Sierra Nevada, Spain
1974	St. Moritz, Switzerland	1997	Sestriere, Italy
1978	Garmisch-Partenkirchen, W Germany	1999	Vail, Colorado
		2001	St. Anton, Switzerland
1982	Schladming, Austria	2003	St. Moritz, Switzerland

Men

DOWNHILL

1950.............Zeno Colo, Italy	1985.............Pirmin Zurbriggen, Switzerland
1954.............Christian Pravda, Austria	1987.............Peter Müller, Switzerland
1958.............Toni Sailer, Austria	1989.............Hansjörg Tauscher, W Germany
1962.............Karl Schranz, Austria	1991.............Franz Heinzer, Switzerland
1966.............Jean-Claude Killy, France	1993.............Urs Lehmann, Switzerland
1970.............Bernard Russi, Switzerland	1996.............Patrick Ortlieb, Austria
1974.............David Zwilling, Austria	1997.............Bruno Kernen, Switzerland
1978.............Josef Walcher, Austria	1999.............Hermann Maier, Austria
1982.............Harti Weirather, Austria	2001.............Hannes Trinkl, Austria
	2003.............Michael Walchhofer, Austria

SLALOM

1950.............Zeno Colo, Italy	1985.............Pirmin Zurbriggen, Switzerland
1954.............Christian Pravda, Austria	1987.............Peter Müller, Switzerland
1958.............Toni Sailer, Austria	1989.............Hansjörg Tauscher, W Germany
1962.............Karl Schranz, Austria	1991.............Franz Heinzer, Switzerland
1966.............Jean-Claude Killy, France	1993.............Urs Lehmann, Switzerland
1970.............Bernard Russi, Switzerland	1996.............Patrick Ortlieb, Austria
1974.............David Zwilling, Austria	1997.............Bruno Kernen, Switzerland
1978.............Josef Walcher, Austria	1999.............Hermann Maier, Austria
1982.............Harti Weirather, Austria	2001.............Hannes Trinkl, Austria
	2003.............Ivica Kostelic, Croatia

GIANT SLALOM

1950.............Zeno Colo, Italy	1985.............Markus Wasmaier, W Germany
1954.............Stein Eriksen, Norway	1987.............Pirmin Zurbriggen, Switzerland
1958.............Toni Sailer, Austria	1989.............Rudolf Nierlich, Austria
1962.............Egon Zimmermann, Austria	1991.............Rudolf Nierlich, Austria
1966.............Guy Périllat, France	1993.............Kjetil André Aamodt, Norway
1970.............Karl Schranz, Austria	1996.............Alberto Tomba, Italy
1974.............Gustavo Thoeni, Italy	1997.............Michael von Grünigen, Switzerland
1978.............Ingemar Stenmark, Sweden	1999.............Marco Büchel, Liechtenstein
1982.............Steve Mahre, United States	2001.............Michael von Grünigen, Switzerland
	2003.............Bode Miller, United States

COMBINED

1982.............Michel Vion, France	1993.............Lasse Kjus, Norway
1985.............Pirmin Zurbriggen, Switzerland	1996.............Marc Girardelli, Luxembourg
1987.............Marc Girardelli, Luxembourg	1997.............Kjetil André Aamodt, Norway
1989.............Marc Girardelli, Luxembourg	1999.............Kjetil André Aamodt, Norway
1991.............Stefan Eberharter, Austria	2001.............Kjetil André Aamodt, Norway
	2003.............Bode Miller, United States

SUPER G

1987.............Pirmin Zurbriggen, Switzerland	1997.............Atle Skaardal, Norway
1989.............Martin Hangl, Switzerland	1999.............Hermann Maier, Austria
1991.............Stefan Eberharter, Austria	Lasse Kjus, Norway
1993.............Cancelled due to weather	2001.............Daron Rahlves, United States
1996.............Atle Skaardal, Norway	2003.............Stephan Eberharter, Austria

Women

DOWNHILL

1950.............Trude Beiser-Jochum, Austria	1985.............Michela Figini, Switzerland
1954.............Ida Schopfer, Switzerland	1987.............Maria Walliser, Switzerland
1958.............Lucile Wheeler, Canada	1989.............Maria Walliser, Switzerland
1962.............Christl Haas, Austria	1991.............Petra Kronberger, Austria
1966.............Erika Schinegger, Austria	1993.............Kate Pace, Canada
1970.............Annerösli Zryd, Switzerland	1996.............Picabo Street, United States
1974.............Annemarie Moser-Pröll, Austria	1997.............Hilary Lindh, United States
1978.............Annemarie Moser-Pröll, Austria	1999.............Renate Götschl, Austria
1982.............Gerry Sorensen, Canada	2001.............Michaela Dorfmeister, Austria
	2003.............Melanie Turgeon, Canada

Women (Cont.)

SLALOM

1950.............Dagmar Rom, Austria	1987.............Erika Hess, Switzerland
1954.............Trude Klecker, Austria	1989.............Mateja Svet, Yugoslavia
1958.............Inger Bjornbakken, Norway	1991.............Vreni Schneider, Switzerland
1962.............Marianne Jahn, Austria	1993.............Karin Buder, Austria
1966.............Annie Famose, France	1996.............Pernilla Wiberg, Sweden
1970.............Ingrid Lafforgue, France	1997.............Deborah Compagnoni, Italy
1974.............Hanni Wenzel, Liechtenstein	1999.............Trine Bakke, Norway
1978.............Lea Sölkner, Austria	2001.............Anja Paerson, Sweden
1982.............Erika Hess, Switzerland	2003.............Janica Kostelic, Croatia
1985.............Perrine Pelen, France	

GIANT SLALOM

1950.............Dagmar Rom, Austria	1987.............Vreni Schneider, Switzerland
1954.............Lucienne Schmith-Couttet, France	1989.............Vreni Schneider, Switzerland
1958.............Lucile Wheeler, Canada	1991.............Pernilla Wiberg, Sweden
1962.............Marianne Jahn, Austria	1993.............Carole Merle, France
1966.............Marielle Goitschel, France	1996.............Deborah Compagnoni, Italy
1970.............Betsy Clifford, Canada	1997.............Deborah Compagnoni, Italy
1974.............Fabienne Serrat, France	1999.............Anita Wachter, Austria
1978.............Maria Epple, W Germany	2001.............Sonja Nef, Switzerland
1982.............Erika Hess, Switzerland	2003.............Anja Paerson, Sweden
1985.............Diann Roffe, United States	

COMBINED

1982,.............Erika Hess, Switzerland	1996 ....Pernilla Wiberg, Sweden
1985.............Erika Hess, Switzerland	1997.............Renate Götschl, Austria
1987.............Erika Hess, Switzerland	1999 ....Pernilla Wiberg, Sweden
1989.............Tamara McKinney, United States	2001 ....Martina Ertl, Germany
1991.............Chantal Bournissen, Switzerland	2003 ....Janica Kostelic, Croatia
1993.............Miriam Vogt, Germany	

SUPER G

1987.............Maria Walliser, Switzerland	1997 ....Isolde Kostner, Italy
1989.............Ulrike Maier, Austria	1999 ....Alexandra Meissnitzer, Austria
1991.............Ulrike Maier, Austria	2001 ....Regine Cavagnoud, France
1993.............Katja Seizinger, Germany	2003 ....Michaela Dorfmeister, Austria
1996 ....Isolde Kostner, Italy	

Note: The 1995 FIS World Alpine Ski Championships were postponed to 1996 due to lack of snow.

A Face in the Crowd

A senior and the captain of the University of New Mexico ski team, Jennifer Delich of Fernie, British Columbia, won the women's giant slalom title at the 2004 NCAA championships. Her victory helped the Lobos win their first NCAA team championship in any sport.

Men

OVERALL

1967	Jean-Claude Killy, France	1986	Marc Girardelli, Luxembourg
1968	Jean-Claude Killy, France	1987	Pirmin Zurbriggen, Switzerland
1969	Karl Schranz, Austria	1988	Pirmin Zurbriggen, Switzerland
1970	Karl Schranz, Austria	1989	Marc Girardelli, Luxembourg
1971	Gustavo Thoeni, Italy	1990	Pirmin Zurbriggen, Switzerland
1972	Gustavo Thoeni, Italy	1991	Marc Girardelli, Luxembourg
1973	Gustavo Thoeni, Italy	1992	Paul Accola, Switzerland
1974	Piero Gros, Italy	1993	Marc Girardelli, Luxembourg
1975	Gustavo Thoeni, Italy	1994	Kjetil André Aamodt, Norway
1976	Ingemar Stenmark, Sweden	1995	Alberto Tomba, Italy
1977	Ingemar Stenmark, Sweden	1996	Lasse Kjus, Norway
1978	Ingemar Stenmark, Sweden	1997	Luc Alphand, France
1979	Peter Lüscher, Switzerland	1998	Hermann Maier, Austria
1980	Andreas Wenzel, Liechtenstein	1999	Lasse Kjus, Norway
1981	Phil Mahre, United States	2000	Hermann Maier, Austria
1982	Phil Mahre, United States	2001	Hermann Maier, Austria
1983	Phil Mahre, United States	2002	Stephan Eberharter, Austria
1984	Pirmin Zurbriggen, Switzerland	2003	Stephan Eberharter, Austria
1985	Marc Girardelli, Luxembourg	2004	Hermann Maier, Austria

DOWNHILL

1967	Jean-Claude Killy, France	1985	Helmut Höflehner, Austria
1968	Gerhard Nenning, Austria	1986	Peter Wirnsberger, Austria
1969	Karl Schranz, Austria	1987	Pirmin Zurbriggen, Switzerland
1970	Karl Schranz, Austria	1988	Pirmin Zurbriggen, Switzerland
	Karl Cordin, Austria	1989	Marc Girardelli, Luxembourg
1971	Bernhard Russi, Switzerland	1990	Helmut Höflehner, Austria
1972	Bernhard Russi, Switzerland	1991	Franz Heinzer, Switzerland
1973	Roland Collumbin, Switzerland	1992	Franz Heinzer, Switzerland
1974	Roland Collumbin, Switzerland	1993	Franz Heinzer, Switzerland
1975	Franz Klammer, Austria	1994	Marc Girardelli, Luxembourg
1976	Franz Klammer, Austria	1995	Luc Alphand, France
1977	Franz Klammer, Austria	1996	Luc Alphand, France
1978	Franz Klammer, Austria	1997	Luc Alphand, France
1979	Peter Müller, Switzerland	1998	Andreas Schifferer, Austria
1980	Peter Müller, Switzerland	1999	Lasse Kjus, Norway
1981	Harti Weirather, Austria	2000	Hermann Maier, Austria
1982	Steve Podborski, Canada	2001	Hermann Maier, Austria
	Peter Müller, Switzerland	2002	Stephan Eberharter, Austria
1983	Franz Klammer, Austria	2003	Stephan Eberharter, Austria
1984	Urs Raber, Switzerland	2004	Stephan Eberharter, Austria

SLALOM

1967	Jean-Claude Killy, France	1985	Marc Girardelli, Luxembourg
1968	Domeng Giovanoli, Switzerland	1986	Rok Petrovic, Yugoslavia
1969	Jean-Noël Augert, France	1987	Bojan Krizaj, Yugoslavia
1970	Patrick Russel, France	1988	Alberto Tomba, Italy
	Alain Penz, France	1989	Armin Bittner, W Germany
1971	Jean-Noël Augert, France	1990	Armin Bittner, W Germany
1972	Jean-Noël Augert, France	1991	Marc Girardelli, Luxembourg
1973	Gustavo Thoeni, Italy	1992	Alberto Tomba, Italy
1974	Gustavo Thoeni, Italy	1993	Tomas Fogdof, Sweden
1975	Ingemar Stenmark, Sweden	1994	Alberto Tomba, Italy
1976	Ingemar Stenmark, Sweden	1995	Alberto Tomba, Italy
1977	Ingemar Stenmark, Sweden	1996	Sebastien Amiez, France
1978	Ingemar Stenmark, Sweden	1997	Thomas Sykora, Austria
1979	Ingemar Stenmark, Sweden	1998	Thomas Sykora, Austria
1980	Ingemar Stenmark, Sweden	1999	Thomas Stangassinger, Austria
1981	Ingemar Stenmark, Sweden	2000	Kjetil André Aamodt, Norway
1982	Phil Mahre, United States	2001	Benjamin Raich, Austria
1983	Ingemar Stenmark, Sweden	2002	Ivica Kostelic, Croatia
1984	Marc Girardelli, Luxembourg	2003	Kalle Palander, Finland
		2004	Rainer Schoenfelder, Austria

Men (Cont.)
GIANT SLALOM

1967 ....Jean-Claude Killy, France	1986 ....Joël Gaspoz, Switzerland
1968 ....Jean-Claude Killy, France	1987 ....Joël Gaspoz, Switzerland
1969 ....Karl Schranz, Austria	Pirmin Zurbriggen, Switzerland
1970 ....Gustavo Thoeni, Italy	1988 ....Alberto Tomba, Italy
1971 ....Patrick Russel, France	1989 ....Pirmin Zurbriggen, Switzerland
1972 ....Gustavo Thoeni, Italy	1990 ....Ole-Cristian Furuseth, Norway
1973 ....Hans Hinterseer, Austria	Günther Mader, Austria
1974 ....Piero Gros, Italy	1991 ....Alberto Tomba, Italy
1975 ....Ingemar Stenmark, Sweden	1992 ....Alberto Tomba, Italy
1976 ....Ingemar Stenmark, Sweden	1993 ....Kjetil André Aamodt, Norway
1977 ....Heini Hemmi, Switzerland	1994 ....Christian Mayer, Austria
Ingemar Stenmark, Sweden	1995 ....Alberto Tomba, Italy
1978 ....Ingemar Stenmark, Sweden	1996 ....Michael von Grünigen, Switzerland
1979 ....Ingemar Stenmark, Sweden	1997 ....Michael von Grünigen, Switzerland
1980 ....Ingemar Stenmark, Sweden	1998 ....Hermann Maier, Austria
1981 ....Ingemar Stenmark, Sweden	1999 ....Michael von Grünigen, Switzerland
1982 ....Phil Mahre, United States	2000 ....Hermann Maier, Austria
1983 ....Phil Mahre, United States	2001 ....Hermann Maier, Austria
1984 ....Ingemar Stenmark, Sweden	2002 ....Frederic Covili, France
Pirmin Zurbriggen, Switzerland	2003 ....Michael von Grünigen, Switzerland
1985 ....Marc Girardelli, Luxembourg	2004 ....Bode Miller, United States

SUPER G

1986 ....Markus Wasmeier, W Germany	
1987 ....Pirmin Zurbriggen, Switzerland	1996 ....Atle Skaardal, Norway
1988 ....Pirmin Zurbriggen, Switzerland	1997 ....Luc Alphand, France
1989 ....Pirmin Zurbriggen, Switzerland	1998 ....Hermann Maier, Austria
1990 ....Pirmin Zurbriggen, Switzerland	1999 ....Hermann Maier, Austria
1991 ....Franz Heinzer, Switzerland	2000 ....Hermann Maier, Austria
1992 ....Paul Accola, Switzerland	2001 ....Hermann Maier, Austria
1993 ....Kjetil André Aamodt, Norway	2002 ....Stephan Eberharter, Austria
1994 ....Jan Einar Thorsen, Norway	2003 ....Stephan Eberharter, Austria
1995 ....Peter Runggaldier, Italy	2004 ....Hermann Maier, Austria

COMBINED

1979 ....Andreas Wenzel, Liechtenstein	1993 ....Marc Girardelli, Luxembourg
1980 ....Andreas Wenzel, Liechtenstein	1994 ....Kjetil André Aamodt, Norway
1981 ....Phil Mahre, United States	1995 ....Marc Girardelli, Luxembourg
1982 ....Phil Mahre, United States	1996 ....Günther Mader, Austria
1983 ....Phil Mahre, United States	1997 ....Kjetil André Aamodt, Norway
1984 ....Andreas Wenzel, Liechtenstein	1998 ....Werner Franz, Austria
1985 ....Andreas Wenzel, Liechtenstein	1999 ....Kjetil André Aamodt, Norway
1986 ....Markus Wasmeier, W Germany	2000 ....Kjetil André Aamodt, Norway
1987 ....Pirmin Zurbriggen, Switzerland	Lasse Kjus, Norway
1988 ....Hubert Strolz, Austria	2001 ....Lasse Kjus, Norway
1989 ....Marc Girardelli, Luxembourg	2002 ....Kjetil André Aamodt, Norway
1990 ....Pirmin Zurbriggen, Switzerland	2003 ....Bode Miller, United States
1991 ....Marc Girardelli, Luxembourg	2004 ....Bode Miller, United States
1992 ....Paul Accola, Switzerland	

Women
OVERALL

1967 ....Nancy Greene, Canada	1986 ....Maria Walliser, Switzerland
1968 ....Nancy Greene, Canada	1987 ....Maria Walliser, Switzerland
1969 ....Gertrud Gabl, Austria	1988 ....Michela Figini, Switzerland
1970 ....Michèle Jacot, France	1989 ....Vreni Schneider, Switzerland
1971 ....Annemarie Pröll, Austria	1990 ....Petra Kronberger, Austria
1972 ....Annemarie Pröll, Austria	1991 ....Petra Kronberger, Austria
1973 ....Annemarie Pröll, Austria	1992 ....Petra Kronberger, Austria
1974 ....Annemarie Moser-Pröll, Austria	1993 ....Anita Wachter, Austria
1975 ....Annemarie Moser-Pröll, Austria	1994 ....Vreni Schneider, Switzerland
1976 ....Rosi Mitermaier, W Germany	1995 ....Vreni Schneider, Switzerland
1977 ....Lise-Marie Morerod, Switzerland	1996 ....Katja Seizinger, Germany
1978 ....Hanni Wenzel, Liechtenstein	1997 ....Pernilla Wiberg, Sweden
1979 ....Annemarie Moser-Pröll, Austria	1998 ....Katja Seizinger, Germany
1980 ....Hanni Wenzel, Liechtenstein	1999 ....Alexandra Meissnitzer, Austria
1981 ....Marie-Thérèse Nadig, Switzerland	2000 ....Renate Götschl, Austria
1982 ....Erika Hess, Switzerland	2001 ....Janica Kostelic, Croatia
1983 ....Tamara McKinney, United States	2002 ....Michaela Dorfmeister, Austria
1984 ....Erika Hess, Switzerland	2003 ....Janica Kostelic, Austria
1985 ....Michela Figini, Switzerland	2004 ....Anja Pärson, Sweden

Women (Cont.)

DOWNHILL

1967 ....Marielle Goitschel, France	1986 ....Maria Walliser, Switzerland
1968 ....Isabelle Mir, France & Olga Pall, Austria	1987 ....Michela Figini, Switzerland
1969 ....Wiltrud Drexel, Austria	1988 ....Michela Figini, Switzerland
1970 ....Isabelle Mir, France	1989 ....Michela Figini, Switzerland
1971 ....Annemarie Pröll, Austria	1990 ....Katrin Gutensohn-Knopf, Germany
1972 ....Annemarie Pröll, Austria	1991..............Chantal Bournissen, Switzerland
1973 ....Annemarie Pröll, Austria	1992 ....Katja Seizinger, Germany
1974 ....Annemarie Moser-Pröll, Austria	1993 ....Katja Seizinger, Germany
1975 ....Annemarie Moser-Pröll, Austria	1994 ....Katja Seizinger, Germany
1976 ....Brigitte Totschnig, Austria	1995 ....Picabo Street, United States
1977 ....Brigitte Totschnig-Habersatter, Austria	1996 ....Picabo Street, United States
1978 ....Annemarie Moser-Pröll, Austria	1997 ....Renate Götschl, Austria
1979 ....Annemarie Moser-Pröll, Austria	1998 ....Katja Seizinger, Germany
1980 ....Marie-Thérèse Nadig, Switzerland	1999 ....Renate Götschl, Austria
1981 ....Marie-Thérèse Nadig, Switzerland	2000 ....Regina Haeusl, Germany
1982 ....Marie-Cecile Gros-Gaudenier, France	2001 ....Isolde Kostner, Italy
1983 ....Doris De Agostini, Switzerland	2002 ....Isolde Kostner, Italy
1984 ....Maria Walliser, Switzerland	2003 ....Michaela Dorfmeister, Austria
1985 ....Michela Figini, Switzerland	2004 ....Renate Götschl, Austria

SLALOM

1967 ....Nancy Greene, Canada	1986 ....Maria Walliser, Switzerland
1968 ....Nancy Greene, Canada	1987 ....Maria Walliser, Switzerland
1969 ....Gertrud Gabl, Austria	1988 ....Michela Figini, Switzerland
1970 ....Michèle Jacot, France	1989 ....Vreni Schneider, Switzerland
1971 ....Annemarie Pröll, Austria	1990 ....Petra Kronberger, Austria
1972 ....Annemàrie Pröll, Austria	1991 ....Petra Kronberger, Austria
1973 ....Annemarie Pröll, Austria	1992 ....Petra Kronberger, Austria
1974 ....Annemarie Moser-Pröll, Austria	1993 ....Anita Wachter, Austria
1975 ....Annemarie Moser-Pröll, Austria	1994 ....Vreni Schneider, Switzerland
1976 ....Rosi Mitermaier, W Germany	1995 ....Vreni Schneider, Switzerland
1977 ....Lise-Marie Morerod, Switzerland	1996 ....Katja Seizinger, Germany
1978 ....Hanni Wenzel, Liechtenstein	1997 ....Pernilla Wiberg, Sweden
1979 ....Annemarie Moser-Pröll, Austria	1998 ....Katja Seizinger, Germany
1980 ....Hanni Wenzel, Liechtenstein	1999 ....Alexandra Meissnitzer, Austria
1981 ....Marie-Thérèse Nadig, Switzerland	2000 ....Renate Götschl, Austria
1982 ....Erika Hess, Switzerland	2001 ....Janica Kostelic, Croatia
1983 ....Tamara McKinney, United States	2002 ....Laure Pequegnot, France
1984 ....Erika Hess, Switzerland	2003 ....Janica Kostelic, Croatia
1985 ....Michela Figini, Switzerland	2004 ....Anja Pärson, Sweden

GIANT SLALOM

1967 ....Nancy Greene, Canada	1986 ....Vreni Schneider, Switzerland
1968 ....Nancy Greene, Canada	1987 ....Vreni Schneider/ Maria Walliser, Switz
1969 ....Marilyn Cochran, United States	1988 ....Mateja Svet, Yugoslavia
1970 ....Michèle Jacot/Françoise Macchi, France	1989 ....Vreni Schneider, Switzerland
1971 ....Annemarie Pröll, Austria	1990 ....Anita Wachter, Austria
1972 ....Annemarie Pröll, Austria	1991 ....Vreni Schneider, Switzerland
1973 ....Monika Kaserer, Austria	1992 ....Carole Merle, France
1974 ....Hanni Wenzel, Liechtenstein	1993 ....Carole Merle, France
1975 ....Annemarie Moser-Pröll, Austria	1994 ....Anita Wachter, Austria
1976 ....Lise-Marie Morerod, Switzerland	1995 ....Vreni Schneider, Switzerland
1977 ....Lise-Marie Morerod, Switzerland	1996 ....Martina Ertl, Germany
1978 ....Lise-Marie Morerod, Switzerland	1997 ....Deborah Compagnoni, Italy
1979 ....Christa Kinshofer, W Germany	1998 ....Martina Ertl, Germany
1980 ....Hanni Wenzel, Liechtenstein	1999 ....Alexandra Meissnitzer, Austria
1981 ....Marie-Thérèse Nadig, Switzerland	2000 ....Michaela Dorfmeister, Austria
1982 ....Irene Epple, W Germany	2001 ....Sonja Nef, Switzerland
1983 ....Tamara McKinney, United States	2002 ....Sonja Nef, Switzerland
1984 ....Erika Hess, Switzerland	2003 ....Anja Pärson, Sweden
1985 ....Maria Keihl, W Germany	2004 ....Anja Pärson, Sweden
..............Michela Figini, Switzerland	

SUPER G

1986 ....Maria Keihl, W Germany	1992 ....Carole Merle, France
1987 ....Maria Walliser, Switzerland	1993 ....Katja Seizinger, Germany
1988 ....Michela Figini, Switzerland	1994 ....Katja Seizinger, Germany
1989 ....Carole Merle, France	1995 ....Katja Seizinger, Germany
1990 ....Carole Merle, France	1996 ....Katja Seizinger, Germany
1991 ....Carole Merle, France	1997 ....Hilde Gerg, Germany

World Cup Season Title Holders (Cont.)

Women (Cont.)

SUPER G (CONT.)

1998	Katja Seizinger, Germany	2002 ....Hilde Gerg, Germany
1999	Alexandra Meissnitzer, Austria	2003 ....Carole Montillet, France
2000	Renate Götschl, Austria	2004 ....Renate Götschl, Austria
2001	Regine Cavagnoud, France	

COMBINED

1979 ....Annemarie Moser-Pröll, Austria
                  Hanni Wenzel, Liechtenstein
1980 ....Hanni Wenzel, Liechtenstein
1981 ....Marie-Thérèse Nadig, Switzerland
1982 ....Irene Epple, W Germany
1983 ....Hanni Wenzel, Liechtenstein
1984 ....Erika Hess, Switzerland
1985 ....Brigitte Oertli, Switzerland
1986 ....Maria Walliser, Switzerland
1987 ....Brigitte Oertli, Switzerland
1988 ....Brigitte Oertli, Switzerland
1989 ....Brigitte Oertli, Switzerland
1990 ....Anita Wachter, Austria
1991 ....Sabine Ginther, Austria

1992 ....Sabine Ginther, Austria
1993 ....Anita Wachter, Austria
1994 ....Pernilla Wiberg, Sweden
1995 ....Pernilla Wiberg, Sweden
1996 ....Anita Wachter, Austria
1997 ....Pernilla Wiberg, Sweden
1998 ....Hilde Gerg, Germany
1999 ....Hilde Gerg, Germany
2000 ....Renate Götschl, Austria
2001 ....Janica Kostelic, Croatia
2002 ....Renate Götschl, Austria
2003 ....Janica Kostelic, Croatia
2004 ....Anja Pärson, Sweden

World Cup Career Victories

Men

DOWNHILL

25..........................Franz Klammer, Austria
19..........................Peter Müller, Switzerland
15..........................Franz Heinzer, Switzerland

SLALOM

40..........................Ingemar Stenmark, Sweden
35..........................Alberto Tomba, Italy
16..........................Marc Girardelli, Luxembourg

GIANT SLALOM

46..........................Ingemar Stenmark, Sweden
23..........................Michael Von Grünigen, Switz
15..........................Alberto Tomba, Italy

SUPER G

20..........................*Hermann Maier, Austria
10..........................Pirmin Zurbriggen, Switzerland
7............................Marc Girardelli, Luxembourg

COMBINED

11..........................Phil Mahre, United States
                          Pirmin Zurbriggen, Switzerland
                          Marc Girardelli, Luxembourg

Women

DOWNHILL

36..........................Annemarie Moser-Pröll, Austria
17..........................Michela Figini, Switzerland
16..........................Katja Seizinger, Germany

SLALOM

34..........................Vreni Schneider, Switzerland
21..........................Erika Hess, Switzerland
16..........................*Janica Kostelic, Croatia

GIANT SLALOM

20..........................Vreni Schneider, Switzerland
16..........................Annemarie Moser-Pröll, Austria
16..........................Anita Wachter, Austria

SUPER G

16..........................Katja Seizinger, Germany
12..........................Carole Merle, France
11..........................*Renate Götschl, Austria

COMBINED

8............................Hanni Wenzel, Liechtenstein
7............................Annemarie Moser-Pröll, Austria
                          Brigitte Oertli, Switzerland

*Active in 2003–04.

U.S. Olympic Gold Medalists

Men

Year	Winner	Event
1980	Phil Mahre	Combined
1984	Bill Johnson	Downhill
1984	Phil Mahre	Slalom
1994	Tommy Moe	Downhill

Women

Year	Winner	Event
1948	Gretchen Fraser	Slalom
1952	Andrea Mead Lawrence	Slalom
1952	Andrea Mead Lawrence	Giant Slalom
1972	Barbara Ann Cochran	Slalom
1984	Debbie Armstrong	Giant Slalom
1994	Diann Roffe-Steinrotter	Super G
1998	Picabo Street	Super G

Figure Skating

Go Figure

Two years before Turin, the 2004 season raised more questions than it answered

BY MERRELL NODEN

THE YEAR KICKED off with a strong sense of déjà vu, much as every U.S. skating season has of late. In January, at the U.S. Figure Skating Championships in Atlanta, Michelle Kwan won the ladies title, displaying the same poise and seemingly effortless grace she'd shown in winning the previous six straight and seven overall. We are tempted to call her "ageless" except that we know that Kwan is 24, still young enough to entertain perfectly reasonable hopes of finally winning the Olympic gold medal that's eluded her in two previous trips to the Games.

Stranger things have happened. If you doubt that, consider the year just passed. In it, we saw the testing of a new scoring system; a meltdown by the usually powerful Russian women; the premature (though possibly temporary) retirement of the reigning Olympic champion; a new skating organization that sued the established International Skating Union as part of a campaign to replace it as the sport's governing body; and a streaker on the ice at the world championships, where you'd think the chilly temperatures might shrink his . . . er . . . zest for such shenanigans.

Choosing not to compete at all this winter was Sarah Hughes, the defending Olympic champion. Despite being only 19 years old at the time of nationals, Hughes quietly disappeared from skating at the end of the 2003 season after finishing sixth at the worlds. She chose instead to finish her freshman year at Yale in relative anonymity. "I always wanted to go to college with my peers. I'm really enjoying this," said Hughes, adding that she does miss the competition. "Hopefully I'll want to skate again, to want to get better."

Hughes's retirement left her coach, Robin Wagner, without a job. In December Wagner took over coaching Sasha Cohen after Cohen dumped her overbearing Russian coach, Tatiana Tarasova. Cohen came to nationals with high hopes that did not dim when she led following the short skate. But during the free skate, she fell on a triple toe and had a poor landing on a triple Lutz. For the third time in her career, she finished second to Kwan, who earned seven 6.0s for presentation but stopped short of committing herself to pursuing Olympic gold in Turin in 2006.

In stark contrast to their performance at last year's nationals, the men skated well, with the six final skaters all earning enthusiastic standing ovations. The competition ended with the crowning of Johnny Weir, at 19 the youngest men's champion since Todd Eldredge in 1991. Weir skated brilliantly, pounding the ice in delight even before he saw his marks, which included a 6.0 for presentation, the first perfect score in the U.S. men's championship in four years.

Unfortunately, the world championships in Dortmund, Germany, were a dose of cold reality for the jubilant Americans. Weir placed fifth and Weiss sixth, far behind winner Evgeny Plushenko of Russia, who won his third world title handily.

In what certainly looked like a case of grade inflation, Plushenko was awarded four perfect 6.0s despite taking a hard fall. One had to wonder what those four judges would have given Plushenko had he stayed on his feet. In all, the staggeringly generous judges at the worlds awarded 43 perfect marks. Change may be arriving just in time.

Or maybe not. Cynics argued that the new, anonymous, computer-based points system did not go far enough and was merely an attempt by the ISU to silence a growing number of critics led by its upstart rival, the World Skating Federation. The WSF, which was founded in 2003 and backed by notable retired skaters like Dick Button and Scott Hamilton, brought suit in mid-December against the ISU, accused it of being a monopoly, one that has threatened "to 'blacklist' or banish anyone connected with the WSF." The ISU brushed the charges aside, but it seemed clear that the new body was determined to clean up the corruption evident at the 2002 Olympics.

In contrast to Plushenko's dominance, the Russian ladies skated abysmally. Irina Slutskaya was their top finisher, in 9th, with teammate Elena Sokolova one place behind her. The only thing in Dortmund more unexpected than their meltdown was the performance of one Ron Bensimhon, a 30-year-old Canadian who took to the ice before Kwan's free skate and stripped off most of his

clothes, claiming he was hoping to "liven up a boring afternoon."

Whether or not the streaker distracted Kwan, it's hard to imagine she could have beaten the stunning performance of Japan's Shizuka Arakawa. The graceful 22-year-old opened her long program with a stunning triple lutz-triple toe-double loop combination and never faltered. For Arakawa, this was nothing short of a miracle comeback. A tremendously talented skater who landed her first triple in elementary school, she had fallen on hard times after winning Japanese national titles in 1998 and '99. She was eighth at last year's world championship and only third at her nationals this year. In March of 2004, she moved to Simsbury, Conn., and began working with Tarasova, who must have taken some satisfaction in watching her new skater beat her old (Cohen, who finished second).

The season was not without drama, but it raised more questions than it answered: Will anyone emerge to challenge Plushenko? Will the defending ladies champ even try to qualify for Turin? Will Kwan? Will Cohen break through? And even if the answer to those last three questions is yes, will any of them be able to beat the breathtaking Arakawa?

MARTIN MEISSNER/AP PHOTO

FOR THE RECORD 2004

World Champions

Dortmund, Germany, March 22–28

Women

1.......Shizuka Arakawa, Japan
2.......Sasha Cohen, United States
3.......Michelle Kwan, United States

Men

1.........Evgeny Plushenko, Russia
1.........Brian Joubert, France
3.........Stefan Lindemann, Germany

Pairs

1.......Tatiana Totmianina/ Maxim Marinin, Russia
2.......Xue Shen/ Hongbo Zhao, China
3.......Qing Pang/ Jian Tong, China

Dance

1.........Tatiana Navka/ Roman Kostomarov, Russia
2.........Albena Denkova/ Maxim Staviyski, Bulgaria
3.........Kati Winkler/ Rene Lohse, Germany

World Figure Skating Championships Medal Table

Country	Gold	Silver	Bronze	Total
Russia	3	0	0	3
China	0	1	1	2
United States	0	1	1	2
Germany	0	0	2	2
Japan	1	0	0	1
Bulgaria	0	1	0	1
France	0	1	0	1

Champions of the United States

Atlanta, January 3–11

Women

1......................Michelle Kwan, Los Angeles FSC
2......................Sasha Cohen, Orange County FSC
3......................Jennifer Kirt, The SC of Boston

Men

1......................Johnny Weir, SC of New York
2......................Michael Weiss, Washington FSC
3......................Matthew Savoie, Illinois Valley FSC

Pairs

1......................Rena Inoue/ John Baldwin,
  All Year FSC
2......................Kathryn Orscher/ Garrett Lucash,
  SC of Hartford/Charter Oak FSC
3......................Tiffany Scott/ Philip Dulebohn,
  Colonial FSC/ U. of Delaware FSC

Dance

1....................Tanith Belbin/ Benjamin Agosto,
  Detroit SC
2......................Melissa Gregory/ Denis Petukhov,
  Broadmoor SC/ Skokie Valley SC
3....................Loren Galler-Rabinowitz/ David Mitchell,
  The SC of Boston

Skating Terminology*

Basic Skating Terms

Edges: The two sides of the skating blade, on either side of the grooved center. There is an inside edge, on the inner side of the leg; and an outside edge, on the outer side of the leg.

Free Foot, Hip, Knee, Side, etc.: The foot a skater is not skating on at any one time is the free foot; everything on that side of the body is then called "free." (See also "skating foot.")

Free Skating (Freestyle): A 4- or 5-minute competition program of free-skating components, choreographed to music, with no set elements. Skating moves include jumps, spins, steps and other linking movements.

Skating Foot, Hip, Knee, Side, etc.: Opposite of the free foot, hip, knee, side, etc. The foot a skater is skating on at any one time is the skating foot; everything on that side of the body is then called "skating."

Toe Picks (Toe Rakes): The teeth at the front of the skate blade, used primarily for certain jumps and spins.

Trace, Tracing: The line left on the ice by the skater's blade.

Jumps

Waltz: A beginner's jump, involving half a revolution in the air, taken from a forward outside edge and landed on the back outside edge of the other foot.

Toe Loop: A one-revolution jump taken off from and landed on the same back outside edge. This jump is similar to the loop jump except that the skater kicks the toe pick of the free leg into the ice upon takeoff, providing added power.

Toe Walley: A jump similar to the toe loop, except that the takeoff is from the inside edge.

Flip: A jump taken off with the toe pick of the free leg from a back inside edge and landed on a back outside edge, with one in-air revolution.

Lutz: A toe jump similar to the flip, taken off with the toe pick of the free leg from a backward outside edge. The skater enters the jump skating in one direction, and concludes the jump skating in the opposite direction. Usually performed in the corners of the rink. Named after inventor Alois Lutz, who first landed the jump in Vienna, 1918.

Salchow: A one-, two- or three-revolution jump. The skater takes off from the back inside edge of one foot and lands backwards on the outside edge of the right foot, the opposite foot from which the skater took off. Named for its originator and first Olympic champion (1908), Sweden's Ulrich Salchow.

Axel: A combination of the waltz and loop jumps, including one-and-a-half revolutions. The only jump begun from a forward outside edge, the Axel is landed on the back outside edge of the opposite foot. Named for its inventor, Norway's Axel Paulsen.

Spins

Spin: The rotation of the body in one place on the ice. Various spins are the back, fast or scratch, sit, camel, butterfly and layback.

Camel Spin: A spin with the skater in an arabesque position (the free leg at right angles to the leg on the ice).

Flying Camel Spin: A jump spin ending in the camel-spin position.

Flying Sit Spin: A jump spin in which the skater leaps off the ice, assumes a sitting position at the peak of the jump, lands and spins in a similar sitting position.

Pair Movements/Techniques

Death Spiral: One of the most dramatic moves in figure skating. The man, acting as the center of a circle, holds tightly to the hand of his partner and pulls her around him. The woman, gliding on one foot, achieves a position almost horizontal to the ice.

Lifts: The most spectacular moves in pairs skating. They involve any maneuver in which the man lifts the woman off the ice. The man often holds his partner above his head with one hand.

Throws: The man lifts the woman into the air and throws her away from him. She spins in the air and lands on one foot.

Twist: The man throws the woman into the air. She spins in the air (either a double- or triple-twist), and he catches her at the landing.

*Compiled by the United States Figure Skating Association.

World Champions

Women

1906	Madge Sayers-Cave, Great Britain	1932	Sonja Henie, Norway
1907	Madge Sayers-Cave, Great Britain	1933	Sonja Henie, Norway
1908	Lily Kronberger, Hungary	1934	Sonja Henie, Norway
1909	Lily Kronberger, Hungary	1935	Sonja Henie, Norway
1910	Lily Kronberger, Hungary	1936	Sonja Henie, Norway
1911	Lily Kronberger, Hungary	1937	Cecilia Colledge, Great Britain
1912	Opika von Meray Horvath, Hungary	1938	Megan Taylor, Great Britain
1913	Opika von Meray Horvath, Hungary	1939	Megan Taylor, Great Britain
1914	Opika von Meray Horvath, Hungary	1940–46	No competition
1915–21	No competition	1947	Barbara Ann Scott, Canada
1922	Herma Plank-Szabo, Austria	1948	Barbara Ann Scott, Canada
1923	Herma Plank-Szabo, Austria	1949	Alena Vrzanova, Czechoslovakia
1924	Herma Plank-Szabo, Austria	1950	Alena Vrzanova, Czechoslovakia
1925	Herma Jaross-Szabo, Austria	1951	Jeannette Altwegg, Great Britain
1926	Herma Jaross-Szabo, Austria	1952	Jacqueline duBief, France
1927	Sonja Henie, Norway	1953	Tenley Albright, United States
1928	Sonja Henie, Norway	1954	Gundi Busch, W Germany
1929	Sonja Henie, Norway	1955	Tenley Albright, United States
1930	Sonja Henie, Norway	1956	Carol Heiss, United States
1931	Sonja Henie, Norway	1957	Carol Heiss, United States

World Champions (Cont.)

Women (Cont.)

1958	Carol Heiss, United States
1959	Carol Heiss, United States
1960	Carol Heiss, United States
1961	No competition
1962	Sjoukje Dijkstra, Netherlands
1963	Sjoukje Dijkstra, Netherlands
1964	Sjoukje Dijkstra, Netherlands
1965	Petra Burka, Canada
1966	Peggy Fleming, United States
1967	Peggy Fleming, United States
1968	Peggy Fleming, United States
1969	Gabriele Seyfert, E Germany
1970	Gabriele Seyfert, E Germany
1971	Beatrix Schuba, Austria
1972	Beatrix Schuba, Austria
1973	Karen Magnussen, Canada
1974	Christine Errath, E Germany
1975	Dianne DeLeeuw, Netherlands
1976	Dorothy Hamill, United States
1977	Linda Fratianne, United States
1978	Annett Poetzsch, E Germany
1979	Linda Fratianne, United States
1980	Annett Poetzsch, E Germany
1981	Denise Biellmann, Switzerland
1982	Elaine Zayak, United States
1983	Rosalynn Sumners, United States
1984	Katarina Witt, E Germany
1985	Katarina Witt, E Germany
1986	Debi Thomas, United States
1987	Katarina Witt, E Germany
1988	Katarina Witt, E Germany
1989	Midori Ito, Japan
1990	Jill Trenary, United States
1991	Kristi Yamaguchi, United States
1992	Kristi Yamaguchi, United States
1993	Oksana Baiul, Ukraine
1994	Yuka Sato, Japan
1995	Chen Lu, China
1996	Michelle Kwan, United States
1997	Tara Lipinski, United States
1998	Michelle Kwan, United States
1999	Maria Butyrskaya, Russia
2000	Michelle Kwan, United States
2001	Michelle Kwan, United States
2002	Irina Slutskaya, Russia
2003	Michelle Kwan, United States
2004	Shizuka Arakawa, Japan

Men

1896	Gilbert Fuchs, Germany
1897	Gustav Hugel, Austria
1898	Henning Grenander, Sweden
1899	Gustav Hugel, Austria
1900	Gustav Hugel, Austria
1901	Ulrich Salchow, Sweden
1902	Ulrich Salchow, Sweden
1903	Ulrich Salchow, Sweden
1904	Ulrich Salchow, Sweden
1905	Ulrich Salchow, Sweden
1906	Gilbert Fuchs, Germany
1907	Ulrich Salchow, Sweden
1908	Ulrich Salchow, Sweden
1909	Ulrich Salchow, Sweden
1910	Ulrich Salchow, Sweden
1911	Ulrich Salchow, Sweden
1912	Fritz Kachler, Austria
1913	Fritz Kachler, Austria
1914	Gosta Sandhal, Sweden
1915–21	No competition
1922	Gillis Grafstrom, Sweden
1923	Fritz Kachler, Austria
1924	Gillis Grafstrom, Sweden
1925	Willy Bockl, Austria
1926	Willy Bockl, Austria
1927	Willy Bockl, Austria
1928	Willy Bockl, Austria
1929	Gillis Grafstrom, Sweden
1930	Karl Schafer, Austria
1931	Karl Schafer, Austria
1932	Karl Schafer, Austria
1933	Karl Schafer, Austria
1934	Karl Schafer, Austria
1935	Karl Schafer, Austria
1936	Karl Schafer, Austria
1937	Felix Kaspar, Austria
1938	Felix Kaspar, Austria
1939	Graham Sharp, Great Britain
1940–46	No competition
1947	Hans Gerschwiler, Switzerland
1948	Dick Button, United States
1949	Dick Button, United States
1950	Dick Button, United States
1951	Dick Button, United States
1952	Dick Button, United States
1953	Hayes Alan Jenkins, United States
1954	Hayes Alan Jenkins, United States
1955	Hayes Alan Jenkins, United States
1956	Hayes Alan Jenkins, United States
1957	David W. Jenkins, United States
1958	David W. Jenkins, United States
1959	David W. Jenkins, United States
1960	Alan Giletti, France
1961	No competition
1962	Donald Jackson, Canada
1963	Donald McPherson, Canada
1964	Manfred Schneldorfer, W Germany
1965	Alain Calmat, France
1966	Emmerich Danzer, Austria
1967	Emmerich Danzer, Austria
1968	Emmerich Danzer, Austria
1969	Tim Wood, United States
1970	Tim Wood, United States
1971	Andrej Nepela, Czechoslovakia
1972	Andrej Nepela, Czechoslovakia
1973	Andrej Nepela, Czechoslovakia
1974	Jan Hoffmann, E Germany
1975	Sergei Volkov, USSR
1976	John Curry, Great Britain
1977	Vladimir Kovalev, USSR
1978	Charles Tickner, United States
1979	Vladimir Kovalev, USSR
1980	Jan Hoffmann, E Germany
1981	Scott Hamilton, United States
1982	Scott Hamilton, United States
1983	Scott Hamilton, United States
1984	Scott Hamilton, United States
1985	Aleksandr Fadeev, USSR
1986	Brian Boitano, United States
1987	Brian Orser, Canada
1988	Brian Boitano, United States
1989	Kurt Browning, Canada
1990	Kurt Browning, Canada
1991	Kurt Browning, Canada
1992	Viktor Petrenko, CIS
1993	Kurt Browning, Canada
1994	Elvis Stojko, Canada
1995	Elvis Stojko, Canada
1996	Todd Eldredge, United States
1997	Elvis Stojko, Canada

Men (Cont.)

1998 ....Alexei Yagudin, Russia	2002 ....Alexei Yagudin, Russia
1999 ....Alexei Yagudin, Russia	2003 ....Evgeny Plushenko, Russia
2000 ....Alexei Yagudin, Russia	2004 ....Evgeny Plushenko, Russia
2001 ....Evgeny Plushenko, Russia	

Pairs

1908 ....Anna Hubler, Heinrich Burger, Germany
1909 ....Phyllis Johnson, James H. Johnson, Great Britain
1910 ....Anna Hubler, Heinrich Burger, Germany
1911 ....Ludowika Eilers, Walter Jakobsson, Germany/Finland
1912 ....Phyllis Johnson, James H. Johnson, Great Britain
1913 ....Helene Engelmann, Karl Majstrik, Germany
1914 ....Ludowika Jakobsson-Eilers, Walter Jakobsson-Eilers, Finland
1915–21 .....No competition
1922 ....Helene Engelmann, Alfred Berger, Germany
1923 ....Ludowika Jakobsson-Eilers, Walter Jakobsson-Eilers, Finland
1924 ....Helene Engelmann, Alfred Berger, Germany
1925 ....Herma Jaross-Szabo, Ludwig Wrede, Austria
1926 ....Andree Joly, Pierre Brunet, France
1927 ....Herma Jaross-Szabo, Ludwig Wrede, Austria
1928 ....Andree Joly, Pierre Brunet, France
1929 ....Lilly Scholz, Otto Kaiser, Austria
1930 ....Andree Brunet-Joly, Pierre Brunet-Joly, France
1931 ....Emilie Rotter, Laszlo Szollas, Hungary
1932 ....Andree Brunet-Joly, Pierre Brunet-Joly, France
1933 ....Emilie Rotter, Laszlo Szollas, Hungary
1934 ....Emilie Rotter, Laszlo Szollas, Hungary
1935 ....Emilie Rotter, Laszlo Szollas, Hungary
1936 ....Maxi Herber, Ernst Bajer, Germany
1937 ....Maxi Herber, Ernst Bajer, Germany
1938 ....Maxi Herber, Ernst Bajer, Germany
1939 ....Maxi Herber, Ernst Bajer, Germany
1940–46 .....No competition
1947 ....Micheline Lannoy, Pierre Baugniet, Belgium
1948 ....Micheline Lannoy, Pierre Baugniet, Belgium
1949 ....Andrea Kekessy, Ede Kiraly, Hungary
1950 ....Karol Kennedy, Peter Kennedy, United States
1951 ....Ria Baran, Paul Falk, W Germany
1952 ....Ria Baran Falk, Paul Falk, W Germany
1953 ....Jennifer Nicks, John Nicks, Great Britain
1954 ....Frances Dafoe, Norris Bowden, Canada
1955 ....Frances Dafoe, Norris Bowden, Canada
1956 ....Sissy Schwarz, Kurt Oppelt, Austria
1957 ....Barbara Wagner, Robert Paul, Canada
1958 ....Barbara Wagner, Robert Paul, Canada
1959 ....Barbara Wagner, Robert Paul, Canada
1960 ....Barbara Wagner, Robert Paul, Canada
1961 ....No competition
1962 ....Maria Jelinek, Otto Jelinek, Canada

1963 ....Marika Kilius, Hans-Jurgen Baumler, W Germany
1964 ....Marika Kilius, Hans-Jurgen Baumler, W Germany
1965 ....Ljudmila Protopopov, Oleg Protopopov, USSR
1966 ....Ljudmila Protopopov, Oleg Protopopov, USSR
1967 ....Ljudmila Protopopov, Oleg Protopopov, USSR
1968 ....Ljudmila Protopopov, Oleg Protopopov, USSR
1969 ....Irina Rodnina, Alexsei Ulanov, USSR
1970 ....Irina Rodnina, Alexsei Ulanov, USSR
1971 ....Irina Rodnina, Sergei Ulanov, USSR
1972 ....Irina Rodnina, Sergei Ulanov, USSR
1973 ....Irina Rodnina, Aleksandr Zaitsev, USSR
1974 ....Irina Rodnina, Aleksandr Zaitsev, USSR
1975 ....Irina Rodnina, Aleksandr Zaitsev, USSR
1976 ....Irina Rodnina, Aleksandr Zaitsev, USSR
1977 ....Irina Rodnina, Aleksandr Zaitsev, USSR
1978 ....Irina Rodnina, Aleksandr Zaitsev, USSR
1979 ....Tai Babilonia, Randy Gardner, United States
1980 ....Maria Cherkasova, Sergei Shakhrai, USSR
1981 ....Irina Vorobieva, Igor Lisovsky, USSR
1982 ....Sabine Baess, Tassilio Thierbach, E Germany
1983 ....Elena Valova, Oleg Vasiliev, USSR
1984 ....Barbara Underhill, Paul Martini, Canada
1985 ....Elena Valova, Oleg Vasiliev, USSR
1986 ....Ekaterina Gordeeva, Sergei Grinkov, USSR
1987 ....Ekaterina Gordeeva, Sergei Grinkov, USSR
1988 ....Elena Valova, Oleg Vasiliev, USSR
1989 ....Ekaterina Gordeeva, Sergei Grinkov, USSR
1990 ....Ekaterina Gordeeva, Sergei Grinkov, USSR
1991 ....Natalia Mishkutienok, Artur Dmitriev, USSR
1992 ....Natalia Mishkutienok, Artur Dmitriev, CIS
1993 ....Isabelle Brasseur, Lloyd Eisler, Canada
1994 ....Evgenia Shishkova, Vadim Naumov, Russia
1995 ....Radka Kovarikova, Rene Novotny, Czech Republic
1996 ....Marina Eltsova, Andrey Buskhov, Russia
1997 ....Mandy Wötzel, Ingo Steuer, Germany
1998 ....Jenni Meno, Todd Sand, United States
1999 ....Elena Berezhnaya, Anton Sikharulidze, Russia
2000 ....Maria Petrova and Aleksei Tikhonov, Russia
2001 ....Jamie Salé and David Pelletier, Canada
2002 ....Xue Shen and Hongbo Zhao, China
2003 ....Xue Shen and Hongbo Zhao, China
2004 ....Tatiana Totmianina and Maxim Marinin, Russia

Dance

1950	Lois Waring, Michael McGean, United States	1973	Ljudmila Pakhomova, Aleksandr Gorshkov, USSR
1951	Jean Westwood, Lawrence Demmy, Great Britain	1974	Ljudmila Pakhomova, Aleksandr Gorshkov, USSR
1952	Jean Westwood, Lawrence Demmy, Great Britain	1975	Irina Moiseeva, Andreij Minenkov, USSR
1953	Jean Westwood, Lawrence Demmy, Great Britain	1976	Ljudmila Pakhomova, Aleksandr Gorshkov, USSR
1954	Jean Westwood, Lawrence Demmy, Great Britain	1977	Irina Moiseeva, Andreij Minenkov, USSR
1955	Jean Westwood, Lawrence Demmy, Great Britain	1978	Natalia Linichuk, Gennadi Karponosov, USSR
1956	Pamela Wieght, Paul Thomas, Great Britain	1979	Natalia Linichuk, Gennadi Karponosov,USSR
1957	June Markham, Courtney Jones, Great Britain	1980	Krisztina Regoeczy, Andras Sallai, Hungary
1958	June Markham, Courtney Jones, Great Britain	1981	Jayne Torvill, Christopher Dean, Great Britain
1959	Doreen D. Denny, Courtney Jones, Great Britain	1982	Jayne Torvill, Christopher Dean, Great Britain
1960	Doreen D. Denny, Courtney Jones, Great Britain	1983	Jayne Torvill, Christopher Dean, Great Britain
1961	No competition	1984	Jayne Torvill, Christopher Dean, Great Britain
1962	Eva Romanova, Pavel Roman, Czechoslovakia	1985	Natalia Bestemianova/ Andrei Bukin, USSR
1963	Eva Romanova, Pavel Roman, Czechoslovakia	1986	Natalia Bestemianova/ Andrei Bukin, USSR
1964	Eva Romanova, Pavel Roman, Czechoslovakia	1987	Natalia Bestemianova/ Andrei Bukin, USSR
1965	Eva Romanova, Pavel Roman, Czechoslovakia	1988	Natalia Bestemianova/ Andrei Bukin, USSR
1966	Diane Towler, Bernard Ford, Great Britain	1989	Marina Klimova/ Sergei Ponomarenko, USSR
1967	Diane Towler, Bernard Ford, Great Britain	1990	Marina Klimova/ Sergei Ponomarenko, USSR
1968	Diane Towler, Bernard Ford, Great Britain	1991	Isabelle Duchesnay/ Paul Duchesnay, France
1969	Diane Towler, Bernard Ford, Great Britain	1992	Marina Klimova/ Sergei Ponomarenko, CIS
1970	Ljudmila Pakhomova, Aleksandr Gorshkov, USSR	1993	Renee Roca/ Gorsha Sur, United States
1971	Ljudmila Pakhomova, Aleksandr Gorshkov, USSR	1994	Oksana Grishuk/ Evgeny Platov, Russia
1972	Ljudmila Pakhomova, Aleksandr Gorshkov, USSR	1995	Oksana Grishuk/ Evgeny Platov, Russia
		1996	Oksana Grishuk/ Evgeny Platov, Russia
		1997	Oksana Grishuk/ Evgeny Platov, Russia
		1998	Anjelika Krylova/Oleg Ovsyannikov, Russia
		1999	Anjelika Krylova/Oleg Ovsyannikov, Russia
		2000	Marina Anissina/ Gwendal Peizerat, France
		2001	Barbara Fusar-Poli/ Maurizio Margaglio, Italy
		2002	Irina Lobacheva/ Ilia Averbukh, Russia
		2003	Shae-Lynn Bourne/ Victor Kraatz, Canada
		2004	Tatiana Navka/Roman Kostomarov, Russia

Champions of the United States

The championships held in 1914, 1918, 1920 and 1921 under the auspices of the International Skating Union of America were open to Canadians, although the competitions were considered to be United States championships. Beginning in 1922, the championships have been held under the auspices of the United States Figure Skating Association.

Women

1914	Theresa Weld, SC of Boston	1931	Maribel Y. Vinson, SC of Boston
1915–17	No competition	1932	Maribel Y. Vinson, SC of Boston
1918	Rosemary S. Beresford, New York SC	1933	Maribel Y. Vinson, SC of Boston
1919	No competition	1934	Suzanne Davis, SC of Boston
1920	Theresa Weld, SC of Boston	1935	Maribel Y. Vinson, SC of Boston
1921	Theresa Weld Blanchard, SC of Boston	1936	Maribel Y. Vinson, SC of Boston
1922	Theresa Weld Blanchard, SC of Boston	1937	Maribel Y. Vinson, SC of Boston
1923	Theresa Weld Blanchard, SC of Boston	1938	Joan Tozzer, SC of Boston
1924	Theresa Weld Blanchard, SC of Boston	1939	Joan Tozzer, SC of Boston
1925	Beatrix Loughran, New York SC	1940	Joan Tozzer, SC of Boston
1926	Beatrix Loughran, New York SC	1941	Jane Vaughn, Philadelphia SC & HS
1927	Beatrix Loughran, New York SC	1942	Jane Vaughn Sullivan, Philadelphia SC & HS
1928	Maribel Y. Vinson, SC of Boston	1943	Gretchen Van Zandt Merrill, SC of Boston
1929	Maribel Y. Vinson, SC of Boston	1944	Gretchen Van Zandt Merrill, SC of Boston
1930	Maribel Y. Vinson, SC of Boston		

Women (Cont.)

1945...........Gretchen Van Zandt Merrill, SC of Boston	1975 ....Dorothy Hamill, SC of New York
1946...........Gretchen Van Zandt Merrill, SC of Boston	1976 ....Dorothy Hamill, SC of New York
1947...........Gretchen Van Zandt Merrill, SC of Boston	1977 ....Linda Fratianne, Los Angeles FSC
1948...........Gretchen Van Zandt Merrill, SC of Boston	1978 ....Linda Fratianne, Los Angeles FSC
1949 ....Yvonne Claire Sherman, SC of New York	1979 ....Linda Fratianne, Los Angeles FSC
1950 ....Yvonne Claire Sherman, SC of New York	1980 ....Linda Fratianne, Los Angeles FSC
1951 ....Sonya Klopfer, Junior SC of New York	1981 ....Elaine Zayak, SC of New York
1952 ....Tenley E. Albright, SC of Boston	1982 ....Rosalynn Sumners, Seattle SC
1953 ....Tenley E. Albright, SC of Boston	1983 ....Rosalynn Sumners, Seattle SC
1954 ....Tenley E. Albright, SC of Boston	1984 ....Rosalynn Sumners, Seattle SC
1955 ....Tenley E. Albright, SC of Boston	1985 ....Tiffany Chin, San Diego FSC
1956 ....Tenley E. Albright, SC of Boston	1986 ....Debi Thomas, Los Angeles FSC
1957...........Carol E. Heiss, SC of New York	1987 ....Jill Trenary, Broadmoor SC
1958 ....Carol E. Heiss, SC of New York	1988 ....Debi Thomas, Los Angeles FSC
1959 ....Carol E. Heiss, SC of New York	1989 ....Jill Trenary, Broadmoor SC
1960 ....Carol E. Heiss, SC of New York	1990 ....Jill Trenary, Broadmoor SC
1961...........Laurence R. Owen, SC of Boston	1991 ....Tonya Harding, Carousel FSC
1962...........Barbara Roles Pursley, Arctic Blades FSC	1992 ....Kristi Yamaguchi, St Moritz ISC
1963...........Lorraine G. Hanlon, SC of Boston	1993 ....Nancy Kerrigan, Colonial FSC
1964...........Peggy Fleming, Arctic Blades FSC	1994 ....Tonya Harding, Portland FSC
1965...........Peggy Fleming, Arctic Blades FSC	1995 ....Nicole Bobek, Los Angeles FSC
1966...........Peggy Fleming, City of Colorado Springs	1996 ....Michelle Kwan, Los Angeles FSC
1967 ....Peggy Fleming, Broadmoor SC	1997 ....Tara Lipinski, Detroit SC
1968...........Peggy Fleming, Broadmoor SC	1998 ....Michelle Kwan, Los Angeles FSC
1969 ....Janet Lynn, Wagon Wheel FSC	1999 ....Michelle Kwan, Los Angeles FSC
1970 ....Janet Lynn, Wagon Wheel FSC	2000 ....Michelle Kwan, Los Angeles FSC
1971 ....Janet Lynn, Wagon Wheel FSC	2001 ....Michelle Kwan, Los Angeles FSC
1972 ....Janet Lynn, Wagon Wheel FSC	2002 ....Michelle Kwan, Los Angeles FSC
1973 ....Janet Lynn, Wagon Wheel FSC	2003 ....Michelle Kwan, Los Angeles FSC
1974 ....Dorothy Hamill, SC of New York	2004 ....Michelle Kwan, Los Angeles FSC

Men

1914 ....Norman M. Scott, WC of Montreal	1953 ....Hayes Alan Jenkins, Cleveland SC
1915–17 .....No competition	1954 ....Hayes Alan Jenkins, Broadmoor SC
1918 ....Nathaniel W. Niles, SC of Boston	1955 ....Hayes Alan Jenkins, Broadmoor SC
1919 ....No competition	1956 ....Hayes Alan Jenkins, Broadmoor SC
1920 ....Sherwin C. Badger, SC of Boston	1957 ....David Jenkins, Broadmoor SC
1921 ....Sherwin C. Badger, SC of Boston	1958 ....David Jenkins, Broadmoor SC
1922 ....Sherwin C. Badger, SC of Boston	1959 ....David Jenkins, Broadmoor SC
1923 ....Sherwin C. Badger, SC of Boston	1960 ....David Jenkins, Broadmoor SC
1924 ....Sherwin C. Badger, SC of Boston	1961 ....Bradley R. Lord, SC of Boston
1925 ....Nathaniel W. Niles, SC of Boston	1962 ....Monty Hoyt, Broadmoor SC
1926 ....Chris I. Christenson, Twin City FSC	1963 ....Thomas Litz, Hershey FSC
1927 ....Nathaniel W. Niles, SC of Boston	1964 ....Scott Ethan Allen, SC of New York
1928 ....Roger F. Turner, SC of Boston	1965 ....Gary C. Visconti, Detroit SC
1929 ....Roger F. Turner, SC of Boston	1966 ....Scott Ethan Allen, SC of New York
1930 ....Roger F. Turner, SC of Boston	1967 ....Gary C. Visconti, Detroit SC
1931 ....Roger F. Turner, SC of Boston	1968 ....Tim Wood, Detroit SC
1932 ....Roger F. Turner, SC of Boston	1969 ....Tim Wood, Detroit SC
1933 ....Roger F. Turner, SC of Boston	1970 ....Tim Wood, City of Colorado Springs
1934 ....Roger F. Turner, SC of Boston	1971 ....John Misha Petkevich, Great Falls FSC
1935 ....Robin H. Lee, SC of New York	1972 ....Kenneth Shelley, Arctic Blades FSC
1936 ....Robin H. Lee, SC of New York	1973 ....Gordon McKellen Jr., SC of Lake Placid
1937 ....Robin H. Lee, SC of New York	1974 ....Gordon McKellen Jr., SC of Lake Placid
1938 ....Robin H. Lee, Chicago SC	1975 ....Gordon McKellen Jr., SC of Lake Placid
1939 ....Robin H. Lee, St Paul FSC	1976 ....Terry Kubicka, Arctic Blades FSC
1940 ....Eugene Turner, Los Angeles FSC	1977 ....Charles Tickner, Denver FSC
1941 ....Eugene Turner, Los Angeles FSC	1978 ....Charles Tickner, Denver FSC
1942 ....Robert Specht, Chicago FSC	1979 ....Charles Tickner, Denver FSC
1943 ....Arthur R. Vaughn Jr., Phila. SC & HS	1980 ....Charles Tickner, Denver FSC
1944–45 .....No competition	1981 ....Scott Hamilton, Philadelphia SC & HS
1946 ....Dick Button, Philadelphia SC & HS	1982 ....Scott Hamilton, Philadelphia SC & HS
1947 ....Dick Button, Philadelphia SC & HS	1983 ....Scott Hamilton, Philadelphia SC & HS
1948 ....Dick Button, Philadelphia SC & HS	1984 ....Scott Hamilton, Philadelphia SC & HS
1949 ....Dick Button, Philadelphia SC & HS	1985 ....Brian Boitano, Peninsula FSC
1950 ....Dick Button, SC of Boston •	1986 ....Brian Boitano, Peninsula FSC
1951 ....Dick Button, SC of Boston	1987 ....Brian Boitano, Peninsula FSC
1952 ....Dick Button, SC of Boston	1988 ....Brian Boitano, Peninsula FSC

Men (Cont.)

1989 ....Christopher Bowman, Los Angeles FSC
1990 ....Todd Eldredge, Los Angeles FSC
1991 ....Todd Eldredge, Los Angeles FSC
1992 ....Christopher Bowman, Los Angeles FSC
1993 ....Scott Davis, Broadmoor SC
1994 ....Scott Davis, Broadmoor SC
1995 ....Todd Eldredge, Detroit SC
1996 ....Rudy Galindo, St Moritz ISC

1997 ....Todd Eldredge, Detroit SC
1998 ....Todd Eldredge, Detroit SC
1999 ....Michael Weiss, Washington FSC
2000 ....Michael Weiss, Washington FSC
2001 ....Timothy Goebel, Winterhurst FSC
2002 ....Todd Eldredge, Los Angeles FSC
2003 ....Michael Weiss, Washington FSC
2004 ....Johnny Weir, SC of New York

Pairs

1914 ......Jeanne Chevalier, Norman M. Scott, WC of Montreal
1915–17 .No competition
1918 ......Theresa Weld, Nathaniel W. Niles, SC of Boston
1919 ......No competition
1920 ......Theresa Weld, Nathaniel W. Niles, SC of Boston
1921 ......Theresa Weld Blanchard, Nathaniel W. Niles, SC of Boston
1922 ......Theresa Weld Blanchard, Nathaniel W. Niles, SC of Boston
1923 ......Theresa Weld Blanchard, Nathaniel W. Niles, SC of Boston
1924 ......Theresa Weld Blanchard, Nathaniel W. Niles, SC of Boston
1925 ......Theresa Weld Blanchard, Nathaniel W. Niles, SC of Boston
1926 ......Theresa Weld Blanchard, Nathaniel W. Niles, SC of Boston
1927 ......Theresa Weld Blanchard, Nathaniel W. Niles, SC of Boston
1928 ......Maribel Y. Vinson, Thornton L. Coolidge, SC of Boston
1929 ......Maribel Y. Vinson, Thornton L. Coolidge, SC of Boston
1930 ......Beatrix Loughran, Sherwin C. Badger, SC of New York
1931 ......Beatrix Loughran, Sherwin C. Badger, SC of New York
1932 ......Beatrix Loughran, Sherwin C. Badger, SC of New York
1933 ......Maribel Y. Vinson, George E. B. Hill, SC of Boston
1934 ......Grace E. Madden, James L. Madden, SC of Boston
1935 ......Maribel Y. Vinson, George E. B. Hill, SC of Boston
1936 ......Maribel Y. Vinson, George E. B. Hill, SC of Boston
1937 ......Maribel Y. Vinson, George E. B. Hill, SC of Boston
1938 ......Joan Tozzer, M. Bernard Fox, SC of Boston
1939 ......Joan Tozzer, M. Bernard Fox, SC of Boston
1940 ......Joan Tozzer, M. Bernard Fox, SC of Boston
1941 ......Donna Atwood, Eugene Turner, Mercury FSC/Los Angeles FSC
1942 ......Doris Schubach, Walter Noffke, Springfield Ice Birds
1943 ......Doris Schubach, Walter Noffke, Springfield Ice Birds
1944 ......Doris Schubach, Walter Noffke, Springfield Ice Birds
1945 ......Donna Jeanne Pospisil, Jean-Pierre Brunet, SC of New York
1946 ......Donna Jeanne Pospisil, Jean-Pierre Brunet, SC of New York

1947 ......Yvonne Claire Sherman, Robert J. Swenning, SC of New York
1948 ......Karol Kennedy, Peter Kennedy, Seattle SC
1949 ......Karol Kennedy, Peter Kennedy, Seattle SC
1950 ......Karol Kennedy, Peter Kennedy, Broadmoor SC
1951 ......Karol Kennedy, Peter Kennedy, Broadmoor SC
1952 ......Karol Kennedy, Peter Kennedy, Broadmoor SC
1953 ......Carole Ann Ormaca, Robin Greiner, SC of Fresno
1954 ......Carole Ann Ormaca, Robin Greiner, SC of Fresno
1955 ......Carole Ann Ormaca, Robin Greiner, St Moritz ISC
1956 ......Carole Ann Ormaca, Robin Greiner, St Moritz ISC
1957 ......Nancy Rouillard Ludington, Ronald Ludington, Commonwealth FSC/ SC of Boston
1958 ......Nancy Rouillard Ludington, Ronald Ludington, Commonwealth FSC/ SC of Boston
1959 ......Nancy Rouillard Ludington, Ronald Ludington, Commonwealth FSC
1960 ......Nancy Rouillard Ludington, Ronald Ludington, Commonwealth FSC
1961 ......Maribel Y. Owen, Dudley S. Richards, SC of Boston
1962 ......Dorothyann Nelson, Pieter Kollen, Village of Lake Placid
1963 ......Judianne Fotheringill, Jerry J. Fotheringill, Broadmoor SC
1964 ......Judianne Fotheringill, Jerry J. Fotheringill, Broadmoor SC
1965 ......Vivian Joseph, Ronald Joseph, Chicago FSC
1966 ......Cynthia Kauffman, Ronald Kauffman, Seattle SC
1967 ......Cynthia Kauffman, Ronald Kauffman, Seattle SC
1968 ......Cynthia Kauffman, Ronald Kauffman, Seattle SC
1969 ......Cynthia Kauffman, Ronald Kauffman, Seattle SC
1970 ......Jo Jo Starbuck, Kenneth Shelley, Arctic Blades FSC
1971 ......Jo Jo Starbuck, Kenneth Shelley, Arctic Blades FSC
1972 ......Jo Jo Starbuck, Kenneth Shelley, Arctic Blades FSC
1973 ......Melissa Militano, Mark Militano, SC of New York
1974 ......Melissa Militano, Johnny Johns, SC of New York/Detroit SC
1975 ......Melissa Militano, Johnny Johns, SC of NY/ Detroit SC

Pairs *(Cont.)*

1976 ......Tai Babilonia, Randy Gardner,
Los Angeles FSC
1977 ......Tai Babilonia, Randy Gardner, LA FSC
1978 ......Tai Babilonia, Randy Gardner,
Los Angeles FSC/Santa Monica FSC
1979 ......Tai Babilonia, Randy Gardner,
Los Angeles FSC/Santa Monica FSC
1980 ......Tai Babilonia, Randy Gardner,
Los Angeles FSC/Santa Monica FSC
1981 ......Caitlin Carruthers, Peter Carruthers,
SC of Wilmington
1982 ......Caitlin Carruthers, Peter Carruthers,
SC of Wilmington
1983 ......Caitlin Carruthers, Peter Carruthers,
SC of Wilmington
1984 ......Caitlin Carruthers, Peter Carruthers,
SC of Wilmington
1985 ......Jill Watson, Peter Oppegard, LA FSC
1986 ......Gillian Wachsman, Todd Waggoner,
SC of Wilmington
1987 ......Jill Watson, Peter Oppegard, Los Angeles FSC
1988 ......Jill Watson, Peter Oppegard,
Los Angeles FSC
1989 ......Kristi Yamaguchi/ Rudy Galindo, St Mortiz ISC

1990 ......Kristi Yamaguchi/ Rudy Galindo, St Mortiz ISC
1991 ......Natasha Kuchiki/ Todd Sand, LA FSC
1992 ......Calla Urbanski/ Rocky Marval,
U of Delaware FSC/SC of New York
1993 ......Calla Urbanski/ Rocky Marval,
U of Delaware FSC/SC of New York
1994 ......Jenni Meno/ Todd Sand,
Winterhurst FSC/Los Angeles FSC
1995 ......Jenni Meno/ Todd Sand,
Winterhurst FSC/Los Angeles FSC
1996 ......Jenni Meno/ Todd Sand,
Winterhurst FSC/Los Angeles FSC
1997 ......Kyoko Ina/ Jason Dungjen, SC of New York
1998 ......Kyoko Ina/ Jason Dungjen, SC of New York
1999 ......Danielle Hartsell/ Steve Hartsell, Detroit SC
2000 ......Kyoko Ina/ John Zimmerman, SC of New
York/Birmingham FSC
2001 ......Kyoko Ina/ John Zimmerman, SC of New
York/Birmingham FSC
2002 ......Kyoko Ina/ John Zimmerman, SC of New
York/Birmingham FSC
2003 ......Tiffany Scott/ Philip Dulebohn, Colonial FSC/
Univ of Delaware FSC
2004 ......Rena Inoue/John Baldwin, All Year FSC

Dance

1914 ......Waltz: Theresa Weld, Nathaniel W. Niles,
SC of Boston
1915–19..No competition
1920 ......Waltz: Theresa Weld, Nathaniel W. Niles,
SC of Boston
Fourteenstep: Gertrude Cheever Porter,
Irving Brokaw, New York SC
1921 ......Waltz and Fourteenstep: Theresa Weld
Blanchard, Nathaniel W. Niles, SC of Boston
1922 ......Waltz: Beatrix Loughran, Edward M.
Howland, New York SC/SC of Boston
Fourteenstep: Theresa Weld Blanchard,
Nathaniel W. Niles, SC of Boston
1923 ......Waltz: Mr. & Mrs. Henry W. Howe,
New York SC
Fourteenstep: Sydney Goode, James B.
Greene, New York SC
1924 ......Waltz: Rosaline Dunn, Frederick Gabel,
New York SC
Fourteenstep: Sydney Goode, James B.
Greene, New York SC
1925 ......Waltz and Fourteenstep: Virginia Slattery,
Ferrier T. Martin, New York SC
1926 ......Waltz: Rosaline Dunn, Joseph K. Savage,
New York SC
Fourteenstep: Sydney Goode, James B.
Greene, New York SC
1927 ......Waltz and Fourteenstep: Rosaline Dunn,
Joseph K. Savage, New York SC
1928 ......Waltz: Rosaline Dunn, Joseph K. Savage,
New York SC
Fourteenstep: Ada Bauman Kelly, George T.
Braakman, New York SC
1929 ......Waltz and Original Dance combined:
Edith C. Secord, Joseph K. Savage,
SC of New York
1930 ......Waltz: Edith C. Secord, Joseph K. Savage,
SC of New York
Original: Clara Rotch Frothingham, George
E. B. Hill, SC of Boston
1931 ......Waltz: Edith C. Secord, Ferrier T. Martin,
SC of New York
Original: Theresa Weld Blanchard, Nathaniel
W. Niles, SC of Boston

1932 ......Waltz: Edith C. Secord, Joseph K. Savage,
SC of New York
Original: Clara Rotch Frothingham, George
E. B. Hill, SC of Boston
1933 ......Waltz: Ilse Twaroschk, Frederick F.
Fleishmann, Brooklyn FSC
Original: Suzanne Davis, Frederick
Goodridge, SC of Boston
1934 ......Waltz: Nettie C. Prantel, Roy Hunt, SC of
New York
Original: Suzanne Davis, Frederick
Goodridge, SC of Boston
1935 ......Waltz: Nettie C. Prantel, Roy Hunt,
SC of New York
1936 ......Marjorie Parker, Joseph K. Savage,
SC of New York
1937 ......Nettie C. Prantel, Harold Hartshorne,
SC of New York
1938 ......Nettie C. Prantel, Harold Hartshorne,
SC of New York
1939 ......Sandy Macdonald, Harold Hartshorne,
SC of New York
1940 ......Sandy Macdonald, Harold Hartshorne,
SC of New York
1941 ......Sandy Macdonald, Harold Hartshorne, SCNY
1942 ......Edith B. Whetstone, Alfred N. Richards, Jr,
Philadelphia SC & HS
1943 ......Marcella May, James Lochead Jr., Skate & Ski Club
1944 ......Marcella May, James Lochead Jr., Skate & Ski Club
1945 ......Kathe Mehl Williams, Robert J. Swenning,
SC of New York
1946 ......Anne Davies, Carleton C. Hoffner Jr.,
Washington FSC
1947 ......Lois Waring, Walter H. Bainbridge Jr.,
Baltimore FSC/Washigton FSC
1948 ......Lois Waring, Walter H. Bainbridge Jr.,
Baltimore FSC/Washington FSC
1949 ......Lois Waring, Walter H. Bainbridge Jr.,
Baltimore FSC/Washington FSC
1950 ......Lois Waring, Michael McGean, Baltimore FSC
1951 ......Carmel Bodel, Edward L. Bodel, St. Moritz ISC
1952 ......Lois Waring, Michael McGean,
Baltimore FSC

Dance (Cont.)

1953 ......Carol Ann Peters, Daniel C. Ryan,
Washington FSC
1954 ......Carmel Bodel, Edward L. Bodel, St Moritz ISC
1955 ......Carmel Bodel, Edward L. Bodel,
St Moritz ISC
1956 ......Joan Zamboni, Roland Junso,
Arctic Blades FSC
1957 ......Sharon McKenzie, Bert Wright,
Los Angeles FSC
1958 ......Andree Anderson, Donald Jacoby, Buffalo SC
1959 ......Andree Anderson Jacoby, Donald Jacoby,
Buffalo SC
1960 ......Margie Ackles, Charles W. Phillips Jr.,
Los Angeles FSC/Arctic Blades FSC
1961 ......Diane C. Sherbloom, Larry Pierce,
Los Angeles FSC/WC of Indianapolis
1962 ......Yvonne N. Littlefield, Peter F. Betts,
Arctic Blades FSC/ Paramount, CA
1963 ......Sally Schantz, Stanley Urban,
SC of Boston/Buffalo SC
1964 ......Darlene Streich, Charles D. Fetter Jr.,
WC of Indianapolis
1965 ......Kristin Fortune, Dennis Sveum,
Los Angeles FSC
1966 ......Kristin Fortune, Dennis Sveum, Los Angeles FSC
1967 ......Lorna Dyer, John Carrell, Broadmoor SC
1968 ......Judy Schwomeyer, James Sladky,
WC of Indianapolis/Genesee FSC
1969 ......Judy Schwomeyer, James Sladky,
WC of Indianapolis/Genesee FSC
1970 ......Judy Schwomeyer, James Sladky,
WC of Indianapolis/Genesee FSC
1971 ......Judy Schwomeyer, James Sladky,
WC of Indianapolis/Genesee FSC
1972 ......Judy Schwomeyer, James Sladky,
WC of Indianapolis/Genesee FSC
1973 ......Mary Karen Campbell, Johnny Johns,
Lansing SC/Detroit SC
1974 ......Colleen O'Connor, Jim Millns, Broadmoor
SC/ City of Colorado Springs
1975 ......Colleen O'Connor, Jim Millns, Broadmoor SC
1976 ......Colleen O'Connor, Jim Millns,
Broadmoor SC
1977 ......Judy Genovesi, Kent Weigle,
SC of Hartford/Charter Oak FSC

1978 ......Stacey Smith, John Summers,
SC of Wilmington
1979 ......Stacey Smith, John Summers,
SC of Wilmington
1980 ......Stacey Smith, John Summers,
SC of Wilmington
1981 ......Judy Blumberg, Michael Seibert,
Broadmoor SC/ISC of Indianapolis
1982 ......Judy Blumberg, Michael Seibert,
Broadmoor SC/ISC of Indianapolis
1983 ......Judy Blumberg, Michael Seibert,
Pittsburgh FSC
1984 ......Judy Blumberg, Michael Seibert,
Pittsburgh FSC
1985 ......Judy Blumberg, Michael Seibert,
Pittsburgh FSC
1986 ......Renee Roca, Donald Adair,
Genesee FSC/Academy FSC
1987 ......Suzanne Semanick, Scott Gregory,
U of Delaware SC
1988 ......Suzanne Semanick, Scott Gregory,
U of Delaware SC
1989 ......Susan Wynne, Joseph Druar,
Broadmoor SC/Seattle SC
1990 ......Susan Wynne, Joseph Druar,
Broadmoor SC/Seattle SC
1991 ....Elizabeth Punsalan/Jerod Swallow, Broadmoor SC
1992 ......April Sargent, Russ Witherby,
Ogdensburg FSC/U of Delaware FSC
1993 ......Renee Roca, Gorsha Sur, Broadmoor SC
1994 ......Elizabeth Punsalan, Jerod Swallow,
Broadmoor SC/Detroit SC
1995 ......Renee Roca, Gorsha Sur, Broadmoor SC
1996 ......Elizabeth Punsalan, Jerod Swallow, Detroit SC
1997 ......Elizabeth Punsalan, Jerod Swallow, Detroit SC
1998 ......Elizabeth Punsalan, Jerod Swallow, Detroit SC
1999 ......Naomi Lang, Peter Tchernyshev, Detroit SC
2000 ......Naomi Lang, Peter Tchernyshev, Detroit SC
2001 ......Naomi Lang, Peter Tchernyshev, Detroit SC
2002 ......Naomi Lang, Peter Tchernyshev, American
Academy FSC
2003 ......Naomi Lang, Peter Tchernyshev, American
Academy FSC
2004 ......Tanith Belbin/Benjamin Agosto, Detroit SC

U.S. Olympic Gold Medalists

Women

1956	Tenley Albright	
1960	Carol Heiss	
1968	Peggy Fleming	
1976	Dorothy Hamill	
1992	Kristi Yamaguchi	
1998	Tara Lipinski	
2002	Sarah Hughes	

Men

1948	Richard Button
1952	Richard Button
1956	Hayes Alan Jenkins
1960	David W. Jenkins
1984	Scott Hamilton
1988	Brian Boitano

Special Achievements

Women successfully landing a triple Axel in competition:
Midori Ito, Japan, 1988 free-skating competition at Aichi, Japan.
Tonya Harding, United States, 1991 U.S. Figure Skating Championship.
Men successfully landing three quadruple jumps in competition:
Timothy Goebel, United States, 1999 Skate America, Colorado Springs (two Salchows and one toe loop).

Miscellaneous Sports

Six-time Tour winner
Lance Armstrong

AP PHOTO/FRANCK PREVEL

Uphill Climb

Lance Armstrong overcame hostile fans, the French Alps, and all comers to win a record sixth straight Tour de France

BY MERRELL NODEN

THIS WAS THE YEAR that Lance Armstrong proved beyond any doubt that he is the greatest cyclist of all time. The 32-year-old Texan won his sixth straight Tour de France, breaking the record of five Tour wins he'd shared with Jacques Anquetil, Eddy Merckx, Bernard Hinault and Miguel Indurain (though only Indurain had won five consecutively).

Just how dominant was he in July? Armstrong beat Tour runnerup Andreas Klöden of Germany and the T-Mobile team by 6 minutes and 19 seconds, and while that was not the biggest winning margin of his career, he made it look strikingly easy. He won five stages—the most he's won in a single Tour—all from Nos. 13 through 19. This year, for the first time, the 9.6-mile climb up L'Alpe d'Huez—a mountain with 21 hairpin turns that is classified as "hors categorie," or beyond category—was contested as a time trial. Armstrong won it, averaging 14.5 miles per hour.

"He is doubtless the greatest rider ever in the Tour de France," summed up Patrice Clerc, president of the Tour.

Of course, he is even more than that, and has been for years. He is the world's most visible, inspirational cancer survivor, a man who seems to have sidestepped death at the last possible moment. It's a role no one

applies for, but one that Armstrong has embraced with the same determination and doggedness he brings to cycling. This year Armstrong launched his WearYELLOW LiveSTRONG wristband campaign, which aims to raise money for the Lance Armstrong Foundation benefitting people living with cancer. Nike, one of his major sponsors, helped by manufacturing eight million rubber wristbands of the same canary yellow as the jersey worn by the Tour leader. Sold for $1 apiece at sporting goods stores or through www.livestrong.org, the wristbands became one of the summer's hippest fashion statements, worn by celebrities (including Matt Damon and Tom Hanks) and average Joes alike. There was also a TV ad running during the summer that showed Armstrong riding past a children's cancer ward and waving to the ecstatic kids in the windows.

Of course, this is too good a story to be enjoyed unbesmirched. There are the rumors of drug use, which have swirled for some time, always unsubstantiated. Armstrong denies them vehemently, pointing out that he is among the most oft-tested athletes in the world and has never failed a test. In 2002 the French government seemed to confirm this when an official investigation found no evidence that Armstrong had cheated.

But that did not quell the rumors, and

PATRICK KOVARIK/AFP/GETTY IMAGES

this year they reached a crescendo. There was at times an ugly mood permeating this year's Tour, and it was set two weeks before the race began, when a book called *L.A. Confidential: The Secrets of Lance Armstrong* came out. Written by David Walsh, a columnist for the London *Sunday Times*, and Pierre Ballester, a French freelance journalist, it contained a number of fairly specific allegations. Most of them came from Emma O'Reilly, a young Irishwoman who served from 1998 to 2000 as the U.S. Postal Service teams' soigneur, a kind of combination gofer and masseuse. Among other allegations, O'Reilly claims to have been asked to dispose of Armstrong's syringes; to have been dispatched to pick up drugs for him while he trained in the Pyrenees in May 1999; and to have been asked by Armstrong for makeup to hide his bruises and needle marks. According to her, Armstrong joked with her, "Emma, you know enough now to bring me down."

Things did not get any better once the Tour began. Fanned by the fallout from France's refusal to support the U.S.-led invasion of Iraq, the ire of many Tour fans fell upon Armstrong. There is bad blood—no pun intended— between the countries, and it spilled out in many places Armstrong rode. Fans screamed "Dopé!" (doper) and "Trucier!" (cheater) when he sailed by. They threw beer and less savory things at him, and painted EPO—for erythropoietin, a drug that boosts the body's production of oxygen-rich red blood cells, thereby increasing endurance—in block letters on the roadway.

Armstrong has never been willing to sit back and take the allegations. He went to court to try to get his denial inserted in the French edition of the book but was turned down by the judge. On the course, he rode with cold determination, and on one occasion found a suitable punishment for one of his tormentors. During the 18th stage he went out of his way to embarrass Filippo Simeoni of Italy, who has filed a defamation suit against Armstrong for calling him a liar for insinuating that Armstrong used drugs. When Simeoni moved away from the peloton to join a small breakaway pack, Armstrong did not hesitate to jump on his rear wheel and follow him up to the other riders, eventually forcing him back to the peloton and depriving him of a chance to win the stage.

Armstrong rode into Paris with the race well in hand, having covered the 2,109 miles in 83 hours, 36 minutes, and two seconds. All that was left was the old—and probably futile—game of trying to determine where exactly Armstrong ranks among the great athletes of all time: Was he the equal of Thorpe or Ruth? How about Jordan? Or Ali? It's hard for Americans to appreciate exactly what the Tour means, so recently have we paid it any attention. But Armstrong's remarkable journey, from cancer ward to storming up L'Alpe d'Huez, adds a dimension few other stories have.

Archery

National Men's Champions

1879...Will H. Thompson	1910...Henry Richardson	1947...Jack Wilson	1978...Darrell Pace
1880...L.L. Pedinghaus	1911...Dr. Robert Elmer	1948...Larry Hughes	1979...Rick McKinney
1881...F.H. Walworth	1912...George Bryant	1949...Russ Reynolds	1980...Rick McKinney
1882...D.H. Nash	1913...George Bryant	1950...Stan Overby	1981...Rick McKinney
1883...Col. Robert Williams	1914...Dr. Robert Elmer	1951...Russ Reynolds	1982...Rick McKinney
1884...Col. Robert Williams	1915...Dr. Robert Elmer	1952...Robert Larson	1983...Rick McKinney
1885...Col. Robert Williams	1916...Dr. Robert Elmer	1953...Bill Glackin	1984...Darrell Pace
1886...W.A. Clark	1919...Dr. Robert Elmer	1954...Robert Rhode	1985...Rick McKinney
1887...W.A. Clark	1920...Dr. Robert Elmer	1955...Joe Fries	1986...Rick McKinney
1888...Lewis Maxson	1921...James Jiles	1956...Joe Fries	1987...Rick McKinney
1889...Lewis Maxson	1922...Dr. Robert Elmer	1957...Joe Fries	1988...Jay Barrs
1890...Lewis Maxson	1923...Bill Palmer	1958...Robert Bitner	1989...Ed Eliason
1891...Lewis Maxson	1924...James Jiles	1959...Wilbert Vetrovsky	1990...Ed Eliason
1892...Lewis Maxson	1925...Dr. Paul Crouch	1960...Robert Kadlec	1991...Ed Eliason
1893...Lewis Maxson	1926...Stanley Spencer	1961...Clayton Sherman	1992...Alan Rasor
1894...Lewis Maxson	1927...Dr. Paul Crouch	1962...Charles Sandlin	1993...Jay Barrs
1895...W.B. Robinson	1928...Bill Palmer	1963...Dave Keaggy Jr.	1994...Jay Barrs
1896...Lewis Maxson	1929...Dr. E.K. Roberts	1964...Dave Keaggy Jr.	1995...Justin Huish
1897...W.A. Clark	1930...Russ Hoogerhyde	1965...George Slinzer	1996...Richard (Butch)
1898...Lewis Maxson	1931...Russ Hoogerhyde	1966...Hardy Ward	Johnson
1899...M.C. Howell	1932...Russ Hoogerhyde	1967...Ray Rogers	1997...Richard (Butch)
1900...A.R. Clark	1933...Ralph Miller	1968...Hardy Ward	Johnson
1901...Will H. Thompson	1934...Russ Hoogerhyde	1969...Ray Rogers	1998...Victor Wunderle
1902...Will H. Thompson	1935...Gilman Keasey	1970...Joe Thornton	1999...Victor Wunderle
1903...Will H. Thompson	1936...Gilman Keasey	1971...John Williams	2000...Richard (Butch)
1904...George Bryant	1937...Russ Hoogerhyde	1972...Kevin Erlandson	Johnson
1905...George Bryant	1938...Pat Chambers	1973...Darrell Pace	2001...Richard (Butch)
1906...Henry Richardson	1939...Pat Chambers	1974...Darrell Pace	Johnson
1907...Henry Richardson	1940...Russ Hoogerhyde	1975...Darrell Pace	2002...Victor Wunderle
1908...Will H. Thompson	1941...Larry Hughes	1976...Darrell Pace	2003...Joseph Bailey
1909...George Bryant	1946...Wayne Thompson	1977...Rick McKinney	2004...Sagar Mistry

National Women's Champions

1879...Mrs. S. Brown	1909...Harriet Case	1941...Ree Dillinger	1974...Doreen Wilber
1880...Mrs. T. Davies	1910...J.V. Sullivan	1946...Ann Weber	1975...Irene Lorensen
1881...Mrs. A.H. Gibbes	1911...Mrs. J.S. Taylor	1947...Ann Weber	1976...Luann Ryon
1882...Mrs. A.H. Gibbes	1912...Mrs. Witwer Tayler	1948...Jean Lee	1977...Luann Ryon
1883...Mrs. M.C. Howell	1913...Mrs. P. Fletcher	1949...Jean Lee	1978...Luann Ryon
1884...Mrs. H. Hall	1914...Mrs. B.P. Gray	1950...Jean Lee	1979...Lynette Johnson
1885...Mrs. M.C. Howell	1915...Cynthia Wesson	1951...Jean Lee	1980...Judi Adams
1886...Mrs. M.C. Howell	1916...Cynthia Wesson	1952...Ann Weber	1981...Debra Metzger
1887...Mrs. A.M. Phillips	1919...Dorothy Smith	1953...Ann Weber	1982...Luann Ryon
1888...Mrs. A.M. Phillips	1920...Cynthia Wesson	1954...Laurette Young	1983...Nancy Myrick
1889...Mrs. A.M. Phillips	1921...Mrs. L.C. Smith	1955...Ann Clark	1984...Ruth Rowe
1890...Mrs. M.C. Howell	1922...Dorothy Smith	1956...Carole Meinhart	1985...Terri Pesho
1891...Mrs. M.C. Howell	1923...Norma Pierce	1957...Carole Meinhart	1986...Debra Ochs
1892...Mrs. M.C. Howell	1924...Dorothy Smith	1958...Carole Meinhart	1987...Terry Quinn
1893...Mrs. M.C. Howell	1925...Dorothy Smith	1959...Carole Meinhart	1988...Debra Ochs
1894...Mrs. Albert Kern	1926...Dorothy Smith	1960...Ann Clark	1989...Debra Ochs
1895...Mrs. M.C. Howell	1927...Mrs. R. Johnson	1961...Victoria Cook	1990...Denise Parker
1896...Mrs. M.C. Howell	1928...Beatrice Hodgson	1962...Nancy	1991...Denise Parker
1897...Mrs. J.S. Baker	1929...Audrey Grubbs	Vonderheide	1992...Sherry Block
1898...Mrs. M.C. Howell	1930...Audrey Grubbs	1963...Nancy	1993...Denise Parker
1899...Mrs. M.C. Howell	1931...Dorothy	Vonderheide	1994...Judy Adams
1900...Mrs. M.C. Howell	Cummings	1964...Victoria Cook	1995...Jessica Carlson
1901...Mrs. C.E.	1932...Ilda Hanchette	1965...Nancy Pfeiffer	1996...Janet Dykman
Woodruff	1933...Madeline Taylor	1966...Helen Thornton	1997...Janet Dykman
1902...Mrs. M.C. Howell	1934...Desales Mudd	1967...Ardelle Mills	1998...Janet Dykman
1903...Mrs. M.C. Howell	1935...Ruth Hodgert	1968...Victoria Cook	1999...Denise Parker
1904...Mrs. M.C. Howell	1936...Gladys Hammer	1969...Doreen Wilber	2000...Karen Scavatto
1905...Mrs. M.C. Howell	1937...Gladys Hammer	1970...Nancy Myrick	2001...Kathie Loesch
1906...Mrs. E.C. Cook	1938...Jean Tenney	1971...Doreen Wilber	2002...Jessica Peterson
1907...Mrs. M.C. Howell	1939...Belvia Carter	1972...Ruth Rowe	2003...Samantha Marino
1908...Harriet Case	1940...Ann Weber	1973...Doreen Wilber	2004...Khatuna Lorig

Chess

World Champions

FIDE

1866–94	Wilhelm Steinitz, Austria
1894–1921	Emanuel Lasker, Germany
1921–27	Jose Capablanca, Cuba
1927–35	Alexander Alekhine, France
1935–37	Max Euwe, Holland
1937–47	Alexander Alekhine, France
1948–57	Mikhail Botvinnik, USSR
1957–58	Vassily Smyslov, USSR
1958–59	Mikhail Botvinnik, USSR
1960–61	Mikhail Tal, USSR
1961–63	Mikhail Botvinnik, USSR
1963–69	Tigran Petrosian, USSR

FIDE

1969–72	Boris Spassky, USSR
1972–75	Bobby Fischer, United States
1975–85	Anatoly Karpov, USSR
1985–93	*Garry Kasparov, USSR
1994–98	Anatoly Karpov, Russia
1999–2000	Alexander Khalifman, Russia
2000–01	Anand Viswanathan, India
2002–04	Ruslan Ponomariov, Ukraine
2004–	Rustam Kasimdzhanov, Uzbekistan

*Kasparov stripped of title by FIDE in 1993.

Professional Chess Association

1993–	Garry Kasparov

United States Champions

1857–71	Paul Morphy	1961–62	Larry Evans	1989	R. Dzindzichashvili
1871–76	George Mackenzie	1962–68	Bobby Fischer		Stuart Rachels
1876–80	James Mason	1968–69	Larry Evans		Yasser Seirawan
1880–89	George Mackenzie	1969–72	Samuel Reshevsky	1990	Lev Alburt
1889–90	Samuel Lipschutz	1972–73	Robert Byrne	1991	Gata Kamski
1890	Jackson Showalter	1973–74	Lubomir Kavale	1992	Patrick Wolff
1890–91	Max Judd		John Grefe	1993	Alex Yermolinsky
1891–92	Jackson Showalter	1974–77	Walter Browne		A. Shabalov
1892–94	Samuel Lipschutz	1978–80	Lubomir Kavalek	1994	Boris Gulko
1894	Jackson Showalter	1980–81	Larry Evans	1995	Patrick Wolff
1894–95	Albert Hodges		Larry Christiansen		Nick DeFirmian
1895–97	Jackson Showalter		Walter Browne		Alexander Ivanov
1897–1906	Harry Pillsbury	1981–83	Walter Browne	1996	Alex Yermolinsky
1906–09	Vacant		Yasser Seirawan	1997	Alex Yermolinsky
1909–36	Frank Marshall	1983	R. Dzindzichashvili	1998	Alex Yermolinsky
1936–44	Samuel Reshevsky	1983	Larry Christiansen	1999	Boris Gulko
1944–46	Arnold Denker		Walter Browne	2000	Joel Benjamin
1946–48	Samuel Reshevsky	1984–85	Lev Alburt	2001	Joel Benjamin
1948–51	Herman Steiner	1986	Yasser Seirawan	2002	Larry Christiansen
1951–54	Larry Evans	1987	Joel Benjamin	2003	Alexander Shabalov
1954–57	Arthur Bisguier		Nick DeFirmian		
1957–61	Bobby Fischer	1988	Michael Wilder		

Curling

World Men's Champions

Year	Country, Skip	Year	Country, Skip	Year	Country, Skip
1972	Canada, Crest Melesnuk	1983	Canada, Ed Werenich	1994	Canada, Rick Folk
1973	Sweden, Kjell Oscarius	1984	Norway, Eigil Ramsfjell	1995	Canada, Kerry Burtnyk
1974	U.S., Bud Somerville	1985	Canada, Al Hackner	1996	Canada, Jeff Stoughton
1975	Switzerland, Otto Danieli	1986	Canada, Ed Luckowich	1997	Sweden, Peter Lindholm
1976	U.S., Bruce Roberts	1987	Canada, Russ Howard	1998	Canada, Wayne Middaugh
1977	Sweden, Ragnar Kamp	1988	Norway, Eigil Ramsfjell	1999	Scotland, Hammy McMillan
1978	U.S., Bob Nichols	1989	Canada, Pat Ryan	2000	Canada, Greg McAulay
1979	Norway, Kristian Soerum	1990	Canada, Ed Werenich	2001	Sweden, Peter Lindholm
1980	Canada, Rich Folk	1991	Scotland, David Smith	2002	Canada, Randy Ferbey
1981	Switzerland, Jurg Tanner	1992	Switzerland, Markus Eggler	2003	Canada, Randy Ferbey
1982	Canada, Al Hackner	1993	Canada, Russ Howard	2004	Sweden, Peja Lindholm

World Women's Champions

Year	Country, Skip	Year	Country, Skip	Year	Country, Skip
1979	Switzerland, Gaby Casanova	1986	Canada, Marilyn Darte	1996	Canada, Marilyn Bodogh
1980	Canada, Marj Mitchell	1987	Canada, Pat Sanders	1997	Canada, Sandra Schmirler
1981	Sweden, Elisabeth Hogstrom	1988	Germany, Andrea Schopp	1998	Sweden, Elisabet Gustafson
1982	Denmark, Marianne Jorgenson	1989	Canada, Heather Houston	1999	Sweden, Elisabet Gustafson
1983	Switzerland, Erika Mueller	1990	Norway, Dordi Nordby	2000	Canada, Kelley Law
1984	Canada, Connie Lallberte	1991	Norway, Dordi Nordby	2001	Canada, Colleen Jones
1985	Canada, Linda Moore	1992	Sweden, Elisabet Johanssen	2002	Scotland, Jackie Lockhart
		1993	Canada, Sandra Peterson	2003	United States, Debbie McCormick
		1994	Canada, Sandra Peterson	2004	Canada, Colleen Jones
		1995	Sweden, Elisabet Gustafson		

U.S. Men's Champions

Year	Site	Winning Club	Skip
1957	Chicago, IL	Hibbing, MN	Harold Lauber
1958	Milwaukee, WI	Detroit, MI	Douglas Fisk
1959	Green Bay, WI	Hibbing, MN	Fran Kleffman
1960	Chicago, IL	Grafton, ND	Orvil Gilleshammer
1961	Grand Forks, ND	Seattle, WA	Frank Crealock
1962	Detroit, MI	Hibbing, MN	Fran Kleffman
1963	Duluth, MN	Detroit, MI	Mike Slyziuk
1964	Utica, NY	Duluth, MN	Robert Magle Jr.
1965	Seattle, WA	Superior, WI	Bud Somerville
1966	Hibbing, MN	Fargo, ND	Joe Zbacnik
1967	Winchester, MA	Seattle, WA	Bruce Roberts
1968	Madison, WI	Superior, WI	Bud Somerville
1969	Grand Forks, ND	Superior, WI	Bud Somerville
1970	Ardsley, NY	Grafton, ND	Art Tallackson
1971	Duluth, MN	Edmore, ND	Dale Dalziel
1972	Wilmette, IL	Grafton, ND	Robert Labonte
1973	Colorado Springs, CO	Winchester, MA	Charles Reeves
1974	Schenectady, NY	Superior, WI	Bud Somerville
1975	Detroit, MI	Seattle, WA	Ed Risling
1976	Wausau, WI	Hibbing, MN	Bruce Roberts
1977	Northbrook, IL	Hibbing, MN	Bruce Roberts
1978	Utica, NY	Superior, WI	Bob Nichols
1979	Superior, WI	Bemidji, MN	Scott Baird
1980	Bemidji, MN	Hibbing, MN	Paul Pustovar
1981	Fairbanks, AK	Superior, WI	Bob Nichols
1982	Brookline, MA	Madison, WI	Steve Brown
1983	Colorado Springs, CO	Colorado Springs, CO	Don Cooper
1984	Hibbing, MN	Hibbing, MN	Bruce Roberts
1985	Mequon, WI	Wilmette, IL	Tim Wright
1986	Seattle, WA	Madison, WI	Steve Brown
1987	Lake Placid, NY	Seattle, WA	Jim Vukich
1988	St. Paul, MN	Seattle, WA	Doug Jones
1989	Detroit, MI	Seattle, WA	Jim Vukich
1990	Superior, WI	Seattle, WA	Doug Jones
1991	Utica, NY	Madison, WI	Steve Brown
1992	Grafton, ND	Seattle, WA	Doug Jones
1993	St. Paul, MN	Bemidji, MN	Scott Baird
1994	Duluth, MN	Bemidji, MN	Scott Baird
1995	Appleton, WI	Superior, WI	Tim Somerville
1996	Bemidji, MN	Superior, WI	Tim Somerville
1997	Seattle, WA	Langdon, ND	Craig Disher
1998	Bismarck, SD	Stevens Pt., WI	Paul Pustovar
1999	Duluth, MN	Superior, WI	Tim Somerville
2000	Ogden, UT	Wisconsin3	Craig Brown
2001	Madison, WI	Washington	Jason Larway
2002	Virginia, MN	Wisconsin2	Paul Pustovar
2003	Utica, NY	Minnesota3	Pete Fenson
2004	Grand Forks, ND	Seattle, WA	Jason Larway

U.S. Women's Champions

Year	Site	Winning Club	Skip
1977	Wilmette, IL	Hastings, NY	Margaret Smith
1978	Duluth, MN	Wausau, WI	Sandy Robarge
1979	Winchester, MA	Seattle, WA	Nancy Langley
1980	Seattle, WA	Seattle, WA	Sharon Kozal
1981	Kettle Moraine, WI	Seattle, WA	Nancy Langley
1982	Bowling Green, OH	Oak Park, IL	Ruth Schwenker
1983	Grafton, ND	Seattle, WA	Nancy Langley
1984	Wauwatosa, WI	Duluth, MN	Amy Hatten
1985	Hershey, PA	Fairbanks, AK	Bev Birklid
1986	Chicago, IL	St Paul, MN	Gerri Tilden
1987	St Paul, MN	Seattle, WA	Sharon Good
1988	Darien, CT	Seattle, WA	Nancy Langley
1989	Detroit, MI	Rolla, ND	Jan Lagasse
1990	Superior, WI	Denver, CO	Bev Behnke
1991	Utica, NY	Houston, TX	Maymar Gemmell
1992	Grafton, ND	Madison, WI	Lisa Schoeneberg
1993	St Paul, MN	Denver, CO	Bev Behnke
1994	Duluth, MN	Denver, CO	Bev Behnke
1995	Appleton, WI	Madison, WI	Lisa Schoeneberg
1996	Bemidji, MN	Madison, WI	Lisa Schoeneberg
1997	Seattle, WA	Arlington, WI	Patti Lank
1998	Bismarck, SD	Wilmette, IL	Kari Erickson
1999	Duluth, MN	Madison, WI	Patti Lank

Curling (Cont.)

U.S. Women's Champions (Cont.)

Year	Site	Winning Club	Skip
2000	Ogden, UT	Nebraska	Amy Wright
2001	Madison, WI	Illinois	Kari Erickson
2002	Virginia, MN	Madison, WI	Patti Lank
2003	Utica, NY	Illinois	Debbie McCormick
2004	Grand Forks, ND	Madison, WI	Patti Lank

Cycling

Professional Road Race World Champions

1927 ....Alfred Binda, Italy	1957 ....Rik Van Steenbergen, Belgium	1981 ....Freddy Maertens, Belgium
1928 ....George Ronsse, Belgium	1958 ....Ercole Baldini, Italy	1982 ....Giuseppe Saronni, Italy
1929 ....George Ronsse, Belgium	1959 ....Andre Darrigade, France	1983 ....Greg LeMond, United States
1930 ....Alfred Binda, Italy	1960 ....Rik van Looy, Belgium	1984 ....Claude Criquielion, Belgium
1931 ....Learco Guerra, Italy	1961 ....Rik van Looy, Belgium	1985 ....Joop Zoetemelk, Holland
1932 ....Alfred Binda, Italy	1962 ....Jean Stablenski, France	1986 ....Moreno Argentin, Italy
1933 ....George Speicher, France	1963 ....Bennoni Beheyt, Belgium	1987 ....Stephen Roche, Ireland
1934 ....Karel Kaers, Belgium	1964 ....Jan Janssen, Holland	1988 ....Maurizio Fondriest, Italy
1935 ....Jean Aerts, Belgium	1965 ....Tommy Simpson, England	1989 ....Greg LeMond, United States
1936 ....Antonio Magne, France	1966 ....Rudi Altig, West Germany	1990 ....Rudy Dhaenene, Belgium
1937 ....Elio Meulenberg, Belgium	1967 ....Eddy Merckx, Belgium	1991 ....Gianni Bugno, Italy
1938 ....Marcel Kint, Belgium	1968 ....Vittorio Adorni, Italy	1992 ....Gianni Bugno, Italy
No competition 1939–45	1969 ....Harm Ottenbros, Netherlands	1993 ....Lance Armstrong, United States
1946 ....Hans Knecht, Switzerland	1970 ....J.P. Monseré, Belgium	1994 ....Luc LeBlanc, France
1947 ....Theo. Middelkamp, Holland	1971 ....Eddy Merckx, Belgium	1995 ....Abraham Olano, Spain
1948 ....Alberic Schotte, Belgium	1972 ....Marino Basso, Italy	1996 ....Johan Museeuw, Belgium
1949 ....Henri Van Steenbergen, Belgium	1973 ....Felice Gimondi, Italy	1997 ....Laurent Brochard, France
1950 ....Alberic Schotte, Belgium	1974 ....Eddy Merckx, Belgium	1998 ....Oskar Camenzind, Switz
1951 ....Ferdinand Kubler, Switzerland	1975 ....Hennie Kuiper, Holland	1999 ....Oscar Gomez Freire, Spain
1952 ....Heinz Mueller, Germany	1976 ....Freddy Maertens, Belgium	2000 ....Romans Vainsteins, Latvia
1953 ....Fausto Coppi, Italy	1977 ....Francesco Moser, Italy	2001 ....Oscar Gomez Freire, Spain
1954 ....Louison Bobet, France	1978 ....Gerri Knetemann, Holland	2002 ....Mario Cipollini, Italy
1955 ....Stan Ockers, Belgium	1979 ....Jan Raas, Holland	2003 ....Igor Astraloa, Spain
1956 ....Rik Van Steenbergen, Belg.	1980 ....Bernard Hinault, France	

Tour DuPont Winners

Year	Winner	Time
1989	Dag Otto Lauritzen, Norway	33 hrs, 28 min, 48 sec
1990	Raul Alcala, Mexico	45 hrs, 20 min, 9 sec
1991	Erik Breukink, Holland	48 hrs, 56 min, 53 sec
1992	Greg LeMond, United States	44 hrs, 27 min, 43 sec
1993	Raul Alcala, Mexico	46 hrs, 42 min, 52 sec
1994	Viatcheslav Ekimov, Russia	47 hrs, 14 min, 29 sec
1995	Lance Armstrong, United States	46 hrs, 31 min, 16 sec
1996	Lance Armstrong, United States	48 hrs, 20 min, 5 sec

Note: Race not held since 1996.

Tour de France Winners

Year	Winner	Time
1903	Maurice Garin, France	94 hrs, 33 min
1904	Henry Cornet, France	96 hrs, 5 min, 56 sec
1905	Louis Trousselier, France	110 hrs, 26 min, 58 sec
1906	Rene Pottier, France	Not available
1907	Lucien Petit-Breton, France	158 hrs, 54 min, 5 sec
1908	Lucien Petit-Breton, France	Not available
1909	Francois Faber, Luxembourg	157 hrs, 1 min, 22 sec
1910	Octave Lapize, France	162 hrs, 41 min, 30 sec
1911	Gustave Garrigou, France	195 hrs, 37 min
1912	Odile Defraye, Belgium	190 hrs, 30 min, 28 sec
1913	Philippe Thys, Belgium	197 hrs, 54 min
1914	Philippe Thys, Belgium	200 hrs, 28 min, 48 sec
1915–18	No race	
1919	Firmin Lambot, Belgium	231 hrs, 7 min, 15 sec
1920	Philippe Thys, Belgium	228 hrs, 36 min, 13 sec
1921	Leon Scieur, Belgium	221 hrs, 50 min, 26 sec
1922	Firmin Lambot, Belgium	222 hrs, 8 min, 6 sec
1923	Henri Pelissier, France	222 hrs, 15 min, 30 sec

Tour de France Winners (Cont.)

Year	Winner	Time
1924	Ottavio Bottechia, Italy	226 hrs, 18 min, 21 sec
1925	Ottavio Bottechia, Italy	219 hrs, 10 min, 18 sec
1926	Lucien Buysse, Belgium	238 hrs, 44 min, 25 sec
1927	Nicolas Frantz, Luxembourg	198 hrs, 16 min, 42 sec
1928	Nicolas Frantz, Luxembourg	192 hrs, 48 min, 58 sec
1929	Maurice Dewaele, Belgium	186 hrs, 39 min, 16 sec
1930	Andre Leducq, France	172 hrs, 12 min, 16 sec
1931	Antonin Magne, France	177 hrs, 10 min, 3 sec
1932	Andre Leducq, France	154 hrs, 12 min, 49 sec
1933	Georges Speicher, France	147 hrs, 51 min, 37 sec
1934	Antonin Magne, France	147 hrs, 13 min, 58 sec
1935	Romain Maes, Belgium	141 hrs, 32 min
1936	Sylvere Maes, Belgium	142 hrs, 47 min, 32 sec
1937	Roger Lapebie, France	138 hrs, 58 min, 31 sec
1938	Gino Bartali, Italy	148 hrs, 29 min, 12 sec
1939	Sylvere Maes, Belgium	132 hrs, 3 min, 17 sec
1940–46	No race	
1947	Jean Robic, France	148 hrs, 11 min, 25 sec
1948	Gino Bartali, Italy	147 hrs, 10 min, 36 sec
1949	Fausto Coppi, Italy	149 hrs, 40 min, 49 sec
1950	Ferdi Kubler, Switzerland	145 hrs, 36 min, 56 sec
1951	Hugo Koblet, Switzerland	142 hrs, 20 min, 14 sec
1952	Fausto Coppi, Italy	151 hrs, 57 min, 20 sec
1953	Louison Bobet, France	129 hrs, 23 min, 25 sec
1954	Louison Bobet, France	140 hrs, 6 min, 5 sec
1955	Louison Bobet, France	130 hrs, 29 min, 26 sec
1956	Roger Walkowiak, France	124 hrs, 1 min, 16 sec
1957	Jacques Anquetil, France	129 hrs, 46 min, 11 sec
1958	Charly Gaul, Luxembourg	116 hrs, 59 min, 5 sec
1959	Federico Bahamontes, Spain	123 hrs, 46 min, 45 sec
1960	Gastone Nencini, Italy	112 hrs, 8 min, 42 sec
1961	Jacques Anquetil, France	122 hrs, 1 min, 33 sec
1962	Jacques Anquetil, France	114 hrs, 31 min, 54 sec
1963	Jacques Anquetil, France	113 hrs, 30 min, 5 sec
1964	Jacques Anquetil, France	127 hrs, 9 min, 44 sec
1965	Felice Gimondi, Italy	116 hrs, 42 min, 6 sec
1966	Lucien Aimar, France	117 hrs, 34 min, 21 sec
1967	Roger Pingeon, France	136 hrs, 53 min, 50 sec
1968	Jan Janssen, Netherlands	133 hrs, 49 min, 32 sec
1969	Eddy Merckx, Belgium	116 hrs, 16 min, 2 sec
1970	Eddy Merckx, Belgium	119 hrs, 31 min, 49 sec
1971	Eddy Merckx, Belgium	96 hrs, 45 min, 14 sec
1972	Eddy Merckx, Belgium	108 hrs, 17 min, 18 sec
1973	Luis Ocana, Spain	122 hrs, 25 min, 34 sec
1974	Eddy Merckx, Belgium	116 hrs, 16 min, 58 sec
1975	Bernard Thevenet, France	114 hrs, 35 min, 31 sec
1976	Lucien Van Impe, Belgium	116 hrs, 22 min, 23 sec
1977	Bernard Thevenet, France	115 hrs, 38 min, 30 sec
1978	Bernard Hinault, France	108 hrs, 18 min
1979	Bernard Hinault, France	103 hrs, 6 min, 50 sec
1980	Joop Zoetemelk, Netherlands	109 hrs, 19 min, 14 sec
1981	Bernard Hinault, France	96 hrs, 19 min, 38 sec
1982	Bernard Hinault, France	92 hrs, 8 min, 46 sec
1983	Laurent Fignon, France	105 hrs, 7 min, 52 sec
1984	Laurent Fignon, France	112 hrs, 3 min, 40 sec
1985	Bernard Hinault, France	113 hrs, 24 min, 23 sec
1986	Greg LeMond, United States	110 hrs, 35 min, 19 sec
1987	Stephen Roche, Ireland	115 hrs, 27 min, 42 sec
1988	Pedro Delgado, Spain	84 hrs, 27 min, 53 sec
1989	Greg LeMond, United States	87 hrs, 38 min, 35 sec
1990	Greg LeMond, United States	90 hrs, 43 min, 20 sec
1991	Miguel Induráin, Spain	101 hrs, 1 min, 20 sec
1992	Miguel Induráin, Spain	100 hrs, 49 min, 30 sec
1993	Miguel Induráin, Spain	95 hrs, 57 min, 9 sec
1994	Miguel Induráin, Spain	103 hrs, 38 min, 38 sec
1995	Miguel Induráin, Spain	92 hrs, 44 min, 59 sec
1996	Bjarne Riis, Denmark	95 hrs, 57 min, 16 sec
1997	Jan Ullrich, Germany	100 hrs, 30 min, 35 sec

Tour de France Winners (Cont.)

Year	Winner	Time
1998	Marco Pantani, Italy	92 hrs, 49 min, 46 sec
1999	Lance Armstrong, United States	91 hrs, 32 min, 16 sec
2000	Lance Armstrong, United States	92 hrs, 33 min, 8 sec
2001	Lance Armstrong, United States	86 hrs, 17 min, 28 sec
2002	Lance Armstrong, United States	82 hrs, 5 min, 12 sec
2003	Lance Armstrong, United States	83 hrs, 41 min, 12 sec
2004	Lance Armstrong, United States	83 hrs, 36 min, 2 sec

Sled Dog Racing

Iditarod

Year	Winner	Time	Year	Winner	Time
1973	Dick Wilmarth	20 days, 00:49:41	1989	Joe Runyan	11 days, 05:24:34
1974	Carl Huntington	20 days, 15:02:07	1990	Susan Butcher	11 days, 01:53:23
1975	Emmitt Peters	14 days, 14:43:45	1991	Rick Swenson	12 days, 16:34:39
1976	Gerald Riley	18 days, 22:58:17	1992	Martin Buser	10 days, 19:17:15
1977	Rick Swenson	16 days, 16:27:13	1993	Jeff King	10 days, 15:38:15
1978	Dick Mackey	14 days, 18:52:24	1994	Martin Buser	10 days, 13:02:39
1979	Rick Swenson	15 days, 10:37:47	1995	Doug Swingley	9 days, 02:42:19
1980	Joe May	14 days, 07:11:51	1996	Jeff King	9 days, 05:43:13
1981	Rick Swenson	12 days, 08:45:02	1997	Martin Buser	9 days, 08:30:45
1982	Rick Swenson	16 days, 04:40:10	1998	Jeff King	9 days, 05:52:26
1983	Dick Mackey	12 days, 14:10:44	1999	Doug Swingley	9 days, 14:31:19
1984	Dean Osmar	12 days, 15:07:33	2000	Doug Swingley	9 days, 00:58:06
1985	Libby Riddles	18 days, 00:20:17	2001	Doug Swingley	9 days, 19:55:50
1986	Susan Butcher	11 days, 15:06:00	2002	Martin Buser	8 days, 22:46:02
1987	Susan Butcher	11 days, 02:05:13	2003	Robert Sorlie	9 days, 15:47:36
1988	Susan Butcher	11 days, 11:41:40	2004	Mitch Seavey	9 days, 12:20:22

Fishing

Saltwater Fishing Records

Species	Weight	Where Caught	Date	Angler
Albacore	88 lb 2 oz	Gran Canaria, Canary Islands	Nov 19, 1977	Siegfried Dickemann
Amberjack, greater	155 lb 12 oz	Bermuda	Aug 16, 1992	Larry Trott
Amberjack, Pacific	104 lb	Baja California, Mexico	July 4, 1984	Richard Cresswell
Angler	126 lb 12 oz	Sognefjorden Hoyanger, Norway	July 4, 1990	Gunnar Thorsteinsen
Barracuda, great	85 lb	Christmas Island, Kiribati	April 11, 1992	John W. Helfrich
Barracuda, Mexican	21 lb	Phantom Isle, Costa Rica	Mar 27, 1987	E. Greg Kent
Barracuda, pickhandle	29 lb 12 oz	Malindi, Kenya	Nov 7, 2002	Paul Gerritsen
Bass, barred sand	13 lb 3 oz	Huntington Beach, California	Aug 29, 1988	Robert Halal
Bass, black sea	10 lb 4 oz	Virginia Beach, Virginia	Jan 1, 2000	Allan P. Paschall
Bass, European	20 lb 14 oz	Cap d'Agde, France	Sept. 8, 1999	Robert Mari
Bass, giant sea	563 lb 8 oz	Anacapa Island, California	Aug 20, 1968	James D. McAdam Jr.
Bass, striped	78 lb 8 oz	Atlantic City, New Jersey	Sept 21, 1982	Albert R. McReynolds
Bluefish	31 lb 12 oz	Hatteras Inlet, North Carolina	Jan 30, 1972	James M. Hussey
Bonefish	19 lb	Zululand, South Africa	May 26, 1962	Brian W. Batchelor
Bonito, Atlantic	18 lb 4 oz	Faial Island, Azores	July 8, 1953	D.G. Higgs
Bonito, Pacific	21 lb 3 oz	Malibu, California	July 30, 1978	Gino M. Picciolo
Cabezon	23 lb	Juan De Fuca Strait, Washington	Aug 4, 1990	Wesley S. Hunter
Cobia	135 lb 9 oz	Shark Bay, Australia	July 9, 1985	Peter W. Goulding
Cod, Atlantic	98 lb 12 oz	Isle of Shoals, New Hampshire	June 8, 1969	Alphonse Bielevich
Cod, Pacific	35 lb	Unalaska Bay, Alaska	June 16, 1999	Jim Johnson
Conger	133 lb 4 oz	South Devon, England	June 5, 1995	Vic Evans
Dolphinfish	87 lb	Papagallo Gulf, Costa Rica	Sept 25, 1976	Manuel Salazar
Drum, black	113 lb 1 oz	Lewes, Delaware	Sept 15, 1975	Gerald M. Townsend
Drum, red	94 lb 2 oz	Avon, North Carolina	Nov 7, 1984	David Deuel
Eel, American	9 lb 4 oz	Cape May, New Jersey	Nov 9, 1995	Jeff Pennick
Eel, marbled	36 lb 1 oz	Durban, South Africa	June 10, 1984	Ferdie van Nooten
Flounder, southern	20 lb 9 oz	Nassau Sound, Florida	Dec 23, 1983	Larenza W. Mungin
Flounder, summer	22 lb 7 oz	Montauk, New York	Sept 15, 1975	Charles Nappi
Grouper, Warsaw	436 lb 12 oz	Destin, Florida	Dec 22, 1985	Steve Haeusler
Halibut, Atlantic	355 lb 6 oz	Valevag, Norway	Oct 20, 1997	Odd Arve Gunderstad

Saltwater Fishing Records (Cont.)

Species	Weight	Where Caught	Date	Angler
Halibut, California	58 lb 9 oz	Santa Rosa Island, California	June 26, 1999	Roger W. Borrell
Halibut, Pacific	459 lb	Dutch Harbor, Alaska	June 11, 1996	Jack Tragis
Jack, crevalle	58 lb 6 oz	Barro do Kwanza, Angola	Dec 10, 2000	Nuno A. P. da Silva
Jack, horse-eye	29 lb 8 oz	Ascencion Island, S Atlantic Ocean	May 28, 1993	Mike Hanson
Jack, Pacific crevalle	39 lb	Playa Zancudo, Costa Rica	Mar 3, 1997	Ingrid Callaghan
Jewfish	680 lb	Fernandina Beach, Florida	May 20, 1961	Lynn Joyner
Kawakawa	29 lb	Isla Clarion, Mexico	Dec 17, 1986	Ronald Nakamura
Lingcod	76 lb 9 oz	Gulf of Alaska, Alaska	Aug 11, 2001	Antwan D. Tinsley
Mackerel, cero	17 lb 2 oz	Islamorada, Florida	Apr 5, 1986	G. Michael Mills
Mackerel, king	93 lb	San Juan, Puerto Rico	Apr 18, 1999	Steve Perez Graulau
Mackerel, narrowbarred	99 lb	Natal, South Africa	Mar 14, 1982	Michael J. Wilkinson
Mackerel, Spanish	13 lb	Ocracoke Inlet, North Carolina	Nov 4, 1987	Robert Cranton
Marlin, Atlantic blue	1,402 lb 2 oz	Vitoria, Brazil	Feb 29, 1992	Paulo R.A. Amorim
Marlin, black	1,560 lb	Cabo Blanco, Peru	Aug 4, 1953	Alfred C. Glassell Jr.
Marlin, Pacific blue	1,376 lb	Kaaiwi Point, Hawaii	May 31, 1982	J.W. de Beaubien
Marlin, striped	494 lb	Tutukaka, New Zealand	Jan 16, 1986	Bill Boniface
Marlin, white	181 lb 14 oz	Vitoria, Brazil	Dec 8, 1979	Evandro Luiz Coser
Permit	60 lb	Ilha do Mel Paranagua, Brazil	Dec 14, 2002	Renato P. Fiedler
Pollock	50 lb	Salstraumen, Norway	Nov 30, 1995	Thor Magnus-Lekang
Pompano, African	50 lb 8 oz	Daytona Beach, Florida	Apr 21, 1990	Tom Sargent
Roosterfish	114 lb	La Paz, Mexico	June 1, 1960	Abe Sackheim
Runner, blue	11 lb 2 oz	Dauphin Island, Alaska	June 28, 1997	Stacey M. Moiren
Runner, rainbow	37 lb 9 oz	Isla Clarion, Mexico	Nov 21, 1991	Tom Pfleger
Sailfish, Atlantic	141 lb 1 oz	Luanda, Angola	Feb 19, 1994	Alfredo de Sousa Neves
Sailfish, Pacific	221 lb	Santa Cruz Island, Ecuador	Feb 12, 1947	Carl W. Stewart
Seabass, white	83 lb 12 oz	San Felipe, Mexico	Mar 31, 1953	Lyal C. Baumgardner
Seatrout, spotted	17 lb 7 oz	Ft. Pierce, Florida	May 11, 1995	Craig F. Carson
Shark, bigeye thresher	802 lb	Tutukaka, New Zealand	Feb 8, 1981	Dianne North
Shark, blue	528 lb	Montauk Point, New York	Aug 9, 2001	Joe Seidel
Shark, grter hammrhd	991 lb	Sarasota, Florida	May 30, 1982	Allen Ogle
Shark, Greenland	1,708 lb 9 oz	Trondheimsfjord, Norway	Oct 18, 1987	Terje Nordtvedt
Shark, porbeagle	507 lb	Caithness, Scotland	Mar 9, 1993	Christopher Bennet
Shark, shortfin mako	1,221 lb	Chatham, Massachusetts	July 21, 2001	Luke Sweeney
Shark, tiger	1,780 lb	Cherry Grove, South Carolina	June 14, 1964	Walter Maxwell
Shark, tope	72 lb 12 oz	Parengarenga Harbor, N.Z.	Dec 19, 1986	Melanie B. Feldman
Shark, white	2,664 lb	Ceduna, Australia	Apr 21, 1959	Alfred Dean
Skipjack, black	26 lb	Baja California, Mexico	Oct 23, 1991	Clifford K. Hamaishi
Snapper, cubera	121 lb 8 oz	Cameron, Louisiana	July 5, 1982	Mike Hebert
Snook, common	53 lb 10 oz	Parismina Ranch, Costa Rica	Oct 18, 1978	Gilbert Ponzi
Spearfish, Mediterr.	90 lb 13 oz	Madeira Island, Portugal	June 2, 1980	Joseph Larkin
Spearfish, longbill	127 lb 13 oz	Puerto Rico, Gran Canaria, Spain	May 20, 1999	Paul Cashmore
Spearfish, shortbill	74 lb 8 oz	Bay of Islands, New Zealand	Mar 16, 1999	Leonie Kai Patterson
Swordfish	1,182 lb	Iquique, Chile	May 7, 1953	Louis Marron
Tarpon	286 lb 9 oz	Rubane, Guinea-Bissau	Mar 20, 2003	Max Domecq
Tautog	25 lb	Ocean City, New Jersey	Jan 20, 1998	Anthony Monica
Tilapia, Mozambique	6 lb 13 oz	Loskop Dam, S Africa	Apr 4, 2003	Eugene C. Kruger
Trevally, bigeye	31 lb 8 oz	Poivre Island, Seychelles	Apr 23, 1997	Les Sampson
Trevally, giant	145 lb 8 oz	Maui, Hawaii	Mar 28, 1991	Russell Mori
Tuna, Atlantic bigeye	392 lb 6 oz	Puerto Rico, Gran Caneria, Spain	July 25, 1996	Dieter Vogel
Tuna, blackfin	45 lb 8 oz	Key West, Florida	May 4, 1996	Sam J. Burnett
Tuna, bluefin	1,496 lb	Aulds Cove, Nova Scotia	Oct 26, 1979	Ken Fraser
Tuna, longtail	79 lb 2 oz	Montague Island, New South Wales, Australia	Apr 12, 1982	Tim Simpson
Tuna, Pacific bigeye	435 lb	Cabo Blanco, Peru	Apr 17, 1957	Russel Lee
Tuna, skipjack	45 lb 4 oz	Baja California, Mexico	Nov 16, 1996	Brian Evans
Tuna, southern bluefin	348 lb 5 oz	Whakatane, New Zealand	Jan 16, 1981	Rex Wood
Tuna, yellowfin	388 lb 12 oz	San Benedicto Is, Mexico	Apr 1, 1977	Curt Wiesenhutter
Tunny, little	35 lb 2 oz	Cape de Garde, Algeria	Dec 14, 1988	Jean Yves Chatard
Wahoo	158 lb 8 oz	Loreto, Baja California, Mexico	June 10, 1996	Keith Winter
Weakfish	19 lb 2 oz	Jones Beach Inlet, New York	Oct 11, 1984	Dennis Rooney
		Delaware Bay, Delaware	May 20, 1989	William E. Thomas
Yellowtail, California	88 lb 3 oz	Alijos Rocks, Baja Calif., Mexico	Jun 21, 2000	Ronald Fujii
Yellowtail, southern	114 lb 10 oz	Tauranga, New Zealand	Feb 5, 1984	Mike Godfrey

Freshwater Fishing Records

Species	Weight	Where Caught	Date	Angler
Barramundi	83 lb 7 oz	Lake Tinaroo, N Queensl'd, Aus.	Sept 23, 1999	David Powell
Bass, largemouth	22 lb 4 oz	Montgomery Lake, Georgia	June 2, 1932	George W. Perry
Bass, rock	3 lb	York River, Ontario	Aug 1, 1974	Peter Gulgin
Bass, shoal	8 lb 12 oz	Apalatchicola River, Florida	Jan 28, 1995	Carl W. Davis
Bass, smallmouth	10 lb 14 oz	Dale Hollow, Tennessee	April 24, 1969	John T. Gorman
Bass, Suwannee	3 lb 14 oz	Suwannee River, Florida	Mar 2, 1985	Ronnie Everett
Bass, white	6 lb 13 oz	Orange, Virginia	July 31, 1989	Ronald Sprouse
Bass, whiterock	27 lb 5 oz	Greers Ferry Lake, Arkansas	Apr 24, 1997	Jerald Shaum
Bass, yellow	2 lb 9 oz	Waverly, Tennessee	Feb 27, 1998	John Chappell
Bluegill	4 lb 12 oz	Ketona Lake, Alabama	Apr 9, 1950	T.S. Hudson
Bowfin	21 lb 8 oz	Florence, South Carolina	Jan 29, 1980	Robert Harmon
Buffalo, bigmouth	70 lb 5 oz	Bastrop, Louisiana	Apr 21, 1980	Delbert Sisk
Buffalo, black	63 lb 6 oz	Mississippi River, Iowa	Aug 14, 1999	Jim Winters
Buffalo, smallmouth	82 lb 3 oz	Athens Lake, Georgia	June 6, 1993	Randy Collins
Bullhead, brown	6 lb 5 oz	Lake Mahopac, New York	Sept 8, 2002	Ray Lawrence
Bullhead, yellow	4 lb 4 oz	Mormon Lake, Arizona	May 11, 1984	Emily Williams
Burbot	18 lb 11 oz	Angenmanalren, Sweden	Oct 22, 1996	Margit Agren
Carp, common	75 lb 11 oz	Lac de St. Cassien, France	May 21, 1987	Leo van der Gugten
Catfish, blue	116 lb 12 oz	Mississippi River, Arkansas	Aug 3, 2001	Charles Ashley Jr.
Catfish, channel	58 lb	Santee-Cooper Reservoir, SC	July 7, 1964	W.B. Whaley
Catfish, flathead	123 lb	Elk City Reservoir, Indep., KS	May 14, 1998	Ken Paulie
Catfish, white	21 lb 8 oz	Gorton Pond, East Lime, CT	Apr 22, 2001	Thomas Urquhart
Char, Arctic	32 lb 9 oz	Tree River, Canada	July 30, 1981	Jeffrey Ward
Crappie, white	5 lb 3 oz	Enid Dam, Mississippi	July 31, 1957	Fred L. Bright
Dolly Varden	20 lb 14 oz	Wulik River, Alaska	July 7, 2001	Raz Reid
Dorado	51 lb 5 oz	Corrientes, Argentina	Sep 27, 1984	Armando Giudice
Drum, freshwater	54 lb 8 oz	Nickajack Lake, Tennessee	Apr 20, 1972	Benny E. Hull
Gar, alligator	279 lb	Rio Grande River, Texas	Dec 2, 1951	Bill Valverde
Gar, Florida	10 lb	Florida Everglades, Florida	Jan 28, 2002	Herbert Ratner Jr.
Gar, longnose	50 lb 5 oz	Trinity River, Texas	July 30, 1954	Townsend Miller
Gar, shortnose	5 lb 12 oz	Rend Lake, Illinois	July 16, 1995	Donna K. Willmert
Gar, spotted	9 lb 12 oz	Lake Mexia, Texas	Apr 7, 1994	Rick Rivard
Grayling, Arctic	5 lb 15 oz	Katseyedie River, Northwest Territories	Aug 16, 1967	Jeanne P. Branson
Inconnu	53 lb	Pah River, Alaska	Aug 20, 1986	Lawrence Hudnall
Kokanee	9 lb 6 oz	Okanagan Lake, Vernon, BC	June 18, 1988	Norm Kuhn
Muskellunge	67 lb 8 oz	Hayward, Wisconsin	July 24, 1949	Cal Johnson
Muskellunge, tiger	51 lb 3 oz	Lac Vieux-Desert, Michigan	July 16, 1919	John Knobla
Peacock, speckled	27 lb	Rio Negro, Brazil	Dec 4, 1994	Gerald (Doc) Lawson
Perch, Nile	230 lb	Lake Nasser, Egypt	Dec 20, 2000	William Toth
Perch, white	3 lb 1 oz	Forest Hill Park, NJ	May 6, 1989	Edward Tango
Perch, yellow	4 lb 3 oz	Bordentown, New Jersey	May 1865	C.C. Abbot
Pickerel, chain	9 lb 6 oz	Homerville, Georgia	Feb 17, 1961	Baxley McQuaig Jr.
Pike, northern	55 lb 1 oz	Lake of Grefeern, W Germany	Oct 16, 1986	Lothar Louis
Redhorse, greater	9 lb 3 oz	Salmon River, Puláski, New York	May 11, 1985	Jason Wilson
Redhorse, silver	11 lb 7 oz	Plum Creek, Wisconsin	May 29, 1985	Neal Long
Salmon, Atlantic	79 lb 2 oz	Tana River, Norway	1928	Henrik Henriksen
Salmon, Chinook	97 lb 4 oz	Kenai River, Alaska	May 17, 1985	Les Anderson
Salmon, chum	35 lb	Edye Pass, Canada	July 11, 1995	Todd A. Johansson
Salmon, coho	33 lb 4 oz	Pulaski, New York	Sep 27, 1989	Jerry Lifton
Salmon, pink	14 lb 13 oz	Monroe, Washington	Sep 30, 2001	Alexander Minerich
Salmon, sockeye	15 lb 3 oz	Kenai River, Alaska	Aug 9, 1987	Stan Roach
Sauger	8 lb 12 oz	Lake Sakakawea, North Dakota	Oct 6, 1971	Mike Fischer
Shad, American	11 lb 4 oz	Connecticut River, Massachusetts	May 19, 1986	Bob Thibodo
Sturgeon, white	468 lb	Benicia, California	July 9, 1983	Joey Pallotta III
Sunfish, green	2 lb 2 oz	Stockton Lake, Missouri	June 18, 1971	Paul M. Dilley
Sunfish, redbreast	1 lb 12 oz	Suwannee River, Florida	May 29, 1984	Alvin Buchanan
Sunfish, redear	5 lb 7 oz	Diverson Canal, Georgia	Nov 6, 1998	Amos M. Gay
Tigerfish, giant	97 lb	Zaire River, Kinshasa, Zaire	July 9, 1988	Raymond Houtmans
Trout, Apache	5 lb 3 oz	Apache Reservation, Arizona	May 29, 1991	John Baldwin
Trout, brook	14 lb 8 oz	Nipigon River, Ontario	July 1916	W.J. Cook
Trout, brown	40 lb 4 oz	Heber Springs, Arkansas	May 9, 1992	Howard (Rip) Collins
Trout, bull	32 lb	Lake Pond Oreille, Idaho	Oct 27, 1949	N.L. Higgins
Trout, cutthroat	41 lb	Pyramid Lake, Nevada	Dec 1925	John Skimmerhorn
Trout, golden	11 lb	Cook's Lake, Wyoming	Aug 5, 1948	Charles S. Reed

Freshwater Fishing Records *(Cont.)*

Species	Weight	Where Caught	Date	Angler
Trout, lake	72 lb	Great Bear Lake, Northwest Territories	Aug 19, 1995	Lloyd Bull
Trout, rainbow	42 lb 2 oz	Bell Island, Alaska	June 22, 1970	David Robert White
Trout, tiger	20 lb 13 oz	Lake Michigan, Wisconsin	Aug 12, 1978	Pete M. Friedland
Walleye	25 lb	Old Hickory Lake, Tennessee	Aug 2, 1960	Mabry Harper
Warmouth	2 lb 7 oz	Yellow River, Holt, Florida	Oct 19, 1985	Tony D. Dempsey
Whitefish, lake	14 lb 6 oz	Meaford, Ontario	May 21, 1984	Dennis Laycock
Whitefish, mountain	5 lb 8 oz	Elbow River, Calgary, Alberta	Aug 1, 1995	Randy Woo
Whitefish, broad	9 lb	Tozitna River, Alaska	July 17, 1989	Al Mathews
Whitefish, round	6 lb	Putahow River, Manitoba	June 14, 1984	Allan J. Ristori
Zander	25 lb 2 oz	Trosa, Sweden	June 12, 1986	Harry Lee Tennison

Greyhound Racing

Annual Greyhound Race of Champions Winners*

Year	Winner (Sex)	Affiliation/Owner	Year	Winner (Sex)	Affiliation/Owner
1982	DD's Jackie (F)	Wonderland Park/ R.H. Walters Jr.	1988	BB's Old Yellow (M)	Supplemental (Southland)/ Margie Bonita Hyers
1983	Comin' Attraction (F)	Rocky Mt. Greyhound Park/ Bob Riggin	1989	Osh Kosh Juliet (F)	Tampa Greyhound Track/ William F. Pollard
1984	Fallon (F)	Tampa Greyhound Track/ E.J. Alderson	1990	Daring Don (M)	Interstate Kennel Club/ Perry Padrta
1985	Lady Delight (F)	Lincoln Greyhound Park/ Julian A. Gay	1991	Mo Kick (M)	Flagler Greyhound Track/ Eric M. Kennon
1986	Ben G Speedboat (M)	Multnomah Kennel Club/ Louis Bennett	1992	Dicky Vallie (M)	Dairyland Greyhound Track/ George Benjamin
1987	ET's Pesky (F)	Supplemental (Flagler)/ Emil Tanis	1993	Mega Morris (M)	Jacksonville Kennel Club/ Ferrell's Kennel

* The Greyhound Race of Champions has not been held since 1993.

Gymnastics

World Champions
MEN
All-Around

Year	Champion, Nation	Year	Champion, Nation	Year	Champion, Nation
1903	Joseph Martinez, France	1938	Jan Gajdos, Czechoslovakia	1983	Dimitri Bilozertchev, USSR
1905	Marcel Lalue, France	1950	Walter Lehmann, Switzerland	1985	Yuri Korolev, USSR
1907	Joseph Czada, Czechoslovakia	1954	Valentin Mouratov, USSR Victor Chukarin, USSR	1987	Dimitri Bilozertchev, USSR
1909	Marcos Torres, France	1958	Boris Shaklin, USSR	1989	Igor Korobchinsky, USSR
1911	Ferdinand Steiner, Czechoslovakia	1962	Yuri Titov, USSR	1991	Grigori Misutin, CIS
1913	Marcos Torres, France	1966	Mikhail Voronin, USSR	1993	Vitaly Scherbo, Belarus
1922	Peter Sumi, Yugoslavia F. Pechacek, Czechoslovakia	1970	Eizo Kenmotsu, Japan	1994	Ivan Ivankov, Belarus
1926	Peter Sumi, Yugoslavia	1974	Shigeru Kasamatsu, Japan	1995	Li Xiaoshuang, China
1930	Josip Primozic, Yugoslavia	1978	Nikolai Andrianov, USSR	1997	Ivan Ivankov, Belarus
1934	Eugene Mack, Switzerland	1979	Alexander Ditiatin, USSR	1999	Nicolae Krukov, Russia
		1981	Yuri Korolev, USSR	2001	Feng Jing, China
				2003	Paul Hamm, United States

Pommel Horse

Year	Champion, Nation	Year	Champion, Nation	Year	Champion, Nation
1930	Josip Primozic, Yugoslavia	1962	Miroslav Cerar, Yugoslavia	1981	Michael Mikolai, East Germany
1934	Eugene Mack, Switzerland	1966	Miroslav Cerar, Yugoslavia	1983	Dmitri Bilozertchev, USSR
1938	Michael Reusch, Switzerland	1970	Miroslav Cerar, Yugoslavia	1985	Valentin Moguilny, USSR
1950	Josef Stalder, Switzerland	1974	Zoltan Magyar, Hungary	1987	Zsolt Borkai, Hungary Dmitri Bilozertchev, USSR
1954	Grant Chaguinjan, USSR	1978	Zoltan Magyar, Hungary		
1958	Boris Shaklin, USSR	1979	Zoltan Magyar, Hungary		

World Champions (Cont.)

MEN (Cont.)

Pommel Horse (Cont.)

Year	Champion, Nation
1989	Valentin Moguilny, USSR
1991	Valeri Belenki, USSR
1992	Pae Gil Su, North Korea
	Vitaly Scherbo, CIS
	Li Jing, China

Year	Champion, Nation
1993	Pae Gil Su, North Korea
1994	Marius Urzica, Romania
1995	Li Donghua, Switzerland
1996	Pae Gil Su, North Korea
1997	Valeri Belenki, Germany

Year	Champion, Nation
1999	Alexei Nemov, Russia
2001	Marius Urzica, Romania
2003	Teng Haibin, China
	Takehiro Kashima, Japan

Floor Exercise

Year	Champion, Nation
1930	Josip Primozic, Yugoslavia
1934	Georges Miesz, Switzerland
1938	Jan Gajdos, Czechoslovakia
1950	Josef Stalder, Switzerland
1954	Valentin Mouratov, USSR
	Masao Takemoto, Japan
1958	Masao Takemoto, Japan
1962	Nobuyuki Aihara, Japan
	Yukio Endo, Japan
1966	Akinori Nakayama, Japan
1970	Akinori Nakayama, Japan

Year	Champion, Nation
1974	Shigeru Kasamatsu, Japan
1978	Kurt Thomas, United States
1979	Kurt Thomas, United States
	Roland Brucker, GDR
1981	Yuri Korolev, USSR
	Li Yuejui, Chi
1983	Tong Fei, China
1985	Tong Fei, China
1987	Lou Yun, China
1989	Igor Korobchinsky, USSR
1991	Igor Korobchinsky, USSR

Year	Champion, Nation
1993	Grigori Misutin, Ukraine
1994	Vitaly Scherbo, Belarus
1995	Vitaly Scherbo, Belarus
1996	Vitaly Scherbo, Belarus
1997	Alexei Nemov, Russia
1999	Alexei Nemov, Russia
2001	Marian Dragulescu, Rom
2003	Paul Hamm, United States
	Jordan Jovtchev, Bulgaria

Rings

Year	Champion, Nation
1930	Emanuel Loffler, Czechoslovakia
1934	Alois Hudec, Czechoslovakia
1938	Alois Hudec, Czechoslovakia
1950	Walter Lehmann, Switzerland
1954	Albert Azarian, USSR
1958	Albert Azarian, USSR
1962	Yuri Titov, USSR
1966	Mikhail Voronin, USSR
1970	Akinori Nakayama, Japan

Year	Champion, Nation
1974	N. Andrianov, USSR
	D. Grecu, Rom.
1978	Nikolai Andrianov, USSR
1979	Alexander Ditiatin, USSR
1981	Alexander Ditiatin, USSR
1983	Dimitri Bilozertchev, USSR
1985	Li Ning, China
	Yuri Korolev, USSR
1987	Yuri Korolev, USSR
1989	Andreas Aguilar, W Ger
1991	Grigory Misutin, USSR

Year	Champion, Nation
1992	Vitaly Scherbo, CIS
1993	Yuri Chechi, Italy
1994	Yuri Chechi, Italy
1995	Yuri Chechi, Italy
1996	Yuri Chechi, Italy
1997	Yuri Chechi, Italy
1999	Zhen Dong, China
2001	Jordan Jovtchev, Bulgaria
2003	Jordan Jovtchev, Bulgaria
	Dimosthenis Tampakos Greece

Parallel Bars

Year	Champion, Nation
1930	Josip Primozic, Yugoslavia
1934	Eugene Mack, Switzerland
1938	Michael Reusch, Switzerland
1950	Hans Eugster, Switzerland
1954	Victor Chukarin, USSR
1958	Boris Shaklin, USSR
1962	Miroslav Cerar, Yugoslavia
1966	Sergei Diamidov, USSR
1970	Akinori Nakayama, Japan
1974	Eizo Kenmotsu, Japan
1978	Eizo Kenmotsu, Japan

Year	Champion, Nation
1979	Bart Conner, United States
1981	Koji Gushiken, Japan
	Alexandr Ditiatin, USSR
1983	Vladimir Artemov, USSR
	Lou Yun, China
1985	Sylvio Kroll, East Germany
	Valentin Moguilny, USSR
1987	Vladimir Artemov, USSR
1989	Li Jing, China
	Vladimir Artemov, USSR
1991	Li Jing, China

Year	Champion, Nation
1992	Li Jin, China
	Alexei Voropaev, CIS
1993	Vitaly Scherbo, Belarus
1994	Huang Liping, China
1995	Vitaly Scherbo, Belarus
1996	Rustam Sharipov, Ukraine
1997	Zhang Jinjing, China
1999	Joo-Hyung Lee, S Korea
2001	Sean Townsend, U.S.
2003	Li Xiao-Peng, China

High Bar

Year	Champion, Nation
1930	Istvan Pelle, Hungary
1934	Ernst Winter, Germany
1938	Michael Reusch, Switzerland
1950	Paavo Aaltonen, Finland
1954	Valentin Mouratov, USSR
1958	Boris Shaklin, USSR
1962	Takashi Ono, Japan
1966	Akinori Nakayama, Japan
1970	Eizo Kenmotsu, Japan
1974	Eberhard Gienger, West Germany

Year	Champion, Nation
1978	Shigeru Kasamatsu, Japan
1979	Kurt Thomas, United States
1981	Alexander Takchev, USSR
1983	Dimitri Bilozertchev, USSR
1985	Tong Fei, China
1987	Dimitri Bilozertchev, USSR
1989	Li Chunyang, China
1991	Li Chunyang, China
	R. Buechner, Germ
1992	Grigori Misutin, CIS
1993	Sergei Kharkov, Russia

Year	Champion, Nation
1994	Vitaly Scherbo, Belarus
1995	Andreas Wecker, Germany
1996	Jesús Carballo, Spain
1997	Jani Tanskanen, Finland
1999	Jesus Carballo, Spain
2001	Vlasios Maras, Greece
2003	Takehiro Kashima, Japan

World Champions (Cont.)
MEN (Cont.)

Vault

Year	Champion, Nation	Year	Champion, Nation	Year	Champion, Nation
1934	Eugene Mack, Switzerland	1978	Junichi Shimizu, Japan	1992	Yoo Ok Youl, South Korea
1938	Eugene Mack, Switzerland	1979	Alexander Ditiatin, USSR	1993	Vitaly Scherbo, Belarus
1950	Ernst Gebendinger, Switzerland	1981	Ralf-Peter Hemmann, East Germany	1994	Vitaly Scherbo, Belarus
1954	Leo Sotornik, Czechoslovakia	1983	Arthur Akopian, USSR	1995	G. Misutin, Ukraine
1958	Yuri Tltov, USSR	1985	Yuri Korolev, USSR		A. Nemov, Russia
1962	Premysel Krbec, Czechoslovakia	1987	Lou Yun, China Sylvio Kroll, East Germany	1996	Alexei Nemov, Russia
1966	Haruhiro Yamashita, Japan	1989	Joerg Behrend, East Germany	1997	Sergei Fedorchenko, Kazakhstan
1970	Mitsuo Tsukahara, Japan			1999	Li Xiao-Peng, China
1974	Shigeru Kasamatsu, Japan	1991	Yoo Ok Youl, South Korea	2001	Marian Dragulescu, Rom
				2003	Li Xiao-Peng, China

WOMEN

All-Around

Year	Champion, Nation	Year	Champion, Nation	Year	Champion, Nation
1934	Vlasta Dekanova, Czechoslovakia	1970	Ludmilla Tourischeva, USSR	1991	Kim Zmeskal, United States
1938	Vlasta Dekanova, Czechoslovakia	1974	Ludmilla Tourischeva, USSR	1993	Shannon Miller, United States
		1978	Elena Mukhina, USSR	1994	Shannon Miller, United States
1950	Helena Rakoczy, Poland	1979	Nelli Kim, USSR	1995	Lilia Podkopayeva, Ukraine
1954	Galina Roudiko, USSR	1981	Olga Bicherova, USSR	1997	Svetlana Khorkina, Russia
1958	Larissa Latynina, USSR	1983	Natalia Yurchenko, USSR	1999	Maria Olaru, Romania
1962	Larissa Latynina, USSR	1985	Elena Shoushounova, USSR Oksana Omeliantchik, USSR	2001	Svetlana Khorkina, Russia
1966	Vera Caslavska, Czechoslovakia	1987	Aurelia Dobre, Romania	2003	Svetlana Khorkina, Russia
		1989	Svetlana Bouguinskaia, USSR		

Floor Exercise

Year	Champion, Nation	Year	Champion, Nation	Year	Champion, Nation
1950	Helena Rakoczy, Poland	1979	Emilia Eberle, Romania	1992	Kim Zmeskal, United States
1954	Tamara Manina, USSR	1981	Natalia Ilenko, USSR	1993	Shannon Miller, United States
1958	Eva Bosakava, Czechoslovakia	1983	Ecaterina Szabo, Romania	1994	Dina Kochetkova, Russia
1962	Larissa Latynina, USSR	1985	Oksana Omeliantchik, USSR	1995	Gina Gogean, Romania
1966	Natalia Kuchinskaya, USSR	1987	Elena Shoushounova, USSR Daniela Silivas, Romania	1996	Gina Gogean, Romania
1970	Ludmilla Tourischeva, USSR	1989	Svetlana Bouguinskaia, USSR Daniela Silivas, Romania	1997	Gina Gogean, Romania
1974	Ludmilla Tourischeva, USSR			1999	Andreea Raducan, Romania
1978	Nelli Kim, USSR Elena Mukhina, USSR	1991	Cristina Bontas, Romania Oksana Tchusovitina, USSR	2001	Andreea Raducan, Romania
				2003	Daiane Dos Santos, Brazil

Uneven Bars

Year	Champion, Nation	Year	Champion, Nation	Year	Champion, Nation
1950	Gertchen Kolar, Austria Anna Pettersson, Sweden	1979	Ma Yanhong, China Maxi Gnauck, East Germany	1991	Gwang Suk Kim, North Korea
1954	Agnes Keleti, Hungary	1981	Maxi Gnauck, East Germany	1992	Lavinia Milosivici, Romania
1958	Larissa Latynina, USSR	1983	Maxi Gnauck, East Germany	1993	Shannon Miller, United States
1962	Irina Pervuschina, USSR	1985	Gabriele Fahrnich, East Germany	1994	Luo Li, China
1966	Natalia Kuchinskaya, USSR			1995	Svetlana Khorkina, Russia
1970	Karin Janz, East Germany	1987	Daniela Silivas, Romania Doerte Thuemmler, East Germany	1996	Svetlana Khorkina, Russia
1974	Annelore Zinke, East Germany			1997	Svetlana Khorkina, Russia
1978	Marcia Frederick, United States	1989	Fan Di, China Daniela Silivas, Romania	1999	Svetlana Khorkina, Russia
				2001	Svetlana Khorkina, Russia
				2003	Chellsie Memmel, U.S. Hollie Vise, United States

World Champions (Cont.)
WOMEN (Cont.)
Balance Beam

Year	Champion, Nation	Year	Champion, Nation	Year	Champion, Nation
1950	Helena Rakoczy, Poland	1979	Vera Cerna, Czechoslovakia	1993	Lavinia Milosovici, Romania
1954	Keiko Tanaka, Japan	1981	Maxi Gnauck, East Germany	1994	Shannon Miller, United States
1958	Larissa Latynina, USSR	1983	Olga Mostepanova, USSR	1995	Mo Huilan, China
1962	Eva Bosakova, Czech.	1985	Daniela Silivas, Romania	1996	Dina Kochetkova, Russia
1966	Natalia Kuchinskaya, USSR	1987	Aurelia Dobre, Romania	1997	Gina Gogean, Romania
1970	Erika Zuchold, East Germany	1989	Daniela Silivas, Romania	1999	E. Zamolodchikova, Russia
1974	Ludmilla Tourischeva, USSR	1991	Svetlana Boguinskaia, USSR	2001	Andreea Raducan, Romania
1978	Nadia Comaneci, Romania	1992	Kim Zmeskal, United States	2003	Fan Ye, China

Vault

Year	Champion, Nation	Year	Champion, Nation	Year	Champion, Nation
1950	Helena Rakoczy, Poland	1979	Dumitrita Turner, Romania	1994	Gina Gogean, Romania
1954	T. Manina, USSR	1981	Maxi Gnauck, East Germany	1995	L. Podkopayeva, Ukraine
	Anna Pettersson, Sweden	1983	Boriana Stoyanova, Bulgaria		Simona Amanar, Rom.
1958	Larissa Latynina, USSR	1985	Elena Shoushounova, USSR	1996	Gina Gogean, Romania
1962	Vera Caslavska, Czech.	1987	Elena Shoushounova, USSR	1997	Simona Amanar, Romania
1966	Vera Caslavska, Czech.	1989	Olesia Durnik, USSR	1999	Jie Ling, China
1970	Erika Zuchold, East Germany	1991	Lavinia Milosovici, Romania	2001	Svetlana Khorkina, Russia
1974	Olga Korbut, USSR	1992	Henrietta Onodi, Hungary	2003	Oksana Chusovitina,
1978	Nelli Kim, USSR	1993	Elena Pískun, Belarus		Uzbekistan

National Champions
MEN
All-Around

Year	Champion	Year	Champion	Year	Champion
1963	Art Shurlock	1976	Kurt Thomas	1991	Chris Waller
1964	Rusty Mitchell	1977	Kurt Thomas	1992	John Roethlisberger
1965	Rusty Mitchell	1978	Kurt Thomas	1993	John Roethlisberger
1966	Rusty Mitchell	1979	Bart Conner	1994	Scott Keswick
1967	Katsuzoki Kanzaki	1980	Peter Vidmar	1995	John Roethlisberger
1968	Yoshi Hayasaki	1981	Jim Hartung	1996	Blaine Wilson
1969	Steve Hug	1982	Peter Vidmar	1997	Blaine Wilson
1970	Makoto Sakamoto	1983	Mitch Gaylord	1998	Blaine Wilson
	Mas Watanabe	1984	Mitch Gaylord	1999	Blaine Wilson
1971	Yoshi Takei	1985	Brian Babcock	2000	Blaine Wilson
1972	Yoshi Takei	1986	Tim Daggett	2001	Sean Townsend
1973	Marshall Avener	1987	Scott Johnson	2002	Paul Hamm
1974	John Crosby	1988	Dan Hayden	2003	Paul Hamm
1975	Tom Beach	1989	Tim Ryan	2004	Paul Hamm
	Bart Conner	1990	John Roethlisberger		

Floor Exercise

Year	Champion	Year	Champion	Year	Champion
1963	Tom Seward	1977	Ron Galimore	1991	Mike Racanelli
1964	Rusty Mitchell	1978	Kurt Thomas	1992	Gregg Curtis
1965	Rusty Mitchell	1979	Ron Galimore	1993	Kerry Huston
1966	Dan Millman	1980	Ron Galimore	1994	Jeremy Killen
1967	Katsuzoki Kanzaki	1981	Jim Hartung	1995	Daniel Stover
	Ron Aure	1982	Jim Hartung	1996	Jay Thornton
1968	Katsuzoki Kanzaki	1983	Mitch Gaylord	1997	Jason Gatson
1969	Steve Hug	1984	Peter Vidmar	1998	Jason Gatson
	Dave Thor	1985	Mark Oates	1999	Jason Gatson
1970	Makoto Sakamoto	1986	Robert Sundstrom	2000	Blaine Wilson
1971	John Crosby	1987	John Sweeney	2001	Sean Townsend
1972	Yoshi Takei	1988	Mark Oates	2002	Morgan Hamm
1973	John Crosby		Charles Lakes	2003	Morgan Hamm
1974	John Crosby	1989	Mike Racanelli	2004	Paul Hamm
1975	Peter Korman	1990	Bob Stelter		

National Champions (Cont.)

MEN (Cont.)

Pommel Horse

Year	Champion	Year	Champion	Year	Champion
1963	Larry Spiegel	1978	Jim Hartung	1992	Chris Waller
1964	Sam Bailie	1979	Bart Conner	1993	Chris Waller
1965	Jack Ryan	1980	Jim Hartung	1994	Mihai Begiu
1966	Jack Ryan	1981	Jim Hartung	1995	Mark Sohn
1967	Paul Mayer/Dave Doty	1982	Jim Hartung	1996	Josh Stein
1968	Katsuoki Kanzaki	1983	Bart Conner	1997	John Roethlisberger
1969	Dave Thor	1984	Tim Daggett	1998	John Roethlisberger
1970	Mas Watanabe	1985	Phil Cahoy	1999	John Roethlisberger
1971	Leonard Caling	1986	Phil Cahoy	2000	John Roethlisberger
1972	Sadao Hamada	1987	Tim Daggett	2001	Brett McClure
1973	Marshall Avener	1988	Kevin Davis	2002	Paul Hamm
1974	Marshall Avener	1989	Kevin Davis	2003	Paul Hamm
1975	Bart Conner	1990	Patrick Kirksey	2004	Brett McClure
1977	Gene Whelan	1991	Chris Waller		

Rings

Year	Champion	Year	Champion	Year	Champion
1963	Art Shurlock	1977	Kurt Thomas	1991	Scott Keswick
1964	Glen Gailis	1978	Mike Silverstein	1992	Tim Ryan
1965	Glen Gailis	1979	Bart Conner	1993	John Roethlisberger
1966	Glen Gailis	1980	Jim Hartung	1994	Scott Keswick
1967	Fred Dennis	1981	Jim Hartung	1995	Paul O'Neill
	Don Hatch	1982	Jim Hartung	1996	Kip Simons
1968	Yoshi Hayasaki		Peter Vidmar	1997	Blaine Wilson
1969	Fred Dennis	1983	Mitch Gaylord	1998	Jeff Johnson
	Bob Emery	1984	Jim Hartung	1999	Blaine Wilson
1970	Makoto Sakamoto	1985	Dan Hayden	2000	Blaine Wilson
1971	Yoshi Takei	1986	Dan Hayden	2001	Sean Townsend
1972	Yoshi Takei	1987	Scott Johnson	2002	Blaine Wilson
1973	Jim Ivicek	1988	Dan Hayden	2003	Blaine Wilson
1974	Tom Weeder	1989	Scott Keswick	2004	Raj Bhavsar
1975	Tom Beach	1990	Scott Keswick		

Vault

Year	Champion	Year	Champion	Year	Champion
1963	Art Shurlock	1978	Jim Hartung	1991	Scott Keswick
1964	Gary Hery	1979	Ron Galimore	1992	Trent Dimas
1965	Brent Williams	1980	Ron Galimore	1993	Bill Roth
1966	Dan Millman	1981	Ron Galimore	1994	Keith Wiley
1967	Jack Kenan	1982	Jim Hartung/Jim Mikus	1995	David St. Pierre
	Sid Jensen	1983	Chris Reigel	1996	Blaine Wilson
1968	Rich Scorza	1984	Chris Reigel	1997	Blaine Wilson
1969	Dave Butzman	1985	Scott Johnson	1998	Brent Klaus
1970	Makoto Sakamoto		Mark Oates	1999	Guard Young
1971	Gary Morava	1986	Scott Wilbanks	2000	Blaine Wilson
1972	Mike Kelley	1987	John Sweeney	2001	Jason Furr
1973	Gary Morava	1988	John Sweeney/Bill Paul	2002	Paul Hamm
1974	John Crosby	1989	Bill Roth	2003	Raj Bhavsar
1975	Tom Beach	1990	Lance Ringnald	2004	David Sender
1977	Ron Galimore				

Parallel Bars

Year	Champion	Year	Champion	Year	Champion
1963	Tom Seward	1971	Brent Simmons	1981	Bart Conher
1964	Rusty Mitchell	1972	Yoshi Takei	1982	Peter Vidmar
1965	Glen Gailis	1973	Marshall Avener	1983	Mitch Gaylord
1966	Ray Hadley	1974	Jim Ivicek	1984	Peter Vidmar
1967	Katsuzoki Kanzaki	1975	Bart Conner		Mitch Gaylord
	Tom Goldsborough	1977	Kurt Thomas		Tim Daggett
1968	Yoshi Hayasaki	1978	Bart Conner	1985	Tim Daggett
1969	Steve Hug	1979	Bart Conner	1986	Tim Daggett
1970	Makoto Sakamoto	1980	Phil Cahoy/Larry Gerard	1987	Scott Johnson

National Champions (Cont.)
MEN (Cont.)

Parallel Bars (Cont.)

Year	Champion	Year	Champion	Year	Champion
1988	D. Hayden/K. Davis	1994	Steve McCain	2000	Trent Wells
1989	Conrad Voorsanger	1995	John Roethlisberger	2001	Sean Townsend
1990	Trent Dimas	1996	Jair Lynch	2002	Sean Townsend
1991	Scott Keswick	1997	Blaine Wilson	2003	Jason Gatson
1992	Jair Lynch	1998	Blaine Wilson	2004	Alexander Artemev
1993	Chainey Umphrey	1999	Jason Gatson		

High Bars

Year	Champion	Year	Champion	Year	Champion
1963	Art Shurlock	1979	Yoichi Tomita	1991	Lance Ringnald
1964	Glen Gailis	1980	Jim Hartung	1992	Jair Lynch
1965	Rusty Mitchell	1981	Bart Conner	1993	Steve McCain
1966	Katsuzoki Kanzaki	1982	Mitch Gaylord	1994	Scott Keswick
1967	Katsuzoki Kanzaki	1983	Mario McCutcheon	1995	John Roethlisberger
	Jerry Fontana	1984	Peter Vidmar	1996	Bill Roth
1968	Yoshi Hayasaki		Tim Daggett	1997	Douglas Stibel
1969	Rich Grisby		Mitch Gaylord	1998	Jason Gatson
1970	Makoto Sakamoto	1985	Dan Hayden	1999	Jamie Natalie
1971	Yoshi Takei	1986	D. Hayden/D. Moriel	2000	Trent Wells
1972	Tom Lindner	1987	David Moriel		Jamie Natalie
1973	John Crosby	1988	Dan Hayden	2001	Daniel Diaz-Luong
1974	Brent Simmons	1989	Tim Ryan	2002	Blaine Wilson
1975	Tom Beach	1990	Trent Dimas	2003	Paul Hamm
1977	Kurt Thomas		Lance Ringnald	2004	Paul Hamm
1978	Kurt Thomas				

WOMEN

All-Around

Year	Champion	Year	Champion	Year	Champion
1963	Donna Schanezer	1976	Denise Cheshire	1991	Kim Zmeskal
1965	Gail Daley	1977	Donna Turnbow	1992	Kim Zmeskal
1966	Donna Schanezer	1978	Kathy Johnson	1993	Shannon Miller
1968	Linda Scott	1979	Leslie Pyfer	1994	Dominique Dawes
1969	Joyce Tanac	1980	Julianne McNamara	1995	Dominique Moceanu
	Schroeder	1981	Tracee Talavera	1996	Shannon Miller
1970	Cathy Rigby McCoy	1982	Tracee Talavera	1997	V. Adler/ K. Powell
1971	Joan Moore Gnat	1983	Dianne Durham	1998	Kristen Maloney
	Linda Metheny	1984	Mary Lou Retton	1999	Kristen Maloney
	Mulvihill	1985	Sabrina Mar	2000	Elise Ray
1972	Joan Moore Gnat	1986	Jennifer Sey	2001	Tasha Schwikert
	Cathy Rigby McCoy	1987	Kristie Phillips	2002	Tasha Schwikert
1973	Joan Moore Gnat	1988	Phoebe Mills	2003	Courtney Kupets
1974	Joan Moore Gnat	1989	Brandy Johnson	2004	Courtney Kupets/
1975	Tammy Manville	1990	Kim Zmeskal		Carly Patterson

Vault

Year	Champion	Year	Champion	Year	Champion
1963	Donna Schanezer	1976	Debbie Wilcox	1990	Brandy Johnson
1965	Gail Daley	1977	Lisa Cawthron	1991	Kerri Strug
1966	Donna Schanezer	1978	Rhonda Schwandt	1992	Kerri Strug
1968	Terry Spencer		Sharon Shapiro	1993	Dominique Dawes
1969	Joyce Tanac	1979	Christa Canary	1994	Dominique Dawes
	Schroeder	1980	J. McNamara/B. Kline	1995	Shannon Miller
	Cleo Carver	1981	Kim Neal	1996	Dominique Dawes
1970	Cathy Rigby McCoy	1982	Yumi Mordre	1997	Vanessa Atler
1971	Joan Moore Gnat	1983	Dianne Durham	1998	Dominique Moceanu
	Adele Gleaves	1984	Mary Lou Retton	1999	Vanessa Atler
1972	Cindy Eastwood	1985	Yolanda Mavity	2000	Kristen Maloney
1973	Roxanne Pierce	1986	Joyce Wilborn	2001	Mohini Bhardwaj
	Mancha	1987	Rhonda Faehn	2002	Elizabeth Tricase
1974	Dianne Dunbar	1988	Rhonda Faehn	2003	Annia Hatch
1975	Kolleen Casey	1989	Brandy Johnson	2004	Liz Tricase

National Champions (Cont.)
WOMEN (Cont.)

Uneven Bars

Year	Champion	Year	Champion	Year	Champion
1963	Donna Schanezer	1976	Leslie Wolfsberger	1991	Elisabeth Crandall
1965	Irene Haworth	1977	Donna Turnbow	1992	Dominique Dawes
1966	Donna Schanezer	1978	Marcia Frederick	1993	Shannon Miller
1968	Linda Scott	1979	Marcia Frederick	1994	Dominique Dawes
1969	Joyce Tanac	1980	Marcia Frederick	1995	Dominique Dawes
	Schroeder	1981	Julianne McNamara	1996	Dominique Dawes
	Lisa Nelson	1982	Marie Roethlisberger	1997	Kristy Powell
1970	Roxanne Pierce	1983	Julianne McNamara	1998	Elise Ray
	Mancha	1984	Julianne McNamara	1999	Jamie Dantzscher
1971	Joan Moore Gnat	1985	Sabrina Mar		Jennie Thompson
1972	Cathy Rigby McCoy	1986	Marie Roethlisberger	2000	Elise Ray
1973	Roxanne Pierce	1987	Melissa Marlowe	2001	Katie Heenan
	Mancha	1988	Chelle Stack	2002	Tasha Schwikert
1974	Diane Dunbar	1989	Chelle Stack	2003	Katie Heenan
1975	Leslie Wolfsberger	1990	Sandy Woolsey	2004	Courtney Kupets

Balance Beam

Year	Champion	Year	Champion	Year	Champion
1963	Leissa Krol	1979	Heidi Anderson	1993	Dominique Dawes
1965	Gail Daley	1980	Kelly Garrison-Steves	1994	Dominique Dawes
1966	Irene Haworth	1981	Tracee Talavera	1995	Doni Thompson
	Linda Scott	1982	Julianne McNamara		Monica Flammer
1968	Linda Scott	1983	Dianne Durham	1996	Dominique Dawes
1969	Lonna Woodward	1984	Pam Bileck	1997	Kendall Beck
1970	Joyce Tanac Schroeder		Tracee Talavera	1998	Dominique Moceanu
1971	Linda Metheny	1986	Angie Denkins	1999	Vanessa Atler
	Mulvihill	1987	Kristie Phillips	2000	Alyssa Beckerman
1972	Kim Chace	1985	Kelly Garrison-Steves		Amy Chow
1973	Nancy Thies Marshall	1988	Kelly Garrison-Steves	2001	Tasha Schwikert
1974	Joan Moore Gnat	1989	Brandy Johnson	2002	Tasha Schwikert
1975	Kyle Gayner	1990	Betty Okino	2003	Hollie Vise
1976	Carrie Englert	1991	Shannon Miller	2004	Courtney Kupets
1977	Donna Turnbow	1992	Kerri Strug		
1978	Christa Canary		Kim Zmeskal		

Floor Exercise

Year	Champion	Year	Champion	Year	Champion
1963	Donna Schanezer	1979	Heidi Anderson	1993	Shannon Miller
1965	Gail Daley	1980	Beth Kline	1994	Dominique Dawes
1966	Donna Schanezer	1981	Michelle Goodwin	1995	Dominique Dawes
1968	Linda Scott	1982	Amy Koopman	1996	Dominique Dawes
1970	Cathy Rigby McCoy	1983	Dianne Durham	1997	Lindsay Wing
1971	Joan Moore Gnat	1984	Mary Lou Retton	1998	Vanessa Atler
	Linda Metheny	1985	Sabrina Mar	1999	Elise Ray
	Mulvihill	1986	Yolanda Mavity	2000	Kristen Maloney
1972	Joan Moore Gnat	1987	Kristie Phillips	2001	Tabitha Yim
1973	Joan Moore Gnat	1988	Phoebe Mills	2002	Tasha Schwikert
1974	Joan Moore Gnat	1989	Brandy Johnson	2003	Ashley Postell
1975	Kathy Howard	1990	Brandy Johnson	2004	Carly Patterson
1976	Carrie Englert	1991	Kim Zmeskal		
1977	Kathy Johnson		Dominique Dawes		
1978	Kathy Johnson	1992	Kim Zmeskal		

National Four-Wall Champions

MEN

1919.....Bill Ranft	1941.....Joe Platak	1963.....Oscar Obert	1985.....Naty Alvarado
1920.....Max Gold	1942.....Jack Clemente	1964.....Jimmy Jacobs	1986.....Naty Alvarado
1921.....Carl Haedge	1943.....Joe Platak	1965.....Jimmy Jacobs	1987.....Naty Alvarado
1922.....Art Shinners	1944.....Frank Coyle	1966.....Paul Haber	1988.....Naty Alvarado
1923.....Joe Murray	1945.....Joe Platak	1967.....Paul Haber	1989.....Poncho Monreal
1924.....Maynard Laswe	1946.....Angelo Trutio	1968.....Stuffy Singer	1990.....Naty Alvarado
1925.....Maynard Laswe	1947.....Gus Lewis	1969.....Paul Haber	1991.....John Bike
1926.....Maynard Laswe	1948.....Gus Lewis	1970.....Paul Haber	1992.....Octavio Silveyra
1927.....George Nelson	1949.....Vic Hershkowitz	1971.....Paul Haber	1993.....David Chapman
1928.....Joe Griffin	1950.....Ken Schneider	1972.....Fred Lewis	1994.....Octavio Silveyra
1929.....Al Banuet	1951.....Walter Plakan	1973.....Terry Muck	1995.....David Chapman
1930.....Al Banuet	1952.....Vic Hershkowitz	1974.....Fred Lewis	1996.....David Chapman
1931.....Al Banuet	1953.....Bob Brady	1975.....Fred Lewis	1997.....Octavio Silveyra
1932.....Angelo Trutio	1954.....Vic Hershkowitz	1976.....Fred Lewis	1998.....David Chapman
1933.....Sam Atcheson	1955.....Jimmy Jacobs	1977.....Naty Alvarado	1999.....David Chapman
1934.....Sam Atcheson	1956.....Jimmy Jacobs	1978.....Fred Lewis	2000.....David Chapman
1935.....Joe Platak	1957.....Jimmy Jacobs	1979.....Naty Alvarado	2001.....Vince Munoz
1936.....Joe Platak	1958.....John Sloan	1980.....Naty Alvarado	2002.....David Chapman
1937.....Joe Platak	1959.....John Sloan	1981.....Fred Lewis	2003.....John Bike
1938.....Joe Platak	1960.....Jimmy Jacobs	1982.....Naty Alvarado	2004.....David Chapman
1939.....Joe Platak	1961.....John Sloan	1983.....Naty Alvarado	
1940.....Joe Platak	1962.....Oscar Obert	1984.....Naty Alvarado	

WOMEN

1980.....Rosemary Bellini	1987.....Rosemary Bellini	1994.....Anna Engele	2000.....Priscilla Shumate
1981.....Rosemary Bellini	1988.....Rosemary Bellini	1995.....Anna Engele	2001.....Anna Christoff
1982.....Rosemary Bellini	1989.....Anna Engele	1996.....Anna Engele	2002.....Priscilla Shumate
1983.....Diane Harmon	1990.....Anna Engele	1997.....Lisa Fraser	2003.....Lisa Gilmore
1984.....Rosemary Bellini	1991.....Anna Engele	1998.....Lisa Fraser	2004.....Yvonne August
1985.....Peanut Motal	1992.....Lisa Fraser	1999.....Anna Christoff	
1986.....Peanut Motal	1993.....Anna Engele		

National Three-Wall Champions

MEN

1950.....Vic Hershkowitz	1964.....Marty Decatur	1978.....Fred Lewis	1992.....John Bike
1951.....Vic Hershkowitz	1965.....Carl Obert	1979.....Naty Alvarado	1993.....Eric Klarman
1952.....Vic Hershkowitz	1966.....Marty Decatur	1980.....Lou Russo	1994.....David Chapman
1953.....Vic Herskkowitz	1967.....Carl Obert	1981.....Naty Alvarado	1995.....David Chapman
1954.....Vic Hershkowitz	1968.....Marty Decatur	1982.....Naty Alvarado	1996.....Vince Munoz
1955.....Vic Hershkowitz	1969.....Marty Decatur	1983.....Naty Alvarado	1997.....Vince Munoz
1956.....Vic Hershkowitz	1970.....Steve August	1984.....Naty Alvarado	1998.....Vince Munoz
1957.....Vic Hershkowitz	1971.....Lou Russo	1985.....Vern Roberts	1999.....Vince Munoz
1958.....Vic Hershkowitz	1972.....Lou Russo	1986.....Vern Roberts	2000.....Vince Munoz
1959.....Jimmy Jacobs	1973.....Paul Haber	1987.....Vern Roberts	2001.....Vince Munoz
1960.....Jimmy Jacobs	1974.....Fred Lewis	1988.....Jon Kendler	2002.....Vince Munoz
1961.....Jimmy Jacobs	1975.....Lou Russo	1989.....John Bike	2003.....Vince Munoz
1962.....Oscar Obert	1976.....Lou Russo	1990.....Vince Munoz	2004.....Sean Lenning
1963.....Marty Decatur	1977.....Fred Lewis	1991.....John Bike	

WOMEN

1981.....Allison Roberts	1987.....Rosemary Bellini	1993.....Anna Engele	1999.....Allison Roberts
1982.....Allison Roberts	1988.....Rosemary Bellini	1994.....Anna Engele	2000.....Priscilla Shumate
1983.....Allison Roberts	1989.....Rosemary Bellini	1995.....Allison Roberts	2001.....Anna Christoff
1984.....Rosemary Bellini	1990.....Rosemary Bellini	1996.....Anna Engele	2002.....Priscilla Shumate
1985.....Rosemary Bellini	1991.....Rosemary Bellini	1997.....Allison Roberts	2003.....Lisa Gilmore
1986.....Rosemary Bellini	1992.....Anna Engele	1998.....Anna Christoff	2004.....Jennifer Schmitt

World Four-Wall Champions

1984...................Merv Deckert, Canada	1994...................David Chapman, United States
1986...................Vern Roberts, United States	1997...................John Bike Jr., United States
1988...................Naty Alvarado, United States	2000...................David Chapman, United States
1991...................Pancho Monreal, United States	2003...................Paul Brady, Ireland

Lacrosse

United States Club Lacrosse Association Champions

1960 ......Mt. Washington Club	1975 ......Mt. Washington Club	1990 ......Mt. Washington Club
1961 ......Baltimore Lacrosse Club	1976 ......Mt. Washington Club	1991 ......Mt. Washington Club
1962 ......Mt. Washington Club	1977 ......Mt. Washington Club	1992 ......Maryland Lacrosse Club
1963 ......University Club	1978 ......Long Island Athletic Club	1993 ......Mt. Washington Club
1964 ......Mt. Washington Club	1979 ......Maryland Lacrosse Club	1994 ......LI-Hofstra Lacrosse Club
1965 ......Mt. Washington Club	1980 ......Long Island Athletic Club	1995 ......Mt. Washington Club
1966 ......Mt. Washington Club	1981 ......Long Island Athletic Club	1996 ......LI-Hofstra Lacrosse Club
1967 ......Mt. Washington Club	1982 ......Maryland Lacrosse Club	1997 ......LI-Hofstra Lacrosse Club
1968 ......Long Island Athletic Club	1983 ......Maryland Lacrosse Club	1998 ......LI-Hofstra Lacrosse Club
1969 ......Long Island Athletic Club	1984 ......Maryland Lacrosse Club	1999 ......New York Athletic Club
1970 ......Long Island Athletic Club	1985 ......LI-Hofstra Lacrosse Club	2000 ......Team Toyota (Baltimore)
1971 ......Long Island Athletic Club	1986 ......LI-Hofstra Lacrosse Club	2001 ......LI Lacrosse Club
1972 ......Carling	1987 ......LI-Hofstra Lacrosse Club	2002 ......Single Source Solutions
1973 ......Long Island Athletic Club	1988 ......Maryland Lacrosse Club	2003 ......Single Source Solutions
1974 ......Long Island Athletic Club	1989 ......LI-Hofstra Lacrosse Club	2004 ......Single Source Solutions

National Lacrosse League Champions*

1987 ......Baltimore Thunder	1993 ......Buffalo Bandits	1999 ......Toronto Rock
1988 ......New Jersey Saints	1994 ......Philadelphia Wings	2000 ......Toronto Rock
1989 ......Philadelphia Wings	1995 ......Philadelphia Wings	2001 ......Philadelphia Wings
1990 ......Philadelphia Wings	1996 ......Buffalo Bandits	2002 ......Toronto Rock
1991 ......Detroit Turbos	1997 ......Rochester Knighthawks	2003 ......Toronto Rock
1992 ......Buffalo Bandits	1998 ......Philadelphia Wings	2004 ......Calgary Roughnecks

*Indoor league formerly known as the Eagle Pro Box Lacrosse League, and the Major Indoor Lacrosse League.

Major League Lacrosse

2001 .....Long Island Lizards	2003 .....Long Island Lizards
2002 .....Baltimore Bayhawks	2004 ......Philadelphia Barrage

Little League Baseball

Little League World Series Champions

Year	Champion	Runner-Up	Score	Year	Champion	Runner-Up	Score
1947	Williamsport, PA	Lock Haven, PA	16–7	1977	Kao-Hsuing, Taiwan	El Cajun, CA	7–2
1948	Lock Haven, PA	St. Petersburg, FL	6–5	1978	Pin-Tung, Taiwan	Danville, CA	11–1
1949	Hammonton, NJ	Pensacola, FL	5–0	1979	Hsien, Taiwan	Campbell, CA	2–1
1950	Houston, TX	Bridgeport, CT	2–1	1980	Hua Lian, Taiwan	Tampa, FL	4–3
1951	Stamford, CT	Austin, TX	3–0	1981	Tai-Chung, Taiwan	Tampa, FL	4–2
1952	Norwalk, CT	Monongahela, PA	4–3	1982	Kirkland, WA	Hsien, Taiwan	6–0
1953	Birmingham, AL	Schenectady, NY	1–0	1983	Marietta, GA	Barahona, D.Rep.	3–1
1954	Schenectady, NY	Colton, CA	7–5	1984	Seoul, S. Korea	Altamonte Sgs, FL	6–2
1955	Morrisville, PA	Merchantville, NJ	4–3	1985	Seoul, S. Korea	Mexicali, Mex.	7–1
1956	Roswell, NM	Merchantville, NJ	3–1	1986	Tainan Park, Taiwan	Tucson, AZ	12–0
1957	Monterrey, Mex.	LaMesa, CA	4–0	1987	Hua Lian, Taiwan	Irvine, CA	21–1
1958	Monterrey, Mex.	Kankakee, IL	10–1	1988	Tai-Chung, Taiwan	Pearl City, HI	10–0
1959	Hamtramck, MI	Auburn, CA	12–0	1989	Trumbull, CT	Kaohsiung, Taiwan	5–2
1960	Levittown, PA	Ft. Worth, TX	5–0	1990	Taipei, Taiwan	Shippensburg, PA	9–0
1961	El Cajon, CA	El Campo, TX	4–2	1991	Tai-Chung, Taiwan	San Ramon Vly, CA	11–0
1962	San Jose, CA	Kankakee, IL	3–0	1992*	Long Beach, CA	Zamboanga, Phil.	6–0
1963	Granada Hills, CA	Stratford, CT	2–1	1993	Long Beach, CA	David Chiriqui, Pan.	3–2
1964	Staten Island, NY	Monterrey, Mex.	4–0	1994	Maracaibo, Venez.	Northridge, CA	4–3
1965	Windsor Locks, CT	Stoney Creek, Can.	3–1	1995	Tainan, Taiwan	Sprint, TX	17–3
1966	Houston, TX	W. New York, NJ	8–2	1996	Kao-Hsuing, Taiwan	Cranston, RI	13–3
1967	West Tokyo, Japan	Chicago, IL	4–1	1997	Guadalupe, Mex.	Mission Viejo, CA	5–4
1968	Osaka, Japan	Richmond, VA	1–0	1998	Toms River, NJ	Kashima, Japan	12–9
1969	Taipei, Taiwan	Santa Clara, CA	5–0	1999	Osaka, Japan	Phenix City, AL	5–0
1970	Wayne, NJ	Campbell, CA	2–0	2000	Maracaibo, Venez.	Bellaire, TX	3–2
1971	Tainan, Taiwan	Gary, IN	12–3	2001	Tokyo, Japan	Apopka, FL	2–1
1972	Taipei, Taiwan	Hammond, IN	6–0	2002	Louisville, KY	Sendai, Japan	1–0
1973	Tainan City, Taiwan	Tucson, AZ	12–0	2003	Tokyo, Japan	Boynton Beach, FL	10–1
1974	Kao-Hsuing, Taiwan	El Cajun, CA	7–2	2004	Willemstad, Curacao	Thousand Oaks, CA	5–2
1975	Lakewood, NJ	Tampa, FL	4–3				
1976	Tokyo, Japan	Campbell, CA	10–3				

*Long Beach declared a 6–0 winner after the international tournament committee determined that Zamboanga City had used players that were not within its city limits.

American Power Boat Association Gold Cup Champions

Year	Boat	Driver	Avg MPH	Year	Boat	Driver	Avg MPH
1904	Standard (June)	Carl Riotte	23.160	1956	Miss Thriftaway	Bill Muncey	96.552
1904	Vingt-et-Un II (Sep)	W. Sharpe Kilmer	24.900	1957	Miss Thriftaway	Bill Muncey	101.787
1905	Chip I	J. Wainwright	15.000	1958	Hawaii Kai III	Jack Regas	103.000
1906	Chip II	J. Wainwright	25.000	1959	Maverick	Bill Stead	104.481
1907	Chip II	J. Wainwright	23.903	1960	No race	—	—
1908	Dixie II	E.J. Schroeder	29.938	1961	Miss Century 21	Bill Muncey	99.678
1909	Dixie II	E.J. Schroeder	29.590	1962	Miss Century 21	Bill Muncey	100.710
1910	Dixie III	F.K. Burnham	32.473	1963	Miss Bardahl	Ron Musson	105.124
1911	MIT II	J.H. Hayden	37.000	1964	Miss Bardahl	Ron Musson	103.433
1912	P.D.Q. II	A.G. Miles	39.462	1965	Miss Bardahl	Ron Musson	103.132
1913	Ankle Deep	Cas Mankowski	42.779	1966	Tahoe Miss	Mira Slovak	93.019
1914	Baby Speed Demon II	Jim Blackton & Bob Edgren	48.458	1967	Miss Bardahl	Bill Shumacher	101.484
				1968	Miss Bardahl	Bill Shumacher	108.173
1915	Miss Detroit	Johnny Milot & Jack Beebe	37.656	1969	Miss Budweiser	Bill Sterett	98.504
				1970	Miss Budweiser	Dean Chenoweth	99.562
1916	Miss Minneapolis	Bernard Smith	48.860				
1917	Miss Detroit II	Gar Wood	54.410	1971	Miss Madison	Jim McCormick	98.043
1918	Miss Detroit II	Gar Wood	51.619	1972	Atlas Van Lines	Bill Muncey	104.277
1919	Miss Detroit III	Gar Wood	42.748	1973	Miss Budweiser	Dean Chenoweth	99.043
1920	Miss America I	Gar Wood	62.022				
1921	Miss America I	Gar Wood	52.825	1974	Pay 'n Pak	George Henley	104.428
1922	Packard Chriscraft	J.G. Vincent	40.253	1975	Pay 'n Pak	George Henley	108.921
1923	Packard Chriscraft	Caleb Bragg	43.867	1976	Miss U.S.	Tom D'Eath	100.412
1924	Baby Bootlegger	Caleb Bragg	45.302	1977	Atlas Van Lines	Bill Muncey	111.822
1925	Baby Bootlegger	Caleb Bragg	47.240	1978	Atlas Van Lines	Bill Muncey	111.412
1926	Greenwich Folly	George Townsend	47.984	1979	Atlas Van Lines	Bill Muncey	100.765
				1980	Miss Budweiser	Dean Chenoweth	106.932
1927	Greenwich Folly	George Townsend	47.662				
				1981	Miss Budweiser	Dean Chenoweth	116.932
1928	No race						
1929	Imp	Richard Hoyt	48.662	1982	Atlas Van Lines	Chip Hanauer	120.050
1930	Hotsy Totsy	Vic Kliesrath	52.673	1983	Atlas Van Lines	Chip Hanauer	118.507
1931	Hotsy Totsy	Vic Kliesrath	53.602	1984	Atlas Van Lines	Chip Hanauer	130.175
1932	Delphine IV	Bill Horn	57.775	1985	Miller American	Chip Hanauer	120.643
1933	El Lagarto	George Reis	56.260	1986	Miller American	Chip Hanauer	116.523
1934	El Lagarto	George Reis	55.000	1987	Miller American	Chip Hanauer	127.620
1935	El Lagarto	George Reis	55.056	1988	Miss Circus Circus	Chip Hanauer & Jim Prevost	123.756
1936	Impshi	Kaye Don	45.735				
1937	Notre Dame	Clell Perry	63.675	1989	Miss Budweiser	Tom D'Eath	131.209
1938	Alagi	Theo Rossi	64.340	1990	Miss Budweiser	Tom D'Eath	143.176
1939	My Sin	Z.G. Simmons Jr.	66.133	1991	Winston Eagle	Mark Tate	137.771
1940	Hotsy Totsy III	Sidney Allen	48.295	1992	Miss Budweiser	Chip Hanauer	136.282
1941	My Sin	Z.G. Simmons Jr.	52.509	1993	Miss Budweiser	Chip Hanauer	141.195
1942–45	—	No race	—	1994	Smokin' Joe Camel	Mark Tate	145.260
1946	Tempo VI	Guy Lombardo	68.132	1995	Miss Budweiser	Chip Hanauer	149.160
1947	Miss Peps V	Danny Foster	57.000	1996	PICO American Dream	Dave Villwock	149.328
1948	Miss Great Lakes	Danny Foster	46.845	1997	Miss Budweiser	Dave Villwock	129.366
1949	My Sweetie	Bill Cantrell	73.612	1998	Miss Budweiser	Dave Villwock	140.309
1950	Slo-Mo-Shun IV	Ted Jones	78.216	1999	Miss PICO	Chip Hanauer	152.591
1951	Slo-Mo-Shun V	Lou Fageol	90.871	2000	Miss Budweiser	Dave Villwock	162.850
1952	Slo-Mo-Shun IV	Stan Dollar	79.923	2001	Miss Tubby's Subs	Michael Hanson	140.519
1953	Slo-Mo-Shun IV	Joe Taggart & Lou Fageol	99.108	2002	Miss Budweiser	Dave Villwock	143.093
				2003	Miss Fox Hills	Mitch Evans	144.152
1954	Slo-Mo-Shun IV	Joe Taggart & Lou Fageol	92.613	2004	Miss Detroit Yacht Club	Nate Brown	141.195
1955	Gale V	Lee Schoenith	99.552				

Hydro-Prop* Annual Champion Drivers

Year	Driver	Boat	Wins	Year	Driver	Boat	Wins
1947	Danny Foster	Miss Peps V	6	1977	Mickey Remund	Miss Budweiser	3
1948	Dan Arena	Such Crust	2	1978	Bill Muncey	Atlas Van Lines	6
1949	Bill Cantrell	My Sweetie	7	1979	Bill Muncey	Atlas Van Lines	7
1950	Dan Foster	Such Crust/DaphneX	2	1980	Dean Chenoweth	Miss Budweiser	5
1951	Chuck Thompson	Miss Pepsi	5	1981	Dean Chenoweth	Miss Budweiser	6
1952	Chuck Thompson	Miss Pepsi	3	1982	Chip Hanauer	Atlas Van Lines	5
1953	Lee Schoenith	Gale II	1	1983	Chip Hanauer	Atlas Van Lines	3
1954	Lee Schoenith	Gale V	4	1984	Jim Kropfeld	Miss Budweiser	6
1955	Lee Schoenith	Gale V/Wha Hoppen	1	1985	Chip Hanauer	Miller American	5
1956	Russ Schleeh	Shanty I	3	1986	Jim Kropfeld	Miss Budweiser	3
1957	Jack Regas	Hawaii Kai III	5	1987	Jim Kropfeld	Miss Budweiser	5
1958	Mira Slovak	Bardah/Miss Buren	3	1988	Tom D'Eath	Miss Budweiser	4
1959	Bill Stead	Maverick	5	1989	Chip Hanauer	Miss Circus Circus	3
1960	Bill Muncey	Miss Thriftway	4	1990	Chip Hanauer	Miss Circus Circus	6
1961	Bill Muncey	Miss Century 21	4	1991	Mark Tate	Winston/Oberto	3
1962	Bill Muncey	Miss Century 21	5	1992	Chip Hanauer	Miss Budweiser	7
1963	Bill Cantrell	Gale V	0	1993	Chip Hanauer	Miss Budweiser	7
1964	Ron Musson	Miss Bardahl	4	1994	Mark Tate	Smokin' Joe Camel	2
1965	Ron Musson	Miss Bardahl	4	1995	Mark Tate	Smokin' Joe Camel	4
1966	Mira Slovak	Tahoe Miss	4	1996	Dave Villwock	PICO American Dream	6
1967	Bill Schumacher	Miss Bardahl	6	1997	Mark Tate	Close Call	1
1968	Bill Schumacher	Miss Bardahl	4	1998	Dave Villwock	Miss Budweiser	8
1969	Bill Sterett Sr.	Miss Budweiser	4	1999	Dave Villwock	Miss Budweiser	8
1970	Dean Chenoweth	Miss Budweiser	4	2000	Dave Villwock	Miss Budweiser	6
1971	Dean Chenoweth	Miss Budweiser	2	2001	Dave Villwock	Miss Budweiser	1
1972	Bill Muncey	Atlas Van Lines	6	2002	Dave Villwock	Miss Budweiser	3
1973	Mickey Remund	Pay 'n Pak	4	2003	Dave Villwock	Miss Budweiser	2
1974	George Henley	Pay 'n Pak	7	2004	Dave Villwock	Miss Budweiser	2
1975	Billy Schumacher	Weisfield's	2				
1976	Bill Muncey	Atlas Van Lines	5				

Hydro-Prop* Annual Champion Boats

Year	Boat	Owner	Wins	Year	Boat	Owner	Wins
1970	Miss Budweiser	Little-Friedkin	4	1988	Miss Budweiser	Bernie Little	4
1971	Miss Budweiser	Little-Friedkin	2	1989	Miss Budweiser	Bernie Little	4
1972	Atlas Van Lines	Joe Schoenith	6	1990	Miss Circus Circus	Bill Bennett	6
1973	Pay 'n Pak	Dave Heerensperger	4	1991	Miss Budweiser	Bernie Little	4
1974	Pay 'n Pak	Dave Heerensperger	7	1992	Miss Budweiser	Bernie Little	7
1975	Pay 'n Pak	Dave Heerensperger	5	1993	Miss Budweiser	Bernie Little	7
1976	Atlas Van Lines	Bill Muncey	5	1994	Miss Budweiser	Bernie Little	4
1977	Miss Budweiser	Bernie Little	3	1995	Miss Budweiser	Bernie Little	5
1978	Atlas Van Lines	Bill Muncey	6	1996	PICO Amer. Dream	Fred Leland	6
1979	Atlas Van Lines	Bill Muncey	7	1997	Miss Budweiser	Bernie Little	5
1980	Miss Budweiser	Bernie Little	5	1998	Miss Budweiser	Bernie Little	8
1981	Miss Budweiser	Bernie Little	6	1999	Miss Budweiser	Bernie Little	8
1982	Atlas Van Lines	Fran Muncey	5	2000	Miss Budweiser	Bernie Little	6
1983	Atlas Van Lines	Muncey-Lucero	3	2001	Miss Budweiser	Bernie Little	1
1984	Miss Budweiser	Bernie Little	6	2002	Miss Budweiser	Bernie Little	3
1985	Miller American	Muncey-Lucero	5	2003	Miss Budweiser	Joe Little	2
1986	Atlas Van Lines	Bernie Little	3	2004	Miss Budweiser	Joe Little	2
1987	Miss Budweiser	Bernie Little	5				

*Formerly known as Unlimited Hydroplane Racing Association.

Polo

United States Open Polo Champions

1904 ......Wanderers	1935 ......Greentree	1963 ......Tulsa	1986 ......Retama II
1905–09..Not contested	1936 ......Greentree	1964 ......Concar Oak	1987 ......Aloha
1910 ......Ranelagh	1937 ......Old Westbury	Brook	1988 ......Les Diables
1911 ......Not contested	1938 ......Old Westbury	1965 ......Oak Brook–	Bleus
1912 ......Cooperstown	1939 ......Bostwick Field	Santa Barbara	1989 ......Les Diables
1913 ......Cooperstown	1940 ......Aknusti	1966 ......Tulsa	Bleus
1914 ......Meadow Brook	1941 ......Gulf Stream	1967 ......Bunntyco–	1990 ......Les Diables
Magpies	1942–45...Not contested	Oak Brook	Bleus
1915 ......Not contested	1946 ......Mexico	1968 ......Midland	1991 ......Grant's Farm
1916 ......Meadow Brook	1947 ......Old Westbury	1969 ......Tulsa Greenhill	Manor
1917–18..Not contested	1948 ......Hurricanes	1970 ......Tulsa Greenhill	1992 ......Hanalei Bay
1919 ......Meadow Brook	1949 ......Hurricanes	1971 ......Oak Brook	1993 ......Gehache
1920 ......Meadow Brook	1950 ......Bostwick	1972 ......Milwaukee	1994 ......Aspen
1921 ......Great Neck	1951 ......Milwaukee	1973 ......Oak Brook	1995 ......Outback
1922 ......Argentine	1952 ......Beverly Hills	1974 ......Milwaukee	1996 ......Outback
1923 ......Meadow Brook	1953 ......Meadow Brook	1975 ......Milwaukee	1997 ......Isla Carroll
1924 ......Midwick	1954 ......C.C.C.–	1976 ......Willow Bend	1998 ......Esque
1925 ......Orange County	Meadow Brook	1977 ......Retama	1999 ......Outback
1926 ......Hurricanes	1955 ......C.C.C.	1978 ......Abercrombie &	2000 ......Outback
1927 ......Sands Point	1956 ......Brandywine	Kent	2001 ......Outback
1928 ......Meadow Brook	1957 ......Detroit	1979 ......Retama	2002 ......Team
1929 ......Hurricanes	1958 ......Dallas	1980 ......Southern Hills	Coca Cola
1930 ......Hurricanes	1959 ......Circle F	1981 ......Rolex A & K	2003 ......C Spear
1931 ......Santa Paula	1960 ......Oak Brook–	1982 ......Retama	2004 ......Isla Carroll
1932 ......Templeton	C.C.C.	1983 ......Ft. Lauderdale	
1933 ......Aurora	1961 ......Milwaukee	1984 ......Retama	
1934 ......Templeton	1962 ......Santa Barbara	1985 ......Carter Ranch	

Top-Ranked Players

The United States Polo Association ranks its registered players from minus 2 to plus 10 goals, with 10-Goal players being the game's best. At present, the USPA recognizes ten 10-Goal and seven 9-Goal players:

10-GOAL	9-GOAL
Mariano Aguerre	Eduardo Novillo Astrada
Miguel Novillo Astrada	Lucas A. Criado
Javier Novillo Astrada	Francisco de Narvaez
Michael Vincent Azzaro	Melo E. Fernandez-Araujo
Adolfo Cambiaso	Carlos Gracida
Bautista Heguy	Guillermo M. Gracida
Eduardo Heguy	Alberto Heguy
Juan Ignacio Merlos	Matias G. Magrini
Sebastian Merlos	Agustin Merlos
Adam Snow	

YET ANOTHER SIGN OF THE APOCALYPSE

A Scottish rugby team quit in the middle of a league match because the players complained that the 43° weather was too cold.

Professional Rodeo Cowboys Association World Champions

All-Around

1929....Earl Thode	1950....Bill Linderman	1969....Larry Mahan	1988....Dave Appleton
1930....Clay Carr	1951....Casey Tibbs	1970....Larry Mahan	1989....Ty Murray
1931....John Schneider	1952....Harry Tompkins	1971....Phil Lyne	1990....Ty Murray
1932....Donald Nesbit	1953....Bill Linderman	1972....Phil Lyne	1991....Ty Murray
1933....Clay Carr	1954....Buck Rutherford	1973....Larry Mahan	1992....Ty Murray
1934....Leonard Ward	1955....Casey Tibbs	1974....Tom Ferguson	1993....Ty Murray
1935....Everett Bowman	1956....Jim Shoulders	1975....Tom Ferguson	1994....Ty Murray
1936....John Bowman	1957....Jim Shoulders	1976....Tom Ferguson	1995....Joe Beaver
1937....Everett Bowman	1958....Jim Shoulders	1977....Tom Ferguson	1996....Joe Beaver
1938....Burel Mulkey	1959....Jim Shoulders	1978....Tom Ferguson	1997....Dan Mortensen
1939....Paul Carney	1960....Harry Tompkins	1979....Tom Ferguson	1998....Ty Murray
1940....Fritz Truan	1961....Benny Reynolds	1980....Paul Tierney	1999....Fred Whitfield
1941....Homer Pettigrew	1962....Tom Nesmith	1981....Jimmie Cooper	2000....Joe Beaver
1942....Gerald Roberts	1963....Dean Oliver	1982....Chris Lybbert	2001....Cody Ohl
1943....Louis Brooks	1964....Dean Oliver	1983....Roy Cooper	2002....Trevor Brazile
1944....Louis Brooks	1965....Dean Oliver	1984....Dee Picket	2003....Trevor Brazile
1947....Todd Whatley	1966....Larry Mahan	1985....Lewis Feild	
1948....Gerald Roberts	1967....Larry Mahan	1986....Lewis Feild	
1949....Jim Shoulders	1968....Larry Mahan	1987....Lewis Feild	

Saddle Bronc Riding

1929....Earl Thode	1950....Bill Linderman	1969....Bill Smith	1988....Clint Johnson
1930....Clay Carr	1951....Casey Tibbs	1970....Dennis Reiners	1989....Clint Johnson
1931....Earl Thode	1952....Casey Tibbs	1971....Bill Smith	1990....Robert Etbauer
1932....Peter Knight	1953....Casey Tibbs	1972....Mel Hyland	1991....Robert Etbauer
1933....Peter Knight	1954....Casey Tibbs	1973....Bill Smith	1992....Billy Etbauer
1934....Leonard Ward	1955....Deb Copenhaver	1974....John McBeth	1993....Dan Mortensen
1935....Peter Knight	1956....Deb Copenhaver	1975....Monty Henson	1994....Dan Mortensen
1936....Peter Knight	1957....Alvin Nelson	1976....Monty Henson	1995....Dan Mortensen
1937....Burel Mulkey	1958....Marty Wood	1977....Bobby Berger	1996....Billy Etbauer
1938....Burel Mulkey	1959....Casey Tibbs	1978....Joe Marvel	1997....Dan Mortensen
1939....Fritz Truan	1960....Enoch Walker	1979....Bobby Berger	1998....Dan Mortensen
1940....Fritz Truan	1961....Winston Bruce	1980....Clint Johnson	1999....Billy Etbauer
1941....Doff Aber	1962....Kenny McLean	1981....B. Gjermundson	2000....Billy Etbauer
1942....Doff Aber	1963....Guy Weeks	1982....Monty Henson	2001....Tom Reeves
1943....Louis Brooks	1964....Marty Wood	1983....B. Gjermundson	2002....Glen O'Neil
1944....Louis Brooks	1965....Shawn Davis	1984....B. Gjermundson	2003....Dan Mortensen
1947....Carl Olson	1966....Marty Wood	1985....B. Gjermundson	
1948....Gene Pruett	1967....Shawn Davis	1986....Bud Munroe	
1949....Casey Tibbs	1968....Shawn Davis	1987....Clint Johnson	

Bareback Riding

1932....Smoky Snyder	1953....Eddy Akridge	1972....Joe Alexander	1991....Clint Corey
1933....Nate Waldrum	1954....Eddy Akridge	1973....Joe Alexander	1992....Wayne Herman
1934....Leonard Ward	1955....Eddy Akridge	1974....Joe Alexander	1993....Deb Greenough
1935....Frank Schneider	1956....Jim Shoulders	1975....Joe Alexander	1994....Marvin Garrett
1936....Smoky Snyder	1957....Jim Shoulders	1976....Joe Alexander	1995....Marvin Garrett
1937....Paul Carney	1958....Jim Shoulders	1977....Joe Alexander	1996....Mark Garrett
1938....Pete Grubb	1959....Jack Buschbom	1978....Bruce Ford	1997....Eric Mouton
1939....Paul Carney	1960....Jack Buschbom	1979....Bruce Ford	1998....Mark Gomes
1940....Carl Dossey	1961....Eddy Akridge	1980....Bruce Ford	1999....Lan LaJeunesse
1941....George Mills	1962....Ralph Buell	1981....J.C. Trujillo	2000....Jeffrey Collins
1942....Louis Brooks	1963....John Hawkins	1982....Bruce Ford	2001....Lan LaJeunesse
1943....Bill Linderman	1964....Jim Houston	1983....Bruce Ford	2002....Bobby Mote
1944....Louis Brooks	1965....Jim Houston	1984....Larry Peabody	2003....Will Lowe
1947....Larry Finley	1966....Paul Mayo	1985....Lewis Feild	
1948....Sonny Tureman	1967....Clyde Vamvoras	1986....Lewis Feild	
1949....Jack Buschbom	1968....Clyde Vamvoras	1987....Bruce Ford	
1950....Jim Shoulders	1969....Gary Tucker	1988....Marvin Garrett	
1951....Casey Tibbs	1970....Paul Mayo	1989....Marvin Garrett	
1952....Harry Tompkins	1971....Joe Alexander	1990....Chuck Logue	

Professional Rodeo Cowboys Association World Champions (Cont.)

Bull Riding

1929....John Schneider	1948....Harry Tompkins	1967....Larry Mahan	1986....Tuff Hedeman
1930....John Schneider	1949....Harry Tompkins	1968....George Paul	1987....Lane Frost
1931....Smokey Snyder	1950....Harry Tompkins	1969....Doug Brown	1988....Jim Sharp
1932....John Schneider	1951....Jim Shoulders	1970....Gary Leffew	1989....Tuff Hedeman
1932....Smokey Snyder	1952....Harry Tompkins	1971....Bill Nelson	1990....Jim Sharp
John Schneider	1953....Todd Whatley	1972....John Quintana	1991....Tuff Hedeman
1933....Frank Schneider	1954....Jim Shoulders	1973....Bobby Steiner	1992....Cody Custer
1934....Frank Schneider	1955....Jim Shoulders	1974....Don Gay	1993....Ty Murray
1935....Smokey Snyder	1956....Jim Shoulders	1975....Don Gay	1994....Daryl Mills
1936....Smokey Snyder	1957....Jim Shoulders	1976....Don Gay	1995....Jerome Davis
1937....Smokey Snyder	1958....Jim Shoulders	1977....Don Gay	1996....Terry West
1938....Kid Fletcher	1959....Jim Shoulders	1978....Don Gay	1997....Scott Mendes
1939....Dick Griffith	1960....Harry Tompkins	1979....Don Gay	1998....Ty Murray
1940....Dick Griffith	1961....Ronnie Rossen	1980....Don Gay	1999....Mike White
1941....Dick Griffith	1962....Freckles Brown	1981....Don Gay	2000....Cody Hancock
1942....Dick Griffith	1963....Bill Kornell	1982....Charles Sampson	2001....Blue Stone
1943....Ken Roberts	1964....Bob Wegner	1983....Cody Snyder	2002....Blue Stone
1944....Ken Roberts	1965....Larry Mahan	1984....Don Gay	2003....Terry West
1947....Wag Blessing	1966....Ronnie Rossen	1985....Ted Nuce	

Calf Roping

1929....Everett Bowman	1950....Toots Mansfield	1969....Dean Oliver	1988....Joe Beaver
1930....Jake McClure	1951....Don McLaughlin	1970....Junior Garrison	1989....Rabe Rabon
1931....Herb Meyers	1952....Don McLaughlin	1971....Phil Lyne	1990....Troy Pruitt
1932....Richard Merchant	1953....Don McLaughlin	1972....Phil Lyne	1991....Fred Whitfield
1933....Bill McFarlane	1954....Don McLaughlin	1973....Ernie Taylor	1992....Joe Beaver
1934....Irby Mundy	1955....Dean Oliver	1974....Tom Ferguson	1993....Joe Beaver
1935....Everett Bowman	1956....Ray Wharton	1975....Jeff Copenhaver	1994....Herbert Theriot
1936....Clyde Burk	1957....Don McLaughlin	1976....Roy Cooper	1995....Fred Whitfield
1937....Everett Bowman	1958....Dean Oliver	1977....Roy Cooper	1996....Fred Whitfield
1938....Burel Mulkey	1959....Jim Bob Altizer	1978....Roy Cooper	1997....Cody Ohl
1939....Toots Mansfield	1960....Dean Oliver	1979....Paul Tierney	1998....Cody Ohl
1940....Toots Mansfield	1961....Dean Oliver	1980....Roy Cooper	1999....Fred Whitfield
1941....Toots Mansfield	1962....Dean Oliver	1981....Roy Cooper	2000....Fred Whitfield
1942....Clyde Burk	1963....Dean Oliver	1982....Roy Cooper	2001....Cody Ohl
1943....Toots Mansfield	1964....Dean Oliver	1983....Roy Cooper	2002....Fred Whitfield
1944....Clyde Burk	1965....Glen Franklin	1984....Roy Cooper	2003...Cody Ohl
1947....Troy Fort	1966....Junior Garrison	1985....Joe Beaver	
1948....Toots Mansfield	1967....Glen Franklin	1986....Chris Lybbert	
1949....Troy Fort	1968....Glen Franklin	1987....Joe Beaver	

Steer Wrestling

1929....Gene Ross	1950....Bill Linderman	1969....Roy Duvall	1988....John W. Jones
1930....Everett Bowman	1951....Dub Phillips	1970....John W. Jones	1989....John W. Jones
1931....Gene Ross	1952....Harley May	1971....Billy Hale	1990....Ote Berry
1932....Hugh Bennett	1953....Ross Dollarhide	1972....Roy Duvall	1991....Ote Berry
1933....Everett Bowman	1954....James Bynum	1973....Bob Marshall	1992....Mark Roy
1934....Shorty Ricker	1955....Benny Combs	1974....Tommy Puryear	1993....Steve Duhon
1935....Everett Bowman	1956....Harley May	1975....F. Shepperson	1994....Blaine Pederson
1936....Jack Kerschner	1957....Clark McEntire	1976....Tom Ferguson	1995....Ote Berry
1937....Gene Ross	1958....James Bynum	1977....Larry Ferguson	1996....Chad Bedell
1938....Everett Bowman	1959....Harry Charters	1978....Byron Walker	1997....Brad Gleason
1939....Harry Hart	1960....Bob A. Robinson	1979....Stan Williamson	1998....Mike Smith
1940....Homer Pettigrew	1961....Jim Bynum	1980....Butch Myers	1999....Mickey Gee
1941....Hub Whiteman	1962....Tom Nesmith	1981....Byron Walker	2000....Frank Thompson
1942....Homer Pettigrew	1963....Jim Bynum	1982....Stan Williamson	2001....Rope Myers
1943....Homer Pettigrew	1964....C.R. Boucher	1983....Joel Edmondson	2002....Sid Steiner
1944....Homer Pettigrew	1965....Harley May	1984....John W. Jones	2003....Teddy Johnson
1947....Todd Whatley	1966....Jack Roddy	1985....Ote Berry	
1948....Homer Pettigrew	1967....Roy Duvall	1986....Steve Duhon	
1949....Bill McGuire	1968....Jack Roddy	1987....Steve Duhon	

Professional Rodeo Cowboys Association World Champions *(Cont.)*

Team Roping

1929....Charles Maggini	1951....Olan Sims	1973....Leo Camarillo	1994....Jake Barnes
1930....Norman Cowan	1952....Asbury Schell	1974....H.P. Evetts	Clay O. Cooper
1931....Arthur Beloat	1953....Ben Johnson	1975....Leo Camarillo	1995....Bobby Hurley
1932....Ace Gardner	1954....Eddie Schell	1976....Leo Camarillo	Allen Bach
1933....Roy Adams	1955....Vern Castro	1977....Jerold Camarillo	1996....Steve Purcella
1934....Andy Jauregui	1956....Dale Smith	1978....Doyle Gellerman	Steve Northcott
1935....Lawrence Conltk	1957....Dale Smith	1979....Allen Bach	1997....Speed Williams
1936....John Rhodes	1958....Ted Ashworth	1980....Tee Woolman	Rich Skelton
1937....Asbury Schell	1959....Jim Rodriguez Jr.	1981....Walt Woodard	1998....Speed Williams
1938....John Rhodes	1960....Jim Rodriguez Jr.	1982....Tee Woolman	Rich Skelton
1939....Asbury Schell	1961....Al Hooper	1983....Leo Camarillo	1999....Speed Williams
1940....Pete Grubb	1962....Jim Rodriguez Jr.	1984....Dee Pickett	Rich Skelton
1941....Jim Hudson	1963....Les Hirdes	1985....Jake Barnes	2000....Speed Williams
1942....Verne Castro	1964....Bill Hamilton	1986....Clay O. Cooper	Rich Skelton
Vic Castro	1965....Jim Rodriguez Jr.	1987....Clay O. Cooper	2001....Speed Williams
1943....Mark Hull	1966....Ken Luman	1988....Jake Barnes	Rich Skelton
Leonard Block	1967....Joe Glenn	1989....Jake Barnes	2002....Speed Williams
1944....Murphy Chaney	1968....Art Arnold	1990....Allen Bach	Rich Skelton
1947....Jim Brister	1969....Jerold Camarillo	1991....Bob Harris	2003....Speed Williams
1948....Joe Glenn	1970....John Miller	1992....Clay O. Cooper	Rich Skelton
1949....Ed Yanez	1971....John Miller	1993....Bobby Hurley	
1950....Buck Sorrels	1972....Leo Camarillo		

Steer Roping

1929....Charles Maggini	1948....Everett Shaw	1967....Jim Bob Altizer	1986....Jim Davis
1930....Clay Carr	1949....Shoat Webster	1968....Sonny Davis	1987....Shaun Burchett
1931....Andy Jauregui	1950....Shoat Webster	1969....Walter Arnold	1988....Shaun Burchett
1932....George Weir	1951....Everett Shaw	1970....Don McLaughlin	1989....Guy Allen
1933....John Bowman	1952....Buddy Neal	1971....Olin Young	1990....Phil Lyne
1934....John McEntire	1953....Ike Rude	1972....Allen Keller	1991....Guy Allen
1935....Richard Merchant	1954....Shoat Webster	1973....Roy Thompson	1992....Guy Allen
1936....John Bowman	1955....Shoat Webster	1974....Olin Young	1993....Guy Allen
1937....Everett Bowman	1956....Jim Snively	1975....Roy Thompson	1994....Guy Allen
1938....Hugh Bennett	1957....Clark McEntire	1976....Marvin Cantrell	1995....Guy Allen
1939....Dick Truitt	1958....Clark McEntire	1977....Buddy Cockrell	1996....Guy Allen
1940....Clay Carr	1959....Everett Shaw	1978....Sonny Worrell	1997....Guy Allen
1941....Ike Rude	1960....Don McLaughlin	1979....Gary Good	1998....Guy Allen
1942....King Merrit	1961....Clark McEntire	1980....Guy Allen	1999....Guy Allen
1943....Tom Rhodes	1962....Everett Shaw	1981....Arnold Felts	2000....Guy Allen
1944....Tom Rhodes	1963....Don McLaughlin	1982....Guy Allen	2001....Guy Allen
1945....Everett Shaw	1964....Sonny Davis	1983....Roy Cooper	2002....Buster Record
1946....Everett Shaw	1965....Sonney Wright	1984....Guy Allen	2003....Guy Allen
1947....Ike Rude	1966....Sonny Davis	1985....Jim Davis	

Note: In 1945–46 champions were crowned only in Steer Roping.

Rowing

National Collegiate Rowing Champions

MEN

1985 ....Harvard	1992 ....Harvard	1999 ....California
1986 ....Wisconsin	1993 ....Brown	2000 ....California
1987 ....Harvard	1994 ....Brown	2001 ....California
1988 ....Harvard	1995 ....Brown	2002 ....California
1989 ....Harvard	1996 ....Princeton	2003 ....Harvard
1990 ....Wisconsin	1997 ....Washington	2004 ....Harvard
1991 ....Pennsylvania	1998 ....Princeton	

WOMEN

1979 ....Yale	1988 ....Washington	1997 ....Washington
1980 ....California	1989 ....Cornell	1998 ....Washington
1981 ....Washington	1990 ....Princeton	1999 ....Brown
1982 ....Washington	1991 ....Boston University	2000 ....Brown
1983 ....Washington	1992 ....Boston University	2001 ....Washington
1984 ....Washington	1993 ....Princeton	2002 ....Brown
1985 ....Washington	1994 ....Princeton	2003 ....Harvard
1986 ....Wisconsin	1995 ....Princeton	2004 ....Brown
1987 ....Washington	1996 ....Brown	

Rugby Union

National Men's Club Championship

Year	Winner	Runner-Up	Year	Winner	Runner-Up
1979	Old Blues (CA)	St. Louis Falcons	1992	Old Blues (CA)	Mystic River (MA)
1980	Old Blues (CA)	St. Louis Falcons	1993	Old Mission Beach AC	Milwaukee
1981	Old Blues (CA)	Old Blue (NY)	1994	Old Mission Beach AC	Life College (GA)
1982	Old Blues (CA)	Denver Barbos	1995	Potomac Athletic Club	Old Mission Beach
1983	Old Blues (CA)	Dallas Harlequins	1996	Old Mission Beach AC	Old Blues (CA)
1984	Dallas Harlequins	Los Angeles	1997	Gentlemen of Aspen	Old Blue (NY)
1985	Milwaukee	Denver Barbos	1998	Gentlemen of Aspen	Old Blue (NY)
1986	Old Blues (CA)	Old Blue (NY)	1999	Gentlemen of Aspen	Golden Gate (CA)
1987	Old Blues (CA)	Pittsburgh	2000	Gentlemen of Aspen	Hayward Griffins
1988	Old Mission Beach AC	Milwaukee	2001	San Mateo	New York AC
1989	Old Mission Beach AC	Philly/Whitemarsh	2002	San Mateo	Austin
1990	Denver Barbos	Old Blues (CA)	2003	Boston Irish Wolfhounds	San Mateo
1991	Old Mission Beach AC	Washington	2004	Boston Irish Wolfhounds	Austin

National Men's Collegiate Championship

Year	Winner	Runner-Up	Year	Winner	Runner-Up
1980	California	Air Force	1993	California	Air Force
1981	California	Harvard	1994	California	Navy
1982	California	Life College	1995	California	Air Force
1983	California	Air Force	1996	California	Penn St
1984	Harvard	Colorado	1997	California	Penn St
1985	California	Maryland	1998	California	Stanford
1986	California	Dartmouth	1999	California	Penn St
1987	San Diego State	Air Force	2000	California	Wyoming
1988	California	Dartmouth	2001	California	Penn St
1989	Air Force	Long Beach	2002	California	Utah
1990	Air Force	Army	2003	Air Force	Harvard
1991	California	Army	2004	California	Cal Poly SLO
1992	California	Army			

World Cup Championship

Year	Winner	Runner-Up	Year	Winner	Runner-Up
1987	New Zealand	France	1999	Australia	France
1991	Australia	England	2003	England	Australia
1995	South Africa	New Zealand			

Rugby League

American National Rugby League Champions

Year	Winner	Runner-Up
1998	Glen Mills Bulls	Philadelphia Bulldogs
1999	Glen Mills Bulls	New Jersey Sharks
2000	Glen Mills Bulls	Philadelphia Fight
2001	Glen Mills Bulls	Media Mantarays
2002	New York Knights	Glen Mills Bulls
2003	Connecticut Wildcats	Glen Mills Bulls
2004	Glen Mills Bulls	Connecticut Wildcats

World Cup Championship

Year	Winner	Runner-Up	Host
1954	Great Britain	France	France
1957	Australia	International Team	Australia
1960	Great Britain	International Team	England
1968	Australia	France	Australia–New Zealand
1970	Great Britain	Australia	England
1972	Australia	Great Britain	France
1975	Australia	England	Worldwide
1977	Australia	Great Britain	Australia–New Zealand
1985–88	Australia	New Zealand	Worldwide
1989–92	Australia	Great Britain	Worldwide
1995	Australia	England	Great Britain
2000	Australia	New Zealand	G Britain-Ireland-France

Sailing

America's Cup Champions

SCHOONERS AND J-CLASS BOATS

Year	Winner	Skipper	Series	Loser	Skipper
1851	America	Richard Brown			
1870	Magic	Andrew Comstock	1–0	Cambria, Great Britain	J. Tannock
1871	Columbia (2–1)	Nelson Comstock	4–1	Livonia, Great Britain	J.R. Woods
	Sappho (2–0)	Sam Greenwood			
1876	Madeleine	Josephus Williams	2–0	Countess of Dufferin, Canada	J.E. Ellsworth
1881	Mischief	Nathanael Clock	2–0	Atalanta, Canada	Alexander Cuthbert
1885	Puritan	Aubrey Crocker	2–0	Genesta, Great Britain	John Carter
1886	Mayflower	Martin Stone	2–0	Galatea, Great Britain	Dan Bradford
1887	Volunteer	Henry Haff	2–0	Thistle, Great Britain	John Barr
1893	Vigilant	William Hansen	3–0	Valkyrie II, Great Britain	William Granfield
1895	Defender	Henry Haff	3–0	Valkyrie III, Great Britain	William Granfield
1899	Columbia	Charles Barr	3–0	Shamrock I, Great Britain	Archie Hogarth
1901	Columbia	Charles Barr	3–0	Shamrock II, Great Britain	E.A. Sycamore
1903	Reliance	Charles Barr	3–0	Shamrock III, Great Britain	Bob Wringe
1920	Resolute	Charles F. Adams	3–2	Shamrock IV, Great Britain	William Burton
1930	Enterprise	Harold Vanderbilt	4–0	Shamrock V, Great Britain	Ned Heard
1934	Rainbow	Harold Vanderbilt	4–2	Endeavour, Great Britain	T.O.M. Sopwith
1937	Ranger	Harold Vanderbilt	4–0	Endeavour II, Great Britain	T.O.M. Sopwith

12-METER BOATS

Year	Winner	Skipper	Series	Loser	Skipper
1958	Columbia	Briggs Cunningham	4–0	Sceptre, Great Britain	Graham Mann
1962	Weatherly	Bus Mosbacher	4–1	Gretel, Australia	Jock Sturrock
1964	Constellation	Bob Bavier & Eric Ridder	4–0	Sovereign, Australia	Peter Scott
1967	Intrepid	Bus Mosbacher	4–0	Dame Pattie, Australia	Jock Sturrock
1970	Intrepid	Bill Ficker	4–1	Gretel II, Australia	Jim Hardy
1974	Courageous	Ted Hood	4–0	Southern Cross, Australia	John Cuneo
1977	Courageous	Ted Turner	4–0	Australia	Noel Robins
1980	Freedom	Dennis Conner	4–1	Australia	Jim Hardy
1983	Australia II	John Bertrand	4–3	Liberty, United States	Dennis Conner
1987	Stars & Stripes	Dennis Conner	4–0	Kookaburra III, Australia	Iain Murray

60-FOOT CATAMARAN vs 133-FOOT MONOHULL

Year	Winner	Skipper	Series	Loser	Skipper
1988	Stars & Stripes	Dennis Conner	2–0	New Zealand	David Barnes

75-FOOT MONOHULL (IACC)

Year	Winner	Skipper	Series	Loser	Skipper
1992	America[3]	Bill Koch	4–1	Il Moro di Vinezia, Italy	Paul Cayard
1995	Black Magic I	Russell Coutts	5–0	Young America, United States	Dennis Conner
2000	New Zealand	Russell Coutts	5–0	Luna Rossa, Italy	Francesco de Angelis
2003	Swiss Alinghi	Russell Coutts	5–0	New Zealand	Dean Barker

Note: Winning entries have been from the United States every year but three: In 1983 an Australian vessel won, and in 1995 and 2000 a vessel from New Zealand won.

Shooting World Champions

Men

50M FREE RIFLE PRONE

1947 .....O. Sannes, Norway
1949 .....A.C. Jackson, U.S.
1952 .....A.C. Jackson, U.S.
1954 .....G. Boa, Canada
1958 .....M. Nordquist
1962 .....K. Wenk, W Germany
1966 .....D. Boyd, U.S.
1970 .....M. Fiess, S. Africa
1974 .....K. Bulan, Czechoslovakia
1978 .....A. Allan, Great Britain
1982 .....V. Danilschenko, USSR
1986 .....S. Bereczky, Hungary
1990 .....V. Bochkarev, USSR
1994 .....Venjie Li, China
1998 .....Thomas Tamas, U.S.
1999 .....Thomas Tamas, U.S.
2000 .....Siarhei Martynau, Belarus
2001 .....Matthew Emmons, U.S.
2002 .....Matthew Emmons, U.S.

AIR RIFLE

1966 .....G. Kümmet, W Germany
1970 .....G. Kusterman, W Germ.
1974 .....E. Pedzisz, Poland
1978 .....O. Schlipf, W. Germany
1979 .....K. Hillenbrand
1981 .....F. Bessy, France
1982 .....F. Rettkowski, E Germ.
1983 .....P. Heberle, France
1985 .....P. Heberle, France
1986 .....H. Riederer, W Germany
1987 .....K. Ivanov, USSR
1989 .....J. P. Amet, France
1990 .....H. Riederer, W Germany
1994 .....Boris Polak, Israel
1998 .....Artem Khadjibekov, Russia
1999 .....Jozef Gonci, Slovakia
2000 .....Artem Khadjibekov, Russia
2001 .....Jason Parker, U.S.
2002 .....Jason Parker, U.S.

THREE POSITION RIFLE

1966 .....M. Thompson, U.S.
1970 .....M. Thompson Murdock, U.S.
1974 .....A. Pelova, Bulgaria
1978 .....W. Oliver, U.S.
1982 .....M. Helbig, E Germany
1986 .....V. Letcheva, Bulgaria
1990 .....V. Letcheva, Bulgaria
1994 .....A. Maloukhina, Russia
1998 .....Sonja Pfeilschifter, Germany
1999 .....Sonja Pfeilschifter, Germany
2000 .....Hong Shan, China
2001 .....Petra Horneber, Germany
2002 .....Petra Horneber, Germany

AIR RIFLE

1970 .....V. Cherkasque, USSR
1974 .....T. Ratkinova, USSR
1978 .....W. Oliver, U.S.
1979 .....K. Monez, U.S.
1981 .....S. Romaristova, USSR
1982 .....S. Lang, W Germany
1983 .....M. Helbig, E Germany
1985 .....E. Forian, Hungary
1986 .....V. Letcheva, Bulgaria
1987 .....V. Letcheva, Bulgaria
1989 .....V. Letcheva, Bulgaria
1990 .....E. Joc, Hungary

MEN'S TRAP

1929 .....De Lumniczer, Hungary
1930 .....M. Arie, U.S.
1931 .....Kiszkurno, Poland
1933 .....De Lumniczer, Hungary
1934 .....A. Montagh, Hungary
1935 .....R. Sack, W Germany
1936 .....Kiszkurno, Poland
1937 .....K. Huber, Finland
1938 .....I. Strassburger, Hungary
1939 .....De Lumniczer, Hungary
1947 .....H. Liljedahl, Sweden
1949 .....F. Rocchi, Argentina
1950 .....C. Sala, Italy
1952 .....P.J. Grossi, Argentina
1954 .....C. Merlo, Italy
1958 .....F. Eisenlauer, U.S.
1959 .....H. Badravi, Egypt
1961 .....E. Mattarelli, Italy
1962 .....W. Zimenko, USSR
1965 .....J.E. Lire, Chile
1966 .....K. Jones, U.S.
1967 .....G. Rennard, Belgium
1969 .....E. Mattarelli, Italy
1970 .....M. Carrega, France
1971 .....M. Carrega, France
1973 .....A. Andrushkin, USSR
1974 .....M. Carrega, France
1975 .....J. Primrose, Canada
1977 .....E. Azkue, Spain
1978 .....E. Vallduvi, Spain
1979 .....M. Carrega, France
1981 .....A. Asanov, USSR
1982 .....L. Giovonnetti, Italy
1983 .....J. Primrose, Canada
1985 .....M. Bednarik,
         Czechoslovakia
1986 ....M. Bednarik,
         Czechoslovakia
1987 .....D. Monakov, USSR

Women

AIR RIFLE (Cont.)

1994 .....Sonja Pfeilschifter, Germany
1998 .....Sonja Pfeilschifter, Germany
1999 .....Sonja Pfeilschifter, Germany
2000 .....Sonja Pfeilschifter, Germany
2001 ....Katerina Kurkova, Czech.
2002 ....Katerina Kurkova, Czech.

SPORT PISTOL

1966 .....N. Rasskazova, USSR
1970 .....N. Stoljarova, USSR
1974 .....N. Stoljarova, USSR
1978 .....K. Dyer, U.S.
1982 .....P. Balogh, Hungary
1986 .....M. Dobrantcheva, USSR
1990 .....M. Logvinenko, USSR
1994 .....Soon Hee Boo, S Korea
1998 .....Yieqing Cai, China
1999 .....Soon Hee Boo, S Korea
2000 .....Lalita Vauhleuskaya,
         Belarus
2001 .....Munkhbayar Dorjsuren,
         Germany
2002 .....Munkhbayar Dorjsuren,
         Germany

AIR PISTOL

1970 .....S. Carroll, U.S.
1974 .....Z. Simonian, USSR

MEN'S TRAP (Cont.)

1989 .....M. Venturini, Italy
1990 .....J. Damne, E Germany
1994 .....Dmitriy Monakov, Ukraine
1995 .....Giovanni Pellielo, Italy
1998 .....Giovanni Pellielo, Italy
1999 .....Joao Rebelo, Portugal
2000 .....Michael Diamond, Australia
2001 ....Michael Diamond, Australia
2002 ....Khaled Almudhaf, Kuwait

THREE POSITION RIFLE

1929 .....O. Ericsson, Sweden
1930 .....Petersen, Denmark
1931 .....Amundson, Norway
1933 .....De Lisle, France
1935 .....Leskinnen, Finland
1937 .....Mazoyer, France
1939 .....Steigelmann, Germany
1947 .....I.H. Erben, Sweden
1949 .....P. Janhonen, Finland
1952 .....Kongshaug, Norway
1954 .....A. Bugdanov, USSR
1958 .....Itkis, USSR
1962 .....G. Anderson, U.S.
1966 .....G. Anderson, U.S.
1970 .....Parkhimovitch, USSR
1974 .....L. Wigger, U.S.
1978 .....E. Svensson, Sweden
1982 .....K. Ivanov, USSR
1986 .....P. Heinz, W Germany
1990 .....E. C. Lee, S Korea
1994 .....P. Kurka, Czech Republic
1998 .....Jozef Gonci, Slovakia
1999 .....Jozef Gonci, Slovakia
2000 .....Jozef Gonci, Slovakia
2001 .....Marcel Bürge, Switz
2002 .....Marcel Bürge, Switz

AIR PISTOL (Cont.)

1978 .....K. Hansson, Sweden
1979 .....R. Fox, U.S.
1981 .....N. Kalinina, USSR
1982 .....M. Dobrantcheva, USSR
1983 .....K. Bodin, Sweden
1985 .....M. Dobrantcheva, USSR
1986 .....A. Völker, E Germany
1987 .....J. Brajkovic, Yugoslavia
1989 .....N. Salukvadse, USSR
1990 .....Jasna Sekaric, Yugoslavia
1994 .....Jasna Sekaric, IOP
1998 .....Dorisuren Munkhbayar,
         Mongolia
1999 .....Nino Salukvadze,
         Georgia
2000 .....Luna Tao, China
2001 .....Olena Kostevych, Ukraine
2002 .....Olena Kostevych, Ukraine

U.S. Champions—Men
MAJOR FAST PITCH

1933..........J.L. Gill Boosters, Chicago	1970..........Raybestos Cardinals, Stratford, CT
1934..........Ke-Nash-A, Kenosha, WI	1971..........Welty Way, Cedar Rapids, IA
1935..........Crimson Coaches, Toledo, OH	1972..........Raybestos Cardinals, Stratford, CT
1936..........Kodak Park, Rochester, NY	1973..........Clearwater (FL) Bombers
1937..........Briggs Body Team, Detroit	1974..........Gianella Bros, Santa Rosa, CA
1938..........The Pohlers, Cincinnati	1975..........Rising Sun Hotel, Reading, PA
1939..........Carr's Boosters, Covington, KY	1976..........Raybestos Cardinals, Stratford, CT
1940..........Kodak Park, Rochester, NY	1977..........Billard Barbell, Reading, PA
1941..........Bendix Brakes, South Bend, IN	1978..........Billard Barbell, Reading, PA
1942..........Deep Rock Oilers, Tulsa	1979..........McArdle Pontiac/Cadillac, Midland, MI
1943..........Hammer Air Field, Fresno	1980..........Peterbilt Western, Seattle
1944..........Hammer Air Field, Fresno	1981..........Archer Daniels Midland, Decatur, IL
1945..........Zollner Pistons, Fort Wayne, IN	1982..........Peterbilt Western, Seattle
1946..........Zollner Pistons, Fort Wayne, IN	1983..........Franklin Cardinals, Stratford, CT
1947..........Zollner Pistons, Fort Wayne, IN	1984..........California Kings, Merced, CA
1948..........Briggs Beautyware, Detroit	1985..........Pay'n Pak, Seattle
1949..........Tip Top Tailors, Toronto	1986..........Pay'n Pak, Seattle
1950..........Clearwater (FL) Bombers	1987..........Pay'n Pak, Seattle
1951..........Dow Chemical, Midland, MI	1988..........TransAire, Elkhart, IN
1952..........Briggs Beautyware, Detroit	1989..........Penn Corp, Sioux City, IA
1953..........Briggs Beautyware, Detroit	1990..........Penn Corp, Sioux City, IA
1954..........Clearwater (FL) Bombers	1991..........Guanella Brothers, Rohnert Park, CA
1955..........Raybestos Cardinals, Stratford, CT	1992..........Natl Health Care Disc, Sioux City, IA
1956..........Clearwater (FL) Bombers	1993..........Natl Health Care Disc, Sioux City, IA
1957..........Clearwater (FL) Bombers	1994..........Decatur Pride, Decatur, IL
1958..........Raybestos Cardinals, Stratford, CT	1995..........Decatur Pride, Decatur, IL
1959..........Sealmasters, Aurora, IL	1996..........Green Bay All-Car, Green Bay, WI
1960..........Clearwater (FL) Bombers	1997..........Green Bay All-Car, Green Bay, WI
1961..........Sealmasters, Aurora, IL	1998..........Meierhoffer-Fleeman, St. Joseph, MO
1962..........Clearwater (FL) Bombers	1999..........Decatur Pride, Decatur, IL
1963..........Clearwater (FL) Bombers	2000..........Meierhoffer, St. Joseph, MO
1964..........Burch Tool, Detroit	2001..........Frontier Players Casino, St. Joseph, MO
1965..........Sealmasters, Aurora, IL	2002..........Frontier Players Casino, St. Joseph, MO
1966..........Clearwater (FL) Bombers	2003..........Farm Tavern, Madison, WI
1967..........Sealmasters, Aurora, IL	2004..........Farm Tavern, Madison, WI
1968..........Clearwater (FL) Bombers	
1969..........Raybestos Cardinals, Stratford, CT	

SUPER SLOW PITCH

1981..........Howard's/Western Steer, Denver, NC	1994..........Bell Corp, Tampa, FL
1982..........Jerry's Catering, Miami, FL	1995..........Lighthouse/Worth, Stone Mt.., GA
1983..........Howard's/Western Steer, Denver, NC	1996..........Ritch's Superior, Windsor Locks, CT
1984..........Howard's/Western Steer, Denver, NC	1997..........Ritch's Superior, Windsor Locks, CT
1985..........Steele's Sports, Grafton, OH	1998..........Lighthouse/Worth, Stone Mt.., GA
1986..........Steele's Sports, Grafton, OH	1999..........Team Easton, Wilmington, NC
1987..........Steele's Sports, Grafton, OH	2000..........Team TPS, Louisville, KY
1988..........Starpath, Monticello, KY	2002..........Long Haul/Taylor Bros./Shen Corp./TPS,
1989..........Ritch's Salvage, Harrisburg, NC	Albertville, MN
1990..........Steele's Silver Bullets, Grafton, OH	2003..........Resmondo/Hagae/Sunbelt/Taylor,
1991..........Sunbelt/Worth, Centerville, GA	Canal Winchester, OH
1992..........Ritch's Superior, Windsor Locks, CT	
1993..........Ritch's Superior, Windsor Locks, CT	

YET ANOTHER SIGN OF THE APOCALYPSE

*The Ukrainian rhythmic gymnastics team
claimed it lost the 2004 European championship
because it was hexed by 15 psychics hired
by the Russian team.*

U.S. Champions—Men (Cont.)

MAJOR SLOW PITCH

1953..........Shields Construction, Newport, KY	1980..........Campbell Carpets, Concord, CA
1954..........Waldneck's Tavern, Cincinnati	1981..........Elite Coating, Gordon, CA
1955..........Lang Pet Shop, Covington, KY	1982..........Triangle Sports, Minneapolis
1956..........Gatliff Auto Sales, Newport, KY	1983..........No. 1 Electric & Heating, Gastonia, NC
1957..........Gatliff Auto Sales, Newport, KY	1984..........Lilly Air Systems, Chicago
1958..........East Side Sports, Detroit	1985..........Blanton's, Fayetteville, NC
1959..........Yorkshire Restaurant, Newport, KY	1986..........Non-Ferrous Metals, Cleveland
1960..........Hamilton Tailoring, Cincinnati	1987..........Starpath, Monticello, KY
1961..........Hamilton Tailoring, Cincinnati	1988..........Bell Corp/FAF, Tampa, FL
1962..........Skip Hogan A.C., Pittsburgh	1989..........Ritch's Salvage, Harrisburg, NC
1963..........Gatliff Auto Sales, Newport, KY	1990..........New Construction, Shelbyville, IN
1964..........Skip Hogan A.C., Pittsburgh	1991..........Riverside Paving, Louisville, KY
1965..........Skip Hogan A.C., Pittsburgh	1992..........Vernon's, Jacksonville, FL
1966..........Michael's Lounge, Detroit	1993..........Back Porch/Destin Roofing, Destin, FL
1967..........Jim's Sport Shop, Pittsburgh	1994..........Riverside RAM/Taylor Bros., Louisville, KY
1968..........County Sports, Levittown, NY	1995..........Riverside/RAM/Taylor/TPS, Louisville, KY
1969..........Copper Hearth, Milwaukee	1996..........Bell 2/Robert's/Easton, Orlando, FL
1970..........Little Caesar's, Southgate, MI	1997..........Long Haul/TPS, Albertville, MN
1971..........Pile Drivers, Virginia Beach, VA	1998..........Chase Mortgage/Easton, Wilmington, NC
1972..........Jiffy Club, Louisville, KY	1999..........Gasoline Heaven/Worth, Commack, NY
1973..........Howard's Furniture, Denver, NC	2000..........Long Haul/TPS, Albertville, MN
1974..........Howard's Furniture, Denver, NC	2001..........New Construction, Shelbyville, IN
1975..........Pyramid Cafe, Lakewood, OH	2002..........Twin States/Worth, Montgomery, AL
1976..........Warren Motors, Jacksonville, FL	2003..........New Construction/B&J/Snap-On,
1977..........Nelson Painting, Oklahoma City	Metamora, IL
1978..........Campbell Carpets, Concord, CA	
1979..........Nelco Mfg Co., Oklahoma City	

YET ANOTHER SIGN OF THE APOCALYPSE

Te Kuiti, a small town in New Zealand,
re-created Pamplona's Running of the Bulls
with 2,000 sheep.

U.S. Champions—Women

MAJOR FAST PITCH

1933..........Great Northerns, Chicago	1969..........Orange (CA) Lionettes
1934..........Hart Motors, Chicago	1970..........Orange (CA) Lionettes
1935..........Bloomer Girls, Cleveland	1971..........Raybestos Brakettes, Stratford, CT
1936..........Nat'l Screw & Mfg., Cleveland	1972..........Raybestos Brakettes, Stratford, CT
1937..........Nat'l Screw & Mfg., Cleveland	1973..........Raybestos Brakettes, Stratford, CT
1938..........J.J. Krieg's, Alameda, CA	1974..........Raybestos Brakettes, Stratford, CT
1939..........J.J. Krieg's, Alameda, CA	1975..........Raybestos Brakettes, Stratford, CT
1940..........Arizona Ramblers, Phoenix	1976..........Raybestos Brakettes, Stratford, CT
1941..........Higgins Midgets, Tulsa	1977..........Raybestos Brakettes, Stratford, CT
1942..........Jax Maids, New Orleans	1978..........Raybestos Brakettes, Stratford, CT
1943..........Jax Maids, New Orleans	1979..........Sun City (AZ) Saints
1944..........Lind & Pomeroy, Portland, OR	1980..........Raybestos Brakettes, Stratford, CT
1945..........Jax Maids, New Orleans	1981..........Orlando (FL) Rebels
1946..........Jax Maids, New Orleans	1982..........Raybestos Brakettes, Stratford, CT
1947..........Jax Maids, New Orleans	1983..........Raybestos Brakettes, Stratford, CT
1948..........Arizona Ramblers, Phoenix	1984..........Los Angeles Diamonds
1949..........Arizona Ramblers, Phoenix	1985..........Hi-Ho Brakettes, Stratford, CT
1950..........Orange (CA) Lionettes	1986..........Southern California Invasion, Los Angeles
1951..........Orange (CA) Lionettes	1987..........Orange County Majestics, Anaheim, CA
1952..........Orange (CA) Lionettes	1988..........Hi-Ho Brakettes, Stratford, CT
1953..........Betsy Ross Rockets, Fresno	1989..........Whittier (CA) Raiders
1954..........Leach Motor Rockets, Fresno	1990..........Raybestos Brakettes, Stratford, CT
1955..........Orange (CA) Lionettes	1991..........Raybestos Brakettes, Stratford, CT
1956..........Orange (CA) Lionettes	1992..........Raybestos Brakettes, Stratford, CT
1957..........Hacienda Rockets, Fresno	1993..........Redding Rebels, Redding, CA
1958..........Raybestos Brakettes, Stratford, CT	1994..........Redding Rebels, Redding, CA
1959..........Raybestos Brakettes, Stratford, CT	1995..........Redding Rebels, Redding, CA
1960..........Raybestos Brakettes, Stratford, CT	1996..........California Commotion, Woodland Hills, CA
1961..........Gold Sox, Whittier, CA	1997..........California Commotion, Woodland Hills, CA
1962..........Orange (CA) Lionettes	1998..........California Commotion, Woodland Hills, CA
1963..........Raybestos Brakettes, Stratford, CT	1999..........California Commotion, Woodland Hills, CA
1964..........Erv Lind Florists, Portland, OR	2000..........Phoenix Storm, Phoenix
1965..........Orange (CA) Lionettes	2001..........Phoenix Storm, Phoenix
1966..........Raybestos Brakettes, Stratford, CT	2002..........Stratford Brakettes, Stratford, CT
1967..........Raybestos Brakettes, Stratford, CT	2003..........Stratford Brakettes, Stratford, CT
1968..........Raybestos Brakettes, Stratford, CT	2004..........Stratford Brakettes, Stratford, CT

MAJOR SLOW PITCH

1959..........Pearl Laundry, Richmond, VA	1982..........Richmond (VA) Stompers
1960..........Carolina Rockets, High Pt, NC	1983..........Spooks, Anoka, MN
1961..........Dairy Cottage, Covington, KY	1984..........Spooks, Anoka, MN
1962..........Dana Gardens, Cincinnati	1985..........Key Ford Mustangs, Pensacola, FL
1963..........Dana Gardens, Cincinnati	1986..........Sur-Way Tomboys, Tifton, GA
1964..........Dana Gardens, Cincinnati	1987..........Key Ford Mustangs, Pensacola, FL
1965..........Art's Acres, Omaha	1988..........Spooks, Anoka, MN
1966..........Dana Gardens, Cincinnati	1989..........Canaan's Illusions, Houston
1967..........Ridge Maintenance, Cleveland	1990..........Spooks, Anoka, MN
1968..........Escue Pontiac, Cincinnati	1991..........Kannan's Illusions, San Antonio, TX
1969..........Converse Dots, Hialeah, FL	1992..........Universal Plastics, Cookeville, TN
1970..........Rutenschruder Floral, Cincinnati	1993..........Universal Plastics, Cookeville, TN
1971..........Gators, Ft. Lauderdale, FL	1994..........Universal Plastics, Cookeville, TN
1972..........Riverside Ford, Cincinnati	1995..........Armed Forces, Sacramento, CA
1973..........Sweeney Chevrolet, Cincinnati	1996..........Spooks, Anoka, MN
1974..........Marks Brothers Dots, Miami	1997..........Taylor's Major Slow Pitch, Glendale, MD
1975..........Marks Brothers Dots, Miami	1998..........Lakerettes, Conneaut Lake, PA
1976..........Sorrento's Pizza, Cincinnati	1999..........Lakerettes, Conneaut Lake, PA
1977..........Fox Valley Lassies, St. Charles, IL	2000..........Premier Motor Sports, Pittsboro, NC
1978..........Bob Hoffman's Dots, Miami	2001..........Shooters/Nike, Orlando, FL
1979..........Bob Hoffman's Dots, Miami	2002..........Diamond Queens, Nashville, TN
1980..........Howard's Rubi-Otts, Graham, NC	2003..........No tournament
1981..........Tifton (GA) Tomboys	

Speed Skating

All-Around World Champions
MEN

1891 .....Joseph F. Donoghue, U.S.	1936 .....Ivar Ballangrud, Norway	1975 .....Harm Kuipers, Netherlands
1893 .....Jaap Eden, Netherlands	1937 .....Michael Staksrud, Nor.	1976 .....Piet Kleine, Netherlands
1895 .....Jaap Eden, Netherlands	1938 .....Ivar Ballangrud, Norway	1977 .....Eric Heiden, U.S.
1896 .....Jaap Eden, Netherlands	1939 .....Birger Wasenius, Finland	1978 .....Eric Heiden, U.S.
1897 .....Jack K. McCulloch, Can.	1947 .....Lassi Parkkinen, Finland	1979 .....Eric Heiden, U.S.
1898 .....Peder Ostlund, Norway	1948 .....Odd Lundberg, Norway	1980 .....Hilbert van der Duin, Neth.
1899 .....Peder Ostlund, Norway	1949 .....Kornel Pajor, Hungary	1981 .....Amund Sjobrand, Norway
1900 .....Edvard Engelsaas, Nor.	1950 .....Hjalmar Andersen, Nor.	1982 .....Hilbert van der Duin, Neth.
1901 .....Franz F. Wathan, Finland	1951 .....Hjalmar Andersen, Nor.	1983 .....Rolf Falk-Larssen, Nor.
1904 .....Sigurd Mathisen, Norway	1952 .....Hjalmar Andersen, Nor.	1984 .....Oleg Bozhev, USSR
1905 .....C. Coen de Koning, Neth.	1953 .....Oleg Goncharenko, USSR	1985 .....Hein Vergeer, Netherlands
1908 .....Oscar Mathisen, Norway	1954 .....Boris Shilkov, USSR	1986 .....Hein Vergeer, Netherlands
1909 .....Oscar Mathisen, Norway	1955 .....Sigvard Ericsson, Swe.	1987 .....Nikolai Guliaev, USSR
1910 .....Nikolai Strunnikov, Russia	1956 .....Oleg Goncharenko, USSR	1988 .....Eric Flaim, U.S.
1911 .....Nikolai Strunnikov, Russia	1957 .....Knut Johannesen, Nor.	1989 .....Leo Visser, Netherlands
1912 .....Oscar Mathisen, Norway	1958 .....Oleg Goncharenko, USSR	1990 .....Johann Olav Koss, Nor.
1913 .....Oscar Mathisen, Norway	1959 .....Juhani Järvinen, Finland	1991 .....Johann Olav Koss, Nor.
1914 .....Oscar Mathisen, Norway	1960 .....Boris Stenin, USSR	1992 .....Roberto Sighel, Italy
1922 .....Harald Strom, Norway	1961 .....Henk van der Grift, Neth.	1993 .....Falko Zandstra, Neth.
1923 .....Klas Thunberg, Finland	1962 .....Viktor Kosichkin, USSR	1994 .....Johann Olav Koss, Nor.
1924 .....Roald Larsen, Norway	1963 .....Jonny Nilsson, Sweden	1995 .....Rintje Ritsma, Netherlands
1925 .....Klas Thunberg, Finland	1964 .....Knut Johannesen, Nor.	1996 .....Rintje Ritsma, Netherlands
1926 .....Ivar Ballangrud, Norway	1965 .....Per Ivar Moe, Norway	1997 .....Ids Postma, Netherlands
1927 .....Bernt Evensen, Norway	1966 .....Kees Verkerk, Neth.	1998 .....Ids Postma, Netherlands
1928 .....Klas Thunberg, Finland	1967 .....Kees Verkerk, Neth.	1999 .....Rintje Ritsma, Netherlands
1929 .....Klas Thunberg, Finland	1968 .....Fred Anton Maier, Nor.	2000 ....Gianni Romme, Netherlands
1930 .....Michael Staksrud, Nor.	1969 .....Dag Fornaes, Norway	2001 ....Rintje Ritsma, Netherlands
1931 .....Klas Thunberg, Finland	1970 .....Ard Schenk, Netherlands	2002 ....Jochem Uytdehaage, Neth.
1932 .....Ivar Ballangrud, Norway	1971 .....Ard Schenk, Netherlands	2003 ....Gianni Romme, Netherlands
1933 .....Hans Engnestangen, Nor.	1972 .....Ard Schenk, Netherlands	2004 .....Chad Hedrick, U.S.
1934 .....Bernt Evensen, Norway	1973 .....Göran Claeson, Sweden	
1935 .....Michael Staksrud, Nor.	1974 .....Sten Stensen, Norway	

WOMEN

1936 .....Kit Klein, U.S.	1965 .....Inga Artamonova, USSR	1987 .....Karin Kania, GDR
1937 .....Laila Schou Nilsen, Nor.	1966 .....Valentina Stenina, USSR	1988 .....Karin Kania, GDR
1938 .....Laila Schou Nilsen, Nor.	1967 .....Stien Kaiser, Netherlands	1989 .....Constanze Moser, GDR
1939 .....Verné Lesche, Finland	1968 .....Stien Kaiser, Netherlands	1990 .....Jacqueline Börner, GDR
1947 .....Verné Lesche, Finland	1969 .....Lasma Kauniste, USSR	1991 .....Gunda Kleemann, Ger.
1948 .....Maria Isakova, USSR	1970 .....Atje Keulen-Deelstra, Neth.	1992 .....Gunda Niemann-Kleemann, Germany
1949 .....Maria Isakova, USSR	1971 .....Nina Statkevich, USSR	
1950 .....Maria Isakova, USSR	1972 .....Atje Keulen-Deelstra, Neth.	1993 .....Gunda Niemann, Germany
1951 .....Eevi Huttunen, Finland	1973 .....Atje Keulen-Deelstra, Neth.	1994 .....Emese Hunyady, Austria
1952 .....Lidia Selikhova, USSR	1974 .....Atje Keulen-Deelstra, Neth.	1995 .....Gunda Niemann, Germany
1953 ....Khalida Shchegoleeva, USSR	1975 .....Karin Kessow, GDR	1996 .....Gunda Niemann, Germany
1954 .....Lidia Selikhova, USSR	1976 .....Sylvia Burka, Canada	1997 .....Gunda Niemann, Germany
1955 .....Rimma Zhukova, USSR	1977 .....Vera Bryndzej, USSR	1997 .....Gunda Niemann, Germany
1956 .....Sofia Kondakova, USSR	1978 .....Tatiana Averina, USSR	1998 .....Gunda Niemann, Germany
1957 .....Inga Artamonova, USSR	1979 .....Beth Heiden, U.S.	1999 .....Gunda Niemann, Germany
1958 .....Inga Artamonova, USSR	1980 .....Natalia Petruseva, USSR	2000 .....Claudia Pechstein, Ger.
1959 .....Tamara Rylova, USSR	1981 .....Natalia Petruseva, USSR	2001 .....Anni Friesinger, Germany
1960 .....Valentina Stenina, USSR	1982 .....Karin Busch, GDR	2002 .....Anni Friesinger, Germany
1961 .....Valentina Stenina, USSR	1983 .....Andrea Schöne, GDR	2003 .....Cindy Klassen, Canada
1962 .....Inga Artamonova, USSR	1984 .....Karin Enke-Busch, GDR	2004 .....Renate Groenewold, Neth
1963 .....Lidia Skoblikova, USSR	1985 .....Andrea Schöne, GDR	
1964 .....Lidia Skoblikova, USSR	1986 .....Karin Kania-Enke, GDR	

Squash

National Men's Champions

HARD BALL		HARD BALL *(Cont.)*		SOFT BALL	
Year	**Champion**	**Year**	**Champion**	**Year**	**Champion**
1907	John A. Miskey	1959	Benjamin H. Heckscher	1983	Kenton Jernigan
1908	John A. Miskey	1960	G. Diehl Mateer Jr.	1984	Kenton Jernigan
1909	William L. Freeland	1961	Henri R. Salaun	1985	Kenton Jernigan
1910	John A. Miskey	1962	Samuel P. Howe III	1986	Darius Pandole
1911	Francis S. White	1963	Benjamin H.	1987	Richard Hashim
1912	Constantine Hutchins		Heckscher	1988	John Phelan
1913	Morton L. Newhall	1964	Ralph E. Howe	1989	Will Carlin
1914	Constantine Hutchins	1965	Stephen T. Vehslage	1990	Syed Jafry
1915	Stanley W. Pearson	1966	Victor Niederhoffer	1991	Hector Barragan
1916	Stanley W. Pearson	1967	Samuel P. Howe III	1992	Phil Yarrow
1917	Stanley W. Pearson	1968	Colin Adair	1993	Phil Yarrow
1918–19	No tournament	1969	Anil Nayar	1994	Roberto Rosales
1920	Charles C. Peabody	1970	Anil Nayar	1995	A. Martin Clark
1921	Stanley W. Pearson	1971	Colin Adair	1996	Mohsen Mir
1922	Stanley W. Pearson	1972	Victor Niederhoffer	1997	A. Martin Clark
1923	Stanley W. Pearson	1973	Victor Niederhoffer	1998	A. Martin Clark
1924	Gerald Roberts	1974	Victor Niederhoffer	1999	David McNeely
1925	W. Palmer Dixon	1975	Victor Niederhoffer	2000	A. Martin Clark
1926	W. Palmer Dixon	1976	Peter Briggs	2001	Damian Walker
1927	Myles Baker	1977	Thomas E. Page	2002	Damian Walker
1928	Herbert N. Rawlins Jr.	1978	Michael Desaulniers	2003	Preston Quick
1929	J. Lawrence Pool	1979	Mario Sanchez	2004	Preston Quick
1930	Herbert N. Rawlins Jr.	1980	Michael Desaulniers		
1931	J. Lawrence Pool	1981	Mark Alger		
1932	Beckman H. Pool	1982	John Nimick		
1933	Beckman H. Pool	1983	Kenton Jernigan		
1934	Neil J. Sullivan II	1984	Kenton Jernigan		
1935	Donald Strachan	1987	Frank J. Stanley IV		
1936	Germain G. Glidden	1988	Scott Dulmage		
1937	Germain G. Glidden	1989	Rodolfo Rodriquez		
1938	Germain G. Glidden	1990	Hector Barragan		
1939	Donald Strachan	1991	Hector Barragan		
1940	A. Willing Patterson	1992	Hector Barragan		
1941	Charles M.P. Britton	1985	Kenton Jernigan		
1942	Charles M.P. Britton	1986	Hugh LaBossier		
1943–45	No tournament	1993	Hector Barragan		
1946	Charles M.P. Britton	1994	Hector Barragan		
1947	Charles M.P. Britton	1995	W. Keen Butcher		
1948	Stanley W. Pearson Jr.	1996	W. Keen Butcher		
1949	H. Hunter Lott Jr.	1997	Rob Hill		
1950	Edward J. Hahn	1998	Rob Hill		
1951	Edward J. Hahn	1999	Rob Hill		
1952	Harry B. Conlon	2000	Thomas Harrity		
1953	Ernest Howard	2001	Rob Hill		
1954	G. Diehl Mateer Jr.	2002	Gary Waite		
1955	Henri R. Salaun	2003	Thomas Harrity		
1956	G. Diehl Mateer Jr.	2004	Thomas Harrity		
1957	Henri R. Salaun				
1958	Henri R. Salaun				

National Women's Champions

HARD BALL		HARD BALL *(Cont.)*		SOFT BALL	
Year	**Champion**	**Year**	**Champion**	**Year**	**Champion**
1928	Eleanora Sears	1965	Joyce Davenport	1983	Alicia McConnell
1929	Margaret Howe	1966	Betty Meade	1984	Julie Harris
1930	Hazel Wightman	1967	Betty Meade	1985	Sue Clinch
1931	Ruth Banks	1968	Betty Meade	1986	Julie Harris
1932	Margaret Howe	1969	Joyce Davenport	1987	Diana Staley
1933	Susan Noel	1970	Nina Moyer	1988	Sara Luther
1934	Margaret Howe	1971	Carol Thesieres	1989	Nancy Gengler
1935	Margot Lumb	1972	Nina Moyer	1990	Joyce Maycock
1936	Anne Page	1973	Gretchen Spruance	1991	Ellie Pierce
1937	Anne Page	1974	Gretchen Spruance	1992	Demer Holleran
1938	Cecile Bowes	1975	Ginny Akabane	1993	Demer Holleran
1939	Anne Page	1976	Gretchen Spruance	1994	Demer Holleran
1940	Cecile Bowes	1977	Gretchen Spruance	1995	Ellie Pierce
1941	Cecile Bowes	1978	Gretchen Spruance	1996	Demer Holleran
1942–46	No tournament	1979	Heather McKay	1997	Demer Holleran
1947	Anne Page Homer	1980	Barbara Maltby	1998	Latasha Khan
1948	Cecile Bowes	1981	Barbara Maltby	1999	Demer Holleran
1949	Janet Morgan	1982	Alicia McConnell	2000	Latasha Khan
1950	Betty Howe	1983	Alicia McConnell	2001	Shabana Khan
1951	Jane Austin	1984	Alicia McConnell	2002	Latasha Khan
1952	Margaret Howe	1985	Alicia McConnell	2003	Latasha Khan
1953	Margaret Howe	1986	Alicia McConnell	2004	Latasha Khan
1954	Lois Dilks	1987	Alicia McConnell		
1955	Janet Morgan	1988	Alicia McConnell		
1956	Betty Howe Constable	1986	Alicia McConnell		
1957	Betty Howe Constable	1987	Alicia McConnell		
1958	Betty Howe Constable	1988	Alicia McConnell		
1959	Betty Howe Constable	1989	Demer Holleran		
1960	Margaret Varner	1990	Demer Holleran		
1961	Margaret Varner	1991	Demer Holleran		
1962	Margaret Varner	1992	Demer Holleran		
1963	Margaret Varner	1993	Demer Holleran		
1964	Ann Wetzel	1994	Demer Holleran		

Note: Tournament not held since 1994.

YET ANOTHER SIGN OF THE APOCALYPSE

*Gatorade is planning to introduce an
"ESPN-flavored" drink.*

Ironman World Championship

Year	MEN Winner	Time	Year	WOMEN Winner	Time
1978	Gordon Haller	11:46	1978	No finishers	
1979	Tom Warren	11:15:56	1979	Lyn Lemaire	12:55
1980	Dave Scott	9:24:33	1980	Robin Beck	11:21:24
1981	John Howard	9:38:29	1981	Linda Sweeney	12:00:32
1982	Scott Tinley	9:19:41	1982	Kathleen McCartney	11:09:40
1982	Dave Scott	9:08:23	1982	Julie Leach	10:54:08
1983	Dave Scott	9:05:57	1983	Sylviane Puntous	10:43:36
1984	Dave Scott	8:54:20	1984	Sylviane Puntous	10:25:13
1985	Scott Tinley	8:50:54	1985	Joanne Ernst	10:25:22
1986	Dave Scott	8:28:37	1986	Paula Newby-Fraser	9:49:14
1987	Dave Scott	8:34:13	1987	Erin Baker	9:35:25
1988	Scott Molina	8:31:00	1988	Paula Newby-Fraser	9:01:01
1989	Mark Allen	8:09:15	1989	Paula Newby-Fraser	9:00:56
1990	Mark Allen	8:28:17	1990	Erin Baker	9:13:42
1991	Mark Allen	8:18:32	1991	Paula Newby-Fraser	9:07:52
1992	Mark Allen	8:09:09	1992	Paula Newby-Fraser	8:55:29
1993	Mark Allen	8:07:46	1993	Paula Newby-Fraser	8:58:23
1994	Greg Welch	8:20:27	1994	Paula Newby-Fraser	9:20:14
1995	Mark Allen	8:20:34	1995	Karen Smyers	9:16:46
1996	Luc Van Lierde	8:04:08	1996	Paula Newby-Fraser	9:06:49
1997	Thomas Hellriegel	8:33:01	1997	Heather Fuhr	9:31:43
1998	Peter Reid	8:24:20	1998	Natascha Badmann	9:24:16
1999	Luc Van Lierde	8:17:17	1999	Lori Bowden	9:13:02
2000	Peter Reid	8:21:01	2000	Natascha Badmann	9:26:17
2001	Tim DeBoom	8:31:18	2001	Natascha Badmann	9:28:37
2002	Tim DeBoom	8:29:56	2002	Natascha Badmann	9:07:54
2003	Peter Reid	8:22:35	2003	Lori Bowden	9:11:55

Note:The Ironman Championship was contested twice in 1982.
Sites: Waikiki Beach (1978–79); Ala Moana Park (1980); Kailua-Kona (since 1981).

U.S. Triathlon National Champions*

Year	MEN Winner	Year	MEN Winner	Year	WOMEN Winner	Year	WOMEN (CONT.) Winner
1984	Scott Molina	1994	Scott Molina	1984	Beth Mitchell	1994	Karen Smyers
1985	Scott Molina	1995	Jeff Devlin	1985	L. Buchanan	1995	Karen Smyers
1986	Scott Molina	1996	Jeff Devlin	1986	K. Hanssen	1996	Susan Latshaw
1987	Mike Pigg	1997	C. Wydoff	1987	K. Hanssen	1997	Sian Welch
1988	Mike Pigg	1998	Hunter Kemper	1988	C. Kaushansky	1998	Siri Lindley
1989	Ken Glah	1999	Hunter Kemper	1989	Jan Ripple	1999	Barb Lindquist
1990	Scott Molina	2000	Marcel Viffian	1990	Karen Smyers	2000	Joanna Zeiger
1991	Mike Pigg	2001	Hunter Kemper	1991	Karen Smyers	2001	Karen Smyers
1992	Mike Pigg	2002	Seth Wealing	1992	Karen Smyers	2002	Barb Lindquist
1993	Bill Braun	2003	Hunter Kemper	1993	Karen Smyers	2003	Laura Reback

*Olympic distances: 1.5 km swim, 40km bike, 10km run.

Volleyball

World Champions
MEN

Year	Winner	Runner-up	Site
1949	Soviet Union	Czechoslovakia	Prague
1952	Soviet Union	Czechoslovakia	Moscow
1956	Czechoslovakia	Soviet Union	Paris
1960	Soviet Union	Czechoslovakia	Rio de Janeiro
1962	Soviet Union	Czechoslovakia	Moscow
1966	Czechoslovakia	Romania	Prague
1970	East Germany	Bulgaria	Sofia, Bulgaria
1974	Poland	Soviet Union	Mexico City
1978	Soviet Union	Italy	Rome
1982	Soviet Union	Brazil	Buenos Aires
1986	United States	Soviet Union	Paris
1990	Italy	Cuba	Rio de Janeiro
1994	Italy	Netherlands	Athens
1998	Italy	Yugoslavia	Tokyo
2002	Brazil	Russia	Buenos Aires

World Champions (Cont.)

WOMEN

Year	Winner	Runner-up	Site
1952	Soviet Union	Poland	Moscow
1956	Soviet Union	Romania	Paris
1960	Soviet Union	Japan	Rio de Janeiro
1962	Japan	Soviet Union	Moscow
1966	Japan	United States	Prague
1970	Soviet Union	Japan	Sofia, Bulgaria
1974	Japan	Soviet Union	Mexico City
1978	Cuba	Japan	Rome
1982	China	Peru	Lima, Peru
1986	China	Cuba	Prague
1990	Soviet Union	China	Beijing
1994	Cuba	Brazil	Sao Paulo, Brazil
1998	Cuba	China	Osaka, Japan
2002	Italy	United States	Berlin

U.S. Men's Open Champions—Gold Division

1928	Germantown, PA YMCA
1929	Hyde Park YMCA, IL
1930	Hyde Park YMCA, IL
1931	San Antonio, TX YMCA
1932	San Antonio, TX YMCA
1933	Houston, TX YMCA
1934	Houston, TX YMCA
1935	Houston, TX YMCA
1936	Houston, TX YMCA
1937	Duncan YMCA, IL
1938	Houston, TX YMCA
1939	Houston, TX YMCA
1940	Los Angeles AC, CA
1941	North Ave. YMCA, IL
1942	North Ave. YMCA, IL
1943–44	No championships
1945	North Ave. YMCA, IL
1946	Pasadena, CA YMCA
1947	North Ave. YMCA, IL
1948	Hollywood, CA YMCA
1949	Downtown YMCA, CA
1950	Long Beach, CA YMCA
1951	Hollywood, CA YMCA
1952	Hollywood, CA YMCA
1953	Hollywood, CA YMCA
1954	Stockton, CA YMCA
1955	Stockton, CA YMCA
1956	Hollywood, CA YMCA Stars
1957	Hollywood, CA YMCA Stars
1958	Hollywood, CA YMCA Stars
1959	Hollywood, CA YMCA Stars
1960	Westside JCC, CA
1961	Hollywood, CA YMCA
1962	Hollywood, CA YMCA
1963	Hollywood, CA YMCA
1964	Hollywood, CA YMCA Stars
1965	Westside JCC, CA
1966	Sand & Sea Club, CA
1967	Fresno, CA VBC
1968	Westside JCC, Los Angeles, CA
1969	Los Angeles, CA YMCA
1970	Chart House, San Diego
1971	Santa Monica, CA YMCA
1972	Chart House, San Diego
1973	Chuck's Steak, Los Angeles
1974	UC Santa Barbara, CA
1975	Chart House, San Diego
1976	Malibu, Los Angeles
1977	Chuck's, Santa Barbara
1978	Chuck's, Los Angeles
1979	Nautilus, Long Beach CA
1980	Olympic Club, San Francisco
1981	Nautilus, Long Beach CA
1982	Chuck's, Los Angeles
1983	Nautilus Pacifica, CA
1984	Nautilus Pacifica, CA
1985	Molten/SSI Torrance, CA
1986	Molten, Torrance, CA
1987	Molten, Torrance, CA
1988	Molten, Torrance, CA
1989	Not held
1990	Nike, Carson, CA
1991	Offshore, Woodland Hills, CA
1992	Creole Six Pack, Elmhurst, NY
1993	Asics, Huntington Beach, CA
1994	Asics/Paul Mitchell, Hunt. Beach, CA
1995	Shakter, Belagarad, Ukraine
1996	POL-AM-VBC, Brooklyn, NY
1997	Canuck Stuff VBC, Calgary
1998	T-Town, Tulsa, OK
1999	Los Angeles Athletic Club,
2000	Paul Mitchell, Huntington Beach, CA
2001	Los Angeles Athletic Club,
2002	Paul Mitchell, Huntington Beach, CA
2003	Paul Mitchell, Huntington Beach, CA
2004	Bameso-l Dig, Dominican Republic

U.S. Women's Open Champions—Gold Division

1949	Eagles, Houston	1979	Mavericks, Los Angeles
1950	Voit #1, Santa Monica, CA	1980	NAVA, Fountain Valley, CA
1951	Eagles, Houston	1981	Utah State, Logan, UT
1952	Voit #1, Santa Monica, CA	1982	Monarchs, Hilo, HI
1953	Voit #1, Los Angeles	1983	Syntex, Stockton, CA
1954	Houstonettes, Houston, TX	1984	Chrysler, Palo Alto, CA
1955	Mariners, Santa Monica, CA	1985	Merrill Lynch, AZ
1956	Mariners, Santa Monica, CA	1986	Merrill Lynch, AZ
1957	Mariners, Santa Monica, CA	1987	Chrysler, Pleasanton, CA
1958	Mariners, Santa Monica, CA	1988	Chrysler, Hayward, CA
1959	Mariners, Santa Monica, CA	1989	Plymouth, Hayward, CA
1960	Mariners, Santa Monica, CA	1990	Plymouth, Hayward, CA
1961	Breakers, Long Beach, CA	1991	Fitness, Champaign, IL
1962	Shamrocks, Long Beach, CA	1992	Nick's Kronies, Chicago
1963	Shamrocks, Long Beach, CA	1993	Nick's Fishmarket, Chicago
1964	Shamrocks, Long Beach, CA	1994	Nick's Fishmarket, Chicago
1965	Shamrocks, Long Beach, CA	1995	Kittleman/Branfield's/Nick's, Chi.
1966	Renegades, Los Angeles	1996	Pure Texas Nuts, Austin, TX
1967	Shamrocks, Long Beach, CA	1997	Kittleman/Branfield's/Nick's, Chi.
1968	Shamrocks, Long Beach, CA	1998	The Exterminators, Barrington, IL
1969	Shamrocks, Long Beach, CA	1999	Dominican Dream Team, Santo Domingo, D.R.
1970	Shamrocks, Long Beach, CA	2000	Dominican Dream Team II, Santo Domingo, D.R.
1971	Renegades, Los Angeles	2001	Dominican Dream Team III, Santo Domingo, D.R.
1972	E Pluribus Unum, Houston		
1973	E Pluribus Unum, Houston	2002	Team Trim, Long Beach, CA
1974	Renegades, Los Angeles	2003	The Exterminators, Barrington, IL
1975	Adidas, Norwalk, CA	2004	U.S.A.-A2, Barrington, IL
1976	Pasadena, TX		
1977	Spoilers, Hermosa, CA		
1978	Nick's, Los Angeles		

Wrestling

United States National Champions
1983

FREESTYLE		FREESTYLE (Cont.)		GRECO-ROMAN (Cont.)	
105.5	Rich Salamone	220	Greg Gibson	136.5	Dan Mello
114.5	Joe Gonzales	Hvy	Bruce Baumgartner	149.5	Jim Martinez
125.5	Joe Corso	Team	Sunkist Kids	163	James Andre
136.5	Rich Dellagatta*			180.5	Steve Goss
149.5	Bill Hugent	**GRECO-ROMAN**		198	Steve Fraser*
163	Lee Kemp	105.5	T.J. Jones	220	Dennis Koslowski
180.5	Chris Campbell	114.5	Mark Fuller	Hvy	No champion
198	Pete Bush	125.5	Rob Hermann	Team	Minn. Wrestling Club

1984

FREESTYLE		FREESTYLE (Cont.)		GRECO-ROMAN (Cont.)	
105.5	Rich Salamone	220	Harold Smith	149.5	Jim Martinez*
114.5	Charlie Heard	Hvy	Bruce Baumgartner	163	John Matthews
125.5	Joe Corso	Team	Sunkist Kids	180.5	Tom Press
136.5	Rich Dellagatta*			198	Mike Houck
149.5	Andre Metzger	**GRECO-ROMAN**		220	No champion
163	Dave Schultz*	105.5	T.J. Jones	Hvy	No champion
180.5	Mark Schultz	114.5	Mark Fuller	Team	Adirondack 3-Style, WA
198	Steve Fraser	136.5	Dan Mello		

1985

FREESTYLE		FREESTYLE (Cont.)		GRECO-ROMAN (Cont.)	
105.5	Tim Vanni	220	Greg Gibson	136.5	Buddy Lee
114.5	Jim Martin	286	Bruce Baumgartner	149.5	Jim Martinez
125.5	Charlie Heard	Team	Sunkist Kids	163	David Butler
136.5	Darryl Burley			180.5	Chris Catallo
149.5	Bill Nugent*	**GRECO-ROMAN**		198	Mike Houck
163	Kenny Monday	105.5	T.J. Jones	220	Greg Gibson
180.5	Mike Sheets	114.5	Mark Fuller	286	Dennis Koslowski
198	Mark Schultz	125.5	Eric Seward*	Team	U.S. Marine Corps

United States National Champions (Cont.)

1986

FREESTYLE

105.5	Rich Salamone
114.5	Joe Gonzales
125.5	Kevin Darkus
136.5	John Smith
149.5	Andre Metzger*
163	Dave Schultz
180.5	Mark Schultz
198	Jim Scherr
220	Dan Severn

FREESTYLE (Cont.)

286	Bruce Baumgartner
Team	Sunkist Kids (Div. I)
	Hawkeye Wrestling Club (Div. II)

GRECO-ROMAN

105.5	Eric Wetzel
114.5	Shawn Sheldon
125.5	Anthony Amado

GRECO-ROMAN (Cont.)

136.5	Frank Famiano
149.5	Jim Martinez
163	David Butler*
180.5	Darryl Gholar
198	Derrick Waldroup
220	Dennis Koslowski
286	Duane Koslowski
Team	U.S. Marine Corps (Div. I)
	U.S. Navy (Div. II)

1987

FREESTYLE

105.5	Takashi Irie
114.5	Mitsuru Sato
125.5	Barry Davis
136.5	Takumi Adachi
149.5	Andre Metzger
163	Dave Schultz*
180.5	Mark Schultz
198	Jim Scherr
220	Bill Scherr

FREESTYLE (Cont.)

286	Bruce Baumgartner
Team	Sunkist Kids (Div. I)
	Team Foxcatcher (Div. II)

GRECO-ROMAN

105.5	Eric Wetzel
114.5	Shawn Sheldon
125.5	Eric Seward
136.5	Frank Famiano

GRECO-ROMAN (Cont.)

149.5	Jim Martinez
163	David Butler
180.5	Chris Catallo
198	Derrick Waldroup*
220	Dennis Koslowski
286	Duane Koslowski
Team	U.S. Marine Corp (Div. I)
	U.S. Army (Div. II)

1988

FREESTYLE

105.5	Tim Vanni
114.5	Joe Gonzales
125.5	Kevin Darkus
136.5	John Smith*
149.5	Nate Carr
163	Kenny Monday
180.5	Dave Schultz
198	Melvin Douglas III
220	Bill Scherr

FREESTYLE (Cont.)

286	Bruce Baumgartner
Team	Sunkist Kids (Div. I)
	Team Foxcatcher (Div. II)

GRECO-ROMAN

105.5	T.J. Jones
114.5	Shawn Sheldon
125.5	Gogi Parseghian*
136.5	Dalen Wasmund

GRECO-ROMAN (Cont.)

149.5	Craig Pollard
163	Tony Thomas
180.5	Darryl Gholar
198	Mike Carolan
220	Dennis Koslowski
286	Duane Koslowski
Team	U.S. Marine Corps (Div. I)
	Sunkist Kids (Div. II)

1989

FREESTYLE

105.5	Tim Vanni
114.5	Zeke Jones
125.5	Brad Penrith
136.5	John Smith
149.5	Nate Carr
163	Rob Koll
180.5	Rico Chiapparelli
198	Jim Scherr*
220	Bill Scherr

FREESTYLE (Cont.)

286	Bruce Baumgartner
Team	Sunkist Kids (Div. I)
	Team Foxcatcher (Div. II)

GRECO-ROMAN

105.5	Lew Dorrance
114.5	Mark Fuller
125.5	Gogi Parseghian
136.5	Isaac Anderson

GRECO-ROMAN (Cont.)

149.5	Andy Seras*
163	David Butler
180.5	John Morgan
198	Michial Foy
220	Steve Lawson
286	Craig Pittman
Team	U.S. Marine Corps (Div. I)
	Jets USA (Div. II)

1990

FREESTYLE

105.5	Rob Eiter
114.5	Zeke Jones
125,5	Joe Melchiore
136.5	John Smith
149.5	Nate Carr
163	Rob Koll
180.5	Royce Alger
198	Chris Campbell*
220	Bill Scherr

FREESTYLE (Cont.)

286	Bruce Baumgartner
Team	Sunkist Kids (Div. I)
	Team Foxcatcher (Div. II)

GRECO-ROMAN

105.5	Lew Dorrance
114.5	Sam Henson
125.5	Mark Pustelnik
136.5	Isaac Anderson

GRECO-ROMAN (Cont.)

149.5	Andy Seras
163	David Butler
180.5	Derrick Waldroup
198	Randy Couture*
220	Chris Tironi
286	Matt Ghaffari
Team	Jets USA (Div. I)
	California Jets (Div. II)

*Outstanding wrestler.

United States National Champions (Cont.)

1991

FREESTYLE
105.5 ....Tim Vanni
114.5 ....Zeke Jones
125.5 ....Brad Penrith
136.5 ....John Smith*
149.5 ....Townsend Saunders
163 ....Kenny Monday
180.5 ....Kevin Jackson
198 ....Chris Campbell
220 ....Mark Coleman

FREESTYLE (Cont.)
286 ....Bruce Baumgartner
Team ....Sunkist Kids (Div. I)
          Jets USA (Div. II)

GRECO-ROMAN
105.5 ....Eric Wetzel
114.5 ....Shawn Sheldon
125.5 ....Frank Famiano
136.5 ....Buddy Lee

GRECO-ROMAN (Cont.)
149.5 ....Andy Seras
163 ....Gordy Morgan
180.5 ....John Morgan*
198 ....Michial Foy
220 ....Dennis Koslowski
286 ....Craig Pittman
Team ....Jets USA (Div. I)
          Sunkist Kids (Div. II)

1992

FREESTYLE
105.5 ....Rob Eiter
114.5 ....Jack Griffin
125.5 ....Kendall Cross*
136.5 ....John Fisher
149.5 ....Matt Demaray
163 ....Greg Elinsky
180.5 ....Royce Alger
198 ....Dan Chaid
220 ....Bill Scherr

FREESTYLE (Cont.)
286 ....Bruce Baumgartner
Team ....Sunkist Kids (Div. I)
          Team Foxcatcher (Div. II)

GRECO-ROMAN
105.5 ....Eric Wetzel
114.5 ....Mark Fuller
125.5 ....Dennis Hall
136.5 ....Buddy Lee*

GRECO-ROMAN (Cont.)
149.5 ....Rodney Smith
163 ....Travis West
180.5 ....John Morgan
198 ....Michial Foy
220 ....Dennis Koslowski
286 ....Matt Ghaffari
Team ....NY Athletic Club (Div. I)
          Sunkist Kids (Div. II)

1993

FREESTYLE
105.5 ....Rob Eiter
114.5 ....Zeke Jones
125.5 ....Brad Penrith
136.5 ....Tom Brands
149.5 ....Matt Demaray
163 ....Dave Schultz*
180.5 ....Kevin Jackson
198 ....Melvin Douglas
220 ....Kirk Trost

FREESTYLE (Cont.)
286 ....Bruce Baumgartner
Team ....Sunkist Kids (Div. I)
          Team Foxcatcher (Div. II)

GRECO-ROMAN
105.5 ....Eric Wetzel
114.5 ....Shawn Sheldon
125.5 ....Dennis Hall*
136.5 ....Shon Lewis

GRECO-ROMAN (Cont.)
149.5 ....Andy Seras
163 ....Gordy Morgan
180.5 ....Dan Henderson
198 ....Randy Couture
220 ....James Johnson
286 ....Matt Ghaffari
Team ....NY Athletic Club (Div. I)
          Sunkist Kids (Div. II)

1994

FREESTYLE
105.5 ....Tim Vanni
114.5 ....Zeke Jones
125.5 ....Terry Brands
136.5 ....Tom Brands
149.5 ....Matt Demaray
163 ....Dave Schultz
180.5 ....Royce Alger
198 ....Melvin Douglas
220 ....Mark Kerr

FREESTYLE (Cont.)
286 ....Bruce Baumgartner*
Team ....Sunkist Kids (Div. I)
          Team Foxcatcher (Div. II)

GRECO-ROMAN
105.5 ....Isaac Ramaswamy
114.5 ....Shawn Sheldon
125.5 ....Dennis Hall
136.5 ....Shon Lewis

GRECO-ROMAN (Cont.)
149.5 ....Andy Seras*
163 ....Gordy Morgan
180.5 ....Dan Henderson
198 ....Derrick Waldroup

GRECO-ROMAN (Cont.)
220 ....James Johnson
286 ....Matt Ghaffari
Team ....Armed Forces (Div. I)
          NY Athletic Club (Div. II)

1995

FREESTYLE
105.5 ....Rob Eiter
114.5 ....Lou Rosselli
125.5 ....Kendall Cross*
136.5 ....Tom Brands
149.5 ....Matt Demaray
163 ....Dave Schultz
180.5 ....Kevin Jackson
198 ....Melvin Douglas
220 ....Kurt Angle

FREESTYLE (Cont.)
286 ....Bruce Baumgartner
Team ....Sunkist Kids (Div. I)
          Team Foxcatcher (Div. II)

GRECO-ROMAN
105.5 ....Isaac Ramaswamy
114.5 ....Shawn Sheldon
125.5 ....Dennis Hall*
136.5 ....Van Fronhofer

GRECO-ROMAN (Cont.)
149.5 ....Heath Sims
163 ....Matt Lindland
180.5 ....Marty Morgan
198 ....Michial Foy
220 ....James Johnson
286 ....Rulon Gardner
Team ....Armed Forces (Div. I)
          Sunkist Kids (Div. II)

*Outstanding wrestler.

United States National Champions *(Cont.)*

1996

FREESTYLE

105.5 ......Rob Eiter
114.5 ......Lou Rosselli
125.5 ......Kendall Cross
136.5 ......Tom Brands
149.5 ......Townsend Saunders
163 ....Kenny Monday
180.5 ......Les Gutches*
198 ....Melvin Douglas
220 ....Kurt Angle

FREESTYLE *(Cont.)*

286 ....Bruce Baumgartner
Team ....Sunkist Kids (Div. I)
............NY Athletic Club (Div. II)

GRECO-ROMAN

105.5 ......Mujaahid Maynard
114.5 ......Shawn Sheldon
125.5 ......Dennis Hall*
136.5 ......Shon Lewis

GRECO-ROMAN *(Cont.)*

149.5 ......Rodney Smith
163 ....Keith Sieracki
180.5 ......Marty Morgan
198 ....Michial Foy
220 ....John Oostendrop
286 ....Matt Ghaffari
Team ....Armed Forces (Div. I)
............Sunkist Kids (Div. II)

1997

FREESTYLE

110 ....Kanamti Soloman
119 ....Zeke Jones
127.75 .....Terry Brands
138.75 .....Carl Kolat
152 ....Lincoln McIlravy*
167.5 ......Dan St. John
187.25 .....Les Gutches
213.75 .....Melvin Douglas

FREESTYLE *(Cont.)*

275.5 ......Tom Erikson
Team ....Sunkist Kids (Div. I)
............NY Athletic Club (Div. II)

GRECO-ROMAN

110 ....Mark Yanagihara
119 ....Broderick Lee
127.75 .....Dennis Hall

GRECO-ROMAN *(Cont.)*

138.75 .....Kevin Bracken
152 ....Chris Saba
167.5 ......Miguel Spencer
187.25 .....Dan Henderson
213.75 .....Randy Couture*
275.5 ......Rulon Gardner
Team ....Armed Forces (Div. I)
............NY Athletic Club (Div. II)

1998

FREESTYLE

119 ....Sam Henson
127.75 .....Tony Purler
138.75 .....Shawn Charles
152 ....Lincoln McIlravy
167.5 ......Steve Marianetti
187.25 .....Les Gutches*
213.75 .....Melvin Douglas

FREESTYLE *(Cont.)*

286 ....Tolly Thompson
Team ....Sunkist Kids (Div. I)
............NY Athletic Club (Div. II)

GRECO-ROMAN

119 ....Shawn Sheldon
127.75 .....Dennis Hall
138.75 .....Shon Lewis

GRECO-ROMAN *(Cont.)*

152 ....Chris Saba
167.5 ......Matt Lindland
187.25 .....Dan Niebuhr*
213.75 .....Jason Klohs
286 ....Matt Ghaffari
Team ....Armed Forces (Div. I)
............Sunkist Kids (Div. II)

1999

FREESTYLE

119 ....Lou Rosselli
127.75 .....Terry Brands
138.75 .....Cary Kolat
152 ....Lincoln McIlravy
167.5 ......Joe Williams
187.25 .....Les Gutches
213.75 .....Dominic Black

FREESTYLE *(Cont.)*

286 ....Stephen Neal*
Team ....Sunkist Kids (Div. I)
............NY Athletic Club (Div. II)

GRECO-ROMAN

119 ....Steven Mays
127.75 .....Dennis Hall
138.75 .....Glen Nieradka

GRECO-ROMAN *(Cont.)*

152 ....David Zuniga
167.5 ......Matt Lindland
187.25 .....Quincey Clark
213.75 .....Randy Couture
286 ....Dremiel Byers*
Team ....Minnesota Storm (Div. I)
............Sunkist Kids (Div. II)

2000

FREESTYLE

119 ....Sammie Henson
127.75 .....Keyy Boumans
138.75 .....Cary Kolat
152 ....Lincoln McIlravy
167.5 ......Brandon Slay*
187.25 .....Les Gutches
213.75 .....Melvin Douglas

FREESTYLE *(Cont.)*

286 ....Kerry McCoy
Team ....Sunkist Kids (Div. I)
............NY Athletic Club (Div. II)

GRECO-ROMAN

119 ....Brandon Paulson
127.75 .....Dennis Hall
138.75 .....Kevin Bracken

GRECO-ROMAN *(Cont.)*

152 ....Heath Sims
167.5 ......Matt Lindland
187.25 .....Quincey Clark*
213.75 .....Jason Gleasman
286 ....Rulon Gardner
Team ....Armed Forces (Div. I)
............Sunkist Kids (Div. II)

*Outstanding wrestler.

United States National Champions (Cont.)

2001

FREESTYLE
119 ....Eric Akin
127.75 .....Eric Guerrero
138.75 .....Bill Zadick
152 ....Ramico Blackmon
167.5 ....Joe Williams
187.25 .....Cael Sanderson*
213.75 .....Dominic Black

FREESTYLE (Cont.)
286 ....Kerry McCoy
Team ....Sunkist Kids (Div. I)
           New York AC (Div. II)

GRECO-ROMAN
119 ....Jeff Cervone
127.75 .....Dennis Hall
138.75 .....Kevin Bracken

GRECO-ROMAN (Cont.)
152 ....Marcel Cooper
167.5 ....Keith Sieracki
187.25 .....Matt Lindland*
213.75 .....Garrett Lowney
286 ....Rulon Gardner
Team ....Army (Div. I)
           Sunkist Kids (Div. II)

2002

FREESTYLE
121 ....Teague Moore
132 ....Eric Guerrero
145.5 ....Bill Zadick
163 ....Joe Williams*
185 ....Cael Sanderson
211.5 ....Tim Hartung
264.5 ....Kerry McCoy

FREESTYLE (Cont.)
Team ....Sunkist Kids (Div. I)
           New York AC (Div. II)

GRECO-ROMAN
121 ....Brandon Paulson
132 ....Glenn Nieradka*
145.5 ....Kevin Bracken

GRECO-ROMAN (Cont.)
163 ....Keith Sieracki
185 ....Ethan Bosch
211.75 .....Garrett Lowney
264.5 ....Dremiel Byers
Team ....Army (Div. I)
           New York AC (Div. II)

2003

FREESTYLE
121 ....Stephen Abas
132 ....Eric Guerrero*
145.5 ....Chris Bono
163 ....Joe Williams
185 ....Cael Sanderson
211.5 ....Daniel Cormier
264.5 ....Kerry McCoy

*Outstanding wrestler.

FREESTYLE (Cont.)
Team ....Sunkist Kids (Div. I)
           Gator WC (Div. II)

GRECO-ROMAN
121 ....Brandon Paulson
132 ....James Gruenwald*
145.5 ....Kevin Bracken

GRECO-ROMAN (Cont.)
163 ....Keith Sieracki
185 ....Brad Vering
211.5 ....Garrett Lowney
264.5 ....Dremiel Byers
Team ....Army (Div. I)
           Air Force (Div. II)

2004

FREESTYLE
121 ....Stephen Abbas
132 ....Eric Guerrero
145.5 ....Jamill Kelly
163 ....Joe Williams
185 ....Lee Fullhart*
211.5 ....Daniel Cormier
264.5 ....Kerry McCoy

*Outstanding wrestler.

FREESTYLE (Cont.)
Team ....Sunkist Kids (Div. I)
           Gator WC (Div. II)

GRECO-ROMAN
121 ....Brandon Paulson
132 ....James Gruenwald
145.5 ....Faruk Sahin

GRECO-ROMAN (Cont.)
163 ....Darryl Christian
185 ....Brad Vering
211.5 ....Justin Ruiz
264.5 ....Dremiel Byers*
Team ....New York AC (Div. I)
           Air Force (Div. II)

Alex the Great

Alex Tsirtsis, a senior at Griffith High in Griffith, Ind., broke the national high school record for consecutive victories with his 221st, at the Hobart Invitational on January 24, 2004. The three-time state champion is ranked No. 2 in the nation at 140 pounds by *Amateur Wrestling News*.

The Sports Market

New Miami Heat big
man Shaquille O'Neal

Market Volatility

Investors continued to be gung-ho for sports-related ventures but, as always, there was no such thing as a sure thing

BY MERRELL NODEN

THE LOS ANGELES Lakers' press release of July 14th began optimistically enough, on a rather forward-looking note: "The Lakers have acquired forward Lamar Odom, forward Caron Butler, forward Brian Grant and a future first-round draft pick from the Miami Heat ... " Then came the real news: " ... for center Shaquille O'Neal."

Only one year after the Laker front office had surrounded O'Neal with a Rushmore of veteran stars including Gary Payton, Karl Malone and Kobe Bryant, the remodeled Laker dynasty was obliterated, flung to the far corners of the basketball universe before it had won a single title. Payton wound up in Boston and the 41-year-old Malone mulled retirement. Coach Phil Jackson, who would have broken Red Auerbach's record of nine career NBA championships if Los Angeles had beaten Detroit in the 2004 finals, also retired. Rudy Tomjanovich took over for Jackson only four days before the big trade. He was left to build a new Laker team around Bryant, whose well-publicized legal dilemma cost him millions in endorsement dollars and more still perhaps in a civil suit still pending.

The Shaq trade and its fallout were the biggest news of the year in sports business. With one trade, the power-shift from West to East—which the Pistons began with their five-game triumph over the Lakers in the finals—was complete, and the fortunes of two teams changed radically. Miami, which had barely finished above .500, became an instant contender in the Eastern Conference, while the once mighty Lakers ... well, the situation is not as dire as it was in Chicago following Michael Jordan's retirement, but the team is definitely in a rebuilding phase.

The Lakers' removal and transcontinental relocation of their cornerstone reinforced the notion that there are no sure things, in sports or in the business of selling sports. In this, SPORTS ILLUSTRATED's 50th year—and ESPN's 25th—the sports world continues to offer tempting, if risky, business opportunities. There is no shortage of rich men willing to lavish money on new teams, like the Charlotte Bobcats of the NBA; on new stadiums, like the two just opened in Philadelphia and

Athens produced a stirring Games, but may face a financial hangover.

those that may soon be springing up all over New York; new networks like College Sports Television; and new pitchmen, like the three Wheaties cover-athletes to emerge from the Olympics, swimmer Michael Phelps, gymnast Carly Patterson and sprinter Justin Gatlin.

Everybody wants in—from a single young football player named Maurice Clarett, who went to court to challenge an NFL rule that requires him to wait three years after high school graduation before entering the NFL draft, to the five big cities competing for the right to host the 2012 Summer Games. Even doctors and hospitals now view sports as a potent advertising tool: According to a front page story in *The New York Times*, competition among medical practices has grown so stiff that some now pay for the right to treat pro athletes, in hopes of using the connection to trumpet their services.

The difference between now and half a century ago is that nobody doubts the investment potential of sports, the vast fortunes they can provide. They should. A study by Robert H. Frank, professor of management and economics at Cornell, called into question the conventional wisdom that college athletic success bolsters alumni donations and attracts better students: Quite the contrary, writes Frank, "There is not a shred of evidence to suggest that cuts in spending on athletics would reduce either donations by alumni or applications."

Indeed, sports are risky business. Ask the people of Greece five years from now what they think of "their" Olympics and they probably won't be singing "Hellas! Hellas!" quite as lustily as they did for those 17 thrilling days in August 2004. That's because the Athens Games cost $9 billion, with $1.5 billion going to security alone. The Greek people will be paying off the debt for years—maybe generations—to come.

Those are scary numbers, sure to winnow the number of cities willing to bid for future Games. (If you doubt it, just ask the citizens of Montreal, who spent years paying for their 1976 Games, and whose Olympic Stadium will stand empty in 2004, following the departure of the beloved Expos, who fled for Washington, D.C., at the end of the baseball season.) Even a huge city like New York, which is one of the five finalists to host the 2012 Games, will have to undertake massive construction projects beforehand. In September, New York City Mayor Michael Bloomberg warned that if the city didn't break ground soon on a new stadium on Manhattan's West Side, it might as well give up hope of getting the Games. The proposed stadium, to cost an estimated $1.4 billion, would become the permanent home of the New York Jets, who were offering to put up $800 million, with the remaining $600 million to come from the city and state coffers. That arrangement drew considerable fire in a city still trying to bounce back economically from the terrorist attacks of September 11, 2001.

And that wasn't the only new stadium being proposed for the New York area. Major League Soccer's MetroStars, whose average crowds of 15,882 (in 2003) have been a poor fit for 80,000-seat Giants Stadium, announced plans to build a soccer-specific stadium in Harrison, N.J. The stadium, which will seat 25,000 and cost $100 million, is expected to open in 2006. In August, the NBA unanimously approved the sale of the New Jersey Nets to a group led by Bruce Ratner, a real estate developer. Ratner plans to move the team to Brooklyn and make it the centerpiece of a $2.5 billion complex of commercial skyscrapers, residential towers and, oh yes, a 19,000-seat basketball arena. The project would occupy 10 acres currently used for storage by the Long Island Railroad.

And up in the Bronx, there was talk—yet again—of building a new stadium for the Yankees. Three years ago Bloomberg's predecessor, Rudy Giuliani, had orchestrated a deal to build an $800 million stadium with a retractable roof in Macombs Dam Park, right across 161st St. from the House that Ruth Built. The cost was to be split by taxpayers and the team. That plan was killed by Bloomberg, who cited the city's budget crunch. Under the new plan, the Yankees would foot the bill for a retro stadium in the same location, with the city and state to kick in an estimated $300 to $400 million for improvements like a new subway stop, a ferry landing and a conference center.

The Yankees also made news for winning their ongoing dispute with Cablevision. The dispute dates to 2002, when Cablevision was the lone cable service of 31 to balk at making the Yankees Entertainment & Sports (YES) Network part of its basic package, proposing instead that it be part of a pricier sports package. YES sued, alleging violations of the Sherman and Clayton Acts. For a time, it seemed the standoff would leave the three million Cablevision subscribers without television access to the Yankees. Mayor Bloomberg and New York state Attorney General Eliot Spitzer stepped in to arrange an interim agreement until the dispute could go to binding arbitration. When it did, in March, it was ruled that Cablevision would have to carry YES as part of its basic programming. But it was not the sweeping victory YES executives had hoped for: YES will receive $1.83 per subscriber, not the $2.00 it had originally demanded. Still, score another one for Yankee owner George Steinbrenner, who owns 60% of YES.

The Yankees' imperious owner aside, anyone who doubts that owning a sports team is a risky investment need only look at the National Hockey League, where owners may reap no profit all season. NHL owners locked out their players just hours after their old contract expired, at 12:01 a.m. on September 16, 2004.

The dispute revolved, as these things often do, around revenue sharing. Claiming that the league had lost $1.8 billion over the past 10 years, NHL commissioner Gary Bettman warned that management would not agree to a deal that didn't include some clearly specified relationship between team revenues and player salaries. The figure of $35 million was proposed as a reasonable cap for each team. NHLPA Executive Director Bob Goodenow answered that the players are "not prepared to entertain a salary cap in any way, shape, measure or form," and the lockout was on. Bettman warned that it might well last the entire season.

That news resulted in significant layoffs in the league's offices in Toronto, New York and Montreal. It also left players scrambling to find somewhere to play. Among the options were the revived World Hockey Association, scheduled to open the season on Oct. 29; a six-team circuit called the Original Stars Hockey League that will feature four-on-four play; the American Hockey League, a minor league whose season begins Oct. 13; and pro leagues in Europe.

Also locked out, though for different reasons, was Maurice Clarett, who two years ago, as a freshman, led Ohio State to the national football title. Clarett's star could scarcely have been brighter following that game—he could have had no idea how

Jarome Iginla and the Calgary Flames played in what could be the last Stanley Cup for a while.

LOU CAPOZZOLA

quickly things would sour. When a joint Ohio State and NCAA investigation determined that he had received improper benefits from a family friend and then lied about it to investigators, Clarett was suspended for the 2003 Ohio State season. He decided to enter the NFL draft, hoping to challenge the NFL's rule requiring players to wait three years following their high school graduation before entering the draft.

U.S. District Judge Shira Scheindlin ruled first and found that the legal issues were so clearly in Clarett's favor that a trial wasn't even necessary. The NFL appealed and won. Twice the Supreme Court turned down Clarett's appeal. While he awaited the results of yet another appeal, Clarett was variously rumored to be working out in California or Texas, and to be contemplating playing in the CFL. If he ultimately wins the case, Clarett could win millions from the NFL. For now, his future was cloudy at best.

One young athlete with a spectacularly bright future is Freddy Adu, the 15-year-old who moved to the U.S. from Ghana at age 7. Adu became the youngest pro athlete in U.S. team sports in more than a century when he signed a four-year contract with Major League Soccer and suited up for D.C. United. Though Adu may have fallen a little short of the ridiculous expectations some had for him, surely he justified his league-high salary of $500,000 by adding an average of 8,000 fans at each of the venues United visited.

MLS also announced that two new franchises would join the league next year, one in Salt Lake City and the other in Los Angeles. The Salt Lake City team, Real Salt Lake, will be run by former NBA executive Dave Checketts and hopes to take draw from both Utah's rapidly growing Hispanic population and its highest per-capita soccer participation rate of any U.S. state. The L.A. team gives the league an instant intra-city rivalry, because MLS already has a team in Los Angeles, the Galaxy. Mexican tycoon Jorge Vergara will own the new L.A. outfit, called Chivas USA, and it will be a North-of-the-border version of his venerable Mexican club Chivas of Guadalajara. The two new teams bring the total of MLS teams to 12.

No one could say what fate awaited the nine-year-old league, but then again, who would have guessed, when the Raiders left Los Angeles in 1995, that nine years later the country's second biggest market would have not one but two soccer franchises and still no football?

Sports business, it seems, is as unpredicable as sport itself.

Baseball Directory

Major League Baseball
Address: 245 Park Avenue
             New York, NY 10167
Telephone: (212) 931-7800
Commissioner: Bud Selig
Chief Operating Officer: Robert DuPuy
Senior VP, Public Relations: Richard Levin
www.majorleaguebaseball.com

Major League Baseball Players Association
Address: 12 East 49th Street, 24th Floor
             New York, NY 10017
Telephone: (212) 826-0808
Executive Director: Donald Fehr
Director of Communications: Greg Bouris
Director of Licensing: Judy Heeter
www.bigleaguers.com

Anaheim Angels
Address: P.O. Box 2000
             Anaheim, CA 92803
Telephone: (714) 940-2000
Stadium (Capacity): Angel Stadium
of Anaheim (45,050)
Owner: Arturo Moreno
General Manager: Bill Stoneman
Manager: Mike Scioscia
Vice President of Communications: Tim Mead
www.angelsbaseball.com

Arizona Diamondbacks
Address: 401 East Jefferson Street
             Phoenix, AZ 85004
Telephone: (602) 462-6500
Stadium (Capacity): Bank One Ballpark (49,033)
CEO: Jeff Moorad
General Manager: Joe Garagiola Jr.
Manager: Al Pedrique
Director of Public Relations: Mike Swanson
www.azdiamondbacks.com

Atlanta Braves
Address: P.O. Box 4064
             Atlanta, GA 30302
Telephone: (404) 522-7630
Stadium (Capacity): Turner Field (50,091)
Vice Chrmn./Sr. Advisor of Time Warner/AOL: Ted Turner
Executive VP & General Manager: John Schuerholz
Manager: Bobby Cox
Director of Public Relations: Jim Schultz
www.atlantabraves.com

Baltimore Orioles
Address: Oriole Park at Camden Yards
             333 W Camden Street
             Baltimore, MD 21201
Telephone: (410) 685-9800
Stadium (Capacity): Oriole Park at Camden Yards
(48,876)
Chairman of the Board/CEO: Peter G. Angelos
Vice Chairman/COO: Joseph E. Foss
Manager: Lee Mazzilli
Director of Public Relations: Bill Stetka
www.theorioles.com

Boston Red Sox
Address: 4 Yawkey Way
             Fenway Park
             Boston, MA 02215
Telephone: (617) 267-9440
Stadium (Capacity): Fenway Park (33,993)
Principal Owner: John W. Henry
Senior VP and General Manager: Theo Epstein
Manager: Terry Francona
Director of Public relations: Glenn Geffner
www.redsox.com

Chicago Cubs
Address: Wrigley Field
             1060 West Addison
             Chicago, IL 60613
Telephone: (773) 404-2827
Stadium (Capacity): Wrigley Field (39,111)
President and CEO: Andrew B. MacPhail
Vice President/GM: Jim Hendry
Manager: Dusty Baker
Director of Media Relations: Sharon Pannozzo
www.cubs.com

Chicago White Sox
Address: Comiskey Park
             333 West 35th Street
             Chicago, IL 60616
Telephone: (312) 674-1000
Stadium (Capacity): U.S. Cellular Field (47,098)
Chairman: Jerry Reinsdorf
General Manager: Kenny Williams
Manager: Ozzie Guillen
VP of Communications: Scott Reifert
www.whitesox.com

Cincinnati Reds
Address: 100 Main Street
             Cincinnati, OH 45202
Telephone: (513) 765-7000
Stadium (Capacity): Great American Ball Park
(42,256)
CEO/General Partner: Carl Lindner
COO: John L. Allen
General Manager: Dan O'Brien
Managing Executive: John L. Allen
Manager: Dave Miley
Director of Media Relations: Rob Butcher
www.cincinnatireds.com

Cleveland Indians
Address: Jacobs Field
             2401 Ontario Street
             Cleveland, OH 44115-4003
Telephone: (216) 420-4200
Stadium (Capacity): Jacobs Field (43,368)
President and CEO: Lawrence J. Dolan
Executive VP and General Manager: Mark Shapiro
Manager: Eric Wedge
Director of Media Relations: Bart Swain
www.indians.com

Colorado Rockies
Address: 2001 Blake Street
             Denver, CO 80205
Telephone: (303) 292-0200
Stadium (Capacity): Coors Field (50,449)
Chairman and CEO: Charles K. Monfort
President: Keli McGregor
General Manager and Executive VP: Dan O'Dowd
Manager: Clint Hurdle
Senior Director of Communications/PR: Jay Alves
www.coloradorockies.com

Detroit Tigers
Address: Comerica Park
             2100 Woodward Avenue
             Detroit, MI 48201
Telephone: (313) 962-4000
Stadium (Capacity): Comerica Park (40,120)
Owner: Mike Ilitch
President and GM: Dave Dombrowski
Manager: Alan Trammell
Sr. Director of Communications: Cliff Russell
www.detroittigers.com

Florida Marlins
Address: 2267 Dan Marino Boulevard
             Miami, FL 33056
Telephone: (305) 626-7400
Stadium (Capacity): Pro Player Stadium (36,331)
Owner: Jeffrey H. Loria
President: David Samson
Senior VP and General Manager: Larry Beinfest
Manager: Jack McKeon
VP of Communications/Broadcasting:P.J. Loyello
www.floridamarlins.com

Houston Astros
Address: P.O. Box 288
             Houston, TX 77001
Telephone: (713) 259-8000
Stadium (Capacity): Minute Maid Park (40,950)
Chairman: Drayton McLane
President of Baseball Operations: Tal Smith
Manager: Phil Garner
Director of Media Relations: Jimmy Stanton
www.astros.com

Kansas City Royals
Address: P.O. Box 419969
             Kansas City, MO 64141
Telephone: (816) 921-8000
Stadium (Capacity): Kauffman Stadium (40,785)
Owner and Chairman of the Board: David D. Glass
General Manager: Allard Baird
Manager: Tony Peña
Vice President, Broadcasting/PR: David Witty
www.kcroyals.com

Los Angeles Dodgers
Address: 1000 Elysian Park Avenue
             Los Angeles, CA 90012-1199
Telephone: (323) 224-1500
Stadium (Capacity): Dodger Stadium (56,000)
Chairman: Frank McCourt
President and COO: Bob Graziano
Executive VP/GM: Paul DePodesta
Manager: Jim Tracy
Director Public Relations: John Olguin
www.dodgers.com

Milwaukee Brewers
Address: 1 Brewers Way
             Milwaukee, WI 53214
Telephone: (414) 902-4400
Stadium (Capacity): Miller Park (41,900)
Chairman: Wendy A. Selig-Prieb
General Manager: Doug Melvin
Manager: Ned Yost
Director of Media Relations: Jon Greenberg
www.milwaukeebrewers.com

Minnesota Twins
Address: 34 Kirby Puckett Place
             Minneapolis, MN 55415
Telephone: (612) 375-1366
Stadium (Capacity): Hubert H. Humphrey
 Metrodome (48,678)
Owner: Carl Pohlad
General Manager: Terry Ryan
Manager: Ron Gardenhire
Manager of Media Relations: Sean Harlin
www.twinsbaseball.com

Montreal Expos
Address: P.O. Box 500 Station M
             Montreal, Quebec H1V 3P2 Canada
Telephone: (514) 253-3434
Stadium (Capacity): Olympic Stadium (46,500)
President: Tony Tavares

Montreal Expos *(Cont.)*
Vice President and General Manager: TBA
Manager: Frank Robinson
Director, Media Services: Monique Giroux
www.montrealexpos.com

New York Mets
Address: Shea Stadium
             123-01 Roosevelt Ave.
             Flushing, NY 11368
Telephone: (718) 507-6387
Stadium (Capacity): Shea Stadium (56,749)
Owner: Fred Wilpon
General Manager: Omar Minaya
Manager: TBA
VP of Media Relations: Jay Horwitz
www.mets.com

New York Yankees
Address: Yankee Stadium
             Bronx, NY 10451
Telephone: (718) 293-4300
Stadium (Capacity): Yankee Stadium (57,746)
Principal Owner: George Steinbrenner
Chief Operating Officer: Lonn Trost
VP/General Manager: Brian Cashman
Manager: Joe Torre
Director of Media Relations: Rick Cerone
www.yankees.com

Oakland Athletics
Address: 7000 Coliseum Way
             Oakland, CA 94621
Telephone: (510) 638-4900
Stadium (Capacity): Network Associates Coliseum
(43,662)
Owners: Steve Schott and Ken Hofmann
President: Michael Crowley
General Manager: Billy Beane
Manager: Ken Macha
Baseball Information Manager: Mike Selleck
www.oaklandathletics.com

Philadelphia Phillies
Address: P.O. Box 7575
             Philadelphia, PA 19101-7575
Telephone: (215) 463-6000
Stadium (Capacity): Citizens Bank Park 43,500
Chairman: Bill Giles
President: David P. Montgomery
Vice President and General Manager: Ed Wade
Manager: TBA
Vice President, Public Relations: Larry Shenk
www.phillies.com

Pittsburgh Pirates
Address: P.O. Box 7000
             Pittsburgh, PA 15212
Telephone: (412) 323-5000
Stadium (Capacity): PNC Park (37,898)
CEO and Managing General Partner: Kevin McClatchy
Senior VP and General Manager: Dave Littlefield
Manager: Lloyd McClendon
Director of Media Relations: Jim Trdinich
www.pirateball.com

St. Louis Cardinals
Address: Busch Stadium/ 250 Stadium Plaza
             St. Louis, MO 63102
Telephone: (314) 421-3060
Stadium (Capacity): Busch Stadium (49,814)
President: Mark Lamping
Senior Vice President and GM: Walt Jocketty
Manager: Tony LaRussa
Director of Media Relations: Brian Bartow
www.stlcardinals.com

San Diego Padres
Address: P.O. Box 122000
               San Diego, CA 92112
Telephone: (619) 283-4494
Stadium (Capacity): PETCO Park (46,000)
Chairman: John Moores
General Manager: Kevin Towers
Manager: Bruce Bochy
Director of Media Relations: Luis Garcia
www.padres.com

San Francisco Giants
Address: 24 Willie Mays Plaza
               San Francisco, CA 94107
Telephone: (415) 972-2000
Stadium (Capacity): SBC Park (41,503)
President/Managing General Partner: Peter Magowan
General Manager: Brian Sabean
Manager: Felipe Alou
Manager of Media Relations: Jim Moorehead
www.sfgiants.com

Seattle Mariners
Address: P.O. Box 4100
               Seattle, WA 98104
Telephone: (206) 346-4000
Stadium (Capacity): SAFECO Field (47,116)
Chairman and CEO: Howard Lincoln
General Manager: Bill Bavasi
Manager: TBA
Director of Baseball Information: Tim Hevly
www.seattlemariners.com

Tampa Bay Devil Rays
Address: One Tropicana Drive
               St. Petersburg, FL 33705
Telephone: (727) 825-3137
Stadium (Capacity): Tropicana Field (43,761)
Managing General Partner/CEO: Vincent J. Naimoli
Senior VP and General Manager: Chuck LaMar
Manager: Lou Piniella
Vice President, Public Relations: Rick Vaughn
www.devilrays.com

Texas Rangers
Address: P.O. Box 90111
               Arlington, TX 76004
Telephone: (817) 273-5222
Stadium (Capacity): Ameriquest Field (49,115)
Owner: Thomas O. Hicks
General Manager: John Hart
Manager: Buck Showalter
Senior VP, Communications: John Blake
www.texasrangers.com

Toronto Blue Jays
Address: SkyDome
               1 Blue Jays Way, Suite 3200
               Toronto, Ontario M5V 1J1 Canada
Telephone: (416) 341-1000
Stadium (Capacity): SkyDome (45,100)
President/CEO: Paul Godfrey
Senior Vice President/GM: J.P. Ricciardi
Manager: John Gibbons
Directo of Communications: Jay Stenhouse
www.bluejays.com

Pro Football Directory

National Football League
Address: 280 Park Avenue
               New York, NY 10017
Telephone: (212) 450-2000
Commissioner: Paul Tagliabue
www.nfl.com

NFL Players Association
Address: 2021 L Street, N.W.
               Washington, D.C. 20036
Telephone: (202) 463-2200
Executive Director: Gene Upshaw
Director of Communications: Carl Francis
www.nflpa.org

Arizona Cardinals
Address: P.O. Box 888
               Phoenix, AZ 85001
Telephone: (602) 379-0101
Stadium (Capacity): Sun Devil Stadium (73,377)
President and Owner: Bill Bidwill
VP of Football Operations: Rod Graves
Head Coach: Dennis Green
Director of Public Relations: Mark Dalton
www.azcardinals.com

Atlanta Falcons
Address: 4400 Falcon Park Way
               Flowery Branch, GA 30542
Telephone: (770) 965-3115
Stadium (Capacity): Georgia Dome (71,149)
Owner and CEO: Arthur Blank
President and GM: Rich McKay
Coach: Jim Mora Jr.
Director of Communications: Aaron Salkin
www.atlantafalcons.com

Baltimore Ravens
Address: 11001 Owings Mills Blvd.
               Owings Mills, MD 21117
Telephone: (410) 654-6200
Stadium (Capacity): M & T Bank Stadium(69,084)
Owner/CEO: Art Modell
President/COO: David Modell
Coach: Brian Billick
VP of Public Relations: Kevin Byrne
www.baltimoreravens.com

Buffalo Bills
Address: One Bills Drive
               Orchard Park, NY 14127
Telephone: (716) 648-1800
Stadium (Capacity): Ralph Wilson Stadium (73,967)
Chairman: Ralph C. Wilson Jr.
President and General Manager: Tom Donohoe
Coach: Mike Mularkey
Vice President of Communications: Scott Berchtold
www.buffalobills.com

Carolina Panthers
Address: Ericsson Stadium
               800 South Mint St.
               Charlotte, NC 28202
Telephone: (704) 358-7000
Stadium (Capacity): Bank of America Stadium (73,367)
Founder and Owner: Jerry Richardson
President: Mark Richardson
General Manager: Marty Hurney
Coach: John Fox
Director of Communications: Charlie Dayton
www.panthers.com

Chicago Bears
Address: 1000 Football Drive
Lake Forest, IL 60045
Telephone: (847) 295-6600
Stadium (Capacity): Soldier Field (61,500)
Chairman: Michael McCaskey
President/CEO: Ted Phillips
Coach: Lovie Smith
Director of Public Relations: Scott Hagel
www.chicagobears.com

Cincinnati Bengals
Address: One Paul Brown Stadium
Cincinnati, OH 45202
Telephone: (513) 621-3550
Stadium (Capacity): Paul Brown Stadium (65,327)
President: Mike Brown
Executive Vice President: Katherine Blackburn
Coach: Marvin Lewis
VP of Communications: Julia Payne
www.bengals.com

Cleveland Browns
Address: 76 Lou Groza Boulevard
Berea, OH 44017
Telephone: (440) 891-5000
Stadium (Capacity): Cleveland Browns Stadium
(73,200)
Owner: Randy Lerner
VP Player Personnel/Football Dev.: Pete Garcia
Coach: Butch Davis
Exec. Director of Communications: Todd Stewart
www.clevelandbrowns.com

Dallas Cowboys
Address: One Cowboys Parkway
Irving, TX 75063
Telephone: (972) 556-9900
Stadium (Capacity): Texas Stadium (65,639)
Owner, President and General Manager: Jerry Jones
Coach: Bill Parcells
Public Relations Director: Rich Dalrymple
www.dallascowboys.com

Denver Broncos
Address: 13655 Broncos Parkway
Englewood, CO 80112
Telephone: (303) 649-9000
Stadium (Capacity): INVESCO Field at Mile High
(76,125)
President and Chief Executive Officer: Pat Bowlen
General Manager: Ted Sundquist
Coach: Mike Shanahan
VP of Public Relations: Jim Saccomano
www.denverbroncos.com

Detroit Lions
Address: 222 Republic Drive
Allen Park, MI 48101
Telephone: (313) 216-4000
Stadium (Capacity): Ford Field (65,000)
Owner/Chairman: William Clay Ford
President/CEO: Matt Millen
Coach: Steve Mariucci
Director of Media Relations: Matt Barnhart
www.detroitlions.com

Green Bay Packers
Address: 1265 Lombardi Avenue
Green Bay, WI 54304
Telephone: (920) 496-5700
Stadium (Capacity): Lambeau Field (72,515)
President: Bob Harlan
Executive VP/GM/Coach: Mike Sherman
Executive Director of Public Relations: Jeff Blumb
www.packers.com

Houston Texans
Address: Two Reliant Park
Houston, TX 77054
Telephone: (832) 667-2000
Stadium (Capacity): Reliant Stadium (71,054)
Chairman and CEO: Robert C. McNair
Senior VP and General Manager: Charley Casserly
Coach: Dom Capers
Media Realtions Manager: Rocky Harris
www.houstontexans.com

Indianapolis Colts
Address: P.O. Box 535000
Indianapolis, IN 46253
Telephone: (317) 297-2658
Stadium (Capacity): RCA Dome (56,127)
Owner and Chief Executive Officer: Jim Irsay
President: Bill Polian
Senior Executive Vice President: Pete Ward
Coach: Tony Dungy
Vice President of Public Relations: Craig Kelley
www.colts.com

Jacksonville Jaguars
Address: One Alltel Stadium Place
Jacksonville, FL 32202
Telephone: (904) 633-6000
Stadium (Capacity): Alltel Stadium (73,000)
Owner: J. Wayne Weaver
Vice President and CFO: Bill Prescott
Senior VP of Football Operations: Paul Vance
Coach: Jack Del Rio
VP of Communications and Media: Dan Edwards
www.jaguars.com

Kansas City Chiefs
Address: One Arrowhead Drive
Kansas City, MO 64129
Telephone: (816) 920-9300
Stadium (Capacity): Arrowhead Stadium (79,451)
Founder: Lamar Hunt
CEO, President and General Manager: Carl Peterson
Coach: Dick Vermeil
Public Relations Director: Bob Moore
www.kcchiefs.com

Miami Dolphins
Address: 7500 S.W. 30th Street
Davie, FL 33314
Telephone: (954) 452-7000
Stadium (Capacity): Pro Player Stadium (75,540)
Chairman of the Board/Owner: H. Wayne Huizenga
General Manager: Rick Spielman
Head Coach: Dave Wannstedt
Senior VP Media Relations: Harvey Greene
www.miamidolphins.com

Minnesota Vikings
Address: 9520 Viking Drive
Eden Prairie, MN 55344
Telephone: (952) 828-6500
Stadium (Capacity): HHH Metrodome (64,121)
Owner: Red McCombs
President: Gary Woods
Coach: Mike Tice
Public Relations Director: Bob Hagan
www.vikings.com

New England Patriots
Address: Gillette Stadium
1 Patriot Place, Foxboro, MA 02035
Telephone: (508) 543-8200
Stadium (Capacity): Gillette Stadium (68,436)
Owner and Chairman: Robert K. Kraft
Vice Chairman: Jonathan Kraft
Coach: Bill Belichick
Director of Media Relations: Stacey James
www.patriots.com

New Orleans Saints
Address: 5800 Airline Drive
Metairie, LA 70003
Telephone: (504) 733-0255
Stadium (Capacity): Louisiana Superdome (68,390)
Owner: Tom Benson
GM of Football Operations: Mickey Loomis
Head Coach: Jim Haslett
Director of Media Relations: Greg Bensel
www.neworleanssaints.com

New York Giants
Address: Giants Stadium
East Rutherford, NJ 07073
Telephone: (201) 935-8111
Stadium (Capacity): Giants Stadium (80,242)
President and co-CEO: Wellington T. Mara
Chairman and co-CEO: Preston Robert Tisch
Senior VP and General Manager: Ernie Accorsi
Coach: Tom Coughlin
Vice President of Communications: Pat Hanlon
www.giants.com

New York Jets
Address: 1000 Fulton Avenue
Hempstead, NY 11550
Telephone: (516) 560-8100
Stadium (Capacity): Giants Stadium (80,062)
Owner: Robert Wood Johnson IV
General Manager: Terry Bradway
Coach: Herman Edwards
VP of Public Relations: Ron Colangelo
www.newyorkjets.com

Oakland Raiders
Address: 1220 Harbor Bay Parkway
Alameda, CA 94502
Telephone: (510) 864-5000
Stadium (Capacity): Network Assoc. Coliseum (63,132)
Owner: Al Davis
Executive Assistant: Al LoCasale
Coach: Norv Turner
Director of Public Relations: Mike Taylor
www.raiders.com

Philadelphia Eagles
Address: NovaCare Complex
1 NovaCare Way
Philadelphia, PA 19145
Telephone: (215) 463-2500
Stadium (Capacity): Lincoln Financial Field (68,532)
Chairman: Jeffrey Lurie
Exec. VP of Football Operations/Coach: Andy Reid
Director of Football Media Services: Derek Boyko
www.philadelphiaeagles.com

Pittsburgh Steelers
Address: 3400 South Water Street
Pittsburgh, PA 15203
Telephone: (412) 432-7800
Stadium (Capacity): Heinz Field (64,350)
Chairman: Dan Rooney
Director of Football Operations: Kevin Colbert
Coach: Bill Cowher
Director of Communications: Ron Wahl
www.steelers.com

St. Louis Rams
Address: One Rams Way
St. Louis, MO 63045
Telephone: (314) 982-7267
Stadium (Capacity): Edward Jones Dome (66,000)
Owner and Chairman: Georgia Frontiere
President: John Shaw
Coach: Mike Martz
Director of Public Relations: Duane Lewis
www.stlouisrams.com

San Diego Chargers
Address: Qualcomm Stadium
4020 Murphy Canyon Road
San Diego, CA 92123
Telephone: (858) 874-4500
Stadium (Capacity): Qualcomm Stadium (71,500)
Chairman: Alex G. Spanos
President and CEO: Dean A. Spanos
Executive VP and General Manager: A.J. Smith
Coach: Marty Schottenheimer
Director of Public Relations: Bill Johnston
www.chargers.com

San Francisco 49ers
Address: 4949 Centennial Boulevard
Santa Clara, CA 95054
Telephone: (408) 562-4949
Stadium (Capacity): 3Com Park (69,734)
Owner: Denise DeBartolo-York
Owner: John York
General Manager: Terry Donahue
Coach: Dennis Erickson
Public Relations Director: Kirk Reynolds
www.49ers.com

Seattle Seahawks
Address: 11220 N.E. 53rd Street
Kirkland, WA 98033
Telephone: (425) 827-9777
Stadium (Capacity): Qwest Field (67,000)
Owner: Paul Allen
President: Bob Whitsitt
General Manager: Bob Ferguson
Coach: Mike Holmgren
Director of Public Relations: Dave Pearson
www.seahawks.com

Tampa Bay Buccaneers
Address: One Buccaneer Place
Tampa, FL 33607
Telephone: (813) 870-2700
Stadium (Capacity): Raymond James Stadium (66,321)
Owner: Malcolm Glazer
General Manager: Bruce Allen
Coach: Jon Gruden
Communications Manager: Jeff Kamis
www.buccaneers.com

Tennessee Titans
Address: 460 Great Circle Road
Nashville, TN 37228
Telephone: (615) 565-4000
Stadium (Capacity): The Coliseum (68,798)
Owner: K.S. Adams Jr.
General Manager: Floyd Reese
Coach: Jeff Fisher
Director of Media Relations: Robbie Bohren
www.titansonline.com

Washington Redskins
Address: 21300 Redskins Park Drive
Ashburn, VA 20147
Telephone: (703) 726-7000
Stadium (Capacity): Fedex Field (86,484)
Owner: Daniel M. Snyder
VP of Football Operations: Vinny Cerrato
Coach: Joe Gibbs
Director of Public Relations: Michelle Tessier
www.redskins.com

Other Leagues

Canadian Football League
Address: 50 Wellington Street East - 3rd Floor
            Toronto, Ontario M5E1C8 Canada
Telephone: (416) 322-9650
Commissioner:Tom E.S. Wright
Senior VP, Business Operations/Treasurer: James E.
Grundy
Director of Football Media: Shawn Lackie
www.cfl.ca

NFL EUROPE
Address: 280 Park Avenue
            New York, NY 10017
Telephone: (212) 450-2000
Managing Direotrors: John Beake and Jim Connolly
Chief Operating Officer: Dan Margoshes (London)
Director of Communications: David Tossel
www.nfleurope.com

Pro Basketball Directory

National Basketball Association

National Basketball Association
Address: 645 Fifth Avenue
            New York, NY 10022
Telephone: (212) 826-7000
Commissioner: David Stern
Deputy Commissioner: Russell Granik
Sr. VP of Communications: Brian McIntyre
www.nba.com

National Basketball Association Players Association
Address: 2 Penn Plaza
            Suite 2430
            New York, NY 10121
Telephone: (212) 655-0880
Executive Director: William Hunter
www.nbpa.com

Atlanta Hawks
Address: One CNN Center
            Atlanta, GA 30303
Telephone: (404) 827-3800
Arena (Capacity): Philips Arena (19,445)
Owner: Atlanta Spirit, LLC
President and CEO: Bernie Mullin
General Manager: Billy Knight
Coach: Mike Woodson
VP of Communications: Arthur Triche
www.hawks.com

Boston Celtics
Address: 151 Merrimac Street
            Boston, MA 02114
Telephone: (617) 523-6050
Arena (Capacity): FleetCenter (18,624)
CEO and Managing Partner: Wyc Grousbeck
Executive Dir. of Basketball Operations: Danny Ainge
Coach: Doc Rivers
Director of Media Relations: Bill Bonsiewicz
www.celtics.com

Charlotte Bobcats
Address: 100 Hive Drive
            Charlotte, NC 28217
Telephone: (704) 357-0252
Arena (Capacity): Charlotte Coliseum (23,319)
Owner: Robert L. Johnson
General Manager and Coach: Bernie Bickerstaff
Director of Public Relations: Scott Leightman
www.bobcatsbasketball.com

Chicago Bulls
Address: 1901 W. Madison Street
            Chicago, IL 60612
Telephone: (312) 455-4000
Arena (Capacity): United Center (21,711)
Chairman: Jerry Reinsdorf
Executive VP of Basketball Operations: John Paxson
Coach: Scott Skiles
Senior Director of Media Services: Tim Hallam
www.bulls.com

Cleveland Cavaliers
Address: One Center Court
            Cleveland, OH 44115
Telephone: (216) 420-2000
Arena (Capacity): Gund Arena (20,562)
Chairman: Gordon Gund
President and GM: Jim Paxson
Coach: Paul Silas
Director of Public Relations: Amanda Mercado
www.cavs.com

Dallas Mavericks
Address: 2500 Victory Avenue
            Dallas, TX 75219
Telephone: (214) 665-4660
Arena (Capacity): American Airlines Center (19,200)
Owner: Mark Cuban
General Manager and Head Coach: Don Nelson
President of Basketball Operations: Donn Nelson
Sr. VP of Marketing/Communications: Matt Fitzgerald
www.dallasmavericks.com

Denver Nuggets
Address: Pepsi Center
            1000 Chopper Circle
            Denver, CO 80204
Telephone: (303) 405-1100
Arena (Capacity): Pepsi Center (19,099)
Owner: E. Stanley Kroenke
General Manager: Kiki Vandeweghe
Coach: Jeff Bzdelik
Director of Media Relations: Eric Sebastian
www.nuggets.com

Detroit Pistons
Address: The Palace of Auburn Hills
            Two Championship Drive
            Auburn Hills, MI 48326
Telephone: (248) 377-0100
Arena (Capacity): The Palace of Auburn Hills (22,076)
Owner: William M. Davidson
President of Basketball Operations: Joe Dumars
Coach: Larry Brown
VP of Public Relations: Matt Dobek
www.pistons.com

National Basketball Association *(Cont.)*

Golden State Warriors

Address: 1011 Broadway
            Oakland, CA 94607-4019
Telephone: (510) 986-2200
Arena (Capacity): The Arena in Oakland (19,596)
Owner and CEO: Christopher Cohan
Executive VP of Basketball Operations: Chris Mullin
Coach: Mike Montgomery
Director of Public Relations: Raymond Ridder
www.gs-warriors.com

Houston Rockets

Address: Two Greenway Plaza, Suite 400
            Houston, TX 77046
Telephone: (713) 627-3865
Arena (Capacity): Toyota Center (18,300)
Owner: Leslie Alexander
President and CEO: George Postolos
General Manager: Carroll Dawson
Coach: Jeff Van Gundy
Director of Team Communications: Nelson Luis
www.rockets.com

Indiana Pacers

Address: 125 S. Pennsylvania Street
            Indianapolis, IN 46204
Telephone: (317) 917-2500
Arena (Capacity): Conseco Fieldhouse (18,345)
Owners: Melvin Simon and Herbert Simon
CEO/President: Donnie Walsh
President of Basketball Operations: Larry Bird
Head Coach: Rick Carlisle
Media Relations Director: David Benner
www.pacers.com

Los Angeles Clippers

Address: The Staples Center
            1111 S. Figueroa Street - St. 1100
            Los Angeles, CA 90015
Telephone: (213) 742-7500
Arena (Capacity): The Staples Center (18,964)
Owner: Donald T. Sterling
Vice President of Basketball Operations: Elgin Baylor
Coach: Mike Dunleavy
Vice President of Communications: Joe Safety
www.clippers.com

Los Angeles Lakers

Address: 555 North Nash Street
            El Segundo, CA 90245
Telephone: (310) 426-6000
Arena (Capacity): The Staples Center (18,997)
Owner: Dr. Jerry Buss
General Manager: Mitch Kupchak
Coach: Rudy Tomjanovich
Director of Public Relations: John Black
www.lakers.com

Memphis Grizzlies

Address: 175 Toyota Plaza - Suite 150
            Memphis TN 38103
Telephone: (901) 888-4667
Arena (Capacity): FedEx Forum (18,400)
Majority Owner: Michael E. Heisley
President of Basketball Operations: Jerry West
General Manager: Dick Versace
Coach: Hubie Brown
Director of Media Relations: Kirk Clayborn
www.grizzlies.com

Miami Heat

Address: American Airlines Arena
            601 Biscayne Boulevard
            Miami, FL 33132
Telephone: (786) 777-4328
Arena (Capacity): American Airlines Arena (16,500)
Managing General Partner: Micky Arison
President: Pat Riley
President/GM of Basketball Operations: Randy Pfund
Coach: Stan Van Gundy
VP of Sports Media Relations: Tim Donovan
www.heat.com

Milwaukee Bucks

Address: The Bradley Center
            1001 N. Fourth Street
            Milwaukee, WI 53203
Telephone: (414) 227-0500
Arena (Capacity): The Bradley Center (18,717)
Owner: Herb Kohl
General Manager: Larry Harris
Coach: Terry Porter
Public Relations Director: Cheri Hanson
www.bucks.com

Minnesota Timberwolves

Address: 600 First Avenue North
            Minneapolis, MN 55403
Telephone: (612) 673-1600
Arena (Capacity): Target Center (19,006)
Owner: Glen Taylor
VP of Basketball Operations: Kevin McHale
Coach: Phil (Flip) Saunders
Director of Communications: Ted Johnson
www.timberwolves.com

New Jersey Nets

Address: 390 Murray Hill Parkway
            East Rutherford, NJ 07073
Telephone: (201) 935-8888
Arena (Capacity): Continental Airlines Arena (20,049)
Owner: Bruce Ratner
General Manager: Ed Stefanski
Coach: Lawrence Frank
Director of Public Relations: Gary Sussman
www.njnets.com

New Orleans Hornets

Address: 1501 Girod Street
            New Orleans, LA 70113
Telephone: (504) 301-4000
Arena (Capacity): New Orleans Arena (18,500)
Majority Owner: George Shinn
Co-Owner: Ray Wooldridge
Coach: Byron Scott
VP of Public Relations: Harold Kaufman
www.hornets.com

New York Knicks

Address: Madison Square Garden
            Two Pennsylvania Plaza
            New York, NY 10121
Telephone: (212) 465-5867
Arena (Capacity): Madison Square Garden (19,763)
Owner: ITT/Sheraton and Cablevision
Chairman: James Dolan
President of Basketball Operations: Isiah Thomas
Coach: Lenny Wilkens
Vice President of Public Relations: Joe Favorito
www.nyknicks.com

National Basketball Association (Cont.)

Orlando Magic
Address: Two Magic Place
8701 Maitland Summit Blvd.
Orlando, FL 32810
Telephone: (407) 916-2400
Arena (Capacity): TD Waterhouse Centre (17,248)
Owner: Rich DeVos
Senior Executive Vice President: Pat Williams
General Manager: John Weisbrod
Coach: Johnny Davis
Director of Media Relations: Joel Glass
www.orlandomagic.com

Philadelphia 76ers
Address: First Union Center
3601 South Broad Street
Philadelphia, PA 19148
Telephone: (215) 339-7600
Arena (Capacity): Wachovia Center (20,444)
Chairman: Ed Snider
General Manager: Billy King
Coach: Jim O'Brien
VP of Communications: Karen Frascona
www.sixers.com

Phoenix Suns
Address: 201 East Jeffreson Street
Phoenix, AZ 85004
Telephone: (602) 379-7900
Arena (Capacity): America West Arena (19,023)
Chairman/CEO and Managing General Partner: Jerry Colangelo
President and General Manager: Bryan Colangelo
Coach: Mike D'Antoni
VP of Basketball Communications: Julie Fie
www.suns.com

Portland Trail Blazers
Address: One Center Court
Suite 200
Portland, OR 97227
Telephone: (503) 234-9291
Arena (Capacity): Rose Garden Arena (19,980)
Chairman of the Board: Paul Allen
President: Steve Patterson
General Manager: John Nash
Coach: Maurice Cheeks
Executive Director of Communications: Mike Hanson
www.blazers.com

Sacramento Kings
Address: One Sports Parkway
Sacramento, CA 95834
Telephone: (916) 928-0000
Arena (Capacity): ARCO Arena (17,317)
Owners: Joe and Gavin Maloof
President of Basketball Operations: Geoff Petrie
Coach: Rick Adelman
Director of Media Relations: Troy Hanson
www.kings.com

San Antonio Spurs
Address: SBC Center
100 Montana
San Antonio, TX 78203
Telephone: (210) 554-7787
Arena (Capacity): SBC Center (18,500)
Chairman: Peter Holt
General Manager: R.C. Buford
Head Coach : Gregg Popovich
Director of Media Services: Tom James
www.spurs.com

Seattle SuperSonics
Address: 351 Elliott Avenue West
Suite 500
Seattle, WA 98119
Telephone: (206) 281-5847
Arena (Capacity): KeyArena (17,072)
Owner: The Basketball Club of Seattle, LLC
Chairman: Howard Schultz
President/CEO: Wally Walker
General Manager: Rick Sund
Coach: Nate McMillan
Director of Public Relations: Marc Moquin
www.supersonics.com

Toronto Raptors
Address: 40 Bay Street, Suite 400
Toronto, Ontario M5J 2X2 Canada
Telephone: (416) 815-5600
Arena (Capacity): Air Canada Centre (19,800)
Owner: Maple Leaf Sports and Entertainment, Ltd.
General Manager: Rob Babcock
Coach: Sam Mitchell
Director of Media Relations: Jim Labumbard
www.raptors.com

Utah Jazz
Address: 301 West So. Temple
Salt Lake City, UT 84101
Telephone: (801) 325-2500
Arena (Capacity): Delta Center (19,911)
Owner: Larry H. Miller
President: Dennis Haslam
VP of Basketball Operations: Kevin O'Connor
Coach: Jerry Sloan
Director of Media Relations: Kim Turner
www.utahjazz.com

Washington Wizards
Address: 601 F Street NW
Washington D.C. 20004
Telephone: (202) 661-5000
Arena (Capacity): MCI Center (20,173)
Owner: Abe Pollin
President of Basketball Operations: Ernie Grunfeld
Coach: Eddie Jordan
Director of Public Relations: Nicole Hawkins
www.washingtonwizards.com

Women's National Basketball Association

Women's National Basketball Association
Address: 645 Fifth Avenue
             New York, NY 10022
Telephone: (212) 688-9622
President: Valerie B. Ackerman
Dir. of Basketball Communications: John Maxwell
www.wnba.com

Charlotte Sting
Address: 100 Hive Drive
             Charlotte, NC 29217
Telephone: (704) 357-0252
Arena (Capacity): Charlotte Coliseum (12,843)
Owner Robert Johnson
Coach: Trudi Lacey
Director of Public Relations: Karen Kase
www.charlottesting.com

Connecticut Sun
Address: One Mohegan Sun Blvd.
             Uncasville, CT 06382
Telephone: (877) 786-8499
Arena (Capacity): Mohegan Sun Arena (9,341)
CEO: Mitchell Etess
General Manager: Chris Sienko
Coach: Mike Thibault
Media Relations Manager: Bill Tavares
www.connecticutsun.com

Detroit Shock
Address: 2 Championship Drive
             Auburn Hills, MI 48326
Telephone: (248) 377-0100
Arena (Capacity): The Palace of Auburn Hills (19,000)
Managing Partner: William Davidson
President: Tom Wilson
Head Coach: Bill Laimbeer
Director of Media Relations: Dennis Sampier
www.detroitshock.com

Houston Comets
Address: Two Greenway Plaza, Suite 400
             Houston, TX 77046-3865
Telephone: (713) 627-9622
Arena (Capacity): Toyota Center (18,500)
President: Leslie L. Alexander
Coach and General Manager: Van Chancellor
Director of Media Relations: Nelson Luis
www.houstoncomets.com

Indiana Fever
Address: 125 S. Pennsylvania Street
             Indianapolis, IN 46204
Telephone: (317) 917-2500
Arena (Capacity): Conseco Field House (18,345)
President: Donnie Walsh
Chief Operating Officer: Kelly Krauskopf
Coach: Brian Winters
Director of Media Relations: Kevin Messenger
www.wnba.com/fever

Los Angeles Sparks
Address: 555 Nash Street
             El Segundo, CA 90245
Telephone: (310) 330-2434
Arena (Capacity): Staples Center (19,282)
Chairman: Dr. Jerry Buss
General Manager: Virginia (Penny) Toler
Coach: Karleen Thompson
Media Relations Director: Kristal Shipp
www.lasparks.com

Minnesota Lynx
Address: Target Center
             600 First Avenue North
             Minneapolis, MN 55403
Telephone: (612) 673-8400
Arena (Capacity): Target Center (19,006)
Owner: Glen Taylor
Coach: Suzie McConnell Serio
Public Relations Manager: Mike Cristaldí
www.wnba.com/lynx/

New York Liberty
Address: Two Penn Plaza
             New York, NY 10121
Telephone: (212) 465-5867
Arena (Capacity): Madison Square Garden (19,763)
GM and Vice President: Carol Blazejowski
Coach: Pat Coyle
VP of Marketing and Communications: Amy Scheer
www.nyliberty.com

Phoenix Mercury
Address: 201 East Jefferson Street
             Phoenix, AZ 85004
Telephone: (602) 514-8333
Arena (Capacity): America West Arena (10,746)
Chairman and CEO: Jerry Colangelo
General Manager: Seth Sulka
Coach: Carrie Graf
Media Relations Director: Tami Nealy
www.phoenixmercury.com

Sacramento Monarchs
Address: One Sports Parkway
             Sacramento, CA 95834
Telephone: (916) 455-4647
Arena (Capacity): ARCO Arena (17,317)
Owner: Maloof Family
President: John Thomas
GM and Coach: John Whisenant
Manager of Media Relations: Kimberly Williams
www.sacramentomonarchs.com

San Antonio Silver Stars
Address: One SBC Center
             San Antonio, TX 78219
Telephone: (210) 444-5050
Arena (Capacity): SBC Center (18,500)
Owner: Spurs Sports & Entertainment
COO: Clarissa Davis-Wrightsil
Coach: Shell Dailey
Media Services Manager: Kris Davis
www.sanantoniosilverstars.com

Women's National Basketball Association *(Cont.)*

Seattle Storm
Address: 351 Elliott Avenue West
            Suite 500
            Seattle, WA 98119
Telephone: (206) 281-5800
Arena (Capacity): Key Arena (12,000)
Owners: The Basketball Club of Seattle LLC
Chairman: Howard Schultz
Coach: Anne Donovan
Director, Public Relations: Valerie O'Neil
www.wnba.com/storm

Washington Mystics
Address: MCI Center
            601 F Street, NW
            Washington, DC 20004
Telephone: (202) 661-5000
Arena (Capacity): MCI Center (19,093)
Chairman: Abe Pollin
President: Susan O'Malley
Coach: Michael Adams
Director, Public Relations: Dyani Gordon
www.washingtonmystics.com

Hockey Directory

National Hockey League
Address: 1251 Avenue of the Americas
            47th floor
            New York, NY 10020-1198
Telephone: (212) 789-2000
Commissioner: Gary Bettman
President of NHL Enterprises: Ed Horne
Executive VP and Dir. of Hockey Operations: Colin Campbell
VP of Media Relations: Frank Brown
www.nhl.com

National Hockey League Players Association
Address: 777 Bay Street, Suite 2400
            Toronto, Ontario M5G 2C8 Canada
Telephone: (416) 313-2300
Executive Director: Bob Goodenow
www.nhlpa.com

Mighty Ducks of Anaheim
Address: Arrowhead Pond of Anaheim
            2695 Katella Avenue
            Anaheim, CA 92806
Telephone: (714) 940-2900
Arena (Capacity): Arrowhead Pond of Anaheim (17,174)
Chairman and Governor: Jay Rasulo
Senior VP and Interim GM: Al Coates
Coach: Mike Babcock
Director of Communications: Alex Gilchrist
www.mightyducks.com

Atlanta Thrashers
Address: 1 CNN Center
            P.O. Box 15538
            Atlanta, GA 30348
Telephone: (404) 827-5300
Arena (Capacity): Philips Arena (18,545)
Owner: Atlanta Spirit, LLC
Governor: Bruce Levenson
VP and General Manager: Don Waddell
Coach: Bob Hartley
Senior VP Communications: Tom Hughes
www.atlantathrashers.com

Boston Bruins
Address: One Fleet Center Place, Suite 250
            Boston, MA 02114-1303
Telephone: (617) 624-1900
Arena (Capacity): FleetCenter (17,565)
Owner and Governor: Jeremy M. Jacobs
Alternative Governor and President: Harry Sinden
VP/General Manager and Alt. Governor: Mike O'Connell
Coach: Mike Sullivan
Director of Media Relations: Heidi Holland
www.bostonbruins.com

Buffalo Sabres
Address: HSBC Arena
            One Seymour H. Knox III Plaza
            Buffalo, NY 14203
Telephone: (716) 855-4100
Arena (Capacity): HSBC Arena (18,690)
Owner: B. Thomas Golisano
General Manager: Darcy Regier
Coach: Lindy Ruff
VP of Communications: Michael Gilbert
www.sabres.com

Calgary Flames
Address: Pengrowth Saddledome
            555 Saddledome Rise, SE
            Calgary, Alberta T2G 2W1
Telephone: (403) 777-2177
Arena (Capacity): Pengrowth Saddledome (17,409)
Owners: Harley N. Hotchkiss, N. Murray Edwards, Alvin G. Libin, Allan P. Markin, J.R. "Bud" McCaig, Byron J.Seaman, Daryl K. Seaman, Clayton H. Riddell
President and CEO: Ken King
General Manager and Coach: Darryl Sutter
Director of Communications: Peter Hanlon
www.calgaryflames.com

Carolina Hurricanes
Address: 1400 Edwards Mill Road
             Raleigh, NC 27607
Telephone: (919) 467-7825
Arena (Capacity): RBC Center (18,730)
Owner: Peter Karmanos
CEO and General Manager: Jim Rutherford
VP/Assistant General Manager: Jason Karmanos
Coach: Peter Laviolette
Director of Media Relations: Mike Sundheim
www.carolinahurricanes.com

Chicago Blackhawks
Address: United Center
             1901 W. Madison Street
             Chicago, IL 60612
Telephone: (312) 455-7000
Arena (Capacity): United Center (20,500)
President: William W. Wirtz
Senior Vice President/GM: Robert Pulford
Coach: Brian Sutter
Executive Director of Communications: Jim DeMaria
www.chicagoblackhawks.com

Colorado Avalanche
Address: Pepsi Center
             1000 Chopper Circle
             Denver, CO 80204
Telephone: (303) 405-1100
Arena (Capacity): Pepsi Center (18,007)
Owner and Governor: E. Stanley Kroenke
Alt. Governor, President and General Manager: Pierre Lacroix
Coach: Joel Quenneville
VP of Communications and Team Services:
  Jean Martineau
www.coloradoavalanche.com

Columbus Blue Jackets
Address: 200 West Nationwide Boulevard
             Columbus, OH 43215
Telephone: (614) 246-4625
Arena (Capacity): Nationwide Arena (18,136)
Owner: John H. McConnell
President, GM and Coach: Doug MacLean
Coach: Dave King
Director of Communications: Todd Sharrock
www.bluejackets.com

Dallas Stars
Address: 211 Cowboys Parkway
             Irving, TX 75063
Telephone: (972) 831-2401
Arena (Capacity): American Airlines Center (18,532)
Owner: Thomas O. Hicks
General Manager: Doug Armstrong
Coach: Dave Tippett
Director of Media Relations: Mark Janko
www.dallasstars.com

Detroit Red Wings
Address: Joe Louis Arena
             600 Civic Center Drive
             Detroit, MI 48226
Telephone: (313) 396-7444
Arena (Capacity): Joe Louis Arena (20,056)
Owner and Governor: Mike Ilitch
Owner, Secretary and Treasurer: Marian Ilitch
Senior Vice President/Alt. Governor: Jim Devellano
General Manager: Ken Holland
Coach: Dave Lewis
Senior Director of Communications: John Hahn
www.detroitredwings.com

Edmonton Oilers
Address: 11230 110th Street
             Edmonton, Alberta T5G 3H7
Telephone: (780) 414-4000
Arena (Capacity): Skyreach Centre (16,839)
Owner: Edmonton Investors Group
President and CEO: Patrick LaForge
General Manager: Kevin Lowe
Coach: Craig MacTavish
VP of Public Relations, Hockey: Bill Tuele
www.edmontonoilers.com

Florida Panthers
Address: 1 Panther Parkway
             Sunrise, FL 33323
Telephone: (954) 835-7000
Arena (Capacity): Office Depot Center (19,250)
Chairman of the Board/CEO: Alan Cohen
Alternate Governor: William A. Torrey
General Manager: Mike Keenan
Coach: Jaques Martin
VP of Communications: Randy Sieminski
www.floridapanthers.com

Los Angeles Kings
Address: The Staples Center
             1111 South Figueroa Street
             Los Angeles, CA 90015
Telephone: (213) 742-7100
Arena (Capacity): The Staples Center (18,118)
Owners: Philip Anschutz and Edward P. Roske Jr.
President and Governor: Tim Leiweke
Vice President and GM: Dave Taylor
Coach: Andy Murray
Director of Media Relations: Mike Altieri
www.lakings.com

Minnesota Wild
Address: 317 Washington Street
             St. Paul, MN, 55102
Telephone: (651) 602-6000
Arena (Capacity): Excel Energy Center (18,064)
Chairman: Bob Naegele Jr.
General Manager: Doug Risebrough
Coach: Jacques Lemaire
VP of Communications/Broadcasting: Bill Robertson
www.wild.com

Montreal Canadiens
Address: Bell Centre
           1260 de la Gauchetiere West
           Montreal, Quebec H3B 5E8 Canada
Telephone: (514) 932-2582
Arena (Capacity): Bell Centre (21,273)
Owner: George N. Gillett Jr.
President and Governor: Pierre Boivin
Executive VP and General Manager: Bob Gainey
Coach: Claude Julien
Director of Communications: Donald Beauchamp
www.canadiens.com

Nashville Predators
Address: Gaylord Entertainment Center
           501 Broadway
           Nashville, TN 37203
Telephone: (615) 770-2300
Arena (Capacity): Gaylord Entertainment Center
(17,113)
Owner, Chairman and Governor: Craig Leipold
President, COO: Jack Diller
Executive VP of Hockey Operations/GM: David Poile
Coach: Barry Trotz
Director of Communications: Ken Anderson
www.nashvillepredators.com

New Jersey Devils
Address: Continental Airlines Arena, PO Box 504
           East Rutherford, NJ 07073
Telephone: (201) 935-6050
Arena (Capacity): Continental Airlines Arena (19,040)
Owners: Ray Chambers, Louis Katz and George
  Steinbrenner
CEO, President and GM: Lou Lamoriello
Coach: Pat Burns
Director of Public Relations: Jeff Altstadter
www.newjerseydevils.com

New York Islanders
Address: 1535 Old Country Road
           Plainview, NY 11803
Telephone: (516) 501-6700
Arena (Capacity): Nassau Coliseum (16,234)
Owners: Charles Wong and Sanjay Kumar
Senior VP of Operations and Alt. Governor: Michael J.
  Picker
General Manager/Alt. Governor: Mike Milbury
Coach: Steve Stirling
VP of Communications: Chris Botta
www.newyorkislanders.com

New York Rangers
Address: Madison Square Garden
           2 Pennsylvania Plaza
           New York, NY 10121
Telephone: (212) 465-6000
Arena (Capacity): Madison Square Garden (18,200)
Owner: Cablevision
President and General Manager: Glen Sather
Coach: Tom Renney
VP of Public Relations: John Rosasco
www.newyorkrangers.com

Ottawa Senators
Address: The Corel Centre
           1000 Palladium Drive
           Ottawa, Ontario K2V 1A5 Canada
Telephone: (613) 599-0250
Arena (Capacity): The Corel Centre (18,500)
Owner, Governor and Chairman: Eugene Melnyk

Ottawa Senators *(Cont.)*
President and Chief Executive Officer: Roy Mlakar
General Manager: John Muckler
Coach: Bryan Murray
VP of Communications: Phil Legault
www.ottawasenators.com

Philadelphia Flyers
Address: First Union Center
           3601 South Broad Street
           Philadelphia, PA 19148
Telephone: (215) 465-4500
Arena (Capacity): Wachovia Center (19,523)
Majority Owner: Comcast Spectacor
Chairman: Ed Snider
President: Ron Ryan
General Manager: Bob Clarke
Coach: Ken Hitchcock
Sr. Director of Communications: Zack Hill
www.philadelphiaflyers.com

Phoenix Coyotes
Address: Glendale Arena
           9400 W. Maryland Avenue
           Glendale, AZ 85305
Telephone: (623) 772-3200
Arena (Capacity): Glendale Arena (17,653)
Chairman and Governor: Steve Ellman
Managing Partner and Alt. Governor: Wayne Gretzky
VP and General Manager: Michael Barnette
Coach: Bob Francis
VP of Media and Player Relations: Richard Nairn
www.phoenixcoyotes.com

Pittsburgh Penguins
Address: Mellon Arena
           66 Mario Lemieux Place
           Pittsburgh, PA 15219
Telephone: (412) 642-1300
Arena (Capacity): Mellon Arena (16,958)
Owner: Mario Lemieux (Lemieux Ownership Group)
General Manager: Craig Patrick
Coach: Eddie Olczyk
Director of Media Relations: Keith Wehner
www.pittsburghpenguins.com

St. Louis Blues
Address: Savvis Center
           1401 Clark Avenue
           St. Louis, MO 63103
Telephone: (314) 622-2500
Arena (Capacity): Savvis Center (20,022)
President and Chief Executive Officer: Mark Sauer
Senior VP and General Manager: Larry Pleau
Coach: Mike Kitchen
Director of Communications: Chuck Menke
www.stlouisblues.com

San Jose Sharks
Address: HP Pavillion at San Jose
           525 West Santa Clara Street
           San Jose, CA 95113
Telephone: (408) 287-7070
Arena (Capacity): HP Pavillion at San Jose (17,496)
Owner: San Jose Sports And Entertainment
  Enterprises
President and CEO: Greg Jamison
Executive VP and General Manager: Doug Wilson
Coach: Ron Wilson
Director of Media Relations: Ken Arnold
www.sjsharks.com

Tampa Bay Lightning

Address: 401 Channelside Drive
            Tampa, FL 33602
Telephone: (813) 301-6600
Arena (Capacity): Ice Palace (19,758)
Owner: Palace Sports & Entertainment/Bill Davidson
and David Hermelin
CEO and Governor: Tom Wilson
General Manager: Jay Feaster
Coach: John Tortorella
VP of Public Relations: Bill Wickett
www.tampabaylightning.com

Toronto Maple Leafs

Address: Air Canada Centre
            40 Bay Street - St. 400
            Toronto, Ontario M5J 2X2 Canada
Telephone: (416) 815-5500
Arena (Capacity): Air Canada Centre (18,819)
Chairman: Lawrence M. Tanenbaum
President and CEO: Richard Peddie
GM: John Ferguson
Coach: Pat Quinn
Director of Media Relations: Pat Park
www.mapleleafs.com

Vancouver Canucks

Address: General Motors Place/800 Griffiths Way
            Vancouver, B.C. V6B 6G1
Telephone: (604) 899-4600
Arena (Capacity): General Motors Place (18,422)
Chairman and Governor: John E. McCaw Jr.
President and CEO: Stanley McCammon
Chief Operating Officer: David Cobb
Senior VP/GM: David Nonis
Coach: Marc Crawford
Manager of Media Relations: Chris Brumwell
www.canucks.com

Washington Capitals

Address: 401 Ninth Street, NW
            Suite 750
            Washington, DC 20004
Telephone: (202) 266-2200
Arena (Capacity): MCI Center (18,672)
Majority Owner and Chairman: Ted Leonsis
Owner and President: Richard M. Patrick
VP and General Manager: George McPhee
Coach: Glen Hanlon
Manger of Media Relations: Brian Potter
www.washingtoncaps.com

Olympic Sports Directory

United States Olympic Committee

Address: Olympic House
            1 Olympic Plaza
            Colorado Springs, CO 80909
Telephone: (719) 632-5551
Acting CEO: Jim Scherr
Chief Communications Officer: Darryl Seibel
www.usolympicteam.com

U.S. Olympic Training Centers

Address: 1 Olympic Plaza
            Colorado Springs, CO 80909
Telephone: (719) 632-5551
Director: John Smith

Address: 421 Old Military Road
            Lake Placid, NY 12946
Telephone: (518) 523-2600
Director: Jack Favro

Address: 2800 Olympic Parkway
            Chula Vista, CA 91915
Telephone: (619) 656-1500
Director: Patrice Milkovich
www.olympic.org

International Olympic Committee

Address: Chateau de Vidy
            Case Postale 356
            CH-1007 Lausanne, Switzerland
Telephone: 41-21-621-6111
President: Jacques Rogge
Director General: Francois Carrard
www.olympic.org

Torino Olympic Organizing Committee for the 2006 Winter Games

Address: Via Nizza 262/58
            10126 Torino (Italy)
Telephone: 39 011 63 10 511
President: Valentino Castellani
Press Operations: Cristiano Carlutti
(XX Winter Games; Feb 10–26, 2006)
www.torino2006.org

Beijing Olympic Organizing Committee for the 2008 Summer Games

Address: 24 Dongsi Shitao Street
            Beijing, China 100007
Telephone: (8610) 65282009
(XXVIII Summer Games; Aug 8–24, 2008)
www.beijing-olympic.org.cn

U.S. Olympic Organizations

National Archery Association (NAA)

Address: 1 Olympic Plaza
            Colorado Springs, CO 80909
Telephone: (719) 866-4576
President: Mark Miller
Executive Director: Brad Camp
Media Relations: Mary Beth Vorwerk
www.usarchery.org

USA Badminton (USAB)

Address: 1 Olympic Plaza
            Colorado Springs, CO 80909
Telephone: (719) 866-4808
President: Don Chew
Executive Director: Dan Cloppas
Media Contact: Barb Kissick
www.usabadminton.org

U.S. Olympic Organizations *(Cont.)*

USA Baseball
Address: P.O. Box 1131
             Durham, NC 27702
Telephone: (919) 474-8721
Chairman: Lindsay Burbage
Executive Director/CEO: Paul V. Seiler
Director of Communications: David Fanucchi
www.usabaseball.com

USA Basketball
Address: 5465 Mark Dabling Blvd.
             Colorado Springs, CO 80918
Telephone: (719) 590-4800
President: Tom Jernstedt
Executive Director: Jim Tooley
Assistant Executive Director for Public Relations:
 Craig Miller
www.usabasketball.com

U.S. Biathlon Association (USBA)
Address: 29 Ethan Allen Avenue
             Colchester, VT 05446
Telephone: (802) 654-7833
President: Bob Pokelwaldt
Executive Director: Claire DelNegro
PR and Media Manager: Tom LaDue
www.usbiathlon.org

U.S. Bobsled and Skeleton Federation
Address: P.O. Box 828
             Lake Placid, NY 12946
Telephone: (518) 523-1842
President: Jim Morris
Executive Director: Matt Roy
Media and PR Director Director: Julie Urbansky
www.usabobsledandskeleton.org

USA Boxing, Inc.
Address: 1 Olympic Plaza
             Colorado Springs, CO 80909
Telephone: (719) 866-4506
President: Dr. Robert Voy
Executive Director: Eric Parthen
Director of PR and Media: Julie Goldsticker
www.usaboxing.org

U.S. Canoe and Kayak Team
Address: 230 South Tryon Street - Suite 220
             Charlotte, NC 28202
Telephone: (704) 348-4330
President: Anne Blanchard
Executive Director: David Yarborough
Media/Communications: Luke Dieker
www.usacanoekayak.org

USA Cycling
Address: 1 Olympic Plaza
             Colorado Springs, CO 80909
Telephone: (719) 866-4581
President: Jim Ochowicz
Chief Executive Officer: Gerard Bisceglia
Director of Communications: Andy Lee
www.usacycling.org

United States Diving, Inc. (USD)
Address: Pan American Plaza, Suite 430
             201 South Capitol Avenue
             Indianapolis, IN 46225
Telephone: (317) 237-5252
President: Dave Burgering
Executive Director: Todd Smith
Director of Communications: Kelli Servizzi
www.usdiving.org

U.S. Equestrian Team (USET)
Address: Pottersville Rd.
             Gladstone, NJ 07934
Telephone: (908) 234-1251
Executive Director: Bonnie Jenkins
Director of Communications: Marty Bauman
www.uset.org

U.S. Fencing Association (USFA)
Address: 1 Olympic Plaza
             Colorado Springs, CO 80909
Telephone: (719) 866-4511
President: Stacey Johnson
Executive Director: Michael Massik
Media Relations Director: Cynthia Bent
www.usfencing.org

U.S. Field Hockey Association (USFHA)
Address: 1 Olympic Plaza
             Colorado Springs, CO 80909-5773
Telephone: (719) 866-4567
President: Sharon Taylor
Executive Director: Sheila Walker
Sport and Public Information Director:
 Howard Thomas
www.usfieldhockey.com

U.S. Figure Skating Association
Address: 20 First Street
             Colorado Springs, CO 80906
Telephone: (719) 635-5200
President: Chuck Foster
Director of Media Relations: Lindsay DeWall
www.usfsa.org

USA Gymnastics
Address: Pan American Plaza, Suite 300
             201 South Capitol Avenue
             Indianapolis, IN 46225
Telephone: (317) 237-5050
Chairman of the Board: Ron Froehlich
President: Robert Colarossi
Director of Public Relations: Steve Penny
www.usa-gymnastics.org

USA Hockey
Address: 1775 Bob Johnson Drive
             Colorado Springs, CO 80906
Telephone: (719) 576-8724
President: Ron DeGregorio
Executive Director: Doug Palazzari
Manager of Media and PR: TBA
www.usahockey.com

U.S. Olympic Organizations *(Cont.)*

United States Judo, Inc. (USJ)
Address: 1 Olympic Plaza Suite 202
          Colorado Springs, CO 80909
Telephone: (719) 866-4730
President: Dr. Ronald Tripp
Executive Director: William Rosenberg
www.usjudo.org

U.S. Luge Association (USLA)
Address: 35 Church Street
          Lake Placid, NY 12946
Telephone: (518) 523-2071
President: Doug Bateman
Executive Director: Ron Rossi
Public Relations Manager: Jon Lundin
www.usaluge.org

U.S. Modern Pentathlon Association
Address: 5407 Bandera Road - Suite 512
          San Antonio, TX 78238
Telephone: (210) 229-2004
President: Ralph Bender
Executive Director: Robert Marbut Jr.
www.usmpa.home.texas.net

U.S. Racquetball Association
Address: 1685 West Uintah
          Colorado Springs, CO 80904
Telephone: (719) 635-5396
President: Randy Stafford
Executive Director: Jim Hiser
Public Relations Coordinator: Ryan John
www.usra.org

USA Roller Sports
Address: 4730 South Street
          P.O. Box 6579
          Lincoln, NE 68506
Telephone: (402) 483-7551
President: George Kolibaba
Communications Director: Bill Wolf
www.usarollersports.org

U.S. Rowing
Address: Pan American Plaza, Suite 400
          201 South Capitol Avenue
          Indianapolis, IN 46225
Telephone: (317) 237-5656/ 1 (800) 314-4769
Executive Director: John Dane
Press Contact: Brett Johnson
www.usrowing.org

U.S. Sailing Association
Address: 15 Maritime Drive
          P.O. Box 1260
          Portsmouth, RI 02871
Telephone: (401) 683-0800
President: Dave Rosekrans
Executive Director: Nick Craw
Communications Manager: Marlieke de Lange Eaton
Olympic Yachting Director: Jonathan R. Harley
www.ussailing.org

USA Shooting
Address: 1 Olympic Plaza
          Colorado Springs, CO 80909
Telephone: (719) 866-4670
Chairman of the Board: Dr. James Lally
Executive Director: Robert K. Mitchell
Media and Public Relations: Sara Greenlee
www.usashooting.com

U.S. Ski and Snowboard Association
Address: P.O. Box 100
          Park City, UT 84060
Telephone: (435) 649-9090
Chairman: Chuck Ferries
President and CEO: Bill Marolt
V.P. of Communications and Media: Tom Kelly
www.usskiteam.com

U.S. Soccer Federation (USSF)
Address: 1801-1811 South Prairie Avenue
          Chicago, IL 60616
Telephone: (312) 808-1300
President: Robert Contiguglia
Secretary General: Dan Flynn
Director of Communications: Jim Moorhouse
www.ussoccer.com

Amateur Softball Association (ASA)
Address: 2801 N.E. 50th Street
          Oklahoma City, OK 73111
Telephone: (405) 424-5266
President: H. Franklin Taylor III
Executive Director: Ron Radigonda
Director of Communications: Brian McCall
www.softball.org

U.S. Speed Skating
Address: P.O. Box 450639
          Westlake OH 44145
Telephone: (440) 899-0128
President: Fred Benjamin
Executive Director: Katie Marquard
Public Relations Director: Melissa Scott
www.usspeedskating.org

U.S. Swimming, Inc. (USS)
Address: 1 Olympic Plaza
          Colorado Springs, CO 80909
Telephone: (719) 866-4578
President: Ron Van Pool
Executive Director: Chuck Wielgus
Public Relations Director: Mary Wagner
www.usa-swimming.org

U.S. Synchronized Swimming, Inc. (USSS)
Address: Pan American Plaza, Suite 901
          201 South Capitol Avenue
          Indianapolis, IN 46225
Telephone: (317) 237-5700
President: Betty Hazle
Executive Director: Terry Harper
Media Relations Director: Mandy Harlan
www.usasynchro.org

U.S. Table Tennis Association (USTTA)
Address: 1 Olympic Plaza
          Colorado Springs, CO 80909
Telephone: (719) 866-4583
Executive Director: Teodor Gheorghe
President: Sheri Pittman
Director of Media and PR: Debbie Doney
www.usatt.org

U.S. Taekwondo Union (USTU)
Address: 1 Olympic Plaza, Suite 405
          Colorado Springs, CO 80909
Telephone: (719) 866-4632
President: Sang Lee
Executive Director: R. Jay Warwick
Media and Communications Director: Chris Condron
www.ustu.org

U.S. Olympic Organizations *(Cont.)*

USA Team Handball
Address: 1 Olympic Plaza
                Colrado Springs, CO 80909
Telephone: (719) 866-4036
President: Bob Djokovich
Executive Director: Mike Cavanaugh
www.usateamhandball.org

U.S. Tennis Association
Address: 70 West Red Oak Lane
                White Plains, NY 10604
Telephone: (914) 696-7000
President: Alan G. Schwartz
Executive Director: Lee Hamilton
Director Marketing/Communications: David Newman
www.usta.com

USA Track & Field (formerly TAC)
Address: 1 RCA Dome, Suite 140
                Indianapolis, IN 46225
Telephone: (317) 261-0500
President: Bill Roe
Chief Executive Officer: Craig A. Masback
Director of Communications: Jill Geer
www.usatf.org

USA Volleyball
Address: 715 South Circle Drive
                Colorado Springs, CO 80910
Telephone: (719) 228-6800
President: Albert M. Monaco Jr.
Interim CEO: Howard Klostermann
Manager of Media Relations: Paul Soriano
www.usavolleyball.org

United States Water Polo (USWP)
Address: 1631 Mesa Avenue - Suite 1A
                Colorado Springs, CO 80906
Telephone: (719) 634-0699
President: Rich Foster
Executive Director: Tom Seitz
Media Director: Eric Velazquez
www.usawaterpolo.com

USA Weightlifting
Address: 1 Olympic Plaza
                Colorado Springs, CO 80909
Telephone: (719) 866-4508
President: Dennis Snethen
Executive Director and Media Contact: Wesley
  Barnett
www.usaweightlifting.org

USA Wrestling
Address: 6155 Lehman Drive
                Colorado Springs, CO 80918
Telephone: (719) 598-8181
President: Bruce Baumgartner
Executive Director: Rich Bender
Director of Communications: Gary Abbott
www.usawrestling.org

Affiliated Sports Organizations

Amateur Athletic Union (AAU)
Address: Walt Disney World Resort; P.O. Box 22409
                Lake Buena Vista, FL 32830-1000
Telephone: (407) 934-7200
President: Bobby Dodd
Media Contact: Melissa Wilson
www.aausports.org

U.S. Curling Association (USCA)
Address: 1100 Center Point Drive
                P.O. Box 866
                Stevens Point, WI 54481
Telephone: (715) 344-1199
President: Mark Swandby
Executive Director: David Garber
Communications Director: Rick Patzke
www.usacurl.org

USA Karate Federation
Address: 1300 Kenmore Boulevard
                Akron, OH 44314
Telephone: (330) 753-3114
President: George Anderson
www.usakarate.org

U.S. Orienteering Federation
Address: P.O. Box 1444
                Forest Park, GA 30298
Telephone: (404) 363-2110
President: Chuck Ferguson
Executive Director: Robin Shannonhouse
Marketing and Public Relations VP: Sherry Litasi
Publicity telephone: (303) 694-4914
www.us.orienteering.org

U.S. Squash Racquets Association
Address: 23 Cynwyd Road
                P.O. Box 1216
                Bala Cynwyd, PA 19004
Telephone: (610) 667-4006
President: Ken Stillman
Vice President: Charlie Johnson
www.us-squash.com

USA Triathlon
Address: 1365 Graden of the Gods Road
                Colorado Springs, CO 80907
Telephone: (719) 597-9090
President: Brad Davison
Executive Director: TBA
Communications Director: B. J. Hoeptner Evans
www.usatriathlon.org

USA Waterski
Address: 1251 Holy Cow Road
                Polk City, FL 33868
Telephone: (863) 324-4341
President: Andrea Plough
Executive Director: Steve McDermeit
Public Relations Manager: Scott Atkinson
www.usawaterski.org

Championship Auto Racing Teams (CART)
Address: 5350 Lakeview Parkway South Drive
            Building 36 - Inner Park/Park 100
            Indianapolis, IN 46268
Telephone: (317) 715-4100
President: Dick Eidswick
VP of PR and Communications: Wendy Gabers
www.cart.com

Indy Racing League
Address: 4565 West 16th Street
            Indianapolis, IN 46222
Telephone: (317) 484-6526
President and Founder: Tony George
Director of Media Relations: Ron Green
www.indyracing.com

International Motor Sports Association
Address: 1394 Broadway Avenue
            Braselton, GA 30517
Telephone: (706) 658-2120
President: Scott Atherton
Executive Director: Doug Robinson
www.imsaracing.net

National Association for Stock Car Auto Racing (NASCAR)
Address: 1801 W International Speedway Blvd.
            Daytona Beach, FL 32114-1243
Telephone: (386) 253-0611
CEO/Chairman: Brian France
President: Mike Helton
VP of Corporate Communications: Jim Hunter
www.nascar.com

National Hot Rod Association
Address: 2035 East Financial Way
            Glendora, CA 91741
Telephone: (626) 914-4761
President: Tom Compton
VP of PR and Communications: Jerry Archambeault
www.nhra.com

Professional Bowlers Association LLC
Address: 719 Second Avenue - Suite 701
            Seattle, WA 98104
Telephone: (206) 332-9688
Commissioner: Fred Schreyer
Director of Corporate Communications: Beth Marshall
www.pba.com

U.S. Chess Federation
Address: 3054 Route 9 W
            New Windsor, NY 12553
Telephone: (845) 562-8350
President: Beatriz Marinello
Executive Director: George De Feis
Media Relations: Anne Ashton
www.uschess.org

International Game Fish Association
Address: 300 Gulf Stream Way
            Dania Beach, FL 33004
Telephone: (954) 927-2628
President: Rob Kramer
www.igfa.org

Ladies Professional Golf Association
Address: 100 International Golf Drive
            Daytona Beach, FL 32124
Telephone: (386) 274-6200
Commissioner: Ty Votaw
Director of Media Relations: Connie Wilson
www.lpga.com

PGA Tour
Address: 112 PGA Tour Boulevard
            Ponte Vedra Beach, FL 32082
Telephone: (904) 285-3700
Commissioner: Tim Finchem
Senior VP of Communications: Bob Combs
www.pgatour.com

Professional Golfers' Association of America
Address: 100 Avenue of the Champions
            Box 109601
            Palm Beach Gardens, FL 33410-9601
Telephone: (561) 624-8400
President: M.G. Orender
Director of Public Relations: Julius Mason
www.pgaonline.com

United States Golf Association
Address: P.O. Box 708, Golf House
            Liberty Corner Road
            Far Hills, NJ 07931-0708
Telephone: (908) 234-2300
President: Fred S. Ridley
Director of Media Relations: Craig Smith
www.usga.org

U.S. Handball Association
Address: 2333 North Tucson Boulevard
            Tucson, AZ 85716
Telephone: (520) 795-0434
President: Bob Hickman
Executive Director: Vern Roberts
Director of Public Relations: Mark Carpenter
www.ushandball.org

Breeders' Cup Limited
Address: 2525 Harrodsburg Road
            PO Box 4230
            Lexington, KY 40504
Telephone: (859) 223-5444
President: D. G. Van Clief Jr.
Media Relations Director: James Gluckson
Director of Marketing: Damon Thayer
www.breederscup.com

The Jockeys' Guild, Inc.
Address: P.O. Box 150
            Monrovia, CA 91017
Telephone: (866) 465-6257
Chairman of the Board: Tomey Swan

Thoroughbred Racing Associations of America
Address: 420 Fair Hill Drive, Suite 1
            Elkton, MD 21921
Telephone: (410) 392-9200
Executive Vice President: Chris Scherf
www.tra-online.com

National Thoroughbred Racing Association

Address: 800 Third Avenue - Suite 901
            New York, NY 10022
Telephone: (212) 230-9500
Senior VP/Mrkting & Industry Rels: Keith Chamblin
www.ntra.com

United States Trotting Association

Address: 750 Michigan Avenue
            Columbus, OH 43215
Telephone: (614) 224-2291
Executive Vice President: Fred J. Noe
Director of Publicity: John Pawlak
www.ustrotting.com

Iditarod Trail Committee

Address: P.O. Box 870800; Wasilla, AK 99687
Telephone: (907) 376-5155
Executive Director: Stan Hooley
Race Director: Joanne Potts
www.iditarod.com

U.S. Lacrosse

Address: 113 W University Parkway
            Baltimore, MD 21210
Telephone: (410) 235-6882
Executive Director: Steven B. Stenersen
www.lacrosse.org

Little League Baseball, Inc.

Address: P.O. Box 3485
            Williamsport, PA 17701
Telephone: (570) 326-1921
President & CEO: Stephen D. Keener
Senior Communications Executive: Lance Van Auken
www.littleleague.org

U.S. Polo Association

Address: 771 Corporate Drive, Suite 505
            Lexington, KY 40503
Telephone: (859) 219-1000
Chairman: Jack Shelton
www.uspolo.org

American Powerboating Association

Address: 17640 Nine Mile Road
            Eastpointe, MI 48021
Telephone: (586) 773-9700
Executive Administrator: Gloria Urbin
www.apba-racing.com

Professional Rodeo Cowboys Association

Address: 101 Pro Rodeo Drive
            Colorado Springs, CO 80919
Telephone: (719) 593-8840
Commissioner: Steven J. Hatchell
Director of Communications: Leslie King
www.prorodeo.com

USA Rugby Football Union

Address: 1033 Walnut Street
            Suite 200
            Boulder, CO 80302
Telephone: (719) 637-1022
President: Neal Brendel
CEO: Doug Arnot
Communications Director: Deborah Engen
www.usarugby.org

The United Soccer Leagues

Address: 14497 North Dale Mabry Highway, Ste 201
            Tampa, FL 33618
Telephone: (813) 963-3909
President and A-League Commissioner: Francisco
    Marcos
Director of Public Relations:Gerald Barnhart
www.uslsoccer.com

Major League Soccer

Address: 110 East 42nd Street, Suite 1000
            New York, NY 10017
Telephone: (212) 687-1400
Commissioner: Don Garber
Director of Communications: Trey Fitzgerald
www.mlsnet.com

Major Indoor Soccer League

Address: 1175 Post Road East
            Westport, CT 06880
Telephone: (203) 222-4900
Commissioner: Steve Ryan
Director of Communications: Jay Cavallo
www.misl.net

Women's United Soccer Association

Address: 6205 Peachtree Dunwoody Road
            Atlanta, GA 30328
Telephone: (678) 645-0800
Commissioner: Tony DiCicco
Director of Public Relations: Shaun May
www.wusa.com

Association of Tennis Professionals Tour

Address: 201 ATP Tour Boulevard
            Ponte Vedra Beach, FL 32082
Telephone: (904) 285-8000
Chief Executive Officer: Mark Miles
VP of Comm. and Media Relations: Greg Sharko
www.atptour.org

COREL WTA Tour (Women's Tennis)

Address: One Progress Plaza - Suite 1500
            St. Petersburg, FL 33701
Telephone: (727) 895-5000
Chief Executive Officer: Larry Scott
Director of Corporate Communications: Darrell Fry
www.wtatour.com

Association of Volleyball Professionals

Address: 6100 Center Drive - 9th Floor
            Los Angeles, CA 90045
Telephone: (310) 426-8000
Public Relations: Debbie Rubio, The Robbins Group
    (818) 776-1244
www.avptour.com

MINOR LEAGUES

Baseball (AAA)

National Association of Professional Baseball Leagues

Address: 201 Bayshore Drive S.E. - P.O. Box A
            St. Petersburg, FL 33731
Telephone: (727) 822-6937
President: Mike Moore
Director of Media Relations: Jim Ferguson
www.minorleaguebaseball.com

MINOR LEAGUES *(Cont.)*

Baseball (AAA) *(Cont.)*

International League
Address: 55 South High Street, Suite 202
             Dublin, OH 43017
Telephone: (614) 791-9300
President: Randy Mobley
www.ilbaseball.com

Pacific Coast League
Address: 1631 Mesa Avenue
             Colorado Springs, CO 80906
Telephone: (719) 636-3399
President: Branch Rickey
www.pclbaseball.com

Hockey

American Hockey League
Address: 1 Monarch Place Suite 2400
             Springfield, MA 01144
Telephone: (413) 781-2030
President, CEO & Treasurer: David A. Andrews
VP of Hockey Operations: Jim Mill
Director of Media: Jason Chaimovitch
www.theahl.com

Halls of Fame Directory

National Baseball Hall of Fame and Museum
Address: P.O. Box 590/25 Main Street
             Cooperstown, NY 13326
Telephone: (607) 547-7200
President: Dale Petroskey
Senior Vice President: Bill Haase
V.P. of Communications and Education: Jeff Idelson
www.baseballhalloffame.org

Naismith Memorial Basketball Hall of Fame
Address: 1000 West Columbus Avenue
             Springfield, MA 01105
Telephone: (413) 781-6500
President and CEO: John L. Doleva
VP of Marketing and Sales: Dan O'Keefe
www.hoophall.com

International Bowling Museum and Hall of Fame
Address: 111 Stadium Plaza
             St. Louis, MO 63102
Telephone: (314) 231-6340
Executive Director: Gerald Baltz
Marketing Director: Jim Baer
www.bowlingmuseum.com

National Boxing Hall of Fame
Address: 1 Hall of Fame Drive
             Canastota, NY 13032
Telephone: (315) 697-7095
President: Donald Ackerman
Executive Director: Edward Brophy
www.ibhof.com

Professional Football Hall of Fame
Address: 2121 George Halas Drive NW
             Canton, OH 44708
Telephone: (330) 456-8207
Executive Director: John Bankert
Vice President of Public Relations: Joe Horrigan
www.profootballhof.com

LPGA Hall of Fame
Address: 100 International Golf Drive
             Daytona Beach, FL 32124
Telephone: (386) 274-6200
Commissioner: Ty Votaw
Director of Media Relations: Connie Wilson
www.lpga.com

Hockey Hall of Fame
Address: 30 Yonge Street.BCE Place
             Toronto, Ontario Canada M5E 1X8
Telephone: (416) 360-7735
Chairman: William Hay
President & COO: Jeff Denomme
Director of Marketing and Facility Services: Craig Baines
www.hhof.com

National Museum of Racing and Hall of Fame
Address: 191 Union Avenue
             Saratoga Springs, NY 12866
Telephone: (518) 584-0400
Executive Director: Peter Hammell
Assistant Director: Catherine Maguire
Communications Officer: Richard Hamilton
www.racingmuseum.org

National Soccer Hall of Fame
Address: Wright Soccer Campus
             18 Stadium Circle
             Oneonta, NY 13820
Telephone: (607) 432-3351
President: Will Lunn
www.soccerhall.org

International Swimming Hall of Fame
Address: 1 Hall of Fame Drive
             Fort Lauderdale, FL 33316
Telephone: (954) 462-6536
President: Dr. Samuel J. Freas
Media Contact: Preston Levi
www.ishof.org

International Tennis Hall of Fame
Address: 194 Bellevue Avenue
             Newport, RI 02840
Telephone: (401) 849-3990
CEO: Mark Stenning
Marketing Manager: Kat Anderson
www.tennisfame.com

National Track & Field Hall of Fame
Address: 216 Ft. Washington Avenue
             The Armory Foundation
             New York, NY 10032
Telephone: (317) 261-0500
Chief Executive Officer: Craig Masback
Director of Communications: Jill Geer
www.usatf.org

Sporting Venues

STADIUM MAPS COURTESY OF TICKETMASTER

BASEBALL

Anaheim Angels
P.O. Box 2000
Anaheim, CA 92803
(714) 940-2000
Stadium: Angel Stadium
of Anaheim

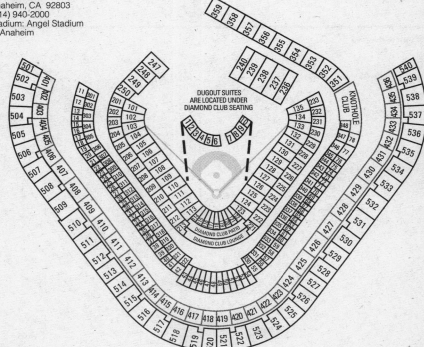

Arizona Diamondbacks

401 East Jefferson Street
Phoenix, AZ 85004
(602) 462-6500
Stadium: Bank One Ballpark

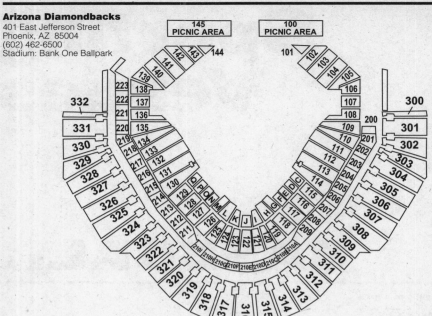

Atlanta Braves

P.O. Box 4064
Atlanta, GA 30302
(404) 522-7630
Stadium: Turner Field

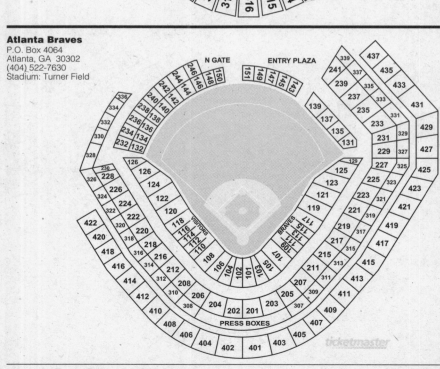

Baltimore Orioles

333 W Camden Street
Baltimore, MD 21201
(410) 685-9800
Stadium: Oriole Park
  at Camden Yards

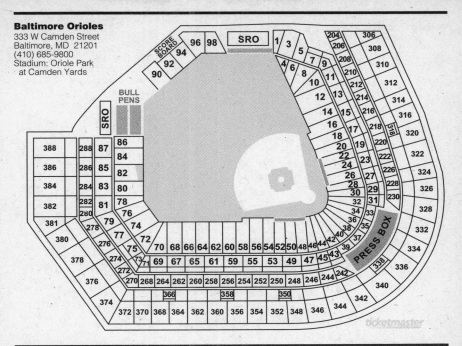

Boston Red Sox

4 Yawkey Way
Boston, MA 02215
(617) 267-9440
Stadium: Fenway Park

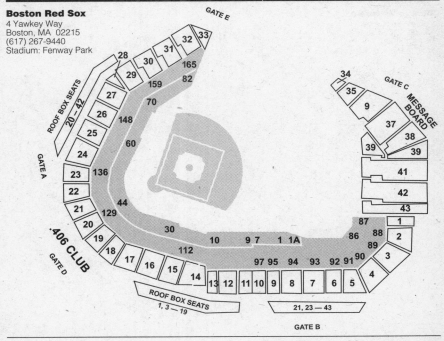

Chicago Cubs

1060 West Addison
Chicago, IL 60613
(773) 404-2827
Stadium: Wrigley Field

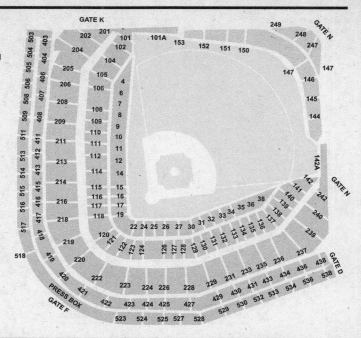

Chicago White Sox

333 West 35th Street
Chicago, IL 60616
(312) 674-1000
Stadium: U.S. Cellular Field

Cincinnati Reds
100 Main Street
Cincinnati, OH 45202
(513) 765-7000
Stadium: Great American Ball Park

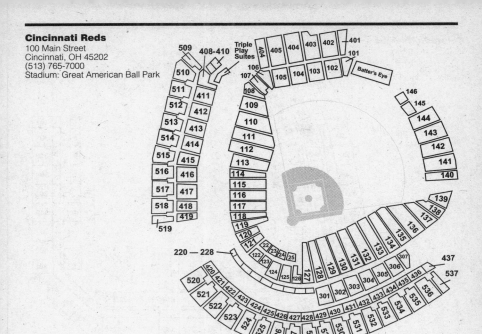

Cleveland Indians
2401 Ontario Street
Cleveland, OH 44115-4003
(216) 420-4200
Stadium: Jacobs Field

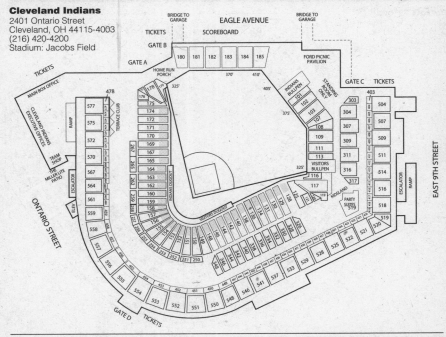

Colorado Rockies

2001 Blake Street
Denver, CO 80205
(303) 292-0200
Stadium: Coors Field

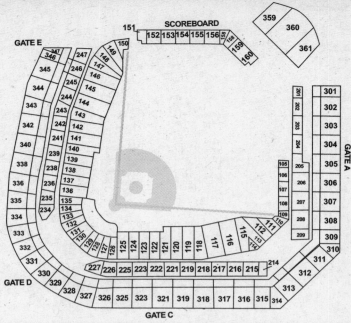

Detroit Tigers

2100 Woodward Avenue
Detroit, MI 48201
(313) 962-4000
Stadium: Comerica Park

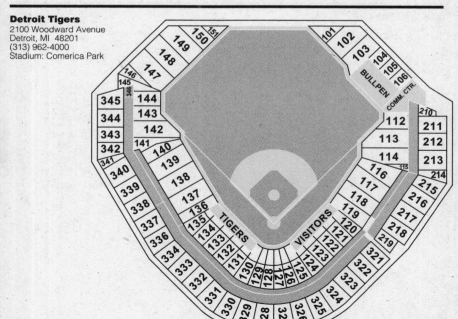

ticketmaster

Florida Marlins

2267 Dan Marino Boulevard
Miami, FL 33056
(305) 626-7400
Stadium: Pro Player
 Stadium

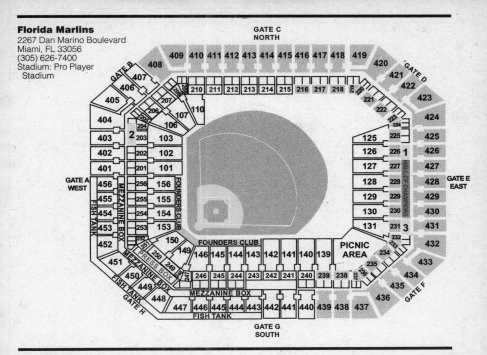

Houston Astros

P.O. Box 288
Houston, TX 77001
(713) 259-8000
Stadium:
 Minute Maid Park

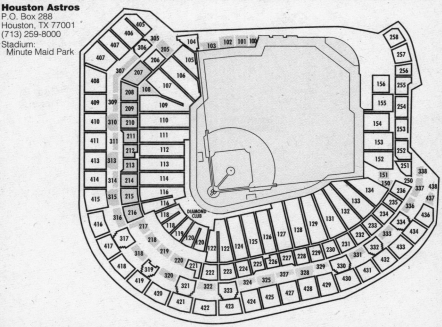

Kansas City Royals

P.O. Box 419969
Kansas City, MO 64141
(816) 921-8000
Stadium: Kauffman Stadium

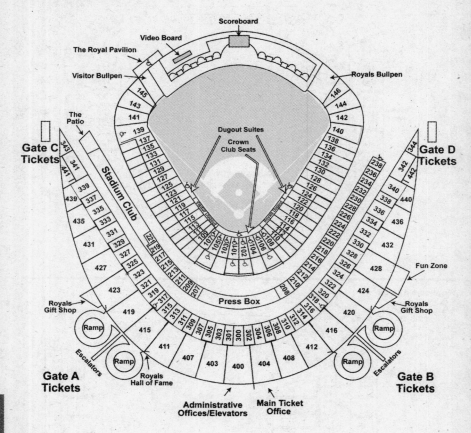

Los Angeles Dodgers

1000 Elysian Park Avenue
Los Angeles, CA 90012-1199
(323) 224-1500
Stadium: Dodger Stadium

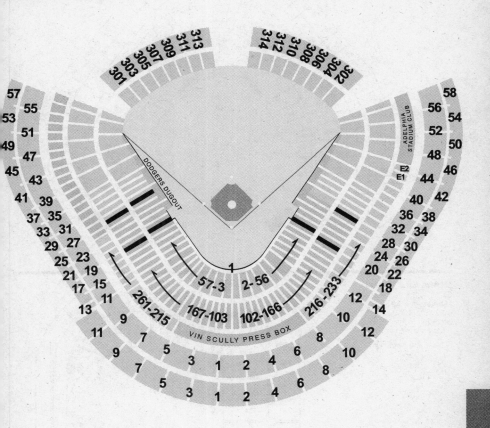

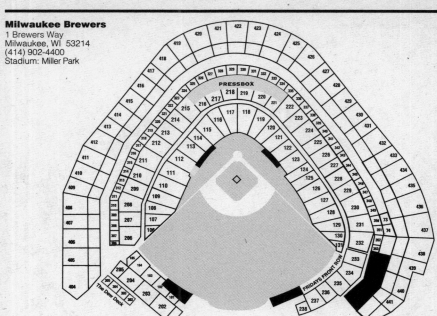

Milwaukee Brewers

1 Brewers Way
Milwaukee, WI 53214
(414) 902-4400
Stadium: Miller Park

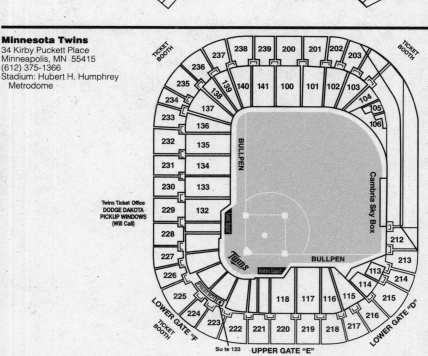

Minnesota Twins

34 Kirby Puckett Place
Minneapolis, MN 55415
(612) 375-1366
Stadium: Hubert H. Humphrey
  Metrodome

Montreal Expos
P.O. Box 500 Station M
Montreal, Quebec H1V 3P2 Canada
(514) 253-3434
Stadium:
  Olympic Stadium

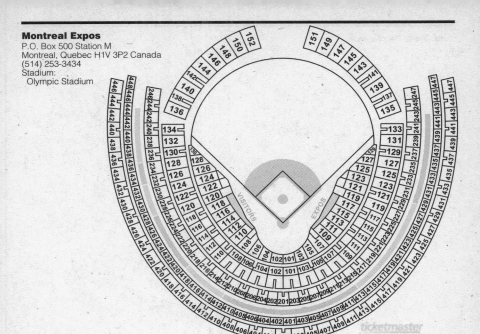

New York Mets
123-01 Roosevelt Ave.
Flushing, NY 11368
(718) 507-6387
Stadium: Shea Stadium

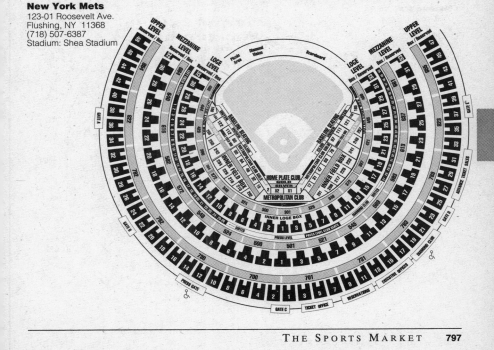

New York Yankees

Bronx, NY 10451
(718) 293-4300
Stadium: Yankee Stadium

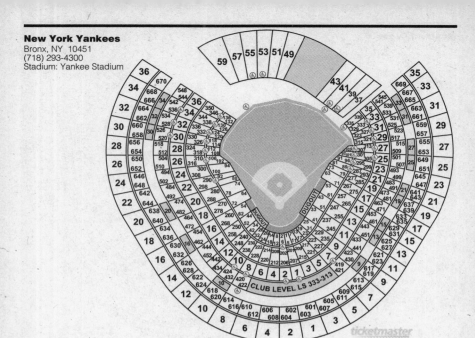

Oakland A's

7000 Coliseum Way
Oakland, CA 94621
(510) 638-4900
Stadium: Network
 Associates Coliseum

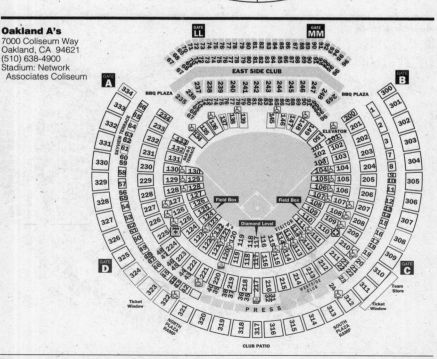

Philadelphia Phillies

P.O. Box 7575
Philadelphia, PA 19101-7575
(215) 463-6000
Stadium: Citizens Bank Park

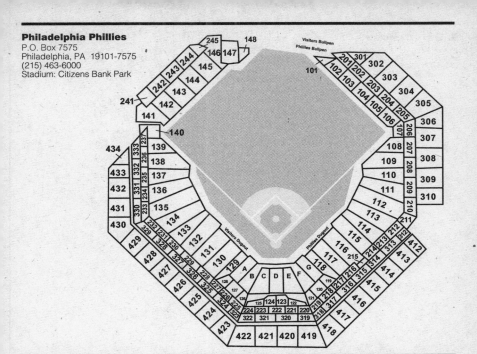

Pittsburgh Pirates

P.O. Box 7000
Pittsburgh, PA 15212
(412) 323-5000
Stadium: PNC Park

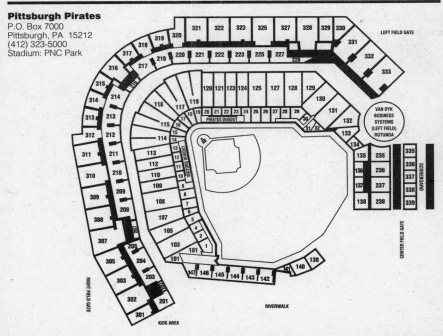

St Louis Cardinals

250 Stadium Plaza
St. Louis, MO 63102
(314) 421-3060
Stadium: Busch Stadium

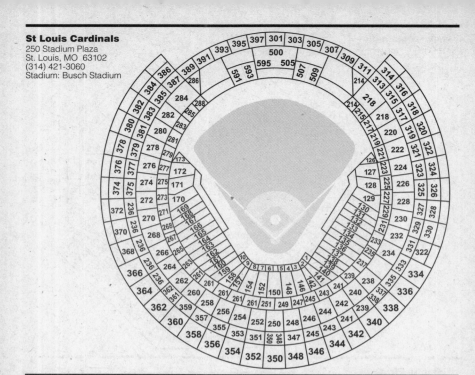

San Diego Padres

P.O. Box 122000
San Diego, CA 92112
(619) 283-4494
Stadium: Petco Park

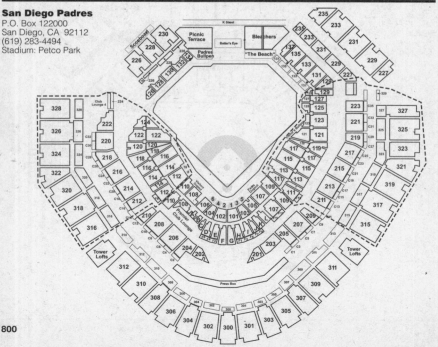

San Francisco Giants
24 Willie Mays Plaza
San Francisco, CA 94107
(415) 972-2000
Stadium: SBC Park

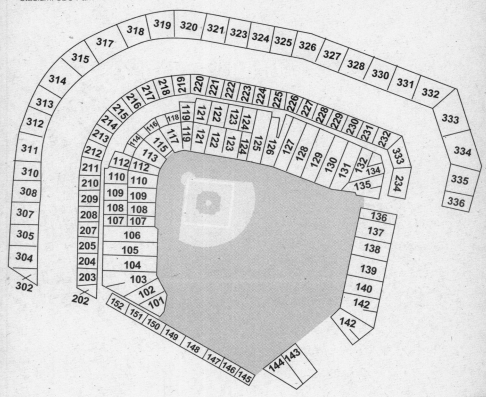

Seattle Mariners
P.O. Box 4100
Seattle, WA 98104
(206) 346-4000
Stadium: SAFECO Field

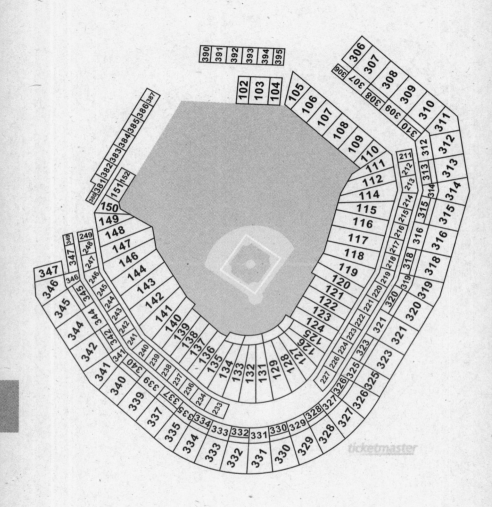

Tampa Bay Devil Rays
One Tropicana Drive
St. Petersburg, FL 33705
(727) 825-3137
Stadium: Tropicana Field

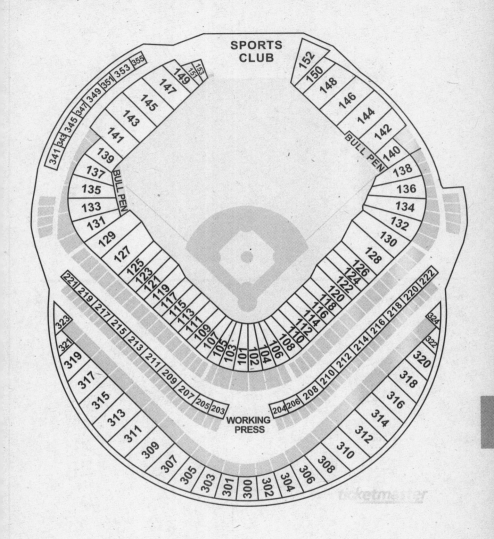

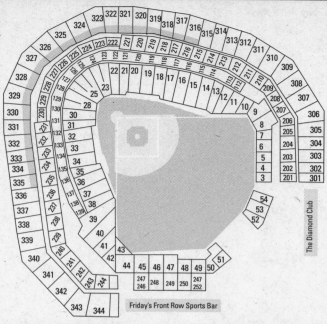

Texas Rangers
P.O. Box 90111
Arlington, TX 76004
(817) 273-5222
Stadium:
Ameriquest Field
in Arlington

The Diamond Club

Friday's Front Row Sports Bar

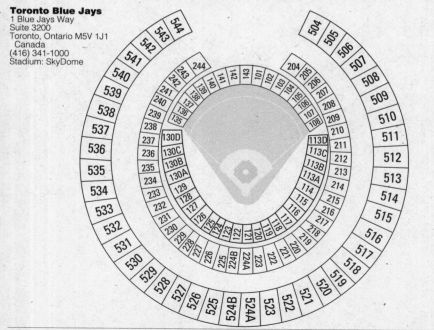

Toronto Blue Jays
1 Blue Jays Way
Suite 3200
Toronto, Ontario M5V 1J1
 Canada
(416) 341-1000
Stadium: SkyDome

BASKETBALL

Atlanta Hawks
One CNN Center
Atlanta, GA 30303
Telephone: (404) 827-3800
Arena: Philips Arena

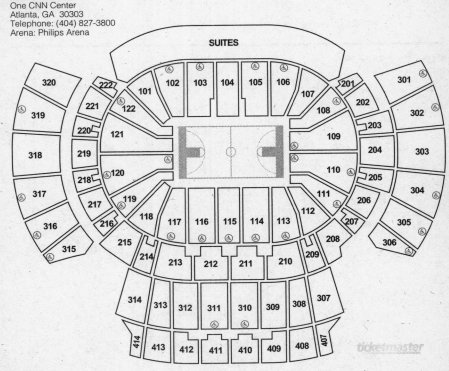

SUITES

Boston Celtics

151 Merrimac Street
Boston, MA 02114
Telephone: (617) 523-6050
Arena: FleetCenter

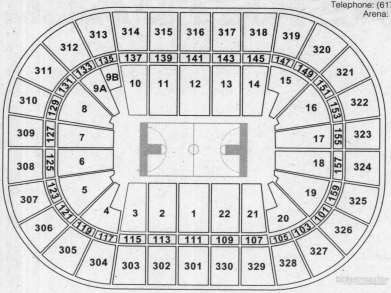

New Orleans Hornets

1501 Girod Street
New Orleans, LA 70113
Telephone: (504) 301-4000
Arena: New Orleans Arena

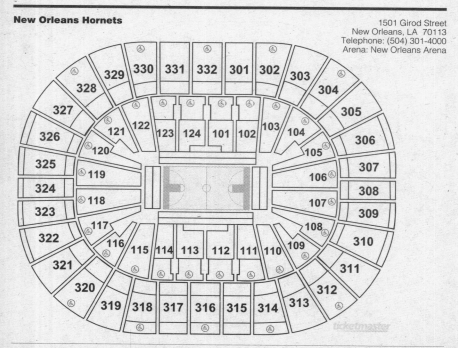

Chicago Bulls

1901 W. Madison Street
Chicago, IL 60612
Telephone: (312) 455-4000
Arena: United Center

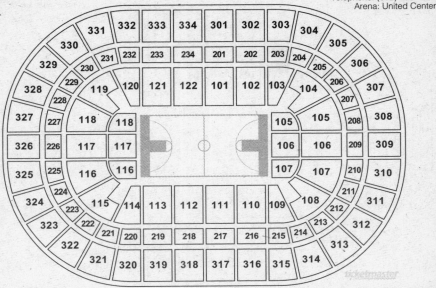

Cleveland Cavaliers

One Center Court
Cleveland, OH 44115
Telephone: (216) 420-2000
Arena: Gund Arena

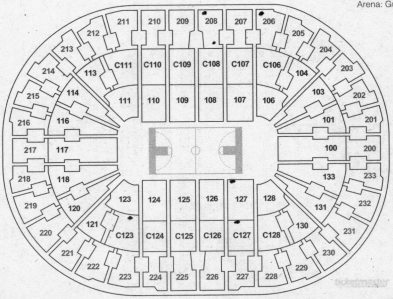

Dallas Mavericks

2500 Victory Avenue
Dallas, TX 75201
Telephone: (214) 665-4660
Arena: American Airlines Center

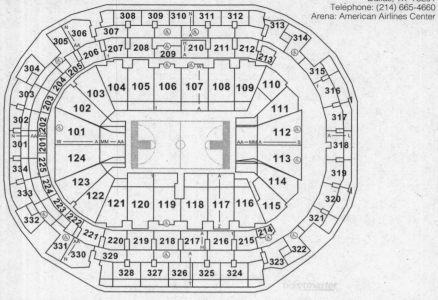

Denver Nuggets

1000 Chopper Circle
Denver, CO 80204
Telephone: (303) 405-1100
Arena: Pepsi Center

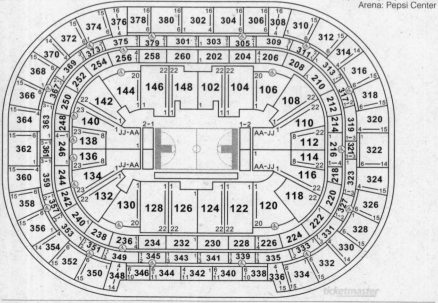

Detroit Pistons

Two Championship Drive
Auburn Hills, MI 48326
Telephone: (248) 377-0100
Arena: The Palace of Auburn Hills

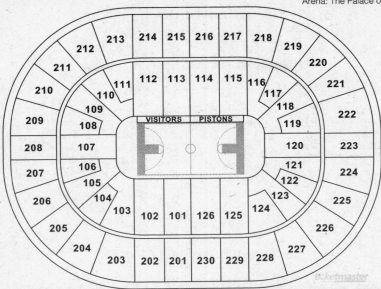

Golden State Warriors

1011 Broadway
Oakland, CA 94607-4019
Telephone: (510) 986-2200
Arena: The Arena in Oakland

Houston Rockets

Two Greenway Plaza, Suite 400
Houston, TX 77046
Telephone: (713) 627-3865
Arena: Compaq Center

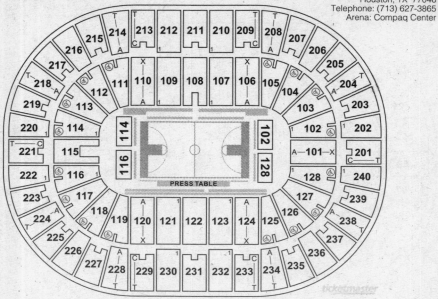

Indiana Pacers

125 S. Pennsylvania Street
Indianapolis, IN 46204
Telephone: (317) 917-2500
Arena: Conseco Fieldhouse

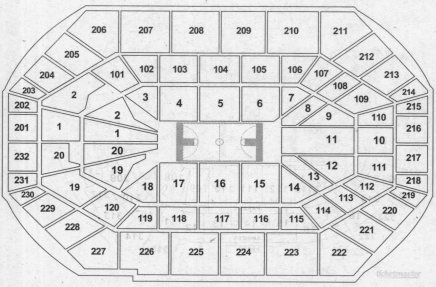

Los Angeles Clippers

1111 S. Figueroa Street - St. 1100
Los Angeles, CA 90015
Telephone: (213) 742-7500
Arena: The Staples Center

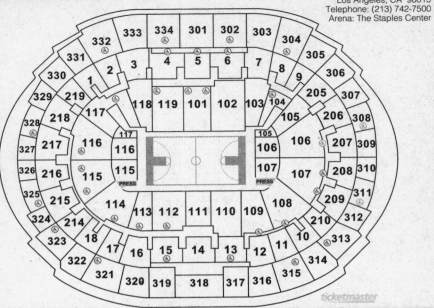

Los Angeles Lakers

555 North Nash Street
El Segundo, CA 90245
Telephone: (310) 426-6000
Arena: The Staples Center

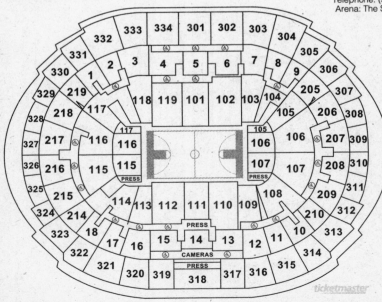

Memphis Grizzlies

60 Madison Street /10th Floor
Memphis, TN 38103
Telephone: (901) 205-1234
Arena: FedEx Forum

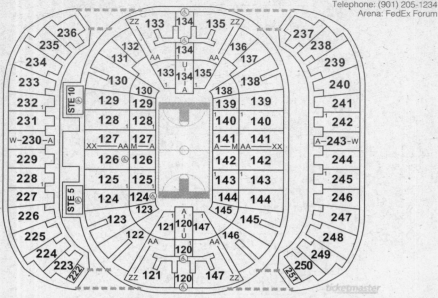

Miami Heat

601 Biscayne Boulevard
Miami, FL 33132
Telephone: (786) 777-4328
Arena: American Airlines Arena

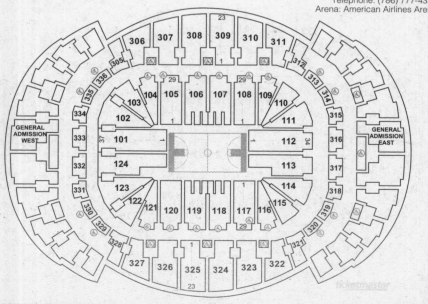

Milwaukee Bucks

1001 N. Fourth Street
Milwaukee, WI 53203
Telephone: (414) 227-0500
Arena: The Bradley Center

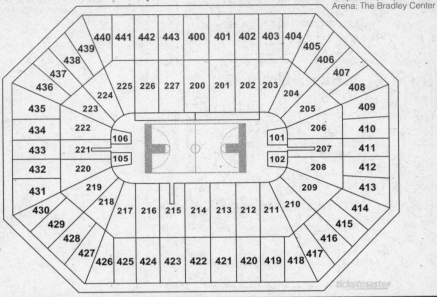

Minnesota Timberwolves

600 First Avenue North
Minneapolis, MN 55403
Telephone: (612) 673-1600
Arena: Target Center

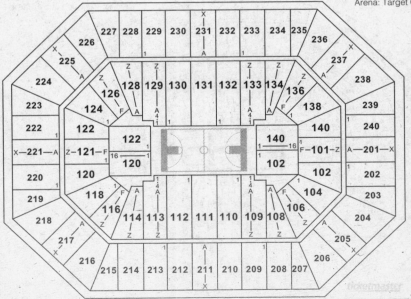

New Jersey Nets

390 Murray Hill Parkway
East Rutherford, NJ 07073
Telephone: (201) 935-8888
Arena: Continental Airlines Arena

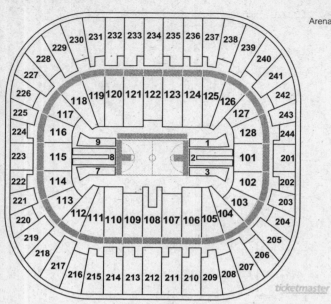

New York Knickerbockers

Two Pennsylvania Plaza
New York, NY 10121
Telephone: (212) 465-5867
Arena: Madison Square Garden

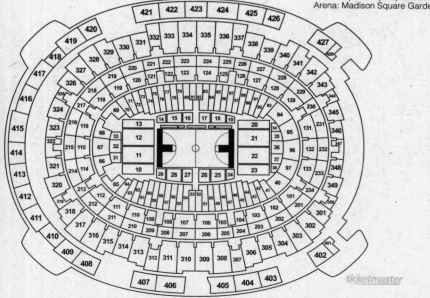

Orlando Magic

Two Magic Place
8701 Maitland Summit Blvd.
Orlando, FL 32810
Telephone: (407) 916-2400
Arena: TD Waterhouse Centre

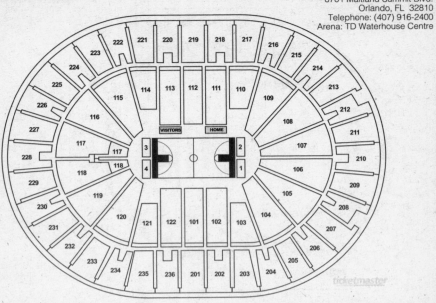

Philadelphia 76ers

3601 South Broad Street
Philadelphia, PA 19148
Telephone: (215) 339-7600
Arena: First Union Center

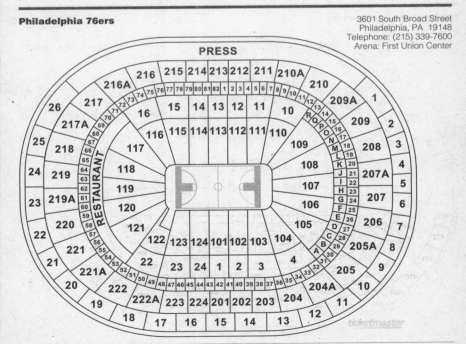

Phoenix Suns

P.O. Box 1369
Phoenix, AZ 85001 ·
Telephone: (602) 379-7900
Arena: America West Arena

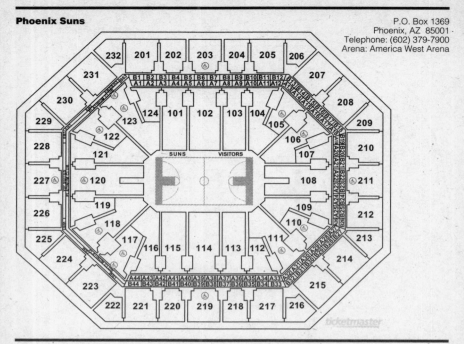

Portland Trail Blazers

One Center Court
Suite 200
Portland, OR 97227
Telephone: (503) 234-9291
Arena: Rose Garden Arena

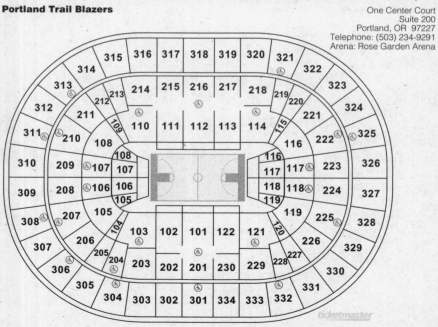

Sacramento Kings

One Sports Parkway
Sacramento, CA 95834
Telephone: (916) 928-0000
Arena: ARCO Arena

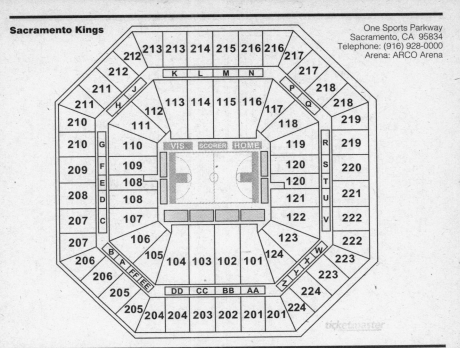

San Antonio Spurs

100 Montana
San Antonio, TX 78203
Telephone: (210) 554-7787
Arena: Alamodome

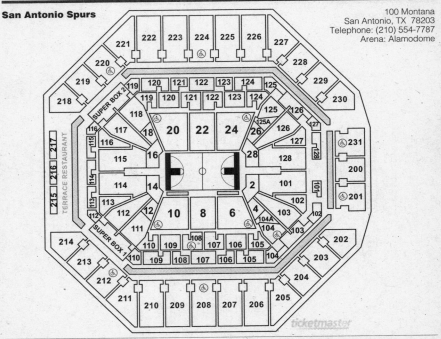

Seattle SuperSonics

351 Elliott Avenue West
Suite 500
Seattle, WA 98119
Telephone: (206) 281-5847
Arena: KeyArena

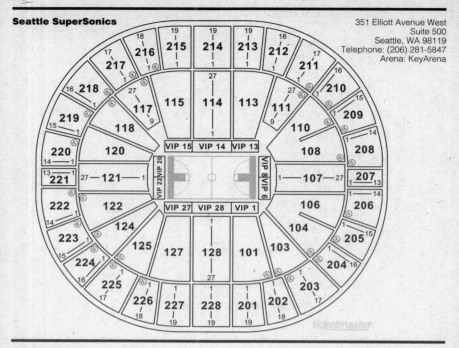

Toronto Raptors

40 Bay Street, Suite 400
Toronto, Ontario M5J 2X2 Canada
Telephone: (416) 815-5600
Arena: Air Canada Centre

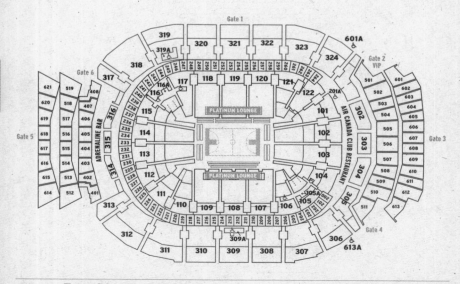

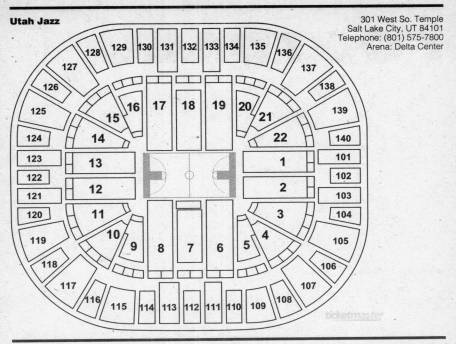

Utah Jazz

301 West So. Temple
Salt Lake City, UT 84101
Telephone: (801) 575-7800
Arena: Delta Center

Washington Wizards

601 F Street NW
Washington D.C. 20004
Telephone: (202) 661-5000
Arena: MCI Center

FOOTBALL

Arizona Cardinals
Sun Devil Stadium
ASU Campus Fifth Street
Tempe, AZ 85281
(602) 379-0101

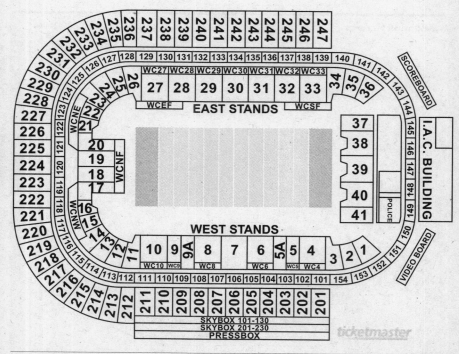

Atlanta Falcons

Georgia Dome
One Georgia Dome Dr.
Atlanta, GA 30313
(770) 965-3115

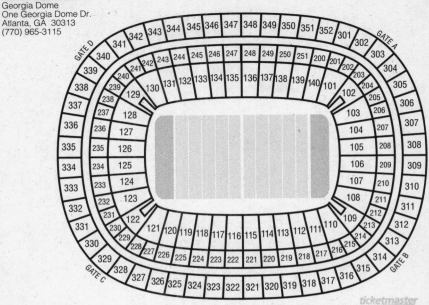

Baltimore Ravens

M&T Bank Stadium
1101 Russell St.
Baltimore, MD 21230
(410) 654-6200

Buffalo Bills

Ralph Wilson Stadium
One Bills Drive
Orchard Park, NY 14127
(716) 648-1800

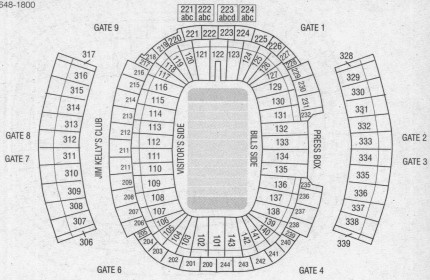

Carolina Panthers

Bank of America Stadium
800 South Mint St.
Charlotte, NC 28202
(704) 358-7000

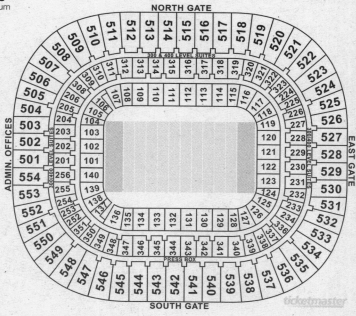

Chicago Bears
Soldier Field
16th St. at Lakeshore Dr.
Chicago, IL 60605
(847) 295-6600

Cincinnati Bengals
Paul Brown Stadium
One Paul Brown Stadium
Cincinnati, OH 45202
(513) 621-3550

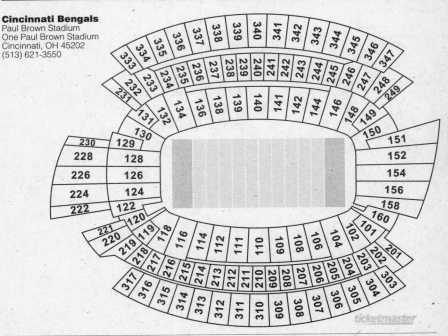

Cleveland Browns

Cleveland Browns Stadium
1085 W. 3rd St.
Cleveland, OH 44114
(440) 891-5000

Dallas Cowboys

Texas Stadium
2401 E. Airport Freeway
Irving, TX 75062
(972) 556-9900

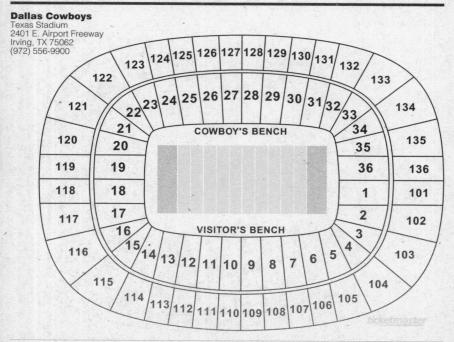

Denver Broncos
INVESCO Field at Mile High
1701 Bryant St.
Denver, CO 80204
(303) 649-9000

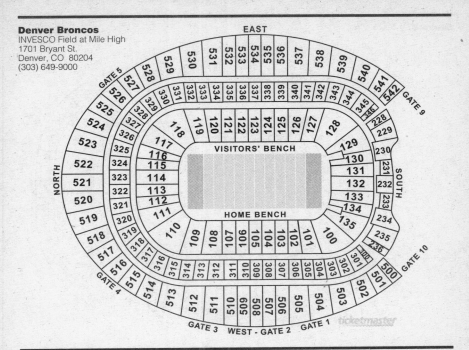

Detroit Lions
Ford Field
2000 Brush St.
Detroit, MI 48226
(313) 216-4000

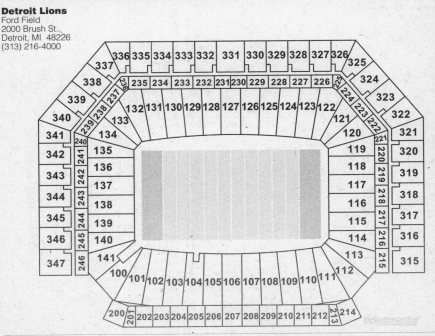

Green Bay Packers

Lambeau Field
1265 Lombardi Avenue
Green Bay, WI 54304
Telephone: (920) 496-5700

Houston Texans

Reliant Stadium
One Reliant Park
Houston, TX 77054
(832) 667-2000

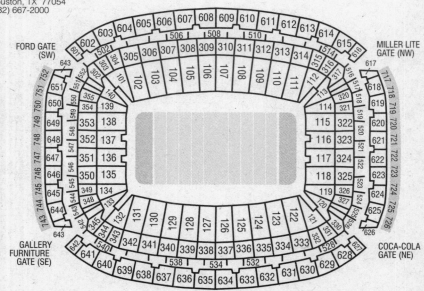

Indianapolis Colts
RCA Dome
200 S. Capitol Ave.
Indianapolis, IN 46225
(317) 297-2658

Jacksonville Jaguars
Alltel Stadium
1400 E. Duvall St.
Jacksonville, FL 32202
(904) 633-6000

Kansas City Chiefs

Arrowhead Stadium
One Arrowhead Drive
Kansas City, MO 64129
(816) 920-9300

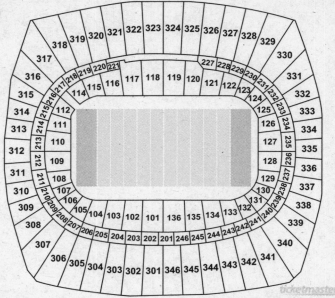

Miami Dolphins

Pro Player Stadium
2269 Dan Marino Blvd.
Miami, FL 33056
(954) 452-7000

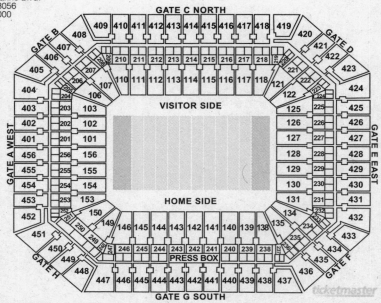

Minnesota Vikings
HHH Metrodome
500 11th Ave. South
Minneapolis, MN 55415
(952) 828-6500

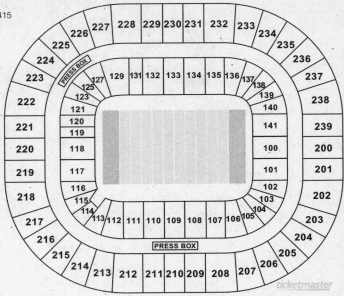

New England Patriots
Gillette Stadium
One Patriot Place
Foxborough, MA 02035
(508) 543-8200

New Orleans Saints
Louisiana Superdome
1500 Podyras St.
New Orleans, LA 70112
(504) 733-0255

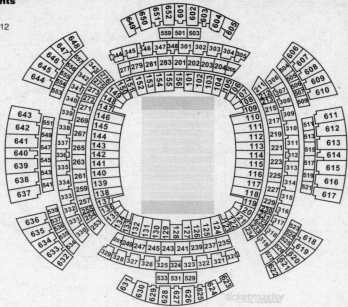

New York Giants
New York Jets
Giants Stadium
50 Route 120
East Rutherford, NJ 07073
(201) 935-8111

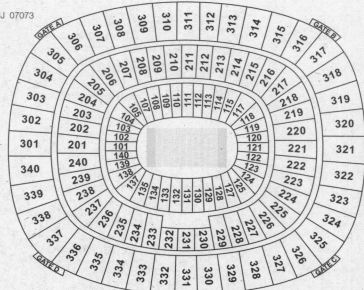

Oakland Raiders

Network Associates Coliseum
7000 Coliseum Way
Oakland, CA 94621
(510) 864-5000

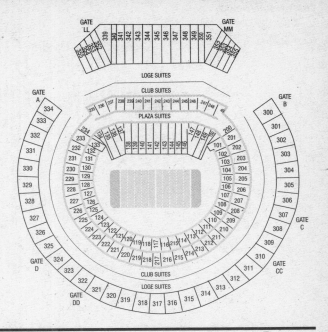

Philadelphia Eagles

Lincoln Financial Field
3551 Broad St.
Philadelphia, PA 19148
(215) 463-2500

Pittsburgh Steelers

Heinz Field
100 Art Rooney Ave.
Pittsburgh, PA 15212
(412) 432-7800

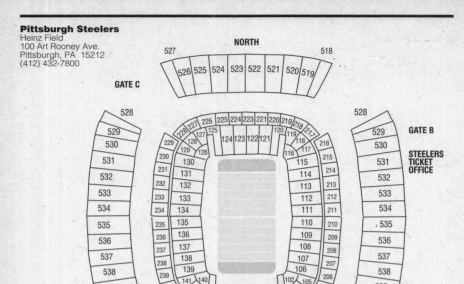

St. Louis Rams

Edward Jones Dome
701 Convention Plaza
St. Louis, MO 63101
(314) 982-7267

San Diego Chargers

Qualcomm Stadium
9449 Friars Rd.
San Diego, CA 92108
(858) 874-4500

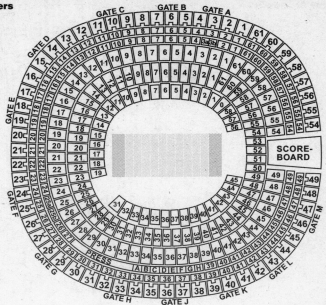

San Francisco 49ers

3Com Park
Jamestown and Harney Way
San Francisco, CA 94124
(408) 562-4949

Seattle Seahawks
Qwest Field
800 Occidental Ave. South
Seattle, WA 98104
(425) 827-9777

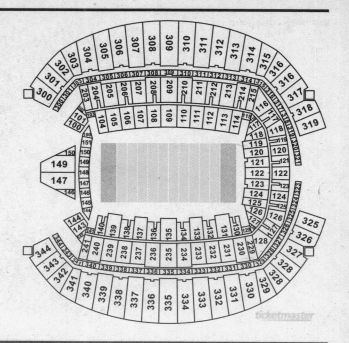

Tampa Bay Buccaneers
Raymond James Stadium
4201 N. Dale Mabry Hwy.
Tampa, FL 33607
(813) 870-2700

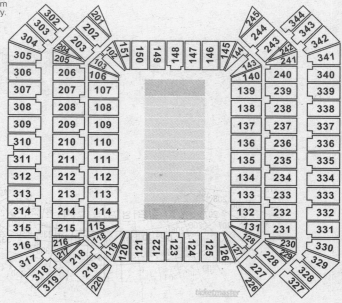

Tennessee Titans

The Coliseum
One Titans Way
Nashville, TN 37219
(615) 565-4000

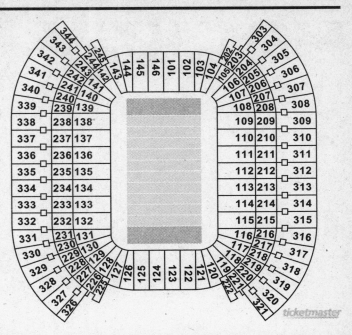

ticketmaster

Washington Redskins

Fedex Field
1600 Ralijon Rd.
Landover, MD 20785
(703) 726-7000

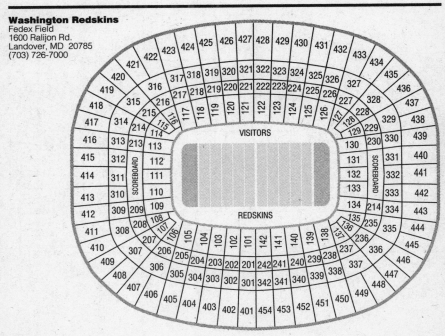

HOCKEY

Mighty Ducks of Anaheim
2695 Katella Avenue
Anaheim, CA 92806
Telephone: (714) 940-2900
Arena: Arrowhead Pond of Anaheim

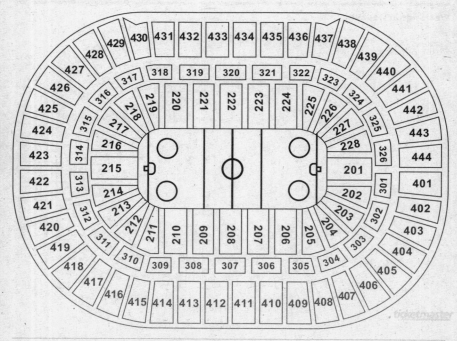

Atlanta Thrashers

1 CNN Center
P.O. Box 15538
Atlanta, GA 30348
Telephone: (404) 827-5300
Arena: Philips Arena

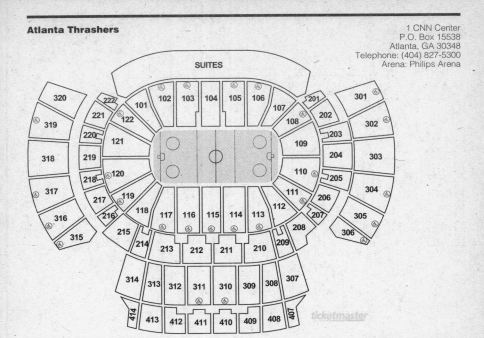

Boston Bruins

One FleetCenter, Suite 250
Boston, MA 02114-1303
Telephone: (617) 624-1900
Arena: FleetCenter

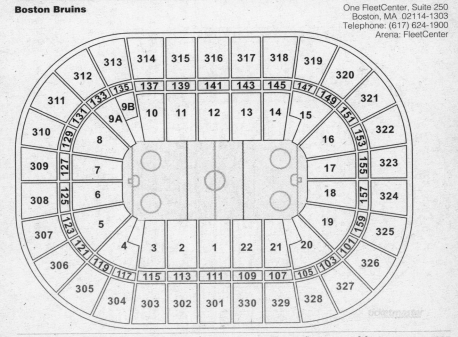

One Seymour H. Knox III Plaza
Buffalo, NY 14203
Telephone: (716) 855-4100
Arena: HSBC Arena

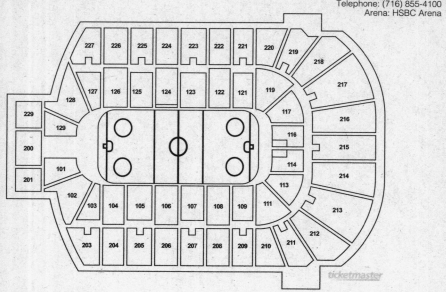

Calgary Flames

555 Saddledome Rise, SE
Calgary, Alberta T2G 2W1
Telephone: (403) 777-2177
Arena: Pengrowth
Saddledome

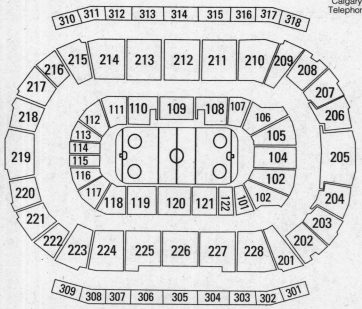

Carolina Hurricanes

1400 Edwards Mill Road
Raleigh, NC 27607
Telephone: (919) 467-7825
Arena: Entertainment and
Sports Arena

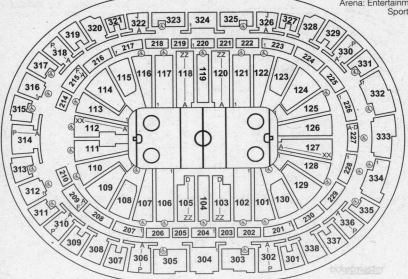

Chicago Blackhawks

1901 W. Madison Street
Chicago, IL 60612
Telephone: (312) 455-7000
Arena: United Center

Colorado Avalanche

1000 Chopper Circle
Denver, CO 80204
Telephone: (303) 405-1100
Arena: Pepsi Center

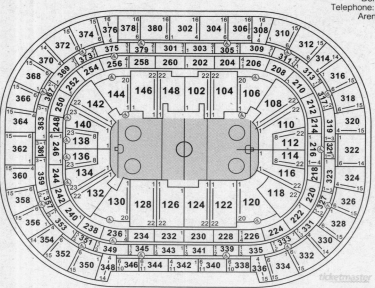

Columbus Blue Jackets

200 West Nationwide Boulevard
Columbus, OH 43215
Telephone: (614) 246-4625
Arena: Nationwide Arena

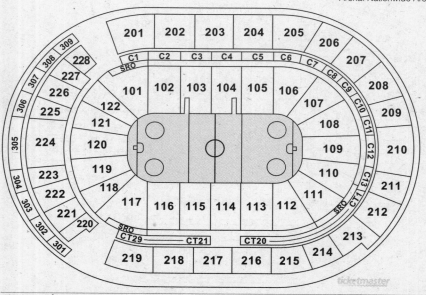

Dallas Stars

211 Cowboys Parkway
Irving, TX 75063
Telephone: (972) 831-2401
Arena: American Airlines
Center

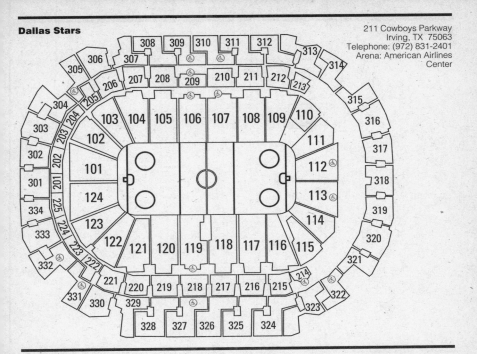

Detroit Red Wings

600 Civic Center Drive
Detroit, MI 48226
Telephone: (313) 396-7544
Arena: Joe Louis Arena

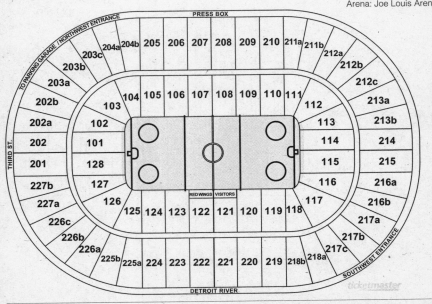

Edmonton Oilers

11230 110th Street
Edmonton, Alberta T5G 3H7
Telephone: (780) 414-4000
Arena: Skyreach Centre

Florida Panthers

1 Panther Parkway
Sunrise, FL 33323
Telephone: (954) 835-7000
Arena: National Car Rental Center

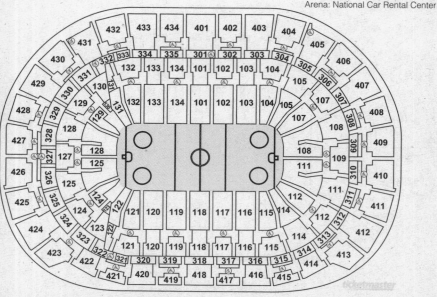

Los Angeles Kings

1111 South Figueroa Street
Los Angeles, CA 90037
Telephone: (213) 742-7100
Arena: The Staples Center

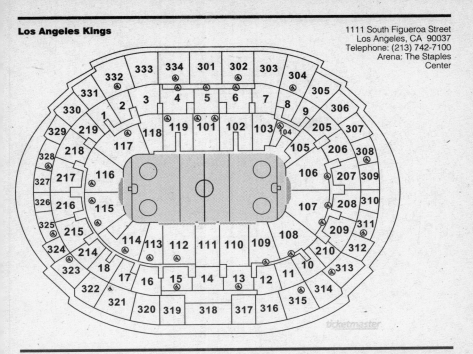

Minnesota Wild

317 Washington Street
St. Paul, MN, 55102
Telephone: (651) 602-6000
Arena: Excel Energy Center

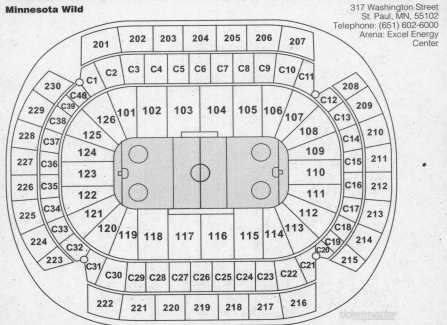

Montreal Canadiens

1260 de la Gauchetiere West
Montreal, Quebec H3B 5E8 Canada
Telephone: (514) 932-2582
Arena: Molson Centre

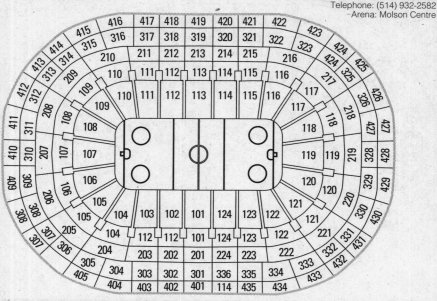

Nashville Predators

501 Broadway
Nashville, TN 37203
Telephone: (615) 770-2300
Arena: Gaylord Entertainment
Center

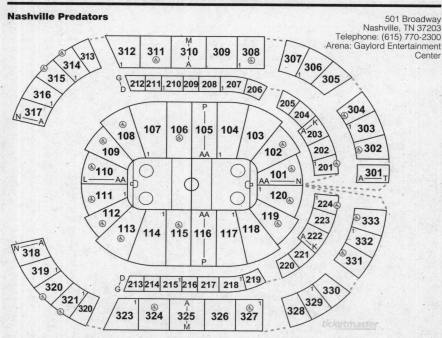

New Jersey Devils

P.O. Box 504
East Rutherford, NJ 07073
Telephone: (201) 935-6050
Arena: Continental Airlines Arena

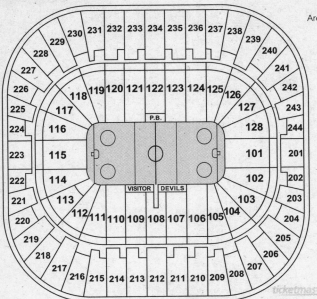

New York Islanders

1535 Old Country Road
Plainview, NY 11803
Telephone: (516) 501-6700
Arena: Nassau Coliseum

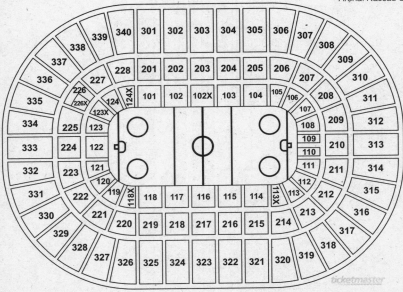

New York Rangers

2 Pennsylvania Plaza
New York, NY 10121
Telephone: (212) 465-6000
Arena: Madison Square
Garden

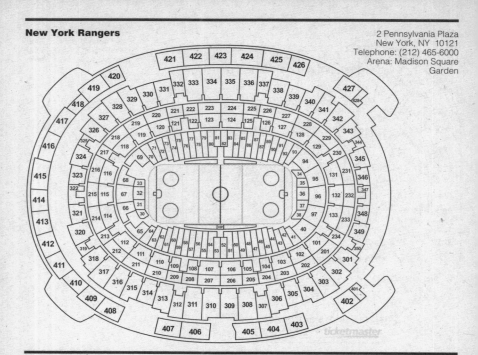

Ottawa Senators

1000 Palladium Drive
Ottawa, Ontario K2V 1A5 Canada
Telephone: (613) 599-0250
Arena: The Corel Centre

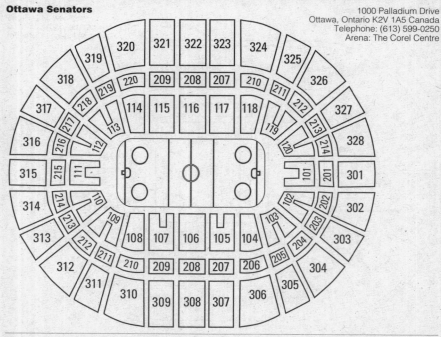

Philadelphia Flyers

3601 South Broad Street
Philadelphia, PA 19148
Telephone: (215) 465-4500
Arena: First Union Center

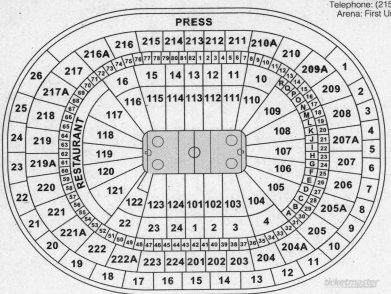

Phoenix Coyotes

9400 W. Maryland Avenue
Glendale, AZ 85305
Telephone: (623) 772-3200
Arena: Glendale Arena

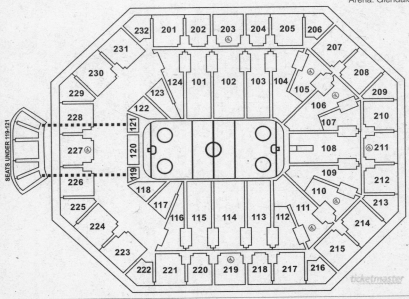

Pittsburgh Penguins

66 Mario Lemieux Place
Pittsburgh, PA 15219
Telephone: (412) 642-1300
Arena: Mellon Arena

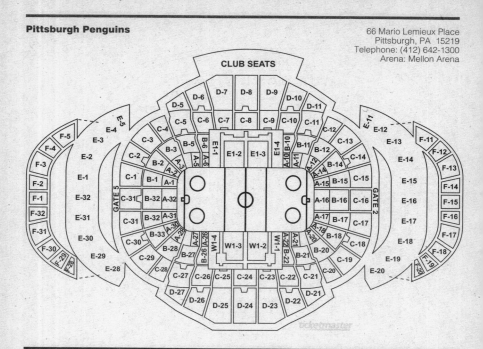

St. Louis Blues

1401 Clark Avenue
St. Louis, MO 63103
Telephone: (314) 622-2500
Arena: Savvis Center

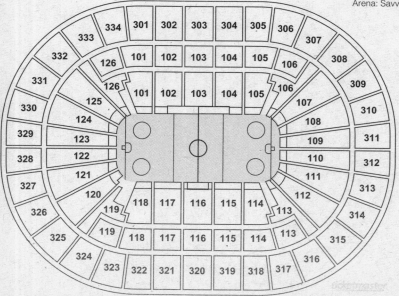

San Jose Sharks

525 West Santa Clara Street
San Jose, CA 95113
Telephone: (408) 287-7070
Arena: Compaq Center at
San Jose

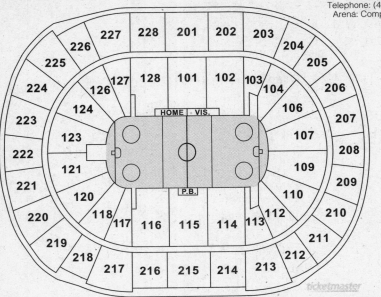

Tampa Bay Lightning

401 Channelside Drive
Tampa, FL 33602
Telephone: (813) 229-2658
Arena: Ice Palace

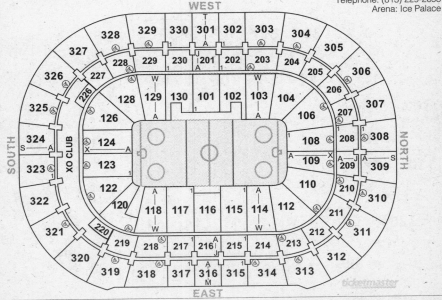

Toronto Maple Leafs

40 Bay Street - St. 400
Toronto, Ontario M5J 2X2 Canada
Telephone: (416) 815-5500
Arena: Air Canada Centre

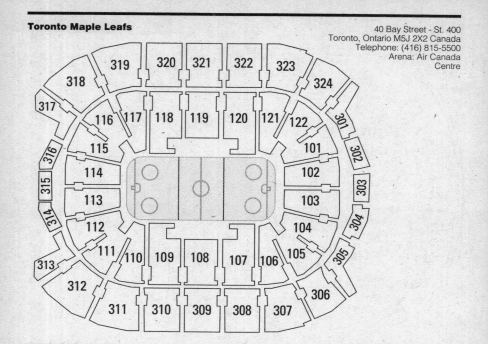

Vancouver Canucks

800 Griffiths Way
Vancouver, B.C. V6B 6G1
Telephone: (604) 899-4600
Arena: General Motors Place

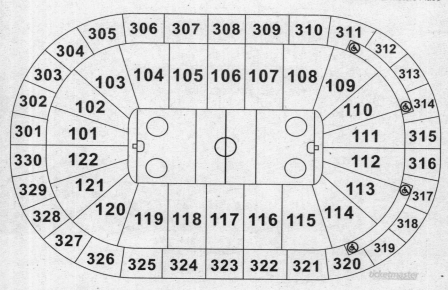

Awards

MICHAEL O'NEAL

FOR THE RECORD · Year by Year

Athlete Awards

Sports Illustrated Sportsman of the Year

1954	Roger Bannister, Track and Field
1955	Johnny Podres, Baseball
1956	Bobby Morrow, Track and Field
1957	Stan Musial, Baseball
1958	Rafer Johnson, Track and Field
1959	Ingemar Johansson, Boxing
1960	Arnold Palmer, Golf
1961	Jerry Lucas, Basketball
1962	Terry Baker, Football
1963	Pete Rozelle, Pro Football
1964	Ken Venturi, Golf
1965	Sandy Koufax, Baseball
1966	Jim Ryun, Track and Field
1967	Carl Yastrzemski, Baseball
1968	Bill Russell, Pro Basketball
1969	Tom Seaver, Baseball
1970	Bobby Orr, Hockey
1971	Lee Trevino, Golf
1972	B.J. King, Tennis/ J. Wooden, Bask
1973	Jackie Stewart, Auto Racing
1974	Muhammad Ali, Boxing
1975	Pete Rose, Baseball
1976	Chris Evert, Tennis
1977	Steve Cauthen, Horse Racing
1978	Jack Nicklaus, Golf
1979	Terry Bradshaw, Pro Football
	Willie Stargell, Baseball
1980	U.S. Olympic Hockey Team
1981	Sugar Ray Leonard, Boxing
1982	Wayne Gretzky, Hockey
1983	Mary Decker, Track and Field

1984	Mary Lou Retton, Gymnastics
	Edwin Moses, Track and Field
1985	Kareem Abdul-Jabbar, Pro Basketball
1986	Joe Paterno, Football
1987	Athletes Who Care:
	Bob Bourne, Hockey
	Kip Keino, Track and Field
	Judi Brown King, Track and Field
	Dale Murphy, Baseball
	Chip Rives, Football
	Patty Sheehan, Golf
	Rory Sparrow, Pro Basketball
	Reggie Williams, Pro Football
1988	Orel Hershiser, Baseball
1989	Greg LeMond, Cycling
1990	Joe Montana, Pro Football
1991	Michael Jordan, Pro Basketball
1992	Arthur Ashe, Tennis
1993	Don Shula, Pro Football
1994	Bonnie Blair, Speed Skating
	Johann Olav Koss, Speed Skating
1995	Cal Ripken Jr, Baseball
1996	Tiger Woods, Golf
1997	Dean Smith, College Basketball
1998	Mark McGwire, Sammy Sosa, Baseball
1999	U.S. Women's Soccer Team
2000	Tiger Woods, Golf
2001	C. Schilling/ R. Johnson, Baseball
2002	Lance Armstrong, Cycling
2003	Tim Duncan/ David Robinson, Bask

Associated Press Athletes of the Year

	MEN	WOMEN
1931	Pepper Martin, Baseball	Helene Madison, Swimming
1932	Gene Sarazen, Golf	Babe Didrikson, Track and Field
1933	Carl Hubbell, Baseball	Helen Jacobs, Tennis
1934	Dizzy Dean, Baseball	Virginia Van Wie, Golf
1935	Joe Louis, Boxing	Helen Wills Moody, Tennis
1936	Jesse Owens, Track and Field	Helen Stephens, Track and Field
1937	Don Budge, Tennis	Katherine Rawls, Swimming
1938	Don Budge, Tennis	Patty Berg, Golf
1939	Nile Kinnick, Football	Alice Marble, Tennis
1940	Tom Harmon, Football	Alice Marble, Tennis
1941	Joe DiMaggio, Baseball	Betty Hicks Newell, Golf
1942	Frank Sinkwich, Football	Gloria Callen, Swimming
1943	Gunder Haegg, Track and Field	Patty Berg, Golf
1944	Byron Nelson, Golf	Ann Curtis, Swimming
1945	Bryon Nelson, Golf	Babe Didrikson Zaharias, Golf
1946	Glenn Davis, Football	Babe Didrikson Zaharias, Golf
1947	Johnny Lujack, Football	Babe Didrikson Zaharias, Golf
1948	Lou Boudreau, Baseball	Fanny Blankers-Koen, Track and Field
1949	Leon Hart, Football	Marlene Bauer, Golf
1950	Jim Konstanty, Baseball	Babe Didrikson Zaharias, Golf
1951	Dick Kazmaier, Football	Maureen Connolly, Tennis
1952	Bob Mathias, Track and Field	Maureen Connolly, Tennis
1953	Ben Hogan, Golf	Maureen Connolly, Tennis
1954	Willie Mays, Baseball	Babe Didrikson Zaharias, Golf
1955	Hopalong Cassidy, Football	Patty Berg, Golf
1956	Mickey Mantle, Baseball	Pat McCormick, Diving
1957	Ted Williams, Baseball	Althea Gibson, Tennis
1958	Herb Elliott, Track and Field	Althea Gibson, Tennis
1959	Ingemar Johansson, Boxing	Maria Bueno, Tennis
1960	Rafer Johnson, Track and Field	Wilma Rudolph, Track and Field
1961	Roger Maris, Baseball	Wilma Rudolph, Track and Field
1962	Maury Wills, Baseball	Dawn Fraser, Swimming
1963	Sandy Koufax, Baseball	Mickey Wright, Golf
1964	Don Schollander, Swimming	Mickey Wright, Golf
1965	Sandy Koufax, Baseball	Kathy Whitworth, Golf
1966	Frank Robinson, Baseball	Kathy Whitworth, Golf
1967	Carl Yastrzemski, Baseball	Billie Jean King, Tennis
1968	Denny McLain, Baseball	Peggy Fleming, Skating
1969	Tom Seaver, Baseball	Debbie Meyer, Swimming

Associated Press Athletes of the Year *(Cont.)*

	MEN	WOMEN
1970	George Blanda, Pro Football	Chi Cheng, Track and Field
1971	Lee Trevino, Golf	Evonne Goolagong, Tennis
1972	Mark Spitz, Swimming	Olga Korbut, Gymnastics
1973	O.J. Simpson, Pro Football	Billie Jean King, Tennis
1974	Muhammad Ali, Boxing	Chris Evert, Tennis
1975	Fred Lynn, Baseball	Chris Evert, Tennis
1976	Bruce Jenner, Track and Field	Nadia Comaneci, Gymnastics
1977	Steve Cauthen, Horse Racing	Chris Evert, Tennis
1978	Ron Guidry, Baseball	Nancy Lopez, Golf
1979	Willie Stargell, Baseball	Tracy Austin, Tennis
1980	U.S. Olympic Hockey Team	Chris Evert Lloyd, Tennis
1981	John McEnroe, Tennis	Tracy Austin, Tennis
1982	Wayne Gretzky, Hockey	Mary Decker, Track and Field
1983	Carl Lewis, Track and Field	Martina Navratilova, Tennis
1984	Carl Lewis, Track and Field	Mary Lou Retton, Gymnastics
1985	Dwight Gooden, Baseball	Nancy Lopez, Golf
1986	Larry Bird, Pro Basketball	Martina Navratilova, Tennis
1987	Ben Johnson, Track and Field	Jackie Joyner-Kersee, Track and Field
1988	Orel Hershiser, Baseball	Florence Griffith Joyner, Track and Field
1989	Joe Montana, Pro Football	Steffi Graf, Tennis
1990	Joe Montana, Pro Football	Beth Daniel, Golf
1991	Michael Jordan, Pro Basketball	Monica Seles, Tennis
1992	Michael Jordan, Pro Basketball	Monica Seles, Tennis
1993	Michael Jordan, Pro Basketball	Sheryl Swoopes, Basketball
1994	George Foreman, Boxing	Bonnie Blair, Speed Skating
1995	Cal Ripken Jr, Baseball	Rebecca Lobo, Basketball
1996	Michael Johnson, Track and Field	Amy Van Dyken, Swimming
1997	Tiger Woods, Golf	Martina Hingis, Tennis
1998	Mark McGwire, Baseball	Se Ri Pak, Golf
1999	Tiger Woods, Golf	U.S. Women's Soccer Team
2000	Tiger Woods, Golf	Marion Jones, Track and Field
2001	Barry Bonds, Baseball	Jennifer Capriati, Tennis
2002	Lance Armstrong, Cycling	Serena Williams, Tennis
2003	Lance Armstrong, Cycling	Annika Sörenstam, Golf

James E. Sullivan Award

Presented annually by the AAU to the athlete who "by his or her performance, example and influence as an amateur, has done the most during the year to advance the cause of sportsmanship."

1930	Bobby Jones, Golf	1964	Don Schollander, Swimming
1931	Barney Berlinger, Track and Field	1965	Bill Bradley, Basketball
1932	Jim Bausch, Track and Field	1966	Jim Ryun, Track and Field
1933	Glenn Cunningham, Track and Field	1967	Randy Matson, Track and Field
1934	Bill Bonthron, Track and Field	1968	Debbie Meyer, Swimming
1935	Lawson Little, Golf	1969	Bill Toomey, Track and Field
1936	Glenn Morris, Track and Field	1970	John Kinsella, Swimming
1937	Don Budge, Tennis	1971	Mark Spitz, Swimming
1938	Don Lash, Track and Field	1972	Frank Shorter, Track and Field
1939	Joe Burk, Rowing	1973	Bill Walton, Basketball
1940	Greg Rice, Track and Field	1974	Rich Wohlhuter, Track and Field
1941	Leslie MacMitchell, Track and Field	1975	Tim Shaw, Swimming
1942	Cornelius Warmerdam, Track	1976	Bruce Jenner, Track and Field
1943	Gilbert Dodds, Track and Field	1977	John Naber, Swimming
1944	Ann Curtis, Swimming	1978	Tracy Caulkins, Swimming
1945	Doc Blanchard, Football	1979	Kurt Thomas, Gymnastics
1946	Arnold Tucker, Football	1980	Eric Heiden, Speed Skating
1947	John B. Kelly Jr, Rowing	1981	Carl Lewis, Track and Field
1948	Bob Mathias, Track and Field	1982	Mary Decker, Track and Field
1949	Dick Button, Skating	1983	Edwin Moses, Track and Field
1950	Fred Wilt, Track and Field	1984	Greg Louganis, Diving
1951	Bob Richards, Track and Field	1985	Joan B.-Samuelson, T & F
1952	Horace Ashenfelter, Track and Field	1986	Jackie Joyner-Kersee, T & F
1953	Sammy Lee, Diving	1987	Jim Abbott, Baseball
1954	Mal Whitfield, Track and Field	1988	Florence Griffith Joyner, Track
1955	Harrison Dillard, Track and Field	1989	Janet Evans, Swimming
1956	Pat McCormick, Diving	1990	John Smith, Wrestling
1957	Bobby Morrow, Track and Field	1991	Mike Powell, Track and Field
1958	Glenn Davis, Track and Field	1992	Bonnie Blair, Speed Skating
1959	Parry O'Brien, Track and Field	1993	Charlie Ward, Football, Basketball
1960	Rafer Johnson, Track and Field	1994	Dan Jansen, Speed Skating
1961	Wilma Rudolph, Track and Field	1995	Bruce Baumgartner, Wrestling
1962	Jim Beatty, Track and Field	1996	Michael Johnson, Track and Field
1963	John Pennel, Track and Field		

James E. Sullivan Award (Cont.)

1997	Peyton Manning, Football
1998	Chamique Holdsclaw, Basketball
1999	Kelly and Coco Miller, Basketball
2000	Rulon Gardner, Wrestling
2001	Michelle Kwan, Figure Skating
2002	Sarah Hughes, Figure Skating
2003	Michael Phelps, Swimming

The Sporting News Sportsman of the Year

1968	Denny McLain, Baseball
1969	Tom Seaver, Baseball
1970	John Wooden, Basketball
1971	Lee Trevino, Golf
1972	Charles O. Finley, Baseball
1973	O.J. Simpson, Pro Football
1974	Lou Brock, Baseball
1975	Archie Griffin, Football
1976	Larry O'Brien, Pro Basketball
1977	Steve Cauthen, Horse Racing
1978	Ron Guidry, Baseball
1979	Willie Stargell, Baseball
1980	George Brett, Baseball
1981	Wayne Gretzky, Hockey
1982	Whitey Herzog, Baseball
1983	Bowie Kuhn, Baseball
1984	Peter Ueberroth, LA Olympics
1985	Pete Rose, Baseball
1986	Larry Bird, Pro Basketball
1987	No award
1988	Jackie Joyner-Kersee, T & F
1989	Joe Montana, Pro Football
1990	Nolan Ryan, Baseball
1991	Michael Jordan, Pro Basketball
1992	Mike Krzyzewski, Basketball
1993	Pat Gillick/Cito Gaston, Baseball
1994	Emmitt Smith, Pro Football
1995	Cal Ripken Jr, Baseball
1996	Joe Torre, Baseball
1997	Michael Jordan, Basketball
1998	Mark McGwire, Baseball
1999	New York Yankees, Baseball
2000	Kurt Warner/ Marshall Faulk, Football
2001	Curt Schilling, Baseball
2002	Tyrone Willingham, Football
2003	Jack McKeon, Baseball Dick Vermeil, Football

United Press International Male and Female Athlete of the Year

	MEN	WOMEN
1974	Muhammad Ali, Boxing	Irena Szewinska, Track and Field
1975	Joao Oliveira, Track and Field	Nadia Comaneci, Gymnastics
1976	Alberto Juantorena, Track and Field	Nadia Comaneci, Gymnastics
1977	Alberto Juantorena, Track and Field	Rosie Ackermann, Track and Field
1978	Henry Rono, Track and Field	Tracy Caulkins, Swimming
1979	Sebastian Coe, Track and Field	Marita Koch, Track and Field
1980	Eric Heiden, Speed Skating	Hanni Wenzel, Alpine Skiing
1981	Sebastian Coe, Track and Field	Chris Evert Lloyd, Tennis
1982	Daley Thompson, Track and Field	Marita Koch, Track and Field
1983	Carl Lewis, Track and Field	Jarmila Kratochvilova, Track and Field
1984	Carl Lewis, Track and Field	Martina Navratilova, Tennis
1985	Steve Cram, Track and Field	Mary Decker Slaney, Track and Field
1986	Diego Maradona, Soccer	Heike Drechsler, Track and Field
1987	Ben Johnson, Track and Field	Steffi Graf, Tennis
1988	Matt Biondi, Swimming	Florence Griffith Joyner, Track and Field
1989	Boris Becker, Tennis	Steffi Graf, Tennis
1990	Stefan Edberg, Tennis	Merlene Ottey, Track and Field
1991	Michael Jordan, Pro Basketball	Monica Seles, Tennis
1992	Mario Lemieux, Hockey	Monica Seles, Tennis
1993	Michael Jordan, Pro Basketball	Steffi Graf, Tennis
1994	Nick Price, Golf	Bonnie Blair, Speed Skating
1995	Cal Ripken Jr, Baseball	Steffi Graf, Tennis

Note: Award not given since 1995.

Dial Award

Presented by the Dial Corporation to the male and female national high school athlete/scholar of the year.

	BOYS	GIRLS
1979	Herschel Walker, Football	No award
1980	Bill Fralic, Football	Carol Lewis, Track and Field
1981	Kevin Willhite, Football	Cheryl Miller, Basketball
1982	Mike Smith, Basketball	Elaine Zayak, Skating
1983	Chris Spielman, Football	Melanie Buddemeyer, Swimming
1984	Hart Lee Dykes, Football	Nora Lewis, Basketball
1985	Jeff George, Football	Gea Johnson, Track and Field
1986	Scott Schaffner, Football	Mya Johnson, Track and Field
1987	Todd Marinovich, Football	Kristi Overton, Water Skiing
1988	Carlton Gray, Football	Courtney Cox, Basketball
1989	Robert Smith, Football	Lisa Leslie, Basketball
1990	Derrick Brooks, Football	Vicki Goetze, Golf
1991	Jeff Buckey, Football, Track and Field	Katie Smith, Basketball, Volleyball, Track
1992	Jacque Vaughn, Basketball	Amanda White, Track and Field, Swimming
1993	Tiger Woods, Golf	Kristin Folkl, Basketball
1994	Taymon Domzalski, Basketball	Shannon Miller, Gymnastics
1995	Brent Abernathy, Baseball	Shea Ralph, Basketball
1996	Grant Irons, Football	Grace Park, Golf
1997	Ronald Curry, Football	Michelle Kwan, Figure Skating

Note: Award not given since 1997.

Profiles

Maddux the Magnificent | BY TOM VERDUCCI

Sports Illustrated

There was, it turned out,
life after football....
A heartbreak of a life

WHERE HAVE YOU GONE, Joe Namath?

BY MARK KRIEGEL

CARL IWASAKI

AUGUST 9, 2004 www.si.com
AOL Keyword: Sports Illustrated

Football Hall of Famer Joe Namath

Profiles

Henry Aaron (b. 2-5-34): Baseball OF. "Hammerin' Hank." Alltime leader in HR (755) and RBI (2,297); third in hits (3,771). 1957 MVP. Led league in HR and RBI four times each, runs scored three times, hits and batting average twice. No. 44, he had 44 homers four times. Had 40+ HR eight times; 100+ RBI 11 times; .300+ average 14 times. All-Star 24 times . Career span 1954–76; jersey number retired by Atlanta and Milwaukee.

Kareem Abdul-Jabbar (b. 4-16-47): Born Lew Alcindor. Basketball C. Alltime leader points scored (38,387), field goals attempted (28,307), field goals made (15,837); second alltime blocked shots (3,189); third alltime rebounds (17,440). Won six MVP awards (1971–72, 1974, 1976–77, 1980). Career scoring average was 24.6, rebounding average 11.2. Ten-time All-Star, All-Defensive team five times. 1970 Rookie of the Year. Played on six championship teams; was playoff MVP in 1971, 1985. Career span 1969–88 with Milwaukee, Los Angeles. Also played on three NCAA championship teams with UCLA; tournament MVP 1967–69; Player of the Year two times.

Affirmed (b. 2-21-75, d. 1-12-01): Thoroughbred race horse. Triple Crown winner in 1978 with jockey Steve Cauthen aboard. Trained by Laz Barrera.

Andre Agassi (b. 4-29-70): Tennis player. Won 1999 French Open to become fifth man in history to win all four Grand Slams. Won '92 Wimbledon, '94 and '99 U.S. Opens and '95, '00, '01 and '03 Australian Opens. Ranked No. 1 in 1995 and again in '99.

Troy Aikman (b. 11-21-66): Football QB. Quarterbacked Cowboys to three Super Bowl titles (XXVII, XXVIII, XXX). MVP of Super Bowl XXVII, in which he completed 22 of 30 passes for 273 yards and four TDs with no interceptions. Spent entire career (1989–2000) with Dallas Cowboys, passing for 32,942 yards and 171 TDs.

Michelle Akers (b. 2-1-66): Soccer player. Charter member of U.S. women's national team. Scored first goal ever for U.S. women's team on 8-21-85 against Denmark. Second alltime leading scorer in U.S. women's national team history (105 goals). Member of Women's World Cup champion team in 1991, '99, and third-place team in '95. Member of Olympic champion team in 1996. Battled chronic fatigue syndrome.

Tenley Albright (b. 7-18-35): Figure skater. Gold medalist at 1956 Olympics, silver medalist at 1952 Olympics. World champion two times (1953, 1955) and U.S. champion five consecutive years (1952–56).

Grover Cleveland Alexander (b. 2-26-1887, d. 11-4-50): Baseball RHP. Tied for third alltime in career wins (373), second in shutouts (90). Won 30+ games three times, 20+ games six other times. Set rookie record with 28 wins in 1911. Career span 1911–30 with Philadelphia (NL), Chicago (NL), St. Louis (NL).

Vasili Alexeyev (b. 1942): Soviet weightlifter. Gold medalist at two consecutive Olympics in 1972, 1976. World champion eight times.

Muhammad Ali (b. 1-17-42): Born Cassius Clay. Boxer. Heavyweight champion three times (1964–67, 1974–78, 1978–79). Stripped of title in 1967 because he refused to serve in the Vietnam War. Career record 56–5 with 37 KOs. Defended title 19 times. Also light heavyweight gold medalist at 1960 Olympics. Battles Parkinson Syndrome.

Phog Allen (b. 11-18-1885, d. 9-16-74): College basketball coach. Ninth alltime in coaching wins (746); .739 career winning percentage. Won 1952 NCAA championship. Spent most of his career from 1920 to '56 with Kansas.

Bobby Allison (b. 12-3-37): Auto racer. Third alltime in NASCAR victories (84). Won Daytona 500 three times (1978, 1982, 1988). NASCAR champion in 1983.

Naty Alvarado (b. 7-25-55): Mexican-born handball player. "El Gato (The Cat)." Won a record 11 U.S. pro four-wall handball titles, starting in 1977.

Lance Alworth (b. 8-3-40): Football WR. "Bambi" led AFL in receiving in 1966, '68 and '69. 200+ years in a game five times in career, a record. Gained 100+ yards in a game 41 times. In 1965 gained 1,602 yards receiving. Career span 1962–70 with San Diego and 1971–72 with Dallas. Elected to Pro Football Hall of Fame 1978.

Gary Anderson (b. 7-16-59): Football K. Four-time Pro Bowl kicker (1983, '85, '93, '98). NFL's alltime leading scorer (2,133 pts). Made league record 40 consecutive FGs in 1997–98 season. Made every field goal and extra point attempt during the 1998–99 season.

Sparky Anderson (b. 2-22-34): Baseball manager. Only manager to win World Series in both leagues (Cincinnati, 1975–76, Detroit, 1984); only manager to win 100 games in both leagues. Elected to Hall of Fame in 2000.

Willie Anderson (b. 1880, d. 1910): Scottish golfer. Won U.S. Open four times (1901 and an unmatched three straight, 1903–05). Also won four Western Opens between 1902 and 1909.

Mario Andretti (b. 2-28-40): Auto racer. The only driver in history to win the Daytona 500 (1967), the Indy 500 (1969) and a Formula One world championship (1978). Second alltime in CART victories (52). Twelve career Formula One victories. USAC/CART champion four times (consecutively 1965–66, 1969, 1984).

Earl Anthony (b. 4-27-38, d. 8-14-01): Bowler. Won PBA National Championship six times, more than any other bowler (consecutively 1973–75, 1981–83) and Tournament of Champions two times (1974, 1978). First bowler to top $1 million in career earnings. Bowler of the Year six times (consecutively 1974–76, 1981–83). Won 41 career PBA titles.

Said Aouita (b. 11-2-60): Track and field. Moroccan set world records in 2,000 meters (4:50.81 in 1987), and 5,000 meters (12:58.39 in 1987). 1984 Olympic champion in 5,000; 1988 Olympic third place in 800.

Al Arbour (b. 11-1-32): Hockey D-coach. Led NY Islanders to four consecutive Stanley Cup championships (1980–83). Also played on three Stanley Cup champions: Detroit, Chicago and Toronto, from 1953 to 1971.

Eddie Arcaro (b. 2-19-16, d. 11-14-97): Horse racing jockey. The only jockey to win the Triple Crown two times (aboard Whirlaway in 1941, Citation in 1948). Rode Preakness Stakes winner (1941, 1948, consecutively 1950–51, 1955, 1957) and Belmont Stakes winner (consecutively 1941–42, 1945, 1948, 1952, 1955) six times each and Kentucky Derby winner five times (1938, 1941, 1945, 1948, 1952). 4,779 career wins.

Nate Archibald (b. 9-2-48): Basketball player. "Tiny" only by NBA standards at 6' 1", 160 pounds. Six-time All-Star. Led NBA in scoring (34.0) and assists (11.4) in 1972–73. First team, all-NBA in 1973, '75 and '76. MVP of NBA All-Star Game in 1981. Career span 1970–84 with six teams.

Alexis Arguello (b. 4-19-52): Nicaraguan boxer. Won world titles in three weight classes: featherweight, super featherweight and lightweight. Won first title, WBA featherweight, on 11-23-74 when he KO'd Ruben Olivares in 13. Career record: 88–8, 64 KO.

Henry Armstrong (b. 12-12-12, d. 10-24-88): Boxer. Champion in three different weight classes: featherweight, welterweight, and lightweight. Career record 145-20-9 with 98 KOs (27 consecutively, 1937–38) from 1931 to 1945.

Lance Armstrong (b. 9-18-71): Cyclist. Recovered from testicular cancer to win six straight Tour de France races (1999–04), a record. Two-time winner of Tour DuPont (1995, '96). Won 1993 world championships.

Arthur Ashe (b. 7-10-43, d. 2-6-93): Tennis player. First black man to win U.S. Open (1968, as an amateur), Australian Open (1970) and Wimbledon singles titles (1975). 33 career tournament victories. Member of Davis Cup team 1963–78; captain 1980–85. Stadium at the United States Tennis Center, home of the U.S. Open, named in his honor.

Assault (b. 1943, d. 1971): Thoroughbred race horse. Horse of the Year for 1946 when he won the Triple Crown. Won Kentucky Derby by eight lengths, Preakness by a neck, and the Belmont by three lengths. Trained by Max Hirsch.

Red Auerbach (b. 9-20-17): Basketball coach-executive. 938 career wins. Coached Boston from 1946 to 1965, winning nine championships, eight consecutively. Had .662 career winning percentage, with 50+ wins eight consecutive seasons. Also won seven championships as general manager.

Hobey Baker (b. 1-15-1892, d. 12-21-18): Sportsman. Member of both college football and hockey Halls of Fame. College hockey and football star at Princeton, 1911–14. Fighter pilot in World War I, died in plane crash. College hockey Player of the Year award named in his honor.

Seve Ballesteros (b. 4-9-57): Spanish golfer. Notorious scrambler. Won British Opens in 1979, '84 and '88. Won Masters in 1980 and '83.

Ernie Banks (b. 1-31-31): Baseball SS-1B. "Mr. Cub." Won two consecutive MVP awards, in 1958–59. 512 career HR. League leader in HR, RBI two times each; 40+ HR five times; 100+ RBI eight times; career batting average of .274. Career span 1953–71 with Chicago.

Roger Bannister (b. 3-23-29): Track and field. British runner broke the four-minute mile barrier, running 3:59.4 on 5-6-54.

Red Barber (b. 2-17-08, d. 10-22-92): Sportscaster. TV-radio baseball announcer was the voice of Cincinnati, Brooklyn and NY Yankees. His expressions, such as "sitting in the catbird seat," "pea patch" and "rhubarb," captivated audiences from 1934 to 1966.

Charles Barkley (b. 2-20-63): Basketball F. "The Round Mound of Rebound." Eleven-time All-Star. One

of only four NBA players to amass 20,000 points, 10,000 rebounds, and 4,000 assists. Named one of NBA's greatest 50 players. Leading scorer on the 1992 Olympic team. League MVP for 1992–93 season. Played for Philadelphia, Phoenix, Houston. Career averages: 22.2 ppg, 11.7 rpg.

Rick Barry (b. 3-28-44): Basketball F. Only player in history to win scoring titles in NCAA (Miami (FL), 1965), NBA (San Francisco, 1967) and ABA (Oakland, 1969). Five-time first-team All-NBA. 1966 Rookie of the Year. 1975 playoff MVP with Golden State. Eight-time NBA All-Star. Career scoring average 23.2. Career span 1966–79.

Carmen Basilio (b. 4-2-27): Boxer. Won titles as a welterweight and middleweight. Won welterweight title by TKO of Tony DeMarco in 12 rounds on 6-10-55. Won and then lost middleweight title in two 15-round fights with Ray Robinson. Made three unsuccessful bids to regain middle title. *The Ring* Fighter of the Year for 1957. Career record: 56–16–7, 27 KOs.

Sammy Baugh (b. 3-17-14): Football QB-P. Led NFL in passing six times and punting four times, a record. Holds record for highest career punting average (45.1) and highest season average (51.0 in 1940). Career span 1937–52 with Washington, passing for 21,866 yards and 186 TDs.

Elgin Baylor (b. 9-16-34): Basketball F. Fourth alltime highest scoring average (27.4) in NBA history. Averaged 30+ points three consecutive seasons (1960-63). 1959 Rookie of the Year. 11-time All-Star. Played in eight NBA Finals without winning championship. Career span 1958–71 with Lakers. MVP of 1958 NCAA Tournament with Seattle.

Bob Beamon (b. 8-29-46): Track and field. Gold medalist in long jump at 1968 Olympics with world record leap of 29' 2½" that stood until 1991.

Franz Beckenbauer (b. 9-11-45): West German soccer player. Captain of 1974 World Cup champions and coach of 1990 champions. Also played for NY Cosmos from 1977 to 1980.

Boris Becker (b. 11-22-67): German tennis player. The youngest male player (17, in 1985) to win a Wimbledon singles title. Won three Wimbledon titles (1985–86, 1989), one U.S. Open (1989) and one Australian Open title (1991). Led West Germany to consecutive Davis Cup victories (1988–89).

Chuck Bednarik (b. 5-1-25): Football C-LB. Last of the great two-way players, was named All-Pro at both center and linebacker. Missed only three games in 14 seasons with Philadelphia from 1949–62. Seven-time All-NFL. Two-time All-America at Pennsylvania.

Clair Bee (b. 3-2-1896, d. 5-20-83): Basketball coach. Originated 1-3-1 defense, helped develop three-second rule, 24-second clock. Won 82.7 percent of games as coach for Rider College and Long Island University. Coach, Baltimore Bullets, 1952–54. Author, 23-volume Chip Hilton series for children, 21 nonfiction sports books.

Jean Beliveau (b. 8-31-31): Hockey C. Won MVP award twice (1956, 1964), playoff MVP in 1965. Led league in assists three times, goals two times and points once. 507 career goals, 712 assists. All-Star six times. Played on 10 Stanley Cup champions with Montreal from 1950 to 1971.

Bert Bell (b. 2-25-1895, d. 10-11-59): Football executive. Second NFL commissioner (1946–59). Also owner of Philadelphia (1933–40) and Pittsburgh

(1941–46). Proposed the first NFL draft of college players, in 1936.

James (Cool Papa) Bell (b. 5-17-03, d. 3-7-91): Baseball OF. Legendary foot speed—according to Satchel Paige could flip light switch and be in bed before room was dark. Hit .392 in games against white major leaguers. Career span 1922–46 with many teams of the Negro Leagues, including the Pittsburgh Crawfords and the Homestead Grays. Inducted in the Hall of Fame in 1974.

Lyudmila Belousova/Oleg Protopov (no dates of birth available): Soviet figure skaters. Won Olympic gold medal in pairs competition in 1964 and 1968. Won four consecutive World and European championships (1965–68) and eight consecutive Soviet titles (1961–68).

Deane Beman (b. 4-22-38): Commissioner of the PGA Tour 1974–94. Won British Amateur title in 1959 and U.S. Amateur titles in 1960 and 1963.

Johnny Bench (b. 12-7-47): Baseball C. MVP in 1970, 1972; World Series MVP in 1976; Rookie of the Year in 1968. 389 career HR. League leader in HR two times, RBI three times. Career span 1967–83 with Cincinnati. Elected to Hall of Fame in 1989.

Patty Berg (b. 2-13-18): Golfer. Alltime women's leader in major championships (16), third alltime in career wins (57). Won Titleholders Championship and Western Open seven times each, the most of any golfer. Also won U.S. Women's Amateur (1938) and U.S. Women's Open (1946).

Yogi Berra (b. 5-12-25): Baseball C. Played on 10 World Series winners. Alltime Series leader in games, at-bats, hits and doubles. MVP in 1951 and consecutively 1954–55. 358 career HR. Career span 1946–63, '65. Managed pennant-winning Yankees (1964) and Mets (1973).

Jay Berwanger (b. 3-19-14, d. 6-26-02): College football RB. Won the first Heisman Trophy and named All-America with Chicago in 1935.

Raymond Berry (b. 2-27-33): Football WR. Led NFL in receiving 1958–60. In 13-season career, caught 631 passes, 68 for TDs. Career span 1955–67, all with Baltimore Colts. Coached New England Patriots from 1984–89 with 51–41 record.

George Best (b. 5-22-46): Northern Ireland soccer player. Led Manchester United to European Cup title in 1968. Named England's and Europe's Player of the Year in 1968. Played in North American Soccer League from 1976–81. Frequent troubles with alcohol and gambling shadowed career.

Abebe Bikila (b. 8-7-32, d. 10-25-73): Track and field. Ethiopian barefoot runner won consecutive gold medals in the marathon at Olympics, in 1960 and 1964.

Fred Biletnikoff (b. 2-23-43): Football WR. In 14 pro seasons caught 589 passes for 8,974 yards and 76 TDs. In 1971 led NFL receivers with 61 catches; in '72 led AFC with 58. Career span 1965–78, all with Raiders. Elected to Pro Football Hall of Fame in 1988.

Dmitri Bilozerchev (b. 12-22-66): Soviet gymnast. Won three gold medals at 1988 Olympics. Made comeback after shattering his left leg into 44 pieces in 1985. Two-time world champion (1983, '87). At 16, became youngest to win all-around world championship title in 1983.

Dave Bing (b. 11-24-43): Basketball G. NBA Rookie of Year in 1967. Led NBA in scoring (27.1) in 1968.

MVP NBA All-Star game in 1976. In 12-year career from 1967–78, most of it with Detroit Pistons, averaged 20.3 points. Averaged 24.8 ppg in four years at Syracuse.

Matt Biondi (b. 10-8-65): Swimmer. Won five gold medals, one silver and one bronze at 1988 Olympics. Won one gold and one silver at 1992 Games.

Larry Bird (b. 12-7-56): Basketball F. Won three consecutive MVP awards (1984–86) and two playoff MVP awards (1984, 1986). Rookie of the Year (1980) and All-Star nine consecutive seasons. Led league in free throw percentage four times. Averaged 20+ points 10 times. Career span 1979–92 with Boston. Named College Player of the Year in 1979 with Indiana State. 1997–98 NBA Coach of the Year in first year as coach of Indiana Pacers.

Bonnie Blair (b. 3-18-64): Speed skater. Won gold medal in 500 meters and bronze medal in 1,000 meters at 1988 Olympics. Swept both Olympic events in 1992 and '94. 1989 World Sprint champion. Winner of 1992 Sullivan Award. *Sports Illustrated* 1994 Sportswoman of the Year.

Toe Blake (b. 8-21-12, d. 5-17-95): Hockey LW and coach. Second alltime highest winning percentage (.634) and eighth in wins (500). Led Montreal to eight Stanley Cup championships from 1955 to 1968 (consecutively 1956–60, 1965–66, '68). Also MVP and scoring leader in 1939. Played on two Stanley Cup champions with Montreal from 1932 to 1948.

Doc Blanchard (b. 12-11-24): College football FB. "Mr. Inside." Teamed with Glenn Davis to lead Army to three consecutive undefeated seasons (1944–46) and two consecutive national championships (1944–45). Won Heisman Trophy and Sullivan Award in 1945. All-America three times.

George Blanda (b. 9-17-27): Football QB-K. Alltime leader in seasons played (26), games played (340), and PAT's (943); third in points scored (2,002); kicked 335 field goals. Passed for 26,920 career yards and 236 touchdowns. Tied record with seven touchdown passes on Nov. 19, 1961. AFL Player of the Year (1961) when he threw 36 TDs. Played until age 48. Career span 1949–75 with Chicago, Houston, Oakland.

Fanny Blankers-Koen (b. 4-26-18, d. 1-25-04): Track and field. Dutch athlete won four gold medals at 1948 Olympics, in 100 meters; 200 meters; 80-meter hurdles; and 400-meter relay. She also set world records in high jump (5' 7¼" in 1943), long jump (20' 6" in 1943) and pentathlon (4,692 points in 1951).

Wade Boggs (b. 6-15-58): Baseball 3B. Won five batting titles (1983, consecutively 1985–88); had .350+ average five times, 200+ hits seven times. Won World Series with 1996 Yankees. Career span 1982–99 with Boston, New York Yankees, Tampa Bay; .328 career average, 3,010 hits.

Nick Bolletieri (b. 7-31-31): Tennis coach. Since 1976, has run Nick Bolletieri Tennis Academy in Bradenton, Fla. Former residents of the academy include Andre Agassi, Monica Seles and Jim Courier.

Barry Bonds (b. 7-24-64): Baseball OF. Baseball's single-season home run king, with 73 in 2001. Also produced .863 slugging percentage and 177 walks in 2001, breaking two of Babe Ruth's records, the first of which had stood since 1920. One of three players to top 40 homers (42) and 40 steals (40) in same season (1996). Six-time National League MVP (1990, '92, '93,

'01, '02, '03); Career span 1986–92 with Pittsburgh; 1993– with San Francisco.

Bjorn Borg (b. 6-6-56): Swedish tennis player. Third alltime in Grand Slam singles titles (11—tied with Rod Laver). Set modern record by winning five consecutive Wimbledon titles (1976–80). Won six French Open titles (1974–75, 1978–81). Reached U.S. Open final four times, but title eluded him. 65 career tournament victories. Led Sweden to Davis Cup win in 1975.

Julius Boros (b. 3-3-20, d. 5-28-94): Golfer. Won U.S. Opens in 1952 at Northwood CC in Dallas and in 1963 at The Country Club in Brookline, Mass. Won 1968 PGA Championship at Pecan Valley CC, San Antonio, when 48 years old, making him oldest winner of a major ever. Led PGA money list in 1952 and '55.

Mike Bossy (b. 1-22-57): Hockey RW. Set NHL rookie scoring record of 54 goals in 1978. Scored 50 or more each of first nine seasons. Totaled 573 goals and 1,126 points in 10 seasons (1977–87) with New York Islanders. Elected to Hall of Fame in 1991.

Ralph Boston (b. 5-9-39): Track and field. Long jumper won medals at three consecutive Olympics: gold in 1960, silver in '64, bronze in '68.

Ray Bourque (b. 12-28-60): Hockey D. Highest scoring defenseman in NHL history (1,579 pts). Won five Norris Trophies as NHL's top defenseman. Played in 19 consecutive All-Star games. No. 77. Won first and only Stanley Cup in 2001. Career span 1979–00 with Boston; 2000–01 with Colorado.

Scotty Bowman (b. 9-18-33): Retired in 2002 after leading Detroit to his ninth Stanley Cup title. Alltime leader in regular-season wins (1,244) and playoff wins (223). Coached Montreal, St. Louis, Buffalo, and Detroit. Won Jack Adams Award, Coach of the Year, 1976–77, 1995–96.

Bill Bradley (b. 7-28-43): Basketball F. Played on two NBA championship teams with New York from 1967 to '77. Player of the Year and NCAA tournament MVP in 1965 with Princeton; All-America three times; Sullivan Award winner in 1965. Rhodes scholar. U.S. Senator (D-NJ) 1979–96.

Terry Bradshaw (b. 9-2-48): Football QB. Played on four Super Bowl champions (1974, '75, '78, '79). Named Super Bowl MVP two consecutive seasons (1978–79). 212 career touchdown passes; 27,989 yards passing. Player of the Year in 1978. Career span 1970–83 with Pittsburgh.

Tom Brady (b. 8-3-77): Football QB. Led New England Patriots to Super Bowl victories in 2002 and '04, winning the Super Bowl MVP award in both games. Career span since 2000 with New England.

George Brett (b. 5-15-53): Baseball 3B-1B. Won batting titles in three different decades (1976, '80, '90). MVP in 1980 with .390 batting average. Hit .300+ 11 times. Led league in hits and triples three times. Career span 1973–93, with Kansas City. Career totals: 3,153 hits; 317 HR; 1,595 RBI; batting average .305. Elected to Hall of Fame in 1999.

Bret Hanover (b. 1962, d. 1993): Horse. Son of Adios. Won 62 of 68 harness races and earned $922,616. Undefeated as two-year-old. From total of 1,694 foals, he sired winners of $61 million and 511 horses that have recorded sub-2:00 performances.

Lou Brock (b. 6-18-39): Baseball OF. Second in career stolen bases (938); second highest single-season steals total (118) of modern era. Led league in steals eight times, with 50+ steals 12 consecutive

seasons. Alltime World Series leader in steals (14—tied with Eddie Collins); hit .391 in World Series play. 3,023 career hits. Career span 1961–64 Chicago (NL), 1964–79 St. Louis.

Jim Brown (b. 2-17-36): Football FB. 126 career touchdowns; 12,312 career rushing yards. Led league in rushing a record eight times. His 5.2 yards per carry average is the best ever. Player of the Year four times (1957, '58, '63, '65) and Rookie of the Year in 1957. Rushed for 1,000+ yards in seven seasons, 200+ yards in four games, 100+ yards in 54 other games. Career span 1957–65 with Cleveland; never missed a game. All-America in both football and lacrosse at Syracuse.

Larry Brown (b. 9-14-40): Basketball coach. Led Kansas University to the 1988 NCAA title, and the Detroit Pistons to the 2004 NBA championship. Played on gold-medal–winning 1964 U.S. Olympic team, coached 2004 Olympic team—only U.S. male to both play and coach in the Olympics. Peripatetic coaching career included stints at UCLA, and the NBA's Nuggets, Nets, Spurs, Clippers, Pacers, Sixers and Pistons. First coach in league history to guide six different NBA franchises to the playoffs.

Paul Brown (b. 9-7-08, d. 8-5-91): Football coach. Led Cleveland to 10 consecutive championship games. Won four consecutive AAFC titles (1946–49) and three NFL titles (1950, '54, '55). Coached Cleveland from 1946 to 1962; became first coach of Cincinnati, 1968–75, and then general manager. Career coaching record 222-113-9. Also won national championship with Ohio State in 1942.

Avery Brundage (b. 9-28-1887, d. 5-5-75): Amateur sports executive. President of International Olympic Committee 1952–72. Served as president of U.S. Olympic Committee 1929–53. Also president of Amateur Athletic Union 1928–35. Member of 1912 U.S. Olympic track and field team.

Paul (Bear) Bryant (b. 9-11-13, d. 1-26-83): College football coach. Third in Division I-A football history with 323 wins. Won six national championships (1961, '64, '65, '73, '78, '79) with Alabama. Career record 323–85–17, including four undefeated seasons. Won 15 bowl games. Career span 1945–82 with Maryland, Kentucky, Texas A&M, Alabama.

Sergei Bubka (b. 12-4-63): Track and field. Ukrainian pole vaulter was gold medalist at 1988 Olympics. Only five-time world outdoor champion in any event (1983, '87, '91, '93, '95). First man to vault 20 feet, set world indoor record of 20' 2" on 2-21-93 and world outdoor record of 20' 1½" on 9-20-92.

Don Budge (b. 6-13-15, d. 1-26-00): Tennis player. First player to achieve the Grand Slam, in 1938. Won two consecutive Wimbledon and U.S. singles titles (1937, '38), one French and one Australian title (1938).

Dick Butkus (b. 12-9-42): Football LB. Regarded as greatest middle linebacker in NFL history. Selected to eight Pro Bowls. Career span 1965–73 with Chicago. All-America two times with Illinois. Award recognizing the outstanding college linebacker named in his honor.

Dick Button (b. 7-18-29): Figure skater. Gold medalist at 1948 and 1952 Olympics. World champion five consecutive years (1948–52) and U.S. champion seven consecutive years (1946–52). Sullivan Award winner in 1949.

Walter Byers (b. 3-13-22): Amateur sports executive. First director of NCAA, served from 1952 to 1987.

Frank Calder (b. 11-17-1877, d. 2-4-43): Hockey executive. First commissioner of NHL, served from 1917 to 1943. Rookie of the Year award named in his honor.

Walter Camp (b. 4-7-1859, d. 3-14-25): Football pioneer. Played for Yale in its first football game vs. Harvard on Nov. 17, 1876. Proposed rules such as 11 men per side, scrimmage line, center snap, yards and downs. Founded the All-America selections in 1889.

Roy Campanella (b. 11-19-21; d. 6-26-93): Baseball C. MVP in 1951, '53, '55. Played on five pennant winners; 1955 World Series winner with Brooklyn. Career span 1948–57, ended when paralyzed in car crash.

Earl Campbell (b. 3-29-55): Football RB. Led NFL in rushing three consecutive seasons. Rookie of the Year in 1978. Ran for 19 TDs in 1979 and 1,934 yards in 1980 when he was named league's Player of the Year twice. 9,407 career rushing yards. Career span 1978–85 with Houston, New Orleans. Won Heisman Trophy with Texas in 1977.

John Campbell (b. 4-8-55): Canadian harness racing driver. Alltime leading money winner with over $100 million in earnings. Leading money winner in 1986–90, 1992–95, '98, '00.

Billy Cannon (b. 2-8-37): Football RB. Led Louisiana State to national championship in 1958 and won Heisman Trophy in 1959. Signed contract with both NFL (Los Angeles) and AFL (Houston) teams. Houston won lawsuit for his services. Played in six AFL championship games with Houston, Oakland, Kansas City. Career span 1960–70. Served three-year jail term for 1983 conviction on counterfeiting charges.

Jose Canseco (b. 7-2-64): Baseball OF. One of three players to top 40 homers (42) and 40 steals (40) in same season (1988). AL MVP in 1988, when he also batted .307 with 124 RBI. AL Rookie of the Year in 1986. Career span 1985–01 with seven teams: 462 HRs, 1,407 RBIs, 1,942 K's.

Harry Caray (b. 3-1-17, d. 2-18-98): Sportscaster. TV-radio baseball announcer 1945–97 with St. Louis (NL), Oakland, Chicago (AL) and Chicago (NL). Achieved celebrity status on Cubs' superstation WGN by singing "Take Me Out to the Ball Game" with Wrigley Field fans.

Rod Carew (b. 10-1-45): Baseball 2B-1B. Won seven batting titles (1969, '72–75, '77, '78). Had .328 career average, 3,053 career hits, and .300+ average 15 times. 1977 MVP; 1967 Rookie of the Year. Career span 1967–85; jersey number (29) retired by Minnesota and Anaheim.

Steve Carlton (b. 12-22-44): Baseball LHP. Four Cy Young awards (1972, '77, '80, '82). Second in career strikeouts (4,136). 329 career wins; won 20+ games six times. League leader in wins four times, innings pitched and strikeouts five times each. Struck out 19 batters in one game in 1969. Career span 1965–88 primarily with St. Louis and Philadelphia.

JoAnne Carner (b. 4-21-39): Golfer. Won 42 titles, including U.S. Women's Opens in 1971 and '76 and du Maurier Classic in 1975 and '78. LPGA top earner in 1974, '82, '83. LPGA Player of the Year in 1974, '81, '82. Won five Vare Trophies (1974, '75, '81–83).

Joe Carr (b. 10-22-1880; d. 5-20-39): Football administrator. Instrumental in forming American Professional Football Association in 1920. President of AAFA from 1922 to '39.

Don Carter (b. 7-29-26): Bowler. Won All-Star Tournament four times (1952, '54, '56, '58) and PBA National Championship in 1960. Voted Bowler of the Year six times (1953, '54, '57, '58, '60, '62).

Alexander Cartwright (b. 4-17-1820, d. 7-12-1892): Baseball pioneer. Credited with setting the basic rules of baseball: bases 90 feet apart, nine men per side, three strikes per out and three outs per inning. On June 19, 1846, in what is often cited as the first baseball game, his New York Knickerbockers lost to the New York Nine 23–1 at Elysian Fields in Hoboken, NJ.

Billy Casper (b. 6-24-31): Golfer. Famed putter. Won 51 PGA tournaments. PGA Player of Year in both 1966 and '70. Won Vardon Trophy in 1960, '63, '64, '65 and '68. Won the U.S. Open twice, in 1959 at Winged Foot in Mamaronek, New York, and in 1966 in 18-hole playoff over Arnold Palmer at Olympic Club, San Francisco. Beat Gene Littler in 18-hole playoff to win 1970 Masters.

Tracy Caulkins (b. 1-11-63): Swimmer. Won three gold medals at 1984 Olympics. Won 48 U.S. national titles, more than any other swimmer, from 1978 to 1984. Also won Sullivan Award in 1978.

Steve Cauthen (b. 5-1-60): Jockey. In 1978 became youngest jockey to win Triple Crown, aboard Affirmed. First jockey to top $6 million in season earnings (1977). *Sports Illustrated* Sportsman of Year for 1977. Moved to England in 1979; rode Epsom Derby winners Slip Anchor (1985) and Reference Point (1987).

Evonne Goolagong Cawley (b. 7-31-51): Tennis player. Won four Australian Open titles from 1974 through '77; won 1971 French Open; won Wimbledon in 1971 and '80. Runner-up four straight years at U.S. Open (1973–76), which she never won.

Bill Chadwick (b. 10-10-15): Hockey referee. Spent 16 years as a referee despite vision in only one eye. Developed hand signals to signify penalties. Also former television announcer for the New York Rangers.

Wilt Chamberlain (b. 8-21-36, d. 10-12-99): Basketball C. "The Big Dipper." "The Stilt." Scored 100 points in a single game in 1962. Alltime leader in rebounds (23,924) and rebounding average (22.9). Third in career points (31,419). Alltime single-season leader in points scored (4,029 in 1962), scoring average (50.4 in 1962), rebounding average (27.2 in 1961) and field goal percentage (.727 in 1973). Set record for most rebounds in a game in 1960 (55). Four MVP awards (1960, '66–68); playoff MVP in 1972 and 1960 Rookie of the Year. 13-time All-Star. 30.1 career scoring average. Career span 1959–72 with Philadelphia/Golden State Warriors, Philadelphia 76ers, Los Angeles.

Colin Chapman (b. 1928, d. 12-16-83): Auto racing engineer. Founded Lotus race and street cars, designing the first Lotus racer in 1948. Introduced the monocoque design for Formula One cars in 1962 and ground effects in 1978.

Julio Cesar Chavez (b. 7-12-62): Mexican boxer. Held titles as junior welterweight, lightweight and super featherweight. Career record: 103-6-2 (83 KOs).

Gerry Cheevers (b. 12-7-40): Hockey goalie. Goaltender for Stanley Cup-winning Boston Bruins teams of 1970 and '72. In 12 seasons with Boston had 230-94-74 record with a goals against average of 2.89. Also coached Bruins from 1980–84, with 204-126-46 record. Elected to Hall of Fame 1985.

Cigar (b. 1990): Thoroughbred race horse. Tied Citation's American-record 16-race win-streak with a win on 7-13-96. Won $4 million Dubai World Cup on 3-27-96.

Citation (b. 4-11-45, d. 8-8-70): Thoroughbred race horse. Triple Crown winner in 1948 with jockey Eddie Arcaro aboard. Trained by Ben A. Jones.

King Clancy (b. 2-25-03, d. 11-6-86): Hockey D. Four-time All-Star. Coach, Montreal Maroons, Toronto. Also referee. Trophy named in his honor, recognizing leadership qualities and contribution to community.

Jim Clark (b. 3-4-36, d. 4-7-68): Scottish auto racer. Won 25 career Formula 1 races. Formula 1 champion two times (1963, 1965). Won Indy 500 in 1965. Named Indy 500 Rookie of the Year in 1963. Killed during competition in 1968 at age 32.

Bobby Clarke (b. 8-13-49): Hockey C. Won MVP award three times (1973, '75, '76). 358 career goals, 852 assists. Scored 100+ points three times. Played on two consecutive Stanley Cup champions (1974, '75) with Philadelphia. Career span 1969–84. Also general manager with Philadelphia 1984–90, Minnesota 1991–92, Florida 1993–94, and Philadelphia 1994–.

Roger Clemens (b. 8-4-62): Baseball RHP. Won six Cy Young awards (1986, '87, '91, '97, '98, '01), most by any pitcher. Also 1986 MVP. Has struck out a record 20 batters in one game on two occasions. League leader in ERA six times, strikeouts four times, and wins four times. Won Triple Crown of pitching in 1997 and '98. Won 300th game on June 13, 2003. Career span 1984–96 with Boston; 1997–98 Toronto; 1999–03 NY Yankees; 2004– Houston.

Roberto Clemente (b. 8-18-34, d. 12-31-72): Baseball OF. Killed in plane crash while still an active player. Had 3,000 career hits and .317 career average. Won four batting titles; .300+ average 13 times. 1966 MVP; 1971 World Series MVP. Twelve consecutive Gold Gloves; led league in assists five times. Career span 1955–72 with Pittsburgh.

Ty Cobb (b. 12-18-1886, d. 7-17-61): Baseball OF. Alltime leader in batting average (.366), second in runs scored (2,245) and hits (4,189), fourth in stolen bases (892). 1911 MVP and 1909 Triple Crown winner. Twelve batting titles. Had .400+ average three times, .350+ average 13 other times; 200+ hits nine times. Led league in hits seven times, steals six times and runs scored five times. Career span 1905–28 with Detroit and Philadelphia.

Mickey Cochrane (b. 4-6-03, d. 6-28-62): Baseball C. Second highest career batting average among catchers (.320). MVP in 1928, '34. Had .300+ average eight times. Career span 1925–37 with Philadelphia and Detroit.

Sebastian Coe (b. 9-29-56): Track and field. Two-time Olympic gold medalist in the 1,500 meters (1980, '84). Also won two silver medals in 800 meters at same two Olympics. Set world record in 800 meters (1:41.73 in 1981) and 1,000 meters (2:12.18 in 1981). Served in British Parliament after his running career.

Eddie Collins (b. 5-2-1887, d. 3-25-51): Baseball 2B. 3,311 career hits; .333 career average; .330+ average 12 times. 743 career stolen bases; alltime co-leader in World Series steals (14—tied with Lou Brock); alltime leader in single-game steals (six, twice). 1914 MVP. Career span 1906–30 with Philadelphia (AL), Chicago (AL).

Nadia Comaneci (b. 11-12-61): Romanian gymnast. First ever to score a perfect 10 at Olympics

(on uneven parallel bars in 1976). Won three gold, two silver and one bronze medal at 1976 Olympics. Also won two gold and two silver medals at 1980 Olympics.

Dennis Conner (b. 9-16-42): Sailing. Captain of three America's Cup winners (1980, '87,'88).

Maureen Connolly (b. 9-17-34, d. 6-21-69): Tennis player. "Little Mo." First woman to achieve the Grand Slam, in 1953. Won the U.S. singles title in 1951 at age 16. Thereafter lost only four matches before retiring in 1954 after breaking her leg in a riding accident. Was never beaten in singles at Wimbledon, winning three consecutive titles (1952–54). Won three consecutive U.S. singles titles (1951–53) and two consecutive French titles (1953–54). Also won Australian title (1953).

Jimmy Connors (b. 9-2-52): Tennis player. Alltime men's leader in tournament victories (109). Held men's No. 1 ranking a record 160 consecutive weeks (7-29-74 through 8-16-77). Won five U.S. Open singles titles on three different surfaces (grass 1974, clay 1976, hard 1978, '82, '83). Won two Wimbledon singles titles (1974, '82) further apart than anyone since Bill Tilden. Also won 1974 Australian Open title. Reached Grand Slam final seven other times.

Jim Corbett (b. 9-1-1866; d. 2-18-33): Boxer. "Gentleman Jim." Invented jab. Won heavyweight title on 9-7-1892 with a KO of John Sullivan in 21 rounds; it was first heavyweight title fight using gloves. Lost title when KO'd by Bob Fitzsimmons in 14 on 3-17-1897, then lost two bids to regain it against Jim Jeffries. Career record: 11-4-2, 7 KOs, 2 ND.

Angel Cordero (b. 11-8-42): Jockey. Seventh alltime in wins (7,057) and earnings ($164,561,227). Led yearly earnings three times, in 1976, '82, '83, winning Eclipse Awards in the last two years.

Howard Cosell (b. 3-25-18, d. 4-23-95): Sportscaster. Lawyer–turned–TV-radio sports commentator. Best known for his work on "Monday Night Football." His nasal voice and "tell it like it is" approach made him a controversial figure.

James (Doc) Counsilman (b. 12-28-20, d. 1-4-04): Swimming coach. Coached Indiana from 1957 to 1990. Won six consecutive NCAA championships (1968–73). Career record 287-36-1. Coached U.S. men's team at Olympics in 1964, '76. Swam English Channel in 1979 at age 58.

Count Fleet (b. 3-24-40, d. 12-3-73): Thoroughbred race horse. Triple Crown winner in 1943 with jockey Johnny Longden aboard. Trained by Don Cameron.

Yvan Cournoyer (b. 11-22-43): Hockey RW. "The Roadrunner" had 428 goals and 435 assists during his 15-season career with the Montreal Canadiens. Had 25 or more goals in 12 straight seasons. Played on 10 Stanley Cup championship teams. Elected to Hall of Fame in 1982.

Margaret Smith Court (b. 7-16-42): Australian tennis player. Alltime leader in Grand Slam singles titles (24) and total Grand Slam titles (62). Achieved Grand Slam in 1970 and mixed doubles Grand Slam in 1963 with Ken Fletcher. Won 11 Australian singles titles (1960–66, 1969–71, '73), five French titles (1962, '64, '69, '70, '73), 5 U.S. titles (1962, '65, '69, '70, '73) and three Wimbledon titles (1963, '65, '70). Court also won 19 Grand Slam doubles titles and 19 mixed doubles titles.

Bob Cousy (b. 8-9-28): Basketball G. Led NBA in assists eight consecutive seasons. Averaged 18+ points and named to All-Star team 10 consecutive seasons. 1957 MVP. Played on six championship teams with Boston from 1950 to 1969. Finished career with 6,955 assists; in 1958 had 28 assists in a single game. Also played on 1947 NCAA title team with Holy Cross.

Dave Cowens (b. 10-25-48): Basketball C. NBA co-Rookie of Year in 1971. NBA MVP for 1973. All-Star game MVP in 1973. Career span 1970–71 through 1982–83, all but the last year with the Boston Celtics, averaging 17.6 points and 13.6 rebounds per game. Coached Charlotte 1996–99 and Golden State 2000–01. Elected to Hall of Fame in 1991.

Ben Crenshaw (b. 1-11-52): Golfer. Legendary putter. Won Masters in 1984 and '95. Captain of 1999 U.S. Ryder Cup team.

Johan Cruyff (b. 4-25-47): Dutch soccer player. Led Ajax Amsterdam to three European Cup titles, and guided the Netherlands to the 1974 World Cup final, a 2–1 loss to Germany.

Larry Csonka (b. 12-25-46): Football RB. In 11 seasons rushed for 8,081 yards and 64 TDs. MVP of Super Bowl VIII, when he rushed 33 times for a then Super Bowl-record 145 yards in Miami's 24–7 defeat of Minnesota. Career span 1968–74, '79 with Miami; 1976–78 with New York Giants. Elected to Hall of Fame in 1987.

Billy Cunningham (b. 6-3-43): Basketball player and coach. "Kangaroo Kid." In 11 pro seasons (1965–76) with Philadelphia 76ers and Carolina Cougars, averaged 21.2 points per game. Three-time first-team All-NBA selection (1969–71). 1973 ABA MVP. Coached 76ers to three NBA Finals and the 1983 NBA title. Elected to Hall of Fame in 1985.

Bjørn Dæhlie (b.6-19-67): Norwegian skier. Legendary cross-country skier won a Winter Olympics–record eight gold medals over three Games from 1992 to '98. Won a total of 12 Olympic medals and more than 40 World Cup races.

Chuck Daly (b. 7-20-30): Basketball coach. Coached the 1992 Olympic "Dream Team." Won two consecutive NBA titles with Detroit (1989, '90). Won 50+ games four consecutive seasons. Coached Detroit 1983–92, New Jersey 1992–94, and Orlando 1997–99.

Damascus (b. 1964, d. 1995): Thoroughbred race horse. After finishing third in 1967 Kentucky Derby, won the Preakness, the Belmont, the Dwyer, the American Derby, the Travers, the Woodward and others—12 of 16 starts. Unanimous Horse of the Year in 1967.

Stanley Dancer (b. 7-25-27): Harness racing driver. Only driver to win the Trotting Triple Crown two times (Nevele Pride in 1968, Super Bowl in 1972). Also won Pacing Triple Crown driving Most Happy Fella in 1970. Won The Hambletonian four times (1968, '72, '75, '83). Driver of the Year in 1968.

Tamas Darnyi (b. 6-3-67): Hungarian swimmer. Gold medalist in 200-meter and 400-meter individual medleys at 1988 and '92 Olympics. Won both events at World Championships in 1986 and '91. Set world records in these events at 1991 Championships (1:59.36 and 4:12.36).

Al Davis (b. 7-4-29): Football executive. Owner and general manager of Raiders since 1963. Team has won three Super Bowl championships (1976, '80, '83). Served as AFL commissioner in 1966; helped negotiate AFL–NFL merger. Famously moved Raiders to Los Angeles in 1982 and back to Oakland in 1995.

Ernie Davis (b. 12-14-39, d. 5-18-63): Football RB. Won Heisman Trophy in 1961, the first black man to win the award. All-America three times at Syracuse. First selection in 1962 NFL draft, but became fatally ill with leukemia and never played professionally.

Glenn Davis (b. 12-26-24): College football HB. "Mr. Outside." Teamed with Doc Blanchard to lead Army to three consecutive undefeated seasons (1944–46) and two consecutive national championships (1944, '45). Won Heisman Trophy in 1946. Named All-America three times.

John Davis (b. 1-12-21, d. 7-13-84): Weightlifter. Gold medalist at two consecutive Olympics, 1948, '52. World champion six times.

Terrell Davis (b. 10-28-72): Football RB. One of only four players to rush for more than 2,000 yards in a season (2,008 in 1998). MVP of Super Bowl XXXII, rushing for 157 yards and three TDs for Denver. Forced to retire in 2002 after several knee injuries.

Pete Dawkins (b. 3-8-38): Football RB. 1958 Heisman Trophy winner while at Army. Never played pro football. Attended Oxford on Rhodes scholarship, won two Bronze Stars in Vietnam, rose to brigadier general before leaving Army to become investment banker. Made unsuccessful run for Senate from New Jersey in 1988.

Len Dawson (b. 6-20-35): Football QB. MVP of Super Bowl IV, a 23–7 victory against Minnesota. Threw 239 TDs in his career. Career span 1957–75, the last 13 seasons with Kansas City Chiefs. Elected to Hall of Fame in 1987.

Dizzy Dean (b. 1-16-11, d. 7-17-74): Baseball RHP. 1934 MVP with 30 wins. League leader in strikeouts, complete games four times each. 150 career wins. Arm trouble shortened career after 134 wins by age 26. Career span 1930–41 and 1947 with St. Louis and Chicago (NL).

Dave DeBusschere (b. 10-16-40, d. 5-14-03): Basketball F. NBA first-team All-Defensive Team six straight seasons, 1969–74. Member of NBA champion New York Knicks in 1970 and '73. Career span 1962–74 with Detroit and New York. Career stats: 16.1 ppg, 11.0 rpg. Youngest coach (24) in NBA history. Elected to NBA Hall of Fame in 1982.

Pierre de Coubertin (b. 1-1-1863, d. 9-2-37): Frenchman called the father of the Modern Olympics. President of International Olympic Committee from 1896 to 1925.

Oscar De La Hoya (b. 2-4-73): Boxer. Won title belts in five different weight classes between junior lightweight and junior middleweight divisions. 35–2 with 28 KOs. Won lightweight gold medal at 1992 Olympics in Barcelona.

Jack Dempsey (b. 6-24-1895, d. 5-31-83): Boxer. Heavyweight champ (1919–26), lost title to Gene Tunney and rematch in the famed "long count" bout in 1927. Career record 62-6-10 with 49 KOs from 1914–28.

Gail Devers (b. 11-19-66): Track and field sprinter-hurdler. Won 100 meters at 1992 and '96 Olympics. Successfully completed 100m/100h double at 1993 World Championships, winning 100 in 10.82 and 100 hurdles in American record 12.46. Also won '93 world indoor title in 60 (6.95). Battled Graves disease.

Klaus Dibiasi (b. 10-6-47): Italian diver. Gold medalist in platform at three consecutive Olympics (1968, '72, '76) and silver medalist at 1964 Olympics.

Eric Dickerson (b. 9-2-60): Football RB. Alltime single-season record holder in yards rushing (2,105 in 1984). Retired with 13,259 career rushing yards. Led league in rushing four times. Rushed for 1,000+ yards in seven consecutive seasons; 100+ yards in 61 games, including 12 times in 1984. Rookie of the Year in 1983. Career span 1983–93 with Los Angeles Rams, Indianapolis, Los Angeles Raiders and Atlanta.

Bill Dickey (b. 6-6-07 d. 11-12-93): Baseball C. Lifetime average .313. Hit 202 career home runs. Played on 11 AL All-Star teams. In eight World Series, hit five homers with 24 RBI. Career span 1928–43 and 1946, all with New York (AL). Inducted into Hall of Fame 1954.

Harrison Dillard (b. 7-8-23): Track and field. Only man to win Olympic gold medal in sprint (100 meters in 1948) and hurdles (110 meters in 1952). Sullivan Award winner in 1955.

Joe DiMaggio (b. 11-25-14 d. 3-8-99): Baseball OF. "The Yankee Clipper." Hit safely in record 56 straight games in 1941. MVP in 1939, '41, '47. Had .325 career batting average; .300+ average 11 times; 100+ RBI nine times. League leader in batting average, HR, and RBI two times each. Played on 10 World Series winners with New York (AL). Career span 1936–51.

Mike Ditka (b. 10-18-39): Football TE–Coach. First TE elected to Hall of Fame (1988). NFL Rookie of the Year in 1961. Named to five Pro Bowls. Made 427 catches for 5,812 yards and 43 TDs. Career span 1961–72 with Chicago, Philadelphia and Dallas. Coached Chicago to 46–10 win against New England in Super Bowl XX. Recorded 127–101 record as head coach of Chicago and New Orleans.

Tony Dorsett (b. 4-7-54): Football RB. Fifth leading rusher in NFL history (12,739 yards). Set record for longest run from scrimmage with 99-yard TD run on 1-3-83. Scored 91 career TDs. Rushed for 1,000+ yards in eight seasons. Named Rookie of the Year in 1977. Career span 1977–88 with Dallas, Denver. Graduated from Pittsburgh as alltime NCAA leader in yards rushing (6,082) and won 1976 Heisman Trophy.

Abner Doubleday (b. 6-26-1819, d. 1-26-1893): Civil War hero incorrectly credited as the inventor of baseball in Cooperstown, NY, in 1839.

Clyde Drexler (b. 6-22-62): Basketball G. Nicknamed "The Glide" for his smooth play. Member of U.S. "Dream Team" that won 1992 Olympic gold medal. Career span 1984–1994 with Portland and 1995–98 with Houston, with whom he won his first NBA title in 1995. Career stats: 20.4 ppg, 5.6 apg. Head coach at University of Houston from 1998–00.

Ken Dryden (b. 8-8-47): Hockey G. Goaltender of the Year five times (1973, 1976–79). Playoff MVP as a rookie in 1971, maintained rookie status and named Rookie of the Year in 1972. Led league in goals against average five times. Career record 258-57-74, including 46 shutouts. Career 2.24 goals against average is the modern record. Four playoff shutouts in 1977. Played on six Stanley Cup champions with Montreal from 1970 to 1979.

Don Drysdale (b. 7-23-36, d. 7-3-93): Baseball RHP. Set the major league record—broken in 1988 by Orel Hershiser—of 58 consecutive scoreless innings in 1968. Led NL three times in strikeouts (1959, '60, '62) and once in wins (1962). Won 1962 Cy Young Award with 25–9 mark. Career span of 209–166, with 2,484 K's and 2.95 ERA. Career span 1956–69, all with Dodgers. Inducted into Hall of Fame 1984.

Tim Duncan (b. 4-25-76): Basketball C. 2001 NBA MVP. First-team All-NBA every season in the league (1998–03). 1998 Rookie of the Year. 1999 and 2003 NBA Finals MVP, when he led San Antonio to NBA titles. Also league MVP in '03 Career span 1997– with San Antonio.

Roberto Duran (b. 6-16-51): Panamanian boxer. Champion in three different weight classes: lightweight (1972–79), welterweight (1980, lost rematch to Sugar Ray Leonard in famous "no más" bout) and junior middleweight (1983–84). Career record: 104–15 (69 KOs).

Leo Durocher (b. 7-27-05, d. 10-7-91): Baseball manager. "Leo the Lip." Said "Nice guys finish last." Managed three pennant winners and 1954 World Series winner. Won 2,008 games in 24 years. Led Brooklyn 1939–48; New York (NL) 1948–55; Chicago (NL) 1966–72; and Houston 1972–73.

David Duval (b. 11-9-71): Golfer. Won 2001 British Open. Set record for tour earnings in a single season with $2.6 million in 1998, when he also won Vardon Trophy for lowest scoring average (69.13). Four-time all-America at Georgia Tech.

Tomás Dvorák (b. 5-11-72): Czech decathlete. Broke Dan O'Brien's seven-year-old decathlon world record by 103 points on 7-4-99 in Prague, amassing 8,994 points. Won decathlon bronze medal at Atlanta in '96.

Eddie Eagan (b. 4-26-1898, d. 6-14-67): Only American athlete to win gold medal at Summer and Winter Olympic Games (boxing 1920, bobsled '32).

Alan Eagleson (b. 4-24-33): Hockey labor leader. Founder of NHL Players' Association and its executive director from 1967–92. Resigned from Hall of Fame 3-25-98 and served six months of an 18-month jail sentence for three counts of fraud and theft involving players' insurance premiums.

Dale Earnhardt (b. 4-29-52, d. 2-18-01): Auto racer. "The Intimidator." NASCAR champion seven times (1980, 1986–87, 1990–91, 1993–94). Won 1998 Daytona 500 and 75 other NASCAR races. Died in crash on the final lap of the 2001 Daytona 500.

Stefan Edberg (b. 1-19-66): Swedish tennis player. Won two Wimbledon singles titles (1988, '90), two Australian Open titles (1985, '87) and two U.S. Open titles (1991, '92). Led Sweden to three Davis Cup titles (1984, '85, '87).

Gertrude Ederle (b. 10-23-06): Swimmer. First woman to swim the English Channel, in 1926. Swam 21 miles from France to England in 14:39. Also won three medals at the 1924 Olympics.

Hicham El Gerrouj (b. 9-14-74): Track and field. Morrocan runner broke world record in mile on 7-7-99, clocking 3:43.13 to trim 1.26 seconds from six-year-old previous record. Performance was his fourth world record, in addition to indoor mile, indoor 1,500 and outdoor 1,500. Won two gold medals at 2004 Games.

Herb Elliott (b. 2-25-38): Track and field. Australian runner was gold medalist in 1960 Olympic 1,500 meters in world record 3:35.6. Also set world mile record of 3:54.5 in 1958. Undefeated at 1,500 meters/mile in international competition. Retired at 22.

Ernie Els (b.10-17-69): South African golfer. Two-time U.S. Open winner (1994, '97); first foreign-born player to win the event twice since Alex Smith in 1910. 2002 British Open champion.

John Elway (b. 6-28-60): Football QB. First player taken in 1983 NFL draft. One of two NFL QBs with more than 50,000 passing yards (51,475). 300 career TD passes. Famous for last-minute drives. Won back-to-back Super Bowls (XXXII and XXXIII) after three previous Super Bowl losses. Career span 1983–99 with Denver.

Roy Emerson (b. 11-3-36): Australian tennis player. Second alltime in Grand Slam singles titles (12). Won six Australian titles, five consecutively (1961, 1963–67), two Wimbledon titles (1964, '65), two U.S. titles (1961, '64) and two French titles (1963, '67). Also won 13 Grand Slam doubles titles.

Kornelia Ender (b. 10-25-58): East German swimmer. Won four gold medals at 1976 Olympics and three silver medals at 1972 Olympics.

Julius Erving (b. 2-22-50): Basketball F. "Dr. J." His combined ABA and NBA career points (30,026) rank fifth alltime. Career scoring average of 24.2. Won four MVP awards (1974–76, '81); playoff MVP 1974, '76. All-Star 16 times. Led ABA in scoring three times. Played on three championship teams, with New York (ABA) and Philadelphia (NBA). Career span 1971–86. Elected to Hall of Fame in 1993.

Phil Esposito (b. 2-20-42): Hockey C. "Espo." First to break the 100-point barrier (126 in 1969). Led league in goals six consecutive seasons, points five times and assists three times. Won MVP award two times (1969, '74). 1,590 career points, 717 goals, and 873 assists. Scored 30+ goals 13 consecutive seasons and 100+ points six times. All-Star 10 times. Career span 1963–81 with Chicago, Boston, New York Rangers.

Tony Esposito (b. 4-23-43): Hockey goalie. Brother of Phil. A six-time All-Star during 16-season NHL career, almost all of it with the Chicago Blackhawks. Career GAA of 2.92. Won or shared Vezina Trophy three times. Elected to Hall of Fame in 1988.

Janet Evans (b. 8-28-71): Swimmer. Competed in 1988, '92 and '96 Olympics, winning three gold medals in '88 and one in '92. Set world record in 400-meter freestyle (4:03.85 in 1988), 800-meter freestyle (8:16.22 in 1989) and 1,500-meter freestyle (15:52.10 in 1988). Sullivan Award winner in 1989.

Lee Evans (b. 2-25-47): Track and field. Gold medalist in 400 meters at 1968 Olympics with world record time of 43.86, which stood until 1988.

Chris Evert (b. 12-21-54): Also Chris Evert Lloyd. Tennis player. Second alltime in tournament titles (157). Tied for fourth alltime in women's Grand Slam singles titles (18). Won at least one Grand Slam singles title every year from 1974–86. Won seven French Open titles (1974, '75, '79, '80, '83, '85, '86), six U.S. Open titles (1975–77, '78, '80, '82), three Wimbledon titles (1974, '76, '81) and two Australian Open titles (1982, '84). Reached Grand Slam finals 16 other times. Reached semifinals at 52 of her last 56 Grand Slams.

Weeb Ewbank (b. 5-6-07, d. 11-17-98): Football coach. Only coach to win titles in both the NFL and AFL. Coached Baltimore Colts to classic overtime defeat of New York Giants in 1958 and New York Jets to their stunning 16–7 win over Baltimore in Super Bowl III. Career record of 134-130-7. Career span 1954–62 with Colts and 1963–73 with Jets. Elected to Hall of Fame in 1978.

Patrick Ewing (b. 8-5-62): Basketball C. First NBA "lottery" pick. 1986 Rookie of the Year. A member of two gold-medal winning Olympic teams, including the

1992 "Dream Team." Career span 1985–02 with New York, Seattle, and Orlando; averaged 21.0 ppg, 9.8 rpg. Played in three NCAA title games with Georgetown (1982, '84, '85); tournament MVP in 1984.

Nick Faldo (b. 7-18-57): British golfer. Three-time winner of Masters (1989, '90, '96) and British Open (1987, '90, '92).

Juan Manuel Fangio (b. 6-24-11, d. 7-17-95): Argentine auto racer. 24 Formula 1 victories in just 51 starts. Formula 1 champion five times, the most of any driver (1951, '54–57). Retired in 1958.

Brett Favre (b.10-10-69): Football QB. Won NFL MVP award three years in a row (1995–97). Led Packers to victory in Super Bowl XXXI. Career span 1991– with Atlanta and Green Bay.

Bob Feller (b. 11-3-18): Baseball RHP. Pitched three no-hitters and 12 one-hitters. 266 career wins; 2,581 career strikeouts. Won 20+ games six times. League leader in wins six times, strikeouts seven times, innings pitched five times. Served four years in military during career. Career span 1936–41, 1945–56 with Cleveland.

Tom Ferguson (b. 12-20-50): Rodeo. First to top $1 million in career earnings. All-Around champion six consecutive years (1974–79).

Enzo Ferrari (b. 2-8-1898, d. 8-14-88): Auto racing engineer. Team owner since 1929, he built first Ferrari race car in Italy in 1947 and continued to preside over Ferrari race and street cars until his death. In 68 years of competition, Ferrari's cars have won over 5,000 races.

Herve Filion (b. 2-1-40): Harness racing driver. Alltime leader in career wins (more than 14,000). Driver of the Year 10 times, more than any other driver (consecutively 1969–74, '78, '81, '89).

Rollie Fingers (b. 8-25-46): Baseball RHP. Won 107 games in relief in his career; 341 career saves. 1981 Cy Young and MVP winner; 1974 World Series MVP. Saved six World Series games in his career. Career span 1968–85 with Oakland, San Diego, Milwaukee.

Bobby Fischer (b. 3-9-43): Chess. World champion from 1972 to 1975, the only American to hold title. Never played competitive chess during his reign. Forfeited title to Anatoly Karpov by refusing to play him.

Carlton Fisk (b. 12-26-47): Baseball C. Retired as alltime HR leader among catchers (352) and second in games caught (2,226). 376 career HR, including a record 75 after age 40. Rookie of the Year in 1972 and All-Star 11 times. Hit dramatic 12th-inning HR to win Game 6 of 1975 World Series. Career span 1969–93 with Boston, Chicago (AL). Elected to Hall of Fame in 2000.

Emerson Fittipaldi (b. 12-12-46): Brazilian auto racer. Won Indy 500 in 1989 and '93. Won CART championship in 1989. Formula 1 champion two times (1972, '74).

James Fitzsimmons (b. 7-23-1874, d. 3-11-66): Horse racing trainer. "Sunny Jim." Trained two Triple Crown winners (Gallant Fox in 1930, Omaha in 1935). Trained six Belmont Stakes winners (1930, '32, '35, '36, '39, '55), four Preakness Stakes winners (1930, '35, '55, '57) and three Kentucky Derby winners (1930, '35, '39).

Peggy Fleming (b. 7-27-48): Figure skater. Olympic champion 1968. World champion (1966–68) and U.S. champion (1964–68).

Curt Flood (b. 1-18-38, d. 1-20-97): Baseball OF. Challenged baseball's reserve clause by refusing to be traded after 1969 season. Supreme Court rejected his plea, but baseball was eventually forced to adopt free agency system. Won seven consecutive Gold Gloves from 1963 to 1969. Career batting average of .293. Career span 1956–69 with St. Louis.

Whitey Ford (b. 10-21-26): Baseball LHP. Alltime World Series leader in wins, losses, games started, innings pitched, hits allowed, walks and strikeouts. 236 career wins, 2.75 ERA. Led league in wins and winning percentage three times each; ERA, shutouts, innings pitched two times each. 1961 Cy Young winner and World Series MVP. Career span 1950, 1953–67 with New York Yankees.

Forego (b. 1970, d. 8-27-97): Thoroughbred race horse. Horse of the Year in 1974 (won 8 of 13 starts); '75 (won 6 of 9); and '76 (won 6 of 8). Finished fourth in 1973 Kentucky Derby. Over six years won 34 of 57 starts and $1,938,957.

George Foreman (b. 1-22-48): Boxer. Heavyweight champion (1973–74). Retired in 1977, but returned to the ring in 1987. At age 45, KO'd Michael Moorer to regain heavyweight title. Also heavyweight gold medalist at 1968 Olympics.

Dick Fosbury (b. 3-6-47): Track and field. Gold medalist in high jump at 1968 Olympics. Introduced back-to-the-bar style of high jumping, called the "Fosbury Flop."

Jimmie Foxx (b. 10-22-07, d. 7-21-67): Baseball 1B. Won three MVP awards (1932–33, '38). Fourth alltime highest slugging average (.609), with 534 career HR; hit 30+ HR 12 consecutive seasons, 100+ RBI 13 consecutive seasons. Won Triple Crown in 1933. Led league in HR four times, batting average two times. Career span 1925–45 with Philadelphia, Boston (AL).

A.J. Foyt (b. 1-16-35): Auto racer. Alltime leader in Indy Car victories (67). Won Indy 500 four times (1961, '64, '67, '77), Daytona 500 one time (1972), 24 Hours of Daytona two times (1983, '85) and 24 Hours of LeMans one time (1967). USAC champion seven times, more than any other driver (1960, '61, '63, '64, '67, '75, '79).

William H.G. France (b. 9-26-09, d. 6-7-92): Auto racing executive. Founder of NASCAR and president from 1948–72. Builder of Daytona and Talladega speedways.

Dawn Fraser (b. 9-4-37): Australian swimmer. First swimmer to win gold medal in same event at three consecutive Olympics (100-meter freestyle in 1956, '60, '64). First woman to break the one-minute barrier at 100 meters (59.9 in 1962).

Joe Frazier (b. 1-12-44): Boxer. "Smokin' Joe." Heavyweight champion (1970–73). Best known for his three epic bouts with Muhammad Ali. Career record 32-4-1 with 27 KOs from 1965 to 1976. Also heavyweight gold medalist at 1964 Olympics.

Walt Frazier (b. 3-29-45): Basketball G. "Clyde." Point guard on championship Knick teams of 1970 and '73. First team All-NBA in 1970, '72, '74 and '75. First team All-Defense every year from 1969–'75. Averaged 18.9 points per game in 13-season NBA career. Elected to Hall of Fame in 1986.

Frankie Frisch (b. 9-9-1898, d. 3-12-73): Baseball IF. "The Fordham Flash." Led NL in hits in 1923 (223). NL MVP in 1931. Hit over .300 13 seasons. Scored 100+ runs seven times. Drove in 100+ runs three times. Career .316 batting average. Career span 1919–37 with New York (NL) and St. Louis (NL). Elected to Hall of Fame in 1947.

Dan Gable (b. 10-25-48): Wrestler. Gold medalist in 149–pound division at 1972 Olympics. Two-time NCAA champion (in 1968 at 130 pounds, in 1969 at 137 pounds). Coached Iowa to NCAA championship 15 times (1978–86, 1991–93 and 1995–97).

Clarence Gaines (b. 5-21-23): College basketball coach. "Bighouse." 828 career wins in 46 seasons at Division II Winston-Salem State from 1947–93.

John Galbreath (b. 8-10-1897, d. 7-20-88): Horse racing owner. Owner of Darby Dan Farms from 1935 until his death and baseball's Pittsburgh Pirates from 1946 to 1985. Only man to breed and own winners of both the Kentucky Derby (Chateaugay in 1963 and Proud Clarion in 1967) and the Epsom Derby (Roberto in 1972).

Gallant Fox (b. 3-23-27, d. 11-13-54): Thoroughbred race horse. Triple Crown winner in 1930 with jockey Earle Sande aboard. Trained by James Fitzsimmons. The only Triple Crown winner to sire another Triple Crown winner (Omaha in 1935).

Don Garlits (b. 1-14-32): Auto racer. "Big Daddy." Has won 35 National Hot Rod Association Top Fuel events. Won three NHRA Top Fuel points titles (1975, 1985–86). First Top Fuel driver to surpass 190 mph (1963), 200 mph (1964), 240 mph (1973), 250 mph (1975) and 270 mph (1986). Credited with developing rear-engine dragster.

Haile Gebrselassie (b. 4-18-73): Track and field. Ethiopian distance runner has dominated long distance running since 1993. Holds world records in the 5,000 and 10,000 meters. Gold medalist in the 10,000 at the 1996 and 2000 Olympics.

Lou Gehrig (b. 6-19-03, d. 6-2-41): Baseball 1B. "The Iron Horse." Second alltime in consecutive games played (2,130), leader in grand slam HR (23), third in RBI (1,995) and slugging average (.632). MVP in 1927, '36; won Triple Crown in 1934. .340 career average; 493 career HR. 100+ RBI 13 consecutive seasons. Led league in RBI five times and HR three times. Played on seven World Series winners with New York (AL). Died of disease since named for him. Career span 1923–39.

Bernie Geoffrion (b. 2-16-31): Hockey RW. "Boom Boom" for his powerful slapshot. Won Hart Memorial Trophy for 1960–61. Scored 393 goals and 429 assists in 16 seasons (1950–68), the first 14 with Montreal, the final two with New York. Elected to Hall of Fame 1972.

Eddie Giacomin (b. 6-6-39): Hockey goalie. "Fast Eddie" led NHL goalies in wins for three straight seasons. Shared Vezina Trophy for 1970–71. Career GAA of 2.82. Career span 1965–78 with New York and Detroit.

Althea Gibson (b. 8-25-27, d. 9-28-03): Tennis player. Won two consecutive Wimbledon and U.S. singles titles (1957, '58), the first black player to win these tournaments. Also won the French Open in 1956.

Bob Gibson (b. 11-9-35): Baseball RHP. 1968 Cy Young and MVP award winner with modern National League–best ERA (1.12). Also 1970 Cy Young award winner. Pitched no-hitter in 1971. Record holder for most strikeouts in a World Series game (17); Series MVP in 1964, '67. Won 20+ games five times. 251 career wins; 3,117 strikeouts. Career span 1959–75 with St. Louis.

Josh Gibson (b. 12-21-11, d. 1-20-47): Baseball C. "The Black Babe Ruth." Couldn't play in major leagues because of racial barrier. Credited with 950 HR (75 in 1931, 69 in 1934) and .350 batting average. Had .400+ average two times. Career span 1930–46 with Homestead Grays, Pittsburgh Crawfords.

Kirk Gibson (b. 5-28-57): Baseball OF. Played on two World Series champions (Detroit in 1984 and Los Angeles in 1988). Hit dramatic pinch-hit HR to win Game 1 of 1988 series. MVP in 1988. Career span 1979–94 with Detroit, Los Angeles, Kansas City, Pittsburgh. Also starred in baseball and football at Michigan State.

Frank Gifford (b. 8-16-30): Football RB. NFL Player of Year in 1956 when he rushed for 819 yards and caught 51 passes. Played in seven Pro Bowls. Retired for one season after ferocious hit by Chuck Bednarik. Career span 1952–60 and 1962–64, all with New York (N). Elected to Hall of Fame in 1977.

Rod Gilbert (b. 7-1-41): Hockey RW. Played 16 seasons, all with the New York Rangers (1960–78), and had 406 goals and 615 assists. Elected to Hall of Fame 1982.

Sid Gillman (b. 10-26-11, d. 1-4-03): Football coach. Developed wide-open, pass-oriented style of offense, introduced techniques for situational player substitutions and the study of game films. Won AFL championship (1963) with San Diego Chargers. Career span 1955–59 Los Angeles; 1960–69 Los Angeles/San Diego Chargers; 1973–74 Houston. Lifetime record 123-104-7.

Pancho Gonzales (b. 5-9-28, d. 7-3-95): Tennis player. Won two consecutive U.S. singles titles (1948–49). In 1969, at age 41, beat Charlie Pasarell 22–24, 1–6, 16–14, 6–3, 11–9 in longest Wimbledon match ever (5:12).

Jeff Gordon (b. 8-4-71): Auto racer. NASCAR's alltime money winner. Four-time NASCAR Winston Cup champion (1995, '97, '98, '01). Youngest Winston Cup Series champion in the modern era, winning his first title at age 24. Won 1997 and '99 Daytona 500. Set NASCAR modern record with 13 wins in 1998.

Shane Gould (b. 11-23-56): Australian swimmer. Won three gold medals, one silver and one bronze at 1972 Olympics. Set 11 world records over 23-month period beginning in 1971. Held world record in five freestyle distances ranging from 100 meters to 1,500 meters in late 1971 and 1972. Retired at age 16.

Steffi Graf (b. 6-14-69): German tennis player. Achieved the Grand Slam in 1988. Won four Australian Open singles titles (1988–90, '94), seven Wimbledon titles (1988, '89, 1991–93, '95, '96), six French Open titles (1987, '88, '93, '95, '96, '99) and five U.S. Open titles (1988–89, '93, '95, '96). Held the No. 1 ranking a record 186 weeks. Gold medalist at 1988 Olympics. Second in alltime Grand Slam singles titles (22).

Otto Graham (b. 12-6-21): Football QB. Led Cleveland to 10 championship games in his 10-year career. Played on four consecutive AAFC champions (1946–49) and three NFL champions (1950, '54, '55). Combined league totals: 23,584 yards passing, 174 touchdown passes. Player of the Year two times (1953, '55). Led league in passing six times. Career span 1946–55.

Red Grange (b. 6-13-03, d. 1-28-91): Football HB. "The Galloping Ghost." All-America three consecutive seasons with Illinois (1923–25), scoring 31 touchdowns in 20–game collegiate career. Signed by George Halas of Chicago in 1925, attracted sellout

crowds across the country. Established the first AFL with manager C.C. Pyle in 1926, but league folded after one year. Career span 1925–34 with Chicago, New York.

Rocky Graziano (b. 6-7-22, d. 5-22-90): Boxer. Middleweight champion from 1947–48. Career record 67–13. Endured three brutal title fights against Tony Zale, with Zale winning by KO in 1946 and 1948, and Graziano winning by KO in 1947.

Hank Greenberg (b. 1-1-11, d. 9-4-86): Baseball 1B. 331 career HR (58 in 1938). MVP in 1935, '40. League leader in HR and RBI four times each. Fifth alltime highest slugging average (.605). 100+ RBI seven times. Career span 1933-41, 1945-47 with Detroit, Pittsburgh.

Joe Greene (b. 9-24-46): Football DT. "Mean Joe." Anchored Pittsburgh's famed "Steel Curtain" defense. Selected for Pro Bowl 10 times. Played on four Super Bowl champions (1974, '75, '78, '79). Career span 1969–81 with Pittsburgh.

Maurice Greene (b. 7-23-74): Track and field. Won Olympic gold medals in Sydney in the 100 meters and the 4x100 relay. Held world record for 100 meters for three years after running 9.79 in Athens on 6-16-99.

Forrest Gregg (b. 10-18-33): Football OT/G. Played in then-record 188 straight games from 1956–71. Named all-NFL eight straight years starting in 1960. Career span 1956–71, most of it with Green Bay Packers. Played on winning Packer team in first two Super Bowls. Inducted into Hall of Fame in 1977.

Wayne Gretzky (b. 1-26-61): Hockey C. "The Great One." No. 99. Most dominant player in NHL history. Alltime scoring leader in points (2,795), assists (1,910), and goals (885). Alltime single-season scoring leader in points (215 in 1986), goals (92 in 1982) and assists (163 in 1986). Won nine MVP awards (1980-87, '89). Led league in assists 16 times, scoring 11 times, goals five times. Scored 200+ points four times, 100+ points 10 other times; 70+ goals four consecutive seasons, 50+ goals five other times; 100+ assists 11 consecutive seasons. Playoff MVP two times (1985, '88). Played on four Stanley Cup champions with Edmonton from 1978 to 1988. Career span 1978–99 with Edmonton, Los Angeles, St. Louis, and New York Rangers.

Bob Griese (b. 2-3-45): Football QB. Led Miami to three straight Super Bowls (1971–73), including the 1972 Miami team that went 17–0. Career span 1967–80 with Miami, passing for 25,092 yards and 192 TDs. Elected to Hall of Fame in 1990.

Florence Griffith Joyner (b. 12-21-59, d. 9-21-98): Track and field. Won three gold medals (100 meters, 200 meters, 4x100-meter relay) at 1988 Olympics; Set world record in 100 (10.49) in 1988 and in 200 (21.34) at the 1988 Olympics. Sullivan Award winner in 1988.

Ken Griffey Jr. (b. 11-21-69): Baseball OF. Hit 56 home runs in back-to-back seasons (1997–98). Became youngest man (31 years 261 day) to reach 450 HRs when he connected on 8-9-01. Won AL MVP award in 1997, when he hit .304 with 56 HRs and 147 RBI. 10 Gold Glove Awards. Father Ken Sr. starred with Cincinnati Reds in 1970s. Hit 500th HR in 2004.

Archie Griffin (b. 8-21-54): College football RB. Only player to win the Heisman Trophy two times (1974–75), with Ohio State. Eighth alltime NCAA career yards rushing (5,177). Professional career span 1976–83 with Cincinnati; totaled 2,808 yards rushing and 192 receptions.

Lefty Grove (b. 3-6-00, d. 5-22-75): Baseball LHP. 300 career wins and fifth alltime highest winning percentage (.680). League leader in ERA nine times, strikeouts seven consecutive seasons. Won 20+ games eight times. 1931 MVP. Career span 1925–41 with Philadelphia (AL), Boston (AL).

Tony Gwynn (b. 5-9-60): Baseball OF. Won eight batting titles (1984, 1987–89, 1994–97). League leader in hits six times, with .300+ average 16 times, 200+ hits five times. Career span 1982–01 with San Diego: .338 average, 3,141 hits.

Walter Hagen (b. 12-21-1892, d. 10-5-69): Golfer. Third alltime leader in major championships (11). Won PGA Championship five times (1921, 1924–27), British Open four times (1922, '24, '28, '29) and U.S. Open two times (1914, '19). Won 40 career tournaments.

Marvin Hagler (b. 5-23-54): Boxer. "Marvelous." Middleweight champion (1980–87). Career record 62-3-2 with 52 KOs from 1973–87. Defended title 13 times.

George Halas (b. 2-2-1895, d. 10-31-83): Football owner and coach. "Papa Bear." Alltime leader in seasons coaching (40) and second in wins (324). Career record 324-151-31 intermittently from 1920–1967. Remained as owner until his death. Chicago won a record seven NFL championships during his tenure.

Glenn Hall (b. 10-3-31): Hockey goalie. "Mr. Goalie" was an All-Star in 11 of his 18 seasons. Set record for consecutive games played by a goaltender (502) and ended career with goals against average of 2.51. Won or shared Vezina Trophy three times. Career span 1952–71 with Detroit, Chicago and St. Louis.

Charles Haley (b. 1-6-64): Football DE. Only player in NFL history to be a member of five Super Bowl champions, two with San Francisco (1989, '90) and three with Dallas (1993, '94, '96). Career span 1986–99. Recorded 100.5 career sacks.

Mia Hamm (b. 3-17-72): Soccer player. Alltime leading scorer in U.S. women's national team history. Member of Women's World Cup champion team in 1991, '99, and third-place team in '95. Member of 1996 Olympic champion team. Debuted with national team against China on 8-3-87 as its youngest player ever, at age 15.

Arthur B. (Bull) Hancock (b. 1-24-10, d. 9-14-72): Horse racing owner. Owner of Claiborne Farm and arguably the greatest breeder in history. For 15 straight years, from 1955–69, a Claiborne stallion led the sire list. Foaled at Claiborne Farm were four Horses of the Year (Kelso, Round Table, Bold Ruler and Nashua).

Tom Harmon (b. 9-28-19, d. 3-17-90): Football RB. Won Heisman Trophy in 1940 with Michigan. Triple-threat back led nation in scoring and named All-America two consecutive seasons (1939, '40). Awarded Silver Star and Purple Heart in World War II. Played in NFL with Los Angeles (1946–47).

Franco Harris (b. 3-7-50): Football RB. Holds Super Bowl record for career rushing yards (354). Super Bowl MVP in 1974. Made the "Immaculate Reception" to win 1972 playoff game against Oakland. Played on four Super Bowl champions (1974, '75, '78, '79) with Pittsburgh. Gained 1,000+ yards in nine seasons, 100+ yards in 47 games. Played in eight Pro Bowls. Rookie of the Year in 1972. Career span 1972–84 with Pittsburgh and Seattle. Rushed for 12,120 yards and scored 100 career touchdowns. Elected to the Hall of Fame in 1990.

Leon Hart (b. 11-2-28, d. 9-24-02): Football DE. Won Heisman Trophy in 1949, the last lineman to win the award. Played on three national champions with Notre Dame (1946, '47, '49), and the Irish went undefeated during his four years (36-0-2). Also played on three NFL champions with Detroit. Career span 1950–57.

Bill Hartack (b. 12-9-32): Horse racing jockey. Rode five Kentucky Derby winners (1957, '60, '62, '64, '69), three Preakness Stakes winners (1956, '64, '69) and one Belmont Stakes winner (1960).

Doug Harvey (b. 12-19-24, d. 12-26-90): Hockey D. Defensive Player of the Year seven times (1954–57, 1959–61). Led league in assists in 1954. All-Star 10 times. Played on six Stanley Cup champions with Montreal from 1947–68.

Dominik Hasek (b. 1-29-65): Czech hockey G. Two-time NHL MVP (1997, '98) with Buffalo; six-time Vezina Trophy winner (1994, '95, 1997–99, '01) as top goalie in league. Led NHL with a 1.95 goals-against average in 1993–94, the first sub-2.00 GAA since Bernie Parent in 1974. Topped that with 1.87 GAA in 1998–99. Guided Czech Republic to Olympic gold medal in 1998 at Nagano. Career span 1990–02 with Chicago, Buffalo and Detroit; 2003– Detroit.

Billy Haughton (b. 11-2-23, d. 7-15-86): Harness racing driver. Won the Pacing Triple Crown driving Rum Customer in 1968. Won the Hambletonian four times (1974, '76, '77, '80).

John Havlicek (b. 4-8-40): Basketball F/G. "Hondo" averaged 20.8 points per game over 16-season NBA career, all with Boston. First team All-NBA (1971–74). Member of eight NBA championship teams. Playoff MVP 1974. Member of Ohio State team that won 1960 NCAA title. Elected to Hall of Fame in 1983.

Elvin Hayes (b. 11-17-45): Basketball C. Three-time first-team All-NBA selection (1975, '77, '79). 12-time All-Star (1969–80). Led NBA in scoring (1969) and in rebounding (1970, '74). Played from 1968–84 with San Diego/Houston Rockets and Baltimore/Washington Bullets, averaging 21.0 points and 12.5 rebounds per game. 1968 *Sporting News* College Player of Year as Houston senior. Elected to Hall of Fame in 1989.

Woody Hayes (b. 2-14-13, d. 3-12-87): College football coach. Won three national championship (1954, '57, '68) and four Rose Bowls. Career record 238-72-10, including four undefeated seasons, with Ohio State from 1951–1978. Forced to resign after striking an opposing player during 1978 Gator Bowl.

Marques Haynes (b. 10-3-26): Basketball G. Known as "The World's Greatest Dribbler." Beginning in 1946 barnstormed more than four million miles throughout 97 countries for the Harlem Globetrotters, Harlem Magicians, Meadowlark Lemon's Bucketeers, Harlem Wizards.

Thomas Hearns (b. 10-18-58): Boxer. "Hit Man." Champion in four weight classes: welterweight, super welterweight, middleweight and light heavyweight. Career record: 57–4–1 with 45 KOs.

Eric Heiden (b. 6-14-58): Speed skater. Won five gold medals at 1980 Olympics. World champion three consecutive years (1977–79). Won Sullivan Award in 1980.

Carol Heiss (b. 1-20-40): Figure skater. Gold medalist at 1960 Olympics, silver medalist at 1956 Olympics. World champion five consecutive years (1956–60) and U.S. champion four consecutive years (1957–60). Married 1956 gold medalist Hayes Jenkins.

..ckey Henderson (b. 12-25-57): Baseball OF. Career leader in stolen bases, walks and runs; modern single-season stolen base record holder (stole 130 bases in 1982). Led league in steals 11 times. 1990 MVP. Alltime leader in lead-off HRs. Career span 1979– with nine teams.

Sonja Henie (b. 4-8-12, d. 10-12-69): Norwegian figure skater. Gold medalist at three consecutive Olympics (1928, '32, '36). World champion 10 consecutive years (1927–36).

Orel Hershiser (b. 9-16-58): Baseball RHP. Alltime leader most consecutive scoreless innings pitched (59 in 1988). Cy Young Award winner in 1988 and World Series MVP. Career span 1983–00 with Los Angeles, Cleveland, San Francisco and New York (NL): 204–150, 3.48 ERA.

Foster Hewitt (b. 11-21-02, d. 4-22-85): Hockey sportscaster. In 1923, aired one of hockey's first radio broadcasts. Became the voice of hockey in Canada on radio and later television. Famous for the phrase, "He shoots ... he scores!"

Tommy Hitchcock (b. 2-11-00, d. 4-19-44): Polo. 10-goal rating 18 times in his 19-year career from 1922–40. Killed in plane crash in World War II.

Lew Hoad (b. 11-23-34): Australian tennis player. Won two Wimbledon singles titles (1956, '57). Also won French title and Australian title in 1956, but failed to achieve the Grand Slam when defeated at Forest Hills by countryman Ken Rosewall.

Ben Hogan (b. 8-13-12, d. 7-25-97): Golfer. Third alltime in career wins (63). Won U.S. Open four times (1948, '50, '51, '53), the Masters (1951, '53) and PGA Championship (1946, '48) two times each and British Open once (1953). PGA Player of the Year four times (1948, '50, '51, '53).

Marshall Holman (b. 9-29-54): Bowler. Won 21 PBA titles between 1975–88. Had leading average in 1987 (213.54) and was named PBA Bowler of the Year.

Nat Holman (b. 10-18-1896, d. 2-12-95): College basketball coach. Only coach in history to win NCAA and NIT championships in same season, in 1950 with CCNY; 423 career wins, a .689 winning percentage.

Larry Holmes (b. 11-3-49): Boxer. Heavyweight champion (1978–85). Career record 69–6 with 44 KOs from 1973–02. Defended title 21 times.

Lou Holtz (b. 1-6-37): Football coach. Has led four different programs to Top 20 seasons. Coached Notre Dame to national championship in 1988 and a 12–0 record with a 34–21 win over West Virginia in Fiesta Bowl. 12-8-2 career record in bowl games. Career span 1969–75 at William & Mary and N Carolina St; 1977–96 at Arkansas, Minnesota and Notre Dame; and 1999– at S Carolina.

Evander Holyfield (b. 10-19-62): Boxer. Only man to win the heavyweight title four times. Won heavyweight belt for the first time on Oct. 25, 1990, when he KO'd James (Buster) Douglas in Las Vegas. Fought three epic bouts with Riddick Bowe and two memorable clashes with Mike Tyson (Tyson was disqualified in the rematch for biting Holyfield's ears, severing one of them.)

Red Holzman (b. 8-10-20; d. 11-13-98): Basketball coach. Led New York to NBA titles in 1970 and '73. NBA Coach of the Year in 1970. After two-year coaching stints with Milwaukee and St. Louis, coached

New York from 1968–82. Career record: 696–604. Elected to Hall of Fame in 1985.

Harry Hopman (b. 8-12-06, d. 12-27-85): Australian tennis coach. As nonplaying captain, led Australia to 15 Davis Cup titles between 1950–69. Mentor to Lew Hoad, Ken Rosewall, Rod Laver and John Newcombe.

Willie Hoppe (b. 10-11-1887, d. 2-1-59): Billiards. Won 51 world championship matches from 1904–52.

Rogers Hornsby (b. 4-27-1896, d. 1-5-63): Baseball 2B. Second alltime in career batting average (.358), won seven batting titles, including with .424 average in 1924. Led league in slugging nine times. Triple Crown winner in 1922, '25; MVP award winner in 1925, '29. 2,930 hits and 1,584 RBI's from 1915–37 with five teams, including St. Louis (NL).

Paul Hornung (b. 12-23-35): Football RB–K. Led league in scoring three consecutive seasons, including a record 176 points in 1960 (15 touchdowns, 15 field goals, 41 extra points). Player of the Year in 1961. Career span 1957–66 with Green Bay. Suspended for 1963 season by Pete Rozelle for gambling. Also won Heisman Trophy in 1956 with Notre Dame.

Gordie Howe (b. 3-31-28): Hockey RW. Second alltime in goals (801), first in years played (26) and games (1,767). Finished career with 1,850 points and 1,049 assists. Won MVP award six times (1952, '53, '57, '58, '60, '63). Led league in scoring six times, goals five times and assists three times. All-Star 12 times. Played on four Stanley Cup champions with Detroit from 1946–71. Teamed with sons Mark and Marty in the WHA with Houston and New England from 1973–79, in NHL with Hartford in 1980.

Carl Hubbell (b. 6-22-03, d. 11-21-88): Baseball LHP. 253 career wins. MVP in 1933, '36. League leader in wins and ERA three times each. Won 24 consecutive games from 1936–37. Struck out Ruth, Gehrig, Foxx, Simmons and Cronin consecutively in 1934 All-Star game. Pitched no-hitter in 1929. Career span 1928–43 with New York (NL).

Sam Huff (b. 10-4-34): Football LB. Made 30 interceptions. Career span 1956–69 with New York Giants and Washington. Elected to Hall of Fame in 1982.

Bobby Hull (b. 1-3-39): Hockey LW. "The Golden Jet." Led league in goals seven times and points three times. 610 career goals. Won MVP award two consecutive seasons (1965, '66). Son Brett won MVP award in 1991, the only father and son to be so honored. All-Star 10 times. Career span 1957–72 with Chicago, 1973–80 with Winnipeg of WHA.

Brett Hull (b. 8-9-64): Hockey RW. Son of Bobby Hull. Won Hart Memorial Trophy for 1990–91 season. Scored Stanley Cup–winning goal for Dallas in third overtime of Game 6 against Buffalo in 1999. Career span 1986– with Calgary, St. Louis, Dallas and Detroit.

Jim (Catfish) Hunter (b. 4-8-46, d. 9-9-99): Baseball RHP. 1974 Cy Young award winner. Won 20+ games five consecutive seasons. Led league in wins and winning percentage two times each, ERA one time. 250+ innings pitched eight times. Pitched perfect game in 1968. Member of five World Series champions for Oakland and New York (AL). Career span 1965–79.

Don Hutson (b. 1-31-13, d. 6-26-97): Football WR. Finished his career as alltime leader in touchdown receptions (99). Led league in pass receptions eight times, receiving yards seven times and scoring five consecutive seasons. Caught at least one pass in 95 consecutive games. Player of the Year two consecutive seasons (1941, '42). Career span 1935–45 with Green Bay.

Hank Iba (b. 8-6-04; d. 1-15-93): College basketball coach. Coached Oklahoma A&M (which became Oklahoma State) from 1934–70. Team won NCAA titles in 1945 and '46. 767 career wins is seventh alltime.

Jackie Ickx (b. 1-1-45): Belgian auto racer. Won the 24 Hours of LeMans a record six times (1969, 1975–77, '81, '82) before retiring in 1985.

Punch Imlach (b. 3-15-18, d. 12-1-87): Hockey coach. 467 wins. With Toronto from 1958–69. Won four Stanley Cup championships (1962–64, 1967).

Miguel Induráin (b. 7-16-64): Cyclist. Won five consecutive Tours de France (1991–95), a feat unequaled until Lance Armstrong matched in 2003.

Juli Inkster (b.6-24-60): Golfer. 28 career victories. Became only the second woman ever to win all four of the LPGA's modern majors when she won the LPGA Championship on 6-27-99. Inducted to LPGA Hall of Fame in 1999.

Bo Jackson (b. 11-30-62): Baseball OF and Football RB. Only person in history to be named to baseball All-Star game and football Pro Bowl game. 1985 Heisman Trophy winner at Auburn. 1989 MLB All-Star game MVP. Signed with football's LA Raiders in 1988. Retired 1994 following hip replacement surgery.

Joe Jackson (b. 7-16-1889, d. 12-5-51): Baseball OF. "Shoeless Joe." Third alltime highest career batting average (.356), with .300+ average 11 times. One of the "Eight Men Out" banned from baseball for throwing 1919 World Series. Career span 1908–20 with Cleveland, Chicago (AL).

Phil Jackson (b. 9-17-45): Basketball F-Coach. Coached the Lakers to their third straight NBA Championship in 2002, his ninth as a coach. Won six titles as coach of Chicago (1991–93, 1996–98). Best winning percentage in NBA history (726–258, .738). Spent 13 years as a scrappy forward in the NBA, winning an NBA title with New York in 1973.

Reggie Jackson (b. 5-18-46): Baseball OF. "Mr. October." Alltime leader in World Series slugging percentage (.755). 1977 Series MVP, hit three HR in final game on three consecutive pitches. 563 career HR total is eighth best alltime. Led league in HR four times. 1973 MVP. Alltime strikeout leader (2,597). In a 12-year period played on 10 first-place teams, five World Series winners. Career span 1967–87 with Oakland, Baltimore, New York (AL) and California. Inducted to Baseball Hall of Fame in 1993.

Bruce Jenner (b. 10-28-49): Track and Field. Set decathlon world record (8,634) in winning gold medal at 1976 Olympics. Sullivan Award winner in 1976.

John Henry (b. 1975): Thoroughbred race horse. Sold as yearling for $1,100, the gelding was Horse of the Year in 1981 and 1984 and retired with then-record $6,597,947 in winnings.

Ben Johnson (b. 12-30-61): Track and field. Canadian sprinter set world record in 100 meters (9.83 in 1987). Won event at 1988 Olympics in 9.79, but gold medal revoked for failed drug test. Both world records revoked for steroid usage. Suspended for life after testing positive for elevated testosterone level at an indoor meet in Montreal on 1-17-93.

Earvin (Magic) Johnson (b. 8-14-59): Basketball G. Retired Nov. 7, 1991 after being diagnosed with HIV, the virus that causes AIDS. Returned to Lakers Feb '96 at age 36. Finished career second alltime in assists (10,141). MVP award three times (1987, '89, '90) and playoff MVP in 1980, '82 and '87. Played on five championship teams with Los Angeles. All-Star eight consecutive seasons. League leader in assists four times, steals two times, free throw percentage once. Career stats: 19.5 ppg, 11.2 apg, 7.2 rpg. Also won NCAA championship and named tournament MVP in 1979 with Michigan State.

Jack Johnson (b. 3-31-1878, d. 6-10-46): Boxer. First black heavyweight champion (1908–15). Career record 78-8-12 with 45 KOs from 1897–28.

Jimmy Johnson (b. 7-16-43): Football coach. Won two straight Super Bowls (1993, '94) as Dallas coach. Career record of 89–66 with Dallas and Miami. Led Miami (FL) to collegiate national championship in 1987. One of only three men to win college and NFL championships.

Michael Johnson (b. 9-13-67): Track and field. First man to win gold medals in both the 200 and 400 at the Olympics (1996). Broke 17-year-old 200-meter world record (19.66) at 1996 U.S. Olympic trials, then further lowered mark to 19.32 at Atlanta. Repeated in the 400 meters at the 2000 Sydney Games. Anchored U.S. 4x400 team at 1993 World Championship to world record of 2:54.29.

Randy Johnson (b. 9-10-63): Baseball LHP. Six-foot, 10-inch fireballer is tallest player in Major League history. Won Cy Young Award five times (1995, '99, 2000, '01, '02). Won "pitching triple crown" in 2002, leading league in wins, ERA and strikeouts. Led Arizona Diamondbacks to 2001 World Series victory, winning Series MVP award along with teammate Curt Schilling. Pitched no-hitter on 6-2-90 for Seattle against Oakland; pitched perfect game on 5-18-04 for Arizona against Atlanta. Career span 1988–89 with Montreal; 1989–98 Seattle; 1998 Houston; 1999– Arizona.

Walter Johnson (b. 11-6-1887, d. 12-10-46): Baseball RHP. "Big Train." Alltime leader in shutouts (110), second in wins (416), fourth in losses (279) and third in innings pitched (5,914). His record of 3,509 career strikeouts lasted for 56 years. 2.17 career ERA. MVP in 1913, '24. Won 20+ games 12 times. League leader in strikeouts 12 times, ERA five times, wins six times. Pitched no-hitter in 1920. Career span 1907–27 with Washington.

Ben A. Jones (b. 12-31-1882, d. 6-13-61): Horse racing trainer. Trained Triple Crown winner (Whirlaway in 1941). Trained six Kentucky Derby winners, more than any other trainer (1938, '41, '44, '48, '49, '52), two Preakness Stakes winners (1941, '44) and one Belmont Stakes winner (1941).

Bobby Jones (b. 3-17-02, d. 12-18-71): Golfer. Achieved golf's only recognized Grand Slam in 1930. Second alltime in major championships (13). Won U.S. Amateur five times, more than any golfer (1924, '25, '27, '28, '30), U.S. Open four times (1923, '26, '29, '30), British Open three times (1926, '27, '30) and British Amateur (1930). Also designed Augusta National course, site of the Masters, and founded the tournament. Winner of Sullivan Award in 1930.

K.C. Jones (b. 5-25-32): Basketball G-coach. Member of eight straight NBA-championship Boston teams in his nine season career from 1958–67. Averaged 7.4 points and 4.3 assists per game. Coached Celtics from 1983–88, with 308–102 regular season record and 65–37 playoff record with NBA titles in 1984 and '86.

Robert Trent Jones (b. 6-20-06, d. 6-14-00): English-born golf course architect designed or remodeled over 500 courses, including Baltusrol, Hazeltine, Oak Hill and Winged Foot. In the mid-60s five straight U.S. Opens were played on courses designed or remodeled by Jones.

Roy Jones Jr. (b.1-16-69): Boxer. Won titles as middleweight, super middleweight and light heavyweight. Career record: 49–2, 38 KOs. Won controversial silver medal at the 1988 Olympics in Seoul despite dominating his South Korean opponent in the final. Awarded Val Barker Trophy as outstanding boxer of '88 Games.

Sam Jones (b. 6-24-33): Basketball G. Played 12 seasons with Boston (1958–69), who won NBA title every year from 1959–66, plus 1968 and '69. Averaged 17.7 points per game. Elected to Hall of Fame in 1983.

Michael Jordan (b. 2-17-63): Basketball G. "Air." Arguably greatest player of all time. Led Bulls to six NBA titles (1991–93; 1996–98). Tied with Wilt Chamberlain for lead in career scoring average (30.1 ppg), and record holder for most points scored in a playoff game (63 in 1986). Guided Bulls to an NBA-record 72 wins in 1995–96. Led league in scoring a record 10 seasons, steals three times. League MVP in 1988, '91, '92, '96 and '98; Finals MVP in 1991–93 and 1996–98; Rookie of the Year in 1985. Career span 1984–93, 1995–98 with Chicago; 2001–03 with Washington. College Player of the Year in 1984. Played on NCAA title team with North Carolina in 1982. Member of gold medal-winning 1984 and '92 Olympic teams. Played minor league baseball in 1994.

Jackie Joyner-Kersee (b. 3-3-62): Track and field. Gold medalist in heptathlon and long jump at 1988 Olympics and in the former at the 1992 Olympics. Set heptathlon world record (7,291 points) at 1988 Olympics. Also won silver medal in heptathlon at 1984 Games and bronze in long jump at 1992 and '96 Olympics. Sullivan Award winner in 1986.

Alberto Juantorena (b. 3-12-51): Track and field. Cuban was gold medalist in 400 and 800 meters at 1976 Olympics.

Wang Junxia (b. 1963): Chinese distance runner. Broke four world records in six days in Sept. 1993. Broke 10,000 (29:31.78) on Sept 8; ran 1,500 in 3:51.92 in finishing second to countrywoman Qu Yunxia's world record of 3:50.46 on Sept 11; ran 3,000 record of 8:12.19 in heats on Sept 12 and lowered it to 8:06.11 on Sept 13. Won gold in 5,000 and silver in 10,000 at 1996 Olympics.

Sonny Jurgensen (b. 8-23-34): Football QB. In 18 seasons, passed for 32,224 yards and 255 TDs. Led NFL in passing both 1967 and '69. Career span 1957–74 with Philadelphia and Washington. Elected to Hall of Fame in 1983.

Duke Kahanamoku (b. 8-24-1890, d. 1-22-68): Swimmer. Won a total of five medals (3 gold and two silver) at three Olympics in 1912, '20, '24. Introduced the crawl stroke to America. Surfing pioneer and water polo player. Later sheriff of Honolulu.

Al Kaline (b. 12-19-34): Baseball OF. 3,007 career hits and 399 career HR. As a 20-year-old in 1955, became youngest player to win batting title, with .340 average. Had .300+ average nine times. Played in 18 All-Star games. Career span 1953–74 with Detroit.

Anatoly Karpov (b. 5-23-61): Soviet chess player. First world champion to receive title by default, in 1975, when Bobby Fischer chose not to defend his crown. Champion until 1985 when beaten by Garry Kasparov. Recognized by FIDE as champion in 1994.

Garry Kasparov (b. 4-13-63): Born Garik Weinstein. Chess player. World champion from 1985 to 1993 when stripped of title by FIDE. Won six-game series against IBM computer, Deep Blue, in 1996. Lost to improved version of Deep Blue in 1997.

Kip Keino (b. 1-17-40): Track and field. Kenyan was gold medalist in 1,500 meters at 1968 Olympics and in steeplechase at 1972 Olympics.

Jim Kelly (b. 2-14-60): Football QB. Led Buffalo to four straight Super Bowls—all losses. Career passer rating of 84.4. Led NFL in passing in 1990. In 11 NFL seasons passed for 35,467 yards and 237 TDs. Career span 1983–96 with Houston (USFL) and Buffalo Bills.

Kelso (b. 1957, d. 1983): Thoroughbred race horse. Gelding was Horse of the Year five straight years (1960–64). Finished in the money in 53 of 63 races. Career earnings $1,977,896.

Harmon Killebrew (b. 6-29-36): Baseball 3B-1B. 573 career HR total is seventh most alltime. 100+ RBI nine times, 40+ HR eight times. League leader in HR six times and RBI four times. 1969 MVP. 100+ walks and strikeouts seven times each. Career span 1954–75 with Washington and Minnesota.

Jean Claude Killy (b. 8-30-43): French skier. Won three gold medals at 1968 Olympics. World Cup overall champion two consecutive years (1967, '68).

Ralph Kiner (b. 10-27-22): Baseball OF. Led league in HR seven consecutive seasons. Third in alltime HR frequency (7.1 HR every 100 at bats). 369 career HR, with 50+ HR two times. 100+ RBI and runs scored in same season six times; 100+ walks six times. Career span 1946–55 with Pittsburgh, Chicago (NL), and Cleveland.

Billie Jean King (b. 11-22-43): Tennis player. Won a record 20 Wimbledon titles, including six singles titles (1966–68, '72, '73, '75). Won four U.S. singles titles (1967, '71, '72, '74), and singles titles at Australian Open (1968) and French Open (1972). Won 27 Grand Slam doubles titles—total of 39 Grand Slam titles is third alltime. Helped found the women's pro tour in 1970, serving as president of the Women's Tennis Association two times. Helped form Team Tennis.

Nile Kinnick (b. 7-9-18, d. 6-2-43): College football RB. Won the Heisman Trophy in 1939 with Iowa. Premier runner, passer and punter was killed in plane crash during routine Navy training flight. Stadium in Iowa City named in his honor.

Tom Kite (b. 12-9-49): Golfer. Winner of 19 career PGA Tour events, including the 1992 U.S. Open at Pebble Beach. Led PGA in scoring average in 1981 and '82. PGA Player of Year in 1989, when he won a then-record $1,395,278. Ryder Cup captain in 1997.

Franz Klammer (b. 12-3-54): Austrian alpine skier. Greatest downhiller ever. Gold medalist in downhill at 1976 Olympics. Also won four World Cup downhill titles (1975–78).

Bob Knight (b. 10-25-40): College basketball coach. Won three NCAA championships with Indiana in 1976, '81, '87. Coached U.S. Olympic team to gold medal in 1984. Fired by Indiana in 2000 after a series of disputes with the media, ex-players, students, and the university. Hired by Texas Tech in 2001, took team to 2003 NIT semifinals. Career span since 1966 with Army, Indiana and Texas Tech.

Olga Korbut (b. 5-16-55): Soviet gymnast. First ever to complete backward somersault on balance beam. Won three gold medals at 1972 Olympics.

Johann Olav Koss (b.10-29-68): Speed Skater. Norwegian won three gold medals at 1994 Olympics in Lillehammer, with world records in the 1,500, 5,000 and 10,000 meters. Won 1,500 meter gold medal and 10,000 meter silver medal in 1992 Games at Albertville.

Sandy Koufax (b. 12-30-35): Baseball LHP. Cy Young Award winner three times (1963, '65, '66); and MVP in 1963; World Series MVP in 1963, '65. Pitched four no-hitters, including one perfect game. League leader in ERA five consecutive seasons, strikeouts four times. Won 25+ games three times. Career record 165–87, with 2.76 ERA. Career span 1955–66 with Brooklyn/Los Angeles.

Jack Kramer (b. 8-1-21): Tennis player. Won two consecutive U.S. singles titles (1946, '47) and one Wimbledon title (1947). Also won six Grand Slam doubles titles. Served as executive director of Association of Tennis Professionals from 1972–75.

Ingrid Kristiansen (b. 3-21-56): Track and field. Norwegian runner is only person—male or female—to hold world records in 5,000 meters (14:37.33 set in 1986), 10,000 meters (30:13.74 set in 1986) and marathon (2:21:06 set in 1985). Also won Boston Marathon two times (1986, '89) and New York City Marathon once (1989).

Bob Kurland (b. 12-23-24): College basketball player. 6' 10¼" center on Oklahoma A&M teams that won NCAA titles in 1945 and '46. Consensus All-America and NCAA tournament MVP in both 1945 and '46. Led nation in scoring in 1946. His habit of swatting shots off rim led to creation of goaltending rule in 1945. Won gold medals in both 1948 and '52 Olympics. Turned down lucrative pro offers, playing instead for Phillips 66 Oilers AAU team.

Michelle Kwan (b. 7-7-80): Figure skater. Six-time U.S. champion (1996, 1998–02), four-time world champion (1996, '98, '00, '01); silver medalist in 1998 Olympics and bronze medalist in Salt Lake City in 2002.

Rene Lacoste (b. 7-2-05, d. 10-12-96): French tennis player. "The Crocodile." One of France's "Four Musketeers" of the 1920s. Won three French singles titles (1925, '27, '29), two consecutive U.S. titles (1926, '27) and two Wimbledon titles (1925, '28). Also designed casual shirt with embroidered crocodile that bears his name.

Marion Ladewig (b. 10-30-14): Bowler. Won All-Star Tournament eight times (1949–52, '54, '56, '59, '63) and WPBA National Championship once (1960). Also voted Bowler of the Year nine times (1950–54, 1957–59, '63).

Guy Lafleur (b. 9-20-51): Hockey RW. Won MVP award two consecutive seasons (1977, '78), playoff MVP in 1977. Scored 50+ goals and 100+ points six consecutive seasons. Led league in points scored three consecutive seasons, goals and assists one time each. 560 career goals, 793 assists. Played on five Stanley Cup champions with Montreal from 1971–85.

Curly Lambeau (b. 4-9-1898; d. 6-1-65): Football QB and coach. Quarterback for Packers team in early

1920s. Record of 212-106-21 in his 29 seasons (1921–49) as Packer coach, winning three NFL titles in 1929–31.

Jack Lambert (b. 7-8-52): Football LB. Anchored Pittsburgh's famed "Steel Curtain" defense. Selected for Pro Bowl nine times. Played on four Super Bowl champions (1974, '75, '78, '79) with Pittsburgh from 1974–84. Elected to Hall of Fame 1990.

Jake LaMotta (b. 7-10-21): Boxer. "The Bronx Bull." Subject of *Raging Bull*, a film by Martin Scorsese, starring Robert DeNiro. Won middleweight title by knocking out Marcel Cerdan in 10 on 6-16-49. Lost title to Ray Robinson, who KO'd him in 13 on 2-13-51. Career record: 83–19–4, 30 KOs.

Kenesaw Mountain Landis (b. 11-20-1866, d. 11-25-44): Baseball's first and most powerful commissioner from 1920–44. By banning the eight "Black Sox" involved in the fixing of the 1919 World Series, he restored public confidence in the integrity of baseball.

Tom Landry (b. 9-11-24, d. 2-12-00): Football coach. Third alltime in wins (270). The first coach in Dallas history, from 1960–88. Led team to 13 division titles, seven championship games and five Super Bowls. Won two Super Bowl championships (1971, '77). Career record 270-178-6.

Dick (Night Train) Lane (b. 4-16-28, d. 1-29-02): Football DB. Third alltime in interceptions (68) and second in interception yardage (1,207). Set record with 14 interceptions as a rookie in 1952. Career span 1952–65 with Los Angeles, Chicago Cardinals, Detroit.

Joe Lapchick (b. 4-12-00, d. 8-10-70): Basketball C–coach. One of the first big men in basketball, member of New York's Original Celtics. Coached St. John's (1936–47, 1956–65) to four NIT titles. Coached New York Knicks, 1947–56.

Steve Largent (b. 9-28-54): Football WR. Retired as alltime leader in pass receptions (819), and TD receptions (100). 177 consecutive games with reception, 10 seasons with 50+ receptions and eight seasons with 1,000+ yards receiving. Career span 1976–89 with Seattle. Oklahoma congressman from 1994–01.

Don Larsen (b. 8-7-29): Baseball RHP. Pitched only perfect game in World Series history, for New York (AL) on 10-8-56, beating the Dodgers 2–0; named World Series MVP. Career span 1953–67 for many teams.

Tommy Lasorda (b. 9-22-27): Baseball manager. Spent nearly his entire minor and major league career in Dodgers organization as a pitcher, coach and manager. Managed Dodgers 1977–96, winning four pennants and two World Series (1981, '88). Only three men managed one baseball team longer. Coached U.S. Olympic baseball team to the gold medal at the 2000 Sydney Games.

Rod Laver (b. 8-9-38): Australian tennis player. "Rocket." Only player to achieve the Grand Slam twice (as an amateur in 1962 and as a pro in 1969). Third alltime in men's Grand Slam singles titles (11—tied with Bjorn Borg). Won four Wimbledon titles (1961, '62, '68, '69), three Australian titles (1960, '62, '69), two U.S. titles (1962, '69) and two French titles (1962, '69). Also won eight Grand Slam doubles titles. First player to earn $1 million in prize money. 47 career tournament victories. Member of undefeated Australian Davis Cup team from 1959–62.

Andrea Mead Lawrence (b. 4-19-32): Skier. Gold medalist in slalom and giant slalom at 1952 Olympics.

Bobby Layne (b. 12-19-26; d. 12-1-86): Football QB. Led Detroit to NFL championships in both 1952 and '53. In 1952 led NFL in every passing category. Career span 1948–62, most with Detroit. Elected to Hall of Fame in 1967.

Sammy Lee (b. 8-1-20): Diver. Gold medalist at two consecutive Olympics (highboard in 1948, '52); bronze medalist in springboard at 1948 Olympics. Won the 1953 Sullivan Award. Also 1960 U.S. Olympic diving coach.

Jacques Lemaire (b. 9-7-45): Hockey C–Coach. As center for Montreal from 1967–79 was part of eight Stanley Cup winning teams. Over 12 seasons, all with Montreal, scored 366 goals and had 469 assists. Elected to Hall of Fame in 1984. Coached New Jersey to their first Stanley Cup in 1995.

Mario Lemieux (b. 10-5-65): Hockey C. Won MVP award in 1988, '93, '96. Playoff MVP in 1991. Led league in points five seasons and goals scored three seasons, assists one season. Rookie of the Year in 1985. Won 1992–93 scoring title despite sitting out six weeks to receive treatment for Hodgkin's disease, a form of cancer. Sat out 1994–95 season, returned in '95–96 to lead league in scoring and become second fastest player to score 500 career goals. Awarded ownership of Penguins in a settlement in 1999, and returned to the ice in 2001, when he scored 35 goals in 43 games. Career span 1984–94, 1995–97, 2001– with Pittsburgh.

Greg LeMond (b. 6-26-61): Cyclist. First American to win Tour de France; won event three times (1986, '89, '90). Recovered from hunting accident to win in 1989.

Ivan Lendl (b. 3-7-60): Tennis player. Second most alltime men's career tournament victories (94). Won three consecutive U.S. Open singles titles (1985–87) and three French Open titles (1984, '86, '87). Also won two Australian Open singles titles (1989, '90). Reached Grand Slam final nine other times.

Suzanne Lenglen (b. 5-24-1899, d. 7-4-38): French tennis player. Lost only one match from 1919–26. Won six Wimbledon singles and doubles titles (1919–23, '25). Won six French singles and doubles titles (1920–23, '25, '26).

Sugar Ray Leonard (b. 5-17-56): Boxer. Champion in five weight classes: welterweight, junior middleweight, middleweight, super middleweight and light heavyweight. Career record 36-3-1 with 25 KOs from 1977–97, including comeback loss to Hector Camacho at the age of 41. Also light welterweight gold medalist at 1976 Olympics.

Carl Lewis (b. 7-1-61): Track and field. Held world record for 100 meters (9.86), set at 1991 World Championships in Tokyo. Duplicated Jesse Owens's feat by winning four gold medals at 1984 Olympics (100 and 200 meters, 4x100-meter relay and long jump). Won 1996 Olympic long jump gold at age 35, giving him nine career gold medals and making him just the second track and field athlete (along with Al Oerter) to win four Olympic golds in a single event. Sullivan Award winner in 1981.

Nancy Lieberman-Cline (b. 7-1-58): Basketball G. Three-time All-America at Old Dominion. Player of the Year (1979, '80). Olympian in 1976. Promoter of women's basketball: played in WPBL, WABA. First woman to play basketball in a men's professional league (USBL, 1986). Joined WNBA in 1997, retired in '98 to become GM/coach of the Detroit Shock.

Bob Lilly (b. 7-26-39): Football DT. Dallas Cowboys' first ever draft pick, first Pro Bowl player and first all-NFL choice. Made all-NFL eight times. Career span 1961–74, all with Dallas. Elected to Hall of Fame in 1980.

Tara Lipinski (b. 6-10-82): Figure skater. In 1998 at Nagano eclipsed Sonja Henie as the youngest individual Winter Olympic champion in history when, at 15, she won the women's figure skating gold medal. Also won U.S. and world championships in 1997.

Sonny Liston (b. 5-8-32, d. 12-30-70): Boxer. Heavyweight champion from 1962–64. Won title by KO of Floyd Patterson. Lost title when TKO'd by Cassius Clay (Muhammad Ali) and then lost rematch when KO'd in first round. Career record: 50–4, 39 KOs.

Vince Lombardi (b. 6-11-13, d. 9-3-70): Football coach. Highest alltime winning percentage (.740). Career record 105-35-6. Won five NFL championships and two consecutive Super Bowl titles with Green Bay from 1959–67. Coached Washington in 1969. Super Bowl trophy named in his honor.

Johnny Longden (b. 2-14-07, d. 2-14-03): Horse racing jockey. Rode Triple Crown winner Count Fleet in 1943. 6,032 career wins.

Nancy Lopez (b. 1-6-57): Golfer. 48 career LPGA Tour wins. LPGA Player of the Year four times (1978, '79, '85, '88). Winner of LPGA Championship three times (1978, '85, '89). Member of the LPGA Hall of Fame.

Greg Louganis (b. 1-29-60): Diver. Gold medalist in platform and springboard at two consecutive Olympics (1984, '88). World champion five times (platform in 1978, '82, '86; springboard in 1982, '86). Also Sullivan Award winner in 1984.

Joe Louis (b. 5-13-14, d. 4-12-81): Boxer. "The Brown Bomber." Longest title reign of any heavyweight champion (11 years, nine months) from 1937–49. Career record 63–3 with 49 KOs from 1934–51. Defended title 25 times.

Jerry Lucas (b. 3-30-40): Basketball F. Three-time first-team All-NBA (1965, '66, '68). Averaged 17.0 points and 15.6 rebounds per game from 1963–74 with Cincinnati, San Francisco and New York. Averaged over 20 points and 20 rebounds a game while at Ohio State. In 1960 member of both NCAA championship team and gold-medal winning U.S. Olympic team. Elected to Hall of Fame in 1979.

Sid Luckman (b. 11-21-16, d. 7-5-98): Football QB. Played on four NFL champions (1940, '41, '43, '46) with Chicago. Player of the Year in 1943. Tied record with seven touchdown passes in one game in 1943. All-Pro six times. 137 career touchdown passes. Career span 1939–50. Also All-America with Columbia.

Jon Lugbill (b. 5-27-61): Whitewater canoe racer. Won five world singles titles from 1979–89.

Hank Luisetti (b. 6-16-16, d. 12-17-02): Basketball F. The first player to use the one-handed shot. All-America at Stanford three consecutive years from 1936–38.

D. Wayne Lukas (b. 9-2-35): Horse racing trainer. Former college basketball coach and quarter horse trainer. Won six straight Triple Crown races from 1994–96, including all three Triple Crown races in 1995, the first trainer to accomplish that feat with multiple horses (Thunder Gulch and Timber County). Trained horses that have won 13 Triple Crown races—four Kentucky Derbys, five Preakness' and four

Belmonts—and three Horses of the Year (Lady's Secret in 1986, Criminal Type in 1990, and Charismatic in 1999).

Connie Mack (b. 2-22-1862, d. 2-8-56): Born Cornelius McGillicuddy. Baseball manager. Managed Philadelphia for 50 years (1901–50) until age 87. All-time leader in games (7,755), wins (3,731) and losses (3,948). Won nine pennants and five World Series (1910, '11, '13, '29, '30).

Greg Maddux (b. 4-14-66): Baseball P. Won 15 or more games in 15 straight seasons (1988–02). Four-time Cy Young Award winner (1992–95). Led league in wins three times, ERA four times. 12 Gold Gloves. Won 300th game on 8-7-04. Career span 1986– with Chicago (NL) and Atlanta.

Larry Mahan (b. 11-21-43): Rodeo. All-around champion six times (1966–70, '73).

Frank Mahovlich (b. 1-10-38): Hockey LW. Winner of Calder Trophy for top rookie for 1957–58 season. In 18 NHL seasons with Toronto, Detroit and Montreal, had 533 goals and 570 assists. Played for six Stanley Cup winners. Elected to Hall of Fame 1981.

Phil Mahre (b. 5-10-57): Skier. Gold medalist in slalom at 1984 Olympics (twin brother Steve won silver medal). World Cup champion three consecutive years (1981–83).

Joe Malone (b. 2-28-1890, d. 5-15-69): Hockey F. "Phantom Joe." Led the NHL in its first season, 1917–18, with 44 goals in 20 games with Montreal. Led league in scoring two times (1918, '20). Holds NHL record with most goals scored, single game (7) in 1920.

Karl Malone (b. 7-24-63): Basketball F. "The Mailman." Finished 2003–04 season with 36,928 career points scored. Two-time NBA MVP (1997, '99). 11-time first-team All-NBA (1989–99). All-Star MVP, 1989, 1993 (shared with John Stockton). All-Rookie team, 1986. Member of 1992 and '96 Olympic teams. Career span 1985–2003 with Utah, 2003–04 with Los Angeles.

Moses Malone (b. 3-23-55): Basketball C. Three-time NBA MVP (1979, '82, '83). Playoff MVP in 1983, when he led Philadelphia to the NBA title. First-ballot Hall of Famer retired with 8,531 career free throws made, 16,212 rebounds and 27,409 points scored. Four-time first-team All-NBA. Led league in rebounding six times, five consecutively. Went directly to pros from high school. Career span 1974–95 with nine teams, including Houston and Philadelphia.

Hermann Maier (b.12-7-72): Austrian skier. Recovered from spectacular crash in the downhill to win two gold medals at 1998 Olympics in Nagano. Won 1998 Super G, Giant Slalom and overall World Cup season titles.

Man o' War (b. 1917, d. 1947): Thoroughbred race horse. Won 20 of 21 races 1919–20. Only loss was in 1919 in Sanford Stakes to Upset. Passed up Derby but won both Preakness and Belmont. Winner of $249,465. Sire of War Admiral, 1937 Triple Crown winner.

Mickey Mantle (b. 10-20-31, d. 8-13-95): Baseball OF. Won three MVP awards (1956, '57, '62); won Triple Crown in 1956. 536 career HR. Greatest switch hitter in history. Played in 20 All-Star games. Alltime World Series leader in HR (18), RBI (40) and runs scored (42). No. 7 was a member of seven World Series winners with New York (AL). Career span 1951–68.

Diego Maradona (b. 10-30-60): Argentine soccer player. Led Argentina to 1986 World Cup victory and to 1990 World Cup finals. Led Naples to Italian League titles (1987, '90), Italian Cup (1987) and to UEFA Cup title (1989). Throughout 1980s often acknowledged as best player in the world. Tested positive for cocaine and suspended by FIFA and Italian Soccer Federation for 15 months in March 1991. Failed drug test in 1994 World Cup and suspended before second round.

Pete Maravich (b. 6-22-47, d. 1-5-88): Basketball G. "Pistol Pete." Alltime NCAA leader in points scored (3,667), scoring average (44.2) and games scoring 50+ points (28, including then Division I record 69 points in 1970). Alltime single-season leader in points scored (1,381) and scoring average (44.5) in 1970. NCAA scoring leader and All-America three consecutive seasons 1968–70 with Louisiana State. Averaged 20+ points eight times as a pro, leading the league in scoring in 1977. All-Star five times. Averaged 24.2 points per game from 1970–79 with Atlanta, New Orleans/Utah and Boston.

Gino Marchetti (b. 1-2-27): Football DE. Played in Pro Bowl every year from 1955–65, except 1958 when he broke right ankle tackling Frank Gifford in Colts' 23–17 win over the Giants. Career span 1952–66, almost all with Baltimore. Inducted into Hall of Fame in 1972.

Rocky Marciano (b. 9-1-23, d. 8-31-69): Boxer. Heavyweight champion (1952–56). Career record 49–0 with 43 KOs from 1947 to 1956. Only heavyweight to retire as undefeated champion.

Juan Marichal (b. 10-24-37): Baseball RHP. 243 career wins, 2.89 career ERA. Won 20+ games six times; 250+ innings pitched eight times; 200+ strikeouts six times. Pitched no-hitter in 1963. Career span 1960–75, mostly with San Francisco. Elected to Hall of Fame in 1983.

Dan Marino (b. 9-15-61): Football QB. Set alltime single-season record for yards passing (5,084) and touchdown passes (48) in 1984. Passed for 4,000+ yards five other seasons. Career totals: 61,361 yards passing, 420 touchdown passes, first alltime in both categories. Career span 1983–00 with Miami.

Roger Maris (b. 9-10-34, d. 12-14-85): Baseball OF. Broke Babe Ruth's alltime single-season HR record with 61 in 1961. Won consecutive MVP awards and led league in RBI 1960–61. Career span 1957–68 with Kansas City, New York (AL), St. Louis.

Billy Martin (b. 5-16-28, d. 12-25-89): Baseball 2B–manager. Volatile manager was hired and fired by Minnesota, Detroit, Texas, New York (AL) (five times!) and Oakland from 1969–88. Career record: 1253–1013. Won World Series with New York as manager in 1977 and as player four times.

Pedro Martinez (b. 10-25-71): Baseball P. Three Cy Young Awards (1997, '99, '00). Became second pitcher to win Cy Young Awards in both leagues in 1999. Became first pitcher in 25 years to have more than 300 Ks and ERA below 2.00 in 1997. Led league in ERA and strikeouts three times each. Started 1999 All-Star Game and was named MVP after striking out first four batters. Career span 1992– with Los Angeles, Montreal and Boston.

Eddie Mathews (b. 10-13-31, d. 2-18-01): Baseball 3B. 512 career HR and 30+ HR nine consecutive seasons. League leader in HR two times, walks four times. Career span 1952–68, mostly with Milwaukee.

Christy Mathewson (b. 8-12-1880, d. 10-7-25): Baseball RHP. Third alltime most wins (373, tied with

Grover Alexander) and shutouts (79); career ERA 2.13. Led league in wins five times; won 30+ games four times and 20+ games nine other times. Led league in ERA and strikeouts five times each. Pitched two no-hitters. Pitched three shutouts in 1905 World Series. Career span 1900–16 with New York.

Bob Mathias (b. 11-17-30): Track and field. At age 17, youngest to win gold medal in decathlon at 1948 Olympics. First decathlete to win gold medal at consecutive Olympics (1948, '52). Also won Sullivan Award in 1948.

Ollie Matson (b. 5-1-30): Football RB. Versatile runner totalled 12,884 combined yards rushing, receiving and kick returning. Scored 73 career touchdowns, including a 105-yard kickoff return on 10-14-56, the second longest ever. Career span 1952–66 with Chicago Cardinals, Los Angeles, Detroit, Philadelphia. Also won bronze medal in 400 meters at 1952 Olympics. Elected to Hall of Fame in 1972.

Roland Matthes (b. 11-17-50): German swimmer. Gold medalist in 100-meter and 200-meter backstroke at two consecutive Olympics (1968, '72). Set 16 world records from 1967–73.

Don Maynard (b. 1-25-37): Football WR. Retired in 1973 as the NFL's alltime leading receiver. In 15 seasons, 10 with the New York Jets, caught 633 passes for 11,834 yards and 88 TDs. Averaged 18.7 yards per catch for career. Elected to Hall of Fame in 1987.

Willie Mays (b. 5-6-31): Baseball OF. "Say Hey Kid." MVP in 1954, '65; Rookie of the Year in 1951. Retired with third-most career HR (660); hit 50+ HR two times, 30+ HR nine other times. Led league in HR four times. 100+ RBI 10 times; 100+ runs scored 12 consecutive seasons. 3,283 career hits. Led league in stolen bases four consecutive seasons. 30 HR and 30 steals in same season two times and first man in history to hit 300+ HR and steal 300+ bases. Won 11 consecutive Gold Gloves; set record for career putouts by an outfielder and league record for total chances. His catch in the 1954 World Series off the bat of Vic Wertz called the greatest ever. Career span 1951–73 with New York/San Francisco and New York (NL).

Bill Mazeroski (b. 9-5-36): Baseball 2B. Hit dramatic ninth-inning home run in Game 7 to win 1960 World Series, first of only two Series' to end on a home run. Won eight Gold Gloves. Led league in assists nine times, double plays eight times and putouts five times. Inducted to Hall of Fame in 2001. Career 1956–72 with Pittsburgh; 2,016 hits, 138 HR, .260 avg.

Joe McCarthy (b. 4-21-1887, d. 1-3-78): Baseball manager. Alltime highest winning percentage among managers for regular season (.615). First manager to win pennants in both leagues (Chicago (NL), 1929, New York (AL), 1932). From 1926–50 his teams won seven World Series and nine pennants.

Mark McCormack (b. 11-6-30, d. 5-16-03): Sports marketing agent. Founded International Management Group in 1962. Also author of best-selling business advice books.

Pat McCormick (b. 5-12-30): Diver. Gold medalist in platform and springboard at two consecutive Olympics (1952, '56). Also won Sullivan Award in 1956.

Willie McCovey (b. 1-10-38): Baseball 1B. Led NL in HRs three times (1963, '68, '69) and in RBI twice (1968, '69). 521 career homers. .270 career average. Hit 18 grand slams. Rookie of Year 1959. NL MVP in

1969. Career span 1959–80 with San Francisco, San Diego and Oakland. Elected to Hall of Fame in 1986.

John McEnroe (b. 2-26-59): Tennis player. Third alltime men's most career tournament victories (77). Won four U.S. Open singles titles (consecutively 1979–81, '84) and three Wimbledon titles (1981, '83, '84). Also won eight Grand Slam doubles titles. Led U.S. to five Davis Cup victories (1978, '79, '81, '82, '92).

John McGraw (b. 4-7-1873, d. 2-25-34): Baseball manager. Second alltime in games (4,801) and wins (2,784). Guided New York (NL) to three World Series titles and 10 pennants from 1902–32.

Mark McGwire (b. 10-1-63): Baseball 1B. Broke Roger Maris's 37-year-old single-season HR record with 70 in 1998. Rookie of the Year in 1987, when he hit rookie record 49 home runs. Hit 30+ HR 12 times, 40+ HR six times, 50+ HR four straight years (1996–99). Member of 1984 U.S. Olympic baseball team. Had 583 career HRs and 1,414 RBIs with Oakland and St. Louis from 1986–01.

Denny McLain (b. 3-29-44): Baseball RHP. Last pitcher to win 30+ games in a season (Detroit, 1968); won 20+ games two other times. Won two consecutive Cy Young Awards (1968 '69). Led league in innings pitched two times. Served 2½-year jail term for 1985 conviction of extortion, racketeering and drug possession. Re-entered prison in 1997 on fraud conviction. Career span 1963–72, mostly with Detroit.

Mary T. Meagher (b. 10-27-64): Swimmer. "Madame Butterfly." Won three gold medals at 1984 Olympics (100-meter butterfly, 200-meter butterfly and 400-medley relay). In 1981 set world records in 100-meter butterfly (57.93) and 200-meter butterfly (2:05.96).

Rick Mears (b. 12-3-51): Auto racer. Has won Indy 500 four times (1979, '84, '88, '91) and been CART champion three times (1979, '81, '82). Named Indy 500 Rookie of the Year in 1978.

Eddy Merckx (b. 1945): Belgian cyclist. Won five Tours de France, including four in a row (1969–72).

Mark Messier (b. 1-18-61): Hockey C. Two-time Hart Trophy (MVP) winner. Won Stanley Cups with Edmonton (1984, '85, '87, '88, '90) and New York Rangers (1994). Third alltime in scoring (1,804 pts), fourth in assists (1,146) and seventh in goals scored (658). Career span 1979– with Edmonton, New York Rangers and Vancouver.

Cary Middlecoff (b. 1-6-21, d. 9-1-98): Golfer. Won 40 PGA tournaments, including 1955 Masters and U.S. Opens in 1949 and '56. Won 1956 Vardon Trophy. Also a dentist.

George Mikan (b. 6-18-24): Basketball C. The first dominant big man in professional basketball. Averaged 20+ points per game and named to All-Star team six consecutive seasons. Led league (NBA and NBL) in scoring six times. Played on five championship teams in six years (1949–54) with Minneapolis. Also played on 1945 NIT championship team with DePaul. All-America three times. Served as ABA Commissioner from 1968–69.

Stan Mikita (b. 5-20-40): Hockey C. Won MVP award two consecutive seasons (1967, '68). 926 career assists, 1,467 career points. Led league in assists four straight seasons and points four times. 541 career goals. All-Star six times. Career span 1958–80 with Chicago.

Del Miller (b. 7-5-13; d. 8-19-96): Harness racing driver. Raced in eight decades, beginning in 1929, the longest career of any athlete. Won The Hambletonian in 1950.

Marvin Miller (b. 4-14-17): Labor negotiator. Union chief of MLB Players Association from 1966–84. Led strikes in 1972 and '81. Negotiated five labor contracts that increased minimum salary and pension fund, allowed for agents and arbitration, and brought about the end of the reserve clause and the start of free agency.

Art Monk (b. 12-5-57): Football WR. Caught 940 passed for 12,721 yards and 68 TDs during his career. Set NFL single season record with 106 catches in 1984. Career span 1980–95 with Washington, New York Jets and Philadelphia.

Earl Monroe (b. 11-21-44): Basketball G. "The Pearl" played 13 seasons (1967–80) with Baltimore and New York. NBA Rookie of Year in 1968. Four-time All-Star. Member of 1973 NBA championship Knicks team. Averaged 18.8 points a game. Elected to Basketball Hall of Fame 1989.

Joe Montana (b. 6-11-56): Football QB. Second alltime highest-rated passer (92.3); 40,551 career passing yards and 273 TD passes. Won four Super Bowl championships (1981, '84, '88, '89) with San Francisco. Named Super Bowl MVP three times (1981, '84, '89). Player of the Year in 1989. Voted to eight Pro Bowls. Led his teams to 31 fourth-quarter comebacks. Also led Notre Dame to national championship in 1977. Career span 1979–94 with San Francisco and Kansas City. Elected to Hall of Fame in 2000.

Carlos Monzon (b. 8-7-42, d. 1-8-95): Argentine boxer. Longest title reign of any middleweight champion (6 years, nine months) from 1970–77. Career record 89-3-9 with 61 KOs from 1963–77. Won 82 consecutive bouts from 1964–77. Defended title 14 times. Retired as champion.

Helen Wills Moody (b. 10-6-05, d. 1-1-98): Tennis player. Third alltime in women's Grand Slam singles titles (19). Her eight Wimbledon titles are second most alltime (1927–30, '32, '33, '35, '38). Won seven U.S. titles (1923–25, 1927–29, '31) and four French titles (1928–30, '32). Also won 12 Grand Slam doubles titles.

Archie Moore (b. 12-13-16 d. 12-9-98): Boxer. "The Mongoose." Longest title reign of any light heavyweight champion (9 years, one month) from 1952–62. Career record 199-26-8 with an alltime record 145 KOs from 1935–65. Retired at age 52.

Davey Moore (b. 11-1-33; d. 3-23-63): Boxer. Won featherweight title by KO of Kid Bassey in 13 on 3-18-59. Five successful defenses of title, before losing it on 3-21-63 to Sugar Ramos who KO'd him in 10. Died two days after fight of brain damage suffered during fight. Career record: 58-7-1, 30 KOs.

Noureddine Morceli (b. 2-20-70). Algerian track and field middle distance runner. Set world record for mile (3:44.39) in Rieti, Italy, on 9-5-93. Set world record for 1,500 (3:28.86) on 9-5-92. World champion at 1,500 in 1991, '93 and '95. Won gold medal at 1996 Olympics in Atlanta. Only man ever to rank first in the world at 1,500/mile four straight years (1990–93).

Joe Morgan (b. 9-19-43): Baseball 2B. Sparkplug for Cincinnati's Big Red Machine in the 1970s. Won two MVP awards (1975, '76). 10-time All-Star. Amassed 1,865 career walks, 689 stolen bases. 100+ walks and runs scored eight times each; 40+ stolen bases nine times. Won five Gold Gloves. Retired at second alltime in games played by 2nd baseman (2,527).

Career span 1963–84 with Houston, Cincinnati, San Francisco, Philadelphia and Oakland.

Willie Mosconi (b. 6-27-13; d. 9-16-93): Pocket billiards player. Won world title a record 15 straight times between 1941–57. Once pocketed 526 balls without a miss.

Edwin Moses (b. 8-31-55): Track and field. Gold medalist in the 400-meter hurdles at two Olympics (1976, '84); bronze medalist at 1988 Olympics. Won 122 consecutive races from 1977–87. Set four world records in 400-meter hurdles. Won the Sullivan Award in 1983.

Marion Motley (b. 6-5-20 d. 6-27-99): Football FB. All-time AAFC leader in yards rushing (3,024). Led NFL in rushing once. Combined league totals: 4,712 yards rushing, 39 touchdowns. Played for four consecutive AAFC champions (1946–49) and one NFL champion (1950). Career span with Cleveland 1946–1953.

Shirley Muldowney (b. 6-19-40): Drag racer. First woman to win the Top Fuel championship, which she won three times (1977, '80, '82).

Anthony Munoz (b. 8-19-58): Football OT. Probably the greatest offensive tackle ever. Made Pro Bowl a record-tying 11 times. Career span 1980–92 with Cincinnati. Elected to Hall of Fame 1998.

Isaac Murphy (b. 4-16-1861, d. 2-12-1896): Horse racing jockey. Top jockey of his era, Murphy, who was black, won three Kentucky Derbys (aboard Buchanan in 1884, Riley in 1890 and Kingman in 1891).

Eddie Murray (b. 2-24-56): Baseball 1B. One of greatest switch-hitters in baseball history. 100+ RBI six seasons and 30+ HRs five seasons. Retired with 3,255 hits, 504 HRs and 1,917 RBI—eighth alltime and most ever by switch hitter. Career span 1977–97 with Baltimore, Los Angeles, New York (NL), Cleveland and Anaheim. Inducted into Baseball Hall of Fame in 2003.

Jim Murray (b. 12-29-19; d. 8-16-98): Sportswriter. Won Pulitzer Prize in 1990. Named Sportswriter of the Year 14 times. Columnist for *Los Angeles Times* 1961–98.

Ty Murray (b. 10-11-69): Rodeo cowboy. All-around world champion, 1989–94, and '98. Set single-season earnings record in 1990 ($213,771). Rookie of the Year in 1988. At 20, became youngest man ever to win national all-around title in 1989.

Stan Musial (b. 11-21-20): Baseball OF–1B. "Stan the Man." Had .331 career batting average and 475 career HR. MVP award winner (1943, '46, '48). 3,630 career hits; 725 career doubles. Won seven batting titles. Led league in hits six times, slugging average five times, doubles eight times. Had .300+ batting average 17 times, 200+ hits six times, 100+ RBI 10 times, and 100+ runs scored 11 times. 24-time All-Star. Career span 1941–63 with St. Louis.

John Naber (b. 1-20-56): Swimmer. Won four gold medals and one silver medal at 1976 Olympics. Sullivan Award winner in 1977.

Bronko Nagurski (b. 11-3-08, d. 1-7-90): Football FB. Punishing runner played on three NFL champions (1932, '33, '43) with Bears. 2,778 career yards with Chicago from 1930–37 and 1943.

James Naismith (b. 11-6-1861, d. 11-28-39): Invented basketball in 1891 while an instructor at YMCA Training School in Springfield, Mass. Refined the game while a professor at Kansas from 1898–37. Hall of Fame is named in his honor.

Joe Namath (b. 5-31-43): Football QB. "Broadway Joe." Super Bowl MVP in 1968 after he guaranteed victory for New York. 173 career touchdown passes. Led league in yards passing three times, including 4,007 yards in 1967. Player of the Year, 1968; Rookie of the Year, 1965. Career span 1965–77 with New York Jets and Los Angeles.

Ilie Nastase (b. 7-19-46): Romanian tennis player. "Nasty" for his unruly deportment on court. Beat Arthur Ashe to win 1972 U.S. Open title. Won 1973 French Open. Twice Wimbledon runner-up (to Stan Smith in 1972 and Bjorn Borg in 1976).

Martina Navratilova (b. 10-18-56): Tennis player. Fourth in women's Grand Slam singles titles (18—tied with Chris Evert). Won a record nine Wimbledon titles, including six consecutively (1978, '79, 1982–87, '90). Won four U.S. Open titles (1983, '84, '86, '87), three Australian Open titles (1981, '83, '85) and two French Open titles (1982, '84). Reached Grand Slam final 13 other times. Also won 40 Grand Slam doubles titles. Her total of 58 Grand Slam titles is second alltime to Margaret Court. Set mark for longest winning streak with 74 matches in 1984. Also won the doubles Grand Slam in 1984 with Pam Shriver. Won 109 consecutive doubles matches with Shriver from 1983–85.

Byron Nelson (b. 2-14-12): Golfer. Won 52 career tournaments, including 11 consecutively in 1945. Won the Masters (1937, '42) and PGA Championship (1940, '45) two times each and U.S. Open once (1939).

Ernie Nevers (b. 6-11-03, d. 5-3-76): Football FB. Set alltime pro single game record for points scored (40) and touchdowns (six) on 11-28-29. Career span 1926–31 with Duluth and Chicago. Also a pitcher with St. Louis (AL), surrendered two of Babe Ruth's 60 home runs in 1927. All-America at Stanford, earned 11 letters in four sports.

John Newcombe (b. 5-23-44): Australian tennis player. Won three Wimbledon singles titles (1967, '70, '71), two U.S. titles (1967, '73) and two Australian Open titles (1973, '75). Also won 17 Grand Slam doubles titles.

Pete Newell (b. 8-31-15): College basketball coach. Despite coaching only 13 seasons, 1947–60, was first coach to win NIT, NCAA and Olympic crowns. Led San Francisco to 1949 NIT title, Cal to 1959 NCAA title, and the 1960 U.S. Olympic basketball team that included Jerry Lucas, Oscar Robertson and Jerry West to gold medal. Overall collegiate coaching record of 234–123.

Jack Nicklaus (b. 1-21-40): Golfer. "The Golden Bear." Alltime leader in major championships (20). Second alltime in career wins (70). Won Masters six times, more than any golfer (1963, '65, '66, '72, '75, '86—at age 46, the oldest player to win event), PGA Championship five times (1963, '71, '73, '75, '80), U.S. Open four times (1962, '67, '72, '80), British Open three times (1966, '70, '78) and U.S. Amateur twice (1959, '61). PGA Player of the Year five times (1967, '72, '73, '75, '76). Also NCAA champion with Ohio State in 1961.

Ray Nitschke (b. 12-29-36 d. 3-8-98): Football LB. Defensive signal-caller for the great Green Bay teams of the '60s. Voted Packer MVP by teammates after 1967 season. MVP of the 1962 NFL title game. Career span 1958–72 with Green Bay.

Chuck Noll (b. 1-5-32): Football coach. Only coach to win four Super Bowls (1975, '76, '79, '80). Coaching career 1969–91 with Pittsburgh; 209-156-1.

Greg Norman (b. 2-10-55): Golfer. "The Shark" led PGA in winnings in 1986, '90, '95, '96. Won Vardon Trophy twice, 1989, '90. Won two British Opens (1986, '93) but is more famous for his heartbreaking losses. PGA Player of the Year 1996.

James D. Norris (b. 11-6-06, d. 2-25-66): Hockey executive. Owner of the Detroit Red Wings from 1933–43 and Chicago from 1946–66. Teams won four Stanley Cup championships (1936, '37, '43, '61). Defensive Player of the Year award named in his honor. Also a boxing promoter, operated International Boxing Club from 1949–58.

Paavo Nurmi (b. 6-13-1897, d. 10-2-73): Track and field. Finnish middle- and long-distance runner won a total of nine gold medals at three Olympics in 1920, '24, '28.

Matti Nykänen (b. 7-17-63): Finnish ski jumper. Three-time Olympic gold medalist. Won 90-meter jump (1984, '88) and 70-meter jump (1988). World champion on 90-meter jump in 1982. Won four World Cups (1983, '85, '86, '88).

Dan O'Brien (b. 7-18-66): Track and field decathlete. Won world decathlon title in 1991, '93, '95. Set world decathlon record of 8,891 in Talence, France, on 9-4/5-92, that stood for seven years. Heavily favored to win 1992 Olympic decathlon but missed making U.S. team when he no-heighted in pole vault at U.S. Olympic Trials. Redeemed himself with gold medal at 1996 Olympics in Atlanta.

Parry O'Brien (b. 1-28-32): Track and field. Shot-putter who revolutionized the event with his "glide" technique and won Olympic gold medals in 1952 and '56, silver in '60. Set 10 world records from 1953–59, topped by a put of 63' 4" in 1959. Sullivan Award winner in 1959.

Al Oerter (b. 8-19-36): Track and field. Gold medalist in discus at four consecutive Olympics (1956, '60, '64, '68), setting Olympic record each time. First to break the 200-foot barrier, throwing 200' 5" in 1962.

Sadaharu Oh (b. 5-20-40): Baseball 1B in Japanese league. 868 career HR in 22 seasons for the Tokyo Giants. Led league in HR 15 times, RBI 13 times, batting five times and runs 13 consecutive seasons. Awarded MVP nine times; won two consecutive Triple Crowns and nine Gold Gloves.

Hakeem Olajuwon (b. 1-21-63): Basketball C. From Nigeria. Alltime NBA career leader in blocked shots (3,830). Became the first player to be named NBA MVP, NBA Defensive Player of the Year and NBA Finals MVP in the same season as Houston won its first NBA championship in 1994. Led NCAA in FG %, rebounding and blocked shots in 1984 at Houston. Member of 1996 U.S. Olympic team. Career span 1984–2002 with Houston and Toronto; 21.8 ppg, 11.1 rpg.

Merlin Olsen (b. 9-15-40): Fooball DT. Part of Los Angeles's "Fearsome Foursome" defensive line. Named to Pro Bowl 14 straight times. Career span 1962–76, all with the Los Angeles Rams. Elected to Hall of Fame 1982.

Omaha (b. 1932, d. 1959): Thoroughbred race horse. Won Triple Crown in 1935. Trained by Sunny Jim Fitzsimmons.

Mark O'Meara (b. 1-13-57): Golfer. Has 16 career PGA Tour victories, including the 1998 Masters and British Open, at age 41. Tour rookie of the year in 1981; won 1979 U.S. Amateur.

Shaquille O'Neal (b. 3-6-72): Basketball C. "Shaq." Three-time NBA Finals MVP after leading the Lakers to back-to-back-to-back NBA Finals victories (2000–02). Was named MVP of the regular season, All-Star game, and playoffs in 1999–2000. Led league in scoring in 1995 and 2000, and in field goal percentage in 1994, 1998–02. Top pick of Orlando in 1992 NBA draft. NBA Rookie of the Year 1993. Member of 1996 U.S. Olympic team. Led NCAA in blocked shots in 1992 as an All-American at Louisiana State. Career span 1992–2004 with Orlando and Los Angeles Lakers. Signed with Miami in 2004.

Bobby Orr (b. 3-20-48): Hockey D. Defensive Player of the Year more than any other player, eight consecutive seasons (1968–75). Won MVP award three consecutive seasons (1970–72), playoff MVP two times (1970, '72). Also Rookie of the Year in 1967. Led league in assists five times and scoring two times. Career span 1966–77 with Boston.

Mel Ott (b. 3-2-09, d. 11-21-58): Baseball OF. 511 career HR, 1,861 RBI, .304 batting average. League leader in HR and walks six times each. 100+ RBI nine times and 100+ walks ten times. Career span 1926–47 with New York (NL).

Jim Otto (b. 1-5-38): Football C. Number 00 started every game (210) in his 15-year career (1960–74) with Oakland. Inducted to Hall of Fame in 1980.

Kristin Otto (b. 1966): German swimmer. Won six gold medals for East Germany at 1988 Olympics.

Jesse Owens (b. 9-12-13, d. 3-31-80): Track and field. Gold medalist in four events (100 meters and 200 meters; 4x100-meter relay and long jump) at 1936 Olympics. At the 1935 Big 10 championship set or equaled six world record in 70 minutes, including 100 yards, long jump, 220-yard low hurdles and 220 dash.

Alan Page (b. 8-7-45): Football DT. First defensive player to be named NFL Player of the Year, in 1972. Played in 236 straight games, including four Super Bowls. Four-time NFC Defensive Player of Year. Career span 1967–81 with Minnesota and Chicago. Now sits on Minnesota Supreme Court.

Satchel Paige (b. 7-7-06, d. 6-8-82): Baseball RHP. Alltime greatest black pitcher, didn't pitch in major leagues until 1948 at age 42 with Cleveland. Oldest pitcher in major league history at age 59 with Kansas City in 1965. Pitched in the Negro leagues from 1926–50 with Birmingham Black Barons, Pittsburgh Crawfords and Kansas City Monarchs. Estimated career record is 2,000 wins, 250 shutouts, 30,000 strikeouts, 45 no-hitters.

Se Ri Pak (b. 9-28-77): South Korean golfer. 16 career LPGA Tour victories. 1998 LPGA Rookie of the Year for winning the first two majors she ever entered, the LPGA Championship and the U.S. Open.

Arnold Palmer (b. 9-10-29): Golfer. Fourth alltime in career wins (60). Won the Masters four times (1958, '60, '62, '64), British Open two consecutive years (1961, '62) and U.S. Open (1960) and U.S. Amateur (1954) once each. PGA Player of the Year two times (1960, '62). First golfer to surpass $1 million in career earnings. Also won Seniors Championship two times (1980, '84) and U.S. Senior Open once (1981).

Jim Palmer (b. 10-15-45): Baseball RHP. 268 career wins, 2.86 ERA. Won three Cy Young Awards (1973, '75, '76). Won 20+ games eight times. Led league in wins three times, innings pitched four times, ERA two times. Never allowed a grand slam HR. Pitched on six World Series teams with Baltimore, including shutout at age 20. Pitched no-hitter in 1969. Career span 1965–84 with Baltimore.

Bernie Parent (b. 4-3-45): Hockey G. Alltime leader for wins in a season (47 in 1974). Goaltender of the Year, playoff MVP, league leader in wins, goals against average and shutouts two consecutive seasons (1974–75). Career record 270-197-121, including 55 shutouts. Career 2.55 goals against average. Tied record of four playoff shutouts in 1975. Played on two consecutive Stanley Cup champions (1974–75). Career span 1965–79 with Philadelphia.

Brad Park (b. 7-6-48): Hockey D. Seven-time All-Star. In 17 seasons with the New York Rangers, Boston and Detroit (1968–85) scored 213 goals and had 683 assists. Elected to Hall of Fame 1988.

Jim Parker (b. 4-3-34): Football T/G. All-NFL four times at guard, four times at tackle. First full-time offensive lineman inducted to Hall of Fame, in 1973. Career span 1957–67, all with Baltimore. Winner of 1956 Outland Trophy as Ohio State senior.

Joe Paterno (b. 12-21-26): College football coach. Finished 2004 season with 339 career wins. Has won two national championships (1982, '86) with Penn State since 1966. Career record 327-96-3, including five undefeated seasons. Has also won 20 bowl games.

Lester Patrick (b. 12-30-1883, d. 6-1-60): Hockey coach. Led New York Rangers to three Stanley Cup championships (1928, '33, '40). Originated the NHL's farm system and developed playoff format.

Floyd Patterson (b. 1-4-35): Boxer. Heavyweight champion two times (1956–59, 1960–62). First heavyweight to regain title, in rematch with Ingemar Johansson. Career record 55-8-1 with 40 KOs from 1952–72. Also middleweight gold medalist at 1952 Olympics.

Walter Payton (b. 7-25-54, d. 11-1-99): Football RB. "Sweetness." Retired as alltime leader in yards rushing (16,726). Gained 1,000+ yards rushing in 10 seasons. 110 career rushing touchdowns (110). 125 career touchdowns. Seven-time All-Pro. Player of the Year two times (1977, '85). Led league in rushing five consecutive seasons. Career span 1975–87 with Chicago.

Pelé (b. 10-23-40): Born Edson Arantes do Nascimento. Brazilian soccer player. Soccer's great ambassador. Played on three World Cup winners with Brazil (1958, '62, '70). Helped promote soccer in U.S. by playing with New York Cosmos from 1975–77. Scored 1,281 goals in 22 years.

Willie Pep (b. 9-19-22): Boxer. Featherweight champion two times (1942–48, 1949–50). Lost title to Sandy Saddler, won it back in rematch, then lost it to Saddler again. Master tactician: legend has it he once won a round without throwing a punch. Career record 230-11-1 with 65 KOs from 1940–66. Won 73 consecutive bouts from 1940–43. Defended title nine times.

Gil Perreault (b. 11-13-50): Hockey C. NHL Rookie of the Year in 1970–71. Five-time All-Star. Scored 512 goals and had 814 assists in career from 1970–87 with Buffalo. Elected to Hall of Fame in 1990.

Fred Perry (b. 5-18-09, d. 2-2-95): British tennis player. Won three consecutive Wimbledon singles titles (1934–36), the last British man to win the tournament. Also won three U.S. titles (1933, '34, '36), one French title (1935) and one Australian title (1934).

Gaylord Perry (b. 9-15-38): Baseball RHP. First pitcher to win Cy Young Award in both leagues (Cleveland 1972, San Diego 1978). 314 career wins,

3,534 strikeouts. 20+ wins five times; 200+ strikeouts eight times; 250+ innings pitched 12 times. Pitched no-hitter in 1968. Admitted to throwing a spitter. Career span 1962–83 with eight teams.

Bob Pettit (b. 12-12-32): Basketball F. First player in history to break 20,000-point barrier (20,880 career points scored). 26.4 career scoring average; 16.2 rebound avg. MVP in 1956 and 1959; Rookie of the Year in 1955. All-Star 10 consecutive seasons. Led league in scoring two times, rebounding once. Career span 1954–64 with St. Louis.

Richard Petty (b. 7-2-37): Auto racer. Alltime leader in NASCAR victories (200). Seven-time Daytona 500 winner (1964, '66, '71, '73, '74, '79, '81) and NASCAR season points champion (1964, '67, '71, '72, '74, '75, '79), the most of any driver in both categories. First stock car racer to reach $1 million in earnings. Son of Lee Petty, three-time NASCAR champion. Retired after 1992 season.

Laffit Pincay Jr. (b. 12-29-46): Jockey. Only jockey with more than 9,000 career victories. Among the top money-winners of all time, with more than $215,000,000 in career earnings. Won five Eclipse Awards as outstanding jockey. Rode one Kentucky Derby winner (Swale), and three Belmont winners (Conquistador Cielo, Cavaet, Swale).

Scottie Pippen (b. 9-25-65): Basketball F. Won six NBA titles with Chicago (1991–93, 1996–98). Three-time first-team All-NBA (1994–96). Named to NBA's first-team All-Defensive team six times. Named MVP of the 1994 NBA All-Star Game. Member of 1992 and '96 gold medal-winning U.S. Olympic basketball teams. Career span 1987–2004 with Chicago, Houston and Portland.

Jacques Plante (b. 1-17-29, d. 2-27-86): Hockey G. First goalie to wear a mask. Third alltime in wins (435) and second lowest modern goals against average (2.38). Goaltender of the Year seven times, more than any other goalie (consecutively 1955–59, '61, '68). Won MVP award in 1961. Led league in goals against average eight times, wins six times and shutouts four times. Was on six Stanley Cup champions with Montreal from 1952–62 and played for four other teams until retirement in 1972.

Gary Player (b. 11-1-35): South African golfer. Won the Masters (1961, '74, '78) and British Open (1959, '68, '74) three times each, PGA Championship two times (1962, '72) and U.S. Open (1965). Also won Seniors Championship three times (1986, '88, '90) and U.S. Senior Open two consecutive years (1987, '88).

Sam Pollock (b. 12-15-25): Hockey executive. As general manager of Montreal from 1964–78 won nine Stanley Cup championships (1965, '66, '68, '69, '71, '73, '76, '78).

Denis Potvin (b. 10-29-53): Hockey D. Seven-time All-Star during 15-season career (1973–88), all with New York Islanders. Won Calder Trophy for 1973–74 season. Won Norris Trophy three times. Captained Islanders to four Stanley Cup championships. Elected to Hall of Fame in 1991.

Mike Powell (b. 11-10-63): Track and field. Long jumper broke Bob Beamon's 23-year-old world record at 1991 World Championships in Tokyo with a jump of 29' 4½". Won silver in 1992 Olympics.

Steve Prefontaine (b. 1-25-51, d. 5-30-75): Track and field. Distance runner killed in car accident at age 24. Held every American record from 2,000 meters to

10,000 meters at the time of his death. At age 21, finished fourth in the 5,000 meters at the 1972 Olympics in Munich after leading with less than 600 meters to go.

Annemarie Moser-Pröll (b. 3-27-53): Austrian skier. Gold medalist in downhill at 1980 Olympics. World Cup overall champion six times, more than any other skier (1971–75, '79).

Alain Prost (b. 2-24-55): French auto racer. Second alltime in Formula 1 victories (51). Formula 1 champion four times (1985–86, '89, '93).

Jack Ramsay (b. 2-21-25): Basketball coach. Coached 11 seasons at St. Joseph's University, with 234–72 record. Overall record of 864–783 as NBA coach. Coach of NBA champion 1977 Portland Trail Blazers. Elected to Hall of Fame 1992.

Jean Ratelle (b. 10-3-40): Hockey C. In 21-season career (1960–81) with the New York Rangers and Boston, scored 491 goals and had 776 assists. Twice won Lady Byng Trophy. Elected to Hockey Hall of Fame in 1985.

Willis Reed (b. 6-25-42): Basketball C. Most noted for his dramatic return to the court on 5-8-70, in the seventh and deciding game of the 1970 NBA Finals against Los Angeles. Playoff MVP of both New York championship teams, in 1970 and '73. NBA Rookie of Year in 1965. NBA MVP in 1970. Played 10 seasons (1965–74), all with New York. Career average of 18.7 points a game. Elected to Hall of Fame in 1981.

Harold Henry (Pee Wee) Reese (b. 7-23-18 d. 8-14-99): Baseball SS. Played for six pennant-winning Brooklyn teams. Led NL in runs scored in 1949, with 132. Career span 1940–58 with Brooklyn; .269 avg., 2,170 hits, 1,338 runs, 232 SB. Elected to Hall of Fame in 1984.

Mary Lou Retton (b. 1-24-68): Gymnast. Won all-around gold with a perfect 10 on her final vault at the 1984 Olympics in Los Angeles. Also won one silver and two bronze medals at those Games.

Grantland Rice (b. 11-1-1880, d. 7-13-54): Sportswriter. Legendary figure during sport's Golden Age of the 1920s. Wrote "For when the one great Scorer comes/ To write against your name/ He writes not that you won or lost/ But how you played the game." Also named the 1924–25 Notre Dame backfield the "Four Horsemen."

Jerry Rice (b. 10-13-62): Football WR. Alltime leader in touchdowns, touchdown receptions, receptions, receiving yards and in consecutive games with a TD reception (13 in 1988). Player of the Year in 1987 and led league in scoring (138 points on 23 touchdowns). Super Bowl MVP in 1989 with record 215 receiving yards on 11 catches. Also set Super Bowl record with three touchdown receptions in 1990 and in 1995. Career span 1985– with San Francisco and Oakland.

Henri Richard (b. 2-29-36): Hockey C. "The Pocket Rocket." Won 11 Stanley Cup championships with Montreal. Four-time All-Star. Career span 1955–75.

Maurice Richard (b. 8-4-21, d. 5-27-00): Hockey RW. "The Rocket." First player to score 50 goals in a season, in 1945. Led league in goals five times. 544 career goals. MVP in 1947. All-Star eight times. Tied playoff record for most goals in a game (five on March 23, 1944). Won eight Stanley Cups with Montreal 1942–59.

Bob Richards (b. 2-2-26): Track and field. The only pole vaulter to win gold medal at two consecutive Olympics (1952, '56). Also won Sullivan Award in 1951.

Branch Rickey (b. 12-20-1881, d. 12-9-65): Baseball executive. Integrated major league baseball in 1947 by signing Jackie Robinson to a contract with the Brooklyn Dodgers. Conceived of minor league farm system in 1919 at St. Louis; instituted batting cage and sliding pit.

Pat Riley (b. 3-20-45): Basketball coach. Coached Los Angeles to four NBA championships (1981, '85, '87, '88). Coach of the Year three times (1990, '93, '97) for three different teams. Led New York to NBA Finals in 1994. Coached teams to 50+ wins 13 years in a row. Coaching career 1984–2003 with Los Angeles, New York and Miami.

Cal Ripken Jr. (b. 8-24-60): Baseball SS–3B. Broke Lou Gehrig's record for most consecutive games played (2,131) on 9-5-95; streak ended at 2,632 games on 9-20-98. Two-time AL MVP (1983, '91). Rookie of the Year in 1982. 19-time All-Star. Set record for consecutive errorless games by a shortstop (95 in 1990). Hit 20+ HRs in 10 consecutive seasons. Career span 1981–01 with Baltimore; .276 avg., 431 HR, 1,695 RBI, 3,184 hits.

Glenn (Fireball) Roberts (b. 1-20-31, d. 7-2-64): Auto racer. Won 34 NASCAR races. Died as a result of a fiery accident in the World 600 at Charlotte Motor Speedway in May 1964. At the time of his death Roberts had won more major races than any other driver in NASCAR history.

Oscar Robertson (b. 11-24-38): Basketball G. "The Big O." Only player in NBA history to average a triple-double for an entire season (1962). Rookie of the Year in 1961, MVP in 1964, and nine-time first-team All-NBA (1961–69). Led league in assists eight times. Averaged 30+ points six times in seven seasons. MVP of NBA All-Star three times (1961, '64, '69). Career span 1960–74 with Cincinnati and Milwaukee; 9,887 career assists; 26,710 points, 25.7 ppg. Also College Player of the Year, All-America and NCAA scoring leader three consecutive seasons from 1958–60 with Cincinnati. Third all-time NCAA highest scoring average (33.8).

Brooks Robinson (b. 5-18-37): Baseball 3B. Alltime leader in assists, putouts, double plays and fielding average among 3rd basemen. Won 16 consecutive Gold Gloves. Led league in fielding average a record 11 times. MVP in 1964—led league in RBI—and MVP in 1970 World Series. Career span 1955–77 with Baltimore; .267 avg, 2,848 hits, 1,357 RBI.

David Robinson (b. 8-6-65): Basketball C. "The Admiral." Three-time Olympian (1988, '92, '96), and 1995 NBA MVP. One of only two players to win an NBA rebounding title (1991), a blocked shots title (1992) and a scoring title (1994). Four-time first-team All-NBA. All-American at Navy where he led the NCAA in both rebounding (13.0) and blocked shots (5.91) in 1986. 1990 NBA Rookie of the Year. Career span 1989–2003 with San Antonio.

Eddie Robinson (b. 2-13-19): College football coach. Retired with alltime college record 408 career wins through 1941–97 at Division I-AA Grambling State.

Frank Robinson (b. 8-31-35): Baseball OF–manager. Only player to win MVP awards in both leagues (Cincinnati, 1961, Baltimore, 1966). Won

Triple Crown and World Series MVP in 1966. Rookie of the Year in 1956. Fifth in career HR (586). Became first black manager in major leagues, with Cleveland in 1975. Career span 1956–76 with Cincinnati, Baltimore, Los Angeles, California and Cleveland; .294 avg., 1,812 RBI, 2,943 hits, 1,829 runs.

Jackie Robinson (b. 1-13-19, d. 10-24-72): Baseball 2B. Broke the color barrier as first black player in major leagues in 1947 with Brooklyn. 1947 Rookie of the Year; 1949 MVP with league-leading .342 batting average. Led league in stolen bases two times; stole home 19 times. Played on six pennant winners with Brooklyn, 1947–56; .311 avg., 137 HR, 947 runs, 197 SB. Elected to Hall of Fame in 1962. No. 42 retired by every team in the major leagues.

Larry Robinson (b. 6-2-51): Hockey D. Twice won Norris Trophy as NHL's top defenseman. Member of six Montreal teams that won Stanley Cup. Awarded Conn Smythe Trophy as MVP of 1978 Stanley Cup. Career span 1972–92, all but the last three with Montreal. Coached New Jersey to Stanley Cup in 2000.

Sugar Ray Robinson (b. 5-3-21, d. 4-12-89): Born Walker Smith Jr. Boxer. Called best pound-for-pound boxer ever. Welterweight champ (1946–51) and middleweight champ five times. Career record: 174-19-6 with 109 KOs from 1940–65. Won 91 consecutive bouts from 1943–51. Fifteen losses came after age 35.

Knute Rockne (b. 3-4-1888, d. 3-31-31): College football coach. Won national championship three times (1924, '29, '30). Alltime highest winning percentage (.881). Career record 105-12-5, including five undefeated seasons, with Notre Dame from 1918–30.

Bill Rodgers (b. 12-23-47): Track and field. Won the Boston and New York City marathons four times each between 1975–80.

Dennis Rodman (b. 5-13-61): Basketball F. Won seven consecutive NBA rebounding titles (1992–98). Won two NBA titles with Detroit (1989, '90) and three with Chicago (1996–98). NBA Defensive Player of the Year (1990, '91). Career span 1986–00, mostly with Detroit and Chicago; 7.3 ppg, 13.1 rpg.

Chi Chi Rodriguez (b. 10-23-35): Golfer. Led senior money list for 1987 ($509,145). Won eight events during PGA career that began in 1960.

Art Rooney (b. 1-27-01; d. 8-25-88): Owner of Pittsburgh Steelers. Bought team in 1933 and ran it until his death in 1988. Elected to Hall of Fame in 1964.

Murray Rose (b. 1-6-39) Australian swimmer. Won three gold medals (including 400- and 1,500-meter freestyle) at 1956 Olympics. Also won one gold, one silver and one bronze medal at 1960 Olympics.

Pete Rose (b. 4-14-41): Baseball OF-IF. "Charlie Hustle." Baseball's alltime hits leader (4,256), who was banned from the game for life in 1989 for his gambling activities and, thus, is ineligible for the Hall of Fame. Had 44-game hitting streak in 1978. 1963 Rookie of the Year; 1973 MVP; 1975 World Series MVP. Won three batting titles, and led the league in hits seven times, runs scored four times and doubles five times. Alltime leader in games played (3,562) and at bats (14,053); second in doubles (746); fifth in runs scored (2,165). Career span 1963–86 with Cincinnati, Philadelphia and Montreal; .303 avg., 160 HR, 1,314 RBI. Manager of Cincinnati from 1984–89. Served five-month jail term for tax evasion in 1990.

Ken Rosewall (b. 11-2-34): Australian tennis player. Won Grand Slam singles titles at ages 18 and 35. Won four Australian titles (1953, '55, '71, '72), two French titles (1953, '68) and two U.S. titles (1956, '70). Reached four Wimbledon finals, but title eluded him.

Art Ross (b. 1-13-1886, d. 8-5-64): Hockey D–coach. Improved design of puck and goal net. Manager-coach of Boston, 1924–45, won Stanley Cup, 1938–39. The Art Ross Trophy is awarded to the NHL scoring champion.

Donald Ross (b. 1873, d. 4-26-48): Scottish-born golf course architect. Trained at St. Andrews under Old Tom Morris. Designed over 500 courses, including Pinehurst No. 2 course and Oakland Hills.

Patrick Roy (b. 10-5-65): Hockey G. Retired as alltime leader in career wins for a goalie (551). Won Vezina Trophy three times. Won Conn Smythe Trophy three times (1986, '93, '01). Career span 1984–2003 with Montreal and Colorado.

Pete Rozelle (b. 3-1-26, d. 12-6-96): Football executive. Fourth NFL commissioner, served from 1960–89. During his term, league expanded from 12 to 28 teams. Created Super Bowl in 1966 and negotiated merger with AFL. Devised plan for revenue sharing of lucrative TV monies among owners. Presided during players' strikes of 1982 and '87.

Wilma Rudolph (b. 6-23-40, d. 11-12-94): Track and field. Gold medalist in three events (100 , 200 and 4 x100-meter relay) at 1960 Olympics. Also won Sullivan Award in 1961.

Adolph Rupp (b. 9-2-01, d. 12-10-77): College basketball coach. Second alltime in NCAA wins (876) and winning percentage (.822). Won four NCAA championships (1948, '49, '51, '58). Career span 1930–72 with Kentucky.

Amos Rusie (b. 5-3-1871, d. 12-6-42): Baseball RHP. Fastball was so intimidating that in 1893 the pitching mound was moved back 5' 6" to its present distance of 60' 6". Led league in strikeouts and walks five times each. Career record 246–174, 3.07 ERA with New York (NL) from 1889–1901.

Bill Russell (b. 2-12-34): Basketball C. Won MVP award five times (1958, 1961–63, '65). Played on 11 championship teams with Boston (1957, 1959–66, '68, '69). Player-coach 1968–69 (league's first black coach). Second alltime in career rebounds (21,620) and rebounding average (22.5); second-highest single-game rebounding total (51 in 1960). Led league in rebounding four times. Career span 1956–69 with Boston. 15.1 ppg, 4.3 apg. Also played on two NCAA championship teams with San Francisco in 1955–56; tournament MVP in 1955. Member of gold medal-winning 1956 Olympic team.

Babe Ruth (b. 2-6-1895, d. 8-16-48): Born George Herman Ruth. Baseball P–OF. "The Bambino," "The Sultan of Swat." Most dominant player in history. Alltime leader in slugging average (.690), HR frequency (8.5 HR every 100 at bats); Hit 714 career HR, 2,211 RBI, and 2,056 walks. Hit 54 HR in 1920, more than any other team in the American League. 1923 MVP. 60 HR in 1927, a record that stood for 34 years. Second alltime in World Series HR (15), including his "called shot" off Charlie Root in 1932. Began career as a pitcher: 94 career wins and 2.28 ERA. Won 20+ games two times; ERA leader in 1916. Played on 10 pennant winners, seven World Series winners (three with Boston, four with New York (AL)). Sold to Yankees in 1920 (Boston hasn't won World

Series since). Career span 1914–35 with Boston, New York (AL) and Boston (NL); .342 avg., 2,873 hits.

Nolan Ryan (b. 1-31-47): Baseball RHP. Pitched seven no-hitters. Alltime leader in career strikeouts (5,714) and walks (2,795). League leader in strikeouts 11 times, shutouts three times, ERA two times. 300+ strikeouts six times, including season record of 383 in 1973. Career span 1966–93 with New York (NL), California, Houston and Texas; 324–292, 3.19 ERA. Elected to Hall of Fame 1999.

Jim Ryun (b. 4-29-47): Track and field. Youngest ever to run sub-four-minute mile (3:59.0 at 17 years, 37 days). Set two world records in mile (3:51.3 in 1966 and 3:51.1 in 1967) and one in 1,500 (3:33.1 in 1967). Plagued by bad luck at Olympics; won silver medal in 1968 1,500 meters despite mononucleosis; was bumped and fell in 1972. Won Sullivan Award in 1967.

Toni Sailer (b. 11-17-35): Austrian skier. Won gold medals in 1956 Olympics in slalom, giant slalom and downhill, the first skier to accomplish the feat.

Juan Antonio Samaranch (b. 7-17-20): Amateur sports executive. From 1980–01, Spaniard served as president of International Olympic Committee.

Pete Sampras (b. 8-12-71): Tennis player. Alltime leader in men's Grand Slam singles titles (14). First player in ATP rankings history to hold No. 1 ranking for six consecutive years. Won 64 tournament titles.

Joan Benoit Samuelson (b. 5-16-57): Track and field. Gold medalist in first ever women's Olympic marathon (1984). Won Boston Marathon two times (1979, '83). Sullivan Award winner in 1985.

Barry Sanders (b. 7-16-68): Football RB. Third player in NFL history to rush for over 2,000 yards (2,053 in 1997). Led league in rushing four times (1990, '94, '96, '97). Rushed for 1,000+ yards in each of his 10 pro seasons. Retired abruptly in 1999, ranked second alltime in career rushing yards (15,269). NCAA single-season leader in yards rushing (2,628 in 1988), when he won the Heisman Trophy at Oklahoma State.

Gene Sarazen (b. 2-27-02 d. 5-13-99): Golfer. Won PGA Championship three times (1922, '23, '33), U.S. Open two times (1922, '32), British Open once (1932) and the Masters once (1935). His win at the Masters included golf's most famous shot, a double eagle on the 15th hole of the final round. Won 38 career tournaments. Also won Seniors Championship two times (1954, '58). Pioneered the sand wedge in 1930.

Glen Sather (b. 9-2-43): Hockey coach and general manager. 464 regular season wins. Led Edmonton to four Stanley Cup championships (1984, '85, '87, '88) from 1979–89 and 1993–94. Also played for six teams from 1966–76.

Terry Sawchuk (b. 12-28-29, d. 5-31-70): Hockey G. Alltime leader in shutouts (103); second in wins (447). Career 2.52 goals against average. Goaltender of the Year four times (1951–52, '54, '64). Led league in wins and shutouts three times and goals against average two times. Rookie of the Year in 1950. Tied record of four playoff shutouts in 1952. Played on four Stanley Cup champions with Detroit and Toronto from 1949–69.

Gale Sayers (b. 5-30-43): Football RB. Alltime leader in kickoff return average (30.6). Scored 56 career touchdowns, including a rookie record 22 in 1965. Tied record with six touchdowns in one game on 12-12-65. Led league in rushing and gained 1,000+ yards rushing two times. Rookie of the Year in 1965.

Career span 1965–71 with Chicago cut short due to knee injury. Also All-America two times with Kansas.

Dolph Schayes (b. 5-19-28): Basketball player. Retired as NBA's all-time leading scorer (19,249 pts). First-team All-NBA six times. Over stretch of 10 years played in 706 consecutive games. Career span 1948–64 with Syracuse and Philadelphia; 18.2 ppg. College star at NYU. Elected to Hall of Fame 1972.

Bo Schembechler (b. 4-1-29): Football coach. In 21 seasons at Michigan from 1969–89, had a 194-48-5 record. Overall college coaching record 234-65-8.

Mike Schmidt (b. 9-27-49): Baseball 3B. Won three MVP awards (1980, '81, '86). 548 career home runs. Led league in HR eight times, slugging average five times, and RBI and walks four times each. Won 10 Gold Gloves. Career span 1972–89 with Philadelphia; .267 avg., 1,506 runs, 1,595 RBI. Elected to the Hall of Fame in 1995.

Don Schollander (b. 4-30-46): Swimmer. Won four gold medals (including 100- and 400-meter freestyle) at 1964 Olympics; won one gold and one silver medal at 1968 Olympics. Also won Sullivan Award in 1964.

Dick Schultz (b. 9-5-29): Amateur sports executive. Second executive director of the NCAA, served from 1987–93. Also served as athletic director at Cornell (1976–81) and Virginia (1981–87).

Seattle Slew (b. 1974; d. 5-7-02): Thoroughbred race horse. Horse of the Year for 1977, when he won the Triple Crown, winning the Kentucky Derby by 1¾ lengths; the Preakness by 1½; and the Belmont by 4. In three-year career from 1976–78, won 14 of 17 starts.

Tom Seaver (b. 11-17-44): Baseball RHP. "Tom Terrific." 311 career wins, 2.86 ERA. Cy Young Award winner three times (1969, '73, '75) and Rookie of the Year 1967. Struck out 3,640 batters in his career. Led league in strikeouts five times, winning percentage four times and wins and ERA three times each. Won 20+ games five times; 200+ strikeouts 10 times. Struck out 19 batters in one game in 1970, including the final 10 in succession. Pitched no-hitter in 1978. Career span 1967–86 with New York (NL), Cincinnati, Chicago (AL), Boston.

Secretariat (b. 3-30-70, d. 10-4-89): Thoroughbred race horse. Triple Crown winner in 1973 with jockey Ron Turcotte aboard. Ran fastest Kentucky Derby and Belmont Stakes ever. Trained by Lucien Laurin.

Katja Seizinger (b. 5-10-72): German skier. Won downhill gold medals in 1994 at Lillehammer and '98 at Nagano. Won Giant Slalom bronze medal at Nagano. 1998 World Cup champion in downhill, Super G and overall. 32 World Cup victories in downhill and Super G.

Monica Seles (b. 12-2-73): Tennis player. Won three consecutive French Open singles titles (1990–92), four Australian Open titles (1991–93, '96) and two U.S. Open titles (1991, '92). Seles's 1993 season ended on 4-30 when she was stabbed in the back by a deranged fan while seated during a changeover in a tournament in Hamburg, Germany; also missed 1994 season. Returned to tennis in 1995, reached U.S. Open final.

Bill Sharman (b. 5-25-26): Basketball G. First team All-Star four straight years 1956–59. Led NBA in free throw percentage every year from 1953–57, and in 1959 and '61. All-Star Game MVP in 1955. Career span 1950–61 with Washington and Boston; 17.8 ppg, 88.3 FT%. NBA Coach of the Year in 1972, when his Lakers won NBA title. Elected to Hall of Fame in 1974.

Wilbur Shaw (b. 10-31-02, d. 10-30-54): Auto racer. Won Indy 500 three times in four years (1937, '39, '40). AAA champion two times (1937, '39). Also pioneered the use of the crash helmet after suffering skull fracture in 1923 crash.

Patty Sheehan (b. 10-27-56): Golfer. Won back-to-back LPGA championships (1983, '84). Won 1992 and '94 U.S. Women's Opens, '93 LPGA title, '96 Nabisco. 1983 LPGA Player of Year. Vare Trophy winner in 1984. Qualified for Hall of Fame in 1993.

Fred Shero (b. 10-23-25, d. 11-24-90): Hockey coach. Fourth alltime highest winning percentage (.612). Led Philadelphia to two Stanley Cup championships (1974, '75). Former New York Rangers defender (1947–50) coached Philadelphia and New York from 1971–81; 390-225-119.

Bill Shoemaker (b. 8-19-31 d. 10-12-03): Horse racing jockey. Second alltime in wins (8,833). Rode Belmont Stakes winner five times (1957, '59, '62, '67, '75), Kentucky Derby winner four times (1955, '59, '65, '86—at age 54, the oldest jockey to win Derby) and Preakness Stakes winner two times (1963, '67). Also won Eclipse Award in 1981.

Eddie Shore (b. 11-25-02, d. 3-16-85): Hockey D. Won MVP award four times (1933, '35, '36, '38). All-Star seven times. Played on two Stanley Cup champions with Boston from 1926–40.

Frank Shorter (b. 10-31-47): Track and field. Gold medalist in marathon at 1972 Olympics, the first American to win the event since 1908. Olympic silver medalist in 1976 marathon. Sullivan Award winner in 1972.

Jim Shoulders (b. 5-13-28): Rodeo. 16 career titles. All-Around champion five times (1949, 1956–59).

Don Shula (b. 1-4-30): Football coach. Retired as alltime NFL leader in wins (347). Won two consecutive Super Bowl championships (1972, '73) with Miami, including NFL's only undefeated season in 1972. Also reached Super Bowl four other times. Career span 1963–95 with Baltimore and Miami.

Al Simmons (b. 5-22-02; d. 5-26-56): Baseball OF. "Bucketfoot Al" for hitting stance. Named AL MVP for 1929, when he led league with 157 RBI. Led league in batting average in 1930 (.381) and '31 (.390). Career span 1924–44 with several teams, including Philadelphia (AL); .334 avg., 307 HR. Elected to Hall of Fame in 1953.

O.J. Simpson (b. 7-9-47): Born Orenthal James. Football RB. "Juice." First man to top 2,000 yards rushing in one season (2,003 in 1973). 11,236 career yards rushing. Led league in rushing four times. Gained 1,000+ yards rushing five consecutive seasons. Player of the Year three times (1972, '73, '75). Gained 200+ yards rushing in a game a record six times. Scored 61 career touchdowns, including 23 in 1975. Also won Heisman Trophy with USC in 1968.

Sir Barton (b. 1916, d. 1937): Thoroughbred. In 1919, before they were linked as the Triple Crown, became first horse to win the Kentucky Derby, the Preakness and the Belmont. Won eight of 13 starts as 3-year-old.

George Sisler (b. 3-24-1893, d. 3-26-73): Baseball 1B. Set record in 1920 with 257 hits in one season. League leader two times, banged out 200+ hits six times. Won two batting titles, including the 1922 crown with a .420 average; averaged .400+ two times and .300+ 11 other times. Career span 1915–30 with St. Louis (NL); .340 avg. and 2,812 hits.

Mary Decker Slaney (b. 8-4-58): Track and field. American record holder in five events ranging from 800 to 3,000 meters. Won 1,500 and 3,000 meters at World Championships in 1983. Lost chance for medal at 1984 Olympics when she tripped and fell after contact with Zola Budd. Won Sullivan Award in 1982. Competed in 1996 Olympics at age 37.

Bruce Smith (b. 6-18-63): Football DE. Alltime NFL leader in sacks (200). Played in four consecutive Super Bowls with Buffalo (1991–94), all losses. Career span 1985– with Buffalo and Washington.

Dean Smith (b. 2-28-31): College basketball coach. Alltime leader in wins (879); seventh alltime highest winning percentage (.776). Alltime most NCAA tournament appearances (27), reached Final Four 11 times. Won NCAA championship in 1982 and '93. Coached 1976 Olympic team to gold medal. Career span 1962–97 with North Carolina. 1997 *Sports Illustrated* Sportsman of the Year.

Emmitt Smith (b. 5-15-69): Football RB. Led NFL in rushing four times (1991, '92 , '93, '95). Set NFL record with 25 TDs in 1995. Named MVP of Super Bowl XXVIII, when he ran for 132 yards in a 30–13 Dallas victory over Buffalo. Career span 1990–2002 with Dallas, 2003– Arizona; in 2002, passed Walter Payton as the NFL's alltime leading rusher.

Ozzie Smith (b. 12-26-54): Baseball SS. "The Wizard of Oz." May be the best defensive shortstop in history. Holds alltime record for most assists in a season among shortstops (621 in 1980). Career double-play and assist leader among shortstops. 14-time All-Star. Won 13 consecutive Gold Gloves. Career span 1978–96 with San Diego and St. Louis; .262 avg., 2,460 hits, 580 SB.

Red Smith (b. 9-25-05, d. 1-15-82): Sportswriter. Won Pulitzer Prize in 1976. After Grantland Rice, the most widely syndicated sports columnist. His literary essays appeared in the *New York Herald Tribune* from 1945–71 and the *New York Times* from 1971–82.

Stan Smith (b. 12-14-46): Tennis. Won 39 tournaments in career, including 1972 Wimbledon in five sets over Ilie Nastase. Won 1971 U.S. Open over Jan Kodes and amateur version of U.S. Open in 1969. 1970 won inaugural Grand Prix Masters. Inducted to Tennis Hall of Fame in 1987.

Tommie Smith (b. 6-5-44): Track and field. Won 1968 Olympic 200 meters in world record of 19.83, then was expelled from Olympic Village, along with bronze medalist John Carlos, for raising black-gloved fist and bowing head during playing of national anthem to protest racism in U.S.

Conn Smythe (b. 2-1-1895, d. 11-18-80): Hockey executive. As general manager with Toronto from 1929–61 won seven Stanley Cup championships (1932, '42, '45, '47–49, '51). Award for playoff MVP named in his honor.

Sam Snead (b. 5-27-12, 5-23-02): Golfer. Alltime leader in career wins (81). Won the Masters (1949, '52, '54) and PGA Championship (1942, '49, '51) three times each and British Open (1946). Runner-up at U.S. Open four times, but title eluded him. PGA Player of the Year in 1949. Won Seniors Championship six times, more than any golfer (1964, '65, '67, '70, '72, '73).

Peter Snell (b. 12-17-38): Track and field. New Zealand runner was gold medalist in 800 meters at two consecutive Olympics (1960 and 1964). Also gold medalist in 1,500 meters at 1964 Olympics. Twice broke world mile record; broke world 800 record once.

Duke Snider (b. 9-19-26): Baseball OF. Holds NL record with 11 home runs and 26 RBI in World Series play. Played on six pennant winners with Brooklyn. Hit 40+ HR five consecutive seasons and 100+ RBI six times. Career span 1947–64 with Brooklyn/LA, New York (NL) and San Francisco; .295 average, 407 HR and 1,333 RBI.

Sammy Sosa (b. 11-12-68): Baseball RF. Followed Mark McGwire in eclipsing Roger Maris's single-season HR mark in 1998. Lost HR race to McGwire that season but won MVP with .308 average, 66 HR, 134 runs, 158 RBI. In 2001, became first man to hit 60+ home runs in three seasons. Career span 1989– with Texas, Chicago (AL) and Chicago (NL).

Javier Sotomayor (b. 10-13-67): Track and field. Cuban high jumper broke the 8-foot barrier with world record jump of 8' 0" in 1989. Set record of 8' ½" in 7-27-93 in Salamanca, Spain.

Warren Spahn (b. 4-23-21): Baseball LHP. Alltime leader in wins by a lefthander (363); 20+ wins 13 times. League leader in wins eight times, complete games nine times, strikeouts four consecutive seasons, innings pitched four times and ERA three times. 1957 Cy Young award. 63 career shutouts. Pitched two no-hitters after age 39. Career span 1942–65, all but last year with Boston/Milwaukee Braves.

Tris Speaker (b. 4-4-1888, d. 12-8-58): Baseball OF. Alltime leader in doubles (792), fifth in hits (3,514) and fifth in batting average (.345). One batting title (.386 in 1916), but .375+ average six times. League leader in doubles eight times, hits two times and HR and RBI one time each. 200+ hits four times, 40+ doubles 10 times and 100+ runs scored seven times. MVP in 1912. Career span 1907–28, mostly with Boston (AL) and Cleveland.

Michael Spinks (b. 7-13-56): Boxer. Defeated Larry Holmes for the heavyweight championship of the world on 9-22-85. Lost title to Mike Tyson in 91 seconds on 6-27-88. Won world light heavyweight title on 7-18-81 and defended it nine times before moving up to heavyweight division. 1976 Olympic middleweight champion.

Mark Spitz (b. 2-10-50): Swimmer. Won a record seven gold medals (two in freestyle, two in butterfly, three in relays) at 1972 Olympics, setting world record in each event. Also won two gold medals, one silver and one bronze medal at 1968 Olympics. Sullivan Award winner in 1971.

Amos Alonzo Stagg (b. 8-16-1862, d. 3-17-65): College football coach. 314 career wins. Won national title with Chicago in 1905. Coach of the Year with Pacific in 1943 at age 81. Five undefeated seasons. Career span 1892–46. Only person elected to both college football and basketball Halls of Fame. Played in the first basketball game in 1891.

Willie Stargell (b. 3-6-40, d. 4-9-01): Baseball OF–1B. "Pops" achieved a 1979 MVP triple crown, winning NL regular season, playoff and World Series MVP awards. Led NL in homers in 1971 and '73. Career span 1962–82 with Pittsburgh; .282 avg., 475 HR, 1,540 RBI. Elected to Hall of Fame in 1988.

Bart Starr (b. 1-9-34): Football QB. Played on three NFL champions (1961, '62, '65) and first two Super Bowl champions (1966, '67) with Green Bay. Also named MVP of first two Super Bowls. Player of the Year in 1966. Led league in passing three times. Career span 1956–71 with Green Bay; 24,718 passing yards, 152 TDs. Also coached Green Bay to 53-77-3 record from 1975–83.

Roger Staubach (b. 2-5-42): Football QB. Led Dallas to six NFC Championships, four Super Bowls and two Super Bowl titles (1971, '77). Player of the Year and Super Bowl MVP in 1971. Also led league in passing four times. Won Heisman Trophy with Navy as a junior in 1963. Served four-year military obligation before turning pro. Career span 1969–79 with Dallas; 22,700 passing yards, 153 TDs passing.

Jan Stenerud (b. 11-26-42): Football K. Scored 1,699 career NFL points. Converted 373 field goals in 558 attempts. Career span 1967–85 with Kansas City, Green Bay and Minnesota. First pure kicker inducted to Hall of Fame, 1991.

Casey Stengel (b. 7-30-1890, d. 9-29-75): Baseball manager. "The Ol' Perfesser." Managed New York (AL) to 10 pennants and seven World Series titles (five consecutively) in 12 years from 1949–60. Alltime leader in World Series games (63), wins (37) and losses (26). Platoon system was his trademark strategy, Stengelese his trademark language ("You could look it up."). Managed New York (NL) from 1962–65. Jersey number (37) retired by Yankees and Mets. Career mark: 1,905-1,842 (.508).

Ingemar Stenmark (b. 3-18-56): Swedish skier. Gold medalist in slalom and giant slalom at 1980 Olympics. World Cup overall champion three consecutive years (1976–78).

Woody Stephens (b. 9-1-13 d. 8-22-98): Horse racing trainer. Trained two Kentucky Derby winners (Cannonade, who won the 100th Derby in 1974 and Swale in 1984) and five straight Belmont winners from 1982–86, starting with 1982 Horse of the Year Conquistador Cielo.

David Stern (b. 9-22-42): Fourth NBA commissioner. Has served since 1984. Oversaw unprecedented growth of league. Owners rewarded him with five-year, $40-million contract extension in 1996.

Jackie Stewart (b. 6-11-39): Scottish auto racer. Fifth alltime in Formula 1 victories (27); Formula 1 champion three times (1969, '71, '73). Also Indy 500 Rookie of the Year in 1966. Retired in 1973.

Payne Stewart (b. 1-3-57, d. 10-25-99): Golfer. Two-time U.S. Open champion (1991, '99), also won 1989 PGA Championship. Killed in plane crash.

John Stockton (b. 3-26-62): Basketball G. Alltime leader in assists (15,177) and steals (3,128). Set single-season assist record (1,164) in 1990–91. Led NBA in assists a record nine consecutive times (1988–96). 10-time All-Star, consecutively 1989–97, 2000. Co-MVP (with Karl Malone) of 1993 All-Star Game. Member of 1992 and '96 Olympic teams. Career span 1984–2003 with Utah; 13.2 ppg, 10.7 rpg.

Picabo Street (b. 4-3-71): Skier. Won silver medal in downhill at 1994 Olympics in Lillehammer and gold in Super G at '98 Games in Nagano. World Cup downhill champion in 1995 and '96. Nine career World Cup victories.

John L. Sullivan (b. 10-15-1858, d. 2-2-18): Boxer. Last bareknuckle champion. Heavyweight title holder (1882–92), lost to Jim Corbett. Career record 38-1-3 with 33 KOs from 1878–92.

Paul Tagliabue (b. 11-24-40): Football executive. Fifth NFL commissioner, has served since 1989.

Anatoli Tarasov (b. 1918, d. 6-23-95): Hockey coach. Orchestrated Soviet Union's emergence as a hockey power. Won nine consecutive world amateur championships (1963–71) and three Olympic gold medals in 1964, '68, '72.

Fran Tarkenton (b. 2-3-40): Football QB. Hall of Famer retired with 342 touchdown passes, 47,003 yards passing, 6,467 pass attempts and 3,686 pass completions. Player of the Year in 1975. Career span 1961–78 with Minnesota, New York Giants.

Lawrence Taylor (b. 2-4-59): Football LB. Revolutionized the linebacker position. Retired as the alltime leader in sacks. Named to Pro Bowl a record 10 consecutive seasons. Player of the Year in 1986. Played on two Super Bowl champions with New York Giants (1986, '90). Career span 1981–93 with New York. Elected to Hall of Fame 1999.

Isiah Thomas (b. 4-30-61): Basketball G. Point guard for Detroit team that won NBA title in 1989 and '90. All-NBA First Team 1984–86. NBA All-Star Game MVP in 1984 and '86. Led NBA in assists (13.9) in 1984–85; finished career with 9,061 assists. Career span 1981–94 with Detroit; 19.2 ppg, 9.3 apg. GM of Toronto Raptors 1995–97. Coached Indiana Pacers 2000–03. Member of Indiana University team that won 1981 NCAA title.

Thurman Thomas (b. 5-15-66): Football RB. Rushed for 1,000+ yards eight years in a row (1989–96). Led AFC in rushing in 1990 and 1991. Career span 1988–01 with Buffalo and Miami; 12,074 yards, 88 TDs.

Daley Thompson (b. 7-30-58): Track and field. British decathlete was gold medalist at two consecutive Olympics in 1980 and '84. At 1984 Olympics set world record (8,847 points) that lasted eight years.

John Thompson (b. 9-2-41): College basketball coach. Former Boston Celtic coached at Georgetown (1973–99), where he mentored Patrick Ewing, Alonzo Mourning and Dikembe Mutombo. Won NCAA title in 1984, runner-up in '82 and '85. Career record: 596–239.

Bobby Thomson (b. 10-25-23): Baseball OF. Three-time All-Star who hit dramatic "shot heard 'round the world" off of Ralph Branca to win NL pennant for New York (NL) in 1951. The Giants had come from 13½ games behind Brooklyn to tie Brooklyn and force a three-game playoff. Career span 1946–60 with New York (NL), Milwaukee, Chicago (NL), Boston and Baltimore; .270, 264 HR, 1,026 RBI.

Ian Thorpe (b. 10-13-82): Australian swimmer. "Thorpedo." As a 17-year-old, won gold medal in the 400-meter freestyle and silver in the 200 free at 2000 Olympics in Sydney. World record holder in both events heading into 2004 games in Athens. Also won gold medals at Sydney in the 400- and 800-meter freestyle relays.

Jim Thorpe (b. 5-28-1888, d. 3-28-53): Sportsman. Gold medalist in decathlon and pentathlon at 1912 Olympics. Played pro baseball with New York (NL) and Cincinnati 1913–19, and pro football with several teams 1919–26. Stripped of gold medals when it was discovered he had played pro baseball, and they were restored only after his death. Also All-America two times with Carlisle.

Dick Tiger (b. 8-14-29; d. 12-14-71): Nigerian boxer. Born Richard Ihetu. Two-time middleweight champ, also won light heavyweight title. Fighter of the Year for 1962 and '65. Elected to Boxing Hall of Fame 1974.

Bill Tilden (b. 2-10-1893, d. 6-5-53): Tennis player. "Big Bill." Won seven U.S. singles titles, six consecutively (1920–25, '29) and three Wimbledon titles (1920, '21, '30). Also won six Grand Slam doubles titles. Led U.S. to seven consecutive Davis Cup victories (1920–26).

Ted Tinling (b. 6-23-10; d. 5-23-90): British tennis couturier. The premier source of women's tennis fashion, from Suzanne Lenglen to Steffi Graf—most notable creation: the frilled lace panties worn by Gorgeous Gussy Moran at Wimbledon in 1949.

Y.A. Tittle (b. 10-24-26): Football QB. Two-time NFL Most Valuable Player (1961, '63). Set NFL record with 36 TD passes in 1963. Career span 1948–64 with Baltimore, San Francisco and New York Giants; 33,070 yards, 242 TD. Inducted into Hall of Fame 1971.

Jayne Torvill/Christopher Dean (b. 10-7-57/ b. 7-27-58): British figure skaters. Won four consecutive ice dancing world championships (1981–84) and Olympic ice dancing gold medal (1984). Won world professional championships in 1985. Won Olympic ice dancing bronze in 1994.

Vladislav Tretiak (b. 4-25-52): Hockey G. Led USSR to gold medals at Olympics in 1972, '76, '84. Played on 13 world amateur champions from 1970–84.

Lee Trevino (b. 12-1-39): Golfer. Won U.S. Open (1968, '71), British Open (1971, '72) and PGA Championship (1974, '84) two times each. PGA Player of the Year in 1971. Also won U.S. Senior Open in 1990. First Senior $1 million season.

Emlen Tunnell (b. 3-29-25, d. 7-23-75): Football S. Alltime leader in interception return yardage with 1,282 and second in interceptions (79). All-Pro nine times. Career span 1948–61 with New York Giants and Green Bay.

Gene Tunney (b. 5-25-1897, d. 11-7-78): Boxer. Heavyweight champion (1926–28). Defeated Jack Dempsey two times, including famous "long count" bout. Career record 65-2-1 with 43 KOs from 1915–28. Retired as champion.

Ted Turner (b. 11-19-38): Sportsman. Skipper who successfully defended the America's Cup in 1977. Also owner of the Atlanta Braves since 1976 and Hawks since '77. Founded the Goodwill Games in 1986.

Mike Tyson (b. 6-30-66): Boxer. Became boxing's youngest heavyweight champion (20 years, 144 days) by knocking out Trevor Berbick in 1986. Lost crown in devastating upset to James (Buster) Douglas in 1990. Served three years in prison (1992–95) for rape. Regained piece of heavyweight title but lost it to Evander Holyfield in 1996. He "lost it" again in their rematch in 1997, when he was disqualified for biting Holyfield's ears.

Johnny Unitas (b. 5-7-33, d. 9-11-02): Football QB. Set record by throwing TD passes in 47 consecutive games (1956–60). Three-time NFL MVP (1959, '64, '67). Led league in TD passes four consecutive seasons. Career span 1956–72 with Baltimore and San Diego; 290 TD passes, 40,239 passing yards.

Al Unser Sr. (b. 5-29-39): Auto racer. Won Indy 500 four times (1970, '71, '78, '87). Retired with 39 career CART victories. USAC/CART champion three times (1970, '83, '85). Brother of Bobby.

Bobby Unser (b. 2-20-34): Auto racer. Won Indianapolis 500 three times (1968, '75, '81). Retired with 35 career victories. USAC champion twice (1968, '74). Brother of Al Sr.

Harold S. Vanderbilt (b. 7-6-1884, d. 7-4-70): Sailor. Owner and skipper who successfully defended the America's Cup three consecutive times, in 1930, '34 and '37.

Glenna Collett Vare (b. 6-20-03, d. 2-2-89): Golfer. Won U.S. Women's Amateur six times, more than any golfer (1922, '25, '28–30, '35).

Bill Veeck (b. 2-9-14, d. 1-2-86): Baseball owner. From 1946–80, owned ballclubs in Cleveland, St. Louis (AL) and Chicago (AL). In 1948, Cleveland became baseball's first team to draw two million in attendance. That year Veeck integrated AL by signing Larry Doby and Satchel Paige. A brilliant promoter, Veeck sent midget Eddie Gaedel up to bat for St. Louis in 1951.

Guillermo Vilas (b. 8-17-52): Tennis. Argentine won 50 straight matches in 1977. In '77 won French Open, where he beat Brian Gottfried, and the U.S. Open, where he beat Jimmy Connors. Also won Australian Open twice, 1978–79.

Lasse Viren (b. 7-22-49): Track and field. Finnish runner was gold medalist in 5,000 and 10,000 meters at two consecutive Olympics (1972, '76).

Virginia Wade (b. 7-10-45): Tennis. Beloved in Britain, Wade won three major titles, most notably Wimbledon in 1977, its centenary year, where she triumphed over Betty Stove. Also won 1968 U.S. Open, '72 Australian Open, and doubles titles in '73 at the Australian, French and U.S. Opens, all with Margaret Smith Court.

Honus Wagner (b. 2-24-1874, d. 12-6-55): Baseball SS. Had .327 career batting average, 3,415 hits and eight batting titles. Averaged .300+ 15 consecutive seasons. Led league in RBI four times, with 100+ RBI nine times. Third alltime in triples (252) and league leader in doubles eight times. 703 career stolen bases, league leader in steals five times. Career span 1897–1917 with Pittsburgh.

Grete Waitz (b. 10-1-53): Track and field. Norwegian runner won New York City Marathon a record nine times (1978–80, '82–86, '88). Won the women's marathon at the 1983 World Championship.

Jersey Joe Walcott (b. 10-31-14, d. 2-25-94): Boxer. Heavyweight champion from 1951–52. Won title at age 37 on fifth attempt before surrendering it to Rocky Marciano. Later became sheriff of Camden, NJ.

Doak Walker (b. 1-1-27, d. 9-27-98): Football HB. Led NFL in scoring two times, his first and final seasons. All-Pro five times. Played on two consecutive NFL champions (1952–53) with Detroit. Career span 1950–55. Also won Heisman Trophy as a junior in 1948. All-America three consecutive seasons with SMU.

Herschel Walker (b. 3-3-62): Football RB. 1982 Heisman Trophy winner signed with the New Jersey Generals of the USFL in '83. Gained 5,562 rushing yards and scored 61 touchdowns in three seasons before league folded. Entered NFL in 1986 with Dallas and led league in rushing yards in 1988. Career span 1983–97 with New Jersey (USFL), Dallas, Minnesota, Philadelphia and New York Giants; 13,787 rushing yards and 143 TD (both leagues).

Bill Walsh (b. 11-30-31): Football coach. Led San Francisco to three Super Bowl wins, after the 1981, '84, '88 seasons. Career record with 49ers from

1979–88, 102-63-1. Perfected short-passing offense with quarterback Joe Montana.

Bill Walton (b. 11-5-52): Basketball C. College Player of the Year three consecutive seasons (1972–74). Played on two NCAA championship teams (1972, '73) with UCLA; tournament MVP twice (1972, '73). Sullivan Award winner in 1973. NBA MVP in 1978, playoff MVP in '77. Led league in rebounding and blocks in 1977. Career span 1974–86 with Portland, San Diego and Boston; 13.3 ppg, 10.5 rpg.

War Admiral (b. 1934, d. 1959): Thoroughbred race horse. A son of Man o' War, won Triple Crown and Horse of the Year honors in 1937.

Paul Warfield (b. 11-28-42): Football WR. Five-time All-NFL, averaged sensational 20.1 yards per catch during his career. Played on two Super Bowl–winning Miami teams. Career span 1964–77 with Cleveland and Miami; 427 receptions for 8,565 yards and 85 TDs. Inducted into Hall of Fame 1983.

Glenn (Pop) Warner (b. 4-5-1871, d. 9-7-54): College football coach. Fourth alltime in wins (319). Won three national championships with Pittsburgh (1916, '18) and Stanford (1926). Career record 319-106-32 with six teams from 1896–38.

Tom Watson (b. 9-4-49): Golfer. Winner of British Open five times (1975, '77, '80, '82, '83), the Masters two times (1977, '81) and U.S. Open once (1982). PGA Player of the Year six times, more than any golfer (1977–80, '82, '84).

Dick Weber (b. 12-23-29): Bowler. Won All-Star Tournament four times (1962, '63, '65, '66). Voted Bowler of the Year three times (1961, '63, '65). Won 31 career PBA titles.

Johnny Weismuller (b. 6-2-04, d. 1-21-84): Swimmer. Won three gold medals (including 100- and 400-meter freestyle) at 1924 Olympics and two gold medals at the 1928 Olympics. Also played Tarzan in the movies.

Jerry West (b. 5-28-38): Basketball G. "Mr. Clutch." 10 time first-team All-NBA; All-Defensive Team four times; 1969 playoff MVP. Led league in assists and scoring one time each. Career span 1960–72 with Los Angeles; 27.0 ppg, 6.7 apg. All-America two times with West Virginia. Played on 1960 gold medal-winning Olympic team. Guided the Lakers to seven NBA championships as either a general manager or a consultant from 1980 to 2001.

Whirlaway (b. 4-2-38, d. 4-6-53): Thoroughbred race horse. Triple Crown winner in 1941 with jockey Eddie Arcaro aboard. Trained by Ben A. Jones.

Byron (Whizzer) White (b. 6-8-17, d. 4-15-02): Football RB. Led NFL in rushing two times (Pittsburgh in 1938, Detroit in '40). Led NCAA in scoring and rushing with Colorado in 1937; named All-America. United States Supreme Court justice 1962–93.

Reggie White (b. 12-19-62): Football DE. "Minister of Defense." Retired as alltime NFL leader in sacks (198). Set a Super Bowl record with three sacks against New England in Super Bowl XXXI. He played in 13 Pro Bowls. Career span: 1984–01 with Memphis Showboats (USFL), Philadelphia, Green Bay and Carolina.

Charles Whittingham (b. 4-13-13 d. 4-20-99): Thoroughbred race horse trainer. Nicknamed "Bald Eagle" after losing his hair to tropical disease in World War II. Led yearly earnings list for trainers in 1970–73, '75, '81, '82. Won three Eclipse Awards and trained

two Horses of the Year (Ack Ack in 1971 and Ferdinand in 1987).

Kathy Whitworth (b. 9-27-39): Golfer. Alltime LPGA leader with 88 tour victories, including six majors. Won LPGA Championship in 1967, '71 and '75. Won Titleholders Championship (extinct major) in 1965 and '66. Won Western Open (extinct major) in 1967. Won Vare Trophy every year from 1965–72, except '68. LPGA Player of Year from 1966–69 and 1971–73.

Hoyt Wilhelm (b. 7-26-23, d. 8-23-02): Baseball RHP. Threw knuckleball until age 48. Career 2.52 ERA, 227 saves. Hit home run in his first at bat (never hit another) and pitched no-hitter in 1958. Career span 1952–72 with nine teams.

Bud Wilkinson (b. 4-23-15 d. 2-9-94): Football coach. Coached Oklahoma to NCAA record 47 consecutive wins (1953–57). Won three national championships (1950, '55, '56) with Oklahoma, where he coached from 1947–1963. Won Orange Bowl four times and Sugar Bowl two times. Career record 145-29-4, including four undefeated seasons. Also coached St. Louis of NFL in 1978–79.

Billy Williams (b. 6-15-38): Baseball OF. "Sweet Swinging." Six-time All-Star and the 1961 NL Rookie of the Year. Career span 1959–76 with Chicago (NL) and Oakland; .290 avg., 426 HR, 1,475 RBI. Elected to Hall of Fame in 1987.

Ted Williams (b. 8-30-18, d. 7-5-02): Baseball OF. "The Splendid Splinter." Last player to hit .400 (.406 in 1941). MVP in 1946, '49 and Triple Crown winner in 1942, '47. Retired with career batting average of .344, along with 2,019 walks and a .634 slugging average. Won six AL batting titles, and led the league in HR and RBI four times each. Had .300+ average 15 consecutive seasons; 100+ RBI and runs scored nine times each; 30+ HR eight times; and 100+ walks 11 times. Lost nearly five seasons to military service. Career span 1939–42 and 1946–60 with Boston; 521 career HR.

Hack Wilson (b. 4-26-1900; d. 11-23-48): Baseball OF. Stood 5' 6" but weighed 210. Had five astounding seasons 1926–30, before alcohol ruined his career. Best was 1930 when he hit .356, scored 146 runs, hit a NL record 56 homers and drove in 190, which is still the major league record. Career span 1923–34 with several teams. Elected to Hall of Fame in 1979.

Dave Winfield (b. 10-3-51): Baseball OF. Drafted out of Univ. of Minnesota by baseball, basketball and football teams. Drove in 100+ runs five times, and led the NL in 1979 with 118. Derided by George Steinbrenner as "Mr. May," but hit clutch double to win 1992 World Series for Toronto. Career span 1973–95 with San Diego, New York (AL), California, Toronto, Minnesota and Cleveland; .283 avg., 465 HR, 3,110 hits, 1,833 RBI and 1,669 runs. Inducted into Hall of Fame in 2001.

Major W.C. Wingfield (b. 10-16-1833, d. 4-18-12): British tennis pioneer. Credited with inventing the game of tennis, which he called "Sphairistike" or "sticky" and patented in February 1874.

Colonel Matt Winn (b. 6-30-1861, d. 10-6-49): General manager of Churchill Downs from 1904 until his death; made Kentucky Derby premier U.S. race.

Katarina Witt (b. 12-3-65): East German figure skater. Gold medalist at 1984 and '88 Olympics. Also world champion four times (1984, '85, '87, '88).

John Wooden (b. 10-14-10): College basketball coach. Coached UCLA to 10 NCAA championships in 12 years (1964, '65, '67–73, '75). Record winning streak of 88 games (1971–74). 664 career wins and fourth highest career winning percentage (.804). First member of basketball Hall of Fame as coach and player. Career span 1949–75 with UCLA. 1932 College Player of the Year at Purdue.

Tiger Woods (b. 12-30-75): Golfer. Produced the Tiger Slam in 2000–01, an unofficial Grand Slam during which he won four consecutive professional majors. Holds the tournament record for best scores at the Masters, the U.S. Open, the PGA Championship and the British Open. Became the youngest winner of the Masters in 1997, when he shot a record-270 to win by a record 12 strokes. Became the youngest player to win all four major tournaments ('99 PGA, '00 U.S. Open, '00 British Open). Also won three straight U.S. Junior Amateur titles (1991–93) and three straight U.S. Amateur titles (1994–96). Then took the PGA tour by storm, winning six of his first 21 tournaments. Already has 34 PGA Tour victories (including eight majors) and has won more money ($32,687,252) than any golfer in history. 1996 and 2000 *Sports Illustrated* Sportsman of the Year.

Mickey Wright (b. 2-14-35): Golfer. Second alltime in career wins (82) and major championships (13; tied with Louise Suggs). Won the U.S. Open four times (1958, '59, '61, '64), the LPGA Championship four times (1958, '60, '61, '63), and the Western Open three times (1962, '63, '66).

Kristi Yamaguchi (b.7-12-71): Figure skater. Olympic champion in 1992. Back-to-back world champion (1991, '92).

Cale Yarborough (b. 3-27-40): Auto racer. Won Daytona 500 four times (1968, '77, '83, '84). 83 career victories. NASCAR champion three consecutive years (1976–78).

Carl Yastrzemski (b. 8-22-39): Baseball OF. "Yaz." 1967 MVP and Triple Crown winner. Three batting titles. Second alltime in games played (3,308) and sixth in walks (1,845). Career span 1961–83 with Boston; .285 avg., 3,419 hits, 452 HR and 1,844 RBI.

Cy Young (b. 3-29-1867, d. 11-4-55): Baseball RHP. Alltime leader in wins (511), innings pitched (7,354⅔) and complete games (749); fourth in shutouts (76). Had 2.63 career ERA. Pitched three no-hitters, including a perfect game in 1904. Career span 1890–1911 with Cleveland and Boston (AL).

Steve Young (b. 10-11-61): Football QB. Career passer rating of 96.8. Led the league in passing six times. Led 49ers to victory in Super Bowl XXIX of which he was MVP for tossing a record six TD passes. Two-time NFL MVP (1992 and '94). Repeated concussions forced his retirement in 2000. Career span 1984–00 with Los Angeles Express (USFL), Tampa Bay and San Francisco; 33,124 yards, 232 TD passes; rushed for 43 TD.

Robin Yount (b. 9-16-55): Baseball OF–SS. Won AL MVP as a shortstop (1982) and a centerfielder (1989). Became Milwaukee's shortstop at 18, Career span 1974–93 with Milwaukee; .285 avg., 3,142 hits, 251 HR and 583 2B. Elected to Hall of Fame 1999.

Steve Yzerman (b. 5-9-65): Hockey C. Won three Stanley Cups with Red Wings (1997, '98, '02). Won Conn Smythe trophy in 1998. Scored 100+ points six consecutive seasons (1987–93). Career span 1983– with Detroit.

Babe Didrikson Zaharias (b. 6-26-14, d. 9-27-56): Sportswoman. Commonly called the greatest female athlete of all time, Zaharias was the Gold medalist in the 80-meter hurdles and javelin throw at the 1932 Olympics; she also won the silver medal in the high jump (her gold medal jump was disallowed for using the then-illegal western roll). Became a golfer in 1935 and won 12 major titles, including U.S. Open three times (1948, '50, '54—a year after cancer surgery). Also helped found the LPGA in 1949.

Tony Zale (b. 5-29-13, d. 3-20-97): Boxer. Born Anthony Zaleski. "The Man of Steel." Two-time middleweight champ. Fought Rocky Graziano for title three times in 21 months, winning twice. 67-18-2 with 44 KOs. Elected to Boxing Hall of Fame 1958.

Emil Zatopek (b. 9-19-22, d. 11-21-00): Track and field. Czech runner became only athlete to win gold medal in 5,000 and 10,000 meters and marathon, at 1952 Olympics. Also gold medalist in 10,000 meters at '48 Olympics.

Zinedine Zidane (b. 6-23-72): French soccer player. "Zizou." Led France to 1998 World Cup title; scored two goals in 3–0 win over Brazil in the final. Led Juventus to 1998 Italian League title and to '98 European Cup final. 1998 FIFA World Player of the Year. Led France to 2000 European Championship.

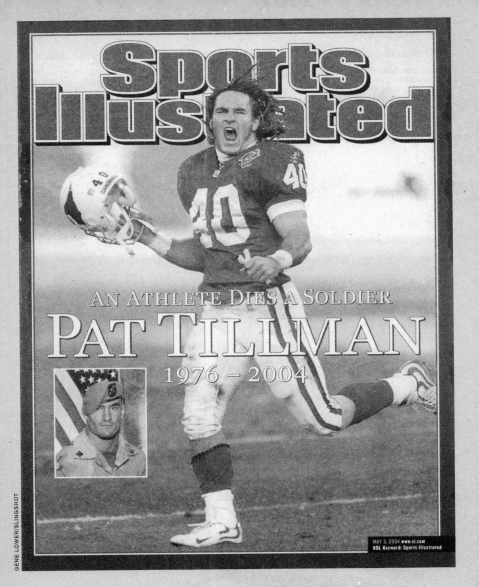

Sports Illustrated

AN ATHLETE DIES A SOLDIER

PAT TILLMAN

1976 – 2004

MAY 3, 2004 www.si.com
AOL Keyword: Sports Illustrated

Obituaries

**Pat Tillman
1976–2004**

George Bamberger, 80, baseball player, pitching coach and manager. *As the Orioles' pitching coach from 1968 to '77, Bamberger mentored 18 20-game winners, including four in '71. Hall of Famer Jim Palmer, who won 20 games for Bamberger seven times, remembers him:*

"George had flawless mechanics. If I ever got out of sync, I used to visualize him throwing batting practice. But with us—his "boys"—he didn't preach mechanics. He had a sixth sense of what a pitcher needed to be better, and he knew it could be different for each guy. There were a few hard rules, but everybody was unique, and he understood that. George's great strength was he didn't overcoach. There's no place for panic on the mound. Teams mirror their coaches, and George was unflappable. Remember that he was a coach for Earl Weaver, who could drive you crazy. George was almost deaf in his right ear, and he used to sit to Earl's left. Once someone asked how he put up with Weaver's histrionics. George said, 'Huh?' It was the perfect answer, and theirs was the perfect marriage. Earl would say bizarre things, like asking George to go to the mound to tell Dave McNally to either throw the ball harder or make it curve more. Later I said, 'George, you didn't really tell him that, did you?' He said, 'No, we talked about golf.'

"Bambi was unassuming, a guy from Staten Island with the accent to boot. One winter when I lived in Baltimore, I bought a house, and he helped me put in a storage area. He was a master wood craftsman. He didn't have to, but there he was, putting in ceiling tiles with me. And that's what made him a great coach: He knew what you needed on and off the field."

In North Redington Beach, Fla., of colon cancer, April 4, 2004.

Earl Battey, 68, baseball player. *A four-time All-Star catcher with the Twins in the 1960s, Battey hit .270 in 13 major league seasons. SI writes:*

"Battey had a reputation as one of the game's toughest players. In Game 3 of the 1965 World Series against the Dodgers, he was chasing a foul ball when he ran into a railing, Adam's apple first. Though barely able to turn his neck, he threw out five runners in the final four games, including Maury Wills twice. 'There are two requisites to being a catcher,' the 6' 1", 220-pound Battey once joked. 'You've to be big and you've got to be dumb, and I qualify on both counts.' "

In Ocala, Fla., of cancer, Nov. 15, 2003.

Fanny Blankers-Koen, 85, track and field legend. *At the age of 30, after having competed in the 1936 Olympics as a teenager and then started a family, Fanny Blankers-Koen returned to international competition at the London Games of 1948. Inspired by a British track coach who said she was too old to win, Blankers-Koen won four gold medals in those Games, an Olympic feat that remains unmatched by any woman to this day. In 1999, the IAAF, the international governing body for track and field, named Blankers-Koen the greatest female athlete of the 20th century. SI's Brian Cazaneuve writes:*

" Francina Koen was 18 when at the 1936 Berlin Games she experienced her first Olympic highlight: approaching U.S. legend Jesse Owens and asking for an autograph. The shy Dutch teenager placed sixth in the 100-meter dash in Berlin [and fifth in both the long jump and 400-meter relay.—*Ed.*], but lost the decade of her athletic prime to a World War and two cancelled Olympics. At the 1948 London Games, Koen won an unprecedented four gold medals, though she nearly went home midway through the competition after European tabloids criticized her for not being a proper housewife and mother. Koen had won the 100 meters and 80-meter hurdles in London when she told her husband and coach, Jan Blankers, that she wanted to return to Holland to be with their two sons. After Blankers convinced her that she would regret leaving, 'The Flying Dutchwoman' captured gold medals in the 200 meters and 4 x 100-meter relay. She might have won more medals, but the world-record holder in the long jump and high jump and Dutch champ in the javelin was limited to three individual events by IOC rules. After the Games, Koen returned home a national heroine; local fans honored her achievement by giving her the gift of a bicycle so she wouldn't have to run so much. Until her death at age 85, Blankers-Koen lived in Amsterdam, where she played tennis and rode her bike daily."

In Amsterdam, from undisclosed causes, Jan. 25, 2004.

Bill Braucher, 77, sportswriter. *SI writes:*

"Braucher helped lure coach Don Shula to the Dolphins from the Colts, planting the seeds that would lead to one of the NFL's great dynasties." In 1970, Miami owner Joe Robbie wanted to talk to Shula about his coaching vacancy but was forbidden to under the NFL's tampering rules. So Robbie had Braucher, a *Miami Herald* columnist who, like Shula, was a graduate of John Carroll University, make the contact. (Apparently, the NFL saw through the ruse, docking the Dolphins a first-round draft pick when Shula took the job.) 'He was instrumental in me coming here, and that's something that changed my life,' Shula said."

In Miami, Fla., of lung caner, March 26, 2004.

Harry (the Cat) Brecheen, 89, baseball player. *A lefthander, Brecheen is one of 13 pitchers to win three games in a World Series. SI writes:*

"Pitching for the Cardinals in Game 2 of the 1946 Series, Brecheen, nicknamed for his slick fielding, shut out the Red Sox 3–0 on four hits and singled in the game's first run. He won Game 6 with a complete-game seven-hitter and, as a reliever, got the final six outs in Game 7. Brecheen won 133 games in a 12-year career, including 20 in '48."

In Ada, Okla., of undisclosed causes, Jan. 17, 2004.

Ken Brett, 55, baseball player. *Brett's 14-year career (he went 83–85 with a 3.93 ERA) began with the Red Sox in '67, the year he became the youngest pitcher to appear in a World Series. Hall of Famer George Brett recalls the older brother he called Kemer.*

"I might never have become a ballplayer if not for Kemer. It's easier to make it if someone close to you has made it: You think, If he can make it, so can I. One summer in high school, I spent a week with him in Boston. I'd go to the clubhouse, sit in the dugout, watch batting practice and we'd walk back to his apartment together, maybe stopping off for a sandwich. I mean, he was single in Boston, Jim Lonborg was his next-door neighbor and he had his 16-year-old brother tagging along. But Kemer didn't mind.

"He was as competitive as there was. He was pitching for the Angels in '77 when he started a fight against my team, the Royals. Amos Otis was batting with runners on second and third, and Kemer got the sign to walk him intentionally. Amos was standing with his bat on his shoulder, and he yelled, "Throw me a strike, you big p----!" Kemer threw one as hard as he could behind Amos's head, the ball went to the backstop, and Cookie Rojas came in from third. My brother ran to the plate to cover and tackled Cookie, a real Dick Butkus tackle. The dugouts emptied, Kemer was fighting Amos, and I had to wonder, What do I do? Try to kick Amos's ass, or my brother's? (I ended up standing around, trying to break things up.) Kemer got tossed, and after the inning I ran through the tunnel under the stadium to California's clubhouse. Kemer had scratches all over his neck and face. I asked what Cookie had done to deserve the tackle. Kemer said, 'At the last second I realized what I had done, and I didn't want him to score.'

"He was a great brother and a great husband and if I can do half as well raising my three kids as he did as a father I'll be happy. I loved being kemer's teammate on the Royals, in '80 and '81. The first game he pitched, he came out of the bullpen, and I was standing on the mound with Jamie Quirk, our catcher. The gate in rightfield opened, and out came my brother, running, sticking his arms out and veering left, veering right like a plane. I said to Jamie, 'Now I know why he's been on 10 teams.' Kemer's career wasn't what we expected. He was arguably the best player in Southern California in high school. But after he blew out his elbow in '68 and had surgeries, he was never the same. I never heard him complain, though. I asked him once, 'Aren't you tired of getting traded?' He said, 'Do you know how many places I've been, how many great guys I've met? I wouldn't trade places with anyone in the game.' "

In Spokane, Wash., of brain cancer, Nov 18, 2003.

Roosevelt Brown, 71, football player. *A Hall of Fame offensive tackle, Brown helped the New York Giants to six NFL title games in his career, which lasted from 1953 to '65. SI's Paul Zimmerman remembers the eight-time All-NFL selection:*

"The phlebitis in his legs, which ended Brown's career at 33, had forced him to watch practice from one of those portable golf seats. As he sat observing a line drill at Giants training camp a few years ago, surveying 300-pounders belly-bumping each other, I asked him what he thought of modern offensive-line techniques. Brown, a member of the scouting department, gave a little snort without taking his eyes off the field.

" 'Techniques?' he said. 'What techniques? There isn't any technique anymore.'

"As a player Brown brought stylishness and grace to a position known for its brutality. He was a month short of his 21st birthday when he played his first game for the Giants, lining up at left tackle. He had been a two-time wrestling captain at Morgan State, and he carried 245 pounds, which grew to 255 in his later years, on a 29-inch waist. (Not that he was a little man. When he joined the Giants, they had only two heavier players.) His technique and body control were dazzling, but even more remarkable was his ability to pull and lead the sweeps of Eddie Price or Frank Gifford or Alex Webster around the left side. Guards were supposed to pull, not tackles. Pro football didn't see another pulling tackle until Ron Mix of the Chargers in 1960, and it hasn't seen one since. (They didn't measure 40 times in those days, but I'd guess Brown's was in the 4.7 range.) And Brown wouldn't just get out in front of the play, he would cut down his man like a scythe. Giants fans would start cheering as soon as they saw his number 79 flying around the end, looking for a target. It wasn't every day that a crowd cheered for an offensive lineman, but Rosey Brown, a proud and fierce warrior, might have been the best ever."

In Columbus, N.J., of a heart attack, June 9, 2004.

Ivan Calderon, 41, baseball player.

An outfielder who played for Seattle, Chicago (AL), Montreal and Boston, Calderon hit .272 during his 10-year career. He was killed in an attack in a store near his home in Loiza, Puerto Rico. Two gunmen entered, and without saying a word shot Calderon in the back several times.

In Loiza, Puerto, Rico, of gunshot wounds, Dec. 27, 2003.

Ken Caminiti, 41, baseball player.

Voted the National League's most valuable player in 1996 after a season in which he hit 40 home runs, batted .326 and drove in 130 runs, Caminti, a third baseman, led San Diego to the World Series two seasons later. The Padres were swept by the Yankees that year, but, having guided the team to its first Series since 1984, Caminiti's place in the franchise's history was secure.

He will also be remembered for his well-publicized struggles with drug addiction and for his admission, in a 2002 interview with SPORTS ILLUSTRATED, that he used steroids during his MVP season of '96. Caminiti alleged during that interview that half of the players in the major leagues were using steroids. Six days before his death, Caminiti admitted in a Houston courtroom that he had violated his probation by testing positive for cocaine in September 2004. An autopsy was pending at press time.

In the Bronx, N.Y., of a heart attack, Oct. 10, 2004.

James (Doc) Counsilman, 83, swimming coach. *The swim coach at Indiana University for 34 years, Counsilman mentored dozens of U.S. swimming stars, including the legendary Mark Spitz, who, before winning a record seven gold medals at the 1972 Olympics, helped Counsilman's Hoosiers to four consecutive NCAA swimming titles—in the midst of an Indiana run of six straight. SI writes:*

"Counsilman coached U.S. swimmers to 21 gold medals in the 1964 and '76 Olympics and led Indiana to 23 Big Ten championships as the Hoosiers' coach from 1957 to '90. As a teenager, Counsilman taught himself to swim in fish hatcheries in his hometown of St. Louis. After a stint in the Army in World War II—he was awarded the Distinguished Flying Cross after flying 32 missions—he graduated from Ohio State, then earned a doctorate in human performance from Iowa. (His dissertation was on the crawl.) He later applied Bernoulli's principle of fluid mechanics to determine that the optimal stroke involved bending the arm, a discovery that revolutionized the sport. (His 1968 book, *The Science of Swimming*, is still the sport's bible.) Even as he coached, Counsilman remained a competitive swimmer. In '79, just before he became, at 58, the oldest person to swim the English Channel, he said, 'I don't mind getting old. I just don't want to get old before my time.' "

In Bloomington, Ind., of Parkinson's disease, Jan. 4, 2004.

Yinka Dare, 32, basketball player. *After leaving George Washington University following his sophomore year, Dare, a seven-foot center born and raised in*

Nigeria, was the 14th player selected in the 1994 NBA draft. He went to the Nets, but Dare never lived up to his potential, spending most of two seasons on the New Jersey bench, and finishing with career averages of 2.1 points and 2.6 rebounds a game in 110 NBA games.

In Englewood, N.J., of a heart attack, Jan 9, 2004.

Dick Durrance, 89, skier. *SI writes*:
"Dick Durrance won so many skiing championships that the U.S. Ski Association put his profile on the medal it awarded for national titles. (He won five in 1939 and turned the medals into a necklace for his wife, Miggs.) Durrance missed out on a chance to win an Olympic medal when the '40 Games were canceled because of World War II, during which he trained ski-borne troops of the 10th Mountain Division. After the war he moved to Apsen, Colo., where he helped turn what had been a desolate mining town into a top ski resort by cutting new trails and designing the race course that hosted the '50 world championship. He also directed more than 40 skiing films. 'His real significance to American skiing was that he bridged the gap between [the U.S.] and Europe, where the technique was far more advanced,' said John Fry, a former editor of *Ski Magazine*. 'What Dick brought was a racing turn that was ahead of his time.' "

In Carbondale, Colo., of natural causes, June 13, 2004.

Gertrude Ederle, 97, swimmer. *SI writes*:
"In 1926, Gertrude Ederle became the first woman to swim the English Channel. Upon her return to New York City, the 19-year-old daughter of a Bronx butcher received a ticker tape parade that was attended by two million people. President Calvin Coolidge proclaimed her 'America's best girl,' and a song, *Trudy*, was written in her honor.

"Ederle learned to swim on the New Jersey shore, near her parents' summer cottage, and went on to win gold in the 4 x 100-meter freestyle relay at the 1924 Olympics. Still, London bookies were offering 5-to-1 odds against her making it across when, on the morning of Aug. 6, she covered herself with lanolin and sheep grease, put on her bathing suit and entered the Channel at Cape Gris-Nez. She set her stroke rhythm to *Let Me Call You Sweetheart*, a waltz her sister played on a Victrola aboard the tug that accompanied her. 'When I looked up at the support boat and saw the American flag flying, tattered by the wind, I'd just dig a little deeper,' she told the *Los Angeles Times* in 1984. Fourteen hours and 31 minutes after she set out—nearly two hours faster than any of the five men who had swum the Channel—she reached Kingsdown, England, where bonfires and thousands of fans awaited. Ederle went on to tour the vaudeville circuit, swimming on stage in a giant tank. But she lost her hearing, which had been deteriorating since a bout of childhood measles, in 1930 and retreated from the spotlight, teaching swimming to deaf children in New York City, where she lived until moving to a New Jersey nursing home. She never married. 'Everybody [said] it couldn't be done,' she said in 2001. 'Every time somebody said that, I wanted to prove it could be.' "

In Wyckoff, N.J., of natural causes, Nov. 30, 2003.

Otto Graham, 82, football player. *A man whose name has to be included in any discussion of the greatest quarterbacks of all time, Otto Graham led the Cleveland Browns to 10 consecutive title games from 1946 to '55. The Hall of Famer led Cleveland to victory in seven of those 10 championship games. SI's Paul Zimmerman writes:*

"Watching Graham and his Browns in the All-America Football Conference was to see a brand of football that was way ahead of its time. The NFL, in the late 1940s, was shaking off the traces of the single wing. The T formation was still a learning experience. Pass protection was primitive, and quarterbacks completed less than 50% of their passes. But the Browns, whose offensive line employed [coach] Paul Brown's technique of cup blocking and chanted 'Nobody touches Graham' as they broke the huddle, helped make Otto the most precise and meticulous passer the game had ever seen. In 1953 he connected on 64.7% of his throws.

"Cleveland breezed through four AAFC titles before joining the NFL in 1950. That year, at one of the keynote games in league history, the Browns played the two-time NFL champion Eagles in Philadelphia. I sat in the end zone and watched Graham play the defenders like violins, working the corners with comeback routes off quick, timed squareouts and, when they loosened up, hitting them up the middle with 238-pound fullback Marion Motley. The final score was 35–10. 'It was those comebacks off the quick outs that killed 'em,' Graham told me years later. 'They were something I worked out with my receivers, Dante Lavelli and Mac Speedie. Throw the timed pattern, but have them break back toward me at the end of it. Defensive backs couldn't react to that.'

"What he didn't mention was that it took utmost accuracy to make the whole thing work, and until John Unitas and Joe Montana arrived no one was as accurate as Graham. One story was about how one of his teammates bent a wire coat hanger into a diamond shape one day and challenged Graham to throw a football through it from 15 feet away. He went 10 for 10.

"He played in the NFL for six years and reached the championship game in each one, and his effect on his teammates was electric. They just never felt they could lose a game he was quarterbacking. How would I rate him, alltime? Top five, along with Montana, Unitas Sammy Baugh, Sid Luckman and John Elway. But no one was as great a winner as Graham."

In Sarasota, Fla., of a heart aneurysm, Dec. 17, 2003.

Matthew Gribble, 41, swimmer. *An Olympic swimmer and former world-record holder in the 100-meter butterfly, Matthew Gribble was killed in an automobile accident in Florida. SI writes:*

"In 1982, Gribble upset heavily favored Michael Gross of Germany in the World Games, then set a world record the next year that stood for 11 months. At the '84 Olympics, though, a back injury slowed Gribble, who didn't advance past his preliminary heat in his final competitive race. 'Matt was the type of guy who was always real quiet,' said Kurt Wienants, Gribble's teammate at the University of Miami, where Gribble's 100-meter-butterfly record still stands. 'Then he would just show up on the block and be amazing.' "

Near Miami, Fla., of injuries sustained in a car accident, March 21, 2004.

Albert Heppner, 29, race walker. *After failing to qualify for the 2004 U.S. Olympic team, Albert Heppner apparently committed suicide. SI writes:*

"Heppner finished fifth at the 50-km Olympic trials on Feb. 15, 2004, in Chula Vista, Calif., even though he held a two-minute lead 30 kilometers into the race.

After fading dramatically ('I just started falling apart,' he said later. 'I've never crashed like I did today.') Heppner collapsed at the finish and was taken by stretcher to a holding area, where he soon recovered. Three days later police discovered his car abandoned by the road near the Pine Valley Bridge, where he and his teammates often went hiking. They found Heppner's body the next morning in a gorge, 200 feet below. Heppner, who would have had another chance to qualify for the Olympics at a meet in May, took up race walking in 1989 as a high schooler in Maryland. By '99, after competing at Wisconsin, he was the U.S.'s second-ranked 50-km race walker. In 2000 he withdrew from the Olympic trials in Sacramento, suffering from hypothermia in the frigid, wet conditions. An aspiring journalist who was studying at San Diego State, Heppner trained at the Olympic Training Center in Chula Vista and was known for the way he embraced new teammates. 'Al was the self-appointed welcoming committee and the most outgoing, fun-loving guy on the team,' said Curt Clausen, who won the Feb. 15 race.'This is impossible to understand.' "

Near Chula Vista, Calif., from injuries sustained in a fall from the edge of a gorge, Feb. 19, 2004.

Sidney James, 97, managing editor, SI. *When* Sports Illustrated *launched in 1954, the man at the helm was former* Life *magazine editor Sidney James. SI's Walter Bingham remembers him:*

"If there is a word to describe Sidney L. James, Sports Illustrated's first managing editor, it is *enthusiastic.* He would respond to written story suggestions with GOLLY, GEE WHIZ or WOW scribbled to the side. Sid, who died last week at 97, never met a sports story he didn't like, partly because he came to the job as an innocent in the business.

"In his younger years he had been a reporter for the *St. Louis Post Dispatch* and then an editor at LIFE, where in 1952 he had been instrumental in publishing Ernest Hemingway's *The Old Man and the Sea.* When Henry R. Luce, TIME's founder, contemplated whether or not to launch a sports magazine, he asked Ernie Haverman, a trusted colleague, if it was a good idea. Haverman sent Luce an 11-page memo detailing why it wouldn't work. Sid said it would.

"In those early days, beginning in August 1954, the magazine covered the full spectrum of sports—rodeo, canoeing, trapshooting and yes, baseball, football and golf. Eddie Mathews may have been on SI's first cover, but he was quickly followed by a grouping of colorful golf bags, a woman knee-deep in the ocean surf and, in time, the Yale bulldog. It was Sid's belief that something in sports touched everyone.

"During his six years as managing editor, James presided over the birth of the infamous SI jinx. In 1957 he ran a cover that said WHY OKLAHOMA IS UNBEATABLE. The next week the Sooners' 47-game winning streak came to an end. He also coaxed contributions from such literary all-stars as Hemingway and John Steinbeck. William Faulkner offered his impressions of the 1955 Kentucky Derby; Robert Frost observed the 1956 baseball All-Star Game. . . .

"A few years ago, Sid, long retired and living in California, was asked if he would consider attending an SI reunion in New York City. He declined because of age but said that somewhere in the archives was a speech of Luce's saying that without Sid James, there never would have been a Sports Illustrated. No reason to argue.

In Alameda, Calif., of undisclosed causes, March 11, 2004.

Edmund Joyce, 87, athletic director. *The Reverend Edmund Joyce served as chairman of the board of athletics at Notre Dame from 1952 to '87. SI writes:*

"During his tenure Joyce oversaw a successful program—the Irish won three national football championships and went to the 1978 Final Four—but he was also influential outside of South Bend. In 1977 he was awarded the Distinguished American Award by the College Football Hall of Fame, and he regularly spoke at NCAA conventions. 'Every delegate would be in that hall, and you could hear a pin drop,' said former Irish basketball coach Digger Phelps of Joyce's speeches. 'And his messages were always . . . student first, athlete second. He never deviated from that.'."

In South Bend, Ind., of complications from a stroke, May 2, 2004.

Roque Maspoli, 86, soccer player.

Roque Maspoli stood—and leaped and soared and stretched—between the pipes for Uruguay when it upset Brazil 2–1 in the final of the 1950 World Cup. With an astonishing—and astonished—crowd of 200,000 fans looking on in Rio de Janeiro, Maspoli came up with spectacular save after spectacular save to repel the home team, which had scored 13 goals in its previous two games. "Maspoli performed acrobatic prodigies in goal," English soccer historian Brian Glanville wrote in 1973. "Time and again, [Brazil's] Zizinho, Ademir and Jair, that terrifying trio, worked their sinuous way through the blue walls of Uruguay's defense. Time and again . . . an interception by the flying Maspoli frustrated them."

In Montevideo, Uruguay, of undisclosed causes, Feb. 22, 2004.

Brian Maxwell, 51, runner and inventor. *A former world-class marathoner, Brian Maxwell went on to found PowerBar Inc., a leader in the increasingly popular field of on-the-go sports bars. SI writes:*

"Maxwell's dyspepsia spawned a billion-dollar-a-year industry: Stricken with stomach problems during a 1983 race, he became determined to find a low-fat food that could be consumed before, or even during, an endurance event. He set to work in the kitchen of his Berkeley apartment with Bill Vaughn, a Cal biochemist, and Jennifer Biddulph, a student of food science who later became Maxwell's wife. In 1986 PowerBar was born. While the bars could be difficult to chew—'Put 'em under your arm, that softens 'em up,' former quarterback Steve Young once advised—they gained wide popularity. In 2000 Maxwell sold the company for a reported $375 million to Nestle SA. He donated millions to Cal, where a statue of him and Jennifer stands near the track and field venue."

In Ross, Calif., of a heart attack, March 19, 2004.

Norris McWhirter, 78, world-record book editor.

Norris McWhirter launched the first Guinness World Records *with his twin brother, Ross, in the mid-1950s. Since then the series has become the gold standard for settling bets in pubs the world over, chock full of obscure records, little-known facts and oddball figures. SI writes:*

"The McWhirters, sons of a British newspaper editor who brought home 150 papers a week, worked as sportswriters before starting a business that sold obscure facts and figures to newspapers and advertising agencies. Their work caught the attention of Sir Hugh Beaver, the managing director of the

Guinness brewery, who a few years earlier while hunting had gotten into a heated argument over which was the fastest game bird in Europe—the golden plover or the red grouse.

"Believing people might be interested in a reference work that would resolve such disputes, Beaver commissioned the brothers to compile a collection of world records. The first, relatively slender edition of the McWhirters' book, containing 8,000 entries, came out in August 1955 and was an immediate hit. In its 49 years the Guinness book has sold more than 100 million copies, settled countless bar bets and inspired attention seekers around the world to grow a 56-inch thumbnail and spend 14 minutes spinning a frying pan on one finger. The McWhirters, who became public figures in the wake of the book's success, used their visibility to advocate conservative causes. In 1975 Ross offered rewards totaling $102,000 for the capture of IRA terrorists responsible for a series of London bombings. He was assassinated outside his home shortly afterward, and the IRA claimed responsibility.

"Norris, who presided over the continuing growth of the book (the most recent edition was translated into 37 languages) retired as *Guinness* editor in 1985. 'He was a human dynamo,' Roger Bannister, a close friend, told *The New York Times* in late April. 'My family and I will miss him more than I can say.' "

In Wiltshire, England, of a heart attack, April 19, 2004.

Bob Murphy, 79, broadcaster. Bob Murphy called Mets games on radio and television from the team's inception in 1962 to 2003. With his distinctive voice and signature turns of phrase, including his "happy recaps" of Mets victories, Murphy could make even promotional copy for regional milk purveyor Dairylea sound interesting, to say nothing of the baseball action he so deftly narrated. "It's like losing a brother," said Mets announcer and former big-league slugger Ralph Kiner, who with Murphy and Lindsey Nelson formed the team's first broadcast crew. Murphy called his final game in September 2003.

In Palm Beach, Fla., of lung cancer, Aug. 3, 2004.

Gayle Olinekova, 50, distance runner. *In the Jan. 5, 1981, issue of SI, Gayle Olinekova's ripplingly muscled legs were crowned "the greatest legs ever to stride the earth." Twenty-three years later, SI writes:*

"At the 1980 New Orleans Marathon, Olinekova, who began racing as a teen in Toronto, ran what was then the third-fastest time for a woman marathoner (2:35:12) despite her unusually stocky 5'6", 125-pound frame. 'The Twiggy look is history,' she said in '81. Originally a sprinter, Olinekova embarked on a drifter's life in Europe after missing the '72 Canadian Olympic team. At one point she was sleeping in the high jump pit at Rome's Stadio Olimpico, where she trained during the day. She returned to North America in '74 and began lengthening her runs, qualifying for the 1980 Moscow Olympics in the 1,500 meters before Canada boycotted the Games. About that time she said, 'I decided to go crazy with weights.' She also subsisted on a highly unorthodox diet, eating almost nothing but fruit. Olinekova settled near L.A., became a chiropractor, and wrote five books promoting healthy lifestyles."

In Thousand Oaks, Calif., of cancer, Nov. 26, 2003.

Marco Pantani, 34, cyclist. *The last man to win the Tour de France before Lance Armstrong began his six-year run, Marco Pantani often raced with a bandanna on his head and hoops in his ears, earning the nickname "the Pirate." SI writes:*

"One of the sport's best climbers, the lithe Pantani never got to defend his title after being thrown out of the 1999 Giro d'Italia when a blood test raised suspicions of doping. He went into seclusion for a year, but returned to the Tour de France in 2000. During a mountain stage that year Lance Armstrong, who was leading overall, pulled up at the finish line to let Pantani win. Pantani took offense, adding fuel to a rivalry that reached a low in '02 when Pantani said of Armstrong and his battle with testicular cancer, 'he is a great rider but not a great champion. He's clever at making the most of his sickness.' Pantani finished a strong 14th in the May 2003 Giro but later entered a treatment center for depression. Though several bottles of antidepressants were found in the hotel room where Pantani's body was found, investigators ruled out suicide.

In Rimini, Italy, of cardiac arrest, Feb 14, 2004.

George Peoples, 43, football player. A former running back at Auburn and in the NFL with New England and Tampa Bay, Peoples was found dead in a Tampa, Fla., motel room. He was named offensive player of the year at Auburn in 1981, and was selected in the eighth round of the '82 NFL draft by the Dallas Cowboys. He spent three seasons in the league, getting cut by the Bucs before the '85 season. Peoples had several brushes with the law after his playing days, and struggled with cocaine addiction for years.

In Tampa, Fla., of undisclosed causes, Nov. 23, 2003.

Marge Schott, 75, baseball franchise owner. *Marge Schott held controlling interest in the Cincinnati Reds from 1984 until '99, when Major League Baseball forced her to give up everyday control after she made offensive remarks—including calling outfielder Eric Davis one of her "million dollar n-----s." Davis, who played for the Reds from 1984–91 and in '96, remembers the woman who mixed caring (she donated millions to charity) with controversy:*

"I met Marge and her Saint Bernard, Schottzie, my rookie year. It was the first time I'd ever seen a dog on a [major league] baseball field. But that was her. She tried to make the team a family. She wanted the fans involved. A lot of times she didn't express it that way, but she truly cared.

"On those teams there were black and white and Dominican players. And she didn't go out of her way to degrade somebody because of his race. After I was traded to the Dodgers and those comments came out about me in 1992, I got a lot of calls from black leaders about what I should do. But I took what she said with a grain of salt.

"When you drink, you speak your mind a lot and you get into situations where the wrong people are listening. That's what got her in trouble. But her comments live on because I still hear them today when people ask me about Marge. It's unfortunate because deep down inside she wasn't a bad person.

"She brought me out of retirement and back to the Reds in 1996. I played another five years for other teams, but every time I came to Cincinnati, I had a conversation with Marge. I would call her periodically just to say hello because we were friends. The last time I saw her was in 2002, when the Reds played their last homestand at Riverfront Stadium. She called me *Honey*. It was her favorite word. She called everybody *Honey*."

In Cincinnati, of undisclosed causes, March 2, 2004.

Warren Spahn, 82, baseball player. *A pitcher with a famously high leg kick in his delivery, Warren Spahn was the winningest lefthander in major league history. He was a first-ballot Hall of Famer, and he won at least 20 games a season 13 times, threw two no-hitters and made the National League All-Star team 14 times in his 21-year career, which was spent mostly with the Boston and Milwaukee Braves. Appearing in the pages of SI, Boys of Summer author Roger Kahn writes:*

"Warren Spahn seldom forgot a name, a face, a batter's tendencies or an insult. More than once he recalled the trauma of his major league debut as an obscure 20-year-old lefthander with the wartime Boston Braves. It was 1942, and Casey Stengel, managing Boston to a seventh-place finish, summoned Spahn from the bullpen to face the Dodgers' Pee Wee Reese. 'Kid,' Stengel said, 'this hitter has been beaned and got his skull broke. I want you to throw your first two pitches at his head.'

"Spahn was a magnificent competitor, but he was also a sportsman. He threw two fastballs shoulder-high inside, neither near Reese's head, then walked the Brooklyn shortstop. Stengel made his bent-legged way back to the mound. 'Yer outta the game,' he said, 'and when you get to the dugout, keep walking till you reach the clubhouse. There's gonna be a bus ticket there back to Hartford. You'll never win in the major leagues. You got no guts.' Proceeding with this narrative long afterward, Spahn uttered a put-down for the ages. 'A few years later,' he said, 'after I won the Bronze Star during the Battle of the Bulge. . . .'

"Nor did Spahn's story finish there. Stengel moved on and won five World Series for the Yankees. Spahn would go on to win 363 games, more than any other lefthander. The two crossed paths again, in 1965, when Spahn's pitching days were almost done and Stengel was managing the Mets into the cellar. Spahn was pounded in a few starts, and Stengel complained, 'The hitters jump on him so quick, I can't get him outta there fast enough.' Summing up not so long ago, Spahn said, exercising his fine and occasionally malicious wit, 'I pitched for Casey Stengel both before and after he was a genius.'

"I'd suggest that Warren Edward Spahn was the most intelligent person ever named for Warren Gamaliel Harding, perhaps our most limited president. Spahnie's study of pitching was as profound as that of the immortal Christy Mathewson. 'Home plate is 17 inches wide,' Spahn liked to point out. 'All I asked for were the two inches on each corner. The hitters could have the 13 inches in between. I didn't throw there.' He was very fast when young but evolved into a master of the slider and the changeup. 'Batting is timing,' he said. 'Pitching is upsetting timing.'

"Few who saw Spahn will forget the arcing grace of his windup. His strong arms pumped far back, and as he rocked, his right leg kicked high before he threw. His motion was unique and fluid, a sort of pitching equivalent to Stan Musial's swing. 'Musial was the hardest man to to fool,' Spahn said. 'He had an average of .314 against me, but I never brooded when Stan hit me. The time to worry was when some .250 hitter knocked my cap off with a line drive.'

"Like many good soldiers, Spahn didn't like to discuss his wartime adventures, much less dwell on how he won his medal. When I asked about his battlefield promotion from enlisted man to lieutenant, he said lightly, 'Hell, in the Bulge they were running out of officers.' He went on, 'After you've tried to sleep in frozen tank ruts within the range of Nazi guns, every day you get to play baseball is a breeze.'

"During a recent gathering in Cooperstown, I introduced him to my wife and said, 'After a game Mr. Spahn remembered each one of the 125 pitches he had thrown, where it was, what it was and the sequence.' The praise made Spahn uncomfortable. 'That's nothing special, Mrs. Kahn,' he said. 'After all, pitching is what I did.' "

In Broken Arrow, Okla., of undisclosed causes, Nov. 24, 2003.

Dernell Stenson, 25, baseball player. *A third-round-draft pick in the 1996 major league draft, taken by the Boston Red Sox, Dernell Stenson worked his way through the minor leagues and played 37 games for the Cincinnati Reds in 2003, hitting a home run in his last big-league game. SI's George Dohrmann writes:*

"Allegedly the victim of a murder in Arizona, where he had been playing fall baseball, Reds outfielder Dernell Stenson was buried in his hometown of LaGrange, Ga., last week. About 1,000 people attended the Nov. 10, 2003, funeral, including Ken Griffey Jr., Barry Larkin and 50 others from the Reds organization. Police arrested four men in connection with the crime, which is believed to have stemmed from a robbery attempt.

"On Nov. 4 pitcher Joe Valentine and two other Reds walked into Sugar Daddy's, a Scottsdale bar frequented by Arizona Fall League players, at around 11:30 p.m. and saw Stenson alone at the bar. 'We were walking outside to the patio and Dernell said he'd see us back there,' Valentine said. 'But we didn't see him. . . . We didn't get a goodbye, which was definitely unusual.' Two hours later police found Stenson's body lying six miles away, in a Chandler street. He had been shot in the head and chest and run over; a trail of blood ran more than 50 feet, indicating he had been dragged by a car. Stenson is the first active major leaguer to be slain since 1978, when Angels outfielder Lyman Bostock was shot.

" 'He had so much to look forward to,' said Stenson's older brother James Stenson Jr. 'It is so hard for my mother and all of us to understand.' Dernell, 25, had planned to spend the off-season in Indianapolis with his longtime girlfriend. But when a roster spot opened, Stenson—who hit .247 with three homers and 13 RBIs in 37 games for Cincinnati in 2003—went to the Scottsdale Scorpions, where he had been batting .394. Drafted out of LaGrange High by the Red Sox in the third round in 1996, Stenson 'was considered the heir apparent to Mo Vaughn,' said Reds player development director Tim Naehring, a former Red Sox player. But he struggled at first base, was moved to the outfield at Triple A Pawtucket and Boston put him on waivers in February. The Reds claimed him and sent him to Double A. The demotion stung the shy Stenson, yet he never complained and was rewarded when injuries to Reds outfielders led to a promotion. 'His dream was to play in the major leagues,' said his mother, Cora. 'At least he got a chance to realize his dream.' "

In Chandler, Ariz., of gunshot wounds, Nov. 5, 2003.

Pat Tillman, 27, football player. *After graduating summa cum laude with a 3.84 grade-point average from Arizona State University, Pat Tillman, an all-Pac 10 linebacker, was drafted by the Arizona Cardinals in the seventh round of the 1998 NFL draft. A special teams player at first, Tillman—who led the Sun Devils to the 1997 Rose Bowl and was the '98 Pac10 defensive player of the year—eventually won a starting spot at* safety with the Cardinals. Deeply affected by the terrorist attacks against the U.S. on Sept. 11, 2001, Tillman, who came from a family of veterans, gave up his $3.6 million contract with Arizona to enlist in the U.S. military. SI's Gary Smith writes:

". . . Here in Spera, where the enemy slipped across the Pakistani border a few miles to the east to infest the cliff heads and steep thickets of pine, 27-year-old Army Ranger Sgt. Pat Tillman had no need anymore to lie in bed imagining what a soldier's last gasps sounded and looked like. No reason now to dig at himself in the dark, wondering what right he had to live off the sacrifice of relatives and strangers who'd fought in American wars.

"He and the thin detail of Rangers and Afghani fighters in his patrol would be in deep trouble if Muslim militants lay in wait tonight. The nearest U.S. firebase was in Khost, about 30 miles away. The density of trees and tortured geometry of the terrain made it nearly impossible for the Predator drones circling high overhead to detect the enemy and give warning, or for the Chinook choppers back at base to stage a swift rescue.

"But there was no longer any lying back in the razor-wire-ringed bases where Special Forces had crouched through much of 2003. Operation Mountain Storm had begun. The Pakistani military was squeezing Islamic extremists out of sanctuaries in the east and through the mountain corridors into Afghanistan. The grim chore of the 2nd Battalion of the 75th Army Ranger Regiment was to patrol these twisting gorges, to cut down insurgents on the move, to live in mud-brick villages among the locals who might spill secrets. To find the big dog suspected to be lying low in the region—Taliban chief Mullah Mohammed Omar—and maybe the even bigger one, al-Qaeda No. 2 man Ayman al-Zawahiri, or the biggest one of all, Osama bin Laden. Pat Tillman had left Fort Lewis, Wash., three weeks before and joined Mountain Storm with his 26-year-old brother, Kevin, two Rangers assigned to separate units but near enough, a few times a week, to look into each other's eyes. . . .

"[After the terrorist attacks on the World Trade Center and the Pentagon] Kevin, an infielder in the Cleveland Indians organization, was dead-set. He was going to quit the minor leagues and give up his dream, a life in the bigs, to enlist and attempt to become an Army Ranger. But how, everyone in America would wonder, could Pat do that too? How could he walk away from a three-year, $3.6 million contract with the Arizona Cardinals and end up in a region so riddled with risk that Afghanis themselves trembled to enter unless they belonged to the local tribe? .

"Pat rattled along the dirt road in the lead pickup truck with his fellow Rangers, allied Afghani soldiers following in a vehicle just behind. For him the question had always been different: How could he not? . . .

"[After making the decision to enlist] the Tillman brothers made the Rangers. . . .'I can't stop smiling,' Pat's old college coach, Bruce Snyder, told The Miami Herald at the time, 'and I'm not sure why.'

"Pat called home from the Baghdad airport in the summer of 2003 during a 3½-month Rangers road trip. He began the conversation with his father by reading a list of things about which they couldn't speak, leaving virtually nothing about which they could.

"Pat returned to the States but kept his distance and his silence as the world offered movie and book deals and awards for courage, the covers of magazines and Wheaties boxes. . . .

"He couldn't do it. He couldn't possibly hold himself above his Ranger mates, bouncing in this truck through the mountains of Afghanistan on April 22, 2004, three weeks after he and his brother had been summoned back to the Middle East. . . .

"A tribesman rode with them, a Taliban sympathizer. He was a plant who had offered to take the Rangers to a hidden enemy arms dump. Instead he was leading them into a trap. That's what Taliban sources would report two days later, after the air ripped just outside of Spera at half past seven and everything went to hell.

"The Rangers scrambled out of their vehicles as they came under ambush and charged the militants on foot. Suddenly Pat was down, Pat was dying. Two other U.S. soldiers were wounded, and a coalition Afghani fighter was killed in a firefight that lasted 15 or 20 minutes before the jihadists melted away. That's what the American military says.

"Pat's truck hit a land mine, and he died from wounds caused by the explosion. That's what an Afghani coalition commander says. [The Army's final report stated that Tillman was probably killed by so-called friendly fire during the engagement. He was posthumously awarded the Silver Star for combat valor.—Ed.] Either way, on April 26, Kevin made the long flight home with his brother's body.

"The news whistled through America's soul and raised the hair on the back of its neck. . . .

"The mist of human motive is as dense as the fog of war. Pat Tillman may have died in the Middle East last April because it was the only place on earth where he could get a good night's sleep. But anytime a man listens to his inner voice, refuses to wall it off with all the mortar and bricks that his culture can possibly offer, it's a moment to stand in wonder as well as to weep.

"Elizabeth McKenrick, the wife of 4th Ranger Training Battalion Commander Terry McKenrick, couldn't help herself on April 23rd. As a rule she shields her three children from newscasts about the war because otherwise she knows that the next time their dad is shipped from Fort Benning, Ga., to the Middle East, she won't stand a chance of convincing them he'll return home. But when she saw the TV report about Pat Tillman, she called her nine-year-old to her side. 'Listen,' she said. 'Listen to the story of what this man did.' "

In Spera, Afghanistan, from gunshot wounds, April 22, 2004.

Sid Smith, 78, hockey player. *A forward with the Maple Leafs in the 1940s and '50s, Sid Smith led Toronto to three Stanley Cups. SI writes:*

"Smith, whose 12-year career ended in 1958, twice won the Lady Byng Memorial Trophy as the NHL's most gentlemanly player. But he was also a scoring threat. In Game 2 of the 1949 Stanley Cup finals he had a hat trick in a 3–1 win over Detroit, and upon his retirement, only three active players—Gordie Howe, Maurice Richard and Ted Lindsay—had scored more than his 186 goals."

In Wasaga Beach, Ont., after a lengthy illness, April 29, 2004.

Ralph Wiley, 52, sportswriter. *Ralph Wiley started as a senior writer at SI in 1982. SI Writes:*

"During his nine years as a writer at SI, Wiley wrote more than 20 cover stories, marked by aggressive reporting and astute observation. But Wiley—who also wrote books and plays and was a contributor on ESPN's The Sports Reporters—was best known for his boxing profiles, enriched by his lifelong love of the sport and his keen political awareness."

In Orlando, Fla., of heart failure, June 13, 2004.